# WILEY

# GAAP
## 2009

Interpretation and Application of
GENERALLY ACCEPTED
ACCOUNTING PRINCIPLES

**Subscriber
Update
Service**

## BECOME A SUBSCRIBER!
### *Did you purchase this product from a bookstore?*

If you did, it's important for you to become a subscriber. John Wiley & Sons, Inc. may publish, on a periodic basis, supplements and new editions to reflect the latest changes in the subject matter that you ***need to know*** in order stay competitive in this ever-changing industry. By contacting the Wiley office nearest you, you'll receive any current update at no additional charge. In addition, you'll receive future updates and revised or related volumes on a 30-day examination review.

If you purchased this product directly from John Wiley & Sons, Inc., we have already recorded your subscription for this update service.

To become a subscriber, please call **1-877-762-2974** or send your name, company name (if applicable), address, and the title of the product to:

mailing address:  **Supplement Department
John Wiley & Sons, Inc.
One Wiley Drive
Somerset, NJ 08875**

e-mail: **subscriber@wiley.com**
fax: **1-732-302-2300**
online: **www.wiley.com**

For customers outside the United States, please contact the Wiley office nearest you:

Professional & Reference Division
John Wiley & Sons Canada, Ltd.
22 Worcester Road
Etobicoke, Ontario M9W 1L1
CANADA
Phone: 416- 236-4433
Phone: 1-800-567-4797
Fax: 416-236-4447
Email: canada@jwiley.com

John Wiley & Sons Australia, Ltd.
33 Park Road
P.O. Box 1226
Milton, Queensland 4064
AUSTRALIA
Phone: 61-7-3859-9755
Fax: 61-7-3859-9715
Email: brisbane@johnwiley.com.au

John Wiley & Sons, Ltd.
The Atrium
Southern Gate, Chichester
West Sussex, PO19 8SQ
ENGLAND
Phone: 44-1243 779777
Fax: 44-1243 775878
Email: customer@wiley.co.uk

John Wiley & Sons (Asia) Pte. Ltd.
2 Clementi Loop #02-01
SINGAPORE 129809
Phone: 65-64632400
Fax: 65-64634604/5/6
Customer Service: 65-64604280
Email: enquiry@wiley.com.sg

# WILEY

# GAAP
## 2009

Interpretation and Application of
GENERALLY ACCEPTED
ACCOUNTING PRINCIPLES

Barry J. Epstein
Ralph Nach
Steven M. Bragg

WILEY

JOHN WILEY & SONS, INC.

For general information on our other products and services, please contact our Customer Care Department within the US at 800-762-2974, outside the US at 317-572-3993 or fax 317-572-4002.

Wiley also publishes its books in a variety of electronic formats. Some content that appears in print may not be available in electronic books. For more information about Wiley products, visit our Web site at www.wiley.com.

**ISBN 978-0470-28606-7**

Printed in the United States of America
10 9 8 7 6 5 4 3 2 1

# CONTENTS

# PREFACE

*GAAP: Interpretation and Application* provides analytical explanations and copious illustrations of all current generally accepted accounting principles. The book integrates principles promulgated by all the relevant standard-setting bodies—the FASB, including its Emerging Issues Task Force's consensus summaries, discussion issues, and staff positions, and the AICPA's Accounting Standards Executive Committee (AcSEC). These materials are synthesized into a user-oriented topical format, eliminating the need for readers to first be knowledgeable about the names or numbers of the salient professional standards.

The principal intended audience for the book is the practitioner, with the primary objective being to assist in resolving the myriad practical problems faced in applying GAAP. Accordingly, meaningful, realistic examples abound, guiding users in the application of GAAP to complex fact situations that must be dealt with in the real world practice of accounting In addition to this emphasis, a major strength of the book is that it does explain the theory of GAAP in sufficient detail to serve as a valuable adjunct to accounting textbooks. Much more than merely a reiteration of currently promulgated GAAP, it provides the user with the underlying conceptual basis for the rules, to facilitate the process of reasoning by analogy that is so necessary in dealing with the complicated, fast-changing world of commercial arrangements and transaction structures. It is based on the authors' belief that proper application of GAAP demands an understanding of the logical underpinnings of all its technical requirements.

Each chapter of this book, or major section thereof, provides an overview discussion of the perspective and key issues associated with the topics covered; a listing of the professional pronouncements which guide practice; and a detailed discussion of the concepts and the accompanying examples. A comprehensive disclosure checklist, following the main text, offers practical guidance to preparing financial statements in accordance with GAAP, with supplemental insights into SEC-mandated disclosures as needed. Also included is a comprehensive comparison of GAAP to International (IFRS) standards, increasingly the norm for entities reporting outside the US and, possibly soon, for US-based entities as well. This book also contains a comprehensive index, and an exhaustive listing of professional pronouncements, keyed to both this book and to the newly developed codification of accounting standards prepared by the FASB.

The authors' wish is that this book will serve preparers, practitioners, faculty, and students, as a reliable reference tool, to facilitate their understanding of, and ability to apply, the complexities of the authoritative literature. Comments from readers, both as to errors and omissions and as to proposed improvements for future editions, should be addressed to Barry J. Epstein, c/o John Wiley & Sons, Inc., 155 N. 3rd Street, Suite 502, DeKalb, Illinois 60115, prior to May 15, 2009, for consideration for the 2010 edition.

Barry J. Epstein
Ralph Nach
Steven M. Bragg
August 1, 2008

# ABOUT THE AUTHORS

**Barry J. Epstein,** PhD, CPA, is a partner with Chicago-based Russell Novak & Company, LLP, where he specializes in technical consultation on accounting and auditing matters and corporate governance, and maintains a national practice as a consulting and testifying expert for commercial and other litigation matters, including accountants' malpractice, contractual dispute resolution, damages modeling, and white-collar criminal defense. He has previously served in senior technical and litigation consulting positions with several regional and national CPA firms, and as a corporate finance executive and college professor. Dr. Epstein has authored or coauthored six books (including *Wiley IFRS Interpretation and Application*), hundreds of professional education courses, several articles in business or professional journals, and a weekly business column for an international newspaper. He has served on several state and national technical committees, including the AICPA's Board of Examiners, served as chair of the Illinois CPA Society's senior accounting technical committee, and held teaching positions at several universities. Dr. Epstein received his doctorate from the University of Pittsburgh, and also holds degrees from DePaul University and the University of Chicago. He is a member of the Illinois CPA Society, the AICPA, and the American Accounting Association.

**Ralph Nach,** CPA, is a Senior Consultant with AuditWatch, part of Thompson Reuters, for which he writes, teaches, and consults on a wide range of accounting, auditing, and financial reporting matters. He has been a practitioner for over thirty years, during which he has served in capacities including accountant, auditor, quality control director, peer reviewer, educator, chief learning officer, and consultant for several public accounting firms, including Arthur Anderson LLP. Most recently Mr. Nach served as a partner in the National Office of Audit and Accounting of McGladrey & Pullen, LLP. He is a former adjunct lecture in graduate accounting and finance at Northwestern University in Evanston, Illinois. Mr. Nach holds a BSBA with honors from the Walter E. Heller School of Business Administration of Roosevelt University in Chicago, and is a licensed CPA in Illinois. Mr. Nach has coauthored several other books and speaks nationally on accounting, auditing, and financial reporting topics. He is a member of the American Institute of Certified Public Accountants, the Information Systems Audit and Control Association (ISACA), the Illinois CPA Society, where he has served as a chairman and/or member of numerous committees, and an associate member of the Association of Certified Fraud Examiners.

**Steven Bragg,** CPA, CMA, CIA, CPIM, has been the chief financial officer or controller of four companies, as well as a consulting manager at Ernst & Young and auditor at Deloitte & Touche. He received a master's degree in finance from Bentley College, an MBA from Babson College, and a Bachelor's degree in Economics from the University of Maine. He is the author of 28 books, including *Accounting Best Practices*, *The Ultimate Accountants' Reference*, and *Controllership*. He has been the two-time president of the Colorado Mountain Club. He resides with his wife and two daughters in Centennial, Colorado. Sign up for his free accounting best practices newsletter at www.stevebragg.com.

# AUTHORITATIVE ACCOUNTING PRONOUNCEMENTS

Listed below are all of the authoritative accounting pronouncements currently in effect as we go to press. The current text refers to the FASB's *Accounting Standards—Current Text,* which is divided into two volumes: General Standards and Industry Standards. These volumes as well as two volumes of Original Pronouncements may be ordered from the AICPA (800-862-4272) or FASB (203-847-0700). The Emerging Issues Task Force Abstracts, which are in a separate book, may be ordered from the FASB. AICPA Statements of Position by the Accounting Standards Executive Committee may be ordered from the AICPA. These are available individually or in the publication entitled *AICPA Technical Practice Aids.* Places in this text where the pronouncements are discussed may be found by referencing the last column in the listings below.

### Abbreviations for Accounting Pronouncements and Other References

The following is a key to the abbreviations used throughout the book to refer to authoritative pronouncements and other references:

| *Abbreviation* | *Source\** | *Pronouncement* |
|---|---|---|
| AAER | SEC | Accounting and Auditing Enforcement Release |
| AAG | AcSEC | Accounting and Auditing Guides |
| AIN | AICPA | Accounting Interpretation |
| APB | APB | Opinions |
| ARB | CAP | Accounting Research Bulletins |
| ASR | SEC | Accounting Series Release |
| AUG | AcSEC | AICPA General or Industry-Specific Audit Guide |
| CON | FASB | Statements of Financial Accounting Concepts |
| D | EITF | Discussions of Technical Matters |
| DIG | DIG | FAS 133 Implementation Issue |
| EITF | EITF | Issue and/or Consensus Position |
| FAS | FASB | Statements of Financial Accounting Standards |
| FIN | FASB | Interpretation |
| FSP | FASB | Staff Position |
| FTB | FASB | Technical Bulletin |
| IAS | IASC | International Accounting Standard |
| IFRS | IASB | International Financial Reporting Standard |
| IRC | US Congress | The Internal Revenue Code (Statute) |
| PB | AcSEC | Practice Bulletin |
| Q&A | FASB | FASB Staff Implementation Guide |
| SAB | SEC | Staff Accounting Bulletin |
| SAS | ASB | Statement of Auditing Standards |
| SOP | AcSEC | Statement of Position |
| SOX | US Congress | The Sarbanes-Oxley Act of 2002 |

\* *Standard setters and regulators cited above*

| | |
|---|---|
| AICPA | *American Institute of Certified Public Accountants* |
| AcSEC | *AICPA Accounting Standards Executive Committee* |
| APB | *Accounting Principles Board* |
| ASB | *Auditing Standards Board* |
| CAP | *Committee on Accounting Procedure* |
| DIG | *Derivatives Implementation Group* |
| EITF | *Emerging Issues Task Force* |
| FASB | *Financial Accounting Standards Board* |
| IASB | *International Accounting Standards Board* |
| IASC | *International Accounting Standards Committee* |
| SEC | *US Securities and Exchange Commission* |

---

* *Missing numbers throughout this listing represent pronouncements that have been completely superseded.*

---

**Financial Accounting Standards Board**
**Statements of Financial Accounting Concepts (CON)(1978-2007)**

| | | |
|---|---|---|
| 1 | Objectives of Financial Reporting by Business Enterprises | 30, 31 |
| 2 | Qualitative Characteristics of Accounting Information | 28, 32, 33 |
| 4 | Objectives of Financial Reporting by Nonbusiness Organizations | |
| 5 | Recognition and Measurement in Financial Statements of Business Enterprises | 28, 34, 106, 355, 357, 648, 656, 1197 |
| 6 | Elements of Financial Statements | 27, 28, 29, 34, 35, 37, 44, 45, 71, 72, 86, 250, 251, 387, 439, 595, 597, 606, 608, 620, 656, 667, 761, 1002, 1067, 1071 |
| 7 | Using Cash Flow Information and Present Value in Accounting Measurements | 28, 37, 38, 39, 41, 165, 172, 217, 451, 459, 472, 596, 659, 697, 706, 802, 820, 956, 1248 |

---

**Emerging Issues Task Force Issues (1984-2007)**

| Number * | Title | Status | GAAP Interp. & Applic. page reference |
|---|---|---|---|
| 84-5 | Sale of Marketable Securities with a Put Option | Partially nullified by FAS 140; see also FAS 133 and FIN 45. | 519 |
| 84-10 | LIFO Conformity of Companies Relying on Insilco Tax Court Decision | Guidance provided by AICPA Issues Paper on LIFO Accounting, issued 11/30/84. See also Issue 84-24. | |
| 84-15 | Grantor Trusts Consolidation | No consensus, see FIN 46(R). | |
| 84-17 | Profit Recognition on Sales of Real Estate with Graduated Payment Mortgages and Insured Mortgages | Consensus reached. See Issue 87-9. | 393, 411 |
| 84-18 | Stock Option Pyramiding | Nullified by FAS 123(R) except for entities within the scope of para. 83 of the Statement. | |
| 84-19 | Mortgage Loan Payment Modifications | Consensus reached. | 1172, 1184 |
| 84-23 | Leveraged Buyout Holding Company Debt | No consensus reached. Guidance provided by SEC *Staff Accounting Bulletin 73*. Disclosure guidance provided by FAS 133. | |
| 84-34 | Permanent Discount Restricted Stock Purchase Plans | Nullified by FAS 123(R) except for entities within the scope of para. 83 of the Statement. | |

---

\* *Missing numbers throughout this listing represent pronouncements that have been completely superseded.*

*(EITF cont.)*

*(EITF cont.)*

| Number | Title | Status | GAAP Interp. & Applic. page reference |
|---|---|---|---|
| 98-13 | Accounting by an Equity Method Investor for Investee Losses When the Investor Has Loans to and Investments in Other Securities of the Investee | Consensus reached. See also Issue 99-10 and D-84. FIN 46(R) mentioned. | 510, 543, 544 |
| 98-14 | Debtor's Accounting for Changes in Line-of-Credit or Revolving-Debt Arrangements | Consensus reached. | |
| 98-15 | Structured Notes Acquired for a Specific Investment Strategy | Consensus reached. | 510, 576 |
| 99-1 | Accounting for Debt Convertible into the Stock of a Consolidated Subsidiary | Consensus reached | 250, 752, 772 |
| 99-2 | Accounting for Weather Derivatives | Consensus reached. | 250, 266 |
| 99-4 | Accounting for Stock Received from De-mutualization of Insurance Companies | Consensus reached. | 1217, 1225 |
| 99-5 | Accounting for Pre-Production Costs Related to Long-Term Supply Arrangements | Consensus reached. See FAS 144. | 434, 440 |
| 99-7 | Accounting for an Accelerated Share Re-purchase Program | Consensus reached; affected by FAS 141. | 1003, 1023 |
| 99-8 | Accounting for Transfers of Assets That Are Derivative Instruments but That Are Not Financial Assets | Consensus reached; see also FAS 133 and FAS 140. | 510, 576 |
| 99-9 | Effect of Derivative Gains and Losses on the Capitalization of Interest | Consensus reached; see also FAS 133. | 434, 442 |
| 99-10 | Percentage Used to Determine the Amount of Equity Method Losses | Consensus reached. See also Issue 02-14. | 510, 543, 544, 546 |
| 99-12 | Determination of the Measurement Date for the Market Price of Acquirer Securities Issued in a Purchase Business Combination | Consensus reached. | 641, 722 |
| 99-13 | Application of EITF Issue 97-10, *The Effect of Lessee Involvement in Asset Construction*, and FASB Interpretation 23, *Leases of Certain Property Owned by a Governmental Unit or Authority*, to Entities That Enter into Leases with Governmental Entities. | Consensus reached. See FIN 45 and 46(R). | 801, 859 |
| 99-15 | Accounting for Decreases in Deferred Tax Asset Valuation Allowances Established in a Purchase Business Combination As a Result of a Change in Tax Regulations | Consensus reached. | 641, 721, 904 |
| 99-16 | Accounting for Transactions with Elements of Research and Development Arrangements | Consensus reached. See also FIN 46(R). | 434, 506 |
| 99-17 | Accounting for Advertising Barter Transactions | Consensus reached. | 166 |
| 99-19 | Reporting Revenue Gross as a Principal Versus Net as an Agent | Consensus reached. Also see SAB 101 and D-85. | 304, 422, 423, 566, 570, 571 |
| 99-20 | Recognition of Interest Income and Impairment on Certain Investments | Consensus reached | 216, 262, 510, 563, 577 |

## EITF DISCUSSION OF TECHNICAL MATTERS

Listed below are EITF documents that contain discussion by the Emerging Issues Task Force of technical matters that have long-term relevance and do not relate specifically to a numbered EITF Issue. The more important of these are briefly annotated.

| Number | Title |
|---|---|
| D-8 | Accruing Bad-Debt Expense at Inception of a Lease |

This establishes that the former practice of accruing a bad debt provision at least inception, which would then be offset by unearned income consistent with other initial direct costs, is inappropriate.

**D-10**    Required Use of Interest Method in Recognizing Interest Income

This clarified that other interest recognition methods (Rule of 78s, etc.) would not be acceptable alternatives to the (effective rate) interest method.

**D-11**    Impact of Stock Market Decline

This addressed the need for disclosure of post-balance-sheet date events in the specific context of the sharp stock market decline which occurred in late 1987.

**D-12**    Foreign Currency Translation—Selection of Exchange Rate When Trading Is Temporarily Suspended

**D-21**    Phase-in Plans When Two Plants Are Completed at Different Times but Share Common Facilities

**D-23**    Subjective Acceleration Clauses and Debt Classification

This clarified the distinctions between FAS 6, dealing with classification of short-term debt as noncurrent under defined circumstances, and FTB 79-3, which addresses the potential need to classify long-term debt having a subjective acceleration clause as current.

**D-24**    Sale-Leaseback Transactions with Continuing Involvement

This responded to several specific circumstances illustrating application of the FAS 98 requirement that precludes sale-leaseback accounting (with attendant gain or loss recognition) when there is any continuing involvement by the seller other than that of a normal lessee.

**D-27**    Accounting for the Transfer of Excess Pension Assets to a Retiree Health Care Benefits Account

This states that the transfer of excess pension assets, whether or not made pursuant to the Revenue Reconciliation (Tax) Act of 1990, should be recognized as a negative contribution to the pension fund and a positive contribution to the health care plan; no gain or loss arises from this transaction.

**D-30**    Adjustment Due to Effect of a Change in Tax Laws or Rates

This simply reinforced the FAS 109 requirement that the effect of changes in laws or rates is to be recognized when enacted.

**D-31**    Temporary Differences Related to LIFO Inventory and Tax-to-Tax Differences

This clarified that differences between tax and book LIFO inventory valuations must be tax effected. It also reinforced the rule that only book tax differences are temporary differences under FAS 109; thus differences between "outside basis" and "inside basis" would not give rise to deferred taxes to be recognized in the financial statements.

**D-32**    Intraperiod Tax Allocation of the Tax Effect of Pretax Income from Continuing Operations

This item states that while the tax effect of pretax income from continuing operations would not be affected by other items (e.g., extraordinary items) on the income statement, the tax effect of a loss from continuing operations would consider the tax effects of other items, per paragraph 140 of FAS 109.

**D-33**    Timing of Recognition of Tax Benefits for Prereorganization Temporary Differences and Carryforwards

This expands the requirements under FAS 109, relevant to pre- and postacquisition carryforwards, to also apply to pre- and postreorganization carryforwards.

**D-34**    Accounting for Reinsurance: Questions and Answers about FASB Statement 113

**D-35**    FASB Staff Views on Issue 93-6, *Accounting for Multiple-Year Retrospectively-Rated Contracts by Ceding and Assuming Enterprises*

**D-36**    Selection of Discount Rates Used for Measuring Defined Benefit Pension Obligations and Obligations of Postretirement Benefit Plans other than Pensions

This sets forth the SEC's position that discount rates be reflective of current rates as of the balance sheet date.

| *Number* | *Title* |
|---|---|
| D-83 | Accounting for Payroll Taxes Associated with Stock Option Exercises |

This states the staff position, with regard to the tax implications of exercises of employee stock options, that payroll taxes, even though directly related to the appreciation on stock options, are operating expenses and should be reflected as such in the statement of operations.

D-84    Accounting for Subsequent Investments in an Investee After Suspension of Equity Method Loss Recognition When an Investor Increases Its Ownership Interest from Significant Influence to Control through a Market Purchase of Voting Securities

The SEC staff addressed a fact pattern in which a subsequent investment was made in an equity method investee after there had been a suspension of equity method loss recognition in accordance with APB 18. In such a circumstance, the excess over fair value of underlying net assets is to be allocated to all identifiable tangible and intangible assets of the investee in accordance with the FAS 141 (which superseded APB 16, but did not change the purchase method accounting to be applied).

D-85    Application of Certain Transition Provisions in SEC Staff Accounting Bulletin No. 101

This provides interpretive guidance regarding the need for retroactive application of certain elements of SAB 101 (dealing with revenue recognition, and more particularly with regard to two issues: The factors to be considered in determining whether revenue should be presented on a gross or net basis in an income statement; and retailers' presentation of revenue from sales of leased or licensed departments.) Retroactive application was not required, but in the alternative a cumulative effect presentation under the provisions of APB 20 was necessary. (Subsequently, a deferred implementation date was granted for the provisions of SAB 101.)

D-86    Issuance of Financial Statements

This addresses the matter of when financial statements are considered to be "issued," which is important in the context of responsibility for false or misleading information filed with the SEC. According to SEC staff, financial statements are "issued" as of the date they are distributed for general use and reliance in a form and format that complies with generally accepted accounting principles (GAAP) and, in the case of annual financial statements, that contain an audit report that indicates that the auditors have complied with generally accepted auditing standards (GAAS) in completing their audit. Issuance of financial statements then would generally be the earlier of when the annual or quarterly financial statements are widely distributed to all shareholders and other financial statement users or filed with the SEC. The issuance of an earnings release does not constitute issuance of financial statements because the earnings release would not be in a form and format that complies with GAAP and GAAS.

D-87    Determination of the Measurement Date for Consideration Given by the Acquirer in a Business Combination When That Consideration Is Securities other than Those Issued by the Acquirer

Regarding the date that should be used to measure the consideration given by the acquirer to shareholders of an acquired company in a purchase business combination when that consideration is securities other than those issued by the acquirer, these should be measured on the date the business combination is consummated. Measurement at the consummation date also avoids issues associated with fixing the value of investment securities when FAS 115 or APB 18 requires the carrying value of the investment to be adjusted for changes in fair value or operating results of the investee, respectively.

D-89    Accounting for Costs of Future Medicare Compliance Audits

Commitments by health care providers for the future performance of compliance audits, made in settlement agreements arising from Medicare fraud allegations, do not create liabilities under the definition set forth in FASB Concepts Statement 6. Accordingly, accrual of the present value of these future costs at the time of such agreements would not be appropriate under GAAP.

When forfeitable, unvested equity instruments are issued to a nonemployee (e.g., vendor), notwithstanding the existence of substantial penalties for nonperformance, the shares should not be considered to have been issued until performance later occurs. Measurement date is not to be recognized, therefore, at the date of issuance.

Certain performance fees are earned if defined benchmarks are exceeded (e.g., S&P 500 index for investment managers) which are generally measured on an annual basis, thus raising a concern over interim reporting. The SEC prefers that revenues not be accrued on an interim basis when later changes could result in this revenue being reduced or eliminated for the year as a whole. However, it is acceptable to accrue revenue on an interim basis to the extent that the formula provides for compensation in the event of termination on those dates. The accounting policy disclosures must set forth the manner in which revenues are being recognized. In no case can revenues be recognized based upon a projection of future performance; under SAB 101 the fee revenue must be fixed or determinable prior to recognition for financial reporting purposes.

Push-down (or "new basis") accounting is required by the SEC if an entity becomes substantially wholly owned by another entity as a result of a single or a related series of transactions whereby at least 95% of the common stock is acquired. Such accounting is permitted, not required, if from 80% to 95% of the shares are acquired. Push-down accounting is prohibited if less than 80% of the shares are obtained in the transaction(s). This would be true even if the wholly owned status was intended to be temporary (e.g., when minority shares are to be sold to new investors). In making a determination of whether an entity has become "substantially wholly owned," it is appropriate to aggregate holdings of investors which "mutually promoted" the acquisition and which "collaborate" on control of the investee. To overcome the rebuttable presumption that investors are acting in concert in such situations, a number of criteria (relating to independence, risk of ownership, absence of subsequent collaboration, etc.) are set forth.

Per SEC rules, equity that is not "permanent" (i.e., that can be redeemed by the holder's demand or by conditions not under the issuer's control) must be displayed outside of the equity section of the balance sheet. (There are no similar requirements under general GAAP, however.) The potential effects of normal liquidation events, however, do not necessitate such presentation. Determining whether securities are subject to redemption at the holder's option is fact-specific and my not be obvious in some instances. If securities must be redeemed if, for example, a registration statement is not filed by a defined date, or if there is noncompliance with debt covenants, inclusion as equity would be prohibited. Similarly, if the preferred stock is subject to a change-in-control provision and the preferred holders control a majority of votes on the board of directors, the preferred stock would be excludable from equity. Where redemption values vary over time, the stock should be presented at its redemption amount at the balance sheet date, which may or may not involve accretion over time (by the interest method, generally), depending on its terms.

### AICPA STATEMENTS OF POSITION (1974-2007)

## Audit and Accounting Guides

## OTHER GAAP SOURCES

**Issues Papers of the Accounting Standards Division**

Issues Papers of the AICPA's Accounting Standards Division primarily identify financial accounting and reporting issues that the Division believed needed addressing by the Financial Accounting Standards Board. These pronouncements constitute generally accepted accounting principles but are not mandatory.

| | |
|---|---|
| Accounting for Changes in Estimates | 12/15/78 |
| Joint Venture Accounting | 7/17/79 |
| Accounting by Investors for Distributions Received in Excess of Their Investment in a Joint Venture (Addendum to Joint Venture Accounting issues paper) | 10/8/79 |
| "Push Down" Accounting | 10/30/79 |
| Accounting in Consolidation for Issuances of a Subsidiary Stock | 6/30/80 |
| Certain Issues That Affect Accounting for Minority Interest in Consolidated Financial Statements | 3/17/81 |
| The Acceptability of "Simplified LIFO" for Financial Reporting Purposes | 10/14/82 |
| Computation of Premium Deficiencies in Insurance Enterprises | 3/26/84 |
| Identification and Discussion of Certain Financial Accounting and Reporting Issues Concerning LIFO Inventories | 11/30/84 |
| Accounting for Options | 3/6/86 |
| The Use of Discounting in Financial Reporting for Monetary Items with Uncertain Terms other than Those Covered by Existing Authoritative Literature | 9/9/87 |
| Quasi Reorganizations | 10/28/88 |

**Practice Bulletins**

| | | |
|---|---|---|
| 1. | Purpose and Scope of AcSEC Practice Bulletins and Procedures for Their Issuance | |
| | ACRS Lives and GAAP | 11/23/81 |
| | Accounting by Colleges and Universities for Compensated Absences | 9/13/82 |
| | ADC Arrangements | 2/10/86 |
| 2. | Elimination of Profits Resulting from Intercompany Transfers of LIFO Inventories | 11/87 |
| 4. | Accounting for Foreign Debt/Equity Swaps | 5/88 |
| 5. | Income Recognition on Loans to Financially Troubled Countries | 7/88 |
| 6. | Amortization of Discounts on Certain Acquired Loans | 8/89 |
| 8. | Application of FASB Statement 97 to Insurance Enterprises | 11/90 |
| 11. | Accounting for Preconfirmation Contingencies in Fresh Start Reporting | 3/94 |
| 13. | Direct Response Advertising and Probable Future Benefits | 12/94 |
| 14. | Accounting and Reporting by Limited Liability Companies and Limited Liability Partnerships | 4/95 |
| 15. | Accounting by the Issuer of Surplus Notes | 1/95 |

**Web sites**

See page 26.

# 1 RESEARCHING GAAP MATTERS

## DEVELOPMENT OF GAAP

### What Is GAAP?

*The phrase "generally accepted accounting principles" is a technical accounting term that encompasses the conventions, rules, and procedures necessary to define accepted accounting practice at a particular time. It includes not only broad guidelines of general application, but also detailed practices and procedures. Those conventions, rules, and procedures provide a standard by which to measure financial presentations.* Auditing Standards Board (ASB), AU Section 411

Generally accepted accounting principles (GAAP) are concerned with the measurement of economic activity, the time when such measurements are to be made and recorded, the disclosures surrounding this activity, and the preparation and presentation of summarized economic information in the form of financial statements. GAAP develops when questions arise about how to best accomplish those objectives—measurement, timing of recognition, disclosure, or presentation. In response to those questions, GAAP is either prescribed in official pronouncements of authoritative bodies empowered to create it, or it originates over time through the development of customary practices that evolve when authoritative bodies fail to respond. Thus, GAAP is a reaction to and a product of the economic environment in which it develops. As such, the development of accounting and financial reporting standards has lagged the development and creation of increasingly intricate economic structures and transactions.

There are two broad categories of accounting principles—recognition and disclosure. Recognition principles determine the timing and measurement of items that enter the accounting cycle and impact the financial statements. These are quantitative standards that require economic information to be reflected numerically.

Disclosure principles deal with factors that are not always numeric. Disclosures involve qualitative information that is an essential ingredient of a full set of financial statements. Their absence would make the financial statements misleading by omitting information relevant to the decision-making needs of the reader. Disclosure principles complement recognition principles by explaining assumptions underlying the numerical information and providing additional information on accounting policies, contingencies, uncertainties, etc., which are essential to fully understand the performance and financial condition of the reporting enterprise.

### Who Created GAAP?

From time to time, the bodies given responsibility for the promulgation of GAAP have changed, and indeed more than a single such body has often shared this responsibility. GAAP established by all earlier standard-setting bodies, to the extent not withdrawn or superseded, remains in effect at the present time. These bodies are described in the following paragraphs.

**Committee on Accounting Procedure (CAP).** The first serious attempt to create formalized generally accepted accounting principles began in 1930, primarily as a consequence of the stock market crash of 1929 and the widespread perception that an absence of uniform and stringent financial reporting requirements had contributed to the rampant stock market speculation of the preceding decade that culminated with that crash. (Previously, GAAP had largely been defined by academic writings and general industry practices.) The American Institute of Accountants, (which in 1957 was renamed the American Institute of Certified Public Accountants [AICPA]), created a special committee to work with the New York Stock Exchange toward the goal of establishing standards for accounting procedures. The special committee recommended five rules to the Exchange that were published in 1938 as Accounting Research Bulletin (ARB) 1 of the Committee on Accounting Procedure. The Committee subsequently published 51 such bulletins, including Accounting Research Bulletin 43, which consolidated and superseded Bulletins 142. (A listing of the Accounting Research Bulletins and other standards that have not been completely superseded appears at the front of this publication, together with references to the pages of *Wiley GAAP* that discuss those pronouncements.) The Committee also attempted to achieve uniformity in accounting terminology. However, the Committee's limited resources and lack of serious research efforts in support of its pronouncements were questioned in the late 1950s, particularly as a number of very complex controversial topics loomed on the horizon.

**Accounting Principles Board.** The profession's response was to substitute, under its auspices, the Accounting Principles Board (APB) for the Committee on Accounting Procedure. This was done to facilitate the development of principles, which were to be based primarily on the research of a separate division of the AICPA, the Accounting Research Division. Under this strategy, the Division was to undertake extensive research, publish its findings, and then permit the Accounting Principles Board to take the lead in the discussions that would ensue concerning accounting principles and practices. The Board's authority was enforced primarily through prestige and Rule 203 of the AICPA Code of Professional Conduct. Furthermore, formal approval of Board issuances by the Securities and Exchange Commission (SEC) gave additional support to its activities.

During the Board's fourteen years of existence, it issued 31 authoritative opinions and 4 nonauthoritative statements. They dealt with amendments of Accounting Research Bulletins, opinions on the form and content of financial statements, and issuances requiring changes in both the recognition and disclosure principles of the profession. However, the Board did not make use of the efforts of the Accounting Research Division, which published fifteen research studies during its lifetime. Both the Board and the Division acted independently in selecting topics for their respective agendas. The Board issued pronouncements in areas where little research had been done, and the Division performed research studies without seeking to be all-inclusive or exhaustive in analysis. The Accounting Principles Board did not, ultimately, operate differently or more effectively than had the Committee on Accounting Procedure.

**Financial Accounting Standards Board.** As a result of these operational problems, in 1971 the AICPA appointed the "Wheat Study Group" chaired by Francis M. Wheat, a former SEC commissioner. The Wheat Study Group was charged with examining the standard-setting process and making recommendations regarding the form and structure of the standard-setting process as well as whether standard setting should reside in the government or in the private sector. Based on the recommendations of this group, the Financial Accounting Standards Board (FASB) was formed in 1972. The Board consists of seven full-time members; they have diverse backgrounds with three coming from public accounting, two from private industry, and one each from academia and from an oversight body. The Board is assisted by a staff of professionals who conduct research and work directly with the Board.

FASB is recognized as authoritative through Financial Reporting Release 1 of the Securities and Exchange Commission and through Rule 203 of the AICPA Code of Professional Conduct.

FASB is an independent body relying on the Financial Accounting Foundation for selection of its members and approval of its budgets. FASB is supported by the sale of its publications and by fees assessed on all public companies based on their market capitalizations. (The imposition of this fee was established by the Sarbanes-Oxley Act and replaces the voluntary private-sector contributions that previously supported the Foundation. The change was made to allay any public concerns about the FASB's perceived independence from contributors.) The Board of Trustees of the Foundation is composed of members of

> American Accounting Association
> American Institute of Certified Public Accountants
> CFA Institute
> Financial Executives International
> Government Finance Officers Association
> Institute of Management Accountants
> National Association of State Auditors, Comptrollers, and Treasurers
> Securities Industry Association

The Board issues several types of pronouncements.[1] The most important of these are Statements of Financial Accounting Standards and Interpretations, which are used to clarify or elaborate on existing Statements or pronouncements of predecessor bodies. Standards and Interpretations constitute category A GAAP, which also includes FASB staff positions—a relatively new form of guidance—and the Board's FAS 133 implementation issues. Technical Bulletins, which are category B GAAP, usually address issues not covered directly by existing standards and are primarily used to provide guidance where it is not expected to be costly or create a major change. Bulletins are discussed at Board meetings and subject to Board veto. Both Bulletins and Interpretations are designed to be responsive to implementation and practice problems on relatively narrow subjects (the last Bulletin was issued in 2001; that role will now apparently be filled by FASB staff positions, a substantial number of which have already been produced).

The FASB staff can issue implementation guides and staff positions, which are category D GAAP. In a question-and-answer format, implementation guides address specific questions that arise when a standard is initially issued. Staff positions are responses to questions on appropriate application of FASB literature that are expected to have widespread relevance. The questions addressed in implementation guides and staff positions are submitted by phone, letter, or through the FASB Web site's technical inquiry service. Implementation guides and staff positions are drafted by the staff and issued provided that a majority of the FASB Board members do not object. In addition, staff positions must be exposed on the FASB Web site for a 30-day comment period before issuance.

**American Institute of Certified Public Accountants (AICPA).** The Accounting Standards Executive Committee (AcSEC) is the senior technical committee at the AICPA. It is composed of fifteen volunteer members, representative of industry, academia, analysts, and both national and regional public accounting firms. All AcSEC members are CPAs and members of the AICPA.

AcSEC is authorized to set accounting standards and to speak for the AICPA on accounting matters. The accounting standards that AcSEC issues are prepared largely through the work of AICPA committees and task forces. AcSEC issues Statements of Position (SOPs) and industry audit and accounting guides, which are reviewed and cleared by the FASB and thus constitute category B GAAP. SOPs provide guidance on financial accounting and reporting issues. Industry audit and accounting guides provide guidance to auditors in examining and reporting on financial statements of entities in specific industries and provide standards on accounting problems unique to a particular industry. AcSEC Practice Bulletins (category C GAAP) usually provide guidance on very narrowly defined accounting issues. Until recently, the standards issued by AcSEC addressed topics broadly applicable to all industries in addition to industry-specific topics. Effective November 2002, FASB reclaimed the sole authority to promulgate general-purpose GAAP, relegating AcSEC to the issuance of industry-specific accounting and auditing standards.

---

[1] *To date, the FASB has issued 161 Statements on Financial Accounting Standards, 48 Interpretations, 51 Technical Bulletins, as well as over 60 Staff Positions and over 30 implementation compilations. In addition, FASB has devoted substantial time and resources toward developing a Conceptual Framework for Financial Accounting, which has resulted in the issuance of 7 Concepts Statements, 6 of which are still in effect and discussed later in this chapter. (FASB is currently pursuing a complete review of the Concepts Statements as part of its convergence efforts with IASB.) (Since a number of standards have been superseded or withdrawn, the number of standards, interpretations, etc., which remain in force are somewhat fewer than the total issued. The preponderance of currently effective GAAP is the product of the FASB, and not of its predecessors, although a number of such older standards remain in effect.)*

**Emerging Issues Task Force (EITF).** The Emerging Issues Task Force (EITF) was formed in 1984 by the FASB in order to assist the Board in identifying current or emerging issues and implementation problems before divergent practices become entrenched. The guidance provided is often on narrow issues that are of immediate interest and importance. Task Force members are drawn primarily from public accounting firms but also include individuals who would be aware of issues and practices that should be considered by the group. The Task Force meets every other month with nonvoting representatives of the SEC and the FASB attending for discussion purposes.

For each agenda item, an issues paper is developed by members, their firms, or the FASB staff. After discussion by the Task Force, a consensus may be reached on the issue, in which case the consensus is referred to the FASB for ratification at its next scheduled meeting. If no consensus is reached, the problem may end up on the Board agenda or be resolved by the SEC, or the issue will remain unresolved with no standard-setting organization currently considering it. These issues may be in especially narrow areas having little broad-based interest. Occasionally, FASB may include a narrow issue in the scope of a broader project and reaffirm or supersede the work of the Task Force.

FASB publishes a volume of EITF Abstracts, which are summaries of each issue paper and the results of Task Force discussion. The listing of Issues in the front section of *Wiley GAAP* identifies the status of all matters considered by EITF to the date of this publication.

Although EITF pronouncements are technically category C GAAP, they are so specialized that generally there is no category A or B GAAP covering the respective topics. The SEC believes that a Task Force consensus is GAAP for public companies, and they will question any accounting that differs from it. In addition, the SEC believes that the EITF supplies a public forum to discuss accounting concerns and assist in providing advice. Thus, they are supportive of the Task Force's work.

The EITF also previously published Discussion Issues, which are FASB staff announcements and SEC staff announcements regarding technical matters that are deemed important by the FASB or SEC staff, but that do not relate specifically to a numbered EITF issue. These announcements were designed to help provide guidance on the application of relevant accounting pronouncements. A listing of the EITF Discussion Issues, with a short summary of each, appears at the front of *Wiley GAAP*, following the listing of the EITF Issues. It is anticipated that no further discussion issues will be issued by EITF, however.

**Other sources.** Not all GAAP has resulted from a deliberative process and the issuance of pronouncements by authoritative bodies. Certain principles and practices evolved into current acceptability without adopted standards. For example, depreciation methods such as straight-line and declining balance are both acceptable, as are inventory costing methods such as LIFO and FIFO. There are, however, no definitive pronouncements that can be found to state this. Furthermore, there are many disclosure principles that evolved into general accounting practice because they were originally required by the SEC in documents submitted to them. Among these are reconciling the actual rate with the statutory rate used in determining income tax expense, when not otherwise obvious from the financial statements themselves. Even much of the content of balance sheets and income statements has evolved over the years without adopted standards.

Following about five years' effort, FASB essentially completed its project to codify GAAP, which will eliminate the multilevel hierarchy in favor of a bifurcation between authoritative and nonauthoritative guidance. In early 2008, FASB initiated a one-year verification phase of this Codification, during which time its constituents are being encouraged to provide feedback on whether its content accurately reflects existing US GAAP for nongovernmental entities. Until this trial period has elapsed, users have been advised that the Codification content has not been approved as authoritative and, therefore, users have been requested to verify research results using their existing resources for the currently effective literature.

As an interim step, the GAAP hierarchy, which has been defined in the auditing literature, was to be moved from SAS 69 to a new FASB standard. A "near-final draft" of this standard was published in September 2006. Changes from the present hierarchy were to include expanding the sources of category A GAAP to include accounting principles that are issued after being subject to FASB's due process.

According to this near-final FASB Statement, the proposed new hierarchy document is being considered because of the complexity of the long-standing hierarchy set forth by SAS 69, because that hierarchy was directed to auditors rather than reporting entities, and because of the anomaly of ranking FASB concepts statements lower than industry practices, although the former are subject to due process while the latter are not. The draft standard still relegates concepts statements to the lowest level in the five-level hierarchy, but gives these primacy over all others in that level.

A further provision of this draft standard holds that financial statements that depart materially from principles set forth in the GAAP hierarchy could not be represented as being in conformity with GAAP. This important change would apparently supersede the "Rule 203 exception" which allows for rare situations where departure from GAAP actually is believed warranted in the interest of fair presentation of the reporting entity's financial position or results of operations. (A similar "true and fair view" exception exists under IFRS.)

No further action has been taken on the proposed FASB statement on the GAAP hierarchy as of mid 2008.

## How Is GAAP Created?

The FASB and AICPA adhere to rigorous "due process" when creating new guidance in category A and category B GAAP. The goal is to involve constituents who would be affected by the newly issued guidance so that the standards created will result in information that reports economic activity as objectively as possible without attempting to influence behavior in any particular direction. Ultimately, however, the guidance is the judgment of the FASB or the AICPA, based on research, public input, and deliberation. The FASB's due process procedures are described below. The AICPA follows similar procedures in its projects.

The FASB receives requests for new standards from all parts of its diverse constituency, including auditors, industry groups, the EITF, and the SEC. Requests for action include both suggestions for new topics and suggestions for reconsideration of existing pronouncements. For each major project it adds to its technical agenda, the FASB begins by appointing an advisory task force of approximately fifteen outside experts. Care is taken to ensure that various points of view are represented on the task force. The task force meets with and advises the Board and staff on the definition and scope of the project and the nature and extent of any additional research that may be needed. The FASB and its staff then debate the significant issues in the project and arrive at tentative conclusions. As it does so, the FASB and its staff study existing literature on the subject and conduct or commission any additional research as needed. The task force meetings and the Board meetings are open to public observation and a public record is maintained. Many of these proceedings are also available by live or archived audio Webcast as well as via telephone.

If the accounting problem being considered by the Board is especially complex, the FASB will begin by publishing a Discussion Memorandum or another discussion document. The discussion document generally sets forth the definition of the problem, the scope of the project, and the financial accounting and reporting issues; discusses research findings and relevant literature; and presents alternative solutions to the issues under consideration and the arguments and implications relative to each. It is distributed to interested parties by request and is available on the FASB Web site. The document is prepared by the FASB staff with the advice and assistance of the task force. It specifies a deadline for written comments and often contains an invitation to present viewpoints at a public hearing.

Any individual or organization may request to speak at the public hearing, which is conducted by the FASB and the staff assigned to the project. Public observers are welcome. After each individual speaks, the FASB and staff ask questions. Questions are based on written material submitted by the speakers prior to the hearing as well as on the speaker's oral comments. In addition to the hearing, the staff analyzes all the written comments submitted. The FASB members study this analysis and read the comment letters to help them reach conclusions. The hearing transcript and written comments become part of the public record.

After the comment letters and oral presentations responding to the discussion document are considered, formal deliberations begin. (If the accounting problem is not as complex and no discussion document was issued, the due process begins at this point.) The FASB deliberates at meetings that are open to public observation, although observers do not participate in the discussions. The agenda for each meeting is announced in advance. Prior to each Board meeting, the staff presents a written analysis and recommendations of the issues to be discussed. During the meeting, the staff presents orally a summary of the written materials and the Board discusses each issue presented. The Board meets as many times as is necessary to resolve the issues.

When the Board has reached tentative conclusions on all the issues in the project, the staff prepares an Exposure Draft. The Exposure Draft sets forth the Board's conclusions about the proposed standards of financial accounting and reporting, the proposed effective date and method of transition, background information, and an explanation of the basis for the Board's conclusions. The Board reviews, and if necessary, revises, the Exposure Draft. Then, a vote is taken about whether the Exposure Draft can be published for public comment. A majority of the Board members must vote to approve an Exposure Draft for issuance for comment. If four votes are not obtained, the FASB holds additional meetings and redrafts the Exposure Draft.

Any individual or organization can provide comments about the conclusions in the Exposure Draft during the exposure period, which is generally sixty days or more. The Board may also decide to have a public hearing to hear constituents' views. At the conclusion of the comment period, all comment letters and oral presentations are analyzed by the staff, and the Board members read the letters and the staff analysis. Then, the Board is ready to re-deliberate the issues, with the goal of issuing final accounting standards.

As in the earlier process, all Board meetings are open to the public. During these meetings, the Board considers the comments received and may revise their earlier conclusions. If substantial modifications are made, the Board will issue a revised Exposure Draft for additional public comment. If so, the Board also may decide that another public hearing is necessary. When the Board is satisfied that all reasonable alternatives have been adequately considered, the staff drafts a final pronouncement for the Board's vote. Four votes are required for adoption of a pronouncement. Once issued, the standards become GAAP after the effective date stated in the pronouncement.

## The Hierarchy of GAAP

Under GAAP as it has been constituted over a number of decades, a number of standard-setting and standard-interpreting bodies (including, as of mid-2008, FASB, AICPA's AcSEC, and EITF) issue pronouncements which have, to varying degrees, the force of requirements that financial statement preparers must follow. The multiplicity of standard-setting entities made it necessary to set forth a hierarchy, so that preparers and auditors would have a set of behavioral rules to follow in selecting from overlapping or seemingly contradictory rules. This hierarchy was actually set forth by the auditing literature, but will be replaced by an interim accounting standard (probably in 2008) and, shortly thereafter, will be made moot by the promulgation of the codification of GAAP. Under the forthcoming codification, all extant standards will be incorporated into a single document, and former distinctions among levels of the GAAP hierarchy will be eliminated. Future GAAP pronouncements will be styled as modifications to or replacements of existing portions of this codification, and will not exist as freestanding standards, interpretations, amendments, or staff positions. This will represent a very fundamental change to the structure of the body of GAAP, and will require substantial changes to how preparers and others undertake to stay abreast of evolving GAAP.

Under precodification GAAP, the determination of which accounting principle is applicable under a particular set of conditions requires an appreciation of the hierarchy of GAAP. The hierarchy was developed to assist the researcher in identifying the different sources of GAAP and to provide a means of resolving potential conflicts between standards by providing differing levels of authority. In AU 411 (SAS 69), the ASB identified the following as the sources of established generally accepted accounting principles:

A. Accounting principles promulgated by a body designated by the AICPA Council to establish such principles, pursuant to rule 203 [ET section 203.01] of the AICPA Code of Professional Conduct.

B. Pronouncements of bodies, composed of expert accountants, that deliberate accounting issues in public forums for the purpose of establishing accounting principles or describing existing accounting practices that are generally accepted, provided those pronouncements have been exposed for public comment and have been cleared by a body referred to in category A.

C. Pronouncements of bodies, organized by a body referred to in category A and composed of expert accountants, that deliberate accounting issues in public forums for the purpose of interpreting or establishing accounting principles or describing existing accounting practices that are generally accepted, or pronouncements referred to in category B that have been cleared by a body referred to in category A but have not been exposed for public comment.

D. Practices or pronouncements that are widely recognized as being generally accepted because they represent prevalent practice in a particular industry, or the knowledgeable application to specific circumstances of pronouncements that are generally accepted.

Compliance with accounting pronouncements included in category A is mandatory. Auditors are not to express an unqualified opinion on financial statements if the financial statements contain a material departure from category A pronouncements unless, due to unusual circumstances, adherence to the pronouncements would make the statements misleading. Rule 203 implies that application of officially established accounting principles almost always results in fair presentation in conformity with generally accepted accounting principles, but this is not an absolute prohibition of departures from promulgated GAAP.

If an accounting treatment is not specified by a pronouncement covered by Rule 203, accountants and auditors are required to progress through the hierarchy to categories B, C, or D, in that sequence, and use the treatment specified by the source in the highest category. If an accounting pronouncement in category B, C, or D is relevant to the circumstances, accountants or auditors must follow that pronouncement or be able to justify the conclusion that another treatment is generally accepted.

Departures from promulgated GAAP justified as being necessary in order for the financial statements to not be misleading (the so-called "Rule 203 exception") have been very rarely observed in practice, but are clearly permitted under current standards. As of mid-2008, survival of this exception is in doubt, since the proposed FASB statement on the GAAP hierarchy would eliminate this exception. That is, departures from promulgated GAAP would cause financial statements to be deemed not in conformity with GAAP and, if the effect of the departure is material, not worthy of an unqualified auditors' opinion. Note that there are two reasons for the likely removal of this option. First, it pertains to the auditors' expression of an opinion, and not, as currently constituted, to the preparers' selection among accounting principles or methods. Second, in order for US GAAP to converge with IFRS (which does not have an exact equivalent to this exception), it was deemed necessary to eliminate it.

For financial statements of entities other than governmental entities[2]

a. Category A, officially established accounting principles, consists of Financial Accounting Standards Board (FASB) Statements of Financial Accounting Standards (denoted as FAS in this book) and Interpretations (denoted as FIN), Accounting Principles Board (APB) Opinions, and AICPA Accounting Research Bulletins (ARB). As discussed later in this chapter, FASB has proposed that its FASB Staff Positions (FSP) and Derivatives Implementation Group Issues (DIG) also be classified in Category A.

b. Category B consists of FASB Technical Bulletins (FTB) and, if cleared by the FASB, AICPA Industry Audit and Accounting Guides and AICPA Statements of Position (SOP).

---

[2] *The description of a governmental entity, which was agreed to in a joint meeting of the FASB and GASB Boards in 1996, states*

> *Public corporations and bodies corporate and politic are governmental organizations. Other organizations are governmental organizations if they have one or more of the following characteristics:*
>
> a. *Popular election of officers or appointment (or approval) of a controlling majority of the members of the organization's governing body by officials of one or more state or local governments;*
> b. *The potential for unilateral dissolution by a government with the net assets reverting to a government; or*
> c. *The power to enact and enforce a tax levy.*
>
> *Furthermore, organizations are presumed to be governmental if they have the ability to issue directly (rather than through a state or municipal authority) debt that pays interest exempt from federal taxation. However, organizations possessing only that ability (to issue tax-exempt debt) and none of the other governmental characteristics may rebut the presumption that they are governmental if their determination is supported by compelling relevant evidence.*

*This publication does not describe GAAP for governmental entities. Readers interested in learning more should consult the publication* **Wiley GAAP for Governments.**

    c.   Category C consists of AICPA Accounting Standards Executive Committee (AcSEC) Practice Bulletins (PB) that have been cleared by the FASB and consensus positions of the FASB Emerging Issues Task Force (EITF).

    d.   Category D includes AICPA accounting interpretations (AIN), implementation guides (Qs and As) published by the FASB staff, and practices that are widely recognized and prevalent either generally or in the industry.

If financial statement preparers are unable to locate relevant guidance using one of the above sources of established accounting principles, other accounting literature may be considered. These sources include FASB Statements of Financial Accounting Concepts, AICPA Issues Papers, International Financial Reporting Standards of the International Accounting Standards Board and of its predecessor, the International Accounting Standards Committee, Governmental Accounting Standards Board (GASB) Statements, Interpretations and Technical Bulletins, Federal Accounting Standards Advisory Board (FASAB) Statements, Interpretations, and Technical Bulletins, pronouncements of other professional associations or regulatory agencies, Technical Information Service Inquiries and Replies included in AICPA Technical Practice Aids, and accounting textbooks, handbooks and articles. The use of those other sources depends upon their relevance to the particular circumstances, the specificity of the guidance, and the general recognition of the author or issuing organization as an authority. This would mean that FASB publications in this category are to be considered more influential in establishing an acceptable accounting practice than an accounting textbook. Relying on guidance in this category requires the exercise of professional judgment and a broader search of literature sources than would be true in the other four categories.

Note, in particular, that the FASB Concepts Statements are not included in the levels A-D of the GAAP hierarchy, at present. Thus, the guidance in those statements do not take precedence over the various promulgated GAAP. Nonetheless, SAS 69 (current source of the hierarchy) identifies the Concepts Statements as the first of the group of other literature that should be consulted to guide practice in the absence of definitive guidance from a source explicitly cited in the hierarchy. The proposed adoption of a GAAP hierarchy by FASB, superseding that found in the current auditing literature, would effectively elevate the Concepts Statements to level A GAAP. (Note further that FASB is currently reviewing the six extant Concepts Statements with the announced intention of producing a new conceptual framework document.)

Readers should pay close attention to both the relocation of the GAAP hierarchy from the auditing to the accounting literature, and to the replacement of the GAAP hierarchy by the codification. If (as expected) the codification is approved by FASB, all GAAP references will change, not merely for new pronouncements, but for the entire extant body of GAAP. Future editions of this book will reflect such changes when they become official.

## Materiality

Materiality as a concept has great significance in understanding, researching, and implementing GAAP. Each Statement of Financial Accounting Standards (FAS) issued by the FASB concludes by stating that the provisions of the statement are not applicable to immaterial items.

Materiality is defined by the FASB as the magnitude of an omission or misstatement in the financial statements that makes it probable that a reasonable person relying on those financial statements would have been influenced by the omitted information or made a different judgment if the correct information had been known. However, due to its inherent subjectivity, the definition does not provide definitive guidance in distinguishing material information from immaterial information. The individual accountant must exercise professional judgment in evaluating information and concluding on its materiality. Materiality as a criterion has both quantitative and qualitative aspects, and items should not be deemed *immaterial* unless all potentially applicable quantitative and qualitative aspects are given full consideration and found not relevant.

Quantitatively, materiality has been defined in relatively few pronouncements, which is a testament to the great difficulty of setting precise measures for materiality. For example, in FAS 131, *Disclosures about Segments of an Enterprise and Related Information,* a material segment or customer is defined as representing 10% or more of the reporting entity's revenues (although, even given this rule, qualitative considerations may cause smaller segments to be deemed reportable). The Securities and Exchange Commission has in various of its pronouncements defined materiality as 1% of total assets for receivables from officers and stockholders, 5% of total assets for separate balance sheet disclosure of items, and 10% of total revenue for disclosure of oil and gas producing activities.

Although materiality judgments have traditionally been primarily based on quantitative assessments, the nature of a transaction or event can affect a determination of whether that transaction or event is material. For example, a transaction that, if recorded, changes a profit to a loss or changes compliance with ratios in a debt covenant to noncompliance would be material even if it involved an otherwise immaterial amount. Also, a transaction that might be judged immaterial if it occurred as part of routine operations may be material if its occurrence helps meet certain objectives. For example, a transaction that allows management to achieve a target or obtain a bonus that otherwise would not become due would be considered material, regardless of the actual amount involved.

Another factor in judging materiality is the degree of precision that may be attained when making an estimate. For example, accounts payable can usually be estimated more accurately than a possible loss from the incurrence of an asset retirement obligation. An error that would be material in estimating accounts payable might be acceptable in estimating the retirement obligation.

Certain events or transactions may be deemed material because of their nature, regardless of the dollar amounts involved, and thus require disclosure under any circumstances. Offers to buy or sell assets for more or less than book value, litigation proceedings against the company pursuant to price-fixing or antitrust allegations, and active negotiations regarding their settlement can have a material impact on the enterprise's future profitability and, thus, are all examples of items that would not be capable of being evaluated for materiality based solely upon numerical calculations.

It is clear that materiality, as traditionally defined by the accounting and auditing establishment, may no longer align with the definition implicitly applied by financial statement users, including the SEC and other regulatory authorities. Given the epidemic of financial reporting frauds in the late 1990s and early 2000s, it became clear that a more nuanced and complex definition of materiality was probably required. In general, a decision regarding the application of GAAP (e.g., the choice of a nonstandard costing or revenue recognition method for a particular transaction) should be viewed as being immaterial only if all conceivable effects, such as the impact on common financial statement ratios or trends, are expected to be truly immaterial. A strict application of a quantitative threshold—say, 5% of net income—should be avoided, and once a materiality level is established, it should be strictly maintained in the face of identified errors or warranted adjustments in amounts greater than what had been defined.

The SEC, in its Staff Accounting Bulletin 99 (SAB 99), provides a useful discussion of this issue. Although not strictly applicable to nonpublic preparers of financial statements, this guidance is worthy of consideration by all accountants and auditors. Among other things, SAB 99 notes that deliberate application of nonacceptable accounting methods cannot be justified merely because the impact on the financial statements is deemed to be immaterial. SAB 99 also usefully reminds preparers and others that materiality has both quantitative and qualitative dimensions, which must both be given full consideration. More recently, Staff Accounting Bulletin 108 (SAB 108) has added to the literature of materiality with its discussion of considerations applicable to prior period restatements. (See discussion in Chapter 5.)

### The Crisis of Confidence Regarding GAAP

Over approximately the past decade, GAAP as a body of standards, and the standard-setting process itself, have increasingly come under attack. A notable string of accounting scandals unfolded in the late 1990s and early 2000s, and as one consequence the entire US financial reporting system was put under the microscope by the nation's leaders, the international financial community, the media, and the general public. What resulted was not only landmark legislation in the form of the Sarbanes-Oxley Act, but also a thorough and ongoing self-examination undertaken by all accountants—from CEOs to auditors to regulators to standard setters.

In 2001, Enron Corp., one of the world's biggest companies at the time, publicly acknowledged that it had failed to comply with existing accounting requirements in at least two areas—sales of stock to special-purpose entities (SPE) and nonconsolidation of certain SPE. This noncompliance caused material overstatements of assets, shareholders' equity, and net income, and the concealment of substantial debt obligations for several years. As a result, Enron's stock price fell to under twenty-five cents per share. As the ensuing events unfolded, public policy discussions and media criticisms of GAAP, of standard setting in the private sector, and of the accounting profession reached unprecedented levels. The criticisms centered primarily on the failure of financial statements to warn investors of the impending collapse of Enron, and on the lack of independence and objectivity of a self-regulating profession that offers both consulting and auditing services to its clients.

Numerous other high-profile business failures and accounting scandals also occurred or came to light during this period. Many involved aggressive accounting by large, formerly well-regarded entities. A watershed event was the revelation of massive $11 billion fraud by WorldCom, which led directly to the enactment of the far-reaching Sarbanes-Oxley Act.

**The Sarbanes-Oxley Act of 2002.** The result of these business failures and accounting scandals was the Sarbanes-Oxley Act, which included among its provisions the following sweeping changes:

1.  Established the Public Company Accounting Oversight Board (PCAOB), to oversee the audits of public companies that are subject to the securities laws of the United States (referred to as "issuers") and to establish auditing, quality control, ethics, independence, and other standards relating to the auditing of the financial statements of issuers. Three of the five PCAOB members cannot be and must not have been certified public accountants.

2.  Placed severe limits on an audit firm's ability to provide nonaudit services to its issuer audit clients.

3.  Established a requirement that the CEO and the CFO of each issuer certify in each periodic report to the SEC

    a.  The appropriateness of the financial statements and disclosures and
    b.  That those financial statements and disclosures fairly present, in all material respects, the operational and financial condition of the issuer.

4. Required the SEC to conduct a study of off-balance-sheet transactions and the use of special-purpose entities, and to report its recommendations to Congress.
5. Required the GAO to conduct a study regarding the consolidation of public accounting firms since 1989, including the present and future impact of the consolidation, and the solutions to any problems it discovers.

Another important provision of the Sarbanes-Oxley Act, set forth in Section 404, increases corporate management's responsibility for assessing the effectiveness of internal control over financial reporting. Operational management, as well as financial management, must be more cognizant of their joint responsibility for quality financial reporting. Management's methods for assessing internal control will, and should, vary from company to company. Corporate management must assess the risk of material financial statement misstatement along two dimensions: (1) Inherent risk—the susceptibility of one or more financial statement assertions to a material misstatement, and (2) Fraud risk—the risk of material misstatement due to fraudulent financial reporting or theft of assets.

The principal regulatory focus of the Sarbanes-Oxley Act is on auditors and corporate management, which is appropriate because the Enron, WorldCom, and other scandals were primarily the result of management fraud and audit failures, rather than faulty accounting standards. However, there are several requirements of the Act that have the possibility of affecting GAAP and its standards setters.

First, the Act defines the required characteristics of an accounting standards-setting body. For the time being, standards will continue to be set by FASB, as the SEC reaffirmed in 2003 that it will continue to acknowledge FASB's pronouncements as being generally accepted. However, FASB is expected to announce some changes to demonstrate that it "has adopted procedures to ensure prompt consideration, by majority vote of its members, of changes to accounting principles necessary to reflect emerging accounting issues and changing business practices" and "considers, in adopting accounting principles. . . the extent to which international convergence on high quality accounting standards is necessary or appropriate."

Second, the Act requires that the SEC conduct a study on the adoption by the United States financial reporting system of a principles-based accounting system. The study

> *shall include an examination of—(i) the extent to which principles-based accounting and financial reporting exists in the United States; (ii) the length of time required for change from a rules-based to a principles-based financial reporting system; (iii) the feasibility of and proposed methods by which a principles-based system may be implemented; and (iv) a thorough economic analysis of the implementation of a principles-based system.*

That study was released in 2003 and can be found on the Special Studies section of the SEC's Web site (www.sec.gov). Briefly, it found that the oft-cited distinction between rules-based and principles-based standards was largely illusory, inasmuch as high-quality financial reporting standards must be (and have generally been) based on sound principles, but that a pure, principles-only set of standards, without practical guidance, would not serve the public interest.

**Principles-based standards.** Some have suggested that rules-based accounting standards contributed to the Enron, WorldCom and other collapses. It is true that certain detailed rules found under US GAAP (e.g., capital lease requirements such as the 90% test) have encouraged carefully constructed evasions (e.g., 89% leases), which often provoke even more detailed rules, followed by yet more "engineered" transactions and reporting stratagems. Some observers suggested that the answer to the problems of "gaming the rules" and the ever-increasing complexity of resulting standards might have been found in embracing a principles-based, as opposed to a rules-based, approach to standards setting. To some (limited) extent, the standards published by the International Accounting Standards Board exhibited that characteristic, and some therefore argued that a movement toward principles-based standards might be facilitated by the convergence of US GAAP and international standards.

The idea of a principles-based approach to US standard setting is not new. FASB's conceptual framework, summarized later in this chapter, contains the body of principles that underlies US accounting and reporting. The FASB has used the conceptual framework in developing its accounting standards for more than twenty years. However, FASB has sometimes bowed to pressure to provide exceptions to its principles in order to achieve "desired" accounting results (e.g., to limit the volatility of reported earnings, as with current pension accounting requirements under FAS 87). Indeed, it is probably the existence of multiple exceptions to the promulgated standards, more than any failure to ground these in general principles, that has opened the door to various reporting practices that, in certain circumstances, permitted the conduct of financial reporting frauds.

If a principles-based approach were implemented by FASB, accounting standards would continue to be developed from the conceptual framework (which is currently under revision), but the principles would apply more broadly than under existing standards. That is, there would be fewer exceptions to the principles in the standards. In addition, FASB, EITF, and AICPA would provide less interpretive and implementation guidance for applying the standards because the overall principle would ostensibly provide the necessary foundation for the answer with such guidance being considered superfluous. Exceptions would be extremely limited under a principles-based approach. In addition, a principles-based approach requires accountants to exercise good professional judgment and to resist the urge to seek specific answers and rulings on every implementation issue. It also would require that the SEC and users of financial information accept the consequences of applying professional judgment, which means there would undoubtedly be some divergence in practice, resulting in some loss of comparability of the financial statements of reporting enterprises.

FASB issued for public comment a proposal for a principles-based approach to US standard setting in 2002, followed by a public roundtable meeting with respondents to the proposal. Many respondents agreed on the need for standards that emphasize principles over detailed rules and report the economic substance of transactions or events. However, many concluded that complex rules are primarily driven by increasingly complex economic transactions (e.g., the explosive growth in the use of hedging and financial derivatives), and that there is no way to return to a simpler time or to simpler GAAP. Also, many respondents expressed concern about using principles-based standards in the current legal and regulatory-environment. The well-known penchant for litigation means that, as former Federal Reserve Board Chairman Paul Volcker observed, "(T)he American tradition is to have clear and definite rules, so firms can defend themselves from the hoards of lawyers who stand ready to sue auditors for making a bad judgment."

As of mid-2008, it appears that the debate over rules- or principles-based standards may be implicitly resolved by either the full convergence of US GAAP with IFRS or, in what was formerly thought to be unlikely but which is now deemed to be a very real possibility, having IFRS supersede US GAAP. The fact that well over 100 other nations have opted to endorse IFRS (at least for publicly held companies' financial reporting), with as many as another 50 taking steps to have IFRS supersede their respective national GAAP regimes, coupled with the possible granting of permission for IFRS-based reporting by US companies registered with the SEC, makes this further development increasingly probable, in the authors' view.

**Standards overload.** The recent criticisms of rules-based standards join earlier criticisms about the complexity of accounting standards. Some accountants complain about "standards overload," saying that there are too many accounting standards, which are individually too complex to be understood and implemented, and that too many organizations (SEC, FASB, EITF, AICPA, etc.) are empowered to issue these pronouncements. Complaints regarding standards overload are not new, and with about 161 FASB Statements and myriad other standards (including hundreds of EITF Issues), these complaints must be given credence. However, the solution, if there is one, is not obvious. Nor is it clear that financial reporting frauds, audit failures, or other such phenomena have been the result of this overload. Overwhelmingly, frauds result from the deliberate misapplication of GAAP, and not from an inability on the part of preparers and auditors to comprehend the requirements of the standards.

Some say that a solution would be to reduce and simplify GAAP, especially for entities having characteristics suggesting that the risk of misleading the users of the financial statements might be low. For example, some recommend a size test, with smaller entities following a subset of the standards that are mandated for larger entities (a system now used in the UK, and being proposed by IASB as well). Even this simple suggestion has complications, however; size could arguably be determined by assets, revenues, net worth, or number of owners. Others recommend that public entities, regardless of size, follow a more comprehensive set of standards than privately owned businesses.

Those who disagree say that differing standards would reduce the quality of financial reporting. For example, if decisions about which entities should follow which standards were made using a single criterion for all standards (such as size or ownership), some entities that engage heavily in a certain type of transaction (e.g., derivative financial instruments) might not be subject to the standards for that transaction—even though the recognition, measurement, and disclosure of those transactions was critical to understanding the financial condition and results of operations of the entity. To solve that problem, criteria would need to be based in some way on the underlying subject matter of the standard, which would result in an accountant having to examine each standard to determine if it would apply to a particular entity. That could compound the standards overload problem rather than solve it.

This so-called "big GAAP vs. little GAAP" debate has raged off and on for many decades. When advocates of differential standards are challenged, however, they typically have been unable to identify alternative recognition or measurement principles for large (or public) entities vs. those for smaller (or privately held) entities. Generally, at best, certain disclosures are cited as candidates for slimming down in financial statements of the smaller or private companies. The proposed IASB standard for nonpublicly accountable reporting entities (inaccurately being referred to as smaller and medium-sized entities) would eliminate some alternative but acceptable practices, but would nonetheless allow those entities access to the full range of acceptable practices if so desired. In short, there may be less than meets the eye to this entire controversy.

In fact, the FASB has endeavored in recent years to offer somewhat differentiated standards for disclosures. FAS 126 exempts nonpublic companies from certain financial instrument disclosures if the entity's total assets are less than $100 million and the entity has not held or issued any derivative financial instruments. Nonpublic companies also are not required to disclose earnings per share (FAS 128), segment information (FAS 131), or certain pension and postretirement information (FAS 132R). These exemptions have not, however, been widely hailed as representing significant progress against the perceived problem of standards overload.

To obtain better insight into these issues, in early 2004, the AICPA formed a Private Company Financial Reporting Task Force and charged it with conducting empirical research on the needs of preparers and users of private company financial statements and how well

GAAP was meeting those needs, and developing recommendations based upon the results of the study.

The results of its research were mixed. As should have been expected, there were significant perceptual differences between the owner/managers of reporting entities, independent CPA practitioners, and external users. For example, when asked if they would consider it useful for GAAP reporting to be different in certain respects for small companies, the owner/managers' "yes" responses averaged between 57% and 62% (depending on size of their companies), the practitioners' responses between 73% and 77%, the sureties 44%, investors/venture capital firms 46%, and lender/creditors 69%. These results show the tension that exists in the marketplace between financial statement users' voracious needs for information provided for their decision-making purposes on the one hand, and the expense borne by the reporting entities responsible for preparing those financial statements and for obtaining independent assurance on them on the other hand.

The results of the Task Force's research indicated a moderately high to high rating regarding the overall value of GAAP financial statements to users (primarily lenders, sureties, and equity investors). However, many GAAP accounting or disclosure requirements were rated low by all of the constituents with respect to relevance or usefulness in decision making. These included such topics as pension and postretirement plans; variable interest entities, and share-based payments (FAS123[R] had not yet become effective when the survey was conducted). Based on this and other data revealed by their study, the Task Force concluded that these particular requirements were not meeting the needs of the various constituents of private company reporting and that this would support the need for development of differential GAAP.

In the authors' opinion, this conclusion is based on incomplete information, and we believe that if a similar research study were conducted by polling preparers, auditors, and users of large and public company financial statements, most or all of these same GAAP requirements would be identified as being of limited relevance and usefulness. That is, the authors believe the fundamental problem to be more universal than just "big GAAP/little GAAP." A more holistic reexamination of the GAAP reporting model is necessary in the light of an environment that includes such rampant abuses as earnings manipulation and many other visible failures of GAAP financial statements to fully and truthfully inform stakeholders about the precariousness of their investments.

In addition to the recommendation regarding differential GAAP, the Task Force also recommended changes to the standard-setting model to address the needs of private companies and offered alternatives such as

- Changing the composition of FASB and the Financial Accounting Foundation (FAF) to increase participation from the private company financial statement community
- FAF establishment of a private company standards setter under its jurisdiction
- Creation of a private company standards setter outside the jurisdiction of the FAF

In early 2008, certain of these changes came to fruition, when FAF announced that, as of mid-2008, membership of FASB was to be reduced to five from seven, with simple majority voting being retained. The issue of greater involvement by the financial statement community has been dealt with, in a fashion, by requiring that board members possess investment experience broadly defined. The membership of the oversight body, FAF, is to be optionally increased, and the number and breadth of organizations invited to nominate their trustees will be expanded.

**FASB initiatives.** In 2002, FASB embarked on a multiple-year, phased initiative to simplify and codify GAAP and make it more easily searchable and retrievable. As noted above, this effort has resulted in a draft codification being made available for user testing in 2008, with full implementation expected by 2009.

In another part of the project, FASB has attempted to reduce the complexity of accounting standards by reducing the number of standard-setting bodies that issue authoritative accounting pronouncements. FASB changed the process of the EITF to give FASB more direct involvement with its agenda, deliberations, and conclusions. Two FASB board members were added to the EITF Agenda Committee and FASB is now required to ratify each EITF consensus at a public board meeting before the consensus officially becomes GAAP. Also, FASB and the AICPA agreed that AcSEC would cease issuing Statements of Position that create broadly applicable GAAP, instead limiting its work to specialized industry accounting standards. FASB intends to collaborate with representatives from the EITF, AICPA, and SEC to develop a model for deciding if additional authoritative standards are necessary on a given topic and then how to most effectively segregate duties among those bodies with respect to issuing those standards.

FASB also wants to more thoroughly assess the cost-benefit relationships of proposed standards; presumably, complex standards are more costly to implement, and thus the costs are more likely to outweigh the expected benefits to users. If so, enactment would be less probable. To understand the costs of a proposed standard, FASB intends to actively engage its constituents in a discussion of the costs as a formal step in the Board's due process. To understand more fully the benefits of a proposed standard, FASB has created a User Advisory Council, a group of forty professionals representing a variety of investment and analytical disciplines, which will be consulted on specific projects as well as helping the Board formulate its overall agenda. During 2004, FASB also established a Small Business Advisory Committee (SBAC) in order to obtain additional needed input from its small business constituents.

In 2005, the FASB and AICPA separately issued Exposure Drafts proposing to move the nongovernmental GAAP Hierarchy, discussed earlier in this chapter, from the auditing literature to the accounting literature. In connection with this change, the Exposure Drafts also designated FASB Staff Positions (FSP) and Derivatives Implementation Group Issues (DIG) as "Level A" GAAP.

FASB acknowledged that this proposal (still not finalized as of mid-2008) was transitional in nature. Its long-range plan was to reduce the number of levels in the hierarchy to just two, authoritative and nonauthoritative, and this will be achieved when the codification is finally promulgated. In addition, at the conclusion of its current projects on codification and retrieval and on its conceptual framework, FASB expects to address any inconsistencies in guidance that make the current four-tier structure necessary and to address the role of its Statements of Financial Accounting Concepts in the hierarchy.

Although these FASB initiatives are viewed by many as a step in the right direction, it remains to be seen whether they successfully answer criticisms of standards overload. The financial environment is increasingly complex and litigious, which makes a lessening of the burden of GAAP unlikely in the near term.

**IASB initiatives.** While the debate in the US continues over the need for simplified "small GAAP," the international standard setter, IASB, has proposed a comprehensive standard that would (much like an earlier, and apparently successful, UK GAAP initiative) capture the key guidance for entities having no public reporting responsibilities (of whatever size), streamlining some existing standards and culling alternatives that are deemed, for whatever reason, nonapplicable to these nonpublic reporting entities. A controversial proposal, the Exposure Draft (available at www.iasb.org/Current+Projects/IASB+Projects/Small +Mediumsized+Entities/Exposure+Drafts+forSmall+Mediumsized+Entities.htm) was open for comments until October 1, 2007, and is still being debated as of mid-2008. It is highly likely that the SME proposal, or a close approximation thereof, will be enacted before year-end 2008. The strongest argument against this (or any similar) proposal is that it is the natures of the business transactions (e.g., those involving derivatives, guarantees, compound instruments having attributes of debt and equity) that should dictate the required accounting, and that even smaller or nonpublic entities engaging in such transactions should be bound by proper financial reporting standards. On the other side of the argument are those who claim that modern GAAP has become too complex for preparers, auditors, and users, particularly when addressing financial statements of smaller, less-sophisticated companies, thus justifying the use of streamlined standards.

**The AICPA and its diminished influence.** In the aftermath of the various financial reporting scandals previously discussed, many in the business and accounting communities criticized the AICPA for not proactively and forthrightly acknowledging systematic shortcomings in both the financial reporting and auditing realms and for not taking a visible leadership role in developing proposed solutions regarding their remediation. This perception that the AICPA was "sitting on the sidelines" as these scandals unfolded undoubtedly contributed to the creation, by the Sarbanes-Oxley Act, of the Public Company Accounting Oversight Board and its charge to oversee the auditing profession with respect to the audits of issuers. The PCAOB assumed the AICPA's previous responsibilities for ethics, independence, quality control, continuing professional education, peer review, and auditing standards as they relate to auditors of public company issuers.

Under these circumstances, the AICPA was (and still is) in danger of being rendered irrelevant as a standard setter and, no less, as a standard bearer for the profession. Its auditing standards board (ASB) has continued to issue pronouncements that are binding on auditors of nonissuers while the PCAOB has diverged from the AICPA's auditing standards by issuing its own standards. This provides fodder for debate regarding the advisability of "big GAAS, little GAAS." To the detriment of the auditing profession, the ultimate resolution of this conflict might be left to the judiciary if, as is quite conceivable, a nonissuer audit failure is alleged to have occurred that the plaintiff alleges might have been prevented had the auditor followed the PCAOB standards instead of the Auditing Standards Board standards.

**Alleged harmful effects of standards.** In general, reporting entities have not welcomed proposals for new standards, since these inevitably involve change, costs of implementation, and, perhaps, a period of confusion while the marketplace assimilates the new information. In addition, the business community often claims that FASB does not understand the economic impact of new standards on their businesses. It complains that the implementation of certain accounting standards will harm business' ability to compete in the global marketplace and will impede its ability to raise debt or equity capital on favorable terms.

Two early examples of such resistance were the issuance of FAS 43 (compensated absences) and FAS 106 (postretirement benefits). In both cases, the business community said that the new standard would force it to reduce benefits to employees—and in some cases it did just that. The counterargument was perhaps more impressive, however: as a consequence of formerly failing to fully account for the actual economics of promises made or benefits granted, companies were misled regarding their true financial condition, which, once exposed, resulted in changes in behavior that were arguably long overdue. Managers were harmed by their former ignorance and by the delay; they were not hurt by the truth. (Proposed changes to accounting for pensions and other postemployment benefits, discussed in Chapter 16, will inevitably also trigger much anguish and again, quite possibly, reductions in promised benefits).

In two recent cases, dissatisfaction with proposed standards escalated to the point where the business community asked the federal government to intervene. When, in the mid-1990s, FASB proposed that the value of stock options granted to employees be reflected as an expense in the financial statements, the business community, and particularly technology firms, loudly claimed that the proposed recognition would have a dramatic and negative economic effect. First, the argument went, it would force them to discontinue issuing stock options, which would prevent the companies from compensating valuable employees. Second, to the extent options were granted and reflected in expense, it would cause the firms' costs of capital to increase significantly because of lower levels of reported profitability. Finally, it would put US firms at a competitive disadvantage to foreign companies that did not have to expense the value of stock options (or were not offering this benefit to employees).

Before that battle ended, "sense of the House" and "sense of the Senate" resolutions had been introduced, objecting to FASB's tentative conclusions, and a bill had been introduced that would have, if enacted, precluded the recognition of the value of stock options as an expense as a matter of law. This debate threatened not only the stock-based compensation standard, but also the future of accounting standard setting in the private sector itself. That concern contributed to FASB's decision to issue FAS 123 with only a requirement for disclosure of the value of stock options, with recognition and measurement optionally continuing under prior (APB 25) rules. Not surprisingly, virtually all publicly held companies continued to utilize the "implicit value" approach of APB 25, even though FAS 123 clearly stated that the "fair value" approach was preferable GAAP. (Interestingly, after the Enron and WorldCom scandals, and the resulting Sarbanes-Oxley legislation, some companies began to voluntarily expense options, and FASB responded by issuing an Exposure Draft in March 2004, later finalized as FAS123(R), that requires companies to expense share-based compensation.

Later, when FASB was pursuing its derivative financial instruments project, the business community again approached the Congress with a request for it to intercede in the debate. Although the federal government was not as quick to intervene in this instance, FASB was again criticized by several members of Congress and by their staff. To have been thus criticized and, in part, thwarted by influential government officials twice in a span of five years might have proved to be detrimental as the Congress considered legislation in response to the collapse of Enron Corp. However, standard setting in the private sector, and the supremacy of FASB in the standard-setting role, appear to have survived those challenges, at least for the immediate future. It remains to be seen how, if at all, convergence with—or possible supersession by—IFRS might be responded to by those who wish to see a more prominent role by government in the financial reporting standard-setting sphere.

## The Business Reporting Research Project

Beginning in 1998, FASB undertook research on business reporting (which has been defined to include both financial and nonfinancial information), with the goal of identifying the types of information businesses were already voluntarily providing, and the means used to deliver it.

FASB produced four reports setting forth results of this project as follows:

1.  *Update of Electronic Distribution of Business Reporting Information—Survey of Business Reporting Research Information on Companies' Internet Sites (May 2002)*, an update of the report issued in 2000, which describes the reporting of business information over the Internet and identifies notable practices.

2. *Improving Business Reporting: Insights into Voluntary Disclosures* (January 2001), which identifies the kinds of business information that corporations in eight selected industries are reporting outside of their financial statements.

3. *GAAPSEC Disclosure Requirements* (March 2001), which identifies redundancies between GAAP and SEC disclosure requirements and ways to eliminate them.

4. *Business and Financial Reporting: Challenges from the New Economy* (April 2001), which examines the perceived "disconnect" between information provided in financial statements ("old economy" financial reporting) and the information needs of investors and creditors ("new economy" financial reporting).

The FASB business reporting research project appears, as of mid-2008, to no longer be an active undertaking.

Other projects and proposals have followed, produced by accounting standards-related bodies and others, including a number of private-sector and academic proposals worthy of attention. Most recently, a far-reaching set of changes to financial reporting has been proposed by the CFA Institute (*A Comprehensive Business Reporting Model: Financial Reporting for Investors* [draft, October 2005], which, among other things, strongly endorses universal use of fair value information). However, to this date, there have been no fundamental changes in financial reporting requirements or expectations. Perhaps the most promising currently ongoing effort is FASB's *Financial Statement Presentation* (originally, *Financial Performance Reporting*) project, preliminary views on which are expected to be unveiled in late 2008. A joint undertaking with the International Accounting Standards Board (IASB), this is intended to establish standards for the presentation of information in financial statements that would improve the usefulness of that information in assessing the financial performance of an entity.

This project is to focus on form and content, classification and aggregation, and display of specified items and summarized amounts on the face of the financial statements. That includes determining whether to require the display of certain items determined to be key measures or necessary for the calculation of key measures. The project will not address management discussion and analysis (MD&A found in SEC filings) or the reporting of pro forma earnings in press releases or other communications outside financial statements. Also, it will not address segment information or matters of recognition or measurement of items in financial statements. As of mid-2008, a number of tentative decisions have been made by FASB and IASB, but much work remains to be done on this project.

This project is discussed in somewhat more detail in Chapter 3.

## RESEARCHING GAAP PROBLEMS

The research procedures presented here are intended to serve as a general model for approaching research on accounting issues or questions you may have. These procedures are only intended as an illustration of the process, not as a "cookbook" approach. These procedures should be refined and adapted to each individual fact situation.

### Research Procedures

### Step 1: Identify the Problem

It has been observed that the act of defining a problem provides a large fraction of the solution to the problem. This certainly applies to the domain of researching financial reporting issues, as well. Most often it is found that incorrect answers (e.g., regarding the proper way to report revenue-producing activities) flow from improper definition of the actual question to be resolved. Provisional definitions of problems should be vigorously challenged *before* attempting to search for solutions. The process to be employed is to

- Gain an understanding of the problem or question.
- Challenge the tentative definition of the problem and revise, as necessary.
- Problems and research questions can arise from new authoritative pronouncements, changes in a firm's economic operating environment, or new transactions, as well as from the realization that the problem had not been properly defined in the past.
- It is important to remember that research can be performed before or after the critical event has occurred.  However, if proposed transactions and potential economic circumstances are anticipated, more deliberate attention can be directed at finding the correct solution, and certain proposed transactions having deleterious reporting consequences might be avoided altogether or structured more favorably.
- If little is known about the subject area, it may be useful to consult general reference sources (e.g., *Journal of Accountancy, CPA Journal, Business Week*) to become more familiar with the topic and build up some "economic horse sense" in the area (i.e., the basic what, why, how, when, who, where).  Web-based research vastly expands the ability to gather useful information.
- If you are a preparer/auditor, ensure that you have sufficiently determined whether the issue you are researching is a GAAP issue or an auditing issue so that your search is directed to the appropriate literature.
- With the ongoing process of convergence with IFRS (and possible IFRS adoption) a reality, it will be wise to consider not merely short-term implications under US GAAP, but longer-term potential ramifications if changes are made to existing GAAP.

### Step 2: Analyze the Problem

- Identify critical factors, issues, and questions that relate to the research problem.
- What are the options?  Brainstorm possible alternative accounting treatments.  Note that alternatives continue to narrow both under US GAAP and also due to ongoing efforts to converge to IFRS.
- What are the goals of the transaction?  Are these goals compatible with full and transparent disclosure and recognition?  Evolving GAAP and IFRS will both place greater emphasis on "transparency" in financial reporting.
- What is the economic substance of the transaction, irrespective of the manner in which it appears to be structured?
- What limitations or factors can impact the accounting treatment?

### Step 3: Refine the Problem Statement

- Clearly articulate the critical issues in a way that will facilitate research and analysis.

### Step 4: Identify Plausible Alternatives

- Plausible alternative solutions are based upon prior knowledge or theory.
- Additional alternatives may be identified as steps 5-7 are completed.
- The purpose of identifying and discussing different alternatives is to be able to respond to key accounting issues that arise out of a specific situation.
- The alternatives are the potential methods of accounting for the situation from which only one will ultimately be chosen.
- Exploring alternatives is important because many times there is no single cut-and-dried financial reporting solution to the situation.
- Ambiguity often surrounds many transactions and related accounting issues and, accordingly, the accountant and business advisor must explore the alternatives and use professional judgment in deciding on the proper course of action.

- Remember that other accountants may reasonably disagree with the judgment used or conclusions made, but this does not necessarily mean they are right.

**Step 5: Develop a Research Strategy**

- Determine which authorities or literature need to be searched. Often it will be necessary to search all authoritative literature (FASB, EITF, SEC, AICPA, etc.) as well as current reporting practices (e.g., annual reports).
- Generate keywords or phrases that will form the basis of an electronic search.
- Consider trying a broad search to

  - Assist in developing an understanding of the area,
  - Identify appropriate search terms, and
  - Identify related issues and terminology.

- Consider trying very precise searches to identify if there is authoritative literature directly on point.

**Step 6: Search Authoritative Literature (described in additional detail below)**

- This step involves implementation of the research strategy through searching, identifying, and locating applicable information.

  - Research published GAAP.
  - Research using *Wiley GAAP*.
  - Research other literature.
  - Research practice.
  - Use theory.
  - Find analogous events and/or concepts that are reasonably similar.

**Step 7: Evaluation**

- Analyze and evaluate all of the information obtained.
- This evaluation should lead to the development of a solution or recommendation. Again it is important to remember that steps 3-7 describe activities that will interact with each other and lead to a more refined process in total, and a more complete solution. These steps may involve several iterations.

**Search Authoritative Literature (Step 6) —Further Explanation**

The following sections discuss in more detail how to search authoritative literature as outlined in Step 6.

**Researching authoritative sources of GAAP.** Begin with the publications that set forth the accounting standards in the GAAP hierarchy—the FASB, the AICPA, and the EITF (and for public companies, the SEC).

FASB publishes both loose leaf and bound sets of books, as well as CDROMs, of the *Current Text* and the *Original Pronouncements*. The former integrates all of the currently recognized category A GAAP alphabetically in topic order (e.g., Accounting Changes, Business Combinations, etc.). The AICPA Research Bulletins, APB Opinions, and FASB Statements and Interpretations have been combined in this integrated document. Supplemental guidance from the AICPA Accounting Interpretations and FASB Technical Bulletins is also incorporated. All these materials have been edited down from the original pronouncements and thus may lack the precision that can be obtained only from the unedited version. Each paragraph in the *Current Text* is referenced to the pronouncement from which it is drawn, which is useful for research or follow-up. The first volume of the *Current Text* deals with general standards, while the second contains standards for specialized industries. Descriptive materials, including reasons for conclusions, are absent from the *Current Text*.

The *Original Pronouncements* contains all of the AICPA Accounting Research Bulletins, APB Opinions, the FASB Standards, Interpretations, Concepts Statements, and Technical Bulletins. Paragraphs containing accounting principles that have been superseded or dropped are shaded to alert the user. All changes are identified in detail on a status page placed at the beginning of each pronouncement, which can also assist the user in finding other relevant materials.

Generally, if a quick answer to a specific question is needed, the *Current Text* can be accessed readily. If a fuller understanding of the answer and the reasons underlying it are required, the *Original Pronouncements* may be preferable. In many cases, both sources should be consulted.

FASB also publishes the *EITF Abstracts* (category C GAAP). Each EITF issue discussed by the Task Force is included in the book, regardless of whether a consensus was reached, in the order in which they were added to the EITF agenda. A status section at the end of each issue indicates whether the consensus has been superseded or remains relevant and whether any additional EITF discussion is planned. Many issues are discussed a number of times, and in some cases consensuses are withdrawn or modified in subsequent considerations of a given issue. Accordingly, care must be exercised because, unlike FASB Statements, for example, issues addressed in EITF consensuses can evolve without adequate notice that they have been affected by subsequently issued standards.

*EITF Abstracts* also includes EITF Discussion Issues, which are FASB or SEC staff announcements of positions taken on issues that have yet to be resolved, or even addressed, by the EITF or other standard-setting bodies. While not within the GAAP hierarchy, these do represent current thinking on the particular topic and should be given due consideration in resolving practice problems. The more important of these are covered in this book.

FASB staff issues application guidance (like that found in FASB Staff Implementation Guides and EITF Discussion Issues) through FASB Staff Positions (which it intends to belong to category A GAAP). The staff positions are initially communicated through the FASB Web site (www.fasb.org) and remain there until incorporated into printed FASB literature. FASB staff positions are answers to questions about appropriate application of FASB literature expected to be of widespread relevance to constituents and for which the FASB staff believes that there is only one acceptable answer. The more important of these are covered in this book.

The AICPA publishes all its outstanding Statements of Position and Practice Bulletins in *AICPA Technical Practice Aids*. That book is organized in a manner similar to FASB's *Original Pronouncements*, with the SOP and Practice Bulletins included in the order in which they were issued. There are 26 audit and accounting guides, which are listed at the front of this publication following the AICPA Statements of Position. These publications are available in soft-cover, loose-leaf binder, and electronically on the Internet or CD-ROM.

There are also several commercial services that provide electronic Web-based access to all promulgated GAAP. The great advantage of electronic access is that information can be randomly accessed, so a search by topic will yield a plethora of potentially useful leads. The "fuzzy search" option is quite forgiving of poorly articulated search terms, most often leading the researcher to relevant materials even when the seeker is not clear about what is actually being sought.

**Researching using *Wiley GAAP*.** This publication can assist in researching generally accepted accounting principles for the purpose of identifying technical answers to specific inquiries. You can begin your search in one of two ways: by using the contents page at the front of *Wiley GAAP* to determine the chapter in which the answer to your question is likely to be discussed, or by using the index at the back of this publication to identify specific pages of the publication that discuss the subject matter relating to your question. The path chosen depends in part on how specific the question is; an initial reading of the chapter or relevant section thereof will provide a broader perspective on the subject. For example, if one wanted to know how to account for receivables pledged as collateral, it would be best to start with Chapter 5. However, if one's interest was limited to securitizations of credit card portfolios, it might be better to search the index, because securitizations are a very specialized type of transaction involving receivables, addressed in only a few pages of the text.

Each chapter in this publication is organized in the following manner:

- A chapter table of contents on the first page of the chapter
- Perspective and Issues, providing an overview of the chapter contents and noting any current controversy or proposed GAAP changes affecting the chapter's topics
- A box listing the Sources of GAAP
- Definition of Terms, defining any specialized terms unique to the chapter's subject matter
- Concepts, Rules, and Examples, setting forth the detailed guidance and examples

After reading the relevant portions of this publication, the Sources of GAAP box can be used to find the authoritative pronouncements related to the topic so that these can be appropriately understood and cited in documenting your research findings and conclusions. Upon identifying these pronouncements, refer to the Authoritative Accounting Pronouncements section preceding this chapter, which lists all authoritative pronouncements currently in effect in numerical order. The listed pronouncements are referenced both to the *Current Text* published by FASB and to pages in this publication. Using this list, one can crossreference to or from this publication to both the original pronouncements and/or the *Current Text*. Likewise, the reader familiar with the professional literature can use the listing of authoritative accounting pronouncements to quickly locate the pages in this publication relevant to each specific pronouncement. The reader can therefore locate more detail on each topic covered in this publication, and also be aware of those few, highly specialized topics and pronouncements not covered within this publication.

The current status of each EITF Issue is indicated—that is, whether superseded, resolved, or consensus reached by the EITF, or whether further discussion is pending. Explanations of EITF Issues are integrated in the chapter text to facilitate a logical flow, enhance readability, and increase the likelihood that the researcher will find the information relevant to his or her issue logically grouped together in the most easily retrievable manner.

**Researching nonpromulgated GAAP.** Researching nonpromulgated GAAP consists of reviewing pronouncements in areas similar to those being researched, reading accounting literature mentioned in the GAAP hierarchy as "other sources" to be used when sources at levels A through D do not exist, and careful reading of the relevant portions of the FASB Conceptual Framework summarized later in this chapter. Understanding concepts and intentions espoused by accounting experts can give the essential clues to a logical formulation of alternatives and conclusions regarding problems that have not yet been addressed by the standard-setting bodies.

Both the AICPA and FASB publish a myriad of nonauthoritative literature. FASB publishes the documents it uses in its due process: Discussion Memorandums, Invitations to Comment, Exposure Drafts, and Preliminary Views as well as minutes from its meetings. It also publishes research reports, newsletters, and implementation guidance. The AICPA publishes its Exposure Drafts, as well as Technical Practice Aids, Issues Papers, comment letters on proposals of other standard-setting bodies, and the monthly periodical, *Journal of Ac-*

*countancy.* Technical Practice Aids are answers published by the AICPA Technical Information Service to questions about accounting and auditing standards. AICPA Issues Papers are research documents about accounting and reporting problems that the AICPA believes should be resolved by FASB. They provide information about alternative accounting treatments used in practice. These two AICPA publications, which are not approved by FASB, have no authoritative status, but those who depart from their guidance should be prepared to justify that departure based upon the facts and circumstances of the particular situation. Listings of FASB and AICPA publications are available at their Web sites. (A list of Web site addresses is located at the end of this chapter.)

The Securities and Exchange Commission issues Staff Accounting Bulletins and makes rulings on individual cases that come before it, which create and impose accounting standards on those whose financial statements are to be submitted to the Commission. The SEC, through acts passed by Congress, has been given broad powers to prescribe accounting practices and methods for all statements filed with it.

The International Accounting Standards Board (IASB) publishes its standards, interpretations, the *Framework for the Preparation and Presentation of Financial Statements*, and project archives. Summaries of the standards and interpretations and the project archives are available at the Board's Web site, along with instructions for purchasing the complete standards, interpretations, and other materials.

The American Accounting Association (AAA) is an organization consisting primarily of accounting educators. It is devoted to encouraging research into accounting theory and practice. The issuances of the AAA tend to be normative, that is, prescribing what GAAP ought to be like, rather than explaining current standards. However, the monographs, committee reports, and *The Accounting Review* published by the AAA may be useful sources for research into applicable accounting standards.

Governmental agencies such as the Government Accountability Office, the Federal Accounting Standards Advisory Board, and the Cost Accounting Standards Board have certain publications that may assist in researching written standards. Also, industry organizations and associations may be other helpful sources.

Certain publications are helpful in identifying practices used by entities that may not be promulgated as standards. The AICPA publishes an annual survey of the accounting and disclosure policies of many public companies in *Accounting Trends and Techniques* and maintains a library of financial statements that can be accessed through a computerized search process (NAARS). EDGAR (Electronic Data Gathering, Analysis, and Retrieval) publishes the SEC filings of public companies, which includes the companies' financial statements. Through selection of keywords and/or topics, these services can provide information on how other entities resolved similar problems.

**Internet-based research sources.** There has been and continues to be an information revolution affecting the exponential growth in the volume of materials, authoritative and nonauthoritative, that are available on the Internet. A listing of just a small cross-section of these sources follows:

## Accounting Web sites

| | | |
|---|---|---|
| *AICPA Online* | http://www.aicpa.org | Includes accounting news section; CPE information; section on professional ethics; information on relevant Congressional/Executive actions; online publications, such as the *Journal of Accountancy*; Accounting Standards Executive Committee; also has links to other organizations; includes links to authoritative standards for nonissuers including auditing standards, attestation standards, and quality control standards |
| *American Accounting Association* | http://www.aaahq.org | Accounting news; publications; faculty information; searchable; links to other sites |
| *FASB* | http://www.fasb.org | Information on FASB; includes list of new Pronouncements/Statements; summaries of selected projects; summaries/status of all FASB Statements. Due to funding provided by PCAOB, FASB now posts its statements, interpretations, staff positions, and newly issued EITF issues on its Web site. |
| *GASB* | http://www.gasb.org | Information on GASB; new GASB documents; summaries/status of all GASB statements; proposed Statements; Technical Bulletins; Interpretations |
| *International Accounting Standards Board (IASB)* | http://www.iasb.org.uk | Information on the IASB; lists of Pronouncements, Exposure Drafts, project summaries, and conceptual framework |
| *NASBA* | http://www.nasba.org | National State Boards of Accountancy; includes listings of registered CPE sponsors and links to state boards of accountancy as well as standards governing continuing professional education that it jointly issues with the AICPA |
| *PCAOB* | http://www.pcaobus.org | Sections on rulemaking, standards (including the interim auditing, attestation, quality control, ethics, and independence standards), enforcement, inspections and oversight activities |
| *Rutgers Accounting Web* | http://www.accounting.rutgers.edu | Includes links to journals and publications, software, publishers, educational institutions, government agencies, and information regarding continuous auditing initiatives |
| *SEC* | http://www.sec.gov | SEC digest and statements; EDGAR searchable database; information on current SEC rulemaking; links to other sites |
| *WebCPA* | http://www.webcpa.com | Breaking news regarding the profession, links to regulators, taxing agencies, associations, and agencies |

**Example of how to solve a GAAP problem.** As an example of how to solve a GAAP problem, let us examine how the FASB and its staff approached a question raised by the Edison Electric Institute (EEI) in the project that eventually led to FAS 143, *Asset Retirement Obligations*.

The EEI requested that the FASB add a project to its agenda to determine the appropriate accounting for removal costs, such as the costs of nuclear decommissioning and similar costs affecting other industries. At the time this was raised, the existing accounting practices for removal costs were inconsistent as to the criteria used for recognition, measurement, and the presentation of the obligation in the financial statements. Some entities did not recognize any obligations for removal costs until actually incurred. Other entities estimated the cost of retiring the asset and accrued a portion of that amount each period as an expense, with an offsetting liability, so that when the asset was retired a liability for the full amount of the removal costs would already be on the ledger. Still others recognized the expense but displayed the credit side of the entry as a contra asset rather than a liability.

FASB looked for an analogous situation and found one in FAS 19, *Financial Accounting and Reporting by Oil and Gas Producing Companies.* Paragraph 37 of that standard states that "estimated dismantlement, restoration, and abandonment cost shall be taken into account in determining amortization and depreciation rates." The effect of that paragraph was that the credit side of the entry was to accumulated depreciation, which could result in an accumulated depreciation amount that exceeded the cost of the asset. There was no recognition of an obligation to dismantle and restore the property (a liability). Instead the focus was on achieving a particular pattern of expense recognition. Because the amount of the obligation that the entity had incurred was not a central concern under FAS 19, the FASB (which embraced a balance sheet orientation in its conceptual framework, which was issued after FAS 19 was promulgated) rejected it and sought another solution.

FASB considered the definition of a liability in paragraphs 36-40 of CON 6 to determine whether nuclear decommissioning and similar asset retirements could be considered liabilities of the entities owning the assets. Since the first characteristic of a liability—that an entity has "a present duty or responsibility to one or more other entities that entails settlement by probable future transfer or use of assets at a specified or determinable date, on occurrence of a specified event, or on demand"—would be met when an entity is required by current laws, regulations, or contracts to settle an asset retirement obligation upon retirement of the asset, FASB concluded that accounting for this liability would be the central goal of the new standard.

In some situations, the duty or responsibility to remove the asset is created by an entity's own promise. In other situations, the duty or responsibility is created by circumstances in which an entity finds itself bound to perform, and others are justified in relying on the entity to perform. Thus, in its initial deliberations, the FASB decided that entities should report both legal and constructive obligations in their financial statements. Paragraph 36 of CON 6, which defines the essential characteristics of a liability, recognizes both types of obligations. It states

*...although most liabilities rest generally on a foundation of legal rights and duties, existence of a legally enforceable claim is not a prerequisite for an obligation to qualify as a liability if for other reasons the entity has the duty or responsibility to pay cash, to transfer other assets, or to provide services to another entity.*

Paragraph 40 of CON 6 provides further insight. It states

*Liabilities stemming from equitable or constructive obligations are commonly paid in the same way as legally binding contracts, but they lack the legal sanction that characterizes most liabilities and may be binding primarily because of social or moral sanctions or custom. An equitable obligation stems from ethical or moral constraints rather than from rules of common or statute law....*

During its due process, FASB heard from constituents that without improved guidance for determining whether a constructive obligation exists, inconsistent application of the final standard would result. After further consideration of the qualitative characteristics of reliability and comparability found in CON 2, and the recognition characteristic of reliability in CON 5, the FASB decided to confine recognition only to legal obligations, including legal obligations created under the doctrine of promissory estoppel.

FASB also considered the second characteristic of a liability, that "the duty or responsibility obligates a particular entity, leaving it little or no discretion to avoid the future sacrifice." It concluded that an asset retirement obligation had that characteristic.

FASB considered the third and final characteristic of a liability, that "the transaction or other event obligating the entity has already happened." It concluded that an entity must look to the nature of the duty or responsibility to assess whether the obligating event has occurred. FASB provides the example of a nuclear power facility: although the operator assumes responsibility for decontamination upon receipt of a license, it is not until the facility is operated and contamination occurs that there is an obligating event.

When contemplating the manner in which the asset retirement obligation could be measured, FASB was guided by CON 7. In that concepts statement, FASB concluded that "the only objective of present value, when used in accounting measurements at initial recognition and fresh-start measurements, is to estimate fair value." Based on this, FASB determined that an asset retirement obligation should be measured at fair value, but in the (typical) absence of quoted market prices or prices for similar liabilities, entities should use present value techniques to measure the liability.

In deciding upon the appropriate designation of the debit offsetting the entry recording the obligation, FASB first made reference to the definition of an asset under CON 6. FASB concluded that capitalized asset retirement costs would not qualify for presentation as a separate asset because no separate future economic benefit flows from these costs. Thus, asset retirement costs do not meet the definition of an asset in paragraph 25 of CON 6. However, FASB observed that current accounting practice includes in the historical-cost basis of an asset all the costs that are necessary to prepare the asset for its intended use. FASB concluded that the requirement for capitalization of the asset retirement cost as part of the historical cost of the asset and then depreciating that asset both (1) obtains a measure of cost that more closely reflects the entity's total investment in the asset, and (2) permits the allocation of that cost to expense in the periods over which the related asset would be expected to provide benefits.

Thus, in this actual situation, by reasoning from analogous situations and applying established accounting concepts, FASB was able to develop an important new standard. In a like manner, solutions to GAAP practice problems can be reached. Those solutions will serve the reporting entity in achieving GAAP-compliant financial reporting until a standards-setting body resolves the problem by issuing authoritative guidance.

## The Conceptual Framework

FASB has issued seven pronouncements (six of which remain extant) called Statements of Financial Accounting Concepts (CON) in a series designed to constitute a foundation of financial accounting standards. This conceptual framework is designed to prescribe the nature, function, and limits of financial accounting and to be used as a guideline that will lead to consistent standards. These conceptual statements do not establish accounting standards or disclosure practices for particular items. They are not enforceable under the AICPA Code of Professional Conduct.

FASB's conceptual framework is intended to serve as the foundation upon which the Board can construct standards that are both sound and internally consistent. The fact that the framework was intended to guide FASB in establishing standards is embodied in the preface to each of the Concepts Statements. The preface to CON 6 states

> *The Board itself is likely to be the most direct beneficiary of the guidance provided by the Statements in this series. They will guide the Board in developing accounting and reporting standards by providing the Board with a common foundation and basic reasoning on which to consider merits of alternatives.*

The conceptual framework is also intended for use by the business community to help understand and apply standards and to assist in their development. This goal is also mentioned in the preface to each of the Concepts Statements, as this excerpt from CON 6 shows.

> *However, knowledge of the objectives and concepts the Board will use in developing standards also should enable those who are affected by or interested in financial accounting standards to understand better the purposes, content, and characteristics of information provided by financial accounting and reporting. That knowledge is expected to enhance the usefulness of, and confidence in, financial accounting and reporting. The concepts also may provide some guidance in analyzing new or emerging problems of financial accounting and reporting in the absence of applicable authoritative pronouncements.*

The FASB Special Report, *The Framework of Financial Accounting Concepts and Standards* (1998), states that the conceptual framework should help solve complex financial accounting or reporting problems by

- *Providing a set of common premises as a basis for discussion;*
- *Providing precise terminology;*
- *Helping to ask the right questions;*
- *Limiting areas of judgment and discretion and excluding from consideration potential solutions that are in conflict with it; and*
- *Imposing intellectual discipline on what traditionally has been a subjective and ad hoc reasoning process.*

Of the seven CON, the fourth, *Objectives of Financial Reporting by Nonbusiness Organizations*, is not covered here due to its specialized nature.

**Components of the conceptual framework.** The components of the conceptual framework for financial accounting and reporting include objectives, qualitative characteristics, elements, recognition, measurement, financial statements, earnings, funds flow, and liquidity. The relationship between these components is illustrated in the following diagram reproduced from a FASB Invitation to Comment, *Financial Statements and Other Means of Financial Reporting.*

In the diagram, components to the left are more basic and those to the right depend on components to their left. Components are closely related to those above or below them.

The most basic component of the conceptual framework is the objectives. The objectives underlie the other phases and are derived from the needs of those for whom financial information is intended. The qualitative characteristics are the criteria to be used in choosing and evaluating accounting and reporting policies.

Elements of financial statements are the components from which financial statements are created. They include assets, liabilities, equity, investments by owners, distributions to owners, comprehensive income, revenues, expenses, gains, and losses. In order to be included in financial statements, an element must meet criteria for recognition and possess a characteristic that can be reliably measured.

**Conceptual Framework
for Financial Accounting and Reporting**

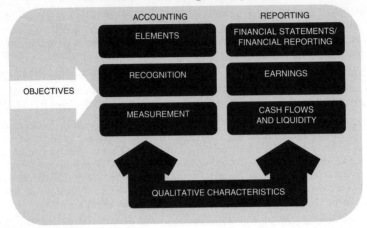

Reporting or display considerations is concerned with what information should be provided, who should provide it, and where it should be displayed. How the financial statements (financial position, earnings, and cash flow) are presented is the focal point of this part of the conceptual framework project.

A Statement of Financial Accounting Concepts (CON) does not establish GAAP. Since GAAP may be inconsistent with the principles set forth in the conceptual framework, the FASB expects to reexamine existing accounting standards. Until that time, a CON does not require a change in existing GAAP. CON do not amend, modify, or interpret existing GAAP, nor do they justify departing from GAAP based upon interpretations derived from them.

FASB is currently pursuing several projects affecting the conceptual framework and the GAAP hierarchy. As to the latter, FASB expects to revise the existing hierarchy, now consisting of four levels or categories (plus a catchall fifth level of nonpromulgated guidance, such as from textbooks or scholarly writings, but also including the concepts statements) to a dichotomy between authoritative and nonauthoritative guidance. In the near term, FASB intends to elevate concepts statements to "level A" GAAP. This is indicative of a greater awareness of the relevance of the concepts statements as guidance for making accounting decisions. As numerous older accounting standards have evolved and been superseded by new requirements, such as mandates for the wider use of fair value information within the financial statements, the principles espoused in CON no longer seem as divergent from actual practice, and may more usefully serve as actual, authoritative guides to practice.

### CON 1: Objectives of Financial Reporting by Business Enterprises

CON 1 identifies the objectives (purposes) of financial reporting and indicates that these objectives apply to all financial reporting; they are not limited to financial statements. Financial reporting includes the financial statements and other forms of communication that provide accounting information (corporate annual reports, prospectuses, annual reports filed with the Securities and Exchange Commission, news releases, and management forecasts).

CON 1 identifies three objectives of financial reporting. The first objective is to provide information that is useful in making business and economic decisions. Users of financial information are divided into internal and external groups. Internal users include management and directors of the business enterprise. Internal reports tend to provide information that is more detailed than the information available to or used by external users. External users include both individuals who have or intend to have a direct economic interest in a business and those who have an indirect interest because they advise or represent those individuals with a direct interest. These users include owners, lenders, suppliers, potential investors and creditors, employees, customers, financial analysts and advisors, brokers, underwriters, stock exchanges, lawyers, economists, taxing authorities, regulatory authorities, legislators, financial press and reporting agencies, labor unions, trade associations, business researchers, teachers, students, and the public. CON 1 is directed at general-purpose external financial reporting by a business enterprise as it relates to the ability of that enterprise to generate favorable cash flows. External users' needs are emphasized because these users lack the authority to obtain the financial information they want and need from an enterprise. Thus, external users must rely on the information provided to them by management.

The second objective of financial reporting is to provide understandable information that will aid investors and creditors in predicting the future cash flows of a firm. Investors and creditors want information about cash flows because the expectation of cash flows affects a firm's ability to pay interest and dividends, which in turn affects the market price of that firm's stocks and bonds.

The third objective of financial reporting is to provide information relative to an enterprise's economic resources, the claims to those resources (obligations), and the effects of transactions, events, and circumstances that change resources and claims to resources. A description of these informational needs follows:

- **Economic resources, obligations, and owners' equity.** This information provides the users of financial reporting with a measure of future cash flows and an indication of the firm's strengths, weaknesses, liquidity, and solvency.

- **Economic performance and earnings.** Past performance provides an indication of a firm's future performance. Furthermore, earnings based upon accrual accounting provide a better indicator of economic performance and future cash flows than do current cash receipts and disbursements. Accrual basis earnings are a better indicator because a charge for recovery of capital (depreciation/amortization) is made in determining these earnings. The relationship between earnings and economic performance results from matching the costs and benefits (revenues) of economic activity during a given period by means of accrual accounting. Over the life of an enterprise, economic performance can be determined by net cash flows or by total earnings since the two measures would be equal.

- **Liquidity, solvency, and funds flows.** Information about cash and other funds flows from borrowings, repayments of borrowings, expenditures, capital transactions, economic resources, obligations, owners' equity, and earnings may aid the user of financial reporting information in assessing a firm's liquidity or solvency.

- **Management stewardship and performance.** The assessment of a firm's management with respect to the efficient and profitable use of the firm's resources is usually made on the basis of economic performance as reported by periodic earnings. Because earnings are affected by factors other than current management performance, earnings may not be a reliable indicator of management performance.

- **Management explanations and interpretations.** Management is responsible for the efficient use of a firm's resources. Thus, it acquires knowledge about the enterprise and its performance that is unknown to the external user. Explanations by management concerning the financial impact of transactions, events, circumstances, uncertainties, estimates, judgments, and any effects of the separation of the results of operations into periodic measures of performance enhance the usefulness of financial information.

## CON 2: Qualitative Characteristics of Accounting Information

The purpose of financial reporting is to provide decision makers with useful information. When accounting choices are to be made by individuals or by standard-setting bodies, those choices should be based upon the usefulness of that information to the decision-making process. This CON identifies the qualities or characteristics that make information useful in the decision making process. It also establishes a terminology and set of definitions to provide a greater understanding of the characteristics. The following diagram from CON 2 summarizes the qualitative characteristics of accounting information:

### A Hierarchy of Accounting Qualities

**Usefulness for decision making.** This is the most important characteristic of information. Information must be useful to be beneficial to the user. To be useful, accounting information must be both relevant and reliable. Both of these characteristics are affected by the completeness of the information provided.

**Relevance.** Information is relevant to a decision if it makes a difference to the decision maker in his/her ability to predict events or to confirm or correct expectations. Relevant information will reduce the decision maker's assessment of the uncertainty of the outcome of a decision even though it may not change the decision itself. Information is relevant if it provides knowledge concerning past events (feedback value) or future events (predictive value) and if it is timely. Disclosure requirement information is relevant because it provides information about past events and it improves the predictability of future events. The predictive value of accounting information does not imply that such information is a prediction. The predictive value refers to the utility that a piece of information has as an input into a predictive model. Although timeliness alone will not make information relevant, information must be timely to be relevant. It must be available before it loses its ability to influence the decision maker.

**Reliability.** Financial statements are an abstraction of the activities of a business enterprise. They simplify the activities of the actual firm. To be reliable, financial statements must portray the important financial relationships of the firm itself. Information is reliable if it is verifiable and neutral and if users can depend on it to represent that which it is intended to represent (representational faithfulness).

Information may not be representationally faithful if it is biased. Bias is the tendency for an accounting measure to be consistently too high or too low. Bias may arise because the measurer does not use the measurement method properly or because the measurement method does not represent what it purports to represent.

**Verifiability** means that several independent measures will obtain the same accounting measure. An accounting measure that can be repeated with the same result (consensus) is desirable because it serves to detect and reduce measurer bias. Cash is highly verifiable. Inventories and depreciable assets tend to be less verifiable because alternative valuation methods exist. The direct verification of an accounting measure would serve to minimize measurer bias and measurement bias. The verification of the procedures used to obtain the measure would minimize measurer bias only. Finally, verifiability does not guarantee representational faithfulness or relevance.

The characteristic of neutrality means that accounting information should serve to communicate without attempting to influence behavior in a particular direction. This does not mean that accounting should not influence behavior or that it should affect everyone in the same way. It means that information should not favor certain interest groups.

To be useful, accounting information should be comparable. The characteristic of comparability allows the users of accounting information to assess the similarities and differences either among different entities for the same time period or for the same entity over different time periods. Comparisons are usually made on the basis of quantifiable measurements of a common characteristic. Therefore, to be comparable, the measurements used must be reliable with respect to the common characteristic. Noncomparability can result from the use of different inputs, procedures, or systems of classification. Noncomparability can also arise when the data measurements lack representational faithfulness.

The characteristic of consistency also contributes to information usefulness. Consistency is an interperiod comparison that requires the use of the same accounting principles from one period to another. Although a change of an accounting principle to a more preferred method results in inconsistency, the change is acceptable if the effect of the change is disclosed. Consistency does not insure comparability. If the measurements used are not representationally faithful, comparability will not be achieved.

**Trade-offs.** Although it is desirable that accounting information contain the characteristics that have been identified above, not all of these characteristics are compatible. Often, one characteristic may be obtained only by sacrificing another. The trade-offs that must be made are determined on the basis of the relative importance of the characteristics. This relative importance, in turn, is dependent upon the nature of the users and their particular needs.

**Constraints.** The qualitative characteristics of useful accounting information are subject to two constraints: the materiality and the relative cost benefit of that information. An item of information is material and should be reported if it is significant enough to have an effect on the decision maker. Materiality requires judgment. It is dependent upon the relative size of an item, the precision with which the item can be estimated, and the nature of the item. No general standards of materiality are provided (although an appendix to CON 2 lists several guidelines that have been applied).

Accounting information provides the user with certain benefits. Associated with this benefit, however, is the cost of using that information and of providing it to the user. Information should be provided only if its benefits exceed its cost. Unfortunately, it is difficult to value the benefit of accounting information. It is also difficult to determine whether the burden of the cost of disclosure and the benefits of such disclosure are distributed fairly.

**Role of conservatism.** Conservatism is a reaction to uncertainty. For many years, accountants have been influenced by conservatism. Conservatism in accounting may mislead users if it results in a deliberate understatement of net assets and net income. Such understatement is undertaken to minimize the risk of uncertainty to outside lenders. Unfortunately, such understatements often lead to overstatements in subsequent years, produce biased financial statements, and conflict with the characteristics of representational faithfulness, neutrality, and comparability.

## CON 3: Elements of Financial Statements of Business Enterprises.

CON 3 was replaced by CON 6. CON 6 carried forward essentially all of the concepts in CON 3, then added the elements unique to the financial statements of not-for-profit organizations.

## CON 5: Recognition and Measurement in Financial Statements of Business Enterprises

CON 5 indicates that financial statements are the principal means of communicating useful financial information. A full set of such statements contains

- Financial position at end of the period
- Earnings for the period
- Comprehensive income for the period
- Cash flows during the period
- Investments by and distributions to owners during the period

Financial statements result from simplifying, condensing, and aggregating transactions. Therefore, no one financial statement provides sufficient information by itself and no one item or part of each statement can summarize the information.

A statement of financial position provides information about an entity's assets, liabilities, and equity. Earnings is a measure of entity performance during a period. It is similar to net income but excludes accounting adjustments from earlier periods such as cumulative effect changes in accounting principles. Comprehensive income comprises all recognized changes in equity other than those arising from investments by and distributions to owners. A statement of cash flows reflects receipts and payments of cash by major sources and uses including operating, financing, and investing activities. The investments by and distributions to owners reflect the capital transactions of an entity during a period.

Income is determined by the concept of financial capital maintenance which means that only if the money amount of net assets increases during a period (excluding capital transactions) is there a profit. For recognition in financial statements, subject to both cost benefit and materiality constraints, an item must meet the following criteria:

1. Definition—Meet the definition of an element in financial statements
2. Measurability—Have a relevant attribute measurable with sufficient reliability
3. Relevance
4. Reliability

Items reported in the financial statements are based on historical cost, replacement cost, market value, net realizable value, and present value of cash flows. Price level changes are not recognized in these statements and conservatism guides the application of recognition criteria.

## CON 6:  Elements of Financial Statements

CON 6 defines ten interrelated elements that are used in the financial statements of business enterprises.

1.  Assets—Probable future economic benefits obtained or controlled by a particular entity as a result of past transactions or events
2.  Liabilities—Probable future sacrifices of economic benefits arising from present obligations of a particular entity to transfer assets or provide services to other entities in the future as a result of past transactions or events
3.  Equity (net assets) —The residual interest in the assets that remains after deducting its liabilities.  In a business enterprise, equity is the ownership interest.
4.  Revenues—Inflows or other enhancements of assets of an entity or settlement of its liabilities (or a combination of both) from delivering or producing goods, rendering services, or other activities that constitute the entity's ongoing major and central operations
5.  Expenses—Outflows or other using up of assets or incurrences of liabilities (or a combination of both) from delivering or producing goods, rendering services, or carrying out other activities that constitute the entity's ongoing major and central operations
6.  Gains—Increases in equity (net assets) from peripheral or incidental transactions of an entity and from all other transactions and other events and circumstances affecting the entity except those that result from revenues or investments by owners
7.  Losses—Decreases in equity (net assets) from peripheral or incidental transactions of an entity and from all other transactions and other events and circumstances affecting the entity except those that result from expenses or distributions to owners
8.  Comprehensive income—The change in equity of a business enterprise during a period from transactions and other events and circumstances from sources other than investments by owners or distributions to owners
9.  Investments by owners—Increases in equity of a particular business enterprise resulting from transfers to it for the purpose of increasing ownership interests
10. Distributions to owners—Decreases in the equity of a particular business enterprise resulting from transferring assets, rendering services, or incurring liabilities to owners

The various elements articulate; that is, a change in one element causes an offsetting change in another item of the same type or causes another element to change by the same amount.  For example, a purchase of a building for cash and a mortgage note increases an asset (building), decreases another asset (cash), and increases a liability (mortgage note).  A diagram from CON 6 that illustrates the articulation of the elements is included below.

All transactions and other events and circumstances that affect a business enterprise during a period

**A.** All changes in assets and liabilities not accompanied by changes in equity

1. Ex-changes of assets for assets
2. Ex-changes of liabilities for liabilities
3. Acquisitions of assets by incurring liabilities
4. Settlements of liabilities by transferring assets

**B.** All changes in assets or liabilities accompanied by changes in equity

1. Comprehensive income

a. Revenues
b. Gains
c. Expenses
d. Losses

2. All changes in equity from transfers between a business enterprise and its owners

a. Investments by owners
b. Distributions to owners

**C.** Changes within equity that do not affect assets or liabilities

In this publication, assets, liabilities, and equity are described more fully in Chapter 2. Revenues, expenses, gains, losses, and comprehensive income are described in Chapter 3. Investments by owners and distributions to owners are described in Chapter 17.

CON 6 also defines several significant financial accounting and reporting terms that are used in the Concepts Statements (and FASB pronouncements issued after the Concepts Statements). An event is a happening of consequence to an entity. It can be an internal event (the use of raw materials) or an external event with another entity (the purchase of labor) or with the environment in which the business operates (a technological advance by a competitor). A transaction is a particular kind of event. It is an external event that involves transferring something of value to another entity. Circumstances are a condition, or set of conditions, that create situations that might otherwise have not occurred and might not have been anticipated. Accrual accounting attempts to record the financial effects on a entity of transactions and of other events and circumstances that have consequences for the entity in the periods in which those transactions, events, and circumstances occur rather than in the periods in which cash is received or paid by the entity. Thus, accrual accounting is based not only on cash transactions but also on credit transactions, bartering, changes in prices, changes in the form of assets or liabilities, and other transactions, events and circumstances that involve no current cash transfers but will have cash consequences in the future. Accrual is the accounting process of recognizing the effects of future cash receipts and payments in the current period. Deferral is the accounting process of recognizing a liability resulting from a current cash receipt or an asset resulting from a current cash payment. Realization is the process of converting noncash assets into cash. Recognition is the process of formally incorporating a transaction or other event into the financial statements. Matching is the simultaneous recognition of the revenues and expenses that result directly and jointly from the same transaction or other event. Allocation is the process of assigning expenses to periods when the transactions or events that cause the using up of the benefits cannot be identified or when the cause can be identified but the actual amount of benefit used up cannot be reliably measured.

CON 6 also discusses the elements used in the financial statements of not-for-profit organizations. Of the ten elements, seven are used by not-for-profit organizations. The three elements omitted are investments by owners, distributions to owners, and comprehensive income. They are omitted because not-for-profit organizations do not have owners. The seven remaining elements are defined for not-for-profit organizations the same as they are for business enterprises. The net assets (equity) of not-for-profit organizations is divided into three classes—unrestricted, temporarily restricted, and permanently restricted—based on the existence or absence of donor-imposed restrictions. A portion of Chapter 24 describes the accounting and reporting of not-for-profit organizations.

## CON 7: Using Cash Flow Information and Present Value in Accounting Measurements

CON 7 provides a framework for using estimates of future cash flows as the basis for accounting measurements either at initial recognition or when assets are subsequently remeasured at fair value (fresh-start measurements). It also provides a framework for using the interest method of amortization. It provides the principles that govern measurement using present value, especially when the amount of future cash flows, their timing, or both are uncertain. However, it does not address recognition questions, such as which transactions and events should be valued using present value measures or when fresh-start measurements are appropriate.

Fair value is the objective for most measurements at initial recognition and for fresh-start measurements in subsequent periods. At initial recognition, the cash paid or received (historical cost or proceeds) is usually assumed to be fair value, absent evidence to the contrary. For fresh-start measurements, a price that is observed in the marketplace for an essentially similar asset or liability is fair value. If purchase prices and market prices are available, there is no need to use alternative measurement techniques to approximate fair value. However, if alternative measurement techniques must be used for initial recognition and for fresh-start measurements, those techniques should attempt to capture the elements that when taken together would comprise a market price if one existed. The objective is to estimate the price likely to exist in the marketplace if there were a marketplace—fair value.

CON 7 states that the only objective of using present value in accounting measurements is fair value. It is necessary to capture, to the extent possible, the economic differences in the marketplace between sets of estimated future cash flows. A present value measurement that fully captures those differences must include the following elements:

1. An estimate of the future cash flow, or in more complex cases, series of future cash flows at different times
2. Expectations about possible variations in the amount or timing of those cash flows
3. The time value of money, represented by the risk-free rate of interest
4. The risk premium—the price for bearing the uncertainty inherent in the asset or liability
5. Other factors, including illiquidity and market imperfections

**How CON 7 measures differ from previously utilized present value techniques.** Previously employed present value techniques typically used a single set of estimated cash flows and a single discount (interest) rate. In applying those techniques, adjustments for factors 2. through 5. described in the previous paragraph are incorporated in the selection of the discount rate. In the CON 7 approach, only the third factor listed (the time value of money) is included in the discount rate; the other factors cause adjustments in arriving at risk-adjusted expected cash flows. CON 7 introduces the probability-weighted, expected cash flow approach, which focuses on the range of possible estimated cash flows and estimates of their respective probabilities of occurrence.

Previous techniques used to compute present value used estimates of the cash flows most likely to occur. CON 7 refines and enhances the precision of this model by weighting different cash flow scenarios (regarding the amounts and timing of cash flows) by their estimated probabilities of occurrence and factoring these scenarios into the ultimate determination of fair value. The difference is that values are assigned to the cash flows other than the most likely one. To illustrate, a cash flow might be $100, $200, or $300 with probabilities of 10%, 50%, and 40%, respectively. The most likely cash flow is the one with 50% probability, or $200. The expected cash flow is $230 [=($100 × .1) + ($200 × .5) + ($300 × .4)].

The CON 7 method, unlike previous present value techniques, can also accommodate uncertainty in the timing of cash flows. For example, a cash flow of $10,000 may be received in one year, two years, or three years with probabilities of 15%, 60%, and 25%, respectively. Traditional present value techniques would compute the present value using the most likely timing of the payment—two years. The example below shows the computation of present value using the CON 7 method. Again, the expected present value of $9,030 differs from the traditional notion of a best estimate of $9,070 (the 60% probability) in this example.

| | | |
|---|---|---|
| Present value of $10,000 in 1 year discounted at 5% | $9,523 | |
| Multiplied by 15% probability | | $1,428 |
| Present value of $10,000 in 2 years discounted at 5% | $9,070 | |
| Multiplied by 60% probability | | 5,442 |
| Present value of $10,000 in 3 years discounted at 5% | $8,638 | |
| Multiplied by 25% probability | | 2,160 |
| Probability weighted expected present value | | $9,030 |

**Measuring liabilities.** The measurement of liabilities involves different problems from the measurement of assets; however, the underlying objective is the same. When using present value techniques to estimate the fair value of a liability, the objective is to estimate the value of the assets required currently to (1) settle the liability with the holder or (2) transfer the liability to an entity of comparable credit standing. To estimate the fair value of an entity's notes or bonds payable, accountants look to the price at which other entities are willing to hold the entity's liabilities as assets. For example, the proceeds of a loan are the price that a lender paid to hold the borrower's promise of future cash flows as an asset.

The most relevant measurement of an entity's liabilities should always reflect the credit standing of the entity. An entity with a good credit standing will receive more cash for its promise to pay than an entity with a poor credit standing. For example, if two entities both promise to pay $750 in three years with no stated interest payable in the interim, Entity A, with a good credit standing, might receive about $630 (a 6% interest rate). Entity B, with a poor credit standing, might receive about $533 (a 12% interest rate). Each entity initially records its respective liability at fair value, which is the amount of proceeds received—an amount that incorporates that entity's credit standing.

Present value techniques can also be used to value a guarantee of a liability. Assume that Entity B in the above example owes Entity C. If Entity A were to assume the debt, it would want to be compensated $630—the amount that it could get in the marketplace for its promise to pay $750 in three years. The difference between what Entity A would want to take the place of Entity B ($630) and the amount that Entity B receives ($533) is the value of the guarantee ($97).

**Interest method of allocation.** CON 7 describes the factors that suggest that an interest method of allocation should be used. It states that the interest method of allocation is more relevant than other methods of cost allocation when it is applied to assets and liabilities that exhibit one or more of the following characteristics:

a.  The transaction is, in substance, a borrowing and lending transaction.
b.  Period-to-period allocation of similar assets or liabilities employs an interest method.
c.  A particular set of estimated future cash flows is closely associated with the asset or liability.
d.  The measurement at initial recognition was based on present value.

**Accounting for changes in expected cash flows.** If the timing or amount of estimated cash flows changes and the asset or liability is not remeasured at a fresh-start measure, the interest method of allocation should be altered by a catch-up approach. That approach adjusts the carrying amount to the present value of the revised estimated future cash flows, discounted at the original effective interest rate.

**Application of present value tables and formulas.**

*Present value of a single future amount.* To take the present value of a single amount that will be paid in the future, apply the following formula; where *PV* is the present value of $1 paid in the future, *r* is the interest rate per period, and *n* is the number of periods between the current date and the future date when the amount will be realized.

$$PV = \frac{1}{(1+r)^n}$$

In many cases the results of this formula are summarized in a present value factor table.

| (n) Periods | 2% | 3% | 4% | 5% | 6% | 7% | 8% | 9% | 10% |
|---|---|---|---|---|---|---|---|---|---|
| 1 | 0.9804 | 0.9709 | 0.9615 | 0.9524 | 0.9434 | 0.9346 | 0.9259 | 0.9174 | 0.9091 |
| 2 | 0.9612 | 0.9426 | 0.9246 | 0.9070 | 0.8900 | 0.8734 | 0.8573 | 0.8417 | 0.8265 |
| 3 | 0.9423 | 0.9151 | 0.8890 | 0.8638 | 0.8396 | 0.8163 | 0.7938 | 0.7722 | 0.7513 |
| 4 | 0.9239 | 0.8885 | 0.8548 | 0.8227 | 0.7921 | 0.7629 | 0.7350 | 0.7084 | 0.6830 |
| 5 | 0.9057 | 0.8626 | 0.8219 | 0.7835 | 0.7473 | 0.7130 | 0.6806 | 0.6499 | 0.6209 |

### Example

Suppose one wishes to determine how much would need to be invested today to have $10,000 in 5 years if the sum invested would earn 8%. Looking across the row with n = 5 and finding the present value factor for the r = 8% column, the factor of 0.6806 would be identified. Multiplying $10,000 by 0.6806 results in $6,806, the amount that would need to be invested today to have $10,000 at the end of 5 years. Alternatively, using a calculator and applying the present value of a single sum formula, one could multiply $10,000 by $1/(1+.08)^5$, which would also give the same answer—$6,806.

*Present value of a series of equal payments (an annuity).* Many times in business situations a series of equal payments paid at equal time intervals is required. Examples of these include payments of semiannual bond interest and principal or lease payments. The present value of each of these payments could be added up to find the present value of this annuity, or alternatively a much simpler approach is available. The formula for calculating the present value of an annuity of $1 payments over *n* periodic payments, at a periodic interest rate of *r* is

$$PV \text{ Annuity} = \frac{\left(1 - \frac{1}{(1+r)^n}\right)}{r}$$

The results of this formula are summarized in an annuity present value factor table.

| (n) Periods | 2% | 3% | 4% | 5% | 6% | 7% | 8% | 9% | 10% |
|---|---|---|---|---|---|---|---|---|---|
| 1 | 0.9804 | 0.9709 | 0.9615 | 0.9524 | 0.9434 | 0.9346 | 0.9259 | 0.9174 | 0.9091 |
| 2 | 1.9416 | 1.9135 | 1.8861 | 1.8594 | 1.8334 | 1.8080 | 1.7833 | 1.7591 | 1.7355 |
| 3 | 2.8839 | 2.8286 | 2.7751 | 2.7233 | 2.6730 | 2.6243 | 2.5771 | 2.5313 | 2.4869 |
| 4 | 3.8077 | 3.7171 | 3.6299 | 3.5460 | 3.4651 | 3.3872 | 3.3121 | 3.2397 | 3.1699 |
| 5 | 4.7135 | 4.5797 | 4.4518 | 4.3295 | 4.2124 | 4.1002 | 3.9927 | 3.8897 | 3.7908 |

### Example

Suppose four annual payments of $1,000 will be needed to satisfy an agreement with a supplier. What would be the amount of the liability today if the interest rate the supplier is charging is 6% per year? Using the table to get the present value factor, the n = 4 periods row, and the 6% column, gives you a factor of 3.4651. Multiply this by $1,000 and you get a liability of $3,465.10 that should be recorded. Using the formula would also give you the same answer with r = 6% and n = 4.

Caution must be exercised when payments are not to be made on an annual basis. If payments are on a semiannual basis n = 8, but *r* is now 3%. This is because *r* is the periodic interest rate, and the semiannual rate would not be 6%, but half of the 6% annual rate. Note that this is somewhat simplified, since due to the effect of compound interest 3% semiannually is slightly more than a 6% annual rate.

**Example of the relevance of present values.** A measurement based on the present value of estimated future cash flows provides more relevant information than a measurement based on the undiscounted sum of those cash flows. For example, consider the following four future cash flows, all of which have an undiscounted value of $100,000:

1. Asset A has a fixed contractual cash flow of $100,000 due tomorrow. The cash flow is certain of receipt.
2. Asset B has a fixed contractual cash flow of $100,000 due in twenty years. The cash flow is certain of receipt.
3. Asset C has a fixed contractual cash flow of $100,000 due in twenty years. The amount that ultimately will be received is uncertain. There is an 80% probability that the entire $100,000 will be received. There is a 20% probability that $80,000 will be received.
4. Asset D has an *expected* cash flow of $100,000 due in twenty years. The amount that ultimately will be received is uncertain. There is a 25% probability that $120,000 will be received. There is a 50% probability that $100,000 will be received. There is a 25% probability that $80,000 will be received.

Assuming a 5% risk-free rate of return, the present values of the assets are

1. Asset A has a present value of $99,986. The time value of money assigned to the one-day period is $14 [$100,000 × .05/365 days]
2. Asset B has a present value of $37,689 [$100,000/$(1 + .05)^{20}$]
3. Asset C has a present value of $36,181 [$(100,000 × .8 + 80,000 × .2)/(1 + .05)^{20}$]
4. Asset D has a present value of $37,689 [($120,000 × .25 + 100,000 × .5 + 80,000 × .25)/(1 + .05)^{20}$]

Although each of these assets has the same undiscounted cash flows, few would argue that they are economically the same or that a rational investor would pay the same price for each. Investors require compensation for the time value of money. They also require a risk premium. That is, given a choice between Asset B with expected cash flows that are certain and Asset D with cash flows of the same expected amount that are uncertain, investors will place a higher value on Asset B, even though they have the same expected present value. CON 7 says that the risk premium should be subtracted from the expected cash flows before applying the discount rate. Thus, if the risk premium for Asset D was $500, the risk-adjusted present values would be $37,500 {[($120,000 × .25 + 100,000 × .5 + 80,000 × .25) − 500]/$(1 + .05)^{20}$}.

**Practical matters.** Like any accounting measurement, the application of an expected cash flow approach is subject to a cost-benefit constraint. The cost of obtaining additional information must be weighed against the additional reliability that information will bring to the measurement. As a practical matter, an entity that uses present value measurements often has little or no information about some or all of the assumptions that investors would use in assessing the fair value of an asset or a liability. Instead, the entity must use the information that is available to it without undue cost and effort when it develops cash flow estimates. The entity's own assumptions about future cash flows can be used to estimate fair value using present value techniques, as long as there are no contrary data indicating that investors would use different assumptions. However, if contrary data exist, the entity must adjust its assumptions to incorporate that market information.

# 2 BALANCE SHEET

## PERSPECTIVE AND ISSUES

Balance sheets (also known as statements of financial position) present information about assets, liabilities, and owners' equity (depending on the type of reporting enterprise, this is referred to as shareholders' equity, net assets, members' equity, or partners' capital) and their relationships to each other. They reflect an enterprise's resources (assets) and its financing structure (liabilities and equity) in conformity with generally accepted accounting principles. The balance sheet reports the aggregate effect of transactions at a point in time, whereas the statements of income, retained earnings, comprehensive income, and cash flows all report the effect of transactions occurring during a specified period of time such as a month, quarter, or year.

For years, users of financial statements put more emphasis on the income statement than on the balance sheet. Investors' main concern was the short-run maximization of earnings per share. During the late 1960s and early 1970s, the future prospects of business enterprises were largely judged based on measures of earnings growth. But the combination of inflation and recession during the 1970s and the emphasis in FASB's Conceptual Framework Project on the asset-liability approach to accounting theory brought about a rediscovery of the balance sheet. This shift toward emphasis on the balance sheet has marked a departure from the traditional transaction-based concept of income toward a capital maintenance concept espoused by economists. Under this approach to income measurement, the amount of beginning net assets would be compared to the amount of ending net assets, and the difference would be adjusted for dividends and capital transactions. Only to the extent that an enterprise maintained its net assets (after adjusting for capital transactions) would income be earned. By using a capital maintenance concept, it was asserted that investors would theoretically be better able to predict the overall profit potential of the reporting enterprise.

The balance sheet is studied in order to assess the enterprise's liquidity, financial flexibility, ability to pay its debts when due, and to distribute cash to its investors to provide an acceptable rate of return. An enterprise's liquidity refers to the extent to which it holds cash or cash equivalents in the normal course of operating its business. The concept of financial flexibility is broader than the concept of liquidity. Financial flexibility is a company's ability to take effective actions to alter the amounts and timing of its cash flows so it can respond to unexpected needs and opportunities. Financial flexibility includes the ability to raise new equity capital or to borrow additional amounts by, for example, utilizing unused lines of credit.

The rights of the shareholders and other suppliers of capital (bondholders and other creditors) of an enterprise are many and varied. The disclosure of these rights is an important objective in the presentation of financial statements. The rights of shareholders and creditors are mutually exclusive claims against the assets of the enterprise, and the rights of creditors (liabilities) take precedence over the rights of shareholders (equity). Both sources of capital are concerned with two basic rights: the right to share in the cash or property disbursements (interest and dividends) and the right to share in the assets in the event of liquidation.

Although a balance sheet presents an enterprise's financial position, it does not purport to report its value. It cannot for reasons that include

- The values of certain assets, such as human resources, secret processes, and competitive advantages are not included in a balance sheet despite the fact that they have value and will generate future cash flows.
- The values of other assets are measured at historical cost, rather than market value, replacement cost, or specific value to the enterprise. For example, property and equipment are measured at original cost reduced by depreciation, but the underlying assets' value can significantly exceed that adjusted cost and the assets may continue to be productive even though fully depreciated in the accounting records.
- The values of most liabilities are measured at the present value of cash flows at the date the liability was incurred rather than at the current market rate. When market rates increase, the increase in value of a liability payable at a fixed interest rate that is below market is not recognized in the balance sheet. Conversely, when interest rates decrease, the loss in value of a liability payable at a fixed rate in excess of the market rate is not recognized.

In recent years, FASB standards have increasingly employed fair value as the relevant measure for items presented in the balance sheet. For example, FAS 115, *Accounting for Certain Investments in Debt and Equity Securities,* changed the relevant measure for most investments in securities to fair value from the lower of cost or market. FAS 133, *Accounting for Derivative Instruments and Hedging Activities,* requires derivative financial instruments, whether asset or liabilities, to be reported at fair value which, prior to that pronouncement, were not reported on the balance sheet at all. FAS 157, *Fair Value Measurements,* improves the consistency and comparability of the fair value measurements appearing in the balance sheet. Measuring more assets and liabilities at fair value enhances the ability of a balance sheet to report a measure that more closely approximates the enterprise's value.

In many industries, it is common for the balance sheet to be divided into classifications based on the length of the enterprise's operating cycle. Assets are classified as "current" if they are reasonably expected to be converted into cash, sold, or consumed either within one year or within one operating cycle, whichever is longer. Liabilities are classified as "current" if they are expected to be liquidated through the use of current assets or incurring other current liabilities. The excess or deficiency of current assets over or under current liabilities, which is referred to as net working capital, identifies, if positive, the relatively liquid portion of the enterprise's capital that is potentially available to serve as a buffer for meeting unexpected obligations arising within the ordinary operating cycle of the business.

In some industries, the concept of working capital has little importance and the balance sheet is not classified. Such industries include broker-dealers, investment companies, real estate companies, and utilities. Personal financial statements are unclassified for the same reason.

| Sources of GAAP | | | | | | |
|---|---|---|---|---|---|---|
| *ARB* | *APB* | *FAS* | *FIN* | *FTB* | *EITF* | *CON* |
| 43, Ch. 2, 3A | 6,10, 12, 21, 22 | 5, 6, 12, 57,78, 95, 115,130, 141(R), 150, 157, 160 | 8, 39, 45 | 793 | 02-1 | 6 |

## DEFINITIONS OF TERMS

**Assets.** Probable future economic benefits obtained or controlled by a particular enterprise as a result of past transactions or events (CON 6).

The following three characteristics must be present for an item to qualify as an asset:

1. The asset must provide probable future economic benefit that enables it to provide future net cash inflows.
2. The enterprise must be able to receive the benefit and restrict others' access to it.
3. The event that provides the enterprise with the right to receive the benefit has occurred.

All three characteristics must be present for an item to meet the definition of an asset. Assets have other characteristics, but those characteristics are not essential to the definition. For example, most assets are exchangeable, legally enforceable, or tangible. But an item can still be an asset even if it cannot be exchanged, provided that the enterprise that owns it can use it in a manner that generates future cash flows or other benefits. Similarly, rights to an item need not be legally enforceable if the rights can be enforced in other ways, such as by using social or moral persuasion. Finally, assets need not be tangible. Securities, patents, and similar ownership rights are assets despite the fact that they cannot be touched or seen.

The characteristic possessed by all assets is service potential (also called future economic benefit); the ability to directly or indirectly provide services or benefits to the owner of the asset, usually in the form of future cash inflows. Once recognized, an asset remains on the balance sheet until it is exchanged for another asset, used to settle a liability, its future economic benefits are used up, or it no longer is expected to provide future benefits (e.g., obsolescence of inventory or impairment of long-lived assets).

**Liabilities.** Probable future sacrifices of economic benefits arising from present obligations of an enterprise to transfer assets or provide services to others in the future as a result of past transactions or events (CON 6).

The following three characteristics must be present for an item to qualify as a liability:

1.  A liability requires that the enterprise settle a present obligation by the probable future transfer of an asset on demand, when a specified event occurs, or at a particular date.
2.  The obligation cannot be avoided.
3.  The event that obligates the enterprise has occurred.

Liabilities usually result from transactions in which enterprises obtain economic resources. For example, trade accounts payable result from purchasing raw materials; salaries and wages payable result from employees providing services, and notes payable result from borrowing cash from a lender. Other liabilities may arise from nonreciprocal transfers such as the declaration of dividends payable to the owners of the enterprise or the pledging of assets as a contribution to a charitable organization. An enterprise may incur a liability involuntarily. A liability may be imposed on the enterprise by government or by the court system in the form of taxes, fines, or levies. A liability may arise from changes in prices or interest rates.

Liabilities are imposed by agreement, by law, by court, by equitable or constructive obligation, and by business ethics and custom. Liabilities may be legally enforceable or they may be equitable obligations that arise from social, ethical, or moral requirements.

Liabilities are reflected on the balance sheet until the enterprise is no longer responsible for discharging them. Most liabilities are discharged either by transferring an asset or incurring another liability. However, some liabilities simply expire. For example, warranty liabilities are estimates of goods that will be returned for repair or replacement or cash that will have to be paid to a dissatisfied customer. At the end of the warranty period, any remaining liability simply is removed from the balance sheet.

Some financial instruments that have historically been reported as equity are now reported as liabilities. These include mandatorily redeemable financial instruments issued in the form of shares, a financial instrument that includes an obligation to repurchase the issuer's equity shares, and obligations requiring issuance of equity shares based on various limiting criteria. This change has been quite controversial, and indeed certain provisions of the standard (FAS 150) have been indefinitely postponed as to effective date (see Chapter 19 for discussion).

**Equity.** Equity is the residual interest in the assets of the enterprise that remains after deducting its liabilities. In a business enterprise, as distinguished from a not-for-profit organization or governmental unit, the equity represents the interest of its owners (CON 6).

Equity is increased by owners' investments and by comprehensive income, and it is reduced by distributions to the owners. Equity of a business enterprise is the source of its distributions to the owners; all such distributions of enterprise assets to owners are voluntary. Because equity is a residual (the net amount of assets less liabilities), equity is affected by all transactions and events that increase or decrease assets without increasing or decreasing liabilities by the same amount.

A diagram reproduced from CON 6 that appears in the "Researching GAAP Problems" section of Chapter 1 illustrates this relationship. For example, issuing a bond does not change equity because the increase in the asset (cash) is the same as the increase in the liability (bonds payable). Paying interest on the bond does change equity. The decrease in the asset (cash) is not offset by a corresponding decrease in the liability (bonds payable).

In practice, the distinction between equity and liabilities may be difficult to ascertain. Securities such as convertible debt and preferred stock may have characteristics of both equity (residual ownership interest) and liabilities (nondiscretionary future sacrifices). For such items, the objective of accounting standards is to ensure that transactions that are similar in substance are reported in a similar manner by different enterprises, irrespective of their form.

**Valuation allowance.** The valuation allowance is a separate item on a balance sheet (or disclosed in the notes to the financial statement) that reduces or increases the carrying amount of an asset or a liability. It is neither an asset nor a liability in its own right; it is merely a mechanism used to adjust the carrying amount of the related asset or liability. For example, an estimate of uncollectible amounts reduces the carrying amount of an account receivable, while a bond premium increases the carrying amount of bonds payable.

## CONCEPTS, RULES, AND EXAMPLES

### Limitations of a Balance Sheet

Although a balance sheet shows an enterprise's *financial position* at a point in time, it does not purport to report the value of the enterprise at that date. There are several reasons why this is so. One limitation of the balance sheet is that many assets and liabilities are reported at historical transaction prices (referred to as "historical cost"), that are used because they are objective and capable of being independently verified. Historical costs, however, will only equal fair value at the time of the actual transaction; thereafter, the two will almost always differ.

Many accountants and analysts believe that the balance sheet would be more useful if the assets were restated to reflect current values. These current values might or might not be market related, and might simply be presented as historical cost adjusted for the changing value of the dollar due to inflation. However, for some assets and liabilities, cost already closely approximates current fair value. The cost of monetary assets such as cash, short-term investments, and receivables closely approximates their current fair values. The cost of current liabilities, which are liabilities that require either a current asset or another current liability to liquidate, is payable in a short period and closely approximates current values. If they were to be discounted to their present value, any discount amount would likely be immaterial because of the short time period before payment is due.

For other assets and liabilities, cost can significantly differ from current value. Productive assets such as property, plant, equipment, and amortizable intangibles are reported at cost net of accumulated depreciation, depletion, or amortization. Those amounts may differ from their current values to the enterprise (value in use) or to others (exit or net realizable values). Long-term liabilities are recorded as the discounted value of future payments to be made under contract. On the issuance date of fixed-rate debt, the interest rate equals the market rate and current value equals balance sheet cost. However, as time passes and the market interest rate fluctuates, the recorded cost will differ from the current value.

Although assets are often stated at historical cost, if events or changes in circumstances indicate a permanent and material decline in fair value, generally accepted accounting principles usually require immediate recognition of the economic loss. In contrast, appreciation in fair value is normally recognized for accounting purposes only when actually realized in an arm's-length transaction (e.g., a sale). However, the recent trend in newly issued financial accounting standards has been to reflect increases as well as decreases in the fair values of assets and liabilities in the financial statements. FAS 115 and FAS 133 require that debt securities, most equity securities, and derivative financial instruments be reported at fair value. Reporting liabilities at fair value is less common under current GAAP, but there are certain exceptions, including mandatorily redeemable preferred stock, which is classified as debt per FAS 150 and measured initially and subsequently at fair value.

Another limitation of the balance sheet is that, with respect to the presentation of certain assets and liabilities, it ignores the effects of the time value of money. Although certain receivables and payables may be discounted (APB 21), most assets and liabilities are stated at carrying amounts that are not determined by reference to the expected timing of the related cash inflows or outflows that will ultimately occur.

In the historical cost balance sheet, estimates are frequently used to determine the carrying/book values of many of the assets. Estimates are used in determining the collectibility of receivables, salability of inventory, and useful lives of long-term assets. All of these estimates affect the amount presented in the balance sheet; for example, estimated uncollectible accounts are deducted from accounts receivable to reflect the estimated net realizable value displayed in the balance sheet. While estimates are necessary in order to record the effects of economic events in the appropriate accounting period, these estimates require informed, good-faith judgments for which there is little practical guidance provided in authoritative accounting literature.

A final limitation of the balance sheet is that it ignores items that are of financial value to the enterprise but that cannot be objectively determined. For example, internally generated goodwill, a skilled and trained workforce, and secret processes are potential sources of substantial financial value sometimes, in our knowledge-based economy, far exceeding the recorded value of recognized assets. However, because these values are not objectively and verifiably measurable, current accounting principles and practices prohibit their presentation on the balance sheet. Presently, only assets obtained in market transactions are recorded in the accounting records of an enterprise.

## Form of Balance Sheet

The format of a balance sheet is not specified by any authoritative pronouncement. Instead, formats and titles have developed as a matter of tradition and, in some cases, through industry practice.

Two basic formats are used.

1. The balanced format, in which the sum of the amounts for liabilities and equity are added together on the face of the statement to illustrate that assets equal liabilities plus equity
2. The less frequently presented equity format, which shows totals for assets, liabilities, and equity but no sums illustrating that assets less liabilities equals equity

Those two formats can take one of two forms.

1. The account form, presenting assets on the left-hand side of the page and liabilities and equity on the right-hand side
2. The report form, which is a top-to-bottom or running presentation

The three elements customarily displayed in the heading of a balance sheet are

1. The legal name of the enterprise whose financial position is being presented
2. The title of the statement (e.g., balance sheet or statement of financial position)
3. The date of the statement (or statements, if multiple dates are presented for comparative purposes)

The enterprise's legal name appears in the heading exactly as specified in the document that created it (e.g., the certificate of incorporation, partnership agreement, LLC operating agreement, etc.). The legal form of the enterprise is often evident from its name when the name includes such designations as "incorporated," "LLP," or "LLC." Otherwise, the legal form is either captioned as part of the heading or disclosed in the notes to the financial statements. A few examples are as follows:

**ABC Company**
(a general partnership)

**ABC Company**
(a sole proprietorship)

**ABC Company**
(a division of DEF, Inc.)

The use of the titles "balance sheet," "statement of financial position," or "statement of financial condition" infer that the statement is presented using generally accepted accounting principles. If, instead, some other comprehensive basis of accounting, such as income tax basis or cash basis is used, the financial statement title must be revised to reflect this variation. The use of a title such as "Statements of Assets and Liabilities—Income Tax Basis" is necessary to differentiate the financial statement being presented from a GAAP balance sheet.

The last day of the fiscal period is used as the statement date. Usually, this is a month-end date unless the enterprise uses a fiscal reporting period always ending on a particular day of the week such as Friday or Sunday. In these cases, the balance sheet would be dated accordingly (i.e., December 26, October 1, etc.).

Balance sheets generally are uniform in appearance from one period to the next with consistently followed form, terminology, captions, and patterns of combining insignificant items. If changes in the manner of presentation are made when comparative statements are presented, the prior year's information is to be restated to conform to the current year's presentation.

### Assets

Assets, liabilities, and shareholders' equity are separated in the balance sheet so that important relationships can be shown and attention can be focused on significant subtotals.

**Current assets.** Per ARB 43, Chapter 3, current assets are cash and other assets that are reasonably expected to be realized in cash or sold or consumed during the normal operating cycle of the business. When the normal operating cycle is less than one year, a one-year period is used to distinguish current assets from noncurrent assets. When the operating cycle exceeds one year, the operating cycle will serve as the proper period for purposes of current asset classification. When the operating cycle is very long, the usefulness of the concept of current assets diminishes. The following items are classified as current assets:

1. **Cash and cash equivalents** include cash on hand consisting of coins, currency, undeposited checks; money orders and drafts; demand deposits in banks; and certain short-term, highly liquid investments. Any type of instrument accepted by a bank for deposit would be considered to be cash. Cash must be available for withdrawal on demand. Cash that is restricted as to withdrawal, such as certificates of deposit, would not be included with cash because of the time restrictions. Also, cash must be available for current use in order to be classified as a current asset. Cash that is restricted in use would not be included in cash unless its restrictions will expire within the operating cycle. Cash restricted for a noncurrent use, such as cash designated for the purchase of property or equipment, would not be included in current assets. Per FAS 95, cash equivalents include short-term, highly liquid investments that (1) are readily convertible to known amounts of cash and (2) are so near their maturity (maturities of three months or less from the date of purchase by the enterprise) that they present negligible risk of changes in value because of changes in

interest rates. US Treasury bills, commercial paper, and money market funds are all examples of cash equivalents. Chapter 7 discusses cash in more detail.

2.  **Short-term investments** are readily marketable securities acquired through the use of temporarily idle cash. To be classified as current assets, management must be willing and able to sell the security to meet current cash needs or the investment must mature within one year (or the operating cycle, if longer). These securities are accounted for under FAS 115. Securities classified as trading securities under FAS 115 must be reported as current assets. Securities classified as held-to-maturity or available-for-sale are reported as either current or noncurrent depending upon management's intended holding period, the security's maturity date (if any), or both. It is not necessary to show the FAS 115 classification on the face of the balance sheet. Short-term investments can be combined into a single line if the classification details appear in the notes to the financial statements. The balance sheet presentation might be as follows:

| | |
|---|---|
| Marketable securities | $xxx |

Chapter 8 discusses short-term investments in more detail.

3.  **Receivables** include accounts and notes receivable, receivables from affiliated enterprises, and officer and employee receivables. The term "accounts receivable" is generally understood to represent amounts due from customers arising from transactions in the ordinary course of business (sometimes referred to as "trade receivables"). Valuation allowances, if any, are to be clearly stated. Estimates of needed allowances for uncollectibility may be based on historical correlations of bad debt experience as a percentage of sales or based on a direct credit quality analysis of the receivables. Valuation allowances to reflect the time value of money (discounts) are reported with the related receivable. If material, the different components that comprise receivables are to be separately stated. Receivables pledged as collateral are to be disclosed in the notes to the financial statements. The receivables section of a balance sheet might be presented as follows:

| | |
|---|---|
| Receivables: | |
| Accounts | $xxx |
| Notes | xxx |
| | xxx |
| Less allowance for uncollectible accounts | (xxx) |
| | xxx |
| Affiliated companies | xxx |
| Officers and employees | xxx |
| | $xxx |

Chapter 7 discusses receivables in more detail.

4.  **Inventories** are goods on hand and available for sale. The basis of valuation and the method of pricing are to be disclosed. One form of presentation is as follows:

| | |
|---|---|
| Inventories—at the lower of cost or market (specific identification) | $xxx |

In the case of a manufacturing concern, raw materials, work in process, and finished goods are stated separately on the balance sheet or disclosed in the notes to the financial statements. Customarily, the components of manufacturing inventories are stated in order of their readiness for sale and ultimate conversion to cash—that is, finished goods are ready for sale, work in process is closer to being finished than raw materials and, of course, raw materials have not yet been placed into production. A sample form of presentation is as follows:

Inventories:

|  |  |
|---|---|
| Finished goods | $xxx |
| Work in process | xxx |
| Raw materials | xxx |
|  | $xxx |

Chapter 9 discusses inventories in more detail.

5. **Prepaid expenses** are amounts paid in advance to secure the use of assets or the receipt of services at a future date. Prepaid expenses will not be converted to cash, but they are classified as current assets because, if not prepaid, they would have required the use of current assets during the coming year (or operating cycle, if longer). Prepaid rent and prepaid insurance are the most common examples of prepaid expenses. Chapter 7 discusses prepaid expenses in more detail.

**Noncurrent assets.** Excluded from the classification of current assets are assets that will not be realized in cash during the next year (or operating cycle, if longer). The following assets would be classified as noncurrent assets:

1. **Long-term investments** are investments that are intended to be held for an extended period of time (longer than one operating cycle). The following are the three major types of long-term investments:

   a. **Debt and equity securities** are stocks, bonds, and long-term notes receivable. Securities that are classified as available-for-sale or held-to-maturity investments under FAS 115 would be classified as long-term if management intended to hold them for more than one year. Under FAS 115, the categories of these securities (held-to-maturity versus available-for-sale) need not be reported on the face of the balance sheet if they are reported in the notes to the financial statements. The securities section of the balance sheet could be presented as follows:

Long-term investments:

|  |  |  |
|---|---|---|
| Investments in A company common stock |  | $xxx |
| Notes receivable | $ xxx |  |
| Less discount on notes receivable | (xxx) | xxx |
| Investment in B company bonds |  | xxx |
|  |  | $xxx |

   b. **Tangible assets** not currently used in operations (e.g., land purchased as an investment and held for sale).

   c. **Investments held in special funds** (e.g., sinking funds, pension funds, amounts held for plant expansion, and cash surrender values of life insurance policies).

   Chapter 12 describes investments in more detail.

2. **Property, plant, and equipment** are assets of a durable nature that are used in the production or sale of goods, sale of other assets, or rendering of services rather than being held for sale (e.g., machinery and equipment, buildings, furniture and fixtures, natural resources, and land). These are disclosed with related accumulated depreciation/depletion as follows:

|  |  |
|---|---|
| Property, plant, and equipment | $xxx |
| Less accumulated depreciation | (xxx) |
|  | $xxx |
| or |  |
| Property, plant, and equipment (net of $xxx accumulated depreciation) | $xxx |

Accumulated depreciation may be shown in total or by major classes of depreciable assets. In addition to showing this amount on the balance sheet, the notes to the financial statements are to disclose the amounts of major classes of depreciable assets, by nature or function, at the balance sheet date. Assets under capital leases are separately disclosed. A general description of the method or methods used in computing depreciation with respect to major classes of depreciable assets (APB 12) is also to be included in the notes to financial statements. Chapter 11 discusses property, plant, and equipment and Chapter 16 discusses capital leases in more detail.

3. **Intangible assets** include legal and/or contractual rights that are expected to provide future economic benefits and purchased goodwill. The technical definition of goodwill is that it represents the excess of the cost of an acquired enterprise over the net of the fair values assigned to its identifiable assets and liabilities. Practically, goodwill represents the amount by which the acquirer believes the acquiree enterprise's fair value as a whole exceeds the net fair value of its assets and liabilities. Goodwill is only recognized as an asset when acquired in a business combination; internally generated goodwill is not recognized. Patents, copyrights, logos, and trademarks are examples of rights that are recognized as intangible assets. Intangible assets with finite useful lives are amortized to expense over those lives. Generally, the amortization of an intangible asset is credited directly to the recorded amount of the asset although it is acceptable to use an accumulated amortization valuation allowance. Intangible assets with indefinite economic useful lives are tested for impairment at least annually. Chapter 13 discusses goodwill in more detail. Chapter 11 discusses other intangible assets.

4. **Other assets.** Other assets is an all-inclusive heading which incorporates assets that do not fit neatly into any of the other asset categories (e.g., long-term prepaid expenses, deposits made to purchase equipment, deferred income tax assets (net of any required valuation allowance), bond issue costs, noncurrent receivables, and restricted cash).

## Liabilities

Liabilities are displayed on the balance sheet in the order of expected payment. The distinction between current and noncurrent assets and liabilities generally rests upon both the ability and intent of the enterprise to liquidate or not to liquidate within the traditional one-year time frame or the operating cycle, if longer.

**Current liabilities.** Per ARB 43, Chapter 3, obligations are classified as current if their liquidation is reasonably expected to require the use of existing resources properly classifiable as current assets or to create other current obligations. Obligations that are due on demand or that are callable at any time by the lender are classified as current regardless of the intent of the enterprise or lender. The following items are classified as current liabilities:

1. **Accounts payable.** Accounts payable is normally comprised of amounts due to suppliers (vendors) for the purchase of goods and services used in the ordinary course of running a business.

2. **Trade notes payable** are also obligations that arise from the purchase of goods and services. They differ from accounts payable because the supplier or vendor finances the purchase on terms longer than the customary period for trade payables. The supplier or vendor generally charges interest for this privilege. If interest is not charged, it is imputed in accordance with APB 21. (Imputed interest is discussed further in Chapter 15.) A valuation allowance is used to reduce the carrying amount of the note for the resulting discount as follows:

| | | |
|---|---|---|
| Notes payable, net of imputed interest of $xx | | $ xxx |
| or | | |
| Notes payable | $ xxx | |
| Less discounts | (xxx) | $ xxx |

3. **Dividends payable** are obligations to distribute cash or other assets to shareholders that arise from the declaration of dividends by the enterprise's board of directors.

4. **Advances and deposits** are collections of cash or other assets received in advance to ensure the future delivery of goods or services. Advances and deposits are classified as current liabilities if the goods and services are to be delivered within the next year (or the operating cycle, if longer). Advances and deposits include such items as advance rentals and customer deposits. Certain advances and deposits are sometimes captioned as deferred or unearned revenues.

5. **Agency collections and withholdings** are liabilities that arise because the enterprise acts as an agent for another party. Employee tax withholdings, sales taxes, and wage garnishments are examples of agency collections.

6. **Current portion of long-term debt** is the portion of a long-term obligation that will be settled during the next year (or operating cycle, if longer) by using current assets. Generally, this amount includes only the payments due within the next year under the terms of the underlying agreement. However, if the enterprise has violated a covenant in a long-term debt agreement and, as a result, the investor is legally entitled to demand payment, the entire debt amount is classified as current unless the lender formally (in writing) waives the right to demand repayment of the debt for a period in excess of one year (or one operating cycle, if longer). In two cases, obligations to be paid in the next year are not classified as current liabilities. Debt expected to be refinanced through another long-term issue and debt that will be retired through the use of noncurrent assets, such as a bond sinking fund, are treated as noncurrent liabilities because the liquidation does not require the use of current assets or the creation of other current liabilities.

7. **Accrued expenses** represent estimates of expenses incurred on or before the balance sheet date that have not yet been paid and that are not payable until a succeeding period within the next year. Examples of accrued expenses include salaries, vacation pay, interest, and retirement plan contributions.

Chapter 14 discusses current liabilities in more detail.

**Noncurrent liabilities.** Obligations that are not expected to be liquidated within one year (or the current operating cycle, if longer) are classified as noncurrent. The following items would be classified as noncurrent:

1. **Notes and bonds payable** are obligations that will be paid in more than one year (or one operating cycle, if longer). Most notes and bonds require periodic payments of interest, and some require periodic payments of principal. If the stated rate of interest on a note or bond is different than the market rate on the day the note or bond is issued, the proceeds from issuance will differ from the face amount of the note or bond. If the market rate is higher than the stated rate, the bonds will be issued at a discount, which means that the proceeds are less than the face amount. If the market rate is lower than the stated rate, the bonds will be issued at a premium, which means that the proceeds exceed the face amount. Valuation allowances are used to adjust the carrying value of the debt to reflect the resulting discount or premium, as shown below.

| | | |
|---|---|---|
| Notes payable, including premium of $xx | | $xxx |
| or | | |
| Notes payable | $xxx | |
| Plus premium | $xxx | $xxx |

Discounts and premiums are amortized using the effective-interest-rate method, which results in a constant interest rate over the life of the debt. Chapter 15 discusses notes and bonds payable in more detail.

2. **Capital lease obligations** are contractual obligations that arise from obtaining the use of property or equipment via a capital lease contract. Chapter 16 discusses lease obligations.

3. **Written put options on the option writer's (issuer's) equity shares and forward contracts to purchase an issuer's equity shares that require physical or net cash settlement** are classified as liabilities on the issuer's balance sheet. The obligation is classified as noncurrent unless the date at which the contract will be settled is within the next year (or operating cycle, if longer). These contracts are discussed further in Chapter 15.

4. **Certain financial instruments that embody an unconditional obligation to issue a variable number of equity shares and financial instruments other than outstanding shares that embody a conditional obligation to issue a variable number of equity shares** are classified as a liability in the issuer's balance sheet. The obligation is classified as noncurrent unless the date at which the financial instrument will be settled is within the next year (or operating cycle, if longer). Chapter 15 discusses these financial instruments.

5. **Contingent obligations** are recorded when it is probable that an obligation will occur as the result of a past event. In most cases, a future event will eventually confirm the amount payable, the payee, or the date payable. Examples of contingent obligations are lawsuits that have not been settled, product warranty obligations, guarantees of indebtedness (other than the obligation to stand ready to perform, which is a noncontingent liability), and agreements to repurchase an asset or make future payments. The classification of a contingent liability as current or noncurrent depends on when the confirming event will occur and how soon afterwards payment must be made. Contingencies are discussed further in Chapter 14.

6. **Mandatorily redeemable shares** are recorded as liabilities per FAS 150. A mandatory redemption clause requires common or preferred stock to be redeemed (retired) at a specific date(s) or upon occurrence of an event which is uncertain as to timing although ultimately certain to occur. This feature is in contrast to callable preferred stock, which may be redeemed at the issuing corporation's option and which is appropriately categorized as equity. The obligation is classified as noncurrent unless the date at which the shares must be redeemed is within the next year (or operating cycle, if longer). See Chapters 15 and 19 for additional discussion of these securities.

7. **Other noncurrent liabilities** include defined benefit pension obligations, postemployment obligations, and postretirement obligations. These reflect the long-term obligations of the enterprise to provide future retirement, insurance, or other benefits to employees as a result of their past service. Those obligations are described in more detail in Chapter 18. Deferred income taxes are liabilities to pay income taxes in the future that result from differences between the carrying amounts of assets and liabilities for income tax and financial reporting purposes. Chapter 17 discusses deferred income taxes.

## Offsetting Assets and Liabilities

In general, assets and liabilities are not permitted to be offset against each other unless certain specified criteria are met. FIN 39 permits offsetting only when all of the following conditions are met that constitute a right of setoff:

1. Each of the two parties owes the other determinable amounts (although they may be in different currencies and bear different rates of interest).
2. The enterprise has the right to set off the amount it owes against the amount owed to it by the other party.
3. The enterprise intends to set off the two amounts.
4. The right of setoff is legally enforceable.

In particular cases, state laws or bankruptcy laws may impose restrictions or prohibitions against the right of setoff. Furthermore, when maturities differ, only the party with the nearest maturity can offset, because the party with the later maturity must settle in the manner determined by the party with the earlier maturity.

The offsetting of cash or other assets against a tax liability or other amounts due to governmental bodies is acceptable only under limited circumstances. When it is clear that a purchase of securities is in substance an advance payment of taxes payable in the near future and the securities are acceptable for the payment of taxes, amounts may be offset. Primarily this occurs as an accommodation to governmental bodies that issue tax anticipation notes in order to accelerate the receipt of cash from future taxes.

For forwards, interest rate swaps, currency swaps, options, and other conditional or exchange contracts, the conditions for the right of offset must exist or the fair value of contracts in a loss position cannot be offset against the fair value of contracts in a gain position. Nor can accrued receivable amounts be offset against accrued payable amounts. If, however, there is a master netting arrangement, then fair value amounts recognized for forwards, interest or currency swaps, options, or other such contracts may be offset without being subject to the conditions previously specified.

FIN 41 permits the offset of amounts recognized as payables in repurchase agreements against amounts recognized as receivables in reverse repurchase agreements with the same counterparty. If certain conditions are met, an enterprise may, but is not required to, offset the amounts recognized. The additional conditions are

1. The repurchase agreements and the reverse repurchase agreements must have the same explicit settlement date.
2. The repurchase agreements and the reverse repurchase agreements must be executed in accordance with a master netting agreement.
3. The securities underlying the repurchase agreements and the reverse repurchase agreements exist in "book entry" form.
4. The repurchase agreements and the reverse repurchase agreements will be settled on a securities transfer system that transfers ownership of "book entry" securities, and banking arrangements are in place so that the enterprise must only keep cash on deposit sufficient to cover the net payable.
5. The same account at the clearing bank is used for the cash inflows of the settlement of the reverse repurchase agreements and the cash outflows in the settlement of the repurchase agreements.

## Stockholders' Equity

Owners' equity represents the residual interest in the assets of the enterprise after liabilities are subtracted from assets. In a corporation, shareholders' equity arises from three sources: contributed (paid-in) capital, retained earnings, and accumulated other comprehensive income. Shareholders' equity is discussed further in Chapter 19.

**Contributed capital.** Contributed, or paid-in capital is the amount of equity invested in a corporation by its owners. It consists of capital stock and additional paid-in capital. Contributed capital arises from the issuance of common and preferred stock to investors, from transactions by the corporation in its own stock (for example, treasury stock, stock dividends, conversion of convertible bonds) and from the donation of assets or services.

**Capital stock.** Capital stock is the par or stated value of preferred and common shares. In the past, capital stock was the legal capital of the corporation—the amount that could not be distributed to shareholders so that the interest of creditors would be protected. In recent years, some states have changed their laws so that legal capital includes additional paid-in capital (i.e., in those states the distinction between the capital stock and additional paid-in capital is not recognized). The face of the balance sheet often provides information about the type of issues, the par or stated value per share, and the number of shares authorized, issued, and outstanding. For preferred stock, the liquidation preferences and features (e.g., whether participating, cumulative, convertible, or callable) are also shown, as follows:

| | |
|---|---|
| 6% cumulative preferred stock, $100 par value, callable at $115, 10,000 shares authorized and outstanding, aggregate liquidation preference in liquidation of $xxx | $xxx |
| Common stock, $10 par value per share, 2,000,000 shares authorized, 1,500,000 shares issued and outstanding | $xxx |

**Additional paid-in capital.** There are two major categories of additional paid-in capital.

1. Paid-in capital in excess of par/stated value, which is the difference between the actual issue price of the shares and the shares' par/stated value. Amounts in excess are disclosed separately for common stock and each issue of preferred stock as follows:

   | | |
   |---|---|
   | Additional paid-in capital—6% preferred stock | $xxx |
   | Additional paid-in capital—common stock | $xxx |

2. Paid-in capital from other transactions, which includes treasury stock, retirement of stock, stock dividends recorded at market, lapse of stock purchase warrants, conversion of convertible bonds in excess of the par value of the stock, and any other additional capital from the company's own stock transactions.

**Retained earnings.** Retained earnings are the cumulative net income of the corporation from the date of its inception (or reorganization) to the date of the financial statements, less the cumulative distributions to shareholders either directly (dividends) or indirectly (treasury stock).

In the past, the board of directors of a corporation would appropriate (set aside) a portion of retained earnings for a special purpose and indicate on the face of the balance sheet or in the notes to the financial statements that the appropriated amount was unavailable for dividends. That practice is uncommon today.

**Accumulated other comprehensive income.** Other comprehensive income is the change in equity of a business enterprise during a period that arises from sources other than net income and transactions with its owners. Under current accounting standards, its accumulated components include net unrealized holding gains and losses on investments classified as available-for-sale securities (FAS 115), the effective portion of the gain or loss on derivative instruments designated and qualified as either cash-flow hedges or hedges of forecasted foreign-currency-denominated transactions (FAS 133), the excess of minimum pension liability over unrecognized prior service cost (FAS 87), and unrealized gains (losses) on foreign currency translations (FAS 52). The components of accumulated other comprehensive income are shown either in the statement of changes in shareholders' equity or in the shareholders' equity section of the balance sheet, as follows:

| | | |
|---|---|---|
| Accumulated other comprehensive income | | |
| Foreign currency translation adjustments | $xxx | |
| Pension liability adjustment | xxx | |
| Unrealized gains on securities | xxx | xxx |

**Treasury stock.** Treasury stock represents shares of the corporation's stock that have been issued, repurchased by the corporation, and that have not been retired or canceled. These shares have no voting rights and are not entitled to receive dividends. Treasury stock is traditionally shown as the last item (a deduction) within the shareholders' equity section. (In very limited circumstances involving employee compensation plans, treasury stock can be shown as an asset.) The number of shares and the method of valuation are generally shown, as follows:

Treasury stock, 1,000 shares at cost                                 $ xxx

## Partners' Capital

Partnership balance sheets are the same as corporate entities except for the equity section. In a partnership, this section is usually referred to as partners' capital. Although each individual partner's capital need not be displayed, the totals for each class of partner, general or limited, are separately presented. Loans to or from partners are displayed as assets and liabilities of the partnership and not as reductions of or additions to partners' capital. Payments of interest to partners on loans are properly classified as expenses on the income statement. Payments to partners representing a distribution of partnership earnings computed, in accordance with the partnership agreement, as a percentage of the partner's capital are analogous to corporate dividends and are therefore reflected as distributions of capital rather than as interest. Similarly, because a partner is not an employee of the partnership, amounts allocated to that partner in exchange for services rendered are considered capital distributions rather than expenses. However, in an attempt to emulate corporate financial reporting, some partnerships, with adequate disclosure, do display such payments as expenses.

**Members' equity.** A limited liability company (LLC) presents its equity using the caption "members' equity." In accordance with PB 14, the equity attributable to each class of member is to be separately stated on the face of the balance sheet or disclosed in the notes to the financial statements. Notwithstanding the legal limits on the members' liability, in the event that the LLC's cumulative losses and distributions exceed its members' collective capital investment, a deficit in members' equity is to be reflected. PB 14 permits presentation by the LLC of components of members' equity that are similar to those of corporate entities such as accumulated undistributed earnings (analogous to retained earnings).

## Alternative Balance Sheet Segmentation

Besides classifying balance sheets into current and noncurrent assets and liabilities, there are other segmentation schemes that GAAP requires for various reporting purposes, depending upon the circumstances. Since these requirements do not utilize a common taxonomy, the following explanation will be referenced throughout *Wiley GAAP*.

Classification of assets (and sometimes liabilities also) may be required for the presentation of segment information under FAS 131. This requirement only applies to publicly held entities, although nonpublic companies may also elect to make segment disclosures.

Under FAS 131, it will be necessary to identify operating segments and reportable segments of the business. (Terms are defined below.)

A different classification strategy is required for purposes of testing for impairment of goodwill, under FAS 142. This standard created the concept of the reporting unit as a basis for making an impairment evaluation.

Yet another term, a business, was defined in EITF 98-3 and was often used as a threshold criterion of what could not be considered a special-purpose entity (as addressed in various standards, including FAS 140). The consensus under EITF 98-3 has been nullified by FAS 141(R), which adopts an essentially identical definition.

Finally, another classification system is invoked under FAS 144 in assessing the realizability of long-lived assets for the purpose of determining whether those assets are impaired. This standard established the concepts of asset groups and disposal groups.

The graphic below has been developed to illustrate how these different classification schemes overlap. It is possible that a given enterprise, if it reports segment data and if it has goodwill from a business combination on its balance sheet, may be required to apply most or all of these taxonomies in meeting its financial reporting obligations—to disclose segment information, to test for goodwill impairment, and to test for impairment of long-lived assets other than goodwill.

**Definitions (with references to professional standards and the chapter of *Wiley GAAP* that addresses the associated topic).**

**Operating segment** (FAS 131, Chapter 22)—A component of an enterprise engaged in business activity for which it may earn revenues and incur expenses, about which separate financial information is available that is evaluated regularly by the chief operating decision makers in deciding how to allocate resources and in assessing performance.

**Reportable segment** (FAS 131, Chapter 22)—A segment is considered to be reportable if it is significant to the enterprise as a whole. A segment is regarded as significant if it satisfies any one of the three quantitative tests prescribed by FAS 131.

**Reporting unit** (FAS 142, Chapter 11)—A reporting unit is an operating segment or one level below an operating segment (referred to as a component). A component of an operating segment is a reporting unit if the component constitutes a business for which discrete financial information is available and segment management regularly reviews the operating results of that component. However, two or more components of an operating segment are to be aggregated and deemed a single reporting unit if the components have similar economic characteristics. An operating segment is deemed to be a reporting unit if all of its components are similar, if none of its components is a reporting unit, or if it comprises only a single component.

**Business** (FAS 141[R], Chapter 13)—A *business* is an integrated set of activities and assets that is capable of being conducted and managed for the purpose of providing a return in the form of dividends, lower costs, or other economic benefits directly to investors or other owners, members, or participants.

**Asset group** (FAS 144, Chapter 11)—The lowest level of assets to be held and used, for which identifiable cash flows are largely independent of the cash flows of other groups of assets and liabilities.

**Disposal group** (FAS 144, Chapters 3 and 11)—Assets to be disposed of together as a group in a single transaction and the liabilities directly associated with those assets that will be transferred in the transaction.

The Parent Holding Company

*Owns subsidiaries, land and headquarters building that they all use*

| Subsidiary 1 Division a Business i | Subsidiary 2 Business iv | Subsidiary 3 Business v 2 Product Lines | Subsidiary 4 2 Similar Businesses Business vi | Subsidiary 5 2 Similar Businesses Business viii | Subsidiary 6 Business ix | Subsidiary 7 2 Nonsimilar Businesses Business x |
|---|---|---|---|---|---|---|
| Asset Group (a) | Asset Group (d) with Primary Asset | Asset Group (e) and Disposal Group (f) | Asset Group (g) | Asset Group (i) | Asset Group (j) | Asset Group (k) |
| Reporting Unit (1) | Reporting Unit (2) | Reporting Unit (3) | Reporting Unit (4) | Reporting Unit (5) | | Reporting Unit (6) |
| Division b — Business ii: Asset Group (b); Business iii: Asset Group (c) | | | Business vii Asset Group (h) | | | Business xi Asset Group (l) Reporting Unit (7) |
| Operating Segment A | | Operating Segment B | Operating Segment C | Operating Segment D | | Operating Segment E |
| Reportable Segment I | | | Reportable Segment II | Reportable Segment III | | Reportable Segment IV |

## Disclosures

In addition to the measurement accounting principles that guide the values placed on the elements included in the balance sheet, there are accounting principles specifying the informative disclosures that are necessary because, without the information they provide, the financial statements would be misleading.

The following five disclosure techniques are used in varying degrees in contemporary financial statements:

1. Parenthetical explanations
2. Notes to the financial statements
3. Cross-references
4. Valuation allowances (sometimes referred to as "contra" amounts)
5. Supporting schedules

**Parenthetical explanations.** Information is sometimes disclosed by means of parenthetical explanations appended to the appropriate balance sheet caption. For example

| | |
|---|---|
| Common stock ($10 par value, 200,000 shares authorized, 150,000 issued) | $1,500,000 |

Parenthetical explanations have an advantage over both notes to the financial statements and supporting schedules. Parenthetical explanations place the disclosure prominently in the body of the statement instead of in a note or schedule where it is more likely to be overlooked.

**Notes to financial statements.** If the information cannot be disclosed in a relatively short and concise parenthetical explanation, a note disclosure is used. For example

| | |
|---|---|
| Inventories (see note 1) | $2,550,000 |

The notes to the financial statements would contain the following:

**Note 1:** Inventories are stated at the lower of cost or market. Cost is determined using the first-in, first-out (FIFO) method.

**Cross-references.** Cross-referencing is used when there is a direct relationship between two accounts on the balance sheet. For example, among the current assets, the following might be shown if $1,500,000 of accounts receivable were pledged as collateral for a $1,200,000 bank loan:

| | |
|---|---|
| Accounts receivable pledged as collateral on bank loan payable | $1,500,000 |

Included in the current liabilities would be the following:

| | |
|---|---|
| Bank loan payable—collateralized by accounts receivable | $1,200,000 |

**Valuation allowances.** Valuation allowances are used to reduce or increase the carrying amounts of certain assets and liabilities. Accumulated depreciation reduces the carrying value of property, plant, and equipment, and a bond premium (discount) increases (decreases) the face value of a bond payable as shown in the following illustrations:

| | | |
|---|---|---|
| Equipment | $18,000,000 | |
| Less accumulated depreciation | (1,625,000) | $16,375,000 |
| Bonds payable | $20,000,000 | |
| Less discount on bonds payable | (1,300,000) | $18,700,000 |
| Bonds payable | $20,000,000 | |
| Add premium on bonds payable | 1,300,000 | $21,300,000 |

**Supporting schedules.** A supporting schedule might be used to provide additional detail about an item in the financial statements. For example, consolidating schedules might be included in addition to the basic consolidated financial statements or a five-year summary of selected financial data might be included. In general, supporting schedules are not used to provide information required by GAAP because those schedules are not part of the basic financial statements and are typically subjected to only limited procedures by auditors.

**Accounting policies.** There are many different methods of valuing assets, recognizing revenues, and assigning costs. Financial statement users must be aware of the accounting policies used by enterprises so that sound economic decisions can be made. Per APB 22, the disclosures are to identify and describe the accounting principles followed by the enterprise and methods of applying those principles that materially affect the determination of financial position, changes in cash flows, or results of operations. The accounting policies disclosure is to encompass those accounting principles and methods that involve the following:

1. Selection from acceptable alternatives
2. Principles and methods peculiar to the industry
3. Unique applications of GAAP

The accounting policies disclosure need not duplicate information provided elsewhere in the financial statements. The accounting policies usually appear in a separate section called "Summary of Significant Accounting Policies" or as the first note of the notes to the financial statements.

**Related parties.** According to FAS 57, *Related-Party Disclosures*, financial statements are required to disclose material related-party transactions other than compensation arrangements, expense allowances, or other similar items that occur in the ordinary course of business.

A related party is essentially any party that controls or can significantly influence the management or operating policies of the company to the extent that the company may be prevented from fully pursuing its own interests. Related parties include affiliates, investees accounted for by the equity method, trusts for the benefit of employees, principal owners, management, and immediate family members of owners or management.

Transactions with related parties are to be disclosed even if there is no accounting recognition made for such transactions (e.g., a service is performed without payment). Disclosures are not permitted to assert that the terms of related-party transactions were essentially equivalent to arm's-length dealings unless those claims can be substantiated. If the financial position or results of operations of the reporting enterprise could change significantly because of common control or common management, disclosure of the nature of the ownership or management control is required, even if there were no transactions between the entities.

The disclosures are to include

1. The nature of the relationship
2. A description of transactions and the effects of those transactions reflected in the financial statements for each period for which an income statement is presented
3. The dollar amount of transactions for each period for which an income statement is presented and the effects of any change in the terms of such transactions as compared to the terms used in prior periods
4. Amounts due to and from related parties as of the date of each balance sheet presented, together with the terms and manner of settlement

**Comparative statements.** In order to increase the usefulness of financial statements, many enterprises include financial statements for one or more prior years in their annual reports. Some also include five- or ten-year summaries of condensed financial information. These comparative financial statements allow investment analysts and other interested readers to perform comparative analysis of pertinent information. ARB 43, Chapter 2, states the presentation of comparative financial statements in annual reports enhances the usefulness of such reports and brings out more clearly the nature and trends of current changes affecting the enterprise. That presentation emphasizes the fact that the statements for a series of periods are far more significant than those for a single period and that the accounts for one period are but an installment of what is essentially a continuous history. (Note that, while comparative financial statements are presently required under US GAAP, it is highly likely that this will become a requirement as the FASB moves to converge its standards with those of IASB, the international standard setter.)

**Subsequent events.** The balance sheet is dated as of the last day of the fiscal period, but a period of time usually elapses before the financial statements are issued. During this period, significant events or transactions may have occurred that materially affect the company's financial position. These events and transactions are called subsequent events. The omission of disclosure of significant events occurring between the balance sheet date and issuance date of the financial statements could mislead the reader who is otherwise unaware of those events.

There are two types of subsequent events (which, curiously, are defined not in the accounting standards, but in the auditing literature, by SAS 1, *Subsequent Events*). The first type are events that provide additional evidence about conditions that existed at the date of the balance sheet and which affect the estimates inherent in the process of preparing financial statements. The second type are events that provide evidence with respect to conditions that did not exist at the date of the balance sheet but arose subsequent to that date. The first type results in adjustments of the financial statements. The second type does not require adjustment of the financial statements but may require disclosure in order to keep the financial statements from being misleading. Disclosure can be made in the form of explanatory notes, sometimes supplemented with pro forma statements.

**Examples of subsequent events**

1. A loss on an uncollectible trade account receivable that results from a customer's deteriorating financial condition, which led to bankruptcy subsequent to the balance sheet date, would be indicative of conditions existing at the balance sheet date, thereby calling for adjustment of the financial statements before their issuance. On the other hand, a loss on an uncollectible trade account receivable resulting from a customer's major casualty, such as a fire or flood subsequent to the balance sheet date, would not be indicative of conditions existing at the balance sheet date, and the adjustment of the financial statements would not be appropriate. However, if the amount is material, disclosure would be required.

2. A settlement of a lawsuit would require adjustment of the financial statements if the event that gave rise to the claim occurred prior to the balance sheet date. However, only disclosure is required if the event that gave rise to the claim occurred after the balance sheet date, and then only if the amount involved were expected to be material.

3. The second type of events (those not existing at the balance sheet date) that require disclosure but not adjustment include the following:

    a. Sale of a bond or capital stock issue
    b. Purchase of a business
    c. Loss of plant or inventories as a result of fire or flood
    d. Gains or losses on certain marketable securities

**Contingencies.** A contingency is defined in FAS 5 as an existing condition, situation, or set of circumstances involving uncertainty as to possible gain or loss. The uncertainty will ultimately be resolved when one or more future events occur or fail to occur. Resolution of the uncertainty may confirm the acquisition of an asset, the reduction of a liability, the loss or impairment of an asset, or the incurrence of a liability.

If it is probable that an asset has been impaired or that a liability has been incurred at the date of the financial statements and the amount of that loss can be reasonably estimated, the loss is accrued by a charge to earnings and the recognition of a liability. Contingencies requiring accrual are discussed more fully in Chapter 14.

However, if it is only reasonably possible that a future event will confirm that an asset was impaired or a liability had been incurred at the balance sheet date, an enterprise must disclose the contingency if the amount involved could have a material effect on the financial statements. The disclosure is to include the nature of the contingency and either an estimate of the amount of the loss or the range of possible losses. If an estimate of loss cannot be made, that fact must be disclosed.

If the likelihood is remote that a loss has been incurred, no disclosure is necessary in most circumstances. However, guarantees of the indebtedness of others, guarantees to repurchase receivables or other assets, and obligations of commercial banks under standby letters of credit are always disclosed, irrespective of the likelihood of future performance on the part of the enterprise. The required disclosure is to include the nature and amount of the guarantee.

FIN 45, *Guarantor's Accounting and Disclosure Requirements for Guarantees, Including Indirect Guarantees of Indebtedness of Others,* explains that guarantees actually embody two separate obligations, (1) the contingent obligation to perform under the guarantee in the event of nonperformance by the party whose obligation is guaranteed, and (2) an obligation to be ready to perform, referred to as a standby obligation, during the period that the guarantee is in effect. As a result of this bifurcation of the obligation, many guarantees are now required to be recognized as liabilities on the balance sheet. Discussion of the recognition and disclosure of guarantees is included in Chapter 14.

An estimated gain from a gain contingency usually is not reflected in the balance sheet or income statement because doing so might recognize revenue prior to its realization. Adequate disclosure of the gain contingency is to be made, but care must be taken to avoid misleading implications as to the likelihood of realization. For example, if the enterprise may be able to recover some portion of an incurred loss by proceeding against a third party, that fact might be disclosed.

**Commitments.** All significant contractual commitments are to be disclosed in the notes to the financial statements. For example, lease contract provisions, pension obligations, requirements contracts, bond indenture covenants, commitments to purchase or construct new facilities, and employee share-based compensation plans are to be clearly disclosed in the notes.

### Risks and Uncertainties

AICPA Statement of Position 94-6, *Disclosure of Certain Significant Risks and Uncertainties,* requires disclosure in financial statements about risks and uncertainties existing as of the date of those statements that could significantly affect the amounts reported in the near term. Near term is defined as a period of time not to exceed one year from the date of the financial statements. The four areas of disclosure required by SOP 94-6 are risks and uncertainties relating to the nature of the enterprise's operations, use of estimates in the preparation of financial statements, certain significant estimates, and vulnerability due to certain concentrations.

**Nature of operations.** SOP 94-6 requires that enterprises disclose the major products or services that they sell or provide, the principal markets that they serve, and the location of those markets.

If an enterprise operates in more than one industry, it must disclose all industries it is operating within as well as the relative importance of each industry. The basis for determining the relative importance of each industry (assets, revenue, or earnings) is also to be disclosed. Quantification is not required in disclosures about the nature of operations. Comparisons of relative importance for enterprises operating in more than one business can be conveyed by the use of words such as predominantly, equally, or major.

**Use of estimates in the preparation of financial statements.** Financial statements must include an explanation that the preparation of financial statements in accordance with GAAP requires the use of estimates by management. The purpose of this disclosure is to clearly alert users to the pervasiveness of estimates.

**Certain significant estimates.** SOP 94-6 requires disclosures regarding estimates used in valuing assets, liabilities, or gain or loss contingencies if both of the following conditions are met:

1. It is at least reasonably possible that the estimate of the effect on the financial statements of a condition, situation, or set of circumstances that existed at the date of the financial statements will change in the near term due to one or more future confirming events.
2. The effect of the change would be material to the financial statements.

For the purposes of determining materiality, it is not the amount of an estimate that determines whether an item is material and must be disclosed, but rather the effect of using a different estimate that determines materiality.

The disclosure is to indicate the nature of the uncertainty and that it is reasonably possible that the estimate will change in the near term. SOP 94-6 is separate from and does not change FAS 5, *Accounting for Contingencies.* If an estimate is covered under FAS 5 as a loss contingency, the disclosure also is to include an estimate of the possible range of loss, or state that an estimate cannot be made. Disclosure of any factors that would make an estimate sensitive to change is encouraged but not required.

Many enterprises use risk-reduction techniques to mitigate losses. If the effect of a change in the estimate is unlikely to be material because of risk-reduction techniques, the enterprise is encouraged, but not required, to disclose the uncertainty as well as the relevant risk-reduction techniques.

**Examples of items that may be based on estimates that are particularly sensitive to change in the near term (SOP 94-6)**

1. Inventory subject to rapid technological obsolescence
2. Specialized equipment subject to technological obsolescence
3. Valuation allowances for deferred income tax assets based on future taxable income
4. Capitalized motion picture film production costs
5. Capitalized computer software costs
6. Deferred policy acquisition costs of insurance enterprises
7. Valuation allowances for commercial and real estate loans
8. Environmental remediation-related obligations
9. Litigation-related obligations
10. Contingent liabilities for guarantees of other enterprises' obligations
11. Amounts reported for long-term obligations, such as amounts reported for pensions and postemployment benefits
12. Net proceeds recoverable, the provisions for expected loss to be incurred, or both, on disposition of a business or assets
13. Amounts reported for long-term contracts

**Current vulnerability due to concentrations.** Vulnerability from concentrations occurs when enterprises fail to diversify in order to mitigate risk. Financial statements must disclose such concentrations if management knows prior to issuance of the financial statements that all of the following conditions exist (SOP 94-6):

1.  The concentration exists at the date of the financial statements.
2.  The concentration makes the enterprise vulnerable to the risk of a near-term severe impact.
3.  It is at least reasonably possible that the events that could cause the severe impact will occur in the near term.

**Examples of concentrations that require disclosure (SOP 94-6)**

1.  Concentrations in the volume of business transacted with a particular customer, supplier, lender, grantor, or contributor
2.  Concentrations in revenue from particular products, services, or fundraising events
3.  Concentrations in the available sources of supply of materials, labor, services, or of licenses or other rights used in the enterprise's operations
4.  Concentrations in the market or geographic area in which an enterprise conducts its operations

The potential for severe impact can occur as the result of the total or partial loss of a business relationship, price or demand changes, loss of patent protection, changes in the availability of a resource or right, or the disruption of operations in a market or geographic area. For purposes of SOP 94-6, it is always considered reasonably possible in the near term that any customer, grantor, or contributor will be lost and that operations located outside an enterprise's home country will be disrupted.

For concentrations of labor subject to collective bargaining agreements and concentrations of operations outside an enterprise's home country, the following additional disclosures are required (SOP 94-6):

1.  For labor subject to collective bargaining agreements, disclosure is to include both the percentage of the labor force covered by collective bargaining agreements and the percentage of the labor force covered by collective bargaining agreements that will expire within one year.
2.  For operations located outside the enterprise's home country, disclosure is to include the carrying amounts of net assets and the geographic areas in which they are located.

## Forthcoming Changes to Financial Statement Presentation Standards

While the set of basic financial statements that have been mandated under GAAP—with the adoption of the cash flow statement requirement in the late 1980s being the last major change—is not likely to change, *per se*, it is quite possible that the form and content of the financial statements may be altered as a result of an ongoing FASB/IASB joint project expected to come to fruition in the next year or so. This is partly in response to proposals offered by the user community, in particular from financial analysts, who have argued that more meaningful information could be displayed by a more comprehensive use of the "operating-investment-financing" trichotomy already familiar from its usage in the cash flow statement.

The FASB project, *Financial Statement Presentation*, which has been ongoing since 2001, has, as of early 2008, reached a number of important, albeit tentative, conclusions. The project has been divided into several phases, only the first of which has thus far been completed, with a discussion document for the second phase expected in mid-2008.

The conclusions expressed thus far include the following:

1.  That a complete set of financial statements be required to display balance sheets at both the beginning and the end of the reporting period (beginning balance sheets are not currently required).

2. That a statement that shows (for the reporting period) the changes in assets and liabilities other than those arising from transactions with owners in their capacity as owners and that includes display of the currently required subtotal net income be made a requirement. Such a statement would be referred to as a statement of earnings and comprehensive income (see commentary in Chapter 3).

3. That there be a required statement that shows the changes in assets and liabilities arising from transactions with owners in their capacity as owners, which would be referred to as a statement of changes in equity (see commentary in Chapter 3).

4. That a statement of cash flows continue to be required (see Chapter 4).

Another tentative decision reached is to require comparative financial statements—which has long been encouraged, since single period financial statements are deemed to be less readily interpreted by users. However, in conjunction with the tentative decision to require both beginning and ending balance sheets, this means that a basic set of financial statements, should this proposal be enacted, would require at least three balance sheets.

The proposed change in the presentation requirements for financial statements would have as a key objective the separating of the reporting entity's financing activities from its business and other activities, and the further separating of the entity's financing activities into transactions with owners, in their capacity as owners, from all of its other financing activities. It would thus expand upon the typology of cash flows first imposed by FAS 95 (described in Chapter 4), although the implications of such a distinction for the balance sheet are perhaps less obvious than for the "flow" statements (notably, the income statement). According to FASB, the financing section in the statement of financial position would include financial assets and financial liabilities that management deems to be part of the financing of the entity's business activities. Amounts relating to financing liabilities would be presented in the financing liabilities category and amounts relating to financing assets would be presented in the financing assets category in each of the financial statements.

In determining whether an asset or liability would be included in the financing section of the balance sheet, a reporting entity would consider whether the item is interchangeable with other sources of financing and whether the item could be characterized as independent of specific business activities. Thus, for nonfinancial institution reporting entities, financing section display of cash, bank loans, available-for-sale financial instruments, bonds, and leases, plus financial instruments held to hedge any of these items, would generally be appropriate.

Reportedly, the current thinking is that there would be a newly devised *equity* section in the statement of cash flows to report changes in items displayed in the equity section of the balance sheet, although this preliminary conclusion could well change before a final standard is enacted.

Regarding the investing category in a revamped balance sheet, this would include assets and liabilities that would not be related to financing the entity's business activities that management views as integral to its main business activities. All the changes to investing assets and liabilities would be presented in the investing category in the statement of comprehensive income and the statement of cash flows. For example, available-for-sale investments and instruments used to hedge these investments would require investing classification under the contemplated rules.

The operating category of the redesigned balance sheet would include assets and liabilities related to the core operations of the reporting entity. The accounting policies note to the financial statements would be used to define the basis for classification of the assets and liabilities, and any change in that basis would be deemed a change in accounting policy, to be implemented by means of retroactive application.

Expanded information regarding liquidity may also be mandated by a new standard on financial statement presentation, if the FASB and IASB maintain their current views during the remainder of deliberations. It is unclear whether this will result in new or revised informative disclosures, or in requirements that directly impact the balance sheet and other financial statements.

The second phase of the financial statement presentation project addresses more fundamental issues for presentation of information on the faces of financial statements. According to FASB, topics being dealt with include

1.  Developing principles for aggregating and disaggregating information in each financial statement
2.  Defining the totals and subtotals to be reported in each financial statement (which might include categories such as business and financing)
3.  Deciding whether components of other comprehensive income should be recycled/reclassified to profit or loss and, if so, the characteristics of the transactions and events that should be recycled and when recycling should occur
4.  Reconsidering FAS 95, *Statement of Cash Flows* (as well as the corresponding international standard, IAS 7), including whether to require the use of the direct or indirect method

FASB has indicated that a discussion stage document will be released in mid-2008 to address the aforementioned issues.

The final phase of the FASB's project, still in the very preliminary stage, will address the presentation and display of interim financial information in US GAAP (and IASB may reconsider its corresponding rule, IAS 34), and will reportedly include

1.  Which, if any, financial statements should be required in an interim financial report
2.  Whether entities should be allowed to present the financial statements in an interim financial report in a condensed format; if so, whether the Boards should provide guidance on how to condense the information
3.  What comparative periods, if any, should be required or allowed in interim financial reports, and when, if ever, should twelve-month-to-date financial statements be required or allowed in interim financial reports
4.  Whether guidance for nonpublic companies should differ from guidance for public companies

Any new pronouncements regarding financial statement presentation will (at least in the near term) apply only to business entities (both public and nonpublic ones), but will not apply to nonbusiness entities (not-for-profit organizations or defined benefit plans). Both FASB and the international standard setter, IASB, are currently attempting to develop a principles-based standard that will apply equally to all business entities. They will also potentially consider whether the standard should include different presentation provisions for a limited scope of entities (e.g., financial institutions).

It will address the organization and presentation of financial information on the face of the financial statements but will not address recognition or measurement guidance provided in other standards for individual assets, liabilities, or transactions.

Furthermore, it will address all the financial statements that constitute a complete set of financial statements.

It will address the necessity for totals and subtotals in the financial statements, including the net income/profit or loss subtotal, and will assess whether to change the mechanism of recycling used today.

It will not, however, include a comprehensive review of the notes to the financial statement, albeit it may necessitate certain amendments to existing disclosure requirements. On the other hand, if FASB and IASB are unable to achieve stated objectives by making changes to the face of financial statements, they may choose to develop new disclosure requirements.

The financial statement presentation project will not address management discussion and analysis or management commentary (i.e., the narratives commonly accompanying financial statements, as required for SEC registrants). Neither is it currently planned that this project will address pro forma measures; segment reporting requirements; financial ratios (except earnings per share [EPS] and other per-share amounts); forecasts of information; nonfinancial ratios or other nonfinancial information; nor financial statements for specific industries (except for considering how the decisions in the project may affect the financial statements of financial institutions).

## Example of Balance Sheet Classification and Presentation

The classification and presentation of information in a balance sheet may be highly aggregated, highly detailed, or anywhere in between. In general, highly aggregated balance sheets are used in annual reports and other presentations provided to the public. Highly detailed balance sheets are used internally by management. The following highly aggregated balance sheet includes only a few line items. The additional details required by generally accepted accounting principles are found in the notes to the financial statements. Note that both of the following examples reflect current financial reporting standards, and have not been modified to incorporate any of the proposed changes suggested in the current FASB/IASB deliberations.

**ABC Corporation**
**Balance Sheet**
**December 31, 2009**

*Assets*

| | |
|---|---|
| Current assets | xxx |
| Long-term investments | xxx |
| Property, plant, and equipment, net | xxx |
| Deferred income tax assets | xxx |
| Goodwill | xxx |
| Intangible and other assets | xxx |
| Total assets | xxx |

*Liabilities and Shareholders' Equity*

| | |
|---|---|
| Current liabilities | xxx |
| Deferred income tax liabilities | xxx |
| Long-term debt | xxx |
| Total liabilities | xxx |
| Capital stock | xxx |
| Additional paid-in capital | xxx |
| Retained earnings | xxx |
| Accumulated other comprehensive income | xxx |
| Total shareholders' equity | xxx |
| Total liabilities and shareholders' equity | xxx |

The following comprehensive balance sheet includes more line items (for details about specific assets and liabilities) than are found in most balance sheets.

**ABC Corporation**
**Balance Sheet**
**December 31, 2009**

*Assets*
*Current assets:*
Cash and bank deposits:

| | | | |
|---|---|---|---|
| Restricted to current bond maturity | $xxx | | |
| Unrestricted | xxx | $xxx | |

Short-term investments:

| | | | |
|---|---|---|---|
| Marketable equity securities (trading) | | xxx | |
| Marketable debt securities (available-for-sale) | | xxx | |
| Refundable income taxes | | xxx | |
| Receivables from affiliates | | xxx | |
| Accounts receivable | xxx | | |
| Less allowance for uncollectible accounts | (xxx) | xxx | |
| Notes receivable due in 2010 | xxx | | |
| Less discounts on notes receivable | (xxx) | xxx | |
| Installment notes receivable due in 2010 | | xxx | |
| Interest receivable | | xxx | |
| Creditors' accounts with debit balances | | xxx | |
| Advances to employees | | xxx | |

Inventories (carried at the lower of cost or market using FIFO):

| | | | |
|---|---|---|---|
| Finished goods | xxx | | |
| Work in process | xxx | | |
| Raw materials | xxx | xxx | |

Deferred income taxes (net of valuation allowance of $xxx)
Prepaid expenses:

| | | | |
|---|---|---|---|
| Prepaid rent | xxx | | |
| Prepaid insurance | xxx | xxx | |
| Total current assets | | | $xxx |

*Long-term investments:*

| | | |
|---|---|---|
| Investments in equity securities (available-for-sale) | xxx | |
| Investments in bonds (held-to-maturity) | xxx | |
| Investments in equity securities (at cost, plus equity in undistributed net earnings since acquisition) | xxx | |
| Investments in unused land and facilities | xxx | |
| Cash surrender value of officers' life insurance policies | xxx | |
| Sinking fund for bond retirement | xxx | |
| Plant expansion fund | xxx | |
| Total long-term investments | | $xxx |

*Property, plant, and equipment:*

| | | |
|---|---|---|
| Land | $xxx | |
| Buildings (including capitalized interest of $xxx) | xxx | |
| Machinery and equipment | xxx | |
| Furniture and fixtures | xxx | |
| Assets under capital leases | xxx | |
| Leasehold improvements | xxx | |
| Less accumulated depreciation and amortization | (xxx) | |
| Total property, plant, and equipment | | xxx |

*Intangible assets net of amortization:*

| | | |
|---|---|---|
| Goodwill of acquired businesses | $xxx | |
| Patents | xxx | |
| Trademarks | xxx | |
| Total intangible assets, net | | xxx |

*Other assets:*

| | | |
|---|---|---|
| Installment notes due after 2010 | $xxx | |
| Unamortized bond issue costs | xxx | |
| Deferred income taxes (net of valuation allowance of $xxx) | | xxx |
| Total other noncurrent assets | | xxx |
| Total assets | | $xxx |

*Liabilities and Shareholders' Equity*
*Current liabilities:*

| | | |
|---|---:|---:|
| Current maturities of long-term debt | $xxx | |
| Current maturities of capital lease obligations | xxx | |
| Commercial paper and other short-term notes payable | xxx | |
| Accounts payable | xxx | |
| Accrued salaries, wages, and commissions | xxx | |
| Payroll taxes withheld and accrued | xxx | |
| Employee 401(k) contributions withheld | xxx | |
| Accrued rent | xxx | |
| Income taxes payable | xxx | |
| Sales taxes payable | xxx | |
| Dividends payable | xxx | |
| Rent revenue collected in advance | xxx | |
| Other advances from customers | xxx | |
| Deferred income taxes | xxx | |
| Short-term portion of accrued warranty costs | xxx | |
| Other accrued liabilities | <u>xxx</u> | |
|    Total current liabilities | | $xxx |

*Noncurrent liabilities:*

| | | | |
|---|---:|---:|---:|
| Notes payable due after 2010 | $xxx | | |
|   Plus unamortized note premium | <u>xxx</u> | $xxx | |
| Long-term bonds: | | | |
|   10% debentures due 2018 | xxx | | |
|   9 1/2% collateralized obligations maturing serially to 2011 | xxx | | |
|   8% convertible subordinated debentures due 2022 | xxx | | |
|     Less unamortized discounts net of premiums | <u>(xxx)</u> | xxx | |
| Accrued pension cost | | xxx | |
| Capital lease obligations | | xxx | |
| Asset retirement obligations (net of accumulated accretion of $xxx) | | xxx | |
| Deferred income taxes | | xxx | |
| Long-term portion of accrued warranty costs | | <u>xxx</u> | |
|     Total noncurrent liabilities | | | <u>xxx</u> |
| Total liabilities | | | $<u>xxx</u> |

*Shareholders' equity:*
*Capital stock:*

| | | |
|---|---:|---:|
| $12.50 convertible preferred stock, $100 stated value, 200,000 shares authorized, 175,000 outstanding | $xxx | |
| 12% cumulative preferred stock, $100 stated value, callable at $115, 100,000 shares authorized and outstanding | xxx | |
| Common stock, $10 stated value, 500,000 shares authorized, 450,000 issued, 15,000 held in treasury | xxx | |
| Common stock subscribed 10,000 shares | xxx | |
| Less: Subscriptions receivable | <u>(xxx)</u> | $xxx |

*Additional paid-in capital:*

| | | |
|---|---:|---:|
| From 12% cumulative preferred | xxx | |
| From common stock | xxx | |
| From treasury stock transactions | xxx | |
| From stock dividends | xxx | |
| From expiration of share options | xxx | |
| Warrants outstanding | <u>xxx</u> | xxx |

*Retained earnings*

| | |
|---|---:|
| | xxx |

*Accumulated other comprehensive income:*

| | | |
|---|---:|---:|
| Net unrealized loss on available-for-sale securities | (xxx) | |
| Unrealized loss from foreign currency translation | (xxx) | |
| Excess of minimum pension liability over unrecognized prior service cost | <u>(xxx)</u> | (xxx) |
| *Less: Treasury stock at cost* | | (<u>xxx</u>) |
| Total shareholders' equity | | $<u>xxx</u> |
| Total liabilities and shareholders' equity | | $<u>xxx</u> |

# 3 STATEMENTS OF INCOME AND COMPREHENSIVE INCOME

## PERSPECTIVE AND ISSUES

A primary focus of financial reporting is to provide information about an entity's performance that is useful to present and potential investors, creditors, and others when they are making financial decisions. In financial reporting, performance is primarily measured by net income and its components, which are provided in the income statement. Although information in the income statement is information about past performance, investors, creditors, and others use that information to predict future performance.

In contrast to the balance sheet, which provides information about an entity at a point in time, an income statement provides information about a period of time. It reflects information about the transactions and other events occurring within the period. Most of the weaknesses of an income statement are a result of its periodic nature. Entities are continually creating and selling goods and services, and at any single point in time some of those processes will be incomplete. Thus, measurement of net income for a period involves estimates. The degree of completion of inventories, the amounts of inventories that have been manufactured or purchased but ultimately will not be sold, and the amounts of goods and services that have been sold but ultimately will not result in cash receipts are just of few of the many estimates that must be made in order to present an income statement. The entity's ability (or inability) to make these estimates is reflected in the performance measure for the period.

Historically, performance was measured only by the income statement. During the 1990s, a second performance measure was introduced—comprehensive income—which was a concept first set forth in CON 3 in 1980 (which was superseded by CON 6 in 1985). Comprehensive income is a more inclusive notion of performance than net income. It includes all recognized changes in equity that occur during a period except those resulting from investments by owners and distributions to owners. Thus, included in comprehensive income but excluded from net income are foreign currency adjustments, unrealized changes in the fair value of available-for-sale securities, the effective portion of the gain or loss on derivative instruments designated and qualified as either a cash-flow hedging item or a hedge of a forecasted foreign-currency-denominated transaction, and minimum pension liability adjustments. Because comprehensive income includes the effects on an entity of economic events largely outside of its management's control, some have said that net income is a measure of management's performance and comprehensive income is a measure of entity performance.

The requirement to report comprehensive income in addition to net income is another step in the movement toward the capital maintenance concept of income mentioned in Chapter 2. Under that concept of income, income is earned only if the entity's net assets at the end of the period exceed its net assets at the beginning of the period after excluding the effects of transactions with owners. A capital maintenance concept of income is more consistent with investors' expectations that an investment should generate more financial resources than were invested, although, unless all assets and liabilities were reported at their respective fair values, this is at best an imperfect approximation of true economic income.

Instead of, or in addition to, net income or comprehensive income, some companies are using "pro forma earnings" and other measures to report corporate performance. The practice has generated debate and confusion because companies calculate and report those "earnings" using definitions that vary from company to company (and sometimes even within the same company from quarter to quarter). In response to growing concerns about this practice, and as a proximate result of the enactment of the Sarbanes-Oxley Act of 2002, in January 2003, the SEC adopted a new disclosure regulation, Regulation G, that requires public companies that disclose or release non-GAAP financial measures (all of which have been loosely referred to as pro forma earnings) to include in that same disclosure or release a presentation of the most directly comparable GAAP financial measure, along with a reconciliation of the disclosed non-GAAP measure to the most directly comparable GAAP financial measure. FASB and its international equivalent, IASB, are conducting a joint project on financial performance reporting to improve the usefulness of this information and converge US GAAP and IFRS (discussed in this chapter).

| Sources of GAAP | | | | | | |
|---|---|---|---|---|---|---|
| *ARB* | *APB* | *FAS* | *FTB* | *EITF* | *SOP* | *FSP* |
| 43, Ch. 2 | 9, 16, 18, 20, 30 | 7, 15, 16, 101, 128, 130, 133, 141(R), 142, 144, 145, 156, 160 | 85-6 | 87-4, 87-24, 00-9, 00-10, 01-10, 01-13, 03-13, 06-3 | 98-5 | 146-1 |

## DEFINITIONS OF TERMS

**Component of an entity.** The operations and cash flows that can be clearly distinguished, operationally and for financial reporting purposes, from the rest of the entity. All of the following are components of an entity:

1. A reportable segment, which is a segment considered to be significant to an enterprise's operations; a segment that has passed one of three 10% tests (assets, revenues, or operating profit or loss) or has been identified as being reportable through other criteria (FAS 131)

2.  An operating segment, which is a component of an enterprise that may earn revenues and incur expenses, and about which separate financial information is available that is evaluated regularly by the chief operating decision maker in deciding how to allocate resources and in assessing performance (FAS 131)
3.  A reporting unit, which is an operating segment or one level below an operating segment (FAS 142)
4.  A subsidiary
5.  An asset group, which is the lowest level for which identifiable cash flows are largely independent of the cash flows of other groups of assets and liabilities (FAS 144)

**Comprehensive income.** The change in equity of a business enterprise during a period from transactions and other events and circumstances from nonowner sources. It includes all changes in equity during a period, except those resulting from investments by owners and distributions to owners (CON 6).

**Development stage enterprise.** An entity that is devoting substantially all its efforts to establishing itself as a new business and either its principal operations have not commenced or its principal operations have commenced but have not generated a significant amount of revenue.

**Distribution to owners.** Decreases in net assets of a particular enterprise resulting from the entity transferring assets, rendering services, or incurring liabilities to owners.

Distributions to owners reduce the ownership interest of the receiving owners in the entity and reduce the net assets of the entity by the amount of the distribution. Such transactions are displayed in the statement of changes in equity.

**Expenses.** Decreases in assets or increases in liabilities during a period resulting from delivery of goods, rendering of services, or other activities constituting the reporting entity's central operations (CON 6).

**Extraordinary item.** Events and transactions that are distinguished by their unusual nature and by the infrequency of their occurrence (APB 30).

**Gains.** Increases in equity (net assets) from peripheral or incidental transactions of an entity and from all other transactions and other events and circumstances affecting the entity during a period except those that result from revenues or investments by owners (CON 6).

**Investments by owners.** Increases in net assets of a particular enterprise resulting from transfers to it of something valuable to obtain or increase ownership interests (or equity) in it.

Investments by owners may be in the form of assets, services, or the payment of entity liabilities. These investments are displayed in the statement of changes in equity. The purchase of an ownership interest from another owner is not a net investment because such a transfer does not increase the net assets of the entity.

**Losses.** Decreases in equity (net assets) from peripheral or incidental transactions of an entity from all other transactions and other events and circumstances affecting the entity during a period except those that result from expenses or distributions to owners (CON 6).

**Realization.** The process of converting noncash resources and rights into money or, more precisely, the sale of an asset for cash or claims to cash (CON 6).

**Recognition.** The process of formally recording or incorporating an item in the financial statements of an entity (CON 6).

**Revenues.** Increases in assets or decreases in liabilities during a period from delivering goods, rendering services, or other activities constituting the enterprise's central operations (CON 6).

# CONCEPTS, RULES, AND EXAMPLES

## Limitations of the Income Statement

Economists have generally adopted a wealth maintenance concept of income. Under this concept, income is the maximum amount that can be consumed during a period and still leave the enterprise with the same amount of wealth at the end of the period as existed at the beginning. Wealth is determined with reference to the current market values (fair values) of the net productive assets at the beginning and end of the period. Therefore, the economists' definition of income would fully incorporate market value changes (both increases and decreases in wealth) in the determination of periodic income.

Accountants, on the other hand, have generally defined income by reference to specific events that give rise to recognizable elements of revenue and expense during a reporting period. The events that produce reportable items of revenue and expense are a subset of economic events that determine economic income. Many changes in the market values of wealth components are deliberately excluded from the measurement of accounting income, but are included in the measurement of economic income.

The discrepancy between accounting and economic measures of income is primarily the result of accountants' concerns for reliability and measurability. Those concerns have traditionally served to prevent revenue and gains from being recognized until an acceptable level of assurance is obtained about the existence and amount of those revenues and gains. In general, accountants do not recognize revenues or gains until they are realizable—convertible into known amounts of cash or claims to cash.

However, some gains are realizable but are still not reported in net income. Holding gains on certain debt and equity investments are readily convertible into known amounts of cash. Those gains are currently excluded from net income for two reasons. First, many consider net income to be a measure of management's performance, and holding gains and losses result from market fluctuations that are outside the control of management. To report holding gains and losses in net income decreases the ability to use that measure to judge management performance. Second, many entities that purchase large amounts of investments finance those investments with liabilities, earning money from the spread (the difference between the investment return and the borrowing costs). Including in net income unrealized holding gains and losses on only the investments, and not the related liabilities, could cause volatility in earnings that is not representative of how those entities are impacted by economic events.

Notwithstanding the traditional adherence to historical cost bases for most assets and almost all liabilities, FASB is currently working on a project that could lead to reporting certain liabilities at fair value. If this approach ultimately is accepted, future changes in accounting standards may eliminate this as a point of distinction between accounting and economic measures of income.

Another reason for the discrepancy between accounting and economic measures of income is the periodic nature of the income statement. Both accountants and economists realize that the earnings process occurs throughout the various stages of production, sales, and final delivery of the product. However, the difficulty in measuring the precise rate at which this earnings process is taking place has led accountants to conclude that income should normally be recognized only when it is fully realized. *Realization* generally implies that the enterprise producing the item has completed all of its obligations relating to the product and that collection of the resulting receivable is assured beyond reasonable doubt. A system of revenue recognition based on realization provides a way of dealing with the periodic nature of the income statement.

The economic measure of income would be relatively simple for an entity to apply on a life-cycle basis. Economic income would be measured by the difference between its wealth at the termination point versus its wealth at the origination date, plus withdrawals or other distributions and minus additional investments over the course of the entity's life. However, applying the same measurement strategy to discrete fiscal periods, as accountants do, is substantially more difficult. Allocating earnings to individual years, quarters, or months requires both estimates and use of judgment. Consequently, accountants have preferred that there be unambiguous guidelines for revenue recognition. These have generally permitted revenue recognition only at the completion of the earnings cycle, with a notable exception for long-term construction-type contracts.

Accountants have moved closer to an economic measure of income by introducing the measure "comprehensive income" into the financial statements. Comprehensive income is the change in equity resulting from all sources other than distributions to owners and investments by owners. Thus, its definition is similar to economic income. However, because of the realization and recognition concerns discussed earlier, comprehensive income remains a subset of economic income.

Whether economic income, comprehensive income, net income, or some other measure is the appropriate measure of income is partially dependent upon the perspective of the party doing the measuring. From the perspective of the outside investors taken as a whole, income might be defined as earnings before any payments to those investors, including bondholders and preferred stockholders as well as common shareholders. On the other hand, from the perspective of the common shareholders, income might better be defined as earnings after payments to other investors, including creditors and preferred shareholders. Analysts regularly use earnings before interest, income taxes, depreciation, and amortization (known as EBITDA) as a surrogate measure for economic income, although this can easily be criticized. Perhaps the best accounting can do is provide the broadest possible measure (comprehensive income) and include in the financial statements information that allows each reader to compute the measure that is most meaningful to him or her.

## Recognition and Measurement

**Revenues.** Revenues represent actual or expected cash inflows that result from an entity's central operations. Revenues are generally recognized at the culmination of the earnings process—when the entity has substantially completed all it must do to be entitled to future cash inflows (or to retain cash already transferred). Most often, an exchange transaction indicates that revenues have been earned. Merchandise is delivered or services are rendered to a customer, resulting in the receipt of cash or the right to receive cash in the future. Revenues are generally measured by the values of the assets exchanged (or liabilities incurred). When, as is typically the case, the entity generating revenue is responsible for collecting sales or other taxes from the customers, to be later paid to the governmental authorities, these taxes may either be reported as part of gross revenue (and also as expense), or the taxes may be omitted from the income statement altogether (i.e., reporting revenues net of tax). EITF 06-3 clarifies that this is a choice between acceptable accounting principles, to be applied consistently. Chapter 10 discusses revenue recognition in more detail.

Revenues are commonly distinguished from gains for three reasons. Revenues result from an entity's central operations; gains result from incidental or peripheral activities of the entity. Revenues are usually earned; gains result from nonreciprocal transactions (such as winning a lawsuit or receiving a gift) or other economic events for which there is no earnings process. Revenues are reported gross; gains are reported net.

The existence of an exchange transaction generally is critical to the accounting recognition of revenue. However, an exchange transaction is viewed in a broader sense than the legal concept of a sale. Whenever an exchange of rights and privileges takes place, an exchange transaction is deemed to have occurred. For example, interest revenue and interest expense are earned or incurred ratably over a period without a discrete transaction taking place. Accruals are recorded periodically in order to reflect the interest realized by the passage of time. In a like manner, the percentage-of-completion method recognizes revenue based upon the measure of progress on a long-term construction project. The earnings process is considered to occur simultaneously with the measure of progress (e.g., the incurrence of costs).

The timing of revenue recognition also varies based on the realizability of the future cash flows. For example, the production of certain commodities takes place in an environment in which the ultimate realization of revenue is so assured that revenue can be recognized upon the completion of the production process. At the opposite extreme is the situation in which an exchange transaction has taken place, but significant uncertainty exists as to the ultimate collectibility of the amount. For example, in certain sales of real estate, where the down payment percentage is extremely small and the security for the buyer's notes is minimal, revenue is often not recognized until the time collections are actually received.

The revenue recognition system that is based on realization has worked reasonably well over the years. However, new types of transactions, products, and services have challenged that system. In most recent years, revenue recognition issues top the list of reasons for financial reporting restatements, or closely trail improper use of reserves for that dubious honor. In 2002, FASB added a major revenue recognition project to its agenda. That project may lead to a new accounting standard on revenue recognition generally and also might involve amending the related guidance on revenues and liabilities in certain of the Board's Concepts Statements.

As of mid-2008, preliminary views document was being promised by FASB, which it states will describe a single contract-based revenue recognition model that has two different measurement approaches. The expectation is that this will be a convergent approach with IASB. Chapter 10 provides more information about FASB's project and about revenue recognition under special circumstances.

**Expenses.** Expenses represent actual or expected cash outflows that result from an entity's central operations. Expenses are generally recognized when an asset either is consumed in an entity's central operations or is no longer expected to provide the level of future benefits expected when that asset was recognized.

Expenses are commonly distinguished from losses for three reasons. Expenses result from an entity's central operations; losses result from incidental or peripheral activities of the entity. Expenses are often incurred during the earnings process; losses often result from nonreciprocal transactions (such as thefts or fines) or other economic events unrelated to an earnings process. Expenses are reported gross; losses are reported net.

Although many cash outflows are recognized directly as expenses, this accounting is often done for expediency since most expenses are first assets, if only for a brief moment. Measuring the consumption of assets is done by one of three pervasive measurement principles: associating cause and effect, systematic and rational allocation, or immediate recognition.

Some costs, such as materials and direct labor consumed in the manufacturing process, are relatively easy to identify with the related revenue elements. The matching principle requires that all expenses incurred in the generation of revenue should be recognized in the same accounting period as the related revenues are recognized. Thus, those cost elements are included in inventory and expensed as cost of sales when a product is sold and revenue from the sale is recognized. That process is associating cause and effect.

Other costs are more closely associated with specific accounting periods. In the absence of a cause and effect relationship, the asset's cost should be allocated to the accounting periods benefited in a systematic and rational manner. This form of expense recognition involves assumptions about the expected length of benefit and the relationship between benefit and cost of each period. Depreciation of plant, property, and equipment, amortization of intangibles, and allocation of rent and insurance are examples of costs that are recognized by the use of a systematic and rational method.

The costs of advertising are expensed either as costs are incurred or the first time the advertising takes place (e.g., when the television advertisement is aired or printed copy is published), if later (SOP 93-7). However, there are two exceptions

1. Direct-response advertising

   a. Whose primary purpose is to elicit sales to customers who could be shown to have responded specifically to the advertising, and
   b. That results in probable future economic benefits; and

2. Expenditures for advertising costs that are made subsequent to recognizing revenues related to those costs.

Expenditures for direct-response advertising are deferred if both of the conditions listed above are met. The future benefits to be received are the future revenues arising as a direct result of the advertising. The company is required to provide entity-specific persuasive evidence that there is a linkage between the direct-response advertising and these future benefits. These costs are then amortized over the period in which the future benefits are expected to be received.

Advertising expenditures are sometimes made subsequent to the recognition of revenue (such as in "cooperative advertising" arrangements with customers). In order to achieve proper matching, these costs are to be estimated, accrued, and charged to expense when the related revenues are recognized.

All other costs are normally expensed in the period in which they are incurred. This includes costs for which no clear-cut future benefits can be identified, costs that were recorded as assets in prior periods but for which no remaining future benefits can be identified, and costs for which no rational allocation scheme can be devised.

The general approach for recognizing expenses is first to attempt to match costs with the related revenues. Next, a method of systematic and rational allocation should be attempted. If both of those measurement principles are inappropriate, the cost should be immediately expensed.

Expenses do not include distributions to owners. Expenses of a corporation are easily identified and separated from distributions to stockholders. In both the sole proprietorship and partnership form of entity, the identification process can be more difficult. Items such as interest or salaries paid to partners or owners may be thought of as distributions of profits rather than expenses. However, many entities adopt the philosophy that financial reporting should be the same regardless of legal form (economic substance takes precedence over legal form). Under the corporate form of business, interest on stockholder loans and salaries paid to stockholders are clearly classified as expenses and not as distributions. Accordingly, these items may be treated as expenses for both partnerships and sole proprietorships. However, full disclosure and consistency of financial reporting treatment would be required. Circumstances may involve treating certain payments, such as guaranteed salaries, as expenses while classifying other "salaries" as profit distributions.

**Gains and losses.** Gains are increases in equity resulting from transactions and economic events other than those that generate revenues or are investments from owners. Losses are decreases in equity resulting from transactions and economic events other than those that generate expenses or are distributions to owners. Gains and losses result from an entity's peripheral transactions (e.g., sale of used equipment), from economic events outside of the control of management (e.g., holding gains on securities), or from nonreciprocal transactions (e.g., lawsuit settlements, fines, and thefts).

Gains and losses are often described in financial statements by their sources, for example, realized gains (losses) on sale of securities or earthquake loss. They are usually measured at net amounts. For example, gains (losses) from sales of assets are measured by subtracting the unexpired cost of the asset from the proceeds, and holding gains (losses) are measured by subtracting the value at the beginning of the period from the value at the end of the period.

Gains often result from transactions and other events that involve no earnings process; therefore, in terms of recognition, it is more significant that the gain be realized or realizable than earned. Losses are recognized when it becomes evident that future economic benefits of a previously recognized asset have been reduced or eliminated, or that a liability has been incurred without associated economic benefits.

**Other comprehensive income.** Comprehensive income is the change in equity that results from revenue, expenses, gains, and losses during a period, as well as any other recognized changes in equity that occur for reasons other than investments by owners and distributions to owners.

Other comprehensive income (comprehensive income less net income) is defined to include the effects of foreign currency translation, minimum pension liability adjustments, the effective portion of the gain or loss on derivative instruments designated and qualified as either a cash-flow hedging item or a hedge of a forecasted foreign-currency-denominated transaction, and unrealized gains and losses on certain investments in debt and equity securities. Other comprehensive income is recognized and measured in accordance with the accounting pronouncement that deems it part of other comprehensive income. Thus, foreign currency adjustments are recognized and measured in accordance with FAS 52 (Chapter 23); additional pension liabilities are recognized and measured in accordance with FAS 87 (Chapter 18); hedges are recognized and measured in accordance with FAS 133 (Chapter 8) and unrealized gains and losses are recognized and measured in accordance with FAS 115 (Chapter 12). In general, those items are recognized and measured whenever a complete set of financial statements is prepared.

## Format of Statements of Income and Comprehensive Income

The basic order of presentation of information in an income statement (or statement of income and comprehensive income) is defined by a series of accounting pronouncements, as shown by the diagram below. Other than in the section "income from continuing operations," the display of revenues, expenses, gains, losses, and other comprehensive income is predetermined by authoritative pronouncement. Only within income from continuing operations does tradition and industry practice determine the presentation.

The sections containing information about other comprehensive income and comprehensive income, shown in the shaded area on the diagram, can be presented in a combined statement of income and comprehensive income. Alternatively, that information can be reported in a stand-alone statement of comprehensive income or in an expanded statement of changes in stockholder's equity. In FAS 130, FASB encourages the use of either a combined statement in which other comprehensive income appears below net income or a stand-alone statement that begins with net income. Regardless of the reporting location chosen, totals for net income, other comprehensive income, and comprehensive income must appear in the statement, and the statement must be of the same prominence as other financial statements. Information about other comprehensive income cannot be presented only in the notes to financial statements. For ease of reading, this publication uses the term "income statement" to include a combined statement of income and comprehensive income.

| *Statement of Income and Comprehensive Income* | *Report net of tax?* | *Reference* |
|---|---|---|
| **Income from continuing operations**<br>Sales or service revenues<br>Costs of goods sold<br>Operating expenses<br>Remaining excess of fair value over cost of acquired net assets in a<br>    business combination<br>Gains and losses<br>Other revenues and expenses<br>Items that are unusual or infrequent, but not both<br>Income tax expense related to continuing operations | No | APB 30<br><br><br><br>FAS 141(R) |
| **Results from discontinued operations**<br>Income (loss) from operations of a discontinued component<br>Gain (loss) from disposal of a discontinued component | Yes | FAS 144,<br>FAS 16 |
| **Extraordinary items**<br>Items that are both unusual and infrequent<br>Investor's share of an equity method investee's extraordinary item | Yes | APB 9, APB 30,<br>FAS 101,<br>FTB 85-6 |
| **Net income** | | |
| **Other comprehensive income**<br>Foreign currency adjustments<br>Unrealized gains (losses) on securities<br>Minimum pension liability<br>Gains/losses on cash-flow hedging items<br>Gains/losses on hedges of forecasted foreign-currency-denominated<br>    transactions<br>Income tax related to other comprehensive income (if components are<br>    not shown net of tax) | Optional | FAS 130,<br>FAS 133 |
| **Comprehensive income** | | |
| **Earnings per share information** | | FAS 128 |

*NOTE: Alternatively, information in the shaded area can be presented as a separate statement or in a statement of changes in stockholders' equity.*

The three items that are shown in the heading of an income statement are

1.   The name of the entity whose results of operations is being presented
2.   The title of the statement
3.   The period of time covered by the statement

The entity's legal name should be used and supplemental information could be added to disclose the entity's legal form as a corporation, partnership, sole proprietorship, or other form if that information is not apparent from the entity's name. The use of the titles "Income Statement," "Statement of Income and Comprehensive Income," "Statement of Operations," or "Statement of Earnings" denotes preparation in accordance with generally accepted accounting principles. If another comprehensive basis of accounting were used, such as the cash or income tax basis, the title of the statement would be modified accordingly. "Statement of Revenue and Expenses—Income Tax Basis" or "Statement of Revenue and Expenses—Modified Cash Basis" are examples of such titles.

The date of an income statement must clearly identify the time period involved, such as "Year Ending March 31, 2009." That dating informs the reader of the length of the period covered by the statement and both the starting and ending dates. Dating such as "The Period Ending March 31, 2009" or "Through March 31, 2009" is not useful because of the lack of precision in those titles. Income statements are rarely presented for periods in excess of one year but are frequently seen for shorter periods such as a month or a quarter. Entities whose operations form a natural cycle may have a reporting period end on a specific day (e.g., the last Friday of the month). These entities should head the income statement "For the 52 Weeks Ended March 27, 2009" (each week containing seven days, beginning on a Saturday and ending on a Friday). Although that fiscal period includes only 364 days (for most years), it is still considered an annual reporting period.

Income statements generally should be uniform in appearance from one period to the next. The form, terminology, captions, and pattern of combining insignificant items should be consistent. If comparative statements are presented, the prior year's information should be restated to conform to the current year's presentation if changes in presentation are made.

Aggregation of items should not serve to conceal significant information, such as netting revenues against expenses or combining dissimilar types of resources, expenses, gains, or losses. The category "other or miscellaneous expense" should contain, at maximum, an immaterial total amount of aggregated insignificant items. Once this total approaches 10% of total expenses, some other aggregations with explanatory titles should be selected.

## Income from Continuing Operations

The section "income from continuing operations" includes all revenues, expenses, gains, and losses that are not required to be reported in other sections of an income statement.

There are two generally accepted formats for the presentation of income from continuing operations: the single-step and the multiple-step formats.

In the single-step format, items are classified into two groups: revenues and expenses. The operating revenues and other revenues are itemized and summed to determine total revenues. The cost of goods sold, operating expenses, and other expenses are itemized and summed to determine total expenses. The total expenses (including income taxes) are deducted from the total revenues to arrive at income from continuing operations.

**Example of single-step format for income from continuing operations**

| | | |
|---|---|---|
| Revenues: | | |
| Sales (net of discounts and returns and allowances) | $xxx | |
| Gain on sale of equipment | xxx | |
| Interest income | xxx | |
| Dividend income | xxx | $xxx |
| Expenses: | | |
| Cost of goods sold | $xxx | |
| Selling expenses | xxx | |
| General and administrative expenses | xxx | |
| Interest expense | xxx | xxx |
| Income from continuing operations | | xxx |

Some believe that a multiple-step format enhances the usefulness of information about an entity's performance by reporting the interrelationships of revenues and expenses, using subtotals to report significant amounts. In a multiple-step format, operating revenues and expenses are separated from nonoperating revenues and expenses to provide more information concerning the firm's primary activities. This format breaks the revenue and expense items into various intermediate income components so that important relationships can be shown and attention can be focused on significant subtotals. Some examples of common intermediate income components are as follows:

1. **Gross profit (margin)**—The difference between net sales and cost of goods sold.
2. **Operating income**—Gross profit less operating expenses.
3. **Income before income taxes**—Operating income plus any other revenue items and less any other expense items.

**Example of a multiple-step format for income from continuing operations**

| | | | |
|---|---|---:|---:|
| Sales: | | | |
| Sales | | | $xxx |
| Less: Sales discounts | | $xxx | |
| Sales returns and allowances | | xxx | (xxx) |
| Net sales | | | $xxx |
| Cost of goods sold | | | xxx |
| Gross profit | | | $xxx |
| Operating expenses: | | | |
| Selling expenses | | | |
| Sales salaries | $xxx | | |
| Commissions | xxx | | |
| Advertising expense | xxx | | |
| Delivery expense | xxx | | |
| Selling supplies expense | xxx | | |
| Depreciation of store furniture and equipment | xxx | $xxx | |
| General and administrative expenses | | | |
| Officers' salaries | $xxx | | |
| Office salaries | xxx | | |
| Bad debts expense | xxx | | |
| Office supplies expense | xxx | | |
| Depreciation of office furniture and fixtures | xxx | | |
| Depreciation of building | xxx | | |
| Insurance expense | xxx | | |
| Utilities expense | xxx | xxx | |
| Total operating expense | | | (xxx) |
| Operating income | | | $xxx |
| Other revenues: | | | |
| Dividend income | | $xxx | |
| Gain on business acquisition ("bargain purchase") | | xxx | |
| Interest income | | xxx | xxx |
| Other expenses: | | | |
| Interest expense | | | (xxx) |
| Income from continuing operations | | | $xxx |

The following items of revenue, expense, gains, and losses are included within income from continuing operations:

1. **Sales or service revenues** are charges to customers for the goods and/or services provided during the period. This section should include information about discounts, allowances, and returns in order to determine net sales or net revenues.
2. **Cost of goods sold** is the cost of the inventory items sold during the period. In the case of a merchandising firm, net purchases (purchases less discounts, returns, and allowances plus freight-in) are added to beginning inventory to obtain the cost of goods available for sale. From the cost of goods available for sale amount, the ending inventory is deducted to obtain the cost of goods sold.

**Example of calculation of cost of goods sold of a merchandising company**

| | | | |
|---|---|---:|---:|
| Beginning inventory | | | $xxx |
| Add: Purchases | | $xxx | |
| Freight-in | | xxx | |
| Cost of purchases | | xxx | |
| Less: Purchase discounts | $xx | | |
| Purchase returns and allowances | xx | (xxx) | |
| Net purchases | | | xxx |

| | |
|---|---|
| Cost of goods available for sale | xxx |
| Less:   Ending inventory | (xxx) |
| Cost of goods sold | $xxx |

A manufacturing company computes the cost of goods sold in a slightly different way.  This requires that the company first computes the costs of goods manufactured, which can be computed as follows:

**Example of computation of cost of goods manufactured**

| | | |
|---|---|---|
| Direct materials inventory, beginning of period | $xxx | |
| Purchases of materials (including freight-in and deducting purchase discounts) | xxx | |
| Total direct materials available | $xxx | |
| Direct materials inventory, end of period | (xxx) | |
| Direct materials used | | $xxx |
| Direct labor | | xxx |
| Factory overhead: | | |
|     Depreciation of factory equipment | $xxx | |
|     Utilities | xxx | |
|     Indirect factory labor | xxx | |
|     Indirect materials | xxx | |
|     Other overhead items | xxx | xxx |
| Manufacturing cost incurred during the period | | $xxx |
| Add:  Work in process, beginning of period | | xxx |
| Less:  Work in process, end of period | | (xxx) |
| Cost of goods manufactured during the period | | $xxx |

Once the cost of goods manufactured has been calculated, the cost of goods sold can be computed.  The cost of goods manufactured is added to the beginning inventory to arrive at cost of goods available for sale.  The ending inventory is then deducted from the cost of goods available for sale to determine the cost of goods sold.

**Example of computation of cost of goods sold of a manufacturing company**

| | |
|---|---|
| Finished goods inventory, beginning of period | $xxx |
| Add:  Cost of goods manufactured during the period | xxx |
| Cost of goods available for sale | $xxx |
| Less:  Finished goods inventory, end of period | (xxx) |
| Cost of goods sold during the period | $xxx |

3. **Operating expenses** are primary recurring costs associated with central operations (other than cost of goods sold) that are incurred in order to generate sales.  Operating expenses are normally reported in the following two categories:

   a.   Selling expenses
   b.   General and administrative expenses

Selling expenses are those expenses directly related to the company's efforts to generate sales (e.g., sales salaries, commissions, advertising, delivery expenses, depreciation of store furniture and equipment, and store supplies).  General and administrative expenses are expenses related to the general administration of the company's operations (e.g., officers and office salaries, office supplies, depreciation of office furniture and fixtures, telephone, postage, accounting and legal services, and business licenses and fees).

4. **Gains and losses** result from the peripheral transactions of the entity. If immaterial, they are usually combined and shown with the normal, recurring revenues and expenses.  If they are individually material, they should be disclosed on a separate line.  Examples are write-downs of inventories and receivables, effects of a strike,

gains and losses on the disposal of equipment, and gains and losses from exchange or translation of foreign currencies. Holding gains on available-for-sale securities are included in other comprehensive income rather than income from continuing operations.

5.  **Other revenues and expenses** are revenues and expenses not related to the central operations of the company (e.g., interest revenues and expenses, and dividend revenues).

6.  **Unusual or infrequent** items are items that are either unusual or infrequent, but not both. They should be reported as a separate component of income from continuing operations. Under FAS 141(R), the excess of the fair value net assets acquired in a business combination over the fair value of consideration given will henceforth be recognized immediately in net income. The standard is not explicit regarding the location in the income statement where this is to be reported, but it is no longer to be reported as an extraordinary item, suggesting that it should be included in other income from continuing operations.

7.  **Goodwill impairment losses** are presented as a separate line item in the income from continuing operations section of the income statement. FAS 142 prohibits the amortization of goodwill and instead requires that goodwill be tested for impairment at least annually. If goodwill is found to be impaired, it is to be written down to fair value. The resultant loss must be included in the operations section of the income statement. However, if a goodwill impairment loss is associated with a discontinued operation, the loss is included (on a net-of-tax basis) within the results of discontinued operations.

8.  **Exit or disposal activity costs** are included in income from continuing operations before income taxes. Exit or disposal activities are restructurings and other activities that materially change the scope of business undertaken by an entity or the manner in which a business is conducted. If a subtotal such as "income from operations" is presented, the costs of exit or disposal activities will normally be included in that subtotal. However, if the costs are associated with exit or disposal activities that involve a discontinued operation, they are to be included in the results of discontinued operations (see below). If an entity's responsibility to settle the liability associated with an exit or disposal activity is removed or discharged, the related costs are reversed through the same line item(s) in the income statement that were used when those costs were initially recognized. (Exit or disposal activities are discussed in more detail later in this chapter.)

9.  **Income tax expense** related to continuing operations is that portion of the total income tax expense applicable to continuing operations.

The section ends in a subtotal that varies depending upon the existence of discontinued operations and extraordinary items. The effects of changes in accounting principles, which under prior GAAP (APB 20) were most commonly reported as special items in the income statement, are now (under FAS 154, addressed in Chapter 5) to be dealt with by *retrospective application* to all prior periods being presented. For example, the subtotal is usually titled "income from continuing operations" only when there is a section for discontinued operations in one of the years presented. If there is only a section for extraordinary items, the subtotal is usually titled "income before extraordinary items." The titles are adjusted accordingly if more than one of the sections are necessary. If there are no discontinued operations or extraordinary items, the subtotal is titled "net income."

### Examples of the format for presentation of various income statement items

**Discontinued operations and an extraordinary item**

| | | |
|---|---|---|
| Income (loss) from continuing operations | | $ xxx |
| Discontinued operations | | |
| Income (loss) from operations of Division Z, | | |
| less applicable income taxes of $xxx | $xxx | |
| Income (loss) on disposal of Division Z, less | | |
| applicable income taxes of $xxx | <u>xxx</u> | <u>xxx</u> |
| Income (loss) before extraordinary item | | $ xxx |
| Extraordinary item, less applicable income | | |
| taxes of $xxx (Note __) | | <u>xxx</u> |
| Net income | | $ <u>xxx</u> |
| Per share of common stock* | | |
| Income (loss) from continuing operations | | $x.xx |
| Net income | | $<u>x.xx</u> |

**Discontinued operations only**

| | | |
|---|---|---|
| Income (loss) from continuing operations | | $ xxx |
| Discontinued operations | | |
| Income (loss) from operations of Division Z, | | |
| less applicable income taxes of $xxx | $xxx | |
| Income (loss) on disposal of Division Z, less | | |
| applicable income taxes of $xxx | <u>xxx</u> | <u>xxx</u> |
| Net income | | $ <u>xxx</u> |
| Per share of common stock* | | |
| Income (loss) from continuing operations | | $x.xx |
| Net income | | $<u>x.xx</u> |

**Extraordinary item only**

| | |
|---|---|
| Income (loss) before extraordinary item | $ xxx |
| Extraordinary item, less applicable income taxes of $xxx (Note __) | xxx |
| Net income | $ <u>xxx</u> |
| Per share of common stock* | |
| Income (loss) before extraordinary item | $x.xx |
| Net income | $<u>x.xx</u> |

*\* These examples assume that per share amounts of discontinued operations and extraordinary items are shown in the notes.*

## Results from Discontinued Operations

FAS 144 has changed the standards on reporting for long-lived assets to be disposed of, as well as the qualifying conditions for reporting discontinued operations. Reporting of discontinued operations was originally set forth by APB 30.

APB 30 required that a discontinued operation be a segment of the business in order to qualify for the special financial statement presentation afforded to such operations. By contrast, under FAS 144 the reporting requirements apply to a "component of an entity." A component of an entity is distinguishable from the rest of the entity because it has its own operations and cash flows. A component may be a reportable segment, an operating segment, a reporting unit, a subsidiary, or an asset group. Refer to the discussion of alternative balance sheet segmentation and the accompanying diagram in Chapter 2 for further guidance.

If a component of an entity is either classified as held-for-sale or has been disposed of during the period, the results of its operations are reported in discontinued operations, if *both* of the following conditions are met:

1. The operations and cash flows of the component have been or will be removed from the ongoing operations of the entity as a result of the disposal transaction, *and*

2. The entity will have no significant continuing involvement in the operations of the component after the disposal transaction.

The conditions that must be met for a component to be classified as held-for-sale are set forth in Chapter 11.

EITF 03-13 provides guidance in applying these two criteria. The determination of whether the operations and cash flows of a disposed component have been or will be eliminated from the ongoing operations of the entity depends on (1) whether continuing cash flows have been or are expected to be recognized and, if so, (2) whether those continuing cash flows are direct or indirect. Continuing cash flows are cash inflows or outflows that are recognized by the ongoing entity and are associated with activities involving a disposed component. If continuing cash flows are recognized, the determination as to whether those continuing cash flows are direct or indirect is based on their nature and significance. If any continuing cash flows are determined to be direct, the cash flows have not been eliminated and the operations of the component are not to be presented as a discontinued operation.

EITF 03-13 also concluded that continuing involvement in the operations of the disposed component would provide the ongoing entity with the ability to influence the operating and (or) financial policies of the disposed component. The retention of risk or the ability to obtain benefits associated with the ongoing operations for the disposed component might indicate that the ongoing entity has the ability to influence the operating and (or) financial policies of the disposed component, resulting in a finding of continuing involvement. The determination as to whether the continuing involvement is significant would be based on quantitative and qualitative assessments from the perspective of the disposed component. The assessment is to consider all types of continuing involvement, individually and in the aggregate.

The assessment period commences when the component initially meets the criteria for classification as held for sale or is actually disposed of. The assessment period ends one year from the date of the actual disposal. During this assessment period, each time it issues financial statements, management of the ongoing entity is to consider whether any significant events or circumstances had occurred that might cause its original assessment with respect to whether both criteria for classification as discontinued operations are expected to be met. If a significant event or circumstance occurs during the assessment period that results in management assessing that both criteria are no longer expected to be met by the end of the assessment period, the operations of the component are not to be presented as discontinued operations. Consequently, it is possible that, during the assessment period, amounts may be classified into and out of discontinued operations based upon reassessments necessitated by the occurrence of events or circumstances.

### Examples of determination of whether to report discontinued operations

Software Solutions Plus develops and sells software for several markets. It has a children's educational line, a children's game line, a business office line, and a desktop publishing line. The product line is the lowest level at which the operations and cash flows can be clearly distinguished by management. Thus, each product line is an operating segment and a component of the entity.

### Case 1

Software Solutions Plus decides to exit the game business and commits to a plan to sell the children's game line. The assets and liabilities of the product line are classified as held-for-sale at that date. Software Solutions Plus will have no continuing involvement with the children's game software after the sale is closed. In addition, Software Solutions Plus has decided that it will not develop any new computer games for the children's market. In this case, the conditions are met to report the children's game line as a discontinued operation.

**Case 2**

Instead of exiting the children's game business entirely as in Case 1, Software Solutions Plus decides to keep its game programmers on its staff and have them develop new children's games. However, instead of selling the games to the home market via distributors as it had been doing, each existing and newly developed game will be marketed and sold to other software game companies. Software Solutions Plus will not provide technical support for any particular game software after it is sold. In this case, although Software Solutions Plus will not have any continuing involvement with the games after they are sold, it will continue to have revenues and expenses related to the children's game product line. Thus, the first of the two conditions required for discontinued operations treatments is not met. The change in the manner of marketing the line cannot be reported in discontinued operations.

**Case 3**

Software Solutions Plus decides to discontinue developing and selling its graphics drawing program product, which is part of the desktop publishing product line. In this case, because the graphics drawing program product is not a component of the entity on its own, but instead is part of the component desktop publishing product line, the sale of the graphics drawing program cannot be reported in discontinued operations.

**Case 4**

Software Solutions Plus commits to a plan to sell the desktop publishing line to another software company. The assets and liabilities of the product line are classified as held-for-sale at that date. As part of the sales agreement, Software Solutions Plus will receive a sizable royalty for each program sold and will provide technical support to the buyer's programming staff and to customers for the next three years. In this case, because Software Solutions Plus will continue to receive cash flows from the product line and will continue to have significant involvement with the product line after the product line is sold, the sale of the desktop publishing product line cannot be reported in discontinued operations. In the third year after the sale, Software Solutions Plus should reassess whether the conditions necessary to report the activity in discontinued operations have been met.

In the period in which a component of an entity is either classified as held-for-sale or has been disposed of, the results of operations of that component and any gain or loss recognized on disposal is reported as a separate component of income, before extraordinary items and the cumulative effect of accounting changes (if any). The income statements of any prior periods being presented should be restated to also reflect the results of operations of the component as discontinued operations. All amounts should be reported less applicable income taxes (benefits), as shown in the example below.

**Example of income statement presentation for discontinued operations**

|  | *2009* | *2008* |
|---|---|---|
| Income from continuing operations before income taxes | $ 598 | $ 583 |
| Income taxes | 239 | 233 |
| Income from continuing operations | 359 | 350 |
| Discontinued operations (Note ___) | | |
| Loss from operations of discontinued component | 1,165 | 1,045 |
| Loss on disposal of discontinued component | 167 | |
| Income tax benefit | (532) | (418) |
| Loss on discontinued operations | 800 | 627 |
| Net income | $ (441) | $ (282) |

This example shows the loss on disposal on the face of the income statement. Alternatively, the amount can be shown in the notes to the financial statements, as long as the disclosure identifies the caption in the income statement in which the loss is included.

General corporate overhead may not be allocated to discontinued operations. Interest expense, however, is to be allocated to discontinued operations if, as a result of a disposal transaction, the buyer assumes debt of the seller/reporting entity or, as a result of the disposal transaction, the reporting entity is required to repay debt (EITF 87-24). Allocation to discontinued operations of other consolidated interest is permitted but not required. If the corporation decides to allocate other consolidated interest, EITF 03-13 provides guidance regarding the maximum amount and methods of allocation.

**Computing the gain or loss on disposal.** To compute the loss (or gain) on disposal, the entity must first compute the fair value of the component; less the cost to sell it. Costs to sell are the incremental direct costs to transact the sale. In other words, costs to sell result directly from the decision to sell the component, are essential to the sales transaction, and would not have been incurred by the entity absent the decision to sell the component. Examples of costs to sell are broker commissions, legal fees, title transfer fees, and closing costs. In the limited situations in which the sale will occur more than one year after the component is classified as held-for-sale, the costs to sell should be discounted to present value. (For more information about long-lived assets held for sale, see Chapter 11.)

Next, the entity must compute the carrying value of the component. The carrying amounts of assets (other than long-lived assets) and liabilities are first adjusted in accordance with GAAP, and any adjustments are excluded from the gain or loss from disposal. For example, if trade accounts receivable are being sold as part of a component, the adequacy of the valuation allowance would be assessed as of the date the component is classified as held-for-sale, and any adjustment needed to bring the allowance to the proper balance would be included in bad debt expense. Similarly, if the sale of the component includes assumption of bonds payable, the accumulated amortization of any premium or discount on those bonds would be brought up to date, and this adjustment would be included in interest expense.

The gain or loss on disposal is computed by comparing the total carrying amount to the fair value net of costs to sell. A loss is recognized in the period in which the component is classified as held-for-sale if the total carrying amount exceeds the fair value less costs to sell. On the other hand, if the fair value less costs to sell exceeds the carrying amount (that is, there is a gain on disposal), the gain is not recognized until the actual sale occurs. Fair value, as defined in FAS 157, is essentially the price the seller would receive on the open market for a product.

Under FAS 144, losses from operations of the component subsequent to the date the component is classified as held-for-sale are to be recognized in the period in which they are incurred. That is, expected future losses are not accrued prior to being incurred, since doing so would result in the creation of a liability (reserve) which fails to meet the definition in CON 6.

### Example of computing the gain or loss on disposal

Today's Telecommunications has decided to close its pager division, which is a component of the reporting entity. It has committed to a plan to sell the assets and liabilities of the division and has properly reclassified the division as held-for-sale at that date. The following conditions apply:

- The division has incurred $1,750 losses from operations from the beginning of the year to the date it was reclassified as held-for-sale.
- The fair value of the assets and liabilities of the division are $10,775.
- Brokers' commissions and other costs to sell are estimated to be $1,650.
- The carrying value of the assets and liabilities of the division is $12,525 before the GAAP adjustments (depreciation, amortization, adjustment of valuation accounts, and similar periodic adjustments) are made.
- The GAAP adjustments reduce the carrying value of the assets and liabilities by $125.

- Losses from operations of the division from the date it is classified as held-for-sale to the end of the fiscal year are $580. (This loss does not include the GAAP adjustments noted above.)
- Anticipated future losses from operations of the division from the end of this fiscal year to the expected sales date are $1,999.
- The tax rate is 40%.

The income statement presentation of discontinued operations would be

Discontinued operations (Note ___)

| | |
|---|---|
| Loss from operations of discontinued division, net of tax of $982 | $1,473 |
| Loss on disposal of discontinued division, net of tax of $1,310 | 1,965 |
| Loss on discontinued operations | $3,438 |

The loss from operations of the discontinued pager division is the sum of the $1,750 loss incurred prior to the date the assets and liabilities were classified as held-for-sale, plus the $125 GAAP adjustments that were recorded, plus the $580 loss incurred from the date the division was classified as held-for-sale to the end of the fiscal year. The sum ($2,455) less the tax effects of $982 ($2,455 × 40%) is the loss from operations of $1,473.

The loss on disposal is the difference between the carrying value of the division and its fair value less costs to sell. The carrying value of the division is $12,400 ($12,525 less the GAAP adjustments of $125). The fair value of the division less costs to sell is $9,125 ($10,775 fair value less costs to sell of $1,650). The difference of $3,275 less the tax effects of $1,310 ($3,275 × 40%) is the loss on disposal of $1,965. The anticipated future losses from operations of the division will be reported in discontinued operations in the future period in which they occur. They are not included in the loss on disposal in the current fiscal year.

**Future periods.** Subsequent to the fiscal year in which the assets and liabilities of a component are classified as held-for-sale, the discontinued operations section of an income statement includes

1. Results of operations of the discontinued component
2. Certain adjustments that are directly related to the disposal of a component of an entity, such as

   a. Resolution of contingencies associated with the terms of the disposal transaction, such as purchase price adjustments and indemnification issues with the purchaser
   b. Resolution of contingencies associated with the operations of the component prior to its disposal, such as environmental or product warranty obligations retained by the seller
   c. Settlement of employee benefit plan obligations directly associated with the disposal transaction that occur no later than one year after the disposal transaction. (See the discussion of settlements and curtailments of plan liabilities in Chapter 18.)

When adjustments of this nature occur, they should be classified separately in discontinued operations of the current period and the notes to the financial statements should disclose the nature and amount of these adjustments.

### Example of discontinued operations in a future period

Continuing the previous example, the sale of Today's Telecommunications' pager division, which is a component of the entity, closed in the year subsequent to the fiscal year in which the assets and liabilities were classified as held-for-sale.

- The actual sales price less costs to sell was $9,725.
- The net carrying value of the assets and liabilities on the date of sale was $12,225.
- The loss from operations from the end of the fiscal year to the date of sale was $2,045.
- The tax rate is 40%.

The income statement presentation of discontinued operations would be

Discontinued operations (Note ____)
| | |
|---|---|
| Loss from operations of discontinued division, net of tax of $818 | 1,227 |
| Gain on disposal of discontinued division, net of tax of $310 | 465 |
| Loss on discontinued operations | 762 |

The loss from operations of the discontinued pager division is the $2,045 less the tax effects of $818 ($2,045 × 40%).

The loss on disposal is the difference between the carrying value of the division and its sales price less the loss recognized in the prior period. The carrying value of the division was $12,225; the sales price less costs to sell was $9,725, for an actual loss of $2,500. The loss recognized in the prior period was $3,275, so an adjustment of $775 ($2,500 less $3,275) is necessary. The tax effects on the adjustment are $310 ($775 × 40%), so the net adjustment is a gain of $465 ($775 − $310).

## Extraordinary Items

An event or transaction should be presumed to be an ordinary and usual activity (and thus, not to be described as extraordinary) unless the event or transaction is both of an unusual nature and infrequent in its occurrence.

**Unusual nature.** To meet this criterion, the underlying event or transaction should possess a high degree of abnormality and be of a type clearly unrelated to, or only incidentally related to, the ordinary and typical activities of the reporting entity, taking into account the environment in which it operates.

In determining whether an event or transaction is of an unusual nature, the following special characteristics of the reporting entity are considered:

1. Type and scope of operations
2. Lines of business
3. Operating policies
4. Industry (or industries) in which the reporting entity operates
5. Geographic locations of its operations
6. Nature and extent of government regulation

An event that is of an unusual nature for one reporting entity can be an ordinary and usual activity of another because of the above characteristics. Whether an event or transaction is beyond the control of management is irrelevant in the determination of whether it is of an unusual nature.

**Infrequency of occurrence.** To satisfy this requirement, the underlying event or transaction should be of a type that would not reasonably be expected to recur in the foreseeable future, again taking into account the environment in which the reporting entity operates.

**Items specifically included or excluded from extraordinary items.** Accounting pronouncements have specifically required the following items to be presented as extraordinary, irrespective of whether they meet the criteria stated above:

1. The investor's share of an investee's extraordinary item when the investor uses the equity method of accounting for the investee (APB 18).
2. The net effect of adjustments relating to the discontinuation of the application of FAS 71 by a public utility or other reporting entity with regulated operations (FAS 101).
3. The remaining excess of the fair value of acquired net assets over their cost pursuant to FAS 141. Chapter 13 provides additional information about the excess over cost in a business combination transaction.

4.  Estimated losses recognized due to obligations under the Coal Industry Retiree Health Benefit Act of 1992 (EITF 92-13).

Material gains and losses from the extinguishment of debt and gains from troubled debt restructurings previously were items specifically required to be classified as extraordinary. FAS 145 rescinded that requirement, so those gains and losses are now evaluated using the unusual and infrequent criteria described above. In addition, EITF 00-9 clarifies that, by analogy, these same criteria are to be used to evaluate the classification of gains or losses arising from adjustments to the carrying amount of debt required by the hedge accounting requirements of FAS 133.

The following items are, by definition, *not* extraordinary items:

1.  Write-down or write-off of receivables, inventories, equipment leased to others, or intangible assets
2.  Foreign currency gains and losses
3.  Gains and losses on the disposal of a segment of a business
4.  Gains and losses from sale or abandonment of property, plant, or equipment used in operations
5.  Effects of a strike
6.  Adjustments of accruals on long-term contracts
7.  Losses and costs incurred as a result of the September 11, 2001 terrorist attacks (EITF 01-10)

Per FTB 85-6, neither the cost incurred by a company to defend itself from a takeover attempt nor the cost incurred as part of a "standstill" agreement meet the criteria for extraordinary classification as discussed in APB 30.

**Presentation.** Extraordinary items should be segregated from the results of ordinary operations and be shown net of taxes in a separate section of the income statement, following "discontinued operations." If more than one extraordinary item occurs during a period, they should be reported separately or details should be included in the notes to the financial statements.

**Example of the income statement presentation for extraordinary items**

An extraordinary item would be presented as follows:

| | |
|---|---:|
| Income before extraordinary items | $xxx |
| Extraordinary items (less applicable income taxes of $__) (Note __) | xxx |
| Net income | $xxx |

## Accounting Changes

A change in accounting principle results from adoption of a generally accepted accounting principle different from the one previously used for reporting purposes. The term accounting principle includes not only accounting principles and practices, but also the methods of applying them. Changes in accounting principles (or the method of applying them) must be justified by those who make the change (the entity's management), unless they are made in order to comply with a FASB position.

Prior to the adoption of FAS 154, which was part of the FASB's efforts to converge US GAAP to IFRS, many accounting changes were to be accounted for by including in the income statement, in the period of change, a special charge or credit for the cumulative effect of the change on retained earnings, due to applying the new method implicitly to all prior periods' earnings. FAS 154 requires instead that the new method be retrospectively applied, so that all prior periods' financial statements being presented (i.e., comparative financial statements) be restated. The cumulative effect on years prior to the first comparative period is an adjustment to opening retained earnings. See Chapter 5 for a detailed discussion of accounting changes.

## Other Comprehensive Income

Under current accounting standards, other comprehensive income includes foreign currency adjustments, unrealized changes in the fair value of available-for-sale securities, the effective portion of the gain or loss on derivative instruments designated and qualified as either a cash-flow hedge or a hedge of a forecasted foreign-currency-denominated transaction, and minimum pension liability adjustments. FAS 130 requires that the components of other comprehensive income along with totals for net income, other comprehensive income, and comprehensive income must appear in a statement of the same prominence as other financial statements. (However, an entity that has no items of other comprehensive income in any period presented is required to report only net income.) Presenting those required amounts in a combined statement of income and comprehensive income is only one of three permissible methods. The other two are discussed later in this chapter.

Some items impact other comprehensive income in one period and then affect net income in the same or a later period. For example, an unrealized holding gain on an available-for-sale security is included in other comprehensive income in the period in which the market fluctuation occurs. Later, perhaps years later, the security is sold and the realized gains are included in net income. An adjustment to the unrealized holding gain component of other comprehensive income is necessary to avoid double counting the gain—once in net income in the current year and also in other comprehensive income in the earlier period. Adjustments of that type are called reclassification adjustments. The process of including in net income an item previously reported in other comprehensive income is often referred to as "recycling."

Usually, a sale triggers the need for a reclassification adjustment. The sale of an available-for-sale security in the current period triggers the need for an adjustment for the gains (losses) that had been included in other comprehensive income in a prior period. Likewise, the sale of an investment in a foreign entity triggers an adjustment for foreign currency items that had been included in other comprehensive income previously (i.e., accumulated translation gains or losses). Amounts accumulated in other comprehensive income from cash flow hedges are reclassified into earnings in the same period(s) in which the hedged forecasted transactions (such as a forecasted sale) affects earnings. If it becomes probable that the forecasted transaction will not occur, the net gain or loss in accumulated other comprehensive income must be immediately reclassified. An adjustment is also necessary upon the complete (or substantially complete) liquidation of an investment in a foreign entity. Only minimum pension liabilities will not require reclassification adjustments (because they will not be reported in net income in any future period).

Reclassification adjustments can be presented on the face of the statement with the components of other comprehensive income or can be netted against the related component and with details of the reclassification being provided in the notes to the financial statements.

The tax effects of items reported in other comprehensive income must also be included in other comprehensive income. The items of other comprehensive income can be reported either net of related tax effects on the face of the statement or gross with the tax effects related to all components reported on a single, separate line. If gross reporting is used, the notes to the financial statements must disclose the tax effects related to each component (if there is more than one component). The following examples illustrate the two presentations.

### Example of the "net of tax" presentation

**Hypothetical Corporation**
**Statement of Income and Comprehensive Income**
**For the Year Ended December 31, 2009**
**($000 omitted)**

| | | |
|---|---:|---:|
| Sales | | $395,400 |
| (details omitted) | | |
| Net earnings | | 83,250 |
| Other comprehensive income | | |
| Foreign currency translation adjustment, net of $5,100 tax | | 11,900 |
| Unrealized gain on securities: | | |
|   Unrealized holding gains arising during period, net of $7,500 tax | 17,500 | |
|   Less:  Reclassification adjustment, net of $1,500 tax, for gain included | | |
|     currently in net income | (3,500) | 14,000 |
| Cash flow hedges | | |
|   Net derivative losses arising during the period, net of $4,800 tax | (11,200) | |
|   Less:  Reclassification adjustment for losses included currently in net in- | | |
|     come, net of $7,762 tax | 18,113 | 6,913 |
| Minimum pension liability adjustment, net of $1,950 tax | | (4,550) |
|   Other comprehensive income | | 28,263 |
| Comprehensive income | | $111,513 |

### Example of the "gross of tax" presentation

**Hypothetical Corporation**
**Statement of Income and Comprehensive Income**
**For the Year Ended December 31, 2009**
**($000 omitted)**

| | | |
|---|---:|---:|
| Sales | | $395,400 |
| (details omitted) | | |
| Net earnings | | 83,250 |
| Other comprehensive income | | |
| Foreign currency translation adjustment | | 17,000 |
| Unrealized gains on securities: | | |
|   Unrealized holding gains arising during period | 25,000 | |
|   Less:  Reclassification adjustment for gain included currently in net in- | | |
|     come | (5,000) | 20,000 |
| Cash flow hedges | | |
|   Net derivative losses arising during the period | (16,000) | |
|   Less:  Reclassification adjustment for losses included currently in net in- | | |
|     come | 25,875 | 9,875 |
| Minimum pension liability adjustment | | (6,500) |
| Tax effects of items included in other comprehensive income | | (12,112) |
| Other comprehensive income | | 28,263 |
| Comprehensive income | | $111,513 |

If the "gross" approach illustrated above were utilized, it would also be necessary to present in the notes to the financial statements details regarding the allocation of the tax effects to the several items included in other comprehensive income.  An example of that note disclosure follows.

### Note X:  Income Taxes

The tax effects of items included in other comprehensive income for the year ended December 31, 2009, are as follows:

| | Before-tax amount | Tax expense (benefit) | Net-of-tax amount |
|---|---:|---:|---:|
| Foreign currency translation adjustments | $17,000 | $ 5,100 | $11,900 |
| Unrealized gains on securities: | | | |
|   Unrealized holding gains arising during period | 25,000 | 7,500 | 17,500 |
|   Reclassification adjustment | (5,000) | (1,500) | (3,500) |
|   Net unrealized holding gains | 20,000 | 6,000 | 14,000 |

| | Before-tax amount | Tax expense (benefit) | Net-of-tax amount |
|---|---|---|---|
| Cash flow hedges: | | | |
| Net derivative losses arising during the period | (16,000) | 4,800 | (11,200) |
| Reclassification adjustment | 25,875 | (6,913) | 18,113 |
| Net effects of cash flow hedges | 9,875 | (2,113) | 6,913 |
| Minimum pension liability adjustment | (6,500) | (1,950) | (4,550) |
| Other comprehensive income | $40,375 | $12,112 | $28,263 |

## Earnings Per Share

Earnings per share (EPS) is a measure often used in evaluating a firm's stock price and in assessing the firm's future earnings and ability to pay dividends. Because of the importance of earnings per share, the profession has concluded that it should be disclosed on the face of the income statement.

Earnings per share is a very compact indicator of a company's performance. In order to assess quality of earnings, FAS 128 requires presentation of *basic earnings per share* on the face of the income statement for public-market issued common stock or potential common stock (such as options, warrants, convertible securities or contingent stock agreements). Shares outstanding are determined by the weighted-average method. Earnings are defined as both income from continuing operations and net income available to common stockholders. Thus, dividends declared on preferred stock and dividends for the period on cumulative preferred stock, whether or not earned or paid, are deducted from both income from continuing operations and net income before computing per share amounts.

**Diluted earnings per share** is computed similarly to basic earnings per share but the number of shares outstanding is adjusted to include the number of additional common shares that would be issued if the potentially dilutive shares had been issued.

Entities with simple capital structures, that is, only common stock, should display basic earnings per share for both continuing operations and net income on the face of the income statement. All other entities are required to display both basic and diluted per share amounts for both continuing operations and net income. For discontinued operations, extraordinary items, or cumulative effect of an accounting change, basic and diluted per share amounts may be either reported on the face of the income statement or disclosed in the notes. More details on the per share calculations can be found in Chapter 20.

### Example of the presentation and computation of earnings per share

Assume that 100,000 shares were outstanding throughout the year.

**ABC Company**
**Income Statement**
**For the Year Ended December 31, 2009**

| | | |
|---|---|---|
| Sales | | $2,000,000 |
| Cost of goods sold | | 750,000 |
| Gross profit | | $1,250,000 |
| Selling and administrative expenses | | 500,000 |
| Income from operations | | $ 750,000 |
| Other revenues and expense | | |
| Interest income | $40,000 | |
| Interest expense | (30,000) | 10,000 |
| Income before unusual or infrequent items and income taxes | | $ 760,000 |
| Unusual or infrequent items: | | |
| Loss from permanent impairment of value of manufacturing facilities | | (10,000) |
| Income from continuing operations before income taxes | | $ 750,000 |
| Income taxes | | 300,000 |
| Income from continuing operations | | $ 450,000 |

Discontinued operations:
    Loss from operations of Division X, including loss on disposal of
       $100,000 and income tax benefit of $20,000             $30,000
Income before extraordinary item                    $ 420,000
Extraordinary item—loss from earthquake less applicable income tax
  benefit of $38,000                         (72,000)
    Net income                           $ 348,000
    Basic EPS computation
      Income from continuing operations ($450,000/100,000)      $     4.50
          Extraordinary items* ($72,000/100,000)                (0.72)
          Discontinued operations* ($30,000/100,000)           (0.30)
     Net income available for common stockholders        $     3.48

 * *May be shown in the notes to the financial statements.*

## Prior Period Adjustments

Traditionally there has been a concern that unless all income and expense items first being recognized are included in the current period's income statement, financial statement users would be inclined to place unjustifiably low emphasis on the matter. Put another way, the fear was that the use of prior period adjustments would offer preparers a means of effectively concealing what might be important events or changes in estimates from users. For that reason, current GAAP strictly limits the use of prior period adjustments.

FAS 16 defines a prior period adjustment and clearly states that only the following items are to be excluded from the determination of net income for the current period:

1. The correction of an error in the financial statements of a prior period
2. Adjustments that result from realization of income tax benefits of preacquisition operating loss carryforwards of purchased subsidiaries

APB 9 specifies the recording and presentation of a prior period adjustment. When prior period adjustments are recorded, the resulting effects on the net income of prior periods shall be disclosed in the year in which the adjustments are made. The adjustments are reported at both their gross amount and net of applicable income taxes. If the statements are presented for only a single period, then the beginning balance of retained earnings is restated to reflect the effects of the correction or change. When comparative statements are presented, adjustments should be made of the amounts of net income (and the components thereof) and retained earnings balance (as well as other affected balances) for all of the periods included in the financial statements.

FAS 141(R) has limited the circumstances under which revisions to deferred tax benefit recognition can be effected following a business acquisition, as described in Chapter 13. Within the newly defined limit, however, adjustment of a prior period's financial statements may still occur.

FAS 154 addresses corrections of errors and establishes that use of the term "restatement" now is only appropriate for corrections of errors. An example of the accounting presentation for a prior period adjustment appears in Chapter 5.

## Statement of Income and Retained Earnings

An acceptable practice is to combine the income statement and the statement of retained earnings into a single statement called the Statement of Income and Retained Earnings. The income statement is prepared in the normal manner. The beginning balance in retained earnings is added to the net income (loss) figure. Declared dividends are deducted to obtain the retained earnings ending balance.

**Example of a statement of income and retained earnings**

Baker, Inc.
Statement of Income and Retained Earnings
For the Year Ended December 31, 2009

| | | |
|---|---:|---:|
| Sales | | $2,482 |
| Cost of goods sold | | 1,489 |
| Gross margin on sales | | $ 993 |
| Operating expenses | | |
| Selling expenses | $ 220 | |
| Administrative expenses | 255 | 475 |
| Income from operations | | $ 518 |
| Other revenues/gains (expenses/losses) | | |
| Interest revenue (expense)—net | $ (40) | |
| Gain on sale of investment in ABC Company | 100 | |
| Gain on translation of foreign currencies | 20 | 80 |
| Income before unusual or infrequent items | | $ 598 |
| Unusual or infrequent items: | | |
| Write-down of property and equipment | $ (20) | |
| Loss from permanent impairment of value of distributing facility | (50) | (70) |
| Income from continuing operations before provision for income taxes | | $ 528 |
| Provision for income taxes | | 211 |
| Income from continuing operations | | $ 317 |
| Discontinued operations: | | |
| Loss from operations of discontinued Division Z (less applicable taxes of $466) | $ (699) | |
| Loss on disposal of Division Z (less applicable taxes of $67) | (100) | (799) |
| Loss before extraordinary items | | $ (482) |
| Extraordinary loss from earthquake (less applicable income tax benefit of $70) | | (165) |
| Net loss | | $ (647) |
| Retained earnings, January 1, 2009 | $1,900 | |
| Prior period adjustment: | | |
| Correction of depreciation error (less applicable income taxes of $28) | (42) | |
| Adjusted retained earnings, January 1, 2009 | | 1,858 |
| Deduct dividends: | | |
| Preferred stock | $ (40) | |
| Common stock | (30) | (70) |
| Retained earnings, December 31, 2009 | | $1,141 |
| Per share amounts (100 shares)* | | |
| Income from continuing operations | | $ 3.17 |
| Net loss | | $ (6.47) |

* *Assumes other per share amounts are included in notes to financial statements.*

## Reporting Comprehensive Income in a Statement other than a Combined Statement of Income and Comprehensive Income

Entities are not required to present information about comprehensive income in a combined statement of income and comprehensive income. Instead, they need only to present the components of other comprehensive income along with totals for net income, other comprehensive income, and comprehensive income in a statement of the same prominence as other financial statements. Thus, two other alternatives are available.

1. In an expanded statement of changes in stockholder's equity, or
2. In a stand-alone statement of comprehensive income

In FAS 130, FASB encourages the use of either a combined statement of income and comprehensive income or a stand-alone statement that begins with net income. In practice, the expanded statement of changes in stockholder's equity is also widely used.

## Example of presentation of comprehensive income in the statement of changes in stockholders' equity

If comprehensive income is reported in the statement of changes in stockholders' equity, there are several formats that can be employed to accomplish this goal. Each of these modes of presentation is somewhat cumbersome, primarily because one element of comprehensive income (earnings) must be added to retained earnings while another (comprehensive income) is not.

Consider the case of Leisuretime Industries, which has preferred and common shares outstanding, and also has two classes of other comprehensive income. If Leisuretime Industries chooses to report comprehensive income in the statement of changes in stockholders' equity (rather than in either a freestanding statement of comprehensive income or combined statement of earnings and comprehensive income), one of two formats might be selected. These are illustrated below.

**Leisuretime Industries**
**Statement of Changes in Stockholders' Equity**
**For the Year Ended December 31, 2009**
**($000 omitted)**

|  | Preferred stock | Common stock | Compre-hensive income | Retained earnings | Accumu-lated other compre-hensive income | Total |
|---|---|---|---|---|---|---|
| Balances, January 1, 2009 | $500,000 | $4,500,000 |  | $715,600 | $ (5,950) | $5,709,650 |
| Comprehensive income |  |  |  |  |  |  |
| Net income |  |  | $66,760 | 66,760 |  |  |
| Other comprehensive income: |  |  |  |  |  |  |
| Foreign currency translation adjustments, net of tax |  |  | 3,000 |  |  |  |
| Unrealized gains on securities: |  |  |  |  |  |  |
| Unrealized holding gains arising during period, net of tax |  |  | 23,000 |  |  |  |
| Less: reclassification adjustment, net of tax, for gain included in net income |  |  | (5,500) |  |  |  |
| Other comprehensive income |  |  | 20,500 |  | 20,500 |  |
| Comprehensive income |  |  | $87,260 |  |  | 87,260 |
| Proceeds from issuance of shares | 50,000 | 200,000 |  |  |  | 250,000 |
| Dividends paid |  |  |  | (24,825) |  | (24,825) |
| Balances, December 31, 2009 | $550,000 | $4,700,000 |  | $757,535 | $14,550 | $6,022,085 |

**Leisuretime Industries**
**Statement of Changes in Stockholders' Equity**
**For the Year Ended December 31, 2009**
**($000 omitted)**

|  | Preferred stock | Common stock | Retained earnings | Foreign currency translation | Unrealized gains on securities | Total |
|---|---|---|---|---|---|---|
| Balances, January 1, 2009 | $500,000 | $4,500,000 | $715,600 | $(9,275) | $ 3,325 | $5,709,650 |
| Comprehensive income |  |  |  |  |  |  |
| Net income |  |  | 66,760 |  |  | 66,760 |
| Other comprehensive income: |  |  |  |  |  |  |
| Foreign currency translation adjustments, net of tax |  |  |  | 3,000 |  | 3,000 |
| Unrealized gains on securities: |  |  |  |  |  |  |
| Unrealized holding gains arising during period, net of tax |  |  |  |  | 23,000 | 23,000 |

| | Preferred stock | Common stock | Retained earnings | Foreign currency translation | Unrealized gains on securities | Total |
|---|---|---|---|---|---|---|
| Less: reclassification adjustment, net of tax, for gain included in net income | | | | | (5,500) | (5,500) |
| Other comprehensive income | | | | | | 20,500 |
| Comprehensive income | | | | | | 87,260 |
| Proceeds from issuance of shares | 50,000 | 200,000 | | | | 250,000 |
| Dividends paid | | | (24,825) | | | (24,825) |
| Balances, December 31, 2009 | $550,000 | $4,700,000 | $757,535 | $(6,275) | $20,825 | $6,022,085 |

## Pro Forma Earnings

During the late 1990s and early 2000s, companies increasingly made reference in press releases and published materials to an alternative measure of performance, loosely (if inaccurately) referred to as "pro forma earnings." (The term "pro forma" more properly suggests that amounts that are not actual historical results are being cast in the form of a report on historical performance—e.g., when after a midyear business acquisition the full year's results are presented as if the merger had occurred on January 1. This is not, however, the case with the more controversial recent usage of this term.) This practice has generated controversy and confusion because there is no standard definition for "pro forma earnings." Different reporting entities can, and have, defined pro forma earnings on a wide range of ad hoc bases, and sometimes a given entity fails even to consistently define this amount from period to period.

The reporting of pro forma earnings proliferated over the years preceding the enactment of Sarbanes-Oxley and the subsequent promulgation of Regulation G by the SEC. Often, even when GAAP-basis earnings are stated in the same announcement as the pro forma measure, it is the latter which receives most of the attention. In a number of instances, pro forma earnings have been based on very aggressive exclusions of operating costs and, sometimes, the inclusion of onetime gains. Such practices ultimately came to be widely recognized as being misleading and inappropriate, and popular sentiment turned against employment of such devices.

Some companies defended their use of pro forma calculations as merely responding to the marketplace's need for a measure that gives insight into the company's future performance. Pro forma earnings, they said, were necessary to compensate for deficiencies in GAAP. Because GAAP-basis net income is affected by various noncash charges and credits, as well as by nonrecurring gains and losses, some argued that this traditional measure may not provide investors with the most meaningful and accurate guide to the entity's future results of operations. They held that investors needed access to a number that measures only the performance of the reporting entity's ongoing "normalized" operations. As with many arguments, there was probably an element of truth to this assertion.

However, assuming for the moment that GAAP-basis net income is a flawed indicator of future performance, their argument would have had greater validity if a standardized pro forma measure had been promulgated by the accounting profession or uniformly applied by the investment community. Such a standard definition does not exist, however. Despite the lack of standardization, there has been an increasing willingness on the part of investors to accept the pro forma expressions without understanding what they are or how they have been computed.

For reporting entities, part of the allure of pro forma earnings is that it can be defined to exclude some or all of a range of "unusual" items. Not surprisingly, most of the excluded items have been charges, such as those for worker layoffs, restructurings, assets impairments, and inventory obsolescence. Even if truly not expected to recur annually, many of these charges are quite normal and may be anticipated to recur at irregular intervals in the life of a given business. Furthermore, many such charges can be viewed as "catch-ups" for under-recognition of expenses in earlier periods, and since those charges would have been fully reflected in current earnings, the subsequent period's catch-up should, logically, also be included in the current period measure of operating results.

A further practice, which is improper but unfortunately has not been uncommon, has been for reporting entities to opportunistically charge off an exaggerated loss in the current period, perhaps in connection with such randomly occurring events as discontinued operations. The loss is then excluded from pro forma earnings. The excess reserves (sometimes referred to as "cookie jar reserves") then become available to be drawn down in future periods, as the provided-for expenses fail to materialize in the amounts reserved. The draw-downs of the excess reserves increase net income in future periods, but those draw-downs will not be excluded from pro forma earnings the way the original loss had been. The result will be to boost both GAAP-basis net income and pro forma earnings in future years. (This is not, however, to suggest that all companies that announce pro forma earnings use "cookie jar reserves" to commit financial fraud. However, investors' acceptance of undefined measures of earnings increases the temptation to engage in irregularities that misstate the results of operations, and surveys have found consistently that misapplication of reserve accounting has been either the most, or second-most, common reason for subsequently announced restatements of previously announced results of operations.)

The SEC adopted Regulation G to curtail the use of pro forma earnings statements. Regulation G states that a public company, or a person acting on its behalf, is not to make public a non-GAAP financial measure that, taken together with the information accompanying that measure, either contains an untrue statement of a material fact or omits a material fact that would be necessary to make the presentation of the non-GAAP financial measure not misleading. Further, Regulation G requires a public company that discloses or releases a non-GAAP financial measure to include in that disclosure or release a presentation of the most directly comparable GAAP financial measure and a reconciliation of the disclosed non-GAAP measure to that directly comparable GAAP financial measure.

The regulations also prohibit certain non-GAAP measures from inclusion in SEC filings. Public companies must not

1.  Exclude from non-GAAP liquidity measures charges or liabilities that required, or will require, cash settlement, or would have required cash settlement absent an ability to settle in another manner. However, earnings before interest and taxes (EBIT) and earnings before interest, taxes, depreciation, and amortization (EBITDA) are permissible.

2.  Create a non-GAAP performance measure that eliminates items identified as non-recurring, infrequent, or unusual if the nature of the excluded item is such that it is (a) reasonably likely to recur within two years or (b) similar to a charge or gain that occurred within the prior two years.

3.  Present non-GAAP financial measures on the face of the registrant's financial statements prepared in accordance with GAAP or in the accompanying notes.

4.  Present non-GAAP financial measures on the face of any pro forma financial information required to be disclosed by Article 11 of Regulation S-X (e.g., business combinations or disposals).

5.  Use titles or descriptions of non-GAAP financial measures that are the same as, or confusingly similar to, titles or descriptions used for GAAP measures.

The SEC's action has served to curb the abuse of pro forma earnings measures, but it does little to standardize the measures in use. Others, however, have proposed approaches to standardize the computation of pro forma earnings. For example, the rating agency Standard & Poors (S&P) has introduced a measure that it will use in its COMPUSTAT database, in its US equity indices, and in its financial statement analysis. It has denoted this measure as "core earnings." S&P defines core earnings as net income, as defined by GAAP, specifically *including* these items

- Employee stock option grant expenses
- Restructuring charges from ongoing operations
- Write-downs of depreciable or amortizable operating assets
- Pension costs
- Purchased research and development

And specifically *excluding* these items

- Discontinued operations
- Extraordinary items
- Impairment of goodwill charges
- Gains and losses from asset sales
- Pension gains
- Unrealized gains and losses from hedging activities
- Merger and acquisition fees
- Litigation settlements

S&P's definition may help investors and also serve to reverse, or at least constrain, the expanding use of subjectively defined, alternative income measures. Although there may be a demand for a performance measure other than net income or comprehensive income, such a measure will not be useful unless it is standardized so that comparisons can be confidently made among different entities or within the same entity over time.

The FASB's *Financial Statement Presentation* project (originally, *Reporting Financial Performance*), discussed in Chapter 2 and below, may eventually serve to further reduce the abuses inherent in the use of alternative measures of performance commonly known as "pro forma."

## Development Stage Enterprises

FAS 7 indicates that development stage enterprises should prepare their financial statements in accordance with the same GAAP applicable to established operating entities. FAS 7 indicated that specialized accounting practices are unacceptable and that accounting treatment should be governed by the nature of the transaction rather than the age of the entity. FAS 7 also provided that a development stage enterprise should disclose certain additional information that would alert readers to the fact that the company is in the development stage. Disclosure requirements include

1. All disclosures applicable to operating entities
2. Identification of the statements as those of a development stage enterprise
3. Disclosure of the nature of development stage activities
4. A balance sheet that, in the equity section, includes the cumulative net losses since inception
5. An income statement showing current period revenue and expense as well as the cumulative amount from the inception of the entity
6. A statement of cash flows showing cash flows for the period as well as those from inception

7. A statement of stockholders' equity showing the following from the enterprise's inception:

   a. For each issuance, the date and number of equity securities issued for cash or other consideration

   b. For each issuance, the dollar amounts (per share and in total) assigned to the consideration received for equity securities

   c. For each issuance involving noncash consideration, the nature of the consideration and the basis used in assigning the valuation

8. For the first period in which an enterprise is no longer a development stage enterprise, it shall disclose that in prior periods the entity was a development stage enterprise. If comparative statements are presented, the foregoing disclosure presentations (2-7) need not be shown.

FIN 7 allows parent or equity method investor companies to capitalize or defer some development stage company costs that would have to be expensed by the development stage company. Costs may be deferred if recoverable within the entire entity.

### Reporting on the Costs of Start-Up Activities

SOP 98-5 provides guidance on financial reporting of start-up costs and organization costs and requires such costs to be expensed as incurred. Start-up costs are defined as one-time activities related to opening a new facility, introducing a new product or service, conducting activities in a new territory, pursuing a new class of customer, initiating a new process in an existing facility, or some new operation. Those costs are variously referred to as preopening costs, preoperating costs, organization costs, and start-up costs. Routine ongoing efforts to improve existing quality of products, services, or facilities are not start-up costs. Other costs, related to specific activities listed below, are excluded from the SOP and should be accounted for in accordance with other existing authoritative literature. These include

1. Costs of acquiring or constructing long-lived assets and getting them ready for their intended uses. (However, the costs of using long-lived assets that are allocated to start-up activities [for example, depreciation of equipment] are within the scope of the SOP.)

2. Costs of acquiring or producing inventory

3. Costs of acquiring intangible assets. (However, the costs of using intangible assets that are allocated to start-up activities [for example, amortization of a purchased patent] are within the scope of the SOP.)

4. Costs related to internally developed assets (for example, internal-use computer software costs). (However, the costs of using those assets that are allocated to start-up activities are within the scope of the SOP.)

5. Costs that are within the scope of FAS 2, *Accounting for Research and Development*, and FAS 71, *Accounting for the Effects of Certain Types of Regulation*

6. Costs of fund-raising incurred by not-for-profit organizations

7. Costs of raising capital

8. Costs of advertising

9. Costs incurred in connection with existing contracts as stated in SOP 81-1, *Accounting for Performance of Construction-Type and Certain Production-Type Contracts.*

10. Costs of merger or acquisition activities

11. Costs of ongoing customer acquisition, such as policy acquisition costs and loan origination costs

## Exit and Disposal (Restructuring) Costs

Restructuring costs have received a good deal of attention in recent years because of revelations of abuses that have characterized these charges as "big bath" write-offs but which have been used to create "cookie jar" reserves later employed to smooth future earnings.

Restructuring charges are costs that are incurred or will be incurred in connection with a plan of action that will materially change the scope of business undertaken by an entity or the manner in which a business is conducted. They typically include costs such as employee benefits, costs associated with product line elimination or relocation, costs for new systems development or acquisitions, retraining costs, and losses on asset impairment and dispositions. A series of FASB and EITF pronouncements address the costs commonly recognized in restructurings. They are

1. FAS 13, which discusses the accounting for a termination of a capital lease (Chapter 16).
2. FAS 87 and 88, which discuss an employer's accounting for pension plans (Chapter 18).
3. FAS 106, which discusses an employer's accounting for postretirement benefits other than pensions (Chapter 18).
4. FAS 112, which discusses an employer's accounting for postemployment benefits (Chapter 18).
5. FAS 144, which discusses the accounting for long-lived assets that will be disposed of, including discontinued operations (Chapter 11).
6. EITF 95-3, which discusses costs associated with exiting a company newly acquired in a business combination (Chapter 13).
7. EITF 95-14 and 96-5, which discuss costs in anticipation of a business combination (Chapter 13).
8. FAS 146, which discusses the accounting for certain onetime termination benefits, costs to terminate contracts other than capital leases, and costs to consolidate facilities or relocate employees (this chapter).
9. EITF 87-4, which discusses the application of SEC Staff Accounting Bulletin 67 (this chapter).

**Employee termination benefits.** In 2002, FAS 146, *Accounting for Costs Associated with Exit or Disposal Activities*, superseded the guidance provided in EITF 94-3, *Liability Recognition for Certain Employee Termination Benefits and Other Costs to Exit an Activity (Including Certain Costs Incurred in a Restructuring)*. In general, the liability for employee termination benefits is recognized under FAS 146 in a manner similar to, but not exactly the same as, it was under EITF 94-3.

FAS 146 applies to termination benefits provided to current employees that are involuntarily terminated under the terms of a benefit arrangement that applies for a specified termination event or for a specified future period. Those benefits are referred to as onetime termination benefits. If an entity has a history of providing similar benefits to employees involuntarily terminated in earlier events, the benefits are presumed to be part of an ongoing benefit arrangement (rather than a onetime benefit arrangement) unless there is evidence to the contrary.

Specifically excluded from consideration are employee termination benefits

1. Paid pursuant to the terms of an ongoing employee benefit plan, regardless of whether the plan was preexisting or is newly created
2. Paid under the terms of an individual deferred compensation agreement

A onetime benefit arrangement first exists at the date the plan of termination meets *all* of the following criteria:

1. Management approves and commits to the termination plan.
2. The termination plan specifies the number of employees to be terminated, their job classifications or functions, and their locations, as well as the expected completion date.
3. The termination plan establishes the terms of the benefit arrangement in sufficient detail that employees are able to determine the type and amount of benefits that they will receive if they are involuntarily terminated.
4. Actions required to complete the plan indicate that significant changes to the plan are unlikely.
5. The terms of the plan have been communicated to employees (the communication date).

The timing of recognition of the liability for onetime termination benefits depends on whether the employees are required to render service beyond a minimum retention period. The minimum retention period is the notification period that an entity is required to provide to employees in advance of a termination event as a result of law, statute, or contract, or in the absence of a legal notification period, the minimum retention period cannot exceed sixty days.

If employees are entitled to receive the termination benefits regardless of when they leave or if employees will not be retained to render service beyond the minimum retention period, the liability for the termination benefits is recognized and measured at its fair value at the communication date.

If employees are required to render service until they are terminated in order to receive the termination benefit and will be retained beyond the minimum retention period, the liability for the termination benefits is measured at its fair value at the communication date and recognized ratably over the service period.

### Examples of the determination of the minimum retention period and recognition

Master Mobile Communications announces that it will close its Donnybrook plant and terminate all 120 employees there. The terms of the plan meet the criteria above. There are three major groups of employees: management, union workers, and nonunion workers. Management is required to stay and render service until the plant's closing, which is four months from now, and each of the twelve management employees will receive $10,000. The union workers' contract states that they must be notified ninety days in advance before they can be terminated. The union workers will be terminated in ninety days. The termination benefit for each of the fifty union employees is one week per every six months of employment. The nonunion workers can leave at any time within the next three months and still collect the termination benefit. Each of the fifty-eight nonunion employees will receive a termination benefit of $1,000 for each year of service. There is no state statute specifying a notification period.

### Case 1:  Management

Management is required to work until termination, so it is necessary to determine whether the service period is beyond the minimum retention period. There is no state statute specifying a notification period, but the Worker Adjustment and Retraining Act, which applies to entities with over 100 employees, requires a sixty-day notification period for this plant's closing. Thus, the minimum retention period is sixty days. Management must work beyond the minimum retention period, so the $120,000 liability (12 × $10,000) is recognized at $30,000 per month for the next four months. Present value techniques are not necessary to measure the liability because the discount period is so short that the face amount would not differ materially from the fair value.

### Case 2:  Union employees

The union employees' contract requires a ninety-day notification period, so the minimum retention period for these employees is ninety days.  The union workers will be terminated at the end of the ninety-day period, so they will not be required to work beyond the minimum retention period.  If the total of the termination benefits for the fifty union employees is $142,500, a liability of $142,500 is recognized at the communication date.  Present value techniques are not necessary to measure the liability because the discount period is so short that the face amount would not differ materially from the fair value.

### Case 3:  Nonunion workers

Nonunion workers are not required to work until the termination date to collect the termination benefit.  Therefore, it is not necessary to determine the minimum retention period for these employees.  If the 58 nonunion employees have 230 years of service among them, a liability of $230,000 is recognized at the communication date.  Present value techniques are not necessary to measure the liability because the discount period is so short that the face amount would not differ materially from the fair value.

If subsequent to the communication date there are changes in either the timing or amount of the expected termination benefit cash flows, the cumulative effect of the change should be computed and reported in the same line item(s) in the income statement in which the costs were initially reported.  If present value techniques were used to measure the initial liability, the same credit-adjusted risk-free rate should be used to remeasure the liability.

Changes in the liability due to the passage of time (accretion) are recognized as accretion expense in the income statement.  If employees are not required to provide services or are required to provide services only during the minimum retention period, accretion expense is charged for the passage of time after the communication date.  If employees are required to provide services beyond the minimum retention period, accretion expense is charged for the passage of time after the termination date.  Accretion expense should not be titled interest expense or be considered interest costs subject to capitalization.

According to FSP 146-1, if newly offered benefits represent a revision to an ongoing arrangement that is not limited to a specified termination event or to a specified future period, the benefits represent an enhancement to an ongoing benefit arrangement.  Therefore, these benefits are to be accounted for under the provisions of one or more of the following pronouncements:

- FAS 87—Pensions
- FAS 88—Settlements and Curtailments
- FAS 106—Postretirement Benefits other than Pensions
- FAS 112—Postemployment Benefits

If a plan of termination changes, and employees that were expected to be terminated within the minimum retention period are retained to render service beyond that period, the liability amount should be recomputed as though it had been known at the initial communication date that those employees would be required to render services beyond the minimum retention period.  The cumulative effect of the change is recognized as a change in the liability and reported in the same line item(s) in the income statement in which the costs were initially reported.  The remainder of the liability is recognized ratably from the date of change to the termination date.

If a plan of termination includes both voluntary and involuntary termination benefits, a liability for the involuntary benefits is recognized as described above.  A liability for the incremental voluntary benefits (the excess of the voluntary benefit amount over the involuntary benefit amount) is recognized in accordance with FAS 88 (Chapter 18).  That is, if the benefits are special termination benefits offered only for a short period of time, the liability is recognized when the employees accept the offer and the amount can be reasonably estimated. If, instead, the voluntary termination benefits are contractual termination benefits (for example, required by a union contract or a pension contract) the liability is recognized when it is probable that employees will be entitled to benefits and the amount can be reasonably estimated.

**Contract termination and other costs to exit an activity.** In addition to employee termination costs, an entity may incur contract termination costs, relocation costs, plant consolidation costs, and other costs associated with the exit or disposal activity. FASB rejected the EITF 94-3 consensus that an entity's commitment to a plan, by itself, creates a present obligation to others that meets the definition of a liability. Instead, FAS 146 sets forth the following standards for recognition.

A liability for the costs to terminate a contract before the end of its term is recognized and measured at its fair value when the entity actually terminates the contract in accordance with the contractual term (e.g., by written notice).

A liability for the costs that will continue to be incurred under a contract for its remaining term without economic benefit to the entity is recognized and measured at its fair value when the entity ceases using the right conveyed by the contract (the cease-use date). If the contract is an operating lease, the fair value of the liability should be determined based on the remaining lease rentals, reduced by estimated sublease rentals, even if the entity does not intend to find a sublease. However, remaining operating lease payments should not be reduced to an amount less than zero by the estimated sublease payments.

A liability for other costs associated with the exit or disposal activity should be recognized when the liability is incurred, which is generally when the goods or services associated with the activity are received. The liability should not be recognized before it is incurred even if the costs are incremental and a direct result of the exit or disposal plan.

**Reporting and disclosure.** The costs of exit or disposal activities must be included in income from continuing operations before income taxes. If the subtotal "income from operations" is presented, the costs must be included in that subtotal. If the costs are associated with exit or disposal activities that involve a discontinued operation, they are included in the results of discontinued operations. If an entity's responsibility to settle the liability associated with an exit or disposal activity is removed or discharged, the related costs are reversed through the same line item(s) in the income statement that were used when those costs were initially recognized.

The following information should be disclosed in the period in which an exit or disposal plan is initiated, and in each period until the activity is completed:

1. A description of the activity and the expected completion date.
2. For each of the major categories of costs (e.g., onetime termination benefits, contract termination costs, and other costs), the amount expected to be incurred, the amount incurred during the period, and the cumulative amount incurred to date, in total for the entity and for each reportable segment (Chapter 22).
3. For each of the major categories of costs, a reconciliation of the beginning and ending liability balances, showing separately the costs incurred during the period, the costs paid or otherwise settled during the period, and any adjustments.
4. The reasons for any adjustments to the liability amounts.
5. The line items(s) in the income statement in which the exit or disposal costs are aggregated.

6.  If a liability for a cost associated with the exit or disposal activity is not recognized because the amount cannot be reasonably estimated, that fact and the reasons therefor.

**Forthcoming Changes to Financial Statement Presentation Standards**

FASB has been pursuing a project on a topic—now referred to as *financial statement presentation*, but previously known as *financial performance reporting*—for several years. It focuses on form and content, classification and aggregation, and display of specified items and summarized amounts on the face of the financial statements. The scope includes determining whether to require the display of certain items determined to be key measures or necessary for the calculation of key measures. Of interest are all display matters, not limited to those conveying information about the entity's income or expense. This project is being pursued in cooperation with the IASB, and one central objective of this joint effort is to converge the two standard-setters' financial statement display requirements.

The project does not address the management discussion and analysis materials often found (and required under SEC rules), or the reporting of so-called pro forma earnings in press releases or other communications outside financial statements. Neither does it include consideration of segment information or matters of recognition or measurement of items in financial statements.

Among the issues likely to be resolved by this project, tentative conclusions reached as of early 2008 are as follows:

1.  That a single statement of comprehensive income that includes a subtotal similar to the existing subtotal "net income from continuing operations" would be mandated under US GAAP. Tentatively, this statement of earnings and comprehensive income would report the changes in assets and liabilities other than those arising from transactions with owners in their capacity as owners, and which would include the currently required subtotal *net income*.

2.  That each financial statement would need to be given the same degree of prominence as all others. By requiring that a single statement of earnings and comprehensive income be presented, the current choice among three means of presenting comprehensive income, as illustrated earlier in this chapter, would be eliminated.

3.  That comparative information consisting at a minimum of a complete set of financial statements for two annual periods (the current and prior annual period) would be required. FASB has also tentatively determined that it will allow (but not provide guidance on) voluntary presentation of financial information beyond the required minimum (i.e., beyond a complete set of financial statements for two annual periods).

4.  To continue to require presentation of per share information within the financial statements. It has been concluded by FASB, preliminarily, that presentation of basic and diluted earnings per share (EPS) on the face of the statement of earnings and comprehensive income will continue to be the only required per share measure, and that disclosure of basic and diluted comprehensive income per share in notes to financial statements will continue to be permitted but not required. Furthermore, disclosure of the weighted-average number of shares used as the denominator in calculating per share metrics in notes to financial statements will continue to be required.

5.  It is also likely that extraordinary item presentation (which in recent years has been quite narrowly defined and thus increasingly infrequently observed) will be fully

eliminated, although there would still be identification of extraordinary items, albeit not permitted to be displayed as "below the line" special items.

6. The definition of discontinued operations will be narrowed somewhat, and financial statement display will no longer be on a "net of tax" basis in the income statement. In the revamped statement of cash flows, discontinued operations will become a stand-alone major caption, as will income taxes.

The proposed requirement for a combined statement of earnings and comprehensive income appears to be the most significant of the likely new mandates, but the need for a "beginning balance sheet" would also be a marked departure from current GAAP. Indeed, it is more commonly observed that there are a greater number of "flow statements" (e.g., the income statement) presented than "stock" statements (the balance sheet), as that follows from SEC rules (e.g., non–small business filers report two years' balance sheets and three years' income statements). If the tentative conclusions on the FASB project hold firm, this situation will in fact be reversed (but not for SEC filings unless its rules are changed).

In addition to the foregoing matters, described by FASB as being intended to address narrow differences between existing US GAAP and IFRS (the international standards), FASB is addressing more substantive matters pertaining to financial statement presentation, including the following:

1. Developing consistent principles for aggregating and disaggregating information in each financial statement.

2. Defining the totals and subtotals to be reported in each financial statement (which might involve establishing new, definitive categories, such as business and financing).

3. Determining whether components of other comprehensive income should be recycled to profit or loss (the current practice) and, if so, the characteristics of the transactions and events that should be recycled and when recycling should occur.

4. Reconsideration of FAS 95, including whether to require the use of the direct or indirect method. (See Chapter 4.)

5. Which financial statements, if any, should be required to be presented in an interim financial report.

6. Whether condensed presentation of financial statements required in an interim financial report should be permitted, and whether FASB should provide guidance related to how the information may be condensed.

7. What comparative periods, if any, should be permitted in interim financial reports and whether twelve-months-to-date (rolling twelve months) financial statements should be required or permitted.

8. Whether guidance for nonpublic companies should differ from that for public companies.

Regarding these latter matters, FASB has tentatively concluded that a single standard that would apply broadly to all business entities should be developed. It plans to first develop a reporting model that would apply broadly to all for-profit entities other than financial institutions, then to address reporting by financial institutions. It has also concluded, tentatively, that a financing category should be included on the face of the statement of earnings and comprehensive income, and that the definition for a financing category should be developed before any other category, such as operating. This definition will be applicable to all entities, excluding financial institutions.

See further details about the FASB financial statement presentation project in Chapter 2.

# 4 STATEMENT OF CASH FLOWS

## PERSPECTIVE AND ISSUES

FAS 95, as amended, establishes standards for cash flow reporting. A statement of cash flows is a required part of a complete set of financial statements for business enterprises and not-for-profit organizations. Only defined benefit plans, certain other employee benefit plans, and highly liquid investment companies that meet specified conditions are not required to present the statement.

The primary purpose of the statement of cash flows is to provide information about cash receipts and cash payments of an entity during a period. A secondary purpose is to provide information about the entity's investing and financing activities during the period.

Specifically, the statement of cash flows helps investors and creditors assess

1. Ability to generate future positive cash flows
2. Ability to meet obligations and pay dividends
3. Reasons for differences between net income and net cash receipts and payments
4. The cash and noncash aspects of investing and financing transactions on an entity's financial position

CON 1 states that "financial reporting should provide information that is useful to present and potential investors, creditors, and other users for making rational investment and credit decisions." Since the ultimate objective of investment and credit decisions is the maximization of net cash inflows, information for assessing the amounts, timing, and uncertainty of prospective cash flows is needed. CON 5 concludes that financial statements must show cash flows during the period in order to be complete.

FAS 159 has amended FAS 95 to end the requirement that cash flows arising in connection with investments classified as trading securities under FAS 115 be included in operating activities. Following this amendment, cash flows involving trading securities are to be classified based on the nature of, and purpose for which, the financial assets or liabilities are acquired or incurred.

| Sources of GAAP | | |
|---|---|---|
| *CON* | *EITF* | *FAS* |
| 1, 5 | 95-13, 02-6 | 95, 102, 104, 115, 117, 123(R), 133, 149, 159 |

## DEFINITIONS OF TERMS

**Cash equivalents.** Short-term, highly liquid investments that (1) are readily convertible to known amounts of cash and (2) are so near their maturity (maturity of three months or less from the date of purchase by the enterprise) that they present negligible risk of changes in value because of changes in interest rates. Treasury bills, commercial paper, and money market funds are all examples of cash equivalents.

**Direct method.** A method which derives the net cash provided by operating activities from the components of operating cash receipts and payments as opposed to adjusting net income for items not affecting cash.

**Financing activities.** The transactions a firm engages in to acquire and repay capital (e.g., borrowings, sale of capital stock, repayments, etc.).

**Indirect (reconciliation) method.** A method which derives the net cash provided by operating activities by adjusting net income for revenue and expense items not resulting from cash transactions.

**Investing activities.** The transactions the firm engages in which affect its investments in noncurrent assets (e.g., purchase or sale of plant, property, and equipment).

**Operating activities.** The transactions not classified as financing or investing activities, generally involving producing and delivering goods or providing services.

## CONCEPTS, RULES, AND EXAMPLES

### Cash Focus

The statement of cash flows includes only inflows and outflows of cash and cash equivalents. Cash equivalents include any short-term highly liquid investments (see definition for criteria) used as a temporary investment of idle cash. The effects of investing and financing activities that do not result in receipts or payments of cash are to be reported in a separate schedule immediately following the statement or in the notes to the financial statements. The reasoning for not including noncash items in the statement of cash flows and placing them in a separate schedule is that it preserves the statement's primary focus on cash flows from operating, investing, and financing activities. Thus, if a transaction is part cash and part noncash, only the cash portion is reported in the body of the statement of cash flows.

### Classification of Cash Receipts and Disbursements

The statement of cash flows requires classification of cash receipts and cash disbursements into three categories.

**Investing activities** include the acquisition and disposition of (1) long-term productive assets or (2) securities held in available-for-sale or held-to-maturity portfolios that are not considered cash equivalents. Investing activities also include the lending of money and the collection on loans.

FAS 102, as amended by FAS 115, had mandated that cash flows were to be classified as *operating* cash flows if they originated from the purchase or sale of loans, debt, or equity instruments acquired specifically for resale and are carried at market value in a trading account. However, as recently amended by FAS 159, FAS 95 no longer requires operating classification of such cash flows. Rather, classification is to be determined with reference to the nature of, and purpose for which, the related financial assets and financial liabilities were acquired or incurred. In other words, it will be necessary to evaluate the facts and circumstances of each situation, rather than applying a mechanical prescription.

**Financing activities** result from transactions with owners and lenders that provide financial resources to the reporting entity or return or repay those resources to those owners and lenders. The financing activities of not-for-profit organizations also include receiving contributions from donors that require the resources to be used for long-term purposes, such as an endowment restricted for the purchase of long-lived assets.

**Operating activities** include all transactions that are not classified as investing or financing activities. Operating activities include delivering or producing goods for sale and providing services. Most income tax-related cash flows are classified as operating activities. Note, however, that FAS 123(R) amended FAS 95 to require that certain cash flows relating to the portion of income tax expense associated with share-based compensation are classified as financing activities. FAS 123(R) is discussed in Chapter 19 and its income tax provisions are discussed in Chapter 17.

The following are examples of the classification of cash inflows and outflows within the statement of cash flows:

|  | *Operating* | *Investing* | *Financing* |
|---|---|---|---|
| Cash Inflows | • Receipts from sale of goods or services | • Principal collections from loans and sales of other entities' debt instruments* | • Proceeds from issuing stock (or other ownership interests) |
|  | • Sale of loans, debt, or equity instruments carried in a trading portfolio | • Sale of equity instruments* of other enterprises and from returns of investment in those instruments | • Proceeds from issuing debt (short-term or long-term) |
|  | • Returns on loans (interest)<br>• Returns on equity securities (dividends) | • Sale of property, plant, and equipment | • Not-for-profits' donor-restricted cash gifts that are limited to long-term purposes |
|  |  |  | • Income tax benefits received due to increases in the fair value of equity instruments issued in share-based payment arrangements |
| Cash Outflows | • Payments for inventory | • Loans made and acquisitions of other entities' debt instruments* | • Payment of dividends |
|  | • Payments to employees and other suppliers | • Purchase of equity instruments* of other enterprises | • Repurchase of entity's stock |

| | | |
|---|---|---|
| • Payments of income taxes including cash that would have been paid for income taxes if the reporting entity had not received an income tax benefit due to increases in the fair value of equity instruments issued in share-based payment arrangements<br>• Payments of interest<br>• Purchase of loans, debt, or equity instruments carried in trading portfolio<br>• Payments of asset retirement obligations (EITF 02-6) | • Purchase of property, plant, and equipment | • Repayment of debt principal, including capital lease obligations |

\* *Held in available-for-sale or held-to-maturity portfolios*

Disclosure of the following noncash investing and financing activities may be appended to the statement or reported in the accompanying notes:

- Acquiring an asset through a capital lease or by incurring long-term debt
- Conversion of debt to equity
- Exchange of noncash assets or liabilities for other noncash assets or liabilities
- Issuance of ownership shares to acquire assets
- Obtaining an investment asset or a building by receiving a contribution

The following example reveals the classification of cash receipts and disbursements into the investing and financing activities of a statement of cash flows (though without detail of the required operating activities section):

**Liquid Corporation**
**Statement of Cash Flows**
**For the Year Ended December 31, 2009**

| | | |
|---|---|---|
| Net cash flows from operating activities | | $ xxx |
| Cash flows from investing activities: | | |
|     Purchase of property, plant, and equipment | $(xxx) | |
|     Sale of equipment | xx | |
|     Collection of notes receivable | xx | |
|         Net cash used in investing activities | | (xx) |
| Cash flows from financing activities: | | |
|     Sale of common stock | xxx | |
|     Repayment of long-term debt | (xx) | |
|     Reduction of notes payable | (xx) | |
|         Net cash provided by financing activities | | xx |
| Effect of exchange rate changes on cash | | xx |
| Net increase (decrease) in cash | | $ xxx |
| Cash and cash equivalents at beginning of year | | xxx |
| Cash and cash equivalents at end of year | | $xxx |
| Schedule of noncash financing and investing activities: | | |
|     Conversion of bonds into common stock | | $ xxx |
|     Property acquired under capital leases | | xxx |
| | | $ xxx |

## Operating Activities Presentation

**Direct vs. indirect.** The operating activities section of the statement of cash flows can be presented under the direct or indirect method. However, the FASB has expressed a preference for the direct method of presenting net cash from operating activities. Despite frequently voiced preferences of the user community for the direct method presentation, the indirect method has always been vastly preferred by preparers. An ongoing FASB project on financial statement presentation by business enterprises may very well eliminate, at long last, the acceptability of the indirect method, as noted later in this chapter.

The *direct method* shows the items that affected cash flow. Cash received and cash paid are presented, as opposed to converting accrual-basis income to cash flow information. At a minimum, entities using the direct method are required to report the following classes of operating cash receipts and payments:

1. Cash collected from customers
2. Interest and dividends received
3. Other operating cash receipts
4. Cash paid to employees and other suppliers
5. Interest paid
6. Income taxes paid including separate identification of the cash that would have been paid if the reporting entity had not received an income tax benefit resulting from increases in the fair value of its shares associated with share-based compensation arrangements.
7. Other operating cash payments

The direct method allows the user to clarify the relationship between the company's net income and its cash flows. For example, payments of expenses are shown as cash disbursements and are deducted from cash receipts. In this way, the user is able to recognize the cash receipts and cash payments for the period. The information needed to prepare the operating activities section using the direct method can often be obtained by converting information already appearing in the balance sheet and income statement. Formulas for conversion of various income statement amounts for the direct method of presentation from the accrual basis to the cash basis are summarized below.

| Accrual basis | Additions | Deductions | Cash basis |
|---|---|---|---|
| Net sales | + Beginning A/R | − Ending A/R<br>   AR written off | = Cash received from<br>   customers |
| Cost of goods sold | + Ending inventory<br>   Beginning A/P | − Manufacturing depreciation and<br>   amortization<br>   Beginning inventory<br>   Ending A/P | = Cash paid to suppliers |
| Operating expenses | + Ending prepaid<br>   expenses<br>   Beginning accrued<br>   expenses | − Sales and administrative<br>   depreciation and amortization<br>   Beginning prepaid expenses<br>   Ending accrued expenses payable<br>   Bad debts expense | = Cash paid for operating<br>   expenses |

When the direct method is used, a separate schedule reconciling net income to net cash flows from operating activities must also be provided. That schedule reports the same information as the operating activities section prepared using the indirect method. Therefore, a firm must prepare and present both the direct and indirect methods when using the direct method for reporting cash from operating activities.

The *indirect method* is the most widely used presentation of cash from operating activities, primarily because it is easier to prepare. It focuses on the differences between net income and cash flows. The indirect format begins with net income, which is obtained directly from the income statement. Revenue and expense items not affecting cash are added or deducted to arrive at net cash provided by operating activities. For example, depreciation and amortization would be added back because they reduce net income without affecting cash.

The statement of cash flows prepared using the indirect method emphasizes changes in the components of most current asset and current liability accounts. Changes in inventory, accounts receivable, and other current accounts are used to determine the cash flow from operating activities. It is important to note that the change in accounts receivable should be calculated using the balances net of the allowance account in order to ensure that write-offs of uncollectible accounts are treated properly. Other adjustments under the indirect method include changes in the account balances of deferred income taxes and the income (loss) from investments reported using the equity method. However, short-term borrowing used to purchase equipment would be classified as a financing activity.

The following diagram may facilitate understanding of the adjustments to net income necessary for converting accrual-based net income to cash-basis net income when using the indirect method. The diagram is simply an expanded balance sheet equation.

| | Current assets* | − | Noncurrent assets | = | Current liabilities | + | Long-term liabilities | + | Income | Accrual income adjustment to convert to cash flow |
|---|---|---|---|---|---|---|---|---|---|---|
| 1. | Increase | | | = | | | | | Increase | Decrease |
| 2. | Decrease | | | = | | | | | Decrease | Increase |
| 3. | | | | = | Increase | | | | Decrease | Increase |
| 4. | | | | = | Decrease | | | | Increase | Decrease |

\* Other than cash and cash equivalents

For example, using Row 1, a credit sale would increase accounts receivable and accrual-basis income but would not affect cash. Therefore, its effect must be removed from the accrual income in order to convert to cash income. The last column indicates that the increase in a current asset balance must be deducted from income to obtain cash flow. Using Row 2, a decrease in a current asset, such as prepaid rent, indicates that net income was decreased by rent expense, without a cash outflow in the current period. Thus, the decrease in prepaid rent would be added back to convert to cash income.

Similarly, using Row 3, an increase in a current liability must be added to income to obtain cash flows (e.g., accrued wages are on the income statement as an expense, but they do not require cash; the increase in wages payable must be added back to remove this non-cash expense from accrual-basis income). Using Row 4, a decrease in a current liability, such as accounts payable, indicates that cash was used but the expense was incurred in an earlier period. Thus, the decrease in accounts payable would be subtracted to include this disbursement in cash income.

If the indirect method is chosen, then the amount of interest and income tax paid must be included in the related disclosures.

The major drawback to the indirect method involves the user's difficulty in comprehending the information presented. This method does not show the sources or uses of cash. Only adjustments to accrual-basis net income are shown. In some cases the adjustments can be confusing. For instance, the sale of equipment resulting in an accrual-basis loss would require that the loss be added to net income to arrive at net cash from operating activities. (The loss was deducted in the computation of net income, but because the sale will be shown as an investing activity, the loss must be added back to net income.)

Although the indirect method is more commonly used in practice, the authors believe that the direct method is preferable. It portrays both the amounts of cash provided by and used in the reporting entity's operations, instead of presenting net income and reconciling items. The direct method reports only the items that affect cash flow (inflows/outflows of cash) and ignores items that do not affect cash flow (depreciation, gains, etc.). The general formats of both the direct method and the indirect method are shown below.

**Direct method**

| | | |
|---|---:|---:|
| Cash flows from operating activities: | | |
| Cash received from sale of goods | $xxx | |
| Cash interest received | xxx | |
| Cash dividends received | xxx | |
| Cash provided by operating activities | | $xxx |
| Cash paid to suppliers | (xxx) | |
| Cash paid for operating expenses | (xxx) | |
| Cash interest paid | (xxx) | |
| Cash paid for taxes | (xxx) | |
| Cash disbursed for operating activities | | (xxx) |
| Net cash flows from operating activities | | $xxx |

**Indirect method**

| | |
|---|---:|
| Cash flows from operating activities: | |
| Net income | $ xx |
| Add/deduct items not affecting cash: | |
| Decrease (increase) in accounts receivable | (xx) |
| Depreciation expense | xx |
| Increase (decrease) in accounts payable | xx |
| Decrease (increase) in inventories | xx |
| Loss on sale of equipment | xx |
| Net cash flows from operating activities | $xxx |

## Other Requirements

**Gross vs. net basis.** The emphasis in the statement of cash flows is on gross cash receipts and payments. For instance, reporting the net change in bonds payable would obscure the financing activities of the entity by not disclosing separately cash inflows from issuing bonds and cash outflows from retiring bonds. In a few circumstances, netting of cash flows is allowed. Items having quick turnovers, large amounts, and short maturities may be presented as net cash flows if the cash receipts and payments pertain to (1) investments (other than cash equivalents), (2) loans receivable, and (3) debts (original maturity of three months or less).

**Extraordinary items and discontinued operations.** FAS 95 permits, but does not require, separate disclosure of cash flows related to extraordinary items and to discontinued operations. If an entity chooses to disclose this information, disclosure must be consistent for all periods affected.

**Cash flow per share.** This information may *not* be displayed in the financial statements of a reporting entity because the FASB does not want the cash flow statement to have equal status with the income statement. If a single cash flow per share amount were reported, it would conflate operating cash flows with those from investing and financing activities, and thus not represent a meaningful construct in any event.

## Entities Exempt from Providing a Statement of Cash Flows

Per FAS 102, a statement of cash flows is not required for a defined benefit pension plan that presents the financial information under the guidelines of FAS 35. Other employee benefit plans are exempted, provided that the financial information presented is similar to the requirements of FAS 35. Investment enterprises or a common trust fund held for the collective investment and reinvestment of moneys are not required to provide a statement of cash flows if the following conditions are met:

1. Substantially all of the entity's investments are highly liquid.
2. The entity's investments are carried at market value.

3.  The entity has little or no debt, based on average debt outstanding during the period, in relation to average total assets.
4.  The entity provides a statement of changes in net assets.

## Net Reporting by Financial Institutions

Per FAS 104, banks, savings institutions, and credit unions are allowed to report net cash receipts and payments for the following:

1.  Deposits placed with other financial institutions
2.  Withdrawals of those deposits
3.  Time deposits accepted
4.  Repayments of time deposits
5.  Loans made to customers
6.  Principal collections of loans made to customers

## Not-for-Profit Organizations

FAS 117 requires not-for-profit organizations to include a statement of cash flows in a complete set of financial statements. The statement of cash flows is prepared as it is for business enterprises with the following differences:

1.  The indirect method of reporting cash flows from operations (or reconciliation of net income to net cash flows from operations required when the direct method is used) is prepared beginning with the change in net assets.
2.  Investing activities also include receiving contributions that are restricted by the donor to the purchase or improvement of long-lived assets or for long-term investment such as permanent or term endowment.
3.  Noncash activities include gifts of long-lived assets and gifts of securities held for long-term investment.

## Reporting Hedging Transactions

Per FAS 104, as amended by FAS 133, the cash flows resulting from derivative instruments that are accounted for as fair value hedges or cash flow hedges may be classified as the same type of cash flows as the hedged items provided that the accounting policy is disclosed. However, if the derivative instrument used to hedge includes at inception an other-than-insignificant financing element, all cash inflows and outflows of the derivative instrument are reported by the borrower as cash flows from financing activities. A derivative that at inception includes off-market terms, or requires up-front cash payment, or both, often contains a financing element. A derivative instrument is viewed as including a financing element if its contractual terms have been structured to ensure that net payments will be made by one party in the earlier periods of the derivative's term and subsequently returned by the counterparty in the later periods (other than elements that are inherent in at-the-money derivative instruments with no prepayments). If for any reason hedge accounting is discontinued, then any cash flows subsequent to the date of discontinuance are classified consistent with the nature of the instrument.

## Reporting Foreign Currency Cash Flows

If an entity has foreign currency transactions or foreign operations, it should translate the foreign currency cash flows using exchange rates in effect at the time of the cash flows. A weighted-average exchange rate for the period can be used for the translation if the result is substantially the same. The effect of changes in exchange rates on any cash balances held in foreign currencies should be shown as a separate part of the reconciliation of the change in cash and cash equivalents during the period. An example of reporting the effect of exchange rate changes is shown in the statement of cash flows in the "Classification" section of this chapter.

Noncash exchange gains and losses recognized in net income should be reported as a separate item when reconciling net income and operating activities.

For a more detailed discussion of the exchange rate effects on the statement of cash flows, see Chapter 23.

## Preparation of the Statement

Under a cash and cash equivalents basis, the changes in the cash account and any cash equivalent account is the "bottom line" figure of the statement of cash flows. Using the 2008 and 2009 balance sheets shown below, an increase of $25,000 can be computed. This is the difference between the totals for cash and treasury bills between 2008 and 2009 ($41,000 – $16,000).

When preparing the statement of cash flows using the direct method, gross cash inflows from revenues and gross cash outflows to suppliers and for expenses are presented in the operating activities section.

In preparing the reconciliation of net income to net cash flow from operating activities (indirect method), changes in all accounts (other than cash and cash equivalents) that are related to operations are additions to or deductions from net income to arrive at net cash provided by operating activities.

A T-account analysis may be helpful when preparing the statement of cash flows. A T-account is set up for each account, and beginning (2008) and ending (2009) balances are taken from the appropriate balance sheet. Additionally, a T-account for cash and cash equivalents from operating activities and a master or summary T-account of cash and cash equivalents should be used.

### Example of preparing a statement of cash flows

The financial statements below will be used to prepare the statement of cash flows.

**Johnson Company**
**Balance Sheets**
**December 31, 2009 and 2008**

|  | *2009* | *2008* |
|---|---|---|
| *Assets* | | |
| *Current assets:* | | |
| Cash | $ 37,000 | $ 10,000 |
| Treasury bills | 4,000 | 6,000 |
| Accounts receivable—net | 9,000 | 11,000 |
| Inventory | 14,000 | 9,000 |
| Prepaid expenses | 10,000 | 13,000 |
| Total current assets | $ 74,000 | $ 49,000 |
| *Noncurrent assets:* | | |
| Investment in available-for-sale securities | 7,500 | 15,000 |
| Add (less) adjustment for changes in fair value | 1,000 | (3,000) |
| Investment in XYZ (35%) | 16,000 | 14,000 |
| Patent | 5,000 | 6,000 |
| Leased asset | 5,000 | -- |
| Property, plant, and equipment | 39,000 | 37,000 |
| Less accumulated depreciation | (7,000) | (3,000) |
| Total assets | $140,500 | $115,000 |

|  | 2009 | 2008 |
|---|---|---|
| **Liabilities** | | |
| *Current liabilities:* | | |
| Accounts payable | $ 2,000 | $ 12,000 |
| Notes payable—current | 9,000 | -- |
| Interest payable | 3,000 | 2,000 |
| Dividends payable | 5,000 | 2,000 |
| Income taxes payable | 2,180 | 1,000 |
| Lease obligation | 700 | -- |
| Total current liabilities | 21,880 | 17,000 |
| *Noncurrent liabilities:* | | |
| Deferred tax liability | 9,360* | 4,920* |
| Bonds payable | 10,000 | 25,000 |
| Lease obligation | 4,300 | -- |
| Total liabilities | $ 45,540 | $ 46,920 |
| **Stockholders' equity** | | |
| Common stock, $10 par value | $ 33,000 | $ 26,000 |
| Additional paid-in capital | 16,000 | 3,000 |
| Retained earnings | 45,320 | 41,000 |
| Accumulated other comprehensive income | | |
| Net unrealized loss on available-for-sale securities | 640 | (1,920) |
| Total stockholders' equity | $ 94,960 | $ 68,080 |
| Total liabilities and stockholders' equity | $140,500 | $115,000 |

\* *Net of deferred tax asset ($540) and ($1,080) respectively.*

**Johnson Company**
**Statement of Earnings and Comprehensive Income**
**For the Year Ended December 31, 2009**

| | | |
|---|---|---|
| Sales | | $100,000 |
| Other income | | 8,500 |
| | | $108,500 |
| Cost of goods sold, excluding depreciation | | 60,000 |
| Selling, general, and administrative expenses | | 12,000 |
| Depreciation | | 8,000 |
| Amortization of patents | | 1,000 |
| Interest expense | | 2,000 |
| | | $ 83,000 |
| Income before taxes | | $ 25,500 |
| Income taxes: | | |
| Current | $6,180 | |
| Deferred | 3,000 | 9,180 |
| Net income | | $ 16,320 |
| Other comprehensive income, net of tax | | |
| Unrealized gains on securities: | | |
| Unrealized holding gains (less applicable income taxes of $900) | | 1,600 |
| Add reclassification adjustment (less applicable income taxes of $540) | | 960 |
| Total other comprehensive income | | $ 2,560 |
| Comprehensive income | | $ 18,880 |

### Additional information (all relating to 2009)

1. Equipment costing $6,000 with a book value of $2,000 was sold for $5,000.
2. The company received a $3,000 dividend from its investment in XYZ, accounted for under the equity method and recorded income from the investment of $5,000 that is included in other income.
3. The company issued 200 shares of common stock for $5,000.
4. The company signed a note payable for $9,000.
5. Equipment was purchased for $8,000.
6. The company converted $15,000 bonds payable into 500 shares of common stock. The book value method was used to record the transaction.

7. A dividend of $12,000 was declared.
8. Equipment was leased on December 31, 2009. The principal portion of the first payment due December 31, 2010, is $700.
9. The company sold half of their available-for-sale investments during the year for $8,000. The fair value of the remaining available-for-sale investments was $8,500 on December 31, 2009.
10. The income tax rate is 36%.

**Summary of Cash and Cash Equivalents**

| Inflows | | Outflows | |
|---|---|---|---|
| (d) | 5,000 | | |
| | | 8,000 | (g) |
| (h) | 5,000 | 9,000 | (i) |
| (n) | 9,000 | | |
| (s) | 8,000 | | |
| (t) | 15,000 | | |
| | 42,000 | 17,000 | |
| | | 25,000 | Net increase in cash |
| | 42,000 | 42,000 | |

**Cash and Cash Equivalents—Operating Account**

| | | | |
|---|---|---|---|
| (a) | 16,320 | | |
| (b) | 8,000 | | |
| (c) | 1,000 | 3,000 | (d) |
| (e) | 3,000 | 5,000 | (f) |
| (f) | 3,000 | | |
| (j) | 2,000 | 5,000 | (k) |
| (l) | 3,000 | 10,000 | (m) |
| (o) | 1,000 | | |
| (p) | 1,180 | 500 | (s) |
| | 38,500 | 23,500 | |
| | | 15,000 | (t) |
| | 38,500 | 38,500 | |

**Accounts Receivable (net)**

| | | | |
|---|---|---|---|
| 11,000 | | | |
| | | 2,000 | (j) |
| 9,000 | | | |

**Inventory**

| | | | |
|---|---|---|---|
| | 9,000 | | |
| (k) | 5,000 | | |
| | 14,000 | | |

**Prepaid Expenses**

| | | | |
|---|---|---|---|
| 13,000 | | | |
| | | 3,000 | (l) |
| 10,000 | | | |

**Investment in AFS Securities**

| | | | |
|---|---|---|---|
| 15,000 | | | |
| | | 7,500 | (s) |
| 7,500 | | | |

**Adjustment for Changes in FV of AFS Securities**

| | | | |
|---|---|---|---|
| | | 3,000 | |
| (s) | 1,500 | | |
| (s) | 2,500 | | |
| | 1,000 | | |

**Investment in XYZ**

| | | | |
|---|---|---|---|
| | 14,000 | | |
| (f) | 5,000 | 3,000 | (f) |
| | 16,000 | | |

**Patent**

| | | | |
|---|---|---|---|
| 6,000 | | | |
| | | 1,000 | (c) |
| 5,000 | | | |

**Leased Equipment**

| | | | |
|---|---|---|---|
| (r) | 5,000 | | |
| | 5,000 | | |

**Property, Plant, & Equipment**

| | | | |
|---|---|---|---|
| 37,000 | | | |
| | | 6,000 | (d) |
| (g) | 8,000 | | |
| 39,000 | | | |

**Accumulated Depreciation**

| | | | |
|---|---|---|---|
| | | 3,000 | |
| | | 8,000 | (b) |
| (d) | 4,000 | | |
| | | 7,000 | |

**Accounts Payable**

| | | | |
|---|---|---|---|
| | | 12,000 | |
| (m) | 10,000 | | |
| | | 2,000 | |

**Notes Payable**

| | | | |
|---|---|---|---|
| | | 9,000 | (n) |
| | | 9,000 | |

**Interest Payable**

| | | | |
|---|---|---|---|
| | | 2,000 | |
| (o) | 1,000 | 2,000 | (o) |
| | | 3,000 | |

**Dividends Payable**

| | | | |
|---|---|---|---|
| | | 2,000 | |
| (i) | 9,000 | 12,000 | (i) |
| | | 5,000 | |

**Income Taxes Payable**

| | | | |
|---|---|---|---|
| | | 1,000 | |
| (p) | 5,000 | 6,180 | (p) |
| | | 2,180 | |

**Deferred Tax Liability (Net)**

| | | | |
|---|---|---|---|
| | | 4,920 | |
| | | 3,000 | (e) |
| | | 540 | (s) |
| | | 900 | (s) |
| | | 9,360 | |

**Bonds Payable**

| | | | |
|---|---|---|---|
| | | 25,000 | |
| (q) | 15,000 | | |
| | | 10,000 | |

| Lease Obligation | | | Common Stock | | | Addl. Paid-in Capital | |
|---|---|---|---|---|---|---|---|
| | 5,000 (r) | | | 26,000 | | | 3,000 |
| | 5,000 | | | 2,000 (h) | | | 3,000 (h) |
| | | | | 5,000 (q) | | | 10,000 (q) |
| | | | | 33,000 | | | 16,000 |

| Retained Earnings | | | Unrealized Gain (Loss) on AFS Securities | |
|---|---|---|---|---|
| | 41,000 | | 1,920 | |
| | 16,320 (a) | | | 960 (s) |
| (i)  12,000 | | | | 1,600 (s) |
| | 45,320 | | | 640 |

## Explanation of entries

a.  Cash and Cash Equivalents—Operating activities is debited for $16,320 (net income) and the credit is to Retained Earnings.

b.  Depreciation is not a cash flow; however, depreciation expense was deducted to arrive at net income. Therefore, Accumulated Depreciation is credited and Cash and Cash Equivalents—Operating activities is debited.

c.  Amortization of patents is another expense not requiring cash; therefore, Cash and Cash Equivalents—Operating activities is debited and Patent is credited.

d.  The sale of equipment (additional information, item 1.) resulted in a $3,000 gain. The gain is computed by comparing the book value of $2,000 with the sales price of $5,000. Cash proceeds of $5,000 are an inflow of cash. Since the gain was included in net income, it must be deducted from net income to determine cash provided by operating activities. This is necessary to avoid counting the $3,000 gain both in cash provided by operating activities and in investing activities. The following entry would have been made on the date of sale:

| | | |
|---|---|---|
| Cash | 5,000 | |
| Accumulated depreciation ($6,000 – $2,000) | 4,000 | |
| Property, plant, and equipment | | 6,000 |
| Gain on sale of equipment ($5,000 – $2,000) | | 3,000 |

Adjust the T-accounts as follows:  debit Summary of Cash and Cash Equivalents for $5,000, debit Accumulated Depreciation for $4,000, credit Property, Plant, and Equipment for $6,000, and credit Cash and Cash Equivalents—Operating activities for $3,000. Note that per FAS 95, the *gross* gain, not the net of tax gain, is removed from operating activities. The tax effect on this gain is left in operating activities.

e.  The deferred income tax liability account shows an increase of $4,440. The $3,000 increase that pertains to amounts reported in the income statement must be added to income from operations. Although the $3,000 was deducted as part of income tax expense in determining net income, it did not require an outflow of cash. Therefore, debit Cash and Cash Equivalents—Operating activities and credit Deferred Taxes. The other two amounts in the deferred tax liability account are covered below, under paragraph "p."

f.  Item 2. under the additional information indicates that the investment in XYZ is accounted for under the equity method. The investment in XYZ had a net increase of $2,000, which is the result of the equity in the earnings of XYZ of $5,000 and the receipt of a $3,000 dividend. Dividends received (an inflow of cash) would reduce the investment in XYZ, while the equity in the income of XYZ would increase the investment without affecting cash. The journal entries would have been

| | | |
|---|---|---|
| Cash (dividend received) | 3,000 | |
| Investment in XYZ | | 3,000 |
| Investment in XYZ | 5,000 | |
| Equity in earnings of XYZ | | 5,000 |

The dividend received ($3,000) is an inflow of cash, and the equity earnings are not. Debit Investment in XYZ for $5,000, credit Cash and Cash Equivalents—Operating activities for

$5,000, debit Cash and Cash Equivalents—Operating activities for $3,000, and credit Investment in XYZ for $3,000.

g.  The Property, Plant, and Equipment account increased because of the purchase of $8,000 (additional information, item 5.). The purchase of assets is an outflow of cash. Debit Property, Plant, and Equipment for $8,000 and credit Summary of Cash and Cash Equivalents.

h.  The company sold 200 shares of common stock during the year (additional information, item 3.). The entry for the sale of stock was

| | | |
|---|---|---|
| Cash | 5,000 | |
| Common stock (200 shares × $10) | | 2,000 |
| Additional paid-in capital | | 3,000 |

This transaction resulted in an inflow of cash. Debit Summary of Cash and Cash Equivalents $5,000, credit Common Stock $2,000, and credit Additional Paid-in Capital $3,000.

i.  Dividends of $12,000 were declared (additional information, item 7.). Only $9,000 was actually paid in cash, resulting in an ending balance of $5,000 in the Dividends Payable account. Therefore, the following entries were made during the year:

| | | |
|---|---|---|
| Retained earnings | 12,000 | |
| Dividends payable | | 12,000 |
| Dividends payable | 9,000 | |
| Cash | | 9,000 |

These transactions result in an outflow of cash. Debit Retained Earnings $12,000 and credit Dividends Payable $12,000. Additionally, debit Dividends Payable $9,000 and credit Summary of Cash and Cash Equivalents $9,000 to indicate the cash dividends paid during the year.

j.  Accounts Receivable (net) decreased by $2,000. This is added as an adjustment to net income in the computation of cash provided by operating activities. The decrease of $2,000 means that an additional $2,000 cash was collected on account above and beyond the sales reported in the income statement. Debit Cash and Cash Equivalents—Operating activities and credit Accounts Receivable for $2,000.

k.  Inventories increased by $5,000. This is subtracted as an adjustment to net income in the computation of cash provided by operating activities. Although $5,000 additional cash was spent to increase inventories, this expenditure is not reflected in accrual-basis cost of goods sold. Debit Inventory and credit Cash and Cash Equivalents—Operating activities for $5,000.

l.  Prepaid Expenses decreased by $3,000. This is added back to net income in the computation of cash provided by operating activities. The decrease means that no cash was spent when incurring the related expense. The cash was spent when the prepaid assets were purchased, not when they were expensed on the income statement. Debit Cash and Cash Equivalents—Operating activities and credit Prepaid Expenses for $3,000.

m.  Accounts Payable decreased by $10,000. This is subtracted as an adjustment to net income. The decrease of $10,000 means that an additional $10,000 of purchases were paid for in cash; therefore, income was not affected but cash was decreased. Debit Accounts Payable and credit Cash and Cash Equivalents—Operating activities for $10,000.

n.  Notes Payable increased by $9,000 (as listed under additional information, item 4.). This is an inflow of cash and would be included in the financing activities. Debit Summary of Cash and Cash Equivalents and credit Notes Payable for $9,000.

o.  Interest Payable increased by $1,000, but interest expense reported on the income statement was $2,000. Therefore, although $2,000 was expensed, only $1,000 cash was paid ($2,000 expense – $1,000 increase in interest payable). Debit Cash and Cash Equivalents—Operating activities for $1,000 for the noncash portion, debit Interest Payable for $1,000 for the cash portion, and credit Interest Payable for $2,000 for the expense.

p.  The following entry was made to record the incurrence of the tax liability:

| | | |
|---|---|---|
| Income tax expense | 9,180 | |
| Income taxes payable | | 6,180 |
| Deferred tax liability | | 3,000 |

Therefore, $9,180 was deducted in arriving at net income. The $3,000 credit to Deferred Income Taxes was accounted for in entry e. above. The $6,180 credit to Taxes Payable does not, however, indicate that $6,180 cash was paid for taxes. Since Taxes Payable increased $1,180, only $5,000 must have been paid and $1,180 remains unpaid. Debit Cash and Cash Equivalents—Operating activities for $1,180, debit Income Taxes Payable for $5,000, and credit Income Taxes Payable for $6,180.

q.  Item 6. under the additional information indicates that $15,000 of bonds payable were converted to common stock. This is a *noncash* financing activity and should be reported in a separate schedule. The following entry was made to record the transaction:

| | | |
|---|---|---|
| Bonds payable | 15,000 | |
| Common stock (500 shares × $10 par) | | 5,000 |
| Additional paid-in capital | | 10,000 |

Adjust the T-accounts with a debit to Bonds Payable, $15,000; a credit to Common Stock, $5,000; and a credit to Additional Paid-in Capital, $10,000.

r.  Item 8. under the additional information indicates that leased equipment was acquired on the last day of 2009. This is also a noncash financing activity and should be reported in a separate schedule. The following entry was made to record the lease transaction:

| | | |
|---|---|---|
| Leased asset | 5,000 | |
| Lease obligation | | 5,000 |

s.  The company sold half of its available-for-sale investments during the year for $8,000 (additional information, item 9.). The entry for the sale of the investments was

| | | |
|---|---|---|
| Cash | 8,000 | |
| Investment in available-for-sale securities | | 7,500 |
| Gain on sale of investments | | 500 |

This transaction resulted in an inflow of cash. Debit Summary of Cash and Cash Equivalents $8,000, credit Investment in Available-for-Sale Securities $7,500, and credit Cash and Cash Equivalents—Operating activities $500. The following additional journal entries were made:

| | | |
|---|---|---|
| Adjustment for changes in FV | 1,500 | |
| Other comprehensive income ($1,500 × 64%) | | 960 |
| Deferred tax liability ($1,500 × 36%) | | 540 |

To adjust the allowance account for the sale, one-half of the amounts provided at the end of 2008 must be taken off the books when the related securities are sold.

| | | |
|---|---|---|
| Adjustment for changes in FV | 2,500 | |
| Unrealized gain on available-for-sale securities ($2,500 × 64%) | | 1,600 |
| Deferred tax liability ($2,500 × 36%) | | 900 |

The change in FV of the remaining securities at year-end (as listed under additional information, item 9.) must be adjusted. The book value of the securities before the adjustment above is $6,000 ($7,500 − $1,500). The fair value of the securities is $8,500. An adjustment of $2,500 is necessary.

t.  The cash and cash equivalents from operations ($15,000) is transferred to the Summary of Cash and Cash Equivalents.

All of the changes in the noncash accounts have been accounted for and the balance in the Summary of Cash and Cash Equivalents account of $25,000 is the amount of the year-to-year increase in cash and cash equivalents. The formal statement may now be prepared using the T-account, Summary of Cash and Cash Equivalents. The alphabetic characters in the statement below refer to the entries in that T-account. The following statement of cash flows is prepared under the direct method. The calculations for gross receipts and gross payments needed for the direct method are shown below the statement.

**Johnson Company**
**Statement of Cash Flows**
**For the Year Ended December 31, 2009**

*Cash flow from operating activities*

| | | | |
|---|---|---|---|
| Cash received from customers | $102,000 | | |
| Dividends received | 3,000 | | |
| Cash provided by operating activities | | | $105,000 |
| Cash paid to suppliers | $ 75,000 | | |
| Cash paid for expenses | 9,000 | | |
| Interest paid | 1,000 | | |
| Income taxes paid | 5,000 | | |
| Cash paid for operating activities | | | (90,000) |
| Net cash flow provided by operating activities | | (t) | $ 15,000 |

*Cash flow from investing activities*

| | | | |
|---|---|---|---|
| Sale of equipment | 5,000 | (d) | |
| Sale of investments | 8,000 | (s) | |
| Purchase of property, plant, and equipment | (8,000) | (g) | |
| Net cash provided by investing activities | | | 5,000 |

*Cash flow from financing activities*

| | | | |
|---|---|---|---|
| Sale of common stock | $ 5,000 | (h) | |
| Increase in notes payable | 9,000 | (n) | |
| Dividends paid | (9,000) | (i) | |
| Net cash provided by financing activities | | | 5,000 |
| Net increase in cash and cash equivalents | | | $ 25,000 |
| Cash and cash equivalents at beginning of year | | | 16,000 |
| Cash and cash equivalents at end of year | | | $ 41,000 |

*Calculation of amounts for operating activities section*

Cash received from customers = Net sales + Beginning A/R – Ending A/R
$100,000 + $11,000 – $9,000 = $102,000

Cash paid to suppliers = Cost of goods sold + Beginning A/P – Ending A/P + Ending inventory – Beginning inventory
$60,000 + $12,000 – $2,000 + $14,000 – $9,000 = $75,000

Cash paid for operating expenses = Operating expenses + Ending prepaid expenses – Beginning prepaid expenses – Depreciation expense (and other noncash operating expenses)
$12,000 + $8,000 + $1,000 + $10,000 – $13,000 – $8,000 – $1,000 = $9,000

Interest paid = Interest expense + Beginning interest payable – Ending interest payable
$2,000 + $2,000 – $3,000 = $1,000

Taxes paid = Income taxes + Beginning income taxes payable – Ending income taxes payable – Change in deferred income taxes—operating portion
$9,180 + $1,000 – $2,180 – $3,000 = $5,000

When a statement of cash flows is prepared using the direct method of reporting operating cash flows, the reconciliation of net income to operating cash flows must also be provided. The T-account, Cash and Cash Equivalents—Operating Activities is used to prepare the reconciliation. The alphabetic characters in the reconciliation below refer to the entries in the T-account.

*Reconciliation of net income to net cash provided by operating activities*

| | | | |
|---|---|---|---|
| Net income | | (a) | $16,320 |
| Add (deduct) items not using (providing) cash: | | | |
| Depreciation | 8,000 | (b) | |
| Amortization | 1,000 | (c) | |
| Gain on sale of equipment | (3,000) | (d) | |
| Increase in deferred taxes | 3,000 | (e) | |
| Equity in XYZ | (2,000) | (f) | |
| Decrease in accounts receivable | 2,000 | (j) | |
| Increase in inventory | (5,000) | (k) | |
| Decrease in prepaid expenses | 3,000 | (l) | |
| Decrease in accounts payable | (10,000) | (m) | |
| Increase in interest payable | 1,000 | (o) | |

| | | | |
|---|---|---|---|
| Increase in income taxes payable | 1,180 | (p) | |
| Gain on sale of AFS securities | (500) | (s) | (1,320) |
| Net cash flow provided by operating activities | | (t) | $15,000 |
| **Schedule of noncash transactions** | | | |
| Conversion of bonds into common stock | | (q) | $15,000 |
| Acquisition of leased equipment | | (r) | $ 5,000 |

## Statement of Cash Flows for Consolidated Entities

A consolidated statement of cash flows must be presented when a complete set of consolidated financial statements is issued. The consolidated statement of cash flows would be the last statement to be prepared as the information to prepare it will come from the other consolidated statements (consolidated balance sheet, income statement, and statement of retained earnings). The preparation of these other consolidated statements is discussed in Chapter 13.

The preparation of a consolidated statement of cash flows involves the same analysis and procedures as the statement for an individual entity with a few additional items. When the indirect method is used, the additional noncash transactions relating to the business combination such as the differential amortization must also be reversed and all transfers to affiliates must be eliminated, as they do not represent cash inflows or outflows of the consolidated entity.

All unrealized intercompany profits should have been eliminated in preparation of the other statements. Any income or loss allocated to noncontrolling parties would need to be added back, as it would have been eliminated in computing consolidated net income but does not represent a true cash outflow or inflow. Finally, only dividend payments that are not intercompany should be recorded as cash outflows in the financing activities section.

In preparing the operating activities section of the statement by the indirect method following a purchase business combination, the changes in assets and liabilities related to operations since acquisition should be derived by comparing the consolidated balance sheet as of the date of acquisition with the year-end consolidated balance sheet. These changes will be combined with those for the acquiring company up to the date of acquisition as adjustments to net income. The effects due to the acquisition of these assets and liabilities are reported under investing activities.

## Forthcoming Changes to Financial Statement Presentation Standards

As discussed in Chapters 2 and 3, the currently active FASB project (which is being pursued in conjunction with IASB), *Financial Statement Presentation*, will likely result in expanding the use of the categorizations long used to describe cash flows—operating, investing, and financing—to some or all of the other basic financial statements. The major change to the cash flow statement, if current thinking holds, would be to require the use of the direct method of reporting operating cash flows. As set forth earlier in this chapter, FAS 95 favored the use of the direct method, but the vast majority of all reporting entities have continued to employ the indirect method, which is generally defended as being less costly to prepare.

There is also a possibility that the required disclosure of noncash investing and financing activities might be relocated, although this remains an open matter for further debate.

Another likely change in the statement of cash flows will eliminate the concept of cash equivalents, thereby restricting reporting to actual changes in cash. Presumably cash equivalents would be merged with other short-term investments, and changes in such investments would be reported in the cash flow statement based on nature and intent of acquisition, as required under FAS 159, for those investments measured at fair value.

Current thinking on the format and content of the statement of cash flows is that, if changes are to be made, operating and investing cash flows will become subsections of a new major category to be denoted as "business." Cash flows associated with discontinued operations would be separately set forth in a newly established caption. Financing cash flows would be presented, as now, in a separate major category. Finally, cash flows relating to equity transactions and those pertaining to income taxes would also be uniquely categorized. A preliminary views or similar discussion-stage document is expected by year-end 2008.

The increased visibility of the cash flows from discontinued operations would be, if enacted, a response to complaints that have been voiced by the user community regarding interpretation of currently provided discontinued operations data; if adopted, the definition of discontinued operations would be narrowed and tax effects would no longer be associated with discontinued operations. (In the proposed cash flow presentation, all income taxes would be reported as such, in a separate major category, without intraperiod allocation.)

# 5 ACCOUNTING POLICIES, CHANGES, AND RESTATEMENTS

## PERSPECTIVE AND ISSUES

Under US GAAP, management is granted the flexibility of choosing between or among certain alternative methods of accounting for the same economic transactions, although over time the range of choices has narrowed and will likely be further reduced. Examples of the availability of such choices are provided throughout this publication, in such diverse areas such as alternative cost-flow assumptions used to account for inventory and cost of sales, different methods of depreciating long-lived assets, and varying methods of identifying operating segments. The professional literature (in the areas of accounting principles, auditing standards, quality control standards, and professional ethics) is emphatic that, in choosing among the various alternatives, management is to select principles and apply them in a manner that results in financial statements that faithfully represent economic substance over form and that are fully transparent to the user.

Changes in accounting can be necessitated over time due to changes in the assumptions and estimates underlying the application of accounting principles and methods of applying them, changes in the principles defined as acceptable by a standards-setting authority, or other types of changes.

The accounting and disclosure of changes in accounting for given transactions are issues that have confronted the accounting profession for a great many years. The matter is particularly sensitive because of the impact on financial statement analysis, particularly of the trend or longitudinal variety, of altering the methods of accounting for specific transactions, and of disclosing the effects of those changes.

From a managerial perspective as well, changes in the accounting for given transactions can have a profound influence on investing and operational decisions. Financial statement analysis and management decision making both generally presume the consistency and comparability of financial statements across periods and among entities within industry groupings. Any type of accounting change potentially can create inconsistency, and since some change is inevitable, the challenge is to present the effects of the change in a manner that is most readily comprehended by users of financial statements, who may impose various adjustments of their own in their efforts to make the information comparable for analysis purposes.

This concern is exacerbated by the fact that events of the late 1900s and early 2000s created a crisis of confidence about the accuracy of financial reports and the credibility of the parties associated with preparing and auditing them. The number and magnitude of restatements of previously issued financial statements raised disturbing questions about management manipulation, and about the possible complicity of, or at least negligence by, the external auditors. The enactment of the Sarbanes-Oxley Act of 2002 and the restructuring of oversight of, and standard setting for, the auditing profession were two consequences of this series of unfortunate developments. The move to "converge" US GAAP and international accounting standards—and the real possibility that IFRS may supersede US GAAP, at least for publicly held companies—are further indicators of the premium now being placed on accurate, transparent, and uniform financial reporting.

When contemplating a potential change in accounting principle, a primary focus of management should be to consider its effect on financial statement comparability. This should not, however, dissuade preparers from adopting preferable accounting standards, where otherwise warranted.

As one result of the joint FASB-IASB effort to converge US GAAP and International Financial Reporting Standards (IFRS), FASB in 2005 issued FAS 154, *Accounting Changes and Error Corrections*, which superseded APB 20 and essentially conformed US GAAP practice to that under international financial reporting standards. FAS 154 requires retrospective application of a newly adopted accounting policy for most changes in accounting principle, including changes in accounting principle required by newly issued pronouncements. FASB did, however, retain the right to require different transition provisions for changes in accounting principle mandated by the future issuance of new pronouncements, should it deem such differences to be appropriate.

In another significant alteration, FAS 154 also requires the reporting of a change in depreciation, amortization, or depletion *method* as a change in an accounting *estimate* rather than a change in *principle,* as had been required under APB 20. This type of change is not effected by retrospectively adjusting prior financial statements.

An accounting change is defined as a change in either

1. Accounting principle
2. Accounting estimate
3. Reporting entity

While the correction of an error in previously issued financial statements is not considered an accounting change, per se, this subject is also dealt with by FAS 154, which for the first time expressly restricts the use of the term "restatement" to describe corrections of prior period errors, in order to avoid any ambiguity regarding whether an error is involved in a particular change to previously issued financial statements.

FAS 154 retains and restates from predecessor standard APB 20 the underlying presumption that, in preparing financial statements, an accounting principle, once adopted, should not be changed in accounting for events and transactions of a similar type. This consistent use of accounting principles is intended to enhance the utility of financial statements. The presumption that a reporting entity should not change an accounting principle may be overcome only if management justifies the use of an alternative acceptable accounting principle on the basis that it is actually preferable.

FAS 154 does not provide a definition of preferability or criteria by which to make such assessments, so this remains a matter of professional judgment. Because there is no universally agreed-upon set of objectives for external financial reporting, what is preferable for one industry or company is not necessarily considered preferable for another. This may serve to perpetuate some of the same reporting inconsistencies that existed prior to the issuance of FAS 154 and even prior to its predecessor standard, APB 20.

SAS 69 (discussed in Chapter 1) requires that an entity adopt the accounting principles set forth in pronouncements with effective dates after March 15, 1992. An entity initially applying an accounting principle after that date (including those making an accounting change) must follow the applicable GAAP hierarchy set forth in SAS 69. An entity following an established accounting principle that was effective on or before March 15, 1992, need not change its accounting until a new pronouncement is issued. (Note that the hierarchy of GAAP may change in the near-term future, as FASB completes its codification project, and the specification of the GAAP hierarchy is removed from the auditing literature. As an interim measure, a "near final" FASB Statement, simply moving the current SAS 69 requirements to accounting literature, was exposed in 2006, but has not yet been issued in final form.)

In 2003, the FASB staff began issuing FASB Staff Positions (abbreviated in this publication as FSP and discussed more fully in Chapter 1) to provide guidance on the application of its authoritative literature. Unless otherwise specified, FSP are effective for new transactions or arrangements entered into after the beginning of the first fiscal quarter following the date of final posting of the FSP to the FASB Web site (http://www.FASB.org). FSP are included in the FAS 154 definition of "accounting pronouncement" and, thus, in the rare instance that an FSP is silent regarding transition, the reporting entity will be required to retrospectively apply the new FSP to all prior periods.

| Sources of GAAP | | | |
|---|---|---|---|
| *APB* | *FAS* | *FIN* | *EITF* |
| 9, 22, 28 | 16, 111, 154, 157, 159 | 1 | 06-9 |

## DEFINITIONS OF TERMS

**Accounting change.** Under FAS 154, an accounting change is one of three types of modifications that affect a reporting entity's accounting principles and practices, or their application. The three types of accounting changes are: (1) a change in accounting principle from one generally accepted accounting principle to another alternative that is considered preferable, (2) a change in an accounting estimate, and (3) a change in the reporting entity. Although, technically, corrections of errors in prior periods' financial statements (now referred to exclusively as "restatements"), are not accounting changes, their treatment is also governed by FAS 154.

**Accounting policies.** The accounting principles of a reporting entity and the methods of applying them. Management is required to adopt the accounting policies that result in a fair, full, and complete presentation of financial position, results of operations, and cash flows in the financial statements of the reporting entity.

**Accounting principle.** A methodology used to measure and report the monetary effects of economic events in financial statements. Acceptable accounting principles are either prescribed by a recognized standard-setting body in an authoritative pronouncement or, in the absence of a relevant pronouncement, are predominantly followed by entities that engage in transactions of a similar nature or operate in a particular industry or profession. In the context of FAS 154, accounting principles encompass both accounting practices and the methods of applying them.

**Change in accounting estimate.** A revision of an accounting measurement based on the occurrence of new events, additional experience, subsequent developments, better insight, and improved judgment. Refining previously made estimates is an inherent part of the accounting process.

**Change in accounting estimate effected by a change in accounting principle.** A change in accounting estimate that is inseparable from the effect of a related change in accounting principle (for example, a change in depreciation method).

**Change in accounting principle.** A change from one generally accepted accounting principle to another generally accepted accounting principle, including the methods of applying the principles. This does not include selection and adoption of an accounting principle to account for the substance and/or form of events (1) occurring for the first time in the operations of a given reporting entity or (2) that had occurred in the past but that were previously considered immaterial. A change in accounting principle can also occur when an authoritative standards setter issues a new standard that renders an existing accounting principle no longer acceptable.

**Change in reporting entity.** A special type of change in accounting principle that results in financial statements that, in effect, are those of a different reporting entity. Financial statements are prepared for an entity that is different from the one reported on in previous financial statements. Specifically excluded from this type of accounting change are business combinations under FAS 141 and consolidation of variable interest entities under FIN 46R.

**Comparability.** The quality of information that enables users to identify similarities in and differences between two sets of economic circumstances. Normally, comparability is a quantitative assessment of a common characteristic.

**Consistency.** Conformity from period to period with unchanging policies and procedures. Consistency enhances the utility of financial statements to users by facilitating analysis and understanding of comparative accounting data.

**Cumulative catch-up.** A method used to reflect a change in accounting estimate whereby the results of the change are recognized in the statement of income of the period of the change.

**Cumulative effect.** The difference between the retained earnings balance at the beginning of the year in which a change is reported and the beginning retained earnings balance that would have been reported if the new principle had been applied retrospectively in all prior periods that would have been affected.

**Errors.** Mathematical mistakes, mistakes in applying accounting principles, oversight or misuse of available facts, and use of unacceptable GAAP.

**Restatement.** The revision of previously issued financial statements in order to correct an error made in preparing them (see definition of "errors" above). Under FAS 154, this term is only to be used in the context of error corrections, and not to describe any other types of financial statement changes.

# CONCEPTS, RULES, AND EXAMPLES

## Accounting Policies

The reporting entity's management is responsible for adopting and adhering to the highest quality accounting policies possible. APB 22 requires management, in discharging this responsibility, to adopt accounting principles and methods of applying them that are "the most appropriate in the circumstances to present fairly financial position, results of operations, and cash flows in accordance with generally accepted accounting principles." APB 22 requires management to disclose, in the notes to the financial statements, a description of all significant accounting policies of the reporting entity. This requirement applies even in reporting situations where one or more of the basic financial statements has been omitted. In theory, if only one method of accounting for a type of transaction is acceptable under GAAP, it is not necessary to explicitly cite it in the accounting policies note, although many entities do routinely identify all accounting policies affecting the major financial statement captions.

A listing of accounting policies commonly disclosed by reporting entities follows (the listing is not intended to be all-inclusive):

- Advertising costs
- Advertising, direct response arrangements
- Cash equivalents
- Changes in accounting policies
- Combined financial statements, principles of combination
- Concentrations of credit risk, major customers and/or suppliers
- Consolidated financial statements, principles of consolidation
- Consolidated financial statements, variable interest entities
- Deferred income taxes
- Deferred income taxes, undistributed earnings of subsidiaries and/or joint ventures
- Derivatives and hedging activities
- Fair value elections, methods, assumptions, inputs used
- Financial instruments
- Fiscal year, 52-53 week year
- Fiscal year, difference between fiscal year used for financial reporting and income tax purposes
- Foreign currency translation
- Foreign sales corporations
- Goodwill
- Guarantees
- Impairment of long-lived assets, goodwill, other intangibles, investments, etc.
- Income taxes, deposit to retain fiscal year
- Income taxes, nonaccrual by flow-through entity
- Income taxes, liability for unrecognized income tax positions
- Intangibles, amortizable and/or nonamortizable
- Interest capitalization
- Internal-use software
- Inventories
- Investments, cost method
- Investments, debt and marketable equity securities including reclassifications between portfolios
- Investments, equity method
- Long-term contracts

- Nature of operations
- Not-for-profits; restrictions that are satisfied in the year they originate
- Operating cycle
- Out-of-pocket costs (typically for service businesses)
- Pension and other postretirement or postemployment plans
- Property and equipment, depreciation and amortization
- Property and equipment, changes from held-and-used to held-for-sale
- Rebates
- Receivables, past due, interest and late charges, determination of allowance for bad debts
- Reclassifications
- Revenue recognition, lessor leasing activities
- Revenue recognition, long-term contract accounting
- Revenue recognition, methods for each significant product or service
- Revenue recognition, multiple-element arrangements
- Revenue recognition, product returns
- Revenue recognition, real estate (time-sharing) sales (e.g., installment cost recovery, full accrual)
- Revenue recognition, software sold or otherwise marketed
- Share-based payment arrangements
- Shipping and handling costs
- Start-up costs
- Syndication costs
- Use of estimates
- Warranties

The "summary of significant accounting policies" is customarily, but not necessarily, the first note disclosure included in the financial statements. A more all-encompassing title such as "Nature of business and summary of significant accounting policies" is frequently used.

It is not necessary to repeat details provided elsewhere in the disclosures in the accounting policy disclosure. Many preparers simply cross-reference accounting policy disclosures to relevant details provided in other notes to the financial statements.

### Alternatives and Elections under GAAP

Confusion abounds in the preparer and user communities regarding what alternatives are available to account for the same or similar transactions, and under which circumstances those alternatives are appropriate. Over the years, in order to facilitate consistent, comparable reporting between entities and between periods, FASB has been reducing the number of alternative accounting principles or methods of applying them. This trend should continue as FASB converges its authoritative literature with international standards (IFRS). The remainder of this section will discuss the alternatives most commonly encountered in practice. Each alternative includes parenthetical reference to the primary governing GAAP and to the chapter of this publication where the relevant issues are discussed in greater detail.

**Advertising costs (SOP 93-7; Chapter 3).** AcSEC, in SOP 93-7, categorized the costs of media advertising (e.g., television, radio, newspapers, direct mail) into two broad categories: production costs and communication costs. Except for direct response advertising costs, the costs of advertising are accounted for as follows:

**Production costs**—Management can elect an accounting policy of expensing production costs either when the costs are incurred or the first time that the advertising takes place. If management chooses to defer these costs, they may only be deferred (recorded as an asset) if the advertising is expected to occur. If it is subsequently decided not to run the advertising, all deferred production costs are to be reversed and recorded as expense in the period that the decision is made.

**Communication costs**—These costs are generally expensed when the cost is incurred (i.e., when the television or radio advertising is broadcast or when the print advertising is published). An exception is provided for cooperative advertising arrangements. This is, in essence, an arrangement whereby a supplier reimburses its customer for all or a portion of the customer's costs of advertising the supplier's products. In most cases, the supplier's revenues from sale of its products to its customers have been earned prior to when it is obligated to reimburse the customer for the advertising. When this is the case, the supplier is required to accrue the cooperative advertising reimbursement and recognize it as an expense in the same period as the related revenues are recognized.

An example is provided, later in this chapter, to illustrate how to report a change in accounting principle with respect to accounting for advertising costs.

**Fair value option (FAS 159; Chapter 6).** In 2007, FASB issued FAS 159, *The Fair Value Option for Financial Assets and Financial Liabilities*. This standard (discussed in detail in Chapter 6) permits reporting entities (including not-for-profit organizations) to elect to measure many financial assets and liabilities at fair value, with changes in fair value reflected in earnings (or another performance indicator, if applicable) as they occur. FAS 159 offers substantial flexibility to management in making the fair value election in that the election generally may be applied by individual instrument.

By offering reporting entities an option to apply fair value accounting to selected financial assets and liabilities, the risk of opportunistic application had to be dealt with. One dissenter to the enactment of this standard raised the objection that "...an instrument-by-instrument option that results in partial adoption of fair values...significantly reduces the relevance of the resulting reporting by failing to portray the earnings effects of financial (and other) instruments' exposures in the same reporting period and increases users' costs in processing the information by introducing treatment alternatives that reduce the comparability of reported results within and across reporting entities and line items."

To compensate for this admitted shortcoming, in adopting FAS 159, the electing entity is required to make substantial new disclosures and to simultaneously adopt FAS 157, *Fair Value Measurements*, which also includes additional disclosure requirements. See Chapter 6 for a comprehensive discussion of these standards and a description of the complex effective date and early adoption provisions.

**Functional currency (FAS 52; Chapter 23).** Management's determination of a reporting entity's functional currency is based on identification of the "primary economic environment in which the entity operates." This determination can, in many cases, be relatively straightforward. However, FASB acknowledged that this might not always be obvious. When this is the case, management must exercise judgment as to which functional currency will most faithfully portray the entity's economic performance. Once management makes the functional currency decision regarding a foreign entity, that decision is to be used consistently unless there are subsequent changes in the economic facts and circumstances that indicate clearly that there has been a change in that entity's functional currency. Should this occur, however, this is not considered to be a change in accounting principle.

The determination of a foreign entity's functional currency dictates which method of foreign currency translation is required to be used with respect to that entity. If the foreign entity's functional currency is its local currency, the current rate method is required to be used to translate its financial statements. If, instead, the foreign entity's functional currency is the US dollar, the remeasurement method is required.

**Inventory cost flow assumptions (ARB 43; Chapter 9).** Inventory may be costed by means of specific identification or by application of one of several acceptable alternative cost-flow assumptions, which are

1. First-in, first-out (FIFO),
2. Last-in, first-out (LIFO), and
3. Weighted-average

The adoption of a cost-flow assumption is not an all-or-nothing proposition. For example, management may choose to elect LIFO for certain types of inventory and FIFO or weighted-average for other types. Each of the assumptions has advantages and disadvantages and will yield different results.

In electing to use a particular cost-flow assumption, there are other policy matters that must be decided. Particularly in the use of LIFO, which originated as an income tax concept, the Internal Revenue Service (Form 970, *Application to Use the LIFO Method*) requires an electing taxpayer to provide details of the manner in which it is applying the method. For example, a taxpayer electing to use dollar-value LIFO must specify, among other things

1. How it defines "items" in the inventory,
2. The method it will use to determine LIFO pools and a description of the types of items that will be included in each pool,
3. The method that will be used to compute the LIFO value of each dollar-value pool (e.g., double-extension, link-chain, or index method),
4. The method that will be used to determine the current year cost of goods in closing inventories and to value any LIFO increments in the pool(s), and
5. If the taxpayer is using the Inventory Price Index Computation (IPIC) Method (either using link-chain IPIC or double-extension IPIC), the Bureau of Labor Statistics (BLS) price index table that will be used.

Changing one or more of the above conventions used to apply the LIFO method would constitute a change in accounting principle that, under FAS 154, would require *retroactive* application to all prior periods for which it is practical to do so. This is true even though both before and after the change, the reporting entity uses the LIFO method.

The future of LIFO inventory costing may be some doubt, given the FASB commitment to "converge" with IFRS, and given the possibility that IFRS may in fact supersede US GAAP in the not-too-distant future. Specifically, IFRS eliminated LIFO as an acceptable costing method several years ago, on the grounds that it does not realistically describe the flow of goods except in highly unusual circumstances. In the US, LIFO costing was embraced primarily because it was advantageous in inflationary periods for tax reporting purposes, and the LIFO conformity rule necessitated simultaneous use for GAAP financial reporting. The expectation is that there will be pressure for changes to tax law to de-couple tax reporting from GAAP financial reporting. At the same time, there is renewed agitation to eliminate LIFO from tax rules, to eliminate what has been a tax deferral strategy by corporate taxpayers. The outcome of these various debates is not yet clear.

**Depreciation of long-lived assets (ARB 43; Chapter 11).** Management is responsible for choosing a method of depreciating its long-lived assets that systematically allocates the cost of the asset (reduced by any residual or salvage value) to expense over the periods benefited by the use of those assets. In determining the appropriate method of depreciation, estimated useful life, and salvage value to assign to particular types of assets, management considers the nature of the assets, the manner or pattern in which they are expected to be used, nature, timing and extent of expected wear and tear, potential loss of productivity in later years of use, likelihood of technological obsolescence, etc.

Based on these considerations, a number of alternative methods of depreciation are available such as

1. Straight-line
2. Declining balance (e.g., double-declining balance)
3. Sum-of-the-years' digits
4. Group or composite methods
5. Present value methods
6. Units of production

Management also may elect to use certain conventions in applying the chosen depreciation methods. For example, many reporting entities adopt a convention of taking one-half of the annual depreciation computed for newly acquired assets in the year of acquisition and one-half in the final year or the year of subsequent disposition. Another convention adopted by some companies is to use an accelerated method of depreciation during the early years of use and then switch to straight-line depreciation over the remaining useful life at a defined point, in order to fully depreciate the asset over its useful life.

Subsequent change to the method of depreciation or the manner in which it is applied is considered a change in accounting estimate effected by a change in accounting principle. When management determines that such a change is required, the change is accounted for prospectively in the current and any future periods affected. Retrospective application to prior periods' financial statements is not permitted. However, unlike other changes in accounting estimate, management is required to justify the change on the basis of the revised depreciation method being considered preferable to the former method.

**Long-term construction contracts (SOP 81-1, AAG-Construction Contractors; Chapter 10).** The two primary methods of accounting for long-term construction contracts are completed-contract and percentage-of-completion. The appropriate method for a particular reporting entity depends on whether or not management is able to dependably estimate cost to complete and extent of progress towards completion of its construction contracts. Under SOP 81-1, there is a rebuttable presumption that management is capable of making these estimates and that, therefore, the percentage-of-completion method is the preferable method of accounting. When circumstances warrant, management may elect to use the percentage-of-completion method as its primary method of accounting for long-term construction contracts and still apply the competed-contract method of accounting to contracts that meet certain specified criteria. When this is the case, the facts and circumstances are to be fully disclosed in the notes to the financial statements.

**Share-based payment arrangements (FAS 123[R]; Chapter 19).** In accounting for share-based payment arrangements, management has a number of policy decisions to make including

1. The method(s) and models used to value share-based payment arrangements such as whether to use a lattice model or a closed-form model such as the Black-Scholes-Merton model. Management may elect to use different valuation models for different types of instruments.
2. The share price to be used as the "current" share price in estimating fair value on the grant date (e.g., the closing share price or the share price at another specified time),
3. Subject to a specified minimum amount (floor), whether to recognize compensation cost for awards with service conditions and graded vesting schedules (a) on a straight-line basis over the requisite service period for each portion of the award as it separately vests as if the award were, in effect, separate awards, or (b) on a

straight-line basis over the requisite service period for the whole award. Once elected, this policy must be followed consistently for all similar awards.

4. The method to be used to compute the initial pool of excess tax benefits available on adoption of FAS 123(R).
5. For nonpublic companies

   a. Whether to measure all liability awards at fair value, calculated value, or intrinsic value
   b. Whether to measure equity awards at fair value or calculated value

## Initial Adoption Decisions

Upon formation of a business or nonprofit organization, management makes decisions regarding the adoption of accounting policies, based on the types of activities in which the entity engages and the industry and environment in which it operates. Certain types of events and transactions are subject to GAAP that permits choices to be made from among alternative, acceptable accounting treatments. The principles selected from among the available alternatives and the methods of applying those principles constitute the reporting entity's accounting policies.

Management initially adopts accounting principles at two distinct times

1. Upon formation of the reporting entity
2. Upon the occurrence of a new type of event or transaction that had either not happened in the past or had previously been judged to be immaterial

Once the initial adoption decisions are made, the users of the financial statements expect a reporting entity's financial statements to be prepared consistently over time. This facilitates comparisons across periods and among different reporting entities.

## Accounting Changes

There are legitimate reasons why a reporting entity would change its accounting, either voluntarily or because it is required to do so

1. Changing to an existing alternative accounting principle that management deems to be preferable to the one it is currently following
2. Adopting a newly issued accounting principle
3. Refining an estimate made in the past as a result of further experience and better information
4. Correcting an error made in previously issued financial statements. Although technically not an "accounting change" as defined in GAAP literature, this involves restating previously issued financial statements and is also governed by FAS 154.

To facilitate accurate analysis, it is important for management of the reporting entity to adequately inform the financial statement users when one or more of these changes is made, and to provide sufficient information to enable the reader to distinguish the effects of the change from other factors affecting results of operations.

FAS 154, *Accounting Changes and Error Corrections*, was issued in 2005 in order to more closely conform the treatment of accounting changes under US GAAP to international financial reporting standards under IAS 8 (see Appendix B, *International vs. US Accounting Standards*). It applies to financial statements of commercial businesses and not-for-profit organizations as well as historical summaries and other presentations derived from them that include one or more periods reflecting an accounting change or error correction.

FAS 154 became effective for accounting changes and error corrections made in fiscal years beginning after December 15, 2005 (i.e., for calendar 2006 and later periods).

Each of the types of accounting changes and the proper treatment prescribed for them is discussed in detail in the following sections.

## Change in Accounting Principle

Management is permitted to change from one generally accepted accounting principle to another only when (1) it voluntarily decides to do so and can justify the use of the alternative accounting principle as being preferable to the principle currently being followed, or (2) it is required to make the change as a result of a newly issued accounting pronouncement. If the change is being made voluntarily, the financial statements of the period of change are to include disclosure of the nature of and reason for the change and an explanation of why management believes the newly adopted accounting principle is preferable. In accordance with FIN 1, this preferability assessment is required to be made from the perspective of financial reporting, and not solely from an income tax perspective. Thus, favorable income tax consequences alone do not justify making a change in financial reporting practices.

According to FAS 154, the term *accounting principle* includes not only the accounting principles and practices used by the reporting entity, but also its methods of applying them. FIN 1 elaborates on this by stating that a change in the components used to cost a firm's inventory is considered a change in accounting principle and, therefore, is only permitted when the new inventory costing method is preferable to the former method.

**Preferability.** As stated, management is only permitted to voluntarily change the reporting entity's accounting principles when the newly employed principle is preferable to the principle it is replacing. The independent auditors are then charged with concurring with management's assessment. If the auditors do not believe management has provided reasonable justification for the change, AU §508.51 requires the auditors to express either a qualified or adverse opinion, depending on the materiality of the effects of the unacceptable accounting principle on the financial statements.

When management of a public company voluntarily changes the registrant's accounting principles, a letter from the registrant's independent public accountants is required to be filed with the SEC. This "preferability letter" is to be included as an exhibit in 10-Q and 10-K filings (Regulation S-K Item 601, Exhibit 18) and must indicate whether the change in principle or practice (or method of applying that principle or practice) is to an acceptable alternative that, in the auditors' judgment, is preferable under the circumstances.

**Retrospective application.** FAS 154 provides that changes in accounting principle be reflected in financial statements by retrospective application to all prior periods presented unless it is impracticable to do so. This is a significant departure from the predecessor standard, APB 20, which had required current accounting for such changes, using the cumulative effect method. FAS 154 points out, however, that in the future when new accounting principles are issued, those pronouncements will include specific provisions regarding transitioning to the new principles that are to be followed by adopting entities. Thus, future standards may still provide for adoption using cumulative effect adjustments, if FASB believes this to be the most beneficial method of transition. The new default method, however, will be retrospective restatement, whereas previously the default procedure was to recognize a cumulative effect adjustment in current results of operations.

Retrospective application is accomplished by the following steps:

At the beginning of the first period presented in the financial statements,

Step 1 -　　Adjust the carrying amounts of assets and liabilities for the cumulative effect of changing to the new accounting principle on periods prior to those presented in the financial statements.

Step 2 -　　Offset the effect of the adjustment in Step 1 (if any) by adjusting the opening balance of retained earnings (or other components of equity or net assets, as applicable to the reporting entity).

For each individual prior period that is presented in the financial statements,

Step 3 -　　Adjust the financial statements for the effects of applying the new accounting principle to that specific period.

**Example of retrospective application of a new accounting principle**

In 1998, upon the incorporation of Newburger Company, its management elected to recognize advertising costs as incurred. Newburger has been consistently following that policy in its financial statements. In 2009, Newburger's management reviewed its accounting policies and concluded that application of its current policy was resulting in substantial costs associated with the production of television advertising being recognized in financial reporting periods that preceded the periods in which the related revenues were earned. Consequently, management decided to change Newburger's policy to elect to expense advertising costs the first time the advertising takes place as permitted by SOP 93-7, *Reporting on Advertising Costs*. Additional assumptions follow:

- As has been its policy in the past, Newburger plans to issue comparative financial statements presenting two years, 2009 and 2008.
- Newburger does not engage in direct-response advertising activities (SOP 93-7).
- A combined federal and state income tax rate of 40% was in effect for all relevant periods.
- Prior to the change in accounting principle, there were no temporary differences or loss carryforwards and, thus, there were no deferred income tax assets or liabilities.
- Advertising costs are deductible for income tax purposes when incurred and, therefore, upon adoption of the new accounting policy, Newburger will have a temporary difference between the book and income tax bases of its asset, deferred advertising costs. These advertising costs that are being recognized in the financial statements in the year after they are deducted on Newburger's income tax return represent a future taxable temporary difference that will give rise to a deferred income tax liability.
- The financial statements originally issued as of and for the years ended December 31, 2008 and 2007, prior to the adoption of the new accounting principle are presented below with advertising-related captions shown separately for illustrative purposes.

**Newburger Company**
**Statements of Income and Retained Earnings**
**Prior to Change in Accounting Principle**
**Years Ended December 31, 2008 and 2007**

|  | *2008* | *2007* |
|---|---|---|
| Sales | $ 2,300,000 | $ 2,000,000 |
| Cost of sales | (850,000) | (750,000) |
| Gross profit | 1,450,000 | 1,250,000 |
| Advertising expense | 65,000 | 55,000 |
| Other selling, general and administrative expenses | 385,000 | 445,000 |
|  | 450,000 | 500,000 |
| Income from operations | 1,000,000 | 750,000 |
| Other income (expense) | 11,000 | 10,000 |
| Income before income taxes | 1,011,000 | 760,000 |
| Income taxes | (404,000) | (304,000) |
| Net income | 607,000 | 456,000 |
| Retained earnings, beginning of year | 13,756,000 | 14,500,000 |
| Dividends | (1,400,000) | (1,200,000) |
| Retained earnings, end of year | $12,963,000 | $13,756,000 |

**Newburger Company**
**Balance Sheets**
**Prior to Change in Accounting Principle**
**December 31, 2008 and 2007**

| | 2008 | 2007 |
|---|---|---|
| **Assets** | | |
| Current assets | | |
| Cash and cash equivalents | $ 2,200,000 | $ 2,400,000 |
| Deferred advertising cost | -- | -- |
| Prepaid expenses | 125,000 | 120,000 |
| Other current assets | 22,000 | 20,000 |
| Total current assets | 2,347,000 | 2,540,000 |
| Property and equipment | 10,729,000 | 11,311,000 |
| Total assets | $13,076,000 | $13,851,000 |
| **Liabilities and Stockholders' Equity** | | |
| Deferred income taxes | $ -- | $ -- |
| Other current liabilities | 35,000 | 12,000 |
| Total current liabilities | 35,000 | 12,000 |
| Noncurrent liabilities | 65,000 | 70,000 |
| Total liabilities | 100,000 | 82,000 |
| Stockholders' equity | | |
| Common stock | 13,000 | 13,000 |
| Retained earnings | 12,963,00 | 13,756,000 |
| Total stockholders' equity | 12,976,000 | 13,769,000 |
| Total liabilities and stockholders' equity | $13,076,000 | $13,851,000 |

**Newburger Company**
**Statements of Cash Flows**
**Prior to Change in Accounting Principle**
**Years Ended December 31, 2008 and 2007**

| | 2008 | 2007 |
|---|---|---|
| **Operating activities** | | |
| Net income | $ 607,000 | $ 456,000 |
| Depreciation | 715,000 | 715,000 |
| Deferred income taxes | -- | -- |
| Gain on sale of property and equipment | -- | -- |
| Changes in | | |
| Deferred advertising costs | -- | -- |
| Prepaid expenses | (5,000) | 1,000 |
| Other current assets | (2,000) | 1,500 |
| Other current liabilities | 23,000 | 900 |
| Net cash provided by operating activities | 1,338,000 | 1,174,400 |
| **Investing activities** | | |
| Property and equipment | | |
| Acquisition | (133,000) | (120,000) |
| Proceeds from sale | -- | -- |
| Net cash used for investing activities | (133,000) | (120,000) |
| **Financing activities** | | |
| Dividends paid to stockholders | (1,400,000) | (1,200,000) |
| Long-term debt | | |
| Borrowed | -- | -- |
| Repaid | (5,000) | (5,000) |
| Net cash used for financing activities | (1,405,000) | (1,205,000) |
| Decrease in cash and cash equivalents | (200,000) | (150,600) |
| Cash and cash equivalents, beginning of year | 2,400,000 | 2,550,600 |
| Cash and cash equivalents, end of year | $2,200,000 | $2,400,000 |

Step 1 -    Adjust the carrying amounts of assets and liabilities at the beginning of the first period presented in the financial statements (January 1, 2008, in this example).

for the cumulative effect of changing to the new accounting principle on periods prior to those presented in the financial statements.

In this example, the preparer refers to the previously issued 2007 financial statements presented above. Assume the following data regarding advertising costs at December 31, 2007/January 1, 2008:

| | |
|---|---|
| Costs incurred during 2007 for advertising that will not take place for the first time until 2008 | $25,000 |
| Deferred income tax liability that would have been recognized at December 31, 2007, computed at 40% of the temporary difference | (10,000) |
| Net adjustment to beginning assets and liabilities | $15,000 |

Step 2 - Offset the effect of the adjustment in Step 1 by adjusting the opening balance of retained earnings (or other components of equity or net assets, as applicable to the reporting entity).

The $15,000 net effect of the adjustment in Step 1 is presented in the statement of income and retained earnings as an adjustment to the January 1, 2008 retained earnings as previously reported at December 31, 2007.

Step 3 - Adjust the financial statements of each individual prior period presented for the effects of applying the new accounting principle to that specific period.

In this case, the following adjustments are necessary to adjust the 2008 financial statements for the period-specific effects of the change in accounting principle:

| Cost incurred in | Year the advertising was first run | |
|---|---|---|
| 2007 | 2008 | $ 25,000 |
| 2008 | 2009 | (45,000) |
| Pretax, period-specific adjustment to advertising costs at 12/31/07 | | (20,000) |
| × 40% income tax effect | | 8,000 |
| Effect on 2008 net income | | $(12,000) |

Adjustments to the 2008 financial statements for the period-specific effects of retrospective application of the new accounting principle are

**Adjustments to 2008 financial statements**

| | Deferred advertising costs | Deferred income tax liability | Advertising expense | Income tax expense |
|---|---|---|---|---|
| Balance at 12/31/08 prior to adjustment | $ -- | $ -- | $65,000 | $404,000 |
| Adjustment to opening balances from retrospective application to 2008 | 25,000 | 10,000 | -- | -- |
| Advertising costs incurred in 2007, first run in 2008 | (25,000) | -- | 25,000 | -- |
| Advertising costs incurred in 2008, first run in 2009 | 45,000 | -- | (45,000) (20,000) | -- |
| Income tax effect of net adjustment to 2008 advertising expense (40%) | -- | 8,000 | -- | 8,000 |
| Adjusted amounts for 2008 financial statements | $45,000 | $18,000 | $45,000 | $412,000 |

The adjusted comparative financial statements, reflecting the retrospective application of the new accounting principle, follow.

**Newburger Company**
**Statements of Income and Retained Earnings**
**Reflecting Retrospective Application of Change in Accounting Principle**
**Years Ended December 31, 2009 and 2008**

| | 2009 | 2008 as adjusted |
|---|---|---|
| Sales | $ 2,700,000 | $ 2,300,000 |
| Cost of sales | 995,000 | 850,000 |

| | 2009 | 2008 as adjusted |
|---|---|---|
| Gross profit | 1,705,000 | 1,450,000 |
| Advertising expense | 66,000 | 45,000 |
| Other selling, general, and administrative expenses | 423,000 | 385,000 |
| | 489,000 | 430,000 |
| Income from operations | 1,216,000 | 1,020,000 |
| Other income (expense) | 9,000 | 11,000 |
| Income before income taxes | 1,225,000 | 1,031,000 |
| Income taxes | 490,400 | 412,000 |
| Net income | 734,600 | 619,000 |
| Retained earnings, beginning of year, as originally reported | | 13,756,000 |
| Adjustment for retrospective application of new accounting principle (Note X) | | 15,000 |
| Retained earnings, beginning of year, as adjusted | 12,990,000 | 13,771,000 |
| Dividends | 1,600,000 | 1,400,000 |
| Retained earnings, end of year | $12,124,600 | $12,990,000 |

**Newburger Company**
**Balance Sheets**
**Reflecting Retrospective Application of Change in Accounting Principle**
**Years Ended December 31, 2009 and 2008**

| | 2009 | 2008 as adjusted |
|---|---|---|
| **Assets** | | |
| Current assets | | |
| Cash and cash equivalents | $ 2,382,000 | $ 2,200,000 |
| Deferred advertising costs | 16,000 | 45,000 |
| Prepaid expenses | 123,000 | 125,000 |
| Other current assets | 21,000 | 22,000 |
| Total current assets | 2,542,000 | 2,392,000 |
| Property and equipment | 9,800,000 | 10,729,000 |
| Total assets | $12,342,000 | $13,121,000 |
| **Liabilities and stockholders' equity** | | |
| Deferred income taxes | $ 6,000 | $ 18,000 |
| Other current liabilities | 36,000 | 35,000 |
| Total current liabilities | 42,400 | 53,000 |
| Noncurrent liabilities | 162,000 | 65,000 |
| Total liabilities | 204,400 | 118,000 |
| Stockholders' equity | | |
| Common stock | 13,000 | 13,000 |
| Retained earnings | 12,124,600 | 12,990,000 |
| Total stockholders' equity | 12,137,600 | 13,003,000 |
| Total liabilities and stockholders' equity | $12,342,000 | $13,121,000 |

**Newburger Company**
**Statements of Cash Flows**
**Reflecting Retrospective Application of Change in Accounting Principle**
**Years Ended December 31, 2009 and 2008**

| | 2009 | 2008 as adjusted |
|---|---|---|
| **Operating activities** | | |
| Net income | $ 734,600 | $ 619,000 |
| Depreciation | 725,000 | 715,000 |
| Deferred income taxes | (11,600) | 8,000 |
| Gain on sale of property and equipment | (1,200,000) | -- |
| Changes in | | |
| Deferred advertising costs | 29,000 | (20,000) |
| Prepaid expenses | 2,000 | (5,000) |
| Other current assets | 1,000 | (2,000) |
| Other current liabilities | 1,000 | 23,000 |
| Net cash provided by operating activities | $ 281,000 | $1,338,000 |

|  | 2009 | 2008 as adjusted |
|---|---|---|
| ***Investing activities*** | | |
| Property and equipment | | |
|     Acquisition | (1,096,000) | (133,000) |
|     Proceeds from sale | 2,500,000 | -- |
| Net cash provided by (used for) investing activities | 1,404,000 | (133,000) |
| ***Financing activities*** | | |
| Dividends paid to stockholders | (1,600,000) | (1,400,000) |
| Long-term debt | | |
|     Borrowed | 105,000 | -- |
|     Repaid | (8,000) | (5,000) |
| Net cash used for financing activities | (1,503,000) | (1,405,000) |
| Increase (decrease) in cash and cash equivalents | 182,000 | (200,000) |
| Cash and cash equivalents, beginning of year | 2,200,000 | 2,400,000 |
| Cash and cash equivalents, end of year | $2,382,000 | $2,200,000 |

It is important to note that, in presenting the previously issued financial statements for 2008, the caption "as adjusted" is included in the column heading. Prior to the issuance of FAS 154, many preparers used the caption "as restated." FAS 154 explicitly defines a restatement as a revision to previously issued financial statements to correct an error. Therefore, to avoid misleading the financial statement reader, use of the terms restatement or restated are to be limited to prior period adjustments to correct errors as discussed later in this chapter.

***Indirect effects.*** The example above only reflects the direct effects of the change in accounting principle, net of the effect of income taxes. Changing accounting principles sometimes results in indirect effects from legal or contractual obligations of the reporting entity, such as profit sharing or royalty arrangements that contain monetary formulas based on amounts in the financial statements. In the preceding example, if Newburger Company had an incentive compensation plan that required it to contribute 15% of its pretax income to a pool to be distributed to its employees, the adoption of the new accounting policy would potentially require Newburger to provide additional contributions to the pool computed as

|  | *Pretax effect of retroactive application* | *Contractual rate* | *Indirect effect* |
|---|---|---|---|
| Prior to | | | |
| 2008 | $25,000 | 15% | $3,750 |
| 2008 | (20,000) | 15% | (3,000) |
|  | | | $ 750 |

Contracts and agreements are often silent regarding how such a change might affect amounts that were computed (and distributed) in prior years. Management of Newburger Company might have discretion over whether to make the additional contributions. Further, it would probably consider it undesirable to reduce the 2008 incentive compensation pool because of an accounting change of this nature, and it might thus decide for valid business reasons not to reduce the pool under these circumstances.

FAS 154 specifies that irrespective of whether the indirect effects arise from an explicit requirement in the agreement or are discretionary, if incurred they are to be recognized in the period in which the reporting entity makes the accounting change, which is 2009 in the example above.

**Impracticability exception.** All prior periods presented in the financial statements are required to be adjusted for the retroactive application of the newly adopted accounting principle, unless it is impracticable to do so. FASB recognized that there are certain circumstances when there is a change in accounting principle when it will not be feasible to compute (1) the retroactive adjustment to the prior periods affected or (2) the period-specific adjustments relative to periods presented in the financial statements presented.

In order for management to assert that it is impracticable to retrospectively apply the new accounting principle, one or more of the following conditions must be present:

1.   Management has made a reasonable effort to determine the retrospective adjustment and is unable to do so.
2.   If it were to apply the new accounting principle retrospectively, management would be required to make assumptions regarding its intent in a prior period that would not be able to be independently substantiated.
3.   If it were to apply the new accounting principle retrospectively, management would be required to make significant estimates of amounts for which it is impossible to develop objective information that would have been available at the time the original financial statements for the prior period (or periods) were issued to provide evidence of circumstances that existed at that time regarding the amounts to be measured, recognized, and/or disclosed by retrospective application.

***Inability to determine period-specific effects.*** If management is able to determine the adjustment to beginning retained earnings for the cumulative effect of applying the new accounting principle to periods prior to those presented in the financial statements, but is unable to determine the period-specific effects of the change on all of the prior periods presented in the financial statements, FAS 154 requires the following steps to adopt the new accounting principle:

1.   Adjust the carrying amounts of the assets and liabilities for the cumulative effect of applying the new accounting principle at the beginning of the earliest period presented for which it is practicable to make the computation.
2.   Any offsetting adjustment required by applying step 1. is made to beginning retained earnings (or other applicable components of equity or net assets) of that period.

***Inability to determine effects on any prior periods.*** If it is impracticable to determine the cumulative effect of adoption of the new accounting principle on any prior periods, the new principle is applied prospectively as of the earliest date that it is practicable to do so. The most common example of this occurs when management of a reporting entity decides to change its inventory costing assumption from first-in, first-out (FIFO) to last-in, first-out (LIFO), as illustrated in the following example:

**Example of change from FIFO to LIFO**

During 2009 Warady Inc. decided to change the method used for pricing its inventories from FIFO to LIFO. The inventory values are as listed below using both FIFO and LIFO methods. Sales for the year were $15,000,000 and the company's total purchases were $11,000,000. Other expenses were $1,200,000 for the year. The company had 1,000,000 shares of common stock outstanding throughout the year.

*Inventory values*

|  | *FIFO* | *LIFO* | *Difference* |
|---|---|---|---|
| 12/31/08 Base year | $ 2,000,000 | $2,000,000 | $    -- |
| 12/31/09 | 4,000,000 | 1,800,000 | 2,200,000 |
| Variation | $ 2,000,000 | $ ( 200,000) | $ 2,200,000 |

The computations for 2009 would be as follows:

|  | FIFO | LIFO | Difference |
|---|---|---|---|
| Sales | $15,000,000 | $15,000,000 | $_____-- |
| Cost of goods sold |  |  |  |
|     Beginning inventory | 2,000,000 | 2,000,000 | -- |
|     Purchases | 11,000,000 | 11,000,000 | -- |
|     Goods available for sale | 13,000,000 | 13,000,000 | -- |
|     Ending inventory | 4,000,000 | 1,800,000 | 2,200,000 |
|  | 9,000,000 | 11,200,000 | (2,200,000) |
| Gross profit | 6,000,000 | 3,800,000 | 2,200,000 |
| Other expenses | 1,200,000 | 1,200,000 | -- |
| Net income | $ 4,800,000 | $ 2,600,000 | $2,200,000 |

The following is an example of the required disclosure in this circumstance:

**Note A:  Change in Method of Accounting for Inventories**

During 2009, management changed the company's method of accounting for all of its inventories from first-in, first-out (FIFO) to last-in, first-out (LIFO). The change was made because management believes that the LIFO method provides a better matching of costs and revenues.  In addition, with the adoption of LIFO, the company's inventory pricing method is consistent with the method predominant in the industry.  The change and its effect on net income ($000 omitted except for per share amounts) and earnings per share for 2009 are as follows:

|  | Net income | Earnings per share |
|---|---|---|
| Net income before the change | $4,800 | $4.80 |
| Reduction of net income due to the change | 2,200 | 2.20 |
| Net income as adjusted | $2,600 | $2.60 |

Management has not retrospectively applied this change to prior years' financial statements because beginning inventory on January 1, 2009, using LIFO is the same as the amount reported on a FIFO basis at December 31, 2008.  As a result of this change, the current period's financial statements are not comparable with those of any prior periods. The FIFO cost of inventories exceeds the carrying amount valued using LIFO by $2,200,000 at December 31, 2009.

**Changing or eliminating differences in fiscal year-end.**  The EITF reached a consensus in Issue 06-9, that the following scenarios constitute voluntary changes in accounting principle that are subject to the accounting and disclosure rules in FAS 154:

1.   A consolidated entity changes its fiscal year-end to alter or eliminate a difference between its year-end and the fiscal year-end of the entity that consolidates it in its financial statements (the parent or FIN 46 primary beneficiary).
2.   An investee that is accounted for by an investor using the equity method changes its fiscal year-end to alter or eliminate a difference between its year-end and the fiscal year-end of the equity method investor.

The EITF, in its discussion of this topic, emphasizes the fact that, under FAS 154, retrospective application is not required if it is impracticable to do so.

**Disclosure of Prospective Changes in GAAP**

**Disclosing the impact of newly established GAAP that has not yet become effective.**  The accounting principles used in the reporting entity's financial statements may comply with GAAP as of the reporting date but those principles may become unacceptable at a specified future date due to the issuance of a new accounting standard that is not yet effective.  If the new GAAP, when adopted, is expected to materially affect the future financial statements, it is necessary to inform the users of the current financial statements about the future change.  The objective of such a disclosure is to ensure that the financial statements are not misleading and that the users are provided adequate information to assess the significance of adopting the new GAAP on the reporting entity's future financial statements.

Independent auditors are required to evaluate the adequacy of disclosure of the future change in accounting principle (AU §9410). In some cases, the effect of the future change will be so pervasive as to necessitate the presentation of pro forma financial data to supplement the historical financial statements. The pro forma data would present the effects of the future adoption as if it had occurred at the balance sheet date. The pro forma data may be presented in a column next to the historical data, in the notes to the financial statements, or separately accompanying the basic historical financial statements. Disclosure may also be needed of other future effects that may be triggered by the adoption of the new GAAP, such as adverse effects on the reporting entity's compliance with its debt covenants.

The best source of guidance in determining the form and content of these disclosures is SEC Staff Accounting Bulletin 74 (SAB 74, which was subsequently included in the SEC codification of SABs as Topic 11M). While this guidance is applicable to public companies, it also can be interpreted to apply to nonpublic companies under category D of the GAAP hierarchy, as "practices that are widely recognized and prevalent." Under this requirement management is to disclose

1. A brief description of the new standard.
2. The date the reporting entity is required to adopt the new standard.
3. If the new standard permits early adoption and the reporting entity plans to do so, the date that the planned adoption will occur.
4. The method of adoption that management expects to use. If this determination has not yet been made, then a description of the alternative methods of adoption that are permitted by the new standard.
5. The impact that the new standard will have on reported financial position and results of operations. If management has quantified the impact, then it is to disclose the estimated amount. If management has not yet determined the impact or if the impact is not expected to be material, this is to be disclosed.

The SEC staff also encourages the following additional disclosures:

1. The potential impact of adoption on such matters as loan covenant compliance, planned or intended changes in business practices, changes in availability of or cost of capital, etc.
2. Newly issued standards that are not expected to materially affect the reporting entity should nevertheless be disclosed with an accompanying statement that adoption is not expected to have a material effect on the reporting entity.
3. When the newly issued standard only affects disclosure and the future disclosures are expected to be significantly different from the current disclosures, it is desirable to provide the reader with details.

**Proposed GAAP.** There is no requirement under GAAP or under SEC rules to disclose the potential effects of standards that have been proposed but not yet issued. If management wishes to voluntarily disclose information that it believes will provide the financial statement users with useful, meaningful information, the SEC provides guidance (§501.11 of the Codification of Financial Reporting Policies) on how to present this information, either in narrative form or as pro forma information, in a manner that "is reasonable, balanced and not misleading." In its guidance, the SEC notes that it may be reasonable to cover only those proposals where, based on the standard setter's published agenda, adoption appears imminent. When management chooses to make these disclosures, the disclosures should

1. Provide a brief description of the proposed standard.
2. Explain the purpose of the disclosures, the basis of presentation, and any significant assumptions made in preparing them.
3. Discuss, in a balanced manner,

    a. The positive and negative effects of applying the proposed standard,
    b. The effects the proposed standard would have had on prior results of operations,
    c. The potential effects of the proposed standard on future periods,
    d. The effects that can be quantified, and
    e. The effects, if any, that cannot be quantified.

4. Address the entire proposed standard, not just certain aspects of it.
5. Limit any disclosures that quantify the effects of the proposed standard to covering only the most recent fiscal year.
6. Warn the readers that the final standard, when and if issued, could differ from the proposal that was used as a basis for these disclosures and that, as a result, the actual application of any final standard could result in effects different than those disclosed.
7. If necessary for a fair and balanced presentation, provide information regarding more than one proposed standard. There is a risk to the reporting entity that the disclosure may appear to be incomplete or misleading if it discusses the effects of one significant proposed standard but not another.

### Reclassifications

Occasionally, a company will choose to change the way it applies an accounting principle that results in a change in the way that a particular financial statement caption is displayed or in the individual general ledger accounts that comprise a caption. These reclassifications may occur for a variety of reasons that include

1. In management's judgment, the revised methodology more accurately reflects the economics of a type or class of transaction.
2. An amount that was immaterial in previous periods and combined with another number has become material and warrants presentation as a separately captioned line item.
3. Due to changes in the business or the manner in which the financial statements are used to make decisions, management deems a different form of presentation to be more useful or informative.

In order to maintain comparability of financial statements when such changes are made, the financial statements of all periods presented must be reclassified to conform to the new presentation.

Such reclassifications, which usually affect only the statement of income, do not affect reported net income or retained earnings for any period since they result in simply recasting amounts that were previously reported. Normally a reclassification will result in an increase in one or more reported numbers with a corresponding decrease in one or more other numbers. In addition, these changes reflect changes in the application of accounting principles either for which there are multiple alternative treatments, or for which GAAP is silent and thus management has discretion in presentation.

Reclassifications are not explicitly dealt with in GAAP but nevertheless do commonly occur in practice. The following examples are adapted from actual notes that appeared in the summary of significant accounting policies of publicly held companies:

**Example 1**

Effective January 1, 2009, the company removed the impact of intellectual property income, gains and losses on sales and other-than-temporary declines in market value of certain investments, realized gains and losses on certain real estate activity, and foreign currency transaction gains and losses from the caption, "Selling, General and Administrative Expenses" in the Consolidated Statement of Income. Custom development income was also removed from the "Research, Development, and Engineering" caption on the Consolidated Statement of Income. Intellectual property and custom development income are now presented in a separate caption in the Consolidated Statement of Income. The other items listed above are now included as part of "Other Income and Expense." Results of prior periods have been reclassified to conform to the current year presentation.

**Example 2**

Effective January 1, 2009, management has elected to reclassify certain expenses in its consolidated statements of income. Costs of the order entry function and certain accounting and information technology services have been reclassified from cost of sales to selling, general, and administrative expense. Costs related to order fulfillment have been reclassified from selling, general, and administrative expense to cost of sales. These reclassifications resulted in a decrease to cost of sales and an increase to selling, general, and administrative expense of $31.8 million, and $36.2 million for the years ended December 31, 2008 and 2007, respectively.

## Change in Accounting Estimate

The preparation of financial statements requires frequent use of estimates for such items as asset service lives, salvage values, lease residuals, asset impairments, collectibility of accounts receivable, warranty costs, pension costs, etc. Future conditions and events that affect these estimates cannot be estimated with certainty. Therefore, changes in estimates will be inevitable as new information and more experience is obtained. FAS 154 requires that changes in estimates be recognized currently and prospectively, as did APB 20, the predecessor standard. The effect of the change in accounting estimate is accounted for in "(a) the period of change if the change affects that period only or (b) the period of change and future periods if the change affects both." The reporting entity is precluded from retrospective application, restatement of prior periods, or presentation of pro forma amounts as a result of a change in accounting estimate.

For example, on January 1, 2009, a machine purchased for $10,000 was originally estimated to have a ten-year useful life and a salvage value of $1,000. On January 1, 2014 (five years later), the asset is expected to last another ten years and have a salvage value of $800. As a result, both the current period (the year ending December 31, 2009) and subsequent periods are affected by the change. Annual depreciation expense over the estimated remaining useful life is computed as follows:

| | |
|---|---:|
| Original cost | $10,000 |
| Less estimated salvage (residual) value | (1,000) |
| Depreciable amount | 9,000 |
| Accumulated depreciation, based original assumptions (10-year life) | |
| 2009 | 900 |
| 2010 | 900 |
| 2011 | 900 |
| 2012 | 900 |
| 2013 | 900 |
| | 4,500 |

| | |
|---|---|
| Carrying value at 1/1/2014 | 5,500 |
| Revised estimate of salvage value | (800) |
| Depreciable amount | 4,700 |
| Remaining useful life at 1/1/2014 | 10 years |
| | $ 470 depreciation per year |

Effect on 2014 net income        $470 – $900 = $430 increase

## Note A:  Change in Accounting Estimate.

During 2014, management assessed its estimates of the useful lives and residual values of the Company's machinery and equipment. Management revised its original estimates and currently estimates that its production equipment acquired in 2009 and originally estimated to have a 10-year useful life and a residual value of $1,000 will have a 15-year useful life and a residual value of $800. The effects of reflecting this change in accounting estimate on the 2014 financial statements are as follows:

Increase in

| | |
|---|---|
| Income from continuing operations and net income | $430.00 |
| Earnings per share (for public companies)* | $ 0.02 |

 * *Assuming 25,000 shares were outstanding for all of 2014*

As another example, the industry in which ABC Company operates suffers a significant downturn, resulting in a decline in the financial condition of its customers, and a noticeable worsening of the days required to collect its accounts receivable. ABC had formerly provided an amount equal to 2% of its credit sales as an increment to the bad debt allowance, resulting in a current balance in the allowance of $105,000. However, the new economic conditions mandate an immediate change to a 4% allowance. Accordingly, ABC provides an additional $105,000 in the current period to increase the previously recorded allowance to meet the new 4% estimate, and also begins providing 4% in the bad debt allowance on all new credit sales. Both of these adjustments are reflected in current period expense, even though the increased allowance on existing receivables pertains to sales made (in part) in a prior reporting period, because the change in estimate was made in the current period based on new circumstances that arose in that period—specifically, the declining credit standing of its customers.

Accounting for long-term construction contracts under the percentage-of-completion method necessarily involves ongoing revisions to estimates of total contract revenue, total contract cost, and extent of progress toward project completion. These revisions represent changes in accounting estimate and, in accordance with SOP 81-1, *Accounting for Performance of Construction-Type and Certain Production-Type Contracts*, the change in estimate is accounted for using the cumulative catch-up method. This is applied by

1.  Computing the percentage of completion, earned revenues, cost of earned revenues, and gross profit on a contract-to-date basis at the balance sheet date using the reporting entity's consistently applied accounting policy for the contract and reflecting the revised estimates.
2.  Reflecting in the current period's earned revenue and cost of earned revenue the difference between the newly computed contract-to-date results computed in 1. and those amounts recognized in previous periods.

This results in the effect of the change in accounting estimate being reflected in the current period statement of income, and prospectively accounting for the contract using the revised assumptions.

An impairment of a long-lived asset, as described by FAS 144, is not a change in accounting estimate. Rather, it is an event that is to be treated as an operating expense of the period in which it is recognized, in effect as additional depreciation. (See further discussion in Chapter 11.)

## Change in Accounting Estimate Effected by a Change in Accounting Principle

In order to change certain accounting estimates, management must adopt a new accounting principle or change the method it uses to apply an accounting principle. In contemplating such a change, management would not be able to separately determine the effects of changing the accounting principle from the effects of changing its estimate. The change in estimate is accomplished by changing the method.

Under FAS 154, a change in accounting estimate that is effected by a change in accounting principle is to be accounted for in the same manner as a change in accounting estimate, that is, prospectively in the current and future periods affected. However, because management is changing the company's accounting principle or method of applying it, the new accounting principle, as previously discussed, must be preferable to the accounting principle being superseded.

Management may decide, for example, to change its depreciation method for certain types of assets from straight-line to an accelerated method such as double-declining balance to recognize the fact that those assets are more productive in their earlier years of service because they require less downtime and do not require repairs as frequently. Such a change is permitted by FAS 154 only if management justifies it based on the fact that using the new method is preferable to the old one, in this case because it more accurately matches the costs of production to periods in which the units are produced.

A distinction is made in FAS 154, however, for entities that elect to apply a depreciation method that results in accelerated depreciation until the point during the useful life of the depreciable asset when it is useful to change to straight-line depreciation in order to fully depreciate the asset over the remaining term. At this point, the remaining carrying value (net book value) is depreciated using the straight-line method over its remaining useful life. FAS 154 (as did the predecessor standard, APB 20) provides that, if this method is consistently followed by the reporting entity, the changeover to straight-line depreciation is not considered to be an accounting change.

## Change in Reporting Entity

An accounting change resulting in financial statements that are, in effect, of a different reporting entity than previously reported on, is retrospectively applied to the financial statements of all prior periods presented in order to show financial information for the new reporting entity for all periods. The change is also retrospectively applied to previously issued interim financial information.

The following qualify as changes in reporting entity:

1. Consolidated or combined financial statements in place of individual entities' statements
2. A change in the members of the group of subsidiaries that comprise the consolidated financial statements
3. A change in the companies included in combined financial statements

Specifically *excluded* from qualifying as a change in reporting entity are

1. A business combination accounted for by the purchase method and
2. Consolidation of a variable interest entity under FIN 46(R).

## Error Corrections

Errors are sometimes discovered after financial statements have been issued. Errors result from mathematical mistakes, mistakes in the application of GAAP, or the oversight or misuse of facts known or available to the accountant at the time the financial statements were prepared. Errors can occur in recognition, measurement, presentation, or disclosure. A change from an unacceptable (or incorrect) accounting principle to a correct principle is also considered a correction of an error, and thus not as a change in accounting principle. Such a change should not be confused with the preferability determination discussed earlier that involves two or more acceptable principles. An error correction pertains to the recognition that a previously used method was not an acceptable method at the time it was employed.

The essential distinction between a change in estimate and the correction of an error depends upon the availability of information. An estimate requires revision because by its nature it is based upon incomplete information. Later data will either confirm or contradict the estimate and any contradiction will require revision of the estimate. An error results from the misuse of existing information available at the time and is discovered at a later date. However, this discovery is not as a result of additional information or subsequent developments.

FAS 154 specifies that, when correcting an error in prior period financial statements, the term "restatement" is to be used. That term is exclusively reserved for this purpose so as to effectively communicate to users of the financial statements the reason for a particular change in previously issued financial statements.

Restatement consists of the following steps:

Step 1 -   Adjust the carrying amounts of assets and liabilities at the beginning of the first period presented in the financial statements for the cumulative effect of correcting the error on periods prior to those presented in the financial statements.

Step 2 -   Offset the effect of the adjustment in Step 1 (if any) by adjusting the opening balance of retained earnings (or other components of equity or net assets, as applicable to the reporting entity) for that period.

Step 3 -   Adjust the financial statements of each individual prior period presented for the effects of correcting the error on that specific period (referred to as the period-specific effects of the error).

**Example of prior period adjustment**

Assume that Truesdell Company had overstated its depreciation expense by $50,000 in 2007 and $40,000 in 2008, both due to mathematical mistakes. The errors affected both the financial statements and the income tax returns in 2007 and 2008 and are discovered in 2009.

Truesdell's balance sheets and statements of income and retained earnings as of and for the year ended December 31, 2008, prior to the restatement were as follows:

**Truesdell Company**
**Statement of Income and Retained Earnings**
**Prior to Restatement**
**Year Ended December 31, 2008**

|                                               | *2008*      |
|-----------------------------------------------|-------------|
| Sales                                         | $2,000,000  |
| Cost of sales                                 |             |
| Depreciation                                  | 750,000     |
| Other                                         | 390,000     |
|                                               | 1,140,000   |
| Gross profit                                  | 860,000     |
| Selling, general, and administrative expenses | 450,000     |
| Income from operations                        | 410,000     |
| Other income (expense)                        | 10,000      |
| Income before income taxes                    | 420,000     |
| Income taxes                                  | 168,000     |
| Net income                                    | 252,000     |
| Retained earnings, beginning of year          | 6,463,000   |
| Dividends                                     | (1,200,000) |
| Retained earnings, end of year                | $5,515,000  |

**Truesdell Company**
**Balance Sheet**
**Prior to Restatement**
**December 31, 2008**

|  | *2008* |
|---|---|
| *Assets* | |
| Current assets | $2,540,000 |
| Property and equipment | |
|    Cost | 3,500,000 |
|    Accumulated depreciation and amortization | (430,000) |
|  | 3,070,000 |
| Total assets | $5,610,000 |
| *Liabilities and stockholders' equity* | |
| Income taxes payable | $     -- |
| Other current liabilities | 12,000 |
| Total current liabilities | 12,000 |
| Noncurrent liabilities | 70,000 |
| Total liabilities | 82,000 |
| Stockholders' equity | |
|    Common stock | 13,000 |
|    Retained earnings | 5,515,000 |
| Total stockholders' equity | 5,528,000 |
| Total liabilities and stockholders' equity | $5,610,000 |

The following steps are followed to restate Truesdell's prior period financial statements:

Step 1 -   Adjust the carrying amounts of assets and liabilities at the beginning of the first period presented in the financial statements for the cumulative effect of correcting the error on periods prior to those presented in the financial statements.

        The first period presented in the financial statements is 2008. At the beginning of that year, $50,000 of the mistakes had been made and reflected on both the income tax return and financial statements. Assuming a flat 40% income tax rate and ignoring the effects of penalties and interest that would be assessed on the amended income tax returns, the following adjustment would be made to assets and liabilities at January 1, 2008:

| | |
|---|---|
| Decrease in accumulated depreciation | $50,000 |
| Increase in income taxes payable | (20,000) |
| | $30,000 |

Step 2 -   Offset the effect of the adjustment in Step 1 by adjusting the opening balance of retained earnings (or other components of equity or net assets, as applicable to the reporting entity) for that period.

        Retained earnings at the beginning of 2008 will increase by $30,000 as the offsetting entry resulting from Step 1.

Step 3 -   Adjust the financial statements of each individual prior period presented for the effects of correcting the error on that specific period (referred to as the period-specific effects of the error).

        The 2008 prior period financial statements will be corrected for the period-specific effects of the restatement as follows:

| | |
|---|---|
| Decrease in depreciation expense and accumulated depreciation | $40,000 |
| Increase in income tax expense and income taxes payable | (16,000) |
| Increase 2008 net income | $24,000 |

The restated financial statements are presented below.

**Truesdell Company**
**Statements of Income and Retained Earnings**
**As Restated**
**Years Ended December 31, 2009 and 2008**

|  | 2009 | 2008 restated |
|---|---|---|
| Sales | $2,100,000 | $2,000,000 |
| Cost of sales |  |  |
| Depreciation | 740,000 | 710,000 |
| Other | 410,000 | 390,000 |
|  | 1,150,000 | 1,100,000 |
| Gross profit | 950,000 | 900,000 |
| Selling, general, and administrative expenses | 460,000 | 450,000 |
| Income from operations | 490,000 | 450,000 |
| Other income (expense) | (5,000) | 10,000 |
| Income before income taxes | 485,000 | 460,000 |
| Income taxes | 200,000 | 184,000 |
| Net income | 285,000 | 276,000 |
| Retained earnings, beginning of year, as originally reported | 5,569,000 | 6,463,000 |
| Restatement to reflect correction of depreciation (Note X) | -- | 30,000 |
| Retained earnings, beginning of year, as restated | 5,569,000 | 6,493,000 |
| Dividends | (800,000) | (1,200,000) |
| Retained earnings, end of year | $5,054,000 | $5,569,000 |

**Truesdell Company**
**Balance Sheet**
**As Restated**
**December 31, 2009 and 2008**

|  | 2009 | 2008 restated |
|---|---|---|
| *Assets* |  |  |
| Current assets | $2,840,000 | $2,540,000 |
| Property and equipment |  |  |
| Cost | 3,750,000 | 3,500,000 |
| Accumulated depreciation and amortization | (1,050,000) | (340,000) |
|  | 2,700,000 | 3,160,000 |
| Total assets | $5,540,000 | $5,700,000 |
| *Liabilities and stockholders' equity* |  |  |
| Income taxes payable | $50,000 | $ 36,000 |
| Other current liabilities | 110,000 | 12,000 |
| Total current liabilities | 160,000 | 48,000 |
| Noncurrent liabilities | 313,000 | 70,000 |
| Total liabilities | 473,000 | 118,000 |
| Stockholders' equity |  |  |
| Common stock | 13,000 | 13,000 |
| Retained earnings | 5,054,000 | 5,569,000 |
| Total stockholders' equity | 5,067,000 | 5,582,000 |
| Total liabilities and stockholders' equity | $5,540,000 | $5,700,000 |

When restating previously issued financial statements, management is to disclose

1. The fact that the financial statements have been restated
2. The nature of the error
3. The effect of the restatement on each line item in the financial statements
4. The cumulative effect of the restatement on retained earnings (or other applicable components of equity or net assets)

    a.   At the beginning of the earliest period presented in comparative financial statements or

    b.   At the beginning of the period in single-period financial statements

  5.   The effect on net income, both gross and net of income taxes

    a.   For each prior period presented in comparative financial statements or

    b.   For the period immediately preceding the period presented in single-period financial statements

  6.   For public companies (or others electing to report earnings per share data), the effect of the restatement on affected per-share amounts for each prior period presented.

These disclosures need not be repeated in subsequent periods.

The correction of an error in the financial statements of a prior period discovered subsequent to their issuance is reported as a prior period adjustment in the financial statements of the subsequent period. In some cases, however, this situation necessitates the recall or withdrawal of the previously issued financial statements and their revision and reissuance.

## Evaluating Uncorrected Misstatements

Misstatements, particularly if detected after the financial statements have been produced and distributed, may under certain circumstances be left uncorrected. This decision is directly impacted by judgments about materiality, an important concept discussed in Chapter 1. The financial statement preparer is expected to exercise professional judgment in determining the level of materiality to apply in order to cost-effectively prepare full, complete, and accurate financial statements in a timely manner. However, there have been instances where the materiality concept has been used to rationalize the noncorrection of errors that should have been dealt with, and indeed even to excuse errors known when first committed. The fact that the concept of materiality has sometimes been abused led to the promulgation of further guidance relative to error corrections.

Although independent auditors are charged with obtaining sufficient evidence to enable them to provide the financial statement user with reasonable assurance that management's financial statements are free of material misstatement, the financial statements are primarily the responsibility of the preparers. Certain auditing literature is therefore germane to the preparers' consideration of matters such as error corrections and application of materiality guidelines. These matters are further explored in the following paragraphs.

**Types of misstatements.** Preparers of financial statements obviously will need to have control procedures to reduce the risk of accounting errors being committed and not detected. From the auditors' perspective, it is required that the examination be conducted in a manner that will provide reasonable assurance of detecting material misstatements, including those resulting from errors. Auditors will evaluate both known misstatements and likely misstatements (i.e., those projected to exist based on sample data gathered during the audit), as defined in SAS 107 of the auditing literature. Known misstatements arise from

  1.   Incorrect selection or application of accounting principles
  2.   Errors in gathering, processing, summarizing, interpreting, or overlooking relevant data
  3.   An intent to mislead the financial statement user to influence their decisions
  4.   To conceal theft

Likely misstatements arise from

1. Differences in judgment between management and the auditor regarding accounting estimates where the amount presented in the financial statements is outside the range of what the auditor believes is reasonable
2. Amounts that the auditor has projected (the statistical term "extrapolated" is also used in this context) based on the results of performing statistical or nonstatistical sampling procedures on a population

Under auditing standards, auditors are responsible for accumulating all known and likely misstatements except those that, in the auditors' judgment, are trivial or inconsequential. In forming judgments regarding the triviality of misstatements, auditors consider whether the misstatement individually or when aggregated with other similar amounts would be considered immaterial to the financial statements. Despite many efforts to develop a firm definition of materiality that have been made by academicians and the profession over the decades, a universally agreed-upon definition of materiality remains elusive, and thus a matter for professional judgment (although the legal definition, of being likely to affect the conclusion reached by a decision maker, remains useful).

Auditors are expected to communicate known and likely misstatements to management in a timely manner, distinguishing between these categories. Timely communication is important in order to provide management the opportunity to evaluate whether they concur that the items are misstatements and to determine whether to adjust the financial statements or request that the auditor obtain additional evidence.

Auditors are obligated by professional standards to request that management record adjustments to correct all known misstatements, other than those deemed to be trivial. Because some of these may be based on audit sampling results, some management may either resist because there is inherent distrust of projections, or because it will not be clear how corrections can be recorded when the error items cannot be specifically identified.

Likely misstatements are treated as follows:

1. If the likely misstatement results from a projection to the population from examination of a sample, auditors will request management to examine the relevant population from which the sample was drawn. This might be a class of transactions, an account balance, or the information required to be presented in a disclosure. The purpose of the requested examination is for management to identify and correct misstatements in the remaining population, (i.e., the items [units] in the population that the auditors did not select for detailed testing). For example, the auditor may identify a misstatement caused by an error in inventory pricing relative to raw materials. Management would be requested, in this case, to reexamine the entire raw materials inventory to determine whether it includes other misstatements and to correct any other misstatements found as a result of the reexamination.
2. If the likely misstatement results from differences in estimates—such as the magnitude of the amount needed for the allowance for uncollectible accounts receivable—the auditors should request that management review the methods and assumptions used to develop their estimate.

Ultimately, management is responsible for deciding how to respond to auditors' requests and whether it wishes to correct some or all of the misstatements brought to its attention by the auditors. Both the auditors and management, in assessing the impact of uncorrected misstatements, are required to assess materiality both quantitatively and qualitatively, from the standpoint of whether a financial statement user would be misled if a misstatement were not corrected or if, in the case of informative disclosure errors, full disclosure was not made. Qualitative considerations include (but are not limited to) whether the misstatement

1. Arose from estimates or from items capable of precise measurement and, if the misstatement arose from an estimate, the degree of precision inherent in the estimation process
2. Masks a change in earnings or other trends
3. Hides a failure to meet analysts' consensus expectations for the reporting entity
4. Changes a loss to income or vice versa
5. Concerns a segment or other portion of the reporting entity's business that has been identified as playing a significant role in operations or profitability
6. Affects compliance with loan covenants or other contractual commitments
7. Increases management's compensation by affecting a performance measure used as a basis for computing it
8. Involves concealment of an unlawful transaction

**Misstatements from prior years.** Management, with the concurrence of the reporting entity's auditors, may have decided to not correct misstatements that occurred in one or more prior years because, in their judgment at the time, the financial statements were not materially misstated. Two methods of making that materiality assessment—sometimes referred to as the "rollover" and the "iron curtain" methods—have been widely used in practice. These are described and illustrated in the following paragraphs.

The *rollover method* quantifies a misstatement as its originating or reversing effect on the *current period's* statement of income, irrespective of the potential effect on the balance sheet of one or more prior periods' accumulated uncorrected misstatements.

The *iron curtain method,* on the other hand, quantifies a misstatement based on the *accumulated uncorrected amount* included in the current, end-of-period balance sheet, irrespective of the year (or years) in which the misstatement originated.

Each of these methods, when considered separately, has strengths and weaknesses, as follows:

| *Method* | *Focuses on* | *Strength* | *Weakness* |
|---|---|---|---|
| Rollover | Current period income statement | Focuses on whether the income statement of the current period is materially misstated assuming that the balance sheet is not materially misstated | Material misstatement of the balance sheet can accumulate over multiple periods |
| Iron curtain | End of period balance sheet | Focuses on ensuring that the balance sheet is not materially misstated irrespective of the year or years in which a misstatement originated | Does not consider whether the effect of correcting a balance sheet misstatement that arose in one or more periods is material to the current period income statement |

**Guidance for SEC registrants.** The SEC staff issued SAB 108, *Considering the Effects of Prior Year Misstatements in Current Year Financial Statements,* in order to address how registrants (i.e., publicly held corporation) are to evaluate misstatements. SAB 108 prescribes that if a misstatement is material to *either* the income statement or balance sheet, it is to be corrected in a manner set forth in the bulletin and illustrated in the example and diagram below.

### Example

Lenny Payne, the CFO of Flamingo Industries, is preparing the company's 2009 financial statements. The company has consistently overstated its accrued liabilities by following a policy of accruing the entire audit fee it will pay its independent auditors for auditing the financial statements for the reporting year, even though approximately 80% of the work is performed in, and is thus an expense of, the following year.

Due to regular increases in audit fees, the overstatement of liabilities at 12/31/2009 has accumulated as follows:

| Year ended 12/31 | Amount of misstatement originating during year | End-of-year accumulated misstatement |
|---|---|---|
| 2005 | $15 | $15 |
| 2006 | 5 | 20 |
| 2007 | 5 | 25 |
| 2008 | 5 | 30 |
| 2009 | 10 | 40 |

Lenny has consistently used the rollover approach to assess materiality and, in all previous years, had judged the amount of the misstatement that originated during that year to be immaterial. The guidance in SAB 108 is illustrated in the following decision diagram:

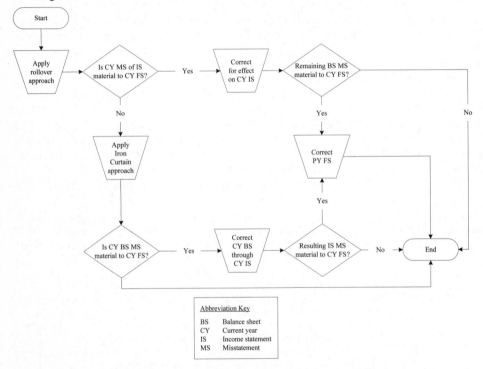

Following the decision tree, Lenny analyzes the misstatement as follows:

1. Applying the *rollover* approach, as he had done consistently in the past, Lenny computes the misstatement as the $10 that originated in 2009. In his judgment, this amount is immaterial to the 2009 income statement.

2. Applying the *iron curtain* approach, Lenny evaluates whether the accumulated misstatement of $40 materially misstates the balance sheet at 12/31/2009. Lenny believes that, considering both quantitative and qualitative factors, the misstatement has grown to the point where it does result in a materially misstated balance sheet.

According to SAB 108 and as shown on the diagram, Lenny would record an adjustment to correct the balance sheet as follows:

|  | *Debit* | *Credit* |
| --- | --- | --- |
| Accrued professional fees | 40,000 |  |
| Professional fees (general and administrative expenses) |  | 40,000 |

*To correct balance sheet by reversing misstated accrual for audit fees not yet incurred.*

Upon review of the effect of the correcting entry, Lenny believes that recording the entry will result in a material misstatement to the 2009 income statement. Consequently, to avoid this result, the prior years' financial statements of Flamingo Industries would, under normal circumstances, be required to be restated as previously discussed in the section of this chapter covering error corrections. This would be the case even if the adjustment to the prior year financial statements was, and continues to be, immaterial to those financial statements. The SEC would not, however, require Flamingo Industries to amend previously filed reports; instead, registrants are permitted to make the correction in the next filing submitted to the SEC that includes the prior year financial statements.

In addition, the SEC provided transition relief for certain reporting entities initially adopting SAB 108. The SEC staff indicated in SAB 108 that in the following circumstances the FAS 154 requirement for prior period restatement would be waived:

1. The reporting entity's initial registration statement was effective on or before November 15, 2006, and
2. Management had, in the past, properly applied its pervious method of evaluating misstatements (either iron curtain or rollover), including consideration of all relevant qualitative factors (which the SEC set forth in SAB 99, *Materiality*)

Registrants that meet these criteria are permitted to reflect the results of initial application of SAB 108 as a cumulative effect adjustment to retained earnings as of the beginning of the fiscal year. Disclosures are required of

1. The nature and amount of each individual error correction included in the cumulative effect adjustment,
2. When and how each error arose, and
3. The fact that the errors had been previously considered to be immaterial.

The SEC encouraged early adoption of this guidance in any report for an interim period ending in the first fiscal year ending after November 15, 2006, that is filed after September 13, 2006, the publication date of SAB 108. If the cumulative effect adjustment occurs in an interim period other than the first interim period, the SEC waived the requirement that previously filed interim reports for that fiscal year be amended. Instead, comparative information presented for interim periods of the first year subsequent to initial application are to be adjusted to reflect the cumulative effect adjustment as of the beginning of the fiscal year of initial application. The adjusted results are also required to be included in the disclosures of selected quarterly information that are required by Regulation S-K, Item 302.

Entities that do not meet the criteria to use the cumulative effect adjustment are required to follow the provisions of FAS 154 that require restatement of all prior periods presented in the filing.

**Guidance for private entities.** FASB had proposed the issuance of a proposed FSP FAS 154-a, *Considering the Effects of Prior-Year Misstatements When Quantifying Misstatements in Current-Year Financial Statements,* in early 2007. If it had been issued as proposed, the FSP would have, in essence, adopted SAB 108 for all nongovernmental reporting entities that are not subject to SAB 108, including not-for-profit organizations. It would have, in common with SAB 108, permitted a onetime cumulative effect adjustment to retained earnings upon initial application, if management had previously evaluated misstatements for materiality using both quantitative and relevant qualitative factors using either the rollover method or the iron curtain method (but not both).

FASB subsequently decided to not issue this FSP, and removed the project from its agenda. Notwithstanding this development, readers are reminded that SABs offer useful guidance even for nonregistrants and their auditors. In the authors' opinion, these bulletins would be among the nonauthoritative literature to be considered when deliberating application of GAAP in the absence of authoritative guidance found in higher levels of the formal GAAP hierarchy (discussed in Chapter 1).

### Interim Reporting Considerations

If a change in accounting principle is made in an interim period, the change is made using the same methodology for retrospective application discussed and illustrated earlier in this chapter. Management is precluded from using the impracticability exception to avoid retrospective application to prechange interim periods of the same fiscal year in which the change is made. Thus, if it is impracticable to apply the change to those prechange interim periods, the change can only be made as of the beginning of the following fiscal year. FASB believes this situation will rarely occur in practice.

APB 28 requires that interim financial reports disclose any changes in accounting principles or the methods of applying them from those that were employed in

1. The prior fiscal year;
2. The comparable interim period of the prior fiscal year; and
3. The preceding interim periods of the current fiscal year.

The disclosures required by FAS 154 for changes in accounting principle are to be made, in full, in the financial statements of the interim period in which the change is made.

**Public companies.** When a public company adopts a new standard in an interim period, the APB 28 disclosures cited above are to be supplemented, as applicable, with all disclosures required by the newly adopted standard to be included in annual financial statements. If the change is made in a period other than the first quarter, prior filings are not required to be amended; however, adjustment of each prior quarter's results is to be included in the filing for the quarter in which the new principle is being adopted. If the newly adopted standard requires retrospective application to all prior periods, the prior interim quarters are also to be presented on an adjusted basis.

In addition, a special disclosure rule applies to a public company that

1. Changes accounting principles in the fourth quarter of a fiscal year;
2. Regularly reports interim financial information; and
3. Does not separately disclose in its annual report (or in a separate report) the minimum summarized information required by APB 28 for the fourth quarter of the fiscal year.

When all three of these conditions are present, management is required to disclose in a note to the annual financial statements the effects of the change on interim period results.

## Summary of Accounting Changes and Error Corrections

| Type and description of change or correction | *Treatment in financial statements, historical summaries, financial highlights, and other similar presentations of businesses and not-for-profit organizations* | | |
|---|---|---|---|
| | *Retrospective application to all periods presented* [1] | *Affects period of change and, if applicable, future periods* | *Restatement of all prior period financial statements presented* |
| **Accounting Changes** | | | |
|    Change in accounting principle | ✓ | | |
|       *New principle required to be preferable* | | | |
|    Change in accounting estimate | | ✓ | |
|    Change in accounting estimate effected by a change in accounting principle | | ✓ | |
|       *New principle required to be preferable* | | | |
|    Change in reporting entity [2] | ✓ | | |
| **Restatements** [3] | | | |
|    Correction of errors in previously issued financial statements | | | ✓ |

---

[1] *FAS 154 provides an exception to the requirement for retroactive restatement when it is impracticable to make the restatement. This exception is only permitted to be used under specified conditions.*

[2] *This is generally limited to (a) presentation of consolidated or combined financial statements instead of financial statements of individual entities, (b) a change in the specific subsidiaries making up a group of entities for which consolidated financial statements are presented, and (c) changing the entities included in combined financial statements.* **Neither a business combination under FAS 141(R) nor consolidation of a variable interest entity under FIN 46(R) is considered a change in reporting entity.**

[3] *The word "restatement" is only to be used to describe and/or present corrections of prior period errors.*

# 6 FAIR VALUE

## PERSPECTIVE AND ISSUES

The communities of financial statement preparers, users, auditors, standard setters, and regulators have engaged in a long-standing debate regarding the relevance, transparency, and decision-usefulness of financial statements prepared under the current US GAAP "mixed attribute" model for measuring assets and liabilities. The debate has become even more heated due to the recent economic turmoil in credit markets.

Financial statement users advance the argument that they are not being properly informed about the economic impact on the reporting entity of gains and losses associated with changes in the fair values of assets and liabilities that it owns or owes. They assert that, had they been provided this information, they might well have made different decisions regarding investing in, lending to, or entering into business transactions with the reporting entities.

Others argue that transparent reporting of fair values creates "pro-cyclicality," whereby the reporting of fair values has the effect of directly influencing the economy and potentially causing great harm. These arguments are countered by fair value advocates, who state their belief that the extended economic malaise that afflicted Japan since the late 1980s was exacerbated by the lack of transparency in its commercial banking system, which allowed its banks to avoid recognizing losses on loans of questionable credit quality.

FASB has been on record for more than a decade regarding its long-term goal of having all financial assets and liabilities reported at fair value. That said, it has taken a very cautious, incremental approach towards attaining this goal. Its projects with respect to fair value have been conducted in multiple phases over long periods of time; they have involved a full complement of discussion memoranda, invitations to comment, preliminary views documents, public hearings, deliberations, and redeliberations. Certain modest disclosure standards were promulgated and later rescinded and replaced by other standards, but comprehensive requirements for full fair value reporting of financial instruments remained on the horizon.

There are, in the authors' opinion, many reasons for this deliberate, incremental approach to reaching the goal of full adoption of fair value measurement for financial instruments. These reasons include

1.  *Project interdependencies*—Many of the projects on FASB's agenda have implications that affect fair value measurements and disclosures. Notable among them are

    a.  The commitment to converge US GAAP with international standards (IFRS),
    b.  The joint development of a new conceptual framework with the IASB,
    c.  The development of new formats for the basic financial statements, to respond to user criticisms regarding the usefulness of the current model, and
    d.  Pressure on FASB to reduce complexity of existing standards and to address calls from private company stakeholders to provide relief from the costs associated with the preparation of financial statements.

2.  *Preoccupation with other important priorities*—In recent years, FASB has been dealing with a succession of complex, controversial, politically charged issues that required urgent attention due to the volatility of the business environment and financial markets, as well as a general deterioration in the legal and regulatory climate in reaction to a series of high-profile frauds and business failures. Among these issues were

    a.  Share-based payments
    b.  Special-purpose entities and off-balance-sheet financing
    c.  Derivatives and hedging
    d.  Recognition of guarantee obligations
    e.  Business combinations of businesses, not-for-profit organizations, and mutual enterprises including determination of when voting ownership is not indicative of the party that controls an entity
    f.  Recognition, measurement, and disclosures related to uncertain income tax positions
    g.  Pensions and other postemployment benefits
    h.  Leases

3.  *Technical complexities encountered in resolving practice issues*—After completing the initial phase of a lengthy project to distinguish liabilities from equity, and issuing FAS 150, *Accounting for Certain Financial Instruments with Characteristics of Both Liabilities and Equity*, it became necessary to indefinitely postpone the effective date of certain of its provisions as a result of unintended consequences that would have occurred if the standard had been implemented as written.[1]

---

[1] *FAS 150 contains a provision requiring reporting entities that issue mandatorily redeemable common stock to classify these instruments as liabilities in the balance sheet. Implementation of this provision adversely affected many privately held businesses whose common stock was subject to "buy-sell" agreements that obligated the reporting entity to redeem the owners' stock upon the event of their death. Application of FAS 150 would have required that 100% of these companies' equity be classified as liabilities, causing many of them to be in violation of restrictive debt covenants, or leaving them unable to obtain credit enhancements such as guarantees, letters of credit, or surety bonds.*

4.  *The current political and economic environment*—Those who are seeking to assign blame for the current turmoil in credit markets have focused on several areas of GAAP that may have been contributing factors, such as

    a.  Qualifying special-purpose entities (QSPEs) under FAS 140, and their exemption from the consolidation requirements of FIN 46(R), and
    b.  Inconsistencies between specialized accounting rules that apply to different types of enterprises

Amidst all this controversy and all of these distractions, FASB and its international counterpart, the IASB, still firmly believe that, at a minimum, financial instruments are best measured and reported at fair value, and both standard setters are proceeding under that assumption.

FAS 157 contributes to FASB's goal by providing a unified definition of fair value, related guidance on measurement, and enhanced disclosure requirements to inform financial statement users about the fair value measurements included in the financial statements, the methods and assumptions used to estimate them, and the degree of observability of the inputs used in management's estimation process. FAS 157 does not impose any new fair value requirements (i.e., those not already identified under existing GAAP) but it does describe how to accomplish such measurements. The standard retains the exceptions that exist in current GAAP that apply when, in management's judgment, it is not practical to estimate fair value. In such instances, management is required to inform the reader in an explanatory note to the financial statements that it is unable to estimate fair value and the reasons that such an estimate cannot be made. FAS 157 amends numerous existing standards by, in many cases, simply deleting definitions of fair value contained in those standards that conflict with the FAS 157 definition.

While FAS 157 continued in the tradition of incrementally moving towards fair value accounting, FAS 159 provides a radical leap forward in encouraging voluntary adoption of fair value accounting for financial assets and liabilities within its scope. FASB took a controversial approach by allowing management of qualifying entities, subject to certain limitations, to elect to measure financial assets and liabilities at fair value in the balance sheet and recognize changes in fair value in earnings in the period in which they occur. Management is given an extraordinary amount of discretion in selecting the assets and/or liabilities for which it chooses to make this election. In general, the election is made on an individual contract basis. This conclusion resulted in strong dissents from two board members believing that, even with the additional disclosures mandated by FAS 159 (in tandem with the new disclosures required by FAS 157), this selective approach would reduce comparability between similar enterprises— and even between different years' financial statements of the electing enterprise. In addition, the flexibility permitted coupled with early adoption alternatives permitted under the standard provided loopholes that could enable management having questionable motives to financially engineer reported results to avoid recognizing losses on other-than-temporarily impaired investments in current earnings by, in effect, shifting the losses to the transition adjustment to beginning retained earnings associated with adoption of FAS 159.

In June 2007, FASB announced the formation of a Valuation Resource Group (VRG) to provide it with input with respect to issues relating to the application of FAS 157, including alternative views and practical solutions. The VRG, as presently constituted, consists of 25 members, including representatives of large audit firms, valuation experts, financial statement preparers, private equity investors, and the London-based International Valuation Standards Committee. In addition, meetings are attended by observers from the SEC, PCAOB, IASB, and AICPA. VRG meetings, the first of which was held in October 2007, are closed to the public and minutes are not being distributed inasmuch as the group is not authorized to set standards or make authoritative decisions. The FASB staff facilitates VRG meetings and is charged with evaluating information gathered from the meetings to determine which, if any, issues raised by the VRG merit the consideration of FASB as additions to its technical agenda.

This chapter provides the reader/researcher with

1. A discussion of the current state of the mixed-attribute model
2. An explanation of the new fair value measurement model provided by FAS 157, *Fair Value Measurements*
3. An explanation of the provisions of FAS 159, *The Fair Value Option for Financial Assets and Financial Liabilities,* and the various elections it permits management to make
4. Illustrations of financial statement formats and comprehensive disclosures that integrate with the disclosures required by previously issued and still effective authoritative literature regarding financial instruments and fair value

It should be assumed that additional applications of fair value accounting will be forthcoming. Among the extensions of fair value being considered for the next phase of the project (and in connection with other FASB projects) are

1. Permitting election of the fair value option for certain *non*financial assets and *non*financial liabilities and the deposit liabilities of depository institutions which were excluded from the scope of FAS 159
2. Fundamentally changing hedge accounting from the current model to a model more consistent with FAS 159
3. Reconsideration of the model in FAS 150 for distinguishing between liabilities and equity

| | | | | Sources of GAAP | | | | |
|---|---|---|---|---|---|---|---|---|
| *APB* | *FAS* | *FIN* | *FTB* | *EITF* | *SOP* | *FSP* | *AAG* | |
| 18 | 107, 115, | 46(R) | 85-4 | 96-19 | 05-1 | FTB 85-4-1, | AAG-HC | |
| | 117, 124, | | | | | FAS 157-1, | | |
| | 126, 133, | | | | | FAS 157-2 | *CON* | |
| | 141, | | | | | | 7 | |
| | 141(R), | | | | | | | |
| | 155, 156, | | | | | | | |
| | 157, 159, | | | | | | | |
| | 160, 161 | | | | | | | |

## DEFINITIONS OF TERMS

**Active market.** A market in which transactions occur with sufficient frequency and volume to provide pricing information on an ongoing basis.

**Bond.** A debt instrument evidencing a transaction whereby a borrower (referred to as the bond's issuer) agrees to pay a sum of money at a designated future date plus periodic interest payments at the stated rate. The contract between the issuer and the bondholder (also known as the holder or investor) is referred to as an indenture. Bonds are used by commercial enterprises; municipalities; federal, state and foreign governments; colleges and universities; hospitals; and other entities to finance a wide variety of activities or special projects.

**Exit price.** *For valuing assets,* the price that a reporting entity that holds the asset would hypothetically receive by selling it on the measurement date. *For valuing liabilities,* the price that a hypothetical marketplace participant would pay to transfer the liability on the measurement date. Hypothetically, the amount that the holder of a reporting entity's debt would receive to transfer its interest in the reporting entity's liability to another market participant on the measurement date.

**Fair value.** The price that would be received to sell an asset or paid to transfer a liability in an orderly transaction between market participants at the measurement date. Although GAAP literature has primarily focused on fair value in the context of assets and liabilities, the definition also applies to instruments classified in equity.

**Financial asset.** Cash, evidence of an ownership interest in an entity, or a contract that conveys to one entity a right (1) to receive cash or another financial instrument from a second entity or (2) to exchange other financial instruments on potentially favorable terms with the second entity.

**Financial instrument with off-balance-sheet risk.** A financial instrument has off-balance-sheet risk of accounting loss if the risk of accounting loss to the entity can exceed the amount recognized as an asset, if any, or if the ultimate obligation can exceed the amount that is recognized as a liability in the statement of financial position.

**Financial liability.** A contract that imposes on one entity an obligation (1) to deliver cash or another financial instrument to a second entity or (2) to exchange other financial instruments on potentially unfavorable terms with the second entity.

**Firm commitment.** A binding, legally enforceable agreement between unrelated parties that includes

1. All significant terms including the quantity of goods or services to be exchanged, a fixed price, and the transaction's timing. The fixed price may be denominated in the reporting entity's functional currency or in a foreign currency. It might also be stated as a specified interest rate or effective yield.
2. A disincentive for nonperformance sufficient to make performance probable.

**Highest and best use.** The use of an asset by market participants that would maximize its value or the value of the group of assets in which those market participants would use it. An asset is valued using one of the following approaches:

1. *In-use.* This approach is used if the maximum value would be provided to market participants by using the asset in combination with other assets *as a group.* The asset could be used as it is installed and configured at the measurement date or in a different configuration. An *in-use* fair value measurement is based on the price that would be received by the reporting entity on the measurement date in a current transaction to sell the asset along with the other assets in the group using consistent assumptions regarding the highest and best use of all of the assets in the group.
2. *In-exchange.* This approach is used if the maximum value would be provided to market participants from the asset on a standalone basis. An *in-exchange* fair value measurement is based on the price that would be received on the measurement date in a current transaction to sell the asset individually and not as part of a group of assets.

**Market participants.** Buyers and sellers in the principal or most advantageous market for an asset or liability who are

1. Independent of the reporting entity (i.e., other than related parties)
2. Knowledgeable to the extent that they have a reasonable understanding about the asset or liability and the transaction based on all available information, including information that is obtainable through the performance of usual and customary due diligence efforts
3. Able to buy or sell the asset or liability

4.  Willing to enter into a transaction for the asset or liability (i.e., they are not under duress that would force or compel them to enter into the transaction)

**Most advantageous market.** From the standpoint of a reporting entity that does not have access to the principal market (see definition below) for an asset or liability, the market in which the reporting entity would sell the asset for the maximum amount or transfer the liability for the minimum amount, taking into consideration the costs of executing the transaction in the respective markets. Although transaction costs are considered in making a determination of the market that is most advantageous, such costs are not to be factored into the fair value valuation determined by reference to that market.

**Net realizable value.** The amount of cash anticipated to be produced in the normal course of business from an asset, net of any direct costs of the conversion into cash.

**Orderly transaction.** A sale or transfer by the reporting entity that holds an asset or owes a liability that

- Is not a forced liquidation or distress sale
- Assumes exposure of the asset or liability to the market for a period prior to the measurement date to facilitate marketing activities that are usual and customary for transactions involving such assets or liabilities

**Principal market.** From the standpoint of the reporting entity, the market that it would use to sell the asset or transfer the liability that has the highest volume of transactions and level or activity for the asset or liability. If there is a principal market for an asset or liability, fair value is required to be determined by reference to that market, even if the reporting entity could receive a more favorable price in a different market. This is the case even if the price is not directly observable and, instead, is determined using a valuation technique with assumptions (inputs) derived from market data.

## CONCEPTS, RULES, AND EXAMPLES

### The Mixed Attribute Model

Under longstanding US GAAP, assets, liabilities, and equity are measured and presented on a reporting entity's balance sheet by applying a disjointed, inconsistent assortment of accounting methods. This current state of affairs is sometimes referred to as the "mixed attribute model." The following table summarizes the current state of the mixed-attribute model and the effects of FAS 157 and FAS 159 (if any) on specified assets and liabilities of reporting entities that are not financial institutions, investment companies, or insurance companies.

**Assets**

| Key* | Caption | Customary measurement attribute |
| --- | --- | --- |
| A | Cash and cash equivalents | Cost, approximating fair value |
| E | Accounts receivable (with terms not exceeding one year) | Estimated net realizable value |

**Liabilities and Equity**

| Key* | Caption | Customary measurement attribute |
| --- | --- | --- |
| E | Notes and bonds payable | Unpaid principal adjusted for accrued interest, unamortized premium or discount, unamortized debt issue costs |
| A,E | Accounts payable | Contractual price agreed upon by the parties; depending on the contractual terms, often will approximate fair value |

**Assets**

| Key* | Caption | Customary measurement attribute |
|---|---|---|
| E | Notes, loans and accounts receivable with terms exceeding one year | Unamortized principal due less allowance for credit losses; also subject to evaluation for impairment when holder considers it probable that it will be unable to collect all amounts due in accordance with the contractual terms |
| N | Inventory | Lower of cost or market using FIFO, LIFO, average cost, or specific identification |
| N | Deposits | Cost less portion applied by the holder or for which no future benefits are expected |
| E | Investments in debt and marketable equity securities including those held by a not-for-profit organization | Trading and available-for-sale securities at fair value; held-to-maturity securities at amortized cost subject to evaluation for other-than-temporary impairment |
| E | Investments, cost method | Historical cost less dividends received by the investor in excess of the investee's net accumulated earnings since the date of acquisition by the investor, and subject to evaluation for other-than-temporary impairment |
| E | Investments, equity method | Historical cost adjusted to recognize the investor's share of investee income and losses, dividend distributions, and amortization of difference between investor cost and underlying net assets of the investee ("equity method goodwill"); subject to evaluation for other-than-temporary impairment |

**Liabilities and Equity**

| Key* | Caption | Customary measurement attribute |
|---|---|---|
| A | Payroll taxes withheld and accrued; sales taxes payable | Amounts due to taxing authorities; due to short periods during which these amounts are outstanding, they usually approximate fair value without being discounted to their present value |
| N | Income tax liabilities currently payable | Amounts due to taxing authorities based on positions claimed on income tax returns filed or to be filed |
| N | Unrecognized income tax positions | Amounts due to taxing authorities for income tax positions claimed or to be claimed on tax returns that exceed the maximum amount that is more than 50% probable of being sustained upon audit |
| N | Deferred income taxes | Future taxable temporary differences multiplied by the effective tax rate expected to apply upon their future reversal |
| N | Accrued expenses | Expenses incurred or allocated to operations that have not yet been invoiced by the supplier or provider and are not yet currently payable |
| E | Warranty obligations | Estimated costs expected to be incurred over the warranty period |

| **Assets** | | | **Liabilities and Equity** | | |
|---|---|---|---|---|---|
| | | *Customary* | | | *Customary* |
| *Key\** | *Caption* | *measurement attribute* | *Key\** | *Caption* | *measurement attribute* |
| A | Derivatives | Fair value (depending on the measurement, the derivative can be an asset in one period and a liability in another period) | N | Deferred compensation arrangements, pensions, other postemployment benefits | Subject to highly complex GAAP that, in general, accrues the cost of the benefits to be provided in the future in a manner that results in compensation cost being recognized in the periods benefiting from the services provided, including factors for the time value of money, various actuarial assumptions relevant to the measurement, and when the arrangement is funded and based on assumptions regarding future investment returns |
| N | Prepaid expenses | Cost less amounts consumed in operations or allocated to operations based on the passage of time | E | Guarantee liabilities | Initially recognized at fair value; reduced during the life of the guarantee as the guarantor is discharged from the obligation to stand ready to perform |
| N | Deferred income taxes | Future deductible temporary differences and carryforwards multiplied by the effective tax rate expected to apply upon their future reversal and less a valuation allowance for the portion, if any, that is not more than 50% probable of being realized. | N | Asset retirement obligations | Initially recognized as the expected present value of the future cost associated with a legal obligation to retire an asset or group of assets; generally increased in subsequent periods for accretion of interest on the obligation |
| N | Property and equipment held and used | Cost less accumulated depreciation subject to evaluation for impairment upon the occurrence of certain events and circumstances | N | Contingencies | If probable that a liability has been incurred and amount is reasonably estimable, the estimated settlement amount |
| N | Property and equipment held for sale | Fair value less cost to sell | | | |
| N | Cash surrender value of life insurance | Amount realizable under the contract at the balance sheet date net of outstanding policy loans | | | |

**Assets**

| Key* | Caption | Customary measurement attribute |
|------|---------|----------------------------------|
| N | Goodwill | Arises in business combinations: FAS 141: The excess of the purchase price over the fair values of identifiable tangible and intangible net assets acquired; subject to annual impairment tests; FAS 141(R): The excess of the consideration transferred plus the fair value of any noncontrolling interest in the acquiree at the acquisition date over the fair values of the identifiable net assets acquired; In both cases, goodwill is subject to annual impairment testing |
| N | Other intangible assets | Fair value at initial recognition; subject to considerations as to whether the intangible is amortizable and whether impaired; Under FAS 141(R) this category includes in-process research and development assets acquired in a business combination |

**Liabilities and Equity**

| Key* | Caption | Customary measurement attribute |
|------|---------|----------------------------------|

*ABBREVIATION KEY:*

E—*Generally eligible for fair value election under FAS 159*
A—*Already stated at fair value or an amount that approximates fair value*
N—*Not eligible for fair value election or to be measured at fair value on a recurring basis*

Further complicating this state of affairs is the current state of specialized industry accounting rules. A commercial bank holding a debt instrument is subject to FAS 115, *Accounting for Certain Investments in Debt and Equity Securities*, and thus would consider whether the debt instrument is held for trading purposes, is available for sale, or is expected to be held to maturity. Depending on how the instrument is classified, the bank would report the security at either fair value or at amortized cost. Furthermore, if the instrument is classified as available-for-sale or held-to-maturity, changes in fair value will not be recognized in the income statement while the bank holds the instrument, unless it becomes impaired and that impairment is considered "other-than-temporary."

An investment banking enterprise, however, that holds the same security would measure the security at fair value and recognize all changes in fair value, whether increases or decreases, in net income in the period they occur.

## Objectives

Since the late 1980s, FASB has been pursuing a stated goal that would require all financial instruments and many other assets and liabilities to be stated at each balance sheet date at fair value with changes from period to period recognized as gains or losses in the statement of income. The pursuit of this goal has resulted in a succession of standards that have increased the number of fair value measurements required by GAAP and, to provide more transparency to users, increased the scope and complexity of the related disclosures required.

In December 1991, with the issuance of FAS 107, *Disclosures about Fair Value of Financial Instruments,* the term "fair value" was coined to replace the previously used term "market value" (for which the term "fair market value" was sometimes used interchangeably) in authoritative accounting literature. This change was made to emphasize the fact that, even in the absence of active primary markets for an asset or liability, the asset or liability can be valued by reference to prices and rates from secondary markets as well. Over time, this concept has been expanded further to include the application of various fair value estimation models, such as the discounted probability-weighted expected cash flow model first introduced in CON 7.

As these broader fair value concepts were evolving in the literature and in practice, the preexisting "market-based" literature had not been revised. Further, the concepts and definitions of fair value were not consistently understood or applied in similar situations by similar reporting entities.

FAS 157 was issued in September 2006 in order to

- Establish a single, consistent GAAP definition of fair value
- Provide uniform, consistent guidance on how to measure fair value including the establishment of a hierarchical fair value measurement framework that classifies measurement inputs based on their level of market observability
- Expand the information required to be provided to financial statement users about fair value measurements

In FAS 157, FASB asserts that it is not mandating new fair value measurements, but rather is only providing "clarification" regarding the application of these measurements in the existing literature.

**Definition.** Fair value is defined in FAS 157 as the price that would be received to sell an asset or paid to transfer a liability in an orderly transaction between market participants at the measurement date. FAS 157 elaborates that an "orderly transaction" is a hypothetical transaction assumed to take place on the measurement date with the item being valued having been exposed to the market for the usual and customary period of time for transactions involving such assets or liabilities in order to provide sufficient time for marketing activities. Further, an orderly transaction is not a sale where the seller is under duress (e.g., a forced liquidation or distress sale).

Fair value measurements are to be considered from the perspective of a market participant that holds the asset or owes the liability. Thus, the objective of measuring fair value is to determine an exit price: the price that would be received to sell an asset or the price that would be paid to transfer the liability. This concept will be explained and illustrated later in this chapter.

**Scope.** In pursuing an incremental approach, FAS 157 contained scope exceptions for certain, highly-complex specialized applications.

1. Share-based payments (FAS 123 [R])
2. Measurement models that are based on vendor-specific objective evidence (VSOE) such as

    a. Multiple-deliverable arrangements
    b. Software revenue recognition
    c. Software stored on another entity's hardware

3. Market value[2] of inventory for the purposes of applying the lower of cost or market model to measure inventory realizability.

After issuance of FAS 157, constituents of FASB observed an inconsistency between the objective of the pronouncement—to measure fair value based on an exit price—and the fair value measurement objective in paragraph 5 (c)(ii) of FAS 13, *Accounting for Leases*. The lease standard provides guidance that, when the lessor is not a manufacturer or dealer, the fair value of the leased property at the inception of the lease will ordinarily be its cost (an *entry* price as opposed to the FAS 157 requirement to use an *exit* price). In addition, constituents have expressed concerns regarding the application of FAS 157 to estimated residual values of leased assets. After receiving this feedback, FASB was concerned that application of FAS 157 might cause unintended consequences with respect to changing the classification of leases under the FAS 13 model.

As a result, the Board approved the issuance on February 14, 2008, of FSP FAS 157-1, *Application of FASB Statement No. 157 to FASB Statement No. 13 and Other Accounting Pronouncements That Address Fair Value Measurements for Purposes of Lease Classification or Measurement under Statement 13*. The FSP amends FAS 157 to include a scope exception excluding from its provisions FAS 13 and other accounting pronouncements that address fair value measurements for purposes of lease classification or measurement. Notably, however, the scope exception does not apply to lease assets acquired and lease liabilities assumed in a business combination that are required to be measured at fair value under FAS 141(R) or its immediate predecessor, FAS 141.

In issuing the FSP, FASB acknowledges that, temporarily, while it is engaged in a joint project with the IASB to reconsider lease accounting, the term "fair value" as used in the context of lease accounting will differ from its meaning within the context of other fair value applications, where the applicable accounting is governed by FAS 157.

FSP FAS 157-1 is effective upon the initial adoption of FAS 157. Reporting entities that applied FAS 157 consistent with the provisions of the FSP would continue to apply the provisions of the FSP from the date of initial adoption of FAS 157. Reporting entities that did not apply FAS 157 in a manner consistent with the FSP are to apply the provisions of the FSP retrospectively to the date of initial adoption of FAS 157.

In addition to the scope exceptions listed above, FAS 157 retains the exceptions included in GAAP that tacitly acknowledge that it is sometimes not practical to estimate fair value without "undue cost or effort." When this is the case, however, management is required to inform the users of the financial statements that it has invoked this exception, as well as the reasons that it believes making fair value measurements would be impractical. This exception applies to certain measurements made in connection with the following matters:

| GAAP measurement category | Primary GAAP (as amended and/or interpreted) |
| --- | --- |
| Advertising barter transactions | EITF 99-17 |
| Asset retirement obligations | FAS 143/FIN 47 |
| Business combinations | FAS 141 and FAS 141(R) |
| Contributions made and received | FAS 116 |
| Exit and disposal activities | FAS 146 |

---

[2] *The term "market" in the context of inventories has a very specialized definition quite different from its use in the fair value literature. When considering whether inventories have been stated at the lower of cost or market, market is generally considered to be replacement cost; however, for the purpose of this computation, market is not permitted to exceed a defined ceiling (net realizable value) or be less than a defined floor (net realizable value less a normal markup). Inventories are discussed in detail in Chapter 9.*

| GAAP measurement category | Primary GAAP (as amended and/or interpreted) |
|---|---|
| Financial instrument disclosures | FAS 107 |
| Guarantees | FIN 45 |
| Nonmonetary transactions | APB 29/FAS 153 |
| Not-for-profit organizations | AAG-NFP |
| Pensions | FAS 87 |
| Postemployment benefits other than pensions | FAS 106 |
| Puttable marketable securities | EITF 85-40 |
| Transfers of financial assets | FAS 140 |

## Measurement Principles and Methodologies

It is helpful to break down the measurement process under FAS 157 into a series of steps. Although not necessarily performed in a linear manner, the following procedures and decisions need to be applied and made, in order to value an asset or liability at fair value under FAS 157. Each of the steps will be discussed in greater detail.

1. *Identify the item to be valued and the unit of account.* Specifically identify the asset or liability, including the unit of account to be used for the measurement.
2. *Determine the principal or most advantageous market and the relevant market participants.* From the reporting entity's perspective, determine the principal market in which it would sell the asset or transfer the liability. In the absence of a principal market, consider the most advantageous market for the asset or the liability. Once the principal or most advantageous market is identified, determine the characteristics of the market participants. It is not necessary that specifically named individuals or enterprises be identified for this purpose.
3. *Select the valuation premise to be used for asset measurements.* If the item being measured is an asset, determine the valuation premise to be used by evaluating whether marketplace participants would judge the highest and best use of the asset utilizing an "in-use" valuation premise or an "in-exchange" valuation premise.
4. *Consider the risk assumptions applicable to liability measurements.* If the item being measured is a liability, identify the key assumptions that market participants would make regarding nonperformance risk including, but not limited to, the reporting entity's own credit risk (credit standing).[3]
5. *Identify available inputs.* Identify the key assumptions that market participants would use in pricing the asset or liability, including assumptions about risk. In identifying these assumptions, referred to as "inputs" by FAS 157, maximize the inputs that are observable (i.e., that are based on market data available from sources independent of the reporting entity). In so doing, assess the availability of relevant, reliable market data for each input that significantly affects the valuation, and identify the level of the new fair value input hierarchy in which it is to be categorized.

---

[3] *At the time this publication went to press, FASB was engaged in redeliberating a proposed Staff Position, FSP FAS 157-c, the purpose of which is to clarify the application of FAS 157 to liabilities. Based on the results of the FASB's deliberations to date, the proposed FSP would amend FAS 157 to specify that the best measurement of the fair value of an entity's liability is the price at which that liability is traded as an asset. The proposed FSP would allow management of the reporting entity to measure fair value of a liability for which a quoted price is not available at the amount that the entity would receive as proceeds if it were to issue that liability at the measurement date. The authors strongly encourage the reader/researcher to monitor the status of this project on the FASB Web site (www.fasb.org) as it progresses, to ensure that any effect a final FSP might have on the application of fair value measurement principles applicable to liabilities is fully considered in applying the guidance provided in this and other affected chapters.*

6. *Select the appropriate valuation technique(s).* Based on the nature of the asset or liability being valued, and the types and reliability of inputs available, determine the appropriate valuation technique or combination of techniques to use in valuing the asset or liability. The three broad categories of techniques are the market approach, the income approach, and the cost approach.
7. *Make the measurement.* Measure the asset or liability.
8. *Determine amounts to be recognized and information to be disclosed.* Determine the amounts and information to be recorded, classified, and disclosed in interim and annual financial statements

**Item identification and unit of account.** In general, the same unit of account at which the asset or liability is aggregated or disaggregated by applying other applicable GAAP pronouncements is to be used for fair value measurement purposes. FAS 157 prohibits adjustment to the valuation for a "blockage factor." A blockage factor is an adjustment made to a valuation that takes into account the fact that the investor holds a large quantity (block) of shares relative to the market trading volume in those shares. The prohibition applies even if the quantity held by the reporting entity exceeds the market's normal trading volume—and that, if the reporting entity were, hypothetically, to place an order to sell its entire position in a single transaction, that transaction could affect the quoted price.

**Principal or most advantageous market and market participants.** FAS 157 requires the person performing the valuation to maximize the use of assumptions (inputs) that are observable from market data obtained from sources independent of the reporting entity. In making a fair value measurement, management is to assume that the asset or liability is exchanged in a hypothetical, orderly transaction between market participants at the measurement date. To characterize the exchange as orderly, it is assumed that the asset or liability will have been exposed to the market for a sufficient period of time prior to the measurement date to enable marketing activities to occur that are usual and customary with respect to transactions involving such assets or liabilities. It is also to be assumed that the transaction is not a forced transaction (e.g., a forced liquidation or distress sale).

FASB had tentatively concluded that fair value should be measured by reference to the most advantageous market for the asset or liability being measured. Two concerns were raised by FASB constituents regarding this tentative conclusion:

1. The US Securities and Exchange Commission (SEC), in ASR 118,[4] requires registered investment companies to obtain quoted market prices from "the exchange on which the security is principally traded" which might not always be the most advantageous market.
2. If FAS 157 required management to use the most advantageous market to measure fair value, it would mean that management would be required to continuously evaluate prices for multiple assets and liabilities across all possible markets with observable prices to determine which market yielded the best price. While technology can enable such a process, FASB acknowledged that it would not be cost effective to do so.

Given these concerns and FASB's belief that the principal market will generally also be the most advantageous market for the item being measured, FAS 157, as issued, specifies that if there is a principle market for an asset or liability (determined under ASR 118 or otherwise), the measure of fair value is to be the price in that market (whether directly observ-

---

[4] *Codified by topic in SEC Financial Reporting Releases (FRR) paragraph 404.03 et seq.*

able or determined indirectly using a valuation technique), even if the price in a different market is potentially more advantageous at the measurement date.

Management is to identify the *principal market* for the asset or liability, if such a market exists. If the entity has access to more than one market, the principal market is the market in which the reporting entity would sell the asset or transfer the liability that has the greatest volume and activity level for the asset or liability. The greater volume of activity ensures that the measurement is based on multiple transactions potentially between multiple counterparties, and is thus more representative of fair value than if the measurement were based on less extensive data.

Note that the determination of the principal market is made from the perspective of the reporting entity. Thus, different reporting entities engaging in different specialized industries, or with access to different markets, might not have the same principal market for an identical asset or liability. Inputs from the principal market are to be used irrespective of whether the price is directly observable or determined through the use of a valuation technique.

If there is no principal market for an asset or liability from the perspective of the reporting entity, then management is to use the most advantageous market for the measurement. The most advantageous market is the market that the reporting entity has the ability to access at the measurement date, in which it would maximize the price it receives from the sale of an asset or would minimize the price it pays to transfer a liability. In determining the most advantageous market, management considers transaction costs. However, once the most advantageous market had been identified, transaction costs are not used to adjust the market price used for the purposes of the fair value measurement.

FAS 157 provides a typology of markets that potentially exist for assets or liabilities.

1. *Active exchange market.* A market in which closing prices are readily available and that generally represent fair value (e.g., NYSE Euronext, Toronto Stock Exchange, London Stock Exchange, Hong Kong Stock Exchange).

2. *Dealer market.* A market in which parties (dealers referred to as market makers) stand ready to buy or sell a particular investment for their own account at bid and ask prices that they quote. The bid price is the price the dealer is willing to pay to purchase the investment and the ask price is the price at which the dealer is willing to sell the investment. In these markets, these bid and ask prices are typically more readily available than closing prices characteristic of active exchange markets. By using their own capital to finance and hold an inventory of the items for which they "make a market," these dealers provide the market with liquidity. Examples of dealer markets in the US are "over-the-counter" markets that publicly report prices through the National Association of Securities Dealers Automated Quotations Systems (NASDAQ) or Pink Sheets LLC, and the market for US Treasury securities. Dealer markets also exist for various financial and nonfinancial assets and liabilities, including commodities and used equipment.

3. *Brokered market.* These markets use "brokers" or intermediaries to match buyers with sellers. Brokers do not trade for their own account and do not hold an inventory in the security. The broker knows the bid and asked prices of the potential counterparties to the transaction but the counterparties are unaware of each other's price requirements. Prices of consummated transactions are sometimes available privately or as a matter of public record. Brokered markets include electronic communication networks that match buy and sell orders, as well as commercial and residential real estate markets. In some cases, each of the counterparties is aware of the

other's identity, while in other cases, their indentities are not disclosed by the broker.

4. *Principal-to-principal market*. A market in which the counterparties negotiate directly and independently without an intermediary. Because no intermediary or exchange is involved, little if any information about these transactions is released to the public.

Market participants in the principal or most advantageous market are buyers and sellers that

1. Are unrelated third parties
2. Have the ability to enter into a transaction for the asset or liability
3. Have the motivation to voluntarily enter into a transaction for the asset or liability without being forced to do so under duress
4. Are knowledgeable about the asset or liability since they would posses a reasonable understanding of the asset or liability and the terms of the transaction based on all available information including information obtainable through the performance of usual and customary due diligence procedures

The person determining the measurement is not required to identify specific individuals or enterprises that would potentially be market participants. Instead, it is important to identify the distinguishing characteristics of participants in the particular market by considering factors specific to the asset or liability being measured, the market identified, and the participants in that market with whom the reporting entity would enter into a transaction for the asset or liability.

**Measurement considerations when markets become illiquid or less liquid**. At the time many entities were in the process of adopting FAS 157, those same entities were experiencing the effects of a tumultuous credit market in the US and abroad. The previously active markets for certain types of securities became illiquid or less liquid. Questions arose regarding whether transactions occurring in less liquid markets with less frequent trades might cause those market transactions to be considered forced or distress sales, thus rendering valuations made using those prices not indicative of the actual fair value of the securities. In order to respond to these concerns, the Center for Audit Quality (CAQ), a nonprofit group based in Washington, D.C., closely affiliated with the AICPA, issued a white paper on October 3, 2007, entitled, "Measurements of Fair Value in Illiquid (or Less Liquid) Markets."[5]

The white paper indicates that an imbalance between supply and demand can occur when there are more sellers than buyers for a particular instrument and that imbalance can result in "forcing prices down." Transactions in markets affected by this situation where there is a lack of equilibrium between buyers and sellers are not considered to be forced or distressed transactions as contemplated by FAS 157 (or, for that matter, by the standards that preceded FAS 157). The white paper cites a 2004 SEC Accounting and Auditing Enforcement Release[6] in which the Commission imposed a cease-and-desist order on a registrant because the registrant departed from using established market-based valuation methods when it believed that supply and demand were not "in reasonable balance."

One of the practices covered by the cease-and-desist order involved the valuation of bonds, primarily in the telecommunications industry, that were contained in a high-yield bond portfolio near the end of 2000 when the telecommunications industry was experiencing

---

[5]   *http://www.aicpa.org/caq/download/WP Measurements of FV in Illiquid Markets.pdf*

[6]   *AAER No. 2132; US Securities and Exchange Commission; November 4, 2004;*
      *http://sec.gov/litigation/admin/34-50632.htm*

significant turmoil (liquidations, reorganizations, and bankruptcy filings resulting from factors such as overexpansion of capacity in anticipation of business growth that never materialized). The registrant, a financial services firm, believed that market conditions rendered third-party price quotations unreliable and, rather than use such quotations in its fair value measurements, decided to take a "longer view of the market" and use management's own subjective opinion regarding the value of the bonds.

According to the SEC, the registrant in effect, "valued its positions at the price at which it *thought* a willing buyer and seller *should* enter into an exchange, rather than at the price at which a willing buyer and a willing seller *would* enter into a current exchange." (Emphasis added.) The situation cited in the release was exacerbated by the fact that the registrant had valued some of the same high-yield bonds held in the portfolios of its own mutual funds using a lower valuation.

Under FAS 157, orderly transactions are occurring in the marketplace for an asset or liability when knowledgeable buyers and sellers independent of the reporting entity are willing and able to transact, and are motivated to transact without being forced to do so. If orderly transactions are occurring in a manner that is usual and customary for the asset or liability, then the transactions are not to be characterized as forced or distress sales. Just because transaction volume in a market drops significantly from prior periods does not necessarily mean that the market is no longer active. The white paper asserts that persuasive evidence would be required to establish that an observable transaction is a forced or distressed transaction and, furthermore, it is inappropriate to assume that all transactions in a relatively illiquid market are forced or distressed transactions.

**Selection of the valuation premise for asset measurements.** The measurement of the fair value of an asset is to assume the highest and best use of that asset by market participants. Generally, the highest and best use is the way that market participants would be expected to deploy the asset (or a group of assets within which they would the asset) that would maximize the value of the asset (or group). This highest and best use assumption might differ from the way that the reporting entity is currently using the asset or group of assets or its future plans for using it (them).

At the measurement date, the highest and best use must be physically possible, legally permissible, and financially feasible. Determination of the highest and best use of the asset will establish which of the two valuation premises to use in measuring the asset's fair value, the in-use valuation premise, or the in-exchange valuation premise.

*Strategic buyers and financial buyers.* FAS 157 differentiates between two broad categories of market participants that would potentially buy an asset or group of assets.

1. *Strategic buyers* are market participants whose acquisition objectives are to use the asset or group of assets (the "target") to enhance the performance of their existing business by achieving benefits such as additional capacity, improved technology, managerial, marketing, or technical expertise, access to new markets, improved market share, or enhanced market positioning. Thus, a strategic buyer views the purchase as a component of a broader business plan and, as a result, a strategic buyer may be willing to pay a premium to consummate the acquisition and may, in fact, be the only type of buyer available with an interest in acquiring the target. Ideally, from the standpoint of the seller, more than one strategic buyer would be interested in the acquisition which would create a bidding situation that further increases the selling price.

2. *Financial buyers* are market participants who seek to acquire the target based on its merits as a standalone investment. A financial buyer is interested in a return on its investment over a shorter time horizon, often three to five years, after which time

their objective would typically be to sell the target. An attractive target is one that offers high growth potential in a short period of time resulting in a selling price substantially higher than the original acquisition price. Therefore, even at acquisition, a financial buyer is concerned with a viable exit strategy. A financial buyer, unlike a strategic buyer, typically does not possess a high level of industry or managerial expertise in the target's industry. Transactions involving financial buyers are often highly leveraged when the economic environment is such that the cost of debt is lower than the cost of equity.

**The in-use valuation premise.** This premise assumes that the maximum fair value to market participants is the price that would be received by the reporting entity (seller) assuming the asset would be used by the buyer with other assets as a group and further, that the other assets in the group would be available to potential buyers. The target might continue to be used as presently installed or may be configured in a different manner by the buyer. The assumptions regarding the level of aggregation (or disaggregation) of the asset and other associated assets may be different than the level used in applying other accounting pronouncements. Thus, in considering highest and best use and the resulting level of aggregation, the evaluator is not constrained by how the asset may be assigned by the reporting entity to a reportable or operating segment under FAS 131, a business under EITF 98-3[7], a reporting unit under FAS 142, or an asset or disposal group under FAS 144. The assumptions regarding the highest and best use of the target should normally be consistent for all of the assets included in the group within which it would be used. Generally, the market participants whose highest and best use of an asset or group of assets would be "in-use" are characterized as strategic buyers, as previously described.

**The in-exchange valuation premise.** This premise assumes that the maximum fair value to market participants is the price that would be received by the reporting entity (seller) assuming the asset would be sold principally on a stand-alone basis. Generally, the market participants whose highest and best use of an asset or group of assets would be "in-use" are characterized as strategic buyers, as previously described.

**Risk assumptions when valuing a liability.** Many accountants, analysts, and others find the concept of computing fair value of liabilities and recognizing changes in fair value as they occur to be counterintuitive. Consider the case when a reporting entity's own credit standing declines (a "bad thing"). A fair value measurement that incorporates the effect of this decline in credit rating would result in a decline in the fair value of the liability and a resultant increase in stockholders' equity (a "good thing"). The justification provided in FAS 157 (and by quoting from CON 7) is that

> A change in credit standing represents a change in the relative positions of the two classes of claimants (shareholders and creditors) to an entity's assets. If the credit standing diminishes, the fair value of creditors' claims diminishes. The amount of shareholders' residual claims to the entity's assets may appear to increase but that increase is probably offset by losses that may have occasioned the decline in credit standing. Because shareholders usually cannot be called on to pay a corporation's liabilities, the amount of their residual claims approaches, and is limited by zero. Thus a change in the position of borrowers necessarily alters the position of shareholders, and vice versa.

As FAS 157 was originally drafted and issued, fair value measurements of liabilities assume that a hypothetical transfer to a market participant occurs on the measurement date. In

---

[7] *EITF 98-3 was nullified by FAS 141(R) effective at the beginning of the first annual reporting period beginning on or after December 15, 2008. FAS 141(R) simplified the definition of a business which will result in more asset acquisitions being characterized as business combinations, including enterprises that are in the development stage.*

measuring the fair value of a liability, the evaluator is to assume that the reporting entity's obligation to its creditor (i.e., the counterparty to the obligation) will continue at and after the measurement date (i.e., the obligation will not be repaid or settled prior to its contractual maturity). This being the case, this hypothetical transfer price would most likely represent the price that the current creditor (holder of the debt instrument) could obtain from a market-place participant willing to purchase the debt instrument in a transaction involving the original creditor assigning its rights to the purchaser. In effect, the hypothetical market participant that purchased the instrument would be in the same position as the current creditor with respect to expected future cash flows (or expected future performance, if the liability is not settleable in cash) from the reporting entity.

The evaluator is to further assume that the nonperformance risk related to the obligation would be the same before and after the hypothetical transfer occurs. Nonperformance risk is the risk that the obligation will not be fulfilled. It is an all-encompassing concept that includes the reporting entity's own credit standing but also includes other risks associated with the nonfulfillment of the obligation. For example, a liability to deliver goods and/or perform services may bear nonperformance risk associated with the ability of the debtor to fulfill the obligation in accordance with the timing and specifications of the contract. Further, nonperformance risk increases or decreases as a result of changes in the fair value of credit enhancements associated with the liability (e.g., collateral, credit insurance, and/or guarantees).

Reporting entities have reported to the FASB staff that they have experienced various operational difficulties in applying FAS 157 to fair value measurements of liabilities. Many businesses do not issue bonds in public debt markets and are not privy to the amounts that would be realized by their creditors for transferring or securitizing their debt to other market participants. FASB constituents also have asserted that the price that one investor pays another investor to purchase a debt instrument held as an asset would not be indicative of an exit price that the debtor would be required to pay to induce another party to assume the debt in a hypothetical exit transaction.

To respond to these concerns, the FASB staff issued Proposed FSP FAS 157-c, *Measuring Liabilities under FASB Statement No. 157,* on January 18, 2008. The one-month comment period ended on February 18, 2008, and FASB was still redeliberating the proposed FSP as this publication went to press. Based on the results of the redeliberations to date, the following tentative conclusions were reached:

1. The best measurement of fair value for an entity's liability is the price at which that liability is traded as an asset. Thus, a quoted, unadjusted price for the identical liability (and the identical unit of account) in an active market is the best evidence of fair value for that liability; this measurement would be equally valid for both the obligor of the liability and the asset holder.
2. In the absence of a quoted price for the identical liability in an active market, management of the reporting entity may measure the fair value of a liability at the price it would receive if it were to issue that liability at the measurement date.

*NOTE: It is important for the reader to note that this valuation concept is not the same as the concept of the incremental borrowing rate used in accounting for leases. The incremental borrowing rate assumes that the borrower is incurring debt in addition to its existing debt. The valuation concept that would be used in the proposed FSP assumes that the borrower either did not owe the liability being measured as of the measurement date or refinanced it with the same repayment terms and remaining number of payments.*

### Example of measuring a liability absent a quoted market price (based on proposed FSP)

Gomberg Development Inc. (GDI) owed a commercial bank $2,679,824 at 12/31/2009 (the measurement date). When the loan was originated on 12/31/2006, it bore a fixed rate of 9.25% which, at the time, represented the lender's prime rate plus two percent. The original principal amount was $3,000,000 and the loan was to be repaid over a 15-year term with monthly payments of $30,876 of principal and interest.

In order to disclose the fair value of its financial instruments in accordance with FAS 107 (GDI does not qualify for the exemption from this disclosure because it is counterparty to derivative financial instruments), it needs to measure the fair value of this debt.

As is usually the case in private lending transactions, there is no available market information at 12/31/09, the measurement date, regarding the amount that GDI would be required to pay an unrelated counterparty with similar credit standing to assume its debt.

Alternatively, GDI's management contacts local lending institutions and inquires about the availability of terms to refinance its existing debt based on current interest rates and its current credit standing. GDI's management determines (and contemporaneously documents) that based on an improvement in its credit standing, it could obtain $2.7 million of replacement financing at 6% on the measurement date, which represents the lender's prime rate of 5% plus an additional 1%.

Management calculates the fair value of the loan at 12/31/2009 by solving for the present value of 144 remaining payments of $30,876, discounted at 6%, which yields $3,164,010. The logic behind this result from the standpoint of GDI is that due to a favorable change in interest rates and in its own credit standing, the fair value of its debt has increased. It would be more attractive for a counterparty to purchase the existing debt from the originating lender since the yield on the loan exceeds yields based on 12/31/2009 interest rates for investments with similar risk characteristics.

The FASB Staff proposed that the FSP be applied prospectively effective on the later of (1) the beginning of the first reporting period ending after the issuance date of the FSP or (2) the beginning of the period in which an entity initially applies FAS 157. Earlier application would not be permitted. The effect of initial application would be included as a change in fair value in the period of adoption. The authors recommend that readers/researchers monitor the status of this project on the FASB Web site (www.fasb.org) as it progresses to ensure that any effect a final FSP might have on the application of fair value measurement principles to liabilities is fully considered in applying the guidance we provide in this and other affected chapters.

**Inputs.** For the purpose of fair value measurements, inputs are the assumptions that market participants would use in pricing an asset or liability, including assumptions regarding risk. An input is either observable or unobservable. Observable inputs are either directly observable or indirectly observable. FAS 157 requires the evaluator to maximize the use of observable inputs and minimize the use of unobservable inputs.

An observable input is based on market data obtainable from sources independent of the reporting entity. An unobservable input reflects assumptions made by management of the reporting entity with respect to assumptions it believes market participants would use to price an asset or liability based on the best information available under the circumstances.

FAS 157 provides a fair value input hierarchy (see diagram below) to serve as a framework for classifying inputs based on the extent to which they are based on observable data.

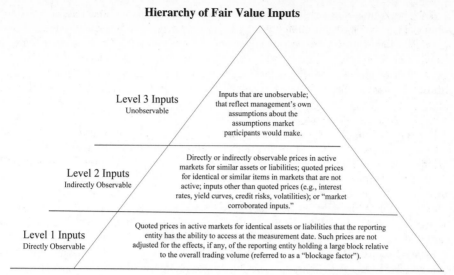

**Hierarchy of Fair Value Inputs**

Level 3 Inputs
Unobservable

Inputs that are unobservable; that reflect management's own assumptions about the assumptions market participants would make.

Level 2 Inputs
Indirectly Observable

Directly or indirectly observable prices in active markets for similar assets or liabilities; quoted prices for identical or similar items in markets that are not active; inputs other than quoted prices (e.g., interest rates, yield curves, credit risks, volatilities); or "market corroborated inputs."

Level 1 Inputs
Directly Observable

Quoted prices in active markets for identical assets or liabilities that the reporting entity has the ability to access at the measurement date. Such prices are not adjusted for the effects, if any, of the reporting entity holding a large block relative to the overall trading volume (referred to as a "blockage factor").

*Level 1 inputs.* Level 1 inputs are considered the most reliable evidence of fair value and are to be used whenever they are available. These inputs consist of quoted prices in active markets for identical assets or liabilities. The active market must be one in which the reporting entity has the ability to access the quoted price at the measurement date. To be considered an active market, transactions for the asset or liability being measured must occur frequently enough and in sufficient volume to provide pricing information on an ongoing basis.

If a market price at the exact measurement date is not readily available, or is available but not representative of fair value because the market is not active or because events occurring after the last available quoted price would have affected fair value at the measurement date[8], the quoted price is to be adjusted to more accurately reflect fair value. As discussed previously, in order for a market to be considered active, it must have a sufficient volume of transactions to provide quoted market prices that are the most reliable measure of fair value. Markets experiencing reduced transaction volumes are still considered active if transactions are occurring frequently enough on an ongoing basis to provide reliable pricing information. FAS 157 requires that quoted prices from active markets (Level 1 inputs) be used whenever they are available. The use of Level 2 or Level 3 inputs is generally prohibited when Level 1 inputs are available.

Even if management were to conclude that a reduction in transaction volume in a particular market rendered that market inactive (i.e., the market is unable to provide reliable pricing information) the observable transactions that were occurring in that market would still be considered Level 2 inputs which need to be taken into account by management in its measurements of fair value. Management is required to establish and consistently apply a policy for identifying events that potentially affect its fair value measurements.

---

[8] *Examples of such events that could occur after the close of a market but prior to the measurement date would include principal-to-principal transactions or brokered trades about which the evaluator has access to reliable information, or announcements made in press conferences, shareholders meetings, or in regulatory filings.*

If the reporting entity holds a large number of similar assets and liabilities (such as a pool of debt securities), and quoted prices are not accessible with respect to each individual asset and/or liability in a cost-effective manner to enable timely financial reporting, management may choose to substitute, as a practical expedient, an alternative pricing model that does not rely exclusively on quoted prices such as using a matrix pricing model for debt securities. The use of a pricing model as an alternative to directly pricing each asset or liability in the group will require management to characterize the measurement in its entirety as a level lower than Level 1 in the hierarchy.

Under no circumstances, however, is management to adjust the quoted price for blockage factors. Blockage adjustments arise when an entity holds a position in a single financial instrument that is traded on an active market that is relatively large in relation to the market's daily trading volume. While there is no common agreement as to how large a position would constitute a "block" of a particular instrument, FASB unconditionally prohibits any adjustment as a result of blockage, even if the market's normal daily trading volume is insufficient to absorb the quantity held by the reporting entity and irrespective of whether the placing of an order to sell the position in a single transaction might affect the quoted price.

*Level 2 inputs.* Level 2 inputs are quoted prices for the asset or liability (other than those included in Level 1) that are either directly or indirectly observable. Level 2 inputs are to be considered when quoted prices for the identical asset or liability are not available. If the asset or liability being measured has a contractual term, a Level 2 input must be observable for substantially the entire term. These inputs include

1. Quoted prices for *similar* assets or liabilities in active markets
2. Quoted prices for identical or similar assets or liabilities in markets that are *not active*. As discussed in the previous section, these markets may not be considered active because

   a. They have an insufficient volume or frequency of transactions for the asset or liability
   b. Prices are not current
   c. Quotations vary substantially over time
   d. Quotations vary substantially among market makers (e.g., in some brokered markets)
   e. Insufficient information is released publicly (e.g., a principal-to-principal market)

3. Inputs other than quoted prices that are observable for the asset or liability (e.g., interest rates and yield curves observable at commonly quoted intervals; volatilities; prepayment speeds; loss severities; credit risks; and default rates)
4. Inputs that are derived principally from or corroborated by observable market data that, through correlation or other means, are determined to be relevant to the asset or liability being measured (market-corroborated inputs)

Adjustments made to Level 2 inputs necessary to reflect fair value, if any, will vary depending on an analysis of specific factors associated with the asset or liability being measured. These factors include

1. Condition
2. Location
3. Extent to which the inputs relate to items comparable to the asset or liability
4. Volume and level of activity in the markets in which the inputs are observed

Depending on the level of the fair value input hierarchy in which the inputs used to measure the adjustment are classified, an adjustment that is significant to the fair value measurement in its entirety could render the measurement a Level 3 measurement.

During the turmoil experienced in credit markets beginning in early 2008, a holder of collateralized mortgage obligations (CMOs) backed by a pool of subprime mortgages might determine that no active market exists for the CMOs. Management might use an appropriate ABX credit default swap index for subprime mortgage bonds[9] to provide a Level 2 fair value measurement input in measuring the fair value of the CMOs.

*Level 3 inputs.* Level 3 inputs are unobservable inputs. These are necessary when little, if any, market activity occurs for the asset or liability. Level 3 inputs are to reflect management's own assumptions about the assumptions regarding an exit price that a market participant holding the asset or owing the liability would make including assumptions about risk. The best information available in the circumstances is to be used to develop the Level 3 inputs. This information might include internal data of the reporting entity. Cost-benefit considerations apply in that management is not required to "undertake all possible efforts" to obtain information about the assumptions that would be made by market participants. Attention is to be paid, however, to information available to management without undue cost and effort and, consequently, management's internal assumptions used to develop unobservable inputs are to be adjusted if such information contradicts those assumptions.

*Inputs based on bid and ask prices.* Quoted bid prices represent the maximum price at which market participants are willing to buy an asset; quoted ask prices represent the minimum price at which market participants are willing to sell an asset. If available market prices are expressed in terms of bid and ask prices, management is to use the price within the bid-ask spread (the range of values between bid and ask prices) that is most representative of fair value irrespective of where in the fair value hierarchy the input would be classified. FAS 157 permits the use of pricing conventions such as midmarket pricing as a practical alternative for determining fair value measurements within a bid-ask spread.

*Classifying inputs.* Classification of inputs as to the level of the hierarchy in which they fall serves two purposes. First, it provides the evaluator with a means of prioritizing assumptions used as to their level of objectivity and verifiability in the marketplace. Second, as discussed later in this chapter, the hierarchy provides a framework to provide informative disclosures that enable readers to assess the reliability and market observability of the fair value estimates embedded in the financial statements.

In making a particular measurement of fair value, the inputs used may be classifiable in more than one of the levels of the hierarchy. When this is the case, the inputs used in the fair value measurement in its entirety are to be classified in the level of the hierarchy in which the lowest level input that is significant to the measurement is classified.

It is important to assess available inputs and their relative classification in the hierarchy prior to selecting the valuation technique or techniques to be applied to measure fair value for a particular asset or liability. The objective, in selecting from among alternative calculation techniques, would be to select the technique or combination of techniques that maximizes the use of observable inputs. FASB clarifies, however, that the intended use of the hierarchy is to prioritize the inputs themselves, not the valuation techniques in which they are used.

**Valuation techniques.** In measuring fair value, management is to employ one or more valuation techniques consistent with the market approach, the income approach, and/or the

---

[9] *ABX indices are disseminated by Markit Group Limited, a London-based consortium of 16 large banks and four hedge funds that provides credit derivative pricing data, valuations, and trade processing services.*

cost approach. As previously discussed, the selection of a particular technique (or techniques) to measure fair value is to be based on its appropriateness to the asset or liability being measured as well as the sufficiency and observability of inputs available.

In certain situations, such as when using Level 1 inputs, use of a single valuation technique will be sufficient. In other situations, such as when valuing a reporting unit, management may need to use multiple valuation techniques. When doing so, the results yielded by applying the various techniques are to be evaluated and appropriately weighted based on judgment as to the reasonableness of the range of results. The objective of the weighting is to determine the point within the range that is most representative of fair value.

Management is required to consistently apply the valuation techniques it elects to use to measure fair value. It would be appropriate to change valuation techniques or how they are applied if the change results in fair value measurements that are equally or more representative of fair value. Situations that might give rise to such a change would be when new markets develop, new information becomes available, previously available information ceases to be available, or improved techniques are developed. Revisions that result from either a change in valuation technique or a change in the application of a valuation technique are to be accounted for as changes in accounting estimate under FAS 154. Curiously, however, FASB exempted such changes from the disclosure requirements under FAS 154 that apply to other changes in accounting estimate.

*Market approaches.* Market approaches to valuation use information generated by actual market transactions for identical or comparable assets or liabilities (including a business in its entirety). Market approach techniques often will use market multiples derived from a set of comparable transactions for the asset or liability or similar items. The evaluator will need to consider both qualitative and quantitative factors in determining the point within the range that is most representative of fair value. An example of a market approach is matrix pricing. This is a mathematical technique used primarily for the purpose of valuing debt securities without relying solely on quoted prices for the specific securities. Matrix pricing uses factors such as the stated interest rate, maturity, credit rating, and quoted prices of similar issues to develop the issue's current market yield.

*Income approaches.* Techniques classified as income approaches measure fair value based on current market expectations about future amounts (such as cash flows or net income) and discount them to an amount in measurement date dollars. Valuation techniques that follow an income approach include the Black-Scholes-Merton model (a closed-form model) and binomial or lattice models (an open-form model), which use present value techniques, as well as the multiperiod excess earnings method that is used in fair value measurements of certain intangible assets such as in-process research and development.

*Cost approaches.* Cost approaches are based on quantifying the amount required to replace an asset's remaining service capacity (i.e., the asset's current replacement cost). A valuation technique classified as a cost approach would measure the cost to a market participant (buyer) to acquire or construct a substitute asset of comparable utility, adjusted for obsolescence. Obsolescence adjustments include factors for physical wear and tear, improvements to technology, and economic (external) obsolescence. Thus, obsolescence is a broader concept than financial statement depreciation which simply represents a cost allocation convention and is not intended to be used as a valuation technique.

**Measurement considerations.**

*Initial recognition.* When the reporting entity first acquires an asset or incurs (or assumes) a liability in an exchange transaction, the transaction price represents an entry price, the price paid to acquire the asset and the price received to assume the liability. Fair value measurements are based not on entry prices, but rather on exit prices; the price that would be received to sell the asset or paid to transfer the liability. While entry and exit prices differ conceptually, in many cases they may be identical and can be considered to represent fair value of the asset or liability at initial recognition. This is not always the case, however, and in assessing fair value at initial recognition, management is to consider transaction-specific factors and factors specific to the assets and/or liabilities that are being initially recognized. Examples of situations where transaction price is not representative of fair value at initial recognition include

1. Related-party transactions
2. Transactions occurring under duress such as a forced or liquidation transaction
3. The exchange transaction occurs in a market different from the principal or most advantageous market in which the reporting entity would sell the asset or transfer the liability. An example of this situation is when the reporting entity is a securities dealer that enters into transactions in different markets depending on whether the counterparty is a retail customer or another securities dealer.
4. Different units of account that apply to the transaction price and the assets/liabilities being measured. This can occur, for example, where the transaction price includes other elements besides the assets/liabilities that are being measured such as unstated rights and privileges that are subject to separate measurement or when the transaction price includes transaction costs (see discussion below).

*Transaction costs.* Transaction costs are the incremental direct costs that would be incurred to sell an asset or transfer a liability. While, as previously discussed, transaction costs are considered in determining the market that is most advantageous, they are not used to adjust the fair value measurement of the asset or liability being measured. FASB excluded them from the measurement because they do not represent an attribute of the asset or liability being measured.

*Transportation costs.* If an attribute of the asset or liability being measured is its location, the price determined in the principal or most advantageous market is to be adjusted for the costs that would be incurred by the reporting entity to transport it to or from that market.

## Fair Value Disclosures

Substantial disclosures regarding fair value are required by many different pronouncements that comprise authoritative GAAP literature. In the preparation of the financial statements, these disclosures are often placed in different informative notes including descriptions of the entity's accounting policies, financial instruments, impairment, derivatives, pensions, revenue recognition, share-based compensation, risks and uncertainties, certain significant estimates, etc. FAS 157 requires additional quantitative and qualitative disclosures. FAS 157 encourages, but does not require management to combine its fair value disclosures with other required disclosures such as the financial instrument disclosures required by FAS 107. In addition, FAS 157 encourages disclosure of information about other similar measurements that are not intended to represent fair value such as inventories measured at the lower of cost or market. FAS 157 uses a hybrid principles-based approach and rules-based approach to detailing the fair value disclosures it requires. It provides the following high-level disclosure objectives:

1. For assets and liabilities measured at fair value on a recurring basis subsequent to their initial recognition, management is to provide information that will enable financial statement users to assess the inputs used to develop those measurements and, further, for measurements using significant unobservable (Level 3) inputs, the effect of those measurements on earnings for the period.

2. For assets and liabilities measured at fair value on a nonrecurring basis subsequent to their initial recognition, management is to provide information that will enable financial statement users to assess the inputs used to develop those measurements.

To operationalize these objectives, FAS 157 provides the following required disclosures. The quantitative disclosures are required to be presented in a tabular format. Unless otherwise specified, the disclosures are required to be made in each interim and annual period.

**Disclosures required to be made with respect to assets and liabilities measured at fair value on a recurring basis in periods subsequent to initial recognition.** Disclose separately for each major category of assets and liabilities

1. The amount of the fair value measurements at the reporting date
2. The level within the fair value hierarchy in which the fair value measurements fall in their entirety; separately disclosing the amounts of fair value measurements that use quoted prices in active markets for identical assets or liabilities (Level 1), significant other observable inputs (Level 2), and significant unobservable inputs (Level 3)
3. For those fair value measurements using significant unobservable (Level 3) inputs, a reconciliation of the beginning and ending balances, separately stating changes during the period attributable to

    a. Total realized and unrealized gains or losses for the period segregating those gains or losses included in income (or changes in net assets of a not-for-profit organization) and a description of where those gains or losses are reported in the statement of income (or statement of activities of a not-for-profit organization)

    (1) The unrealized gains or losses included in this disclosure that relate to assets and liabilities still held at the balance sheet date and
    (2) A description of where, in the statement of income, those unrealized gains or losses are reported

    b. Purchases, sales, issuances, and settlements (net)
    c. Transfers in and/or out of Level 3 (e.g., due to changes in the observability of significant inputs)

    Note that, for the purposes of this reconciliation, derivative assets and liabilities are permitted to be presented net.
4. In the first interim period of the fiscal year of adoption and subsequently in annual financial statements, the valuation techniques used to measure fair value and a discussion of changes in valuation techniques, if any, during the period

**Disclosures required to be made with respect to assets and liabilities measured at fair value on a nonrecurring basis in periods subsequent to initial recognition (such as impaired assets).** Disclose separately for each major category of assets and liabilities

1. Fair value measurements recorded during the period and the reasons for the measurements
2. The level within the fair value hierarchy in which the fair value measurements fall in their entirety; separately disclosing the amounts of fair value measurements that use quoted prices in active markets for identical assets or liabilities (Level 1), significant other observable inputs (Level 2), and significant unobservable inputs (Level 3)
3. For fair value measurements using significant unobservable (Level 3) inputs, a description of the inputs and the information used to develop them

4.  In the first interim period of the fiscal year of adoption and subsequently in annual financial statements, the valuation techniques used to measure fair value and discussion of changes in valuation techniques used to measure similar assets and/or liabilities in prior periods

**Enhanced disclosures regarding derivative instruments and hedging activities.** To respond to concerns regarding lack of transparency regarding reporting entities' derivatives and hedging activities, FASB issued FAS 161, *Disclosures about Derivative Instruments and Hedging Activities,* in March 2008. FAS 161 will be effective for financial statements issued for fiscal years and interim periods beginning after November 15, 2008, with early application encouraged.

FAS 161 establishes a disclosure framework intended to enhance the understanding of financial statement users about

1.  How and why the reporting entity uses derivative instruments,
2.  How derivative instruments and related hedged items are accounted for, and
3.  How derivative instruments and related hedged items affect the reporting entity's financial position, financial performance, and cash flows.

Included in the extensive new disclosures is a requirement that every interim and annual financial statement include quantitative disclosures presented in a tabular format, detailing substantial information regarding the location in the financial statements and the fair value amounts of derivatives reported on the balance sheet. Those fair value amounts are to be presented gross, even if the derivatives are subject to master netting arrangements and are permitted to be presented net on the balance sheet. Derivatives and hedging transactions are discussed in detail in Chapter 8, and the newly required disclosures are included in the Disclosure Checklist in Appendix A.

### Effective Date and Transition

As originally issued, FAS 157 was to be fully effective for financial statements issued for fiscal years beginning after November 15, 2007, and interim periods within those fiscal years. FASB encouraged early adoption but only for fiscal years during which the reporting entity had not yet issued interim or annual financial statements. In addition, if the management of the reporting entity elected to adopt FAS 159, *The Fair Value Option for Financial Assets and Financial Liabilities*, prior to its scheduled effective date (described later in this chapter), the reporting entity was also required to simultaneously adopt the requirements of FAS 157.

On February 12, 2008, FASB adopted FSP FAS 157-2 which provides a limited one-year delay of the effective date for certain limited provisions of FAS 157. The FASB's intent in adopting the delay is to allow it (and its constituents) additional time to resolve issues that may have arisen in the initial application of FAS 157. The delay is not available to any reporting entity that had already issued interim or annual financial statements reflecting the application of the measurement and disclosure provisions of FAS 157 prior to the issuance of the FSP on February 12, 2008. Those entities are required to continue to apply the provisions of FAS 157 in their entirety.

The delay applies to nonfinancial assets and nonfinancial liabilities except for items recognized or disclosed at fair value in the reporting entity's financial statements on a recurring basis (at least annually).

With respect to eligible items, application of FAS 157 may be delayed until fiscal years beginning after November 15, 2008, and interim periods within those fiscal years.

Nonfinancial assets and nonfinancial liabilities are defined in the FSP as all assets and liabilities that *do not* meet the definition of a financial asset or financial liability in paragraph 6 of FAS 159 (see "Definitions of Terms" at the beginning of this chapter).

Examples of items to which the deferral applies include the following (not all-inclusive):

1. Items measured at fair value on a recurring basis but not necessarily recognized or disclosed in the financial statements at fair value

    a. Reporting units measured at fair value in the first step of an annual goodwill impairment test
    b. Indefinite-lived intangible assets measured at fair value for impairment assessment purposes under FAS 142

2. Items measured at fair value on a nonrecurring basis

    a. Nonfinancial assets and nonfinancial liabilities initially measured at fair value in a business combination or other new basis event that are not measured at fair value in subsequent periods
    b. Nonfinancial long-lived assets (or asset groups) measured at fair value in performing an impairment assessment under FAS 144
    c. Asset retirement obligations that are initially measured at fair value under FAS 143 but are not required to be remeasured on a recurring basis
    d. Nonfinancial liabilities associated with exit or disposal activities initially measured at fair value under FAS 146

3. Items measured at fair value on a nonrecurring basis but not necessarily recognized or disclosed in the financial statements at fair value—nonfinancial assets and nonfinancial liabilities measured at fair value in the second step of a goodwill impairment test

Examples of items to which the deferral *does not* apply include the following (not all-inclusive):

1. Financial assets and financial liabilities initially measured at fair value in a business combination or other new basis event irrespective of whether they are to be measured at fair value in subsequent periods
2. Eligible items under paragraph 7 of FAS 159, *The Fair Value Option for Financial Assets and Financial Liabilities*, that are recognized or disclosed at fair value on a recurring basis
3. Financial instruments within the scope of FAS 107, *Disclosures about Fair Value of Financial Instruments*, irrespective of whether they are recognized in the financial statements
4. Financial and nonfinancial derivatives within the scope of FAS 133, *Accounting for Derivative Instruments and Hedging Activities*
5. Servicing assets and servicing liabilities within the scope of FAS 156, *Accounting for Servicing of Financial Assets,* including situations where management has elected the amortization method as the subsequent measurement attribute, because the fair value is required to be disclosed on a recurring basis
6. Loans measured for impairment using the practical expedient in FAS 114, *Accounting by Creditors for Impairment of a Loan* (based on the fair value of the collateral if the loan is collateral dependent), even if the collateral is nonfinancial

Entities that elect the one-year deferral are required to include the following disclosures in all interim and annual financial statements it issues until FAS 157 is fully applied to all assets and liabilities covered by its scope:

1. The fact that the reporting entity has only partially applied FAS 157, and
2. Each major category of assets and liabilities that are recognized or disclosed at fair value for which the entity has not applied FAS 157

## FAS 159, *The Fair Value Option for Financial Assets and Financial Liabilities*

**Introduction.** Five months after the issuance of FAS 157, in February 2007, FASB followed with FAS 159, *The Fair Value Option for Financial Assets and Financial Liabilities*, which encourages reporting entities to optionally elect to use fair value to measure eligible assets and liabilities in their financial statements. Electing entities would obtain relief from the onerous and complex documentation requirements that apply to certain hedging transactions under FAS 133 while reducing the financial statement effects of volatility caused by differing measurement methods for qualifying assets and related liabilities. FAS 159 applies to businesses and not-for-profit organizations and provides management of these entities substantial discretion in electing to measure eligible assets and liabilities at fair value.

**Eligible financial assets and financial liabilities.** The following items are eligible for the election (also see the summary table in the section of this chapter, entitled "The Mixed Attribute Model"):

1. All recognized financial assets and financial liabilities except

    a. Investments in subsidiaries required to be consolidated by the reporting entity
    b. Interests in variable interest entities required to be consolidated by the reporting entity[10]
    c. Financial assets recognized under leases
    d. Employers' and plans' obligations (unfunded or underfunded liabilities) or assets (representing net overfunded positions) for

        (1) Pension benefits
        (2) Other postretirement benefits (including health care and life insurance benefits)
        (3) Postemployment benefits
        (4) Other deferred compensation, termination, and share-based payment arrangements such as employee stock option plans; employee stock purchase plans; compensated absences; and exit and disposal activities

    e. Financial assets and financial liabilities under leases (this exception does not, however, apply to a guarantee of a third-party lease obligation or a contingent obligation associated with cancellation of a lease)
    f. Deposit liabilities, withdrawable on demand, of banks; saving and loan associations; credit unions; and other similar depository institutions
    g. Financial instruments that are, in whole or in part, classified by the issuer as a component of stockholders' equity (including "temporary equity," also sometimes referred to as "mezzanine") such as a convertible debt security with a noncontingent beneficial conversion feature.

2. Firm commitments that would otherwise not be recognized at inception and that involve only financial instruments. And example is a forward purchase contract for a loan that is not readily convertible to cash. The commitment involves only financial

---

[10] *Under FAS 141(R), consolidated variable interest entities are referred to as subsidiaries in the same manner as consolidated voting interest entities.*

instruments (the loan and cash) and would not be recognized at inception since it does not qualify as a derivative.

3. A written loan commitment
4. Rights and obligations under insurance contracts or warranties that are not financial instruments[11] but whose terms permit the insurer (warrantor) to settle claims by paying a third party to provide goods and services to the counterparty (insured party or warranty claimant)
5. A host financial instrument resulting from bifurcating an embedded nonfinancial derivative instrument from a nonfinancial hybrid instrument under FAS 133, *Accounting for Derivative Instruments and Hedging Activities*, paragraph 12 (subject to the scope exceptions listed above.). An example would be an instrument in which the value of the bifurcated embedded derivative is payable in cash, services, or merchandise but the host debt contract is only payable in cash.

**Flexibility of application.** FAS 159 provides management with substantial flexibility in electing the fair value option (FVO). Once elected, however, the election is irrevocable unless, as discussed later in this section, a new election date occurs. The election can be made for a single eligible item without electing it for other identical items subject to the following limitations:

1. If the FVO is elected with respect to an investment otherwise required to be accounted for under the equity method of accounting, the FVO election is to be applied to all of the investor's financial interests in the same entity (equity and debt, including guarantees) that are eligible items.
2. If a single contract with a borrower (such as a line of credit or construction loan) involves multiple advances to that borrower and those advances lose their individual identity and are aggregated with the overall loan balance, the FVO is only permitted to be elected to apply to the larger overall loan balance and not individually with respect to each individual advance.
3. If the FVO is applied to an eligible insurance or reinsurance contract, it is also required to be applied to all claims and obligations under the contract.
4. If the FVO is elected for an eligible insurance contract (base contract) for which integrated or nonintegrated contract features or coverages (some of which are referred to as "riders") are issued either concurrently or subsequently, the FVO is required to be applied to those features and coverages. The FVO is not permitted to be elected for only the nonintegrated contract features and coverages, even though they are accounted for separately under SOP 05-1, *Accounting by Insurance Enterprises for Deferred Acquisition Costs in Connection with Modifications or Exchanges of Insurance Contracts.*[12]

Other than as provided in 1. and 2. above, management is not required to apply the FVO to all instruments issued or acquired in a single transaction. The lowest level of election, however, is at the single legal contract level. A financial instrument that is, in legal form, a

---

[11] *Insurance contracts that require or permit the insurer to settle claims by providing goods or services instead of by paying cash are not, by definition, financial instruments. Similarly, warranties that require or permit the warrantor to settle claims by providing goods and services in lieu of cash do not constitute financial instruments.*

[12] *SOP 05-1 defines a nonintegrated contract feature in an insurance contract as a feature in which the benefits provided are not related to or dependent on the provisions of the base contract. For the purposes of applying the FVO election, neither an integrated nor a nonintegrated contract feature or coverage qualifies as a separate instrument.*

single contract is not permitted to be separated into component parts for the purpose of electing the FVO. For example, an individual bond is the minimum denomination of that type of debt security.

An investor in an equity security of a particular issuer may elect the FVO for its entire investment in that equity security including any fractional shares issued by the investee in connection, for example, with a dividend reinvestment plan.

Management of an acquirer, parent company, or primary beneficiary[13] decides whether to elect the FVO with respect to the eligible items of an acquiree, subsidiary, or consolidated variable interest entity. That decision, however, only applies in the consolidated financial statements. FVO choices made by management of an acquiree, subsidiary, or variable interest entity continue to apply in their separate financial statements should they choose to issue them.

**Timing of the election.** Management may elect the FVO for an eligible item in one of two ways.

1. Based on an established policy for specified types of eligible items that it follows consistently, or
2. On the date of occurrence of one of the following events:

   a. The entity initially recognizes the item.
   b. The entity enters into an eligible firm commitment.
   c. Financial assets previously required to be reported at fair value with unrealized gains and losses included in income due to the application of specialized accounting principles cease to qualify for that accounting treatment (e.g., a subsidiary subject to the AAG on investment companies transfers a security to another subsidiary of the same parent that is not subject to the AAG).
   d. The accounting treatment for an investment in another entity changes because

      (1) The investment becomes subject to the equity method of accounting (and, for example, had previously been accounted for under FAS 115, *Accounting for Certain Investments in Debt and Equity Securities*, or under the FVO)
      (2) The investor ceases to consolidate a subsidiary or variable interest entity but retains an interest in the entity

   e. An event requires an eligible item to be remeasured at fair value at the time that the event occurs but does not require fair value measurements to be made at each subsequent reporting date. Among the events that require initial fair value measurement or subsequent fair value remeasurement of this kind are

      (1) Business combinations,
      (2) Consolidation or deconsolidation of a subsidiary or variable interest entity, and
      (3) Significant modifications of debt, as defined in EITF 96-19, *Debtor's Accounting for a Modification or Exchange of Debt Instruments*.

      Specifically excluded from being considered an eligible event are

      (1) Recognition of impairment under lower-of-cost-or-market accounting, or
      (2) Other-than-temporary impairment

---

[13] *Under FAS 141(R) a primary beneficiary is referred to as a parent in the same manner as a company that consolidates a voting interest entity.*

**Financial statement presentation and disclosure.**

*Balance sheet.* FAS 159 requires the reporting entity to report assets and liabilities for which the FVO was elected in a manner that separates those amounts from carrying amounts of similar assets and liabilities measured using another measurement method. Two alternatives are provided.

1. Present the aggregate fair value and non–fair value amounts on the same balance sheet line and parenthetically provide the amount measured at fair value that is included in the aggregate amount.
2. Present two separate line items to display the fair value and non–fair value carrying amounts.

In the authors' opinion, the manner in which the first alternative is illustrated in FAS 159 could potentially confuse or mislead readers.

> Private equity investments ($75 at fair value)                $125

This caption could easily be misunderstood by the reader to mean that the reporting entity holds private equity investments with an aggregate carrying value of $125 whose fair value has declined to $75 thus implying a $50 unrealized loss. In fact, this caption is intended to convey the fact that the reporting entity holds private equity investments with an aggregate carrying value of $125 and that the $125 is comprised of $75 valued at fair value in accordance with an election of the FVO and $50 using another measurement attribute such as the cost method or equity method.

If using parenthetical disclosure, it would be less misleading if the amount were presented as follows:

> Private equity investments
> ($75 measured at fair value; $50 measured using the equity method)        $125

This can get cumbersome and is still confusing. It becomes even more unwieldy when considering the fact that reporting entities customarily present two or three years' comparative balance sheets and that not-for-profit organizations often use tabular formats for their statements of financial position that present separate columns for unrestricted net assets, temporarily restricted net assets, and permanently restricted net assets.

Another source of confusion is the fact that existing GAAP requires certain items (such as derivatives, trading securities, and available-for-sale securities) to be stated at fair value without consideration of the FVO. Therefore, it is conceivable that a single balance sheet will contain financial instruments that are stated at fair value due to a requirement in GAAP, financial instruments that are stated at fair value due to management's election of the FVO, and financial instruments that are stated using some other attribute such as cost method, equity method, or, as is permitted for investments in certain debt securities, using amortized cost. When this is the case, the reporting entity may wish to use a format such as the one shown below.

**Young Aviation Chopper and Helicopter Works, Inc.**
**Consolidated Balance Sheet (Unclassified for Illustrative Purposes)**
**December 31, 2009**

| | Amounts measured under the company's customary accounting policies at other than fair value | Amounts required to be measured at fair value or whose carrying values approximate fair value | Eligible amounts measured at fair value at management's election | Total |
|---|---|---|---|---|
| **Assets** | | | | |
| Cash and cash equivalents | | $ 38 | | $ 38 |
| Accounts receivable | $ 97 | | | 97 |
| Notes receivable | 400 | | $150 | 550 |
| Inventory | 134 | | | 134 |
| Investments | | | | |
| Trading securities | | 115 | | 115 |
| Securities available-for-sale | | 75 | | 75 |
| Securities held-to-maturity | 32 | | | 32 |
| Derivatives | | 60 | | 60 |
| Private equity | 50 | | 75 | 125 |
| Property and equipment, net | 10 | | | 10 |
| Other assets | 20 | | | 20 |
| Total assets | $ 743 | $288 | $225 | $1,256 |
| **Liabilities** | | | | |
| Borrowings under short-term line of credit | $ 128 | | | $ 128 |
| Long-term debt | 140 | | $ 60 | 200 |
| Accounts payable | | $110 | | 110 |
| Accrued liabilities | 130 | | | 130 |
| Other liabilities | 555 | | | 555 |
| Total liabilities | 953 | 110 | 60 | 1,123 |
| **Stockholders' equity** | | | | |
| Common stock | 4 | | | 4 |
| Additional paid-in capital | 88 | | | 88 |
| Retained earnings | 42 | | | 42 |
| Accumulated other comprehensive income | (1) | — | — | (1) |
| Total stockholders' equity | 133 | -- | -- | 133 |
| Total liabilities and stockholders' equity | $1,086 | $110 | $ 60 | $1,256 |

Many variations can be derived from this method of presentation. For example, subtotals are only necessary to be presented for the total column since the notes to the financial statements provide fair value totals by major class. The financial statement preparer may wish to augment this presentation by including a column that subtotals all amounts stated at fair value irrespective of whether they are subject to the FVO election.

Separate sections of assets and liabilities could contain separate line items enumerating the eligible items within each for which the FVO was elected by management.

**Statement of cash flows.** FAS 159 requires cash receipts and cash payments related to items measured at fair value to be classified in the statement of cash flows according to their nature and purpose. This requirement necessitated an amendment to FAS 95, *Statement of Cash Flows*, which had previously required cash receipts and payments associated with trading securities to be classified as being from (or for) investing activities. Inexplicably, however, FAS 159 leaves the provision of FAS 95 unchanged that requires returns on investments (interest and dividends) to be accounted for as operating activities.

**Disclosure objectives.** Consistent with the approach in FAS 157, FAS 159 provides financial statement preparers with the principal objectives associated with fair value option disclosures and then sets forth in detail the disclosures FASB deems necessary to meet the objective. The principal objectives are to facilitate comparisons (1) between entities that choose different measurement attributes for similar assets and liabilities, and (2) between assets and liabilities in the financial statements of an entity that elects to use different measurement attributes for similar assets and liabilities. FASB indicates that it expects the disclosures to result in

1.  Information sufficient to enable financial statement users to understand

    a.  The reasons why management elected or partially elected the FVO
    b.  How changes in fair values affected net income for the period
    c.  The differences between fair values and contractual cash flows for certain items

2.  The information that would have been required to be disclosed about certain items (e.g., equity-method investments, nonperforming loans) absent the FVO election

Although not required by FAS 159, FASB encourages management to present the disclosures it requires in combination with related fair value disclosures required to be disclosed by other pronouncements (such as FAS 107 and FAS 157).

Unless otherwise indicated, all of the required disclosures are to be included in both interim and annual financial statements.

***Items for which disclosures are required.*** The disclosures required by FAS 159 apply to items measured under the FVO as well as under the option provided by FAS 155, *Accounting for Certain Hybrid Financial Instruments,* that permits management, in applying FAS 133 to the initial recognition of a host contract with an embedded derivative, to irrevocably elect to initially and subsequently measure the hybrid financial instrument in its entirety at fair value with changes in fair value recognized in net income.

***Items for which disclosures are not required.*** The disclosures required by FAS 159 do not apply to the following items. However, any existing disclosures required by the cited pronouncements continue to be required under GAAP.

1.  Investments in securities classified as trading securities under FAS 115, *Accounting for Certain Investments in Debt and Equity Securities*
2.  Life settlement contracts measured at fair value pursuant to FSP FTB 85-4-1, *Accounting for Life Settlement Contracts by Third-Party Investors*
3.  Servicing rights measured at fair value under FAS 156, *Accounting for Servicing of Financial Assets*

***Disclosures required as of each interim and annual balance sheet date.***

1.  The reasons that management elected the FVO for each eligible item or group of similar eligible items
2.  If management elected the FVO for some but not all of the eligible items within a group of similar eligible items

    a.  A description of the items in the group and the reasons for partial election
    b.  Information sufficient to enable users to understand how the group of similar items relates to the individual line items presented on the balance sheet

3.  For each balance sheet line item that includes one or more items for which the FVO was elected

    a.  Information sufficient to enable users to understand how each balance sheet line item relates to major categories of assets and liabilities presented in accordance with the fair value disclosure requirements of FAS 157 discussed previously in this chapter. Those requirements include providing the reader information regarding the level or levels of the fair value hierarchy in which the assumptions used to measure fair value (referred to as "inputs") are derived.

b.   The aggregate carrying amount of items included in each balance sheet line item, if any, that are not eligible for the FVO

4.   The difference between the aggregate fair value and the aggregate unpaid principal balance of

a.   Loans and long-term receivables (other than securities subject to FAS 115) with contractual principal amounts and for which the FVO has been elected

b.   Long-term debt instruments that have contractual principal amounts and for which the FVO has been elected

5.   For loans held as assets for which the FVO has been elected

a.   The aggregate fair value of loans on nonaccrual status if the entity's policy is to recognize interest income separately from other changes in fair value

b.   The aggregate fair value of loans that are 90 or more days past due

c.   The difference between the aggregate fair value and the aggregate unpaid principal balance for loans that are 90 or more days past due, in nonaccrual status, or both

6.   For investments that, absent election of the FVO, would have been accounted for under the equity method, the following disclosures from APB 18, *The Equity Method of Accounting for Investments in Common Stock*[14]

a.   Financial statements of the investor are to disclose parenthetically, in the notes to the financial statements, or in separate statements or schedules

(1)   The name of each investee and percentage of ownership of its common stock, and

(2)   The accounting policies of the investor with respect to investments in common stock.

b.   When investments in common stock of corporate joint ventures or other investments accounted for under the equity method are, in the aggregate, material in relation to the investor's financial position and results of operations, it may be necessary to present in the notes or in separate statements, either individually or in groups, summarized information as to assets, liabilities, and results of operations of the investees.

***Disclosures required about items for which the fair value option has been elected for each interim and annual period for which an income statement is presented.***

1.   For each line item in the statement of financial position, the amounts of gains and losses from changes in fair value included in net income during the period and the specific line in the income statement on which those gains and losses are reported. FAS 159 permits management to meet this requirement by aggregating these disclosures with respect to items for which the FVO was elected with the amounts of

---

[14]   *APB 18 indicates that management of the investor is to evaluate the significance of an investment to its financial position and results of operations in determining the extent of disclosures necessary to inform the reader of the financial position and results of operations of an investee. If the investor holds more than one investment in common stock, it may be appropriate to provide disclosures wholly or partially on an aggregate basis.*

gains and losses from changes in fair value with respect to other items measured at fair value as required by other authoritative literature.

2. A description of how interest and dividends are measured and where they are reported in the statement of income.[15]

3. With respect to gains and losses included in net income during the period attributable to changes in instrument-specific credit risk associated with loans and other receivables held as assets.

   a. The estimated amount or such gains or losses
   b. How the gains or losses were determined

4. For liabilities with fair values that have been significantly affected during the reporting period by changes in instrument-specific credit risk

   a. The estimated amount of gains and losses from changes in fair value included in net income attributable to changes in the instrument-specific credit risk
   b. How the gains and losses were determined
   c. Qualitative information regarding the reasons for those changes

***Other required disclosures.***

1. In annual financial statements only, the methods and significant assumptions used to estimate the fair value of items for which the FVO was elected.[16]

2. If management elects the FVO upon the occurrence of an event where (a) an investment newly becomes subject to the equity method, (b) a subsidiary or variable interest entity that the investor previously consolidated ceases to qualify for consolidation but the investor continues to hold common stock in the entity, or (c) an eligible item is required to be measured or remeasured at fair value at the time of the event but is not required to be subsequently measured at each succeeding reporting date, the following disclosures are required in the financial statements covering the period of the election:

   a. Qualitative information about the nature of the event
   b. Quantitative information by balance sheet line item indicating which line items in the income statement include the effect on net income of initially electing the FVO for the item.

***Special provisions applicable to not-for-profit organizations.*** Not-for-profit organizations (NFPs) are to apply FAS 159 in the same manner as commercial enterprises with the following exceptions:

1. Where provisions of FAS 159 refer to an income statement, those references should be replaced by references to a statement of activities, statement of changes in net assets, or statement of operations.

2. References to earnings or net income should be replaced with references to changes in net assets unless the NFP is a health-care organization subject to the AICPA Au-

---

[15] *FAS 159 is silent with respect to the methods to be used for measuring and reporting dividend income, interest income, and interest expense associated with items for which the FVO has been elected.*

[16] *While FAS 107,* **Disclosures about Fair Value of Financial Instruments,** *already required reporting entities to annually disclose the methods and significant assumptions used to estimate the fair value of financial instruments, this disclosure requirement expands that disclosure to include instruments that are outside the scope of FAS 107 such as certain insurance contracts for which the FVO was elected.*

dit and Accounting Guide, *Health Care Organizations*. Because NFP health care organizations present performance indicators that are analogous to income from continuing operations of business enterprises, they are to report unrealized gains and losses on items for which the FVO has been elected within the performance indicator or as a part of discontinued operations, as applicable under the circumstances. In accordance with FAS 117, *Financial Statements of Not-for-Profit Organizations*, NFPs may present such gains and losses either within or outside other intermediate measures of operations unless the gains or losses are part of discontinued operations. NFP health care organizations are permitted to present such unrealized gains or losses that are not part of discontinued operations as a part of any intermediate measures of operations that are presented as a component of the performance indicator.

3.  The disclosure requirements presented above under the caption, "Disclosures required about items for which the fair value option has been elected for each interim and annual period for which an income statement is presented" are to apply not only to the effect on performance indicators or other intermediate measures of operations that may be presented, but also with respect to the effect on the change in each of the classes of net assets, as applicable (unrestricted, temporarily restricted, and permanently restricted).

**Example of disclosure under FAS 157 and FAS 159 combined with FAS 107 disclosures**

The following example does not purport to illustrate all of the disclosure requirements specified within the standards. Instead, it is presented to illustrate how the financial statement preparer might organize the required tabular disclosures by integrating the FAS 107 disclosures regarding the fair value of financial instruments with the FAS 157 and FAS 159 disclosures discussed in this chapter.

**Young Aviation Chopper and Helicopter Works, Inc.**
**Notes to Financial Statements**
**December 31, 2009**

Note X, Fair values of financial assets and liabilities

(000 Omitted)

| Description | Total carrying amount in balance sheet 12/31/09 | FAS 107 estimated fair value | Assets/ liabilities measured at fair value 12/31/09 | Fair Value Measurements at 12/31/09 — Measured Using | | | Year Ended 12/31/09 — Changes in fair values for items elected to be measured at fair value and the caption in which they are included in the statement of income | | | | |
| | | | | Quoted prices in active markets for identical assets (Level 1) | Significant other observable inputs (Level 2) | Significant unobservable inputs (Level 3) | Trading gains and losses | Other gains and losses | Interest income on notes | Interest expense on long-term debt | Total changes in fair values included in earnings |
|---|---|---|---|---|---|---|---|---|---|---|---|
| **Asset Category** | | | | | | | | | | | |
| Investments | | | | | | | | | | | |
| Trading | $115 | $115 | $115 | $105 | $10 | -- | $10 | -- | -- | -- | $10 |
| Available-for-sale | 75 | 75 | 75 | 75 | -- | -- | -- | -- | -- | -- | -- |
| Derivatives | 60 | 60 | 60 | 25 | 15 | 20 | -- | (3) | -- | -- | (3) |
| Private equity | 125 | 138 | 75 | -- | 25 | 50 | -- | (18) | -- | -- | (18) |
| Notes receivable | 550 | 500 | 150 | -- | 100 | 50 | -- | -- | 30 | -- | 30 |
| **Liability Category** | | | | | | | | | | | |
| Long-term debt | (200) | (206) | (60) | (30) | (10) | (20) | -- | 13 | -- | (4) | 9 |

Private equity investments for which the fair value option was elected represent investments that would otherwise be accounted for using the equity method of accounting. See Note 1, Summary of Significant Accounting Policies for disclosures regarding the methods and assumptions used to value each major class of financial assets and liabilities.

**Effective date.** FAS 159 was effective as of the beginning of each reporting entity's first fiscal year beginning after November 15, 2007. Special early adoption provisions applied, however, except as those provisions permitted, the statement was not to be applied retrospectively to fiscal years beginning prior to the effective date.

**Early adoption.** Management was permitted to adopt SFAS 159 and elect the FVO for existing eligible items as of the beginning of a fiscal year beginning on or before November 15, 2007, if it met the following conditions:

1. Management also adopted all of the requirements of FAS 157 at the early adoption date of FAS 159 (the first day of the fiscal year of early adoption) or earlier.

2. At the time management chose to early adopt FAS 159, it had not yet issued financial statements of the reporting entity including required notes to those financial statements, for any interim period of the fiscal year that included the early adoption date.

3. The choices to apply or not to apply the FVO to eligible items existing at the early adoption date were retroactive to that early adoption date.

4. For eligible items with an election date occurring after the early adoption date but before management's choice to apply early, the election for those items was retroactive to their election date.

5. All other requirements that would normally have applied as of the required effective date also applied as of the early adoption date.

6. Management's choice to adopt early was to be made after FASB issued FAS 159 in February 2007, but within 120 days of the beginning of the fiscal year of adoption. Thus, the deadlines for the early election by management were as follows:

| *Fiscal year* | | *FAS 159* |
|---|---|---|
| *Beginning* | *Ending* | *early election deadline* |
| 3/1/2007 | 2/29/2008 | 6/29/2007 |
| 4/1/2007 | 3/31/2008 | 7/30/2007 |
| 5/1/2007 | 4/30/2008 | 8/29/2007 |
| 6/1/2007 | 5/31/2008 | 9/29/2007 |
| 7/1/2007 | 6/30/2008 | 10/29/2007 |
| 8/1/2007 | 7/31/2008 | 11/29/2007 |
| 9/1/2007 | 8/31/2008 | 12/30/2007 |
| 10/1/2007 | 9/30/2008 | 1/29/2008 |
| 11/1/2007 | 10/31/2008 | 2/29/2008 |

# 7 CASH, RECEIVABLES, AND PREPAID EXPENSES

## PERSPECTIVE AND ISSUES

Assets displayed on the balance sheet are the resources available to the reporting entity to support its current and future operations. To provide information about liquidity, the assets are often divided into current and noncurrent assets. Current assets consist of cash and other assets that are reasonably expected to be realized in cash or sold or consumed during the normal operating cycle of the business. When the normal operating cycle is less than one year, a one-year period is used to distinguish current assets from noncurrent assets. If the operating cycle exceeds one year, the operating cycle is the proper period to use for current asset identification. When information about current assets is accompanied by information about current liabilities, readers of the financial statements can assess the amount of net working capital (current assets less current liabilities) possessed by the reporting entity and its *current ratio* (current assets divided by current liabilities). Each of those measures provides useful, and different, information about the liquidity of the reporting entity—that is, its ability to satisfy current obligations as they become due in the normal course of business.

Current assets usually include cash, short-term investments, receivables, inventory, and prepaid expenses. This chapter discusses cash, receivables, and prepaid expenses. Chapter 8 discusses short-term investments, and Chapter 9 discusses inventory. This chapter also discusses the standards in FAS 140, *Accounting for Transfers and Servicing of Financial Assets and Extinguishments of Liabilities.* Because of certain recent developments associated with the off-balance sheet accounting for certain securitizations (e.g., various subprime mortgage and collateralized debt obligations) FASB appears committed to making revisions to certain aspects of this standard by the end of 2008, which readers should deep abreast of. Discussion of FAS 140 is included in this chapter because that standard describes the proper accounting for sales of receivables to third parties and the use of receivables as collateral in secured borrowings. This chapter also includes FAS 140's standards for repurchase agreements and securities lending. Although those two types of transfers usually involve investments, they are discussed in this chapter because the same underlying theory—the financial components approach—is used for those transactions as is used for transfers involving receivables. FAS 140's standards for extinguishment of debt are set forth in Chapter 15.

Recognition and measurement of cash is generally straightforward. However, it is necessary to inform readers of the financial statements about any limitations on the ability to use cash in current operations.

Trade receivables and other customary trade term receivables that are due in no longer than one year are measured at outstanding face value (principal) adjusted for any write-offs and the allowance for doubtful accounts, provided that management has the intent and ability to hold those receivables for the foreseeable future or until maturity or payoff. Loans receivable that management will hold until maturity or payoff are valued at outstanding principal adjusted for any write-offs, the allowance for loan losses, any deferred fees or costs on originated loans, and any unamortized premiums of discounts on purchased loans.

If a receivable is due on terms exceeding one year, the proper valuation is the present value of future payments to be received, computed by using an interest (discount) rate commensurate with the risks involved, as of the date of the receivable's creation. In many situations where an explicit interest rate is provided, the rate commensurate with the risks involved is the rate stated in the agreement between the payee and the obligor. However, if the receivable is noninterest-bearing or if the rate stated in the agreement is not indicative of the market rate for a debtor of similar creditworthiness under similar terms, interest must be imputed at the market rate. The resulting discount is amortized as additional interest income over the life of the agreement, per APB 21.

Receivables that are pledged or assigned to a lender as collateral for a lending agreement remain under the control of the reporting entity and therefore remain on its balance sheet, as does the debt incurred under the borrowing arrangement. It is necessary, however, to inform readers of the financial statements about the pledge or assignment.

As an alternative to borrowing against the value of the receivables, customer obligations are sometimes sold in order to generate cash before their due dates. If the transferor has no continuing involvement with the transferred assets or with the transferee, it is clear that a sale has taken place, and a gain or loss on sale is measured and recognized. However, in many cases, the transferor of the receivables has continuing involvement with the transferred assets because it sells the receivables with recourse for uncollectible amounts, retains an interest in the receivables, or agrees to service the receivables after the sale. The greater the control that the transferor retains over the receivables, the more likely that the transfer will be accounted for as a secured borrowing rather than a sale.

Under the financial components approach used in FAS 140, a sale is recognized only if control over the transferred assets is relinquished in fact. A determination that control has been surrendered is made if three criteria are all met. If control has been surrendered, the reporting entity recognizes the financial and servicing assets (if any) it controls and liabilities (if any) it assumes, and removes from its accounting records the carrying value of any assets surrendered and liabilities extinguished. The same accounting and the same three criteria are applied to all transfers of financial assets, regardless of type. Thus, the standards apply to sales of receivables with recourse, sales of receivables with retained interests or servicing, securitizations (the transformation of the receivables into securities that are sold to other investors), repurchase agreements (a "sale" of a security accompanied by an agreement to "repurchase" it at a future date), and securities lending agreements.

If control has not been surrendered, the transfer of financial assets is accounted for as a secured borrowing. The accounting for the collateral by the debtor and the secured party depends on whether the debtor has defaulted and the nature of the rights and obligations that result from the collateral agreement. If the secured party (the lender) has the right to sell or repledge the collateral, then the debtor reports that asset in its balance sheet separately from other assets not so encumbered. If the secured party does in fact sell the collateral, it recognizes the proceeds from the sale and its obligation to return the collateral. Accounting for the sale of the collateral is also subject to the standards set forth by FAS 140. If the original debtor defaults on the secured borrowing agreement, thereby forfeiting the right to redeem the collateral, the lender will recognize the collateral as its asset, measured at fair value, or, if it has already sold the collateral, derecognize its obligation to return the collateral; concurrently, the debtor will derecognize the collateral, as it no longer has an equitable claim to it.

| | | Sources of GAAP | | | |
|---|---|---|---|---|---|
| *ARB* | *APB* | *FAS* | *FTB* | *SOP* | *EITF* |
| 43, Ch. 1A | 6, 21 | 5, 6, 65, 91, | 01-1 | 01-6 03-3 | 88-11, 88-22, 88-23, 92-2, |
| 43, Ch 3A | | 114, 115, 133, | | | 02-9, D-51, D-63, D-65, |
| | | 140, 155, 156 | | | D-66, D-69 |
| | | | | | |
| *FSP* | *FIN* | | | | |
| 140-1, | 14, 45, | | | | |
| 140-2 | 46(R) | | | | |
| 140-3 | | | | | |

## DEFINITIONS OF TERMS

**Accounts receivable.** Amounts due from customers for goods or services provided in the normal course of business operations.

**Aging the accounts.** Computation of the adjustment for uncollectibility of accounts receivable outstanding at the end of the period based upon the length of time the accounts have been unpaid.

**Assignment.** The formal procedure for collateralization of borrowings through the use of accounts receivable. It normally does not involve debtor notification.

**Beneficial interests.** Rights to receive all or portions of specified cash inflows to a trust or other entity.

**Cash.** Coins and currency on hand and balances in checking accounts available for immediate withdrawal.

**Cash equivalents.** Short-term, highly liquid investments that are readily convertible to known amounts of cash and are so near their maturity that they present negligible risk of changes in value due to changes in interest rates. Examples include treasury bills, commercial paper, and money market funds.

**Collateral.** Personal or real property used to secure the performance of a loan or other obligation. Upon default of the obligation the collateral may be sold by the lender in order to satisfy the obligation.

**Current assets.** Those assets that are reasonably expected to be realized in cash or sold or consumed within a year or within the normal operating cycle of the reporting entity, if longer than a year.

**Factoring.** The outright sale of accounts receivable to a third-party financing entity. The sale may be with or without recourse.

**Financial asset.** Cash, evidence of an ownership interest in an entity, or a contract that conveys to another entity a right to (1) receive cash or a financial instrument from a first entity, or (2) exchange other financial instruments on potentially favorable terms with the first entity.

**Financial liability.** A contract that imposes on one entity a contractual obligation to (1) deliver cash or a financial instrument to another entity, or (2) exchange other financial instruments on potentially unfavorable terms with another entity.

**Interest-only strip.** The contractual right to receive some or all of the interest due on a financial instrument without the rights to receive the principal.

**Net realizable value.** The amount of cash anticipated to be produced in the normal course of business from an asset, net of any direct costs of the conversion into cash.

**Operating cycle.** The average time between the acquisition of materials or services and the cash realization from the sale of products or services produced using the acquired materials or services.

**Percentage-of-sales method.** Computing the adjustment for uncollectible accounts receivable based on the historical relationship between bad debts and gross credit sales.

**Pledging.** Using an asset as collateral for borrowings. It generally refers to borrowings secured by accounts receivable.

**Recourse.** The right of a transferee (factor) to receive payment from the transferor of receivables for uncollectible accounts, prepayments by the debtors, merchandise returns, or other defects in the eligibility of the receivables.

**Securitization.** The transformation of receivables into securities that are sold to other investors.

**Servicing asset.** A contract to service financial assets that provides the servicer with estimated future revenues (e.g., fees, late charges) that more than adequately compensate the servicer for performing the service.

**Servicing liability.** A contract to service financial assets that provides the servicer with estimated future revenues (e.g., fees, late charges) that are not expected to adequately compensate the servicer for performing the service.

**Transfer.** Conveyance of a noncash financial asset by or to someone other than issuer of financial asset.

## CONCEPTS, RULES, AND EXAMPLES

### Cash

To be included as cash in the balance sheet, funds must be represented by coins, currency, undeposited checks, money orders, drafts, and demand deposits that are immediately available without restriction. Cash that is restricted as to use would not be included with cash unless the restrictions on it expire within the year (or the operating cycle, if longer). Thus, cash contractually required to be held in a sinking fund is classified as a current asset if it will be used to retire the current portion of long-term debt. However, if material, it would be reported on a separate line rather than included with cash. Cash in a demand deposit account that is being held for the retirement of long-term debts that do not mature currently is excluded from current assets and shown as a noncurrent investment. Cash in transit to the reporting entity (e.g., checks already mailed by the customer) cannot be included in cash because it is not under the control of the reporting entity.

It has long been common to see the caption "Cash and Cash Equivalents" in the balance sheet. That caption includes other forms of near-cash as well as demand deposits and liquid, short-term securities. Cash equivalents must be available upon demand in order to justify inclusion. However, a current joint FASB-IASB project, addressing financial statement presentation, might restore the prominence of "cash," excluding equivalents, by dispensing with the concept of cash and equivalents. Such a change would affect both the balance sheet and the statement of cash flows, as these two financial statements must articulate.

**Compensating balances.** An entity will often be required to maintain a minimum amount of cash on deposit, generally in connection with having a borrowing arrangement with a financial institution (compensating balance). The purpose of this balance may be to substitute for service fees foregone by the bank (or fees at a rate less than market) or simply to increase the yield on a loan to the lender. Since most organizations must maintain a certain working balance in their cash accounts simply to handle routine transactions and to cushion against unforeseen variations in the demand for cash, borrowers often will not find compensating balance arrangements objectionable. Nevertheless, the compensating balance is not available for unrestricted use and penalties will result if it is used. If material, the portion of the reporting entity's cash account that is a compensating balance must be segregated and shown as a separate caption on the balance sheet, and this should be included in noncurrent assets if related borrowings are noncurrent liabilities. If the borrowings are current liabilities or if the compensating balance reduces fees that would have been incurred in the next year, it is acceptable to show the compensating balance as a separately captioned current asset.

**Example of compensating balance disclosure**

The Arkansas Billboard Company (ABC) has obtained a short-term, $10 million line of credit with Premier Bank. The loan agreement with Premier includes a requirement that ABC maintain a compensating balance of 5% of the maximum amount of the line of credit (5% × $10 million = $500,000). ABC also has a loan with First National Bank involving a single balloon payment of $200,000 due in two years, and requiring a compensating balance of 10%. (10% × $200,000 = $20,000) At year-end, ABC has cash balances of $782,000 at Premier and $28,000 at First National. ABC's reporting of cash on its balance sheet is as follows:

| *Current assets:* | |
| --- | --- |
| Cash | 290,000 |
| Restricted cash compensating balances | 500,000 |
| | |
| *Noncurrent assets:* | |
| Restricted cash compensating balances | 20,000 |

**Cash not immediately available.** Cash in savings accounts subject to a statutory notification requirement and cash in certificates of deposit maturing during the current operating cycle or within one year may be included as current assets but, if material, is to be separately captioned in the balance sheet to avoid the misleading implication that these funds are available immediately upon demand. Typically, such items will be included in the short-term investments caption, but these could be labeled as time deposits or restricted cash deposits.

**Overdrafts.** A reporting entity may issue checks with a dollar value exceeding the balance in its checking account. If the excess amount of these checks over the checking account balance has not yet cleared the bank, the overage is called a book overdraft, since the overdraft only exists in the reporting entity's accounting records. For reporting purposes, although the bank is yet unaware of this situation, the overdraft is reported as a liability, since the checks have already been released and are thus no longer under the control of the reporting entity. If the checks have cleared the bank, and the bank has advanced the reporting entity the funds (sometimes marketed as "automatic overdraft protection"), then this borrowing is also reported as a liability.

**Petty cash.** Petty cash and other imprest cash accounts are usually combined in financial statements with other cash accounts.

## Receivables

**Types of receivables.** Accounts receivable, open accounts, or trade accounts are agreements by customers to pay for services received or merchandise obtained. Notes receivable are formalized obligations evidenced by written promissory notes. Other categories of receivables include trade acceptances, third-party instruments, and amounts due from officers, shareholders, employees, or affiliated companies. The latter categories of receivables generally arise from cash advances but could result from sales of merchandise or the provision of services. The nature of amounts due from trade customers is often different from that of balances receivable from related parties, such as employees or shareholders. Thus, generally accepted accounting principles require that the different classes of receivables be separately identified either on the face of the balance sheet itself, or in the notes thereto.

Receivables due within one year (or one operating cycle, if longer) generally should be presented at outstanding face value (principal amount), adjusted for any write-offs already taken and valuation allowances. Valuation allowances adjust the carrying amount of receivables downward because not all of those receivables will ultimately be realized as cash. For example, valuation allowances are reported for amounts estimated to be uncollectible and also for the estimated returns, allowances, and other discounts to be taken by customers prior to or at the time of payment. In practice, the deductions that should be made for estimated returns, allowances, and trade discounts are usually deemed to be immaterial and such adjustments are rarely made. However, if it is known that sales are recorded for merchandise that is shipped "on approval" and available data suggests that a sizable proportion of such sales are returned by the customers, then the estimated future returns must be accrued. Similarly, material amounts of anticipated discounts and allowances are to be recorded in the period of sale.

### Example of different classes of receivables

Snowy Winters & Sons is a purveyor of fine books about the Alaskan heartland. Its total ending receivable balance is $420,000. The receivable balance is affected by the following items:

- The allowance for uncollectible accounts receivable is $17,000, reflecting a historical rate of bad debts equal to 4% of receivables.
- It ships books on a subscription basis, resulting in a 15% return rate. Winters has recorded an allowance for returns of $63,000.
- It offers an early payment discount of 1%, which is generally taken. Winters maintains a 1% early payments allowance of $4,200 to reflect this arrangement.
- One large customer, Anchorage Book Company (ABC), is delinquent in its payments, so the collections department has converted ABC's outstanding balance of $58,000 into a short-term note receivable, payable over ten months at a 12% interest rate.
- The Winters legal staff has won a lawsuit from which the company can expect to receive a total of $12,000, payable over two years.
- Early Winters, the family patriarch, borrowed $15,000 from the company to purchase an antique dogsled.

Snowy Winters' controller reports this information on the Winters balance sheet in the following manner:

| | | |
|---|---:|---:|
| Accounts receivable, trade | 335,000 | |
| Less: Allowances for doubtful accounts | (17,000) | |
| Returns allowance | (63,000) | |
| Early payment for discount allowance | (4,200) | 250,800 |
| Receivables due from officers | | 15,000 |
| Notes receivable due in current year | | 58,000 |
| | | |
| Noncurrent receivables | | |
| Claims receivable (litigation settlement to be | | |
| collected over two years) | | 12,000 |

**Valuation allowance for uncollectible amounts.** The recording of a valuation allowance for anticipated uncollectible amounts is almost always necessary. The direct write-off method, in which a receivable is charged off only when it is clear that it cannot be collected, is unsatisfactory since it overstates assets and also results in a mismatching of revenues and expenses. (Note that the direct charge-off method may be required for tax purposes, but if so, this results in temporary differences for which interperiod tax allocation will generally be required.) Proper matching, which remains a valid financial reporting objective, can only be achieved if bad debts are recorded in the same fiscal period as the revenues to which they are related. Since the amount of uncollectible accounts is not known with certainty, however, an estimate must generally be made.

There are two popular estimation techniques. One, the percentage-of-sales method, is principally oriented towards achieving the best possible matching of revenues and expenses. The other method, aging the accounts, is more inclined toward the presentation of the correct net realizable value of the trade receivables in the balance sheet. Both methods are acceptable under GAAP, and are widely employed.

For the percentage-of-sales method, historical data are analyzed to ascertain the relationship between bad debts and credit sales. The derived percentage is then applied to the current period's sales revenues in order to arrive at the appropriate debit to bad debts expense for the year. The offsetting credit is made to allowance for uncollectible accounts (often still referred to as the reserve for bad debts). When specific customer accounts are subsequently identified as uncollectible, they are written off against this allowance.

**Example of percentage-of-sales method**

| | |
|---|---|
| Total credit sales for year: | $7,500,000 |
| Bad debt ratio from prior years or other data source: | 1.75% of credit sales |
| Computed year-end adjustment for bad debts expense: | $131,250 ($7,500,000 × .0175) |

The entry required is

| | | |
|---|---:|---:|
| Bad debts expense | 131,250 | |
| Allowance for uncollectible receivables | | 131,250 |

Care must be taken to ensure that the bad debt ratio computed will be representative of uncollectibility of the current period's credit sales. A ratio based on historical experience may require an adjustment to reflect the current economic climate. For example, if a large percentage of customers are concentrated in a geographic area that is experiencing an economic downturn, the rate of default may increase over that previously suffered. Changes in credit terms and in customer mix may also affect the relationship between sales and bad debts, and should be given consideration in determining the bad debt percentage to be applied to current period credit sales. In practice, these relationships evolve slowly over time and may not always be observed over the short term.

When aging the accounts, an analysis is prepared of the customer receivables at the balance sheet date. Each customer's balance is categorized by the number of days or months the underlying invoices have remained outstanding. Based on the reporting entity's past experience or on other available statistics, such as industry trends, historical bad debts percentages are applied to each of these aggregate amounts, with larger percentages being applied to the older accounts. The end result of this process is a computed total dollar amount that implies the proper ending balance in the allowance for uncollectible receivables at the balance sheet date. The computed amount is compared to the balance in the valuation account, and an adjustment is made for the differences. Thus, the adjustment needed will be an amount other than the amount computed by the aging.

**Example of the aging method**

|  | | *Age of accounts* | | |
| --- | --- | --- | --- | --- |
|  | *Under 30 days* | *30-90 days* | *Over 90 days* | *Total* |
| Gross receivables | $1,100,000 | $425,000 | $360,000 | |
| Bad debt percentage | 0.5% | 2.5% | 15% | |
| Provision required | $ 5,500 | $ 10,625 | $ 54,000 | $70,125 |

The credit balance required in the allowance account is $70,125. Assuming that a debit balance of $58,250 already exists in the allowance account (from charge-offs during the year that exceeded the credit balance in the allowance account at the previous year-end), the necessary entry is

| | | |
| --- | --- | --- |
| Bad debts expense | 128,375 | |
|    Allowance for uncollectible receivables | | 128,375 |

Both of the estimation techniques should produce approximately the same result over the course of a number of years. Nonetheless, these adjustments are based upon estimates and will never precisely predict ultimate results. When facts subsequently become available to indicate that the amount provided as an allowance for uncollectible accounts was incorrect, an adjustment classified as a change in estimate is made, unless this was the consequence of a failure to consider facts available at the time the estimate was made, in which case a correction of an accounting error will have to be recognized (see Chapter 5). For discussion of impairments of loans receivable and troubled debt restructurings, see Chapter 15.

**Imputed interest.** If a receivable is due on terms exceeding one year, the proper valuation is the present value of future payments to be received, determined by using an interest rate commensurate with the risks involved at the date of the receivable's creation. In many situations the interest rate commensurate with the risks involved is the rate stated in the agreement between the payee and the debtor. However, if the receivable is noninterest-bearing or if the rate stated in the agreement is not indicative of the market rate for a debtor of similar creditworthiness under similar terms, interest is imputed at the market rate. A valuation allowance is used to adjust the face amount of the receivable to the present value at the market rate. The balance in the valuation allowance is amortized as additional interest income so that interest income is recognized using a constant rate of interest over the life of the agreement. Initial recording of such a valuation allowance also results in the recognition of an expense, typically (for customer receivables) reported as selling expense or as a contra-revenue item (sales discounts).

APB 21 specifies when and how interest is to be imputed when the receivable is noninterest-bearing or the stated rate on the receivable is not reasonable. It applies to transactions conducted at arm's length between unrelated parties, as well as to transactions in which captive finance companies offer favorable financing to increase sales of related companies. APB 21 divides receivables into three categories for discussion: notes issued solely for cash, notes issued for cash and a right or privilege, and notes issued in exchange for property, goods, or services.

When a note is issued solely for cash, its present value is necessarily assumed to be equal to the cash proceeds. The interest rate is that rate which equates the cash proceeds received by the borrower to the amounts to be paid in the future. For example, if a borrower agrees to pay $1,060 in one year in exchange for cash today of $1,000, the interest rate implicit in that agreement is 6%. A valuation allowance of $60 is applied to the face amount ($1,060) so that the receivable in included in the balance sheet at its present value ($1,000).

When a note receivable that bears an unrealistic rate of interest is issued in exchange for cash, an additional right or privilege is usually granted, unless the transaction was not conducted at arm's length. If there was an added right or privilege involved, the difference between the present value of the receivable and the cash advanced is the value assigned to the right or privilege. It will be accounted for as an addition to the cost of the products purchased for the purchaser/lender, and as additional revenue to the debtor.

### Example of accounting for a note issued for both cash and a contractual right

1. Schwartz borrows $10,000 from Weiss via an unsecured five-year note. Simple interest at 2% is due at maturity.
2. Schwartz agrees to sell Weiss a car for $15,000, which is less than its market price.
3. The market rate of interest on a note with similar terms and a borrower of similar creditworthiness is 10%.

The present value factor for an amount due in five years at 10% is .62092. Therefore, the present value of the note is $6,830 [= ($10,000 principal + $1,000 interest at the stated rate) × .62092]. According to APB 21, the $3,170 (= $10,000 – $6,830) difference between the present value of the note and the face value of the note is regarded as part of the cost/purchase price of the car. The following entry would be made by Weiss to record the transaction:

| | | |
|---|---|---|
| Note receivable | 10,000 | |
| Car | 18,170 | |
| Cash | | 25,000 |
| Discount on note receivable | | 3,170 |

The discount on note receivable is amortized using the effective interest method, as follows:

| | *Effective interest (10%)* | *Stated interest (2%)* | *Amortization* | *Note and interest receivable* |
|---|---|---|---|---|
| 01/01/09 | | | | 6,830 |
| 01/01/10 | 683 | 200 | (483) | 7,513 |
| 01/01/11 | 751 | 200 | (551) | 8,264 |
| 01/01/12 | 826 | 200 | (626) | 9,091 |
| 01/01/13 | 909 | 200 | (709) | 10,000 |
| 01/01/14 | 1,000 | 200 | (800) | 11,000 |

The entry for the first year would be

| | | |
|---|---|---|
| Discount on note receivable | 483 | |
| Interest receivable | 200 | |
| Interest revenue | | 683 |

When a note is issued in exchange for property, goods, or services and the transaction is entered into at arm's length, the stated interest rate is presumed to be fair unless (1) no interest rate is stated, (2) the stated rate is unreasonable, (3) the face value of the note receivable is materially different from fair value of the property, goods, or services received, or (4) the face value of the note receivable is materially different from the current market value of the note at the date of the transaction. According to APB 21, when the rate on the note is not fair, the note is to be recorded at the fair market value of the property, goods, or services sold or the market value of the note, whichever is the more clearly determinable. The difference is recorded as a discount or premium and amortized to interest income.

**Example of accounting for a note exchanged for goods**

1.  Green sells Brown inventory that has a fair market value of $8,573.
2.  Green receives a two-year noninterest-bearing note having a face value of $10,000.

In this situation, the fair market value of the consideration is readily determinable and, thus, represents the amount at which the note is to be recorded. The following entry would be made by Green:

| | | |
|---|---|---|
| Notes receivable | 10,000 | |
|    Discount on notes receivable | | 1,427 |
|    Sales revenue | | 8,573 |

The discount will be amortized to interest expense over the two-year period using the interest rate implied in the transaction, which is 8%. The present value factor is .8573 ($8,573/$10,000). Using a present value table for amount due in two years, .8573 is located under the 8% rate.

If neither the fair value of the property, goods, or services sold nor the fair value of the note receivable is determinable, then the present value of the note must be determined using an imputed market interest rate. This rate will then be used to establish the present value of the note by discounting all future payments on the note at that rate. General guidelines for determining the appropriate interest rate, which are provided by APB 21, include the prevailing rates of similar instruments with debtors having similar credit ratings and the rate the debtor could obtain for similar financing from other sources. Other factors to be considered include any collateral or restrictive covenants involved, the current and expected prime rate, and other terms pertaining to the instrument. The objective is to approximate the rate of interest that would have resulted if an independent borrower and lender had negotiated a similar transaction under comparable terms and conditions. This determination is as of the issuance date, and any subsequent changes in market interest rates are irrelevant.

Additional discussion about present value techniques, including additional examples, is found in Chapter 15.

**Lending and financing activities, including trade receivables.** Receivables generally arise from extending credit to others. Banks, savings institutions, finance companies, credit unions, and mortgage companies are generally thought of as the types of entities that extend credit. However, all entities that sell on credit to customers (that is, trade receivables) also extend credit, however briefly. SOP 01-6, *Accounting by Certain Entities (Including Entities with Trade Receivables) That Lend to or Finance the Activities of Others,* sets standards for the recognition, measurement, presentation, and disclosure of financing and lending transactions of all types.

The scope of SOP 01-6 is very broad. The only financing and lending transactions exempt from the standards established by this SOP are those (1) of entities that report receivables at fair value with gains and losses included in earnings or (2) that are subject to a category (a) standard that conflicts with the guidance in the SOP. The provisions of the SOP are discussed below, at the end of this chapter, and further in Chapter 25.

If the reporting entity has the intent and ability to hold trade receivables or loans for the foreseeable future or until maturity or payoff, those receivables are reported in the balance sheet at outstanding principal (face) amount less any write-offs and allowance for uncollectible receivables. Loans originated by the reporting entity are reported net of deferred fees or costs of originating them, and purchased loans are reported net of any unamortized premium or discount. Once a decision has been made to sell loans, those loans are transferred to a held-for-sale category on the balance sheet and reported at the lower of cost or fair value. Any amount by which cost exceeds fair value is accounted for as a valuation allowance.

When a trade receivable or loan is deemed uncollectible, the balance is written off against the allowance for uncollectible receivables. Recoveries of loans and trade receivables that were previously written off are recorded when received—either by a credit directly to earnings or by a credit to the allowance for uncollectible receivables. A credit loss on a financial instrument with off-balance-sheet risk is recorded as a liability rather than being included in a valuation allowance netted against a recognized financial instrument. When settled, the credit loss is deducted from the liability.

SOP 01-6 also includes standards for recognizing fees related to receivables. Delinquency fees are to be recognized when chargeable, provided that collectibility is reasonably assured. Prepayment fees are not to be recognized until prepayments have occurred. Rebates of finance charges due because payments are made earlier than required are to be recognized when the receivables are prepaid and are accounted for as adjustments to interest income.

### Example of delinquency fees, prepayment fees, and rebates

The DitchWay Company sells a ditch digging machine called the DitchMade that contractors use to lay utility lines and pipes. DitchWay invoices customers a standard monthly fee for two years, using a book of 24 preprinted invoices, after which they receive title to their DitchMade machines. The DitchMade machine is patent-protected and unique, so contractors must purchase from DitchWay. If a contractor makes a late payment, DitchWay bills them a $150 late fee. Since DitchWay can withhold title to the equipment if all fees are not received, the collection of these fees is reasonably assured. Its entry to record a late fee follows:

| | | |
|---|---|---|
| Accounts receivable | 150 | |
| Income—delinquency fees | | 150 |

One contractor enters bankruptcy proceedings. It has accumulated $450 of unpaid delinquency fees by the time it enters bankruptcy. DitchWay uses the following entry to eliminate the fees from its accounts receivable:

| | | |
|---|---|---|
| Bad debt reserve | 450 | |
| Accounts receivable | | 450 |

DitchWay's sale agreement recognizes that its billing schedule is essentially a series of loan payments with an implied interest rate of 12%. About 20% of all contractors obtain better financing elsewhere and prepay their invoices in order to reduce the interest payment. DitchWay charges a flat $500 prepayment fee when a prepayment occurs. Though the proportion of early payments is predictable, DitchWay cannot recognize prepayment fees until each prepayment actually occurs. One contractor makes a prepayment, so DitchWay records the following entry:

| | | |
|---|---|---|
| Accounts receivable | 500 | |
| Income—prepayment fees | | 500 |

The DitchWay sales agreement also states that, when a contractor prepays an invoice, it should pay the full amount of the invoice, even if paid early, and DitchWay will rebate the unearned portion of the interest expense associated with the early payment. In one case, a contractor prepays a single $2,500 invoice for which the original sales entry was as follows:

| | | |
|---|---|---|
| Accounts receivable | 2,500 | |
| Interest income | | 450 |
| Revenue | | 2,050 |

The amount of interest to be rebated back to the contractor is $225, which DitchWay records with the following entry:

| | | |
|---|---|---|
| Interest income—rebated | 225 | |
| Cash | | 225 |

The use of the contra account, interest income—rebated, provides the reporting entity with greater control and information for management purposes. However, the debit could be made directly to interest income if these enhancements are not useful.

**Pledging, assigning, and factoring receivables.** An organization can alter the timing of cash flows resulting from sales to its customers by using its accounts receivable as collateral for borrowings or by selling the receivables outright. A wide variety of arrangements can be structured by the borrower and lender, but the most common are pledging, assignment, and factoring.

Pledging is an agreement in which accounts receivable are used as collateral for loans. The customers whose accounts have been pledged are not aware of this event, and their payments are still remitted to the original entity to which the debt was owed. The pledged accounts merely serve as security to the lender, giving comfort that sufficient assets exist to generate cash flows adequate in amount and timing to repay the debt. However, the debt is paid by the borrower whether or not the pledged receivables are collected and whether or not the pattern of their collection matches the payments due on the debt.

The only accounting issue relating to pledging is that of adequate disclosure. The accounts receivable, which remain assets of the borrowing entity, continue to be shown as current assets in its financial statements but must be identified as having been pledged. This identification can be accomplished either parenthetically or by note disclosures. Similarly, the related debt should be identified as having been collateralized by the receivables.

### Example of disclosure for pledged receivables

*Current assets:*
Accounts receivable ($3,500,000 of which has been pledged as collateral
for bank loans), net of allowance for doubtful accounts of $600,000      8,450,000
*Current liabilities:*
Bank loans payable (collateralized by pledged accounts receivable)      2,700,000

A more common practice is to include the disclosure in the notes to the financial statements. Since the borrower has not surrendered control of the pledged receivables, it continues to carry the pledged receivables as its assets (FAS 140). (More complex collateral arrangements are described in the section "Accounting for collateral" later in this chapter.)

The assignment of accounts receivable is a more formalized transfer of the receivables to the lending institution. The lender investigates the specific receivables that are being proposed for assignment and will approve those that it deems worthy as collateral. Usually customers are not aware that their accounts have been assigned and they continue to forward their payments to the original obligee (the borrowing entity). In some cases, the assignment agreement requires that collection proceeds be immediately delivered to the lender. The borrower is, however, the primary obligor of the debt and is required to make timely payment on the debt whether or not the receivables are collected as anticipated. The borrowing is with recourse, and the general credit of the borrower is pledged to the payment of the debt.

Since the lender knows that not all the receivables will be collected on a timely basis by the borrower, only a fraction of the face value of the receivables will be advanced as a loan to the borrower. Typically, this amount ranges from 70 to 90%, depending upon the credit history and collection experience of the borrower.

Assigned accounts receivable remain the assets of the borrower and continue to be presented in its financial statements, with appropriate disclosure of the assignment similar to that illustrated for pledging. Prepaid finance charges would be recorded as a prepaid expense and amortized to expense over the period to which the charges apply.

In the typical case involving the assignment of receivables, the borrower retains control of the receivables, and it is clear that the transaction is a secured borrowing rather than a sale. If it is unclear whether the borrower has retained control of the receivables, a determination must be made as to whether to account for the transfer as a sale or as a secured borrowing.

Making that determination is discussed later in this chapter in the section titled "Transfers of Financial Assets under FAS 140."

Factoring traditionally involves the outright sale of receivables to a finance company known as a factor. These arrangements involve (1) notification to the customer to remit future payments to the factor and (2) the transfer of receivables to the factor without recourse to the transferor. The factor assumes the risk of an inability to collect. Thus, once a factoring arrangement is completed, the transferor has no further involvement with the accounts, except for a return of merchandise.

In its simplest form, the receivables are sold and the difference between the cash received and the carrying value is recognized as a gain or loss.

### Example of accounting for the factoring of receivables without recourse

Thirsty Corp. enters into an agreement with Rich Company to sell a group of its receivables without recourse for $180,055. A total face value of $200,000 accounts receivable (against which a 5% allowance had been recorded) are involved. The entries required are as follows:

| | | |
|---|---|---|
| Cash | 180,055 | |
| Allowance for bad debts (200,000 × .05) | 10,000 | |
| Loss on sale of receivables | 19,945 | |
|     Bad debts expense | | 10,000 |
|     Accounts receivable | | 200,000 |

The classic variety of factoring provides two financial services to the business: it permits the reporting entity to obtain cash earlier than waiting for customers to pay, and it transfers the risk of bad debts to the factor. The factor is compensated for each of these services. Interest is charged based on the anticipated length of time between the date the factoring arrangement is consummated and the expected collection date of the receivables sold. A fee is charged based upon the factor's anticipated bad debt losses.

### Example of accounting for the factoring of receivables without recourse

Thirsty Corp. enters into an agreement with Rich Company to sell a group of its receivables without recourse. The receivables have a total face value of $200,000 (against which a 5% allowance had been recorded). The factor will charge 20% interest computed on the weighted-average time to maturity of the receivables of thirty-six days plus a 3% fee.

The entries required are as follows:

| | | |
|---|---|---|
| Cash | 180,055 | |
| Allowance for bad debts (200,000 × .05) | 10,000 | |
| Interest expense (or prepaid) (200,000 × .20 × 36/365) | 3,945 | |
| Factoring fee (200,000 × .03) | 6,000 | |
| Loss on sale of receivables | 10,000 | |
|     Bad debts expense | | 10,000 |
|     Accounts receivable | | 200,000 |

The interest expense, factor's fee and loss can be combined into a $19,945 loss on the sale of receivables.

Some companies factor receivables as a means of transferring bad debt risk, but leave the cash on deposit with the factor until the weighted-average due date of the receivables, thereby avoiding interest charges. This arrangement is still referred to as factoring, since the customer receivables have been sold. However, the borrowing entity does not receive cash but instead records a new receivable, usually captioned "Due from Factor." This receivable, in contrast to the original customer receivables, is essentially without risk and is presented in the balance sheet without a deduction for estimated uncollectible receivables.

Merchandise returns are normally the responsibility of the transferor, who must then make the appropriate settlement with the factor. To protect against the possibility that merchandise returns will diminish the total of receivables to be collected, a factor will frequently advance only a portion of the face amount of the factored receivables (less any interest and factoring fee deductions). The factor will retain a certain fraction of the total proceeds relating to the portion of sales that are anticipated to be returned by customers. This sum is known as the factor's holdback. When merchandise is returned to the transferor, an entry is made offsetting the receivable from the factor. At the end of the return privilege period, any remaining holdback will become due and payable to the transferor.

### Example of accounting for the factoring of receivables without recourse

1. Thirsty Corp. enters into an agreement with Rich Company to sell a group of its receivables without recourse. The receivables have a total face value of $200,000 (against which a 5% allowance had been recorded). The factor will charge 20% interest computed on the weighted-average time to maturity of the receivables of thirty-six days plus a 3% fee. A 5% holdback will also be retained.
2. Thirsty's customers return for credit $4,800 of merchandise.
3. The customer return privilege period expires and the remaining holdback is paid to the transferor.

The entries required are as follows:

| | | | |
|---|---|---:|---:|
| 1. | Cash | 180,055 | |
| | Allowance for bad debts (200,000 × .05) | 10,000 | |
| | Interest expense (or prepaid) (200,000 × .20 × 36/365) | 3,945 | |
| | Factoring fee (200,000 × .03) | 6,000 | |
| | Factor's holdback receivable | | |
| | [$10,000/($10,000 + $190,000) × $190,000] | 9,500 | |
| | Loss on sale of receivables | 500 | |
| | Bad debts expense | | 10,000 |
| | Accounts receivable | | 200,000 |

The interest expense, factor's fee and loss can be combined into a $10,445 charge to loss on the sale of receivables.

| | | | |
|---|---|---:|---:|
| 2. | Sales returns and allowances | 4,800 | |
| | Factor's holdback receivable | | 4,800 |
| 3. | Cash | 5,200 | |
| | Factor's holdback receivable | | 4,700 |
| | Loss on sale of receivables | | 500 |

The factor's holdback receivable recorded by the seller is required by FAS 140 to be an allocation of the carrying value of the receivables ($190,000) between the assets sold (the receivables) and the assets retained (the holdback) based on their relative fair values at the date of the factoring agreement. The factor holds back 5% of the face value ($200,000) for a total of $10,000. Upon settlement the loss or gain recorded at the origination of the factoring arrangement needs to be adjusted because the factor pays the remaining holdback of $5,200 ($10,000 holdback – $4,800 returns) in settlement of an asset with a carrying value of $4,700 ($9,500 – $4,800).

Factoring results in a transfer of title to the factored receivables. Where there is a no recourse provision or other continuing involvement with the receivables, the removal of the receivables from the borrower's balance sheet is clearly warranted.

Another variation is known as factoring with recourse. Accounting for factoring with recourse requires a determination of whether the transfer is a sale or a secured borrowing. That determination is made by applying FAS 140.

## Transfers of Financial Assets under FAS 140

If receivables or other financial assets are transferred to another entity and the transferor has no continuing involvement with the transferred assets or with the transferee, it is clear that a sale has taken place, the asset should be derecognized, and a gain or loss on the sale is to be measured and recognized. However, in many cases, the transferor of the receivables has some form of continuing involvement with the transferred assets, either because it sells the receivables with recourse for uncollectible amounts, it retains an interest in the receivables, or it agrees to service the receivables after the sale. The more control that the transferor retains over the receivables, the more the transfer appears to be in substance a secured borrowing rather than a sale.

FAS 140 established the procedures used to determine whether a transfer of financial assets is a sale or a secured borrowing. The standard uses a financial components approach in which a single financial asset is viewed as a mix of component assets (controlled economic benefits) and component liabilities (obligations for probable future sacrifices of economic benefits). The focus is on who controls the components and whether that control has changed as a result of a given transfer. If the transferor has surrendered control of the transferred assets, the transfer is a sale. If the transferor retains control of the transferred assets, the transfer is a secured borrowing.

In order to be accounted for as an actual transfer (i.e., disposition) of financial assets, the transferred assets must be isolated from the transferor (put presumptively out of reach of the transferor's creditors); each transferee or holder of beneficial interest must be granted the right to pledge or exchange the transferred assets; and the transferor cannot maintain effective control over the assets. All conditions must be satisfied for derecognition accounting by the transferor to be appropriate.

Derecognition of financial liabilities by a debtor can be properly reflected only if the obligation is extinguished, which requires that either the debt is retired (paid off) or the debtor is legally released from being the primary obligor by either the counterparty or by judicial action (e.g., in bankruptcy proceedings). These conditions are discussed in the following paragraphs (financial assets) and in Chapter 14 (financial liabilities).

**Scope.** FAS 140 applies to transfers of noncash financial assets by and to an entity other than the issuer of the financial asset. Thus, a transfer includes selling a receivable, transferring a receivable to a trust, or using a receivable as security for a loan. A transfer includes neither the origination of a receivable, the settlement of a receivable, nor the restructuring of a receivable in a troubled debt restructuring because those transactions are transfers involving the issuer of the receivable.

Among the types of transfers of financial assets for which FAS 140 establishes standards are

- Transfers of receivables with recourse (factoring with recourse)
- Transfers of undivided partial interests in receivables (retained interests)
- Transfers of receivables with servicing retained
- Transfers of minimum lease payments under sales-type and direct financing leases and any related guaranteed residual
- Securitizations
- Repurchase agreements
- Securities lending
- Transfers of receivables as collateral

The foregoing types of transactions are discussed in this chapter. In addition, FAS 140 sets standards for extinguishments of liabilities, which are discussed in Chapter 15.

Examples of items included in the scope of FAS 140 are the accounting for

1. Beneficial interests in a securitization trust that holds nonfinancial assets such as securitized stranded costs or similar imposed rights (unless a third party must consolidate the trust).
2. A litigation judgment that is enforceable and contractually reduced to a fixed payment schedule.
3. Transfer of an equity method investment unless subject to EITF 01-2 (similar productive assets) or EITF 98-8 (sale of real estate).
4. A forward contract on a financial instrument that may be net settled or physically settled by exchange for cash or some other financial asset.
5. Recognized financial instruments that may be either financial assets or financial liabilities at some point (e.g., forward or swap contracts), must meet the criteria applicable to derecognition of financial assets *and* financial liabilities to be derecognized.
6. Dollar rolls in connection with the transfer of existing securities.
7. Transfers of investments in subsidiaries that have not been consolidated because the parent carries the investment at fair value (e.g., an investment company).

The following items are *excluded* from the scope of FAS 140:

1. The right to receive the minimum lease payments under an operating lease since it is an unrecognized financial asset.
2. Transfers of servicing rights that are contractually separated from the serviced assets because they are nonfinancial assets.
3. Payment of cash or conveyances of noncash financial assets in partial or full settlement of a debt. An origination, settlement, or restructuring of a receivable is not a transfer since it does not involve a conveyance of a noncash financial asset by or to someone other than the issuer.
4. Acquisition of treasury shares by exchanging noncash financial assets, because it is an investment by or a distribution to owners.
5. Desecuritization of securities into loans or other financial assets.
6. Securitized stranded costs of electric utilities (although enforceable rights) are not considered financial assets since they arise from an imposition of tax rather than a contractual agreement.
7. Contingent receivables from litigation before terms are reduced to a contract.
8. Transfer of ownership interest in a consolidated subsidiary if the subsidiary's assets are not all financial assets.
9. Recognized derivatives that are nonfinancial assets (an option to purchase commodities) at the date of transfer.
10. Dollar rolls when the underlying securities do not yet exist or are to be announced (TBA GNMA rolls).
11. Transfers of unguaranteed residual values on transfers of sales-type or direct financing lease receivables.

**Surrender of control.** A transfer of financial assets (or a portion of a financial asset) is a sale if the transferor surrenders control over those assets in exchange for consideration. However, control is not surrendered to the extent that the consideration received is a beneficial interest in the transferred assets. For example, a transferor's exchange of one form of beneficial interests in a trust for an equivalent, but different, form in the same transferred financial assets cannot be accounted for as a sale. If the trust initially issued the beneficial interests, the exchange is not even considered to be a transfer under FAS 140. A proposed amendment to FAS 140, *Accounting for Transfers of Financial Assets*, was first exposed in

2003, further exposed in revised form in 2005, and remains under deliberation as of mid-2008. Given recent subprime and other lending concerns, which in part arise from securitization practices involving complex structures employing off-balance-sheet accounting, this project is expected to receive renewed attention in the latter part of 2008. Elimination of *qualified* SPE status is deemed a likely outcome, although this is by no means a certainty.

The existing standard specifies that control is deemed to have been surrendered by the transferor only if all of the following conditions are met.

*NOTE: Proposed amendments to these criteria, currently under consideration by FASB, are set forth in italics in the following:*

1.  The assets transferred are beyond the reach of the transferor and its affiliates (to be amended to specify consolidated affiliates that are not an SPE or other bankruptcy-remote entity), its creditors, potential bankruptcy trustees or other receivers, except for an affiliate that is a qualifying special-purpose entity (QSPE).

    *NOTE: FIN 46(R) introduced the concept of variable interest entities, or VIE, which largely superseded the concept of SPE, but entities that met the criteria for qualifying special-purpose entities, or QSPE, under FAS 140 continue to be so classified. That is, by definition QSPEs are not VIEs and are not subject to consolidation.*

    *NOTE: Largely as a consequence of the subprime mortgage lending and collateralized debt obligation (CDO) developments of late 2007 and early 2008, FASB has signaled its intent to reexamine the use of QSPEs, and there is a reasonable expectation that QSPEs may be eliminated as a vehicle for off-balance-sheet financing, perhaps by the end of 2008.*

2.  The transferee (or if the transferee is a QSPE, each holder of its beneficial interests) has the right to pledge or exchange the assets (or beneficial interests) it received, and no condition both (1) constrains the transferee (or holder) from taking advantage of its right to pledge or exchange and (2) provides more than a trivial benefit to the transferor.

    *NOTE: This will be expanded to state that if the transaction involves a series of steps intended to isolate the transferred assets, each entity that receives the transferred financial assets is a transferee, and thus each transfer must meet the foregoing conditions.*

3.  The transferor (or its consolidated affiliates, per the proposed amendment) does not maintain effective control over the transferred assets. A transferor maintains effective control if (1) an agreement both entitles and obligates the transferor to repurchase or redeem the assets before their maturity or (2) the transferor has the ability to unilaterally cause the holder to return specific assets. If the transferor can cause the holder to return assets only through a cleanup call, that ability does not indicate effective control. (A cleanup call is an option to purchase the remaining transferred financial assets, or the remaining beneficial interests in a QSPE if the amount of outstanding assets or beneficial interests falls to a prespecified level at which the cost of servicing those assets or beneficial interests becomes burdensome in relation to the benefits of servicing.)

4.  The proposed amendment to FAS 140 will further stipulate that the isolation analysis must take into account any arrangement or agreement that is undertaken in connection with the transfer, even if not consummated at the time of the transfer.

5.  The proposed amendment to FAS 140 will also specify that, if the transferee is a QSPE, no arrangement or agreement is to be made between any holder of beneficial interests issued by the QSPE and the transferor or its consolidated affiliates that would have resulted in not isolating the assets transferred if such arrangement or agreement had been between the QSPE itself, rather than its beneficial interest

holders. (A revised Exposure Draft issued in 2005 remains outstanding as of mid-2008.)

All available evidence is to be assessed to determine if transferred assets would be beyond the reach of the powers of a bankruptcy trustee (or equivalent). It is irrelevant to this determination that the possibility of bankruptcy is remote at the date of the transfer. Instead, the transferor must endeavor to isolate the assets in the event of bankruptcy, however unlikely that eventuality may be. In many cases, transferors use two transfers to isolate the transferred assets. First, it transfers the assets to a wholly owned corporation that is designed in a way that prevents the transferor or its creditors from reclaiming the assets (or makes the possibility that they can reclaim them remote). Next, the wholly owned corporation transfers the assets to a trust. The trust is prevented from undertaking any business other than management of the assets and from incurring any liabilities. (Thus, there are no creditors to force bankruptcy of the trust.)

A determination that the transferred assets are beyond the reach of a bankruptcy trustee may require a legal opinion regarding the application of the laws of the relevant jurisdiction. Such legal opinions commonly address whether a "true sale" has occurred, and in practice different attorneys may reach different conclusions regarding a given transaction. If a transfer is to an affiliated entity, the legal opinion would also have to address whether the transferee did not need to be consolidated (i.e., that it was a QSPE). There is nothing under GAAP that makes obtaining a "true sale" opinion an absolute necessity, however.

The existence of setoff rights does not impede the finding of a "true sale." In practice, while setoff rights may exist for the transferor and transferee, if either the obligor under the transferred financial asset (e.g., debtor under transferred receivable) or the transferor entity enters bankruptcy, the transferee might have only an unsecured claim, notwithstanding the nominal right of setoff.

Assets transferred by a bank or other financial institution that is subject to possible receivership by the FDIC can be considered isolated from the transferor even if the FDIC or another creditor can require their return, provided that the return can only occur in receivership, after a default, and in exchange for a payment of, at a minimum, principal and interest earned at the contractual yield to the date the investors are paid. (That rule does not apply to situations in which the transferor can require return of the assets in exchange for payment of principal and interest earned at the contractual yield to the date the investors are paid. In those cases the assets are not isolated from the transferor.) FTB 01-1, *Effective Date for Certain Financial Institutions of Certain Provisions of Statement 140 Related to the Isolation of Transferred Financial Assets*, deferred application of the isolation criterion for banks and certain other financial institutions until periods beginning after December 31, 2001. FTB 01-1 also gave those institutions up to five years of additional transition time to comply with this criterion regarding transfers of assets to certain securitization master trusts, under defined conditions.

A transferee has control of transferred assets if there is the unconstrained right to both pledge and exchange the assets. In actual practice it may be more difficult to discern whether the transferee has control if it can pledge the transferred assets but cannot sell them. The key to a determination of control by a transferee with the right to pledge *or* exchange the assets rests on whether the transferee obtains all or most of the cash inflows that are the primary economic benefits of the pledged or exchanged assets. Generally, the right of first refusal, prohibition of a sale to competitors, and the requirement to obtain transferor permission that won't be unreasonably withheld (judgment is necessary in this case) to sell or pledge won't preclude accounting as a sale. Agreements that constrain the transferee from pledge or exchange are to be accounted for as secured borrowings.

**Maintaining effective control.** The criteria set forth by FAS 140 must be met in order for a transfer to be accounted for as a sale, and the formal criteria identified in the body of the standard are affected by the expanded implementation guidance included in Appendix A to the standard. If the transferor maintains effective control, the transfer is accounted for as a secured borrowing and not as a sale.

The transferor must not be able to unilaterally take back the transferred assets. Therefore, a call option, a forward purchase contract, or a removal of accounts provision will in most cases defeat the determination that a sale has taken place. The transferor cannot take back the transferred assets even through the liquidation of the VIE or QSPE. For example, a transferor that holds a residual interest in a QSPE must be precluded from participating in any auction that QSPE may hold at the termination of its existence because presumably it would be willing to pay a price above any other bidder because it would receive any excess over fair value back via its residual interest.

A transferor maintains effective control over the transferred assets, and thus cannot account for the transfer as a sale, if a repurchase or redemption agreement meets all of the following conditions:

1.  The assets covered by the agreement must be the same or substantially the same as the transferred assets. In order to meet this condition, the assets transferred and those to be repurchased or redeemed must meet all of the following conditions:

    a.  The same primary obligor or, in the case of government-guaranteed instruments, the same guarantor and terms of the guarantee. (If the asset is debt guaranteed by a sovereign government, central bank, government-sponsored enterprise or agency thereof, the guarantor and the terms of the guarantee must be the same.)
    b.  Identical form and type providing the same risks and rights
    c.  The same maturity, or, in the case of mortgage-backed pass-through or pay-through securities, have similar remaining weighted-average maturities that provide approximately the same market yield
    d.  Identical contractual interest rates
    e.  Similar collateral
    f.  The same aggregate unpaid principal amount or principal amounts that are within accepted "good delivery" standards for the type of security being transferred

2.  The transferor is able to repurchase or redeem the assets on substantially the agreed terms even if the transferee were to default. In order to meet this condition, the transferor must, during the entire term of the contract, have obtained cash or other collateral sufficient to fund substantially the entire cost of purchasing replacement assets from others. For example, a contractual provision that terminates a repurchase agreement immediately if the value of the collateral become insufficient to fund substantially all of the cost of purchasing replacement assets would satisfy the requirement, as would a margining provision.

3.  The redemption or repurchase agreement is executed concurrently with the transfer of the assets and requires repurchase or redemption prior to maturity at a fixed or determinable price.

FSP FAS 140-3, *Accounting for Transfers of Financial Assets and Repurchase Financing Transactions*, addresses situations where the original transferee subsequently transfers the financial assets back to the original transferor as collateral for a borrowing arrangement under a repurchase arrangement. The issue is whether this violates the surrender of control criterion of FAS 140, obviating the ability of the original transferor to record the transfer as a sale. FSP FAS 140-3 establishes criteria under which the secured borrowing could be evaluated separately from the initial transfer for purposes of determining proper accounting.

Under the provisions of this staff position, the transferor and transferee are to separately account for a transfer of a financial asset and a related repurchase financing arrangement only if the two transactions have a valid and distinct business or economic purpose for being entered into separately, *and* the repurchase financing does not result in the transferor regaining control over the financial asset. The valid business purpose criterion excludes obtaining favorable accounting treatment. To qualify for separate accounting treatment, the initial transfer of a financial asset and the repurchase financing entered into either contemporaneously with, or in contemplation of, each other must meet *all* of the following conditions at inception of the transaction:

1. The initial transfer and the repurchase financing are not contractually contingent on each other, so that the pricing and performance of either the transfer or the repurchase financing will not be dependent on the terms and execution of the other.
2. The repurchase financing provides the initial transferor with recourse to the transferee upon default, which must leave the transferor exposed to the credit risk of the transferee or its affiliates, and not only exposed to the market risk of the transferred financial asset.
3. The transferee's agreement to repurchase the previously transferred financial asset is at a fixed price (generally related to the agreed interest rate on the amount financed) and not at fair value.
4. The financial asset is readily obtainable in the marketplace, and the transfer and repurchase financing are executed at market rates, and not circumvented by embedding off-market terms in a separate transaction contemplated at the time of the initial transfer or the repurchase financing.
5. The maturity date of the repurchase financing is earlier than that of the financial asset.

If the transaction satisfies each of the above-noted conditions, the initial transfer should be evaluated to determine if, without consideration of the repurchase financing, it meets the requirements for sale accounting under SFAS 140. Also, the transferor and transferee should analyze the repurchase financing as a repurchase agreement, with both parties using the same criteria.

On the other hand, if the transactions do not meet all of these conditions, the initial transfer and repurchase financing should be evaluated as a linked transaction to determine whether it meets the requirements in FAS 140 for sale accounting. If the linked transaction does not qualify for sale accounting, the linked transactions should be accounted for based on the economic substance of the combined transactions. Typically, these will represent a forward contract, to be accounted for in accordance with FAS 133.

Readers should also be alert to the possibility that the status of qualified special-purpose entities (QSPE) may be changed significantly, largely due to the reaction to the subprime lending problems that surfaced in 2007 and 2008. One possible outcome is that QSPE may be eliminated entirely. FASB will be making some decisions on this and related matters as early as year-end 2008.

**Accounting for transfers.** Upon any transfer (whether accounted for as a sale or as a secured borrowing), the transferor will allocate, based on relative fair values at the date of transfer, the previous carrying amount between the retained interests, if any, and the assets transferred. Retained interests are interests in the transferred assets over which control has not been given up by the transferor. They include servicing assets and liabilities, undivided interests in the transferred assets, and beneficial interests in assets transferred to a qualifying special-purpose entity in a securitization.

If a sale, the transferor (seller) is to

1. Derecognize all assets sold
2. Recognize all assets obtained (including cash, options, swaps, etc.) and liabilities incurred (including forward commitments and servicing liabilities) in consideration as proceeds
3. Measure assets controlled and liabilities incurred at fair value initially if they are part of the proceeds of the sale (new assets and liabilities, which could include cash, put or call options held or written—such as guarantee or recourse obligations, forward commitments, swaps, beneficial interests, and servicing liabilities). If it is not practical to estimate the fair value of the assets, the transferor will record those assets at zero. If it is not practical to estimate the fair value of the liabilities, the transferor will not recognize any gain on the transaction and will record liabilities at the greater of

    a. Excess fair value of the assets obtained minus the fair value of the liabilities incurred, over the carrying value of the assets transferred or
    b. The amount to be recorded in conjunction with FAS 5 and FIN 14 that represents the minimum amount in an estimated range of a probable liability.

4. Recognize gains or losses in earnings.

All financial asset transfers not meeting the sale criteria are required to be accounted for as secured borrowings with collateral (or another security interest) pledged.

**Other qualifying SPE issues.** FAS 140 sets forth certain conditions that must be met for a trust or other legal entity to be considered a qualifying special-purpose entity (QSPE). One condition is that a QSPE may hold only passive derivative financial instruments that pertain to beneficial interests issued or sold to parties other than the transferor, its affiliates, or its agents. (Note that, in the context of the recent subprime mortgage crisis, the strict requirement that the QSPE act only in a passive capacity has been blamed for the inability of banks and other financial institutions to respond in a proactive way, e.g., by restructuring the terms of troubled debt.)

Another set of requirements established by FAS 140 defines when a derivative financial instrument pertains to beneficial interests issued (other than another derivative financial instrument). It states this will be satisfied only if the derivative instrument

1. Is entered into (a) when the beneficial interests are issued by the QSPE to parties other than the transferor, its affiliates, or its agents or sold to such other parties after being issued by the QSPE to the transferor, its affiliates, or its agents or (b) when a passive derivative financial instrument needs to be replaced upon occurrence of an event or circumstance (specified in the legal documents that established the SPE or created the beneficial interests in the transferred assets that it holds) outside the control of the transferor, its affiliates, or its agents, for example, when the counterparty to the derivative defaults or is downgraded below a specified threshold;
2. Has a notional amount that does not initially exceed the amount of those beneficial interests and is not expected to exceed them subsequently; and
3. Has characteristics that relate to, and partly or fully but not excessively counteract, some risk associated with those beneficial interests or the related transferred assets.

The FASB limited the notional amount of the derivatives in a QSPE to the amount of beneficial interests held by parties other than the transferor, its affiliates, or its agents (outside parties) in order to prevent a transferor from avoiding the requirements of FAS 133 by transferring derivatives to a QSPE that relate to its own beneficial interests in the QSPE. According to FAS 140, "The Board noted that if the transferor wanted to enter into derivative instruments pertaining to the beneficial interests it holds, it could accomplish that by entering into such derivative instruments on its own behalf, which would be accounted for under FAS 133." The basis for requiring that the derivatives not excessively counteract the risks associated with the beneficial interests held by parties other than the transferor or its affiliates was to preclude a QSPE from holding a derivative that does not pertain to the beneficial interests held by outside parties.

However, questions have since arisen in practice which caused FASB to issue a staff position, FSP 140-2, *Clarification of the Application of Paragraphs 40(b) and 40(c) of FASB Statement No. 140*, to clarify application of the original provisions of FAS 140. This FSP holds that

> *The requirements of paragraphs (b) and (c), above, must be met when beneficial interests are initially issued by the QSPE, or when a passive derivative financial instrument needs to be replaced upon the occurrence of a specified event outside the control of the transferor, its affiliates, or its agents. Assessing whether the requirements of paragraphs (b) and (c), above, are met is to be based on an analysis of the expected assets of the QSPE and the expected amount of beneficial interests held by outside parties over the expected life of the qualifying SPE. However, unexpected subsequent events outside the control of the transferor, its affiliates, or its agents (e.g., prepayments of assets of the QSPE), that were not contemplated by an analysis of the expected assets of the QSPE and the expected amount of beneficial interests held by outside parties when the beneficial interests of the QSPE were issued would not impair the qualified status of the QSPE.*
>
> *Purchases of previously issued beneficial interests by a transferor, its affiliates, or its agents from outside parties that are held temporarily and are classified as trading securities are not to be considered when determining whether the requirements of paragraphs (b) and (c), above, are met.*
>
> *Furthermore, any remedial action taken by the QSPE to "rebalance" the derivative amount with the amount of beneficial interests held by parties other than the transferor, its affiliates, or its agents must be taken in accordance with the terms and activities specified in the governing documents of the QSPE at the time it was originally established. That is, all activities must continue to meet the permitted activities limitations of FAS 140. In this regard, activities include, but are not limited to, the selection of a derivative counterparty, the determination of the notional amount, and the timing of the amortization of the notional amount and must be considered with the activities specified in the legal document that established the SPE.*

**Measuring assets and liabilities after completion of a transfer.** FAS 140 addresses initial recognition and measurement but, except for servicing, does not address subsequent measurement. Existing GAAP must be used for that purpose. For example

1. Interest-only strips, retained interests in securitizations, loans, other receivables, or other financial assets that can contractually be prepaid or otherwise settled in such a way that the holder would not recover substantially all of its recorded investment (except for derivative instruments that are within the scope of FAS 133) are to be subsequently measured like investments in debt securities classified as available-for-sale or trading under FAS 115, and thus at fair value.

2. Equity securities that have readily determinable fair values are subsequently measured in accordance with FAS 115, at fair value (either available-for-sale or trading).

3. Debt securities are subsequently measured in accordance with FAS 115, FAS 65 (mortgage-backed securities) or EITF 99-20 (purchased and retained beneficial interests in securitized financial assets).

4. Derivative financial instruments are subsequently measured in accordance with FAS 133.

If it was initially impracticable to measure the fair value of an asset or liability but it later becomes practicable, the transferor does not remeasure the asset or liability (or the gain or loss) under FAS 140 unless it is a servicing asset or liability. (FAS 156, *Accounting for Servicing of Financial Assets*, has revised accounting for servicing assets and liabilities; this is discussed in detail later in this chapter.) However, adjustment of the carrying value may be required by other standards, such as FAS 115.

The provisions of FAS 140 apply to a wide range of transfers of financial instruments. Some of those are discussed in the following paragraphs.

**Transfers of receivables with recourse.** Classic factoring involves the outright sale of receivables and, notwithstanding the existence of a "holdback" intended to deal with returns and allowances, are accounted for as sales. However, some entities have such a poor history of uncollectible accounts that factors are only willing to purchase their accounts if a substantial fee is collected to compensate for the risk. If the company believes that the receivables are of a better quality than the factor has assessed them, a way to avoid excessive factoring fees is to sell these receivables with recourse. This variation of factoring is, in substance, an assignment of receivables with notification to the affected customers (whereas traditional assignment does not include notification of debtors).

*Structure of transfer.* In a transfer of receivables with recourse, the transferor is obligated to make payments to the transferee or to repurchase receivables sold upon the occurrence of an uncertain future event. Typically, recourse provisions compensate the transferee for uncollectible accounts (sometimes amounts over a defined threshold), but they can also be written to compensate the transferee for such uncertain future events as prepayments of receivables subject to discounts or that are interest bearing, merchandise returns, or other events that change the anticipated cash flows from the receivables.

The effect of a recourse provision on the application of FAS 140's surrender of control provisions may vary by jurisdiction and by the level of recourse provided. For example, in some jurisdictions, full recourse will not place the receivables beyond the reach of the transferor and its creditors, while a limited recourse provision may have this result. Thus, some transfers of receivables with recourse will meet the criteria of FAS 140 and be accounted for as sales; other transfers will fail the criteria and be accounted for as secured borrowings. The remaining discussion in this section relates to scenarios where the arrangement qualifies for sales treatment.

*Applicability of FAS 133 or FIN 45.* In order for the recourse provision to be exempt from derivatives accounting, it must meet *all three* of the following criteria:

1. The contract provides for payments to be made solely to reimburse the guaranteed party (the factor) for failure of the debtor to satisfy its obligations to make required payments, when due at prespecified payment dates or at dates that are earlier due to acceleration caused by a default. For the purposes of meeting this criterion, the debtor's obligation cannot be due under a contract that is accounted for as a derivative.

2. Payment under the recourse provision is made only if the debtor's obligation under 1. above is past due.

3.  At the date of inception of the factoring arrangement and subsequently throughout the term of the arrangement, the factor will be exposed to the risk of nonpayment through direct or indirect ownership of the guaranteed receivable.

If the recourse provision fails any of the three above criteria, it is considered a derivative and is accounted for by the transferor under the provisions of FAS 133, discussed in detail in Chapter 8.

Another accounting issue to consider is whether the recourse provision is considered a guarantee under FIN 45. FIN 45, which is discussed in detail in Chapter 14, provides that a contract that contingently requires the guarantor to make payments to the guaranteed party (in this case the factor) based on the nonoccurrence of a scheduled payment under a contract is considered a guarantee. The determination that the recourse obligation is a guarantee does not affect the measurement of that obligation because the measurement rules of FIN 45 are identical with the measurement rules for a recourse obligation that is not considered a guarantee. However, it is important to determine the applicability of that interpretation because FIN 45 requires additional disclosures not demanded by FAS 140.

***Computing gain or loss.*** In computing the gain or loss to be recognized at the date of a transfer of receivables that meets the criteria of FAS 140, the borrower (transferor) must take into account the anticipated chargebacks from the transferee. This action requires an estimate by the transferor, based on its past experience. Adjustments are to be made at the time of sale to record the recourse obligation for the estimated effects of any bad debts, prepayments by customers (where the receivables are interest-bearing or where cash discounts are available), and any defects in the eligibility of the transferred receivables. In computing this recourse obligation, the transferor is to consider all probable credit losses over the life of the transferred receivables. The recourse obligation is to be measured at its fair value on the date of sale.

EITF 92-2, as modified by subsequent pronouncements, specifies that a present value method is acceptable for estimating fair value if the timing of the future cash flows are reasonably estimable. In applying a present value method, the estimated future cash flows are to be discounted using a discount rate at which the liability could be settled in an arm's-length transaction (i.e., a risk-adjusted rate versus a risk-free rate). Subsequent accruals to adjust the discounted amount are to be discounted at the interest rate inherent in determining the initial recourse obligation. FAS 140, as is the case with a great number or recently issued pronouncements, expresses a preference for the use of the CON 7 probability-weighted expected cash flow model over the more traditional discounting of the single point estimate of the most probable or most likely cash flows. This model is discussed and illustrated in Chapter 1.

### Example of accounting for the transfer of receivables with recourse

1.  Thirsty Corp. enters into an agreement with Rich Company to sell a group of its receivables with a face value of $200,000 on which a 5% allowance for uncollectible accounts had been recorded. Rich Company (the factor) will charge 20% interest computed on the weighted-average time to maturity of the receivables of thirty-six days and a 3% fee. A 5% holdback will also be retained.
2.  Generally, 40% of Thirsty's customers take advantage of a 2% cash discount.
3.  The factor accepts the receivables subject to recourse for nonpayment.
4.  In this jurisdiction, the transfer qualifies as a sale.

Under FAS 140, Thirsty must record the recourse liability. It has accepted the obligation for all credit losses and has, in effect, guaranteed the receivables. The recourse obligation is measured as the estimate of uncollectibles (5% of face value).

The entry required to record the sale is

| | | |
|---|---|---|
| Cash | 180,055 | |
| Allowance for bad debts | 10,000 | |
| Interest expense (200,000 × .20 × 36/365) | 3,945 | |
| Factoring fee (200,000 × .03) | 6,000 | |
| Factor's holdback receivable | | |
|    [$10,000/($10,000 + $190,000) × $190,000] | 9,500 | |
| Loss on sale of receivables | 2,100 | |
|     Due to factor for discounts (200,000 × .40 × .02) | | 1,600 |
|     Accounts receivable | | 200,000 |
|     Recourse obligation | | 10,000 |

Simplified, the entry is

| | | |
|---|---|---|
| Cash | 180,055 | |
| Allowance for bad debts | 10,000 | |
| Factor's holdback receivable (9,500 – 1,600) | 7,900 | |
| Loss on sale of receivables (3,945 + 6,000 + 2,100) | 12,045 | |
|     Accounts receivable | | 200,000 |
|     Recourse obligation | | 10,000 |

The accounts receivable net of the allowance for uncollectible accounts (a valuation allowance) is removed from the transferor's accounting records as it has been sold. Previously accrued bad debts expense is not reversed, however, as the transferor still expects to incur that expense through the recourse provision of the factoring agreement. (Alternatively, the bad debts expense could have been reversed and the new charge to loss on sale will have to be increased by $10,000.) The loss on sale of receivables is the sum of the interest charged by the factor ($3,945), the factor's fee ($6,000), the expected chargeback for cash discounts to be taken ($1,600), and the difference between the holdback receivable at face value and at carrying value ($500). The factor's holdback receivable is a retained interest in the receivables transferred, and it is measured by allocating the original carrying amount ($190,000) between the assets sold ($190,000) and the assets retained ($10,000).

If, subsequent to the sale of the receivables, the actual experience relative to the recourse terms differs from the provision made at the time of the sale, a change in an accounting estimate results. It is accounted for prospectively, as are all changes in accounting estimates, and therefore will be reflected as an additional gain or loss in the subsequent period. These changes are not to be deemed corrections of errors or other retroactive adjustments.

If the above facts apply, but the transfer does not qualify as a sale, the borrower's entry will be

| | | |
|---|---|---|
| Cash | 180,055 | |
| Interest expense (or prepaid) | 3,945 | |
| Factoring fee | 6,000 | |
|     Factor borrowing payable | | 190,000 |

In a secured borrowing, the accounts receivable continue to be recognized by the borrower. Both the accounts receivable and the factor borrowings payable must be cross-referenced on the face of the balance sheet or in the notes to the financial statements. The accounting for the collateral under FAS 140 depends upon the terms of the collateral agreement. Accounting for collateral is discussed later in this chapter.

**Retained interests.** Interests in transferred assets that are not a part of the proceeds of a sale are considered retained interests that are still under the control of the transferor. Retained interests include undivided interests for which control has not been given up by the transferor, servicing assets and liabilities, and beneficial interests in assets transferred to a qualifying special-purpose entity in a securitization. (Note that FAS 156 amended FAS 140 with regard to the accounting for servicing assets and liabilities, as explained later in this chapter.) In general, the more extensive an interest that the transferor of assets retains, the less likely the transaction will be classified as a sale and the more likely the transaction will be classified as a secured borrowing. The primary reason for this result is that in a true sale, the transferor no longer bears the risks or reaps the rewards associated with the transferred assets. If a determination cannot be made between classification as proceeds of a sale or as retained interests, the asset is classified as proceeds and measured at fair value.

Retained interests are measured by allocating the carrying value of the transferred assets before the transfer between the assets sold (if any) and the assets retained based on their relative fair values on the date of transfer. EITF 88-11 (as modified by subsequent pronouncements) specifies that the carrying value allocated is to be exclusive of any amounts included in an allowance for loan losses. Any gain recognized upon a partial sale of a loan is not to exceed the gain that would be recognized if the entire loan were sold. If the transferor retains a servicing contract, a portion of the carrying value is allocable to either a servicing asset retained or a servicing liability undertaken since FAS 140 requires all entities servicing financial assets for others to recognize either a servicing asset or servicing liability for each servicing contract.

Relative fair value determinations are to incorporate assumptions regarding interest rates, defaults, and prepayments that marketplace participants would make, as well as the expected timing of cash flows. This allocation must be applied to all transfers that have retained interests, regardless of whether or not they qualify as sales. It should be noted that this fair value allocation may result in a relative change in financial reporting basis unless the fair values are proportionate to their carrying values. Thus, the gain or loss from any sale component could also be affected.

The retained interests continue to be the transferor's assets since control of these assets has not been transferred. Thus, the retained interest is considered continuing control over a previously owned asset (although the form may have changed). It is not to be remeasured at fair value, nor is a gain or loss recognized on it.

### Example: Sale of partial interest in receivables

*Facts Given*

| | |
|---|---|
| Receivables' fair value | $16,500 |
| Receivables' book value | 15,000 |

Seller sells 80% of receivables and agrees to service them. The benefits of servicing are just adequate to compensate for the servicing, thus there is no servicing asset or liability to be recognized.

| | *FV* | *80% FV* | *20% FV* | *Allocated 80% BV\** | *Allocated 20% BV\** |
|---|---|---|---|---|---|
| Receivables sold | $16,500 | $13,200 | | $12,000 | |
| Retained amount (20%) | | | $3,300 | | $3,000 |

\* *Allocated based on the relative fair values.*

*Seller's Journal Entry*

| | | |
|---|---|---|
| Cash | 13,200 | |
|     Receivables | | 12,000 |
|     Gain | | 1,200 |

Seller reports retained amount at $3,000, which is defined by book value, not fair value.

### Examples: Sale of loans with various types of retained interests

*Facts Given Applicable to All Examples Below (Each Example Is Independent)*

| | |
|---|---|
| Loans' fair value and amount of cash proceeds | $16,500 |
| Loans' book value | 15,000 |
| Fair value of recourse obligation | (900) |
| Fair value of call option\* on portfolio of $16,500 | 800 |
| Fair value of interest rate swap on portfolio of $16,500 | 700 |

\* *An option that permits the seller/transferor to repurchase the same or similar loans.*

### Seller's Journal Entries

1.  Sale only

| | | |
|---|---|---|
| Cash | 16,500 | |
|     Loans | | 15,000 |
|     Gain | | 1,500 |

2.  Sale with recourse obligation

| | | |
|---|---|---|
| Cash | 16,500 | |
|     Loans | | 15,000 |
|     Recourse obligation | | 900 |
|     Gain | | 600 |

3.  Sale with recourse obligation and call option to purchase the loans sold or similar loans

| | | |
|---|---|---|
| Cash | 16,500 | |
| Call option | 800 | |
|     Loans | | 15,000 |
|     Recourse obligation | | 900 |
|     Gain | | 1,400 |

4.  Sale with recourse obligation, call and swap (seller provides floating interest rate return although the underlying loans are at fixed interest rate terms)

| | | |
|---|---|---|
| Cash | 16,500 | |
| Call option | 800 | |
| Interest rate swap | 700 | |
|     Loans | | 15,000 |
|     Recourse obligation | | 900 |
|     Gain | | 2,100 |

5.  Partial sale with recourse obligation, call and swap. Seller sells 80% of loans.

| | FV | 80% FV | 20% FV | Allocated 80% BV* | Allocated 20% BV* |
|---|---|---|---|---|---|
| Loans | $16,500 | $13,200 | | $11,579 | |
| Call | 800 | 640 | | 561 | |
| Swap | 700 | 560 | | 491 | |
| Recourse obligation | (900) | (720) | | (631) | |
| Retained amount (20%) | | | $ 3,420 | | $3,000 |
| | $17,100 | $13,680 | $ 3,420 | $12,000 | $3,000 |

| | | |
|---|---|---|
| Cash | 13,200 | |
| Call | 640 | |
| Swap | 560 | |
|     Loans | | 12,000 |
|     Recourse obligation | | 720 |
|     Gain | | 1,680 |

Seller reports retained amount of receivables at $3,000, at book value.

\* *Allocated based on the relative fair values.*

In some transfers of receivables, the transferor provides credit enhancement (similar to a recourse provision) by retaining a beneficial interest that absorbs the credit risk. If there is no liability beyond the transferor's retained subordinated interests, the retained interest is initially measured at allocated carrying value based on relative fair value, and no recourse liability is necessary. The retained interest would be subsequently measured like other retained interests held in the same form.

Cash reserve accounts and subordinated beneficial interests created as credit enhancements are retained interests and are accounted for as such even if the seller collects the proceeds and deposits a portion in the cash reserve account. (New asset credit enhancements such as financial guarantees and credit derivatives are measured at the fair value of the amount to benefit the transferor.) Paragraphs 68-70 provide guidance on estimating fair values and are to be used in the case of credit enhancements.

One possible method of estimating fair value of a credit enhancement is the cash-out method. Using that method, cash flows are discounted from the date the credit enhancement asset becomes available to the transferor (i.e., when the cash in the credit enhancement account is expected to be paid out to the transferor). The present value can be computed using an expected present value technique with a risk-free rate or a "best estimate" technique with an appropriate discount rate. Among other transferor assumptions, time period of restrictions, reinvestment income, and potential losses due to uncertainties must be included. FAS 140 does not provide guidance concerning subsequent measurement of credit enhancements.

FSP 140-1, *Accounting for Accrued Interest Receivable Related to Securitized and Sold Receivables under Statement 140*, holds that if the right to collect accrued interest and fees receivable (AIR) is transferred with receivables to a qualifying special-purpose entity (QSPE), those rights are one of the components of the sale transaction and are accounted for as a retained beneficial interest (presumably to the extent that cash flows from the AIR will return to the transferor). Because the AIR cannot be contractually prepaid or settled in such a way that the transferor would not recover substantially all of its recorded investment, the beneficial interest is not required to be subsequently measured like an investment in debt securities classified as available for sale or trading under FAS 115.

**Servicing.** FAS 140 specified the accounting for all separately recognized servicing assets and liabilities. FAS 156 significantly modified that accounting, offering reporting entities a onetime option to reclassify certain financial assets categorized as available-for-sale to trading, in order to achieve more accurate matching of gains and losses on servicing obligations and those assets used, effectively, to hedge certain risks associated with holding servicing rights.

Servicing of financial assets can include such activities as

1. Collecting payments (principal, interest, and escrows)
2. Paying taxes and insurance from escrows
3. Monitoring delinquencies
4. Foreclosing
5. Investing funds temporarily prior to their distribution
6. Remitting fees to guarantors, trustees, and service providers
7. Accounting for and remitting distributions to holders of beneficial interests

Although inherent in holding most financial assets, servicing is a distinct asset or liability only when separated contractually from the underlying financial asset. The servicing asset usually results either from separate purchase or assumption of rights or from securitization with retained servicing. Servicers normally receive a defined percentage for performing these services (e.g., one-fourth of 1% on outstanding loan balances). Servicers' obligations are contractually specified. Servicing is subject to significant risks due to the effects of change in interest rates and debtors' propensity for prepayment of the related obligations.

When a transferor undertakes a duty to service the transferred financial assets, it recognizes either a servicing asset or a servicing liability unless the benefits of servicing neither exceed nor are less than the compensation to be received, in which case there is neither an asset nor liability to record (which would occur only in rare circumstances). Where the contractually agreed compensation is greater than the objective value of servicing, an asset is recognized, while if lower than the value, a liability is recorded.

Adequate compensation for servicing is determined by the marketplace. The concept of adequate compensation is judged by requirements that would be imposed by a new or outside servicer. It includes profit demanded by the marketplace and does not vary with the specific servicing costs of the servicer. Thus, it would not be acceptable to use a given servicer's cost plus a profit margin to estimate the fair value of a servicing asset or liability to be recognized by that particular servicer.

In general, servicing is associated with loans—most commonly, with mortgage loans—and as interest rates change the value of servicing contracts will also change, sometimes dramatically so. For example, if interest rates decline, debtors will have a greater propensity to prepay, reducing the amount of future servicing fees to be earned, and thus causing the value of the servicing contract to shrink. Conversely, if interest rates rise, the likelihood of prepayments declines, increasing the value of servicing contracts.

Other changes in economic conditions may also impact the value of servicing arrangements. Some entities having servicing contracts will attempt to hedge these risks by holding financial assets, the value of which will move in the opposite direction of the servicing contracts. Under FAS 140, financial reporting generally did not allow these offsetting effects to be accurately matched in periodic earnings; FAS 156 is intended, in part, to improve this accounting outcome.

Typically, the benefits are more than adequate compensation for the servicing and the servicing contract results in an asset. The benefits to be reaped by the servicer include

1.  Fees
2.  Late charges
3.  Float
4.  Other income

If the above benefits are not expected to provide adequate compensation, the contract results in a liability. With regard to the sale of assets, a servicing liability would reduce the net proceeds and would affect the gain or loss calculation.

If servicing is retained when the related assets are transferred, under FAS 140, any resulting servicing assets were to be measured at book value allocated based on relative fair values of loans and servicing at the date of sale, if practical. Servicing liabilities undertaken, servicing assets purchased, and servicing liabilities assumed were measured at fair value. Under FAS 156, *Accounting for Servicing of Financial Assets*, however, separately recognized servicing assets and liabilities are both to be initially recognized at fair values, and—optionally—may also be remeasured at each subsequent reporting date at fair values. This standard thus altered the gain or loss recognition arising in connection with the sale of financial assets with retained servicing, when contrasted to past practice under FAS 140.

The remainder of this discussion is based on FAS 156.

FAS 156 requires that servicing assets or liabilities must be given recognition whenever the entity undertakes a commitment to provide servicing of financial assets, such as loans. This may arise when the entity transfers assets in a "true sale" situation (i.e., when gain or loss on the transfer is recognized, in contrast to transfers that are only secured borrowings). It will also arise when the reporting entity transfers financial assets into a QSPE in a guaranteed mortgage securitization transaction where the transferor retains all the resulting securities and categorizes them as available-for-sale or trading securities under FAS 115. Additionally, it can arise from independent acquisitions or assumptions of servicing rights or obligations unrelated to financial assets of the reporting entity or its consolidated affiliates.

In sharp contrast to practice under FAS 140, the new standard requires that all servicing assets and liabilities be initially recorded at fair values. The only exception permitted occurs when it is not practicable to do this (i.e., when fair values cannot be assessed). In subsequent reporting periods, the servicer may either use the amortization method or the fair value remeasurement method of accounting for the servicing assets and liabilities. Under the amortization method, servicing assets or liabilities are amortized in proportion to and over the period of estimated net servicing income or net servicing loss; servicing assets are to be assessed for any impairment, and servicing liabilities are assessed for increased obligation based on fair value at each reporting date. Under the fair value measurement method, servicing assets or servicing liabilities are adjusted up or down to fair value at each reporting date, and changes in fair value are included in earnings in the period in which the changes occur.

A reporting entity that elects to subsequently measure a class of separately recognized servicing assets and servicing liabilities at fair value should apply that election prospectively to all new and existing separately recognized servicing assets and servicing liabilities within those classes that a servicer elects to subsequently measure at fair value. This election cannot be applied on a contract-by-contract basis.

Adoption of FAS 156 must occur in the first fiscal year beginning after September 15, 2006. The effect of remeasuring an existing class of separately recognized servicing assets and servicing liabilities at fair value should be reported as a cumulative-effect adjustment to retained earnings as of the beginning of the fiscal year and should be separately disclosed.

FAS 156 provides reporting entities with recognized servicing rights with an *optional* onetime reclassification of available-for-sale securities to trading securities, without calling into question the treatment of other available-for-sale securities under FAS 115, provided that the available-for-sale securities are identified as offsetting the entity's exposure to changes in fair value of servicing assets or servicing liabilities that a servicer elects to subsequently measure at fair value. Note that this election is not available relative to servicing assets or liabilities that will be accounted for by the amortization method. Any gains and losses associated with the reclassified securities that are included in accumulated other comprehensive income at the time of the reclassification should be reported as a cumulative-effect adjustment to retained earnings as of the beginning of the fiscal year that an entity adopts FAS 156. The carrying amount of reclassified securities and the effect of that reclassification on the cumulative-effect adjustment should be separately disclosed.

The purpose of reclassifying financial assets to trading is to have the changes in fair values reported in current earnings, rather than in other comprehensive income. Including fair value changes in current income will tend to offset, albeit not perfectly, the income effects of changes in the servicing assets and liabilities being accounted for at fair value. There is no need to test for hedging effectiveness, in contrast to hedge accounting under FAS 133, although FAS 156 does require that these assets be identified as being useful in this regard.

Finally, FAS 156 requires that servicing assets and liabilities that are being accounted for at fair value must be segregated from those being accounted for by the amortization method. This can be accomplished by using separate financial statement captions, or by footnote disclosures.

### Example: Sale of receivables with servicing asset retained by transferor

*Facts*

| | |
|---|---|
| Receivables' fair value, without servicing | $16,500 |
| Receivables' book value | 15,000 |
| Servicing liability of $16,500 portfolio | 800 |

Partial sale of receivables with servicing liability (i.e., excess cost to provide servicing over fees anticipated) retained. Seller sells 80% of receivables.

| | FV | 80% FV | 20% FV | Receivables allocated 80% BV* | Receivables allocated 20% BV* |
|---|---|---|---|---|---|
| Receivables sold | $16,500 | $13,200 | | $12,000 | |
| Servicing asset** | 800 | 640 | | | |
| Retained amount (20%) | | | $3,460 | | $3,000 |
| | $17,300 | $13,840 | $3,460 | $12,000 | $3,000 |

\* Allocated based on the relative fair values.
\*\* Initially measured at fair value, if practicable per FAS 156.

### Journal Entry

| | | |
|---|---|---|
| Cash | 13,200 | |
| Servicing asset | 640 | |
| Receivables | | 12,000 |
| Gain | | 1,840 |

Seller reports retained receivables at $3,000 (book value) and the servicing liability at its fair value of $640.

### Example: Sale of receivables with servicing liability retained by transferor

#### Facts Given

| | |
|---|---|
| Receivables' fair value, without servicing | $16,500 |
| Receivables' book value | 15,000 |
| Servicing (liability) for $16,500 portfolio | (500) |

Partial sale of receivables with servicing liability (i.e., excess cost to provide servicing over fees anticipated) retained. Seller sells 80% of receivables.

| | FV | 80% FV | 20% FV | Receivables allocated 80% BV* | Receivables allocated 20% BV* |
|---|---|---|---|---|---|
| Receivables sold | $16,500 | $13,200 | | $12,000 | |
| Servicing liability** | (500) | (400) | | | |
| Retained amount (20%) | | | $3,300 | | $3,000 |
| | $16,000 | $12,800 | $3,300 | $12,000 | $3,000 |

\* Allocated based on the relative fair values.
\*\* Initially measured at fair value, if practicable, per FAS 156.

### Journal Entry

| | | |
|---|---|---|
| Cash | 13,200 | |
| Servicing liability | | 400 |
| Receivables | | 12,000 |
| Gain | | 800 |

Seller reports retained receivables at $3,000 (book value) and the servicing obligation at its fair value of $400.

FAS 140, as amended by FAS 156, imposes standards for both initial measurement and subsequent measurement of servicing assets and liabilities. Specifically, servicing assets or servicing liabilities from each contract are to be accounted for separately as follows:

1. Assets are to be reported separately from liabilities. They are not to be netted, since there is no right of offset.
2. Initially measure retained servicing assets and liabilities at fair values at date of sale or securitization.
3. Initially measure at fair value all purchased servicing assets, assumed servicing liabilities, and servicing liabilities undertaken in a sale or securitization.
4. Account separately for interest-only strips (future interest income from serviced assets that exceeds servicing fees).

5. Either amortize servicing assets and liabilities in proportion to and over the period of estimated net servicing income (the excess of servicing revenues over servicing costs), or adjust to fair value at each reporting date. However, if amortization is employed, impairment of servicing assets and increased obligation of servicing obligations must be accounted for, as described in the following point.

6. Evaluate and measure impairment of servicing assets as follows:

   a. Stratify recognized servicing assets based on predominant risk (asset size, type, interest rate, term, location, date of organization, etc.)

   b. Recognize impairment through a valuation allowance for individual stratum in the amount of the excess of carrying value over fair value.

   c. Adjust the valuation allowances to reflect subsequently needed changes. Excess fair value for a stratum is not recognized.

7. If amortization of servicing liabilities is employed, it is done in proportion to and over the period of net servicing loss (excess of servicing costs over servicing revenues). In cases where subsequent changes have increased the fair value of the servicing liability above the carrying value, an increased liability and a loss are recognized.

8. If servicing assets and liabilities are reported at fair value, changes in value are to be included in periodic earnings as they occur.

In remeasuring servicing assets for impairment, this is to be based on the fair value of the contracts and not on the gain or loss from carrying out the terms of the contracts. FAS 140 (paragraph 63) requires that entities separately evaluate and measure impairment of designated strata of servicing assets. Stratification requires that judgment be used when selecting the most important characteristic. FAS 140 does not require that either the most predominant risk characteristic or more than one predominant risk characteristic be used to stratify the servicing assets for purposes of evaluating and measuring impairment. Different stratification criteria may be used for FAS 140 impairment testing and for FAS 133 grouping of similar assets to be designated as a hedged portfolio in a fair value hedge. The stratum selected is to be used consistently; a change is to be accounted for as a change in estimate under FAS 154. The change and reasons for the change are to be included in the disclosures made in accordance with paragraph 17 of FAS 140.

A servicing liability accounted for by the amortization method, on the other hand, is to be remeasured for increases in fair value, which would be recognized as a loss. Similar to the accounting for changes in a valuation allowance for an impaired asset, increases in the servicing obligation may be recovered, but the obligation cannot be adjusted to less than the amortized measurement of its initially recognized amounts.

The fair value of a servicing asset or liability at date of transfer is best measured by quoted market prices for similar servicing responsibilities. There is the potential for significantly different estimates of fair value when a quoted market price is not available. The transferor is to analyze all available information to obtain the best estimate of the fair value of the servicing contract. These include

1. The amount that would result in a current transaction between willing parties other than in a forced or liquidation sale
2. The legitimacy of the offer
3. The third party's specific knowledge about relevant factors
4. The experience of the broker with similar contracts
5. The price of other parties that have demonstrated an interest

6. The right to benefit from cash flows of potential future transactions (late charges, ancillary revenue, etc.)
7. The nature of the assets being serviced

In cases where there are few servicing contracts purchased or sold, present value methods may be used for estimating the fair value of servicing. Disclosure is required of the methods and significant assumptions followed to determine the estimate of fair value (unless not practicable) of recognized servicing assets and liabilities.

**Examples: Sale of receivables with servicing asset retained**

*Facts Given Applicable to Both Examples Below (Each Example Is Independent)*

| | |
|---|---:|
| Receivables' fair value | $16,500 |
| Receivables' book value | 15,000 |
| Servicing asset fair value on portfolio of $16,500 | 700 |
| Recourse obligation on portfolio of $16,500 | (900) |

1. Receivables sold, with servicing asset retained, no recourse obligation on receivables.

*Journal Entry*

| | | |
|---|---:|---:|
| Cash | 16,500 | |
| Servicing asset | 700 | |
| Receivables | | 15,000 |
| Gain on transfer | | 2,200 |

2. Partial sale of receivables with servicing asset retained and recourse obligation. Seller sells 80% of receivables.

| | FV | 80% FV | 20% FV | Allocated 80% BV* | Allocated 20% BV* |
|---|---:|---:|---:|---:|---:|
| Receivables sold | $16,500 | $13,200 | | $12,000 | |
| Servicing asset | 700 | 560 | | | |
| Recourse obligation | (900) | (720) | | | |
| Retained amount (20%) | | | $3,300 | | $3,000 |
| | $16,300 | $13,040 | $3,300 | $12,000 | $3,000 |

\* *Allocated based on the relative fair values of the receivables sold and retained.*

*Journal Entry*

| | | |
|---|---:|---:|
| Cash | 13,200 | |
| Servicing asset | 560 | |
| Receivables | | 12,000 |
| Recourse obligation | | 720 |
| Gain on transfer | | 1,040 |

Seller reports retained receivables at $3,000 (book value) and servicing asset at $560, the fair value of servicing the 80% of the portfolio that has been transferred.

In the unlikely circumstance that it is not practicable to measure the fair value of servicing at the date of transfer, the transferor must evaluate whether a liability has been incurred and does not automatically assume that an asset exists. If it is determined that a liability does not exist, then a value of zero is assigned to the servicing asset that cannot be measured. If it is determined that a liability does exist, a valuation technique using discounted cash flows is used to estimate its fair value.

**Example: Estimate of fair values is not practical**

Entity A sells loans with a recourse obligation to repurchase any delinquent loans and retains the servicing, which is expected to provide more than adequate compensation for performance.

|  | Case I | Case II |
|---|---|---|
|  | *Asset fair value* | *Liability fair value* |
|  | *cannot be determined* | *cannot be determined* |
| Loans' fair value | $16,500 | $16,500 |
| Loans' book value | 15,000 | 15,000 |
| Fair value of servicing asset | ? | 700 |
| Fair value of recourse obligation | (900) | ? |

**Proceeds**

|  | | |
|---|---|---|
| Cash | $16,500 | $16,500 |
| Less: Recourse obligation | (900) | ? |
| Net proceeds | $15,600 | $16,500 |

**Allocation of book value based on fair value of assets**

|  | FV | % | BV allocated | FV | % | BV allocated |
|---|---|---|---|---|---|---|
| Loans sold | $15,600 | 100 | $15,000 | $16,500 | 96 | $14,400 |
| Servicing assets | 0 | 0 | 0 | 700 | 4 | 600 |
|  | $15,600 | 100 | $15,000 | $17,200 | 100 | $15,000 |

**Journal Entries**

|  | | | | |
|---|---|---|---|---|
| Cash | 16,500 | | 16,500 | |
| Servicing asset | 0 | | 600 | |
| Loans | | 15,000 | | 15,000 |
| Recourse obligation | | 900 | | 2,100 |
| Gain | | 600 | | 0 |

In Case I, it is not practicable to measure the fair value of servicing, but it is known that the servicing is expected to provide at least adequate compensation. Thus, servicing is an asset and not a liability. If it is not practicable to measure the fair value of an asset, that asset is measured at zero. In Case II, it is not practicable to measure the fair value of the recourse obligation. If it is not practicable to measure the fair value of a liability, no gain is to be recorded on the sale. The liability is recorded at the greater of (1) the excess fair value of the assets obtained minus the fair value of the liabilities incurred over the carrying value of the assets transferred or (2) the amount to be recorded in conjunction with FAS 5 and FIN 14. In Case II, the liability is recognized at the excess fair value.

Subcontracting the servicing to another entity is not accounted for under FAS 140 because it does not involve a transfer. It is to be accounted for under other existing guidance (noting that executory contracts generally do not receive financial statement recognition under GAAP).

In the unusual case that servicing assets are assumed without a cash payment, the facts and circumstances will determine how the transaction is recorded. For example, the servicing asset may represent consideration for goods or services provided by the transferee to the transferor of the servicing. The servicing assets also might be received in full or partial satisfaction of a receivable from the transferor of the servicing. Another possibility is that the transferor (the party providing servicing) is in substance making a capital contribution to the transferee (the party receiving the servicing) in exchange for an increased ownership interest. Additionally, the possibility that there is an overstatement of the value of the servicing by the transferee must be carefully considered.

The amount to be paid to a replacement servicer under the terms of the servicing contract is not relevant to the determination of adequate compensation. This amount could, however, be relevant for determining the contractually specified servicing fees.

Rights to future income from serviced assets that exceed contractually specified servicing fees are accounted for as a servicing asset, an interest-only strip, or both, depending on whether the servicer would continue to receive the value of the right to future income if a replacement servicer started servicing the assets. Generally, the value of the right to receive future cash flows from ancillary sources such as late fees is included with the servicing asset if retention of the right depends on servicing being performed satisfactorily.

An interest-only strip does not depend on satisfactory performance of servicing, and any portion that would continue to be received if servicing were shifted to a replacement servicer would be accounted for separately as a financial asset. FAS 156 specifies that interest-only strips or other interests that continue to be held by the transferor in securitizations, loans, other receivables, or other financial assets that can be prepaid or otherwise settled in such a way that the entity might not recover its investment are to be subsequently remeasured as an investment in debt securities classified as available-for-sale or trading under FAS 115.

### Example of rights to future income from serviced assets

The NorthStar Bank sells a portion of its loan portfolio, but retains the obligation to service the loans and the rights to a portion of any future interest income. Accounting for the servicing asset will be on the amortization method permitted by FAS 156. NorthStar records a servicing asset of $148,000 and an interest-only strip receivable of $68,000 (based on the fair value of its retention of a portion of interest proceeds) as part of the sale transaction. The total book value of loans sold is $3,000,000, for which it receives total payment of $2,900,000. The entry to record these assets as part of the sale is

| | | |
|---|---|---|
| Servicing asset | 148,000 | |
| Interest-only strip receivable | 68,000 | |
| Cash | 2,900,000 | |
| Loans | | 3,000,000 |
| Gain on transfer of receivables | | 116,000 |

The $3,000,000 of loans to be serviced will be contractually terminated at different times, so the estimated net servicing income and related amortization of the servicing asset will decline in accordance with the following schedule:

| | Year 1 | Year 2 | Year 3 | Year 4 | Year 5 |
|---|---|---|---|---|---|
| Estimated net servicing income | $120,000 | $109,000 | $82,000 | $53,000 | $19,000 |
| Percent of total estimated servicing income | 31% | 28% | 21% | 14% | 6% |
| Annual amortization of servicing asset | $45,880 | $41,440 | $31,080 | $20,720 | $8,880 |

Thus, the entry to record amortization of the servicing asset in Year 1 follows:

| | | |
|---|---|---|
| Amortization—servicing asset | 45,880 | |
| Servicing asset | | 45,880 |

NorthStar retains a portion of the interest income to which it is due under the original loan sale agreement. The initial interest income retention is for $23,000, and is recorded as follows:

| | | |
|---|---|---|
| Cash | 23,000 | |
| Interest-only strip receivable | | 23,000 |

At the beginning of Year 4, NorthStar sells its servicing business to a third party, but retains the interest-only strip receivable, whose balance has now declined to $17,500. The entry to eliminate the remaining unamortized balance of the servicing asset, covering Years 4 and 5, follows:

| | | |
|---|---|---|
| Amortization—servicing asset | 29,600 | |
| Servicing asset | | 29,600 |

Since the interest-only strip receivable is no longer dependent on NorthStar's satisfactory servicing activities, it shifts the remaining balance of this receivable into an available-for-sale investment account, as shown in the following entry:

| | | |
|---|---|---|
| Investment in debt securities—available-for-sale | 17,500 | |
| Interest-only strip receivable | | 17,500 |

Some organizations transfer servicing rights on loans to third parties. SOP 01-6 provides criteria to be considered when evaluating whether the transfer qualifies as a sale, the first three of which are cited by reference to EITF 95-5, which is discussed in Chapter 8.

1. Has title passed?
2. Have substantially all risks and rewards of ownership been irrevocably passed to the buyer?
3. Are any protection provisions retained by the seller considered minor and are they reasonably estimable?
4. Has the seller received written approval from the investor (if required)?
5. Is the buyer a currently approved seller/servicer and not at risk of losing approved status?
6. If the sale is seller-financed

   a. Has the buyer made a nonrefundable deposit large enough to demonstrate a commitment to pay the remaining sales price?
   b. Does the note receivable from the buyer provide full recourse to the buyer?

7. Is the seller adequately compensated in accordance with a subservicing agreement for any short-duration, temporary servicing provided?

If the servicing rights sold are on loans that are retained, the carrying amount is allocated between servicing rights and loans retained using the relative fair value method prescribed by FAS 140.

**Changes resulting in transferor regaining control of financial assets sold.** If a transferor is required to re-recognize financial assets in which it holds a beneficial interest because the transferor's contingent right (for example, a removal of accounts provision, known as ROAP, or other contingent call option on the transferred financial assets) becomes exercisable, no gain or loss is recognized. The transferor continues to account for its beneficial interest in those assets apart from the re-recognized assets. That is, the beneficial interest is not combined with and accounted for with the re-recognized assets. A gain or loss may be recognized upon the exercise of a ROAP or similar contingent right with respect to the "repurchased" portion of the transferred assets that were sold if the ROAP or similar contingent right held by the transferor is not accounted for as a derivative under Statement 133 and is not at-the-money. The exercise would result in a recombination of the beneficial interest with the repurchased assets.

If a transferor is required to rerecognize financial assets because the SPE becomes nonqualifying, no gain or loss is recognized with respect to the "repurchase" by the transferor of the financial assets originally sold that remain outstanding in the SPE (or the portion thereof if the transferor retained a partial interest in those assets). The fair value of the re-recognized assets will equal the fair value of the liability assumed by the transferor because the transferor is contractually required to pass on all of the cash flows from the re-recognized assets to the SPE for distribution in accordance with the contractual documents governing the SPE. The transferor continues to account for its beneficial interest in those assets, if any, apart from the re-recognized assets.

Under no circumstances is a valuation allowance initially recorded for assets (loans) that are re-recognized at their fair value.

The accounting for the servicing asset related to the previously sold financial assets does not change because the transferor, as servicer, is still contractually required to collect the asset's cash flows for the benefit of the SPE and otherwise service the assets. The transferor continues to recognize the servicing asset and assess the asset for impairment as required by FAS 140 (EITF 02-9).

**Sales-type and direct financing lease receivables.** Lessors' lease receivables are composed of two components: minimum lease payments and residual values. Minimum lease payments are requirements for lessees to pay cash, and thus are financial assets subject to

FAS 140 if transferred. Residual values are the rights to the leased equipment at the end of the lease. If the residual value is guaranteed at the inception of the lease, the right is a financial asset subject to FAS 140 if transferred. If the residual value is not guaranteed (or if it is guaranteed after the inception of the lease), transfers of that residual value are not subject to FAS 140. When entities sell lease receivables, the gross investment of the lease is allocated between minimum lease payments, residual values guaranteed at inception, and residual values not guaranteed at inception. If the reporting entity retains servicing rights, it also records a servicing asset or liability if appropriate. FAS 140 does not apply to sales of operating lease payments.

### Example of sale of interest in lease payments

Lucky Leasing sells a senior interest in the guaranteed cash flows of a financing lease for $12,200. It retains a subordinated interest in the guaranteed cash flows and the residual value that is not guaranteed. The lease has the following components:

|  | *Face value* | *Present value* |
| --- | --- | --- |
| Minimum lease payments | $ 8,350 | $ 7,000 |
| Guaranteed residual value | 7,000 | 5,875 |
| Residual value not guaranteed | 1,400 | 1,175 |
| Total investment in lease | $16,750 | $14,050 |

The present values are computed using the implicit lease rate. The fair value of the subordinated interest retained is $1,200. Lucky Leasing receives no explicit compensation for servicing the lease, but it estimates that the benefits of servicing are just adequate to compensate it for its servicing responsibilities (that is, there is no servicing asset or liability). The allocation of the carrying amount for the interest sold is as follows:

|  | *Fair value* | *Allocated cost* |
| --- | --- | --- |
| Senior interest sold | $12,200 | $11,722 |
| Subordinated interest retained | 1,200 | 1,153 |
| Totals | $13,400 | $12,875 |

The entry to record the sale would be as follows:

| | | |
| --- | --- | --- |
| Cash | 12,200 | |
| Subordinated interest | 1,153 | |
| Residual value | 1,175 | |
| Net investment in lease | | 14,050 |
| Gain on sale | | 478 |

**Securitizations.** Entities that generate a large number of similar receivables, such as mortgages, credit card receivables, or car loans, sometimes securitize those receivables. Securitization is the transformation of the receivables into securities that are sold to other investors. For example, mortgages can be converted into mortgage-backed securities, which entitle the investors to receive specific cash flows generated by the mortgages. With an established market, issuance of the securities can cost less than using the receivables as collateral for a borrowing. Because QSPE assets are isolated from a possible transferor's bankruptcy, the QSPE's credit quality is enhanced and the financing costs on the debt are reduced. For even lower financing costs, the QSPE can obtain credit enhancements in the form of recourse debt, subordinate assignments, or guarantees. Additionally, the resulting securities are more liquid than the underlying receivables. Securitizations are accounted for as sales only if (1) a qualified special-purpose entity is used to buy the assets, (2) each holder of its beneficial interests has the right to pledge or exchange the beneficial interest and there is no condition that both constrains the holder from taking advantage of that right and provides more than a trivial benefit to the transferor, and (3) the transferor does not maintain effective control over the assets.

The transferor (also called issuer or sponsor) forms a securitization mechanism (separate corporation or a trust, referred to as a qualifying special-purpose entity [QSPE]) to buy the assets and to issue the securities. The securitization mechanism then generates beneficial interests in the assets or resulting cash flows that are sold to investors with the sales proceeds used to pay the transferor/sponsor for the transferred assets. The form of the securities chosen depends on such things as the nature of the assets, income tax considerations, and returns to be received. The securities issued by the SPE may consist of a single class of interests with the characteristics of equity or multiple classes of interests, some having debt characteristics and others equity characteristics. A properly structured QSPE is not to be consolidated in the financial statements of the transferor or its affiliates. (Note that, although FIN 46(R) creates the concept of *variable interest entities*, or VIE, which largely replaces the earlier concept of special-purpose entities, the concept of *qualifying special-purpose entities*, or QSPE, as established by FAS 140, continues unchanged as of mid-2008, although FASB is likely to alter or eliminate QSPE accounting, perhaps as early as year-end 2008.)

For example, a transferor originates long-term loans and accumulates them on its balance sheet (referred to as warehousing). When the group of loans reaches a sufficient size, the loans are sold to a QSPE. During the accumulation phase, the transferor finances the cost of holding the loans with prearranged lines of credit, known as warehouse lines. Often the transferor hedges the price risk of the loans as they await sale. This is referred to as an on-balance-sheet warehousing.

Alternatively, a transferor may use a properly structured off-balance-sheet warehousing to securitize assets. In an off-balance-sheet warehouse, the transferor creates a temporary securitization vehicle. A bank typically extends credit to the securitization vehicle in the form of a variable-funding note. Using the proceeds of the note, the vehicle acquires loans from the transferor as they are originated. The principal of the note increases, up to a ceiling, as the transferor transfers additional loans to the securitization vehicle. When the loans have reached the ceiling amount of the note, the bank puts the note back to the securitization vehicle, forcing the vehicle to sell the loans to a permanent QSPE to raise the cash to pay the note.

Payments by the securitization mechanism are usually classified as pay-through, pass-through or revolving-period. In a pay-through, cash flows from the assets pay off the debt securities. The assets are essentially collateral. In a pass-through, undivided interests are issued and the investors share in the net cash flows. In a revolving-period, undivided interests are issued, but until liquidation, the net cash flows are split between buying additional assets and paying off investors. During the reinvestment period, principal repayments are reinvested in additional receivables generated by the debtors whose receivables were securitized. Under EITF 88-22, as modified by subsequently issued pronouncements, any gain recognized by the transferor/sponsor on the sale of credit card or other receivables to a QSPE is limited to amounts relating to receivables existing at the date of sale. This prevents the transferor/sponsor from recognizing additional gains on transfers that are anticipated to occur during the specified reinvestment period. In computing gain or loss on the initial transfer, the transferor/sponsor recognizes costs estimated to be incurred for all future servicing activities including the costs of servicing the receivables expected to be sold during the reinvestment period. If the initial sale results in a gain, the costs associated with the receivables to be sold during the reinvestment period may be recorded as an asset and allocated to expense using a systematic and rational method over the initial and reinvestment periods.

A QSPE is considered qualified if it meets the criteria set forth by FAS 140. In general, those criteria require that the SPE remain on "autopilot" after its creation. The QSPE is required to be a passive custodian for the benefit of the holders of its beneficial interests. All of the QSPE's responses to changes in business conditions must be predetermined and spelled out in the agreements that create the QSPE. The QSPE cannot make business decisions, nor can it direct an agent to make business decisions on its behalf. The four criteria are

1. The QSPE is demonstrably distinct from the transferor. To be demonstrably distinct, the transferor, its affiliates, or its agents cannot unilaterally dissolve the SPE and either

   a. At least 10% of the fair value of its beneficial interests is held by parties other than the transferor, its affiliates, or its agents or
   b. The transfer is a guaranteed mortgage securitization. A guaranteed mortgage securitization is a securitization of mortgage loans that is within the scope of FAS 65 and includes a substantive guarantee by a third party.

2. The permitted activities of the QSPE

   a. Must be significantly limited
   b. Must have been entirely specified in the legal documents that established the QSPE or created the beneficial interests in the transferred assets it holds
   c. May be significantly changed only with the approval of a majority of the holders of the beneficial interests not including the transferor, its affiliates, or its agents

3. The QSPE may hold only

   a. Financial assets that are passive in nature. A financial asset is passive only if holding the asset requires no decisions of the holder other than decisions inherent in servicing. For example, an equity instrument is not passive if the SPE is permitted to choose how to vote the shares, and an investment accounted for by the equity method is not passive since that method is used when the investor has the ability to exercise significant influence over that investment.
   b. Passive derivative instruments related to beneficial interests issued or sold to parties other than the transferor, its affiliates, or its agents. Options to call or put are not passive investments, since they require a decision as to whether to exercise the rights. Interest rate swaps, caps, and floors are passive derivative instruments.
   c. Financial assets that would reimburse the QSPE if the servicer failed to adequately perform or if others failed to pay timely. The financial assets must have been entered into when the QSPE was created, when assets were transferred to it, or when it issued beneficial interests.
   d. Servicing rights related to the financial assets it holds
   e. Nonfinancial assets obtained in connection with the collection of financial assets it holds (but the QSPE may hold them only temporarily)
   f. Cash collected from financial assets it holds
   g. Investments purchased pending distribution to holders of beneficial interests, provided that those investments are appropriate for that purpose. For example, the investments must be relatively risk-free and have a maturity date no later than the expected distribution date.

4. The QSPE can sell or dispose of noncash financial assets only in automatic response to one of the following conditions:

   a. Occurrence of an event that causes the fair value of those financial assets to decline by a specified degree below the fair value of those assets when the QSPE obtained them. The occurrence of the event must be outside the control of the transferor, its affiliates, or its agents. The nature of the event must be specified in the legal documents that established the QSPE or created the beneficial interests in the transferred assets it holds.

b. Exercise of a right to put a beneficial interest back to the QSPE by a beneficial interest holder other than the transferor, its affiliates, or its agents

c. Exercise by the transferor of a call or a removal-of-accounts provision ("ROAP"), provided that the exercise is specified in the legal documents that established the QSPE, transferred assets to the QSPE, or created the beneficial interests in the transferred assets it holds. Care must be exercised in designing a call or a ROAP because it can be construed as giving the transferor the ability to unilaterally cause the holder to return specific assets (and thus the transfer will not be a sale). In general, any call or ROAP that allows the transferor to specify the assets to be removed or that are conditioned upon an event within the transferor's control (such as a transferor's decision to exit a product line) will cause the transfer to fail the FAS 140 criteria. Calls or ROAPs that allow the transferor to remove defaulted receivables are permitted, as are those that allow limited access for random removal of excess assets.

d. Termination of the QSPE or maturity of the beneficial interests in those financial assets on a fixed or determinable date that was specified at the inception

5. The QSPE can make decisions inherent in servicing the transferred assets. For example

   a. A QSPE that performs servicing can restructure or "work out" a loan, as long as its discretion is significantly limited and the parameters of that discretion are fully described in the legal documents that established the QSPE or that created the beneficial interests in the transferred assets. However, the QSPE cannot initiate a new lending to the borrower as a result of the workout. Nor can the QSPE have the ability to determine whether to restructure (or work out) the loan versus disposing of the loan, since that decision is generally not automatic because it requires use of judgment and estimates.

   b. A QSPE can pay certain expenses (e.g. property taxes or insurance) that are the responsibility of the debtor if the debtor fails to pay them.

   c. A QSPE can advance funds to make timely payments to the holders of the beneficial interests and later reimburse itself for those advances.

   d. A QSPE can decide whether to initiate foreclosure proceedings, as long as its discretion is significantly limited and the parameters of that discretion are fully described in the legal documents that established the QSPE or that created the beneficial interests in the transferred assets.

   e. A QSPE can decide how to dispose of foreclosed assets that it temporarily holds, as long as its discretion is significantly limited and the parameters of that discretion are fully described in the legal documents that established the QSPE or that created the beneficial interests in the transferred assets.

   f. A QSPE can decide how to dispose of defaulted loans only if a servicing agreement that was in effect when the QSPE was established describes specific conditions in which the servicer is required to dispose of a loan. In other words, the QSPE must have no choice but to dispose of the defaulted loan when the described conditions occur.

FIN 46(R), which was intended to curb the use of unconsolidated nonqualified SPE structures, excludes QSPE from the definition of a variable interest entity (VIE). Under FIN 46(R), a QSPE is not permitted to be consolidated by the asset transferor or its affiliates. If, however, the SPE does not qualify as a QSPE or as a formerly qualifying SPE ("FQSPE") under FAS 140, it would not be exempt from the consolidation and disclosure requirements of FIN 46(R). In addition, a beneficial interest holder (BIH) in a QSPE or FQSPE could potentially be required to consolidate the trust if the BIH has the unilateral ability to either cause the trust to liquidate or to change the trust so that it no longer qualifies as a QSPE or FQSPE.

The issuance of FIN 46(R), created an incentive to convert former SPE to QSPE, thereby avoiding the need for consolidation. FASB addressed this concern in several projects it pursued, one of which, FAS 156 (discussed above), was finalized in early 2006.

Various financial components arise from securitizations. Examples include servicing contracts, interest-only strips, retained interests, recourse obligations, options, swaps, and forward contracts. All controlled assets and liabilities must be recognized under FAS 140.

### Example of a securitization deal involving four classes of securities

| | |
|---|---:|
| Principal of loans held by the securitizer/transferor | $10,000,000 |
| Accrued interest on loans held by the securitizer/transferor | 230,000 |
| Deferred origination costs of loans held by the securitizer/transferor | 100,000 |
| Deferred origination fees of loans held by the securitizer/transferor | (200,000) |
| Loss allowance on loans held by the securitizer/transferor | (250,000) |
| Net carrying amount of loans | $ 9,880,000 |

Classes of securities issued and prices:

| | Principal | Price | Fair value |
|---|---:|---:|---:|
| Class A | $9,000,000 | 100 | $ 9,000,000 |
| Class B | 1,000,000 | 90 | 900,000 |
| Interest-only strip (retained) | | | 150,000 |
| Residual class (retained) | | | 100,000 |
| Total fair value | | | $10,150,000 |

Servicing is retained by the transferor and has a fair value of $75,000
Transaction costs are $100,000
Proceeds are $9,800,000 ($9,000,000 Class A + $900,000 Class B − $100,000 costs)

Allocation of carrying value:

| | Fair value | Percent | Allocation | Sold | Retained |
|---|---:|---:|---:|---:|---:|
| Class A | $ 9,000,000 | 88.0 | $8,696,332 | $8,696,332 | |
| Class B | 900,000 | 8.8 | 869,633 | 869,633 | |
| Interest-only strip | 150,000 | 1.5 | 144,939 | | $144,939 |
| Residual class | 100,000 | 1.0 | 96,626 | | 96,626 |
| Servicing | 75,000 | .7 | 72,470 | | 72,470 |
| Total | $10,225,000 | 100.0 | $9,880,000 | $9,565,965 | $314,035 |

The entry to record the sale would be as follows:

| | | |
|---|---:|---:|
| Cash | 9,800,000 | |
| Interest-only strip | 144,939 | |
| Residual class | 96,626 | |
| Servicing asset | 72,470 | |
| Loan loss allowance | 250,000 | |
| Deferred origination fees | 200,000 | |
| Loans receivable | | $10,000,000 |
| Interest receivable | | 230,000 |
| Deferred origination costs | | 100,000 |
| Gain on sale of loans | | 234,035 |

The entry to mark the securities retained to fair value under FAS 115 would be

| Interest-only strip | 5,061 | |
|---|---|---|
| Residual class | 3,374 | |
| Comprehensive income (unless trading) | | 8,435 |

Just as it is necessary to distinguish new assets, which are recorded at fair value, from retained interests, which are recorded at allocated carrying value, when accounting for a transfer to another enterprise, it is necessary to do so when accounting for a transfer to a QSPE. In certain securitization transactions, more than one transferor contributes assets to a single QSPE. A transferor treats the beneficial interests it receives in a securitization that commingles assets from more than one transferor as

1. New assets to the extent that the sources of the cash flows to be received by the transferor are assets transferred by another entity
2. Retained interests to the extent that the sources of the cash flows are assets transferred by the transferor
3. New assets to the extent that any derivatives, guarantees, or other contracts were entered into by the QSPE to "transform" the transferred assets. (They are new because they were entered into by the QSPE rather than transferred into the QSPE by another entity.)

After a securitization, the beneficial interests held by the transferor either are in the form of securities that are accounted for under FAS 115 or are required to be accounted for as available-for-sale securities or trading securities in accordance with FAS 140. Thus, the transferor must classify the beneficial interests into one of the FAS 115 categories. If beneficial interests held by the transferor after the transfer convey rights to the same cash flows as the transferor was entitled to receive from securities that it transferred to the QSPE, the FAS 115 classification of the beneficial interests is the same as the securities held before the transfer. For example, if prior to the transfer the debt securities were accounted for as available-for-sale securities in accordance with FAS 115, the beneficial interests are to be classified as available-for-sale securities if the transferor receives the cash flows from those securities via its beneficial interest. In contrast, if the transferred assets were not Statement 115 securities prior to the transfer but the beneficial interests were issued in the form of debt securities or in the form of equity securities that have readily determinable fair values, then the transferor has the opportunity to decide the appropriate FAS 115 classification at the date of the transfer.

Revolving-period securitizations present some unique issues because they contain an implicit forward contract to sell new receivables during the revolving period. The forward contract may become valuable to the transferor or burdensome depending upon how interest rates and market conditions change. The value of the implicit forward contract arises from the difference between the rate promised to the holders of the beneficial interests and the market rate of return on similar investments. For example, if the agreed-upon rate to holders is 5% and the market rate is 7%, the forward contract's value to the transferor is 2% of the amount of the investment for each year remaining in the revolving period after the initially transferred receivables are collected. When receivables are sold to a revolving-period securitization trust, gain or loss recognition is limited to receivables that exist and have been sold. Similarly, servicing assets or liabilities are limited to servicing receivables that exist and have already been transferred. As proceeds from collection of the receivables are used to purchase new receivables for the trusts, each additional transfer is treated as a separate sale, with its own gain or loss calculation. Those additional transfers also can result in recognition of additional servicing assets and liabilities.

FAS 140 does not address the accounting for desecuritization of securities into loans or other financial assets. EITF Topic D-51, *The Applicability of FASB Statement No. 115 to Desecuritizations of Financial Assets*, addresses that issue. That staff announcement states that the guidance in FAS 140 is to be extended by analogy to desecuritizations. Thus, the transfer of securities or beneficial interests in a securitized pool of financial assets in which the transferor receives in exchange only the financial assets underlying those securities or beneficial interests would not be accounted for as a sale.

### Example of revolving period securitizations

The Mason-Dixon Auto Sales Company enters into a revolving-period securitization agreement to sell $100,000 of its car loan receivables each month to the Meridian QSPE for a four-year period. Meridian guarantees a 5% rate of return to its investors for the entire four-year period. Mason-Dixon will continue to service all receivables sold to Meridian. If Mason-Dixon can create new car loans at interest rates greater than 5%, then it can recognize the difference between the actual interest rate and the rate issued to Meridian's investors as an interest-only strip.

At the end of the first month, Mason-Dixon sells $100,000 of principal on car loan receivables to Meridian, as well as $600 of accrued interest on the loans. Thus, the net carrying amount of the loans sold is $100,600. Mason-Dixon retains receivables servicing, which has a fair value of $6,000, as well as an interest-only strip receivable that recognizes the difference between the 5% guaranteed interest rate paid to Meridian's investors and the average 7% actual interest rate on the loan receivables, which has a fair value of $8,000 at the sale date.

The initial sale includes transaction costs of $5,000, which are deducted from the cash paid by Meridian to Mason-Dixon. The following entry by Mason-Dixon records the sale transaction:

| | | |
|---|---|---|
| Cash | 95,600 | |
| Interest-only strip receivable | 8,000 | |
| Servicing asset | 6,000 | |
| Loans receivable | | 100,000 |
| Interest receivable | | 600 |
| Gain on sale of loans | | 9,000 |

At the end of the next month, Mason-Dixon sells another $100,000 of receivables to Meridian, as well as $350 of accrued interest on the loans. Thus, the net carrying amount of the second group of loans is $100,350. The lower accrued interest is due to a drop in the actual interest rate on this second block of loans, which averages 4% and is below the 5% guaranteed Meridian's investors. The fair value of the servicing asset associated with these loans is $6,000. The following calculation allocates the fair value of the various elements of the transaction to the net carrying amount of the loans:

| | *Fair value* | *Percent* | *Allocation* |
|---|---|---|---|
| Loans | $100,000 | 98.0 | $98,343 |
| Interest-only strip | (4,000) | (3.9) | (3,914) |
| Servicing asset | 6,000 | 5.9 | 5,921 |
| Totals | $102,000 | 100.0 | $100,350 |

This second sale also includes transaction costs of $5,000, which are deducted from the cash paid to Mason-Dixon. The following entry records the sale transaction:

| | | |
|---|---|---|
| Cash | 95,350 | |
| Servicing asset | 6,000 | |
| Loss on sale of loans | 3,000 | |
| Interest-only strip receivable | | 4,000 |
| Loans receivable | | 100,000 |
| Interest receivable | | 350 |

**Proposed changes to accounting for transfers of financial assets.** FASB exposed a draft standard, *Qualifying Special-Purpose Entities and Isolation of Transferred Assets*, in 2003, which was intended to amend FAS 140 to revise or clarify the derecognition requirements for financial assets and the initial measurement of interests related to transferred financial assets that are retained or acquired by a transferor. A revised Exposure Draft, *Accounting for Transfers of Financial Assets*, was issued in 2005 and remains outstanding and an active project as of mid-2008.

This draft standard, if adopted, would amend FAS 140 in several important ways.

1. It would require that the isolation analysis defined under FAS 140 consider any arrangement or agreement made in connection with a transfer even if it was not entered into at the time of the transfer.

2. It would require that if the transferee is a qualifying SPE, no arrangement or agreement is made between any holder of beneficial interests issued by the QSPE and the transferor, or its consolidated affiliates or agents that would have caused the assets not to be isolated as required by paragraphs 9(a) and 9(d) of FAS 140 if the same arrangement or agreement had involved the QSPE instead of its beneficial interest holders.

3. It would define a *participating interest* as a portion of a financial asset that (a) conveys proportionate ownership rights with priority under the law that is equal to the priority of each other participating interest, (b) involves no recourse to or subordination by any participating interest holder, and (c) does not entitle any participating interest holder to receive cash before any other participating interest holder.

4. It would establish the following conditions for reporting a transfer of a portion (or portions) of a financial sale:

   (a) The transferred portion (or portions) and any portion retained by the transferor must be participating interests as described in paragraph 8(a) of FAS 140 as amended.

   (b) The transferred portion (or portions) must meet the conditions for surrender of control in paragraph 9 of FAS 140 as amended.

   If the transfer does not meet those conditions, sale accounting can be achieved only by transferring an entire financial asset or group of financial assets to a QSPE or other entity that is not consolidated with the transferor and the entire transferred financial asset(s) must meet the conditions of paragraph 9 of FAS 140 as amended.

5. It would replace the term *retained interest* with other, more specific terms. The two most prevalent types of interests that are described in the proposed standard are *transferor's beneficial interests* and *participating interests retained by the transferor.* A transferor's beneficial interest is a beneficial interest received by a transferor as part of the proceeds from a sale of financial assets to a qualifying SPE. A participating interest retained by the transferor represents the transferor's ownership interest (or share of ownership) in a financial asset that has been divided according to the requirements for participating interest specified in paragraph 3(a) of the proposed standard. Some of the other types of interest referred to as retained interests in FAS 140 include *servicing rights, rights to a portion of the interest from a transferred financial asset* or *transferred participating interest,* and *cash collateral accounts.* In the proposed standard, each of those types of interest is referred to either specifically or as other interests received (or held) by the transferor. Except for a transferor's participating interest, a servicing right, and cash or other collateral posted by the transferor, all of the interests called retained interests in FAS 140 are considered new assets to the transferor by the proposed standard.

6. It would require that a transferor's beneficial interest be initially measured at fair value.

7.  It would require that for an SPE with the ability to roll over (i.e., to retire and reissue) beneficial interests to meet the conditions to be a QSPE, no party, (including that party's consolidated affiliates or agents) may have two or more involvements with the QSPE that provide that party with the opportunity to obtain a more-than-trivial incremental benefit relative to the benefit that would be obtained if separate parties had those same involvements.

8.  It would prohibit a QSPE from holding equity instruments unless those instruments result from efforts to collect the transferred financial assets, in which case they may be held only temporarily.

9.  It would prohibit financial assets transferred to any entity (including a QSPE) from being derecognized by the transferor unless the financial assets are isolated from the transferor and its consolidated affiliates, except for certain bankruptcy-remote affiliates. Any arrangement made in connection with a transfer must be considered even if the arrangement is not entered into at the time of the transfer.

This project remains active, and readers should be alert to further developments regarding this matter, as there is a reasonable likelihood that changes will be made to it during FASB's redeliberation process. Thus, the final standard, if and when issued, may differ from the elements discussed above. As of mid-2008, FASB appears inclined to remove the concept of QSPE from FAS 140 as well as from FIN 46(R), and is also intending to amend the derecognition criteria of FAS 140 to clarify and improve the isolation and effective control criteria of that standard.

**Repurchase agreements.** Repurchase agreements are used to obtain short-term use of funds. Under the terms of a repurchase agreement the transferor transfers a security to a transferee in exchange for cash. Concurrently, the transferor agrees to reacquire the security at a future date for an amount equal to the cash exchanged and an interest factor. Many repurchase agreements are for short terms, often overnight.

It is necessary to determine if the repurchase agreement meets the requirements described in the section, "Surrender of control." Usually the critical determination is whether the repurchase agreements gives the transferor effective control over the transferred assets. That determination is made by applying the criteria described in the section, "Maintaining effective control." In most cases, if the repurchase is required prior to the maturity of the security transferred and the cash transferred is sufficient to repurchase the assets if the transferee defaults, the transferor retains effective control and the agreement is accounted for as a secured borrowing. For example, fixed-coupon and dollar-roll repurchase agreements, and other contracts under which the securities to be repurchased need not be the same as the securities sold, qualify as borrowings if the return of substantially the same securities as those transferred is assured. However, if a transferor does not maintain control over the transferred assets and other criteria in FAS 140 are met, the transfer is accounted for as a sale and a forward commitment. FSP FAS 140-3, discussed earlier in this chapter, addresses situations where a transferee transfers the assets back to the transferor in a repurchase financing arrangement, which (depending on meeting criteria specified in that staff position) may or may not interfere with derecognition of the assets by the original transferor.

### Example of a repurchase agreement

Mighty Manufacturing has $1,995,000 excess cash that it desires to invest for a 7-day period. It transfers the cash to Lion Bank in exchange for $2,000,000 of commercial paper. At the end of the 7-day period, Lion Bank agrees to repurchase the commercial paper for $1,996,500. Mighty Manufacturing does not have the right to sell or pledge the commercial paper during the 7-day period.

The entries to record the origination of the agreement are as follows:

| *Mighty Manufacturing* | | | *Lion Bank* | | |
|---|---|---|---|---|---|
| Investment | 1,995,000 | | Cash | 1,995,000 | |
| Cash | | 1,995,000 | Short-term payable | | 1,995,000 |

The entries to record the termination of the agreement seven days later are as follows:

| *Mighty Manufacturing* | | | *Lion Bank* | | |
|---|---|---|---|---|---|
| Cash | 1,996,500 | | Short-term payable | 1,995,000 | |
| Investment | | 1,995,000 | Interest expense | 1,500 | |
| Interest income | | 1,500 | Cash | | 1,996,500 |

**Securities lending transactions.** Broker-dealers and other financial services companies initiate securities lending transactions when they need to obtain specific securities to cover a short sale or a customer's failure to deliver securities sold. The transferor/lender provides the securities to the transferee/borrower in exchange for "collateral," usually in an amount greater than the fair value of the borrowed securities. This collateral is commonly cash but could alternatively be other securities or standby letters of credit.

When the collateral is cash, the transferor/lender invests the cash during the period that the security is loaned. The investment return on the cash collateral is larger than the fees paid by the lender under the agreement (the rebate). Because the cash collateral is usually valued daily and adjusted frequently for changes in the market value of the underlying securities, the transaction has very low credit risk.

In determining whether to account for a securities lending transaction as a sale or a secured borrowing, the same criteria used for other asset transfers are applied. Many securities lending transactions are accompanied by an agreement that entitles and obligates the transferor/lender to repurchase or redeem the transferred assets before their maturity. Thus, the transferor maintains effective control over the securities lent. If that is the case, the transaction is accounted for as a secured borrowing. The following is an example of a securities lending transaction accounted for as a secured borrowing:

**Example: Securities lending transaction (30 days)**

| | |
|---|---|
| Fair value of loaned security | $16,500 |
| Book value of loaned security | 16,500 |
| Collateral (cash) | 16,995 |
| Transferor/lender's return from investing cash | 5% |
| Transferor/lender's rebate to transferee/borrower | 4% |

*Transferor/lender's journal entries*

*At date of loan:*

| | | |
|---|---|---|
| Securities pledged | 16,500 | |
| Securities | | 16,500 |
| *To record transfer of securities as a loan* | | |

| | | |
|---|---|---|
| Cash | 16,995 | |
| Loan agreement payable | | 16,995 |
| *To record receipt of cash collateral* | | |

| | | |
|---|---|---|
| Money market instrument | 16,995 | |
| Cash | | 16,995 |
| *To invest cash collateral* | | |

*At end of 30 days:*

| | | |
|---|---|---|
| Cash | 17,065 | |
| Interest income | | 70 |
| Money market instrument | | 16,995 |
| *To transfer cash from money market and record interest earned* | | |

| | | |
|---|---|---|
| Securities | 16,500 | |
| Securities pledged | | 16,500 |

*To record securities returned by transferee/borrower*

| | | |
|---|---|---|
| Loan agreement payable | 16,995 | |
| Interest rebate | 56 | |
| Cash | | 17,051 |

*To return cash collateral and pay rebate*

**Accounting for collateral.** Accounting for collateral depends both on whether the secured party has the right to sell or repledge the collateral and on whether the debtor has defaulted. Ordinarily, the transferor should carry the collateral as an asset and the transferee does not record the pledged asset.

The collateral provisions of FAS 140 apply to all transfers (repurchase agreements, dollar-roll, securities lending, etc.) of financial assets pledged as collateral and accounted for as a secured borrowing. The provisions do not apply to the accounting for cash in secured borrowing transactions.

If the secured party (transferee) has the right to sell or repledge the collateral, then the debtor (transferor) reclassifies the asset used as collateral and reports it in the balance sheet separately from other assets not similarly encumbered. That is, the debtor (transferor) continues to hold the collateral assets as its own, and the secured party (transferee) does not recognize the collateral asset. If the secured party (transferee) sells the collateral, it recognizes the proceeds from the sale and the obligation to return the collateral to the debtor (transferor).

Although collateral is required to be reclassified and reported separately by the transferor if the transferee has the right to sell or repledge the collateral, that requirement does not change the transferor's measurement of the collateral. The same measurement principles are to be used as before the transfer and the collateral is not derecognized. The subsequent measurement of the transferee's obligation to return the collateral in securities borrowing and resale agreement transactions is not addressed by FAS 140.

If the transferor defaults and is not entitled to the return of the collateral, it is to be derecognized by the transferor. If not already recognized, the transferee records its asset at fair value.

### Example of accounting for collateral

Deep Water Marine enters into a loan arrangement with Key West Bank for $4,700,000, using one of its submersibles as collateral. The loan terms are monthly interest payments at an annual rate of 9%, followed by a balloon payment in five years for the entire amount of the principal. The submersible has a book value of $4,250,000, net of accumulated depreciation of $500,000, and a fair value of $4,650,000. Deep Water misses its first loan payment, so the parties renegotiate the loan agreement, allowing Key West the right to resell the submersible. Deep Water records this change by separately listing the submersible in the property, plant, and equipment section of its balance sheet in the following manner:

| | |
|---|---|
| Equipment used as collateral with right of sale (net of accumulated depreciation of $500,000) | $4,250,000 |

Two months after the loan initiation date, Deep Water defaults on the note and enters bankruptcy proceedings, so Key West takes possession of the submersible. Deep Water records the default with the following entry:

| | | |
|---|---|---|
| Loan payable | 4,700,000 | |
| Accrued interest payable | 70,500 | |
| Accumulated depreciation | 500,000 | |
| Fixed assets—equipment | | 4,750,000 |
| Gain on loan defaults | | 520,500 |

Foreclosure of the Deep Water loan is certain. The estimated cost to sell the submersible is a 2% commission, or $93,000, which Key West includes in the following entry to record its ownership of the submersible ($4,650,000 fair value net of $93,000 commission):

| | | |
|---|---|---|
| Repossessed assets | 4,557,000 | |
| Bad debt expense | 213,500 | |
|     Interest receivable | | 70,500 |
|     Loans receivable | | 4,700,000 |

Key West sells the submersible for $4,500,000, net of all sales costs. It records the transaction with the following entry:

| | | |
|---|---|---|
| Cash | 4,500,000 | |
| Loss on asset sale | 57,000 | |
|     Repossessed assets | | 4,557,000 |

**Financial assets subject to prepayment.** FAS 140 requires interest-only strips, loans, other receivables, or retained interests in securitizations to be measured like investments in debt securities. If they can be contractually prepaid or settled in a way that precludes recovery of substantially all of the recorded investment, they are classified as available-for-sale or trading under FAS 115 (i.e., they generally cannot be treated as held-to-maturity debt instruments). Only assets meeting all of the FAS 115 requirements and acquired late enough in life that, even if prepaid, the holder would recover substantially all of its recorded investment may be initially classified as held-to-maturity. The probability of prepayment or settlement is not relevant to the classification under FAS 115.

Although financial assets that do not meet the securities definition of FAS 115 must be measured in the same manner as investments under FAS 115, other provisions of that Statement (disclosures, etc.) are not required to be applied.

**Accounting for acquired loans and related standby commitment fees.**

*Decline in credit quality.* SOP 03-3 addresses the accounting for the differences between contractual and expected future cash flows of acquired (i.e., nonoriginated) loans when these differences are attributable, at least in part, to a decline in the debtor's credit quality subsequent to loan inception.

Under SOP 03-3, which is applicable to all nongovernmental entities including not-for-profit organizations, purchased loans are displayed at the initial investment amount on the balance sheet. The amount of any discount is not displayed on the balance sheet nor does the acquirer carry over an allowance for loan losses established by the seller. This prohibition applies equally to stand-alone purchases of loans and to those that occur as part of purchase business combinations.

When loans are acquired with evidence of deterioration in credit quality since origination, the acquirer is required to estimate the cash flows expected to be collected on the loan. This estimation is to be performed both at the purchase date and again periodically over the lives of the loans. Cash flows in excess of the initial investment (purchase price) expected to be collected are recognized as yield; this is referred to as "accretable yield." On the other hand, contractual cash flows in excess of expected cash flows (the nonaccretable difference) are not recognized as yield.

The accounting for changing expectations regarding future cash flows depends on whether these are decreases or increases. If, subsequent to acquisition, there are decreases in the probable cash flows, impairments are to be recognized in the current period's income statement. In other words, such a development cannot be handled prospectively, as a yield adjustment, over the remaining lives of the loans.

By contrast, probable increases in subsequent flows expected to be collected are recognized prospectively as a yield adjustment. In cases where a new, higher yield on a loan is established (due to a probable increase in cash flows to be collected), that yield is to be used as the effective interest rate in any later impairment test.

If loans are refinanced or restructured after acquisition, these cannot be accounted for as new loans, unless these are troubled debt restructurings, addressed by FAS 15, FAS 114, and FAS 115.

Acquired loans are not to be aggregated for purposes of determining evidence of post-origination credit deterioration. Rather, each loan, even if purchased in a pool, must be individually evaluated. However, subsequent pooling or aggregation of smaller-balance homogeneous loans is allowed for purposes of recognition, measurement, and disclosure. To be accounted for in the aggregate, loans must have a common credit risk (such as past due status or credit score) and have a common predominant risk characteristic (such as type of loan or date of origination). Furthermore, aggregation is limited to loans purchased in the same fiscal quarter.

SOP 03-3 does not provide general guidance as to the recognition of income, because that guidance does not exist for originated loans. However, income recognition will still be prohibited on loans for which an investor expects to substantially improve the collateral for resale or expects to use the collateral in operations.

Variable loans with index rate decreases, contractual cash flow decreases, and expected cash flow decreases are to be evaluated based on the change in expected cash flows attributable to the decrease in index rates. Those changes are recognized prospectively, rather than as impairments. The decrease in expected cash flows due to index rate decreases must be ascertained, and those changes are to be evaluated against the loan's contractual payments receivable, which must be calculated based on the index rate as it changes over the life of the loan.

***Standby commitment fees.*** Some entities agree to purchase loans at a stated price in return for a standby commitment fee. If the settlement date of a standby commitment to purchase loans is reasonable (i.e., within a normal loan commitment period), then the commitment fee is recognized in accordance with FAS 91. In general, FAS 91 requires the fee to be recognized as a yield adjustment over the life of the loan (or group of loans) purchased. If the commitment expires unexercised, the fee is recognized as income upon its expiration. FAS 91 provides two exceptions to the general rule.

1. If, based on the reporting entity's experience with similar arrangements, there is a remote likelihood that the commitment will be exercised, the fee is amortized as service fee income using the straight-line method over the commitment period. Should the commitment be exercised, the remaining unamortized portion of the fee is recognized as a yield adjustment over the life of the loan.
2. If the commitment fee is determined on a retrospective basis as a percentage of the unused portion of an available line of credit, the commitment fee is to be recognized as service fee income on the determination date if

   a. The commitment fee percentage is nominal compared to the stated interest rate on any related borrowing under the line of credit, and
   b. Borrowings under the line of credit will bear the market rate of interest on the date of the loan.

If the settlement date is not within a reasonable period, or if the reporting entity does not have the intent and ability to accept delivery without selling assets, the standby commitment is accounted for as a written put option. That is, the standby commitment fee is recorded as a liability. Thereafter, the liability is reported at the greater of the initial standby commitment fee or the fair value of the written put option, with the offsetting entry reported in current operations.

**Disclosures**

**SOP 01-6.** SOP 01-6 includes disclosure requirements for all entities involved in financing activities (including trade receivables).

1. The following amounts must be reported separately on the face of the balance sheet:

    a. The amount of receivables held for sale

    b. The amount of foreclosed or repossessed assets, which can be included in the other assets category if the notes to the financial statements disclose the amount

2. The balance sheet or notes are to report

    a. Separately, each major category of loans and trade receivables

    b. The allowance for doubtful accounts or loan losses

    c. Any unearned income, unamortized premiums or discounts, and any net unamortized deferred fees and costs related to loans or trade receivables

    d. The recorded investment in loans (and trade receivables, if applicable) on non-accrual status, as of each balance sheet presented

    e. The recorded investment in loans (and trade receivables, if applicable) on accrual status that are past due ninety days or more, as of each balance sheet presented

    f. The carrying amount of financial instruments that serve as collateral for borrowings

3. The "summary of significant accounting principles" note is to include the following:

    a. The basis for accounting for trade receivables, loans receivable, and lease financings, including those held for sale

    b. Whether aggregate or individual asset basis is used in determining the lower of cost or fair value of nonmortgage loans held for sale

    c. The classification and method of accounting for receivables that can be contractually prepaid or otherwise settled in a way that the reporting entity would not recover substantially all of its recorded investment

    d. The method for recognizing interest income on loan and trade receivables, including related fees and costs, and the method of amortizing net deferred fees or costs

    e. The accounting policies and methodology used to estimate the allowance for doubtful accounts and/or loan losses, including the factors that influenced management's judgment (such as existing economic conditions and historical losses)

    f. The accounting policies and methodology used to estimate any liability for off-balance-sheet credit losses, including the factors that influenced management's judgment

    g. The policy for placing loans (and trade receivables, if applicable) on nonaccrual status

    h. The policy for recording payments received on loans (and trade receivables, if applicable) that are in nonaccrual status

    i. The policy for resuming interest accruals on loans that are in nonaccrual status

    j. The policy for charging off uncollectible trade receivables and loans

k.  Whether past due or delinquency status is based on how recently payments have been made or on contractual terms

4.  The aggregate amount of gains or losses on sales of loans or trade receivables (including the amounts of adjustments to record receivables held for sale at the lower of cost or fair value) are to be presented separately in the financial statements or disclosed in the notes.

**FAS 140.**  FAS 140 disclosures include

1.  For collateral

    a.  If the reporting entity has entered into repurchase agreements or securities lending transactions, its policy for requiring collateral or other security
    b.  If the reporting entity has pledged any of its assets as collateral that are not reclassified and separately reported on the balance sheet, the carrying amount and classification of those assets on the date on the most recent balance sheet
    c.  If the reporting entity has accepted collateral that it is permitted by contract or custom to sell or repledge, the fair value of that collateral as of the date of each balance sheet, the portion of that collateral that it has sold or repledged, and the sources and uses of that collateral

2.  Description of items for which it is not practicable to estimate fair value and reasons why it is not practicable

3.  For servicing assets and liabilities

    a.  Amounts recognized and amortized during the period
    b.  Fair value recognized, method and assumptions used to estimate fair value
    c.  Risk characteristics used to stratify recognized servicing assets in order to measure impairments
    d.  Valuation allowance and all related activity for each period for which results of operations are reported

4.  If the reporting entity has securitized any financial assets during any period presented and accounted for that securitization as a sale, it must disclose the following information for each major asset type (e.g., mortgage loans, auto loans, credit card receivables):

    a.  Accounting policies for initially measuring the retained interests
    b.  The method used in measuring the fair value of the retained interests and the key assumptions used in that measurement (at a minimum, assumptions about discount rates, expected prepayments, expected weighted-average life of prepayable assets, anticipated credit losses)
    c.  A description of the reporting entity's continuing involvement with the assets securitized
    d.  The amount of the gain or loss from sale of the assets in the securitization
    e.  Cash flows between the QSPE and the reporting entity

5.  If the reporting entity has retained interests in securitized financial assets at the most recent balance sheet presented, it must disclose the following information for each major asset type (e.g., mortgage loans, auto loans, credit card receivables)

    a.  Accounting policy for subsequently measuring the retained interests
    b.  The method used in measuring the fair value of the retained interests and the key assumptions used in that measurement (at a minimum, assumptions about discount rates, expected prepayments, expected weighted-average life of pre-

payable assets, anticipated credit losses, expected static pool losses, if applicable)

   c.   A sensitivity analysis or stress test showing the hypothetical effect on the fair value of the retained interests of two or more unfavorable variations from the expected level for each key assumption (computed independently of any other change in the key assumptions) and a description of the objectives, methodology, and limitations of the sensitivity analysis or stress test

   d.   For the securitized assets and any other financial assets managed with them, the total principal amount, the portion derecognized, the portion remaining, and delinquencies as of the end of the period, and the credit losses, net of recoveries, during the period. This disclosure is to exclude securitized assets that the reporting entity manages but with which it does not have any other continuing involvement.

   e.   Average balances during the period for the securitized assets and any other financial assets managed with them. (This disclosure is not required but merely encouraged.)

**SOP 03-3.** Additional disclosures required by this SOP for acquirers of loans

1.   How prepayments on loans are accounted for
2.   For loans acquired through purchase, including in a business combination, separately for loans accounted for as debt securities, and for those not accounted for as debt securities

   a.   The outstanding balance (undiscounted cash flows owed)
   b.   The carrying amount at the beginning of the period
   c.   The carrying amount at the end of the period
   d.   A reconciliation of the amount of accretable yield at the beginning of the period to the amount of accretable yield at the end of the period
   e.   For loans acquired in the current period

      (1)  The contractually required payments receivable
      (2)  The cash flows expected to be collected
      (3)  The fair value at acquisition
      (4)  The carrying amount of any acquired loans that are in nonaccrual status

   f.   The carrying amount of all loans in nonaccrual status
   g.   For loans not accounted for as debt securities

      (1)  The amount of any expense recognized for impairment
      (2)  The amount of any reduction in a valuation allowance for losses that results from an increase in cash flows previously expected to be collected
      (3)  The amount of the allowance for uncollectible loans at the beginning of the period
      (4)  The amount of the allowance for uncollectible loans at the end of the period

## Prepaid Expenses

**Types of prepaid expenses.** Prepaid expenses are amounts paid to secure the use of assets or the receipt of services at a future date or continuously over one or more future periods. Prepaid expenses will not be converted to cash, but they are classified as current assets because, if not prepaid, they would have required the use of current assets during the coming year (or operating cycle, if longer). Examples of items that are often prepaid include dues, subscriptions, maintenance agreements, memberships, licenses, rents, and insurance.

The examples of prepaid expenses cited in the previous paragraph are unambiguous. This is, however, not always the case. In negotiating union labor contracts, the parties may agree that the union employees will be entitled to receive a lump-sum cash payment or series of payments in exchange for agreeing to little or no increase in the employees' base wage rate. These lump-sum arrangements ordinarily do not require the employee to refund any portion of the lump sum to the employer in the event that the employee terminates employment during the term of the labor agreement. Further, it is assumed by the parties that, upon termination of a union member, the employer will replace that individual with another union member at the same base wage rate to whom no lump sum would be due. Management believes that the lump-sum payment arrangement will reduce or eliminate raises during the contract term and that these lump-sum payments will benefit future periods. In order to record these lump sums as prepaid expenses, EITF 88-23 specifies that, based on a careful review of the facts and circumstances around the contract and negotiations, the payments must clearly benefit a future period in the form of a lower base wage rate than would otherwise have been in effect. Further, the amortization period is not permitted to extend beyond the term of the union contract. The presumption of replacing terminating union members with other union members at the same wage rate is essential to this conclusion and, thus, this accounting treatment is only applicable to union contracts and is not permitted to be applied by analogy to account for individual employment contracts or other compensation arrangements. The SEC observer to the EITF's proceedings noted that accounting for this transaction as a prepaid expense is only appropriate when there is no evidence of any kind that the lump-sum payment or payments are related to services rendered in the past.

**Amortization.** Prepaid expenses are amortized to expense on a ratable basis over the period during which the benefits or services are received. For example, if rent is prepaid for the quarter at the beginning of the quarter, two months of the rent will be included in the prepaid rent account. At the beginning of the second month, the equivalent of one month's rent (half the account balance) would be charged to rent expense. At the beginning of the third month, the remaining prepayment would be charged to rent expense.

### Example of prepaid expenses

The PipeTrak Company starts using geographical information systems (GIS) software to track the locations of the country's pipeline infrastructure under a contract for the Department of Homeland Security. It pays maintenance fees on three types of GIS software, for which the following maintenance periods are covered:

| Software name | Maintenance start date | Maintenance duration | Maintenance fee |
|---|---|---|---|
| Culture Data (CD) | February | Annual | $4,800 |
| Map Layering (ML) | April | Semiannual | 18,000 |
| Land Grid (LG) | June | Quarterly | 6,000 |

It initially records these fee payments as prepaid expenses. PipeTrak's controller then uses the following amortization table to determine the amount of prepaid expenses to charge to expense each month:

| Software | Feb | Mar | Apr | May | Jun | Jul | Aug | Sep | Oct | Nov | Dec |
|---|---|---|---|---|---|---|---|---|---|---|---|
| CD | 400 | 400 | 400 | 400 | 400 | 400 | 400 | 400 | 400 | 400 | 400 |
| ML | | | 3,000 | 3,000 | 3,000 | 3,000 | 3,000 | 3,000 | | | |
| LG | | | | | 2,000 | 2,000 | 2,000 | | | | |
| Totals | 400 | 400 | 3,400 | 3,400 | 5,400 | 5,400 | 5,400 | 3,400 | 400 | 400 | 400 |

In June, PipeTrak records the following entry to charge a portion of its prepaid software maintenance to expense:

| | | |
|---|---|---|
| Software maintenance expense | 5,400 | |
| Prepaid expenses | | 5,400 |

# 8 SHORT-TERM INVESTMENTS AND FINANCIAL INSTRUMENTS

## PERSPECTIVE AND ISSUES

Reporting entities have an unprecedented variety of financial products available to them to meet their short-term (and long-term) investing and risk management goals. These products have differing characteristics and present the investor with a wide range of returns and, of course, a wider range of risks. Many of these are useful as hedging tools, as well.

GAAP has evolved slowly, deliberately, and sometimes reactively to the emergence of new financial vehicles and their increasing complexity. Initial efforts in this regard focused primarily on informing financial statement readers about the risks and uncertainties inherent in these investments. This was achieved by providing disclosures that accompanied financial statements, but that did not formally recognize the investments as assets or liabilities, and also did not recognize their inherent volatility in the income statement. This approach thus did not fully provide the needed transparency and proved an inadequate substitute for full financial statement recognition.

FAS 133, *Accounting for Derivative Instruments and Hedging Activities,* governs the accounting for derivatives. Scores of interpretations have since been issued by a special implementation guidance task force (the Derivatives Implementation Group or DIG) established by FASB. Derivatives literature is exceedingly complex, which is largely a consequence of the rules establishing "special accounting" for hedging. Limited accounting relief (i.e., simplified accounting) for certain types of hedging activities may be provided by applying FAS 159, *The Fair Value Option for Financial Assets and Financial Liabilities* that will become effective during 2008. In addition, FASB and IASB are conducting other projects designed to simplify and converge accounting for financial instruments, derivatives, and hedging. Accountants therefore must be particularly alert to changes in these requirements.

FAS 133 applies to all entities and requires that all derivative instruments (DI) be recognized as either assets or liabilities on the balance sheet at their respective fair values. Gains and losses on DI which are *not* designated as hedges are always to be recognized currently in earnings (in the case of a not-for-profit entity, in the change in net assets). Special accounting (effectively, the deferral of gains or losses) for derivatives is permissible only when the instrument has been designated as a hedge, and then only to the extent that the hedge is effective. Depending upon which of the conditions specified in the standard are met, a derivative will be specifically designated as either a hedge of fair value changes, of cash flows, or of certain foreign currency exposures.

Hedges of the changes in fair value can be associated with a recognized asset or liability or of an unrecognized firm commitment. In a fair value hedge, gains and losses of both the DI and the hedged item are recognized currently in earnings. In the case of a perfectly effective hedge, these gains and losses will fully offset each period, but more typically this result will not be achieved. There will thus be a residual charge or credit to earnings each period that the hedge position is in place.

Cash flows hedges, on the other hand, pertain to forecasted transactions. The effective portions of these hedges are initially reported in other comprehensive income and are reclassified into earnings only later, when the forecasted transactions affect earnings. Any ineffective portions of the hedges are reported currently in earnings. (Fair value and cash flow hedges are addressed in detail in this chapter.)

Hedges of the foreign currency exposure of a net investment in a foreign operation also qualify for special accounting treatment. In a foreign currency net investment hedge, the gain or loss is reported in other comprehensive income as part of the cumulative translation adjustment. In the case of foreign currency hedges of unrecognized firm commitments, the gain or loss is reported the same way as a fair value hedge. A gain or loss on a foreign currency hedge that is associated with an available-for-sale security will also be reported the same way as a fair value hedge. Finally, a gain or loss arising from a hedge relating to a foreign currency denominated forecasted transaction is reported in the same way as a cash flow hedge. (These hedges are discussed in this chapter and in Chapter 23.)

Not-for-profit entities (NFP) are not permitted to use hedge accounting for forecasted transactions. This is because NFP do not report *other comprehensive income*—all such items are included in the statement of activity, which provides an all-inclusive measure of changes in net assets for the period. In other regards, however, FAS 133 requirements are fully applicable to NFP.

A nonderivative financial instrument generally cannot be designated as a hedge. An exception, however, occurs when that instrument is denominated in a foreign currency and is designated as a hedge of a net investment in a foreign operation or an unrecognized firm commitment.

Hedge effectiveness must be demonstrated if the accounting set forth in FAS 133 is to be employed. This does not require perfect effectiveness (which is almost never attainable in practice), but the standard is not explicit regarding the degree of effectiveness that must be attained to justify the use of special hedge accounting. The method to be used for assessing the effective and ineffective portions of a hedge must be established at the inception of the hedge and must be consistent with the approach actually used by the reporting entity for managing risk. Should a hedge fail to meet a minimum threshold of effectiveness, it is to be dedesignated, and hedge accounting ceases.

Rules pertaining to the recognition of transfers of financial assets and to the extinguishments of financial liabilities have gone through several changes over the years. Under the provisions of FAS 140, *Accounting for Transfers and Servicing of Financial Assets and Extinguishments of Liabilities*, subsequent to a transfer of financial assets an entity recognizes the financial and servicing assets it controls and the liabilities it has incurred, derecognizes those financial assets over which control has been surrendered, and derecognizes liabilities which have been extinguished. Multiple criteria pertaining to surrender of control must all be met for sale treatment to apply. Derivatives and liabilities resulting from a transfer of financial assets are measured at fair value. FAS 140 established requirements for "qualified special-purpose entities (QSPE)," which remain an exception to the more general, and also highly complex, requirements applicable to what are now called "variable interest entities."

FAS 115 remains GAAP regarding passive investments in all debt securities and in those equity securities that have a readily determinable fair value. It classifies these securities into one of three categories: held-to-maturity, trading, or available-for-sale. The first of these can only be applied to debt securities, which are then to be reported at amortized cost. The trading category can include both debt and equity securities, which are to be reported at fair value, via charges or credits included in current earnings. The available-for-sale category is used for those investments that do not fit in either of the other two classifications; these are also reported at fair value in the balance sheet, although changes in fair value are not reflected in current earnings.

FAS 115 did not change the accounting for financial liabilities and it does not apply to DI. In the case of an investment subject to this standard with an embedded derivative, the host instrument is accounted for under FAS 115 and the embedded derivative is accounted for under FAS 133.

FAS 107, as amended by FAS 133, requires entities to disclose the fair value of *all* (i.e., both recognized and unrecognized) financial instruments for which it is practicable to estimate values, including liabilities. Pertinent descriptive information regarding the instrument is to be disclosed if an estimate of fair value cannot be made without incurring excessive costs. Certain types of financial instruments—including pensions, postretirement benefits, deferred compensation, insurance contracts, lease contracts, and warranty obligations—are excluded from the requirements of this standard. FAS 107 also requires disclosure of concentrations of credit risk for all financial instruments.

FAS 126 amended FAS 107 to make disclosures optional for entities that

1. Have total assets less than $100 million on the balance sheet date; and
2. Have not held or issued any derivative financial instruments during the reporting period; and
3. Are nonpublic

The definition of nonpublic entities used in FAS 126 (and specified under other GAAP) has been expanded by FSP FAS 126-1 to include entities that are conduit bond obligors.

These are entities that benefited from a state or local governmental unit issuing bonds on its behalf to provide the entity with needed financing. The conduit bond obligor is fully responsible for repayment of the principal and interest on the bonds (referred to by such terms as industrial revenue bonds or private activity bonds) as well as any financial reporting obligations imposed as a result of the issuance.

As a general principle, the offsetting of assets and liabilities is not permitted under GAAP. However, when a right of setoff exists—defined as a debtor's legal right to discharge debt owed to another party by applying against the debt an amount the other party owes to the debtor—offsetting is allowed. FIN 39 and FIN 41 make another exception in the case of multiple forward swap, and similar contracts executed with the same party under master netting arrangements. The conditions to be met are

1. Each of the two parties owes the other determinable amounts.
2. The reporting party has the right to set off.
3. The reporting party intends to set off.
4. The right of setoff is enforceable at law.

Confusing and often conflicting definitions of fair value, which appeared throughout GAAP, have been eliminated and replaced by a single definition provided by FAS 157, *Fair Value Measurements*. FAS 157 will be effective for fiscal years beginning after November 15, 2007, and for interim periods within those fiscal years. Besides standardizing the definition of fair value, FAS 157 also provides measurement guidance and new disclosure requirements. Full coverage of FAS 157 and FAS 159 is provided in Chapter 6.

Chronic complaints about the quality of disclosures as prescribed by FAS 133 have resulted in the 2008 imposition of FAS 161, *Disclosures about Derivative Instruments and Hedging Activities*, which provides for enhanced disclosures about (1) how and why an entity uses derivative instruments, (2) how derivative instruments and related hedged items are accounted for under FAS 133 and its related interpretations, and (3) how derivative instruments and related hedged items affect the reporting entity's financial position, financial performance, and cash flows.

| Sources of GAAP | | | | |
|---|---|---|---|---|
| *ARB* | *APB* | *FAS* | *FIN* | *EITF* |
| 43, Ch. 3A | 22 | 52, 65, 80, 95, 102, 107, 109, 111, 112, 115, 123, 126, 127, 130, 133, 137, 138, 140, 145, 149, 155, 157, 159, 161 | 39, 41 | 85-9, 86-25, 86-28, 86-40, 87-12, 87-30, 89-18, 90-17, 95-5, 96-11, 96-12, 99-1, 99-2, 00-19, 01-6, 02-2, 02-3, 03-1, 03-11, D-11, D-39, D-50, D-73, D-102, D-109 |
| | | | *FTB* 94-1 | |
| | | | *SOP* 03-3 | |
| | | *FSP* FAS 115-1, 124-1 | | |

## DEFINITIONS OF TERMS

**Bifurcation.** Separation of an embedded derivative instrument from the host contract so that separate accounting can be applied to the embedded derivative instrument.

**Carrying amount (value).** The amount at which securities are measured and reported on the reporting entity's balance sheet by applying the appropriate GAAP.

**Contractual obligations.** All contractual obligations that are financial instruments meet the definition of a liability set forth in CON 6, *Elements of Financial Statements*. Some may not be recognized as liabilities in financial statements (i.e., they may be "off-balance-sheet") because they fail to meet some other criterion for recognition. For some financial instruments, the obligation is owed to or by a group of entities rather than a single entity.

**Contractual rights.** All contractual rights that are financial instruments meet the definition of asset set forth in CON 6. Some may not be recognized as assets in financial statements (may be "off-balance-sheet") because they fail to meet some other criterion for recognition. For some financial instruments, the obligation is held by or due from a group of entities rather than a single entity.

**Cost (of a security).** The original purchase price plus all costs incidental to the acquisition (e.g., brokerage fees and taxes) unless a new cost basis is assigned as a result of a decline in fair value which is other than temporary.

**Derivative instruments.** In FAS 133, derivative instruments are defined by their three distinguishing characteristics. Specifically, derivative instruments are financial instruments or other contracts that have

1. One or more underlyings and one or more notional amounts (or payment provisions or both);
2. No initial net investment or a smaller net investment than required for contracts expected to have a similar response to market changes; and
3. Terms that require or permit

    a. Net settlement
    b. Net settlement by means outside the contract
    c. Delivery of an asset that results in a position substantially the same as net settlement

In contrast to prior GAAP, FAS 133 defines derivative instruments by reference to specific characteristics, rather than in terms of classes or categories of financial instruments. These distinctive features are believed to distinguish the fundamental nature of derivative instruments such as options and futures.

**Equity security.** Any security (defined below) that evidences an ownership interest in an entity or the right to acquire or dispose of such an ownership interest in an entity for a fixed or determinable price. Equity securities include common or preferred stock, warrants, stock rights, call options, or put options. Equity securities do not include convertible debt or preferred stock that, by their terms, either must be redeemed by the issuer or is redeemable at the option of the investor.

**Equity securities with readily determinable fair values.** Equity securities (see definition above) that meet one of the following criteria:

1. Sales prices or bid-and-asked quotations are available currently on an SEC-registered securities exchange or in an over-the-counter market whose prices or quotations are publicly reported by the National Association of Securities Dealers' Automated Quotations Systems (NASDAQ) or by Pink Sheets LLC.
2. For equity securities traded exclusively in a foreign market, the foreign market is of comparable breadth and scope to one of the US markets mentioned in 1. above.
3. For equity securities representing investments in mutual funds, the fair value per share or per unit is determined and published, and is used as the basis for current transactions.

Equity securities that otherwise meet one of the above criteria that are restricted as to transfer from their current holder to another party are included in the scope of this definition if the restriction terminates within one year. In accordance with FAS 157, *Fair Value Measurements*, the fair values of these securities are to be measured based on the quoted price of an otherwise unrestricted security of the same issuer, adjusted for the effect of the restriction.

**Fair value.** The price that would be received to sell an asset or paid to transfer a liability in an orderly transaction between market participants at the measurement date.

**Financial asset.** A financial asset is defined as

1. Cash,
2. Evidence of an ownership interest in an entity, or
3. A contractual right that conveys to one entity a right

   a. To receive cash or another financial asset from another entity, or
   b. To exchange other financial instruments on potentially favorable terms with the other entity.

**Financial instrument.** As defined by FAS 107, *Disclosures about Fair Value of Financial Instruments,* a financial instrument is

1. Cash,
2. Evidence of an ownership interest in an entity, or
3. A contract that meets both of the following criteria:

   a. Imposes on one entity a contractual obligation

      (1) To deliver cash or another financial instrument to a second entity or
      (2) To exchange other financial instruments on potentially unfavorable terms with the second entity, and

   b. Conveys to that second entity a contractual right

      (1) To receive cash or another financial instrument from the first entity, or
      (2) To exchange other financial instruments on potentially favorable terms with the first entity.

The FAS 107 definition was intended to encompass both financial assets and liabilities. Attempting to meet these twin objectives rendered the definition difficult to comprehend, however. FAS 157 provided separate definitions of financial assets and financial liabilities, as summarized herein, which aid the accountant charged with applying GAAP in practice.

**Financial liability.** A contractual obligation of an entity

1. To deliver cash or another financial asset to another entity or
2. To exchange other financial instruments on potentially unfavorable terms with the other entity.

**Firm commitment.** An agreement with an unrelated party, binding on both parties and usually legally enforceable, having the following attributes:

1. The agreement specifies all significant terms including the timing of the transaction, the quantity to be exchanged, and a fixed price. The fixed price can be expressed in the entity's functional currency or in a foreign currency. The fixed price can also be expressed as a specified interest rate or specified effective yield.
2. The agreement includes a disincentive for nonperformance sufficient to make contractual performance probable.

**Forecasted transaction.** A transaction that is expected to occur for which there is no firm commitment. Because no transaction or event has yet occurred, when the transaction or event does occur, it will be at the prevailing market price.

**Initial net investment.** A derivative instrument is one where the initial net investment is zero or is less than the notional amount (possibly plus a premium or minus a discount). This characteristic refers to the relative amount of investment. Derivative instruments allow the holder an opportunity to take part in the rate or price change without owning the underlying asset or owing the actual liability.  If an amount approximating the notional amount must be invested or received, it is not a derivative instrument.  The two basic forms of derivative instruments are futures and options.  The futures contract involves little or no initial net investment.  Settlement is usually near the delivery date.  Call options, when purchased, require a premium payment that is less than the cost of purchasing the equivalent number of shares.  Even though this distinguishing characteristic is the result of the action by only one of the parties, it determines the application for both.

FAS 149 amended FAS 133 to specify that if the initial net investment in the contract, after adjusting for the time value of money, is less by more than a nominal amount, then an initial net investment that would be commensurate with the amount that would be exchanged either to acquire the asset related to the underlying or to incur the obligation related to the underlying, the threshold condition for classification as a derivative is met.  The amount of the asset acquired or liability incurred, for purpose of this determination, should be comparable to the *effective* notional amount of the contract.  The effective notional amount is the stated notional amount adjusted for any leverage factor.

**Net settlements.**  To qualify as a derivative instrument, one of the following settlement criteria must be met:

1. No delivery of an asset equal to the notional amount is required.  For example, an interest rate swap does not involve delivery of the instrument in which the notional amount is expressed.
2. Delivery of an asset equal to the notional amount is required of one of the parties, but an exchange (or other market mechanism, institutional arrangement or side agreement) facilitates net settlement.  For example, a call option has this attribute.
3. Delivery by one of the parties of an asset equal to the notional amount is required but the asset is either readily convertible to cash (as with a contract for the delivery of a marketable equity security), or is required but that asset is itself a derivative instrument (as is the case for a swaption [an option on a swap]).

This characteristic means that the derivative instrument can be settled by a net delivery of assets (the medium of exchange does not have to be cash).  Contract terms based on changes in the price or rate of the notional that implicitly or explicitly require or permit net settlement qualify.  Situations where one of the parties can liquidate their net investment or be relieved of the contract rights or obligations without significant transaction costs because of a market arrangement (broadly interpreted) or where the delivered asset can be readily converted to cash also meet the requirements for net settlement.  It is assumed that an exchange-traded security is readily converted to cash.  Thus, commodity-based contracts for gold, oil, wheat, etc. are now included under this standard.  The convertible to cash condition requires an active market and consideration of interchangeability and transaction volume.  Determining if delivery of a financial asset or liability equal to the notional amount is a derivative instrument may depend upon whether it is readily convertible into cash.  Different accounting will result if the notional is not readily converted to cash. Using the notional as collateral does not necessarily mean it is readily convertible to cash.

**Normal purchases and sales.**  Contracts without a settlement provision and without a market mechanism to facilitate net settlement; or which require delivery of nonfinancial assets that constitute normal purchases or normal sales of the reporting entity.

**Notional amount.**  The notional amount (or payment provision) is the referenced units of measure associated with the underlying asset or liability, such as shares of stock, principal amount, face value, stated value, basis points, barrels of oil, etc.  It may be that amount plus a premium or minus a discount.  The interaction of the price or rate (underlying) with the referenced associated asset or liability (notional amount) determines whether settlement is required and, if so, the amount.

**Other-than-temporary decline.** A downward movement in the value of a marketable equity security for which there are known causes. The decline indicates a remote likelihood of a price recovery.

**Security.** A security is defined as one of the following:

1. A share, participation, or other interest in an enterprise or in property of the issuer, or
2. An obligation of the issuer that

    a. Is represented by an instrument issued in bearer or registered form or is registered in books maintained to record transfers by or on behalf of the issuer,

    b. Is of a type commonly dealt in on securities exchanges or markets or, when represented by an instrument, is commonly recognized in any area in which it is issued or dealt in as an investment medium, and

    c. Is either one of a class or series or, by its terms, is divisible into a class or series of shares, participations, interests, or obligations

**Short-term investments.** Securities or other assets acquired with excess cash, having ready marketability and intended by management to be liquidated, if necessary, within the current operating cycle.

**Temporary decline.** A downward fluctuation in the fair value of a security that has no known causes that suggest the decline will not reverse in the future.

**Underlying.** An underlying is commonly a specified price or rate such as a stock price, interest rate, currency rate, commodity price, or a related index. However, any variable (financial or physical) with (1) observable changes or (2) objectively verifiable changes such as a credit rating, insurance index, climatic or geological condition (temperature, rainfall) qualifies. Unless it is specifically excluded, a contract based on any qualifying variable is accounted for under FAS 133 if it has distinguishing characteristics 2. and 3. above.

**Unrealized gain (loss).** The unrealized difference between the fair value of a short-term investment and its carrying value.

**Valuation allowance.** An account used to adjust the carrying value of equity securities to fair value. The offset is either a gain or loss account (for trading securities) or a contra equity account (for available-for-sale securities).

## CONCEPTS, RULES, AND EXAMPLES

### Short-Term Investments

Short-term (or temporary) investments usually consist of debt securities and equity securities with readily determinable fair values. Accordingly, investments that are held for purposes of control of another entity or pursuant to an ongoing business relationship, for example, stock held in a supplier, would be excluded from current assets and would instead be listed as other assets or long-term investments (discussed in detail in Chapter 12).

**Debt securities and equity securities with readily determinable fair values.** FAS 115, *Accounting for Certain Investments in Debt and Equity Securities*, governs the accounting for all debt securities and for equity securities with readily determinable fair values.

| *Included in the scope of FAS 115* | *Excluded from the scope of FAS 115* |
|---|---|
| All debt including loans that meet the FAS 115 definition of a "security," even if the loan involved a modification of terms in connection with a troubled debt restructuring (FTB 94-1) | Unsecuritized loans |
| Mortgage-backed securities | Equity securities that, absent election of the fair value option permitted by FAS 159, would be required to be accounted for using the equity method |
| Equity securities with readily determinable fair values | Investments in consolidated entities |
| Rights to purchase equity securities (e.g., warrants and call options) or to sell equity securities (e.g., put options) | Not-for-profit organizations (subject, instead to FAS 124) |
| An instrument otherwise subject to FAS 115 that contains an embedded derivative subject to FAS 133. The host instrument remains within the scope of FAS 115 | Derivatives subject to FAS 133 |
| Cooperatives and mutual enterprises including credit unions, and mutual insurance companies | Reporting entities subject to specialized industry requirements that substantially all their investments be stated at fair value with changes in fair value recognized currently in income (e.g. brokers and dealers in securities; employee benefit plans; investment companies) |
| | Transaction gains or losses on held-to-maturity foreign-currency-denominated debt securities (accounted for under FAS 52) |

FAS 115 requires all debt securities and equity securities with readily determinable fair values to be placed into one of three categories.

**Classification of Debt Securities and Equity Securities with Readily Determinable Fair Values**

| *Category* | *Type* | *Characteristics* | *Reported on balance sheet* | *Reported in income* |
|---|---|---|---|---|
| 1. Held-to-maturity | Debt | Positive intent and ability to hold until maturity | Amortized cost | Interest Realized gains and losses |
| 2. Trading | Debt or equity | Bought and held principally to sell short-term | Fair value | Interest and dividends Realized gains and losses Unrealized gains and losses |
| 3. Available-for-sale | Debt or equity | Neither held-to-maturity nor trading securities | Fair value Unrealized gains and losses to accumulated other comprehensive income (component of equity) | Interest and dividends Realized gains and losses |

If a classified balance sheet is presented, the debt and equity securities owned by an entity are to be grouped into current and noncurrent portfolios. By definition, all trading securities are classified as current assets. The determination of current or noncurrent status for individual held-to-maturity and individual available-for-sale securities is made on the basis of whether or not the securities are considered working capital available for current operations (ARB 43, chapter 3A).

**Fair value readily determinable.** The fair value of an equity security is considered readily determinable if

1. Sales prices or bid-and-ask quotations are currently available on SEC-registered exchanges or in an over-the-counter market publicly reported by the National Association of Securities Dealers Automated Quotation System (NASDAQ) or by Pink Sheets LLC. Unless qualified for sale within one year, restricted stock does not meet this definition.
2. It is traded on a foreign market of comparable breadth and scope to one of the US markets identified above.
3. It represents an interest in a mutual fund and fair value per unit (share) is determined and published and is the basis for current transactions.

**Classification.** Classification is to be made at the time of the initial acquisition of the investment. The appropriateness of classification is to be reassessed at each reporting date.

**Held-to-maturity debt securities.** If an entity has both the *positive intent* and the *ability* to hold debt securities to maturity, they are measured and presented at amortized cost. In general, transfers to or from this category are not permitted. In those rare circumstances when there are transfers or sales of securities in this category, disclosure must be made of the following in the notes to the financial statements for each period for which the results of operations are presented:

1. Amortized cost
2. Realized or unrealized gain or loss
3. Circumstances leading to the decision to sell or transfer

Isolated, nonrecurring, and unusual events that could not have been reasonably anticipated may cause a sale or transfer without calling the originally determined intent or ability to hold into question. Other changes in circumstances that are not considered inconsistent include

1. Material deterioration in creditworthiness of the issuer
2. Elimination or reduction of tax-exempt status of interest through a change in tax law
3. Major business disposition or combination
4. Statutory or regulatory changes that materially modify what a permissible investment is or the maximum level of the security to be held
5. Downsizing in response to a regulatory increase in the industry's capital requirements
6. A material increase in risk weights for regulatory risk-based capital purposes

The held-to-maturity category does not include securities available for sale in response to a need for liquidity or changes in

1. Market interest rates
2. Foreign currency risk
3. Funding sources and terms
4. Yield and availability of alternative investments
5. Prepayment risk

For asset-liability management purposes, similar or identical securities may be classified differently depending upon intent and ability to hold.

Under FAS 140, securities such as interest-only strips, which can be settled in a manner that could cause the recorded amounts to not be substantially recovered, cannot be classified as held-to-maturity. Dependent upon the circumstances these are to be categorized as either trading or available-for-sale.

For a discussion of the treatment of foreign-currency-denominated held-to-maturity securities and permissible hedging strategies under FAS 133, see Chapter 23.

***Maturity date.*** The sale of a security within three months of its maturity meets the requirement to hold to maturity since the interest rate risk is substantially diminished. Likewise, if a call is considered probable, a sale within three months of that date meets the requirement. The sale of a security after collection of at least 85% of the principal outstanding at acquisition (due to prepayments or to scheduled payments of principal and interest in equal installments) also qualifies since the "tail" portion no longer represents an efficient investment due to the economic costs of accounting for the remnants. Scheduled payments are not required to be equal for variable-rate debt.

### Example of held-to-maturity debt securities

The 12/31/08 debt security portfolio categorized as held-to-maturity is as follows:

| Security | Maturity value | Amortized cost | Assumed fair value |
|---|---|---|---|
| DEF 12% bond, due 12/31/09 | $ 10,000 | $10,320 | $10,200 |
| PQR mortgage-backed debt, due 12/31/11 | $100,000 | $92,000 | $90,000 |
| JKL 8% bond, due 12/31/15 | $ 10,000 | $ 8,929 | $ 9,100 |

The balance sheet would report all the securities in this category at amortized cost and would classify them as follows:

| Security | Maturity date | Balance sheet | Classification |
|---|---|---|---|
| DEF | 12/31/09 | $10,320 | Current |
| PQR | 12/31/11 | 92,000 | Noncurrent |
| JKL | 12/31/15 | 8,929 | Noncurrent |

Interest income, including premium and discount amortization, is included in income. Any realized gains or losses are also included in income.

**Trading securities.** If an entity has debt and/or equity securities (with readily determinable fair value) that it intends to actively and frequently buy and sell for short-term profits, those securities are classified as trading securities. Unless classified as held-to-maturity securities, under FAS 65 mortgage-backed securities held for sale require classification as trading securities. The securities in this category are required to be carried at fair value on the balance sheet as current assets. All applicable interest and dividends, realized gains and losses, and unrealized gains and losses on changes in fair value are included in income from continuing operations.

### Example of accounting for trading securities

The year one current trading securities portfolio is as follows:

| Security | Cost | Fair value | Difference (fair value minus cost) |
|---|---|---|---|
| ABC | $1,000 | $ 900 | $(100) |
| MNO calls | 1,500 | 1,700 | 200 |
| STU | 2,000 | 1,400 | (600) |
| XYZ 7% bond | 2,500 | 2,600 | 100 |
| | $7,000 | $6,600 | $(400) |

A $400 adjustment is required in order to recognize the decline in fair value. The entry required is

| | | |
|---|---|---|
| Unrealized loss on trading securities | 400 | |
| Trading securities—MNO calls | 200 | |
| Trading securities—XYZ 7% bond | 100 | |
| Trading securities—ABC | | 100 |
| Trading securities—STU | | 600 |

The unrealized loss would appear on the income statement as part of other expenses and losses. Dividend income and interest income (including premium and discount amortization) is included in income. Any realized gains or losses from the sale of securities are also included in income.

An alternative to direct write-up and write-down of securities is the use of an asset valuation allowance account to adjust the portfolio totals. In the above example, the entry would be

| | | |
|---|---|---|
| Unrealized loss on trading securities | 400 | |
|     Valuation allowance (contra asset) | | 400 |

The valuation allowance of $400 would be deducted from historical cost to obtain a fair value of $6,600 for the trading securities on the balance sheet.

All trading securities are classified as current assets and the balance sheet would appear as follows:

*Current assets:*
Trading securities at fair value (cost = $7,000)        $6,600

The year two current trading portfolio is as follows:

| Security | New securities cost | Old securities X1 fair value | X2 fair value | Difference* |
|---|---|---|---|---|
| ABC | | $ 900 | $1,000 | $100 |
| DEF Puts | $1,500 | | 1,500 | 0 |
| STU | | 1,400 | 1,800 | 400 |
| VWX | 2,700 | | 2,800 | 100 |
| | $4,200 | $2,300 | $7,100 | $600 |

\* *Difference = X2 fair value – (Cost or X1 fair value)*

A $600 adjustment is required in order to recognize the increase in fair value. The entry required is

| | | |
|---|---|---|
| Trading securities—ABC | 100 | |
| Trading securities—STU | 400 | |
| Trading securities—VWX | 100 | |
|     Unrealized gain on trading securities | | 600 |

The unrealized gain would appear on the income statement as part of other income.

**Example of accounting for a realized gain**

1. The same information as given in the above example for year one
2. In year two, the MNO calls are sold for $1,600 and the XYZ 7% bonds are sold for $2,700.

The entry required to record the sale is

| | | |
|---|---|---|
| Cash | 4,300 | |
| Realized loss on sale of trading securities | 100 | |
|     Realized gain on sale of trading securities | | 100 |
|     Trading securities—MNO calls (X1 fair value) | | 1,700 |
|     Trading securities—XYZ 7% bonds (X1 fair value) | | 2,600 |

Under the valuation allowance method, the current trading portfolio would appear as follows:

| Security | Cost | X2 fair value |
|---|---|---|
| ABC | $1,000 | $1,000 |
| DEF Puts | 1,500 | 1,500 |
| STU | 2,000 | 1,800 |
| VWX | 2,700 | 2,800 |
| | $7,200 | $7,100 |

The required entries to recognize the increase in fair value and the realized gain are

| | | |
|---|---|---|
| Valuation allowance | 300 | |
|     Unrealized gain on trading securities | | 300 |

*To adjust the valuation allowance to reflect the unrealized loss of $100 at the end of year two on the remaining trading portfolio*

| | | |
|---|---|---|
| Cash | 4,300 | |
| Trading securities—MNO calls (Cost) | | 1,500 |
| Trading securities—XYZ 7% bonds (Cost) | | 2,500 |
| Realized gain on sale of trading securities | | 300 |

The balance sheet under both methods would appear as follows:

*Current assets:*

Trading securities at fair value (cost = $7,200)          $7,100

**Available-for-sale securities.** Investments in debt securities and in equity securities with a readily determinable fair value that are *not* classified as either trading securities or held-to-maturity are classified as available-for-sale. The securities in this category are required to be carried at fair value on the balance sheet. The determination of current or noncurrent status for individual securities depends on whether the securities are considered working capital (ARB 43, chapter 3A).

Other than the possibility of having some noncurrent securities on the balance sheet, the major difference between trading securities and available-for-sale securities is the handling of unrealized gains and losses. Unlike trading securities, the *unrealized* gains and losses are excluded from net income. Instead, they are reported in other comprehensive income per FAS 130. All applicable interest (including premium and discount amortization) and any realized gains or losses from the sale of securities are included in income from continuing operations.

### Example of available-for-sale equity securities

Bonito Corporation purchases 2,500 shares of equity securities at $6 each, which it classifies as available-for-sale. At the end of one year, the quoted market price of the securities is $4, which rises to $9 at the end of the second year, when Bonito sells the securities. The company has an incremental tax rate of 25%. The calculation of annual gains and losses follows:

| | *Gain/(loss) before tax* | *Tax on gain/(loss)* | *Gain/(loss) net of tax* |
|---|---|---|---|
| End of Year 1 | (5,000) | (1,250) | (3,750) |
| End of Year 2 | 12,500 | 3,125 | 9,375 |
| Net gain | 7,500 | 1,875 | 5,625 |

Bonito reports these gains and losses in net income and other comprehensive income in the indicated years as follows:

| | *Year 1* | *Year 2* |
|---|---|---|
| Net income: | | |
| Gain on sale of securities | | $7,500 |
| Income tax expense | | (1,875) |
| Net gain realized in net income | | 5,625 |
| | | |
| Other comprehensive income: | | |
| Gain/(loss) on available-for-sale securities | | |
| arising during period, net of tax | $(3,750) | 9,375 |
| Reclassification adjustment, net of tax | | (5,625) |
| Other comprehensive income net gain/(loss) | (3,750) | 3,750 |

### Example of available-for-sale debt securities

Bonito Corporation purchases 10,000 bonds of Easter Corporation maturing in 6 years, at a price of $95.38, and classifies them as available-for-sale. The bonds have a par value of $100 and pay interest of 7% annually. At the price Bonito paid, the effective interest rate is 8%. The calculation of the bond discount follows:

| | | |
|---|---|---|
| Maturity value of bonds receivable | | $1,000,000 |
| Present value of $1,000,000 due in 6 years at 8% | | |
| (multiplier = 0.63017) | 630,170 | |
| Present value of $70,000 interest payable annually | | |
| for 6 years at 8% annually (multiplier = 4.6229) | 323,600 | |
| Purchase price of bonds | | 953,770 |
| Discount on bonds payable | | 46,230 |

The complete table of interest income and discount amortization calculations for the remaining life of the bonds follows:

| Year | Beginning value | Interest received | Recognized interest income* | Discount amortization | Ending value |
|---|---|---|---|---|---|
| 1 | $953,800 | $70,000 | $76,304 | 6,304 | 960,104 |
| 2 | 960,104 | 70,000 | 76,808 | 6,808 | 966,912 |
| 3 | 966,912 | 70,000 | 77,353 | 7,353 | 974,265 |
| 4 | 974,265 | 70,000 | 77,941 | 7,941 | 982,206 |
| 5 | 982,206 | 70,000 | 78,576 | 8,576 | 990,782 |
| 6 | 990,782 | 70,000 | 79,218 | 9,218 | 1,000,000 |

\* *(Beginning value)* × *(Effective interest rate of 8%)*

At the end of Year 1, the quoted market price of the bonds is $98, and it is $94 at the end of Year 2. The company has an incremental tax rate of 25%. The following table calculates the before-tax and after-tax holding gains and losses on the investment.

| Year | Ending carrying value | Ending fair value | Holding gain/(loss) | Income tax | Net of tax |
|---|---|---|---|---|---|
| 1 | $960,104 | $980,000 | $19,896 | 4,974 | 14,922 |
| 2 | 966,912 | 940,000 | (26,912) | (6,728) | (20,184) |
| Net | | | (7,016) | (1,754) | (5,262) |

Bonito sells the bonds at the end of Year 2, and reports these gains and losses in net income and other comprehensive income in the indicated years as follows:

| | Year 1 | Year 2 |
|---|---|---|
| Net income: | | |
| Interest income | 76,304 | 76,808 |
| Loss on sale of bonds | | (7,016) |
| Income tax expense | (19,076) | (17,448) |
| Net gain/(loss) realized in net income | 57,228 | 52,344 |
| | | |
| Other comprehensive income: | | |
| Gain/(loss) on available-for-sale securities | | |
| arising during period, net of tax | 14,922 | (20,184) |
| Reclassification adjustment, net of tax | | 5,262 |
| Other comprehensive income net gain/(loss) | 14,922 | (14,922) |

**Deferred income tax effects.** The recognition of unrealized gains and losses for financial statement purposes is likely to have deferred income tax effects. See the discussion in Chapter 12.

**Transfers between categories.** Fair value is used for transfers between categories. When the security is transferred, any unrealized holding gains and losses are accounted for in the following manner:

1. **From trading**—Already recognized and not to be reversed
2. **Into trading**—Recognize immediately in income
3. **Available-for-sale debt security into held-to-maturity**—Continue to report the unrealized holding gain or loss at the transfer date as other comprehensive income and amortize the gain or loss over the investment's remaining life as an adjustment of yield in the same manner as a premium or discount. The transferred-in security will probably record a premium or discount since fair value is used. Thus, the two amortizations will tend to cancel each other on the income statement.

4. **Held-to-maturity debt security into available-for-sale**—Recognize in other comprehensive income per FAS 130. Few transfers are expected from the held-to-maturity category.

See examples of accounting for transfers between portfolios in Chapter 12. Note that transfers are expected to be rare in occurrence and indeed may have significant, negative consequences, such as the "tainting" of other held-to-maturity investments when an asset in that category is transferred or sold before maturity.

**Other-than-temporary impairment.** The consensus guidance set forth in EITF 03-01, *The Meaning of Other-Than-Temporary Impairment and Its Application to Certain Investments* (as amended and effectively superseded by FSP FAS 115-1 and FAS 124-1) addresses an important but previously imprecisely described matter: the meaning of "other-than-temporary" impairment.

Investments within the scope of EITF 03-01 are

1. Cost-method investments in equity securities,
2. Debt and equity securities subject to FAS 115 including host instruments from which embedded derivatives have been bifurcated (separated) under FAS 133,
3. Debt and equity securities subject to FAS 124 when the holder of the investment reports a "performance indicator" as defined in the AAG, *Health Care Organizations.*

The amended pronouncement sets forth a multistep process for evaluating whether a security is impaired and, if so, whether the impairment is deemed to be other than temporary.

*Unit of accounting.* The unit of accounting to be used for the purpose of performing these steps is the individual security level. This is defined as the level and method of aggregation used by the reporting entity to measure realized and unrealized gains and losses on its debt and equity securities. An example of an acceptable method of aggregation would be for the reporting entity to consider equity securities of an issuer that carry the same CUSIP number[1] that were purchased in separate trade lots to be considered together on an average cost basis.

In considering whether the issuer (i.e., borrower or debtor) of a debt security can prepay or settle the security in a manner that would result in the investor not recovering substantially all of its cost, the investor is not permitted to combine separate contracts such as a debt security and a guarantee or other credit enhancement.

*Cost-method equity investments.* Special rules apply to cost-method investments because, by definition, they do not have readily determinable fair values. These rules are discussed in detail in Chapter 12.

*Step 1: Determining whether the investment is impaired.* The first step is to determine whether the investment is impaired. Impairment is determined by comparing the fair value of the investment to its adjusted cost. For this purpose, cost is adjusted for any applicable accretion, amortization, hedging adjustments, and previous write-downs caused by other-than-temporary impairment. If adjusted cost exceeds fair value, the investment is impaired.

*Step 2: Evaluating whether the impairment is other than temporary.* If an investment is determined to be impaired by applying Step 1, management is to evaluate whether it considers the impairment to be other than temporary by considering all available evidence. In lieu

---

[1] *CUSIP is an acronym for the **Committee on Uniform Security Identification Procedures** of the American Bankers Association (ABA). The committee developed a nine-digit numbering system for uniquely identifying US government, municipal, and corporate securities. The first six digits identify the issuer of the securities and the remaining three digits uniquely identify the particular issue.*

of providing guidance on how to make this determination, the FSP refers the reader to "pertinent guidance" contained in the following accounting and auditing literature:

- FAS 115, paragraph 16 and the FASB Implementation Guide, *A Guide to Implementation of Statement 115 on Accounting for Certain Investments in Debt and Equity Securities*
- ABP 18, *The Equity Method of Accounting for Investment in Common Stock*, paragraph 6
- SEC Staff Accounting Bulletin Topic 5M (formerly SAB 59), *Other-than-temporary impairment of Certain Investments in Debt and Equity Securities*
- EITF 99-20, *Recognition of Interest Income and Impairment on Purchased Beneficial Interests and Beneficial Interests That Continue to Be Held by a Transferor in Securitized Financial Assets*
- SAS 92, *Auditing Derivative Instruments, Hedging Activities, and Investments in Securities* and the companion AICPA Audit Guide

Notable in paragraph 16 of FAS 115, cited above, is a footnote that refers the reader to the SEC's SAB 59 which, in essence, provides that it is the refutable presumption that impairments of investments are indeed "other than temporary" and thus (in the case of available-for-sale and held-to-maturity investments) such declines in value would have to be reported currently in results of operations, unless there were positive evidence to support the alternative contention (i.e., that the impairment instead was merely temporary in nature), and thus—in the case of held-to-maturity investments—not to be recognized at all. A similar approach is applicable to the evaluation of impairments of equity-method investments.

For equity securities, this criterion will automatically be met, unless the investor has both the intent and ability to hold the investment for a period of time sufficient for a forecasted recovery in fair value to the cost of the investment, and evidence indicating the likelihood of a recovery outweighs evidence to the contrary. Ability and intent must be evaluated in light of the entity's working capital and other needs, any regulatory limitations it faces, the issuer's ability to settle the security, and other factors. A history of selling investments before recovery of fair value would suggest that, for that reporting entity, the decline in fair value should be seen as other than temporary.

*Step 3: Accounting for impairment that is other than temporary.* If, as a result of the evaluation performed in Step 2, management determines that the impairment of an investment is other than temporary, an impairment loss is recognized as a charge to earnings for the difference between the carrying value of the investment and its fair value at the balance sheet date of the reporting period in which the determination is made. The full amount of the impairment write-down is recognized even if, subsequent tot the balance sheet date and prior to the issuance of the financial statements, a portion of the impairment loss is recovered due to an increase in the fair value of the investment. The impaired value becomes the new cost basis, from which recoveries in value may not be given recognition—in distinct contrast to the accounting prescribed for temporary declines in value.

When debt securities are deemed to have been other-than-temporarily impaired, and the carrying value is accordingly reduced, the amount and timing of income recognition in subsequent periods would then be governed by the provisions of SOP 03-3, *Accounting for Certain Loans or Debt Securities Acquired in a Transfer.* This SOP is discussed in detail in the *Banking and Thrift* section of Chapter 25; briefly, it holds that purchased loans, and loans or debt instruments that have been written down to impaired values, are to be displayed at the initial investment (impaired value) amount on the balance sheet. The amount of the downward adjustment is not to be displayed. Given the evidence of deterioration in credit quality since origination, the reporting entity will be required to estimate the cash flows expected to be collected on the debt instrument; this is to be done both at the purchase date and again periodically over the terms of the debt instruments. Cash flows in excess of the adjusted carrying (impaired) value expected to be collected are to be recognized as yield, and are referred to as "accretable yield." If, subsequently, there are decreases in the probable cash flows, further impairments are to be recognized. Probable increases in subsequent cash flows expected to be collected are recognized *prospectively* as a yield adjustment.

### Example of impairment of available-for-sale securities

Bonito Corporation purchases 5,000 shares of Southern Star Corporation's common stock at $8 per share, for a total investment of $40,000, and classifies the investment as available-for-sale. The following events occur:

- Towards the end of Year 1, Southern experiences a significant decline in its earnings performance and related credit rating due to the loss of a key customer, resulting in a drop in the common stock price to $4. Bonito's management feels that the price decline is temporary, and so records the loss in other comprehensive income.
- The stock price drops to $3 at the end of Year 2, due to Southern's inability to generate replacement sales. Bonito's management now feels that the price decline is other than temporary, and records the loss in net income.
- The stock price increases in Year 3 to $5, which is reflected in other comprehensive income.

Bonito's incremental income tax rate is 30%. Its calculation of annual gains and losses follows:

| | Stock price | Gain/(loss) before tax | Tax effect of gain/(loss) | Gain/(loss) net of tax |
|---|---|---|---|---|
| End of Year 1 | $4 | $(20,000) | $6,000 | $(14,000) |
| End of Year 2 | $3 | (5,000) | 1,500 | (3,500) |
| End of Year 3 | $5 | 10,000 | (3,000) | 7,000 |
| Net (loss) | | $(15,000) | $4,500 | $(10,500) |

The effects of Bonito's reporting of these events are reflected in the following table:

| | Year 1 | Year 2 | Year 3 |
|---|---|---|---|
| Net income: | | | |
| Loss on other-than-temporary impairment of available-for-sale investment | | $(25,000) | |
| Income tax expense | | 7,500 | |
| Net gain/(loss) realized in net income | | $(17,500) | |
| | | | |
| Other comprehensive income: | | | |
| Gain/(loss) on available-for-sale securities arising during period, net of tax | $(14,000) | $(3,500) | $7,000 |
| Reclassification adjustment, net of tax | | 17,500 | |
| Other comprehensive income net gain/(loss) | $(14,000) | $14,000 | $7,000 |

**Cash flow statement.** Cash flows resulting from sales, purchases or maturity of securities are to be accounted for as follows:

1. Held-to-maturity — Investing activity
2. Available-for-sale — Investing activity
3. Trading — Classify based on the nature and purpose for which the securities were acquired

This was mandated by FAS 159, discussed in detail in Chapter 6, which was effective as of the beginning of the reporting entity's first fiscal year that begins after 11/15/2007

Cash flows from 1. and 2. above are required to be reported gross (cash inflows from gross proceeds separately from outflows for purchase of investments) for each security classification.

Irrespective of the classification of the above cash flows from (or for) purchases, sales, and maturities of investments, FAS 95 requires that cash inflows representing "…returns on loans, other debt instruments of other entities, and equity securities-interest and dividends" be classified as operating activities (FAS 95 as amended, ¶22b). At the time that FAS 95 was balloted, three of the seven members of FASB dissented because they believed that "…interest and dividends received are returns on investments in debt and equity securities that should be classified as cash inflows from investing activities."

**Option contracts.** Call and put options can serve as valuable hedging instruments or as highly leveraged speculative investments. Options give one party, the *holder,* the right but not the obligation to either buy (call) or sell (put) a fixed quantity of an instrument at a defined price. The counterparty, known as the *writer* of the option, has no choice to make and must perform if called upon to do so by the holder.

One call contract gives the holder the right to buy 100 shares of the underlying security at a specific exercise price, regardless of the market price. The seller (writer) of the call, on the other hand, must sell the security to the buyer at that specified exercise price, regardless of the market price. For example, assume a Dreamy July 35 call has a quoted market price of $6 (per share or $600 per contract). These facts indicate that a buyer that pays $600 to a seller for a call has the right to purchase 100 shares of Dreamy at any time until July (typically, the end of trading on the third Friday of the month quoted) for $35 per share. The buyer can exercise this right at any time until it expires. The writer of the call must stand ready to deliver 100 shares to the buyer for $35 per share until expiration. Typically, the holder expects the market price to rise and the writer expects the market price to stay the same or to fall.

A put is the opposite of a call. A put gives the holder of the put the right to sell the underlying security at the exercise price regardless of the market price. It gives the writer of the put the obligation to buy at the exercise price, if so demanded by the holder. Typically, the holder of a put option expects the market price to fall, and the writer expects the market price to stay the same or to rise.

There are many compound options used by traders and investors, all of which consist of combinations of one or more calls and puts, in some cases having differing expiration dates. Strips, straps, straddles, and spreads are combinations and/or variations of the basic call and the basic put. These and other compound instruments should be analyzed in terms of their constituent elements, and accounted for accordingly.

**Example**

Writer D owns 100 shares of Dreamy at a cost of $75 per share and sells 1 Dreamy July 35 call to Holder E at $6. The following positions result if the market price:

|  |  | Position | |
|---|---|---|---|
|  |  | *Writer (D)* | *Holder (E)* |
| 1. | Stays at 35 and there is no exercise | +$600 | –$600 |

D receives the $600 premium and E pays for the right to call the stock. If the market price doesn't move, the option expires; E is out $600 and D collects it.

|  |  |  |  |
|---|---|---|---|
| 2. | Rises to 55 and there is an exercise | +$600 | +$1,400 |
|  | and immediate sale | (0 + $600) | ($2,000 – $600) |

If the price rises to $55 per share and the security is called, D sells the security to E at $35 ($0 profit on the shares) and is effectively $600 (the amount of the premium) better off. E, however, buys the security at $35 per share and immediately sells it for $55 per share. E gains $2,000 from the security sale less the $600 premium, and so is $1,400 better off.

| | | | |
|---|---|---|---|
| 3. | Falls to 15 and there is no exercise | –$1,400 | –$600 |
| | | (– $2,000 + $600) | (0 – $600) |

If the market price falls to $15 per share, D incurs an effective $2,000 decrease in value of the shares held, less the $600 premium received. E does not exercise the option and loses the premium paid.

The issue in accounting for options is whether cost or fair value—or some combination—is to be used in accounting for the option itself and for the associated underlying security. For instance, assume M buys 100 shares of XYZ at $15 per share and the security price immediately moves to $25 per share. At this point, M buys a November 25 put contract at $100 for the contract. M has effectively hedged and guaranteed a minimum profit of $900 [(100 shares x $10) – ($1 x 100 shares)] regardless of market price movement, since XYZ can be sold for $25 per share until the third Friday in November. If the price continues upward, the put will expire unexercised and M will continue to benefit point for point. If the price stays the same, M locks in a profit of $900. If the price falls, M has locked in a profit of $900. The question is whether, under this fact pattern, both the option and the security can be accounted for at historical cost or at fair value or at some combination of the two.

Before the promulgation of FAS 133, FAS 115 had been the only relevant guidance, and it was not really definitive. FAS 115 established the requirements for accounting for investments. Theoretically, therefore, FAS 115 only applied to *purchased* puts and calls, since *written* options are liabilities, not investments. Likewise, cash settled options and equity indexed options do not represent ownership interests and debt securities options are not covered by FAS 115. In the absence of formal standards, however, numerous aspects of the issue had been addressed by the EITF. The result was that options were usually carried at fair value. This practice problem was resolved with the issuance of FAS 133.

**Other guidance on accounting for investments.** A number of specialized issues arising in connection with short-term (or other) investments have been addressed by the EITF. These matters are summarized in the following paragraphs.

EITF 86-40 holds that investments in open-end mutual funds that invest in US government securities are to be reported at fair value per FAS 115. Investments in mutual funds that invest solely in US government debt securities are deemed to be equity investments (since it is the shares of the fund, and not the ultimate debt securities, that are owned), and therefore cannot be classified as held-to-maturity investments.

EITF 96-11 addresses the accounting for certain forward contracts and purchased options to acquire securities covered by FAS 115. It applies only when the terms require physical settlement. It stipulates that forward contracts and purchased options, which are not classified as derivatives, having no intrinsic value at acquisition, are to be designated and accounted for as prescribed by FAS 115. These forwards and options would not be eligible for designation as hedging instruments.

EITF 96-12 deals with the complex area of "structured notes," in particular with the matters of recognition of interest income and of balance sheet classification of such instruments. According to this consensus, when recognizing interest income on structured note securities in an available-for-sale or held-to-maturity portfolio, the retrospective interest method is to be used if three conditions are satisfied. These conditions are

1. Either the original investment amount or the maturity amount of the contractual principal is at risk

2. Return of investment on note is subject to volatility arising from either

  a. No stated rate or stated rate that is not a constant percentage or in same direction as changes in market-based interest rates or interest rate index, or

  b. Fixed or variable coupon rate is lower than that for interest for traditional notes with similar maturity and a portion of potential yield is based on occurrence of future circumstances or events

3. Contractual maturity of bond is based on a specific index or on occurrence of specific events or situations outside the control of contractual parties

This consensus does not apply to structured note securities that, by their nature, subject the holder to reasonably possible loss of all or substantially all of the original invested amount (other than due to debtor failure to pay amount owed). In those instances, the investment is to be carried at fair value with changes in value recognized in current earnings.

The retrospective interest method requires that periodic income be measured by reference to the change in amortized cost from period beginning to period end, plus any cash received during the period. Amortized cost is determined with reference to the conditions applicable as of the respective balance sheet date. Other than temporary declines in fair value would also have to be recognized in earnings, consistent with FAS 115 requirements for held-to-maturity investments.

EITF 96-15 had previously held that total changes in fair value of foreign-currency-denominated available-for-sale (AFS) debt securities were to be reported in stockholders' equity. However, the subsequently issued FAS 133 prohibited the use of a foreign-currency-denominated liability as a hedge of an AFS debt security. Thus, in a fair hedge of an AFS debt instrument, any gain or loss on the currency derivative will have to be reported in current earnings, not in other comprehensive income, as will any foreign currency portion of the gain or loss on the debt security.

A relatively recent development has been the creation of "weather derivatives," which were addressed by EITF 99-2. At issue was whether such contracts should be reported under accrual accounting, under settlement accounting, under insurance accounting, marked to fair value through earnings at each reporting date, or under some other method. Also at issue was whether the accounting for these derivatives should vary based on the type of contract. Past practice has been diverse.

FAS 133 provides that contracts that are not exchange-traded are not subject to the requirements of that statement if settlement is based on a climatic or geological variable or on some other physical variable. Any derivative based on a physical variable that eventually becomes exchange-traded automatically becomes subject to the requirements of FAS 133.

The EITF consensus is that an entity that enters into a non-exchange-traded forward-based weather derivative in connection with nontrading activities is to account for the contract by applying an "intrinsic value method." The intrinsic value method computes an amount based on the difference between the expected results from an upfront allocation of the cumulative strike and the actual results during a period, multiplied by the contract price (for example, dollars per heating degree day). The use of external statistical sources, such as the National Weather Service, is necessary in applying this technique.

Furthermore, the EITF concluded that an entity that purchases a nonexchange-traded option-based weather derivative in connection with nontrading activities is to amortize to expense the premium paid (or due) and apply the intrinsic value method to measure the contract at each interim balance sheet date. The premium asset is to be amortized in a rational and systematic manner.

Also, it was decided that all entities that sell or write a non-exchange-traded option-based weather derivative are to initially recognize the premium as a liability and recognize any subsequent changes in fair value currently in earnings (the premium would not be amortized).

The EITF observed that a purchased or written weather derivative may contain an "embedded" premium or discount when the contract terms are not consistent with current market terms. In those circumstances, the premium or discount is to be quantified, removed from the calculated benchmark strike, and accounted for as noted above.

Finally, the EITF reached a consensus that all weather derivative contracts entered into under trading or speculative activities are to be accounted for at their fair value, with subsequent changes in fair value reported currently in earnings.

## Financial Instruments

**Terminology and scope.** FAS 107 provided a definition of financial instruments that is intended to cover both financial assets and liabilities. Attempting to make the definition all-encompassing made it difficult to understand and apply in practice. FAS 159, *The Fair Value Option for Financial Assets and Financial Liabilities*, assists in that endeavor by providing separate definitions of financial assets and financial liabilities. These definitions are provided earlier in this chapter in the section entitled Definitions of Terms. Financial assets are discussed in this chapter; financial liabilities are discussed in Chapter 14.

**Types of financial assets.** The term "financial assets" encompasses a wide range of instruments including, but not limited to

| | |
|---|---|
| Accounts receivable | General partnership interests |
| Beneficial interests in trusts | Limited partnership interests |
| Cash | LLC member interests |
| Certificates of deposit | Municipal bonds |
| Commercial paper | Mutual fund shares or units |
| Common and preferred stock | Notes and loans receivable |
| Corporate bonds | US Government securities |

An unconditional contractual obligation whose economic benefit or sacrifice is to be the receipt or delivery of a financial instrument other than cash is to be considered a financial instrument. For example, a note that is payable in US Treasury bonds gives an issuer the contractual obligation to deliver and gives a holder the contractual right to receive bonds, not cash. But because the bonds represent obligations of the US Treasury to pay cash, they are considered financial instruments. Therefore, the note is also a financial instrument to both the holder of the note and the issuer of the note.

Another type of financial instrument is one that gives an entity the *contractual right* or obligation to exchange other financial instruments on *potentially* favorable or unfavorable terms. An example of this type of financial instrument would be a call option to purchase a specific US Treasury note for $100,000 in six months. The option *holder* has a contractual right, but not obligation, to exchange the financial instrument on potentially favorable terms. Six months later, if the fair value of the note exceeds $100,000, the holder will exercise the option because the terms are favorable (the option is now "in the money"). The *writer* of the call option has a contractual obligation to exchange financial instruments on potentially unfavorable terms if the holder exercises the option. The writer is normally compensated for accepting this obligation by being paid a premium, which it keeps whether or not the option is exercised.

A put option to sell a Treasury note has similar effects, although the change in fair values making it worthwhile to exercise the option will be a decline, rather than an increase. The holder of the put option, as with the call option, effectively has an unlimited profit potential and no risk of loss (the only sunk cost is the premium paid), whereas the writer of the option has unlimited risk of loss and only a fixed amount of income.

Options, such as those discussed here, are derivative financial instruments because their fair value depends upon the value of the underlying. A bank's commitment to lend $100,000 to a customer at a fixed rate of 10% any time during the next six months at the customer's option is also a derivative financial instrument, since its value would vary as market interest rates change. It is an option, with the potential borrower being the holder and the bank being the writer (the parties are collectively referred to as the "counterparties").

An interest rate swap is a series of forward contracts to exchange, for example, fixed cash payments for variable cash receipts. The cash receipts are computed by multiplying a specified floating-rate market index by a notional amount of principal. An interest rate swap is both a contractual right and a contractual obligation of both counterparties.

**Exclusions.** Excluded from financial instrument classification are options and contracts that contain the right or obligation to exchange a financial instrument for a physical asset, such as bushels of wheat. For example, two entities enter a sale-purchase contract in which the purchaser agrees to take delivery of wheat or gold six months later and pay the seller $100,000 at the time of delivery. The contract is not a financial instrument because it requires the delivery of wheat or gold, which are not financial instruments.

Also excluded from financial instrument classification are contingent items that may ultimately require the payment of cash but that are not contractual. An example would be a contingent liability for tort judgments payable. However, when such an obligation becomes enforceable and is reduced to a fixed payment schedule, it then would be considered to be a financial instrument.

**Derivative financial instruments.** Derivative financial instruments (DFI) are financial instruments whose fair value correlates to a specified benchmark such as stock prices, interest rates, mortgage rates, currency rates, commodity prices, or some other agreed-upon reference (these are called "underlyings"). Option contracts and forward contracts are the two basic forms of derivatives, and they can be either publicly or privately traded. Forward contracts have symmetrical gain and loss characteristics—that is, they provide exposure to both losses and gains from market movements, although generally there is no initial premium to be paid. Forward contracts are usually settled on or near the delivery date by paying or receiving cash, rather than by physical delivery. On the other hand, option contracts have asymmetrical loss functions: they provide little or no exposure to losses (beyond the premium paid) from unfavorable market movements, but can provide large benefits from favorable market movements. Both forwards and options have legitimate roles to play in hedging programs, if properly understood and carefully managed.

Typical derivative financial instruments *include*

1. Option contracts
2. Interest rate caps
3. Interest rate floors
4. Fixed-rate loan commitments
5. Note issuance facilities
6. Letters of credit
7. Forward contracts
8. Forward interest rate agreements
9. Interest rate collars
10. Futures
11. Swaps
12. Instruments with similar characteristics

DFI *exclude* all on-balance-sheet receivables and payables including

1. Mortgage-backed securities
2. Interest-only obligations
3. Principal-only obligations
4. Indexed debt

5. Other optional characteristics incorporated within those receivables and payables (such as convertible bond conversion or call terms)

In addition, DFI *exclude* contracts that either

1. Require exchange for a nonfinancial commodity or
2. Permit settlement by delivering a nonfinancial commodity

Thus, most product (petroleum, grain, etc.) futures contracts would be excluded from the definition of DFI, while swaps (if settled in cash) would be included.

As with other financial instruments, derivatives can be acquired either for investment purposes or for speculation. For enterprises which are not in the business of speculation, however, the typical purpose of DFI is to manage risk, such as that associated with stock price movements, interest rate variations, currency fluctuations, and commodity price volatility. The parties involved tend to be brokerage firms, financial institutions, insurance companies, and large corporations, although any two or more entities of any size can hold or issue derivatives. Even small companies often engage in hedging, most commonly for risk arising from importing and exporting denominated in foreign currencies.

The DFI are contracts which are intended to protect or hedge one or more of the parties from adverse movement in the underlying base, which can be a financial instrument position held by the entity or a commitment to acquire same at some future date, among others. Unfortunately, these protections or hedges are rarely perfect and sometimes the hedge, once established, is later modified, even indirectly—such as by disposing of the underlying position while retaining the former hedge—so that the DFI becomes in effect a speculative position. The DFI themselves can become risky and, if leveraged, small adverse price or interest rate variations can produce significant losses. Thus, instead of providing protection, many DFI have actually generated losses and the failure to manage these instruments properly has contributed to a popular perception that hedging itself is a suspect activity.

The financial engineering efforts common in recent decades resulted in the creation of a wide range of derivative instruments, from easily understood interest rate swaps (exchanging variable- or floating-rate debt for fixed-rate debt) and interest rate caps (limiting exposure to rising interest rates) to such complicated "exotics" as structured notes, inverse floaters, and interest-only strips. Prior to FAS 133, most of these were not given formal balance sheet recognition, resulting in great accounting risk (i.e., risk of loss in excess of amounts reported in the financial statements). Over time, various disclosure requirements were imposed, but these did not deal with the fundamental issues of recognition and measurement. In hindsight it is clear that the failure to explicitly account for many of these derivative instruments contributed to the failure to effectively manage investments in derivatives. FAS 133 superseded the various prior requirements while incorporating most of the earlier disclosure rules.

### Accounting for Derivatives and Hedging Transactions Per FAS 133: An Overview

Following a lengthy period of development, FAS 133 was implemented beginning in 2000. This standard, while far more comprehensive than any of the predecessors discussed above, is still not an all-inclusive standard on the accounting for all financial instruments. FAS 133 addresses the accounting for derivatives (which formerly presented the most intractable financial reporting problems) and continues, in much modified form, the practice of "special accounting" for hedges, which would not be necessary if a universal fair value financial reporting rule were imposed.

Fair values are defined in FAS 133 as they were in FAS 107, discussed above. The new standard will resolve a number of previous inconsistencies and other inadequacies found in previous standards, including

- The effects of derivative instruments were not easily understood, were often not properly displayed in the financial statements, and, sometimes, were not even recognized in the financial statements.
- The available accounting guidance was incomplete. Many derivative instruments were carried off balance sheet.
- The accounting guidance was inconsistent. There was different measurement of various derivative instruments, and different qualifications for alternative types of hedging.
- The guidance that did exist was difficult to apply. There was a variety of sources and no single comprehensive approach had been defined.

FAS 133 requires standardized accounting and reporting for all derivative instruments (including derivatives which are embedded in other instruments) and for hedging activities.

**Underlying principles.**   There are four key principles underlying the new standard.

1. Derivative instruments are assets and liabilities.
2. The fair value of derivative instruments is the only relevant measure to be reported.
3. Only true assets and liabilities are reported as such. Gains and losses from derivative instruments are not separate liabilities or assets and are not to be reported as such.
4. Only designated qualifying items that are effectively offset by changes in fair value or cash flows during the term of the hedge are eligible to use the special accounting for hedging.

Derivative instruments represent rights and obligations, and these must be reported as assets and liabilities at fair value (which reflects the current cash equivalent). Gains and losses on derivative instruments not designated as hedges are recognized in earnings (or as a change in net assets, in the case of not-for-profit enterprises). The ability to apply hedge accounting requires that specified criteria be met, because of its elective nature and because of its reliance on management intent. Strategic risk hedges do not meet the qualifying criteria. Thus, hedge accounting is limited to relationships involving derivative instruments and certain foreign currency denominated instruments that are designated as hedges and meet the qualifying criteria.

**Contracts not subject to FAS 133.**   The following contracts are considered exceptions and are not subject to the requirements of FAS 133:

1. **Regular-way security trades**—Delivery of a security readily convertible to cash within the time period generally established by marketplace regulations or conventions where the trade takes place rather than by the usual procedure of an individual enterprise. Contracts for the delivery of securities that are not readily convertible to cash are not subject to FAS 133's provisions because net settlement would not be possible.

   For example, most trades of equity securities in the US require settlement in three business days. If an individual contract requires settlement in more than three business days (even if this is normal for a particular entity), this exception would not apply, unless (per FAS 149, which amended FAS 133) the reporting entity is required to account for such transactions on a trade-date basis. This exception also applies to when-issued and to-be-announced securities, if there is no other way to purchase or sell them and if the trade will settle within the shortest period permitted.

   Based on the foregoing, the following may be excluded: forward purchases or sales of to-be-announced securities, and when-issued, as-issued, or if-issued securities.

2. **Normal purchases and normal sales**—Contracts for future delivery of assets (other than derivative instruments or financial instruments) that are readily convertible to cash and for which there is no net settlement provision and no market mechanism to ease net settlement. Terms must be consistent with normal transactions and quantities must be reasonable in relation to needs. All relevant factors are to be considered. An example would include contracts similar to binding purchase orders. However, take or pay contracts that require little or no initial net investment, and that have products readily convertible to cash that do not qualify as normal purchases, would be a derivative instrument, and not an exception.

   The purpose of the "normal purchases and normal sales" definition was to exclude certain routine types of transactions from the required accounting as derivative instruments. FAS 138 expanded this exemption to include certain contracts which do contain net settlement or market mechanisms if it is judged probable, at the inception and throughout the duration of such contracts, that they will not in fact settle net and will instead result in physical delivery. Notwithstanding, this more broadly based exemption from the accounting requirements of FAS 133, certain contracts will not qualify for exemption in any case; these include contracts the price of which are based on an underlying that is not clearly and closely related to the assets being sold or purchased, and those requiring cash settlement for any gains or losses or otherwise settled net on a periodic basis. Documentary evidence is required to support the use of the expanded exemption from the FAS 133 provisions.

   FAS 149 has further addressed the "normal purchases and sales" provisions of FAS 133. Under the amendment, power purchase or sales agreements (whether forwards, options, or some combination thereof) pertaining to delivery of electricity qualify for this exception only if a series of conditions are all met. The contracts cannot permit net settlement, but must require physical delivery, and must be capacity contracts, as differentiated from ordinary option contracts. For the seller, the quantities deliverable under the contracts must be quantities normally to be sold; for the buyer, quantities must be those normally to be used or sold, and the buyer must be an entity which is contractually obligated to maintain sufficient capacity to meet the needs of its customers. Certain additional requirements, and further exceptions, are set forth by FAS 149.

   Counterparties may reach different conclusions as to whether the contracts are a derivative instrument. Asymmetrical results are acceptable (i.e., the exception may apply to one party but not the other).

3. **Certain insurance contracts**—Contracts where the holder is only compensated when an insurable event (other than price or rate change) takes place and

   a. The value of the holder's asset or liability is adversely changed or
   b. The holder incurs a liability.

   For example, contracts generally not considered to be derivative instruments include those within the scope of FAS 60, 97, and 113, traditional life insurance, and traditional property and casualty insurance policies.

   Most traditional insurance contracts will not be derivative instruments. Some, however, can include embedded derivatives that must be accounted for separately. For example, embedded derivatives may be found in indexed annuity contracts, variable life and annuity contracts, and property and casualty contracts involving changes in currency rates.

4. **Certain financial guarantee contracts**—Contracts that call for payments only to reimburse for a loss from debtor failure to pay when due. However, a credit-

indexed contract requiring payment for changes in credit ratings (an underlying) would not be an exception.

5. **Certain contracts that are not exchange traded**—Contracts with underlyings based on one of the following:

   a. Climatic, geological or other physical variable: for example, inches of rain or heating-degree days;

   b. Value or price involving a nonfinancial asset not readily converted to cash or a nonfinancial liability that does not require delivery of an asset that is readily converted to cash; or

   c. Specified volumes of revenue of one of the parties: examples are royalty agreements or contingent rentals based on related sales.

   In the case of a mixture of underlyings, some of which are exceptions, the predominant characteristic of the combined variable of the contract is the determinant. If there is a high correlation with the behavior of the excepted variables above, it is an exception and if there is a high correlation with the nonexcepted variables, it is a derivative instrument.

6. **Derivatives that serve as impediments to sales accounting**—A derivative instrument that affects the accounting for the transfer of an asset. For example, a call option on transferred assets under FAS 140 would prevent accounting for the transfer as a sale. This is necessary, since recognizing the call as a derivative instrument would result in double counting. For instance, a lessor guarantee of the residual value may prevent the accounting for a sales-type lease.

In addition to the foregoing, the following are not considered derivative instruments:

1. Contracts issued or held that are both

   a. Indexed to the enterprise's own stock, and

   b. Classified in shareholders' equity.

   Derivative instruments are assets or liabilities. Items properly accounted for in shareholders' equity are thus excluded from the definition of derivatives. Contracts that can or must be settled through issuance of an equity instrument but that are indexed in part or in full to something other than the enterprise's own stock are considered derivative instruments if they qualify and they are to be classified as assets or liabilities. Some of these kinds of items will be revisited later by the FASB.

2. Contracts issued in connection with stock-based compensation arrangements as addressed in FAS 123(R).

   Many instruments under FAS 123(R) are classified in shareholder equity. The FASB felt that those properly classified as liabilities have been adequately addressed.

3. Contracts issued as contingent consideration in a business combination under FAS 141.

   Contracts in a business combination that are similar to, but are not accounted for as contingent consideration under FAS 141, are subject to this standard as derivative instruments or embedded derivative instruments.

The exceptions for the above three issued contracts are not applicable to the counterparties.

**Embedded derivative instruments.** A reporting entity is not allowed to circumvent the requirements of FAS 133 recognition and measurement by embedding a derivative instrument in another contract. If these embedded derivative instruments would otherwise be subject to FAS 133, they are included in its scope. However, some common compound instruments that generally have been widely employed for some time, and where the derivative component bears a close economic relationship to the host contract, are excluded from FAS 133 for practical reasons.

*Embedded derivative instruments* are defined as explicit or implicit terms affecting (1) the cash flows or (2) the value of other exchanges required by contract in a way similar to a derivative instrument (one or more underlying can modify the cash flows or exchanges). An embedded derivative instrument is to be separated from the host contract and accounted for separately as a derivative instrument by both parties if and only if *all* the three following criteria are met:

1.  Risks and economic characteristics are not clearly and closely related to those of the *host contract*;
2.  The hybrid instrument is not required to be measured at fair value under GAAP with changes reported in earnings; and
3.  A separate instrument with the same terms as the embedded derivative instrument would be accounted for as a derivative instrument. For this condition, the initial net investment of the hybrid instrument is not the same as that for the embedded derivative instrument.

The foregoing three conditions for the separate accounting for embedded derivatives are explained in the following paragraphs.

*Risks and economic characteristics are not clearly and closely related to those of the host contract.* If the underlying is an interest rate or interest rate index that changes the net interest payments of an interest-bearing contract, it is considered clearly and closely related unless one of the following conditions exist:

1.  The hybrid instrument can be settled contractually in a manner that permits any possibility whatsoever that the investor would not recover substantially all of the initial recorded investment.
2.  The embedded derivative instrument could under any possibility whatsoever

    a.  At least double the investor's initial rate of return (ROR) on the host contract and
    b.  Could also result in a ROR at least twice the market return for a similar contract (same host contract terms and same debtor credit quality).

The date acquired (or incurred) is the assessment date for the existence of the above conditions. Thus, the issuer and an acquirer in a secondary market could account for the instrument differently because of different points in time.

### Example of embedded instruments which are separately accounted for

Assuming that the host contract is a debt instrument, the following are considered not to be clearly and closely related and would normally have to be separated out as embedded derivatives:

1.  Interest rate indexes, floors, caps and collars not meeting the criteria for exclusion (see below);
2.  Leveraged inflation-indexed interest payments or rentals;
3.  Calls and puts that do not accelerate repayment of the principal but require a cash settlement equal to the option price at date of exercise. Subsequently added options that cause one party to be exposed to performance or default risk by different parties for the embedded option than for the host contract;
4.  Term extending options where there is no reset of interest rates;
5.  Equity-indexed interest payments;
6.  Commodity-indexed interest or principal payments;

7. A convertible debt conversion option for the investor if it qualifies as a derivative instrument (readily convertible to cash, etc.); and

8. A convertible preferred stock conversion option if the terms of the preferred stock (not the conversion option) are more similar to debt (a cumulative fixed rate with a mandatory redemption feature) than to equity (cumulative, participating, perpetual).

**Example of embedded instruments which are not separately accounted for**

Assuming that the host contract is a debt instrument, the following are considered to be clearly and closely related and would not normally have to be separated out as embedded derivative instruments:

1. Interest rate indexes (see below);
2. Interest rate floors, caps and collars, if at issuance

    a. The cap is at or above the current market price (or rate) and/or
    b. The floor is at or below the current market price (or rate)

3. Nonleveraged inflation-indexed interest payments or rentals
4. Credit-sensitive payments (interest rate resets for debtor creditworthiness)
5. "Plain-vanilla" servicing rights not containing a separate embedded derivative instrument
6. Calls and puts that can accelerate repayment of principal unless

    a. The debt involves substantial premium or discount (zero coupon) and
    b. The call or put is only contingently exercisable (not exercisable unless default occurs) and is indexed only to credit risk or interest rates.

7. Term-extending options if the interest rate is concurrently reset to approximately the current market rate for the extended term and the host contract had no initial significant discount
8. Contingent rentals based on a variable interest rate

Based on the foregoing, calls and puts embedded in equity instruments are normally accounted for as follows:

1. Investor—Both the call and the put are embedded derivative instruments.
2. Issuer—Only the put could be an embedded derivative instrument. The put and the call would not be embedded derivative instruments if they are both

    a. Indexed to the issuing entity's own stock and
    b. Classified in shareholders' equity.

*The hybrid instrument is not required to be measured at fair value under GAAP with changes reported in earnings.* For example, most unsettled foreign currency transactions are subject to FAS 52. Gains or losses are recognized in earnings and thus instruments of this nature are not considered embedded derivative instruments. Trading and available-for-sale securities that have cash flows denominated in a foreign currency also are not considered embedded derivative instruments.

*A separate instrument with the same terms as the embedded derivative instrument would be accounted for as a derivative instrument.* For this condition, the initial net investment of the hybrid instrument is not the same as that for the embedded derivative instrument.

To illustrate, a convertible debt conversion option for the issuer would not be an embedded derivative instrument since a separate option with the same terms would not be a derivative instrument because it is indexed to the issuer's own stock and would be classified in shareholders' equity.

Another example would involve convertible preferred stock. A convertible preferred stock conversion option would not be an embedded derivative instrument if the terms of the preferred stock (not the conversion option) bear greater similarity to equity (e.g., cumulative, participating, perpetual) than to debt (i.e., a cumulative fixed rate with a mandatory redemption feature).

Interest-only strips and principal-only strips are specifically not subject to this standard assuming (1) the original financial instrument did not contain an embedded derivative instrument and (2) they don't incorporate any new terms from the original. In addition, foreign currency derivative instruments are specifically not separated from the host contract if (1) the currency of the primary economic environment is the functional currency of one of the parties or (2) the good or service price is routinely denominated in that currency in international commerce.

If an embedded derivative instrument is separated from the host, the accounting is as follows:

1. The embedded derivative instrument is accounted for based on FAS 133; and
2. The host contract is accounted for based on GAAP for that instrument, without the embedded derivative instrument.

If the embedded derivative instrument cannot be reliably identified and measured separately, the entire contract must be measured at fair value with the gain or loss recognized in income. In this case, the contract cannot be designated as a hedging instrument.

Gains and losses of derivative instruments not designated as hedges are recognized in earnings or, for a not-for-profit organization, in the change in net assets.

The SEC's position, as articulated in EITF D-109, is that in performing an evaluation of an embedded derivative feature, the consideration of the economic characteristics and risks of the host contract should be based on all of the stated or implied substantive terms and features of the hybrid financial instrument. In evaluating the stated and implied substantive terms and features, the existence or omission of any single term or feature is not necessarily determinative of the economic characteristics and risks of the host contract (i.e., whether the nature of the host contract is more akin to a debt instrument or more akin to an equity instrument). Although the consideration of an individual term or feature may be weighted more heavily in the evaluation, judgment is required based upon an evaluation of all the relevant terms and features.

**Hybrid financial instruments.** By definition, financial instruments that contain embedded derivatives are known as hybrid financial instruments. As issued, FAS 133 contained an exception to exclude interest-only and principal-only strips from the definition of an embedded derivative. FASB has issued FAS 155, *Accounting for Certain Hybrid Financial Instruments,* to simplify the accounting for such hybrid financial instruments by permitting fair value remeasurement for any hybrid financial instrument that contains an embedded derivative that otherwise would require bifurcation under FAS 133. FAS 155 narrows the scope exception for interest-only and principal-only strips on debt instruments to include only such strips representing rights to receive a specified portion of the contractual interest or principal cash flows.

Per FAS 133, if an embedded instrument requiring separation (because the close correlation criterion noted above is not met) from its host, but it cannot be reliably identified and measured, the entire contract must be measured at fair value. As amended by FAS 155, upon recognition of a hybrid instrument that would otherwise require separation into a derivative and a host, the reporting entity may elect irrevocably to measure, on an instrument-by-instrument basis, the entire hybrid instrument at fair value. The changes in fair value will be reported currently in earnings. Such an election must be supported either by concurrent documentation or by a preexisting documented policy supporting automatic election.

This fair value election is also available for remeasurement with respect to previously recognized financial instruments upon the occurrence of a business combination, a significant modification of debt, or other qualifying remeasurement event, where a new basis of accounting may be created.

Fair value measurements will often differ because they exclude transaction costs, which are included in many historical cost-based accounting entries. (For example, the fair value of stock just purchased on an exchange is lower than cost.) FAS 155 holds that any difference at inception of a recognized hybrid financial instrument for which the fair value election is applied and the transaction price is *not* to be included in current earnings (and thus is retained in the asset carrying amount) unless estimated fair value has been determined (1) from a quoted price in an active market, (2) from comparison to other observable current market transactions, or (3) using a valuation technique that incorporates observable market data.

According to FAS 155, the holder of an interest in securitized financial assets (other than holders of strips or related claims to cash flows) is to determine whether the interest is a free-standing derivative or contains an embedded derivative that would be required to be separated from the host contract and accounted for separately under FAS 133. That determination is to be based on an analysis of the contractual terms of the interest in securitized financial assets. This, in turn, requires understanding the nature and amount of assets, liabilities, and other financial instruments that constitute the complete securitization transaction. It is expected that the holder of an interest in securitized financial assets will obtain sufficient information about the payoff structure and the payment priority of the interest to make a determination about whether an embedded derivative exists.

Changes in cash flows that are attributable to changes in the creditworthiness of an interest resulting from securitized financial assets and liabilities (including derivative contracts) that represent the assets or liabilities that are held by the issuer are not to be considered an embedded derivative under FAS 155. The concentration of credit risk in the form of subordination of one financial instrument to another is also not to be considered an embedded derivative under the new standard.

FAS 155 further amends FAS 133 to require balance sheet segregation of those hybrid financial instruments that are being measured at fair value. This can be accomplished either by (1) the display of separate line items for fair value and non–fair value carrying amounts, or (2) parenthetical disclosure of fair value carrying amounts included in the aggregate of all carrying amounts. Also, disclosure must be made of the effect on earnings of changes in the fair value of recognized hybrid financial instruments.

The changes made by this standard are generally effective in 2007. The fair value election for hybrid financial instruments that had previously been bifurcated under the provisions of FAS 133 can also be applied upon initial adoption of FAS 155.

## Hedging Activities—General Requirements

**Overview.** Matters relating to hedging activities constitute the core of the new standard and represent the most difficult accounting issues. While the standard requires that all derivatives be reported at fair value in the balance sheet, the changes in fair value will be reported in different ways depending on the nature and effectiveness of the hedging activities to which they are related, if held for hedging purposes. FAS 133 identifies changes in the fair values of derivatives as being the result of (1) effective hedging, (2) ineffective hedging, or (3) unrelated to hedging. Furthermore, the hedging itself can be related to the fair value of an existing asset or liability or of a firm commitment, the cash flow associated with forecasted transactions, or foreign currency exposures.

After meeting specified conditions, a qualified derivative may be specifically designated as a total or partial (expressed as a percentage where the risk exposure profile is the same as that in the whole derivative) hedge of

1.  Changes in the fair value of

    a.  A recognized asset or liability, or
    b.  An unrecognized firm commitment.

    In a fair value hedge, all gains and losses (of both the derivative instrument and the hedged item) are recognized in earnings in the period of change.

2.  Variable cash flows of a forecasted transaction.

    In a cash flow hedge, the effective portion of the hedge is reported in other comprehensive income and is reclassified into earnings when the forecasted transaction affects earnings.

3.  Foreign currency exposure of

    a.  A net investment in a foreign operation

    In a foreign currency net investment hedge, the gain or loss is reported in other comprehensive income as part of the cumulative translation adjustment to the extent that it is effective.

    b.  An unrecognized firm commitment

    In a foreign currency unrecognized firm commitment hedge, the gain or loss is reported the same way as a fair value hedge (see category 1., above).

    c.  An available-for-sale security

    In a foreign currency available-for-sale security hedge, the gain or loss is reported the same way as a fair value hedge (see category 1., above).

    d.  A foreign currency denominated forecasted transaction.

    In a foreign currency denominated forecasted transaction hedge, the gain or loss is reported in the same way as a cash flow hedge (see category 2., above).

Hedge portions that are not effective are reported in earnings immediately.

A nonderivative financial instrument cannot generally be designated as a hedge. One exception, however, occurs when that instrument is denominated in a foreign currency and is designated as a hedge under 3a. or 3b. above. Not-for-profit enterprises cannot use hedge accounting for forecasted transactions.

**Effectiveness—General observations.** The method used for assessing the effective and ineffective portions of a hedge must be defined at the time of designation, must be used throughout the hedge period and must be consistent with the approach used for managing risk. Similar hedges should usually be assessed for effectiveness in a similar manner unless a different method can be justified. If an improved method is identified and is to be applied prospectively to an existing hedge, that hedge must be discontinued. The new method can then be designated and a new hedge relationship can be established.

Factors to be included in the effectiveness assessment must be specified at inception. The effect of all excluded factors and ineffective amounts are to be included in earnings. For example, if an option contract hedge is assessed for effectiveness based on changes in the option's intrinsic value, the change due to the time value of the contract would be excluded from the effectiveness assessment and that amount would be included in earnings. As another example, differences in key terms between the hedged item and the hedging instrument such as notional amounts, maturities, quantities, location or delivery dates would cause ineffectiveness and that amount would be included in earnings.

**Fair Value Hedges**

The change in the fair value of an entire financial asset or liability for a period is computed as the fair value at the end of the period, adjusted to exclude changes in fair value

(1) from payments received or made (partial recoveries or settlements) and (2) from the passage of time, minus the fair value at the beginning of the period.

**Qualifications.** To qualify as a fair value hedge, both the hedged items and the designated hedging instruments must meet all of the following criteria:

1. At the hedge's origin, formal documentation exists of the

    a. Hedging relationship;
    b. Risk management objectives;
    c. Strategy for undertaking the hedge;
    d. Identification of the hedged item, the hedging instrument, the nature of the risk being hedged, the method of assessing effectiveness and the components (if any) that are excluded (such as time value) from the effectiveness assessment; and the
    e. Reasonable method to be used in recognizing in earnings the asset or liability representing the gain or loss in the case of a hedged firm commitment.

2. The hedging relationship is expected to be highly effective in producing offsetting fair value changes throughout the hedge period. This relationship must be assessed at least every three months and each time financial statements or earnings are reported.

3. If hedging with a written option, the combination must provide as much potential for gains from positive fair value changes as potential for losses from negative fair value changes. If a net premium is received, a combination of options is considered a written option. The combination of a written option and some other nonoption derivative is also considered a written option.

Unless foreign currency is involved, a nonderivative instrument cannot be designated as a hedging instrument.

According to FAS 133, an asset or liability will be eligible for designation as a hedged item in a fair value hedge (to which a hedging position will be related, for purposes of reporting gain or loss) if the hedged item is specifically identified as all or a specific portion of a recognized asset or liability, or an unrecognized firm commitment; is exposed to fair value changes that are attributable to the hedged risk such that earnings would be affected; and is not either remeasured at fair value for financial reporting purposes, or an equity-method investment, or an equity method or minority interest in a consolidated subsidiary, a firm commitment related to the foregoing, or an equity instrument issued by the entity. Other limitations also apply, affecting held-to-maturity debt securities and nonfinancial assets.

More specifically, to be eligible for designation as a hedged item, an asset or liability must meet all of the following criteria:

1. The single item (or portfolio of similar items) must be specifically identified as hedging all or a specific portion.

    a. If similar items are aggregated and hedged, each item has to share the risk exposure that is being hedged (i.e. each individual item must respond in a generally proportionate manner to the change in fair value).
    b. A specific portion must be one of the following:

        (1) A percentage of the total asset, liability, or portfolio;
        (2) One or more selected contractual cash flows: for instance, the present value of the interest payments due in the first two years of a four-year debt instrument;
        (3) An embedded put, call, cap, or floor that does not qualify as an embedded derivative in an existing asset or liability; or

      (4)  Residual value in a lessor's net investment in a sales-type or direct financing lease.

2.    The item has an exposure to fair value changes that could affect earnings (this does not apply to not-for-profit enterprises).

3.    The item is not

    a.    Remeasured with changes reported currently in earnings; for example, a foreign currency denominated item;

    b.    An APB 18 equity-method investment or an equity investment in a consolidated subsidiary;

    c.    A minority interest;

    d.    A firm commitment to enter into a business combination or to acquire or dispose of

        (1)  A subsidiary;

        (2)  A minority interest; or

        (3)  An equity method investee; or

    e.    An entity-issued equity interest classified in stockholders' equity.

4.    The item is not a held-to-maturity debt security (or similar portfolio) unless the hedged risk is for something other than for fair value changes in market interest rates or foreign exchange rates; examples include hedges of fair value due to changes in the obligor's creditworthiness, and hedges of fair value due to changes in a prepayment option component.

5.    If the item is a nonfinancial asset or liability (other than a recognized loan servicing right or a nonfinancial firm commitment with financial components), the designated hedged risk is the fair value change of the total hedged item (at its actual location, if applicable); FAS 133 stipulates that the price of a major ingredient cannot be used, and the price of a similar item at a different location cannot be used without adjustment.

6.    If the item is a financial asset or liability, a recognized loan servicing right or a nonfinancial firm commitment with financial components, the designated hedge risk is the risk of changes in fair value from fair value changes in

    a.    The total hedged item;

    b.    Market interest rates;

    c.    Related foreign currency rates;

    d.    The obligor's creditworthiness; or

    e.    Two or more of the above, other than a.

Prepayment risk for a financial asset cannot be hedged, but an option component of a prepayable instrument can be designated as the hedged item in a fair value hedge. Embedded derivatives have to be considered also in designating hedges. For instance, in a hedge of interest rates, the effect of an embedded prepayment option must be considered in the designation of the hedge.

**Reporting gains and losses from fair value hedges.** The accounting for qualifying fair value hedges' gains and losses is as follows:

- On the hedging instrument, gains and losses are recognized in earnings.
- On the hedged item, gains and losses are recognized in earnings, even if they would normally be included in other comprehensive income if not hedged. For example, gains and losses on an available-for-sale security would be taken into income, if this is

being hedged. The carrying amount of the hedged item is adjusted by the gains and losses resulting from the hedged risk.

Differences between the gains and losses on the hedged item and the hedging instrument are either due to amounts excluded from the assessment of hedging effectiveness, or are due to ineffectiveness. These gains and losses are to be recognized currently in earnings.

### Example

An available-for-sale security carrying amount is adjusted by the amount resulting from the hedged risk, a fair value hedge.

| | |
|---|---|
| Hedged item: | Available-for-sale security |
| Hedging instrument: | Put option |
| Underlying: | Price of the security |
| Notional amount: | 100 shares of the security |

On July 1, 2009, Company XYZ purchased 100 shares of Widgetworks at a cost of $15 per share and classified it as an available-for-sale security. On October 1, 2009, Company XYZ purchased for $350 an at-the-money put on Widgetworks with an exercise price of $25 and an expiration date of April 2010. This put purchase locks in a profit of $650 ($1,000 spread in market price less $350 cost of the put), if the price stays at $25 or goes lower, but allows continued profitability if the price of the Widgetworks stock continues to go up. Company XYZ specifies that only the intrinsic value of the option is to be used to measure effectiveness. Thus, the time value decreases in the fair value of the put will be charged against the income of the period. Company XYZ then documents the hedge's strategy, objectives, hedging relationships, and method of measuring effectiveness. The following table shows the fair value of the hedged item and the hedging instrument.

**Case 1**

| Hedged Item | *10/1/09* | *12/31/09* | *3/31/10* | *4/17/10* |
|---|---|---|---|---|
| Widgetworks share price | $ 25 | $ 22 | $ 20 | $ 20 |
| Number of shares | 100 | 100 | 100 | 100 |
| Total | $2,500 | $2,200 | $2,000 | $2,000 |
| **Hedging Instrument** | | | | |
| Put option (100 shares) | | | | |
| Intrinsic value | $ 0 | $ 300 | $ 500 | $ 500 |
| Time value | 350 | 215 | 53 | 0 |
| Total | $ 350 | $ 515 | $ 553 | $ 500 |
| **Intrinsic Value** | | | | |
| **Gain (Loss) on Put** | $ 0 | $ 300 | $ 200 | $ 0 |

**Entries: Income Tax Effects and Transaction Costs Are Ignored**

| | | | | |
|---|---|---|---|---|
| 7/1/09 | Purchase: | Available-for-sale security | 1,500 | |
| | | Cash | | 1,500 |
| 9/30/09 | End of Quarter: | Valuation allowance—available-for-sale security | 1,000 | |
| | | Other comprehensive income | | 1,000 |
| 10/1/09 | Put Purchase: | Put option | 350 | |
| | | Cash | | 350 |
| 12/31/09 | End of Year: | Put option | 300 | |
| | | Hedge gain (intrinsic value gain) | | 300 |
| | | Hedge loss | 135 | |
| | | Put option (time value loss) | | 135 |
| | | Hedge loss | 300 | |
| | | Valuation allowance—available-for-sale security (market value loss) | | 300 |

**Partial Balance Sheet**
**Effect of Hedging Relationships**
**December 31, 2009**
**Dr (Cr)**

| | |
|---|---:|
| Cash | $(1,850) |
| Available-for-sale securities | 1,200 |
| Plus:  Valuation allowance | 1,000 |
| Put option | 515 |
| Other comprehensive income | (1,000) |
| Retained earnings | 135 |

**Entries**

| | | | | |
|---|---|---|---:|---:|
| 3/31/10 | End of Quarter: | Put option | 200 | |
| | | Hedge gain (intrinsic value changes) | | 200 |
| | | Hedge loss | 162 | |
| | | Put option (time value loss) | | 162 |
| | | Hedge loss | 200 | |
| | | Available-for-sale security (market value loss) | | 200 |
| 4/17/10 | Put Expires: | Put option | 0 | |
| | | Hedge gain (intrinsic value changes) | | 0 |
| | | Hedge loss | 53 | |
| | | Put option (time value changes) | | 53 |
| | | Hedge loss | 0 | |
| | | Available-for-sale security (market value changes) | | 0 |

**Partial Balance Sheet**
**Effect of Hedging Relationships**
**April 17, 2010 (Expiration of put)**
**Dr (Cr)**

| | |
|---|---:|
| Cash | $(1,850) |
| Available-for-sale securities | 1,500 |
| Plus:  Valuation allowance | 500 |
| Put option | 500 |
| Other comprehensive income | (1,000) |
| Retained earnings | 350 |

At or before expiration, an in-the-money put must be sold or exercised.  Assuming that it is sold, the entry would be

| | | |
|---|---:|---:|
| Cash | 500 | |
| Put option | | 500 |

On the other hand, if the put is exercised, the entry would be

| | | |
|---|---:|---:|
| Cash (exercise price) | 2,500 | |
| Other comprehensive income | 1,000 | |
| Available-for-sale security | | 1,500 |
| Valuation allowance | | 500 |
| Put option | | 500 |
| Gain on sale | | 1,000 |

The net effect on retained earnings of the hedge and sale is a net gain of $650 ($1,000 – $350).

### Case 2

| Hedged Item | 10/1/09 | 12/31/09 | 3/31/10 | 4/17/10 |
|---|---|---|---|---|
| Widgetworks share price | $ 25 | $ 28 | $ 30 | $ 31 |
| Number of shares | 100 | 100 | 100 | 100 |
| Total | $2,500 | $2,800 | $3,000 | $3,100 |
| **Hedging Instrument** | | | | |
| Put option (100 shares) | | | | |
| Intrinsic value | $ 0 | $ 0 | $ 0 | $ 0 |
| Time value | 350 | 100 | 25 | 0 |
| Total | $ 350 | $ 100 | $ 25 | $ 0 |
| **Intrinsic Value Gain (Loss) on Put** | $ 0 | $ 0 | $ 0 | $ 0 |

### Entries: Income Tax Effects and Transaction Costs Are Ignored

| | | | | |
|---|---|---|---|---|
| 7/1/09 | Purchase: | Available-for-sale security | 1,500 | |
| | | Cash | | 1,500 |
| 9/30/09 | End of Quarter: | Valuation allowance— | | |
| | | available-for-sale security | 1,000 | |
| | | Other comprehensive income | | 1,000 |
| 10/1/09 | Put Purchase: | Put option | 350 | |
| | | Cash | | 350 |
| 12/31/09 | End of Year: | Put option | 0 | |
| | | Hedge gain (intrinsic value gain) | | 0 |
| | | Hedge loss | 250 | |
| | | Put option (time value loss) | | 250 |
| | | Valuation allowance—available-for-sale security | 300 | |
| | | Hedge gain (market value gain) | | 300 |

### Partial Balance Sheet
### Effect of Hedging Relationships
### December 31, 2009
### Dr (Cr)

| | |
|---|---|
| Cash | $(1,850) |
| Available-for-sale securities | 1,500 |
| Plus: Valuation allowance | 1,300 |
| Put option | 100 |
| Other comprehensive income | (1,000) |
| Retained earnings | (50) |

### Entries

| | | | | |
|---|---|---|---|---|
| 3/31/10 | End of Quarter: | Put option | 0 | |
| | | Hedge gain (intrinsic value change) | | 0 |
| | | Hedge loss | 75 | |
| | | Put option (time value loss) | | 75 |
| | | Valuation allowance—available-for-sale security | 200 | |
| | | Hedge gain (market value gain) | | 200 |
| 4/17/10 | Put Expires: | Put option | 0 | |
| | | Hedge gain (intrinsic value change) | | 0 |
| | | Hedge loss | 25 | |
| | | Put option (time value change) | | 25 |
| | | Valuation allowance—available-for-sale security | 100 | |
| | | Hedge gain (market value change) | | 100 |

**Effect of Hedging Relationships**
**April 17, 2010 (Expiration of put)**
**Dr (Cr)**

| | |
|---|---:|
| Cash | $(1,850) |
| Available-for-sale securities | 1,500 |
|    Plus: Valuation allowance | 1,600 |
| Put option | 0 |
| Other comprehensive income | (1,000) |
| Retained earnings | (250) |

The put expired unexercised and Company XYZ must decide whether to sell the security. If it continues to hold, normal FAS 115 accounting would apply. If it continues to hold and a new put is purchased, the above example would be applicable again with the present position as a starting point. If the security is sold, the entry would be

| | | |
|---|---:|---:|
| Cash (fair value) | 3,100 | |
| Other comprehensive income | 1,000 | |
|    Available-for-sale security | | 1,500 |
|    Valuation allowance | | 1,600 |
|    Gain on sale | | 1,000 |

**Measuring the effectiveness of fair value hedges.** Although there are specific conditions applicable to the hedge type (fair value or cash flow), in general, the assumption of no ineffectiveness in a hedging relationship between an interest-bearing financial instrument and an interest rate swap (or a compound hedging instrument composed of an interest rate swap and a mirror-image call or put option) can be made if all of the following conditions are met:

1. The principal amount of the interest-bearing asset or liability being hedged and the notional amount of the swap match;
2. The fair value of the swap is zero at inception, if the hedging instrument is solely an interest rate swap. If the hedging instrument is a compound derivative containing the swap and a mirror-image call or put, the premium for the option must be paid or received in the same manner as the premium on the option embedded in the hedged item, and further conditions must be met depending on whether the premium on the option element of the hedged item was paid upon inception or over the life of the instrument.
3. The net settlements under the swap are computed the same way on each settlement date;
4. The financial instrument is not prepayable, but this criterion does not apply to an interest-bearing asset or liability that is prepayable only due to an embedded call option when the hedging instrument is a compound derivative composed of a swap and a mirror-image call option; and
5. The terms are typical for those instruments and don't invalidate the assumption of effectiveness.
6. The maturity date of the instrument and the expiration date of the swap match;
7. No floor or ceiling on the variable interest rate of the swap exists; and
8. The interval (three to six months or less) between repricings is frequent enough to assume the variable rate is a market rate.

The fixed rate on the hedged item is not required to exactly match the fixed rate on the swap. The fixed and variable rates on the swap can be changed by the same amount. As an example, a swap payment based on LIBOR and a swap receipt based on a fixed rate of 5% can be changed to a payment based on LIBOR plus 1% and a receipt based on 6%.

Under FAS 133, a "shortcut method" is permitted to be used to compute fair value adjustments, which produces the same reporting results as when the method illustrated above has been applied. This shortcut is only appropriate for a fair value hedge of a fixed-rate asset or liability using an interest rate swap and only with the assumption of no ineffectiveness is appropriate (i.e., if the criteria above have been met.[2] The FASB's decision to redefine interest rate risk (by permitting "benchmark rate" hedging in FAS 138) necessitated that is also address the effect on the shortcut method for fair value hedges and cash flow hedges.

For fair value hedges, an assumption of no ineffectiveness is invalidated when the interest rate index embodied in the variable leg of the interest rate swap is different from the benchmark interest rate being hedged. In situations in which the interest rate index embodied in the variable leg of the swap has greater credit risk than that embodied in the benchmark interest rate, the effect of the change in the swap's credit sector spread over that in the benchmark interest rate would represent hedge ineffectiveness because it relates to an unhedged risk (credit risk) rather than to the hedged risk (interest rate risk).

In situations in which the interest rate index embodied in the variable leg of the swap has less credit risk than that embodied in the benchmark interest rate, the effect of the change in a certain portion of the hedged item's spread over the swap interest rate would also represent hedge ineffectiveness. In order for an entity to comply with an assumption of no ineffectiveness, the index on which the variable leg of the swap is based must match the benchmark interest rate designated as the interest rate risk being hedged for the hedging relationship.

**Discontinuance of a fair value hedge.** The accounting for a fair value hedge should not continue if any of the events below occur.

1.  The criteria are no longer met;
2.  The derivative instruments expire or are sold, terminated or exercised; or
3.  The designation is removed.

If the fair value hedge is discontinued, a new hedging relationship may be designated with a different hedging instrument and/or a different hedged item, as long as the criteria established in FAS 133 are met.

**Ineffectiveness of a fair value hedge.** Unless the shortcut method is applicable, the reporting entity must assess the hedge's effectiveness at the inception of the hedge and at least every three months thereafter. In addition, FAS 133 requires that at the inception of the hedge the method to be used to assess hedge effectiveness must be identified. To comply, the reporting entity should decide which changes in the derivative's fair value will be considered in assessing the effectiveness of the hedge, and the method to be used to assess hedge effectiveness. Regarding the former, some derivative instruments (options) have two components: intrinsic value and time value. The intrinsic value of a call option is the excess, if any, of the market price over the strike or exercise price; the intrinsic value of an option recognizes that the price of the underlying item may move above the strike price (for a call) or below the strike price (for a put) during the exercise period. The enterprise elects to measure effectiveness either including or excluding time value; it must do so consistently once the designation is made.

---

[2]   *The steps in the shortcut method are as follows:*

    *a.*   *Determine the difference between the fixed rate to be received on the swap and the fixed rate to be paid on the bonds.*

    *b.*   *Combine that difference with the variable rate to be paid on the swap.*

    *c.*   *Compute and recognize interest expense using that combined rate and the fixed-rate liability's principal amount. (Amortization of any purchase premium or discount on the liability also must be considered, although that complication is not incorporated in this example.)*

    *d.*   *Determine the fair value of the interest rate swap.*

    *e.*   *Adjust the carrying amount of the swap to its fair value and adjust the carrying amount of the liability by an offsetting amount.*

Hedge effectiveness must be assessed in two different ways—in *prospective* considerations and in *retrospective* evaluations. FAS 133 provides flexibility in selecting the method the entity will use in assessing hedge effectiveness, but an entity should assess effectiveness for similar hedges in a similar manner and that the use of different methods for similar hedges should be justified.

Prospectively, the entity must, at both inception and on an ongoing basis, be able to justify an expectation that the relationship will he highly effective in achieving offsetting changes in fair value over future periods. That expectation can be based upon regression or other statistical analysis of past changes in fair values or on other relevant information. Retrospectively, the entity must, at least quarterly, determine whether the hedging relationship has been highly effective in having achieved offsetting changes in fair value through the date of periodic assessment. That assessment can also be based upon regression or other statistical analysis of past changes in fair values, as well as on other relevant information. If at inception the entity elects to use the same regression analysis approach for both prospective and retrospective effectiveness evaluations, then during the term of that hedging relationship those regression analysis calculations should generally incorporate the same number of data points. As an alternative to using regression or other statistical analysis, an entity could use the dollar-offset method to perform the retrospective evaluations of assessing hedge effectiveness.

FAS 133 does not define hedging effectiveness quantitatively. However, it is useful in this regard to contemplate the similar international accounting standard, IAS 39. That standard specifies that a hedge is normally regarded as highly effective if, at inception and throughout the life of the hedge, the enterprise can expect that the change in fair values of the hedging instrument and the hedged item will "almost fully offset." In addition, the standard requires that actual results be within a range of 80–125%. Interpretive guidance to that standard suggests that the appropriateness of any method of assessing hedge effectiveness depends on the nature of the risk being hedged and the type of hedging instrument used. Any method of assessing effectiveness must be reasonable and consistent with other similar hedges unless different methods are explicitly justified.

Logic suggests that the approach used under IAS 39 could also be applied under FAS 133, with a range of 80–125% being defined as effectiveness for hedge accounting purposes. This guidance has always appeared reasonable, particularly in the absence of any quantitative criteria for hedge effectiveness under US GAAP. As US GAAP further converges with—or even becomes superseded by—IFRS, applying its guidance regarding hedge effectiveness only makes more sense as time passes.

**Impairment.** All assets or liabilities designated as fair value hedges are subject to the normal GAAP requirements for impairment. Those requirements are to be applied, however, only after the carrying amounts have been adjusted for the period's hedge accounting. Since the hedging instrument is a separate asset or liability, its fair value is not considered in applying the impairment criteria to the hedged item.

## Cash Flow Hedges

The second major subset of hedging arrangements relate to uncertain future cash flows, as contrasted with hedged items engendering uncertain fair values. A derivative instrument may be designated as a hedge to the exposure of fluctuating expected future cash flows produced by a particular risk. The exposure may be connected with an existing asset or liability or with a forecasted transaction.

**Qualifications.** To qualify as a cash flow hedge, both the hedged items and the designated hedging instruments must meet all of the following criteria:

1.  At the hedge's origin, formal documentation exists of the

    a.  Hedging relationship;
    b.  Risk management objectives;
    c.  Strategy for undertaking the hedge; and
    d.  Identification of the hedged transaction, the hedging instrument, the nature of the hedged risk, the method of assessing effectiveness and the components (if any) that are excluded (such as time value) from the effectiveness assessment.

2.  Documentation must include

    a.  All relevant details;
    b.  The specific nature of any asset or liability involved;
    c.  When (date on or period within) a forecasted transaction is expected to occur; and
    d.  The expected currency amount (exact amount of foreign currency being hedged) or expected quantity (specific physical quantities such as number of items, weight, etc.) of a forecasted transaction. If a price risk is being hedged in a forecasted sale or purchase, the hedged transaction cannot

        (1)  Be specified solely in terms of expected currency amounts; or
        (2)  Be specified as a percentage of sales or purchases.

    The current price of the transaction should be identified and the transaction should be described so that it is evident that a given transaction is or is not the hedged transaction. For instance, a forecasted sale of the first 2,000 units in January is proper, but the forecasted sale of the last 2,000 units is not because they cannot be identified when they occur—the month has to end before the last units sold can be identified.

3.  The hedging relationship is expected to be highly effective in producing offsetting cash flows throughout the hedge period. This relationship must be assessed at least every three months and each time financial statements or earnings are reported.

4.  If hedging with a written option, the combination must provide at least as much potential for positive cash flow changes as exposure to negative cash flow changes. A derivative that results from the combination of a written option and another nonoption derivative is also considered a written option.

5.  A link must be used to modify interest receipts or payments of a recognized financial asset or liability from one variable rate to another variable rate. It has to be between a designated asset (or group of similar assets) and a designated liability (or group of similar liabilities) and it has to be highly effective. A link occurs when the basis of one leg of an interest rate swap is the same as the basis of the interest rate receipt of a designated asset and the basis of the other leg of the swap is the same as the basis of the interest payments for a designated liability.

A nonderivative instrument cannot be designated as a hedging instrument for a cash flow hedge.

In addition to the above, to be eligible for designation as a cash flow hedge, a forecasted transaction must meet all of the following criteria:

1.  The single transaction (or group of individual transactions) must be specifically identified. If individual transactions are grouped and hedged, each has to share the same risk exposure that is being hedged (i.e. each individual transaction must respond in a proportionate manner to the change in cash flow). Thus, a forecasted

sale and a forecasted purchase cannot both be included in the same group of transactions.

2. The occurrence is probable.
3. It is a transaction with an external party (unless a foreign currency cash flow hedge) and it has an exposure to cash flow changes that could affect earnings.
4. The transaction is not to be remeasured under GAAP with changes reported in earnings; for example, foreign currency denominated items would be excluded for this reason. Forecasted sales on credit and forecasted accrual of royalties on probable future sales are not considered the forecasted acquisition of a receivable. Also, if related to a recognized asset or liability, the asset or liability is not remeasured under GAAP with changes in fair value resulting from the hedged risk reported in earnings.
5. The item is not a held-to-maturity debt security (or similar portfolio) unless the hedged risk is for something other than for cash flow changes in market interest rates, as for example, in a hedge of cash flow changes due to an obligor's creditworthiness or default.
6. It does not involve

   a. A business combination;
   b. A parent company's interest in consolidated subsidiaries;
   c. A minority interest;
   d. An equity-method investment; or
   e. An entity-issued equity interest classified in stockholders' equity.

7. If it involves a purchase or sale of a nonfinancial asset, the hedged risk is

   a. The change in the functional-currency-equivalent cash flows resulting from changes in the related foreign currency rates; or
   b. The change in cash flows relating to the total hedged purchase or sales price (at its actual location, if applicable); for example, the price of a similar item at a different location cannot be used.

8. If it involves a purchase or sale of a financial asset or liability or the variable cash flow of an existing financial asset or liability, the hedged risk is the risk of changes in cash flow of

   a. The total hedged item;
   b. Market interest rates;
   c. Related foreign currency rates;
   d. Obligor's creditworthiness or default; or
   e. Two or more of the above, other than a.

Prepayment risk for a financial asset cannot be hedged.

**Gains and losses from cash flow hedges.** The accounting for qualifying cash flow hedges' gains and losses is as follows:

1. The effective portion of the gain or loss on the derivative instrument is reported in other comprehensive income.
2. The ineffective portion of the gain or loss on the derivative instrument is reported in earnings.
3. Any component excluded from the computation of the effectiveness of the derivative instrument is reported in earnings.
4. Accumulated other comprehensive income from the hedged transaction should be adjusted to the lesser (in absolute amounts) of the following:

a.   The cumulative gain or loss on the derivative from the creation of the hedge minus any component excluded from the determination of hedge effectiveness and minus any amounts reclassified from accumulated other comprehensive income into earnings;

b.   The portion of the cumulative gain or loss on the derivative needed to offset the cumulative change in expected future cash flow on the transaction from the creation of the hedge minus any amounts reclassified from accumulated other comprehensive income into earnings.

The adjustment of accumulated other comprehensive income should recognize in other comprehensive income either a part or all of the gain or loss on the adjustment of the derivative instrument to fair value.

5.   Any remaining gain or loss is reported in earnings.

**Reclassifications to earnings.**  In the period that the hedged forecasted transaction affects earnings, amounts in accumulated other comprehensive income should be reclassified into earnings.  If the transaction results in an asset or liability, amounts in accumulated other comprehensive income should be reclassified into earnings when the asset or liability affects earnings through cost of sales, depreciation, interest expense, etc.  Any time that a net loss on the combined derivative instrument and the hedged transaction is expected, the amount that isn't expected to be recovered should immediately be reclassified into earnings.

### Example of a "plain vanilla" interest rate swap

On July 1, 2009, Abbott Corp. borrows $5 million with a fixed maturity (no prepayment option) of June 30, 2013, carrying interest at prime + 1/2%.  Interest only is due semiannually.  At the same date, it enters into a "plain vanilla" type swap arrangement, calling for fixed payments at 8% and receipt of prime + 1/2%, on a notional amount of $5 million.  At that date prime is 7.5%, and there is no premium due on the swap arrangement.

This swap qualifies as a cash flow hedge under FAS 133, and it is appropriate to assume no ineffectiveness, since the criteria set forth in that standard are all met.

*NOTE: These criteria are that: the notional amount of the swap and the principal amount of the debt are equal; the fair value of the swap at inception is zero; the formula for computing net settlements under the swap is constant during its term; the debt may not be prepaid; all interest payments on the debt are designated as being hedged and no payments beyond the term of the swap are so designated; there is no floor or cap on the variable rate of the debt that is not likewise designated for the swap; the repricing dates of the swap match those of the variable rate debt; and the same index is designated for the hedging instrument and the underlying obligation.*

Accordingly, as rates change over the term of the debt and of the swap arrangement, changes in the value of the swap are reflected in other comprehensive income, and the swap will appear on the balance sheet as an asset or liability at fair value.  As the maturity of the debt approaches, the value of the swap will converge on zero.  Periodic interest expense in the income statement will be at the effective rate of 8%.

Assume that the prime rate over the four-year term of the loan, as of each interest payment date, is as follows, along with the fair value of the remaining term of the interest rate swap at those dates:

| Date | Prime rate (%) | Fair value of swap* |
|---|---|---|
| December 31, 2009 | 6.5 | $ - 150,051 |
| June 30, 2010 | 6.0 | - 196,580 |
| December 31, 2010 | 6.5 | - 111,296 |
| June 30, 2011 | 7.0 | - 45,374 |
| December 31, 2011 | 7.5 | 0 |
| June 30, 2012 | 8.0 | 23,576 |
| December 31, 2012 | 8.5 | 24,038 |
| June 30, 2013 | 8.0 | 0 |

\*  *Fair values are determined as the present values of future cash flows resulting from expected interest rate differentials, based on the current prime rate, discounted at 8%.*

Regarding the fair values presented in the foregoing table, it should be assumed that the fair values are precisely equal to the present value, at each valuation date (assumed to be the interest payment dates), of the differential future cash flows resulting from utilization of the swap. Future variable interest rates (prime + 1/2%) are assumed to be the same as the existing rates at each valuation date (i.e., there is no basis for any expectation of rate changes, and therefore the best estimate is that the current rate will persist over time). The discount rate, 8%, is assumed to be constant over time.

Thus, for example, the fair value of the swap at December 31, 2009, would be the present value of an annuity of seven payments (the number of remaining semiannual interest payments due) of $25,000 each (pay 8%, receive 7%, based on then-existing prime rate of 6.5%) to be made to the swap counterparty, discounted at an annual rate of 8% (using 4% for the semiannual discounting, which is a slight simplification). This computation yields a present value of a stream of seven $25,000 payments to the swap counterparty amounting to $150,051 at December 31, 2009, which is a liability to be reported by the entity at that date. The offset is a debit to other comprehensive income, since the hedge is (presumably) judged to be 100% effective in this case. Semiannual accounting entries will be as follows:

**December 31, 2009**

| | | |
|---|---|---|
| Interest expense | 175,000 | |
| Accrued interest (or cash) | | 175,000 |

*To accrue or pay semiannual interest on the debt at the variable rate of prime + 1/2% (7.0%)*

| | | |
|---|---|---|
| Interest expense | 25,000 | |
| Accrued interest (or cash) | | 25,000 |

*To record net settlement on swap arrangement [8.0 - 7.0%]*

| | | |
|---|---|---|
| Other comprehensive income | 150,051 | |
| Swap contract | | 150,051 |

*To record the fair value of the swap contract as of this date (a net liability because fixed rate payable to counterparty of 8% exceeds floating rate receivable from counterparty of 7%)*

**June 30, 2010**

| | | |
|---|---|---|
| Interest expense | 162,500 | |
| Accrued interest (or cash) | | 162,500 |

*To accrue or pay semiannual interest on the debt at the variable rate of prime + 1/2% (6.5%)*

| | | |
|---|---|---|
| Interest expense | 37,500 | |
| Accrued interest (or cash) | | 37,500 |

*To record net settlement on swap arrangement [8.0 - 6.5%]*

| | | |
|---|---|---|
| Other comprehensive income | 46,529 | |
| Swap contract | | 46,529 |

*To record the fair value of the swap contract as of this date (increase in obligation because of further decline in prime rate)*

**December 31, 2010**

| | | |
|---|---|---|
| Interest expense | 175,000 | |
| Accrued interest (or cash) | | 175,000 |

*To accrue or pay semiannual interest on the debt at the variable rate of prime + 1/2% (7.0%)*

| | | |
|---|---|---|
| Interest expense | 25,000 | |
| Accrued interest (or cash) | | 25,000 |

*To record net settlement on swap arrangement [8.0 - 7.0%]*

| | | |
|---|---|---|
| Other comprehensive income | 150,051 | |
| Swap contract | | 150,051 |

*To record the fair value of the swap contract as of this date (decrease in obligation due to increase in prime rate*

### June 30, 2011

| | | |
|---|---|---|
| Interest expense | 187,500 | |
| Accrued interest (or cash) | | 187,500 |

*To accrue or pay semiannual interest on the debt at the variable rate of prime + 1/2% (7.5%)*

| | | |
|---|---|---|
| Interest expense | 12,500 | |
| Accrued interest (or cash) | | 12,500 |

*To record net settlement on swap arrangement [8.0 - 7.5%]*

| | | |
|---|---|---|
| Swap contract | 65,922 | |
| Other comprehensive income | | 65,922 |

*To record the fair value of the swap contract as of this date (decrease in obligation due to further increase in prime rate)*

### December 31, 2011

| | | |
|---|---|---|
| Interest expense | 200,000 | |
| Accrued interest (or cash) | | 200,000 |

*To accrue or pay semiannual interest on the debt at the variable rate of prime + 1/2% (8.0%)*

| | | |
|---|---|---|
| Interest expense | 0 | |
| Accrued interest (or cash) | | 0 |

*To record net settlement on swap arrangement [8.0 - 8.0%]*

| | | |
|---|---|---|
| Swap contract | 45,374 | |
| Other comprehensive income | | 45,374 |

*To record the fair value of the swap contract as of this date (further increase in prime rate to the original rate of inception of the hedge eliminates fair value of the derivative)*

### June 30, 2012

| | | |
|---|---|---|
| Interest expense | 212,500 | |
| Accrued interest (or cash) | | 212,500 |

*To accrue or pay semiannual interest on the debt at the variable rate of prime + 1/2% (8.5%)*

| | | |
|---|---|---|
| Receivable from counterparty (or cash) | 12,500 | |
| Interest expense | | 12,500 |

*To record net settlement on swap arrangement [8.0 – 8.5%], counterparty remits settlement*

| | | |
|---|---|---|
| Swap contract | 23,576 | |
| Other comprehensive income | | 23,576 |

*To record the fair value of the swap contract as of this date (increase in prime rate creates net asset position for derivative)*

### December 31, 2012

| | | |
|---|---|---|
| Interest expense | 225,000 | |
| Accrued interest (or cash) | | 225,000 |

*To accrue or pay semiannual interest on the debt at the variable rate of prime + 1/2% (9.0%)*

| | | |
|---|---|---|
| Receivable from counterparty (or cash) | 25,000 | |
| Interest expense | | 25,000 |

*To record net settlement on swap arrangement [8.0 – 9.0%], counterparty remits settlement*

| | | |
|---|---|---|
| Swap contract | 462 | |
| Other comprehensive income | | 462 |

*To record the fair value of the swap contract as of this date (increase in asset value due to further rise in prime rate)*

### June 30, 2013 (Maturity)

| | | |
|---|---|---|
| Interest expense | 212,500 | |
| Accrued interest (or cash) | | 212,500 |

*To accrue or pay semiannual interest on the debt at the variable rate of prime + 1/2% (8.5%)*

| | | |
|---|---|---|
| Receivable from counterparty (or cash) | 12,500 | |
| Interest expense | | 12,500 |

| | | |
|---|---|---|
| Other comprehensive income | 24,038 | |
| Swap contract | | 24,038 |

*To record the fair value of the swap contract as of this date (value declines to zero as expiration date approaches)*

### Example of an option on an interest rate swap

The facts of this example are a variation on the previous example. Abbott Corp. anticipates as of June 30, 2009, that as of June 30, 2011, it will become a borrower of $5 million with a fixed maturity four years hence (June 30, 2015). Based on its current credit rating, it expects to be able to borrow at prime + 1/2%. As of June 30, 2009, it is able to purchase, for a single payment of $25,000, a "swaption" (an option on an interest rate swap), calling for fixed pay at 8% and variable receipt at prime + 1/2%, on a notional amount of $5 million, for a term of four years. The option will expire in two years. At June 30, 2009, prime is 7.5%.

*NOTE: The interest rate behavior in this example differs somewhat from the prior example, to better illustrate the "one-sidedness" of options, versus the obligation under a swap arrangement or other futures and forwards.*

It will be assumed that the time value of the swaption expires ratably over the two years.

This swaption qualifies as a cash flow hedge under FAS 133. However, while the change in fair value of the contract is an effective hedge of the cash flow variability of the prospective debt issuance, the premium paid is a reflection of the time value of money and is thus to be expensed ratably over the period that the swaption is outstanding.

The table below gives the prime rate at semiannual intervals including the two-year period prior to the debt issuance, plus the four years during which the forecasted debt (and the swap, if the option is exercised) will be outstanding, as well as the fair value of the swaption (and later, the swap itself) at these points in time.

| Date | Prime rate (%) | Fair value of swaption/swap* |
|---|---|---|
| December 31, 2009 | 7.5 | $ 0 |
| June 30, 2010 | 8.0 | 77,925 |
| December 31, 2010 | 6.5 | 0 |
| June 30, 2011 | 7.0 | - 84,159 |
| December 31, 2011 | 7.5 | 0 |
| June 30, 2012 | 8.0 | 65,527 |
| December 31, 2012 | 8.5 | 111,296 |
| June 30, 2013 | 8.0 | 45,374 |
| December 31, 2013 | 8.0 | 34,689 |
| June 30, 2014 | 7.5 | 0 |
| December 31, 2014 | 7.5 | 0 |
| June 30, 2015 | 7.0 | 0 |

\* *Fair value is determined as the present value of future expected interest rate differentials, based on the current prime rate, discounted at 8%. An "out of the money" swaption is valued at zero, since the option does not have to be exercised. Since the option is exercised on June 30, 2011, the value at that date is recorded, although negative.*

The value of the swaption contract is only recorded (unless and until exercised, of course, at which point it becomes a contractually binding swap) if it is positive, since if "out of the money" the holder would forego exercise in most instances and thus there is no liability by the holder to be reported. (This example is an illustration of the opposite, however, as despite having a negative value the option holder determines that exercise is advisable.) At June 30, 2010, for example, the swaption is an asset, since the reference variable rate (prime + 1/2% or 8.5%) is greater than the fixed swap rate of 8%, and thus the expectation is that the option will be exercised at expiration. This would, if present rates hold steady, which is the naïve assumption, result in a series of eight semiannual payments from the swap counterparty in the amount of $12,500. Discounting this at a nominal 8%, the present value as of the debt origination date (to be June 30, 2011) would be $84,159, which, when further discounted to June 30, 2010, yields a fair value of $77,925.

Note that the following period (December 31, 2010) prime drops to such an extent that the value of the swaption evaporates entirely (actually goes negative, which will not be reported since the holder is under no obligation to exercise it), and the carrying value is therefore eliminated. At expiration, the holder does (for this example) exercise, notwithstanding a negative fair value, and from that point forward the fair value of the swap will be reported, whether positive (an asset) or negative (a liability).

As noted above, assume that, at the option expiration date, despite the fact that prime + 1/2% is below the fixed pay rate on the swap, the management of Abbott Corp. is convinced that rates will climb over the four-year term of the loan, and thus exercises the swaption at that date. Accounting journal entries over the six years are as follows:

**June 30, 2009**

| | | |
|---|---|---|
| Swaption contract | 25,000 | |
|     Cash | | 25,000 |

*To record purchase premium on swaption contract*

**December 31, 2009**

| | | |
|---|---|---|
| Loss on hedging transaction | 6,250 | |
|     Swaption contract | | 6,250 |

*To record change in time value of swaption contract—charge premium to income since this represents payment for time value of money, which expires ratably over two-year term*

**June 30, 2010**

| | | |
|---|---|---|
| Swaption contract | 77,925 | |
|     Other comprehensive income | | 77,925 |

*To record the fair value of the swaption contract as of this date*

| | | |
|---|---|---|
| Loss on hedging transaction | 6,250 | |
|     Swaption contract | | 6,250 |

*To record change in time value of swaption contract—charge premium to income since this represents payment for time value of money, which expires ratably over two-year term*

**December 31, 2010**

| | | |
|---|---|---|
| Other comprehensive income | 77,925 | |
|     Swaption contract | | 77,925 |

*To record the change in fair value of the swaption contract as of this date; since contract is "out of the money," it is not written down below zero (i.e., a net liability is not reported)*

| | | |
|---|---|---|
| Loss on hedging transaction | 6,250 | |
|     Swaption contract | | 6,250 |

*To record change in time value of swaption contract—charge premium to income since this represents payment for time value of money, which expires ratably over two-year term*

**June 30, 2011**

| | | |
|---|---|---|
| Other comprehensive | 84,159 | |
|     Swap contract | | 84,159 |

*To record the fair value of the swap contract as of this date—a net liability is reported since swap option was exercised*

| | | |
|---|---|---|
| Loss on hedging transaction | 6,250 | |
|     Swaption contract | | 6,250 |

*To record change in time value of swaption contract—charge premium to income since this represents payment for time value of money, which expires ratably over two-year term*

**December 31, 2011**

| | | |
|---|---|---|
| Interest expense | 200,000 | |
|     Accrued interest (or cash) | | 200,000 |

*To accrue or pay interest on the debt at the variable rate of prime + 1/2% (8.0%)*

| | | |
|---|---|---|
| Interest expense | 0 | |
|     Accrued interest (or cash) | | 0 |

*To record net settlement on swap arrangement [8.0 – 8.0%]*

| | | |
|---|---|---|
| Swap contract | 84,159 | |
|     Other comprehensive income | | 84,159 |

*To record the change in the fair value of the swap contract as of this date*

**June 30, 2012**

| | | |
|---|---|---|
| Interest expense | 212,500 | |
|     Accrued interest (or cash) | | 212,500 |

*To accrue or pay interest on the debt at the variable rate of prime + 1/2% (8.5%)*

| | | |
|---|---|---|
| Receivable from counterparty (or cash) | 12,500 | |
|     Interest expense | | 12,500 |

*To record net settlement on swap arrangement [8.0 – 8.5%]*

| | | |
|---|---|---|
| Swap contract | 65,527 | |
|     Other comprehensive income | | 65,527 |

*To record the fair value of the swap contract as of this date*

**December 31, 2012**

| | | |
|---|---|---|
| Interest expense | 225,000 | |
|     Accrued interest (or cash) | | 225,000 |

*To accrue or pay interest on the debt at the variable rate of prime + 1/2% (9.0%)*

| | | |
|---|---|---|
| Receivable from counterparty (or cash) | 25,000 | |
|     Interest expense | | 25,000 |

*To record net settlement on swap arrangement [8.0 – 9.0%]*

| | | |
|---|---|---|
| Swap contract | 45,769 | |
|     Other comprehensive income | | 45,769 |

*To record the fair value of the swap contract as of this date*

**June 30, 2013**

| | | |
|---|---|---|
| Interest expense | 212,500 | |
|     Accrued interest (or cash) | | 212,500 |

*To accrue or pay interest on the debt at the variable rate of prime + 1/2% (8.5%)*

| | | |
|---|---|---|
| Receivable from counterparty (or cash) | 12,500 | |
|     Interest expense | | 12,500 |

*To record net settlement on swap arrangement [8.0 – 8.5%]*

| | | |
|---|---|---|
| Other comprehensive income | 65,922 | |
|     Swap contract | | 65,922 |

*To record the change in fair value of the swap contract as of this date (declining prime rate causes swap to lose value)*

**December 31, 2013**

| | | |
|---|---|---|
| Interest expense | 212,500 | |
|     Accrued interest (or cash) | | 212,500 |

*To accrue or pay interest on the debt at the variable rate of prime + 1/2% (8.5%)*

| | | |
|---|---|---|
| Receivable from counterparty (or cash) | 12,500 | |
|     Interest expense | | 12,500 |

*To record net settlement on swap arrangement [8.0 – 8.5%]*

| | | |
|---|---|---|
| Other comprehensive income | 10,685 | |
|     Swap contract | | 10,685 |

*To record the fair value of the swap contract as of this date (decline is due to passage of time, as the prime rate expectations have not changed from the earlier period)*

**June 30, 2014**

| | | |
|---|---|---|
| Interest expense | 200,000 | |
|     Accrued interest (or cash) | | 200,000 |

*To accrue or pay interest on the debt at the variable rate of prime + 1/2% (8.0%)*

| | | |
|---|---|---|
| Receivable from counterparty (or cash) | 0 | |
|     Interest expense | | 0 |

*To record net settlement on swap arrangement [8.0 – 8.0%]*

| | | |
|---|---|---|
| Other comprehensive income | 34,689 | |
|     Swap contract | | 34,689 |

*To record the decline in the fair value of the swap contract to zero as of this date*

**December 31, 2014**

| | | |
|---|---|---|
| Interest expense | 200,000 | |
| Accrued interest (or cash) | | 200,000 |

*To accrue or pay interest on the debt at the variable rate of prime + 1/2% (8.0%)*

| | | |
|---|---|---|
| Receivable from counterparty (or cash) | 0 | |
| Interest expense | | 0 |

*To record net settlement on swap arrangement [8.0 – 8.0%]*

| | | |
|---|---|---|
| Swap contract | 0 | |
| Other comprehensive income | | 0 |

*No change to the zero fair value of the swap contract as of this date*

**June 30, 2015 (Maturity)**

| | | |
|---|---|---|
| Interest expense | 187,500 | |
| Accrued interest (or cash) | | 187,500 |

*To accrue or pay interest on the debt at the variable rate of prime + 1/2% (7.5%)*

| | | |
|---|---|---|
| Interest expense | 12,500 | |
| Accrued interest (or cash) | | 12,500 |

*To record net settlement on swap arrangement [8.0 – 7.5%]*

| | | |
|---|---|---|
| Other comprehensive income | 0 | |
| Swap contract | | 0 |

*No change to the zero fair value of the swap contract, which expires as of this date*

**Effectiveness of cash flow hedges.** The assumption of no ineffectiveness in a cash flow hedge between an interest-bearing financial instrument and an interest rate swap can be assumed if all of the following conditions are met:

1. The principal amount and the notional amount of the swap match;
2. The fair value of the swap is zero at origin;
3. The net settlements under the swap are computed the same way on each settlement date;
4. The financial instrument is not prepayable; and
5. The terms are typical for those instruments and don't invalidate the assumption of effectiveness.
6. All variable rate interest payments or receipts on the instrument during the swap term are designated as hedged and none beyond that term;
7. No floor or cap on the variable rate of the swap exists unless the variable rate instrument has one. If the instrument does, the swap must have a comparable (not necessarily equal) one;
8. Repricing dates match; and
9. The index base for the variable rates match.

The variable rate on the instrument is not required to exactly match the variable rate on the swap. The fixed and variable rates on the swap can be changed by the same amount.

### Example of using options to hedge future purchase of inventory

Friendly Chemicals Corp. uses petroleum as a feedstock from which it produces a range of chemicals for sale to producers of synthetic fabrics and other consumer goods. It is concerned about the rising price of oil and decides to hedge a major purchase it plans to make in mid-2009. Oil futures and options are traded on the New York Mercantile exchange and other markets; Friendly decides to use options rather than futures because it is only interested in protecting itself from a price increase; if prices decline, it wishes to reap that benefit rather than suffer the loss which would result from holding a futures contract in a declining market environment.

At December 31, 2009, Friendly projects a need for ten million barrels of crude oil of a defined grade to be purchased by mid-2010; this will suffice for production through mid-2011. The current world price for this grade of crude is $164.50 per barrel, but prices have been rising recently. Management desires to limit its crude oil costs to no higher than $165.75 per barrel, and accordingly purchases, at a cost of $2 million, an option to purchase up to ten million barrels at a cost of $165.55 per barrel (which, when added to the option premium, would make the total cost $165.75 per barrel if the full ten million barrels are acquired), at any time through December 2010.

Management has studied the behavior of option prices and has concluded that changes in option prices which relate to time value are not correlated to price changes and hence are ineffective in hedging price changes. On the other hand, changes in option prices which pertain to pricing changes (intrinsic value changes) are highly effective as hedging vehicles. The table below reports the value of these options, analyzed in terms of time value and intrinsic value, over the period from December 2009 through December 2010.

|  |  | *Fair value of option relating to* | |
| --- | --- | --- | --- |
| *Date* | *Price of oil/barrel* | *Time value\** | *Intrinsic value* |
| December 31, 2009 | $164.50 | $2,000,000 | $      0 |
| January 31, 2010 | 164.90 | 1,900,000 | 0 |
| February 28, 2010 | 165.30 | 1,800,000 | 0 |
| March 31, 2010 | 165.80 | 1,700,000 | 2,500,000 |
| April 30, 2010 | 166.00 | 1,600,000 | 4,500,000 |
| May 31, 2010 | 165.85 | 1,500,000 | 3,000,000 |
| June 30, 2010\*\* | 166.00 | 700,000 | 2,250,000 |
| July 31, 2010 | 165.60 | 650,000 | 250,000 |
| August 31, 2010 | 165.50 | 600,000 | 0 |
| September 30, 2010 | 165.75 | 550,000 | 1,000,000 |
| October 31, 2010 | 165.80 | 500,000 | 1,250,000 |
| November 30, 2010 | 165.85 | 450,000 | 1,500,000 |
| December 31, 2010\*\*\* | 165.90 | 400,000 | 1,750,000 |

\*   *This example does not address how the time value of options would be computed in practice.*
\*\*  *Options for five million barrels exercised; remainder held until end of December, then sold.*
\*\*\* *Values cited are immediately prior to sale of remaining options.*

At the end of June 2010, Friendly Chemicals exercises options for five million barrels, paying $165.55 per barrel for oil selling on the world markets for $166.00 each. It holds the remaining options until December, when it sells these for an aggregate price of $2.1 million, a slight discount to the nominal fair value at that date.

The inventory acquired in mid-2010 is processed and included in goods available for sale. Sales of these goods, in terms of the five million barrels of crude oil which were consumed in their production, are as follows:

| *Date* | *Equivalent barrels sold in month* | *Equivalent barrels on hand at month end* |
| --- | --- | --- |
| June 30, 2010 | 300,000 | 4,700,000 |
| July 31, 2010 | 250,000 | 4,450,000 |
| August 31, 2010 | 400,000 | 4,050,000 |
| September 30, 2010 | 350,000 | 3,700,000 |
| October 31, 2010 | 550,000 | 3,150,000 |
| November 30, 2010 | 500,000 | 2,650,000 |
| December 31, 2010 | 650,000 | 2,000,000 |

Based on the foregoing facts, the journal entries prepared on a monthly basis (for illustrative purposes) for the period December 2009 through December 2010 are as follows:

**December 31, 2009**

| | | |
| --- | --- | --- |
| Option contract | 2,000,000 | |
|    Cash | | 2,000,000 |

*To record purchase premium on option contract for up to ten million barrels of oil at price of $165.55 per barrel*

**January 31, 2010**

| | | |
|---|---|---|
| Loss on hedging transaction | 100,000 | |
| Option contract | | 100,000 |

*To record change in time value of option contract—charge premium to income since this represents payment for time value of money, which expires ratably over two-year term and does not qualify for hedge accounting treatment*

| | | |
|---|---|---|
| Option contract | 0 | |
| Other comprehensive income | | 0 |

*To reflect change in intrinsic value of option contracts (no value at this date)*

**February 28, 2010**

| | | |
|---|---|---|
| Loss on hedging transaction | 100,000 | |
| Option contract | | 100,000 |

*To record change in time value of option contract—charge premium to income since this represents payment for time value of money, which expires ratably over two-year term and does not qualify for hedge accounting treatment*

| | | |
|---|---|---|
| Option contract | 0 | |
| Other comprehensive income | | 0 |

*To reflect change in intrinsic value of option contracts (no value at this date)*

**March 31, 2010**

| | | |
|---|---|---|
| Loss on hedging transaction | 100,000 | |
| Option contract | | 100,000 |

*To record change in time value of option contract—charge premium to income since this represents payment for time value of money, which expires ratably over two-year term and does not qualify for hedge accounting treatment*

| | | |
|---|---|---|
| Option contract | 2,500,000 | |
| Other comprehensive income | | 2,500,000 |

*To reflect change in intrinsic value of option contracts*

**April 30, 2010**

| | | |
|---|---|---|
| Loss on hedging transaction | 100,000 | |
| Option contract | | 100,000 |

*To record change in time value of option contract—charge premium to income since this represents payment for time value of money, which expires ratably over two-year term and does not qualify for hedge accounting treatment*

| | | |
|---|---|---|
| Option contract | 2,000,000 | |
| Other comprehensive income | | 2,000,000 |

*To reflect change in intrinsic value of option contracts (further increase in value)*

**May 31, 2010**

| | | |
|---|---|---|
| Loss on hedging transaction | 100,000 | |
| Option contract | | 100,000 |

*To record change in time value of option contract—charge premium to income since this represents payment for time value of money, which expires ratably over two-year term and does not qualify for hedge accounting treatment*

| | | |
|---|---|---|
| Other comprehensive income | 1,500,000 | |
| Option contract | | 1,500,000 |

*To reflect change in intrinsic value of option contracts (decline in value)*

**June 30, 2010**

| | | |
|---|---|---|
| Loss on hedging transaction | 800,000 | |
| Option contract | | 800,000 |

*To record change in time value of option contract—charge premium to income since this represents payment for time value of money, which expires ratably over two-year term and does not qualify for hedge accounting treatment; since one-half the options were exercised in June, the remaining unexpensed time value of that portion is also entirely written off at this time*

| | | |
|---|---|---|
| Option contract | 1,500,000 | |
| Other comprehensive income | | 1,500,000 |

*To reflect change in intrinsic value of option contracts (further increase in value) **before** accounting for exercise of options on five million barrels*

| | |
|---|---|
| June 30 intrinsic value of options before exercise | 4,500,000 |
| Allocation to oil purchased at $165.55 | 2,250,000 |
| Remaining intrinsic value of option | 2,250,000 |

The allocation to exercised options will be maintained in other comprehensive income until transferred to cost of goods sold as a contra cost, as the five million barrels are sold, at the rate of 45¢ per equivalent barrel ($166.00 – $165.55).

| | | |
|---|---|---|
| Inventory | 827,750,000 | |
| Cash (or accounts payable) | | 827,750,000 |

*To record purchase of five million barrels of oil at option price of $165.55/barrel*

| | | |
|---|---|---|
| Inventory | 2,250,000 | |
| Option contract | | 2,250,000 |

*To increase the recorded value of the inventory to include the fair value of options given up (exercised) in acquiring the oil (taken together, the cash purchase price and the fair value of options surrendered add to $166 per barrel, the world market price at date of purchase)*

| | | |
|---|---|---|
| Cost of goods sold | 49,800,000 | |
| Inventory | | 49,800,000 |

*To record cost of goods sold (300,000 barrels at $166) before amortizing deferred hedging gain in other comprehensive income*

| | | |
|---|---|---|
| Other comprehensive income | 135,000 | |
| Cost of goods sold | | 135,000 |

*To amortize deferred hedging gain at rate of 45¢ per barrel sold*

**July 31, 2010**

| | | |
|---|---|---|
| Loss on hedging transaction | 50,000 | |
| Option contract | | 50,000 |

*To record change in time value of option contract—charge premium to income since this represents payment for time value of money, which expires ratably over two-year term, and does not qualify for hedge accounting treatment*

| | | |
|---|---|---|
| Other comprehensive income | 2,000,000 | |
| Option contract | | 2,000,000 |

*To reflect change in intrinsic value of remaining option contracts (decline in value)*

| | | |
|---|---|---|
| Cost of goods sold | 41,500,000 | |
| Inventory | | 41,500,000 |

*To record cost of goods sold (250,000 barrels at $166) before amortizing deferred hedging gain in other comprehensive income*

| | | |
|---|---|---|
| Other comprehensive income | 112,500 | |
| Cost of goods sold | | 112,500 |

*To amortize deferred hedging gain at rate of 45¢ per barrel sold*

**August 31, 2010**

| | | |
|---|---|---|
| Loss on hedging transaction | 50,000 | |
|     Option contract | | 50,000 |

*To record change in time value of option contract—charge premium to income since this represents payment for time value of money, which expires ratably over two-year term, and does not qualify for hedge accounting treatment*

| | | |
|---|---|---|
| Other comprehensive income | 250,000 | |
|     Option contract | | 250,000 |

*To reflect change in intrinsic value of remaining option contracts (decline in value to zero)*

| | | |
|---|---|---|
| Cost of goods sold | 66,400,000 | |
|     Inventory | | 66,400,000 |

*To record cost of goods sold (400,000 barrels at $166) before amortizing deferred hedging gain in other comprehensive income*

| | | |
|---|---|---|
| Other comprehensive income | 180,000 | |
|     Cost of goods sold | | 180,000 |

*To amortize deferred hedging gain at rate of 45¢ per barrel sold*

**September 30, 2010**

| | | |
|---|---|---|
| Loss on hedging transaction | 50,000 | |
|     Option contract | | 50,000 |

*To record change in time value of option contract—charge premium to income since this represents payment for time value of money, which expires ratably over two-year term, and does not qualify for hedge accounting treatment*

| | | |
|---|---|---|
| Option contract | 1,000,000 | |
|     Other comprehensive income | | 1,000,000 |

*To reflect change in intrinsic value of remaining option contracts (increase in value)*

| | | |
|---|---|---|
| Cost of goods sold | 58,100,000 | |
|     Inventory | | 58,100,000 |

*To record cost of goods sold (350,000 barrels at $166) before amortizing deferred hedging gain in other comprehensive income*

| | | |
|---|---|---|
| Other comprehensive income | 157,500 | |
|     Cost of goods sold | | 157,500 |

*To amortize deferred hedging gain at rate of 45¢ per barrel sold*

**October 31, 2010**

| | | |
|---|---|---|
| Loss on hedging transaction | 50,000 | |
|     Option contract | | 50,000 |

*To record change in time value of option contract—charge premium to income since this represents payment for time value of money, which expires ratably over two-year term, and does not qualify for hedge accounting treatment*

| | | |
|---|---|---|
| Option contract | 250,000 | |
|     Other comprehensive income | | 250,000 |

*To reflect change in intrinsic value of remaining option contracts (further increase in value)*

| | | |
|---|---|---|
| Cost of goods sold | 91,300,000 | |
|     Inventory | | 91,300,000 |

*To record cost of goods sold (550,000 barrels at $166) before amortizing deferred hedging gain in other comprehensive income*

| | | |
|---|---|---|
| Other comprehensive income | 247,500 | |
|     Cost of goods sold | | 247,500 |

*To amortize deferred hedging gain at rate of 45¢ per barrel sold*

**November 30, 2010**

| | | |
|---|---|---|
| Loss on hedging transaction | 50,000 | |
|    Option contract | | 50,000 |

*To record change in time value of option contract—charge premium to income since this represents payment for time value of money, which expires ratably over two-year term, and does not qualify for hedge accounting treatment*

| | | |
|---|---|---|
| Option contract | 250,000 | |
|    Other comprehensive income | | 250,000 |

*To reflect change in intrinsic value of remaining option contracts (further increase in value)*

| | | |
|---|---|---|
| Cost of goods sold | 83,000,000 | |
|    Inventory | | 83,000,000 |

*To record cost of goods sold (500,000 barrels at $166) before amortizing deferred hedging gain in other comprehensive income*

| | | |
|---|---|---|
| Other comprehensive income | 225,000 | |
|    Cost of goods sold | | 225,000 |

*To amortize deferred hedging gain at rate of 45¢ per barrel sold*

**December 31, 2010**

| | | |
|---|---|---|
| Loss on hedging transaction | 50,000 | |
|    Option contract | | 50,000 |

*To record change in time value of option contract—charge premium to income since this represents payment for time value of money, which expires ratably over two-year term, and does not qualify for hedge accounting treatment*

| | | |
|---|---|---|
| Option contract | 250,000 | |
|    Other comprehensive income | | 250,000 |

*To reflect change in intrinsic value of remaining option contracts (further increase in value) before sale of options*

| | | |
|---|---|---|
| Cost of goods sold | 107,900,000 | |
|    Inventory | | 107,900,000 |

*To record cost of goods sold (650,000 barrels at $166) before amortizing deferred hedging gain in other comprehensive income*

| | | |
|---|---|---|
| Other comprehensive income | 292,500 | |
|    Cost of goods sold | | 292,500 |

*To amortize deferred hedging gain at rate of 45¢ per barrel sold*

| | | |
|---|---|---|
| Cash | 2,100,000 | |
| Loss on sale of options | 50,000 | |
|    Option contract | | 2,150,000 |
| Other comprehensive income | 1,750,000 | |
|    Gain on sale of options | | 1,750,000 |

*To record sale of remaining option contracts; the cash price was $50,000 lower than carrying value of asset sold (options having unexpired time value of $400,000 plus intrinsic value of $1,750,000), but transfer of other comprehensive income to income recognizes formerly deferred gain; since no further inventory purchases are planned in connection with this hedging activity, the unrealized gain is taken into income*

Note that at December 31, 2010, other comprehensive income has a remaining credit balance of $900,000, which represents the deferred gain pertaining to the two million equivalent barrels of oil in inventory. As this is sold, the other comprehensive income will be transferred to cost of goods sold as a reduction of cost of sales.

**Discontinuance of a cash flow hedge.** The accounting for a cash flow hedge should not continue if any of the events below occur.

1. The criteria are no longer met;
2. The derivative instrument expires or is sold, terminated or exercised; or
3. The designation is removed by management.

The net gain or loss in accumulated other comprehensive income should remain there until it is properly reclassified when the hedged transaction affects earnings. If it is probable that the original forecasted transactions won't occur, the net gain or loss in accumulated other comprehensive income should immediately be reclassified into earnings.

If the cash flow hedge is discontinued, a new hedging relationship may be designated with a different hedging instrument and/or a different hedged item as long as the criteria established in FAS 133 are met.

**Ineffectiveness of a cash flow hedge.** In assessing the effectiveness of a cash flow hedge, the time value of money generally will need to be considered, if significant in the circumstances. Doing so becomes especially important if the hedging instrument involves periodic cash settlements. For example, a *tailing strategy* with futures contracts is a situation in which an entity likely would reflect the time value of money. When employing such a strategy, the entity adjusts the size or contract amount of futures contracts used in a hedge so that earnings (or expense) from reinvestment (or funding) of daily settlement gains (or losses) on the futures do not distort the results of the hedge. To assess offset of expected cash flows when a tailing strategy has been used, an entity could reflect the time value of money, possibly comparing the present value of the hedged forecasted cash flow with the results of the hedging instrument.

As with fair value hedges, FAS 133 does not provide a quantitative definition of hedging effectiveness for cash flow hedges. Again, it is useful in this regard to contemplate the similar international accounting standard, IAS 39, which specifies that a hedge is regarded as highly effective if, at inception and throughout the life of the hedge, the enterprise can expect that the change in cash flows of the hedging instrument and the hedged item will "almost fully offset." Actual results within a range of 80–125% could reasonably be expected to qualify as effective.

**Impairment.** All assets or liabilities designated as cash flow hedges are subject to normal GAAP requirements for impairment. Those requirements are to be applied, however, after hedge accounting has been applied for the period. Since the hedging instrument is a separate asset or liability, its expected cash flow or fair value is not considered in applying the impairment criteria to the hedged item. If an impairment loss or recovery on a hedged forecasting asset or liability is recognized, any offsetting amount should be immediately reclassified from accumulated other comprehensive income into earnings.

**Expanded application of interest rate hedging.** FAS 138 amended FAS 133 to permit the use of hedge accounting where the interest rate being hedged is the "benchmark interest rate." As used in the standard, this rate will be either the risk-free rate (i.e., that applicable to direct Treasury borrowings) or the LIBOR swap rate. LIBOR-based swaps in fact are the most commonly employed interest rate hedging vehicles, and it was the persistence of requests made to the FASB's derivatives implementation group regarding the application of hedge accounting to such swaps that resulted in this amendment.

The FASB has thus concluded that, with respect to the separation of interest rate risk and credit risk, the risk of changes in credit sector spread and any credit spread attributable to a specific borrower should be encompassed in credit risk rather than interest rate risk. Under such an approach, an entity would be permitted to designate the risk of changes in the risk-free rate as the hedged risk, and any spread above that rate would be deemed to reflect credit risk. The Board concluded that considering all the effects of credit risk together was more understandable and more operational than this distinction between interest rate risk and credit risk that was at first set forth in the implementation guidance for FAS 133.

FAS 138 requires that all contractual cash flows be used in determining the changes in fair value of the hedged item when benchmark interest rates are being employed. In other words, cash flows pertaining to the portion of interest payments which is related to the entity's credit risk (the risk premium over the benchmark rate) cannot be excluded from the computation.

The accounting for an interest rate hedge using a benchmark rate is very similar to that illustrated beginning on page 288 of this chapter. However, the variable rate used, rather than reflecting the credit riskiness of the party doing the hedging (which was prime + 1/2% in that illustration), would instead be the benchmark rate (e.g., the rate on Treasury five-year notes). Since changes in the benchmark rate might not exactly track the changes in the underlying instrument (due to changes in the "credit spread" which are a reflection of changes in the underlying party's perceived credit risk), the hedge will likely be imperfect, such that a net gain or loss will be reflected in periodic earnings.

### Foreign Currency Hedges

The FASB's basic objectives in hedge accounting for foreign currency exposure are

1. To continue to permit the hedge accounting required under FAS 52; and
2. To increase the consistency of accounting guidance by broadening the scope of hedges that are eligible for this treatment.

Unlike FAS 52, this standard allows hedges of forecasted foreign currency transactions, including some intercompany transactions. Hedging foreign currency intercompany cash flows with foreign currency options is a common practice and was permitted under prior GAAP. FAS 133 modified that accounting rule to permit using other derivative instruments (forward contracts, etc.), on the grounds that the accounting for all derivative instruments should be the same.

FAS 133 precluded hedge accounting for an asset or liability that is remeasured for changes in price attributable to the risk being hedged when those changes are reported currently in earnings. It also precluded fair value or cash flow hedge accounting for foreign currency risk associated with any asset or liability that is denominated in a foreign currency and remeasured into the functional currency under FAS 52. Subsequently, the FASB considered removing the preclusion for any asset or the liability denominated in a foreign currency because, even though the transaction gain or loss on the undesignated asset or liability and the change in fair value of the undesignated derivative were reported currently in earnings, different measurement criteria were used for each instrument, which created volatility in earnings. It eventually decided to permit all recognized foreign-currency-denominated assets and liabilities for which a foreign currency transaction gain or loss is recognized in earnings to be hedged items.

Designated hedging instruments and hedged items qualify for fair value hedge accounting and cash flow hedge accounting under FAS 138 only if all of the criteria in FAS 133 for fair value hedge accounting and cash flow hedge accounting are met. The FASB concluded that fair value hedges could be used for all recognized foreign-currency-denominated asset or liability hedging situations and that cash flow hedges could be used for recognized foreign-currency-denominated asset or liability hedging situations in which all of the variability in the functional-currency-equivalent cash flows are eliminated by the effect of the hedge. Remeasurement of the foreign-currency-denominated assets and liabilities will continue to be based on the guidance in FAS 52, which requires remeasurement based on spot exchange rates, regardless of whether a fair value hedging relationship or a cash flow hedging relationship exists.

**Foreign currency net investment hedge.** Either a derivative instrument or a nonderivative financial instrument (that can result in a foreign currency transaction gain or loss under FAS 52) can be designated as a hedge of a foreign currency exposure of a net investment in a foreign operation. The gain or loss from the designated instrument to the extent that it is effective is reported as a translation adjustment. The hedged net investment is accounted for under FAS 52.

### Example of a foreign currency net investment hedge

Auburn Corporation has invested $15 million in a subsidiary in Germany, and for which the euro is the functional currency. The initial exchange rate is €1.2:$1, so the initial investment is worth €18,000,000. Auburn issues a debt instrument for €12 million and designates it as a hedge of the German investment. Auburn's strategy is that any change in the fair value of the loan attributable to foreign exchange risk should offset any translation gain or loss on 2/3 of Auburn's German investment.

At the end of the year, the exchange rate changes to €0.8:$1. Auburn uses the following calculation to determine the translation gain on its net investment:

€18,000,000/$0.8 = $22,500,000 less €18,000,000/$1.2 = $15,000,000 = $7,500,000

Auburn uses the following calculation to determine the translation loss on its euro-denominated debt:

€12,000,000/$0.8 = $15,000,000 less €12,000,000/$1.2 = $10,000,000 = $5,000,000

Auburn creates the following entries to record changes in the value of the translation gain on its investment and translation loss in its debt, respectively:

| | | |
|---|---|---|
| Investment in subsidiary | 7,500,000 | |
|     Cumulative translation adjustment (equity) | | 7,500,000 |
| Cumulative translation adjustment (equity) | 5,000,000 | |
|     Euro-denominated debt | | 5,000,000 |

The net effect of these translation adjustments is a net increase in Auburn's investment of $2,500,000. In the following year, the exchange rates do not change, and Auburn sells its subsidiary for $17.5 million. Auburn's tax rate is 30%. Its reporting annual gains and losses follows:

| | *Year 1* | *Year 2* |
|---|---|---|
| Net income: | | |
|     Gain on sale of investment in ABC Company | | $2,500,000 |
|     Income tax expense | | (750,000) |
|     Net gain realized in net income | | 1,750,000 |
| Other comprehensive income: | | |
|     Foreign currency translation adjustment, net of tax | $1,750,000 | |
|     Reclassification adjustment, net of tax | | (1,750,000) |
| Other comprehensive income net gain/(loss) | $1,750,000 | $(1,750,000) |

**Foreign currency unrecognized firm commitment hedge.** Either a derivative instrument or a nonderivative financial instrument (that can result in a foreign currency transaction gain or loss under FAS 52) can be designated as a fair value hedge of an unrecognized firm commitment (or a specific portion) attributable to foreign currency. If the criteria are met, this hedging relationship is accounted for as a fair value hedge. (An example appears in Chapter 23.)

**Foreign currency available-for-sale security hedge.** Only a derivative instrument can be designated as a fair value hedge of an available-for-sale debt security (or a specific portion) attributable to foreign currency. If the criteria are met, this hedging relationship is accounted for as a fair value hedge. For an available-for-sale equity security to be accounted for as a fair value hedge, it must meet all of the fair value hedge criteria and the following two requirements:

1. The security cannot be traded on an exchange (or similar marketplace) denominated in the investor's functional currency; and

2. Dividends (or other cash flows) to the holders must be denominated in the same foreign currency as that expected to be received upon the sale of the security.

If the available-for-sale equity security qualifies as a foreign currency hedge, the change in fair value from foreign exchange risk is reported in earnings and not in other comprehensive income.

Any gain or loss on a designated nonderivative hedging instrument from foreign currency risk is determined under FAS 52 (as the increase or decrease in functional currency cash flows produced by the change in spot exchange rates) and is reported in earnings along with the change in the carrying amount of the hedged firm commitment.

**Foreign-currency-denominated forecasted transaction.** Only a derivative instrument can be designated as a cash flow hedge of a foreign-currency-denominated forecasted transaction. The parties to this transaction can either be external or intercompany. To qualify for hedge accounting, all of the following criteria must be met:

1. An operating unit with foreign currency exposure is a party to the derivative instrument;
2. The transaction is denominated in a currency that is not the functional currency;
3. All of the criteria for a cash flow hedge are met (with the possible exception of allowing a qualifying intercompany transaction); and
4. If a group of individual transactions is involved, both an inflow and an outflow of foreign currency cannot be included in the same group.

If the foregoing criteria are met, this hedging relationship is accounted for as a cash flow hedge.

**Using certain intercompany derivatives as hedging instruments in cash flow hedges of foreign currency risk in the consolidated financial statements.** FAS 138 has amended FAS 133 to permit the use of intercompany derivatives as the hedging instruments in cash flow hedges of foreign currency risk in the consolidated financial statements, if those intercompany derivatives are offset by unrelated third-party contracts on a net basis. The new standard defines an "internal derivative" as a foreign currency derivative contract that has been entered into with another member of a consolidated group and which can be a hedging instrument in a foreign currency cash flow hedge of a forecasted borrowing, purchase, or sale or an unrecognized firm commitment in the consolidated financial statements only if the following two conditions are satisfied. First, from the perspective of the member of the consolidated group using the derivative as a hedging instrument, specific criteria for foreign currency cash flow hedge accounting are satisfied. Second, the members of the consolidated group who are not using the derivative as a hedging instrument must either (1) enter into a derivative contract with an unrelated third party to offset the exposure that results from that internal derivative or (2) if certain defined conditions are met, enter into derivative contracts with unrelated third parties that would offset, on a net basis for each foreign currency, the foreign exchange risk arising from multiple internal derivative contracts.

**Other guidance on accounting for financial instruments.** Several EITF consensuses offer additional guidance on these matters. EITF 02-2, which was never finalized, addresses whether separate contracts that meet the definition of financial instruments should be combined for accounting purposes. When entities enter into multiple contracts that individually meet the definition of a financial instrument under FAS 133, but for which the financial reporting impact of recording those contracts separately may be different from the impact of recording those contracts on a combined basis, the preliminary sense is that two or more financial instruments should be required to be combined for accounting purposes if *all* of the following four criteria are met:

1. The transactions or contracts are with the same counterparties (or are structured through an intermediary).
2. The transactions or contracts are entered into in contemplation of one another.
3. The separate transactions or contracts share at least one underlying, and changes in that underlying (holding the prices of all other underlyings constant) result in at least one substantially offsetting change in fair value for those transactions or contracts.
4. The structure of the arrangement (separate contracts) does not serve a substantive business purpose that is fundamentally unrelated to the accounting (that is, the business purpose is not directly or indirectly based on the accounting result) and that could not have been accomplished in a single contact or transaction.

Due to the passage of time, it does not appear that EITF 02-2 will be finalized, and therefore the preliminary position merely serves to provide insight into this accounting issue. A final consensus on this topic, if ever reached, would likely include exceptions (e.g., for treasury functions commonly having multiple transactions with the same counterparties on a daily basis). In any event, as a consequence of the issuance of FAS 150, the tentative consensus on this Issue could only be applicable to situations to which FAS 150 does not apply.

EITF 02-3 is directed at the accounting for derivative contracts held for trading purposes and contracts involved in energy trading and risk management activities. This was addressed, in part, in response to the Enron financial reporting scandal. EITF revisited the wisdom of permitting mark-to-market accounting for energy trading contracts, particularly where such contracts had no quoted market prices or current similar transactions. In predecessor EITF 00-17, it had been held that valuation models, including options-pricing models, could be used to determine fair value, albeit only in the absence of market transactions. Also at issue were the matters of whether (1) recognizing unrealized gains (or losses) at the inception of such contracts and (2) gross or net presentation of gains and losses (whether realized or unrealized) would be appropriate.

EITF concluded that energy contracts should not be marked to fair value. It determined, as well, that the common practice of carrying energy physical inventories at fair value had no basis under GAAP, unless so provided under higher-level GAAP. Furthermore, net presentation of gains and losses derived from derivatives is required under FAS 133, even if physical settlement occurs, if the derivatives are held for trading purposes (as that term is defined in FAS 115). It was also decided that a derivative held for trading purposes may be designated as a hedging instrument, if the FAS 133 criteria are all met, on a prospective basis (i.e., from date of the consensus), notwithstanding the FAS 133 prohibition on designation of derivative instruments held for trading as "hedges."

EITF 03-11 addressed whether realized gains or losses on derivative contracts that are *not* held for trading purposes should be presented gross or net in the income statement irrespective of whether the derivative is designated as a hedging instrument.

A consensus was reached that determining whether realized gains and losses on physically settled derivative contracts *not* held for trading purposes should be reported in the income statement on a gross or net basis is a matter of judgment that depends on the relevant facts and circumstances. Consideration of the facts and circumstances should be made in the context of the various activities of the entity, and not based solely on the terms of the individual contracts. For making an evaluation of the facts and circumstances in order to determine whether an arrangement should be reported on a gross or net basis, EITF noted that the economic substance of the transaction as well as the guidance set forth in APB 29 relative to nonmonetary exchanges and the gross versus net reporting indicators provided in Issue 99-19 may be considered. The economic substance of the transaction should be given precedence over its legal form.

EITF Topic D-102 addresses documentation of the method that is used to measure hedge ineffectiveness under FAS 133. FAS 133 implies that an entity must document, at inception of a hedge, the method that will be used to measure hedge ineffectiveness (in addition to the method to be used to assess effectiveness) in order to meet the documentation requirements of the standard. In a staff announcement addressing the documentation requirements for all types of hedges—fair value, cash flow, and net investment hedges, the FASB has stated that formal documentation is required, at the inception of a hedge, of the hedging relationship and the entity's risk management objective and strategy for undertaking the hedge, including identification of

1. The hedging instrument,
2. The hedged item or transaction,
3. The nature of the risk being hedged,
4. The method that will be used to retrospectively and prospectively assess the hedging instrument's effectiveness, and
5. The method that will be used to measure hedge ineffectiveness.

## Organizations That Do Not Report Earnings

Not-for-profits or other organizations not reporting earnings recognize gains or losses on nonhedging derivative instruments and hedging instruments as a change in net assets. Changes in the carrying amount of the hedged items are also recognized as a change in net assets.

Organizations that do not report earnings cannot use cash flow hedges. If the hedging instrument is a foreign currency net investment hedge, it is accounted for in the same manner as described above.

## Summary of Accounting for Hedges

| | | *Type of hedge—FAS 133* | |
| --- | --- | --- | --- |
| *Attribute* | *Fair value* | *Cash flow* | *Foreign currency (FC)* |
| Types of hedging instruments permitted | Derivatives | Derivatives | Derivatives or nonderivatives depending on the type of hedge |
| Balance sheet valuation of hedging instrument | Fair value | Fair value | Fair value |
| Recognition of gain or loss on changes in value of hedging instrument | Currently in earnings | Effective portion currently as a component of other comprehensive income (OCI) and reclassified to earnings in future period(s) that fore-casted transaction affects earnings | **FC denominated firm commitment** Currently in earnings **Available-for-sale security (AFS)** Currently in earnings **Forecasted FC transaction** Same as cash flow hedge |

| Attribute | Fair value | _Type of hedge—FAS 133_ | |
| | | Cash flow | Foreign currency (FC) |
| --- | --- | --- | --- |
| | | Ineffective portion currently in earnings | **Net investment in a foreign operation** OCI as part of the cumulative translation adjustment to the extent it is effective as a hedge |
| Recognition of gain or loss on changes in the fair value of the hedged item | Currently in earnings | Not applicable; these hedges are not associated with recognized assets or liabilities | **FC denominated firm commitment** Currently in earnings **Available-for-sale security (AFS)** Currently in earnings **Forecasted FC transaction** Not applicable; same as cash flow hedge |

## Disclosures

### Financial instrument disclosures.

*Fair value disclosures.* Certain reporting entities are required to disclose the fair values of all (recognized and unrecognized) financial instruments that it is practicable to estimate, including liabilities. Pertinent descriptive information as to the fair value of the instrument is to be presented if an estimate of fair value cannot actually be made without incurring excessive costs.

These fair value disclosures are optional under FAS 126 for entities that

1. Have total assets less than $100 million on the balance sheet date; and
2. Did not hold or issue any derivative financial instruments during the reporting period; and
3. Are not considered to be public enterprises under the new, expanded definition provided in FSP FAS 126-1.[3]

FAS 157, *Fair Value Measurements*, issued in late 2006, provides a greatly expanded set of guidelines for determining fair value in a variety of fact circumstances. This standard does not impose fair value requirements beyond what already exists under GAAP, but rather provides the tools with which to make the already-required measurements.

FAS 157 (covered in greater detail in Chapter 6) was effective for financial statements for fiscal years beginning after November 15, 2007, and interim periods included in those fiscal years. Reporting entities were encouraged to implement FAS 157 prior to its effective date as long as financial statements had not been issued for any interim periods during the earlier fiscal year.

---

[3] *The definition of a public entity has been expanded to include reporting entities that are the debtor under conduit debt securities traded in domestic or foreign exchange or over-the-counter market, including local or regional markets. These securities, sometimes referred to as industrial revenue bonds, are defined as certain limited-obligation revenue bonds, certificates of participation, or similar debt instruments that are issued by a state or local governmental entity with the objective of assisting the reporting entity in obtaining financing. While the conduit debt securities bear the name of the governmental authority issuer, the issuer is often not obligated for the repayment of the debt other than providing resources to the obligor under the terms of a separate lease or loan agreement. In addition, the conduit bond obligor is responsible for any future financial reporting requirements imposed as a condition of the issuance of the securities.*

FAS 157 emphasizes that fair value measurements are *not* to be made on an entity-specific basis. Therefore, a fair value measurement is expected to include all of the assumptions that market participants would use in pricing the asset or liability, and exclude factors specific to the reporting entity, if information is available that indicates that market participants would exclude those factors. Simply put, this means that fair value is what the market (if there is one) says an asset or liability is worth, absent unique features or interests that a given holder might bring to its use or satisfaction. FAS 157, applies to all fair value measurements called for under other GAAP except for (1) share-based payment transactions (FAS 123[R]), (2) fair value measurements that prescribe the use of vendor-specific objective evidence (VSOE) (e.g., multiple-deliverable arrangements under EITF 00-21, software revenue recognition under SOP 97-2) and, (3) inventory pricing.

Fair value measurements of assets are to reflect the "highest and best use" value which, depending on the circumstances, might involve an "in-use valuation premise or an "in-exchange valuation premise."

Market-derived prices are not permitted to be adjusted due to the quantity of the position held relative to the trading volume of the security. This is referred to as a "blockage factor" since it is derived from the size of the "block" of securities held by the reporting entity. Notably, this is the first time that GAAP has extended this requirement to fair value measurements made by entities subject to the specialized accounting requirements of the AICPA Audit and Accounting Guides for broker-dealers and investment companies.

Guidance is also provided regarding the consideration of the effects of restrictions associated with securities in determining their fair value.

If the carrying amount for trade receivables and payables approximates their fair values (which is normally the case), no disclosure is required.

If an estimate of fair value cannot be made without incurring excessive costs, management is to disclose

1. Information pertinent to estimating fair value such as carrying amount, effective interest rate, and maturities
2. The reasons why estimating fair value is not practicable

Chapter 6 provides comprehensive guidance on measuring and disclosing fair values of financial and nonfinancial instruments, when required or permitted by GAAP.

**Derivatives disclosures.** FAS 133 imposed new requirements for specific disclosures about derivative instruments and nonderivative instruments designated and qualifying as hedging instruments. FAS 161 has expanded these disclosures to ameliorate certain deficiencies noted by users of financial statements. Specifically required by FAS 133 were the objectives for holding or issuing the instruments, which have been modified by FAS 161, which requires that the objectives for using derivative instruments be disclosed in terms of underlying risk and accounting designation, which is deemed to better convey the purpose of derivative use in terms of the risks that the reporting entity is intending to manage. The purpose is to communicate with statement users the context needed to understand the objectives, the strategies for achieving them, the risk management policy and a description of items or transactions that are hedged for each of the following:

1. Fair value hedges;
2. Cash flow hedges;
3. Foreign currency net investment hedges; and
4. All other derivatives.

Derivative instruments not designated as hedges are to have the purpose of their activity disclosed. Qualitative disclosures concerning the use of derivative instruments are encouraged, particularly in a context of overall risk management strategies employed by the entity. The FASB also encourages disclosure of similar quantitative information about other non-derivative financial instruments or nonfinancial assets and liabilities related by activity to derivative instruments.

FAS 161 requires disclosing the fair values of derivative instruments and their gains and losses in a tabular format, which should provide a more complete picture of the location in the reporting entity's financial statements of both the derivative positions existing at period end and the effect of using derivatives during the reporting period. Also, disclosing information about credit-risk-related contingent features is expected to provide information on the potential effect on an entity's liquidity from using derivatives. FAS 161 requires—for the first time—cross-referencing within the footnotes, which should help users of financial statements locate important information about derivative instruments.

***Hedge disclosures.*** In addition to the above, for every reporting period for which a complete set of financial statements is issued, there are required disclosures by hedge type.

***Fair value hedges.*** For all designated and qualified instruments and the related hedged items that give rise to foreign currency transaction gains or losses under FAS 52, disclosure is required of the net gain or loss included in earnings, a description of where it is reported, and the amounts due to

1. Hedge ineffectiveness;
2. Components that were excluded from the assessment of effectiveness; and
3. Hedged firm commitments that no longer qualify as hedges.

***Cash flow hedges.*** For all designated and qualified instruments and the related hedged items in cash flow hedges, the following are disclosed:

1. The net gain or loss in earnings, a description of where it is reported, and the amounts due to

   a. Hedge ineffectiveness; and
   b. Components that were excluded from the assessment of effectiveness;

2. A description of events that will result in reclassification of amounts in accumulated other comprehensive income to earnings and the net amount expected to be reclassified during the next twelve months;
3. The maximum length of time of any cash flow hedges of forecasted transactions (excluding those relating to payment of variable interest on existing financial instruments); and
4. The amount reclassified from accumulated other comprehensive income into earnings because a cash flow hedge was discontinued due to it being probable that the original forecasted transactions would not occur.

FAS 161, in addition to the existing requirement for disclosures of information by accounting designation, requires that qualitative information be provided by *underlying risks*. The following illustrates the implementation of these qualitative requirements, including volume of activity, and also includes a nontabular presentation of the quantitative information about the hedged items in fair value hedges.

**Example of disclosure of objectives and strategies for using derivative instruments by underlying risk**

Utopia Company is exposed to certain risks relating to its ongoing business operations. The primary risks managed by using derivative instruments are commodity price risk and interest rate risk. Forward contracts on various commodities are entered into to manage the price risk associated with forecasted purchases of materials used in Utopia's manufacturing process. Interest rate swaps are entered into to manage interest rate risk associated with the Utopia's fixed-rate borrowings.

FAS 133 requires companies to recognize all derivative instruments as either assets or liabilities at fair value in the statement of financial position. In accordance with such requirements, Utopia designates commodity forward contracts as cash flow hedges of forecasted purchases of commodities and interest rate swaps as fair value hedges of fixed-rate borrowings.

**Cash flow hedges.** For derivative instruments that are designated and qualify as a cash flow hedge, the effective portion of the gain or loss on the derivative is reported as a component of other comprehensive income and reclassified into earnings in the same period or periods during which the hedged transaction affects earnings. Gains and losses on the derivative representing either hedge ineffectiveness or hedge components excluded from the assessment of effectiveness are recognized in current earnings.

As of December 31, 2009, Utopia had the following outstanding commodity forward contracts that were entered into hedge forecasted purchases:

| Commodity | Number of metric tons |
|---|---|
| Copper | 30,000 |
| Palladium | 6,000 |
| Nickel | 75,000 |

**Fair value hedges**. For derivative instruments that are designated and qualify as a fair value hedge, the gain or loss on the derivative as well as the offsetting loss or gain on the hedged item attributable to the hedged risk are recognized in current earnings.

Utopia includes the gain or loss on the hedged items (that is, fixed-rate borrowings) in the same line item—interest expense—as the offsetting loss or gain on the related interest rate swaps as follows:

| Income statement classification | Gain/loss on swaps | Gain/loss on borrowings |
|---|---|---|
| Interest expense | $350,000 | $(22,000) |

As of December 31, 2009, the total notional amount of the Utopia's receive-fixed/pay-variable interest rate swaps was $12.6 million.

**Example of disclosure in tabular format of fair value amounts, and gains and losses on derivative instruments and related hedged items**

*Tabular Disclosures of (a) Fair Values of Derivative Instruments in a Statement of Financial Position and (b) the Effect of Derivative Instruments on the Statement of Financial Performance*

**Fair Values of Derivative Instruments**

| *In millions of dollars* | *Asset Derivatives* | | | |
|---|---|---|---|---|
| As of December 31 | *2009* | | *2008* | |
| | *Balance sheet location* | *Fair value* | *Balance sheet location* | *Fair value* |
| **Derivatives designated as hedging instruments under FAS 133** | | | | |
| Interest rate contracts | Other assets | $xx,xxx | Other assets | $xx,xxx |
| Foreign exchange contracts | Other assets | xx,xxx | Other assets | xx,xxx |
| Equity contracts | Other assets | xx,xxx | Other assets | xx,xxx |
| Commodity contracts | Other assets | xx,xxx | Other assets | xx,xxx |
| Credit contracts | Other assets | xx,xxx | Other assets | xx,xxx |
| Other contracts | Other assets | xx,xxx | Other assets | xx,xxx |
| **Total derivatives designated as hedging instruments under FAS 133** | | $xx,xxx | | $xx,xxx |

| | Balance sheet location | Fair value | Balance sheet location | Fair value |
|---|---|---|---|---|
| **Derivatives not designated as hedging instruments under FAS 133** [a] | | | | |
| Interest rate contracts | Other assets | $xx,xxx | Other assets | $xx,xxx |
| Foreign exchange contracts | Other assets | xx,xxx | Other assets | xx,xxx |
| Equity contracts | Other assets | xx,xxx | Other assets | xx,xxx |
| Commodity contracts | Other assets | xx,xxx | Other assets | xx,xxx |
| Credit contracts | Other assets | xx,xxx | Other assets | xx,xxx |
| Other contracts | Other assets | xx,xxx | Other assets | xx,xxx |
| **Total derivatives not designated as hedging instruments under FAS 133** | | $xx,xxx | | $xx,xxx |
| **Total derivatives** | | $xx,xxx | | $xx,xxx |

| *In millions of dollars* *As of December 31* | *Liability Derivatives* | | | |
|---|---|---|---|---|
| | **2009** | | **2008** | |
| | *Balance sheet location* | *Fair value* | *Balance sheet location* | *Fair value* |
| **Derivatives designated as hedging instruments under FAS 133** | | | | |
| Interest rate contracts | Other liabilities | $xx,xxx | Other liabilities | $xx,xxx |
| Foreign exchange contracts | Other liabilities | xx,xxx | Other liabilities | xx,xxx |
| Equity contracts | Other liabilities | xx,xxx | Other liabilities | xx,xxx |
| Commodity contracts | Other liabilities | xx,xxx | Other liabilities | xx,xxx |
| Credit contracts | Other liabilities | xx,xxx | Other liabilities | xx,xxx |
| Other contracts | Other liabilities | xx,xxx | Other liabilities | xx,xxx |
| **Total derivatives designated as hedging instruments under FAS 133** | | $xx,xxx | | $xx,xxx |
| **Derivatives not designated as hedging instruments under FAS 133** [a] | | | | |
| Interest rate contracts | Other liabilities | $xx,xxx | Other liabilities | $xx,xxx |
| Foreign exchange contracts | Other liabilities | xx,xxx | Other liabilities | xx,xxx |
| Equity contracts | Other liabilities | xx,xxx | Other liabilities | xx,xxx |
| Commodity contracts | Other liabilities | xx,xxx | Other liabilities | xx,xxx |
| Credit contracts | Other liabilities | xx,xxx | Other liabilities | xx,xxx |
| Other contracts | Other liabilities | xx,xxx | Other liabilities | xx,xxx |
| **Total derivatives not designated as hedging instruments under FAS 133** | | $xx,xxx | | $xx,xxx |
| **Total derivatives** | | $xx,xxx | | $xx,xxx |

[a] *See footnote XX for additional information on the Utopia Company's purpose for entering into derivatives not designated as hedging instruments and its overall risk management strategies.*

**The Effect of Derivative Instruments on the Statement of Financial Performance for the Years Ended December 31, 2009 and 2008**

| *Derivatives in FAS 133 fair value hedging relationships* | *Location of gain or (loss) recognized in income on derivative* [a] | *Amount of gain or (loss) recognized in income on derivative* | |
|---|---|---|---|
| | | *2009* | *2008* |
| Interest rate contracts | Interest income/(expense) | $xx,xxx | $xx,xxx |
| Foreign exchange contracts | Foreign currency gain/(loss) | xx,xxx | xx,xxx |
| Equity contracts | Other income/ (expense) | xx,xxx | xx,xxx |
| Commodity contracts | Other income/(expense) | xx,xxx | xx,xxx |
| Credit derivatives | Other income/(expense) | xx,xxx | xx,xxx |
| Other contracts | Other income/(expense) | xx,xxx | xx,xxx |
| Total | | $xx,xxx | $xx,xxx |

| *Derivatives in FAS 133 cash flow hedging relationships* | *Amount of gain on (loss) recognized in OCI on derivative (effective portion)* | |
|---|---|---|
| | *2009* | *2008* |
| Interest rate contracts | $xx,xxx | $xx,xxx |
| Foreign exchange contracts | xx,xxx | xx,xxx |
| Equity contracts | xx,xxx | xx,xxx |
| Commodity contracts | xx,xxx | xx,xxx |
| Credit derivatives | xx,xxx | xx,xxx |
| Other contracts | xx,xxx | xx,xxx |
| Total | $xx,xxx | $xx,xxx |

| *Location of gain or (loss) reclassified from accumulated OCI into income (effective portion)* [a] | *Amount of gain or (loss) reclassified from accumulated OCI into income (effective portion)* | |
|---|---|---|
| | *2009* | *2008* |
| Interest income/(expense) | $xx,xxx | $xx,xxx |
| Sales/Revenue | xx,xxx | xx,xxx |
| Other Income/(expense) | xx,xxx | xx,xxx |
| Cost of sales | xx,xxx | xx,xxx |
| Other income/(expense) | xx,xxx | xx,xxx |
| Other income/(expense) | xx,xxx | xx,xxx |
| | $xx,xxx | $xx,xxx |

| *Location of gain or (loss) recognized in income on derivative (ineffective portion and amount excluded from effectiveness testing)* [a] | *Amount of gain or (loss) recognized in income on derivative (ineffective portion and amount excluded from effectiveness testing)* [d] | |
|---|---|---|
| | *2009* | *2008* |
| Other income/(expense) | $xx,xxx | $xx,xxx |
| Other income/(expense) | xx,xxx | xx,xxx |
| Other income/(expense) | xx,xxx | xx,xxx |
| Other income/(expense) | xx,xxx | xx,xxx |
| Other income/(expense) | xx,xxx | xx,xxx |
| Other income/(expense) | xx,xxx | xx,xxx |
| | $xx,xxx | $xx,xxx |

| *Derivatives in FAS 133 net investment hedging relationships* | *Amount of gain or (loss recognized in OCI on derivative (effective portion)* | |
|---|---|---|
| | *2009* | *2008* |
| Foreign exchange contracts | $xx,xxx | $xx,xxx |

| *Location of gain or (loss) reclassified from accumulated OCI into income (effective portion)* | *Amount of gain or (loss recognized in OCI on derivative (effective portion)* | |
|---|---|---|
| | *2009* | *2008* |
| Gain or (loss) on sale of subsidiary | $xx,xxx | $xx,xxx |

| *Location of gain or (loss) recognized in income on derivative (ineffective portion and amount excluded from effectiveness testing)* [a] | *Amount of gain or (loss) recognized in income on derivative (ineffective portion and amount excluded from effectiveness testing)* [d] | |
|---|---|---|
| | *2009* | *2008* |
| Other income/(expense) | $xx,xxx | $xx,xxx |

| *Derivatives not designated as hedging instruments under FAS 133* [b, c] | *Location of gain or (loss) recognized in income on derivative* [a] | *Amount of gain or (loss) recognized in income on derivative* | |
|---|---|---|---|
| | | *2009* | *2008* |
| Interest rate contracts | Other income/ (expense) | $xx,xxx | $xx,xxx |
| Foreign exchange contracts | Other income/ (expense) | xx,xxx | xx,xxx |
| Equity contracts | Other income/ (expense) | xx,xxx | xx,xxx |
| Commodity contracts | Other income/(expense) | xx,xxx | xx,xxx |
| Credit derivatives | Other income/(expense) | xx,xxx | xx,xxx |
| Other contracts | Other income/(expense) | xx,xxx | xx,xxx |
| Total | | $xx,xxx | $xx,xxx |

[a] *If gains and losses associated with a type of contract (for example, interest rate contracts) are displayed in multiple line items in the income statement, the entity is required to disclose the amount included in each line item.*

[b] *See footnote XX for additional information on the Utopia Company's purpose for entering into derivatives not designated as hedging instruments and its overall risk management strategies.*

[c] *For alternative disclosures about "trading derivatives," see separate table for trading activities in footnotes to the financial statements.*

[d] *The amount of gain or (loss) recognized in income represents $XXX related to the ineffective portion of the hedging relationships and $XXX related to the amount excluded from the assessment of hedge effectiveness.*

**Example of tabular disclosure of nondesignated/nonqualifying derivative instruments that are included in an entity's trading activity**

When the reporting entity elects the alternative disclosure for gains and losses on derivative instruments included in its trading activities, a format such as the following may be elected for use.

Note that many entities already include the required information about their trading activities in other disclosures within the financial statements, in which case it would now need to provide a cross-reference from the derivative footnote to other footnotes in which trading derivative-related information is included.

**The Effect of Trading Activities on the Statement of Financial Performance for the Years Ended December 31, 2009 and 2008**

| Type of Instrument | Trading Revenue | |
| --- | --- | --- |
| | 2009 | 2008 |
| Fixed income/interest rate | $xx,xxx | $xx,xxx |
| Foreign exchange | xx,xxx | xx,xxx |
| Equity | xx,xxx | xx,xxx |
| Commodity | xx,xxx | xx,xxx |
| Credit | xx,xxx | xx,xxx |
| Other | xx,xxx | xx,xxx |
| Total | $xx,xxx | $xx,xxx |

**Example of disclosure of contingent features in derivative instruments**

This example illustrates the disclosure of credit-risk-related contingent features in derivative instruments.

**Contingent Features**

Certain of Utopia Company's derivative instruments contain provisions that require Utopia's debt to maintain an investment grade credit rating from each of the major credit rating agencies. If Utopia's debt were to fall below investment grade, it would be in violation of these provisions, and the counterparties to the derivative instruments could request immediate payment or demand immediate and ongoing full overnight collateralization on derivative instruments in net liability positions.

The aggregate fair value of all derivative instruments with credit-risk-related contingent features that are in a liability position on December 31, 2009, is $XX million for which Utopia has posted collateral of $X million in the normal course of business. If the credit-risk-related contingent features underlying these agreements were triggered on December 31, 2009, Utopia would be required to post an additional $XX million of collateral to its counterparties.

***Foreign currency net investment hedges.*** For all such designated and qualified instruments that give rise to foreign currency transaction gains or losses under FAS 52, the net gain or loss that is included in the cumulative translation adjustment.

***Comprehensive income.*** The net gain or loss from cash flow hedges on derivative instruments reported in other comprehensive income must be shown as a separate classification. Accumulated other comprehensive income disclosures should show separately the following:

1. Beginning and ending accumulated derivative instrument gain or loss;
2. Net change from current period hedging transactions; and
3. Net amount of reclassifications to earnings.

# 9 INVENTORY

## PERSPECTIVE AND ISSUES

The accounting for inventories is a major consideration for many entities because of its significance to both the income statement (cost of goods sold) and the balance sheet (current assets). Inventories are defined in ARB 43, Chapter 4 as

*...those items of tangible personal property which are held for sale in the ordinary course of business, are in the process of production for such sale, or are to be currently consumed in the production of goods or services to be available for sale.*

The complexity of accounting for inventories arises from factors that include

1. The high volume of activity (or turnover) and the associated challenges of keeping accurate, up-to-date records.
2. Choosing from among various cost flow alternatives that are permitted by GAAP.
3. Ensuring compliance with complex US income tax laws and regulations when electing to use the last-in, first-out (LIFO) method.
4. Monitoring and properly accounting for adjustments necessitated by applying the lower of cost or market method to the inventory.

There are two types of entities for which the accounting for inventories is relevant. The merchandising entity (generally referred to as a retailer, dealer, or wholesaler/distributor) purchases inventory for resale to its customers. The manufacturer buys raw materials, and processes those raw materials using labor and equipment into finished goods that are then sold to its customers. While the production process is progressing, the costs of the raw materials, salaries and wages paid to the labor force (and related benefits), depreciation of the machinery, and an allocated portion of the manufacturer's overhead are accumulated by the accounting system as work in process (WIP). Finished goods inventory is the completed product which is on hand awaiting shipment or sale.

In the case of either type of entity we are concerned with answering the same basic questions.

1.  At what point in time should the items be included in inventory (ownership)?
2.  What costs incurred should be included in the valuation of inventories?
3.  What cost flow assumption should be used?
4.  At what value should inventories be reported (determination of the lower of cost or market, or LCM)?

ARB 43, Chapter 4, as amended by FAS 151, discusses the definition, valuation, and classification of inventory. APB 28 addresses the measurement and classification of inventories during interim periods. FAS 48 governs revenue recognition when the buyer has the right to return the product and is covered in depth in Chapter 10 of this book. FAS 49 addresses product financing arrangements. Finally, APB 29 (as amended by FAS 153) addresses exchanges of nonmonetary assets and is covered in Chapter 11.

| Sources of GAAP | | | | |
|---|---|---|---|---|
| *ARB* | *APB* | *FAS* | *EITF* | *PB* |
| 43, Ch. 4 | 20, 28, 29 | 48, 49, 151, 153 | 86-46, 04-6, 04-13 | 2 |

## DEFINITIONS OF TERMS

**Base stock.** Based on the theory that a minimal level of inventory is a permanent investment, the amount maintained indefinitely on the balance sheet at its historical cost.

**Ceiling.** In lower of cost or market (LCM) computations, market (replacement cost, as defined below) cannot be higher than the ceiling (net realizable value, as defined below).

**Consignments.** A marketing method in which the consignor ships goods to the consignee, who acts as an agent for the consignor in selling the goods. The inventory remains the property of the consignor until sold by the consignee.

**Cost.** The accumulated amount of expenditures and charges incurred directly or indirectly to acquire and/or produce items of inventory and to move them to the location from which they will be sold or held for sale.

**Direct (variable) costing.** This method includes only variable manufacturing costs in the cost of ending finished goods inventory. This method is not acceptable for financial reporting or income tax purposes.

**Dollar-value LIFO.** A variation of conventional LIFO in which layers of inventory are priced in dollars adjusted by price indices instead of being priced at unit prices.

**Double-extension.** A method used to compute the LIFO conversion price index. The index indicates the relationship between the base-year and current prices in terms of a percentage.

**Finished goods.** A manufacturer's completed but unsold products.

**First-in, first-out (FIFO).** A cost flow assumption; the first goods purchased or produced are assumed to be the first goods sold.

**Floor.** In lower of cost or market computations, market is limited to net realizable value less a normal profit, called the floor. Market (replacement cost) cannot be below the floor.

**Full absorption (full costing).** In accordance with GAAP, this method includes all direct and indirect manufacturing costs (fixed and variable) in the cost of finished goods inventory.

**Goods in transit.** Merchandise that is in the process of being shipped from seller to buyer and that is en route at a particular point in time.

**Gross profit.** The result of subtracting cost of sales from net sales. Also referred to as "gross margin."

**Gross profit method.** A method used in interim periods to estimate the amount of ending inventory based on the cost of goods available for sale, sales, and the expected gross profit percentage.

**Inventory.** Those items of tangible personal property that are (1) held for sale in the normal course of business (finished goods), (2) in the process of being produced for that purpose (work in process), or (3) to be used in the production of such items (raw materials).

**Inventory layer.** Under the LIFO method, an increase in inventory quantity during a period.

**Last-in, first-out (LIFO).** A cost flow assumption; the last goods purchased are assumed to be the first goods sold.

**LIFO conformity rule.** A statutory requirement that, in the US, if the LIFO method is used for income tax purposes, it must also be used for financial reporting purposes.

**LIFO liquidation.** The permanent elimination of all or part of the LIFO base or old inventory layers when inventory quantities decrease. This inventory decrement can distort gross profit, operating income, and net income since old costs are being reflected in cost of goods sold and matched against current revenues.

**LIFO reserve.** The difference, at a specified date, between inventory valued using LIFO and inventory valued using the method the company uses for internal management or reporting purposes.

**LIFO retail.** An inventory costing method which combines the LIFO cost flow assumption and the retail inventory method.

**Link-chain.** A method of applying dollar-value LIFO by developing a single cumulative index. This method may be used instead of double-extension only when there are substantial changes in product lines over the years.

**Lower of cost or market.** Inventories are required to be valued at the lower of cost or market. Market is generally considered to be replacement cost; however, for the purpose of this computation, market is not permitted to exceed the ceiling (net realizable value) or be less than the floor (net realizable value less a normal markup).

**Markdown.** A decrease in selling price below original retail price.

**Markdown cancellation.** An increase in selling price after a markdown that does not adjust the selling price to an amount that exceeds the original retail price.

**Markup.** An increase in selling price above original retail price.

**Markup cancellation.** A decrease in selling price after a markup to an amount that is not below the original retail price.

**Moving or weighted-average.** An inventory costing method used in conjunction with a perpetual inventory system. A weighted-average cost per unit is recomputed after every purchase. Cost of goods sold is recorded at the most recent moving average cost.

**Net realizable value.** The selling price of an item, less selling costs and costs to complete.

**Parking transaction.** An arrangement which attempts to remove inventory and a current liability from the balance sheet. See **product financing arrangement**.

**Periodic inventory system.** An inventory system where actual quantities are determined and recorded inventories adjusted as a result of a physical count taken at set intervals.

**Perpetual inventory system.** An inventory system where records of inventory quantities are maintained and updated as transactions occur.

**Product financing arrangement.** An arrangement whereby a firm buys inventory for another firm which agrees to purchase the inventory over a certain period at specified prices which include handling and financing costs.

**Purchase commitment.** A noncancelable commitment to purchase goods. Losses on such commitments are recognized when the contract price exceeds fair value, even if this occurs prior to delivery.

**Raw materials.** For a manufacturing firm, materials on hand awaiting entry into the production process.

**Replacement cost.** The cost to reproduce an inventory item by purchase or manufacture. In lower of cost or market computations, the term market means replacement cost, subject to the ceiling and floor limitations defined above.

**Retail method.** An inventory costing method that uses a cost ratio to reduce ending inventory valued at retail to cost.

**Shrinkage.** The situation arising when the number of units of an inventory item physically counted at a point in time is less than the number of units purported to be on hand according to the enterprise's perpetual inventory records. Shrinkage can result from a combination of theft, spoilage, and errors in the perpetual records.

**Specific identification.** An inventory system where the seller identifies which specific items are sold and which remain in ending inventory.

**Standard costs.** Predetermined unit costs, which are acceptable for financial reporting purposes if adjusted periodically to reflect current conditions and if their use approximates the results that would be obtained by applying one of the recognized cost flow assumptions.

**Weighted-average.** An inventory costing method where ending inventory and cost of goods sold are priced at the weighted-average cost of all items available for sale.

**Work in process (WIP).** For a manufacturing firm, the inventory of partially completed products.

## CONCEPTS, RULES, AND EXAMPLES

### Ownership of Goods

Generally, in order to obtain an accurate measurement of inventory quantity, it is necessary to determine when title legally passes between buyer and seller. The exception to this general rule arises from situations when the buyer assumes the significant risks of ownership of the goods prior to taking title and/or physical possession of the goods. Substance over form in this case would dictate that the inventory is an asset of the buyer and not the seller, and that a purchase and sale of the goods be recognized by the parties irrespective of the party that holds legal title.

The most common error made in this area is to assume that an entity has title only to the goods it physically holds. This may be incorrect in two ways: (1) goods held may not be owned, and (2) goods that are not held may be owned. Four issues affect the determination of ownership: (1) goods in transit, (2) consignment arrangements, (3) product financing arrangements, and (4) sales made with the buyer having the right of return.

**Goods in transit.** At year-end, any goods in transit from seller to buyer must be included in one of those parties' inventories based on the conditions of the sale. Such goods are included in the inventory of the firm financially responsible for transportation costs. This responsibility may be indicated by shipping acronyms such as FOB, which is used in overland shipping contracts, or FAS, CIF, C&F, and ex-ship, which are used in maritime contracts.

The term FOB is an abbreviation of "free on board." If goods are shipped FOB destination, transportation costs are paid by the seller and title does not pass until the carrier delivers the goods to the buyer. These goods are part of the seller's inventory while in transit. If goods are shipped FOB shipping point, transportation costs are paid by the buyer and title passes when the carrier takes possession of the goods. These goods are part of the buyer's inventory while in transit. The terms FOB destination and FOB shipping point often indicate a specific location at which title to the goods is transferred, such as FOB Cleveland. This means that the seller retains title and risk of loss until the goods are delivered to a common carrier in Cleveland who will act as an agent for the buyer. The rationale for these determinations originates in agency law, since transfer of title is conditioned upon whether the carrier with physical possession of the goods is acting as an agent of the seller or the buyer.

A seller who ships FAS (free alongside) must bear all expense and risk involved in delivering the goods to the dock next to (alongside) the vessel on which they are to be shipped. The buyer bears the costs of loading and shipment. Title passes when the carrier, as agent for the buyer, takes possession of the goods.

In a CIF (cost, insurance, and freight) contract the buyer agrees to pay in a lump sum the cost of the goods, insurance costs, and freight charges. In a C&F (cost and freight) contract, the buyer promises to pay a lump sum that includes the cost of the goods and all freight charges. In either case, the seller must deliver the goods to the buyer's agent/carrier and pay the costs of loading. Both title and risk of loss pass to the buyer upon delivery of the goods to the carrier.

A seller who delivers goods ex-ship bears all expense and risk until the goods are unloaded, at which time both title and risk of loss pass to the buyer.

### Examples of goods in transit

The Meridian Vacuum Company is located in Santa Fe, New Mexico, and obtains compressors from a supplier in Hong Kong. The standard delivery terms are free alongside (FAS) a container ship in Hong Kong harbor, so that Meridian takes legal title to the delivery once possession of the goods is taken by the carrier's dockside employees for the purpose of loading the goods on board the ship. When the supplier delivers goods with an invoiced value of $120,000 to the wharf, it e-mails an advance shipping notice (ASN) and invoice to Meridian via an electronic data interchange (EDI) transaction, itemizing the contents of the delivery. Meridian's computer system receives the EDI transmission, notes the FAS terms in the supplier file, and therefore automatically logs it into the company computer system with the following entry:

| | | |
|---|---|---|
| Inventory | 120,000 | |
| Accounts payable | | 120,000 |

The goods are assigned an "In Transit" location code in Meridian's perpetual inventory system. When the compressor eventually arrives at Meridian's receiving dock, the receiving staff records a change in inventory location code from "In Transit" to a code designating a physical location within the warehouse.

Meridian's secondary compressor supplier is located in Vancouver, British Columbia, and ships overland using free on board (FOB) Santa Fe terms, so the supplier retains title until the shipment arrives at Meridian's location. This supplier also issues an advance shipping notice by EDI to inform Meridian of the estimated arrival date, but in this case Meridian's computer system notes the FOB Santa Fe terms, and makes no entry to record the transaction until the goods arrive at Meridian's receiving dock.

**Consignment arrangements.** In consignment arrangements, the consignor ships goods to the consignee, who acts as the agent of the consignor in trying to sell the goods. In some consignments, the consignee receives a commission and is, in effect, acting as an agent of the consignor. In other arrangements, the consignee "purchases" the goods simultaneously with the sale of the goods to the customer. Goods on consignment are included in the inventory of the consignor and excluded from the inventory of the consignee.

### Example of a consignment arrangement

The Portable Handset Company (PHC) ships a consignment of its cordless phones to a retail outlet of the Consignee Corporation. PHC's cost of the consigned goods is $3,700. PHC shifts the inventory cost into a separate inventory account to track the physical location of the goods. The entry follows:

|                             |       |       |
|-----------------------------|-------|-------|
| Consignment out inventory   | 3,700 |       |
|     Finished goods inventory |       | 3,700 |

A third-party shipping company ships the cordless phone inventory from PHC to Consignee. Upon receipt of an invoice for this $550 shipping expense, PHC charges the cost to consignment inventory with the following entry:

|                           |     |     |
|---------------------------|-----|-----|
| Consignment out inventory | 550 |     |
|     Accounts payable |     | 550 |

*To record the cost of shipping goods from the factory to Consignee*

Consignee sells half the consigned inventory during the month for $2,750 in credit card payments, and earns a 22% commission on these sales, totaling $605. According to the consignment arrangement, PHC must also reimburse Consignee for the 2% credit card processing fee, which is $55 ($2,750 × 2%). The results of this sale are summarized as follows:

| | |
|---|---:|
| Sales price to Consignee's customer earned on behalf of PHC | $2,750 |
| Less: Amounts due to Consignee in accordance with arrangement | |
|     22% sales commission | (605) |
|     Reimbursement for credit card processing fee | (55) |
| | (660) |
| Due to PHC | $2,090 |

Upon receipt of the monthly sales report from Consignee, PHC records the following entries:

|                      |       |       |
|----------------------|-------|-------|
| Accounts receivable  | 2,090 |       |
| Cost of goods sold   | 55    |       |
| Commission expense   | 605   |       |
|     Sales |       | 2,750 |

*To record the sale made by Consignee acting as agent of PHC, the commission earned by Consignee and the credit card fee reimbursement earned by Consignee in connection with the sale*

|                           |       |       |
|---------------------------|-------|-------|
| Costs of goods sold       | 2,125 |       |
|     Consignment out inventory |       | 2,125 |

*To transfer the related inventory cost to cost of goods sold, including half the original inventory cost and half the cost of the shipment to consignee [($3,700 + $550 = $4,250) × ½ = $2,125]*

**Product financing arrangements.** FAS 49 addresses the issues involved with product financing arrangements. A product financing arrangement is a transaction in which an entity (referred to as the "Sponsor") simultaneously sells and agrees to repurchase inventory to and from a financing entity. The repurchase price is contractually fixed at an amount equal to the original sales price plus the financing entity's carrying and financing costs. The purpose of the transaction is to enable the sponsor enterprise to arrange financing of its original purchase of the inventory. The various steps involved in the transaction are illustrated by the diagram below.

1. In the initial transaction the sponsor "sells" inventoriable items to the financing entity in return for the remittance of the sales price and at the same time agrees to repurchase the inventory at a specified price (usually the sales price plus carrying and financing costs) over a specified period of time.
2. The financing entity borrows from a bank (or other financial institution) using the newly purchased inventory as collateral.
3. The financing entity remits the proceeds of its borrowing to the sponsor and the sponsor presumably uses these funds to pay off the debt incurred as a result of the original purchase.
4. The sponsor then, over a period of time as funds become available, repurchases the inventory from the financing entity for the specified price plus carrying and financing costs.

FASB ruled that the substance of this transaction is that of a borrowing transaction, not a sale. That is, the transaction is, in substance, no different from the sponsor directly obtaining third-party financing to purchase inventory. FAS 49 specifies that the proper accounting by the sponsor is to record a liability in the amount of the selling price when the funds are received from the financing entity in exchange for the initial transfer of the inventory. The sponsor proceeds to accrue carrying and financing costs in accordance with its normal accounting policies. These accruals are eliminated and the liability satisfied when the sponsor repurchases the inventory. The inventory is not removed from the balance sheet of the sponsor and a sale is not recorded. Thus, although legal title has passed to the financing entity, for purposes of measuring and valuing inventory, the inventory is considered to be owned by the sponsor.

### Example of a product financing arrangement

The Medieval Illumination Company (MIC) has borrowed the maximum amount it has available under its short-term line of credit. MIC obtains additional financing by selling $280,000 of its candle inventory to a third party financing entity. The third party obtains a bank loan at 6% interest to pay for its purchase of the candle inventory, while charging MIC 8% interest and $1,500 per month to store the candle inventory at a public storage facility. As MIC obtains candle orders, it purchases inventory back from the third party, which in turn authorizes the public warehouse to drop ship the orders directly to MIC's customers at a cost of $35 per order. Since this is a product financing arrangement, MIC cannot remove the candle inventory from its accounting records or record revenue from sale of its inventory to the third party. Instead, the following entry records the initial financing arrangement:

| | | |
|---|---|---|
| Cash | 280,000 | |
| Short-term debt | | 280,000 |

After one month, MIC records accrued interest of $1,867 ($280,000 × 8% interest × 1/12 year) on the loan, as well as the monthly storage fee of $1,500, as shown in the following entry:

| | | |
|---|---|---|
| Interest expense | 1,867 | |
| Storage expense | 1,500 | |
| Accrued interest | | 1,867 |
| Accounts payable | | 1,500 |

On the first day of the succeeding month, MIC receives a prepaid customer order for $3,800. The margin on the order is 40% and, therefore, the related inventory cost is $2,280. MIC pays the third party $2,280 to buy back the required inventory as well as $35 to the public storage facility to ship the order to the customer, and records the following entries:

| Short-term debt | 2,280 | |
| Cash | | 2,280 |
| *To repurchase inventory from the third-party financing entity* | | |
| | | |
| Cash | 3,800 | |
| Sales | | 3,800 |
| *To record the sale to the customer* | | |
| | | |
| Cost of goods sold | 2,280 | |
| Inventory | | 2,280 |
| *To record the cost of the sale to the customer* | | |
| | | |
| Freight out | 35 | |
| Accounts payable | | 35 |
| *To record the cost of fulfilling the order* | | |

FAS 49 identifies variations of the terms of the above arrangement that also meet the criteria for being accounted for as product financing arrangements.

1.  The third-party financing entity purchases the inventory directly from the sponsor's supplier (instead of from the sponsor) with a simultaneous agreement to sell the inventory to the sponsor.
2.  The sponsor enters into an agreement with a third-party financing entity to control the disposition of product that has been purchased by the third party either from the sponsor or from the sponsor's supplier.

**Sales made with the buyer having the right of return.** Another issue requiring special consideration exists when a buyer is granted a right of return, as defined by FAS 48. The seller must consider the propriety of recognizing revenue at the point of sale under such a situation (this topic is discussed in detail in Chapter 10). The sale is recorded only when six specified conditions are met including the condition that the future amount of returns can be reasonably estimated by the seller. If a reasonable estimate cannot be made, then the sale is not recorded until the earlier of the expiration date of the return privilege or the date when all six conditions are met. Similar to product financing costs, this situation results in the seller continuing to include the goods in its measurement and valuation of inventory even though legal title has passed to the buyer.

## Accounting for Inventories

A major objective of accounting for inventories is the matching of appropriate costs to the period in which the related revenues are earned in order to properly compute gross profit, also referred to as gross margin. Inventories are recorded in the accounting records using either a periodic or perpetual system.

In a periodic inventory system, inventory quantities are determined by physical count. The quantity of each item counted is then priced using the cost flow assumption that the enterprise had adopted as its accounting policy for that type of inventory. Cost of goods sold is computed by adding beginning inventory and net purchases (or cost of goods manufactured) and subtracting ending inventory.

Alternatively, a perpetual inventory system keeps a running total of the quantity (and possibly the cost) of inventory on hand by maintaining subsidiary inventory records that reflect all sales and purchases as they occur. When inventory is purchased, inventory (rather than purchases) is debited. When inventory is sold, the cost of goods sold and corresponding reduction of inventory are recorded.

Using a periodic inventory system necessitates the taking of physical inventory counts to determine the quantity of inventory on hand at the end of a reporting period. In order to facilitate accurate annual financial statements, in practice physical counts are performed at least annually on the last day of the fiscal year.

If the enterprise maintains a perpetual inventory system, it must regularly and systematically verify the accuracy of its perpetual records by physically counting inventories and comparing the quantities on hand with the perpetual records. GAAP does not provide explicit requirements regarding the timing and frequency of physical counts necessary to verify the perpetual records; however there is a US income tax requirement (IRC§471[b][1]) that a taxpayer perform "...a physical count of inventories at each location on a regular and consistent basis...." The purpose of this requirement is to enable the taxpayer to support any tax deductions taken for inventory shrinkage if it elects not to take a complete physical inventory at all locations on the last day of the fiscal year. The IRS, in its Rev. Proc. 98-29, provided a "retail safe harbor method" that permits retailers to deduct estimated shrinkage where the retailer takes physical inventories at each location at least annually.

## Valuation of Inventories

The primary basis of accounting for inventories is cost. Cost is defined in ARB 43, Chapter 4, as the sum of the applicable expenditures and charges directly or indirectly incurred in bringing an article to its existing condition and location.

This definition allows for a wide interpretation of the costs to be included in inventory.

**Raw materials and merchandise inventory.** For raw materials and merchandise inventory which are purchased outright, the identification of cost is relatively straightforward. The cost of these purchased inventories will include all expenditures incurred in bringing the goods to the point of sale and converting them to a salable condition. These costs include the purchase price, transportation costs (freight-in), insurance while in transit, and handling costs charged by the supplier.

### Example of recording raw material costs

Aruba Bungee Cords, Inc. (ABC) purchases rubber bands, a raw material that it uses in manufacturing its signature product. The company typically receives delivery of all its raw materials and uses them in manufacturing its finished products during the winter, and then sells its stock of finished goods in the spring. The supplier invoice for a January delivery of rubber bands includes the following line items:

| | |
|---|---:|
| Rubber band (1,681 pounds at $3 per pound) | $5,043 |
| Shipping and handling | 125 |
| Shipping insurance | 48 |
| Sales tax | 193 |
| Total | $5,409 |

Since ABC is using the rubber bands as raw materials in a product that it resells, it will not pay the sales tax. However, both the shipping and handling charge and the shipping insurance are required for ongoing product acquisition, and so are included in the following entry to record receipt of the goods:

| | | |
|---|---|---|
| Inventory raw materials | 5,216 | |
| Accounts payable | | 5,216 |

*To record purchase of rubber bands and related costs ($5,043 + $125 + $48)*

On February 1, ABC purchases a $5,000, two-month shipping insurance policy (paradoxically, this type of policy is sometimes referred to as "inland marine" coverage) that applies to all incoming supplier deliveries for the remainder of the winter production season, allowing it to refuse shipping insurance charges on individual deliveries. Since the policy insures all inbound raw materials deliveries (not just rubber bands), it is too time-consuming to charge the cost of this policy to individual raw material deliveries using specific identification, and accordingly, the controller can estimate a flat charge per delivery based on the number of expected deliveries during the two-month term of the insurance policy as follows:

$5,000 insurance premium + 200 expected deliveries during the policy term = $25 per delivery and then charge each delivery with $25 as follows:

| | | |
|---|---|---|
| Inventory—raw materials | 25 | |
| Prepaid insurance | | 25 |

*To allocate cost of inland marine coverage to inbound insured raw materials shipments*

In this case, however, the controller determined that shipments are expected to occur evenly during the two-month policy period and therefore will simply make a monthly standard journal entry as follows:

| | | |
|---|---|---|
| Inventory—raw materials | 2,500 | |
| Prepaid insurance | | 2,500 |

*To amortize premium on inland marine policy using the straight-line method*

Note that the controller must be careful, under either scenario, to ensure that perpetual inventory records appropriately track unit costs of raw materials to include the cost of shipping insurance. Failure to do so would result in an understatement of the cost of raw materials inventory on hand at the end of any accounting period.

Purchases can be recorded at their gross amount or net of any allowable discount. If recorded gross, the discounts taken represent a reduction in the purchase cost for purposes of determining cost of goods sold. On the other hand, if they are recorded net, any lost discounts are treated as a financial expense, not as cost of goods sold. The net method is considered to be theoretically preferable, but the gross method is simpler and, thus, more commonly used. Either method is acceptable under GAAP, provided that it is consistently applied.

***Inventory exchanges.*** Some enterprises enter into transactions to acquire inventory by exchanging items of their inventory with the supplier. For exchange transactions occurring in fiscal periods beginning on or before June 15, 2005, APB 29 specified that the exchange be evaluated as to whether it resulted in the "culmination of an earning process." If for example, the inventory items exchanged were products held for sale in the ordinary course of the same line of business in order to facilitate sales to customers of either of the exchanging parties (or both), then the exchange itself did not constitute the culmination of an earning process. Consequently, no profit or loss would have been recognized as a result of the exchange transaction and the acquired items would have been recorded at the book value of the items given up.

Exchange transactions occurring in fiscal periods beginning after June 15, 2005, are subject to the amendments to APB 29 that were made by FAS 153, *Exchanges of Nonmonetary Assets.* FAS 153 eliminates the "culmination of an earning process" criteria and replaces it with a test of commercial substance. However, the new standard retains the accounting treatment described above for exchange transactions whose purpose is to facilitate sales to customers that are not a party to the exchange. In part, promulgation of FAS 153 was stimulated by the desire to converge with corresponding practice under International Financial Reporting Standards, under which nonmonetary exchanges are generally accounted for at fair values, with gain or loss recognized currently, and so-called "book value swaps" are rarely justified. (See Chapter 11.)

***Inventory purchases and sales with the same counterparty.*** Some enterprises sell inventory to another party from which they also acquire inventory in the same line of business. EITF 04-13 states that such situations should be considered to be a single transaction when there is a legal requirement for an inventory transfer between the parties to be offset by another inventory transfer, irrespective of the use of separate invoices and cash settlements for each individual transaction. The following conditions are indicators that offsetting inventory transactions should be treated as a single transaction, even in the absence of a legal requirement for offsetting inventory transfers.

- There is a specific legal right by both parties to offset their payment and receivable obligations to each other.
- Inventory purchases and sales between the counterparties are simultaneous.
- Inventory purchases and sales between the counterparties are at off-market prices.
- There is a strong likelihood that the counterparties will engage in reciprocal inventory transactions.

**Example of counterparty inventory transfers**

The Recording Artists Equipment Company (RAEC) maintains an inventory of microphones, preamplifiers, and related recording equipment for its professional musician clientele, while the Podcaster Supply Company (PSC) stocks mixer hardware and software for its customers. The two companies enter into an agreement whereby RAEC ships excess quantities of its microphone and preamplifier inventory to PSC for sale by PSC to its customers, while PSC may ship an equivalent value of its mixers to RAEC for sale by RAEC to its customers. Historically, PSC has always delivered an equivalent quantity of mixers to RAEC. Each transaction is separately documented and settled in cash at wholesale prices. These transfers should be treated as a single transaction, since there is a strong likelihood that reciprocal inventory transfers will occur, and because RAEC is obligated to accept inventory transfers from PSC that are of an equivalent value to its shipments to PSC.

***Inventory hedges.*** One notable exception to recording inventories at cost is provided by the hedge accounting requirements of FAS 133. If inventory has been designated as the hedged item in a fair value hedge, changes in the fair value of the hedged inventory are recognized on the balance sheet as they occur, with the offsetting charge or credit recognized currently in earnings. Hedging is discussed in detail in Chapter 8.

**Manufacturing inventories.** Inventory cost in a manufacturing enterprise is to include both acquisition and production costs. This concept is commonly referred to as full absorption or full costing. As a result, the WIP and finished goods inventories include direct materials, direct labor, and an appropriately allocated portion of indirect production costs referred to as indirect overhead.

Under full absorption costing, indirect overhead costs—costs that are incidental to and necessary for production—are allocated to goods produced and, to the extent those goods are uncompleted or unsold at the end of a period, are included in ending WIP or finished goods inventory, respectively. Indirect overhead costs include such costs as

- Depreciation and cost depletion
- Repairs
- Maintenance
- Factory rent and utilities
- Indirect labor
- Normal rework labor, scrap, and spoilage
- Production supervisory wages
- Indirect materials and supplies
- Quality control and inspection
- Small tools not capitalized

Indirect overhead is comprised of two elements, variable and fixed overhead. FAS 151 clarifies that variable overhead is to be allocated to work-in-process and finished goods based on the actual usage of the production facilities. Fixed overhead, however, is to be allocated to work-in-process and finished goods based on the normal expected capacity of the enterprise's production facilities with the overhead rate recomputed in instances when actual production exceeds the normal capacity. Initially, this may appear to be an inconsistent accounting method; however, the use of this convention ensures that the inventory is not recorded at an amount in excess of its actual cost as illustrated in the following example:

## Example of allocating fixed overhead to units produced

Brewed Refreshment Plant, Inc. (BRP), located in Washington, D.C., has historically produced between 3,200 and 3,800 barrels of beer annually with its average production approximating 3,500 barrels. This average takes into account its normal number of work shifts and the normal operation of its machinery adjusted for downtime for normal maintenance and recalibration. BRP's average capacity and overhead costs (partial list) are presented below.

| | | |
|---|---|---|
| (a) Normal expected annual productive capacity | | <u>3,500</u> barrels |
| Fixed overhead costs (partial list): | | |
| Depreciation of machinery | $600 | |
| Factory rent | 800 | |
| Plant superintendent | <u>80</u> | |
| (b) Total fixed overhead to allocate | <u>$1,480</u> | |
| (c) Fixed overhead rate per barrel produced (b. ÷ a.) | $ <u>0.4229</u> per barrel | |

*Scenario 1:* The Washington Nationals major-league baseball team outperforms expectations; since BRP's beer is sold at the Nationals' stadium, BRP substantially increases production beyond the normal level expected.

| | |
|---|---|
| Actual production level | <u>4,500</u> barrels |

If BRP were to apply fixed overhead using the rate based on its normal productive capacity, the calculation would be as follows:

4,500 barrels produced × $0.4229 per barrel = $1,903 of overhead applied

This would result in an over-allocation of $423, the difference between the $1,903 of overhead applied and the $1,480 of overhead actually incurred. This violates the lower of cost or market principle since the inventory would be valued at an amount that exceeded its actual cost. Therefore, BRP applied FAS 151 and recomputed its fixed overhead rate as follows:

1,480 fixed overhead incurred ÷ Revised production level of 4,500 barrels = $0.3289 per barrel

*Scenario 2:* The Washington Nationals experience a cold, rainy summer and worse-than-expected attendance. If production lags expectations and BRP only produces 2,500 barrels of beer, the original overhead rate is not revised. The fixed overhead is allocated as follows:

2,500 barrels produced × $0.4229 per barrel = $1,057 of overhead applied

Per FAS 151, when production levels decline below the original expectation, the fixed overhead rate is not recomputed. The $423 difference between the $1,480 of actual fixed overhead incurred and the $1,057 of overhead applied is accounted for as an expense in the period incurred.

For the purpose of determining normal productive capacity, it is expected that capacity will vary from period to period based on enterprise-specific or industry-specific experience. Management is to formulate a judgment regarding a reasonable range of normal production levels expected to be achieved under normal operating conditions.

The enterprise may incur unusually large expenses resulting from idle facilities, excessive waste, spoilage, freight, or handling costs. FAS 151 clarifies that when this situation occurs, the abnormal portion of these expenses is to be treated as a cost of the period incurred and not to be allocated to inventory.

Generally, interest costs incurred during the production of inventory are not capitalized under FAS 34. A complete discussion regarding the capitalization of interest costs is provided in Chapter 11.

Selling costs do not constitute production costs. General and administrative expenses are typically not allocated to production. However, there may be circumstances in which certain general and administrative expenses are related to the production process and are therefore allocable to the WIP and finished goods inventories.

### Example of variable and fixed overhead allocation

The InCase Manufacturing Company (IMC) uses injection molding to create two types of plastic CD cases—regular size and mini, on a seven-day, three-shift production schedule. During the current month, it records the following overhead expenses:

| | | | |
|---|---|---|---|
| Depreciation of machinery | $232,000 | Rent | $36,000 |
| Indirect labor | 208,000 | Repairs | 12,000 |
| Indirect materials | 58,000 | Small tools | 28,000 |
| Maintenance | 117,000 | Scrap and spoilage | 49,000 |
| Production supervisory wages | 229,000 | Utilities | 37,000 |
| Quality control | 82,000 | | |

IMC's controller analyzed scrap and spoilage statistics and determined that abnormal losses of $32,000 were incurred due to a bad batch of plastic resin pellets. She adjusted scrap and spoilage expense by charging the cost of those pellets to cost of goods sold during the current period, resulting in a reduced scrap and spoilage expense of $17,000. Also, the rent cost includes a $6,000 lease termination penalty payable to the lessor of a vacant factory. Since this cost is considered an exit or disposal activity under FAS 146, it does not benefit production and is therefore charged directly to expense in the current period.

For allocation purposes, IMC's controller elects to group the adjusted overhead expenses into two cost pools. Pool #1 contains all expenses related to machinery operation, which includes depreciation, indirect labor, indirect materials, maintenance, rent, repairs, small tools, and utilities. Pool #2 contains all expenses related to production runs, which includes production supervisory wages, quality control, scrap, and spoilage. The following three journal entries record (1) the recognition of excess scrap and unused facilities in the current period, (2) the allocation of costs to the machinery cost pool, and (3) the allocation of costs to the production runs cost pool:

| | | |
|---|---|---|
| Cost of goods sold expense | 38,000 | |
|     Scrap and spoilage expense | | 32,000 |
|     Rent expense | | 6,000 |
| | | |
| Overhead pool #1—Machinery operation | 722,000 | |
|     Depreciation | | 232,000 |
|     Indirect labor | | 208,000 |
|     Indirect materials | | 58,000 |
|     Maintenance | | 117,000 |
|     Rent | | 30,000 |
|     Repairs | | 12,000 |
|     Small tools | | 28,000 |
|     Utilities | | 37,000 |
| | | |
| Overhead pool #2—Production runs | 328,000 | |
|     Production supervisory wages | | 229,000 |
|     Quality control | | 82,000 |
|     Scrap and spoilage | | 17,000 |

Since the costs in overhead pool #1 are centered on machine usage, the controller elects to use the total operating hours used for the production of each product as the allocation basis for that pool. The accumulated production hours by machine for the past month are as follows:

| *Machinery type* | *Regular CD production hours* | *Mini CD production hours* |
|---|---|---|
| 50-ton press | 0 | 710 |
| 55-ton press | 310 | 290 |
| 70-ton press | 480 | 230 |
| 85-ton press | 690 | 0 |
| Total hours | 1,480 | 1,230 |
| Percentage of total hours | 55% | 45% |

Since the costs in overhead pool #2 are centered on production volume, the controller decides to use the total pounds of plastic resin pellets used for production during the month as the allocation basis for that cost pool. The total plastic resin usage, adjusted for spoilage, was 114,000 pounds of resin for the regular CD cases and 76,000 pounds for the mini CD cases, which is a percentage split of 60% for regular CD cases and 40% for mini CD cases.

With the calculation of allocation bases completed, the split of overhead costs between the two products follows:

|  | *Total costs in pool* | *55% regular CD allocation* | *45% mini CD allocation* |
|---|---|---|---|
| Overhead pool #1 | 722,000 | 397,100 | 324,900 |

|  | *Total costs in pool* | *60% regular CD allocation* | *40% mini CD allocation* |
|---|---|---|---|
| Overhead pool #2 | 328,000 | 196,800 | 131,200 |

Thus, the total overhead allocated to regular CD cases is $593,900 (397,100 + 196,800), while the total overhead allocated to mini CD cases is $456,100 (324,900 + 131,200). Of the case quantities produced, 85% of the regular CD cases and 70% of the mini CD cases were sold during the month, with the remainder being transferred into finished goods inventory. IMC's controller uses these percentages to apportion the cost of allocated overhead between the cost of goods sold and finished goods inventory, as shown in the following entry:

| | | |
|---|---|---|
| Cost of goods sold–regular CD cases | 504,815 | |
| Cost of goods sold–mini CD cases | 319,270 | |
| Finished goods inventory–regular CD cases | 89,085 | |
| Finished goods inventory–mini CD cases | 136,830 | |
|     Overhead pool #1–Machinery operation | | 722,000 |
|     Overhead pool #2–Production runs | | 328,000 |

**Determining inventory cost.** The theoretical basis for valuing inventories and cost of goods sold requires assigning production and/or acquisition costs to the specific goods to which they relate. This method of inventory valuation is usually referred to as specific identification. Specific identification is generally not practical as the product will generally lose its separate identity as it passes through the production and sales process. Exceptions to this would arise in situations involving small inventory quantities with high unit value and low turnover rate such as automobiles or heavy machinery. Because of the limited applicability of specific identification, it is necessary to make certain assumptions regarding the cost flows associated with inventory. Although these cost flow assumptions are used for accounting purposes, they may or may not reflect the actual physical flow of the inventory.

**Cost flow assumptions.** The most common cost flow assumptions used are specified in ARB 43, Chapter 4: (1) first-in, first-out (FIFO), (2) last-in, first-out (LIFO), and (3) weighted-average. Additionally, there are variations in the application of each of these assumptions which are commonly used in practice.

In selecting which cost flow assumption to adopt as its accounting policy for a particular type of industry, management should consider a variety of factors. First, the industry norm should be examined as this will facilitate intercompany comparison by financial statement users. The appropriateness of using a particular cost flow assumption will vary depending on the nature of the industry and the expected economic climate. The appropriate method in a period of rising prices differs from the method that is appropriate for a period of declining prices. Each of the foregoing assumptions and their relative advantages or disadvantages are discussed below. Examples are provided to enhance understanding of the application.

**First-in, first-out (FIFO).** The FIFO method of inventory valuation assumes that the first goods purchased are the first goods used or sold, regardless of the actual physical flow. This method is thought to most closely parallel the physical flow of the units in most industries. The strength of this cost flow assumption lies in the inventory amount reported on the balance sheet. Because the earliest goods purchased are the first ones removed from the inventory account, the remaining balance is composed of items priced at more recent cost. This yields results similar to those obtained under current cost accounting on the balance sheet. However, the FIFO method does not necessarily reflect the most accurate income figure as older, historical costs are being charged to cost of goods sold and matched against current revenues.

The following example illustrates the basic principles involved in the application of FIFO:

|  | Units available | Units sold | Actual unit cost | Actual total cost |
|---|---|---|---|---|
| Beginning inventory | 100 | -- | $2.10 | $210 |
| Sale | -- | 75 | -- | -- |
| Purchase | 150 | -- | 2.80 | 420 |
| Sale | -- | 100 | -- | -- |
| Purchase | 50 | -- | 3.00 | 150 |
| Total | 300 | 175 |  | $780 |

Given this data, the cost of goods sold and ending inventory balance are determined as follows:

|  | Units | Unit cost | Total cost |
|---|---|---|---|
| Cost of goods sold | 100 | $2.10 | $210 |
|  | 75 | 2.80 | 210 |
|  | 175 |  | 420 |
| Ending inventory | 50 | 3.00 | 150 |
|  | 75 | 2.80 | 210 |
|  | 125 |  | 360 |
| Totals | 300 |  | $780 |

Notice that the total of the units in cost of goods sold and ending inventory, as well as the sum of their total costs, is equal to the goods available for sale and their respective total costs.

The FIFO method provides the same results under either the periodic or perpetual inventory tracking system.

**Last-in, first-out (LIFO).** The LIFO method of inventory valuation assumes that the last goods purchased are the first goods used or sold. This allows the matching of current costs with current revenues and provides the best measure of gross profit. However, unless costs remain relatively unchanged over time, the LIFO method will usually misstate the ending inventory balance sheet amount because LIFO inventory usually includes costs of acquiring or manufacturing inventory that were incurred in earlier periods. LIFO does not usually follow the physical flow of merchandise or materials. However, the matching of physical flow with cost flow is not an objective of accounting for inventories.

LIFO accounting is actually an income tax concept. Consequently, the rules regarding the application of the LIFO method are not set forth in US GAAP, but rather, are found in the US Internal Revenue Code (IRC) §472. US Treasury regulations provide that any taxpayer that maintains inventories may select LIFO application for any or all inventoriable items. This election is made with the taxpayer's income tax return on Form 970 after the close of the first tax year that the taxpayer intends to use (or expand the use of) the LIFO method. Partial adoption of LIFO is allowed for both accounting and income tax purposes.

The quantity of ending inventory on hand at the beginning of the year of election is termed the "base layer." This inventory is valued at actual (full absorption) cost, and unit cost for each inventory item is determined by dividing total cost by the quantity on hand. At the end of the initial and subsequent years, increases in the quantity of inventory on hand are referred to as increments, or LIFO layers. These increments are valued individually by applying one of the following costing methods to the quantity of inventory representing a layer:

1.   The actual cost of the goods most recently purchased or produced
2.   The actual cost of the goods purchased or produced in order of acquisition
3.   An average unit cost of all goods purchased or produced during the current year

4. A hybrid method that more clearly reflects income (for income tax purposes, this method must meet with the approval of the IRS Commissioner)

Thus, after using the LIFO method for five years, it is possible that an enterprise could have ending inventory consisting of the base layer and five additional layers (or increments) provided that the quantity of ending inventory increased every year.

The single goods (unit) LIFO approach is illustrated in the following example:

Rose Co. is in its first year of operation and elects to use the periodic LIFO method of inventory valuation. The company sells only one product. Rose applies the LIFO method using the order of current year acquisition cost. The following data are given for years 1 through 3:

| | | Units | | | Purchase cost | |
| | Beginning | | | Ending | | |
| Year 1 | inventory | Purchased | Sold | inventory | Unit cost | Total cost |
|---|---|---|---|---|---|---|
| Purchase | | 200 | | | $2.00 | $400 |
| Sale | | | 100 | | -- | -- |
| Purchase | | 200 | | | 3.00 | 600 |
| Sale | | | 150 | | -- | -- |
| | -- | 400 | 250 | 150 | | |
| | | | | | | |
| Year 2 | | | | | | |
| Purchase | | 300 | | | $3.20 | $960 |
| Sale | | | 200 | | -- | -- |
| Purchase | | 100 | | | 3.30 | 330 |
| | 150 | 400 | 200 | 350 | | |
| | | | | | | |
| Year 3 | | | | | | |
| Purchase | | 100 | | | $3.50 | $350 |
| Sale | | | 200 | | -- | -- |
| Sale | | | 100 | | -- | -- |
| | 350 | 100 | 300 | 150 | | |

In year 1 the following occurred:

1. The total goods available for sale were 400 units.
2. The total sales were 250 units.
3. Therefore, the ending inventory was 150 units.

The ending inventory is valued at the earliest current year acquisition cost of $2.00 per unit. Thus, ending inventory is valued at $300 (150 × $2.00).

Another way to look at this is to analyze both cost of goods sold and ending inventory.

| | Units | Unit cost | Total cost |
|---|---|---|---|
| Cost of goods sold | 200 | $3.00 | $600 |
| | 50 | 2.00 | 100 |
| | 250 | | $700 |
| Ending inventory | 150 | 2.00 | $300 |

Note that the base-year cost is $2.00 and that the base-year level is 150 units. Therefore, if ending inventory in the subsequent period exceeds 150 units, a new layer (or increment) will be created.

| Year 2 | Units | Unit cost | Total cost | |
|---|---|---|---|---|
| Cost of goods sold | 100 | $3.30 | $330 | |
| | 100 | 3.20 | 320 | |
| | 200 | | $650 | |
| Ending inventory | 150 | 2.00 | $300 | Base-year layer |
| | 200 | 3.20 | 640 | Year 2 increment |
| | 350 | | $940 | |

If ending inventory exceeds 350 units in the next period, a third layer (increment) will be created.

| *Year 3* | *Units* | *Unit cost* | *Total cost* | |
|---|---|---|---|---|
| Cost of goods sold | 100 | $3.50 | $350 | |
| | 200 | 3.20 | 640 | |
| | 300 | | $990 | |
| Ending inventory | 150 | 2.00 | $300 | Base-year layer |

Notice how the decrease (decrement) of 200 units in year 3 eliminated the entire year 2 increment. Thus, any year 4 increase in the quantity of inventory would result in a **new** increment which would be valued at year 4 prices.

In situations where the ending inventory decreases from the level established at the close of the preceding year, the enterprise experiences a decrement or LIFO liquidation. Decrements reduce or eliminate previously established LIFO layers. Once any part of a LIFO layer has been eliminated, it cannot be reinstated after year-end. For example, if in its first year after the election of LIFO an enterprise establishes a LIFO layer (increment) of ten units, then in the next year inventory decreases by four units leaving the first layer at six units, the enterprise is not permitted in any succeeding year to increase the number of units in the first year layer back up to the original ten units. The quantity in the first layer remains at a maximum of six units subject to further reduction if decrements occur in future years. Any unit increases in future years will create one or more new layers. The effect of LIFO liquidations in periods of rising prices is to transfer, from ending inventory into cost of goods sold, costs that are below the current cost being paid. Thus, the resultant effect of a LIFO liquidation is to increase income for both accounting and income tax purposes. Because of this, LIFO is most commonly used by companies in industries in which levels of inventories are consistently maintained or increased over time.

LIFO liquidations can be either voluntary or involuntary. A voluntary liquidation occurs when an enterprise deliberately lets its inventory levels drop. Voluntary liquidations may be desirable for a number of reasons. Management might consider the current price of purchasing the goods to be too high, a smaller quantity of inventory might be needed for efficient production due to conversion to a "just-in-time" production model, or inventory items may have become obsolete due to new technology or transitions in the enterprise's product lines.

Involuntary LIFO liquidations stem from reasons beyond the control of management, such as a strike, material shortages, shipping delays, etc. Whether voluntary or involuntary, all LIFO liquidations result in a corresponding increase in income in periods of rising prices.

To determine the effect of the liquidation, management must compute the difference between actual cost of sales and what cost of sales would have been had the inventory been reinstated. The Internal Revenue Service has ruled that this hypothetical reinstatement must be computed under the company's normal pricing procedures for valuing its LIFO increments. In the above example the effect of the year 3 LIFO liquidation would be computed as follows:

Hypothetical inventory reinstatement

$$200 \text{ units @ } \$3.50 - \$3.20 = \$60$$

Hypothetically, if there had been an increment instead of a decrement in year 3 and the year 2 inventory layer had remained intact, 200 more units (out of the 300 total units sold in year 3) would have been charged to cost of goods sold at the year 3 price of $3.50 instead of the year 2 price of $3.20. Therefore, the difference between $3.50 and the actual amount charged to cost of sales for these 200 units liquidated ($3.20) measures the effect of the liquidation.

The following is considered acceptable GAAP disclosure in the event of a LIFO liquidation:

> During 2009, inventory quantities were reduced below their levels at December 31, 2008. As a result of this reduction, LIFO inventory costs computed based on lower prior years' acquisition costs were charged to cost of goods sold. If this LIFO liquidation had not occurred and cost of sales had been computed based on the cost of 2009 purchases, cost of goods sold would have increased by approximately $xxx and net income decreased by approximately $xx or $x per share.

Applying the unit LIFO method requires a substantial amount of recordkeeping. The recordkeeping becomes more burdensome as the number of products increases. For this reason a "pooling" approach is often used to compute LIFO inventories.

Pooling is the process of grouping items which are naturally related and then treating this group as a single unit in determining LIFO cost. Because the ending inventory normally includes many items, decreases in one item can be offset by increases in others, whereas under the unit LIFO approach a decrease in any one item results in a liquidation of all or a portion of a LIFO layer.

Complexity in applying the pooling method arises from the income tax regulations. These regulations require that the opening and closing inventories of each type of good be compared. In order to be considered comparable for this purpose, inventory items must be similar as to character, quality, and price. This qualification has generally been interpreted to mean identical. The effect of this interpretation is to require a separate pool for each item under the unit LIFO method. To provide a simpler, more practical approach to applying LIFO and allow for increased use of LIFO pools, election of the dollar-value LIFO method is permitted.

***Dollar-value LIFO.*** Dollar-value LIFO may be elected by any taxpayer. Under the dollar-value LIFO method of inventory valuation, the cost of inventories is computed by expressing base-year costs in terms of total dollars rather than specific prices of specific units. The dollar-value method also provides an expanded interpretation of the use of LIFO pools. Increments and decrements are treated the same as under the unit LIFO approach but are reflected only in terms of a *net* increment or liquidation for the entire pool.

***Identifying pools.*** Three alternatives exist for determining pools under dollar-value LIFO: (1) the natural business unit method, (2) the multiple pooling method, and (3) pools for wholesalers, retailers, jobbers, etc.

The natural business unit is defined by the existence of separate and distinct processing facilities and operations and the maintenance of separate income (loss) records. The concept of the natural business unit is generally dependent upon the type of product being produced, not the various stages of production for that product. Thus, the pool of a manufacturer can (and will) contain raw materials, WIP, and finished goods. The three examples below, adapted from the treasury regulations, illustrate the application of the natural business unit concept.

**Example 1**

A corporation manufactures, in one division, automatic clothes washers and dryers of both commercial and domestic grade as well as electric ranges and dishwashers. The corporation manufactures, in another division, radios and television sets. The manufacturing facilities and processes used in manufacturing the radios and television sets are distinct from those used in manufacturing the automatic clothes washers, etc. Under these circumstances, an enterprise consisting of two business units and two pools would be appropriate: one consisting of all of the LIFO inventories involved with the manufacture of clothes washers and dryers, electric ranges and dishwashers and the other consisting of all the LIFO inventories involved with the production of radios and television sets.

**Example 2**

A taxpayer produces plastics in one of its plants. Substantial amounts of the production are sold as plastics. The remainder of the production is shipped to a second plant of the taxpayer for the production of plastic toys which are sold to customers. The taxpayer operates its plastics plant and toy plant as separate divisions. Because of the different product lines and the separate divisions, the taxpayer has two natural business units.

**Example 3**

A taxpayer is engaged in the manufacture of paper. At one stage of processing, uncoated paper is produced. Substantial amounts of uncoated paper are sold at this stage of processing. The remainder of the uncoated paper is transferred to the taxpayer's finishing mill where coated paper is produced and sold. This taxpayer has only one natural business unit since coated and uncoated paper are within the same product line.

The treasury regulations require that a pool consist of all items entering into the entire inventory investment of a natural business unit, unless the taxpayer elects to use the multiple-pooling method.

The multiple-pooling method is the grouping of "substantially similar" items. In determining substantially similar items, consideration is given to the processing applied, the interchangeability, the similarity of use, and the customary practice of the industry. While the election of multiple pools will necessitate additional recordkeeping, it may result in a better estimation of gross profit and periodic net income.

According to Reg. §1.472-8(c), inventory items of wholesalers, retailers, jobbers, and distributors are to be assigned to pools by major lines, types, or classes of goods. The natural business unit method may be used with permission of the Commissioner.

All three methods of pooling allow for a change in the components of inventory over time. New items which properly fall within the pool may be added, and old items may disappear from the pool, but neither will necessarily cause a change in the total dollar value of the pool.

***Computing dollar-value LIFO.*** The purpose of the dollar-value LIFO method of valuing inventory is to convert inventory priced at end-of-year prices to that same quantity of inventory priced at base-year (or applicable LIFO layer) prices. The dollar-value method achieves this result through the use of a conversion price index. The inventory computed at current year cost is divided by the appropriate index to arrive at its base-year cost. The main computational focus is on the determination of the conversion price index. There are four types of methods that can be used in the computation of the ending inventory amount of a dollar-value LIFO pool: (1) double-extension, (2) link-chain, (3) indexing, and (4) alternative LIFO for automobile dealers.

***Double-extension method.*** This method was originally developed to compute the conversion price index. It involves extending the entire quantity of ending inventory for the current year at both base-year prices and end-of-year prices to arrive at a total dollar value for each, hence the title "double-extension." The dollar total computed at end-of-year prices is then divided by the dollar total computed at base-year prices to arrive at the index, usually referred to as the conversion price index. This index indicates the relationship between the base-year and current prices in terms of a percentage. Each layer (or increment) is valued at its own percentage. Although a representative sample is allowed (meaning that not all of the items need to be double-extended; this is discussed in more detail under indexing), the recordkeeping under this method is very burdensome. The base-year price must be maintained for each inventory item. Depending upon the number of different items included in the inventory of the enterprise, the necessary records may be too detailed to keep past the first year or two.

The following example illustrates the double-extension method of computing the LIFO value of inventory. The example presented is relatively simple and does not attempt to incorporate all of the complexities of LIFO inventory accounting.

### Example

Isaacson, Inc. uses the dollar-value method of LIFO inventory valuation and computes its price index using the double-extension method. Isaacson has a single pool which contains two inventory items, A and B. Year 1 is the company's initial year of operations. The following information is given for years 1 through 4:

| | Ending inventory | Ending quantity (units) and current unit price | | | |
|---|---|---|---|---|---|
| | *current prices* | *A* | | *B* | |
| *Year* | | | | | |
| 1 | $100,000 | 5,000 | $6.00 | 7,000 | $10.00 |
| 2 | 120,300 | 6,000 | 6.30 | 7,500 | 11.00 |
| 3 | 122,220 | 5,800 | 6.40 | 7,400 | 11.50 |
| 4 | 133,900 | 6,200 | 6.50 | 7,800 | 12.00 |

In year 1 there is no computation of an index; the index is 100%. The LIFO cost is the same as the actual current year cost. This is the base year.

In year 2 the first step is to double-extend the quantity of ending inventory at base-year and current year costs.

| *Item* | *Quantity* | Base-year *cost/unit* | *Extended* | Current year *cost/unit* | *Extended* |
|---|---|---|---|---|---|
| A | 6,000 | $ 6.00 | $ 36,000 | $ 6.30 | $ 37,800 |
| B | 7,500 | 10.00 | 75,000 | 11.00 | 82,500 |
| | | | $111,000 | | $ 120,300* |

* *When using the double-extension method and extending **all** of the inventory items to arrive at the index, this number must equal the ending inventory at current prices. If a sampling method is used (as discussed under indexing), this number **divided by** your ending inventory at current prices is the percentage sampled.*

Now we can compute the conversion price index which is

$$\frac{\text{Ending inventory at current year prices}}{\text{Ending inventory at base-year prices}}$$

In this case  $\dfrac{120,300}{111,000} = 108.4\%$ (rounded)

Next, compute the year 2 layer at base-year cost by taking the current year-ending inventory at base-year prices (if you only extend a sample of the inventory, this number is arrived at by dividing the ending inventory at current year prices by the conversion price index) of $111,000 and subtracting the base-year cost of $100,000. In year 2 we have an increment (layer) of $11,000 valued at base-year costs.

The year 2 layer of $11,000 at base-year cost must be converted so that the layer is valued at the prices in effect when it came into existence (i.e., at year 2 prices). This is done by multiplying the increment at base-year cost ($11,000) by the rounded conversion price index (1.084). The result is the year 2 layer at LIFO prices.

| | |
|---|---|
| Base-year layer | $100,000 |
| Year 2 layer ($11,000 × 1.084) | 11,924 |
| | $111,924 |

In year 3 the same basic procedure is followed.

| *Item* | *Quantity* | Base-year *cost/unit* | *Extended* | Current year *cost/unit* | *Extended* |
|---|---|---|---|---|---|
| A | 5,800 | $ 6.00 | $ 34,800 | $ 6.40 | $ 37,120 |
| B | 7,400 | 10.00 | 74,000 | 11.50 | 85,100 |
| | | | $108,800 | | $122,220 |

There has been a decrease in the base-year cost of the ending inventory ($111,000 −$108,800 = $2,200) which is referred to as a decrement. A decrement results in the decrease (or elimination) of previously provided layers. In this situation, the computation of the index is not necessary as there is no LIFO layer that requires a valuation. If a sampling approach has been used, the index is needed to arrive at the ending inventory at base-year cost and thus determine if there has been an increment or decrement.

Now the ending inventory at base-year cost is $108,800. The base-year cost layer is still intact at $100,000, so the cumulative increment is $8,800. Since this is less than the $11,000 increment of year 2, no additional increment is established in year 3. The LIFO cost of the inventory is shown below.

| | |
|---|---|
| Base-year layer | $100,000 |
| Year 2 layer ($8,800 × 1.084) | 9,539 |
| | $109,539 |

The fourth year then follows the same steps.

| | | Base-year | | Current year | |
|---|---|---|---|---|---|
| *Items* | *Quantity* | *cost/unit* | *Extended* | *cost/unit* | *Extended* |
| A | 6,200 | $ 6.00 | $ 37,200 | $ 6.50 | $ 40,300 |
| B | 7,800 | 10.00 | 78,000 | 12.00 | 93,600 |
| | | | $115,200 | | $133,900 |

The conversion price index is 116.2% (133,900/115,200).

A current year increment exists because the ending inventory at base-year prices in year 4 of $115,200 exceeds the year 3 number of $108,800. The current year increment of $6,400 must be valued at year 4 prices. Thus, the LIFO cost of the year 4 inventory is

| | |
|---|---|
| Base-year layer | $100,000 |
| Year 2 layer ($8,800 × 1.084) | 9,539 |
| Year 4 layer ($6,400 × 1.162) | 7,437 |
| | $116,976 |

It is important to point out that once a layer is reduced or eliminated it is never reinstated (as with the year-2 increment) after year-end.

***Link-chain method.*** Since the double-extension method computations are arduous even if only a few items exist in the inventory, consider the complexity that arises when there is a constant change in the inventory mix or when there is a large number of inventory items. The link-chain method of applying dollar-value LIFO was developed to mitigate the effects of this complexity.

Consider the situation where the components of inventory are constantly changing. The regulations require that any new products added to the inventory be recorded at base-year prices. If these are not available, then the earliest cost available after the base year is used. If the item was not in existence in the base year, the taxpayer may reconstruct the base cost, using a reasonable method to determine what the cost would have been if the item had been in existence in the base year. Finally, as a last resort, the current year purchase price can be used. While this does not appear to be a problem on the surface, imagine a base period which is twenty-five to fifty years in the past. The difficulty involved with finding the base-year cost may require using a more current cost, thus eliminating some of the LIFO benefit. Imagine a situation faced by a company in a "hi-tech" industry where inventory is continually being replaced by newer, more advanced products. The effect of this rapid change under the double-extension method (because the new products did not exist in the base period) is to use current prices as base-year costs. When inventory has such a rapid turnover, the overall LIFO advantage becomes diluted as current and base-year costs are often identical. This situation necessitated the development of the link-chain method.

The link-chain method was originally developed for (and limited to) those companies that wanted to use LIFO but, because of a substantial change in product lines over time, were unable to reconstruct or maintain the historical records necessary to make accurate use of the double extension method. It is important to note that the double-extension and link-chain methods are not elective alternatives for the same situation. For income tax purposes, the link-chain election requires that substantial changes in product lines be evident over the years, and may not be elected solely because of its ease of application. The double-extension and index methods must be demonstrably impractical in order to elect the link-chain method. However, an enterprise may use different computational techniques for financial reporting and income tax purposes. Therefore, the link-chain method could be used for financial reporting purposes even if a different application is used for income tax purposes. Obviously, the recordkeeping burdens imposed by using different LIFO methods for GAAP and income tax purposes (including the deferred income tax accounting that would be required for the temporary difference between the GAAP and income tax bases of the LIFO inventories) would make this a highly unlikely scenario.

The link-chain method is the process of developing a single cumulative index which is applied to the ending inventory amount priced using beginning-of-the-year costs. Thus, the index computed at the end of each year is "linked" to the index from all previous years. A separate cumulative index is used for each pool regardless of the variations in the components of these pools over the years. Technological change is accommodated by the method used to calculate each current year's index. The index is calculated by double-extending a representative sample of items in the pool at both beginning-of-year prices and end-of-year prices. This annual index is then applied to (multiplied by) the previous period's cumulative index to arrive at the new current year cumulative index.

An example of the link-chain method is shown below. The end-of-year costs and inventory quantities used are the same as those used in the double-extension example.

Assume the following inventory data for years 1-4 for Dickler Distributors, Inc. Year 1 is assumed to be the initial year of operation for the company. The LIFO method is elected on the first income tax return. Assume that A and B constitute a single pool.

| | *Ending inventory* | *Cost per unit* | | *Extension* | |
| *Product* | *quantity* | *Beg. of yr.* | *End of yr.* | *Beginning* | *End* |
| Year 1 | | | | | |
| A | 5,000 | N/A | $ 6.00 | N/A | $ 30,000 |
| B | 7,000 | N/A | 10.00 | N/A | 70,000 |
| | | | | | $100,000 |
| Year 2 | | | | | |
| A | 6,000 | $ 6.00 | 6.30 | $ 36,000 | $ 37,800 |
| B | 7,500 | 10.00 | 11.00 | 75,000 | 82,500 |
| | | | | $111,000 | $120,300 |
| Year 3 | | | | | |
| A | 5,800 | 6.30 | 6.40 | $ 36,540 | $ 37,120 |
| B | 7,400 | 11.00 | 11.50 | 81,400 | 85,100 |
| | | | | $117,940 | $122,220 |
| Year 4 | | | | | |
| A | 6,200 | 6.40 | 6.50 | $ 39,680 | $ 40,300 |
| B | 7,800 | 11.50 | 12.00 | 89,700 | 93,600 |
| | | | | $129,380 | $133,900 |

The initial year (base year) does not require the computation of an index under any LIFO method. The base-year index will always be 1.00.

Thus, the base-year inventory layer is $100,000 (the end-of-year inventory stated at base-year cost). The second year requires the first index computation. Notice that in year 2 our extended totals are

| *Product* | *Beginning-of-year prices* | *End-of-year prices* |
| A | $ 6,000 | $ 37,800 |
| B | 75,000 | 82,500 |
| | $ 111,000 | $ 120,300 |

The year 2 index is 1.084 (120,300/111,000). This is the same as computed under the double-extension method because the beginning-of-the-year prices reflect the base-year price. This will not always be the case, as sometimes new items may be added to the pool, causing a change in the index. Thus, the cumulative index is the 1.084 current year index multiplied by the preceding year index of 1.00 to arrive at a link-chain index of 1.084.

This index is then used to restate the inventory to base-year cost by dividing the inventory at end-of-year prices by the cumulative index: $120,300/1.084 = $111,000. The determination of the LIFO increment or decrement is then basically the same as the double-extension method. In year 2 the increment (layer) at base-year cost is $11,000 ($111,000 – 100,000). This layer must be valued at the prices effective when the layer was created, or extended at the cumulative index for that year. This results in an ending inventory at LIFO cost of

|  | *Base-year cost* | *Index* | *LIFO cost* |
|---|---|---|---|
| Base-year layer | $100,000 | 1.000 | $100,000 |
| Year 2 layer | 11,000 | 1.084 | 11,924 |
|  | $111,000 |  | $111,924 |

The index for year 3 is computed as follows:

|  | *Beginning-of-year prices* | *End-of-year prices* |
|---|---|---|
| A | $ 36,540 | $ 37,120 |
| B | 81,400 | 85,100 |
|  | $117,940 | $122,220 |

$$122,220/117,940 = 1.036$$

The next step is to determine the cumulative index which is the product of the preceding year's cumulative index and the current year index, or 1.123 (1.084 × 1.036). The new cumulative index is used to restate the inventory at end-of-year dollars to base-year cost. This is accomplished by dividing the end-of-year inventory by the new cumulative index. Thus, current inventory at base-year cost is $108,833 ($122,220 ÷ 1.123). In this instance we have experienced a decrement (a decrease from the prior year's $111,000). The determination of ending inventory is

|  | *Base-year cost* | *Index* | *LIFO cost* |
|---|---|---|---|
| Base-year layer | $100,000 | 1.000 | $100,000 |
| Year 2 layer | 8,833 | 1.084 | 9,575 |
| Year 3 layer | -- | 1.123 | -- |
|  | $108,833 |  | $109,575 |

Finally, the same steps are performed for the year 4 computation. The current year index is 1.035 (133,900/129,380). The new cumulative index is 1.162 (1.035 × 1.123). The base-year cost of the current inventory is $115,232 (133,900/1.162). Thus, LIFO inventory at the end of year 4 is

|  | *Base-year cost* | *Index* | *LIFO cost* |
|---|---|---|---|
| Base-year layer | $100,000 | 1.000 | $100,000 |
| Year 2 layer | 8,833 | 1.084 | 9,575 |
| Year 3 layer | -- | 1.123 | -- |
| Year 4 layer | 6,399 | 1.162 | 7,435 |
|  | $115,232 |  | $117,010 |

Notice how even though the numbers used were the same as those used in the double-extension example, the results were different (year 4 inventory under double-extension was $116,976), however, not by a significant amount. It is much easier to keep track of beginning-of-the-year prices than base-year prices, but perhaps more importantly, it is easier to establish beginning-of-the-year prices for new items than to establish their base-year price. This latter reason is why the link-chain method is so much more desirable than the double-extension method. However, before electing or applying this method, a company must be able to establish a sufficient need as defined in the treasury regulations.

***Indexing methods.*** Indexing methods can basically be broken down into two types: (1) an internal index and (2) an external index.

The internal index is merely a variation of the double-extension method. The regulations allow for the use of a statistically valid representative sample of the inventory to be double-extended. The index computed from the sample is then used to restate the inventory to base-year cost and to value the new layer.

The external index method, referred to in treasury regulations as the Inventory Price Index Computation (IPIC) Method, involves using indices published by the US Department of Labor's Bureau of Labor Statistics (BLS)[1] and applying them to specified categories of inventory included in the taxpayer's LIFO pools.

*Alternative LIFO method for automobile dealers.* Beginning in 1992, a simplified dollar-value method became available for use by retail automobile dealers for valuing inventory of new automobiles and light-duty trucks. The use of this method and its acceptance for income tax purposes is conditioned on the application of several LIFO submethods, definitions and special rules. The reader is referred to Rev. Proc. 92-79 for a further discussion of this method.

*LIFO accounting literature.* GAAP for the application of LIFO has been based upon income tax rules rather than on financial accounting pronouncements. LIFO is cited in GAAP as an acceptable inventory method but specific rules regarding its implementation are not provided. The income tax regulations, as discussed below, do provide specific rules for the implementation of LIFO and require financial statement conformity. For this reason, income tax rules have essentially defined the financial accounting treatment of LIFO inventories. In recognition of the lack of authoritative accounting guidelines in the implementation of LIFO, the AICPA's Accounting Standards Division formed a task force on LIFO inventory problems to prepare an Issues Paper on this topic. "Identification and Discussion of Certain Financial Accounting and Reporting Issues Concerning LIFO Inventories," issued in 1984, identifies financial accounting issues resulting from the use of LIFO and includes advisory guidance on resolving them. Issues Papers, however, do not establish authoritative standards of financial accounting. The guidance provided by the task force is described below.

1. **Specific goods vs. dollar-value.** Either the specific goods approach or dollar-value approach to LIFO is acceptable for financial reporting. Disclosure of whether the specific goods or dollar-value approach is used is not required.

2. **Pricing current year purchases.** Three approaches to pricing LIFO inventory increments are available under income tax regulations—earliest acquisition price, latest acquisition price, and average acquisition price. The earliest acquisition price approach is the most compatible with financial reporting objectives, but all three are acceptable for financial reporting.

3. **Quantity to use to determine price.** The price used to determine the inventory increment should be based on the cost of the quantity or dollars of the increment rather than on the cost of the quantity or dollars equal to the ending inventory. Disclosure of which approach is used is not required.

4. **Disclosure of LIFO reserve or replacement cost.** The LIFO reserve or replacement cost and its basis for determination should be disclosed for financial reporting.

5. **Partial adoption of LIFO.** If a company changes to LIFO, it should do so for all of its inventories. Partial adoption should only be allowed if there exists a valid business reason for not fully adopting LIFO. A planned gradual adoption of LIFO over several time periods is considered acceptable if valid business reasons exist (lessening the income statement effect of adoption in any one year is not a valid

---

[1] *For more information see http://www.bls.gov*

business reason). Where partial adoption of LIFO has been justified, the extent to which LIFO has been adopted should be disclosed. This can be disclosed by indicating either the portion of the ending inventory priced on LIFO or the portion of cost of sales resulting from LIFO inventories.

6. **Methods of pooling.** An entity should have valid business reasons for establishing its LIFO pools. Additionally, the existence of a separate legal entity that has no economic substance is not reason enough to justify separate pools. Disclosure of details regarding an entity's pooling arrangements is not required.

7. **New items entering a pool.** New items should be added to a pool based on what the items would have cost had they been acquired in the base period (reconstructed cost) rather than based on their current cost. The reconstructed cost should be determined based on the most objective sources available including published vendor price lists, vendor quotes, and general industry indexes. Where necessary, the use of a substitute base year in making the LIFO computation is acceptable. Disclosure of the way that new items are priced is not required.

8. **Dollar-value index.** The required index can be developed using two possible approaches, the unit cost method or the cost component method. The unit cost method measures changes in the index based on the weighted-average increase or decrease in the unit costs of raw materials, work in process, and finished goods inventory. The cost component method, on the other hand, measures changes in the index by the weighted-average increase or decrease in the component costs of material, labor, and overhead that make up ending inventory. Either of these methods is acceptable.

9. **LIFO liquidations.** The effects on income of LIFO inventory liquidations should be disclosed in the notes to the financial statements. A replacement reserve for the liquidation should not be provided. When an involuntary LIFO liquidation occurs, the effect on income of the liquidation should not be deferred.

   When a LIFO liquidation occurs, there are three possible ways to measure its effect on income.

   a. The difference between actual cost of sales and what cost of sales would have been had the inventory been reinstated under the entity's normal pricing procedure

   b. The difference between actual cost of sales and what cost of sales would have been had the inventory been reinstated at year-end replacement cost

   c. The amount of the LIFO reserve at the beginning of the year which was credited to income (excluding the increase in the reserve due to current year price changes)

   The first method is considered preferable. Disclosure of the effect of the liquidation should give effect only to pools with decrements (i.e., there should be no netting of pools with decrements against other pools with increments).

10. **Lower of cost or market.** The most reasonable approach to applying the lower of cost or market rules to LIFO inventory is to base the determination on groups of inventory rather than on an item-by-item approach. A pool constitutes a reasonable grouping for this purpose. An item-by-item approach is permitted by authoritative accounting literature, particularly for obsolete or discontinued items.

   For companies with more than one LIFO pool, it is permissible to aggregate the pools in applying the lower of cost or market test if the pools are similar. Where the pools are significantly dissimilar, aggregating the pools is not appropriate.

   Previous write-downs to market value of the cost of LIFO inventories should be reversed after a company disposes of the physical units of the inventory for which reserves were provided. The reserves at the end of the year should be based on a new computation of cost or market.

11. **LIFO conformity and supplemental disclosures.** A company may present supplemental non-LIFO disclosures within the historical cost framework. If nondiscretionary variable expenses (i.e., profit sharing based on earnings) would have been different based on the supplemental information, then the company should give effect to such changes. Additionally, the supplemental disclosure should reflect the same type of income tax effects as required by generally accepted accounting principles in the primary financial statements.

    A company may use different LIFO applications for financial reporting than it uses for income tax purposes. Any such differences should be accounted for as temporary differences with the exception of differences in the allocation of cost to inventory in a business combination. Any differences between LIFO applications used for financial reporting and those used for income tax purposes need not be disclosed beyond the requirements of FAS 109.

12. **Interim reporting and LIFO.** The Task Force's conclusions on interim reporting of LIFO inventory are discussed in Chapter 21.

13. **Different financial and income tax years.** A company with different fiscal year-ends for financial reporting and income tax reporting should make a separate LIFO calculation for financial purposes using its financial reporting year as a discrete period for that calculation.

14. **Business combinations accounted for by the purchase method.** Inventory acquired in a business combination accounted for by the purchase method will be recorded at fair value at the date of the combination. The acquired company may be able to carry over its prior basis for that inventory for income tax purposes, causing a difference between GAAP and income tax basis. An adjustment should be made to the fair value of the inventory only if it is reasonably estimated to be liquidated in the future. The adjustment would be for the income tax effect of the difference between income tax and GAAP basis.

    Inventory acquired in such a combination should be considered the LIFO base inventory if the inventory is treated by the company as a separate business unit or a separate LIFO pool. If instead the acquired inventory is combined into an existing pool, then the acquired inventory should be considered as part of the current year's purchases.

15. **Changes in LIFO applications.** A change in a LIFO application is a change in accounting principle. LIFO applications refer to the approach (i.e., dollar value or specific goods), computational technique, or the numbers or contents of the pools.

The AICPA's Practice Bulletin 2 provides guidance for intercompany transfers. The focus of this bulletin is the LIFO liquidation effect caused by transferring inventories which in turn create intercompany profits. This liquidation can occur when (1) two components of the same taxable entity transfer inventory, for example, when a LIFO method component transfers inventory to a non-LIFO component, or (2) when two separate taxable entities that consolidate transfer inventory, even though both use the LIFO method.

This LIFO liquidation creates profit which must be eliminated along with other intercompany profits.

*LIFO income tax rules and restrictions.* As discussed previously, most of the rules and regulations governing LIFO originate in the US Internal Revenue Code and the related regulations, revenue rules, revenue procedures, and judicial decisions. Taxpayers electing to use the LIFO inventory method are subject to myriad rules and restrictions such as

1. The inventory is to be valued at cost regardless of market value (i.e., application of the lower of cost or market rule is not allowed).

2. Changes in the LIFO reserve can potentially cause the taxpayer to be subject to alternative minimum tax (AMT) or increase the amount of AMT.

3. Corporations that use the LIFO method whose stockholders subsequently elect to be taxed as an "S" Corporation are required to report as income their entire LIFO reserve resulting in a special tax under IRC §1363(d) that is payable in four annual installments. The "S" Corporation is, however, permitted to retain LIFO as its inventory accounting method after the election.

4. Once elected, the LIFO method must continue to be used consistently in future periods. A taxpayer is permitted, subject to certain restrictions, to revoke its LIFO election in accordance with Rev. Proc. 99-49. After revocation however, the taxpayer is precluded from reelecting LIFO for a period of five taxable years beginning with the year of the change. For GAAP purposes, a change to or from the LIFO method is accounted for as a change in accounting principle under FAS 154 (see Chapter 5).

A unique rule regarding LIFO inventories is referred to as the LIFO Conformity Rule. A taxpayer may not use a different inventory method in reporting profit or loss of the entity for external financial reports. Thus, if LIFO is elected for income tax purposes, it must also be used for accounting purposes.

Treasury regulations permit certain exceptions to this general rule. Among the exceptions allowable under the regulations are the following:

1. The use of an inventory method other than LIFO in presenting information reported as a supplement to or explanation of the taxpayer's primary presentation of income in financial reports to outside parties. [Reg. §1.472-2(e)(1)(i)]

2. The use of an inventory method other than LIFO to determine the value of the taxpayer's inventory for purposes of reporting the value of such inventory as an asset on the balance sheet. [Reg. §1.472-2(e)(1)(ii)]

3. The use of an inventory method other than LIFO for purposes of determining information reported in internal management reports. (Reg. §1.472-2[e][1][iii])

4. The use of an inventory method other than LIFO for financial reports covering a period of less than one year. (Reg. §1.472- 2[e][1][iv])

5. The use of lower of LIFO cost or market to value inventories for financial statements while using LIFO cost for income tax purposes. (Reg. §1.472-2[e][1][v])

6. For inventories acquired by a corporation in exchange for issuing stock to a stockholder that, immediately after the exchange is considered to have control (a section 351 transaction), the use of the transferor's acquisition dates and costs for GAAP while using redetermined LIFO layers for tax purposes. (Reg. §1.472-2[e][1][vii])

7. The inclusion of certain costs (under full absorption) in inventory for income tax purposes, as required by regulations, while not including those same costs in inventory under GAAP (full absorption). (Reg. §1.472-2[e][8][i])

8. The use of different methods of establishing pools for GAAP purposes and income tax purposes. (Reg. §1.472-2[e][8][ii])

9. The use of different determinations of the time sales or purchases are accrued for GAAP purposes and tax purposes. (Reg. §1.472-2[e][8][xii])

10. In the case of a business combination, the use of different methods to allocate basis for GAAP purposes and income tax purposes. (Reg. §1.472-29[e][8][xiii])

Another important consideration in applying the LIFO conformity rule is the law concerning related corporations. In accordance with the Tax Reform Act of 1984, all members of the same group of financially related corporations are treated as a single taxpayer when applying the conformity rule. Previously, taxpayers were able to circumvent the conformity rule by having a subsidiary on LIFO, while the non-LIFO parent presented combined non-LIFO financial statements. This is a violation of the conformity requirement [Sec. 472(g)].

**Weighted-average and moving-average.** Another method of inventory valuation involves averaging and is commonly referred to as the weighted-average method. This method is permitted for financial reporting purposes but is not permitted for income tax purposes (Rev. Ruling 71-234).

Under this method the cost of goods available for sale (beginning inventory plus net purchases) is divided by the number of units available for sale to obtain a weighted-average cost per unit. Ending inventory and cost of goods sold are then priced at this average cost. As an example, assume the following data:

|  | Units available | Units sold | Actual unit cost | Actual total cost |
|---|---|---|---|---|
| Beginning inventory | 100 | -- | $2.10 | $210 |
| Sale | -- | 75 | -- | -- |
| Purchase | 150 | -- | 2.80 | 420 |
| Sale | -- | 100 | -- | -- |
| Purchase | 50 | -- | 3.00 | 150 |
| Total | 300 | 175 | | $780 |

The weighted-average cost per unit is $780/300, or $2.60. Ending inventory is 125 units (300 – 175) at $2.60, or $325; cost of goods sold is 175 units at $2.60, or $455.

When the weighted-average assumption is applied using a perpetual inventory system, the average cost is recomputed after each purchase. This process is referred to as a moving average. Cost of goods sold is recorded using the most recent average. This combination is called the moving-average method and is applied below to the same data used in the weighted-average example above.

|  | Units on hand | Purchases in dollars | Cost of sales in dollars | Inventory total cost | Inventory moving-average unit cost |
|---|---|---|---|---|---|
| Beginning inventory | 100 | $ -- | $ -- | $210.00 | $2.10 |
| Sale (75 units @ $2.10) | 25 | -- | 157.50 | 52.50 | 2.10 |
| Purchase (150 units, $420) | 175 | 420.00 | -- | 472.50 | 2.70 |
| Sale (100 units @ $2.70) | 75 | -- | 270.00 | 202.50 | 2.70 |
| Purchase (50 units, $150) | 125 | 150.00 | -- | 352.50 | 2.82 |

Cost of goods sold is 75 units at $2.10 and 100 units at $2.70, or $427.50.

**Comparison of cost flow assumptions.** Of the three cost flow assumptions, FIFO and LIFO produce the most extreme results, while results from using the weighted-average method generally fall somewhere in between. The selection of one of these methods involves a detailed analysis of the organization's objectives, industry practices, current and expected future economic conditions, and most importantly, the needs of the intended users of the financial statements.

The following table compares the relative effects of using FIFO and LIFO cost assumptions on the balance sheet and statement of income under differing economic conditions:

| Changes in price levels | Relative effect on balance sheet | | Relative effect on statement of income | |
|---|---|---|---|---|
| | *FIFO* | *LIFO* | *FIFO* | *LIFO* |
| Inflation (i.e., rising prices) | Higher inventory carrying value | Lower inventory carrying value | Lower cost of sales; higher gross profit and net income | Higher cost of sales; lower gross profit and net income |
| Deflation (i.e., falling prices) | Lower inventory carrying value | Higher inventory carrying value | Higher cost of sales; lower gross profit and net income | Lower cost of sales; higher gross profit and net income |

In periods of rising prices the LIFO method is generally thought to best fulfill the objective of providing the clearest measure of periodic net income. It does not, however, provide an accurate estimate of inventory cost in an inflationary environment. However, this shortcoming can usually be overcome by providing additional disclosures in the notes to the financial statements. In periods of rising prices a prudent business should use the LIFO method because it will result in a decrease in the current income tax liability when compared to other alternatives. In a deflationary period, the opposite is true.

FIFO is a balance-sheet-oriented costing method. It gives the most accurate estimate of the current cost of inventory during periods of changing prices. In periods of rising prices, the FIFO method will result in higher income taxes than the other alternatives, while in a deflationary period FIFO provides for a lesser income tax burden. However, a major advantage of the FIFO method is that it is not subject to all of the complex regulations and requirements of the income tax code that govern the use of LIFO.

The average methods do not provide an estimate of current cost information on either the balance sheet or income statement. The average methods are not permitted to be used for income tax purposes and therefore, their use for financial reporting purposes would necessitate the use of FIFO for income tax reporting purposes since LIFO requires financial statement conformity.

Although price trends and underlying objectives are important to consider in selecting a cost flow assumption, other considerations are the risk of experiencing unintended liquidations of LIFO layers, as well as the effects of the chosen method on cash flow, capital maintenance, collateral requirements, and restrictive covenants imposed by lenders, etc.

It should be noted that there is some question about the future of LIFO for inventory costing purposes. Few have ever defended LIFO as a realistic cost flow assumption, and without the LIFO conformity rule imposed under US tax law, most accountants would have supported another method of costing, probably FIFO, as being more representationally faithful for financial reporting purposes. Under International Financial Reporting Standards, LIFO is not permitted. Now that FASB and IASB are formally committed to converge their respective financial reporting standards, there will be pressure on FASB to derecognize LIFO as appropriate for financial reporting purposes. The logical strategy would be to seek repeal of the LIFO conformity rule, thereby permitting LIFO for tax purposes without forcing the financial statements to report under a costing method that does not describe real economic events. To date, there has been little discussion of this issue, which would appear to be an impediment to full convergence of the standards.

**Lower of cost or market (LCM).** As stated in ARB 43, Chapter 4

*...a departure from the cost basis of pricing the inventory is required when the utility of the goods is no longer as great as its cost.... Where there is evidence that the utility of goods...will be less than cost...the difference should be recognized as a loss of the current period.*

Loss of utility can occur for a variety of reasons including damage, spoilage, obsolescence, changes in market prices, etc. The application of LCM is a means of attempting to measure loss of utility and recognize the effects in the period in which this occurs.

The term "market" means current replacement cost not to exceed a ceiling of net realizable value (selling price less reasonably estimable costs of completion and disposal) or be less than a floor of net realizable value adjusted for a normal profit margin.

LCM is not applied in conjunction with the LIFO method of inventory valuation for income tax purposes. However, it is important to note that LCM/LIFO is applied for financial reporting purposes. Such application gives rise to a temporary difference in the carrying value of inventory between financial statements and income tax returns. LCM/LIFO for financial reporting was discussed earlier in this chapter.

LCM may be applied to either the entire inventory or to each individual inventory item. The primary objective for selecting between the alternative methods of applying the LCM rule is to select the one which most clearly reflects periodic income. The rule is most commonly applied to the inventory on an item-by-item basis. The reason for this application is twofold.

1. It is required by income tax purposes unless it involves practical difficulties, and
2. It provides the most conservative valuation of inventories, because decreases in the value of one item are not offset by increases in the value of another.

The application of these principles is illustrated in this example. Assume the following information for products A, B, C, D, and E:

| *Item* | *Cost* | *Replacement cost* | *Est. selling price* | *Cost to complete* | *Normal profit percentage* | *Normal profit amount* |
|------|------|------|------|------|------|------|
| A | $2.00 | $1.80 | $ 2.50 | $0.50 | 24% | $0.60 |
| B | 4.00 | 1.60 | 4.00 | 0.80 | 24% | 0.96 |
| C | 6.00 | 6.60 | 10.00 | 1.00 | 18% | 1.80 |
| D | 5.00 | 4.75 | 6.00 | 2.00 | 20% | 1.20 |
| E | 1.00 | 1.05 | 1.20 | 0.25 | 12.5% | 0.15 |

First, determine the market value and then compare this to historical cost. Market value is equal to the replacement cost, but cannot exceed the net realizable value (NRV) nor be below net realizable value less the normal profit percentage.

## Market Determination

| *Item* | *Cost* | *Replacement cost* | *NRV (ceiling)* | *NRV less profit (floor)* | *Market* | *LCM* |
|------|------|------|------|------|------|------|
| A | $2.00 | $1.80 | $2.00 | $1.40 | $1.80 | $1.80 |
| B | 4.00 | 1.60 | 3.20 | 2.24 | 2.24 | 2.24 |
| C | 6.00 | 6.60 | 9.00 | 7.20 | 7.20 | 6.00 |
| D | 5.00 | 4.75 | 4.00 | 2.80 | 4.00 | 4.00 |
| E | 1.00 | 1.05 | 0.95 | 0.80 | 0.95 | 0.95 |

NRV (ceiling) equals selling price less costs of completion (e.g., item A: $2.50 – .50 = $2.00). NRV less profit (floor) is self-descriptive (e.g., item A: $2.50 – .50 –.60 = $1.40). Market is replacement cost unless lower than the floor or higher than the ceiling. Note that market must be designated before LCM is determined. Finally, LCM is the lower of cost or market value.

Replacement cost is a valid measure of the future utility of the inventory item since increases or decreases in the enterprise's purchase price generally foreshadow related increases or decreases in the price at which it is able to sell the item. The ceiling and the floor provide safeguards against the recognition of either excessive profits or excessive losses in future periods in those instances where the selling price and replacement cost do not move in the same direction in a proportional manner. The ceiling avoids the recognition of additional losses in the future when the selling price is falling faster than replacement cost. Without the ceiling constraint, inventories would be carried at an amount in excess of their net realizable value. The floor avoids the recognition of abnormal profits in the future when replacement cost is falling faster than the selling price. Without the floor, inventories would be carried at a value less than their net realizable value minus a normal profit.

The loss from writing inventories down to LCM is generally reflected on the income statement in cost of goods sold. If material, the loss must be separately captioned in the income statement. While GAAP is not explicit as to presentation, it would appear that this adjustment could either be displayed as a separately identified charge within cost of goods sold, or as an administrative expense. The write-down is recorded as a debit to a loss account and a credit either to an inventory or a valuation allowance account.

**Inventory estimation methods.** There are instances in which an accountant must estimate the value of inventories without an actual physical count. Some of the estimation methods used to accomplish this are the retail method, the LIFO retail method, and the gross profit method. These methods are not cost flow assumptions like LIFO and FIFO but rather, they are computational methods that have been devised to assist in estimating inventory cost under the relevant cost flow assumption.

*Retail method.* The retail method is used by retailers to estimate the cost of their ending inventory. The retailer can either take a physical inventory at retail prices or estimate ending retail inventory and then use a computed cost-to-retail ratio to convert the ending inventory priced at retail to its estimated cost. This method eliminates the process of going back to original vendor invoices or other documents in order to determine the original cost for each inventoriable item. The retail method can be used under any of the three cost flow assumptions discussed earlier: FIFO, LIFO, or average cost. As with ordinary FIFO or average cost, the LCM rule is also applied when either one of these two cost assumptions is used in conjunction with the retail method.

The key to applying the retail method is determining the cost-to-retail ratio. The calculation of this ratio varies depending upon the cost flow assumption selected. The cost-to-retail ratio provides a measure of the relationship between the cost of goods available for sale and the retail price of these same goods. This ratio is used to convert the ending retail inventory back to cost. The computation of the cost-to-retail ratio for the FIFO and average cost methods is described below. The use of the LIFO cost flow assumption with this method is discussed in the succeeding section.

1. **FIFO cost**—The FIFO method assumes that the ending inventory is made up of the latest purchases. Therefore, beginning inventory is excluded from the computation of the cost-to-retail ratio, and the computation uses the cost of current year net purchases divided by their retail value adjusted for both net markups and net markdowns as will be further explained and illustrated.

2. **FIFO (LCM)**—The computation is basically the same as FIFO cost except that markdowns are excluded from the computation of the cost-to-retail ratio.

3. **Average cost**—Average cost assumes that ending inventory consists of all goods available for sale. Therefore, the cost-to-retail ratio is computed by dividing the cost of goods available for sale (Beginning inventory + Net purchases) by the retail value of these goods adjusted for both net markups and net markdowns.

4. **Average cost (LCM)**—Is computed in the same manner as average cost except that markdowns are excluded from the calculation of the cost-to-retail ratio.

A simple example illustrates the computation of the cost-to-retail ratio under both the FIFO cost and average cost methods in a situation where no markups or markdowns exist.

| | FIFO cost | | Average cost | |
|---|---|---|---|---|
| | *Cost* | *Retail* | *Cost* | *Retail* |
| Beginning inventory | $100,000 | $ 200,000 | $100,000 | $ 200,000 |
| Net purchases | 500,000 (a) | 800,000 (b) | 500,000 | 800,000 |
| Total goods available for sale | $600,000 | 1,000,000 | $600,000 (c) | 1,000,000 (d) |
| Sales at retail | | (800,000) | | (800,000) |
| Ending inventory—retail | | $ 200,000 | | $ 200,000 |

| Cost-to-retail ratio | $\dfrac{\text{(a) } 500,000}{\text{(b) } 800,000}$ = 62.5% | | $\dfrac{\text{(c) } 600,000}{\text{(d) } 1,000,000}$ = 60% | |
|---|---|---|---|---|

Ending inventory—cost
200,000 × 62.5%  $ 125,000
200,000 × 60%  $ 120,000

Note that the only difference in the two examples is the numbers used to calculate the cost-to-retail ratio.

The lower of cost or market aspect of the retail method is a result of the treatment of net markups and net markdowns. Net markups (markups less markup cancellations) are net increases above the original retail price, which are generally caused by changes in supply and demand. Net markdowns (markdowns less markdown cancellations) are net decreases below the original retail price. An approximation of lower of cost or market is achieved by including net markups but excluding net markdowns from the cost-to-retail ratio.

To understand this approximation, assume a toy is purchased for $6, and the retail price is set at $10. It is later marked down to $8. A cost-to-retail ratio including markdowns would be $6 divided by $8 or 75%, and ending inventory would be valued at $8 times 75%, or $6 (original cost). The logic behind including markdowns in the cost-to-retail ratio is the assumption that these inventories would eventually be marked down and that markdowns are a normal part of business for this enterprise and/or these types of inventories. A cost-to-retail ratio excluding markdowns would be $6 divided by $10 or 60%, and ending inventory would be valued at $8 times 60%, or $4.80 (LCM). The logic behind excluding markdowns from the cost-to-retail ratio is that the enterprise did not expect to mark these inventory items down and that this is not a normal occurrence. The write-down to $4.80 reflects the loss in utility which is evidenced by the reduced retail price.

The application of the lower of cost or market rule is illustrated for both the FIFO and average cost methods in the example below. Remember, if the markups and markdowns below had been included in the previous example, both would have been included in the cost-to-retail ratio.

| | FIFO cost (LCM) | | Average cost (LCM) | |
|---|---|---|---|---|
| | *Cost* | *Retail* | *Cost* | *Retail* |
| Beginning inventory | $100,000 | $ 200,000 | $100,000 | $ 200,000 |
| Net purchases | 500,000 (a) | 800,000 (b) | 500,000 | 800,000 |
| Net markups | -- | 250,000 (b) | -- | 250,000 |
| Total goods available for sale | $600,000 | 1,250,000 | $600,000 (c) | 1,250,000 (d) |
| Net markdowns | | (50,000) | | (50,000) |
| Sales at retail | | (800,000) | | (800,000) |
| Ending inventory—retail | | $ 400,000 | | $ 400,000 |

| Cost-to-retail ratio | $\dfrac{\text{(a) } 500,000}{\text{(b) } 1,050,000}$ = 47.6% | | $\dfrac{\text{(c) } 600,000}{\text{(d) } 1,250,000}$ = 48% | |
|---|---|---|---|---|

Ending inventory—LCM
400,000 × 47.6%  $ 190,400
400,000 × 48%  $ 192,000

Under the FIFO (LCM) method all of the markups are considered attributable to the current period purchases. While this is not necessarily accurate, it provides the most conservative estimate of the ending inventory.

There are a number of additional issues that affect the computation of the cost-to-retail ratio. Purchase discounts and freight-in affect only the cost column in this computation. The sales figure that is subtracted from the adjusted cost of goods available for sale in the retail column must be gross sales after adjustment for sales returns. Sales discounts are not included in the computation. If sales are recorded gross, then deduct the gross sales figure. If sales are recorded net, then both the recorded sales and sales discount must be deducted to give the same effect as deducting gross sales. Normal spoilage is generally allowed for in the enterprise's pricing policies, and for this reason it is deducted from the retail column after the calculation of the cost-to-retail ratio. Abnormal spoilage, on the other hand, is deducted from both the cost and retail columns before the cost-to-retail calculation as it could otherwise distort the ratio. It is then generally reported as a separate loss, either within cost of goods sold or administrative expenses. Abnormal spoilage generally arises from a major theft or casualty, while normal spoilage is usually due to shrinkage or breakage. These determinations and their treatments will vary depending upon the enterprise's policies.

When applying the retail method, separate computations are made for any departments that experience significantly higher or lower gross profit margins. Distortions arise in applying the retail method when a department sells goods with gross profit margins that vary in a proportion different from the gross profit margins of goods purchased during the period. In this case, the cost-to-retail percentage would not be representative of the mix of goods in ending inventory. Also, manipulations of income are possible by planning the timing of markups and markdowns.

The retail method is an acceptable method of estimating inventories under FIFO (LCM) for income tax purposes. Income tax regulations require valuation at lower of cost or market (except for LIFO) and regular and consistent physical counts of inventory at each location.

**LIFO retail method.** As with other LIFO methods, treasury regulations are the governing force behind the LIFO retail method. The regulations differentiate between a "variety" store which is required to use an internally computed index and a "department" store which is permitted to use a price index published by the Bureau of Labor Statistics. The computation of an internal index was previously discussed in the dollar-value LIFO section. It involves applying the double-extension method to a representative sample of the ending inventory. Selection of an externally published index is to be in accordance with the treasury regulations.

The steps used in computing the value of ending inventory under the LIFO retail method are listed below and then applied in an example for illustrative purposes.

1. Calculate (or select) the current year conversion price index. Recall that in the base year this index will be 1.00.
2. Calculate the value of the ending inventory at both cost and retail. Remember, as with other LIFO methods, income tax regulations do not permit the use of LCM, so both markups and markdowns are included in the computation of the cost-to-retail ratio. However, the beginning inventory is excluded from goods available for sale at cost and at retail.
3. Restate the ending inventory at retail to base-year retail. Divide the current ending inventory at retail by the current year index determined in step 1.
4. Layers are then treated as they were for the dollar-value LIFO example presented earlier. If the ending inventory restated to base-year retail exceeds the previous year's amount at base-year retail, a new layer is established.
5. The computation of LIFO cost is the last step and requires multiplying each layer at base-year retail by the appropriate price index and multiplying this product by the cost-to-retail ratio in order to arrive at the LIFO cost for each layer.

The following example illustrates a two-year period to which the LIFO retail method is applied. The first period represents the first year of operations for the company and is its base year.

**Year 1**

Step 1—Because this is the base year, there is no need to compute an index, as it will always be 1.00.

Step 2—

| | Cost | Retail |
|---|---|---|
| Beginning inventory | $ -- | $ -- |
| Purchases | 582,400 | 988,600 |
| Markups | -- | 164,400 |
| Markdowns | -- | (113,000) |
| Subtotal | 582,400 | 1,040,000 |
| Total goods available for sale | $582,400 | 1,040,000 |
| Sales—at retail | | 840,000 |
| Ending year 1 inventory—at retail | | $ 200,000 |

Cost-to-retail ratio $\dfrac{\text{(a) } 582,400}{\text{(b) } 1,040,000} = 56\%$

Ending inventory at cost
$200,000 × 56%    $112,000

Step 3—Because this is the base year, the restatement to base-year cost is not necessary; however, the computation would be $200,000/1.00 = $200,000.

Steps 4
and 5—The determination of layers is again unnecessary in the base year; however, the computation would take the following format:

| | Ending inventory at base-year retail | Conversion price index | Cost-to-retail ratio | LIFO cost |
|---|---|---|---|---|
| Base year ($200,000/1.00) | $200,000 | 1.00 | 0.56 | $112,000 |

**Year 2**

Step 1—We make the assumption that the computation of an internal index yields a result of 1.12 (obtained by double-extending a representative sample).

Step 2—

| | Cost | Retail |
|---|---|---|
| Beginning inventory | $112,000 | $ 200,000 |
| Purchases | 716,300 | 1,168,500 |
| Markups | -- | 87,500 |
| Markdowns | -- | (21,000) |
| Subtotal | $716,300 | 1,235,000 |
| Total goods available for sale | | 1,435,000 |
| Sales—at retail | | 1,171,800 |
| Ending year 2 inventory—at retail | | $ 263,200 |

Cost-to-retail ratio $\dfrac{716,300}{1,235,000} = 58\%$

Step 3—The restatement of ending inventory at current year retail to base-year retail is done using the index computed in step 1. In this case it is $263,200/1.12 = $235,000.

Steps 4
and 5—There is a LIFO layer in year 2 because the $235,000 inventory at base-year retail exceeds the year 1 amount of $200,000.

The computation of the LIFO cost for each layer is shown below.

|  | Ending inventory at base-year retail | Conversion price index | Cost-to-retail ratio | LIFO cost |
|---|---|---|---|---|
| Base year |  |  |  |  |
| ($200,000/1.00) | $200,000 | 1.00 | 0.56 | $112,000 |
| Year 2 layer | 35,000 | 1.12 | 0.58 | 22,736 |
|  | $235,000 |  |  |  |
| Ending year 2 inventory at LIFO cost |  |  |  | $134,736 |

The treatment of subsequent increments and decrements is the same for this method as it is for the regular dollar-value method.

*Gross profit method.* The gross profit method is used to estimate ending inventory when a physical count is not taken. It can also be used to evaluate the reasonableness of a given inventory amount. Assume the following data:

| Beginning inventory | $125,000 |
|---|---|
| Net purchases | 450,000 |
| Sales | 600,000 |
| Estimated gross profit percentage | 32% |

Ending inventory is estimated as follows:

| Beginning inventory | $125,000 |
|---|---|
| Net purchases | 450,000 |
| Cost of goods available for sale | 575,000 |
| Cost of goods sold [$600,000 – (32% × $600,000)] or (68% × $600,000) | 408,000 |
| Estimated ending inventory | $167,000 |

The gross profit method is used for interim reporting estimates, for conducting analytical review procedures by independent accountants in audits and review engagements, and for estimating inventory lost in fires or other catastrophes. The method is not acceptable, however, for either income tax or annual financial reporting purposes.

*Standard costs.* Standard costs are predetermined unit costs used by manufacturing firms for planning and control purposes. Standard costs are often used to develop approximations of GAAP inventories for financial reporting purposes. The use of standard cost approximations in financial reporting is acceptable only if adjustments to the standards are made periodically to reflect current conditions and if their use approximates the results that would be obtained by directly applying one of the recognized cost flow assumptions.

**Example of standard costing**

The Bavarian Clock Company (BCC) uses standard costing to value its FIFO inventory. One of its products is the Men's Chronometer wristwatch, for which the following bill of materials has been constructed:

| Part description | Quantity | Cost |
|---|---|---|
| Titanium watch casing | 1 | $212.25 |
| Leather strap | 1 | 80.60 |
| Scratch resistant crystal bezel | 1 | 120.15 |
| Double timer shock-resistant movement | 1 | 42.80 |
| Multilingual instruction sheet | 1 | 0.80 |
| Ornamental box | 1 | 2.75 |
| Overhead charge | 1 | 28.00 |
| Total |  | $487.35 |

The industrial engineering department designed the following labor routing for assembly of the Men's Chronometer and determined the standard process times:

| Labor routing description | Quantity/ minutes | Labor type | Cost/ minute | Cost |
|---|---|---|---|---|
| Quality review of raw materials received | 3.5 | Quality assurance | $0.42 | $ 1.47 |
| Attach strap to casing | 7.5 | Watch maker | 0.79 | 5.93 |
| Insert movement in casing | 10.8 | Watch maker | 0.79 | 8.53 |
| Attach bezel | 3.2 | Watch maker | 0.79 | 2.53 |
| Final quality review and testing | 11.0 | Quality assurance | 0.42 | 4.62 |
| Insert into packing case | 1.5 | Assembler | 0.13 | .20 |
| Total | 37.5 | | | $ 23.28 |

Thus, the total standard cost of the Men's Chronometer is $510.63 ($487.35 material and overhead cost + $23.28 labor cost). At the beginning of December, there are 1,087 Men's Chronometers in finished goods inventory, which are recorded at standard cost, resulting in a beginning inventory valuation of $555,054.81 (= $510.63 × 1,087 units).

During December, BCC records actual material costs of $1,915,312.19, actual labor costs of $111,844.40, and actual overhead costs of $124,831.55 related to the Men's Chronometer, which are charged to the inventory account. During the month, BCC manufactures 4,105 Men's Chronometers and ships 4,385, leaving 807 units in finished goods inventory. At a standard cost of $510.63 per unit, this results in a month-end finished goods inventory balance of $412,078.41. The monthly charge to cost of goods sold is calculated as follows:

| | |
|---|---|
| Beginning inventory at standard cost | $ 555,054.81 |
| + Actual material costs incurred | 1,915,312.19 |
| + Actual labor costs incurred | 111,844.40 |
| + Actual overhead costs incurred | 124,831.55 |
| – Ending inventory at standard cost | (412,078.41) |
| = Cost of goods sold | $2,294,964.54 |

At month-end, the purchasing manager conducts his quarterly review of the bill of materials and determines that the cost of the bezel has permanently increased by $4.82, bringing the total standard bezel cost to $124.97 and therefore the total standard cost of the Men's Chronometer to $515.45. This increases the value of the ending inventory by $3,889.74 ($4.82 standard cost increase × 807 units in finished goods inventory), to $415,968.15, while reducing the cost of goods sold to $2,291,074.80. The following entry records the month-end inventory valuation at standard cost:

| | | |
|---|---|---|
| Cost of goods sold | 2,291,074.80 | |
|     Finished goods inventory | | 2,291,074.80 |

As a cross-check, BCC's controller divides the cost of goods sold by the total number of units shipped, and arrives at an actual unit cost of $522.48, as opposed to the standard costs of $515.45. The variance from the standard cost is $7.03 per unit, or a total of $30,826.55. Upon further investigation, she finds that overnight delivery charges of $1,825 were incurred for a shipment of watch casings, while there was a temporary increase in the cost of the leather strap of $2.83 for a 1,000-unit purchase, resulting in an additional charge of $2,830. She elects to separately track these excess material-related costs with the following entry:

| | | |
|---|---|---|
| Material price variance | 4,655.00 | |
|     Cost of goods sold | | 4,655.00 |

In addition, the production staff incurred overtime charges of $16,280 during the month. Since overtime is not included in the labor routing standard costs, the controller separately tracks this information with the following entry:

| | | |
|---|---|---|
| Labor price variance | 16,280.00 | |
|     Cost of goods sold | | 16,280.00 |

Finally, the controller determines that some costs comprising the overhead cost pool exceeded the budgeted overhead cost during the month, resulting in an excess charge of $9,891.55 to the Men's Chronometer cost of goods sold. She separates this expense from the cost of goods sold with the following entry:

| Overhead price variance | 9,891.55 | |
| Cost of goods sold | | 9,891.55 |

Her variance analysis has identified all causes of the $30,826.55 cost overage, as noted in the following table:

| Total cost of goods sold | $2,291,074.80 |
| – Standard cost of goods sold | (2,260,248.25) |
| – Material price variance | (4,655.00) |
| – Labor price variance | (16,280.00) |
| – Overhead price variance | (9,891.55) |
| = Remaining unresolved variance | -- |

As explained previously, variances resulting from abnormal costs incurred are considered period costs and, thus, are not allocated to inventory.

### Other valuation methods.

*Base stock.* The base stock method assumes that a certain level of inventory investment is necessary for normal business activities and is, therefore, permanent. The base stock inventory is carried at historical cost. Decreases in the base stock are considered temporary and are charged to cost of goods sold at replacement cost. Increases are carried at current year costs. The base stock approach is seldom used in practice since it is not allowed for income tax purposes, and the LIFO method yields similar results.

*Direct costing.* An alternative to full absorption costing is direct costing. Direct costing (also referred to as variable costing) requires classifying only direct materials, direct labor, and variable production overhead as inventory costs. Under this method, all fixed costs are accounted for as period costs. The exclusion of all overhead from inventory costs is not an acceptable accounting method for GAAP or under the US Treasury Regulations for income tax purposes.

*Relative sales value.* Relative sales (or net realizable) values are used to assign costs to inventory items purchased or manufactured in groups. This method is applicable to joint products, subdivided assets such as real estate lots, and basket purchases.

For example, products A and B have the same processes performed on them up to the split-off point. The total cost incurred to this point is $80,000. This cost can be assigned to products A and B using their relative sales value at the split-off point. If A could be sold for $60,000 and B for $40,000, the total sales value is $100,000. The cost would be assigned on the basis of each product's relative sales value. Thus, A would be assigned a cost of $48,000 (60,000/100,000 × 80,000) and B a cost of $32,000 (40,000/100,000 × 80,000).

### Differences between GAAP and Income Tax Accounting for Inventories

**Full absorption costing—income tax.** Prior to the Tax Reform Act of 1986 (TRA 1986), production costing for GAAP and for income tax purposes were very similar. However, TRA 1986 included provisions referred to as Uniform Capitalization (UNICAP) which changed inventory costing for income tax purposes by requiring certain additional indirect costs that are not capitalizable under GAAP be capitalized rather than expensed for income tax purposes. TRA 1986 requires that manufacturers capitalize rather than expense these additional items:

1. Depreciation and amortization in excess of that reported in financial statements
2. Percentage depletion in excess of cost
3. Rework labor, scrap, and spoilage costs
4. Allocable general and administrative costs related to the production function

For income tax purposes, these costs, as well as the indirect production costs listed above for inventory costing under GAAP, are allocated to the WIP and finished goods inventories. Examples of general and administrative costs that must be allocated include payroll department costs, wages of security guards, and the president's salary. The difference between the GAAP and tax inventory carrying values is a temporary difference, which requires deferred income tax accounting (discussed in Chapter 17).

**Uniform capitalization rules—income tax vs. GAAP.** TRA 1986 established the UNICAP rules for inventory costs for tax purposes. The Emerging Issues Task Force reached a consensus in its Issue 86-46 that capitalizing a cost for income tax purposes does not, by itself, indicate that it is preferable or even appropriate to capitalize the cost for financial reporting purposes. Although a cost may be required to be capitalized for income tax purposes, management must analyze the individual facts and circumstances based on the nature of its operations and industry practice to determine whether to capitalize the cost for financial reporting purposes.

**Inventory capitalization for retailers/wholesalers—income tax vs. GAAP.** Prior to TRA 1986, retailers and wholesalers recorded their inventory as the invoice price plus the cost of applicable sales tax and freight-in under both GAAP and income tax law. TRA 1986 applied UNICAP to certain retailers and wholesalers and introduced a requirement that additional costs be capitalized. Inventories of retailers/wholesalers whose average annual gross receipts for the preceding three years are $10 million or less are exempt from applying UNICAP.

The costs which must be capitalized have been divided into two categories. The first category is direct costs and includes the inventory invoice price plus transportation. Also included in direct costs is the cost of labor for purchasing, storing, and handling inventory items. The second category is indirect costs and consists of any costs that directly benefit or are incurred because of the performance of a resale activity. The following types of indirect costs must be capitalized under UNICAP:

1. Off-site storage or warehousing
2. Purchasing
3. Handling, processing, assembly, and repackaging
4. Allocable general and administrative costs related to the above three functions

The indirect costs are allocated between inventory and cost of goods sold by using traditional methods (specific identification, standard costing methods, etc.) or one of three simplified methods. Temporary differences require deferred income tax accounting as discussed in Chapter 17.

**Other Inventory Topics**

**Purchase commitments.** Purchase commitments generally are not recognized in the financial statements because they are executory in nature. However, disclosure in the notes to the financial statements is required for firm purchase commitments that are material in amount.

If at a balance sheet date the contract price of these commitments exceeds the market value, the estimated loss is accrued and reported as a loss in the income statement. This results in recognition of the loss before the inventory is actually purchased.

**Inventories valued at selling price.** In exceptional cases, inventories may be reported at sales price less estimated disposal costs. Such treatment is justified when cost is difficult to determine, quoted market prices are available, marketability is assured, and units are interchangeable. Precious metals, certain agricultural products, and meat are examples of inventories valued in this manner. When inventory is valued above cost, revenue is recognized before the time of sale. Naturally full disclosure in the financial statements is required.

**Stripping costs incurred during production in the mining industry.** The EITF reached a consensus in EITF 04-6 that stripping costs incurred during a mine's production phase are to be accounted for as variable production costs and, therefore allocated to inventory. This consensus was limited to stripping costs incurred during the period when inventory is being produced (i.e., extracted) and did not address the accounting for these costs when incurred during the preproduction phase of the mine.

**Interim reporting.** The principles used to determine ending inventory and cost of goods sold in annual reports are also used in interim reports, although four exceptions are allowed (under APB 28). These are

1. The gross profit method may be used to estimate cost of goods sold and ending inventory.
2. When LIFO layers are liquidated during the interim period but are expected to be replaced by year-end, cost of goods sold is adjusted to reflect current costs rather than older LIFO costs.
3. Temporary market declines need not be recognized if substantial evidence exists that market prices will recover. If LCM losses are recorded in one or more interim periods and are recovered by year-end, the recovery is recognized as a fourth-quarter gain.
4. Planned standard cost variances expected to reverse by year-end are not recognized.

See a complete discussion of interim financial reporting in Chapter 21.

# 10 REVENUE RECOGNITION— EVOLVING PRINCIPLES AND SPECIALIZED APPLICATIONS

# REVENUE RECOGNITION — GENERAL PRINCIPLES

**Revenue recognition concerns.** The principles guiding recognition of revenues for financial reporting purposes are central to GAAP and in most instances are unambiguous and straightforward. In fact, the underlying principles have not changed in decades, although FASB is deliberating fundamental changes, thereto, grounded in an assets-and-liabilities approach. However, while the basic principles are uncomplicated, it is nonetheless true that a large fraction of financial reporting frauds over the period beginning about 1995 were the result of misapplications, often deliberate, of revenue recognition practices prescribed under GAAP. Apart from outright fraud (e.g., recording nonexistent transactions), there were several factors contributing to this unfortunate state of affairs.

First, business practices have continued to grow increasingly complex, involving, among other things, a marked shift from manufacturing to a services-based economy, where the proper timing for revenue recognition is often more difficult to ascertain. Second, there has been an undeniable increase in the willingness of managers, whose compensation packages are often directly linked to the company's stock price and reported earnings, to "stretch" accounting rules to facilitate earnings management. This has particularly been the case where GAAP requirements have been vague, complex or abstruse. And third, it has been well documented that, too often, independent auditors have been willing to accommodate managements' wishes, particularly in the absence of specific rules under GAAP to support a denial of such requests. These actions have often had disastrous consequences, if not immediately, then in the longer run.

Errors or deliberate distortions involving revenue recognition fall into two categories: situations in which revenue legitimately earned is reported in the incorrect fiscal (financial reporting) period, often referred to as "cutoff" errors, and situations in which revenue is recognized although never actually earned. Given the emphasis on periodic reporting (e.g., quarterly earnings announcements in the case of publicly held entities), even simple "cutoff" errors can have enormous impact, notwithstanding the fact that these should tend to offset over several periods. As a practical matter, all instances of improper revenue recognition are very serious, and these constitute a challenge to all accountants attempting to properly interpret and apply GAAP, including independent auditors.

**Types of supporting documentation.** The various rules with respect to recognition of revenue for different types of transactions have evolved over a long period of time and have been created in a piecemeal fashion by different standard setters in differing economic environments. There are now more than 140 pieces of authoritative literature, at all levels of the GAAP hierarchy, dealing with various aspects of revenue recognition, contributing perhaps to the confusion that may have resulted in at least some of the misapplications of GAAP.

**Revenue recognition—general guidelines.** In terms of currently enforceable guidance, under long-established GAAP, revenue, whether from the sale of product or provision of services, is to be recognized only when it has been earned. According to CON 5, *Recognition and Measurement in Financial Statements of Business Enterprises*,

> ...(a)n entity's revenue-earning activities involve delivering or producing goods, rendering services, or other activities that constitute its ongoing major or central operations, and revenues are considered to have been earned when the entity has substantially accomplished what it must do to be entitled to the benefits represented by the revenues.

In other words, in order to be recognized revenue must be realized or realizable, and it must have been earned.

CON 5 notes that "the two conditions (being realized or realizable, and being earned) are usually met by the time product or merchandise is delivered or services are rendered to customers, and revenues from manufacturing and selling activities and gains and losses from sales of other assets are commonly recognized at time of sale (usually meaning delivery)." Moreover, "if services are rendered or rights to use assets extend continuously over time (for example, interest or rent), reliable measures based on contractual prices established in ad-

vance are commonly available, and revenues may be recognized as earned as time passes."
In other words, for most traditional and familiar types of transactions, the point at which it is
appropriate to recognize revenue will be quite clear.

The SEC, reflecting on the conceptual foundation for revenue recognition, observed first
in Staff Accounting Bulletin 101, and then in its replacement, SAB 104, that

> ...*revenue generally is realized or realizable and earned when* **all** *of the following criteria
> are met:*
>
> 1.   *There is persuasive evidence that an arrangement exists*
> 2.   *Delivery has occurred or services have been rendered*
> 3.   *The seller's price to the buyer is fixed or determinable, and*
> 4.   *Collectibility is reasonably assured*

Note that, while SEC rules and "unofficial" guidance are not necessarily to be deemed
GAAP for nonpublic companies, to the extent that these provide insights into standards
found in the GAAP hierarchy, they should always be viewed as relevant guidance and followed, absent other, contradictory rules established under GAAP. In the absence of any
other source found in the GAAP hierarchy, SEC pronouncements may represent the best
thinking on the subject and are considered authoritative for all reporting entities.

With regard to the four criteria set forth above, consideration should be directed at the
following discussion, which is drawn partially from SAB 101 and SAB 104.

First, regarding persuasive evidence of an arrangement, attention must be paid to the
customary manner in which the reporting entity engages in revenue-producing transactions
with its customers or clients. Since these transactions are negotiated between the buyer and
seller and can have unique or unusual terms, there are (and can be) no absolute standards.
Thus, for an enterprise that traditionally obtains appropriate documentation (purchase orders,
etc.) from its customers before concluding sales to them, advance deliveries to customers,
even if later ratified by receipt of the proper paperwork, would not be deemed a valid basis
for revenue recognition at the time of delivery.

When evaluating purported revenue transactions, the substance of the transactions must
always be considered, and not merely their form. It has become increasingly commonplace
to "paper over" transactions in ways that can create the basis for inappropriate revenue recognition. For example, transactions that are actually consignment arrangements might be
described as "sales" or as "conditional sales," but revenue recognition would not be appropriate until the consigned goods are later sold to a third-party purchaser.

Careful analysis of the rights and obligations of the parties and the risks borne by each at
various stages of the transactions should reveal when and whether an actual sale has occurred
and whether revenue recognition is warranted. In general, if the buyer has a right to return
the product in question, coupled with a deferred or conditional payment obligation and/or
significant remaining performance obligations by the seller, revenue will not be recognizable
by the seller at the time of initial delivery. Similarly, if there is an implicit or explicit obligation by the seller to repurchase the item transferred, a real sales transaction has not occurred. The buyer must assume the risks of ownership in all cases if revenue is to be recognized.

With regard to whether delivery has occurred or services have been rendered, ownership
and risk taking must have been transferred to the buyer if revenue is to be recognized by the
seller. Thus, if the seller is holding goods for delivery to the buyer because the buyer's receiving dock workers are on strike and no deliveries are being accepted, revenue generally
cannot be recognized in the reporting period, even if these delayed deliveries are made subsequent to period end. (There are limited exceptions to this general principle, typically in-

volving a written request from the buyer for delayed delivery under a "bill and hold" arrangement, having a valid business purpose.)

Delivery, as used here, implies more than simply the physical relocation of the goods to the buyer's place of business. Rather, it means that the goods have actually been accepted by the customer, which, depending on the terms of the relevant contract, could be conditioned on whether inspection, testing, and/or installation have been completed, and the buyer has committed to pay for the items purchased. For revenue recognition to be justified, substantial performance of the terms of delivery must have occurred, and if any terms remain uncompleted, there should be a basis grounded on historical experience to assume that these matters will be satisfactorily attended to.

In some instances there are multiple "deliverables"; in such cases, revenue is not recognized for any given element if later deliverables are essential for the functionality of the already delivered element. In other situations, such as in various licensing arrangements, physical "delivery" may occur well before product usage by the buyer can take place (e.g., software for the future year's tax preparation delivered before the current year end), and revenue is not to be recognized prior to the initial date of expected use by the buyer.

In the case of many service transactions, large up-front fees are often charged, nominally in recognition of the selling of a membership, the signing of a contract, or for enrolling the customer in a program. (For example, initiation fees to join a health club where the terms of membership also obligate the member to pay ongoing fees.) Unless the services provided to the customer at inception are substantial, the presumption is that the revenue received has not been earned, but rather must be deferred and recognized, usually ratably, over the period that substantive services are provided. Thus, initiation fees are amortized over the membership period.

The seller's price to the buyer is fixed or determinable when a customer does not have the unilateral right to terminate or cancel the contract and receive a cash refund. Depending on customary practice, extended return privileges might imply that this condition has not been met in given circumstances. Prices that are conditional on the occurrence of future events are not fixed or determinable from the perspective of revenue recognition.

In theory, until the refund rights have expired, or the specified future events have occurred, revenue should not be recognized. As a practical matter, however, assuming that the amount of refunds can be reliably estimated (based on past experience, industry data, etc.), revenues, net of expected refunds, can be recognized on a pro rata basis. Absent this ability to reliably estimate, however, revenue recognition is deferred.

The final factor, reasonable assurance of collectibility, implies that the accrual for bad debts (uncollectible accounts receivable) can be estimated with reasonable accuracy, both to accomplish proper periodic matching of revenue and expenses, and to enable the presentation of receivables at net realizable value, as required under GAAP. An inability to accomplish this objective necessitates deferral of revenue recognition—generally until collection occurs, or at least until it becomes feasible to estimate the uncollectible portion with sufficient accuracy.

An extreme situation, calling for not merely accrual of losses from estimated uncollectible receivables, is to defer revenue recognition entirely until collectibility is assured (or actually achieved). The most conservative accounting alternative, first set forth in ARB 43 and then again cited in CON 5, is to record revenue only as collected. It states "(i)f collectibility of assets received for product, services, or other assets is doubtful, revenues and gains *may* be recognized on the basis of cash received." (Emphasis added.) The permissive language, which (it must be assumed) was deliberately selected in preference to a mandatory exhortation (e.g., "must"), suggests that even in such a situation this hyperconservative departure from accrual accounting is not truly prescriptive, but is a possible solution to a fact-specific set of circumstances.

### Evolving Problems in Revenue Recognition

Certain of the more attention-getting problems in applying the general principles of revenue recognition are discussed in the following paragraphs.

**Financial statement presentation: gross vs. net.** In general, it is well established that reporting on a "gross" basis is appropriate when the entity takes ownership of the goods being sold to its customers, with the risks and rewards of ownership accruing to it. For example, if the entity runs the risk of obsolescence or spoilage during the period it holds the merchandise, gross reporting would normally be appropriate. On the other hand, if the entity merely acts as an agent for the buyer or seller from whom it earns a commission, then "net" reporting would be more appropriate.

In recent years there have been increasing reports of enterprises that inflate revenues reported in their income statements by reporting transactions on a "gross" basis, notwithstanding that the entity's real economic role is as an agent for buyer and/or seller. This distortion became widespread in the case of Internet commerce-based "dot-com companies" and other start-up and innovative businesses typically not reporting earnings, for which market valuations were heavily influenced by absolute levels of and trends in gross revenues. Reporting revenues "gross" rather than "net" often had an enormous impact on the perceived value of those enterprises.

Factors to consider in determining whether sales are properly reported "gross" or "net" include

1. Whether the entity acts as a principal or an agent in the transactions
2. Whether the entity takes title to the property
3. Whether the entity has the normal risks and rewards of ownership
4. Whether the entity acts as an agent or broker (including performing services, in substance, as an agent or broker) with compensation on a commission or fee basis

**Reporting taxes collected as revenue.** Most businesses must collect certain taxes which must subsequently be transmitted to governmental bodies, making the entity in effect an agent of the state. The most obvious example of this situation is the imposition of sales taxes, which are almost universally applicable to retail merchandise transactions and, increasingly, to service transactions as well. Historically accounting practice has varied, with some entities reporting gross revenue inclusive of taxes—which are then later reported as expenses when remitted—while other entities report revenue net of these taxes, treating them as purely a balance sheet event. EITF 06-3 confirms that either methodology is acceptable, and if material, should be defined in the accounting policies note to the financial statements. As an elective accounting policy, accordingly, any change in method should be justified as being warranted as a means of improving financial reporting.

**Barter transactions.** Barter transactions (nonmonetary exchanges, as described in APB 29 and FAS 153) are not a problem, assuming that they represent the culmination of an earnings process. However, in recent years there have been many reports of transactions that appear to have been concocted merely to create the illusion of revenue-generating activities. Examples include advertising swaps engaged in by some entities, most commonly "dot-com" enterprises, and the excess capacity swaps of fiber optic communications concerns under "indefeasible right to use" agreements. Both of these and many other situations involved immediate recognition of revenues coupled with deferred recognition of costs, and typically in aggregate were equal exchanges not providing profits to either party. Furthermore, these examples do not represent culminations of the normal earnings process (e.g., fiber-optic networks were built in order to sell communications services to end users, not for the purpose of swapping capacity with other similar operations).

In hindsight, most observers can see why these and many other aggressive reporting practices deviated from established or implied GAAP; although there are still some who insist that because GAAP failed to explicitly address these precise scenarios, the accounting for the transactions was open to interpretation. Since GAAP (even the highly rules-based US GAAP) cannot possibly hope to overtly address all the various innovative transaction structures that exist and will be invented, it is necessary to apply basic principles and reason by analogy to newly emerging circumstances. Of great importance to financial statement preparers (and internal and external auditors) is obtaining a thorough understanding of the nature and normal operations of the business enterprise being reported upon, application of "substance over form" reasoning, and the goal of faithfully representing the economics of transactions.

**Channel stuffing.** Many difficult issues of revenue recognition involve practices that may or may not involve GAAP departures, depending on the situation-specific facts and circumstances. Channel stuffing is a prime example of this issue, where sales are actually made prior to the period-end cutoff but may have been stimulated by "side agreements," such as a promise to customers of extended return privileges or more liberal credit terms. In such circumstances, there might be a greater likelihood that a substantial portion of these sales may be subsequently nullified, as unrealistically large orders inevitably lead to later large returns made for full credit.

For purposes of financial reporting under GAAP, valuation allowances should be established for expected sales returns and allowances. (In practice, however, this is rarely done because the amounts involved are immaterial, unlike the amounts of the more familiar allowances for uncollectible accounts.) The use of valuation accounts for anticipated returns and allowances is dictated by both the matching concept (recording returns and allowances in the same fiscal period in which the revenue is recognized) as well as by the requirement to present accounts receivable at net realizable value. When the potential product returns are not subject to reasonable estimation (as when a sales promotion effort of the type just described is first being attempted by the reporting entity) but could be material, it might not be permissible to recognize revenues at all, pending subsequent developments (FAS 48). Furthermore, from the SEC's perspective, factors such as the following could require deferral of revenues at the time goods are shipped to customers, pending resolution of material uncertainties.

1. Significant levels of product inventory in the distribution channel
2. Lack of "visibility" into, or the inability to determine or observe, the levels of inventory in a distribution channel and the current level of sales to end users
3. Expected introductions of new products that may result in the technological obsolescence of, and larger than expected returns of, current products
4. The significance of a particular distributor to the company's (or a reporting segment of the company's) business, sales and marketing
5. The newness of a product
6. The introduction of competitors' products with superior technology or greater expected market acceptance could affect market demand and changing trends in that demand for an entity's products

**Mischaracterization of extraordinary or unusual transactions as components of gross revenue.** Not all revenue recognition errors and frauds involve questions of when or if revenue should be recognized. In some instances, classification in the income statement is of greater concern. While matters in this group often do not result in a distortion of net results of operations, they can seriously distort important indicators of performance trends. When this occurs, it most often involves reporting unusual or infrequent gains on sales of segments or specific assets as revenue from product or service transactions. A variation on this involves reporting unusual gains as offsets to one or more categories of operating expenses, similarly distorting key financial ratios and other indicators, again without necessarily invalidating the net income measure.

Over the years, the range of items for which extraordinary item classification is permitted has been sharply curtailed. FASB is still, as of mid-2008, pursuing a joint project with IASB that will, if it culminates in a standard consistent with current plans, eliminate the extraordinary classification completely. However, while this would eliminate the potential for abuse described in the preceding paragraph, misclassification of income or expense items would continue to constitute a fraud risk.

**Mischaracterizing transactions as involving "arm's-length" third parties, thus justifying unwarranted gain recognition.** Transfers of inventory or other assets to a related entity typically defers gain or income recognition until subsequent transfer to an "arm's-length" party. In some cases, sales have been disguised as being to unrelated entities with gain being recognized, when in fact the "buyer" was a nominee of the seller, or the financing was provided or guaranteed by the seller, or the "buyer" was a "variable interest entity" that failed to meet the complex and changing requirements under GAAP required for gain recognition. Depending upon the facts of the situation, this can result in gains being improperly recognized, or the gross amount of the transaction being improperly recognized in the seller/transferor's financial statements.

**Selling undervalued assets to generate reportable gains.** This issue again ranges from deliberate but real economic transactions that have as a goal the inflation of reportable revenues or gains, to misrepresented events having no economic substance but the same objective. Among the former is the deliberate invasion of low-cost LIFO inventory "layers," which boosts gross margins and net profits for the period, albeit at the cost of having to later replenish inventories with higher-cost goods. To the extent that this depletion of lower-cost inventory really occurs, there is no GAAP alternative to reflecting these excess profits currently, although the threat of full disclosure may prove to be somewhat of a deterrent.

Regarding the latter category, in some instances the ability to generate gains could indicate that errors occurred in recording a previous transaction. Thus, large gains flowing from the sale of assets recently acquired in a purchase business combination transaction could well mean the purchase price allocation process was flawed. If this is true, a reallocation of purchase price would be called for, and some or all of the apparent gains would be eliminated.

Related to the foregoing is the strategy of retiring outstanding debt in order to generate reportable gains. In periods of higher-than-historically-typical interest rates, lenders will often agree to early extinguishment of outstanding low-coupon obligations at a discount, hence creating accounting gains for the borrower, albeit replacement debt at current yields will result in higher interest costs over future years. To the extent the debt is really retired, however, this is a real economic event, and the consequent gain is reported in current earnings under GAAP. This issue is discussed in more detail in Chapter 15.

**Deliberate misstatement of percentage of completion on long-term construction contracts.** Under SOP 81-1 (detailed later in this chapter), profits on certain long-term construction-type contracts are recognized ratably over the period of construction. An obvious and often easy way to distort periodic results of operations is to deliberately over- or understate the degree to which one or more discrete projects has been completed as of period end. This, coupled with the difficulty and importance of estimating remaining costs to be incurred to complete each project, makes profit recognition under this required method of accounting challenging to verify.

## Disclosures

APB 22 requires disclosures of "…important judgments as to appropriateness of principles relating to the recognition of revenue." SAB 101 expressed the opinion of the SEC staff that because revenue recognition generally involves the exercise of judgment, companies are always required to disclose their revenue recognition policies. SAB 101 also provided that, when applicable, the notes to the financial statements are to include disclosure of

1. The revenue recognition policy for each material type of transaction
2. If the company enters into multiple-element sales arrangements (e.g., bundling of related products and/or services), the method of accounting for each element and the method used to determine each element and value it
3. Material changes in estimates of returns in accordance with FAS 48 (e.g., changing the percentage of sales used to establish the allowance).

In addition, SEC Regulation S-X requires that each of the following categories of revenue (and the related costs), if applicable, be stated separately on the face of the income statement:

1. Sales of tangible products (net of discounts, returns, and allowances)
2. Income from rentals
3. Revenue from services
4. Other revenues

In addition to the foregoing, the financial statement preparer should consider the applicability of FAS 57, *Related-Party Disclosures,* and SOP 94-6, *Disclosure of Certain Significant Risks and Uncertainties.* (See Chapter 2.)

## Specialized Applications

The remainder of this chapter discusses specialized principles that have been established for accounting for the following types of transactions:

1. Long-term construction contracts
2. Service revenues
3. Sales when collection is uncertain
4. Revenue recognition when right of return exists
5. Profit recognition on real estate sales
6. Real estate operations
7. Franchising
8. Other special accounting and reporting issues

Each of these sections may be read as an individual unit.

## LONG-TERM CONSTRUCTION CONTRACTS

### PERSPECTIVE AND ISSUES

Accounting for long-term construction contracts involves questions as to when revenue is to be recognized and how to measure the revenue to be recorded. The basic GAAP governing the recognition of long-term contract revenue is contained in ARB 45, *Long-Term Construction-Type Contracts,* AcSEC Statement of Position 81-1, *Accounting for Performance of Construction-Type and Certain Production-Type Contracts,* and the AICPA *Audit and Accounting Guide for Construction Contractors.*[1] In accordance with SAS 69, Accounting Research Bulletins (ARB) are "category A" (the highest level) GAAP, and SOP 81-1 and the Audit and Accounting Guide are "category B" GAAP.

The accounting for long-term construction contracts is complicated by the need to rely upon estimates of revenues, costs to be incurred, and progress toward completion.

| Sources of GAAP | | | | |
|---|---|---|---|---|
| *CON* | *ARB* | *APB* | *FAS* | *SOP* |
| 5 | 45 | 20 | 109 | 81-1, 98-5 |

## DEFINITIONS OF TERMS

**Back charges.** Billings for work performed or costs incurred by one party (the biller) that, in accordance with the agreement, should have been performed or incurred by the party billed.

**Change order.** A legal document executed by a contractor and customer (which can be initiated by either) that modifies selected terms of a contract (e.g., pricing, timing and scope of work) without the necessity of redrafting the entire contract.

**Claims.** Amounts in excess of the agreed contract price that a contractor seeks to collect from customers for customer-caused delays, errors in specifications and designs, unapproved change orders, or other causes of unanticipated costs. (SOP 81-1)

**Combining contracts.** Grouping two or more contracts into a single profit center for accounting purposes.

**Completed-contract method.** A method of accounting that recognizes revenue only after the contract is complete.

**Cost-to-cost method.** A percentage-of-completion method used to determine the extent of progress toward completion on a contract. The ratio of costs incurred from project inception through the end of the current period (numerator) to the total estimated costs of the project (denominator) is applied to the contract price (as adjusted for change orders) to determine total contract revenue earned to date.

**Estimated cost to complete.** The anticipated additional cost of materials, labor, subcontracting costs, and indirect costs (overhead) required in order to complete a project at a scheduled time.

**Percentage-of-completion method.** A method of accounting that recognizes revenue on a contract as work progresses.

**Precontract costs.** Costs incurred before a contract has been accepted (e.g., architectural designs, purchase of special equipment, engineering fees, and start-up costs).

**Profit center.** A unit for the accumulation of revenues and costs for the measurement of contract performance.

**Progress billings on long-term contracts.** Requests for partial payments sent to the customer in accordance with the terms of the contract at agreed-upon intervals as various project milestones are reached.

**Segmenting contracts.** Dividing a single contract or group of contracts into two or more profit centers for accounting purposes.

**Subcontractor.** A second-level contractor who enters into a contract with a prime (general) contractor to perform a specific part or phase of a construction project.

**Substantial completion.** The point at which the major work on a contract is completed and only insignificant costs and potential risks remain.

---

[1] *The SOP is included as an appendix to the Audit and Accounting Guide.*

**Work-in-progress (WIP).** The accumulated construction costs of the project that have been incurred since project inception.

## CONCEPTS, RULES, AND EXAMPLES

Long-term construction contract revenue is recognizable over time as construction progresses rather than at the completion of the contract. This "as earned" approach to revenue recognition is justified because under most long-term construction contracts both the buyer and the seller (contractor) obtain legally enforceable rights. The buyer has the legal right to require specific performance from the contractor and, in effect, has an ownership claim to the contractor's work in progress. The contractor, under most long-term contracts, has the right to require the buyer to make progress payments during the construction period. The substance of this business activity is that revenue is earned continuously as the work progresses.

### Methods of Accounting

ARB 45 describes the two generally accepted methods of accounting for long-term construction contracts.

#### The percentage-of-completion method.

*The percentage-of-completion method recognizes income as work on a contract (or group of closely related contracts) progresses. The recognition of revenues and profits is generally related to costs incurred in providing the services required under the contract.*

Under this method, *work-in-progress* (WIP) is accumulated in the accounting records. At any point in time if the cumulative billings to date under the contract exceed the amount of the WIP plus the portion of the contract's estimated gross profit attributable to that WIP, then the contractor recognizes a current liability captioned "billings in excess of costs and estimated earnings." This liability recognizes the remaining obligation of the contractor to complete additional work prior to recognizing the excess billing as revenue.

If the reverse is true, that is, the accumulated WIP and gross profit earned exceed billings to date, then the contractor recognizes a current asset captioned "costs and estimated earnings in excess of billings." This asset represents the portion of the contractor's revenues under the contract that have been earned but not yet billed under the contract provisions. Where more than one contract exists, these assets and liabilities are determined on a project-by-project basis, with the accumulated assets and liabilities being separately stated on the balance sheet. Assets and liabilities are not offset unless a right of offset exists. Thus, the net debit balances for certain contracts are not ordinarily offset against net credit balances for other contracts. An exception may exist if the balances relate to contracts that meet the criteria for combining described in SOP 81-1 and discussed later in this section.

Under the percentage-of-completion method, income is not based on cash collections or interim billings. Cash collections and interim billings are based upon contract terms that do not necessarily measure contract performance.

#### The completed-contract method. Per ARB 45

*The* completed-contract method *recognizes income only when the contract is complete, or substantially complete.*

Under this method, contract costs and related billings are accumulated in the accounting records and reported as deferred items on the balance sheet until the project is complete or substantially complete. A contract is regarded as substantially complete if remaining costs of completion are immaterial. When the accumulated costs (WIP) exceed the related billings, the excess is presented as a current asset (inventory account). If billings exceed related costs, the difference is presented as a current liability. This determination is also made on a project-by-project basis with the accumulated assets and liabilities being separately stated on the balance sheet. An excess of accumulated costs over related billings is presented as a current asset, and an excess of accumulated billings over related costs is presented in most cases as a current liability.

**Preferability assessment.** SOP 81-1 deems the percentage-of-completion method to be preferable when estimates are reasonably dependable and the following conditions exist:

1. Contracts executed by the parties include provisions that clearly specify the enforceable rights regarding goods or services to be provided and received by the parties, the consideration to be exchanged, and the manner and terms of settlement.
2. The buyer can be expected to satisfy his or her obligations under the contract.
3. The contractor can be expected to perform his or her contractual obligations.

SOP 81-1 presumes that contractors generally have the ability to produce estimates that are sufficiently dependable to justify the use of the percentage-of-completion method of accounting. Persuasive evidence to the contrary is necessary to overcome this presumption.

The principal advantage of the completed-contract method is that it is based on final results, whereas the percentage-of-completion method is dependent upon estimates for unperformed work. The principal disadvantage of the completed-contract method is that when the period of a contract extends into more than one accounting period, there will be an irregular recognition of income.

These two methods are not equally acceptable alternatives for the same set of circumstances. ARB 45 states that, in general, when estimates of costs to complete and extent of progress toward completion of long-term contracts are reasonably dependable, the percentage-of-completion method is preferable. When lack of dependable estimates or inherent hazards cause forecasts to be doubtful, the completed-contract method is preferable.

The completed-contract method may also be acceptable when a contractor has numerous relatively short-term contracts and when results of operations do not vary materially from those that would be reported under the percentage-of-completion method.

Based on the contractor's individual circumstances, a decision is made as to whether to apply completed-contract or percentage-of-completion accounting as the entity's basic accounting policy. If warranted by different facts and circumstances regarding a particular contract or group of contracts, that contract or group of contracts is to be accounted for under the other method with accompanying financial statement disclosures of this departure from the normal policy.

## Costs Incurred

**Precontract costs.** Precontract costs are costs incurred before a contract has been entered into, with the expectation of the contract being accepted and thereby recoverable through future billings. Precontract costs include architectural designs, costs of learning a new process, and any other costs that are expected to be recovered if the contract is accepted. SOP 98-5, *Reporting on the Costs of Start-Up Activities,* requires that precontract costs be expensed as incurred, as they are the equivalent of start-up costs in other types of businesses. Consequently, precontract costs are not permitted to be included in WIP. Contract costs incurred after the acceptance of the contract are costs incurred towards the completion of the project and are accumulated in work-in-progress (WIP).

If precontract costs are incurred in connection with a current contract in anticipation of obtaining additional future contracts, those costs are nevertheless accounted for as costs of the current contract. If such costs are not incurred in connection with a current contract, then they must be expensed as incurred. There is no look-back provision in this standard. A contractor may not retroactively record precontract costs as WIP if a contract is subsequently executed.

**Contract costs.** Contract costs are costs identifiable with or allocable to specific contracts. Generally, contract costs include all direct costs such as direct materials, direct labor, and any indirect costs (overhead) allocable to the contracts. Contract costs can be broken down into two categories: costs incurred to date and estimated costs to complete.

The company may choose to defer costs related to producing excess goods in anticipation of future orders of the same item. Costs associated with excess production can be treated as inventory if the costs are considered recoverable.

**Estimated costs to complete.** These are the anticipated costs required to complete a project at a scheduled time. They are comprised of the same elements as the original total estimated contract costs and are based on prices expected to be in effect when the costs will be incurred.

The latest estimates are used to determine the progress towards completion. SOP 81-1 provides the practices to be followed when estimating costs to complete.

Systematic and consistent procedures are to be used. These procedures are to be correlated with the cost accounting system in order to facilitate a comparison between actual and estimated costs. Additionally, the determination of estimated total contract costs is to identify the significant cost elements.

Estimated costs are to reflect any expected price increases. These expected price increases are not "blanket provisions" for all contract costs, but rather specific provisions for each specific type of cost. Expected increases in each of the cost elements such as wages, materials, and overhead items are considered separately.

Finally, estimates of costs to complete are to be reviewed periodically to reflect new information. Estimates of costs are to be examined for price fluctuations and reviewed for possible future problems, such as labor strikes or direct material delivery delays.

Accounting for contract costs is similar to accounting for inventory. Costs necessary to ready the asset for sale (transfer of possession and occupancy by the customer) are recorded in WIP as incurred. WIP includes both direct and indirect costs but not general and administrative expenses or selling expenses since, by definition, they are not identifiable with a particular contract and are therefore treated as period costs. However, general and administrative expenses may be included in contract costs under the completed contract method since this could result in better matching of revenues and costs, especially in years when no contracts were completed.

**Subcontractor costs.** Since a contractor may not be able to perform all facets of a construction project, one or more subcontractors may be engaged. Amounts earned by the subcontractor are included in contract costs as the work is completed. These amounts are directly attributable to the project and included in WIP, similar to direct materials and direct labor.

**Back charges.** Contract costs may require adjustment for back charges. A back charge is a billing by the contractor to a subcontractor (or a reduction in the amount due to that subcontractor under the subcontract) for costs incurred by the contractor to complete or correct work that the contract stipulated was to have been performed by the subcontractor. These charges are often disputed by the parties involved.

### Example of a back charge situation

The subcontract (the contract between the general contractor and the subcontractor) obligates the subcontractor to raze a building and prepare the land for construction of a replacement building. The general contractor had to clear away debris left by the subcontractor before construction could begin. The general contractor expects to be reimbursed for the work since it was required to be performed by the subcontractor. The contractor back charges the subcontractor for the costs of debris removal.

The contractor treats the back charge as a receivable from the subcontractor (or a reduction in the amount payable to the subcontractor) and reduces contract costs by the amount recoverable. If the subcontractor disputes the back charge, the cost becomes a claim. Claims are an amount in excess of the agreed contract price or amounts not included in the original contract price that the contractor seeks to collect. Claims are only recorded as additional contract revenue if the requirements set forth in SOP 81-1 are met.

The subcontractor records the back charge as a payable and as additional contract costs if it is probable the amount will be paid. If the amount or validity of the liability is disputed, the subcontractor considers the probable outcome in order to determine the proper accounting treatment.

## Types of Contracts

Four types of contracts are distinguished based on their pricing arrangements: (1) fixed-price or lump-sum contracts, (2) time-and-materials contracts, (3) cost-type contracts, and (4) unit-price contracts.

Fixed-price contracts are contracts for which the price is not usually subject to adjustment because of costs incurred by the contractor. The contractor bears the risks of cost overruns.

Time-and-materials contracts are contracts that provide for payments to the contractor based on direct labor hours at fixed rates and the contractor's cost of materials.

Cost-type contracts provide for reimbursement of allowable or otherwise defined costs incurred plus a fee representing profits. Some variations of cost-plus contracts are (1) cost-without-fee: no provision for a fee, (2) cost-plus-fixed-fee: contractor reimbursed for costs plus provision for a fixed fee, and (3) cost-plus-award-fee: same as (2) plus provision for an award based on performance. The contract price on a cost-type contract is determined by the sum of the reimbursable expenditures and a fee. The fee is the profit margin (revenue less direct expenses) to be earned on the contract.

Unit-price contracts are contracts under which the contractor is paid a specified amount for every unit of work performed.

Contract costs (incurred and estimated to complete) are used to compute the gross profit or loss recognized. Under the percentage-of-completion method, gross profit or loss is recognized each period. The revenue recognized is matched against the contract costs incurred (similar to cost of goods sold) to determine gross profit or loss. Under the completed contract method, the gross profit or loss is determined at the substantial completion of the contract, and no revenue or contract costs are recognized until this point.

Additionally, inventoriable costs (accumulated in WIP) are never to exceed the net realizable value (NRV) of the contract. When contract costs exceed their NRV, they must be written down, requiring a contract loss to be recognized in the current period (this will be discussed in greater detail later). This is similar to accounting for inventory.

### Example of contract types

Domino Construction Inc. enters into a government contract to construct an early warning radar dome. The contract amount is for $1,900,000, on which Domino expects to incur costs of $1,750,000 and earn a profit of $150,000. Costs expected to be incurred on the project are

| | |
|---|---|
| Concrete pad | $ 175,000 |
| Pad installation labor | 100,000 |
| Radar dome | 1,150,000 |
| Dome installation labor | 325,000 |
| Total cost | $1,750,000 |

This is a two-month project, where a concrete pad is installed during the first month and a prefabricated dome is assembled on the pad during the second month. To comply with bank loan agreements, complete GAAP-basis financial statements are prepared by Domino at each month-end. Domino encounters problems pouring the concrete pad, requiring its removal and reinstallation. The extra cost incurred is $175,000. During the second month, in order to meet the completion deadline, Domino spends an extra $35,000 on overtime for the dome construction crew. Domino records different billable amounts and profits under the following five contract scenarios:

1. *Fixed-price contract.* At the end of the first month of work, Domino has already lost all of its profit and expects to incur an additional loss of $25,000. It then incurs an additional loss of $35,000 in the second month. Domino issues one billing upon completion of the project. Its calculation of losses on the contract follows:

|  | Month 1 | Month 2 |
| --- | --- | --- |
| Total billing at completion | $1,900,000 | $1,900,000 |
| – Expected total costs | (1,750,000) | (1,925,000) |
| – Additional costs | (175,000) | (35,000) |
| + Loss already recorded | -- | 25,000 |
| = Loss to record in current period | $ (25,000) | $ (35,000) |

2. *Cost-plus-fixed fee.* Domino completes the same project, but bills it to the government at cost at the end of each month, as well as a $150,000 fixed fee at the end of the project that is essentially a project management fee and which comprises all of Domino's profit. The project completion entry follows:

|  | Month 1 | Month 2 | Totals |
| --- | --- | --- | --- |
| Expected material costs | $175,000 | $1,150,000 | $1,325,000 |
| + Additional material costs | 175,000 | -- | 175,000 |
| + Expected labor costs | 100,000 | 325,000 | 425,000 |
| + Additional labor costs | -- | 35,000 | 35,000 |
| + Fixed fee | -- | 150,000 | 150,000 |
| = Total billing | $450,000 | $1,660,000 | $2,110,000 |

3. *Cost-plus-award.* Domino completes the same cost-plus-fixed-fee contract just described, but also bills the government an additional $50,000 for achieving the stipulated construction deadline, resulting in a total profit of $200,000. The project completion entry follows:

|  | Month 1 | Month 2 | Totals |
| --- | --- | --- | --- |
| Expected material costs | $175,000 | $1,150,000 | $1,325,000 |
| + Additional material costs | 175,000 | -- | 175,000 |
| + Expected labor costs | 100,000 | 325,000 | 425,000 |
| + Additional labor costs | -- | 35,000 | 35,000 |
| + Fixed fee | -- | 150,000 | 150,000 |
| + Timely completion bonus | -- | 50,000 | 50,000 |
| = Total billing | $450,000 | $1,710,000 | $2,160,000 |

4. *Time-and materials contract with no spending cap.* Domino completes the same project, but bills all costs incurred at the end of each month to the government. The additional material cost of the concrete pad is billed at cost, while the overtime incurred is billed at a standard hourly rate with a 25% markup. Domino's profit is contained within the markup on its labor billings. Domino records a profit on the project of $115,000 on total billings of $2,075,000. Its calculation of profits on the contract follows:

|  | Month 1 | Month 2 | Totals |
| --- | --- | --- | --- |
| Expected material costs | $175,000 | $1,150,000 | $1,325,000 |
| + Additional material costs | 175,000 | -- | 175,000 |
| + Expected labor costs | 100,000 | 325,000 | 425,000 |
| + Additional labor costs | -- | 35,000 | 35,000 |
| + 25% profit on labor costs billed | 25,000 | 90,000 | 115,000 |
| = Total billing | $475,000 | $1,600,000 | $2,075,000 |

5. *Time and material contract with spending cap.* Domino completes the same time-and-materials project just described, but the contract authorization is divided into two task orders; one authorizes a spending cap of $450,000 on the concrete pad installation, while the second task order caps spending on the radar dome at $1,500,000. Domino records a

loss of $10,000 on total billings of $1,950,000. Its calculation of profits on the contract follows:

|  | *Month 1* | *Month 2* | *Totals* |
|---|---|---|---|
| Expected material costs | $175,000 | $1,150,000 | $1,325,000 |
| + Additional material costs | 175,000 | -- | 175,000 |
| + Expected labor costs | 100,000 | 325,000 | 425,000 |
| + Additional labor costs | -- | 35,000 | 35,000 |
| + 25% profit on labor costs billed | 25,000 | 90,000 | 115,000 |
| − Spending cap limitation | (25,000) | (100,000) | (125,000) |
| = Total billing | $450,000 | $1,500,000 | $1,950,000 |

## Revenue Measurement

In practice, various methods are used to measure the extent of progress toward completion. The most common methods are the cost-to-cost method, efforts-expended method, units-of-delivery method, and units-of-work-performed method. Each of these methods of measuring progress on a contract can be identified as either an input or output measure.

The input measures attempt to identify progress on a contract in terms of the efforts devoted to it. The cost-to-cost and efforts-expended methods are examples of input measures. Under the cost-to-cost method, the percentage of completion is estimated by comparing total costs incurred from the inception of the job to date (numerator) to total costs expected for the entire job (denominator).

Output measures are made in terms of results by attempting to identify progress toward completion by physical measures. The units-of-delivery and units-of-work-performed methods are examples of output measures. Under both of these methods, an estimate of completion is made in terms of achievements to date.

Both input and output measures have drawbacks in certain circumstances. A significant problem of input measures is that the relationship between input and productivity is only indirect; inefficiencies and other factors can cause this relationship to change. A particular drawback of the cost-to-cost method is that costs of uninstalled materials and other up-front costs may produce higher estimates of the percentage-of-completion because of their early incurrence. These costs are excluded from the cost-to-cost computation or allocated over the contract life when it appears that a better measure of contact progress will be obtained.

A significant problem of output measures is that the cost, time, and effort associated with one unit of output may not be comparable to that of another. For example, because of the cost of the foundation, the costs to complete the first story of a twenty-story office building can be expected to be greater than the costs of the remaining nineteen floors.

Because ARB 45 recommends that "recognized income [is to] be that percentage of estimated total income...that incurred costs to date bear to estimated total costs," the cost-to-cost method has become one of the most popular measures used to determine the extent of progress toward completion.

Under the cost-to-cost method, the percentage of revenue to recognize can be determined by the following formula:

$$\left( \frac{\text{Cost to date}}{\text{Cost to date} + \text{Estimated costs to complete}} \times \frac{\text{Contract}}{\text{price}} \right) - \frac{\text{Revenue}}{\text{previously recognized}} = \frac{\text{Current}}{\text{revenue recognized}}$$

By slightly modifying this formula, current gross profit can also be determined.

$$\left( \frac{\text{Cost to date}}{\text{Cost to date} + \text{Estimated costs to complete}} \times \frac{\text{Expected total}}{\text{gross profit}} \right) - \frac{\text{Gross profit}}{\text{previously recognized}} = \frac{\text{Current gross}}{\text{profit earned}}$$

### Example of percentage-of-completion (cost-to-cost) and completed-contract methods with profitable contract

Assume a $500,000 contract that requires three years to complete and incurs a total cost of $405,000. The following data pertain to the construction period:

| | Year 1 | Year 2 | Year 3 |
|---|---|---|---|
| Costs incurred during the period | $150,000 | $210,000 | $ 45,000 |
| Cumulative costs incurred to date | 150,000 | 360,000 | 405,000 |
| Estimated costs yet to be incurred at year-end | 300,000 | 40,000 | -- |
| Estimated total costs | 450,000 | 400,000 | -- |
| Progress billings made during the year | 100,000 | 370,000 | 30,000 |
| Cumulative billings to date | 100,000 | 470,000 | 500,000 |
| Collections of billings | 75,000 | 300,000 | 125,000 |

### Journal Entries Common to Completed-Contract and Percentage-of-Completion Methods

| | Year 1 | | Year 2 | | Year 3 | |
|---|---|---|---|---|---|---|
| Work-in-progress | 150,000 | | 210,000 | | 45,000 | |
| Cash, payables, etc. | | 150,000 | | 210,000 | | 45,000 |
| Contract receivables | 100,000 | | 370,000 | | 30,000 | |
| Billings on contracts | | 100,000 | | 370,000 | | 30,000 |
| Cash | 75,000 | | 300,000 | | 125,000 | |
| Contract receivables | | 75,000 | | 300,000 | | 125,000 |

### Journal Entries for Completed-Contract Method Only

| | | | | | Year 3 | |
|---|---|---|---|---|---|---|
| Billings on contracts | | | | | 500,000 | |
| Cost of revenues earned | | | | | 405,000 | |
| Contract revenues earned | | | | | | 500,000 |
| Work-in-progress | | | | | | 405,000 |

### Journal Entries for Percentage-of-Completion Method Only

| | Year 1 | | Year 2 | | Year 3 | |
|---|---|---|---|---|---|---|
| Cost of revenues earned | 150,000 | | 210,000 | | 45,000 | |
| Work-in-progress | | 150,000 | | 210,000 | | 45,000 |
| Billings on contracts | 100,000 | | 370,000 | | 30,000 | |
| Contract revenues earned | | 166,667 | | 283,333 | | 50,000 |
| Costs and estimated earnings in excess of billings on uncompleted contracts | 66,667 | | 66,667 | | | |
| Billings in excess of costs and estimated earnings on uncompleted contracts | | | | 20,000 | 20,000 | |

### Income Statement Presentation

| | Year 1 | Year 2 | Year 3 | Total |
|---|---|---|---|---|
| **Percentage-of-completion** | | | | |
| Contract revenues earned | $166,667* | $283,333** | $ 50,000*** | $ 500,000 |
| Cost of revenues earned | (150,000) | (210,000) | (45,000) | (405,000) |
| Gross profit | $ 16,667 | $ 73,333 | $ 5,000 | $ 95,000 |
| **Completed-contract** | | | | |
| Contract revenues earned | -- | -- | $ 500,000 | $ 500,000 |
| Cost of revenues completed | -- | -- | (405,000) | (405,000) |
| Gross profit | -- | -- | $ 95,000 | $ 95,000 |

$$* \quad \frac{\$150,000}{450,000} \quad x \quad 500,000 \quad = \quad \$166,667$$

$$** \quad \left( \frac{\$360,000}{400,000} \quad x \ 500,000 \right) \quad - \quad 166,667 \quad = \quad \$283,333$$

$$*** \quad \left( \frac{\$405,000}{405,000} \quad x \ 500,000 \right) \quad - \quad 166,667 \quad - \quad 283,333 \quad = \quad \$50,000$$

*Balance Sheet Presentation*

|  | Year 1 | Year 2 | Year 3 |
|---|---|---|---|
| **Percentage-of-completion** |  |  |  |
| Current assets: |  |  |  |
| Contract receivables | $25,000 | $ 95,000 | * |
| Costs and estimated earnings in excess of billings on uncompleted contracts | 66,667 |  |  |
| Current liabilities: |  |  |  |
| Billings in excess of costs and estimated earnings on uncompleted contracts, year 2 |  | 20,000 |  |
| **Completed-contract** |  |  |  |
| Current assets: |  |  |  |
| Contract receivables | $25,000 | $ 95,000 | * |
| Costs in excess of billings on uncompleted contracts |  |  |  |
| Work-in-progress | 150,000 |  |  |
| Less billings on long-term contracts | (100,000) | $50,000 |  |
| Current liabilities: |  |  |  |
| Billings in excess of costs on uncompleted contracts, year 2 ($470,000 – 360,000) |  | $110,000 |  |

\* *Since the contract was completed, there are no balance sheet amounts at the end of year 3.*

Some contractors adopt an accounting policy of not recognizing any gross profit on a contract that is less than 10% complete. This election is usually made for two reasons.

1. The contractor is qualified to make and has made the election permitted by Internal Revenue Code §460(b)(5) to defer the recognition of such gross profit for US federal income tax purposes and wishes to avoid computational differences between applying the percentage-of-completion method for financial reporting and tax purposes, and

2. The contractor believes that this policy is prudent given the uncertainties associated with a contract that is so close to inception.

The GAAP effect of such a policy is usually immaterial and the accountant normally need not be concerned about it being a departure from GAAP.

### Contract Losses

When the current estimate of total contract costs exceeds the current estimate of total contract revenues, a provision for the entire loss on the entire contract is made. Losses are recognized in the period in which they become evident under either the percentage-of-completion method or the completed-contract method. The loss is computed on the basis of the total estimated costs to complete the contract, including the contract costs incurred to date plus estimated costs (use the same elements as contract costs incurred) to complete. The loss is presented as a separately captioned current liability on the balance sheet.

In any year when a percentage-of-completion contract has an expected loss, the amount of the loss reported in that year is computed as follows:

Reported loss = Total expected loss + All profit previously recognized

**Example of percentage-of-completion and completed-contract methods with loss contract**

Using the previous information, if the estimated costs yet to be incurred at the end of year two were $148,000, the total expected loss is $8,000 [$500,000 – (360,000 + 148,000)], and the total loss reported in year two would be $24,667 ($8,000 + 16,667). Under the completed-contract method, the loss recognized is simply the total expected loss, $8,000.

| Journal entry at end of year 2 | Percentage-of-completion | Completed-contract |
|---|---|---|
| Loss on uncompleted long-term contract (expense) | 24,667 | 8,000 |
| Estimated loss on uncompleted contract (liability) | 24,667 | 8,000 |

**Profit or Loss Recognized on Contract**
**(Percentage-of-Completion Method)**

| | Year 1 | Year 2 | Year 3 |
|---|---|---|---|
| Contract price | $500,000 | $500,000 | $500,000 |
| Estimated total costs: | | | |
| Costs incurred contract-to-date | $150,000 | $360,000 | $506,000* |
| Estimated costs yet to be incurred | 300,000 | 148,000 | -- |
| Estimated total costs for the three-year period, actual for year 3 | $450,000 | $508,000 | $506,000 |
| Estimated gross profit (loss), actual for year 3 | 50,000 | (8,000) | (6,000) |
| **Summary of Effect on Results of Operations** | | | |
| Current end-of-year estimate of gross profit (loss) actual for year 3 | -- | $ (8,000) | $ (6,000) |
| Accumulated effect of gross profit (loss) recognized in prior years | -- | 16,667 | (8,000) |
| Effect on gross profit (loss) recognized in current year | -- | $ (24,667) | $ 2,000 |

\* *Assumed*

**Profit or Loss Recognized on Contract**
**(Completed-Contract Method)**

| | Year 1 | Year 2 | Year 3 |
|---|---|---|---|
| Contract price | $500,000 | $500,000 | $500,000 |
| Estimated total costs: | | | |
| Costs incurred to date | $150,000 | $360,000 | $506,000* |
| Estimated cost yet to be incurred | 300,000 | 148,000 | -- |
| Estimated total costs for the three-year period, actual for year 3 | $450,000 | $508,000 | $506,000 |
| Estimated profit (loss), inception-to-date, actual for year 3 | $ 50,000 | $ (8,000) | $ (6,000) |
| Loss previously recognized | -- | -- | $ (8,000) |
| Amount of estimated income (loss) recognized in the current period, actual for year 3 | -- | $ (8,000) | $ 2,000 |

\* *Assumed*

Upon completion of the project during year 3, it can be seen that the actual loss was only $6,000 ($500,000 – $506,000); therefore, the estimated loss provision was overstated in previous years by $2,000. However, since this is a change of an estimate, the $2,000 difference must be handled prospectively; consequently, $2,000 of income is recognized in year 3 ($8,000 loss previously recognized – $6,000 actual loss).

## Combining and Segmenting Contracts

The profit center for accounting purposes is usually a single contract, but under some circumstances the profit center may be a combination of two or more contracts, a segment of a contract or a group of combined contracts. The contracts must meet requirements in SOP 81-1 in order to combine, or segment; otherwise, each individual contract is presumed to be the profit center.

For accounting purposes, a group of contracts may be combined if they are so closely related that they are, in substance, parts of a single project with an overall profit margin. Per SOP 81-1, a group of contracts may be combined if the contracts

1. Are negotiated as a package in the same economic environment with an overall profit margin objective.
2. Constitute an agreement to do a single project.

3. Require closely interrelated construction activities.
4. Are performed concurrently or in a continuous sequence under the same project management.
5. Constitute, in substance, an agreement with a single customer.

Segmenting a contract is a process of breaking up a larger unit into smaller units for accounting purposes. If the project is segmented, revenues are assigned to the different elements or phases to achieve different rates of profitability based on the relative value of each element or phase to the estimated total contract revenue. According to SOP 81-1, a project may be segmented if all of the following steps were taken and are documented and verifiable:

1. The contractor submitted bona fide proposals on the separate components of the project and on the entire project.
2. The customer had the right to accept the proposals on either basis.
3. The aggregate amount of the proposals on the separate components approximated the amount of the proposal on the entire project.

A project that does not meet the above criteria may still be segmented if all of the following are applicable:

1. The terms and scope of the contract or project clearly call for the separable phases or elements.
2. The separable phases or elements of the project are often bid or negotiated separately in the marketplace.
3. The market assigns different gross profit rates to the segments because of factors such as different levels of risk or differences in the relationship of the supply and demand for the services provided in different segments.
4. The contractor has a significant history of providing similar services to other customers under separate contracts for each significant segment to which a profit margin higher than the overall profit margin on the project is ascribed.
5. The significant history with customers who have contracted for services separately is one that is relatively stable in terms of pricing policy rather than one unduly weighted by erratic pricing decisions (responding, for example, to extraordinary economic circumstances or to unique customer-contractor relationships).
6. The excess of the sum of the prices of the separate elements over the price of the total project is clearly attributable to cost savings incident to combined performance of the contract obligations (for example, cost savings in supervision, overhead, or equipment mobilization). Unless this condition is met, segmenting a contract with a price substantially less than the sum of the prices of the separate phases or elements is inappropriate even if the other conditions are met. Acceptable price variations are allocated to the separate phases or elements in proportion to the prices ascribed to each. In all other situations a substantial difference in price (whether more or less) between the separate elements and the price of the total project is evidence that the contractor has accepted different profit margins. Accordingly, segmenting is not appropriate, and the contracts are the profit centers.
7. The similarity of services and prices in the contract segments and services and the prices of such services to other customers contracted separately are documented and verifiable.

Note that the criteria for combining and segmenting are to be applied consistently to contracts with similar characteristics and in similar circumstances.

## Joint Ventures and Shared Contracts

Especially large or risky contracts are sometimes shared by more than one contractor. When the owner of the contract requests competitive bids, many contractors will form syndicates or joint ventures in order to bid on and successfully obtain a contract that each contractor individually could not perform.

When this occurs, a separate set of accounting records is maintained for the joint venture. If the percentages of interest for each of the participants are identical in more than one contract, the joint venture might keep its records in the same manner as it would if it was simply another construction company. Usually, the joint venture is for a single contract and ends upon completion of that contract.

A joint venture is a type of partnership, organized for a limited purpose. An agreement of the parties and the terms of the contract successfully bid upon will determine the nature of the accounting records. Income statements are usually cumulative statements showing totals from date of contract inception until reporting date. Each participant records its share of the amount from the venture's income statement less its previously recorded portion of the venture's income as a single line item similar to the equity method for investments. Similarly, balance sheets of each participant present a single line asset balance, "investment in and advances to joint ventures." In most cases, footnote disclosure is similar to the equity method and presents condensed financial statements of material joint ventures.

## Accounting for Change Orders

Change orders are modifications of specifications or provisions of an original contract. Contract revenue and costs are adjusted to reflect change orders that are approved by the contractor and customer. According to SOP 81-1, accounting for a change order depends on the scope and price of the change.

If the scope and price have both been agreed to by the customer and contractor, contract revenue and cost are both adjusted to reflect the change order.

According to SOP 81-1, accounting for unpriced change orders depends on their characteristics and the circumstances in which they occur. Under the completed-contract method, costs attributable to unpriced change orders are deferred as contract costs if it is probable that total contract costs, including costs attributable to the change orders, will be recovered from contract revenues. Recovery is deemed probable if the future event or events are likely to occur.

Per SOP 81-1, the following guidelines apply when accounting for unpriced change orders under the percentage-of-completion method:

1. If it is not probable that the costs will be recovered through a change in the contract price, costs attributable to unpriced change orders are treated as costs of contract performance in the period in which the costs are incurred.
2. If it is probable that the costs will be recovered through a change in the contract price, the costs are deferred (excluded from the costs of contract performance) until the parties have agreed on the change in contract price, or alternatively, treated as costs of contract performance in the period in which they are incurred with a corresponding increase to contract revenue in the amount of the costs incurred.
3. If it is probable that the contract price will be adjusted by an amount that exceeds the costs attributable to the change order and both of the following apply:

    a. The amount of the excess can be reliably estimated, and
    b. Realization of the full contract price adjustment is probably beyond a reasonable doubt,

the original contract price is adjusted for the full amount of the adjustment as the costs are recognized.

However, since the substantiation of the amount of future revenue is difficult, satisfaction of the condition of "realization beyond a reasonable doubt" should only be considered satisfied in circumstances in which an entity's historical experience provides such assurance or in which an entity has received a bona fide pricing offer from a customer and records only the amount of the offer as revenue.

## Accounting for Contract Options

Per SOP 81-1, an addition or option to an existing contract is treated as a separate contract if any of the following circumstances exist:

1. The product or service to be provided differs significantly from the product or service provided under the original contract.
2. The price of the new product or service is negotiated without regard to the original contract and involves different economic judgments.
3. The products or services to be provided under the exercised option or amendment are similar to those under the original contract, but the contract price and anticipated contract cost relationship are significantly different.

If the addition or option does not meet the above circumstances, the contracts are combined unless the addition or option does not meet the criteria for combining, in which case it is treated as a change order.

## Accounting for Claims

Claims represent amounts in excess of the agreed-upon contract price that a contractor seeks to collect from customers for unanticipated additional costs. The recognition of additional contract revenue relating to claims is appropriate if it is probable that the claim will result in additional revenue and if the amount can be reliably estimated. SOP 81-1 specifies that all of the following conditions must exist in order for the probable and estimable requirements to be satisfied:

1. The contract or other evidence provides a legal basis for the claim; or a legal opinion has been obtained, stating that under the circumstances there is a reasonable basis to support the claim.
2. Additional costs are caused by circumstances that were unforeseen at the contract date and are not the result of deficiencies in the contractor's performance.
3. Costs associated with the claim are identifiable or otherwise determinable and are reasonable in view of the work performed.
4. The evidence supporting the claim is objective and verifiable, not based on management's "feel" for the situation or on unsupported representations.

When the above requirements are met, revenue from a claim is recorded only to the extent that contract costs relating to the claim have been incurred.

When the above requirements are not met, SOP 81-1 states that a contingent asset is disclosed in accordance with FAS 5.

## Accounting Changes

Prior to the issuance of FAS 154, the methodology prescribed for reporting a change in the method of accounting for long-term construction contracts had been defined by APB 20 as a special change in principle requiring retroactive treatment and restatement of previous financial statements. FAS 154 superseded APB 20, and adopted retroactive restatement as the standard methodology to be used for accounting for changes in accounting principle, including changes in the accounting for long-term construction contracts. (See Chapter 5 for further discussion.)

Revisions in revenue, cost, and profit estimates or in measurements of the extent of progress toward completion are changes in accounting estimates. These changes are accounted for prospectively in order for the financial statements to fully reflect the effects of the latest available estimates.

### Deferred Income Taxes

Deferred income taxes resulting from temporary differences are classified in accordance with FAS 109, *Accounting for Income Taxes*. Contract-related deferred income taxes result from the use of a method of income recognition for income tax purposes different from the method used for financial reporting purposes. (Refer to Chapter 17 for further discussion of deferred income taxes.)

## SERVICE REVENUES

### PERSPECTIVE AND ISSUES

Services represent over half of the transactions completed in the US economy, but there are no official pronouncements that provide specific accounting standards for them. Accounting for service transactions has evolved primarily through industry practice, and as a result, different accounting methods have developed to apply the fundamental principles of revenue and cost recognition. In fact, different accounting methods are used by similar entities for practically identical transactions.

FASB is currently pursuing a major project addressing revenue recognition, which would resolve the accounting for service transactions. It is anticipated that this project will be ongoing through 2008. In the interim, until definitive standards regarding revenue recognition are promulgated, this section can still provide relevant guidance on service industry issues. In addition, the guidance provided by the SEC in Staff Accounting Bulletin 101 and its replacement, SAB 104, discussed in the introductory materials to this chapter, is highly relevant to accounting for service transactions and should be deemed pertinent to accounting even by nonpublic reporting entities, inasmuch as it reflects the current thinking by an authoritative source of GAAP.

| Sources of GAAP | | | |
|---|---|---|---|
| *Other* | *FTB* | *EITF* | *SOP* |
| * | 90-1 | 91-9, 01-14 | 98-5 |

\* *SEC Staff Accounting Bulletins 101 and 104*

### DEFINITIONS OF TERMS

**Collection method.** A method that recognizes revenue when cash is collected.

**Completed performance method.** A method that recognizes revenue after the last significant act has been completed.

**Direct costs.** Costs that are related specifically to the performance of services under a contract or other arrangement.

**Indirect costs.** Costs that are incurred as a result of service activities that are not directly allocable to specific contracts or customer arrangements.

**Initiation fee.** A onetime, up-front charge that gives the purchaser the privilege of using a service or facilities.

**Installation fee.** A onetime, up-front charge for making equipment operational so that it functions as intended.

**Out-of-pocket costs.** Costs incurred incidental to the performance of services that are often reimbursable to the service firm by the customer either at actual cost or at an agreed-upon rate (e.g., meals, lodging, airfare, taxi fares, etc.).

**Precontract or preengagement costs.** Costs incurred prior to execution of a service contract or engagement letter.

**Product transaction.** A transaction between a seller and a purchaser in which the seller supplies tangible merchandise to the purchaser.

**Proportional performance method.** A method that recognizes revenue on the basis of the number of acts performed in relation to the total number of acts to be performed.

**Service transaction.** A transaction between a seller and a purchaser in which the seller performs work, or agrees to maintain a readiness to perform work, for the purchaser.

**Specific performance method.** A method that recognizes revenue after one specific act has been performed.

## CONCEPTS, RULES, AND EXAMPLES

The AICPA has defined service transactions as follows:

*...transactions between a seller and a purchaser in which, for a mutually agreed price, the seller performs, agrees to perform, agrees to perform at a later date, or agrees to maintain readiness to perform an act or acts, including permitting others to use enterprise resources that do not alone produce a tangible commodity or product as the principal intended result.*

Generally accepted accounting principles require that revenue generally be recognized when (1) it is realized or realizable and (2) it has been earned. With respect to service transactions, the AICPA concluded

*...revenue from service transactions [is to] be based on performance, because performance determines the extent to which the earnings process is complete or virtually complete.*

In practice, performance may involve the execution of a defined act, a set of similar or identical acts, or a set of related but not similar or identical acts. Performance may also occur with the passage of time. Accordingly, one of the following four methods can serve as a guideline for the recognition of revenue from service transactions:

1. The specific performance method
2. The proportional performance method
3. The completed performance method
4. The collection method

### Service vs. Product Transactions

Many transactions involve the sale of a tangible product and a service; therefore, for proper accounting treatment, it must be determined whether the transaction is primarily a service transaction accompanied by an incidental product, primarily a product transaction accompanied by an incidental service, or a sale in which both a service transaction and a product transaction occur. The following criteria apply:

1. **Service transactions.** If the seller offers both a service and a product in a single transaction and if the terms of the agreement for the sale of the service are worded in such a manner that the inclusion or exclusion of the product would not change the total transaction price, the product is incidental to the rendering of the service; the

transaction is a service transaction that is accounted for in accordance with one of the four methods presented. For example, fixed-price equipment maintenance contracts that include parts at no additional charge are service transactions.

2. **Product transactions.** If the seller offers both a service and a product in a single transaction and if the terms of the agreement for the sale of the product are worded in such a manner that the inclusion or exclusion of the service would not change the total transaction price, the rendering of the service is incidental to the sale of the product; the transaction is a product transaction that is accounted for as such. For example, the sale of a product accompanied by a guarantee or warranty for repair is considered a product transaction.

3. **Service and product transactions.** If the seller offers both a product and a service and the agreement states the product and service are separate elements such that the inclusion or exclusion of the service would vary the total transaction price, the transaction consists of two components: a product transaction that is accounted for separately as such, and a service transaction that is accounted for in accordance with one of the four accepted methods.

### Revenue Recognition Methods

Once a transaction is determined to be a service transaction, one of the following four methods is used to recognize revenue. The method chosen is to be based on the nature and extent of the service(s) to be performed.

1. **Specific performance method.** The specific performance method is used when performance consists of the execution of a single act. Revenue is recognized at the time the act takes place. For example, a stockbroker records sales commissions as revenue upon the sale of a client's investment.

2. **Proportional performance method.** The proportional performance method is used when performance consists of a number of identical or similar acts.

   a. If the service transaction involves a specified number of identical or similar acts, an equal amount of revenue is recorded for each act performed. For example, a refuse disposal company recognizes an equal amount of revenue for each weekly removal of a customer's garbage.

   b. If the service transaction involves a specified number of defined but not identical or similar acts, the revenue recognized for each act is based on the following formula:

   $$\frac{\text{Direct cost of individual act}}{\substack{\text{Total estimated direct costs} \\ \text{of the transaction}}} \times \substack{\text{Total revenues from} \\ \text{complete transaction}}$$

   For example, a correspondence school that provides lessons, examinations, and grading would use this method. If the measurements suggested in the preceding equation are impractical or not objectively determinable, revenue is recognized on a systematic and rational basis that reasonably relates revenue recognition to service performance.

   c. If the service transaction involves an unspecified number of acts over a fixed time period for performance, revenue is recognized over the period during which the acts will be performed by using the straight-line method unless a better method of relating revenue and performance is appropriate. For example, a health club might recognize revenue on a straight-line basis over the term of a member's membership. Many professional service firms record revenues on their engagements on an "as-performed basis" by valuing labor time, as expended, at a standard hourly billing rate and accumulating these amounts as an asset, work-in-progress (WIP). For periodic reporting, ending balances of WIP (and the related revenue recognized) must be adjusted by recording valuation allowances for unbillable or unrealizable WIP.

**Example of proportional performance revenue recognition**

The Cheyenne Snow Removal Company enters into a contract with the Western Office Tower to plow its parking lot. The contract states that Cheyenne will receive a fixed payment of $500 to clear Western's central parking lot whenever snowfall exceeds two inches. Following an unusually snowy winter, Western elects to cap its snow removal costs by tying Cheyenne into an annual $18,000 fixed price for snow removal, no matter how many snow storms occur. Snowfall is not predictable by month, and can occur over as much as a six-month period. Western pays the full amount in advance, resulting in the following entry by Cheyenne:

|                        |        |        |
|------------------------|--------|--------|
| Cash                   | 18,000 |        |
|     Customer advances  |        | 18,000 |

Though Cheyenne could recognize revenue on a straight-line basis though the contract period, it chooses to tie recognition more closely to actual performance with the proportional performance method. Its total estimated direct cost through the contract period is likely to be $12,600, based on its average costs in previous years. There is one snowstorm in October, which costs Cheyenne $350 for snow removal under the Western contract. Cheyenne's revenue recognition calculation in October is

$$\frac{\$350 \text{ direct cost}}{\$12,600 \text{ total direct cost}} \times \$18,000 \text{ total revenue} = \$500 \text{ revenue recognition}$$

Thus, Cheyenne recognizes a gross margin of $150 during the month. By the end of February, Cheyenne has conducted snow removal 28 times at the same margin, resulting in revenue recognition of $14,000 and a gross margin of $4,200. Cheyenne's cumulative entry for all performance under the Western contract to date is as follows:

|                        |        |        |
|------------------------|--------|--------|
| Customer advances      | 14,000 |        |
| Direct labor expense   | 9,800  |        |
|     Revenue            |        | 14,000 |
|     Cash               |        | 9,800  |

In March, Cheyenne removes snow 12 more times at a cost of $4,200. Its initial revenue recognition calculation during this month is

$$\frac{\$4,200 \text{ direct cost}}{\$12,600 \text{ total direct cost}} \times \$18,000 \text{ total revenue} = \$6,000 \text{ revenue recognition}$$

However, this would result in total revenue recognition of $20,000, which exceeds the contract fixed fee by $2,000. Accordingly, Cheyenne only recognizes sufficient revenue to maximize the contract cap, resulting in a loss of $200 for the month.

|                        |       |       |
|------------------------|-------|-------|
| Customer advances      | 4,000 |       |
| Direct labor expense   | 4,200 |       |
|     Revenue            |       | 4,000 |
|     Cash               |       | 4,200 |

3. **Completed performance method.** The completed performance method is used when more than one act must be performed and when the final act is so significant to the entire transaction taken as a whole that performance cannot be considered to have taken place until the performance of that final act occurs. For example, a moving company packs, loads, and transports merchandise; however, the final act of delivering the merchandise is so significant that revenue is not recognized until the goods reach their intended destination. If the services are to be performed in an in-

determinable number of acts over an indeterminable period of time and if an objective measure for estimating the degree to which performance has taken place cannot be found, revenue is recognized under the completed performance method.

4. **Collection method.** The collection method is used in circumstances when there is a significant degree of uncertainty surrounding the collection of service revenue. Under this method, revenue is not recognized until the cash is collected. For example, personal services may be provided to a customer whose ability to pay is uncertain.

## Expense Recognition

GAAP, in general, requires that costs be recognized as expense in the period that the revenue with which they are associated is recognized (the matching principle). Costs are deferred only when they are expected to be recoverable from future revenues. When applying these principles to service transactions, special consideration must be given to the different types of costs that might arise. The major classifications of costs arising from service transactions are as follows:

1. **Precontract or preengagement costs.** These are costs that are incurred before the service contract (or engagement letter in many professional services firms) has been executed between the parties. They can include legal fees for negotiating contract terms, costs of credit investigations, and the salaries and benefits of individuals involved in negotiating contracts with prospective clients. (See the related discussion in the long-term construction contracts section of this chapter.)

2. **Direct costs.** Costs that are specifically attributable to providing service under a specific contract or contracts. For example, service labor and repair parts on a fixed-price maintenance contract.

3. **Indirect costs.** Costs that are incurred as a result of all service activity but that are not directly allocable to any specific contracts or engagements.

4. **Out-of-pocket costs.** Costs incurred incidental to the performance of services that are often reimbursable to the service firm by the customer either at actual cost or at an agreed-upon rate (e.g., meals, lodging, airfare, taxi fare, etc.).

5. **Overhead.** General costs of running the business that do not fall into any of the above categories, often referred to as selling, general, and administrative expenses. These include uncollectible receivables, advertising, sales commissions, and facilities costs (depreciation, rent, maintenance, etc.).

**Accounting treatment.** The costs listed above are accounted for as follows:

1. **Precontract or preengagement costs.** Expense as incurred as start-up costs under SOP 98-5 under all of the service revenue recognition methods.

2. **Direct costs.** Expense as incurred under all of the service revenue recognition methods because of the close correlation between the amount of direct costs incurred and the extent of performance achieved. Direct costs incurred prior to performance, referred to as initial direct costs (e.g., expendable materials purchased for use on the job/engagement that are purchased and held by the service enterprise as a form of inventory), are deferred and recorded as prepayments (or supplies inventory, depending on the nature of the item). Under the specific performance or completed performance methods, these costs are recognized as expenses at the time of service performance at the point that revenue is recognized. Under the proportional performance method, initial direct costs are charged to expense in proportion to the recognition of service revenue (i.e., by applying the ratio of revenues recognized in the period to total expected revenues over the life of the contract).

3. **Indirect costs.** Under all of the revenue recognition methods, indirect costs are expensed as incurred.

4. **Out-of-pocket costs.** Under all of the revenue recognition methods, out-of-pocket costs are expensed as incurred with the related client billings presented as revenue in the statement of income.

5. **Overhead.** Under all of the revenue recognition methods, overhead is expensed as incurred.

**Losses on service transactions** are recognized when direct costs incurred to date plus estimated remaining direct costs of performance exceed the current estimated net realizable revenue from the contract. The loss (given as the Direct costs incurred to date + Estimated remaining direct costs – Estimated realizable revenue) is first applied to reduce any recorded deferred costs to zero, with any remaining loss recognized on the income statement and credited to an estimated liability.

### Initiation and Installation Fees

Many service transactions also involve the charging of a nonrefundable initiation or activation fee with subsequent periodic payments for future services and/or a nonrefundable fee for installation of equipment essential to providing future services with subsequent periodic payments for the services. These nonrefundable fees may, in substance, be partly or wholly advance charges for future services.

**Initiation or activation fees.** If there is an objectively determinable value for the right or privilege granted by the fee, that value is recognized as revenue on the initiation date. Any related direct costs are recognized as expense on the initiation date. If the value of the right or privilege cannot be objectively determined, the fee is recorded as a liability for future services and recognized as revenue in accordance with one of the revenue recognition methods.

**Installation fees.** If the equipment and its installation costs are essential for the service to be provided and if customers cannot normally purchase the equipment in a separate transaction, the installation fee is considered an advance charge for future services. The fee is recognized as revenue over the estimated service period. The costs of installation and the installed equipment are amortized over the period the equipment is expected to generate revenue. If customers can normally purchase the equipment in a separate transaction, the installation fee is part of a product transaction that is accounted for separately as such.

#### Example of installation fees

Vintner Corporation has invented a nitrogen injection device for resealing opened wine bottles, calling it NitroSeal. The device is especially useful for restaurants, which can seal wine bottles opened for customers who want to take home unfinished wine. Because the NitroSeal device is massive, Vintner pays a third party to install each unit for a fixed fee of $200, charging restaurants a $300 nonrefundable installation fee plus a monthly fee for a 20-month cancelable contract. The initial entries to record an installation charge from a supplier and related installation billing to a customer are as follows:

| | | |
|---|---|---|
| Installation asset | 200 | |
|     Accounts payable | | 200 |
| Accounts receivable | 300 | |
|     Unearned installation fees (liability) | | 300 |

Vintner recognizes the installation revenue and associated installation expense for each installation in 1/20 increments to match the contract length, each with the following entry:

| | | |
|---|---|---|
| Unearned installation fees | 15 | |
|    Installation revenue | | 15 |
| Installation expense | 10 | |
|    Installation asset | | 10 |

A customer cancels its contract with Vintner after 5 months. As a result, Vintner accelerates all remaining amortization on the installation asset and recognizes all remaining unearned installation fees at once, using the following entries:

| | | |
|---|---|---|
| Unearned installation fees | 225 | |
|    Installation revenue | | 225 |
| Installation expense | 150 | |
|    Installation asset | | 150 |

If the service contract had included a clause for a refundable installation fee, then cancellation after five months would still have resulted in immediate acceleration of amortization on the installation asset. However, the unearned installation revenue could not be recognized. Instead, the following entry would have recorded the return of the installation fee:

| | | |
|---|---|---|
| Unearned installation fees | 225 | |
|    Cash | | 225 |

### Recommended Disclosures—Not Required by GAAP

1. The revenue recognition method used and its justification
2. Information concerning unearned revenues
3. Information concerning deferred costs
4. Periods over which services are to be performed

### Other Guidance to Accounting for Service Transactions

Several extant EITF consensuses and other formal literature provide guidance to the accounting for service transactions. These are discussed in the following paragraphs.

**Freight services in process.** EITF 91-9 addresses the manner in which revenue and expense pertaining to freight services in process as of the balance sheet date are to be given financial statement recognition. It holds that recognition of revenue when freight is received from the shipper or when freight leaves the carrier's terminal, with expenses recognized as incurred, is not acceptable accounting.

**Reporting reimbursable costs.** While not limited to service providers, a common situation for many professional service providers is the incurrence of costs that are later billed to clients, with or without a mark-up over actual cost. Examples of out-of-pocket expenses include meals, lodging, airfare, taxi fares, etc. Prior practice had been varied, with many reporting entities showing reimbursements, implicitly as offsets to expenses; others reported such reimbursements as revenue. While the net effect on reported earnings was the same under either approach, certain key performance measures, such as gross revenue, could vary considerably depending on choice of accounting method. EITF 01-14 mandates that any billings for out-of-pocket costs are to be classified as revenue in the statement of income and not as a reduction in expenses. This guidance is equally applicable whether expenses are billed to clients (1) as a pass-through, (i.e., at actual cost to the service firm without a markup), (2) at a marked-up amount, or (3) are included in the billing rate or negotiated price for the services.

**Separately priced extended warranties.** Extended warranties provide additional protection beyond that of the manufacturer's original warranty, lengthen the period of coverage specified in the manufacturer's original warranty, or both. Similarly, a product maintenance contract is an agreement for services to maintain a product for a certain length of time. Clearly, revenue recognition at inception is not acceptable, and it is often impossible to estimate the actual pattern of service that will be provided to the customers over the terms of the contracts. FTB 90-1 directs that revenue from these contracts be deferred and recognized on a straight-line basis unless evidence exists that costs are incurred on some other basis. If so, revenue is allocated to each period using the ratio of the period's cost to estimated total cost.

Direct costs of obtaining extended warranty or maintenance contracts are to be capitalized and recognized as expense in the ratio that revenues recognized each period bear to total anticipated revenues from the respective contracts. Any other costs are charged to expense as incurred. Losses on these contracts are recognized immediately if the sum of the future costs and remaining unamortized direct acquisition costs exceed the related unearned revenue. When recognizing a loss, any unamortized acquisition costs are first charged to expense, and a liability for any remaining loss is then recorded.

### Example of a separately priced product maintenance contract

Salomon Heating enters into a four-year product maintenance contract with Everly Manufacturing, under which Salomon will conduct preventive maintenance and repairs to Everly's heating systems. Under the contract terms, Salomon bills Everly $1,000 during each month of the contract period, and recognizes the billed amount as revenue at once. This equates to straight-line recognition of the total contract amount.

Salomon incurred a $4,000 legal expense in writing the contract with Everly, as well as a $1,600 commission, both of which it defers and amortizes over the contract period. During the first month of work, Salomon incurs direct costs of $650 in wages, as well as $200 of repair-related materials. Its charge to expense entry follows:

| | | |
|---|---|---|
| Cost of goods sold—materials | 200 | |
| Cost of goods sold—labor | 650 | |
| Legal expense | 83 | |
| Commission expense | 33 | |
|     Inventory—spare parts | | 200 |
|     Cash | | 650 |
|     Deferred legal costs | | 83 |
|     Deferred commission costs | | 33 |

At the end of two years, Salomon realizes that it must rebuild Everly's boiler. The rebuild will cost $10,000, while all expected future maintenance work will cost an additional $20,000. Unamortized legal costs equal $2,000 and unamortized commissions equal $800, while unearned revenue is $24,000. Salomon must recognize a loss of $8,800, which is the difference between all expected costs of $32,800 and unearned revenue of $24,000. To do so, Salomon accelerates all remaining amortization of the capitalized legal and commission assets, and recognizes a liability for the remainder of the loss with the following entry:

| | | |
|---|---|---|
| Commission expense | 800 | |
| Legal expense | 2,000 | |
| Loss on contractual obligation | 6,000 | |
|     Deferred commission costs | | 800 |
|     Deferred legal costs | | 2,000 |
|     Unfulfilled contractual obligations (liability) | | 6,000 |

Salomon rebuilds Everly's boiler at the expected cost of $10,000. Since this is one-third of the remaining costs to be incurred under the contract, Salomon recognizes one-third of the $6,000 unfulfilled contractual obligation that was used to offset the loss, and charges the rest of the cost to expense with the following entry:

| | | |
|---|---|---|
| Unfulfilled contractual obligations (liability) | 2,000 | |
| Cost of goods sold—labor | 8,000 | |
|     Cash | | 10,000 |

# SALES WHEN COLLECTION IS UNCERTAIN

## PERSPECTIVE AND ISSUES

Under GAAP, revenue recognition customarily does not depend upon the collection of cash. Accrual accounting techniques normally record revenue at the point of a credit sale by establishing a receivable. When uncertainty arises surrounding the collectibility of this amount, the receivable is appropriately adjusted by establishing a valuation allowance. In some cases, however, the collection of the sales price may be so uncertain that an objective measure of ultimate collectibility cannot be established. When such circumstances exist, the seller either uses the installment method or the cost recovery method to recognize the transaction (APB 10). Both of these methods allow for a deferral of gross profit until cash has been collected.

An installment transaction occurs when a seller delivers a product or performs a service and the buyer makes periodic payments over an extended period of time. Under the installment method, revenue recognition is deferred until the period(s) of cash collection. The seller recognizes both revenues and cost of sales at the time of the sale; however, the related gross profit is deferred to those periods in which cash is collected. Under the cost recovery method, both revenues and cost of sales are recognized at the time of the sale, but none of the related gross profit is recognized until the entire cost of sales has been recovered. Once the seller has recovered all cost of sales, any additional cash receipts are recognized as revenue. APB 10 does not specify when one method is preferred over the other. However, the cost recovery method is more conservative than the installment method because gross profit is deferred until all costs have been recovered; therefore, it is appropriate for situations of extreme uncertainty.

| Sources of GAAP | |
|:---:|:---:|
| *APB* | *CON* |
| 10 | 3 |

## DEFINITIONS OF TERMS

**Cost recovery method.** The method of accounting for an installment basis sale whereby the gross profit is deferred until all cost of sales has been recovered.

**Deferred gross profit.** The gross profit from an installment basis sale that will be recognized in future periods.

**Gross profit rate.** The percentage computed by dividing gross profit by revenue from an installment sale.

**Installment method.** The method of accounting for a sale whereby gross profit is recognized in each period in which cash from the sale is collected.

**Installment sale.** A sales transaction for which the sales price is collected through the receipt of periodic payments over an extended period of time.

**Net realizable value.** The portion of the recorded amount of an asset expected to be realized in cash upon its liquidation in the ordinary course of business.

**Realized gross profit.** The gross profit recognized in the current period.

**Repossessions.** Merchandise sold by a seller under an installment arrangement that the seller physically takes back after the buyer defaults on the payments.

## CONCEPTS, RULES, AND EXAMPLES

### The Installment Method

The installment method was developed in response to the increasing incidence of sales contracts that allowed buyers to make payments over several years. As the payment period becomes longer, the risk of loss resulting from uncollectible accounts increases; consequently, circumstances surrounding a receivable may lead to considerable uncertainty as to whether payments will actually be received. Under these circumstances, the uncertainty of cash collection dictates that revenue recognition be deferred until the actual receipt of cash.

The installment method can be used in most sales transactions for which payment is to be made through periodic installments over an extended period of time and the collectibility of the sales price cannot be reasonably estimated. This method is applicable to the sales of real estate (covered in the last section of this chapter), heavy equipment, home furnishings, and other merchandise sold on an installment basis. Installment method revenue recognition is not in accordance with accrual accounting because revenue recognition is not normally based upon cash collection; however, its use is justified in certain circumstances on the grounds that accrual accounting may result in "front-end loading" (i.e., all of the revenue from a transaction being recognized at the point of sale with an improper matching of related costs). For example, the application of accrual accounting to transactions that provide for installment payments over periods of ten, twenty, or thirty years may underestimate losses from contract defaults and other future contract costs.

**Applying the installment method.** When a seller uses the installment method, both revenue and cost of sales are recognized at the point of sale, but the related gross profit is deferred to those periods during which cash will be collected. As receivables are collected, a portion of the deferred gross profit equal to the gross profit rate times the cash collected is recognized as income. When this method is used, the seller must compute each year's gross profit rate and also must maintain records of installment accounts receivable and deferred revenue that are separately identified by the year of sale. All general and administrative expenses are normally expensed in the period incurred.

The steps to use in accounting for sales under the installment method are as follows:

1.  During the current year, record sales and cost of sales in the regular manner. Record installment sales transactions separately from other sales. Set up installment accounts receivable identified by the year of sale (e.g., Installment Accounts Receivable—2009).
2.  Record cash collections from installment accounts receivable. Care must be taken so that the cash receipts are properly identified as to the year in which the receivable arose.
3.  At the end of the current year, transfer installment sales revenue and installment cost of sales to deferred gross profit properly identified by the year of sale. Compute the current year's gross profit rate on installment sales as follows:

$$\text{Gross Profit rate} = 1 - \left( \frac{\text{Cost of installment sales}}{\text{Installment sales revenue}} \right)$$

Alternatively, the gross profit rate can be computed as follows:

$$\text{Gross profit rate} = \frac{\text{Installment sales revenue} - \text{Cost of installment sales}}{\text{Installment sales revenue}}$$

4. Apply the current year's gross profit rate to the cash collections from the current year's installment sales to compute the realized gross profit from the current year's installment sales.

$$\text{Realized gross profit} \; = \; \frac{\text{Cash collections from the}}{\text{current year's installment sales}} \; \times \; \frac{\text{Current year's}}{\text{gross profit rate}}$$

5. Separately apply each of the previous years' gross profit rates to cash collections from those years' installment sales to compute the realized gross profit from each of the previous years' installment sales.

$$\text{Realized gross profit} \; = \; \frac{\text{Cash collections from the}}{\text{previous years' installment sales}} \; \times \; \frac{\text{Previous years'}}{\text{gross profit rate}}$$

6. Defer the current year's unrealized gross profit to future years. The deferred gross profit to carry forward to future years is computed as follows:

$$\frac{\text{Deferred gross}}{\text{profit (2009)}} \; = \; \frac{\text{Ending balance installment}}{\text{account receivable (2009)}} \; \times \; \frac{\text{Gross profit rate}}{\text{(2009)}}$$

**Example of the installment method of accounting**

|  | *2009* | *2010* | *2011* |
|---|---|---|---|
| Sales on installment | $400,000 | $450,000 | $600,000 |
| Cost of installment sales | (280,000) | (337,500) | (400,000) |
| Gross profit on sales | $120,000 | $112,500 | $200,000 |
|  |  |  |  |
| Cash collections: |  |  |  |
| 2009 sales | $150,000 | $175,000 | $ 75,000 |
| 2010 sales |  | $200,000 | $125,000 |
| 2011 sales |  |  | $300,000 |

Accounting entries are made for steps 1 and 2 above using this data; the following computations are required for steps 3-6:

Step 3 — Compute the current year's gross profit rate.

|  | *2009* | *2010* | *2011* |
|---|---|---|---|
| Gross profit on sales | $120,000 | $112,500 | $200,000 |
| Installment sales revenue | $400,000 | $450,000 | $600,000 |
| Gross profit rate | 30% | 25% | 33 1/3% |

Step 4 — Apply the current year's gross profit rate to cash collections from current year's sales.

| *Year* | *Cash collections* |  | *Gross profit rate* |  | *Realized gross profit* |
|---|---|---|---|---|---|
| 2009 | $150,000 | × | 30% | = | $ 45,000 |
| 2010 | 200,000 | × | 25% | = | 50,000 |
| 2011 | 300,000 | × | 33 1/3% | = | 100,000 |

Step 5 — Separately apply each of the previous years' gross profit rates to cash collections from that year's installment sales.

*In Year 2010*

| *From year* | *Cash collections* |  | *Gross profit rate* |  | *Realized gross profit* |
|---|---|---|---|---|---|
| 2009 | $175,000 | × | 30% | = | $52,500 |

*In Year 2011*

| *From year* | *Cash collections* |  | *Gross profit rate* |  | *Realized gross profit* |
|---|---|---|---|---|---|
| 2009 | $ 75,000 | × | 30% | = | $22,500 |
| 2010 | 125,000 | × | 25% | = | 31,250 |
|  |  |  |  |  | $53,750 |

Step 6 — Defer the current year's unrealized gross profit to future years.

12/31/09

| | | |
|---|---|---|
| Deferred gross profit (2009) = ($400,000 – 150,000) × 30% | = | $ 75,000 |

12/31/10

| | | |
|---|---|---|
| Deferred gross profit (2010) = ($450,000 – 200,000) × 25% | = | $ 62,500 |
| Deferred gross profit (2009) = ($400,000 – 150,000 – 175,000) × 30% | = | 22,500 |
| | | $ 85,000 |

12/31/11

| | | |
|---|---|---|
| Deferred gross profit (2011) = ($600,000 – 300,000) × 33 1/3% | = | $100,000 |
| Deferred gross profit (2010) = ($450,000 – 200,000 – 125,000) × 25% | = | 31,250 |
| | | $131,250 |

**Financial statement presentation.** If installment sales transactions represent a significant portion of the company's total sales, the following three items of gross profit would, theoretically, be reported on the company's income statement:

1. Total gross profit from current year's sales
2. Realized gross profit from current year's sales
3. Realized gross profit from prior years' sales

An income statement using the previous example would be presented as follows (assume all sales are accounted for by the installment method):

**Jordan Equipment Company**
**Partial Income Statement**
**For the Years Ending December 31**

| | *2009* | *2010* | *2011* |
|---|---|---|---|
| Sales | $400,000 | $450,000 | $600,000 |
| Cost of sales | (280,000) | (337,500) | (400,000) |
| Gross profit on current year's sales | 120,000 | 112,500 | 200,000 |
| Less deferred gross profit on current year's sales | (75,000) | (62,500) | (100,000) |
| Realized gross profit on current year's sales | 45,000 | 50,000 | 100,000 |
| Plus gross profit realized on prior years' sales | -- | 52,500 | 53,750 |
| Total gross profit on sales | $ 45,000 | $102,500 | $153,750 |

However, when a company recognizes only a small portion of its revenues using the installment method, the illustrated presentation of revenue and gross profit may be confusing. Therefore, in practice, some companies simply report the realized gross profit from installment sales by displaying it as a single line item on the income statement as follows:

**Stevens Furniture Company**
**Partial Income Statement**
**For the Year Ended December 31, 2009**

| | |
|---|---|
| Sales | $ 2,250,000 |
| Cost of sales | (1,350,000) |
| Gross profit on sales | 900,000 |
| Gross profit realized on installment sales | 35,000 |
| Total gross profit on sales | $ 935,000 |

The balance sheet presentation of installment accounts receivable depends upon whether installment sales are a normal part of operations. If a company sells most of its products on an installment basis, installment accounts receivable are classified as a current asset because the operating cycle of the business (the length of which is to be disclosed in the notes to the financial statements) is the average period of time covered by its installment contracts. If installment sales are not a normal part of operations, installment accounts receivable that are not to be collected for more than a year (or the length of the company's operating cycle, if different than a year) are reported as noncurrent assets. In all cases, to avoid confusion, it is desirable to fully disclose the year of maturity next to each group of installment accounts receivable as illustrated by the following example:

*Current assets:*
Accounts receivable
| | | |
|---|---|---|
| Customers | $180,035 | |
| Less allowance for uncollectible accounts | (4,200) | |
| | 175,835 | |
| Installment accounts—collectible in 2010 | 26,678 | |
| Installment accounts—collectible in 2011 | 42,234 | $244,747 |

Accounting for deferred gross profit is addressed in CON 6 which states that deferred gross profit is not a liability. The reason is that the seller company is not obligated to pay cash or provide services to the customer. Rather, the deferral arose because of the uncertainty surrounding the collectibility of the sales price. CON 6 goes on to say, "deferred gross profit on installment sales is conceptually an asset valuation—that is, a reduction of an asset." However, in practice, deferred gross profit is generally presented either as unearned revenue classified in the current liability section of the balance sheet or as a deferred credit displayed between liabilities and equity.

Following the guideline in CON 6, the current asset section would be presented as follows (using information from the Jordan Equipment example and assuming a 12/31/11 balance sheet):

| | | | | |
|---|---|---|---|---|
| Installment accounts receivable | (2010) | $125,000 | | |
| Installment accounts receivable | (2011) | 300,000 | $ 425,000 | |
| Less: Deferred gross profit | (2010) | $ 31,250 | | |
| Deferred gross profit | (2011) | 100,000 | (131,250) | $293,750 |

**Interest on installment method receivables.** The previous examples ignored interest, a major component of most installment sales contracts. It is customary for the seller to charge interest to the buyer on the unpaid installment receivable balance. Generally, installment contracts call for equal payments, each with an amount attributable to interest on the unpaid balance and the remainder to the installment receivable balance. As the maturity date nears, a smaller amount of each installment payment is attributable to interest and a larger amount is attributable to principal. Therefore, to determine the amount of gross profit to recognize, the interest must first be deducted from the installment payment and then the difference (representing the principal portion of the payment) is multiplied by the gross profit rate as follows:

Realized gross profit = (Installment payment – Interest portion) × Gross profit rate

The interest portion of the installment payment is recorded as interest revenue at the time of the cash receipt. Appropriate accounting entries are required to accrue interest revenue when the collection dates do not correspond with the period end.

To illustrate the accounting for installment sales contracts involving interest, assume that Genrich Equipment Company sells a machine for $5,000 on December 31, 2008, to a customer with a dubious credit history. The machine cost Genrich $3,750. The terms of the agreement require a $1,000 down payment on the date of the sale. The remaining $4,000 is payable in equal annual installments of $1,401.06, including 15% annual interest, at the end of each of the next four years.

For each payment it receives, Genrich must compute the portion to record as interest revenue with the remaining portion of the payment (the principal) to be applied to reduce the installment account receivable balance. Gross profit is only recognized on the principal portion of each payment that is applied to reduce the installment receivable balance. The following schedule illustrates that gross profit is recognized on the entire down payment (which contains no element of interest revenue), whereas the annual installment payments are separated into their interest and principal portions with gross profit only being recognized on the latter portion.

**Schedule of Cash Receipts**

| Date | Cash (debit) | Interest revenue (credit) | Installment accounts receivable (credit) | Installment accounts receivable balance | Realized gross profit |
|------|-----|-----|-----|-----|-----|
| 12/31/08 | | | | $5,000.00 | |
| 12/31/08 | $1,000.00 | $    -- | $1,000.00 | 4,000.00 | $  250.00a |
| 12/31/09 | 1,401.06 | 600.00b | 801.06c | 3,198.94d | 200.27e |
| 12/31/10 | 1,401.06 | 479.84 | 921.22 | 2,277.72 | 230.31 |
| 12/31/11 | 1,401.06 | 341.66 | 1,059.40 | 1,218.32 | 264.85 |
| 12/31/12 | 1,401.06 | 182.74 | 1,218.32 | -- | 304.57 |
| | $6,604.24 | $1,604.24 | $5,000.00 | | |
| | | | Total realized gross profit | | $1,250.00 |

Gross profit rate = 1 – ($3,750/5,000) = 25%

[a] $1,000 × 25% = $250
[b] $4,000 × 15% = $600
[c] $1,401.06 – 600 = $801.06

[d] $4,000 – 801.06 = $3,198.94
[e] $801.06 × 25% = $200.27

**Bad debts and repossessions.** The standard accounting treatment for uncollectible accounts is to accrue a bad debt loss in the year of sale by estimating the amount expected to be uncollectible. This treatment is consistent with the accrual and matching concepts. However, just as revenue recognition under the accrual basis is sometimes abandoned for certain installment basis sales, the accrual basis of recognizing bad debts is also sometimes abandoned.

When the installment method is used, it is usually appropriate to recognize bad debts by the direct write-off method (i.e., bad debts are not recognized until the receivable has been determined to be uncollectible). This practice is acceptable because most installment contracts contain a provision that allows the seller to repossess the merchandise when the buyer defaults on the installment payments. The loss on the account may be eliminated or reduced because the seller has the option of reselling the repossessed merchandise. To write off an uncollectible installment receivable, the following three steps are followed:

1.  The installment account receivable and the deferred gross profit are eliminated.
2.  The repossessed merchandise is recorded as used inventory at its net realizable value. Net realizable value is resale value less any selling or reconditioning costs. The repossessed asset is recorded at this fair value because any asset acquired is recorded at the best approximation of its fair value.
3.  Bad debt expense and a gain or loss on repossession are recognized. The bad debt expense or repossession gain or loss is the difference between the unrecovered cost (installment account receivable minus deferred gross profit) and the net realizable value of the repossessed merchandise.

To illustrate, assume that Marcie Company determined that a $3,000 installment receivable is uncollectible. The deferred gross profit ratio on the original sale was 30%; thus, $900 deferred gross profit exists ($3,000 × 30%). If the repossessed equipment has a $1,500 net realizable value, a $600 repossession loss (or bad debt expense) should be recorded.

| | |
|---|---|
| Installment account receivable | $ 3,000 |
| Less deferred gross profit | (900) |
| Unrecovered cost | 2,100 |
| Less net realizable value of repossessed equipment | (1,500) |
| Repossession loss | $  600 |

Marcie Company would record this loss by making the following entry:

| | | |
|---|---|---|
| Deferred gross profit | 900 | |
| Inventory—repossessed merchandise | 1,500 | |
| Repossession loss | 600 | |
| Installment account receivable | | 3,000 |

## The Cost Recovery Method

The cost recovery method does not recognize any income on a sale until the cost of the item sold has been fully recovered through cash receipts. Once the seller has recovered all costs, any subsequent cash receipts are included in income. The cost recovery method is used when the uncertainty of collection of the sales price is so great that even use of the installment method cannot be justified.

Under the cost recovery method, both revenues and cost of sales are recognized at the point of sale, but the related gross profit is deferred until all costs of sales have been recovered. Each installment must also be divided between principal and interest, but unlike the installment method where a portion of the principal recovers the cost of sales and the remainder is recognized as gross profit, all of the principal is first applied to recover the cost of the asset sold. After all costs of sales have been recovered, any subsequent cash receipts are realized as gross profit. The cost recovery method can be illustrated by using the information from the Genrich Company example used in the section "interest on installment method receivables." If Genrich used the cost recovery method, gross profit would be realized as follows:

### Schedule of Cash Receipts

| Date | Cash (debit) | Deferred interest income (credit)* | Installment accounts receivable (credit) | Installment accounts receivable balance | Unrecovered cost | Realized gross profit | Realized interest revenue |
|---|---|---|---|---|---|---|---|
| 12/31/08 | | | | $5,000.00 | $3,750.00 | | |
| 12/31/08 | $1,000.00 | $  -- | $1,000.00 | 4,000.00 | 2,750.00 | $  -- | $  -- |
| 12/31/09 | 1,401.06 | 600.00 | 801.06 | 3,198.94 | 1,948.94 | -- | -- |
| 12/31/10 | 1,401.06 | 479.84 | 921.22 | 2,277.72 | 1,027.72 | -- | -- |
| 12/31/11 | 1,401.06 | (31.68) | 1,059.40 | 1,218.32 | -- | -- | 373.34** |
| 12/31/12 | 1,401.06 | (1,048.16) | 1,218.32 | -- | -- | 1,250.00 | 1,230.90*** |
| | $6,604.24 | | $5,000.00 | | | $1,250.00 | $1,604.24 |

\* *Interest received in 2009 and 2010 is credited to deferred interest income since the cost of the asset was not recovered until 2011.*

\** *Computed as cash received of $1,401.06 less the portion representing unrecovered cost of $1,027.72 = $373.34. Since this amount exceeds the interest paid by the customer for the year of $341.66, the remaining $31.68 reduces deferred interest income.*

\*** *Computed as cash received of $1,401.06 less the portion applied to principal of $1,218.32 = $182.74 plus the remaining deferred interest income of $1,048.16.*

The accounting entries to record the foregoing are as follows (in whole dollars):

*Debit (Credit)*

| | 2008 | 2009 | 2010 | 2011 | 2012 | Totals |
|---|---|---|---|---|---|---|
| *Initial Sale and Down Payment:* | | | | | | |
| Cash | 1,000 | | | | | |
| Installment accounts receivable | 4,000 | | | | | |
| Inventory | (3,750) | | | | | |
| Deferred gross profit | (1,250) | | | | | |
| *Annual Payments:* | | | | | | |
| Cash | | 1,401 | 1,401 | 1,401 | 1,401 | 5,604 |
| Installment accounts receivable | | (801) | (921) | (1,059) | (1,219) | (4,000) |
| Deferred interest income | | (600) | (480) | 32 | 1,048 | -- |
| Interest income | | | | (374) | (1,230) | (1,604) |
| Deferred gross profit | | | | | 1,250 | 1,250 |
| Recognized gross profit (revenue) | | | | | (1,250) | (1,250) |

# REVENUE RECOGNITION WHEN RIGHT OF RETURN EXISTS

## PERSPECTIVE AND ISSUES

In some industries it is common practice for customers to have the right to return a product to the seller for a credit or refund. However, for companies that experience a high ratio of returned merchandise to sales, the recognition of the original sale as revenue is questionable. In fact, certain industries have found it necessary to defer revenue recognition until the return privilege has substantially expired. Sometimes the return privilege expires soon after the sale, as in the newspaper and perishable food industries. In other cases, the return privilege may last over an extended period of time, as in magazine and textbook publishing and equipment manufacturing. The rate of return normally is directly related to the length of the return privilege. An accounting issue arises when the recognition of revenue occurs in one period while substantial returns occur in later periods.

FAS 48, *Revenue Recognition When Right of Return Exists,* reduced the diversity in the accounting for revenue recognition when such rights exist.

| Sources of GAAP |
|:---:|
| *FAS* |
| 5, 48 |

## DEFINITIONS OF TERMS

**Deferred gross profit.** The gross profit from a sale that is recognized in future periods because of the uncertainty surrounding the collection of the sales price.

**Return privilege.** A right granted to a buyer by express agreement with a seller or by customary industry practice that allows the buyer to return merchandise to the seller within a stated period of time.

## CONCEPTS, RULES, AND EXAMPLES

FAS 48 provides criteria for recognizing revenue on a sale in which a product may be returned (as a matter of contract or a matter of industry practice), either by the ultimate consumer or by a party who resells the product to others. Paragraph 6 states the following:

> If an enterprise sells its product but gives the buyer the right to return the product, revenue from the sales transaction [is] recognized at time of sale only if all of the following conditions are met:
>
> a.　The seller's price to the buyer is substantially fixed or determinable at the date of sale.
> b.　The buyer has paid the seller, or the buyer is obligated to pay the seller and the obligation is not contingent on resale of the product.
> c.　The buyer's obligation to the seller would not be changed in the event of theft or physical destruction or damage of the product.
> d.　The buyer acquiring the product for resale has economic substance apart from that provided by the seller.
> e.　The seller does not have significant obligations for future performance to directly bring about the resale of the product by the buyer.
> f.　The amount of future returns can be reasonably estimated. For purposes of this statement "returns" do not include exchanges by ultimate customers of one item for another of the same kind, quality, and price.

If all of the above conditions are met, the seller recognizes revenue from the sales transaction at the time of the sale and any costs or losses expected in connection with returns are accrued in accordance with FAS 5, *Accounting for Contingencies.* FAS 5 states that estimated losses from contingencies are accrued and charged to income when it is both probable that an asset has been impaired or a liability has been incurred, and the amount of loss can be reasonably estimated.

The interplay between FAS 48 and FAS 5 needs further explanation. Although FAS 48 requires under condition f. that the amount of returns be reasonably estimated, it does not reference the standard to the FAS 5 loss accrual criteria (see Chapter 14). Accordingly, a strict interpretation of both FAS 48 and FAS 5 would indicate that only when the conditions for loss accrual under FAS 5 are met (i.e., the loss is both probable and reasonably estimable) would the condition f. above under FAS 48 also be met, and both sales and estimated returns can be recognized. However, a more literal interpretation of FAS 48 indicates that, by not cross-referencing FAS 5, the FASB intended that the sole criterion for return accrual under FAS 48 be the "reasonably estimated" condition f. Then, whether losses are probable or reasonably possible, they would be accrued under FAS 48 and the sales would also be recognized. If the likelihood of losses is remote, no disclosure is required under FAS 5, and condition f. under FAS 48 would be achieved and revenue would be recognized with no need to record an allowance for estimated returns. Under this theory, only if returns cannot be reasonably estimated, would recognition of revenue be precluded under FAS 48, regardless of whether losses are probable or reasonably possible.

### Example of sale with right of return

Assume that Lipkis, Inc. began the sale of its new textbook on computer programming in 2009 with the following results: On December 1, 2009, 2,000 textbooks with a sales price of $45 each and total manufacturing costs of $30 each are delivered to school bookstores on account. The bookstores have the right to return the textbooks within four months of delivery date. Payments when the books are sold. Payments and returns for the initial deliveries are as follows:

|  | Cash receipts | | Returns | |
| --- | --- | --- | --- | --- |
|  | *Units* | *Amount* | *Units* | *Amount* |
| November 2009 |  |  |  |  |
| December 2009 | 600 | $27,000 | -- | -- |
| January 2010 | 500 | 22,500 | 40 | $1,800 |
| February 2010 | 400 | 18,000 | 90 | 4,050 |
| March 2010 | 300 | 13,500 | 30 | 1,350 |
|  | 1,800 | $81,000 | 160 | $7,200 |

Lipkis, Inc. has had similar agreements with the bookstores in the past and has experienced a 15% return rate on similar sales.

**Requirements for revenue recognition met.** If all six of the requirements were met, the following journal entries would be appropriate:

| 12/1/09 | Accounts receivable | 90,000 | |
| --- | --- | --- | --- |
|  | Sales (2,000 units × $45 per unit) | | 90,000 |
|  | *To record sale of 2,000 textbooks* | | |
| 12/31/09 | Cash (600 units × $45 per unit) | 27,000 | |
|  | Accounts receivable | | 27,000 |
|  | *To record cash receipts for the month* | | |
|  | Cost of sales | 60,000 | |
|  | Inventory (2,000 units × $30 per unit) | | 60,000 |
|  | *To record cost of goods sold for the month* | | |
|  | Sales (15% × 2,000 units × $45 per unit) | 13,500 | |
|  | Cost of sales (15% × 2,000 units × $30 per unit) | | 9,000 |
|  | Deferred gross profit on estimated returns (15% × 2,000 units × $15 per unit) | | 4,500 |
|  | *To record estimate of returns* | | |
| 1/1/10 to 3/31/10 | Cash | 54,000 | |
|  | Accounts receivable | | 54,000 |
|  | *To record cash receipts* | | |

| | | | |
|---|---|---|---|
| | Inventory (160 units × $30 per unit) | 4,800 | |
| | Deferred gross profit on estimated returns | 2,400 | |
| | Accounts receivable (160 units × $45 per unit) | | 7,200 |
| | *To record actual returns* | | |
| 3/31/10 | Cost of sales (140 units × $30 per unit) | 4,200 | |
| | Deferred gross profit on estimated returns | 2,100 | |
| | Sales (140 units × $45 per unit) | | 6,300 |
| | *To record expiration of return privileges and adjust estimate to actual* | | |

The revenue and cost of goods sold recognized in 2009 are based on the number of units expected to be returned, 300 (15% × 2,000 units). The net revenue recognized is $76,500 (85% × 2,000 units × $45 per unit) and the cost of goods sold recognized is $51,000 (85% × 2,000 units × $30 per unit). The deferred gross profit balance is carried forward until either the textbooks are returned or the return privilege expires.

**Requirements for revenue recognition not met.** If all of the six conditions are not met, revenue and cost of sales from the sales transactions must be deferred until either the return privilege has substantially expired or the point when all the conditions are subsequently met is reached, whichever comes first.

If the facts in the Lipkis case were altered so that the bookstores were not required to pay Lipkis until the later of the date the books were actually sold, or the expiration date of the return privilege, condition b. would not be met until the store remitted payment. The following entries would be required. The return privilege is, of course, assumed to be lost by the store when the books are sold to final customers.

| | | | |
|---|---|---|---|
| 12/1/09 | Inventory on consignment | 60,000 | |
| | Inventory | | 60,000 |
| | *To record shipment of 2,000 units to retail bookstores on consignment (2,000 units × $30 = $60,000)* | | |
| 12/31/09 | Cash (600 units × $45 per unit) | 27,000 | |
| | Sales | | 27,000 |
| | *To record cash receipts for December* | | |
| | Cost of sales (600 units × $30 per unit) | 18,000 | |
| | Inventory on consignment | | 18,000 |
| | *To record cost of goods sold for December* | | |
| 1/1/10 to 3/31/10 | Cash | 54,000 | |
| | Sales (1,200[*] units × $45 per unit) | | 54,000 |
| | *To record cash receipts* | | |
| | Cost of sales (1,200 units × $30 per unit) | 36,000 | |
| | Inventory on consignment | | 36,000 |
| | *To record cost of goods sold on cash receipts* | | |
| | Inventory (160 units × $30 per unit) | 4,800 | |
| | Inventory on consignment | | 4,800 |
| | *To record product returns* | | |
| 3/31/10 | Accounts receivable (40 units × $45 per unit) | 1,800 | |
| | Sales | | 1,800 |
| | *To record expiration of return privilege on remaining units* | | |
| | Cost of sales (40[**] units × $30 per unit) | 1,200 | |
| | Inventory on consignment | | 1,200 |
| | *To record cost of goods sold on products for which return privilege expired* | | |

[*] *1,800 units paid for – 600 units paid for in December*
[**] *2,000 units sold – 160 units returned – 1,800 units paid for*

# PROFIT RECOGNITION ON REAL ESTATE SALES

## PERSPECTIVE AND ISSUES

The substance of a sale of any asset is that the transaction unconditionally transfers the risks and rewards of ownership to the buyer. However, the economic substance of many real estate sales is that the risks and rewards of ownership have not been clearly transferred. The turbulent and cyclical environments in the real estate and debt markets have led to the evolution of many complex methods of financing real estate transactions. For example, in some transactions the seller, rather than an independent third party, finances the buyer, while in others, the seller may be required to guarantee a minimum return to the buyer or continue to operate the property for a specified period of time. In many of these complex transactions, the seller still has some association with the property even after the property has been sold. The question that must be answered in these transactions is: At what point does the seller become disassociated enough from the property that profit may be recognized on the transaction?

Accounting for sales of real estate is governed by FAS 66. FIN 43 clarifies that sales of real estate under FAS 66 include property that has improvements or integral equipment not movable without incurring significant costs. Due to the complex nature of these real estate transactions, FAS 66 is very detailed and complex. The purpose of this section is to present the guidelines that need to be considered when analyzing nonretail real estate transactions. FAS 98 dealing with sales-type real estate leases and sales-leaseback real estate transactions is covered in Chapter 16.

A specialized situation involving the sale of real estate pertains to time-share projects, which are addressed by SOP 04-2, as discussed in this chapter. A sister pronouncement, FAS 152, also discussed, has effected the amendments to FAS 66 and FAS 67 necessary to implement the requirements of the SOP.

| Sources of GAAP | | | | |
| --- | --- | --- | --- | --- |
| *FAS* | *FIN* | *EITF* | *FSP* | *SOP* |
| 66, 98, 152 | 43 | 84-17, 86-6, 86-7, 87-9, 88-12, 88-24, 89-14, 94-2, 95-7, 98-8, 00-13, 06-8, 07-6 | 144-1 | 75-2, 78-9, 92-1, 04-2 |

## DEFINITIONS OF TERMS

**Buy-sell agreement.** A contractual arrangement that gives both investors in a jointly owned entity the ability to offer to buy the other's interest.

**Continuing investment.** Payments that the buyer is contractually required to pay on its total debt for the purchase price of the property.

**Cost recovery method.** A method which defers the recognition of gross profit on a real estate sale until the seller recovers the cost of the property sold.

**Deposit method.** A method which records payments by the buyer as deposits rather than a sale. The seller continues to report the asset and related debt on the balance sheet until the contract is canceled or until the sale has been achieved.

**First mortgage (primary debt).** The senior debt the seller has on the property at the time the buyer purchases the property. A first mortgage lender (mortgagee) has foreclosure rights superior to those of second (or junior) mortgage lenders (i.e., proceeds from sale of the foreclosed property are used first to repay the first mortgage lender in full with only the remainder available to satisfy the junior lenders' balances).

**Full accrual method.** A method that recognizes all profit from a real estate sale at the time of sale.

**Initial investment.** The sales value received by the seller at the time of sale. It includes a cash down payment, buyer's notes supported by an irrevocable letter of credit, and payments by the buyer to third parties to reduce or eliminate the seller's indebtedness on the property.

**Installment method.** A method that recognizes revenue on the basis of payments made by the buyer on debt owed to the seller and payments by the buyer to the holder of primary debt. Each payment is apportioned between profit and cost recovery.

**Lien.** A claim or charge a creditor has on property which serves as security for payment of debt by the debtor.

**Minimum initial investment.** The minimum amount that an initial investment must equal or exceed so that the criterion for using the full accrual method is met.

**Partial sale.** A sale in which the seller retains an equity interest in the property or has an equity interest in the buyer.

**Property improvements.** An addition made to real estate, usually consisting of buildings but that may also include any permanent structure such as streets, sidewalks, sewers, utilities, etc.

**Reduced profit method.** A method which recognizes profit at the point of sale, but only a reduced amount. The remaining profit is deferred to future periods.

**Release provision.** An agreement that provides for the release of property to the buyer. This agreement releases the property to the buyer free of any previous liens.

**Sales value.** The sales price of the property increased or decreased for other consideration in the sales transaction that are, in substance, additional sales proceeds to the seller.

**Subordination.** The process by which a party's rights are ranked below the rights of others.

## CONCEPTS, RULES, AND EXAMPLES

### Real Estate Sales other than Retail Land Sales

**FAS 66 scope.** FAS 66, *Accounting for Sales of Real Estate*, established standards applicable to all real estate sales for all types of businesses. However, variations in applying this Statement in practice suggested that additional guidance was needed. FIN 43 clarified that FAS 66 is consistent with the sale-leaseback requirements of FAS 98, *Accounting for Sales and Leasebacks*.

FIN 43 explicitly states that real estate sales transactions under FAS 66 include real estate with property enhancements or integral equipment. This Interpretation defines property improvements and integral equipment as "any physical structure or equipment attached to real estate or other parts thereof, that cannot be removed and used separately without incurring significant cost." Examples include an office building or manufacturing plant.

This interpretation also identifies transactions excluded from the provisions of FAS 66 as follows:

1. A sale of improvements or integral equipment with no sale or plans for a sale of the land.
2. A sale of stock, net assets of a business, or a segment of a business which contain real estate except in cases in which an "in-substance" real estate sale occurs.
3. Securities accounted for under FAS 115.

**Profit recognition methods.** Profit from real estate sales is recognized in full, provided the following:

1.  The profit is determinable (i.e., the collectibility of the sales price is reasonably assured or the amount that will not be collectible can be estimated).
2.  The earnings process is virtually complete, that is, the seller is not obliged to perform significant activities after the sale to earn the profit.

When both of these conditions are satisfied, the method used to recognize profits on real estate sales is referred to as the full accrual method. If both of these conditions are not satisfied, recognition of all or part of the profit is postponed.

For real estate sales, the collectibility of the sales price is reasonably assured when the buyer has demonstrated a commitment to pay. This commitment is supported by a substantial initial investment, along with continuing investments that give the buyer a sufficient stake in the property such that the risk of loss through default motivates the buyer to honor its obligations to the seller. Collectibility of the sales price is also assessed by examining the conditions surrounding the sale (e.g., credit history of the buyer; age, condition, and location of the property; and history of cash flows generated by the property).

The full accrual method is appropriate and profit is recognized in full at the point of sale for real estate transactions when all of the following criteria are met:

1.  A sale is consummated.
2.  The buyer's initial and continuing investments are adequate to demonstrate a commitment to pay for the property.
3.  The seller's receivable is not subject to future subordination.
4.  The seller has transferred to the buyer the usual risks and rewards of ownership in a transaction that is in substance a sale, and the seller does not have a substantial continuing involvement in the property.

On sales in which an independent third party provides all of the financing for the buyer, the seller is most concerned that criterion 1. is met. For such sales, the sale is usually consummated on the closing date. When the seller finances the buyer, the seller must analyze the economic substance of the agreement to ascertain that criteria 2., 3., and 4. are also met (i.e., whether the transaction clearly transfers the risks and rewards of ownership to the buyer).

EITF 88-24 provides the following guidelines for a seller of real estate to follow when considering the various forms of financing that may be applicable to the transaction:

1.  The FAS 66 conditions for obtaining sufficient initial and continuing investment from the buyer before full accrual profit recognition is allowed must be applied unless the seller receives as the full sales value of the property

    a.  Cash without any seller contingent liability on any debt on the property incurred or assumed by the buyer,
    b.  The buyer's assumption of the seller's existing nonrecourse debt on the property,
    c.  The buyer's assumption of all recourse debt on the property with the complete release of the seller from those obligations, or
    d.  Any combination of such cash and debt assumption.

2.  In computing the buyer's initial investment, debt incurred by the buyer that is secured by the property is not considered part of the buyer's initial investment. This is true whether the debt was incurred directly from the seller or other parties or indirectly through assumption. Payments to the seller from the proceeds of such indebtedness are not included as part of the buyer's initial investment.

3.  If the transaction does not qualify for full accrual accounting and, consequently, is being accounted for using installment, cost recovery or reduced profit methods, payments made on debt described in 2. above are not considered to be buyer's cash payments. However, if the profit deferred under the applicable method exceeds the outstanding amount of seller financing and the outstanding amount of buyer's debt secured by the property for which the seller is contingently liable, the seller recognizes the excess in income.

**Consummation of a sale.** A sale is considered consummated when the following conditions are met:

1.  The parties are bound by the terms of a contract.
2.  All consideration has been exchanged.
3.  Any permanent financing for which the seller is responsible has been arranged.
4.  All conditions precedent to closing have been performed.

When a seller is constructing office buildings, condominiums, shopping centers, or similar structures, item 4. may be applied to individual units rather than the entire project. These four conditions are usually met on or after closing, not at the point the agreement to sell is signed or at a preclosing meeting. Closing refers to the final steps of the transaction (i.e., when consideration is paid, the mortgage is secured, and the deed is delivered or placed in escrow). If the consummation criteria have not been satisfied, the seller uses the deposit method of accounting until all of the criteria are met (i.e., the sale has been consummated).

**Adequacy of the buyer's initial investment.** Once the sale is consummated, the next step is to determine whether the buyer's initial investment adequately demonstrates a commitment to pay for the property and the reasonable likelihood that the seller will collect it. This determination is made by comparing the buyer's initial investment to the sales value of the property. FAS 66 specifically details items that are includable as the initial investment and the minimum percentages that the initial investment must bear to the sales value of the property. In order to make the determination of whether the initial investment is adequate, the sales value of the property must also be computed.

**Computation of sales value.** The sales value of property in a real estate transaction is computed as follows:

|   | Stated sales price |
|---|---|
| + | Proceeds from the issuance of an exercised purchase option |
| + | Other payments that are, in substance, additional sales proceeds (e.g., management fees, points, prepaid interest, or fees required to be maintained in advance of the sale that will be applied against amounts due to the seller at a later point) |
| – | A discount that reduces the buyer's note to its present value |
| – | Net present value of services seller agrees to perform without compensation |
| – | Excess of net present value of services seller performs over compensation that seller will receive |
| = | Sales value of the property |

**Composition of the initial investment.** Sales transactions are characterized by many different types of payments and commitments made between the seller, buyer, and third parties; however, the buyer's initial investment only includes the following:

1.  Cash paid to the seller as a down payment
2.  Buyer's notes given to the seller that are supported by irrevocable letters of credit from independent lending institutions
3.  Payments by the buyer to third parties that reduce existing indebtedness the seller has on the property
4.  Other amounts paid by the buyer that are part of the sales value

5. Other consideration received by the seller that can be converted to cash without recourse to the seller; for example, other notes of the buyer

FAS 66 specifically states that the following items are not included as initial investment:

1. Payments by the buyer to third parties for improvements to the property
2. A permanent loan commitment by an independent third party to replace a loan made by the seller
3. Funds that have been or will be loaned, refunded, or directly or indirectly provided to the buyer by the seller or loans guaranteed or collateralized by the seller for the buyer

**Size of initial investment.** Once the initial investment is computed, its size must be compared to the sales value of the property. To qualify as an adequate initial investment, the initial investment must be equal to at least a major part of the difference between usual loan limits established by independent lending institutions and the sales value of the property. The minimum initial investment requirements for real estate sales (other than retail land sales) vary depending upon the type of property being sold. The following table from FAS 66 provides the limits for the various properties:

| *Type of property* | *Minimum initial investment expressed as a percentage of sales value* |
|---|---|
| **Land** | |
| Held for commercial, industrial, or residential development to commence within two years after sale | 20 |
| Held for commercial, industrial, or residential development to commence more than two years after sale | 25 |
| **Commercial and Industrial Property** | |
| Office and industrial buildings, shopping centers, and so forth: | |
| Properties subject to lease on a long-term lease basis to parties with satisfactory credit rating; cash flow currently sufficient to service all indebtedness | 10 |
| Single-tenancy properties sold to a buyer with a satisfactory credit rating | 15 |
| All other | 20 |
| Other income-producing properties (hotels, motels, marinas, mobile home parks, and so forth): | |
| Cash flow currently sufficient to service all indebtedness | 15 |
| Start-up situations or current deficiencies in cash flow | 25 |
| **Multifamily Residential Property** | |
| Primary residence: | |
| Cash flow currently sufficient to service all indebtedness | 10 |
| Start-up situations or current deficiencies in cash flow | 15 |
| Secondary or recreational residence: | |
| Cash flow currently sufficient to service all indebtedness | 15 |
| Start-up situations or current deficiencies in cash flow | 25 |
| **Single-Family Residential Property (including condominium or cooperative housing)** | |
| Primary residence of the buyer | 5[a] |
| Secondary or recreational residence | 10[a] |

[a] *If collectibility of the remaining portion of the sales price cannot be supported by reliable evidence of collection experience, the minimum initial investment [is to] be at least 60% of the difference between the sales value and the financing available from loans guaranteed by regulatory bodies such as the Federal Housing Authority (FHA) or the Veterans Administration (VA), or from independent, established lending institutions. This 60% test applies when independent first-mortgage financing is not utilized and the seller takes a receivable from the buyer for the difference between the sales value and the initial investment. If independent first mortgage financing is utilized, the adequacy of the initial investment on sales of single-family residential property [is] determined [as described in the next paragraph].*

Lenders' appraisals of specific properties often differ. Therefore, if the buyer has obtained a permanent loan or firm permanent loan commitment for maximum financing of the property from an independent lending institution, the minimum initial investment must be the greater of the following:

1. The minimum percentage of the sales value of the property specified in the above table or
2. The lesser of
   a. The amount of the sales value of the property in excess of 115% of the amount of a newly placed permanent loan or firm loan commitment from a primary lender that is an independent established lending institution
   b. 25% of the sales value

To illustrate the determination of whether an initial investment adequately demonstrates a commitment to pay for property, consider the following example:

**Example determining adequacy of initial investment**

Marcus, Inc. exercised a $2,000 option for the purchase of an apartment building from Rubin, Inc. The terms of the sales contract required Marcus to pay $3,000 of delinquent property taxes, pay a $300,000 cash down payment, assume Rubin's recently issued first mortgage of $1,200,000, and give Rubin a second mortgage of $500,000 at a prevailing interest rate.

Step 1 — Compute the sales value of the property.

| | |
|---|---:|
| Payment of back taxes to reduce Rubin's liability to local municipality | $    3,000 |
| Proceeds from exercised option | 2,000 |
| Cash down payment | 300,000 |
| First mortgage assumed by Marcus | 1,200,000 |
| Second mortgage given to Rubin | 500,000 |
| Sales value of the apartment complex | $2,005,000 |

Step 2 — Compute the initial investment.

| | |
|---|---:|
| Cash down payment | $300,000 |
| Payment of back taxes to reduce Rubin's liability to local municipality | 3,000 |
| Proceeds from exercised option | 2,000 |
| | $  305,000 |

Step 3 — Compute the minimum initial investment required.

    a.    The minimum percentage of the sales value of the property as specified in the table is $200,500 (= $2,005,000 × 10%).

    b.    1.    The amount of the sales value of the property in excess of 115% of the recently placed permanent mortgage is $625,000 (sales value of $2,005,000 − $1,380,000 [= 115% of $1,200,000]).

           2.    25% of the sales value ($2,005,000) is $501,250.

The lesser of b.1 and b.2 is b.2, $501,250. The greater of a. and b. is b., $501,250. Therefore, to record this transaction under the full accrual method (assuming all other criteria are met), the minimum initial investment must be equal to or greater than $501,250. Since the actual initial investment is only $305,000, all or part of the recognition of profit from the transaction must be postponed.

If the sale has been consummated but the buyer's initial investment does not adequately demonstrate a commitment to pay, the transaction is accounted for using the installment method when the seller is reasonably assured of recovering the cost of the property if the buyer defaults. However, if the recovery of the cost of the property is not reasonably assured should the buyer default or if the cost has been recovered and the collection of additional amounts is uncertain, the cost recovery or deposit method is used.

**Adequacy of the buyer's continuing investments.** The collectibility of the buyer's receivable must be reasonably assured; therefore, for full profit recognition under the full accrual method, the buyer must be contractually required to pay each year on its total debt for the purchase price of the property an amount at least equal to the level annual payment that would be needed to pay that debt (both principal and interest) over a specified period. This period is no more than twenty years for land, and no more than the customary amortization term of a first mortgage loan by an independent lender for other types of real estate. For continuing investment purposes, the contractually required payments must be in a form that is acceptable for an initial investment. If the seller provides funds to the buyer, either directly or indirectly, these funds must be subtracted from the buyer's payments in determining whether the continuing investments are adequate.

The indebtedness on the property does not have to be reduced proportionately. A lump-sum (balloon) payment will not affect the amortization of the receivable as long as the level annual payments still meet the minimum annual amortization requirement. For example, a land real estate sale may require the buyer to make level annual payments at the end of each of the first five years and then a balloon payment at the end of the sixth year. The continuing investment criterion is met provided the level annual payment required in each of the first five years is greater than or equal to the level annual payment that would be made if the receivable were amortized over the maximum twenty-year (land's specified term) period.

**Continuing investment not qualifying.** If the sale has been consummated and the minimum initial investment criteria have been satisfied but the continuing investment by the buyer does not meet the stated criterion, the seller recognizes profit by the reduced profit method at the time of sale if payments by the buyer each year will at least cover both of the following:

1. The interest and principal amortization on the maximum first mortgage loan that could be obtained on the property
2. Interest, at an appropriate rate, on the excess of the aggregate actual debt on the property over such a maximum first mortgage loan

If the payments by the buyer do not cover both of the above, the seller recognizes profit by either the installment or cost recovery method.

**Release provisions.** An agreement to sell real estate may provide that part or all of the property sold will be released from liens by payment of an amount sufficient to release the debt or by an assignment of the buyer's payments until release. In order to meet the criteria of an adequate initial investment, the investment must be sufficient both to pay the release on property released and to meet the initial investment requirements on property not released. If not, profit is recognized on each released portion as if it were a separate sale when a sale has been deemed to have taken place.

**Seller's receivable subject to future subordination.** The seller's receivable should not be subject to future subordination. Future subordination by a primary lender would permit the lender to obtain a lien on the property, giving the seller only a secondary residual claim. This subordination criterion does not apply if either of the following occur:

1. A receivable is subordinate to a first mortgage on the property existing at the time of sale.
2. A future loan, including an existing permanent loan commitment, is provided for by the terms of the sale and the proceeds of the loan will be applied first to the payment of the seller's receivable.

If the seller's receivable is subject to future subordination, profit is recognized using the cost recovery method. The cost recovery method is justified because the collectibility of the sales price is not reasonably assured in circumstances when the receivable may be subordinated to amounts due to other creditors.

**Seller's continuing involvement.** Sometimes sellers continue to be involved with property for periods of time even though the property has been legally sold. The seller's involvement often takes the form of profit participation, management services, financing, guarantees of return, construction, etc. The seller does not have a substantial continuing involvement with property unless the risks and rewards of ownership have been clearly transferred to the buyer.

If the seller has some continuing involvement with the property and does not clearly transfer substantially all of the risks and rewards of ownership, profit is recognized by a method other than the full accrual method. The method chosen is determined by the nature and extent of the seller's continuing involvement. As a general rule, profit is only recognized at the time of sale if the amount of the seller's loss due to the continued involvement with the property is limited by the terms of the sales contract. In this event, the profit recognized at this time is reduced by the maximum possible loss from the continued involvement.

**Leases involving real estate.** FAS 98 dealing with sales-type real estate leases and sale-leaseback real estate transactions is covered in Chapter 16.

**Profit-sharing, financing, and leasing arrangements.** In real estate sales, it is often the case that economic substance takes precedence over legal form. Certain transactions, though possibly called sales, are in substance profit-sharing, financing, or leasing arrangements and are accounted for as such. These include situations in which

1. The seller has an obligation to repurchase the property, or the terms of the transaction allow the buyer to compel the seller to repurchase the property or give the seller an option to do so.
2. The seller is a general partner in a limited partnership that acquires an interest in the property sold and holds a receivable from the buyer for a significant part (15% of the maximum first-lien financing) of the sales price.
3. The seller guarantees the return of the buyer's investment or a return on that investment for an extended period of time.
4. The seller is required to initiate or support operations, or continue to operate the property at its own risk for an extended period of time.

**Options to purchase real estate property.** Often a buyer will buy an option to purchase land from a seller with the hopeful intention of obtaining a zoning change, building permit, or some other contingency specified in the option agreement. Proceeds from the issue of an option by a property owner (seller) are accounted for by the deposit method. If the option is exercised, the seller includes the option proceeds in the computation of the sales value of the property. If the option is not exercised, the seller recognizes the option proceeds as income at the time the option expires.

**Partial sales of property.** Per FAS 66, "a sale is a partial sale if the seller retains an equity interest in the property or has an equity interest in the buyer." Profit on a partial sale may be recognized on the date of sale if the following occur:

1. The buyer is independent of the seller.
2. Collection of the sales price is reasonably assured.
3. The seller will not be required to support the operations of the property on its related obligations to an extent greater than its proportionate interest.

If the buyer is not independent of the seller, the seller may not be able to recognize any profit that is measured at the date of sale (see the following Buy-sell agreements section).

If the seller is not reasonably assured of collecting the sales price, the cost recovery or installment method is used to recognize profit on the partial sale.

A seller who separately sells individual units in condominium projects or time-sharing interests recognizes profit by the percentage-of-completion method on the sale of individual units or interests if all of the following criteria are met:

1. Construction is beyond a preliminary stage (i.e., engineering and design work, execution of construction contracts, site clearance and preparation, excavation, and completion of the building foundation have all been completed).
2. The buyer is unable to obtain a refund except for nondelivery of the units or interest.
3. Sufficient units have been sold to assure that the entire property will not revert to being rental property.
4. Sales prices are collectible.
5. Aggregate sales proceeds and costs can be reasonably estimated.

The deposit method is used to account for these sales up to the point all the criteria are met for recognition of a sale.

**Buy-sell agreements.** The EITF 07-6 consensus states that a buy-sell clause is not a prohibited form of continuing involvement precluding partial sales treatment, but only if (1) the buyer can act independently from the seller, or if (2) the seller is not compelled to reacquire the other investor's interest in the jointly owned entity. The decision is judgmental, requiring consideration of numerous factors.

Factors to consider in determining whether the buyer cannot act independently from the seller are (1) the presence of a predetermined buy-sell price, (2) the seller has a strategic necessity barring it from relinquishing its ownership rights to the buyer, (3) the seller has business arrangements with the jointly owned entity that economically require it to reacquire the real estate to avoid losing economic benefits or escaping negative consequences of the arrangements, or (4) tax implications compelling the seller to acquire the buyer's interest in the entity.

Factors to consider in determining if the buyer can compel the seller to repurchase the property include (1) the buyer is financially unable to acquire the seller's interest, (2) the buy-sell clause contains a specified rate of return for either party, (3) the buyer has a strategic necessity requiring it to sell its interest to the seller, (4) the buyer is legally restricted from acquiring the seller's interest, (5) the buyer cannot realize its economic interest by sale to a third party, due to the integration of the real estate into the seller's business, or (6) tax implications compelling the buyer to sell its interest to the seller.

**Selection of method.** If a loss is apparent (e.g., the carrying value of the property exceeds the sum of the deposit, fair value of unrecorded note receivable, and the debt assumed by the buyer), then immediate recognition of the loss is required.

The installment method is used if the full accrual method cannot be used due to an inadequate initial investment by the buyer, provided that recovery of cost is reasonably assured if the buyer defaults. The cost recovery method or the deposit methods are used if such cost recovery is not assured.

The reduced profit method is used when the buyer's initial investment is adequate but the continuing investment is not adequate, and payments by the buyer at least cover the sum of (1) the amortization (principal and interest) on the maximum first mortgage that could be obtained on the property and (2) the interest, at an appropriate rate, on the excess of aggregate debt over the maximum first mortgage.

### Methods of Accounting for Real Estate Sales other than Retail Land Sales

**Full accrual method.** This method of accounting for nonretail sales of real estate is appropriate when all four of the recognition criteria have been satisfied. The full accrual method is simply the application of the revenue recognition principle. A real estate sale is recognized in full when the profit is determinable and the earnings process is virtually complete. The profit is determinable when the first three criteria have been met (the sale is consummated, the buyer has demonstrated a commitment to pay, and the seller's receivable is not subject to future subordination). The earnings process is virtually complete when the fourth criterion has been met (the seller has transferred the risks and rewards of ownership and does not have a substantial continuing involvement with the property). If all of the criteria have not been met, the seller records the transaction by one of the following methods as indicated by FAS 66:

1. Deposit
2. Cost recovery
3. Installment
4. Reduced profit
5. Percentage-of-completion (see the section on Long-Term Construction Contracts in this chapter)

Profit under the full accrual method is computed by subtracting the cost basis of the property surrendered from the sales value given by the buyer. Also, the computation of profit on the sale includes all costs incurred that are directly related to the sale, such as accounting and legal fees.

**Installment method.** Under the installment method, each cash receipt and principal payment by the buyer on debt assumed with recourse to the seller consists of part recovery of cost and part recovery of profit. The apportionment between cost recovery and profit is in the same ratio as total cost and total profit bear to the sales value of the property sold. Therefore, under the installment method, the seller recognizes profit on each payment that the buyer makes to the seller and on each payment the buyer makes to the holder of the primary debt. When a buyer assumes debt that is without recourse to the seller, the seller recognizes profit on each payment made to the seller and on the entire debt assumed by the buyer. The accounting treatment differs because the seller is subject to substantially different levels of risk under the alternative conditions. For debt that is without recourse, the seller recovers a portion, if not all, of the cost of the asset surrendered at the time the buyer assumes the debt.

### Example of the installment method

Assume Tucker sells to Price a plot of undeveloped land for $2,000,000. Price will assume, with recourse, Tucker's existing first mortgage of $1,000,000 and also pay Tucker a $300,000 cash down payment. Price will pay the balance of $700,000 by giving Tucker a second mortgage payable in equal installments of principal and interest over a ten-year period. The cost of the land to Tucker was $1,200,000 and Price will commence development of the land immediately.

1. Computation of sales value:

| | |
|---|---|
| Cash down payment | $ 300,000 |
| First mortgage | 1,000,000 |
| Second mortgage | 700,000 |
| Sales value | $2,000,000 |

2. Computation of the initial investment:

| | |
|---|---|
| Cash down payment | $ 300,000 |

3. Computation of the minimum required initial investment:

a. $400,000 ($2,000,000 × 20%)
b. 1) $850,000 [$2,000,000 − (115% × 1,000,000)]
   2) $500,000 ($2,000,000 × 25%)

The minimum initial investment is $500,000 since b.2) is less than b.1) and b.2) is greater than a.

The initial investment criterion has not been satisfied because the actual initial investment is less than the minimum initial investment. Therefore, assuming the sale has been consummated and Tucker is reasonably assured of recovering the cost of the land from Price, the installment method is to be used. The gross profit to be recognized over the installment payment period by Tucker is computed as follows:

| | |
|---|---|
| Sales value | $ 2,000,000 |
| Cost of land | (1,200,000) |
| Gross profit | $    800,000 |

The gross profit percentage to apply to each payment by Price to Tucker and the primary debt holder is 40% ($800,000/$2,000,000).

If Price also pays $50,000 of principal on the first mortgage and $70,000 of principal on the second mortgage in the year of sale, Tucker would recognize the following profit in the year of sale:

| | |
|---|---|
| Profit recognized on the down payment ($300,000 × 40%) | $120,000 |
| Profit recognized on the principal payments: | |
| First mortgage ($50,000 × 40%) | 20,000 |
| Second mortgage ($70,000 × 40%) | 28,000 |
| Total profit recognized in year of sale | $168,000 |

Note that Tucker recognizes profit only on the payment applicable to the first mortgage. This is because Tucker may be called upon to satisfy the liability on the first mortgage if Price defaults.

If Tucker's first mortgage was assumed without recourse, Tucker would recognize the following profit in the year of sale:

| | |
|---|---|
| Profit recognized on the down payment ($300,000 × 40%) | $120,000 |
| Profit recognized on Price's assumption of Tucker's first mortgage without recourse | |
| ($1,000,000 × 40%) | 400,000 |
| Profit recognized on the principal payment of the second mortgage ($70,000 × 40%) | 28,000 |
| Total profit recognized in year of sale | $548,000 |

The income statement (or related footnotes) for the period of sale includes the sales value received, the gross profit recognized, the gross profit deferred, and the costs of sale. In future periods when further payments are made to the buyer, the seller realizes gross profit on these payments. This amount is presented as a single line item in the revenue section of the income statement.

If, in the future, the transaction meets the requirements for the full accrual method of recognizing profit, the seller may change to that method and recognize the remaining deferred profit as income at that time.

**Cost recovery method.** When the cost recovery method is used (e.g., when the seller's receivable is subject to subordination or the seller is not reasonably assured of recovering the cost of the property if the buyer defaults), no profit is recognized on the sales transaction until the seller has recovered the cost of the property sold. If the buyer assumes debt that is with recourse to the seller, profit is not recognized by the seller until the cash payments by the buyer, including both principal and interest on debt due the seller and on debt assumed by the buyer, exceed the seller's cost of the property sold. If the buyer assumes debt that is without recourse to the seller, profit may be recognized by the seller when the cash payments by the buyer, including both principal and interest on debt due the seller, exceed the difference between the seller's cost of the property and the nonrecourse debt assumed by the buyer.

For the cost recovery method, principal collections reduce the seller's related receivable, and interest collections on such receivable increase the deferred gross profit on the balance sheet.

**Example of the cost recovery method**

Assume that on January 1, 2009, Simon, Inc. purchased undeveloped land with a sales value of $365,000 from Davis Co. The sales value is represented by a $15,000 cash down payment, Simon assuming Davis's $200,000 first mortgage (10%, payable in equal annual installments over the next twenty years), and Simon giving Davis a second mortgage of $150,000 (12%, payable in equal annual installments over the next ten years). The sale has been consummated, but the initial investment is below the minimum required amount and Davis is not reasonably assured of recovering the cost of the property if Simon defaults. The cost of the land to Davis was $300,000. The circumstances indicate the cost recovery method is appropriate. The transaction is recorded by Davis as follows:

| 1/1/09 | Notes receivable | 150,000 | |
|---|---|---|---|
| | First mortgage payable | 200,000 | |
| | Cash | 15,000 | |
| | Revenue from sale of land | | 365,000 |
| | Revenue from sale of land | 365,000 | |
| | Land | | 300,000 |
| | Deferred gross profit | | 65,000 |

Case 1 — The first mortgage was assumed with recourse to Davis. Immediately after the sale, the unrecovered cost of the land is computed as follows:

| Land | $300,000 |
|---|---|
| Less: Cash down payment | (15,000) |
| Unrecovered cost | $285,000 |

The note (second mortgage) is reported as follows:

| Note receivable | $150,000 | |
|---|---|---|
| Less: Deferred gross profit | (65,000) | $ 85,000 |

At the end of the year Simon pays $26,547.64 ($8,547.64 principal and $18,000.00 interest) on the second mortgage note and $23,491.94 ($3,491.94 principal and $20,000.00 interest) on the first mortgage. At 12/31/09 the unrecovered cost of the land is computed as follows:

| Previous unrecovered cost | | $285,000.00 |
|---|---|---|
| Less: Note receivable payment | $26,547.64 | |
| First mortgage payment | 23,491.94 | (50,039.58) |
| Unrecovered cost | | $234,960.42 |

The receivable is reported on the 12/31/09 balance sheet as follows:

| Note receivable ($150,000 – 8,547.64) | $141,452.36 | |
|---|---|---|
| Less: Deferred gross profit ($65,000 + 18,000) | 83,000.00 | $58,452.36 |

Case 2 — The first mortgage is assumed without recourse to Davis. The reporting of the note is the same as Case 1; however, the unrecovered cost of the property is different. Immediately after the sale, the unrecovered cost of the property is computed as follows:

| Land | | $300,000 |
|---|---|---|
| Less: Cash down payment | | (15,000) |
| Nonrecourse debt assumed by Simon | | (200,000) |
| Unrecovered cost | | $ 85,000 |

After Simon makes the payments at the end of the year, the unrecovered cost is computed as follows:

| Previous unrecovered cost | $85,000.00 |
|---|---|
| Less: Notes receivable payment | 26,547.64 |
| Unrecovered cost | $58,452.36 |

For the cost recovery method, the income statement for the year the real estate sale occurs includes the sales value received, the cost of the property given up, and the gross profit deferred. In future periods, after the cost of the property has been recovered, the income statement includes the gross profit earned as a separate revenue item.

If, after accounting for the sale by the cost recovery method, circumstances indicate that the criteria for the full accrual method are satisfied, the seller may change to the full accrual method and recognize any remaining deferred gross profit in full.

**Deposit method.** When the deposit method is used (e.g., when the sale is, in substance, the sale of an option and not real estate), the seller does not recognize any profit, does not record a receivable, continues to report in its financial statements the property and the related existing debt even if the debt has been assumed by the buyer, and discloses that those items are subject to a sales contract. The seller also continues to recognize depreciation expense on the property for which the deposits have been received, unless the property has been classified as held for sale (per FAS 144). Cash received from the buyer (initial and continuing investments) is reported as a deposit on the contract. However, some amounts of cash may be received that are not subject to refund, such as interest on the unrecorded principal. These amounts are used to offset any carrying charges on the property (e.g., property taxes and interest on the existing debt). If the interest collected on the unrecorded receivable is refundable, the seller records this interest as a deposit before the sale is consummated and then includes it as a part of the initial investment once the sale is consummated. If deposits on retail land sales are eventually recognized as sales, the interest portion of the deposit is separately recognized as interest income. For contracts that are cancelled, the nonrefundable amounts are recognized as income and the refundable amounts returned to the depositor at the time of cancellation.

As stated, the seller's balance sheet continues to present the debt assumed by the buyer (this includes nonrecourse debt) among its other liabilities. However, the seller reports any principal payments on the mortgage debt assumed as additional deposits, while correspondingly reducing the carrying amount of the mortgage debt.

### Example of a deposit transaction

Elbrus Investments enters into two separate property acquisition transactions with the Buena Vista Land Company.

1. Elbrus pays a $50,000 deposit and promises to pay an additional $800,000 to buy land and a building in an area not yet properly zoned for the facility Elbrus intends to construct. Final acquisition of the property is contingent upon these zoning changes. Buena Vista does not record the receivable, and records the deposit with the following entry:

| | | |
|---|---|---|
| Cash | 50,000 | |
|     Customer deposits | | 50,000 |

Part of the purchase agreement stipulates that Buena Vista will retain all interest earned on the deposit, and that 10% of the deposit is nonrefundable. Buena Vista earns 5% interest on Elbrus' deposit over a period of four months, resulting in $208 of interest income that is offset against the property tax expenses of the property with the following entry:

| | | |
|---|---|---|
| Cash | 208 | |
|     Property tax expense | | 208 |

Immediately thereafter, the required zoning changes are turned down, and Elbrus cancels the sales contract. Buena Vista returns the refundable portion of the deposit to Elbrus and records the nonrefundable portion as income with the following entry:

| | | |
|---|---|---|
| Customer deposits | 50,000 | |
|     Income from contract cancellation | | 10,000 |
|     Cash | | 40,000 |

2.  Elbrus pays a $40,000 deposit on land owned and being improved by Buena Vista. Elbrus immediately begins paying $5,000/month under a four-year, 7% loan agreement totaling $212,000 of principal payments, and agrees to pay an additional $350,000 at closing, subject to the land being approved for residential construction. After two months, Buena Vista has earned $167 of refundable interest income on Elbrus' deposit and has been paid $7,689 of refundable principal and $2,311 of refundable interest on the debt. Buena Vista records these events with the following entry:

| | | |
|---|---|---|
| Cash | 10,167 | |
| Customer deposits | | 10,167 |

The land is approved for residential construction, triggering sale of the property. Buena Vista's basis in the property is $520,000. Buena Vista uses the following entry to describe completion of the sale:

| | | |
|---|---|---|
| Cash | 350,000 | |
| Note receivable | 204,311 | |
| Customer deposits | 50,167 | |
| Gain on asset sale | | 84,478 |
| Land | | 520,000 |

**Reduced profit method.** The reduced profit method is appropriate when the sale has been consummated and the initial investment is adequate but the continuing investment does not clearly demonstrate the buyer's willing commitment to pay the remaining balance of the receivable. For example, a buyer may purchase land under an agreement in which the seller will finance the sale over a thirty-year period. FAS 66 specifically states twenty years as the maximum amortization period for the purchase of land; therefore, the agreement fails to meet the continuing investment criteria.

Under the reduced profit method, the seller recognizes a portion of the profit at the time of sale with the remaining portion recognized in future periods. The amount of reduced profit recognized at the time of sale is determined by discounting the receivable from the buyer to the present value of the lowest level of annual payments required by the sales contract over the maximum period of time specified for that type of real estate property (twenty years for land and the customary term of a first mortgage loan set by an independent lending institution for other types of real estate). The remaining profit is recognized in the periods that lump-sum or other payments are made.

### Example of the reduced profit method

Assume Levinson, Inc. sells a parcel of land to Raemer Co. Levinson receives sales value of $2,000,000. The land cost $1,600,000. Raemer gave Levinson the following consideration:

| | |
|---|---|
| Cash down payment | $ 500,000 |
| First mortgage note payable to an independent lending institution (payable in equal installments of principal and 12% interest, $133,887 payable at the end of each of the next twenty years) | 1,000,000 |
| Second mortgage note payable to Levinson (payable in equal installments of principal and 10% interest, $53,039 payable at the end of each of the next thirty years) | 500,000 |
| Total sales value | $2,000,000 |

The amortization term of the second mortgage (seller's receivable) exceeds the twenty-year maximum permitted by FAS 66. It is assumed that the payments by the buyer will cover the interest and principal on the maximum first mortgage loan that could be obtained on the property and interest on the excess aggregate debt on the property over such a maximum first mortgage loan; consequently, the reduced profit method is appropriate. It is also assumed that the market interest rate on similar agreements is 14%.

The present value of $53,039 per year for twenty years at the market rate of 14% is $351,278 ($53,039 × 6.623).

The gross profit on the sale ($400,000) is reduced by the difference between the face amount of the seller's receivable ($500,000) and the reduced amount ($351,278) or $148,722. The profit recognized at the time of sale is the sales value less the cost of the land less the difference between the face amount of the receivable and the reduced amount. Therefore, the reduced profit recognized on the date of sale is computed as follows:

| | | |
|---|---|---|
| Sales value | | $ 2,000,000 |
| Less: | Cost of land | (1,600,000) |
| | Excess | (148,722) |
| | Reduced profit | $   251,278 |

Under the reduced profit method, the seller amortizes its receivable at the market rate, not the rate given on the second mortgage. The receivable's carrying balance is zero after the specified term expires (in this case, twenty years). The remaining profit of $148,722 is recognized in the years after the specified term expires as the buyer makes payments on the second mortgage (years twenty-one through thirty).

## Profit Recognition on Retail Land Sales

A single method of recognizing profit is applied to all consummated sales transactions within a project.

**Full accrual method.** The full accrual method of accounting is applied if all of the following conditions are met and a sale can be recorded:

1.  **Expiration of refund period.** The buyer has made the down payment and each required subsequent payment until the period of cancellation with refund has expired. That period is the longest period of those required by local law, established by the seller's policy, or specified in the contract.
2.  **Sufficient cumulative payments.** The cumulative payments of principal and interest equal or exceed 10% of the contract sales price.
3.  **Collectibility of receivables.** Collection experience for the project in which the sale is made or for the seller's prior projects indicates that at least 90% of the contracts in the project in which the sale is made that are in force six months after sale will be collected in full. The collection experience with the seller's prior projects may be applied to a new project if the prior projects have

    a.  The same characteristics (type of land, environment, clientele, contract terms, sales methods) as the new project
    b.  A sufficiently long collection period to indicate the percentage of current sales of the new project that will be collected to maturity

    A down payment of at least 20% is an acceptable indication of collectibility.

4.  **Nonsubordination of receivables.** The receivable from the sale is not subject to subordination to new loans on the property except that subordination by an individual lot buyer for home construction purposes is permissible if the collection experience on those contracts is the same as on contracts not subordinated.
5.  **Completion of development.** The seller is not obligated to complete improvements of lots sold or to construct amenities or other facilities applicable to lots sold.

**Percentage-of-completion method.** The percentage-of-completion method is used if criteria 1., 2., 3., and 4. above are met, and full accrual criteria are not met (criterion 5. is not satisfied). However, additional criteria (6. and 7.) must be satisfied.

6.  **There has been progress on improvements.** The project's improvements progressed beyond preliminary stages and the work apparently will be completed according to plan. Some indications of progress are

    a.  The expenditure of funds
    b.  Initiation of work

c.   Existence of engineering plans and work commitments
d.   Completion of access roads and amenities such as golf courses, clubs, and swimming pools

Additionally, there should be no indication of significant delaying factors, such as the inability to obtain permits, contractors, personnel, or equipment. Finally, estimates of costs to complete and extent of progress toward completion should be reasonably dependable.

7.  **Development is practical.** There is an expectation that the land can be developed for the purposes represented and the properties will be useful for those purposes; restrictions, including environmental restrictions, will not seriously hamper development; and that improvements such as access roads, water supply, and sewage treatment or removal are feasible within a reasonable time period.

**Installment method.** The installment method is appropriate if criteria a. and b. are met, full accrual criteria are not met, and the seller is financially capable, as shown by capital structure, cash flow, or borrowing capacity. If the transaction subsequently meets the requirements for the full accrual method, the seller is permitted to change to that method. This would be a change in accounting estimate. This method may be changed to the percentage-of-completion method when all of the criteria are met.

**Deposit method.** If a retail land sale transaction does not meet any of the above criteria, the deposit method is appropriate.

### Time-Share Transactions

A major segment of the real estate industry has evolved in recent decades to market and sell time-shares, whereby parties acquire the right to use property (typically, resort condominiums or other vacation-oriented property) for a fixed number of weeks per year (known as intervals). While a vast variety of property types and transaction structures exist, there are certain common features and complexities that have challenged the accounting profession. Time-sharing transactions are characterized by the following:

1.   Volume-based, homogeneous sales
2.   Seller financing
3.   Relatively high selling and marketing costs
4.   Upon default, recovery of the time-sharing interval by the seller and some forfeiture of principal by the buyer.

The standard setters (in this case, a joint effort by FASB and AcSEC) resolved the issues and produced detailed guidance to accounting for time-share transactions. FAS 152 amended FAS 66 (covered in the preceding discussion) and FAS 67 (addressed in the following section of this chapter) to make reference to the guidance provided by SOP 04-2. Specifically, FAS 66 has been amended to provide that time-share transactions are to be accounted for as nonretail land sales, and FAS 67 has been amended to exclude time-share transactions from certain provisions otherwise applicable to incidental rental operations.

**Accounting for time-share transactions.** SOP 04-2, *Accounting for Real Estate Time-Sharing Transactions,* provides guidance for a seller's accounting for real estate time-sharing transactions, including

1.   Fee simple transactions in which nonreversionary title and ownership of the real estate pass to the buyer or an SPE
2.   Transactions in which title and ownership of all or a portion of the real estate remain with the seller

3. Transactions in which title and ownership of all or a portion of the real estate pass to the buyer and subsequently revert to the seller or transfer to a third party
4. Transactions by a time-share reseller

The major conclusions of this very detailed, specialized standard are as follows:

*Profit recognition.* A time-share seller should recognize profit on time-sharing transactions as set forth by the provisions of FAS 66 that specify the accounting for other than retail land sales. In order to justify recognizing profit, nonreversionary title must be transferred. If title transfer is reversionary, on the other hand, the seller must account for the transaction as if it were an operating lease.

For a time-sharing transaction to be accounted for as a sale, it must meet the following criteria:

1. The seller transfers nonreversionary title to the time-share;
2. The transaction is *consummated*;
3. The buyer makes cumulative payments (excluding interest) of at least 10% of the sales value of the time-share; and
4. Sufficient time-shares would have been sold to reasonably assure that the units will not become rental property.

*Effect of sales incentives.* The SOP requires that certain sales incentives provided by a seller to a buyer to consummate a transaction are to be recorded separately, by reducing the stated sales price of the time-share by the excess of the fair value of the incentive over the amount paid by the buyer. For purposes of testing for buyer's financial commitment as set forth under FAS 66, the seller must reduce its measurement of the buyer's initial and continuing investments by the excess of the fair value of the incentive over the stated amount the buyer pays, except in certain situations in which the buyer is required to make specific payments on its note in order to receive the incentive.

*Reload transactions.* A reload transaction is considered to be a separate sale of a second interval, and the second interval is accounted for in accordance with the profit recognition guidance of FAS 66. For an upgrade transaction, that guidance is applied to the sales value of the new (upgrade) interval, and the buyer's initial and continuing investments from the original interval are included in the profit recognition tests related to the new interval.

*Uncollectibles.* The term uncollectibles is used in SOP 04-2 to include all situations in which, as a result of credit issues, a time-share seller collects less than 100% of the contractual cash payments of a note receivable, except for certain transfers of receivables to independent third parties by the seller. An estimate of uncollectibility that is expected to occur should be recorded as a reduction of revenue at the time that profit is recognized on a time-sharing sale recorded under the full accrual or percentage-of-completion method. Historical and statistical perspectives are used in making such a determination of anticipated uncollectible amounts. Subsequent changes in estimated uncollectibles should be recorded as an adjustment to estimated uncollectibles and thereby as an adjustment to revenue. Under the relative sales value method, the seller effectively does not record revenue, cost of sales, or inventory relief for amounts not expected to be collected. There generally is no accounting effect on inventory when, as expected, a time-share is repossessed or otherwise reacquired.

*Cost of sales.* The seller should account for cost of sales and time-sharing inventory in accordance with the relative sales value method.

*Costs charged to current period expense.* All costs incurred to sell time-shares would be charged to expense as incurred except for certain costs that are

- Incurred for tangible assets used directly in selling the time-shares;
- Incurred for services performed to obtain regulatory approval of sales; or

- Direct and incremental costs of successful sales efforts under the percentage-of-completion, installment, reduced profit, or deposit methods of accounting.

***Incidental operations.*** Rental and other operations during holding periods, including sampler programs and minivacations, should be accounted for as incidental operations. This requires that any excess of revenue over costs be recorded as a reduction of inventory costs.

***VIEs and other complex structures.*** The accounting treatment for more complex time-sharing structures such as time-sharing special-purpose entities (VIEs, formerly known as *special-purpose entities*, or SPEs), points systems, and vacation clubs should be determined using the same profit recognition guidance as for simpler structures, provided that the time-sharing interest has been sold to the end user. For balance sheet presentation purposes, a VIE should be viewed as an entity lacking economic substance and established for the purpose of facilitating sales if the VIE structure is legally required for purposes of selling intervals to a class of nonresident customers, and the VIE has no assets other than the time-sharing intervals and has no debt. In those circumstances, the seller should present on its balance sheet as time-sharing inventory the interests in the VIE not yet sold to end users.

***Continuing involvement by seller or related entities.*** If the seller, seller's affiliate, or related party operates an exchange, points, affinity, or similar program, the program's operations constitute continuing involvement by the seller, and the seller should determine its accounting based on an evaluation of whether it will receive compensation at prevailing market rates for its program services.

### Other Guidance to Accounting for Real Estate Sales Transactions

FIN 43 states that sales of integral equipment are within the scope of FAS 66, and thus the determination of whether equipment is integral is an important one. A determination of whether equipment to be leased is integral is also necessary to enable lessors to determine the proper accounting for sales-type leases. EITF 00-13 states that this determination is to be made based on two factors. The first is the significance of the cost to remove the equipment from its existing location (which would include any costs of repairing the damage done to that location by the act of removal). The second is the decrease in value of the equipment that results from its removal (which is, at a minimum, the cost to ship and reinstall the equipment at a new site). The nature of the equipment and whether others can use it is considered in determining whether there would be any further diminution in fair value. When the combined total of the cost to remove and any further diminution of value exceeds 10% of the fair value of the equipment (installed), the equipment is to be deemed integral equipment, and thus accounted for under the provisions of FAS 66.

FASB Staff Position 144-1 deals with the question of whether a valuation allowance previously established for a loan which is collateralized by a long-lived asset should be carried forward after the asset is foreclosed due to loan default. It holds that, when such a loan is foreclosed, any valuation allowance established for the foreclosed loan should not be carried over as a separate element of the cost basis for purposes of accounting for the long-lived assets under FAS 144. Rather, upon foreclosure the lender must measure the long-lived asset received in full satisfaction of a receivable at fair value less cost to sell as prescribed by FAS 15. Application of FAS 15 results in the identification of a new cost basis for the long-lived asset received in full satisfaction of a receivable.

Staff Position 144-1 also addresses the limitation on gain recognition when an impaired asset obtained by means of foreclosure later recovers some value. FAS 144 states that "a loss shall be recognized for any initial or subsequent write-down to fair value less cost to sell. A gain shall be recognized for any subsequent increase in fair value less cost to sell, but not in excess of the cumulative loss previously recognized (for a write-down to fair value less cost to sell)." Thus gain recognition is limited to the cumulative extent that losses have been recognized while the assets were accounted for as long-lived assets under FAS 144. Put differently, FAS 144 does not allow the lender to "look back" to lending impairments measured and recognized under FAS 5, FAS 15, or FAS 114, for purposes of measuring the cumulative loss previously recognized. "Recovery" of losses not recognized is thus not permitted.

EITF 84-17 discusses the application of FAS 66 to graduated payment mortgages. Graduated payment mortgages for which negative principal amortization is recognized do not meet the continuing investment tests in FAS 66 and thus full profit is not to be recognized immediately. In related EITF 87-9, mortgage insurance is not to be considered the equivalent of an irrevocable letter of credit in determining whether profit is to be recognized, and the purchase of such insurance is not in itself a demonstration of commitment by the buyer to honor its obligation to pay for the property. The sole exception to this rule is that for all FHA (Federal Housing Administration) and VA (Veteran's Administration) insured loans, profits may be recognized under the full accrual method.

EITF 86-6 deals with antispeculation clauses sometimes found in land sale agreements, requiring the buyer to develop the land in a specific manner or within a specific period of time and giving the seller the right, but not the obligation, to reacquire the property when the condition is not met. This option does not preclude recognition of a sale if the probability of the buyer not complying is remote.

EITF 86-7 addresses the timing of income recognition when a homebuilder enters into a contract to build a home on its own lot, relinquishing title to both the lot and the home at closing. It states that profit recognition is not appropriate until the conditions specified in FAS 66 have been met. Deposit accounting is to be used for both the land and building activity until the conditions are met.

EITF 88-12 addresses the situation in which a homeowner's equity interest in property is pledged as security for a note and finds that this cannot be included as part of the buyer's initial investment in determining whether profit can be recognized under FAS 66.

EITF 88-24 deals with a range of possible forms of financing and the implications of each for profit recognition under FAS 66. The following guidelines are to be used by a seller of real estate in applying FAS 66:

1.  In determining whether a transaction qualifies for accounting using the full accrual method of profit recognition, the initial and continuing investment requirements of FAS 66 must be considered unless the seller has unconditionally received all amounts due and is not at risk related to the financing.

2.  In determining the buyer's initial investment, payments made on debt incurred by the buyer that is secured by the property (irrespective of whether the debt is incurred directly from the seller or other parties or indirectly by assumption) is not part of the initial investment. Also excluded from the initial investment are payments made to the seller out of the proceeds from debt described in the preceding sentence.

3.  Under the installment method, cost recovery method, and reduced-profit recognition methods, payments described in 2. above are not considered to be cash payments from the buyer. If, however, the deferred profit under the method applied under FAS 66 exceeds the sum of (1) the outstanding amount of seller financing, and (2) the outstanding amount of the buyer's debt secured by the property for which the seller is contingently liable, the excess amount is recognized as income by the seller.

EITF 89-14 deals with the proper valuation for repossessed real estate which is recorded at the lower of the net receivable due to the seller at foreclosure or the fair value of the property. SOP 92-3 provides further guidance and states that, after foreclosure, foreclosed assets are carried at the lower of fair value (less costs to sell) or cost.

EITF 94-2 addresses the proper treatment of minority interests in certain real estate investment trusts. It holds that the net equity of the operating partnership (after the contributions of the sponsor and the REIT) multiplied by the sponsor's ownership percentage in the operating partnership represents the amount to be initially reported as the minority interest in the REIT's consolidated financial statements. In related Issue 95-7, it was held that, if a minority interest balance is negative, the related charge in the REIT's income statement would be the greater of the minority interest holder's share of current earnings or the amount of distributions to the minority interest holder during the year. Any excess is to be credited directly to equity until elimination of the minority interest deficit that existed at the formation of the REIT. Other REIT accounting matters are also addressed in this Issue, including a consensus that subsequent acquisitions by the REIT, for cash, of a sponsor's minority interest in an operating partnership are accounted for consistent with the accounting for formation of the REIT.

The matter of appropriate accounting for transfers of investments that are in substance real estate was addressed by EITF 98-8, which held that in such circumstances the accounting is to follow FAS 66. Thus transfers of acquisition, development, and construction loans (ADC loans), which are deemed in substance real estate under EITF 84-4, are subject to this consensus, and transfers of marketable investments in a REIT which are accounted for under FAS 115 are to be accounted for per FAS 140.

EITF 06-8 addresses the applicability of a buyer's continuing investment to an entity's recognition of revenue when selling condominium units. An entity can assess the collectibility of the sales price as per FAS 66 by requiring the buyer to either make additional payments during the construction term at least equal to the level annual payments that would be required to fund principal and interest on a customary mortgage for the remaining purchase price of the property, or increase the minimum initial investment by an equivalent aggregate amount. If these criteria cannot be met, then the seller should record the transaction under the deposit method.

Several AICPA Statements of Position (SOPs) deal with real estate topics, also. SOP 75-2 addresses the accounting practices of real estate investment trusts, and requires that interest income is not to be recorded when it is unreasonable to expect collection. It further holds that commitment fees are to be amortized over the combined commitment and loan period. Provisions of this SOP that dealt with loan losses and property valuation have, however, been effectively superseded by FAS 114 and FAS 144, respectively.

SOP 78-9, specifying the accounting for investments in real estate ventures, has been widely applied in practice—even to the extent that its guidance has been analogized to other equity investment situations. It requires that owners of real estate ventures should generally use the equity method of accounting to account for their investments. However, limited partners may have such a minor interest and have no influence or control, in which case the cost method would instead be appropriate.

According to SOP 78-9, if losses exceed the investment, the losses are to be recognized regardless of any increase in the estimated fair value of the venture's assets. Losses in excess of the amount of the investment are a liability. Losses which cannot be borne by certain investors require the remaining investors to use FAS 5 to determine their share of any additional loss. Limited partners are not required to record losses in excess of investment. As usual, if investors do not recognize losses in excess of investment, the equity method is resumed only after the investor's share of net income exceeds the cumulative net losses not recognized previously.

The SOP also notes that venture agreements may designate different allocations for profits, losses, cash distributions and cash from liquidation. Accounting for equity in profits and losses therefore requires careful consideration of allocation formulas because the substance over form concept requires equity method accounting to follow the ultimate cash allocations.

Contributions of real estate to a venture as capital are recorded by the investor at cost, and cannot result in the recognition of a gain, since a capital contribution does not represent the culmination of the earnings process.

SOP 78-9 states that interest on loans and advances that are, in substance, capital contributions and so are accounted for as distributions and not interest.

In SOP 92-1, the related topic of appropriate accounting for real estate syndication income is addressed. This SOP applies to all income recognition from real estate syndication activities. FAS 66 applies to profit and loss recognition on sales of real estate by syndicators to partnerships. SOP 92-1 requires that the same concepts be applied to the syndicators— even though they may have never owned the property.

Under the provisions of 92-1, all fees charged by syndicators are includable in the determination of sales value, as required by FAS 66, except for syndication fees and fees for which future services must be performed. Syndication fees are recognized as income when the earning process is complete and collectibility is reasonably assured. If fees are unreasonable, they are to be adjusted, and the sales price of the real estate is to be appropriately adjusted as well. If a partnership interest is received by the syndicator, the value is included in the test of fee reasonableness. If it is part of the fee, the syndicators are to account for this interest as a retained interest from the partial sale of real estate in conformity with FAS 66. Fees for future services are recognized when the service is rendered.

Fees received from blind pool transactions are recognized ratably as the syndication partnership invests in property but only to the extent that the fees are nonrefundable. If syndicators are exposed to future losses from material involvement or from uncertainties regarding collectibility, income is deferred until the losses can be reasonably estimated. For purposes of determining the FAS 66 requirement concerning the buyer's initial and continuing investment for profit recognition, before cash received by syndicators can be allocated to initial and continuing investment, it is allocated to (1) unpaid syndication fees until such fees are paid in full, and (2) amounts previously allocated to fees for future services (to the extent such services have already been performed when the cash is collected). If syndicators receive or retain partnership interests that are subordinated, these are accounted for as participations in future profits without risk of loss.

## REAL ESTATE OPERATIONS

### PERSPECTIVE AND ISSUES

FAS 67, *Real Estate: Accounting for Costs and Initial Rental Operations of Real Estate Projects,* specifies the accounting for various costs in acquiring and developing real estate projects. It does not apply to

1. Real estate developed by an entity for its own use rather than for sale or rental
2. Initial direct costs of leases (discussed in Chapter 16)
3. Costs directly related to manufacturing, merchandising or service activities rather than real estate activities
4. Rental operations in which the predominant rental period is less than a month

FAS 67 does address the accounting for costs of real estate whether rented or sold.

| Sources of GAAP | | | |
|---|---|---|---|
| *FAS* | *EITF* | *SOP* | *FSP* |
| 67, 144, 152 | 85-27, 95-6 | 04-2 | 144-1 |

## DEFINITIONS OF TERMS

**Amenities.** Features of or enhancements made to real estate projects that enhance the attractiveness of the property to potential tenants or purchasers. Amenities include golf courses, utility plants, clubhouses, swimming pools, tennis courts, indoor recreational facilities, and parking facilities.

**Common costs.** Costs that relate to two or more units within a real estate project.

**Costs incurred to rent real estate projects.** Includes costs of model units and their furnishings, rental facilities, semipermanent signs, rental brochures, advertising, "grand openings," and rental overhead including rental salaries.

**Costs incurred to sell real estate projects.** Includes costs of model units and their furnishings, sales facilities, sales brochures, legal fees for preparation of prospectuses, semipermanent signs, advertising, "grand openings," and sales overhead including sales salaries.

**Fair value.** The amount in cash or cash equivalent value of other consideration that a real estate parcel would yield in a current sale between a willing buyer and a willing seller (other than in a forced or liquidation sale). The fair value of a parcel is affected by its physical characteristics, ultimate use, and the time required to make such use of the property considering access, development plans, zoning restrictions, and market absorption factors.

**Incidental operations.** Revenue-producing activities engaged in during the holding or development period to reduce the cost of developing the property for its intended use, as distinguished from activities designed to generate a profit or a return from the use of the property.

**Incremental costs of incidental operations.** Costs that would not be incurred except in relation to the conduct of incidental operations. Interest, taxes, insurance, security, and similar costs that would be incurred during the development of a real estate project regardless of whether incidental operations were conducted are not incremental costs.

**Incremental revenue from incidental operations.** Revenues that would not be earned except in relation to the conduct of incidental operations.

**Indirect project costs.** Costs incurred after the acquisition of the property, such as construction administration, legal fees, and various office costs, that clearly relate to projects under development or construction.

**Net realizable value.** The estimated selling price in the ordinary course of business less estimated costs of completion, holding, and disposal.

**Phase.** A parcel on which units are to be constructed concurrently.

**Preacquisition costs.** Costs related to a property that are incurred for the express purpose of, but prior to, obtaining that property. Examples may be costs of surveying, zoning or traffic studies, or payments to obtain an option on the property.

**Project costs.** Costs clearly associated with the acquisition, development, and construction of a real estate project.

**Relative fair value before construction.** The fair value of each land parcel in a real estate project in relation to the fair value of the other parcels in the project, exclusive of value added by on-site development and construction activities.

# CONCEPTS, RULES, AND EXAMPLES

## Preacquisition Costs

Payments are generally capitalized if they relate to an option to obtain the real property or if all of the following conditions are met:

1. Costs are directly identified with the property.
2. Costs would be capitalized if the property already were acquired.
3. Acquisition of the option or property is probable. The purchaser wants the property and believes it to be available for sale and has the ability to finance its acquisition.

Once capitalized, these costs are project costs which, if not receivable in the future, or if the property is not acquired are to be recognized as expense.

## Taxes and Insurance

Real estate taxes and insurance are capitalized as property costs only when the property is undergoing activities necessary to get the property ready for its intended use. After the property is substantially complete and ready for its intended use such items are expensed.

## Project Costs

Costs that are identifiable and clearly associated with acquisition, development, and construction of a real estate project are capitalized as a cost of the project.

Indirect costs that relate to several projects are capitalized and allocated to these projects. Overhead costs that do not clearly relate to any project (i.e., general and administrative expenses) are expensed as incurred.

## Amenities

The costs in excess of anticipated proceeds of amenities that are to be sold or transferred in connection with the sale of individual units are treated as common costs of the project.

The costs of amenities that are to be sold separately or retained by the developer are capitalized with those costs in excess of estimated fair value treated as common costs. Fair value is determined as of the expected date of substantial physical completion and the amounts allocated to the amenity are not to be revised later. The sale of the amenity results in a gain or loss when the selling price differs from the fair value less accumulated depreciation.

Costs of amenities are allocated among land parcels benefited for which development is probable. The fair value of a parcel is affected by its physical characteristics, its highest and best use, and the time and cost required to make such use of the property. Before completion and availability for use, operating income or loss is an adjustment to common costs. After such date, operating income or loss is included in the income statement.

## Incidental Operations

Revenue from incidental operations is netted with the costs of such operations and any excess of incremental revenue over incremental costs reduces capitalized project costs. If such costs exceed revenues, the excess is recognized as expense as incurred.

## Allocation of Costs

Capitalized costs are allocated by specific identification. If this is not feasible, then costs prior to construction are allocated by the relative fair value of each parcel before construction and construction costs are allocated by the relative sales value of each unit.

If estimation of relative values is impractical, allocation may be based on square footage or another area method, or by using other appropriate methods.

### Revisions of Estimates

Estimates made and cost allocations are to be reviewed at least annually until the project is substantially complete and available for sale. Costs are revised and reallocated as required for changes in current estimates.

### Abandonment and Change in Use

Abandonment of a project requires all capitalized costs to be expensed and not reallocated to other components of the project or other projects. Real estate dedicated to governmental units is not deemed abandoned and its costs are treated as project common costs.

Changes in use require that costs incurred and expected to be incurred that exceed the estimated value of the required project (when substantially complete and ready for intended use) be charged to expense. If no formal plan for the project exists, then project costs in excess of current net realizable value are expensed.

### Selling Costs

Costs incurred to sell are capitalized if they are

1. Reasonably expected to be recovered from sale of the project or from incidental operations, and
2. Incurred for tangible assets used directly throughout the selling period to assist the selling process or incurred for services required to obtain regulatory approval of sales.

Other costs may be capitalized as prepaid expenses if directly associated with sales, cost recovery is reasonably expected from sales and the full accrual method cannot be used.

All other costs are expensed in the period incurred. Capitalized costs are expensed in the period in which the related revenue is earned.

### Rental Costs

Costs related to and reasonably expected to be recoverable from future rental operations are capitalized. This excludes initial direct costs as defined and described in accounting for leases. Costs that do not qualify for capitalization are expensed as incurred.

Capitalized costs are amortized over the term of the lease, if directly related to a specific operating lease, or over the period of expected benefit. Amortization begins when the project is substantially completed and available for occupancy. Estimated unrecoverable amounts are expensed when it is probable that the lease will be terminated.

A project is substantially completed and available for occupancy when tenant improvements are completed or after one year from the end of major construction activity. Then normal operations take place with all revenues and costs (including depreciation and other amortized costs) recognized in the income statement. If part of a project is occupied but other parts are not yet complete, completed portions are considered separate projects.

### Impairment and Recoverability

As discussed in Chapter 11, real estate projects must be evaluated, when warranted by events and circumstances, to determine whether their carrying value is recoverable from estimated future cash flows. FAS 144 provides guidance on grouping assets that are being held and used into "asset groups" and assets being held for sale into "disposal groups" for the purpose of the evaluation of recoverability and impairment computations. FAS 144 applies to real estate held for development and sale, property to be developed in the future, and property currently undergoing development.

Generally, under FAS 144, recoverability is evaluated at the "lowest level for which identifiable cash flows are largely independent of the cash flows of other assets and liabilities." If a project has identifiable elements with separate cash flows such as residential and commercial, or houses and condominiums, then each element is evaluated separately and not combined for the whole project. Projects are not combined in order to avoid recognizing impairment of one of the components.

Once impairment losses are recognized on property, similar to inventory, a new cost basis is adopted and future recoveries in value are not recognized.

### Other Guidance to Accounting for Real Estate Operations

EITF 85-27 holds that when a seller of real estate agrees to make up any rental shortfalls for a period of time, payments to and receipts from the seller are adjustments to the cost of the property and will affect future depreciation charges.

EITF 95-6 addresses the accounting by a real estate investment trust (REIT) in a service corporation (SC). In determining a REIT's accounting for its investment in an SC, the SC must be evaluated as a potential variable interest entity (VIE) under FIN 46(R) (discussed in detail in Chapter 13). If the SC is subject to FIN 46(R), this consensus does not apply to the determination of the REIT's accounting. If, however, the SC is not subject to FIN 46(R), this consensus continues to apply to the determination of the method of accounting that the REIT should use to record its investment (consolidation, equity method, or cost method). The EITF includes a list of factors that indicate that the equity method of accounting is to be used. Regardless of the method of accounting used by a REIT for its investment in an SC, the SC is not considered an independent third party for the purpose of capitalizing lessor initial direct costs under FAS 91. Consequently, leasing costs capitalized by a REIT as initial direct costs may not exceed the amounts allowable if the REIT had incurred the costs directly.

As noted in the preceding section of this chapter, SOP 04-2 addresses the accounting for time-share operations. Concurrent with the issuance of SOP 04-2, FASB issued FAS 152 to amend FAS 66 and FAS 67 to take explicit notice of the applicability of the SOP. Regarding matters otherwise governed by FAS 67, the SOP establishes accounting requirements for incidental operations. In particular, rental and other operations during holding periods, including sampler programs and minivacations, are to be accounted for as incidental operations. The excess, if any, of revenue over costs of such operations is to be recorded as a reduction of inventory costs.

## FRANCHISING: ACCOUNTING BY FRANCHISORS

### PERSPECTIVE AND ISSUES

Franchising has become a popular growth industry with many businesses seeking to sell franchises as their primary income source and individuals seeking to buy franchises and become entrepreneurs. How to recognize revenue on the individual sale of franchise territories and on the transactions that arise in connection with the continuing relationship between the franchisor and franchisee are prime accounting issues.

The AICPA published an industry accounting guide, *Accounting for Franchise Fee Revenue,* in 1973, from which the FASB extracted the principles it used to prepare FAS 45, having the same title.

| Sources of GAAP |
| :---: |
| *FAS* |
| 45 |

## DEFINITIONS OF TERMS

**Area franchise.** An agreement that transfers franchise rights within a geographical area permitting the opening of a number of franchised outlets. The number of outlets, specific locations, and so forth are decisions usually made by the franchisee.

**Bargain purchase.** A transaction in which the franchisee is allowed to purchase equipment or supplies for a price that is significantly lower than their fair value.

**Continuing franchise fee.** Consideration for the continuing rights granted by the franchise agreement and for general or specific services during its term.

**Franchise agreement.** A written business agreement that meets the following principal criteria:

1.  The relation between the franchisor and franchisee is contractual, and an agreement, confirming the rights and responsibilities of each party, is in force for a specified period.
2.  The continuing relation has as its purpose the distribution of a product or service, or an entire business concept, within a particular market area.
3.  Both the franchisor and the franchisee contribute resources for establishing and maintaining the franchise. The franchisor's contribution may be a trademark, a company reputation, products, procedures, labor, equipment, or a process. The franchisee usually contributes operating capital as well as the managerial and operational resources required for opening and continuing the franchised outlet.
4.  The franchise agreement outlines and describes the specific marketing practices to be followed, specifies the contribution of each party to the operation of the business, and sets forth certain operating procedures that both parties agree to comply with.
5.  The establishment of the franchised outlet creates a business entity that will, in most cases, require and support the full-time business activity of the franchisee.
6.  Both the franchisee and the franchisor have a common public identity. This identity is achieved most often through the use of common trade names or trademarks and is frequently reinforced through advertising programs designed to promote the recognition and acceptance of the common identity within the franchisee's market area.

**Franchisee.** The party who has been granted business rights (the franchise) to operate the franchised business.

**Franchisor.** The party who grants business rights (the franchise) to the party (the franchisee) who will operate the franchised business.

**Initial franchise fee.** Consideration for establishing the franchise relationship and providing some agreed-upon initial services. Occasionally, the fee includes consideration for initially required equipment and inventory, but those items usually are the subject of separate consideration. The payment of an initial franchise fee or a continuing royalty fee is not a necessary criterion for an agreement to be considered a franchise agreement.

**Initial services.** Common provision of a franchise agreement in which the franchisor usually will agree to provide a variety of services and advice to the franchisee, such as the following:

1.  Assistance in the selection of a site. The assistance may be based on experience with factors such as traffic patterns, residential configurations, and competition.

2. Assistance in obtaining facilities, including related financing and architectural and engineering services. The facilities may be purchased or leased by the franchisee, and lease payments may be guaranteed by the franchisor.
3. Assistance in advertising, either for the individual franchisee or as part of a general program
4. Training of the franchisee's personnel
5. Preparation and distribution of manuals and similar material concerning operations, administration, and recordkeeping
6. Bookkeeping and advisory services, including setting up the franchisee's records and advising the franchisee about income taxes, real estate taxes, and other taxes, or about local regulations affecting the franchisee's business
7. Inspection, testing, and other quality control programs

## CONCEPTS AND RULES

### Franchise Sales

Franchise operations are generally subject to the same accounting principles as other commercial enterprises. Special issues arise out of franchise agreements, however, which require the application of special accounting rules.

Revenue is recognized, with an appropriate provision for bad debts, when the franchisor has substantially performed all material services or conditions. Only when revenue is collected over an extended period of time and collectibility cannot be predicted in advance would the use of the cost recovery or installment methods of revenue recognition be appropriate. Substantial performance means

1. The franchisor has no remaining obligation to either refund cash or forgive any unpaid balance due.
2. Substantially all initial services required by the agreement have been performed.
3. No material obligations or conditions remain.

Even if the contract does not require initial services, the pattern of performance by the franchisor in other franchise sales will impact the time period of revenue recognition. This can delay such recognition until services are either performed or it can reasonably be assured they will not be performed. The franchisee operations will be considered as started when such substantial performance has occurred.

If initial franchise fees are large compared to services rendered and continuing franchise fees are small compared to services to be rendered, then a portion of the initial fee is deferred in an amount sufficient to cover the costs of future services plus a reasonable profit, after considering the impact of the continuing franchise fee.

#### Example of initial franchise fee revenue recognition

Shanghai Oriental Cuisine sells a Quack's Roast Duck franchise to Toledo Restaurants. The franchise is renewable after two years. The initial franchise fee is $50,000, plus a fixed fee of $500 per month. In exchange, Shanghai provides staff training, vendor relations support, and site selection consulting. Each month thereafter, Shanghai provides $1,000 of free local advertising. Shanghai's typical gross margin on franchise startup sales is 25%.

Because the monthly fee does not cover the cost of monthly services provided, Shanghai defers a portion of the initial franchise fee and amortizes it over the two-year life of the franchise agreement, using the following calculation:

| | | |
|---|---|---|
| Cost of monthly services provided $1000 × 24 months | = | $24,000 |
| ÷ Markup to equal standard 25% gross margin | = | .75 |
| = Estimated revenue required to offset monthly services provided | = | $32,000 |
| Less: Monthly billing to franchise $500 × 24 months | = | $12,000 |
| = Amount of initial franchise fee to be deferred | = | $20,000 |

Shanghai's entry to record the franchise fee deferral follows:

| | | |
|---|---|---|
| Franchise fee revenue | 20,000 | |
| Unearned franchise fees (liability) | | 20,000 |

Shanghai recognizes 1/24 of the unearned franchise fee liability during each month of the franchise period on a straight-line basis, which amounts to $833.33 per month.

## Area Franchise Sales

Sometimes franchisors sell territories rather than individual locations. In this event, the franchisor may render services to the area independent of the number of individual franchises to be established. Under this circumstance, revenue recognition for the franchisor is the same as stated above. If, however, substantial services are performed by the franchisor for each individual franchise established, then revenue is recognized in proportion to mandatory service. The general rule is that when the franchisee has no right to receive a refund, all revenue is recognized. It may be necessary for revenue recognition purposes to treat a franchise agreement as a divisible contract and allocate revenue among existing and estimated locations. Future revisions to these estimates will require that remaining unrecognized revenue be recorded in proportion to remaining services expected to be performed.

### Example of revenue recognition for area franchise sales

Shanghai Oriental Cuisine sells an area Quack's Roast Duck franchise to Canton Investments for $40,000. Under the terms of this area franchise, Shanghai is solely obligated to provide site selection consulting services to every franchise that Canton opens during the next twelve months, after which Canton is not entitled to a refund. Canton estimates that it will open 12 outlets sporadically throughout the year. Shanghai estimates that it will cost $2,500 for each site selection, or $30,000 in total. Based on the initial $40,000 franchise fee, Shanghai's estimated gross margin is 25%. Canton's initial payment of $40,000 is recorded by Shanghai with the following entry:

| | | |
|---|---|---|
| Cash | 40,000 | |
| Unearned franchise fees (liability) | | 40,000 |

After six months of preparation, Canton requests that four site selection surveys be completed. Shanghai completes the work at a cost of $10,000 and uses the following entry to record both the expenditure and related revenue:

| | | |
|---|---|---|
| Unearned franchise fees (liability) | 13,333 | |
| Franchise fee revenue | | 13,333 |
| Site survey expense | 10,000 | |
| Accounts payable | | 10,000 |

By the end of the year, Shanghai has performed ten site selection surveys at a cost of $25,000 and recognized revenue of $33,333, leaving $6,667 of unrecognized revenue. Since Canton is no longer entitled to a refund, Shanghai uses the following entry to recognize all remaining revenue, with no related expense:

| | | |
|---|---|---|
| Unearned franchise fees (liability) | 6,667 | |
| Franchise fee revenue | | 6,667 |

### Other Relationships

Franchisors may guarantee debt of the franchisee, continue to own a portion of the franchise, or control the franchisee's operations. Revenue is not recognized until all services, conditions, and obligations have been performed.

In addition, the franchisor may have an option to reacquire the location. Accounting for initial revenue is to consider the probability of exercise of the option. If the expectation at the time of the agreement is that the option is likely to be exercised, the entire franchise fee is deferred and not recognized as income. Upon exercise, the deferral reduces the recorded investment of the franchisor.

An initial fee may cover both franchise rights and property rights, including equipment, signs, and inventory. A portion of the fee applicable to property rights is recognized to the extent of the fair value of these assets. However, fees relating to different services rendered by franchisors are generally not allocated to these different services because segregating the amounts applicable to each service could not be performed objectively. The rule of revenue recognition when all services are substantially performed is generally upheld. If objectively determinable separate fees are charged for separate services, then recognition of revenue can be determined and recorded for each service performed.

Franchisors may act as agents for the franchisee by issuing purchase orders to suppliers for inventory and equipment. These are not recorded as sales and purchases by the franchisor; instead, consistent with the agency relationship, receivables from the franchisee and payables to the supplier are reported on the balance sheet of the franchisor. There is, of course, no right of offset associated with these amounts, which are to be presented gross.

### Continuing Franchise and Other Fees

Continuing franchise fees are recognized as revenue as the fees are earned. Related costs are expensed as incurred. Regardless of the purpose of the fees, revenue is recognized when the fee is earned and receivable. The exception is when a portion of the fee is required to be segregated and used for a specific purpose, such as advertising. The franchisor defers this amount and records it as a liability. This liability is reduced by the cost of the services received.

Sometimes, the franchisee has a period of time where bargain purchases of equipment or supplies are granted by the contract. If the bargain price is lower than other customers pay or denies a reasonable profit to the franchisor, a portion of the initial franchise fee is deferred and accounted for as an adjustment of the selling price when the franchisee makes the purchase. The deferred amount is either the difference in the selling price among customers and the bargain price, or an amount sufficient to provide a reasonable profit to the franchisor.

### Costs

Direct and incremental costs related to franchise sales are deferred and recognized when revenue is recorded. However, deferred costs cannot exceed anticipated future revenue, net of additional expected costs.

Indirect costs are expensed as incurred. These usually are regular and recurring costs that bear no relationship to sales.

### Repossessed Franchises

If, for any reason, the franchisor refunds the franchise fee and obtains the location, previously recognized revenue is reversed in the period of repossession. If a repossession is made without a refund, there is no adjustment of revenue previously recognized. However, any estimated uncollectible amounts are to be provided for and any remaining collected funds are recorded as revenue.

### Business Combinations

Business combinations where the franchisor acquires the business of a franchisee are accounted for in accordance with the requirements of FAS 141(R).

No adjustment of prior revenue is made since the financial statements are not retroactively consolidated in recording a business combination. Care must be taken to ensure that the purchase is not a repossession. If the transaction is deemed to be a repossession, it is accounted for as described in the above section.

## OTHER SPECIAL ACCOUNTING AND REPORTING ISSUES

| Sources of GAAP |
| :---: |
| *EITF* |
| 99-19, 00-8, 00-21, 01-9, 02-16, 3-10, 06-1 |

As discussed in the opening section of the chapter, guidance on the proper accounting for revenue under US GAAP remains diverse, without one self-contained authoritative source of prescriptive advice. While FASB is attempting to address this (and might fundamentally revise the foundations for revenue recognition if the "balance sheet oriented" standard being debated is ultimately promulgated), at the current time practitioners must be familiar with, and able to apply, a large number of standards. The major categories of revenue generating transactions, for which specialized accounting standards have been developed, have been addressed in the earlier sections of this chapter. In the following paragraphs, various miscellaneous requirements contained in EITF consensuses are discussed.

**Reporting revenue gross as a principal versus net as an agent.** A longstanding issue in financial reporting has been whether certain entities more accurately convey the nature of their operations by reporting as revenue only the "net" amount they retain when acting effectively as an agent for another entity. While in some situations the answer is obvious, in other cases it has been less clear. Historically this may not have been an urgent issue to be resolved, since users of financial statements were deemed capable of deriving correct inferences regardless of the manner of presentation of the income statement. However, in recent years an unfortunate trend developed, whereby analysts and others cited only revenue growth as an indicator of the entity's success, making the question of income statement presentation of revenue somewhat more important.

EITF 99-19 provides guidance on whether an entity is an agent for a vendor-manufacturer, and thus recognizes the net retainage (commission) for serving in that capacity, or whether that entity is a seller of goods (i.e., acting as a principal), and thus should recognize revenue for the gross amount billed to a customer and an expense for the amount paid to the vendor-manufacturer.

The consensus identifies the following factors to be considered when determining whether revenue is to be reported as the net retainage (hereinafter, "net") or the gross amount billed to a customer ("gross"). None of the indicators are presumptive or determinative, although the relative strength of each indicator is to be considered.

- Is the company the primary obligor in the arrangement; that is, is the company responsible for the fulfillment of the order, including the acceptability of the product or service to the customer? If the company, rather than a supplier, is responsible, that fact is a strong indicator that the company record revenue gross. Responsibility for arranging transportation for the product is not responsibility for fulfillment. If a supplier is responsible for fulfillment, including the acceptability to the customer, that fact indicates that the company recognizes only the net retainage.

- Does the company have general inventory risk? General inventory risk exists if a company takes title to a product before the product is ordered by a customer or will take title to the product if the customer returns it (provided that the customer has a right of return). In considering this indicator, arrangements with a supplier that reduce or mitigate the company's risk level are to be considered. Unmitigated general inventory risk is a strong indicator that the company recognizes revenue gross.

- Does the company have physical loss inventory risk? Physical loss inventory risk exists if the title to the product is transferred to the company at the shipping point and then transferred to the customer upon delivery. Physical loss inventory risk also exists if a company takes title to the product after the order is received but before the product is transferred to the shipper. While less persuasive than general inventory risk, this indicator provides some evidence that a company record revenue gross.

- Does the company establish the selling price? If a company establishes the selling price, that fact may indicate that the company recognizes revenue gross.

- Is the amount earned by the company fixed? If a company earns a fixed amount per transaction or if it earns a percentage of the selling price, that fact may indicate that the company report revenue net.

- Does the company change the product or perform part of the service? If a company changes the product (beyond packaging) or performs part of the service ordered by the customer such that the selling price is greater as a result of the company's efforts, that fact is indicative that a company recognize revenue gross. Marketing skills, market coverage, distribution system, or reputation are not to be evaluated in determining whether the company changes the product or performs part of the service.

- Does the company have multiple suppliers for the product or service ordered by the customer? If a company has the discretion to select the supplier, that fact may indicate that the company record revenue gross.

- Is the company involved in determining the nature, type, characteristics or specifications of the product or service by the customer? If so, that fact may indicate that the company record revenue gross.

- Does the company have credit risk for the amount billed to the customer? Credit risk exists if a company must pay the supplier after the supplier performs, regardless of whether the customer has paid. If the company has credit risk, this fact provides weak evidence that the company record revenue gross. If the supplier assumes the credit risk, the company is to record revenue net.

EITF 99-19 includes thirteen examples to assist in the implementation of the consensus.

**Accounting by a grantee for an equity instrument to be received in conjunction with providing goods or services.** The accounting for such equity issuances by the reporting entity is addressed by SFAS 123(R), discussed in Chapter 19. EITF 00-8 has resolved the proper accounting by the recipient of such payments.

In exchange for goods or services, an entity (the grantee) may receive equity instruments that have conversion or exercisability terms that vary based on future events, such as attainment of sales levels or a successful initial public offering. This issue describes the appropriate accounting if FAS 123(R) does not apply because the instruments received have underlyings based on either the grantee's or issuer's performance.

The grantee measures the fair value of the equity instruments received using the stock price and measurement assumptions as of the earlier of two dates. The first date is the date on which the grantee and the issuer reach a mutual understanding of both the terms of the equity-based compensation and the goods to be delivered (or services to be performed). The second date is the date at which the performance necessary to earn the equity is completed by the grantee, that is, the grantee's rights have vested.

If the terms of the equity agreement are dependent on the achievement of a market condition, the fair value of the instrument is to include the effects on fair value of the commitment to change the terms if the market condition is met. Pricing models are available to value path-dependent equity instruments.

If the terms of the equity agreement are dependent on the achievement of certain performance goals (beyond those that initially established the goods to be delivered or services to be performed), the fair value of the instrument is computed without the effects of the commitment to change the terms if the goals are met. If those goals are subsequently met, the fair value is adjusted to reflect the new terms and the adjustment is reported as additional revenue (as described in the Share-Based Payments section in Chapter 19).

**Revenue arrangements with multiple deliverables.** Another longstanding difficulty has been identifying authoritative guidance germane to the accounting for revenue arrangements (product or service sales) having more than one "deliverable." Many instances of aggressive accounting—where all or most of the total revenue was recognized at the time of delivery of the first of multiple deliverables—came to light in the financial reporting abuses of the late 1990s and early 2000s. EITF 00-21 comprehensively addressed these complex issues, and represents the only universally applicable guidance extant. (SAB 101, issued before EITF 00-21, contained a great deal of specific guidance, but this was substantially eliminated in replacement SAB 104, with EITF 00-21 being granted recognition as the set of requirements for these types of transactions.)

*Perspective and issues.* Vendors may offer customers many related and unrelated products and services sold together ("bundled") or separately. The prices assigned to the various elements of a particular transaction or series of transactions on the seller's invoices and the timing of issuing those invoices are not always indicative of the actual earning of revenue on the various elements of these transactions. This consensus provides guidance on how to measure consideration received from complex, multi-element arrangements and how to allocate that consideration between the different deliverables contained in the arrangement.

*Terms used in EITF 00-21.* The guidance in the standard is extensive and complex, due to the complex nature of the underlying revenue transactions. A number of key terms are used in the standard, defined as follows:

- **Contingent amount.** The portion of the total consideration to be received by a vendor under a multiple deliverable arrangement that would be realized by the vendor only if specified performance conditions were met or additional deliverables were provided to the customer.
- **Noncontingent amount.** The portion of the total consideration to be received by a vendor under a multiple deliverable arrangement that is not subject to any additional performance requirements that the vendor must meet.
- **Refund rights.** The legal right of a customer to obtain a concession or recover all or a portion of the consideration paid to a vendor under a multiple deliverable arrangement.
- **Relative fair value method.** A technique for allocating the total consideration to be received by a vendor under a multiple deliverable arrangement to each separate unit of accounting based on the ratio of the fair value of each separate unit of accounting to the total fair values of all of the separate units of accounting.
- **Residual method.** A technique for determining the portion of the total consideration to be received by a vendor under a multiple deliverable arrangement to be allocated to

the units of accounting that have been delivered by subtracting the fair values of the undelivered items from the total consideration to be received.

- **Stand-alone value.** The value that a specific product or service (deliverable) has to a customer without considering other products or services that might accompany it as part of a multiple deliverable arrangement. In order to have value to a customer on a stand-alone basis, a deliverable must be either sold separately by any vendor or be separately resalable by the customer whether or not there is an observable market for the deliverable.

- **Vendor-specific objective evidence (VSOE).** The price that a vendor charges for a specific product or service (deliverable) when it is sold separately. If the deliverable is not currently being sold separately, a price that is established by management possessing the authority may be used under the condition that it is considered probable that the established price will not change prior to the separate market introduction of the deliverable.

***Summary of guidance provided by EITF 00-21.*** Arrangements between vendors and their customers often include the sale of multiple products and services (deliverables). A multiple deliverable arrangement (MDA) can be structured using fixed, variable, or contingent pricing or combinations thereof. Product delivery and service performance can occur at different times, and in different locations and customer acceptance can be subject to various return privileges, or performance guarantees.

The consensuses in EITF 00-21 provide guidance on

1. How a vendor determines whether an MDA consists of a single unit of accounting or multiple units of accounting
2. Allocating MDA consideration to multiple units of accounting
3. Measuring MDA consideration

In applying the consensuses, it is to be presumed that separate contracts executed at or near the same time with the same entity or related parties were negotiated as a package and are to be considered together in determining how many units of accounting are contained in an MDA. That presumption can be overcome by sufficient contradictory evidence.

The consensuses collectively apply to all deliverables (i.e., products, services, and rights to use assets) covered by contractually binding written, oral, or implied arrangements.

Excluded from the scope of the consensus are the following:

1. Criteria for the timing of revenue recognition for a unit of accounting. Existing authoritative literature governs these determinations.
2. Arrangements where, conditioned upon the vendor's revenue from the customer exceeding certain cumulative levels or the customer continuing its relationship with the vendor for a specified time period

   a. The vendor offers free or discounted products or services in the future or
   b. The vendor provides specified future cash rebates or refunds.

3. Arrangements involving the sale of award credits by a "broad-based loyalty program operator." (Presumably this exception refers to airline frequent-flyer or similar customer loyalty programs.)
4. Accounting for the direct costs incurred by a vendor relative to an MDA.

***Basic principles established.*** EITF 00-21 set forth three basic principles, the application of which are the subject of the discussion that follows:

1. MDA are divided into separate *units of accounting* if the deliverables included in the arrangement meet all three of the criteria presented in the table below.

2. Subject to certain limits regarding contingent amounts to be received under the MDA, *relative fair values* are used to allocate MDA proceeds to the separate units of accounting.
3. The revenue recognition criteria to be applied are determined *separately* for each unit of accounting.

**Units of accounting.** The following table summarizes the criteria used in determining units of accounting for MDA within the scope of these consensuses and is adapted from a decision diagram contained in the EITF Abstract:

| | Criteria | Outcome | Result |
|---|---|---|---|
| 1. | Does the delivered item have stand-alone value to the customer? | Yes | Go to criteria 2 |
| | | No | Do not separate item |
| 2. | Does objective and reliable evidence exist regarding the fair value of the undelivered items? | Yes | Go to criteria 3 |
| | | No | Do not separate item |
| 3. | If the MDA includes a general right of return with respect to the delivered item, is delivery of the undelivered items probable and substantially controlled by the vendor? | Yes or Not Applicable | Delivered item is a separate unit of accounting |
| | | No | Do not separate item |

This separability evaluation is to be applied consistently to MDA that arise under similar circumstances or that possess similar characteristics. The evaluation is to be performed at the inception of the MDA and upon delivery of each item.

If consideration is allocated to a deliverable that does not qualify as a separate unit of accounting, then the reporting entity is required to

1. Combine the amount allocated to the deliverable with the amounts allocated to all other undelivered items included in the MDA and
2. Determine revenue recognition for the combined items as a single unit of accounting.

*Measurement and allocation of MDA consideration.* The following decision diagram summarizes the factors to consider in measuring and allocating MDA consideration:

**Measuring and Allocating MDA Consideration**

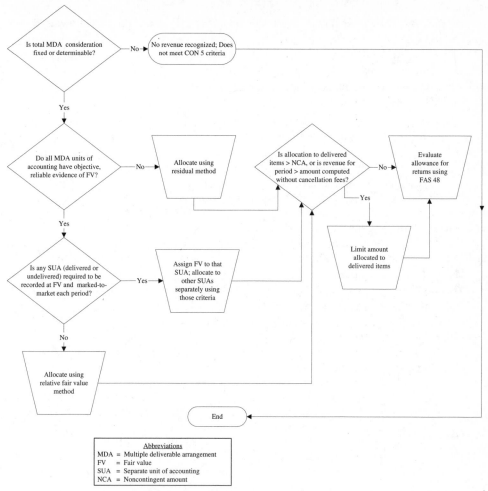

Abbreviations
MDA = Multiple deliverable arrangement
FV  = Fair value
SUA = Separate unit of accounting
NCA = Noncontingent amount

The determination of whether total MDA consideration is fixed or determinable disregards the effects of refund rights or performance bonuses, if any.

After applying the criteria set forth in the decision diagram, the vendor may recognize an asset representing the cumulative difference, from inception of the MDA, between amounts recognized as revenue and amounts received or receivable from the customer (this is analogous to the asset "costs and estimated earnings in excess of billings" which is used in long-term construction accounting). The amount of such assets may not exceed the total amounts to which the vendor is legally entitled under the MDA including fees that would be earned upon customer cancellation. The amount recognized as an asset would be further limited if the vendor did not intend to enforce its contractual rights to obtain such cancellation fees from the customer.

In measuring fair value, it is presumed that a separately stated sales price included in the sales contract for a deliverable is not representative of that deliverable's separate fair value. Rather, the best evidence of fair value is vendor-specific objective evidence (VSOE) of the sales price of the deliverable on a stand-alone basis. Use of VSOE, when available, to determine fair value is always preferable. Otherwise, third-party evidence of fair value is an acceptable substitute.

*Disclosures.* The financial statements of a vendor are to include the following disclosures, when applicable:

1. The nature of the vendor's MDAs including provisions relative to performance, cancellation, termination, or refund.
2. The vendor's accounting policy with respect to the recognition of revenue from MDAs (e.g., whether deliverables are separable into units of accounting).

*Transition.* The guidance in EITF 00-21 was effective for transactions entered into in fiscal periods beginning after June 15, 2003. In May 2003, EITF clarified the application of the consensus in situations in which higher-level GAAP guidance also exists, particularly when higher-level guidance deals with certain of the deliverables in a given MDA, but not with others. To the extent that a reporting entity had applied the guidance of EITF 00-21 prior to the May 2003 additions, implementation of the new guidance would be accounted for as implementation of a new standard, with appropriate transition accounting as the cumulative effect of an accounting change (as described in EITF Topic D-1).

With regard to the guidance in EITF 00-21, the consensus holds that when higher-level accounting literature offers guidance to parts of the MDA, the following rules apply:

1. Higher-level literature provides guidance regarding the determination of separate units of accounting and how to allocate arrangement consideration to those separate units of accounting, the arrangements or the deliverable(s) that is within the scope of that literature should be accounted for in accordance therewith, rather than the guidance in EITF 00-21.
2. If higher-level literature provides guidance requiring separation of deliverables within the scope of higher-level literature from deliverables not within the scope of higher-level literature, but does not specify how to allocate total consideration to each separate unit of accounting, the allocation is to be performed according to relative fair values, using the reporting entity's best estimate of the fair value of those deliverable(s) within the scope of higher-level literature and those not within its scope. Subsequent accounting (i.e., the identification of separate units of accounting and the allocation of values) for the value allocated to the deliverable(s) not subject to higher-level literature would be governed by the provisions of EITF 00-21.
3. If higher-level literature provides no guidance regarding the separation of the deliverables within the scope of higher-level literature from those deliverables that are not or the allocation of arrangement consideration to deliverables within the scope of the higher-level literature and to those that are not, then the guidance in EITF 00-21 should be followed for purposes of such separation and allocation. In that case, it is possible that a deliverable subject to the guidance of higher-level literature does not meet the criteria set forth by EITF 00-21 to be considered a separate unit of accounting. If so, the arrangement consideration allocable to such deliverable should be combined with the amount allocable to the other applicable undelivered item(s) within the arrangement. The appropriate recognition of revenue would then be determined for those combined deliverables as a single unit of accounting.

**Accounting for consideration given by a vendor to a customer.** Previously, there had been several narrower issues addressed by discrete EITF consensuses. EITF 01-9 resolved and codified the following predecessors:

EITF 01-9 provides guidance regarding the recognition, measurement, and income statement display of consideration given by a vendor to purchasers of the vendor's products. This consideration can be provided to a purchaser at any point along the distribution chain, irrespective of whether the purchaser receiving the consideration is a direct or indirect customer of the vendor. Examples of arrangements include, but are not limited to, sales incentive offers labeled as discounts, coupons, rebates, and "free" products or services as well as arrangements referred to as slotting fees, cooperative advertising, and buydowns. The issue does not apply to

1. Coupons, rebates, and other forms of rights for free or significantly discounted products or services received by a customer in a prior exchange transaction that were accounted for by the vendor as a separate deliverable in that prior exchange, or

2. An offer to a customer, in connection with a current revenue transaction, for free or discounted products or services that is redeemable by the customer at a future date without a further exchange transaction with the vendor. Covered by EITF 00-21, summarized above.

The issue also does not discuss the accounting for offers of free or discounted products or services that are exercisable after a customer has completed a specified cumulative level of revenue transactions or remained a customer for a specified time period (for example, "point" and loyalty programs).

EITF 01-9 contains the following separately addressed issues:

1. Cash consideration given by a vendor to a customer is presumed to be a reduction of selling price and is classified as a reduction of revenue when recognized in the vendor's income statement. That presumption is overcome and the consideration is classified as a cost incurred if, and to the extent that, both of the following conditions are met:

   a. The vendor receives, or will receive, an identifiable benefit (goods or services) in exchange for the consideration. In order to meet this condition, the identified benefit must be of a type that the vendor could have acquired in an exchange transaction with a party other than a purchaser of its products or services, that is, that the benefit must be separable from the sale of the vendor's goods or services, and

   b. The vendor can reasonably estimate the fair value of that identifiable benefit. If the amount of consideration paid by the vendor exceeds the estimated fair value of the benefit received, that excess amount is classified as a reduction of revenue when recognized in the vendor's income statement.

   If the consideration is a "free" product or service or anything other than cash (including "credits" that the customer can apply against trade amounts owed to the vendor) or equity instruments, the cost of the consideration is characterized as an expense (as opposed to a reduction of revenue) when recognized in the vendor's income statement. The consensus contains fifteen examples of the application of this issue to various fact scenarios.

2. The amounts representing reduced revenue are classified as expense only if a vendor can demonstrate that classification of those amounts as a reduction of revenue results in negative revenue for a specific customer on a cumulative basis (that is, since the inception of the overall relationship between the vendor and the customer). However, classification as an expense would not be appropriate if a supply arrangement exists that either

   a. Provides the vendor with the right to be a provider of a certain type or class of goods or services for a specified period of time and it is probable that the customer will order the vendor's goods or services, or

   b. Requires the customer to order a minimum amount of goods or services from the vendor in the future, except to the extent that the consideration given exceeds future revenue from the customer under the arrangement.

3. If the consideration (in the form of products, services, or cash) offered voluntarily by a vendor and without charge to customers can be used or becomes exercisable by a customer as a result of a single exchange transaction, and that consideration will not result in a loss on the sale, the vendor recognizes the "cost" of the consideration at the later of the following:

   a. The date the related revenue is recognized by the vendor, or

   b. The date the sales incentive is offered. (For example, a vendor recognizes a liability for a mail-in rebate coupon that requires proof of purchase, based on the estimated amount of refunds or rebates that will be claimed by customers.)

4. If the consideration (in the form of products, services, or cash) offered voluntarily by a vendor and without charge to customers can be used or becomes exercisable by a customer as a result of a single exchange transaction, and that consideration results in a loss on the sale, a vendor does not recognize a liability prior to the date on which the related revenue is recognized (this would be improper matching). However, the offer of consideration in an amount that will result in a loss on the sale of a product may indicate an impairment of existing inventory.

5. If a vendor offers a customer a rebate or refund of a specified amount of cash consideration that is redeemable only if the customer completes a specified cumulative level of purchases or remains a customer for a specified time, the vendor recognizes the cost of the offer in a systematic and rational manner over the period in which the underlying revenue transactions that qualify the customer for the rebate or refund take place. Measurement of the total rebate or refund obligation is based on the estimated number of customers that will ultimately earn and claim rebates or refunds under the offer. If the amount cannot be reasonably estimated, the maximum potential amount is to be recognized.

**Accounting by a customer (including a reseller) for certain consideration received from a vendor.** EITF 02-16 addresses accounting issues similar to EITF 01-9, but from the standpoint of how the vendor's customer—either the end user or a reseller of the vendor's products or services—is to account for cash consideration it receives from its vendor.

In general, there is a rebuttable presumption that cash consideration received from a vendor is a purchase-price concession that should be recognized by the customer as a reduction of cost of goods sold (and/or the inventory of unsold units). This presumption is overcome if payment of the consideration is for either

1. **Delivery of goods and/or services.** Payment to the customer in exchange for goods or services delivered to the vendor is accounted for by the customer as revenue. In order for the customer to recognize revenue, the goods and/or services must be "suf-

ficiently separable" from the customer's purchase of the vendor's products by meeting two criteria.

  a.  The customer would have obtained the goods and/or services from a party other than the vendor and

  b.  The customer is able to reasonably estimate the fair value of the goods and/or services provided to the vendor.

Any excess of cash consideration received by the customer over the fair value of the goods and/or services delivered to the vendor reduces the customer's cost of sales.

2.  **Reimbursement of costs.** A reimbursement of the customer's specific incremental, identifiable costs incurred to sell the vendor's products or services which is accounted for by the customer as a reduction of that cost. To the extent the cash consideration received exceeds the actual cost being reimbursed, the excess reduces cost of sales and/or inventory.

Vendors sometimes enter into binding arrangements that offer customers specified amounts of cash rebates or refunds payable in the future only if the customer remains a customer for a specified period of time, or purchases a specified cumulative dollar amount of goods or services from the vendor. In general, these arrangements are to be recorded by the customer as reductions of cost of sales by systematically allocating a portion of the benefits to be received to each transaction that results in progress toward meeting the target that results in earning the benefit. In order to use this pro rata accounting, however, the amount of the refund must be both probable and reasonably estimable (as those terms are defined in FAS 5). EITF provided indicators that, if present, may impair the customer's ability to determine that the refund is both probable and estimable.

1.  The rebate or refund applies to purchases that are to occur over a "relatively long period" (undefined in the consensus)

2.  An absence of historical experience with similar products or changed circumstances that make historical experience irrelevant

3.  A past history of significant adjustments to expected rebates or refunds

4.  Susceptibility of the product to significant external factors such as technological obsolescence or changes in demand

If the rebate or refund is not considered both probable and estimable, it is not recognized by the customer until it is fully earned by reaching the specified milestone (e.g., the dollar amount of cumulative purchases is reached or the time period for remaining a customer has expired).

Changes in a customer's estimate of the amount of future rebates or refunds, and retroactive changes by a vendor to a previous offer are recognized using a "cumulative catch-up adjustment." This is accomplished by the customer immediately charging or crediting cost of sales in an amount that will adjust the cumulative amounts recognized under the arrangement to the changed terms. Of course, if any portion of the adjustment impacts goods still in the customer's inventory, that portion would adjust the valuation of the inventory and not cost of sales.

The SEC observer to the EITF's proceedings cautioned registrants to consider whether certain transactions between vendors and customers (e.g., simultaneous agreements between the parties to purchase equal amounts of each other's goods) are covered by the provisions of APB 29 regarding nonmonetary exchanges that are not the culmination of an earning process.

**Applying the foregoing guidance to sales incentives offered by manufacturers to consumers.** The standard described immediately above is applicable to situations in which cash consideration is received by a customer from a vendor, and is presumed to be a reduction of the prices of the vendor's products or services. Such incentives are to be characterized as a reduction of cost of sales when recognized in the customer's income statement. There are other instances, however, where consideration is a reimbursement for incentives offered to end users (e.g., retail customers) honored by the vendor's customer (retailer). The common example is coupons given to end users to be redeemed at the retailers offering the vendor's products for sale.

EITF 03-10 reached a consensus that sales incentive arrangements that meet all of certain defined criteria are not subject to the guidance in Issue 02-16. The criteria are

1.   The incentive can be tendered by a consumer at resellers that accept manufacturer's incentives in partial (or full) payment of the price charged by the reseller for the vendor's product;
2.   The reseller receives a direct reimbursement from the vendor (or a clearinghouse authorized by the vendor) based on the face amount of the incentive;
3.   The terms of reimbursement to the reseller for the vendor's sales incentive offered to the consumer are not influenced by or negotiated in conjunction with any other incentive arrangements between the vendor and the reseller, but rather, may only be determined by the terms of the incentive offered to consumers; and
4.   The reseller is subject to an agency relationship with the vendor, whether expressed or implied, in the sales incentive transaction between the vendor and the consumer.

Sales incentives that do not meet all of the foregoing criteria are subject to the guidance in EITF 01-9 and EITF 02-16, as applicable.

**Accounting for consideration given by a service provider to a manufacturer or reseller.** There are cases, such as in the cell phone service industry, where companies provide services to their customers under arrangements that require the customers to purchase equipment in order to utilize those services. In order to spur demand, the companies provide incentives to the equipment manufacturers or resellers to reduce the selling price of the equipment. The accounting for this situation is addressed by EITF 06-1, which states that, if the consideration given by the service provider to the manufacturer or reseller can be linked contractually to the benefit received by the service provider's customers, then the service provider can use the guidance noted above in EITF 01-9 to properly characterize the consideration paid. If the form of consideration to be paid to the service provider's customers is not cash or the service provider does not control the type of consideration paid, then the service provider should record such payments as an expense. If the form of consideration to be paid to the service provider's customers is cash (such as a mail-in rebate), then the service provider should record such payments as a reduction of revenue. The service provider should disclose the nature of the incentive program and the amounts recognized in the statement of operations for the incentive program and their classification for each period presented.

# 11 LONG-LIVED ASSETS

## PERSPECTIVE AND ISSUES

Long-lived assets are those expected to provide an economic benefit to the reporting entity for a number of future periods. GAAP regarding long-lived assets involves the determination of the appropriate amounts at which to initially record the assets—which amounts will include costs associated with any legal obligations to eventually retire the assets and the cost of interest incurred during construction. In addition, determinations must be made of the appropriate method to be used to allocate those amounts over the periods to be benefited, subsequent increases in carrying value attributable to changes in the estimates of retirement costs to be incurred, the measurement of impairment losses, and the accounting for assets to be disposed of rather than kept in service.

Long-lived assets are primarily operational assets and are classified into two basic types: tangible and intangible. Tangible assets have physical substance and are categorized as follows:

1. Depreciable
2. Depletable
3. Other tangible assets

Intangible assets have no physical substance. Their value is based on the rights or privileges to which the reporting entity is entitled.

Most of the accounting issues associated with long-lived assets involve proper measurement and timing of the transactions. Adequate consideration must be given to the economic substance of the transaction.

All entities are required to review long-lived assets and certain identifiable intangible assets for impairment whenever circumstances and situations change such that there is an indication that the carrying amount may not be recoverable. If, upon review, the undiscounted future cash flows (without interest charges) are less than the carrying amount, the carrying amount is reduced to fair value and an impairment loss is recognized. This fair value is considered the new cost basis and is not subject to subsequent adjustment except for depreciation and further impairment. Thus, there is no restoration of previously recognized impairment losses. With some exceptions, this standard also applies to rate-regulated assets. Thus, costs excluded by a regulator from the reporting entity's rate base would be recognized as impairment costs.

Long-lived assets to be disposed of by sale are presented on the balance sheet as "held for sale" and valued at their carrying amount, or their fair value less cost to sell, whichever is less. In subsequent periods, increases in value may be recognized but only to the extent of cumulative losses recognized in the past. Depreciation is not recorded for assets held for sale.

| | | | Sources of GAAP | | | |
|---|---|---|---|---|---|---|
| *ARB* | *APB* | *FAS* | *FIN* | *EITF* | *SOP* | *FSP* |
| 43, | 1, 6, 17, | 2, 15, 34, 42, 58, | 30, 33, | 89-13, 90-8, 91-10, | 96-1, | FAS 142-3, |
| Ch. 9: 44 | 29, 30 | 62, 68, 109, 141, | 47 | 93-11, 95-23, 99-5, | 98-1 | FAS 143-1, |
| | | 141(R), 142, | | 99-9, 99-16, 00-2, | | FAS 144-1, |
| | | 143, 144, 146, | | 01-2, 01-5, 02-7, | | FAS 146-1, |
| | | 147, 153, 157, | | 02-13, 03-13, 04-6, | | FAS 157-2, |
| | | 160 | | 05-6, 07-3 | | AUG AIR-1 |

*Other: Accounting Research Monograph 1*

## DEFINITIONS OF TERMS

**Amortization.** The periodic charge to income that results from a systematic and rational allocation of cost over the life of an intangible asset. Analogous to depreciation of tangible assets.

**Asset acquisition.** A transaction whereby the assets purchased and liabilities assumed do not constitute a business (defined below).

**Asset group.** The lowest level for which identifiable cash flows are largely independent of the cash flows associated with other assets and liabilities.

**Asset retirement obligation.** A legal obligation associated with the retirement of a tangible long-lived asset that results from its acquisition, construction, development, and/or normal operation.

**Book value.** The cost of a long-lived asset less the related accumulated depreciation or amortization to the date of measurement. Sometimes referred to as *net* book value.

**Boot.** The monetary consideration given or received in an asset exchange.

**Business.** An integrated set of activities and assets capable of being conducted and managed in order to provide a return directly to investors, members, participants, or other owners in the form of dividends, lower costs, or other economics benefits. An entity in its development stage that has not yet commenced its planned principal operations that meets this definition is considered to be a business.

**Depreciation.** The periodic charge to income that results from a systematic and rational allocation of cost over the life of a tangible asset. Analogous to amortization of intangible assets. Depreciation is only a method of cost allocation, not a means of determining or presenting current valuation of assets.

**Disposal group.** A group of assets to be disposed of in a single transaction as a group, and the liabilities directly associated with those assets that will be transferred with them.

**Dividends-in-kind.** Dividends paid to stockholders from assets of the corporation other than cash.

**Exchange.** A reciprocal transfer between the reporting entity and another entity that results in the acquisition of assets or services, or the satisfaction of liabilities through a transfer of assets, services, or obligations. In order for a transfer to be considered an exchange transaction, the transferor is not permitted to have substantial continuing involvement in the transferred asset that results in the transferee not obtaining the usual risks and rewards of ownership of the transferred asset.

**Fixed assets.** Those assets that are used in a productive capacity, are tangible (have physical substance), are relatively long-lived, and provide future benefit that is readily measurable. Sometimes referred to as property, plant, and equipment.

**Foreclosure.** A legal action taken by a party that holds a security interest in one or more assets to terminate the owner's interest in those assets. Upon termination of the owner's interest, the secured party obtains legal title to the assets in order to sell them, with the sales proceeds applied to partially or fully satisfy the secured debt.

**Goodwill.** An asset that represents the future economic benefits that arise from other assets acquired in a business combination that are not identified individually or recognized separately. Under FAS 141(R), goodwill is measured as the excess of (1) the aggregate of the fair value of consideration transferred plus the fair value of any noncontrolling interest over (2) the fair value of the net amount of identifiable assets acquired less liabilities assumed.

**Impairment.** The condition that exists when a long-lived asset's carrying amount is not expected to be recoverable over the remainder of its expected life. Fixed assets and intangibles with a finite useful life are evaluated for impairment under FAS 144. Goodwill and indefinite life intangibles are evaluated for impairment under FAS 142.

**Implied fair value.** The excess of the fair value of a reporting unit, as a whole, over the fair values that would be assigned to its assets and liabilities in a purchase business combination at the date of measurement.

**Intangible assets.** Those assets that provide future economic benefit but have no physical substance. Examples include goodwill, patents, copyrights, etc.

**Legal obligation.** An obligation that a party is required to settle as a result of an existing or enacted law, statue, ordinance, or written or oral contract or by legal construction of a contract under the doctrine of promissory estoppel (see definition below).

**Monetary assets.** Assets whose amounts are fixed in terms of units of currency. Examples are cash, accounts receivable, and notes receivable.

**Nonmonetary assets.** Assets other than monetary assets. Examples are inventories; investments in common stock; and property, plant, and equipment.

**Nonmonetary transactions.** Exchanges and nonreciprocal transfers that involve little or no monetary assets or liabilities.

**Nonreciprocal transfer.** A transfer of assets or services in one direction, either from the reporting entity to its owners or to another entity, or from owners or another entity to the reporting entity. A reporting entity's reacquisition of its own outstanding stock is a nonreciprocal transfer.

**Primary asset.** The depreciable long-lived asset (or amortizable intangible asset) that is the most significant component asset from which an asset group derives its cash-flow generating capacity.

**Productive assets.** Assets held for or used in the production of goods or services. Productive assets include an investment in another entity if the investment is accounted for by the equity method but exclude an investment not accounted for by that method.

**Promissory estoppel.** A legal doctrine whereby a court of law will enforce a promise made by one party (the promisor) to another party who relied on the promise (the promisee) even though no formal contract exists between the two parties or no consideration was exchanged.

**Retirement.** The removal from service of a long-lived asset by sale, abandonment, recycling, or other disposal on an other-than-temporary basis. Retirement can occur before or at the end of the asset's useful life. However, retirement does not include the temporary idling of an asset.

**Similar productive assets.** Productive assets that are of the same general type, that perform the same function, or that are employed in the same line of business.

## CONCEPTS, RULES, AND EXAMPLES

### Fixed Assets

Fixed assets (sometimes referred to as "property, plant, and equipment," "tangible long-lived assets," or as "plant assets") are tangible property used in a productive capacity that will benefit the reporting entity for a period longer than one year.

Among the accounting issues that can arise in accounting for fixed assets are

1. Determination of the amounts at which to initially record the assets, whether acquired through purchase or nonmonetary exchange; or through construction by the reporting entity. Fixed assets can be acquired individually, in groups, or as a part of a business combination. They can also be acquired through foreclosure.
2. Whether management capitalizes discrete assets in groups or separately capitalizes the major individual components of individual assets (unit of account)
3. The proper accounting for postacquisition costs incurred with respect to the assets during their useful lives
4. The rate and pattern of allocation of amounts capitalized to the proper periods, including, if applicable, periods during which the assets become impaired
5. Events that cause the assets to be reclassified to or from categories such as held and used, held for sale, or idle
6. Derecognition—the recording of sale, exchange, retirement and/or disposal of the assets at or before the end of their productive life

### Cost considerations.

*Initial acquisition cost.* Upon acquisition, the reporting entity capitalizes all the costs necessary to deliver the asset to its intended location and prepare it for its productive use. Examples of such costs relative to personal property include

1. Sales, use, excise, and other taxes imposed on the purchase
2. Import duties
3. Finders' fees
4. Freight costs and related shipping insurance
5. Storage and handling costs
6. Installation and setup costs
7. Testing and breaking-in costs
8. Foundations and other costs related to providing proper support for the asset
9. Costs of reconditioning assets that are purchased used in order to prepare them for use

When the asset consists of one or more buildings, capitalized costs include such expenditures as

1. Demolition of preexisting structures occupying the land as well as costs related to excavating, grading, or filling the land to ready it for the new structure
2. Contract price paid to the general contractor and subcontractors
3. Architectural and engineering costs
4. Building permits
5. Costs of renovating a preexisting purchased building to convert it for use by the buyer

*Accounting for assets acquired in a group.* It is important to differentiate the acquisition of assets in a group from a business combination. To aid the practitioner in this endeavor, FAS 141(R), *Business Combinations*, provides that, if the assets acquired and liabilities assumed constitute a "business," the transaction is a business combination; otherwise, it is accounted for as an asset acquisition.

To simplify this determination, FAS 141(R) revised the definition of a business previously set forth in EITF 98-3, which was nullified with the issuance of the new standard. The revised definition of a business is

> ...*an integrated set of activities and assets that is capable of being conducted and managed for the purpose of providing a return in the form of dividends, lower costs, or other economic benefits directly to investors or other owners, members, or participants.*[1]

Significantly, the revised definition does not

1. Require that outputs be present, although they frequently are present
2. Require that a business be self-sustaining. Rather it emphasizes that the activities and assets be *capable* of providing a return. Thus, an entity that is in its development stage and has not yet commenced its planned principal operations that otherwise meets the definition is considered to be a business. Development State Enterprises are discussed in greater detail in Chapter 3.

FAS 141(R), discussed in detail in Chapter 13, is to be applied prospectively to business combinations for which the acquisition date is on or after the beginning of the first annual

---

[1] *FASB Statement No. 141(R), **Business Combinations**; Financial Accounting Standards Board, Norwalk, CT: December 2007; Paragraph 3d.*

reporting period beginning on or after December 15, 2008. Earlier application is not permitted.

When a reporting entity acquires assets and assumes liabilities that do not constitute a business, the transaction is accounted for as an asset acquisition. Assets acquired in an asset acquisition are initially recognized at their cost to the acquirer including related transaction costs. The cost of assets acquired as a group is allocated to the individual assets acquired or liabilities assumed based on their relative fair values. Goodwill is not to be recognized in a transaction of this nature.

If assets are transferred between entities under common control, the entity receiving the net assets or equity interests initially recognizes the assets and liabilities transferred at their carrying amounts to the transferring entity at the transfer date. If there is a difference between the carrying amounts of the net assets transferred and their historical cost of the parent company because, for example, push-down accounting had not been applied, EITF 90-5 provides that the financial statements of the recipient entity are to reflect the transferred assets and liabilities at the historical cost of the parent of the entities under common control.

***Unit of accounting.*** No specific guidance is provided in GAAP as to the unit of accounting to be used by management in capitalizing long-lived assets. Management might choose, with respect to assets it acquires or constructs, to aggregate individually identifiable assets and record them as if they were a single asset, and then depreciate them accordingly. Conversely, management might choose, with respect to longer-lived assets such as buildings or aircraft, to disaggregate the purchase price and separately record and depreciate the asset's major components over each component's own, individually determined estimated useful life. (Note that there may be significant tax advantages to separately accounting for components.)

Absent specific guidance regarding such practices, it is important that the financial statements provide sufficient information regarding the reporting entity's policies regarding capitalization of fixed assets and the criteria used by management to determine whether to record specified categories of assets in groups and/or by component. These policies are to be followed consistently, once adopted, with any future voluntary, postadoption changes in the policies subject to FAS 154, *Accounting Changes and Error Corrections.*

***Postacquisition costs.*** Many different terms are used to describe costs that occur subsequent to initial acquisition including, but not limited to, the following:

| | | | |
|---|---|---|---|
| Addition | Overhaul | Rehabilitation | Retrofitting |
| Alteration | Planned major maintenance | Renovation | Turnaround |
| Betterment | Rearrangement | Repair | |
| Improvement | Redevelopment | Replacement | |
| Maintenance | Refurbishment | Retooling | |

Irrespective of the terminology used to describe a cost, the proper accounting treatment depends on a careful analysis of whether the cost is expected to provide future benefits to the reporting entity and, if so, the nature of those expected benefits.

*Costs that increase the value of the asset.* If the cost adds to the existing asset, in effect a new asset has been acquired that is subject to the same capitalization considerations applied in recognizing the original asset. As a practical expedient, most reporting entities establish a dollar threshold under which such costs are charged to expense, irrespective of their purpose (e.g., all costs under $1,500 are charged to expense). This is done under the assumption that the costs of capitalizing and depreciating the item far exceed the benefits to users of the financial statements. In effect, these items are considered to be immaterial to the financial statements, both individually and in the aggregate.

*Costs that increase the future service potential of the asset.* If the cost increases the future service potential of the asset, it is accounted for in one of the following manners, depending on the individual facts and circumstances:

1. *Costs that do not extend the overall useful life of the asset.* If a portion of the original asset is being replaced, theoretically, the carrying value, if any, of the corresponding portion of the asset that is being replaced (cost less accumulated depreciation and less any impairment charges recognized in prior periods) should be removed from the accounting records and recorded as a loss in the period of the replacement. This accounting is seldom used in practice because, in general, accounting records for fixed assets are not maintained in the painstaking detail necessary to determine the carrying value of the individual components that comprise each asset. Instead, most companies will capitalize the replacement components under the rationale that the portion of the asset being replaced would have been depreciated sufficiently based on the useful life of the host asset so that at the time of replacement, little or no carrying value would remain to be removed.

2. *Costs that extend the overall useful life of the asset.* If, as a result of incurring a cost, the useful life of the host asset is extended without increasing its productivity or capacity, it has been suggested that the costs be recorded as a charge to accumulated depreciation, rather than capitalizing them as additions to fixed assets. Recording the transaction in this manner effectively recovers previously recognized depreciation and has the same effect on the net carrying value as capitalizing the addition. This treatment is seldom used in practice and has little theoretical appeal unless it is accompanied by a prospective change in the remaining estimated useful life of the host asset.

*Planned major maintenance activities.* The AICPA Industry Audit Guide, *Audits of Airlines* (AUG AIR), issued by the AICPA in 1981, had permitted airlines to estimate and accrue the future costs of overhauling engines and airframes as required by regulations of the US Federal Aviation Administration (FAA). Following this method, an air carrier would, upon acquisition of an aircraft, estimate the number of hours from inception until when the first major overhaul would be required to be performed in order to recertify the aircraft with the FAA. As those hours were flown, the carrier would use an hourly rate to accrue the estimated overhaul cost and charge the cost to expense. Upon actual performance of the overhaul, the actual costs would be charged to the accrued overhaul cost with any difference between estimate and actual being charged or credited to expense.

FASB concluded that application of this method resulted in recognition of a liability in periods prior to the occurrence of an event that obligated the entity to perform the overhaul. Until the performance of the overhaul is actually required to be performed, the reporting entity will not have incurred a present obligation to perform the overhaul and, therefore, under the CON 6 definition of a liability, the liability had not yet been incurred as the hours were flown.

FASB was also concerned that other commercial enterprises were applying a similar accrue-in-advance method by analogizing their own facts and circumstances to the air carriers whose accounting was prescribed by the AUG. Consequently, in September 2006, it issued FSP AUG AIR-1, *Accounting for Planned Major Maintenance Activities*, which prohibits the use, in both interim and annual financial statements, of the accrue-in-advance method of accounting for planned major maintenance activities. The scope of the FSP includes the airline industry and all other industries. Thus, this method of accounting is no longer permitted.

*Reinstallations and rearrangements.* If, as a result of these activities, the reporting entity expects to obtain benefits that extend into future years arising from improved production efficiency or reduced production costs, the reinstallation or rearrangement costs can be capitalized and depreciated. If the activities are not expected to provide those future benefits, the costs are to be recognized as expense as incurred.

*Relocation.* The costs of moving a fixed asset to a new location at which it will operate in the same manner and with the same functionality as it did at its former location does not result in any future benefits, and therefore the costs of dismantlement, packaging/crating, shipping, and reinstallation are to be recognized as expenses as incurred.

*Repairs and maintenance.* If a cost does not extend an asset's useful life, increase its productivity, improve its operating efficiency, or add additional production capacity, the cost is to be recognized as an expense as incurred.

**Construction of tangible assets for internal use.** All direct costs (labor, materials, payroll, and related benefit costs) of constructing an entity's own tangible fixed assets are capitalized. However, a degree of judgment is involved in allocating costs between indirect costs—a reasonable portion of which are allocable to construction costs—and general and administrative costs, which under GAAP must be treated as period costs.

The FASB has not addressed this issue, and the AICPA has issued conflicting guidance regarding cost capitalization. In SOP 81-1, the AICPA (in the context of long-term construction contracts) indicated that, in order for costs to be capitalized (rather than be treated as period costs), they should be "... clearly related to production either directly or by an allocation based on their discernible future benefits." Later in that same pronouncement, illustrative examples of capitalizable costs are provided with a qualifier "in *some circumstances*, support costs such as central preparation and processing of payrolls [are allocable as indirect costs]."

Subsequently, in SOP 98-1, (addressing the capitalization of costs of software self-developed for internal use), the AICPA indicated that "general and administrative costs *and overhead costs* should not be capitalized as costs of internal-use software." The distinction between the two conflicting rules may be due to the former being applicable to tangible assets and the latter to intangible software costs, although both types of internally constructed assets are subject to interest capitalization during the production period.

Prudence suggests that management establish a carefully reasoned policy that is consistently followed and fully disclosed in the notes to the financial statements, in sufficient detail to unambiguously inform the user about the methods used and amounts involved.

**Preproduction costs of molds, dies, and other tools.** Manufacturers often incur costs referred to as preproduction costs, related to products that they will provide to their customers under long-term supply arrangements. EITF 99-5 reached the following consensuses with respect to these costs:

1. Costs of design and development of products to be sold under long-term supply arrangements are expensed as incurred.
2. Costs of design and development of molds, dies, and other tools that the supplier will own and that will be used in producing the products under the long-term supply arrangement are capitalized as part of the molds, dies, and other tools (subject to a FAS 144 recoverability assessment when one or more impairment indicators is present, as discussed later in this chapter). There is an exception, however, for molds, dies, and other tools involving new technology, which are expensed as incurred as research and development costs under FAS 2.
3. If the molds, dies, and other tools described in 2. above are *not to be owned* by the supplier, then their costs are expensed as incurred unless the supply arrangement

provides the supplier the noncancelable right (as long as the supplier is performing under the terms of the supply arrangement) to use the molds, dies, and other tools during the term of the supply arrangement.

4. If there is a legally enforceable contractual guarantee for reimbursement of design and development costs that would otherwise be expensed under these consensuses, the costs are recognized as an asset as incurred. Such a guarantee must contain reimbursement provisions that are objectively measurable and verifiable. The consensus contains examples illustrating this provision.

Under these consensuses, preparers are encouraged (and SEC registrants are required) to disclose the following information:

1. The accounting policy for preproduction design and development costs.
2. The aggregate amounts of

    a. Assets recognized pursuant to agreements providing for contractual reimbursement of preproduction design and development costs.
    b. Assets recognized for molds, dies, and other tools that the supplier owns.
    c. Assets recognized for molds, dies, and other tools that the supplier does not own.

It is important to note that the above provisions do not apply to assets acquired in a business combination that are used in research and development activities. Instead, such assets are accounted for in accordance with FAS 141(R), which amended FAS 2 to permit recognition of in-process research and development assets.

*Interest cost.* The recorded amount of an asset includes all of the costs necessary to get the asset set up and functioning properly for its intended use, including interest.

The principal purposes accomplished by the capitalization of interest costs are

1. To obtain a more accurate measurement of the costs associated with the investment in the asset
2. To achieve a better matching of costs related to the acquisition, construction, and development of productive assets to the future periods that will benefit from the revenues that the assets generate

All assets that require a time period to get ready for their intended use should include a capitalized amount of interest. However, accomplishing this level of capitalization would usually violate a reasonable cost/benefit test because of the added accounting and administrative costs that would be incurred. In many such situations, the effect of interest capitalization would be immaterial. Accordingly, interest cost is only capitalized as a part of the historical cost of the following qualifying assets when such interest is considered to be material, which normally implies that construction or creation occurs over extended periods of time. Common examples include

1. Assets constructed for an entity's own use or for which deposit or progress payments are made
2. Assets produced as discrete projects that are intended for lease or sale
3. Equity-method investments when the investee is using funds to acquire qualifying assets for principal operations that have not yet begun

Generally, inventories and land that are not undergoing preparation for intended use are not qualifying assets. When land is being developed, it is a qualifying asset. If land is developed for lots, the capitalized interest cost is added to the cost of the land. The capitalized interest will then be properly matched against revenues when the lots are sold. If, however, the land is developed for a building, then the capitalized interest cost is added to the cost of the building, in which case the capitalized interest will be matched against related revenues as the building is depreciated.

The capitalization of interest costs does not apply to the following situations:

1. When routine inventories are produced in large quantities on a repetitive basis
2. When the effects of capitalization would not be material, compared to the effect of expensing interest
3. When qualifying assets are already in use or ready for use
4. When qualifying assets are not being used and are not awaiting activities to get them ready for use
5. When qualifying assets are not included in a consolidated balance sheet
6. When principal operations of an investee accounted for under the equity method have already begun
7. When regulated investees capitalize both the cost of debt and equity capital
8. When assets are acquired with grants and gifts restricted by the donor to the extent that funds are available from those grants and gifts

*The amount of interest to be capitalized.* Interest cost includes the following:

1. Interest on debt having explicit interest rates (fixed or floating)
2. Interest related to capital leases
3. Interest required to be imputed on payables (i.e., those due in over one year, per APB 21)

The most appropriate rate to use as the capitalization rate is the rate applicable to specific new debt resulting from the need to finance the acquired assets. If there is no specific new debt, the capitalization rate is a weighted-average of the rates of the other borrowings of the entity. This latter case reflects the fact that the previously incurred debt of the entity could be repaid if not for the acquisition of the qualifying asset. Thus, indirectly, the previous debt is financing the acquisition of the new asset and its interest is part of the cost of the new asset. The selection of borrowings to be used in the calculation of the weighted-average of rates requires judgment. The amount of interest to be capitalized is that portion which could have been avoided if the qualifying asset had not been acquired. Thus, the capitalized amount is the incremental amount of interest cost incurred by the entity to finance the acquired asset.

If the reporting entity uses derivative financial instruments as fair value hedges to affect its borrowing costs, EITF 99-9 specifies that the interest rate to use in capitalizing interest is to be the effective yield that takes into account gains and losses on the effective portion of a derivative instrument that qualifies as a fair value hedge of fixed interest rate debt. The amount of interest subject to capitalization could include amortization of the adjustments of the carrying amount of the hedged liability under FAS 133, if the entity elects to begin amortization of those adjustments during the period in which interest is eligible for capitalization. Any ineffective portion of the fair value hedge is not reflected in the capitalization rate. During the deliberations with respect to EITF 99-9, the FASB staff expressed a belief that when variable-rate interest on a specific borrowing is associated with an asset under construction and capitalized as part of the cost of that asset, the amounts in accumulated other comprehensive income related to a cash flow hedge of the variability of that interest are to be reclassified into earnings over the depreciable life of the constructed asset, since that depreciable life coincides with the amortization period for the capitalized interest cost on the debt.

Once the appropriate rate has been established, the base to which that rate is to be applied is the average amount of accumulated net capital *expenditures* incurred for qualifying assets during the relevant time frame. Capitalized costs and expenditures are not the same terms. Theoretically, a capitalized cost financed by a trade payable for which no interest is recognized is not a capital expenditure to which the capitalization rate is applied. Reasonable approximations of net capital expenditures are acceptable, however, and capitalized costs are generally used in place of capital expenditures unless there is expected to be a material difference.

If the average capitalized expenditures exceed the specific new borrowings for the time frame involved, then the *excess* expenditures are multiplied by the weighted-average of rates and not by the rate associated with the specific debt. This requirement more accurately reflects the interest cost incurred by the entity to acquire the fixed asset.

The interest being paid on the debt may be simple or compound. Simple interest is computed on the principal alone, whereas compound interest is computed on the principal *and* on any interest that has not been paid. Most fixed assets will be acquired with debt subject to compound interest. Compound interest can be computed using compound interest tables or computer software.

The total amount of interest actually incurred by the entity is the ceiling for the amount of interest cost capitalized. The amount capitalized cannot exceed the amount actually incurred during the period involved. On a consolidated basis, the ceiling is defined as the total of the parent's interest cost plus that of the consolidated subsidiaries. If financial statements are issued separately, the interest cost capitalized is limited to the amount that the separate entity has incurred, and that amount includes interest on intercompany borrowings. The interest incurred is a gross amount and is not netted against interest earned except in cases involving externally restricted tax-exempt borrowings.

### Example of accounting for capitalized interest costs

1. On January 1, 2009, Daniel Corp. contracted with Rukin Company to construct a building for $2,000,000 on land that Daniel had purchased years earlier.
2. Daniel Corp. was to make five payments in 2009 with the last payment scheduled for the date of completion, December 31, 2009.
3. Daniel Corp. made the following payments during 2009:

| | |
|---|---|
| January 1, 2009 | $ 200,000 |
| March 31, 2009 | 400,000 |
| June 30, 2009 | 610,000 |
| September 30, 2009 | 440,000 |
| December 31, 2009 | 350,000 |
| | $2,000,000 |

4. Daniel Corp. had the following debt outstanding at December 31, 2009:

a. A 12%, three-year note dated 1/1/09 with interest compounded quarterly. Both principal and interest due 12/31/12 (relates specifically to building project).     $850,000

b. A 10%, ten-year note dated 12/31/03 with simple interest payable annually on December 31.     $600,000

c. A 12%, five-year note dated 12/31/05 with simple interest payable annually on December 31.     $700,000

The amount of interest to be capitalized during 2009 is computed as follows:

#### *Average Accumulated Expenditures*

| *Date* | *Expenditure* | *Capitalization period** | *Average accumulated expenditures* |
|---|---|---|---|
| 1/1/09 | $ 200,000 | 12/12 | $200,000 |
| 3/31/09 | 400,000 | 9/12 | 300,000 |
| 6/30/09 | 610,000 | 6/12 | 305,000 |
| 9/30/09 | 440,000 | 3/12 | 110,000 |
| 12/31/09 | 350,000 | 0/12 | -- |
| | $2,000,000 | | $915,000 |

\* *The number of months between the date expenditures were made and the date interest capitalization stops (December 31, 2009).*

***Potential Interest Cost to Be Capitalized***

| | | | |
|---|---|---|---|
| ($850,000 × 1.12551)* − $850,000 | = | $106,684 |
| $\underline{65,000}$ × .1108** | = | $\underline{7,202}$ |
| $\underline{\$915,000}$ | | $\underline{\$113,886}$ |

\* *The principal, $850,000, is multiplied by the factor for the future amount of $1 for four periods (quarterly compounding) at 3% to determine the amount of principal and interest due in 2009.*

\*\* *Weighted-average interest rate:*

| | *Principal* | *Interest* |
|---|---|---|
| 10%, ten-year note | $ 600,000 | $60,000 |
| 12%, five-year | $\underline{700,000}$ | $\underline{84,000}$ |
| | $\underline{\$1,300,000}$ | $\underline{\$144,886}$ |

$$\frac{\text{Total interest}}{\text{Total principal}} = \frac{\$144,000}{\$1,300,000} = \underline{11.08}\% \text{ weighted-average interest rate}$$

The actual interest is

| | | |
|---|---|---|
| 12%, three-year note [($850,000 × 1.12551) − $850,000] | = | $106,684 |
| 10%, ten-year note ($600,000 × 10%) | = | 60,000 |
| 12%, five-year note ($700,000 × 12%) | = | $\underline{84,000}$ |
| Total interest | | $\underline{\$250,684}$ |

The interest cost to be capitalized is the lesser of $113,886 (avoidable interest) or $250,684 (actual interest), which is $113,886. The remaining $136,798 ($250,684 − $113,886) is expensed during 2009.

***Determining the time period for interest capitalization.*** Three conditions must be met before capitalization commences.

1. Necessary activities are in progress to get the asset ready to function as intended
2. Qualifying asset expenditures have been made
3. Interest costs are being incurred

As long as these conditions continue, interest costs are capitalized.

Necessary activities are interpreted in a very broad manner. They start with the planning process and continue until the qualifying asset is substantially complete and ready to function. Brief, normal interruptions do not stop the capitalization of interest costs. However, if the entity intentionally suspends or delays the activities for some reason, interest costs are not capitalized from the point of suspension or delay until substantial activities regarding the asset resume.

If the asset is completed in parts, the capitalization of interest costs stops for each part as it becomes ready. An asset that must be entirely complete before the parts can be used capitalizes interest costs until the total asset becomes ready.

Interest costs continue to be capitalized until the asset is ready to function as intended, even in cases where lower of cost or market rules are applicable and market is lower than cost. The required write-down is increased accordingly.

*Capitalization of interest costs incurred on tax-exempt borrowings.* If qualifying assets have been financed with the proceeds from tax-exempt, externally restricted borrowings, and if temporary investments have been purchased with those proceeds, a modification is required. The interest costs incurred from the date of borrowing must be reduced by the interest earned on the temporary investment in order to calculate the ceiling for the capitalization of interest costs. This procedure is followed until the assets financed in this manner are ready. When the specified assets are functioning as intended, the interest cost of the tax-exempt borrowing becomes available to be capitalized by other qualifying assets of the entity. Portions of the tax-exempt borrowings that are not restricted are eligible for capitalization in the normal manner.

*Assets acquired with gifts or grants.* Qualifying assets that are acquired with externally restricted gifts or grants are not subject to capitalization of interest. The principal reason for this treatment is the concept that there is no economic cost of financing when a gift or grant is used in the acquisition.

*Summary of interest capitalization requirements.* The diagram on the following page summarizes the accounting for interest capitalization.

***Real estate special assessments.*** The laws of various states permit the formation of Tax Increment Financing Entities (TIFEs). Although their structure and characteristics differ between jurisdictions, TIFEs are generally special taxing districts established to finance and operate infrastructure owned by the municipality, such as roads, water mains, electric lines, sewers, etc. These infrastructure improvements are used to revitalize a discrete geographic area by facilitating the private development of adjoining residential and commercial real estate. The TIFE or, absent a TIFE, the municipality typically issues bonds to finance the construction of the infrastructure improvements. The bonds may offer investors favorable after-tax yields by qualifying for tax-exempt status under IRC §141. Generally, the bonds are repaid from special assessments specifically designated for this purpose by the TIFE (or the municipality) such as user fees, tolls, sales taxes, real estate taxes, hotel bed taxes, etc.

**SUMMARY OF ACCOUNTING FOR INTEREST CAPITALIZATION**

Besides paying for the debt service, these special assessments also fund ongoing operating costs such as routine infrastructure repairs and maintenance. The infrastructure improvements made with the bond proceeds directly benefit the adjoining property owners and, in fact, the terms of these arrangements are often jointly negotiated between residential and commercial real estate developers and the municipality as an inducement to the developer to invest in a local development project.

Depending on an analysis of the specific facts and circumstances including the relevant statute, ordinance, bond indenture, and other legal documents, the property owner or developer may potentially be required to record a liability for

1. A liability for a special assessment by the TIFE or municipality if that assessment is levied on each individual property owner at an amount that is fixed or determinable and that covers a determinable period of time (EITF 91-10).
2. A guarantee liability under FIN 45 if, for example, it has

   a. Contractually agreed to cover all or a portion of any shortfalls in the required annual debt service of the bond obligations of the issuing TIFE or municipality.
   b. Pledged company assets as collateral for the bond obligations.
   c. Provided a letter of credit or other credit enhancements to support all or a portion of the bond obligations.

   *NOTE:*

   *1.  FIN 45, para. 10 provides that, at the inception of the guarantee, the guarantor may be required under FAS 5 to recognize a liability for a contingent loss. In the circumstances described here, this would result in the developer or property owner recording the TIFE or municipality debt as their own obligation. In fact, EITF 91-10 specifies that if the property owner is constructing facilities for its own use or operation, the presence of any of the factors a. – c. would create a presumption that the TIFE debt be recognized as a company obligation.*

   *2.  Consolidation of the TIFE by the property owner or developer will most likely be prohibited under FIN 46(R) since governmental organizations and financing entities established by governmental organizations are exempt from consolidation unless the property owner or developer is using the arrangement in an attempt to circumvent FIN 46(R).*

The literature cited above is silent regarding how to record the offsetting debit associated with recording these obligations and whether or not the debt represents an amount to be capitalized as a long-lived asset. During the deliberations on this topic, alternative views were expressed. For example, one view was to treat a debit to record the TIFE debt as an investment in the TIFE and amortize the investment as a charge to expense as the bonds are repaid and/or the related development is sold.

In the authors' opinion, the accounting for the debit depends on whether the property is being developed for sale or lease by a real estate developer or is being developed for the reporting entity's own use.

Real estate developers follow the guidance in FAS 67, *Accounting for Costs and Initial Rental Operations of Real Estate Projects*. Under FAS 67, the developer capitalizes any portion allocable to the production period as part of the cost of the property being developed. The remaining portion is charged to expense because it is attributable to the period after the project is substantially complete and ready for intended use.

Reporting entities developing the property for their own use are not included in the scope of FAS 67 and, therefore need to consider the best of the available alternatives. The authors favor analogizing from FAS 67 and the literature on interest capitalization on self constructed assets, and accordingly following the same accounting as described in the previous paragraph.

**Asset retirement obligations.** FAS 143 established standards for measuring the future cost to retire an asset and recognizing that cost in the financial statements as a liability, and correspondingly, as part of the depreciable cost of the asset.

The provisions of the statement do not apply to

1. Temporary idling of long-lived assets
2. Obligations arising solely from a plan to sell or otherwise dispose of long-lived assets covered by FAS 144 (discussed later in this chapter)
3. Obligations resulting from the improper operation of assets (e.g., penalties and fines such as those described in SOP 96-1, *Environmental Remediation Liabilities*)
4. Minimum lease payments or contingent rentals of a lessee under FAS 13
5. Costs of activities required to prepare an asset for an alternative use
6. The costs of replacement parts (unless there is a legal obligation to dispose of them)

The standard applies to *legal obligations* associated with the *retirement* of tangible long-lived assets that result from their acquisition, construction, development, and/or normal operation. Lessee capital lease assets and lessor assets that are leased under operating leases are also subject to these rules.

For the purposes of applying FAS 143, a legal obligation is "an obligation that a party is required to settle as a result of an existing or enacted law, statute, ordinance, or written or oral contract or by legal construction of a contract under the doctrine of *promissory estoppel*." Promissory estoppel is a legal doctrine whereby a court of law will enforce a promise made by one party (the promisor) to another party (the promisee) even though no formal contract exists between the two parties or no consideration was exchanged. This situation can arise when a party (the promisee) relies on a promise to his or her detriment and the person making the promise (the promisor) should have reasonably expected the promisee to rely on the promise. The court will, in these cases, "estop" (prevent) the promisor from asserting that s/he has no obligation because s/he should have anticipated that the promise would be relied upon.

***Asset retirement obligations requiring recognition.*** When an entity acquires, constructs, and operates assets, it often incurs obligations that are unavoidable. Much of the discussion in FAS 143 pertains to specialized industry applications such as offshore oil platforms, nuclear power plants, mining operations, landfills, and underground storage tanks. However, the criteria of the statement are intended to apply to situations encountered more frequently in practice, such as in the following examples.

### Examples of the scope of FAS 143

Example 1—Leased premises. In accordance with the terms of a lease, the lessee is obligated to remove its specialized machinery from the leased premises prior to vacating those premises, or to compensate the lessor accordingly. The lease imposes a legal obligation on the lessee to remove the asset at the end of the asset's useful life or upon vacating the premises, and therefore this situation would be covered by FAS 143.

Example 2—Owned premises. The same machinery described in example 1 is installed in a factory that the entity owns. At the end of the useful life of the machinery, the entity will either incur costs to dismantle and remove the asset or will leave it idle in place. If the entity chooses to do nothing and not remove the equipment, this would adversely affect the fair value of the premises should the entity choose to sell the premises on an "as is" basis. Conceptually, to apply the matching principle in a manner consistent with example 1, the cost of asset retirement should be recognized systematically and rationally over the productive life of the asset and not in the period of retirement. However, in this example, there is no *legal obligation* on the part of the owner of the factory and equipment to retire the asset and, thus, this would *not* be covered by FAS 143.

Example 3—Promissory estoppel. Assume the same facts as in example 2. In this case, however, the owner of the property sold to a third party an option to purchase the factory, exercisable at the end of five years. In offering the option to the third party, the owner verbally represented that the factory would be completely vacant at the end of the five-year option period and that all machinery, furniture and fixtures would be removed from the premises. The property owner would reasonably expect that the purchaser of the option relied to the purchaser's detriment (as evidenced by the financial sacrifice of consideration made in exchange for the option) on the representation that the factory would be vacant. This would trigger promissory estoppel and the owner's obligation would be covered by FAS 143.

### Example of timing of recognition

Phyl Corporation owns and operates a chemical company. At its premises, it maintains underground tanks used to store various types of chemicals. The tanks were installed when Phyl Corporation purchased its facilities seven years prior. On February 1, 2009, the governor of the state signed a law requiring removal of such tanks when they are no longer being used. Since the law imposes a legal obligation on Phyl Corporation, upon enactment, recognition of an asset retirement obligation (ARO) would be required.

### Example of ongoing additions to the obligation

Joyce Manufacturing Corporation (JMC) operates a factory. As part of its normal operations it stores production byproducts and used cleaning solvents on site in a reservoir specifically designed for that purpose. The reservoir and surrounding land, all owned by JMC, are contaminated with these chemicals. On February 1, 2009, the governor of the state signed a law requiring cleanup and disposal of hazardous waste from an already existing production process upon retirement of the facility. Upon enactment of the law, immediate recognition would be required for the ARO associated with the contamination that had already occurred. In addition, liabilities will continue to be recognized over the remaining life of the facility as additional contamination occurs.

*Accounting considerations.* This standard and the interpretation of it in FIN 47 raise several important accounting issues that require careful consideration.

*Recognition and allocation.* Upon initial recognition, the entity records an increase to the carrying amount of the related long-lived asset and an offsetting liability. The entity then depreciates the combined cost of the asset and the capitalized asset retirement obligation using a systematic and rational allocation method over the period during which the long-lived asset is expected to provide benefits, taking into consideration any expected salvage value. Conceptually, this standard is an application of the matching principle in that the total investment in the asset, including the cost of its eventual retirement, is charged to expense over the periods benefited. Depending on the pattern and timing of obligating events, an entity could, under this standard, capitalize an amount of asset retirement cost during a period and, in the same period, allocate an equal amount to depreciation expense. It is important to note that, for the purpose of capitalizing interest under FAS 34, these additions to the carrying amounts of long-lived assets are not considered expenditures.

*Impairment.* Retirement obligations added to the carrying amounts of long-lived assets must be included in those carrying amounts for the purpose of testing those assets for impairment. In estimating future cash flows under the impairment standard, the cash flows related to settling the liability for an asset retirement obligation are to be excluded from both the undiscounted cash flows used to assess the recoverability of the asset's carrying amount and the discounted cash flows used to measure the asset's fair value.

*Measurement.* Asset retirement obligations are initially measured at fair value. Fair value (as defined in FAS 157, *Fair Value Measurements*, and discussed in detail in Chapter

6) is the price that would be paid to transfer the liability in an orderly transaction between market participants at the measurement date. This measurement is not based on the amount that the reporting entity (the obligor) would be required to pay to settle the liability on the measurement date (which would be difficult, if not impossible, to estimate in the absence of a market for the transfer of such obligations). Rather, the measurement assumes that the reporting entity remains the obligor under the ARO and that the obligee has transferred its rights by selling them to a hypothetical market participant on the measurement date. In determining the price it would be willing to pay for the rights associated with the ARO, a third-party market participant would consider the risk of nonperformance of the reporting entity, since that entity will continue to be the obligor after the measurement date. Thus, the fair value measurement of the obligation, under FAS 157, takes into consideration the reporting entity's own risk of nonperformance that includes, but is not limited to, the effect of its own credit standing.

FAS 157 amended FAS 143 to conform its fair value guidance to the new, uniform guidance regarding measuring fair value that is applicable throughout GAAP. In this amendment FASB acknowledges that

> *Rarely, if ever, would there be an observable rate of interest for a liability that has cash flows similar to an asset retirement obligation being measured. In addition, an asset retirement obligation usually will have uncertainties in both timing and amount. In that circumstance, employing a discount rate adjustment technique, where uncertainty is incorporated into the rate, will be difficult, if not impossible.*

This lack of observability means that management, in order to estimate the ARO, will be required to use an expected present value technique that uses its own assumptions regarding the necessary adjustment for market risk. These are referred to as "Level 3 inputs" by FAS 157.

At the time this publication went to press, FASB was engaged in redeliberating a proposed Staff Position, FSP FAS 157-c, the purpose of which is to clarify the application of FAS 157 to liabilities. The authors strongly encourage the reader/researcher to monitor the status of this project on the FASB Web site (www.fasb.org) as it progresses to ensure that any effect a final Staff Position might have on the application of fair value measurement principles to ARO and other liabilities is fully considered in applying the guidance we provide in this and other affected chapters.

*Initially applying an expected present value method.* Appendix B of FAS 157 provides two alternative methods for determining expected present value that are discussed in detail in Chapter 6. To apply Method 1, management adjusts the expected cash flows for market risk by incorporating a cash risk premium in them and uses a risk-free interest rate to discount the risk-adjusted expected cash flows. To apply Method 2, management does not adjust the expected cash flows, but instead adjusts the risk-free interest rate by incorporating a risk premium in it.

As discussed later in this section, Method 1 cannot be used to estimate the expected present value of an ARO due to computational difficulties that cannot be overcome. As a result, the following discussion, adapted from FAS 143, uses Method 2 to illustrate the estimation of expected present value.

Management begins by estimating a series of cash flows that reflect its marketplace estimates of the cost and timing of performing the required retirement activities. Marketplace amounts are those amounts that would be expended by the entity to hire a third party to perform the work or that a third-party would pay for the right to receive the cash flows should a market exist for the transfer of such obligations. Explicit assumptions are to be developed and incorporated in the estimates about all of the following matters:

1. The costs that a third party would incur in performing the necessary tasks associated with retiring the asset.
2. Additional amounts that the third party would include in pricing the work (or the transfer price it would pay for the right to receive the cash flows) related to such factors as inflation, overhead, equipment charges, profit margins, anticipated technological advances, and offsetting cash inflows, if any.
3. The extent to which the amount of the third party's costs or their timing might differ under various future scenarios and the relative probabilities of those scenarios actually occurring.
4. The price that the third party would demand and could expect to receive for bearing the uncertainties and unforeseeable circumstances inherent in the obligation. This is referred to as a *market-risk premium*.

If data is available regarding assumptions that marketplace participants would make that contradicts management's own assumptions, management must adjust its assumptions accordingly. For example, if the costs of labor in the marketplace exceed those of the entity, the higher marketplace costs are to be used in the cash flow estimates. Even if the entity can and will retire the asset using internal resources, the obligation must be computed as if a third party will be retained to perform the work, including provisions for recovery of the contractor's overhead and profit.

The discount rate to be used in the present value calculations is the *credit-adjusted risk-free rate* that adjusts a risk-free rate of interest for the effects of the entity's own credit standing. The risk-free interest rate is the interest rate on monetary assets with maturity dates or durations that coincide with the period covered by the estimated cash flows associated with the ARO. When the measurement involves cash flows denominated in US dollars, the yield curve for US Treasury securities is used.

In adjusting the risk-free rate for the entity's credit standing, the entity takes into account the effects on the fair value estimate of all terms, collateral, and existing guarantees. In FAS 157, FASB indicated that it believed, when it issued FAS 143, that it would be more practical for management to reflect an estimate of its own credit standing as an adjustment to the risk-free rate rather than as an adjustment to the expected cash flows. In fact, based on the model FASB chose to account for subsequent upward and downward changes in the ARO, FAS 143 would not be operational unless the adjustment for credit-standing was made to the risk-free interest rate.

As a practical matter, for companies whose debt is not rated by a bond-rating agency, the adjustment for credit standing may be difficult to establish. For such companies, the incremental borrowing rate used for lease testing (see Chapter 16) may serve as an acceptable approximation of the credit-adjusted risk-free rate.

The ARO may be incurred in one or more of the entity's reporting periods. Each period's incremental liability incurred is recognized as a separate liability and is estimated using these principles based on market and interest rate assumptions existing in the period of subsequent recognition.

FIN 47 clarified that an asset retirement obligation is required to be recognized when incurred (or acquired), even if uncertainty exists regarding the timing and/or method of eventually settling the obligation. In effect, FIN 47 distinguishes between a contingency and an uncertainty. If the obligation to perform the retirement activities is unconditional, the fact that uncertainty exists regarding the timing and/or method of retirement does not relieve the reporting entity of the requirement to estimate and record the obligation if, in fact, it is reasonably estimable. The assumptions regarding the probabilities of the various outcomes used in the computation are to take into account that uncertainty. An ARO is considered reasonably estimable if

1. It is evident that the obligation's fair value is included in an asset's acquisition price,
2. An active market exists for the transfer of the obligation, or
3. Sufficient information is available to enable the use of the CON 7 expected present value technique to estimate the obligation.

Sufficient information is considered to be available to reasonably estimate the obligation if either

1. The settlement date and method of settlement have been specified by others (e.g., the end of a lease term or the end of a statutory period) or
2. Information is available to reasonably estimate

   a. The settlement date or range of potential settlement dates
   b. The settlement method or potential settlement methods
   c. The probabilities of occurrence of the dates and methods in a. and b.

The information necessary to make these estimates can be based on the reporting entity's own historical experience, industry statistics or customary practices, management's own intent, or estimates of the asset's economic useful life. In the authors' opinion, it would be difficult for management to credibly justify that reasonable estimates of these matters cannot be made. Even if management concludes that this is not the case, and that sufficient information does not exist to record the obligation at inception, management is expected to continuously consider whether this remains true in future accounting periods, and to recognize the obligation in the first period when sufficient information becomes available to enable the fair value estimate.

*Accounting in subsequent periods.* After the initial period of ARO recognition, the liability will change as a result of either the passage of time or revisions to the original estimates of either the amounts of estimated cash flows or their timing. Such changes can arise due to the effects of inflation, changes in the probabilities used in the original estimate, changes in interest rates, changes in laws, regulations, statutes, and contracts.

The entity recognizes these changes to the liability by first adjusting the carrying amount of the liability for changes due to the passage of time and then, if applicable, for changes due to revisions in either amounts or timing of estimated cash flows. Changes due to the passage of time increase the carrying amount of the liability because there are fewer periods remaining from the initial measurement date until the settlement date and, thus, the present value of the discounted future settlement amount increases. These changes are recorded as a period cost called *accretion expense* and classified separately in the operating section of the statement of income (or not-for-profit statement of activities). Accretion is computed using an interest method of allocation which results in periodic accretion expense that represents a level effective interest rate applied to the carrying amount of the liability at the beginning of each period. The effective interest rate used to calculate accretion is the credit-adjusted risk-free rate or rates (or incremental borrowing rate) applied when the liability or portion of the liability (as explained below) was initially measured and recognized. Accretion expense is not combined with interest expense, and is not considered interest cost for the purpose of applying the interest capitalization criteria of FAS 34.

Changes in the ARO that result from changes in the estimates of the timing or amounts of future cash flows are accounted for differently for increases and decreases. If the expected present value increases, the increase gives rise to a new obligation accounted for separately just as the ARO was originally measured but using current market value assumptions, and the current credit-adjusted risk-free rate. Thus, over time, a particular long-lived asset may have multiple layers of obligations associated with it which are based on different assumptions measured at different dates during the asset's useful life. The incremental obligation is recorded by increasing the recorded ARO and capitalizing the additional cost as a part of the carrying amount of the related long-lived asset. If multiple layers have been recorded and it is not practical to separately identify the period (or layer) to which subsequent revisions in estimated cash flows relate, the statement permits the use of a *weighted-average credit-adjusted risk-free rate* to measure the change in the liability resulting from that revision.

If, however, the expected present value subsequently decreases, the difference between the remeasured amount and the carrying amount of the liability (after adjustment for inception-to-date accretion) is recorded as a gain in the current period. In this case, the previously recognized layers of liabilities are reduced pro rata so as not to affect the overall effective rate of accretion over the remaining life of the obligation.

For the purposes of measurement in subsequent periods, in the unlikely event that an entity originally determined its ARO based on available market prices rather than using the expected present value method, it would be required to determine the undiscounted cash flows embedded in that market price. This process is analogous to computing the rate of interest implicit in a lease.

FAS 143 does not require detailed cash flow estimates every reporting period but rather allows the entity to exercise judgment as to when facts and circumstances indicate that the initial estimate requires updating.

If the increase in carrying amount of the affected long-lived asset resulting from the remeasurement of ARO in a subsequent period impacts only that period, then the increase is fully depreciated in that period. Otherwise, the increase is depreciated in the period of change and future periods as a change in estimate in accordance with FAS 154 (see Chapter 5). Both depreciation and accretion are classified as operating expenses in the statement of income.

**Other provisions.** Other provisions of FAS 143 affect the calculation of the credit-adjusted rate as well as how it is to be applied by rate-regulated entities.

*Funding and assurance provisions.* Factors such as laws, regulations, public policy, the entity's creditworthiness, or the sheer magnitude of the future obligation may cause an entity to be required to provide third parties with assurance that the entity will be able to satisfy its ARO in the future. Such assurance is provided using such instruments as surety bonds, insurance policies, letters of credit, guarantees by other entities, establishment of trust funds, or by custodial arrangements segregating other assets dedicated to satisfying the ARO. Although providing such means of assurance does not satisfy the underlying obligation, the credit-adjusted interest rate used in calculating the expected present value is adjusted for the effect on the entity's credit standing of employing one or more of these techniques.

*Rate-regulated entities.* Many rate-regulated entities (as defined in FAS 71 and discussed in Chapter 25) follow current specialized accounting that capitalizes costs not otherwise afforded that treatment under GAAP. These entities recover these additional costs in the rates that they charge their customers. These additional capitalized costs may or may not meet the definition of ARO under FAS 143. The differences in the amounts and timing of assets and liabilities between GAAP and regulatory accounting used for rate-making purposes give rise to temporary differences and the resultant deferred income tax accounting.

FAS 143 provides that, if the criteria in FAS 71 are met, the rate-regulated entity is to recognize a regulatory asset or liability for differences in the timing of recognition of the period costs associated with ARO for financial reporting and rate-making purposes. Accounting for the ARO arising from closed or abandoned long-lived assets of rate-regulated entities is covered by FAS 90.

*Disclosures.* The following information about ARO is required to be disclosed in the financial statements.

1. A general description of the ARO and the related long-lived assets
2. A description of how the fair value of the ARO was determined (e.g., by using an expected present value method or some other market-based valuation technique)
3. The funding policy, if any, for ARO
4. The fair value of assets dedicated to satisfy the liability, if any
5. A reconciliation of the beginning and ending aggregate carrying amount of the liability showing separately the changes attributable to

   a. The liability incurred in the current period
   b. The liability settled in the current period
   c. Accretion expense, and
   d. Revisions in expected cash flows

6. An explanation of any significant changes in the ARO not otherwise apparent in other disclosures required by the statement
7. If the fair value of an ARO is not considered reasonably estimable, that fact and the reasons why management believes this to be the case

To supplement the disclosures described above, FAS 157, *Fair Value Measurements*, requires additional disclosures with respect to assets and liabilities measured at fair value on a nonrecurring basis. These additional disclosures are set forth in detail in Chapter 6 and in the Disclosure Checklist in Appendix A.

When FAS 157 was originally issued, it was to be effective for interim and annual financial statements issued for fiscal years beginning after November 15, 2007. Subsequent to its issuance, however, FASB received feedback that implementation difficulties were arising with respect to fair value measurements of nonfinancial assets and liabilities acquired or incurred in connection with business combinations. Further difficulties were reported with respect to determining impairment since these determinations often rely on inputs that are not observable in active markets.

In response to these concerns, FASB approved its Staff Position, FSP FAS 157-2, on February 12, 2008, which became effective on that date. The FSP deferred for one year the application of FAS 157 to nonfinanical assets and liabilities recognized or disclosed at fair value in an entity's financial statements on a nonrecurring basis.

It is important to note, however, that

1. The delay does not apply to entities that had already issued interim or annual financial statements that applied the FAS 157 measurement and disclosure provisions. These entities are required to continue applying all of the provisions of FAS 157.
2. Entities that avail themselves of the delay are required to make the following supplemental disclosures until FAS 157 is fully applied:

   a. The fact that management has only partially applied FAS 157, and
   b. Each major category of assets and liabilities recognized or disclosed at fair value for which management has not yet applied FAS 157.

**Example—initial measurement and recognition**

Gerald Corporation constructs and places into service on January 1, 2009, specialized machinery on premises that it leases under a fifteen-year lease. The machinery cost $1,750,000 and has an estimated useful life of ten years. Gerald Corporation is contractually obligated, under the terms of the lease, to remove the machinery from the premises when it is no longer functional. Gerald is unable to obtain current market-related information regarding the costs of settling the liability at inception and, therefore, chooses to estimate the initial fair value of the ARO using an expected present value technique. The significant assumptions used by Gerald in applying this technique are as follows:

1. Labor costs are based on prevailing wage rates in that geographic area that a contractor would pay to hire qualified workers. Gerald assigns probability assessments to the range of cash flow estimates as follows:

| Cash flow estimate | Probability assessment | Expected cash flows for labor costs |
|---|---|---|
| $40,000 | 25% | $10,000 |
| 60,000 | 50 | 30,000 |
| 75,000 | 25 | 18,750 |
| | 100% | $58,750 |

2. Based on its own experience, which Gerald believes is indicative of local market conditions, Gerald estimates that a contractor will apply a 75% rate to labor costs to charge for overhead and equipment usage and that, based on published industry statistics for the region, a contractor would add a markup of 8% to the combined labor, overhead, and equipment costs.
3. Since the eventual dismantlement and removal will be occurring ten years later, Gerald expects that a contractor would receive a market-risk premium of 5% of the expected cash flows adjusted for inflation. This premium is to compensate the contractor for assuming the risks and uncertainties of contracting now for a project ten years later.
4. The risk-free rate of interest as evidenced by the price of zero-coupon US Treasury instruments that mature in ten years is 4.5%. Gerald adjusts that rate by 2.5% to reflect the effect of its credit standing as evidenced by its incremental borrowing rate of 7%. Therefore, the credit-adjusted risk-free rate used to compute the expected present value is 7%.
5. Gerald assumes an average rate of inflation of 3.5% over the ten-year period.

The ARO is initially measured as follows as of January 1, 2009:

| | Expected cash flows as of January 1, 2009 |
|---|---|
| Expected cash flows for labor costs | $ 58,750 |
| Allocated overhead and equipment charges (75% × $58,750) | 44,063 |
| Contractor's markup [8% × ($58,750 + $44,063)] | 8,225 |
| Expected cash flows before inflation adjustment | 111,038 |
| Average annual compounded inflation rate of 3.5% for 10 years ($1.035^{10}$) | × 1.4106 |
| Expected cash flows adjusted for inflation | 156,630 |
| Market-risk premium (5% × $156,630) | 7,832 |
| Expected cash flows adjusted for market risk | 164,462 |
| Present value using credit-adjusted risk-free rate of 7% for 10 years, compounded annually | $ 83,604 |

On January 1, 2009, Gerald would record the initial ARO as follows:

| | | |
|---|---|---|
| Machinery and equipment | 83,604 | |
| ARO liability | | 83,604 |

**Example—accounting in subsequent periods**

Assuming the same facts as above, during the ten year life of the machinery, Gerald would record entries to recognize accretion and depreciation as follows (assuming no remeasurement of the ARO is required):

| Year | Liability balance as of January 1 | Annual accretion | Liability balance as of December 31 |
|------|----------------------------------|------------------|-------------------------------------|
| 2009 | $ 83,604 | $ 5,852 | $ 89,456 |
| 2010 | 89,456 | 6,262 | 95,718 |
| 2011 | 95,718 | 6,700 | 102,418 |
| 2012 | 102,418 | 7,169 | 109,587 |
| 2013 | 109,587 | 7,671 | 117,258 |
| 2014 | 117,258 | 8,208 | 125,466 |
| 2015 | 125,466 | 8,783 | 134,249 |
| 2016 | 134,249 | 9,397 | 143,646 |
| 2017 | 143,646 | 10,055 | 153,701 |
| 2018 | 153,701 | 10,761 | 164,462 |

### Entries to record annual accretion

The accretion for each year presented in the table is recorded as follows:

| | | |
|---|---|---|
| Accretion expense (presented on the income statement as part of operating expense) | xx,xxx | |
|     Asset retirement obligation | | xx,xxx |

### Depreciation computations

| | |
|---|---|
| Acquisition cost of asset | $ 1,750,000 |
| Capitalized ARO | 83,604 |
| Adjusted carrying amount of asset | $ 1,833,604 |
| Estimated salvage value (assumed) | 100,000 |
| | $ 1,733,604 |
| Estimated useful life | ÷ 10 years |
| Annual depreciation expense | $    173,360 |

### Entry to record annual depreciation

| | | |
|---|---|---|
| Depreciation expense | 173,360 | |
|     Accumulated depreciation | | 173,360 |

### Settlement of ARO

On December 31, 2018, Gerald uses its internal workforce to dismantle and dispose of the machinery and incurred costs as follows:

| | |
|---|---|
| Labor | $ 70,000 |
| Internally allocated overhead and equipment charges (75% of labor) | 52,500 |
| Total costs incurred | 122,500 |
| ARO liability | 164,462 |
| Gain on settlement of ARO | $   41,962 |

Note that, because Gerald chose to perform the retirement activities using its own workforce, the "market approach" mandated by FAS 143 and FAS 157 does not achieve an even matching of the total costs of acquisition and retirement to the periods benefited. The period of the retirement reflects a gain on settlement that would not have occurred had Gerald hired a contractor to perform the work instead of using its own employees.

***Electronic equipment waste obligations.*** The FASB staff has issued a position (FSP) on FAS 143 that prescribes the proper treatment of electronic equipment waste obligations (FSP FAS 143-1). This FSP addresses a directive issued by the European Union, under which the electronic equipment waste management obligation for products put on the market on or prior to August 13, 2005, resides with the commercial user until the equipment is replaced, at which time the waste management obligation may be shifted to the producer of the replacement equipment. If the user does not replace the equipment, then the obligation remains with the user. The waste obligation for electronic equipment acquired subsequent to August 13, 2005, shall be borne solely by the producers of the new electronic equipment.

The FSP states that a commercial user of electronic equipment acquired on or prior to August 13, 2005, must capitalize an asset retirement cost, as outlined in FAS 143, by increasing the carrying amount of the related asset by the same amount as the liability associated with the waste disposal obligation. If the asset is subsequently replaced, the obligation is shifted to the producer of the replacement equipment, so the user must calculate that portion of the payment to the replacement equipment producer relating to the transfer of the ARO, and eliminate the associated liability from its balance sheet, while recognizing a gain or loss based on the difference between the liability on the sale date and that portion of the payment related to the ARO. Meanwhile, the producer of the new asset recognizes revenue for the total amount of the sale, less the fair value of the ARO.

**Environmental remediation costs.** Environmental remediation costs, the costs of cleaning up environmental contamination, are generally expensed as incurred as operating expenses (SOP 96-1). The exceptions to this general rule that result in capitalizing these costs are as follows:

1. If the costs result from legal obligations associated with the eventual retirement of an asset or group of assets they will be capitalized as an asset retirement obligation (ARO) as discussed and illustrated in the previous section of this chapter (FAS 143).

2. If the costs do not qualify as ARO, but they meet one of the following criteria, they may be capitalized (EITF 89-13 and EITF 90-8) subject to reduction for impairment, if warranted:

    a. The costs extend the life, increase the capacity, or improve the safety or efficiency of property owned by the reporting entity.
    b. The costs mitigate or prevent future environmental contamination while also improving the property compared with its condition when originally constructed or acquired by the reporting entity.
    c. The cost of treating property acquired with a known asbestos problem is capitalized as part of the acquisition cost of the property if the costs are incurred within a reasonable time period after acquisition.
    d. The costs of treating an already owned property for asbestos are capitalized as a betterment.
    e. The costs are incurred in preparing for sale a property that is currently held for sale (the application of this criterion must be balanced with the limitation in FAS 144 regarding assets held for sale being carried at the lower of carrying value or, fair value less cost to sell).

With respect to c. and d. above, SEC registrants are required to disclose any significant exposure for asbestos treatment in the management discussion and analysis (MD&A).

Environmental costs associated with the improper operation or use of an asset (e.g., penalties and fines) are specifically excluded from the accounting guidance with respect to ARO and, should they be incurred, under SOP 96-1, they would most likely not qualify to be capitalized under GAAP.

**Nonmonetary transactions.** Several variants of noncash transactions are governed by APB 29 as amended by FAS 153.

*Scope.* The following types of transactions are not treated as nonmonetary transactions:

1. Exchanges of businesses required to be accounted for as business combinations under FAS 141(R) or its predecessor, FAS 141.

2. Transfers between reporting entities under common control such as between a parent company and its subsidiaries; between two subsidiaries of the same parent; or between a corporate joint venture and the venturers.

3. Issuance of equity in the reporting entity in exchange for nonmonetary assets or the performance of services (governed, instead, by the provisions of FAS 123[R]).
4. Stock dividends or stock splits.
5. Involuntary conversions where monetary proceeds are received for the nonmonetary assets stolen, seized, or destroyed, irrespective of whether the proceeds are reinvested in other nonmonetary assets.
6. Assets of the reporting entity exchanged for equity interests in another entity.
7. Certain types of transactions of oil and gas producing companies whose accounting is included in the scope of FAS 19, *Financial Accounting and Reporting by Oil and Gas Producing Companies.*
8. Transfers of financial assets within the scope of FAS 140, *Accounting for Transfers and Servicing of Financial Assets and Extinguishments of Liabilities.*

***Types of nonmonetary transactions.*** There are three types of nonmonetary transactions identified in APB 29.

1. *Nonreciprocal transfers to owners*—Examples include dividends-in-kind, nonmonetary assets exchanged for common stock, split-ups, and spin-offs.
2. *Nonreciprocal transfers with nonowners*—Examples include charitable donations of property either made or received by the reporting entity, and contributions of land by a state or local government to a private enterprise for the purpose of construction of a specified structure.
3. *Nonmonetary exchanges*—Examples include exchanges of inventory for productive assets, exchanges of inventory for similar products, and exchanges of productive assets.

***General rule.*** The primary accounting issue in nonmonetary transactions is the determination of the amount to assign to the nonmonetary assets transferred to or from the reporting entity.

The general rule is that the accounting for nonmonetary transactions is based on the fair values of the assets involved. The definition of fair value in APB 29 has been conformed to the uniform definition prescribed by FAS 157. FAS 157 appended guidance to APB 29 that provides that when one of the parties to a nonmonetary transaction could have elected to receive cash in lieu of the nonmonetary asset, the amount of cash that would have been received may be the best evidence of the fair value of the nonmonetary assets exchanged. FAS 157 left intact, however, the guidance in APB 29 that, in general, the fair value of the asset surrendered should be used to value the exchange unless the fair value of the asset received is more clearly evident of the fair value.

***Exceptions to the general rule.*** If either of the following conditions applies, the accounting for the nonmonetary transaction is based on the recorded amount (i.e., book value) of the nonmonetary asset relinquished, reduced, if applicable, by any preexchange impairment in its value.

1. If both the fair value of the asset being relinquished and the fair value of the asset being received are not reasonably determinable, the recorded amount (i.e., book value adjusted for any applicable impairment) of the asset being relinquished may be the only amount available to objectively measure the transaction. The fair value is not considered determinable within reasonable limits if there are major uncertainties with respect to the amount that would be realized for an asset.
2. An exchange of a product or property held for sale in the ordinary course of business for a product or property to be sold in the same line of business to facilitate sales to customers other than the parties to the exchange.

> *NOTE: FAS 153 eliminated what had been a commonly invoked exception set forth by APB 29, under which exchanges of productive assets not held for sale in the ordinary course of business were recognized at the book value of the asset(s) given up. FAS 153 replaced this with a more limited exception for transactions that lack commercial substance, as discussed below. FAS 153 also clarified that a transfer of a nonmonetary asset will not qualify as an exchange if the transferor has substantial continuing involvement in the transferred assets that results in the transferee not obtaining the usual risks and rewards associated with ownership of the transferred assets.*

**Nonreciprocal transfers.** The valuation of most nonreciprocal transfers is based upon the fair value of the nonmonetary asset given up, unless the fair value of the nonmonetary asset received is more clearly evident. This will result in recognition of gain or loss on the difference between the fair value assigned to the transaction and the carrying value of the asset surrendered.

The valuation of nonmonetary assets distributed to owners of the reporting entity in a spin-off or other form of reorganization or liquidation is based on the recorded amounts, again after first recognizing any warranted reduction for impairment. Other nonreciprocal transfers to owners are accounted for at fair value if (1) the fair value of the assets distributed is objectively measurable, and (2) that fair value would be clearly realized by the distributing reporting entity in an outright sale at or near the time of distribution to the owners.

### Example of accounting for a nonreciprocal transfer with a nonowner

1.  Jacobs Corporation donated depreciable property with a book value of $10,000 (cost of $25,000 less accumulated depreciation of $15,000) to a charity during the current year.
2.  The property had a fair value of $17,000 at the date of the transfer.

The transaction is valued at the fair value of the property transferred, and any gain or loss on the transaction is recognized on the date of the transfer. Thus, Jacobs recognizes a gain of $7,000 ($17,000 – $10,000) in the determination of the current period's net income. The entry to record the transaction would be as follows:

| | | |
|---|---|---|
| Charitable donations | 17,000 | |
| Accumulated depreciation | 15,000 | |
| Property | | 25,000 |
| Gain on donation of property | | 7,000 |

Note that the gain on disposition of the donated property is reported as operating income in accordance with FAS 146 and is not to be presented in the "other income" section of the income statement.

**Nonmonetary exchanges.** Prior to FAS 153, a distinction was made between nonmonetary exchanges involving dissimilar or similar assets, the accounting for which differed quite dramatically. For the most part, such a distinction is no longer critical, since FAS 153 mandates a universal fair value measurement strategy, with limited exceptions.

*Dissimilar assets.* If an exchange involves dissimilar assets, it is to be considered the culmination of the earnings process. The general rule is to value the transaction at the *fair value* of the asset given up, *unless the fair value of the asset received is more clearly evident,* and to recognize gain or loss on the difference between the fair value and carrying value of the asset. If cash is given in addition to the nonmonetary asset, that is referred to as "boot."

### Example of an exchange involving dissimilar assets and no boot

1.  Brian, Inc. exchanges a forklift with a book value of $2,500 (original cost of $4,800, less accumulated depreciation of $2,300 at the transaction date) with Emma & Co. for tooling with a fair value of $3,200.
2.  No boot is exchanged in the transaction.
3.  The fair value of the forklift is not readily determinable.

In this case, Brian, Inc. has a realized gain of $700 ($3,200 – $2,500) on the exchange, using the fair value of the asset received, since the value of the asset given up cannot be ascertained. Because the exchange involves dissimilar assets, the earnings process is deemed to have been culminated. The gain is included in the determination of Brian's net income and income from operations (i.e., it does not qualify for extraordinary treatment). The entry to record the transaction is as follows:

| | | |
|---|---|---|
| Tooling | 3,200 | |
| Accumulated depreciation—forklift | 2,300 | |
| Forklift | | 4,800 |
| Gain on exchange of forklift (operating income) | | 700 |

*Commercial substance.* A nonmonetary exchange is subjected to a test to determine whether or not it has "commercial substance." If determined to have commercial substance, the exchange is recorded at the fair value of the transferred asset. If the transaction is determined not to have commercial substance, the exchange is recognized using the recorded amount of the exchanged asset or assets, reduced for any applicable impairment of value.

To determine commercial substance, the reporting entity estimates whether, after the exchange, it will experience changes in (1) its expected cash flows because of changes in amounts, timing, and/or risks (these factors are collectively referred to as the "configuration" of the expected future cash flows), *or* (2) the entity-specific value of the assets received differs from the entity-specific value of the assets transferred. If the changes in either (1) or (2) are significant relative to the fair values of the assets exchanged, the transaction is considered to have commercial substance. *Entity-specific value* is a concept defined in CON 7 that substitutes assumptions that an entity makes with respect to its own future cash flows for the corresponding assumptions that marketplace participants would make with respect to cash flows. The commercial substance criterion is *not* met if a transaction is structured to achieve income tax benefits in order to achieve a specific outcome for financial reporting purposes.

**Example of an exchange involving similar assets and no boot**

Company presidents Able and Baker agree to swap copiers, since each needs certain printing features only available on the other company's copier. Able's copier has a book value of $18,000 (cost of $24,000 less depreciation of $6,000). Both copiers have a fair value of $24,000. In testing for the commercial substance of the transaction, there is no difference in the fair values of the assets exchanged, nor are Able's future cash flows expected to significantly change as a result of the transfer. Under FAS 153, exchanges of similar assets which do not alter expected future cash flows are deemed to lack commercial substance, and are accounted for at book value. As a result of the trade, Able has the following *unrecognized* gain:

| | |
|---|---|
| Fair value of Able copier given to Baker | $24,000 |
| Book value of Able copier to be given to Baker | 18,000 |
| Total gain (unrecognized) | $ 6,000 |

The entry by Able to record this transaction is as follows:

| | | |
|---|---|---|
| Fixed assets—Office equipment | 18,000 | |
| Accumulated depreciation—Office equipment | 6,000 | |
| Fixed assets—Office equipment | | 24,000 |

Able elects to depreciate its newly acquired copier over four years with an assumed salvage value of zero, which computes to monthly depreciation of $375. If Able had recorded the fair value of the incoming copier at $24,000, this would have required a higher monthly depreciation rate of $500. Thus, the unrecognized gain on the transaction is actually being recognized through ongoing reduced monthly depreciation charges.

Able immediately exchanges its newly-acquired copier for one owned by Charlie. However, the fair value of the copier owned by Charlie is $30,000, as compared to the $24,000 fair value of Able's copier (which is being carried at $18,000, the carryforward basis of its predecessor). In testing for the commercial substance of the transaction, there is determined to be a significant difference in the entity-specific values of the assets exchanged, so in accordance with the provisions of FAS 153 Able must record a gain on the transaction based on the difference in the fair values of the exchanged assets. This is done with the following entry:

| | | |
|---|---|---|
| Fixed assets—Office equipment | 30,000 | |
| Fixed assets—Office equipment | | 18,000 |
| Gain on disposal of office equipment | | 12,000 |

Note that the full gain from both exchanges is now being recognized, since the carryforward book value of the original copier was used as the book value of the first-acquired trade, and that carryforward amount is now being compared to the fair value of the latest trade.

Able elects to depreciate the newly acquired copier over four years with no salvage value, resulting in monthly depreciation of $625. After ten months, Able trades his newly acquired copier to Echo. The book value has now dropped to $23,750 (cost of $30,000 less depreciation of $6,250); however, due to technology advances, its fair value has declined to $20,000. This final trade has no commercial substance, in the FAS 153-defined sense, since cash flows will not materially vary as between the use of these two machines. While, under FAS 153, fair value accounting would not be employed in an exchange of similar assets lacking commercial substance, impairments must be recognized per FAS 144. Were this not done, the new asset would be recognized at an amount in excess of its realizable amount (fair value). Able has the following impairment loss resulting from the transaction, which must be fully recognized in the current period:

| | |
|---|---|
| Fair value of Able copier to be given to Echo | $20,000 |
| Book value of Able copier to be given to Echo | (23,750) |
| Total loss (recognized) | $ (3,750) |

The entry by Able to record this transaction is as follows:

| | | |
|---|---|---|
| Fixed assets—Office equipment | 20,000 | |
| Accumulated depreciation—Office equipment | 6,250 | |
| Loss on asset disposal | 3,750 | |
| Fixed assets—Office equipment | | 30,000 |

A single exception to the nonrecognition rule for similar assets occurs when the exchange involves both a monetary and nonmonetary asset being exchanged for a similar nonmonetary asset. The monetary portion of the exchange is termed *boot*. When boot is at least 25% of the fair value of the exchange, the exchange is considered a monetary transaction and both parties record the exchange at fair value. When boot less than 25% is received in an exchange, only the boot portion of the earnings process is considered to have culminated. The portion of the gain applicable to the boot is considered realized and is recognized in the determination of net income in the period of the exchange.

The formula for the recognition of the gain in an exchange involving boot of less than 25% of fair value is expressed as follows:

$$\frac{\text{Boot}}{\text{Boot} + \text{Fair value of nonmonetary asset received}} \times \text{Total gain indicated} = \text{Gain recognized}$$

**Example of an exchange involving similar assets and boot**

Amanda Excavating exchanges one of its underutilized front loaders with Dorothy Diggers, another excavator, for a bulldozer.

These assets are carried on the respective companies' balance sheets as follows:

| | Amanda *(front loader)* | Dorothy *(bulldozer)* |
|---|---|---|
| Cost | $75,000 | $90,000 |
| Accumulated depreciation | 7,500 | 15,000 |
| Net book value | $67,500 | $75,000 |
| Fair (appraised) value | $60,000 | $78,000 |

The terms of the exchange require Amanda to pay Dorothy $18,000 cash (boot). Boot represents approximately 23% of the fair value of the exchange computed as follows:

|  | Amount | Percent of total |
|---|---|---|
| Fair value of front loader | $60,000 | 77% |
| Cash consideration (boot) | 18,000 | 23% |
| Total consideration | $78,000 | 100% |

Note that as the payer of boot, Amanda does not recognize a gain. As a receiver of boot that is less than 25% of the fair value of the consideration received, Dorothy recognizes a pro rata gain that is computed as follows:

Total gain = $78,000 consideration – $75,000 net book value of bulldozer = $3,000

Portion of gain to be recognized by Dorothy

$$\frac{\$18,000 \text{ boot}}{\$18,000 \text{ boot} + \$60,000 \text{ fair value of}} = 23\% \times \$3,000 \text{ gain} = \$690 \text{ gain recognized}$$
nonmonetary asset received = $78,000

The accounting entries to record this transaction by Amanda and Dorothy are as follows:

|  | Amanda | | Dorothy | |
|---|---|---|---|---|
|  | Debit | Credit | Debit | Credit |
| Excavating equipment | 10,500 |  |  | 32,310 |
| Accum. depreciation—excavating equipment | 7,500 |  | 15,000 |  |
| Cash |  | $18,000 | 18,000 |  |
| Recognized gain | -- | -- | -- | 690 |
|  | 18,000 | $18,000 | 33,000 | 33,000 |

Amanda records the increase in the carrying value of its excavating equipment to account for the difference between the $78,000 fair value of the bulldozer received and the $67,500 carrying value of the front loader exchanged. The accumulated depreciation on the front loader is reversed since, from the standpoint of Amanda, it has no accumulated depreciation on the bulldozer at the date of the exchange.

Dorothy records the cash received, removes the previously recorded accumulated depreciation on the bulldozer, records the $690 gain attributable to the boot as computed above and records the difference as an adjustment to the carrying value of its excavating equipment.

After recording the entries above, the carrying values of the exchanged equipment would be as follows:

|  | Amanda (bulldozer) | Dorothy (front loader) |
|---|---|---|
| Net book value exchanged | $67,500 | $75,000 |
| Cash paid (received) | 18,000 | (18,000) |
| Gain recognized |  | $ 690 |
| Carrying value of asset received | $85,500 | $57,690 |

*Exchange of product or property held for sale for productive assets.* An exchange of goods held for sale in the ordinary course of business for property and equipment to be used in the production process, even if they pertain to the same line of business, is recorded at fair value.

*Exchanges involving monetary consideration (boot).* As noted above, if boot is 25% or more of the fair value of an exchange, the transaction is considered a monetary transaction. In that case, both parties record the transaction at fair value. If the boot is less than 25%, the payer of the boot does not recognize a gain and the receiver of the boot must follow the pro rata recognition guidance in APB 29, para. 22. See below for rules regarding exchanges with boot involving real estate.

Gain on a *monetary* exchange that involves transfer by one entity of its ownership of a controlled asset, group of assets, or business to another entity in exchange for a noncontrolling ownership interest in the other entity is accounted for consistent with the guidance above for similar *nonmonetary* exchanges.

*Exchanges of real estate involving monetary consideration (boot).* A transaction that involves the exchange of similar real estate and boot of 25% or more of the fair value of the exchange is recorded with two separate components, a monetary component and a nonmonetary component. The allocation is made based on the relative fair values of the monetary and nonmonetary portions at the time of the transaction. The party that receives the boot accounts for the monetary component of the transaction under FAS 66 as the equivalent of a sale of an interest in the underlying real estate and the nonmonetary component of the transaction based on the recorded amount (reduced, if applicable, for any impairment in value) of the nonmonetary asset relinquished. For the party that pays the boot, the monetary component is accounted for as an acquisition of real estate, and the nonmonetary component is accounted for based on the recorded amount (reduced, if applicable, for any impairment in value).

There had been some difficulty noted in practice in distinguishing exchanges of similar assets (and also simple acquisitions of productive assets not involving exchanges) from exchanges of businesses (and direct purchase of businesses). The rules governing accounting for exchanges or purchases of productive assets materially differ from acquisitions of businesses (e.g., goodwill would only be recognized in connection with the latter class of transaction, and under APB 29 certain nonmonetary exchanges are recorded at book value) and thus clarification was required.

EITF 98-3, as partially nullified by FAS 153, had addressed this issue, albeit in a relatively complex manner. It defined a business as a self-sustaining integrated set of activities and assets conducted and managed for the purpose of providing a return to investors. A business consists of (1) inputs, (2) processes applied to those inputs, and (3) resulting outputs that are used to generate revenues. Each of these criteria was further defined by EITF 98-3. For a transferred set of activities and assets to have been deemed a business, it must have contained essentially all of the inputs and processes necessary for it to continue to conduct normal operations after the transferred asset is separated from the transferor, which included the ability to sustain a revenue stream by providing its outputs to customers. If these criteria were not satisfied, the assets did not comprise a business and FAS 141 would not have applied to the acquisition.

FAS 141(R) was issued in December 2007. It superseded FAS 141 and fully nullified EITF 98-3. As discussed earlier in this chapter, FAS 141(R) simplified the definition of a business and clarified that an entity in its development stage that has not yet commenced its planned principal operations that otherwise meets the definition is considered to be a business. Development stage enterprises are discussed in greater detail in Chapter 3.

FAS 141(R), discussed in detail in Chapter 13, is to be applied prospectively to business combinations for which the acquisition date is on or after the beginning of the first annual reporting period beginning on or after December 15, 2008. Earlier application is not permitted.

*Barter transactions.* Through third-party barter exchanges, many commercial enterprises exchange their goods and services to obtain barter credits that can be used in lieu of cash to obtain goods and services of other members of the barter exchange.

EITF 93-11 specifies that APB 29 applies to barter transactions and that the basis for recording them is the fair value of the nonmonetary asset given up. Ordinarily, this fair value measurement should not be higher than its carrying value.

Impairment, if applicable, is to be recorded before the exchange. Thus, a new cost basis is established and a loss is recognized on the income statement. If an operating lease is involved, impairment is measured as the amount of remaining lease costs in excess of the fair value of the probable sublease rentals for the remaining lease term. FAS 157 provides guidance with respect to the determination of fair value.

The value of barter credits assigned to the transaction by the exchange are not used to measure fair value unless they can be converted to cash in the short term or there are independent existing market prices available for items to be received for the barter credits.

After the exchange, impairment is recorded if the carrying amount exceeds the fair value of the barter credits or if the business determines that the barter credits will expire unused.

***Involuntary conversions.*** An involuntary conversion results from the forced disposition of property due to casualty, theft, condemnation, or threat of condemnation. Upon involuntary conversion, the owner of the asset forfeits it and potentially receives proceeds from filing a property/casualty insurance claim or from condemnation awards.

Certain conditions may occur which necessitate the involuntary conversion of a nonmonetary asset into a monetary asset. FIN 30, *Accounting for Involuntary Conversions of Nonmonetary Assets to Monetary Assets,* specifies that involuntary conversions of nonmonetary assets to monetary assets are monetary transactions, and the resulting gain or loss is recognized in the period of conversion. It makes no difference that the monetary assets received are immediately reinvested in nonmonetary assets.

This rule does not apply to an interim period involuntary conversion of LIFO inventories that are intended to be replaced but have not yet been replaced by year-end (discussed in detail in Chapter 21).

***Deferred income taxes.*** A difference between the amount of gain or loss recognized for financial reporting purposes and that recognized for income tax purposes constitutes a temporary difference. The difference in the gain or loss recognized results in a difference between the income tax basis and the financial reporting basis of the asset received. The difference in the gain or loss reverses as a result of the annual charge to depreciation. The proper treatment of temporary differences is discussed in Chapter 17.

***Summary.*** In some situations, the fair value of the asset cannot be determined. If the fair value is not determinable, the book values of the assets involved are to be used as the valuation measure.

The situations involving the exchange of nonmonetary assets are summarized in the following diagram.

## Nonmonetary Transactions

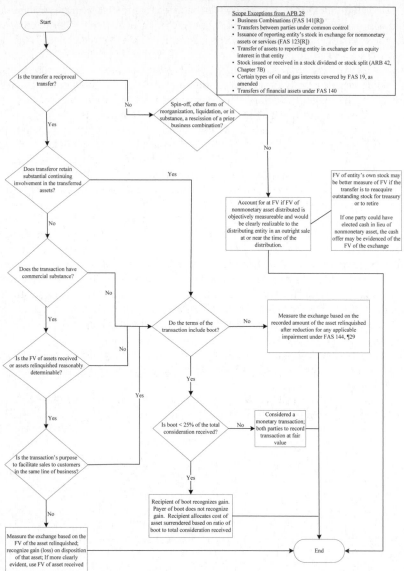

**Depreciation and depletion.** The costs of fixed assets are allocated to the periods they benefit through depreciation or depletion. The method of depreciation chosen is that which results in a systematic and rational allocation of the cost of the asset (less its residual or salvage value) over the asset's expected useful life. The estimation of useful life takes a number of factors into consideration, including technological change, normal deterioration, and actual physical usage. The method used is to be selected based on either a function of time (e.g., technological change or normal deterioration) or as a function of actual physical usage.

*Depreciation methods based on time.* Each of the examples below is based on the following facts:

Michele Corporation purchased a production machine and placed it in service on January 1, 2009. The machine cost $100,000, has an estimated salvage value of $10,000, and an estimated useful life of five years.

1. Straight-line method—Depreciation expense is recognized evenly over the estimated useful life of the asset.

   **Formula**

   a. Compute the straight-line depreciation rate as

   $$\frac{1}{\text{Estimated useful life}}$$

   b. Multiply the depreciation rate by the cost less estimated salvage value.

   **Example**

   a. Straight-line depreciation = $\frac{1}{5}$ = 20% per year

   b. 20% × ($100,000 – $10,000) = $18,000 annual depreciation

2. Accelerated methods—Depreciation expense is higher in the early years of the asset's useful life and lower in the later years. These methods are more appropriate than straight-line if the asset depreciates more quickly or has greater production capacity in the earlier years than it does as it ages. They are also sometimes used on the theory that maintenance and repair costs typically increase as assets age; therefore, in conjunction with accelerated depreciation total ownership costs (depreciation, maintenance and repairs) will approximate straight-line.

   a. Declining balance—Annual depreciation is computed by multiplying the book value at the beginning of the fiscal year by a multiple of the straight-line rate of depreciation as computed above.

      **Formula**

      Double-declining balance (ceases when the book value = the estimated salvage value)

      2 × Straight-line depreciation rate × Book value at the beginning of the year

      **Example**

| Year | Net book value, beginning of year | Double-declining balance depreciation computed as 2 × SL rate × beginning NBV | Net book value, end of year |
|------|------|------|------|
| 1 | $100,000 | $40,000 | $60,000 |
| 2 | 60,000 | 24,000 | 36,000 |
| 3 | 36,000 | 14,400 | 21,600 |
| 4 | 21,600 | 8,640 | 12,960 |
| 5 | 12,960 | 2,960 | 10,000 limited by salvage value |
| Total | | $90,000 | |

   b. Sum-of-the-years' digits (SYD) depreciation

      **Formula**

      (Cost – Estimated salvage value) × Applicable percentage

      $$\text{Applicable percentage} = \frac{\text{Number of years of estimated life remaining at the beginning of the year}}{\text{SYD}}$$

      $$\text{SYD} \quad \frac{n(n+1)}{2} \quad \text{where n = estimated useful life}$$

**Example**

$$SYD = \frac{5(5+1)}{2} = 15$$

This formula yields the sum of each year of the estimated useful life

$$1 + 2 + 3 + 4 + 5 = 15$$

| Year | Remaining estimated useful life at beginning of year | SYD | Applicable percentage | Annual depreciation |
|------|------------------------------------------------------|-----|-----------------------|---------------------|
| 1 | 5 | 15 | 33.33% | $30,000 |
| 2 | 4 | 15 | 26.67 | 24,000 |
| 3 | 3 | 15 | 20.00 | 18,000 |
| 4 | 2 | 15 | 13.33 | 12,000 |
| 5 | 1 | 15 | 6.67 | 6,000 |
| Totals | | | 100.00% | $90,000 |

3. Present value methods—Depreciation expense is lower in the early years and higher in the later years. The rate of return on the investment remains constant over the life of the asset. Time value of money formulas are used.

   a. Sinking fund—Uses the future value of an annuity formula.
   b. Annuity fund—Uses the present value of an annuity formula.

**Partial-year depreciation.** When an asset is either acquired or disposed of during the year, the full-year depreciation calculation is prorated between the accounting periods involved.

### Example of partial-year depreciation

Ginger Corporation, a calendar-year entity, acquired a machine on June 1, 2009, which cost $40,000 with an estimated useful life of four years and a $2,500 salvage value. The depreciation expense for each full year of the asset's life is calculated as

| | Straight-line | Double-declining balance | | | | Sum-of-years' digits | | |
|--------|------------------|--------------------------|-----------|---------|------|----------------------|---------|----------|
| Year 1 | 37,500* ÷ 4 = 9,375 | 50% × | 40,000 = | 20,000 | 4/10 | × 37,500* | = | 15,000 |
| Year 2 | 9,375 | 50% × | 20,000 = | 10,000 | 3/10 | × 37,500 | = | 11,250 |
| Year 3 | 9,375 | 50% × | 10,000 = | 5,000 | 2/10 | × 37,500 | = | 7,500 |
| Year 4 | 9,375 | 50% × | 5,000 = | 2,500 | 1/10 | × 37,500 | = | 3,750 |
| | 37,500 | | | 37,500 | | | | 37,500 |

*  *(40,000 – 2,500)*

Because the first full year of the asset's life does not coincide with the company's fiscal year, the amounts shown above must be prorated as follows:

| | Straight-line | Double-declining balance | | | | Sum-of-years' digits | | |
|------|---------------------------|--------------------------|-----------|---------|------|----------------------|---------|----------|
| 2009 | 7/12 × 9,375 = 5,469 | 7/12 × | 20,000 = | 11,677 | 7/12 | × 15,000 | = | 8,750 |
| 2010 | 9,375 | 5/12 × | 20,000 = | 8,333 | 5/12 | × 15,000 | = | 6,250 |
| | | 7/12 × | 10,000 = | 5,833 | 7/12 | × 11,250 | = | 6,563 |
| | | | | 14,166 | | | | 12,813 |
| 2011 | 9,375 | 5/12 × | 10,000 = | 4,167 | 5/12 | × 11,250 | = | 4,687 |
| | | 7/12 × | 5,000 = | 2,917 | 7/12 | × 7,500 | | 4,375 |
| | | | | 7,084 | | | | 9,062 |
| 2012 | 9,375 | 5/12 × | 5,000 = | 2,083 | 5/12 | × 7,500 | = | 3,125 |
| | | 7/12 × | 2,500 = | 1,458 | 7/12 | × 3,750 | = | 2,188 |
| | | | | 3,541 | | | | 5,313 |
| 2013 | 5/12 × 9,375 = 3,096 | 5/12 × | 2,500 = | 1,042 | 5/12 | × 3,750 | = | 1,562 |
| | 37,500 | | | 37,500 | | | | 37,500 |

As an alternative to proration, an entity may follow any one of several simplified conventions.

1. Record a full year's depreciation in the year of acquisition and none in the year of disposal.
2. Record one-half year's depreciation in the year of acquisition and one-half year's depreciation in the year of disposal.

***Depreciation method based on actual physical usage—Units of production.*** Depreciation is based upon the number of units produced by the asset in a given year.

$$\text{Depreciation rate} = \frac{\text{Cost less salvage value}}{\substack{\text{Estimated number of units to} \\ \text{be produced by the asset over} \\ \text{its estimated useful life}}}$$

$$\substack{\text{Units of production} \\ \text{depreciation}} = \text{Depreciation rate} \times \substack{\text{Number of units produced} \\ \text{during the current year}}$$

***Other depreciation methods.*** In addition to the foregoing, a group (composite) method is sometimes used. This method averages the service lives of a number of assets using a weighted-average of the units and depreciates the group or composite as if it were a single unit. A group consists of similar assets, while a composite is made up of dissimilar assets.

$$\text{Depreciation rate} = \frac{\substack{\text{Sum of the straight-line} \\ \text{depreciation of individual assets}}}{\text{Total asset cost}}$$

Depreciation expense: Depreciation rate × Total group (composite) cost

Gains and losses are not recognized on the disposal of an asset but are netted into accumulated depreciation.

***Depletion.*** Depletion is the annual charge for the use of natural resources. The depletion base includes all development costs such as exploring, drilling, excavating, and other preparatory costs. The amount of the depletion base charged to periodic income is determined by the following formula:

$$\frac{1}{\text{Total expected recoverable units}} \times \text{Depletion base} \times \text{Units sold}$$

The unit depletion rate is revised frequently due to the uncertainties surrounding the recovery of natural resources. The revision is made prospectively; the remaining undepleted cost is allocated over the remaining expected recoverable units.

**Example of depletion**

The Cheyenne Oil Company drills a well in the Denver Basin oil field. It incurs the following development costs to do so:

| | |
|---|---:|
| Land acquisition | $172,000 |
| Land preparation (road and drill pad) | 38,000 |
| Well drilling | 301,000 |
| Trunk line construction | 29,000 |
| Estimated site restoration cost | 50,000 |
| Total | $590,000 |

A considerable amount of extraction equipment is also positioned at the well, but since it can be moved among well sites and is therefore not a fixed part of this well, it is depreciated separately.

The entire $590,000 is capitalized. Cheyenne's geologists calculate that the well has proven reserves of 250,000 barrels of crude oil. In the first year of production, the well produces 45,000 barrels of oil. The depletion charge for the first year of operation follows:

$$\frac{1}{250{,}000 \text{ barrels of proven reserves}} \times \$590{,}000 \times 45{,}000 \text{ barrels produced}$$

$$= \$106{,}200, \text{ which is the depletion charge of } \$2.36 \text{ per barrel extracted}$$

During the second year of the well's operation, Cheyenne's engineers revise the remaining number of proven reserves upward by 20,000 barrels, based on improved oil recovery techniques. Also, due to new environmental laws, the estimated site restoration cost increases by $10,000, increasing the depletion base to $600,000. Total production for the second year is 62,000 barrels of oil. The depletion charge for the first year is not retroactively changed, but changes in cost and estimated total production are rather accounted for prospectively. The depletion calculation for the second year follows:

$$\frac{1}{225{,}000 \text{ barrels of proven reserves remaining}} \times \$493{,}800 \times 62{,}000 \text{ barrels produced}$$

$$= \$136{,}069, \text{ which is the depletion charge of } \$2.19 \text{ per barrel extracted}$$

These depletion expenses leave $357,731 of capitalized costs yet to be amortized over remaining proven reserves of 163,000 barrels, representing a future depletion charge of $2.19 per barrel.

**Income tax methods.** Income tax deductions for depreciation, including accelerated deductions under Section 179 are not in accordance with generally accepted accounting principles because, in general, they are not based on estimated useful lives and do not allocate cost to future periods benefited on a systematic and rational basis. Therefore, differences between financial statement and income tax depreciation result in temporary differences between the carrying values of the long-lived assets for income tax and financial reporting purposes. These temporary differences are taken into account in the calculation of deferred income taxes, as discussed in Chapter 17.

*Pre-1981 depreciation.* Assets placed in service prior to 1981 are depreciated based on the asset's useful life and cannot be depreciated below their salvage value. The depreciation method used depends upon the type of property and whether it was new or used when it was placed in service.

*Accelerated Cost Recovery System.* Assets placed in service between 1981 and 1986 are depreciated under the Accelerated Cost Recovery System (ACRS). ACRS ignores salvage value. Thus, the asset's entire income tax basis is depreciable over the specified recovery period to be used for each class of asset. Property is placed into classes and the depreciation method and life for each class is specified. Election of optional depreciation methods was also permitted. Depreciation deductions are calculated by multiplying the asset's unadjusted basis by the specified depreciation percentage for the related time period. The depreciation percentage will depend upon the asset's class, recovery year, depreciation method and convention.

*Modified Accelerated Cost Recovery System.* For assets placed in service after 1986, income tax depreciation is calculated using the Modified Accelerated Cost Recovery System (MACRS) which also ignores salvage value and divides assets into classes. Depreciation deductions are calculated by multiplying the asset's unadjusted basis by the appropriate depreciation percentage. The percentages are based on the type of property, class life, depreciation method, and convention. Depreciation deductions are limited for certain assets such as listed property (primarily automobiles). Optional depreciation methods may also be elected.

*Additional deductions available in year placed in service.* In order to provide incentives to businesses to invest in long-lived, tangible assets, the Internal Revenue Code (IRC) includes provisions that provide for aggressive deductibility of their costs in the year of acquisition. These deductions are taken prior to computing depreciation as described above and, of course, the amount of the deductions reduces the depreciable basis of the affected assets.

Internal Revenue Code Section 179 allows taxpayers to deduct, in the tax year placed in service, up to $128,000 of costs of qualified acquisitions for tax years beginning in 2008. Absent future legislative adjustments, this amount will be increased by an inflation adjustment in the years 2009-2010 and then reverts to a maximum annual deduction of $25,000 for tax years beginning in 2011 and thereafter without adjustment for inflation. The availability of this benefit begins phasing out, dollar-for-dollar, for companies acquiring more than $510,000 of qualified property during tax years beginning in 2008. This phase-out is also inflation adjusted for 2009-2010, after which it is scheduled to revert to a non-inflation-adjusted annual limitation of $200,000 in 2011.

Income tax depreciation will differ in amount from financial statement depreciation because of differences in treatment of salvage value, recovery methods, recovery periods, and the use of conventions for assets placed in service during the year.

The difference between income tax depreciation and financial statement depreciation is reported as a reconciling item (referred to as a "Schedule M-1 adjustment") on a corporation's US federal income tax return.

**Impairment and disposal.** FAS 144, *Accounting for the Impairment or Disposal of Long-Lived Assets,* applies to long-lived assets of businesses and not-for-profit organizations. Long-lived assets include assets to be held or used, or to be disposed of.

The GAAP rules for measuring and recording impairment of assets are not uniform for all assets or for all specialized industries. The table below distinguishes between those assets subject to the general impairment standard and those for which different, specialized rules apply.

### Subject to General Impairment Standard (FAS 144)

Assets associated with discontinued operations
Cable television plant
Capitalized interest costs
Capitalized motion picture film costs
Development stage enterprises' assets
Financial institutions' depositor-relationship, borrower-relationship, and credit cardholder intangibles (These intangibles had been subject to specialized impairment standards prior to the issuance of FAS 147 in 2002)
Real estate
Software developed or obtained for internal use
Title plant costs of title insurance and title abstract companies, and title agents
Web site development costs

### Subject to Specialized Impairment Standard(s)

Broadcasters' program rights
Computer software to be sold, leased, or otherwise marketed
Deferred income tax assets
Equity method or cost-method investments
Financial institutions' servicing assets
Financial instruments
Goodwill
Intangible assets of motor carriers
Loans receivable
Mortgage servicing rights
Recording masters in the recorded music industry

**Split between General and Specialized Impairment Standards**

| *Subject to general impairment standard* | *Subject to specialized impairment standard* |
| --- | --- |
| Public utilities and certain other regulated enterprises | Abandoned plants and disallowed plant costs of regulated enterprises |
| Intangibles that are amortized | Intangibles that are not amortized |
| Lessee capital leases | Lessor direct financing, sales-type, and leveraged leases |
| Lessor assets subject to operating leases | |
| Proved properties and wells of oil and gas producing companies with related facilities and equipment that are accounted for using the successful efforts method of accounting | Unproved properties of oil and gas producing companies |
| All insurance assets except deferred insurance policy acquisition costs | Deferred insurance policy acquisition costs |

***Impairment of long-lived assets to be held and used.*** *Impairment* is the condition that exists when the carrying amount of a long-lived asset (or asset group, as defined in the statement) exceeds its fair value. Impairment losses are only recognized when the carrying amount of the impaired asset (or asset group) is not recoverable. Recoverability is determined by comparing the carrying amount of the asset (or asset group) on the date it is being evaluated for recoverability to the sum of the *undiscounted* cash flows expected to result from its use and eventual disposition. It is important to note that under FAS 144, an asset's carrying value can exceed its fair value (thus technically it could be considered to be impaired) and yet, if the carrying value is recoverable from expected future cash flows from its use and disposition, as defined, no impairment loss is recognized.

FAS 144 uses "events and circumstances" criteria to determine when, if at all, an asset (or asset group) is evaluated for recoverability. Thus, there is no set interval or frequency for recoverability evaluation, unlike the annual requirement for testing goodwill for impairment. FAS 144 provides a list of examples of events or changes in circumstances that indicate the carrying amount of an asset (asset group) *may* not be recoverable and thus is to be evaluated for recoverability.

1. A significant decrease in the market price of a long-lived asset (asset group)
2. A significant adverse change in the extent or manner in which a long-lived asset (asset group) is being used or in its physical condition
3. A significant adverse change in legal factors or in the business climate that could affect the value of a long-lived asset (asset group), including an adverse action or assessment by a regulator
4. An accumulation of costs significantly in excess of the amount originally expected for the acquisition or construction of a long-lived asset (asset group)
5. A current period operating or cash flow loss combined with a history of operating or cash flow losses or a projection or forecast that demonstrates continuing losses associated with the use of a long-lived asset (asset group)
6. A current expectation that, more likely than not, a long-lived asset (asset group) will be sold or otherwise disposed of significantly before the end of its previously estimated useful life

The list of events and circumstances above is not intended to be all-inclusive. Rather, it is intended to provide examples of situations that warrant evaluation of an asset or group of assets for recoverability to determine whether an impairment loss must be recognized. Financial statement preparers are required to consider, for each interim and annual reporting period, the applicability of these indicators or others that might be applicable in the circumstances. Reliance should not be placed on "disclosure checklists" for this purpose as they are not designed to be used to determine the correct application of GAAP recognition and measurement requirements.

Under FAS 144, if the carrying amount of an asset or asset group (in use or under development) is evaluated and found not to be recoverable (carrying amount exceeds the gross, undiscounted cash flows from use and disposition), then an impairment loss must be recognized. The impairment loss is measured as the excess of the carrying amount over the asset's (or asset group's) fair value.

Fair value (as defined by FAS 157)[2] is the price that the reporting entity would receive to sell the asset on the measurement date in an orderly transaction between market participants in the principal (or most advantageous) market for the asset. In order to measure fair value, management must determine the asset's (or group of assets') highest and best use which may not coincide with the manner that the reporting entity is currently using it. Fair value measurements are discussed and illustrated in detail in Chapter 6.

In conjunction with the recoverability evaluation, it may also be necessary to review the appropriateness of the method of depreciation (amortization) and depreciable (amortizable) lives of the asset or group of assets. If, as a result of that review the remaining useful life of the asset (group) is revised, the revised useful life is used to develop the cash flow estimates used to evaluate recoverability. Changes to the accounting method (e.g., from straight-line to accelerated depreciation), however, would be made prospectively after the application of FAS 144.

FAS 144 introduced the concept of the *asset group*, defined as the lowest level for which identifiable cash flows are largely independent of the cash flows of other assets and liabilities.

An asset group could be

- The whole company
- An operating segment as defined by FAS 131
- A reporting unit as defined by FAS 142
- A business
- A part of a business (such as a division or department)

By reference to asset groups shown in the diagram in the section of Chapter 2 under the caption *Alternative Balance Sheet Segmentation*

- Asset group (a) is a single division of a subsidiary
- Asset groups (b) and (c) are each separate businesses that comprise another division of the same subsidiary
- Asset group (d) is an entire subsidiary consisting of a single business
- Asset group (e) is a product line that is part of a larger business and, after the disposal of disposal group (f), will constitute an entire operating segment
- Asset groups (g) and (h) are each separate businesses that comprise a subsidiary

If a long-lived asset cannot be assigned to any asset group because it does not have identifiable cash flows largely independent of other long-lived assets individually or in asset groups (such as a corporate headquarters), then that asset is evaluated for recoverability by reference to all assets and liabilities of the entity.

---

[2] *FSP FAS 157-2 provided a limited deferral of the effective date of FAS 157 to fiscal years beginning after November 15, 2008, and interim periods within those fiscal years. The deferral applies to nonfinanical assets and liabilities, except for those items recognized or disclosed at fair value in an entity's statements on a recurring basis (at least annually).*

The assets and liabilities in the group that are neither long-lived assets nor goodwill are separately identified. Since those assets and liabilities are not subject to the provisions of FAS 144, the GAAP applicable to their valuation is applied *before* applying FAS 144 to the group. For example, allowances for uncollectible accounts receivable and inventory obsolescence are recorded as necessary.

In assessing the composition of asset groups, there must be awareness of the interrelationship between FAS 144 and FAS 142, *Goodwill and Other Intangible Assets*. Goodwill can only be assigned to an asset group that is being evaluated for recoverability if the asset group is either a reporting unit or includes a reporting unit.

For the purposes of recoverability evaluation, future cash flows are defined as cash inflows less the associated cash outflows directly associated with and that are expected to arise as a direct result of the use and eventual disposition of the asset group excluding interest that is recognized as a period expense when incurred.

The estimate of future cash flows

- Is based on all available evidence
- Incorporates assumptions that marketplace participants would use in their estimates of fair value when that information is available without undue cost or effort; otherwise, the entity incorporates its own assumptions, including the "highest and best use" of the asset (or group)
- Is to be consistent with assumptions used by the entity for comparable periods such as internal budgets and projections, accruals related to incentive compensation plans, or information communicated to others
- Is made for the remaining estimated useful life of the asset (or the primary asset of an asset group) to the entity

  NOTE: *The primary asset is the long-lived asset being depreciated (or intangible asset being amortized) that is the most significant component asset from which the group derives its cash-flow generating capacity. The primary asset cannot be land or nonamortized intangible assets. If the primary asset does not have the longest useful life of the long-lived assets in the group, cash flow estimates must assume that the entire group will be sold at the end of the primary asset's useful life.*

- Takes into account future expenditures necessary to complete an asset under development including interest capitalized under FAS 34
- Includes future outflows necessary to maintain the existing service potential of all or a component of the asset or group of assets
- Excludes cash flows for future capital expenditures that increase the service potential of a long-lived asset or group of assets
- Is required to take into account the likelihood of possible cash flow outcomes if alternative courses of action are being contemplated, or if ranges of cash flows are estimated to occur under different scenarios

  NOTE: *FAS 144, as issued, stopped short of requiring the expected present value method set forth in CON 7. Subsequently, upon the issuance of FAS 157 in 2006, FAS 144 was amended to indicate that, when uncertainties exist with respect to timing and amount of future cash flows, using an expected present value technique will be the appropriate way to estimate fair value. Pursuant to FSP FAS 157-2, nonfinancial assets measured at fair value on a nonrecurring basis will be subject to FAS 157 in fiscal years beginning after November 15, 2008, and interim periods within those fiscal years.*

If an asset group is found to have sustained an impairment loss, the loss is only applied to reduce the carrying amounts of the long-lived asset or assets in the group. In general, the loss is allocated to the long-lived assets in the group based on their relative carrying values.

However, the carrying value of any individual asset in the group that has a fair value that is separately identifiable without "undue cost or effort" is not to be reduced below that fair value.

After recognition of impairment losses, the adjusted carrying amounts of the impaired long-lived assets constitute their new cost bases. Depreciation (amortization) is recognized prospectively over their remaining estimated useful lives. The adjustment to carrying values to reflect an impairment loss may never be restored.

**Example of impairment** (Refer to the diagram in Chapter 2 under the section, *Alternative Balance Sheet Segmentation.*)

The Parent Holding Company (PHC) owns and operates seven businesses, primarily engaged in the manufacturing and distribution of food and beverages. All of the businesses are headquartered in the same building that is owned by PHC. Additional facts are as follows:

- Due to general economic conditions and the failure, in 2009, of several high-tech startups in the city in which PHC is headquartered, the local commercial real estate market is depressed. PHC's headquarters building has eight years remaining in its expected useful life and its carrying value is $4,500,000. PHC has substantial excess space in the building, which it does not expect to need in the foreseeable future. PHC management expects the real estate market to remain depressed for the next two years and when the market recovers, it will consider selling the building and either leasing or purchasing a smaller facility in the area.

- Subsidiary 2 operates a South American bottling plant that produces a line of carbonated beverages that is sold exclusively on that continent. A large increase in sugar prices during 2009 has resulted in lower margins and, due to partial price increases, a 30% decrease in units sold during the year. The plant operates in a building that Subsidiary 2 leases under an operating lease with five years remaining. The primary asset owned by Subsidiary 2 is what it refers to as its "bottling line" which consists of equipment that mixes ingredients, adds carbon dioxide, and fills and caps the bottles. The bottling line has a remaining useful life of four years. The other assets in the asset group have remaining useful lives of seven years. Subsidiary 2 has been profitable for the past three years (2006 – 2008) but is showing a small operating loss for 2009. Additional information regarding Subsidiary 2 follows:

| | Bottling line (primary asset) | Asset B | Asset C | Totals |
|---|---|---|---|---|
| Net book value | $87,000 | $19,000 | $17,000 | $123,000 |
| Remaining life | 4 years | 7 years | 7 years | |
| Expected cash inflows, net of outflows | | | | |
| 2010 | | | | 4,000 |
| 2011 | | | | 6,000 |
| 2012 | | | | 7,000 |
| 2013 | | | | 8,000 |
| From assumed disposition—end of 2013 | | | | 75,000 |
| Total expected net operating cash flows | | | | $100,000 |

- PHC is in the process of preparing its consolidated financial statements for the year ended December 31, 2009. Thus far, normal depreciation of PHC and its subsidiaries' fixed assets has been recorded and impairment has not yet been considered.

*Analysis.*

Step 1—*Identify asset groups.* This has been diagrammed in the exhibit in Chapter 2. Note that the headquarters building cannot be assigned to any specific asset group since it does not generate independent cash flows. Therefore, its potential impairment is assessed at the PHC level on a consolidated basis.

Step 2—*Consider the applicability of impairment indicators.* Assess each of PHC's asset groups (and on a consolidated basis), as to whether the example events and circumstances provided by FAS 144 or any other events and circumstances indicate that

PHC's long-lived assets may be impaired. Based on the decline in the local real estate market, it would be presumed that the market price of the headquarters building has declined, and thus the building should be evaluated for recoverability. Analysis of the situation of Subsidiary 2 is more complex. Two of the factors in FAS 144 warrant consideration. First, it could be argued that the increase in sugar prices constitutes a significant adverse change in the business climate. This might be mitigated if management believed the price increase to be a short-term condition and assuming this belief was supportable by past experience. Second, the current period operating loss should be considered. Since there has not been a history of such losses, the relevance of this factor depends on management's forecast of future results. If Subsidiary 2 were forecast to continue to experience operating losses, this would indicate that the asset group needs to be evaluated for recoverability. For the purposes of this example, we will assume that continuing losses are forecast.

Step 3—*Evaluate recoverability.* Two recoverability evaluations are required, one for the headquarters building and the other for the asset group represented by Subsidiary 2. Since the headquarters building is not allocable to an asset group, its recoverability is evaluated using consolidated cash flows that include the cash flows of Subsidiary 2. Thus, the recoverability evaluation for Subsidiary 2 is performed first.

Subsidiary 2's recoverability evaluation is performed by reference to the four-year remaining useful life of the bottling line, its primary asset. The cash flows used to evaluate recoverability are required to assume that the asset group will be sold in its entirety at the end of four years.

Comparison of the sum of the undiscounted expected cash flows from use and disposition of $100,000 to the carrying amount of $123,000 indicates that the carrying amount of the asset group will not be fully recoverable. Therefore, the asset group is impaired.

The recoverability evaluation for the building is performed using an estimate of expected cash flows, weighted for the probabilities as to whether management will pursue the sale of the facility when the local economy recovers in two years, versus retaining it for the remaining eight years of its expected useful life. In addition, depending on different scenarios of future economic conditions and business performance by PHC's businesses, different levels of cash flows could result both from operations and from disposition. Acknowledging the inherent uncertainties associated with predicting future results and the subjectivity involved in the estimation process, management formulated its best judgment regarding the probabilities of the best, worst, and most-likely scenarios.

### Estimate of Future Cash Flows

| Course of action | Use of the asset (consolidated basis) | Disposition of the asset | Total | Probability assessment | Probability-weighted possible cash flows |
|---|---|---|---|---|---|
| Sale at the end of 2 years | $100,000 | $3,500,000 | $3,600,000 | 20% | $720,000 |
| | 130,000 | 4,600,000 | 4,730,000 | 60% | 2,838,000 |
| | 150,000 | 4,600,000 | 4,750,000 | 20% | 950,000 |
| | | | | 100% | $4,508,000 |
| Sale at the end of 8 years | $410,000 | $4,000,000 | $4,410,000 | 20% | $882,000 |
| | 550,000 | 4,700,000 | 5,250,000 | 60% | 3,150,000 |
| | 620,000 | 4,800,000 | 5,420,000 | 20% | 1,084,000 |
| | | | | 100% | $5,116,000 |

Upon review of the analysis above, management determined that it is 70% probable that it will sell the building at the end of two years. Consequently, the expected cash flows from the use and disposition of the building are as follows:

| Course of action | Probability-weighted possible cash flows | Probability assessment for course of action | Undiscounted expected cash flows |
|---|---|---|---|
| Sale at the end of 2 years | $4,508,000 | 70% | $3,155,600 |
| Sale at the end of 8 years | 5,116,000 | 30% | 1,534,800 |
| | | 100% | $4,690,400 |

Comparison of the undiscounted expected cash flows or $4,690,400 per above to the $4,500,000 carrying value of the building at December 31, 2009, indicates that the carrying value of the building is expected to be fully recoverable, and thus the building is not impaired.

As a result of the above analysis, management may decide upon one of the alternative courses of action. If so, the expected cash flows from that course of action would be used in the recoverability evaluation since it would no longer be necessary to probability-weight the outcomes.

Step 4—*Compute impairment, if any.* Market information regarding the asset group of Subsidiary 2 is not available "without undue cost and effort." Management elects to use the traditional present value of estimated cash flows method to estimate fair value because it believes that uncertainty regarding the timing and amounts of cash flows is minimal (but, if this were not the case, management would use an *expected present value* technique to make this estimate). This estimation method is referred to in FAS 157 as a *discount rate adjustment* technique. Using this technique requires

- A single set of most-likely cash flows that includes assumptions regarding the likelihood of occurrence or nonoccurrence of events that potentially influence the estimated amounts
- A discount rate approximating a market rate of return based on observable rates of return for comparable assets traded in the same market as the asset or group of assets being measured

The 8% interest rate used for this illustration is assumed to be a rate commensurate with the risks involved (unlike the risk-free rate sometimes used in applying an expected present value technique). The computation is as follows:

| Year | Net cash flows | Present value at 8% | Carrying value of asset group | Impairment adjustment required |
|---|---|---|---|---|
| 2010 | $ 4,000 | $ 3,704 | | |
| 2011 | 6,000 | 5,144 | | |
| 2012 | 7,000 | 5,557 | | |
| 2013–Use | 8,000 | 5,880 | | |
| 2013–Sale | 75,000 | 55,127 | | |
| | $100,000 | $75,412 | $123,000 | $47,588 |

| Asset | Carrying value | Pro rata allocation factor | Allocation of impairment loss | Tentative adjusted carrying amount |
|---|---|---|---|---|
| Bottling line | $ 87,000 | 71% | $33,660 | $53,340 |
| Asset B | 19,000 | 15% | 7,351 | 11,649 |
| Asset C | 17,000 | 14% | 6,577 | 10,423 |
| Total | $123,000 | 100% | $47,588 | $75,412 |

Note that the adjusted carrying amount is captioned "tentative." This is because Subsidiary 2 was able to obtain a quoted market price of $16,000 for Asset B. FAS 144 specifies that assets are not to be reduced to an amount below their fair value. To obtain the proper result, the impairment loss requires reallocation among the assets comprising the asset group.

| Asset | Tentative adjusted carrying amount | Pro rata reallocation factor | Reallocation of excess impairment loss | Adjusted carrying amount |
|---|---|---|---|---|
| Bottling line | $53,340 | 84% | $(3,640) | $49,700 |
| Asset C | 10,423 | 16% | (711) | 9,712 |
| Subtotal | 63,763 | 100% | (4,351) | |
| Asset B | 11,649 | | 4,351 | 16,000 |
| Total | $75,412 | | $ -- | $75,412 |

Step 5—*Record the impairment adjustment.* The entry to record impairment in the accounting records of Subsidiary 2 is as follows:

| | | |
|---|---|---|
| Impairment loss (operating section of income statement) | 47,588 | |
| Accumulated depreciation—Machinery and equipment | | 47,588 |

*To adjust the carrying value of the bottling line and related assets to reflect an impairment loss for 2009.*

**Other impairment considerations.** Besides the foregoing, other issues arise as a consequence of applying the impairment rules.

*Going concern.* The example above included an estimate of cash flows at the entity level to assess whether the building was impaired. If the estimate had indicated that the building was impaired, management must consider whether the cash flows estimated for at least the ensuing year will be sufficient for the entity to continue as a going concern. Disclosure in the financial statements of management's plans may be required under SAS 59, *The Auditor's Consideration of an Entity's Ability to Continue as a Going Concern.* In connection with the FASB's initiative to codify all authoritative GAAP in a single searchable database (the "codification"), going concern and liquidation basis disclosures are expected to be migrated from the auditing literature to the codification in April 2009.

*Significant estimates.* If, in the example above, the expected cash flows used to assess the recoverability of the building were closer to the building's $4,500,000 carrying value, consideration is given to the applicability of SOP 94-6, *Disclosure of Certain Significant Risks and Uncertainties.* The assumptions used in the cash flow estimates could be considered, under that SOP, significant estimates for which it is reasonably possible changes could occur in the near term (the ensuing year) and, consequently, disclosure would be required.

*Treatment of certain site restoration/environmental exit costs.* EITF 95-23 discusses how, for the purpose of performing the recoverability evaluation under FAS 144, to treat the costs of future site restoration or closure (referred to as "environmental exit costs") that may be incurred if the asset is sold, abandoned, or ceases operations. To conform to FAS 144, references to an "asset" are also applicable to an "asset group."

FAS 143, discussed earlier in this chapter, requires asset retirement obligations recognized as liabilities to be included as part of the capitalized cost of the related asset and, to avoid double-counting, the cash settlement of those liabilities to be excluded from the expected future cash flows used to evaluate recoverability under FAS 144. If the asset retirement costs have not yet been recognized under FAS 143 because the obligation is being incurred over more than one reporting period during the useful life of the asset, then the cash flows for those unrecognized costs are to be included in the expected future cash flows.

The cash flows for environmental exit costs that are not recorded as liabilities under SOP 96-1, *Environmental Remediation Liabilities,* may not occur until the end of the asset's life if the asset ceases to be used or may be delayed indefinitely as long as management retains ownership of the asset and chooses not to sell or abandon it. Consequently, the EITF reached a consensus that management's intent regarding future actions with respect to the asset is to be taken into account in determining whether to include or exclude these cash flows from the computation of the expected future cash flows used to evaluate recoverability under FAS 144. If management is contemplating alternative courses of action to recover the carrying amount of the asset or if a range is estimated for the amount of possible future cash flows, the likelihood (probability) of these possible outcomes is to be considered in connection with the recoverability evaluation under FAS 144.

EITF 95-23 provides examples illustrating situations where cash flows for environmental exit costs not recognized as liabilities under SOP 96-1 are either included in or excluded from the undiscounted expected future cash flows used to evaluate a long-lived asset or group of assets for recoverability under FAS 144.

*Deferred income taxes.* Impairment losses are not deductible for US federal income tax purposes. Consequently, financial statement recognition of these losses will result in differences between the carrying amounts of the impaired assets used for financial reporting purposes and income tax purposes. These differences are considered temporary differences and are accounted for under the provisions of FAS 109 as discussed in Chapter 17.

*Comparison of accounting and impairment rules.* The following diagram summarizes and compares the rules affecting the accounting for tangible and intangible long-lived assets.

**Summary and Comparison of Accounting and Impairment Rules**

| Attribute | PP&E* | Amortizable intangibles | Nonamortizable intangibles | Goodwill |
|---|---|---|---|---|
| Useful life? | Estimated useful life or, for leasehold improvements, the lesser of that life or the term of the lease | | Indefinite | |
| Consider residual or salvage value? | Yes | Yes—with either 3rd party commitment or ready market | No | |
| Capitalize interest if self-constructed? | Yes | | | |
| Recoverability evaluation or impairment test? | Recoverability evaluation | | Impairment test | Special 2-step impairment test |
| Frequency | When events and circumstances warrant | | At least annually; more often if events and circumstances warrant | |
| Change between amortizable and nonamortizable | | Test for impairment, adjust if required | | |
| Subsequent increases recognized? | No | | | |
| Level of aggregation for impairment purposes | Asset group or disposal group | | Unit of accounting as specified by EITF 02-7 | Reporting unit |

\* *Includes property, plant, and equipment, internal-use software, and Web site development costs.*

**Long-lived assets to be disposed of by sale.** An asset may be disposed of individually or as part of a disposal group. A disposal group is a group of assets to be disposed of in a single transaction as a group and the liabilities directly associated with those assets that will be transferred with those assets (e.g., environmental obligations, warranty obligations associated with a product line, etc.).

Long-lived assets (or disposal groups) are classified as held-for-sale in the period in which *all* of the following six criteria are met:

1. Management possessing the necessary authority commits to a plan to sell the asset (disposal group)
2. The asset (disposal group) is immediately available for sale on an "as is" basis (i.e., in its present condition subject only to usual and customary terms for the sale of such assets)
3. An active program to find a buyer and other actions required to execute the plan to sell the asset (disposal group) have commenced

4. An assessment of remaining actions required to complete the plan indicates that it is unlikely that significant changes will be made to the plan or that the plan will be withdrawn

5. Sale of the asset (disposal group) is probable, as that term is used in the context of FAS 5 (i.e., likely to occur), and transfer of the asset (disposal group) is expected to qualify for recognition as a completed sale within one year

   *NOTE: Certain exceptions to the one-year requirement are set forth in FAS 144 for events and circumstances beyond the entity's control that extend the period required to complete the sale.*

6. The asset (disposal group) is being actively marketed for sale at a price that is reasonable in relation to its current fair value

A newly acquired long-lived asset (disposal group) that is being held for sale is to be classified as held-for-sale on the date of acquisition if

- It meets criteria 5. above (subject to the same exceptions noted in 5.), *and*
- Any other of the required criteria that are not met at the date of acquisition will probably be met within a short period (approximately three months or less) of acquisition.

If the criteria are met after the balance sheet date but prior to issuance of the entity's financial statements, the long-lived asset is to continue to be classified as held-and-used at the balance sheet date. Appropriate subsequent events disclosures would be included in the financial statements in accordance with AICPA Statement on Auditing Standards 1, AU Section 560, *Subsequent Events.* In connection with the FASB's initiative to codify all authoritative GAAP in a single searchable database (the "codification"), guidance with respect to subsequent events is expected to be migrated from the auditing literature to the codification in April 2009.

Long-lived assets (disposal groups) classified as held-for-sale are measured at the lower of their carrying amount or fair value less cost to sell. A loss is recognized for any initial or subsequent write-down to fair value less cost to sell. A gain is recognized for any subsequent increase in fair value less cost to sell, but recognized gains may not exceed the cumulative losses previously recognized. Long-lived assets that are classified as held-for-sale are presented separately on the balance sheet.

Cost to sell consists of costs that directly result from the sales transaction that would not have been incurred if no sale were transacted. Cost to sell includes brokerage commissions, legal fees, title transfer fees, and other closing costs that must be incurred prior to transfer of legal title to assets. Prior to measurement of fair value less cost to sell, the entity adjusts the carrying amounts of any assets included in the disposal group not covered by FAS 144 including any goodwill.

The entity may not accrue, as part of cost to sell, expected future losses associated with operating the long-lived asset (disposal group) while it is classified as held-for-sale. Costs associated with the disposal, including costs of consolidating or closing facilities, are only recognized when the actual costs are incurred. If the exception to the one-year requirement applies (permitted when there are certain events and circumstances beyond the entity's control), and the sale is expected to occur in more than one year, the cost to sell is discounted to its present value.

Long-lived assets (disposal groups) held for sale are not to be depreciated (amortized) while being presented under the held-for-sale classification. Interest and other expenses related to the liabilities of a held-for-sale disposal group are accrued as incurred.

If, at any time after meeting the criteria to be classified as held-for-sale, the asset (disposal group) no longer meets those criteria, the long-lived asset (disposal group) is to be reclassified from held-for-sale to held-and-used, measured at the *lower of*

- Carrying value prior to classification as held-for-sale, adjusted for any depreciation (amortization) that would have been recognized had the asset (disposal group) continued to be classified as held-and-used, or
- Fair value at the date of the subsequent decision not to sell the asset (disposal group).

The adjustment required to the carrying amount of an asset (disposal group) being reclassified from held-for-sale to held-and-used is included in income from continuing operations in the period that the decision is made not to sell. FASB concluded that impairment losses from long-lived assets to be held and used, gains or losses recognized on long-lived assets to be sold, and other costs associated with exit or disposal activities (as defined in FAS 146 and discussed in detail in Chapter 3) should be accounted for consistently. Therefore, if the entity reports a measure of operations (e.g., income from operations), these amounts are reported in operations unless they qualify as discontinued operations, as explained below. The income statement classification of these amounts is to be consistent with the accounting policy for classifying the depreciation of the underlying assets per the following examples:

| | |
|---|---|
| Machinery and equipment used in production | Cost of goods sold |
| Office equipment | General and administrative |
| Trucks and delivery equipment | General and administrative or, if a separate category of expenses, selling expense |
| Combination factory/office building | Allocate between cost of goods sold, and general and administrative in the same manner as depreciation |

If a component of an entity (as defined below) is reclassified as held-and-used, the results of that component that had previously been reported in discontinued operations are reclassified and included in income from continuing operations for all periods presented.

Upon removal of an individual asset or liability from a disposal group classified as held-for-sale, the remaining part of the group is to be evaluated as to whether it still meets all six of the criteria to be classified as held-for-sale. If all of the criteria are still met, then the remaining assets and liabilities will continue to be measured and accounted for as a group. If not all of the criteria are met, then the remaining long-lived assets are to be measured individually at the lower of their carrying amounts or fair value less cost to sell at that date. Any assets that will not be sold are reclassified as held-and-used as described above.

### Example of long-lived assets to be disposed of by sale

The Hewitt Candy Company chooses to stop sales of its candy cane product line, and accordingly shifts the $840,000 carrying cost (i.e., book value) of its candy cane twister equipment into a held-for-sale account. After several months of trying to close a sale of the equipment, Hewitt's controller notes that the fair value of the twister equipment is now $855,000. However, after projected sale costs that include commissions, legal fees, and title transfer fees are included, the net fair value is only $825,000. The controller accordingly writes down the equipment cost to $825,000 with the following entry:

| | | |
|---|---|---|
| Loss on fair value adjustment | 15,000 | |
| Equipment held-for-sale | | 15,000 |

After another two months, the controller notes that the equipment's fair value, net of estimated disposition costs, has increased to $860,000. Though this represents a gain of $35,000 over the adjusted carrying cost of the equipment, he can only recognize a gain up to the amount of all previously recorded losses, which he does with the following entry:

| | | |
|---|---|---|
| Equipment held-for-sale | 15,000 | |
| Gain on fair value adjustment | | 15,000 |

Six months after the twister equipment is classified as held-for-sale, Hewitt's management concludes that it will wait for better market conditions to sell the equipment. Hewitt's controller reclassifies the equipment as held-and-used with the following entry:

| | | |
|---|---|---|
| Equipment | 840,000 | |
| Equipment held-for-sale | | 840,000 |

Prior to its classification as held-for-sale, the equipment had been depreciated on a straight-line basis over a ten-year life span using an original equipment base cost of $1.2 million, so $60,000 would otherwise have been incurred while the equipment was classified as held-for-sale; this would have reduced the equipment's net carrying cost (i.e., book value) from $840,000 to $780,000. Since this is lower than the estimated fair value of $860,000 as of the date when the decision was made to halt sale activities, the controller records the following entry:

| | | |
|---|---|---|
| Depreciation—equipment | 60,000 | |
| Accumulated depreciation—equipment | | 60,000 |

After four more months, Hewitt receives an unsolicited cash offer of $875,000 for the twister equipment, which it accepts. During these additional four months, the equipment has been depreciated by a further $40,000. Hewitt's controller records the sale with the following entry:

| | | |
|---|---|---|
| Cash | 875,000 | |
| Accumulated depreciation—equipment | 460,000 | |
| Equipment held-and-used | | 1,200,000 |
| Gain on equipment sale | | 135,000 |

***Long-lived assets to be disposed of other than by sale.*** Long-lived assets may be abandoned, exchanged, or distributed to owners in a spin-off. Until the actual disposal occurs, the assets continue to be classified on the balance sheet as "held and used." During that period prior to disposal, they are subject to conventional impairment rules applicable to assets held and used.

Abandoned assets are considered disposed of under FAS 144 when they cease to be used. Temporary idling of an asset, however, is not considered abandonment. At the time an asset is abandoned, FAS 144 prescribes that its carrying amount be adjusted to its salvage value, if any, but not less than zero (i.e., a liability cannot be recorded upon abandonment).

If the entity commits to a plan to abandon the asset before the end of its previously estimated useful life, the depreciable life is revised in accordance with the rules governing a change in estimate under FAS 154 and depreciation of the asset continues until the end of its shortened useful life.

If a long-lived asset is to be disposed of either by spinning it off to owners of the company or in an exchange transaction for a similar productive long-lived asset, the disposal is recognized when the actual exchange or spin-off occurs. If that asset (group) is evaluated for recoverability while held and used and before the disposal, the estimates of future cash flows are to assume that the disposal will not occur and that the asset will continue to be held and used for the remainder of its useful life. Two separate impairment losses might be recognized in this scenario.

1. An impairment loss for the asset while it is held and used
2. An additional impairment loss if, upon exchange or spin-off, which are recorded under APB 29 at the asset's recorded amount, the recorded amount/carrying value exceeds fair value

***Discontinued operations.*** FASB believed that financial statement users would benefit from expanded application of the accounting and disclosure provisions for discontinued operations originally set forth in APB Opinion 30. Consequently, FAS 144 eliminated the previous requirement that a discontinued operation qualify as a segment of the business. To facilitate this change, FAS 144 introduced the concept of a "component of an entity." A component of an entity is distinguishable from the rest of the entity because it has its own operations and cash flows. It may be a reportable segment or operating segment (as defined by FAS 131), a reporting unit (as defined by FAS 142), a subsidiary, or an asset group.

If a component of an entity is either classified as held-for-sale or has been disposed of during the period, the results of its operations are to be reported in discontinued operations if *both* of the following conditions are met:

- The operations and cash flows of the component have been or will be eliminated from the ongoing operations of the entity as a result of the disposal transaction
- The entity will not have significant continuing involvement in the operations of the component after the disposal transaction

*The assessment period.* The assessment of these conditions in light of certain fact situations has been the source of some confusion in practice. EITF 03-13 attempts to provide clarification and examples of appropriate application. Management's assessment is to be based on all facts and circumstances including management's intent and ability to (1) eliminate the disposed component's cash flows from its ongoing operations and (2) not have significant continuing involvement in the operations of the disposed component. The assessment is to include significant events or circumstances that occur during the period from the balance sheet date to the date of issuance of the financial statements.

The assessment period commences at the date that the component initially meets the criteria to be classified as held-for-sale (discussed earlier in this chapter) or is disposed of. The assessment period ends one year from the date that the component is actually disposed of. During the year between disposal and the end of the assessment period, management is to consider whether any significant events or circumstances had occurred that potentially would change its current assessment. If such an event or circumstance occurs, management is to perform a reassessment to determine if it still expects to meet the two conditions. If the results of the reassessment are that management no longer expects to meet the two conditions by the end of the assessment period, the disposed component's operations are not to be presented as discontinued operations. If the reassessment indicates the opposite, that management expects to meet both conditions by the end of the assessment period, the component's operations are to be presented as discontinued operations. Each change in assessment that occurs during the assessment period will require reclassification of the operations for all periods presented in comparative financial statements.

If events or circumstances occur that are beyond the control of the reporting entity that extend the period required to meet the two conditions, the assessment period may extend beyond one year from the date of disposal provided that management (1) responds to the situation by taking the necessary actions, and (2) expects to successfully meet the two conditions.

The following discussion will analyze each of the conditions separately from the standpoint of management of the "ongoing entity," defined as the remaining operations of a reporting entity after it has disposed of a component or classified a component as held-for-sale.

*Elimination of the component's operations and cash flows.* Management of the ongoing entity is to assess whether any continuing cash flows have been generated or are expected to be generated. Continuing cash flows are cash inflows and/or outflows generated by the ongoing entity that are associated with activities involving the component that was disposed of or classified as held-for-sale. Cash inflows and/or outflows are assessed for this purpose in the same manner as under FAS 144 in assessing the recoverability of assets to be held and used.

*Direct vs. indirect cash flows.* If continuing cash flows have occurred or are expected to occur, their nature and significance must be evaluated to determine whether they are considered direct or indirect. The evaluation of whether the cash flows are direct or indirect is to be made by management by considering its expectations based on the best information available. If all of the significant continuing cash flows are direct, the first condition in FAS 144 is not met and the operations of the component are to be presented as part of continuing operations in the financial statements of the ongoing entity. If, however, all of the significant continuing cash flows are indirect, those cash flows are considered to have been eliminated from the ongoing entity and the component will have met the first of the two conditions for classification as a discontinued operation in the income statement of the ongoing entity.

Examples of cash flows that are considered indirect include but are not limited to

1. Interest income earned from seller financing associated with the disposal
2. Contingent consideration associated with a business combination
3. Dividends earned on investments
4. Royalties received based on passive interests in the operations of the disposed component

Cash flows are direct if they result from the ongoing entity's substantive continuation of the component's revenue-producing and/or cost-generating activities subsequent to the disposal transaction.

Significant cash inflows of the ongoing entity are direct if they result from a

1. Migration of revenues from the disposed component after the disposal transaction or
2. Continuation of revenue-producing activities by the ongoing entity through its active involvement with the disposed component after the disposal transaction

Significant cash outflows of the ongoing entity are direct if they result from a

1. Migration of costs from the disposed component after the disposal transaction or
2. Continuation of cost-generating activities by the ongoing entity through its active involvement with the disposed component after the disposal transaction

*Migration of revenues and costs.* Migration in this context refers to the expectation of management that the ongoing entity will continue to sell products or services similar to those of the disposed component to the disposed component's specific customers and that, in so doing, will continue to generate related revenues and/or incur related expenses. EITF 03-13 indicates that there is a rebuttable presumption that revenues and/or costs have migrated to the ongoing entity if, after the disposal transaction, the ongoing entity continues to sell a similar product or service, as defined in the Consensus. This presumption can be overcome by an analysis of specific facts and circumstances such as differences between the products or services or the markets in which they are provided.

*Continuation of revenue-producing and cost-generating activities.* Continuation of activities occurs when the ongoing entity remains actively involved with the disposed component after the disposal occurs. This can be evidenced, for example, by the continuation of predisposal purchases or sales of products or services between the ongoing entity and the disposed component or a related party.

*Determining significance of continuing cash flows.* EITF 03-13 prescribes a with-and-without approach to determining whether continuing cash flows are considered significant. The determination of significance is to be made separately for gross cash inflows and gross cash outflows. Naturally, if gross cash inflows are determined to be significant, it is not necessary to determine the significance of gross cash outflows since it will already have been determined that the operations of the disposed-of component do not qualify for classification as discontinued operations in the financial statements of the ongoing entity.

Management makes the determination of the significance of cash inflows by comparing its estimate of the ongoing entity's cash inflows expected to result from the migration of the disposed component's sales after the disposal with a hypothetical estimate of what the cash inflows of the disposed component would have been had the disposal transaction not occurred. For the purpose of this estimate, the hypothetical cash inflows of the disposed component are to include cash inflows arising from external, third-party transactions and intercompany transactions as if they had been transactions between unrelated parties.

*Significance of continuing involvement.* EITF 03-13 defines continuing involvement as the ability of the ongoing entity to influence the operating and/or financial policies of the disposed component. This determination is to be based on both quantitative and qualitative assessments made from the standpoint of the disposed component. The ongoing entity's retention of risk or ability to obtain benefits from the ongoing operations associated with the disposed component is not, by itself, conclusive of the ability to influence. Management is to evaluate individually and in the aggregate, ownership interests, contractual arrangements, and other arrangements. Ownership interests include common stock, in-substance common stock as defined in EITF 02-14, or a call option to acquire an interest in the disposed component. Ownership interests consisting of only common stock accounted for under the cost method or only of in-substance common stock do not constitute significant continuing involvement.

In evaluating contractual or other arrangements, the following factors are to be considered:

1. Significance of the contract or arrangement in the context of the disposed component's overall operations.
2. The extent of involvement of the ongoing entity in the disposed component's operations.
3. The rights that the contract or arrangement conveys to each of the parties.
4. The pricing terms included in the contract or arrangement.

The following circumstances are not considered to constitute continuing cash flows or continuing involvement:

1. Resolution of transaction-related contingencies—Subsequent resolution of contingencies related to the disposal transaction such as adjustments to the purchase price and enforcement of any indemnification provisions in the disposal agreement.
2. Resolution of operating contingencies—Subsequent resolution of contingencies related to the operations of the disposed component that existed prior to the disposal such as environmental and product warranty obligations that were retained by the seller (the ongoing entity).
3. Settlement of employee benefit plan obligations—Settlement of pension and other postemployment benefit-related obligations that are directly related to the disposal transaction.

In a period in which a component of an entity is either classified on the balance sheet as held-for-sale or has been disposed of, the entity's income statement *for current and prior periods* is to report the component's results of operations (including gains or losses related to transfer of the asset from the held and used to the held-for-sale category) as discontinued operations, net of applicable income taxes or benefit. Future losses may not be anticipated and accrued and are to be recognized in the period in which they are incurred. Placement in the income statement is illustrated in Chapter 3.

The gain or loss on disposal is permitted to be disclosed either on the face of the statement of income or in the notes to the financial statements.

In subsequent periods, certain adjustments may arise that affect amounts previously reported in discontinued operations. Examples of such adjustments include

- Resolution of contingencies associated with the terms of the disposal such as purchase price adjustments and indemnification issues with the purchaser
- Resolution of contingencies associated with the operation of the component prior to its disposal such as environmental or product warranty obligations retained by the seller
- Settlement of employee benefit plan obligations directly associated with the disposal transaction (generally settlements and curtailments of plan liabilities as contemplated by FAS 88)

When adjustments of this nature occur, they are classified separately in discontinued operations of the current period and the notes to the financial statements are to disclose the nature and amount of these adjustments.

Assets and liabilities of a disposal group classified as held-for-sale are presented separately in their respective sections of the balance sheet. Offsetting of these amounts is not permitted.

**Example of discontinued operations reporting**

The Hewitt Candy Company sells its entire candy cane production line, recognizing a gain of $155,000 on the transaction prior to applicable taxes of $54,000. During the year in which the sale was completed, Hewitt lost $23,000 on its operation of the candy cane line, while it also lost $72,000 during the preceding year. Applicable tax reductions during these years were $8,000 and $25,000, respectively. It reports these results in the following portion of its income statement:

|  | 20X0 | 20X1 |
|---|---|---|
| Discontinued operations: | | |
| Loss from operations of discontinued candy cane division (net of applicable taxes of $25,000 and $8,000) | $(47,000) | $(15,000) |
| Gain on disposal of candy cane division (net of applicable taxes of $54,000) | -- | 101,000 |

A clause in the sale agreement stipulates that Hewitt must reimburse the buyer for any maintenance problems found in the equipment. In the following year, the two parties negotiate a payment by Hewitt of $39,000 to address claims made under this clause. The applicable tax reduction associated with this payment is $14,000. It reports these results in the following portion of its income statement:

|  | 20X0 | 20X1 | 20X2 |
|---|---|---|---|
| Discontinued operations: | | | |
| Loss from operations of discontinued candy cane division (net of applicable taxes of $25,000 and $8,000) | $(47,000) | $(15,000) | -- |
| Gain on disposal of candy cane division (net of applicable taxes of $54,000) | -- | 101,000 | -- |
| Adjustment to gain on disposal of candy cane division (net of applicable taxes of $14,000) | -- | -- | $(25,000) |

*Long-lived assets temporarily idled.* The only reference in FAS 144 to the temporary idling of long-lived assets is the provision that prohibits recognizing temporary idling as abandonment. At a minimum, however, if material assets are temporarily idled, the following considerations apply:

1. Idling constitutes a "significant adverse change in the extent or manner in which . . ." the asset (or asset group) is being used, which is an indicator requiring a recoverability evaluation under FAS 144.

2. The estimates of future cash flows used in performing the recoverability evaluation are to consider, on a probability-weighted basis, the range of outcomes under consideration by management regarding when the asset will be returned to service, sold, or abandoned.

3. Idle property and equipment is to be clearly and unambiguously captioned and segregated on the balance sheet from both the "held-and-used" and "held-for-sale" categories since it does not qualify for either classification, with appropriate disclosure of the relevant circumstances.

4. As part of the ongoing review of the appropriateness of useful lives, the remaining useful life of the idle equipment is to be reassessed.

5. Evaluation by management of whether temporary suspension of depreciation or amortization of the asset is warranted until it is returned to service.

**Foreclosed assets obtained in troubled debt restructurings.** In general, assets obtained by a lender pursuant to foreclosure are recorded at their fair values at the time of the restructuring. To the extent that the foreclosed assets include long-lived assets that will be sold in full satisfaction of the debt, those assets are to be recorded in accordance with FAS 144 at fair value, less cost to sell. If the amount recognized does not fully satisfy the debt, the lender records a loss computed as

Recorded investment in the receivable – Fair value, less cost to sell = Loss

To the extent that the loss is not offset by a valuation allowance, it is included in net income for the period of the restructuring.

The recorded investment in the receivable may have been recorded net of a valuation allowance for uncollectibility or as face amount of the receivable adjusted for such items as accrued interest and unamortized premium, discount, finance charges, or loan acquisition costs. The recorded investment in the receivable may also reflect previous direct write-downs.

If the fair value of the foreclosed assets only partially satisfy the outstanding debt, the creditor is to follow FAS 114 (discussed in detail in Chapters 15 and 25) after first reducing the recorded investment in the receivable by the fair value less cost to sell of the foreclosed assets.

Note that substance over form is an important consideration in determining the applicability of this accounting protocol. Even if formal foreclosure proceedings do not occur, if a troubled debt restructuring results in the lender obtaining physical custody of assets of the borrower that had been pledged as collateral to satisfy all or a portion of the outstanding debt, the transaction is accounted for in the same manner as a foreclosure, as previously described.

Subsequent to the restructuring, the lender accounts for foreclosed assets in the same manner as assets acquired in exchange for cash. FSP FAS 144-1 specifies that the valuation allowance for a loan collateralized by a long-lived asset is not to be carried over as a separate element of the cost basis of that long-lived asset received in full satisfaction of a receivable in a troubled debt restructuring. The valuation allowance for the loan also is not to be included in the amount of cumulative losses previously recognized when computing the amount of gain that can be recognized under FAS 144 if the value of the collateral subsequently increases.

**Reporting and disclosures.** With respect to the impairment of long-lived assets to be held and used, the following disclosures are required:

1. A description of the impaired long-lived asset (or asset group) and the facts and circumstances that led to the impairment

2. The amount of the impairment loss and the caption in the income statement (or not-for-profit statement of activities) in which it is included, if not presented separately on the face of the income statement

3. The method or methods used to determine fair value (e.g., quoted market prices as described in the forthcoming FASB standard on fair value measurements, market prices for similar assets, or other valuation techniques)

4. For public companies, the segment in which the impaired long-lived asset or asset group is reported under FAS 131

With respect to long-lived assets and disposal groups to be disposed of, and other exit and disposal activities, disclosures for the period in which the activity is initiated and any subsequent periods until completion of the activity are to include

1. A description of the exit or disposal activity, including

   a. The facts and circumstances that led to the expected exit or disposal,

   b. The expected manner and timing of the activity, including its expected date of completion,

   c. If not separately presented on the face of the balance sheet, the carrying amount or amounts of the major classes of assets and liabilities included as part of a disposal group (public companies are also required to disclose which segment or segments includes each disposal group)

2. The gain or loss recognized for any initial or subsequent write-downs to fair value less cost to sell and, if not separately presented on the face of the income statement, the caption in the income statement or the statement of activities that includes the gain or loss

3. The following information for each major category of costs to be incurred in connection with the activity (e.g., onetime termination benefits, contract termination costs, and other costs):

   a. Costs incurred during the period

   b. Cumulative costs incurred from inception to balance sheet date

   c. Total costs expected to be incurred

   d. A reconciliation of changes in the liability during the period including

      (1) Liability at the beginning of the period

      (2) Costs incurred and charged to expense during the period

      (3) Costs paid or otherwise settled during the period

      (4) Adjustments made to the liability, if any, and the reasons the adjustments were necessary

4. The income statement (or statement of activities) captions that include the costs in 3.

5. If any costs incurred that are associated with exit or disposal activities have not been accrued because the fair value of the liability is not reasonably estimable, that fact and the reasons such an estimate cannot be made

6. With respect to discontinued operations, if applicable

   a. The amounts of revenue and pretax profit or loss reported in discontinued operations

   b. For each discontinued operation that generates continuing cash flows

      (1) The nature of activities that result in the continuing cash flows

      (2)  The period of time that the continuing cash flows are expected to be generated

      (3)  The principal factors that led to the conclusion that the expected cash flows are not direct cash flows of the disposed component

  c.  For each discontinued operation in which the ongoing entity will engage in a continuation of activities

      (1)  In the period in which operations are initially classified as discontinued, the types of continuing involvement that the ongoing entity will have after the disposal transaction

      (2)  If there will be a continuation of revenues and expenses between the ongoing entity and the discontinued component that were eliminated in consolidation prior to the disposal, the amount of the intercompany revenues and expenses that were eliminated for all periods presented in the financial statements.

7.  If assets are reclassified from the held-for-sale category to the held-and-used category during the period, a description of the facts and circumstances that led to the decision to change the plan to sell the asset or group of assets and the effect on the results of operations for the period in which the decision is made and any prior periods presented

8.  For each reportable segment of a public company, the following information about the costs of exit or disposal activities:

  a.  Costs incurred during the period

  b.  Cumulative costs incurred from inception to balance sheet date, net of any adjustments to the liability, with the reasons the adjustments were necessary

  c.  Total costs expected to be incurred

## Intangible Assets

The range of intangibles is perhaps more clearly understood today than it was in the past, and there is more pressure to improve the relevance of financial reporting in light of changing business and economic conditions. For manufacturing companies the primary assets typically are tangible, such as buildings and equipment. For financial institutions the major assets are financial instruments. For high-technology, knowledge-based companies, however, the primary assets are intangible (e.g., patents and copyrights) and for professional service firms the key assets may be "soft" resources such as knowledge bases and client relationships. Overall, enterprises for which intangible assets constitute a large and growing component of total assets are a rapidly growing part of the economy. Intangible assets are defined as both current and noncurrent assets that lack physical substance. Specifically excluded, however, are financial instruments and deferred income tax assets. Goodwill is not considered an identifiable intangible asset, and accordingly, under FAS 142, is accounted for differently from identifiable intangibles. Goodwill is the preeminent unidentifiable intangible, and this characteristic (i.e., the lack of identifiability) has been determined by the FASB to be the critical element in the definition of goodwill. Accordingly, identifiable intangible assets that are reliably measurable are recognized and reported separately from goodwill.

    **Leasehold improvements.** Leasehold improvements result when tangible physical enhancements are made to property by or on behalf of the lessee of real estate. By law, when improvements are made to real property and those improvements are permanently affixed to the property, the title to those improvements automatically transfers to the owner of the property. The rationale behind this is that the improvements, when permanently affixed, are inseparable from the rest of the real estate.

As a result of this automatic title transfer, the lessee's interest in the improvements is not a direct ownership interest but rather it is an intangible right to use and benefit from the improvements during the term of the lease. Consequently, the capitalized costs incurred by a lessee in constructing improvements to property that it leases represent an intangible asset analogous to a license to use them. Thus, when allocating the costs of leasehold improvements to the periods benefited, the expense is referred to as amortization (as used in the context of amortization of intangibles) and not depreciation.

A frequently encountered issue with respect to leasehold improvements relates to determination of the period over which they are to be amortized. Normally, the cost of long-lived assets is charged to expense over the estimated useful lives of the assets. However, the right to use a leasehold improvement expires when the related lease expires, irrespective of whether the improvement has any remaining useful life. Thus, the appropriate useful life for a leasehold improvement is the lesser of the useful life of the improvement or the term of the underlying lease. EITF 05-6 reinforces this concept by requiring that leasehold improvements acquired in a business combination or leasehold improvements completed well after commencement of a lease agreement be amortized over the lesser of the useful life of the leasehold improvement or a time period that includes required lease periods as well as reasonably assured lease renewal periods.

Some leases contain a fixed, noncancelable term and additional renewal options. When considering the term of the lease for the purposes of amortizing leasehold improvements, normally only the initial fixed noncancelable term is included. There are exceptions to this general rule that arise out of the application of GAAP to the lessee's accounting for the lease. If a renewal option is a bargain renewal option, then it is probable at the inception of the lease that it will be exercised and, therefore, the option period is included in the lease term for purposes of determining the amortizable life of the leasehold improvements. Additionally, under the definition of the lease term there are other situations where it is probable that an option to renew for an additional period would be exercised. These situations include periods for which failure to renew the lease imposes a penalty on the lessee in such amount that a renewal appears, at the inception of the lease, to be reasonably assured. Other situations of this kind arise when an otherwise excludable renewal period precedes a provision for a bargain purchase of the leased asset or when, during periods covered by ordinary renewal options, the lessee has guaranteed the lessor's debt on the leased property.

In deciding whether to include the period covered by a renewal option in the calculation of the amortizable life of the leasehold improvements, the lessee must be consistent with the interpretation of renewal options included in the minimum lease payment calculations made to determine whether the lease is a capital or operating lease.

### Example

Marcie Corporation occupies a warehouse under a five-year operating lease commencing January 1, 2009, and expiring December 31, 2013. The lease contains three successive options to renew the lease for additional five-year periods. The options are not bargain renewals as they call for fixed rentals at the prevailing fair market rents that will be in effect at the time of exercise. When the initial calculation was made to determine whether the lease is an operating lease or a capital lease, only the initial noncancelable term of five years was included in the calculation. Consequently, for the purpose of determining the amortizable life of any leasehold improvements made by Marcie Corporation, only the initial five-year term is used. If Marcie Corporation decides, at the beginning of year four of the lease, to make a substantial amount of leasehold improvements to the leased property, it could be argued that it would now be probable that Marcie would exercise one or more of the renewal periods, since not doing so would impose the substantial financial penalty of abandoning expensive leasehold improvements. This would trigger accounting for the lease by treating the period or periods for which it is likely that the lessee will renew as a new agreement and require testing to determine whether the lease, prospectively, qualifies as a capital or operating lease.

The SEC has provided the following guidance on the proper accounting treatment by a lessee for incentives or allowances provided by a lessor to a lessee under an operating lease[3]:

1. The incentives are not permitted to be netted against the leasehold improvements they were intended to subsidize. Instead, they are to be recorded as deferred rent and amortized as reductions to lease expense over the lease term.
2. The leasehold improvements are to be recorded gross, at their cost, and amortized as discussed above.
3. The lessee's cash flow statement is to reflect the cash received from the lessor as an incentive or allowance as cash provided by operating activities and the acquisition of the leasehold improvements as cash used for investing activities.

Lease accounting is discussed in detail in Chapter 16.

**Software developed for internal use.** SOP 98-1 provides guidance on accounting for the costs of internally developed software. Software must meet two criteria to be accounted for as internally developed software. First, the software's specifications must be designed or modified to meet the reporting entity's internal needs, including costs to customize purchased software. Second, during the period in which the software is being developed, there can be no plan or intent to market the software externally, although development of the software can be jointly funded by several entities that each plan to use the software internally.

In order to justify capitalization of related costs, it is necessary for management to conclude that it is probable that the project will be completed and that the software will be used as intended. Absent that level of expectation, costs must be expensed currently as research and development costs (discussed in detail later in this chapter). Entities which engage in both research and development of software for internal use and for sale to others must carefully identify costs with one or the other activity, since the former is (if all conditions are met) subject to capitalization, while the latter is expensed as research and development costs until technological feasibility is demonstrated, per FAS 86. (See Chapter 25 for a discussion of software developed internally for sale or lease.)

*Costs subject to capitalization.* Cost capitalization commences when an entity has completed the conceptual formulation, design, and testing of possible project alternatives, including the process of vendor selection for purchased software, if any. These early-phase costs (referred to as "preliminary project stage" in SOP 98-1) are analogous to research and development costs and must be expensed as incurred. These cannot be later restored as assets if the development proves to be successful.

Costs incurred subsequent to the preliminary project stage that meet the criteria under GAAP as long-lived assets are capitalized and amortized over the asset's expected economic life. Capitalization of costs begins when both of two conditions are met. *First,* management having the relevant authority authorizes and commits to funding the project and believes that it is probable that it will be completed and that the resulting software will be used as intended. *Second,* the conceptual formulation, design, and testing of possible software project alternatives (i.e., the preliminary project stage) have all been completed.

---

[3] *Letter from SEC Chief Accountant to the chairman of the AICPA Center for Public Company Audit Firms (CPCAF) dated February 7, 2005; http://www.sec.gov/info/accountants/staffletters/cpcaf020705.htm*

Costs capitalized include those of the application development stage of the software development process. These include coding and testing activities and various implementation costs. In particular, the SOP notes that such costs are limited to (1) external direct costs of materials and services consumed in developing or obtaining internal-use computer software; (2) payroll and payroll-related costs for employees who are directly associated with and who devote time to the internal-use computer software project to the extent of the time spent directly on the project; and (3) interest cost incurred while developing internal-use computer software, consistent with the provisions of FAS 34.

General and administrative costs, overhead costs, and training costs are expensed as incurred. Even though these may be costs which are associated with the internal development or acquisition of software for internal use, under GAAP those costs relate to the period in which they are incurred. The issue of training costs is particularly important, since internal-use computer software purchased from third parties often includes, as part of the purchase price, training for the software (and often fees for routine maintenance as well). Per the SOP, when the amount of training or maintenance fees is not specified in the contract, entities are required to allocate the cost among training, maintenance, and amounts representing the capitalizable cost of computer software. Training costs are recognized as expense as incurred. Maintenance fees are recognized as expense ratably over the maintenance period.

SOP 98-1 provides examples of when computer software is acquired or developed for internal use. Some of these are: when modifications are made to software controlling robots acquired for use in the manufacturing process; software is developed for cash management, payroll processing, or accounts payable system purposes; a bank develops an online account status inquiry system for customers to utilize; a travel agency invests in software to give it access to an airline reservation system; a communications provider develops computerized systems to manage customer services such as voice mail; or when a publisher invests in computerized systems to produce a product which is then sold to customers.

On the other hand, software which does not qualify under the standard as being for internal use includes software sold by a robot manufacturer to purchasers of its products; the cost of developing programs for microchips used in automobile electronic systems; software developed for both sale to customers and internal use; computer programs written for use in research and development efforts; and costs of developing software under contract with another entity.

***Impairment.*** Impairment of capitalized internal-use software is recognized and measured in accordance with the provisions of FAS 144 in the same manner as tangible long-lived assets and other amortizable intangible assets. Circumstances which might suggest that an impairment has occurred and that would trigger a recoverability evaluation include (1) a realization that the internal-use computer software is not expected to provide substantive service potential; (2) a significant change in the extent or manner in which the software is used; (3) a significant change has been made or is being anticipated to the software program; or (4) the costs of developing or modifying the internal-use computer software significantly exceed the amount originally expected. These conditions are analogous to those generically set forth by FAS 144.

In some instances, ongoing software development projects will become troubled before being discontinued. SOP 98-1 provides that management needs to assess the likelihood of successful completion of projects in progress. When it becomes no longer probable that the computer software being developed will be completed and placed in service, the asset should be written down to the lower of the carrying amount or fair value, if any, less costs to sell. Importantly, it is a rebuttable presumption that any uncompleted software has a zero fair value. SOP 98-1 provides indicators that the software is no longer expected to be completed and placed in service. These include (1) a lack of expenditures budgeted or incurred for the project; (2) programming difficulties that cannot be resolved on a timely basis; (3) significant cost overruns; (4) information indicating that the costs of internally developed software will significantly exceed the cost of comparable third-party software or software products, suggesting that management intends to obtain the third-party software instead of completing the internal development effort; (5) the introduction of new technologies which increase the likelihood that management will elect to obtain third-party software instead of completing the internal project, and (6) a lack of profitability of the business segment or unit to which the software relates or actual or potential discontinuation of the segment.

*Amortization.* As for other long-lived assets, the cost of computer software developed or obtained for internal use should be amortized in a systematic and rational manner over its estimated useful life. The intangible nature of the asset contributes to the difficulty of developing a meaningful estimate, however. Among the factors to be weighed are the effects of obsolescence, new technology, and competition. Management would especially need to consider if rapid changes are occurring in the development of software products, software operating systems, or computer hardware, and whether it intends to replace any technologically obsolete software or hardware.

Amortization commences for each module or component of a software project when the software is ready for its intended use, without regard to whether the software is to be placed in service in planned stages that might extend beyond a single reporting period. The SOP stipulates that computer software is deemed ready for its intended use after substantially all testing has been completed.

*Other matters.* In some cases internal-use software is later sold or licensed to third parties, notwithstanding the original intention of management that the software was acquired or developed solely for internal use. In such cases, SOP 98-1 provides that any proceeds received are to be applied first as a reduction of the carrying amount of the software. No profit is recognized until the aggregate proceeds from sales exceed the carrying amount of the software. After the carrying value is fully recovered, any subsequent proceeds are recognized in revenue as earned.

### Example of software developed for internal use

The Da Vinci Invention Company employs researchers based in countries around the world. The far-flung nature of its operations makes it extremely difficult for the payroll staff to collect timesheets, so the management team authorizes the design of an in-house, Web-based timekeeping system. The project team incurs the following costs:

| Cost type | Charged to expense | Capitalized |
|---|---|---|
| Concept design | $ 2,500 | |
| Evaluation of design alternatives | 3,700 | |
| Determination of required technology | 8,100 | |
| Final selection of alternatives | 1,400 | |
| Software design | | $ 28,000 |
| Software coding | | 42,000 |
| Quality assurance testing | | 30,000 |
| Data conversion costs | 3,900 | |
| Training | 14,000 | |
| Overhead allocation | 6,900 | |
| General and administrative costs | 11,200 | |
| Ongoing maintenance costs | 6,000 | |
| Totals | $57,700 | $100,000 |

Thus, the total capitalized cost of this development project is $100,000. The estimated useful life of the timekeeping system is five years. As soon as all testing is completed, Da Vinci's controller begins amortizing using a monthly charge of $1,666.67. The calculation follows:

$100,000 capitalized cost ÷ 60 months = $1,666.67 amortization charge

Once operational, management elects to construct another module for the system that issues an e-mail reminder for employees to complete their timesheets. This represents significant added functionality, so the design cost can be capitalized. The following costs are incurred:

| Labor type | Labor cost | Payroll taxes | Benefits | Total cost |
|---|---|---|---|---|
| Software developers | $11,000 | $ 842 | $1,870 | $13,712 |
| Quality assurance testers | 7,000 | 536 | 1,190 | 8,726 |
| Totals | $18,000 | $1,378 | $3,060 | $22,438 |

The full $22,438 amount of these costs can be capitalized. By the time this additional work is completed, the original system has been in operation for one year, thereby reducing the amortization period for the new module to four years. The calculation of the monthly straight-line amortization follows:

$22,438 capitalized cost ÷ 48 months = $467.46 amortization charge

The Da Vinci management then authorizes the development of an additional module that allows employees to enter time data into the system from their cell phones using text messaging. Despite successfully passing through the concept design stage, the development team cannot resolve interface problems on a timely basis. Management elects to shut down the development project, requiring the charge of all $13,000 of programming and testing costs to expense in the current period.

After the system has been operating for two years, a Da Vinci customer sees the timekeeping system in action and begs management to sell it as a stand-alone product. The customer becomes a distributor, and lands three sales in the first year. From these sales Da Vinci receives revenues of $57,000, and incurs the following related expenses:

| Expense type | Amount |
|---|---|
| Distributor commission (25%) | $14,250 |
| Service costs | 1,900 |
| Installation costs | 4,300 |
| Total | $20,450 |

Thus, the net proceeds from the software sale is $36,550 ($57,000 revenue less $20,450 related costs). Rather than recording these transactions as revenue and expense, the $36,550 net proceeds are offset against the remaining unamortized balance of the software asset with the following entry:

| | | |
|---|---|---|
| Revenue | $57,000 | |
| Fixed assets—software | | $36,550 |
| Commission expense | | 14,250 |
| Service expense | | 1,900 |
| Installation expense | | 4,300 |

At this point, the remaining unamortized balance of the timekeeping system is $40,278, which is calculated as follows:

| | |
|---|---|
| Original capitalized amount | $100,000 |
| + Additional software module | 22,438 |
| – 24 months amortization on original capitalized amount | (40,000) |
| – 12 months amortization on additional software module | (5,610) |
| – Net proceeds from software sales | (36,550) |
| Total unamortized balance | $40,278 |

Immediately thereafter, Da Vinci's management receives a sales call from an application service provider who manages an Internet-based timekeeping system. The terms offered are so good that the company abandons its in-house system at once and switches to the ASP system. As a result of this change, the company writes off the remaining unamortized balance of its timekeeping system with the following entry:

| | | |
|---|---|---|
| Accumulated depreciation | 45,610 | |
| Loss on asset disposal | 40,278 | |
| Fixed assets—software | | 85,888 |

**Web site development costs.** The costs of developing a Web site, including the costs of developing services that are offered to visitors (e.g., chat rooms, search engines, e-mail, calendars, and so forth), are often quite significant. The SEC staff had expressed the opinion that a large portion of those costs should be accounted for in accordance with AICPA SOP 98-1, *Accounting for the Costs of Computer Software Developed or Obtained for Internal Use*, which sets forth certain conditions which must be met before costs may be capitalized.

In EITF 00-2, the Task Force reached a consensus that costs incurred in the planning stage must be expensed as incurred. The cost of software used to operate a Web site must be accounted for consistent with SOP 98-1, unless a plan exists to market the software externally, in which case FAS 86 governs. Costs incurred to develop graphics (broadly defined as the "look and feel" of the Web page) are included in software costs, and thus accounted for under SOP 98-1 or FAS 86, as noted in the foregoing. However, the accounting for costs of content development were not addressed by the EITF. Costs of operating Web sites are accounted for in the same manner as other operating costs analogous to repairs and maintenance.

EITF 00-2 includes a detailed exhibit stipulating how a variety of specific costs are to be accounted for consistent with this consensus.

**Initial recognition and measurement of intangibles assets.** Intangibles acquired individually or with a group of other assets[4] are initially recognized and measured based on their fair values. Fair value, consistent with FAS 157, is determined based on the assumptions that market participants would use in pricing the asset. Even if the reporting entity does not intend to use an intangible asset in a manner that is its highest and best use, the intangible is nevertheless measured at its fair value. Although the implementation guidance with respect to initial accounting for an exchange transaction refers to determining the cost of the assets acquired, APB 29 notes that, generally, cost is measured based on the fair value of the consideration provided or the fair value of the net assets acquired, whichever is more reliably measureable.

The aggregate amount assigned to a group of assets acquired is to be allocated to the individual assets acquired based on their relative fair values. Goodwill is prohibited from being recognized in an asset acquisition.

Although a reporting entity can purchase intangibles that were developed by others, US GAAP, dating back to APB 17 issued in 1970, continues to maintain a strict prohibition against capitalizing costs of internally developing, maintaining, or restoring intangibles, including goodwill. The only exceptions to this general rule are leasehold improvements, software developed for internal use, and Web site development costs, as discussed previously in this chapter.

*Amortization and impairment considerations.* Many intangible assets are based on rights that are conveyed legally by contract, statute, or similar means. For example, governments grant franchises or similar rights to taxi companies, cable companies, and hydroelectric plants; and companies and other private-sector organizations grant franchises to automobile dealers, fast-food outlets, and professional sports teams. Other rights, such as airport landing rights, are granted by contract. Some of those franchises or similar rights are for finite terms, while others are perpetual. Many of those with finite terms are routinely renewed, absent violations of the terms of the agreement, and the costs incurred for renewal are minimal. Many such assets are also exchangeable, and the prices at which they trade reflect expectations of renewal at minimal cost. However, for others, renewal is not assured, and their renewal may entail substantial cost.

---

[4] *See discussion of **accounting for assets acquired in a group** earlier in this chapter.*

Trademarks, service marks, and trade names may be registered with the government for a period of twenty years and are renewable for additional twenty-year periods as long as the trademark, service mark, or trade name is used continuously. (Brand names, often used synonymously with trademarks, are typically not registered and thus the required attribute of control will be absent.) The US government now grants copyrights for the life of the creator plus fifty years. Patents are granted by the government for a period of seventeen years but may be effectively renewed by adding minor modifications that are patented for additional seventeen-year periods. Such assets also are commonly exchangeable.

If no legal, regulatory, contractual, competitive, economic, or other factors limit the useful life of an intangible asset to the reporting entity, the useful life of the asset is considered to be indefinite (which, of course, is not the same as unlimited or infinite).

Identifiable intangible assets having indefinite useful economic lives supported by clearly identifiable cash flows are not subject to regular periodic amortization. Instead, the carrying amount of the intangible is tested for impairment annually, and again between annual tests if events or circumstances warrant such a test. An impairment loss is recognized if the carrying amount exceeds the fair value. Furthermore, amortization of the asset commences when evidence suggests that its useful economic life is no longer deemed indefinite.

FSP FAS 142-3, *Determination of the Useful Life of Intangible Assets,* was issued in April 2008 to address an inconsistency in practice in the length of useful lives of recognized intangibles determined under FAS 142 and the period of expected cash flows used to measure the fair value of the intangible asset upon its acquisition in a business combination when the arrangement includes renewal or extension terms. Generally, the useful life that had been determined under FAS 142 was shorter than the measurement period used to determine fair value. The FASB staff attributed the inconsistency to the level of negotiations necessary to renew or extend the arrangements and/or the inclusion in the expected cash flow estimates of *implicit* renewal or extension terms.

Under the FSP, the reporting entity is to consider its own historical experience in renewing or extending similar arrangements in determining the assumptions regarding renewal or extension. These assumptions, nevertheless, are to be adjusted for entity-specific factors specified in FAS 142:

1. The entity's expected use of the asset
2. The expected useful life of another asset or asset group to which the useful life of the intangible asset may be related
3. Any provisions contained in applicable law, regulation, or contract that may limit the useful life
4. The entity's own historical experience in renewing or extending similar arrangements if such experience is consistent with the intended use of the intangible asset by the reporting entity, and irrespective of whether those similar arrangements contained explicit renewal or extension provisions. In the absence of such historical experience, management is to consider the assumptions that market participants would use about the renewal or extension consistent with their highest and best use of the asset, and adjusted for relevant entity-specific factors.
5. The effects of obsolescence, demand, competition, and other economic factors such as

   a. Stability of the industry
   b. Known technological advances,
   c. Legislative action that results in an uncertain or changing regulatory environment, and
   d. Expected changes in distribution channels

6.   The level of maintenance expenditures that would be required to obtain the expected future cash flows from the asset.

An income approach is commonly used to measure the fair value of an intangible asset. The period of expected cash flows used to measure fair value of the intangible, adjusted for applicable entity-specific factors, is to be considered by management in determining the useful life of the intangible for amortization purposes.

EITF 02-7 provides guidance about when it is appropriate to combine into a single "unit of accounting" for impairment testing purposes, separately recorded indefinite-life intangibles, whether acquired or internally developed.

The assets may be combined into a single unit of accounting for impairment testing if they are operated as a single asset and, as such, are inseparable from one another. The EITF provided indicators to use in evaluating the individual facts and circumstances to exercise judgment.

**Indicators that indefinite-lived intangibles are to be combined as a single unit of accounting**

1.   The intangibles will be used together to construct or enhance a single asset.
2.   If the intangibles had been part of the same acquisition, they would have been recorded as a single asset.
3.   The intangibles, as a group, represent "the highest and best use of the assets" (e.g., they could probably realize a higher sales price if sold together than if they were sold separately). Indicators pointing to this situation are

     a.   The unlikelihood that a substantial portion of the assets would be sold separately, or
     b.   The fact that, should a substantial portion of the intangibles be sold individually, there would be a significant reduction in the fair value of the remaining assets in the group.

4.   The marketing or branding strategy of the entity treats the assets as being complementary (e.g., a trademark and its related trade name, formulas, recipes, and patented or unpatented technology can all be complementary to an entity's brand name).

**Indicators that indefinite-lived intangibles are not to be combined as a single unit of accounting**

1.   Each separate intangible generates independent cash flows.
2.   In a sale, it would be likely that the intangibles would be sold separately. If the entity had previously sold similar assets separately, this would constitute evidence that combining the assets would not be appropriate.
3.   The entity is either considering or has already adopted a plan to dispose of one or more of the intangibles separately.
4.   The intangibles are used exclusively by different asset groups (as defined in FAS 144).
5.   Differing useful economic lives.

EITF 02-7 provided additional guidance regarding the "unit of accounting" determination.

1.   Goodwill and finite-lived intangibles are not permitted to be combined in the "unit of accounting" since they are subject to different impairment rules.

2.  If the intangibles collectively constitute a business, they may not be combined into a unit of accounting.
3.  If the unit of accounting includes intangibles recorded in the separate financial statements of consolidated subsidiaries, it is possible that the sum of impairment losses recognized in the separate financial statements of the subsidiaries will not equal the consolidated impairment loss.

    *NOTE: Although counterintuitive, this situation can occur when*

    1.  *At the separate subsidiary level, an intangible asset is impaired since the cash flows from the other intangibles included in the unit of accounting that reside in other subsidiaries cannot be considered in determining impairment, and*
    2.  *At the consolidated level, when the intangibles are considered as a single unit of accounting, they are not impaired.*

4.  Should a unit of accounting be included in a single reporting unit, that same unit of accounting and associated fair value is to be used in computing the implied fair value of goodwill for measuring any goodwill impairment loss.

Identifiable intangible assets, such as franchise rights, customer lists, trademarks, patents and copyrights, and licenses are to be amortized over their expected useful economic life, even if that life exceeds the former forty-year ceiling, with required impairment reviews of their recoverability when necessitated by changes in facts and circumstances in the same manner as set forth in FAS 144 for tangible long-lived assets. FAS 144 also requires consideration of the intangible's residual value (analogous to salvage value for a tangible asset) in determining the amount of the intangible to amortize. Residual value is defined as the value of the intangible to the entity at the end of its (entity-specific) useful life reduced by any estimated disposition costs. The residual value of an amortizable intangible is assumed to be zero unless the intangible will continue to have a useful life to another party after the end of its useful life to its current holder, and one or both of the following criteria are met:

1.  The current holder has received a third-party commitment to purchase the intangible at the end of its useful life, *or*
2.  A market for the intangible exists and is expected to continue to exist at the end of the asset's useful life as a means of determining the residual value of the intangible by reference to marketplace transactions.

A broadcast license which, while nominally subject to expiration in five years, might be indefinitely renewable at little additional cost to the broadcaster. If cash flows can be projected indefinitely, and assuming a market exists for the license, no amortization is to be recorded until such time as a finite life is predicted. However, impairment is required to be tested at least annually to ensure that the asset is carried at no more than its fair value.

The foregoing examples all addressed identifiable intangibles, which are recognized in the financial statements when purchased separately or in connection with a business combination. There are other intangibles, which are deemed to not be identifiable because they cannot be reliably measured. The Statement uses technological know-how and an assembled workforce as examples of such intangible assets. Intangibles that cannot be separately identified are considered integral components of goodwill.

**Goodwill.** FAS 141(R) provides the following definition of goodwill:

> *Goodwill is an asset representing the future economic benefits arising from other assets acquired in a business combination that are not individually identified and separately recognized.*[5]

---

[5] *Statement of Financial Accounting Standards No. 141(R)*, **Business Combinations**, *Financial Accounting Standards Board: Norwalk, CT; December 2007; paragraph 3j.*

Goodwill is generally afforded special accounting treatment because it is neither separately identifiable nor transferable. Goodwill arising from combinations between two or more not-for-profit organizations or in an acquisition of a for-profit enterprise by a not-for-profit organization continues to be outside the scope of FAS 141(R), while FASB continues work on a separate project currently on its agenda regarding these types of transactions.

FAS 142 originally exempted unidentifiable intangible assets recognized in an acquisition of a bank or thrift institution under FAS 72. However, with the issuance of FAS 141(R), FAS 72 was nullified and the exemption removed from the literature.

Initially, goodwill is recognized in a business combination at the acquisition date, as the excess of 1. over 2. below:

1. The aggregate of

    a. The consideration transferred; generally accounted for at fair value at the acquisition date,
    b. The fair value of any noncontrolling interest in the acquiree, and
    c. If the business combination was achieved in stages (sometimes referred to as step-acquisition), the acquisition-date fair value of the equity interest in the acquiree previously held by the acquirer.

2. The net of the amounts of identifiable assets acquired and liabilities assumed measured at the acquisition date in accordance with FAS 141(R).

Goodwill is not to be amortized. Goodwill is, however, subject to unique impairment testing techniques. Therefore, FAS 144 is not applied to goodwill and goodwill associated with acquisitions of tangible property and equipment is not tested for impairment in tandem with that property and equipment.

The impairment test for goodwill is performed at the level of the reporting unit. A reporting unit is an operating segment or one level below an operating segment. The diagram in the section of Chapter 2 captioned, *Alternative Balance Sheet Segmentation* illustrates how different groupings in a business can be characterized as reporting units and is accompanied by definitions of reporting units, operating segments, and other organizational groupings. The reporting entity may internally refer to reporting units by such terms as business units, operating units, or divisions. Determination of reporting units is largely dependent on how the business is managed and its structure for reporting and management accountability. The Statement acknowledges that an entity may have only one reporting unit which would, of course, result in the goodwill impairment test being performed at the entity level. This can occur when the entity has acquired a business that it has integrated with its existing business in such a manner that the acquired business is not separately distinguishable as a reporting unit.

On the date an asset is acquired or a liability is assumed, it is to be assigned to a reporting unit if it meets both of the following conditions:

1. The asset will be used in or the liability is related to the operations of a reporting unit
2. The asset or liability will be considered in determining the fair value of the reporting unit

The methodology used is to be reasonable and supportable and is to be applied similarly to how aggregate goodwill is determined in a purchase business combination. Net assets include assets and liabilities that are recognized as "corporate" items if they, in fact, relate to the operations of the reporting unit (e.g., environmental liabilities associated with land owned by a reporting unit, and pension assets and liabilities attributable to employees of a reporting unit). Executory contracts (e.g., operating leases, contracts for purchase or sale, construction contracts) are considered part of net assets only if the amount reflected in the acquirer's financial statements is based on a fair value measurement subsequent to entering into the contract. To illustrate, if an acquiree had a preexisting operating lease on either favorable or unfavorable terms as compared to its fair value on the date of acquisition, the acquirer would recognize, in its purchase price allocations, an asset or liability for the fair value of the favorable or unfavorable terms, respectively. FAS 142 distinguishes between accounting for this fair value of an otherwise unrecognized executory contract and prepaid rent or rent payable which generally have carrying values that approximate their fair values.

The annual goodwill impairment test may be performed at any time during the fiscal year as long as it is done consistently at the same time each year. Each reporting unit is permitted to establish its own annual testing date. Additional impairment tests are required between annual impairment tests if: (1) warranted by a change in events and circumstances, *and* (2) it is more likely than not that the fair value of the reporting unit is below its carrying amount. If indicators exist requiring impairment testing of goodwill, impairment testing of nonamortizable intangibles, and/or recoverability evaluation of tangible long-lived assets or amortizable intangibles, the other assets are tested/evaluated first and any impairment loss recognized prior to testing goodwill for impairment.

FAS 142 provides examples of events or circumstances that require goodwill of a reporting unit to be tested for impairment between annual tests.

1. A significant adverse change in legal factors or in the business climate
2. An adverse action or assessment by a regulator
3. Unanticipated competition
4. A loss of key personnel
5. An expectation that it is more likely than not that a reporting unit or a significant portion of it will be sold or otherwise disposed of *or* the allocation of a portion of goodwill to a business to be disposed of
6. The necessity of performing a FAS 144 recoverability test of a significant asset group within a reporting unit
7. The recognition of a goodwill impairment loss in the financial statements of a subsidiary that is a component of a reporting unit

Similar to the list of events and circumstances in FAS 144, this list is not intended to be all-inclusive. Other indicators may come to the attention of management that would indicate that goodwill impairment testing be performed between annual tests.

***Performing the impairment test.*** Goodwill is impaired when its implied fair value is less than its carrying amount. The actual determination of whether goodwill is impaired is made as follows:

1. Compare the fair value of the reporting unit as a whole to its carrying value including goodwill. If the reporting unit's fair value exceeds its carrying value, goodwill is not impaired and no further computations are required. If, however, the carrying value of the reporting unit exceeds its fair value, the second step of the impairment test is required.
2. Determine whether and by how much goodwill is impaired as follows:

    a. Estimate the *implied fair value* of goodwill.
    b. Compare the implied fair value of goodwill to its carrying amount.
    c. If the carrying amount of goodwill exceeds its implied value, it is impaired and is written down to the implied fair value.

The implied fair value of goodwill is the excess of the fair value of the reporting unit as a whole, over the fair values that would be assigned to its assets and liabilities in a purchase business combination.

Consistent with long-standing practice in GAAP, upon recognition of an impairment loss, the adjusted carrying amount of goodwill becomes its new cost basis, and future restoration of the written down amount is prohibited.

The *fair value of a reporting unit* is defined (in an amendment to FAS 142 made by FAS 157) as the price that would be received to sell the unit as a whole in an orderly transaction between market participants at the measurement date. The determination of the implied fair value of goodwill is based on the assumption that the fair value of a reporting unit as a whole will differ from the fair value of its identifiable net assets. This is the general principle that gives rise to goodwill in the first place. The acquirer assigns additional value to the acquiree (as evidenced by a purchase price that exceeds the collective fair values of the assets and liabilities to be acquired) based on the acquirer's perceived ability to take advantage of synergies and other benefits that flow from its control over the acquiree.

Market capitalization of a publicly traded business unit is computed based on a quoted market price per share that does not consider any advantages that might inure to an acquirer in a situation where control is obtained. For this reason, FAS 142 cautions that the market capitalization of a reporting unit with publicly traded stock may not be representative of its fair value. Presumably, estimating the fair value of a privately held business using earnings multiples derived from publicly traded companies in the same line of business might have the same limitation.

FAS 142 also prescribes that when a significant portion of a reporting unit is comprised of an acquired entity, the same techniques and assumptions used to determine the purchase price of the acquisition are to be used to measure the fair value of the reporting unit unless such techniques and assumptions are not consistent with the objective of measuring fair value.

For the purposes of determining the fair value of a reporting unit, the relevant facts and circumstances are to be carefully evaluated with respect to whether to assume that the reporting unit could be bought or sold in a taxable or nontaxable transaction. The factors to consider in making the evaluation are set forth in EITF 02-13.

1. The assumptions that marketplace participants would make in estimating fair value
2. The feasibility of the assumed structure considering

    a. The ability to sell the reporting unit in a nontaxable transaction, and
    b. Any limits on the entity's ability to treat a sale as a nontaxable transaction imposed by income tax laws or regulations, or corporate governance requirements.

3. Whether the assumed structure would yield the best economic after-tax return to the (hypothetical) seller for the reporting unit.

Prior to the issuance of FAS 141(R), only goodwill attributable to the parent was recognized in the consolidated financial statements. If a reporting unit is not wholly owned by the reporting entity, the fair value of that reporting unit and the implied fair value of goodwill are to be determined in the same manner as prescribed by FAS 141(R). If the reporting unit includes goodwill that is solely attributable to the parent, any impairment loss would be attributed entirely to the parent. If, however, the reporting unit's goodwill is attributable to both the parent and the noncontrolling interest, the impairment loss would need to be allocated to both the parent and the noncontrolling interest in a rational manner. The same logic applies to gain or loss on disposal of all or a portion of a reporting unit. When that reporting unit is disposed of, the gain or loss on disposal is to be attributed to both the parent and to the non-controlling interest.

For the purpose of goodwill impairment testing, the carrying value of a reporting unit is to include deferred income taxes irrespective of whether fair value of the reporting unit was determined assuming taxable or nontaxable treatment.

FAS 142 permits the carryforward of a previous determination of the fair value of the reporting unit if *all three* of the following conditions are met:

1. There has been no significant change in the composition of the assets and liabilities of the reporting unit.
2. The previously computed fair value of the reporting unit exceeded its carrying amount by a substantial margin (undefined in the FAS).
3. Based on any events occurring or changes in circumstances since the previous computation, the likelihood is remote that the reporting unit's current value is below its carrying amount.

The *fair value of an asset (or liability)* is the amount at which the asset (or liability) could be sold (transferred) in an orderly transaction between market participants at the measurement date. Quoted market prices in active markets are considered the best evidence of fair value and are to be used if available. If quoted market prices are not available, the estimate of fair value is to be based on the best information available including prices for similar assets and liabilities or the results of applying available valuation techniques. Such techniques include expected present value methods, option pricing models, matrix pricing, option-adjusted spread models, and fundamental analysis. The weight to be given to evidence gathered in the valuation process is to be proportional to the ability to objectively observe it. When an estimate is in the form of a range of either the amount or timing of estimated future cash flows, the likelihood of possible outcomes is to be considered (i.e., probability weightings are assigned in order to estimate the most likely outcome).

The measurement techniques and assumptions used to estimate the fair values of the reporting unit's net assets are to be consistent with those used to measure the fair value of the reporting unit as a whole. For example, estimates of the amounts and timing of cash flows used to value the significant assets of the reporting unit are to be consistent with those assumptions used to estimate such cash flows at the reporting unit level when a cash flow model is used to estimate the reporting unit's fair value as a whole.

For the purpose of computing the implied fair value of reporting unit goodwill, assumptions must be made as to the income tax bases of the reporting unit's assets and liabilities in order to compute any relevant deferred income taxes. If the computation of the reporting unit's fair value in step 1 of the goodwill impairment test assumed that the reporting unit was structured as a taxable transaction, then new income tax bases are used. Otherwise the existing income tax bases are used (EITF 02-13).

### Example of the impairment test

Spectral Corporation acquires FarSite Binocular Company for $5,300,000; of this amount, $3,700,000 is assigned to a variety of assets, with the remaining $1,600,000 assigned to goodwill, as noted in the following table:

| | |
|---|---|
| Purchase price | $ 5,300,000 |
| – Accounts receivable | (450,000) |
| – Inventory | (750,000) |
| – Production equipment | (1,000,000) |
| – Acquired formulas and processes | (1,500,000) |
| = Goodwill | $ 1,600,000 |

The asset allocation related to acquired formulas and processes is especially critical to the operation, since it refers to the use of a proprietary lens coating system that allows FarSite's binoculars to yield exceptional clarity in low-light conditions. This asset is being depreciated over ten years.

One year after the acquisition date, the FarSite division has recorded annual cash flow of $1,450,000; assuming the same cash flow for the next five years, the present value of the expected cash flows, discounted at the corporate cost of capital of 8%, is roughly $5,789,000. Also, an independent appraisal firm assigns a fair value of $3,600,000 to FarSite's identifiable assets. With this information, the impairment test follows:

| | |
|---|---|
| FarSite division's fair value | $5,789,000 |
| – Fair value of identifiable assets | (3,600,000) |
| = Implied fair value of goodwill | $2,189,000 |

Though the implied fair value of FarSite's goodwill has increased, Spectral's controller cannot record this increase.

A few months later, Spectral's management learns that a Czech optics company has created a competing optics coating process that is superior to and less expensive than FarSite's process. Since this will likely result in a reduction in FarSite's fair value below its carrying amount, Spectral conducts another impairment test. Management assumes that the forthcoming increase in competition will reduce the expected present value of its cash flows to $3,900,000. In addition, the appraisal firm now reduces its valuation of the acquired formulas and processes asset by $1,200,000. The revised impairment test follows:

| | |
|---|---|
| FarSite division's fair value | $3,900,000 |
| – Fair value of identifiable assets | (2,400,000) |
| = Implied fair value of goodwill | 1,500,000 |
| – Carrying amount of goodwill | 1,600,000 |
| = Impairment loss | $ (100,000) |

Since the implied fair value of goodwill is $100,000 less than its current carrying amount, Spectral's controller uses the following entry to record reduction in value:

| | | |
|---|---|---|
| Impairment loss | 100,000 | |
| Goodwill | | 100,000 |

In addition, Spectral's controller writes down the value of the acquired formulas and processes by the amount recommended by the appraisal firm with the following entry:

| | | |
|---|---|---|
| Impairment loss | 1,200,000 | |
| Accumulated depreciation | | 1,200,000 |

A year later, FarSite's research staff discovers an enhancement to its optical coating process that will restore FarSite's competitive position against the Czech firm. However, Spectral's controller cannot increase the carrying cost of the acquired formulas and processes or goodwill to match their newly increased fair value and implied fair value, respectively.

***Negative goodwill—FAS 141.*** Negative goodwill results from situations (sometimes referred to as "bargain purchases") where the fair values of the net assets acquired in a business combination exceed the purchase price and is discussed in detail in Chapter 13. FAS 141 requires that negative goodwill first be allocated pro rata to reduce amounts assigned to the acquired assets including in-process research and development. Assets that are not reduced by negative goodwill are

- Financial assets (except equity-method investments)
- Assets to be disposed of by sale
- Deferred income tax assets
- Prepaid assets related to pension or other postretirement benefit plans
- Any other current assets

After applying the negative goodwill to reduce the values assigned to the assets permitted to be adjusted, if negative goodwill still remains, FAS 141 prescribes that it be recognized as an extraordinary gain in the period in which the business combination is initially recognized. However, two exceptions are provided to this general rule.

- When an extraordinary gain is recognized prior to completion of the purchase price allocations, the subsequent change necessitated by completion of the allocations is also recognized as either an extraordinary gain or loss in the period that the purchase price allocation is finalized.
- If the purchase price includes a provision for contingent consideration (e.g., a subsequent adjustment to the purchase price based on the acquiree attaining certain postacquisition levels of sales or pretax income), the remaining negative goodwill is recorded as a deferred credit until the contingency is resolved. In the period in which the contingency is resolved, any remaining negative goodwill is reclassified from the deferred credit to an extraordinary gain.

***Negative goodwill—FAS 141(R).*** FAS 141(R) dramatically changes the accounting for a bargain purchase. Under FAS 141(R),[6] management of the acquirer is required to reassess whether it correctly identified all of the assets acquired and liabilities assumed and, if applicable, recognize the additional assets or liabilities identified in that reassessment. In addition, acquirer management is to review the procedures it used to measure the amounts of all of the following items recognized at the acquisition date under FAS 141(R), if applicable:

1. Identifiable assets acquired and liabilities assumed,
2. Noncontrolling interest in the acquiree
3. The acquirer's previously held equity interest in the acquiree in a business combination achieved in stages, and
4. The consideration transferred.

The purpose of conducting the review is to ensure that all information available at the acquisition date was properly considered in the measurement process.

After conducting the completeness reassessment and measurement review described above, if an excess still remains, the acquirer is to recognize that excess as a gain on the acquisition date and that gain is not characterized as an extraordinary gain.

***Other goodwill considerations.*** Other provisions included in FAS 142 include the following:

- Equity method goodwill continues to be recognized under APB 18 and is not subject to amortization. This goodwill is not tested for impairment under FAS 142, but rather, is tested under APB 18. This test considers whether the fair value of the underlying investment has declined and whether that decline is "other than temporary."
- Goodwill of a reporting unit that is fully disposed of is included in the carrying amount of the net assets disposed of in computing the gain or loss on disposal.
- If a significant portion of a reporting unit is disposed of, the goodwill of that unit is required to be tested for impairment. In performing the impairment test, only the net assets to be retained after the disposal are included in the computation. If, as a result of the test, the carrying amount of goodwill exceeds its implied fair value, the excess carrying amount is allocated to the carrying amount of the net assets disposed of in computing the gain or loss on disposal and, consequently, is not considered an impairment loss.

---

[6] *To be applied prospectively to business combinations with acquisition dates on or after the beginning of the first annual reporting period beginning on or after December 15, 2008.*

In order to provide financial statement users with transparent information about goodwill, separate line item treatment is required as follows:

- **Balance sheet (statement of financial position)**—The aggregate amount of goodwill included in assets is captioned separately from other assets and may not be combined with other intangibles.
- **Income statement**—The aggregate amount of goodwill impairment losses is captioned separately in the operating section unless associated with discontinued operations.

## Research and Development Costs—Prior to FAS 141(R)

Research and development (R&D) are defined as follows:

1. Research is the planned search or critical investigation aimed at the discovery of new knowledge with the hope that such knowledge will be useful in developing a new product or service or a new process or technique or in bringing about a significant improvement to an existing product or process.
2. Development is the translation of research findings or other knowledge into a plan or design for a new product or process or for a significant improvement to an existing product or process whether intended for sale or use.

There are three ways in which R&D costs are incurred by a business.

1. Purchase of R&D from other entities
2. Conducting R&D for others under a contractual arrangement
3. Conducting R&D activities for the benefit of the reporting entity

The accounting treatment relative to R&D depends upon the nature of the cost. R&D costs incurred in the ordinary course of operations consist of materials, equipment, facilities, personnel, and indirect costs that can be attributed to research or development activities. These costs are expensed in the period in which they are incurred unless they have alternative future uses.

Examples of such R&D costs include

1. Laboratory research to discover new knowledge
2. Formulation and design of product alternatives

    a. Testing for product alternatives
    b. Modification of products or processes

3. Preproduction prototypes and models

    a. Tools, dies, etc. for new technology
    b. Pilot plants not capable of commercial production

4. Engineering activity until the product is ready for manufacture

Examples of costs that are not considered R&D would include

1. Engineering during an early phase of commercial production
2. Quality control for commercial production
3. Troubleshooting during a commercial production breakdown
4. Routine, ongoing efforts to improve products
5. Adaptation of existing capacity for a specific customer or other requirements
6. Seasonal design changes to products
7. Routine design of tools, dies, etc.
8. Design, construction, startup, etc. of equipment except that used solely for R&D

In many cases, entities will pay other parties to perform R&D activities on their behalf. In applying substance over form in evaluating these arrangements, a financial reporting result cannot be obtained indirectly if it would not have been permitted if accomplished directly. Thus, if costs incurred to engage others to perform R&D activities that, in substance, could have been performed by the reporting entity itself, those costs must be expensed as incurred. On the other hand, if the payment is to acquire intangibles for use in R&D activities, and these assets have other uses, then the expenditure is capitalized and accounted for in accordance with FAS 142.

When R&D costs are incurred as a result of contractual arrangements, the nature of the agreement dictates the accounting treatment of the costs involved. The key determinant is the transfer of the risk associated with the R&D expenditures. If the business receives funds from another party to perform R&D and is obligated to repay those funds regardless of the outcome, a liability must be recorded and the R&D costs expensed as incurred. In order to conclude that a liability does not exist, the transfer of the financial risk must be substantive and genuine.

### Example of research and development

The TravelBins Corporation is developing a hard-shell plastic ski case on wheels. It assigns two staff to the design of the case, as well as a product design consultant, and also contracts with a Portuguese firm to develop suitable molds for the main case and ancillary parts. The company works its way through 17 product development and production activities before it is satisfied that the new ski case is ready for general distribution. The following matrix shows where costs are charged as various steps are completed:

| Step No. | Activity | Charge to R&D expense | Charge to production overhead | Move to inventory | Capitalize |
|---|---|---|---|---|---|
| 1 | Cost of product design consultant | xxx | | | |
| 2 | Salaries related to design of the ski case | xx | | | |
| 3 | Purchase of design computers and rapid proto-typing machines | | | | xxx |
| 4 | Allocation of indirect development costs | xxx | | | |
| 5 | Cost of preliminary test molds | xxx | | | |
| 6 | Cost of building in which test facility is housed | | | | xxx |
| 7 | Cost of resin pellets acquired for test runs | | | xxx | |
| 8 | Scrapped cases from test runs | xxx | | | |
| 9 | Good-quality cases from test runs | | | xxx | |
| 10 | Cost of independent stress test firm | xxx | | | |
| 11 | Patent filing cost | | | | xxx |
| 12 | Cost to defend patent | | | | xxx |
| 13 | Cost of final mold | | | | xxx |
| 14 | Machine set-up time | | xxx | | |
| 15 | Quality control during commercial production | | xxx | | |
| 16 | Routine mold adjustments | | xxx | | |
| 17 | Production engineering to reduce scrap rate | | xxx | | |

The cost of design computers and building are capitalized, since they can be used independently from the product development process. The cost of the final mold is capitalized and amortized over the life of the mold, while patent costs are capitalized and amortized over the life of the product (which may extend past the life of the first mold). The cost of the plastic resin and good-quality ski cases can be transferred to inventory for use in regular production and for sale to customers, respectively.

**In-process research and development.** Immediate write-off of purchased in-process research and development costs was required under FAS 141 prior to its rescission and replacement by FAS 141(R), discussed later in this section.

There had been concern that acquirers were aggressively allocating large portions of the purchase price of the acquiree company to in-process R&D that was then written off at acquisition date. To the extent that this practice resulted in mischaracterizing these costs, it resulted in a reduction of the goodwill recorded in connection with the business combination. This practice would likely result in distorted earnings in future periods that potentially could have borne goodwill impairment costs. It also would distort future periods' performance measurements such as return on assets and return on equity.

All parties associated with the preparation of (and/or, under new SEC rules, the certification of) the financial statements should consider the reasonableness of any such write-offs and the possibility of a challenge by the SEC.

### Research and Development Costs—FAS 141(R)

Intangible assets acquired in a business combination that are used in research and development activities are to be recognized as indefinite-lived intangibles until the associated research and development efforts are either completed or abandoned. This treatment is afforded R&D assets irrespective of whether they are considered to have an alternative future use.

While these assets are considered to have an indefinite life, they are not to be amortized but, rather, are to be tested for impairment annually, or more frequently if events or changes in circumstances indicate the assets might be impaired. Upon completion or abandonment of the R&D efforts, management is to determine the remaining useful life of the assets and commence amortization in accordance with the guidance in FAS 142, as amended.

Temporarily idling of R&D assets is treated consistently with other temporarily idled assets; that is, they are not to be accounted for as abandoned.

In order to operationalize these changes, FAS 141(R) amended FAS 2, *Accounting for Research and Development Costs,* by providing a scope exception for tangible and intangible R&D assets acquired in a business combination. The amendment provides the following accounting rules for R&D assets after their initial recognition, based on whether they are tangible or intangible:

1. Tangible assets acquired in a business combination that are used in R&D activities are to be accounted for in accordance with their nature,
2. Intangible assets acquired in a business combination that are used in R&D activities are accounted for in accordance with FAS 142, as amended.

**Nonrefundable advance payments related to future R&D activities.** Entities conducting R&D activities may make payments in advance for goods or services to be used in R&D activities. Often, these payment arrangements involve a specific R&D project and the R&D activities to be performed generally have no alternative future use at the time the arrangements are entered into. All or a portion of the advance payment may be nonrefundable to the entity conducting the R&D activities. For example, if the R&D project does not advance to a stage where the goods or services that were paid for in advance are necessary, the entity conducting the R&D activities will not recover its advance payments.

The EITF reached a consensus in Issue 07-3 that nonrefundable advance payments are to be deferred and capitalized. As the related goods are delivered and services performed, the capitalized amounts are to be recognized as expense. On a continuous basis, management is to evaluate whether it expects the goods to be delivered or services rendered and to charge the capitalized advance payments to expense when there no longer is an expectation of future benefits.

The scope of the consensus is limited to nonrefundable advance payments for goods to be used or services to be rendered in future R&D activities pursuant to an executory contractual arrangement where the goods or services have no alternative future use. Refundable advance payments are not included in the scope of the consensus.

The consensus is effective for financial statements issued for fiscal years beginning after December 15, 2007, and interim periods within those fiscal years.

**Sponsored research and development activities.** EITF 99-16 discusses the accounting for a transaction in which a sponsor creates a wholly owned subsidiary with cash and rights to certain technology originally developed by the sponsor, and receives from the newly created subsidiary two classes of stock. The sponsor then distributes one of the classes of stock (e.g., Class A) to its stockholders. This class of stock has voting rights. Under a purchase option, the sponsor has the right, for a specified period of time, to repurchase all the Class A stock distributed to the stockholders for an exercise price approximating the fair value of the Class A shares. The class retained by the sponsor (e.g., Class B) conveys essentially no financial interest to the sponsor and has no voting rights other than certain blocking rights. The certificate of incorporation prohibits the subsidiary from changing its capital structure, from selling any significant portion of its assets, and from liquidating or merging during the term when the purchase option is outstanding.

The sponsor and the subsidiary enter into a development contract that requires the subsidiary to spend all the cash contributed by the sponsor for research and development activities mutually agreed upon with the sponsor. The subsidiary has no employees other than its CEO. The subsidiary contracts with the sponsor to perform, on behalf of the sponsor, all of the research and development activities under the development contract.

The sponsor accounts for the research and development contract as follows:

- The sponsor reclassifies the cash contributed to the subsidiary as restricted cash when the Class A shares are distributed to its stockholders.
- The distribution of the Class A shares by the sponsor to its stockholders is accounted for as a dividend based on the fair value of the shares distributed.
- In the financial statements of the sponsor, the Class A shares are presented similar to a minority interest.
- The sponsor recognizes research and development expense as the research and development activities are conducted.
- The research and development expense recognized by the sponsor is not allocated to the Class A shares in determining net income or in calculating earnings per share.
- If the Class A purchase option is exercised, the sponsor accounts for the purchase as the acquisition of a minority interest.
- If the Class A purchase option is not exercised by its expiration date, the sponsor reclassifies the Class A stock to additional paid-in capital as an adjustment of the original dividend.

The effect of the above guidance is quite similar to what would be achieved by consolidating the subsidiary. In fact, this consensus predated the issuance of FIN 46 and FIN 46(R) which would require consolidation of many special-purpose entities used in R & D arrangements. FIN 46(R) is discussed and illustrated at length in Chapter 13.

# 12 LONG-TERM INVESTMENTS

## PERSPECTIVE AND ISSUES

The appropriate accounting for noncurrent (or long-term) investments in equity and debt securities is normally dependent upon the degree of marketability (liquidity) of the investment, management's intentions regarding the holding period, and (in the case of equity investments only) the investor's ownership percentage.

For "passive" investments in marketable equity securities, generally defined as those circumstances where the investor holds less than a 20% interest in the investee, FAS 115, *Accounting for Certain Investments in Debt and Equity Securities*, requires that the investment be reported at fair value. Such equity investments must be classified at the acquisition date as being held for trading purposes or as being "available-for-sale." While fair value (what was historically referred to as "mark-to-market" or "fair market value") accounting is prescribed in either case, only for trading securities will the change in fair value be reflected on the income statement in the current period. For investments in equity securities that are classified as "available-for-sale," unrealized gains and losses are classified in an equity account referred to as accumulated other comprehensive income, after being reported as a component of other comprehensive income per FAS 130, *Reporting Comprehensive Income*. If however, there is a decline in fair value of the "available-for-sale" securities that is considered "other-than-temporary," this adjustment is charged to net income in the current period.

A special situation arises when an entity acquires loans that had been originated by another entity, and an intervening decline occurs in the obligor's creditworthiness. Under SOP 03-3, *Accounting for Certain Loans or Debt Securities Acquired in a Transfer,* the accounting for these acquired loans—which may be either loans receivable or debt securities—will be based on the expected future cash flows to be received, rather than on the nominal or contractual amounts of the obligations. The acquirees of these loans will often be financial institutions, but the requirements of SOP 03-3 are equally applicable to all entities, including not-for-profit organizations that invest in loans or debt securities.

When an investor has significant influence over an investee, the investor is no longer considered to be a passive investor, and the equity method must be used to account for the investment. Generally, significant influence is deemed to exist when the investor owns between 20 to 50% of the investee's voting shares, although APB 18, *The Equity Method of Accounting for Investments in Common Stock,* contemplates circumstances where such influence is present with under 20% ownership, or conversely is absent with holdings of 20% or greater. Over 50% is a strong indicator of control, and under the provisions of FAS 94, *Consolidation of All Majority-Owned Subsidiaries,* full consolidation of the investee's financial statements is mandatory unless the investor lacks control. The equity method involves increasing the original cost of the investment by the investor's pro rata share of the investee's net income, and decreasing it for the investor's share of the investee's net losses and for dividends paid.

Equity method accounting has been referred to as "one-line consolidation," because the net result of applying APB 18 on reported net income and on net worth should be identical to what would have occurred had full consolidation been applied. Thus, to the extent that the cost of acquiring the investment exceeds the fair value of the investor's share of the investee's underlying net assets, the excess must be accounted for in a manner analogous to the accounting prescribed for goodwill. Therefore, FAS 142, *Goodwill and Other Intangible Assets,* impacts the application of the equity method of accounting because the portion of the purchase cost identified as representing goodwill is not subject to amortization.

This chapter also discusses the accounting for investments in marketable equity securities with readily determinable fair values and in debt securities as prescribed by FAS 115. Under FAS 115, fair value-based reporting was embraced to a greater extent than previously, although the use of the accumulated other comprehensive income account did postpone income statement recognition of some of these changes in value, resulting in a smoothing effect on net income. Debt securities for which the reporting entity's management has both the intent and ability to hold to maturity are accounted for under FAS 115 at their amortized historical cost; and while unrealized gains and losses on these investments are excluded from reported net income, they are subject to more disclosure in the financial statements than had been the case in the past. Problematic in adhering to the model prescribed by FAS 115 and the related interpretive literature is the determination of whether a given decline in value is temporary or "other than temporary" in nature, an issue which for available-for-sale and held-to-maturity investments results in substantially differing financial reporting consequences.

The advent of FAS 159, *The Fair Value Option for Financial Assets and Financial Liabilities,* may make these operational difficulties moot should management avail itself of elections available under that standard to measure certain specified financial assets and liabilities at fair value with changes in fair value recognized currently in net income. FAS 159, when effective (or adopted early) will give management unprecedented flexibility in electing to measure eligible financial assets and financial liabilities at fair value on a contract-by-contract basis. Comprehensive coverage of this important pronouncement along with FAS 157, *Fair Value Measurements,* is provided in Chapter 6.

FAS 115 applies to most industries except those for which fair value reporting is strictly required, such as brokers and dealers in securities, investment companies, and employee benefit plans. Furthermore, FAS 115 does not apply to not-for-profits, the accounting for which is governed by the provisions of FAS 124, *Accounting for Certain Investments Held by Not-for-Profit Organizations,* which prescribes fair value reporting for all categories of investments, including debt instruments that are being held to maturity. The graphic below summarizes the distinctions for financial reporting purposes of varying levels of ownership in and/or control of an investee entity.

**Equity Investments**

*Percentage of voting ownership*

| 0% | 5% | | 20% | | 50% | | 100% |

*Presumed level of economic influence*

| M i n o r | Little or no influence | Significant Influence | Voting Control |
|---|---|---|---|

*Valuation basis used in investor balance sheet when investor does not control investee*

| Cost method (APB 18) or fair value election (FAS 159) | Equity method (APB 18) or fair value election (FAS 159) |
|---|---|

*Consolidated balance sheet presentation*

*Voting interest entities*

| Cost method (APB 18) or optional fair value election (FAS 159) | Equity method (APB 18) or optional fair value election (FAS 159) | Consolidation (ARB 51; FAS 94) *Investor is presumed to control subsidiary and is thus considered its parent* |
|---|---|---|

*Variable interest entities FIN 46(R)*

| Consolidation (FIN 46[R]) *Primary beneficiary is considered parent and VIE is considered subsidiary* |
|---|

| Sources of GAAP | | | | | | |
|---|---|---|---|---|---|---|
| *APB* | *ARB* | *FAS* | *FIN* | *EITF* | *SOP* | *FSP* |
| 17, 18, 23 | 43 | 52, 94, 107, 109, 115, 126, 130, 133, 140, 142, 144 157 159 | 35, 46(R) | 84-5, 85-40, 89-4, 96-10, 97-7, 98-7, 98-13, 98-15, 99-8, 99-10, 99-20, 00-1, 00-6, 02-14, 02-18, 03-16, 04-5, 06-9, 07-1, D-39, D-46, D-68 | 78-9, 03-3 | FAS 144-1, SOP 78-9-1, APB 18-1, FAS 115-1 and 124-1, FTB 85-4-1 |

## DEFINITIONS OF TERMS

**Analogous entity.**  An enterprise, such as certain limited liability companies, that has governance provisions that are functionally equivalent to those of a corporation.

**Available-for-sale securities.**  Investments (debt or equity) that are classifiable neither as held-to-maturity nor as trading.

**Collaborative arrangement.**  A contractual agreement between two or more parties to conduct specified joint operating activities in which the parties are active participants that are exposed to risks and entitled to rewards based on the commercial success of the activities. The activities that are the subject of the arrangement (referred to as "endeavors") are not primarily conducted through a separate legal entity created for that purpose.

**Corporate joint venture.**  A corporation formed, owned, and operated by two or more businesses (venturers) as a separate and discrete business or project (venture) for their mutual benefit.

**Cost method.**  A method of accounting for an investment whereby the investor recognizes only dividends received from the investee as income.

**Differential.** The difference between the carrying value of a common stock investment and the book value of the underlying net assets of the investee.

**Equity method.** An accounting method used by an investor that obtains significant influence but does not possess control of the investee. Application of the equity method includes recognition of the investor's proportionate share of the investee's net income or loss, dividends, and any changes in the investment percentage in the investee by the investor.

**Equity method goodwill.** The excess of the cost of the acquired interest in an investee over the sum of the amounts assigned to the investee's identifiable net assets.

**Held-to-maturity securities.** Investments in debt securities that the entity has both the ability and the intent to hold to maturity.

**Investee.** An enterprise that issued voting stock that is held by an investor.

**Investee capital transaction.** The purchase or sale by the investee of its own common shares, which alters the investor's ownership interest and is accounted for by the investor as if the investee were a consolidated subsidiary.

**Investor.** A business enterprise that holds an investment in voting stock of another enterprise.

**Joint venture.** A legal entity owned and operated by two or more businesses referred to as the venturers organized for the purpose of a separate business activity or project that mutually benefits the venturers.

**Life settlement contract.** A contract between the owner of a life insurance policy and a third-party investor where (1) the investor does not have an insurable interest in the life of the insured, (2) the investor conveys consideration to the policy owner in an amount that exceeds the policy's cash surrender value, and (3) upon the death of the insured, the face value of the policy is paid to the investor.

**Other comprehensive income.** Revenues, expenses, gains and losses that under generally accepted accounting principles are included in comprehensive income but excluded from net income.

**Protective rights**. Rights granted by contract or law that entitle a minority owner to veto or block certain actions of the majority owner. In the context of EITF 96-16, *Investor's Accounting for an Investee When the Investor Has a Majority of the Voting Interest but the Minority Shareholder or Shareholders Have Certain Approval or Veto Rights,* all rights that vest with a minority owner are considered protective in nature; however if the protective rights are not also considered to be "substantive participation rights" (see definition below), then the existence of protective rights will not overcome the presumption that the holder of the majority voting interest controls the entity. Examples of protective rights that are not also considered substantive participating rights include but are not limited to the minority interest holder having the ability to block the following actions by the majority interest holder:

1. Amendments to the investee's articles of incorporation or LLC articles of organization
2. Pricing on transactions between the majority voting interest holder and the investee and other related party transactions
3. Liquidation of the investee or a decision to enter the investee into bankruptcy or other receivership
4. Acquisitions and dispositions of assets not expected to occur in the ordinary course of business
5. Issuance or repurchase of equity interests

**Significant influence.** The ability of the investor to affect the financial or operating policies of the investee; it is presumed to exist when there is at least 20% voting common stock ownership by the investor.

**Substantive kick-out rights.** Limited partners' ability dissolve (liquidate) a limited partnership or otherwise remove the general partners. To be considered substantive, kick-out rights must meet *both* the following criteria:

1. The kick-out rights can be exercised by a single limited partner or a vote of a simple majority (or lower percentage)[1] of the limited partners, voting interests held by parties

   a. Other than the general partners,
   b. Entities under common control with the general partners, or
   c. A general partner and other parties acting on behalf of the general partners or a general partner.

2. The limited partners who hold the kick-out rights are not limited from exercising those rights by any significant barriers including, but not limited to

   a. The kick-out rights are subject to conditions making it unlikely that they will be exercisable (e.g., conditions that narrowly limit the timing of the exercise).
   b. Financial penalties or operational barriers associated with dissolving (liquidating) the limited partnership or replacing the general partners that would act as a significant disincentive for dissolution (liquidation) or removal.
   c. The absence of an adequate number of qualified replacement general partners or the inadequacy of the compensation for the purpose of attracting a qualified replacement.
   d. The absence of an explicit, reasonable mechanism in the limited partnership agreement or in the applicable laws and regulations, by which the limited partners holding the rights can call for and conduct a vote to exercise their rights.
   e. The inability of the limited partners holding the rights to obtain the information necessary to exercise them.

**Substantive participating rights.** Substantive participating rights are legal or contractual provisions that provide partners, individually or in the aggregate, with effective involvement in significant partnership financial and operating decisions expected to be made in the ordinary course of conducting the partnership's business.[2,3] When the owners of a corporation or analogous entity with minority voting rights possess substantive participating rights, the minority owners will be considered to have overcome the presumption that the owner of the majority of the voting rights controls the investee entity.

In EITF 96-16, the Task Force provided two examples (not considered to be all-inclusive) of minority rights to effectively participate in corporate actions that are both protective rights and substantive participating rights:

---

[1] *The examples of the voting tests that operationalize this requirement are set forth in EITF 04-5, para 7a. and footnotes 10 and 11.*

[2] *The concept of participating rights is not the same as "protective rights." To some extent, all rights possessed by partners, including participating rights, are protective in nature. However, some rights are protective of the partners' interests while not entitling the partners to participate in routine decision making.*

[3] *The ordinary course of business excludes self-dealing transactions with the other partners.*

1. Selecting, terminating, and setting the compensation of management responsible for implementation of the investee's policies and procedures, and
2. Operating and capital decisions of the investee, including budgets, in the ordinary course of business.

**Trading securities.** Investments (debt or equity) which the entity intends to sell in the near term, and which are usually acquired as part of an established strategy to buy and sell, thereby generating profits based on short-term price movements.

**Undistributed investee earnings.** The investor's share of investee net income in excess of dividends paid.

## CONCEPTS, RULES, AND EXAMPLES

### Fair Value Measurements, Disclosures, and Elections

As early as June 1998, FASB stated in FAS 133 that "Fair value is the most relevant measure for financial instruments and the only relevant measure for derivative instruments." FASB's work in this area since that time has largely focused on removing the technical barriers and incrementally converging with international standards.

In September 2006, it issued FAS 157, *Fair Value Measurements,* followed in February 2007 by FAS 159, *The Fair Value Option for Financial Assets and Financial Liabilities.* FAS 157 furthered the cause of fair value by establishing a single definition to replace the disparate definitions that had previously existed throughout GAAP and providing a framework for informing financial statement readers about the source and level of subjectivity (or observability) of the inputs used in the measurement process.

FAS 159 provides management with unprecedented flexibility in electing, on a contract-by-contract basis, to use fair value to measure specified financial assets *and liabilities* in the financial statements of the reporting entity with the effects of changes in fair value being recognized currently in net income (or other performance indicator, as applicable).

Not surprisingly, both standards contain substantial additional disclosure requirements to inform financial statement readers of a myriad of details, to enable assessment of the extent and manner to which fair value measurements are used throughout the financial statements.

In March 2008, FASB issued FAS 161, *Disclosures about Derivative Instruments and Hedging Activities,* to amend FAS 133 and require extensive new disclosures regarding how and why the reporting entity uses derivative instruments; how those instruments and any related hedged items are accounted for; and how they affect financial position, financial performance, and cash flows. FAS 161 is effective for financial statements issued for fiscal years and interim periods beginning after November 15, 2008 with early application encouraged.

Chapter 6 provides comprehensive coverage of the important topic of fair value. It is recommended that readers/researchers refer to Chapter 6 in tandem with this chapter (and with respect to other financial instruments covered in Chapter 8) to better understand the interplay between these standards and other applicable authoritative literature.

### Equity Securities

The accounting for investments in equity securities has been debated for many years. Historical cost had traditionally been prescribed for investments where the investor did not exercise control (i.e., had no more than a 50% voting interest). The threshold for the use of historical cost was later reduced to only those circumstances where significant influence was not a factor, presumptively defined as under a 20% voting interest. The equity method, promulgated by APB 18, is the prescribed method of accounting for investments where significant influence over investee actions is held by the investor.

The trend in recent accounting thought favors a market (or fair) value approach. There are many reasons why users of financial statements as well as standard setters (including the SEC) have increasingly focused on the fair value approach, including the enhanced availability of fair value information, and the concern that adherence to the historical cost model provided management and investors with less relevant decision information, which may have contributed to business failures, particularly those of financial institutions.

FAS 115 is applicable to almost all reporting entities, except those whose specialized accounting practice has already been to account for all investments at fair value. FAS 115 is also inapplicable to not-for-profit enterprises, although a separate standard, FAS 124, requires not-for-profits to account for all investments in debt and equity securities at fair value, with the changes in value taken into reported changes in net assets currently. All marketable equity securities (except those accounted for by the equity method, discussed later in this chapter) are to be classified at acquisition as being either for trading purposes or as available-for-sale. Trading securities are those that are acquired with the intention of being sold in the near term with the general objective of realizing profits from short-term price movements. While a time criterion is not established, a persistent practice of active and frequent trading would be suggestive of the fact that new acquisitions of marketable equity securities are intended to be traded. If management does not commit to an intention to trade, and it cannot be demonstrated that the securities are being held for trading, the investments are to be categorized as available-for-sale.

The distinction between these classifications is important. While equity securities in either category are reported at fair value, it is only the changes in value for the trading securities that are recognized in net income of the current period. Thus, holding gains and losses are accounted for as if realized, in the case of trading securities. In contrast, changes in value for securities held in the available-for-sale portfolio are not recognized in net income of the period in which they occur. The only exceptions will be for entities for which specialized industry accounting practices have long prescribed a pure mark-to-market approach, with all changes in fair value reflected in current income. These industries include securities broker-dealers, employee benefit plans, and investment companies.

Under FAS 115, fair value of an equity security is considered to be determinable if it is quoted in an organized trading exchange or, generally, in over-the-counter trading. Restricted stock is, by definition, not traded and hence fair values are not readily determinable, but stock that is subject to "Rule 144" or similar restrictions, which are due to expire within one year, is not deemed to be restricted for purposes of applying FAS 115. Stock traded only on foreign exchanges is included in the definition if the markets are comparable in breadth and scope to those in the US. Fair values for investments in mutual funds are generally considered to be determinable.

For available-for-sale equity securities, balance sheet presentation is identical to that for trading securities—current fair value. However, unless there has been a permanent impairment in the value of those securities, the change in fair value is excluded from current net income. Instead, the change in value is reported as a separate component of stockholders' equity captioned "accumulated other comprehensive income," with the current period's change being included in other comprehensive income.

FAS 115 imposed this mode of reporting changes in the fair value of available-for-sale equity securities because of the expectation that most investments intended to be held for an indeterminate period will experience predominantly temporary fluctuations that, over time, may tend to largely offset. Thus, the belief was that interim fluctuations in value would not necessarily be indicative of the long-term economic impact from holding the investments, and accordingly, including these changes currently in net income could be misleading.

While others have argued that the goal of periodic financial reporting should be to report the economic events of the period being presented, without concealing or "smoothing" the results, FASB ultimately agreed with those who favored the longer-term view. Notwithstanding substantial sentiment in favor of adopting a pure fair value approach, with gains and losses on all financial instruments being reported in current period net income, FASB's deliberations resulted in a standard that preserved many attributes of traditional historical cost concepts; the subsequent adoption of FAS 130, requiring the display of comprehensive income, somewhat ameliorated the potentially misleading implications of omitting these changes from net income. However, making the determination of the accounting for certain transactions dependent upon management intent, rather than on objectively verifiable circumstances, remains a concern for the accounting profession, as well as posing a challenge for auditors.

While this argument was persuasive when FAS 115 was issued in 1993, it has largely fallen out of favor with users of financial statements who increasingly, although not universally, favor the transparency of full fair value accounting for financial instruments, with all changes in fair value reflected currently in net income.

### Example of accounting for investments in equity securities

Assume that Ralph Corporation purchases the following equity securities for investment purposes during 2009:

| Security description | Acquisition cost | Value at year-end |
|---|---|---|
| 1,000 sh. Bell Steel common | $ 34,500 | $ 37,000 |
| 2,000 sh. Whammer pfd. "A" | 125,000 | 109,500 |
| 1,000 sh. Hilltopper common | 74,250 | 88,750 |

Assume that, at the respective dates of acquisition, management of Ralph Corporation designated the Bell Steel and Hilltopper investments as being for trading purposes, while the Whammer shares were designated as having been purchased for long term investment purposes. Accordingly, the entries to record the purchases were as follows:

| | | |
|---|---|---|
| Investment in equity securities—held-for-trading | 108,750 | |
| Cash | | 108,750 |
| Investment in equity securities—available-for-sale | 125,000 | |
| Cash | | 125,000 |

At year-end, both portfolios are adjusted to fair value; the decline in Whammer preferred stock, series A, is judged to be a temporary market fluctuation rather than a permanent decline. The entries to adjust the investment accounts at December 31, 2009, are

| | | |
|---|---|---|
| Investment in equity securities—held-for-trading | 17,000 | |
| Gain on holding equity securities | | 17,000 |
| Unrealized loss on securities—available-for-sale (other comprehensive income) | 15,500 | |
| Investment in equity securities—available-for-sale | | 15,500 |

Thus, the change in value of the portfolio of trading securities is recognized currently in net income, whereas the change in the value of the available-for-sale securities is reflected directly in a component of stockholders' equity captioned "accumulated other comprehensive income," after being reported in other comprehensive income.

## Transfers between Available-for-Sale and Trading Categories

A major reason for the development of FAS 115 was the concern that under the prior rules there had been too many instances where management had been able to deliberately affect reported net income by careful selection of portfolio securities to be sold in a given period. The practice, typically known as "gains trading," was widely blamed for misleading financial reporting, primarily by financial institutions (which generally hold much more substantial investment portfolios than do industrial enterprises). In a gains trading situation, reporting entities seeking additional net income would sell securities from the nontrading portfolio having low carrying values versus current market values; since these had not previously been marked-to-market, the gain would be reported in current income. In a variation on this process, securities held in a trading account, but suffering declining value, would be transferred to a nontrading portfolio, thus averting a charge against net income.

FAS 115 was intended to curtail the abuses described above. However, by basing accounting on management's expression of its intent, FAS 115 failed to fully preclude such abuses, apart from imposing more stringent limitations on transfers among classifications and prohibiting the use of the "held-to-maturity" classification once it has been "tainted" by sales out of that portfolio.

Under FAS 115, transfers from one of the three portfolio classifications to any other are expected to be very uncommon. Thus, securities purchased for the trading portfolio would be so classified because it was management's intent to seek advantage in short-term price movements; the fact that management does not in fact dispose of those investments quickly would not necessarily mean that the original categorization was improper or that an expressed changed intent should be honored by an accounting entry. While transfers out of the trading category are not completely prohibited, these would have to be supported by facts and circumstances making the assertion of changed intent highly credible.

Transfers among portfolios are accounted for at fair value as of the date of the transfer. Generally, investments in the trading category transferred to the available-for-sale category warrant no further recognition of gain or loss, as the investments have already been marked to market. The only exception is that, if the investment accounts, as a practical matter, have not been updated for fair values since the latest balance sheet date, any changes since that time will need to be recognized at the date the transfer occurs. The fair value at the date of transfer becomes the new "cost" of the equity security in the available-for-sale portfolio.

### Example of a transfer between trading and available-for-sale portfolios

Ralph Corporation's investment in Hilltopper common stock was assigned to the trading portfolio and at December 31, 2009, was marked to its fair value of $88,750. Assume that in April 2010 management now determines that this investment will not be traded, but rather will continue to be held indefinitely. Under the criterion established by FAS 115, this investment now belongs in the available-for-sale portfolio. Assume also that the fair value at the date this decision is made is $92,000, and that no book adjustments have been made since the one that recognized the value increase to $88,750. The entry to record the transfer from the trading to the available-for-sale portfolio is

| | | |
|---|---|---|
| Investment in equity securities—available-for-sale | 92,000 | |
| Investment in equity securities—held-for-trading | | 88,750 |
| Gain on holding equity securities | | 3,250 |

Unrealized gains and losses on trading securities are always recognized in income, and in this example the additional increase in fair value since the last "mark-to-market" adjustment, $3,250, is recognized at the time of the transfer to the available-for-sale portfolio. Further gains after this date, however, will not be recognized in net income, but rather will be included in other comprehensive income per FAS 130.

For securities being transferred into the trading category, any unrealized gain or loss (recorded in the accumulated other comprehensive income account, as illustrated above) is deemed to be realized at the date of the transfer. Also, any fair value changes since the date of the most recent balance sheet may need to be recognized at this time.

### Example of a transfer between available-for-sale and trading portfolios

The investment in Whammer preferred stock was held in the available-for-sale portfolio and in March 2010 was adjusted to a fair value of $112,000 (as illustrated above). The increase from adjusted cost ($109,500, after a permanent impairment in value had been recognized) was reflected in other comprehensive income, rather than in net income, given that the security was not at the time being held for trading. Now assume that, in June 2010, a decision is made to try to sell the investment in the short term. This means that the holding of Whammer stock will be treated as being in the trading portfolio. Further, the value of the shares held at the date of this decision is $114,700. The entry to record the transfer from available-for-sale to trading and the "realization" of the increased value at that date is as follows:

| | | |
|---|---|---|
| Investment in equity securities—held-for-trading | 114,700 | |
| Unrealized gain on securities—available-for-sale (other comprehensive income) | | 2,500 |
| Investment in equity securities—available-for-sale | 112,000 | |
| Gain on holding equity securities (an income statement account) | | 5,200 |

The recognized gain at the time of transfer, in this case, is the sum of the previously unrecognized gain that had been recorded in the additional equity account ($2,500) plus the further gain not yet given any recognition in the investor's financial statements ($2,700). Note that the elimination of the additional equity representing the previously reported unrealized gain will be included in comprehensive income in the current period as a debit, since the additional equity account is being reversed at this time. On the other hand, had there been a decline since the date of the last balance sheet, the gain to be recognized at the date of this transfer would have been the net of the previous, unrecognized gain, and the later loss; if the loss exceeded the earlier gain, a net loss would be recognized at this point. Any further gains or losses after the transfer to the trading portfolio will be handled as earlier described (i.e., recognized in income currently).

## Presentation of Investments in Equity Securities

Investments in equity securities that are held for trading are presented as current assets in classified balance sheets. Investments that are available for sale may be either current or noncurrent, depending upon the reporting entity's intentions. For purposes of reporting in the statement of cash flows, all purchases and sales of trading securities must be included in the operations section, while those of available-for-sale investments are to be shown as part of investing activities.

FAS 115 requires specific disclosures of the components of a reporting entity's portfolios of investments. For available-for-sale securities, a classification by type of security is necessary: equity securities will be grouped together in this disclosure, and thus distinguished from debt securities. Furthermore, aggregate fair values, gross unrealized holding gains and gross unrealized holding losses are also to be disclosed as of the date of each balance sheet being presented.

For each income statement presented, proceeds from the sales of available-for-sale securities and gross realized gains and losses must be disclosed. Further, the basis upon which the gains or losses were determined (e.g., average cost, specific identification, etc.) must be disclosed. In addition, the notes must identify gross gains or losses included in net income resulting from transfers of securities from the available-for-sale to the trading portfolio, and the net change in unrealized gains or losses recognized by an adjustment of the accumulated other comprehensive income account.

## Fair Value Considerations

**Changes in fair value after the balance sheet date.** Under GAAP, events occurring after the balance sheet date are generally not reflected in the balance sheet. However, disclosure may be necessary if, absent that information, the user of the financial statements would be misled. While not addressed explicitly by FAS 115, presumably material changes in fair value occurring subsequent to the date of the balance sheet but prior to issuance of the financial statements should be disclosed.

Sometimes changes in value can be indicative of the underlying cause of the price fluctuations. Of most interest here would be declines in value of available-for-sale securities held at the balance sheet date which suggest that an "other than temporary" impairment has occurred. If the decline actually occurred after year-end as evidenced by a bankruptcy filing, then the event would be disclosed but not reflected in the year-end balance sheet. However, in some instances, the subsequent decline would be seen as a "confirming event" which provided evidence that the classification or other treatment of an item on the balance sheet was incorrect. Thus, if a decline in the fair value of available-for-sale securities at the balance sheet date had been accounted for as temporary (and hence reported in other comprehensive income) a further decline after the balance sheet date might suggest that the decline as of the balance sheet date had, in fact, been a permanent impairment. Note that any further value decline after year-end would not be recorded in the financial statements; the only question to be addressed is whether the decline that occurred prior to year-end should have been treated as a permanent impairment rather than as a temporary market fluctuation.

If it is clear that the impairment at year-end had, in fact, been other than temporary in nature, then the financial statements are to be adjusted to reflect this loss in net income. Absent sufficient basis to reach this conclusion, the appropriate course of action is to not adjust the statements, but merely to disclose the (material) change in fair value that occurred subsequent to year-end including, if appropriate, a statement to the effect that the later decline was deemed to be an other-than-temporary impairment, and will be reflected in the net income of the next year's financial statements. It should also be made clear that the decline occurring prior to year-end was not considered to be an other-than-temporary impairment at that time.

The FASB staff noted that when an entity has decided to sell a security classified as available-for-sale having a fair value less than cost at year-end, and it does not reasonably expect a recovery in value before the sale is to occur, then a write-down for an other than temporary decline is prescribed. This would most obviously be necessary if the actual sales transaction, anticipated at year-end, occurs prior to the issuance of the financial statements.

**Deferred income tax effects of changes in the fair value of debt and marketable equity securities.** Unrealized gains or losses on holdings of marketable securities are not recognized for income tax purposes until realized through a sale. Thus, the gains or losses that are included in the financial statements (either in the income statement or in other comprehensive income) are temporary differences as defined by FAS 109. Under this standard, the income tax effects of all temporary differences are recognized in the financial statements as deferred income tax assets or deferred income tax liabilities, with an additional requirement that an allowance be provided for deferred income tax assets that are "more likely than not" not going to be realized. Accordingly, adjustments to the carrying value of debt or equity investments included in either the trading or available-for-sale portfolios for changes in fair value will give rise to deferred income taxes, as will any recognition of "other-than-temporary" declines in the value of debt securities being held to maturity.

For gains or losses recognized in connection with holdings of investments classified as trading, since the fair value changes are recognized in net income currently, the deferred income tax effects of those changes will also be presented in the income statement.

**Example of deferred income taxes on investments in debt and marketable equity securities**

Odessa Corp. purchased Zeta Company bonds for the purpose of short-term speculation, at a cost of $100,000. At year-end, the bonds had a fair value of $75,000. Odessa has a 40% effective income tax rate. The entries to record the fair value adjustment and the related income tax effect are

| | | |
|---|---|---|
| Loss on holding of trading securities | 25,000 | |
|     Investment in debt securities—trading portfolios | | 25,000 |
| Deferred income tax benefit | 10,000 | |
|     Provision for income taxes | | 10,000 |

On the other hand, if the investment in Zeta Company bonds had been classified (at the date of acquisition, or subsequently if the intentions had been revised) as available-for-sale, the adjustment to fair value would have been reported in other comprehensive income, and not included in net income. Accordingly, the income tax effect of the adjustment would also have been included in other comprehensive income. The entries would have been as follows:

| | | |
|---|---|---|
| Unrealized loss on securities—available-for-sale | 25,000 | |
|     Investment in debt securities—available-for-sale (other comprehensive income) | | 25,000 |
| Deferred income tax benefit | 10,000 | |
|     Unrealized loss on securities—available-for-sale (other comprehensive income) | | 10,000 |

Finally, if the investment in Zeta Company bonds had been made with the intention and ability to hold to maturity, recognition of the decline in value would have depended upon whether it was judged to be temporary or other than temporary in nature. If the former, no recognition would be given to the decline, and hence there would be no deferred income tax effect either. If deemed to be other than temporary, the investment would need to be written down, with the loss included in net income. Accordingly, the income tax effect would also be reported in the income statement. The entries would be as follows:

| | | |
|---|---|---|
| Loss on decline of securities—held-to-maturity | 25,000 | |
|     Investment in debt securities—held-to-maturity | | 25,000 |
| Deferred income tax benefit | 10,000 | |
|     Provision for income taxes | | 10,000 |

An other-than-temporary decline in value in securities available for sale would also have been recognized in net income (not merely in other comprehensive income), and accordingly the income tax effect of that loss would have been reported in net income.

As with all other transactions or events giving rise to deferred income tax assets, an evaluation must be made as to whether the entity would be "more likely than not" to ultimately realize the income tax benefit so recorded. To the extent that it was concluded that some or all of the deferred income tax asset would not be realized, an allowance would be recorded, with the offset being either to the current income tax provision (if the income tax effect of the timing difference was reported in net income) or to other comprehensive income (if the income tax effect had been reported there).

Deferred income taxes will also be recorded in connection with unrealized gains recognized due to changes in the fair value of debt or equity investments. Deferred income tax liabilities will be reported in the balance sheet, and the corresponding income tax provision will be reported in the income statement (for fair value gains arising from holdings of securities in the trading portfolio) or in other comprehensive income (for fair value changes relative to available-for-sale investments).

**Sale of equity securities with a put option.** In certain circumstances, a reporting entity sells marketable securities that it holds, but writes a put option such that the acquirer may force it to repurchase the securities. EITF 84-5 and EITF 85-40 addressed this matter, but its consensuses were partially modified by FAS 140, which holds that the existence of the put, or the probability that it will be exercised, only affects the determination of whether the transfer is to be accounted for as a sale or as a borrowing if the marketable security is not readily obtainable. In most typical situations, the existence of the put will not impact sale recognition (using the criteria of FAS 140), but in relatively rare circumstances, when the put as written is "deep in money" that it makes it probable that the transferee (buyer) will exercise it, sale recognition may not be warranted. The likelihood of put option exercise is assessed only when the put is written; it is not to be reassessed later. Thus, the accounting for the sale of the securities is determined at the date of sale, and is not subject to later revision.

**Accounting for hedges of the foreign currency risk inherent in an available-for-sale equity security.** Some investments, such as those registered on foreign exchanges, have inherent foreign exchange risk associated with them. If these investments are categorized as available-for-sale, value changes may include the effects of both market and exchange rate changes. In some cases, the entity will enter into foreign exchange hedging to protect against exchange rate risk; the issue then is whether transaction gains or losses on forward contract should be included in contra equity account for available-for-sale securities' unrealized gains or losses. It was agreed that the gain or loss is to be shown in the same (other comprehensive income) account if it is associated with the securities' price change. Foreign exchange risk is inherent only if two conditions are met: securities are not traded on an exchange denominated in reporting entity's functional currency; and dividends or other cash flows are all denominated in foreign currency.

### Debt Securities

Historically, accounting for marketable investments in debt securities was not well developed in the professional literature. In fact, the principal guidance concerning long-term investments in debt instruments was found in ARB 43, which stipulated that the amortized cost method be used, absent a substantial, other than temporary decline in value.

FAS 115 applies to both equity and debt instruments held as investments, and prescribes fair value accounting for all except debt instruments being held to maturity. For those investments, amortized historical cost is generally preserved as the measurement principle.

FAS 115 requires that investments in debt securities be classified upon acquisition as belonging to one of three portfolios: trading, available-for-sale, or held-to-maturity. The first of these is characterized by frequent purchase and sale activities, with the general objective of realizing profits from short-term price movements, which in the case of investments in debt instruments will largely be the result of changes in market interest rates but which may also be affected by market perceptions of credit risk. Since intention is the prime criterion applied, even a paucity of sales activity does not necessarily mean that specific debt securities acquired during a period do not belong in the trading portfolio.

The held-to-maturity category is the most restrictive of the three; debt instruments can be so classified only if the reporting entity has both the positive intent and the ability to hold the securities for that length of time. A mere intent to hold an investment for an indefinite period is not adequate to permit such a classification. On the other hand, a variety of isolated causes may necessitate transferring an investment in a debt security from the held-to-maturity category without calling into question the investor's general intention to hold other similarly classified investments to maturity. Among these are declines in the creditworthiness of a particular investment's issuer or a change in income tax law or regulations. On the other hand, sales of investments that were classified as held-to-maturity for other reasons will raise doubts about the entity's assertions regarding these and other similarly categorized securities. For this reason, transfers from or sales of held-to-maturity securities should be very rare.

Accounting for debt securities that are held for trading and those that are available for sale is based on fair value. For balance sheet purposes, increases or decreases in value are reflected by adjustments to the asset account; such adjustments are to be determined on an individual security basis. Changes in the values of debt securities in the trading portfolio are recognized in net income immediately, while most changes in the values of debt securities in the available-for-sale category are reported in other comprehensive income rather than being included in net income. The only exception is for declines that are deemed to be other than temporary, in which case the loss is recognized currently in net income. Once the investment is written down for a decline that is other than temporary, subsequent increases are reported only in changes to the contra equity account; increases cannot be accounted for as "recoveries" of previous declines. (See "Other-than-Temporary Impairment of Investments Available for Sale" in the discussion of equity investments, above, for an example.)

There had been some confusion regarding the applicability of FAS 115, which was resolved by the issuance of FTB 94-1. The problem arose from the "grandfathering" provision of FAS 114, permitting debt restructured prior to that standard's effective date to be accounted for consistent with the provisions of FAS 15, which FAS 114 superseded. The concern was that this might have suggested that FAS 115 could not be applied to restructured loans that qualified as debt securities. However, FTB 94-1 made it clear that FAS 115 applies to all loans which qualify as debt securities, and that the "grandfathering" provision would not be applicable in such circumstances. In other words, the provisions of FAS 115 take precedence over those of FAS 114, in situations where FAS 115 applies.

**Transfers of debt securities among categories.** Transfer of any given security between categories is accounted for at fair value. If the transfer is from the trading category, there is no further income statement effect since the fair value-based gains or losses have already been reported. If the transfer is to the trading category, the unrealized gain or loss is recognized immediately. Depending on whether the transfer is from the available-for-sale or the held-to-maturity category, such unrealized gain or loss would have been included in the accumulated other comprehensive income account on the balance sheet, after having been reported as an element of other comprehensive income, or would not have been reported at all prior to the transfer.

If the debt security is being transferred from held-to-maturity to the available-for-sale category, the unrealized gain or loss, not previously reflected in the investment account, will be added to the appropriate accumulated other comprehensive income account at the date of transfer and reported in other comprehensive income. If a security is being transferred from available-for-sale to held-to-maturity, the unrealized holding gain or loss previously accrued will continue to be maintained in the accumulated other comprehensive income account, but now will be amortized to income over the period until maturity as an adjustment of yield, using the effective interest method. The fair value as of the date of transfer to the held-to-maturity classification, net of any subsequent amortization of the discrepancy between fair value and maturity or par value as of the transfer date, will be the new "cost" for purposes of the disclosures required by FAS 115.

### Example of accounting for debt securities

Marcie Corporation purchases the following debt securities as investments in 2009:

| *Issue* | *Face value* | *Price paid** |
|---|---|---|
| Dukane Chemical 8% due 2013 | $200,000 | $190,000 |
| Forwall Pharmaceutical 9.90% due 2025 | 500,000 | 575,000 |
| Luckystrike Mining 4% due 2011 | 100,000 | 65,000 |

\* Accrued interest is ignored in these amounts; the normal entries for interest accrual and receipt are assumed.

Management has informed us that Marcie's objectives differed among the various investments; the Dukane bonds are considered to be suitable as a long-term investment, with the intention that they will be held until maturity. The Luckystrike bonds are a speculation; the significant discount from par value was seen as very attractive, despite the low coupon rate. Management believes the bonds were depressed because mining stocks and bonds have been out of favor, but believes the economic recovery will lead to a surge in market value, at which point the bonds will be sold for a quick profit.  The Forwall Pharmaceutical bonds are deemed a good investment, but with a maturity date sixteen years in the future, management is unable to commit to holding these to maturity.

Based on the foregoing, the appropriate accounting for the three investments in bonds would be as follows:

### Dukane Chemical 8% due 2013

Account for these as held-to-maturity; maintain at historical cost, with discount ($10,000) to be amortized over term to maturity (assumed to be four years, for an amortization of $2,500 per year[4]).

### Forwall Pharmaceutical 9.90% due 2025

Account for these as available-for-sale, since neither the held-for-trading nor held-to-maturity criteria apply.  These are to be reported at fair value at each balance sheet date, with any unrealized gain or loss included in the additional/contra equity account, unless an "other-than-temporary" decline occurs.

### Luckystrike Mining 4% due 2011

As an admitted speculation, these are accounted for as part of the trading category, and also reported at fair value on the balance sheet.  All adjustments to carrying value will be included in net income each year, irrespective of whether the fluctuations are deemed to be temporary.

Transfers between categories are to be accounted for at fair value at the date of the transfer.  Consider the following events.

1.  Marcie management decides in 2010, when the Forwall bonds have a fair value of $604,500, that the bonds will be disposed of in the short term, hopefully when the price hits $605,000.  The bonds are presently carried on the books at $580,000, which was the fair value at the time the year-end 2009 financial statements were being prepared.  Based on this description of the decision, the bonds are to be transferred to the trading portfolio at a "cost" of $604,500.  The entry to record this would be the following:

| | | |
|---|---:|---:|
| Investment in debt securities—held-for-trading | 604,500 | |
| Unrealized gain on holding debt securities as investment | 5,000 | |
|     Investment in debt securities—available-for-sale | | 580,000 |
|     Gain on holding debt securities | | 29,500 |

The previously unrealized gain (reflected in the write-up of the investment from original cost, $575,000, to the fair value at year-end 2009, $580,000) is now "realized" for financial reporting purposes, as is the further rise in value from $580,000 to $604,500 at the time the portfolio transfer takes place.

2.  Assume that at year-end 2009 the investment in the Forwall bonds is still held, and the fair value has declined to $602,000.  Management's intentions regarding this holding have not changed since the decision to transfer to held-for-trading.  The year-end adjustment will be

| | | |
|---|---:|---:|
| Loss on holding debt securities | 2,500 | |
|     Investment in debt securities—held-for-trading | | 2,500 |

The market decline is reflected in net income in 2009, since the bonds are in the held-for-trading portfolio.

3.  Now, assume that in 2010, management determines that a major investment in plant renewal and expansion will likely be necessary by the year 2012, based on a detailed capital budget

---

[4]  *Technically, GAAP requires that the discount be amortized using an effective interest method that produces a constant percentage yield over the life of the bond.  In the case of Dukane Chemical, this would result in amortization of approximately $2,452 in 2009, $2,484 in 2010, $2,516 in 2011, and $2,548 in 2013 using annual compounding and an effective annual rate of 1.291%.  For the purposes of this example, straight-line amortization has been used because the results are not materially different.*

prepared. With this in mind, Marcie Corporation determines that the holding of Forwall Pharmaceutical bonds would be an excellent vehicle to provide for these future cash needs, and accordingly concludes to hold these to maturity. At the time this decision is made, the fair value of the bonds is quoted at $603,000. The entry to record the transfer from held-for-trading to held-to-maturity is as follows:

| | | |
|---|---|---|
| Investment in debt securities—held-to-maturity | 603,000 | |
| Investment in debt securities held-for-trading | | 602,000 |
| Gain on holding debt securities | | 1,000 |

The bonds are again transferred at fair value, which in this case gives rise to a $1,000 recognized gain.

4.  In 2010 Marcie management also made a decision about its investment in Dukane Chemical bonds. These bonds, which were originally designated as held-to-maturity, were accounted for at amortized historical cost. Assume the amortization in 2009 was $2,000 (because the bonds were not held for a full year), so that the book value of the investment at year-end 2009 was $192,000. In 2010, at a time when the value of these bonds was $198,000, management concluded that it was no longer certain that they would be held to maturity, and therefore transferred this holding to the available-for-sale portfolio. The entry to record this would be

| | | |
|---|---|---|
| Investment in debt securities—available-for-sale | 198,000 | |
| Unrealized gain on holding debt securities as investment | | 6,000 |
| Investment in debt securities—held-to-maturity | | 192,000 |

The transfer is at fair value, but since the bonds are being transferred into the available-for-sale category (for which unrealized gains and losses are recorded in an additional or contra equity account), the gain at this date, $6,000, is not recognized in net income, but rather will be reported in other comprehensive income.

5.  In 2011, for the same reason management determined to hold the Forwall Pharmaceuticals bonds to maturity, it also reverses its prior decision regarding the Dukane Chemical bond holding. It now professes an intention to hold these until their maturity, in 2013. At the date this decision is made, the Dukane bonds are quoted at $195,000. Assume that the value at year-end 2010 had been $198,000, so no adjustment was needed at that time to the carrying value of the investment. Again the transfer will be recorded at fair value.

| | | |
|---|---|---|
| Investment in debt securities—held-to-maturity | 195,000 | |
| Unrealized gain on holding debt securities as investment | 3,000 | |
| Investment in debt securities—available-for-sale | | 198,000 |

The unrealized gain previously recognized in an equity account is partially eliminated, since fair value at the date of this transfer is less than the previously recorded amount. The change in this equity account must be reported as other comprehensive income for the period in which this portfolio reclassification occurs. The remaining balance in the additional/contra equity account (whether a net debit or credit) is accounted for as additional premium or discount, and is amortized over the remaining term to maturity. GAAP mandates that the effective yield method be used, but for this example, assume that the discount will be amortized over the remaining two years on the straight-line basis (if this difference from the effective yield method is not material, this would be an acceptable practice). Thus, the actual discount as measured by the spread between the new carrying value, $195,000, and face value to be received at maturity, $200,000, plus the additional discount measured by the unrealized gain reported in the equity section of $3,000, gives a total discount amounting to $8,000 to be amortized over the remaining two years. This $8,000, when added to the $2,000 discount amortized in 2010 (when the bonds were in the original held-to-maturity portfolio), equals $10,000, which is the discount between the face value, $200,000 and the price paid by Marcie Corporation ($190,000).

Note that the illustrated reclassification of the Dukane Chemical bonds from the held-to-maturity to the available-for-sale portfolios would, in most instances, have serious adverse consequences for Marcie. Under FAS 115, classification as held-to-maturity can only occur when, at acquisition, management has both the intent and the ability to maintain the investment until maturity. A sale prior to maturity is taken as an indication that its intent was not truly present, and accordingly, use of the held-to-maturity classification for any other investments will be precluded, unless the sale before maturity is precipitated by certain events.

These are

1. Evidence of a substantial deterioration in the issuer's creditworthiness, placing the entity at jeopardy from any further holding of the investment
2. A tax law change affecting the tax-exempt status of the investment holding
3. A major business acquisition or disposition necessitating portfolio changes to maintain the entity's interest rate risk posture
4. For banks or thrifts, a change in regulatory capital requirements such that a significant downsizing is necessitated, including disposition of the bond portfolio, and
5. A significant increase in risk weighting (under bank and thrift capital rules) of the held-to-maturity investments, again necessitating dispositions of these investments

Other isolated, nonrecurring, and unusual events and circumstances might also suffice to justify disposal of these investments without "tainting" the remaining held-to-maturity portfolio or precluding its future use by the entity, but these would be rare occurrences.

While a transfer from the held-to-maturity to the available-for-sale portfolios would not be a sale, it would be demonstrative of an intent or willingness to dispose of the investment, which would be equally suggestive of an earlier misrepresentation of management's intent regarding those investments. While FAS 115 is silent on this, the same strictures affecting an outright sale of these portfolio investments should be assumed to apply to a transfer to the available-for-sale category. In other words, while not prohibited, such transfers would be very rare and carry an accounting risk for the reporting entity.

**Certain transactions that do not impede further use of the held-to-maturity classification.** According to EITF 96-10, as modified by the provisions of FAS 140, transactions involving held-to-maturity investments that are not accounted for as sales do not call into question the classification of investments as held-to-maturity. It should be noted, however, that the most common such transaction, the "wash sale," is explicitly required under FAS 140 to be given sale treatment and, accordingly, will cause the reporting entity to abandon held-to-maturity treatment of other investments held or later acquired. One example of transaction that might avoid sale recognition, and hence preserve use of the held-to-maturity classification by the entity, is bond swaps. However, if intent is to not hold the new security received until maturity, then intent regarding other bond holdings, etc., will be questioned. Desecuritizations will not be treated as sales under EITF 96-10.

**Presentation in the financial statements.** Trading securities must always be grouped with current assets in classified balance sheets, and held-to-maturity investments will be noncurrent (unless the maturity date is within one year). Available-for sale securities may conceivable be classified as either current or noncurrent.

If declines in value are deemed to meet FAS 115's definition of *other than temporary*, then these are to be included in net income in the current period. However, subsequent recoveries cannot be recognized in net income. If available-for-sale investments are written down for such impairments that later reverse, the recovery is accounted for as an increase in fair value to be reflected in the other comprehensive income account, on the balance sheet only. If held-to-maturity investments are similarly written down and later recover some or all of the lost value, the fair value increase will not be reported in the balance sheet at all, although disclosure will generally be made in the notes.

For purposes of reporting in the statement of cash flows, all purchases and sales of trading securities must be included in the operations section, while those of available-for-sale and held-to-maturity investments are to be shown as part of investing activities.

FAS 115 requires specific disclosures of the components of a reporting entity's portfolios of investments. For available-for-sale securities and (separately) for held-to-maturity securities, classification by type of security is necessary; categories of issuers, such as US Treasury, other US agencies, state and municipal governmental units, foreign governmental units, corporations, mortgage-backed, and others are suggested. Aggregate fair values, gross unrealized holding gains, and gross unrealized holding losses must also be disclosed, by major security type, as of the date of each balance sheet being presented.

For the available-for-sale and held-to-maturity portfolios, information about contractual maturities must be presented as of the date of the latest balance sheet presented and must be grouped into at least four categories: within one year; one to five years; five to ten years; and, over ten years. Both fair values and amortized cost of debt securities in each maturity category must be presented.

For each income statement presented, proceeds from the sales of available-for-sale securities, and the gross realized gains and losses resulting from those sales, also must be disclosed. Further, the basis upon which the gains or losses were determined, (e.g., average cost, specific identification, etc.) must be disclosed. In addition, the notes must identify gross gains or losses included in net income resulting from transfers of securities from the available-for-sale to the trading portfolio, and the net change in unrealized gains or losses recognized by an adjustment of the contra equity account.

For sales or transfers from securities categorized as held-to-maturity, the amortized cost amounts, the related gains or losses realized or unrealized, and the circumstances surrounding the decision to sell or to reclassify the investment, are all to be disclosed in the notes to the financial statements for each period for which an income statement is being presented. There is, of course, a presumption that sales or transfers from the held-to-maturity portfolio will be rare occurrences.

## Impairment

**Other-than-temporary declines in fair value.** In general, the determination of whether an investment is impaired hinges on a judgment as to whether a decline in fair value is temporary in nature or is "other than temporary."

While the term " other than temporary" is used in the standards dealing both with passive investments (FAS 115) and those where significant influence over the investee exists (APB 18), this term previously was not formally defined in the authoritative literature.

The Emerging Issues Task Force, in its consensus position EITF 03-1, *The Meaning of Other-Than-Temporary Impairment and Its Application to Certain Investments*, established the meaning of this oft-employed expression and developed guidelines for ascertaining when such impairment has occurred. EITF 03-1 was subsequently nullified and replaced in November, 2005, by FSP FAS 115-1 and FAS 124-1, having the same title. The FSP was initially effective for reporting periods beginning after December 15, 2005, with early application permitted.

**Scope of FSP FAS 115-1 and FAS 124-1.** The guidance in the FSP, by reference to FAS 115, excludes the following:

1. Investments that, absent an election under FAS 159 to use fair value, would be accounted for using the equity method of accounting
2. Investments in consolidated subsidiaries
3. Investments in derivative instruments subject to FAS 133, *Accounting for Derivative Instruments and Hedging Activities*
4. Investments held by reporting entities subject to specialized industry accounting principles that stipulate that substantially all investments in debt and equity securi-

ties be recognized at fair (or market) value with changes in fair value recognized in net income as they occur. These reporting entities include

a. Brokers and dealers in securities
b. Employee benefit plans
c. Investment companies

5. Investments held by not-for-profit organizations subject to FAS 124, *Accounting for Certain Investments Held by Not-for-Profit Organizations,* where the investments are not held by an investor that reports a performance indicator as defined in AAG-*Health Care Organizations.*

Subject to the above exclusions, the FSP applies to investments in

1. Debt securities
2. Equity securities with readily determinable fair values
3. Equity investments accounted for under the cost method

The FSP elaborates by providing the following additional scope guidance:

1. The FSP applies to all equity securities held by insurance companies
2. Investors are not permitted to "look through" the form of investment to the type of securities that are held by the investee. For example, if the investor holds shares of a mutual fund that invests primarily in debt securities, the assessment of impairment under the FSP would not be made for the portfolio of debt securities held by the mutual fund but rather would be made for the mutual fund shares themselves, which are considered equity securities.
3. If the application of FAS 133 (paragraph 12) results in bifurcating an investment into a host instrument and an embedded derivative, the host instrument would be evaluated for impairment under the FSP if it falls within the FSP's scope.
4. The FSP applies to debt and equity securities that are within the scope of FAS 124 and that are held by an investor and that reports a performance indicator.

The FSP establishes a multistep decision process to determine if an investment has been impaired, evaluate whether the impairment is other than temporary, and if determined to be impaired, measure the impairment loss. It also establishes a discrete model for assessing impairment of cost-method investments which present unique challenges since reasonable estimation of their fair value is often not practical or cost effective.

The model set forth in the FSP for investments other than those accounted for using the cost method is as follows:

**Step 1—Determine whether the investment is impaired.** An investment is impaired if its fair value is less than its cost. Cost as defined for this purpose includes adjustments made to the cost basis of an investment for accretion, amortization, previous other-than-temporary impairments, and hedging.[5]

The unit of account used to determine impairment is the individual security level, defined as the level and method of aggregation that the reporting entity uses to measure realized and unrealized gains and losses on its debt and equity securities. For example, management may aggregate all equity securities of an issuer that have the same CUSIP number[6] that were purchased

---

[5] *FAS 133, par. 22(b) indicates that, with respect to a qualifying fair value hedge, the change in fair value of the hedged item that is attributable to the hedged risk is recorded as an adjustment to the carrying amount of the hedged item and is recognized currently in net income.*

[6] *A CUSIP number is a nine-digit alpha numeric identifier used to identify securities traded in public markets. CUSIP is an acronym that stands for "Committee on Uniform Securities Identification Procedures."*

in separate trade lots and use an average cost convention to compute realized or unrealized gains or losses.

In assessing impairment of debt securities, the investor is not permitted to combine separate contracts such as guarantees or other credit enhancements.

The assessment of whether an investment is impaired is to be made for each interim and annual reporting period, subject to special provisions that apply to cost-method investments discussed separately below.

After comparing fair value to cost, if cost exceeds fair value, the investment is considered impaired and the evaluator is to then proceed to step 2 to determine whether the impairment is "other than temporary."

**Step 2—Evaluate whether the impairment is other than temporary.** Instead of providing stand-alone guidance to the evaluator, step 2 of the FSP contains cross-references to other authoritative literature (which contain further cross-references) to be applied to the specific facts and circumstances as applicable:

- FAS 115, paragraph 16
- Q&A FAS 115, *A Guide to Implementation of Statement 115 on Accounting for Certain Investments in Debt and Equity Securities: Questions and Answers* (revised September 2001)
- SEC SAB 59 (Topic 5M in the codification of Staff Accounting Bulletins), *Other-Than-Temporary Impairment of Certain Investments in Debt and Equity Securities*
- SAS 92, *Auditing Derivative Instruments, Hedging Activities, and Investments in Securities* (AU §332)
- AUG *Auditing Derivative Instruments, Hedging Activities, and Investments in Securities*

In synthesizing the guidance contained in these sources, it is important to understand first and foremost that FASB used the phrase "other than temporary" to convey its intent that an impairment in the fair value of a security need not be permanent to be recognized and recorded in the financial statements. Thus, there is a rebuttable presumption that impairment of a security is other than temporary and will require recognition in the period that the impairment occurs.

Management is to evaluate all available evidence regarding the realizability of an investment starting with the premise that the investment may be required to be written down. Many objective and subjective factors can influence this decision and the applicability and relative importance of these factors will vary between types of investments, between reporting entities, and between accounting periods. Professional judgment will naturally be involved given the fact that, in making these judgments, management considers its knowledge and past experience, its evaluation of the extent and duration of the effects of current events, and its expectations and assumptions regarding the future.

Examples of factors that might, either individually or in combination, be indicative of a decline in fair value being other than temporary include, but are not limited to

- Fair value is significantly less than cost and

  - The decline in fair value is due to adverse conditions related to the specific security, to the industry, or to a geographic area
  - The decline has existed for an extended period of time
  - Management does not have both the intent and ability to hold the security for a sufficient period of time to allow for any anticipated recovery in fair value

- The security has been downgraded by a rating agency
- The financial condition of the issuer has worsened
- The issuer has reduced or eliminated dividends
- Scheduled interest payments have not been made
- Subsequent to the end of the reporting period, the reporting entity recorded losses associated with the security
- The occurrence of specific events that might influence the issuer's operations, such as changes in technology that may reduce its earnings potential or the discontinuance of a portion of the business that may affect future earnings potential

In addition to the foregoing, impairment of debt securities can be caused by numerous factors including, but not limited to

- Increases in market interest rates
- Changes in foreign exchange rates
- Changes in perceptions by market participants of the value of credit enhancements such as financial guarantee insurance caused, for example, by a ratings downgrade on the insurer of the securities
- Illiquidity in credit markets that renders the investment unsalable or only saleable in secondary markets at a deep discount from face value

Unless there is persuasive evidence to support a realizable value that equals or exceeds the investment's carrying value, the reporting entity is required to write down the investment to fair value and recognize an impairment loss as a charge to net income in the period in which the investment becomes impaired.

If the impaired security is a debt instrument that was not impaired at acquisition, and the investor believes that, at a subsequent balance sheet date, it is probable that the investor will be unable to collect all amounts due according to the contractual terms of the debt, an other-than-temporary impairment is considered to have occurred.

Generally, if the holder of an available-for-sale debt security decides to sell it at a loss shortly after the balance sheet date and management does not expect the fair value of the security to recover prior to the expected time of sale, the other-than-temporary impairment loss would be recognized as a charge to net income in the period in which the decision is made to sell the security.

**Step 3—If the impairment is other than temporary, recognize an impairment loss equal to the difference between the investment's cost and its fair value.** If, as a result of step 2, management judges the impairment to be other than temporary, the reporting entity recognizes an impairment loss as a charge to net income for the entire difference between the investment's cost and its fair value at the balance sheet date. The impairment measurement is not to include any partial recoveries that might have occurred subsequent to the balance sheet date but prior to issuance of the financial statements.

The reduced carrying amount of the investment becomes that investment's new cost basis. This new cost basis is not to be changed for any subsequent recoveries in fair value. Subsequent recoveries in the fair value of available-for-sale securities are to be included in other comprehensive income; subsequent decreases in fair value are to be evaluated as to whether they are other than temporary in nature; if considered temporary, the decrease is recorded in other comprehensive income; if considered other than temporary, the decrease is to be recognized as a component of net income for the period as previously described.

### Example of other-than temporary impairment of an available-for-sale security

In January 2010 new information comes to the attention of Ralph Corporation management regarding the viability of Whammer Corp. Based on this information, it is determined that the decline in Whammer preferred stock is probably not a temporary one, but rather is other than temporary (i.e., the asset is impaired). FAS 115 prescribes that such a decline be reflected in net income, and the written-down value be treated as the new cost basis. The fair value has remained at the amount last reported, $109,500. Accordingly, the entry to recognize the fact of the investment's permanent impairment is as follows:

| | | |
|---|---|---|
| Loss on holding equity securities | 15,500 | |
|     Unrealized loss on securities—available-for-sale (other comprehensive income) | | 15,500 |

Any subsequent recovery in this value would not be recognized in net income unless realized through a sale of the investment to an unrelated entity in an arm's-length transaction, as long as the investment continues to be categorized as "available-for-sale," as distinct from "held-for-trading." However, if there is an increase in value (not limited to just a recovery of the amount of the loss recognized above, of course) the increase will be added to the investment account and shown in a separate account in stockholder's equity, since the asset is to be marked to fair value on the balance sheet.

It should be noted that the issue of other-than-temporary impairment does not arise in the context of investments held for trading purposes, since unrealized holding gains and losses are immediately recognized without limitation. In effect, the distinction between realized and unrealized gains or losses does not exist for trading securities.

**Example of temporary impairment**

In March 2010 further information comes to management's attention, which now suggests that the decline in Whammer preferred was indeed only a temporary decline; in fact, the value of Whammer now rises to $112,000. Since the carrying value after the recognition of the impairment was $109,500, which is treated as the cost basis for purposes of measuring further declines or recoveries, the increase to $112,000 will be accounted for as an increase to be reflected in the additional stockholders' equity account, as follows:

| | | |
|---|---|---|
| Investment in equity securites—available-for-sale | 2,500 | |
|     Unrealized gain on securities—available-for-sale (other comprehensive income) | | 2,500 |

Note that this increase in value is not recognized in current net income, since the investment is still considered to be available-for-sale, rather than a part of the trading portfolio. Even though the previous decline in Whammer stock was realized in current net income, because judged at the time to be a permanent impairment in value, the recovery cannot be recognized in net income. Rather, the change in value will be included in other comprehensive income and then displayed in an additional equity account.

**Subsequent accounting for debt securities after recognition of other-than-temporary impairment.** After recognizing a loss from other-than-temporary impairment with respect to a debt security, the investor is to treat the security as if it had been purchased on the measurement date on which the impairment was recognized. If the security had been originally purchased at a premium, the impairment charge will either reduce or eliminate the premium or if the impairment is large enough cause the reporting entity to record a discount. If the security had been purchased at its face amount or a discount, the impairment charge will result in recording or increasing the discount.

After recording the adjustment for the impairment, the adjusted premium or discount is to be amortized prospectively over the remaining term of the debt security based on the amount and timing of future estimated cash flows.

**Cost-method investments.** By their nature, cost-method investments normally do not have readily determinable fair values. Consequently, the FSP provides a different model for determining whether a cost-method investment is other-than-temporarily impaired. The determination is made as follows:

1.  If the investor has estimated the investment's fair value (e.g., for the purposes of the disclosures required by FAS 107, *Disclosures about Fair Value of Financial Instruments*, that estimate is to be used to determine if the investment is impaired for those reporting periods in which the investor estimates fair value. If the fair value is less than cost, the investor would proceed to step 2 of the impairment protocol described previously.

2.  For reporting periods in which the investor has not estimated the fair value of the investment, the investor is required to evaluate whether an event or change in circumstances has occurred during the period that may have a significant adverse effect on the fair value of the investment. Such events and circumstances are referred to as impairment indicators and include, but are not limited to

a.   A significant deterioration in the earnings performance, credit rating, asset quality, or business prospects of the investee
b.   A significant adverse change in the economic, regulatory, or technological environment of the investee
c.   A significant adverse change in the general market condition of either the geographic area or the industry in which the investee operates
d.   A solicited or unsolicited bona fide offer to purchase, an offer by the investee to sell, or a completed auction process for the same or similar security for an amount less than the cost of the investment
e.   Factors exist that raise significant concerns regarding the ability of the investee to continue as a going concern, such as negative cash flows from operations, working capital deficiencies, or noncompliance with debt covenants or statutory capital requirements.

If an impairment indicator is present, the investor is required to estimate the investment's fair value and compare the estimated fair value to the cost of the investment. If the fair value is less than cost, the investor is to proceed to step 2, as previously described, to evaluate whether the impairment is other than temporary.

Additionally, if a cost-method investment had previously been evaluated under step 2 as to whether impairment was other than temporary, and the investor had previously concluded that the investment was not other-than-temporarily impaired, the investor is required to continue to make this evaluation by estimating the investment's fair value in each subsequent interim and annual reporting period until either (1) the investment's fair value recovers to an amount that equals or exceeds the cost of the investment, or (2) the investor recognizes an other-than-temporary impairment loss.

**Equity-method investments.** The authoritative requirements stated above do not include in their scope investments accounted for under the equity method of accounting. In early 2004, the EITF discontinued its deliberations on providing a model to use with respect to other-than-temporary impairment of equity-method investments. At the EITF's March 17-18, 2004 meeting, the SEC observer stated that registrants were to continue to "rigorously assess equity-method investments for impairment" and further indicated that the staff of the SEC would, as it had done in the past, continue to object to what it characterized as inappropriate impairment analyses for such investments such as using a FAS 144 undiscounted cash flow approach.

The only guidance in authoritative GAAP with respect to this determination is provided by paragraph 6b of APB 18, circa 1971:

*"A series of operating losses of an investee or other factors may indicate that a decrease in value of the investment has occurred which is other than temporary and which should be recognized even though the decrease in value is in excess of what would otherwise be recognized by application of the equity method."*

In the authors' opinion, the following can be surmised from this discussion:

1.   An investor that holds an equity-method investment should pay close attention to this issue and monitor whether any events or changes in circumstances have occurred that may be indicative of impairment.
2.   Similar to the model for cost-method investments, if any impairment indicators have been identified, management should use its best efforts to estimate the fair value of its investment and compare it to the carrying amount,
3.   If the carrying amount exceeds the fair value, management should consider all evidence that is available without undue cost and effort in order to assess the underly-

ing causes of this condition and whether it considers the impairment to be other than temporary in nature.

4. If impairment is not considered to be other than temporary, management should consider voluntarily making the same disclosures as discussed in the next section that apply to other types of investments that have similar circumstances.

**Disclosures.** The FSP restates and expands certain disclosure requirements from previous standards, primarily to provide financial statement users with a better understanding of why impairments of investments have not been deemed other than temporary (i.e., why a loss associated with the impairment had not been recognized as a charge to current period net income).

The required disclosures are extensive and need to be fully understood by preparers of financial statements. At the date of each annual balance sheet presented, the following quantitative information must be disclosed in a tabular format aggregated by category of investment:

1. The aggregate amount of unrealized losses (that is, the amount by which cost or amortized cost exceeds fair value), and
2. The aggregate related fair value of investments with unrealized losses.

These disclosures are to be further segregated by those investments that have been in a continuous unrealized loss position for less than twelve months and those that have been in a continuous unrealized loss position for twelve months or longer. For purposes of making this distinction, the balance sheet date of the reporting period in which the impairment is identified is used to determine the duration. When interim financial statements are not prepared, the reference point would be the annual balance sheet date of the period during which the impairment was identified. The continuous unrealized loss position ends when either (1) there is recognition of a charge to net income of an other-than-temporary impairment, or (2) the investor becomes aware of a recovery of fair value during the period to at least the cost of the investment.

As of the date of the most recent annual balance sheet, additional narrative must be presented, such that financial statement users will be able to understand the quantitative disclosures, as well as the positive and negative information that management of the reporting entity considered in concluding that impairments were not other than temporary. These disclosures can be aggregated by investment categories, although individually significant unrealized losses generally are not to be aggregated. Disclosure or discussion elements would include

1. The nature of the investment(s)
2. The cause(s) of the impairment(s)
3. The number of investment positions that are in an unrealized loss position
4. The severity and duration of the impairment(s)
5. Other evidence considered by management in reaching the conclusion that the impairment is not other than temporary, for example, citing industry analyst reports, sector credit ratings, volatility of the security's fair value, and/or any other information that management considers relevant.

When the investment(s) is accounted for under the cost method, the reporting entity is required to disclose the following additional information, when applicable, as of each date for which a balance sheet is presented in its *annual* financial statements:

1. The aggregate carrying amount of all cost-method investments,

2. The aggregate carrying amount of cost-method investments that the investor did not evaluate for impairment, and

3. The fact that the fair value of a cost-method investment is not estimated if there are no identified events or changes in circumstances that may have a significant adverse effect on the fair value of the investment, and either

   a. Management determined, as provided under FAS 107, that it is not practicable to estimate the fair value of the investment, or

   b. The investor is exempt from estimating fair value per FAS 126.

### The Equity Method of Accounting for Investments

The equity method, sometimes referred to as "one-line consolidation," permits an entity (investor) owning a percentage of the common stock of another entity (investee) to incorporate its pro rata share of the investee's operating results into its net income. However, rather than include its share of each component (e.g., sales, cost of sales, operating expenses, etc.) in its financial statements, the investor only includes its share of the investee's net income as a separate line item in its income. Note that there are exceptions to this one-line rule. The investor's share of investee extraordinary items and prior period adjustments retain their identities in the investor's income and retained earnings statements and are separately reported if material in relation to the investor's income. It should be noted that the final bottom-line impact on the investor's financial statements is identical whether the equity method or full consolidation is employed; only the amount of detail presented within the statements will differ.

The equity method is not a substitute for consolidation; it is employed where the investor has significant influence over the operations of the investee but lacks control. In general, significant influence is inferred when the investor owns between 20% and 50% of the investee's voting common stock. Any ownership percentage over 50% presumably gives the investor actual voting control, making full consolidation of financial statements necessary. The 20% threshold stipulated in APB 18 is not absolute; circumstances may suggest that significant influence exists even though the investor's level of ownership is less than 20%, or that it is absent despite a level of ownership above 20%. In considering whether significant influence exists, FIN 35 identifies the following factors: (1) opposition by the investee, (2) agreements under which the investor surrenders shareholder rights, (3) majority ownership by a small group of shareholders, (4) inability to obtain desired information from the investee, (5) inability to obtain representation on investee board of directors, etc. Whether sufficient contrary evidence exists to negate the presumption of significant influence is a matter of judgment. Judgment requires a careful evaluation of all pertinent facts and circumstances, over an extended period of time in some cases.

Prior to the issuance of FAS 94, some investors used the equity method in those rare instances in which the investor owned over 50% of the investee's voting common shares but consolidated statements were deemed to be inappropriate (usually because consolidated statements would mask important differences in the financial or operating characteristics as between the investor-parent and the investee-subsidiary). However, FAS 94 eliminated this once popular "nonhomogeneity" justification for not consolidating. This left only temporary control, noncontrol, and foreign exchange restrictions and related reasons as justification for not consolidating majority-owned subsidiaries. FAS 144 eliminated temporary control as a justification for nonconsolidation. As a practical matter, absence of control by the parent is the only remaining reason to not consolidate a majority-owned investee.

Complexities in the use of the equity method arise in several areas.

1. *Differences between the cost at which the investor acquired its shares and the investor's proportionate share of the net assets of the investee.* The cost of the investment to the investor might not be equal to the fair value of the investor's share of the investee's net assets. APB 18 requires these differences to be accounted for in the same manner as if the investee were a consolidated subsidiary. This requires analysis to determine whether the differences are attributable to (a) specific tangible assets whose fair values exceed their carrying values as recorded in the accounting records of the investee, or (b) specifically identifiable intangible assets that are not recognized in the accounting records of the investee because they were internally developed. Any excess remaining after allocating the differences to (a) and/or (b) is analogous to goodwill in a business combination accounted for under the acquisition method (formerly referred to as the purchase method). Since the ultimate income statement effects of applying the equity method of accounting must generally be the same as full consolidation, an adjustment must be made to account for these differentials.

   Further compounding this complexity is the fact that, when FAS 141(R) and FAS 160 become effective, on or after the beginning of the first annual reporting period beginning on or after December 15, 2008, the recognition and measurement rules that apply to these differences arising from the acquisition of new equity-method investments will be required, prospectively, to conform to the revisions in the new standards while previously acquired equity-method investments will continue to follow the previous rules and will not be restated to conform to the new standards.

2. *Deferred income tax accounting.* The equity method is not a recognized tax accounting method under the US Internal Revenue Code (IRC). For income tax purposes, the investor's share of the investee's net income is not recognized until realized through either the payment of dividends or through the sale of the investment. This gives rise to a future taxable temporary difference between the carrying value of the equity-method investment for financial reporting purposes and the income tax basis of the investment. The temporary difference will give rise to recognition of a deferred income tax liability.

3. *Measurement of an equity-method investment when the investor acquires its interest in stages.* Revisions to equity-method measurement rules that apply when the investor acquires its interests in the investee in stages (or steps). These revisions result from amendments made to APB 18 by FAS 141(R) and FAS 160, designed to ensure that equity method accounting treats such staged acquisitions in a manner similar to the way they are treated in the context of business combinations.

Absent these complicating factors, the use of the equity method by the investor is relatively straightforward: the original cost of the investment is increased by the investor's proportionate share of the investee's net income and is decreased by the investor's proportionate share of the investee's net losses and by dividends received. The basic procedure is illustrated below.

**Example of the equity method—a simple case ignoring deferred income taxes**

On January 2, 2009, R Corporation (the investor) acquired 40% of E Company's (the investee) voting common stock on the open market for $100,000. Unless demonstrated otherwise, it is assumed that R Corporation can exercise significant influence over E Company's operating and financing policies. On January 2, E's stockholders' equity consists of the following:

| Common stock, par $1, 100,000 shares authorized, 50,000 shares issued | |
|---|---|
| and outstanding | $ 50,000 |
| Additional paid-in capital | 150,000 |
| Retained earnings | 50,000 |
| Total stockholders' equity | $250,000 |

Note that the cost of E Company common stock was equal to 40% of the book value of E's net assets. Assume also that there is no difference between the book value and the fair value of E Company's assets and liabilities. Accordingly, the balance in the investment account in R's records represents exactly 40% of E's stockholders' equity (net assets). Assume further that E Company reported a 2009 net income of $30,000 and paid cash dividends of $10,000. Its stockholders' equity at year-end would be as follows:

| Common stock, par $1, 100,000 shares authorized, 50,000 shares issued | |
|---|---|
| and outstanding | $ 50,000 |
| Additional paid-in capital | 150,000 |
| Retained earnings | 70,000 |
| Total stockholders' equity | $270,000 |

R Corporation would record its share of the increase in E Company's net assets during 2009 as follows:

| | | |
|---|---|---|
| Investment in E Company | 12,000 | |
|     Equity in E income | | 12,000 |
| *($30,000 × 40%)* | | |
| Cash | 4,000 | |
|     Investment in E Company | | 4,000 |
| *($10,000 × 40%)* | | |

When R's balance sheet is prepared at December 31, 2009, the balance reported in the investment account would be $108,000 (= $100,000 + $12,000 – $4,000). This amount represents 40% of the book value of E's net assets at the end of the year (40% × $270,000). Note also that the equity in E income is reported as a separate caption in R's income statement, typically as a component of income from continuing operations before income taxes.

In computing the deferred income tax effects of income recognized by applying the equity method, the investor must make an assumption regarding the means by which the undistributed earnings of the investee will be realized by the investor. The earnings can be realized either through later dividend receipts or by disposition of the investment at a gain. The former assumption would result in income taxes at the investor's marginal income tax rate on ordinary income (net of the 80% dividends received deduction permitted by the Internal Revenue Code for intercorporate investments of less than 80% but at least 20%; a lower deduction of 70% applies if ownership is below 20%). The latter option would be treated as a capital gain, which is currently taxed at the full corporate income tax rate, since the preferential corporate capital gains rate was eliminated by the 1986 Tax Reform Act.

### Example of the equity method—a simple case including deferred income taxes

Assume the same information as in the example above. In addition, assume that R Corporation has a combined (federal, state, and local) marginal income tax rate of 34% on ordinary income and that it anticipates realization of E Company earnings through future dividend receipts.

R Corporation's current income tax expense associated with its investment is computed based on its current dividends received less the dividends received deduction under IRC §243. Since R owns a 40% interest in E, the applicable percentage for the dividends received deduction is 80%. Note that the dividends received deduction constitutes a permanent difference under FAS 109 that never reverses. The provision for income taxes currently payable is computed as follows:

| | |
|---|---|
| Dividends received | $4,000 |
| Less— dividends received deduction (80%) | 3,200 |
| Taxable income from investment in E | 800 |
| × current combined federal and state tax rate | × 34% |
| Income taxes currently payable | $ 272 |

To compute deferred income taxes under the liability method used in FAS 109, at each reporting date we must determine the temporary difference between the carrying amount of the investment for financial reporting purposes and its tax basis. In this case, this is done as follows:

| | |
|---|---:|
| Carrying value of equity-method investment | |
| for financial reporting purposes | |
| Original cost | $100,000 |
| Equity method earnings | 12,000 |
| Dividends | (4,000) |
| | 108,000 |
| Income tax basis | |
| Original cost | 100,000 |
| Temporary difference | $ 8,000 |

Since R expects to realize this difference in the future through the receipt of dividends, it adjusts the difference for the permanent difference that arises from benefit of the dividends received deduction of 80% of $8,000 or $6,400 thus leaving $1,600 that would be subject to the effective rate that R expects to apply to reversal of the temporary difference, which, as provided in the assumptions above, is 34%. Applying the 34% expected future effective tax rate to the $1,600 taxable portion of the temporary difference would yield a deferred income tax expense (and related liability) of $544. The entry to record these items at December 31, 2009, is as follows:

| | | |
|---|---:|---:|
| Income tax expense—Current | 272 | |
| Income tax expense—Deferred | 544 | |
| Income taxes currently payable | | 272 |
| Deferred income tax liability | | 544 |

*To record provision for income taxes for the year ended 12/31/2009 attributable to equity-method investment in E*

The deferred income tax liability is originally computed with reference to the projected income tax effect of the "temporary difference reversal." It may be subsequently adjusted for a variety of reasons, including changed income tax rates and altered management expectations (see Chapter 17 for a complete discussion).

Notwithstanding FAS 109's requirement that deferred income taxes be adjusted for changed expectations at each subsequent balance sheet date, the actual income tax effect of the temporary difference reversal may still differ from the deferred income tax provided. This difference may occur because the actual income tax effect is a function of the entity's other current items of income and expense in the year of reversal (while FAS 109 requires the use of a projected effective income tax rate, actual rates may differ). It may also result from a realization of the investee's earnings in a manner other than anticipated (assuming that income tax rates on "ordinary" income differ from those on capital gains).

### Example of income tax effects resulting from the sale of an equity-method investment

Assume that in 2010, before any further earnings or dividends are reported by the investee, the investor sells the entire investment for $115,000. The income tax impact is

| | |
|---|---:|
| Selling price | $115,000 |
| Less income tax basis (original cost) | 100,000 |
| Gain | $ 15,000 |
| Capital gain rate (marginal corporate rate) | × 34% |
| Income tax liability | $ 5,100 |

The entries to record the sale, the income tax thereon, and the reversal of the previously provided deferred income taxes on the undistributed 2009 earnings of the investee are as follows:

| | | | |
|---|---|---:|---:|
| 1. | Cash | 115,000 | |
| | Investment in E Company | | 108,000 |
| | Gain on sale of investment | | 7,000 |
| 2. | Income tax expense—Current | 5,100 | |
| | Deferred income tax liability | 544 | |
| | Income taxes payable—Current | | 5,100 |
| | Income tax benefit—Deferred | | 544 |

Note that if the realization through a sale of the investment had been anticipated at the time the 2009 balance sheet was prepared, the deferred income tax liability would have been adjusted (possibly to reflect the entire $5,100 amount of the ultimate obligation), with the offset included in 2009's ordinary income tax expense. The above example explicitly assumes that the sale of the investment was not anticipated prior to 2010.

**Differences in fiscal year.** If the investor and investee have different fiscal years, APB 18 permits the investor to use the most recent financial statements available as long as the lag in reporting is consistent from period to period. Analogizing from ARB 51, the lag period is not to exceed three months.

If the investee changes its fiscal year-end to reduce or eliminate the lag period, EITF 06-9 stipulates that the change be treated as a voluntary change in accounting principle under FAS 154 (discussed in detail in Chapter 5). Although FAS 154 requires such changes to be made by retrospective application to all periods presented, it provides an exception if it is not practical to do so.

**Accounting for a differential between cost of an equity-method investment and the investor's proportionate share of net assets.** The preceding examples ignored one of the major complexities of the equity method; namely, the APB 18 requirement that the investor account for any differential between its cost and its proportionate share of the fair value of the investee's net identifiable assets consistent with the accounting for a business combination under the purchase method prescribed by FAS 141 or, after the effective date of FAS 141(R) and 160, the acquisition method prescribed therein.

In almost all instances, the price paid by an investor to acquire shares of an investee will differ from the corresponding underlying book value (i.e., the investee's net assets per its GAAP-basis financial statements). The differential can be broken down into the following components from the authoritative literature on business combinations:

1. Tangible and intangible assets recognized in the accounting records of the investee at carrying values that are below their fair values
2. Identifiable intangible assets not recognized in the accounting records of the investee because of the longstanding prohibition in GAAP against recognizing internally developed intangibles (with the notable exception of internal-use software). These might include in-process research and development assets, customer lists, and other amortizable or nonamortizable intangibles as discussed in detail in Chapters 11 and 13).
3. Goodwill

Clearly, this means that premiums or discounts versus underlying book values must be identified, analyzed, and dealt with in the accounting for the investment under the equity method. It also means that assets or liabilities not recognized by the investee must be identified and assigned, on a memo basis, the appropriate shares of the investor's purchase cost.

In the simplest example of applying this principle, if fixed assets having appreciated fair values are identified, part of the price paid by the investor must be allocated (in a notational sense only—since the entire investment is presented as a single caption in the investor's financial statements, consistent with the "one-line consolidation" aspect of equity method accounting) to the "step-up" in the values of those assets. Since those assets (other than land) are subject to depreciation, the investor must amortize a part of the investment cost against its share of investee earnings. This can require a costly and time-consuming effort on the part of the investor, particularly when a range of assets having varying depreciable lives is involved, as would almost always be the case.

Under APB 18, any premium paid by the investor that cannot be identified as being attributable to appreciated recognized tangible and intangible assets or unrecognized internally developed intangible assets of the investee is analogous to goodwill. While under prior rules this goodwill component would have been amortized, under FAS 142 this is subject not to amortization but rather to impairment testing. The impairment testing regime to be applied is not, however, that specified in FAS 142, which only pertains to testing by entities which actually record an asset explicitly as goodwill (i.e., the acquirer in a business combination accounted for under FAS 141 under the purchase method or 141[R] under the acquisition method). Equity method investors will continue to assess impairment of investments in investees by considering whether declines in the fair values of those investments, versus carrying values, may be other than temporary in nature as discussed previously in this chapter.

Under the authoritative literature on business combinations that has been in effect since mid-2001, there is an enhanced requirement, applicable to purchase method business combinations (now referred to as the acquisition method) and equity-method investments, to identify intangible assets that must be given separate recognition from goodwill. Previous practice was less stringent, because all intangibles were subject to amortization, with the result that many would-be identifiable intangibles, such as customer relationships, were not separately identified. These overlooked but nevertheless existent intangibles were effectively combined with goodwill and amortized over the period, not exceeding forty years, that is was permissible to assign as the economic life of goodwill. This is no longer permissible. Accordingly, analyzing the purchase cost of an equity-method investment, an investor needs to identify the portions of the premium paid that relate to identifiable intangibles per FAS 142, as well as to goodwill, with appropriate treatments regarding varying amortizable lives or, in some instances, amortization not being recognized due to the assets having indefinite lives.

Although infrequently encountered in practice, the amount paid by the investor for its interest in the investee may imply that there had been a discount, analogous to a bargain purchase in the GAAP that relates to business combinations. In the rare instances where this occurs, this would be treated in the same manner as negative goodwill. Of critical importance when this is the case, is the date on which the investor obtained its interest in the investee as the rules accorded negative goodwill differ between current practice under FAS 141, 142, FAS 141(R), and FAS 160, and the amendments made to FAS 142. These are discussed in greater detail in Chapter 13.

In the following examples, the accounting for equity-method investments involving both positive goodwill and negative goodwill are presented.

### Example of complex case ignoring deferred income taxes—goodwill

Foxen Corporation (FC) acquired 40% of Besser, Inc.'s (BI) shares on January 2, 2009, for $140,000. BI's assets and liabilities at that date had the following book and fair values:

|  | *Book values* | *Fair values* |
|---|---|---|
| Cash | $ 10,000 | $ 10,000 |
| Accounts receivable (net) | 40,000 | 40,000 |
| Inventories (FIFO cost) | 80,000 | 90,000 |
| Land | 50,000 | 40,000 |
| Plant and equipment (net of accumulated depreciation) | 140,000 | 220,000 |
| Total assets | $320,000 | $400,000 |
| Liabilities | $ (70,000) | $ (70,000) |
| Net assets (stockholders' equity) | $250,000 | $330,000 |

The first order of business is the calculation of the differential, as follows:

| | |
|---|---|
| FC's cost for 40% of BI's common | $140,000 |
| Book value of 40% of BI's net assets ($250,000 × 40%) | (100,000) |
| Total differential | $ 40,000 |

Next, the $40,000 is allocated to those individual assets and liabilities for which fair value differs from book value. In the example, the differential is allocated to inventories, land, and plant and equipment, as follows:

| Item | Book value | Fair value | Difference debit (credit) | 40% of difference debit (credit) |
|------|-----------|-----------|--------------------------|----------------------------------|
| Inventories | $ 80,000 | $ 90,000 | $10,000 | $ 4,000 |
| Land | 50,000 | 40,000 | (10,000) | (4,000) |
| Plant and equipment | 140,000 | 220,000 | 80,000 | 32,000 |
| Differential allocated | | | | $32,000 |

Assuming that there are no unrecognized identifiable intangibles included in the allocation, the difference between the allocated differential of $32,000 and the total differential of $40,000 is goodwill of $8,000. Goodwill, as shown by the following computation, represents the excess of the cost of the investment over the fair value of the net assets acquired.

| | |
|---|---|
| FC's cost for 40% of BI's common | $140,000 |
| 40% of the fair value of BI's net assets ($330,000 × 40%) | (132,000) |
| Excess of cost over fair value (goodwill) | $   8,000 |

It is important to note that the allocation of this differential is not recorded formally by either FC or BI. Furthermore, FC, the investor, does not remove the differential from the investment account and recategorize it in its own respective asset categories, since the use of the equity method (one-line consolidation) does not involve the recording of individual assets and liabilities of the investee in the financial statements of the investor. FC leaves the differential of $40,000 in the investment account, as a part of the balance of $140,000 at January 2, 2009. Accordingly, information pertaining to the allocation of the differential is maintained by the investor, but this information is outside the formal accounting system, presumably on a spreadsheet maintained for this purpose.

After the differential has been allocated, the amortization pattern is developed. To develop the pattern in this example, assume that BI's plant and equipment have ten years of useful life remaining and that BI depreciates its fixed assets on a straight-line basis. FC would prepare the following amortization schedule covering the years 2009 through 2011:

| Item | Differential debit (credit) | Remaining useful life | Amortization 2009 | 2010 | 2011 |
|------|----------------------------|----------------------|------|------|------|
| Inventories (FIFO) | $ 4,000 | Sold in 2009 | $4,000 | $   -- | $   -- |
| Land | (4,000) | Indefinite | -- | -- | -- |
| Plant and equipment (net) | 32,000 | 10 years | 3,200 | 3,200 | 3,200 |
| Goodwill | 8,000 | Not relevant | -- | -- | -- |
| Totals | $40,000 | | $7,200 | $3,200 | $3,200 |

Note that the entire differential allocated to inventories is amortized in 2009 because the cost flow assumption used by BI is FIFO. If BI had been using LIFO instead of FIFO, no amortization would take place until BI sold some of the inventory included in the LIFO layer that existed at January 2, 2009. Since this sale could be delayed for many years under LIFO, the differential allocated to LIFO inventories would not be amortized until BI sold more inventory than it manufactured/purchased. Note, also, that the differential (in this example, a negative valuation amount) allocated to BI's land is not amortized, because land is not a depreciable asset. The goodwill component of the differential is not amortized, but instead is evaluated along with the investment as a whole as to whether it is other-than-temporarily impaired.

The amortization of the differential is recorded formally in the accounting system of FC. Recording the amortization adjusts the equity in BI's income that FC recorded based upon BI's income statement. BI's income must be adjusted because it is based upon BI's book values, not upon the cost that FC incurred to acquire its interest in BI. FC would make the following entries in 2009, assuming that BI reported net income of $30,000 and paid cash dividends of $10,000:

| 1. | Investment in BI | 12,000 | |
| | Equity in BI income | | 12,000 |
| | *$30,000 net income × 40% proportionate share* | | |
| 2. | Equity in BI income (amortization of differential) | 7,200 | |
| | Investment in BI | | 7,200 |
| 3. | Cash | 4,000 | |
| | Investment in BI | | 4,000 |
| | *Record dividends received by investor $10,000 × 40%* | | |

The balance in the investment account on FC's records at the end of 2009, after giving effect to these entries is $140,800 [$140,000 + $12,000 – ($7,200 + $4,000)], and BI's stockholders' equity is $250,000 + net income of $30,000 – dividends of $10,000 = $270,000. The investment account balance as reflected by FC, the investee of $140,800 is not equal to $108,000 (40% of $270,000). However, this difference can easily be reconciled, as follows:

| | | |
|---|---|---|
| Balance in investment account at December 31, 2009 | | $140,800 |
| 40% of BI's net assets at December 31, 2009 | | 108,000 |
| Difference at December 31, 2009 | | $ 32,800 |
| Differential at January 2, 2009 | $40,000 | |
| Differential amortized during 2009 | (7,200) | |
| Unamortized differential at December 31, 2009 | | $ 32,800 |

With the passing years, the balance in the investment account approaches the amount representing 40% of the book value of BI's net assets, as the differential is amortized as a component of equity method income or loss. However, since a part of the differential was allocated to land, which is not depreciating, and to goodwill, which is not subject to amortization, the carrying value will most likely never exactly equal the equity in the investee's net assets. However, if the investee disposes of the land, the investor must also eliminate the associated portion of the differential. If the carrying value of the investment becomes impaired and the impairment is considered other than temporary, the goodwill portion of the differential may also be eliminated. Thus, under certain conditions the investor's carrying value may subsequently be adjusted to equal the underlying net asset value, although this outcome is relatively unlikely to occur.

To illustrate how the sale of land would affect equity method procedures, assume that BI sold the land in the year 2015 for $80,000. Since BI's cost for the land was $50,000, it would report a gain of $30,000, of which $12,000 (= $30,000 × 40%) would be recorded by FC, when it records its 40% share of BI's reported net income, ignoring income taxes. However, from FC's viewpoint, the gain on sale of land should have been $40,000 ($80,000 – $40,000) because the cost of the land from FC's perspective was $40,000 at January 2, 2009 (since the allocated fair value of the land was below its book value). Therefore, in addition to the $12,000 share of the gain recorded above, FC should record an additional $4,000 gain [($40,000 – $30,000) × 40%] by debiting the investment account and crediting the equity in BI's income account. This $4,000 debit to the investment account will eliminate the $4,000 differential allocated to land on January 2, 2009, since the original differential was a credit (the fair value of the land was $10,000 less than its book value).

Adjustments to the goodwill portion of the differential are somewhat more complex. APB 18 requires that that difference between cost and underlying book value be accounted for as if the investee were a consolidated subsidiary. An investor is therefore required to determine the individual components that comprise the differential as illustrated above, and this may result in the identification of part of the differential as goodwill (referred to as "equity method goodwill"). Under GAAP, goodwill associated with a business combination is required to be evaluated annually for impairment. FASB decided, however, that equity-method investments would continue to be tested for impairment in accordance with APB 18 (i.e., the equity-method investment as a whole, not the underlying net assets, are to be evaluated for impairment) and that equity method goodwill will not be treated as being separable from the related investment. Accordingly, goodwill is not to be tested for impairment in accordance with the current goodwill and intangible assets standard, FAS 142.

### Example of adjustment of goodwill for other-than-temporary impairment of an equity-method investment—ignoring income taxes

Building on the facts from the previous example, BI's reported net income in 2010 and loss in 2011 are $15,000 and ($12,000), respectively. No dividends are paid by BI after 2009. FC's carrying value, before considering possible impairment in value, as of year end 2011 is computed as follows:

| | |
|---|---:|
| Carrying value of investment, December 31, 2009 | $140,800 |
| FC's interest in BI's 2010 net income ($15,000 × 40%) | 6,000 |
| Amortization of differential between fair value and carrying value | (3,200) |
| Carrying value, December 31, 2010 | 143,600 |
| FC's interest in BI's 2011 net loss ($12,000 × 40%) | (4,800) |
| Amortization of differential between fair value and carrying value | (3,200) |
| Carrying value, December 31, 2011, before considering additional charge for impairment | $135,600 |

If, at December 31, 2011, FC determines that the fair value of its investment in BI has declined to $130,000, and this decline in value is judged to be other than temporary in nature, then FC must, per APB 18, recognize a further loss amounting to $5,600 for the year. Notice that this fair value decline is assessed with reference to the fair (presumably, but not necessarily, market) value of the investment in BI. It would not be determined with specific reference to the value of BI's business operations, in the manner that the implied fair value of goodwill is assessed in connection with business combinations accounted for by the presentation of consolidated financial statements, although a permanent decline in value of the investment would likely be related to the value of BI's operations.

While the standard is silent on this issue, it is reasonable that any recognized decline in value be assigned first to the implicit goodwill component of the investment account. In this example, since the decline, $5,600, is less than the $8,000 goodwill component of the differential, it will be fully absorbed, and future periods' amortization of the differential assigned to other assets will not be affected. On the other hand, if the value decline had exceeded $8,000, the excess would logically have been allocated to the underlying nonmonetary assets of the investee, such that the remaining differential previously identified with plant and equipment might have been reduced or eliminated, thereby altering future amortization on a prospective basis.

The impact of interperiod income tax allocation in the foregoing example is similar to that demonstrated earlier in the simplified example. Under prior GAAP, a complication arose with regard to the portion of the differential allocated to goodwill: since equity method goodwill is not amortizable for income tax purposes it represented a permanent (not a temporary) difference that would not give rise to deferred income taxes. Under current GAAP goodwill rules, unless goodwill has been reduced for financial reporting purposes due to impairment there will be no book-tax difference and hence no deferred income tax issue to be addressed. The other components of the differential in the foregoing example are all temporary differences, with normal deferred income tax implications.

### Example of complex case ignoring deferred income taxes—computation of negative goodwill

The facts in this example are similar to those in the immediately preceding examples, but in this instance the price paid by the investor, Lucky Corp., is less than its proportionate share of the investee's net assets, at fair value. This is analogous to negative goodwill in a business combination, and the accounting for the negative differential between cost and fair value follows that mandated for bargain purchases either under the business combinations and goodwill standards, FAS 141 and FAS 142 or, if the stock is acquired after its effective date, under the bargain purchase provisions of FAS 141(R).

Assume that Lucky Corp. acquired 40% of Compliant Company's shares on January 2, 2009, for a cash payment of $120,000. Compliant Company's assets and liabilities at that date had the following book and fair values:

|                                                    | Book values | Fair values |
|----------------------------------------------------|-------------|-------------|
| Cash                                               | $ 10,000    | $ 10,000    |
| Accounts receivable (net)                          | 40,000      | 40,000      |
| Inventories (FIFO cost)                            | 80,000      | 90,000      |
| Land                                               | 50,000      | 40,000      |
| Plant and equipment (net of accumulated depreciation) | 140,000  | 220,000     |
| Total assets                                       | $320,000    | $400,000    |
| Liabilities                                        | $ (70,000)  | $ (70,000)  |
| Net assets (stockholders' equity)                  | $250,000    | $330,000    |

The first step is to compute the differential, which is as follows:

| | |
|---|---|
| Lucky's cost for 40% of Compliant's common stock | $120,000 |
| Book value of 40% of Compliant's net assets ($250,000 × 40%) | (100,000) |
| Total differential | $ 20,000 |

Next, the $20,000 is allocated, on a preliminary basis, to those individual assets and liabilities for which fair value differs from book value. In the example, the differential is initially allocated to inventories, land, and plant and equipment, as follows:

| Item | Book value | Fair value | Difference debit (credit) | 40% of difference debit (credit) |
|------|-----------|-----------|---------------------------|----------------------------------|
| Inventories | $ 80,000 | $ 90,000 | $10,000 | $ 4,000 |
| Land | 50,000 | 40,000 | (10,000) | (4,000) |
| Plant and equipment | 140,000 | 220,000 | 80,000 | 32,000 |
| Differential allocated | | | | $32,000 |

The difference between the allocated differential of $32,000 and the actual differential of $20,000 is negative goodwill of $12,000. Negative goodwill, as shown by the following computation, represents the excess of the fair value of the net assets acquired over the cost of the investment.

| | |
|---|---|
| Lucky's cost for 40% of Compliant's common stock | $120,000 |
| 40% of the fair value of Compliant's net assets ($330,000 × 40%) | (132,000) |
| Excess of fair value over cost (negative goodwill) | $ 12,000 |

Although the topic is not addressed explicitly by FAS 142, the investor's handling of negative goodwill should track how this would be dealt with by a parent company preparing consolidated financial statements following a "bargain purchase" business combination. It is important to note that the treatment of negative goodwill in this regard will depend on the date on which the investor obtained its interest.

**Example of negative goodwill under FAS 141 and FAS 142**

The $12,000 amount preliminarily identified in the previous example as negative goodwill is to be offset, on a pro rata basis, against all of the acquired assets other than cash and cash equivalents, trade receivables, inventory, financial instruments that are required by U.S. generally accepted accounting principles (GAAP) to be carried on the balance sheet at fair value, assets to be disposed of by sale, and deferred income tax assets. In the present example, the assets qualifying for having negative goodwill allocated against their respective fair values are land and plant and equipment. The negative goodwill, $12,000, will therefore be assigned as follows:

| Item | Preliminary value assignment (40% of fair value) | Preliminary differential assigned | Proportion of qualified costs | Allocation of negative goodwill | Net differential |
|---|---|---|---|---|---|
| Inventories | $ 36,000 | $ 4,000 | 0.0% | 0 | 4,000 |
| Land | 16,000 | (4,000) | 15.4% | (1,848) | (5,848) |
| Plant and equipment | 88,000 | 32,000 | 84.6% | (10,152) | 21,848 |
| Total | $140,000 | $32,000 | 100.0% | (12,000) | $20,000 |

Note that, in the above table, inventories are not qualified to be assigned a portion of the negative goodwill. Both land and plant and equipment, however, are allocated some of the amount preliminarily identified as negative goodwill, notwithstanding that land has already been written down because its fair value was lower than the investee's carrying (i.e., book) value for that asset. The net differential, after offsetting of negative goodwill, is $20,000, which is the excess of the purchase cost, $120,000, over the book value of the underlying net assets of Compliant Company at the date of the transaction.

In this example, the net differential assigned to plant and equipment, $21,848, will be amortized over the next ten years (the average remaining useful life of that asset group), for a charge of $2,185 per year against the earnings from the investee. Land, of course, is not depreciable and thus the total differential, a negative $5,848, will remain until the investee disposes of the land. The amount assigned to inventory, $4,000, will be taken into net income in 2009 because of the FIFO costing convention.

Since the entire amount preliminarily identified as negative goodwill has been successfully offset against qualifying assets, no amount remains to be recognized as an extraordinary gain in 2009, the year in which the investment is made. In the (extremely unlikely) event that the bargain purchase was of such a magnitude that even after offsetting the preliminary amount determined to be negative goodwill there remained an unabsorbed balance, that would have to be reported by Lucky Corp. as an extraordinary gain in 2009, in order to conform to the GAAP requirements applicable to negative goodwill.

Effective prospectively for equity-method investments where the acquisition date is on or after the beginning of the first annual reporting period beginning on or after December 15, 2008, the treatment of negative goodwill arising from a bargain purchase has dramatically changed. Instead of allocating the negative goodwill to certain qualifying assets as illustrated above, any negative goodwill that exists on the acquisition date is to be immediately recognized as a gain in net income of the period of acquisition. Unlike the prior requirements, the gain is not to be characterized as an extraordinary gain but rather is to be included in income from continuing operations. Analogizing to FAS 141(R), management of the investor, prior to recognizing a gain on a bargain purchase, is to reassess whether it correctly identified all of the investee assets and liabilities and make any adjustments necessitated by the reassessment. Management of the investor is then required to review the procedures it used to measure the amounts recognized at acquisition of the interest in the investee. The objective of the review/reassessment is to ensure the all available information that exists on the date the interest is acquired has been appropriately considered in making the necessary measurements.

**Investor share of investee losses in excess of the carrying value of the investment.** As demonstrated in the foregoing paragraphs, the carrying value of an investment which is accounted for by the equity method is increased by the investor's share of investee earnings and reduced by its share of investee losses and by dividends received from the investee. Sometimes the losses are so large that the carrying value is reduced to zero, and this raises the question of whether the investment account should be allowed to "go negative," or whether losses in excess of the investment account should be recognized in some other manner.

In general, an equity-method investment would not be permitted to have a negative (i.e., credit) balance, since this would imply that it represented a liability. In the case of normal corporate investments, the investor would enjoy limited liability and would not be held liable to the investee's creditors should, for instance, the investee become insolvent. For this reason, excess losses of the investee would not be reflected in the financial statements of the investor. The practice is to discontinue application of the equity method when the investment account reaches a zero balance, with adequate disclosure being made of the fact that further investee losses are not being reflected in the investor's earnings. If the investee later returns to profitability, the investor ignores its share of earnings until the previously ignored losses have been fully offset; thereafter, normal application of the equity method is resumed.

There are, however, limited circumstances in which further investee losses would be reflected. Often the investor has guaranteed or otherwise committed to indemnify creditors or other investors in the investee entity for losses incurred, or to fund continuing operations of the investee. Having placed itself at risk in the case of the investee's insolvency, continued application of the equity method is deemed to be appropriate, since the net credit balance in the investment account (reportable as a liability entitled "losses in excess of investment made in investee") would indeed represent an obligation of the investor.

The other situation in which investee losses in excess of the investor's actual investment in common stock of the investee are to be reflected is somewhat more complicated. When the investor has investments consisting of both common stock holdings accounted for under APB 18, and other investments in or loans to the investee, such as in its preference shares (including mandatorily redeemable preferred stock) or debt obligations of the investee, there will not only be further application of APB 18, but also possible interaction between the provisions of APB 18 and those of FAS 114 and/or FAS 115. In addition, there will be the question of the appropriate proportion of the investee's loss to be recognized by the investor—that is, should the investor's share of further investee losses be computed based only on its common stock ownership interest, or would some other measure of economic interest be more relevant?

The Emerging Issues Task Force (in Issues 98-13 and 99-10) has attempted to address the accounting to be applied under the circumstances described in the foregoing paragraph. A principal concern was that an anomaly could develop if, for example, the common shareholdings were being accounted for by application of the equity method (including a suspension of the method when the carrying value declined to zero due to investee losses) while investments in the same investee's debt or preferred shares were being carried at fair value per FAS 115 (assuming that the debt was not being carried at amortized cost due to classification as a held-to-maturity investment). A parallel concern invokes the accounting for loans under FAS 114 when investee debt is being held by the investor.

According to EITF 98-13, the adjusted basis of the other investments (preferred stock, debt, etc.) are to be adjusted for the equity method losses, after which the investor is to apply FAS 114 and 115 to the other investments, as applicable. Those equity method losses are applied to the other investments in reverse order of seniority (that is, the respective priority in liquidation). This sequence is logical because it tracks the risk of investor loss: common shareholders' interests are the first to be eliminated, followed by those of the preferred shareholders, and so on—with debt having the highest claim to investee assets in the event of liquidation. If the investee later becomes profitable, equity method income subsequently recorded (if, as described earlier, any unrecognized losses have first been exceeded) is applied to the adjusted basis of the other investments in reverse order of the application of the equity method losses (i.e., equity method income is applied to the more senior securities first).

In applying this standard, the cost basis of the other investments is taken to mean the original cost of those investments adjusted for the effects of other than temporary write-downs, unrealized holding gains and losses on FAS 115 securities classified as trading, and amortization of any discount or premium on debt securities or loans. The adjusted basis is defined as the cost basis, as adjusted for the FAS 114 valuation allowance account for an investee loan and for the cumulative equity method losses applied to the other investments.

The interaction of APB 18 and FAS 114 and 115 could mean, for example, that investee losses are recognized via a reduction in carrying value of preferred shares, which might then be immediately upwardly adjusted to recognize fair value as of the balance sheet date in accordance with FAS 115. In a situation such as this, the equity method downward adjustment would be a loss recognized currently in net income, while the upward revaluation to fair value would typically be credited to other comprehensive income, and thus excluded from current period net income (unless defined as being held for trading purposes, which would be unusual).

EITF 98-13 addressed only the situation where the investor had the same percentage interests in common stock and all the other equity or debt securities of the investee. However, a further complication can arise when the investor's share in the common stock of the investee is not mirrored in its investment in the other debt or equity securities of the investee that it also holds. While this possibility is discussed in EITF 99-10, GAAP is not definitive regarding the mechanism by which the investor's share of further losses should be recognized in such situations. What is clear, however, is that merely applying the investor's percentage interest in the investee's common stock to the period's loss would not be appropriate in these cases.

In the absence of definitive guidance, two approaches are deemed to be justifiable. The first is to eliminate the carrying value of first, the common stock and then, the other securities of the investee (including loans made to the investee), in reverse order of seniority, as set forth under EITF 98-13. The percentage of the investee's loss to be absorbed against each class of investment other than common stock would be governed by the proportion of that investment held by the investor—and emphatically not by its common stock ownership percentage. The logic is that, if the investor entity were to be harmed by the investee's further losses (once the common stock investment were reduced to zero carrying value), the harm would derive from being forced to take a reduced settlement in a liquidation of the investee, at which point the percentage ownership in separate classes of stock or in holdings of classes of debt would determine the amount of the investor's losses.

The second acceptable approach also takes into account the investor's varying percentage interests in the different equity and debt holdings. However, rather than being driven by the investee's reported loss for the period, the investor's loss recognition is determined by the period-to-period change in its claim on the net assets of the investee, as measured by book value. This approach implicitly assumes that fair values upon a hypothetical liquidation of the investee would equal book values—an assumption which is obviously unlikely to be borne out in any actual liquidation scenario. Nonetheless, given the enormous difficulty of applying this measurement technique to the continuously varying fair values of the investee's assets and liabilities, this was deemed to be a necessary compromise.

Thus, both methods of computing the excess investee losses to be recognized by an investor having more than just a common stock interest in the investee depend on the varying levels of those other investment vehicles. These two alternative, acceptable approaches are described and illustrated below.

**Example of accounting for excess loss of investee when other investments are also held in same entity, when proportions of all investments are identical**

Assume the following facts: Dardanelles Corporation owns 25% of the common stock of Bosporus Company. Dardanelles also owns 25% of Bosporus' preferred shares, and 25% of its commercial debt. Bosporus has $50,000 of debt and $100,000 of preferred stock outstanding.

As of 1/1/2009 the carrying (i.e., book) value of Dardanelles' investment in Bosporus common stock was $12,000, after having applied the equity method of accounting in prior periods, per APB 18. In 2009, 2010, and 2011, Bosporus incurs net losses of $140,000, $50,000 and $30,000, respectively.

As of 1/1/2009, the carrying (book) values of Dardanelles' investment in Bosporus' preferred stock and commercial debt were $25,000 and $12,500, respectively. Due to its continuing losses, the market or fair value of Dardanelles' outstanding preferred shares and its commercial debt decline over the years 2009-2011; Bosporus' portion of these values are as follows:

|  | *Fair value of preferred shares, consistent with FAS 115* | *Fair value of commercial debt, consistent with FAS 114* |
|---|---|---|
| 1/1/2009 | N/A | N/A |
| 12/31/2009 | $20,000 | $12,000 |
| 12/31/2010 | 9,500 | 8,000 |
| 12/31/2011 | 2,000 | 7,000 |

The following table indicates the adjustments that would be made on the books of Dardanelles to record its share of Bosporus' losses in 2009-2011:

|  | Common stock Book value | Preferred stock Book value | Preferred stock Fair value | Commercial debt Book value | Commercial debt Fair value |
|---|---|---|---|---|---|
| 1/1/2009 | $ 12,000 | $ 25,000 | N/A | $ 12,500 | N/A |
| 2009 loss (25% × 140,000 = 35,000) | (12,000) | (23,000) |  | -- |  |
|  |  | 2,000 | $20,000 | 12,500 | $12,000 |
| Adjust pfd. stk. to FMV and debt to FV |  | 18,000 |  | (500) |  |
| **12/31/2009 values** | 0 | 20,000 |  | 12,000 |  |
| 2009 loss (25% × 50,000 = 12,500) |  | (2,000) |  | (10,500) |  |
|  |  | 18,000 | 9,500 | 1,500 | 8,000 |
| Adjust pfd. stk. to FMV and debt to FV |  | (8,500) |  | -- |  |
| **12/31/2010 values** | 0 | 9,500 |  | 1,500 |  |
| 2010 loss (25% × 30,000 = 7,500) |  | -- |  | (1,500) |  |
|  |  | 9,500 | 2,000 | 0 | 7,000 |
| Adjust pfd. stk. to FMV and debt to FV |  | (7,500) |  | -- |  |
| **12/31/2011 values** | $ 0 | $ 2,000 |  | $ 0 |  |

Actual journal entries and explanations for the foregoing are given as follows:

| 12/31/09 | Investee losses | 35,000 |  |
|---|---|---|---|
|  | Investment in Bosporus common stock |  | 12,000 |
|  | Investment in Bosporus preferred stock |  | 23,000 |

*To record Dardanelles' share of Bosporus' loss for the year; the excess over the carrying value of the common stock is used to reduce the carrying value of the preferred shares*

|  | Investment in Bosporus preferred stock | 18,000 |  |
|---|---|---|---|
|  | Unrealized gain on securities available for sale |  |  |
|  | (other comprehensive income) |  | 18,000 |

*Since the fair value of the preferred shares is $20,000, per FAS 115 the carrying value must be upwardly revalued and the adjustment is included in other comprehensive income for the year*

|  | Loss from impairment of loan | 500 |  |
|---|---|---|---|
|  | Investment in Bosporus commercial debt |  | 500 |

*As required by FAS 114, the impairment of the loan to Bosporus must be recognized by a charge against current period net income*

| | | | |
|---|---|---:|---:|
| 12/31/10 | Investee losses | 12,500 | |
| | Investment in Bosporus preferred stock | | 2,000 |
| | Investment in Bosporus commercial debt | | 10,500 |

*To record Dardanelles' share of Bosporus' loss for the year; the excess over the remaining carrying value of the preferred stock (without consideration of the FAS 115 adjustment) is used to reduce the carrying value of the commercial debt held*

| | | | |
|---|---|---:|---:|
| | Unrealized gain on securities available for sale (other comprehensive income) | 8,500 | |
| | Investment in Bosporus preferred stock | | 8,500 |

*Since the fair market value of the preferred shares is not $9,500, the adjustment booked in the prior period must be partially reversed, this adjustment is included in other comprehensive income for the year*

| | | | |
|---|---|---:|---:|
| 12/31/11 | Investee losses | 1,500 | |
| | Investment in Bosporus commercial debt | | 1,500 |

*To record Dardanelles' share of Bosporus' loss for the year; the maximum to be recognized is the carrying value of the commercial debt since the carrying value of common and preferred stock investments have already been reduced to zero*

| | | | |
|---|---|---:|---:|
| | Unrealized gain on securities available for sale (other comprehensive income) | 7,500 | |
| | Investment in Bosporus preferred stock | | 7,500 |

*Since the fair value of the preferred shares are now $2,000, the carrying value must be further reduced, with the adjustment included in other comprehensive income*

It should be noted in the foregoing example that in year 2011 there will be $6,000 of unrecognized investee losses, since as of the end of that year the carrying value of all the investor's investments in the investee will have been reduced to zero, except for the fair value of the preferred stock which is presented pursuant to FAS 115. Also note that the carrying value of the commercial debt is reduced for an impairment in 2009 because the fair value is lower than the cost basis; in later years the fair value exceeds the cost basis, but under FAS 114 net upward adjustments would not be permitted.

**Example of accounting for excess loss of investee when other investments are also held in same entity, when proportions of investments vary—first method: investee's reported loss used as basis for recognition**

When the percentage interest in common stock of the investee is not mirrored by the level of ownership in its other securities, the process of recognizing the investor's share of investee losses becomes much more complex. Per EITF 99-10, there are two acceptable approaches, both of which are illustrated here. The first approach is to recognize the investor's share of investee losses by reducing the various investments held in the investee (common and preferred stock and commercial debt, in this example) by the relevant percentages applicable to each class of investment.

In the following, the same facts as in the preceding example are continued, except that the percentage of ownership in the equity and debt instruments is as follows:

| | Percentage ownership by Dardanelles Corporation |
|---|:---:|
| Common stock | 25% |
| Preferred stock | 50% |
| Commercial debt | 100% |

Note that the fair values of the securities held (using the new assumed percentages of ownership of each class) are as follows:

| | Fair value of preferred shares, consistent with FAS 115 | Fair value of commercial debt, consistent with FAS 114 |
|---|:---:|:---:|
| 1/1/2009 | N/A | N/A |
| 12/31/2009 | $40,000 | $48,000 |
| 12/31/2010 | 19,000 | 32,000 |
| 12/31/2011 | 4,000 | 28,000 |

Given the foregoing, the period-by-period adjustments are summarized in the following table:

| | Common stock | Preferred stock | | Commercial debt | |
|---|---|---|---|---|---|
| | *Book value* | *Book value* | *Fair value* | *Book value* | *Fair value* |
| 1/1/2009 | $ 12,000 | $ 50,000 | N/A | $50,000 | N/A |
| 2009 loss = $140,000 | | | | | |
| Eliminate @ 25% ratio | (12,000) | | | | |
| Reduce preferred @ 50% ratio | | (46,000) | | | |
| | | 4,000 | $40,000 | | $48,000 |
| Adjust pfd. stk. to FMV and debt to FV | | 36,000 | | (2,000) | |
| **12/31/2009 values** | 0 | 40,000 | | 48,000 | |
| 2010 loss = $50,000 | | | | | |
| Eliminate preferred @50% ratio | | (4,000) | | | |
| Reduce commercial debt @ 100% ratio | | | | (42,000) | |
| | | 36,000 | 19,000 | 6,000 | 32,000 |
| Adjust pfd. stk. to FMV and debt to FV | | 17,000 | | -- | |
| **12/31/2010 values** | 0 | 19,000 | | 6,000 | |
| 2011 loss = $30,000 | | | | | |
| Reduce commercial debt @ 100% ratio | | | | (6,000) | |
| | | | 4,000 | 0 | 7,000 |
| Adjust pfd. stk. to FMV and debt to FV | | (15,000) | | -- | |
| **12/31/2011 values** | $ 0 | $ 4,000 | | $ 0 | |

Journal entries and explanations for the adjustments that would be made consistent with the foregoing fact pattern are as follows:

| 12/31/09 | Investee losses | 58,000 | |
|---|---|---|---|
| | Investment in Bosporus common stock | | 12,000 |
| | Investment in Bosporus preferred stock | | 46,000 |

*To record Dardanelles' share of Bosporus' loss for the year; the excess over the carrying value of the common stock is used to reduce the carrying value of the preferred shares based on Dardanelles' 50% ownership interest in the preferred stock outstanding*

| | Investment in Bosporus preferred stock | 36,000 | |
|---|---|---|---|
| | Unrealized gain on securities available for sale (other comprehensive income) | | 36,000 |

*Since the fair value of the preferred shares is $40,000, per FAS 115 the carrying value must be upwardly revalued and the adjustment is included in other comprehensive income for the year*

| | Loss from impairment of loan | 2,000 | |
|---|---|---|---|
| | Investment in Bosporus commercial debt | | 2,000 |

*As required by FAS 114, the impairment of the loan to Bosporus must be recognized by a charge against current period net income*

| 12/31/10 | Investee losses | 46,000 | |
|---|---|---|---|
| | Investment in Bosporus preferred stock | | 4,000 |
| | Investment in Bosporus commercial debt | | 42,000 |

*To record Dardanelles' share of Bosporus' loss for the year; the excess over the remaining carrying value of the preferred stock (without consideration of the FAS 115 adjustment) is used to reduce the carrying value of the commercial debt held*

| | Unrealized gain on securities available for sale (other comprehensive income) | 17,000 | |
|---|---|---|---|
| | Investment in Bosporus preferred stock | | 17,000 |

*Since the fair value of the preferred shares is not $19,000, the adjustment booked in the prior period must be partially reversed, this adjustment is included in other comprehensive income for the year*

| 12/31/11 | Investee losses | 6,000 | |
|---|---|---|---|
| | Investment in Bosporus commercial debt | | 6,000 |

*To record Dardanelles' share of Bosporus' loss for the year; the maximum to be recognized is the carrying value of the commercial debt since the carrying value of common and preferred stock investments have already been reduced to zero*

| Unrealized gain on securities available for sale | | |
|---|---|---|
| (other comprehensive income) | 15,000 | |
| Investment in Bosporus preferred stock | | 15,000 |

*Since the fair value of the preferred shares are now $4,000, the carrying value must be further reduced, with the adjustment included in other comprehensive income*

It should be noted in the foregoing example that the limitation on loss recognition each year is given by reference to the investor's percentage interests in the various classes of equity or debt held. The 2009 loss is allocated between the common and preferred interests. A $12,000, 25% interest in the common stock equates to a total of $48,000 of common stock ($12,000 ÷ 25%). Therefore, if the full $140,000 loss were first allocated to reduce the book value of the common stock, $48,000 would have been applied to reduce that book value to zero. That would leave $92,000 of loss ($140,000 – $48,000) that remains to be allocated to the preferred interests. $92,000 × the 50% preferred interest of the investor is $48,000. Since the carrying value of the preferred stock investment is greater than this amount, the full loss is recognized by the investor proportional to its interest.

Similarly, the investee loss of $50,000 in 2010 is first used to eliminate the remaining carrying value (before the FAS 115 adjustment) of the preferred stock investment, at a 50% ratio. The total of the preferred interests is computed by dividing the remaining carrying value of the preferred stock, $4,000, by the 50% interest that it represents. Therefore, the $8,000 of the $50,000 loss would be allocated to the preferred interests, thus leaving $42,000 to allocate to the commercial debt. Since Dardanelles owns all of this debt issue, the limitation on loss recognition would be the lesser of the remaining loss ($42,000) or the carrying value of the debt (before the FAS 114 adjustment) of $48,000.

Finally, note that in year 2011 there will be $24,000 of unrecognized investee losses, since as of the end of that year the carrying value of all the investor's investments in the investee will have been reduced to zero (except for the fair value of the preferred stock which is presented pursuant to FAS 115).

### Example of accounting for excess loss of investee when other investments are also held in same entity, when proportions of investments vary—second method: investee's reported change in net assets used as basis for recognition

The alternative, equally acceptable approach to investee loss recognition when various equity and debt interests are held in the investee, at varying percentage ownership levels, ignores the investee's reported loss for the period in favor of an indirect approach, making reference to the change in the investor's interest in the investee's reported net assets (net book value). In theory, the results will often be very similar if not identical, but investee capital transactions with other owners (e.g., issuing another series of preferred shares) could impact the loss recognition by the investor under some circumstances. Furthermore, since the investor's cost of its investments in the investee will normally vary from the investee's book value of those investments (e.g., if the investments were acquired in the secondary market), the losses computed by this method may differ from those computed by the first of the two alternative approaches.

To illustrate, again assume all the facts above, including the percentage interests in the immediately preceding example. Also, the condensed balance sheets of Bosporus Corporation as of the relevant dates are given as follows:

|  | *1/1/09* | *12/31/09* | *12/31/10* | *12/31/11* |
|---|---|---|---|---|
| Total assets | $270,000 | $135,000 | $ 90,000 | $ 50,000 |
| Commercial debt | 50,000 | 50,000 | 50,000 | 50,000 |
| Other liabilities | 20,000 | 25,000 | 30,000 | 20,000 |
| Preferred stock | 100,000 | 100,000 | 100,000 | 100,000 |
| Common stock + retained earnings | 100,000 | (40,000) | (90,000) | (120,000) |
| Total liabilities and equity | $270,000 | $135,000 | $ 90,000 | $ 50,000 |

The investor's share of the investee's net assets at these respective dates and the changes to be recognized therein as the investor's share of investee losses for the years 2009–2011 are given below.

| | 1/1/09 | 12/31/09 | 12/31/10 | 12/31/11 |
|---|---|---|---|---|
| | | *(At investee's book values)* | | |
| Investor's shares of: | | | | |
| Commercial debt (100%) | $ 50,000 | $ 50,000 | $ 50,000 | $ 30,000 |
| Preferred stock (50%) | 50,000 | 30,000 | 5,000 | 0 |
| Common stock + retained earnings (25%) | 25,000 | 0 | 0 | 0 |
| Total share of investee's net assets | $125,000 | $ 80,000 | $ 55,000 | $ 30,000 |
| Change in share from prior year (investor's share of investee loss for year) | | $(45,000) | $(25,000) | $(25,000) |

In terms of how the actual investee losses should be recorded by the investor, the EITF guidance is not explicit, but there is no reason to depart from the approach illustrated above. Thus, the investment in Bosporus common stock would be eliminated first, then the investment in the preferred stock, and finally the investment in the debt securities. The provisions of FAS 114 and 115 would have to be adhered to as well, again similar to the illustration above.

One part of the foregoing analysis that may need elaboration is the decision, in 2011, to absorb all the excess investee losses against the investor's interest in the commercial debt. In many cases the commercial debt will be secured or for other reasons have preference over the other liabilities (which would tend to include accruals, trade payables, etc.). Therefore, in an actual liquidation situation the unsecured creditors would be eliminated before the commercial debtholders. However, the purpose of this computation—determining how much of the investee's losses should be reported by the investor—is not predicated on an actual liquidation, but rather is based on a going concern assumption and conservatism. Since the investor in this example owns a major position in the common stock, half of the preferred stock, and all of the debt, presumably if the ongoing losses were indicative of imminent demise the investor would have already put the investee into liquidation or taken other dramatic steps. Since this has not occurred, the appropriate computational strategy, it is believed, is to allocate further losses against the investor's remaining interest, which is in the commercial debt. (If actual liquidation were being contemplated, it would be necessary to consider an even greater write-down of the carrying value of this investment.)

Note that the loss recognized each period differs from that under the previous approach, since the allocation is based on the book values of the various interests on the investee's balance sheet, not the cost basis from the investor's perspective, as detailed below.

| | Common stock | Preferred stock | | Commercial debt | |
|---|---|---|---|---|---|
| | Book value | Book value | Fair value | Book value | Fair value |
| 1/1/2009 | $12,000 | $50,000 | N/A | $ 50,000 | N/A |
| 2009 change in investor's share of investee's net book value = −45,000 | | | | | |
| Eliminate carrying value of common | (12,000) | | | | |
| Reduce carrying value of preferred | | (33,000) | | | |
| | | 17,000 | $40,000 | | $48,000 |
| Adjust pfd. stk. to FMV and debt to FV | | 23,000 | | (2,000) | |
| **12/31/2009 values** | 0 | 40,000 | | 48,000 | |
| 2010 change in investor's share of investee's net book value = −25,000 | | | | | |
| Reduce carrying value of commercial debt | | (17,000) | | (8,000) | |
| | | 23,000 | 19,000 | 40,000 | 32,000 |
| Adjust pfd. stk. to FMV and debt to FV | | (4,000) | | (8,000) | |
| **12/31/2010 values** | 0 | 19,000 | | 32,000 | |
| 2011 change in investor's share of investee's net book value = −25,000 | | | | | |
| Reduce carrying value of commercial debt | | | | (25,000) | |
| | | | 4,000 | 7,000 | 7,000 |
| Adjust pfd. stk. to FMV and debt to FV | | (15,000) | | -- | |
| **12/31/2011 values** | $ 0 | $ 4,000 | | $ 7,000 | |

Journal entries and explanations for the adjustments that would be made consistent with the foregoing fact pattern would be similar to those shown earlier in this section and therefore will not be repeated here.

**Accounting for subsequent investments in an investee after suspension of equity method loss recognition.** As discussed, recognition of investee losses by the investor is suspended when the investment account is reduced to zero, subject to the further reduction in the carrying value of any other investments (preferred stock, debt, etc.) in that investee, as circumstances warrant. In some cases, after the recognition of investee losses is suspended, the investor will make a further investment in the investee, and the question arises whether recognition of some or all of the previously unrecognized investee losses should immediately be given recognition, up to the amount of the additional investment.

The EITF previously addressed (in Topic D-84) the situation where the increased investment in the equity method investee triggered a need to consolidate (i.e., the 50% ownership threshold was exceeded), and cited the SEC's position against further loss recognition. More recently, in EITF 02-18, the situation where the increased investment did not cause control to be assumed, but rather where equity method accounting was specified both before and after the further investment is made (e.g., the investor owned 30% of the investee's common stock previously, and then increased the interest to 35%) has been dealt with.

EITF 02-18 holds that recognition of some or all of the previously unrecognized ("suspended") losses is conditioned on whether the new investment represents funding of prior investee losses. To the extent that it does, the previously unrecognized share of prior losses will be given recognition (i.e., reported in the investor's current period net income). Making this determination requires the use of judgment and is fact-specific, but some of the considerations would be as follows:

- Whether the additional investment is acquired from a third party or directly from the investee, since it is unlikely that funding of prior losses occurs unless funds are infused into the investee;
- The fair value of the consideration received in relation to the value of the consideration paid for the additional investment, with an indicated excess of consideration paid over that received being suggestive of a funding of prior losses;
- Whether the additional investment results in an increase in ownership percentage of the investee, with investments being made without a corresponding increase in ownership or other interests (or, alternatively, a pro rata equity investment made by all existing investors) being indicative of the funding of prior losses; and
- The seniority of the additional investment relative to existing equity of the investee, with investment in subordinate instruments being suggestive of the funding of prior losses.

When additional investments are made in an investee that has experienced losses, the corollary issue of whether the investor has committed to further investments may arise. If such is the case, then yet-unrecognized (suspended) investee losses may also need to be recognized in investor net income currently—in effect, as a loss contingency which is deemed probable of occurrence.

**Example of subsequent investments in investee with losses in excess of original investment**

R Corp. invested $500,000 in an investee, E Company, representing a 40% ownership interest. Investee losses caused R Corp. to completely eliminate the carrying value of this investment, and the recognition of R Corp.'s share of a further $200,000 of E Company losses ($200,000 × 40% = $80,000) was suspended. Later, R Corp. invested another $100,000 in E Company. Application of the criteria above led to the conclusion that one-half of its investment was in excess of the value of the consideration received, and thus the entry to record the further investment would be

| | | |
|---|---|---|
| Investment in E Company stock | 50,000 | |
| Loss on equity-method investment in E Company | 50,000 | |
| Cash | | 100,000 |

If it is determined, however, that R Corp. has "otherwise committed" to further investment in E Company, the investor might have to recognize losses up to the full amount of the suspended losses. The entry might therefore be

| | | |
|---|---|---|
| Investment in E Company stock | 20,000 | |
| Loss on equity-method investment in E Company | 80,000 | |
| Cash | | 100,000 |

**Intercompany transactions between investor and investee.** Transactions between the investor and the investee may require that the investor make certain adjustments when it records its share of the investee earnings. According to the realization concept, profits can be recognized by an entity only when realized through a sale to outside (unrelated) parties in arm's-length transactions (sales and purchases) between the investor and investee. Similar problems, however, can arise when sales of fixed assets between the parties occur. In all cases, there is no need for any adjustment when the transfers are made at book value (i.e., without either party recognizing a profit or loss in its separate accounting records).

In preparing consolidated financial statements, all intercompany (parent-subsidiary) transactions are eliminated. However, when the equity method is used to account for investments, only the profit component of intercompany (investor-investee) transactions is eliminated. This is because the equity method does not result in the combining of all income statement accounts (such as sales and cost of sales), and therefore will not cause the financial statements to contain redundancies. In contrast, consolidated statements would include redundancies if the gross amounts of all intercompany transactions were not eliminated.

Another distinction between the consolidation and equity method situations pertains to the percentage of intercompany profit to be eliminated. In the case of consolidated statements, the entire intercompany profit is eliminated, regardless of the percentage ownership of the subsidiary. However, according to Accounting Interpretation 1 of APB 18, only the investor's pro rata share of intercompany profit is to be eliminated in equity accounting, whether the transaction giving rise to the profit is "downstream" (a sale to the investee) or "upstream" (a sale to the investor). An exception is made when the transaction is not "arm's-length" or if the investee company was created by or for the benefit of the investor. In these cases, 100% profit elimination would be required, unless realized through a sale to a third party before year-end.

### Example of accounting for intercompany transactions

Continue with the basic facts set forth in an earlier example and also assume that E Company sold inventory to R Corporation in 2009 for $2,000 above E's cost. Thirty percent of this inventory remains unsold by R at the end of 2009. E's net income for 2009, including the gross profit on the inventory sold to R, is $15,000; E's income tax rate is 34%. R should make the following journal entries for 2009 (ignoring deferred income taxes):

| | | | |
|---|---|---|---|
| 1. | Investment in E Company | 6,000 | |
| | Equity in E income | | 6,000 |
| | *$15,000 × 40%* | | |
| 2. | Equity in E income (amortization of differential) | 3,200 | |
| | Investment in E Company | | 3,200 |
| 3. | Equity in E income | 158 | |
| | Investment in E Company | | 158 |
| | *$2,000 × 30% × 66% × 40%* | | |

The amount in the last entry needs further elaboration. Since 30% of the inventory remains unsold, only $600 of the intercompany profit remains unrealized at year-end. This profit, net of income taxes, is $396. R's share of this profit ($158) is included in the first ($6,000) entry recorded. Accordingly, the third entry is needed to adjust or correct the equity in the reported net income of the investee.

Eliminating entries for intercompany profits in fixed assets are similar to those in the examples above. However, intercompany profit is realized only as the assets are depreciated by the purchasing entity. In other words, if an investor buys or sells fixed assets from or to an investee at a price above book value, the gain would only be realized piecemeal over the asset's remaining depreciable life. Accordingly, in the year of sale the pro rata share (based on the investor's percentage ownership interest in the investee, regardless of whether the sale is upstream or downstream) of the unrealized portion of the intercompany profit would have to be eliminated. In each subsequent year during the asset's life, the pro rata share of the gain realized in the period would be added to income from the investee.

### Example of eliminating intercompany profit on fixed assets

Assume that Investor Co., which owns 25% of Investee Co., sold to Investee a fixed asset, having a five-year remaining life, at a gain of $100,000. Investor Co. is in the 34% marginal income tax bracket. The sale occurred at the end of 2009; Investee Co. will use straight-line depreciation to amortize the asset over the years 2010 through 2014.

The entries related to the foregoing are

*2009*

| | | | |
|---|---|---|---|
| 1. | Gain on sale of fixed asset | 25,000 | |
| | Deferred gain | | 25,000 |
| | *To defer the unrealized portion of the gain* | | |
| | | | |
| 2. | Deferred income tax benefit | 8,500 | |
| | Income tax expense | | 8,500 |
| | *Income tax effect of gain deferral* | | |

Alternatively, the 2009 events could have been reported by this single entry.

| | | |
|---|---|---|
| Equity in investee income | 16,500 | |
| Investment in Investee Co. | | 16,500 |

*2010 through 2014 (each year)*

| | | | |
|---|---|---|---|
| 1. | Deferred gain | 5,000 | |
| | Gain on sale of fixed assets | | 5,000 |
| | *To amortize deferred gain* | | |
| | | | |
| 2. | Income tax expense | 1,700 | |
| | Deferred income tax benefit | | 1,700 |
| | *Income tax effect of gain realization* | | |

The alternative treatment would be

| | | |
|---|---|---|
| Investment in Investee Co. | 3,300 | |
| Equity in investee income | | 3,300 |

In the above example, the income tax currently paid by Investor Co. (34% × $25,000 taxable gain on the transaction) is recorded as a deferred income tax benefit in 2009 since current income taxes will not be due on the book gain recognized in the years 2010 through 2014. Under provisions of FAS 109, deferred income tax assets are recorded to reflect the income tax effects of all future deductible temporary differences. Unless Investor Co. could demonstrate that future taxable amounts arising from existing future taxable temporary differences exist (or, alternatively, that a net operating loss (NOL) carryback could have been elected), this deferred income tax asset will be offset by an equivalent valuation allowance in Investor Co.'s balance sheet at year-end 2009. Thus, the deferred income tax asset might not be recognizable, net of the valuation allowance, for financial reporting purposes unless other future taxable temporary differences not specified in the example generate future taxable income to offset the net deductible effect of the deferred gain.

*NOTE: The deferred income tax impact of an item of income for book purposes in excess of tax is the same as a deduction for income tax purposes in excess of book.*

**Investee income items separately reportable by the investor.** In the examples thus far, the investor has reported its share of investee income, and the adjustments to this income, as a single item described as equity in investee income. However, when the investee has extraordinary items and/or prior period adjustments that are material, the investor is to report its share of these items separately on its statements of income and retained earnings.

### Example of accounting for separately reportable items

Assume that both an extraordinary item and a prior period adjustment reported in an investee's income and retained earnings statements are individually considered material from the investor's viewpoint.

*Statement of income*

| | |
|---|---:|
| Income before extraordinary item | $ 80,000 |
| Extraordinary loss from earthquake (net of income taxes of $12,000) | (18,000) |
| Net income | $ 62,000 |

*Statement of changes in retained earnings*

| | |
|---|---:|
| Retained earnings at January 1, 2009, as originally reported | 250,000 |
| Add restatement for prior period adjustment—correction of an error made in 2008 (net of income taxes of $10,000) | 20,000 |
| Retained earnings at January 1, 2009, restated | $270,000 |

If an investor owned 30% of the voting common stock of this investee, the investor would make the following journal entries in 2009:

| | | | |
|---|---|---:|---:|
| 1. | Investment in investee company | 24,000 | |
| |     Equity in investee income before extraordinary item | | 24,000 |
| | *$80,000 × 30%* | | |
| 2. | Equity in investee extraordinary loss | 5,400 | |
| |     Investment in investee company | | 5,400 |
| | *$18,000 × 30%* | | |
| 3. | Investment in investee company | 6,000 | |
| |     Equity in investee prior period adjustment | | 6,000 |
| | *$20,000 × 30%* | | |

The equity in the investee's prior period adjustment should be reported on the investor's statement of changes in retained earnings which is often presented in a more all-encompassing format with the statement of changes in stockholders' equity, and the equity in the extraordinary loss is reported separately in the appropriate section on the investor's statement of income.

**Obtaining significant influence subsequent to initial investment.** An investor that holds an investment accounted for using the cost method may subsequently qualify to use the equity method of accounting. This can occur, for example, if the investor acquires additional voting shares or if the investor's voting percentage increases as a result of repurchase of voting stock by the investee.

*Accounting prior to the effective date of FAS 141(R) and FAS 160.* Under long-standing GAAP, APB 18 required that the investor adopt the equity method by retroactively restating the results of operations and retained earnings for all prior periods presented. If the retroactive adjustment was made on or after adoption of FAS 142, the goodwill related to that investment, including goodwill related to step purchases made prior to adoption of FAS 142, were not to be amortized in determining the amount of the retroactive adjustment. Differences between the carrying amount of the investment in common stock of the investee and the investor's proportionate share of the underlying net assets of the investee that did not relate to specific accounts of the investee were to be treated as nonamortizable goodwill under FAS 142.

*Accounting on or after the effective date of FAS 141(R) and FAS 160.* Effective for fiscal years, and interim periods within those fiscal years, beginning on or after December 15, 2008, FAS 141(R) and FAS 160 amended APB 18 so that the accounting for equity-method investments acquired in stages (step-by-step) would be accounted for in a manner consistent with step-by-step acquisitions of consolidated subsidiaries. Consequently, when the investor obtains significant influence it didn't previously have, through the means described above, APB 18, as amended requires that, upon qualifying to use the equity method, the investor is to adjust the investment, results of operations, and retained earnings retroactively *on a step-by-step basis.* This is accomplished by remeasuring the previous cost-method investment in the investee to its fair value at the date the investor qualified to use the equity method (analogous to the acquisition date in a business combination) and recognizing the resulting gain or loss, if any, in current net income. After making this adjustment, the difference between the carrying value of the aggregate investment (the sum of the remeasured cost-method investment and the newly acquired investment) will undoubtedly differ from the investor's proportionate share of the underlying equity in the investee's net assets, with this difference being ascribed to goodwill. The accounting for this equity method goodwill would be as described above for post-FAS 142 goodwill; that is, it would not be amortized in accordance with the provisions of FAS 142.

On a going-forward basis, the investor would apply the equity method of accounting to its investment as previously described, including evaluation, if applicable, of whether any impairment is other-than-temporary in nature.

If the investor's voting interest were to subsequently increase again, but continue to constitute a noncontrolling interest in the investee, the step-by-step method would be reapplied whereby the investor would restate all prior holdings, irrespective of when they were acquired, to their fair value on the date that the additional increase in voting interest occurred and then prospectively apply the equity method in the current and future reporting periods.

**Accounting for a partial sale or additional purchase of an equity-method investment.** This section covers the accounting issues that arise when the investor sells some or all of its equity in the investee, or acquires additional equity in the investee.

### Example of accounting for a discontinuance of the equity method

Assume that an investor owns 10,000 shares (30%) of XYZ Company common stock for which it paid $250,000 ten years ago. On July 1, 2009, the investor sells 5,000 XYZ shares for $375,000. The balance in the investment in XYZ Company account at January 1, 2009, was $600,000. Assume that the original differential between cost and book value has been fully amortized. To calculate the gain (loss) upon this sale of 5,000 shares, it is first necessary to adjust the investment account so that it is current as of the date of sale. Assuming that the investee had net income of $100,000 for the six months ended June 30, 2009, the investor would record the following entries:

| | | | |
|---|---|---|---|
| 1. | Investment in XYZ Company | 30,000 | |
| | Equity in XYZ income | | 30,000 |
| | *$100,000 × 30%* | | |
| 2. | Income tax expense | 2,040 | |
| | Deferred income tax liability | | 2,040 |
| | *$30,000 × 20% × 34%* | | |

The gain upon sale can now be computed, as follows:

| | |
|---|---:|
| Proceeds upon sale of 5,000 shares | $375,000 |
| Book value of the 5,000 shares ($630,000 × 50%) | 315,000 |
| Gain from sale of XYZ common | $ 60,000 |

Two entries will be needed to reflect the sale: one to record the proceeds, the reduction in the investment account, and the gain (or loss) and the other to record the related income tax effects. Remember that the investor must have computed the deferred tax effects of the undistributed earnings of the investee that it had recorded each year, on the basis that those earnings either would eventually be paid as dividends or would be realized as capital gains. When those dividends are ultimately received or when the investment is disposed of, the previously recorded deferred income tax liability must be reversed.

To illustrate, assume that the investor in this example provided deferred income taxes at an effective rate for dividends (considering the 80% exclusion) of 6.8%. The realized capital gain will be taxed at an assumed 34%. For income tax purposes, this gain is computed as $375,000 – $125,000 = $250,000, yielding an income tax effect of $85,000. For accounting purposes, the deferred income taxes already provided are 6.8% × ($315,000 – $125,000), or $12,920. Accordingly, an additional income tax expense of $72,080 is incurred upon the sale, due to the fact that an additional gain was realized for book purposes ($375,000 – $315,000 = $60,000; income tax at 34% = $20,400) and that the deferred income tax previously provided for at dividend income rates was lower than the real capital gains rate [$190,000 × (34% – 6.8%) = $51,680 extra income tax due]. The entries are as follows:

| | | | |
|---|---|---:|---:|
| 1. | Cash | 375,000 | |
| | Investment in XYZ Company | | 315,000 |
| | Gain on sale of XYZ Company stock | | 60,000 |
| 2. | Deferred income tax liability | 12,920 | |
| | Income tax expense | 72,080 | |
| | Income taxes payable—current | | 85,000 |

The gains (losses) from sales of investee stock are reported on the investor's income statement in the "Other income and expense" section, assuming that a multistep income statement is presented.

In this example, the sale of investee stock reduced the percentage owned by the investor to 15%. In such a situation, the investor would discontinue use of the equity method. The balance in the investment account on the date the equity method is suspended ($315,000 in the example) will be accounted for on the basis of fair value, under FAS 115; presumably being reported in the available-for-sale investment portfolio. This accounting principle change does not require the computation of a cumulative effect or any retroactive disclosures in the investor's financial statements. In periods subsequent to this principles change, the investor records cash dividends received from the investment as dividend income and subjects the investment to the appropriate GAAP used to assess "other-than-temporary" impairment. Any dividends received in excess of the investor's share of postdisposal net income of the investee are credited to the investment, rather than to income.

The process of discontinuing the use of the equity method and adopting FAS 115, as necessitated by a reduction in ownership below the significant influence threshold level, does not require retroactive application. However, the opposite situation having the 20% ownership level equaled or exceeded again (or for the first time) is more complex. APB 18 stipulates that this change in accounting principle (i.e., to the equity method) requires that the investment account, results of operations (all periods being presented, current and prior), and retained earnings of the investor company be retroactively adjusted. If the date on which the additional interest is acquired is on or after the beginning of the first annual reporting period beginning on or after December 15, 2008, the retroactive adjustment is made on a step-by-step basis as prescribed in FAS 141(R) for business combinations made in stages.

**Example of accounting for a return to the equity method of accounting—Pre FAS 141(R)**

Continuing the same example, XYZ Company reported net income for the second half of 2009 and all of 2010 respectively, of $150,000 and $350,000; XYZ paid dividends of $100,000 and $150,000 in December of those years. In January 2011, the investor purchased 10,000 XYZ shares for $700,000, increasing its ownership to 45% and thereby necessitating a return to equity method accounting, including retroactive adjustment. The relevant entries are as follows:

| | | | |
|---|---|---|---|
| 1. | Cash | 15,000 | |
| | Income from XYZ dividends | | 15,000 |
| 2. | Income tax expense | 1,020 | |
| | Income taxes payable—current | | 1,020 |

*To record dividend income and income taxes thereon at current effective income tax rate ($15,000 × .068) in 2009*

| | | | |
|---|---|---|---|
| 3. | Cash | 22,500 | |
| | Income from XYZ dividends | | 22,500 |
| 4. | Income tax expense | 1,530 | |
| | Income taxes payable—current | | 1,530 |

*To record dividend income and income taxes thereon ($22,500 × .068) in 2009*

| | | | |
|---|---|---|---|
| 5. | Investment in XYZ Company | 700,000 | |
| | Cash | | 700,000 |

*To record additional investment in XYZ Company*

| | | | |
|---|---|---|---|
| 6. | Investment in XYZ Company | 37,500 | |
| | Retained earnings | | 34,950 |
| | Deferred income tax liability | | 2,550 |

*To adjust investment to reflect equity method accounting*

Entry 6. is the cumulative effect adjustment for 15% of XYZ Company's undistributed earnings for the second half of 2009 and all of 2010. This adjustment is computed as follows:

| | |
|---|---|
| Income earned in 2009 subject to equity method | |
| 2009 income ($100,000 + $150,000) | $250,000 |
| Less income earned through June 30 which is reflected in the investment account through previous use of the equity method | (100,000) |
| 2009 income subject to equity method adjustment | $150,000 |
| Income earned in 2010 subject to the equity method | 350,000 |
| Total income subject to the equity method | $500,000 |
| Less dividends declared in 2009 and 2010 | (250,000) |
| Increase in investee equity since suspension of equity method (undistributed income) | $250,000 |
| Investor's equity during the period July 1, 2009, through December 31, 2010 (cumulative effect) ($250,000 × 15%) | $ 37,500 |

Besides showing the cumulative effect as a prior period adjustment on the retained earnings statement, the investor also must retrospectively adjust the 2009 and 2010 financial statements to reflect the use of the equity method. This means that the dividend income of $15,000 in 2009 and $22,500 in 2010 is to be eliminated to reflect the equity method. Accordingly, the term "dividend income" is eliminated and "equity in investee income" is substituted. Since the equity method was used for half of the year 2009 and equity in investee income was accrued through June 30, the term should already appear on 2009's income statement. However, the equity in investee income will be increased by $22,500, the investor's share of the income for the last six months of 2009 ($150,000 × 15%). The net effect on 2009's income before income taxes is a $7,500 increase ($22,500 increase in equity in investee income less a $15,000 decrease in dividend income). For 2010, the net effect on income before income taxes is $30,000. This results from adding equity in investee income of $52,500 ($350,000 × 15%) and eliminating dividend income of $22,500. In addition to the income statement, the balance sheets at December 31, 2009 and 2010, are adjusted as follows (before income tax effects):

1. Add $7,500 to the investment in investee and the retained earnings balances at December 31, 2009.

2. Add $37,500 to the investment in investee and the retained earnings balances at December 31, 2010.

**Investor accounting for investee capital transactions.** According to APB 18, investee transactions of a capital nature that affect the investor's share of the investee's stockholders' equity are accounted for as if the investee were a consolidated subsidiary. These transactions principally include situations where the investee purchases treasury stock from, or sells unissued shares or reissues treasury shares it holds to, outside shareholders. (If the investor participates in these transactions on a pro rata basis, its percentage ownership will not change and no special accounting will be necessary.) Similar results are obtained when holders of outstanding options or convertible securities acquire investee common shares.

When the investee engages in one of the above capital transactions, the investor's ownership percentage is changed. This gives rise to a gain or loss, depending on whether the price paid (for treasury shares acquired) or received (for shares issued) is greater or lesser than the per share carrying value of the investor's interest in the investee. However, since no gain or loss can be recognized on capital transactions, these purchases or sales will affect additional paid-in capital and/or retained earnings directly, without being reflected in the investor's income statement. This method is consistent with the treatment that would be accorded to a consolidated subsidiary's capital transaction. An exception is that, under certain circumstances, the SEC will permit income recognition based on the concept that the investor is essentially selling part of its investment.

### Example of accounting for an investee capital transaction

Assume R Corp. purchases, on 1/2/09, 25% (2,000 shares) of E Corp.'s outstanding shares for $80,000. The cost is equal to both the book and fair values of R's interest in E's underlying net assets (i.e., there is no differential to be accounted for). One week later, E Corp. buys 1,000 shares of its stock from other shareholders for $50,000. Since the price paid ($50/share) exceeded R Corp.'s per share carrying value of its interest, $40, R Corp. has in fact suffered an economic loss by the transaction. Also, its percentage ownership of E Corp. has increased as the number of shares held by third parties has been reduced.

R Corp.'s new interest in E's net assets is

$$\frac{2{,}000 \text{ shares held by R}}{7{,}000 \text{ shares outstanding}} \times \text{E Corp. net assets}$$

$$.2857 \times (\$320{,}000 - \$50{,}000) = \$77{,}143$$

The interest held by R Corp. has thus been diminished by $80,000 – $77,143 = $2,857. Therefore, R Corp. should make the following entry:

| | | |
|---|---|---|
| Additional paid-in capital (or retained earnings) | 2,857 | |
| Investment in E Corp. | | 2,857 |

R Corp. charges the loss against additional paid-in capital if such amounts have accumulated from past transactions of a similar nature; otherwise the debit is to retained earnings. Had the transaction given rise to a gain it would have been credited to additional paid-in capital only (never to retained earnings) following the prescription in APB 6 that transactions in one's own shares cannot produce net income.

Note that the amount of the charge to additional paid-in capital (or retained earnings) in the entry above can be verified as follows: R Corp.'s share of the posttransaction net equity (2/7) times the "excess" price paid ($50 – $40 = $10) times the number of shares purchased = 2/7 × $10 × 1,000 = $2,857.

**Investor's proportionate share of other comprehensive income items.** FSP APB 18-1 holds that an investor's proportionate share of an investee's equity adjustments for other comprehensive income items (e.g., fair value adjustments to available-for-sale investments) is to be offset against the carrying value of the investment in the investee entity at the time significant influence is lost. To the extent that the offset results in a carrying value of the investment that is less then zero, an investor will (1) reduce the carrying value of the investment to zero; and (2) record the remaining balance in income.

**Exchanges of equity-method investments.** According to EITF 98-7, affirmed by EITF 01-2, an exchange of an equity-method investment for another such investment falls within the scope of APB 29 and is thus to be accounted for at book value, without gain or loss recognition (other than what may be necessary to record impairment, of course).

**Significant influence in the absence of ownership of voting common stock.** APB 18 was written to apply to investments in voting common stock of an investee, and authoritative guidance has been sorely lacking regarding the accounting for investments in other investment vehicles, such as options and warrants, and complex licensing and/or management agreements, where significant influence might also be present. These nontraditional modes of investment, providing the investor with significant influence, have become more common over the years, and thus the need for guidance became acute. In EITF 02-14, *Whether an Investor Should Apply the Equity Method of Accounting to Investments Other Than Common Stock,* the concept of *in-substance common stock* was developed to address the accounting for these alternative investments.

The EITF 02-14 consensus was that a reporting entity that has the ability to exercise significant influence over the operating and financial policies of an investee is to apply the equity method only when it has an investment(s) in common stock and/or an investment that is in-substance common stock. In-substance common stock is an investment in an entity that has risk and reward characteristics that are substantially similar to the investee's common stock. Whether or not significant influence is wielded is a fact question, and criteria are not suggested in this consensus.

Management is to consider certain characteristics when determining whether an investment in an entity is substantially similar to an investment in that entity's common stock. These are conjunctive constraints: thus, if the entity determines that any one of the following characteristics indicates that an investment in an entity is not substantially similar to an investment in that entity's common stock, the investment is not in-substance common stock.

1.  **Subordination.** It must be determined whether the investment has subordination characteristics substantially similar to the investee's common stock. If there are substantive liquidation preferences, the instrument would not be deemed substantially similar to common stock. On the other hand, certain liquidation preferences are not substantive (e.g., when the stated liquidation preference that is not significant in relation to the purchase price of the investment), and would be discounted in this analysis.

2.  **Risks and rewards of ownership.** A reporting entity must determine whether the investment has risks and rewards of ownership that are substantially similar to an investment in the investee's common stock. If an investment is not expected to participate in the earnings (and losses) and capital appreciation (and depreciation) in a manner that is substantially similar to common stock, this condition would not be met. Participating and convertible preferred stocks would likely meet this criterion, however.

3.  **Obligation to transfer value.** An investment is not substantially similar to common stock if the investee is expected to transfer substantive value to the investor and the common shareholders do not participate in a similar manner. For example, if the investment has a substantive redemption provision (for example, a mandatory redemption provision or a non-fair-value put option) that is not available to common shareholders, the investment is not substantially similar to common stock.

In some instances it may be difficult to assess whether the foregoing characteristics are present or absent. EITF 02-14 suggests that, in such circumstances, management of the reporting entity (the investor) is also to analyze whether the future changes in the fair value of the investment are expected to be highly correlated with the changes in the fair value of the investee's common stock. If the changes in the fair value of the investment are not expected to be highly correlated with the changes in the fair value of the common stock, then the investment is not in-substance common stock.

According to EITF 02-14, the determination of whether an investment vehicle is in-substance common stock must be made upon acquisition, if the entity has the ability to exercise significant influence. The assessment is to be revisited if one or more of these occur.

1. The contractual terms of the investment are changed resulting in a change to any of its characteristics described above.
2. There is a significant change in the capital structure of the investee, including the investee's receipt of additional subordinated financing.
3. The reporting entity obtains an additional interest in an investment in which the investor has an existing interest. As a result, the method of accounting for the cumulative interest is based on the characteristics of the investment at the date at which the entity obtains the additional interest (that is, the characteristics that the entity evaluated in order to make its investment decision), and will result in the reporting entity applying one method of accounting to the cumulative interest in an investment of the same issuance.

The mere fact that the investee is suffering losses is not a basis for reconsideration of whether the investment is in-substance common stock.

Upon implementation of the consensus under EITF 02-14, for investments in which the entity has the ability to exercise significant influence over the operating and financial policies of the investee, the reporting entity was to make an initial determination about whether investments existing as of the date of the consensuses in EITF 02-14 are first applied are in-substance common stock. The initial determination was to be based on circumstances that existed on the date of adoption of this Issue, rather than on the date that the investment was made.

EITF 02-14 contains several examples to illustrate the application of the criteria noted above.

### Equity Investments in Corporate Joint Ventures and Noncorporate Entities

In practice, for legal, tax, and financial purposes, a wide variety of noncorporate entities and structures are used to operate businesses, to hold investments in real estate or in other entities, or to undertake discrete projects as joint ventures. These include partnerships (e.g. limited partnerships [LP], general partnerships [GP], limited liability partnerships [LLP],) and limited liability companies (LLC). Practice questions persistently arise regarding whether directly or by analogy, authoritative GAAP literature that applies to corporate structures is also applicable to investors in noncorporate entities.

A series of pronouncements provide guidance regarding different fact situations. The following is an overview of their provisions arranged by type of entity and containing citations to relevant GAAP. Each citation refers to the relevant pronouncement as amended by subsequently issued pronouncements.

**Corporate joint ventures.** Venturers are to account for their investments in corporate joint ventures using the equity method (APB 18, para 16; SOP 78-9, para .04).

**General partnerships.** There is a rebuttable presumption that a general partner that has a majority voting interest is in control of the partnership. If voting rights are indeterminate under the provisions of the partnership agreement or applicable law, the general partner with a majority of the financial interests in the partnership's profits or losses would be presumed to have control. If this presumption is not overcome, the general partner with voting control or the majority financial interest would consolidate the partnership in its financial statements and the other noncontrolling general partners would use the equity method (AIN APB 18-2, SOP 78-9).

Partners holding lesser interests may possess substantive participating rights (as defined in EITF 04-5) granted by a contract, lease, agreement with other partners, or court decree. When the other partners have such rights, the presumption of control by the general partner with the majority voting interest or majority financial interest is overcome. Under those circumstances, the controlling general partner would consolidate the partnership and the noncontrolling general partner would consolidate the partnership and the noncontrolling general partners would use the equity method (SOP 78-9, EITF 04-5).

**Limited partnerships.** The structure of many limited partnerships consists of one investor serving as general partner and having only a small equity interest and the other investors holding limited partnership (or equivalent) interests. The proper accounting for such structures has been the subject of much debate; one of the very few authoritative sources of guidance is SOP 78-9, *Accounting for Investments in Real Estate Ventures,* which formally deals only with certain real estate investments but has been applied by analogy to other investments. EITF 96-16, *Investor's Accounting for an Investee when the Investor Has a Majority of the Voting Interest but the Minority Shareholder or Shareholders Have Certain Approval or Veto Rights,* provided expanded guidance to the appropriate accounting in those circumstances where the majority owner lacks control due to the existence of "substantial participating rights" by minority owners.

If the investor/holder is an entity that is required under GAAP to measure its investment in the limited partnership (LP) at fair value with changes in fair value reported in the income statement, then it follows that applicable specialized guidance with respect to accounting for its investment.

If the investee entity is a variable interest entity (VIE) under the provisions of FIN 46(R), *Consolidation of Variable Interest Entities,* the holders of interests in the entity are to use the GAAP applicable to those interests. If the investor has a controlling financial interest in the VIE, the investor is deemed to be the entity's primary beneficiary (analogous to a parent company) and is required to consolidate the investee in its financial statements.

Noncontrolling interest holders in an LP that is a VIE are to account for their interests using the equity method or the cost method. Limited partner interests that are so minor that the limited partner has virtually no influence over operating and financial policies of the partnership would be accounted for using the cost method (SOP 78-9). In order to be considered to be this minor, the SEC Staff has indicated that an interest would not be permitted to exceed 3-5% (EITF Topic D-46). In practice, this benchmark is also generally accepted for non-SEC registrants since it represents the most authoritative guidance currently available with respect to making this determination.

If the LP is not a VIE and the partners are not subject to specialized industry fair value accounting rules, a determination is made as to whether a single general partner or multiple general partners control the LP. If a single general partner controls the LP, that partner is to consolidate the LP, all other general partners are to apply the equity method of accounting to their investments, and the limited partners will use either the cost method (for minor investments) or the equity method, as previously discussed.

If more than one general partner controls the partnership, EITF 04-5, *Determining Whether a General Partner, or the General Partners as a Group, Controls a Limited Partnership or Similar Entity When the Limited Partners Have Certain Rights,* provides the framework for analyzing the respective legal and contractual rights and privileges associated with each owner/investor's interests to determine control. For the purpose of applying EITF 04-5, entities under common control are considered to be a single general partner. No guidance is offered, however, in EITF 04-5 as to how to determine which of several general partners is to consolidate the partnership.

EITF 04-5 integrates certain concepts from FIN 46(R) into what had been only fragmentary guidance. FIN 46(R) introduced the concept of "kick-out rights" which, when held by limited partners, gave them the right to eject the general partner(s) of the partnership, thereby (often) preventing the general partner(s) from exercising control. EITF 04-5 holds that there is a refutable presumption that general partners in a partnership have control, regardless of their actual ownership percentage, which can be overcome if the limited partners have certain defined abilities.

If the limited partners have the *substantive ability* to dissolve (liquidate) the limited partnership or otherwise remove the general partners without cause—which is referred to as "kick-out rights"—then the general partners will be deemed to lack control over the partnership. In such cases, consolidated financial reporting would not be appropriate, but equity method accounting would almost inevitably be warranted. To qualify, the kick-out rights must be exercisable by a single limited partner or a simple majority (or fewer) of limited partners. Thus, if a super-majority of limited partner votes is required to remove the general partner(s), this would not constitute a substantive ability to dissolve the partnership and would not thwart control by the general partner(s).

There is a range of possible qualifying requirements to exercise kick-out rights that could lead to the conclusion that nominal kick-out rights are ineffective in precluding the general partner(s) from exercising control. EITF 04-5 offers a series of illustrative examples to help the preparer interpret this guidance, and should be consulted to benchmark any real-world set of circumstances. Examples of barriers to the exercise of kick-out rights include

1. Conditions that make it unlikely the rights will be exercisable (e.g., conditions that narrowly limit the timing of the exercise)
2. Financial penalties or operational barriers associated with dissolving (liquidating) the limited partnership or replacing the general partners that would act as a significant disincentive for dissolution (liquidation) or removal
3. The absence of an adequate number of qualified replacements for the general partners or the lack of adequate compensation to attract a qualified replacement
4. The absence of an explicit, reasonable mechanism in the limited partnership agreement or in the applicable laws or regulations, by which the limited partners holding the rights can call for and conduct a vote to exercise those rights
5. The inability of the limited partners holding the rights to obtain the information necessary to exercise them

A limited partner's unilateral right to withdraw is pointedly not equivalent to a kick-out right. However, if the partnership is contractually or statutorily bound to dissolve upon the withdrawal of one partner, that would equate to a kick-out right.

EITF 04-5 also addresses "participating rights" held by the limited partners, which it contrasts to "protective rights" as these were first defined in EITF 96-16. Limited partners' rights (whether granted by contract or by law) that would allow the limited partners to block selected limited partnership actions would be considered protective rights and would not overcome the presumption of control by the general partners(s). Among the actions cited by EITF 04-5 as illustrating protective (not participating) rights are

1.   Amendments to the limited partnership agreement
2.   Pricing on transactions between the general partners and the limited partnership and related self-dealing transactions
3.   Liquidation of the limited partnership initiated by the general partners or a decision to cause the limited partnership to enter bankruptcy or other receivership
4.   Acquisitions and dispositions of assets that are not expected to be undertaken in the ordinary course of business (Note that limited partners' rights relating to acquisitions and dispositions that expected to be made in the ordinary course of the limited partnership's business are participating rights.)
5.   Issuance or repurchase of limited partnership interests

The presence of protective rights would not serve to overcome the presumption of control by the general partner(s). Substantive participating rights, on the other hand, do overcome the presumption of general partner control. Such rights could include

1.   Selecting, terminating, and setting the compensation of management responsible for implementing the limited partnership's policies and procedures
2.   Establishing operating and capital decisions of the limited partnership, including budgets, in the ordinary course of business

EITF 04-5 is emphatic in stating that determination of whether the presumption of general partner control is overcome is a "facts and circumstances" assessment to be made in each unique situation. For example, depending on which decisions are required to be put to a full vote of the partnership (as opposed to being reserved for the general partner), the limited partners may be found to have substantive participating rights. Another important factor weighing on this determination: the relationships among limited and general partners (using FAS 57 related-party criteria).

The assessment of the extent of limited partners' rights and the impact those have on the presumption of general partner(s) control over the partnership (for consolidated financial reporting purposes) is to be made upon initial acquisition of the general partner's interest or formation of the partnership, and again at each financial reporting (balance sheet) date.

*Limited partnerships controlled by the general partners.* As previously stated, the general partners are collectively presumed to be in control of the limited partnership and, if this is substantively the case, the accounting for the general partners depends on whether control of the entity rests with a single general partner. If a single general partner controls the limited partnership, that general partner consolidates the limited partnership in its financial statements. If no single general partner controls the limited partnership, each general partner applies the equity method to account for its interest (EITF 04-5).

Noncontrolling limited partners are to account for their interests using the equity method or by the cost method. As previously discussed, limited partner interests that are so minor (not to exceed 3 to 5 percent) that the limited partner has virtually no influence over operating and financial policies of the partnership would be accounted for using the cost method (SOP 78-9).

*Limited partnerships controlled by the limited partners.* If the presumption of control by the general partners is overcome by applying EITF 04-5 and the limited partners control the partnership, the general partners would use the equity method to account for their interests in the partnership.

If there is a controlling limited partner, that partner would consolidate the limited partnership in its financial statements. Noncontrolling limited partners would follow the same guidance provided above that applies when the general partners control the partnership (i.e., use the equity method unless the interest is minor—in which case the cost method would be used).

**Limited liability companies that maintain a specific ownership account for each investor.** When an LLC maintains individual equity accounts for each member, similar to the structure of a limited partnership, the investor/member is to analogize to the guidance above that applies to accounting for investments in limited partnerships using either the cost method or equity method (EITF 03-16 and, by reference, SOP 78-9 and EITF Topic D-46). In the discussion of EITF 03-16, it was indicated that it might be appropriate to apply this guidance by analogy to other entities that have similar specifically identifiable ownership account structures.

EITF 03-16 provides an exception to this general rule. The scope of the consensus does not include investments in LLCs used as securitization vehicles under FAS 140 that continue to be held by a transferor in a securitization transaction accounted for as a sale. These interests are accounted for as debt securities and categorized as either available-for-sale or trading securities under FAS 115 and are subject to specialized requirements regarding recognition of interest income and impairment (EITF 99-20).

**Limited liability companies that are functionally equivalent to corporations ("analogous entities").** Some LLCs have governance structures that have characteristics that closely resemble those of corporations. These LLCs are not included in the scope of EITF 03-16 summarized above. Instead, membership interests in these LLCs are subject to different criteria to determine the proper accounting treatment to be used in the investor/member's financial statements.

The applicable GAAP relative to LLCs that are analogous entities is EITF 96-16, *Investor's Accounting for an Investee When the Investor has a Majority of the Voting Interest but the Minority Shareholder or Shareholders Have Certain Approval or Veto Rights.* This consensus was revised concurrent with EITF's issuance of the consensus reached in EITF 04-5, described above. Under the revised EITF 96-16, there is a similar rebuttable presumption that the majority voting interest holder(s) are in control of the investee. Management is to exercise judgment based on the relevant facts and circumstances as to whether one or more minority shareholders or members possess rights that individually or in the aggregate provide them with effective participation in the significant decisions expected to be made in the "ordinary course of business." If the minority owner or owners possess substantive participating rights, the presumption of control by the majority owners is overcome and the minority owner or owners are considered to be in control.

Again, the controlling interest holder would be required to consolidate, and the noncontrolling interest holders would apply either the equity method or cost method, depending on the extent of their respective holdings.

**Display in the reporting entity's financial statements when the investee is not a corporation.** Under some circumstances, investor-venturers account for undivided interests in assets by means of pro rata consolidation, including a fraction of each asset category of the investee in the investor's balance sheet, typically commingled with the investor's own assets. This has most commonly occurred in the case of construction joint ventures, and is not a procedure formally defined under GAAP. In EITF 00-1, *Investor Balance Sheet and Income Statement Display under the Equity Method for Investments in Certain Partnerships and Other Ventures,* the issue addressed is whether proportional consolidation can be used to account for an investment in a partnership or a joint venture, as an alternative to full consolidation, equity method accounting, or historical cost.

The consensus was that the pro rata method of consolidation is not appropriate for an investment in an unincorporated legal entity, except when the investee is in either the construction industry or an extractive industry, where there is a longstanding practice of its use. For the purpose of the consensus, an entity is considered to be in an extractive industry only if its activities are limited to the extraction of mineral resources (such as oil and gas exploration and production) and not if its activities involve such related pursuits as refining, marketing, or transporting the extracted mineral resources.

## Collaborative Arrangements

A collaborative arrangement (sometimes referred to in practice as "line-item" joint ventures or "virtual" joint ventures) is a contractual agreement between two or more parties (participants) to jointly conduct business activities for their mutual benefit without the formation of a separate entity in which to conduct the activities. These types of arrangements are commonly used for such purposes as producing motion pictures; designing and developing hardware and/or software; or developing new pharmaceutical drugs.

Determining the proper accounting treatment for the various activities included in these endeavors is the subject of EITF 07-1, *Accounting for Collaborative Arrangements* ratified by FASB on December 12, 2007, effective for annual and interim financial statements issued for fiscal years beginning after December 15, 2008.

**Joint operating activities.** As previously mentioned, collaborative arrangements are used to conduct many different types of business activities. For example, two or more parties may agree to collaborate on joint operation of a facility such as a hospital or long-term care nursing facility. Two professional services firms (e.g., architects, engineers, consultants) may choose to jointly submit a proposal to obtain a new engagement that neither would have the capacity and/or capability to perform on its own. A movie studio may collaborate with another studio because it wants to produce a film starring an actor that is under contract with another studio or two studios may wish to spread the cost (and, of course, the risk) of producing a film. Frequently, in the pharmaceutical industry, two companies engage in a joint operating activity to research, develop, market, manufacture, and/or distribute a drug candidate including the process of obtaining all necessary regulatory approvals in one or more geographic markets.

A collaborative arrangement may involve various types of activities conducted or supervised by the participants including, but not limited to research, development, branding, promotion, sales, marketing, order processing, package design, manufacturing, and distribution. In some collaborative arrangements, a legal entity may be used for certain specified activities or in certain geographic jurisdictions due, for example, to legal restrictions imposed by the jurisdiction.

The participants' roles and responsibilities vary between arrangements but can be structured where certain responsibilities are shared between the participants and other responsibilities are solely the responsibility of one of the participants.

**Scope.** Under EITF 07-1, an activity (referred to as an "endeavor") that is the subject of a joint operating arrangement is characterized as a collaborative arrangement within the scope of the pronouncement if

1. The endeavor involves two or more parties
2. Both (all) of the parties are

    a. Active participants in the endeavor *and*
    b. Exposed to significant risks and rewards that depend on the endeavor's commercial success.

3. The endeavor is not *primarily* conducted through a separate legal entity created for it.

*Active involvement.* In evaluating whether a participant is active with respect to an endeavor, management is to consider the arrangement's specific facts and circumstances. Examples of involvement that could constitute active participation include, but are not limited to:

1. Directing and executing the activities of the endeavor,
2. Participating on a steering committee or other oversight or governance body,
3. Possessing a legal or contractual right to the intellectual property that underlies the endeavor.

Solely providing financial resources to an endeavor would not constitute an active level of involvement for the purposes EITF 07-1.

*Significant risks and rewards.* Management of a participant is to exercise its best judgment in evaluating whether the participant is exposed to significant risks and entitled to significant rewards. Consideration is to be given to the terms and conditions of the arrangement and the facts and circumstances surrounding it including

- The stage of the endeavor's life cycle at which the participant is commencing its involvement
- Management's expectations regarding the duration and extent of its financial participation in relation to the total expected duration and total expected value of the endeavor

Examples of terms and conditions of an arrangement that may indiciate that a participant is not exposed to significant risks or entitled to significant rewards include

- Market rates are paid for services provided by the participant
- Ability of a participant to exit the arrangement without cause and recover all or most of its cumulative economic participation through the exit date
- Limits on the rewards that a participant is entitled to receive
- Allocation of initial profits from the endeavor to only one participant

Frequently, a collaborative arrangement will involve the license of intellectual property with the participants to the arrangement exchanging consideration with respect to the license at the arrangement's inception. The existence of terms of this nature are not necessarily indicative of the participants not being exposed to significant risks or entitled to significant rewards.

*Timing of determination or redetermination.* A participant may become involved in a collaborative arrangement at any time during the life cycle of the endeavor. From the perspective of a participant, determination of whether an endeavor is a collaborative arrangement is to be made at the inception of the arrangement or when the participant initially becomes involved in the arrangement based on the facts and circumstances existing at that time. A participant is to reevaluate whether the arrangement continues to qualify as a collaborative arrangement any time there is a change in a participant's role in the arrangement or a change in a participant's exposure to risks or entitlement to rewards from the arrangement.

**Accounting for transactions conducted in a separate legal entity.** Any transactions associated with the endeavor that are conducted in a separate legal entity are to be accounted for under other applicable accounting pronouncements such as

- Consolidation of voting interest entities—ARB 51,
- Consolidation of variable interest entities—FAS 94, FIN 46(R)
- Joint ventures—See discussion in previous section of this chapter

**Accounting for transactions with unrelated third parties.** A participant in a collaborative arrangement is to recognize revenue earned and costs incurred in transactions with third parties (parties that are not participants to the collaborative arrangement) in its income statement based on whether the participant is serving as a principal or an agent in the transaction under EITF 99-19, *Reporting Revenue Gross as a Principal versus Net as an Agent.* If the transacting participant is considered a principal in the transaction, the revenues and costs are recorded gross. If the transacting participant is considered an agent in the transaction, the revenues and costs are recorded net. Under no circumstances is a participant in a collaborative arrangement permitted to use the equity method of accounting to account for its activities associated with the collaborative arrangement.

EITF 99-19 (discussed in detail in Chapter 10) does not provide a "bright-line" test that definitively would characterize the role of a participant in a transaction. Rather, it provides a series of indicators of gross reporting and a series of indicators of net reporting, the purpose of which is to enable management to analyze the facts and circumstances associated with the transaction to make a well-reasoned determination.

*Indicators of gross reporting (principals).*

- **Participant is primary obligor.** Under EITF 99-19, this is considered to be a "strong indicator" of the participant's role in the transaction.
- **Participant has authority, within reasonable limits, to establish price.** Even when subject to reasonable, preestablished economic constraints, if the participant has the authority to negotiate price with the customer, this may indicate that the participant possesses risks and rewards of a principal to the transaction.
- **Participant involvement in determining specifications.** If the participant has the authority to determine the nature, type, characteristics, or specifications of the products and/or services ordered by the customer, this may be indicative of the participant having primary responsibility for fulfillment. For the purposes of analyzing the applicability of this indicator, the evaluator considers whether the participant makes physical alterations to the product or performs services that add value sufficient to increase the selling price to the customer.
- **Participant performance.** The participant changes the product or performs part of the service.
- **Participant discretion in supplier selection.**
- **Participant exposed to inventory risks.** The participant bears inventory risk in one or both of the following manners:
  - General inventory risk either before the customer places the order or upon the return of the inventory by the customer
  - Specific risk of physical inventory loss after the customer places the order or during shipping of the inventory
- **Participant bears credit risk.**

*Indicators of net reporting (agents).*

- **Participant in not the primary obligor.** The supplier of the goods or services, not the participant, is the primary obligor in the transaction.
- **Participant earnings are fixed.** The amount the participant earns is fixed.

- **Participant is not exposed to credit risk.** The supplier and not the participant bears credit risk in connection with the transaction.

**Accounting for transactions between participants.** In evaluating the income statement characterization of transactions between participants to a collaborative arrangement, management is to consider

- The nature of the arrangement
- The contractual terms of the arrangement
- The nature of the participant's business operations
- Whether the transactions are included in the scope of other authoritative GAAP literature on income statement classification, either directly or by analogy

If no authoritative GAAP is identified that is relevant directly or by analogy, management is to elect a reasonable and rational accounting policy to be consistently applied to all such similar transactions.

**Disclosure.** The following disclosures apply to the entire endeavor characterized as a collaborative arrangement, even if a portion of the endeavor is being conducted through the use of a legal entity.

A participant to a collaborative arrangement is required to disclose in the initial interim or annual period of its participation in the arrangement and all annual periods thereafter

1. Its accounting policy for collaborative arrangements,
2. Information regarding the nature and purpose of the collaborative arrangements in which it participates,
3. Its rights and obligations under the collaborative arrangements,
4. For each period for which an income statement is presented, the income statement classification and amounts attributable to transactions arising from the collaborative arrangement between the participants.

Disclosures are to be made separately for each individually significant collaborative arrangement in which the reporting entity participates.

Curiously, the EITF did not require disclosure of the nature, classification, and amounts of revenues and costs recognized in the income statement from transactions between the participant and third parties. The authors believe that management should voluntarily include such disclosures to supplement the disclosures listed above, as that information is exceedingly relevant to users of the financial statements to enable them to assess the relative significance of the arrangements to the reporting entity's financial performance.

**Transition.** EITF 07-1 is to be adopted through retrospective application to all prior periods presented for all collaborative arrangements existing as of the effective date of the consensus. If it is not practical to retrospectively apply the consensus, management is to disclose both the reasons why reclassifications were not made and the effect of the reclassification on the current period in accordance with FAS 154, paragraph 9. The determination of whether retrospective application is practical is to be made on an arrangement-by-arrangement basis. In the period of initial application, a participant is to disclose

1. A description of the prior period information that has been retrospectively adjusted, if applicable, and
2. The effect of the change on revenue, operating expenses, and any other affected financial statement line items.

**Matters for which guidance is not provided.** Although the consensus is quite complex, the EITF took great pains to point out several matters that are not covered by the consensus and that require careful scrutiny of other authoritative literature and the exercise of professional judgment. The scope of 07-1 specifically excludes

1. Arrangements for which the accounting treatment is addressed by other authoritative literature,
2. Guidance regarding matters such as
   a. Determining the appropriate units of accounting
   b. Determining the appropriate recognition requirements for a given unit of accounting,
   c. The timing of when recognition criteria are considered to have been met.

**Example of a collaborative arrangement**

Leonard Sporting Goods Company (LSG) and Maureen Metals LLC. (MML) contractually agree to codevelop a new set of golf clubs using a special alloy and what they believe to be a revolutionary design. The terms of their Joint Development Agreement (JDA) are as follows:

*LSG responsibilities*

- Conducting all necessary research and development activities associated with the design of the club faces and shafts
- Developing the branding strategy, and designing the logo and product packaging
- Engaging a contract manufacturer and performing or supervising all manufacturing, warehousing, logistics, and order processing functions
- Carrying necessary inventories and insuring them against casualty loss
- Establishing prices, and performing all invoicing, credit checks, and collection activities

*MML responsibilities*

- Conducting all necessary research and development on the development of the experimental alloy
- Handling all press relations and conducting the advertising campaign
- Filing of all patents associated with the product, its design, and materials
- Marketing the product in its home state and six surrounding states; sales orders originating in those states are to be forwarded to LSG for processing, and shipment with LSG responsible for performing all of the activities specified above. In the specified states, MML has limited discretion regarding the pricing of the product.

Other provisions of the JDA include

- All costs and operating profits are to be split by the participants 50%/50%.
- The participants will co-own the intellectual property arising out of the project.
- Due to legal considerations in the Grand Duchy of Leslie, all sales in that jurisdiction are required to be made by a legal entity duly established within its borders. Consequently, when orders are placed for shipment to the Duchy, LSG sells the golf clubs to Duchy Golf Sales Co. (DGS), a corporation chartered in the Duchy to enable DGS to then transact with the sporting goods retailer located in the Duchy. DGS is owned 50% each by LSG and MML who each invested $10,000 upon its incorporation on January 2, 2009.
- On a quarterly basis each participant is to provide the other participant a full accounting for its activities with respect to the endeavor and whichever participant has advanced a net amount in excess of its proportionate share of the operating results is entitled to receive an "equalization payment" from the other participant.

The following summarizes the transactions associated with the endeavor for calendar year 2009, including the final activities necessary to commence production of the product and deliver it to sporting good stores in time for the 2009 holiday selling season.

| (000s omitted) | Total endeavor results (excluding JV) | 50% of endeavor results | Joint venture DGS |
|---|---|---|---|
| Sales | $9,200 | $4,600 | $500 |
| Cost of sales | 5,000 | 2,500 | 300 |
| Gross profit | 4,200 | 2,100 | 200 |
| Operating expenses | | | |
|     Advertising and promotion | 500 | 250 | |
|     Bad debts | 200 | 100 | |
|     Branding, package and logo design | 300 | 150 | |
|     Legal and patent filing fees | 600 | 300 | 50 |
|     Research and development | | | |
|         Alloy and metallurgy | 200 | 100 | |
|         Club faces and shafts | 300 | 150 | |
|     Shipping and delivery | 600 | 300 | 20 |
|         Total operating expenses | 2,700 | 1,350 | 70 |
| Income from operations | $1,500 | | $130 |
| × share of operating results allocable to each participant | ×50% | | |
| | $ 750 | $ 750 | |

The annual "equalization" payment was computed as follows, based on the transactions reported by the participants:

| (000s omitted) | Initially recorded in the accounting records of | |
|---|---|---|
| | LSG | MML |
| Sales | $9,200 | $ -- |
| Cost of sales | 5,000 | -- |
| Gross profit | 4,200 | -- |
| Operating expenses | | |
|     Advertising and promotion | -- | 500 |
|     Bad debts | 200 | -- |
|     Branding, package and logo design | 300 | -- |
|     Legal and patent filing fees | -- | 600 |
|     Research and development | | |
|         Alloy and metallurgy | -- | 200 |
|         Club faces and shafts | 300 | -- |
|     Shipping and delivery | 600 | -- |
|         Total operating expenses | 1,400 | 1,300 |
| Income (loss) from operations prior to equalization | 2,800 | (1,300) |
| Share of operating results per agreement | 750 | 750 |
| Equalization payment (receivable) payable | $2,050 | $(2,050) |

## Analysis

1. *Determine applicability of EITF 07-1.* The endeavor involves 2 parties that are both actively involved and that share equally in both risks and rewards. The existence of the separate entity (DGS) does not disqualify the arrangement since the joint operating activities are not *primarily* conducted through the separate entity. Thus, from the perspective of the participants, the arrangement is considered a collaborative arrangement within the scope of EITF 07-1 for the year ended December 31, 2009.

2. *Determine the accounting for the transactions in the separate legal entity.* DGS has no parent company that controls it via ownership as a voting interest entity or via other financial control as a variable interest entity. Thus, under paragraph 16 of APB 18, each participant is to record its investment in DGS and apply the equity method to account for its investment in the joint venture as follows:

*1/2/2009*

| | | |
|---|---|---|
| Investment in DGS | 10,000 | |
|     Cash | | 10,000 |

*To record initial investment in Duchy Golf Sales Co. joint venture*

*12/31/2009*
Investment in DGS                                                        65
    Equity in earnings of investee (income statement)                       65
*To record 50% interest in the earnings of the joint venture for the year*

3. *Apply EITF 99-19 to determine which of the participants is principal and which is agent.* Analysis under the provisions of EITF 99-19 yields the following results:

| *Indicator (G=Gross; N=Net)* | *LSG* | *MML* |
|---|---|---|
| a. Is primary obligor | G | N |
| b. Has authority, within reasonable limits, to establish price | G | N[*] |
| c. Involved in determining specifications of product or service | G | N |
| d. Changes the product or performs part of the service | G | N |
| e. Has discretion in selection of suppliers | G | N |
| f. Exposed to inventory risks | | |
|    1. General risk before order placed; upon customer return | G | N |
|    2. Specific risk after order placed or during shipping | G | N |
| g. Exposure to credit risk | G | G |
| h. Earnings fixed vs. variable | G | G |

[*]*In six states, MML has limited discretion with respect to sales price*

Under EITF 99-19, the party that is the primary obligor is a strong indicator of the party that serves as principal to the transactions. In addition, all of the other indicators point towards LSG being the principal. This is irrespective of the fact that MML does have limited authority in certain markets to negotiate price. Even in those limited states, LSG serves as the principal to the transaction. Both participants bear credit risk equally and are not limited to a percentage commission since they share equally in the commercial success of the endeavor, thus the applicability of indicators g. and h. is neutral between the parties. Based on the analysis of the above factors, management of both particpants concluded that LSG is the principal to the transactions associated with the collaborative arrangement and MML functions as an agent.

    Note that, in this fact situation, LSG is the principal for all sales other than those made through the joint venture. In some collaborative arrangements, this will not be the case and management will be required to analyze differing sales arrangements to determine separately for each type of arrangement, the party that is the principal. As can be discerned from the analysis above, this involves the exercise of judgment in light of the specific facts and circumstances.

4. *Determine the applicable GAAP for the transactions and elect an appropriate accounting policy to be disclosed and followed consistently.* Management of LSG and MML summarized the various activities, revenues and expenses associated with the arrangement as follows:

| Natural classification | Particip. with primary responsi-bility under JDA | Functional classification | | | | Ongoing, major central operations? | |
|---|---|---|---|---|---|---|---|
| | | Directly earned or incurred as principal in transactions with 3rd party customers | Design and development of product, co-owned intellectual property | Develop-ment of co-owned marketing-related intangibles | Marketing | LSG | MML |
| Sales to sporting goods stores | LSG | x | | | | x | |
| R&D laboratory services; licensing | N/A | | | | | | x |
| Advertising and promotion of product | MML | | | | x | x | |
| Branding, logo, package design | LSG | | | x | | x | |
| Credit, collections, bad debts | LSG | x | | | | x | |
| Filing for patents | MML | | x | | | x | x |
| Manufacturing, delivery, fulfill-ment | LSG | x | | | | x | |
| R&D–Clubs | LSG | | x | | | x | |
| R&D–Metals | MML | | x | | | x | x |

Based on the foregoing analysis, LSG's management determines that since it is the principal under EITF 99-19, LSG is required to present in its income statement, 100% of the sales, and cost of sales, and other related operating expenses that it incurred in connection with the endeavor. It is unable to find any authoritative GAAP that directly or by analogy would address how to account for the equalization payments it is required to make or entitled to receive. It analyzes the components of the payment and reflects them in LSG's income statement as follows:

*Components of Equalization Payment to MML*

> *Presented as additional cost of sales; in effect the sharing of its gross profit with MML results in LSG realizing a reduced margin on its sales of these codeveloped products*

a.  MML share of gross profit                                             $2,100

Reimbursements to MML for LSG share of expenses:

> *These functions were performed under the JDA by MML; LSG elects to pre-sent these as operating expenses; none of the advertising expenses were capitalizable as direct response advertising or required to be deferred prior to the first time the advertising takes place under LSG's accounting policies it adopted under SOP 93-7, **Reporting on Advertising Costs***

b.  Advertising and promotion                                                250

c.  Legal and patent filing fees                                             300

> *LSG records the reimbursement to MML for the metallurgical research and development as additional research and development expense analogous with outsourced contract R&D since its laboratory did not have the experience or capability to perform such research*

| | | |
|---|---|---|
| d. | Research and development alloy and metallurgy | 100 |

Reimbursement from MML for MML share expenses

> *LSG elects to present these reimbursements as reductions of its recorded expenses retaining their character; it believes its arrangement with MML to share half of the endeavor's results provides it the benefit of reduced costs and that the benefits it receives from the equalization payment should be characterized in its income statement as reductions of the expenses it would otherwise have borne on its own without MML's participation.*

| | | |
|---|---|---|
| e. | Bad debts | (100) |
| f. | Branding, package and logo design | (150) |
| g. | Research and development—Club faces and shafts | (150) |
| h. | Shipping and delivery | (300) |
| | Net equalization payment | $2,050 |

**Leonard Sporting Goods Company**
**Statement of Income**
**Ignoring income taxes and other transactions (000s omitted)**
**Year ended 12/31/2009**

| | Prior to application of EITF 07-1 | | Effects of equalization payment | Adjusted income statement |
|---|---|---|---|---|
| Sales | $9,200 | | | $9,200 |
| Cost of sales | | | | |
| Sales to third parties | 5,000 | | | 5,000 |
| Reimbursement to MML as agent | | a | $ 2,100 | 2,100 |
| Total cost of sales | 5,000 | | 2,100 | 7,100 |
| Gross profit | 4,200 | | (2,100) | 2,100 |
| Operating expenses | | | | |
| Advertising and promotion | -- | b | 250 | 250 |
| Bad debts | 200 | e | (100) | 100 |
| Branding, package and logo design | 300 | f | (150) | 150 |
| Legal and patent filing fees | -- | c | 300 | 300 |
| Research and development | | | | |
| Alloy and metallurgy | -- | d | 100 | 100 |
| Club faces and shafts | 300 | g | (150) | 150 |
| Shipping and delivery | 600 | h | (300) | 300 |
| Total operating expenses | 1,400 | | (50) | 1,350 |
| Income (Loss) from operations | 2,800 | | (2,050) | 750 |
| Equity interest in income of investee | 65 | | | 65 |
| Pretax income | $2,865 | | $(2,050) | $ 815 |

MML's management analyzed the facts and circumstances associated with the collaborative arrangement. As a research laboratory, performing research and development activities for other entities under contractual arrangements is part of MML's ongoing major and central operations.[7] MML management reached the conclusion that, since LSG is the principal in the transactions with third parties, MML, as an agent, should not recognize revenue or the related cost of that revenue at their gross amounts nor should it present expenses in the operating expense category in its income statement that are related to these transactions that it considers peripheral. Following this line of reasoning management classifies the activity related to the arrangement as follows:

**Maureen Metals LLC**
**Statement of Income**
**Ignoring income taxes and other transactions (000s omitted)**
**Year ended December 31, 2009**

| | | | |
|---|---:|---:|---:|
| ***Revenues from collaborative arrangement*** | | | |
| MML share of gross profit | | | $2,100 |
| Related expenses net of reimbursements | | | |
|     Advertising and promotion | $500 | $(250) | 250 |
|     Bad debts | | | 100 |
|     Branding, package and logo design | | | 150 |
|     Shipping and delivery | | | 300 |
| | | | 800 |
| Net revenues from collaborative arrangement | | | 1,300 |
| | | | |
| ***Intellectual property design and development*** | | | |
| Legal and patent filing fees | $600 | $(300) | 300 |
| Research and development | | | |
|     Metallurgical | 200 | (100) | 100 |
|     Club faces and shafts | | | 150 |
| | | | 550 |
| Income from operations | | | 750 |
| Equity interest in income of investee | | | 65 |
| Pretax income | | | $ 815 |

Note MML management's position that the costs of developing the intellectual property and protecting it by filing for patents are part of its "ongoing, major, or central operations." Thus, those expenses are not considered directly related to its earnings as agent from the transactions occurring after the product was fully developed and shipments commenced. Although the details are presented for illustrative purposes, the net revenues from the collaborative arrangement could be shown as the first line in the income statement and MML management could elect to voluntarily disclose the details in the notes to the financial statements to better inform the reader regarding the nature and results of the activities associated with the collaborative arrangement.

## Investments in Life Settlement Contracts

A life settlement contract is an agreement executed between a third-party investor and the owner of a life insurance policy where (1) the investor does not have an insurable interest in the life of the insured, (2) the investor pays an amount in excess of the policy's cash surrender value to the policy owner, and (3) upon the death of the insured, the face value of the

---

[7] *The phrase "ongoing, major or central operations" is used in CON 5,* **Recognition and Measurement in Financial Statements of Business Enterprises** *to differentiate activities from those that are incidental or peripheral to the reporting entity. Frequently, financial results from incidental or peripheral activities are presented in "other income and expense" if they are unusual or infrequent in nature whereas the results from ongoing, major, or central operations are shown as components of operating income and expense.*

policy is paid to the investor. These investments may be facilitated by a broker or transacted directly between the investor and the policy owner.

FSP FTB 85-4-1, *Accounting for Life Settlements Contracts by Third-Party Investors,* requires the investor to elect to account for these investments using either the "investment method" or the "fair value method." This irrevocable election is made in one of two ways:

1. On an instrument-by-instrument basis supported by documentation prepared concurrently with acquisition of the investment, or
2. Based on a preestablished, documented policy that automatically applies to all such investments.

**The investment method.** The investor recognizes the initial investment at the transaction price plus all initial direct external costs. Continuing costs (payments of policy premiums and direct external costs, if any) necessary to keep the policy in force are capitalized. Gain recognition is deferred until the death of the insured. At that time the investor recognizes in net income (or other applicable performance indicator) the difference between the carrying amount of the investment and the policy proceeds.

The investor is required to test the investment for impairment upon the availability of new or updated information that indicates that, upon the death of the insured, the expected proceeds from the insurance policy may not be sufficient for the investor to recover the carrying amount of the investment plus anticipated gross future premiums (undiscounted for the time value of money) and capitalizable external direct costs, if any. Indicators to be considered include, but are not limited to

1. A change in the life expectancy of the insured
2. A change in the credit standing of the insurer

As a result of performing an impairment test, if the undiscounted expected cash inflows (the expected proceeds from the policy) are less than the carrying amount of the investment plus the undiscounted anticipated gross future premiums and capitalizable external direct costs, an impairment loss is recognized. The loss is recorded by reducing the carrying value of the investment to its fair value. The fair value computation is to employ current interest rates.

**The fair value method.** The initial investment is recorded at the transaction price. Each subsequent reporting period, the investor remeasures the investment at fair value and recognizes changes in fair value in current period net income (or other relevant performance indicators for reporting entities that do not report net income). Cash outflows for policy premiums and inflows for policy proceeds are to be included in the same financial statement line item as the changes in fair value are reported.

**Balance sheet presentation.** On the face of its balance sheet, the investor is required to differentiate between investments remeasured at fair value and those accounted for using the investment method. This may be accomplished by either

1. Presenting separate line items for each type of investment, or
2. Parenthetical disclosure

**Examples of balance sheet presentation alternatives**

1. Separate line items

   Investments in life settlement contracts measured at
   | | |
   |---|---|
   | Fair value | $xxx,xxx |
   | Initial investment and accumulated costs | $xxx,xxx |

2. Parenthetical disclosure

| | |
|---|---|
| Investments in life settlement contracts | $xxx,xxx |
| (Portion stated at fair value $xxx,xxx) | |

**Income statement presentation.** Investment income attributable to fair value remeasurements is presented on the face of the income statement separately from investment income attributable to contracts accounted for using the investment method. This may be accomplished by either

1. Presenting separate line items for investment income attributable to each type of investment, or
2. Parenthetical disclosure

**Examples of income statement presentation alternatives**

1. Separate line items

| Investment income from life settlement contracts measured at | |
|---|---|
| Fair value | $xx,xxx |
| Initial investment and accumulated costs | $xx,xxx |

2. Parenthetical disclosure

| | |
|---|---|
| Investment income from life settlement contracts | $xxx,xxx |
| (Portion from contracts carried at fair value $xxx,xxx) | |

**Cash flow statement presentation.** Cash inflows and outflows attributable to investments in life settlement contracts are to be classified based on the nature and purpose for which the contracts were acquired.

**Disclosure of accounting policy.** In addition to other applicable GAAP disclosures, the investor is to disclose the policy it follows to account for life settlement contracts including the classification in the cash flow statement of cash inflows and outflows associated with these contracts.

**Disclosures when using the investment method.** For life settlement contracts accounted for under the investment method, the investor is required to disclose the following information based on the remaining life expectancy of the insured individuals:

1. By year, for each of the first five fiscal years ending after the balance sheet date, in total for the years succeeding those first five years, and in the aggregate

    a. The number of life settlement contracts in which it has invested
    b. The carrying value of those contracts
    c. The face value (death benefits) of the life insurance policies covered by those contracts

2. By year, for each of the first five fiscal years ending after the date of the most recent balance sheet presented, the life insurance premiums expected to be paid in order to keep the life insurance policies related to the life settlement contracts in force.
3. If management becomes aware of new or updated information that causes it to change its estimates of the expected timing of its receipt of the proceeds from the investments, it is to disclose the nature of the information and its related effect on the timing of the expected receipt of the policy proceeds. This disclosure is to in-

clude significant effects of the change in estimate on the disclosure described in 1. above.[8]

**Disclosures when using the fair value method.** For life settlement contracts accounted for under the fair value method, the investor is required to disclose the following information based on the remaining life expectancy of the insured individuals:

1. The method(s) and significant assumptions used to estimate the fair value of the contracts, including any mortality assumptions
2. By year, for each of the first five fiscal years ending after the balance sheet date, in total for the years succeeding those first five years, and in the aggregate

    a. The number of life settlement contracts in which it has invested
    b. The carrying value of those contracts
    c. The face value (death benefits) of the life insurance policies covered by those contracts

3. The reasons for changes in its estimates of the expected timing of it s receipt of the proceeds from the investments including significant effects of the change in estimates on the information disclosed in 5. above

**Other disclosures.** For each reporting period for which and income statement is presented

- The gains or losses recognized on investments sold during the period, and
- Unrealized gains or losses recognized during the period with respect to investments that are still held at the balance sheet date.

### Other Guidance on Investments and Related Matters

**Accounting for transfers of assets that are derivative instruments but that are not financial assets.** EITF 99-8 addressed the accounting for certain assets that under FAS 133 are derivative instruments, but that are not financial assets as defined in FAS 140. FAS 140 applies only to transfers of financial assets, even though it is used to account for extinguishments of all liabilities (whether financial or nonfinancial). Prior to this consensus, it had been unclear how transfers of assets that are derivative instruments but that are not financial assets were to be accounted for. EITF 99-8 prescribes that transfers of assets that are derivative instruments and subject to the requirements of FAS 133, but that are not financial assets, are to be accounted for by analogizing to FAS 140. An example would be a transfer to another entity of a derivative instrument, such as a forward contract to purchase gold that requires physical settlement, which is subject to the requirements of FAS 133.

**Structured notes.** Structured notes are debt obligations that are coupled with derivatives, most often related to interest rates or foreign currency exchange rates, such that a prescribed increase or decrease in the reference rate will have a large impact on some defined attribute of the debt obligation, such as its interest rate, maturity value or maturity date. In some instances, two or more such instruments may be acquired, having essentially opposite characteristics, such that, for example, a change in a reference interest rate will cause the fair value on one holding to increase and the other to decrease, by equal amounts. In some instances, this may have been arranged in order to be able to achieve a recognizable loss on the one (losing) investment by selling it, while holding the other (winning) one as an available-for-sale security with unrealized gains reported in other comprehensive income. EITF 98-15

---

[8] *The FSP clarifies that this disclosure requirement does not impose an obligation on management to actively seek out new or updated information in order to update the assumptions used in determining the remaining life expectancy of the life settlement contracts.*

effectively ends this practice by requiring that the related investments be accounted for as a unit while held, but if one is sold the (joint) carrying amount must be allocated based on relative fair values as of the date of sale, consistent with guidance in FAS 140. The consequence is that neither gain nor loss, recognized or included in stockholders' equity, will result from such transactions.

**Recognition of interest income and impairment on purchased and retained beneficial interests in securitized financial assets.** When a reporting entity sells a portion of an asset that it owns, the portion retained becomes an asset separate from the portion sold and separate from the assets obtained in exchange. This is the situation when financial assets such as loans are securitized with certain interests being retained (e.g., a defined portion of contractual cash flows). The entity must allocate the previous carrying amount of the assets sold based on the relative fair values of each component at the date of sale. In most cases, the initial carrying amount (i.e., the allocated cost) of the retained interest will be different from the fair value of the instrument. Furthermore, cash flows from those instruments may be delayed depending on the contractual provisions of the entire structure (for example, cash may be retained in a trust to fund a cash collateral account). The issue addressed by EITF 99-20 was how interest income and impairment should be recognized for retained interests in securitizations that are classified as available-for-sale or as held-to-maturity.

The consensus was that the holder of the beneficial interest is to recognize the excess of all cash flows anticipated at the acquisition transaction date over the initial investment as interest income using the effective yield method. The holder is to update the estimate of cash flows over the life of the beneficial interest. If the estimated cash flows change (but there is still an excess over the carrying amount), the adjustment is accounted for as a change in estimate with the amount of the periodic accretion adjusted over the life of the beneficial interest. If the fair value of the beneficial interest declines below its carrying amount, the reporting entity would apply the impairment guidance in FAS 115. If it is not practicable for a holder/transferor to estimate the fair value of the beneficial interest at the securitization date, interest income is recognized using the cash basis rather than the effective yield method.

If, based on current information and events that the reporting entity anticipates a market participant will use in determining the current fair value of the beneficial interest, there is a change in estimated cash flows, the amount of accretable yield is to be recalculated. If the change in estimated cash flows is adverse, an other-than-temporary impairment would be found to have occurred.

**Accounting for freestanding derivative financial instruments indexed to, and potentially settled in, the stock of a consolidated subsidiary.** EITF Issue 96-13 established a framework for accounting for freestanding derivative instruments that are indexed to, and potentially settled in, a company's own stock. It did not, however, provide guidance on the accounting for freestanding derivative instruments that are indexed to, and potentially settled in, a subsidiary's stock. EITF 00-6 addressed how such contracts should be classified and measured in the consolidated financial statements.

A consensus exists that stock of a subsidiary is not equity of the parent; therefore, derivatives indexed to and to be settled in stock of a subsidiary do not meet FAS 133's exclusion criteria. If derivatives meeting the criteria of FAS 133 (e.g., for net settlement, etc.), these must be accounted for under the provisions of FAS 133, and not of Issue 96-13. The consensus also discusses a number of exceptions based on the criteria set forth in FAS 133.

The EITF reached several consensuses regarding derivatives not within the scope of FAS 133, while also noting that option or forward strike prices and premiums could be indicative of impairments of the parent's investment in subsidiaries—which would need to be assessed using FAS 144. A parent's contract to purchase a subsidiary's (minority held) common stock is not recorded until settled; during the period of the contract, income continues to be allocated to the minority interest. A contract to sell shares in a subsidiary, likewise, is recorded when settled; until that time, income would not be allocated to outside interests (counter parties to the derivative). No consensus was reached regarding written options, however.

### Implications of Accounting for Investments on the Reporting of Comprehensive Income

FAS 130 expanded reporting of the changes in items (other than investments by or distributions to owners) that are reported in the equity section of the balance sheet. Among these items are unrealized gains or losses on securities held in the available-for-sale portfolio, and accordingly changes in these gains or losses must be reported in the statement of comprehensive income or via the other allowable reporting mechanisms described in Chapter 3. These changes may be reported net of income tax or gross, with the income tax effect separately presented within other comprehensive income.

The major complicating factor arising from reporting changes in the unrealized gains or losses of available-for-sale securities derives from the "recycling" of gains or losses when the underlying securities are later sold or transferred into the trading portfolio; either of these events necessitates recognition of the entire gain or loss in net income, including any unrealized gain or loss that might have previously been reported in other comprehensive income (but not in net income). To avoid "double counting" the gain or loss, the amount of gain or loss previously reported in other comprehensive income must be reversed simultaneously with the recognition in net income.

#### Example of "recycling" between accumulated other comprehensive income and net income

To illustrate the "recycling" problem, consider an investment by Zenobia Co. in $500,000 face amount of Vaught Corp. bonds due July 1, 2019, carrying coupons of 8%. The purchase, for a total of $530,000, occurs on July 1, 2009, and the bonds are deemed available for sale, as defined by FAS 115. Per that standard, periodic interest income must be computed by the effective yield method based on the acquisition cost (i.e., the face value net of any premium or discount), but the difference, if any, between amortized cost and fair value as of the balance sheet date must be reported as a contra or additional equity account, with changes being taken into other comprehensive income for the period.

The yield to maturity on the Zenobia bonds is approximately 7.15%; for simplicity, the premium will be amortized straight-line ($1,500 per semiannual interest payment period) in this example, rather than by the effective yield method as is actually required.

Assume that the bonds have a fair value of $522,000 as of year-end 2009 and $527,000 as of year-end 2010. As of March 31, 2011, the value of the bonds is $528,000, at which time they are in fact sold.

Given the foregoing, as of December 31, 2009, the amortized cost basis of the investment would be $530,000 − $1,500 = $528,500. Since the fair value at that date is $522,000, an unrealized loss of $528,500 − $522,000 = $6,500 must be recorded in other comprehensive income, before any income tax effects (which will be ignored here, again for simplicity). Interest income for the half-year ended December 31, 2009, was $20,000 − $1,500 = $18,500 under the simplifying assumption of straight-line amortization, and this would be included in earnings.

At year-end 2010, the bonds have an amortized cost basis of $528,500 − $3,000 = $525,500 vs. a fair value of $527,000. Interest income for the year ended December 31, 2010, included in earnings, was $40,000 − $3,000 = $37,000. A positive adjustment (i.e., income) of $8,000 must be reported in other comprehensive income for 2010 in order to carry the bonds at fair value as of the year-end.

For the three-month period ended March 31, 2011, further premium amortization of $750 must be recorded (along with an interest accrual), which will reduce the bond's amortized cost basis to $525,500 − $750 = $524,750 as of the date of the sale, which is made at the market value of $528,000. For purposes of reporting results of operations for the quarter ended March 31, 2011, a positive other comprehensive income adjustment of $1,750 must be reflected—this is necessary to bring the carrying value of the bonds up to their fair value as of that date. However, since the bonds are sold and a realized gain of $3,250 is to be reported in earnings, a "reclassification adjustment" of the same amount must be included as a negative (i.e., expense) item in other comprehensive income for that period, which will thus cause the net other comprehensive income item pertaining to the bonds held in the available-for-sale portfolio to be a negative $1,500 for the period ended March 31, 2011.

The foregoing is summarized in the following table (it is assumed that the 2011 transaction is reported at year-end):

**Zenobia Co.**
**Selected Portions of Combined Statements of Earnings and Comprehensive Income**
**(ignoring income tax effects)**
**December 31, 2009, 2010, and 2011**

*December 31, 2009*

|  |  |  |
|---|---|---|
|  |  | $    -- |
| Other income and expense: |  |  |
| Interest income (net of premium amortization, $1,500) |  | 18,500 |
|  |  | -- |
| Net earnings |  | -- |
| Other comprehensive income: |  |  |
| Unrealized loss on bonds available for sale |  | (6,500) |
| Total other comprehensive income |  | -- |
| Comprehensive income |  | $    -- |

*December 31, 2010*

|  |  |  |
|---|---|---|
|  |  | $    -- |
| Other income and expense: |  |  |
| Interest income (net of premium amortization, $3,000) |  | 37,000 |
|  |  | -- |
| Net earnings |  | -- |
| Other comprehensive income: |  |  |
| Unrealized gain on bonds available for sale |  | 8,000 |
| Total other comprehensive income |  | -- |
| Comprehensive income |  | $    -- |

*December 31, 2011*

|  |  |  |
|---|---|---|
|  |  | $    -- |
| Other income and expense: |  |  |
| Interest income (net of premium amortization, $750) |  | 9,250 |
| Gain on sale of bonds |  | 3,250 |
|  |  | -- |
| Net earnings |  | -- |
| Other comprehensive income: |  |  |
| Unrealized loss on bonds available for sale | 1,750 |  |
| Less: Reclassification adjustment for gain |  |  |
| realized on sale | (3,250) | (1,500) |
| Total other comprehensive income |  | -- |
| Comprehensive income |  | $    -- |

## Certain Loans or Debt Securities Acquired in Transfers

The preceding discussion has not differentiated between securities investments acquired directly from the issuer and those obtained on the secondary market, since this distinction has not heretofore held implications for financial reporting. However, a new accounting standard, SOP 03-3, *Accounting for Certain Loans or Debt Securities Acquired in a Transfer*, imposes for the first time new accounting requirements for debt instruments acquired in transfers when the purchase price reflects a change in the debtor's credit standing since the original issuance of the instrument. This standard is applicable to all acquirers of loans or debt securities (bonds, securitized loans, etc.), not merely financial institutions, although relatively fewer of commercial or industrial entities would tend to be making such purchases.

Debt instruments (whole loans or loan participations, as well as securities) will generally trade in the secondary market at prices that vary from the amount at which they were issued originally. The prices may be higher or lower than the face amount, depending on the confluence of several factors. Because interest rates change almost continually, it is rare that market rates will correspond to the nominal rate on any given loan or debt security, even if the loan or instrument originally carried a market yield. Furthermore, many instruments are issued at premiums or discounts at inception, for various reasons. In the secondary market, prices will be adjusted continually to reflect current market conditions as they pertain to the loan's (or security's) coupon rate and the credit standing of the issuer/borrower, within the context of market rates of interest and other factors. If current rates are higher than the instrument's coupon (i.e., contractual) rate, it will trade at a discount from par value, while if the current rates are below the coupon rate, it will sell for a premium, if other variables are held constant.

Furthermore, the borrower's creditworthiness may well have changed since the loan was originated or the debt instrument was issued. This also impacts the price at which the loan or security will trade, with a decline in credit standing resulting in a drop in value, and an improvement in credit standing causing a rise in the value of the entity's debt. Creditworthiness pertains to the risk of default, and a number of well-regarded private sector companies closely monitor the outstanding debt of publicly held and private corporations and various governmental agencies and political subdivisions. Examples of rating agencies or measures are Moody's, Standard & Poor's and Fitch's, for publicly held companies and the Fair Isaac credit score for private companies.

Yields on debt instruments may also vary because of macrolevel factors, such as market concerns over industry developments, rather than a change in a given issuer's specific risk of default or a change in general interest rates. For example, during the telecom industry bust of the late 1990s and early 2000s, even well-regarded entities saw prices of their traded debt securities drop substantially due to industry-wide concerns.

Loans or debt securities may trade in the secondary market at their original issuance prices as the coincidental result of offsetting changes in the above-noted variables. Thus, market yields may have declined—which, taken alone, would cause a rise in the price of fixed coupon debt instruments—but concurrently the issuer's creditworthiness may have been reassessed downward by rating agencies—which, absent other events, would cause the price of the debt to decline. In tandem, the credit downgrade may have essentially negated the price response to lower market interest rates. In applying SOP 03-3, it is necessary to refer not simply to the price at which the loan or security has been transferred, in relation to its "par" or original issuance price, but also to examine whether there is information to suggest that there has been a change in the issuer's credit quality since inception of the obligation. Only in the latter circumstance will the provisions of this new standard be applied.

**SOP 03-3 in greater detail.** The purpose of SOP 03-3 is to prescribe the accounting for debt instruments (comprising most loans and debt securities, with certain exceptions) which are acquired via a transfer (i.e., in the secondary market) and which have been affected by changes in credit quality. The standard requires that the accretable yield be determined. This is derived from the relationship between the future cash flows expected to be collected and the price paid for the acquired instrument. The accretable yield is distinguished from the nonaccretable difference, which is generally the excess of the total of contractual future cash flows over the expected cash flows.

Neither the accretable yield nor the nonaccretable difference can be displayed in the financial statements. For example, consider a loan that contractually is obligated to pay a total of $85,000 in future interest and principal, but which can be purchased for $50,000 and is expected to provide future cash flows of only $73,500. The $23,500 ($73,500 − 50,000) spread between the purchase price and the undiscounted expected future cash flows is the accretable yield. The further $11,500 ($85,000 − 73,500) spread between expected and contractual cash flows, however, is the nonaccretable difference, which cannot be given accounting recognition under SOP 03-3. That is, the loan (which is an investment in the hands of the transferee) cannot be recorded or displayed at the higher, $85,000 amount, with a contra account or valuation allowance pertaining to the pretransfer estimated uncollectible amount being reported. Instead, the purchase cost, $50,000, must be the initial representation of this acquired asset, which is later increased by virtue of the accretion of yield (and reduced by collections).

While SOP 03-3 applies to loans and debt securities, there are important exceptions. Derivative instruments are excluded entirely from the scope of the standard, although debt instruments that contain embedded derivatives are not excluded. Also, debt securities that are accounted for at fair value with changes taken into income currently (i.e., those held in trading portfolios) are exempted, since these are not accreted to face value or to an expected level of future cash flows. Similarly, since changes in the fair values of trading and available-for-sale securities held by not-for-profit organizations both are reflected currently in the changes in net assets (the parallel performance measure for not-for-profit entities, roughly corresponding to net income), these are also exempted. Mortgage loans classified by mortgage bankers as held-for-sale (and presented at fair value) are also exempted from the provisions of SOP 03-3.

SOP 03-3 applies to both specific acquisitions of loans or debt securities (e.g., purchases of single loans, pools of loans, or debt securities) and to acquisitions as part of a business combination accounted for under FAS 141. In the case of business acquisitions, while it was sometimes observed in past practice that the gross amount of the loan would be recorded, together with a contra or valuation allowance for the estimated uncollectible portion, this is no longer permitted. SOP 03-3 is explicit that "carryover" of the selling entity's book values is not permitted. A new cost basis is established and, at the date of acquisition, the asset (investment) must reflect the actual cost of the loan or other instrument, without any "grossing up" and without any contra asset being recorded. Any valuation allowance (contra asset) provided *after* acquisition will reflect only the change in value occurring after that date. The transferee's valuation allowance cannot include any changes in value arising while the asset was in the hands of the former owner/transferor of the loan or security.

Upon acquisition the effective yield is to be computed, based on the expected pattern (i.e., timings and amounts) of future cash flows, so that interest can be accreted on the level-yield basis (a constant rate on a changing base). Over the holding term of the investment, expected cash flows may be altered: they may decline due to perceived impairment or may increase due to upgrading of creditworthiness. The accounting for such changes will vary, with decreases in expectations triggering immediate impairment loss recognition, while increases will generally be reported prospectively over the holding period of the instrument. The precise accounting for changes in expected future cash flows also depends, per SOP 03-3, on whether the instrument is accounted for as a loan (under FAS 114), or as a debt security (under FAS 115). These matters are addressed in the following sections.

SOP 03-3 amends PB 6, *Amortization of Discounts on Certain Acquired Loans*, which provided similar guidance. However, under PB 6, changes in expected future cash collections for qualifying loans (described below) resulted in changes to yields recognized prospectively, whereas under the newly established guidance of SOP 03-3, reductions in expected future cash flows will trigger the recognition of a loss in the current reporting period.

**Accounting for investments in loans acquired by transfer.** Loans acquired by transfer (i.e., in the secondary market) are recorded initially at acquisition cost, consistent with a fundamental tenet of GAAP. If the acquisition price differs from the par or face amount (i.e., there is a premium or a discount) the effective yield has to be computed and used to accrete the discount (or, if a premium, amortize it) over the expected term of the instrument. This process is well established under GAAP and is not new with SOP 03-3.

However, if there is evidence of a decline in creditworthiness since the instrument's inception, such that it is deemed probable at the date of transfer that the full amount of contractual cash flows will not be received, the provisions of SOP 03-3 must be applied. In this context, probable is used in the same way as it is under FAS 5, and only if that rather high threshold criterion is satisfied will this standard be invoked. In such cases, the transferee must estimate cash flows to be received, and accrete the initial carrying amount to that amount, rather than to the gross amount of future contractual cash flows. An uncertainty regarding future cash flows that suggests only a possible shortfall versus contractual amounts owed would not qualify under the standard for the accounting set forth in this discussion. (In such a situation, there would be disclosure of reasonably possible contingent losses, and if at a later date the loss is deemed to have become probable, a loss accrual would be recognized per FAS 5.)

The estimation of the amounts of expected future cash flows, and the timing of those cash flows, is obviously a matter of some complexity and inevitable subjectivity. For example, if payments from a credit-impaired obligor are expected to be made, say, fifteen days late on average, this will impact the computed effective yield on the loan and is to be given explicit consideration in ascertaining the effective yield, subject to the usual materiality threshold concerns. The calculation of accretable yield is made at the acquisition date, but, as described below, may later have to be adjusted as expectations regarding future cash flow amounts change. Subsequent reduced expectations of cash flows will result in the recognition of impairment, while expectations of enhanced or improved cash flows may result in reversal of previously recognized impairment (if any), or increased effective yield over the instrument's remaining holding period.

### Basic example of loans acquired via transfer

Assume that Investor Co. acquires a loan with a remaining principal balance of $650,000 on January 1, 2009. The contractual terms of the loan call for interest-only payments, at 9%, annually through December 31, 2013, at which time the full principal balance is due. The debtor's credit rating has been reduced subsequent to the initiation of the borrowing, and the 2008 interest payment was not made when due. Investor Co. pays $500,000 (flat) for the loan and any unpaid interest. The expectation is that the debtor will pay $40,000 at the end of 2009, $60,000 at the end of years 2010 and 2011 (each year), $70,000 at the end of 2012, and $600,000 at the end of 2013. Total projected cash inflows, $830,000, are lower than the contractually due amount, $1,001,000 (including the arrearage for 2008), and the effective yield will be about 12.6%. At transfer, the investment is recorded at cost, as follows:

| | | |
|---|---|---|
| Investment in loan receivable | 500,000 | |
| Cash | | 500,000 |

At the end of 2009, immediately prior to receipt of the payment, the entry to record the accretion for the year, at the effective yield, is

| | | |
|---|---|---|
| Investment in loan receivable | 62,974 | |
| Accretion (interest income) | | 62,974 |

The collection of the anticipated amount at December 31, 2009, is recorded as follows:

| | | |
|---|---|---|
| Cash | 40,000 | |
| Investment in loan receivable | | 40,000 |

Entries for subsequent years' accretion and collections would follow in the same manner. This presumes, of course, that amounts expected to be received indeed are received, and that expectations about the future receipts do not depart from what had been anticipated when the loan was purchased.

The changes in carrying amount and recognition of income over the full five-year period are illustrated in the following chart.

| | A | B | C | D | E |
|---|---|---|---|---|---|
| | *Beginning* | *Cash flows* | | *Reduction (increase)* | *Ending carrying* |
| *Year ending* | *carrying* | *expected to* | *Interest* | *in carrying amount* | *amount of loan* |
| *December 31* | *amount* | *be collected* | *income* | *(B–C)* | *(A–D)* |
| 2009 | $500,000 | $ 40,000 | $ 62,974 | $ (22,974) | $522,974 |
| 2010 | 522,974 | 60,000 | 65,867 | (5,867) | 528,841 |
| 2011 | 528,841 | 60,000 | 66,606 | (6,606) | 535,447 |
| 2012 | 535,447 | 70,000 | 67,438 | 2,562 | 532,885 |
| 2013 | 532,885 | 600,000 | 67,115 | 532,885 | -- |
| | | $830,000 | $330,000 | $500,000 | |

In the foregoing chart total cash collected, $830,000, consisted of $330,000 in interest, accreted at the 12.6% computed yield, and $500,000 return of investment in the loan receivable. Contrast this result with the examples that follow.

### Example with decrease in expected cash flows

If, subsequent to acquisition and computation of effective yield, the expected cash flows associated with a loan are revised downward, SOP 03-3 directs that this be accounted for as an impairment, with the adjustment being such that the previously determined yield percentage is maintained in future periods by applying the constant return to a downwardly adjusted carrying value. While some might argue that a diminished expectation of cash flows would imply a new, lower rate of return, SOP 03-3 instead opts for recognizing an immediate impairment, measured as the then-present value of the stream of cash flow shortfalls being projected. This results in a continuing rate of return equal to the original estimate, but with a step-down in the carrying value of the loan.

To illustrate, using the same basic facts above, assume now that immediately after the 2011 payment is made, Investor Co., revises its expectation of cash flows to be received in 2012 and 2013. It now anticipates zero cash collection in 2011, and only $500,000 at year-end 2013. The present value of these shortfalls—a $70,000 shortage one year hence, followed by a $100,000 shortfall two years later—discounted at the 12.6% yield on the investment computed at the date of transfer, reveals an impairment of $141,039 as of the start of 2012. The entry to record this, given that the investment is treated as a loan rather than as a debt security, is as follows:

| | | |
|---|---|---|
| Bad debt expense | 141,039 | |
| Allowance for uncollectible loan receivable | | 141,039 |

The reduced net carrying value of the loan receivable, which is $394,408 immediately following this adjustment, will continue to accrete at 12.6%, as the following table illustrates:

| | A | B | C | D | E |
|---|---|---|---|---|---|
| | *Beginning* | *Cash flows* | | *Reduction (increase) in* | *Ending carrying* |
| *Year ending* | *carrying* | *expected to* | *Interest* | *carrying amount* | *amount of loan* |
| *December 31* | *amount of loan* | *be collected* | *income* | *(B–C)* | *(A–D)* |
| 2009 | $500,000 | $ 40,000 | $ 62,974 | $ (22,974) | $522,974 |
| 2010 | 522,974 | 60,000 | 65,867 | (5,867) | 528,841 |
| 2011 | 528,841 | 60,000 | 66,606 | (6,606) | |
| 2012* | | | | 141,039 | 394,408 |
| 2013 | 394,408 | -- | 49,675 | (49,675) | 444,083 |
| 2014 | 444,083 | 500,000 | 55,917 | 444,083 | -- |
| | | $660,000 | $301,039 | $500,000 | |

\* *Provision of allowance for estimated uncollectible future cash flows, computed at present value using the effective yield on the loan.*

It will be observed in the foregoing chart that total cash collected, $660,000, consisted of $301,039 in interest, accreted at the 12.6% computed yield, and the recovery of only $358,961 of the $500,000 investment in the loan receivable. In other words, SOP 03-3 treats the decrease in expected cash flows as a loss of principal, accounted for as a bad debt and a provision of a valuation allowance against the $500,000 loan receivable. Note that the decreased cash flow expectation was *not* accounted for as a lowered future return on the investment (which would have resulted in lower interest income recognition in years 2012 and 2013, in this example, coupled with a full recovery of the principal invested).

**Example with decrease in expected cash flows followed by increase in expected cash flows (recovery of uncollectible loan receivable)**

If Investor Co., above, first lowers its expectation regarding future cash flows and then partially reverses its estimate, so that some or all (but not more than all) of the allowance of the uncollectible loan receivable proves unneeded, this is accounted for under SOP 03-3 as a reversal of the valuation allowance account (i.e., as a change in an accounting estimate).

To illustrate, consider again the facts in the basic example, and now assume that in 2011 Investor Co. has the expectation that no interest will be collected in 2012 and that only $500,000 will be collected in 2013. In 2012, however, $20,000 is in fact collected, and Investor Co. then expects a full collection of the $600,000 in 2013 (but no recovery of the $50,000 missed payment in 2012).

The entry to record the reduced expectation of future cash flows at the end of 2010 or beginning of 2011 is as shown previously.

| | | |
|---|---|---|
| Bad debt expense | 141,039 | |
| Allowance for uncollectible loan receivable | | 141,039 |

In 2012, the collection of the $20,000 (when no collection at all was anticipated) coupled with the renewed expectation of collecting $600,000 in 2013 required that some of the previously provided valuation allowance be reversed. The amount of valuation allowance to be restored, per SOP 03-3, is that amount which will result in interest accretion thereafter at the previously determined 12.6% yield through the final collection of the loan. Assuming that the $20,000 collection in December 2012 came as a surprise, the adjustment will be computed with reference to the final remaining collection, $600,000, expected in December 2013, and to the $20,000 unexpected 2014 collection.

The entry to partially restore the carrying value of the loan, net of the valuation allowance, is as follows:

| | | |
|---|---|---|
| Allowance for uncollectible loan receivable | 108,802 | |
| Bad debt expense | | 108,802 |

The computation of the foregoing amount may be somewhat confusing, unless one keeps in mind that the objective of SOP 03-3 is to provide for the reporting of interest income over the full carrying term of the loan receivable, at a constant rate on a changing balance, with that rate being the rate computed at the date of transfer. The only exception, which will be illustrated later in this section, is for situations where the total cash to be collected exceeds the estimate made at the date of transfer; in that case, a higher rate of return is reported in periods after the change in estimate, to avoid the alternative of reporting a gain at the date the new estimate is made. In this example, the anticipated "extra" 2013 collection of $100,000 ($600,000 – $500,000) has a present value at the end of 2012 of $88,802, so this previously provided valuation allowance is no longer needed. Furthermore, the $20,000 collection in 2012 was unexpected, and had previously been fully included in the valuation allowance as being uncollectible, so this too must be reversed. Therefore, the total reversal of valuation allowance is the sum of these two amounts, or $108,802. Alternatively, this can be computed as the adjustment necessary to bring the net carrying value of the loan receivable to the amount of "principal" to be collected in December 2013 (i.e., the present value, discounting at 12.6%, of the expected $600,000 collection).

The net carrying value of the loan receivable will continue to accrete at 12.6%, both after the recognition of the valuation allowance at the end of 2011 and after the partial elimination of the valuation allowance in 2012, as the following table illustrates:

| Year ending December 31 | A Beginning carrying amount of loan | B Cash flows expected to be collected | C Interest income | D Reduction (increase) in carrying amount (B–C) | E Ending carrying amount of loan (A–D) |
|---|---|---|---|---|---|
| 2009 | $500,000 | $ 40,000 | $ 62,974 | $ (22,974) | $522,974 |
| 2010 | 522,974 | 60,000 | 65,867 | (5,867) | 528,841 |
| 2011 | 528,841 | 60,000 | 66,606 | (6,606) | |
| 2011* | | | | 141,039 | 394,408 |
| 2012 | 394,408 | 20,000 | 49,675 | (29,675) | |
| 2012** | | | | (108,802) | 532,885 |
| 2013 | 532,885 | 600,000 | 67,115 | 532,885 | -- |
| | | $780,000 | $312,237 | $500,000 | |

\* *Provision of allowance for estimated uncollectible future cash flows, computed at present value using the effective yield on the loan.*

\*\* *Restoration of a portion of the previously provided allowance, computed at present value using the effective yield on the loan, relative to expected 2013 collection, plus the $20,000 unanticipated collection in 2012 at full accreted amount.*

It will be observed in the foregoing chart that total cash collected, $780,000, consisted of $312,237 in interest, accreted at the 12.6% computed yield, and the recovery of only $467,763 of the $500,000 investment in the loan receivable. As in the immediately preceding example, SOP 03-3 treats the decrease in expected cash flows as a loss of principal, accounted for as a bad debt and a provision of a valuation allowance against the $500,000 loan receivable. In this case, $32,237 of "principal" (i.e., of the amount recognized at the time of transfer) was lost, which is the net of the $141,039 valuation allowance provision in 2011 and the $108,802 recovery recognized in 2012.

Note that in all of the preceding examples the carrying value of the loan receivable continues to earn the computed 12.6% yield throughout the holding period. This was true if the initially estimated future cash flows were all collected as planned, or if changes to the estimated amounts or timings later were made—as long as the total cash to be collected did not exceed the amount originally (i.e., upon transfer to Invest Co.) estimated. In the next example, the collections exceed what was anticipated when the loan was acquired, and this necessitates a different approach to accounting for the interest yield on the investment.

In all cases where an allowance for uncollectible loan amounts has been provided, if the loan is subsequently foreclosed, the lender must measure the long-lived asset received in full satisfaction of a receivable at fair value less cost to sell as prescribed by FAS 15. That standard prescribes that after a troubled debt restructuring, the creditor must account for assets received in satisfaction of a receivable the same as if the assets had been acquired for cash. Accordingly there will be a new cost basis for the long-lived asset received in full satisfaction of a receivable; the valuation allowance would not be carried over as a separate element of the cost basis for purposes of accounting for the long-lived asset under FAS 144 subsequent to foreclosure. This treatment has been confirmed by FSP 144-1.

### Example with increase in expected cash flows

Assume again the basic facts of the investment in the loan receivable made by Investor Co. However, after fully collecting the anticipated amounts in 2009 and 2010, Investor revises its estimates of the amounts to be collected in 2011, 2012, and 2013. Specifically, it now expects to receive $75,000 at the end of 2011 and again at the end of 2012, and to collect the full remaining balance, $650,000, at the end of 2013. SOP 03-3 does not permit recognition of a gain or other income upon making this new estimate, but does instead require that the effective yield be recomputed and that future receipts be allocated between interest income and principal reduction consistent with the new accretable yield.

Note that no entry is required at the time of the new estimate of future cash flows because no gain or loss (or reversal of previously recognized loss) is being affected. As with changes in accounting estimates under FAS 154, this is handled strictly on a prospective basis.

| Year ending December 31 | A Beginning carrying amount of loan | B Cash flows expected to be collected | C Interest income | D Reduction (increase) in carrying amount (B–C) | E Ending carrying amount of loan (A–D) |
|---|---|---|---|---|---|
| 2009 | $500,000 | $ 40,000 | $ 62,974 | $ (22,974) | $522,974 |
| 2010 | 522,974 | 60,000 | 65,867 | (5,867) | 528,841 |
| 2011* | | | | | |
| 2012 | 528,841 | 75,000 | 88,086 | (13,086) | 541,927 |
| 2013 | 541,927 | 75,000 | 90,265 | (15,265) | 557,192 |
| 2014 | 557,192 | 650,000 | 92,808 | 557,192 | -- |
| | | $900,000 | $400,000 | $500,000 | |

* *Based on new expectations regarding future cash flows, a new yield is computed in an amount that equates the present value of expected receipts in 2011-13 to the carrying value at the end of 2010, $528,841. This yield is about 16.7%.*

In the foregoing example, $900,000 in cash is ultimately collected, allocated $400,000 to interest income and $500,000 to recovery of the amount recorded at the date of transfer, which was the sum paid for the loan receivable.

**Accounting for investments in pools of loans acquired by transfer.** Loans that are acquired as a pool present special accounting considerations. Each individual loan must meet the criteria of SOP 03-3 in order to apply the accounting set forth in this standard. Thus, if a group of loans are acquired together and in the aggregate have expected future cash flows in an amount lower than the aggregate contractual cash flows, this does not qualify each of the loans to be accounted for under SOP 03-3. Rather, each loan must be reviewed for impairment due to credit quality, and only those individual loans exhibiting the defined characteristic would be subject to the specified accounting.

After making a determination that each loan in a proposed pool has met the threshold conditions set forth under SOP 03-3 (i.e., that there has been evidence of credit quality deterioration subsequent to the origination, and that it is probable that, as of the transfer date, the transferee will not collect all the contractually required payments), a further determination must be made that the loans share common risk characteristics. Under provisions of SOP 03-3, loans with similar credit risk or risk ratings, and one or more predominant risk characteristics, such as financial asset type, collateral type, size, interest rate, date of origination, term, and geographic location, will be considered to have common risk characteristics. Credit risk can be assessed by reference to publicly available ratings of publicly held companies or by automated ratings such as that produced by Fair Isaac Corporation (FICO scores).

The aggregate cost of the loans to be aggregated is to be apportioned to the loans in the pool in proportion to their respective fair values at date of acquisition. The aggregate accretable yield of the pool is allocated among the loans in this same manner.

Only loans acquired in a given fiscal *quarter* (not year!) are subject to aggregation for financial reporting purposes. Once a pool is established, its integrity must be maintained, and thus loans can only be removed from the pool upon sale, foreclosure, write-off, or settlement. New loans cannot be added to an existing pool. The excess of contractually required cash flows over the acquisition cost of the pool may not be used to offset or absorb changes to anticipated cash flows associated with other loans or pools of loans having other common risk characteristics.

Removal of a loan from a portfolio is effected at the loan's then-carrying value, and accordingly a gain or loss would be reflected in income of the period, measured as the difference between the carrying value and the fair value of the amount received in settlement (e.g., cash or collateral). Any difference between the carrying amount of the loan being removed from the pool and the fair value of the amount received will not impact the percentage yield being used to accrete value on the remainder of the pool.

**Example of an investment in a pool of loans acquired by transfer**

Garfield Corporation acquires the following seven loans for $600,000 during the same fiscal quarter:

| Loan no. | Fair value | Remaining term | Interest rate | FICO score |
|---|---|---|---|---|
| 1 | $53,000 | 4 years | 9% | 450 |
| 2 | 260,000 | 4 years | 6% | 800 |
| 3 | 125,000 | 4 years | 10% | 600 |
| 4 | 78,000 | 4 years | 8% | 480 |
| 5 | 50,000 | 4 years | 7% | 730 |
| 6 | 92,000 | 4 years | 10% | 390 |
| 7 | 67,000 | 4 years | 9% | 340 |
| | $725,000 | | | |

Garfield elects to split these loans into two groups—those having Fair Isaac & Co. (FICO) scores below the minimum Fannie Mae acceptance score of 620, and those above it. Accordingly, loan numbers 2 and 5 are shifted into a separate Pool A, with the remaining loans in Pool B. The $600,000 acquisition cost is allocated to the two pools based on the relative fair values of the loans within the pools, as shown below.

| Pool no. | Aggregate fair value | Proportion of total fair value | Cost allocation |
|---|---|---|---|
| A | $310,000 | 43% | $258,000 |
| B | 415,000 | 57% | 342,000 |
| | $725,000 | 100% | $600,000 |

Garfield expects $117,376 annual payments from the Pool B loans. It determines that the discount rate equating all cash flows expected to be collected with the $342,000 allocated purchase price is 14%. Using the 14% rate, Garfield constructs the following amortization table for Pool B:

| Year | Expected cash receipts | Interest income (14%) | Reduction of carrying amount | Carrying amount |
|---|---|---|---|---|
| Inception | | | | $342,000 |
| 1 | $117,376 | $ 47,880 | $ 69,496 | 272,504 |
| 2 | 117,376 | 38,151 | 79,225 | 193,279 |
| 3 | 117,376 | 27,059 | 90,317 | 102,962 |
| 4 | 117,376 | 14,414 | 102,962 | 0 |
| | $469,504 | $127,504 | $342,000 | |

At the beginning of Year 3, Garfield writes off the remaining balance of Loan 7. Prior to the final payment, Loan 7 has a carrying value of $31,204, as determined by apportioning the carrying amount of Pool B at the end of Year 2 amongst the five loans in the pool based on their relative fair values at the date of acquisition. This apportionment calculation is shown in the following table:

| Loan no. | Fair value at inception | Relative values | Apportionment of year 2 carrying amount |
|---|---|---|---|
| 1 | $ 53,000 | 12.77% | $24,684 |
| 3 | 125,000 | 30.12% | 58,217 |
| 4 | 78,000 | 18.80% | 36,327 |
| 6 | 92,000 | 22.17% | 42,847 |
| 7 | 67,000 | 16.14% | 1,204 |
| | $415,000 | 100.00% | $193,279 |

Garfield records the loan write-off with the following entry:

| | | |
|---|---|---|
| Loss on loan write-off | 31,204 | |
| Investment in loan receivable | | 31,204 |

The following amortization table reflects the removal of Loan 7 from Pool B, along with its proportionate share of the expected cash receipts in Years 3 and 4.

| Year | Expected cash receipts | Interest income (14%) | Reduction of carrying amount | Carrying amount |
|------|------------------------|------------------------|------------------------------|-----------------|
| Inception | | | | $342,000 |
| 1 | $117,376 | $ 47,880 | $ 69,496 | 272,504 |
| 2 | 117,376 | 38,151 | 79,225 | 193,279 |
| Write-off | | | 31,204 | 162,075 |
| 3 | 98,426 | 22,690 | 75,736 | 86,339 |
| 4 | 98,426 | 12,087 | 86,339 | 0 |
| | $431,604 | $120,808 | $342,000 | |

**Accounting for investments in debt securities acquired by transfer.** If the debt instrument acquired in a transfer to be accounted for under SOP 03-3 meets the definition of a security, as set forth in FAS 115 (namely, that it constitutes a share, participation, or other interest that is represented by a registered or bearer instrument or by book entry, and is one of a class or series of participations, interests or obligations), then SOP 03-3 prescribes a slightly different mode of accounting for changes in expected cash flows. In order to conform to FAS 115's requirements, an anticipated downward change in expected future cash flows must be examined to determine whether merely a temporary change in value has occurred, or whether an other than temporary decline has been signaled. While temporary impairment is not impossible, if in fact the transferee of debt securities—the issuer of which had suffered an adverse change in creditworthiness prior to the transfer—now anticipates further reduced cash flows from the security, there is substantial likelihood that the impairment in value is other than temporary. Under FAS 115, other-than-temporary impairment must be recognized by writing down the carrying value of the investment and reflecting the charge in current earnings, whether the security is being held in the available-for-sale portfolio or is being held to maturity.

If, on the other hand, the estimated future cash flows from the debt security are increased from the amounts anticipated at transfer, then similar to what was illustrated above, the accretable yield is to be recomputed and periodic interest income thereafter appropriately adjusted. This is considered a change in accounting estimate under FAS 154.

To illustrate, consider the same facts as set forth above, except now assume that the loan was instead a debt security meeting the definition set forth in FAS 115. When acquired, it was treated as being available for sale, but for this example no changes in value are addressed other than that associated with the changed expectation of cash flows.

### Example of reduction in cash flow expectations

The anticipated cash flows occurred in 2009, 2010, and 2011 but at the beginning of 2012 Investor Co. revises its expectations, and now believes that there will be a zero cash collection in 2012, and only $500,000 at year-end 2013. The present value of these shortfalls—a $70,000 shortage at year-end 2012, followed by a $100,000 gap at year-end 2013—discounted at the same 12.6% rate computed as the yield on the investment at transfer, reveals an impairment of $141,039 as of the start of 2012. The entry to record this, given that the investment is treated as a debt security, rather than as a loan, is as follows:

| | | |
|---|---|---|
| Loss on impairment of investment | 141,039 | |
|     Investment in available-for-sale debt securities | | 141,039 |

Apart from the bookkeeping (writing down the investment directly rather than crediting a contra asset account), the treatment is very similar to that previously presented. Most importantly, the reduced net carrying value of the debt security held as an available for sale security will continue to accrete at 12.6%, as the following table illustrates:

| Year ending December 31 | A Beginning carrying amount of investment | B Cash flows expected to be collected | C Interest income | D Reduction (increase) in carrying amount (B–C) | E Ending carrying amount of investment (A–D) |
|---|---|---|---|---|---|
| 2009 | $500,000 | $ 40,000 | $ 62,974 | $ (22,974) | $522,974 |
| 2010 | 522,974 | 60,000 | 65,867 | (5,867) | 528,841 |
| 2011 | 528,841 | 60,000 | 66,606 | (6,606) | |
| 2011* | | | | 141,039 | 394,408 |
| 2012 | 394,408 | -- | 49,675 | (49,675) | 444,083 |
| 2013 | 444,083 | 500,000 | 55,917 | 444,083 | -- |
| | | $660,000 | $301,039 | $500,000 | |

\* *Write-down of carrying value of investment in debt security, due to reduced expectation of future cash flows, which is judged to be an other-than-temporary impairment, computed at present value using the effective yield on the loan.*

The total cash collected, $660,000, is accounted for as interest income, in the total amount $301,039, and recovery of the "principal" of the investment, net of the impairment recorded in 2011, amounting to $358,961.

### Example with decrease in expected cash flows followed by increase in expected cash flows

Unlike in the earlier examples, where the investment was accounted for as a loan receivable, here the investment is in a debt security accounted for under FAS 115, which prohibits restoring an other than temporary decline in value. For this reason, the write-down was not reflected through a contra asset (allowance) account, and a later improvement in the outlook for future cash flows must instead be accounted for prospectively as a yield adjustment.

Assume, therefore, that Investor Co., first lowers its expectation regarding future cash flows and then partially reverses its estimate, so that some or all of the amount of future cash flow thought not to be forthcoming now again is expected to be received. Specifically, assume that in 2011 Investor Co. has the expectation that no interest will be collected in 2012 and that only $500,000 will be collected in 2013. In 2012, however, $20,000 is in fact collected, and Investor Co. then expects a full collection of the $600,000 in 2013 (but no recovery of the $50,000 missed payment in 2012).

The entry to record the reduced expectation of future cash flows at the end of 2010 or beginning of 2011 is as shown below.

| | | |
|---|---|---|
| Loss on impairment of investment | 141,039 | |
| Investment in available-for-sale debt securities | | 141,039 |

In 2012, the collection of the $20,000 (when no collection at all was anticipated), coupled with the renewed expectation of collecting $600,000 in 2013, requires that the yield through the end of the expected holding period (final payoff, in this case) be recomputed. Assuming that the $20,000 payment for 2012 was received before the financial statements for 2012 have been prepared, it would be appropriate to recompute accretable yield as of the beginning of that year, so that both 2012 and 2013 will report interest income consistent with the pattern of cash flows over that two-year period. The calculated yield on an investment equal to the carrying value at the beginning of 2012 ($394,408), which is expected to generate cash inflows of $20,000 at the end of that year and $600,000 at the end of the next year, is 25.9%, and this is used to accrete yield over the remaining term.

Since this will be reported prospectively, no entry is made as of the beginning of the year (nor would the necessary information have been available), but the entry to record interest income and the accretion for uncollected interest would be as follows:

| | | |
|---|---|---|
| Cash | 20,000 | |
| Investment in available-for-sale debt securities | 82,156 | |
| Interest income | | 102,156 |

The accretion of value is akin to an amortization of discount, and represents interest earned but not received, based on the most recent estimates of future cash flows. It does not represent a recovery of the previously written down carrying value of the investment because of permanent impairment. The complete analysis can be seen in the chart below.

| | A | B | C | D | E |
|---|---|---|---|---|---|
| Year ending December 31 | Beginning carrying amount of investment | Cash flows expected to be collected | Interest income | Reduction (increase) in carrying amount (B–C) | Ending carrying amount of investment (A–D) |
| 2009 | $500,000 | $ 40,000 | $ 62,974 | $ (22,974) | $522,974 |
| 2010 | 522,974 | 60,000 | 65,867 | (5,867) | 528,841 |
| 2011 | 528,841 | 60,000 | 66,606 | (6,606) | |
| 2011* | | | | 141,039 | 394,408 |
| 2012** | 394,408 | 20,000 | 102,156 | (82,156) | 476,564 |
| 2013 | 476,564 | 600,000 | 123,436 | 476,564 | -- |
| | | $780,000 | $421,039 | $500,000 | |

\* *Write-down of carrying value of investment in debt security, due to reduced expectation of future cash flows, which is judged to be an other-than-temporary impairment, computed at present value using the effective yield on the loan.*

\** *Interest is accreted at the new rate of 25.9% hereafter.*

It will be observed in the foregoing chart that total cash collected, $780,000, consisted of $421,039 in interest, accreted, first, at the 12.6% computed yield through the end of 2011, and then at the 25.9% computed yield in light of higher expected cash flows for 2012 and 2013. The remainder of the cash flows, totaling $358,961, was attributable to the recovery of the investment, net of the write-down for impairment in 2011.

In contrast to the example where the investment was accounted for as a loan receivable, here the yield is adjusted prospectively when a recovery in value is observed, and this causes relatively more of the future cash flows to be treated as interest income, and relatively less as recovery of the investment principal.

Note that if no reduction in future cash flows had been anticipated, but if an increase in cash flows was expected at some point during the holding period of the investment, the result, from an accounting standpoint, would be as shown immediately above. The accretable yield would have been computed and recognized prospectively over the remaining holding period of the security.

**Disclosure requirements under SOP 03-3.** The standard sets forth expanded disclosure requirements pertaining to accounting for prepayments. In addition, disclosure is required, separately for instruments accounted for as loans and for those accounted for as debt securities, of outstanding balances and related carrying amounts at the beginning and end of each reporting period; and of the amount of accretable yield at the beginning and end of each period, with reconciliation of additions, accretion, and disposals of loans and for any reclassification between accretable and nonaccretable yields. Also, for loans acquired during the reporting period, disclosure is required of the contractually required payments receivable, expected cash flows associated therewith, and fair values at acquisition dates. For instruments accounted for as loans (not debt securities), the investor must disclose provisions for uncollectible amounts and reversals thereto made during the period, and the amount of the allowance for uncollectible amounts at both the beginning and end of the reporting period.

Finally, if the income recognition method set forth in SOP 03-3 is not applied to any loans within the scope of the standard—because subsequent developments result in placing the loan on nonaccrual status, or because an indeterminate foreclosure date makes computation of accretable yield impossible, for example—disclosure is required of the carrying amount at acquisition and at the end of the reporting date.

# 13 BUSINESS COMBINATIONS AND CONSOLIDATED FINANCIAL STATEMENTS

# PERSPECTIVE AND ISSUES

## Background and Historical Perspective

Historically, one of the most daunting problems facing accountants has been the determination of when it is more informative and meaningful to present the financial statements of multiple enterprises together, as if they were a single economic unit.

Since the issuance of APB 16, *Business Combinations,* in 1970 by FASB's predecessor, the AICPA Accounting Principles Board, practitioners have struggled with many fundamental issues.

FASB has been working intermittently on various projects with respect to business combinations and purchased intangibles since it was founded in 1973. Major standards were finally promulgated in 2001 affecting accounting for business combinations and for intangible assets, including goodwill, and a further major change has been mandated by another new standard issued in 2007.

US GAAP had traditionally permitted two distinct methods of accounting for business combinations. The purchase accounting method required that the actual cost of the acquisition be recognized, including any excess over the amounts allocable to the fair value of identifiable net assets, commonly known as goodwill. The pooling of interests methods, available only when a set of stringent criteria were all met, resulted in combining the book values of the merging entities, without any adjustment to reflect the fair values of acquired assets and liabilities, and without any recognition of goodwill. Since pooling of interests accounting required that the mergers be achieved by means of exchanges of common stock, the use of this method was largely restricted to publicly held acquirers, which greatly preferred poolings since this averted step-ups in the carrying value of depreciable assets and goodwill recognition, the amortization of which would reduce future reported earnings.

Pooling accounting was widely seen as not being indicative of economic reality, since mergers which were "marriages of equals" rarely, if ever, occurred, notwithstanding that this was the theoretical basis for using this method of accounting. Ultimately, the pooling method was eliminated, but gaining support for this change required a significant compromise by FASB on the related matter of goodwill accounting: under the rules established in FAS 141 and FAS 142 goodwill would no longer be amortized, and the impact of business combinations on reported income would often more closely resemble that of the now-banned pooling method than the traditional purchase accounting method. However, although periodic amortization is no longer reported, goodwill must be tested annually for impairment and, when impairment is found to have occurred, goodwill must be written down to fair value, with the adjustment reflected as a charge against the operating income of that period.

Under FAS 141 and FAS 142, all business combinations, except for those involving not-for-profit entities and combinations of entities under common control (e.g., parent/subsidiary and brother/sister mergers), were required to be accounted for as purchases. Goodwill arising from earlier purchase business combinations already amortized was not to be restored, but the unamortized balance as of the effective date of the new standards was no longer subject to amortization. Poolings completed before the effective date of FAS 141 did not, however, need to be restated—and, as a practical matter, developing fair value information about long-ago combinations accounted for as poolings would have been an impossible task.

While goodwill impairment must be regularly assessed, the actual application of FAS 142 results in recognizing goodwill created by the reporting entity subsequent to the purchase combination, to the extent that this replaces or offsets impaired goodwill, so in many cases impairments will not be recognized even when the value of the acquired operations has declined. This approach—which effectively reverses the longstanding ban on recognizing internally created (as opposed to purchased) goodwill—was necessitated by the virtual impossibility of separately identifying elements of goodwill having alternative derivations. Even with this simplified approach, measurement of goodwill impairment is a fairly difficult task, often requiring the services of independent valuation consultants.

The requirements imposed by FAS 141 and 142 significantly differed from those established by International Financial Reporting Standards (IFRS), and both FASB and the IASB acknowledged that their respective standards could be improved and converged. Consequently the two boards conducted a joint project to converge their business combinations standards, which culminated with the issuance in the US of FAS 141(R) and 160, which are to be effective *prospectively* for business combinations for which the acquisition date is on or after the beginning of the first annual reporting period beginning on or after December 15, 2008. IASB issued a revised version of its corresponding standard, IFRS 3, in early 2008. While the revised US standards more closely resemble the International standards, differences still remain between the two, and accountants that are responsible for preparing financial statements using both sets of standards—or are responsible for reconciling or converting financial statements—will still need to be cognizant of these differences.

This chapter addresses the application of the acquisition method of accounting (formerly referred to as the purchase method) for business combinations in detail, and the accounting for goodwill to a lesser extent. Chapter 11 addresses the accounting for all intangible assets, including goodwill, with greater specificity. This chapter retains, in an appendix, the guidance that will ultimately be nullified or amended when FAS 141(R) and FAS 160 become effective, because this guidance still applies to business combinations that predate the effective date of the new standards, and will continue to apply to those business combinations, since they are not required (or permitted) to be restated to conform to the new acquisition-method rules.

While the presentation of consolidated financial statements is required under GAAP, there is no parallel requirement to present combined financial statements for entities under common control (brother/sister entities). However, in certain cases, it is desirable that combined financial statements be prepared for such entities. This process is very similar to an accounting consolidation using the formerly permitted pooling accounting, except that the equity accounts for the combining entities are carried forward intact.

The major accounting issues in business combinations and in the preparation and presentation of consolidated or combined financial statements are as follows:

1.  The proper accounting basis for the assets and liabilities of the combining entities
2.  The accounting for goodwill or negative goodwill, if any exists
3.  The elimination of intercompany balances and transactions in the preparation of consolidated or combined statements

Consolidation of many of what were formerly called "special-purpose entities" (SPE)—now renamed "variable interest entities" (VIE) by FIN 46(R)—has increased substantially under these requirements, which were spurred on by the financial reporting scandals of the early 2000s. Rules governing consolidation of VIE are complex and are continuing to evolve further in response to an ongoing credit market turmoil that is being (as of mid-2008) experienced worldwide.

The accounting for the assets and liabilities of entities acquired in a business combination is largely dependent on the fair values assigned to them at the transaction date. (The now-obsolete pooling method relied upon book values.) FAS 157, *Fair Value Measurements,* introduced a framework for measuring fair value, and its provisions provide important guidance when assigning values as part of a business combination. In essence, it favors valuations determined on the open market, but allows other methodologies if open market valuation is not practicable. The fair value concepts and procedures are discussed in greater detail in Chapter 6.

The accounting procedures for combinations of not-for-profit organizations were not addressed by the original issuance of FAS 141, and still remain unaddressed with the issuance of FAS 141(R). FAS 141(R) did expand the scope of FAS 141 to include mutual entities, and FASB currently plans to issue guidance applicable to not-for-profit mergers and acquisitions in the fourth quarter of 2008.

| **Sources of GAAP** | | | |
|---|---|---|---|
| *APB* | *ARB* | *FAS* | *EITF* |
| 16, 18, 29 | 51 | 94, 140, 141(R), 142, 160 | 85-12, 86-32, 87-21, 91-5, 96-5, 96-16, 97-2, 00-4, 02-5, 02-11, D-101 |
| *FIN* | *SOP* | *FSP* | *FTB* |
| 46(R) | 03-3, 07-1 | 46(R)-1, 46(R)-2, 46(R)-3, 46(R)-4, 46(R)-5, 46(R)-6, 46(R)-7 | 85-6 |

## DEFINITIONS OF TERMS

**Acquiree.** One or more businesses in which an acquirer obtains control in a business combination.

**Acquirer.** An entity that obtains control over one or more businesses in a business combination. When the acquiree is a variable interest entity (VIE), the primary beneficiary of the VIE is always the acquirer.

**Acquisition date.** The date on which control of the acquiree is obtained by the acquirer.

**Acquisition-related costs.** Expenses incurred by an acquirer to enter into a business combination.

**Assembled workforce.** An existing group of employees that permits an acquirer to continue operating a business that it acquires on and after the acquisition date without having to hire and train new employees to perform their functions.

**Asset.** A reporting entity recognizes an asset if both of the following criteria are met at the balance sheet date (CON 6):

1. The reporting entity has obtained or controls future economic benefits that result from transactions or events that occurred in the past.
2. Receipt of those future economic benefits by the reporting entity is probable.

**Business.** An integrated set of assets and activities capable of being conducted and managed in order to provide a return directly to investors or other owners, members, or participants. The return can be in the form of dividends, lower costs, or other economic benefits. A development stage enterprise (FAS 7) is not precluded from qualifying as a business under this definition and the guidance that accompanies it in FAS 141(R).

**Business combination.** A transaction or event that results in an acquirer obtaining control over one or more businesses. It is important to note that transactions that are sometimes referred to as "mergers of equals" or as "true mergers" are nevertheless considered to be business combinations with an acquirer and one or more acquirees.

**Closing date.** The day on which an acquirer legally transfers consideration, acquires the assets, and assumes the liabilities of an acquiree.

**Combined financial statements.** Financial statements that present the collective results of operations and financial position of a group of entities under common management or control as if the group were a single economic entity. The presentation of the combined group excludes the party or parties that control or manage it.

**Consolidated financial statements.** The financial statements of a parent and all of its subsidiaries presented as a single economic entity.

**Consolidated group.** A parent and all of its subsidiaries.

**Contingency.** An existing, unresolved condition, situation, or set of circumstances that will eventually be resolved by the occurrence or nonoccurrence of one or more future events. A potential gain or loss to the reporting entity can result from the contingency's resolution.

**Contingent consideration.** Generally, an acquirer's obligation to transfer additional assets or equity interests to the acquiree's former owners if specified future events occur or conditions are met. The contingent obligation is incurred as part of a business combination in order to obtain control of an acquiree.

Contingent consideration might also arise when the terms of the business combination provide a requirement that the acquiree's former owners return previously transferred assets or equity interests to the acquirer under certain specified conditions.

**Control (or controlling financial interest).** Control of an entity can be obtained either (1) by obtaining ownership of a majority of its outstanding voting interests (the controlled entity being referred to as a voting interest entity), or (2) by obtaining contractual rights to receive the majority of the financial benefits and/or by assuming contractual obligations to bear the majority of the financial consequences that occur in the future from the entity outperforming or underperforming its expectations (the controlled entity being referred to as a variable interest entity or VIE). These conditions are mutually exclusive (i.e., an entity is either a voting interest entity controlled by the holders of a voting majority of its equity or is a variable interest entity controlled individually or collectively by one or more other parties referred to as holders of variable interests). In the latter instance, when a single party has control, the party is referred to as the primary beneficiary of the VIE.

Entities that might otherwise be considered voting interest entities nevertheless might not be controlled by the holders of the majority of the voting interests in situations where, for example, the entity is in legal reorganization, subject to bankruptcy proceedings, or operating subject to governmental restrictions (e.g., foreign exchange restrictions or other controls) that impose uncertainties on the entity whose severity casts significant doubt regarding the voting owner's ability to control the entity.

**Dual-listed corporation** or **Dual-listed company.** A contractual arrangement between two or more businesses in which they agree to retain their separate legal identities while operating as if they were a single economic unit. Unlike a stapling arrangement (defined below), dual listed entities' equity shares are traded separately.

**Equity interests.** In an investor-owned entity, instruments evidencing rights of ownership. In a mutual entity, instruments evidencing ownership, membership, or participation rights.

**Expected losses and expected residual returns.** Expected losses represent the expected negative variability in the fair value of an enterprise's net assets exclusive of variable interests. Expected residual returns represent the expected positive variability in the fair value of an enterprise's net assets exclusive of variable interests. The expected variability (separately defined below and illustrated in this chapter) in an enterprise's net income or loss is included in the determination of expected losses and expected residual returns.

**Expected variability.** When estimating an entity's expected future cash flows in accordance with CON 7, *Using Cash Flow Information and Present Value in Accounting Measurements* (discussed more fully in Chapter 1), a range of probability-weighted expected outcomes is used. Mathematically, this is simply a weighted-average calculation. The expected variability of the cash flows included in that calculation is computed by: (1) computing the difference between each individual estimated outcome and the weighted-average, (2) multiplying each difference computed in the previous step by the probability of occurrence assigned to that individual outcome, and (3) separately summing the positive variations (expected residual returns) and negative variations (expected losses). The absolute value of the expected residual returns will always equal the absolute value of the expected losses. The sum of the absolute values of the expected residual returns and the expected losses represents the expected variability in both directions associated with that estimate of probability-weighted expected cash flows.

**Fair value.** The price that would be received to sell an asset or paid to transfer a liability in an orderly transaction between market participants at the measurement date. Although GAAP literature has primarily focused on fair value in the context of assets and liabilities, the definition also applies to instruments classified in equity.

**Favorable contract.** From the perspective of a counterparty, a contract is favorable if its terms are more lucrative than current market terms.

**Goodwill.** An intangible asset acquired in a business combination that reflects the future economic benefits expected to be derived from the business combination that are not allocated to other individually identifiable, separately recognizable assets acquired.

**Identifiable asset.** An asset that (1) represents a legal and/or contractual right or (2) is separable from the entity that holds it. A legal and/or contractual right is considered identifiable irrespective of whether it is transferrable or separable from the entity or from other rights and obligations. An asset is considered separable if it is capable of being separated or divided from the entity that holds it for the purpose of the asset's sale, transfer, license, rental, or exchange, by itself or together with a related contract, or other identifiable asset, or liability, irrespective of whether management of the entity intends to do so.

**Intangible asset.** A nonfinancial asset that lacks physical substance.

**Liability.** A reporting entity has incurred a liability if both of the following criteria are met at the balance sheet date (CON 6):

1. The reporting entity has a present obligation to sacrifice economic benefits in the future by providing services or transferring assets to others resulting from transactions or events that occurred in the past.
2. The future sacrifice of economic benefits by the reporting entity is probable.

**Market participants.** Buyers and sellers in the principal or most advantageous market for an asset or liability who are

1. Independent of the reporting entity (i.e., they are not related parties).
2. Knowledgeable to the extent that they have a reasonable understanding about the asset or liability and the transaction based on all available information, including information that is obtainable through the performance of usual and customary due diligence efforts.
3. Able to buy or sell the asset or liability.
4. Willing to enter into a transaction for the asset or liability (i.e., they are not under duress that would force or compel them to enter into the transaction).

**More likely than not (MLTN).** A likelihood or probability of more than fifty percent.

**Mutual entity.** An enterprise that is not investor-owned, organized for the purpose of providing dividends, reduced costs, or other economic benefits directly to its owners, members, or participants. Examples of mutual entities include mutual insurance companies, credit unions, and cooperative entities.

**Noncontrolling interest.** The equity or net assets in a subsidiary not directly or indirectly attributable to its parent. Noncontrolling interests were formerly referred to in accounting literature as minority interests.

**Owners.** Holders of ownership interests (equity interests) in investor-owned or mutual entities. Owners include parties referred to as shareholders, partners, proprietors, members, or participants.

**Parent.** An entity that possesses a controlling financial interest in one or more subsidiaries including an entity that is the primary beneficiary of a variable interest entity.

**Primary beneficiary.** A variable interest holder that is required to consolidate a variable interest entity (VIE). Under FAS 141(R), this party is also referred to as a "parent" and the VIE is also referred to as a "subsidiary."

Consolidation is required when the holder of one or more variable interests would absorb a majority of the VIE's expected losses, receive a majority of the VIE's expected residual returns, or both. If one holder would absorb a majority of the VIE's expected losses and another holder would receive a majority of the VIE's expected residual returns, the holder absorbing the majority of the expected losses is the primary beneficiary and is thus required to consolidate the VIE.

**Reacquired right.** A right previously granted by the acquirer to the acquiree that allowed the acquiree to use one or more of the acquirer's assets. The applicable asset may be recognized or unrecognized for accounting purposes in the acquirer/grantor's financial statements.

**Reporting unit.** An operating segment or one level below that (called a component), that is used to perform goodwill impairment testing.

**Reverse acquisition.** An acquisition when one entity, nominally the acquirer, issues so many shares to the former owners of the target entity that they become the majority owners of the successor entity.

**Reverse spin-off.** A spin-off transaction in which the nominal or legal spinnor is to be accounted for as the spinnee, in order to reflect the economic reality of the spin-off transaction.

**Roll-up or Put-together transaction.** A business combination that is effected by two or more entities transferring the net assets of their businesses to a newly formed entity. These transactions can also be effected by the owners of the entities transferring their equity interests in those entities to the newly formed entity.

**Stapling arrangement.** An arrangement in which two or more legal entities contractually agree to combine their securities so that they are quoted at a single price and cannot be traded or transferred independently.

**Step acquisition (a business combination achieved in stages).** A business combination in which the acquirer held an equity interest in the acquiree prior to the acquisition date on which the acquirer obtained control.

**Subordinated financial support.** Variable interests that absorb some or all of an entity's expected losses.

**Subsidiary.** An entity, including unincorporated entities such as partnerships or trusts, in which another entity, referred to as its parent, holds a controlling financial interest. A variable interest entity that is consolidated by a primary beneficiary is also included in this definition.

**Total at-risk equity investment.** The following criteria are set forth in FIN 46(R) for determining the total at-risk equity investment in an entity:

1. *Include* only equity investments that participate significantly in profits and losses, even if the investments have no voting rights.
2. *Exclude* equity interests issued by the entity in exchange for subordinated interests in other variable interest entities.

3. *Exclude* amounts provided to the equity investor (e.g., fees, charitable contributions, or other payments) directly or indirectly by the entity or other parties involved with the entity unless the provider is a parent, subsidiary, or affiliate of the investor that is required to be included in the same set of consolidated financial statements as the investor.

4. *Exclude* amounts financed for the equity investor (e.g., by loans or guarantees of loans) directly by the entity or by other parties involved with the entity, unless the party is a parent, subsidiary, or affiliate of the investor that is required to be included in the same set of consolidated financial statements as the investor.

There is a rebuttable presumption that an equity investment of less than 10% of an entity's total assets is insufficient to permit the entity to finance its activities without additional subordinated financial support. In order to overcome this presumption, one or more of the following conditions must be present:

1. *Performance*—The entity has demonstrated that it can finance its activities without additional subordinated financial support.

2. *Comparability*—The entity's invested equity is at least as much as other entities holding similar assets of similar quality in similar amounts and who operate without additional subordinated financial support.

3. *Reasonable forecast*—Based on reasonable quantitative evidence, the entity's invested equity exceeds the estimate of the entity's expected losses.

This 10% threshold was intended by FASB to apply only in one direction (i.e., an investment of less than 10% is considered insufficient, but an investment of 10% or more is not necessarily presumed to be sufficient). Many entities engaged in high-risk activities, holding high-risk assets, or carrying significant off-balance-sheet exposures require more than 10% equity investment in order to finance their activities. Consequently, irrespective of the 10% threshold, an evaluation must be done to determine whether a particular entity with which the enterprise is involved requires an equity investment of 10% or greater in order to finance its activities without additional subordinated financial support.

**Unfavorable contract.** From the perspective of a counterparty, a contract is unfavorable if its terms are less lucrative than current market terms. An unfavorable contract is not necessarily a contract that will result in a loss to the counterparty.

**Unrealized intercompany profit.** The excess of the transaction price over the carrying value of an item (usually inventory or plant assets) transferred from (or to) a parent to (or from) the subsidiary (or among subsidiaries) and not sold to an outside entity. For purposes of consolidated financial statements, recognition must be deferred until subsequent realization through a transaction with an unrelated party.

**Variable interest.** Ownership, contractual, or other monetary interests in an entity that are either entitled to receive expected positive variability (referred to as expected residual returns) or obligated to absorb expected negative variability (referred to as expected losses).

**Variable interest entity.** An entity for which an analysis of the at-risk investments of the holders of its voting interests would not be effective in establishing the party or parties that hold a controlling financial interest in the entity. This situation arises either (1) because the entity is not adequately capitalized by at-risk equity sufficient to absorb its expected losses or (2) because the at-risk equity holders do not receive or bear all of the financial benefits or detriments that would provide those holders with a controlling financial interest in the entity.

## CONCEPTS, RULES, AND EXAMPLES

### FAS 141(R) and FAS 160 and Convergence with International Standards

On December 4, 2007, FASB released two new standards, FAS 141(R), *Business Combinations* (revised 2007), and FAS 160, *Noncontrolling Interests in Consolidated Financial Statements*. These standards were the product of the first major joint project undertaken by FASB and the International Accounting Standards Board (IASB). In January 2008, IASB published the counterpart international standard, IFRS 3 (revised), *Business Combinations,* and IAS 27 (as revised in 2007), *Consolidated and Separate Financial Statements*. The tandem sets of standards substantially converge US GAAP and International GAAP, however differences still remain between them as the two standards setters did not agree on all of their conclusions (See Appendix B, *International vs. US Accounting Standards,* for a summary of the remaining differences).

### Organization of This Chapter and Its Appendix

In general, FAS 141(R) and FAS 160 prohibit the retrospective remeasurement of business combinations that occurred prior to their effective date. Furthermore, special transition provisions, to apply to mutual entities and guidance applicable to mergers and acquisitions by not-for profit organizations, are not expected to be issued until at least the fourth quarter of 2008. Consequently, guidance included in many of the pronouncements that were nullified or amended by the new standards will continue to apply to those business combinations predating the new standards or to not-for-profit organizations that are awaiting a final determination by FASB as to how, if at all, the changes in FAS 141(R) and FAS 160 might be applied to their combination transactions.

To aid the reader/researcher in navigating this maze, we have divided this chapter into two discrete sections. The main portion of the chapter is devoted to the interpretation and application of FAS 141(R) and 160, and assumes that the nullifications and amendments of predecessor standards that they prescribe have occurred.

To augment the main portion of the chapter to provide the currently applicable guidance to those who still are required to follow it, we have placed guidance regarding the former standards in Appendix A. We recognize this may, to some extent be duplicative, but we believe that this method of organizing the material will result in the most effective and complete research relative to a given aspect of the standards.

### Effective Date and Transition Provisions

FAS 141(R) and FAS 160 are to be applied prospectively to business combinations with acquisition dates on or after the beginning of the first annual reporting period beginning after December 15, 2008. Early application is not permitted. Thus, reporting entities with fiscal years ending December 31, 2009, and thereafter are required to apply the new pronouncements to business combinations made at any time during those fiscal years. Further, reporting entities are not permitted to retrospectively adjust the carrying amounts of assets and liabilities from previously recognized business combinations for the effects of the new pronouncements. Special transition provisions apply to mutual entities and with respect to amendments made to FIN 48 and FAS 109 governing the accounting for current and deferred income taxes, respectively. These are discussed later in this chapter and in Chapter 17, *Income Taxes*.

### Objectives

FAS 141(R) and FAS 160 follow a revised drafting convention, intended to be more principles-based than rules-based in tone. Thus, each major section of these pronouncements is preceded by a prominent statement of the main principles embodied by that section, presented in a bold-faced font for emphasis. It is pointed out, however, that all paragraphs and the appendices containing implementation guidance are of equal authority.

The overriding objective of the new standards is to improve the relevance, representational faithfulness, transparency, and comparability of information provided in financial statements about business combinations and their effects on the reporting entity by establishing principles and requirements with respect to how an acquirer, in its consolidated financial statements

1.  Recognizes and measures identifiable assets acquired, liabilities assumed, and the noncontrolling interest in the acquiree, if any,
2.  Recognizes and measures acquired goodwill or a gain from a bargain purchase,
3.  Determines the nature and extent of disclosures sufficient to enable the reader to evaluate the nature of the business combination and its financial effects on the consolidated reporting entity,
4.  Accounts for and reports noncontrolling interests in subsidiaries, and
5.  Deconsolidates a subsidiary when it ceases to hold a controlling interest in it.

## Scope

Transactions or other events that meet the definition of a business combination are subject to FAS 141(R) and FAS 160. Excluded from the scope of these standards, however, are

1.  Formation of a joint venture
2.  Acquisition of an asset or group of assets that does not represent a business, as that term is newly defined
3.  Combinations between entities or businesses under common control
4.  Combinations between not-for-profit organizations or the acquisition of a for-profit business by a not-for-profit organization, the accounting for which was still being deliberated by FASB when this publication went to press

## Transactions and Events Accounted for as Business Combinations

A business combination results from the occurrence of a transaction or other event that results in an acquirer obtaining control of one or more businesses. This can occur in many different ways that include the following examples individually or in some cases, in combination:

1.  Transfer of cash, cash equivalents, or other assets, including the transfer of assets of another business of the acquirer
2.  Incurring liabilities
3.  Issuance of equity instruments
4.  Obtaining variable interests in an acquiree variable interest entity (VIE) that is a business, resulting in the acquirer becoming the VIE's primary beneficiary/parent, under the provisions of FIN 46(R), *Consolidation of Variable Interest Entities*
5.  By contract alone without the transfer of consideration, such as when

    a.  An acquiree business repurchases enough of its own shares to cause one of its existing investors (the acquirer) to obtain control over it
    b.  There is a lapse of minority veto rights that had previously prevented the acquirer from controlling an acquiree in which it held a majority voting interest
    c.  An acquirer and acquiree contractually agree to combine their businesses without a transfer of consideration between them

## Qualifying as a Business

FASB 141(R) substantively revises the previous definition of a business that was set forth in EITF 98-3, *Determining Whether a Nonmonetary Transaction Involves Receipt of Productive Assets or of a Business*. Further, it amends FIN 46(R), *Consolidation of Variable Interest Entities*, to clarify that the initial consolidation of a VIE that is a business is considered to be a business combination. This effectively provides parity between the accounting for business combinations and any related noncontrolling interests involving voting interest entities and those involving variable interest entities.

In order to be considered a business, an integrated group of activities and assets must be *capable* of being conducted and managed to provide a return directly to investors, *owners, members, or participants*. The return can be in the form of dividends, reduced costs, or other economic benefits. The word *capable* was added to emphasize the fact that the definition does not preclude a development stage enterprise (as defined in FAS 7) from qualifying as a business. *Other owners, members, or participants* were included to emphasize the applicability of FAS 141(R) to mutual entities that previously used the pooling-of-interests method of accounting for business combinations and to noncorporate entities. In addition, the EITF 98-3 requirement that the group of activities and assets be *self-sustaining* was omitted from the new definition.

The definition and related guidance elaborate further that a business consists of inputs and processes applied to those inputs that have the ability to create outputs. Clarification is provided that, while outputs are usually present in a business, they are not required to qualify as a business as long as there is the *ability* to create them.

An input is an economic resource that creates or has the ability to create outputs when one or more processes are applied to it. Examples of inputs include fixed assets, intangible rights to use fixed assets, intellectual property or other intangible assets, and access to markets in which to hire employees or purchase materials.

A process is a system, protocol, convention, or rule with the ability to create outputs when applied to one or more inputs. Processes are usually documented; however, an organized workforce with the requisite skills and experience may apply processes necessary to create outputs by following established rules and conventions. In evaluating whether an activity is a process, FAS 141(R) indicates that functions such as accounting, billing, payroll, and other administrative systems do not meet the definition. Thus, processes are the types of activities that an entity engages in to produce the products and/or services that it provides to the marketplace rather than the internal activities it follows in operating its business.

An output is simply the by-product resulting from applying processes to inputs. An output provides, or has the ability to provide, the desired return to the investors, members, participants, or other owners.

In analyzing a transaction or event to determine whether it is a business combination, it is not necessary that the acquirer retain, postcombination, all of the inputs or processes used by the seller in operating the business. Using the "market participant" approach to analyzing the facts, as defined in FAS 157, *Fair Value Measurements*, if market participants could, for example, acquire the business in an arm's-length transaction and continue to produce outputs by integrating the business with their own inputs and processes, then that subset of remaining inputs and processes still meets the definition of a business from the standpoint of the acquirer.

The guidance in FAS 141(R) provides additional flexibility by providing that it is not necessary that a business have liabilities, although that situation is expected to be rare.

As discussed previously, development stage enterprises are not precluded from meeting the criteria to be a business. This is true even if they do not yet produce outputs. If there are no outputs being produced, the acquirer is to determine whether the enterprise constitutes a business by considering whether it

1. Has started its planned principal activities,
2. Has hired employees,
3. Has obtained intellectual property,
4. Has obtained other inputs,
5. Has implemented processes that could be applied to its inputs,
6. Is pursuing a plan to produce outputs,
7. Will have the ability to obtain access to customers that will purchase the outputs.

It is important to note, however, that it is not required that all of these factors be present for a given set of development stage activities and assets to qualify as a business. Again, the relevant question to ask is whether a market participant would be capable of conducting or managing the set of activities and assets as a business irrespective of whether the seller did so or the acquirer intends to do so.

Finally, FAS 141(R) provided what it acknowledged was circular logic in asserting that, absent evidence to the contrary, if goodwill is included in a set of assets and activities, it can be presumed to be a business. The circularity arises from the fact that, in order to apply GAAP to determine whether to initially recognize goodwill, the accountant would be required to first determine whether there had, in fact, been an acquisition of a business. Otherwise, it would not be permitted to recognize goodwill. It is not necessary, however, that goodwill be present in order to consider a set of assets and activities to be a business.

### Techniques for Structuring Business Combinations

A business combination can be structured in a number of different ways that satisfy the acquirer's strategic, operational, legal, tax, and risk management objectives. Some of the more frequently used structures are

1. One or more businesses become subsidiaries of the acquirer. As subsidiaries, they continue to operate as legal entities.
2. The net assets of one or more businesses are legally merged into the acquirer. In this case, the acquiree entity ceases to exist (in legal vernacular, this is referred to as a statutory merger and normally the transaction is subject to approval by a majority of the outstanding voting shares of the acquiree).
3. The owners of the acquiree transfer their equity interests to the acquirer entity or to the owners of the acquirer entity in exchange for equity interests in the acquirer.
4. All of the combining entities transfer their net assets (or their owners transfer their equity interests into a new entity formed for the purpose of the transaction). This is sometimes referred to as a roll-up or put-together transaction.
5. A former owner or group of former owners of one of the combining entities obtains control of the combined entities collectively.
6. An acquirer might hold a noncontrolling equity interest in an entity and subsequently purchase additional equity interests sufficient to give it control over the investee. These transactions are referred to as step acquisitions or business combinations achieved in stages.
7. A business owner organizes a partnership, S corporation, or LLC to hold real estate. The real estate is the principal location of the commonly owned business and that business entity leases the real estate from the separate entity.

### Accounting for Business Combinations under the Acquisition Method

The acquirer is to account for a business combination using the acquisition method. This term, new to US GAAP, represents an expansion of the now-outdated term, "purchase method." The change in terminology was made in order to emphasize that a business combination can occur even when a purchase transaction is not involved.

The following steps are required to apply the acquisition method:

1. Identify the acquirer.
2. Determine the acquisition date.
3. Identify the assets and liabilities, if any, requiring separate accounting because they result from transactions that are not part of the business combination, and account for them in accordance with their nature and the applicable GAAP.
4. Identify assets and liabilities that require acquisition date classification or designation decisions to facilitate application of GAAP in postcombination financial statements and make those classifications or designations based on (a) contractual terms, (b) economic conditions, (c) acquirer operating or accounting policies, and (d) other pertinent conditions existing at the acquisition date.
5. Recognize and measure the identifiable tangible and intangible assets acquired and liabilities assumed.
6. Recognize and measure any noncontrolling interest in the acquiree.
7. Measure the consideration transferred.
8. Recognize and measure goodwill or, if the business combination results in a bargain purchase, recognize a gain.

**Step 1—Identify the acquirer.** FAS 141(R), as did the predecessor standard, strongly emphasizes the concept that every business combination has an acquirer. In the "basis for conclusions" that accompanies FAS 141(R), FASB asserted that

> ..."true mergers" or "mergers of equals" in which none of the combining entities obtain control of the others are so rare as to be virtually nonexistent...[1]

The determination of the acquirer is based on application of the provisions of ARB 51 (as amended by FAS 160 and interpreted by FIN 46[R]) regarding the party that possesses a controlling financial interest in another entity. While ARB 51 provides, that in general, direct or indirect ownership of a majority of the outstanding voting interests in another entity "...is a condition pointing toward consolidation," this is not an absolute rule to be applied in all cases. In fact, ARB 51 explicitly provides that majority owned entities are not to be consolidated if the majority owner does not hold a controlling financial interest in the entity. Exceptions to the general majority ownership rule include, but are not limited to the following situations:

1. An entity that is in legal reorganization or bankruptcy
2. An entity subject to uncertainties due to government-imposed restrictions, such as foreign exchange restrictions or controls, whose severity casts doubt on the majority interest owner's ability to control the entity
3. If the acquiree is a variable interest entity (VIE), the primary beneficiary of the VIE is always considered to be the acquirer. Accounting for VIEs is discussed later in this chapter.

---

[1] *FAS 141(R), paragraph B35.*

If applying the guidance in ARB 51 does not clearly indicate the party that is the acquirer, FAS 141(R) provides factors to consider in making that determination under different facts and circumstances:

1. *Relative size*—Generally, the acquirer is the entity whose relative size is significantly larger than that of the other entity or entities. Size can be compared by using measures such as assets, revenues, or net income.

2. *Initiator of the transaction*—When more than two entities are involved, another factor to consider (besides relative size) is which of the entities initiated the transaction.

3. *Roll-ups or put-together transactions*—When a new entity is formed to issue equity interests to effect a business combination, one of the preexisting entities is to be identified as the acquirer. If, instead, a newly formed entity transfers cash or other assets, or incurs liabilities as consideration to effect a business combination, that new entity may be considered to be the acquirer.

4. *Nonequity consideration*—In business combinations accomplished primarily by the transfer of cash or other assets, or by incurring liabilities, the entity that transfers the cash or other assets, or incurs the liabilities is usually the acquirer.

5. *Exchange of equity interests*—In business combinations accomplished primarily by the exchange of equity interests, the entity that issues its equity interests is generally considered to be the acquirer. One notable exception that occurs frequently in practice is sometimes referred to as a reverse acquisition, discussed in detail later in this chapter. In a reverse acquisition, the entity issuing equity interests is legally the acquirer, but for accounting purposes is considered the acquiree. There are, however, other factors that should be considered in identifying the acquirer when equity interests are exchanged. These include

    a. *Relative voting rights in the combined entity after the business combination*—Generally, the acquirer is the entity whose owners, as a group, retain or obtain the largest portion of the voting rights in the consolidated entity. This determination must take into consideration the existence of any unusual or special voting arrangements as well as any options, warrants, or convertible securities.

    b. *The existence of a large minority voting interest in the combined entity in the event no other owner or organized group of owners possesses a significant voting interest*—Generally, the acquirer is the entity whose owner or organized group of owners holds the largest minority voting interest in the combined entity.

    c. *The composition of the governing body of the combined entity*—Generally, the acquirer is the entity whose owners have the ability to elect, appoint, or remove a majority of members of the governing body of the combined entity.

    d. *The composition of the senior management of the combined entity*—Generally the acquirer is the entity whose former management dominates the management of the combined entity.

    e. *Terms of the equity exchange*—Generally, the acquirer is the entity that pays a premium over the precombination fair value of the equity interests of the other entity or entities.

**Step 2—Determine the acquisition date.** By definition, the acquisition date is that on which the acquirer obtains control of the acquiree. As discussed previously, this concept of control (or, more precisely, controlling financial interest) is not always evidenced by voting ownership. Thus, control can be obtained contractually by an acquirer absent that party holding any voting ownership interests.

The general rule is that the acquisition date is the date on which the acquirer legally transfers consideration, acquires the assets, and assumes the liabilities of the acquiree. This date, in a relatively straightforward transaction, is referred to as the closing date. Not all transactions are that straightforward, however. All pertinent facts and circumstances are to be considered in determining the acquisition date. The parties to a business combination might, for example, execute a contract that entitles the acquirer to the rights and obligates the acquirer with respect to the obligations of the acquiree prior to the actual date of the closing. Thus, in evaluating economic substance over legal form, the acquirer will have contractually acquired the target on the date it executed the contract.

### Example of acquisition date preceding closing date

In 2005, Fortune Brands, Inc. (FB), a US-based holding company (NYSE Symbol: FO) purchased more than 25 spirit and wine brands and specified distribution assets from a French company. In its annual report, FB disclosed that the acquired assets were transferred to a subsidiary of the seller, in which FB received, in connection with the transaction, economic rights (these were structured as "tracker shares" in the holding subsidiary of the seller) with respect to the acquired assets prior to their actual legal transfer to the company. In addition, FB obtained the contractual right to manage the acquired assets prior to their legal transfer to FB. Among the reasons FB cited for entering into these arrangements was their commercial desire to obtain the economic benefits associated with owning and operating the acquired assets as soon as possible after funding the purchase price for them.

Until the assets were legally transferred to FB, the transaction was accounted for under FIN 46(R), *Consolidation of Variable Interest Entities*, and consequently, FB's interests in the tracker shares of the seller's subsidiary were consolidated since FB was considered the primary beneficiary of that subsidiary. The seller's residual interest in the holding subsidiary was reported in the consolidated financial statements of FB as a noncontrolling interest.[2]

**Step 3—Identify assets and liabilities requiring separate accounting.** FASB 141(R) provides a basic recognition principle that, as of the acquisition date, the acquirer is to recognize, separately from goodwill, the identifiable assets acquired (whether tangible or intangible), the liabilities assumed, and, if applicable, any noncontrolling interest (previously referred to as "minority interest") in the acquiree.

In applying the recognition principle to a business combination, the acquirer may recognize assets and liabilities that had not been recognized by the acquiree in its precombination financial statements. Under FAS 141(R), GAAP continues to permit recognition of acquired intangibles (e.g., patents, customer lists) that would not be granted recognition if they were internally developed.

The pronouncement elaborates on the basic principle by providing that recognition is subject to the following conditions:

1. At the acquisition date, the identifiable assets acquired and liabilities assumed must meet the definitions of assets and liabilities as set forth in CON 6, *Elements of Financial Statements*.[3]

---

[2] *Fortune Brands, Inc. Form 10-K for the fiscal year ended December 31, 2006. US Securities and Exchange Commission Web site. Filing date March 1, 2007.*
*http://www.sec.gov/Archives/edgar/data/789073/000104746907001501/a2176419z10-k.htm/*

[3] *Assets are defined as "probable future economic benefits obtained or controlled by a particular entity as a result of past transactions or events" (CON 6, par. 25). Liabilities are defined as "probable future sacrifices of economic benefits arising from present obligations of a particular entity to transfer assets or provide services to other entities in the future as a result of past transactions or events" (CON 6, par. 35).*

2.  The assets and liabilities recognized must be part of the exchange transaction between the acquirer and the acquiree (or the acquiree's former owners) and not part of a separate transaction or transactions.

***Restructuring or exit activities.*** Frequently, in a business combination, the acquirer's plans include the future exit of one or more of the activities of the acquiree or the termination or relocation of employees of the acquiree. Since these exit activities are discretionary on the part of the acquirer and the acquirer is not obligated to incur the associated costs, the costs do not meet the definition of a liability and are not recognized at the acquisition date. Rather, the costs will be recognized in postcombination financial statements in accordance with FAS 146, *Accounting for Costs Associated with Exit or Disposal Activities*, as amended by FAS 141(R), and discussed in detail in Chapter 3.

***Boundaries of the exchange transaction.*** Preexisting relationships and arrangements often exist between the acquirer and acquiree prior to beginning negotiations to enter into a business combination. Furthermore, while conducting the negotiations, the parties may enter into separate business arrangements. In either case, the acquirer is responsible for identifying amounts that are not part of the exchange for the acquiree. Recognition under the acquisition method is only given to the consideration transferred for the acquiree and the assets acquired and liabilities assumed in exchange for that consideration. Other transactions outside the scope of the business combination are to be recognized by applying other relevant GAAP.

The acquirer is to analyze the business combination transaction and other transactions with the acquiree and its former owners to identify the components that comprise the transaction in which the acquirer obtained control over the acquiree. This distinction is important to ensure that each component is accounted for according to its economic substance irrespective of its legal form.

The imposition of this condition was based on an observation that, upon becoming involved in negotiations for a business combination, the parties may exhibit characteristics of related parties. In so doing, they may be willing to execute agreements designed *primarily* for the benefit of the acquirer of the combined entity that might be designed to achieve a desired financial reporting outcome after the business combination has been consummated. Thus, the imposition of this condition is expected to curb such abuses.

In analyzing a transaction to determine inclusion or exclusion from a business combination, consideration should be given to which of the parties will reap its benefits. If a precombination transaction is entered into by the acquirer, or on behalf of the acquirer, or *primarily* to benefit the acquirer (or to benefit the to-be-combined entity as a whole) rather than for the benefit of the acquiree or its former owners, the transaction most likely would be considered to be a "separate transaction" outside the boundaries of the business combination and for which the acquisition method would not apply.

The acquirer is to consider the following factors, which FASB indicates "are neither mutually exclusive nor individually conclusive," in determining whether a transaction is a part of the exchange transaction or recognized separately:

1.  *Purpose of the transaction*—Typically, there are many parties involved in the management, ownership, operation, and financing of the various entities involved in a business combination transaction. Of course, there are the acquirer and acquiree entities, but there are also owners, directors, management, and various parties acting as agents representing their respective interests. Understanding the motivations of the parties in entering into a particular transaction potentially provides insight into whether or not the transaction is a part of the business combination or a separate transaction.

2. *Initiator of the transaction*—Identifying the party that initiated the transaction may provide insight into whether or not it should be recognized separately from the business combination. FASB believes that if the transaction was initiated by the acquirer, it would be less likely to be part of the business combination and, conversely, if it were initiated by the acquiree or its former owners, it would be more likely to be part of the business combination.

3. *Timing of the transaction*—Examining the timing of the transaction may provide insight into whether, for example, the transaction was executed in contemplation of the future business combination in order to provide benefits to the acquirer or the postcombination entity. FASB believes that transactions that take place during the negotiation of the terms of a business combination may be entered into in contemplation of the eventual combination for the purpose of providing future economic benefits *primarily* to the acquirer of the to-be-combined entity and, therefore, should be accounted for separately.

FAS 141(R) provides the following presumption after analyzing the economic benefits of a precombination transaction:

| *Primarily for the benefit of* | *Transaction likely to be* |
|---|---|
| Acquirer or combined entity | Separate transaction |
| Acquiree or its former owners | Part of the business combination |

FAS 141(R) provides three examples of separate transactions that *are not* to be included in applying the acquisition method, each of which will be discussed in further detail:

1. Reimbursement to the acquiree or its former owners for paying the acquirer's acquisition-related costs,
2. A settlement of a preexisting relationship between acquirer and acquiree, and
3. Compensation to employees or former owners of the acquiree for future services

*Acquisition-related costs.* In a departure from the previous US GAAP for business combinations, acquisition-related costs, under FAS 141(R), are to be charged to expense of the period in which the costs are incurred and the related services received. Examples of these costs include

| | |
|---|---|
| Accounting fees | Internal acquisitions department |
| Advisory fees | Legal fees |
| Consulting fees | Other professional fees |
| Finder's fees | Valuation fees |

FAS 141(R) makes an exception to the general rule with respect to costs to register and issue equity or debt securities. These costs are to be recognized in accordance with other applicable GAAP. Stock issuance costs are normally charged against the gross proceeds of the issuance (See Chapter 19). Debt issuance costs are, under CON 6, to be either treated as a reduction of the amount borrowed or treated as an expense of the period in which they are incurred; however, some reporting entities have treated these costs as deferred charges and amortized them to income during the term of the debt. (See Chapter 15)

*Settlements of preexisting relationships between acquirer and acquiree.* Prior to pursuing a business combination, business may have been transacted between the parties. The nature of the transactions may have been contractual, such as the purchase of goods and/or services, or the licensing of intellectual property. Alternatively, the parties may have had an adversarial relationship whereby they were plaintiff and defendant in pending litigation. If a business combination in effect settles such a preexisting relationship, the acquirer is to recognize a gain or loss measured in the following manner:

1. If the relationship is noncontractual (e.g., litigation), measure at fair value
2. If the relationship is contractual, measure at the lesser of

    a. The amount by which, from the acquirer's perspective, the contract is favorable or unfavorable, or
    b. The amount of any settlement provisions stated in the contract that are available to the counterparty for which the contract is unfavorable.

If 2.b. is less than 2.a., the difference is to be included as part of the accounting for the business combination.

In determining whether a contract is favorable or unfavorable to a party, the terms of the contract are compared to current market terms. It is important to note that a contract can be unfavorable to the acquirer and yet not result in a loss.

The amount of the gain or loss measured as a result of settling a preexisting relationship will, of course, depend on whether the acquirer had previously recognized related assets or liabilities with respect to that relationship.

### Example of settlement of preexisting contractual supplier relationship; contract unfavorable to acquirer

Meyer Corporation (MC) and Henning, Inc. (HI) are parties to a 3-year supply contract that contains the following provisions:

1. MC is required to annually purchase 3,000 flat-panel displays from HI at a fixed price of $400 per unit for an aggregate purchase price of $1,200,000 for each of the three years.
2. MC is required to pay HI the annual $1,200,000 irrespective of whether it takes delivery of all 3,000 units and the required payment is nonrefundable.
3. The contract contains a penalty provision that would permit MC to cancel it at the end of the second year for a lump sum payment of $500,000.
4. In each of the first two years of the contract, MC took delivery of the full 3,000 units.

At December 31, 2008, the supply contract was unfavorable to MC because MC would be able to purchase flat-panel displays with similar specifications and of similar quality from another supplier for $350 per unit. Therefore, in accordance with ARB 43, MC accrued a loss of $150,000 (3,000 units remaining under the firm purchase commitment × $50 loss per unit).

On January 1, 2009, MC acquires HI for $30 million, which reflects the fair value of HI based on what other marketplace participants would be willing to pay. On the acquisition date, the $30 million fair value of HI includes $750,000 related to the contract with MC that consists of

| Identifiable intangibles[4] | $600,000 | Representing the remaining year of the contract, at prevailing market prices |
| Favorable pricing | 150,000 | Representing the portion of the contract price that is favorable to HI and unfavorable to MC |
| | $750,000 | |

HI has no other identifiable assets or liabilities related to the supply contract with MC. MC would compute its gain or loss on settlement of this preexisting relationship as follows:

1. Amount of unfavorability to acquirer (MC) at acquisition date   $150,000
2. Lump-sum settlement amount available to MC   500,000
3. Lesser of 1. or 2.   150,000
4. Amount by which 1. exceeds 2.   N/A

---

[4] *In computing the valuation of HI, these amounts would represent such identifiable customer-related intangible assets as customer contract, related customer relationship, production backlog, etc.*

Since MC had already recognized an unrealized loss on the firm purchase commitment as of December 31, 2008, upon its acquisition of HI, its loss of $150,000 from recognizing the lesser of 1. and 2. above would be offset by the elimination of the liability for the unrealized loss on the firm purchase commitment in the same amount of $150,000. Thus, under these circumstances, MC would have neither a gain nor a loss on the settlement of its preexisting relationship with HI. The entries to record these events are not considered part of the business combination accounting. It is important to note that, from the perspective of MC, when it applies the acquisition method to record the business combination, it will characterize the $600,000 "at-market" component of the contract as part of goodwill and not as identifiable intangibles. This is the case because of the obvious fallacy of MC recognizing customer-relationship intangible assets that represent a relationship with itself.

### Example of settlement of preexisting contractual supplier relationship; contract favorable to acquirer

Using the same facts as the MC/HI example above, assume that, instead of the contract being unfavorable to the acquirer MC, it was unfavorable to HI in the amount of $150,000 and that there was a cancellation provision in the contract that would permit HI to pay a penalty after year two of $100,000 to cancel the remainder of the contract.

On the acquisition date, the $30 million fair value of HI, under this scenario would include $450,000 related to the contract with MC that consists of

| | | |
|---|---|---|
| Identifiable intangibles | $600,000 | Representing the remaining year of the contract, at prevailing market prices |
| Unfavorable pricing | (150,000) | Representing the portion of the contract price that is unfavorable to HI and favorable to MC |
| | $450,000 | |

Under these changed assumptions, MC would not have incurred or recorded an unrealized loss on the firm purchase commitment with HI since the contract terms were favorable to MC. The determination of MC's gain or loss would be as follows:

| | | |
|---|---|---|
| 1. | Amount of favorability to acquirer (MC) at acquisition date | $150,000 |
| 2. | Lump-sum settlement amount available to HI | 100,000 |
| 3. | Lesser of 1. or 2. | 100,000 |
| 4. | Amount by which 1. exceeds 2. | 50,000 |

Under this scenario, unless HI believed that the market would change in the near term, it would be economically advantageous, absent a business combination, for HI to settle the remaining contract at the acquisition date by paying the $100,000 penalty because HI would be able to sell the remaining 3,000 units covered by the contract for an aggregate price of $150,000 more than it was committed to sell those units to MC.

At the acquisition date, MC would record a gain of $100,000 to settle its preexisting relationship with HI. The entry to record the gain is not considered part of the business combination accounting.

In addition, however, since 2. is less than 1., the $50,000 difference is included in the accounting for the business combination, since economically, postcombination, the combined entity will not benefit from that portion of the acquisition date favorability of the contract.

As was the case in the first example, the portion of the purchase price allocated to the contract in the business combination accounting would be accounted for as goodwill for the same reason.

*Contingent payments to employees or former owners of the acquiree.* The acquirer is to assess whether arrangements to make contingent payments to employees or selling owners of the acquiree represent contingent consideration that is part of the business combination transaction or represent separate transactions to be excluded from the application of the acquisition method to the business combination. In general, the acquirer is to consider the reasons why the terms of the acquisition include the payment provision, the party that initiated the arrangement, and when (at what stage of the negotiations) the arrangement was entered into by the parties. When those considerations do not provide clarity regarding whether the transaction is separate from the business combination, the acquirer considers the following indicators:

1. *Postcombination employment*—Consideration is to be given to the terms under which the selling owners will be providing services as key employees of the combined entity. The terms may be evidenced by a formal employment contract, by provisions included in the acquisition documents, or by other documents. If the arrangement provides that the contingent payments are automatically forfeited upon termination of employment, the consideration is to be characterized as compensation for postcombination services. If, instead, the contingent payments are not affected by termination of employment, this would be an indicator that the contingent payments represent additional consideration that is part of the business combination transaction and not compensation for services.

2. *Duration of postcombination employment*—If the employee is contractually bound to remain employed for a period that equals or exceeds the period during which the contingent payments are due, this may be an indicator that the contingent payments represent compensation for services.

3. *Amount of compensation*—If the amount of the employee's compensation that is not contingent is considered to be reasonable in relation to other key employees of the combined entity, this may indicate that the contingent amounts represent additional consideration and not compensation for services.

4. *Differential between amounts paid to employees and selling owners who do not become employees of the combined entity*—If, on a per-share basis, the contingent payments due to former owners of the acquiree that did not become employees are lower than the contingent payments due to the former owners that did become employees of the combined entity, this may indicate that the incremental amounts paid to the employees are compensation.

5. *Extent of ownership*—The relative ownership percentages (e.g., number of shares, units, percentage of membership interest) owned by the selling owners who remain employees of the combined entity serve as an indicator of how to characterize the substance of the contingent consideration. If, for example, the former owners of substantially all of the ownership interests in the acquiree are continuing to serve as key employees of the combined entity, this may be an indicator that the contingent payment arrangement is substantively a profit-sharing vehicle designed with the intent of providing compensation for services to be performed postcombination. Conversely, if the former owners that remained employed by the combined entity collectively owned only a nominal ownership interest in the acquiree and all of the former owners received the same amount of contingent basis on a per-share basis, this may be an indicator that the contingent payments represent additional consideration. In considering the applicability of this indicator, care must be exercised to closely examine the effects, if any, of transactions, ownership interests, and employment relationships, precombination and postcombination, with respect to parties related to the selling owners of the acquiree.

6. *Relationship of contingent arrangements to the valuation approach used*—The payment terms negotiated in many business combinations provide that the amount of the acquisition date transfer of consideration from acquirer to acquiree (or the acquiree's former owners) is computed near the lower end of a range of valuation estimates the acquirer used in valuing the acquiree. Furthermore, the formula for de-

termining future contingent payments is derived from or related to that valuation approach. When this is the case, it may be an indicator that the contingent payments represent additional consideration. Conversely, if the formula for determining future contingent payments more closely resembles prior profit-sharing arrangements, this may be an indicator that the substance of the contingent payment arrangement is to provide compensation for services.

7. *Formula prescribed for determining contingent consideration*—Analyzing the formula to be used to determine the contingent consideration may provide insight into the substance of the arrangement. Contingent payments that are determined on the basis of a multiple of earnings may be indicative of being, in substance, contingent consideration that is part of the business combination transaction. Alternatively, contingent consideration that is determined as a prespecified percentage of earnings would be more suggestive of a routine profit-sharing arrangement for the purposes of providing additional compensation to employees for postcombination services rendered.

8. *Other considerations*—Given the complexity of a business combination transaction and the sheer number and girth of the legal documents necessary to affect it, the financial statement preparer is charged with the daunting, but unavoidable task of performing a comprehensive review of the terms of all of the associated agreements. These can take the form of noncompete agreements, consulting agreements, leases, guarantees, indemnifications, and, of course, the formal agreement to combine the businesses. Particular attention should be paid to the applicable income tax treatment afforded to the contingent payments. The income tax treatment of these payments may be an indicator that tax avoidance was a primary motivator in characterizing them in the manner that they are structured. An acquirer might, for example, simultaneous to a business combination, execute a property lease with one of the key owners of the acquiree. If the lease payments were below market, some or all of the contingent payments to that key owner/lessor under the provisions of the other legal agreements might, in substance, be making up the shortfall in the lease and thus, should be recharacterized as lease payments and accounted for separately from the business combination in the combined entity's postcombination financial statements. If this were not the case, and the lease payments were reflective of the market, this would be an indicator pointing to a greater likelihood that the contingent payment arrangements actually did represent contingent consideration associated with the business combination transaction.

**Step 4—Classify or designate identifiable assets acquired and liabilities assumed.** In order to facilitate the combined entity's future application of GAAP in its postcombination financial statements, management is required to make decisions on the acquisition date relative to the classification or designation of certain items. These decisions are to be based on the contractual terms, economic and other conditions, and the acquirer's operating and accounting policies as they exist *on the acquisition date*. Examples include, but are not limited to, the following:

1. Classification of investments in certain debt and equity securities as trading, available for sale, or held to maturity under FAS 115, *Accounting for Certain Investments in Debt and Equity Securities*
2. Designation of a derivative instrument as a hedging instrument under the provisions of FAS 133, *Accounting for Derivative Instruments and Hedging Activities*
3. Assessment of whether an embedded derivative is to be separated from the host contract under FAS 133

In applying Step 4, specific exceptions are provided for lease contracts and insurance contracts. Generally, these contracts are to be classified by reference to the contractual terms and other factors that were applicable *at their inception* rather than at the acquisition date. If, however, the contracts were modified subsequent to their inception and those modifications would change their classification at that date, then the accounting for the contracts will be determined by the modification date facts and circumstances. Under these circumstances, the modification date could be the same as the acquisition date.

**Step 5—Recognize and measure the identifiable tangible and intangible assets acquired and liabilities assumed.** In general, the acquirer measures the identifiable tangible and intangible assets acquired, liabilities assumed, and, if applicable, noncontrolling interest at fair value on the acquisition date. The following guidance is to be followed in applying the recognition and measurement principles (subject to certain specified exceptions).

*Operating leases.* Irrespective of whether the acquiree is the lessee or lessor, the acquirer is to evaluate, as of the acquisition date, each of the acquiree's operating leases to determine whether its terms are favorable or unfavorable compared to the market terms of leases of identical or similar items. If the lease terms are favorable, the acquirer is to recognize an intangible asset; if the lease terms are unfavorable, the acquirer is to recognize a liability.

Even when the lease is considered to be at market terms, there nevertheless may be an identifiable intangible associated with it. This would be the case if market participants would be willing to pay to obtain it (i.e., to obtain the rights and privileges associated with it). Examples of this situation are leases for favorably positioned airport gates, and prime retail space in an economically favorable location. If, from the perspective of marketplace participants, acquiring the lease would entitle them to future economic benefits that qualify as identifiable intangible assets (discussed later in this chapter), the acquirer would recognize, separately from goodwill, the associated identifiable intangible asset.

*Operating lease assets owned by an acquiree/lessor.* The fair value of assets owned by the acquiree that are subject to operating leases with the acquiree being the lessor are to be measured separately from the underlying lease to which they are subject.

*Assets with uncertain cash flows.* Since fair value measurements take into account the effects of uncertainty regarding the amounts and timing of future cash flows, the acquirer is not to recognize a separate valuation allowance for assets subject to such uncertainties.

*Assets the acquirer plans to idle or to use in a manner that is not their highest and best use.* The measurement of the identifiable assets acquired at fair value is to be made in accordance with the requirements of FAS 157, which is discussed in detail in Chapter 6. One of those requirements is that the measurement is to assume the highest and best use of the asset by market participants. In applying this requirement to assets that are acquired in a business combination, this assumption is to be used even if it differs from the manner in which the acquiree was using the assets or the manner in which the acquirer intends to use the assets. Thus, even if the acquirer intends, for competitive or other business reasons to idle an acquired asset or use it in a manner that is not its highest and best use, the acquirer is still required to initially measure the fair value of that asset using the assumption of its highest and best use and to continue to use that assumption for the purposes of subsequently testing the asset for impairment.

*Identifiable intangibles to be recognized separately from goodwill.* Intangible assets acquired in a business combination are to be  recognized separately from goodwill if they meet either of two criteria to be considered *identifiable*. These criteria are

1. *Separability criterion*—The intangible asset is capable of being separated or divided from the entity that holds it, and sold, transferred, licensed, rented, or exchanged,

regardless of the acquirer's intent to do so. An intangible asset meets this criterion even if its transfer would not be alone, but instead would be accompanied or bundled with a related contract, other identifiable asset, or a liability.

2. *Legal/contractual criterion*—The intangible asset results from contractual or other legal rights. An intangible asset meets this criterion even if the rights are not transferable or separable from the acquiree or from other rights and obligations of the acquiree.

Appendix A to FAS 141(R) carries forward from the original FAS 141 a lengthy, though not exhaustive, listing of intangible assets that FASB believes have characteristics that meet one of these two criteria (legal/contractual or separability). A logical approach in practice would be for the acquirer to first consider whether the intangibles specifically included on the FASB list are applicable to the particular acquiree and then to consider whether there may be other unlisted intangibles included in the acquisition that meet one or both of the criteria for separate recognition.

FAS 141(R) organizes groups of identifiable intangibles into categories related to or based on

1. Marketing
2. Customers or clients
3. Artistic works
4. Contractual
5. Technological

These categorizations are somewhat arbitrary. Consequently, some of the items listed could fall into more than one of the categories. Examples of identifiable intangibles included in each of the categories are as follows:

*Marketing-related intangible assets.*

1. *Newspaper mastheads.* The unique appearance of the title page of a newspaper or other periodical.
2. *Trademarks, service marks, trade names, collective marks, certification marks.* A trademark represents the right to use a name, word, logo, or symbol that differentiates a product from products of other entities. A service mark is the equivalent of a trademark for a service offering instead of a product. A collective mark is used to identify products or services offered by members affiliated with each other. A certification mark is used to designate a particular attribute of a product or service such as its geographic source (e.g., Columbian coffee or Florida orange juice) or the standards under which it was produced (e.g., ISO 9000 Certified).
3. *Trade dress.* The overall appearance and image (unique color, shape, or package design) of a product.
4. *Internet domain names.* The unique name that identifies an address on the Internet. Domain names must be registered with an Internet registry and are renewable.
5. *Noncompetition agreements.* Rights to assurances that companies or individuals will refrain from conducting similar businesses or selling to specific customers for an agreed-upon period of time.

*Customer-related intangible assets.*

1. *Customer lists.* Names, contact information, order histories, and other information about a company's customers, that a third party, such as a competitor or a telemarketing firm would want to use in its own business.

2. *Customer contracts and related customer relationships.* When a company's relationships with its customers arise primarily through contracts and are of value to buyers who can "step into the shoes" of the sellers and assume their remaining rights and duties under the contracts, and which hold the promise that the customers will place future orders with the entity or relationships between entities and their customers for which

   a. The entities have information about the customers and have regular contacts with the customers, and
   b. The customers have the ability to make direct contact with the entity.

3. *Noncontractual customer relationships.* Customer relationships that arise through means such as regular contacts by sales or service representatives, the value of which are derived from the prospect of the customers placing future orders with the entity.

4. *Order or production backlogs.* Unfilled sales orders for goods and services in amounts that exceed the quantity of finished goods and work-in-process on hand for filling the orders.

*Artistic-related intangible assets.*

1. *Plays, operas, ballets.*
2. *Books, magazines, newspapers, and other literary works.*
3. *Musical works such as compositions, song lyrics, and advertising jingles.*
4. *Photographs, drawings, and clip art.*
5. *Audiovisual material including motion pictures, music videos, television programs.*

*Contract-based intangible assets.*

1. *License, royalty, standstill agreements.* License agreements represent the right, on the part of the licensee, to access or use property that is owned by the licensor for a specified period of time at an agreed-upon price. A royalty agreement entitles its holder to a contractually agreed-upon portion of the income earned from the sale or license of a work covered by patent or copyright. A standstill agreement conveys assurances that a company or individual will refrain from engaging in certain activities for specified periods of time.

2. *Advertising contracts.* A contract with a newspaper, broadcaster, or Internet site to provide specified advertising services to the acquiree.

3. *Lease agreements.* (irrespective of whether the acquiree is the lessee or lessor)

4. *Construction permits.* Rights to build a specified structure at a specified location

5. *Construction contracts.* Rights to become the contractor responsible for completing a construction project and benefit from the profits it produces, subject to the remaining obligations associated with performance (including any past-due payments to suppliers and/or subcontractors).

6. *Construction management, service, or supply contracts.* Rights to manage a construction project for a fee, procure specified services at a specified fee, or purchase specified products at contractually agreed-upon prices.

7. *Broadcast rights.* Legal permission to transmit electronic signals using specified bandwidth in the radio frequency spectrum, granted by the operation of communication laws.

8. *Franchise rights.* Legal rights to engage in a trade-named business, to sell a trade-marked good, or to sell a service-marked service in a particular geographic area.

9. *Operating rights.* Permits to operate in a certain manner, such as those granted to a carrier to transport specified commodities.

10. *Use rights.* Permits to use specified land, property, or air space in a particular manner, such as the right to cut timber, expel emissions, or to land airplanes at specified gates at an airport.

11. *Servicing contracts.* The contractual right to service a loan. Servicing entails activities such as collecting principal and interest payments from the borrower, maintaining escrow accounts, paying taxes and insurance premiums when due, and pursuing collection of delinquent payments.

12. *Employment contract.* The right to succeed the acquiree as the employer under a formal contract to obtain an employee's services in exchange for fulfilling the employer's remaining duties, such as payment of salaries and benefits, as specified by the contract.

*Technology-based intangible assets.*

1. *Patented or copyrighted software.* Computer software source code, program specifications, procedures, and associated documentation that is legally protected by patent or copyright.

2. *Mask works.* Software permanently stored on a read-only memory chip as a series of stencils or integrated circuitry. Mask works may be provided statutory protection in some countries.

3. *Unpatented technology.* Access to knowledge about the proprietary processes and workflows followed by the acquiree to accomplish desired business results.

4. *Databases.* Databases are collections of information generally stored digitally in an organized manner. A database can be protected by copyright (e.g., the database contained on the CD-ROM version of this publication). Many databases, however, represent information accumulated as a natural by-product of a company conducting its normal operating activities. Examples of these databases are plentiful and include title plants, scientific data, and credit histories. Title plants (discussed in detail in Chapter 25) represent historical records with respect to real estate parcels in a specified geographic location.

5. *Trade secrets.* Trade secrets are proprietary, confidential information, such as a formula, process, or recipe.

One commonly cited intangible asset deliberately omitted by the FASB from its list of identifiable intangibles is an "assembled workforce." FASB decided that the replacement cost technique that is often used to measure the fair value of an assembled workforce is not a representationally faithful measure of the fair value of the intellectual capital acquired. It was thus decided that an exception to the recognition criteria would be made, and that the fair value of an acquired assembled workforce would remain part of goodwill.

**Research and development assets.** In a significant break from past practice, FAS 141(R) requires the acquirer to recognize and measure all tangible and intangible assets used in research and development (R&D) activities acquired individually or in a group of assets as part of the business combination. This prescribed treatment is to be followed even if the assets are judged to have no alternative future use. These assets are to be measured at their acquisition-date fair values. Fair value measurements, consistent with FAS 157, are to be made based on the assumptions that would be made by market participants in pricing the asset. Assets that the acquirer does not intend to use or intends to use in a manner that is not their highest and best use are, nevertheless, required to be measured at fair value.

*Intangible R&D assets.* Upon initial recognition, the *intangible* R&D assets are to be classified as indefinite-lived assets until the related R&D efforts are either completed or abandoned. In the reporting periods during which the R&D intangible assets are classified as indefinite-lived, they are not to be amortized. Instead, they are to be tested for impairment in the same manner as other indefinite-lived intangibles. Upon completion or abandonment of the related R&D efforts, management is to determine the remaining useful life of the intangibles and amortize them accordingly. In applying these requirements, assets that are temporarily idled are not to be considered abandoned.

*Tangible R&D assets.* Tangible R&D assets acquired in a business combination are to be accounted for according to their nature (e.g., supplies, inventory, depreciable assets).

**Exceptions to the recognition and/or measurement principles.** FAS 141(R) provides certain exceptions to its general principles for recognizing assets acquired and liabilities assumed at their acquisition date fair values. These can be summarized as follows:

| *Nature of exception* | *Recognition* | *Measurement* |
|---|---|---|
| Assets held for sale | | x |
| Contingent assets and liabilities of the acquiree | x | |
| Indemnification assets | x | x |
| Reacquired rights | | x |
| Employee benefits | x | x |
| Share-based payment awards | | x |
| Income taxes | x | x |

*Assets held for sale.* Assets classified as held for sale individually or as part of a disposal group are to be measured at acquisition date fair value less cost to sell consistent with FAS 144, *Accounting for the Impairment or Disposal of Long-Lived Assets* (discussed in detail in Chapter 11).

In postacquisition periods, long-lived assets classified as held for sale are not to be depreciated *or* amortized. If the assets are part of a disposal group (discussed in detail in Chapter 11), interest and other expenses related to the liabilities included in the disposal group are to continue to be accrued.

In determining fair value less cost to sell, it is important to differentiate costs to sell from expected future losses associated with the operation of the long-lived asset or disposal group to which it belongs.

Costs to sell are defined as the incremental direct costs necessary to transact a sale. To qualify as costs to sell, the costs must result directly from the sale transaction, incurring them needs to be considered essential to the transaction, and the costs would not have been incurred by the entity absent the decision to sell the assets. Examples of costs to sell include brokerage commissions, legal fees, title transfer fees, and closing costs necessary to effect the transfer of legal title. Costs to sell are expressly not permitted to include any future losses that are expected to result from operating the assets (or disposal group) while it is classified as held for sale. If the expected timing of the sale exceeds one year from the balance sheet date, which is permitted in limited situations by paragraph 31 of FAS 144, the costs to sell are to be discounted to their present value.

Should a loss be recognized in subsequent periods due to declines in the fair value less cost to sell, such *losses* are permitted to be restored by future periods gains only to the extent to which the losses have been recognized cumulatively from the date the asset (or disposal group) was classified as held for sale.

During its deliberations on FAS 141(R), FASB's tentative conclusion was that assets held for sale *should* be measured in the same manner as other acquired assets—that is, at their acquisition-date fair value. If the final standard had contained this provision, however, it would have caused a practical dilemma because, technically, on the day after the acquisition date, the new consolidated reporting entity would be required to apply paragraph 34 of FAS 144 and write-down the newly acquired assets to their fair value less cost to sell, resulting in recognizing a loss equal to the selling costs. FASB referred to this as a "Day 2 loss." This anomaly could have been remedied by incorporating an amendment to FAS 144 in FAS 141(R), but FASB believed such an amendment should be made in a separate project in order to provide its constituents an opportunity to submit comments on the proposed change.

The FASB thus deemed this treatment to be a *temporary* exception to the measurement principle under FAS 141(R). As of mid-2008, however, FASB and IASB had each removed from their respective agendas similar projects that would have, in the case of the FASB standards, amended FAS 144 to require assets held for sale to be measured at fair value and presumably remove the temporary exception to the measurement principle currently included in FAS 141(R). Thus, this measurement principle exception will not be resolved in the near future.

*Contingent assets and liabilities of the acquiree.* A contingency is defined in FAS 5 as an existing, unresolved condition, situation, or set of circumstances that will eventually be resolved by the occurrence or nonoccurrence of one or more future events. A potential gain or loss to the reporting entity can result from the contingency's resolution.

*Acquisition-date considerations.* For the purposes of determining recognition of a contingent asset or liability by an acquirer under FAS 141(R), contingencies are classified as either contractual or noncontractual in nature.

Examples of contractual contingencies include

- A lessee's obligation to pay additional rent based on a percentage of its sales that exceed a certain base amount, referred to as percentage rent or contingent rent
- A contingent asset representing the contractual right to receive life insurance proceeds upon the death of the insured
- A loan guarantee representing a contingent commitment to repay a loan if the debtor defaults on its obligation
- A product warranty representing a contingent commitment to repair or replace a defective product

Examples of noncontractual contingencies include

- Environmental remediation obligations
- Favorable or unfavorable outcomes from litigation
- Assessments of back taxes, penalties, and interest by a taxing authority
- Penalties and fines imposed by regulators

FASB's conclusions with respect to recognition of contingent assets and liabilities by an acquirer are best illustrated by reference to the decision diagram on the next page.

**Contingent Assets and Liabilities of the Acquiree**

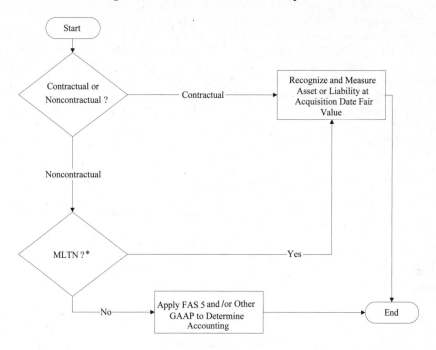

**Definitions from CON 6**

**Asset.** A reporting entity recognizes an asset if both of the following criteria are met at the balance sheet date (CON 6)

1. The reporting entity has obtained or controls future economic benefits that result from transactions or events that occurred in the past.

2. Receipt of those future economic benefits by the reporting entity is probable.

**Liability.** A reporting entity has incurred a liability if both of the following criteria are met at the balance sheet date (CON 6):

1. The reporting entity has a present obligation to sacrifice economic benefits in the future by providing services or transferring assets to others resulting from transactions or events that occurred in the past.

2. The future sacrifice of economic benefits by the reporting entity is probable.

\*MLTN = More Likely Than Not

To make this decision with respect to contingent assets, evaluate whether it is MLTN that the acquirer has obtained or controls future economic benefits as the result of a past transaction or event (criterion 1. from the definition). To make this decision with respect to contingent liabilities, evaluate whether it is MLTN that the acquirer has a present obligation to sacrifice future economic benefits as a result of a past transaction or event (criterion 1. from the definition).

Assets and liabilities arising from contractual contingencies are to be recognized and measured on the acquisition date at their fair value at that date.

If the nature of the contingency is noncontractual, management of the acquirer is required to assess whether

- For a contingent asset, it is more likely than not (MLTN) that the acquirer has obtained, or controls, on the acquisition date, future economic benefits as a result of a past transaction or event, or
- For a contingent liability, it is MLTN that the acquirer has an obligation on the acquisition date to sacrifice future economic benefits as a result of a past transaction or event.

If an asset or liability associated with a noncontractual contingency meets the applicable more-likely-than-not criterion, it is recognized and measured in the same manner as a contractual contingency—that is, it is recognized and measured at its acquisition date fair value.

If a noncontractual contingency does not meet the applicable MLTN criterion, then it is not recognized in the financial statements of the consolidated entity on the acquisition date. Instead, subsequent to the acquisition date, management is to apply other applicable GAAP, including FAS 5, if applicable, in determining how and when to account for the contingency.

The consideration of whether there is a probability of "more likely than not" (i.e., a probability of more than 50%) is to be made in a very specific manner as described above and in the accompanying decision diagram. FASB differentiates the application of MLTN for this purpose from the way in which probability is considered in the definitions of assets and liabilities in CON 6.

| *Financial statement element* | Consideration of probability for the purpose of | |
| --- | --- | --- |
| | *Applying the MLTN recognition criteria in FAS 141(R)* | *Determination of whether an element is an asset or liability in CON 6* |
| *Asset* | Applies to whether, on the acquisition date, the acquirer has obtained or controls future economic benefits as a result of past transactions or events. | Applies to whether the reporting entity will receive economic benefits in the future. |
| *Liability* | Applies to whether, on the acquisition date, the acquirer is obligated to provide services or transfer assets in the future as a result of past transactions or events. | Applies to whether services will be provided or assets transferred by the reporting entity in the future. |

*Post-acquisition considerations.* The subsequent accounting for contingent assets and liabilities of the acquiree that are recognized by the acquirer on the acquisition date depends on the nature and timing of new information received by management of the acquiree regarding the possible outcome of the contingency. In the absence of such information, the acquirer is to continue to account for the asset or liability at acquisition-date fair value. When new information is obtained regarding the contingency's possible outcome, management of the acquirer is to evaluate the information and measure the asset or liability as follows:

1.  A liability is to be measured at the *higher* of

    a.  Acquisition-date fair value, *or*
    b.  The amount that would be recognized if applying FAS 5.

2.  An asset is to be measured at the *lower* of

    c.  Acquisition-date fair value, *or*
    d.  The best estimate of the future settlement amount.

Only upon resolution of a contingency is the acquirer permitted to derecognize an asset or liability that the contingency gives rise to. Thus, derecognition could occur, for example, if the acquirer collects cash, sells the right to receive the future cash flows associated with a contingent asset, or settles a contingent liability in full. Derecognition of a contingent liability is also permitted if the obligation is cancelled or expires.

*Indemnification assets.* Indemnification provisions are usually included in the voluminous closing documents necessary to effect a business combination. Indemnifications are contractual terms designed to fully or partially protect the acquirer from the potential adverse effects of an unfavorable future resolution of a contingency or uncertainty that exists at the acquisition date. Frequently the indemnification is structured to protect the acquirer by limiting the maximum amount of postcombination loss that the acquirer would bear in the event of an adverse outcome. A contractual indemnification provision results in the acquirer obtaining, as a part of the acquisition, an indemnification asset and simultaneously assuming a contingent liability of the acquiree.

*Acquisition-date considerations.* FAS 141(R) requires the acquirer to recognize and measure the indemnification asset using the same measurement basis it uses to measure the indemnified obligation.

In measuring an indemnification asset, management is to take into account any uncertainty in the amounts or timing of expected future cash flows. If the asset is measured at acquisition-date fair value, those effects are included in the measure of fair value and, therefore, a separate valuation allowance is not recognized.

Some indemnifications relate to assets or liabilities that are exceptions to the recognition or measurement principles. Indemnifications may, for example, be related to noncontractual contingencies that do not meet the more-likely-than-not criterion for recognition in the acquisition-date financial statements. Other indemnifications may be related to uncertain income tax positions that are measured, under FIN 48, as the maximum amount that is estimated to be more likely than not of being sustained upon examination by the relevant taxing jurisdiction. In cases such as these, the indemnification asset is to be recognized and measured using assumptions consistent with those used to measure the item being indemnified. Since uncertainty with respect to the collectibility of the indemnification asset is not directly included in its measurement, collectibility is considered separately and, to the extent necessary, reflected in a valuation allowance to reduce the carrying amount of the indemnification asset.

*Postacquisition considerations.* At each reporting date subsequent to the acquisition date, the acquirer is to measure an indemnification asset recognized as part of the business combination using the same basis as the indemnified item, subject to any limitations imposed contractually on the amount of the indemnification. If an indemnification asset is not subsequently measured at fair value (because to do so would be inconsistent with the basis used to measure the indemnified item), management is to assess the collectibility of the asset and, to the extent necessary, a valuation allowance should be established or adjusted. An indemnification asset is derecognized only when the asset is collected, the rights to receive the asset are sold, or the acquirer otherwise loses its right to receive it.

*Reacquired rights.* An acquirer and acquiree may have engaged in preacquisition business transactions such as leases, licenses, or franchises that resulted in the acquiree paying consideration to the acquirer to use tangible and/or intangible assets of the acquirer in the acquiree's business.

*Acquisition-date considerations.* Upon consummation of the business combination, the acquirer may reacquire a previously granted right. Upon reacquisition, the acquirer is to account for the right as an identifiable, amortizable intangible asset separate from goodwill.

If the terms of the contract that give rise to the reacquired right are either favorable or unfavorable to the acquirer compared to current market transactions for identical or similar rights, the acquirer is to recognize a gain or loss computed as the lesser of

1. The amount by which, from the acquirer's perspective, the contract is favorable or unfavorable, or
2. The amount of any settlement provisions stated in the contract that are available to the counterparty for which the contract is unfavorable.

If 2. is less than 1., the difference is to be included as part of the accounting for the business combination.

*Postacquisition considerations.* Reacquired rights recognized at the acquisition date are amortized, postcombination, on the basis of the remaining, unexpired term of the related contract. The remaining contractual term is to be used for this purpose even if market participants would consider potential future contract renewals in determining the fair value of the contract.

Should the acquirer subsequently sell the reacquired right to a third party, the carrying amount of the intangible asset is to be included in the determination of gain or loss on the sale.

*Employee benefits.* Liabilities (and assets, if applicable), associated with acquiree employee benefit arrangements are to be recognized and measured under other GAAP, as applicable.

| *Types of benefits* | *Applicable GAAP* | *Amended by FAS 141(R)* | *Covered in Wiley GAAP Chapter* |
|---|---|---|---|
| Deferred compensation contracts including postretirement benefit aspects of split-dollar life insurance arrangements | APB 12 EITF 06-4 EITF 06-10 | | 18 |
| Compensated absences and sabbatical leaves | FAS 43 EITF 06-2 | | 14 |
| Pensions, plan curtailments, and termination benefits | FAS 87 FAS 88 FAS 158 | x | 18 |
| Postretirement benefits other than pensions including postretirement benefit aspects of split-dollar life insurance arrangements | FAS 106 FAS 158 EITF 06-4 EITF 06-10 | x | 18 |
| Postemployment benefits (benefits provided to inactive or former employees, their beneficiaries, and covered dependents after employment but before retirement) including, but not limited to | FAS 112 | | 18 |
| • Salary continuation<br>• Supplemental unemployment benefits<br>• Severance benefits<br>• Disability-related benefits including workers' compensation<br>• Job training and counseling (e.g., outplacement)<br>• Continuation of benefits such as health care and life insurance | | | |
| Onetime termination benefits | FAS 146 | x | 3, 18 |

In researching the application of these pronouncements, it is important to consider the amendments to them made by FAS 141(R). For example,

1. FAS 87, *Employer's Accounting for Pensions*, and FAS 106, *Employers' Accounting for Postretirement Benefits other than Pensions*, are amended to clarify that

   a. The acquirer is to recognize, as part of the business combination, an asset or liability that represents the funded status of a single-employer defined benefit pension plan and/or a single-employer defined benefit postretirement plan. In determining the funded status, the acquirer is to disregard the effects of expected plan amendments, terminations, or curtailments that it has no obligation to make at the acquisition date.

b.   The projected benefit obligation assumed for a single-employer defined benefit pension plan or the accumulated postretirement benefit obligation assumed for a single-employer defined benefit postretirement plan are to reflect any other necessary changes in assumptions based on an assessment by the acquirer of relevant future events.

c.   If the acquiree participates in a multiemployer defined benefit pension or post-retirement plan, and at the acquisition date it is probable that the acquirer will withdraw from that plan, the acquirer is to recognize a withdrawal liability as of the acquisition date under FAS 5.

2.   FAS 146, *Accounting for Costs Associated with Exit or Disposal Activities,* is amended to expand its scope to cover exit activities associated with entities that are acquired in a business combination.

*Acquirer share-based payment awards exchanged for acquiree awards held by its employees.* In connection with a business combination, the acquirer often awards share-based payments to the employees of the acquiree in exchange for the employees' acquiree awards. Obviously, there are many valid business reasons for the exchange, not the least of which is ensuring smooth transition and integration as well as retention of valued employees.

The discussion that follows uses concepts and terminology from FAS 123(R), *Share-Based Payment*, discussed in greater detail in Chapter 19.

*Acquirer not obligated to exchange.* Accounting for the replacement awards under FAS 141(R) is dependent on whether the acquirer is obligated to replace the acquiree awards. The acquirer is obligated to replace the acquiree awards if the acquiree or its employees can enforce replacement through rights obtained from the terms of the acquisition agreement, the acquiree awards, or applicable laws or regulations.

If the acquirer is not obligated to replace the acquiree awards, all of the fair-value-based measure (FVBM)[5] of the replacement awards is recognized as compensation cost in the post-combination financial statements.

### Example of acquirer replacing acquiree awards without the obligation to do so

New Parent, Inc. (NP) acquired New Subsidiary, Inc. (NS) on January 1, 2009. Because of the business combination, the share-based payment awards that had been previously granted by NS to its employees expired on the acquisition date.

Although NP was not obligated, legally or contractually to replace the expired awards, its Board of Directors approved a grant of NP awards designed so that the employees of NS would not be financially disadvantaged by the acquisition transaction.

Since the replacement awards were voluntary on the part of NP, the fair-value-based measure of the replacement award is attributed wholly to the postcombination consolidated financial statements of NP and Subsidiary.

*Acquirer obligated to replace acquiree awards.* If the acquirer is obligated to replace the awards of the acquiree, either all or a portion of the fair-value-based measure of the replacement awards is included in measuring the consideration transferred by the acquirer in the business combination. To the extent a portion of the replacement awards is not allocated to consideration transferred, it is accounted for as compensation for postcombination services in the acquirer's consolidated financial statements.

---

[5]   *Although the accompanying guidance uses the term "fair-value-based measure" to refer to the measurement of share-based awards, the guidance also applies to awards of both the acquirer and acquiree that are measured using either the calculated value method or intrinsic value method.*

For the purposes of illustrating the allocation computations, the following conventions and abbreviations are used:

| | |
|---|---|
| $FVBM_{RA}$ | Acquisition date fair-value-based measure of acquirer replacement award |
| $FVBM_{AA}$ | Acquisition date fair-value-based measure of acquiree award that is being replaced by the acquirer |
| $RSP_{AA}$ | Original requisite service period[6] of acquiree awards at their grant date |
| $RSP_{RA}$ | Requisite service period of the acquirer replacement awards at acquisition date |
| $CRSP_{AA}$ | Portion of requisite service period completed at the acquisition date by employees under the acquiree awards |
| TSP | Total service period—the service period already satisfied by the employees at the acquisition date under the acquiree awards plus the requisite service period, if any, required by the acquirer replacement awards |
| PRE | Portion of $FVBM_{RA}$ attributable to precombination services performed by the employees of the acquiree |
| PCC | Postcombination compensation cost |

$$TSP = CRSP_{AA} + RSP_{RA}$$

The following steps are followed to determine the portion of the fair-value-based measure of the replacement award that is to be included as part of the consideration transferred by the acquirer:

1. Compute both $FVBM_{RA}$ and $FVBM_{AA}$ by following the provisions of FAS 123(R), as discussed in detail in Chapter 19.
2. Compute the portion of the replacement award that is attributable to precombination services rendered by the acquiree's employees as follows:

   a. If $RSP_{AA} > TSP$, then

   $$PRE = FVBM_{AA}\left(\frac{CRSP_{AA}}{RSP_{AA}}\right)$$

   b. If $RSP_{AA} \leq TSP$, then

   $$PRE = FVBM_{AA}\left(\frac{CRSP_{AA}}{TSP}\right)$$

3. Compute the portion of the nonvested replacement award attributable to postcombination service as follows:

   $$PCC = FVBM_{RA} - PRE$$

   This amount is to be recognized as compensation cost in the postcombination financial statements since, at the acquisition date, the requisite service conditions had not been met.

The following examples are adapted from FAS 141(R), Appendix A.

---

[6] *The term "requisite service period" includes explicit, implicit, and derived service periods during which employees are required to provide services in exchange for the award. These terms are defined in FAS 123(R), discussed in detail in Chapter 19.*

**Example of acquirer replacement awards requiring no postcombination services exchanges for fully vested acquiree awards where the employees have rendered all required services by the acquisition date**

New Parent, Inc. (NP) acquired New Subsidiary, Inc. (NS) on January 1, 2009. In accordance with the acquisition agreement, NP agreed to replace share-based awards that had previously been issued by NS. Details are as follows:

|  |  | *a. Acquiree Awards* | *b. Acquirer Awards* |
|---|---|---|---|
| 1. | Acquisition date fair-value-based measure of awards | $FVBM_{AA} = \$100$ | $FVBM_{RA} = \$110$ |
| 2. | Original requisite service period of acquiree awards at their grant date | $RSP_{AA} = 4$ years | -- |
| 3. | Portion of 2a. completed by the acquisition date by employees of the acquiree | $CRSP_{AA} = 4$ years | -- |
| 4. | Requisite service period of acquirer replacement awards at the acquisition date | -- | $RSP_{RA} = 0$ |
| 5. | Total service period (3a. + 4b.) | -- | $TSP = 4$ years |
| 6. | The greater of the total service period (5b.) or the original requisite service period of the acquiree awards (2a.) | -- | 4 years |

Since the acquiree's employees had completed all of the services required under the prior awards, applying the formula yields a result that attributes 100% of the fair value of the acquiree award that is being replaced to precombination services rendered.

$$PRE = \quad 1a. \quad \left( \frac{3a.}{6b.} \right)$$

$$PRE = \quad \$100 \quad \left( \frac{4 \text{ years}}{4 \text{ years}} \right)$$

$$PRE = \quad \$100$$

The $100 result, attributed to precombination services, is included by the acquirer in its computation of the consideration transferred in exchange for control of the acquiree.

The final step in the computation is to account for the difference between the acquisition date fair values of the replacement awards and the acquiree awards as follows:

| | |
|---|---|
| Fair value of replacement awards—$FVBM_{RA}$ | $110 |
| – Allocated to consideration per above | 100 |
| Additional compensation cost recognized immediately in postcombination financial statements | $ 10 |

This result illustrates the basic principle in FAS 141(R) that any excess of FVBMRA over the $FVBM_{AA}$ is to be attributed to postcombination services and recognized as compensation cost in the postcombination financial statements.

**Example of acquirer replacement awards requiring performance of postcombination services exchanged for acquiree awards for which all requisite services had been rendered by the acquiree's employees as of the acquisition date**

The acquisition agreement referred to in the previous example governing the NP acquisition of NS that occurred on January 1, 2009, contained the following provisions regarding exchange of outstanding NS awards at acquisition date for NP replacement awards:

|   | | *a. Acquiree Awards* | *b. Acquirer Awards* |
|---|---|---|---|
| 1. | Acquisition date fair-value-based measure of awards | $FVBM_{AA} = \$100$ | $FVBM_{RA} = \$100$ |
| 2. | Original requisite service period of acquiree awards at their grant date | $RSP_{AA} = 4$ years | -- |
| 3. | Portion of 2a. completed by the acquisition date by employees of the acquiree (the acquiree employees in this example had actually completed a total of 7 years of services by the acquisition date) | $CRSP_{AA} = 4$ years | -- |
| 4. | Requisite service period of acquirer replacement awards at the acquisition date | -- | $RSP_{RA} = 1$ year |
| 5. | Total service period (3a. + 4b.) | -- | TSP = 5 years |
| 6. | The greater of the total service period (5b.) or the original requisite service period of the acquiree awards (2a.) | -- | 5 years |

Even though the acquiree's employees had completed all of the requisite service required by the acquiree's awards three years prior to the acquisition, the imposition of an additional year of required service by the acquirer's replacement awards results in an allocation between precombination compensation cost and postcombination compensation cost as follows:

$$PRE = \quad 1a. \quad \left( \frac{3a.}{6b.} \right)$$

$$PRE = \$100 \quad \left( \frac{4 \text{ years}}{5 \text{ years}} \right)$$

$$PRE = \quad \$80$$

The $80 result, attributed to precombination services, is included by the acquirer in its computation of the consideration transferred in exchange for control of the acquirer.

The $20 difference between the $100 fair value of the replacement awards and the $80 allocated to precombination services (and included in consideration transferred) is accounted for as compensation cost in the postcombination consolidated financial statements of NP and Subsidiary under the provisions of FAS 123(R).

**Example of acquirer replacement awards requiring performance of postcombination services exchanged for acquiree awards with remaining unsatisfied requisite service period as of the acquisition date**

The acquisition agreement referred to in the previous examples governing the NP acquisition of NS that occurred on January 1, 2009, contained the following provisions regarding exchange of outstanding NS awards at acquisition date for NP replacement awards:

|   | | *a. Acquiree Awards* | *b. Acquirer Awards* |
|---|---|---|---|
| 1. | Acquisition date fair-value-based measure of awards | $FVBM_{AA} = \$100$ | $FVBM_{RA} = \$100$ |
| 2. | Original requisite service period of acquiree awards at their grant date | $RSP_{AA} = 4$ years | -- |
| 3. | Portion of 2a. completed by the acquisition date by employees of the acquiree | $CRSP_{AA} = 2$ years | -- |
| 4. | Requisite service period of acquirer replacement awards at the acquisition date | -- | $RSP_{RA} = 1$ year |
| 5. | Total service period (3a. + 4b.) | -- | TSP = 3 years |
| 6. | The greater of the total service period (5b.) or the original requisite service period of the acquiree awards (2a.) | -- | 4 years |

The portion of the fair-value-based measure of the replacement awards attributable to pre-combination services already rendered by the acquiree employees is computed as follows:

$$PRE = \quad 1a. \quad \left( \frac{3a.}{6b.} \right)$$

$$PRE = \quad \$100 \quad \left( \frac{2\ years}{4\ years} \right)$$

$$PRE = \quad \$50$$

Based on the computation above, at the acquisition date, NP, the acquirer, includes $50 as consideration transferred to obtain control of NS, the acquiree. The remaining $50 is attributed to postcombination services and, accordingly, recognized as compensation cost in the consolidated postcombination financial statements of NP and Subsidiary.

**Example of acquirer replacement awards that do not require postcombination services exchanged for acquiree awards for which the acquiree's employees had not yet completed all of the requisite services by the acquisition date**

The acquisition agreement referred to in the previous examples governing the NP acquisition of NS that occurred on January 1, 2009, contained the following provisions regarding exchange of outstanding NS awards at acquisition date for NP replacement awards:

|   |   | *a. Acquiree Awards* | *b. Acquirer Awards* |
|---|---|---|---|
| 1. | Acquisition date fair-value-based measure of awards | $FVBM_{AA} = \$100$ | $FVBM_{RA} = \$100$ |
| 2. | Original requisite service period of acquiree awards at their grant date | $RSP_{AA} = 4$ years | -- |
| 3. | Portion of 2a. completed by the acquisition date by employees of the acquiree | $CRSP_{AA} = 2$ years | -- |
| 4. | Requisite service period of acquirer replacement awards at the acquisition date | -- | $RSP_{RA} = 0$ |
| 5. | Total service period (3a. + 4b.) | -- | TSP = 2 years |
| 6. | The greater of the total service period (5b.) or the original requisite service period of the acquiree awards (2a.) | -- | 4 years |

Under this scenario, the terms of the awards previously granted by NS, the acquiree, did not contain a change-in-control provision that would have fully vested them upon the acquisition by NP. If this had been the case, the outcome would be the same as the example above where neither the acquiree awards nor the replacement rewards required the completion of any service on the part of the acquiree's employees.

Since, at the acquisition date, the acquiree employees had completed only two out of the four years of required services and the replacement awards do not extend the duration of services required postcombination, the total service period (TSP) in 5b. is the 2 years already completed by the acquiree's employees under their original awards in 3a. ($CRSP_{AA}$).

The portion of the fair-value-based measure of the replacement awards attributable to pre-combination services already rendered by the acquiree employees is computed as follows:

$$PRE = \quad 1a. \quad \left( \frac{3a.}{6b.} \right)$$

$$PRE = \quad \$100 \quad \left( \frac{2\ years}{4\ years} \right)$$

$$PRE = \quad \$50$$

Consequently, $50 of the fair-value-based measure of the replacement awards is attributable to precombination services already performed by the acquiree employees and is, therefore, included in computing the consideration transferred in exchange for obtaining control of the acquiree.

The remaining $50 of the fair-value-based measure of the replacement awards is attributable to postcombination service. However, since the acquiree's employees are not required to provide any postcombination services under the terms of the replacement awards, the entire $50 is immediately recognized by NP, the acquirer, in its postcombination consolidated financial statements.

Although not illustrated in the preceding examples, FAS 141(R) requires the acquirer to estimate the number of its replacement awards for which the requisite service is expected to occur. To the extent that service is not expected to occur due to employees terminating prior to meeting the replacement award's requisite service requirements, the portion of the fair-value-based measure of the replacement awards included in consideration transferred in the business combination is to be reduced accordingly.

If the replacement award is subject to a graded vesting schedule, the acquirer is to recognize the related compensation cost in accordance with its policy election for other awards in accordance with FAS 123(R), paragraph 42. Compensation cost is either (1) recognized using the "graded vesting attribution method" that separates the award into tranches according to the year in which they vest and treats each tranche as if it had been a separate award, or (2) recognized using a straight-line attribution method over the graded vesting period. If option (2) is elected, compensation cost at any date must equal at least the amount attributable to options that actually vested on or before that date.

Finally, it is important to note that the same requirements for apportioning the replacement award between precombination and postcombination service apply to replacement awards that are classified as equity or as liabilities. All post-acquisition-date changes in the fair-value-based measure of liability awards (and their related income tax effects) are recognized in the acquirer's postcombination financial statements in the periods in which the changes occur.

*Income taxes.* The final exception to the general fair-value-based recognition and measurement provisions of FAS 141(R) is the accounting for income taxes. Since recognition and measurement of income tax assets and liabilities under US GAAP has not historically used fair value measurement or discounted present value techniques, FASB was loath to make fundamental changes to this complex area of accounting. In addition, FASB and IASB are currently pursuing a joint project to converge US and International accounting standards with respect to accounting for income taxes, and that project will be subject to the Boards' due process procedures that provide constituents an opportunity to provide feedback.

FAS 141(R), however, did amend FAS 109 and FIN 48 in order to accommodate the new business combinations framework. The remainder of this section is devoted to describing the provisions of those standards and other related interpretive guidance related to accounting for income taxes in connection with business combinations. Accounting for income taxes is covered in detail in Chapter 17.

*Basic principle.* The basic principle that applies to income tax accounting in a business combination (carried forward without change by FAS 141[R]) is that the acquirer is to recognize, as of the acquisition date, deferred income tax assets or liabilities for the future effects of temporary differences and carryforwards of the acquiree that either

1. Exist on the acquisition date *or*
2. Are generated by the acquisition itself

FAS 141(R) also amends FIN 48 to clarify its applicability to business combinations as follows:

1.  In computing the acquisition date amount of currently payable or refundable income taxes from a particular taxing jurisdiction, management is to apply the recognition and measurement provisions of FIN 48 to evaluate the amounts to record relative to prior income tax positions taken by the acquiree.
2.  As a result of management's evaluation of prior tax positions and the amounts recognized in 1., management is to adjust the income tax bases used in computing the deferred income tax assets and liabilities associated with the business combination at the acquisition date.
3.  New information regarding the facts and circumstances that existed at the acquisition date that comes to the attention of management regarding those income tax positions is treated as follows:

    a.  If the information results in a change during the measurement period, the adjustment is made to goodwill. If goodwill is reduced to zero, any remaining portion of the adjustment is recorded as a bargain purchase gain.
    b.  If the information results in a post-measurement-period change, the change is accounted for in the same manner as any other FIN 48 changes.

FIN 48 is discussed in detail in Chapter 17.

*Valuation allowances.* To the extent applicable, deferred income tax assets are to be reduced by a valuation allowance for the portion of the asset not deemed more-likely-than-not to be realized.

On the acquisition date, any benefits of future deductible temporary differences or net operating loss carryforwards (NOLs) of an acquired entity are to be recognized if the acquirer is permitted to utilize those benefits on a consolidated income tax return under the existing income tax law. The income tax benefits will be recorded gross with an offsetting valuation allowance if it is more likely than not that the deferred income tax asset will not be realized by the reporting entity (for example, if it is estimated that there will not be sufficient future taxable income to utilize the NOL prior to its expiration).

Some jurisdictions restrict the future use of income tax benefits of the acquiree and only permit those benefits to be applied to subsequent taxable income generated by the acquiree even though the entities are permitted to file a consolidated income tax return. When this is the case, or when the acquiree is expected to file a separate income tax return, management of the consolidated reporting entity is to assess the need for a valuation allowance for those benefits based only on the acquiree's separate past and expected future taxable income.

As a result of the acquisition and the permissibility of filing a consolidated income tax return in a particular jurisdiction, the acquirer may be able to use future taxable income generated by the acquiree to obtain the tax benefits of its own net operating loss carryforwards for which the acquirer had previously recognized a valuation allowance. If, based on the weight of available evidence, management of the acquirer concludes that its previously recognized valuation allowance can be reduced or eliminated, the adjustment is not considered part of the accounting for the business combination. Instead, the benefit is recognized as a component of income tax expense in the period of the acquisition.

Post-acquisition-date changes in a valuation allowance with respect to an acquiree's deferred income tax asset are to be recognized as follows:

1.  If the change in judgment occurs during the measurement period (as defined in FAS 141[R]) that is not to exceed one year from the acquisition date, and results from new information bearing on facts and circumstances that existed at the acquisition date, the change is to be recognized as an adjustment to goodwill. Should the ad-

justment reduce goodwill to zero, the acquirer is to recognize any further reduction in the valuation allowance as a gain from a bargain purchase.

2. If the change in judgment occurs subsequent to the measurement period, it is reported as an increase or decrease in income tax expense or benefit of the period in which the judgment changed. Exceptions to this treatment are provided for changes attributable to dividends on unallocated shares of an Employee Stock Ownership Plan (ESOP), employee stock options, and certain quasi reorganizations. Accounting for these exceptions results in adjustments directly to contributed capital rather than to income tax expense.

*Goodwill.* Historically, amortization of goodwill was not an allowable deduction for US federal income tax purposes. To the extent that goodwill amortization is nondeductible in any applicable taxing jurisdiction, the nondeductible goodwill does not represent a temporary difference between GAAP and tax and consequently does not give rise to deferred income taxes.

The 1993 Tax Reconciliation Act amended US federal income tax law to permit the amortization of goodwill and other specified acquired intangibles over a statutory 15-year period (IRC §197). The method of determining the amount of goodwill to recognize for income tax purposes, however, differs from the method prescribed by FAS 141(R) for financial reporting purposes. Further complicating matters, other taxing jurisdictions to which the reporting entity is subject may not recognize goodwill amortization as deductible. This can result in onerous recordkeeping of book/tax differences in the carrying amounts of goodwill in each of the major jurisdictions in which the reporting entity is taxed.

When goodwill amortization is tax-deductible in a particular jurisdiction, it does result in a temporary difference between the income tax basis and GAAP carrying amount of the goodwill. GAAP goodwill is only written off if it becomes partially or fully impaired whereas tax goodwill is subject to periodic amortization until its income tax basis is reduced to zero.

Since goodwill represents a residual amount after considering all identifiable assets acquired and liabilities assumed in the business combination, any deferred income tax asset associated with goodwill would necessarily have to be computed in order to determine the residual. Thus, FASB prescribed the use of a simultaneous equation method to compute goodwill net of the deferred income tax asset associated with it. In order to operationalize this requirement, FAS 141(R) amended paragraph 262 and added paragraph 263 to FAS 109 to describe and illustrate it. This matter is more fully discussed and examples are provided in Chapter 17.

**Step 6—Recognize and measure any noncontrolling interest in the acquiree.** The term "noncontrolling interest" replaces the term, "minority interest" to refer to the portion of the acquiree, if any, that is not controlled by the parent. The term "minority interest" became an inadequate descriptor because, under FAS 141(R) and FIN 46(R), *Consolidation of Variable Interest Entities*, an entity can possess a controlling financial interest in another entity without possessing a majority of the voting interests of that entity. Thus it would be inaccurate, in many cases, to refer to the party that does not possess a controlling financial interest as a "minority" since that party could, in fact, hold a majority of the voting equity of the acquiree.

FAS 141(R) requires the noncontrolling interest in the acquiree to be measured at fair value at the acquisition date. If the acquirer is not acquiring all of the shares in the acquiree and there is an active market for the remaining outstanding shares in the acquiree, the acquirer may be able to use the market price to measure the fair value of the noncontrolling interest. Otherwise, the acquirer would measure fair value using other valuation techniques.

In applying the appropriate valuation technique to determine the fair value of the non-controlling interest, it is likely that there will be a difference in the fair value per share of that interest and the fair value per share of the controlling interest. This difference arises from what has been referred to as a "minority interest discount" applicable to the noncontrolling shares. Obviously, an investor would be unwilling to pay the same amount per share for equity shares in an entity that did not convey control of that entity than it would pay for shares that did convey control.

### Example of fair value of noncontrolling interest adjusted for minority interest discount

Shirley Corporation (SC) is considering acquiring an 80% interest in Jake Industries Inc. (JI), a privately held corporation. SC engages a valuation specialist to determine the fair value of JI whose shares do not trade in an active market.

The specialist's findings with respect to JI as a whole were as follows:

| | |
|---|---|
| Aggregate fair value of JI | $15 million |
| Number of outstanding shares | 375,000 |
| Aggregate fair value per share | $40 |

In valuing the noncontrolling interest, however, the specialist made the following additional assumptions:

| | |
|---|---|
| Aggregate fair value per share | $ 40 |
| Estimated minority interest discount per share | 10 |
| Estimated fair value per share of noncontrolling interest | $30 |
| | |
| Fair value of noncontrolling interest | |
|     Fair value per noncontrolling share | $30 |
|     × # of noncontrolling shares outstanding | × 75,000 |
| | $2,250,000 |

It is important to note from this analysis that, from the perspective of the acquirer, the computation of the acquisition-date fair value of the noncontrolling interest in the acquiree is not computed by simply multiplying the same fair value per share that the acquirer used to value the entity by the percentage voting interest retained collectively by the noncontrolling stockholders. Such a simplistic calculation would have yielded a different result:

$15 million aggregate fair value × 20% noncontrolling shares = $3 million.

If this method had been used, the noncontrolling interest would be overvalued by $750,000 (the difference between $3 million and $2,250,000.

FAS 160 settles the controversial issue of how the noncontrolling interest is to be classified in the consolidated balance sheet by requiring that it be reported within the equity section, separately from the equity of the parent company, and clearly identified with a caption such as "noncontrolling interest in subsidiaries." Should there be noncontrolling interests attributable to more than one consolidated subsidiary, the amounts may be aggregated in the consolidated balance sheet.

Only equity-classified instruments issued by the subsidiary may be classified as equity in this manner. If, for example, the subsidiary had issued a financial instrument that, under applicable GAAP, was classified as a liability in the subsidiary's financial statements, that instrument would not be classified as a noncontrolling interest since it does not represent an ownership interest.

**Step 7—Measure the consideration transferred.** In general, consideration transferred by the acquiree is measured at its acquisition-date fair value. Examples of consideration that could be transferred include cash, other assets, a business, a subsidiary of the acquirer, contingent consideration, common or preferred equity instruments, options, and warrants. The aggregate consideration transferred is the sum of the following elements measured at the acquisition date:

1.  The fair value of the assets transferred by the acquirer,
2.  The fair value of the liabilities incurred by the acquirer to the former owners of the acquiree, and
3.  The fair value of the equity interests issued by the acquirer subject to the measurement exception discussed earlier in this chapter for the portion, if applicable, of acquirer share-based awards exchanged for awards held by employees of the acquiree that is included in consideration transferred.

To the extent the acquirer transfers consideration in the form of assets or liabilities with carrying amounts that differ from their fair values at the acquisition date, the acquirer is to remeasure them at fair value and recognize a gain or loss on the acquisition date. If, however, the transferred assets or liabilities remain within the consolidated entity postcombination with the acquirer retaining control of them, no gain or loss is recognized, and the assets or liabilities are measured at their carrying amounts to the acquirer immediately prior to the acquisition date. This situation can occur, for example, when the acquirer transfers assets or liabilities to the entity being acquired rather than to its former owners.

The structure of the transaction may involve the exchange of equity interests between the acquirer and either the acquiree or the acquiree's former owners. If the acquisition-date fair value of the acquiree's equity interests is more reliably measurable than the equity interests of the acquirer, the fair value of the acquiree's equity interests is to be used to measure the consideration transferred.

**Contingent consideration.** Contingent consideration arrangements in connection with business combinations can be structured in many different ways and can result in the recognition of either assets or liabilities under FAS 141(R). In either case, the acquirer is to include contingent assets and liabilities as part of the consideration transferred, measured at acquisition-date fair value.

If the contingent consideration includes a future payment obligation, that obligation is to be classified as either a liability or equity under the provisions of

- FAS 150, *Accounting for Certain Financial Instruments with Characteristics of Both Liabilities and Equity*,
- EITF 00-19, *Accounting for Derivative Financial Instruments Indexed to, and Potentially Settled in, a Company's Own Stock, or*
- Other applicable GAAP

The acquirer is to carefully consider information obtained subsequent to the acquisition-date measurement of contingent consideration. Additional information obtained during the measurement period that relates to the facts and circumstances that existed at the acquisition date result in measurement period adjustments to the recognized amount of contingent consideration and a corresponding adjustment to goodwill or gain from bargain purchase. Changes that result from events occurring after the acquisition date, such as meeting a specified earnings target, reaching a specified share price, or reaching an agreed-upon milestone on a research and development project, do not constitute measurement period adjustments. Changes in the fair value of contingent consideration that do not result from measurement period adjustments are to be accounted for as follows:

1.  If the contingent consideration is classified as equity, it is not to be remeasured and subsequent settlement of the contingency is to be reflected within equity.
2.  If the contingent consideration is classified as an asset or liability, it is to be remeasured at fair value at each reporting date until resolution of the contingency. Changes in the fair value between reporting dates are to be recognized in net income unless the arrangement is a hedging instrument for which FAS 133, as amended by

FAS 141(R) requires the changes to be initially recognized in other comprehensive income.

**Step 8—Recognize and measure goodwill or gain on a bargain purchase.** The last step in applying the acquisition method is the measurement of goodwill or a gain from a bargain purchase. Goodwill represents an intangible that is not specifically identifiable. It results from situations when the amount the acquirer is willing to pay to obtain its controlling interest exceeds the aggregate recognized values of the net assets acquired measured following the principles of FAS 141(R). Goodwill's elusive nature as an unidentifiable, residual asset means that it cannot be measured directly but rather can only be measured by reference to the other amounts measured as a part of the business combination:

| | | |
|---|---|---|
| GW | = | Goodwill |
| NG | = | Negative goodwill |
| NI | = | Noncontrolling interest in the acquiree, if any, measured at fair value |
| CT | = | Consideration transferred, generally measured at acquisition-date fair value |
| PE | = | Fair value of the acquirer's previously held interest in the acquiree if the acquisition was achieved in stages |
| NA | = | Net assets acquired at the acquisition date—consisting of the identifiable assets acquired and liabilities assumed, measured as described in this chapter |
| (CT + NI + PE) – NA | = | GW or (NG) |

Thus, when application of the formula yields an excess of the consideration transferred, noncontrolling interest, and fair value of previously held interests over the net assets acquired, the acquirer has paid a premium for the acquisition and that premium is characterized as goodwill.

When the opposite is true, that is, when the formula yields a negative result, sometimes referred to as negative goodwill, the acquirer has, in fact, obtained a bargain purchase, as the value the acquirer obtained in the exchange exceeded the fair value of what it surrendered.

In a business combination in which no consideration is transferred, the acquirer is to use one or more valuation techniques to measure the acquisition-date fair value of its interest in the acquiree and substitute that measurement in the formula for "CT," the consideration transferred. The techniques selected require the availability of sufficient data to properly apply them and are to be appropriate for the circumstances. If more than one technique is used, management of the acquirer is to evaluate the results of applying the techniques including the extent of data available and how relevant and reliable the inputs (assumptions) used are. Guidance on the use of valuation techniques is provided in FAS 157, *Fair Value Measurements*, discussed in detail in Chapter 6.

*Bargain purchases.* If the computation above results in negative goodwill, this constitutes a "bargain purchase." Under FAS 141(R), a bargain purchase is recognized in net income as an acquisition-date gain. Unlike the predecessor standard, the gain is not characterized as an extraordinary gain. Rather, it is considered part of income from continuing operations.

Given the complexity of the computations involved, FASB prescribed a verification protocol for management to follow if the computation preliminarily results in a bargain purchase. If the computation initially yields a bargain purchase, management of the acquirer is to perform the following procedures before recognizing a gain on the bargain purchase:

1. Perform a completeness review of the identifiable tangible and intangible assets acquired and liabilities assumed to reassess whether all such items have been correctly identified. If any omissions are found, recognize the assets and liabilities that had been omitted.
2. Perform a review of the procedures used to measure all of the following items. The objective of the review is to ensure that the acquisition-date measurements appropriately considered all available information available at the acquisition date:

   a. Identifiable assets acquired
   b. Liabilities assumed
   c. Consideration transferred
   d. Noncontrolling interest in the acquiree, if applicable
   e. Acquirer's previously held equity interest in the acquiree for a business combination achieved in stages

***Measurement period.*** More frequently than not, management of the acquirer does not obtain all of the relevant information needed to complete the acquisition-date measurements in time for the issuance of the first set of interim or annual financial statements subsequent to the business combination. If the initial accounting for the business combination has not been completed by that time, the acquirer is to report provisional amounts in the consolidated financial statements for any items for which the accounting is incomplete. FAS 141(R) provides for a "measurement period" during which any adjustments to the provisional amounts recognized at the acquisition date are to be retrospectively adjusted to reflect new information that management obtains regarding facts and circumstances existing as of the acquisition date. Information that has a bearing on this determination must not relate to postacquisition events or circumstances. The information is to be analyzed to determine whether, if it had been known at the acquisition date, it would have affected the measurement of the amounts recognized as of that date.

In evaluating whether new information obtained is suitable for the purpose of adjusting provisional amounts, management of the acquirer is to consider all relevant factors. Critical in this evaluation is the determination of whether the information relates to facts and circumstances as they existed at the acquisition date or instead, the information results from events occurring after the acquisition date. Relevant factors include

1. The timing of the receipt of the additional information, *and*
2. Whether management of the acquirer can identify a reason that a change is warranted to the provisional amounts.

Obviously, information received shortly after the acquisition date has a higher likelihood of relevance to acquisition-date circumstances than information received months later.

### Example of consideration of new information obtained during the measurement period

Krupp Industries, Inc. (KI) acquired Miller Motor Works Corp. (MMW) on January 2, 2009. In the first quarter 2009 consolidated financial statements of Krupp Industries and Subsidiary, it assigned a provisional fair value of $40 million to an asset group consisting of a factory and related machinery that manufactures engines used in large trucks and sport utility vehicles (SUVs).

As of the acquisition date, the average cost of gasoline in the markets served by the customers of MMW was $4.30 per gallon. For the first four months subsequent to the acquisition, the per-gallon price of gasoline was relatively stable and only fluctuated slightly up or down on any given day. Upon further analysis, management was able to determine that, during that four-month period, the production levels of the asset group and related order backlog did not vary substantially from the acquisition date.

In May, 2009, however, due to an accident on May 3, 2009, at a large US refinery, the average cost per gallon skyrocketed to more than $6.00 a gallon. As a result of this huge spike in the price of fuel, MMW's largest customers either canceled orders or sharply curtailed the number of engines they had previously ordered.

*Scenario 1:* On April 15, 2009, management of KI signed a sales agreement with Joshua International (JI) to sell the asset group for $30 million. Given the fact that management was unable to identify any changes that occurred during the measurement period that would have accounted for a change in the acquisition-date fair value of the asset group, management determines that it will retrospectively reduce the provisional fair value assigned to the asset group to $30 million.

*Scenario 2:* On May 15, 2009, management of KI signed a sales agreement with Joshua International (JI) to sell the asset group for $30 million. Given the intervening events that affected the price of fuel and the demand for MMW's products, management determines that the $10 million decline in the fair value of the asset group from the provisional fair value it was originally assigned resulted from those intervening changes and, consequently does not adjust the provisional fair value assigned to the asset group at the acquisition date.

In addition to adjustments to provisional amounts recognized, the acquirer may determine during the measurement period that it omitted recognition of additional assets or liabilities that existed at the acquisition date. During the measurement period, any such assets or liabilities identified are also to be recognized and measured on a retrospective basis.

In determining adjustments to the provisional amounts assigned to assets and liabilities, management should be alert for interrelationships between recognized assets and liabilities. For example, new information that management obtains that results in an adjustment to the provisional amount assigned to a liability for which the acquiree carries insurance could also result in an adjustment, in whole or in part, to a provisional amount recognized as an asset representing the claim receivable from the insurance carrier. In addition, as discussed in this chapter and Chapter 17, changes in provisional amounts assigned to assets and liabilities frequently will also affect temporary differences between the items' income tax basis and GAAP carrying amount, which in turn will affect the computation of deferred income assets and liabilities.

Adjustments to the provisional amounts that are made during the measurement period are recognized retrospectively as if the accounting for the business combination had actually been completed as of the acquisition date. This will result in the revision of comparative information included in the financial statements for prior periods including any necessary adjustments to depreciation, amortization, or other effects on net income or other comprehensive income related to the adjustments.

The measurement period ends on the earlier of

1. The date management of the acquirer receives the information it seeks regarding facts and circumstances as they existed at the acquisition date or learns that it will be unable to obtain any additional information, *or*
2. One year after the acquisition date.

After the end of the measurement period, the only revisions that are permitted to be made to the initial acquisition date accounting for the business combination are restatements for corrections of prior period errors in accordance with FAS 154, *Accounting Changes and Error Corrections,* discussed in detail in Chapter 5.

**Additional guidance in applying the acquisition method.** Due to the complexity of many business combinations and the varying structures used to effect them, FASB provided supplemental guidance to aid practitioners in applying the standard.

*Business combinations achieved in stages (step acquisitions).* A step acquisition is a business combination in which the acquirer held an equity interest in the acquiree prior to the acquisition date on which it obtained control.

FAS 141(R) requires the acquirer to remeasure its previous holdings of the acquiree's equity at acquisition date fair value. Any gain or loss on remeasurement is recognized in earnings on that date.

If the acquirer had previously recognized changes in the carrying amount of the acquiree's equity in other comprehensive income (e.g., because the investment was classified as available for sale), that amount is to be reclassified and included in the computation of the acquisition date gain or loss from remeasurement.

### Example of a step acquisition.

On 12/31/2008, Finestone Corporation (FC) owns 5% of the 30,000 outstanding voting common shares of Kitzes Industries (KI). On FC's 12/31/2008 balance sheet, it classified its investment in KI as available for sale. On 3/31/2009, FC acquired additional equity shares in KI sufficient to provide FC with a controlling interest in KI and, thus, become KI's parent company.

The following table summarizes FC's initial holdings in KI, the subsequent increase in those holdings, and the computation of the gain on remeasurement at the acquisition date of 3/31/2009:

| Date | # of Shares | Percent interest | Per share Cost | Per share Fair value | Aggregate investment Cost | Aggregate investment Fair value | Unrealized appreciation included in accumulated other comprehensive income |
|------|-------------|------------------|------|------------|-----------|------------|------------|
| 12/31/2008 | 1,500 | 5% | $10 | $16 | $ 15,000 | $ 24,000 | $9,000 |
| 3/31/2009 | 21,000 | 70% | 20 | 20 | 420,000 | 420,000 | |
| | 22,500 | 75% | | | | | |

Computation of gain (loss) on remeasurement at acquisition date:

| | |
|---|---|
| Fair value per share on 4/1/2009 | $ 20 |
| Number of preacquisition shares | × 1,500 |
| Aggregate fair value of preacquisition shares on 4/1/2009 | 30,000 |
| Carrying amount of preacquisition shares on 4/1/2009 | 24,000 |
| Appreciation attributable to the 1st quarter of 2009 | 6,000 |
| Pre-2009 appreciation reclassified from accumulated OCI | 9,000 |
| Gain on remeasurement of KI stock on 3/31/2009 | $ 15,000 |

***Business combinations achieved without the transfer of consideration.*** The reason that FAS 141(R) discontinued use of the term "purchase method" and coined the new term "acquisition method" was to emphasize that a purchase is not the only means by which one entity can obtain control over another entity. Examples of acquisitions that are *not* the result of a purchase transaction include

1. Repurchase by the acquiree of a sufficient amount of its own outstanding shares to enable an existing investor to obtain control and, in effect, become an acquirer.
2. The expiration of minority veto rights where those rights had previously prevented an investor holding the majority of the voting equity from controlling the investee.
3. Execution of a contract between acquirer and acquiree in which the parties agree to combine their businesses without the transfer of consideration and without the acquirer holding any equity interests in the acquiree, either precombination or thereafter. Two variations of this type of business combination are

   a. A stapling arrangement in which two entities agree contractually that each of their respective equity securities be traded or transferred together. The combined securities are referred to as stapled securities because they cannot be traded or transferred independently and market quotations are only available at a single, stapled price.

    b.   A dual-listing company structure (DLC) in which two companies, pursuant to provisions included in their bylaws, articles of incorporation, or articles of association agree to operate as if they were a single economic entity while each retains its separate legal identity. Under a DLC structure, unlike a stapling arrangement, the two companies' shares are traded and quoted separately.

In a business combination achieved solely by contract, the acquirer, in its postcombination financial statements, is to account for the equity interests in the acquiree that it does not hold as a noncontrolling interest in the acquiree. This treatment is required even when it results in 100% of the equity interests in the acquiree being attributed to the noncontrolling interest holders.

    **Changes in the parent's ownership interest in a subsidiary.** Subsequent to a business combination, the parent may increase or decrease its ownership percentage in the acquiree/subsidiary.

    *Changes not affecting control.* The parent company may purchase or sell shares of the subsidiary after the acquisition date without affecting the determination that it controls the subsidiary. In addition, the subsidiary may issue new shares or repurchase some of its own shares as treasury stock or for retirement.

    Changes in the parent's ownership interest that do not affect the determination that the parent retains a controlling financial interest in the subsidiary are accounted for as equity transactions with no gain or loss recognized in consolidated net income or in other comprehensive income. The carrying amount of the noncontrolling interest in the subsidiary is to be adjusted to reflect the change in ownership interest. Any difference between the fair value of the consideration received or paid in the transaction and the amount by which the noncontrolling interest is adjusted is to be recognized in equity attributable to the parent.

    In the case of a subsidiary that has accumulated other comprehensive income (AOCI), if there is a change in the parent's ownership interest, the carrying amount of AOCI is to be adjusted through a corresponding charge or credit to equity attributable to the parent.

    *Changes resulting in loss of control.* If a parent company ceases to have a controlling financial interest in a subsidiary, the parent is required to deconsolidate the subsidiary as of the date on which its control ceased. Examples of situations that can result in a parent being required to deconsolidate a subsidiary include

1.   Sale by the parent of all or a portion of its ownership interest in the subsidiary resulting in the parent no longer holding a controlling financial interest,
2.   Expiration of a contract that granted control of the subsidiary to the parent,
3.   Issuance by the subsidiary of stock that reduces the ownership interest of the parent to a level not representing a controlling financial interest,
4.   Loss of control of the subsidiary by the parent because the subsidiary becomes subject to control by a governmental body, court, administrator, or regulator.

If a parent effects a deconsolidation of a subsidiary through a nonreciprocal transfer to owners such as through a spinoff transaction, the transaction is accounted for under APB 29, *Accounting for Nonmonetary Transactions.* Otherwise, the parent is to account for the deconsolidation by recognizing, in net income, a gain or loss attributable to the parent. The gain or loss is measured as follows:

| FVCR | = | Fair value of consideration received, if any |
|------|---|----------------------------------------------|
| FVNIR | = | Fair value of any noncontrolling investment retained by the former parent at the deconsolidation date |

CVNI   =   Carrying value of the noncontrolling interest in the former subsidiary on the deconsolidation date, including any accumulated other comprehensive income attributable to the noncontrolling interest

CVAL   =   Carrying value of the former subsidiaries assets and liabilities at the deconsolidation date.

(FVCR + FVNIR + CVNI) − CVAL   =   Deconsolidation Gain (Loss)

Should the parent's loss of controlling financial interest occur through two or more transactions, management of the former parent is to consider whether the transactions should be accounted for as a single transaction. In evaluating whether to combine the transactions, management of the former parent is to consider all of the terms and conditions of the transactions as well as their economic impact. The presence of one or more of the following indicators may lead to management concluding that it should account for multiple transactions as a single transaction:

1. The transactions are entered into simultaneously or in contemplation of one another,
2. The transactions, when considered in tandem, are in substance a single transaction designed to achieve an overall commercial objective,
3. The occurrence of one transaction depends on the occurrence of at least one other transaction,
4. One transaction, when considered on its own merits, does not make economic sense, but when considered together with the other transaction or transactions would be considered economically justifiable.

Obviously, this determination requires the exercise of sound judgment and attention to economic substance over legal form.

**Allocation of net income and other comprehensive income to the parent and noncontrolling interest.** In preparing consolidated financial statements, the parent is to eliminate 100% of the intercompany income or loss. This elimination is not affected by the existence of a noncontrolling interest since the consolidated financial statements purport to present the financial position and economic performance of a single economic entity. The elimination of the intercompany income or loss may be allocated between the parent and noncontrolling interests.

Revenues, expenses, gains, losses, net income or loss, and other comprehensive income are to be reported in the consolidated financial statements at the consolidated amounts that include amounts attributable to the owners of the parent company and the noncontrolling interest. Net income or loss, and other comprehensive income or loss, are to be allocated to the parent and the noncontrolling interest.

Losses allocated to the parent and to the noncontrolling interest may exceed their respective interests in the equity of the subsidiary. When this occurs, and if it continues to occur in subsequent periods, the excess as well as any further losses are to continue to be allocated to the parent and noncontrolling interest even if this allocation results in a deficit balance in noncontrolling interest.

## Disclosures

The disclosure requirements of the new standards are quite extensive and, for the reader's convenience, are presented in detail in the disclosure checklist in Appendix A to this publication.

## Other Changes Made by FAS 141(R) and 160

**Variable interest entities (VIEs).** Several important changes have been made that affect VIEs. Additional changes are expected to be forthcoming shortly. FASB has been pursuing a "fast-track" project to reexamine VIE accounting along with accounting for securitized assets and qualified special-purpose entities (QSPE) under FAS 140. FASB is under extreme pressure to act quickly with respect to these matters due to perceptions by regulators and some marketplace participants that these standards may have played a contributory role in the deterioration of credit markets currently being experienced in the US and other parts of the world.

*Terminology.* The new standards amend the definitions of parent and subsidiary to encompass variable interest entities. Thus, the primary beneficiary of a variable interest entity will henceforth be referred to as the parent, and the VIE itself will be referred to as a subsidiary.

*Definition of a business.* The revised definition of a business provided by FAS 141(R) will provide limited simplification in performing the qualitative analysis required by FIN 46(R). More entities are expected to qualify as businesses under the revised definition, but it is still unclear as to the effect, if any, this might have, for example, in decreasing the number of entities that might be required to be consolidated as VIEs.

*Definition of noncontrolling interests.* FIN 46(R), as amended, provides that the term "noncontrolling interests" as used in the context of VIEs has the same meaning as in FAS 160, *Noncontrolling Interests in Consolidated Financial Statements.* FAS 160 defines a noncontrolling interest as the portion of equity (or net assets) in a subsidiary (VIE) that is not directly or indirectly attributable to the parent (primary beneficiary). Thus parent companies of subsidiaries that are variable interest entities will be required, as described earlier in this chapter, to fully record the noncontrolling interest's share of VIE losses even if recording these losses results in a deficit in noncontrolling interest. Further, the consolidated financial statements are to reflect noncontrolling interests as part of the equity section of the balance sheet rather than in liabilities or mezzanine.

*Initial measurement provisions.* The initial measurement provisions of FIN 46(R), as amended, provide that

1. When the primary beneficiary of the VIE and the VIE are under common control, the primary beneficiary is to initially measure the assets, liabilities and noncontrolling interests of the VIE at their carrying amounts in the accounting records of the entity that controls the VIE or the amounts at which they would be carried by the controlling entity if that entity issued GAAP financial statements.

2. When the primary beneficiary of the VIE and the VIE are not under common control

    a. The initial consolidation of a VIE that is a business (as that definition was revised by FAS 141([R]), discussed above, is a business combination transaction and, accordingly, is to be accounted for in accordance with the provisions of FAS 141(R).

    b. If an entity becomes the primary beneficiary of a VIE that is *not* a business

        (1) The primary beneficiary is to initially measure and recognize the assets and liabilities of the VIE, except for goodwill, in accordance with FAS 141(R). However, any assets and liabilities transferred to the VIE by the primary beneficiary at, after, or shortly before the date the entity became the primary beneficiary are to be initially measured at the same amounts at which the assets and liabilities would have been measured if they had not been transferred. No gain or loss is to be recognized as a result of such transfers.

        (2) The primary beneficiary is to recognize a gain or loss for the difference between (a) the fair value of any consideration paid, the fair value of any

noncontrolling interests, and the reported amount of any previously held interests and (b) the net amount of the VIE's identifiable assets and liabilities recognized and measured under the provisions of FAS 141(R). *Goodwill is not to be recognized if the VIE is not a business.*

**Disclosures.** The primary beneficiary (parent) of a VIE (subsidiary) that is a business is required to make all of the applicable informative disclosures required by FAS 141(R). The primary beneficiary of a VIE that is not a business is to disclose (in addition to the other extensive disclosures required by FIN 46[R]) the amount of gain or loss recognized on the initial consolidation of the VIE/subsidiary.

## APPENDIX
## STANDARDS APPLICABLE TO PRE-2009 BUSINESS COMBINATIONS

| | | | | |
|---|---|---|---|---|
| **Sources of GAAP** | | | | |
| *APB* | *ARB* | *FAS* | *FTB* | *EITF* |
| 16, 18, | 51 | 94, 140, | 85-5, | 85-12, 86-32, 87-21, 88-16, 90-5, 90-12, |
| 29 | | 141, 142 | 85-6 | 90-13, 91-5, 93-7, 95-3, 95-8, 96-5, |
| | | | | 96-7, 96-16, 97-2, 97-8, 97-15, 98-1, |
| | | | | 98-3, 99-12, 99-15, 00-4, 01-3, 02-5, 02-11, |
| | | | | 02-17, 04-1, D-54, D-100, D-101 |
| *FIN* | | *FSP* | | *SOP* |
| 46(R) | | 46(R)-1, 46(R)-2, 46(R)-3, | | 03-3 |
| | | 46(R)-4, 46(R)-5 | | |

## DEFINITIONS OF TERMS

**Accounting consolidation.** The process of combining the financial statements of a parent company and one or more legally separate and distinct subsidiaries.

**Acquisition.** One enterprise pays cash, or issues stock or debt, for all or part of the voting stock of another enterprise. The acquired enterprise remains intact as a separate legal entity. The parent-subsidiary relationship is accounted for as a purchase, and it is referred to as an acquisition.

**Combination.** Any transaction whereby one enterprise obtains control over the assets and properties of another enterprise, regardless of the resulting form of the enterprise emerging from the combination transaction.

**Combined financial statements.** Financial statements presenting the financial position and/or results of operations of legally separate entities, related by common ownership, as if they were a single entity.

**Consolidated financial statements.** Consolidated statements presenting, primarily for the benefit of the shareholders and creditors of the parent company, the results of operations and the financial position of a parent company and its subsidiaries essentially as if the group were a single enterprise with one or more branches or divisions.

**Consolidation.** A new enterprise is formed to acquire two or more other enterprises through an exchange of voting stock. The acquired enterprises then cease to exist as separate legal entities.

**Control.** Generally, the ability of one entity to direct the activities of another, so as to accomplish the former entity's objectives. Control may be present even absent majority ownership.

**Controlling financial interest.** The at-risk equity investors hold a controlling financial interest in an entity if they collectively

1. Have voting or similar rights (such as the rights of a common stockholder, general partner, or LLC member) to make decisions, directly or indirectly, about the entity's activities that significantly affect the entity's success.

   *NOTE: If none of the investors hold these rights, this criterion is not satisfied. In addition, if some investors' voting rights are not proportional to their obligations to absorb the entity's expected losses, or to receive the entity's expected residual rewards, or both **and** substantially all of the entity's activities involve or are conducted on behalf of an investor that has disproportionately few voting rights, this criterion is not satisfied.*

2.  Are obligated to absorb the entity's expected losses. If the investors are directly or indirectly protected from these losses or guaranteed a return by the entity (or by other parties involved with the entity), this criterion is not satisfied.

3.  Are entitled to receive the entity's expected residual returns. If the investors' return is limited by (a) the entity's governing documents, (b) arrangements with other variable interest holders (e.g., holders of debt, beneficial interests, etc.) or (c) the entity itself, this criterion is not satisfied.

If any one of these three criteria is absent, the at-risk equity investors collectively lack a controlling financial interest and, therefore, only have a controlling voting interest.

**Entity concept.** A method of preparing consolidated financial statements of a parent and majority-owned subsidiary that involves restatement of net assets of the subsidiary to fair value at the date of acquisition for *both* majority and noncontrolling interests.

**Equity investment.** An interest in an entity that, under GAAP, is reportable as equity on the entity's balance sheet. The practical application of this definition to certain types of instruments (e.g., mandatorily redeemable preferred stock) was affected by the issuance of FAS 150, *Accounting for Certain Financial Instruments with Characteristics of Both Liabilities and Equity.*

**Goodwill.** The excess of the cost of an acquisition price over the fair value of acquired net assets which is recorded as an asset and written down only when, and if, impairment is identified and measured, based on future events and conditions.

**Merger.** One enterprise acquires all of the net assets of one or more other enterprises through an exchange of stock, payment of cash or other property, or the issuance of debt instruments.

**Negative goodwill.** Properly known as the "excess of fair value over cost of acquired net assets." This amount represents the *net* excess of fair value of the net assets of a business acquisition, after allocation as a pro rata reduction of the amounts that otherwise would be assigned to all of the acquired assets other than cash and cash equivalents, trade receivables, inventory, financial instruments that are required to be carried on the balance sheet at fair value, assets to be disposed of by sale, and deferred tax assets. This excess is generally reported as an extraordinary gain in the period in which the business combination is initially recognized, unless the purchase price involves contingent consideration, in which case it is reported as a deferred credit until the contingency is resolved.

**Noncontrolling interest.** Sometimes referred to as minority interest, any remaining outstanding voting stock of a subsidiary not purchased by the acquiring enterprise.

**Parent company concept.** A method of preparing consolidated financial statements of a parent and majority-owned subsidiary that involves restatement of net assets of the subsidiary to fair value at the date of acquisition for *only* the majority interest.

**Preacquisition contingencies.** Uncertainties existing at the date of an acquisition accounted for by the purchase method that, if resolved within one year of the acquisition, result in a reallocation of the purchase price.

**Purchase method.** The accounting method used for a business combination that recognizes that one combining entity was acquired by another. It establishes a new basis of accountability for the acquiree.

**Purchased preacquisition earnings.** An account used to report the earnings of a subsidiary attributable to percentage ownership acquired at the interim date in the current reporting period.

**Related parties and de facto principals and agents.** In determining whether a holder of an interest in a variable interest entity (VIE) is the VIE's primary beneficiary, the holder and its related parties are treated collectively as a single party. For this purpose, FIN 46(R) expands the definition of related parties from FAS 57 to include additional parties that act as "de facto agents or principals" of the variable interest holder including

1.  A party unable to finance its operations without receiving subordinated financial support from the VIE interest holder such as another VIE of which the holder is the primary beneficiary.
2.  A party the received its interests in the VIE as a contribution or loan from the holder.
3.  An officer, employee, or member of the governing board of the holder.
4.  A party that has agreed not to sell, transfer, or encumber its interest in the entity without prior approval of the holder when that agreement could constrain that party's ability to manage the economic risks or realize the economic rewards with respect to its interests in the VIE to which it would otherwise be entitled.
5.  A party with a close business relationship to the holder such as the relationship between a professional service provider (e.g., an attorney, accountant, banker, consultant, etc.) and one of its significant clients.

Upon the application of this related-party attribution rule, if two or more related parties (including de facto agents or principals) hold variable interests in the same VIE for which the parties collectively would be the primary beneficiary, a determination is required of which party will individually be considered the primary beneficiary (i.e., will consolidate the VIE in its financial statements). The party whose activities are most closely associated with the VIE is deemed to be the primary beneficiary. Among the factors that are to be considered when making this determination are

1.  The existence of principal/agency relationships between members of the related-party group.
2.  The significance of the VIE's activities to the members of the related-party group.
3.  The relationship of the members of the related-party group to the VIE's activities.
4.  The exposure of a member of the related-party group to the VIE's expected losses.
5.  The design (structure) of the VIE.

**Subsidiary.** An enterprise that is controlled, directly or indirectly, by another enterprise.

## CONCEPTS, RULES, AND EXAMPLES

### Purchase Accounting under FAS 141

Business combinations (of whatever legal form) involving unrelated entities (i.e., those not under common control), are required to be accounted for using the purchase method of accounting. The only current exceptions to this rule are not-for-profit entities or mutual enterprises, whose consolidation accounting is currently being deliberated by FASB. The long-standing option in US GAAP to treat certain transactions, meeting a series of restrictive criteria, as "poolings of interests "no longer exists for newly transacted business combinations. Purchase accounting is an application of the cost principle, whereby assets obtained are accounted for at the price that was paid (which, in an arm's-length transaction, represents fair value). A purchase transaction gives rise to a new basis of accounting for the purchased assets and liabilities.

Pooling has been banned outright, effective for transactions initiated after June 30, 2001. The use of grossly disparate methods of accounting for what could be almost identical economic transactions was no longer seen as being conceptually defensible, despite widespread use not only in the US but in many other nations as well (although, in recent years, the use of pooling had been sharply curtailed by many nations' accounting standards). Though defended by some (principally publicly held entities that generally were able to structure stock-swap acquisitions and which were often very driven by the desire to avert future goodwill amortization charges that would reduce reported earnings) all transactions must now be accounted for as purchases.

FAS 141, *Business Combinations*, continues the definition of "initiated" originally found in APB 16: it is the earlier of (1) the date that the major terms of a plan, including the ratio of exchange of stock, are announced publicly or otherwise formally made known to the stockholders of any one of the combining companies, or (2) the date that stockholders of a combining company are notified in writing of an exchange offer. Purchase accounting must be used for acquisitions initiated after June 30, 2001. The other provisions of FAS 141 (e.g., strengthened rules for identification and separate recognition of intangibles other than goodwill, discussed later in this chapter) are effective for acquisitions completed after June 30, 2001; thus these requirements are applicable to transactions that may have been initiated earlier.

FAS 141 replaced APB 16, while largely retaining the guidance in that standard pertaining to purchase business combinations. FAS 142, *Goodwill and Other Intangible Assets*, superseded APB 17 and arguably mitigates to a great extent the perceived negative impact of banning pooling by dropping the requirement to amortize goodwill arising from business acquisitions accounted for as purchases. (Goodwill is addressed later in this chapter and also in Chapter 11.)

**Cost allocation, goodwill, and negative goodwill.** The major purchase business combinations accounting issue is how to allocate the purchase cost to the various assets and liabilities acquired. Where the legal form of combination is a merger or consolidation, the acquirer records all the acquired assets and assumed liabilities at their fair values (not the acquired entity's book values). If the actual cost exceeds the fair values of the tangible and identifiable intangible net assets acquired, this excess is recorded as an intangible asset (goodwill). Under FAS 142, goodwill is no longer subject to periodic amortization, but rather, will be subject to periodic evaluation for impairment. It is expected that many, if not most, purchase business combinations will involve the recognition of goodwill.

Requirements for goodwill accounting now differ markedly from what was mandated under the prior rules (APB 17). They also differ from what appeared to be the goal of the FASB's original proposal, under which pooling accounting was to have been eliminated and goodwill arising from purchases was to have been amortized over twenty years or less. At that time, FASB rejected the notion of not subjecting goodwill to periodic amortization, and it noted that the conceptual alternative, conducting periodic assessments of goodwill impairment, would be hindered by the absence of cash flows directly identifiable with goodwill. Nonetheless, faced with strident opposition to the proposed elimination of pooling of interests accounting, FASB first proposed a compromise that would have retained goodwill amortization and reported it "below the line" (i.e., as a nonoperating expense). Ultimately FASB reached an accommodation which eliminated the longstanding requirement to amortize goodwill, substituting impairment testing, which it had earlier said would be unworkable.

Far less common than transactions giving rise to goodwill are "bargain purchases," where the cost of the acquisition is actually less than the fair value of the net assets acquired. Under FAS 142, this deficiency of cost under fair value is first allocated as a pro rata reduction of the amounts that otherwise would be assigned to the acquired assets other than cash and cash equivalents, trade receivables, inventory, financial instruments that are required to be carried on the balance sheet at fair value, assets to be disposed of by sale, and deferred income tax assets.

If the initially recorded amounts of these acquired assets are entirely eliminated, the excess, commonly, if somewhat misleadingly, called "negative goodwill," is generally recognized immediately as an extraordinary gain. In cases in which there are contingent consideration issues (discussed below), however, the negative goodwill will be carried as a deferred credit on the balance sheet, until the contingency is resolved. To the extent that some or all of the contingency has to be settled by the acquirer (i.e., via payment of cash or distribution of other assets), it is charged against this deferred credit, with any ultimate remaining balance being reported as a gain.

*NOTE: Under prior GAAP, the offset was against all noncurrent assets, other than marketable securities, with any residual being deferred and amortized in the manner of positive goodwill. In practical terms, the new requirement is very close to the superseded one.*

The logical foundation for gain recognition in bargain purchases is the belief that the very act of consummating the acquisition gives rise to income. This contradicts the principle that income results only from the use of assets, not their mere purchase. However, if care is given to accurate measurement of fair values, and the bargain is of such a great magnitude (unlikely to occur, in reality) that the allocated fair values of most noncurrent assets is entirely offset by the negative goodwill, with an excess yet remaining, then a gain has probably indeed been achieved by the acquirer. By giving this residual gain prominence in the income statement by requiring that it be categorized as extraordinary, rather than included in operations or in other income, the risk of misleading users of the financial statements is reduced.

**Accounting for mergers.** If the acquisition form of combination is used, the acquired entity maintains a separate legal and accounting existence and all assets and liabilities remain, in the records of the acquiree, at their premerger book values. However, when an accounting consolidation is performed (i.e., when consolidated financial statements are prepared), exactly the same results are obtained as those outlined above (i.e., assets and liabilities are adjusted to fair values, and goodwill is recorded). In terms of how the parent-level (i.e., consolidated) financial statements are presented, there is absolutely no difference between acquisition combinations and outright mergers.

When less than 100% of the stock of the acquired entity is owned by the acquirer, a complication arises in the preparation of consolidated statements, and a noncontrolling interest (discussed below) must be computed.

When one entity is acquired by another, whether by outright merger or via a stock holding, a distinguishing characteristic of the purchase accounting method is that none of the equity accounts of the acquired entity (including its retained earnings) will appear on the acquirer's accounting records or on the consolidated financial statements. In other words, ownership interests of the acquired entity's shareholders are not continued after the merger, consolidation, or combination (acquisition) takes place.

In some transactions there is a continuity of ownership, as when, for example, shareholders in one entity exchange their shares for stock of the other (acquiring) entity. Previously, if a number of restrictive conditions were met, these transactions would be accounted for as poolings of interests, and (with some limitations) the equity of both combining enterprises would be carried forward to the postcombination balance sheets. Despite the appearance of being "mergers of equals," however, the vast preponderance of these transactions were acquisitions of one entity by the other. Under current GAAP, pooling accounting has been eliminated, and the acquiree's equity accounts cannot be carried forward under any circumstances.

In determining which entity is the acquirer in transactions involving two or more enterprises, the new standard stresses that consideration be given to all pertinent facts, with emphasis on the relative voting rights in the combined enterprise and the composition of the board of directors and the senior management of the combined enterprise. In determining which of the shareholder groups retained or received the larger portion of the voting rights in the combined enterprise, the existence of any major voting blocks, unusual or special voting arrangements, and options, warrants, or convertible securities needs to be considered. Even if a new enterprise is formed to issue stock to effect a business combination (sometimes referred to as a consolidation), one of the existing combining enterprises must, on the basis of the evidence available, be deemed the acquirer.

**Determining fair values.** The purchase method requires that a determination be made of the fair value of each of the acquired company's identifiable tangible and intangible assets and of each of its liabilities, as of the date of combination. The determination of these fair values is crucial for proper application of the purchase method. FAS 141 carried forward the guidance previously found in APB 16, with some elaboration. The list below indicates how this is to be accomplished for various assets and liabilities.

1. Marketable securities—Fair values, which, for trading and available for sale securities, are already reflected in the acquiree's balance sheet
2. Receivables—Present values of amounts to be received determined by using current interest rates, less allowances for uncollectible accounts and collection costs, if applicable
3. Inventories

    a. Finished goods and merchandise inventories—Estimated selling prices less the sum of the costs of disposal and a normal profit
    b. Work in process inventories—Estimated selling prices less the sum of the costs of completion, costs of disposal, and a normal profit
    c. Raw material inventories—Current replacement cost

4. Property, plant, and equipment

    a. If expected to be used in operations—Current replacement costs for similar capacity unless the expected future use of the assets indicates a lower value to the acquirer
    b. If expected to be sold—Fair value less cost to sell

5. Identifiable intangible assets and other assets (such as land, natural resources, and nonmarketable securities)—Appraised (fair) value
6. Liabilities (such as notes and accounts payable, long-term debt, warranties, claims payable)—Present value of amounts to be paid determined at appropriate current interest rates
7. Single-employer defined benefit pension plans—Liabilities for a projected benefit obligation (PBO) in excess of the fair value of plan assets (or, conversely, assets representing the fair value of plant assets in excess of PBO) are to be determined pursuant to FAS 87, *Employers' Accounting for Pensions*
8. Single-employer defined benefit postretirement plans—Liabilities for accumulated postretirement benefit obligations (APBO) in excess of the fair value of plan assets (or, conversely, assets representing the fair value of plan assets in excess of APBO) are to be determined pursuant to FAS 106, *Employers' Accounting for Postretirement Benefits other than Pensions*

FASB Statement 157, *Fair Value Measurements,* offers detailed guidance on the criteria to be employed in determining fair values in a variety of applications, including purchase business combinations. A key provision of the standard is the elimination of any entity-specific valuations (e.g., unique value in use to the acquiring entity), in favor of objectively determinable valuations (e.g., relying upon market-based values). This standard is discussed in detail in Chapter 6.

**In-process research and development.** One of the more controversial items, from an accounting perspective, that might be acquired in business combinations is "in-process research and development." As business acquisitions increasingly are consummated in order to obtain intangible assets possessed by acquirees, this matter has been more commonly encountered, and the apparent inconsistency between GAAP requirements and the motivations for such transactions has been the subject of much debate. Currently, FASB is considering changes to extant requirements that would have a significant impact, as described below.

Under longstanding GAAP, research and development costs (R&D) must be expensed as incurred. This requirement, which dates to the mid-1970's, was imposed in recognition of the great difficulty in assessing the value retained after R&D expenditures are made. Before these rules, many entities capitalized a wide range of intangibles resulting from R&D, only to periodically have to acknowledge the impairment or utter worthlessness of accumulated costs via a large, and unwelcome, charge against earnings. Under US GAAP, therefore, both research and development costs must be fully expensed as incurred; no deferral is permitted.

As an alternative to engaging in its own research and/or development, an acquirer can purchase another entity that has previously incurred and expensed substantial sums for research and development. These transactions are increasingly encountered; in some instances, much or most of the price paid for the acquisition is for the value of the acquiree's previous R&D efforts. To preclude capitalization of these indirect R&D expenditures, FIN 4 clearly states that the acquirer must expense that portion of the purchase price since, were this to be recorded as an acquired asset, it would create a "back door" for R&D capitalization which is prohibited by FAS 2.

While the traditional concern had been that acquiring entities would attempt to capitalize in-process research and development, in more recent years the opposite situation has more frequently arisen; that is, excessive portions of purchase premiums were attributed to in-process research and development and then immediately expensed, thereby reducing the allocation to goodwill and averting future amortization charges. With the new "no amortization" requirement, the expectation is that the motivation for exaggerated allocations to in-process research and development will abate. However, the new standard emphasizes again that appropriate allocation of the purchase cost to in-process research and development is required, and that this must be immediately expensed by the acquiring entity.

While in-process research and development costs must be expensed immediately upon acquisition, under current GAAP (but see below for discussion of possible changes), the value of this R&D continues to play an important financial reporting role due to the new requirement that goodwill be regularly tested for impairment. Specifically, under the provisions of FAS 142, a determination must be made of the implied fair value of goodwill, which is compared to the recorded amount of goodwill for purposes of ascertaining whether, and by how much, goodwill has been impaired. The process, which is identical to the purchase price allocation procedure used in a purchase business combination, involves the allocation of the overall fair value of a reporting unit to all assets and liabilities and unrecognized intangibles (including in-process R&D) as if the unit had been acquired as of the date of the impairment test.

Thus, the value of in-process R&D remains of vital concern to those responsible for accurate financial reporting as long as goodwill remains a recognized asset. Only to the extent that there is an excess of the aggregate fair value over amounts assigned to individual assets/liabilities will there be an implied fair value of goodwill. Were the analysis not done in this manner, the entire (and overstated) residual amount would be allocated to goodwill, which logically would not be truly comparable to the recorded amount of the goodwill, thereby impeding the impairment testing of goodwill.

### Example

Purchaser Corp. acquired Attractive Co. in 2007 for $3.4 million. The purchase price was properly allocated to assets acquired and liabilities assumed, including an allocation of $240,000 to in-process R&D, which was properly expensed as of the acquisition date. A residual value of $500,000 was assigned to goodwill. The operations of the former Attractive Co. became a separate reporting unit within the consolidated company.

In 2008, to test for possible impairment, Purchaser management assessed the fair value of the former Attractive Co. operations—using information about comparable operations and economic characteristics, including market multiples of earnings—at $2.75 million. As of that date, the recorded (book) value of the reporting unit's net assets, excluding goodwill, was $2,400,000, and goodwill continued at its original $500,000 recorded value. Because the estimated fair value of the reporting unit is less than its book value, FAS 142 requires the computation of the fair values of the individual assets and liabilities of the reporting unit to determine if its goodwill is impaired.

Management assigns an aggregate fair value of $2.4 million to the net identifiable tangible and intangible assets excluding goodwill, and also estimates that the in-process R&D has an economic (fair) value of $210,000. Since the residual fair value, [$2.75 million less ($2.4 million + $210,000) = $140,000], is less than the recorded amount of goodwill ($500,000), an impairment of ($500,000 – $140,000 =) $360,000 must be recognized by Purchaser Corp. as an operating expense in 2008.

Note that had the fair value of acquired in-process R&D, $210,000, been excluded from the foregoing analysis, the residual fair value would have been computed as $2.75 million – $2.4 million = $350,000; in that case, since recorded goodwill was $500,000, the impairment of goodwill would have only been $150,000. This result would have been erroneous because it would have ignored a real, albeit unrecognized, asset of the reporting unit (i.e., the in-process R&D). This would result in overstating goodwill by the $210,000 of in-process R&D, recognizing and erroneously captioning an asset for which such recognition is prohibited by GAAP.

**Identifying all intangibles.** Prior to undertaking the purchase price allocation, the acquiring enterprise must review the purchase consideration, if other than cash, to ensure that it has been appropriately valued. It must also carefully identify all of the assets acquired and liabilities assumed, including intangible assets. As the move to a "knowledge-based economy" accelerates, an increasing share of the purchase cost for business acquisitions will pertain to intangible assets, adding to valuation challenges as time goes on.

Intangibles cannot expediently be classified as part of goodwill, as was often done under prior standards, since the newly prescribed treatment for goodwill is not mirrored in the accounting for other intangibles. An identifiable intangible asset will be recognized separately from goodwill if it meets the asset recognition criteria in CON 5, and if either (1) control over the future economic benefits of the asset results from contractual or other legal rights (referred to as the "legal/contractual" criterion) or (2) the intangible asset is capable of being separated or divided and sold, transferred, licensed, rented, or exchanged (referred to as the "separability" criterion). Furthermore, even if the intangible asset cannot be sold, transferred, licensed, rented, or exchanged individually, it would still meet the separability criterion if it could be sold, transferred, licensed, rented, or exchanged along with a related contract, asset, or liability.

FAS 141 lists the intangibles to be separately recognized, along with the terms over which amortization is generally to be applied, with certain exceptions for those intangibles having indefinite lives, such as perpetually renewable broadcast licenses, which are maintained at cost (subject to potential impairment write-downs) until a finite life can be ascertained, if ever. These intangibles generally fall into one of a set of categories, such as customer- or market-based assets (e.g., customer lists, newspaper mastheads, and trade-marked brand names); contract-based assets (e.g., covenants not to compete, broadcast rights); artistic-based assets (e.g., plays, other literary works, musical compositions); and technology-based assets (e.g., title plant, databases, computer software). Except for indefinite life intangibles, identifiable intangibles are to be amortized over their estimated useful lives, defined as the period over which the intangible asset is expected to directly or indirectly generate cash flows for the entity. (See Chapter 11 for a complete discussion.)

The standards demand that all identifiable assets acquired and liabilities assumed in a business combination, whether or not recorded separately in the financial statements of the acquired enterprise, are to be assigned a portion of the total cost of the acquisition, based on their respective fair values as of the date of acquisition. Fair value—the amount a seller would receive on the open market (as per FAS 140) for the asset—will not necessarily correspond to the perceived value to the acquirer, based on the acquirer's planned use of the asset, which was the implicit cost allocation basis under the now-superseded APB 16. A hierarchy of methods available for the determination of fair value is outlined in FASB Statement 157, *Fair Value Measurements*, but interestingly, the income tax basis of an asset or liability is not to be considered in determining its fair value. Given that the residual asset, goodwill, will not be amortized and thus might (unless impaired) remain on the balance sheet indefinitely, the emphasis on accurate and complete valuation of all other identifiable intangibles, which are subject to amortization, is necessary to prevent goodwill's overstatement.

**Duplicate assets and assets to be disposed of.** While all assets are to be carefully evaluated, it is equally important to note that assets having no value are to be assigned no allocated cost. A typical example arises when facilities of the acquired entity duplicate those of the acquirer and accordingly are to be disposed of. The cost allocated to these facilities is equal to the estimated net salvage value, zero if no salvage value is expected, or a negative amount equal to the estimated costs of disposal, if warranted. The EITF has approved the allocation of "holding costs" to assets to be disposed of when debt from the business acquisition is to be paid down from the proceeds of such asset sales. In effect, the value assigned to such assets to be sold is the present value of the estimated selling price; interest incurred on debt used to finance these assets is then charged to the asset rather than to interest expense until the disposition actually occurs. On the other hand, if facilities of the acquired entity duplicate and are superior to facilities of the purchaser, with the intention that the latter will be disposed of, fair value must be allocated to the former. Eventual disposition of the redundant facilities of the acquirer may later result in a recognized gain or loss. This would fall into the general category of indirect costs of acquisition, which are not capitalizable or allocable to assets acquired in the purchase business combination.

The EITF has reached a similar conclusion with regard to entire subsidiaries of acquired entities (EITF 87-11 and 90-6). In such situations, the expected cash flows from the subsidiary's operations, through the expected date of disposition (but not longer than one year from the acquisition date), are considered in the purchase price allocation process. Ideally, operations of the subsidiary, including the cost of borrowed funds, if relevant, will not impact the acquirer's income statement, absent changes in estimates or altered plans for its disposition. Failure to achieve the planned disposition within one year, however, will result in all further operating results, including borrowing costs, being reported in the consolidated statement of income for future periods. Any difference between the subsidiary's carrying value at the disposition date and the proceeds of the disposition is treated as a re-allocation of the original purchase price of the business combination. If, however, the difference arises from identifiable events that occur after the merger date, gain or loss is reported at the disposition date.

**Income tax accounting implications of purchase business combinations.** Accounting for the income tax implications of purchase business combinations changed substantially with the issuance of FAS 109. Prior to that, any existing deferred income tax benefits or liabilities of the acquired entity, or any deferred income tax effects created by the purchase transaction itself (e.g., due to different income tax and financial reporting bases of the acquired assets or liabilities), were not recognized as such in the postacquisition consolidated balance sheet of the acquirer. Instead, these income tax effects were deemed to be components of the valuation process whereby the total purchase cost was allocated to the acquired identifiable assets and liabilities and, when necessary, to goodwill or negative goodwill. Accordingly, purchased assets and liabilities were recorded on a net-of-tax basis under APB 16.

Under FAS 109, the net-of-tax method was eliminated. Instead, asset and liability fair values are assigned "gross," and income tax effects, if any, are recorded as deferred income tax assets and/or liabilities. Under the FAS 109 "asset and liability" approach to deferred income tax accounting (detailed in Chapter 17), deferred income tax assets and liabilities are computed and adjusted at the date of each balance sheet. Therefore, any deferred income taxes of an acquired entity, or any deferred income taxes generated by the acquisition transaction itself, are recognized in recording the purchase business combination.

**Other costs of business combinations.** Direct costs of a business acquisition (e.g., finders' fees) are part of the cost to be allocated to tangible and intangible assets, including goodwill. However, stock registration and related expenses are offset against the proceeds (credits) of the stock issuance. Indirect costs are simply expensed in the period when the combination is effected. (Note, however, that likely revisions to acquisition accounting promised by FASB for mid-2007 in its forthcoming Statement, *Business Combinations*, will require that acquisition costs be expensed immediately, and will prohibit adding these to capitalized costs, since these costs add no value to the combined entity and thus fail to meet the criteria for asset recognition.)

In some instances, there are alternative ways to handle certain costs, influencing their treatment as either direct or indirect costs of a business acquisition. For example, if a prospective acquiree company has employee stock options outstanding that were being accounted for under now-superseded APB 25, and it pays the employees to settle the options prior to the acquisition, then (per APB 25, as later interpreted by the EITF in 84-13 and 85-45) compensation expense must be recognized. On the other hand, if the employees exercise their options and then have their shares purchased by the acquirer (or exchanged for stock in the acquirer), there is no compensation expense, but instead this is reported as an additional cost of the purchase.

Costs related to a takeover defense by a prospective acquiree company are not capitalized, but are expenses of the period incurred. However, the EITF has suggested that if the costs are related to a "going private" transaction, these expenses may be classified as an extraordinary item in the statement of income.

In some takeover defense strategies, a target company will repurchase some of its own shares, generally at a price higher than that being offered by the prospective acquirer. Although generally the cost of repurchased stock is simply charged to treasury stock, there is the recognition that excessive repurchase costs are not always related to the "fair value" of the stock. When the price paid explicitly contains consideration for the seller's agreement not to purchase any further shares (a "standstill agreement"), this excess cost must be expensed (per FTB 85-6), with only the fair value of the shares themselves being charged to the treasury stock account. The EITF did not reach a consensus about the treatment of excessive costs of treasury shares absent explicit payment for other services. However, the SEC favors expensing any excess costs. As a general rule, judgment should be applied in evaluating each circumstance.

### Example of purchase transaction—goodwill

Jorie Corp. acquired all of the common stock of Balkin Boiler Manufacturing Co. on January 2, 2007, at a cost of $32 million, consisting of $15 million in cash and the balance represented by a long-term note to former Balkin stockholders.  As of January 2, 2007, immediately prior to the transaction, Balkin's balance sheet is as follows, with both book and fair values indicated ($000 omitted):

|  | Book value | Fair value |  | Book value | Fair value |
|---|---|---|---|---|---|
| Cash | $ 1,000 | $ 1,000 | Current liabilities | $26,200 | $26,200 |
| Accounts receivable, net | 12,200 | 12,000 | Long-term debt | 46,000 | 41,500 |
| Inventory | 8,500 | 9,750 | Guarantee of debt | -- | 75 |
| Other current assets | 500 | 500 |  |  |  |
| Property, plant, and equipment, net | 38,500 | 52,400 |  |  |  |
| Customer list | -- | 1,400 |  |  |  |
| Patents | 2,400 | 3,900 |  |  |  |
| In-process research and development | -- | 8,600 | Stockholders' equity (deficit) | (9,100) | 21,775 |
| Totals | $63,100 | $89,550 |  | $63,100 | $89,550 |

The fair value of inventory exceeded the corresponding book value because Balkin had been using LIFO for many years to cost its inventory, and actual replacement cost was therefore somewhat higher than carrying value at the date of the acquisition.  The long-term debt's fair value was slightly lower than carrying value (cost) because the debt carries a fixed interest rate and the market rates have risen since the debt was incurred.  Consequently, Balkin benefits economically by having future debt service requirements that are less than they would be if it were to borrow at current rates.  Conversely, of course, the fair value of the lender's note receivable has declined since it now represents a loan payable at less than market rates.  Finally, the fair value of Balkin's receivables have also declined from their carrying amount, due to both the higher market rates of interest and to the greater risk of uncollectibility because of the change in ownership.  The higher interest rates impact the valuation in two ways: (1) when computing the discounted present value of the amounts to be received, the higher interest rate reduces the computed present value, and (2) the higher interest rates may serve as an incentive for customers to delay payments to Balkin rather than borrow the money to repay the receivables, with that delay resulting in cash flows being received later than anticipated thus causing the present value to decline.

Balkin's customer list has been appraised at $1.4 million and is a major reason for the company's acquisition by Jorie.  Having been internally developed over many years, the customer list is not recorded as an asset by Balkin, however.  The patents have been amortized down to $2.4 million in Balkin's accounting records, consistent with GAAP, but an appraisal finds that on a fair value basis the value is somewhat higher.

Similarly, property, plant, and equipment has been depreciated down to a book value of $38.5 million, but has been appraised at a sound value (that is, replacement cost new adjusted for the fraction of the useful life already elapsed) of $52.4 million.

A key asset being acquired by Jorie, albeit one not formally recognized by Balkin, is the in-process research and development (IPR&D), which pertains to activities undertaken over a period of several years aimed at making significant process and product improvements which would enhance Balkin's market position and will be captured by the new combined operations.  It has been determined that duplicating the benefits of this ongoing R&D work would cost Jorie $8.6 million.  The strong motivation to make this acquisition, and to pay a substantial premium over book value, is based on Balkin's customer list and its IPR&D.  Balkin has previously expensed all R&D costs incurred, as required under FAS 2.

Balkin had guaranteed a $1.5 million bank debt of a former affiliated entity, but this was an "off the books" event since, under FIN 45, guarantees issued between corporations under common control are exempt from recognition.  The actual contingent obligation has been appraised as having a fair value (considering both the amount and likelihood of having to honor the commitment) of $75,000.

Thus, although Balkin's balance sheet reflects a stockholders' deficit (including the par value of common stock issued and outstanding, additional paid-in capital, and accumulated deficit) of $9.1 million, the value of the acquisition, including the IPR&D, is much higher. The preliminary computation of goodwill is as follows:

| | | |
|---|---:|---:|
| Purchase price | | $32,000,000 |
| Net working capital | $(2,950,000) | |
| Property, plant, and equipment | 52,400,000 | |
| Customer list | 1,400,000 | |
| Patents | 3,900,000 | |
| In-process research and development | 8,600,000 | |
| Guarantee of indebtedness of others | (75,000) | |
| Long-term debt | (41,500,000) | 21,775,000 |
| Goodwill (excess of cost over fair value) | | $10,225,000 |

Under FIN 4, the fair value allocated to the in-process research and development must be immediately expensed. All other assets and liabilities are recorded by Jorie at the allocated fair values, with the excess cost being assigned to goodwill. The entry to record the purchase (for preparation of consolidated financial statements, for example) is as follows:

| | | |
|---|---:|---:|
| Cash | 1,000,000 | |
| Accounts receivable, net | 12,000,000 | |
| Inventory | 9,750,000 | |
| Other current assets | 500,000 | |
| Property, plant, and equipment | 52,400,000 | |
| Customer list | 1,400,000 | |
| Patents | 3,900,000 | |
| Goodwill | 10,225,000 | |
| Research and development expense | 8,600,000 | |
| Current liabilities | | 26,200,000 |
| Guarantee of indebtedness of others | | 75,000 |
| Long-term debt | | 41,500,000 |
| Notes payable to former stockholders | | 17,000,000 |
| Cash | | 15,000,000 |

Note that, while the foregoing example is for a stock acquisition, an asset and liability acquisition would be accounted for in the exact same manner. Also, since the debt is recorded at fair value, which will often differ from face (maturity) value, the resulting differential (premium or discount) must be amortized using the effective yield method from acquisition date to the maturity date of the debt, and thus there will be differences between actual payments of interest and the amounts recognized in the income statements as interest expense. Finally, note that property, plant, and equipment is recorded "net"—that is, the allocated fair value becomes the "cost" of these assets; accumulated depreciation previously recorded in the accounting records of the acquired entity does not carry forward to the postacquisition financial statements of the consolidated entity.

**Example of purchase transaction—negative goodwill**

Haglund Corp. acquires, on March 4, 2008, all the capital stock of Foster Co. for $800,000 in cash. A formerly successful enterprise, Foster had recently suffered from declining sales and demands for repayment of its outstanding bank debt, which were threatening its continued existence. Haglund management perceived an opportunity to make a favorable purchase of a company operating in a related line of business, and accordingly made this modest offer, which was accepted by the stockholders of Foster, the acquiree. Foster's balance sheet at the date of acquisition is as follows, with both book and fair values indicated ($000 omitted):

|  | Book value | Fair value |  | Book value | Fair value |
|---|---|---|---|---|---|
| Cash | $ 800 | $ 800 | Current liabilities | $ 2,875 | $ 2,875 |
| Accounts receivable, net | 3,600 | 3,400 | Long-term debt | 11,155 | 11,155 |
| Inventory | 1,850 | 1,800 |  |  |  |
| Property, plant, and equipment | 6,800 | 7,200 | Stockholders' equity |  |  |
| Net operating loss carryforwards | -- | 2,400 | (deficit) | (980) | 1,570 |
| Totals | $13,050 | $15,600 |  | $13,050 | $15,600 |

Foster had provided a valuation allowance for the deferred income tax asset attributable to the net operating loss carryforward benefit, since recurring and increasing losses made it more likely than not that these benefits would not be realized, consistent with GAAP (FAS 109). Haglund Corp., which is highly profitable, is in the same line of business, and intends to continue Foster's operations, expects to be able to realize these benefits, and therefore will have no valuation allowance against this asset.

Thus, although Foster's balance sheet reflects a stockholders' deficit (including outstanding common stock, additional paid-in capital and accumulated deficit) of $980,000, the value of the acquisition is much higher, and furthermore the acquirer is able to negotiate a bargain purchase. The preliminary computation of negative goodwill is as follows:

| Net working capital | $ 3,125,000 |  |
|---|---|---|
| Property, plant, and equipment | 7,200,000 |  |
| Net operating loss carryforward | 2,400,000 |  |
| Long-term debt | (11,155,000) | 1,570,000 |
| Purchase price |  | 800,000 |
| Negative goodwill (excess of fair value over cost) |  | $ 770,000 |

Under FAS 141, the negative goodwill is first used to offset all acquired assets other than cash and cash equivalents, trade receivables, inventory, financial instruments that are required to be carried on the balance sheet at fair value, assets to be disposed of by sale, and deferred income tax assets, on a pro rata basis. In the present instance, only the property, plant, and equipment are available for this offsetting (the NOL benefits are equivalent to deferred income tax assets under FAS 109; see further discussion in Chapter 17). The entry to record the purchase before allocating negative goodwill is therefore as follows:

| Cash | 800,000 |  |
|---|---|---|
| Accounts receivable, net | 3,400,000 |  |
| Inventory | 1,800,000 |  |
| Property, plant, and equipment | 7,200,000 |  |
| Deferred income tax asset | 2,400,000 |  |
| Current liabilities |  | 2,875,000 |
| Long-term debt |  | 11,155,000 |
| Cash |  | 800,000 |
| Negative goodwill |  | 770,000 |

The entry to record the offsetting of the negative goodwill is as follows:

| Negative goodwill | 770,000 |  |
|---|---|---|
| Property, plant, and equipment, net |  | 770,000 |

Since the negative goodwill is fully absorbed by the property, plant, and equipment, there will be no residual to recognize in earnings.

### Example of purchase transaction—excess negative goodwill

The facts are similar to the immediately preceding example, except that Foster Co.'s long-term debt amounts to only $3,155,000 (book and fair values) as of the date of the acquisition transaction. This results in such a large amount of negative goodwill that an excess remains after property, plant, and equipment are reduced to zero. This excess negative goodwill is reported in the period in which the acquisition occurs as an extraordinary gain.

Foster's balance sheet at the date of acquisition is as follows, with both book and fair values indicated ($000 omitted):

|  | Book Value | Fair Value |  | Book Value | Fair Value |
|---|---|---|---|---|---|
| Cash | $ 800 | $ 800 | Current liabilities | $ 2,875 | $ 2,875 |
| Accounts receivable, net | 3,600 | 3,400 | Long-term debt | 3,155 | 3,155 |
| Inventory | 1,850 | 1,800 |  |  |  |
| Property, plant, and equipment, net | 6,800 | 7,200 |  |  |  |
| Net operating loss carryforwards | -- | 2,400 | Stockholders' equity | 7,020 | 9,570 |
| Totals | $13,050 | $15,600 |  | $13,050 | $15,600 |

The preliminary computation of negative goodwill is as follows:

| Net working capital | $3,125,000 |  |
|---|---|---|
| Property, plant, and equipment | 7,200,000 |  |
| Net operating loss carryforward | 2,400,000 |  |
| Long-term debt | (3,155,000) | 9,570,000 |
| Purchase price |  | 800,000 |
| Negative goodwill (excess of fair value over cost) |  | $8,770,000 |

The entry to record the purchase before allocating negative goodwill is therefore as follows:

| Cash | 800,000 |  |
|---|---|---|
| Accounts receivable, net | 3,400,000 |  |
| Inventory | 1,800,000 |  |
| Property, plant, and equipment | 7,200,000 |  |
| Deferred income tax asset | 2,400,000 |  |
| Current liabilities |  | 2,875,000 |
| Long-term debt |  | 3,155,000 |
| Cash |  | 800,000 |
| Negative goodwill |  | 8,770,000 |

The entry to record the offsetting of the negative goodwill is as follows:

| Negative goodwill | 8,770,000 |  |
|---|---|---|
| Property, plant, and equipment, net |  | 7,200,000 |
| Extraordinary item—gain on purchase |  | 1,570,000 |

Since the negative goodwill is not fully absorbed by the property, plant, and equipment, there will be a residual to recognize in earnings. Under GAAP, this is presented as an extraordinary item (net of the related income tax effects, not computed here) in the income statement.

However, if the transaction provided for a contingent purchase price (e.g., based on meeting earnings targets over the next several years), the excess negative goodwill ($1,570,000 in this example) would be recorded on the balance sheet as a deferred credit, not subject to amortization, until the contingency was resolved. To the extent an increase in the purchase price resulted, that would reduce (or, at the extreme, fully eliminate) the negative goodwill. Any remaining negative goodwill after the contingent purchase price has been resolved will be reported in the period of final resolution as an extraordinary gain.

## Determining if an Acquisition Is a Business Combination

Before applying FAS 141 it is necessary to conclude that the acquisition constitutes a business, as opposed to being a group of productive assets. EITF 98-3 addresses this particular issue and offers a set of criteria, all of which must be met in order for the acquiree to meet the definition of a business. A business is defined as

*...a self-sustaining integrated set of activities and assets conducted and managed for the purpose of providing a return to investors. A business consists of (a) inputs, (b) processes applied to those inputs, and (c) resulting outputs that are used to generate revenues. For a transferred set of activities and assets to be deemed a business, it must contain all of the inputs and processes necessary for it to continue to conduct normal operations after the transferred set is separated from the transferor, which includes the ability to sustain a revenue stream by providing its outputs to customers.*

According to EITF 98-3, the necessary inputs include (1) long-lived assets, including intangible assets, or right to the use of long-lived assets; (2) intellectual property; (3) the ability to obtain access to necessary materials or rights; and (4) employees. Note that the presence of intellectual property does not necessarily imply that intangible assets had been recognized for financial reporting purposes by the acquiree, and in many cases intangibles might not even be assigned values by the acquirer applying FAS 141.

Processes represent the existence of systems, standards, protocols, conventions, and rules that act to define the processes necessary for normal, self-sustaining operations, such as (1) strategic management processes, (2) operational processes, and (3) resource management processes.

Outputs are the ability to obtain access to the customers that purchase the outputs of the transferred set.

According to EITF 98-3, a transferred set of activities and assets fails the definition of a business if it excludes one or more of the above items such that it is not possible for the set to continue normal operations and sustain a revenue stream by providing its products and/or services to customers. Exclusion of minor items that does not prevent the transferred set from continuing normal operations does not prevent classification of the acquired assets and activities as a business. The assessment of whether excluded items are only minor should be made without regard to the attributes of the transferee and should consider such factors as the uniqueness or scarcity of the missing element, the time frame, the level of effort, and the cost required to obtain the missing element. If goodwill is present in a transferred set of activities and assets, it should be presumed that the excluded items are minor and that the transferred set is a business, since goodwill is associated with an ongoing business and not with individual productive assets.

Importantly, the assessment of whether a transferred set of assets and operations constitutes a business should be made without regard to how the acquirer intends to use the transferred set. It is not relevant whether the transferee will actually operate the transferred set of assets and operations on a stand-alone basis or intends to continue using the transferred set in the same manner as did the transferor. The acquired operations can be restructured, integrated with the acquirer's operations, and reengineered in various ways without interfering with the determination that it was a business combination, if all criteria are satisfied.

There is also no threshold for numbers of individual assets to be obtained to qualify as a business. However, EITF 98-3 notes that if essentially all but a *de minimis* amount of the fair value of the transferred set of activities and assets is represented by a single tangible or identifiable intangible asset, the concentration of value is an indicator that an asset rather than a business is being received. It cites 3% as being a working definition of *de minimis*.

As described by EITF 98-3, the actual determination of whether a transferred set of assets and activities is or is not a business is a three-step process. These are

1. Identify the elements included in the transferred set of assets and activities.
2. Compare the identified elements in the transferred set to the complete set of elements necessary for the transferred set to conduct normal operations, to identify any missing elements.
3. If there are missing elements, make an assessment as to whether the missing elements lead to a conclusion that the transferred set is not a business. That assessment is based on the degree of difficulty or the level of investment (relative to the fair value of the transferred set) necessary to obtain access to or to acquire the missing elements.

If the degree of difficulty and level of investment necessary to obtain access to or to acquire the missing elements are not significant, the missing elements may be deemed minor, thus not impeding classification as a business acquisition. The determination requires the exercise of judgment and is dependent on the particular facts and circumstances. EITF 98-3 offers a series of illustrative examples to suggest how to apply the three-step test to determine if an acquisition is a business combination or merely the purchase of assets.

The provisions in EITF 98-3 as they relate to nonmonetary exchanges of similar productive assets under APB 29 have been nullified by FAS 153, *Exchanges of Nonmonetary Assets,* which became effective for exchanges of nonmonetary assets occurring in fiscal periods beginning after June 15, 2005.

### Goodwill

**Identifiable and unidentifiable intangible assets.** Ending the acceptability of pooling of interests accounting was accompanied by an even more fundamental change in the accounting for goodwill. FASB first prepared to demand accelerating amortization of goodwill over a period shorter than the previously permitted forty years while precluding impairment testing, but then changed its mind and decided to prohibit any form of amortization in favor of the formerly rejected intermittent testing for impairment—and thus an entirely new methodology was introduced.

The asset commonly known as goodwill is a subset of the broader subject, intangible asset accounting. FAS 142 addresses the accounting for all intangibles and raises the bar for delineating among different types of intangibles (i.e., distinguishing those separately identifiable intangibles having finite lives, those arguably having indefinite lives, and goodwill, which is unique in being "unidentifiable" and having an indeterminate life which makes periodic amortization impossible, in the FASB's current view). Chapter 11 discusses intangibles other than goodwill in great detail. Accordingly, this subject will only be addressed in the present chapter to the extent that the recognition and measurement of identifiable intangibles acquired in a purchase business combination impacts upon the measurement of goodwill, which is normally understood as being the residual asset after the assignment of purchase cost to all other assets and liabilities.

CON 5, *Recognition and Measurement in Financial Statements of Business Enterprises,* states that an asset is recognized if it meets the definition of an asset (found in CON 6, *Elements of Financial Statements*), has a relevant attribute measurable with sufficient reliability, and the information about it is representationally faithful, verifiable, neutral (i.e., it is reliable), and capable of making a difference in user decisions (i.e., it is relevant). In a business acquisition, any acquired identifiable intangible asset (e.g., patents, customer lists, etc.) must be recognized separately from goodwill when it meets these CON 5 asset recognition criteria, and additionally meets either of the following two criteria:

1. *Legal/contractual*—Control over the future economic benefits of the asset results from contractual or other legal rights (regardless of whether those rights are transferable or separable from other rights and obligations), or
2. *Separability*—The asset is capable of being separated or divided and sold, transferred, licensed, rented, or exchanged (regardless of whether there is an intent to do so or whether a market currently exists for that asset)—or, if it cannot be individually sold, etc., it is capable of being sold, transferred, licensed, rented or exchanged along with a related contract, asset, or liability.

All intangible assets acquired from other enterprises or individuals, whether singly, in groups, or as part of a business combination, are recognized initially and are measured based on their respective fair values. (Note that the initially determined fair value may be reduced in the case of business combinations with which negative goodwill is associated, as illustrated above.) Under the provisions of FAS 142, serious effort must be directed to identifying the various intangibles acquired.

**Useful economic life.**  Reliably measurable identifiable intangible assets, with the exception of those meeting the criteria for nonamortization (explained below), must be amortized over their respective useful economic lives.  Useful economic life is the period over which the asset is expected to contribute (whether directly or indirectly) to cash flows of the entity.  Factors to be considered in estimating the useful economic life of an intangible asset to an enterprise include

1.  Legal, regulatory, or contractual provisions that may limit the maximum useful life;
2.  Legal, regulatory, or contractual provisions that may enable renewal or extension of the asset's legal or contractual life (provided there is evidence to support renewal or extension without substantial cost and without materially modifying the original terms);
3.  The effects of obsolescence, demand, competition, and other economic factors (such as the stability of the industry, the rate of technological change, expected changes in distribution channels, and the existence of uncertainty over future legal and/or regulatory changes);
4.  The expected useful life of assets or groups of assets of the enterprise to which the useful life of the asset may parallel (such as mineral rights to depleting assets);
5.  The expected use of the intangible asset by the enterprise; and
6.  The level of maintenance expenditure required to obtain the expected future economic benefits from the asset.

In those instances where an intangible asset is determined to have an indefinite useful economic life, it will not be amortized until its life is determined to be finite at a later date.  An example of such an asset would be a broadcast license, expiring in five years, but which may be renewed indefinitely at little cost.  If the acquirer intends to renew the license indefinitely, and there is evidence to support its ability to do so, and the cash flows related to that license are expected to continue indefinitely, then no amortization would be recognized until such time as these criteria are no longer met.

**Residual value.**  Typically, the entire fair value assigned to an intangible asset will be subject to amortization, although in some instances a residual value may be determined, which reduces the amortizable basis.  The residual value of an amortizable intangible is assumed to be zero unless the useful life to the acquiring enterprise is shorter than the intangible asset's useful economic life, and either (1) the acquiring enterprise has a commitment from a third party to purchase the asset at the end of its useful life, or (2) the residual value can be determined by reference to an observable market for that asset and that market is expected to exist at the end of the asset's useful life.  The method of amortization is to reflect the pattern in which the economic benefits of the intangible asset are to be consumed; absent the ability to ascertain this, straight-line amortization is applied.  However, if impairment (determined by application of the FAS 144 criteria) is later determined, the carrying amount will be written down to the impaired amount.

**Allocation to goodwill.**  After completing the purchase price allocation, any residual of cost over fair value of the net identifiable assets and liabilities is assigned to the unidentifiable asset, goodwill.  Formerly subject to mandatory amortization, this now is not permitted to be amortized at all, by any allocation scheme and over any useful life.  Impairment testing, using a methodology at variance with that set forth in FAS 144 (which, however, continues in effect for all other types of long-lived assets and intangibles other than goodwill), must be applied periodically, and any computed impairment will be presented as a separate line item in that period's income statement, as a component of income from continuing operations (unless associated with discontinued operations, in which case, the impairment would, net of income tax effects, be combined with the remaining effects of the discontinued operations).

If all other acquired assets have been identified (including, at the moment the transactions occurs, in-process research and development, which is then immediately expensed) and properly valued, by process of elimination. The remaining excess purchase price can be assigned to no asset other than goodwill.

The decision to eliminate the requirement for amortization was based on the recognition that any assigned useful life would be entirely arbitrary. The FASB recognized that not all goodwill declines in value and that any decline in value would rarely occur on a straight-line basis. Furthermore, FASB found during its field testing of the revised proposal that the estimation (albeit, indirectly) of future cash flows associated with goodwill (which is critical to implementation of an impairment testing approach) was feasible, contrary to earlier doubts. Finally, elimination of periodic amortization charges against earnings was a political price the FASB was willing to pay in order to secure its primary goal, elimination of the pooling-of-interests method of accounting for business combinations.

**Impairment of goodwill.** Given the decision to end the practice of amortization of goodwill, it became necessary to develop a mechanism for ensuring that the amount presented in the financial statements would not exceed the goodwill's estimated fair value at any point in time. This goal is generally consistent with the rules underlying those governing the balance sheet presentation of other long-lived assets.

For example, unlike tangible fixed assets, goodwill is impossible to separately identify and, if the ongoing business is successful, will tend to regenerate itself or be replaced by new internally generated goodwill. Historically, of course, goodwill could only achieve financial statement recognition in the limited situation of being purchased (i.e., internally generated goodwill was not recognizable for financial reporting purposes). However, any strategy for testing for impairment will inevitably be confounded by the existence, along with the purchased goodwill, of internally generated goodwill created subsequent to the date of the business combination. FASB concluded that it would be impossible to track "acquisition-specific" goodwill for impairment testing purposes and accordingly endorsed a major departure from the traditional prohibition against recognition of internally generated intangibles. This approach still results in an inconsistency, however, since only entities that have purchased goodwill in the past will be permitted to recognize the internally generated replacement goodwill to avoid impairment write-downs. Entities that internally generate goodwill but that have not entered into prior purchase business combinations are still prohibited from capitalizing that new goodwill and from presenting it as an asset on their balance sheets.

The impairment testing approach endorsed by FAS 142 reasons that "anomalies that result from the differences in how acquired goodwill and internally generated goodwill are accounted for...justify a departure from the current model of accounting." Thus, it concluded, as long as the total goodwill identifiable with the "reporting unit" to which acquisition-based goodwill was assigned can be shown to have a fair value exceeding the book value of the goodwill arising from the acquisition (which means apples are to be compared with oranges), no impairment will be found. This represents a major departure from prior accounting practice.

A reporting unit is defined in FAS 142 as an operating segment or a component of an operating segment that is one level below the operating segment as a whole. In order for a component to be considered a reporting unit it must

1. Constitute a business as defined in EITF 98-3, *Determining Whether a Nonmonetary Transaction Involves Receipt of Productive Assets or of a Business*, and
2. Have available discrete financial information regarding its operating results that is regularly reviewed by segment management.

A reporting unit is defined by reference to an operating segment, which is a term used in FAS 131. This definition applies equally to publicly held and privately held companies, even though nonpublic entities are exempted from reporting segment information.

Chapter 2, in the section entitled, "Alternative Balance Sheet Segmentation," provides a diagram of how an organizational structure could be analyzed to determine its reporting units and provides definitional guidance regarding terminology used in the authoritative GAAP literature.

**Measurement procedures for impairment.** FASB recognized that goodwill impairment testing could not be effected by the same mechanical approach as FAS 144 sets forth for other long-lived assets. The reason is that the potentially very long-enduring cash flows emanating from goodwill would obviate the usefulness of FAS 144's "undiscounted cash flows" threshold test for impairment. In other words, it is computationally impossible to forecast undiscounted cash flows from the use and eventual disposition of an asset that has an indefinite life. In essence, the cash flows would continue into perpetuity and, thus, goodwill would never be deemed to be impaired.

Accordingly, FASB devised a unique impairment testing protocol for goodwill. Since direct measurement of the fair value of goodwill is clearly impossible, FASB concluded that a method similar to the method of allocating the purchase price to the net assets acquired in a business combination would be used to indirectly measure the value of goodwill subsequent to its acquisition date. Thus, it decided that the fair value of the net assets of a reporting unit be subtracted from the fair value of that reporting unit to determine the implied fair value of goodwill.

The fair value of the net assets of the reporting unit can be measured in a variety of ways. Direct market observation, as outlined in FAS 157, *Fair Value Measurements,* is certainly the most objective method, but in the absence of that information, other techniques can be substituted. CON 7 sets forth an "expected present value technique" which uses the sum of probability-weighted present values in a range of estimated cash flows adjusted for risk, all discounted using the same interest rate convention. FASB has indicated that such a technique is a more effective measurement tool than was the traditional present value approach, especially in situations in which the timing or the amount of estimated cash flows is uncertain, as is the case in measuring nonfinancial assets and liabilities.

In order to operationalize an approach that incorporates the values of the recognized assets and liabilities, the FASB concluded that all of the assets and liabilities of an acquired entity (including goodwill) that will be used in the operations of a reporting unit would be allocated to that reporting unit as of the acquisition date. For many business entities, this required changes to internal management accounting: for example, many of them had not previously allocated liabilities such as pension and environmental obligations below the corporate or entity level. To the extent these liabilities relate to one or more reporting unit or units, they are now included in the determination of the fair value of the recognized net assets of that unit or units.

Under FAS 131, the standard that sets forth the segment reporting required of publicly held corporations, "corporate" assets and liabilities are not assigned to any operating segment. Goodwill had often been included in these unallocated corporate assets. The impairment testing process, however, could not proceed if a similar approach were adhered to, and accordingly under FAS 142 goodwill and all other related assets and liabilities are assigned to reporting units for purposes of testing goodwill for impairment. The amount of goodwill allocated to each segment is required to be disclosed in the notes to the financial statements of publicly held enterprises.

Goodwill impairment testing is a two-step process (as is impairment testing under FAS 144, although these two standards differ fundamentally in their respective approaches). In the first step, the possibility of impairment is assessed by comparing the fair value of the "reporting unit" taken as a whole to its carrying (book) value. If the fair value of the reporting unit exceeds its book value, there is no need for further analysis, since no impairment will be found to have occurred.

If, however, the carrying value exceeds fair value, a second step must be performed to indicate whether goodwill is impaired and, it if is impaired, by how much. In the second step, the recorded goodwill is compared to its implied fair value, computed in the same manner as when completing a business combination's "purchase price allocation." Thus, the fair value of the reporting unit is allocated to all the unit's assets and liabilities (including any unrecognized intangibles, according to the standard, even though this raises a question of noncomparability with book value), including, as a residual, goodwill. If the amount thus assigned to goodwill (its implied fair value) is less than its carrying value, the excess book value must be written off as an impairment expense. No other adjustments are to be made to the carrying values of any of the reporting unit's other assets or liabilities.

Unlike FAS 144's impairment measurement requirements, which use net (i.e., discounted) present values (or, when there is uncertainty regarding amounts or timing of future cash flows, probability-weighted expected present values) to actually measure the magnitude of any indicated impairment, the goodwill impairment approach uses a pseudo–purchase price allocation methodology. Implicitly, of course, the present value of future cash flow estimation techniques described above are incorporated in the impairment model, since the overall fair value of the reporting unit, and the fair values of some or all of the individual assets and liabilities, may be measured using these techniques.

**Initial assessment of goodwill's fair value.** In order to facilitate periodic assessments of possible impairment, it is necessary that a "benchmark assessment" be made. This benchmark assessment is performed in conjunction with most significant acquisitions, regardless of how much goodwill arises from that acquisition. Similarly, a benchmark assessment is performed in conjunction with a reorganization of an entity's reporting structure.

The benchmark assessment involves identifying the valuation model to be used, documenting key assumptions, and measuring the fair value of the reporting unit. In determining how goodwill is to be assigned to "reporting units," a reasonable and supportable approach must be adopted. In general, goodwill is assigned consistent with previous recognition of goodwill and with the reporting units to which the acquired assets and liabilities had been assigned. Goodwill assigned to a reporting unit is measured by the difference between the fair value of the entire reporting unit and the collective sum of the fair values of the reporting unit's assets, net of its liabilities.

In practice, consideration of the "synergistic" effects of business acquisitions may also be necessary (i.e., if other reporting units are expected to benefit from an acquired reporting unit, some or all of the acquired goodwill might be assignable to the other units). For example, a purchase may give a division of the acquirer access to a market niche benefiting one of its existing operating units, even if all the tangible and other intangible assets are assigned to other parts of the enterprise. If the goodwill allocation is based on the existence of such synergies, a "with and without" calculation is then used (i.e., it will be necessary to compare the fair value of the reporting unit before the acquisition to that after it).

Goodwill may also be split among two or more reporting units of the acquirer. Any allocation method used is to be consistently applied and the logic for doing so documented.

While it may be costly to accomplish, this benchmark assessment is necessary to ensure that the entity has identified and documented all key assumptions and tested the outputs of the selected valuation model for reasonableness prior to actually testing goodwill for impairment. Furthermore, measuring the fair value of the reporting unit as part of the benchmark assessment will provide management with a "reality check" on whether the amount of goodwill assigned to the reporting unit is reasonable, by comparing the fair value of the reporting unit with its carrying (book) value. If the fair value of the reporting unit is found to be less than its carrying amount, the goodwill allocation methodology should be reassessed, and the selected valuation model and the assumptions underpinning the initial valuation critically reexamined. In those cases where the indicated fair value of the reporting unit is still less than its carrying amount, goodwill would be tested for impairment.

Under FAS 142, a two-step testing protocol is prescribed. The first step is to compare the reporting unit's carrying amount (book value) to the unit's fair value. If fair value exceeds carrying value, there is no impairment and no need for further analysis. On the other hand, if carrying value exceeds estimated fair value, it becomes necessary to formally test for impairment; that is, to apply the second step as described in the following section.

**Ongoing testing for impairment of goodwill.** FASB's original intent was to mandate goodwill impairment testing on an "events and circumstances" basis, similar to the approach used in FAS 144 for depreciable or amortizable long-lived assets. This approach was discarded in favor of a requirement for annual impairment testing, although interim testing also remains necessary when an event or circumstance occurs between annual tests that suggests that the fair value of a reporting unit might have declined below its carrying value. Examples of such occurrences include an adverse change in the business climate or market, a legal factor, an action by regulators, the introduction of new competition, or a loss of key personnel. Goodwill is also required to be tested for impairment on an interim basis when it is deemed "more likely than not" that a reporting unit or a significant portion of a reporting unit will be sold or otherwise disposed of, and furthermore, when a significant asset group within a reporting unit is required to be reviewed for recoverability because of the events and circumstances triggers included in FAS 144. Annual testing, however, is not triggered by such circumstances, but rather, is required in all cases.

The SEC has indicated that it will likely raise concerns if a registrant is found to have frequently changed the date of its annual goodwill impairment test, especially if it appears that the change in testing dates has been made with the intent of accelerating or delaying an impairment charge.

Assuming the step-one analysis (comparing fair value to carrying value for any reporting unit which includes goodwill) reveals the possibility of impairment, the step-two exercise, impairment testing, must be performed. Because of the nature of goodwill, FASB rejected the use of the impairment testing technique of FAS 121 (which was later superseded by the similar FAS 144) and instead crafted a unique methodology.

The two-step testing regime requires as the first step that a threshold test be applied: is the fair value of the reporting unit greater than, or less than, its carrying value? If the fair value is lower than the carrying value, impairment is suggested. The impairment, however, is not validly measured by the shortfall computed in step one, because to do so would effectively be to adjust the carrying value of the entire reporting unit to the lower of cost or market.

Under FAS 142, impairment is the condition that exists when the carrying amount of goodwill exceeds its implied fair value. Implied fair value, in turn, is the excess of the fair value of a reporting unit as a whole over the individual fair values assigned to its assets and liabilities. Once the fair value of a reporting unit is determined, the fair value of the goodwill component of that unit's net assets must be computed; this is then compared to the carrying value of that goodwill, to ascertain if any impairment loss is to be recognized. For the purpose of making this determination, fair value of a reporting unit is the amount at which the unit as a whole could be bought or sold in a current transaction between willing parties.

The second step of the process is as follows:

1.  It is necessary to allocate the fair value of the reporting unit to all assets and liabilities, and to any unrecognized intangibles (including in-process R&D), as if the unit had been acquired at the measurement date. Any excess of fair value over amounts assigned to net assets (including the unrecognized assets such as in-process research and development) is the implied fair value of goodwill.
2.  The implied fair value of goodwill is compared to its carrying amount (book value). If the carrying amount of the goodwill is greater than its implied fair value, a write-down of the carrying amount is required. Once written down, goodwill cannot later be written back up, even if later tests show that the fair value has recovered and exceeds carrying value.

### Example of goodwill impairment testing

Armand Heavy Industries is a holding company that has two reporting units that were acquired as wholly owned subsidiaries consequent to purchase business combinations after the effective date of FAS 142. Armand's relevant reporting units are Bardige Diesel Engines and Ciarcia Transmissions. Upon acquisition of the two businesses (which are operated as subsidiaries), Armand recorded the assets and liabilities at fair values and recognized the excess of the purchase prices over these assigned fair values as goodwill.

At December 31, 2008, the carrying values of the assets and liabilities are as follows:

|  | *(Amounts in millions)* | |
| --- | --- | --- |
|  | *Bardige Diesel* | *Ciarcia Transmissions* |
| Cash | $ 20 | $ 10 |
| Accounts receivable | 100 | 20 |
| Inventories | 10 | 700 |
| Land, buildings, and equipment | 1,400 | 1,800 |
| Identifiable intangibles | 300 | 0 |
| Goodwill | 400 | 200 |
| Accounts payable | (80) | (300) |
| Long-term debt | (300) | (400) |
| Totals | $1,850 | $2,030 |

Summary income statement information for the two companies for the year ended December 31, 2008, is as follows:

|  | *(Amounts in millions)* | |
| --- | --- | --- |
|  | *Bardige Diesel* | *Ciarcia Transmissions* |
| Revenues | $1,000 | $800 |
| Pre-tax income | $ 200 | $120 |
| Net income | $ 120 | $ 30 |

It is Armand's policy to perform its annual goodwill impairment testing for both reporting units as of December 31.

The following data is available, at reasonable cost, to management of Armand:

### Bardige Diesel

There are no comparable publicly held companies that have similar economic characteristics to this operation. However, management is able to develop reasonably supportable estimates of expected future cash flows associated with the group of assets. That computation yielded a fair value for Bardige Diesel of $1,700.

### Ciarcia Transmissions

A competitor of Ciarcia Transmissions, the Gaffen Gearbox Company, is publicly held and traded on the NASDAQ. Its stock has consistently sold at a multiple of 3 times revenues. Management of Armand Heavy Industries believes that the stock price is fairly representative of the fair value of Gaffen Gearbox, and accordingly that using the multiple in assessing the value of Ciarcia will result in a fair estimate.

| | *(Amounts in millions)* | |
|---|---|---|
| | *Bardige Diesel* | *Ciarcia Transmissions* |
| Fair value of reporting unit | $1,700 | $2,400 |
| Carrying amount of reporting unit including goodwill | 1,850 | 2,030 |
| Fair value over (under) carrying value | $ (150) | $ 370 |

Step 1—Test for potential impairment. Compare fair value of the reporting unit to its carrying amount, including goodwill.

   a.  In the case of Bardige Diesel, the carrying amount exceeds the fair value of the reporting unit, and thus the goodwill of this reporting unit must be tested further to determine whether it is impaired.
   b.  In the case of Ciarcia Transmissions, the fair value of the reporting unit exceeds the carrying value, and thus the goodwill of this reporting unit is not impaired and no further testing is required.

Step 2—Measure the amount of the impairment loss. For Bardige Diesel, management used the guidance in FAS 141 on business combinations and computed the implied value of goodwill and resulting impairment loss as follows:

| | *(Amounts in millions)* | |
|---|---|---|
| | *Carrying value* | *Fair value* |
| Cash | $ 20 | $ 20 |
| Accounts receivable | 100 | 90 |
| Inventories | 10 | 8 |
| Land, buildings, and equipment | 1,400 | 1,200 |
| In-process research and development | -- | 100 |
| Identifiable intangibles | 300 | 350 |
| Customer lists | -- | 100 |
| Goodwill | 400 | NA |
| Accounts payable | (80) | (80) |
| Long-term debt | (300) | (280) |
| Total (net) carrying value | $1,850 | |
| Total (net) fair value assigned to assets and liabilities | | 1,508 |
| Fair value of reporting unit | | 1,700 |
| Implied fair value of goodwill | | 192 |
| Carrying value of goodwill | | 400 |
| Impairment loss | | $ 208 |

As indicated above, Ciarcia Transmissions does not have to proceed to Step 2 because its goodwill was found in Step 1 not to be impaired.

**Circumstances under which detailed annual testing may be waived.** Obviously, annual assessments of impairment can become very extended, and possibly expensive, exercises. In recognition of this fact, the FASB prescribed limited circumstances in which the risk of impairment would be quite low, and therefore the fair value of each reporting unit would not have to be recomputed in a year when they apply. To qualify for this exception, there must not have been changes to the components of the reporting unit since the previous fair value computation; when last measured, the fair value amount must have exceeded the carrying amount of the reporting unit by a substantial margin; and there must be no evidence to suggest that the current fair value of the reporting unit may be less than its current carrying amount.

**Timing of annual testing.** The annual impairment tests need not be performed at fiscal year-ends. Instead, the fair value measurement for each reporting unit could be performed any time during the fiscal year, as long as that measurement date is used consistently from year to year. Different measurement dates can be used for different reporting units. Once elected, however, a reporting unit's annual impairment measurement date is not permitted to be changed.

### Other impairment testing considerations.

*Impairment of identifiable long-lived assets.* Testing for impairment of goodwill in accordance with FAS 142 may intersect with evaluating long-lived assets for impairment, as prescribed by FAS 144. GAAP requires that assets other than goodwill be evaluated for impairment first, and any adjustments necessitated by this evaluation made before testing for goodwill impairment. In some cases, possible impairment of long-lived assets may only be discovered as the goodwill impairment testing is progressing; in such instances, the goodwill impairment testing is ceased and other impairment issues fully addressed before returning to the goodwill impairment testing procedures.

#### Example—Evaluation of other assets necessitated by goodwill impairment testing

Using the same facts as given above for Armand Heavy Industries, the step two comparison of fair values to carrying values yielded a fair value of land, buildings, and equipment of $1,200 which is less than the carrying value of those assets. FAS 144 (as discussed in detail in Chapter 11) requires management to evaluate whether the carrying values of long-lived assets are recoverable when events or changes in circumstances indicate that this may be in doubt. One of the triggering events given as an example in FAS 144 is a significant decrease in the market price of a long-lived asset or asset group. Therefore, since this factor is present, management is required to evaluate the recoverability of those assets.

Management ceased its goodwill impairment testing and estimated the future cash flows (without discounting) from using and disposing of its long-lived assets (which consisted of a single asset group) and determined that these future cash flows aggregated $1,500,000 for the remaining estimated useful lives of the assets. The following comparison was made to the assets' carrying values:

| | |
|---|---:|
| Future cash flows over remaining estimated lives from use and disposition | $1,500,000 |
| Carrying value | 1,400,000 |
| Excess (deficiency) of cash flows over carrying value | $ 100,000 |

Note the following anomalies that arise from this set of facts:

1. Because the gross, undiscounted cash flows from use and disposition of the asset group exceed the carrying value of the asset group, the group is not considered to be impaired even though its fair value has declined below its carrying value.
2. If the amount of the estimated future cash flows had been even slightly below the carrying value, say $1,390,000, the assets would be considered impaired.
3. If the assets were determined to be impaired, the carrying value would be required to be written down to fair value, which in this example is $1,200,000, and this write-down would be recognized prior to the resumption of goodwill impairment testing.

**Tiered structures.** Another possibly complicating factor is the existence of "tiered" structures, with goodwill reflected in the financial statements of a subsidiary entity. In such a circumstance, it is necessary to test for goodwill impairment at the subsidiary reporting unit level in the same manner as goodwill is tested by the parent entity. This subsidiary level test must to be made prior to making the test at the parent company level. If an impairment loss is recognized at the subsidiary level, consideration must be given to the question of whether it is "more likely than not" that the event that gave rise to the impairment loss at the subsidiary level would also reduce the fair value of the consolidated reporting unit or units in which the subsidiary's reporting unit with impaired goodwill resides, to an amount below its carrying amounts. If this is deemed not "more likely than not" to have occurred, then there is no need to test further. On the other hand, if it is deemed to be "more likely than not" that a fair value deficit might also impact the consolidated reporting unit(s), then there is a need to test for impairment at the consolidated reporting unit level. It is possible for the subsidiary to recognize an impairment loss but for the consolidated reporting unit not to recognize a further loss—if the excess fair value of the other operations included in the consolidated reporting unit effectively offsets the deficit value flowing from the subsidiary's portion of that unit.

**Display of goodwill and of goodwill impairment.** The aggregate amount of goodwill is to be presented as a separate line item in the statement of financial position (balance sheet). Traditionally, in classified balance sheets, goodwill is an "other" noncurrent asset, distinguished from property, plant, and equipment.

The aggregate amount of goodwill impairment losses is generally to be presented as a separate line item in the operating section of the income statement. The exception to this rule is when the goodwill impairment loss is associated with a discontinued operation, in which case the impairment loss will be included, on a net-of-tax basis, within the results of discontinued operations. The portion of goodwill associated with net assets to be disposed of is recognized as part of the gain or loss on disposal and is not included in the calculation of impairment loss.

Disclosures about business combinations are to include the primary reason for the acquisition, including a description of the factors that contributed to a purchase price that reflects a premium that results in recognition of goodwill or a discount that results in recognition of an extraordinary gain (negative goodwill). If goodwill is material in relation to the total cost of a business acquisition, disclosure is required of the amount of acquired goodwill. The amount of acquired goodwill related to each segment (only for those entities that are required to report segment information) and the amount of acquired goodwill that is deductible for income tax purposes must also be disclosed.

For each period for which a balance sheet is presented, the notes to the financial statements must disclose the changes in the carrying amount of goodwill during the period. This must include the amount of goodwill acquired, the amount of impairment loss recognized, and the amount of goodwill included in the gain or loss on disposal of all or a portion of a reporting unit. For publicly held entities, this information is to be provided for each segment, and disclosure is to be made of any significant changes in the allocation of goodwill by segment.

For each goodwill impairment loss recognized, disclosure must be made of the following information: a description of the facts and circumstances leading to the impairment; a description of the reporting unit for which the impairment loss is recognized, the adjusted carrying amount of goodwill of that reporting unit, and the amount of the impairment loss; if applicable, the fact that the impairment loss is an estimate that has not yet been finalized, with the reasons therefore and, in subsequent periods, the nature and amount of any significant adjustments made to the initial estimate of the impairment loss; and, when salient, the segment to which the impaired goodwill pertains.

In the period in which an excess over cost related to an acquisition (i.e., negative goodwill) is recognized as an extraordinary gain, it will be shown net of income tax, as set forth by APB 30.

**Special requirements for disposal of segments or other operations containing goodwill.** When a significant portion of a reporting unit is disposed of, goodwill is allocated based on the relative fair values of the portion of the reporting unit being disposed of and the portion of the reporting unit remaining. An impairment test of the goodwill in the remaining (i.e., not disposed of) portion of the reporting unit would be required after the allocation of goodwill to ensure that the reporting unit can support the remaining goodwill.

Goodwill is allocated to a portion of a reporting unit being disposed of only when that portion constitutes a business. However, the allocation approach is not to be used when the business being disposed of is not classified as held-for-sale and was never integrated into the reporting unit. In that scenario, since the operating unit's identity and the original goodwill are still intact, all of the goodwill associated with that business would be included in the determination of the gain or loss on disposal.

The relative fair value allocation approach is also used to determine how goodwill is to be allocated when an entity reorganizes its reporting structure.

**Other impairment considerations.** In some instances a reporting unit may consist of multiple asset groups, and an event might occur that would necessitate an evaluation to determine if the carrying values of some, but not all, long-lived assets of that reporting unit are fully recoverable, per FAS 144. In between required annual goodwill impairment tests, that same event that triggered the recoverability review of an asset group under FAS 144, might or might not require an interim impairment test of reporting unit goodwill, since the criteria differ between the two pertinent standards. Under FAS 142, should a recoverability review be required for a significant asset group within the reporting unit, management must assess whether the triggering event would, more likely than not, also result in a reduction of the fair value of that reporting unit.

Under FAS 142, the reporting unit is the unit of measurement for goodwill, and thus the reporting unit is the lowest level of assets with which goodwill can be associated. Therefore, goodwill cannot be associated with lower-level asset groups, and there is no need to allocate or otherwise associate reporting unit goodwill with asset groups when those assets are tested for impairment.

### Example of the interrelationship between FAS 142 and FAS 144

By reference to the Chapter 2 diagram, "Alternative Balance Sheet Segmentation," the Parent Holding Company's (PHC) Subsidiaries 5 and 6 include two asset groups. PHC's last annual goodwill impairment testing date for Subsidiaries 5 and 6 was November 30, 2007. At March 31, 2008, an evaluation for recoverability is required for Asset Group (j) due to the incurrence of an operating loss for business ix that contains those assets coupled with the forecasted continuation of such losses for the foreseeable future. When PHC initially made the benchmark assessment of its goodwill and allocated the portion of goodwill that relates to reporting unit (5), all of that goodwill was related to Business viii, which is a self-contained asset group whose assets are not required to be reviewed for recoverability at March 31, 2008, and which has significantly outperformed the expectations that PHC originally had for it upon its initial acquisition. Consequently, management believes it unlikely that the poor financial results of business ix which contains Asset Group (j) would result in a reduction in the fair value of the reporting unit as a whole to an amount below its carrying value. Consequently, it is not necessary for PHC to perform a goodwill impairment test at March 31, 2008.

Goodwill may be an asset of a consolidated subsidiary, and the subsidiary may also prepare and present financial statements on a stand-alone basis (for example, to provide to creditors of, and noncontrolling stockholders in, that subsidiary). The subsidiary might constitute part of a reporting unit at the parent company level (by reference to the Chapter 2 diagram captioned "Alternative Balance Sheet Segmentation," for example, this is the case with Subsidiary 5). Per FAS 142, impairment must be tested annually at the subsidiary level when stand-alone financial statements of the subsidiary are produced, whether the subsidiary is publicly held or private. As discussed earlier, for consolidated financial reporting purposes, an impairment loss at the subsidiary level would not automatically be "pushed up," but testing for impairment at the level of the parent's reporting unit that contains that subsidiary would require consideration due to the indicator of possible impairment. If management considers it more likely than not that the goodwill impairment loss recognized by the subsidiary that is a component of a reporting unit would reduce the fair value of that reporting unit to an amount less than its carrying amount, then the goodwill of that reporting unit is to be tested for impairment at the date the subsidiary recognizes its goodwill impairment loss. Upon testing, however, it might be the case that impairment would be found not to exist; this would be the result of the reporting unit's fair value exceeding its carrying value, probably because other component parts of that reporting unit had appreciated in value, thereby offsetting the reduction in value of the subsidiary.

## Noncontrolling Interests

When a company acquires some, but not all, of the voting stock of another entity, the shares held by third parties represent a minority or noncontrolling interest in the acquired company. This occurs when the acquisition form of business combination is employed. A legal merger or consolidation would give the acquirer a 100% interest in whatever assets it obtained from the selling entity. Under GAAP, if a parent company owns more than half of another entity (majority ownership creating presumptive control), the two are generally to be consolidated for financial statement purposes. The only remaining exception to this rule occurs when the parent company does not have control over the subsidiary, such as in situations where the subsidiary is in bankruptcy or reorganization, or subject to severe restrictions imposed by a domestic or foreign government. The noncontrolling interest in the assets and earnings of the consolidated entity must also be accounted for, however.

When consolidated statements are prepared, the full amount of assets and liabilities (in the balance sheet) and income and expenses (in the income statement) of the subsidiary are generally presented. Accordingly, offsetting amounts must be shown for the portion of these items that does not belong to the parent company. In the balance sheet this offset is normally a credit shown as a separate caption in stockholders' equity, representing the noncontrolling interest in consolidated net assets equal to the noncontrolling percentage ownership in the net assets of the subsidiary, based on preacquisition book values. (Note that a likely forthcoming FASB pronouncement, *Business Combinations*, will require that all net assets be restated to fair value upon a business combination, including the noncontrolling interest's portion, in a departure from current practice.)

Some entities choose to present minority (noncontrolling) interest between liabilities and stockholders' equity; however CON 6, *Elements of Financial Statements*, points out that such noncontrolling interests do not meet the definition of a liability and that they represent residual interests in components of the consolidated entity. (Likely future pronouncements from FASB will require that noncontrolling interests be reported only in the equity section.)

Although less likely, a debit balance in noncontrolling interest could result when the subsidiary has a deficit in its stockholders' equity and when there is reason to believe that the noncontrolling owners will make additional capital contributions to erase that deficit. This situation sometimes occurs where the entities are closely held and the noncontrolling owners are related parties having other business relationships with the parent company and/or its stockholders. In most other circumstances, a debit in noncontrolling interest would be charged against parent company retained earnings under the concept that the loss will be borne by that company. Although some believe that this debit should be added to goodwill on the consolidated balance sheet instead, it might be difficult to demonstrate that this would not result in an overstatement of total assets.

In the income statement, the noncontrolling interest in the income (or loss) of a consolidated subsidiary is shown as a deduction from (or an addition to) consolidated net income. As above, if the noncontrolling interest in the net assets of the subsidiary has already been reduced to zero, and if a net debit noncontrolling interest will not be recorded (the usual case), then the noncontrolling interest in any further losses is also not recorded. (However, this must be explained in the notes to the financial statements.) Furthermore, if past noncontrolling losses have not been recorded, the noncontrolling interest in current profits will not be recognized until the aggregate of such profits equals the aggregate unrecognized losses. This closely parallels the rule for equity method accounting recognition of profits and losses.

Under current GAAP (FAS 141) goodwill arising from a purchase of less than 100% of the acquiree is valued at the difference between the purchase price paid by the acquirer and the acquirer's proportionate share of the fair values of the identifiable net assets acquired. The computational approach used to implement the parent company theory is called the partial goodwill method. Under this method, the noncontrolling interest is reported based on the book value of the subsidiary. (Note that under provisions of the forthcoming *Business Combinations* standard for the application of purchase accounting, this accounting will be superseded by a complete adoption of fair value accounting for partial business combinations, under which the acquired entity will be fully revalued at fair value, including recognition of the noncontrolling interest's share of identifiable net assets and implied goodwill.)

An example of currently applicable accounting procedures follows:

On January 1, 2008, Andes Company acquires a 90% interest in Baker Company in exchange for 5,400 shares of its $10 par value stock having a total market value of $120,600.

Details regarding the book values and fair values of the net assets acquired are as follows:

| Item | Book value (BV) | Fair value (FV) | Difference between BV and FV |
|------|-----------------|-----------------|------------------------------|
| Cash | $ 37,400 | $ 37,400 | $ -- |
| Accounts receivable (net) | 9,100 | 9,100 | -- |
| Inventories | 16,100 | 17,100 | 1,000 |
| Equipment | 50,000 | 60,000 | 10,000 |
| Accumulated depreciation | (10,000) | (12,000) | (2,000) |
| Patents | 10,000 | 13,000 | 3,000 |
| Accounts payable | (6,600) | (6,600) | -- |
| Total | $106,000 | $118,000 | $12,000 |

Note that the book value of the net assets of Baker Company may be computed by one of the following two methods:

1. Subtract the book value of the liability from the book values of the assets.

$$112,600 - 6,600 = 106,000$$

2. Add the book values of the components of Baker Company stockholders' equity.

$$50,000 + 15,000 + 41,000 = 106,000$$

The balance sheets of Andes and Baker are presented below as of January 1, 2008, immediately preceding the purchase.

**Andes Company and Baker Company**
**Balance Sheets at 1/1/08**
(Immediately before combination)

| | Andes Company | Baker Company |
|---|---|---|
| **Assets** | | |
| Cash | $ 30,900 | $ 37,400 |
| Accounts receivable (net) | 34,200 | 9,100 |
| Inventories | 22,900 | 16,100 |
| Equipment | 200,000 | 50,000 |
| Less accumulated depreciation | (21,000) | (10,000) |
| Patents | -- | 10,000 |
| Total assets | $267,000 | $112,600 |

|  | Andes Company | Baker Company |
|---|---|---|
| **Liabilities and stockholders' equity** |  |  |
| Accounts payable | $ 4,000 | $ 6,600 |
| Bonds payable, 10% | 100,000 | -- |
| Common stock, $10 par value | 100,000 | 50,000 |
| Additional paid-in capital | 15,000 | 15,000 |
| Retained earnings | 48,000 | 41,000 |
| Total liabilities and stockholders' equity | $267,000 | $112,600 |

The working paper for preparing a consolidated balance sheet at the date of acquisition is presented below. The first two columns are the trial balances of Andes Company and Baker Company immediately following the acquisition.

**Andes Company and Baker Company Consolidated Working Papers**
**For Date of Combination—1/1/08**

*90% interest*

|  | [1] Andes Company | [2] Baker Company (book value) | [3] Debit | [4] Credit | [5] Noncontrolling interest | [6] Consolidated balances |
|---|---|---|---|---|---|---|
| **Balance sheet, 1/1/08** |  |  |  |  |  |  |
| Cash | $ 30,900 | $ 37,400 |  |  |  | $ 68,300 |
| Accounts receivable, net | 34,200 | 9,100 |  |  |  | 43,300 |
| Inventories | 22,900 | 16,100 | 900b |  |  | 39,900 |
| Equipment | 200,000 | 50,000 | 9,000b |  |  | 259,000 |
| Accumulated depreciation | (21,000) | (10,000) |  | $ 1,800b |  | (32,800) |
| Investment in stock of Baker Company | 120,600 |  |  | 120,600a |  |  |
| Difference between cost and book value |  |  | 25,200b | 25,200b |  |  |
| Excess of cost over fair value (goodwill) |  |  | 14,400b |  |  | 14,400 |
| Patents |  | 10,000 | 2,700b |  |  | 12,700 |
| Total assets | $387,600 | $112,600 |  |  |  | $404,800 |
| Accounts payable | $ 4,000 | $ 6,600 |  |  |  | $ 10,600 |
| Bonds payable | 100,000 |  |  |  |  | 100,000 |
| Common stock | 154,000 | 50,000 | 45,000a |  | $ 5,000 | 154,000 |
| Additional paid-in capital | 81,600 | 15,000 | 13,500a |  | 1,500 | 81,600 |
| Retained earnings | 48,000 | 41,000 | 36,900a |  | 4,100 | 48,000 |
| Noncontrolling interest |  |  |  |  | $10,600 | 10,600 |
| Total liabilities and equity | $387,600 | $112,600 | $147,600 | $147,600 |  | $404,800 |

1. Record investment in Andes Company's accounting records (entry already reflected in column [1] above).

    The entry by Andes Company to record the 90% purchase-acquisition was

| Investment in stock of Baker Company | 120,600 |  |
|---|---|---|
|     Common stock |  | 54,000 |
|     Additional paid-in capital |  | 66,600 |

*To record the issuance of 5,400 shares of $10 par value stock to acquire a 90% interest in Baker Company*

Although common stock is used for the consideration in our example, Andes Company could have used debentures, cash, or any other form of consideration acceptable to Baker Company's stockholders to make the purchase. This entry is identical to the first entry in the preceding example using the entity theory/full goodwill method.

2. Difference between investment cost and book value

    The difference between the investment cost and the parent company's equity in the net assets of the subsidiary is computed as follows:

| Investment—FV of 5,400 shares of Andes issued | | $120,600 |
|---|---|---|
| Common stock | $50,000 × 90% = | 45,000 |
| Additional paid-in capital | 15,000 × 90% = | 13,500 |
| Retained earnings | 41,000 × 90% = | 36,900 |
| Andes' share—Baker net assets/stockholders' equity | | 95,400 |
| Differential | | $25,200 |

This difference is due to several undervalued assets and to unrecorded goodwill. The allocation procedure is similar to that for a 100% purchase; however, in this case, the parent company obtained a 90% interest, and thus, will only recognize 90% of the difference between the fair values and book values of the subsidiary's assets, not 100%. The allocation is presented as follows:

**Allocation of the Differential**

| Item | Book value (BV) | Fair value (FV) | Difference between BV and FV | Ownership percentage | Percentage share of difference between BV and FV |
|---|---|---|---|---|---|
| Cash | $ 37,400 | $ 37,400 | $ -- | | |
| Accounts receivable (net) | 9,100 | 9,100 | -- | | |
| Inventories | 16,100 | 17,100 | 1,000 | 90% | $ 900 |
| Equipment | 50,000 | 60,000 | 10,000 | 90% | 9,000 |
| Accumulated depreciation | (10,000) | (12,000) | (2,000) | 90% | (1,800) |
| Patents | 10,000 | 13,000 | 3,000 | 90% | 2,700 |
| Accounts payable | (6,600) | (6,600) | -- | | |
| Total | $106,000 | $118,000 | $12,000 | | |

| | |
|---|---|
| Amount of difference between purchase price and share of book value allocated to revaluation of net assets | 10,800 |
| Total differential per above | 25,200 |
| Remainder allocated to goodwill | $14,400 |

The equipment has a book value of $40,000 ($50,000 less 20% depreciation of $10,000). An appraisal concluded that the equipment's replacement cost new was $60,000 less 20% accumulated depreciation of $12,000 resulting in a net fair value of $48,000.

Goodwill is proven by the following computation:

| | | |
|---|---|---|
| Purchase price paid by Andes | | $120,600 |
| Fair value of net assets acquired | $118,000 | |
| Percentage interest acquired | × 90% | 106,200 |
| Excess of purchase price over fair value of net assets acquired | | $ 14,400 |

Noncontrolling interest is proven by the following computation:

| | |
|---|---|
| Fair value of net assets acquired | $118,000 |
| Percentage interest retained by former controlling stockholders | × 10% |
| Noncontrolling interest | $ 11,800 |

3. Consolidating entries on working paper

The basic reciprocal accounts are the investment in subsidiary account on the parent's books and the subsidiary's stockholders' equity accounts. Only the parent's share of the subsidiary's accounts may be eliminated as reciprocal accounts. The remaining 10% portion is allocated to the noncontrolling interest. The workpaper entry to eliminate the basic reciprocal accounts is as follows:

Entry a:

| | | |
|---|---|---|
| Capital stock—Baker Co. | 45,000 | |
| Additional paid-in capital—Baker Co. | 13,500 | |
| Retained earnings—Baker Co. | 36,900* | |
| Differential | 25,200 | |
|     Investment in stock of Baker Co.—Andes Co. | | 120,600 |

* *($41,000 × 90% = $36,900)*

Note that only 90% of Baker Company's stockholders' equity accounts are eliminated. Also, an account called "differential" is debited in the working paper entry. The differential account is a temporary account to record the difference between the cost of the investment in Baker Company in the parent's accounting records and the book value of the parent's interest (90% in this case) from the subsidiary's accounting records.

The next step is to allocate the differential to the specific assets by making the following workpaper entry:

Entry b:

| | | |
|---|---:|---:|
| Inventory | 900 | |
| Equipment | 9,000 | |
| Patents | 2,700 | |
| Goodwill | 14,400 | |
|     Accumulated depreciation | | 1,800 |
|     Differential | | 25,200 |

This entry reflects the allocations prepared in step 2. and recognizes the parent's share of the asset revaluations. The noncontrolling interest column is the 10% interest of Baker Company's net assets owned by third parties. Under current GAAP, there is no step-up for the noncontrolling interest's share of the excess of the fair value of net assets over book value.

The foregoing examples do not include any other intercompany balances as of the date of consolidation. If any such balances existed, they would be eliminated to fairly present the financial position of the consolidated entity. Several examples of the elimination of other reciprocal amounts will be shown later in the illustration of the preparation of consolidated financial statements subsequent to the date of acquisition.

## Consolidated Statements in Subsequent Periods

The same concepts employed to prepare a consolidated balance sheet at the date of acquisition are applicable to later consolidated statements. Where a noncontrolling interest exists, income in subsequent periods must be allocated to it. The exact nature of the worksheet entries depends on whether the parent is maintaining its accounting records of the investment in a subsidiary using the cost method or equity method (which are acceptable alternatives since the consolidated financial statements will be identical under either method). The equity method is often used when a separate, parent-only column is included in consolidating financial statements.

In addition to the eliminating entries for the parent's recorded investment and subsidiary stockholders' equity, other eliminations will be needed when there are intercompany balances or transactions resulting from parent-subsidiary loans (advances), sales of inventory items (whether or not these occurred at a profit to the seller), sales of fixed assets at other than net book value, and bond transactions or transactions in stock other than voting common shares. The selected items in the following example will demonstrate the accounting issues applicable to all such intercompany items and the proper handling of these items in the consolidation workpapers.

### Example of a consolidation in subsequent periods

The basic facts of the Andes Company-Baker Company case have already been presented. Additional information is as follows:

1.  Andes Company uses the equity method to record changes in the value of its investment in Baker.
2.  During 2008, Andes Company sold merchandise to Baker Company for $20,000 that originally cost Andes Company $15,000. This is referred to as a downstream sale. On December 31, 2008, Baker Company's inventory included merchandise purchased from Andes Company at a cost to Baker Company of $12,000.

3. Also during 2008, Andes Company purchased $18,000 of merchandise from Baker Company. This is referred to as an upstream sale. Baker Company uses a normal markup of 25% above its cost. Andes Company's ending inventory includes $10,000 of the merchandise acquired from Baker Company.

4. Baker Company reduced its intercompany account payable to Andes Company to a balance of $4,000 as of December 31, 2008, by making a payment of $1,000 on December 30. This $1,000 payment was still in transit on December 31, 2008, and thus, had not yet been received by Andes.

5. On January 2, 2008, Baker Company acquired equipment from Andes Company for $7,000. The equipment was originally purchased by Andes Company for $5,000 and had a book value of $4,000 at the date of sale to Baker Company. The equipment had an estimated remaining life of four years as of January 2, 2008, and is being depreciated using the straight-line method, with no estimated salvage value.

6. On December 31, 2008, Baker Company purchased for $44,000, 50% of the outstanding bonds issued by Andes Company. The bonds mature on December 31, 2013, and were originally issued at par. The bonds pay interest annually on December 31 of each year, and the interest was paid to the prior investor immediately before Baker Company's purchase of the bonds.

The worksheet for the preparation of consolidated financial statements as of December 31, 2008, is presented below.

The balance shown in the parent's accounting records as "investment in subsidiary" at the financial statement date should be reconciled to ensure the parent company made the proper entries under the method of accounting used to account for its investment.

An analysis of the investment in Baker at December 31, 2008, is as follows:

|  | Investment in Stock of Baker Company | | |
|---|---|---|---|
| Original cost, 1/1/08 | 120,600 | | |
| % of Baker Co.'s 2008 income ($9,400 × 90%) | 8,460 | 3,600 | % of Baker Co.'s 2008 dividends paid ($4,000 × 90%) |
| Balance, 12/31/08 | 125,460 | | |

Any errors would require correcting entries before the consolidation process is continued. Correcting entries are posted by the appropriate company; eliminating entries are not recorded by either company.

The difference between the cost of the investment and the book value of the net assets acquired was determined and allocated in the preparation of the date of acquisition consolidated balance sheet presented earlier. The same computations are used in preparing financial statements for as long as the investment is owned. Since FASB has currently expressed its preference for the entity theory/full goodwill method, the illustration of that method is carried forward for the purpose of this example.

The following adjusting and eliminating entries are required to prepare consolidated financial statements as of December 31, 2008, and for the year then ended. The number or letter in parentheses to the left of the entry corresponds to the key used on the worksheet.

Step 1 —Complete the transaction for any intercompany items in transit at the end of the year.

| (a) | Cash | 1,000 | |
| | Accounts receivable— subsidiary | | 1,000 |

This adjusting entry will now properly present the financial positions of both companies by eliminating the timing difference.

Step 2 —Prepare the eliminating entries.

| (a) | Sales | 38,000 | |
| | Cost of sales | | 38,000 |

Total intercompany sales of $38,000 include $20,000 in a downstream transaction sold from Andes Company to Baker Company and $18,000 in an upstream transaction sold from Baker Company to Andes Company.

(b) 

| | | |
|---|---|---|
| Cost of sales | 5,000 | |
|     Inventory | | 5,000 |

The ending inventories are overstated because of the unrealized gross profit from the intercompany sales. The debit to cost of goods sold is required because a decrease in ending inventory will increase cost of goods sold to be deducted on the income statement. Supporting computations for the entry are as follows:

| | *In ending inventory of* | |
|---|---|---|
| | *Andes Company* | *Baker Company* |
| Intercompany sales not resold, at selling price | $10,000 | $12,000 |
| Cost basis of remaining intercompany merchandise | | |
|   From Baker to Andes (÷ 125%) | (8,000) | |
|   From Andes to Baker (÷ 133 1/3%) | | (9,000) |
| Unrealized gross profit | $ 2,000 | $ 3,000 |

*NOTE: When preparing consolidated workpapers for 2009 (the next fiscal period), an additional eliminating entry will be required if the goods in 2008's ending inventory are sold to outsiders during 2009. The additional entry will recognize the profit for 2009 that was eliminated as unrealized in 2008. This entry is necessary since the entry at the end of 2008 was made only on the worksheet and not recorded in the accounting records of either Andes or Baker. The 2009 entry would be as follows:*

| | | |
|---|---|---|
| Retained earnings—Baker Co., 1/1/09 | 2,000 | |
| Retained earnings—Andes Co., 1/1/09 | 3,000 | |
|     Cost of goods sold, 2009 | | 5,000 |

(c)

| | | |
|---|---|---|
| Accounts payable—Parent | 4,000 | |
|     Accounts receivable—Subsidiary | | 4,000 |

This entry eliminates the remaining intercompany receivable/payable owed by Baker Company to Andes Company. This eliminating entry is necessary to avoid overstating the consolidated entity's balance sheet. The receivable/payable is not extinguished, and Baker Company must still transfer $4,000 to Andes Company in the future.

(d)

| | | |
|---|---|---|
| Gain on sale of equipment | 3,000 | |
|     Equipment | | 2,000 |
|     Accumulated depreciation | | 250 |
|     Depreciation expense | | 750 |

This entry eliminates the gain on the intercompany sale of the equipment, eliminates the overstatement of equipment, and removes the excess depreciation taken on the gain. Supporting computations for the entry are as follows:

| | *Cost* | *At date of intercompany sale accum. depr.* | *2008 depr. ex.* | *End-of-period accum. depr.* |
|---|---|---|---|---|
| Original basis | | | | |
|   (to seller, Andes Co.) | $5,000 | $(1,000) | $ 1,000 | $(2,000) |
| New basis | | | | |
|   (to buyer, Baker Co.) | 7,000 | -- | 1,750 | (1,750) |
| Difference | $(2,000) | | $( 750) | $ 250 |

If the intercompany sale had not occurred, Andes Company would have depreciated the remaining book value of $4,000 over the estimated remaining life of four years. However, since Baker Company's acquisition price ($7,000) was more than Andes Company's undepreciated basis in the asset ($4,000), the depreciation recorded by Baker Company will include part of the unrealized intercompany profit. The equipment must be reflected on the consolidated balance sheet at its original cost to the consolidated entity. Therefore, the write-up of $2,000 in the equipment, the excess depreciation of $750, and the gain of $3,000 all must be eliminated in consolidation. The ending balance of accumulated depreciation must be shown at what it would have been if the intercompany equipment transaction had not occurred. In future periods, a retained earnings adjustment will be used instead of adjusting the gain since the gain is a 2008 transaction; however, concepts with respect to adjusting accumulated depreciation and the related expense will be extended to include the additional periods.

| (e) | Bonds payable | 50,000 | |
| | Investment in bonds of Andes Company | | 44,000 |
| | Gain on debt extinguishment | | 6,000 |

This entry eliminates the book value (the par value of the bonds) of Andes Company's debt against the bond investment account of Baker Company. To the consolidated entity, this transaction is shown as a retirement of debt even though Andes Company still owes the outstanding intercompany debt to Baker Company. For the purpose of this example, it is assumed that Baker Company is accounting for its investment in the bonds as being held-to-maturity under FAS 115 and, therefore, accounting for the investment at amortized cost. In future periods, Baker Company will amortize the discount, ultimately, upon maturity, bringing the recorded investment up to its par (maturity) value. Retained earnings will be used in future eliminating entries instead of the gain since the gain is a 2008 event.

| (f) | Equity in subsidiary's net income—Andes Co. | 8,460 | |
| | Dividends paid—Baker Co. | | 3,600 |
| | Investment in stock of Baker Co. | | 4,860 |

This eliminating entry adjusts the carrying value of the investment in Baker back to its balance at the beginning of the period and also eliminates the subsidiary's net income. The elimination is computed as follows:

| | | |
|---|---|---|
| Baker's net income of $9,400 × 90% attributable to Andes | = | $   8,460 |
| Baker's dividends paid of $4,000 × Andes' 90% share | = | $   3,600 |
| Andes' investment in Baker at 12/31/08 | | $125,460 |
| Andes' original recorded investment in Baker | | 120,600 |
| Effects of Andes' 2008 equity method accounting | | $   4,860 |

| (g) | Goodwill | 16,000 | |
| | Inventories | 1,000 | |
| | Equipment | 10,000 | |
| | Patents | 3,000 | |
| | Common stock—Baker Company | 50,000 | |
| | Additional paid-in capital—Baker Company | 15,000 | |
| | Retained earnings—Baker Company | 41,000 | |
| | Accumulated depreciation | | 2,000 |
| | Noncontrolling interest | | 13,400 |
| | Investment in Baker | | 120,600 |

This entry eliminates Baker Company's stockholders' equity at the beginning of the year, 1/1/08, reflects 100% of the imputed goodwill associated with Baker, revalues the acquired assets at their acquisition date fair values, reflects the noncontrolling interests of the formerly controlling stockholders of Baker, and eliminates Andes' 1/1/08 investment in Baker. Note that the changes in these amounts during the year were eliminated in entry (f) above. Also note that this entry is identical with the 1/1/08 revaluation and elimination entry 2. in the example of recording the acquisition at 1/1/08 using the entity theory/full goodwill method.

(h)  Cost of sales                                              1,000
     Depreciation expense                                       2,000
     Other operating expenses—patent amortization               300
         Inventory                                                         1,000
         Accumulated depreciation                                          2,000
         Patents (or contra asset, accumulated amortization)                 300

The elimination entry amortizes the revaluations to fair value made in entry (g). The inventory has been sold and, therefore, becomes part of cost of goods sold. Goodwill is not amortized, but will be tested annually for possible impairment. The remaining revaluations will be amortized as follows:

|                  | *Revaluation* | *Amortization period* | *Annual amortization* |
|------------------|---------------|-----------------------|-----------------------|
| Equipment (net)  | $8,000        | 4 years               | $2,000                |
| Patents          | 3,000         | 10 years              | 300                   |

Amortization will continue to be made on future worksheets. For example, at the end of the next year (2009), the amortization entry (h) would be as follows:

Retained earnings                                              3,300
Depreciation expense                                           2,000
Other operating expenses—patent amortization                   300
    Inventory                                                             1,000
    Accumulated depreciation                                              4,000
    Patents (or contra asset, accumulated amortization)                     600

The $3,300 debit to retained earnings is an aggregation of the prior period's charges affecting the income statement ($1,000 + $2,000 + $300). During subsequent years, some accountants prefer reducing the allocated amounts in entry (g) for prior periods' charges. In this case, the amortization entry in future periods would reflect just that period's amortization.

In adjusting for the noncontrolling interest in the consolidated entity's equity and earnings, the following guidelines are to be observed:

1.  The entire subsidiary's stockholders' equity section is eliminated in the basic eliminating entry. The noncontrolling interest's share of the subsidiary's stockholders' equity is presented separately.

2.  The entire amounts of intercompany transactions and balances are eliminated. For example, all receivables/payables and sales/cost of sales with a 90% subsidiary are eliminated.

3.  For intercompany transactions in inventory and fixed assets, the possible effect on noncontrolling interest depends on whether the original transaction affected the subsidiary's income statement. Noncontrolling interest is adjusted only if the subsidiary is the selling entity (upstream sales). In this case, the noncontrolling interest is adjusted for its percentage ownership of the common stock of the subsidiary. The noncontrolling interest is not adjusted for unrealized profits on downstream sales. The effects of downstream transactions are confined solely to the parent's (i.e., controlling) ownership interests.

The noncontrolling interest's share of the subsidiary's net income is shown as a deduction on the consolidated income statement since 100% of the subsidiary's revenues and expenses are consolidated, even though the parent company owns less than a 100% interest. For this example, the noncontrolling interest deduction on the income statement is computed as follows:

| | |
|---|---:|
| Baker Company's reported income | $9,400 |
| Less unrealized profit on an upstream inventory sale | (2,000) |
| Baker Company's income for consolidated financial statement purposes | 7,400 |
| Noncontrolling interest share | × 10% |
| Noncontrolling interest share of Baker net income | $ 740 |

**Andes Company and Baker Company Consolidated Working Papers**
**Year Ended December 31, 2008**

*Consolidation of 90% owned subsidiary*
*first year, subsequent to acquisition, equity method used by Parent; Entity theory/full goodwill method*

| | Andes Company | Baker Company | Adjustments and eliminations Debit | Adjustments and eliminations Credit | Noncontrolling interest | Consolidated balances |
|---|---:|---:|---:|---:|---:|---:|
| **Income statements for year ended 12/31/08** | | | | | | |
| Sales | $750,000 | $420,000 | $ 38,000[a] | | | $1,132,000 |
| Cost of sales | 581,000 | 266,000 | 5,000[b] 1,000[h] | $ 38,000[a] | | 815,000 |
| Gross profit | 169,000 | 154,000 | | | | 317,000 |
| Depreciation and interest expense | 28,400 | 16,200 | 2,000[h] | 750[d] | | 45,850 |
| (Gain) loss on sale of equipment | (3,000) | | 3,000[d] | | | |
| Other operating expenses | 117,000 | 128,400 | 300[h] | | | 245,700 |
| Total operating expenses and gain | 142,400 | 144,600 | | | | 291,550 |
| Income from operations | 26,600 | 9,400 | | | | 25,450 |
| Gain on debt extinguishment | | | | 6,000[e] | | 6,000 |
| Equity in subsidiary's income | 8,460 | | 8,460[f] | | | |
| Noncontrolling income ($7,400 × 10%) | | | | | $ 740 | (740) |
| Net income | $ 35,060 | $ 9,400 | $ 57,760 | $ 44,750 | $ 740 | $ 30,710 |
| **Statement of retained earnings for the year ended 12/31/08** | | | | | | |
| 1/1/08 retained earnings | | | | | | |
| Andes Company | $ 48,000 | | | | | $ 48,000 |
| Baker Company | | $ 41,000 | $ 41,000[g] | | | |
| Add net income (from above) | 35,060 | 9,400 | 57,760 | $ 44,750 | $ 740 | 30,710 |
| Total | 83,060 | 50,400 | 98,760 | 44,750 | 740 | 78,710 |
| Deduct dividends paid | 15,000 | 4,000 | | 3,600[f] | 400 | 15,000 |
| Balance, 12/31/08 | $ 68,060 | $ 46,400 | $ 98,760 | $ 48,350 | $ 340 | $ 63,710 |
| **Balance sheet, 12/31/08** | | | | | | |
| Cash | $ 45,300 | $ 6,400 | $ 1,000[l] | | | $ 52,700 |
| Accounts receivable, trade (net) | 38,700 | 12,100 | | | | 50,800 |
| Accounts receivable, subsidiary | 5,000 | | | $ 1,000[l] 4,000[c] | | |
| Inventories | 38,300 | 20,750 | 1,000[g] | 5,000[b] 1,000[h] | | 54,050 |
| Equipment | 195,000 | 57,000 | 10,000[g] | 2,000[d] | | 260,000 |
| Accumulated depreciation | (35,200) | (18,900) | | 250[d] 2,000[g] 2,000[h] | | (58,350) |
| Investment in stock of Baker Company | 125,460 | | | 4,860[f] 120,600[g] | | |
| Goodwill | | | 16,000[g] | | | 16,000 |
| Investment in held-to-maturity bonds of Andes Company | | 44,000 | | 44,000[e] | | |

| | Andes Company | Baker Company | Adjustments and eliminations Debit | Credit | Noncontrolling interest | Consolidated balances |
|---|---|---|---|---|---|---|
| Patents (net) | | 9,000 | 3,000g | 300h | | 11,700 |
| Total assets | $412,560 | $130,350 | | | | $386,900 |
| | | | | | | |
| Accounts payable, trade | $ 8,900 | $ 14,950 | | | | $ 23,850 |
| Accounts payable, parent | | 4,000 | 4,000c | | | |
| Bonds payable | 100,000 | | 50,000e | | | 50,000 |
| Total liabilities | 108,900 | 18,950 | | | | 73,850 |
| Common stock | 154,000 | 50,000 | 50,000g | | | 154,000 |
| Additional paid-in capital | 81,600 | 15,000 | 15,000g | | | 81,600 |
| Retained earnings (from above) | 68,060 | 46,400 | 98,760 | 48,350 | $340 | 63,710 |
| Noncontrolling interest | | | | 13,400g | $340 | 13,740 |
| Total stockholders' equity | 303,660 | 111,400 | | | | 313,050 |
| | | | | | | |
| Total liabilities and stockholders' equity | $412,560 | $130,350 | $48,760 | $48,760 | $ 0 | $386,900 |

## Other Accounting Issues in Business Combinations

**Contingent consideration.** Many business acquisitions include contingent consideration features, which require, if specified conditions are later met, that additions to the purchase price be paid either in cash, or in shares of the acquiring entity. The presence of contingent consideration provisions in an acquisition arrangement must be addressed, both at the time of the acquisition and later, if and when contingent consideration is earned and paid.

Under FAS 141, contingent consideration was not deemed part of the cost of the acquisition until the contingency (e.g., future earnings) was later resolved. (But see exception in following paragraph.) However, under FAS 141(R), as described in this chapter, the estimated fair value of such contingent payments is to be incorporated into the purchase price determination. The following comments apply to requirements under FAS 141.

At the date of the acquisition, under FAS 141, contingent consideration is important to the extent that it precludes immediate recognition of an extraordinary gain arising from the excess of "negative goodwill" over the amounts allocable to reduce the carrying values of various assets (all assets other than cash, receivables, inventory, financial instruments carried on the balance sheet at fair value, assets to be disposed of by sale, and deferred income tax assets). Under GAAP, if such an excess exists, it is to be classified as a deferred credit, not taken into earnings, until the contingency regarding the purchase price has been resolved.

In truth, only a small fraction of business combinations are true "bargain purchases," and of these, it is expected that only a minute portion will result in such a large amount of negative goodwill that an excess will remain after offsetting against the qualified assets. Of those, an even smaller proportion will relate to transactions in which contingent consideration is to be paid, and thus for which the deferral of what otherwise would be immediately recognized as extraordinary gain would be prescribed.

The accounting for the subsequent payment of the added (i.e., contingent) consideration depends upon whether the contingency was related to the earnings of the acquired entity or to the fair value of the original consideration package given by the acquirer.

In the former instance, commonly referred to as an "earn-out" provision, a subsequent payment of added cash, stock, or any other valuable consideration will require a revaluation of the purchase price. This revaluation possibly could alter the amounts allocable to certain (mostly noncurrent) assets (where cost in the original purchase transaction was less than fair value acquired (i.e., a "bargain purchase") and the difference was offset against those assets), or could result in an increased amount of goodwill being recognized. The effects of a revaluation are handled prospectively (i.e., the additional depreciation of fixed assets is allocated to the remaining economic lives of those items) without making any adjustment to postacquisition periods' results already reported.

In the latter case, the event triggering the issuance of additional shares is a decline in fair value of the original purchase package. Additional shares of the acquirer's stock are issued in order to restore the value of the consideration to the amount intended by the parties at the date of the transaction. According to FAS 141, this does not alter the total cost of the transaction for accounting recognition purposes, even though further consideration is later transferred to the former owners of the acquiree. The total value of the purchase would not be changed and, thus, no alteration of amounts allocated to the various assets and liabilities acquired would be needed. However, the issuance of extra shares of common stock will typically require that the allocation between the common stock and the additional paid-in capital accounts be adjusted, if the shares carry par or stated values.

In rare instances, contingent consideration based on the value of the securities used to effect the acquisition may involve transactions in which common stock was not used. If part of the original purchase price had been paid in bonds or other debt instruments, the reallocation might affect the premium or discount recognized on the debt, which would have an impact on future earnings as these accounts are subsequently amortized.

**Net operating loss carryforwards of an acquired entity.** An entity acquired in a purchase business combination may have a net operating loss carryforward (NOL) that will be available for use by the acquiring entity. While prior GAAP generally prohibited recognition of the income tax benefit of NOL, under FAS 109, deferred income tax assets including NOL are given recognition. Under this standard, benefits related to acquired NOL are reported in the acquirer's balance sheet (as are deferred income tax assets arising from any other future deductible temporary differences). A valuation allowance is also recorded if realization of the NOL is not considered "more likely than not."

As discussed more fully in Chapter 17, recognition "for the first time" of the benefits of NOL (acquired in a purchase business combination at a date subsequent to the purchase) is accomplished by reducing recorded goodwill to zero. Next, if further acquired NOL are realized, other identifiable intangible assets acquired in the same transaction are reduced to zero. Any excess over this amount is reflected as an adjustment to current period deferred income tax expense or benefit. "For the first time" means that a valuation allowance has been reduced or eliminated, either because the probability of realization has been reassessed or because the income tax benefits have, in fact, been realized in the current period.

**Preacquisition contingencies.** At the time a business combination is consummated, the purchase price must be allocated to acquired assets and assumed liabilities in accordance with their respective fair values, with any excess purchase price being assigned to goodwill (if fair value exceeds cost, the cost deficiency is allocated primarily against noncurrent assets, with any remainder treated as "negative goodwill" and, in general, recognized as an extraordinary gain at the date of the acquisition). In some cases, however, the fair values of certain assets (e.g., those to be disposed of) may not be known with precision, and the amounts of certain estimated or contingent liabilities (such as outstanding warranty or litigation claims) may also be subject to a high degree of uncertainty. FAS 141 provides for a "look back" to reallocate the purchase price when these contingencies are ultimately resolved. However, under FAS 141 there is a limited allocation period, usually deemed to be one year, during which a reallocation can be effected; thereafter, resolutions of preacquisition contingencies are treated as current period events and reported in net income of that period.

An exception to this rule exists in the case of income tax uncertainties existing at the date of the business combination. Resolution of these must be accounted for in accordance with FAS 109, which stipulates that such adjustments are to be applied to increase or decrease the remaining balance of goodwill attributable to that business combination; if goodwill is reduced to zero, the remaining amount is first used to reduce other noncurrent intangible assets from the same acquisition to zero, and any excess beyond that amount is recorded as an adjustment to the deferred income tax expense or benefit for the period of resolution. Thus, the resolution of these specific income tax uncertainties cannot result in a general reallocation of the purchase price, as are other resolutions of preacquisition contingencies.

**Changes in controlling interest.** The parent's ownership interest can change as a result of purchases or sales of the subsidiary's common shares by the parent, or as a consequence of capital transactions consummated by the subsidiary itself. The latter circumstance is generally handled precisely as demonstrated in the equity method discussion in Chapter 12, (see pages 554-556). If the parent's relative book value interest in the subsidiary changes, gains or losses are treated as incurred in an entity's own treasury stock transactions. Gains are credited to additional paid-in capital; losses are charged to any previously created additional paid-in capital or, absent that, to retained earnings. However, in financial statements of its registrants, the SEC requires that the parent company recognize a gain on a transaction when a subsidiary sells shares to outside interests at a price greater than the parent's carrying amount.

When the parent's share of ownership increases through the purchase of additional stock in the subsidiary, the cost of the newly acquired stock is debited to the asset, "investment in subsidiary," with a corresponding credit to cash. An issue arises in the preparation of consolidated income statements when the change in ownership takes place midperiod. Consolidated statements are to be prepared based on the ending ownership level.

### Example of a consolidation with a change in the majority interest

Assume that Andes Company increased its ownership of Baker Company from 90% to 95% on October 1, 2008. The investment was acquired at book value of $5,452.50 determined as follows:

| | | |
|---|---:|---:|
| Baker Company common stock outstanding at 10/1/08 | | $50,000 |
| Additional paid-in capital, 10/1/08 | | 15,000 |
| Retained earnings at 10/1/08 | | |
| Balance, 1/1/08 | $41,000 | |
| Net income for nine months ($9,400 × .75) | 7,050* | |
| Preacquisition dividends paid | (4,000) | 44,050 |
| | | 109,050 |
| | | × 5% |
| Book value acquired | | $5,452.50 |

\* *Assumes income was earned evenly over the year.*

The consolidated net income attributable to Andes' interests for 2008 would reflect a net of

| | | | | | | | |
|---|---|---|---|---|---|---|---:|
| 90% | × | $9,400 | × | 12/12 | = | | $8,460.00 |
| 5% | × | $9,400 | × | 3/12 | = | | 117.50 |
| 95% | | | | | | | $8,577.50 |

The preacquisition dividends ($4,000 × 90%) would have been recorded by Andes as follows:

| | | |
|---|---:|---:|
| Cash | 3,600.00 | |
| Investment in Baker company | | 3,600.00 |

Andes would apply the equity method to record its share of the consolidated net income as follows:

| | | |
|---|---:|---:|
| Investment in Baker company | 8,577.50 | |
| Equity in subsidiary's income | | 8,577.50 |

The interim stock purchase results in a new caption, **purchased preacquisition earnings**, being presented on the consolidated income statement. This caption represents the percentage of the subsidiary's income earned, in this case, on the 5% stock interest from January 1, 2008, to October 1, 2008. The basic eliminating entries would be based on the 95% ownership as follows:

| | | |
|---|---|---|
| Equity in subsidiary's income—Andes Co. | 8,577.50 | |
| Dividends paid—Baker Co. | | 3,600.00 |
| Investment in Baker Co. | | 4,977.50 |
| Goodwill | 16,000.00 | |
| Inventories | 1,000.00 | |
| Equipment | 10,000.00 | |
| Patents | 3,000.00 | |
| Common stock—Baker Co. | 50,000.00 | |
| Additional paid-in capital—Baker Co. | 15,000.00 | |
| Retained earnings—Baker Co. ** | 40,800.00 | |
| Purchased preacquisition earnings*** | 352.50 | |
| Accumulated depreciation | | 2,000.00 |
| Investment in stock of Baker Co.—Andes Co. **** | | 120,600.00 |
| Noncontrolling interest***** | | 13,552.50 |

| | |
|---|---|
| ** *$41,000 beginning 2008 balance* | *$41,000* |
| *Less preacquisition dividend of 5% x $4,000* | *(200)* |
| *Retained earnings available, as adjusted* | *$40,800* |
| *** *5% × $9,400 × 9/12 = $352.50* | |
| **** *Original cost, 1/1/08, for 90% interest* | *$120,600* |
| ***** *Noncontrolling interest consists of:* | |
| *Originally recognized amount* | *$13,400.00* |
| *Allocated share of earnings 1/1/08 – 10/1/08* | |
| *($9,400 × 75% × 10% = $705)* | *705.00* |
| *Share of preacquisition dividends through 10/1/08* | |
| *($4,000 × 10% = $400)* | *(400.00)* |
| *Sale of 50% preacquisition retained net income to Andes* | |
| *[($705 – $400) × 50% = $152.50]* | *(152.50)* |
| | *$13,552.50* |

Purchased preacquisition earnings are shown as a deduction, along with noncontrolling interest, to arrive at consolidated net income. Purchased preacquisition earnings are used only with interim acquisitions when applying the purchase accounting method.

**Requirement that all majority-owned subsidiaries be consolidated.** It has been a general assumption under GAAP that when one entity is owned outright or a majority of its voting interests are controlled by another entity (the parent company), the most meaningful representation of the parent company's real financial position and economic performance will be through the presentation of consolidated financial statements. This presumption dates from the issuance in 1959 of ARB 51, *Consolidated Financial Statements*, which stopped short of absolutely requiring that consolidated financial reporting be employed. Over the ensuing years, a number of excuses for not fully consolidating certain subsidiaries arose, leading to substantial diversity of reporting practices. This in turn resulted in FASB issuance of FAS 94, *Consolidation of All Majority-Owned Subsidiaries*.

The practice of excluding some or all subsidiaries from the parent company's financial statements was variously justified due to the parent's lack of absolute control over the affairs of the subsidiary, whether because of legal restrictions or due to the relationship with noncontrolling owners, as well as when control was present but expected to be only temporary. More controversial, if less widely understood, were situations where "off-balance-sheet financing" was accomplished through the use of majority or wholly owned leasing, factoring, or other financing subsidiaries that were then excluded from the parent's financial statements. The actual justification given for excluding these entities from the consolidated financial statements, particularly in the cases of highly leveraged financing subsidiaries, was that consolidation of such "nonhomogeneous" operations would distort the parent's key financial and operating statistics, such as the working capital ratio and gross profit margin.

FAS 94 significantly narrowed, but did not totally eliminate, the ability of entities to exclude majority-owned subsidiaries from parent company financial statements. Most importantly, the "nonhomogeneity" argument could no longer be used to exclude leasing, real estate, financing, insurance, or other subsidiary operations. Under FAS 94, all majority-owned subsidiaries were to be consolidated, unless (1) control over the subsidiary was expected to be temporary in nature, or (2) control could be shown to not reside with the majority owner.

FAS 144 further restricted decisions to not consolidate majority-owned subsidiaries by eliminating the "temporary control" exception. Thus, currently, only demonstrable lack of ability to control the majority-owned subsidiary can justify excluding it from the parent company's consolidated financial statements.

Separate financial statements of entities that are majority owned by other companies (i.e., its subsidiaries) are still permitted to be issued. In fact, noncontrolling stockholders and other interested parties (creditors, vendors, or customers, as well as regulatory authorities) might, in many instances, receive little useful disaggregated information from the parent company's consolidated financial statements. However, if the reporting subsidiary itself had one or more majority-owned subsidiaries of its own, these would be consolidated in the financial statements of the first-tier subsidiary.

Majority-owned subsidiaries that are not consolidated due to the absence of control by a parent company will generally be accounted for using the equity method (discussed in detail in Chapter 11). Analysis of the specific facts and circumstances (e.g., whether the parent has significant influence, even if not actual control) will determine whether the equity method is appropriate.

### Combined Financial Statements

When a group of entities is under common ownership, control, or management, it is often useful to present combined (or combining—showing the separate as well as the combined entities) financial statements. In this situation, the economic substance of the nominally independent entities' combined operations may be more important to financial statement users than is the legal form of those enterprises. When consolidated statements are not presented, combined statements may be used to show the financial position, or operating results, of a group of companies that are each subsidiaries of a common parent.

According to ARB 51, the process of preparing combined statements is virtually the same as consolidations employing the previously permitted pooling-of-interests method. The major exception is that the equity section of the combined balance sheet will incorporate the equity sections of both of the combining entities. However, only a single combined retained earnings amount need be presented.

**Example of the stockholders' equity section of a combined financial statement**

**Lanushka Ltd. and Scully Enterprises, Inc.**
**Combined Balance Sheet**
**December 31, 2008**

*Stockholders' equity*

|  |  |
|---|---:|
| Capital stock: |  |
| Preferred, $100 par, authorized 90,000 shares, issued 5,000 shares | $  500,000 |
| Common, $50 par, authorized 100,000 shares, issued 60,000 shares | 3,000,000 |
| Common, $10 par, authorized 250,000 shares, issued 100,000 shares | 1,000,000 |
| Additional paid-in capital | 650,000 |
| Retained earnings | 3,825,000 |
|  | $8,975,000 |

### Combinations of Entities under Common Control

FAS 141 explicitly does not apply to combinations of entities under common control (parent and subsidiary, brother-sister corporations, etc.). Mergers among such affiliated entities must be accounted for "as if" poolings. This treatment is consistent with the concept of poolings as combinations of common stockholder interests. Notwithstanding the banning of pooling of interests accounting under current GAAP, this prescription still remains in effect.

A question arises, however, when a parent (Company P) transfers ownership in one of its subsidiaries (Company B) to another of its subsidiaries (Company A) in exchange for additional shares of Company A. If P's carrying value of its investment in B differs from B's book value, there appears to be a requirement for A to reflect its new investment in B at B's book value, rather than at P's cost (or equity) basis.

EITF 90-5 resolved this apparent conflict by stating that A's carrying value for the investment in B is to be P's basis, not B's book value. Furthermore, if A subsequently retires the interests of noncontrolling owners of B, the transaction is to be accounted for as a purchase, whether it is effected through a stock issuance by A or by a cash payment to the selling shareholders.

The EITF further concluded (in Issue 90-13) that when a purchase transaction is closely followed by a "sale" of the parent's subsidiary to the newly acquired (target) entity, these two transactions are to be viewed as a single transaction. Accordingly, the parent recognizes gain or loss on the sale of its subsidiary to the target company, to the extent of noncontrolling interest in the target entity. As a result, there will be a new basis (step-up) not only for the target company's assets and liabilities, but also for the subsidiary company's net assets. Basis is stepped up to the extent of noncontrolling participation in the target entity to which the subsidiary company was transferred.

### Combinations of Mutual Enterprises and Not-for-Profit Organizations

**Mutual enterprises.** Acquisitions of an investor-owned entity by a mutual enterprise and acquisitions of a mutual enterprise by an investor-owned entity are fully subject to the requirements of FAS 141. Historically, combinations of mutual enterprises (of which mutually owned savings and loan associations had been the most prominent) had been accounted for as poolings of interests, since there was normally no exchange of cash or other assets as consideration for the transaction. Also, the identity of the "acquirer" was difficult to ascertain in such transactions. Under the provisions of FAS 141, pooling accounting has been eliminated, and in every business combination one party must be identified as the acquirer.

APB 16 and 17 continue to be applicable to combinations of two or more mutual enterprises until such time as FASB is able to provide guidance on how it will meet its stated objective of including mutual enterprises in the scope of FAS 141.

**Not-for-profit organizations.** As with mutual enterprise mergers, many not-for-profit organization combinations are characterized by an absence of cash or other consideration being paid by the presumptive acquirer. Also, many of these combinations have traditionally been accounted for as poolings, which is banned under FAS 141. The acquisition of a not-for-profit organization by a business enterprise is already within the scope of FAS 141. The FASB is currently pursuing a project designed to provide guidance regarding combinations of not-for-profit organizations and the treatment of goodwill and other intangible assets acquired in a merger or acquisition. In the interim, such combinations are subject to the requirements of SOP 94-3, *Reporting of Related Entities by Not-for-Profit Organizations.*

### Accounting for Leveraged Buyouts

One of the most complex accounting issues to have arisen over the past several decades has been the appropriate accounting for a leveraged buyout (LBO). At the center of this issue is the question of whether a new basis of accountability has been created by the LBO transaction. If so, then a step-up in the reported value of assets and/or liabilities is warranted.

If not, the carryforward bases of the predecessor entity continues to be reported in the company's financial statements.

The EITF has addressed leveraged buyouts, first in 86-16, then in 88-16 and 90-12. The EITF's conclusion was that partial or complete new basis accounting is appropriate only when the transaction is characterized by a change in control of voting interest. EITF 88-16 established a series of mechanical tests by which this change in interest is to be measured. Three groups of interests were identified: shareholders in the newly created company, management, and shareholders in the old company (who may or may not also have an interest in the new company). Depending upon the relative interests of these groups in the old entity (OLDCO) and in the new enterprise (NEWCO), there will be either, (1) a finding that the transaction was a purchase (new basis accounting applies) or (2) that it was a recapitalization or a restructuring (carryforward basis accounting applies).

Among the tests that the EITF decreed to determine proper accounting for any given LBO transaction is the "monetary test." This test requires that at least 80% of the net consideration paid to acquire OLDCO interests must be monetary. In this context, monetary means cash, debt, and the fair value of any equity by securities given by NEWCO to selling shareholders of OLDCO. Loan proceeds provided OLDCO to assist in the acquisition of NEWCO shares by NEWCO shareholders are excluded from this definition. If the portion of the purchase that is effected through monetary consideration is less than 80%, but other criteria of EITF 88-16 are satisfied, there will be a step up. This step up will be limited to the percentage of the transaction represented by monetary consideration.

EITF 88-16 presents an extensive series of examples illustrating the circumstances that would and would not meet the purchase accounting criteria to be employed in LBO. These examples should be consulted as needed when addressing an actual LBO transaction accounting issue.

### Reverse Acquisitions

Reverse acquisitions are stock transactions that occur when one entity (the nominal acquirer) issues so many of its shares to the former owners of another entity (the nominal acquiree) that they become the majority owners of the resultant combined enterprise. The consequence of such a transaction is that the legal and accounting treatments will diverge, with the nominal acquiree being the acquirer for financial reporting purposes. While often the nominal acquirer will adopt the acquiree's name, thus alerting users of the statements to the nature of the organizational change, this does not necessarily occur, and, in any event, it will be critical that the financial statements contain sufficient disclosure so that users are not misled. This will be important particularly in the periods immediately following the transaction, and especially when comparative financial statements are presented which include some periods prior to the acquisition, since comparability will be affected.

A typical reverse acquisition would occur when a "shell" enterprise, which often is a publicly held but dormant company, merges with an operating company, which often will be nonpublic. The objective is for the operating entity to "go public" without the usual time consuming and expensive registration process. However, reverse acquisitions are not limited to such situations, and there have been many such transactions involving two public or two nonpublic companies. The nominal acquirer may have substantial operations of its own, although of lesser scope or with lower growth prospects than those of the nominal acquiree.

A number of difficult questions arise in reverse acquisitions, and GAAP does not provide definitive guidance on these important issues. The SEC has provided some direction that, under the hierarchy of GAAP, are viewed as definitive absent higher level "official" indicators from other standard setters. Among the matters to be considered, and which will be discussed in the following paragraphs, are these:

1.  What circumstances signal a reverse acquisition?
2.  How should the consolidated financial statements be presented in the subsequent periods?
3.  How should the purchase cost be computed and allocated in a reverse acquisition?
4.  What would the shareholders' equity section of the balance sheet be immediately following the reverse acquisition?
5.  What would be the impact on computation of earnings per share?
6.  How will noncontrolling interest be presented in the financial statements?

Reverse acquisitions occur when the former shareholders of the nominal acquiree become the majority owners of the postacquisition consolidated enterprise, and most commonly this will result when a stock-for-stock swap occurs. Under prior rules, if all of the twelve restrictive conditions set forth in the now-superseded APB 16 were met, the transaction would be accounted for as a pooling, thus obviating the concerns noted above. Under FAS 141, however, poolings are prohibited and all business combinations will be accounted for as purchases. Unless the combining entities were under common control prior to the transaction (in which case the transaction is accounted for in the manner of a pooling, continuing the exception first established by Interpretation 39 under APB 16), purchase accounting is required for all reverse acquisitions.

If the former owners of the nominal acquiree in a purchase business combination become the majority owners of the consolidated enterprise following the transactions, it will be deemed to have been a reverse acquisition. Following a reverse acquisition, consolidated financial statements will be presented. Although the financial statements will be identified as being those of the nominal acquirer (which will be the legal owner of the nominal acquiree), in substance these will be the financial statements of the acquiree company, with the assets and liabilities, and revenues and expenses, of the nominal acquirer being included effective with the date of the transaction. Put another way, the legal parent company will be deemed to be a continuation of the business of the legal subsidiary, notwithstanding the formal structure of the transaction or the name of the successor enterprise. For this reason, if the legal parent (nominally the acquirer) does not change its name to that of the acquiree, it would be appropriate for the financial statement titles to be captioned in a way that most clearly communicates the substance of the transaction to the readers. For example, the statements may be headed "ABC Company, Inc.—successor to XYZ Corporation."

Given the foregoing, it is clear that the stockholders' equity section of the posttransaction consolidated balance sheet is to be that of the acquiree, not the acquirer, with appropriate modification for the new shares issued in the transaction and ancillary adjustments, if any. Comparative financial statements for earlier periods, if presented, are to be consistent, meaning that these would be the financial statements of the nominal acquiree. Since in some instances the acquiree's name is different than that shown in the heading, care must be taken to fully communicate with the readers. The fact that the prior period's financial information identified as being that of the legal parent is really that of the nominal acquiree obviously is extremely pertinent to a reader's understanding of these statements.

Consistent with the accounting imposed on other purchase business combinations, the cost of reverse acquisitions is measured at the fair value of the net assets acquired, or the value of the consideration paid, if more apparent. A special rule is that, if fair value cannot be determined for the issuer's stock, and the transaction is valued at the fair value of the issuer's net assets, no goodwill is recognized in the transaction. In addition, in the special case of a publicly held shell company and a privately held acquiree, the SEC has ruled that no goodwill can be recognized in any event. Clearly, in such instances there is substantial doubt about the true existence of goodwill and unusual difficulty in valuing the transaction, and this prohibition is prudent under the circumstances.

If the fair value of the shares of the nominal acquiree (which becomes the legal subsidiary after the transaction is completed) is used to determine the cost of the purchase, it is suggested that a calculation be made to determine the number of shares that the acquiree would have issued in order to provide the same level of ownership in the combined entity to the shareholders of the nominal acquirer as they have as a consequence of the reverse acquisition. The fair value of the number of shares thus determined is used to value the transaction, as illustrated later in this section.

In some instances, the market price of acquiree shares may not be fairly indicative of the value of the transaction. In such cases, the most feasible alternative would be to use the fair value of all the outstanding shares of the ostensible acquirer, prior to the transaction, to value the purchase transaction. In some instances, adjustments would have to be made for trading volume, price fluctuations, etc., to most accurately reflect the substance of the acquisition.

In other cases, particularly where the acquirer is a dormant shell entity, market price of its shares may not be meaningful. If it is possible to determine, utilizing the fair value of the net assets of the acquirer may be a more meaningful technique.

Whatever technique is employed under the circumstances, the total purchase cost is to be allocated to the net assets of the acquirer (not the acquiree) following the principles set forth in FAS 141. If the purchase cost exceeds the fair value of net identifiable assets, the excess is allocated to goodwill, which will be tested for impairment as explained elsewhere in this chapter, and written down or eliminated when and if impairment is detected. The financial statements of the consolidated enterprise following the reverse acquisition would reflect the assets and liabilities of the nominal acquirer at fair value, and those of the nominal acquiree at historical cost.

Since for financial reporting purposes the nominal acquiree is the parent company, the retained earnings or deficit of the acquiree will be carried forward in the equity section of the successor entity's balance sheet. The retained earnings or deficit of the nominal acquirer will not be presented. The amount shown for paid-in capital would be valued in terms of the issued capital of the nominal acquiree (the new subsidiary), plus the cost of the acquisition as described above and illustrated below. However, in the actual financial statement, which must reflect the legal structure of the transaction, paid-in capital would be expressed in terms of the legal parent company, which was the nominal acquirer. An example of accounting for a reverse acquisition follows.

Assume that Agoura Corp., which is the nominal acquirer that becomes the legal parent company, issues shares in exchange for the outstanding common stock of Belmar Co., Inc., which is the nominal acquiree which becomes the legal subsidiary of Agoura. For accounting purposes, this will be a reverse acquisition such that Belmar is the actual acquirer.

The balance sheets of the two entities at the end of 2008 and as of September 30, 2009, the date of the transaction, are given as follows:

|  | *Agoura Corporation* | |
|  | *December 31, 2008* | *September 30, 2009* |
|---|---|---|
| Current assets | $   800,000 | $1,000,000 |
| Plant, property, and equipment, net | 2,400,000 | 2,600,000 |
|  | $3,200,000 | $3,600,000 |
| Current liabilities | $   400,000 | $   600,000 |
| Long-term debt | 600,000 | 400,000 |
| Deferred tax liabilities | 200,000 | 200,000 |
|  | 1,200,000 | 1,200,000 |

|                                              | *Agoura Corporation* | |
| -------------------------------------------- | *December 31, 2008* | *September 30, 2009* |
| Stockholders' equity                         |             |             |
| 8% redeemable preferred stock, 2,000 shs.    | 200,000     | 200,000     |
| Common stock, 100,000 shs.                   | 600,000     | 600,000     |
| Retained earnings                            | 1,200,000   | 1,600,000   |
|                                              | $3,200,000  | $3,600,000  |

|                                              | *Belmar Company, Inc* | |
| -------------------------------------------- | *December 31, 2008* | *September 30, 2009* |
| Current assets                               | $2,500,000  | $1,750,000  |
| Plant, property and equipment, net           | 5,000,000   | 7,500,000   |
|                                              | $7,500,000  | $9,250,000  |
|                                              |             |             |
| Current liabilities                          | $1,250,000  | $1,500,000  |
| Long-term debt                               | 1,750,000   | 2,000,000   |
| Deferred tax liabilities                     | 500,000     | 750,000     |
|                                              | 3,500,000   | 4,250,000   |
| Stockholders' equity                         |             |             |
| Common stock, 60,000 shs.                    | 1,500,000   | 1,500,000   |
| Retained earnings                            | 2,500,000   | 3,500,000   |
|                                              | $7,500,000  | $9,250,000  |

Agoura had net income of $400,000 for the nine months ended September 30, 2008, while Belmar Co. enjoyed earnings of $1,000,000 for that period. Neither company paid any dividends during this period.

The fair value of each share of Belmar common stock was $100 at the date of the acquisition. Agoura shares were quoted at $24 on the date.

Agoura's identifiable net assets had fair values equal to their respective book values, with the exception of the plant, property and equipment, which were appraised at $3,000,000 at September 30, 2008.

In effecting the acquisition, Agoura issues 150,000 new shares of its common stock to the owners of Belmar in exchange for all outstanding Belmar shares. Thus, former Belmar owners become the owners of a majority of the common stock of Agoura after this transaction.

To compute the cost of the reverse acquisition, the number of shares of the nominal acquiree entity, Belmar, which would have had to have been issued to acquire the nominal acquirer, Agoura, must be computed. This is done as follows:

| | |
| --- | ---: |
| Actual Agoura shares issued to former Belmar owners | 150,000 |
| Agoura shares outstanding prior to transaction | 100,000 |
| Total Agoura shares outstanding after transaction | 250,000 |
| Fraction held by former Belmar owners (150,000/250,000) | 60% |
| Number of Belmar shares outstanding before transaction | 60,000 |
| Number of Belmar shares that could have been issued in transaction if 60% of total would have remained with original Belmar shareholders | 40,000 |

If Belmar had issued 40,000 of its shares to effect the acquisition of Agoura, the cost would have been (given the fair value of Belmar shares at September 30, 2008) $100 × 40,000 = $4,000,000. This purchase cost would have been allocated to Agoura's assets and liabilities as follows:

| | | |
| --- | ---: | ---: |
| Current assets                             |          | $1,000,000 |
| Plant, property and equipment              |          | 3,000,000  |
|                                            |          | $4,000,000 |
| Current liabilities                        | $600,000 |            |
| Long-term debt                             | 400,000  |            |
| Deferred tax liabilities                   | 200,000  | 1,200,000  |
|                                            |          | 2,800,000  |
| 8% redeemable preferred stock, 2,000 shares |         | 200,000    |
|                                            |          | 2,600,000  |
| Cost of purchase (from above)              |          | 4,000,000  |
| Goodwill to be recognized                  |          | $1,400,000 |

From the foregoing, the information needed to construct a consolidated balance sheet as of the date of the transaction, September 30, 2008, can be determined.

**Agoura Corporation**
**Consolidated Balance Sheet**
**September 30, 2008**

| | |
|---|---:|
| Current assets | $ 2,750,000 |
| Plant, property and equipment, net | 10,500,000 |
| Goodwill | <u>1,400,000</u> |
| | <u>$14,650,000</u> |
| | |
| Current liabilities | $ 2,100,000 |
| Long-term debt | 2,400,000 |
| Deferred tax liabilities | <u>950,000</u> |
| | 5,450,000 |
| | |
| Stockholders' equity | |
|    8% redeemable preferred stock, 2,000 shares | 200,000 |
|    Common stock, 100,000 shares | 5,500,000 |
|    Retained earnings | <u>3,500,000</u> |
| | <u>9,200,000</u> |
| | <u>$14,650,000</u> |

Computing earnings per share after a reverse acquisition poses special problems, particularly so in the year in which the transaction occurs and in any subsequent years when comparative financial statements are presented that include those of pretransaction periods. For this purpose, the number of shares outstanding for the period from the beginning of the current reporting year until the date of the reverse acquisition is the number of shares issued by the nominal acquirer (the legal parent company) to the shareholders of the nominal acquiree. For the period after the transaction, the number of shares considered to be outstanding is the actual number of shares of the legal parent company outstanding during that period. The average number of shares outstanding for the full year being reported upon would be computed by averaging these two amounts. Other appropriate adjustments would be made to deal with changes in numbers of shares issued during the period, as is done under other circumstances (as described in Chapter 20), if necessary. Under the current standard for computing earnings per share (FAS 128), the calculation of basic earnings per share (replacing the former measure, primary earnings per share) is simplified for all entities.

Earnings per share for any earlier periods presented for comparative purposes is likewise complicated by the occurrence of a reverse acquisition. The number of shares issued by the legal parent (i.e., the nominal acquirer) in the reverse acquisition transaction would be used to make this calculation.

Continuing with the Agoura-Belmar acquisition example above, earnings per share can be computed. Assume that consolidated net income for the year ended December 31, 2008, after deducting preferred dividends, equals $1,600,000. This includes Belmar Co., Inc. earnings for the full year 2008, plus Agoura Corp. earnings from the date of acquisition, September 30, 2008, until year-end. Remember that, notwithstanding that the new entity is called Agoura, from an accounting perspective this is Belmar Company.

Earnings per share would thus be computed as follows:

| | |
|---|---:|
| Number of shares outstanding from September 30, 2008 | 250,000 |
| Number of shares deemed outstanding before September 30—the number of Agoura shares issued to Belmar | 150,000 |

Average number of shares

$$[(150,000 \times 9) + (250,000 \times 3)] \div 12 = 175,000$$

Earnings per share for 2007

$$\$1,600,000 \div 175,000 = \$9.14 \text{ per share}$$

For 2008, assuming Belmar alone had earnings of $1,400,000 for the year, earnings per share would be

$1,400,000 ÷ 150,000 = $9.33 per share

Finally, there is the question of noncontrolling interest. In a reverse acquisition situation, the noncontrolling interest is comprised of the former shareholders of the legal subsidiary who do not exchange their shares for those of the new parent company, but continue on as stockholders in the legal subsidiary entity. Note that this holds even though from the accounting perspective they are shareholders in an entity that acquired another company. In other words, the identity of the noncontrolling interest is determined by the legal structure of the transaction, not the accounting substance. Since the net assets of the legal subsidiary (but substantive parent) are included in the consolidated financial statements at the old book values, noncontrolling interest is likewise computed based on the book value of the legal subsidiary's net assets.

For example, in the present case all shareholders of Belmar might not agree to tender their shares in exchange for Agoura stock, and if so they will continue on as noncontrolling owners of the legal subsidiary, Belmar, after it is nominally acquired by Agoura Corp. To illustrate, consider these assumed facts.

Agoura offered 2.5 shares for each share of Belmar common stock. In the example above, 150,000 shares of Agoura were exchanged for 60,000 Belmar shares. Now, however, assume that owners of 4,000 Belmar shares decline to participate in this transaction, so Agoura issues only 140,000 shares in exchange for 56,000 Belmar shares. After the exchange, former Belmar owners hold 140,000 of a total of 240,000 Agoura Corp. shares, or 58.33% of the total outstanding; still a majority and thus enough to define this as a reverse acquisition.

The cost of the purchase is computed similar to what was illustrated above. Since the owners of 56,000 Belmar shares participated and the transaction resulted in these owners obtaining a 58.33% interest in the successor entity, the calculation of the number of Belmar shares hypothetically required to be issued in a "straight" acquisition of Agoura is as follows:

56,000 shares outstanding ÷ .5833 = 96,000 total shares after transaction

96,000 total shares − 56,000 shares outstanding = 40,000 new shares to be issued

Thus, it can be seen that the cost of the purchase, determined in the manner that is necessary when a reverse acquisition takes place, remains 40,000 × $100 = $4,000,000 even given the existence of the noncontrolling interest.

The noncontrolling interest is 4,000 shares ÷ 60,000 shares = 6.6667%. It consists, as of the acquisition date, of 6.6667% of the book value of Belmar common stock and retained earnings, as follows:

| | | | |
|---|---|---|---|
| 6.6667% × $1,500,000 | = | $100,000 | |
| 6.6667% × $3,500,000 | = | 233,310 | |
| Total noncontrolling interest | | $333,310 | |

The consolidated balance sheet at the acquisition date would differ from that shown above only as follows: a noncontrolling interest of $333,310 would be presented (under current GAAP, as a liability, as equity, or in a semiequity account); common stock would be only $5,400,000, comprised of 93.33% (1 − 6.66667%) of Belmar's $1,500,000, plus the $4 million purchase cost); and retained earnings would be only 93.33% or Belmar's pretransaction balance of $3.5 million, or $3,266,655. All other asset and liability account balances would be identical to the presentation above.

## Spin-Offs

Occasionally an entity disposes of a wholly or partially owned subsidiary or of an investee by transferring it unilaterally to the entity's shareholders. The proper accounting for such a transaction, generally known as a spin-off, depends upon the percentage of the company that is owned.

If the ownership percentage is relatively minor, 25% for example, the transfer to stockholders would be viewed as a "dividend in kind" and would be accounted for at the fair value of the property (i.e., shares in the investee) transferred.

However, when the entity whose shares are distributed is majority or wholly owned, the effect is not merely to transfer a passive investment, but to remove the operations from the former parent and to vest them with the parent's shareholders. This transaction is a true spin-off transaction, not merely a property dividend. APB 29 requires that spin-offs and other similar nonreciprocal transfers to owners be accounted for at the recorded book values of the assets and liabilities transferred.

If the operations (or subsidiary) being spun off are distributed during a fiscal period, it may be necessary to estimate the results of operations for the elapsed period prior to spin-off in order to ascertain the net book value as of the date of the transfer. Stated another way, the operating results of the subsidiary to be disposed of are included in the reported results of the parent through the actual date of the spin-off.

In most instances, the subsidiary being spun off will have a positive net book value. This net worth represents the cost of the nonreciprocal transfer to the owners, and, like a dividend, will be reflected as a charge against the parent's retained earnings at the date of spin-off. In other situations, the operations (or subsidiary) will have a net deficit (negative net book value). Since it is unacceptable to recognize a credit to the parent's retained earnings for other than a culmination of an earnings process, the spin-off is recorded as a credit to the parent's paid-in capital. In effect, the stockholders (the recipients of the spun-off subsidiary) have made a capital contribution to the parent company by accepting the operations having a negative book value. As with other capital transactions, this would not be presented in the income statement, but only in the statement of changes in stockholders' equity (and in the statement of cash flows).

## Reverse Spin-Offs

The preceding section has discussed the normal spin-off situation, where an entity (now being referred to as the spinnor) transfers assets into a new legal spun-off entity (the spinnee) and distributes the shares of the spinnee to its shareholders, without the surrender by the shareholders of any stock of the spinnor. As noted, this transaction is accounted for at book value under APB 29.

In other situations, the spinnee will be the continuing entity. The issue is whether to account for a spin-off as a reverse spin-off based on the substance instead of the legal form of the transaction. In a reverse spin-off, the legal spinnee is treated as though it were the spinnor for accounting purposes (accounting spinnor). This parallels the considerations applicable to reverse acquisitions, discussed earlier in this chapter. It is further complicated, however, by the fact that the determination of the accounting spinnor and spinnee may have significant implications with regard to the reporting of discontinued operations in accordance with FAS 144. The accounting spinnee is reported as a discontinued operation by the accounting spinnor if the spinnee is a component of an entity and meets the conditions for such reporting contained in FAS 144.

In EITF 02-11, a consensus was expressed that reverse spin-off accounting (whereby the legal spinnee is treated as the accounting spinnor, etc.) is appropriate when it results in the most accurate depiction of the substance of the transaction for shareholders and other users of the financial statements. Whether this is appropriate however, is a matter of judgment and must be based on all the facts and circumstances. Absent convincing evidence of the existence of a reverse spin-off, the presumption will be that normal spin-off accounting (whereby the legal spinnee is treated as the accounting spinnee, etc.) is to be applied.

Factors that suggest that reverse spin-off accounting is warranted would include factors such as these.

**Relative size.** Generally, in a reverse spin-off, the accounting spinnor (legal spinnee) is larger than the accounting spinnee (legal spinnor). This determination will be based on a comparison of the assets, revenues, and earnings of the two entities. There are no established "bright lines" that are used to determine which entity is the larger of the two, however.

**Relative fair values.** Generally, in a reverse spin-off, the fair value of the accounting spinnor (legal spinnee) is greater than that of the accounting spinnee (legal spinnor).

**Senior management.** Typically, in a reverse spin-off, the accounting spinnor (legal spinnee) retains the senior management of the formerly combined entity, defined to include the chairman of the board, chief executive officer, chief operating officer, chief financial officer, and those divisional heads reporting directly to them, or the executive committee if one exists.

**Length of time to be held.** Normally, in a reverse spin-off, the accounting spinnor (legal spinnee) is held for a longer period than the accounting spinnee (legal spinnor). A proposed or approved plan of sale for one of the separate entities concurrent with the spin-off may, therefore, identify that entity as the accounting spinnee.

The determination of which entities are the accounting spinnor and spinnee, respectively, has significant implications. In a spin-off, the net book value of the spinnee is treated, in effect, as a dividend distribution to the shareholders of the spinnor. Since the net book value of these entities will differ from each other, the amount of the reduction to retained earnings of the surviving reporting entity (the accounting spinnor) will be affected by this determination. EITF 02-11 offers several examples of fact patterns which support spin-off or reverse spin-off determinations.

## Push-Down Accounting

For a number of years, the matter of what is commonly called "push down" accounting (but which is also known as "new basis accounting") had been on the FASB's technical agenda. It received scant attention notwithstanding the SEC's long-held position that, under narrowly defined circumstances, push-down accounting is to be applied. Since 2000 this matter has received renewed attention and may be jointly dealt with by the FASB and the International Accounting Standards Board.

Under new basis accounting, the amounts allocated to various assets and liabilities can be adjusted to reflect the arm's-length valuation reflected in a significant transaction, such as the sale of a majority interest in the entity. For example, the sale of 90% of the shares of a company by one shareholder to a new investor—which under the entity concept would not alter the accounting by the company itself—would, under new basis accounting, be "pushed down" to the entity. The logic is that, as under purchase method accounting for business combinations, the most objective gauge of "cost" is that arising from a recent arm's-length transaction.

Traditionally, GAAP has not permitted new basis accounting, in part because of the practical difficulty of demonstrating that the reference transaction was indeed arm's-length in nature. (Obviously, the risk is that a series of sham transactions could be used to grossly distort the "cost" and hence carrying values of the entity's assets, resulting in fraudulent financial reporting.) Also heavily debated has been where the threshold should be set (a 50% change in ownership, an 80% change, etc.) to denote when a significant event had occurred that would provide valid information on the valuation of the entity's assets and liabilities for financial reporting purposes.

In its deliberations on this subject, the FASB has agreed that a transfer of control over assets from one entity to a joint venture is an event which should result in gain recognition (where warranted) in the financial statements of the transferor, and that a new basis of accountability would be established for those assets. This is a marked departure from past practice, under which a transfer of appreciated assets to a joint venture or partnership (e.g., a transfer of land to a building partnership) was to be accounted for at book value.

Many of the more general issues of push-down accounting (those applicable to traditional business acquisitions) have yet to be dealt with. For example, proponents of push-down accounting point out that in a purchase business combination a new basis of accounting is established, and that this new basis should be pushed down to the acquired entity and should be used when presenting that entity's own, separate financial statements. However, practical problems remain: for example, while push-down makes some sense in the case where a major block of the investee's shares is acquired in a single free-market transaction, if new basis accounting were to be used in the context of a series of step transactions, continual adjustment of the investee's carrying values for assets and liabilities would be necessary. Furthermore, the price paid for a fractional share of ownership of an investee may not always be meaningfully extrapolated to a value for the investee company as a whole.

The SEC's position has been that push-down accounting would be required if 95% or more of the shares of the company have been acquired (unless the company has outstanding public debt or preferred stock that may impact the acquirer's ability to control the form of ownership of the company); that it would be permitted, but not mandated, if 80% to 95% has been acquired; and it would be prohibited if less than 80% of the company is acquired.

While there is no requirement under GAAP to apply the push-down concept, the SEC position is substantial authoritative support and can be referenced even for nonpublic company financial reporting. It would be defensible in any instance where there is a change in control and/or a change in ownership of a majority of the common shares, when separate financial statements of the subsidiary are to be presented. Full disclosure is to be made of the circumstances whenever push-down accounting is applied.

### Example of push-down accounting

Assume that Pullup Corp. acquires, in an open market arm's-length transaction, 90% of the common stock of Pushdown Co. for $464.61 million. At that time, Pushdown Co.'s net book value was $274.78 million (for the entire company). Book and fair values of selected assets and liabilities of Pushdown Co. as of the transaction date are summarized as follows ($000,000 omitted):

| | Book value | | Fair value of | Excess of |
|---|---|---|---|---|
| | *100% of entity* | *90% interest* | *90% interest* | *FV over book* |
| *Assets* | | | | |
| Receivables | $ 24.6 | $ 22.14 | $ 29.75 | $ 7.61 |
| Inventory | 21.9 | 19.71 | 24.80 | 5.09 |
| Property, plant & equipment, net | 434.2 | 390.78 | 488.20 | 97.42 |
| All others | 223.4 | 201.06 | 201.06 | 0.00 |
| Additional goodwill | | | 120.00 | 120.00 |
| Total assets | $704.1 | $633.69 | $863.81 | $230.12 |
| *Liabilities* | | | | |
| Bonds payable | 104.9 | 94.41 | 88.65 | 5.76 |
| All other liabilities | 325.0 | 292.50 | 310.55 | 18.05 |
| Total liabilities | 429.9 | 386.91 | 399.20 | 12.29 |

*Wiley GAAP 2009*

|  | Book value | | Fair value of | Excess of |
|  | 100% of entity | 90% interest | 90% interest | FV over book |
|---|---|---|---|---|
| **Equity** | | | | |
| Preferred stock | 40.0 | 36.00 | 36.00 | 0.00 |
| Common stock | 87.4 | 78.66 | 78.66 | 0.00 |
| Revaluation surplus* | | | 217.83 | 217.83 |
| Retained earnings | 146.8 | 132.12 | 132.12 | 0.00 |
| Total equity | 274.2 | 246.88 | 464.61 | 217.83 |
| Liabilities + Equity | $704.1 | $633.69 | $863.81 | $230.12 |

\* *Net premium paid over book value by arm's-length of "almost all" common stock*

Assuming that "new basis" accounting is deemed to be acceptable and meaningful, since Pushdown Co. must continue to issue separate financial statements to its creditors and holders of its preferred stock, and also assuming that a revaluation of the share of ownership that did not change hands (i.e., the 10% noncontrolling interest in this example) should not be revalued based on the majority transaction, the entries by the subsidiary (Pushdown Co.) for purposes only of preparing stand-alone financial statements would be as follows:

| | | |
|---|---|---|
| Accounts receivable | 7,610,000 | |
| Inventory | 5,090,000 | |
| Plant, property and equipment (net) | 97,420,000 | |
| Goodwill | 120,000,000 | |
| Discount on bonds payable | 5,760,000 | |
| Other liabilities | | 18,050,000 |
| Paid-in capital from revaluation | | 217,830,000 |

The foregoing entry would only be made for purposes of preparing separate financial statements of Pushdown Co. If consolidated financial statements of Pullup Corp. are also presented, essentially the same result will be obtained. The additional paid-in capital account would be eliminated against the parent's investment account, however, since in the context of the consolidated financial statements this would be a cash transaction rather than a mere accounting revaluation.

There is also a body of opinion holding that the separate financial statements of Pushdown Co. in this example should be "grossed up" for the imputed premium that would have been achieved on the transfer of the remaining 10% ownership interest. This is less appealing, however, given the absence of a "real" transaction involving that last 10% ownership stake, making the price at which it would have traded somewhat speculative.

The foregoing example obviously also ignored the tax effects of the transaction. Since the step-ups in carrying value would not, in all likelihood, alter the corresponding tax bases of the assets and liabilities, deferred tax effects would also require recognition. This would be done following the procedures set forth at FAS 109, as described fully in Chapter 17.

## Non-Sub Subsidiaries

Another issue that has concerned accountants and the SEC is the popularity of what have been called "non-sub subsidiaries." This situation arises when an entity plays a major role in the creation and financing of what is often a start-up or experimental operation, but does not take an equity position at the outset. For example, the sponsor might finance the entity by means of convertible debt or debt with warrants entitling it to the later purchase of common shares. The original equity in such arrangements is often provided by the creative or managerial talent engaged in the new entity's operations, who generally exchange their talents for an equity interest. If the operation prospers, the sponsor will exercise its rights and obtain a majority voting stock position; if the operation fails, the sponsor presumably avoids reflecting the losses in its financial statements.

While this strategy may seem to avoid the requirements of equity method accounting or consolidation based on majority voting ownership, the economic substance of the arrangement clearly suggests that the operating results of the sponsored entity be reflected as a subsidiary in the consolidated financial statements of the sponsor who, in substance, is fulfilling the customary role of a parent, even absent ownership of voting stock.

The entities described above are often similar in structure and purpose to what were formerly called "special-purpose entities" or "special-purpose vehicles" and which have now been identified as "variable interest entities." These VIE have been widely discussed in recent years, as their use has grown exponentially for such valid purposes as securitizations, but also for less worthy objectives, including concealing the existence of debt which might represent the moral, if not necessarily the legal, obligations of the reporting entity. These matters are described in the next section.

### Variable Interest Entities

**Introduction and background information.** As previously discussed, ARB 51, *Consolidated Financial Statements*, issued over 40 years ago, provides the primary authority for determining when presentation of consolidated financial statements is required. The rationale underlying ARB 51 is that consolidated financial statements are more informative to users when one enterprise directly or indirectly holds a "controlling financial interest" in one or more other enterprises. ARB 51 went on to stipulate that the usual condition that best evidenced which party held a controlling financial interest was the party that held a majority voting interest.

This general rule requiring consolidation by a party holding a majority of the voting interests is still operational today and the foregoing discussion of consolidations and business combinations provided extensive guidance regarding parent/subsidiary relationships in the context of the parent holding a majority voting interest in the subsidiary. The subsidiary in this relationship is sometimes referred to as a voting interest entity.

Since the issuance of ARB 51, however, managers and their advisors have devised many new and creative types of ownership structures, financing arrangements, financial instruments, and business relationships. Many, if not most of these arrangements were originated to accomplish legitimate business objectives. Some of the arrangements were designed with the express intent of establishing financial control over assets or operations while the sponsoring entity avoided the establishment of voting control that served as the determinant of consolidation.

Examples of such arrangements abound and have been discussed in previous sections of this chapter. Perhaps no such type of financial arrangement or structure, however, has received the level of negative publicity as the special-purpose entity (SPE). The primary authoritative pronouncement that addressed SPE is FAS 140, *Accounting for Transfers and Servicing of Financial Assets and Extinguishments of Liabilities*, which is discussed in detail in Chapter 7. In the context of FAS 140 (and the predecessor standard, FAS 125, where the definition originated) an SPE is narrowly defined as a trust or other legal vehicle to which a transferor transfers a portfolio of financial assets (such as mortgage loans, commercial loans, credit card debt, automobile loans, and other groups of homogenous borrowings).

Commonly SPE have been organized as trusts or partnerships (flow-through entities, in order to avoid double incidence of corporate income taxation), and the outside equity participant was ultimately defined as having as little as 3% of the total assets of the SPE at risk (this was not established by GAAP, but rather evolved somewhat by default and has been subject to varying interpretation under different sets of conditions).

In a process called a securitization, the SPE typically issues and sells securities that represent beneficial interests in the cash flows from the portfolio. The proceeds the SPE receives from the sale of the securities are used to purchase the portfolio from the transferor. The cash flows received by the SPE from the dividends, interest, redemptions, principal repayments, and/or realized gains on the financial assets are used to pay a return to the investors in the SPE's securities. By transferring packages of such loans to an SPE, these assets can be legally isolated and made "bankruptcy proof" (and thus made more valuable as collateral for other borrowings); various types of debt instruments can thus be used, providing the sponsor with fresh resources to fund future lending activities. SPE within the scope of FAS 140 are limited to entities that hold financial assets. SPE are sometimes used, however, to hold nonfinancial assets such as real estate, machinery, or energy contracts.

**Use of special-purpose entities under prior GAAP.** SPE had their origin in the rules for consolidation, which historically were based on the existence of majority ownership of one enterprise by another. While the substitution of control for ownership had been contemplated as a means of limiting the use of SPE to evade consolidation requirements, practical difficulties in defining control had kept this project from fruition for many years.

As discussed previously, SPE achieved "level A GAAP" status by virtue of being somewhat obliquely addressed in FAS 125, which dealt with transfers of financial assets (and later was superseded by the very similar FAS 140). The concept of a "qualified" SPE (QSPE) also arose from this standard, denoting that SPE can participate in "true sales" of financial assets under FAS 125/140, to be accounted for as sales rather than as secured borrowings.

Importantly, in order for the sponsor to avoid consolidating the SPE, the outside equity participant was required to have *control,* which—although customarily not invoked under GAAP as the criterion for consolidation—was established as the key determinant for sponsor nonconsolidation of an SPE. Where an SPE was controlled by parties other than the sponsor, and there was significant risk capital invested by them, consolidation of the SPE in the sponsor's financial statements could be avoided.

**Problems in past practice.** With benefit of hindsight, it is clear that the rules for SPE evolved in a way that left too much to chance and to the influence of highly interested parties. As a result, notwithstanding the arguably important role that SPE may have played in the financial marketplace, SPE came to be widely used to accomplish financial reporting manipulations. Thus, the "outside" equity participants often funded their "independent capital contributions" with debt obtained from lenders to the sponsor, or via debt indirectly guaranteed by the sponsor, some of whom evaded disclosure of their positions as guarantors by means of imaginative interpretations of GAAP, particularly of FAS 5.

Furthermore, sponsors engaged in transactions with SPE that often resulted in the sponsors recognizing large amounts of income. In some instances, complex sets of guarantees and option arrangements had the effect of causing these gains to be reversible. In the most egregious transactions, sponsors were able to recoup reportable gains from economic events and transactions that could never have supported income recognition if engaged in directly by the entity, even extending to recognizing fair value changes in the sponsor's own capital stock.

It is clear that SPE do serve various tax, legal, and strategic corporate objectives, but whether the exclusion of SPE from their sponsor's consolidated financial statements had, under prior rules, any accounting legitimacy, remains an open question. In other words, in setting forth a representation of an entity's economic position and the results of its operations, the validity of excluding events or transactions that are in fact integral to the entity's current position and future prospects, merely because these have been "walled off" by a legal structure, was doubtful. Simply put, the issue is whether economic substance is to be presented, regardless of legal form.

**FASB's response.** After the public revelations regarding Enron and its use of SPE to hide its true financial condition, FASB recognized the need to augment the existing consolidations model to take into account financial arrangements where parties other than the holders of a majority of the voting interests exercise financial control over another entity. Thus, it undertook a project to issue an interpretation of ARB 51 to broaden its scope.

In its deliberations on these issues, FASB decided not to refer to entities within the scope of the eventual interpretation as SPE. This decision underscores the fact that the type of entity to which the interpretation applies is more broadly defined than entities that qualify as SPE involved in securitization transactions or even SPE that hold nonfinancial assets. Thus, an entity within the scope of the interpretation may or may not have formerly been referred to as an SPE.

FASB coined the term variable interest entity (VIE) to designate an entity that is financially controlled by one or more parties that do not hold a majority voting interest. A party that possesses the majority of this financial control, if there is one, is referred to as the VIE's primary beneficiary.

**Scope exceptions.** The following are excluded from the scope of FIN 46(R):

1. Not-for-profit organizations as defined in FAS 117, para 168, (including not-for-profit health care organizations subject to the AICPA AAG, *Health Care Organizations*) unless the organization was organized to avoid VIE status
2. Employer/sponsors of employee benefit plans including ESOP, pension, profit sharing, 401(k), postretirement, and postemployment plans
3. Enterprises subject to SEC Regulation S-X Rule 6-03(c)(1) (investment companies, mutual funds) may only consolidate an entity subject to the same regulation.
4. Separate accounts of life insurance entities
5. A "qualifying special-purpose entity" (QSPE) or a "formerly qualifying SPE" (FQSPE) under the provisions of FAS 140, *Accounting for Transfers and Servicing of Financial Assets and Extinguishments of Liabilities*, are not to be consolidated by entities and their affiliates who transfer financial assets to them
6. Enterprises holding variable interests in a QSPE or FQSPE are not to consolidate that entity unless the holder has the unilateral ability to cause the entity's liquidation or change the entity so that it ceases to meet the conditions of FAS 140 to be considered a QSPE or FQSPE
7. A governmental organization
8. A nongovernmental financing entity established by a governmental organization unless the financing entity is being used to circumvent FIN 46(R) to avoid consolidation
9. An entity created prior to December 31, 2003, for which, after expending "exhaustive efforts," management of the variable interest holder is unable to obtain information needed to determine whether the entity is a VIE, determine whether the holder is the primary beneficiary, or make the required consolidating/eliminating entries required by FIN 46(R)

   *NOTE: With respect to this exception, however, management of the variable interest holder is required to continue to make these efforts after initial adoption of FIN 46(R). If the variable interest holder significantly participated in the design/redesign of the entity, it would be unusual for it to be able to contend that it was unable to obtain the necessary information.*

10. An entity that qualifies to be treated as a business, as defined below (the definition included in FIN 46(R) was adapted from EITF 98-3, *Determining Whether a Nonmonetary Transaction Involves Receipt of Productive Assets or a Business*). However, this scope exception does not apply and the entity would be required to be evaluated as to whether it is a VIE by the holders of its variable interests if any one or more of the following conditions exists:

a. The variable interest holder and/or its related parties/de facto agents[7] (de facto agents are discussed later in this chapter) participated significantly in the design or redesign of the entity. This factor is not considered when the entity is an operating joint venture jointly controlled by the variable interest holder, and either an independent party or a franchisee.

b. The design of the entity results in substantially all of its activities either involving or being conducted on behalf of the variable interest holder and its related parties.

c. Based on the relative fair values of interests in the entity, the variable interest holder and its related parties provide more than half of its total equity, subordinated debt, and other forms of subordinated financial support.

d. The entity's activities relate primarily to one or both of the following:

(1) Single-lessee leases

11. Securitizations or other forms of asset-backed financings

**Definition of a business.** A business is defined, in the context of FIN 46(R) as

*...a self-sustaining integrated set of activities and assets conducted and managed for the purpose of providing a return to investors. A business consists of (a) inputs, (b) processes applied to those inputs, and (c) resulting outputs that are used to generate revenues. For a set of activities and assets to be a business, it must contain all of the inputs and processes necessary for it to conduct normal operations, which include the ability to sustain a revenue stream by providing its outputs to customers.*

In evaluating whether an entity is a business, consideration must be given to unique factors relating to the industry and the activities being performed including

**Inputs**

1. Fixed assets either owned or leased
2. Intangibles either owned or licensed
3. Access to materials or rights needed to perform its activities
4. Employees

**Processes**

1. Strategic management
2. Operations
3. Resource management

**Outputs**

1. Access to customers (clients)

A three-step process is provided in order to assess whether a set of activities ("set") qualifies as a business.

1. Identify elements included in the "set" (i.e., determine the existing inputs, processes, and outputs).

2. Compare the elements identified in 1. with the elements necessary for the set of activities to be conducted as a normal business operation.

3. If any elements are missing, assess the degree of effort or investment relative to the fair value of the set of activities needed to acquire or gain access to the missing

---

[7] *Only for the purposes of applying factor a. above, de facto agents exclude parties that require the variable interest holder's prior approval to sell, transfer, or encumber their interest in the entity.*

elements.  If a significant effort or investment would be required, it can be concluded that the set of activities is not a business; conversely, a de minimis amount of effort or investment to supply the missing elements would lead to the conclusion that the set of activities is a business.

**Interpretation 46(R): accounting for variable interest entities (VIE).**  FIN 46(R) substantially alters the consolidations model to which accountants had long been accustomed.  Under FIN 46(R), variable interest entities that have a primary beneficiary, as defined, must be consolidated in the general-purpose financial statements of that primary beneficiary, regardless of the extent of ownership (or lack of it) by that entity.  FIN 46(R) introduces a number of new terms and concepts in the attempt to explain and operationalize the accounting for VIE.

*Expected variability.*  When estimating an entity's expected future cash flows in accordance with CON 7, *Using Cash Flow Information and Present Value in Accounting Measurements* (discussed more fully in Chapter 1), a range of probability-weighted expected outcomes is used.  Mathematically, this is simply a weighted-average calculation.  The following example illustrates the mathematical concept of expected variability:

### Example of expected variability of cash flows

Mided Mining Company is computing the probability-weighted expected future cash flows from operating and disposing of a tunnel boring machine that has a remaining estimated useful life of three years.  This estimate was necessitated by FAS 144 which requires an evaluation, when certain events or circumstances occur, of whether the future cash flows associated with the use and disposal of long-lives assets are sufficient to recover their carrying value over their estimated remaining depreciable lives.  Because of uncertainty regarding the amounts and timing of the cash flows, Mided's management used the CON 7 probability-weighted expected cash flow model with the following results:

| | *2008* | *2009* | *2010* | *3-year outcome* | *Probability of occurrence* | *Probability-weighted expected outcome* |
|---|---|---|---|---|---|---|
| Expected outcome 1 | $3,500 | $3,200 | $2,700 | $9,400 | 20% | $1,880 |
| Expected outcome 2 | 4,000 | 3,900 | 3,700 | 11,600 | 45% | 5,220 |
| Expected outcome 3 | 4,300 | 4,100 | 4,000 | 12,400 | 30% | 3,720 |
| Expected outcome 4 | 4,400 | 4,700 | -- | 9,100 | 5% | 455 |
| | | | | | 100% | |
| Probability-weighted expected cash flows (weighted-average) | | | | | | $11,275 |

The $11,275 weighted-average, undiscounted, is compared to the carrying value of the tunnel boring machine to determine whether or not the carrying value is fully recoverable.  The weighted-average consists of four different outcomes, each with its own estimated probability of occurrence.  Since these amounts represent management's best estimates, management deems it possible that, at the end of the three-year period, any one of these outcomes could actually occur.  When management considers the individual probability of occurrence for each of the four outcomes estimated above, the analysis yields the following results:

| | [1] *3-year outcome* | [2] *Probability-weighted expected outcome* | [3] *[1] – [2] Variation* | [4] *Probability of occurrence* | [5] *[3] × [4] Probability-weighted variation* | *Positive variation* | *Negative variation* |
|---|---|---|---|---|---|---|---|
| Expected outcome 1 | $9,400 | $11,275 | $(1,875) | 20% | $(375) | $ -- | $(375) |
| Expected outcome 2 | 11,600 | 11,275 | 325 | 45% | 146 | 146 | -- |

| | [1] | [2] Probability-weighted expected outcome | [3] [1] – [2] *Variation* | [4] Probability of *occurrence* | [5] [3] × [4] Probability-weighted *variation* | Positive *variation* | Negative *variation* |
|---|---|---|---|---|---|---|---|
| | *3-year outcome* | | | | | | |
| Expected outcome 3 | 12,400 | 11,275 | 1,125 | 30% | 338 | 338 | -- |
| Expected outcome 4 | 9,100 | 11,275 | (2,175) | 5% | (109) | -- | (109) |
| | | | | 100% | | $484 | $(484) |

Careful examination of the above analysis yields the following conclusions:

1. Variations naturally occur between expected outcomes and actual outcomes.
2. Because the expected outcome is calculated as an average, some of the amounts used to compute it will be higher than the average and some will be lower than the average.
3. When the individual variations are computed and each is multiplied by its probability of occurrence, the absolute value of the sum of the positive variations will exactly equal the absolute value of the sum of the negative variations.
4. When these two absolute values are summed ($484 + $484 = $968 in the example above), the result, the total variability in both directions is called the expected variability of the cash flows.
5. The higher the expected variability of a set of cash flow estimates, the higher the level of risk and uncertainty associated with the estimate.

Further interpretation of this concept is provided in FSP FIN 46(R)-6, where the analysis of expected variability is based on the following two-step approach: (1) Determine the nature of an entity's risks, which shall at least include the areas of credit, interest rates, foreign currency exchange, commodity prices, equity prices, and operations, and then (2) determine the extent of the variability the entity was designed to pass through to its interest holders by reviewing its activities, contract terms, terms of issued interests, how those interests were negotiated, and the parties participating in the entity's design.

*Variable interests.* Ownership, contractual, or other monetary interests in an entity that are either entitled to receive expected positive variability (referred to as expected residual returns) or obligated to absorb expected negative variability (referred to as expected losses). Variable interests are identified by thoroughly analyzing the assets, liabilities, and contractual arrangements of an entity to determine whether each item being analyzed creates variability or absorbs/receives variability. Favorable changes in the fair value of the entity's net assets and contractual arrangements that create variability comprise expected residual returns which result from estimated outcomes in which the entity outperforms the probability-weighted expected results. Unfavorable changes in the fair value of the entity's net assets and contractual arrangements that create variability comprise expected losses which result from estimated outcomes in which the entity underperforms the probability-weighted expected results.

Appendix B of FIN 46(R) provides examples of potential variable interests. Each of the items below is potentially an explicit or implicit variable interest in an entity or in specified assets of an entity. Upon analysis of the specific facts, circumstances, and contract terms, the financial statement preparer is charged with determining whether a particular item either absorbs expected losses or receives expected residual returns (collectively referred to as expected variability) or both. The absorbing/receiving of variability is the sole determinant of whether an interest is a variable interest and, in analyzing specific situations, the degree of variability can differ widely for each item.

1. At-risk equity investments in a VIE
2. Investments in subordinated debt instruments issued by a VIE
3. Investments in subordinated beneficial interests issued by a VIE
4. Guarantees of the value of VIE assets or liabilities
5. Written put options on the assets of a VIE or similar obligations that protect senior interests from suffering losses
6. Forward contracts to sell assets owned by the entity at a fixed price
7. Stand-alone or embedded derivative instruments including total return swaps and similar arrangements
8. Contracts or agreements for fees to be paid to a decision maker (These are generally deemed to absorb variability unless the relationship between the entity and the decision maker meets specified criteria to be considered an employee/employer relationship or a "hired service provider" relationship, in which case the arrangement would not be deemed to create a variable interest. In this case, the fees would be included in computations of expected variability.)
9. Other service contracts with nondecision makers
10. Operating leases that include residual value guarantees and/or lessee option to purchase the leased property at a specified price
11. Variable interests of one VIE in another VIE
12. Interests retained by a transferor of financial assets to a VIE

As previously stated, although all of these examples potentially qualify as variable interests, they differ widely in terms of the extent of their variability which has a direct effect on the likelihood of their causing their holders to be considered the primary beneficiary of the VIE. Note that an interest can qualify as a variable interest but the entity in which the interest is held may not qualify as a variable interest entity. Careful analysis of the facts and circumstances is necessary to determine the economics of a particular situation.

*Implicit variable interests.* One of the most misunderstood provisions of FIN 46(R) is referred to as an implicit variable interest. The FASB Staff attempted to clarify this matter in FSP FIN 46(R)-5.

As discussed in Chapter 16, a party which did not explicitly issue a direct guarantee of another party's obligation can, nevertheless, be held to be an implicit guarantor of that obligation and thus, under FIN 46(R), hold a variable interest in the party whose debt is implicitly guaranteed.

Consider the situation where the principal shareholder of a company personally guarantees a mortgage on the premises that the company occupies and leases from a related LLC whose sole member is the lessee's principal shareholder. Normally, the rent payments due under the related-party lease are structured to provide sufficient cash flow to the lessor to enable it to meet its debt service under the mortgage. If the lessee were to become delinquent under its rent obligations to the lessor, the lessor would not have sufficient cash flow to enable it to make the payments due under its mortgage which would cause a loan delinquency or default.

Should this occur, the following scenarios could occur:

1. The lender could repossess the property and sell it to pay off the loan
2. The lender could enforce the guarantee and compel the shareholder to pay off the loan on behalf of the lessor or, at least to make the delinquent payments on behalf of the lessor to cure the default, or
3. The lessee could sell off assets or borrow money from its stockholder or a third party to enable it to pay its delinquent rent, thereby enabling the lessor to make its delinquent mortgage payments.

Scenario 1. would not be a desirable outcome, as the lessor would lose title to its property and the lessee, in default on its rent, could end up without the premises in which it operates its business since, upon sale of the property, the successor owner would potentially terminate the lease for nonpayment.

Under scenario 2. if the shareholder were to pay the delinquent mortgage payment on behalf of the lessor, the transactions would be recorded as follows:

**Lessor Accounting Records**

|  | Debit | Credit |
|---|---|---|
| Rent receivable | xxx | |
| Rental income | | xxx |
| *To record delinquent rent due from lessee* | | |
| | | |
| Mortgage payable | xxx | |
| Loan payable—Member | | xxx |
| *To record mortgage payment made on behalf of LLC by its member as a loan payable to the member* | | |

**Lessee Accounting Records**

|  | | |
|---|---|---|
| Rent expense | xxx | |
| Rent payable | | xxx |
| *To record delinquent rent due to lessor* | | |

Scenario 3. would be recorded as follows (assuming that the lessee obtains additional funds from its principal shareholder):

**Lessee Accounting Records**

|  | Debit | Credit |
|---|---|---|
| Cash | xxx | |
| Loan payable—shareholder | | xxx |
| *To record loan from shareholder* | | |
| | | |
| Rent payable | xxx | |
| Cash | | xxx |
| *To record rent payment* | | |

**Lessor Accounting Records**

|  | Debit | Credit |
|---|---|---|
| Cash | xxx | |
| Rental income | | xxx |
| *To record rent received from lessee* | | |
| | | |
| Mortgage interest | xxx | |
| Mortgage payable | xxx | |
| Cash | | xxx |
| *To record mortgage payment* | | |

The outcomes of scenarios 2. and 3. are very similar. Under scenario 2., the shareholder/member will have a loan receivable from the thinly capitalized LLC that depends solely on the delinquent corporation for its cash flow. In scenario 2., the lessee will have to raise cash in an amount sufficient to fund the LLC's repayment of its loan to the shareholder/member and keep the mortgage current. Since the LLC is dependent upon the lessee for its cash flow, the lessee has implicitly incurred an obligation to fund the LLC's loan repayment to the shareholder/member. It is, of course, in the best interest of the lessee to fund this since it entitles the lessee to continue to benefit from the use of the leased property and, contractually, the lessee is already obligated to pay the delinquent rent.

Under scenario 3., the shareholder/member will have a loan receivable from a lessee that is experiencing difficulty in meeting its rent obligations. The lessee will have substituted a presumably interest-bearing loan payable to its shareholder for a noninterest-bearing rent payable obligation to the LLC and will, as in scenario 2., be obligated to raise cash sufficient to repay its shareholder and fund its rent obligations under the lease. In effect, the lessee will have used its available credit that it could have used for other operating purposes to help provide financial support to the LLC that would otherwise have insufficient capital to be self-sustaining. Again, implicitly, the lessee is functioning as a guarantor of the LLC's mortgage indebtedness by its willingness to provide the cash flow necessary for the LLC to meet its obligations.

Based on the foregoing analysis, in substance the lessee is the holder of an implicit variable interest in the lessor in the form of an implicit guarantee of the lessor's mortgage debt. Due to the fact that the implicit guarantee exposes the lessee/variable interest holder to the expected losses of the lessor, the lessor/LLC's sole member (and at-risk equity holder) is not the only party that potentially would absorb expected losses of the lessor.

***Expected losses and expected residual returns.*** Expected losses represent the expected negative variability in the fair value of an enterprise's net assets exclusive of variable interests. Expected residual returns represent the expected positive variability in the fair value of an enterprise's net assets exclusive of variable interests. The expected variability in an enterprise's net income or loss is included in the determination of its expected losses and expected residual returns.

**VIE defined.** Variable interest entities include, under FIN 46(R), any entity which, by design, satisfies one of the following characteristics:

1.  The total equity investment at risk is not sufficient to permit the entity to finance its activities without additional subordinated financial support from either the existing equity holders or other parties. That is, the equity investment at risk is not sufficient to absorb all of the expected losses of the entity. For this purpose, the total equity investment at risk

    a.  Includes only equity investments in the entity that participate significantly in profits and losses even if those investments do not carry voting rights.
    b.  Does not include equity interests that the entity issued in exchange for subordinated interests in other variable interest entities.
    c.  Does not include amounts provided to the equity investor directly or indirectly by the entity or by other parties involved with the entity (for example, by fees, charitable contributions, or other payments), unless the provider is a parent, subsidiary, or affiliate of the investor that is required to be included in the same set of consolidated financial statements as the investor.
    d.  Does not include amounts financed for the equity investor (for example, by loans or guarantees of loans) directly by the entity or by other parties involved with the entity, unless that party is a parent, subsidiary, or affiliate of the investor that is required to be included in the same set of consolidated financial statements as the investor.

or

2.  As a group the holders of the equity investment at risk lack any one of the following three characteristics of a controlling financial interest:

    a.  The direct or indirect ability through voting or similar rights to make decisions about an entity's activities that affect the entity's success. The investors do not have that ability through voting rights or similar rights if no owners hold voting rights or similar rights (such as those of a common stockholder in a corporation or a general partner in a partnership).
    b.  The obligation to absorb the expected losses of the entity. The investor or investors do not have that obligation if they are directly or indirectly protected

from absorbing the expected losses or are guaranteed a return by the entity it-self or by other parties with whom the entity is involved.

c. The right to receive the expected residual returns of the entity. The investors do not have that right if their return is limited to a specified maximum amount by the entity's governing documents or arrangements with other variable interest holders or with the entity.

The equity investors as a group also are considered to lack characteristic 2.a. if, upon consideration of those investors' at-risk equity investments and all other interests in the entity (1) the voting rights of some investors are not proportional to their obligations to absorb the entity's expected losses, to receive the entity's expected residual returns, or both, and (2) substantially all of the entity's activities (for example, lending activities, or asset acquisitions) either involve or are conducted on behalf of an investor that has disproportionately few voting rights.

In other words, VIE are generally thinly capitalized entities that carry risks of economic losses or possibilities of economic gains beyond what the nominal owner (the "equity participant") could absorb or will be able to benefit from, respectively. If a party provides "subordinated financial support" to the entity that exposes it to absorbing the majority of the VIE's expected losses, or entitles it to receive the majority of the VIE's expected residual returns, or both, it is generally deemed to be the primary beneficiary of that VIE and will be required to consolidate the VIE as its subsidiary, irrespective of how much, if any equity investment it has in the VIE.

**Initial determination of VIE status.** Whether or not an entity qualifies as a VIE is initially determined when an entity obtains its variable interest in that entity. This determination is based on the circumstances existing at that date, taking into account future changes that are required in existing governing documents and contractual arrangements. It is not necessary, however, for an interest holder to make this determination if both of the following conditions exist:

1. It is apparent that the holder's interest would not be a significant variable interest, and
2. The holder, its related parties, and its de facto agents (as specified below) were not significant participants in the design or redesign of the entity.

**Related-party considerations in determining the primary beneficiary.** Many SPE structures made use of related-party relationships, which did not, however, automatically necessitate consolidation (although disclosures were required under GAAP). For the purpose of a variable interest holder determining whether it is the primary beneficiary of a VIE, FIN 46(R) expands the definition of related parties that is set forth in FAS 57, *Related-Party Disclosures*, to include additional parties that act as "de facto agents" or "de facto principals" of the variable interest holder. The following table sets forth the related parties as prescribed by FAS 57 as well as additional related parties designated by FIN 46(R) for this purpose:

| *Related parties FAS 57* | *De facto principals/agents FIN 46(R)* |
|---|---|
| • Affiliates—Parties that directly or indirectly, through one or more intermediaries control, are controlled by, or are under common control with the variable interest holder | • Parties that cannot finance their operations without subordinated financial support from the variable interest holder (e.g., another VIE of which the variable interest holder is the primary beneficiary) |
| • Equity method investees of the variable interest holder | • Parties that received their interest in the VIE as a contribution or loan from the variable interest holder |

- Employee benefit trusts (e.g., pension and profit-sharing trusts) when the variable interest holder/plan sponsor or members of its management manage the plan or serve as the plan trustee
- Principal owners of the variable interest holder (owners of record or beneficial owners of > 10% of the variable interest holder's voting interests) and members of their immediate families
- Management of the variable interest holder and members of their immediate families
- Transacting parties where one party controls or significantly influences the management or operating policies of the other to the extent that it might be prevented from fully pursuing its own separate interests
- Other parties that have an ownership interest in one of the transacting parties; or control, or significantly influence the management or operating policies of the transacting parties to the extent that one or more of the transacting parties might be prevented from fully pursuing its own separate interests

- Officers and employees of the variable interest holder
- Members of the governing board of the variable interest holder
- Parties that have agreements not to sell, transfer, or pledge their interests in the VIE as collateral without the prior approval of the variable interest holder where that prior approval right constrains that party's ability to manage the economic risks or realize the economic rewards from its interests
- Parties with a close business relationship to the variable interest holder such as the relationship of a professional service provider to one of its significant clients.

These related-party attribution rules under FIN 46(R) will require consolidation of many of the currently popular SPE structures, unless the VIE is well capitalized and such subordinated support vehicles as loan guarantees are dispensed with.

If two or more related parties (including de facto principals/agents specified above) hold variable interests in the same VIE, and the aggregate variable interests held by those parties would, if held by a single party, identify that party as the primary beneficiary, then the member of the related-party group that is most closely associated with the VIE is the primary beneficiary that is required to consolidate the VIE as a subsidiary in its financial statements. In determining which party is most closely associated with the VIE, all relevant facts and circumstances are to be considered including

1. Whether there is a principal/agent relationship between parties within the related-party group
2. The relationship of the activities of the VIE to each of the parties in the related-party group
3. The significance of the VIE's activities to each of the parties in the related-party group
4. The extent of a party's exposure to the expected losses of the VIE
5. The structure of the VIE

**Reconsideration of VIE status.** Once an initial determination is made as to whether an entity is a variable interest entity (as opposed to a voting interest entity), that initial determination need not be reconsidered unless one or more of the following circumstances occurs:

1. A change is made to the VIE's governing documents or contractual arrangements that results in changes in either the characteristics or sufficiency of the at-risk equity investment in the VIE.
2. As a result of a return of some or all of the equity investment to the equity investors, other interests become exposed to the VIE's expected losses.
3. There is an increase in the VIE's expected losses that results from the entity engaging in activities or acquiring assets that were not anticipated at either the inception of the entity or a later reconsideration date.
4. There is a decrease in the VIE's expected losses due to the entity modifying or curtailing its activities.
5. Additional at-risk equity is invested in the VIE.

FIN 46(R) specifically excludes a troubled debt restructuring (as defined and discussed in Chapter 15) from being an event requiring reconsideration of VIE status.

**Determination and redetermination of whether an interest holder is the primary beneficiary.** A holder of a variable interest initially determines whether it is the primary beneficiary of a VIE in conjunction with the initial determination that the entity is a VIE, that is, when the holder initially obtains its interest in the entity. This initial determination of whether an interest holder is the primary beneficiary (irrespective of whether the holder is or is not considered to be the primary beneficiary) needs to be reconsidered when the changes are made to the entity's governing documents or contractual arrangements that result in a reallocation of the obligation to absorb expected losses or the right to receive expected residual returns of the VIE between the existing primary beneficiary and other unrelated parties. A variable interest holder that had previously determined that it was the VIE's primary beneficiary is required to reconsider its initial decision to consolidate that VIE if (1) it sells or otherwise disposes of all or part of its variable interest to unrelated parties, or (2) if the VIE issues new variable interests to parties other than the primary beneficiary or the primary beneficiary's related parties.

If a variable interest holder had, upon obtaining its interest, determined that it was not the primary beneficiary of a VIE, it is to reconsider this determination it if obtains additional variable interests in the VIE.

As is the case with the determination of whether an entity is a VIE, the initial or subsequent determination of its primary beneficiary is not affected by a troubled debt restructuring.

**Variable interests in "silos."** A party may hold a variable interest in specific assets of a VIE (e.g., a guarantee or a subordinated residual interest). In computing expected losses and expected residual returns, a holder of a variable interest in specified assets of a VIE must determine if the interest it holds qualifies as an interest in the VIE itself. The variable interest is considered an interest in the VIE itself if either (1) the fair value of the specific assets is more than half of the total fair value of the VIE's assets or (2) the interest holder has another significant variable interest in the entity as a whole.

If the interests are deemed to be interests in the VIE itself, the expected losses and expected residual returns associated with the variable interest in the specified assets are treated as being associated with the VIE.

If the interests are not deemed to be interests in the VIE itself, the interests in the specified assets are treated as a separate VIE (referred to as a "silo") if the expected cash flows from the specified assets (and any associated credit enhancements, if applicable) are essentially the sole source of payment for specified liabilities or specified other interests. Under this scenario, expected losses and expected residual returns associated with the silo assets are accounted for separately to the extent that the interest holder either absorbs the VIE's expected losses or is entitled to receive its expected residual returns. Any excess of expected losses or expected residual returns not borne by (received by) the variable interest holder is considered attributable to the entity as a whole.

If one interest holder is required to consolidate a silo of a VIE, other VIE interest holders are to exclude the silo from the remaining VIE.

**Consolidation requirements.** An entity must consolidate a VIE of which it is the primary beneficiary. The variable interest holder that is the primary beneficiary of a VIE holds a variable interest (or combination of variable interests) that will absorb a majority of the entity's expected losses, receive a majority of the entity's expected residual returns, or both. The rights and obligations conveyed by the reporting entity's variable interests and the relationship of its variable interests with variable interests held by other parties must be weighed to determine whether its variable interests will absorb a majority of a VIE's expected losses, receive a majority of the entity's expected residual returns, or both. Note that absorbing losses is more important than receiving residual returns: thus, if one entity will absorb a majority of a VIE's expected losses and another (unrelated) entity will receive a majority of the VIE's expected residual returns, the entity absorbing a majority of the losses must consolidate the VIE.

If there are other (noncontrolling) interests, which are analogous to minority interests, these are shown in the consolidated balance sheet just as minority interests are under GAAP, and likewise a share of the operating results of the VIE are allocated to the noncontrolling interests in the consolidated statements of income (operations).

FIN 46(R) provides a 10% equity threshold test which in practice is confusing and unworkable. The interpretation indicates that an at-risk equity investment of less than 10% of the entity's total assets is presumptively not considered sufficient to permit the entity to finance its activities without obtaining additional subordinated financial support but then goes on to provide that the presumption of insufficiency can be overcome by either quantitative analysis, qualitative analysis, or both. Consequently, financial statement preparers could mistakenly rely on the 10% presumption to conclude that an entity with less than 10% at-risk equity is a VIE, when in fact, further analysis would contradict that conclusion. Conversely, the interpretation indicates that it is also possible that an entity can require at-risk equity of more than 10% in order to sufficiently finance its activities. Consequently, the financial statement preparer also cannot rely on meeting or exceeding the 10% threshold as conclusive proof that the entity is sufficiently capitalized to avoid being characterized as a VIE.

FIN 46(R) greatly changes past practice. Currently, enterprises generally have been consolidated in financial statements because one enterprise controls the other through a majority of voting interests. FIN 46(R) requires existing unconsolidated variable interest entities to be consolidated by their primary beneficiaries if the entities do not effectively disperse risks among parties involved. Variable interest entities that effectively disperse risks will not be consolidated unless a single party holds an interest or combination of interests that effectively recombines risks that were previously dispersed.

**Example of application of FIN 46(R).** To explain the approach required by FIN 46(R), consider one of the more common SPE situations under prior GAAP, that of a synthetic lease. A synthetic lease is a financing transaction whereby an independent third-party lessor (i.e., unrelated to the lessee) constructs or acquires an existing single-tenant property and leases it to a lessee. The synthetic lease transaction is generally structured with a short lease term so that the lessee accounts for it as an operating lease under GAAP notwithstanding the fact that, for federal income tax purposes, it is treated as a "financing" which results in the lessee/taxpayer capitalizing the leased asset and deducting depreciation and interest. This arrangement achieves the lessee's objective by removing the related debt obligation from its balance sheet. The lessee commits to a fixed schedule of rental payments, say for five years, so over that time there will be only a single amount for annual cash flows paid each year. The lease calls for the lessor to pay the lessee any excess of the fair value of the asset at lease termination date over its book value, plus a fixed rate of return to the lessor's owners. However, if the fair value of the asset is less than the book value plus the fixed rate of return, the lessee agrees to pay the lessor for any shortfall. Thus, there is cash flow variability created by this residual value guarantee by the lessee, making the lease structure potentially a VIE.

Assume the rental will be $50,000 per year for this example. Thus, the average (expected) cash flow each of those years will be the contractual amount. The fair value of the annual cash flow in any year will be the amount defined under CON 7, which is essentially the discounted present value of the lease payment. Assume 6% is the relevant discount rate, and rents are paid annually in arrears. The fair value of year one rent is then $50,000 \div 1.06 = \$47,170$; the corresponding amount for year two rent is $50,000 \div 1.06^2 = \$44,500$; etc. Since this amount is fixed, there are no expected residual rewards or expected losses from the rental stream in each of the years one through five.

*NOTE: See Chapter 16 for more complex lease examples involving VIE and decision diagrams useful in analyzing VIE.*

However, it is estimated that at the lease termination date there may be a range of fair values for the asset. Also, the lessor is entitled to a cumulative return on investment. It is now necessary to compute, separately, the expected (i.e., probability-weighted) fair values of the shortfall amount and the excess value amount. For simplicity, assume only three discrete outcomes are estimated to be possible.

1. The asset is sold for an amount that falls short of the book value plus the promised rate of return, for a net shortfall of $20,000;
2. The asset is sold for a net gain, after guaranteed return to the lessor, of $10,000; or
3. The asset is sold for a net gain of $40,000.

The relative probabilities of the three outcomes have been assessed at 40%, 35%, and 25%, respectively.

The expected residual cash flow to (or from) the lessee is given as $-20,000(.40) + \$10,000(.35) + \$40,000(.25) = \$5,500$.

Using these amounts, the expected loss (the single negative outcome) and the expected residual return (the sum of the two positive outcomes) can be computed. These are the foregoing individual cash flow amounts less the expected cash flows, weighted by the respective probabilities.

$$\text{Expected loss} = \$-20,000 - \$5,500 = \$-25,500(.40) = \$-10,200$$

$$\text{Expected residual return} = [\$10,000 - \$5,500 = \$4,500(.35) = \$1,575] + [\$40,000 - \$5,500 = \$34,500(.25) = \$8,625] = \$10,200$$

Note that the expected loss equals the expected residual returns, as it must, since the arithmetic average (mean) was used to compute the deviations of each projected outcome. Since the expected loss based on expected cash flow will be borne by the lessee if it occurs, and the expected residual based on expected cash flows will be paid to the lessee if one or the other occurs, the lessee is the primary beneficiary.

The actual computation would be based on the fair value of the expected cash flows. In this case, the expected fair value of the loss is given as $\$-10,200 \div (1.06)^5 = \$-7,622$. The expected fair value of the expected residual rewards is $7,622.

The total expected variability of the lease arrangement is therefore $15,244 (all earlier years' rental streams had zero variability), and the lessee absorbs all of this.

Note that in real-life situations there may be many other complications, such as rentals based on variables such as sales of product, etc. In an actual situation, with a wide range of possible cash flows each period, the computations will be more challenging. However, it might be possible in many cases to immediately conclude qualitatively, based on analysis of the risks, rewards, and relationships that the VIE is indeed to be consolidated, in which case these calculations will be unnecessary. Also, in some situations the VIE will have a range of assets and multiple parties with whom it is in contractual arrangements, which is a complication addressed somewhat by the standard, but which requires more analysis.

**Initial measurement.** Assets, liabilities, and noncontrolling interests of newly consolidated VIE generally will be initially measured at their fair values. However, there is a (logical) exception for assets and liabilities transferred to a VIE by its primary beneficiary; these will continue to be measured as if they had not been transferred (i.e., at book value in the transferor/primary beneficiary's hands). Were this rule not imposed, a reporting entity could create gains merely by transfer of assets to a VIE, violating a basic principle of revenue recognition.

In general, FIN 46(R) applies the concepts regarding initial measurement and recognition of goodwill or negative goodwill that are found in FAS 141, *Business Combinations*, summarized as follows:

|  | *Measurement or recognition issue* | *Applicable requirement per FIN 46(R) to be followed by primary beneficiary (PB)* |
|---|---|---|
| 1. | Measurement date | Date that holder of variable interest(s) first becomes the primary beneficiary |
| 2. | Measurement amount for assets, liabilities and noncontrolling interests | Fair value (FV) on measurement date |
| 3. | Measurement amount exception for enterprises under common control and assets and liabilities consolidated shortly after transfer from primary beneficiary to the VIE | Carrying value (net book value or NBV) in the accounting records of the enterprise that controls the VIE with no gain or loss recognized on account of transfer to a VIE |
| 4. | Excess of<br>FV of VIE assets + NBV of assets transferred by the PB to the VIE<br>*Over*<br>FV of consideration paid + NBV of previously held interests + FV of VIE liabilities and noncontrolling interests | Pro rata adjustment to newly consolidated VIE nonmonetary assets, as required by FAS 141 when negative goodwill results from a business combination. Any remaining amount, after the pro rata adjustment, is an extraordinary gain in the period of initial consolidation |
| 5. | Excess of<br>FV of consideration paid + NBV of previously held interests + FV of VIE liabilities and noncontrolling interests<br>*Over*<br>FV of VIE identifiable assets + NBV of identifiable assets transferred by the PB to the VIE | If the VIE is a business, as defined, recognized as goodwill<br>If the VIE is not a business, recognized as an extraordinary loss in the period of initial consolidation |

The following examples clarify application of the rules described in the preceding paragraphs:

**Case One**

First, assume that Client Corporation enters into an operating lease with an unrelated VIE, Non-Affiliate Corp., and that Non-Affiliate Corporation has a building with book value of

$12,000,000, fair value of $10,500,000 and an outstanding mortgage balance of $11,000,000 (assumed to be the mortgage's fair value). Assume that, due to the terms of the lease arrangement, the criteria for consolidation under FIN 46(R) are met, and that Client Corporation has no equity interest (even using the FIN 46[R] related-party criteria) in Non-Affiliate Corp. Client Corporation would consolidate the building on its balance sheet at its fair value of $10.5 million, reflect debt of $11 million, and because Non-Affiliate Corp. qualifies as a business under the definition provided by FIN 46(R), record goodwill of $500,000. Noncontrolling interest would be recorded at zero, since at this date there is no value to its interest.

### Case Two

If, instead, the fair value of the building were $12.5 million, then the consolidation entry would reflect the building at $12.5 million, the debt at $11 million, and the noncontrolling interest (which happens to also be the 100% equity holder in the VIE) at $1.5 million, since all residual interest will go to those parties.

### Case Three

Same facts as above, but now assume Client Corporation has a 25% interest in Non-Affiliate Corporation, and again the fair value of the building is $12.5 million. Recordation as follows would initially seem appropriate: debit building $12.5 million, credit mortgage payable $11 million, credit noncontrolling interest ($1.5 million × .75 =) $1.125 million, credit Client Corporation's equity (paid-in capital, representing the investment made in the building corporation) for ($1.5 million × .25 =) $375,000. However, this is wrong, since it effectively recognizes a gain on the increase in value of the building ($12.5 million fair value less $12 million book value). Under FIN 46(R) the primary beneficiary cannot recognize this gain, and therefore the primary beneficiary's percentage share of the excess fair value over its carrying value ($500,000 × .25 =) $125,000, must be used to reduce the recorded value of the building. The proper entry is: debit building $12,375,000 ($12,500,000 fair value – primary beneficiary's share of appreciation of $125,000 = $12,375,000), credit mortgage payable $11 million, credit noncontrolling interest ($1.5 million × .75 =) $1.125 million, and credit Client Corporation's equity ($375,000 – $125,000 =) $250,000.

After initial measurement, the assets, liabilities, and noncontrolling interests of a consolidated variable interest entity will be accounted for as if the entity were consolidated based on majority voting interests. In some circumstances, earnings of the variable interest entity attributed to the primary beneficiary arise from sources other than investments in equity of the entity.

**Disclosures.** The primary beneficiary of a VIE is required to disclose (1) the nature, purpose, size, and activities of the VIE, (2) the carrying amount and classification of consolidated assets that are collateral for the VIE's obligations, and (3) any lack of recourse by creditors (or beneficial interest holders) of a consolidated VIE to the general credit of the primary beneficiary. If an enterprise holds a significant variable interest in a VIE of which it is not the primary beneficiary, it is required to disclose (1) the nature of its involvement with the VIE and when that involvement began, (2) the nature, purpose, size, and activities of the VIE, and (3) the reporting enterprise's maximum exposure to loss as a result of its involvement with the VIE.

If a reporting enterprise does not consolidate a VIE because it is unable, after exhaustive efforts, to obtain the necessary information, it is required to make the following disclosures:

1.   The number of entities to which FIN 46(R) is not being applied and the reason why the required information is unavailable,
2.   The nature, purpose, size (if available), and activities of the entity or entities excluded and the nature of the reporting enterprise's involvement with them,
3.   The reporting enterprise's maximum exposure to loss due to its involvement with the entity or entities, and

4. The amounts of income, expense, purchases, sales, or other measures of activity between the reporting enterprise and the VIE for all periods presented. If, in the first set of financial statements to which FIN 46(R) applies, it is not practicable to provide the information for prior periods that are presented for comparative purposes, then that information may be omitted.

If the reporting enterprise consolidates multiple, similarly structured VIE, the informative disclosures may be aggregated for these similar VIE as long as separate information would not be deemed to provide material information to a financial statement user.

If the VIE engages in activities covered by FAS 140, *Accounting for Transfers and Servicing of Financial Assets and Extinguishments of Liabilities*, the disclosures required by FAS 140 regarding the VIE are required to be in the same note to the financial statements as the disclosures enumerated above.

**Exceptions to VIE consolidation requirements.** While FIN 46(R) is expected to require the consolidation of VIE engaged in leasing, and in a wide range of other transactions, including financial transactions, such as securitizations, it specifically permits off-balance-sheet financial vehicles known as qualified special purpose entities (QSPE) to continue to be nonconsolidated entities. These are widely used by corporations and financial institutions and consolidation of QSPE would have been enormously disruptive to the capital markets.

Prior to the issuance of FAS 125, the accounting for financial SPE was guided by analogizing from EITF 90-15, although that standard specifically stated that it applied only to leasing transactions. In fact, SPE were not even formally defined in the accounting literature. In practice, it was generally observed that SPE were designated as any entity that does not qualify as a "business" as that term is defined in EITF 98-3 (and has been adapted in FIN 46(R), as described earlier in this chapter). Generally, if an entity meets the definition of a business, the special nonconsolidation rules for SPE did not apply. However, this was not universally agreed, and an entity that qualified as a business under Issue 98-3 could also have been an SPE, at least in the opinion of some of those involved in standard setting.

The SEC has decreed that for an SPE to remain unconsolidated by the sponsor, and for sale recognition (where relevant) by the sponsor/transferor to be appropriate, "the majority owner of the SPE must be an independent third party who has made a substantive capital investment in the SPE, has control of the SPE, and has substantive risks and rewards of ownership of the assets of the SPE (including residuals). This became known as the "risks and rewards" analysis approach, which became the de facto standard until the issuance of FAS 125.

Rules regarding SPE changed again with the issuance of a comprehensive standard, FAS 125, which was replaced by yet another comprehensive standard, FAS 140. These deal with financial assets only, and establish the new concept of a qualifying SPE.

FAS 125 replaced the "risks and rewards" approach with a focus on "control over financial assets." Note that FAS 125 addressed transfers of financial assets, and was therefore not germane to transfers of other operating assets (plant and equipment, patents and copyrights, etc.). It introduced the concept of the qualifying SPE (QSPE), which was an SPE which

1. *Is a trust, corporation, or other legal vehicle whose activities are permanently limited by the legal documents establishing the SPE to*

   *-Holding title to transferred financial assets*
   *-Issuing beneficial interests*
   *-Collecting cash proceeds from and otherwise servicing the assets held*
   *-Distributing proceeds to the holders of its beneficial interests*

2. *Has standing at law distinct from the transferor*

Thus, one could say that QSPE were intended as a subset of SPE. In order for transfers of financial assets to SPE to be accounted for as sales (true sales), and thus for gain recognition to be appropriate (when otherwise warranted by the facts), the SPE transferee must be a QSPE. The consolidation requirements under EITF 90-15 and EITF Topic D-14 remained in effect for all transactions other than those involving QSPE or subject to FAS 125 (e.g., for nonfinancial assets, for transfers to related parties, etc.). FAS 125 did not explicitly address the need for sponsors to consolidate QSPE, but clearly if gain recognition would be appropriate consolidation could not be mandated, since that would obviate gain recognition (because upon consolidation, intercompany transactions, gains, etc., are all eliminated).

FAS 140 entirely replaced FAS 125, although most of the guidance remained identical. One reason for issuing the new standard was dissatisfaction with FAS 125's treatment of SPE. FAS 140 added new guidance with regard to defining the circumstances in which an SPE can be considered qualifying; circumstances in which the assets held by a qualifying SPE are to appear in the consolidated financial statements of the transferor; circumstances in which sale accounting is precluded if transferred financial assets can be removed from an SPE by the transferor; and other matters.

QSPE under FAS 140 were more narrowly defined. To be deemed a QSPE

*A qualifying SPE is a trust or other legal vehicle that meets all of the following conditions:*

a.  *It is demonstrably distinct from the transferor,*

b.  *Its permitted activities (1) are significantly limited, (2) were entirely specified in the legal documents that established the SPE or created the beneficial interests in the transferred assets that it holds, and (3) may be significantly changed only with the approval of the holders of at least a majority of the beneficial interests held by entities other than any transferor, its affiliates, and its agents,*

c.  *It may hold only*

 i)  *Financial assets transferred to it that are passive in nature;*

 ii)  *Passive derivative financial instruments that pertain to beneficial interests (other than another derivative financial instrument) issued or sold to parties other than the transferor, its affiliate, or its agents;*

 iii)  *Financial assets (for example, guarantees or rights to collateral) that would reimburse it if others were to fail to adequately service financial assets transferred to it or to timely pay obligations due to it and that it entered into when it was established, when assets were transferred to it, or when beneficial interests (other than derivative financial instruments) were issued by the SPE;*

 iv)  *Servicing rights related to financial assets that it holds;*

 v)  *Temporarily, nonfinancial assets obtained in connection with the collection of financial assets that it holds; and*

 vi)  *Cash collected from assets that it holds and investments purchased with that cash pending distribution to holders of beneficial interests that are appropriate for that purpose (that is, money-market or other relatively risk-free instruments without options and with maturities no later than the expected distribution date).*

d.  *If it can sell or otherwise dispose of noncash financial assets, it can do so only in automatic response to one of the following conditions:*

 i)  *Occurrence of an event or circumstance that (a) is specified in the legal documents that established the SPE or created the beneficial interests in the transferred assets that it holds; (b) is outside the control of the transferor, its affiliates, or its agents; and (c) causes, or is expected at the date of transfer to cause, the fair value of those financial assets to decline by a specified degree below the fair value of those assets when the SPE obtained them;*

ii) *Exercise by a beneficial interest holder (other than the transferor, its affiliates, or its agents) of a right to put that holder's beneficial interest back to the SPE;*

iii) *Exercise by the transferor of a call or "replacement of accounts provision" specified in the legal documents that established the SPE, transferred assets to the SPE, or created the beneficial interests in the transferred assets that it holds; or*

iv) *Termination of the SPE or maturity of the beneficial interests in those financial assets on a fixed or determinable date that is specified at inception.*

FAS 140 provided detailed guidance addressing the matters of the QSPE's need to be demonstrably distinct from the transferor; the necessary limitation on its permitted activities; limitations on what assets the QSPE can hold; and the limitations on sales or other dispositions of the assets by the QSPE. When all conditions are met, the QSPE is not consolidated in the financial statements of the sponsor.

Of interest is that the threshold level of an outside equity under FAS 140 was set at 10%. As the FASB stated, "if at least 10% of the interests in the transferred assets (or 10% of the interests in a series in the master trust) were currently held by third parties and if the transferor could not unilaterally dissolve the SPE, that is sufficient evidence to demonstrate that the SPE is demonstrably distinct from the transferor, its affiliates, or its agents." FASB settled on the 10% level "not because it was grounded in any particular literature, but because it appeared sufficient to demonstrate that the transferee is distinct from the transferor."

The accounting for VIE meeting the QSPE rules of FAS 140 continue to be governed by that standard and are not impacted by the imposition of FIN 46(R). However, FASB may further revise VIE accounting, and this area is ripe for ongoing evolution.

### Example of consolidation under FIN 46(R)

In practice, the most common situations requiring consolidation under FIN 46(R) will involve related-party leases as discussed in detail in Chapter 16. Consequently, this example uses a structured related-party lease to illustrate application of the consolidation provisions of FIN 46(R).

Arielle Aromatics Ltd. (AAL) is a manufacturer of aromatherapy products that is 100% owned by Arielle Stone. AAL's headquarters and manufacturing plant are leased pursuant to an operating lease with an S Corporation, Myles' Management, Inc (MMI) owned by Arielle's brother, Myles.

AAL's headquarters building and the land on which it is built are the only assets owned by MMI. They have been pledged as collateral for a mortgage loan which is guaranteed by a corporate guarantee of AAL and a personal guarantee of Arielle.

MMI has been determined to be a variable interest entity (VIE) and AAL its primary beneficiary.

The following is the consolidating worksheet at December 31, 2008:

**Arielle Aromatics Ltd. and Subsidiary**
**Consolidated Worksheet**
**Year Ending December 31, 2008**

| *(000 omitted)* | | | **Adjustments and Eliminations** | | Noncontrolling | |
| --- | --- | --- | --- | --- | --- | --- |
| | *AAL* | *MMI* | *Debit* | *Credit* | *interest* | *Consolidated* |
| Statement of income: | | | | | | |
| Revenues | | | | | | |
| Sales | $ 6,400 | | | | | $ 6,400 |
| Rental income | | $1,200[a] | $1,200 | | | -- |
| Cost of sales | 3,800 | ___ | | | | 3,800 |
| Gross profit | 2,600 | 1,200 | 1,200 | | | 2,600 |
| Depreciation | 100 | 230 | | | | 330 |
| Rent expense | 1,200 | | | $1,200[a] | | -- |
| Interest expense | 200 | 400 | | | | 600 |
| Other expenses | 300 | -- | | | | 300 |

*(000 omitted)* **Adjustments and Eliminations**

| | AAL | MMI | Debit | Credit | Noncontrolling interest | Consolidated |
|---|---|---|---|---|---|---|
| Total operating expenses and interest | 1,800 | 630 | | 1,200 | | 1,230 |
| Income before noncontrolling interest share | 800 | 570 | 1,200 | 1,200 | | 1,370 |
| Noncontrolling interest share of income | | | | | $570 | (570) |
| Net income | $ 800 | $ 570 | $1,200 | $1,200 | $570 | $ 800 |
| **Statement of retained earnings:** | | | | | | |
| Retained earnings, beginning | | | | | | |
| AAL | $ 1,200 | | | | | $1,200 |
| MMI | | $ -- | | | | -- |
| Add net income (from above) | 800 | 570 | $1,200 | $1,200 | $570 | 800 |
| Deduct dividends paid | (100) | (500) | | | (500) | (100) |
| Retained earnings, ending | $ 1,900 | $ 70 | $1,200 | $1,200 | $ 70 | $ 1,900 |
| **Balance sheet:** | | | | | | |
| Cash | $ 2,100 | | | | | $ 2,100 |
| Accounts receivable, trade (net) | 7,500 | | | | | 7,500 |
| Rentals receivable | | $100 | b | $100 | | -- |
| Inventories | 1,100 | | | | | 1,100 |
| Land | | 1,000 | | | | 1,000 |
| Depreciable property and equipment | 1,200 | 7,000 | | | | 8,200 |
| Accumulated depreciation | (300) | (230) | | | | (530) |
| Total assets | $11,600 | $7,870 | | 100 | | $19,370 |
| Notes and mortgages payable | $5,000 | $6,900 | | | | $11,900 |
| Accounts payable, trade | 4,400 | | | | | 4,400 |
| Rent payable | 100 | b | $100 | | | -- |
| Total liabilities | 9,500 | 6,900 | 100 | | -- | 16,300 |
| Common stock | 200 | 900 | | | 900 | 200 |
| Retained earnings (from above) | 1,900 | 70 | 1,200 | 1,200 | $970 | 1,900 |
| Noncontrolling interest | | | | | 970 | 970 |
| Total stockholder's equity | 2,100 | 970 | 1,200 | 1,200 | | 3,070 |
| Total liabilities and stockholders' equity | $11,600 | $7,870 | $1,300 | $1,200 | | $19,370 |

The consolidating entries posted to the December 31, 2008 worksheet are as follows:

a.

| | Debit | Credit |
|---|---|---|
| Rental income | 1,200 | |
| Rental expense | | 1,200 |

*To eliminate intercompany rental income and rental expense at December 31, 2008*

b.

| | Debit | Credit |
|---|---|---|
| Rental payable | 100 | |
| Rentals receivable | | 100 |

*To eliminate intercompany rent receivable and rent payable at December 31, 2008*

The consolidation process is relatively straightforward. The effects of the related-party lease, the rental income and expense and intercompany receivable and payable are eliminated so that, on a consolidated basis, the financial statements reflect the building, mortgage debt, depreciation, and interest expense.

The only difference between this consolidation under FIN 46(R) and a conventional consolidation of a voting interest entity in accordance with ARB 51, is the noncontrolling interest allocation. ARB 51, para. 14 specifies that the elimination of intercompany profit or loss is allocable proportionately to the majority and minority (controlling and noncontrolling) interests. In this example, however, the controlling interest holder, AAL, has no legal claim on the profit of MMI since MMI's profit or loss is legally allocable to its equity owner. If this example had been a conventional consolidation of a voting interest entity, the effect of eliminating the rental income from MMI would be a remaining MMI loss of $630 computed as follows:

| | |
|---|---:|
| MMI net income | $ 570 |
| Effect of elimination of rental income | (1,200) |
| MMI net loss after elimination of intercompany rental income | $ (630) |

FIN 46(R) provides a special rule that the effect of eliminating fees or other sources of income or expense between the primary beneficiary and the consolidated VIE is to be allocated to the primary beneficiary and not to the noncontrolling interest computed as follows and illustrated above:

| | |
|---|---:|
| Net loss of VIE | $ (630) |
| FIN 46(R) adjustment to allocate rental expense to primary beneficiary | 1,200 |
| Adjusted VIE net income allocable to noncontrolling interest | $ 570 |

The net income allocation to the noncontrolling interest shown above is reduced by the dividends paid to the noncontrolling interest as follows:

| | |
|---|---:|
| Adjusted VIE net income allocable to noncontrolling interest | $570 |
| Dividend paid to noncontrolling interest | (500) |
| Noncontrolling interest retained earnings | 70 |
| Noncontrolling interest common stock | 900 |
| Total noncontrolling interest | $970 |

The results of the consolidation can be summarized as

| | |
|---|---:|
| Primary beneficiary rent expense | $1,200 |
| VIE | |
|     Depreciation | 230 |
|     Interest | 400 |
| | 630 |
| Net effect, allocable to noncontrolling interest | $ 570 |

Consolidated net income of $800 is the same as the primary beneficiary's net income since the entire $570 of VIE net income is allocated to the noncontrolling interest. The results, however, can have a profound effect on the way that the financial statements portray the leverage of the primary beneficiary to users, which might be the difference between AAL meeting or violating its loan covenants.

| Debt to equity ratio | |
|---|---|
|     Primary beneficiary | 4.5:1 |
|     Consolidated | 5.3:1 |

Certain practical matters require consideration in the case of consolidating VIEs.

1. *VIE without GAAP financial statements.* Many VIEs structured as shown in this example had not previously prepared financial statements. Prior to consolidating the VIE with the primary beneficiary, the VIE's accounting records must be adjusted to eliminate any differences between GAAP and the basis on which the VIE reports for income tax purposes.

2. *Lack of prior independent CPA involvement with VIE.* VIEs that had not been subject to financial reporting in the past obviously had not needed to engage an independent CPA to perform a compilation, review, or audit engagement. Upon consolidation, the consolidated financial statements including the VIE's financial position and results of operations will be subject to the same level of service as the financial statements of the primary beneficiary.

3. *Interaction with FIN 45.* FIN 45, *Guarantor's Accounting and Disclosure Requirements for Guarantees, Including Indirect Guarantees of Indebtedness of Others,* requires guarantors to recognize a liability at inception for the obligations embodied in the guarantee. In the example above, the guarantee of the VIE's mortgage by the primary beneficiary would be exempt from the initial recognition and measurement provision of FIN 45 be-

cause the guarantee is analogous to a parent guarantee of its subsidiary's debt to a third party, which is specifically exempted from the recognition and measurement provisions of FIN 45. However, the guarantee is not exempt from the disclosure requirements of FIN 45 and FAS 5.

4. *General-purpose financial statements.* In the example, AAL is the "parent" company. It would be precluded by ARB 51 from issuing separate, general purpose financial statements that exclude MMI since this would be a GAAP departure; however, nothing precludes MMI from issuing separate subsidiary-only financial statements.

## Disclosure Requirements

In the period in which a material business combination is completed, the notes to the acquirer's financial statements must disclose the following information:

1. The name and a brief description of the acquiree, together with the percentage of voting shares acquired

2. The period for which the results of the acquiree's operations are included in the income statement of the acquirer

3. The cost of the transaction and, if applicable, the number of shares of stock issued or issuable, the value assigned to those shares, and the basis for determining that value

4. Contingent payments, options, or commitments specified in the acquisition agreement and the accounting treatment that will be followed should any such contingency occur

5. A condensed balance sheet disclosing the following for each major asset and liability caption of the acquiree:

   a. The book value as reflected in the acquiree's financial records at the date of acquisition before fair value adjustments

   b. The fair values assigned at the date of acquisition (including, if pertinent, how negative goodwill was allocated to preliminarily determined asset fair values)

6. For any purchase price allocation that has not been finalized, that fact and the reasons therefore and, in subsequent periods, the nature and amount of any material adjustments made to the initial allocation of the purchase price; and

7. If the amount assigned to goodwill or to other intangible assets acquired is significant in relation to the total cost of the acquired enterprise

   a. The amount of acquired goodwill

   b. The amount of acquired goodwill related to each segment (for entities that are required to report segment information in accordance with FAS 131)

   c. The amount of acquired goodwill that is deductible for income tax purposes

The notes to the financial statements of the acquirer also must disclose the following information in the period in which individually immaterial business combinations have been completed, if material in the aggregate:

1. The number of entities acquired and a brief description of the acquirees;

2. The aggregate cost of the acquisitions, the number of shares of stock issued or issuable, and the value assigned to those shares;

3. The aggregate amount of any contingent payments, options, or commitments and the accounting treatment that will be followed should any such contingency occur (if potentially significant in relation to the aggregate cost of the acquirees); and

4. Information pertaining to recorded goodwill, if the aggregate amount assigned to goodwill or to other intangible assets acquired is significant in relation to the aggregate cost of the acquirees.

Notes to the financial statements also must disclose, for any material business combination completed after the balance sheet date but before the financial statements are issued, information similar to that for completed transactions, above.

For each period for which a statement of financial position is presented, the notes to the financial statements also are to disclose the changes in the carrying amount of goodwill during the period. That would include the amount of goodwill acquired, the amount of impairment loss recognized, and the amount of goodwill included in the gain or loss on disposal of all or a portion of a reporting unit. Entities that report segment information in accordance with FAS 131 are to provide that information for each segment, disclosing any significant changes in the allocation of goodwill by segment.

When goodwill impairment losses are recognized, disclosure is required of

1. The facts and circumstances leading to the impairment;
2. The reporting unit for which the impairment loss is recognized, the adjusted carrying amount of goodwill of that reporting unit, and the amount of the impairment loss;
3. If relevant, the fact that the impairment loss estimate has yet to be finalized, the reasons therefore and, in subsequent periods, the nature and amount of any significant adjustments made to the initial estimate of the impairment loss; and
4. The segment to which the impaired goodwill relates (for entities that are required to report segment information in accordance with FAS 131).

In the period in which an excess over cost related to an acquisition is recognized as an extraordinary gain, it will be presented net of tax, as required under the provisions of APB 30, with appropriate disclosure in the notes to the financial statements.

## INTERPRETIVE GUIDANCE

The complexity of business combinations and the related accounting has necessitated the issuance of numerous interpretive pronouncements. To assist in conducting research and finding the relevant guidance, these pronouncements are categorized as follows:

### Common Control

**Definition of "common control" in applying FAS 141.** FAS 141 does not provide a definition of the term "common control." Nevertheless, this did not prevent FASB from excluding combinations of entities under common control from being subject to fair value purchase accounting requirements. In EITF 02-5, the Task Force was unable to reach a consensus regarding this definition. The discussion of this matter included in the EITF Abstract of that issue, however, indicates the SEC Staff position that common control only exists between or among separate entities in the following situations:

1. An individual or entity holds more than 50% of the voting ownership interests of each entity,
2. Immediate family members (defined below) hold more than 50% of the voting ownership interests of each entity with no evidence present that those family members will not vote their shares identically, and
3. A group of shareholders holds more than 50% of the voting ownership interests of each entity, and there is an agreement documented contemporaneously in writing to vote the majority of the entities' shares identically.

For the purpose of this determination, immediate family members include a married couple and their children, but not their grandchildren. Entities that are owned in varying combinations by living siblings and their children are to be carefully considered regarding the substance of the ownership and voting relationships.

**Exchanges of ownership between commonly controlled entities.** EITF 90-5 stipulates that there is no step up in a transfer of a subsidiary from a parent company to another of its subsidiaries, and that the recipient subsidiary's basis in the new subsidiary will be the same as was the parent company's. However, a buyout of noncontrolling interests by the subsidiary is to be accounted for as a purchase transaction, whether effected by cash or by a stock transaction.

**Change in accounting basis in master limited partnership transactions.** EITF 87-21, as modified by FAS 141, addresses the following types of transactions used to create master limited partnerships (MLP):

1. Roll-up—The combination of two or more separate limited partnerships into one MLP.
2. Drop-down—A sponsor (usually a corporation) transfers specified assets to a limited partnership, units of which are then sold to the public.
3. Roll-out—Same as a drop-down except that instead of selling units to the public, the units are distributed to the stockholders of the sponsor.
4. Reorganization—An entity transfers all of its assets into an MLP and then the transferor terminates its existence.

The key consideration in analyzing the facts and circumstances of the transaction is whether the transaction is covered by the scope of FAS 141. Generally, transactions in which entities transfer net assets or the entities' owners transfer their equity interests to a newly formed entity (referred to as roll-up or put-together transactions) are included in the scope of FAS 141 and would be subject to the prescribed accounting for purchase business combinations. However if the transaction is considered to be a transfer of net assets or exchange of equity interests between entities under common control, it is excluded from the scope of FAS 141 and is recorded in a manner similar to the formerly permitted poolings-of-interest.

The consensuses reached in EITF 87-21, as modified for the issuance of FAS 141, were

1. A new basis of accounting is not appropriate in a roll-up where no cash is involved in the transaction and where the general partner was also the general partner in any of the former limited partnerships involved in the roll-up. The Task Force also specified that, in recording a roll-up, the related transaction costs are to be charged to expense in a manner similar to the accounting for poolings-of-interest under APB 16.
2. A new basis of accounting is not appropriate in a drop-down in which

   a. The sponsor receives 1% of the units in the MLP as the general partner and 24% of the units as a limited partner,
   b. The other 75% of the units are being sold to the public, and
   c. The partnership agreement requires a two-thirds votes of the limited partners to replace the general partner.

3. A new basis of accounting is not appropriate in any roll-out, and
4. A new basis of accounting is not appropriate in a reorganization.

The SEC Observer to the Task Force proceedings specified that the SEC staff would not object to a new basis being recognized in a drop-down to the extent of the percentage change in ownership as long as

1. The MLP sells 80% or more of the partnership units to the public, and
2. The limited partners have the ability to replace the general partner through a "reasonable vote."

**Simultaneous common control mergers.** EITF 90-13 addresses situations in which a parent company obtains control of a target company, then spins one of its previously owned subsidiaries off to the target in exchange for more shares in the target (i.e., the old subsidiary becomes a "grandchild" after the series of transactions). The consensuses reached were as follows, as updated for the issuance of FAS 141:

1. When the transfer of the subsidiary to the target was negotiated in tandem with the parent's obtaining its controlling interest in the target, the two transactions are to be considered as one transaction and, therefore, the transfer is not considered to be between entities under common control.
2. The transaction is to be accounted for by the parent under the provisions of EITF 01-2 as a partial sale of the subsidiary to the noncontrolling interest holders of the target with a resulting gain or loss recognized as well as a partial acquisition of the target.
3. A step-up in basis is permitted to the extent of a change in control, both with respect to the acquisition of the target and the sale of the subsidiary to the target.
4. The accounting for a spin-off of the old subsidiary to the target company is to be accounted for as "reverse acquisition" of the target by the subsidiary. Under reverse acquisition accounting, the subsidiary is substantively considered to have acquired an interest in the target. This results in the subsidiary's assets and liabilities being carried at fair value in the target's financial statements to the extent acquired by the target. The subsidiary, however, does not, in its separate financial statements, revalue its own assets and liabilities since no gain or loss is recognized at the target-subsidiary level.

### Contingent Consideration

**Contingent consideration paid to the acquiree's shareholders.** Whether contingent consideration based on earnings is to be accounted for as an adjustment of the purchase price or as compensation for services, for the use of property, or for profit sharing depends on the facts and circumstances of each case. EITF 95-8 provides factors that can assist in making this determination relate to the terms of continuing employment, components of shareholder group, reasons for the contingent payment provisions, the formula used for determining contingent consideration, and other agreements and issues. For example, if compensation other than contingent payments is set at a reasonable level, this supports treatment of the contingent payments as an additional purchase price.

**Indirect contingent consideration.** EITF 97-8 deals with indirect contingent consideration arrangements in which the contingency is based either on earnings or a guaranteed value of the securities issued to effect the combination. The reason this consideration is considered indirect is because the consideration is not included in the combination agreement but, rather, is embedded in a security or in the form of a separate, freestanding financial instrument.

EITF 97-8, as modified by subsequently issued pronouncements, holds that if the security or separate financial instrument is publicly traded or indexed to a publicly traded security, it is to be recorded by the acquirer/issuer at fair value on the acquisition date. If not publicly traded or indexed to a publicly traded security, the acquirer/issuer is to record the contingent consideration in accordance with FAS 141; that is, when the contingency is resolved. If the security or financial instrument is considered a guarantee under FIN 45, the acquirer/issuer is also subject to the guarantor disclosure requirements of that pronouncement.

FAS 150 specifies that the acquirer/issuer recognize post-acquisition-date changes in the fair value of publicly traded freestanding financial instruments issued as consideration in a business combination. This accounting is followed irrespective of whether the financial instruments are contingent or noncontingent.

**Contingencies based on security prices.** The terms of a business combination may include a stipulation that the acquirer will pay cash or other consideration to the seller if the securities issued by acquirer to effect the business combination are not worth an agreed-upon amount at a specified future date.

Depending on the specifics of the contract, the guaranteed minimum value of the securities could be less than the issuance-date value of the securities which is referred to as a "below-market guarantee." The consensus specifies that for a below-market guarantee, there is no adjustment to the cost of the acquisition, as cost is computed as the fair value of unconditional securities issued on the date of combination. In order to determine the proper accounting for the contingent consideration, the issuer for the securities must analyze the character of the instruments to determine whether they are within the scope of FAS 150. FAS 150 applies to certain freestanding financial instruments that are settleable by the issuance of a variable number of the issuer's equity shares. If the instruments are hybrid instruments containing an embedded derivative, FAS 150 does not apply because the instruments are not a derivative in their entirety. Irrespective of whether the issuer records the securities as liabilities or equity, the contingent consideration arrangement will be subject to the additional disclosures required for guarantors by FIN 45.

EITF 97-15 provides several examples of target value contingent arrangements. One such example is as follows:

- Acquirer, Inc. purchases Seller Co. by issuing 100,000 shares of stock
- The fair value of the stock is $10 per share on the acquisition date, making the aggregate fair value of the stock on the acquisition date $10 × 100,000 = $1,000,000
- As part of the acquisition agreement, Acquirer agrees to issue additional shares three years after the acquisition date if, at that later date, the aggregate fair value of the stock has not appreciated to a target value of at least $2,000,000 ($20 per share) on the following sliding scale:

| Per share price of acquirer shares 3 years after acquisition | Number of additional shares to be issued |
|:---:|:---:|
| $16 | 25,000 |
| $17 | 18,750 |
| $18 | 12,500 |
| $19 | 6,250 |
| $20 | -- |

Note that this example does not result in Seller receiving a guaranteed minimum price since no matter how much the price of Acquirer's shares declines below $16 per share, the number of shares that Seller would be entitled to receive does not increase.

EITF 97-15 sets forth the following formula for computing the acquisition cost when the contingency arrangement does not result in a guaranteed minimum amount of total consideration, which is the lesser of the target value or

(Maximum # of shares potentially issuable) × (Acquisition date fair value per share)

In the example given, the target value is $2,000,000 and the computation of the maximum number of shares × acquisition date fair value per share is computed as

$$125,000 \text{ shares} \times \$10 \text{ per share} = \$1,250,000$$

Since $1,250,000 is less than the target amount, the cost of the acquisition would be recorded at an aggregate amount of $1,250,000 on the acquisition date.

**Valuation of assumed debt.** FAS 141 requires cost allocation to be based on the fair values of assets and liabilities, with the fair value of liabilities being computed using present value. An issue arises because present value ≠ fair value in some cases, such as when a prepayment option affects fair value but present value would often ignore this contingent change in future cash flows. EITF 98-1 holds that fair value is to be used, even if ≠ present value of cash flows. Since market values may not be available, some use of a present value method may be required, but the value of option features, etc., must be included in the calculation.

### Exit and Disposal Activities

**Recognition of termination benefits or changing benefit plan assumptions in anticipation of a business combination.** Termination costs to be incurred from an anticipated business combination are not to be accrued even if the business combination is deemed probable. EITF 96-5 provides that these costs may only be recognized when the business combination is actually consummated.

**Exiting activities and integrating operations.** EITF 95-3 sets forth the consensuses regarding the accounting for certain costs incurred when an acquirer, Company A, in connection with its acquisition of Company B plans to incur certain costs of exiting activities and integrating operations.

EITF specified that a plan to exit an activity of an acquired company exists if it meets all of the following conditions:

1. On the date that the acquisition is consummated, management with the appropriate level of authority has begun to assess and formulate a plan to exit the activity.
2. The assessment of which of the acquiree company's activities to exit is completed and the exit plan finalized, approved, and committed to by the combined company on the earlier of the soonest possible date after consummation, or one year after the consummation date.
3. The exit plan specifically identifies

   a. The activities of the acquired company that will not be continued
   b. The locations of those activities
   c. The method of disposition
   d. All significant actions needed to complete the plan
   e. The expected date of completion of the plan

4. Actions required by the plan commence as soon as possible after the plan is finalized, and
5. The period of time necessary to complete the plan makes it unlikely that the plan will undergo significant changes

The Task Force reached a consensus that a cost resulting from a plan to exit an activity of an acquired company is to be recognized as a liability on the date the acquisition is consummated only if the cost is not associated with or incurred to generate revenues to the combined entity after the consummation date and it meets either of the following criteria:

1. The cost represents an amount to be incurred by the combined company under a contractual obligation of the acquiree that predated the consummation date and either will

   a. Continue after completion of the plan with no economic benefit to the combined company, or
   b. Result in the combined company incurring a cancellation penalty to terminate the obligation.

2. The cost

   a. Has no future economic benefit to the combined company,
   b. Is incremental to other costs incurred either by the acquirer or the acquiree in the conduct of preconsummation date activities, and
   c. Will be incurred as a direct result of the plan to exit an activity of the acquired company.

Costs associated with a plan to involuntarily terminate or relocate employees of the acquiree are recognized as a liability assumed on the date the business combination was consummated and included in the allocation of acquisition cost if all of the following conditions are met:

1. On the date that the acquisition is consummated, management with the appropriate level of authority has begun to assess and formulate a plan to involuntarily terminate or relocate employees of the acquiree.
2. The assessment of which of the acquiree company's employees will be involuntarily terminated or relocated is completed and the plan of termination or relocation is finalized, approved, and committed to by the combined company on the earlier of the soonest possible date after consummation, or one year after the consummation date.
3. On or before the time specified in 2., above, the termination or relocation arrangement has been communicated to the employees of the acquiree in sufficient detail to enable them to determine the type and amount of benefits that they would be entitled to receive if terminated or relocated.
4. The exit plan specifically identifies with respect to the acquiree employees to be terminated or relocated

   a. The number of employees affected,
   b. Their job classification or function, and
   c. Their locations.

5. Actions required by the plan will commence as soon as possible after the plan is finalized, and
6. The period of time necessary to complete the plan makes it unlikely that the plan will undergo significant changes.

These adjustments are not considered preacquisition contingencies under FAS 141.

If later settled for less than the amount initially accrued, the savings are accounted for as a reduction in the purchase price of the acquiree, which usually means goodwill recorded on the acquisition is reduced. If settled for greater than the amount initially accrued, and determined within one year of the acquisition date, the excess is accounted for as an increase in the purchase price of the acquiree, which usually means goodwill recorded on the acquisition is increased. If an excess settlement is not determined within one year of acquisition, it is to be recorded as an expense of the period in which it is determined.

Any costs relating to activities or employees of the acquiree not meeting the specified conditions are considered indirect and general acquisition expenses under FAS 141. Per FTB

85-5, costs related to assets or employees of the acquirer are not costs of the acquisition and thus are prohibited from being included as part of the purchase price allocation process; instead, these costs are required to be reflected in the income statement when incurred. The consensus also identified certain disclosures to be made under these circumstances, including a description of plans to exit activities, possible reallocation of purchase transactions, etc.

## Impairment

**Determination of reporting units.** Whether a component of an operating segment is a reporting unit for purposes of applying FAS 142, for purposes of applying the requirement to determine goodwill impairment depends on whether the component functions as a business, whether discrete financial information is available about that component, whether it is accountable to and in regular contact with segment managers, and whether it is qualitatively distinct from other components of the operating segment. It is possible that components aggregated for purposes of reporting under FAS 131 could be separate for purposes of applying FAS 142 (EITF D-101).

## Income Tax Considerations

**Income tax uncertainties.** EITF 93-7 holds that all income tax uncertainties (such as uncertainties about the allocation of purchase price to individual assets and liabilities for tax purposes in a taxable business combination, uncertainties about carryforwards in a nontaxable combination, and uncertainties about preacquisition tax returns of the acquired entity) existing at the time of a purchase business combination are to be accounted for under the provisions of FAS 109, not under the provisions of FAS 38 (preacquisition contingencies). Any such adjustments are to be applied to increase or decrease the remaining balance of goodwill attributable to that business combination; if goodwill is reduced to zero, the remaining amount is used to reduce other noncurrent intangible assets from the same acquisition to zero, with any excess taken to income.

**Deferred income taxes on acquired in-process R&D.** Per FIN 4, the purchase price allocated in a purchase business combination to research and development costs must be expensed immediately. At issue is whether, under FAS 109, a deferred tax liability must be allocated to the initial (pre-write-off) basis difference between tax and book bases. EITF 96-7 held that since the write-off occurs prior to the measurement of deferred taxes, no deferred taxes are to be assigned.

**Decrease in valuation allowances as a result of a change in income tax regulations.** Consolidated income tax return regulations issued in 1999 changed the rules for utilizing certain net operating loss carryovers and carrybacks (NOLC). These regulations eliminated the requirement to apply the limitations on the separate return limitation year losses to situations in which a change in ownership as defined in IRC §382 has occurred within six months of a target company becoming a member of a consolidated group.

This change in income tax regulations required an entity to reevaluate the need for an existing valuation allowance for deferred income tax assets relating to NOLC acquired in a prior purchase business combination. The specific question was whether the effect of the adjustment should be (1) included in operations or (2) applied first to reduce to zero any goodwill related to the acquisition, second to reduce to zero other noncurrent intangible assets related to the acquisition, and third to reduce income tax expense.

EITF 99-15 requires the effect of a change in income tax law or regulation that results in a decrease in a valuation allowance that initially was recorded in the allocation of the purchase price in a purchase business combination to be included in income from continuing operations. The consensus applies to any reduction in the valuation allowance that otherwise would not have been recognized except for the change in income tax law or regulation, regardless of whether the valuation allowance is reduced in the period of the income tax law change or in a subsequent period.

### Leveraged Buyouts (LBO)

**Cost basis.** One of the most complex accounting areas, EITF 88-16 stipulates how to compute the new cost basis after an LBO transaction. A consensus was reached that a new basis is to be recognized only when there is a change in the voting control from the former entity to the post-LBO entity; that a "substance over form" rule applies when seeking to determine if there had in fact been a change in control; and that a "monetary test" is established whereby fair value can only be used if at least 80% of the fair value of consideration paid to make the acquisition is monetary in nature.

EITF 90-12 prescribes the use of the partial purchase (step acquisition accounting) method, even if retained earnings are eliminated as a consequence.

### Measurement and Allocation

**Measurement date for the market price of acquirer securities issued.** EITF 99-12 provides that the measurement of the fair value of the marketable equity securities issued by the acquirer to effect a business combination is to be made based on the market price of those securities for a very short period of time, such as a few days before and after the terms of the acquisition are agreed to and announced. The determination of this period should not be influenced by the need to obtain approvals of the combination from regulators and/or shareholders.

If the transaction involves a hostile tender offer, the measurement date is established upon the announcement of the proposed transaction and the tender of a sufficient number of shares to make the offer binding, or when the proposed acquisition becomes nonhostile as a result of an agreement by the target company to the purchase price.

If, as a result of further negotiations or the execution of a revised acquisition agreement, the purchase price is substantively changed (either the number of shares to be issued or the amount of other consideration), a new measurement date is to be established on the date of the change.

In some cases, the initial acquisition agreement includes a formula that potentially changes the number of acquirer's shares to be issued or other consideration to be paid. Under these circumstances, the measurement date is the first date on which the number of the acquirer's shares and the amount of other consideration become fixed without being subject to further revision in accordance with the formula. The Task Force noted, however, that the measurement period should not include any dates after the date the business combination is consummated.

**Recognition of customer relationship intangible assets.** EITF 02-17 addresses the propriety of separate recognition of customer relationship intangibles in a business combination. EITF concluded that the contractual-legal and the separability criteria do not restrict the use of certain assumptions that would be used in estimating the fair value of an intangible asset. Thus, if the parties to the business combination believe that an existing contractual relationship with a customer will be renewed, this is considered in making the purchase price allocation to that asset, once the threshold for recognition (i.e., the contractual right) has been identified. It furthermore concluded that the guidance in FAS 141 that states "if an entity establishes relationships with its customers through contracts, those customer relationships would arise from contractual rights," applies if an entity has a practice of establishing contracts with customers, regardless of whether a contract is in existence at the date of acquisition. However, in assigning fair value to the relationship, the lack of a current contract would likely be considered, even if recognition is warranted. Finally, consensus was reached that an order or a production backlog arising from contracts such as purchase or sales orders (even if the purchase or sales orders are cancelable) would be considered a contract.

**Separating goodwill and other intangibles.** Under FAS 141, intangible assets other than goodwill resulting from business combinations are to be separately accounted for, but under prior GAAP (APB 17) it was not uncommon for intangibles thus obtained to be aggregated as goodwill, since the accounting was identical. The transition provisions for FAS 142 permit disaggregating intangibles, but only to the extent that separate accounting records (even if aggregated for financial reporting purposes) had been maintained. The amount of purchase cost allocated to goodwill and other intangible assets cannot be redetermined as part of this process, however. A failure to properly separate formerly aggregated intangibles would potentially distort subsequent determinations of goodwill impairment, since under FAS 141 this determination is based on the value of goodwill after fully assigning purchase cost to all intangibles, including those not formally recognized (EITF D-100).

**Deferred revenue of the acquiree.** EITF 01-3 addresses recognition by an acquirer of deferred revenue previously accounted for by an acquired entity as a liability under GAAP, noting that the fair value requirement for liability recognition under FAS 141 does not correspond to the customary revenue recognition rules for ongoing businesses.

In the case of revenue deferred because the acquiree entity had a performance obligation, the conclusion was that in the context of a purchase business combination, recognition of a performance obligation liability would only be appropriate when the acquirer has a legal obligation (either contractually or by operation of consumer rights laws in the applicable legal jurisdiction) to provide goods, services, the right to use assets, or some other consideration to customers of the acquiree. Other types of obligations that are recognizable by the acquirer might be general rights of return under FAS 48 or contractual price protection provisions.

Absent this legal obligation, the deferred revenue is not recognized as a liability of the acquirer. Revenue arrangements in business combinations might also result in the recognition of an asset (for the customer relationship) and a liability (deferred revenue); these are not permitted to be netted.

**Preexisting relationships between the parties.** EITF 04-1 resolves a number of issues regarding how to account for business combinations involving parties that had preexisting relationships. When two parties with preexisting relationships enter into a business combination, it is to be considered a multiple-element transaction with the business combination being one element and the settlement of the preexisting relationship being the other element.

*Executory contracts.* The effective settlement of a preexisting executory contract between the parties to a business combination is measured at the lesser of

1. The amount by which the contract is either favorable or unfavorable to the acquirer when compared to the terms of current market transactions for the same or similar items, or
2. Any contractually stated settlement provisions available to the counterparty to which the contract is unfavorable.

To the extent that the settlement amount in 2. is less than the "off-market component" in 1., the difference is to be included as part of the business combination.

*Rights to use intangible assets.* An acquirer may have previously granted to the acquiree the right to use its intangible assets, whether recognized or unrecognized. For example, the acquiree may have been granted the right to use the acquirer's logo or service mark under a franchise agreement. As a result of the acquisition the acquirer is, in effect, reacquiring that right. If the contract containing the reacquired right is either favorable or unfavorable when compared to the current market for the same or similar rights, the acquirer is to record a settlement gain or loss measured at the lesser of

1. The amount by which the contract is either favorable or unfavorable to market terms from the acquirer's perspective, or
2. Any contractually stated settlement provisions available to the counterparty to which the contract is unfavorable.

To the extent that the settlement amount in 2. is less than the "off-market component" in 1., the difference is to be included as part of the business combination.

The reacquired right, exclusive of any settlement gain or loss computed in accordance with the method described in the previous paragraph, is to be recognized as an intangible separate from goodwill.

***Lawsuits.*** In connection with a business combination, the effective settlement of either a lawsuit or threatened litigation is to be measured at fair value with a gain or loss recognized in the acquirer's consolidated statement of income, except where the accounting is specified in a different manner in other authoritative GAAP literature.

***Disclosures.*** In a business combination between parties that had a preexisting relationship, the following disclosures are required:

1. The nature of the preexisting relationship
2. The amounts related to the settlement of the preexisting relationship, if any, and the valuation methods used to measure those amounts
3. The amount of settlement gain or loss recognized and how it is classified in the consolidated income statement

## Noncontrolling (Minority) Interest

**Accounting by majority owner for a derivative indexed to the noncontrolling interest in that subsidiary.** After the issuance of FAS 150, the scope of EITF 00-4 has been narrowed considerably. The still-effective provisions of EITF 00-4 address only a single scenario where the parent company holds 80% of its subsidiary's equity shares with the remaining 20% owned by an unrelated noncontrolling interest holder. The noncontrolling interest holder sells its interest to a new party that simultaneously enters into a put option to sell the 20% interest to the parent at a stated future price and date with the parent having a call option to buy the 20% interest under those same terms (i.e., the fixed price of the call option and the fixed price of the put option are the same). Finally, the put and call options are not covered by the scope of FAS 150 because they are embedded in the noncontrolling interest shares and those shares are not mandatorily redeemable.

Under EITF 00-4, the put and call options are viewed on a combined basis with the noncontrolling interest and accounted for as a financing of the parent's purchase of the noncontrolling interest. The parent consolidates 100% of the subsidiary and attributes the stated yield that it earns under the combined derivative and noncontrolling interest position as interest expense (i.e., it accretes the financing to the strike price of the options over the period from their issuance until settlement). This accounting is to be followed even if the exercise prices of the put and call are not equal, as long as they do not differ significantly.

## Nonmonetary Transactions

### Exchanges of similar productive assets.

*NOTE: The guidance from EITF 98-3 described in this section with respect to similar productive assets was partially nullified by the issuance of FAS 153, discussed fully in Chapter 10. FAS 153 elimi-*

nated the exception to fair value for exchanges of similar productive assets and substituted a new exception for exchange transactions lacking commercial substance. *This discussion is retained in its original form as it applies to nonmonetary exchanges predating the effective date of FAS 153, which was for nonmonetary asset exchanges occurring in fiscal periods beginning after June 15, 2005.*

APB 29 states that nonmonetary exchanges are generally to be reported at fair value, but the exchange of productive assets are to be recorded at the carrying value of the assets relinquished. FAS 141, however, uses a fair value approach, to account for business combinations. Some exchanges (e.g., of radio stations or other groups of operating assets) may be viewed as being either nonmonetary exchanges or business combinations. EITF 98-3 defines a business as a self-sustaining integrated set of activities and assets conducted and managed for the purpose of providing a return to investors. It consists of (1) inputs, (2) processes applied to those inputs, and (3) resulting outputs that are used to generate revenues. Each of these criteria is further defined by EITF 98-3. For a transferred set of activities and assets to be deemed a business, it must contain all of the inputs and processes necessary for it to continue to conduct normal operations after the transferred set is separated from the transferor, which includes the ability to sustain a revenue stream by providing its outputs to customers. If these criteria are not satisfied, the assets do not comprise a business and FAS 141 would not apply to an acquisition.

**Exchanges of investments accounted for under the cost method or under FAS 115.** EITF 91-5 addresses three issues regarding a transaction structured as follows:

1. Company A and Company B enter into a purchase business combination.
2. Company A, the acquirer as defined in FAS 141, exchanges its equity shares with the investors holding 100% of Company B's outstanding shares.
3. After the exchange, Company A's shareholders hold the majority of the shares of the combined entity.
4. Shares of the combined entity continue to be publicly traded after the business combination.

The first consensus was that a former investor in Company B who had accounted for the investment in Company B using the cost method or under FAS 115 would record the transaction at fair value.

The second consensus was that an investor in Company A who had accounted for the investment in Company A using the cost method or under FAS 115 would continue to carry the investment in the same manner as it had prior to the business combination (i.e., at historical cost if accounted for under the cost method and at fair value if subject to FAS 115). The third consensus was that the results in the first and second consensuses would not be different if an investor in Company B has also held an investment in Company A prior to the business combination.

### Specialized Accounting Principles

Specialized accounting principles that are appropriately applied at a subsidiary company level are also to be used in the consolidated financial statements (EITF 85-12).

### Subsidiary Accounting and Transactions

**Early extinguishment of subsidiary's mandatorily redeemable preferred stock.** A wholly owned subsidiary issues mandatorily redeemable preferred stock (MRPS) that is subsequently purchased by the parent company prior to the mandatory redemption date (i.e., as an early extinguishment). The EITF considered this scenario and reached a consensus in EITF 86-32, though its guidance was partially nullified by FAS 150.

If the MRPS qualifies as a "mandatorily redeemable financial instrument" under FAS 150, the stock is accounted for as a liability of the subsidiary. Amounts paid or to be paid by the parent company to the former holders of the MRPS in excess of the initial measurement amount are to be accounted for as interest cost.

If the MRPS contains a redemption feature but does not qualify as a mandatorily redeemable financial instrument under FAS 150, FAS 140 provides criteria for determining whether the liability has been extinguished and APB 26 requires the parent company to account for any difference between the redemption price and the carrying amount as a gain or loss on extinguishment of the subsidiary's liability (EITF 86-32).

## Variable Interest Entities and Other Exceptions to Consolidation by Majority Voting Interests

**Variable interests in specified assets of VIE.** Certain variable interests in specified assets of a variable interest entity (VIE) are required to be treated by their holder as separate variable interest entities, sometimes referred to as "silos," "virtual VIEs," or "deemed entities." FSP FIN 46(R)-1 specifies that if any parties other than the variable interest holder and the secured lender have rights or obligations with respect to the specified assets or the cash flows from those assets, the specified assets and related liabilities are not to be treated as a silo for accounting purposes.

**Calculating expected losses.** FSP FIN 46(R)-2 clarifies and illustrates the fact that all entities have "expected losses" as that term is defined in FIN 46(R); even when the entity has never experienced a net loss and does not expect to ever experience one. The term "expected losses" is based on the variability in the fair value of the entity's net assets exclusive of variable interests and not on the anticipated amount or variability of the net income or loss.

**Evaluation of decision making through voting or similar rights.** The holders of the equity investment at risk (the equity group) have the ability to make decisions about an entity's activities if they hold all voting or similar rights. Conversely, the equity group would lack the ability to make decisions if it holds no voting or similar rights.

In situations in which the equity group and another party (or parties) outside the equity group have the ability to make or participate in making decisions about the entity, FSP FIN 46(R)-3 specifies that emphasis should be placed on

1. The ability of the equity group to make decisions that have a significant impact on the success of the entity, and
2. The extent to which the equity group absorbs expected losses and receives expected residual returns of the entity.

If the equity group has the ability to make decisions that have a significant impact on the success of the entity and the equity group has an obligation to absorb expected losses and the right to receive expected residual returns, the equity group likely has the "direct or indirect ability to make decisions about an entity's activities through voting rights or similar rights."

The greater the equity as compared to the expected losses of the entity, the less likely that the equity group would surrender the direct or indirect ability to make decisions about an entity's activities to another party outside the equity group. Further, if the amount of at-risk equity is sufficient to absorb expected losses, the risks of another party outside the equity group may be significantly mitigated by the amount of the equity group's investment.

FSP 46(R)-3 also clarifies that it was not the intent of FASB that all franchisor/franchisee relationships qualify as VIE. A distinction is drawn between the decision-making authority that a franchisee typically holds with respect to the success of the business and the decision-making authority that a franchisor typically retains with respect to the protection of its brand image. The latter authority does not generally limit the franchisee's authority over the normal operations of its business and thus would not preclude the franchisee's investors from being judged to hold decision-making authority through voting or other rights.

**Leasing transactions involving special-purpose entities.** FSP FIN 46(R)-4 clarifies the applicability of the accounting guidance provided in EITF 96-21 with respect to the accounting for contingent loss accruals by a lessee who has guaranteed the lessor's residual under an operating lease. The guidance in the EITF continues to be applicable when the lessee is not the primary beneficiary of a VIE lessor. If the lessee is the primary beneficiary, the EITF guidance does not apply since any such loss accrual would eliminate in consolidation.

**Majority investor's accounting when the minority shareholder(s) have certain approval or veto rights.** EITF 96-16 deals with situations in which the majority owner of an entity does not exercise control and thus, under FAS 94, potentially should not consolidate the investee. The situation arises when the minority owners have rights such as approval of management compensation, selection or termination of management, or the establishment of operating and capital policies and procedures. Collectively, these approval or veto powers are referred to as "substantive participating rights," and are contrasted to "protective rights" such as those relating to entering bankruptcy proceedings, or to major acquisitions or dispositions of assets. The EITF concluded that a finding that the majority owner lacks control depends on the facts and circumstances, and that its lack of control is generally related to the minority owner's ability to effectively participate in decisions in the "ordinary course of business." In the view of the EITF, a minority owner's protective rights would not be sufficient to overcome the presumption of majority control, while substantive participating rights would overcome that presumption.

The Task Force further concluded that a number of other factors must be considered in reaching a conclusion on the matter of a possible negating of majority owner control. Among these are the relative size of majority and minority interests (the greater the disparity, the more likely the minority's rights are only protective in nature); the mechanisms of governance (which decisions are reserved to stockholders as opposed to being made by the directors); other possible relationships between the majority and minority owners; and the likelihood of occurrence of decision-making situations in which the minority would have the right to significantly participate.

The consensuses in this issue were reached prior to the issuance of FIN 46(R), which sets forth criteria to determine when financial control does not reside in the majority voting owners of an entity because the entity (referred to as a variable interest entity or VIE) does not have sufficient subordinated financial support to enable it to be self-supporting. If an entity is considered a VIE under FIN 46(R), it is not subject to this consensus. If, however, the shareholders of an entity are considered to exercise financial control under FIN 46(R), the entity would not be considered a VIE even if the entity is not controlled by the majority voting interest holders because of minority veto rights as described in this issue.

**Physician practice management entities and certain other entities with contractual management arrangements.**

*Scope.* EITF 97-2 applies to contractual management relationships (CMR) between entities operating in the health care industry including the practices of medicine, dentistry, veterinary science, and chiropractic medicine (collectively referred to as physician practices) and entities engaged in managing the operations of physician practices (physician practice management entities or PPMs) where

1. The physician practice is not a variable interest entity (VIE) subject to the requirements of FIN 46(R) and

2. In which the PPM does not own a majority of the outstanding voting equity shares of the physician practice either because the PPM does not elect to do so or because the PPM is precluded by law from that ownership

Both the EITF and its SEC Observer observed that there may be analogous contractual arrangements in other industries to which the consensuses in this issue may be applicable.

***Controlling financial interest.*** A PPM is considered to have a controlling financial interest in a non-VIE physician practice via a contractual management agreement, and thus trigger required consolidation under FAS 94 if six criteria set forth in EITF 97-2 are met.

1. The term of the CMR is either the entire remaining legal life of the physician practice or a period of ten years or more.
2. The CMR may only be terminated by the physician practice because of the PPM's gross negligence, fraud, other illegal acts, or bankruptcy.
3. The PPM has exclusive decision-making authority with respect to

   a. Ongoing, major, or central operations of the physician practice (except the dispensing of medical services). This exclusive decision-making authority is required to encompass

      (1) Scope of services,
      (2) Patient acceptance policies and procedures,
      (3) Contract negotiation and execution,
      (4) Establishment and approval of operating and capital budgets, and
      (5) Issuance of debt if debt financing is an ongoing, major, or central source of financing used by the physician practice.

4. Total compensation of the licensed medical professionals and the ability to establish and implement guidelines for their selection, hiring, and termination.
5. The PPM has a significant financial interest in the physician practice that both can be unilaterally sold or transferred by the PPM, and
6. Provides the PPM with the right to receive income from both ongoing fees and proceeds from the sale of its interest in the physician practice in amounts that fluctuate due to the physician practice's operating performance and changes in fair value.

# 14 CURRENT LIABILITIES AND CONTINGENCIES

## PERSPECTIVE AND ISSUES

The balance sheet bifurcation of assets and liabilities into current and noncurrent segments allows net working capital (defined as current assets minus current liabilities) to be readily perceived. Working capital, which is the relatively liquid portion of total entity capital, can be used to determine the ability of an entity to repay obligations as they become due in the ordinary course of business. Working capital assumes a going-concern concept. If the entity is to be liquidated in the near future, this mode of balance sheet classification of assets and liabilities is generally inappropriate.

ARB 43, Chapter 3, defines current liabilities as those obligations whose liquidation is reasonably expected to require the use of existing resources properly classifiable as current assets or the creation of other current liabilities. This definition excludes from the current liability classification any currently maturing obligations that will be satisfied by using long-term assets and currently maturing obligations expected to be refinanced.

The offsetting of assets and liabilities is almost entirely prohibited under GAAP. However, under certain narrowly defined circumstances, where a right of setoff actually exists, netting for financial reporting purposes is acceptable, as described in this chapter.

FASB has declared, as a long-term goal, that all financial liabilities are to be recognized in the balance sheet at fair values, rather than at amounts based on their historical cost. The proper calculation of fair value, as presented in FAS 157, is described in detail in Chapter 6. Under FAS 159, an entity has the option to record its current liabilities at fair value. This option is addressed in detail in Chapters 8 and 12. Under FAS 141(R), acquirers are required to record contract-related contingencies at their fair values. However, most entities continue to measure their current liabilities at their settlement value, which is the amount of cash (or its equivalent amount of other assets) that will be paid to the creditor to liquidate the obligation during the current operating cycle. Accounts payable, dividends payable, salaries payable, and other current obligations are measured at settlement value because they require the entity to pay a determinable amount of cash. If a current liability is near its payment date, there will be only an insignificant risk of changes in fair value because of changes in market conditions or the entity's credit standing, and settlement value and fair value will be essentially the same.

Other current liabilities are measured at the proceeds received when the obligation arose. Liabilities that are measured this way generally require the entity to discharge the obligation by providing goods or services rather than by paying cash. Liabilities that require the entity to provide goods or services, rather than cash, are not financial instruments and thus are not a target of the fair value measurement option presented in FAS 159. Subscriptions payable, deposits payable, and deferred revenues are examples of current liabilities measured by reference to proceeds received. (However, significant changes could result from the FASB's ongoing revenue recognition project, which appears likely to adopt a "balance sheet" orientation to the definition of revenue and the timing of its recognition. As part of this project, some revisions to the definition of liabilities are being contemplated. A complete discussion of this project is found in Chapter 10).

Although measurement of current liabilities is generally straightforward, some liabilities are difficult to measure because of uncertainties. Uncertainties regarding whether an obligation exists, how much of an entity's assets will be needed to settle the obligation, and when the settlement will take place can impact whether, when, and for how much an obligation will be recognized in the financial statements. FAS 5 is the primary standard that describes accounting for potential liabilities in circumstances involving uncertainties. It requires a liability to be recognized if it is (1) probable that an obligation has been incurred because of a transaction or event happening on or before the date of the financial statements and (2) the amount of the obligation can be reasonably estimated. Thus, uncertainties about the existence of an obligation need not be resolved before the liability is recorded. For example, estimated settlement amounts for ongoing lawsuits are recognized prior to a court's decision if it is probable that the outcome will be unfavorable. Further, difficulty in measuring an obligation is not, by itself, a reason for not recording a liability if the amount can be estimated. For example, warranty obligations are commonly recognized as liabilities even though the number of claims and the amount of each claim are unknown at the time of the sale of the item under warranty. Although future events will eventually resolve the uncertainties (the warranty claims will be paid and the lawsuit will be settled), the liabilities are required to be recognized before all of the uncertainties are resolved so that relevant information is provided on a timely basis.

FAS 5, as interpreted by FIN 34, long had required disclosures about direct and indirect guarantees of the indebtedness of others. FIN 45 now requires that certain obligations arising from guarantees be recorded as liabilities. FIN 45 is discussed in detail in this chapter.

| **Sources of GAAP** | | | | | | | |
|---|---|---|---|---|---|---|---|
| *ARB* | *APB* | *FAS* | *FIN* | *FTB* | *EITF* | *SOP* | *FSP* |
| 43, | 6, 10, | 5, 6, | 8, 14, 39, | 79-3 | 85-20, 86-5, | 96-1 | FIN 45-1, |
| Ch. 3, | 21 | 11, 43, | 41, 45 | | 86-15, 86-30, | | FIN 45-2, |
| 50 | | 48, 78, | | | 95-22, 03-12, | | FIN 45-3 |
| | | 112, | | | 06-2, D-77 | | |
| | | 141(R) | | | | | |

## DEFINITIONS OF TERMS

**Accumulated benefits.** Employee benefits that can be carried over into the next year but that expire upon termination of employment.

**Contingency.** An existing condition, situation, or set of circumstances involving uncertainty as to possible gain or loss that will ultimately be resolved when one or more future events occur or fail to occur.

**Current liabilities.** Obligations whose liquidation is reasonably expected to require the use of existing resources properly classified as current assets or the creation of other current liabilities. Obligations that are due on demand or will be due on demand within one year or the operating cycle, if longer, are current liabilities. Long-term obligations callable because of the debtor's violation of a provision of the debt agreement are current liabilities unless specific FAS 78 conditions are met.

**FICA.** Social security taxes levied upon both employees and employers.

**FUTA.** Social security tax levied upon employers to finance the administration of federal unemployment benefit programs.

**Indirect guarantee of indebtedness of others.** A guarantee under an agreement that obligates one entity to transfer funds to a second entity upon the occurrence of specified events under conditions whereby (1) the funds are legally available to the creditors of the second entity, and (2) those creditors may enforce the second entity's claims against the first entity.

**Operating cycle.** The average length of time necessary for an enterprise to convert inventory to receivables to cash.

## CONCEPTS, RULES, AND EXAMPLES

ARB 43, Chapter 3, contains several examples of current liabilities. It also contains broad general descriptions of the types of items to be shown as current liabilities. These obligations can be divided into those where

1.  Both the amount and the payee are known;
2.  The payee is known but the amount may have to be estimated;
3.  The payee is unknown and the amount may have to be estimated; and
4.  The liability has been incurred due to a loss contingency.

Examples of each of the foregoing types of current liabilities are discussed in the following sections.

### Amount and Payee Known

**Accounts payable** arise primarily from the acquisition of materials and supplies to be used in the production of goods or in conjunction with the providing of services. APB 21 states that payables that arise from transactions with suppliers in the normal course of business and that are due in customary trade terms not to exceed one year may be stated at their face amount rather than at the present value of the required future cash flows.

**Notes payable** are more formalized obligations that may arise from the acquisition of materials and supplies used in operations or from the use of short-term credit to purchase capital assets (APB 21 also applies to short-term notes payable).

**Dividends payable** become a liability of the enterprise when the board of directors declares a cash dividend. Since declared dividends are usually paid within a short period of time after the declaration date, they are classified as current liabilities.

**Unearned revenues or advances** result from customer prepayments for either performance of services or delivery of product. They may be required by the selling enterprise as a condition of the sale or may be made by the buyer as a means of guaranteeing that the seller will perform the desired service or deliver the product. Unearned revenues and advances should be classified as current liabilities at the balance sheet date if the services are to be performed or the products are to be delivered within one year or the operating cycle, whichever is longer.

**Refundable deposits** may be received to cover possible future damage to property. Many utility companies require security deposits. A deposit may be required for the use of a reusable container. Refundable deposits are classified as current liabilities if the firm expects to refund them during the current operating cycle or within one year, whichever is longer.

**Accrued liabilities** have their origin in the end-of-period adjustment process required by accrual accounting. Commonly accrued liabilities include wages and salaries payable, benefits payable, interest payable, and taxes payable. In addition an employer may have a current obligation for the employer portion of FICA tax and FUTA (unemployment) tax. Payroll taxes are not legal liabilities until the associated payroll is actually paid.

**Agency liabilities** result from the legal obligation of the enterprise to act as the collection agent for customer or employee taxes owed to various federal, state, or local government units. Examples of agency liabilities include sales taxes, income taxes withheld from employee paychecks, and employee FICA contributions.

**Product financing liabilities** originate when an entity sells and agrees to repurchase its inventory with the repurchase price equal to the original sales price plus the carrying and financing costs. The purpose of this transaction is to allow the seller to arrange financing on the original purchase of the inventory. The transaction is accounted for as a borrowing rather than as a sale. Chapter 9 provides more information about product financing arrangements.

**Current maturing portion of long-term debt** is shown as a current liability if the obligation is to be liquidated by using assets classified as current. However, if the currently maturing debt is to be liquidated by using other than current assets (i.e., by using a sinking fund that is properly classified as a noncurrent investment), then these obligations should be classified as long-term liabilities.

**Obligations that, by their terms, are due on demand** (FAS 78) or will be due on demand within one year (or operating cycle, if longer) from the balance sheet date, even if liquidation is not expected to occur within that period, are classified as current liabilities.

Noncurrent debt may be due on demand under certain circumstances. FAS 78 requires that long-term obligations that contain call provisions be classified as current liabilities, if as of the balance sheet date one of the following occurs:

1. The debtor is in violation of the agreement and that violation makes the obligation callable.
2. The debtor is in violation of the agreement and that violation, unless cured within the grace period specified in the agreement, makes the obligation callable.

However, if circumstances arise that effectively negate the creditor's right to call the obligation, the obligation may be classified as long-term. Examples are

1. The creditor has waived the right to call the obligation caused by the debtor's violation or the creditor has subsequently lost the right to demand repayment for more than one year (or operating cycle, if longer) from the balance sheet date.
2. Obligations contain a grace period for remedying the violation, and it is probable that the violation will be cured within the grace period. In these situations, the circumstances must be disclosed.

**Demand notes having scheduled repayment terms.** In some instances, a loan will call for scheduled payments and, in the alternative, state that it is due on demand or may be affected by a subjective acceleration clause. According to EITF 86-5, an obligation is considered due on demand even if a debt agreement specifies repayment terms, if the creditor can demand payment at any time. This situation is distinguished from a subjective acceleration clause, which is addressed by FTB 79-3.

**Increasing-rate debt.** EITF 86-15 addresses debt instruments that mature at a defined, near-term date, but which can be continually extended (renewed) for a defined longer period at the option of the debtor, with predefined increases in the interest rate as extensions are elected. These arrangements commonly are known as "increasing-rate notes." The effective outstanding term of the debt should be estimated after considering plans, ability and intent to service the debt. Based upon this term, the borrower's periodic interest rate should be determined by the use of the interest method. Thus, a constant yield will be computed and additional interest will be accrued during the earlier portions of the final term.

Debt interest costs should be amortized over the estimated outstanding term of the debt. Any excess accrued interest resulting from paying the debt before the estimated maturity date is an adjustment of interest expense. It may not be treated as an extraordinary item.

According to EITF 86-15, the classification of the debt as current or noncurrent should be based on the source of repayment. Thus, this classification need not be consistent with the period used to determine the periodic interest cost. For example, the time frame used for the estimated outstanding term of the debt could be a year or less, but because of a planned long-term refinancing agreement the noncurrent classification could be used.

Furthermore, the term-extending provisions of the debt instrument should be evaluated to ascertain whether they constitute a derivative financial instrument under provisions of FAS 133. If so, the derivative element is in all likelihood not "clearly and closely related" to the host instrument (the debt), and thus would have to be reported separately and carried at fair value.

**Long-term obligations that contain subjective acceleration clauses** are classified as current liabilities if circumstances (such as recurring losses or liquidity problems) indicate that the clause will be exercised and payment will be due within one year (or one operating cycle). If, instead, the likelihood of the acceleration of the due date were remote, the obligation would be reported as long-term debt. Situations between the two extremes require disclosure (FTB 79-3).

**Classification of long-term obligations when there are violations of covenants.** Most commercial debt agreements contain a range of financial covenants. The failure to meet these often provides the lender with the contractual right to accelerate the due date, commonly to make the full amount due and payable on demand. Unless a waiver is obtained in such a situation, the balance sheet would have to reflect the nominally long-term debt as a current liability, which in turn might create going concern issues for management and the outside auditors to address and report on.

While a complete waiver, effectively a promise by the lender to not exercise its rights under the financial covenants for at least one year from the balance sheet date, makes it possible to continue presenting the debt as noncurrent, great care must be exercised in interpreting the substance of such an agreement. In practice, many waivers are not effective and cannot form the basis for continued accounting for the debt as noncurrent. For example, a waiver "as of" the current balance sheet date provides no real comfort, since the lender is entitled to assert its rights as soon as the very next day. Likewise, a waiver pending the next scheduled submission of a borrower's covenant compliance letter (generally quarterly, possibly monthly) offers no assurance that the borrower will successfully meet its obligations, and hence affords no basis for presentation of the debt as noncurrent.

According to EITF 86-30, the lender waives that right for a period greater than one year (but retains the requirements to meet the covenant in the future), the reporting entity (i.e., the debtor) should classify the debt as noncurrent unless both (1) a covenant violation has occurred at the balance sheet date or would have occurred absent a loan modification and (2) it is probable that the borrower will be unable to comply with the covenant at measurement dates within the next twelve months.

**Classification of borrowings outstanding under certain revolving credit agreements.** EITF 95-22 applies to borrowings outstanding under a revolving credit agreement that includes both a subjective acceleration clause and a requirement to maintain a lockbox into which the borrower's customers send remittances that are then used to reduce the debt outstanding. These borrowings are short-term obligations and are classified as current liabilities unless the entity has the intent and ability to refinance the revolving credit agreement on a long-term basis (i.e., the conditions in FAS 6 are met). However, if the lockbox is a "springing" lockbox, which is a lockbox agreement in which remittances from the borrower's customers are forwarded to its general bank account and do not reduce the debt outstanding until and unless the lender exercises the subjective acceleration clause, the obligations are long-term since the remittances do not automatically reduce the debt outstanding if the acceleration clause has not been exercised.

**Short-term obligations expected to be refinanced** may be classified as noncurrent liabilities if the conditions specified in FAS 6 all are met. FAS 6 states that an entity may reclassify currently maturing debt (other than obligations arising from transactions in the normal course of business that are due in customary terms) as long-term, provided that the entity intends to refinance the obligation on a long-term basis and its intent is supported by either of the following:

1. Post-balance-sheet-date issuance of a long-term obligation or equity securities. After the date of the entity's balance sheet but before that balance sheet is issued, long-term obligations or equity securities have been issued for the purpose of refinancing the short-term obligations on a long-term basis.
2. Refinancing agreement. Before the balance sheet is issued, the entity has entered into a financing agreement that clearly permits the entity to refinance the short-term obligation on a long-term basis on terms that are readily determinable.

If reclassification of the maturing debt is based upon the existence of a refinancing agreement, then FAS 6 requires the following:

1. The refinancing agreement is noncancelable and will not expire within one year or operating cycle of the balance sheet date.
2. The replacement debt will not be callable except for violation of a provision of the refinancing agreement with which compliance is objectively determinable or measurable.
3. The entity is not in violation of the terms of the refinancing agreement.
4. The lender or investor is financially capable of honoring the refinancing agreement.

Under the provisions of FAS 6, the amount of currently maturing debt to be reclassified cannot exceed the amount raised by the replacement debt or equity issuance, nor can it exceed the amount specified in the refinancing agreement. If the amount specified in the refinancing agreement can fluctuate, then the maximum amount of debt that can be reclassified is equal to a reasonable estimate of the minimum amount expected to be available on any date from the due date of the maturing obligation to the end of the fiscal year. If no estimate can be made of the minimum amount available under the financing agreement, then none of the maturing debt can be reclassified as long-term. If debt or other agreements limit the ability of the organization to fully utilize the proceeds of the refinancing agreement (for example, a clause in another debt agreement sets a maximum debt-to-equity ratio), then only the amount that can be drawn without violating the limitations expressed in those other agreements can be reclassified to long-term. FIN 8 states that if an entity uses current assets after the balance sheet date to liquidate a current obligation, and then replaces those current assets by issuing either equity securities or long-term debt before the issuance of the balance sheet, the currently maturing debt must still be classified as a current liability.

### Example of short-term obligations to be refinanced

The Madison Warehousing Company has obtained a $3,500,000 bridge loan to assist it in completing a new public warehouse. All construction is completed by the balance sheet date, after which Madison has the following three choices for refinancing the bridge loan:

- Enter into a 30-year fixed-rate mortgage for $3,400,000 at 7% interest, leaving Madison with a $100,000 obligation to fulfill from short-term funds. Under this scenario, Madison reports as current debt the $100,000, as well as the $50,000 portion of the mortgage due within one year, with the remainder of the mortgage itemized as long-term debt. The presentation follows:

| | |
|---|---|
| *Current liabilities:* | |
| Short-term notes | 100,000 |
| Current portion of long-term debt | 50,000 |
| | |
| *Noncurrent liabilities:* | |
| 7% mortgage note due in 20XX | 3,350,000 |

- Pay off the bridge loan with Madison's existing variable-rate line of credit (LOC), which expires in two years. The maximum amount of the LOC is 80% of Madison's accounts receivable. Over the two-year remaining term of the LOC, the lowest level of qualifying accounts receivable is expected to be $2,700,000. Thus, only $2,700,000 of the debt can be classified as long-term, while $800,000 is classified as a short-term obligation. The presentation follows:

| | |
|---|---|
| *Current liabilities:* | |
| Short-term note—variable rate line of credit | 800,000 |
| | |
| *Noncurrent liabilities:* | |
| Variable rate line of credit due in 20XX | 2,700,000 |

- Obtain a 10% loan from Madison's owner, with a balloon payment due in five years. Under the terms of this arrangement, the owner can withdraw up to $1,500,000 of funding at any time, even though $3,500,000 is currently available to Madison. Under this approach, $1,500,000 is callable, and therefore must be classified as a short-term obligation. The remainder is classified as long-term debt. The presentation follows:

| | |
|---|---|
| *Current liabilities:* | |
| Short-term note—majority stockholder | 1,500,000 |
| | |
| *Noncurrent liabilities:* | |
| 10% balloon note payable to majority stockholder, due in 20XX | 2,000,000 |

## Payee Known but Amount May Have to Be Estimated

**Taxes payable** includes federal, state, and local income taxes. The amount of income taxes payable is an estimate because the tax laws and rates in effect when the accrual is determined may differ from the tax laws and rates in effect when the taxes ultimately are paid. Temporary differences in recognition and measurement between accounting standards and tax laws create deferred tax liabilities (and deferred tax assets). The portion deemed currently payable must be classified as a current liability. The remaining amount is classified as a long-term liability.

**Property taxes payable** represents the unpaid portion of an entity's obligation to a state or other taxing authority that arises from ownership of real property. ARB 43, Chapter 10 indicates that the most acceptable method of accounting for property taxes is a monthly accrual of property tax expense during the fiscal period of the taxing authority for which the taxes are levied. The fiscal period of the taxing authority is the fiscal period that includes the assessment or lien date.

A liability for property taxes payable arises when the fiscal year of the taxing authority and the fiscal year of the entity do not coincide or when the assessment or lien date and the actual payment date do not fall within the same fiscal year. For example, XYZ Corporation is a calendar-year corporation that owns real estate in a state that operates on a June 30 fiscal year. In this state, property taxes are assessed and become a lien against property on July 1, although they are not payable until April 1 and August 1 of the next calendar year. XYZ Corporation would accrue an expense and a liability on a monthly basis beginning on July 1. At year-end (December 31), the firm would have an expense for six months' property tax on their income statement and a current liability for the same amount.

**Bonus payments** may require estimation since the amount of the bonus may be affected by the entity's net income for the year, by the income taxes currently payable, or by other factors. Additional estimation is necessary if bonus payments are accrued on a monthly basis for purposes of interim financial reporting but are determinable only annually by using a formula whose values are uncertain until shortly before payment.

**Compensated absences** refer to paid vacation, paid holidays, paid sick leave, and other paid leaves of absence. FAS 43 states that an employer must accrue a liability for employee's compensation of future absences if all of the following conditions are met:

1.  The employee's right to receive compensation for future absences is attributable to employee services already rendered.
2.  The right vests or accumulates.
3.  Payment of the compensation is probable.
4.  The amount of the payment can be reasonably estimated.

If an employer is required to compensate an employee for unused vacation, holidays, or sick days even if employment is terminated, then the employee's right to this compensation is said to vest. Accrual of a liability for nonvesting rights depends on whether the unused rights expire at the end of the year in which earned or accumulate and are carried forward to succeeding years. If the rights expire, a liability for future absences should not be accrued at year-end because the benefits to be paid in subsequent years would not be attributable to employee services rendered in prior years. If unused rights accumulate and increase the benefits otherwise available in subsequent years, a liability should be accrued at year-end to the extent that it is probable that employees will be paid in subsequent years for the increased benefits attributable to the accumulated rights and the amount can be reasonably estimated.

FAS 43 allows an exception for employee paid sick days that accumulate but do not vest. No accrued liability is required for sick days that only accumulate. However, an accrual may be made. The Board stated that these amounts are rarely material and the low reliability of estimates of future illness coupled with the high cost of developing these estimates indicates that accrual is not necessary. The required accounting should be determined by the employer's actual administration of sick pay benefits. If the employer routinely lets employees take time off when they are not ill and allows that time to be charged as sick pay, then an accrual should be made.

Pay for other employee leaves of absence that represent time off for past services (jury duty, personal days) should be considered compensation subject to accrual. Pay for employee leaves of absence that will provide future benefits and that are not attributable to past services rendered would not be subject to accrual. FAS 43 does not provide guidance as to whether accruals should be based on current pay rates or expected future rates of pay and does not provide guidance regarding discounting of the accrual amounts.

EITF 06-2 states that liabilities for so-called sabbatical leaves or other similar benefit arrangements that require the completion of a minimum service period, and for which the benefit does not increase with additional years of service, accumulate pursuant to FAS 43 for arrangements in which the individual continues to be a compensated employee and is not required to perform duties for the entity during the absence. Therefore, assuming all of the other conditions set forth above are met, the compensation cost associated with a sabbatical or other similar arrangement must be ratably accrued over the presabbatical periods of service.

EITF 06-2 specifies that transition to this requirement (that is, accrual of previously unrecognized liabilities) can be either via a cumulative effect (i.e., catch-up) adjustment in the period of adoption (years beginning after 2006), or by restatement of earlier periods' results of operations. If by the former method, disclosure must be made of the cumulative effect of the change on retained earnings or other components of equity or net assets in the statement of financial position.

If transition is effected by the latter method, the reporting entity should include the recognition of

1. The cumulative effect of the change to the new accounting principle on periods prior to those presented reflected in the carrying amounts of assets and liabilities as of the beginning of the first period presented;
2. The cumulative effect of the change on retained earnings or on other components of equity or net assets in the statement of financial position; and
3. Adjustments to financial statements for each individual prior period presented to reflect the period-specific effects of applying the new accounting principle.

When restatement is elected, disclosures will be required of the following:

1. A description of the prior-period information that has been retrospectively adjusted;
2. The effects of the change on income from continuing operations, net income (or other appropriate captions of changes in the applicable net assets or performance indicator), any other affected financial statement line items, and any affected per-share amounts for any prior periods retrospectively adjusted; and
3. The cumulative effect of the change on retained earnings or on other components of equity or net assets in the statement of financial position as of the beginning of the earliest period presented.

FAS 112 specifies the use of the four conditions of FAS 43 to identify the need to accrue an obligation for postemployment benefits other than pensions. Postemployment benefits other than pensions are benefits paid after termination of employment but before retirement to or on behalf of former or inactive employees, their beneficiaries, and covered dependents. Examples of those benefits are salary continuation agreements, supplemental unemployment compensation, severance benefits, workers' compensation and other disability-related payments, job training or job placement services and continuation of health care or life insurance benefits after employment. If the four conditions in FAS 43 are met, a liability is accrued. If one or more of the conditions are not met, the employer should assess whether a liability should be accrued under FAS 5. If neither FAS 43 nor FAS 5 is applicable because the amount cannot be reasonably estimated, this fact must be disclosed.

### Payee Unknown and the Amount May Have to Be Estimated

**Sales incentives** are usually offered by an enterprise to increase product sales. They may require the purchaser to accumulate a specified number of miles, points, box tops, wrappers, or other proofs of purchase. They may or may not require the payment of a cash amount. If the incentive offer terminates at the end of the current period but has not been completely accounted for, or if it extends into the next accounting period, a current liability for the estimated number of redemptions that are expected in the future period would be recorded. If the incentive offer extends for more than one accounting period, the estimated liability must be divided into a current portion and a long-term portion. See Chapter 10 for a discussion of EITF 01-9 for additional information about accounting for and disclosure of sales incentives.

### Example of an accrued sales incentive

Sonoma Airlines, a specialty airline offering flights to California's wine producing regions, offers frequent flier miles to its passengers. Anyone remitting 15,000 mileage points earns a free flight on Sonoma, which costs the airline $120 per flight granted, or approximately $0.008 per mileage point remitted. In April, the airline granted 23,000,000 mileage points, having a total value of $184,000 (23,000,000 miles flown × 0.008). Sonoma's history of mileage claims remitted over the past 12 months has been that 40% of all mileage points are eventually remitted. Thus, Sonoma records the following liability in April, based on recognition of 40% of the total value of mileage points granted:

| | | |
|---|---|---|
| Passenger transportation expense | 73,600 | |
| Unremitted mileage points liability | | 73,600 |

Also in April, 8,475,000 mileage points are remitted by Sonoma passengers for free flights. The cost of these remittances is as follows:

| | | |
|---|---|---|
| Mileage points remitted | | 8,475,000 |
| Cost per mileage point | × | $ 0.008 |
| Total liability reduction | = | $67,800 |

Sonoma records the liability reduction with the following entry:

| | | |
|---|---|---|
| Unremitted mileage points liability | 67,800 | |
| Passenger transportation expense | | 67,800 |

The actual cost of transportation of passengers paid or accrued by Sonoma at the time the flights occur is thus reduced by the amount accrued at the time the points currently being redeemed were awarded.

A year later, Sonoma finds that the mileage points remittance rate has risen from 40% to 42%. At this time, there are 163,000,000 mileage points outstanding. Sonoma records a liability for the incremental increase of 2% in the remittance level with the following entry:

| | | |
|---|---|---|
| Passenger transportation expense | 26,080 | |
| Unremitted mileage points liability | | 26,080 |

The entry is based on the following calculation:

| | | |
|---|---|---|
| Mileage points outstanding | | 163,000,000 |
| Net increase in percentage | × | 2% |
| Cost per mileage point | × | $ 0.008 |
| Total liability | = | $26,080 |

Sonoma receives an offer to sell 20,000,000 mileage points to the Wine Connoisseur branded credit card, which in turn sells the points to its card holders in exchange for purchases made with its credit card. The sale price is $0.005 per mile sold, resulting in the following entry:

| | | |
|---|---|---|
| Cash | 100,000 | |
| Revenue | | 100,000 |

Sonoma must also record the related cost of this transaction. Based on its estimated 42% mileage points remittance rate and $0.008 cost per mileage point, Sonoma arrives at the following estimated cost of the transaction:

| | | |
|---|---|---|
| Mileage points sold | | 20,000,000 |
| Mileage remittance percentage | × | 42% |
| Cost per mileage point | × | $ 0.008 |
| Total estimated cost | = | $67,200 |

Sonoma records the following entry to record the expense associated with the mileage point sale:

| | | |
|---|---|---|
| Passenger transportation expense | 67,200 | |
|    Unremitted mileage points liability | | 67,200 |

**Product warranties** providing for repair or replacement of defective products may be sold separately or may be included in the sale price of the product. If the warranty extends into the next accounting period, a current liability for the estimated amount of warranty expense expected in the next period must be recorded. If the warranty spans more than the next period, the estimated liability must be partitioned into a current and long-term portion. FIN 45, discussed more fully later in this chapter, requires disclosure of product warranties in the notes to financial statements. Entities are required to disclose the following information:

1. The nature of the product warranty, including how the warranty arose and the events or circumstances in which the entity must perform under the warranty.
2. The entity's accounting policy and methodology used to determine its liability for the product warranty, including any liability (such as deferred revenue) associated with an extended warranty.
3. A reconciliation of the changes in the aggregate product warranty liability for the reporting period. The reconciliation must include five components: (1) the beginning aggregate balance of the liability, (2) the reductions in the liability caused by payments under the warranty, (3) the increase in the liability for new warranties issued during the period, (4) the change in the liability for adjustments to estimated amounts to be paid under preexisting warranties, and (5) the ending aggregate balance of the liability.
4. The nature and extent of any recourse provisions or available collateral that would enable the entity to recover the amounts paid under the warranties, and an indication (if estimable) of the approximate extent to which the proceeds from recovery or liquidation would be expected to cover the maximum potential amount of future payments under the warranty.
5. The disclosures required by FAS 57 if the warranties are granted to benefit related parties. (See Chapter 2 for a discussion of related-party disclosures.)

A proposed FASB staff position would also require the above disclosures for an indemnification clause included by a software vendor-licensor in a software licensing agreement that indemnifies the licensee against liability and damages (including legal defense costs) arising from any claims of patent, copyright, trademark or trade secret infringement by the software vendor's software.

### Example of product warranty expense

The Churnaway Corporation manufactures clothes washers. It sells $900,000 of washing machines during its most recent month of operations. Based on its historical warranty claims experience, it reserves an estimated warranty expense of 2% of revenues with the following entry:

| | | |
|---|---|---|
| Warranty expense | 18,000 | |
|    Reserve for warranty claims | | 18,000 |

During the following month, Churnaway incurs $10,000 of actual labor and $4,500 of actual materials expenses to repair warranty claims, which it charges to the warranty claims reserve with the following entry:

| | | |
|---|---|---|
| Reserve for warranty claims | 14,500 | |
|    Labor expense | | 10,000 |
|    Materials expense | | 4,500 |

Churnaway also sells three-year extended warranties on its washing machines that begin once the initial one-year manufacturer's warranty is completed. During one month, it sells $54,000 of extended warranties, which it records with the following entry:

| | | |
|---|---|---|
| Cash | 54,000 | |
| Unearned warranty revenue | | 54,000 |

This liability is unaltered for one year from the purchase date, after which the extended warranty servicing period begins. Churnaway recognizes the warranty revenue on a straight-line basis over the 36 months of the warranty period, using the following entry each month:

| | | |
|---|---|---|
| Unearned warranty revenue | 1,500 | |
| Warranty revenue | | 1,500 |

**Future product returns** are accrued if a buyer has a right to return the product purchased and the sale is recognized currently. An accrual for returns must reduce both revenue and the associated cost of sales (FAS 48). In the relatively unlikely situation where the reporting entity is unable to make a reasonable estimate of the amount of future returns, the sale cannot be recognized until the return privilege has expired or conditions permit the loss to be estimated, at which point it would become reportable. Examples of factors that might impair the ability to reasonably estimate a loss are

1. Susceptibility of the product to technological or other obsolescence
2. A lengthy period over which returns are permitted
3. Absence of experience with returns on similar products sold to similar markets
4. Sales are few, significant, and have unique terms (rather than a large number of relatively homogeneous sales of small dollar amounts).

**Example of future product returns**

The SnoJet Company manufactures high-powered snowmobiles, for which it issues a six-month return policy to its distributors. It recently developed the XTR Pro model, which is an incremental enhancement of earlier models, with more horsepower and a tighter suspension. Given its similarity to earlier models, SnoJet's management is comfortable in extending the historical product return rate of 10% to sales of the XTR Pro model. In February, SnoJet sold $840,000 of XTR Pro snowmobiles which have an associated cost of $504,000 (a 60% cost of goods sold). At the same time, the company records $84,000 (10% of gross sales) in an allowance for sales returns, resulting in the following income statement presentation:

| | |
|---|---|
| Sales | $840,000 |
| Less: sales returns | (84,000) |
| Net sales | $756,000 |

Note that, to fully comply with the requirements of FAS 48, a reserve for the cost of the estimated product should also be provided, with a corresponding reduction of cost of sales, as follows:

| | |
|---|---|
| Cost of sales | $504,000 |
| Less: cost of sales on estimated returns | (50,400) |
| Net cost of sales | $453,600 |

In the following month, ten XTR Pro models are returned to SnoJet. The revenue originally recorded on their sale was $24,000, with associated cost of goods sold of $14,400. However, there is some damage to the models, which will require $3,000 to repair. SnoJet records the transaction with the following entry:

| | | |
|---|---|---|
| Allowance for sales returns | 24,000 | |
| Inventory—rework | 11,400 | |
| Loss—returned inventory damage | 3,000 | |
| Accounts receivable | | 24,000 |
| Allowance for cost of sales on product returns | | 14,400 |

SnoJet develops an entirely new, jet-powered snowmobile, called the JetPro, which requires the substantial redesign of its basic snowmobile platform. Also, it is to be sold strictly to professional snowmobile racers with whom the company has minimal sales experience, with sale terms allowing returns onl y within the first two months. In the first month, SnoJet has $150,000 of JetPro sales, for which the related cost of goods sold is $100,000. Given the sales return uncertainty associated with this model, SnoJet records no revenue during the first month, waiting until the second month for the product return policy to expire before recording any revenue. In the first month, its entry to record JetPro sales is

| | | |
|---|---|---|
| Accounts receivable | 150,000 | |
| Unearned revenue | | 150,000 |
| Inventory—customer location | 100,000 | |
| Finished goods inventory | | 100,000 |

At the end of the second month, after the right of return has expired, SnoJet uses the following entry to record the sale and its related profit:

| | | |
|---|---|---|
| Unearned revenue | 150,000 | |
| Revenue | | 150,000 |
| Cost of goods sold | 100,000 | |
| Inventory—customer location | | 100,000 |

Note that the decision not to record revenues until after the risk of product returns has lapsed is relatively unusual in practice, and will be dependent on careful consideration of all the facts and circumstances.

**Environmental remediation liabilities.** Obligations arising from pollution of the environment have become a major cost for businesses. SOP 96-1 sets forth a very detailed description of relevant laws, remediation provisions and other pertinent information, which is useful to auditors as well as to reporting entities. In terms of accounting guidance, the SOP provides that FAS 5 is the principal standard to be interpreted in the context of environmental obligations (e.g., determining the threshold for accrual of a liability, etc.) and its sets "benchmarks" for liability recognition. The benchmarks for the accrual and evaluation of the estimated liability (i.e., the stages which are deemed to be important to ascertaining the existence and amount of the liability) are

1. The identification and verification of an entity as a potentially responsible party (PRP), since the SOP stipulates that accrual should be based on the premise that expected costs will be borne by only the "participating potentially responsible parties" and that the "recalcitrant, unproven and unidentified" PRP will not contribute to costs of remediation
2. The receipt of a "unilateral administrative order"
3. Participation, as a PRP, in the remedial investigation/feasibility study (RI/FS)
4. Completion of the feasibility study
5. Issuance of the Record of Decision (RoD)
6. The remedial design through operation and maintenance, including postremediation monitoring

The amount of the liability that is to be accrued is affected by the entity's allocable share of liability for a specific site, and by its share of the amounts related to the site that will not be paid by the other PRP or the government. The categories of costs to be included in the accrued liability include incremental direct costs of the remediation effort itself, as well as the costs of compensation and benefits for employees directly involved in the remediation effort. The SOP indicates that costs are to be estimated based on existing laws and technologies, and are not to be discounted to estimated present values unless timing of cash payments is fixed or reliably determinable.

Incremental direct costs will include such items as fees paid to outside law firms for work related to the remediation effort, costs relating to completing the RI/FS, fees to outside consulting and engineering firms for site investigations and development of remedial action plans and remedial actions, costs of contractors performing remedial actions, government oversight costs and past costs, the cost of machinery and equipment dedicated to the remedial actions that do not have an alternative use, assessments by a PRP group covering costs incurred by the group in dealing with a site, and the costs of operation and maintenance of the remedial action, including costs of postremediation monitoring required by remedial action plan.

SOP 96-1 states that potential recoveries cannot be offset against the estimated liability, and further notes that any recovery recognized as an asset should be reflected at fair value, which implies that only the present value of future recoveries can be recorded. It also stipulates that environmental clean up costs are not unusual in nature, and thus cannot be shown as extraordinary items in the income statement. Furthermore, it is presumed that the costs are operating in nature, and thus cannot normally be included in "other income and expense" category of the income statement, either. Disclosure of accounting policies regarding recognition of the liability and of any related asset (for recoveries from third parties) are also needed, where pertinent.

## Contingencies

FAS 5 defines a contingency as an existing condition, situation, or set of circumstances involving uncertainty as to possible gain or loss. The uncertainty will ultimately be resolved when one or more future events occur or fail to occur. FAS 5 defines the different levels of probability as to whether or not future events will confirm the existence of a loss as follows:

1. **Probable**—The future event or events are likely to occur.
2. **Reasonably possible**—The chance of the future event or events occurring is more than remote but less than likely.
3. **Remote**—The chance of the future event or events occurring is slight.

Professional judgment is required to classify the likelihood of the future events occurring. All relevant information that can be acquired concerning the uncertain set of circumstances needs to be obtained and used to determine the classification.

FAS 5 states that a loss must be accrued if *both* of the following conditions are met:

1. It is probable that an asset has been impaired or a liability has been incurred at the date of the financial statements.
2. The amount of loss can be reasonably estimated.

**Loss contingency.** Loss contingencies are recognized only if there is an impairment of an asset or the incurrence of a liability as of the balance sheet date. Examples of possible loss contingencies include

1. Collectibility of receivables
2. Warranty liabilities and product defects
3. Loss due to fire, explosion, or other hazards
4. Expropriation of assets
5. Litigation, claims, and assessments
6. Incurred but not reported (IBNR) claims if the entity insures its risk of loss with a claims-made policy
7. Exposures under multiple-year retrospectively rated insurance contacts
8. Catastrophic losses by insurance and reinsurance entities
9. The contingent obligations under guarantees
10. Obligations under standby letters of credit
11. Repurchase agreements

12. Withdrawal from a multiemployer plan
13. Consideration for a failed registration statement

Events that give rise to loss contingencies that occur after the balance sheet date (i.e., bankruptcy or expropriation) but before issuance of the financial statements may require disclosure so that statement users are not misled. Note disclosures or pro forma financial statements may be prepared as supplemental information to show the effect of the loss.

It is not necessary that a single amount be identified. A range of amounts is sufficient to indicate that some amount of loss has been incurred and should be accrued. The amount accrued is the amount within the range that appears to be the best estimate. If there is no best estimate, the minimum amount in the range should be accrued since it is probable that the loss will be at least this amount (FIN 14). The maximum amount of loss should be disclosed. If future events indicate that the minimum loss originally accrued is inadequate, an additional loss should be accrued in the period when this fact becomes known. This accrual is a change in estimate, not a prior period adjustment.

When a loss is probable and no estimate is possible, these facts should be disclosed in the current period. The accrual of the loss should be made in the earliest period in which the amount of the loss can be estimated. Accrual of that loss in future periods is a change in estimate. It is not a prior period adjustment.

If the occurrence of the loss is reasonably possible, the facts and circumstances of the possible loss and an estimate of the amount, if determinable, should be disclosed. (See also Chapter 2.) If the occurrence of the loss is remote, no accrual or disclosure is usually required.

When a public company cannot estimate the reasonably likely impact of a contingent liability, but a range of amounts are determinable, the SEC requires disclosure of those amounts. Disclosure of contingencies for public companies should also include quantification of the related accruals and adjustments, costs of legal defense, and reasonably likely exposure to additional loss, as well as the assumptions that management has made about those amounts, and the extent to which the resulting estimates of loss are sensitive to changes in those assumptions.

**Acquisition-related contingencies.** FAS 5 does not generally apply when determining which contingent assets or liabilities are to be recognized as of the date of an acquisition. Instead, under provisions of FAS 141(R), the acquirer recognizes at their acquisition date fair values the assets acquired and liabilities assumed that arise from contract related contingencies. For noncontractual contingencies, the acquirer shall assess as of the acquisition date whether it is more likely than not that a contingency shall result in an asset or liability; if so, the acquirer recognizes the acquisition-date asset or liability at its fair value. A noncontractual contingency that does not meet the more-likely-than-not criterion is to be treated as previously described under FAS 5.

If the acquirer later obtains new information about the expected outcome of an acquisition-related contingency, it should then measure each liability at the higher of its acquisition-date fair value or the amount that would be recognized under FAS 5. Each acquisition-related contingent asset should be reported at the lower of its acquisition-date fair value or the best estimate of its future settlement amount.

**Unasserted claims or assessments.** It is not necessary to disclose loss contingencies for an unasserted claim or assessment where there has been no manifestation of an awareness of possible claim or assessment by a potential claimant unless it is deemed probable that a claim will be asserted and a reasonable possibility of an unfavorable outcome exists. Under the provisions of FAS 5, general or unspecified business risks are not loss contingencies and, therefore, no accrual is necessary. Appropriations of retained earnings may be used for these risks as long as no charge to income is made to establish the appropriation. Disclosure of these business risks may be required under SOP 94-6 (see Chapter 2).

**Estimate vs. contingency.** Distinguishing between an estimate and a contingency can be difficult because both involve an uncertainty that will be resolved by future events. However, an estimate exists because of uncertainty about the amount of a loss resulting from an event requiring an acknowledged accounting recognition. The event has occurred and the effect is known, but the amount itself is uncertain. For example, depreciation is an estimate, but not a contingency because the actual fact of physical depreciation is acknowledged, although the amount is obtained by an assumed accounting method.

In a contingency, the amount is also usually uncertain, although that is not an essential characteristic. Instead, the uncertainty lies in whether the event has occurred (or will) and what the effect, if any, on the enterprise would be. Collectibility of receivables is a contingency because it is uncertain whether a customer will not pay at a future date, although it is probable that some customers will not pay. Similar logic would hold for obligations related to product warranties. That is, it is uncertain whether a product will fail, but it is probable that some will fail within the warranty period.

Other contingencies are rarely recognized until specific events confirming their existence occur. Every business risks loss by fire, explosion, government expropriation or casualties in the ordinary course of business. To the extent those losses are not (or cannot be) insured, the risks are contingencies. Because those events are often random in their occurrence, uncertainty surrounds whether the future event confirming the loss will or will not take place. The passage of time usually resolves the uncertainty. Until the event confirming the loss occurs (or is probable of occurrence) and the amount of the loss can be reasonably estimated, the potential loss is not recognized in financial statements.

The most difficult area of contingencies is litigation. Accountants must rely on attorneys' assessments concerning the likelihood of such events. Unless the attorney indicates that the risk of loss is remote or slight, or that the loss if it occurs would be immaterial to the company, disclosure in financial statements is necessary and an accrual may also be necessary. In practice, attorneys are loathe to state that the risk of loss is remote, as that term is defined by FAS 5, although the likelihood of obtaining a definitive response to lawyers' letters under SAS 12 is improved if the auditors explicitly cite a materiality threshold. In cases where judgments have been entered against the reporting entity, or where the attorney gives a range of expected losses or other amounts and indicates that an unfavorable outcome is probable, accruals of loss contingencies for at least the minimum point of the range must be made. In most cases, however, an estimate of the contingency is unknown and the contingency is reflected only in footnotes.

Accruals for contingencies, including those arising in connection with litigation, are limited under GAAP to expected losses resulting from events occurring prior to the balance sheet date. One unresolved issue, addressed in EITF Discussion Topic D-77, is whether expected legal costs to be incurred in connection with a loss contingency (that is being accrued) could be accrued as well. Apparently, GAAP would permit such an accrual, but practice is varied, and in any event the decision to do so would need to be disclosed in the financial statements and applied consistently.

## Guarantees

While disclosures of at least some guarantees had been common under provisions of FAS 5, the economic significance of such arrangements had rarely been measured or disclosed in the past. FIN 45 significantly alters past practice by requiring that the fair value of guarantees be recognized as a liability. Subsequently, FASB has issued three staff positions (FSP) interpreting the guidance of FIN 45.

FIN 45 applies to guarantee contracts that contingently require the guarantor to make payments (either in cash, financial instruments, shares of its stock, other assets, or in services) to the guaranteed party based on any of the following circumstances:

1. Changes in a specified interest rate, security price, commodity price, foreign exchange rate, index of prices or rates, or any other variable, including the occurrence or nonoccurrence of a specified event that is related to an asset or liability of the guaranteed party. For example, the provisions apply to the following, as cited by FIN 45:

   a. A financial standby letter of credit
   b. A market value guarantee on either securities (including the common stock of the guaranteed party) or a nonfinancial asset owned by the guaranteed party
   c. A guarantee of the market price of the common stock of the guaranteed party
   d. A guarantee of the collection of the scheduled contractual cash flows from individual financial assets held by a variable interest entity (VIE)
   e. A guarantee granted to a business or its owners that the revenue received by the business will equal or exceed some stated amount

   The last stated example, above, was added to FIN 45 by FSP FIN 45-3, *Application of FIN 45 to Minimum Revenue Guarantees Granted to a Business or Its Owners.* One common example of this type of situation is where a hospital lures a doctor to open a practice in an under-served community with a guarantee of fee income for an initial period. FIN 45 has been amended to make explicit that these types of assurances are guarantees under FIN 45 and must be given accounting recognition.

2. Another entity's failure to perform under an obligating agreement. For example, the provisions apply to a performance standby letter of credit, which obligates the guarantor to make a payment if the specified entity fails to perform its nonfinancial obligation.

3. The occurrence of a specified event or circumstance (an indemnification agreement), such as an adverse judgment in a lawsuit or the imposition of additional taxes due to either a change in the tax law or an adverse interpretation of the tax law, provided that the guarantor is an entity other than an insurance or reinsurance company.

4. The occurrence of specified events under conditions whereby payments are legally available to creditors of the guaranteed party and those creditors may enforce the guaranteed party's claims against the guarantor under the agreement (an indirect guarantee of the indebtedness of others).

FIN 45 does *not* apply to

1. Commercial letters of credit and other loan commitments
2. Subordination on arrangements in securitization transactions
3. A lessee's guarantee of the residual value of leased property
4. A guarantee contract or an indemnification agreement that is issued by either an insurance or a reinsurance company
5. Contingent rents
6. Vendor rebates (by the guarantor) based on either the sales revenues of or the number of units sold by the guaranteed party
7. Guarantees that prevent the guarantor from recognizing either the sale of the asset underlying the guarantee or the profits from that sale

8. Guarantees arising from pension plans, vacation pay arrangement, deferred compensation contracts, and stock issued to employees

FIN 45's requirement to recognize an initial liability does not apply to the following types of guarantees (i.e., these guarantees are subject only to FIN 45's disclosure requirements):

1. A guarantee that is accounted for as a derivative instrument at fair value
2. A contract that guarantees the functionality of nonfinancial assets that are owned by the guaranteed party (product warranties)
3. Contingent consideration in a business combination
4. A guarantee that requires the guarantor to issue its own equity shares
5. A guarantee by an original lessee that has become secondarily liable under a new lease that relieved the original lessee of the primary obligation under the original lease
6. A guarantee issued between parents and their subsidiaries or between corporations under common control
7. A parent's guarantee of a subsidiary's debt to a third party
8. A subsidiary's guarantee of a parent's debt to a third party or the debt of another subsidiary of the parent
9. Software licenses which contain an "indemnification clause" protecting the licensee from liabilities and damages that might arise if the licensor's software is subject to a claim of patent, copyright, or trade secret infringement (per FSP 45-1, *Accounting for Intellectual Property Infringement Indemnifications under FASB Interpretation No. 45, "Guarantor's Accounting and Disclosure Requirements for Guarantees, Including Indirect Guarantees of Indebtedness of Others"*).

FIN 45 establishes the notion that a guarantee actually consists of two distinct components. These two obligations have quite different accounting implications. The first of these is a noncontingent obligation, namely, the obligation to stand ready to perform over the term of the guarantee in the event that the specified triggering events or conditions occur. The second element, which is a contingent obligation, is the obligation to make future payments if those triggering events or conditions occur. At the inception of a guarantee, the guarantor would recognize a liability for both the noncontingent and contingent obligations at their fair values. However, in the unusual circumstance that a liability is recognized under FAS 5 for the contingent obligation (i.e., because it is deemed probable of occurrence and reasonable of estimation that the guarantor will pay), the liability to be initially recognized for the noncontingent obligation would only be the portion, if any, of the guarantee's fair value not already recognized to comply with FAS 5.

It is important to stress that this does not mean that the guarantor records the entire face amount of the guarantee; rather, it is the fair value that would be recognized. When a guarantee is issued in a stand-alone, arm's-length transaction with an unrelated party, the fair value of the guarantee (and thus the amount to be recognized as a liability) is the premium received by the guarantor. When a guarantee is issued as part of another transaction (such as the sale or lease of an asset) or as a contribution to an unrelated party, the fair value of the liability is measured by the premium that would be required by the guarantor to issue the same guarantee in a stand-alone, arm's-length transaction with an unrelated party.

In practice, if the likelihood that the guarantor will have to perform is judged to be only "possible" or "remote," the only amount to be reported will be the fair value of the noncontingent obligation to stand ready to perform. If, however, the contingency is probable of occurrence and can be reasonably estimated under FAS 5, that amount must be reported and the liability to be reported, in total, under the guarantee arrangement will be the greater of (1) the fair value computed as explained above, or (2) the amount computed in accordance with FAS 5's provisions.

FAS 157 deleted language that referenced the application of the CON 7 present value methodology in FIN 45. In the authors' view, this is because, in the context of guarantees given (e.g., by sellers of merchandise) the probability-weighted cash flow estimates would be difficult to develop, unless the guarantor engages in a large volume of such arrangements. However, present value of cash flows is one acceptable means of estimating fair value, although is might involve so-called "level 3" (i.e., unobservable) inputs, and thus would rank at the bottom of the FAS 157 fair value hierarchy.

Since, in the authors' opinion, in the absence of other, better input data, such as the pricing of insurance to assume the risk of performing on the guarantee, the probability-weighted present value of possible future cash flows could serve as useful input to determining the fair value of guarantees made, the following example is presented.

**Example of estimating the fair value of a guarantee using CON 7 when recognition under FAS 5 would not be otherwise required**

Big Red Company guarantees a $1,000,000 debt of Little Blue Company for the next three years in conjunction with selling equipment to Little Blue. Big Red evaluates its risk of payment as follows:

(1) There is no possibility that Big Red will pay during year 1.
(2) There is a 15% chance that Big Red will pay during year 2. If it has to pay, there is a 30% chance that it will have to pay $500,000 and a 70% chance that it will have to pay $250,000.
(3) There is a 20% chance that Big Red will pay during year 3. If it has to pay, there is a 25% chance that it will have to pay $600,000 and a 75% chance that it will have to pay $300,000.

The expected cash flows are computed as follows:

Year 1    100% chance of paying $0 = $0
Year 2    85% chance of paying $0 and a 15% chance of paying (.30 × $500,000 + .70 × $250,000 =) $325,000 = $48,750
Year 3    80% chance of paying $0 and a 20% chance of paying (.25 × $600,000 + .75 × $300,000 =) $375,000 = $75,000

The present value of the expected cash flows is computed as the sum of the years' probability-weighted cash flows, here assuming an appropriate discount rate of 8%.

| | | |
|---|---|---|
| Year 1 | $0 × 1/1.08 = | $ 0 |
| Year 2 | $48,750 × 1/(1.08)$^2$ = | 41,795 |
| Year 3 | $75,000 × 1/(1.08)$^3$ = | 59,537 |
| Fair value of the guarantee | | $101,332 |

Based on the foregoing, a liability of $101,332 would be recognized at inception. This would reduce the net selling price of the equipment sold to Little Blue, thereby reducing the profit to be reported on the sale transaction.

**Example of estimating the fair value of a guarantee using CON 7 when recognition under FAS 5 is also required**

Assume the same basic facts as in the foregoing example, but now also assume that it has been determined that there is a 60% likelihood that the buyer will eventually default and, after legal process, Big Red will have to repay debt amounting to $400,000 at the end of the fifth year. Assume also that a likelihood of 60% is deemed to make this contingent obligation "probable" under FAS 5. The present value of that payment is $272,233, but FAS 5 does not address or seemingly anticipate the application of present value methods. Thus, it would appear that accrual of the full $400,000 expected loss is required, unaffected by expected timing or by the probability

(60%, in this example) that it will occur. Since this amount exceeds the amount computed under FIN 45, no additional amount would be recognized in connection with the noncontingent obligation to stand ready to perform.

If, instead of the immediate foregoing facts, the probable repayments were estimated to be $75,000, then the liabilities to be recognized would total $101,322, of which $75,000 would be required to satisfy the provisions of FAS 5, and the incremental amount, $26,332, would be attributed to the noncontingent obligation.

The entry to record the liability depends upon the circumstances under which the guarantee arose. If the guarantee was issued in a stand-alone transaction for a premium, the offset would be to the asset accepted for the premium's payment (most likely, cash or a receivable). If the guarantee was issued in conjunction with the sale of assets, the proceeds would be allocated between the sale of the asset and the guarantee obligation, so that the profit (loss) on the sale of the asset would be reduced (increased). If the guarantee was issued in conjunction with the formation of a business accounted for under the equity method, the offset would be an increase in the carrying amount of the investment. If the guarantee was issued to an unrelated party for no consideration, an immediate expense would be recognized. If a residual value guarantee was provided by a lessee-guarantor, the offset would be reported as prepaid rent and then amortized over the term of the lease to rent expense. The residual value of equipment by the manufacturer is recognized by the manufacturer as an asset (included in the seller/lessor's net investment in lease).

After initial recognition, the liability is adjusted as the guarantor either is released from risk or is subject to increased risk. FIN 45 does not specify the accounting for guarantees subsequent to initial recognition, and there is no requirement to reassess the fair value of the guarantee after inception. In fact, according to FSP 45-2, *Whether FASB Interpretation No. 45, "Guarantor's Accounting and Disclosure Requirements for Guarantees, Including Indirect Guarantees of Indebtedness of Others," Provides Support for Subsequently Accounting for a Guarantor's Liability at Fair Value,* FIN 45 only addresses measurement of a guarantor's liability at the inception of the guarantee and fair value should only be used in subsequent accounting for the guarantee if the use of that method can be justified under other authoritative guidance. FIN 45 cannot be cited to support adjustments to fair value subsequent to initial recognition.

However, if the guarantor is subsequently released from risk, that logically could be recognized in one of three ways, in the authors' opinion, although no guidance is provided by FIN 45. First, the liability could simply be written off at its expiration or settlement. Second, the liability could be amortized systematically over the guarantee period. Third, the liability might be adjusted to reflect changing fair value, which presumably declines over time as the risk of having to perform decreases. Furthermore, changes dictated by the provisions of FAS 5 (e.g., as a previously "remote" contingency becomes a "probable" one) must be accounted for under that standard, apart from the requirements of FIN 45.

**Fees for guaranteeing a loan.** According to EITF 85-20, fees received for guaranteeing another entity's obligation should be ratably taken into income over the guarantee period, rather than at the time of receipt, consistent with other standards governing service fee income recognition. The consensus also stressed that the guarantor should perform ongoing assessments of the probability of loss related to the guarantee and recognize a liability if the conditions in FAS 5 are met. Now that FIN 45 has been issued and become fully effective, an initial recognition of the stand-ready obligation under the guarantee is required. The contingent aspect of the guarantee would be recognized if the conditions defined by FAS 5 are met.

**Impact of FIN 45 on revenue recognition on sales with a guaranteed minimum resale value.** EITF 95-1 had held that manufacturers are precluded from recognizing sales of equipment when they provide purchasers with guarantees of resale value, unless the criteria for sales-type lease accounting are met. It stated that minimum lease payments, used to ascertain whether a given lease would be an operating or sales-type (capital) lease, were to include the difference between initial proceeds and guaranteed amount. Subsequently, FIN 45 was issued, requiring that the fair value of a guarantee be explicitly recognized. EITF 03-12 clarifies the effect of FIN 45 on the situation described above.

According to EITF 03-12, the fair value of the resale value guarantee will not be recognized by the manufacturer, because FIN 45 does not apply to an asset of the guarantor. Given that the manufacturer would report the residual value as an asset, the guarantee does not fall within the domain of FIN 45.

**Disclosure requirements.** A guarantor is now required to disclose the following information about each guarantee, or each group of similar guarantees, even if the likelihood of the guarantor's having to make any payments under the guarantee were deemed remote:

1. The nature of the guarantee, including how the guarantee arose and the events or circumstances that would require the guarantor to perform under the guarantee
2. The maximum potential amount of future payments (undiscounted) under the guarantee
3. The carrying amount of the liability, if any, for the guarantor's obligations under the guarantee, including any amount recognized under FAS 5
4. The nature and extent of any recourse provisions or available collateral that would enable the guarantor to recover the amounts paid under the guarantee, and an indication of the approximate extent to which the proceeds from recoveries or liquidation would be expected to cover the maximum potential amount of future payments under the guarantee
5. The fair value of financial guarantees issued, if the entity is required to disclose the fair value of financial instruments under the provisions of FAS 107 as amended by FAS 126. (See Chapter 8 for a discussion of which entities are required to disclose the fair value of financial instruments.)
6. The disclosures required by FAS 57 if the guarantees are made to benefit related parties. (See Chapter 2 for a discussion of related-party disclosures.)

## Offsetting of Assets and Liabilities

APB 10 states that offsetting of assets and liabilities is improper except where a right of setoff exists. A right of setoff is a debtor's legal right to discharge debt owed to another party by applying against the debt an amount the other party owes to the debtor. FIN 39 and FIN 41 describe certain conditions, which if met, allow but do not require an entity to offset the amounts recognized. The entity's choice to offset or not must be applied consistently. (FIN 39 and FIN 41 are discussed further in Chapter 2.)

# 15 LONG-TERM LIABILITIES

## PERSPECTIVE AND ISSUES

Long-term (or noncurrent) liabilities are liabilities that will be paid or otherwise settled over a period of more than one year, or if longer, greater than one operating cycle. This chapter discusses accounting for bonds, long-term notes payable, mandatorily redeemable shares, and obligations to issue or repurchase the entity's own shares. Other common types of long-term liabilities are lease obligations (Chapter 16), deferred income taxes (Chapter 17), pension and deferred compensation plan obligations (Chapter 18), and contingencies (Chapter 14).

The appropriate valuation of long-term debt at the date of issuance is the present value of the future payments, using an interest rate commensurate with the risks involved. In many situations this is the rate stated in the agreement between the borrower and the creditor. However, in other situations the debt may be noninterest-bearing, or the rate stated in the agreement may not be indicative of the rate applicable to a borrower having similar creditworthiness and debt having similar terms. In other words, the rate stated in the agreement is not commensurate with the risks involved. To reflect the liability at the appropriate value, interest must be imputed at the market rate, and the resulting premium or discount is amortized as interest over the life of the agreement (per APB 21).

Debt remains on the books of the debtor until it is extinguished. In most cases, a debt is extinguished at maturity, when the required principal and interest payments have been made and the debtor has no further obligation to the creditor. In other cases, the debtor may desire to extinguish the debt before its maturity. For example, if market interest rates are falling, a debtor may choose to issue debt at the new lower rate and use the proceeds to retire older higher-interest-rate debt. FAS 140 states that a debt is extinguished if either of two conditions is met.

1. The debtor pays the creditor and is relieved of its obligation for the liability.
2. The debtor is legally released from being the primary obligor under the liability, either judicially or by the creditor.

FASB continues to pursue a project, *Accounting for Transfers of Financial Assets*, which addresses several liability extinguishment issues. Among these is the possible clarification or replacement of the FAS 140 criterion, above, that directs extinguishment accounting when the debtor is "legally released from being the primary obligor," since this expression is not legally defined. The project will also consider whether FAS 140 criteria should be applied to liabilities which are not within the scope of that standard. The most recent Exposure Draft was issued in 2005.

If a debtor experiences financial difficulties before the debt is repaid, a creditor may need to recognize an impairment of the debt. Under FAS 114, an impairment of the debt is recognized when the present value of the expected future cash flows discounted at the debt's original effective interest rate is less than the recorded investment in the debt. If for economic or legal reasons related to the debtor's financial difficulties, the creditor grants the debtor concessions that would not otherwise have been granted, the debtor must determine how to recognize the effects of the troubled debt restructuring (FAS 15).

Some debt is issued with terms that allow it to be converted to an equity instrument (common or, less often, preferred stock) at a future date. When issued, under current GAAP, no value is attributed to the conversion feature. When the debt is converted, the stock issued is generally valued at the carrying value of the debt (APB 14). In certain situations, a debtor will modify the conversion privileges after issuance of the debt in order to induce prompt conversion of the debt into equity, in which case the debtor must recognize an expense for this consideration (FAS 84).

Debt can also be issued with stock warrants, which allow the holder to purchase a stated number of common shares at a certain price within a defined time period. If debt is issued with detachable warrants, the proceeds of issuance are allocated between the two financial instruments (APB 14).

FAS 150 requires an issuer to report (1) mandatorily redeemable shares, (2) financial instruments that obligate the issuer to repurchase its shares, and (3) financial instruments that obligate the issuer to issue a variable number of shares as liabilities. This can have a major impact on the entity's balance sheet and on key financial ratios by which it is judged as to its solvency and financial stability.

The issuance of FAS 150 concluded the first phase of FASB's redeliberations of an earlier Exposure Draft. Other aspects of the proposed standards would require that the proceeds from the issuance of a compound instrument, such as convertible debt or debt issued with warrants, be allocated to liability and equity components, to be separately presented in the balance sheet. FASB believes that such a presentation provides a more faithful representation of the rights and obligations embedded in compound instruments than does the current practice of presenting the instruments entirely as liabilities or entirely as equity. A discussion of the proposed standard is found later in this chapter.

Through-put contracts, take-or-pay contracts, and other unconditional purchase obligations are sometimes used instead of debt to finance a capital project or a joint venture. These agreements may or may not be recognized on the balance sheet. Entities are required to disclose information about those types of obligations in the notes to the financial statements (FAS 47).

Short-term obligations that are expected to be refinanced and therefore classified as long-term debt per FAS 6 are discussed in Chapter 14.

| | | | | Sources of GAAP | | |
|---|---|---|---|---|---|---|
| *APB* | *FAS* | *FIN* | *FTB* | *EITF* | *SOP* | *FSP* |
| 14, 21, 26 | 5, 6, 15, 47, 84, 114, 118, 140, 145, 150 | 8 | 79-3, 80-1, 80-2, 81-6 | 85-17, 85-29, 87-19, 88-18, 90-19, 96-19, 98-5, 99-1, 00-19, 00-27, 01-1, 02-4, 02-15, 03-7, 04-8, 05-1, 05-2, 05-7, 05-8, 06-6, 06-7, D-10, D-23, D-61, D-98 | 97-1 | FAS 129-1 FAS 150-1 FAS 150-2 FAS 150-3 EITF 00-19-1 |

## DEFINITIONS OF TERMS

**Amortization.** The process of allocating an amount to expense over the periods benefited.

**Bond.** A written agreement whereby a borrower agrees to pay a sum of money at a designated future date plus periodic interest payments at the stated rate.

**Bond issue costs.** Costs related to issuing a bond (i.e., legal, accounting, underwriting fees, printing, and registration costs).

**Book value approach.** Recording the stock issued from a bond conversion at the carrying value of the bonds converted.

**Callable bond.** A bond in which the issuer reserves the right to call and retire the bond prior to its maturity.

**Carrying value.** The face amount of a debt issue increased or decreased by the applicable unamortized premium or discount plus unamortized issue costs.

**Collateral.** Asset(s) pledged to settle the obligation to repay a loan.

**Contingently convertible.** Convertible securities where either the exercisability of the conversion feature or the conversion price are dependent upon the occurrence or nonoccurrence of some defined event (e.g., an IPO or change in control).

**Convertible debt.** Debt that may be converted into common or preferred stock at the holder's option after specific criteria are met.

**Covenant.** A clause in a debt contract written for the protection of the lender that outlines the rights and actions of the parties involved when certain conditions occur (e.g., when the debtor's current ratio declines beyond a specified level).

**Debenture.** Long-term debt not secured by collateral.

**Discount.** Created when a debt instrument is issued for less than face value and occurs when the stated rate on the instrument is less than the market rate at the time of issue.

**Effective interest method.** Amortizing the discount or premium to interest expense so as to result in a constant rate of interest when applied to the amount of debt outstanding at the beginning of any given period.

**Effective rate.** See **market rate**.

**Face value.** The stated amount or principal due on the maturity date.

**Freestanding financial instrument.** A financial instrument that is entered into separately and apart from any of the entity's other financial instruments or equity transactions, or that is entered into in conjunction with some other transaction and is legally detachable and separately exercisable.

**Imputation.** The process of interest rate approximation that is accomplished by examining the circumstances under which the note was issued.

**Issuer.** The entity that issued a financial instrument or may be required under the terms of a financial instrument to issue its equity shares.

**Long-term debt.** Probable future sacrifices of economic benefits arising from present obligations that are not currently payable within one year or the operating cycle of the business, whichever is longer.

**Mandatorily redeemable shares.** Any of various financial instruments issued in the form of shares that embody an unconditional obligation requiring the issuer to redeem the instrument by transferring its assets at a specified or determinable date (or dates) or upon an event that is certain to occur.

**Market rate.** The current rate of interest available for obligations issued under the same terms and conditions by an issuer of similar credit standing.

**Market value approach.** Recording the stock issued from a bond conversion at the current market price of the bonds converted or the stock issued.

**Maturity date.** The date on which the face value (principal) of the bond or note becomes due.

**Maturity value.** See **face value**.

**Monetary value.** What the fair value of the cash, shares, or other instruments that a financial instrument obligates the issuer to convey to the holder would be at the settlement date under specified market conditions.

**Net settlement.** A form of settling a financial instrument under which the party with a loss delivers to the party with a gain cash (net cash settlement) or shares of stock (net share settlement) with a current fair value equal to the gain.

**Physical settlement.** A form of settling a financial instrument under which (1) the party designated in the contract as the buyer delivers the full stated amount of cash or other financial instruments to the seller and (2) the seller delivers the full stated number of shares of stock or other financial instruments or nonfinancial instruments to the buyer.

**Premium.** Created when a debt instrument is issued for more than its face value and occurs when the stated rate on the instrument is greater than the market rate at the time of issue.

**Principal.** See **face value**.

**Secured debt.** Debt that has collateral to satisfy the obligation if not repaid (e.g., a mortgage on specific property).

**Serial bond.** Debt whose face value matures in installments.

**Stated rate.** The interest rate written on the face of the debt instrument.

**Straight-line method.** The method of amortizing the premium or discount to interest expense such that there is an even allocation of interest expense over the life of the debt.

**Take-or-pay contract.** A contract in which a purchaser of goods agrees to pay specified fixed or minimum amounts periodically in return for products, even if delivery is not taken. It results from a project financing arrangement where the project produces the products.

**Through-put agreement.** An agreement similar to a take-or-pay contract except a service is provided by the project under the financing arrangement.

**Troubled debt restructure.** Occurs when the creditor, for economic or legal reasons related to the debtor's financial difficulties, grants a concession to the debtor (deferment or reduction of interest or principal) that it would not otherwise consider.

**Unconditional purchase obligation.** An obligation to transfer a fixed or minimum amount of funds in the future or to transfer goods or services at fixed or minimum prices.

**Yield rate.** See **market rate**.

## CONCEPTS, RULES, AND EXAMPLES

### Notes and Bonds

**Notes** are a common form of exchange in business transactions for cash, property, goods, and services. Notes represent debt issued to a single investor without intending for the debt to be broken up among many investors. A note's maturity, usually lasting one to seven years, tends to be shorter than that of a bond.

Bonds are primarily used to borrow funds from the general public or institutional investors when a contract for a single amount (a note) is too large for any one lender to supply. Dividing up the amount needed into $1,000 or $10,000 units makes it easier to sell the bonds. Bonds also result from a single agreement.

Notes and bonds share common characteristics. They both are promises to pay sums of money at designated maturity dates, plus periodic interest payments at stated rates. They each feature written agreements stating the amounts of principal, the interest rates, when the interest and principal are to be paid, and the restrictive covenants, if any, that must be met.

The interest rate is affected by many factors, including the cost of money, the business risk factors, and general and industry-specific inflationary expectations. The stated rate on a note or bond often differs from the market rate at the time of issuance. When this occurs, the present value of the interest and principal payments will differ from the maturity, or face value. (For a complete discussion of present value techniques see Chapter 1.) If the market rate exceeds the stated rate, the cash proceeds will be less than the face value of the debt because the present value of the total interest and principal payments discounted back to the present yields an amount that is less than the face value. Because an investor is rarely willing to pay more than the present value, the bonds must be issued at a discount. The discount is the difference between the issuance price (present value) and the face, or stated, value of the bonds. This discount is then amortized over the life of the bonds to increase the recognized interest expense so that the total amount of the expense represents the actual bond yield. When the stated rate exceeds the market rate, the bond will sell for more than its face value (at a premium) to bring the effective rate to the market rate. Amortization of the premium over the life of the bonds will decrease the total interest expense.

When the market and stated rates are equivalent at the time of issuance, no discount or premium exists and the instrument will sell at its face value. Changes in the market rate subsequent to issuance are irrelevant in determining the discount or premium or its amortization.

All commitments to pay (and receive) money at a determinable future date are subject to present value techniques and, if necessary, interest imputation with the exception of the following:

1. Normal accounts payable due within one year
2. Amounts to be applied to purchase price of goods or services or that provide security to an agreement (e.g., advances, progress payments, security deposits, and retentions)
3. Transactions between parent and subsidiary
4. Obligations payable at some indeterminable future date (e.g., warranties)

5. Lending and depositor savings activities of financial institutions whose primary business is lending money
6. Transactions where interest rates are affected by prescriptions of a governmental agency (e.g., revenue bonds, tax exempt obligations, etc.)

APB 21 specifies when and how interest is to be imputed when a debt is either noninterest-bearing or the stated rate is not reasonable. APB 21 divides debt into three categories for discussion. The diagram on the following page illustrates the accounting treatment for the three types of debt.

**Notes issued solely for cash.** When a note is issued solely for cash, its present value is assumed to be equal to the cash proceeds. The interest rate is that rate equating the cash proceeds to the amounts to be paid in the future. For example, a $1,000 note due in three years that sells for $889 has an implicit rate of 4% (= $1,000 × .889, where .889 is the present value factor at 4% for a lump sum due three years hence). This implicit rate, 4%, is to be used when amortizing the discount.

In most situations, a bond will be issued at a price other than its face value. The amount of the cash exchanged is equal to the total of the present values of all the future interest and principal payments. The difference between the cash proceeds and the face value is recorded as a premium if the cash proceeds are greater than the face value or a discount if they are less. The journal entry to record a bond issued at a premium follows:

| | | |
|---|---|---|
| Cash | (proceeds) | |
| Bonds payable | | (face value) |
| Premium on bonds payable | | (difference) |

**Example of bonds issued for cash**

Enterprise Autos issues $100,000 of 10-year bonds bearing interest at 10%, paid semiannually, at a time when the market demands a 12% return from issuers with similar credit standings. The proceeds of the bond issuance would be $88,500, which is computed as follows:

| | |
|---|---|
| Present value of 20 semiannual interest payments of $5,000 discounted at 12% (6% semiannually: factor = 11.4699) | $57,300 |
| Present value of $100,000 due in 10 years, discounted at 12% compounded semiannually (factor = .31180) | 31,200 |
| Present value of bond issuance | $88,500 |

The journal entry would be

| | | |
|---|---|---|
| Cash | 88,500 | |
| Discount on bonds payable | 11,500 | |
| Bonds payable | | 100,000 |

**Notes issued for cash and a right or privilege.** Often when a note bearing an unrealistic rate of interest is issued in exchange for cash, an additional right or privilege is granted, such as the issuer agreeing to sell merchandise to the purchaser at a reduced rate. The difference between the present value of the receivable and the cash loaned is regarded as an addition to the cost of the products purchased for the purchaser/lender and as unearned revenue to the seller/issuer. This treatment stems from an attempt to match revenue and expense in the proper periods and to differentiate between those factors that affect income from operations and income or expense from nonoperating sources. In the situation above, the purchaser/lender will amortize the discount (difference between the cash loaned and the present value of the note) to interest income over the life of the note, and the contractual right to purchase inventory at a reduced rate will be allocated to inventory (or cost of sales) as the right expires. The seller/issuer of the note will amortize the discount to interest expense over the life of the note, and the unearned revenue will be recognized in sales as the products are sold to the purchaser/lender at the reduced price. Because the discount is amortized on a different basis than the contractual right, net income for the period is also affected.

**ACCOUNTING FOR MONETARY ASSETS AND LIABILITIES**

**Example of accounting for a note issued for both cash and a contractual right**

1. Miller borrows $10,000 via a noninterest-bearing three-year note from Krueger.
2. Miller agrees to sell $50,000 of merchandise to Krueger at less than the ordinary retail price for the duration of the note.
3. The market rate of interest on a note with similar payment terms and a borrower of similar creditworthiness is 10%.

According to APB 21, the difference between the present value of the note and the face value of the loan is to be regarded as part of the cost of the products purchased under the agreement. The present value factor for an amount due in three years at 10% is .75132. Therefore, the present value of the note is $7,513 (= $10,000 × .75132). The $2,487 (= $10,000 – $7,513) difference between the face value and the present value is to be recorded as a discount on the note payable and as unearned revenue on the future purchases by the debtor. The following entries would be made by the debtor (Miller) and the creditor (Krueger) to record the transaction:

| *Miller* | | | *Krueger* | | |
|---|---|---|---|---|---|
| Cash | 10,000 | | Note receivable | 10,000 | |
| Discount on note payable | 2,487 | | Contract right with supplier | 2,487 | |
| Note payable | | 10,000 | Cash | | 10,000 |
| Unearned revenue | | 2,487 | Discount on note receivable | | 2,487 |

The discount on note payable (and note receivable) is to be amortized using the effective interest method, while the unearned revenue account and contract right with supplier account are amortized on a pro rata basis as the right to purchase merchandise is used up. Thus, if Krueger purchased $20,000 of merchandise from Miller in the first year, the following entries would be necessary:

| *Miller* | | | *Krueger* | | |
|---|---|---|---|---|---|
| Unearned revenue | | | | | |
| [$2,487 × (20,000/50,000)] | 995 | | Inventory (or cost of sales) | 995 | |
| Sales | | 995 | Contract right with supplier | | 995 |
| Interest expense | 751 | | Discount on note receivable | 751 | |
| Discount on note payable | | | Interest revenue | | 751 |
| ($7,513 × 10%) | | 751 | | | |

The amortization of unearned revenue and contract right with supplier accounts will fluctuate with the amount of purchases made. If there is a balance remaining in the account at the end of the loan term, it is amortized to the appropriate account in that final year.

**Noncash transactions.** When a note is issued for consideration such as property, goods, or services, and the transaction is entered into at arm's length, the stated interest rate is presumed to be fair unless (1) no interest rate is stated; (2) the stated rate is unreasonable; or (3) the face value of the debt is materially different from the consideration involved or the current market value of the note at the date of the transaction. According to APB 21, when the rate on the note is not considered fair, the note is to be recorded at the "fair market value of the property, goods, or services received or at an amount that reasonably approximates the market value of the note, whichever is the more clearly determinable." When this amount differs from the face value of the note, the difference is to be recorded as a discount or premium and amortized to interest expense.

**Example of accounting for a note exchanged for property**

1. Alexis sells Brett a machine that has a fair market value of $7,510.
2. Alexis receives a three-year noninterest-bearing note having a face value of $10,000.

In this situation, the fair market value of the consideration is readily determinable and, thus, represents the amount at which the note is to be recorded. The following entry by Brett is necessary:

| | | |
|---|---|---|
| Machine | 7,510 | |
| Discount on notes payable | 2,490 | |
| Notes payable | | 10,000 |

The discount will be amortized to interest expense over the three-year period using the interest rate implied in the transaction. The interest rate implied is 10%, because the factor for an amount due in three years is .75132, which when applied to the $10,000 face value results in an amount equal to the fair value of the machine.

If the fair market value of the consideration or note is not determinable, then the present value of the note must be determined using an imputed interest rate. This rate will then be used to establish the present value of the note by discounting all future payments on the note at this rate. General guidelines for imputing the interest rate, which are provided by APB 21, include the prevailing rates of similar instruments from creditors with similar credit ratings and the rate the debtor could obtain for similar financing from other sources. Other determining factors include any collateral or restrictive covenants involved, the current and expected prime rate, and other terms pertaining to the instrument. The objective is to approximate the rate of interest that would have resulted if an independent borrower and lender had negotiated a similar transaction under comparable terms and conditions. This determination is as of the issuance date, and any subsequent changes in interest rates would be irrelevant.

**Example of accounting for a note exchanged to property**

1. Alexis sells Brett a used machine. The fair market value is not readily determinable.
2. Alexis receives a three-year noninterest-bearing note having a face value of $20,000. The market value of the note is not known.
3. Brett could have borrowed the money for the machine's purchase from a bank at a rate of 10%.

In this situation, the fair market value of the consideration is not readily determinable, so the present value of the note is determined using an imputed interest rate. The rate used is the rate at which Brett could have borrowed the money—10%. The factor for an amount due in three years at 10% is .75132, so the present value of the note is $15,026. The following entry by Brett is necessary:

| | | |
|---|---|---|
| Machine | 15,026 | |
| Discount on notes payable | 4,974 | |
| Notes payable | | 20,000 |

**Accounting by participating mortgage loan borrowers.** Certain mortgage loan agreements provide, generally in exchange for a lower interest rate, that the lender shares in price appreciation of the property securing the loan. Other arrangements provide that the lender receives a share of the earnings or cash flows from the commercial real estate for which the loan was made. SOP 97-1 establishes the borrower's accounting for a participating mortgage loan if the lender participates in increases in the market value of the mortgaged real estate project, the results of operations of that mortgaged real estate project, or both. It requires that certain disclosures be made in the financial statements. In addition, this SOP requires the following:

1. At origination, if the lender is entitled to participate in appreciation in the market value of the mortgaged real estate project, the borrower should determine the fair value of the participation feature and should recognize a participation liability for that amount. A corresponding debit should then be recorded to a debt-discount account. The debt discount should be amortized by the interest method, using the effective interest rate. The net result is to include the expected cost of the participating feature in the periodic interest cost associated with the loan.
2. A the end of each reporting period, the balance of the participation liability should be adjusted if necessary, so that the liability equals the fair value of the participation feature at that point in time. The corresponding debit or credit should be adjusted to the related debt-discount account. The revised discount should then be amortized prospectively.

**Redeemable instruments.** EITF D-61 addressed the classification of certain long-term debt that is subject to a demand from the holder for redemption, subject to a best efforts attempt by the issuer to remarket that date. Thus, there is a possibility that the demand for redemption would not be honored, although a bank letter of credit is also provided as additional security for the lender. Notwithstanding that possibility, this debt must be reported as a current obligation.

**Sales of future revenue.** EITF 88-18 deals with the situation in which a reporting entity receives an initial payment from another party in exchange for a promised stream of royalties or other revenue-based receipts from a defined business, which could be a segment or product line of the reporting entity. Arguably, the up-front payment could be seen as an advance against the future payments, or as a borrowing by the reporting entity. Clearly, of course, the payment is not revenue to the reporting entity.

EITF concluded that the initial receipt would be accounted for as either debt or deferred revenue, depending on the facts and circumstances of the transaction. This EITF identifies six factors that would cause the amounts to be recorded as debt, rather than as deferred income. Theses factors are

1. The transaction does not purport to be a sale.
2. The reporting entity has significant continuing involvement in the generation of the cash flows due the other party (referred to as the investor in this consensus).
3. The transaction is cancelable by either party through payment of a lump sum or other transfer of assets by the entity.
4. The investor's rate of return is implicitly or explicitly limited by the terms of the transaction.
5. Variations in the reporting entity's revenue or income underlying the transaction have only a trifling impact on the investor's rate of return.
6. The investor has any recourse to the reporting entity relating to the payments due to the investor.

Amounts recorded as debt should be amortized under the interest method and amounts recorded as deferred income should be amortized under the units-of-revenue method. The proceeds classified as foreign-currency-denominated debt would be subject to recognition of foreign currency transaction (exchange) gains and losses under FAS 52.

FAS 133 established cash flow hedge accounting for hedges of the variability of the functional currency equivalent of future foreign-currency-denominated cash flows. If the proceeds are classified as deferred income, this would be a nonmonetary liability. Thus, no foreign exchange gains or losses would arise under FAS 52.

## Effective Interest Method

The effective interest method is the preferred method of accounting for a discount or premium arising from a note or bond. Under the effective interest method, the discount or premium is amortized over the life of the debt in such a way as to result in a constant rate of interest when applied to the amount outstanding at the beginning of any given period. Therefore, interest expense is equal to the market rate of interest at the time of issuance multiplied by this beginning figure. The difference between the interest expense and the cash paid represents the amortization of the discount or premium.

Amortization tables are often created at the time of the bond's issuance to provide amounts necessary when recording the entries relating to the debt issue. They also provide a check of accuracy since the final values in the unamortized discount or premium and carrying value columns should be equal to zero and the bond's face value, respectively.

### Example of applying the effective interest method

1.  A 3-year, 12%, $10,000 bond is issued at 1/1/2009, with interest payments semiannually.
2.  The market rate is 10%.

The amortization table would appear as follows:

| Date | Credit cash | Debit int. exp. | Debit prem. | Unamort. prem. bal. | Carrying value |
|---|---|---|---|---|---|
| 1/1/09 | | | | $507.61 | $10,507.61[a] |
| 7/1/09 | $ 600.00[b] | $ 525.38[c] | $ 74.62[d] | 432.99[e] | 10,432.99[f] |
| 1/1/10 | 600.00 | 521.65 | 78.35 | 354.64 | 10,354.64 |
| 7/1/10 | 600.00 | 517.73 | 82.27 | 272.37 | 10,272.37 |
| 1/1/11 | 600.00 | 513.62 | 86.38 | 185.99 | 10,185.99 |
| 7/1/11 | 600.00 | 509.30 | 90.70 | 95.29 | 10,095.29 |
| 1/1/12 | 600.00 | 504.71[g] | 95.29 | -- | 10,000.00 |
| | $3,600.00 | $3,092.39 | $507.61 | | |

(a)  PV of principal and interest payments at 5% for 6 periods

$10,000(.74622) = $ 7,462.20
$ 600(5.07569) = 3,045.41
$10,507.61

(b)  $10,000.00 × .12 × one-half year

(c)  $10,507.61 × .10 × one-half year
(d)  $600.00 – $525.38
(e)  $507.61 – $74.62
(f)  $10,507.61 – $74.62
     (or $10,000 + $432.99)
(g)  Rounding error = $.05

Although the effective interest method is the preferred method of amortizing a discount or premium, the straight-line method may be used if the results are not materially different. The amortized portion is equal to the total amount of the discount or premium divided by the life of the debt from issuance in months multiplied by the number of months the debt has been outstanding that year. Interest expense under the straight-line method is equal to the cash interest paid plus the amortized portion of the discount or minus the amortized portion of the premium.

When the interest date does not coincide with the year-end, an adjusting entry must be made to recognize the proportional share of interest payable and the amortization of the discount or premium. Within the amortization period, the discount or premium can be amortized using the straight-line method.

If bonds or notes are issued between interest payment dates, the interest and the amortization must be computed for the period between the sale date and the next interest date. The purchaser usually pays the issuer for the amount of interest that has accrued since the last payment date. That payment is recorded as a payable by the issuer. At the next interest date, the issuer pays the purchaser as though the bond had been outstanding for the entire interest period. The discount or premium is also amortized for the short period.

### Example of note issued between payment dates

On June 1, 2009, Acme Manufacturing issues a $100,000 7% bond with a three-year life at 104 (i.e. at 104% of face value). Interest is payable on July 1 and January 1. The computation of the premium would be

| | |
|---|---|
| Proceeds | $104,000 |
| Face value | 100,000 |
| Premium | $ 4,000 |

The entry to record the bond issuance and the receipt of interest from the purchaser would be

| | | |
|---|---|---|
| Cash | 106,967 | |
| Bonds payable | | 100,000 |
| Premium on bonds | | 4,000 |
| Interest payable | | 2,967 |

The bonds will be outstanding for two years and seven months. An effective interest rate must be computed that will equate the present value of the future principal and interest payments to the cash received. Using a spreadsheet facilitates the trial and error process. Many inexpensive calculators with financial functions also do this calculation. Alternatively, present value tables can be used to compute the value, as shown below.

First, compute the present value of the interest and principal payments as of 7/1/09 using a guess of 5% annually.

Present value of an annuity due of $3,500 for six periods @ 2.5% = 3,500 × 5.6458 =      19,760
Present value of a single payment of $100,000 in five periods @2.5% = 100,000 × .88385 =    88,385
                                                                          108,145

Then, compute the present value of that result one month earlier (at June 1, 2009) using the same interest rate.

Present value of a single payment of $108,145 in one month = 108,145/[1+(.05/12)] = 107,696

The result is more than the cash received ($106,967), so we know that the interest rate must be higher than 5%. Repeat the calculation at a 6% annual rate.

Present value of an annuity due of $3,500 for six periods @3% = 3,500 × 5.5797 =      19,529
Present value of a single payment of $100,000 in five periods @3% =100,000 × .86261 =    86,261
                                                                          105,790

Present value of a single payment of $105,790 in one month = 105,790/[1+(.06/12)] = 105,263

The result is less than the cash received ($106,967), so we know the rate is between 5 and 6%. By interpolation, we determine that the rate is 5.3%.

$$\frac{107,696 - 106,967}{107,696 - 105,263}$$ × (6% − 5%) = .2996%, which is added to 5% to get the effective rate.

The amortization of the $4,000 premium would be as follows:

|  | Cash paid (received) | Interest at 5.3% annually | Amortization | Interest payable | Bond payable |
|---|---|---|---|---|---|
|  |  |  |  |  | 104,000 |
| 06/01/09 | (2,967) |  |  | 2,967 | 104,000 |
| 07/01/09 | 3,500 | 459 | 74 | (2,967) | 103,926 |
| 01/01/10 | 3,500 | 2,754 | 746 |  | 103,180 |
| 07/01/10 | 3,500 | 2,734 | 765 |  | 102,415 |
| 01/01/11 | 3,500 | 2,714 | 786 |  | 101,629 |
| 07/01/11 | 3,500 | 2,693 | 807 |  | 100,822 |
| 01/01/12 | 103,500 | 2,672 | 822 |  | 100,000 |

The entry to record the first interest payment would be

| Interest payable | 2,967 |  |
|---|---|---|
| Interest expense | 459 |  |
| Premium on bonds | 74 |  |
|     Cash |  | 3,500 |

Costs may be incurred in connection with issuing bonds. Examples include legal, accounting, and underwriting fees; commissions; and engraving, printing, and registration costs. These costs theoretically should be treated as either an expense in the period incurred or a reduction in the related amount of debt, in much the same manner as a discount (CON 6). These costs do not provide any future economic benefit and, therefore, should not be an asset. Since these costs reduce the amount of cash proceeds, they in effect increase the effective interest rate and probably should be accounted for the same as an unamortized discount. However, in practice, issue costs are treated as deferred charges and amortized using the straight-line method. (FASB, as part of convergence efforts being undertaken with the IASB, has proposed that issuance costs be defined as the incremental costs directly attributable to issuance of an instrument that would not have been incurred if the instrument had not been issued. It would also require that the issuance costs be accounted for as a reduction of the proceeds of issuance.)

**Extinguishment of Debt**

Management may reacquire or retire outstanding debt before its scheduled maturity. This decision is usually caused by changes in present or expected interest rates or in cash flows.

In-substance defeasance (irrevocably placing assets in a trust that is to be used solely to service the remaining debt payments) does not result in the extinguishment of a liability. Except for items excluded by FAS 140, a liability is removed from the balance sheet only if

1. The creditor is paid and the debtor is relieved of the obligation.
2. The debtor is released legally either by the creditor or judicially from being the primary obligor.

FASB had been pursuing a project through its *Accounting for Transfers of Financial Assets* Exposure Draft to clarify the phrase "legally released from being the primary obligor," which is not a legally defined term and thus may be subject to varying interpretations. Although the FASB staff has made recommendations for improved language, FASB has not acted on these and has instead indicated that it will pursue this issue in the context of a broader review of FAS 140's extinguishment criteria. FASB has concluded that a derecognition model based solely on legal principles would be inappropriate because of representational faithfulness and operationalizability concerns, and instead is attempting to identify and describe indicators of performance that subsequently might be used to develop models for either derecognition or measurement of performance obligations.

If a debtor becomes secondarily liable, through a third-party assumption and a release by the creditor, the original debtor becomes a guarantor. A guarantee obligation, based on the probability that the third party will pay, is to be recognized and initially measured at fair value. The amount of guarantee obligation increases the loss or reduces the gain recognized on extinguishments. Guarantees are discussed in Chapter 14.

Some financial instruments can have characteristics of either assets or liabilities depending on market conditions (forward contracts, swap contracts, and written commodity options). To be derecognized, those instruments must not only meet the two criteria above, but must also meet the surrender of control criteria of FAS 140 (Chapter 8).

**Debtor's accounting for a modification or exchange of debt instruments other than in a troubled debt restructuring.** An exchange of debt instruments with substantially different terms is a debt extinguishment and should be accounted for in accordance with FAS 140. Any substantial modification in the terms of an existing debt, other than for a troubled debt restructuring, should similarly be reported as a debt extinguishment.

An exchange or modification is considered substantial when the present value of cash flows under the new debt instrument is at least 10% different from the present value of the remaining cash flows under the terms of the original instrument. For the purpose of the 10% test, the effective interest rate of the original debt instrument is used as the discount rate.

Cash flows can be affected by changes in principal amounts, interest rates, maturity, or by fees exchanged between the parties. Substantial change can also result from changes in the following provisions:

1. Recourse or nonrecourse features
2. Priority of the obligation
3. Collateralized or noncollateralized features
4. Debt covenants and/or waivers
5. The guarantor
6. Option features

*Assuming the 10% test is met and the debt instrument are deemed to be substantially different,* the new investment should be initially recorded at fair value and that amount should be compared to the book value of the old debt to determine debt extinguishment gain or loss to be recognized, as well as the effective rate of the new instrument. Fees paid by the debtor to the creditor or received by the debtor from the creditor should be included in determining debt extinguishment gain or loss. Additionally, any costs incurred with third parties should be amortized using the interest method in a manner similar to that used for debt issue costs.

*Assuming the 10% test is not met and the debt instruments are not deemed to be substantially different,* then the new effective interest is to be determined based on the carrying amount of the original instrument and the revised cash flows. Fees paid by the debtor to the creditor or received by the debtor from the creditor should be amortized as an adjustment to interest expense over the remaining term of the modified debt instrument using the interest method. Additionally, any costs incurred with third parties should be expensed as incurred.

**Gain or loss on debt extinguishment.** According to APB 26, the difference between the net carrying value and the price paid to acquire the debt instruments is to be recorded as a gain or loss. If the acquisition price is greater than the carrying value, a loss exists. A gain is generated if the acquisition price is less than the carrying value. These gains or losses are to be recognized in the period in which the retirement took place. Previously, material gains and losses from debt extinguishment were mandatorily classified as extraordinary items in the income statement. However, FAS 145 eliminated that requirement. Debt extinguishment gains and losses now will be reported as extraordinary only if the criteria of APB 30 are met—that is, if the event creating the gain or loss is both unusual and infrequently occurring. It is expected that extinguishments of debt will rarely, if ever, meet these dual criteria. Hence, gains and losses on debt extinguishments will be reported in earnings before extraordinary items.

The unamortized premium or discount and issue costs should be amortized to the acquisition date and recorded prior to the determination of the gain or loss. If the extinguishment of debt does not occur on the interest date, the interest payable accruing between the last interest date and the acquisition date must also be recorded.

**Example of accounting for the extinguishment of debt**

1. A 10%, 10-year, $200,000 bond is dated and issued on 1/1/09 at 98, with the interest payable semiannually.
2. Associated bond issue costs of $14,000 are incurred.
3. Four years later, on 1/1/13, the entire bond issue is repurchased at 102 (i.e., 102% of face value) and is retired.
4. At 1/1/13 the unamortized discount using the effective interest rate of 10.325% is $2,858.

| | | |
|---|---|---|
| Reacquisition price [(102%) × $200,000] | | $204,000 |
| Net carrying amount: | | |
| Face value | $200,000 | |
| Unamortized discount | (2,858) | |
| Unamortized issue costs [14,000 × (6/10)] | (8,400) | 188,742 |
| Loss on bond repurchase | | $ 15,258 |

## Troubled Debt Restructurings

Troubled debt restructurings are defined by FAS 15 as situations in which the creditor, for economic or legal reasons related to the debtor's financial difficulties, grants the debtor a concession that would not otherwise be granted. As explained in EITF 02-4, no single characteristic or factor, taken alone, is determinative of whether a modification of terms or an exchange of a debt instrument is a troubled debt restructuring under FAS 15. Thus, making this determination requires the exercise of judgment. EITF 02-4 poses two questions to assist in making a determination of whether FAS 15 applies in a particular instance.

- Is the debtor experiencing financial difficulty?
- Has the creditor granted a concession?

Both of these questions must be answered in the affirmative for FAS 15 to be applicable. EITF 02-4 has provided guidance on these matters.

**Is the debtor experiencing financial difficulty?** If the debtor's creditworthiness has deteriorated since the debt was originally issued, the debtor should evaluate whether it is experiencing financial difficulties. The following factors are indicators that this may be the case:

- The debtor is in default on some of its debt
- The debtor has declared, or is in the process of declaring, bankruptcy
- There is doubt as to whether the debtor is a going concern
- The debtor's securities have been or are likely to be delisted
- The debtor forecasts that its entity-specific cash flows are insufficient to service the debt through its maturity in accordance with its terms
- The debtor cannot obtain resources at the current market rates for nontroubled debtors except through existing creditors

If both of the following factors are present, it would be concluded that the debtor is not experiencing financial difficulty:

- The creditors agree to restructure the old debt solely to reflect either (1) a decrease in the current interest rates for the debtor, or (2) an increase in the debtor's creditworthiness
- The debtor is currently servicing the old debt and can obtain funds to repay the old debt at the current market rate for a nontroubled debtor

**Has the creditor granted a concession?** The creditor has granted a concession if the debtor's effective borrowing rate on the restructured debt is less than the effective borrowing rate immediately prior to the restructuring. The effective borrowing rate should give effect to all the terms of the restructured debt, including options, warrants, guarantees, and so forth. If the debtor is restructuring the debt for a second time, the effective borrowing rate of the new debt should be compared to the effective borrowing rate of the original debt.

However, in any of the following four situations, a concession granted by the creditor does not automatically qualify as a restructuring:

1. The fair value of the assets or equity interest accepted by a creditor from a debtor in full satisfaction of its receivable is at least equal to the creditor's recorded investment in the receivable.
2. The fair value of the assets or equity interest transferred by a debtor to a creditor in full settlement of its payable is at least equal to the carrying value of the payable.
3. The creditor reduces the effective interest rate to reflect a decrease in current interest rates or a decrease in the risk, in order to maintain the relationship.
4. The debtor, in exchange for old debt, issues new debt with an interest rate that reflects current market rates.

FTB 81-6 notes that FAS 15 does not apply to debtors in bankruptcy unless the restructuring does not result from a general restatement of the debtor's liabilities in bankruptcy proceedings. That is, FAS 15 applies only if the debt restructuring is isolated to the creditor.

A troubled debt restructuring can occur one of two ways. The first is a settlement of the debt at less than the carrying amount. The second is a continuation of the debt with a modification of terms (i.e., a reduction in the interest rate, face amount, accrued interest owed, or an extension of the payment date for interest or face amount). Accounting for such restructurings is prescribed for both debtors and creditors. FTB 80-2 points out that the debtor and creditor must separately apply FAS 15 to the specific fact situation since the tests are not necessarily symmetrical and it is possible for one or the other, but not both, to have a troubled debt restructuring when the debtor's carrying amount and the creditor's recorded investment differ. FAS 114, as amended by FAS 118, specifies the accounting by creditors for troubled debt restructurings involving a modification of terms.

**Debtors.** If the debt is settled by the exchange of assets, a gain is recognized in the period of transfer for the difference between the carrying amount of the debt (defined as the face amount of the debt increased or decreased by applicable accrued interest and applicable unamortized premium, discount, or issue costs) and the consideration given to extinguish the debt. A two-step process is used: (1) any noncash assets used to settle the debt are revalued at fair market value and the associated ordinary gain or loss is recognized and (2) the debt restructuring gain is determined and recognized. The gain or loss is evaluated under the unusual and infrequent criteria of APB 30, which are discussed in Chapter 3. (Automatically classifying the gain or loss as an extraordinary item was eliminated by FAS 145, although this may still be done in the unlikely circumstances that the criteria set forth in APB 30 are met.) If stock is issued to settle the liability, the stock is recorded at its fair market value (FAS 15).

### Example 1: Settlement of debt by exchange of assets

Assume the debtor company transfers land having a book value of $70,000 and a fair market value of $80,000 in full settlement of its note payable. The note has a remaining life of five years, a principal balance of $90,000, and related accrued interest of $10,000 is recorded. The following entries are required to record the settlement:

|  | *Debtor* |  |
|---|---|---|
| Land | 10,000 | |
|    Gain on transfer of assets | | 10,000 |
| Note payable | 90,000 | |
| Interest payable | 10,000 | |
|    Land | | 80,000 |
|    Gain on settlement of debt | | 20,000 |

If the debt is continued with a modification of terms, it is necessary to compare the total future cash flows of the restructured debt (both principal and stated interest) with the carrying value of the original debt. If the total amount of future cash payments is greater than the carrying value, no adjustment is made to the carrying value of the debt. However, a new lower effective interest rate must be computed. This rate makes the present value of the total future cash payments equal to the present carrying value of debt and is used to determine interest expense in future periods. The effective interest method must be used to compute the expense. If the total future cash payments of the restructured debt are less than the present carrying value, the current debt should be reduced to the amount of the future cash flows and a gain should be recognized. No interest expense would be recognized in subsequent periods, since only the principal is being repaid.

According to FAS 15, a troubled debt restructuring that involves only a modification of terms is accounted for *prospectively*. Thus, there is no change in the carrying value of the liability unless the carrying amount of the original debt exceeds the total future cash payments specified by the new agreement.

If the restructuring consists of part settlement and part modification of payments, the part settlement is accounted for first and then the modification of payments.

### Example 2: Restructuring with gain/loss recognized (payments are less than carrying value)

Assume that the note has a principal balance of $90,000, accrued interest of $10,000, an interest rate of 5%, and a remaining life of five years. The interest rate is reduced to 4%, the principal is reduced to $72,500, and the accrued interest at date of restructure is forgiven.

Future cash flows (after restructuring):

| | | |
|---|---|---|
| Principal | | $ 72,500 |
| Interest (5 years × $72,500 × 4%) | | 14,500 |
| Total cash to be paid | | $ 87,000 |
| | | |
| Amount prior to restructure | | |
| ($90,000 principal + $10,000 accrued interest) | | (100,000) |
| Debtor's gain | | $ 13,000 |

The following entries need to be recorded by the debtor to reflect the terms of the agreement:

*Beginning of Year 1*

| | | |
|---|---|---|
| Interest payable | 10,000 | |
| Note payable | 3,000 | |
| Gain on restructure of debt | | 13,000 |

*End of Years 1-5*

| | | |
|---|---|---|
| Note payable | 2,900 | |
| Cash | | 2,900 |

*NOTE: $14,500 ÷ 5 yrs. = $2,900; No interest expense is recorded in this case.*

*End of Year 5*

| | | |
|---|---|---|
| Note payable | 72,500 | |
| Cash | | 72,500 |

### Example 3: Restructuring with no gain/loss recognized (payments exceed carrying value)

Modify Example 2 as follows:

Assume the $100,000 owed is reduced to a principal balance of $95,000. The interest rate of 5% is reduced to 4%.

Future cash flows (after restructuring):

| | | |
|---|---|---|
| Principal | | $ 95,000 |
| Interest (5 years × $95,000 × 4%) | | 19,000 |
| Total cash to be received | | $ 114,000 |
| | | |
| Amount prior to restructure | | |
| ($90,000 principal + $10,000 accrued interest) | | (100,000) |
| Interest expense/revenue over 5 years | | $ 14,000 |

In this example, a new effective interest rate must be computed such that the present value of the future payments equals $100,000. A trial and error approach is used to calculate the effective interest rate that discounts the $95,000 principal and the $3,800 annual interest payments to $100,000, the amount owed prior to restructuring.

#### Trial and Error Calculation

| | (n = 5, i = 2.5%) | (n = 5, i = 3%) |
|---|---|---|
| PV of ordinary annuity | 4.64583 | 4.57971 |
| PV of 1 | .88385 | .86261 |

2.5%: (.88385 × $95,000) + (4.64583 × $3,800) = $101,620
3%: (.86261 × $95,000) + (4.57971 × $3,800) = $ 99,351

*Interpolation:*

$$\left[ \frac{101,620 - 100,000}{101,620 - \ \ 99,351} \right] \times (3\% - 2.5\%) = .357\%$$

New effective rate = 2.5% + .357% = 2.857%

*Interest amortization schedule:*

| Year | Cash | Interest at effective rate | Reduction in carrying value | Carrying amount |
|------|------|----------------------------|------------------------------|-----------------|
|      |      |                            |                              | $100,000        |
| 1    | $ 3,800(a) | $2,857(b)            | $ 943(c)                     | 99,057          |
| 2    | 3,800 | 2,830                     | 970                          | 98,087          |
| 3    | 3,800 | 2,802                     | 998                          | 97,089          |
| 4    | 3,800 | 2,774                     | 1,026                        | 96,063          |
| 5    | 3,800 | 2,745                     | 1,055                        | 95,000*         |
|      | $19,000 |                         |                              |                 |

\* Rounded
(a) $3,800 = $95,000 × .04
(b) $2,857 = $100,000 × 2.857%
(c) $943 = $3,800 − $2,857

The following entries are made by the debtor to recognize the cash payments in the subsequent periods:

**End of Year 1**

| | | |
|---|---|---|
| Note payable ($3,800 − $2,857 | 943 | |
| Interest expense ($100,000 × .02857) | 2,857 | |
| Cash | | 3,800 |

**End of Year 5**

| | | |
|---|---|---|
| Note payable | 95,000 | |
| Cash | | 95,000 |

When the total future cash payments may exceed the carrying amount of the liability, no gain or loss is recognized on the books of the debtor unless the maximum future cash payments are less than the carrying amount of the debt. For example, if the debtor is required to make interest payments at a higher rate if its financial condition improves before the maturity of the debt, the debtor should assume that the larger payments would have to be made. The contingent payments would be included in the total future cash payments for comparison with the carrying amount of the debt. If the future cash payments exceed the carrying amount, a new effective interest rate should be determined. The new rate should be the rate that equates the present value of the future cash payments with the carrying amount of the liability. Interest expense and principal reduction are then recognized as the future cash payments are made.

### Example 4: Contingent payments

Modify Example 2 as follows: The new agreement states that if financial condition at maturity improves as specified, an additional principal payment of $15,000 is required and additional 1% of interest must be paid in arrears for years 4 and 5.

| | |
|---|---|
| Future cash payments: | |
| Required principal per agreement | $ 72,500 |
| Required interest per agreement (5 years × $72,500 × 4%) | 14,500 |
| Contingent principal payment | 15,000 |
| Contingent interest payments (2 years × 72,500 × 1%) | 1,450 |
| | $103,450 |
| Amount prior to restructure ($90,000 + $10,000) | (100,000) |
| | $ 3,450 |

When computing the new effective interest rate, only as many contingent payments as are needed to make the future cash payments exceed the carrying value are included in the calculation. Thus, the contingent principal payment would be included, but the contingent interest would not. The contingent interest payments would be recognized using the same criteria as are used in FAS 5; that is, the payments are recognized when they are both probable and reasonably estimable.

**Substituted debtors in a troubled debt restructuring.** EITF 87-19 addressed the situation of a sale of real estate collateral by a debtor in a troubled debt situation, with the acquirer assuming the obligation to the creditor (the reporting entity), such that the fair value of the obligation (the present value of payments, less than the net investment) was less than the creditor's carrying value of the loan receivable. In such circumstances, the creditor would be required to recognize a loss in the amount by which the net investment in the loan exceeds the fair value of the payments to be received. The fair value of the payments should be recorded as an asset by the creditor.

**FAS 114 creditors.** FAS 114, as amended by FAS 118, applies to all creditors, to all troubled debt restructurings involving a modification of terms, and to all loans except

1. Groups of similar small balance loans that are collectively evaluated
2. Loans measured at fair value or lower of cost or fair value
3. Leases
4. FAS 115 debt securities

If it is probable that a creditor will not collect all amounts (principal and interest) owed to the degree specified in the loan agreement, a loan is considered impaired. A delay does not impair the loan if the creditor collects all amounts due (including accrued interest during the delay at the contractual rate).

An impaired loan can be measured on a loan-by-loan basis in any of the following ways:

1. Present value of expected future cash flows using the loan's original effective interest rate (the contractual interest rate adjusted for premium or discount and net deferred loan costs or fees at acquisition or origination)
2. Loan's observable market price
3. Fair value of the collateral if the loan is collateral dependent (repayment expected to be provided by the collateral). If foreclosure is probable, this measurement must be used.

Other measurement considerations include

1. Costs to sell, on a discounted basis, if they will reduce cash flows to satisfy the loan
2. Creation of or adjustment to a valuation allowance account with the offset to bad-debt expense if the recorded investment is greater than the impaired loan measurement
3. If the contractual interest rate varies based on changes in an independent factor, the creditor can choose between

    a. Calculating the effective interest on the factor as it changes over the loan's life, or
    b. Calculating the effective interest as fixed at the rate in effect at the date of impairment.

    The choice must be consistently applied. Projections of factor changes should not be made.
4. Cash flow estimates should be the creditors' best estimate based on reasonable and supportable assumptions
5. Significant changes occurring in measurement values require recalculation and adjustment of the valuation allowance. Net carrying amount of the loan should not exceed the recorded investment.

After impairment, creditors use existing methods to record, measure, and display interest income. If the existing policy results in a recorded investment less than fair value, no additional impairment is recognized.

Under FAS 114, the creditor would account for the earlier examples as follows:

## Example 1

| | | |
|---|---|---|
| Land | 80,000 | |
| Bad debt expense | 20,000 | |
|     Note receivable | | 90,000 |
|     Interest receivable | | 10,000 |

## Example 2

Future cash flows (after restructuring) at the agreement's original effective interest rate

|  |  | 5% 5 yrs<br>PV Factor |
|---|---|---|
| Principal | $ 56,806 | ($72,500 × .78353) |
| Interest | 12,555 | ($ 2,900 × 4.32948) |
| Total present value | $ 69,361 | |
| | | |
| Amount prior to restructure ($90,000<br>   principal + $10,000 accrued interest) | (100,000) | |
| Creditor's loss | $( 30,639) | |

### Beginning of Year 1

| | | |
|---|---|---|
| Bad debt expense | 30,639 | |
|     Interest receivable | | 10,000 |
|     Valuation allowance | | 20,639 |

### End of Year 1

| | | |
|---|---|---|
| Cash | 2,900 | |
| Valuation allowance | 568 | |
|     Bad debt expense (or interest<br>      income) | | 3,468 (69,361 × .05) |

### End of Year 2

| | | |
|---|---|---|
| Cash | 2,900 | |
| Valuation allowance | 596 | |
|     Bad debt expense (or interest<br>      income) | | 3,496 [(69,361 + 568) =<br>69,929 × .05] |

### End of Year 3

| | | |
|---|---|---|
| Cash | 2,900 | |
| Valuation allowance | 626 | |
|     Bad debt expense (or interest<br>      income) | | 3,526 [(69,929 + 596) =<br>70,525 × .05] |

### End of Year 4

| | | |
|---|---|---|
| Cash | 2,900 | |
| Valuation allowance | 658 | |
|     Bad debt expense (or interest<br>      income) | | 3,558 [(70,525 + 626) =<br>71,151 × .05] |

### End of Year 5

| | | |
|---|---|---|
| Cash | 2,900 | |
| Valuation allowance | 691 | |
|     Bad debt expense (or interest<br>      income) | | 3,591 [(71,151 + 658) =<br>71,809 × .05] |
| Cash | 72,500 | |
| Valuation allowance | 17,500 | |
|     Note receivable | | 90,000 |

## Example 3

Future cash flows (after restructuring) at the agreement's original effective interest rate

|  |  | 5% 5 yrs<br>PV Factor |
|---|---|---|
| Principal | $ 74,435 | ($95,000 × .78353) |
| Interest | 16,452 | ($ 3,800 × 4.32948) |
| **Total** present value | $ 90,887 | |

|  |  | 5% 5 yrs<br>PV Factor |
|---|---|---|
| Amount prior to restructure ($90,000<br>    principal + $10,000 accrued interest) | (100,000) |  |
| Creditor's loss | $( 9,113) |  |

**Beginning of Year 1**

| Bad debt expense | 9,113 |  |
|---|---|---|
| Note receivable—new | 95,000 |  |
|     Note receivable—old |  | 90,000 |
|     Interest receivable |  | 10,000 |
|     Valuation allowance |  | 4,113 |

**End of Year 1**

| Cash | 3,800 |  |
|---|---|---|
| Valuation allowance | 744 |  |
|     Bad debt expense (or interest income) |  | 4,544 (90,887 × .05) |

**End of Year 2**

| Cash | 3,800 |  |
|---|---|---|
| Valuation allowance | 781 |  |
|     Bad debt expense (or interest income) |  | 4,581 [(90,887 + 744) =<br>    91,631 × .05] |

**End of Year 3**

| Cash | 3,800 |  |
|---|---|---|
| Valuation allowance | 821 |  |
|     Bad debt expense (or interest income) |  | 4,621 [(91,631 + 781) =<br>    92,412 × .05] |

**End of Year 4**

| Cash | 3,800 |  |
|---|---|---|
| Valuation allowance | 862 |  |
|     Bad debt expense (or interest income) |  | 4,662 [(92,412 + 821) =<br>    93,233 × .05] |

**End of Year 5**

| Cash | 3,800 |  |
|---|---|---|
| Valuation allowance | 905 |  |
|     Bad debt expense (or interest income) |  | 4,705 [(93,233 + 862) =<br>    94,095 × .05] |
| Cash | 95,000 |  |
|     Note receivable |  | 95,000 |

## Convertible Debt

Bonds are frequently issued with the right to convert into common stock of the company at the holder's option. Convertible debt is typically used for two reasons. First, when a specific amount of funds is needed, convertible debt often allows a lesser number of shares to be issued (assuming conversion) than if the funds were raised by directly issuing the shares. Thus, less dilution occurs. Second, the conversion feature allows debt to be issued at a lower interest rate and with fewer restrictive covenants than if the debt was issued without it.

This dual nature of debt and equity, however, creates a question as to whether the equity element should receive separate recognition. Support for separate treatment is based on the assumption that this equity element has economic value. Since the convertible feature tends to lower the rate of interest, a portion of the proceeds should be allocated to this equity feature. FASB concurred, and it issued proposed standards under a "Liabilities and Equity" project that would, among other things, require convertible debt to be divided into its liability components and equity components. Those components would be separately presented in the balance sheet. If issued (the draft remains outstanding as of early 2008), those standards would replace that under APB 14, which require that the instrument be reported as either all debt or all equity. (FASB is now waiting for another round of comments in early 2008.) For more details, see the discussion of the proposed standards later in this chapter.

Features of convertible debt typically include (1) a conversion price 15-20% greater than the market value of the stock when the debt is issued; (2) conversion features (price and number of shares) which protect against dilution from stock dividends, splits, etc.; and (3) a callable feature at the issuer's option, which is usually exercised once the conversion price is reached (thus forcing conversion or redemption).

Convertible debt also has its disadvantages. If the stock price increases significantly after the debt is issued, the issuer would have been better off by simply issuing the stock. Additionally, if the price of the stock does not reach the conversion price, the debt will never be converted (a condition known as overhanging debt).

When convertible debt is issued and the conversion price is greater than the market value of the stock on the issuance date, no value is apportioned to the conversion feature when recording the issue (APB 14). The debt and its interest are reported as if it were a nonconvertible debt. Upon conversion, the stock may be valued at either the book value or the market value of the bonds.

If the book value approach is used, the new stock is valued at the carrying value of the converted bonds. This method is widely used since no gain or loss is recognized upon conversion, and the conversion represents the transformation of contingent shareholders into shareholders. It does not represent the culmination of an earnings cycle. The primary weakness of this method is that the total value attributed to the equity security by the investors is not given accounting recognition.

### Example of book value method

Assume that a $1,000 bond with an unamortized discount of $50 and a market value of $970 is converted into 10 shares of $10 par common stock whose market value is $97 per share. Conversion using the book value method is recorded as follows:

| | | |
|---|---|---|
| Bonds payable | 1,000 | |
| Discount on bonds payable | | 50 |
| Common stock | | 100 |
| Additional paid-in capital | | 850 |

The alternative market value approach assumes the new stock issued is valued at market (i.e., the market price of the stock issued or the market price of the bonds converted, whichever is more easily determinable). A gain (loss) occurs when the market value of the stocks or bonds is less (greater) than the carrying value of the bond.

### Example of the market value method

Assume the same facts as the example above. The entry to record the conversion is

| | | |
|---|---|---|
| Bonds payable | 1,000 | |
| Loss on redemption (ordinary) | 20 | |
| Discount on bonds payable | | 50 |
| Common stock | | 100 |
| Additional paid-in capital | | 870 |

The weakness of this method is that a gain or loss can be reported as a result of an equity transaction. Only the existing shareholders are affected, as their equity will increase or decrease, but the firm as a whole is unaffected. For this reason, the market value approach is not widely used.

When convertible debt is retired, the transaction is handled in the same manner as nonconvertible debt: the difference between the acquisition price and the carrying value of the bond is reported currently as a gain or loss.

**Accrued interest upon conversion of convertible debt.** Per EITF 85-17, if terms of the convertible debt instrument provide that any accrued interest at the date of conversion is forfeited by the former debt holder, the accrued interest (net of income tax) from the last payment date to the conversion date should be charged to interest expense and credited to capital as a part of the cost basis of the securities issued.

**Convertible bonds with a "premium put."** Some convertible bonds contain mutually exclusive features, with one obviously being the right to convert to the issuer's common or preferred stock. In some instances the other feature is the right, usually on specified dates before or at the stated maturity of the debt, to cause the issuer to repurchase the debt at a price higher than par or the issuance price. This is known as a "premium put" feature. An early consensus on EITF 85-29 held that the issuer should accrue a liability for the put premium over the period from the date of issuance to the initial put date, and that this accrual should continue regardless of market value changes. It further held if the put expires unexercised and if—as would be highly likely if the holders chose to ignore the right to put the debt back to the issuer—the market value of the common stock exceeds the put price at expiration date, the put premium should be credited to additional paid-in capital. Additionally, it held that if the put were to expire unexercised (in the situation where the debt maturity is later than the last put exercise date) and if the put price exceeds the market value of the common stock at that date, the put premium should be amortized as a yield adjustment over the remaining term of the debt, reducing interest cost.

FASB later issued FAS 133. An embedded put is a derivative instrument subject to that standard. FAS 133 "grandfathered" permission for entities not to account separately for embedded premium puts in pre-1998 or pre-1999 hybrid instruments issued at par; the consensus in EITF 85-29 was to continue to apply to an entity which elected not to separately account for the embedded derivative. However, separate accounting was required for convertible debt not "grandfathered" under this provision, and thus, FAS 133 does apply to more recently issued convertible debt having premium put features.

Yet later, FASB issued FIN 45, requiring explicit recognition of guarantees at their inceptions (see Chapter 14 for complete discussion of this topic). A premium put is a form of guarantee arrangement, and thus the fair value of the put must now be recognized at the date of issuance of the convertible debt bearing this feature, unless the put is accounted for as a derivative (and thus also recorded at fair value) under FAS 133. As a practical matter, in either case a liability will be recognized for the fair value of the put option embedded in the convertible debt.

Under FAS 133 this derivative financial instrument will be marked to fair value at each financial reporting date. Whether the adjustment increases or decreases the recorded amount from one period to the next depends largely on the price performance of the issuer's stock, since increasing value of the stock raises the likelihood of conversion and thus decreases the perceived value of the put option. In the authors' opinion, any adjustment to the carrying value of the put option should result in adjustments to the entity's interest expense for the period.

**Debt convertible into the stock of a consolidated subsidiary.** According to EITF 99-1, in the consolidated financial statements, (1) debt issued by a consolidated subsidiary that is convertible into that subsidiary's stock and (2) debt issued by a parent company that is convertible into the stock of a consolidated subsidiary should be accounted for in accordance with APB 14. That is, no portion of the proceeds from the issuance of the debt should be accounted for as attributable to the conversion feature. EITF 99-1 did not apply to convertible debt instruments that require a cash settlement by the issuer of an in-the-money conversion feature, that provide the holder an option to receive cash for an in-the-money conversion feature, or that have a beneficial conversion feature.

**Accounting for a convertible instrument granted or issued to a nonemployee.** EITF 01-1 describes the accounting for a convertible instrument that is used to pay a nonemployee for goods or services if that instrument contains a nondetachable conversion option. The measurement date under EITF 96-18 should be used to measure the intrinsic value of the conversion option rather than the commitment date. The proceeds from issuing the instrument for purposes of determining whether a beneficial conversion option exists is the fair value of the instrument or the fair value of the goods and services received, whichever is more reliably measured. The fair value of the convertible instrument can be measured by applying FAS 123, as interpreted by EITF 96-18. (For details, see Chapter 19.) Once the convertible instrument is issued, distributions paid or payable are financing costs rather than adjustments of the cost of the goods or services received.

If a purchaser of a convertible instrument that contains an embedded beneficial conversion option provides goods or services to the issuer under a separate contract, the contracts should be considered separately unless the separately stated pricing is not equal to fair value. If not equal to fair value, the terms of the respective transactions should be adjusted. The convertible instrument should be recognized at its fair value with a corresponding increase or decrease to the purchase price of the goods or services.

**Convertible bonds with issuer option to settle for cash upon conversion.** EITF 90-19 addressed a variant of convertible bonds which give the issuer (the reporting entity) the option of settling for cash, rather than stock, at the time conversion is elected by holders. In some versions of this arrangement, the debtor would be obligated to settle in cash, based on the stock price at the conversion date. In others, the issuer would have the option to deliver shares or cash based on the contractual conversion rate, or more complex formulae might cause partial settlement in cash.

The consensuses in EITF 90-19 have been largely nullified by FAS 133. That standard requires that in the situation of a mandatory cash settlement upon conversion, the embedded derivative (which is a cash-settled written call option) has to be accounted for separately from the debt, and changes in the derivative's fair value will be reported currently in earnings. When the conversion option can be settled in stock, however, the embedded derivative is indexed only to the issuer's stock and thus, under EITF 00-19 would not be separately accounted for.

If a convertible bond is issued with terms that require the issuer to satisfy the obligation (the amount accrued to the benefit of the holder exclusive of the conversion spread) in cash and to satisfy the conversion spread (the excess conversion value over the accreted value) in either cash or stock, the debt should be accounted for like convertible debt (that is, as a combined instrument under current GAAP) if the conversion spread meets the requirements of EITF 00-19. If the conversion spread feature does not meet those provisions, FAS 133 requires that the embedded derivative be separated from the debt host contract and accounted for by the issuer separately as a derivative instrument.

If a convertible bond is issued with terms that permit the issuer to satisfy the entire obligation in either stock or cash, the bond should be accounted for as conventional convertible debt. If the holder exercises the conversion and the issuer pays cash, the debt is extinguished and the issuer should account for the transaction in accordance with APB 26. FAS 145 removed the mandatory extraordinary item treatment for any gain or loss on debt extinguishment, but if the criteria in APB 30 are met (which is thought to be unlikely) extraordinary classification is still possible.

Certain of the issues raised first by EITF 90-19 were later addressed by EITF 03-7. This provides accounting guidance with respect to a financial instrument which contains the following provisions:

- Instrument is convertible at the option of its holder into a fixed number of shares of the issuer's common stock.
- At conversion, the issuer must settle the obligation to the holder as follows:
  - Payment in cash for the accreted value of the obligation (for a zero-coupon obligation, the accreted value is the amount received from the holder at issuance plus interest accreted from date of issuance to date of settlement)
  - Payment in either cash or stock to satisfy the conversion spread (the difference between the conversion value over the accreted value)
- If the holder does not exercise the conversion option, the issuer is obligated to settle the accreted value of the debt in cash at maturity.

Questions have arisen regarding the accounting for the *settlement* of this instrument partially in cash (the recognized liability) and partially in stock (the unrecognized equity instrument). EITF 03-7 reached a consensus that only the cash payment is to be considered in computing gain or loss on settlement of the recognized liability. Shares transferred to the holder to settle the excess conversion spread represented by the embedded equity instrument are not considered part of the settlement of the debt component of the instrument.

### Convertible Securities with Beneficial or Contingent Conversion Features

**Beneficial conversion.** Reporting entities sometimes issue convertible securities (debt or preferred stock) that are "in the money" at the issuance date (i.e., where it would be economically advantageous to the holders if the securities were converted immediately). That type of conversion feature is called an "embedded beneficial conversion feature." Variations of such securities may be converted at a fixed price, a fixed discount to the market price at date of conversion, a variable discount to the market price at conversion, or the conversion price may be dependent upon future events. In addition, the conversion feature can be exercisable at issuance, at a stated date in the future, or upon the happening of a future event (such as an IPO). EITF 98-5 addressed the assorted accounting issues arising for issuers of such securities (the reporting entity or debtor).

In contrast with current GAAP governing convertible securities lacking this feature, embedded beneficial conversion features are valued separately at issuance. The feature is recognized as additional paid-in capital by allocating a portion of the proceeds equal to the intrinsic value of the feature. The intrinsic value is computed at the commitment date as (1) the difference between the conversion price and the fair value of the common stock (or other securities) into which the security is convertible, multiplied by (2) the number of shares into which the security is convertible.

For convertible debt securities, a discount on the debt may result from the allocation of a portion of the proceeds to the conversion feature. That discount should be amortized over the period to the earliest conversion date (modified by EITF 00-27). If conversion can take place immediately, the discount is charged to interest expense at once, rather than being amortized. For convertible preferred securities, any "discount" on issuance is analogous to a dividend to the preferred shareholder and should be recognized as a return to them, using the effective interest method, through the date of the earliest permitted conversion.

If the conversion feature has multiple steps, the computation of the intrinsic value is made using the conversion terms most beneficial to the investor. For example, if the security was convertible at a 10% discount to market price after three months and then at a 25% discount to market price after one year, the 25% discount terms would be used to measure the intrinsic value of the feature. Any resulting discount on the convertible debt would be amortized to the earliest date at which the particular discount (25% in this case) could be achieved (one year). However, at any financial statement date, the cumulative amortization recorded must be the greater of (1) the amount computed using the effective interest method of amortization or (2) the amount of the benefit the investor would receive if the securities were converted at that date. If the securities are converted prior to the full amortization of the discount, the unamortized discount is to be included in the amount transferred to equity upon conversion.

If a convertible debt security having a beneficial feature is extinguished prior to conversion, a portion of the reacquisition price of the debt security is allocated to the beneficial conversion feature. That portion is measured as the intrinsic value of the conversion feature at the extinguishment date. Since the beneficial conversion feature was originally recognized as equity, the redemption or cancellation of this feature would give rise not to gain or loss, but rather to an adjustment within stockholders' equity. For example, if $2,000 of the redemption payment was identified with the beneficial feature to which $1,200 had originally been allocated, the net result would be that the original allocation would be eliminated and an $800 charge would be made against retained earnings (analogous to a loss on a treasury stock transaction). Any residual beyond the allocated cost of redeeming the beneficial conversion feature would be allocated to the retirement of the debt security, and a gain or loss on extinguishment would be reported in current earnings.

**Contingent conversion.** If the security becomes convertible only upon occurrence (or failure to occur) of a future event outside the control of the investor or if the conversion terms change based on the occurrence (or failure to occur) of a future event, the value of the contingent beneficial conversion feature should be measured as of the commitment date, but it is not recognized in the financial statements until the contingency is resolved. This may be combined with a beneficial conversion feature. For example, a debt instrument issued with a conversion feature at 20% below then-market price, to become effective conditioned on the consummation of a planned refinancing, would be contingently convertible with a beneficial feature. According to EITF 98-5, any contingent beneficial conversion feature should be measured at the commitment date, but not reflected in earnings until the contingent condition has been met.

The definition of "conventional contingently convertible debt instrument" was later addressed by EITF 05-2, in order to clarify provisions of EITF 00-19. The issue arises because of one of the requirements under FAS 133—namely, that embedded derivatives be bifurcated and accounted for separately under certain conditions, but with an exception for accounting for conversion privileges by issuers of certain convertible securities. A consensus was that instruments that provide holders the right to convert at a fixed ratio (or equivalent cash value, at the issuer's discretion), for which option exercise is based on either the passage of time or a contingent event are deemed "conventional" for purposes of applying EITF 00-19.

EITF also specified in EITF 06-7 that, when a previously bifurcated conversion option in a convertible debt instrument no longer meets the bifurcation criteria in FAS 133, one should reclassify the fair value of the liability for the conversion option to shareholders' equity. If a debt discount was recognized when the conversion option was bifurcated, then it should continue to be amortized. Disclosure requirements include a description of the changes causing the termination of bifurcation, as well as the amount of the liability reclassified to stockholders' equity.

EITF also directed consideration to convertible securities with beneficial conversion features in EITF 00-27, which addresses a number of issues about the application of

EITF 98-5 to specific situations. The following summarizes the guidance offered in this EITF consensus:

1. If an instrument includes both detachable instruments (e.g., stock purchase warrants) and an embedded beneficial conversion option, the proceeds of issuance should first be allocated among the convertible instrument and the other detachable instruments based on their relative fair values. Then, the EITF 98-5 model should be applied to the amount allocated to the convertible instrument to determine if the embedded conversion option has an intrinsic value.

2. If the conversion price could change upon the occurrence of a future event, assume that there are no changes to the current circumstances except the passage of time. Use the most favorable price that would be in effect if nothing were changed at the conversion date in order to measure the intrinsic value of an embedded conversion option. Changes to the conversion terms that are caused by future events not controlled by the issuer are recognized if and when the trigger event occurs.

3. If there is no intrinsic value to a conversion right at issuance, but the conversion price resets after the commitment date and, upon reset, the conversion price is greater than the fair market value of the underlying stock, the beneficial conversion amount is recognized when the reset occurs. The beneficial conversion amount is measured by the number of shares that will be issued upon conversion multiplied by the decrease in price between the original conversion price and the reset price.

4. The definition of commitment date for purposes of applying EITF 98-5 should be the same as the definition of a firm commitment in FAS 133. If an instrument includes both detachable instruments and an embedded beneficial conversion option, the commitment date should also be used when determining the relative fair values of all the instruments issued.

5. If a convertible instrument has a stated redemption date, a discount resulting from recording a beneficial conversion option should be amortized from the date of issuance to the stated redemption date, regardless of when the earliest conversion occurs. If the instrument has beneficial conversion features, the unamortized discount remaining at the date of conversion should be immediately recognized as interest expense or as a dividend, as appropriate.

6. If the terms of a contingent conversion option do not permit an issuer to compute the number of shares that the holder would receive upon conversion, the issuer should wait until the contingent event occurs and then compute the number of shares that would be received. The number of shares that would be received is compared to the number of shares that would have been received if the contingent event had not occurred to determine the excess number of shares. The number of excess shares multiplied by the stock price as of the commitment date equals the incremental intrinsic value that should be recognized.

7. If an instrument includes a beneficial conversion option that expires at the end of a stated period and the instrument then becomes mandatorily redeemable at a premium, EITF 00-27 held that the proceeds of issuance were to be allocated between the debt and the embedded beneficial conversion features. The debt amount was then to be accreted to the redemption amount over the period to the required redemption date. FAS 150, however, requires that mandatorily redeemable stock be classified as a liability, measured initially at fair value, with a corresponding decrease to equity and no gain or loss recognized. Thus, this situation is no longer governed by EITF 00-27.

8. If interest or dividends are paid in kind, the commitment date for the paid-in-kind securities is the commitment date for the original instrument if the payment in kind is not discretionary. The payment is not discretionary if (1) neither the issuer nor the holder can elect other forms of payment for the interest or dividends and (2) if the original instrument was converted before dividends were declared or interest was accrued, the holder will receive the number of shares as if the accumulated dividends or interest have been paid in kind. If the payment in kind is discretionary, the commitment date for the paid-in-kind securities is the date that the interest is accrued or the dividends are declared.

9. If an issuer issues a convertible instrument as repayment of a nonconvertible instrument, the fair value of the newly issued convertible instrument equals the redemption amount owed at the maturity date of the old debt. That is, the carrying amount of the old debt is the proceeds received for applying EITF 98-5 to the new debt.

Several tentative conclusions were also expressed, but have not been resolved since the date of issuance of EITF 00-27.

1. If a convertible instrument is extinguished prior to its maturity date, no portion of the reacquisition price should be allocated to the conversion option if that option had no intrinsic value at the issuance date.

2. The intrinsic value of a conversion feature at an early extinguishment date of convertible debt is recorded as a decrease in additional paid-in capital, which may result in a reduction in additional paid-in capital that is larger than the amount originally recorded in paid-in capital at issuance.

3. If an entity redeems convertible preferred stock with a beneficial conversion feature, the intrinsic value of the conversion feature that was recorded at issuance is reversed, and the remaining reacquisition price is allocated to the reacquisition of the stock. Any excess of that portion over the carrying amount of the stock is an adjustment to earnings available to common shareholders.

4. If a company issues a warrant that allows the holder to acquire a convertible instrument for a stated price and that warrant is classified as equity, the date used to measure the intrinsic value of the conversion option is the commitment date for the warrant, not its exercise date, provided that the issuer received fair value for the warrant when issued. The deemed proceeds for determining whether a beneficial conversion option exists are equal to the sum of the proceeds received for the warrant and the exercise price of the warrant. If that sum is less than the fair value of the common stock that would be received upon exercise of the convertible instrument that would be obtained upon exercise of the warrant, the excess represents a deemed distribution to the holder of the warrant, which is to be recognized over the life of the warrant. The deemed distribution is limited to the proceeds received for the warrant; that is, if the deemed distribution is larger than the proceeds received, the difference is not recognized until the warrant is exercised. If the issuer received less than fair value for the warrant upon issuance, the exercise date of the warrant should be used to measure the intrinsic value of the conversion option.

5. If a company issues a warrant that allows the holder to acquire a convertible instrument for a stated price and that warrant is classified as a liability, the date used to measure the intrinsic value of the conversion option is the exercise date for the warrant, not its commitment date. The deemed proceeds for determining whether a beneficial conversion option exists are equal to the sum of the fair value of the warrant on the exercise date and the exercise price of the warrant.

6.  If a conversion feature permits the holder to receive both common stock and warrants to acquire common stock, the intrinsic value of the conversion option is measured as the difference between (1) the proceeds allocated to the common stock portion of the conversion feature and (2) the fair value at the commitment date of the common stock to be received by the holder upon conversion.

The guidance in EITF 00-19 should be used to evaluate whether the issuer controls settlement of the conversion feature of convertible preferred stock. If the issuer does not control settlement, the convertible preferred stock is considered temporary equity.

### Example 1: Intrinsic value of a conversion feature—fixed dollar terms

Software Solutions issues $1,000,000 of convertible debt, which is convertible into $10 par common stock at a price of $50 per share. The fair value of the common stock on the commitment date of the issue is $60. The intrinsic value of the conversion feature is computed as follows:

$1,000,000/$50 per share = 20,000 shares to be issued upon conversion
($60 fair value – $50 conversion price) × 20,000 shares = $200,000 intrinsic value

Software Solutions would make the following entry to recognize the issuance of the bonds at 100:

| | | |
|---|---|---|
| Cash | 1,000,000 | |
| Discount on bonds payable | 200,000 | |
| Bonds payable | | 1,000,000 |
| Additional paid-in capital | | 200,000 |

If the price at which the bond is convertible to stock changes over the life of the bond, the intrinsic value should be computed using the terms that are most beneficial to the holder. The most favorable conversion price that would be in effect assuming that there are no changes to the current circumstances except for the passing of time should be used to measure the intrinsic value.

### Example 2: Intrinsic value of a conversion feature—variable terms

American National Biotech issues $1,000,000 of convertible debt, convertible into $10 par common stock at a price 15% below the commitment date market price for years 1 and 2, 20% below the commitment date market price for years 3 to 5, and 25% below the commitment date market price for years 6 to maturity. The fair value of the common stock on the commitment date of the issue is $50. The intrinsic value of the conversion feature is computed as follows:

The most beneficial price is the 25% discount available in years 6 to maturity
That price would be $37.50 ($50 × .75)
$1,000,000/$37.50 per share = 26,667 shares to be issued upon conversion
($50 fair value – $37.50 conversion price) × 26,667 shares = $333,337 intrinsic value

American National Biotech would make the following entry to recognize the issuance of the bonds at 100:

| | | |
|---|---|---|
| Cash | 1,000,000 | |
| Discount on bonds payable | 333,337 | |
| Bonds payable | | 1,000,000 |
| Additional paid-in capital | | 333,337 |

In some cases the conversion price will be dependent on a future event, or the bond becomes convertible only upon the occurrence of a future event. In those cases, the contingent beneficial conversion feature should be measured at the commitment date but not recognized in earnings until the contingency is resolved.

### Example 3: Intrinsic value of a conversion feature—contingent price terms

Major Manufacturing Co. issues $1,000,000 of convertible debt, which is convertible into $10 par common stock at a discount of 20% off of the conversion date market price. The fair value of the common stock on the commitment date of the issue is $50. The intrinsic value of the conversion feature is computed as follows:

Because the conversion percentage is fixed, the intrinsic value is always $250,000.

| | | | | |
|---|---|---|---|---|
| Market price at conversion | $40 | $50 | $60 | $70 |
| Conversion price | $32 | $40 | $48 | $56 |
| Number of shares issued | 31,250 | 25,000 | 20,833 | 17,857 |
| Discount | $8 | $10 | $12 | $14 |
| Intrinsic value | $250,000 | $250,000 | $250,000 | $250,000 |

Major Manufacturing Co. would make the following entry to recognize the issuance of bonds at 100:

| | | |
|---|---|---|
| Cash | 1,000,000 | |
| Discount on bonds payable | 250,000 | |
| Bonds payable | | 1,000,000 |
| Additional paid-in capital | | 250,000 |

### Example 4: Intrinsic value of a conversion feature—contingent conversion

Shoemaker Co. issues $1,000,000 of convertible debt, which is convertible into $10 par common stock at a discount of 25% below the commitment date market price. The fair value of the common stock on the commitment date of the issue is $60, so the conversion price is $45. The debt is convertible only upon an initial public offering. The intrinsic value of the conversion feature is computed as follows:

$1,000,000/$45 per share = 22,222 shares to be issued upon conversion
($60 fair value − $45 conversion price) × 22,222 shares = $333,330 intrinsic value

Shoemaker Co. would not allocate any portion of the proceeds to the conversion feature at issuance. It would make the following entry to recognize the issuance of the bonds at 100:

| | | |
|---|---|---|
| Cash | 1,000,000 | |
| Bonds payable | | 1,000,000 |

Upon the occurrence of an initial public offering, Shoemaker would make the following entry:

| | | |
|---|---|---|
| Discount on bonds payable | 333,330 | |
| Additional paid-in capital | | 333,330 |

### Example 5: Intrinsic value of a conversion feature—contingent conversion with variable terms

Food Franchisers issues $1,000,000 of convertible debt, which is convertible into $10 par common stock at a price of $50. The fair value of the common stock on the commitment date of the issue is $60. The debt is convertible only upon an initial public offering. If the stock's market price is at least 20% higher than the IPO price one year after the IPO, the conversion price will be 70% of the then market price. The intrinsic value of the contingent conversion feature at issuance is computed as follows:

$1,000,000/$50 per share = 20,000 shares to be issued upon conversion
($60 fair value − $50 conversion price) × 20,000 shares = 250,000 intrinsic value

The intrinsic value of the contingent conversion price change is also computed at the commitment date using the assumptions that the IPO price will be the same as the current market price and that the stock price one year after the IPO is 20% higher, as follows:

Contingent conversion price = $60 × 120% × 70% = $50.40
$1,000,000/$50.40 per share = 19,841 shares to be issued upon conversion
($72 fair value − $50.40 conversion price) × 19,841 shares = $428,565 intrinsic value

Food Franchisers would not allocate any portion of the proceeds to the conversion feature at issuance. It would make the following entry to recognize the issuance of the bonds at 100:

| | | |
|---|---|---|
| Cash | 1,000,000 | |
| Bonds payable | | 1,000,000 |

Upon the occurrence of an initial public offering at $55, Food Franchisers would make the following entry:

| | | |
|---|---|---|
| Discount on bonds payable | 250,000 | |
| Additional paid-in capital | | 250,000 |

If the stock price increased to $66 ($55 × 120%), Food Franchisers would make the following entry for the difference between the two intrinsic values:

| | | |
|---|---|---|
| Discount on bonds payable | 178,565 | |
| Additional paid-in capital | | 178,565 |

If a bond with an embedded beneficial conversion feature is extinguished prior to conversion, a portion of the reacquisition price is allocated to the repurchase of the conversion feature. That portion is the intrinsic value of the conversion feature at the extinguishment date, which would be recorded as a decrease in additional paid-in capital. That accounting may result in a reduction in additional paid-in capital that is larger than the amount originally recorded in paid-in capital at issuance. However, no portion of the reacquisition price should be allocated to the conversion feature if that feature had no intrinsic value at the issuance date.

**Example of extinguishment of debt with an embedded conversion feature**

Software Solutions (Example 1, above) repurchases $500,000 face of its debt at 140. At the date of issuance, the following entry had been made relating to the debt which is later extinguished.

| | | |
|---|---|---|
| Cash | 500,000 | |
| Discount on bonds payable | 100,000 | |
| Bonds payable | | 500,000 |
| Additional paid-in capital | | 100,000 |

At the date of the repurchase, the market value of the stock is $85, and the unamortized discount on the debt was $20,000. The intrinsic value of the conversion feature at the date of the repurchase is computed as follows:

$500,000/$50 per share = 10,000 shares to be issued upon conversion
($85 fair value − $50 conversion price) × 10,000 shares = $350,000 intrinsic value

Software Solutions would make the following entry to recognize the retirement of the bonds:

| | | |
|---|---|---|
| Bonds payable | 500,000 | |
| Additional paid-in capital | 350,000 | |
| Discount on bonds payable | | 20,000 |
| Gain on extinguishment of debt | | 130,000 |
| Cash | | 700,000 |

Questions have arisen regarding the accounting for the settlement of this instrument partially in cash (the recognized liability) and partially in stock (the unrecognized equity instrument). EITF 03-7 states that only the cash payment is to be considered in computing gain or loss on settlement of the recognized liability. Shares transferred to the holder to settle the excess conversion spread represented by the embedded equity instrument are not considered part of the settlement of the debt component of the instrument.

**Contingent conversion rights triggered by issuer call.** In some instances a debt instrument may include a contingent conversion privilege that becomes exercisable if the issuer attempts to call the debt before maturity, even if the stated contingency (e.g., the underlying stock price hitting some predefined threshold value) has not occurred, at which time the holders may elect to surrender the debt for cash (perhaps with a call premium, if the indenture contains such a provision) or to convert at a defined ratio for stock. If the debt remains outstanding until scheduled redemption, there will be no opportunity to convert. (Another variant exists where the debt has a contingent conversion feature at inception, e.g., where the debt becomes convertible if some other event, such as a refinancing, occurs, as well as if the issuer attempts to call the debt.)

EITF 05-1 has concluded that no gain or loss should result from the creation of a conversion opportunity caused by the issuer's exercise of its call option, if the debt as originally issued contained a substantive conversion feature. In such circumstances, conversion of the debt to equity—assuming the existence of substantive rights in the original debt issuance—would be accounted for as a book value swap. On the other hand, if the conversion feature had not been substantive, the conversion triggered by the exercise by the issuer of its call option would be accounted for as a debt extinguishment, with the fair value of the equity being issued used to define the cost of the extinguishment. This would create a gain or loss to be recognized in virtually all situations. Such gain or loss is no longer permitted to be reported as extraordinary, however.

EITF 05-1 defines a *substantive* conversion feature as a conversion feature that was, when the debt instrument was first issued, at least *reasonably possible* of being exercisable in the future, absent the issuer's exercise of a call option—where reasonably possible has the same meaning as under FAS 5. In practical terms, evaluation of whether the original conversion feature had been substantive, in the context of the facts and circumstances at the date of issuance, might include consideration of the interest yield of the contingently convertible debt compared to equivalent rates then required for debt lacking that feature, the likelihood of the occurrence of the defined contingent event, and the relative value of the conversion feature versus the related debt instrument.

**Modifications to conversion privileges.** Under provisions of EITF 96-19, the debtor's (issuer's) accounting for a modification of a debt issue or an exchange for another issue was based on whether the modifications were substantial. Based on the results of the analysis, extinguishment of the original debt could be found to have occurred, with financial reporting ramifications. Subsequently, the SEC took a position on this matter which added further complexity. Most recently, EITF has considered whether a change in an embedded conversion option has to be considered in this analysis, which could affect the ultimate determination of whether a debt extinguishment had occurred. The consensus in EITF 05-7 was that the change in fair value of the embedded conversion option would be included in the analysis of the debt modification. (This conclusion necessitated a change to EITF 96-19 to recognize noncash features in the analysis that had previously been based only on expected cash flows.)

EITF 06-6 alters the situation by holding that debt extinguishment accounting be used if (1) the change in the fair value of the embedded conversion option is at least 10% of the carrying value of the original debt instrument just prior to the debt being modified or exchanged, or (2) the debt instrument modification or exchange adds or eliminates a substantive conversion option. If this analysis does not result in extinguishment accounting, then an increase in the fair value of the conversion option would reduce the debt and increase additional paid-in capital, while a decrease in the fair value of the conversion option would not be recognized.

EITF 05-7 also held that the modification of a convertible debt instrument will affect subsequent recognition of interest expense for the associated debt instrument for changes in the fair value of the embedded conversion option. The change in the fair value of an embedded conversion option will be calculated as the difference between the fair value of the embedded conversion option immediately before and after the modification. EITF noted that the value exchanged by the holder for the modification of the conversion option is to be recognized as a discount (or premium) with a corresponding increase (or decrease) in additional paid-in capital.

Finally, EITF 05-7 concluded that issuers should not recognize a beneficial conversion feature or reassess an existing beneficial conversion feature at the date of the modification of a convertible debt instrument.

**Tax effect of accounting for beneficial conversion feature.** The existence of beneficial conversion features, as noted in the preceding discussion, requires that a portion of the proceeds from issuing debt with such an attribute be credited to a paid-in capital account. The offset to this will generally be a discount related to the convertible debt, meaning the book (carrying) value of the debt will differ from the tax basis, since tax law does not recognize the beneficial conversion feature as an equity element. EITF 05-8 has concluded that the difference between the "tax" and "book" bases of the convertible debt is a temporary difference within the meaning of FAS 109, and that deferred tax accounting is accordingly warranted. EITF 05-8 further concluded that the deferred tax effect upon issuance should be included in paid-in capital, to be amortized as the debt discount is amortized to interest expense.

Put simply, "book" interest expense will exceed "tax" interest expense due to the impact of the debt discount amortization, so that "book" net income will be lower than "tax" earnings. The amount of excess current income tax payable (versus what the GAAP-basis financial statements would suggest) is created via the amortization of the deferred tax obligation established in paid-in capital upon issuance of the convertible debt. Upon adoption of EITF 05-8's consensus, retrospective application per FAS 154 is required, meaning that deferred tax must be provided for the yet-unamortized debt discount created when convertible debt with beneficial features was issued in past years, if such debt remains outstanding.

**Disclosure of contingently convertible securities.** Allegations had been raised that disclosures regarding contingently convertible securities have often been inconsistent across companies, and have often been inadequate. To address this problem, FSP 129-1 interprets how the disclosure provisions of FAS 129 apply to contingently convertible securities. FAS 129 applies to all contingently convertible securities, even those that are not included in the computation of diluted EPS. The FSP identifies the qualitative and quantitative terms that must be disclosed so that users can understand the potential impact of conversion, including: events or changes in circumstances that would cause the contingency to be met and features necessary to understand the conversion rights, the conversion price and number of shares, events or changes that could adjust or change any features of the securities, and the manner of settlement upon conversion. Disclosures should indicate whether shares that would be issued upon conversion are included in the calculation of EPS. Disclosures should also include information about derivative transactions related to the securities.

## Induced Conversion of Debt

A special situation exists in which the conversion privileges of convertible debt are modified after issuance. These modifications may take the form of reduced conversion prices or additional consideration paid to the convertible debt holder. The debtor offers these modifications or "sweeteners" to induce prompt conversion of the outstanding debt.

FAS 84 specifies the accounting method used in these situations and only applies when the convertible debt is converted into equity securities. Upon conversion, the debtor must recognize an expense for the excess of the fair value of all the securities and other consideration given over the fair value of the securities specified in the original conversion terms. The reported expense should not be classified as an extraordinary item.

**Determining applicability of FAS 84.** FAS 84 specifies the accounting for "sweeteners" used to induce the conversion of convertible debt. Traditionally, this involves enhancements offered by the debtor to encourage conversions, often motivated by the desire to bring an end to interest payments on the convertible debt. EITF 02-15 addresses the related circumstance of conversions when the enhanced terms are proposed or requested by the creditors/debtholders. In some instances, only the requesting parties are granted the sweetened terms. The consensus states that FAS 84 applies to all conversion of convertible debts that (1) occur pursuant to changed conversion privileges, (2) are exercisable only for a limited period of time, and (3) include the issuance of all of the equity securities issuable pursuant to conversion privileges included in the terms of the debt at issuance for each debt instrument that is converted, regardless of the party that initiates the offer or whether the offer relates to all debtholders.

### Example of induced conversion expense

1. January 1, 2009, XYZ Company issued ten 8% convertible bonds at $1,000 par value without a discount or premium, maturing December 31, 2019.
2. The bonds are initially convertible into no par common stock of XYZ at a conversion price of $25.
3. On July 1, 2013, the convertible bonds have a market value of $600 each.
4. To induce the convertible bondholders to quickly convert their bonds, XYZ reduces the conversion price to $20 for bondholders who convert before July 21, 2013 (within twenty days).
5. The market price of XYZ Company's common stock on the date of conversion is $15 per share.

The fair value of the incremental consideration paid by XYZ upon conversion is calculated for each bond converted before July 21, 2013.

*Value of securities issued to debt holders:*

| | | |
|---|---|---|
| Face amount | $1,000 | per bond |
| ÷ New conversion price | ÷ $20 | per share |
| Number of common shares issued upon conversion | 50 | shares |
| × Price per common share | × $15 | per share |
| Value of securities issued | $ 750 | (a) |
| Face amount | $1,000 | per bond |
| ÷ Original conversion price | ÷ $25 | per share |
| Number of common shares issuable pursuant to original conversion privilege | 40 | shares |
| × Price per share | × $15 | per share |
| Value of securities issuable pursuant to original conversion privileges | $ 600 | (b) |
| Value of securities issued | $ 750 | (a) |
| Value of securities issuable pursuant to the original conversion privileges | 600 | (b) |
| Fair value of incremental consideration | $ 150 | |

The entry to record the debt conversion for each bond is

| | | |
|---|---|---|
| Convertible debt | 1,000 | |
| Debt conversion expense | 150 | |
|     Common stock—no par | | 1,150 |

## Debt Issued with Stock Warrants

Warrants are certificates enabling the holder to purchase a stated number of shares of stock at a certain price within a certain time period. They are often issued with bonds to enhance the marketability of the bonds and to lower the bond's interest rate.

When bonds with detachable warrants are issued, the purchase price must be allocated between the debt and the stock warrants based on relative market values (APB 14). Since two separate instruments are involved, a market value must be determined for each. However, if one value cannot be determined, the market value of the other should be deducted from the total value to determine the unknown value.

**Example of accounting for a bond with a detachable warrant**

1.  A $1,000 bond with a detachable warrant to buy 10 shares of $10 par common stock at $50 per share is issued for $1,025.
2.  Immediately after the issuance the bonds trade at $995 and the warrants at $35.
3.  The market value of the stock is $48.

The relative market value of the bonds is 96.6% [995/(995 + 35)] and the warrant is 3.4% [35/(995 + 35)]. Thus, $34.85(3.4% × $1,025) of the issuance price is assigned to the warrants. The journal entry to record the issuance is

| | | |
|---|---|---|
| Cash | 1,025.00 | |
| Discount on bonds payable | 9.85 | |
|     Bonds payable | | 1,000.00 |
|     Paid-in capital—warrants | | |
|     (or "Stock options outstanding") | | 34.85 |

The discount is the difference between the purchase price assigned to the bond, $990.15 (96.6% × $1,025), and its face value, $1,000. The debt itself is accounted for in the normal fashion.

The entry to record the subsequent future exercise of the warrant would be

| | | |
|---|---|---|
| Cash | 500.00 | |
| Paid-in capital—warrants | 34.85 | |
|     Common stock | | 100.00 |
|     Paid-in capital | | 434.85 (difference) |

Assuming the warrants are not exercised, the journal entry is

| | | |
|---|---|---|
| Paid-in capital—warrants | 34.85 | |
|     Paid-in capital—expired warrants | | 34.85 |

## Debt Issued with Conversion Features and Stock Warrants

EITF 00-27 states that when a debt instrument includes both detachable instruments such as warrants, and an embedded beneficial conversion option, the proceeds of issuance should first be allocated among the convertible instrument and the other detachable instruments based on their relative fair values. Following this, the EITF 98-5 model should be applied to the amount allocated to the convertible instrument to determine if the embedded conversion option has an intrinsic value.

**Example of convertible debt issued with stock warrants**

Cellular Communicators issues $1,000,000 of convertible debt with 100,000 detachable warrants. The debt is convertible into $10 par common stock at a price of $50 per share. At the commitment date of this issuance, the common stock is trading at $46 per share. Immediately after the issuance, the bonds trade at 85 and the warrants trade at $2. The issuance proceeds of $1,000,000 is allocated to the two instruments as follows:

$850,000 /($850,000 + $200,000) × $1,000,000 = $809,524 to the debt
$200,000/($850,000 + $200,000) × $1,000,000 = $190,476 to the warrants

The intrinsic value of the conversion feature is next computed as follows:

$1,000,000/$50 per share = 20,000 shares to be issued upon conversion
The effective conversion price is the bond's allocated proceeds of $809,524 divided by 20,000 shares or $40.48
($46 current fair value of the stock – $40.48 effective conversion price) × 20,000 shares = $110,476, which is the implied discount granted on the bonds in connection with the conversion feature

Cellular Communicators would make the following entry to recognize the issuance of the bonds with warrants at 100:

| | | |
|---|---|---|
| Cash | 1,000,000 | |
| Discount on bonds payable | 110,476 | |
| Bonds payable | | 809,524 |
| Additional paid-in capital | | 110,476 |
| Paid-in capital—warrants | | 190,476 |

There are a wide range of features that may be incorporated into stock purchase warrants and it will often be a challenge to identify the substance of these features, and to then prescribe the proper accounting for each feature. One such example involves warrants that are issued with put options, sometimes called "puttable warrants." Such warrants allow the holder to purchase a fixed number of the issuer's shares at a fixed price (common to all warrants), but also are puttable by the holder at a specified date for a fixed monetary amount that the holder could require the issuer to pay in cash. For example, assume the warrants are issued when the entity's shares are trading at $12, and each warrant permits the purchase of 100 shares at $15 through April 30, 2010. If not previously exercised, the warrant holders can put each warrant back to the issuer for the equivalent of $14 per share, that is, for 100 × ($14 − $12) = $200 per warrant. The warrant holder is thus assured (given the underlying stock price at inception) of at least $2 per share income, and of course may reap a much larger reward if the share price has risen beyond $15 by the expiration date.

FAS 150 applies to all freestanding instruments including those composed of more than one option or forward contract embodying obligations that require or that may require settlement by transfer of assets. The embedded put option in the foregoing example of a warrant does create a liability, since the issuer (the reporting entity) may be called upon to distribute assets (cash) to the holders of those put options. FSP 150-1 states that this is a liability even if the repurchase feature is conditional on a defined contingency in addition to the level of the issuer's share price. The warrant is not an outstanding share and therefore does not meet the exception for outstanding shares set forth by FAS 150.

FSP 150-1 provides examples of put options which are subject to only cash payment and also of those which could be settled by an issuance of stock. The former case is straightforward: the instrument must be classified as a liability if the share price at the reporting date is such that a cash payment would be demanded by the holders of the puttable warrants. If the share price at that date is such that exercise of the warrant would be elected over exercise of the put option, then the warrant would be included in equity, not in liabilities. In other words, classification would depend on current stock price and could change from period to period, although FSP 150-1 is not explicit on this point.

Other put arrangements call for settlement in shares. That is, if advantageous to do so, the warrant holders exercise the warrants and acquire shares, but if the strike price has not been attained at expiration date, the put is exercised and the reporting entity would have to settle, but instead of paying cash it would issue shares having an aggregate value equal to the put amount. Thus, at inception, the number of shares that the puttable warrant obligates the reporting entity to issue can vary, and the instrument must be examined under the provisions of FAS 150 that deal with obligations to issue a variable number of shares. The facts and circumstances must be considered in judging whether the *monetary value* of the obligation to issue a number of shares that varies is predominantly based on a fixed monetary amount known at inception; if so; it is a liability under FAS 150.

Yet another variation, also illustrated by FSP 150-1, is the warrant for the purchase of shares, which shares are puttable. The holder can exercise the warrant and then immediately force the issuer to repurchase the shares thereby issued. The price at which the shares could be put would be defined in the warrant, and the likelihood that the put option would be exercised would vary with the market value of the shares. Obviously, if the shares acquired by exercise of the warrant had a greater market value than the put price, the put would not be invoked. Accordingly, whether these warrants would be classified as equity or liability would depend on the market value of the underlying shares, and this could change from one balance sheet date to the next. However if the shares to be issued upon warrant exercise were to have a mandatory redemption feature, then the warrants would be reportable as liabilities in any case.

FSP 150-1 offers several other examples, illustrating more complex features that may be found in stock purchase warrants which, depending on circumstances, might necessitate classification as liabilities in the balance sheet.

## Through-Put and Take-or-Pay Contracts

Through-put and take-or-pay contracts are sometimes used to help a supplier pay for new facilities, machines, or other expenditures. They are negotiated as a way of arranging financing for the facilities that will produce the goods or provide the services desired by a purchaser. A through-put contract is an agreement between the owner of a transportation facility or manufacturing facility (such as a pipeline) and a purchaser (such as an oil processor) that requires the purchaser to pay specified amounts at future dates to the owner in return for the transportation or manufacture of a product. A take-or-pay contract is similar. It is an agreement between a purchaser and a supplier that requires the purchaser to pay specified amounts at future dates in return for products or services. In both types of contracts, the purchaser is required to make the specified payments even if it does not receive goods or services.

Some of these contracts are reported on the balance sheet as an asset and a liability. Others are not reported. Other than standards relating to recognition of losses on unconditional purchase obligations (ARB 43, chap. 4), there are no standards that require the contracts to be recognized on the balance sheet. However, FAS 47 requires certain disclosures to be made.

### Example of a through-put contract

Aramarck Oil contracts with the Persian Pipeline Company to ship a minimum of three million barrels a month of unprocessed sour crude oil from is Ahwaz oil field in Iran to the pipeline terminus at Char Bahar, an amount which constitutes 1/3 of the capacity of the pipeline. The contract term is twelve years. Under the contract, Aramarck is obligated to pay Persian for 1/3 of the fixed operating costs of the pipeline, depreciation, interest on the $500 million of 5% debt used to finance the pipeline (to be paid off in equal annual payments over twelve years), and a 7% rate of return on equity to Persian. Estimated annual payments are $20 million. Aramarck's disclosure of the agreement follows:

Aramarck has signed an agreement reserving pipeline capacity for twelve years. Under the terms of the agreement, Aramarck is obligated to make the following minimum payments, whether or not it ships through the pipeline:

| | |
|---|---:|
| 2008 through 2012 ($20 million annually) | $100,000,000 |
| Later years | 140,000,000 |
| Total | 240,000,000 |
| Less: Amount representing interest | (58,984,000) |
| Total at present value | $181,016,00 |

## Mandatorily Redeemable Shares and Similar Instruments

FAS 150 requires that shares of stock (typically, but not necessarily, preferred shares) that are issued with mandatory redemption features be reported as liabilities rather than equity instruments. Payments or accruals of "dividends" and other amounts to be paid to holders of such shares are to be reported as interest expense. The only exception to those rules is for shares that are required to be redeemed only upon the liquidation or termination of the issuer, since the fundamental "going concern assumption" underlying GAAP financial statements means that such an eventuality is not given recognition.

After its issuance, FAS 150 was the object of concern and criticism, particularly due to the perceived lack of opportunity to educate financial statement users regarding the potentially large impact on entities' balance sheets—at the extreme, eliminating all (or even *more than all*) of previously reported equity. In response, FASB issued FSP 150-3, which delayed the effective date for nonpublic reporting entities. Specifically, for instruments that are mandatorily redeemable on fixed dates for amounts that either are fixed or are determined by reference to an interest rate index, currency index, or another external index, the classification, measurement, and disclosure provisions of FAS 150 was deferred and became effective for fiscal periods beginning after December 15, 2004.

However, for all other financial instruments that are mandatorily redeemable, the classification, measurement, and disclosure provisions of FAS 150 were deferred *indefinitely*, pending further FASB action. During this deferral period, FASB expressed its plans to reconsider implementation issues and, perhaps, classification or measurement guidance for those instruments in conjunction with its larger, ongoing project on liabilities and equity. As of mid-2008 these matters remain unresolved.

In the authors' opinion, financial statement preparers should not presume that this application of FAS 150 will be rescinded, although that remains a possibility. There would not appear to be a conceptually sound argument for why public entities having such mandatorily redeemable instruments would be required to report these as liabilities, while granting nonpublic ones an exemption. Accordingly, at minimum, nonpublic entities having mandatorily redeemable shares should educate lenders and other financial statement users to the implications of the new standard and, where necessary and feasible, arrange to amend loan agreements containing covenants which would be violated by a sudden, major change in apparent debt/equity ratios. In other cases, it might be wise, or necessary, to revise the underlying shareholder agreements that define the mandatory redemption provisions. For example, "buy sell" agreements might be superseded by agreements between the individual shareholders themselves, providing for buyouts of retiring or deceased shareholders by the other owners, rather than by the entity itself, and thereby averting liability classification.

Note also (as also set forth in FSP 150-3) that deferral of the disclosure requirements under FAS 150, as described above, does not remove the requirements under FAS 129, which requires the disclosure of information about the pertinent rights and privileges of the various securities outstanding, including mandatory redemption requirements.

FSP 150-3 has also deferred indefinitely the *measurement* provisions of FAS 150, both as to the parent in consolidated financial statements and as to the subsidiary that issued the instruments that resulted in mandatorily redeemable noncontrolling interests before November 5, 2003. For those instruments, the measurement guidance for redeemable shares and noncontrolling interests under GAAP (e.g., EITF D-98) continues to apply during the deferral period. However, the *classification* provisions were not deferred.

The SEC subsequently further clarified the interaction between FAS 150 and D-98 for conditionally redeemable shares. Accounting for these shares, prior to the date on which the condition is first met, is not governed by FAS 150, but for a publicly held company the shares would not be permitted to be included in equity. A "mezzanine" classification would be acceptable until the condition is met, at which point reclassification as liabilities is necessary. Reclassification is akin to redemption, to be recognized at fair value via a charge or credit to equity, with concomitant impact on earnings per share computations in the period when the reclassification takes place.

If on the date of adoption the redemption price is greater than the book value of the shares, the company would *recognize a liability* for the redemption price of the shares that are subject to mandatory redemption, reclassifying amounts previously recognized in equity accounts. The difference between the redemption price and amounts previously recorded in equity is reported on the income statement as a cumulative effect transition adjustment loss. If the redemption price exceeds the company's equity balance, the cumulative transition loss should be reported as an excess of liabilities over assets (a deficit in the stockholders' equity section). In the opposite case, it is reported as an excess of assets over liabilities (i.e., as positive equity).

Shares are mandatorily redeemable if the issuer has an unconditional obligation to redeem the shares by transferring its assets at a specified or determinable date (or dates) or upon an event certain to occur (for example, the death of the holder). The obligation to transfer assets must be unconditional—that is, there is no specified event that is outside the control of the issuer that will release the issuer from its obligation. Thus, callable preferred shares, which are redeemable at the issuer's option, and convertible preferred shares, which are redeemable at the holder's option, are not mandatorily redeemable shares.

FAS 150 requires this reporting for all mandatorily redeemable financial instruments, unless the redemption is required to occur only upon the liquidation or termination of the reporting entity. The exception exists because the fundamental *going concern* assumption underlying GAAP financial reporting would be violated if a classification was imposed in GAAP financial statements that presumed or was conditioned on the reporting entity's cessation as a going concern. However, the exception under FAS 150 did not, as issued, extend to mandatorily redeemable financial instruments of a consolidated subsidiary, in the consolidated financial statements of its parent entity. Since it is the *going concern* status of the reporting entity (i.e., the parent) that is of significance, the mandatory redemption feature of the subsidiary's instruments, albeit conditional, was to be reported consistent with FAS 150's provisions. However, subsequently FSP 150-3 has indefinitely postponed the effective date of this provision for noncontrolling interests. This deferral is applicable to both publicly held and nonpublic reporting entities.

### Example of mandatorily redeemable preferred shares

On June 1, 2009, Verde Corporation issues 1,000 shares of mandatorily redeemable 5% preferred stock with a par value $100 for $110,330. The shares are redeemable at $150 on May 31, 2016. At issuance, Verde Corporation recognizes a liability of $110,330.

Some corporations and partnerships, primarily closely held ones, issue shares or units that are redeemed at the death of the holder. If those shares or units represents the only shares or units in the entity, the entity reports those instruments as liabilities and describes them in its statement of financial position as shares (or units) subject to mandatory redemption, to distinguish them from other liabilities. The classification is unaffected by any insurance policies that the entity may have on the holders' lives. The entity presents interest expense and payments to holders of those instruments separately, apart from interest and payments to other creditors in its statements of income and cash flows. The entity also discloses that the instruments are mandatorily redeemable upon the death of the holders.

### Example of shares that are mandatorily redeemable at the death of the holder

Mike and Ike are equal shareholders in M&I's Auto Repair, Inc. Upon the death of either shareholder, the corporation will redeem shares of the deceased for half of the book value of the corporation. The following information would be disclosed in the notes to the financial statements:

All of the corporation's shares are subject to mandatory redemption upon death of the shareholders, and are thus reported as a liability. The liability amount consists of

| | |
|---|---:|
| Common stock—$100 par value, 1,000 shares authorized, issued and outstanding | $100,000 |
| Undistributed earnings attributable to those shares | 50,000 |
| Accumulated other comprehensive income | (2,000) |
| Total liability | $148,000 |

After issuance, the amount of the liability for the mandatorily redeemable shares should be adjusted using the effective interest method if both the amount to be paid and the settlement date are fixed. If either the amount to be paid or the settlement date varies based on specified conditions, the liability is measured subsequently at the amount of cash that would be paid under the conditions specified in the contract if settlement occurred at the reporting date, recognizing the resulting change in that amount from the previous reporting date as interest cost.

### Example of mandatorily redeemable preferred shares (continued)

The effective interest rate, calculated as described in the "Effective Interest Method" section of this chapter, is 8.5%. Continuing the example above, of Verde Corporation, it would recognize the following annual interest expense and liability amounts:

| | Cash paid | Interest at 8.5% annually | Change in liability | Ending liability |
|---|---|---|---|---|
| 06/01/09 | | | | 110,330 |
| 05/31/10 | 5,000 | 9,378 | 4,378 | 114,708 |
| 05/31/11 | 5,000 | 9,750 | 4,750 | 119,458 |
| 05/31/12 | 5,000 | 10,154 | 5,154 | 124,612 |
| 05/31/13 | 5,000 | 10,592 | 5,592 | 130,204 |
| 05/31/14 | 5,000 | 11,067 | 6,068 | 136,271 |
| 05/31/15 | 5,000 | 11,583 | 6,583 | 142,854 |
| 05/31/16 | 155,000 | 12,146 | (142,854) | 0 |

The entry to record the first "dividend" payment would be

| | | |
|---|---|---|
| Interest expense | 9,378 | |
| Liability | | 4,378 |
| Cash | | 5,000 |

If shares have a conditional redemption feature, which requires the issuer to redeem the shares by transferring its assets upon an event not certain to occur, the shares become mandatorily redeemable—and, therefore, become a liability—if that event occurs, the event becomes certain to occur, or the condition is otherwise resolved. The fair value of the shares is reclassified as a liability, and equity is reduced by that amount, recognizing no gain or loss.

Note that when redemption value is based on a notion of fair value, defined in the underlying agreement, the initial recognition of the difference between this computed amount and the corresponding book value will almost inevitably result in a surplus or deficit. In other words, the promised redemption amount, measured at transition and again at each balance sheet date, will not equal the book value of the equity which is subject to redemption. This discrepancy must be reflected in stockholders' equity, even though the redeemable equity is reclassified to a liability. In effect, the redemption arrangement will result in either a residual in equity (assuming redemption were to fully occur at the balance sheet date) or a deficit, because the agreement provides that redeeming shareholders are entitled to more or less than their respective pro rata shares of the book value of their equity claims. This point is reiterated by FSP 150-2, which states that if the redemption price of mandatorily redeemable shares is greater than the book value of those shares, the company should report the excess as a deficit (equity), even though the mandatorily redeemable shares are reported as a liability.

Common shares that are mandatorily redeemable are not included in the denominator when computing basic or diluted earnings per share. If any amounts, including contractual (accumulated) dividends, attributable to shares that are to be redeemed or repurchased have not been recognized as interest expense, those amounts are deducted in computing income available to common shareholders (the numerator of the calculation), consistently with the "two-class" method set forth in FAS 128 (Chapter 20). The redemption requirements for mandatorily redeemable shares for each of the next five years are required to be disclosed in the notes to the financial statements.

EITF Topic D-98 addresses concerns raised by the SEC regarding the financial statement classification and measurement of securities subject to mandatory redemption requirements or whose redemption is outside the control of the issuer. Certain rules of the SEC were withdrawn upon promulgation of FAS 150, but with the postponement of certain aspects of the new standard, questions arose regarding disclosures needed to comply with SEC requirements.

These rules require securities with redemption features that are not solely within the control of the issuer to be classified outside of permanent equity. The SEC staff believes that all of the events that could trigger redemption should be evaluated separately and that the possibility that *any* triggering event that is not *solely* within the control of the issuer could occur—without regard to probability—would require the security to be classified outside of permanent equity. Determining whether an equity security is redeemable at the option of the holder or upon the occurrence of an event that is solely within the control of the issuer can be complex. Accordingly, all of the individual facts and circumstances should be considered in determining how an equity security should be classified.

D-98 offers several examples of complex fact patterns to help registrants in determining whether classification as a liability or as equity would be appropriate.

For example, if a preferred security has a redemption provision stating that it may be called by the issuer upon an affirmative vote by the majority of its board of directors, but the preferred security holders control a majority of the votes of the board of directors through direct representation on the board of directors or through other rights, the preferred security is effectively redeemable at the option of the holder and its classification outside of permanent equity is required. Thus, in assessing such situations, any provision that requires approval by the board of directors cannot be assumed to be within the control of the reporting entity itself. All of the relevant facts and circumstances would have to be considered.

As another example, if a security with a deemed liquidation clause that provides that the security becomes redeemable if the stockholders of the reporting entity (those immediately prior to a merger or consolidation) hold, immediately after such merger or consolidation, stock representing less than a majority of the voting power of the outstanding stock of the surviving corporation, this would not be permanent equity. A purchaser could acquire a majority of the voting power of the outstanding stock, without company approval, thereby triggering redemption.

Securities with provisions that allow the holders to be paid upon occurrence of events that are solely within the issuer's control should thus always be classified outside of permanent equity. Such events include

1. The failure to have a registration statement declared effective by the SEC by a designated date
2. The failure to maintain compliance with debt covenants
3. The failure to achieve specified earnings targets
4. A reduction in the issuer's credit rating

D-98 notes that if a reporting entity issues preferred shares that are conditionally redeemable (e.g., at the holder's option or upon the occurrence of an uncertain event not solely within the company's control), the shares are not within the scope of FAS 150 because there is no unconditional obligation to redeem the shares by transferring assets at a specified or determinable date or upon an event certain to occur. If the uncertain event occurs, the condition is resolved, or the event becomes certain to occur, then the shares become mandatorily redeemable under FAS 150 and would require reclassification to a liability. Under SEC rules, however, these shares cannot be included in permanent equity, and thus would be displayed as a "mezzanine" equity category. Note that mezzanine capital is an SEC reporting concept which has no analog under GAAP rules.

FAS 150 requires that the issuer measure that liability initially at fair value and reduce equity by the amount of that initial measure, recognizing no gain or loss. D-98 observes that this reclassification of shares to a liability is akin to the redemption of such shares by issuance of debt. Similar to the accounting for the redemption of preferred shares, to the extent that the fair value of the liability differs from the carrying amount of the preferred shares, upon reclassification that difference should be deducted from or added to net earnings available to common shareholders in the calculation of earnings per share.

### Obligations to Issue or Repurchase Shares

FAS 150 also requires that certain financial instruments that require an entity to purchase or issue its own equity shares be reported as liabilities. FAS 150 does not apply to financial instruments that are issued as contingent consideration in a business combination (Chapter 13) or obligations under stock-based compensation plans that are accounted for under FAS 123, APB 25, or SOP 93-6 (Chapter 19). It also does not apply to an embedded feature of a financial instrument unless that financial instrument is a derivative in its entirety.

Additional discussion and examples of FAS 150 are found in Chapter 19.

**Obligations to issue shares.** If an entity enters into a contract that requires it or permits it at its discretion to issue a variable number of shares upon settlement, that contract is recognized as a liability if at inception the monetary value of the obligation is based solely or predominantly on one of the following criteria:

1.  A fixed monetary amount known at inception (e.g., a $100,000 payable can be settled by issuing shares worth $100,000 at the then-current market value).
2.  An amount that varies based on something other than the fair value of the issuer's equity shares (for example, a financial instrument indexed to the Dow that can be settled by issuing shares worth the index-adjusted amount at the then-current market value).
3.  Variations inversely related to changes in the fair value of the entity's equity shares (i.e., a written put option that could be net share settled).

Contracts that meet one of the above criteria are recognized at fair value at the date of issuance and at every measurement date afterwards. The changes in the fair value are recognized in earnings unless the contract falls within the scope of FAS 133 and that statement requires the changes to be recognized elsewhere.

#### Example of a contract with a fixed monetary amount known at inception

Numero Uno Corp. purchases equipment worth $100,000 and agrees to pay $110,000 at the end of one year or, at its option, to issue shares worth $112,000. The contract is recognized as a liability at issuance of $100,000. Subsequent to issuance the liability is remeasured at the fair value of the contract, which would be the accreted value of the cash payment amount ($110,000).

**Obligations to repurchase shares.** If an entity (the issuer) enters into a contract that obligates it to transfer assets to either repurchase its own equity shares or to pay an amount that is indexed to the price of its own shares, the contract is to be reported as a liability (or in certain cases, as an asset, if the fair value of the contract is favorable to the issuer). Examples of that type of financial instrument are written put options on the option writer's (issuer's) equity shares, and forward contracts to repurchase an issuer's own equity shares if those instruments require physical or net cash settlement. (If the repurchase obligation is a redemption feature of common or preferred shares issued, see "Mandatorily Redeemable Shares" in this chapter.)

FAS 150 requires that an issuer classify a financial instrument that is within its scope as a liability (or as an asset in some circumstances) because that financial instrument embodies an obligation of the issuer. FAS 150 addresses three types of freestanding financial instruments that embody obligations of the issuer: mandatorily redeemable financial instruments, obligations to repurchase the issuer's equity shares by transferring assets, and certain obligations to issue a variable number of shares. Instruments within the scope of FAS 150 should be classified and measured in accordance with FAS 150 per EITF D-98.

Written put options are measured initially and subsequently at fair value. Forward contracts are initially measured at the fair value of the shares to be repurchased (adjusted by any consideration or unstated rights or privileges) if the contract requires physical settlement for cash. The offset to the liability entry is a debit to equity. Subsequent to issuance, forward contracts are remeasured in one of two ways.

1. If both the amount to be paid and the settlement date are fixed, the contract is measured at the present value of the amount to be paid, computed using the rate implicit in the contract at inception.
2. If either the amount to be paid or the settlement date varies based on specified conditions, the contract is measured at the amount of cash that would be paid under the conditions specified in the contract if settlement occurred at the reporting date.

Under either measure, the amount of the change from the previous reporting date is recognized as interest cost.

### Example of a written put option on a fixed number of shares

Numero Dos Corp. writes a put allowing the purchaser to sell 100 shares of Numero Dos common stock at $20 per share in six months. The purchaser pays Numero Dos $300 for the right to put the 100 shares. Numero Dos's common stock is currently trading at $23. Numero Dos reports a liability of $300. The liability is subsequently remeasured at the fair value of the put option.

### Example of a forward contract with a variable settlement date

Numero Tres Corp. enters into a contract to purchase 200 shares of its subsidiary at $25 in two years. However, if the holder of the shares dies before the settlement date, Numero Tres agrees to purchase the shares at the present value of $25 at the settlement date computed using the then-current prime rate. The shares are currently trading at $22. The liability to repurchase shares is initially reported at $4,400. At each subsequent measurement date, Numero Tres would adjust the liability to the present value of $25 at settlement date using the discount rate implicit in the contract, unless the holder of the shares had died. If the holder of the shares had died, Numero Tres would adjust the liability to the present value of $25 at settlement date using the then-current prime rate. For example, if one year from issuance date the holder is still alive, the liability would be adjusted to $4,690 using the 6.6% rate implicit in the agreement. The adjustment amount of $290 would be charged to interest expense. If instead the holder had died and the prime rate was 5%, the liability would be adjusted to $4,762 ($5,000/1.05) and the adjustment of $362 would be charged to interest expense.

An entity that has entered into a forward contract that requires physical settlement by repurchase of a fixed number of its equity shares of common stock in exchange for cash does not include those shares in the denominator when computing basic or diluted earnings per share. If any amounts, including contractual (accumulated) dividends, attributable to shares that are to be redeemed or repurchased have not been recognized as interest expense, those amounts are deducted in computing income available to common shareholders (the numerator of the calculation), consistently with the "two-class" method set forth in FAS 128 (Chapter 20).

FSP 150-3 postponed the effective date of certain provisions of FAS 150 and, for certain mandatory redemption arrangements of stock *issued* by nonpublic companies, indefinitely postponed implementation, pending the outcome of further FASB deliberations on a range of liability and equity issues. As of early 2008, this remains unresolved.

## Measuring Liabilities at Fair Value

Under GAAP, until extinguished, long-term debt is measured at the amount recorded at the date of issuance, reduced by payments made and adjusted for any amortization since issuance. This historical cost-based approach is not, however, universally viewed as contributing to the most meaningful financial reporting. In recent years, FASB has indicated its belief that more appropriate financial reporting would result if all financial liabilities (and assets) were reported at their respective fair values, rather than at amounts based on historical cost. Fair value of a liability is an estimated market exit price (as defined extensively in Chapter 6), that is, an estimate of the amount that would have been paid if the entity had settled the liability on the balance sheet date.

Many preparers and users of financial statements question the relevance of information about the fair value of a financial liability, given that management does not intend, and may not even be able, to settle the obligation before the stated maturity. In effect, the fair value amounts are purely hypothetical and do not alter the real obligation represented by the cost-based carrying amount of the liability at issue.

On the other hand, under the current reporting model it is entirely possible that an entity will report gains from debt extinguishment as a result of the early retirement of a debt obligation carrying a below-market interest rate, even if that extinguishment is funded by the immediate issuance of debt bearing the current market rate. Notwithstanding that the entity's real economic position has not been improved (and may have been diminished), a gain has been reported, which many would agree is misleading. The following example illustrates this problem.

### Example

Company A and Company B are competitors, they both are publicly held, and both have bonds outstanding. On December 31, 2009, Company A owes $2,000,000 due in 6 years that carries a fixed interest rate of 10%. Company B also owes $2,000,000 due in 6 years, but Company B issued its bonds in a less favorable interest rate environment. Its debt carries an interest rate of 14%. The two companies have equivalent credit ratings. The prevailing market interest rate for both companies changes to 12% on December 31, 2009. Under historical cost-based GAAP, each company will report $2,000,000 of outstanding debt in its statement of financial position dated December 31, 2009. The fair value of Company A's debt at that date is $1,835,500, while the fair value of Company B's debt is $2,164,500—both fair values computed at the present value of the interest and principal payments at the prevailing market rate of 12%.

If Company A paid off its bonds, it would recognize a gain of $164,500 ($2,000,000 – $1,835,500). But for Company A to recognize its gain, it would have had to repay debt that carried a favorable interest rate. Company A would lose its economically advantageous position of being a company with below-market financing. In addition, if Company A had not used $1,835,500 to repay the debt, it could have invested that amount in its own operations and perhaps earned a higher return. Moreover, if Company A continues to need financing, it will have to refinance at the higher current interest rate. Repurchasing its bonds might not have been the best way for Company A to invest its resources, and might have been motivated, in part, by the desire to manage reported earnings in 2009.

If Company B retired its bonds, it would recognize a loss of $164,500 ($2,000,000 – $2,164,500). As an alternative, Company B could leave its bonds outstanding and realize its loss by paying above-market rates during the remaining 6 years of their term. Depending on the available alternative uses of its money, repaying the bonds and relieving future operations of the burden of above-market interest payments may be the best use of its resources, but Company B would suffer a loss as a result—a loss that can be avoided simply by choosing to not repay its debt.

Company A's gain and Company B's loss would be caused by changes in interest rates—not by a decision to repay debt. The existing measurement model for liabilities sometimes provides an incentive for unwise actions. If Company A wanted to report a gain, it could pay off its debt, even though that might not have been the best use of its resources. If Company B wanted to avoid a loss, it could allow its bonds to remain outstanding, even though the best economic decision would have been to retire them.

The effects of financing decisions, including that of leaving existing financing in place, whether made actively or indirectly through inattention, can significantly impact entity performance. Investors and creditors need information that will help them evaluate the effects of an entity's decision to settle a liability or allow it to remain outstanding. From this perspective, it is logical that information based on prices that reflect the market's assessment, under current conditions, of the present values of the future cash flows embodied in an entity's financial instruments would be more relevant for investors' and creditors' decisions than information based on historic, superseded market prices. Those older market prices reflect both an old interest rate and an outdated assessment of the amounts, timing, and uncertainty of future cash flows.

The project to replace historical data about financial liabilities with fair value data continues to be very controversial. Among opponents are financial institutions that would have to reprice virtually the entire balance sheet at each reporting date and that might see a significant increase in periodic earnings volatility (albeit, reflecting economic reality). It is not clear whether FASB will be successful in changing this longstanding tradition of reporting essentially all financial liabilities at historical cost.

### Proposed Standards for Convertible Debt and Debt Issued with Warrants

FASB has proposed (as part of its *Liabilities and Equity* project, which was awaiting another round of comments through mid-2008) new standards for the issuers of convertible debt and other compound financial instruments. It believes that separate balance sheet presentation of liability components and equity components of a compound instrument more faithfully represents the rights and obligations embedded in that instrument than does presenting the instrument entirely as a liability or entirely as equity.

With certain exceptions, the proposed standard would require that proceeds received from the issuance of a compound financial instrument be allocated to its components based on the relative fair values of those components. Under a "relative-fair-value method," the fair value of each of the separately classified components is determined independently of the fair values of the other components. The proceeds of issuing the compound financial instrument are then allocated to the components on a pro rata basis.

If it is impracticable to apply the relative-fair-value method because the fair value of one of the components cannot be reliably determined, the proceeds would be allocated to the components by means of the "with-and-without method." Under that alternative method, the fair value of the compound financial instrument is compared to the fair value of a hypothetical financial instrument that contains all the same components except the specific component being valued. The value of the component or components that can be reliably measured is measured at its fair value determined as if it were freestanding. The value of the remaining component is the difference between the amount assigned to the component(s) that can be reliably measured and the proceeds of issuance of the compound financial instrument.

If a financial instrument contains a component that is a derivative, the proceeds of issuing that financial instrument would be allocated to its components using the with-and-without method, first allocating to the derivative component the amount of proceeds that would be equal to its fair value as if it were freestanding. That is, the value of the nonderivative component is the difference between the amount assigned to the derivative component and the proceeds of issuance of the compound financial instrument.

Because APB 14, which would be superseded by the proposed standards, required use of the relative-fair-value method for allocating the proceeds of debt issued with stock purchase warrants, no changes in accounting for those compound instruments are expected.

Certain financial instruments, in addition to containing a liability component, an equity component, or both, also contain a component that, freestanding, would be classified as an asset. An example of that type of financial instrument is callable convertible debt, which contains a call option, a debt, and a conversion option. Unless the asset component is required by GAAP to be separated (e.g., per FAS 133), the effect of the asset component would be incorporated into the determination of the fair values of the liability component and the equity component.

For purposes of initial measurement of the components of compound financial instruments, the following general rules would be applied under the proposed standard:

- If a compound financial instrument has no component that is an outstanding share of stock, the obligation that is classified as a liability would be considered an unconditional obligation, and the obligation that is classified as equity would be considered a conditional obligation.
- If a compound financial instrument has a component that is an outstanding share of stock (other than mandatorily redeemable stock), the instrument would be considered to be (1) an outstanding equity share and (2) a conditional obligation.

### Example comparing existing and proposed standards—issuance of convertible debt

An entity issues at par 10,000 noncallable bonds, for a total issue proceeds of $10,000,000. Each bond can be converted by the holder into 100 shares of the entity's $10 par common stock. The noncallable bonds contain the following components:

1. An obligation to repay principal
2. An obligation to pay interest periodically
3. An obligation to issue equity shares if the conversion option is exercised

The first two components are liabilities. The third component is an equity component because it requires the issuance of a fixed number of shares. Because none of the components are outstanding shares of stock, the liability components are unconditional. The fair value of comparable nonconvertible debt is $850; the fair value of the conversion feature is $150.

| *Entry upon issuance of the bonds* | *Proposed standards* | *Existing standards* |
|---|---|---|
| Cash | 10,000,000 | 10,000,000 |
| Discounts on bonds payable | 1,500,000 | |
| Bonds payable | 10,000,000 | 10,000,000 |
| Paid-in capital from conversion option | 1,500,000 | |

The discount on the bonds payable would be amortized over the life of the debt instrument using the effective interest method.

The proposed standard also provides guidance on the accounting for costs incurred to issue a financial instrument. Costs incurred to issue a financial instrument would be accounted for as a reduction of the proceeds of issuance before allocation of those proceeds to the components. Issuance costs are only the incremental costs directly attributable to issuance of an instrument that would not have been incurred if the instrument had not been issued.

It would also be required that a gain or loss, if any, on the liability component of convertible debt be recognized in earnings if the debt were extinguished by repayment or by conversion. That gain or loss would be calculated as the difference between the portion of the consideration paid (or in the case of conversion, the fair value of the compound convertible debt instrument at the date of conversion) that is attributed to the liability component and its carrying amount at the date it is extinguished. The amount of consideration or fair value that is attributed to the liability component would be determined using the relative-fair-value method unless the use of that method is impracticable, in which case the with-and-without method would be used.

### Example comparing existing and proposed standards—conversion of convertible debt

Assume that $50,000 face value of the bonds in the previous example are converted when the market price of the convertible bonds is $55,500, the market price of the common stock is $11 per share, and the unamortized discount on those bonds is $6,500. The fair value of comparable nonconvertible debt is $850 per bond; the fair value of the conversion feature is $250.

| | *Proposed* | *Existing standards using* | |
|---|---|---|---|
| *Entry upon conversion of the bonds* | *standards* | *Book value* | *Market value* |
| Bonds payable | 50,000 | 50,000 | 50,000 |
| Paid-in capital from conversion option | 7,114 | | |
| Loss on conversion shares | | | 12,000 |
|    Discount on bonds payable | 6,500 | | 6,500 |
|    Common stock | 50,000 | 50,000 | 50,000 |
|    Additional paid-in capital | | | 5,500 |
|    Gain on conversion of shares | 614 | | |

The gain on conversion under the proposed standards is the difference between the fair value of the liability component on the date of conversion and the carrying value of the liability component. The fair value of the liability component is computed as follows:

$$\$850/(\$850 + \$250) \times \$55,500 = \$42,886$$

The book value of the liability component is $50,000 − $6,500 = $43,500. The gain is $614. The proceeds from issuing the common shares are $50,386, which is the $7,500 from issuance plus the $42,886 value of the liability component surrendered. Those proceeds are recorded in the common stock account ($50,000) and paid-in capital from conversion option ($386, which is the $7,500 initially recorded less the adjustment of $7,114 at the time of conversion).

The proposal discussed above was to have been adopted years ago, but a number of contentious issues remain unresolved as of mid-2008. Accordingly, it is not possible to predict when, or even if, this standard will be adopted. For more information about this proposed standard, see Chapter 19.

# 16 LEASES

## PERSPECTIVE AND ISSUES

### Introductory Discussion

Lease transactions became enormously popular over the years as businesses sought new ways to finance long-lived assets. Leasing offered two attractive advantages: (typically) 100% financing, coupled with (very often) off-the-books obligations. As of 2005, the Securities and Exchange Commission had estimated that, collectively for all publicly held companies, there were approximately $1.3 trillion of off-balance-sheet lease obligations outstanding. FASB is continuing, as of mid-2008, its reexamination of lease accounting and is now anticipating a preliminary views document to be issued in early 2009. FASB, together with the international standard-setting body, IASB, well may decree that all, or nearly all leases (e.g., those over one year in duration) be reported on the balance sheet—as capital leases are under FAS 13 and associated literature today. If this happens, there may well be a significant impact on the leasing industry.

While favorable financial reporting effects certainly stimulated interest in leasing, there are several economic reasons why the lease transaction is considered a viable alternative to outright purchase. These would likely remain strong motivations even if lease accounting rules were to be revised.

1. The lessee (borrower) is frequently able to obtain 100% financing.
2. Income tax benefits may be available to one or both of the parties.
3. The lessor receives the equivalent of interest as well as an asset with some remaining residual value at the end of the lease term.
4. In some cases, equipment or other assets are not available for outright purchase.

A lease agreement involves at least two parties, a lessor and a lessee, and an asset that is to be leased. The lessor, the party that either owns or commits to purchase the asset, agrees to grant the lessee the right to use it for a specified period of time in return for periodic rent payments.

The lease transaction derives its accounting complexity from the number of alternatives available to the parties involved. Leases can be structured to allow differing assignments of income tax benefits associated with the leased asset to meet the objectives of the transacting parties. Leases can be used to transfer ownership of the leased asset, and they can be used to transfer the risks and rewards of ownership. In any event, the substance of the transaction dictates, with certain exceptions, the accounting treatment, irrespective of its legal form. The lease transaction is probably the best example of the accounting profession's substance-over-form argument. If the transaction effectively transfers the risks and rewards of ownership to the lessee, then the substance of the transaction is that of a sale and, accordingly, it is recognized as such for accounting purposes even though the transaction is legally structured as a lease.

FAS 13 first set forth current GAAP for lease accounting over thirty years ago, and its release was followed by numerous pronouncements that interpreted and expanded upon it, which reveals the complexity of the topic. As a result of the extensive additions to the principles related to lease accounting, and the number and extent of changes made to the original pronouncement, it is cumbersome, if not impossible, to research a lease accounting issue by attempting to use the original pronouncements and the amendments thereto. The task of ascertaining the proper accounting for any given fact situation will be hopefully eased by the recently completed FASB codification, which is undergoing field testing as of mid-2008 (see discussion in Chapter 1).

**Variable interest entities.** Notwithstanding the operating-financing dichotomy established by FAS 13, there later developed the practice of using nonsubstantive lessors (which often were related entities) to assist in keeping leases off the balance sheet of lessees. These entities were frequently used to exclude liabilities from the lessee's consolidated balance sheet in order to more favorably portray the lessee's financial condition. An early EITF consensus, Issue 90-15, attempted to deal with nonsubstantive lessors by requiring consolidation in the financial statements of the lessee entity, but for various reasons this did not fully close what appeared to be a loophole in the existing rules. In January 2003, FASB issued FIN 46, *Consolidation of Variable Interest Entities,* which was closely followed by the issuance of a series of interpretive FASB Staff Positions (FSP), the effect of which was to require consolidation of many such lessors. In December 2003, this was replaced by FIN 46(R), which attempted to remediate much of the confusion created by the original interpretation. (A comprehensive discussion of variable interest entities and FIN 46(R) is included in Chapter 13.) Under the provisions of FIN 46(R), many more lessor entities are required to be consolidated with the financial statements of the lessee, especially in situations where the lessor and lessee have common or related-party ownership.

It is necessary for the lessee to first apply FIN 46(R) to evaluate its relationship with the lessor and, in that respect, FIN 46(R) takes precedence over FAS 13 and its many modifications. This is because if FIN 46(R) requires the lessee to consolidate the lessor, the effects of the lease transaction between the parties will be removed from the consolidated financial statements via an eliminating entry and, consequently, the consolidated reporting entity will depreciate the leased asset and reflect all of the costs of acquiring, holding, maintaining, and disposing of the asset. This makes the issue of distinguishing between operating and financial leases moot for any leases between a VIE and its primary beneficiary.

The lessor will, of course, in any separately issued financial statements, account for the lease in accordance with the appropriate lease accounting requirements that would apply absent FIN 46(R). Certain concepts and definitions discussed herein are also explained in Chapter 13 but are repeated and expanded upon here for completeness and further clarification in the context of lease transactions.

## Recent Developments

**Lease accounting restatements.** Responding to a request from the AICPA's Center for Public Company Audit Firms (CPCAF), in early 2005 the SEC Chief Accountant set forth the staff's views ("the SEC Letter") pertaining to the following issues:

1. The life over which to amortize leasehold improvements,
2. Accounting for periods for which, under the lease, no rental payments are due (referred to as "rent holidays"), and
3. Accounting for landlord/tenant incentives.

Following the release of the SEC Letter (available at www.sec.gov) more than 300 public companies announced restatements related to lease accounting corrections. In addition to the public embarrassment caused by the restatements, these also necessitated acknowledgements by the entities of material weaknesses in their internal controls over their financial reporting processes, in accordance with requirements established by the Sarbanes-Oxley Act of 2002. This put lease accounting in the same category as revenue recognition, stock option accounting, and accruals for restructurings and other contingencies, in terms of being associated with error corrections and acknowledged control weaknesses.

As with all SEC staff interpretations, the SEC Letter only purported to interpret GAAP that was already established, not imposing new requirements. As such, the SEC's views should be deemed equally applicable to publicly held and closely held businesses, as well as to not-for-profit organizations. This leads to the inescapable conclusion that similar instances of failure to adhere to GAAP exist within the financial statements of non-SEC registrants, some fraction of which may have not yet have been dealt with by preparers and auditors of those entities.

The required accounting for the issues described in the SEC Letter follows:

1. Leasehold improvements made by a lessee to property it leases under an operating lease are to be amortized over the shorter of their useful lives or the terms of the respective leases. The lease terms used for this purpose are the initial terms of the leases plus any renewal periods for which renewal has been determined to be rea-

sonably assured, as defined by FAS 13, as amended. Leasehold improvements cannot be amortized over longer terms. Leasehold improvements are discussed in detail in Chapter 11.

2.  Rent holidays, which are periods during which no rent is due under an operating lease, typically offered as an inducement for signing a new lease, are to bear a portion of the cost of the operating lease by ratably charging the minimum lease payments under the lease obligation to all periods that are covered by the lease including the holiday period. This is normally done using the straight-line method of allocation, unless another method more accurately represents the time pattern in which the leased property is used. Rent holiday periods cannot be made to appear as not incurring rent expense.

3.  Incentive or allowance payments made by a lessor to a lessee to help fund leasehold improvements are not permitted to be netted against the cost of the leasehold improvements in the lessee's financial statements. Instead, the leasehold improvements are to be recorded gross and amortized as described in issue 1. above. The incentive payment is to be recorded as deferred rent and amortized as reductions to rent expense over the term of the lease. In the lessee's statement of cash flows, the incentive payments are to be classified as cash provided by operating activities and the acquisition of the leasehold improvements is to be classified as cash used for investing activities.

**SEC staff report on off-balance-sheet arrangements.** In mid-2005, the SEC issued its *Report and Recommendations Pursuant to Section 401(c) of the Sarbanes-Oxley Act of 2002 on Arrangements with Off-Balance-Sheet Implications, Special-Purpose Entities, and Transparency of Filings by Issuers* (the "Report"). The Report makes many important recommendations regarding the improvement of US GAAP including standards regarding lease accounting. The Report criticizes the current rules' extensive reliance on bright line tests that it says, for a lessee, "...the accounting can flip between recording no assets and liabilities at lease inception to recording the entire leased asset and entire loan price with only a very small change in economics." The Report urged FASB to undertake a joint project with the International Accounting Standards Board (IASB) to reconsider the accounting for leases. While acknowledging that such a project would be controversial, lengthy and expensive, the Report expressed the SEC staff's belief such a project would be justified by the potential benefits.

**FASB and IASB lease accounting projects.** In mid-2006, FASB announced that it was adding a project to its agenda to reconsider the accounting for leases, and that the project would be conducted jointly with the IASB. The Boards have since tentatively concluded that a "right-of-use" model would be appropriate for recognizing the rights and obligations inherent in a typical noncancelable lease arrangement. This model may also be extended to other arrangements that convey rights to use other entities' assets. A right to use is seen as being generically distinct from both intangible assets and tangible assets similar to the leased item. If this model were adopted, the lessee would recognize an asset representing its right to use the leased property during the lease term and a corresponding liability for its noncancelable obligation to make the lease payments. The lessee, as is currently the case, could also be required to recognize an asset retirement obligation and/or an obligation arising out of a contractual requirement contained in the lease that the leased property be returned to the lessor in a specified condition at the end of the lease term. Questions to be resolved include which initial and subsequent measurements are to be applicable to the right to use, as well as the accounting for options to either extend the lease or cancel it, and for other corollary obligations by the lessee, such as to return the leased property in specified condition and to maintain the property during use.

The lessor would recognize assets for its right to receive payments from the lessee and its interest in the residual value of the leased property at the end of the lease term.

These tentative conclusions have not been fully deliberated and, until they have been exposed for public comment and subject to the Boards' normal due process procedures, they could change substantially. A preliminary views document is now promised for early 2009.

| | | Sources of GAAP | | |
|---|---|---|---|---|
| *FAS* | *FIN* | *FTB* | *EITF* | *FSP* |
| 13, 22, 23, 27, 28, | 19, 21, 23, 24, | 79-10, 79-12, | 85-16, 86-17, | FAS 13-1, |
| 29, 66, 77, 91, 98, | 26, 27, 43, 45, | 79-13, 79-14, | 86-33, 87-7, | FAS 13-2, |
| 140, 141(R), 143, | 46(R), 48 | 79-15, 79-16, | 87-8, 88-21, | FAS 157-1, |
| 144, 145, 146, | | 82-1, 86-2, 88-1 | 89-16, 89-20, | FIN 46(R)-1, |
| 157, 160 | | | 90-14, 90-20, | FIN 46(R)-2, |
| | | | 92-1, 93-8, | FIN 46(R)-3, |
| | | | 95-1, | FIN 46(R)-4, |
| | | | 95-4, 95-17, | FIN 46(R)-5, |
| | | | 96-21, 97-1, | FIN 46(R)-6, |
| | | | 97-10, 98-9, | FIN 46(R)-7 |
| | | | 99-13, | |
| | | | 00-11, 00-13, | |
| | | | 01-8, 03-12, | |
| | | | D-8, D-24, | |
| | | | D-107 | |

## DEFINITIONS OF TERMS

**Bargain purchase option.** A provision allowing the lessee the option of purchasing the leased property for an amount, exclusive of lease payments, which is sufficiently lower than the expected fair value of the property at the date the option becomes exercisable. Exercise of the option must appear reasonably assured at the inception of the lease. GAAP does not offer additional guidance defining "sufficiently lower," in which many factors such as the time value of money, usage, and technological changes influence whether the option fulfills the criteria for a bargain.

**Bargain renewal option.** A provision allowing the lessee the option to renew the lease agreement for a rental payment sufficiently lower than the expected fair rental of the property at the date the option becomes exercisable. Exercise of the option must appear reasonably assured at the inception of the lease.

**Contingent rentals.** Rentals that represent the increases or decreases in lease payments that result from changes in the factors on which the lease payments are based occurring subsequent to the inception of the lease. However, changes due to the pass-through of increases in the construction or acquisition cost of the leased property or for increases in some measure of cost during the construction or preconstruction period are excluded from contingent rentals. Also, provisions that are dependent only upon the passage of time are excluded from contingent rentals. A lease payment that is based upon an existing index or rate, such as the consumer price index or the prime rate, is a contingent payment, and the computation of the minimum lease payments is based upon the index or rate applicable at the inception of the lease.

**Controlling financial interest.** The at-risk equity investors hold a controlling financial interest in an entity if they collectively

1. Have voting or similar rights (such as the rights of a common stockholder or general partner, or LLC member) to make decisions, directly or indirectly, about the entity's activities that significantly affect the entity's success.

*NOTE: If none of the investors hold these rights this criterion is not satisfied. In addition, if some investors' voting rights are not proportional to their obligations to absorb the entity's expected losses, or to receive the entity's expected residual rewards, or both, and substantially all of the entity's activities involve or are conducted on behalf of an investor that has disproportionately few voting rights, this criterion is not satisfied.*

2. Are obligated to absorb the entity's expected losses. If the investors are directly or indirectly protected from these losses or guaranteed a return by the entity (or by other parties involved with the entity) this criterion is not satisfied.
3. Are entitled to receive the entity's expected residual returns. If the investors' return is limited by (a) the entity's governing documents, (b) arrangements with other variable interest holders (e.g., holders of debt, beneficial interests, etc.), or (c) with the entity itself, this criterion is not satisfied.

If any one of these three criteria is absent, the at-risk equity investors collectively lack a controlling financial interest and, therefore, only have a controlling voting interest. The controlling financial interest, in this case, would be held collectively by the variable interest holders.

**Estimated economic life of leased property.** At the inception of the lease, the estimated remaining time, with normal maintenance and repairs, that the property is expected to be economically usable for its intended purpose by one or more users. The economic life will be affected by such factors as technological changes, normal deterioration, and physical usage. Judgments regarding these matters are influenced by knowledge gained from previous experience. The estimated time period is not limited by the lease term.

**Estimated residual value of leased property.** The estimated fair value of the leased property at the end of the lease term.

**Equity investment.** An interest in an entity that under GAAP is reportable as equity on the entity's balance sheet. The practical application of this definition to certain types of instruments (e.g., mandatorily redeemable preferred stock) has been affected by the issuance in May 2003 of FAS 150, *Accounting for Certain Financial Instruments with Characteristics of Both Liabilities and Equity*, and the subsequent partial deferral of certain of its provisions by FSP FAS 150-3.

**Executory costs.** Those costs such as insurance, maintenance, and real estate taxes incurred for the leased property, whether paid by the lessor or lessee. Amounts paid by a lessee as consideration for a guarantee from an unrelated third party of the residual value are also considered executory costs. If executory costs are paid by the lessor, any lessor's profit on those costs is considered in the same manner as the actual executory costs.

**Expected losses and expected residual returns.** Expected losses represent the expected negative variability in the fair value of an enterprise's net assets exclusive of variable interests. Expected residual returns represent the expected positive variability in the fair value of an enterprise's net assets exclusive of variable interests. The expected variability (separately defined below and illustrated in this chapter and Chapter 13) in an enterprise's net income or loss is included in the determination of expected losses and expected residual returns.

**Expected variability.** When estimating an entity's expected future cash flows in accordance with CON 7, *Using Cash Flow Information and Present Value in Accounting Measurements* (discussed more fully in Chapter 1), a range of probability-weighted expected outcomes is computed and discounted to present value. Mathematically, this is simply a weighted-average calculation. The expected variability of the cash flows included in that calculation is computed by: (1) computing the difference between each individual estimated outcome and the weighted-average, (2) multiplying each difference computed in the previous step by the probability of occurrence assigned to that individual outcome, and (3) separately summing the positive (favorable) variations (expected residual returns) and negative (unfavorable) variations (expected losses). The absolute value of the sum of the expected residual returns will always equal the absolute value of the sum of the expected losses. The sum of the absolute values of the expected residual returns and the expected losses represents the expected variability in both directions associated with that estimate of discounted probability-weighted expected cash flows.

**Fair value of leased property.** The price that would be received to sell the property in an orderly transaction on the measurement date between market participants that are not related parties.

When the lessor is a manufacturer or dealer, the fair value of the property at the inception of the lease will ordinarily be its normal selling price net of volume or trade discounts. In some cases, due to market conditions, fair value may be less than the normal selling price or even the cost of the property.

When the lessor is not a manufacturer or dealer, the fair value of the property at the inception of the lease will ordinarily be its cost net of volume or trade discounts. However, if a significant amount of time elapses between the acquisition of the property by the lessor and the inception of the lease, fair value is determined in light of market conditions prevailing at the inception of the lease. Thus, fair value may be greater or less than the cost or carrying amount of the property.

Fair value determinations made for lease classification or measurement purposes are to be performed as defined by FAS 13, not as later set forth by FAS 157, other than as pertains to business combinations accounted for under FAS 141(R). For acquisition accounting applications, FAS 157 is the relevant guidance to be followed.

**Implicit interest rate.** The discount rate that, when applied to the minimum lease payments, excluding that portion of the payments representing executory costs to be paid by the lessor, together with any profit thereon, and the unguaranteed residual value accruing to the benefit of the lessor, causes the aggregate present value at the beginning of the lease term to be equal to the fair value of the leased property to the lessor at the inception of the lease, minus any investment tax credit retained and expected to be realized by the lessor (and plus initial direct costs in the case of direct financing leases).

**Inception of the lease.** The date of the written lease agreement or commitment (if earlier) wherein all principal provisions are fixed and no principal provisions remain to be negotiated.

**Incremental borrowing rate.** The rate that, at the inception of the lease, the lessee would have incurred to borrow over a similar term (i.e., a loan term equal to the lease term) the funds necessary to purchase the leased asset.

**Initial direct costs.**[1] Only those costs incurred by the lessor that are (1) costs to originate a lease incurred in transactions with independent third parties that (a) result directly from and are essential to acquire that lease and (b) would not have been incurred had that leasing transaction not occurred and (2) certain costs directly related to specified activities performed by the lessor for that lease. Those activities are: evaluating the prospective lessee's financial condition; evaluating and recording guarantees, collateral, and other security arrangements; negotiating lease terms; preparing and processing lease documents; and closing the transaction. The costs directly related to those activities include only that portion of

---

[1] *Initial direct costs are offset by nonrefundable fees that are yield adjustments as prescribed in FAS 91, **Accounting for Nonrefundable Fees and Costs Associated with Originating or Acquiring Loans and Initial Direct Costs of Leases**.*

the employees' total compensation and payroll-related fringe benefits directly related to time spent performing those activities for that lease and other costs related to those activities that would not have been incurred but for that lease. Initial direct costs do not include costs related to activities performed by the lessor for advertising, soliciting potential lessees, servicing existing leases, and other ancillary activities related to establishing and monitoring credit policies, supervision, and administration. Initial direct costs do not include administrative costs, rent, depreciation, any other occupancy and equipment costs and employees' compensation and fringe benefits related to activities described in the previous sentence, unsuccessful origination efforts, and idle time.

**Investment company.** A separate legal entity whose business purpose and activities consist of investing in multiple substantive investments pursuant to investment plans that include exit strategies and that expects to obtain from those investments current income, capital appreciation, or both. Consequently, an investment company does not acquire or hold investments for strategic operating purposes. To be considered an investment company, an investor cannot be entitled to receive benefits from its investments that would not be available to other noninvestor entities that are not related parties of the investee. (SOP 07-1).

**Investment tax credit (ITC).** The ITC was an income tax incentive that the US Congress enacted and repealed several times between 1962 and 1986. The ITC resulted in a direct reduction of the taxpayer's income tax that would have been otherwise payable and was computed by multiplying the eligible, tangible long-lived assets placed in service during the tax year by a statutory percentage. The credit was initially enacted in 1962, with the stated goal of providing an incentive to businesses to acquire machinery and equipment in order to raise productivity, maintain the level of employment, and alleviate a serious balance of payments problem that existed at the time. The credit was repealed in 1986 and has not reappeared since that time; however, it is discussed at length in the current GAAP lease literature (that originated with FAS 13 in November 1976) because it was an important economic factor in the terms of many leases initiated at that time. The authors have retained in this chapter the discussion regarding the applicability of ITC to leasing transactions given the fact that, over time, the credit has been enacted, repealed and reinstated several times, and could be a model for future capital investment tax incentives.

**Lease.** An agreement conveying the right to use property, plant, or equipment (land or depreciable assets or both) usually for a stated period of time.

**Lease term.** The fixed noncancelable term of the lease plus the following:

1. Periods covered by bargain renewal options
2. Periods for which failure to renew the lease imposes a penalty on the lessee in an amount such that renewal appears, at the inception of the lease, to be reasonably assured
3. Periods covered by ordinary renewal options during which a guarantee by the lessee of the lessor's debt directly or indirectly related to the leased property is expected to be in effect or a loan from the lessee to the lessor directly or indirectly related to the leased property is expected to be outstanding
4. Periods covered by ordinary renewal options preceding the date that a bargain purchase option is exercisable
5. Periods representing renewals or extensions of the lease at the lessor's option

However, the lease term does not extend beyond the date a bargain purchase option becomes exercisable or beyond the useful life of the leased asset.

**Minimum lease payments.** For the lessee: The payments that the lessee is or can be required to make in connection with the leased property. Contingent rental guarantees by the lessee of the lessor's debt, and the lessee's obligation to pay executory costs are excluded from minimum lease payments. Additionally, if a portion of the minimum lease payments (MLP) representing executory costs is not determinable from the provisions of the lease, an estimate of executory costs is excluded from the calculation of the minimum lease payments. If the lease contains a bargain purchase option, only the minimum rental payments over the lease term and the payment called for in the bargain purchase option are included in minimum lease payments. Otherwise, minimum lease payments include the following:

1. The minimum rental payments called for by the lease over the lease term
2. Any guarantee of residual value at the expiration of the lease term made by the lessee (or any party related to the lessee), whether or not the guarantee payment constitutes a purchase of the leased property. When the lessor has the right to require the lessee to purchase the property at termination of the lease for a certain or determinable amount, that amount is considered a lessee guarantee. When the lessee agrees to make up any deficiency below a stated amount in the lessor's realization of the residual value, the guarantee to be included in the MLP is the stated amount rather than an estimate of the deficiency to be made up. FIN 19 provides additional guidance regarding residual guarantees, as follows:

   a. Lease provisions requiring the lessee to reimburse the lessor for residual value deficiencies due to damage, extraordinary wear and tear, or excessive usage are analogous to contingent rentals since, at the inception of the lease, the amount of the deficiency is not determinable. Therefore, these payments are not included in the MLP as residual value guarantees.
   b. Some leases contain provisions limiting the lessee's obligation to reimburse the lessor for residual value deficiencies to an amount less than the stipulated residual value of the leased property at the end of the lease term. In computing the MLP associated with these leases, the amount of the lessee's guarantee is limited to the specified maximum deficiency the lessee can be required to reimburse to the lessor.
   c. A lessee may contract with an unrelated third party to guarantee the residual for the benefit of the lessor. The MLP can only be reduced by the third party guarantee to the extent that the lessor explicitly releases the lessee from the obligation to make up the deficiency, even if the guarantor defaults. Amounts paid by the lessee to the guarantor are executory costs and are not included in the MLP, and

3. Any payment that the lessee must or can be required to make upon failure to renew or extend the lease at the expiration of the lease term, whether or not the payment would constitute a purchase of the leased property

For the lessor: The payments described above plus any guarantee of the residual value or of the rental payments beyond the lease term by a third party unrelated to either the lessee or lessor (provided the third party is financially capable of discharging the guaranteed obligation).

Noncancelable in this context means that a lease is cancelable only if one of the following conditions is satisfied:

1. The occurrence of some remote contingency
2. The permission of the lessor
3. The lessee enters into a new lease with the same lessor
4. Payment by the lessee of a penalty in an amount such that continuation of the lease appears, at inception, reasonably assured

**Nonrecourse financing.** Lending or borrowing activities in which, in the event of default, the collateral available to the creditor is limited to certain assets specifically agreed to in the loan agreement and does not include the general assets of the debtor.

**Penalty.** Any requirement that is imposed or can be imposed on the lessee by the lease agreement or by factors outside the lease agreement to pay cash, incur or assume a liability, perform services, surrender or transfer an asset or rights to an asset or otherwise forego an economic benefit, or suffer an economic detriment.

**Primary beneficiary.** A variable interest holder that is required to consolidate a variable interest entity (VIE). Consolidation is required when the holder of one or more variable interests would absorb a majority of the VIE's expected losses, receive a majority of the VIE's expected residual returns, or both. If one holder would absorb a majority of the VIE's expected losses and another holder would receive a majority of the VIE's expected residual returns, the holder absorbing the majority of the expected losses is the primary beneficiary and is thus required to consolidate the VIE.

**Profit recognition.** Any method to record a transaction involving real estate, other than the deposit method, or the methods to record transactions accounted for as financing, leasing, or profit-sharing arrangements. Profit recognition methods commonly used to record transactions involving real estate include, but are not limited to, the full accrual method, the installment method, the cost recovery method, and the reduced profit method.

**Related parties.** Entities that are in a relationship where one party has the ability to exercise significant influence over the operating and financial policies of the related party. Examples include the following:

1. A parent company and its subsidiaries
2. An owner company and its joint ventures and partnerships
3. An investor and its investees

The ability to exercise significant influence must be present before the parties can be considered related. Significant influence may also be exercised through guarantees of indebtedness, extensions of credit, or through ownership of debt obligations, warrants, or other securities. If two or more entities are subject to the significant influence of a parent, owner, investor, or common officers or directors, then those entities are considered related to each other.

**Related parties and de facto principals and agents.** In determining whether a holder of an interest in a variable interest entity is the VIE's primary beneficiary, the holder and its related parties are treated collectively as a single party. For this purpose, FIN 46(R) expands the definition of related parties from FAS 57 to include additional parties that act as "de facto agents or principals" of the variable interest holder including

1. A party unable to finance its operations without receiving subordinated financial support from the VIE interest holder such as another VIE of which the holder is the primary beneficiary
2. A party that received its interests in the VIE as a contribution or loan from the holder
3. An officer, employee, or member of the governing board of the holder
4. A party that has agreed not to sell, transfer, or encumber its interest in the VIE without prior approval of the holder when that agreement could constrain the party's ability to manage the economic risks or realize the economic rewards with respect to its interests in the VIE to which it would otherwise be entitled
5. A party with a close business relationship to the holder such as the relationship between a professional service provider (e.g., attorney, accountant, banker, consultant, etc.) and one of its significant clients

Upon the application of this related-party attribution rule, if two or more related parties (including de facto agents or principals) hold variable interests in the same VIE for which the parties collectively would be the primary beneficiary, a determination is required of which party will individually be considered the primary beneficiary (i.e., will consolidate the VIE in its financial statements). The party whose activities are most closely associated with the VIE is deemed to be the primary beneficiary. Among the factors that are to be considered when making this determination are

1. The existence of principal/agency relationships between members of the related-party group
2. The significance of the VIE's activities to the members of the related-party group
3. The relationship of the members of the related-party group to the VIE's activities
4. The exposure of a member of the related-party group to the VIE's expected losses
5. The design (structure) of the VIE

**Renewal or extension of a lease.** The continuation of a lease agreement beyond the original lease term, including a new lease where the lessee continues to use the same property.

**Rent holiday.** A contractual period of time set forth in a lease, during which the lessee is not obligated to pay rent to the lessor, most commonly the first month(s) under the lease.

**Sale-leaseback accounting.** A method of accounting for a sale-leaseback transaction in which the seller-lessee records the sale, removes all property and related liabilities from its balance sheet, recognizes gain or loss from the sale, and classifies the leaseback in accordance with this section.

**Total at-risk investment.** The following criteria are set forth in FIN 46(R) for determining the total at-risk equity investment in an entity:

1. Include only equity investments that participate significantly in profits and losses, even if the investments have no voting rights.
2. Exclude equity interests issued by the entity in exchange for subordinated interests in other variable interest entities.
3. Exclude amounts provided to the equity investor (e.g., fees, charitable contributions, or other payments) directly or indirectly by the entity or other parties involved with the entity unless the provider is a parent, subsidiary, or affiliate of the investor that is required to be included in the same set of consolidated financial statements as the investor.
4. Exclude amounts financed for the equity investor (e.g., by loans or guarantees of loans) directly by the entity or by other parties involved with the entity, unless the party is a parent, subsidiary, or affiliate of the investor that is required to be included in the same set of consolidated financial statements as the investor.

It is a rebuttable presumption that an equity investment of less than 10% of an entity's total assets is insufficient to permit the entity to finance its activities without additional subordinated financial support. In order to overcome this presumption, one or more of the following conditions must be present:

1. Performance—The entity has demonstrated that it can finance its activities without additional subordinated financial support.
2. Comparability—The entity's invested equity is at least as much as other entities holding similar assets of similar quality in similar amounts and who operate without additional subordinated financial support.
3. Reasonable forecast—Based on reasonable quantitative evidence, the entity's invested equity exceeds the estimate of the entity's expected losses.

This 10% threshold was intended by FASB to apply only in one direction (i.e., a less-than 10% investment is considered insufficient but a 10% or more investment is not necessarily presumed to be sufficient). Many entities engaged in high-risk activities, holding high-risk assets, or carrying significant off-balance-sheet exposures require more than 10% equity investment in order to finance their activities. Consequently, irrespective of the 10% threshold, an evaluation must be done to determine whether a particular entity with which the enterprise is involved requires an equity investment of 10% or greater in order to finance its activities without additional subordinated financial support.

**Unguaranteed residual value.** The estimated residual value of the leased property exclusive of any portion guaranteed by the lessee, by any party related to the lessee, or any party unrelated to the lessee. If the guarantor is related to the lessor, the residual value is considered unguaranteed.

**Unrelated parties.** All parties that are not related parties as defined above.

**Variable interest.** Ownership, contractual, or other monetary interests in an entity that are either entitled to received expected favorable variability ("expected residual returns") or obligated to absorb expected unfavorable variability ("expected losses").

**Variable interest entity (VIE).** An entity financially controlled by parties that are not its majority voting owners. Financial control is evidenced by a controlling party being exposed to the majority of the financial risks associated with the VIE performing worse than expected, *or* being entitled to the majority of the rewards associated with the VIE performing better than expected. This situation arises either because (1) the entity's at-risk equity is insufficient to absorb its expected losses *or* (2) because the entity's at-risk equity holders do not meet all three criteria necessary to be considered to possess a controlling financial interest in the entity.

## CONCEPTS, RULES, AND EXAMPLES

### Variable Interest Entities

The complex and evolving rules for lease accounting from the standpoint of the lessee and of the lessor are set forth in this chapter. From the standpoint of the lessee, it is critical for the accountant to first determine whether the relationship between the entities requires consolidation as a variable interest entity (VIE) under FIN 46(R), which is discussed in detail in Chapter 13. If consolidation is required, the effects of the lease recorded by the parties will be eliminated in the consolidated financial statements and the lease accounting will, in effect, be moot from the standpoint of the lessee.

In essence, a VIE is an entity that, by design, is not funded with an amount of at-risk equity sufficient to enable it to sustain itself in the face of reasonably possible losses without obtaining additional support (*"subordinated financial support"*) from existing or additional sources. In practical terms, in the context of leasing, the lessee is at risk for an amount greater than the contractual rental payments—such as for the lessor's debt arising from financing the leased property.

Determination of whether an entity is a VIE involves analysis of the individual facts, circumstances, relationships, structures, risks, and rewards associated with the entity and the parties with whom it is involved. Often, especially when related parties are involved, this analysis can be performed qualitatively without laborious numeric estimates of expected variability. That is because even a superficial review of the relationships and transaction details will reveal that the entity in question is indeed a VIE, or that it clearly is not one.

In more complex situations, however, or when qualitative analysis does not yield a conclusive answer, the holder of one or more variable interests may be required to estimate the present value of the probability-weighted expected cash flows associated with the entity in order to determine the expected variability of the entity's future cash flows as well as the portion of that expected variability that is allocable to the various holders of variable interests.

**Decision diagrams.** The following decision diagrams are used to discuss the illustrative examples of leasing transactions presented in this chapter.

### APPLYING FASB INTERPRETATION 46(R)

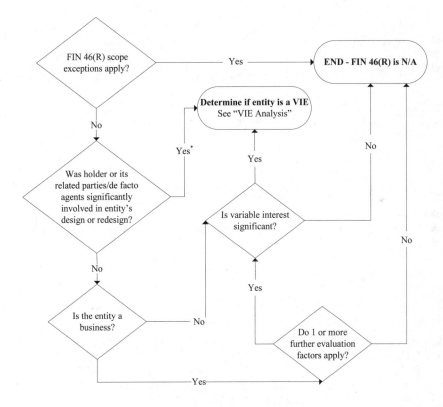

---

\* *This factor is not considered when the entity is an operating joint venture jointly controlled by the variable interest holder, and either an independent party or a franchisee. De facto agents, for this purpose, exclude parties that require the variable interest holder's prior approval to sell, transfer, or encumber their interest in the entity.*

**VIE ANALYSIS**

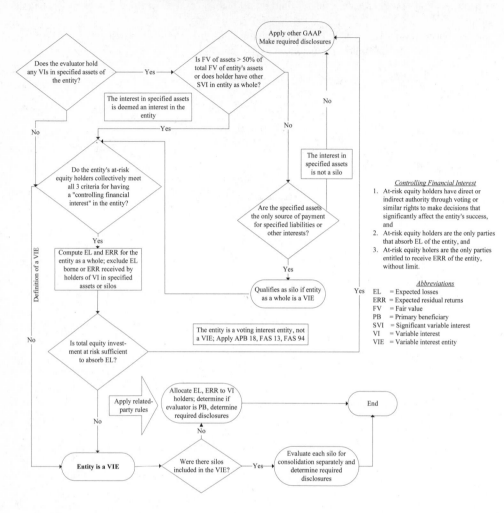

**Entities excluded from the scope of FIN 46(R).** The following scope exceptions are specified in FIN 46(R), as amended by FSP FIN 46(R)-7:

1.  Not-for-profit organizations as defined by FAS 117, para. 168, unless the organization was organized to avoid VIE status
2.  Employer/sponsors of employee benefit plans including ESOP, pension, profit sharing, 401(k), postretirement, and postemployment plans
3.  Separate accounts of life insurance entities
4.  A "qualifying special-purpose entity" (QSPE) or a "formerly qualifying SPE" (FQSPE) under the provisions of FAS 140, *Accounting for Transfers and Servicing of Financial Assets and Extinguishments of Liabilities,* are not to be consolidated by entities and their affiliates who transfer financial assets to them. Note that the entire subject of QSPE accounting is likely to be reexamined and may well be revised by FASB as early as 2009, potentially limiting or eliminating this exemption.

5. Enterprises holding variable interests in a QSPE or FQSPE are not to consolidate that entity unless the holder has the unilateral ability to cause the entity's liquidation or change the entity so that it ceases to meet the conditions set forth by FAS 140 to be considered a QSPE or FQSPE

6. A governmental organization

7. A nongovernmental financing entity established by a governmental organization unless the financing entity is being used to circumvent FIN 46(R) to avoid consolidation

8. An entity created prior to December 31, 2003, for which, after expending "exhaustive efforts," management of the variable interest holder is unable to obtain information needed to determine whether the entity is a VIE, to determine whether the holder is the primary beneficiary, or to make the required consolidating/ eliminating entries required by FIN 46(R).

   *NOTE: With respect to this exception, however, management of the variable interest holder is required to continue to make these efforts after initial adoption of FIN 46(R). If the variable interest holder significantly participated in the design/redesign of the entity, it would be unusual for it to be able to contend that it was unable to obtain the necessary information.*

9. An entity that qualifies to be treated as a business, as defined below (the definition included in FIN 46(R) was adapted from EITF 98-3, *Determining Whether a Nonmonetary Transaction Involves Receipt of Productive Assets or a Business*). However, this scope exception *does not apply* and the entity would be required to be evaluated as to whether it is a VIE by the holders of its variable interests if *any one or more* of the following conditions exists (these are referred to in the decision diagram as "further evaluation factors" for ease of understanding:

   a. The variable interest holder and/or its related parties/de facto agents[2] (de facto agents are discussed later in this chapter) participated significantly in the design or redesign of the entity. This factor is not considered when the entity is an operating joint venture jointly controlled by the variable interest holder, and either an independent party or a franchisee.

   b. The design of the entity results in substantially all of its activities either involving or being conducted on behalf of the variable interest holder and its related parties

   c. Based on the relative fair values of interests in the entity, the variable interest holder and its related parties provide more than half of its total equity, subordinated debt, and other forms of subordinated financial support

   d. The entity's activities relate primarily to one or both of the following:

      (1) Single-lessee leases

      (2) Securitizations or other forms of asset-backed financings

10. When issued, FIN 46(R) provided a scope exception specifying that enterprises subject to SEC Regulation S-X Rule 6-03(c)(1) (investment companies, mutual funds) were only to consolidate an entity subject to the same regulation.

In mid-2007, FASB issued FSP FIN 46(R)-7, *Application of FASB Interpretation No. 46(R) to Investment Companies*, in tandem with AcSEC's issuance of its SOP 07-1, *Clarification of the Scope of the Audit and Accounting Guide, "Investment Companies" and Accounting by Parent Companies and Equity Method Investors for Investments in Investment Companies*.

---

[2] *Only for the purposes of applying factor a. above, de facto agents exclude parties that require the variable interest holder's prior approval to sell, transfer, or encumber their interest in the entity.*

The FSP, by reference to the SOP, amended this scope exception to apply to all investments accounted for at fair value in conformity with the AICPA Audit and Accounting Guide (AAG), *Investment Companies*, as clarified by the new SOP.[3] Therefore, entities that meet the definition of an investment company after adoption of SOP 07-1 will continue to apply investment company accounting to their investments, and those investments will not be subject to the FIN 46(R) consolidation requirements. SOP 07-1 is effective for fiscal years beginning on or after December 15, 2007, with earlier application encouraged.

**Definition of a business.** A business is defined, in the context of FIN 46(R) as

*...a self-sustaining integrated set of activities and assets conducted and managed for the purpose of providing a return to investors. A business consists of (a) inputs, (b) processes applied to those inputs, and (c) resulting outputs that are used to generate revenues. For a set of activities and assets to be a business, it must contain all of the inputs and processes necessary for it to conduct normal operations, which include the ability to sustain a revenue stream by providing its outputs to customers.*

In evaluating whether an entity is a business, consideration must be given to unique factors relating to the industry and the activities being performed including

**Inputs**

1. Fixed assets either owned or leased
2. Intangibles either owned or licensed
3. Access to materials or rights needed to perform its activities
4. Employees

**Processes**

1. Strategic management
2. Operations
3. Resource management

**Outputs**

1. Access to customers (clients)

A three-step process is provided in order to assess whether a set of activities ("set") qualifies as a business:

1. Identify elements included in the "set" (i.e., determine the existing inputs, processes, and outputs.)
2. Compare the elements identified in 1. to the elements necessary for the set of activities to be conducted as a normal business operation.
3. If any elements are missing, assess the degree of effort or investment relative to the fair value of the set of activities needed to acquire or gain access to the missing elements. If a significant effort or investment would be required, it can be concluded that the set of activities is not a business; conversely, a de minimis amount of effort or investment to supply the missing elements would lead to the conclusion that the set of activities is a business.

**Variable interests in "silos."** A party may hold a variable interest in specific assets of a VIE (e.g., a guarantee or a subordinated residual interest). In computing expected losses and expected residual returns, as defined above, a holder of a variable interest in specified assets of a VIE must determine if the interest it holds qualifies as an interest in the VIE itself. The

---

[3] *See the Definitions of Terms section of this chapter for the definition of an investment company as set forth in SOP 07-1.*

variable interest is considered an interest in the VIE itself if either (1) the fair value of the specific assets is more than half of the total fair value of the VIE's assets, or (2) the interest holder has another significant variable interest in the entity as a whole.

If the interests are deemed to be interests in the VIE itself, the expected losses and expected residual returns associated with the variable interest in the specified assets are treated as being associated with the VIE.

If the interests are not deemed to be interests in the VIE itself, the interests in the specified assets are treated as a separate VIE (referred to as a "silo") if the expected cash flows from the specified assets (and any associated credit enhancements, if applicable) are essentially the sole source of payment for specified liabilities or specified other interests. Under this scenario, expected losses and expected residual returns associated with the silo assets are accounted for separately to the extent that the interest holder either bears the expected losses or is entitled to receive the expected returns. Any excess of expected losses or residual returns not borne (received) by the variable interest holder is considered attributable to the entity as a whole.

If one interest holder is required to consolidate a silo of a VIE, other VIE interest holders are to exclude the silo from the remaining VIE.

### Example of application of FIN 46(R) to related-party leases

The most commonly encountered potential VIE situations that occur in practice involve related-party leases. Business owners often organize a partnership or LLC (for this discussion we will assume an LLC) to own property that is leased to a business with the same or similar ownership. The transaction is structured in this manner for a number of reasons that include avoidance of double taxation of the gain on the eventual sale of the property and legal protection of the building from creditors of the operating business in the event of business bankruptcy.

In attempting to avoid lessee capitalization, the lease is often structured with a short initial term (e.g., three years) with the lessee having successive options to renew the lease at similar terms. The building is pledged as collateral under a mortgage with a third-party lender. The lessor entity is thinly capitalized (i.e., it has very little owner-invested equity). Consequently, the lender, besides holding a mortgage on the building as collateral, has further protected its interests by obtaining a loan guarantee from the lessee, an assignment of rents, and a personal guarantee of the owner.

These relationships are illustrated in the following diagram:

**Analysis under FIN 46(R)**

Following the decision diagrams and using the related-party/de facto principal and agent rules included in FIN 46(R)

1. The lessee holds a variable interest in the lessor in the form of the guarantee of the lessor's mortgage debt.
2. The lessor entity is not "scoped out" of FIN 46(R).
3. The lessor entity is a business. It has inputs (owned fixed assets), processes for managing its investment, and outputs relative to access to the lessee.
4. The following "further evaluation factors" apply:

    a. The lessee/variable interest holder and its related parties participated significantly in the design of the lessor.
    b. The design of the lessor LLC results in all of its activities involving and being conducted on behalf of the lessee/variable interest holder.
    c. The lessee/variable interest holder and its related parties provided 100% of the subordinated financial support for the lessor entity.
    d. The lessor entity's activities relate to a single-lessee lease.

5. The lessee/evaluator and its related-party owner were involved in the design of the lessor entity.
6. The lessee's variable interest is assumed to be *significant* for the purpose of this analysis. Fin 46(R) does not provide guidance on making this determination.
7. The lessee's variable interest is in the leased asset.
8. The fair value of the leased asset represents 100% of the total fair value of the lessor's assets and thus is deemed to be an interest in the lessor as a whole versus an interest in just the specified assets of the lessor.
9. The at-risk equity holder of the lessor does not meet the second criterion for being considered to hold a controlling financial interest (i.e., the variable interest holder/lessee could potentially absorb expected losses of the lessor should the lessee be called upon by the lender to perform under the guarantee of the lessor's indebtedness). Note that, in this case, the other two criteria for controlling financial interest are met.
10. As a result of the analysis up to this point, it can be concluded that the lessor is a variable interest entity.
11. No silos exist, since 100% of the fair value of the assets is leased to the single lessee.
12. Application of the related-party/de facto principal and agent rules to the variable interests in the lessor indicates that 100% of the expected losses and expected residual returns from the lessor are allocable to the members of the related-party group (the lessee and the related-party owner of both). Thus, collectively, the lessee and its 100% stockholder are the primary beneficiary of the VIE/lessor. The party most closely associated with the leased property is the lessee who, consequently, is considered the primary beneficiary that is required to consolidate the lessor in its financial statements.

**Other lease terms and provisions.** The following discussion examines the effect that certain changes to the above facts would have on the foregoing conclusions:

*Existence or absence of guarantees.* Even if the stockholder/member's guarantee of the mortgage is not required by the lender and only the lessee guaranteed the debt, the analysis above would be identical. Due to the fact that the lessee/variable interest holder is exposed to the expected losses of the lessor under the terms of the guarantee, the lessor/LLC's sole member (and at-risk equity holder) is not the only party that potentially would absorb expected losses of the lessor.

Conversely, when FIN 46(R) was originally issued, many observers initially believed if the lessee was not required by the lender to guarantee the mortgage, and the only guarantee was that of the stockholder/member, that the absence of an explicit variable interest held by the lessee would preclude the conclusion that the lessor was a VIE.

This situation illustrates one of the most misunderstood provisions of FIN 46(R)—referred to as an *implicit variable interest*—which the FASB Staff attempts to clarify in FSP FIN 46(R)-5.

Even though the lessee did not directly guarantee the debt of the lessor, consideration must be given to the likely scenarios if the lessor/LLC should be close to a default on the mortgage payments. Realistically, what is the likelihood that the sole stockholder/sole member would perform under his or her personal guarantee obligation rather than directing the lessee to pay additional rent sufficient to enable the LLC to keep its mortgage payments current?

Clearly, it would not make economic sense for the sole stockholder/member to perform personally under the guarantee as this would, in substance, result in the stockholder/member making a loan or capital contribution to an otherwise insolvent LLC. Instead, it would logically follow that the best course of action would be for the lessee to pay rent in amounts adequate to fund the LLC's mortgage payments so that the lessee would continue to have use of the leased premises without concern over whether the bank will foreclose on and sell the property to a third party. If the lessee were having difficulty funding the rent payments, its owner would probably authorize it to borrow money or sell assets in order to enable it to do so before its owner used personal funds to perform under the guarantee.

After analyzing this situation, with appropriate attention to the substance rather than simply its form, it can be seen that the lessee is the holder of an implicit variable interest in the lessor in the form of an implicit guarantee of the lessor's mortgage debt.

The remainder of the analysis would be identical to what was presented earlier. Due to the fact that the lessee/variable interest holder is exposed to the expected losses of the lessor under the terms of the implicit guarantee, the lessor/LLC's sole member (and at-risk equity holder) is not the only party that potentially would absorb expected losses of the lessor.

Finally, consider the situation where neither the lessee nor the owner is required to guarantee the debt. A prudent lender would probably not waive both guarantees unless the lessor was sufficiently capitalized by the owner's at-risk equity. That is, there is a presumption that the lessor in such an instance is not a VIE. Under this scenario the lessee would perform the quantitative analysis required to estimate expected losses and estimated residual returns to determine whether the lessor is a VIE and, if it is, whether it is the primary beneficiary.

***Above or below market rentals.*** Rentals due under related-party leases sometimes exceed arm's-length market rentals because the owner is using the lessor as a conduit for the lessee to indirectly provide additional salary or dividends to the owner (characterized as the excess rent).

Under FIN 46(R), an operating lease is generally not considered to be a variable interest unless

1. The lease terms include a lessee residual guarantee of the fair value of the leased asset, since this results in the lessee potentially absorbing estimated negative variability that would otherwise be absorbed by the equity holder of the lessor

2.  The lease terms include an option for the lessee to purchase the property at the end of the lease term at a specified price, since this means that the lessee potentially may receive estimated positive variability that would otherwise be received by the equity holder of the lessor

3.  The lease terms are not indicative of market terms for a similar property in the same geographic location, since this would result in the lessee either receiving estimated positive variability of the lessor (if the lease terms were below market) or absorbing negative variability of the lessor (if the lease terms were above market)

Under each of the foregoing scenarios, the lease is considered a variable interest in determining the primary beneficiary, because the expected losses of the lessor that would be borne by the lessee (the excess of the rentals required over the fair value of the right to use the leased property) exceed the amounts that would have been expected had the rentals been at fair value. Thus, the stockholder/member would not be considered to have a controlling financial interest since s/he was not the only party exposed to the lessor's expected losses.

If the situation reversed, and the rentals were below market amounts, it could be logically concluded that the lessor was absorbing negative variability of the lessee and that, therefore, the lease was a variable interest in the lessee held by the lessor that could potentially result in the lessor being considered the primary beneficiary of the lessee that would necessitate the lessor consolidating the lessee in its financial statements.

**Different organizational structures.** In some instances, the leased property is owned directly by the owner rather than in an LLC or other entity. This reveals an important "loophole" in the provisions of FIN 46(R). The FIN 46(R) definition of a VIE requires that the VIE be a "legal structure used to conduct activities or to hold assets." Examples of these structures identified by FIN 46(R) include corporations, partnerships, limited liability companies, grantor trusts, and other trusts. It does not include a portion of an individual's privately held assets, however. Therefore, if the property is owned personally, it would not be feasible for the lessee to consolidate a personal financial statement of the property owner.

*CAUTIONARY NOTE: Identification of this "loophole" is not intended to serve as a recommendation, and indeed the contrary may be better advice. Many states have estate laws that require the executors of estates of individuals who own property titled in their name to subject those estates to court-supervised probate proceedings in order to ensure that the assets of the deceased individual are appropriately identified and that the title to those assets is unambiguously transferred to the appropriate beneficiary. Probate is a time-consuming and costly process that most astute estate planners advise their clients to avoid.*

*One of the most popular ways to avoid probate is for an individual to transfer the title to all individually owned personal property and real estate to a revocable grantor trust (sometimes called a "living trust"). This trust is an entity that is permitted under the law to hold title to property. The property effectively remains under the control of its former owner since this person, the grantor, is the trustee of the trust.*

*If the owner of the leased property is a grantor trust, the trust is subject to the provisions of FIN 46(R) and, if the trust is determined to be a VIE, it would be required to be consolidated by its primary beneficiary.*

**Renewal options.** FIN 46(R) is silent as to whether a lessee option to renew an operating lease at the end of its initial term is a variable interest. As discussed later in this chapter, renewal options are sometimes required to be included in the minimum lease term for accounting purposes because a nonrenewal election would impose a penalty upon the lessee such that renewal has to be deemed reasonably certain. For this purpose, the implicit penalty could be the abandonment of substantial leasehold improvements constructed by the lessee, or the continuation of a guarantee of the lessor's mortgage obligation notwithstanding nonrenewal. These renewal features are not themselves variable interests because they are considered to be integral parts of the contractual term of the underlying lease. Lease renewal options that cover periods beyond the minimum lease term, however, can be considered to be variable interests.

Renewal options are customarily structured to convey, from the lessor to the lessee, the right to renew the lease at the expiration of its term. As a result of the lessee possessing this right, the lessor is precluded from re-leasing the assets to another party until such time as the lessee decides whether or not it will exercise its option. The existence of the option limits the lessor's ability to lease the space to another tenant. Thus, during the term during which the option is exercisable, there is an adverse effect on the fair value and residual of the leased property. If the option period is not included by the lessee in the minimum lease term, the option conveys to the lessee the right to elect to control and use the leased asset during a period of time when that control and use could have been conveyed by the lessor to another party. In effect, this is a transfer of a portion of the lessor's expected residual rewards to the lessee. This would be true in both related-party and arm's-length leases.

***Other contractual arrangements.*** Leases are often accompanied by other contractual arrangements between the lessee and lessor. Such contractual arrangements can include management, marketing, brokerage, and other types of service agreements. These agreements must be carefully analyzed, as FIN 46(R) provides restrictive rules that often result in such agreements being characterized as variable interests.

All parties affected by these transactions should seek expert professional advice prior to either structuring a new transaction or modifying an existing transaction. For example, adverse income tax consequences could result from the transfer of property from one form of ownership to another.

### Example: Arm's-length leases—computing expected losses and expected residual returns

The application of FIN 46(R) is, of course, not limited to related-party arrangements. The following is an example of the quantitative analysis (versus the qualitative analysis illustrated in the related-party example above) that might be necessary in an arm's-length leasing arrangement.

*NOTE: The terms of the leases below are not intended to represent current market conditions, but rather have been designed to best illustrate the concepts of FIN 46(R).*

Lawrence Lessor, LLC (referred to herein as "the Entity" since it is the entity that the variable interest holders will be evaluating as to whether it is a VIE) is a limited liability company organized specifically for the purpose of building, owning, and operating a single-lessee retail discount warehouse club store on land that it has recently acquired. The store is the only asset owned by the Entity. The 148,000 square foot store will be occupied by Clubco, a nationally known chain that is unrelated to Lawrence Lessor.

The Entity's voting owners (the LLC members) wish only to invest a minimal amount of equity in the Entity and, consequently, the mortgage lender insisted on obtaining a third-party guarantee of the mortgage which Lawrence obtained from an unrelated third-party and paid a premium for.

The terms of the lease with the retailer are as follows: (assumed to be an operating lease):

| | |
|---|---|
| Description of space | 148,000 square foot retail discount warehouse club store |
| Lessee | Clubco Stores, Inc. |
| Initial lease term | Three years |
| Lease commencement date | 1/1/09 |
| Annual base rent | $600,000 |
| Contingent rent | 1% of annual sales over $30 million |
| Purchase options: | $9 million–not a bargain purchase option in accordance with FAS 13 |
| Residual guarantee | Lessee guarantees to lessor that residual value of the building at the end of the lease term will be at least equal to the $7,500,000 fair value of the store land and building at inception or it will pay the lessor the difference |
| Executory costs | All real estate taxes, maintenance, insurance, and common area expenses are to be borne by the lessee |

The construction has been completed, the occupancy permits issued, and the construction financing settled with the proceeds of a 25-year, 6% mortgage loan on December 1, 2008. The mortgage loan is guaranteed by an unrelated third-party guarantor. The store is opening and commencing business on January 1, 2009.

Mortgage details are as follows:

### Summary Amortization Schedule for Mortgage

25-year, 6% mortgage, original principal amount of $7,275,750

| Year | Payments | Interest | Principal | Balance |
|------|----------|----------|-----------|---------|
| Original loan | | | | $7,275,750 |
| 2009 | $562,533 | $433,022 | $129,511 | 7,146,239 |
| 2010 | 562,533 | 425,034 | 137,499 | 7,008,740 |
| 2011 | 562,533 | 416,553 | 145,980 | 6,862,760 |
| | $1,687,599 | $1,274,609 | $412,990 | |

The Entity's recorded aggregate carrying amount of $7,500,000 for the land and building represents the fair value at lease inception with the land's fair value representing 10%, or $750,000.

The rental terms for the store are considered to be at market rates. If the terms were not at market rates, additional expected variability would be assigned to the lease (in addition to the expected variability resulting from the purchase option and residual value guarantee).

Expected cash flows are discounted to their present value using an assumed 3% interest rate representing the interest rate available on risk-free investments. To simplify the example, cash flows are assumed to occur at the end of each annual period for the purpose of discounting them to present value. A copy of the balance sheet from the Entity's annual partnership return at lease inception is as follows:

| Schedule L | Balance Sheets per Books | | | | |
|------------|--------------------------|---|---|---|---|
| **Assets** | | Beginning of tax year | | End of tax year | |
| | | (a) | (b) | (c) | (d) |
| 1. | Cash | | | | 1,000 |
| 2. a. | Trade notes and accounts receivable | | | | |
| b. | Less allowance for bad debts | | | | |
| 3. | Inventories | | | | |
| 4. | US government obligations | | | | |
| 5. | Tax-exempt securities | | | | |
| 6. | Other current assets (*attach schedule*) | | | | |
| 7. | Mortgage and real estate loans | | | | |
| 8. | Other investments (*attach schedule*) | | | | |
| 9. a. | Buildings and other depreciable assets | | | 6,750,000 | |
| b. | Less accumulated depreciation | | | | 6,750,000 |
| 10. a. | Depletable assets | | | | |
| b. | Less accumulated depletion | | | | |
| 11. | Land (net of any amortization) | | | | 750,000 |
| 12. a | Intangible assets (amortizable only) | | | | |
| b | Less accumulated amortization | | | | |
| 13. | Other assets (*attach schedule*) | | | | |
| 14. | Total assets | | | | 7,501,000 |
| | **Liabilities and Capital** | | | | |
| 15. | Accounts payable | | | | |
| 16. | Mortgages, notes, bonds payable in less than 1 year | | | | |
| 17. | Other current liabilities (*attach schedule*) | | | | |
| 18. | All nonrecourse loans | | | | 7,275,750 |
| 19. | Mortgages, notes, bonds payable in 1 year or more | | | | |
| 20. | Other liabilities (*attach schedule*) | | | | |
| 21. | Partners' capital accounts | | | | 225,250 |
| 22. | **Total** liabilities and capital | | | | 7,501,000 |

**Analysis by Clubco** (See the decision diagrams earlier in this chapter.)

1. Clubco holds a variable interest in Lawrence Lessor ("the Entity") in the form of the lease. Expected variability results from the purchase option and the residual value guarantee.
2. The Entity is not scoped out of FIN 46(R).
3. The Entity is a business.
4. Further evaluation factor d. applies; that is, this is a single-lessee lease.
5. Clubco was not involved in the design of the Entity.
6. For illustrative purposes, assume that the purchase option is significant to Clubco.
7. Clubco holds a variable interest in the leased store (the specified assets) in the form of the lease containing a purchase option and residual value guarantee.
8. The fair value of the building leased by Clubco is 100% of the fair value of the Entity's assets. Therefore, Clubco is deemed to hold a variable interest in the Entity as a whole.
9. In applying the test to determine if the members of the LLC/entity have a controlling financial interest (distinguished from a controlling voting interest, which they clearly have), the following results are determined:

    a. The LLC members are the sole voting interest holders and, therefore, meet the voting test.
    b. The LLC members are *not* the only parties that absorb expected losses of the lessor due to the existence of the residual value guarantee provision in the lease that potentially could result in Clubco bearing a portion of the expected losses.
    c. The LLC members are also *not* the only parties entitled to receive the expected residual returns from the property due to the existence of the purchase option provision in the lease that potentially could result in Clubco receiving a portion of the expected residual returns.

10. As a consequence of the analysis up to this point, Clubco can conclude that its variable interest is in a lessor that is a VIE.
11. Since Clubco leases 100% of the fair value of the assets held by entity, there are no silos included therein.
12. To determine whether or not it is the primary beneficiary of the VIE/lessor, Clubco must determine if it either will bear the majority of the expected losses, or receive the majority of the expected residual returns. One form this calculation might take is illustrated below.

**Computation of expected cash flow possibilities for the lease term**

| | 2009 | | | | | |
|---|---|---|---|---|---|---|
| *Probability* | 5% | 15% | 30% | 35% | 10% | 5% |
| *Assumptions* | | | | | | |
| Annual store sales | $25,000,000 | $30,000,000 | $40,000,000 | $50,000,000 | $55,000,000 | $60,000,000 |
| Percentage rent base | $30,000,000 | $30,000,000 | $30,000,000 | $30,000,000 | $30,000,000 | $30,000,000 |
| Percentage rent rate | 1% | 1% | 1% | 1% | 1% | 1% |
| *Possible cash flow outcomes* | | | | | | |
| Rent—Base | $ 600,000 | $ 600,000 | $ 600,000 | $ 600,000 | $ 600,000 | $ 600,000 |
| Rent—Percentage | -- | -- | 100,000 | 200,000 | 250,000 | 300,000 |
| Total rental income | 600,000 | 600,000 | 700,000 | 800,000 | 850,000 | 900,000 |
| Mortgage payments | 562,533 | 562,533 | 562,533 | 562,533 | 562,533 | 562,533 |
| Possible net cash flow | $ 37,467 | $ 37,467 | $ 137,467 | $ 237,467 | $ 287,467 | $ 337,467 |
| Present value, discounted at 3% | $ 36,376 | $ 36,376 | $ 133,463 | $ 230,550 | $ 279,094 | $ 327,638 |

| | **2010** | | | | | |
|---|---|---|---|---|---|---|
| *Probability* | 5% | 15% | 30% | 35% | 10% | 5% |
| *Assumptions* | | | | | | |
| Estimated percentage change in sales | -2.00% | 0.00% | 2.00% | 2.50% | 3.00% | 4.00% |
| Annual store sales | $24,500,000 | $30,000,000 | $40,800,000 | $51,250,000 | $56,650,000 | $62,400,000 |
| Percentage rent base | $30,000,000 | $30,000,000 | $30,000,000 | $30,000,000 | $30,000,000 | $30,000,000 |
| Percentage rent rate | 1% | 1% | 1% | 1% | 1% | 1% |
| *Possible cash flow outcomes* | | | | | | |
| Rent—Base | $ 600,000 | $ 600,000 | $ 600,000 | $ 600,000 | $ 600,000 | $ 600,000 |
| Rent—Percentage | -- | -- | 108,000 | 212,500 | 266,500 | 324,000 |
| Total rental income | 600,000 | 600,000 | 708,000 | 812,500 | 866,500 | 924,000 |
| Mortgage payments | 562,533 | 562,533 | 562,533 | 562,533 | 562,533 | 562,533 |
| Possible net cash flow | $ 37,467 | $ 37,467 | $ 145,467 | $ 249,967 | $ 303,967 | $ 361,467 |
| Present value, discounted at 3% | $ 35,316 | $ 35,316 | $ 137,117 | $ 235,618 | $ 286,518 | $ 340,717 |

| | **2011** | | | | | |
|---|---|---|---|---|---|---|
| *Probability* | 5% | 15% | 30% | 35% | 10% | 5% |
| *Assumptions* | | | | | | |
| Estimated percentage change in sales | -1.00% | 0.00% | 2.50% | 3.50% | 3.75% | 5.00% |
| Annual store sales | $24,255,000 | $30,000,000 | $41,820,000 | $53,043,750 | $58,774,375 | $65,520,000 |
| Percentage rent base | $30,000,000 | $30,000,000 | $30,000,000 | $30,000,000 | $30,000,000 | $30,000,000 |
| Percentage rent rate | 1% | 1% | 1% | 1% | 1% | 1% |
| *Possible cash flow outcomes* | | | | | | |
| Rent—Base | $ 600,000 | $ 600,000 | $ 600,000 | $ 600,000 | $ 600,000 | $ 600,000 |
| Rent—Percentage | -- | -- | 118,200 | 230,438 | 287,744 | 355,200 |
| Total rental income | 600,000 | 600,000 | 718,200 | 830,438 | 887,744 | 955,200 |
| Mortgage payments | 562,533 | 562,533 | 562,533 | 562,533 | 562,533 | 562,533 |
| Possible net cash flow, operations | 37,467 | 37,467 | 155,667 | 267,905 | 325,211 | 392,667 |
| Estimated residual amount | 7,000,000 | 8,000,000 | 9,000,000 | 10,000,000 | 12,000,000 | 13,000,000 |
| Mortgage repayment | 6,862,760 | 6,862,760 | 6,862,760 | 6,862,760 | 6,862,760 | 6,862,760 |
| Possible net sales proceeds | 137,240 | 1,137,240 | 2,137,240 | 3,137,240 | 5,137,240 | 6,137,240 |
| Possible net cash flow | $ 174,707 | $ 1,174,707 | $ 2,292,907 | $ 3,405,144 | $ 5,462,451 | $ 6,529,907 |
| Present value, discounted at 3% | $ 159,881 | $ 1,075,023 | $ 2,098,334 | $ 3,116,189 | $ 4,998,916 | $ 5,975,790 |
| 3-year totals of present value of possible cash flows discounted at 3% | $ 231,573 | $ 1,146,715 | $ 2,368,914 | $ 3,582,357 | $ 5,564,528 | $ 6,644,145 |

Note that, in the forecast for 2011, the effects of the purchase option and residual value guarantee are ignored. They are considered later in the analysis of which variable interest holders participate in expected losses and expected residual returns.

13. Calculation of probability-weighted discounted expected cash flows.

| *Scenario* | *Present value of possible cash flows* | *Estimated probability* | *Discounted probability-weighted expected cash flows* |
|---|---|---|---|
| 1 | $ 231,573 | 5% | $ 11,579 |
| 2 | 1,146,715 | 15% | 172,007 |
| 3 | 2,368,914 | 30% | 710,674 |
| 4 | 3,582,357 | 35% | 1,253,825 |
| 5 | 5,564,528 | 10% | 556,453 |
| 6 | 6,644,145 | 5% | 332,207 |
| | | 100% | $3,036,745 |

This computation uses the expected cash flow methodology prescribed by CON 7, which is also used in estimation of fair value for the purposes of impairment testing of goodwill and tangible long-lived assets, and in computing asset retirement obligations.

14. Calculations of expected losses and expected residual returns (and the related expected variability).

| Scenario | Present value of possible cash flows | Discounted/ probability-weighted expected cash flows | Variance from expected outcome | Estimated probability | Expected Losses | Expected residual returns |
|---|---|---|---|---|---|---|
| 1 | $ 231,573 | $3,036,745 | $(2,805,172) | 5% | $(140,259) | |
| 2 | 1,146,715 | 3,036,745 | (1,890,030) | 15% | (283,505) | |
| 3 | 2,368,914 | 3,036,745 | (667,831) | 30% | (200,349) | |
| 4 | 3,582,357 | 3,036,745 | 545,612 | 35% | | $190,965 |
| 5 | 5,564,528 | 3,036,745 | 2,527,783 | 10% | | 252,778 |
| 6 | 6,644,145 | 3,036,745 | 3,607,400 | 5% | | 180,370 |
| | | | | 100% | $(624,113) | $624,113 |

FIN 46(R) requires consideration of the "expected variability" inherent in the estimate of probability-weighted expected cash flows, in this case $3,036,745. This amount represents a weighted-average of the various expected outcomes multiplied by their respective probabilities. As is always the case when averaging numbers, the sums of the positive and negative differences between each value included in the average and the average itself are always equal. This explains why the expected losses and expected residual returns both equal $624,113. Therefore, the expected variability in both directions is the sum of the two absolute values (i.e., $624,113 + $624,113 = $1,248,226).

Another important point to note is that the terms "expected losses" and "expected residual returns" are not associated with traditional GAAP income or cash flow measures. The entity illustrated above has positive expected cash flows under all six scenarios for all three years. Notwithstanding that fact, the computation shows that it will experience expected losses and expected residual returns—variations from expectation, positive or negative, that could occur as a result of operations or of changes in the fair value of the property. This will always be the case, irrespective of how profitable an entity is or how much cash flow it generates.

15. For each scenario, the facts are analyzed to determine which of the variable interest holders will bear the expected losses. There were no silos included in the VIE, therefore only a single primary beneficiary determination is required. The results of the analysis are aggregated as follows:

| | Expected losses |
|---|---|
| Scenario 1 | $(140,259) |
| Scenario 2 | (283,505) |
| Scenario 3 | (200,349) |
| | $(624,113) |

| Scenario | Estimated residual value of store | Expected losses | Clubco | 3rd-party guarantor | At-risk equity holders of entity | Mortgage Lender | Notes |
|---|---|---|---|---|---|---|---|
| 1 | 7,000,000 | $(140,259) | $(140,259) | | | | $7.5MM guarantee $7 MM residual |
| 2 | 8,000,000 | (283,505) | | | $(283,505) | | |
| 3 | 9,000,000 | (200,349) | | | (200,349) | | |
| Excess of share of losses over equity | | | | (258,604) | (258,604) | | |
| | | $(624,113) | $(140,259) | $(258,604) | $(225,250) | $ -- | |
| | | 100% | 22% | 42% | 36% | 0% | |

Total equity at risk is $225,250 which would not be sufficient for the entity to absorb the expected losses of $624,113 without receiving additional subordinated financial support. Consequently, the Entity (Lawrence Lessor, LLC) by definition is a variable interest entity.

Note that, based on the analysis of the expected losses, no variable interest holder will absorb a majority (>50%) of the Entity's losses. Consequently, the expected residual returns need to be analyzed.

| Scenario | Estimated residual value of store | Expected residual returns | Clubco | At-risk equity holders of entity | Guarantor | Notes |
|---|---|---|---|---|---|---|
| 4 | $10,000,000 | $190,965 | $190,965 | | | Exercise of $9MM Option |
| 5 | 12,000,000 | 252,778 | 252,778 | | | Exercise of $9MM Option |
| 6 | 13,000,000 | 180,370 | 180,370 | | | Exercise of $9MM Option |
| | | $624,113 | $624,113 | | | |
| | | 100% | 100% | | | |

16. Since 100% of the expected residual returns will be received by Clubco, it is the primary beneficiary, the party that is required to consolidate Lawrence Lessor, LLC in its financial statements.

The FASB staff has issued a series of FASB Staff Positions (FSP) providing guidance on the implementation of FIN 46(R). Full coverage of these FSP is provided in Chapter 13, *Business Combinations and Consolidated Financial Statements.*

### Lease or Sale—The Interplay of Lease and Revenue Recognition Accounting

**EITF 01-8, determining whether an arrangement contains a lease.** FAS 13 defines a lease as "an agreement conveying the right to use property, plant, or equipment (land and/or depreciable assets) usually for a stated period of time." EITF 01-8 provides guidance on determining when all or part of an arrangement constitutes a lease.

*Scope of EITF 01-8.* Property, plant, or equipment, as the term is used in FAS 13, includes only land and/or depreciable assets. Therefore, inventory (including equipment parts inventory) cannot be the subject of a lease because inventory is not depreciable. Although specific property, plant, or equipment may be explicitly identified in an arrangement, it is not the subject of a lease if the arrangement can be fulfilled without using the specified property, plant, or equipment. For example, if the owner/seller is obligated to deliver a specified quantity of goods or services but can provide those goods or services using property, plant, or equipment other than that specified in the arrangement, then the arrangement does not contain a lease.

In addition, FAS 13 contains specific scope exceptions with respect to agreements concerning

1. Exploration or exploitation of natural resources (e.g., oil, gas, minerals, and timber).
2. Intangible licensing rights (e.g., motion pictures, plays, manuscripts, patents, and copyrights).

Lease treatment is not precluded in situations where the owner or manufacturer of the property has extended a product warranty that includes a provision for replacement of the property if it is not operating adequately. Similarly, if the arrangement includes a provision permitting the equipment owner the right to substitute other equipment on or after a specified date, irrespective of the reason, the arrangement can still qualify as a lease.

*Right to use property, plant, or equipment.* The right to use the specified property, plant, or equipment is conveyed if any one of the following conditions is met:

- A *party* (for the purpose of this discussion, we will refer to this party, the potential lessee, as "the recipient" of the rights) has the ability or right to operate the property, plant, or equipment or direct others to do so as the recipient specifies, while attaining or controlling more than a minor portion of the output (or service utility),
- The recipient has the ability or right to control physical access to the specified property, plant, or equipment while attaining or controlling more than a minor portion of the output (or other service utility), or
- Analysis of the relevant facts and circumstances indicates that it is remote (as that term is used in FAS 5) that a party (or parties) other than the recipient will attain more

than a minor amount of the output (or other service utility) that will be produced or generated by the specified property, plant, or equipment during the term of the arrangement, *and* the price that the recipient will pay for the output is neither contractually fixed per unit of output nor equal to the market price per unit of output at the time delivery of the output is received.

***Timing of initial assessment and subsequent reassessments.*** The assessment of whether an arrangement contains a lease is to be made at the inception of the arrangement. A reassessment of whether the arrangement contains a lease is to be made only if (a) the contractual terms are modified, (b) a renewal option is exercised or the parties to the arrangement agree on an extension of its term, (c) there is a change in the determination as to whether or not fulfillment of the arrangement is dependent on the property, plant, or equipment that was originally specified, or (d) the originally specified property and equipment undergoes a substantial physical change. Remeasurement/redetermination is not permitted merely because of a change in an estimate made at inception (e.g., the number of expected units of output or the useful life of the equipment).

***Aggregation of separate contracts.*** In applying the EITF guidance, there is a rebuttable presumption that separate contracts between the same parties (or related parties) that are executed on or near the same date were negotiated together as a package.

This issue also provides accounting guidance for any recognized assets and liabilities existing at the time that an arrangement (or a portion of an arrangement) either ceases to qualify as a lease or commences to qualify as a lease due to a reassessment in the circumstances as described above.

**Sales with a guaranteed minimum resale value.** In order to provide sales incentives, manufacturers sometimes include in a sales contract, a guarantee that the purchaser will, upon disposition of the property, receive a minimum resale amount. Upon disposition, the manufacturer either reacquires the property at the agreed-upon minimum price or reimburses the purchaser for any shortfall between the actual sales proceeds and the guaranteed amount.

In EITF 95-1, a consensus was reached that transactions containing guarantees of resale value of equipment by a manufacturer are to be accounted for as leases and not as sales. The minimum lease payments used to determine if the criteria have been met for lessor sales-type lease accounting, described later in this chapter, are computed as the difference between the proceeds received from the transferee/lessee upon initial transfer of the equipment and the amount of the residual value guarantee on its first contractual exercise date.

If the lease is accounted for as an operating lease because it does not qualify for sales-type lease accounting (as discussed and illustrated later in this chapter), the manufacturer/lessor is to record the proceeds received at inception as a liability which is subsequently reduced by crediting revenue pro rata from the inception of the lease until the first guarantee exercise date so that, on that exercise date, the remaining liability is the guaranteed residual amount. If the lessee elects, under the terms of the arrangement, to continue to use the leased asset after the first exercise date, the manufacturer/lessor will continue to amortize the liability for the remaining residual amount to revenue to reduce it further to any remaining guarantee, if applicable.

The foregoing prescribed accounting is followed by manufacturers even when there is dealer involvement in the transaction when it is the manufacturer who is responsible for the guarantee to the purchaser.

In EITF 03-12, a consensus was reached that FIN 45, *Guarantor's Accounting and Disclosure Requirements for Guarantees, Including Indirect Guarantees of Indebtedness of Others,* does not apply to these transactions irrespective of whether they are accounted for as operating leases or sales-type leases because, in either case, the underlying of such a guarantee is an asset owned by the guarantor.

**Equipment sold and subsequently repurchased subject to an operating lease.** EITF 95-4 specifies that if four conditions are satisfied, a manufacturer can recognize a sale at the time its product is transferred to a dealer for subsequent sale to a third-party customer even if this ultimate customer (the dealer's customer) enters into an operating lease agreement with the same manufacturer or the manufacturer's finance affiliate.

1. The dealer must be an independent entity that conducts business separately with manufacturers and customers,
2. The passage of the product from the manufacturer to the dealer fully transfers ownership,
3. The manufacturer (or finance affiliate) has no obligation to provide a lease arrangement for the dealer's customer, and
4. The dealer's customer is in control of selecting which of the many financing options available will be used.

### Lessee Classification

For accounting and reporting purposes the lessee has two possible classifications for a lease.

1. Operating
2. Capital

The proper classification of a lease is determined by the circumstances surrounding the transaction. According to FAS 13, if substantially all of the benefits and risks of ownership have been transferred to the lessee, the lessee records the lease as a capital lease at its inception. Substantially all of the risks or benefits of ownership are deemed to have been transferred if any one of the following criteria is met:

1. The lease transfers ownership to the lessee by the end of the lease term.
2. The lease contains a bargain purchase option.
3. The lease term is equal to 75% or more of the estimated economic life of the leased property, and the beginning of the lease term does not fall within the last 25% of the total economic life of the leased property.
4. The present value (PV) of the minimum lease payments at the beginning of the lease term is 90% or more of the fair value to the lessor less any investment tax credit[4] retained by the lessor. This requirement cannot be used if the lease's inception is in the last 25% of the useful economic life of the leased asset. The interest rate, used to compute the PV, is the incremental borrowing rate of the lessee unless the implicit rate is available and lower. For the purpose of this test, lease structuring fees or lease administration fees paid by the lessee to the lessor are included as part of the minimum lease payments (EITF 96-21).

If a lease agreement meets none of the four criteria set forth above, it is classified as an operating lease by the lessee.

### Lessor Classification

There are four possible classifications that apply to a lease from the standpoint of the lessor.

---

[4] *See the Definitions of Terms at the beginning of this chapter for details regarding the investment tax credit (ITC).*

1. Operating
2. Sales-type
3. Direct financing
4. Leveraged

The conditions surrounding the origination of the lease determine its classification by the lessor. If the lease meets any one of the four criteria specified above for lessees and both of the qualifications set forth below, the lease is classified as either a sales-type lease, direct financing lease, or leveraged lease depending upon the conditions present at the inception of the lease.

1. Collectibility of the minimum lease payments is reasonably predictable
2. No important uncertainties surround the amount of unreimbursable costs yet to be incurred by the lessor under the lease

If a lease transaction does not meet the criteria for classification as a sales-type lease, a direct financing lease, or a leveraged lease as specified above, it is classified by the lessor as an operating lease. The classification testing is performed prior to considering the proper accounting treatment.

It is a common practice in equipment leasing transactions for the lessor to obtain, from an unrelated third party, a full or partial guarantee of the residual value of a portfolio of leased assets. These transactions are structured in such a manner that the third-party guarantor provides a guarantee of the aggregate residual value of the portfolio but does not individually guarantee the residual value of any of the individually leased assets included in that portfolio. To the extent that a specific leased asset's residual value exceeds the guaranteed minimum amount, that excess is used to offset shortfalls relating to other specific leased assets whose residual values are below the guaranteed minimum amount.

In EITF Topic D-107, the SEC staff observer announced the SEC staff's position that the expected proceeds from these types of portfolio residual guarantees are to be *excluded* from minimum lease payments in computing the present value of the minimum lease payments for the purpose of determining the lessor's classification of the lease transaction. The SEC believes this treatment to be appropriate because, under the terms of this portfolio guarantee, the lessor is unable to determine, at lease inception, the guaranteed residual amount of any individually leased asset.

**Distinctions among sales-type, direct financing, and leveraged leases.** A lease is classified as a sales-type lease when the criteria set forth above have been met and the lease transaction is structured in such a way that the lessor (generally a manufacturer or dealer) recognizes a profit or loss on the transaction in addition to interest income. In order for this to occur, the fair value of the property (FV) must be different from the cost (carrying value). The essential substance of this transaction is that of a sale, and thus its name. Common examples of sales-type leases: (1) when a customer of an automobile dealership opts to lease a car in lieu of an outright purchase, and (2) the re-lease of equipment coming off an expiring lease. Note however, that a lease involving real estate must transfer title (i.e., criterion 1. above) by the end of the lease term for the lessor to classify the lease as a sales-type lease.

A direct financing lease differs from a sales-type lease in that the lessor does not realize a profit or loss on the transaction other than interest income. In a direct financing lease, the fair value of the property at the inception of the lease is equal to the cost (carrying value). This type of lease transaction most often involves lessor entities engaged in financing operations. The lessor (a bank, or other financial institution) purchases the asset and then leases the asset to the lessee. This transaction merely replaces the conventional lending transaction where the borrower uses the borrowed funds to purchase the asset. There are many economic reasons why the lease transaction is considered. They are as follows:

1. The lessee (borrower) is able to obtain 100% financing
2. Flexibility of use for the tax benefits
3. The lessor receives the equivalent of interest as well as an asset with some remaining value at the end of the lease term

In summary, it may help to visualize the following chart when considering the classification of a lease from the lessor's standpoint:

One form of a direct financing lease is a leveraged lease which is discussed later in this chapter. This type is mentioned separately because it receives a different accounting treatment by the lessor. A leveraged lease meets all the definitional criteria of a direct financing lease, but differs because it involves at least three parties: a lessee, a long-term creditor, and a lessor (commonly referred to as the equity participant). Other characteristics of a leveraged lease are as follows:

1. The financing provided by the long-term creditor must be without recourse to the general credit of the lessor, although the creditor may hold recourse with respect to the leased property. The amount of the financing must provide the lessor with substantial "leverage" in the transaction.
2. The lessor's net investment declines during the early years and rises during the later years of the lease term before its elimination.

### Lessee Accounting

As discussed in the preceding section, there are two classifications that apply to a lease transaction from the standpoint of the lessee, operating or capital.

**Operating leases.** The accounting treatment accorded an operating lease is relatively simple; the rental payments are charged to expense as the payments are made or become payable. This assumes that the lease payments are being made on a straight-line basis (i.e., an equal payment per period over the lease term).

If the lease agreement calls for either an alternative payment schedule or a scheduled rent increase over the lease term, per FASB Technical Bulletin 85-3, the lease expense is recognized on a straight-line basis over the lease term unless another systematic and rational basis is a better representation of the actual physical usage of the leased property. In addition, the lessor may grant various incentives to the lessee during the lease term such as a rent holiday, or allowances to fund leasehold improvements. Incentives paid to or incurred on behalf of the lessee by the lessor are an inseparable part of the lease agreement. These amounts are recognized as reductions to rental expense on a straight-line basis over the term of a lease as described in the preceding paragraph (FTB 88-1, Issue 2).

In these instances, it is necessary to record either a prepaid asset or a liability depending upon the structure of the payment schedule. If the scheduled increase(s) is due to additional leased property, recognition is to be based on the portion of the leased property that is being utilized with the increased rents recognized over the years that the lessee has control over the use of the additional leased property.

Notice that in the case of an operating lease there is no balance sheet recognition of the leased asset because the substance of the lease is merely that of a rental. There is no reason to expect that the lessee will derive any future economic benefit from the leased asset beyond the lease term.

**Capital leases.** Recall that the classification of a lease is determined prior to the consideration of the accounting treatment. Therefore, it is necessary to first examine the lease transaction against the four criteria (transfer of title, bargain purchase option, 75% of useful life, or 90% of net FV). Should the lease agreement satisfy one of these, it is accounted for as a capital (also referred to as financing) lease.

The lessee records a capital lease as an asset and an obligation (liability) at an amount equal to the present value of the minimum lease payments at the beginning of the lease term. For the purposes of the 90% test, the present value is computed using the incremental borrowing rate of the lessee unless it is practicable for the lessee to determine the implicit rate used by the lessor, and the implicit rate is less than the incremental borrowing rate. The incremental borrowing rate is defined as the rate at lease inception at which the lessee would have been able to borrow over a loan term equivalent to the lease term had it chosen to purchase the leased asset. If the lessee determines a secured borrowing rate that is reasonable and consistent with the financing that would have been used, then, per FTB 79-12, it is acceptable to use a secured borrowing rate.

The asset is recorded at the lower of the present value of the minimum lease payments or the fair value of the asset. When the fair value of the leased asset is less than the present value of the minimum lease payments, the interest rate used to amortize the lease obligation will differ from the interest rate used in the 90% test.

The interest rate used in the amortization will be the same as that used in the 90% test when the fair value is greater than or equal to the present value of the minimum lease payments. For purposes of this computation, the minimum lease payments are considered to be the payments that the lessee is obligated to make or can be required to make excluding executory costs such as insurance, maintenance, and taxes.

The minimum lease payments generally include the minimum rental payments, any guarantee of the residual value made by the lessee, and the penalty for failure to renew the lease, if applicable. If the lease includes a bargain purchase option (BPO), the amount required to be paid under the BPO is also included in the minimum lease payments.

The lease term used in this present value computation is the fixed, noncancelable term of the lease plus the following:

1. All periods covered by bargain renewal options
2. All periods for which failure to renew the lease imposes a penalty on the lessee
3. All periods covered by ordinary renewal options during which the lessee guarantees the lessor's debt on the leased property
4. All periods covered by ordinary renewals or extensions up to the date a BPO is exercisable
5. All periods representing renewals or extensions of the lease at the lessor's option

Remember, if the amount computed as the present value of the minimum lease payments exceeds the fair value of the leased property at the inception of the lease, the amount recorded is limited to the fair value.

The amortization of the leased asset will depend upon how the lease qualifies as a capital lease. If the lease transaction meets the criteria of either transferring ownership, or containing a bargain purchase option, then the asset arising from the transaction is amortized over the estimated useful life of the leased property. If the transaction qualifies as a capital lease because it meets either the 75% of useful life or 90% of FV criteria, the asset is amortized over the lease term. The conceptual rationale for this differentiated treatment arises because of the substance of the transaction. Under the first two criteria, the asset actually becomes the property of the lessee at the end of the lease term (or upon exercise of the BPO). In the latter situations, the title to the property remains with the lessor, and thus, the lessee ceases to have the right to use the property at the conclusion of the lease term.

The leased asset is amortized (depreciated) over the lease term if title does not transfer to the lessee, while the asset is depreciated in a manner consistent with the lessee's normal depreciation policy if the title is to eventually transfer to the lessee. This latter situation can be interpreted to mean that the asset is depreciated over the useful economic life of the leased asset. The treatment and method used to amortize (depreciate) the leased asset is very similar to that used for any other long-lived asset. The amortization entry requires a debit to amortization expense and a credit to accumulated amortization. The leased asset is not amortized below the estimated residual value.

In some instances when the property is to revert back to the lessor, there may be a guaranteed residual value. This is an amount that the lessee guarantees to the lessor. If the FV of the asset at the end of the lease term is greater than or equal to the guaranteed residual amount, the lessee incurs no additional obligation. On the other hand, if the FV of the leased asset is less than the guaranteed residual value, then the lessee must make up the difference, usually with a cash payment. The guaranteed residual value is often used as a tool to reduce the periodic payments by substituting the lump-sum amount at the end of the term that results from the guarantee. In any event the amortization must still take place based on the estimated residual value. This results in a rational and systematic allocation of the expense to the periods of usage and avoids a large loss (or expense) in the last period as a result of the guarantee.

The annual (periodic) rent payments made during the lease term are allocated between a reduction in the obligation and interest expense in a manner such that the interest expense represents the application of a constant periodic rate of interest to the remaining balance of the lease obligation. This is commonly referred to as the effective interest method and is described in APB 21.

The following examples illustrate the treatment described in the foregoing paragraphs.

### Example of accounting for a capital lease—Asset returned to lessor

1. The lease is initiated on 1/1/09 for equipment with an expected useful life of three years. The equipment reverts back to the lessor upon expiration of the lease agreement.
2. The FV of the equipment at lease inception is $135,000.
3. Three payments are due to the lessor in the amount of $50,000 per year beginning 12/31/09. An additional sum of $1,000 is to be paid annually by the lessee for insurance.
4. The lessee guarantees a $10,000 residual value on 12/31/11 to the lessor.
5. Irrespective of the $10,000 residual value guarantee, the leased asset is expected to have only a $1,000 salvage value on 12/31/11.
6. The lessee's incremental borrowing rate is 10%. (The lessor's implicit rate is unknown.)
7. The present value of the lease obligation is as follows:

| | | | | | | |
|---|---|---|---|---|---|---|
| PV of guaranteed residual value | = | $10,000 | × | 7513 * | = | $ 7,513 |
| PV of annual payments | = | $50,000 | × | 2.4869 ** | = | 124,345 |
| | | | | | | $131,858 |

\* *The present value of an amount of $1 due in three periods at 10% is .7513.*
\*\* *The present value of an ordinary annuity of $1 for three periods at 10% is 2.4869.*

The first step in dealing with any lease transaction is to classify the lease. In this case, the lease term is for three years, which is equal to 100% of the expected useful life of the asset. Note that the 90% test is also fulfilled as the PV of the minimum lease payments ($131,858) is greater than 90% of the FV (90% × $135,000 = $121,500). Thus, the lessee accounts for the lease as a capital lease.

In number 7. (above) the present value of the lease obligation is computed. Note that the executory costs (insurance) are not included in the minimum lease payments and that the incremental borrowing rate of the lessee was used to determine the present value. This rate was used because the lessor's implicit rate was not determinable.

*NOTE: In order to have used the implicit rate it would have to have been less than the incremental borrowing rate.*

The entry necessary to record the lease on 1/1/09 is

| | | |
|---|---|---|
| Leased equipment | 131,858 | |
|     Lease obligation | | 131,858 |

Note that the lease is recorded at the present value of the minimum lease payments that, in this case, is less than the FV. If the present value of the minimum lease payments had exceeded the FV, the lease would have been recorded at the FV.

The next step is to determine the proper allocation between interest and reduction of the lease obligation for each lease payment. This is done using the effective interest method as illustrated below.

| Year | Cash payment | Interest expense | Reduction in lease obligation | Balance of lease obligation |
|---|---|---|---|---|
| Inception of lease | | | | $131,858 |
| 2009 | $50,000 | $13,186 | $36,814 | 95,044 |
| 2010 | 50,000 | 9,504 | 40,496 | 54,548 |
| 2011 | 50,000 | 5,452 | 44,548 | 10,000 |

The interest is calculated at 10% (the incremental borrowing rate) of the balance of the lease obligation for each period, and the remainder of each $50,000 payment is allocated as a reduction in the lease obligation. The lessee is also required to pay $1,000 for insurance on an annual basis. The entries necessary to record all payments relative to the lease for each of the three years are shown below.

| | 12/31/09 | | 12/31/10 | | 12/31/11 | |
|---|---|---|---|---|---|---|
| Insurance expense | 1,000 | | 1,000 | | 1,000 | |
| Interest expense | 13,186 | | 9,504 | | 5,452 | |
| Lease obligation | 36,814 | | 40,496 | | 44,548 | |
|     Cash | | 51,000 | | 51,000 | | 51,000 |

The leased equipment recorded as an asset must also be amortized (depreciated). The initial unamortized balance is $131,858; however, as with any other long-lived asset, it cannot be amortized below the estimated residual value of $1,000 (note that it is amortized down to the actual estimated residual value, not the guaranteed residual value). In this case, the straight-line amortization method is applied over a period of three years. This three-year period represents the lease term, not the life of the asset, because the asset reverts back to the lessor at the end of the lease term. Therefore, the following entry will be made at the end of each year:

| | | |
|---|---|---|
| Amortization expense | 43,619 | |
|     Accumulated amortization | | 43,619    [($131,858 – 1,000) ÷ 3] |

Finally, on 12/31/11 we must recognize the fact that ownership of the property has reverted back to the owner (lessor). The lessee made a guarantee that the residual value would be $10,000 on 12/31/11; as a result, the lessee must make up the difference between the guaranteed residual value and the actual residual value with a cash payment to the lessor. The following entry illustrates the removal of the leased asset and obligation from the lessee's accounting records:

| | | |
|---|---|---|
| Lease obligation | 10,000 | |
| Accumulated amortization | 130,858 | |
|     Cash | | 9,000 |
|     Leased equipment | | 131,858 |

The foregoing example illustrated a situation where the asset was to be returned to the lessor. Another situation exists (under BPO or transfer of title) where ownership of the asset is expected to transfer to the lessee at the end of the lease term. Remember that leased assets are amortized over their useful life when title transfers or a bargain purchase option exists. At the end of the lease, the balance of the lease obligation should equal the guaranteed residual value, the bargain purchase option price, or termination penalty for failure to renew the lease.

### Example of accounting for a capital lease—Asset ownership transferred to lessee

1. A three-year lease is initiated on 1/1/09 for equipment with an expected useful life of five years.
2. Three annual lease payments of $52,000 are required beginning on 1/1/09 (note that the payment at the beginning of the year changes the PV computation from the previous example). The lessee pays $2,000 per year for insurance on the equipment and this amount is included in the annual payments.
3. The lessee can exercise a bargain purchase option on 12/31/11 for $10,000. The expected residual value at 12/31/11 is $18,000.
4. The lessee's incremental borrowing rate is 10% (the lessor's implicit rate is unknown).
5. The fair value of the leased property at the inception of the lease is $140,000.

Once again, the classification of the lease must be determined prior to computing the accounting entries to record it. This lease is classified as a capital lease because it contains a BPO. In this case, the 90% test is also fulfilled.

The PV of the lease obligation is computed as follows:

| PV of bargain purchase option | = | $10,000 | × | 7513 * | = $ 7,513 |
|---|---|---|---|---|---|
| PV of annual payments | = | ($52,000 – $2,000) | × | 2.4869 ** | = 136,755 |
| | | | | | $144,268 |

* .7513 is the PV of an amount due in three periods at 10%.
** 2.7355 is the PV of an annuity due for three periods at 10%.

Since the lessee pays $2,000 a year for insurance, this payment is treated as executory costs and excluded from the calculation of the present value of the annual payments. Note that the present value of the lease obligation is greater than the FV of the asset. Because of this, the lease obligation must be recorded at the FV of the leased asset.

| 1/1/09 Leased equipment | 140,000 | |
|---|---|---|
| Obligation under capital lease | | 140,000 |

According to FAS 13, the allocation between interest and principal is determined so that interest expense is computed using a constant periodic rate of interest applied to the remaining balance of the obligation. If the FV of the leased asset is greater than or equal to the PV of the lease obligation, the interest rate used is the same as that used to compute the PV (i.e., the incremental borrowing rate or the implicit rate). In cases such as this when the PV exceeds the FV of the leased asset, a new rate must be computed through a series of manual trial and error calculations. Alternatively, spreadsheet or loan amortization software can be used to solve for the unknown effective interest rate. In this situation the interest rate used was 13.267%. The amortization of the lease takes place as follows:

| Date | Cash payment | Interest expense | Reduction in lease obligation | Balance of lease obligation |
|---|---|---|---|---|
| Inception of lease | | | | $140,000 |
| 1/1/09 | $50,000 | $ -- | $50,000 | 90,000 |
| 1/1/10 | 50,000 | 11,940 | 38,060 | 51,940 |
| 1/1/11 | 50,000 | 6,891 | 43,109 | 8,831 |
| 12/31/11 | 10,000 | 1,169 | 8,831 | -- |

The following entries are required in years 2009 through 2011 to recognize the payment and amortization.

|  |  | 2009 |  | 2010 |  | 2011 |  |
|---|---|---|---|---|---|---|---|
| 1/1 | Insurance expense | 2,000 |  | 2,000 |  | 2,000 |  |
|  | Obligation under capital lease | 50,000 |  | 38,060 |  | 43,109 |  |
|  | Accrued interest payable |  |  | 11,940 |  | 6,891 |  |
|  | Cash |  | 52,000 |  | 52,000 |  | 52,000 |
| 12/31 | Interest expense | 11,940 |  | 6,891 |  | 1,169 |  |
|  | Accrued interest payable |  | 11,940 |  | 6,891 |  | 1,169 |
| 12/31 | Amortization expense | 24,400 |  | 24,400 |  | 24,400 |  |
|  | Accumulated amortization |  | 24,400 |  | 24,400 |  | 24,400 |
|  | [($140,000 – $18,000) ÷ 5 years)] |  |  |  |  |  |  |
| 12/31 | Obligation under capital lease |  |  |  |  | 8,831 |  |
|  | Accrued interest payable |  |  |  |  | 1,169 |  |
|  | Cash |  |  |  |  |  | 10,000 |

## Lessor Accounting

As previously noted, there are four classifications of leases with which a lessor must be concerned. They are operating, sales-type, direct financing, and leveraged.

**Operating leases.** As in the case of the lessee, the operating lease requires a less complex accounting treatment. The payments received by the lessor are recorded as rent revenues in the period in which the payment is received or becomes receivable. As with the lessee, if either the rentals vary from a straight-line basis, the lease agreement contains a scheduled rent increase over the lease term, or the lessor grants incentives to the lessee such as a rent holiday or leasehold improvement allowance, the revenue is recorded on a straight-line basis unless an alternative basis of systematic and rational allocation is more representative of the time pattern of physical usage of the leased property. If the scheduled increase(s) is due to the lessee leasing additional property under a master lease agreement, the increase is allocated proportionally to the additional leased property and recognized on a straight-line basis over the years that the lessee has control over the additional leased property. FTB 88-1 prescribes that, in this case, the total revised rent be allocated between the previously leased property and the additional leased property based on their relative fair values.

The lessor presents the leased property on the balance sheet under the caption "Investment in leased property." This caption is shown with or near the fixed assets of the lessor, and depreciated in the same manner as the lessor's other fixed assets.

Any initial direct costs are amortized over the lease term as the related lease revenue is recognized (i.e., on a straight-line basis unless another method is more representative). However, these costs may be charged to expense as incurred if the effect is not materially different from straight-line amortization.

Any incentives made by the lessor to the lessee are treated as reductions of rent and recognized on a straight-line basis over the term of the lease.

In most operating leases, the lessor recognizes rental income over the lease term and does not measure or recognize any gain or loss on any differential between the fair value of the property and its carrying value. One exception to this rule is set forth in FAS 98. The exception applies when an operating lease involving real estate is not classified as a sales-type lease because ownership to the property does not transfer to the lessee at the end of the lease term. In this case, if at the inception of the lease the fair value of the property is less than its carrying amount, the lessor must recognize a loss equal to that difference at the inception of the lease.

**Sales-type leases.** In accounting for a sales-type lease, it is necessary for the lessor to determine the following amounts:

1. Gross investment
2. Fair value of the leased asset

### 3. Cost

Note that, following the promulgation of FAS 157, there was some confusion over the definition of fair value to be employed for purposes of lease determination and measurement. FSP FAS 157-1 has clarified that FAS 157 does not apply to FAS 13 determinations of lease classifications or measurements. However, FAS 157 is applicable to the determinations to be made in business combinations accounted for under FAS 141(R).

From these amounts, the remainder of the computations necessary to record and account for the lease transaction can be made. The first objective is to determine the numbers necessary to complete the following entry:

| | | |
|---|---|---|
| Lease receivable | xx | |
| Cost of goods sold | xx | |
| Sales | | xx |
| Inventory | | xx |
| Unearned interest | | xx |

The gross investment (lease receivable) of the lessor is equal to the sum of the minimum lease payments (excluding executory costs) plus the unguaranteed residual value. The difference between the gross investment and the present value of the two components of gross investment (minimum lease payments and unguaranteed residual value) is recorded as the unearned interest revenue. The present value is computed using the lease term and implicit interest rate (both of which were discussed earlier). The lease term used in this computation includes any renewal options exercisable at the discretion of the lessor. The resulting unearned interest revenue is to be amortized into income using the effective interest method. This will result in a constant periodic rate of return on the net investment (the net investment is the gross investment less the unearned income).

Recall from our earlier discussion that the fair value (FV) of the leased property is, by definition, equal to the normal selling price of the asset adjusted by any residual amount retained (this amount retained can be exemplified by an unguaranteed residual value, investment credit, etc.). The adjusted selling price used for a sales-type lease is equal to the present value of the minimum lease payments. Thus, we can say that the normal selling price less the residual amount retained is equal to the PV of the minimum lease payments.

The cost of goods sold to be charged against income in the period of the sale is computed as the historic cost or carrying value of the asset (most likely inventory) plus any initial direct costs, less the present value of the unguaranteed residual value. The difference between the adjusted selling price and the amount computed as the cost of goods sold is the gross profit recognized by the lessor at the inception of the lease (sale). Thus, a sales-type lease generates two types of revenue for the lessor.

1. The gross profit on the sale
2. The interest earned on the lease receivable

Note that if the sales-type lease involves real estate, the lessor must account for the transaction under the provisions of FAS 66 in the same manner as a seller of the same property (see Chapter 10).

The application of these points is illustrated in the example below.

#### Example of accounting for a sales-type lease

Price Inc. is a manufacturer of specialized equipment. Many of its customers do not have the necessary funds or financing available for outright purchase. Because of this, Price offers a leasing alternative. The data relative to a typical lease are as follows:

1. The noncancelable fixed portion of the lease term is five years. The lessor has the option to renew the lease for an additional three years at the same rental. The estimated useful life of the asset is ten years.
2. The lessor is to receive equal annual payments over the term of the lease. The leased property reverts back to the lessor upon termination of the lease.
3. The lease is initiated on 1/1/09. Payments are due annually on 12/31 for the duration of the lease term.
4. The cost of the equipment to Price Inc. is $100,000. The lessor incurs costs associated with the inception of the lease in the amount of $2,500.
5. The selling price of the equipment for an outright purchase is $150,000.
6. The equipment is expected to have a residual value of $15,000 at the end of five years and $10,000 at the end of eight years.
7. The lessor desires a return of 12% (the implicit rate).

The first step is to calculate the annual payment due to the lessor. In order to yield the lessor's desired return, the present value (PV) of the minimum lease payments must equal the selling price adjusted for the present value of the residual amount. The present value is computed using the implicit interest rate and the lease term. In this case, the implicit rate is given as 12% and the lease term is eight years (the fixed noncancelable portion plus the renewal period). Thus, the computation would be as follows:

Normal selling price – PV of residual value = PV of minimum lease payments

Or, in this case,

$150,000 – (.40388* × $10,000 = $4,038.80) = 4.96764** × Annual minimum lease payment

$$\frac{\$145,961.20}{4.96764} = \text{Annual minimum lease payment}$$

$29,382.40 = Annual minimum lease payment

\* .40388 is the present value of an amount of $1 due in eight periods at a 12% interest rate.
\*\* 4.96764 is the present value of an annuity of $1 for eight periods at a 12% interest rate.

Prior to examining the accounting implications of the lease, we must first determine the lease classification. Assume that there are no uncertainties regarding the lessor's costs, and the collectibility of the lease payments is reasonably assured. In this example, the lease term is eight years (discussed above) while the estimated useful life of the asset is ten years; thus, this lease is not an operating lease because the lease term covers 80% of the asset's estimated useful life. This exceeds the previously discussed 75% criterion. (Note that it also meets the 90% of FV criterion because the PV of the minimum lease payments of $145,961.20 is greater than 90% of the FV [90% × $150,000 = $135,000]). Next it must be determined if this is a sales-type, direct financing, or leveraged lease. To do this, examine the FV or selling price of the asset and compare it to the cost. Because the two are not equal, this is a sales-type lease.

Next, obtain the figures necessary for the lessor to record the entry. The gross investment is the total minimum lease payments plus the unguaranteed residual value or

($29,382.40 × 8 = $235,059.20) + $10,000 = $245,059.20

The cost of goods sold is the historical cost of the inventory ($100,000) plus any initial direct costs ($2,500) less the PV of the unguaranteed residual value ($10,000 × .40388 = $4,038.80). Thus, the cost of goods sold amount is $98,461.20 (= $100,000 + $2,500 – $4,038.80). Note that the initial direct costs will require a credit entry to record their accrual (accounts payable) or payment (cash). The inventory account is credited for the carrying value of the asset, in this case $100,000.

The adjusted selling price is equal to the PV of the minimum payments, or $145,961.20. Finally, the unearned interest revenue is equal to the gross investment (i.e., lease receivable) less the present value of the components making up the gross investment (the present values of the minimum annual lease payments of $29,382.40 and the unguaranteed residual of $10,000). The computation is [$245,059.20 – ($29,382.40 × 4.96764 = $145,961.20) – ($10,000 × .40388 = 4,038.80) = $95,059.20]. Therefore, the entry necessary for the lessor to record the lease is

| | | |
|---|---|---|
| Lease receivable | 245,059.20 | |
| Cost of goods sold | 98,461.20 | |
| Inventory | | 100,000.00 |
| Sales | | 145,961.20 |
| Unearned interest | | 95,059.20 |
| Accounts payable (initial direct costs) | | 2,500.00 |

The next step in accounting for a sales-type lease is to determine the proper handling of each payment. Both principal and interest are included in each payment. Interest is recognized using the effective interest rate method so that an equal rate of return is earned each period over the term of the lease. This will require setting up an amortization schedule as illustrated below.

| Year | Cash payment | Interest | Reduction in principal | Balance of net investment |
|---|---|---|---|---|
| Inception of lease | | | | $150,000.00 |
| 2009 | $ 29,382.40 | $18,000.00 | $ 11,382.40 | 138,617.00 |
| 2010 | 29,382.40 | 16,634.11 | 12,748.29 | 125,869.31 |
| 2011 | 29,382.40 | 15,104.32 | 14,278.08 | 111,591.23 |
| 2012 | 29,382.40 | 13,390.95 | 15,991.45 | 95,599.78 |
| 2013 | 29,382.40 | 11,471.97 | 17,910.43 | 77,689.35 |
| 2014 | 29,382.40 | 9,322.72 | 20,059.68 | 57,629.67 |
| 2015 | 29,382.40 | 6,915.56 | 22,466.84 | 35,162.83 |
| 2016 | 29,382.40 | 4,219.57 | 25,162.83 | 10,000.00 |
| | $235,059.20 | $95,059.20 | $140,000.00 | |

A few of the columns need to be elaborated upon. First, the net investment is the gross investment (lease receivable) less the unearned interest. Note that at the end of the lease term, the net investment is equal to the estimated residual value. Also note that the total interest earned over the lease term is equal to the unearned interest at the beginning of the lease term.

The entries below illustrate the proper accounting for the receipt of the lease payment and the amortization of the unearned interest in the first year.

| | | |
|---|---|---|
| Cash | 29,382.40 | |
| Lease receivable | | 29,382.40 |
| | | |
| Unearned interest | 18,000.00 | |
| Interest revenue | | 18,000.00 |

Note that there is no entry to recognize the principal reduction. This is done automatically when the net investment is reduced by decreasing the lease receivable (gross investment) by $29,382.40 and the unearned interest account by only $18,000. The $18,000 is 12% (implicit rate) of the net investment. These entries are to be made over the life of the lease.

At the end of the lease term the asset is returned to the lessor and the following entry is required:

| | | |
|---|---|---|
| Asset | 10,000 | |
| Lease receivable | | 10,000 |

**Direct financing leases.** The accounting for a direct financing lease holds many similarities to that for a sales-type lease. Of particular importance is that the terminology used is much the same; however, the treatment accorded these items varies greatly. Again, it is best to preface our discussion by determining our objectives in the accounting for a direct financing lease. Once the lease has been classified, it must be recorded. In order to do this, the following numbers must be obtained:

1. Gross investment
2. Cost
3. Residual value

As noted, a direct financing lease generally involves a leasing company or other financial institution and results in only interest income being earned by the lessor. This is because the FV (selling price) and the cost are equal and, therefore, no profit is recognized on the actual lease transaction. Note how this is different from a sales-type lease that involves both a profit on the transaction and interest income over the lease term. The reason for this difference is derived from the conceptual nature underlying the purpose of the lease transaction. In a sales-type lease, the manufacturer (distributor, dealer) is seeking an alternative means to finance the sale of the product, whereas a direct financing lease is a result of the consumer's need to finance an equipment purchase through a third party. Because the consumer is unable to obtain conventional financing, he or she turns to a leasing company that will purchase the desired asset and then lease it to the consumer. Here the profit on the transaction remains with the manufacturer while the interest income is earned by the leasing company.

Like a sales-type lease, the first objective is to determine the amounts necessary to complete the following entry:

| | | |
|---|---|---|
| Lease receivable | xxx | |
|    Asset | | xxx |
|    Unearned interest | | xx |

The gross investment is still defined as the minimum amount of lease payments exclusive of any executory costs plus the unguaranteed residual value. The difference between the gross investment as determined above and the cost (carrying value) of the asset is to be recorded as the unearned interest income because there is no manufacturer's/dealer's profit earned on the transaction. The following entry would be made to record the initial direct costs:

| | | |
|---|---|---|
| Initial direct costs | xx | |
|    Cash (or accounts payable) | | xx |

The net investment in the lease is defined as the gross investment less the unearned interest income plus the unamortized initial direct costs related to the lease. Initial direct costs are defined in the same way that they were for purposes of the sales-type lease; however, the accounting treatment is different. For a direct financing lease, the unearned lease (interest) income and the initial direct costs are amortized to income over the lease term to yield a constant effective rate of interest on the net investment. Thus, the effect of the initial direct costs is to reduce the implicit interest rate, or yield, to the lessor over the life of the lease.

An example follows that illustrates the preceding principles.

**Example of accounting for a direct financing lease**

Edwards, Inc. needs new equipment to expand its manufacturing operation; however, it does not have sufficient capital to purchase the asset at this time. Because of this, Edwards has employed Samuels Leasing to purchase the asset. In turn, Edwards (the lessee) will lease the asset from Samuels (the lessor). The following information applies to the terms of the lease:

*Lease information*

1. A three-year lease is initiated on 1/1/09 for equipment costing $131,858 with an expected useful life of five years. FV at 1/1/09 of the equipment is $131,858.
2. Three annual payments are due to the lessor beginning 12/31/09. The property reverts back to the lessor upon termination of the lease.
3. The unguaranteed residual value at the end of year three is estimated to be $10,000.
4. The annual payments are calculated to give the lessor a 10% return (implicit rate).
5. The lease payments and unguaranteed residual value have a PV equal to $131,858 (FMV of asset) at the stipulated discount rate.

6. The annual payment to the lessor is computed as follows:

| | | |
|---|---|---|
| PV of residual value | = | $10,000 × .7513[*] = $7,513 |
| PV of lease payments | = | Selling price − PV of residual value |
| | = | $131,858 − 7,513 = $124,345 |

$$\text{Annual payment} = \frac{\$124,345}{PV_3,\ 10\%} = \frac{\$124,345}{2.4869^{**}} = \$50,000$$

[*] .7513 is the PV of an amount due in three periods at 10%.
[**] 2.4869 is the PV of an annuity of $1 for three periods at a 10% interest rate.

7. Initial direct costs of $7,500 are incurred by Samuels in the lease transaction.

As with any lease transaction, the first step must be to determine the proper classification of the lease. In this case, the PV of the lease payments ($124,345) exceeds 90% of the FV (90% × $131,858 = $118,672). Assume that the lease payments are reasonably assured and that there are no uncertainties surrounding the costs yet to be incurred by the lessor.

Next, determine the unearned interest and the net investment in the lease.

| | |
|---|---|
| Gross investment in lease | |
| [(3 × $50,000) + $10,000] | $160,000 |
| Cost of leased property | 131,858 |
| Unearned interest | $ 28,142 |

The unamortized initial direct costs are to be added to the gross investment in the lease and the unearned interest income is to be deducted to arrive at the net investment in the lease. The net investment in the lease for this example is determined as follows:

| | |
|---|---|
| Gross investment in lease | $160,000 |
| Add: Unamortized initial direct costs | 7,500 |
| | $167,500 |
| Less: Unearned interest income | 28,142 |
| Net investment in lease | $139,358 |

The net investment in the lease (Gross investment − Unearned revenue) has been increased by the amount of initial direct costs. Therefore, the implicit rate is no longer 10%. We must recompute the implicit rate. The implicit rate is really the result of an internal rate of return calculation. We know that the lease payments are to be $50,000 per annum and that a residual value of $10,000 is expected at the end of the lease term. In return for these payments (inflows) we are giving up equipment (outflow) and incurring initial direct costs (outflows) with a net investment of $139,358 ($131,858 + $7,500). The only way to manually obtain the new implicit rate is through a trial and error calculation as set up below.

$$\frac{50,000}{(1+i)}\ 1 + \frac{50,000}{(1+i)}\ 2 + \frac{50,000}{(1+i)}\ 3 + \frac{10,000}{(1+i)}\ 3 = \$139,358$$

Where i = implicit rate of interest

This computation is most efficiently performed using either spreadsheet or present value software. In doing so, the $139,358 is entered as the present value, the contractual payment stream and residual value are entered, and the software iteratively solves for the unknown implicit interest rate.

In this case, the implicit rate is equal to 7.008%. Thus, the amortization table would be set up as follows:

| | (a) Lease payments | (b) Reduction in unearned interest | (c) PV × implicit rate (7.008%) | (d) Reduction in initial direct costs (b-c) | (e) Reduction in PVI net invest. (a-b + d) | (f) PVI net invest. in lease $(f)_{(n+1)} = (f)_n − (e)$ |
|---|---|---|---|---|---|---|
| | | | | | | $139,358 |
| 1 | $ 50,000 | $13,186 (1) | $ 9,766 | $3,420 | $ 40,234 | 99,124 |
| 2 | 50,000 | 9,504 (2) | 6,947 | 2,557 | 43,053 | 56,071 |
| 3 | 50,000 | 5,455 (3) | 3,929 | 1,526 | 46,071 | 10,000 |
| | $150,000 | $28,145* | $20,642 | $7,503 | $129,358 | |

* Rounded

(b.1)  $131,858 \times 10\% = \$13,186$
(b.2)  $[\$131,858 - (\$50,000 - 13,186)] \times 10\% = \$9,504$
(b.3)  $\{\$131,858 - [(\$50,000 - 9,504) + (\$50,000 - 13,186)]\} \times 10\% = \$5,455$

Here the interest is computed as 7.008% of the net investment. Note again that the net investment at the end of the lease term is equal to the estimated residual value.

The entry made to initially record the lease is as follows:

| | | |
|---|---|---|
| Lease receivable* [($50,000 × 3) + 10,000] | 160,000 | |
|     Asset acquired for leasing | | 131,858 |
|     Unearned interest | | 28,142 |

\* *Also the "gross investment in lease."*

When the payment of (or obligation to pay) the initial direct costs occurs, the following entry must be made:

| | | |
|---|---|---|
| Initial direct costs | 7,500 | |
|     Cash (or accounts payable) | | 7,500 |

Using the schedule above, the following entries would be made during each of the indicated years:

| | 2009 | | 2010 | | 2011 | |
|---|---|---|---|---|---|---|
| Cash | 50,000 | | 50,000 | | 50,000 | |
|     Lease receivable* | | 50,000 | | 50,000 | | 50,000 |
| Unearned interest | 13,186 | | 9,504 | | 5,455 | |
|     Initial direct costs | | 3,420 | | 2,557 | | 1,526 |
|     Interest revenue | | 9,766 | | 6,947 | | 3,929 |

\* *Also the "gross investment in lease."*

Finally, when the asset is returned to the lessor at the end of the lease term, it must be recorded by the following entry:

| | | |
|---|---|---|
| Used asset | 10,000 | |
|     Lease receivable* | | 10,000 |

\* *Also the "gross investment in lease."*

**Leveraged leases.** One of the more complex accounting subjects regarding leases is the accounting for a leveraged lease. Just as is the case with sales-type and direct financing leases, the classification of the lease by the lessor has no impact on the classification of the lease by the lessee. The lessee simply considers whether the lease qualifies as an operating lease or a capital lease. The lessor's accounting issues, however, are substantially more complex.

In order to qualify as a leveraged lease, a lease agreement must meet the following requirements, and the lessor must account for the investment tax credit (when in effect) in the manner described below.

NOTE: *Failure to do so will result in the lease being classified as a direct financing lease.*

1. The lease must meet the definition of a direct financing lease (the 90% of FV criterion does not apply).[5]
2. The lease must involve at least three parties.

   a. An owner-lessor (equity participant)
   b. A lessee
   c. A long-term creditor (debt participant)

---

[5] *A direct financing lease must have its cost or carrying value equal to the fair value of the asset at the lease's inception. So even if the amounts are not significantly different, leveraged lease accounting may not be used.*

3. The financing provided by the creditor is nonrecourse as to the general credit of the lessor and is sufficient to provide the lessor with substantial leverage.
4. The lessor's net investment (defined below) decreases in the early years and increases in the later years until it is eliminated.

This last characteristic poses the accounting issue.

The leveraged lease arose as a result of an effort to maximize the income tax benefits associated with a lease transaction. In order to accomplish this, it was necessary to involve a third party to the lease transaction (in addition to the lessor and lessee); a long-term creditor. The following diagram[6] illustrates the relationships in a leveraged lease agreement:

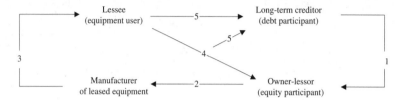

1. The owner-lessor obtains long-term financing from the creditor, generally in excess of 50% of the purchase price. FAS 13 indicates that the lessor must be provided with sufficient leverage in the transaction, therefore the 50%.
2. The owner then uses this financing along with his/her own funds to purchase the asset from the manufacturer.
3. The manufacturer delivers the asset to the lessee.
4. The lessee remits the periodic rent to the lessor.
5. The debt is guaranteed by either using the equipment as collateral, the assignment of the lease payments, or both, depending on the demands established by the creditor.

The FASB concluded that the entire lease agreement be accounted for as a single transaction and not a direct financing lease plus a debt transaction. The feeling was that the latter did not readily convey the lessor's net investment in the lease to the user of the financial statements. Thus, the lessor records the investment as a net amount. The gross investment is calculated as a combination of the following amounts:

1. The rentals receivable from the lessee, net of the principal and interest payments due to the long-term creditor
2. A receivable for the amount of the investment tax credit (ITC) to be realized on the transaction[7]
3. The estimated residual value of the leased asset
4. The unearned and deferred income consisting of

   a. The estimated pretax lease income (or loss), after deducting initial direct costs, remaining to be allocated to income
   b. The ITC remaining to be allocated to income over the remaining term of the lease[7]

---

[6] *Adapted from "A Straightforward Approach to Leveraged Leasing" by Pierce R. Smith,* **The Journal of Commercial Bank Lending,** *July 1973, pp. 40-47.*

[7] *The investment tax credit (ITC) was repealed, effective January 1, 1986. ITC was relevant only for property placed in service prior to this date. We continue to discuss these concepts because Congress has historically reinstated this credit during economic downturns to provide economic stimulus. See the Definitions of Terms section of this chapter for further details.*

The first three amounts described above are readily obtainable; however, the last amount, the unearned and deferred income, requires additional computations. In order to compute this amount, it is necessary to create a cash flow (income) analysis by year for the entire lease term. As described in 4. above, the unearned and deferred income consists of the pretax lease income (Gross lease rentals – Depreciation – Loan interest) and the unamortized investment tax credit. The total of these two amounts for all of the periods in the lease term represents the unearned and deferred income at the inception of the lease.

The amount computed as the gross investment in the lease (foregoing paragraphs) less the deferred taxes relative to the difference between pretax lease income and taxable lease income is the net investment for purposes of computing the net income for the period. In order to compute the periodic net income, another schedule must be completed that uses the cash flows derived in the first schedule and allocates them between income and a reduction in the net investment.

The amount of income is first determined by applying a rate to the net investment. The rate to be used is the rate that will allocate the entire amount of cash flow (income) when applied in the years in which the net investment is positive. In other words, the rate is derived in much the same way as the implicit rate (trial and error), except that only the years in which there is a positive net investment are considered. Thus, income is recognized only in the years in which there is a positive net investment.

The income recognized is divided among the following three elements:

1. Pretax accounting income
2. Amortization of investment tax credit
3. The tax effect of the pretax accounting income

The first two are allocated in proportionate amounts from the unearned and deferred income included in the calculation of the net investment. In other words, the unearned and deferred income consists of pretax lease accounting income and ITC. Each of these is recognized during the period in the proportion that the current period's allocated income is to the total income (cash flow). The last item, the income tax effect, is recognized in income tax expense for the year. The income tax effect of any difference between pretax lease accounting income and taxable lease income is charged (or credited) to deferred income taxes.

When income tax rates change, all components of a leveraged lease must be recalculated from the inception of the lease using the revised after-tax cash flows arising from the revised income tax rates.

If, in any case, the projected cash receipts (income) are less than the initial investment, the deficiency is to be recognized as a loss at the inception of the lease. Similarly, if at any time during the lease period the aforementioned method of recognizing income would result in a future period loss, the loss is to be recognized immediately.

This situation may arise as a result of the circumstances surrounding the lease changing. Therefore, any estimated residual value and other important assumptions must be reviewed on a periodic basis (at least annually). Any change is to be incorporated into the income computations; however, there is to be no upward revision of the estimated residual value.

The following example illustrates the application of these principles to a leveraged lease:

**Example of simplified leveraged lease**

1. A lessor acquires an asset for $100,000 with an estimated useful life of three years in exchange for a $25,000 down payment and a $75,000 three-year note with equal payments due on 12/31 each year. The interest rate is 18%.
2. The asset has no residual value.
3. The PV of an ordinary annuity of $1 for three years at 18% is 2.17427.

4. The asset is leased for three years with annual payments due to the lessor on 12/31 in the amount of $45,000.
5. The lessor uses the ACRS method of depreciation (150% declining balance with a half-year convention in the year placed in service) for income tax purposes and elects to reduce the ITC rate to 4% as opposed to reducing the depreciable basis.
6. Assume a constant income tax rate throughout the life of the lease of 40%.

Chart 1 analyzes the cash flows generated by the leveraged leasing activities. Chart 2 allocates the cash flows between the investment in leveraged leased assets and income from leveraged leasing activities. The allocation requires finding that rate of return, which when applied to the investment balance at the beginning of each year that the investment amount is positive, will allocate the net cash flow fully to net income over the term of the lease. This rate can be found only by a computer program or by an iterative trial and error process. The example that follows has a positive investment value in each of the three years, and thus the allocation takes place in each time period. Leveraged leases usually have periods where the investment account turns negative and is below zero.

Allocating principal and interest on the loan payments is as follows:

$$(\$75,000 \div 2.17427 = \$34,494)$$

| Year | Payment | Interest 18% | Principal | Balance |
|---|---|---|---|---|
| Inception of lease | $ -- | $ -- | $ -- | $75,000 |
| 1 | 34,494 | 13,500 | 20,994 | 54,006 |
| 2 | 34,494 | 9,721 | 24,773 | 29,233 |
| 3 | 34,494 | 5,261 | 29,233 | -- |

**Chart 1**

| | A | | B | | C | | D | | E | | F | | G | | H | | I |
|---|---|---|---|---|---|---|---|---|---|---|---|---|---|---|---|---|---|
| | | | | | | | | | Income | | | | | | Cash | | |
| | | | | | | | | | tax | | | | | | flow | | |
| | | | | | | | Taxable | | payable | | Loan | | | | (A+G-C | | Cumulative |
| | | | | | Interest | | income | | (rcvbl.) | | principal | | | | -E-F) | | cash |
| | Rent | | Depr. | | on loan | | (loss) (A-B-C) | | Dx40% | | payments | | ITC | | | | flow |
| Initial | $ -- | $ | -- | $ | -- | $ | -- | $ | -- | $ | -- | $ | -- | | $(25,000) | | $(25,000) |
| Year 1 | 45,000 | | 25,000 | | 13,500 | | 6,500 | | 2,600 | | 20,994 | | 4,000 | | 11,906 | | (13,094) |
| Year 2 | 45,000 | | 38,000 | | 9,721 | | (2,721) | | (1,088) | | 24,773 | | -- | | 11,594 | | (1,500) |
| Year 3 | 45,000 | | 37,000 | | 5,261 | | 2,739 | | 1,096 | | 29,233 | | -- | | 9,410 | | 7,910 |
| Total | $135,000 | | $100,000 | | $28,482 | | $ 6,518 | | $ 2,608 | | $75,000 | | $4,000 | | $ 7,910 | | |

The chart below allocates the cash flows determined above between the net investment in the lease and income. Recall that the income is then allocated between pretax accounting income and the amortization of the investment credit. The income tax expense for the period is a result of applying the income tax rate to the current periodic pretax accounting income.

The amount to be allocated in total in each period is the net cash flow determined in column H above. The investment at the beginning of year one is the initial down payment of $25,000. This investment is then reduced on an annual basis by the amount of the cash flow not allocated to income.

**Chart 2**

| | 1 | 2 | 3 | 4 | 5 | 6 | 7 |
|---|---|---|---|---|---|---|---|
| | | Cash Flow Assumption | | | | Income Analysis | |
| | Investment | | Allocated | Allocated | | Income | Investment |
| | beginning | Cash | to | to | Pretax | tax | tax |
| | of year | flow | investment | income | income | expense | credit |
| Year 1 | $25,000 | $11,906 | $ 7,964 | $3,942 | $3,248 | $1,300 | $1,994 |
| Year 2 | 17,036 | 11,594 | 8,908 | 2,686 | 2,213 | 885 | 1,358 |
| Year 3 | 8,128 | 9,410 | 8,128 | 1,282 | 1,057 | 423 | 648 |
| | | $32,910 | $25,000 | $7,910 | $6,518 | $2,608 | $4,000 |

Rate of return = 15.77%

1. Column 2 is the net cash flow after the initial investment, and columns 3 and 4 are the allocation based upon the 15.77% rate of return. The total of column 4 is the same as the total of column H in Chart 1.
2. Column 5 allocates column D in Chart 1 based upon the allocations in column 4. Column 6 allocates column E in Chart 1, (and, of course, is computed as 40% of column 5) and column 7 allocates column G in Chart 1 on the same basis.

The journal entries below illustrate the proper recording and accounting for the leveraged lease transaction. The initial entry represents the cash down payment, investment tax credit receivable, the unearned and deferred revenue, and the net cash to be received over the term of the lease.

The remaining journal entries recognize the annual transactions which include the net receipt of cash and the amortization of income.

|  | *Year 1* |  | *Year 2* |  | *Year 3* |  |
|---|---|---|---|---|---|---|
| Rents receivable [Chart 1 (A-C-F)] | 31,518 |  |  |  |  |  |
| Investment tax credit receivable | 4,000 |  |  |  |  |  |
| Cash |  | 25,000 |  |  |  |  |
| Unearned and deferred income |  | 10,518 |  |  |  |  |

*Initial investment, Chart 2 (5+7) totals*

|  | *Year 1* |  | *Year 2* |  | *Year 3* |  |
|---|---|---|---|---|---|---|
| Cash | 10,506 |  | 10,506 |  | 10,506 |  |
| Rent receivable |  | 10,506 |  | 10,506 |  | 10,506 |

*Net for all cash transactions, Chart 1 (A-C-F) line by line for each year*

|  | *Year 1* |  | *Year 2* |  | *Year 3* |  |
|---|---|---|---|---|---|---|
| Income tax receivable (cash) | 4,000 |  |  |  |  |  |
| Investment tax credit receivable |  | 4,000 |  |  |  |  |
| Unearned and deferred income | 5,242 |  | 3,571 |  | 1,705 |  |
| Income from leveraged leases |  | 5,242 |  | 3,571 |  | 1,705 |

*Amortization of unearned income, Chart 2 (5+7) line by line for each year*

The following schedules illustrate the computation of deferred income tax amount. The annual amount is a result of the temporary difference created due to the difference in the timing of the recognition of income for GAAP and income tax purposes. The income for income tax purposes can be found in column D in Chart 1, while the income for GAAP purposes is found in column 5 of Chart 2. The actual amount of deferred income tax is the difference between the income tax computed with the temporary difference and the income tax computed without the temporary difference. These amounts are represented by the income tax payable or receivable as shown in column E of Chart 1 and the income tax expense as shown in column 6 of Chart 2. A check of this figure is provided by multiplying the difference between GAAP income and tax income by the annual rate.

*Year 1*

| Income tax payable | $ 2,600 |  |
|---|---|---|
| Income tax expense | (1,300) |  |
| Deferred income tax (Dr) |  | $1,300 |
| Taxable income | $ 6,500 |  |
| Pretax accounting income | (3,248) |  |
| Difference | $ 3,252 |  |

$3,252 × 40% = $1,300

*Year 2*

| Income tax receivable | $ 1,088 |  |
|---|---|---|
| Income tax expense | 885 |  |
| Deferred income tax (Cr) |  | $1,973 |
| Taxable loss | $ 2,721 |  |
| Pretax accounting income | 2,213 |  |
| Difference | $ 4,934 |  |

$4,934 × 40% = $1,973

|  | *Year 3* |  |  |
|---|---|---|---|
| Income tax payable |  | $ 1,096 |  |
| Income tax expense |  | (423) |  |
| Deferred income tax (Dr) |  |  | $ 673 |
| Taxable income |  | $ 2,739 |  |
| Pretax accounting income |  | (1,057) |  |
| Difference |  | $ 1,682 |  |
| $1,682 × 40% = $673 |  |  |  |

### Interpretive guidance.

*Changes in income tax rates.* FAS 13 requires that the rate of return and allocation of income to be recalculated from the date of inception of a lease and a gain or loss recognized when an important assumption is changed. Per FTB 79-16, the effect on a leveraged lease of a change in the income tax rate is recognized as a gain or loss in the accounting period in which the rate changes. Deferred income taxes relating to the change are recognized in accordance with FAS 109.

*Change or projected changes in the timing of cash flows relative to income taxes applicable to a leveraged lease transaction.* The US Internal Revenue Service (IRS) may challenge the timing of the lessor's income tax deductions related to certain types of leveraged lease transactions.[8] Upon eventual settlement with the IRS regarding these matters, the economics of the lease may be significantly less favorable from the standpoint of the lessor than they were at inception because the originally projected economic benefits resulted heavily from the ability to obtain income tax deductions for accelerated tax depreciation and interest expense that early in the lease term would typically exceed the rental income generated by the lease.

FSP FAS 13-2 amended FAS 13 to provide that the projected timing of income tax cash flows attributable to a leveraged lease is to be reviewed annually during the lease term (or between annual reviews if events or changes in circumstances indicate that a change in timing either has occurred or is projected to occur in the future). Upon review, if the projected timing of the lease's income tax cash flows changes, the lessor will be required to recalculate, from the inception of the lease, the rate of return and the allocation of income to positive investment years in accordance with FAS 13, paragraph 44. The net investment amount is adjusted to the recalculated amount with the change recognized as a gain or loss in the year that the assumptions changed. The pretax gain or loss is to be included in income from continuing operations before income taxes in the same financial statement caption in which leverage lease income is recognized with the income tax effect of the gain or loss reflected in the income tax provision or benefit.

The FSP further provides that the recalculated cash flows are to exclude interest and penalties, advance payments, and deposits to the IRS (and presumably any other relevant state, local, or foreign taxing jurisdiction). The deposits or advance payments are to be included in the projected amount of the settlement with the taxing authority.

The accounting treatment prescribed by the FSP is applicable only to changes or projected changes in the timing of income taxes that are directly attributable to the leveraged lease transaction. EITF 87-8, Issue 10 provides that reporting entities whose tax positions frequently vary between the alternative minimum tax (AMT) and regular tax are not required to annually recalculate the net investment in the lease unless there is an indication that the original assumptions about the leveraged lease's anticipated total after-tax net income were no longer valid.

---

[8] *The transactions that the IRS has reportedly challenged are commonly referred to as Lease In-Lease Out (LILO) and Sale In-Lease Out (SILO) transactions.*

Another factor to consider in the determination of the after-tax cash flows attributable to a leveraged lease transaction is the application of FIN 48, *Accounting for Uncertainty in Income Taxes.* As discussed in detail in Chapter 17, the lessor is required to assess whether it is more likely than not (i.e., there is a greater than 50% chance probability) that the tax positions it takes or plans to take relative to the transaction would be sustained upon examination by the applicable taxing authorities. If the tax positions do not meet that recognition threshold, the tax benefits associated with taking those positions would be excluded from the leveraged lease calculations and, in fact, would give rise to a liability for unrecognized income tax benefits as well as an accrual for any applicable interest and penalties for all open tax years that are within the statute of limitations. This could obviously have a significant impact on the computed rate of return on the investment attributable to the years in which the net investment is positive.

If, however, the tax positions meet the recognition threshold, then they are subject to measurement to determine the maximum amount that is more than 50% probable of being sustained upon examination. The difference between the income tax position taken or planned to be taken on the income tax return (the "as-filed" benefit), and the amount of the benefit measured using the more than 50% computation, along with any associated penalties and interest, is recorded as the liability for unrecognized income tax benefits as previously described.

The only situation in which this liability, penalties, and interest would not be applicable would be if the tax positions were assessed to be highly certain tax positions, as defined in FIN 48. Under those circumstances, the entire tax benefit associated with the lease would be recognized and, of course, no interest or penalties would be recognized.

*Applicability to real estate leases.* The foregoing discussion involved the lease of a manufactured asset. FAS 98 and EITF 85-16 clarify that leases that involve land and buildings or leases in a sale-leaseback transaction potentially qualify as leveraged leases if the criteria to qualify as a leveraged lease are met.

*Applicability to existing assets of the lessor.* At the inception of a lease, the cost or carrying value and the fair value of an asset must be the same for the lease to be classified as a direct financing lease which is a necessary condition for leveraged lease treatment. The carrying amount of an existing asset before any write-down must equal its fair value in order for the lease to be classified as a leveraged lease (FTB 88-1, Issue 3).

*Effect of lessor obligation to make capital contributions.* In some leases, the lessee is granted a rent holiday with its lease payments not commencing until one to two years after lease inception. In order to ensure that there is sufficient cash flow to repay the debt on the leased property, the lessor contractually agrees to make equity contributions to fund the debt repayments during the holiday period. Even though the creditor often has recourse with respect to the general credit of the lessor for these equity contributions, this does not taint the nonrecourse character of the lease financing necessary for leveraged lease classification. In this situation, the lessor's obligation to make the equity contributions is to be recorded as a liability at present value at lease inception. This will increase the lessor's net investment on which it bases its pattern of income recognition (EITF 85-16).

## Real Estate Leases

Real estate leases can be divided into the following four categories:

1. Leases involving land only
2. Leases involving land and building(s)
3. Leases involving real estate and equipment
4. Leases involving only part of a building

**Leases involving only land.**

*Lessee accounting.* If the lease agreement transfers ownership or contains a bargain purchase option, the lessee accounts for the lease as a capital lease, and records an asset and related liability equal to the present value of the minimum lease payments. If the lease agreement does not transfer ownership or contain a bargain purchase option, the lessee accounts for the lease as an operating lease.

*Lessor accounting.* If the lease gives rise to dealer's profit (or loss) and transfers ownership (i.e., title), the lease is classified as a sales-type lease and accounted for under the provisions of FAS 66 in the same manner as a seller of the same property (profit recognition on real estate sales is discussed in detail in Chapter 10). If the lease transfers ownership, both the collectibility and no material uncertainties criteria are met, but does not give rise to dealer's profit (or loss), the lease is accounted for as a direct financing or leveraged lease as appropriate. If the lease does not transfer ownership, but it contains a bargain purchase option and both the collectibility and no material uncertainties criteria are met, the lease is accounted for as a direct financing, leveraged, or operating lease using the same lessor classification criteria as any other lease. If the lease does not meet the collectibility and/or no material uncertainties criteria, the lease is accounted for as an operating lease.

**Leases involving land and building.**

*Lessee accounting.* If the agreement transfers title or contains a bargain purchase option, the lessee accounts for the agreement by separating the land and building components and capitalizing each separately. The land and building elements are allocated on the basis of their relative fair values measured at the inception of the lease. The land and building components are separately accounted for because the lessee is expected to own the real estate by the end of the lease term. The building is amortized over its estimated useful life without regard to the lease term.

When the lease agreement neither transfers title nor contains a bargain purchase option, the fair value of the land must be determined in relation to the fair value of the aggregate property included in the lease agreement. If the fair value of the land is less than 25% of the aggregate fair value of the leased property, then the land is considered immaterial. Conversely, if the fair value of the land is 25% or greater of the fair value of the aggregate leased property, then the land is considered material and the land and building must be treated separately for accounting purposes.

When the land component of the lease agreement is considered immaterial (FV land < 25% of the total FV), the lease is accounted for as a single unit. The lessee capitalizes the lease if one of the following applies:

1.  The term of the lease is 75% or more of the economic useful life of the building.
2.  The present value of the minimum lease payments equals 90% or more of the fair value of the leased real estate less any lessor investment tax credit.

If neither of the above two criteria is met, the lessee accounts for the lease agreement as a single operating lease.

When the land component of the lease agreement is considered material (FV land ≥ 25% of the total FV), the land and building components are separated. By applying the lessee's incremental borrowing rate to the fair value of the land, the annual minimum lease payment attributed to land is computed. The remaining payments are attributed to the building. The division of minimum lease payments between land and building is essential for both the lessee and lessor. The portion of the lease involving the land is always accounted for as an operating lease. The lease involving the building(s) must meet either the 75% or 90% test to be treated as a capital lease. If neither of the two criteria is met, the building(s) are also accounted for as an operating lease.

### Computing the minimum lease payments.

*Construction period lease payments.* Payments made by a lessee during construction of the leased asset and prior to the beginning of the lease term (sometimes called "construction period lease payments") are considered part of the minimum lease payments for the purpose of the 90% of fair value test. These advance payments are to be included in minimum lease payments at their future value, at the beginning of the lease term, with interest accreted using the same interest rate used to discount payments made during the lease term (EITF 96-21).

If the lease is an operating lease, these payments are accounted for as prepaid rent and amortized to expense along with other rental costs over the term of the lease, normally using the straight-line method.

*Residual value guarantees.* If the terms of the lease include a guarantee of the residual value of the leased property by the lessee, that guarantee is to be included in the minimum lease payments and, in accordance with EITF 92-1 is to be allocated entirely to the building. This treatment is consistently followed by both the lessee and the lessor.

*Environmental indemnifications.* An indemnification by the lessee to the lessor for any environmental contamination that the lessee causes during the lease term does not affect the lessee's classification of the lease as capital or operating.

If the lessee's indemnification covers contamination that occurred prior to the lease term, the lessee is to consider, under the FAS 5 criteria for evaluating contingencies, whether the likelihood of loss is considered remote, reasonably possible, or probable before considering any available reimbursements available from insurance companies or other third parties. If the probability of loss is considered remote, then the indemnification does not affect the lessee's classification of the lease. If, however, the probability of loss is either reasonably possible or probable, the transaction is subject to the sale-leaseback provisions of FAS 98 and the lessee will be considered to have purchased, sold, and then leased back the property (EITF 97-1). A lessee providing an indemnification that meets certain criteria under FIN 45 is required to record the indemnification as a guarantee and, in addition, is subject to that pronouncement's disclosure provisions.

*Lessee obligation to maintain financial covenants.* Leases sometimes contain financial covenants similar to those included in loan agreements that obligate the lessee to maintain certain financial ratios. Should the lessee violate these covenants, it is considered an event of default under the lease and the lessor may have a right to put the property to the lessee or require the lessee to make a payment to the lessor. In this case, for the purpose of the 90% of fair value test, the lessee includes in the minimum lease payments the maximum amount it would be required to pay in the event of default unless all of the following conditions exist:

1. The default covenant provision is customary in financing arrangements,
2. The occurrence of the event of default is objectively determinable and is not at the subjective whim of the lessor,
3. The event of default is based on predefined criteria that relate solely to the lessee and its operations, and
4. It is reasonable to assume at the inception of the lease and in considering recent lessee operating trends that the event of default will not occur.

**Lessor accounting.** The lessor's accounting depends on whether the lease transfers ownership, contains a bargain purchase option, or does neither of the two.

If the lease transfers ownership and gives rise to dealer's profit (or loss), the lessor classifies the lease as a sales-type lease and accounts for the lease as a single unit under the provisions of FAS 66 in the same manner as a seller of the same property (see Chapter 10). If the lease transfers ownership, meets both the collectibility and no important uncertainties criteria, but does not give rise to dealer's profit (or loss), the lease is accounted for as a direct financing or leveraged lease as appropriate.

If the lease contains a bargain purchase option and gives rise to dealer's profit (or loss), the lease is classified as an operating lease. If the lease contains a bargain purchase option, meets both the collectibility and no material uncertainties criteria, but does not give rise to dealer's profit (or loss), the lease is accounted for as a direct financing lease or a leveraged lease as appropriate.

If the lease agreement neither transfers ownership nor contains a bargain purchase option, the lessor should follow the same rules as the lessee in accounting for real estate leases involving land and building(s).

However, the collectibility and the no material uncertainties criteria must be met before the lessor can account for the agreement as a direct financing lease, and in no such case may the lease be classified as a sales-type lease (i.e., ownership must be transferred).

The treatment of a lease involving both land and building can be illustrated in the following examples.

### Example of lessee accounting for land and building lease containing transfer of title

1. The lessee enters into a ten-year noncancelable lease for a parcel of land and a building for use in its operations. The building has an estimated remaining useful life of twelve years.
2. The FV of the land is $75,000, while the FV of the building is $310,000.
3. A payment of $50,000 is due to the lessor at the beginning of each of the ten years of the lease.
4. The lessee's incremental borrowing rate is 10%. (The lessor's implicit rate is unknown.)
5. Ownership will transfer to the lessee at the end of the lease.

The present value of the minimum lease payments is $337,951 ($50,000 × 6.75902[9]). The portion of the present value of the minimum lease payments to be capitalized for each of the two components of the lease is computed as follows:

| | | | | | |
|---|---|---|---|---|---|
| FV of land | | | | $ 75,000 | |
| FV of building | | | | 310,000 | |
| Total FV of leased property | | | | $385,000 | |
| Portion of PV allocated to land | $337,951 | × | $\frac{75,000}{385,000}$ | = | $ 65,835 |
| Portion of PV allocated to building | $337,951 | × | $\frac{310,000}{385,000}$ | = | 272,116 |
| Total PV to be capitalized | | | | | $337,951 |

The entry made to initially record the lease is as follows:

| | | |
|---|---|---|
| Leased land | 65,835 | |
| Leased building | 272,116 | |
| Lease obligation | | 337,951 |

Subsequently, the obligation will be decreased using the effective interest method. The leased building will be amortized over its expected useful life.

### Example of lessee accounting for land and building lease without transfer of title or bargain purchase option

Assume the same facts as the previous example except that title does not transfer at the end of the lease.

---

[9] 6.75902 *is the PV of an annuity due for ten periods at 10%.*

The lease is still a capital lease because the lease term is more than 75% of the remaining useful life of the building. Since the FV of the land is less than 25% of the aggregate fair value of the leased property, (75,000/385,000 = 19%), the land component is considered immaterial and the lease is accounted for as a single unit. The entry to record the lease is as follows:

| Leased property | 337,951 | |
|---|---|---|
| Lease obligation | | 337,951 |

Assume the same facts as the previous example except that the FV of the land is $110,000 and the FV of the building is $275,000. Once again title does not transfer.

Because the FV of the land exceeds 25% of the aggregate FV of the leased property (110,000/385,000 = 29%), the land component is considered material and the lease is separated into two components. The annual minimum lease payment attributed to the land is computed as follows:

$$\frac{\text{FV of land}}{\text{PV factor}} \quad \frac{\$110,000}{6.75902^*} \quad = \quad \$16,275$$

\* *6.75902 is the PV of an annuity due for ten periods at 10%.*

The remaining portion of the annual payment is attributed to the building.

| Annual payment | $ 50,000 |
|---|---|
| Less amount attributed to land | (16,275) |
| Annual payment attributed to building | $ 33,725 |

The present value of the minimum annual lease payments attributed to the building is then computed as follows:

| Minimum annual lease payment attributed to building | $ 33,725 |
|---|---|
| PV factor | × 6.75902* |
| PV of minimum annual lease payments attributed to building | $227,948 |

\* *6.75902 is the PV of an annuity due for ten periods at 10%.*

The entry to record the capital portion of the lease is as follows:

| Leased building | 227,948 | |
|---|---|---|
| Lease obligation | | 227,948 |

There is no computation of the present value of the minimum annual lease payment attributed to the land since the land component of the lease is treated as an operating lease. For this reason, each year $16,275 of the $50,000 lease payment will be recorded as land rental expense. The remainder of the annual payment ($33,725) will be applied against the lease obligation using the effective interest method.

**Leases involving real estate and equipment.** FIN 43, issued in 1999, states that sales of integral equipment are within the scope of FAS 66, *Accounting for Sales of Real Estate.* Consequently, the determination of whether equipment is considered to be integral equipment has increased in importance. A determination of whether equipment to be leased is integral is also necessary for proper accounting for sales-type leases by lessors.

According to EITF 00-13, the determination of whether equipment is integral is based on two factors.

1. The significance of the cost to remove the equipment from its existing location (which would include the costs of repairing the damage done to that location by the removal).

2. The decrease in value of the equipment that would result from its removal (which is, at minimum, the cost to ship the equipment to the new site and reinstall it). The nature of the equipment and whether others can use it are considered in determining whether there is further diminution in fair value. When the combined total of the cost to remove and any further diminution of value exceeds 10% of the fair value of the equipment (installed), the equipment is considered integral equipment.

FIN 43, *Real Estate Sales,* clarifies that FAS 66, *Accounting for Sales of Real Estate,* applies to all sales of real estate including real estate with accompanying property improvements or integral equipment. Consistent with FIN 43, EITF 00-11 specifies that when evaluating a lease that includes integral equipment to determine the classification of the lease under FAS 13 (as amended by FAS 98), the equipment is to be evaluated as real estate. EITF 00-11 also provides guidance on evaluating how to determine transfer of ownership of integral equipment when no statutory title registration system exists in the jurisdiction.

When real estate leases also involve equipment or machinery, the equipment component is separated and accounted for as a separate lease agreement by both lessees and lessors. "The portion of the minimum lease payments applicable to the equipment element of the lease shall be estimated by whatever means are appropriate in the circumstances." The lessee and lessor apply the capitalization requirements to the equipment lease independently of accounting for the real estate lease(s). The real estate leases are handled as discussed in the preceding two sections. In a sale-leaseback transaction involving real estate with equipment, the equipment and land are not separated.

Refer to the Profit Recognition on Real Estate Sales section of Chapter 10 for a further discussion of FIN 43, *Real Estate Sales.*

**Leases involving only part of a building.** It is common to find lease agreements that involve only part of a building as, for example, when leasing a floor of an office building or a store in a shopping mall. A difficulty that arises in this situation is that the cost and/or fair value of the leased portion of the whole may not be objectively determinable.

*Lessee accounting.* If the fair value of the leased property is objectively determinable, then the lessee follows the rules and accounts for the lease as described in "Leases involving land and building." If the fair value of the leased property cannot be objectively determined, consider whether the agreement satisfies the 75% test. This calculation is made using the estimated remaining economic life of the building in which the leased premises are located. If the test is met (i.e. the term of the lease is 75% or more of the estimated remaining economic life of the building), the lease is accounted for as a capital lease. If the test is not met, the lease is accounted for as an operating lease.

*Lessor accounting.* From the lessor's position, both the cost and fair value of the leased property must be objectively determinable before the procedures described under "Leases involving land and building" will apply. If either the cost or the fair value cannot be determined objectively, the lessor accounts for the agreement as an operating lease.

**Operating leases with guarantees.** It is important to note that, for any operating lease where the terms include a guarantee of the residual value of the leased asset, two issues require consideration:

1. Since a guarantee constitutes a variable interest in the lessor or in the leased assets, does the guarantee cause the lessee to be the primary beneficiary of the lessor that would be required to consolidate the lessor? (See discussion of FIN 46[R] earlier in this chapter.)
2. Is the guarantee required to be recognized as a liability at inception on the balance sheet of the lessee under FIN 45? (Discussed in Chapter 14.)

**Lessee-incurred real estate development or construction costs.** Lessees sometimes incur real estate development or construction costs prior to executing a lease with the developer/lessor. The lessee records these costs as construction in progress on its balance sheet and any subsequent lease arrangement is accounted for as a sale-leaseback transaction under FAS 98 (EITF 96-21), as discussed in the following section.

## Sale-Leaseback Transactions

Sale-leaseback describes a transaction where the owner of property (seller-lessee) sells the property, and then immediately leases all or part of it back from the new owner (buyer-lessor). These transactions may occur when the seller-lessee is experiencing cash flow or financing problems or because of available income tax advantages. The important consideration in this type of transaction is the recognition of two separate and distinct economic events. It is important to note, however, that in a typical sale-leaseback there is not a change in the party that has the right to use the property. First, there is a sale of property, and second, there is a lease agreement for the same property in which the original seller is the lessee and the original buyer is the lessor. This is illustrated below.

A sale-leaseback transaction is usually structured with the sales price of the asset at or above its current fair value. The result of this higher sales price is higher periodic rental payments over the lease term. The transaction is usually attractive because of the income tax benefits associated with it. The seller-lessee benefits from the higher price because of the increased gain on the sale of the property and the deductibility of the lease payments that are usually larger than the depreciation that was previously being deducted. The buyer-lessor benefits from both the higher rental payments and the larger depreciable income tax basis.

**Retention of rights to use the property.** The accounting treatment from the seller-lessee's point of view will depend upon the extent to which it retains the rights to use the property which can be characterized as one of the following:

1. Substantially all
2. Minor
3. More than minor but less than substantially all

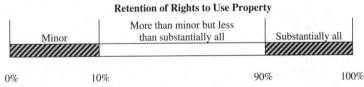

Present value of reasonable leaseback rentals as a percent of the fair value of the asset sold

As depicted in the diagram above, the guideline for the determination of substantially all is based upon the classification criteria presented for the lease transaction. That is, if the present value of fair rental payments is equal to 90% or more of the fair value of the asset sold, the seller-lessee is presumed to have retained substantially all of the rights to use the sold property. The test for retention of minor rights would be to substitute 10% or less for 90% or more in the preceding sentence.

If substantially all the rights to use the property are retained by the seller-lessee, and the agreement meets at least one of the criteria for capital lease treatment, the seller-lessee accounts for the leaseback as a capital lease and any profit on the sale is deferred and amortized in proportion to amortization of the leased asset. If the leaseback is classified as an operating lease, it is accounted for as such, and any profit on the sale is deferred and amortized over the lease term in proportion to gross rental charges. Any loss on the sale would also be deferred unless the loss were perceived to be a real economic loss, in which case the loss would be immediately recognized and not deferred.

If only a minor portion of the rights to use are retained by the seller-lessee, the sale and the leaseback are accounted for separately. However, if the rental payments appear unreasonable based upon the existing market conditions at the inception of the lease, the profit or loss is adjusted so the rentals are at a reasonable amount. The amount created by the adjustment is deferred and amortized over the life of the property if a capital lease is involved or over the lease term if an operating lease is involved.

If the seller-lessee retains more than a minor portion but less than substantially all the rights to use the property, any excess profit on the sale is recognized on the date of the sale. For purposes of this paragraph, excess profit is derived as follows:

1.  If the leaseback is classified as an operating lease, the excess profit is the portion of the profit that exceeds the present value of the minimum lease payments over the lease term including the gross amount of the guaranteed residual value. The seller-lessee uses its incremental borrowing rate to compute the present value of the minimum lease payments. If the implicit rate of interest in the lease is known and lower, it is substituted for the incremental borrowing rate in computing the present value of the minimum lease payments. The present value is amortized over the lease term while that guaranteed residual is deferred until resolution at the end of the lease term.

2.  If the leaseback is classified as a capital lease, the excess profit is the portion of the profit that exceeds the recorded amount of the leased asset.

Executory costs are not to be included in the calculation of profit to be deferred in a sale-leaseback transaction (EITF 89-16). When the fair value of the property at the time of the leaseback is less than its undepreciated cost, the seller-lessee immediately recognizes a loss for the difference. In the example below, the sales price is less than the book value of the property. However, there is no economic loss because the FV is greater than the book value.

| Sales price | Book value | FV and PV |
|---|---|---|
| $85,000 | $90,000 | $100,000 |

($5,000)
Artificial loss

The artificial loss is deferred and amortized as an addition to depreciation.

The diagram below summarizes the accounting for sale-leaseback transactions.

In the above circumstances, when the leased asset is land only, any amortization is recognized on a straight-line basis over the lease term, regardless of whether the lease is classified as a capital or operating lease.

The buyer-lessor accounts for the transaction as a purchase and a direct financing lease if the agreement meets the criteria of either a direct financing lease or a sales-type lease. Otherwise, the agreement is accounted for as a purchase and an operating lease.

**Sale-leaseback involving real estate.** Three requirements are necessary for a sale-leaseback involving real estate (including real estate with equipment) to qualify for sale-leaseback accounting treatment. Those sale-leaseback transactions not meeting the three requirements are accounted for using the deposit method (see Chapter 10) or as a financing. The three requirements are

1. The lease must be a normal leaseback (i.e., it involves active use of the leased property in the seller-lessee's trade or business during the lease term).
2. Payment terms and provisions must adequately demonstrate the buyer-lessor's initial and continuing investment in the property as prescribed by FAS 66.
3. Payment terms and provisions must transfer all the risks and rewards of ownership as demonstrated by a lack of continuing involvement by the seller-lessee.

***Adequacy of initial and continuing investment.*** The buyer-lessor's initial investment is adequate if it demonstrates the buyer-lessor's commitment to pay for the property and indicates a reasonable likelihood that the seller-lessee will collect any receivable related to the leased property. The buyer-lessor's continuing investment is adequate if the buyer is contractually obligated to pay an annual amount at least equal to the amount of the annual payment sufficient to repay the principal and interest over no more than twenty years for land or the customary term of a first mortgage for other real estate.

***Lack of continuing involvement by the seller-lessee.*** Any continuing involvement by the seller-lessee other than normal leaseback disqualifies the lease from sale-leaseback accounting treatment. Some examples of continuing involvement other than normal leaseback include

1. The seller-lessee has an obligation or option (excluding the right of first refusal) to repurchase the property
2. The seller-lessee (or party related to the seller-lessee) guarantees the buyer-lessor's investment or debt related to that investment or a specified return on that investment
3. The seller-lessee is required to reimburse the buyer-lessor for a decline in the fair value of the property below estimated residual value at the end of the lease term based on other than excess wear and tear
4. The seller-lessee remains liable for an existing debt related to the property
5. The seller-lessee's rental payments are contingent on some predetermined level of future operations of the buyer-lessor
6. The seller-lessee provides collateral on behalf of the buyer-lessor other than the property directly involved in the sale-leaseback
7. The seller-lessee provides nonrecourse financing to the buyer-lessor for any portion of the sales proceeds or provides recourse financing in which the only recourse is the leased asset
8. The seller-lessee enters into a sale-leaseback involving property improvements or integral equipment without leasing the underlying land to the buyer-lessor
9. The buyer-lessor is obligated to share any portion of the appreciation of the property with the seller-lessee
10. Any other provision or circumstance that allows the seller-lessee to participate in any future profits of the buyer-lessor or the appreciation of the leased property

The inclusion of a put provision in the lease as a remedy for the occurrence of an event of default under the lease including for lessee noncompliance with financial covenants violates the continuing involvement criteria in FAS 98 when the transaction is part of a sale-leaseback. This would necessitate accounting for the transaction using the deposit method or as a financing depending on the application of FAS 66 to the circumstances (EITF 97-1).

When one member of a consolidated group provides an uncensored guarantee of lease payments for another member of the same consolidated group, this is not held to be continuing involvement on the part of the consolidated group. Therefore, sale-leaseback accounting is appropriate in the consolidated financial statements. In the separate financial statements of the subsidiary/seller-lessee, however, the guarantee is a form of continuing involvement that precludes sale-leaseback accounting because the guarantee provides the buyer-lessor with additional collateral that reduces the buyer-lessor's risk of loss (EITF 90-14).

An uncollateralized irrevocable letter of credit is not a form of continuing involvement that precludes sale-leaseback accounting unless a contract exists between the seller-lessee and third-party guarantor that would create collateral (e.g. right of offset of amounts on deposit). All written contracts between the seller-lessee and the issuer of the letter of credit must be evaluated to determine if other forms of collateral exist (EITF 90-20).

### Example of accounting for a sale-leaseback transaction

To illustrate the accounting treatment in a sale-leaseback transaction, suppose that Seller/Lessee Corporation sells equipment that has a book value of $80,000 and a fair value of $100,000 to Buyer/Lessor Corporation for $100,000 in cash, and then immediately leases it back under the following conditions:

1. The sale date is January 1, 2009, and the equipment has a fair value of $100,000 on that date and an estimated remaining useful life of fifteen years.
2. The lease term is fifteen years, noncancelable, and requires equal rental payments of $13,109 at the beginning of each year.

3. Seller/Lessee Corp. has the option to annually renew the lease at the same rental payments upon expiration of the original lease.
4. Seller/Lessee Corp. has the obligation to pay all executory costs.
5. The annual rental payments provide the Buyer/Lessor Corp. with a 12% return on investment.
6. The incremental borrowing rate of Seller/Lessee Corp. is 12%.
7. Seller/Lessee Corp. depreciates similar equipment on a straight-line basis.

Seller/Lessee Corp. will classify the agreement as a capital lease since the lease term exceeds 75% of the estimated remaining economic life of the equipment, and because the present value of the lease payments ($13,109 × 7.62817[10] = $100,000) is greater than 90% of the fair value of the equipment. Assuming that collectibility of the lease payments is reasonably predictable and that no important uncertainties exist concerning the amount of unreimbursable costs yet to be incurred by Buyer/Lessor Corp., Buyer/Lessor Corp. will classify the transaction as a direct financing lease because the present value of the minimum lease payments is equal to the fair value of $100,000.

Seller/Lessee Corp. and Buyer/Lessor Corp. would make the following journal entries during the first year:

**Upon Sale of Equipment on January 1, 2009**

| *Seller/Lessee Corp.* | | | *Buyer/Lessor Corp.* | | |
|---|---|---|---|---|---|
| Cash | 100,000 | | Equipment | 100,000 | |
| Equipment* | | 80,000 | Cash | | 100,000 |
| Unearned profit on | | | | | |
| sale-leaseback | | 20,000 | | | |
| Leased equipment | 100,000 | | Lease receivable | | |
| Lease obligations | | 100,000 | ($13,109 × 15) | 196,635 | |
| | | | Equipment | | 100,000 |
| | | | Unearned interest | | 96,635 |

\* *Assumes new equipment; for used equipment the accumulated depreciation would also be debited to remove it.*

**To Record First Payment on January 1, 2009\*\***

| *Seller/Lessee Corp.* | | | *Buyer/Lessor Corp.* | | |
|---|---|---|---|---|---|
| Lease obligations | 13,109 | | Cash | 13,109 | |
| Cash | | 13,109 | Lease receivable | | 13,109 |

\*\* *No interest is recorded in connection with the first payment since it is made at the inception of the lease.*

**To Record Incurrence and Payment of Executory Costs**

| *Seller/Lessee Corp.* | | *Buyer/Lessor Corp.* |
|---|---|---|
| Insurance, taxes, etc. | xxx | (No entry) |
| Cash (or accounts payable) | xxx | |

**To Record Amortization Expense on the Equipment, December 31, 2009**

| *Seller/Lessee Corp.* | | *Buyer/Lessor Corp.* |
|---|---|---|
| Amortization expense | 6,667 | (No entry) |
| Accum. amort.— capital | | |
| leases ($100,000 ÷ 15) | 6,667 | |

**To Amortize Profit on Sale-Leaseback by Seller/Lessee Corp., December 31, 2009**

| *Seller/Lessee Corp.* | | *Buyer/Lessor Corp.* |
|---|---|---|
| Unearned profit on sale- | | (No entry) |
| leaseback | 1,333 | |
| Amortization expense | | |
| ($20,000 ÷ 15) | 1,333 | |

---

[10] *7.62817 is the present value of an annuity due for fifteen periods at a 12% interest rate.*

**To Record Interest for 2008, December 31, 2009**

| Seller/Lessee Corp. | | Buyer/Lessor Corp. | |
|---|---|---|---|
| Interest expense | 10,427 | Unearned interest | 10,427 |
| Accrued interest payable | 10,427 | Interest income | 10,427 |

**Partial Lease Amortization Schedule**\*\*

| Date | Cash payment | Interest expense | Reduction of obligation | Lease obligation |
|---|---|---|---|---|
| Inception of lease | | | | $100,000 |
| 1/1/09 | $13,109 | $  -- | $13,109 | 86,891 |
| 1/1/10 | 13,109 | 10,427 | 2,682 | 84,209 |

\*\*  *No interest is recorded in connection with the first payment since it is made at the inception of the lease.*

**Supplemental guidance.**  The following paragraphs provide supplemental guidance regarding the application of sale-leaseback accounting.

***Property sold subject to seller's preexisting operating lease.***  EITF 88-21 considers the situation where the reporting entity is an investor in a partnership that owns property with respect to which the reporting entity is also a lessee under an operating lease that covers all or a portion of the property.  The reporting entity sells its interest in the partnership or the partnership sells the property to an independent party with the preexisting operating lease continuing in effect.

If the leased property is within the scope of FAS 98 (real estate or real estate with integral equipment), EITF 88-21 requires recognition of the transaction as a sale-leaseback if the preexisting lease is significantly modified in connection with the sale.  If no changes are made to the lease or changes are insignificant profit is deferred and recognized in accordance with FAS 66 and 98 for real estate, property improvements, and integral equipment, and FAS 28 for all other property.

The computation of any deferred profit is not affected by the seller-lessee's prior ownership percentage in the property.  In addition, exercise of renewal options or sublease provisions contained in the preexisting lease that were included in the original minimum lease term do not affect the accounting for the transaction.  FAS 98 would apply, however, to renewal options not contained in the original minimum lease term.  These renewal options would be treated as a new lease.  Finally, leases between parties under common control are not considered preexisting leases for this purpose and FAS 98 applies unless one of the parties is a regulated enterprise such as a public utility under the provisions of FAS 71 (EITF 88-21).

***Sale-leaseback of an asset leased to another party.***  A variation of the previous issue arises when a leaseback involves an asset that is personal property falling outside coverage of FAS 98 and either (1) subject to an operating lease or (2) subleased or intended to be subleased to another entity under an operating lease.  The EITF specified that the seller-lessee-sublessor is to account for the transaction by recording the sale, removing the asset from its balance sheet, classifying the leaseback based on the normal criteria for determining lease classification, and recognizing or deferring any gain on the transaction as previously discussed (EITF 93-8).

## Other Lease Issues

**Accounting for a sublease.**  A sublease is an arrangement where the original lessee re-leases the leased property to a third party (the sublessee), and the original lessee acts as a sublessor.  Normally, the nature of a sublease agreement does not affect the original lease agreement, and the original lessee/sublessor retains primary liability to the lessor.

The original lease remains in effect, and the original lessor continues to account for the lease as before.  The original lessee/sublessor accounts for the lease as follows:

1. If the original lease agreement transfers ownership or contains a BPO and if the new lease meets any one of the four specified criteria (i.e., transfers ownership, BPO, 75% test, or 90% test) and both the collectibility and uncertainties criteria, then the sublessor classifies the new lease as a sales-type or direct financing lease; otherwise as an operating lease. In either situation, the original lessee/sublessor continues accounting for the original lease obligation as before.

2. If the original lease agreement does not transfer ownership or contain a BPO, but it still qualifies as a capital lease, then the original lessee/sublessor (with one exception) applies the usual criteria in classifying the new agreement. If the new lease qualifies, the original lessee/sublessor accounts for it as a direct financing lease, with the unamortized balance of the asset under the original lease being treated as the cost of the leased property. However, the original lessee/sublessor should recognize a loss on the sublease if its carrying amount exceeds the total sublease rentals and the estimated residual value (FTB 79-15). The one exception arises when the circumstances surrounding the sublease suggest that the sublease agreement was an important part of a predetermined plan in which the original lessee played only an intermediate role between the original lessor and the sublessee. In this situation, the sublease is classified by the 75% and 90% criteria as well as collectibility and uncertainties criteria. In applying the 90% criterion, the fair value for the leased property is the fair value to the original lessor at the inception of the original lease. Under all circumstances, the original lessee continues accounting for the original lease obligation as before. If the new lease agreement (sublease) does not meet the capitalization requirements imposed for subleases, then the new lease is accounted for as an operating lease.

3. If the original lease is an operating lease, the original lessee/sublessor accounts for the new lease as an operating lease and accounts for the original operating lease as before.

**Example of a direct-financing sublease**

The Silver Pick Mine obtains a $300,000 ore carrier truck under a five-year capital lease at 8% interest. Annual lease payments are $75,137. Silver Pick reduces its lease liability in accordance with the following amortization table:

| Year | Cash payment | Interest | Reduction in principal | Balance of net investment |
|------|------|------|------|------|
| Inception | | | | $300,000 |
| 1 | $75,137 | $24,000 | $51,137 | 248,863 |
| 2 | 75,137 | 19,909 | 55,228 | 193,635 |
| 3 | 75,137 | 15,419 | 59,646 | 133,989 |
| 4 | 75,137 | 10,719 | 64,418 | 69,571 |
| 5 | 75,137 | 5,566 | 69,571 | 0 |
| | $375,685 | $75,685 | $300,000 | |

At the end of Year 2, silver prices drop too low for ongoing mining operations to be profitable, so Silver Pick subleases the ore carrier via a direct financing lease to the Lead Bottom Mine for the remaining three years of the lease at the same interest rate. Silver Pick should use the unamortized balance of $193,635 at the end of Year 2 as the cost basis of the sublease, but Lead Bottom negotiates a lower inception value of $160,000, resulting in the following amortization table:

| Year | Cash payment | Interest | Reduction in principal | Balance of net investment |
|------|------|------|------|------|
| Inception | | | | $160,000 |
| 3 | $62,085 | $12,800 | $49,285 | 110,715 |
| 4 | 62,085 | 8,857 | 53,228 | 57,487 |
| 5 | 62,085 | 4,598 | 57,487 | 0 |
| | $186,255 | $26,255 | $160,000 | |

At the inception of the sublease, Silver Pick records a loss of $39,156 to reflect the negotiated $33,635 drop in the cost basis of the sublease, from $193,635 to $160,000, as well as a reduction of sublease interest income of $5,521, also due to the reduced cost basis. The summary entry for the final three years of Silver Pick's payments under the original lease agreement and its receipts under the sublease follows:

| | Years 3-5 of original lease transaction | | Total of sublease transactions | | Variance |
|---|---|---|---|---|---|
| Lease liability | 193,635 | | 160,000 | | 33,635 |
| Interest expense | 31,776 | | 26,255 | | 5,521 |
| Cash | | 225,411 | 186,255 | | 39,156 |

**Lease escalations.** Virtually all commercial leases contain provisions obligating the lessee to pay the lessor various additional sums, often referred to as lease escalations, that supplement the specified fixed rentals. It is important that the parties to the lease properly classify these payments because the way they are characterized can affect whether the lease is accounted for in the correct manner.

*Escalating base rents.* These are periodic increases in the fixed monthly rentals scheduled to occur at one or more points during the lease term. Escalating base rents are included in minimum lease payments.

Variations of this type of escalation occur when the fixed (or base) rent is structured at inception to include a future escalation based on the expected growth of the lessee requiring it to physically use additional portions of the premises that it was not using at inception or an actual addition or based on the lessee actually adding space or capacity.

FTB 88-1, Issue 1 prescribes the following two rules:

1. If, at the inception of the lease, the lessee takes possession of or controls the physical use of the leased property, all rentals including the escalated rents are to be recognized by the lessee and lessor as rental expense and rental revenue, respectively, on a straight-line basis commencing with the beginning of the lease term.
2. If rents escalate under a master lease agreement because the lessee obtains access to or control of additional leased property at the time of the escalation, the escalated rents are considered by the lessee and lessor as rental expense and rental revenue respectively that is attributable to the newly leased property. This additional rental expense or rental revenue is to be computed based on the relative fair values of the original leased property and the additional leased property as determined at the inception of the lease and allocated to the time periods during which the lessee controls the use of the additional leased property.

*Executory costs.* These represent reimbursements to the lessor of costs associated with owning and maintaining the leased property. The most common executory costs are real estate taxes, insurance, and maintenance. Amounts paid by a lessee as consideration for a guarantee from an unrelated third party of the residual value are also considered executory costs. If executory costs are paid by the lessor, any lessor's profit on those costs is considered in the same manner as the actual executory costs. Executory costs are excluded from minimum lease payments.

*Contingent rentals.* These are additional rentals due that are computed based on changes that occur subsequent to the inception of the lease in factors, other than the passage of time, on which the lease payments were based. Examples of contingent rentals include real estate rentals based on a percentage of the lessee's retail sales over a certain dollar amount (often referred to as percentage rent or overage rent) and equipment rentals based on machine hours of use. One type of escalation that many commercial leases contain is a required rent increase based on increases in an index such as the prime interest rate or the

Consumer Price Index (CPI). Depending on how the terms are structured, these payments might actually consist of two elements that must be separately considered. The portion attributable to the index or rate that was in effect at the inception of the lease (considered part of the minimum lease payments) and the portion representing subsequent increases in that index or rate (considered to be contingent rentals) as illustrated in the following examples.

**Example 1**

A three-year lease requires fixed rentals of $1,000 per month plus $10 for every full percentage point of the prime interest rate or fraction thereof determined as of the beginning of the month. The prime interest rate at the inception of the lease is 6% and on the first day of the fourth month of the lease term the prime interest rate increased to 7%.

At lease inception, the minimum rentals are computed as follows:

$1,000 + ($10 × 6 percentage points = $60) = $1,060 per month × 36 months = $38,160

The increase in rent due at the beginning of the fourth month would be allocated as follows:

| | | | |
|---|---|---|---|
| Minimum rentals: | $10 × 6 percentage points | = | $60 |
| Contingent rentals: | $10 × 1 percentage points | = | 10 |
| | | | $70 |

**Example 2**

Same facts as Example 1 except that the lease requires the lessee to pay fixed rentals of $1,000 per month plus $10 for every full percentage point or fraction thereof that the prime interest rate determined as of the beginning of the month exceeds 6%.

At lease inception, the minimum rentals are computed as follows:

$1,000 per month × 36 months = $36,000

The increase in rent due at the beginning of the fourth month would be allocated as follows:

| | | | |
|---|---|---|---|
| Minimum rentals: | | | $ -- |
| Contingent rentals: | $10 × 1 percentage point | = | 10 |
| | | | $10 |

As illustrated in the examples, amounts determined to be contingent rentals are excluded from minimum lease payments.

As discussed previously, leases for retail space often contain percentage rent provisions that obligate the lessee to pay the lessor a percentage of retail sales over a certain dollar amount. These dollar thresholds are often expressed in terms of annual targets such as one-half of one percent of annual sales over $10 million. This type of lease provision raises the accounting issue of how the lessor and lessee are to account for the lease during the interim periods prior to the attainment of the contractual target.

EITF 98-9 prescribes the accounting as follows:

Lessor: No revenue recognition until the actual target is achieved and surpassed.

Lessee: Recognize contingent rental expense during interim periods if it is probable that the target will be reached by the end of the fiscal year. If, subsequently, the specified target is not met, previously recorded expense is reversed at the time it becomes probable that the target will not be met.

**Lessee involvement in asset construction.** A lessee often has substantial involvement in construction activities with respect to an asset to be leased under a long-term lease agreement. This involvement can take many forms that can include

1. Providing the construction financing directly or indirectly
2. Guaranteeing the construction debt
3. Serving as primary or secondary obligor under construction contracts
4. Acting as the real estate developer or general contractor

5.  Agreeing to purchase the asset if the construction is not completed by a specified date
6.  Agreeing to fund construction cost overruns
7.  Serving as an agent of the lessor for the construction, financing, or ultimate sale of the asset
8.  Agreeing to a date-certain lease that obligates the lessee to commence rental payments on a certain date irrespective of whether the construction is complete by that date

These various forms of involvement raise important substance-over-form considerations that must be carefully considered in light of evolving GAAP literature.

***Construction period rent associated with land and building leases.***  In certain instances, the lessee will delay occupancy or usage of leased property until, for example, leasehold improvements have been completed.  In FSP FAS 13-1, the FASB staff clarifies the fact that a lease coveys to the lessee the right to control the use of property, such as leased land and building, both during and after any construction period necessary to construct leasehold improvements to the property.  Consequently, rental expense is required to be allocated to periods during which construction activities are occurring even though the lessee has not yet commenced operations on the premises.  The FSP further provides that the rentals allocated to the construction period are not to be capitalized as part of the cost of the leasehold improvements but rather are to be recorded as a period expense as a charge against income from continuing operations in the lessee's financial statements.

***Transfer of construction period risks.***  A lessee is considered the owner of a real estate project during its construction period if the lessee bears substantially all of the construction period risks (EITF 97-10).

Under EITF 97-10, if the lessee is determined to bear substantially all of the construction risks, it is considered to be the owner of the asset during the construction period.  If that is the case, then a sale-leaseback of the asset occurs upon the completion of construction and the commencement of the lease term.

The primary test to be used in determining if a lessee has substantially all of the construction period risks is virtually the same as the 90% of fair value test for determining if a lease is to be classified as a capital lease by a lessee.  Beginning with the earlier of the date of the inception of the lease or the date that the construction terms are agreed to, if at any time during the construction period the documents governing the construction project could require, under any circumstance, that the lessee pay 90% or more of the total project costs, excluding land acquisition costs, then the lessee is considered to be the owner of the real estate project during its construction period.

Even if the present value of the lessee's maximum guarantee is less than 90% of total project costs, EITF 97-10 provides six examples of when the lessee would still be considered the owner of a real estate project.

For the purposes of this 90% test, the lessee's maximum guarantee includes any payments the lessee could be required to make in connection with the construction project.  The lessee's maximum guarantee includes, but is not limited to

1.  Lease payments that must be made regardless of when or whether the project is complete
2.  Guarantees of the construction financing
3.  Equity investments made in the owner-lessor or any party related to the owner-lessor
4.  Loans or advances made to the owner-lessor or any party related to the owner-lessor

5. Payments made by the lessee in the capacity of a developer, a general contractor, or a construction manager/agent that are reimbursed less frequently than is normal or customary
6. Primary or secondary obligations to pay project costs under construction contracts
7. Obligations that could arise from being the developer or general contractor
8. An obligation to purchase the real estate project under any circumstances
9. An obligation to fund construction cost overruns
10. Rent or fees of any kind, such as transaction costs, to be paid to or on behalf of the lessor by the lessee during the construction period
11. Payments that might be made with respect to providing indemnities or guarantees to the owner-lessor

The scope of EITF 97-10 includes government-owned property under construction and subject to a future lease of the completed improvements (EITF 99-13).

This consensus was reached in 1998, prior to the issuance of FIN 45 and FIN 46(R) regarding guarantees and variable interest entities, respectively, which can dramatically affect the lessee's conclusions. Any direct or indirect financial interests of the lessee in the leased asset or in the lessor must be analyzed by the lessee to determine if

1. They require accounting recognition as a guarantee obligation under FIN 45.
2. They result in the lessee holding a variable interest in the lessor or in the lessor's specified assets (the project) that potentially could require the lessee to consolidate the lessor as the primary beneficiary of a variable interest entity (VIE) or consolidate the specified assets and related liabilities (referred to as "silo" or a "virtual VIE").

Variable interest entities are discussed earlier in this chapter and in Chapter 13; guarantees are discussed in Chapter 14. If the lessee consolidates the lessor or the project, intercompany transactions and balances will be eliminated in consolidation.

**Change in residual value.** For any of the foregoing types of leases, the lessor is to review the estimated residual value at least annually. If there is a decline in the estimated residual value, the lessor must make a determination as to whether this decline is temporary or permanent. If temporary, no adjustment is required; however, if the decline is other than temporary, then the estimated residual value must be revised to conform to the revised estimate. The loss that arises in the net investment is recognized in the period of decline. Under no circumstance is the estimated residual value to be adjusted to reflect an increase in the estimate. FTB 79-14 clarifies that this prohibition against reflecting an increase in the estimated residual value also extends to increases in the guaranteed portions of the residual value that result from renegotiations between the parties.

**Example of a permanent decline in residual value.**

Hathaway Corporation enters into a sales-type leasing transaction as the lessor of a fire truck. The following table shows key information about the lease:

| | |
|---|---|
| Lease term | 10 years |
| Implicit interest rate | 8% |
| Lease payments | One payment per year |
| Normal selling price | $300,000 |
| Asset cost | $200,000 |
| Residual value | $50,000 |

After one year, immediately after the first lease payment has been received, Hathaway determines that an indicated decline in residual value from $50,000 to $30,000 is other than temporary. The calculation it originally used to determine the annual minimum lease payment follows:

$$\frac{\text{Selling price—(Present value of residual value due in 10 years at 8\% interest} \times \text{residual value)}}{\text{Present value of an annuity of \$1 for 10 years at 8\% interest}}$$

$$= \frac{\$300,000 - (0.46319 \times \$50,000)}{6.71008}$$

$$= \$41,257.33 \text{ Annual minimum lease payment}$$

Hathaway calculates the following reduction in the residual present value of the fire truck, using a multiplier of 0.5002 to obtain the present value of the residual value due in nine years at an interest rate of 8%:

Accreted original residual asset present value = ($50,000) × (Present value of 0.5002) = $25,010

Less: Revised residual asset present value = ($30,000) × (Present value of 0.5002) = $15,006

Equals net change in residual asset present value = ($10,004)

The following table shows the original and revised elements of Hathaway's lease transaction entry:

|  | Initial entry* | Revised residual value | Entry net of Residual value change |
|---|---|---|---|
| Less receivable | 462,572 | 20,000 | 442,572 |
| Cost of goods sold | 176,840 |  | 176,840 |
| Loss on residual reduction |  | 10,004 | 10,004 |
| Inventory | 200,000 |  | 200,000 |
| Sales | 276,840 |  | 276,840 |
| Unearned interest | 162,572 | 9,996 | 152,576 |

\* *Lease receivable = (Total minimum lease payments) + (Residual asset value)*
*Cost of goods sold = (Inventory cost) – (Present value of residual asset value)*
*Sales = (Present value of minimum lease payments)*
*Unearned interest = (Lease receivable) – (Present value of minimum lease payments) – (Present value of residual asset value)*

The following amortization table tracks the net impact of these changes, resulting in a $30,000 residual value at the end of Year 10:

| Year | Cash payment | Interest | Reduction in principal | Balance of net investment |
|---|---|---|---|---|
| Inception |  |  |  | $300,000 |
| 1 | $41,257 | $24,000 | $17,257 | 282,743 |
| Adjustment |  |  | 10,004 | 272,739 |
| 2 | 41,257 | 21,819 | 19,438 | 253,301 |
| 3 | 41,257 | 20,264 | 20,993 | 232,308 |
| 4 | 41,257 | 18,584 | 22,673 | 209,635 |
| 5 | 41,257 | 16,770 | 24,487 | 185,148 |
| 6 | 41,257 | 14,811 | 26,446 | 158,702 |
| 7 | 41,257 | 12,696 | 28,561 | 130,141 |
| 8 | 41,257 | 10,411 | 30,846 | 99,295 |
| 9 | 41,257 | 7,943 | 33,314 | 65,981 |
| 10 | 41,257 | 5,276 | 35,981 | 30,000 |
|  | $412,570 | $152,574 | $270,000 |  |

Thus, net of rounding errors, the total of all payments on the amortization table and the $30,000 revised residual value equals the revised lease receivable of $442,572. Similarly, the total of all interest payments on the amortization table matches the adjusted unearned interest entry.

**Change in the provisions of a lease.** Accounting issues arise when the lessee and lessor agree, subsequent to its inception, to change the provisions of the lease (other than by renewals or term extensions that are discussed later). If, from the standpoint of the lessee, the revised lease terms would have, at the inception of the original lease, resulted in a different lease classification (e.g., operating lease versus capital lease or vice versa), the revised agreement is considered to be a new agreement.

If the original lease was accounted for as a capital lease and the revised lease qualifies for treatment as an operating lease, FAS 13 originally provided that the recorded asset and obligation be eliminated with a gain or loss recognized for the difference. This treatment was amended by FAS 145, effective for transactions occurring after May 15, 2002. Leases subject to the new rules are to be accounted for as sale-leaseback transactions (discussed later in this chapter).

If the original lease was accounted for as an operating lease and the revised lease is a capital lease, then on the date of the revision, the lessee records an asset and an obligation based on the present value of the remaining lease payments (or the fair value of the leased property, if less).

Finally, if the original and revised leases are both capital leases, then the lessee adjusts the recorded asset and obligation by an amount equal to the difference between the present value of the future minimum lease payments under the revised agreement and the recorded balance of the obligation. For the purposes of this calculation, the rate of interest to be used is the rate that was used to record the lease initially. The adjustment is recognized as a gain or loss of the period in which the revision is made.

In the case of either a sales-type or direct financing lease where there is a change in the provisions of a lease, the lease is accounted for by the lessor as discussed below.

Changes in the provisions that affect the amount of the remaining minimum lease payments can result in one of the following three outcomes:

1.  The change does not give rise to a new agreement. A new agreement is defined as a change that, if in effect at the inception of the lease, would have resulted in a different classification.
2.  The change does give rise to a new agreement that would be classified as a direct financing lease.
3.  The change gives rise to a new agreement that would be classified as an operating lease.

If either 1. or 2. occurs, the balance of the minimum lease payments receivable and the estimated residual value (if affected) are adjusted to reflect the effect of the change. The net adjustment is charged (or credited) to unearned income, and the accounting for the lease over its remaining term is adjusted to reflect the change.

If the new agreement is an operating lease, then the remaining net investment (lease receivable less unearned income) is written off and the leased asset is recorded by the lessor at the lower of its cost, present fair value, or carrying value. The net adjustment resulting from these entries is charged (or credited) to income of the period in which the revision is made. Thereafter, the new lease is accounted for as any other operating lease.

The lessee and the lessor may negotiate a shortened lease term and an increase in the lease payments over the revised lease term. EITF 95-17 observes that the nature of the modification is a matter of judgment that depends on the relevant facts and circumstances. If the modification is deemed only a change in future lease payments, the increase is amortized over the remaining term of the modified lease. On the other hand, a modification deemed a termination penalty is to be recognized in the period of modification. Termination penalties are calculated as the excess of the modified lease payments over the original lease payments that would have been required during the shortened lease term.

EITF 95-17 provides that consideration is to be given to (1) the length of the modified lease period compared to the remaining term of the original lease, and (2) the difference between the modified lease payments and comparable market rents in determining whether the modification is a termination penalty.

**Early termination of a lease.** Accounting for premature lease termination from the standpoints of the lessee and lessor follows.

*Lessee accounting.* Discontinuation of business activities in a particular location is considered an exit activity, the accounting for which is specified in FAS 146 (see Chapter 3).

*Operating leases.* In connection with lease termination the lessee may incur (1) costs to terminate the lease prior to the end of its noncancelable term and/or (2) continuing lease costs incurred during the remainder of the lease term for which the lessee receives no economic benefit because the premises are no longer in use. On the date the lessee terminates the lease, the lessee recognizes a liability for the fair value of the termination costs. The termination date is the date that the lessee provides written notice to the lessor in accordance with the notification requirements contained in the lease or the date the lessee and lessor agree to a negotiated early termination.

The fair value of rentals that continue to be incurred under the lease during its remaining term without benefit to the lessee is recognized as a liability on the date that the lessee ceases to use the property (referred to as the cease-use date). Fair value is computed based on the remaining rentals due under the lease, adjusted for any prepaid or deferred rent under the lease, and reduced by estimated sublease rentals that are reasonable to expect for the property. The fair value measurement requires that reasonable sublease rentals be included in the computation even if the lessee does not intend to sublease the property.

In periods subsequent to the recognition of these liabilities but prior to their settlement, changes in fair value are measured using the credit-adjusted risk-free rate of interest (in essence, the lessee's incremental borrowing rate) used to initially measure the liability.

Upon initial recognition of these liabilities, the related costs are recognized in the lessee's income statement as operating expense (or income from continuing operations if no measure of operations is presented) unless required to be presented as part of discontinued operations. The cumulative effects of any subsequent period changes in liabilities that result from changes in the estimates of either the amounts or timing of cash flows are reported in the same income statement caption used to initially recognize the costs. Changes to the liabilities as a result of the passage of time increase their carrying amount and are recorded as accretion expense, which is also considered an operating expense.

*Capital leases.* If the lease is a capital lease, it is subject to the provisions of FAS 144 with respect to long-lived assets to be disposed of other than by sale (see Chapter 11) either individually (in which case the gain or loss is recorded as a component of operating expense) or as part of a disposal group (in which case the gain or loss is presented as a part of discontinued operations). During the time period between the termination date and the cease-use date, the capital lease asset continues to be classified as "held and used," is subject to impairment evaluation, and its remaining carrying value is amortized over that shortened time period.

*Lessor accounting.* Lessor accounting for an early lease termination is as follows.

*Sales-type and direct financing leases.* The lessor records the leased equipment as an asset at the lower of its original cost, present fair value, or current carrying value. The difference between the remaining net investment in the lease and the amount of the adjustment to recognize the leased equipment is reflected in income of the period in which the lease is terminated.

**Example of lessor accounting for the early termination of a sales-type lease**

La Crosse Corporation enters into a sales-type leasing transaction as the lessor of a digital color copier. The following table shows key information about the lease:

| | |
|---|---|
| Lease term | 5 years |
| Implicit interest rate | 8% |
| Lease payments | One payment per year |
| Normal selling price | $80,000 |
| Asset cost | $50,000 |
| Residual value | $10,000 |
| Present value of ordinary annuity of 1 for 5 years at 8% | 3.9927 |
| Present value of 1 due in 5 years at 8% | 0.6806 |

Based on the information in the table, La Crosse calculates an annual minimum lease payment of $18,332, which is reflected in the following amortization table:

| Year | Cash payment | Interest | Reduction in principal | Balance of net investment |
|---|---|---|---|---|
| Inception | | | | $80,000 |
| 1 | $18,332 | $6,400 | $11,932 | 68,068 |
| 2 | 18,332 | 5,445 | 12,887 | 55,181 |
| 3 | 18,332 | 4,414 | 13,918 | 41,263 |
| 4 | 18,332 | 3,301 | 15,031 | 26,232 |
| 5 | 18,332 | 2,100 | 16,232 | 10,000 |
| | $91,660 | $21,660 | $70,000 | |

At the end of Year 3, the lessee cancels the lease. At that time, the fair value of the color copier is $35,000, which is $6,263 less than the $41,263 current carrying value indicated at the end of Year 3 in the amortization table. This change is reflected in the following table, which notes the original and revised elements of La Crosse's lease transaction:

| | Initial entry* | Total of transactions for first 3 years | Lease cancellation entry |
|---|---|---|---|
| Cash | | 54,996 | |
| Lease receivable | 101,660 | 54,996 | 46,664 |
| Cost of goods sold | 43,194 | | |
| Inventory | 50,000 | | 35,000 |
| Sales | 73,194 | | |
| Interest income | | 16,259 | |
| Loss on early lease termination | | | 6,263 |

* Lease receivable = (Total minimum lease payments) + (Residual asset value)
  Cost of goods sold = (Inventory cost) – (Present value of residual asset value)
  Sales = (Present value of minimum lease payments)
  Unearned interest = (Lease receivable) – (Present value of minimum lease payments) – (Present value of residual asset value)

*Operating leases.* Accounting for the leased asset is subject to the provisions of FAS 144. Between the termination date and the cease-use date, the leased asset continues to be presented as held-and-used and depreciated subject to an impairment evaluation that considers the likelihood and timing of replacing the tenant and market rents that would be realized. On the cease-use date, the leased asset is reclassified from held-and-used to the category of idle property and equipment with the associated temporary suspension of depreciation.

Upon receiving notice of termination, the lessor recognizes a receivable for the fair value of any termination fees to be received from the lessee as a result of early cancellation and a corresponding deferred rent liability that is recorded as an adjustment to any previously recorded deferred rent liability or prepaid rent. The remaining rental stream to be received thereafter is recognized on a straight-line basis over the remainder of the time period during which such payments were agreed to continue by adjusting any remaining prepaid rent, deferred rent, and/or unamortized initial direct costs so that they will be fully amortized by the date on which the lessee's payment obligation is fully satisfied.

**Renewal or extension of an existing lease.** The renewal or extension of an existing lease agreement affects the accounting of both the lessee and the lessor. There are two basic situations: (1) the renewal occurs and makes a residual guarantee or penalty provision inoperative or (2) the renewal agreement does not do the foregoing and the renewal is treated as a new agreement. The accounting treatment prescribed under the latter situation for a lessee is as follows:

1.  If the renewal or extension is classified as a capital lease, then the (present) current balances of the asset and related obligation are adjusted by the difference between the present value of the future minimum lease payments under the revised agreement and the (present) current balance of the obligation. The present value of the minimum lease payments under the revised agreement is computed using the interest rate in effect at the inception of the original lease.
2.  If the renewal or extension is classified as an operating lease, then the current balances of the asset and liability are written off and a gain (loss) recognized for the difference. The new lease agreement resulting from a renewal or extension is accounted for in the same manner as other operating leases.

Under the same circumstances, the following treatment is followed by the lessor:

1.  If the renewal or extension is classified as a direct financing lease, then the existing balances of the lease receivable and the estimated residual value are adjusted for the changes resulting from the revised agreement.

    *NOTE: Remember that an upward adjustment to the estimated residual value is not allowed.*

    The net adjustment is charged or credited to unearned income.
2.  If the renewal or extension is classified as an operating lease, then the remaining net investment under the existing sales-type lease or direct financing lease is written off and the leased asset is recorded as an asset at the lower of its original cost, present fair value, or current carrying amount. The difference between the net investment and the amount recorded for the leased asset is charged to income of the period that includes the renewal or extension date. The renewal or extension is then accounted for prospectively as any other operating lease.
3.  If the renewal or extension is classified as a sales-type lease and it occurs at or near the end of the existing lease term, then the renewal or extension is accounted for as a sales-type lease.

    *NOTE: A renewal or extension that occurs in the last few months of an existing lease is considered to have occurred at or near the end of the existing lease term.*

If the renewal or extension causes the guarantee or penalty provision to be inoperative, the lessee adjusts the current balance of the leased asset and the lease obligation to the present value of the future minimum lease payments (according to FAS 13 "by an amount equal to the difference between the PV of the future minimum lease payments under the revised agreement and the present balance of the obligation"). The PV of the future minimum lease payments is computed using the rate used in the original lease agreement.

Given the same circumstances, the lessor adjusts the existing balance of the lease receivable and estimated residual value to reflect the changes of the revised agreement (remember, no upward adjustments to the residual value). The net adjustment is charged (or credited) to unearned income.

### Example of lessor accounting for extension of a sales-type lease

Entré Computers enters into a sales-type leasing transaction as the lessor of a corporate computer system. The following table shows key information about the lease:

| | |
|---|---|
| Lease term | 6 years |
| Implicit interest rate | 10% |
| Lease payments | One payment per year |
| Normal selling price | $240,000 |
| Asset cost | $180,000 |
| Residual value | $450,000 |
| Present value of ordinary annuity of 1 for 6 years at 10% | 4.3553 |
| Present value of 1 due in 6 years at 10% | 0.5645 |

Based on the information in the table, Entré calculates an annual minimum lease payment of $49,273, which is reflected in the following amortization table:

| Year | Cash payment | Interest | Reduction in principal | Balance of net investment |
|---|---|---|---|---|
| Inception | | | | $240,000 |
| 1 | $49,273 | $24,000 | $25,273 | 214,727 |
| 2 | 49,273 | 21,472 | 27,801 | 186,926 |
| 3 | 49,273 | 18,692 | 30,581 | 156,345 |
| 4 | 49,273 | 15,634 | 33,639 | 122,706 |
| 5 | 49,273 | 12,270 | 37,003 | 85,703 |
| 6 | 49,273 | 8,570 | 40,703 | 45,000 |
| | $295,638 | $100,638 | $195,000 | |

After making the Year 3 payment, the lessee requests a lease extension in order to reduce the annual payment amount. To do so, Entré extends the lease duration by two years and assumes the same residual value. Entré calculates the revised annual minimum lease payment under the assumption that the selling price is the balance of the net investment at the end of Year 3, as noted in the preceding amortization table.

$$\frac{\text{Selling price—(Present value of residual value due in 5 years at 10\% interest} \times \text{residual value)}}{\text{Present value of an annuity of \$1 for 5 years at 10\% interest}}$$

$$= \frac{\$156,345 - (0.6209 \times \$45,000)}{3.7908}$$

$$= \$33,873 \text{ Annual minimum lease payment}$$

The revised lease payment and residual value is shown in the following amortization table, which includes both the first three years of the original lease agreement and the full five years of the lease extension agreement:

| Year | Cash payment | Interest | Reduction in principal | Balance of net investment |
|---|---|---|---|---|
| Inception | | | | $240,000 |
| 1 | $49,273 | $24,000 | $25,273 | 214,727 |
| 2 | 49,273 | 21,472 | 27,801 | 186,926 |
| 3 | 49,273 | 18,692 | 30,581 | 156,345 |
| 4 | 33,873 | 15,635 | 18,238 | 138,107 |
| 5 | 33,873 | 13,811 | 20,062 | 118,045 |
| 6 | 33,873 | 11,805 | 22,068 | 95,977 |
| 7 | 33,873 | 9,598 | 24,275 | 71,702 |
| 8 | 33,873 | 7,171 | 26,702 | 45,000 |
| | $317,184 | $122,184 | $195,000 | |

This change is reflected n the following table, which notes the original and revised elements of Entré's lease transaction:

| | Initial entry* | Revised entry | Net entry required |
|---|---|---|---|
| Lease receivable | 340,638 | 362,184 | 21,546 |
| Cost of goods sold | 154,597 | 154,597 | |
| Inventory | 180,000 | 180,000 | |
| Sales | 214,597 | 214,597 | |
| Unearned interest | 100,638 | 122,184 | 21,546 |

> \* Lease receivable = (Total minimum lease payments) + (Residual asset value)
> Cost of goods sold = (Inventory cost) – (Present value of residual asset value)
> Sales = (Present value of minimum lease payments)
> Unearned interest = (Lease receivable) – (Present value of minimum lease payments) – (Present value of residual asset value)

**Leases between related parties.** Leases between related parties are classified and accounted for as though the parties are unrelated, except in cases where it is certain that the terms and conditions of the agreement have been influenced significantly by the fact that the lessor and lessee are related. When this is the case, the classification and/or accounting is modified to reflect the true economic substance of the transaction rather than the legal form. Under FIN 46(R), discussed earlier in this chapter, many related-party lessors will qualify as variable interest entities (VIE). When this is the case, the lessee will present consolidated financial statements that include the lessor's assets, liabilities, and results of operations. The elimination of intercompany transactions and balances will result in the rental expense and rental income being removed from the consolidated financial statements, which will instead reflect the depreciation of the leased asset and the interest expense on any related debt.

FAS 57 requires that the nature and extent of leasing activities between related parties be disclosed. FIN 46(R) requires the following disclosures by the primary beneficiary of a VIE:

1. The nature, purpose, size, and activities of the VIE
2. The carrying amount and classification of consolidated assets that collateralize the VIE's obligations
3. Any lack of recourse that VIE creditors or holders of VIE beneficial interests have to the general credit of the primary beneficiary

**Indemnification provisions in lease agreements.** Some lease agreements contain a provision whereby the lessee indemnifies the lessor on an after-tax basis for certain income tax benefits that the lessor might lose if a change in the income tax law should occur. This situation is discussed in EITF 86-33 which was subsequently modified by FIN 45.

An indemnification agreement of this kind is considered a guarantee that is subject to the recognition and disclosure requirements of FIN 45 discussed in detail in Chapter 14. Any payments that might be required under the indemnification clause are, therefore, not considered contingent rentals.

**Accounting for leases in a business combination.** A business combination, in and of itself, has no effect upon the classification of a lease. However, if, in connection with a business combination, a lease agreement is modified to change the original classification of the lease, it is considered a new agreement and accounted for as previously discussed.

In most cases, a business combination will not affect the previous classification of a lease unless the provisions have been modified as indicated in the preceding paragraph.

The acquiring company applies the following procedures to account for a leveraged lease in a business combination:

1. The classification as a leveraged lease is retained.
2. The net investment in the leveraged lease is assigned a fair value (present value, net of income taxes) based upon the remaining future cash flows. Also, the estimated income tax effects of the cash flows are recognized.

3. The net investment is broken down into three components: net rentals receivable, estimated residual value, and unearned income.

4. Thereafter, the leveraged lease is accounted for as described in the discussion earlier in this chapter.

In a business combination where a lease is acquired that does not conform to FAS 13 (pre-1979), the acquiring company accounts for the lease by retroactively applying FAS 13 at the date of combination.

FAS 141(R) significantly alters the accounting for business combinations. It requires the use of the acquisition method (similar to, but different from, the purchase method employed under FAS 141 and earlier literature), which requires that assets acquired and liabilities assumed in such a transaction be accounted for at fair values. This means, among other things, that capital leases under which the acquiree entity was obligated at the acquisition date are to be revalued at fair value at the date of the acquisition. The amounts of depreciation and interest to be recognized in subsequent periods by the acquirer will accordingly, in most instances, vary from the amounts that would have been recognized by the acquiree absent the business combination.

For example, if the fair value of the leased property under a capital lease is greater than its carrying value (the depreciated capitalized value as of that date), future amortization will be greater than would otherwise have been the case. Given that rental payments will not be altered by the acquisition transaction, this means that the effective interest cost will be reduced. A new effective interest rate will need to be computed in order to properly record the accounting implications of future rental payments, in such a circumstance. Contrariwise, if the fair value of the leased property is lower than its precombination carrying (book) value, the effective interest rate will be greater than had previously been determined.

FAS 141(R) states that the determination of the classification of an existing lease is generally not reassessed at the date of a business combination, and that the determination made at the lease inception is not to be reconsidered. However, if the terms of an operating lease are favorable or unfavorable compared with the market terms of leases of the same or similar items at the acquisition date, accounting ramifications must be addressed. The acquirer in such a circumstance is to recognize an intangible asset if the terms of an operating lease are favorable relative market terms, and is to recognize a liability if the terms are unfavorable relative to market terms.

An identifiable intangible asset may be associated with an operating lease, which may be objectively revealed by market participants' willingness to pay a price for the lease even if its terms are already at market. For example, a lease of gates at an airport or of retail space in a prime shopping area might provide entry into a market or other future economic benefits that qualify as identifiable intangible assets—for example, as a customer relationship. In that situation, the acquirer is to recognize the associated identifiable intangible asset(s). Under FAS 141(R), the identifiable intangible assets acquired in a business combination are to be recognized distinct from goodwill. An intangible asset is *identifiable* if it meets either the separability criterion or the contractual-legal criterion described by FAS 141(R).

If the acquiree in a business combination has assets (e.g., building or equipment) that are subject to operating leases (that is, the acquiree is a lessor), FAS 141(R) directs that such assets are to be recorded at fair value determined without regard to the terms of the associated leases. The extent to which the lease terms are favorable or unfavorable relative to the market at the acquisition date, however, will be reflected in the additional intangible asset or liability to be recognized by the acquirer.

**Accounting for changes in lease agreements resulting from refunding of tax-exempt debt.** Tax-exempt debt is often "refunded" by the issuer of the debt instruments. Refunding is a refinancing that enables the issuer (i.e., a municipality that issued bonds) to take advantage of favorable interest rates. A current refunding is effected when the debt becomes callable and the issuer issues new debt in order to use the proceeds to retire the original debt. An advance refunding is a more complex variation that occurs prior to the call date of the original instruments. It entails issuance of new tax-exempt debt at the lower interest rate with a similar maturity to the original issuance. The proceeds of the new debt are invested in a portfolio of market-traded US Treasury securities and other obligations that effectively "defease" the original bonds (see Chapter 15 for a discussion of debt defeasance). If, during the lease term, a change in the lease results from a refunding by the lessor of tax-exempt debt (including an advance refunding) and (1) the lessee receives the economic advantages of the refunding and (2) the revised agreement can be classified as a capital lease by the lessee and a direct financing lease by the lessor, the change is accounted for as follows:

1. If the change is accounted for as an extinguishment of debt

   a. Lessee accounting. The lessee adjusts the lease obligation to the present value of the future minimum lease payments under the revised agreement. The present value of the minimum lease payments is computed using the interest rate applicable to the revised agreement. Any gain or loss is recognized currently as a gain or loss on the extinguishment of debt in accordance with the provisions of FAS 145 (discussed in detail in Chapter 15).

   b. Lessor accounting. The lessor adjusts the balance of the lease receivable and the estimated residual value, if affected, for the difference in present values between the old and revised agreements. Any resulting gain or loss is recognized currently.

2. If the change is not accounted for as an extinguishment of debt

   a. Lessee accounting. The lessee accrues any costs in connection with the debt refunding that are obligated to be reimbursed to the lessor. These costs are amortized by the interest method over the period from the date of refunding to the call date of the debt to be refunded.

   b. Lessor accounting. The lessor recognizes as revenue any reimbursements to be received from the lessee, for costs paid in relation to the debt refunding. This revenue is recognized in a systematic manner over the period from the date of refunding to the call date of the debt to be refunded.

**Sale or assignment to third parties; nonrecourse financing.** The sale or assignment of a lease or of property subject to a lease that was originally accounted for as a sales-type lease or a direct financing lease will not affect the original accounting treatment of the lease. Any profit or loss on the sale or assignment is recognized at the time of the transaction except under the following two circumstances:

1. When the sale or assignment is between related parties, apply substance versus form provisions presented above under "leases between related parties."

2. When the sale or assignment is with recourse, it is accounted for using the provisions of FAS 77 or FAS 140.

The sale of property subject to an operating lease is not treated as a sale if the seller (or any related party to the seller) retains "substantial risks of ownership" in the leased property. A seller may retain "substantial risks of ownership" by various arrangements. For example, if the lessee defaults upon the lease agreement or if the lease terminates, the seller may arrange to do one of the following:

1. Acquire the property or the lease
2. Substitute an existing lease
3. Secure a replacement lessee or a buyer for the property under a remarketing agreement

A seller does not retain substantial risks of ownership by arrangements where one of the following occurs:

1. A remarketing agreement includes a reasonable fee to be paid to the seller.
2. The seller is not required to give priority to the releasing or disposition of the property owned by the third party over similar property owned by the seller.

When the sale of property subject to an operating lease is not accounted for as a sale because the substantial risk factor is present, it is accounted for as a borrowing. The proceeds are recorded by the seller as an obligation. Rental payments made by the lessee under the operating lease are recorded as revenue by the seller even if the payments are paid to the third-party purchaser. The seller accounts for each rental payment by allocating a portion to interest expense (to be imputed in accordance with the provisions of APB 21), and the remainder to reduce the existing obligation. Other normal accounting procedures for operating leases are applied except that the depreciation term for the leased asset is limited to the amortization period of the obligation.

The sale or assignment of lease payments under an operating lease by the lessor are accounted for as a borrowing as described above.

Nonrecourse financing is a common occurrence in the leasing industry, whereby the stream of lease payments on a lease is discounted on a nonrecourse basis at a financial institution with the lease payments collateralizing the debt. The proceeds are then used to finance future leasing transactions. Even though the discounting is on a nonrecourse basis, FTB 86-2 prohibits the offsetting of the debt against the related lease receivable unless a legal right of offset exists or the lease qualified as a leveraged lease at its inception. The SEC in a Staff Accounting Bulletin has also affirmed this position.

**Money-over-money lease transactions.** A money-over-money lease transaction occurs when an enterprise manufactures or purchases an asset, leases the asset to a lessee and obtains nonrecourse financing in excess of the asset's cost using the leased asset and the future lease rentals as collateral. FTB 88-1, Issue 4 prescribes that this series of transactions should be accounted for as follows:

1. Record the purchase or manufacture of the asset,
2. Record the lease as an operating, direct financing, or sales-type lease as appropriate,
3. Record nonrecourse debt.

The only income that is recognizable by the reporting entity in this transaction would be any manufacturer's or dealer's profit that arises if the lease is classified as a sales-type lease. With respect to balance sheet presentation, offsetting of any assets recorded as a result of the transaction with the nonrecourse debt is not permitted unless a right of setoff exists.

**Wrap-lease transactions.** A wrap-lease transaction (see diagram) occurs when a reporting enterprise

1. Purchases an asset,
2. Leases the asset to a lessee,
3. Obtains nonrecourse financing using the lease rentals and/or the asset as collateral,

4.  Sells the asset to an investor, subject to the lease and the nonrecourse debt, and
5.  Leases the asset back while remaining the substantive principal lessor under the original lease.

If the asset is real estate, the specialized rules with respect to sale-leaseback of real estate set forth in FAS 98 apply (see example of accounting for a sale-leaseback transaction in this chapter).

If the asset is personal property, the accounting would be as follows:

1.  The asset is removed from the accounting records of the original reporting entity,
2.  The leaseback is classified in accordance with the normal criteria for the classification of leases,
3.  Gain on the transaction is recognized or deferred/amortized following the criteria in FAS 13, para. 33, as amended,
4.  The reporting entity reflects the following items on its balance sheet or statement of financial position:

    a.  Any retained interest in the residual value of the leased asset
    b.  Gross sublease receivable
    c.  Note receivable from the investor
    d.  Nonrecourse third-party debt
    e.  Leaseback obligation
    f.  Deferred revenue related to any future remarketing rights for which the remarketing services had not yet been performed

The sublease asset and related nonrecourse debt are not permitted to be offset on the balance sheet unless a right of setoff exists. The governing authoritative literature for wrap-lease transactions is found in EITF 87-7 and FTB 88-1, Issue 5.

**Wrap-Lease Transaction**

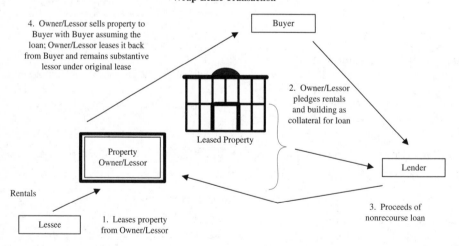

4. Owner/Lessor sells property to Buyer with Buyer assuming the loan; Owner/Lessor leases it back from Buyer and remains substantive lessor under original lease

Buyer

2. Owner/Lessor pledges rentals and building as collateral for loan

Leased Property

Property Owner/Lessor

Lender

Rentals

Lessee

1. Leases property from Owner/Lessor

3. Proceeds of nonrecourse loan

*Cash Flows*

Lessee pays rentals to Lessor.
Lessor pays rentals to Buyer.
Buyer pays loan principal and interest to Lender.

**Transfers of residual value (FAS 140 and FTB 86-2).** Acquisitions of interests in residual values of leased assets may be effected by companies whose primary business is other than leasing or financing. This generally occurs through the outright purchase of the right to own the leased asset or the right to receive the proceeds from the sale of a leased asset at the end of its lease term.

In instances such as these, the rights are recorded by the purchaser at the fair value of the assets surrendered net of the present value of any liabilities assumed, unless the fair value of the residual is more objectively determinable. Increases in the estimated value of the interest in the residual (i.e., residual value accretion) to the end of the lease term are permitted to be recognized only for *guaranteed* residual values because they are financial assets. However, recognition of such increases is prohibited for *unguaranteed* residual values. A nontemporary write-down of a residual value interest (guaranteed/unguaranteed) is recognized as a loss and is not permitted to be subsequently restored. This guidance also applies to lessors who sell the related minimum lease payments but retain the interest in the residual value irrespective of whether the residual is guaranteed.

### Example of the transfer of residual value.

Longbottom Lease Brokers obtains an interest in the residual value of a cable placer truck as a fee for its assistance in leasing the truck to a third party. The fair value of Longbottom's interest in the residual value of the truck is estimated by an appraiser to be $47,000. Since the fair value of Longbottom's interest in the residual value is the most clearly evident valuation, Longbottom uses it as the basis for the following entry:

| | | |
|---|---|---|
| Interest in asset residual value | 47,000 | |
| Revenue—leasing services rendered | | 47,000 |

In another transaction, Longbottom pays $32,000 for the residual value of an aerial truck. Longbottom records the transaction as follows:

| | | |
|---|---|---|
| Interest in asset residual value | 32,000 | |
| Cash | | 32,000 |

After six months, Longbottom appraises its interest in the residual value of both trucks, and finds that the value of the cable placer has declined from $47,000 to $41,000, while the residual value of the aerial truck has increased from $32,000 to $35,000. Longbottom uses the following entry to record the reduction of value in its cable placer truck:

| | | |
|---|---|---|
| Loss on interest in asset residual value | 6,000 | |
| Interest in asset residual value | | 6,000 |

Longbottom records no entry for the $3,000 increase in value of its aerial truck.

**Leases involving government units.** Leases that involve government units (i.e., airport facilities, bus terminal space, etc.) usually contain special provisions that prevent the agreements from being classified as anything but operating leases. These special provisions, referred to as fiscal funding clauses, include the governmental body's authority to abandon a facility at any time during the lease term, thus making its economic life indeterminable. These leases also do not contain a BPO or transfer ownership. The fair value is generally indeterminable because neither the leased property nor similar property is available for sale.

However, leases involving government units are subject to the same classification criteria as nongovernment units, except when all of the following six criteria are met:

*NOTE: If all six conditions are met, the agreement is classified as an operating lease by both lessee and lessor.*

1. A government unit or authority owns the leased property
2. The leased property is part of a larger facility operated by or on behalf of the lessor
3. The leased property is a permanent structure or part of a permanent structure that normally cannot be moved to another location

4.  The lessor, or a higher governmental authority, has the right to terminate the lease at any time under the lease agreement or existing statutes or regulations
5.  The lease neither transfers ownership nor allows the lessee to purchase or acquire the leased property
6.  The leased property or similar property in the same area cannot be purchased or leased from anyone else

If any one of the six conditions that qualify the lease for automatic operating lease treatment is not met, then the lease is evaluated to determine the likelihood of future cancellation. Using the loss contingency criteria from FAS 5, if it is remote (i.e., the chances are slight) that the lease will be canceled, then the lease agreement qualifies as a noncancelable lease and is classified the same as any other such lease with a nongovernmental lessee. Otherwise, the lease is considered to be cancelable and accounted for as an operating lease (FTB 79-10).

**Balance sheet classification.** The balance of the lease payments receivable (lessor) and the lease obligation (lessee) must be allocated between their current and noncurrent portions. First, the current portion is computed at the date of the financial statements as the present value of the lease payments (or receipts) to be paid (received) within twelve months of the balance sheet date. The noncurrent portion is computed as the difference between the current portion and the balance of the lease obligation at the end of the period. The conceptual justification for this treatment is the fact that the total lease obligation is equal to the present value of the future minimum lease payments. Therefore, it follows that the current portion is the present value of the lease payments due within one year while the noncurrent portion is the present value of all other remaining lease payments.

**Summary of Accounting for Selected Items** (See following page)

# TREATMENT OF SELECTED ITEMS IN ACCOUNTING FOR LEASES

| | Lessor | | Lessee | |
|---|---|---|---|---|
| | *Operating* | *Direct financing and sales-type* | *Operating* | *Capital* |
| Initial direct costs | Capitalize and amortize over lease term in proportion to rent revenue recognized (normally SL basis) | Direct financing: Record in separate account; Add to net investment in lease; Compute new effective rate that equates gross amt. of min. lease payments and unguar. residual value with net invest. Amortize so as to produce constant rate of return over lease term. Sales-type: Expense in period incurred as part of cost of sales | N/A | N/A |
| Investment tax credit retained by lessor | N/A | Reduces FV of leased asset for 90% test | N/A | Reduces FV of leased asset for 90% test |
| Bargain purchase option | N/A | Include in: Minimum lease payments 90% test | N/A | Include in: Minimum lease payments 90% test |
| Guaranteed residual value | N/A | Include in: Minimum lease payments 90% test Sales-type: Include PV in sales revenues | N/A | Include in: Minimum lease payments 90% test |
| Unguaranteed residual value | N/A | Include in: "Gross investment in lease" Not included in: 90% test Sales-type: Exclude from sales revenue Deduct PV from cost of sales | N/A | N/A |
| Contingent rentals | Revenue in period earned | Not part of minimum lease payments; revenue in period earned | Expense in period incurred | Not part of minimum lease payments; expense in period incurred |
| Amortization period | Amortize down to estimated residual value over estimated economic life of asset | N/A | N/A | Amortize down to estimated residual value over lease term or estimated economic life[b] |
| Revenue (expense)[a] | Rent revenue (normally SL basis) Amortization (depreciation expense) | Direct financing: Interest revenue on net investment in lease (gross investment less unearned interest income) Sales-type: Dealer profit in period of sale (sales revenue less cost of leased asset) Interest revenue on net investment in lease | Rent expense (normally SL basis)[c] | Interest expense and amortization (depreciation) expense |

a Elements of revenue (expense) listed for the above items are not repeated here (e.g., treatment of initial direct costs).
b If lease has automatic passage of title or bargain purchase option, use estimated economic life; otherwise, use the lease term.
c If payments are not on a SL basis, recognize rent expense on a SL basis unless another systematic and rational method is more representative of use or benefit obtained from the property, in which case, the other method should be used.

# 17 INCOME TAXES

## PERSPECTIVE AND ISSUES

Reporting entities are required to file income tax returns and pay income taxes in the domestic (federal, state, and local) and foreign jurisdictions in which they do business.

GAAP requires that financial statements be prepared on an accrual basis and that, consequently, the reporting entity is required to accrue a liability for income taxes owed or expected to be owed with respect to income tax returns filed or to be filed for all applicable tax years and in all applicable jurisdictions.

A longstanding debate has involved the controversial recognition of benefits (or reduced obligations) related to income tax positions that are uncertain or aggressive and which, if challenged, have a more-than-slight likelihood of not being sustained, resulting in the need to pay additional income taxes, often with interest and—sometimes—penalties added. Preparers have objected to presenting income tax obligations for such positions, often on the not-unreasonable theory that to do so would provide taxing authorities with a "road map" to the challengeable income tax positions taken by the reporting entity. With the June 2006 issuance of FIN 48, *Accounting for Uncertainty in Income Taxes*, uncertain income tax positions were to become subject to formal recognition and measurement criteria, as well as to extended disclosure requirements under GAAP. To respond to the concerns of its private company constituents, FASB granted a one-year deferral of the effective date of FIN 48 for certain nonpublic enterprises. As the end of the deferral period approaches, those same constituents are requesting either an outright exemption for nonpublic enterprises or an additional deferral until the conclusion of an ongoing joint project between the FASB and IASB to converge US GAAP and IFRS income tax accounting standards. FIN 48 is explained and illustrated in detail in this chapter.

The computation of taxable income for the purpose of filing federal, state, and local income tax returns differs from the computation of net income under GAAP for a variety of reasons. In some instances, referred to as temporary differences, the timing of income or expense recognition varies. In other instances, referred to as permanent differences, income or expense recognized for income tax purposes is never recognized under GAAP, or vice versa. An objective under GAAP is to recognize the income tax effects of transactions in the period that those transactions occur. Consequently, deferred income tax benefits and obligations frequently arise in financial statements.

The basic principle is that the deferred income tax effects of all temporary differences (which are defined in terms of differential bases in assets and liabilities under income tax and GAAP accounting) are to be formally recognized. To the extent that deferred income tax assets are of doubtful realizability—are not "more likely than not to be realized"—a valuation allowance is provided, analogous to the allowance for uncollectible receivables.

The process of *inter*period income tax allocation, which gives rise to deferred income tax assets and liabilities, has been required under GAAP for decades, although the measurement philosophy has evolved substantially over the years. As with many accounting measurements, the prescribed methodology has varied depending upon whether the primary objective was accuracy of the balance sheet or of the income statement. While the income statement had long been viewed as being of greatest concern, with the completion of the FASB's current conceptual framework several decades ago the emphasis shifted to the balance sheet. This ultimately precipitated a major change in the interperiod income tax allocation rules, culminating in the issuance of FAS 109 in 1992, which remains in effect.

Under FAS 109, *purchase price allocations* made pursuant to purchase-method business combinations under FAS 141 (and *recognized values* pursuant to acquisition-method business combinations under its replacement standard, FAS 141[R]) are made gross of income tax effects, and any associated income tax benefit or obligation is recognized separately.

FAS 109 was amended by FAS 141(R) effective on or after the first annual reporting period beginning on or after December 15, 2008. As a result of the amendment, post-combination changes in valuation allowances for an acquired entity's deferred income tax assets no longer automatically reduce recorded goodwill and intangibles. Under the new requirements, the accounting depends upon whether the changes occur during or after the expiration of the measurement period.

If the change occurs during the prescribed measurement period, not to exceed one year from the acquisition date, it is first applied to adjust goodwill until goodwill is eliminated, with any excess adjustment remaining being recorded as a gain from a bargain purchase. If the change occurs subsequent to the measurement period, it is recognized in the period of change as a component of income tax expense or benefit, or, in the case of certain specified exceptions, as a direct adjustment to contributed capital. Notably, the transition provisions of FAS 141(R) require this treatment to be applied prospectively after the effective date of the standard, even with respect to acquisitions that were originally recorded under the predecessor standard.

The income tax effects of net operating loss or tax credit carryforwards are treated as deferred income tax assets just like any other deferred income tax benefit. FAS 109 ended the previous treatment of the effect of utilizing a net operating loss in a subsequent year as an extraordinary item in the income statement.

With its balance sheet orientation, FAS 109 requires that the amounts presented be based on the amounts expected to be realized, or obligations expected to be liquidated. Use of an average effective income tax rate convention is permitted, thereby avoiding the computational complexity that made FAS 109's immediate predecessor (FAS 96) so unpopular. The effects of all changes in the balance sheet deferred income tax assets and liabilities flow through the income tax provision in the income statement; consequently, income tax expense is normally not directly calculable based on pretax accounting income in other than the simplest situations.

Discounting of deferred income taxes has never been permitted under GAAP, even though the ultimate realization and liquidation of deferred income tax assets and liabilities is often expected to occur far in the future. The issuance of CON 7, which deals with the use of present value in accounting measurements, did not end this prohibition. In any event, the inability to predict accurately the timing of the realization of deferred income tax benefits or the payment of deferred income tax payments would make discounting very difficult to accomplish.

As this publication was being finalized, FASB and IASB were conducting a joint project on accounting for income taxes, in order to improve the standards in this area and to converge US GAAP and International Financial Reporting Standards. The current project agenda states an expected issuance date of an Exposure Draft in the fourth quarter of 2008, although, as is common, this schedule may be delayed. Progress on the project can be monitored at both the FASB and IASB Web sites.

| Sources of GAAP | | | | | | |
|---|---|---|---|---|---|---|
| *APB* | *FAS* | *Q&A* | *FIN* | *FTB* | *EITF* | *FSP* |
| 16, 17, | 5, 6, 12, | 109 | 18 | 82-1 | 86-9, 86-43, 88-4, 93-13, | FAS 13-2 |
| 20, 23, | 37, 52, | | 48 | | 93-16, 93-17, 94-10, | FAS 109-1 |
| 28 | 109, | | | | 95-10, 95-20, 98-11, | FAS 109-2 |
| | 123(R), | | | | 02-13, 05-8, 06-11, | FAS 126-1 |
| | 141(R) | | | | D-30, D-31, D-32, D-33 | FIN 48-1 |
| | | | | | | FIN 48-2 |

## DEFINITIONS OF TERMS

**Conduit bond obligor.** The party on behalf of whom a state or local government agency raises funds by issuing bonds (commonly referred to as municipal bonds, industrial revenue bonds, or private activity bonds). Interest on the bonds typically is exempt from federal income tax to the investor and in order to qualify for this exemption, the proceeds from the bond must be used by the conduit bond obligor for purposes permitted under the federal income tax code. If the proceeds from the bonds are used to provide funding to multiple parties that participate in a pool (a pooled conduit debt security), all of the individual conduit bond obligors that participate are considered individually to be conduit bond obligors.

**Conduit debt securities.** Certain limited-obligation revenue bonds, certificates of participation, or similar debt instruments issued by a state or local governmental entity (issuer) for the purpose of providing financing for a specific third party (the conduit bond obligor) that is not a part of the issuer's reporting entity. Even though these securities bear the issuer's name, the issuer often has no obligation with respect to the debt other than as provided in a lease or loan agreement with the conduit bond obligor on whose behalf the securities are issued. The conduit bond obligor is responsible for making or funding all principal and interest payments when due and is also responsible for future financial reporting requirements with respect to the securities.

**Deferred income tax asset.** The asset recognized to reflect the expected future benefit available to be realized upon the reversal of deductible temporary differences.

**Deferred income tax liability.** The liability recognized to reflect the expected future income taxes that will be payable upon the reversal of taxable temporary differences.

**Effective settlement.** A conclusion reached by applying criteria specified in FSP FIN 48-1, that a taxing authority has, in effect, made its final determination with respect to the portion of a tax position, if any, that it will accept and that management considers the possibility of further examination or reexamination of any aspect of the position to be remote.

**Future deductible temporary difference.** The difference between the GAAP carrying amount and income tax basis of an asset or liability that will reverse in the future and result in future income tax deductions; these give rise to deferred income tax assets.

**Future taxable temporary difference.** Temporary differences that result in future taxable amounts; that give rise to deferred income tax liabilities.

**Gains and losses included in comprehensive income but excluded from net income.** Certain items which, under GAAP, are events occurring currently but that are reported directly in equity as accumulated other comprehensive income, such as changes in the fair values of available-for-sale portfolios of marketable equity securities.

**Highly certain income tax position.** An income tax position that, based on clear and unambiguous tax law, rulings, regulations and interpretations, has a remote likelihood of being disallowed by the applicable taxing jurisdiction examining it with full possession of all relevant facts.

**Income tax position.** Each judgment that management makes on an income tax return that has been or will be filed that affects the measurement of current or deferred income tax assets and liabilities at an interim or year-end balance sheet date. The effects of taking an income tax position can result in a permanent reduction of income taxes payable or deferral of the payment of income taxes to a future year. The taking of an income tax position can also affect management' estimate of the valuation allowance sufficient to reflect the amount of deferred income tax assets that it believes will be realizable.

**Interperiod tax allocation.** The process of apportioning income tax expense among reporting periods without regard to the timing of the actual cash payments for income taxes. The objective is to reflect fully the income tax consequences of all economic events reported in current or prior financial statements and, in particular, to report the expected future income tax effects of the reversals of temporary differences existing at the reporting date.

**Intraperiod tax allocation.** The process of apportioning income tax expense applicable to a given period between income before extraordinary items and those items required to be shown net of tax such as extraordinary items, discontinued operations, and prior period adjustments.

**Nonpublic enterprise.** An entity (1) whose debt or equity securities are not traded in a public market and (2) is not a conduit bond obligor for conduit debt securities traded in a public market. For the purpose of this definition, a public market can be a domestic or foreign exchange or over-the-counter market, even if the securities are only quoted locally or regionally. It is important to note that GAAP does not contain uniform definitions of public or nonpublic enterprises. Thus, the use of this terminology must be evaluated in the context of the specific standard in which it is used.

**Operating loss carryback or carryforward.** The excess of income tax deductions over taxable income. To the extent that this results in a carryforward, the income tax effect is included in the reporting entity's deferred income tax asset.

**Ordinary income or loss (used in interim accounting for income taxes).** In GAAP this term is defined differently than it is for income tax purposes. For GAAP purposes, ordinary income or loss is computed as pretax income (loss) from continuing operations less: (1) extraordinary items, (2) discontinued operations, (3) cumulative effects of changes in accounting principle, and (4) significant unusual or infrequently occurring items.

**Permanent differences.** Differences between pretax accounting income and taxable income as a result of the treatment accorded certain transactions by the income tax laws and regulations that differ from the accounting treatment. Permanent differences will not reverse in subsequent periods.

**Pretax accounting income.** Income or loss for the accounting period as determined in accordance with GAAP without regard to the income tax expense for the period.

**Public enterprise.** An entity (1) whose debt or equity securities are traded in a public market, (2) that is a conduit bond obligor for conduit debt securities traded in a public market, or (3) whose financial statements are filed with a regulatory agency in preparation for the sale of any class of securities. For the purpose of this definition, a public market can be a domestic or foreign exchange or over-the-counter market, even if the securities are only quoted locally or regionally. It is important to note that GAAP does not contain uniform definitions of public or nonpublic enterprises. Thus, the use of this terminology must be evaluated in the contest of the specific standard in which it is used.

**Taxable income.** The difference between the taxable revenue and deductible expenses as defined by the Internal Revenue Code for a tax period without regard to special deductions (e.g., net operating loss or contribution carrybacks and carryforwards).

**Tax credits.** Reductions in income tax liability as a result of certain expenditures accorded special treatment under the Internal Revenue Code. Examples of such credits are: the Investment Tax Credit, investment in certain depreciable property; the Jobs Credit, payment of wages to targeted groups; the Research and Development Credit, an increase in qualifying R&D expenditures; and others.

**Tax planning strategy.** A representation by management of a planned transaction or series of transactions that would affect the particular future years in which temporary differences will result in taxable or deductible amounts.

**Temporary differences.** In general, differences between income tax and financial reporting bases of assets and liabilities that will result in taxable or deductible amounts in future periods. Temporary differences include "timing differences" as defined by prior GAAP as well as certain other differences, such as those arising from business combinations. Some temporary differences cannot be associated with particular assets or liabilities, but nonetheless do result from events that received financial statement recognition and will have income tax effects in future periods.

**Unrecognized income tax benefits.** The portion of income tax benefits claimed on income tax returns filed or to be filed for which, in management's judgment, realization would not be more than 50% probable should the income tax position be examined by the applicable taxing authority possessing all relevant information.

**Valuation allowance.** The contra asset which is to be reflected to the extent that, in management's judgment, it is "more likely than not" that the deferred income tax asset will not be realized.

## CONCEPTS, RULES, AND EXAMPLES

### Evolution of Accounting for Income Taxes

The differences in the timing of recognition of certain expenses and revenues for income tax reporting purposes versus the timing under GAAP had always been a subject for debates in the accounting profession. The initial debate was over the fundamental principle of whether or not income tax effects of timing difference should be recognized in the financial statements. At one extreme were those who believed that only the amount of income tax currently owed ( as shown on the income tax return for the period) should be reported as periodic income tax expense, on the grounds that potential changes in tax law and the vagaries of the entity's future financial performance would make any projection to future periods speculative. This was the "no allocation" or "flow-through" position. At the other extreme were those who held that the matching principle demanded that reported periodic income tax expense be mechanically related to pretax accounting income, regardless of the amount of income taxes actually currently payable. This was the "comprehensive allocation" argument. The middle ground approach, known as "partial allocation," acknowledged the need for some deferred income tax provision, but only when actual future income tax payments or benefits could be accurately predicted. This debate was settled in the late 1960s: comprehensive income tax allocation became GAAP.

The other key debate was over the measurement strategy to be applied to interperiod income tax allocation. When, in the 1960s and 1970s, accounting theory placed paramount importance on the income statement, with much less interest in the balance sheet, the method of choice was the "deferred method," which invoked the matching principle. The annual income tax provision (consisting of current and deferred portions) was calculated so that it would bear the expected relationship to pretax accounting income; any excess or deficiency of the income tax provision over income taxes payable was recorded as an adjustment to the deferred income tax amounts reflected on the balance sheet. This practice, when applied, resulted in a net deferred income tax debit (subject to some limitations on asset realization) or a net deferred income tax credit, which did not necessarily mean that an asset or liability, as defined under GAAP, actually existed for that reported amount.

By the late 1970s, accounting theory (reflected in FASB's conceptual framework) made the financial reporting priority the statement of financial position (balance sheet). Primary emphasis was placed on the measurement of assets and liabilities—which, under CON 6's definitions, clearly would not include certain deferred income tax benefits or obligations as these were then measured. To compute deferred income taxes consistent with a balance sheet orientation requires use of the "liability method." This essentially ascertains, as of each balance sheet date, the amount of future income tax benefits or obligations that are associated with the reporting entity's assets and liabilities existing at that time. Any adjustments necessary to increase or decrease deferred income taxes to the computed balance, plus or minus the amount of income taxes owed currently, determines the periodic income tax expense or benefit to be reported in the income statement. Put another way, income tax expense is the residual result of several other balance-sheet-oriented computations.

Movement to a balance-sheet-oriented measurement approach began with issuance of FAS 96. This unpopular standard embraced the inherently more straightforward liability approach, but added a number of major complexities to the computation of deferred income taxes, and proved to be unwieldy in practice. It was replaced with FAS 109, under which all deferred income tax assets are given full recognition, whether arising from deductible temporary differences or from net operating loss or tax credit carryforwards.

Under FAS 109 it is necessary to assess whether the deferred income tax asset is realizable. Testing for realization is accomplished by means of a "more-likely-than-not" criterion that indicates whether an allowance is needed to offset some or all of the recorded deferred income tax asset. While the determination of the amount of the allowance may make use of the scheduling of future expected reversals, other methods may also be employed and, in general, FAS 109 is a less rigorous, more flexible standard in regard to the financial statement presentation of deferred income tax assets than was its predecessor.

In summary, interperiod income tax allocation under GAAP is currently based on the liability method, using comprehensive allocation. While this basic principle may be straightforward, there are a number of computational complexities to be addressed. These will be presented in the remainder of this chapter.

An example of application of the liability method of deferred income tax accounting follows.

### Simplified example of interperiod income tax allocation using the liability method

Caitlyn International has no permanent differences in years 2009 through 2011 (these are discussed later in this chapter). The company has only two balance sheet amounts with temporary differences between their income tax and financial reporting bases, property and equipment; and prepaid rent. No consideration is given to the classification of the deferred income tax amounts (i.e., current or long-term) as it is not considered necessary for purposes of this example.

Details of Caitlyn's temporary differences are as follows:

### Caitlyn International Temporary Differences

Prepaid rent future deductible temporary differences

| Basis at December 31 | Tax | GAAP | Future (taxable) deductible amount |
|---|---|---|---|
| 2009 | -- | $(100,000) | $100,000 |
| 2010 | -- | (80,000) | 80,000 |
| 2011 | -- | (125,000) | 125,000 |

### Property and equipment future taxable temporary difference

On January 1, 2009, Caitlyn International purchased $400,000 of property and equipment with a 10-year estimated useful life which, under its normal accounting policy, it depreciates using the straight-line method. For income tax purposes, these assets qualify as 5-year personal property under the General Depreciation System (GDS) and consequently income tax depreciation is computed using the Modified Accelerated Cost Recovery System (MACRS) which is equivalent to double-declining balance depreciation with a half-year assumed for the year placed in service and changing to straight-line depreciation when advantageous to the taxpayer. In addition, as permitted by IRC Section 179, Caitlyn elected to deduct $100,000 of these costs in the year placed in service. By making this election, for the purpose of computing income tax cost recovery, Caitlyn is required to reduce the depreciable basis of the eligible assets by the amount of Section 179 deduction taken during the tax year.

| | 2009 | Tax | GAAP | Future (taxable) deductible amount |
|---|---|---|---|---|
| A | Purchase price of assets | $400,000 | $400,000 | |
| B | Section 179 expense election | 100,000 | -- | |
| C | Adjusted depreciable basis (A – B) | 300,000 | 400,000 | |
| D | Depreciation rate | × 20% | × 10% | |
| E | 2009 depreciation (C × D) | 60,000 | 40,000 | |

| F | Section 179 expense election (B) | 100,000 | -- | |
|---|---|---|---|---|
| G | 2009 depreciation and section 179 (E + F) | 160,000 | 40,000 | |
| H | Basis at 12/31/09 (A – G) | $240,000 | $360,000 | $(120,000) |

*2010*

| I | Depreciation rate | × 32% | × 10% | |
|---|---|---|---|---|
| J | 2010 Depreciation (C × I) | 96,000 | 40,000 | |
| K | Basis at 12/31/10 (H – J) | $144,000 | $320,000 | $(176,000) |

*2011*

| L | Depreciation rate | × 19.2% | × 10% | |
|---|---|---|---|---|
| M | 2011 Depreciation ( C × L) | 57,600 | 40,000 | |
| N | Basis at 12/31/11 (K – M) | $86,400 | $280,000 | $(193,600) |

The computation of deferred income taxes is as follows:

|  | *12/31/2009* | *12/31/2010* | *12/31/2011* |
|---|---|---|---|
| Future deductible temporary difference | | | |
| Prepaid rent | $100,000 | $ 80,000 | $125,000 |
| Future (taxable) temporary difference | | | |
| Property and equipment | (120,000) | (176,000) | (193,600) |
| Net (taxable) deductible temporary difference | (20,000) | (96,000) | (68,600) |
| Effective tax rate | 34% | 34% | 37% |
| Ending deferred income tax asset (liability) | (6,800) | (32,640) | (25,382) |
| Beginning deferred income tax asset (liability) | -- | (6,800) | (32,640) |
| Deferred income tax (expense) benefit | $ (6,800) | $ (25,840) | $ 7,258 |

Note from the computations that, under the liability method, deferred income tax expense or benefit is the amount necessary to adjust the balance sheet to the computed balance. No attempt is made to correlate the amount of deferred income tax expense or benefit to pretax accounting income or loss. Nor is it necessary, as it was under APB 11, to track the amount of each temporary difference that originates or reverses during the year.

## FAS 109 in Greater Detail

While the liability method is conceptually straightforward, in practice there are a number of complexities to be addressed. Income tax accounting remains one of the more difficult areas of accounting practice. In the following pages, these measurement and reporting issues will be discussed in greater detail:

1. Temporary and permanent differences
2. Treatment of net operating loss carryforwards
3. Measurement of deferred income tax assets and liabilities
4. Considering whether a valuation allowance is needed
5. The effect of tax law changes on previously recorded deferred income tax assets and liabilities
6. The effect of a change in the tax status of the reporting entity from taxable to non-taxable or vice versa on previously recognized deferred income tax assets and liabilities
7. The effect of accounting changes for income tax purposes
8. Income tax effects of dividends paid on shares held by Employee Stock Ownership Plans (ESOP)
9. The income tax effects of business combinations at and after acquisition date
10. Intercorporate income tax allocation
11. Separate financial statements of subsidiaries or investees
12. Asset acquisitions
13. Intraperiod income tax allocation
14. Balance sheet classification

15.   Disclosures
16.   Interim reporting

Detailed examples of deferred income tax accounting under FAS 109 are presented throughout the following discussion of these issues.

## Temporary and Permanent Differences

Deferred income taxes are provided for all temporary differences, but not for permanent differences. Thus, it is important to be able to distinguish between the two.

**Temporary differences.** While many typical business transactions are accounted for identically for income tax and financial reporting purposes, there are many others subject to different income tax and accounting treatments, often leading to their being reported in different periods in financial statements than they are reported on income tax returns. The term "timing differences," used under prior GAAP, has been superseded by the broader term "temporary differences" under current rules. Under income statement oriented GAAP, timing differences were said to originate in one period and to reverse in a later period. These involved such common items as alternative depreciation methods, deferred compensation plans, percentage-of-completion accounting for long-term construction contracts, and cash basis versus accrual basis accounting.

The more comprehensive concept of temporary differences, consistent with the modern balance sheet orientation of GAAP, includes all differences between the income tax basis and the financial reporting carrying value of assets and liabilities, if the reversal of those differences will result in taxable or deductible amounts in future years. Temporary differences include all the items formerly defined as timing differences, and other additional items.

Temporary differences under FAS 109 that were defined as timing differences under prior GAAP can be categorized as follows:

**Revenue recognized for financial reporting purposes before being recognized for income tax purposes.** Revenue accounted for by the installment method for income tax purposes, but fully reflected in current GAAP income; certain construction-related revenue recognized using the completed-contract method for income tax purposes, but recognized using the percentage-of-completion method for financial reporting purposes; earnings from investees recognized using the equity method for accounting purposes but taxed only when later distributed as dividends to the investor. These are future taxable temporary differences because future periods' taxable income will exceed GAAP income as the differences reverse; thus they give rise to deferred income tax liabilities.

**Revenue recognized for income tax purposes prior to recognition in the financial statements.** Certain taxable revenue received in advance, such as prepaid rental income and service contract revenue not recognized in the financial statements until later periods. These are future deductible temporary differences, because the costs of future performance will be deductible in the future years when incurred without being reduced by the amount of revenue deferred for GAAP purposes. Consequently, the income tax benefit to be realized in future years from deducting those future costs is a deferred income tax asset.

**Expenses deductible for income tax purposes prior to recognition in the financial statements.** Accelerated depreciation methods or shorter statutory useful lives used for income tax purposes, while straight-line depreciation or longer useful economic lives are used for financial reporting; amortization of goodwill and nonamortizable intangible assets over a 15-year life for income tax purposes while not amortizing them for financial reporting purposes unless they are impaired. Upon reversal in the future, the effect would be to increase taxable income without a corresponding increase in GAAP income. Therefore, these items are future taxable temporary differences, and give rise to deferred income tax liabilities.

**Expenses recognized in the financial statements prior to becoming deductible for income tax purposes.** Certain estimated expenses, such as warranty costs, as well as such contingent losses as accruals of litigation expenses, are not tax deductible until the obligation becomes fixed. In those future periods, those expenses will give rise to deductions on the reporting entity's income tax return. Thus, these are future deductible temporary differences that give rise to deferred income tax assets.

In addition to these familiar and well-understood categories of timing differences, temporary differences include a number of other categories that also involve differences between the income tax and financial reporting bases of assets or liabilities. These include

**Reductions in tax-deductible asset bases arising in connection with tax credits.** Under the provisions of the 1982 income tax act, taxpayers were permitted a choice of either full ACRS depreciation coupled with a reduced investment tax credit, or a full investment tax credit coupled with reduced depreciation allowances. If the taxpayer chose the latter option, the asset basis was reduced for tax depreciation, but was still fully depreciable for financial reporting purposes. Accordingly, this type of election is accounted for as a future taxable temporary difference, that gives rise to a deferred income tax liability.

**Investment tax credits accounted for by the deferral method.** Under GAAP, investment tax credits could be accounted for by either the "flow through" method (full recognition in the period the asset is placed in service, by far the most common method in practice), or by the "deferral" method (recognition in income over the useful lives of the assets giving rise to the credit). Thus, a future deductible temporary difference existed, with which a deferred income tax asset would be associated.

*NOTE: These two categories are no longer of much interest since the investment tax credit was eliminated and is not presently available to taxpayers under current tax law. In the past, however, Congress has reinstated the credit to provide an incentive for businesses to invest in productive equipment. Future reinstatement always remains a possibility, given the cyclical nature of the US economy.*

**Increases in the income tax bases of assets resulting from the indexing of asset costs for the effects of inflation.** Occasionally proposed but never enacted, enacting such a provision to income tax law would allow taxpaying entities to finance the replacement of depreciable assets through depreciation based on current costs, as computed by the application of indices to the historical costs of the assets being remeasured. This reevaluation of asset costs would give rise to future taxable temporary differences that would be associated with deferred income tax liabilities since, upon the eventual sale of the asset, the taxable gain would exceed the gain recognized for financial reporting purposes resulting in the payment of additional tax in the year of sale.

**Certain business combinations accounted for by the purchase method under FAS 141 or the acquisition method under FAS 141(R).** Under certain circumstances, the amounts assignable to assets or liabilities acquired in business combinations will differ from their income tax bases. Such differences may be either taxable or deductible in the future and, accordingly, may give rise to deferred income tax liabilities or assets. These differences are explicitly recognized by the reporting of deferred income taxes in the consolidated financial statements of the acquiring entity. Note that these differences are no longer allocable to the financial reporting bases of the underlying assets or liabilities themselves, as was the case under APB 11's net of tax method.

A financial reporting situation in which deferred income taxes may or may not be appropriate would include life insurance (such as key person insurance) under which the reporting entity is the beneficiary. Since proceeds of life insurance are not subject to income tax under present law, the excess of cash surrender values over the sum of premiums paid will not be a temporary difference under the provisions of FAS 109, if the intention is to hold the policy until death benefits are received. On the other hand, if the entity intends to cash in (surrender) the policy at some point prior to the death of the insured (i.e., it is holding the insurance contract as an investment), which would be a taxable event, then the excess surrender value is in fact a temporary difference, and deferred income taxes are to be provided thereon.

**Temporary differences from share-based compensation arrangements.** FAS 123(R), issued in December 2004, contains intricate rules with respect to accounting for the income tax effects of different types of share-based compensation awards.

The complexity of applying the income tax provisions contained in FAS 123(R) is exacerbated by the complex statutes and regulations that apply under the US Internal Revenue Code (IRC). The American Job Creation Act of 2004 added IRC §409A that contains complicated provisions regarding the timing of taxability of specified amounts deferred under nonqualified deferred compensation plans. In general, amounts deferred under specified types of nonqualified plans are currently includable in gross income to the extent the benefits are not subject to a substantial risk of forfeiture unless certain requirements are met. An incentive stock option (ISO or statutory option governed by IRC §422) is not subject to §409A; however, certain nonqualified stock option (NQSO or nonstatutory) plans are subject to these requirements.

Differences between the accounting rules and the income tax laws can result in situations where the cumulative amount of compensation cost recognized for financial reporting purposes will differ from the cumulative amount of compensation deductions recognized for income tax purposes. Under current income tax law applicable to certain NQSO awards, an employer recognizes an income tax deduction for the intrinsic value of the option on the date that the employee exercises the option. The intrinsic value is computed as the difference between the option's exercise price and the market price of the stock on the date of exercise. Under FAS 123(R) this type of equity award is recognized at the fair value of the options at grant date with compensation cost recognized over the requisite service period. Consequently, during the period from grant date until the end of the requisite service period, the reporting entity is recognizing compensation cost in its financial statements with no corresponding income tax deduction. Because the award described above is accounted for as equity (and not as a liability), the credit that offsets the debit to compensation cost is to additional paid-in capital. This results in a future deductible temporary difference between the carrying amounts of additional paid-in capital for financial reporting and income tax purposes, thus giving rise to a deferred income tax asset and corresponding deferred income tax benefit.

At exercise, to the extent that the income tax deduction based on intrinsic value exceeds the cumulative compensation cost recognized for financial reporting purposes, the income tax effect (the effective income tax rate multiplied by the cumulative difference) is credited to additional paid-in capital rather than being reflected in the income statement as a deferred income tax benefit.

The IRC provides employers the ability to obtain a current income tax deduction for payments of dividends (or dividend equivalents) to employees that hold nonvested shares, share units, or share options that are classified under FAS 123(R) as equity. Under this scenario, the payment of the dividends is charged to retained earnings under FAS 123(R) irrespective of the fact that the employer/reporting entity obtains a tax deduction for the payment as taxable compensation. EITF 06-11 provides that the income tax benefit realized from deducting these payments is to be recorded as an increase to additional paid-in capital and, as explained in depth in the discussion of FAS 123(R) in Chapter 19, included in the pool of excess tax benefits available to absorb tax deficiencies on share-based payment awards.

The consensus reached in EITF 06-11 is to be applied prospectively to income tax benefits resulting from dividends declared in fiscal years beginning after December 15, 2007, and interim periods within those fiscal years. Management is permitted to elect early application at the beginning of a fiscal year for which interim or annual financial statements had not yet been issued. Retrospective application to previously issued financial statements is prohibited. Upon adoption of the consensus, the reporting entity is to disclose in the notes to its financial statements the nature of any change in the accounting policy for treating income tax benefits realized as a result of dividends on share-based payment awards.

**Temporary differences arising from convertible debt with a beneficial conversion feature.** Issuers of debt securities sometimes structure the instruments to include a nondetachable conversion feature. If the terms of the conversion feature are "in-the-money" at the date of issuance, the feature is referred to as a "beneficial conversion feature." Beneficial conversion features are accounted for separately from the host instrument under EITF Issues 00-27 and 98-5.

The separate accounting results in an allocation to additional paid-in capital of a portion of the proceeds received from issuance of the instrument that represents the intrinsic value of the conversion feature calculated at the commitment date, as defined. The intrinsic value is the difference between the conversion price and the fair value of the instruments into which the security is convertible multiplied by the number of shares into which the security is convertible. The convertible security is recorded at its par value (assuming there is no discount or premium on issuance). A discount is recognized to offset the portion of the instrument that is allocated to additional paid-in capital. The discount is accreted from the issuance date to the stated redemption date of the convertible instrument or through the earliest conversion date if the instrument does not include a stated redemption date.

For US income tax purposes, the proceeds are recorded entirely as debt and represent the income tax basis of the debt security, thus creating a temporary difference between the basis of the debt for financial reporting and income tax reporting purposes.

EITF 05-8 specifies that the income tax effect associated with this temporary difference is to be recorded as an adjustment to additional paid-in-capital. It would not be reported, as are most other such tax effects, as a deferred tax asset or liability in the balance sheet.

Other common temporary differences include

**Accounting for investments.** Use of the equity method for financial reporting while using the cost method for income tax purposes.

**Accrued contingent liabilities.** These cannot be deducted for income tax purposes until the liability becomes fixed and determinable.

**Cash basis versus accrual basis.** Use of the cash method of accounting for income tax purposes and the accrual method for financial reporting.

**Charitable contributions that exceed the statutory deductibility limitation.** These can be carried over to future years for income tax purposes.

**Deferred compensation.** Under GAAP, the present value of deferred compensation agreements must be accrued and charged to expense over the employee's remaining employment period, but for income tax purposes these costs are not deductible until actually paid.

**Depreciation.** A temporary difference will occur unless the modified ACRS method is used for financial reporting over estimated useful lives that are the same as the IRS-prescribed recovery periods. This is only permissible for GAAP if the recovery periods are substantially identical to the estimated useful lives.

**Estimated costs** (e.g., warranty expense). Estimates or provisions of this nature are not included in the determination of taxable income until the period in which the costs are actually incurred.

**Goodwill.** For US federal income tax purposes, amortization over fifteen years is mandatory. Amortization of goodwill is no longer permitted under GAAP, but periodic write-downs for impairment may occur, with any remainder of goodwill being expensed when the reporting unit to which it pertains is ultimately disposed of.

**Income received in advance** (e.g., prepaid rent). Income of this nature is includable in taxable income in the period in which it is received, while for financial reporting purposes, it is considered a liability until the revenue is earned.

**Installment sale method.** Use of the installment sale method for income tax purposes generally results in a temporary difference because that method is generally not permitted to be used in accordance with GAAP.

**Long-term construction contracts.** A temporary difference will arise if different methods (e.g., completed-contract or percentage-of-completion) are used for GAAP and income tax purposes.

**Mandatory change from the cash method to the accrual method.** Generally one-fourth of this adjustment is recognized for income tax purposes each year.

**Net capital loss.** C corporation capital losses are recognized currently for financial reporting purposes but are carried forward to be offset against future capital gains for income tax purposes.

**Organization costs.** GAAP requires organization costs to be treated as expenses as incurred. For income tax purposes, organization costs are recorded as assets and amortized over a 60-month period. Also see **Permanent differences** below.

**Uniform cost capitalization (UNICAP).** Income tax accounting rules require manufacturers and certain wholesalers to capitalize as inventory costs, certain costs that, under GAAP are considered administrative costs that are not allocable to inventory.

**Permanent differences.** Permanent differences are book-tax differences in asset or liability bases that will never reverse and therefore, affect income taxes currently payable but do not give rise to deferred income taxes.

Common permanent differences include

**Club dues.** Dues assessed by business, social, athletic, luncheon, sporting, airline and hotel clubs are not deductible for federal income tax purposes.

**Dividends received deduction.** Depending on the percentage interest of the payer owned by the recipient, a percentage of the dividends received by a corporation are nontaxable. Different rules apply to subsidiaries.

**Goodwill—nondeductible.** If, in a particular taxing jurisdiction, goodwill amortization is not deductible, that goodwill is considered a permanent difference and does not give rise to deferred income taxes.

**Lease inclusion amounts.** Lessees of automobiles whose fair value the IRS deems to qualify as a luxury automobile are required to limit their lease deduction by adding to taxable income an amount determined by reference to a table prescribed annually in a revenue procedure.

**Meals and entertainment.** A percentage (currently 50%) of business meals and entertainment costs are not deductible for federal income tax purposes.

**Municipal interest income.** A 100% exclusion is permitted for investment in qualified municipal securities. Note that the capital gains applicable to sales of these securities are taxable.

**Officer's life insurance premiums and proceeds.** Premiums paid for an officer's life insurance policy under which the company is the beneficiary are not deductible for income tax purposes, nor are any death proceeds taxable.

**Organization and start-up costs.** GAAP requires organization and start-up costs to be treated as expenses as incurred. Certain organization and start-up costs are not allowed amortization under the tax code. The most clearly defined are those expenditures relating to the cost of raising capital. Also see temporary differences above.

**Penalties and fines.** Any penalty or fine arising as a result of violation of the law is not allowed as an income tax deduction. This includes a wide range of items including parking tickets, environmental fines, and penalties assessed by the US Internal Revenue Service.

**Percentage depletion.** The excess of percentage depletion over cost depletion is allowable as a deduction for income tax purposes.

**Wages and salaries eligible for jobs credit.** The portion of wages and salaries used in computing the jobs credit is not allowed as a deduction for income tax purposes.

## Treatment of Net Operating Loss Carryforwards

The recognition and measurement of the income tax effects of net operating loss carryforwards under FAS 109 differs materially from how this was dealt with under earlier standards. Historically, it had been presumed that net operating losses would generally not be realizable; accordingly, the income tax effects of carryforwards were not recognized in the financial statements until the future period in which the benefits were realized for income tax purposes. That is, the provision for income taxes in the loss year only reflected the benefit derived, if any, from carrying back the net operating loss to prior years to obtain a refund. Any excess net operating loss available to offset future years' taxable income was not recognized until actually realized. Consequently, the balance sheet would not display a deferred income tax asset relating to the net operating loss carryforward. This treatment was justified in order to report the entity's assets at amounts that did not exceed their estimated net realizable value. (Only in exceptional cases, when realization of the benefits was deemed to be assured beyond a reasonable doubt, was recognition in the loss period permitted.

FAS 96, the first replacement for APB 11, entirely prohibited recognition of net deferred income tax assets to the extent that they exceeded amounts currently refundable through net operating loss carrybacks as of the balance sheet date. This prohibition was based on the view that the display of deferred income tax assets for these benefits would have been tantamount to anticipating future income. Even the narrow "assured beyond a reasonable doubt" exception previously provided was eliminated.

With the imposition of FAS 109, however, all temporary differences and carryforwards have been conferred identical status, and their income tax effects are to be given full recognition on the balance sheet. Specifically, the income tax effects of net operating loss carryforwards are equivalent to the income tax effects of future deductible temporary differences, and the once important distinction between the two has been eliminated. The deferred income tax effects of net operating losses are computed and recorded, but as is the case for all other deferred income tax assets, the need for a valuation allowance must also be assessed (as discussed below). The income tax effects of income tax credit carryforwards (e.g., general business credits, alternative minimum tax credits) are used to increase deferred income tax assets dollar-for-dollar versus being treated in the same manner as future deductible temporary differences as illustrated below.

### Example—Net operating loss carryforwards and income tax credit carryforwards

Casey Corporation has the following future deductible temporary differences and available carryforwards at December 31, 2009:

| | |
|---|---|
| Inventory costs capitalized under Internal Revenue Code §263A | $40,000 |
| Allowance for uncollectible accounts receivable | 20,000 |
| Net operating loss carryforward | 18,000 |
| General business credit carryforward | 14,000 |

Casey's computation of deferred income taxes at December 31, 2009, is as follows:

| | |
|---|---|
| Capitalized inventory costs | $40,000 |
| Allowance for uncollectible accounts receivable | 20,000 |
| Net operating loss carryforward | 18,000 |
| | 78,000 |
| Assumed income tax rate | × 34% |
| | 26,520 |
| General business credit carryforward | 14,000 |
| Deferred income tax asset | $40,520 |

Note the net operating loss is multiplied by the income tax rate to compute its effect on the deferred income tax asset since it is available to reduce future years' *taxable income*. In contrast, the general business credit carryforward is not multiplied by the *income tax* rate since it is available to be used to offset future years' income tax.

The reporting of the current income tax benefit of carrying back net operating losses was also changed by the current standard. FAS 109 provides that the income tax benefits of net operating loss carrybacks and carryforwards, with limited exceptions (discussed below), are to be reported in the same manner as the source of either income or loss in the current year. As used in the standard, the phrase "in the same manner" refers to the classification of the income tax benefit in the income statement (i.e., as income taxes on income from continuing operations, discontinued operations, extraordinary items, etc.) or as the income tax effect of gains included in other comprehensive income but excluded from net income on the income statement. The income tax benefits are not reported in the same manner as the source of the net operating loss carryforward or income taxes paid in a prior year, or as the source of the expected future taxable income that will permit the realization of the carryforward.

For example, if the income tax benefit of a loss that arose in a prior year in connection with an extraordinary item is first given recognition in the current year, the benefit would be allocated to income taxes on income from continuing operations if the benefit offsets income taxes on income from continuing operations in the current year. The expression "first given recognition" means that the net deferred income tax asset, after deducting the valuation allowance, reflects the income tax effect of the loss carryforward for the first time.

Under FAS 109, of course, the gross deferred income tax asset will always reflect all future deductible temporary differences and net operating loss carryforwards in the periods they arise. Thus, first given recognition means that the valuation allowance is eliminated for the first time. If it offsets income taxes on extraordinary income in the current year, then the benefits would be reported in extraordinary items. As another example, the tax benefit arising from the entity's loss from continuing operations in the current year would be allocated to continuing operations, regardless of whether it might be realized as a carryback against income taxes paid on extraordinary items in prior years. The income tax benefit would also be allocated to continuing operations in cases where it is anticipated that the benefit will be realized through the reduction of income taxes to be due on extraordinary gains in future years. (See the discussion of intraperiod income tax allocation later in this chapter.)

Thus, the general rule is that the reporting of income tax effects of net operating losses are driven by the source of the tax benefits in the current period. There are only two exceptions to the foregoing rule. The first exception relates to existing future deductible temporary differences and net operating loss carryforwards which arise in connection with business combinations and for which income tax benefits are first recognized. This exception will be discussed below (see income tax effects of business combinations). As in the preceding paragraph, first recognized means that a valuation allowance (as discussed more fully later in this chapter) provided previously is being eliminated for the first time.

The second exception to the aforementioned general rule is that certain income tax benefits allocable to stockholders' equity are not to be reflected in the income statement. Specifically, income tax benefits arising in connection with contributed capital, employee stock options, dividends paid on unallocated ESOP shares, or temporary differences existing at the date of a quasi reorganization are reported as accumulated other comprehensive income in the stockholders' equity section of the balance sheet and are not included in the income statement.

Certain transactions among stockholders that occur outside the company can affect the status of deferred income taxes. The most commonly encountered of these is the change in ownership of over 50% of the company's stock, which limits or eliminates the company's ability to utilize net operating loss carryforwards, and accordingly requires the reversal of deferred income tax assets previously recognized under FAS 109. Changes in deferred income taxes caused by transactions among stockholders are to be included in current period income tax expense in the income statement, since these are analogous to changes in expectations resulting from other external events (e.g., changes in enacted income tax rates).

However, the income tax effects of changes in the income tax bases of assets or liabilities caused by transactions among stockholders would be included in equity, not in the income statement, although subsequent period changes in the valuation account, if any, would be reflected in income (EITF 94-10).

## Measurement of Deferred Income Tax Assets and Liabilities

**Scheduling of the reversal years of temporary differences.** Under FAS 109 there is no need to forecast (or "schedule") the future years in which temporary differences are expected to reverse except in the most exceptional circumstances. To eliminate the burdensome scheduling requirement of predecessor standard FAS 96, it was necessary to endorse the use of the expected average (i.e., effective) income tax rate to measure the deferred income tax assets and liabilities, and to forgo a more precise measure of marginal tax effects. Scheduling is now encountered primarily (1) when income tax rate changes are to be phased in over multiple years, and (2) in order to determine the classification (current or noncurrent) of a deferred income tax asset arising from a net operating loss carryforward or income tax credit carryforward or to determine whether such a carryforward might expire unused for the purpose of determining the amount of valuation allowance needed (as discussed in the following section of this chapter).

**Determining the appropriate income tax rate.** Currently, C corporations with taxable income between $335,000 and $10,000,000 are taxed at an expected income tax rate equal to the 34% marginal rate, since the effect of the surtax exemption has fully phased out at that level, effectively resulting in a flat tax. Thus, the computation of deferred federal income taxes for these entities is accomplished simply by applying the 34% top marginal rate to all temporary differences and net operating loss carryforwards outstanding at the balance sheet date. This technique is applied to future taxable temporary differences (producing deferred income tax liabilities), and to future deductible temporary differences and net operating loss carryforwards (giving rise to deferred income tax assets). The deferred income tax assets computed must still be evaluated for realizability; some, or all, of the projected income tax benefits may fail the "more-likely-than-not" test and consequently may need to be offset by a valuation allowance.

On the other hand, reporting entities that have historically been taxed at an effective federal income tax rate lower than the top marginal rate compute their federal deferred income tax assets and liabilities by using their expected future effective income tax rates. Consistent with the goal of simplifying the process of calculating deferred income taxes, reporting entities are permitted to apply a single, long-term expected income tax rate, without attempting to differentiate among the years when temporary difference reversals are expected to occur. In any event, the inherent imprecision of forecasting future income levels and the patterns of temporary difference reversals makes it unlikely that a more sophisticated computational effort would produce better financial statements. Therefore, absent such factors as the phasing in of new income tax rates, it is not necessary to consider whether the reporting entity's effective income tax rate will vary from year to year.

The effective income tax rate convention obviates the need to predict the impact of the alternative minimum tax (AMT) on future years. In determining an entity's deferred income taxes, the number of computations may be as few as one, which contrasts markedly with FAS 96, the standard's immediate predecessor.

**Special deductions.** The US income tax code includes economic incentives designed to provide special benefits to certain types of taxpayers and to help stimulate the economy. These special deductions have been quite varied, ranging from statutory depletion deductions for extractive industries to deductions allowed to small insurance companies. A less obscure special deduction results from a provision included in the American Jobs Creation Act of 2004 (AJCA) referred to as the Qualified Production Activities Deduction (AJCA §102). This deduction, effective for taxable years beginning after December 31, 2004, is computed as a specified percentage of the taxpayer's income from qualified domestic production activities for the year. The percentage increases from an initial 3% in 2005 and 2006 to 6% in 2007 through 2009, and finally to 9% for 2010 and later. The computed deduction is subject to certain limitations. For example, the deduction cannot exceed the amount computed by applying the same percentage to taxable income computed prior to considering this deduction nor can the deduction exceed 50% of the wages paid by the taxpayer for the tax year.

In FSP FAS 109-1, the FASB staff clarified that this provision of AJCA is not considered a reduction in the enacted income tax rate for qualified taxpayers because the realization of the income tax benefit is contingent upon the taxpayer, in the future, performing qualified production activities and incurring a sufficient level of wages and profitability. The ability to utilize this special deduction is considered, however, in determining the effective federal income tax rate to apply to future taxable or deductible temporary differences when graduated rates are a significant factor. The future availability of this deduction is also considered in assessing the need for a valuation allowance to reduce a deferred income tax asset.

**Computing deferred income taxes.** The procedure to compute the gross deferred income tax provision (i.e., before addressing the possible need for a valuation allowance) is as follows:

1. Identify all temporary differences existing as of the reporting date. This process is simplified if the reporting entity maintains both GAAP and income tax balance sheets for comparison purposes.
2. Segregate the temporary differences into future taxable differences and future deductible differences. This step is necessary because a valuation allowance may be required to be provided to offset the income tax effects of the future deductible temporary differences and carryforwards, but not the income tax effects of the future taxable temporary differences.
3. Accumulate information about available net operating loss and tax credit carryforwards as well as their expiration dates or other types of limitations, if any.
4. Measure the income tax effect of aggregate future taxable temporary differences by separately applying the appropriate expected income tax rates (federal plus any state, local, and foreign rates that are applicable under the circumstances). Ensure that consideration is given in making these computations to the federal income tax deductibility of income taxes payable to other jurisdictions.
5. Similarly, measure the income tax effects of future deductible temporary differences, including net operating loss carryforwards.

FAS 109 prescribes that separate computations be made for each taxing jurisdiction. In many cases, this level of complexity is not needed and a single, combined effective income tax rate can be used. However, in assessing the need for valuation allowances, it is necessary to consider the entity's ability to absorb deferred income tax benefits against income tax liabilities. Inasmuch as benefits from one tax jurisdiction will not reduce income taxes payable to another tax jurisdiction, separate calculations will be needed in these situations. Also, for purposes of balance sheet presentation (discussed below), offsetting of deferred income tax assets and liabilities is only permissible within the same jurisdiction.

Separate computations are made for each taxpaying component of the primary reporting entity: if a parent company and its subsidiaries are consolidated for financial reporting purposes but file separate income tax returns, the reporting entity comprises a number of components, and the income tax benefits of any one will be unavailable to reduce the income tax obligations of the others.

The principles set forth above are illustrated by the following example.

### Computation of deferred income tax liability and asset—Basic example

Assume that Humfeld Company has a total of $28,000 of future taxable temporary differences, and a total of $8,000 of future deductible temporary differences. There are no available operating loss or tax credit carryforwards. Taxable income is $230,000 and the income tax rate is a flat (i.e., not graduated) 34% for the current year and not anticipated to change in the future. Also assume that there were no deferred income tax liabilities or assets in prior years.

Current income tax expense and income taxes currently payable are computed as taxable income times the current rate ($230,000 × 34% = $78,200). The deferred income tax asset is computed as $2,720 representing 34% of future deductible temporary differences of $8,000. The deferred income tax liability of $9,520 is calculated as 34% of future taxable temporary differences of $28,000. The deferred income tax expense of $6,800 is the net of the deferred income tax liability of $9,520 and the deferred income tax asset of $2,720.

The journal entry to record the required amounts is

| | | |
|---|---|---|
| Current income tax expense | 78,200 | |
| Deferred income tax asset | 2,720 | |
| Income tax expense—deferred | 6,800 | |
| Deferred income tax liability | | 9,520 |
| Income taxes currently payable | | 78,200 |

In 2009, Humfeld Company has taxable income of $411,000, aggregate future taxable and future deductible temporary differences are $75,000 and $36,000, respectively, and the income tax rate remains a flat 34%.

Current income tax expense and income taxes currently payable are each $139,740 ($411,000 × 34%).

Deferred amounts are calculated as follows:

| | *Deferred tax liability* | *Deferred tax asset* | *Income tax expense—deferred* |
|---|---|---|---|
| Required balance at 12/31/09 | | | |
| $75,000 × 34% | $25,500 | | -- |
| $36,000 × 34% | | $12,240 | -- |
| Balances at 12/31/08 | 9,520 | 2,720 | -- |
| Adjustment required | $15,980 | $9,520 | $6,460 |

The journal entry to record the deferred amounts is

| | | |
|---|---|---|
| Deferred income tax asset | 9,520 | |
| Income tax expense—deferred | 6,460 | |
| Deferred income tax liability | | 15,980 |

Because the increase in the liability in 2009 is larger (by $6,460) than the increase in the asset for that year, the result is a deferred income tax expense for 2009.

## The Valuation Allowance for Deferred Income Tax Assets Expected to Be Unrealizable

Under prior GAAP, the presentation of deferred income tax assets in the balance sheet was constrained or prohibited entirely. FAS 109 requires that all deferred income tax assets be given full recognition, subject to the possible provision of an allowance when it is determined that this asset is unlikely to be realized. This approach (providing full recognition on a gross basis, but also providing for a valuation allowance to reduce the recorded asset to the expected realizable amount) conveys the greatest amount of useful information to the users of the financial statements.

In dealing with the question of measurement of the valuation account, FASB could well have been guided by FAS 5, which established the standard for recognizing contingent obligations incurred and impairments of assets. Under FAS 5, the threshold for recognition of impairment would have been that the impairment was deemed to be "probable" of realization. FASB rejected the notion of applying that standard to this measurement situation, and instead developed a new measure, the "more-likely-than-not" criterion. (To date, this criterion has been applied exclusively to the deferred income tax asset issue.)

Under this provision of FAS 109, a valuation allowance is to be provided for that fraction of the computed year-end balances of the deferred income tax assets for which it has been determined that it is more likely than not that the reported asset amount will not be realized. As used in this context, "more likely than not" represents a probability of just over 50%. Since it is widely agreed that the term probable, as used in FAS 5, denotes a much higher probability (perhaps 85% to 90%), the threshold for reflecting an impairment of deferred income tax assets is much lower than the threshold for other assets (i.e., in most cases, the likelihood of a valuation allowance being required is greater than, say, the likelihood that a long-lived asset is impaired).

If a higher threshold had been set (such as FAS 5's "probable"), great diversity could have developed in practice as to the amount of valuation allowances offsetting deferred income tax assets, which would not have been consistent with the goal of comparability of financial statements over time and across entities.

### Establishment of a valuation allowance

Assume that Couch Corporation has a future deductible temporary difference of $60,000 at December 31, 2009. The tax rate is a flat 34%. Based on available evidence, management of Couch Corporation concludes that it is more likely than not that all sources will not result in future taxable income sufficient to realize an income tax benefit of more than $15,000 (25% of the future deductible temporary difference). Also assume that there were no deferred income tax assets in previous years and that prior years' taxable income was inconsequential.

At 12/31/09 Couch Corporation records a deferred income tax asset in the amount of $20,400 ($60,000 × 34%) and a valuation allowance of $15,300 (34% of the $45,000 difference between the $60,000 of future deductible temporary differences and the $15,000 of future taxable income expected to absorb the future tax deduction arising from the reversal of the temporary difference).

The journal entry at 12/31/09 is

| Deferred income tax asset | 20,400 | |
| Valuation allowance | | 15,300 |
| Income tax benefit—deferred | | 5,100 |

The deferred income tax benefit of $5,100 represents that portion of the deferred income tax asset (25%) that, more likely than not, is realizable.

Assume that at the end of 2010, Couch Corporation's future deductible temporary difference has decreased to $50,000 and that Couch now has a net operating loss carryforward of $42,000. The total of the net operating loss carryforward ($42,000) plus the amount of the future deductible temporary difference ($50,000) is $92,000. A deferred income tax asset of $31,280 ($92,000 × 34%) is recognized at the end of 2010. Also assume that management of Couch Corporation concludes that it is more likely than not that $25,000 of the tax asset will not be realized. Thus, a valuation allowance in that amount is required, and the balance in the allowance account of $15,300 must be increased by $9,700 ($25,000 − $15,300).

The journal entry at 12/31/10 is

| Deferred income tax asset | 10,880 | |
| Valuation allowance | | 9,700 |
| Income tax benefit—deferred | | 1,180 |

The deferred income tax asset is debited $10,880 to increase it from $20,400 at the end of 2009 to its required balance of $31,280 at the end of 2010. The deferred income tax benefit of $1,180 represents the net of the $10,880 increase in the deferred income tax asset and the $9,700 increase in the valuation allowance.

While the meaning of the more-likely-than-not criterion is clear (more than 50%), the practical difficulty of assessing whether or not this subjective threshold test is met in a given situation remains. A number of positive and negative factors need to be evaluated in reaching a conclusion as to the necessity of a valuation allowance. Positive factors (those suggesting that an allowance is not necessary) include

1. Evidence of sufficient future taxable income, exclusive of reversing temporary differences and carryforwards, to realize the benefit of the deferred income tax asset
2. Evidence of sufficient future taxable income arising from the reversals of existing future taxable temporary differences (deferred income tax liabilities) to realize the benefit of the deferred income tax asset
3. Evidence of sufficient taxable income in prior year(s) available for realization of a net operating loss carryback under existing statutory limitations
4. Evidence of the existence of prudent, feasible tax planning strategies under management control that, if implemented, would permit the realization of the deferred income tax asset
5. An excess of appreciated asset values over their tax bases, in an amount sufficient to realize the deferred income tax asset
6. A strong earnings history exclusive of the loss creating the deferred tax asset

While the foregoing may suggest that the reporting entity will be able to realize the benefits of the future deductible temporary differences outstanding as of the balance sheet date, certain negative factors must also be considered in determining whether a valuation allowance needs to be established against deferred income tax assets. These factors include

1. A cumulative recent history of losses
2. A history of operating losses, or of net operating loss or tax credit carryforwards that have expired unused
3. Losses that are anticipated in the near future years, despite a history of profitable operations

Thus, the process of evaluating whether a valuation allowance is needed involves the weighing of both positive and negative factors to determine whether, based on the preponderance of available evidence, it is more likely than not that the deferred income tax assets will be realized.

### Example of applying the more-likely-than-not criterion to a deferred income tax asset

Assume the following facts:

1. Foy Corporation reports on a calendar year, and it commenced operations and began applying FAS 109 in 2004.
2. As of the December 31, 2009 balance sheet, it has future taxable temporary differences of $85,000 relating to income earned on equity-method investments; future deductible temporary differences of $12,000 relating to deferred compensation arrangements; a net operating loss carryforward (which arose in 2006) of $40,000; and a capital loss carryforward of $10,000 (which arose in 2009).
3. Foy's expected effective income tax rate for future years is 34% for both ordinary income and net long-term capital gains. Capital losses cannot be offset against ordinary income.

The first steps are to compute the deferred income tax asset and/or liability without consideration of the possible need for a valuation allowance.

*Deferred income tax liability:*

| | |
|---|---|
| Future taxable temporary difference (equity-method investment) | $85,000 |
| Effective tax rate | × 34% |
| Required balance | $28,900 |

*Deferred income tax asset:*

| Future deductible temporary differences and carryforwards: | |
|---|---:|
| Deferred compensation | $12,000 |
| Net operating loss carryforward | 40,000 |
| | 52,000 |
| Effective tax rate | × 34% |
| Required balance (a) | $17,680 |
| Capital loss | $10,000 |
| Effective tax rate | × 34% |
| Required balance (b) | $ 3,400 |

*Total deferred income tax asset:  (a) + (b)*

| Ordinary | $17,680 |
|---|---:|
| Capital | 3,400 |
| Total required balance | $21,080 |

The next step is to consider the need for a valuation allowance to partially or completely offset the deferred income tax asset, based on a "more likely than not" assessment of the asset's realizability. Foy management must evaluate both positive and negative evidence to determine the need for a valuation allowance, if any. Assume that management identifies the following factors that may affect this need:

1. Before the net operating loss (NOL) deduction, Foy reported taxable income of $5,000 in 2009. Management believes that taxable income in future years, apart from NOL deductions, should continue at approximately the same level experienced in 2009.
2. The future taxable temporary differences are not expected to reverse in the foreseeable future as the equity method investee is not expected to incur losses or pay dividends to Foy.
3. The capital loss arose in connection with a securities transaction of a type that is unlikely to recur. The company does not generally engage in activities that have the potential to result in capital gains or losses.
4. Management estimates that certain productive assets have a fair value exceeding their respective income tax bases by about $30,000. The entire gain, if realized for income tax purposes, would result in recapture of depreciation previously taken. Since the current plans call for a substantial upgrading of the company's plant assets, management feels it could easily accelerate those actions in order to realize taxable gains, should it be desirable to do so for income tax planning purposes.

Based on the foregoing information, Foy Corporation management concludes that a $3,400 valuation allowance is required. The reasoning is as follows:

1. There will be some taxable operating income generated in future years ($5,000 annually, based on the earnings experienced in 2009), which will absorb a modest portion of the reversal of the deductible temporary difference ($12,000) and net operating loss carryforward ($40,000) existing at year-end 2009.
2. More importantly, the feasible tax planning strategy of accelerating the taxable gain relating to appreciated assets ($30,000) would certainly be sufficient, in conjunction with operating income over several years, to permit Foy to fully realize the income tax benefits of the future deductible temporary difference and NOL carryover.
3. However, since capital losses can only be carried forward for five years, are only usable to offset future capital gains, and Foy management is unable to project future realization of capital gains, it is more likely than not that the associated tax benefit accrued ($3,400) will not be realized, and thus a valuation allowance must be recorded.

Based on this analysis, an allowance for unrealizable deferred income tax benefits in the amount of $3,400 is established by a charge against the current (2009) income tax provision.

Among the foregoing positive and negative factors to be considered, perhaps the most difficult to fully grasp is that of available income tax planning strategies. Since FAS 109 requires that all available evidence be assessed to determine the need for a valuation allowance, the matter of the cost of implementing those strategies is irrelevant. In fact, there is no limitation regarding strategies that may involve significant costs of implementation, although in computing the amount of valuation allowance needed, any costs of implementation must be netted against the benefits to be derived.

For example, if a gross deferred income tax asset of $50,000 is recorded, and certain strategies have been identified by management which would protect realization of the future deductible item associated with the computed income tax benefit, at an implementation cost of $10,000, then the net amount of income tax benefit which is more likely than not to be realizable would not be $50,000. Rather, it may be only $43,400, which is the gross benefit less the after-tax cost of implementation, assuming a 34% tax rate {$50,000 – [$10,000 × (1 – .34)]}. Accordingly, a valuation allowance of $6,600 is established in this example.

### Impact of a qualifying tax strategy

Assume that Kruse Company has a $180,000 net operating loss carryforward as of 12/31/09, scheduled to expire at the end of the following year. Future taxable temporary differences of $240,000 exist that are expected to reverse in approximately equal amounts of $80,000 in 2010, 2011, and 2012. Kruse Company estimates that taxable income for 2010 (exclusive of the reversal of existing temporary differences and the operating loss carryforward) will be $20,000. Kruse Company expects to implement a qualifying income tax planning strategy that will accelerate the total of $240,000 of taxable temporary differences to 2010. Expenses to implement the strategy are estimated to approximate $30,000. The tax rate is 34%.

In the absence of the income tax planning strategy, $100,000 of the net operating loss carry-forward could be realized in 2010 based on estimated taxable income of $20,000 plus $80,000 of the reversal of future taxable temporary differences. Thus, $80,000 would expire unused at the end of 2010 and the net amount of the deferred income tax asset at 12/31/09 would be recognized as $34,000, computed as $61,200 ($180,000 × 34%) minus the valuation allowance of $27,200 ($80,000 × 34%).

However, by implementing the income tax planning strategy, the deferred income tax asset is calculated as follows:

| Taxable income for 2010: | |
|---|---:|
| Expected amount without reversal of taxable temporary differences | $ 20,000 |
| Reversal of taxable temporary differences due to tax-planning strategy, net of costs | 210,000 |
| | 230,000 |
| Net operating loss to be carried forward | (180,000) |
| Net operating loss expiring unused at 12/31/10 | $___ -- |

The gross deferred income tax asset thus can be recorded at the full benefit amount of $61,200 ($180,000 × 34%). However, a valuation allowance is required for $19,800, representing the net-of-tax effect of the $30,000 in anticipated expenses related to implementation of the strategy. The net deferred income tax asset at 12/31/09 is $41,400 ($61,200 – $19,800). Kruse Company will also recognize a deferred income tax liability of $81,600 at the end of 2009 (34% of the taxable temporary differences of $240,000).

The adequacy of the valuation allowance must be assessed as of each balance sheet date. Adjustments to the amount of the valuation allowance are recorded by a charge against, or a credit to, current earnings, via the current period income tax expense or benefit. Thus, even if the gross amount of future deductible temporary differences has remained constant during a year, income tax expense for that year might be increased or decreased as a consequence of reassessing the adequacy of the valuation allowance at year-end. It is important that these two computational steps be separately addressed: first the computation of the gross deferred income tax assets (the product of the expected effective income tax rate and the total amount of future deductible temporary differences) must be made; then the amount of the valuation allowance to be provided to offset the deferred income tax asset must be assessed (using the criteria set forth above). Although changes in both the deferred income tax asset and valuation allowance affect current period income tax expense, the processes of measuring these two amounts are distinct. Furthermore, FAS 109 requires disclosure of both the gross deferred income tax asset (and also the gross deferred income tax liability) and the change in the valuation allowance for the year. These disclosure requirements underline the need to separately measure these items without offsetting.

## Accounting for Uncertainty in Income Taxes

**Background.** The filing of federal, state, and/or local income tax returns requires management, in consultation with its tax advisors, to make judgments regarding how it will apply intricate and often ambiguous laws, regulations, administrative rulings, and court precedents. If and when the income tax returns are audited by the taxing authority, sometimes years after they are filed, these judgments may be questioned or disallowed all or in part. As a result, management must make assumptions regarding the likelihood of success in defending its judgments in the event of audit in determining the accounting entries necessary to accurately reflect income taxes currently payable and/or refundable. A project was added to FASB's agenda due to diversity in practice regarding how to exercise those judgments and that project resulted in the issuance of FIN 48, *Accounting for Uncertainty in Income Taxes*, in June 2006.

**Effective dates.** FIN 48, as issued, was to become fully effective for years beginning after December 15, 2006.

In response to concerns raised by the FASB Private Company Financial Reporting Committee (PCFRC) and other constituent groups, FASB issued FSP FIN 48-2, *Effective Date of FASB Interpretation No. 48 for Certain Nonpublic Enterprises,* on February 1, 2008. The FSP amended FIN 48 to provide a one-year deferral of its effective date for certain nonpublic enterprises. The deferral applies to nonpublic reporting entities *except* those that

1. Are consolidated by a public enterprise that applies US GAAP
2. Had already issued a full set of US GAAP annual financial statements prior to February 1, 2008 (the issuance date of the FSP)

Entities to which the deferral applies will be required to adopt FIN 48 in annual financial statements for fiscal years beginning after December 15, 2007, with application applying to the *beginning* of the reporting entity's fiscal year.

Those entities that do not qualify for the deferral because they had already issued their annual financial statements prior to the issuance of the FSP are required to continue to apply FIN 48 and my not derecognize any amounts recorded as result of applying the recognition and measurement provisions of the interpretation.

It is important to note that, for the purpose of this FSP, the definition of "nonpublic enterprise" conforms to FAS 109 as amended by FSP FAS 126-1, *Applicability of Certain Disclosure and Interim Reporting Requirements for Obligors for Conduit Debt Securities*, and thus a conduit bond obligor, as defined, is considered a public enterprise and is not eligible for the deferred effective date.

On May 30, 2008, the chair of the PCFRC issued a letter to the chairman of FASB recommending that FASB either provide an outright exemption to private companies from all of the requirements of FIN 48 or, absent that outcome, recommending that FASB indefinitely defer the effective date of FIN 48 for nonpublic companies until the current joint FASB/IASB convergence project on income tax accounting is completed.[1] That project is currently expected to result in an Exposure Draft by the fourth quarter of 2008. The effective date of new requirements, if any are ultimately adopted, would undoubtedly be later than 2008, however.

---

[1] *http://www.pcfr.org/downloads/PCFRC_Recommendation_Letter_Final_FIN_48_5_30_08_(2).pdf*

At the time this publication went to press, FASB had not publicly responded to the PCFRC letter and it is not known whether the FASB is sympathetic to these recommendations.

**Scope.** The term "tax position" is used in FIN 48 to refer to *each* judgment that management makes on an income tax return that has been or will be filed that affects the measurement of current or deferred income tax assets and liabilities at an interim or year-end balance sheet date. Tax positions include

1. Deductions claimed
2. Deferrals of current income tax to one or more future periods
3. Income tax credits applied
4. Characterization as capital gain versus ordinary income
5. Whether or not to report income on an income tax return
6. Whether or not to file an income tax return in a particular jurisdiction

The effects of a tax position can result in a permanent reduction of income taxes payable or deferral of the payment of income taxes to a future year. The taking of a tax position can also affect management's estimate of the valuation allowance sufficient to reflect its estimate of the amount of deferred income tax assets that are realizable.

FIN 48 applies to income taxes accounted for in accordance with FAS 109, and thus does not apply directly or by analogy to other taxes, such as real estate, personal property, sales, excise, or use taxes. The scope of FIN 48 includes any entity potentially subject to income taxes including

- Nonprofit organizations
- Flow-through entities (e.g., partnerships, limited liability companies, and S corporations)
- Entities whose income tax liabilities are subject to 100% credit for dividends paid such as real estate investment trusts (REITs) and registered investment companies.

**Initial recognition and measurement.** FIN 48 uses a two-step approach to recognition and measurement.

*Initial recognition*—Management is to evaluate each tax position as to whether, based on the position's technical merits, it is "more likely than not" that the position would be sustained upon examination by the taxing authority. In making this evaluation, management is required to assume that the tax position will be examined by the taxing authority and that the taxing authority will be provided with all relevant facts and will have full knowledge of all relevant information. Thus, management is prohibited from asserting that a position will be sustained because of a low likelihood that the reporting entity's income tax returns will be examined (a practice that pundits have termed "playing the audit lottery").

The term "more likely than not," consistent with its use in FAS 109, means that there is a probability of more than 50% that the tax position would be sustained upon examination. A judgment of more likely than not represents a positive assertion by management that the reporting entity is entitled to the economic benefits provided by the tax position it is taking. The term "upon examination" includes resolution of appeals or litigation processes, if any, necessary to settle the matter.

It is important to appreciate that this is a new threshold condition for recognition. Unlike the "more likely than not" criterion in FAS 109, which governs the recognition of a valuation allowance to offset all or a portion of deferred income tax assets which have already fully recognized, this establishes a requirement for whether to give any accounting recognition to the income tax effects of questionable tax positions being taken. Failing to meet this threshold test means that, for example, an income tax deduction being claimed would not be accompanied by recognition of a reduction of income tax expense in a GAAP-basis financial statement, and thus that an income tax liability would be required to be reported for the entire tax benefit claimed on the income tax return notwithstanding management's assertion that a deduction claimed on its income tax return was valid.

Positions must be evaluated independently of each other without offset or aggregation. A "unit of account" approach can be taken in this evaluation if it is based on the manner in which management prepares and supports its income tax return and is consistent with the approach that the taxing authority would reasonably be expected to use in conducting an examination.

In considering the technical merits of its tax positions, management is to consider the applicability of the various sources of tax authority (enacted legislation, legislative intent, regulations, rulings, and case law) to the facts and circumstances. Management may also take into account, if applicable, any administrative practices and precedents that are widely understood with respect to the manner that the taxing authority deals specifically with the reporting entity or other similar taxpayers.

*Initial measurement*—If a tax position meets the initial recognition threshold, it is then measured to determine the amount to recognize in the financial statements. The following considerations apply to the measurement process:

1.  Consider if the position is based on clear and unambiguous tax law. If so, and management has a high level of confidence in the technical merits of the position, the position qualifies as a "highly certain tax position" and, consequently, the full benefit would be recognized in the financial statements. Stated in the language of FIN 48, the measurement of the maximum amount of income tax benefit that is more than 50% likely to be realized is 100% of the benefit claimed.

    *NOTE: Management may deem the **amount** of a tax position to be highly certain of being sustained but not highly certain as to the **timing** of the benefit. For example, in deciding whether to record a cost as an expense of the period in which it is incurred or to capitalize it, management may be highly certain that the cost will be deductible in some period but not be highly certain as to whether the proper period to deduct it is in the current period or ratably over multiple future periods. Under these circumstances, management would be required to measure the maximum amount that it believed was more than 50% likely of being sustained in the period that the cost is incurred.*

2.  If it is not highly certain that the full benefit of a position would be sustained in the year claimed, then the amount to be recognized for the tax position is measured as management's *best estimate* of the *maximum* benefit that is more than 50% likely of being realized upon effective settlement with a taxing authority possessing full knowledge of all relevant information. Management is to consider the amounts and probabilities of various settlement outcomes based on the facts, circumstances, and information available at the balance sheet date. As stated above, management must assume that the taxing authority will conduct an examination and may not consider the likelihood of this not occurring in this measurement process.

As explained above, measurement under FIN 48 can be a fairly complex process. It requires that management consider the amounts and probabilities of various effective settlement outcomes. The amount of the income tax benefit to be given financial statement recognition is the largest (i.e., most favorable) estimated outcome that is more than 50% probable, as illustrated in the following example.

**Example of the two-step initial recognition and measurement process**

Menkin Manufacturing planned to claim a $10,000 credit for increasing research activities (R&D credit) on its 2009 corporate income tax return. In consultation with its tax advisor, management believes that a portion of the credit is at risk because of ambiguity regarding the technical merits of the decision to classify certain costs as qualifying to be included in the computation of the credit. Management does believe, however, that it is "more likely than not" that the reporting entity will qualify for all or a portion of the R&D credit, and thus recognition will have to be limited to only a portion of the amount it will be claiming on its income tax return.

Since the credit meets the more-likely-than-not threshold for initial recognition, management must measure the amount to be recognized. It has estimated the range of possible outcomes (i.e., of credit allowed) and related likelihoods as follows:

| Estimated outcome | Probability of occurrence | Cumulative probability of occurrence |
|---|---|---|
| $10,000 | 5% | 5% |
| 8,500 | 35% | 40% |
| 7,500 | 25% | 65% |
| 7,000 | 20% | 85% |
| 6,500 | 10% | 95% |
| 6,000 | 5% | 100% |

The largest outcome above that has a more than 50% cumulative probability of being realized is $7,500, which management has estimated as having a cumulative probability of 65%. Therefore, management would recognize only $7,500 of this tax position in the reporting entity's financial statements. This would result in Menkin Manufacturing reflecting a liability for unrecognized income tax benefits in the amount of $2,500 on its balance sheet as of December 31, 2009.

Note, in the foregoing example, that while the income tax return will claim an R&D credit for the full $10,000, GAAP-basis financial statements will only reflect a credit of $7,500, and thus will report an accrued tax liability of $2,500 pertaining to the credit taken but not likely to be allowed upon examination. The recognition of this liability has created significant controversy in the business community as the liability along with the disclosures required by FIN 48 and discussed later in this chapter arguably provide a "road map" for taxing authorities to use in identifying positions that can be easily challenged. (However, it has been observed that the "Schedule M-3" reconciliation required to accompany corporate tax returns of filers with assets of $10 million or more already does this.) Nonetheless, FIN 48 complies with the GAAP imperative of reporting the entity's assets and liabilities on an appropriate measurement basis. GAAP financial reporting, in other words, is not a tool to be used by management to avoid recording the accounting consequences of the tactical decisions it makes regarding the tax positions it takes.

The following diagram illustrates the application of the recognition and measurement criteria:

**Probability of Position Being Sustained Upon Examination**

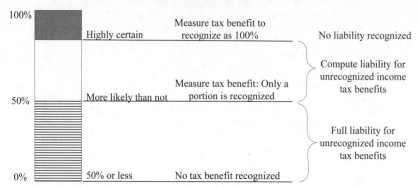

**Interest.** If the relevant taxing jurisdiction requires interest to be paid on income tax underpayments, the reporting entity is to recognize interest expense in the first period that interest would begin to accrue under that jurisdiction's relevant tax law. Interest is to be computed using the following formula:

> Amount of tax position claimed (expected to be claimed) on income tax return
> – Amount of tax position recognized in the financial statements
> _____
> Portion of tax position claimed not recognized in the financial statements
> × Jurisdiction's applicable statutory interest rate
> × Period of time from date that interest first became accruable to reporting date
> _____
> Accrued interest on tax positions taken but not recognized in the financial statements

Thus, if a tax position taken by the reporting entity fails the "more likely than not" recognition test, the presumption is that the position would not be sustained and that the entire tax benefit and associated interest (and penalties, if applicable) are to be recognized as a liability on the balance sheet. Since interest is a period cost for the use of borrowed funds, it must be accrued until the taxing authorities reject the tax position and formally impose the demand for back taxes and interest, or the statute of limitations for the position lapses.

**Penalties.** If upon disallowance on examination, a position would subject the taxpayer to penalty, the reporting entity is to recognize an expense for that penalty in the period it claims or expects to claim the position in its income tax return. That is, the penalty must be accrued as the tax position becomes formalized in a tax filing. An exception is permitted if the positions taken that would be subject to penalty are under the minimum threshold that the jurisdiction uses to assess the penalty. If management later changes its assessment of whether the minimum threshold has been exceeded in a subsequent period, the penalty is to be recognized as an expense in that period.

**Subsequent recognition, derecognition, and measurement.** Judgments regarding initial recognition and measurement are not to be changed based on a reevaluation or reinterpretation of information that was available or should have been available in previous reporting periods. Only if new information becomes available can a new judgment be made. Management's new judgment is to consider the facts, circumstances, and information available at that time. Final certainty is not necessary for this purpose; that is, the position does not have to be subject to final settlement, court ruling, or full resolution to be remeasured.

For tax positions taken by management that do not meet the initial recognition criterion, the benefit becomes recognizable in the first interim period that the position meets any one of the following three conditions:

1. The tax position meets the recognition criterion, and thus its probability of realization is deemed to be more than 50%.
2. The statute of limitations for the relevant taxing authority to examine and challenge the tax position has expired.
3. The tax position is effectively settled through examination, negotiation, or litigation.

In determining whether the condition of "effective settlement" has occurred, FSP FIN 48-1 (issued May 2, 2007) provides that management is to evaluate whether all of the following conditions have been met:

1. The taxing authority has completed its examination procedures including all levels of appeal and administrative reviews that are required by that authority for the specific tax position.
2. Management does not intend to appeal or litigate any aspect of the position included in the completed examination.
3. The possibility of the taxing authority examining or reexamining any aspect of the tax position is remote considering

    a. The authority's policy on reopening closed examinations,
    b. The specific facts and circumstances of the tax position, and
    c. The authority has full knowledge of all relevant information that might cause it to reopen an examination that had been previously closed.

When a taxing authority conducts an examination of a tax year, it may not choose to examine a particular tax position taken by management. Nevertheless, upon completion of the examination and all levels of appeal and review, management is permitted to consider that position effectively settled for that tax year. Management is not permitted, however, to consider that tax position or a tax position similar to it to be settled for any other open periods that were not subject to examination nor is management permitted to use the "effectively settled" criteria for a tax position as a basis for changing its assessment of the technical merits of any tax position taken in other periods.

Tax positions recognized in previous periods that no longer meet the more-likely-than-not criterion are to be reversed ("derecognized," in FASB terminology) in the first period in which that criterion is no longer met. Importantly, it is not permitted that this objective be accomplished through the use of a valuation account or allowance to offset the recorded benefit; rather, it must be recorded as a direct reversal of the previously recorded benefit.

The accounting to record a change in judgment depends on whether the amount subject to change had been previously recognized in a prior annual period or in a prior interim period of the same fiscal year.

According to FIN 48, the effects of changes in tax positions taken in prior annual periods (including related interest and penalties, if any) are to be recognized as a "discrete item" in earnings in the period of change. Although the term "discrete item" is not defined or explained, the authors believe that the intent is for the change to be reported and disclosed in the same manner as the effects of a change in the enacted tax rate. This entails charging or crediting income from continuing operations for the period of change. Presumably, this would not require a separate line item on the face of the income statement (which would give disproportionate attention to the item), but would require separate disclosure in the notes to the financial statements as a significant component of income tax expense attributable to continuing operations, as specified in FAS 109.

Changes occurring in interim periods are accounted for differently. A change in judgment that applies to a tax position taken in a previous interim period of the current fiscal year is considered an integral part of the annual reporting period. Consequently, the effects of the change are recognized prospectively, through an adjustment to the estimated annual effective tax rate, in accordance with APB 28 and FIN 18.

**Classification.** Tax liabilities resulting from applying FIN 48 are current tax obligations. They are *not* to be classified as deferred income tax liabilities unless they are recognized as the result of a future taxable temporary difference created by a tax position that meets the more-likely-than-not criterion.

For reporting entities that present a classified balance sheet, the customary classification rules apply; the portion of income tax obligations recognized that are not deferred income tax liabilities under FAS 109 are classified based on management's judgment regarding whether it anticipates the payment of cash within one year or within the reporting entity's next operating cycle, if it exceeds one year. (Deferred income tax assets and liabilities are classified using the same classification as the assets or liabilities to which they relate or, if they do not relate to specific assets or liabilities, based on the year in which the temporary difference is expected to reverse.) The liability for unrecognized income tax benefits (or reduction in amounts refundable) is not permitted to be combined or netted with deferred income tax assets or liabilities.

FIN 48 provides management policy elections with respect to how it accounts for interest and penalties that are required to be accrued on the liability for unrecognized income tax positions:

| | |
|---|---|
| Interest | Present as additional income taxes or as interest expense |
| Penalties | Present as additional income taxes or in another expense classification |

Management is to elect which of these alternative accounting policies the reporting entity will follow, and then to disclose and consistently apply that policy.

**Applicability to business combinations.** FAS 141(R), *Business Combinations*, amended FIN 48 to clarify that an acquirer is to apply its provisions to income tax positions taken by the acquiree prior to the date of the business combination. Thus, the provisions of FIN 48 apply to the determination of the income tax bases used to compute deferred income tax assets and liabilities as well as amounts of income taxes currently payable to or refundable from taxing authorities.

If a change occurs that affects a preexisting income tax position that was assumed as a part of the acquisition or an income tax position that arose as a result of the acquisition, the change is to be recognized as follows:

1. Changes occurring during the measurement period (as defined in FAS 141[R]) that result from new information regarding facts and circumstances that existed on the acquisition date are recognized as an adjustment to goodwill. Should goodwill be reduced to zero, however, the remaining portion of the adjustment is to be recognized as a gain arising from a bargain purchase, in accordance with FAS 141(R). That standard requires recognition of such gains as part of net income and does not permit characterization as an extraordinary gain, as had been the case with the predecessor standard.
2. All other changes relating to acquired income tax positions are to be accounted for in the same manner as prescribed for other income tax positions.

**Transition.** At adoption, management is required to identify and evaluate all open tax positions existing on the effective date for all years still open under the statute of limitation for all applicable jurisdictions. In a departure from the retroactive application convention set forth in FAS 154 (discussed in detail in Chapter 5), adoption of FIN 48 is to be effected by recognizing a cumulative effect adjustment to the balance of retained earnings as of the beginning of the period of adoption. The adjustment is to be separately stated and not combined with any other such adjustments. Special adoption provisions relate to the effects, if any, of applying the recognition and measurement rules to income tax positions related to business combinations. To the extent that adoption of FIN 48 affects these amounts, a separate cumulative effect adjustment is computed on a before and after basis (i.e., as the difference between the net assets and liabilities recognized before adoption and after adoption of the interpretation).

**Effect on other authoritative literature.** The interpretation amends FAS 5, *Accounting for Contingencies,* to exclude income tax uncertainties from its scope, and provided technical corrections to several other pronouncements.

**Disclosures.** The disclosures required by FIN 48 are discussed later in the chapter along with the disclosures required by other applicable GAAP governing income taxes.

## The Effect of Tax Law Changes on Previously Recorded Deferred Income Tax Assets and Liabilities

**General rules.** The balance-sheet-oriented measurement approach of FAS 109 makes it necessary to reevaluate the deferred income tax asset and liability balances at each year-end. If changes to income tax rates or other provisions of the income tax law (e.g., deductibility of items) are enacted, the effect of these changes must be recognized so that the deferred income tax assets and liabilities are fairly presented on the balance sheet. Any offsetting adjustments are made through the current period's income tax expense or benefit on the income statement; that is, current income tax expense or benefit reflects the income tax effect of current transactions and the revision of previously provided income tax effects for transactions which have yet to reverse.

It might have been argued that the change in the deferred income tax balances should be recognized when first anticipated (e.g., when income tax rate changes are proposed in Congress). However, FASB concluded that it would be more meaningful to report the effects of such changes in the period when the proposed changes in the income tax law have been enacted into law. Enactment is defined by the various taxing jurisdictions; thus for example, federal laws are enacted when the president signs the legislation into law or congress overrides a presidential veto.

This provides a more reliable measure of the impact of such changes and is more consistent with the informational needs of financial statement users.

When income tax rates are revised, this may impact not only the unreversed effects of items which were originally reported in the continuing operations section of the income statement, but also the unreversed effects of items first presented as discontinued operations, extraordinary items, or in other income statement captions. Furthermore, the impact of changes in income tax rates on the accumulated balance of deferred income tax assets or liabilities that arose through charges or credits to other comprehensive income (under FAS 130) is included in income tax expense associated with continuing operations.

For example, if an entity has unrealized gains on holding available-for-sale securities at a time when relevant income tax rates (presumably, the capital gains rates) are lowered, the reduction in the deferred income tax liability associated with these unrealized gains will reduce current period income tax expense associated with continuing operations, despite the fact that the income tax provision was originally reported in other comprehensive income (not net income) and in the equity section of the balance sheet as accumulated other comprehensive income.

**Enactment occurring during an interim period.** When income tax law changes occur during an interim reporting period, the effects are to be reported in the interim period in which enactment occurs. The effects of the changes are included in continuing operations, whatever the source of the temporary differences being impacted. For example, if in the first fiscal quarter of a year an entity accrued a loss relating to discontinued operations, which is not tax deductible until realized, the income tax effect would be shown in the discontinued operations section of the income statement for that quarter. If income tax rates are changed in the third quarter of the same year, the deferred income tax asset recognized in connection with the loss from discontinued operations would then need to be adjusted upward or downward, based on the difference between the newly enacted income tax rates and the previously effective income tax rates. The income statement effect of this adjustment is included with income tax expense pertaining to income from continuing operations in the third quarter.

**Changes in a valuation allowance for an acquired entity's deferred income tax asset.** EITF 99-15 specifies that the effect of a change in income tax law or regulation that results in a decrease in a valuation allowance that initially was recorded in the allocation of the purchase price in a purchase business combination is to be included in income from continuing operations. This applies to any reduction in the valuation allowance that otherwise would not have been recognized except for the change in income tax law or regulation, whether the valuation allowance is reduced in the period of the income tax law change or in a subsequent period.

EITF 99-15 will be nullified with respect to acquisitions made on or after the effective date of FAS 141(R). FAS 141(R) specifies that the acquirer is to recognize changes in a valuation allowance for an acquiree's deferred income tax asset as follows:

1. Changes within the measurement period (defined in FAS 141[R], paragraphs 51-56) resulting from new information regarding facts and circumstances that existed at the acquisition date are to be recognized through an adjustment to goodwill. Should goodwill be reduced to zero, however, the acquirer is to recognize any additional decrease in the valuation allowance as a gain from a bargain purchase in the period of adjustment. The gain, unlike under FAS 141, is not permitted to be characterized as an extraordinary gain.

2. Changes related to elimination of valuation allowances with respect to initial recognition of the following items are afforded special accounting treatment directly affecting equity, rather than current net income:

    a. Temporary differences where the deferred income tax effect is recognized by directly charging or crediting contributed capital (e.g., amounts incurred as stock issuance costs that are treated as deductible expenses for income tax purposes but are accounted for as a reduction of proceeds from the issuance of the stock for financial reporting purposes)

    b. Specified temporary differences between GAAP and income tax accounting that give rise to deferred income tax assets attributable to equity-classified employee stock options are treated as additional paid-in capital under FAS 123(R)

    c. Temporary differences with respect to dividends paid on unallocated shares held by an employee stock ownership plan (ESOP) that are charged to retained earnings

    d. Temporary differences associated with quasi reorganizations (with limited exceptions) that resulted in the deferred income tax benefit directly increasing contributed capital

3. All other changes in the valuation allowance are to be recognized as either an increase to or reduction of income tax expense.

**Special, onetime extension of time to determine effects.** The American Jobs Creation Act of 2004 (AJCA) provided a special, onetime dividends received deduction computed as 85% of certain foreign earnings that were repatriated (i.e., distributed to the US parent or investor by the foreign subsidiary or investee company). This provision was effective for certain foreign earnings repatriated either during the taxpayer's last year beginning prior to October 22, 2004 (the AJCA enactment date) or, alternatively, during the taxpayer's first tax year that began in the first year after enactment. Apparent ambiguity in the wording of this provision of AJCA resulted in requests by taxpayers that Congress or the US Treasury clarify certain of its requirements. The interpretation of these provisions affected decisions made by the management of affected taxpayers regarding when and whether to repatriate or reinvest affected foreign earnings. Until these taxpayers were able to make this assessment and formulate their plans, FSF FAS 109-2 permitted them a onetime exception to the requirement that the effects of this change in the tax law on their deferred income tax assets and liabilities be reflected in the accounting period that included the enactment date. This staff position set forth the accounting and disclosures to be made by affected taxpayers during the period or periods that the evaluation was being made and in the period in which the evaluation was completed. Because of the unique nature of this issue, the FASB staff made it clear that the permissibility of this onetime delay was not to be analogized to other seemingly similar situations.

**Leveraged leases.** When a change in the income tax law is enacted, all components of a leveraged lease must be recalculated from the inception of the lease based upon the revised after-tax cash flows resulting from the change. Differences from the original computation are included in income in the year in which the tax law changes are enacted (EITF 86-43). In making these revised computations, assumptions are to incorporate expectations regarding the effect, if any, of the alternative minimum tax (EITF 87-8).

The US Internal Revenue Service (IRS) may challenge the timing of the lessor's income tax deductions related to certain types of leveraged lease transactions.[2] Upon eventual settlement with the IRS regarding these matters, the economics of the lease may be significantly less favorable from the standpoint of the lessor than they were at inception because the originally projected economic benefits resulted heavily from the ability to obtain income tax deductions for accelerated tax depreciation and interest expense that early in the lease term, would typically exceed the rental income generated by the lease.

FSP FAS 13-2 amended FAS 13 to provide that the projected timing of income tax cash flows attributable to a leveraged lease is to be reviewed annually during the lease term (or between annual reviews if events or changes in circumstances indicate that a change in timing either has occurred or is projected to occur in the future). Upon review, if the projected timing of the lease's income tax cash flows changes, the lessor will be required to recalculate, from the inception of the lease, the rate of return and the allocation of income to positive investment years in accordance with FAS 13, paragraph 44.

The FSP further provides that the recalculated cash flows are to exclude interest and penalties, advance payments, and deposits to the IRS (and presumably any other relevant state, local, or foreign taxing jurisdiction). The deposits or advance payments are to be included in the projected amount of the settlement with the taxing authority.

The accounting treatment prescribed by the FSP is applicable only to changes or projected changes in the timing of income taxes that are directly attributable to the leveraged lease transaction. EITF 87-8, Issue 10, provides that reporting entities whose income tax po-

---

[2] *The transactions that the IRS has reportedly challenged are commonly referred to as Lease In–Lease Out (LILO) and Sale In–Lease Out (SILO) transactions.*

sitions frequently vary between the alternative minimum tax (AMT) and regular tax are not required to annually recalculate the net investment in the lease unless there is an indication that the original assumptions about the leveraged lease's anticipated total after-tax net income were no longer valid.

Another factor to consider in the determination of the after-tax cash flows attributable to leveraged lease transaction is the application of FIN 48. As discussed earlier in this chapter, the lessor is required to assess whether it is more likely than not (i.e., there is a greater than 50% probability) that the income tax positions it takes or plans to take relative to the transaction would be sustained upon examination by the applicable taxing authorities. If the income tax positions do not meet that recognition threshold, the income tax benefits associated with taking those positions would be excluded from the leveraged lease calculations and, in fact, would give rise to a liability for unrecognized income tax benefits as well as an accrual for any applicable interest and penalties for all open tax years that are within the statute of limitations. This could obviously have a significant impact on the computed rate of return on the investment attributable to the years in which the net investment is positive.

If, however, the income tax positions meet the recognition threshold, then they are subject to measurement to determine the maximum amount that is more than 50% probable of being sustained upon examination. The difference between the income tax position taken or planned to be taken on the income tax return (the "as-filed" benefit), and the amount of the benefit measured using the more-than-50% computation, along with any associated penalties and interest is recorded as a liability for unrecognized income tax benefits.

The only situation in which this liability, penalties, and interest would not be applicable would be if the tax positions were assessed to be highly certain tax positions, as defined in FIN 48. Under those circumstances, the entire income tax benefit associated with the lease would be recognized, and of course no interest or penalties would be recognized. Leveraged leases are discussed in detail in Chapter 16.

### Computation of a deferred income tax asset with a change in rates

Assume Campione Company has $80,000 of future deductible temporary differences at the end of 2009, which are expected to result in income tax deductions of approximately $40,000 each on income tax returns for 2010-2011. Enacted tax rates were 50% for years 2006-2009, and are 40% for 2010 and thereafter.

The deferred income tax asset is computed at 12/31/09 under each of the following independent assumptions:

1. If Campione Company expects to offset the future deductible temporary differences against taxable income in years 2010-2011, the deferred income tax asset is $32,000 ($80,000 × 40%).

2. If Campione Company expects to realize an income tax benefit for the future deductible temporary differences by carrying back a loss to pre-2010 tax years to obtain a refund of income taxes previously paid at the higher 50% rate, the deferred income tax asset is $40,000 ($80,000 × 50%).

Assume that Campione Company expects, at the end of 2009, to realize a deferred income tax asset of $32,000 (the first scenario above). Also assume that income taxes payable in *each* of the years 2006-2008 were $8,000 (or 50% of taxable income of $16,000 in each year). Realization of $24,000 (3 years × $8,000 per year) of the $32,000 deferred income tax asset is assured through carryback refunds even if no taxable income is earned in years 2010-2011. Whether a valuation allowance for the remaining $8,000 is needed depends on Campione Company's assessment of the levels of future taxable income.

The foregoing estimate of the *certain* tax benefit, based on a loss carryback to periods of higher tax rates than are statutorily in effect for future periods, should only be utilized when future losses (for income tax purposes) are expected. This restriction applies since the benefit thus recognized (net of any valuation allowance) exceeds benefits that would be available in future periods, when tax rates will be lower.

## Reporting the Effect of Tax Status Changes

The reporting of changes in an entity's income tax status is entirely analogous to the reporting of newly enacted income tax rate changes. Such adjustments typically arise from a change from (or to) taxable status to (or from) "flow through" or nontaxable status. When a previously taxable C corporation elects to become a flow-through entity (an S corporation), the stockholders become personally liable for income taxes on the company's earnings. This liability occurs whether the earnings are distributed to them or not, similar to the taxation of partnerships and limited liability companies.

When the income tax status change becomes effective, the effect of any consequent adjustments to deferred income tax assets and liabilities is reported in current income tax expense. This is always included in the income tax provision relating to continuing operations.

Under FAS 109, deferred income taxes are to be eliminated by reversal through current period income tax expense. Thus, if an entity with a net deferred income tax liability elects S corporation status, it will report an income tax benefit in the continuing operations section of its current income statement.

Similarly, if an S corporation elects to convert to a C corporation, the effect is to assume a net income tax benefit or obligation for unreversed temporary differences existing at the date the change becomes effective. Accordingly, the financial statements for the period in which the change becomes effective will include the effects of the event in current income tax expense. For example, if the entity has unreversed future taxable temporary differences at the date its income tax status change became effective, it reports income tax expense for that period. Conversely, if it had unreversed future deductible temporary differences, a deferred income tax asset (subject to the effects of any valuation allowance necessitated by applying the more-likely-than-not criterion) would be recorded, with a corresponding credit to the current period's income tax expense or benefit in the income statement.

Any entity eliminating an existing deferred income tax asset or liability, or recording an initial deferred income tax asset or liability, must fully explain the nature of the events that transpired to cause this adjustment. This is disclosed in the notes to the financial statements for the reporting period.

S corporation elections may be made prospectively at any time during the year preceding the tax year in which the election is intended to be effective and retroactively up to the 16th day of the 3rd month of the tax year in which the election is intended to be effective. The Internal Revenue Service (IRS) normally informs the electing corporation of whether or not its election has been accepted within 60 days of filing. In practice, however, the IRS seldom denies a timely filed election and such elections are considered essentially automatic. Consequently, if a reporting entity files an election before the end of its current fiscal year to be effective at the start of the following year, it is logical that the income tax effects be reported in current year income. For example, an election by a C corporation to become an S corporation that is filed in December 2009, to be effective at the beginning of the company's next fiscal year, January 1, 2010, would give rise to the elimination of the deferred income tax assets and liabilities at the date of filing, the effect of which would be reported in the 2009 financial statements. No deferred income tax assets or liabilities would appear on the December 31, 2009 balance sheet, and income tax expense or benefit for 2009 would include the effects of the reversals of deferred income tax assets and liabilities that had been previously recognized.

There are two situations that could result in an S corporation continuing to recognize deferred income taxes. The first situation arises when the S corporation operates in one or more states that impose state income taxes on the S corporation in an amount that is material to the financial statements. In this situation, the S corporation should compute and recognize deferred state income tax assets and liabilities in the same manner that a C corporation recognizes them for federal income taxes.

The second situation is referred to as "built-in gains tax." Under current income tax law, a C corporation electing to become an S corporation may have built-in gains, which could result in a future corporate income tax liability, under defined circumstances. In such cases the reporting entity, even though it has become an S corporation, will continue to report a deferred income tax liability related to this built-in gain.

## Reporting the Effect of Accounting Changes for Income Tax Purposes

Occasionally an entity will initiate or be required to adopt changes in accounting that affect income tax reporting, but which will not impact financial statement reporting. Past examples have included the change to the direct write-off method of bad debt recognition (mandated by a change in the income tax law, while the GAAP requirement to recognize an allowance for uncollectible accounts receivable continued in effect for financial reporting); and the adoption of uniform capitalization for valuing inventory for income tax purposes, while continuing to currently expense certain administrative costs not inventoriable under GAAP for financial reporting.

Generally, these mandated changes involve two distinct types of temporary differences. The first of these changes is the onetime, catch-up adjustment which either immediately or over a prescribed time period impacts the income tax basis of the asset or liability in question (net receivables or inventory, in the examples above), and which then reverses as these assets or liabilities are later realized or settled and are eliminated from the balance sheet. The second change is the ongoing differential in the amount of newly acquired assets or incurred liabilities recognized for income tax and financial reporting purposes; these differences also eventually reverse, when the inventory is ultimately sold or the receivables are ultimately collected. This second type of change is the normal temporary difference that has already been discussed. It is the first type of change which differs from those previously discussed in this chapter, and which will now be illustrated.

### Example of adjustment for prospective catch-up adjustment due to change in tax accounting

Blakey Corporation has, at December 31, 2009, accrued interest of $80,000 on its long-term debt. Also assume that expected future taxes will be at a 34% rate and that, effective January 1, 2010, the income tax law is revised to eliminate deductions for accrued but unpaid interest with existing accruals to be taken into income ratably over four years (referred to in tax vernacular as "a four-year spread"). A balance sheet of Blakey Corporation prepared on January 1, 2010, would report

1. A deferred income tax *asset* in the amount of $27,200 (i.e., $80,000 × 34%, which is the income tax effect of future deductions that Blakey will be entitled to take over the succeeding four years for the amount of interest that had been accrued and unpaid at the effective date of the tax law change, taken when specific receivables are written off and bad debts are incurred for income tax purposes);
2. A current income tax liability of $6,800 (one-fourth of the income tax obligation); and a noncurrent income tax liability of $20,400 (three-fourths of the tax income obligation).

The deferred income tax asset is *not* deemed to be identified with the liability, accrued interest (if it were, it would all be reported as a current asset), but rather with the future specific tax benefits expected to be realized from recognizing 25% of the accrual as a deduction in each of the next four years. Accordingly, the deferred income tax asset is categorized as current and noncurrent according to Blakey Corporation's best estimate of the timing of those future income tax benefits.

### Income Tax Effects of Dividends Paid on Shares Held by Employee Stock Ownership Plans (ESOP)

FAS 109 affects the accounting for certain ESOP transactions. Under SOP 93-6, dividends paid on unallocated shares are not considered to be dividends for financial reporting purposes. If used to pay down ESOP debt, these dividends are reported as reductions of debt or of accrued interest; if paid to plan participants, such dividends are reported as compensation cost. GAAP requires that the income tax benefits arising from dividends paid on unallocated shares be consistent with the reporting of those dividends. Thus, if the dividends were included in compensation cost, the tax benefit would be included in the income tax provision associated with continuing operations.

Dividends paid on allocated shares are treated as normal dividends for financial reporting purposes. However, per SOP 93-6, any income tax benefits resulting from these dividend payments are also to be credited to income tax expense reported in continuing operations. In FASB's view, income tax deductible dividends for other than unallocated ESOP-held shares represent an exemption from income tax of an equivalent amount of the payor's earnings. For that reason, it concluded that the income tax effects be reported in continuing operations.

FASB's decision regarding the presentation of the income tax effects of ESOP and other stock compensation plans are fully analogous. Given that both types of plans sometimes result in income tax deductions for amounts not recognized as compensation expense under GAAP, it was determined that the resulting income tax benefits be accounted for consistently.

### Business Combinations

This explanation and illustration of how to apply income tax accounting rules to business combinations, by necessity, must be divided into separate and distinct sections since business combinations are subject to different recognition and measurement rules depending on when the transaction occurred.

Each time FASB has issued standards making major changes to these rules, it has not required reporting entities to retrospectively restate business combinations accounted for under the superseded standards. Thus, a reporting entity that has entered into numerous business combinations over an extended period of time may be applying a plethora of accounting standards to the various subsidiaries it consolidates in its financial statements. It is important to note, however, that upon the effective date of FAS 141(R), discussed later in this section, the acquirer will be required to follow the amendments made to FAS 109 and Fin 48 on a prospective basis for all prior business combinations.

**Poolings of interests.** Upon the issuance of FAS 141, the permissibility of applying poolings of interests accounting was discontinued for business combinations initiated after June 30, 2001. Application of FAS 141 was not retroactive, however, so that reporting entities that had previously recorded poolings were not required to restate those transactions and, consequently, the effects of prior poolings of interests still exist in the financial statements of some companies.

In poolings of interests, the combining entities generally do not adjust the carrying values of their respective assets and liabilities. Reissued or comparative financial statements of periods before the effective date of the combination are restated on a combined basis as if the combining companies had operated together as a single economic unit for all periods presented.

Notwithstanding the general principle of not revising asset or liability carrying amounts, a special rule applies to deferred income tax benefits for which a full or partial valuation allowance had been recognized under the more-likely-than-not criterion of FAS 109.

The standard stipulates that, if one of the combining entities had an unrecognized net deferred income tax benefit (i.e., there was a deferred income tax benefit recognized, gross, which was offset by a valuation allowance), the restated financial statements may or may not reflect the net income tax benefits as an asset. That is, the valuation allowance may be eliminated on a retroactive basis. This treatment depends upon whether the combined entity will be able, under provisions of the income tax laws, to utilize the net operating loss and tax credit carryforwards of the merged companies. If it can do so, then the deferred income tax benefits are recognized in any restated prior period financial statements. If, under the law, the benefits cannot be utilized in a consolidated income tax return or if a consolidated return is not expected to be filed, then the income tax benefits would not be recognized in financial statements restated for the pooling of interests.

Thus, upon recording the pooling, the need for a valuation allowance was subject to a revised analysis, but only the ability to utilize the income tax benefits in a consolidated return was to be considered; other changes in circumstances were handled by adjusting the valuation allowance through current period income tax expense or benefit. This is strictly consistent with the concept of a pooling of interests, in which financial statements are presented for current and prior periods as if the entities had always been combined; had they been combined and had the income tax benefits been available for use in a consolidated return, the valuation allowance would never had been provided.

Under some circumstances, poolings of interests were taxable, meaning that for income tax purposes there was an increase in the income tax basis (referred to as a "step-up") of the net assets of one of the merged (pooled) entities. The differences between the new, stepped-up income tax bases and the carryforward GAAP bases (net book values) utilized for financial reporting purposes are considered future deductible temporary differences giving rise to deferred income tax assets. Whether these assets are recognized is dependent upon whether the more-likely-than-not criterion is met. If the test is not met, a valuation allowance must be established for some or all of the benefits recorded. If a valuation allowance is established, and it is later reduced or eliminated when the likelihood of ultimate realization exceeds the 50% probability threshold, the effect of eliminating the valuation allowance will be reflected in income tax expense or benefit of that period.

**Purchase-method accounting under FAS 141.** Accounting for the income tax effects of business combinations reported as purchases under FAS 141 is one of the more complex aspects of interperiod income tax accounting. The principal complexity relates to the recognition, at the date of the purchase, of the deferred income tax effects of the differences between the income tax and financial reporting bases of the assets and liabilities acquired. Further difficulties arise in connection with the recognition of goodwill or the treatment of negative goodwill from "bargain purchases." In some instances, the reporting entity expects that the ultimate income tax allocation will differ from the initial one (such as when the taxpayer anticipates disallowance by the taxing authorities of an allocation made to identifiable intangibles), and this creates yet another complex accounting matter to be dealt with.

Under GAAP applicable to purchase method accounting prior to FAS 141, a "net of tax" method of valuation had been applied to acquired assets and liabilities. Under this method, the income tax effects resulting from differing income tax and GAAP bases effectively adjusted the carrying values of the corresponding assets and liabilities. Under FAS 109, however, purchase price is allocated on a "gross of tax effects" basis, with separate recognition of the deferred income tax assets and obligations.

Under US federal income tax laws and regulations, business combinations can be either taxable or nontaxable in nature. FAS 109 is applicable to differences between the income tax and financial reporting bases of assets acquired and liabilities assumed in both taxable and nontaxable business combinations.

In a taxable business combination, the total purchase price is allocated to assets and liabilities for both income tax and financial reporting purposes, although under some circumstances these allocations may differ.

In a nontaxable business combination, the predecessor entity's income tax bases for the various assets and liabilities are carried forward for income tax purposes, while for financial reporting purposes the purchase price is allocated to the assets and liabilities acquired. Thus, both taxable and nontaxable business combinations will result in significant differences between the income tax and financial reporting bases of the net assets acquired.

*Acquisition-date accounting using the purchase method under FAS 141.* FAS 109 requires that the income tax effects of the income tax and GAAP basis differences of all assets and liabilities generally be presented as deferred income tax assets and liabilities as of the acquisition date. In general, this "grossing up" of the balance sheet is a straightforward matter.

*Goodwill.* Goodwill arises when a portion of the price paid in a business combination accounted for as a purchase cannot be allocated to identifiable assets, including intangibles. This excess cost is deemed to relate to the unidentifiable intangible asset known as goodwill that is, in practice, associated with the acquired entity's excess earning power.

Historically, goodwill had been subject to mandatory amortization for purposes of GAAP financial reporting over an estimated useful life that was not to exceed 40 years. Until 1993 amortization of goodwill was not deductible for federal income tax purposes. As part of the Omnibus Budget Reconciliation Act of 1993 (OBRA), goodwill became deductible (IRC §197) for federal income tax purposes, with a mandatory fifteen-year straight-line amortization period. Prior to the 1993 income tax law change, goodwill was generally considered to embody a permanent difference between financial statement income and taxable income, rather than a temporary difference, since recovery would come, if at all, only upon sale or dissolution of the entity as a whole. Accordingly, deferred income taxes were not provided under GAAP that was effective at that time.

In 2001, the FASB issued new business combinations and goodwill accounting requirements (FAS 141 and 142), mandating that goodwill no longer be amortized for financial reporting purposes, but rather be subject to periodic impairment testing. (See Chapters 11 and 13 for complete discussions.) Thus, the relationship of GAAP and income tax accounting for goodwill has varied considerably over the years.

Under FAS 141 and 142, the pre-1993 situation was effectively reversed. Goodwill was now amortizable for federal income tax purposes but was no longer amortizable for financial reporting purposes. Goodwill could potentially be charged to GAAP expense sporadically since it must be regularly tested for impairment and to the extent impaired it must be written down or written off immediately.

Thus income tax/GAAP differences under FAS 141 and 142 were deemed temporary differences for which deferred income taxes were recognized for financial reporting under GAAP.

The following timeline summarizes the multiple changes in both GAAP and tax rules with respect to the accounting for goodwill that have added complexity to accounting for business combinations and the deferred income taxes associated with them.

**Timeline of GAAP and Tax Rules with Respect to Goodwill**

| Relevant rule | Applicability | Amortization provisions | Applicability to previously acquired goodwill |
|---|---|---|---|
| **GAAP** | | | |
| ARB 24 codified in ARB 43 | Acquired prior to 11/1/1970 (ARB 24 was issued in 12/1944) | **Nonamortizable** unless an event occurred indicating a loss or limitation of life; if evidence existed that indicated goodwill was losing value or was not perpetual in nature, management could voluntarily write off to expense *or* directly to retained earnings | |
| APB 17 | Acquired after 10/31/1970 | **Amortized** over estimated useful life of 40 years or less using straight-line method unless another method was demonstrably more appropriate | No retrospective application; previously acquired goodwill was to be accounted for under ARB 43 |
| FAS 142 | Acquired in a business combination for which the acquisition date was after June 30, 2001 | **Nonamortizable**, subject to impairment testing at least annually and more frequently if warranted by events and changes in circumstances | Upon adoption of FAS 142, amortization of previously recognized goodwill was required to cease; goodwill was to be assigned to reporting units, intangibles that did not qualify for separate recognition were to be reclassified as goodwill; portions of previously recognized goodwill that qualified for recognition as separate intangibles were reclassified from goodwill |
| **US Federal Income Tax** | | | |
| | Acquired on or before 8/10/93 | **Nonamortizable** | |
| IRC §197 | Acquired after 8/10/93 | **Amortizable** over a 15-year period beginning in the month of acquisition | Previously acquired goodwill was not affected and continued to be nonamortizable |

Since, per FAS 109, temporary differences are those arising from differences between the income tax and financial reporting bases of assets and liabilities, deferred income taxes are to be recognized and measured for goodwill. In general, deductible income taxes amortization of goodwill will create a deferred income tax liability in the financial statements, analogous to that arising from the use of accelerated income tax depreciation. If GAAP goodwill is subsequently reduced to reflect impairment, a portion of the deferred income tax liability will be reversed. Some part of the deferred income tax liability will remain on the balance sheet until the goodwill is ultimately eliminated either through full impairment or when the reporting unit is disposed of or ceases operations.

**Example of computation of deferred income taxes and goodwill resulting from a nontaxable purchase business combination**

Coustan Tacks and Sole Industries Inc. (CTS) acquired substantially all of the assets of Sylvan Shoe Works Inc. (SSW) on January 2, 2008. Following are the facts and assumptions relative to the business combination, the two companies, and the income tax rules that apply:

1. The income tax rate is a flat 34%.
2. The acquisition cost is $500,000.
3. The fair values of the assets acquired total $750,000.
4. The income tax bases of the assets acquired total $600,000.
5. The fair value and income tax bases of the liabilities assumed by CTS in the purchase are $250,000.

6. The difference between the income tax basis and fair values of the assets acquired, $150,000, consists of future taxable temporary differences of $200,000 and future deductible temporary differences of $50,000.

7. There is no doubt as to the realizability of the future deductible temporary differences in this case.

Based on these facts, the GAAP allocation of the purchase price is as follows:

|  | Assets acquired | Liabilities assumed | Deferred tax asset (liability) at rate of 34% |
|---|---|---|---|
| GAAP basis at fair value | $750,000 | $250,000 | |
| Income tax basis | 600,000 | 250,000 | |
| Temporary difference | $150,000 | $     -- | |
| Future deductible temporary differences | $ 50,000 | | 17,000 |
| Future taxable temporary differences | (200,000) | | (68,000) |
| Consideration paid | | 500,000 | |
| Amounts assigned to acquired net assets | | | |
| Assets acquired | 750,000 | | |
| Deferred income tax asset | 17,000 | | |
| | 767,000 | | |
| Liabilities assumed | 250,000 | | |
| Deferred income tax liability | 68,000 | | |
| | 318,000 | 449,000 | |
| Excess consideration allocated to goodwill | | $ 51,000 | |

***Negative goodwill.*** In some purchase business combination situations, "negative goodwill" results from what are often referred to as bargain purchases. These are situations in which the fair value of the net identifiable assets acquired exceeds the purchase price. Under FAS 141 and 142, this excess is first allocated on a pro rata basis to all acquired assets other than cash and cash equivalents, trade receivables, inventory, financial instruments that are required to be carried on the balance sheet at fair value, assets to be disposed of by sale, and deferred income tax assets. This will tend to affect the carrying value of long-lived, mostly depreciable, assets, which will reduce future depreciation charges over the respective lives of those assets. Any excess negative goodwill would then be immediately recognized as an extraordinary gain, as distinct from the earlier requirement that this negative goodwill be amortized over up to forty years.

For income tax purposes, negative goodwill is handled in a manner similar to that under GAAP—the cost bases of nonmonetary long-lived assets are proportionally reduced, and any excess is immediately taxable. Thus, a temporary difference probably did not arise from the accounting treatment applied to negative goodwill for income tax and GAAP purposes. In the past, temporary differences arose from the differential treatments (immediate taxability versus amortization for financial reporting), creating deferred income tax assets in many instances.

The accounting for a taxable purchase business combination is similar to that for a nontaxable one. However, unlike the previous example, in which there were numerous assets with different income tax and financial reporting bases, there are likely to be only a few differences in the case of taxable purchases. Previously, because goodwill was not deductible, attempts were often made by the purchaser to allocate, for income tax purposes, excess purchase cost to other intangibles that were subject to deductible amortization, such as covenants not to compete. Since the 1993 income tax act makes all such intangibles including goodwill amortizable over fifteen years, this motive should no longer be encountered. In practice, the accountant, with assistance from a valuation specialist, is often tasked with analyzing the amount allocated to goodwill for income tax purposes to ensure that due care was taken in identifying acquired intangibles that are recognizable for financial reporting purposes separately from goodwill.

***Exception for permanent basis differences.*** US income tax law contains provisions that allow a parent company that owns a majority interest in a domestic subsidiary to avoid future taxation of the excess of the basis of its investment for financial reporting purposes over its basis in the investment for income tax reporting purposes. For example, if the parent's interest in the subsidiary is 80% or more, the parent is permitted to elect to compute the taxable gain or loss on a liquidation of the subsidiary using the income tax basis of the subsidiary's net assets rather than by reference to the parent company's own income tax basis of its investment in the subsidiary's stock (IRC §332). Another variant is a tax-free statutory merger or consolidation (IRC §368). FAS 109 specifies that deferred income tax assets are only recognized if it is apparent that the temporary difference will reverse in the "foreseeable future."

***In-process research and development.*** To the extent that a portion of the purchase price of a business combination was allocated to in-process research and development, FAS 141 and FAS 142 continued the previous practice of immediately expensing these assets upon their acquisition. EITF 96-7 clarified that this expensing was to be recorded prior to measuring deferred income taxes. This resulted in the allocated in-process research and development having a carrying amount of zero for both financial reporting and income tax reporting purposes. Thus deferred income taxes were not attributed to in-process research and development.

FAS 141(R) rescinded EITF 96-7 and discontinued the longstanding practice of immediately expensing acquired in-process research and development assets. On a prospective basis, for business combinations with acquisition dates on or after the beginning of the first annual reporting period beginning on or after December 15, 2008, the acquirer will be required to recognize all tangible and intangible research and development assets acquired in a business combination. For further details, see the section entitled "Acquisition method accounting under FAS 141(R) and FAS 160" later in this chapter.

***Subsequent accounting.*** One of the attributes which distinguishes FAS 109 from its predecessors is that net deferred income tax benefits are now fully recognized, subject to the possible need for a valuation allowance. This requirement has a major impact on the accounting for business combinations.

In the example presented above, all future deductible temporary differences were assumed to be fully realizable, and therefore the deferred income tax benefits associated with those temporary differences were recorded as of the acquisition date, with no need for an offsetting valuation allowance. However, in other situations, there may be substantial doubt concerning realizability (i.e., it may be considered more likely than not that the future benefits are unrealizable) and accordingly a valuation allowance would be recognized at the date of the purchase business combination. In such an instance, the allocation of the purchase price would reflect this fact, which would result in the allocation of a greater share of the purchase cost to goodwill than would otherwise be the case. Under current GAAP goodwill cannot be amortized for financial reporting purposes, and the difference in accounting for goodwill under GAAP and income tax reporting rules will add to the deferred income tax implications of the business combination.

If, at a date subsequent to the business combination transaction, it is determined that the valuation allowance must be reduced or eliminated, FAS 109 stipulates that the effect of this reduction is applied first to eliminate any goodwill recorded in connection with that business combination. Once goodwill has been reduced to zero, the excess is applied to eliminate any noncurrent identifiable intangible assets acquired in that business combination, and any further excess is reflected in the current period income tax expense or benefit. Thus, in this situation the general rule that changes in the allowance are mated to debits or credits in current period income tax expense from continuing operations is not followed.

The transition provisions of FAS 141(R) relative to income taxes substantially changed the accounting described in the previous paragraph. After the effective date of FAS 141(R),[3] changes in the valuation allowance for acquired deferred income taxes are to be recognized as an adjustment to income tax expense or, in the case of certain items (employee stock options, dividends on unallocated ESOP shares, and certain quasi reorganizations) as an adjustment to contributed capital. This accounting treatment is to be applied prospectively, even if the acquisition occurred prior to the effective date of FAS 141(R).

### Example of subsequent realization of a deferred income tax asset in a purchase business combination

Assume that Michael Company (acquirer) acquired Reba Enterprises (acquiree) on January 2, 2008, for $2,000,000 in cash. There was no goodwill recognized in the transaction. The income tax basis of the net assets was $6,000,000 (i.e., future deductible temporary differences equal $4,000,000).

**Income tax and GAAP bases at acquisition date, 1/1/08**

|  | *Income tax basis* | *GAAP basis* |
|---|---|---|
| Assets | $6,000,000 | $6,000,000 |
| Accrued warranty costs | -- | (4,000,000) |
| Basis, net | $6,000,000 | $2,000,000 |

The $4,000,000 of accrued warranty costs (which is not deductible for income tax purposes until actually paid) is expected to reverse as follows: 2008—$1,500,000; 2009—$1,000,000; After 2009—$1,500,000.

The current and expected future income tax rate is a flat 34% and the law restricts use of the acquiree's future deductible temporary differences and carryforwards to its own future taxable income. The acquiree has incurred tax losses in the past three years and 2008 is also expected to result in a tax loss. Thus, Michael Company management concludes that a valuation allowance for the full amount of the deferred income tax asset is required. However, at the end of 2009, Michael Company, due to improved results, decides that a valuation allowance is no longer necessary.

At the date of acquisition the deferred income tax asset was recorded at $1,360,000 ($4,000,000 × 34%) but with a corresponding valuation allowance for the same amount. At the end of 2008, the deferred income tax asset is $850,000 computed as 34% of $2,500,000 ($4,000,000 original warranty liability – $1,500,000 reversal in 2008), again with a corresponding valuation allowance. At the end of 2009, the deferred income tax asset is $510,000 computed as 34% of $1,500,000 ($4,000,000 original warranty liability – the 2008 reversal of $1,500,000 and the 2009 reversal of $1,000,000).

At the end of 2009, when management determines that a valuation allowance is no longer necessary, elimination of the valuation allowance results in a deferred income tax benefit or in a reduction of deferred income tax expense.

The foregoing facts are summarized as follows:

|  | *Future deductible temporary difference* | *Deferred income tax asset* | *Valuation allowance* | *Deferred income tax expense (benefit)* |
|---|---|---|---|---|
| At acquisition | $4,000,000 | $1,360,000 | $1,360,000 | $ -- |
| 12/31/2008 | 2,500,000 | 850,000 | 850,000 | -- |
| 12/31/2009 | 1,500,000 | 510,000 | -- | (510,000) |

Thus, the journal entries related to deferred income taxes are

***At 1-2-08 (date of acquisition)***

| | | |
|---|---|---|
| Assets acquired | 6,000,000 | |
| Deferred income tax asset | 1,360,000 | |
| Accrued warranty costs | | 4,000,000 |
| Cash | | 2,000,000 |
| Valuation allowance | | 1,360,000 |

---

[3] *On or after the beginning of the first annual reporting period beginning after December 15, 2008.*

*At 12-31-08*

| Deferred income tax benefit | 510,000 | |
| Deferred income tax asset | | 510,000 |

*To reduce the gross deferred income tax asset recognized due to reversal of a portion of the temporary difference.*

| Valuation allowance | 510,000 | |
| Deferred income tax benefit | | 510,000 |

*To reverse the portion of the valuation allowance that related to the prior year's deferred tax asset that reversed in the current year.*

*At 12-31-09*

| Valuation allowance | 850,000 | |
| Deferred income tax asset | | 340,000 |
| Deferred income tax benefit | | 510,000 |

Note that, in the previous example, had goodwill arisen in the acquisition, the accounting would differ based on whether the change in assessment of the valuation allowance occurred before or after the effective date of FAS 141(R).

*Pre-FAS 141(R)* — In the postacquisition period in which the tax benefit is realized, the elimination of the valuation allowance is applied to (1) reduce any goodwill recognized in connection with the acquisition, (2) if the goodwill is reduced to zero, any remaining benefit is used to reduce other noncurrent intangible assets included in the acquisition, and (3) if any benefit remains after (1) and (2), it is recognized as a reduction in income tax expense (or an increase in income tax benefit).

*Post-FAS 141(R)* — If the change occurs during the measurement period and results from new information that bears on facts and circumstances that existed on the acquisition date, the change is recognized by adjusting goodwill. If goodwill is reduced to zero, any excess is recorded currently as a gain from a bargain purchase. Such gains, under FAS 141(R), are no longer characterized as extraordinary.

If the change does not occur during the measurement period, it is reported as a reduction of income tax expense or, if related to dividends on unallocated ESOP shares, employee stock options, or certain quasi reorganizations, as a direct adjustment to contributed capital.

Under FAS 109, the income tax benefits of net operating losses are not distinguished from those arising from future deductible temporary differences. Accordingly, the treatments set forth above for pre- and post-FAS 141(R) are applied here as well. If the benefits are recognized for the first time at a date after the acquisition pre-FAS 141(R) (by reducing or eliminating the valuation allowance), then goodwill arising from the business combination is eliminated, other purchased noncurrent intangibles are reduced to zero, and current income tax expense is reduced. Negative goodwill is neither created nor increased in such circumstances, however.

If, however, the recognition of the benefits occurs after the effective date of FAS 141(R), the benefits do not reduce any assets recorded as a part of the acquisition and, instead, reduce current income tax expense or contributed capital as previously described.

Precisely the same approach is employed in connection with income tax credit carryforwards (investment credit, jobs credit, research and development credit, etc.) which may have existed at the date of the business combination, but which may not have been recognized due to doubtful realizability. While previously the treatments accorded net operating losses and income tax credit carryforwards were dissimilar, under FAS 109 they are identical.

In some instances, entities having unrecognized income tax benefits of net operating losses or income tax credits arising in connection with a purchase business combination may generate other similar income tax benefits after the date of the acquisition. A question in such a circumstance relates to whether a "FIFO" convention should be adopted to guide the recognition of these benefits. While in some instances income tax law may determine the order in which the benefits are actually realized, in other cases the law may not do so. FAS 109 provides that in those latter situations, the benefits realized are to be apportioned, for financial reporting purposes, between pre- and postacquisition income tax benefits. The former are accounted for as above, and the latter reported as reductions of current period income tax expense, consistent with the general rules of FAS 109.

In a period that a subsidiary first meets the criteria in FAS 144 for its operations to be classified as discontinued operations, it becomes apparent that differences between the financial reporting basis and income tax basis of the subsidiary's assets and liabilities will reverse in the foreseeable future. Thus, the parent is to recognize deferred income taxes on the temporary difference between the income tax and financial reporting bases in that period (EITF 93-17).

**Acquisition-method accounting under FAS 141(R) and FAS 160.** FAS 141(R), *Business Combinations (revised 2007),* and its companion standard, FAS 160, *Noncontrolling Interests in Consolidated Financial Statements,* were issued in December 2007. The new standards made substantial changes to the recognition and measurement provisions of the predecessor standards. They also amended both FAS 109 and FIN 48, and those amendments apply not only to business combinations made after the new standards become effective, but also, prospectively, to prior business combinations. FAS 141(R) and FAS 160 are discussed in detail in Chapter 13.

In general, the new standards retain the gross-up approach from FAS 109 whereby deferred income tax assets and liabilities are recorded independently of the acquired assets or assumed liabilities that gave rise to them.

Postcombination changes in a valuation allowance for deferred tax assets of the acquired entity are to be recognized as follows:

1. *Changes during the measurement period*—If a change in the valuation allowance during the measurement period results from new information regarding facts and circumstances existing at the acquisition date, the change is to be recognized as an adjustment to goodwill. If goodwill is reduced to zero by the change, any remaining decrease in the valuation allowance is handled in the same manner as negative goodwill in a bargain purchase; that is, the excess is recorded as a gain. This gain is not to be characterized as an extraordinary gain, as was previously prescribed by FAS 141.

2. *All other changes*—All other changes in the valuation allowance are to be reflected as an increase or decrease in income tax expense in the period of the change or, with respect to the following items, as a charge or credit to the relevant component of equity:

   a. Changes related to tax-deductible costs such as stock issuance costs or debt issuance costs that give rise to temporary GAAP basis/tax basis differences in equity.

   b. Changes related to temporary differences related to employee stock options are to be accounted for in accordance with FAS 123(R), paragraphs 58-63. Accounting for share-based compensation is discussed in Chapter 19.

    c.   Dividends paid on unallocated shares held by an Employee Stock Ownership Plan (ESOP) that are charged to retained earnings. Accounting for stock issued to ESOPs is discussed in Chapter 19.

    d.   Changes that affect deductible temporary differences and carryforwards that existed at the date of certain quasi reorganizations that qualify, under ARB 43, Chapter 7, to be reported as a direct addition to contributed capital upon recognition of the tax benefits in years subsequent to the quasi reorganization. Quasi reorganizations are discussed in Chapter 19.

This treatment of postcombination valuation allowance changes is a departure from the approach taken by FAS 141, which required that when goodwill was exhausted the excess be applied to reduce the carrying values of noncurrent identifiable intangible assets that were part of the acquisition. Only if those assets were collectively reduced to zero did the effect of the change impact current income tax expense or benefit. As stated previously, however, upon the effective date of FAS 141(R), its provisions are to be applied prospectively to all business combinations that were recorded under predecessor standards.

***Assessment of postcombination realizability of deferred income tax assets.*** Some tax jurisdictions permit the acquirer to obtain future income tax benefits in postcombination tax years from utilizing deductible temporary differences or carryforwards of its own or of the acquiree.

If the newly consolidated enterprise expects to file a consolidated income tax return, the acquirer may, upon evaluation of the sufficiency of its valuation allowance, determine that the allowance should change. For example, future taxable income generated by the acquiree may allow the consolidated "taxpayer" to utilize net operating loss carryforwards of the acquirer whose future utilization would have otherwise been doubtful. If this were allowable under the tax law of a jurisdiction, the acquirer is to reduce the valuation allowance accordingly. The reduction of the valuation allowance is not, however, accounted for as part of the accounting for the business combination under the acquisition method. Instead, it is recognized as an income tax benefit as a component of income from continuing operations (or credited directly to equity under the specified circumstances discussed previously).

***Goodwill.*** As previously discussed in the context of prior business combinations standards, few areas of income tax accounting are as complex as the treatment of differences between tax and GAAP goodwill.

The carrying value of goodwill for GAAP and income tax purposes will frequently differ. Examples of reasons for these differences include such items as

*Example items resulting in tax goodwill in excess of GAAP goodwill*

1.   The acquirer and acquiree do not fully analyze the nature of the separately identifiable intangible assets included in the acquisition since all intangible assets, including goodwill, are amortized for US federal income tax purposes using the same 15-year statutory life. Upon review for GAAP purposes, certain intangibles are identified that meet the legal/contractual criterion or the separability criterion and are reclassified from goodwill for GAAP purposes.

2.   Application of FAS 141(R) results in recognition of GAAP assets that are not recognized for income tax purposes such as indemnification assets, or in-process research and development assets. As a result, the residual value allocated to goodwill for GAAP purposes is less than goodwill recognized for income tax purposes.

3.   Postacquisition impairment write-downs of GAAP goodwill that are not deductible for income tax purposes.

*Example items resulting in GAAP goodwill in excess of tax goodwill*

1.  Application of FAS 141(R) results in recognition of GAAP liabilities that are not recognized for income tax purposes, such as preacquisition contingencies or contingent consideration. GAAP recognition of these liabilities reduces the aggregate assigned values with respect to the business combination and increases the residual goodwill recognized for GAAP purposes without affecting the goodwill recognized for income tax purposes.
2.  Over the US federal 15-year statutory life over which goodwill is amortized, the income tax basis of goodwill is reduced annually, whereas for GAAP purposes, the carrying value of goodwill is not reduced unless it is impaired.

FAS 109, as did its predecessor standards, expressly prohibits recognition of a temporary difference or deferred income taxes with respect to goodwill that, in particular taxing jurisdiction, is not deductible.

As amended by FAS 141(R), FAS 109 does, however, prescribe a two-component approach to analyzing differences between GAAP and tax-deductible goodwill to determine whether they give rise to a temporary difference and the related deferred income taxes theron.

*Component 1.* For the purposes of this analysis, the first component of goodwill is the lesser of the amount of goodwill recognized for GAAP purposes or the amount of tax-deductible goodwill recognized for income tax purposes in the particular jurisdiction being analyzed. Obviously, at acquisition, Component 1 goodwill will be the same for GAAP and income tax purposes. However, differences in this component of goodwill that arise in subsequent periods give rise to temporary differences for which deferred income tax assets or liabilities are to be recognized.

*Component 2.* The second component is the excess of the larger goodwill amount that was not allocated to Component 1. In other words, if GAAP goodwill exceeds tax-deductible goodwill, Component 2 would be that excess amount; if tax-deductible goodwill exceeds GAAP goodwill, Component 2 would be that excess amount.

The deferred income tax treatment afforded differences between GAAP goodwill and tax goodwill varies depending on which basis exceeds the other, as illustrated in the following table.

**Recognition of Deferred Income Taxes for GAAP/Tax Differences in Goodwill**

| | *Component 1 goodwill* | *Component 2 goodwill* |
|---|---|---|
| **At acquisition date** | | |
| GAAP goodwill > tax goodwill | At the acquisition date there is no difference between Component 1 GAAP and tax goodwill and, thus, deferred income taxes are not applicable | No deferred income taxes are recognized |
| Tax goodwill > GAAP goodwill | | Deferred income taxes are recognized at acquisition; see examples for how to apply formula to ensure that tax effect of temporary difference is properly considered when computing goodwill or bargain purchase[4] |

---

[4] *Note that in certain circumstances, the formulaic approach illustrated will need to be modified or another computational method substituted. Among these circumstances are situations where (1) the reversal of the temporary differences may be realized for income tax purposes in periods with increasing or decreasing tax rates or (2) where future reversal may be treated as different types of taxable or deductible items (e.g., capital gain vs. ordinary income). In addition, if the acquirer's evaluation of the realizability of a deferred income tax asset necessitates establishing a valuation allowance for all or part of a deferred income tax asset, there may be little, if any effect of deferred income taxes on the amount of goodwill recognized and a trial-and-error method of computation may need to be utilized to determine the amount of the deferred income tax asset to recognize.*

|  | *Component 1 goodwill* | *Component 2 goodwill* |
|---|---|---|
| **Subsequent to acquisition date** | | |
| GAAP goodwill > tax goodwill | | No deferred income taxes are recognized |
| Tax goodwill > GAAP goodwill | As deduction are taken on income tax returns for amortization of goodwill or as impairment charges are recognized under GAAP, changes in this component will give rise to deferred income tax assets or liabilities | If change to Component 2 goodwill occurs during the measurement period as a retrospective adjustment to the provisional amount of goodwill, the acquisition-date deferred income taxes are recomputed accordingly; otherwise all changes subsequent to acquisition will only affect Component 1 and there will be no deferred income tax consequences associated with Component 2 |

### Example of deferred income taxes where tax-deductible goodwill exceeds GAAP goodwill

On January 2, 2009, Butler Soccer Supply (BSS) acquired Spector Sod and Turf (SST) in a taxable acquisition. $14,000 of income tax goodwill was allocable for GAAP purposes to an indefinite-lived intangible asset at acquisition thus causing a difference between the goodwill amounts recognized for purposes of GAAP and income tax reporting.

The effective income tax rate for this jurisdiction expected to apply in all applicable periods is a flat 34%.

The acquisition-date allocations resulted in goodwill being recognized for GAAP and income tax purposes as follows:

| | | |
|---|---|---|
| 1. | Tax-deductible goodwill recognized for income tax purposes | $65,000 |
| 2. | Goodwill recognized for GAAP purposes | 51,000 |
| 3. | Excess of tax-deductible goodwill over GAAP goodwill | $14,000 |

Based on the above, the "components" of goodwill are comprise of

| | *Tax* | *GAAP* |
|---|---|---|
| Component 1 (lesser of 1. or 2. above) | $51,000 | $51,000 |
| Component 2 (excess excluded from Component 1) | 14,000 | -- |
| Total tax basis/GAAP carrying value of goodwill | $65,000 | $51,000 |

As previously discussed, at the acquisition date, Component 1 of goodwill will be the same for tax and GAAP purposes. In future periods, however, as income tax deductions are taken for goodwill amortization, these amounts will differ and that difference will give rise to temporary differences necessitating the recognition of deferred income taxes.

The Component 2 tax-deductible goodwill exceeds GAAP goodwill, representing a future deductible temporary difference that requires recognition of a deferred income tax asset at the acquisition date. Application of this principle, however, can produce computational complexity. In theory, recognition of a deferred income tax asset in connection with recording a business combination results in a reduction of GAAP goodwill since the entry to record the deferred income tax asset would be recorded by debiting the deferred income tax asset and crediting goodwill. That hypothetical credit to goodwill would reduce the difference computed above between GAAP goodwill and tax goodwill and, in circular fashion, would affect the computation of the deferred income tax asset. To avoid this circularity, FAS 141(R) amended FAS 109 to require the following computational method to determine the amount to recognize as a deferred asset:

| | | |
|---|---|---|
| DTA | = | Deferred tax asset |
| TR | = | Tax rate expressed as a percentage |
| PTD | = | Preliminary temporary difference representing the excess of tax goodwill over GAAP goodwill before giving effect to the income tax benefit associated with goodwill |
| DTA | = | $[TR \div (100\% - TR)] \times PTD$ |

Substituting the known amounts per example

| DTA | = | [34% ÷ (100% – 34%)] × $14,000 |
| --- | --- | --- |
| DTA | = | 51.5% × $14,000 |
| DTA | = | $7,212 |

The entry to record the acquisition-date deferred income tax asset is as follows:

*1/2/2009*

| | | |
| --- | --- | --- |
| Deferred income tax asset | 7,212 | |
| Goodwill | | 7,212 |

*To record acquisition-date deferred income tax asset arising from future deductible temporary difference due to excess of the tax basis of deductible goodwill over the carrying amount of goodwill for financial reporting purposes.*

To prove the accuracy of the computations, the deferred income tax asset is computed as follows:

| | | |
| --- | --- | --- |
| Tax goodwill | | $65,000 |
| GAAP goodwill, provisional basis before deferred income tax | $51,000 | |
| Adjustment for deferred income taxes per computation | (7,212) | |
| GAAP goodwill, as adjusted | | 43,788 |
| Future deductible temporary difference | | 21,212 |
| × Effective rate | | 34% |
| | | $7,212 |

On its consolidate income tax return for the year ended December 31, 2009, BSS deducted amortization of goodwill computed as follows:

| | |
| --- | --- |
| Tax basis of goodwill | $65,000 |
| ÷ 15-year statutory amortization period (IRC §197) | 15 |
| Annual deduction for amortization of goodwill | $4,333 |

Assuming that no goodwill impairment was recognized for financial reporting purposes for 2009 and that no valuation allowance was needed to reduce the deferred income tax asset to the amount that is more likely than not realizable, the goodwill temporary difference between income tax basis and GAAP carrying amount at 12/31/2009 is

| | |
| --- | --- |
| Tax basis of goodwill, at acquisition date | $65,000 |
| Less 2009 amortization | 4,333 |
| Tax basis of goodwill at 12/31/2009 | 60,667 |
| GAAP carrying value of goodwill at 12/31/2009 | 43,788 |
| Future deductible temporary difference at 12/31/2009 | 16,879 |
| × Effective tax rate | 34% |
| Deferred income tax asset at 12/31/2009 | 5,739 |
| Deferred income tax asset at acquisition | 7,212 |
| Reduction in deferred asset | $(1,473) |

The entry to record the foregoing is as follows:

*1/31/2009*

| | | |
| --- | --- | --- |
| Deferred income tax expense (income statement) | 1,473 | |
| Deferred income tax asset | | 1,473 |

*To record reduction in deferred income tax asset and related expense attributable to reduction in temporary difference between GAAP and tax goodwill.*

The computation above is easily proven by multiplying the effective tax rate of 34% by the $4,333 change in the future deductible temporary difference, yielding the $1,473 tax effect recorded in the entry.

It is important to note that, on the 2009 consolidated income tax return of BSS and Subsidiary, there will be a deduction for goodwill amortization that will reduce income taxes currently payable that would be recorded as follows, assuming the income tax effects of all other tax positions have been already recorded:

*12/31/2009*

| | | |
|---|---|---|
| Income taxes currently payable or refundable (balance sheet) | 1,473 | |
| Income tax expense or benefit (income statement) | | 1,473 |

*To record current income tax effect of deduction for goodwill amortization.*

Obviously the effects of the two entries offset each other and result in reducing the deferred income tax asset that existed at acquisition date as the income tax benefits are being realized on currently filed income tax returns.

As a practical matter, it would be a rare situation for an acquirer to have gathered all of the information necessary to establish the appropriate values to record the acquisition in time to issue timely financial statements when due. For this reason, FAS 141(R) provides for a measurement period during which provisional amounts initially recognized for the transaction are subject to retrospective adjustment. Any such adjustments are to reflect additional information that the acquirer obtains after the acquisition date that was not previously available. In order for the additional information to be relevant for this purpose, it must provide new information regarding facts and circumstances that existed as of the acquisition date that, if known at the time, would have resulted in different measurements of the amounts recognized as of that date.

In addition to causing revisions to previous measurements, the new information may also result in the recognition of additional assets or liabilities that had not been initially identified or recorded when the provisional entries were made to record the combination. The measurement period ends when management of the acquirer obtains the information it needs to make the final determinations (or determines that such information is not available); however, in no case may the measurement period exceed one year from the acquisition date.

Increases and/or decreases in the provisional amounts during the measurement period are reflected as adjustments to goodwill. These adjustments are made retrospectively as if they had been recorded on the acquisition date. Consequently, information for prior periods that is presented for comparative purposes is to be revised to reflect the adjustments and their effect on other measurements such as depreciation, amortization, and, of course, deferred income taxes.

Subsequent to the measurement period, the only changes that are permitted to the accounting for the business combination are restatements to correct errors in accordance with FAS 154, *Accounting Changes and Error Corrections*, which is discussed in detail in Chapter 5.

*Effect of deferred income tax liabilities arising from goodwill on analysis of the need for a valuation allowance with respect to deferred income tax assets.* In the US, under current federal income tax law, goodwill is amortized over a statutory 15-year life using the straight-line method. The following example illustrates the status of the GAAP tax difference at the end of that 15-year period, assuming no impairment charges are recorded for GAAP.

**Example of effect of income tax goodwill amortization on deferred income taxes**

On January 2, 2009, Melanie Artist Supply, Inc. (MAS) acquired Larry's Paint-by-Number, Inc. (LPBN) in a taxable acquisition. The difference between tax goodwill and GAAP goodwill was as follows (using the same assumptions from the previous "Butler Soccer Supply" example:

| | *Tax* | *GAAP* |
|---|---|---|
| Component 1 | $51,000 | $51,000 |
| Component 2 | 14,000 | -- |
| Total tax basis and GAAP carrying value of goodwill | $65,000 | $51,000 |

Based on the application of the formulaic approach used in the previous example, GAAP goodwill was adjusted as follows at the acquisition date:

|  | *Tax* | *GAAP* |
|---|---|---|
| Component 1 (GAAP adjustment: $51,000 – $7,212) | $51,000 | $43,788 |
| Component 2 | 14,000 | -- |
| Total tax basis and GAAP carrying value of goodwill | $65,000 | $43,788 |

Assuming that there are no impairment charges incurred for GAAP purposes, and income tax amortization is deducted straight-line in each of the 15 succeeding years ($65,000 ÷ 15 years = $4,333 per year) the following summarizes the tax and GAAP balances immediately succeeding the final tax amortization deduction:

| | |
|---|---|
| Carrying value of goodwill for GAAP purposes (same as acquisition date) | $43,788 |
| Income tax basis of goodwill | -- |
| Future taxable temporary difference | 43,788 |
| × Assumed flat effective income tax rate | 34% |
| Deferred income tax liability | $14,888 |

Note that by the end of the 15-year tax amortization period, the acquisition-date deferred income tax asset had fully reversed and had, in fact, become a deferred income tax liability.

In the preceding example, the deferred income tax liability relates to the GAAP carrying value of goodwill that is not amortizable for financial reporting purposes and has an indefinite life. Absent an outright sale or liquidation of the reporting unit, management would be unable to estimate whether the goodwill might give rise to future taxable income prior to the expiration of the statutory net operating loss (NOL) carryforward period which, under current US income tax law is 20 years after the tax year in which the NOL was generated. This same lack of predictability would also apply, for example, to deferred income tax liabilities associated with identifiable, indefinite-life intangibles.

When such a situation arises and management is assessing the realizability of deferred income tax assets to determine the need for a valuation allowance, it would normally not be appropriate to consider the reversal of these types of future taxable temporary differences in assessing whether, in the future, the taxpayer will, more likely than not, be able to generate sufficient taxable income to permit it to obtain the tax benefits associated with its deferred income tax assets. This potentially results in the consolidated reporting entity requiring a full valuation allowance with respect to its deferred income tax assets. If, however, a particular tax jurisdiction were to permit an indefinite carryforward period for an NOL, management would be permitted to consider future reversal of the deferred income tax liability in assessing the need for a valuation allowance.

***Negative goodwill and bargain purchases.*** Chapter 13 discusses in detail the concept of a "bargain purchase" in which the aggregate of the values assigned to the identifiable assets acquired and liabilities assumed exceed the consideration transferred by the acquirer and the noncontrolling interest in the acquiree (if any). This situation can occur when the transaction is a forced sale where the seller is acting under duress if, for example, the seller is at risk because of a personal guarantee of acquiree indebtedness or needs immediate liquidity due to maturing personal debt.

In applying the formulaic approach illustrated in the preceding example, the amount of goodwill recognized for financial reporting purposes may not be sufficient to absorb the adjustment for the amount computed as a deferred income tax asset. When this is the case, the computational approach requires modification as illustrated in the following example.

### Example of deferred income taxes where tax-deductible goodwill exceeds GAAP goodwill and adjustment results in gain from a bargain purchase

On January 2, 2009, Novak Condiments Inc. (NI) acquired Jacobson Pickle Corp. (JP) in a taxable acquisition. The effective income tax rate for this jurisdiction expected to apply in all applicable periods is a flat 34%.

The acquisition-date allocations resulted in goodwill being recognized for GAAP and income tax purposes as follows:

| | | |
|---|---|---|
| 1. | Tax-deductible goodwill recognized for income tax purposes | $251,000 |
| 2. | Goodwill recognized for GAAP purposes | 51,000 |
| 3. | Excess of tax-deductible goodwill over GAAP goodwill | $200,000 |

Based on the above, the "components" of goodwill are comprised of

| | *Tax* | *GAAP* |
|---|---|---|
| Component 1 (lesser of 1. or 2. above) | $51,000 | $51,000 |
| Component 2 (excess excluded from Component 1) | 200,000 | -- |
| Total tax basis and GAAP carrying value of goodwill | $251,000 | $51,000 |

Application of the previously illustrated formula yields the following results:

| DTA | = | Deferred tax asset |
|---|---|---|
| TR | = | Tax rate expressed as a percentage |
| PTD | = | Preliminary temporary difference representing the excess of tax goodwill over GAAP goodwill before giving effect to the income tax benefit associated with goodwill |
| DTA | = | $[TR \div (100\% - TR)] \times PTD$ |

Substituting the known amounts per example

$$DTA = [(34\% \div (100\% - 34\%)] \times \$200,000$$
$$DTA = 51.5\% \times \$200,000$$
$$DTA = \$103,000$$

The deferred tax asset (DTA) computed of $103,000 exceeds the GAAP carrying value initially assigned to goodwill of $51,000. If the DTA were recorded without adjustment, it would result in the elimination of the $51,000 of GAAP goodwill and the recognition of an income tax benefit of $52,000. This would not result in the deferred income tax asset being computed at the rate at which it is expected to be realized when the temporary difference reverses.

| | |
|---|---|
| Acquisition-date basis of goodwill for income tax purposes | $251,000 |
| Acquisition-date carrying value of goodwill for GAAP purposes adjusted for deferred income tax asset | -- |
| Formulaic temporary difference | 251,000 |
| × Effective income tax rate | 34% |
| Deferred income tax asset per "proof" | $ 85,340 |
| Deferred income tax asset as computed | $103,000 |

In order to properly compute the deferred tax adjustment in this case, the formula needs to be modified as follows:

The original formula was

$$DTA = [TR \div (100\% - TR)] \times PTD$$

The formula is modified in order to use the limit imposed by the carrying value of the GAAP-basis goodwill to solve for the PTD as follows:

| | | |
|---|---|---|
| $51,000 (GAAP goodwill) | = | $[TR \div (100\% - TR)] \times PTD$ |
| $51,000 | = | $[34\% \div (100\% - 34\%)] \times PTD$ |
| $51,000 ÷ 51.5% | = | PTD |
| $99,029 | = | PTD |

Using substitution, the adjustment to GAAP goodwill for the deferred income tax asset is computed/proven as follows:

| | | |
|---|---|---|
| $51,000 GAAP goodwill limit | = | $[TR \div (100\% - TR)] \times PTD$ |
| $51,000 | = | $51.5\% \times 99,029$ |

The entry to record the reduction of GAAP goodwill to zero is as follows:

*1/2/2009*

| | | |
|---|---|---|
| Deferred income tax asset | 51,000 | |
|   Goodwill | | 51,000 |

*To record the reduction of goodwill for financial reporting purposes to zero due to the effect of the acquisition-date deferred income tax asset.*

The last step is to compute the gain from bargain purchase that arises as a result of recording the remaining deferred income tax asset.

| | | |
|---|---|---|
| (Original PTD of $200,000 – Revised PTD of $99,029) × 34% | = | gain |
| ($200,000 – $99,029) × 34% | = | gain |
| | = | $34,330 |

The entry to record the remainder of the deferred income tax asset and the gain from bargain purchase is as follows:

*1/2/2009*

| | | |
|---|---|---|
| Deferred income tax asset | 34,330 | |
|   Goodwill | | 34,330 |

*To record the acquisition-date deferred income tax asset attributable to a gain from bargain purchase.*

To prove the accuracy of the computations, the deferred income tax asset is computed as follows:

| | |
|---|---|
| Portion used to reduce GAAP carrying value of goodwill to zero | $51,000 |
| Portion attributable to bargain purchase | 34,330 |
| Total recognized deferred income tax asset | $85,330 |
| Income tax basis of goodwill at acquisition date | $251,000 |
| GAAP carrying value of goodwill as adjusted | -- |
| Temporary difference | 251,000 |
| × Effective income tax rate | 34% |
| | 85,340 |
| Rounding | (10) |
| Total recognized deferred income tax asset | $85,330 |

***In-process research and development assets.*** As previously discussed, the accounting for research and development (R&D) assets acquired in business combinations within the scope of FAS 141(R) substantially differs from prior practice.

For the first time, the standards require the acquirer to recognize all tangible and intangible R&D assets acquired in a business combination at the acquisition date without immediately writing them off to expense. This treatment is afforded these assets *even if they have no alternative future use.* Accounting subsequent to initial recognition is to be accomplished as follows:

1. Tangible R&D assets are to be accounted for based on their nature (e.g., fixed assets to be held and used, inventory, supplies, etc.)
2. Intangible R&D assets are to be classified as indefinite-lived intangibles until the related R&D project is either completed or abandoned.
3. Upon completion or abandonment of the R&D project to which the assets relate, management of the consolidated reporting entity is to determine the estimated remaining useful life of the assets, if any, and amortize their carrying value over that period.
4. As is the case for other long-lived assets, temporarily idled intangible assets are not to be accounted for as abandoned.
5. During the period of time that the assets are considered to be indefinite-lived, they are subject to the same impairment testing rules that apply to other indefinite-lived intangibles.

If income tax law in an applicable taxing jurisdiction requires acquired R&D assets to be written off (deducted) or recognized at an amount that differs from the foregoing GAAP requirements, then the recognition of these assets for financial reporting purposes will result in a future taxable temporary difference and the related deferred income tax liability would be recognized.

### Tax Allocation for Business Investments

As noted in Chapter 12, there are two basic methods for accounting for investments in the common stock of other corporations: (1) the fair value method as set forth in FAS 115, and (2) the equity method, as prescribed by APB 18. The cost method, previously employed for intercorporate investments lacking the attribute of "significant influence" by the investor, is no longer appropriate, except for the exceedingly rare situation when fair value information is absolutely unavailable. If the cost method is used, however, there will be no deferred income tax consequence, since this conforms to the method prescribed for income tax reporting.

The fair value method is used in instances where the investor is not considered to have significant influence over the investee. The ownership threshold generally used to denote significant influence is 20% of ownership; this level of ownership is not considered an absolute (FIN 35), but it will be used to identify the break between application of the fair value and equity methods in the illustrations which follow. In practice, the 20% ownership interest defines the point at which there is a rebuttable presumption that the investor has significant influence, and it is often noted that publicly held companies will establish investment ownership percentages very slightly over or under 20%, presumably to support their desires and decisions to use, or not use, the equity method of accounting for those investments.

Under both the cost and fair value methods, ordinary income is recognized as dividends received by the investor, and capital gains (losses) are recognized upon the disposal of the investment. For income tax purposes, no provision is made during the holding period for the allocable undistributed earnings of the investee. There is no deferred income tax computation necessary when using the cost method because there is no temporary difference. Tax allocation issues pertaining to the use of the fair value method are discussed in Chapter 12.

The equity method is generally required whenever an investor owns 20% or more of an investee or has significant influence over the investee's operations with a lower ownership percentage. Under the equity method, the investment is recorded at cost and subsequently increased by the allocable portion of the investee's net income. The investor's share of the investee's net income is then included in the investor's pretax accounting income. Dividend payments are not included in pretax accounting income but instead are considered to be a reduction in the carrying amount of the investment. For income tax purposes, however, dividends received are the only revenue realized by the investor. As a result, the investor must recognize deferred income tax expense on the undistributed net income of the investee that will be taxed in the future. The current effective GAAP in this area consists of APB 23 and FAS 109, which superseded APB 24 but continues the principles that were set forth therein. These standards are discussed below.

GAAP distinguishes between an investee and a subsidiary and prescribes different accounting treatments for each. An investee is considered to be a corporation whose stock is owned by an investor that holds between 20% and 50% of the outstanding stock. An investee situation occurs when the investor has significant influence but not control over the corporation invested in. A subsidiary, on the other hand, exists when more than 50% of the stock of a corporation is owned by another. This results in a presumption that the investor has direct control over the corporation invested in. APB 23, as amended by FAS 109, governs accounting for the income tax effects of owning subsidiaries.

**Undistributed earnings of a subsidiary.** These accounting requirements are set forth in APB 23, as amended by FAS 109. While the timing of distribution of a subsidiary's net income to its parent may be uncertain, it will eventually occur, whether by means of dividends, or via the disposal of the entity and realization of capital gains. Accordingly, deferred income taxes must be provided, but the amount will be dependent upon the anticipated means of realization, which of course may change over time.

Before FAS 109, an "indefinite reversal" provision in APB 23 permitted reporting entities to avoid recognizing deferred income tax liabilities associated with undistributed subsidiary net income if there was sufficient evidence available to demonstrate that the subsidiary would invest the undistributed net income indefinitely or that distribution was intended to occur in a tax-free liquidation. Under such circumstances, deferred income tax accrual was unnecessary, but expanded disclosures were required.

FAS 109 deleted this provision from APB 23 because, while management controls the timing and circumstances of the distribution of the net income of subsidiaries for income tax purposes, ultimate recognition is a certainty. The same logic also applies to the recognition of deferred income tax assets. The formerly accepted concept of "indefinite reversal" has thus been debunked. However, FAS 109 effectively "grandfathered" certain existing temporary differences for which deferred income taxes were not to be provided, including undistributed net income of domestic subsidiaries or corporate joint ventures if the differences are essentially permanent in nature and arose in fiscal years beginning on or prior to December 15, 1992. The provisions of FAS 109 were to be applied prospectively, without exception, with no need for adjustment for temporary differences arising from ownership of subsidiaries prior to the effective date of that standard.

The magnitude of the income tax effects to be provided depends upon specific application of the income tax laws and management intent. If the law provides a mechanism under which the parent can recover its investment tax-free, deferred income taxes are not provided. For example, under §332 of the Internal Revenue Code (IRC), a parent corporation can liquidate an 80%-or-more-owned subsidiary without recognizing gain or loss for income tax purposes. Also, under IRC §368, a parent can effect a statutory merger or consolidation with its 80%-or-more-owned subsidiary, under which no taxable gain or loss would be recognized.

In other cases, the minimization or avoidance of income taxes can be achieved only if the parent company owns a stipulated share of the subsidiary's stock. A parent owning less than this threshold level of its subsidiary may express its intent to utilize a tax planning strategy to acquire the necessary additional shares to realize this benefit. In evaluating this strategy, the cost of acquiring the additional shares must be considered, and the benefits to be recognized (i.e., a reduced deferred income tax liability) must be offset by the cost of implementing the strategy as discussed earlier in this chapter.

A distinction exists in the application of APB 23 between differences in income tax and financial reporting basis that are considered "inside basis differences" versus "outside basis differences," and this is clarified by EITF 93-16. Certain countries' income tax laws (Italy is cited as an example in the EITF Consensus) allow periodic revaluation of long-lived assets to reflect the effects of inflation with the offsetting credit recorded as equity for income tax purposes. Because this is an internal adjustment that does not result from a transaction with third parties, the additional basis is referred to as "inside basis." Issue 93-16 indicates that the APB 23 indefinite reversal criteria only apply to "outside basis differences," and not to "inside basis differences" arising in connection with ownership of foreign subsidiaries.

Therefore, a deferred income tax liability is to be provided on the amount of the increased inside basis.

Certain foreign countries tax corporate income at rates that differ depending on whether the income is distributed as dividends or retained by the corporation. Upon subsequent distribution of the accumulated earnings, the taxpayer receives a tax credit or refund for the difference between the two rates. In the consolidated financial statements of a parent company, the future income tax credit and the deferred income tax effects related to dividends that will be paid in the future are recognized based on the distributed rate if the parent provided for deferred income taxes because it did not invoke the indefinite reversal criteria of APB 23. If the parent did not provide for deferred income taxes as a result of applying the APB 23 criterion, the undistributed rate is to be used (EITF 95-20). The treatment of the tax credit in the separate financial statements of the foreign company is discussed later in this chapter in the section captioned Separate Financial Statements of Subsidiaries or Investees.

**Undistributed earnings of an investee.** When an entity has an equity method investee, it is presumed to be able to exercise significant influence, but lack control. Because the ability to indefinitely postpone income taxes on the investee's net income would be absent in such a case, in contrast to the parent-subsidiary situation above, GAAP requires full interperiod income tax allocation for the effects of undistributed investee net income. The facts and circumstances involved in each situation, however, will be the final determinant of whether this temporary difference is assumed to be a future dividend or a capital gain for purposes of computing the deferred income tax effect.

### Example of income tax effects from investee company

To illustrate the application of these concepts, assume Parent Company owns 30% of the outstanding common stock of Investee Company and 70% of the outstanding common stock of Subsidiary company. Additional data for Subsidiary and Investee companies for the year 2009 are as follows:

|  | *Investee Company* | *Subsidiary Company* |
|---|---|---|
| Net income | $50,000 | $100,000 |
| Dividends paid | 20,000 | 60,000 |

The following sections illustrate how the foregoing data are used to recognize the income tax effects of the stated events.

The pretax accounting income of Parent Company will include its equity in Investee Company net income equal to $15,000 ($50,000 × 30%). Parent's taxable income, on the other hand, will include dividend income of $6,000 ($20,000 × 30%), reduced by a deduction of 80% of the $6,000, or $4,800. This 80% dividends received deduction is a permanent difference between pretax accounting income and taxable income and is allowed for dividends received from domestic corporations in which the taxpaying corporation's ownership is less than 80% but at least 20%. A lower dividends-received deduction of 70% is permitted when the ownership is less than 20%, and a 100% deduction is provided for dividends received from domestic corporations in which the ownership is 80% to 100%.

In this example, a temporary difference results from Parent's equity ($9,000) in Investee's undistributed income of $30,000 (= $50,000 net income less $20,000 dividends). The amount of the deferred income tax credit in 2009 depends upon the expectations of Parent Company regarding the manner in which the $9,000 of undistributed income will be realized. If the expectation of receipt is via dividends, then the temporary difference is 20% (the net taxable portion, after the dividends received deduction) of $9,000, or $1,800, and the deferred income tax liability associated with this temporary difference in 2009 is the expected effective income tax rate times $1,800. However, if the expectation is that receipt will be through future sale of the investment, then the temporary difference is the full $9,000 and the deferred income tax liability is the current corporate capital gains rate times the $9,000.

The entries below illustrate these alternatives. An assumed tax rate of 34% is used for ordinary income, while a rate of 20% is used for capital gains. It is also assumed that there are no pre-2009 temporary differences to consider. Note that the amounts in the entries below relate only to Investee Company's incremental impact upon Parent Company's income tax assets and liabilities.

| | Expectations for undistributed income | | | |
|---|---|---|---|---|
| | *Dividends* | | *Capital gains* | |
| Income tax expense | 1,020 | | 2,208 | |
| Deferred income tax liability | | 612[b] | | 1,800[c] |
| Income taxes payable | | 408[a] | | 408[a] |

[a]Computation of income taxes payable:

| | |
|---|---|
| Dividend income—30% × ($20,000) | $6,000 |
| Less 80% dividends received deduction | (4,800) |
| Amount included in Parent's taxable income | $1,200 |
| Tax liability—34% × ($1,200) | $ 408 |

[b]Computation of deferred income tax liability (dividend assumption):
Temporary difference:

| | |
|---|---|
| Parent's share of undistributed income—30% × ($50,000 – $20,000 = $30,000) | $9,000 |
| Less 80% dividends received deduction | (7,200) |
| Temporary difference | $1,800 |
| Deferred income tax liability—34% × ($1,800) | $ 612 |

[c]Computation of deferred income tax liability (capital gain assumption):
Temporary difference:

| | |
|---|---|
| Parent's share of undistributed income—same as above | $9,000 |
| Deferred income tax liability—20% × ($9,000) | $1,800 |

### Example of income tax effects from subsidiary

The pretax accounting income of Parent Company will also include equity in Subsidiary income of $70,000 (70% × $100,000). This $70,000 will be included in consolidated pretax income in the Parent's consolidated financial statements. For income tax purposes, Parent and Subsidiary cannot file a consolidated income tax return because the minimum level of control (i.e., 80%) is not present. Consequently, the taxable income of Parent will include dividend income of $42,000 (70% × $60,000), and there will be an 80% dividends received deduction of $33,600. The temporary difference discussed in APB 23 results from Parent's 70% equity ($28,000) in the Subsidiary's undistributed earnings of $40,000. The amount of the deferred income tax liability in 2009 depends upon the expectations of Parent Company as to the manner in which this $28,000 of undistributed income will be received. The same expectations can exist as previously discussed, for Parent's equity in Investee's undistributed earnings (i.e., through future dividend distributions or capital gains).

The entries below illustrate these alternatives. A marginal tax rate of 34% is assumed for dividend income, and a rate of 20% applies to capital gains. It is also assumed that there are no pre-2009 temporary differences to consider. The amounts in the entries below relate only to Subsidiary Company's incremental impact upon Parent Company's income tax assets and liabilities.

| | Expectations for undistributed income | | | |
|---|---|---|---|---|
| | *Dividends* | | *Capital gains* | |
| Income tax expense | 4,760 | | 8,456 | |
| Deferred income tax liability | | 1,904[b] | | 5,600[c] |
| Income taxes payable | | 2,856[a] | | 2,856[a] |

[a]Computation of income taxes payable:

| | |
|---|---|
| Dividend income—70% × ($60,000) | $42,000 |
| Less 80% dividends received deduction | (33,600) |
| Amount included in Parent's taxable income | $ 8,400 |
| Tax liability—34% × ($8,400) | $ 2,856 |

| | *Expectations for undistributed income* | |
|---|---|---|
| | *Dividends* | *Capital gains* |

ᵇComputation of deferred income tax liability (dividend assumption):

Temporary difference:

| | | |
|---|---|---|
| Parent's share of undistributed income—70% × ($40,000) | | $28,000 |
| Less 80% dividends received deduction | | (22,400) |
| | | $ 5,600 |
| Deferred income tax liability—34% × ($5,600) | | $ 1,904 |

ᶜComputation of deferred income tax liability (capital gain assumption):

Temporary difference:

| | | |
|---|---|---|
| Parent's share of undistributed income—70% × ($40,000) | | $28,000 |
| Deferred income tax liability—20% × ($28,000) | | $ 5,600 |

If a parent company owns 80% or more of the voting stock of a subsidiary and the parent consolidates the subsidiary for both financial reporting and income tax purposes, then no temporary differences exist between consolidated pretax income and taxable income. If, in the circumstances noted above, consolidated financial statements are prepared but a consolidated income tax return is not, IRC §243 allows the Parent to take a 100% dividends received deduction. Accordingly, the temporary difference between consolidated pretax income and taxable income is zero if the parent assumes the undistributed income will be realized in dividends.

### Summary of Temporary Differences of Investees and Subsidiaries

*Level of Ownership Interest*

| | 0% | <20% | 50% | >80% | 100% |
|---|---|---|---|---|---|
| ***Accounting*** | | | | | |
| Income recognition | Fair value method | Equity Method | | | |
| Deferred income tax on undistributed earnings | No temporary difference | Temporary difference | | | No temporary difference |
| ***Income tax*** | | | | | |
| Dividends recognized | 30% of dividends received (70% deduction) | 20% of dividends received (80% deduction) | | | None (100% deduction) |

## Separate Financial Statements of Subsidiaries or Investees

**Push-down accounting.** EITF 86-9 addressed a number of issues concerning whether the use of a step-up in the income tax basis of an acquired entity, as permitted by the 1982 tax law, mandated the use of push-down accounting, and the necessary allocation of the income tax provision between parent and subsidiaries if a step-up was not elected. There was a consensus that push-down accounting is not required for non-SEC registrants. In addition, a consensus was reached that, if the acquiree continues to report its net assets on their historical basis, three alternative methods of allocating consolidated income tax expense or benefit are acceptable: (1) allocation to the acquiree on the preacquisition basis; (2) crediting the income tax benefit of basis step-up to the acquiree's stockholders' equity upon realization; and (3) crediting the income tax benefit to the income of the acquirer when realized as a permanent difference.

**Tax credits related to dividend payments.** Some taxing jurisdictions have differing income tax rates that are applied to taxable income based on whether that income is distributed to investors or retained in the business. For example, Germany taxes undistributed profits at a 45% rate and distributed profits at a 30% rate. When previously undistributed profits are distributed, the taxpayer earns an income tax credit for the differential between the two rates. EITF 95-10 specifies that the accounting for the income tax credit in the separate financial statements of the reporting entity paying the dividend is a reduction of income tax expense in the period that the credit is included in its income tax return. During the period of time that the earnings remain undistributed, the rate applied to the temporary difference in computing deferred income taxes is the rate applicable to the undistributed profits (45% in this example).

## Asset Acquisitions

FAS 109 established the principle that the income tax effects of temporary differences related to purchase business combinations are to be "grossed up," in contrast to the older, "net of tax" method which had been previously prescribed by APB 11. However, FAS 109 did not address the accounting for acquisitions of individual assets having different income tax and accounting bases. EITF 98-11, prior to being amended by FAS 141(R) held that the income tax attributes of such an acquisition were to be recorded in a manner similar to the accounting for the income tax effects of negative goodwill under FAS 109 prior to its amendment by FAS 141(R) (i.e., there should not be immediate income statement recognition). Computationally, this involved the use of simultaneous equations or trial and error.

Upon the issuance of FAS 141(R), FASB amended EITF 98-11 to remove inconsistencies between its provisions and amendments made to FAS 109 and FIN 48. As a result of these amendments, the revised EITF 98-11 now provides that in situations where an acquiring entity makes an asset acquisition

1.  When management recognizes a reduction in the reporting entity's valuation allowance that directly results from the asset acquisition, the reduction is not to enter into the accounting for the asset acquisition. The acquiring entity is to reduce the valuation allowance and either recognize the reduction

    a.  As an income tax benefit *or*
    b.  As a credit to contributed capital if related to items such as employee stock options, dividends on unallocated ESOP shares, or certain quasi reorganizations

2.  Any income tax uncertainties existing at the date of acquisition are to be accounted for in accordance with FIN 48, *Accounting for Uncertainty in Income Taxes.*

Unlike the other transition provisions of FAS 141(R), these specific amendments are to be applied to all asset acquisitions irrespective of when they occurred. This application is on a prospective basis after the effective date of FAS 141(R) which is the first annual reporting period beginning on or after December 15, 2008. Under this transition scenario, the acquirer is to recognize

1.  An adjustment to income tax expense (or contributed capital) resulting from post-effective-date changes in a deferred income tax asset valuation allowance
2.  Changes in acquired income tax positions in accordance with FIN 48

## Intraperiod Income Tax Allocation

FAS 109 predominantly deals with the requirements of interperiod income tax allocation (i.e., deferred income tax accounting), but its scope also includes intraperiod income tax allocation. This relates to the matching of various categories of comprehensive income or expense (continuing operations, extraordinary items, corrections of errors, prior period adjustments, etc.) with the income tax effects of those items, as presented in the income (or other financial) statement. The general principle is that the income statement presentation of the effects of income taxes should be the same as items to which the income taxes relate; and in this regard, FAS 109 did not change prior practice. A "with and without" approach is prescribed as the mechanism by which the marginal, or incremental income tax effects of items other than those arising from continuing operations are to be measured. However, under FAS 109 there are some significant departures from past practice, as described in the following paragraphs.

Under prior GAAP, the "with and without" technique was applied in a step-by-step fashion proceeding down the face of the income statement. For example, an entity having continuing operations, discontinued operations, and extraordinary items would calculate income tax expense as follows: (1) Income tax would be computed separately for the aggregate results and for continuing operations. The difference between the two amounts would be allocated to the total of discontinued operations and extraordinary items. (2) Income tax expense would be computed on discontinued operations. The residual amount (i.e., the difference between income tax on discontinued operations and the income tax on the total of discontinued operations and extraordinary items) would then be allocated to extraordinary items. Thus, under the provisions of APB 11, the amount of income tax expense allocated to any given classification in the statement of income (and the other financial statements, if relevant) was partially a function of the location in which the item was traditionally presented in the income and retained earnings statements.

FAS 109 adopted an incremental calculation of income tax expense to be allocated to classifications other than continuing operations. However, rather than applying successive allocations on the "with and without" basis to determine income tax expense or benefit applicable to each succeeding income statement caption, the income tax effects of all items other than continuing operations are allocated pro rata. That is, once income tax expense or benefit allocable to continuing operations is determined, the residual income tax expense or benefit is apportioned to all the other classifications (discontinued operations, et al.) in the ratios that those other items bear, on a pretax basis, to the total of all such items. Furthermore, income tax expense or benefit on income from continuing operations includes not only income taxes on the income earned from continuing operations, as expected, but also the following items:

1. The impact of changes in income tax laws and rates, which includes the effects of such changes on items which were previously reflected directly in stockholders' equity (accumulated other comprehensive income), as described more fully below
2. The impact of changes in the entity's taxable status
3. Changes in estimates about whether the income tax benefits of future deductible temporary differences or net operating loss or tax credit carryforwards are more likely than not to be realizable (i.e., an adjustment to the valuation allowance for such items)
4. The income tax effects of tax-deductible dividends paid to stockholders, as discussed elsewhere in this chapter

Under FAS 109, stockholders' equity is charged or credited directly with the initial income tax effects of items that are reported in stockholders' equity without being presented on the income statement. These items include the following:

1. Corrections of the effects of accounting errors of previous periods

2.  Gains and losses which are defined under GAAP as being part of comprehensive income but are not reported in the income statement, such as foreign currency translation adjustments under FAS 52, and the fair value adjustments applicable to available-for-sale portfolios of debt and marketable equity securities held as investments. As a result of amendments to FAS 109 made by FAS 130, *Reporting Comprehensive Income*, the income tax effects of these types of items will be reported in the same financial statement where other comprehensive income items are reported. As discussed more fully in Chapter 3, these items may be reported either in a stand-alone statement of comprehensive income, a combined statement of income and other comprehensive income, or in an expanded version of the statement of changes in stockholders' equity.

3.  Taxable or deductible increases or decreases in contributed capital, such as offering costs reported under GAAP as reductions of the proceeds of a capital stock offering, but which are either immediately deductible or amortizable for income tax purposes

4.  Increases in the income tax bases of assets acquired in a taxable business combination accounted for as a pooling of interests under GAAP, if an income tax benefit is recognized at the date of the business combination (i.e., if the income tax effects of existing future deductible temporary differences are not fully offset by a valuation allowance at that date)

5.  Expenses incurred in connection with stock issued under provisions of compensatory stock option plans, which are recognized for income tax purposes but are reported for accounting purposes in stockholders' equity under the provisions of APB 25

6.  Dividends paid on unallocated shares held in an ESOP, and that are charged against retained earnings

7.  Deductible temporary differences and net operating loss and tax credit carryforwards that existed at the date of a quasi reorganization

The effects of income tax rate or other income tax law changes on items for which the income tax effects were originally reported directly in stockholders' equity are reported in continuing operations, if they occur in any period after the original event. For example, assume the reporting entity recognized a deferred income tax asset related to an employee stock option program amounting to $34,000 in 2009, based on the estimated future income tax deduction it would receive at the then-current and anticipated future income tax rate of 34%. If the statutory income tax rate is reduced to 25% in 2010 before the temporary difference reverses, the adjustment to the deferred income tax asset ($34,000 − $25,000 = $9,000) is reported in income tax expense or benefit applicable to income from continuing operations in 2010.

### Comprehensive example of the intraperiod income tax allocation process

Assume $50,000 in future deductible temporary differences at 12/31/09; these differences remain unchanged during the current year, 2010.

| | *2010* |
|---|---|
| Income from continuing operations | $400,000 |
| Loss from discontinued operations | (120,000) |
| Extraordinary gain on involuntary conversion (taxable because no replacement property purchased) | 60,000 |
| Correction of error: understatement of depreciation in 2009 | (20,000) |
| Income tax credits | 5,000 |

Income tax rates are: 15% on the first $100,000 of taxable income; 20% on the next $100,000; 25% on the next $100,000; 30% thereafter.

Expected future effective income tax rates were 20% at December 31, 2009, but are judged to be 28% at December 31, 2010.

Retained earnings at December 31, 2009, were $650,000.

Intraperiod tax allocation proceeds as follows:

Step 1 — Income tax on total taxable income of $320,000 ($400,000 – $120,000 + $60,000 – $20,000) is $61,000 computed as follows:

| Taxable income | Income tax rate | Income tax | |
|---|---|---|---|
| $100,000 | 15% | $15,000 | |
| 100,000 | 20% | 20,000 | |
| 100,000 | 25% | 25,000 | |
| 20,000 | 30% | 6,000 | |
| $320,000 | | $66,000 | Income tax before credits |
| | | (5,000) | Tax credit |
| | | $61,000 | Income tax payable |

Step 2 — Income tax on income from continuing operations of $400,000 is $85,000, net of tax credit computed as follows.

| Taxable income | Income tax rate | Income tax | |
|---|---|---|---|
| $100,000 | 15% | $15,000 | |
| 100,000 | 20% | 20,000 | |
| 100,000 | 25% | 25,000 | |
| 100,000 | 30% | 30,000 | |
| $400,000 | | $90,000 | Income tax before credits |
| | | (5,000) | Tax credit |
| | | $85,000 | Income tax payable |

Step 3 — The $24,000 difference is allocated pro rata to discontinued operations, extraordinary gain, and correction of the error in prior year depreciation as follows:

| | Gross amount before tax | Relative % | Allocation of difference |
|---|---|---|---|
| Discontinued operations | $(120,000) | 150% | $36,000 |
| Extraordinary gain | 60,000 | (75%) | (18,000) |
| Error correction | (20,000) | 25% | 6,000 |
| | $ (80,000) | 100% | $24,000 |

Step 4 — The adjustment of the deferred income tax asset, amounting to a $4,000 increase due to an effective tax rate estimate change [$50,000 × (.28 – .20)] is allocated to continuing operations, regardless of the source of the temporary difference.

A summary combined statement of income and retained earnings for 2010 is presented below.

| | | |
|---|---|---|
| Income from continuing operations, before income taxes | | $400,000 |
| Income taxes on income from continuing operations: | | |
| Current | $90,000 | |
| Deferred | (4,000) | |
| Tax credits | (5,000) | 81,000 |
| Income from continuing operations, net | | 319,000 |
| Loss from discontinued operations, net of income tax benefit of $36,000 | | (84,000) |
| Extraordinary gain, net of income tax of $18,000 | | 42,000 |
| Net income | | 277,000 |
| Retained earnings, January 1, 2010 as originally reported | | 650,000 |
| Correction of accounting error, net of income tax effects of $6,000 | | (14,000) |
| Retained earnings, January 1, 2010, as restated | | 636,000 |
| Retained earnings, December 31, 2010 | | $913,000 |

This example does not include items that will, under provisions of FAS 130, be reported in other comprehensive income; the accounting for those is illustrated in Chapter 3.

The income tax effect of a retroactive change in tax rates on current and deferred income tax assets and liabilities is to be determined at the enactment date, using temporary differences and currently taxable income computed as of the date of enactment. The cumulative income tax effect is included in income from continuing operations. Furthermore, the income tax effect of items not included in income from continuing operations (e.g., from discontinued operations) that arose during the current fiscal year and prior to enactment is measured based on the enacted income tax rate at the time the transaction was recognized for financial reporting purposes; the income tax effect of a retroactive change in rates on current or deferred income tax assets or liabilities related to those items is nevertheless included in income from continuing operations (EITF 93-13).

## Balance Sheet Classification

**Deferred income taxes.** A reporting entity that presents a classified balance sheet will classify its deferred income tax liabilities and assets as either current or noncurrent consistent with the classification of the related asset or liability. A deferred income tax asset or liability that is not related to an asset or liability for financial reporting purposes, such as the deferred income tax consequences related to a net operating loss carryforward or income tax credit carryforward, is classified based on the expected reversal or utilization date. These classifications must be made for each separate tax-paying component within each taxing jurisdiction.

Within each of the separate components, the current asset and liability are offset and presented as a single amount, with similar treatment for the noncurrent items. Understandably, offsetting is not permitted for different tax-paying components or for different tax jurisdictions. Thus, a balance sheet may present current and noncurrent deferred income tax assets, along with current and noncurrent deferred income tax liabilities, under certain circumstances.

If the enterprise has recorded a valuation allowance, it must prorate the allowance between current and noncurrent according to the relative size of the gross deferred income tax asset in each classification. The FASB mandated this approach to avoid the necessity of having to estimate which deferred income tax assets would not be recovered.

**Payment to retain fiscal year.** S corporations and partnerships are permitted to elect tax fiscal years other than a calendar year (IRC §444). If the election is made, however, the electing entity is required to make a payment to the Internal Revenue Service in an amount that approximates the income tax that the stockholders (or partners) would have paid on the income for the period between the fiscal year-end elected and the end of the calendar year. This payment, which is not a tax, is recomputed and adjusted annually and is fully refundable to the electing entity in the future upon liquidation, conversion to a calendar tax year-end or a decline in its taxable income to zero. This "required payment" should be accounted for as an asset, analogous to a deposit (EITF 88-4).

## Disclosures

FAS 109 is one of a handful of pronouncements that differentiates between public and nonpublic enterprises with respect to the nature and extent of required disclosures. With the issuance of FSP FAS 126-1 in October 2006, the definition of public enterprises for the purpose of applying certain authoritative GAAP (including FAS 109) was expanded to include enterprises that are conduit obligors for conduit debt securities traded in a domestic or foreign market, including an exchange or over-the-counter market, even if the securities are only marketed locally or regionally (definitions of these terms are included earlier in this chapter). The FSP is to be applied prospectively in fiscal periods beginning after 12/15/2006. Management may elect to retrospectively apply the guidance to all prior periods. If the reporting entity issues interim financial statements, the FSP is to be applied to the first interim period after the date of adoption.

The following disclosures or group of disclosures are applicable in both interim and annual financial statements unless indicated otherwise.

**Balance sheet disclosures.** A reporting entity is required to disclose the components of the net deferred income tax liability or asset recognized in the balance sheet (statement of financial position) as follows:

1. Total of all deferred income tax liabilities
2. Total of all deferred income tax assets
3. Total valuation allowance
4. Net change in the valuation allowance for the period
5. Narrative description of the types of temporary differences and carryforwards that cause significant portions of deferred income tax assets and liabilities. Public enterprises (under the expanded definition prescribed by FSP FAS 126-1 discussed above) are additionally required to disclose the approximate income tax effect (not the separate effect for each jurisdiction) of each temporary difference and carryforward (gross, without consideration of any necessary valuation allowance).

When deferred income tax liabilities are not recognized because of the exceptions provided under APB 23 the following information is to be provided:

1. The types of temporary differences and the events that would cause those temporary differences to become taxable
2. The cumulative amount of each type of temporary difference
3. The amount of unrecognized deferred income tax liability for any undistributed foreign earnings, or a statement that such a determination is not practicable
4. The amount of unrecognized deferred income tax liability for other temporary differences that arose prior to the period for which application of this statement was first required for each of those particular differences

**Income statement disclosures.** FAS 109 places primary emphasis upon the income tax expense or benefit allocated to continuing operations. All significant components of income taxes associated with continuing operations are required to be disclosed for each period for which an income statement is presented. Examples of these components include but are not limited to

1. Current income tax expense or benefit
2. Deferred income tax expense or benefit (exclusive of the effects of other components listed below)
3. General business credits, investment tax credits, or other tax credits
4. Government grants (to the extent recognized as a reduction of income tax expense)
5. The benefits of net operating loss carryforwards
6. Income tax expense that results from allocating certain income tax benefits directly to contributed capital or, if prior to the effective date of FAS 141(R), from allocating them to reduce goodwill or other noncurrent intangible assets of an acquired entity under the prior rules
7. Adjustments to the deferred income tax liability or asset for enacted changes in income tax laws or rates or a change in the tax status of the reporting entity
8. Adjustments to the beginning of year balance of the valuation allowance because of a change in circumstances that causes a change in judgment about the realizability of the related deferred income tax asset in future years (e.g., when an acquirer rec-

ognizes a change in its preacquisition valuation allowance due to income tax benefits it recognizes as a result of a business combination

FAS 109 also requires disclosure of the following:

1. The amounts of income tax expense or benefit allocated to financial statement elements other than continuing operations (e.g., discontinued operations, extraordinary items, other comprehensive income, and retained earnings)
2. The amounts and expiration dates of net operating loss and tax credit carryforwards under the currently enacted tax law
3. The amount of the valuation allowance for which subsequently recognized income tax benefits will be allocated to contributed capital and, if the pre-FAS 141(R) effective date accounting was still applicable, tax benefits that were allocated to reduce goodwill or other noncurrent intangible assets of an acquired entity
4. A narrative description of the nature of significant reconciling items between income tax expense or benefit computed on pretax income from continuing operations by applying the statutory federal income tax rate and the actual amount of such expense or benefit reflected in the financial statements. For the purpose of this disclosure, the federal statutory rate is the regular marginal rate to which ordinary taxable income is subjected (currently 34%) without consideration of the effect of graduated rates, alternative minimum tax rates, or income taxes from other state, local or foreign taxing jurisdictions.
5. Public enterprises (under the expanded definition of public enterprises prescribed by FSP FAS 126-1 discussed previously) are additionally required to provide a reconciliation of the differences described in 4. above using either percentages or dollar amounts.

**Disclosures added by FIN 48.** FIN 48 requires the following additional disclosures. These disclosures are only required in annual financial statements.

1. The accounting policy for whether

    a. Interest on unrecognized income tax positions are included as a component of income tax expense or as a component of interest expense

    b. Penalties on unrecognized income tax positions are included as a component of income tax expense or as a component of another expense category

2. For each annual reporting period presented in the financial statement of the reporting entity

    a. A reconciliation of changes in the liability for unrecognized income tax benefits that includes at a minimum

        (1) The balance at the beginning of the year

        (2) For income tax positions taken during previous periods

            (a) Gross additions
            (b) Gross reductions

        (3) For income tax positions taken during the current period

            (a) Gross additions
            (b) Gross reductions

        (4) Reductions resulting from settlements with taxing authorities
        (5) Reductions resulting from the lapse of the applicable statute of limitations
        (6) The balance at the end of the year

3.  At the date of the latest balance sheet presented

    a.  Disclosures regarding "certain significant estimates" (as required by SOP 94-6 and FAS 5) with respect to items for which it is reasonably possible that there will be a significant increase or decrease in the estimate of the liability for unrecognized income tax benefits within one year of the balance sheet including, at a minimum

        (1) The nature of the uncertainty
        (2) The nature of the event that could occur in the next year that would cause the change
        (3) An estimate of the range of the change that is reasonably possible or, if such an estimate cannot be made, a statement to that effect

4.  The total interest and penalties recognized in each balance sheet and income statement (for not-for-profits, in the statement of financial position and statement of activities, respectively)
5.  A description of the open tax years by major tax jurisdiction
6.  The total amount of unrecognized income tax benefits that, if recognized, would affect the effective income tax rate
7.  In the fiscal year of adoption

    a.  The nature of and reason for the change in accounting principle
    b.  The cumulative effect of the change on retained earnings as of the date of adoption

In the year of adoption, the cumulative effect of initially adopting FIN 48 is to be reported as an adjustment to the opening balance of retained earnings (or other components of equity or net assets).

Note that the year-of-adoption disclosures are not required to be repeated in financial statements of subsequent periods.

**Other disclosures.** If applicable, the following additional disclosures are required:

1.  If there are significant matters that affect the comparability of information between periods presented that are not apparent to a financial statement user from the disclosures described above, the nature of such matters and their effect on the financial statements for the periods presented.
2.  For each period for which an income statement is presented in the separately issued financial statements of a reporting entity that is a member of an affiliated group that files a consolidated income tax return

    a.  The amounts of current and deferred income tax expense included in the statement of income.
    b.  The amounts of any income tax-related balances due to or from other companies in the affiliated group at each balance sheet date.
    c.  A description of the method used by members of the affiliated group to allocate the consolidated current and deferred income tax expense or benefit between them and the nature of any changes, during the years presented, in this method of allocation or the method of determining amounts due to or from affiliates as described in b. above.

3.  Per EITF 00-15 (described later in this chapter), the income tax benefit realized during each period presented from employees' exercise of nonqualified employee stock options. This may be presented as a separate line item in the operating section of the statement of cash flows or in the statement of changes in stockholders' equity.

4. It has become generally accepted, although not explicitly required, to disclose the fact that a reporting entity is not subject to federal income taxes (and state income taxes, if applicable) because it is a flow-through entity (e.g., an S corporation, a limited liability company, or partnership). Public companies are required to disclose this fact as well as the net differences between the income tax bases and financial reporting bases of its assets and liabilities.

## Accounting for Income Taxes in Interim Periods

**Basic rules.** FAS 109 essentially left unchanged the principles applicable to accounting for income taxes in financial statements covering interim periods, established by APB 28 and FIN 18. As set forth in those standards, the appropriate perspective for interim period reporting is to view the interim period as an integral part of the year, rather than as a discrete period. This objective is usually achieved by projecting income for the full annual period, computing the income tax thereon, and applying the "effective rate" to the interim period income or loss, with quarterly (or monthly) revisions to the expected annual results and the income tax effects thereof, as necessary.

While the Board chose to not comprehensively address interim reporting when it deliberated FAS 109, there were certain clear contradictions between APB 28 and the principles of FAS 109, which the Board did address. As discussed in more detail below, these issues were (1) recognizing the income tax benefits of interim losses based on expected net income of later interim or annual periods, (2) reporting the benefits of net operating loss carryforwards in interim periods, and (3) reporting the effects of income tax law changes in interim periods. Other matters requiring interpretation, which were left to the user to address without official guidance, included the classification of deferred income tax assets and liabilities on interim balance sheets and allocation of interim period income tax provisions between current and deferred expense.

The annual computation of income tax expense is based upon the current income taxes payable or refundable as indicated on the income tax return, plus or minus the adjustment necessary to adjust the deferred income tax asset and liability to the proper balances as of the balance sheet date (including consideration of the need for a valuation allowance, as previously discussed). The computation of interim period income tax expense should be consistent with this asset and liability method.

FIN 18 introduced some unfortunate terminology that, although confusing, nevertheless must be understood in the context of interim tax computations. The term "ordinary income" as used in FIN 18 is not the same as that term is used in the income tax law to distinguish capital gains, for example, from operating income and deductions. The FIN 18 definition of "ordinary income" is, formulaically

Pretax income or loss from continuing operations

+/– Extraordinary items
+/– Discontinued operations
+/– Cumulative effects of changes in accounting principle
+/– Significant unusual or infrequently occurring items

This "ordinary income" is used as the denominator in calculating an effective income tax rate to be used to compute income tax expense currently payable for the interim period. Note that pretax income is *not* adjusted for the effects of permanent or temporary differences.

Below is a relatively simple example that illustrates these basic principles:

### Basic example of interim period accounting for income taxes

Boffa, Inc. estimates that pretax accounting income for the full fiscal year ending June 30, 2009, will be $400,000. Boffa does not expect to have any of the items that would adjust its "ordinary income" as defined above either at year-end or during any of its interim quarters. The company expects that it will incur $60,000 of meals and entertainment expenses of which 50% are nondeductible under the current tax law, the annual premium on an officer's life insurance policy is $12,000, and dividend income (from a less than 20% ownership interest) is expected to be $100,000. The company recognized income of $75,000 in the first quarter of the year. The deferred income tax liability arises solely in connection with property and equipment temporary differences; these differences totaled $150,000 at the beginning of the year and are projected to equal $280,000 at year-end after taking into account expected acquisitions and disposals for the remainder of the fiscal year. The graduated statutory income tax rate schedule is provided below. Boffa management used a future expected effective income tax rate of 34% to compute the beginning deferred income tax liability and does not anticipate changing that percentage at the end of the fiscal year. The change in the future taxable temporary difference during the first quarter is $30,000.

Boffa must first calculate its estimated effective income tax rate for the year. This rate is computed using all of the tax planning alternatives available to the company (e.g., tax credits, foreign rates, capital gains rates, etc.).

| | | | |
|---|---|---:|---:|
| Estimated annual pretax accounting income (and "ordinary income" as defined in FIN 18) | | | $ 400,000 |
| Permanent differences: | | | |
| Add: Nondeductible officers' life insurance premium | | $ 12,000 | |
| Nondeductible meals and entertainment | | 30,000 | 42,000 |
| | | | 442,000 |
| Less: Dividends received deduction ($100,000 × 70%) | | | (70,000) |
| | | | 372,000 |
| Less: Change in future taxable temporary difference | | | (130,000) |
| Estimated taxable income for the year | | | $ 242,000 |
| Annual current tax on estimated taxable income (see below) | | | $ 70,530 |
| Effective income tax rate for *current* income tax expense (computed as a percentage of "ordinary income") $70,530/400,000 | | | 17.6% |

| Tax rate schedule | | | Taxable | |
|---|---|---|---|---|
| *At least* | *Not more than* | *Rate* | *income* | *Tax* |
| $ -- | $ 50,000 | 15% | $ 50,000 | $ 7,500 |
| 50,000 | 75,000 | 25% | 25,000 | 6,250 |
| 75,000 | -- | 34% | 167,000 | 56,780 |
| | | | | $70,530 |

Computation of the first quarter current income tax expense.

| | |
|---|---:|
| "Ordinary income" for first quarter | $75,000 |
| Estimated annual effective income tax rate per above | × 17.6% |
| | $13,200 |

This amount can be "proven" as follows:

| | |
|---|---:|
| Annualized current tax computed above | $70,530 |
| Portion of annual tax attributable to first quarter | |
| First quarter pretax income as a % of forecast | |
| $75,000/$400,000 | × 18.75% |
| Result, materially the same as above | $13,224 |

Computation of the first quarter deferred income tax expense (same method as year-end).

| | Future taxable temporary difference | Effective tax rate estimated for reversal year(s) | Computed deferred tax liability |
|---|---|---|---|
| Property and equipment | | | |
| End of first quarter | $180,000 | 34% | $61,200 |
| Beginning of fiscal year | 150,000 | 34% | 51,000 |
| First quarter deferred income tax expense | | | $10,200 |

Recap of first quarter income tax expense.

| | |
|---|---|
| Current | $13,200 |
| Deferred | 10,200 |
| Total | $23,400 |

Finally, the entry necessary to record the income tax expense at the end of the first quarter is as follows:

| | | |
|---|---|---|
| Income tax expense | 23,400 | |
| Income taxes payable—current | | 13,200 |
| Deferred income tax liability | | 10,200 |

In the second quarter, Boffa, Inc. revises its estimate of income for the full fiscal year. It now anticipates only $210,000 of pretax accounting income ("ordinary income"), including only $75,000 of dividend income, because of dramatic changes in the national economy. Other permanent differences are still expected to total $42,000.

| | | |
|---|---|---|
| Estimated annual pretax accounting income (and "ordinary income" as defined in FIN 18) | | $210,000 |
| Permanent differences: | | |
| Add: Nondeductible officers' life insurance premium | $12,000 | |
| Nondeductible meals and entertainment | 30,000 | 42,000 |
| | | 252,000 |
| Less: Dividends received deduction ($75,000 × 70%) | | (52,500) |
| | | 199,500 |
| Less: Change in future taxable temporary difference | | (130,000) |
| Estimated taxable income for the year | | $ 69,500 |
| Annual current tax on estimated taxable income (see below) | | $ 12,375 |
| Effective income tax rate for *current* income tax expense (computed as a percentage of "ordinary income" $12,375/$210,000) | | 5.2% |

| Tax rate schedule | | | Taxable | |
|---|---|---|---|---|
| At least | Not more than | Rate | income | Tax |
| $ -- | $ 50,000 | 15% | $ 50,000 | $ 7,500 |
| 50,000 | 75,000 | 25% | 19,500 | 4,875 |
| | | | $69,500 | $12,375 |

The actual "ordinary income" for the second quarter was $22,000, and the change in the temporary difference was only an additional $10,000. Income tax expense for the second quarter is computed as follows:

Computation of year-to-date and second quarter current income tax expense (benefit).

| | |
|---|---|
| "Ordinary income" for the half year ($75,000 + $22,000) | $97,000 |
| Estimated annual effective income tax rate per above | × 5.2% |
| Year-to-date current income tax expense | $ 5,044 |
| Less: Expense recognized in first quarter | 13,200 |
| Current income tax (benefit) for second quarter | $ (8,156) |

Computation of year-to-date and second quarter deferred income tax expense (benefit).

|  | *Future taxable temporary difference* | *Effective tax rate estimated for reversal year(s)* | *Computed deferred tax liability* |
|---|---|---|---|
| Property and equipment |  |  |  |
| End of second quarter | $190,000 | 34% | $64,600 |
| Beginning of fiscal year | 150,000 | 34% | 51,000 |
| Year-to-date deferred income tax expense |  |  | 13,600 |
| Less: Expense recognized in first quarter |  |  | 10,200 |
| Deferred income tax expense for second quarter |  |  | $ 3,400 |

Recap of second quarter income expense (benefit)

| Current | $(8,156) |
|---|---|
| Deferred | 3,400 |
| Total | $(4,756) |

Under APB 28, and also under the general principle that changes in estimate are reported prospectively (as stipulated by FAS 154), the results of prior quarters are not restated for changes in the estimated effective annual tax rate. Given the current and deferred income tax expense that was recognized in the first quarter, shown above, the following entry is required to record the income taxes as of the end of the second quarter:

| Income taxes payable—current | 8,156 |  |
|---|---|---|
| Income tax expense (benefit) |  | 4,756 |
| Deferred income tax liability |  | 3,400 |

The foregoing illustrates the basic problems encountered in applying GAAP to interim reporting. In the following paragraphs, we discuss some of the items requiring modifications to the approach described above.

**Net operating losses in interim periods.** FIN 18 sets forth the appropriate accounting when losses are incurred in interim periods or when net operating loss (NOL) carryforward benefits are realized during an interim reporting period.

*Carryforward from prior years.* The interim accounting for the utilization of a net operating loss (NOL) carryforward is reflected in one of two ways.

1.  If the income tax benefit of the NOL is expected to be realized as a result of current year "ordinary income," that income tax benefit is included as an adjustment to the effective annual tax rate computation illustrated above.
2.  If the income tax benefit of the NOL is not expected to be realized as described in 1., the benefit is allocated first to reduce year-to-date income tax expense from continuing operations to zero with any excess allocated to other sources of income that would provide the means to utilize the NOL (e.g., extraordinary items, discontinued operations, etc.)

When a valuation allowance is reduced or eliminated because of a revised judgment, the previously unrecognized income tax benefit is included in the income tax expense or benefit of the interim period in which the judgment is revised. An increase in the valuation allowance resulting from a revised judgment would cause a catch-up adjustment to be included in the current interim period's income tax expense from continuing operations. In either situation, the effect of the change in judgment is **not** prorated to future interim periods by means of the effective tax rate estimate.

**Example of interim-period valuation allowance adjustments due to revised judgment**

Camino Corporation has a previously unrecognized $50,000 net operating loss (NOL) carryforward—that is, Camino had previously established a full valuation allowance for the deferred income tax asset arising from the NOL and thus had not previously recognized any deferred income tax benefit associated with the NOL; a flat 40% tax rate for current and future periods is assumed.

Income for the full year (before NOL) is projected to be $80,000, consequently, the management of Camino has revised its judgment as to the future realizability of the NOL. In the first quarter Camino will report a pretax loss of $10,000.

| | |
|---|---|
| Projected annual income | $ 80,000 |
| × Tax rate | 40% |
| Projected tax liability | $ 32,000 |

Accordingly, in the income statement for the first fiscal quarter, the pretax operating loss of $10,000 will give rise to an income tax benefit of $10,000 × 40% = $4,000.

In addition, an income tax benefit of $20,000 ($50,000 NOL × 40%) is recognized, and is included in the current quarter's income tax benefit relating to continuing operations. Thus, the total income tax benefit for the first fiscal quarter will be $24,000 ($4,000 + $20,000).

If Camino's second quarter results in pretax operating income of $30,000, and the expectation for the full year remains unchanged (i.e., operating income of $80,000), the second quarter income tax expense is $12,000 ($30,000 × 40%).

The income tax provision for the fiscal first half-year will be a benefit of $12,000, as follows:

| | |
|---|---|
| Cumulative pretax income through second quarter ($30,000 – $10,000) | $ 20,000 |
| × Effective rate | 40% |
| Income tax provision before recognition of NOL carryforward benefit | 8,000 |
| Benefit of NOL carryforward first recognized in first quarter | (20,000) |
| Total year-to-date tax provision (benefit) | $(12,000) |
| | |
| Consisting of: | |
| First quarter (benefit) | $(24,000) |
| Second quarter expense | 12,000 |
| Year-to-date benefit, per above | $(12,000) |

The foregoing example assumes that during the first quarter Camino's judgment changed as to the full realizability of the previously unrecognized benefit of the $50,000 loss carryforward. Were this not the case, however, the benefit would have been recognized only as actual tax liabilities were incurred (through current period income) in amounts sufficient to offset the NOL benefit.

**Example of recognizing NOL loss carryforward benefit as actual liabilities are incurred**

To illustrate this latter situation, assume the same facts about net income for the first two quarters, and assume now that Camino's judgment about the realizability of the prior period NOL does not change. Tax provisions for the first quarter and first half are as follows:

| | *First quarter* | *First half-year* |
|---|---|---|
| Pretax income (loss) | $(10,000) | $ 20,000 |
| × Effective rate | 40% | 40% |
| Tax provision before recognition of NOL carryforward benefit | $ (4,000) | $ 8,000 |
| Benefit of NOL carryforward recognized | -- | (8,000) |
| Tax provision (benefit) | $ (4,000) | -- |

Notice that recognition of an income tax benefit of $4,000 in the first quarter is based on the expectation of at least a breakeven full year's results. That is, the benefit of the first quarter's loss was deemed more likely than not. Otherwise, no income tax benefit would have been reported in the first quarter.

***Estimated loss for the year.*** When the full year is expected to be profitable, it is irrelevant that one or more interim periods result in a loss, and the expected effective rate for the full year is used to record interim period income tax expense and benefits, as illustrated above. However, when the full year is expected to produce a loss, the computation of the effective annual income tax benefit rate must logically take into account the extent to which a net deferred income tax asset (i.e., the asset less any related valuation allowance) will be recognized at year-end. For the first set of examples, below, assume that the realization of income tax benefits related to NOL carryforwards are not entirely more likely than not. That is, the full benefits will be recognized as deferred income tax assets, but those assets will be offset partially or completely by the valuation allowance.

For each of the following examples we will assume that the Gibby Corporation is anticipating a loss of $150,000 for the fiscal year. The Company's general ledger currently reflects a deferred income tax liability of $30,000; all of the liability will reverse during the fifteen-year carryforward period. Assume future income taxes will be at a 40% rate.

### Example 1

Assume that the company can carry back the entire $150,000 NOL to the preceding three years. The income tax potentially refundable by the carryback would (remember this is only an estimate until year-end) amount to $48,000 (an assumed amount). The effective rate is then 32% ($48,000/150,000).

| | Ordinary income (loss) | | | Tax (benefit) expense | | |
| | Reporting period | Reporting period | Year-to date | Year-to-date | Less previously provided | Reporting period |
|---|---|---|---|---|---|---|
| 1st qtr. | $ (50,000) | $ (50,000) | $(16,000) | $ -- | $(16,000) |
| 2nd qtr. | 20,000 | (30,000) | (9,600) | (16,000) | 6,400 |
| 3rd qtr. | (70,000) | (100,000) | (32,000) | (9,600) | (22,400) |
| 4th qtr. | (50,000) | (150,000) | (48,000) | (32,000) | (16,000) |
| Fiscal year | $(150,000) | | | | $(48,000) |

Note that both the income tax expense (2nd quarter) and benefit are computed using the estimated annual effective rate. This rate is applied to the year-to-date numbers just as in the previous examples, with any adjustment being made and realized in the current reporting period. This treatment is appropriate because the accrual of income tax benefits in the first, third and fourth quarters is consistent with the effective rate estimated at the beginning of the year, in contrast to those circumstances in which a change in estimate is made in a quarter relating to the realizability of income tax benefits not previously provided (or benefits for which full or partial valuation allowances were required).

### Example 2

In this case assume that Gibby Corporation can carry back only $50,000 of the loss and that the remainder must be carried forward. Realization of future taxable income to fully utilize the NOL is not deemed to be more likely than not. The estimated carryback of $50,000 would generate an income tax refund of $12,000 (again assumed). The company is assumed to be in the 40% tax bracket (a flat rate is used to simplify the example). Although the benefit of the NOL carryforward is recognized, a valuation allowance must be provided to the extent that it is more likely than not that the benefit will not be realized. In this example, management has concluded that only 25% of the gross benefit will be realized in future years. Accordingly, a valuation allowance of $30,000 must be established, leaving a net of $10,000 as an estimated realizable income tax benefit related to the carryforward of the projected loss.

$150,000 loss – $50,000 carried back = $100,000 NOL × 40% tax rate = $40,000 benefit × 75% portion deemed unrealizable = $30,000 valuation allowance

Considered in conjunction with the carryback refund of $12,000, the company will obtain a $22,000 income tax benefit relating to the projected current year loss, for an effective income tax benefit rate of 14.7%. The calculation of the estimated annual effective rate is as follows:

| | | | |
|---|---|---|---|
| Expected annual net loss | | | $150,000 |
| Tax benefit from NOL carryback | | $12,000 | |
| Tax benefit of NOL carryforward | | | |
| ($100,000 × 40%) | $40,000 | | |
| Valuation allowance | (30,000) | 10,000 | |
| Total recognized benefit | | | $22,000 |
| Estimated annual effective rate | | | |
| ($22,000 ÷ $150,000) | | | 14.7% |

| Reporting period | Ordinary income (loss) Reporting period | Year-to-date | Tax (benefit) expense Year-to-date Computed | Limited to | Less previously provided | Reporting period |
|---|---|---|---|---|---|---|
| 1st qtr. | $ 10,000 | $ 10,000 | $ 1,470 | $ -- | $ -- | $ 1,470 |
| 2nd qtr. | (80,000) | (70,000) | (10,290) | -- | 1,470 | (11,760) |
| 3rd qtr. | (100,000) | (170,000) | (24,990) | (22,000) | (10,290) | (11,710) |
| 4th qtr. | 20,000 | (150,000) | (22,000) | -- | (22,000) | -- |
| Fiscal year | $(150,000) | | | | | $(22,000) |

In the foregoing, the income tax expense (benefit) is computed by multiplying the year-to-date income or loss by the estimated annual effective rate, and then subtracting the amount of tax expense or benefit already provided in prior interim periods. It makes no difference if the current period indicates an income or a loss, assuming of course that the full-year estimated results are not being revised. However, if the cumulative loss for the interim periods to date exceeds the projected loss for the full year upon which the effective income tax benefit rate had been based, then no further tax benefits can be recorded, as is illustrated above in the benefit for the third quarter.

The foregoing examples cover most of the situations encountered in practice. The reader is referred to Appendix C of FIN 18 for additional examples.

*Operating loss occurring during an interim period.* An instance may occur in which the company expects net income for the year and incurs a net loss during one of the reporting periods. In this situation, the estimated annual effective rate, which was calculated based upon the expected net income figure, is applied to the year-to-date income or loss to arrive at year-to-date income tax expense. The amount previously provided is subtracted from the year-to-date expense to arrive at the expense for the current reporting period. If the current period operations resulted in a loss, then the period will reflect an income tax benefit.

**Income tax provision applicable to interim period nonoperating items.**

*Unusual, infrequent, or extraordinary items.* The financial statement presentation of these items and their related income tax effects are prescribed by FAS 109. Extraordinary items and discontinued operations are to be shown net of their related income tax effects. Unusual or infrequently occurring items are separately disclosed as a component of pretax income, and the income tax expense or benefit is included in the income tax expense from continuing operations. Presenting these items net of tax is strictly prohibited so the reader does not mistake them for extraordinary items.

The interim treatment accorded these items does not differ from the fiscal year-end reporting required by GAAP. However, according to APB 28, these items are not to be included in the computation of the estimated effective annual income tax rate. The opinion also requires that these items be recognized in the interim period in which they occur rather than being prorated equally throughout the year. Examples of the treatment prescribed by the opinion follow later in this section.

Recognition of the income tax effects of a loss due to any of the aforementioned situations is permitted if the benefits are expected to be realized during the year, or if they will be recognizable as a deferred income tax asset at year-end under the provisions of FAS 109.

If a situation arises where realization is not more likely than not in the period of occurrence but becomes assured in a subsequent period in the same fiscal year, the previously unrecognized income tax benefit is reported in income from continuing operations until it reduces the income tax expense to zero, with any excess reported in those other categories of income (e.g., discontinued operations) which provided a means of realization of the tax benefit.

The following examples illustrate the treatment required for reporting unusual, infrequently occurring, and extraordinary items. Again, these items are not to be used in calculating the estimated annual tax rate. For income statement presentation, the income tax expense or benefit relating to unusual or infrequently occurring items is to be included with ordinary income from continuing operations. Extraordinary items are shown net of their applicable tax provision.

The following data apply to the next two examples:

1. Irwin Industries expects fiscal year ending June 30, 2007 income to be $96,000 and net permanent differences to reduce taxable income by $25,500.
2. Irwin Industries also incurred a $30,000 extraordinary loss in the second quarter of the year.

### Example 1

In this case, assume that the loss can be carried back to prior periods and, therefore, the realization of any income tax benefit is assured. Based on the information given earlier, the estimated annual effective income tax rate can be calculated as follows:

| | |
|---|---|
| Expected pretax accounting income | $96,000 |
| Anticipated permanent differences | (25,500) |
| Expected taxable income | $70,500 |

#### Income Tax Calculation "Excluding" Extraordinary Item

| | | | | |
|---|---|---|---|---|
| $50,000 | × | .15 | = | $ 7,500 |
| 20,500 | × | .25 | = | 5,125 |
| $70,500 | | | | $12,625 |

**Effective annual rate** = 13.15% ($12,625 ÷ 96,000)

No adjustment in the estimated annual effective rate is required when the extraordinary, unusual, or infrequent item occurs. The income tax (benefit) applicable to the item is computed using the estimated fiscal year ordinary income and an analysis of the incremental impact of the extraordinary item. The method illustrated below is applicable when the company anticipates operating income for the year. When a loss is anticipated but realization of benefits of NOL carryforwards is not more likely than not, the company computes its estimated annual effective rate based on the amount of tax to be refunded from prior years. The income tax (benefit) applicable to the extraordinary, unusual, or infrequent item is then the decrease (increase) in the refund to be received.

Computation of the income tax applicable to the extraordinary, unusual, or infrequent item is as follows:

| | |
|---|---|
| Estimated pretax accounting income | $96,000 |
| Permanent differences | (25,500) |
| Extraordinary item | (30,000) |
| Expected taxable income | $40,500 |

#### Income Tax Calculation "Including" Extraordinary Item

$40,500 × .15 = $6,075

| | |
|---|---|
| Income tax "excluding" extraordinary item | $12,625 |
| Income tax "including" extraordinary item | 6,075 |
| Income tax benefit applicable to extraordinary, unusual, or infrequent item | $ 6,550 |

| | | | | | | | |
|---|---|---|---|---|---|---|---|
| | | | Income tax (benefit) applicable to | | | | |
| | | *Unusual, in-* | *Ordinary* | | *Unusual, infrequent,* | | |
| | *Ordinary* | *frequent, or* | *income (loss)* | | *or extraordinary item* | | |
| *Reporting* | *income* | *extra-* | *Reporting* | *Year-to-* | *Year-to-* | *Previously* | *Reporting* |
| *period* | *(loss)* | *ordinary item* | *period* | *date* | *date* | *provided* | *period* |
| 1st qtr. | $10,000 | $ -- | $ 1,315 | $ 1,315 | $ -- | $ -- | $ -- |
| 2nd qtr. | (20,000) | (30,000) | (2,630) | (1,315) | (6,550) | -- | (6,550) |
| 3rd qtr. | 40,000 | -- | 5,260 | 3,945 | (6,550) | (6,550) | -- |
| 4th qtr. | 66,000 | -- | 8,680 | 12,625 | (6,550) | (6,550) | -- |
| Fiscal year | $96,000 | $(30,000) | $12,625 | | | | $ (6,550) |

### Example 2

Again, assume that Irwin Industries estimates net income of $96,000 for the year with permanent differences of $25,500 which reduce taxable income. The extraordinary loss of $30,000 cannot be carried back and the ability to carry it forward is not more likely than not. Because no net deferred income tax assets exist, the only way that the loss can be deemed to be realizable is to the extent that current year ordinary income offsets the effect of the loss. As a result, realization of the loss is assured only as, and to the extent that, there is ordinary income for the year.

| | | | Income tax (benefit) applicable to | | | | |
| | | | Ordinary income (loss) | | Unusual, infrequent, or extraordinary item | | |
| Reporting period | Ordinary income (loss) | Unusual, infrequent, or extraordinary item | Reporting period | Year-to-date | Year-to-date | Previously provided | Reporting period |
|---|---|---|---|---|---|---|---|
| 1st qtr. | $ 5,000 | $ -- | $ 658 | $ 658 | $ -- | $ -- | $ -- |
| 2nd qtr. | 20,000 | (30,000) | 2,630 | 3,288 | (3,288)[a] | -- | (3,288) |
| 3rd qtr. | (10,000) | -- | (1,315) | 1,973 | (1,973)[a] | (3,288) | 1,315 |
| 4th qtr. | 81,000 | -- | 10,652 | 12,625 | (6,550)[a] | (1,973) | (4,577) |
| Fiscal year | $96,000 | $(30,000) | $12,625 | | | | $ (6,550) |

[a] *The recognition of the income tax benefit to be realized relative to the unusual, infrequent, or extraordinary item is limited to the lesser of the total income tax benefit applicable to the item or the amount available to be realized. Because realization is based upon the amount of income tax applicable to ordinary income during the period, the year-to-date figures for the income tax benefit fluctuate as the year-to-date income tax expense relative to ordinary income fluctuates. Note that at no point does the amount of the income tax benefit exceed what was calculated above as being applicable to the unusual, infrequent, or extraordinary item.*

***Discontinued operations in interim periods.*** Discontinued operations, according to APB 28, are included as significant, unusual, or extraordinary items. Therefore, the computations described for unusual, infrequent, or extraordinary items will also apply to the income (loss) from the discontinued component of the entity, including any provisions for operating gains (losses) subsequent to the measurement date.

If the decision to dispose of operations occurs in any interim period other than the first interim period, the operating income (loss) applicable to the discontinued component has already been used in computing the estimated annual effective tax rate. Therefore, a recomputation of the total tax is not required. However, the total tax is to be divided into two components.

1. That tax applicable to ordinary income (loss)
2. That tax applicable to the income (loss) from the discontinued component

This division is accomplished as follows: a revised estimated annual effective rate is calculated for the income (loss) from ordinary operations. This recomputation is then applied to the ordinary income (loss) from the preceding periods. The total income tax applicable to the discontinued component is then composed of two items.

1. The difference between the total income tax originally computed and the income tax recomputed on remaining ordinary income
2. The income tax computed on unusual, infrequent, or extraordinary items as described above

### Example

Rochelle Corporation anticipates net income of $150,000 during the fiscal year. The net permanent differences for the year will be $10,000. The company also anticipates income tax credits of $10,000 during the fiscal year. For purposes of this example, we will assume a flat statutory rate of 50%. The estimated annual effective rate is then calculated as follows:

| | |
|---|---|
| Estimated pretax income | $150,000 |
| Net permanent differences | (10,000) |
| Taxable income | 140,000 |
| Statutory rate | 50% |
| Income tax | 70,000 |
| Anticipated credits | (10,000) |
| Total estimated income tax | $ 60,000 |
| Estimated effective rate ($60,000 ÷ 150,000) | 40% |

The first two quarters of operations were as follows:

| | Ordinary income (loss) | | | Tax expense | | |
|---|---|---|---|---|---|---|
| Reporting period | Reporting period | Year-to-date | Year-to-date | Less previously provided | Reporting period |
| 1st qtr | $30,000 | $30,000 | $12,000 | $ -- | $12,000 |
| 2nd qtr. | 25,000 | 55,000 | 22,000 | 12,000 | 10,000 |

In the third quarter, Rochelle made the decision to dispose of Division X. During the third quarter, the company earned a total of $60,000. Upon reclassification of Division X's property and equipment to "held-for-sale" on its balance sheet, the company expects to incur a onetime charge to income of $75,000 and estimates that current year divisional operating losses subsequent to the disposal decision will be $20,000, all of which will be incurred in the third quarter. The company estimates revised ordinary income in the fourth quarter to be $35,000. The two components of pretax accounting income (discontinued operations and revised ordinary income) are shown below.

| | | Division X | |
|---|---|---|---|
| Reporting period | Revised ordinary income | Loss from operations | Asset reclassification |
| 1st qtr. | $ 40,000 | $(10,000) | $ -- |
| 2nd qtr. | 40,000 | (15,000) | -- |
| 3rd qtr. | 80,000 | (20,000) | (75,000) |
| 4th qtr. | 35,000 | -- | -- |
| Fiscal year | $195,000 | $(45,000) | $(75,000) |

Rochelle must now recompute the estimated annual income tax rate. Assume that all the permanent differences are related to the revised continuing operations. However, $3,300 of the tax credits were applicable to machinery used in Division X. Because of the discontinuance of operations, the credit on this machinery would not be allowed. Any recapture of prior period credits must be used as a reduction in the income tax benefit from either operations or the loss on disposal. Assume that the company must recapture $2,000 of the $3,300 investment tax credit that is related to Division X.

The recomputed estimated annual rate for continuing operations is as follows:

| | |
|---|---|
| Estimated (revised) ordinary income | $195,000 |
| Less net permanent differences | (10,000) |
| | $185,000 |
| Tax at statutory rate of 50% | $ 92,500 |
| Less anticipated credits from continuing operations | (6,700) |
| Tax provision | $ 85,800 |
| Estimated annual effective tax rate ($85,800 ÷ 195,000) | 44% |

The next step is to then apply the revised rate to the quarterly income from continuing operations as illustrated below.

|  | Ordinary income | | | Tax provision | | |
|---|---|---|---|---|---|---|
| Reporting period | Reporting period | Year-to-date | Estimated annual effective rate | Year-to-date | Less previously provided | Reporting period |
| 1st qtr. | $ 40,000 | $ 40,000 | 44% | $17,600 | $ -- | $17,600 |
| 2nd qtr. | 40,000 | 80,000 | 44% | 35,200 | 17,600 | 17,600 |
| 3rd qtr. | 80,000 | 160,000 | 44% | 70,400 | 35,200 | 35,200 |
| 4th qtr. | 35,000 | 195,000 | 44% | 85,800 | 70,400 | 15,400 |
| Fiscal year | $195,000 | | | | | $85,800 |

The tax benefit applicable to the operating loss from discontinued operations and the loss from the asset reclassification and remeasurement must now be calculated. The first two quarters are calculated on a differential basis as shown below.

|  | Tax applicable to ordinary income | | Tax (benefit) expense |
|---|---|---|---|
| Reporting period | Previously reported | Recomputed (above) | applicable to Division X |
| 1st qtr. | $12,000 | $17,600 | $ (5,600) |
| 2nd qtr. | 10,000 | 17,600 | (7,600) |
|  |  |  | $ (13,200) |

The only calculation remaining applies to the third quarter tax benefit pertaining to the operating loss and the loss on reclassification of the assets of the discontinued component. The calculation of this amount is made based on the revised estimate of annual ordinary income both including and excluding the effects of the Division X losses. This is shown below.

|  | Loss from operations of Division X | Asset reclassification |
|---|---|---|
| Estimated annual income from continuing operations | $195,000 | $195,000 |
| Net permanent differences | (10,000) | (10,000) |
| Loss from Division X operations | (45,000) | -- |
| Provision for loss on reclassification of Division X assets | -- | (75,000) |
| Total | $140,000 | $110,000 |
| Tax at the statutory rate of 50% | $ 70,000 | $ 55,000 |
| Anticipated credits (from continuing operations) | (6,700) | (6,700) |
| Recapture of previously recognized tax credits as a result of disposal | -- | 2,000 |
| Taxes after effect of Division X losses | 63,300 | 50,300 |
| Taxes computed on estimated income before the effect of Division X losses | 85,800 | 85,800 |
| Tax benefit applicable to Division X | (22,500) | (35,500) |
| Amounts allocable to quarters one and two ($5,600 + $7,600) | (13,200) | -- |
| Tax benefit to be recognized in the third quarter | $ (9,300) | $(35,500) |

The quarterly tax provisions can be summarized as follows:

|  | Pretax income (loss) | | | Tax (benefit) applicable to | | |
|---|---|---|---|---|---|---|
| Reporting period | Continuing operations | Operations of Division X | Loss on asset reclassification | Continuing operations | Operations of Division X | Loss on asset reclassification |
| 1st qtr. | $ 40,000 | $(10,000) | $ -- | $17,600 | $ (5,600) | $ -- |
| 2nd qtr. | 40,000 | (15,000) | -- | 17,600 | (7,600) | -- |
| 3rd qtr. | 80,000 | (20,000) | (75,000) | 35,200 | (9,300) | (35,500) |
| 4th qtr. | 35,000 | -- | -- | 15,400 | -- | -- |
| Fiscal year | $195,000 | $(45,000) | $(75,000) | $85,800 | $(22,500) | $(35,500) |

The following income statement shows the proper financial statement presentation of these discontinued operations. The notes to the statement indicate which items are to be included in the calculation of the annual estimated rate.

**Income Statement**
(FIN 18, Appendix D)

| | | |
|---|---:|---:|
| Net sales* | | $xxxx |
| Other income* | | xxx |
| | | xxxx |
| Costs and expenses | | |
| Cost of sales* | $xxxx | |
| Selling, general, and administrative expenses* | xxx | |
| Interest expense* | xx | |
| Other deductions* | xx | |
| Unusual items* | xxx | |
| Infrequently occurring items* | xxx | xxxx |
| Income (loss) from continuing operations before income taxes and other items listed below | | xxxx |
| Provision for income taxes (benefit)** | | xxx |
| Income (loss) from continuing operations before items listed below | | xxxx |
| Discontinued operations: | | |
| Income (loss) from operations of discontinued Division X (less applicable income taxes of $xxxx) | xxxx | |
| Income (loss) on reclassification of assets of Division X to held-for-sale, (less applicable taxes of $xxxx) | xxxx | xxxx |
| Income (loss) before extraordinary items and cumulative effect of a change in accounting principle | | xxxx |
| Extraordinary items (less applicable income taxes of $xxxx) | | xxxx |
| Cumulative effect on prior years of a change in accounting principle (less applicable income taxes of $xxxx)*** | | xxxx |
| Net income (loss) | | $xxxx |

\*    *Components of ordinary income (loss).*

\*\*   *Consists of total income taxes (benefit) applicable to ordinary income (loss), unusual items and infrequently occurring items.*

\*\*\* *This amount is shown net of income taxes. Although the income taxes are generally disclosed (as illustrated), this is not required.*

# 18 PENSIONS AND OTHER POSTRETIREMENT BENEFITS

## PERSPECTIVE AND ISSUES

This chapter focuses on accounting for postretirement benefits, including single-employer and multiemployer plans, defined benefit pension plans, defined contribution pension plans, and postretirement benefit plans other than pensions, such as those that help fund retiree costs of health care benefits. The accounting for such arrangements has historically been difficult, in large part because the accounting standard setters, influenced by preparers and issuers, have seen fit to include a variety of "smoothing" features that—whatever merits they may have—did necessitate the use of various accruals and deferrals, and the reporting of certain elements within other comprehensive income. Thus, presentation of benefit plan expense and related items has involved lengthy and complex footnotes, and generally at least some "off the financial statement" measurements. Longstanding dissatisfaction with such accounting practices, coupled with FASB's stated goal of converging its standards with those of IASB, is expected to culminate in a revised standard for pension and other postretirement benefit plan accounting that will fully incorporate benefit plan assets and liabilities into the sponsor's statement of financial position, and that will result in periodic benefit plan expense measurement devoid of any "smoothing" devices.

While elimination of all accounting artifacts is the ultimate goal (and one expected to be realized in the near to intermediate term), an interim solution has been provided by FAS 158, which requires, for the first time, that the full extent of over- or underfunding of defined benefit pension plans, and that a lesser measure of the underfunding of other postretirement benefit plans, be displayed on the face of the statement of financial position. For many plan sponsors, this has had the unwelcome effect of reducing or even eliminating stockholders' equity. This outcome was caused by former GAAP provisions that effectively concealed (in the financial statements proper) the reporting entities' obligation for postretirement promises made to employees, relegating such information to the financial statement footnotes.

The provisions of all extant GAAP for pension and other employee benefit plans are explored in detail in the following materials. The expected future developments will also be noted.

FAS 87 specifies the accrual basis of accounting for pension costs. At the time of its narrowly endorsed issuance in 1985, FASB stated that it was not likely to be the final step in the evolution of pension accounting, which it characterized as being in a "transitional stage." FASB acknowledged in the standard that it had made a political compromise when it stated that "recognition in financial statements of [pension assets and liabilities] in their entirety would be too great a change from past practice."

What may have been intended as a transitional stage, however, is now over 23 years old, with the end not yet clearly in sight. Today, decades later, the accounting model remains, in many ways unchanged, although FAS 158 does for the first time require that there be display within the statement of financial position of the funded status of pension and other postretirement benefit plans. The impact of the mandated "smoothing" of gains and losses, the subjective selection of expected asset returns and discount rate, the use of overfunding to affect the entity's reported earnings, and the complexity of information presented in the footnote disclosures, all remain concerns.

FAS 87 continued the three primary and controversial characteristics of its predecessor, APB 8. These are

1.  Delayed recognition (changes are not recognized immediately but are subsequently recognized in a gradual and systematic way)
2.  Reporting net cost (various expense and income items are aggregated and reported as one net amount)
3.  Offsetting assets and liabilities (assets and liabilities are sometimes shown net)

Estimates and averages may be used as long as material differences do not result. Explicit assumptions and estimates of future events must be used for each specified variable included in pension costs and disclosed in the notes to the financial statements.

FAS 87 focuses directly on the terms of the plan to assist in the recognition of compensation cost over the service period of the employees. Whereas the effect of underfunding of defined benefit pension plans was only reflected in plan sponsors' balance sheets to a limited extent, and only if certain conditions occurred, under FAS 87, under recently-imposed FAS 158 the full amount of under- and overfunding of pension plans is to be reported in the statement of financial position. Whereas the underfunding of other defined benefit postretirement plans was not, under provisions of FAS 106, reported in the sponsoring entity's balance sheet, FAS 158 now requires that this be partially or fully reported. These two changes are the major (but not only) improvements flowing from the amendments to FAS 87 and FAS 106 that have been made by FAS 158.

The principal emphasis of FAS 87 is the present value of the pension obligation and the fair value of plan assets. Fair value is addressed, most recently and comprehensively, by FAS 157 and is fully discussed in Chapter 6. The main accounting issues revolve around the expense to recognize on the income statement and the liability to be accrued on the balance sheet. As noted above, the periodic expense to be recognized under current GAAP is a modified version of the actual economic consequence of the employer's commitment to pay future benefits, because of the substantial use of smoothing. (Over the full time horizon, which is measured in decades, all expense does of course get recognized in results of operations.) Also, the amount of liability to be accrued under FAS 87 was previously substantially different from, and less than, the real obligation, but this has been largely resolved by FAS 158, so that the balance sheet will now much more faithfully represent the sponsor's actual obligation, in present value terms.

FAS 88 is closely related to FAS 87. It establishes standards to be followed by sponsors of defined benefit pension plans when obligations are settled, plans are curtailed, or benefits are terminated.

Although there are some major differences in terminology and measurement, other postretirement benefits (commonly referred to as OPEB) accounting basically follows the fundamental framework established for defined benefit pension accounting and applies to all forms of postretirement benefits other than pensions. In most cases, the main focus is on postretirement health care benefits, since that is by far the most costly commitment made by employers to retirees. FAS 106 considers OPEB to be a form of deferred compensation and requires accrual accounting. The terms of the individual contract govern the accrual of the employer's obligation for deferred compensation and the cost is attributed to employee service periods until full eligibility to receive benefits is attained. The employer's obligation for OPEB is fully accrued when the employee attains full eligibility for all expected benefits.

For reasons explained later in this chapter, display in the balance sheet of the effects of underfunding of OPEB was not required by FAS 106. As amended by FAS 158, however, some or all of the underfunded postretirement benefit obligations will now be displayed in the statement of financial position.

FAS 132, *Employers' Disclosures about Pensions and Other Postretirement Benefits*, revised and standardized these disclosures by using a separate but parallel format, eliminating less useful information, requiring some additional data deemed useful by analysts, and allowing some aggregation of presentation. FAS 132 did not alter the recognition and measurement aspects of FAS 87, 88, and 106, but it did amend the disclosure requirements of those standards. FAS 132(R) subsequently added further disclosure requirements, and FAS 158 made yet further changes. Amended FAS 132(R) forms the basis for the discussion in this chapter.

The complex accounting and disclosure requirements under the aforementioned standards have proved to be a source of frustration for even seasoned analysts of financial statements. In addition, dramatic changes in the values of investments held by defined benefit plans—including both the large value increases of the late 1990s and the subsequent drastic declines of the early 2000s—coupled with sometimes aggressive assumptions about expected returns and discount rates, which were slow to be adjusted as market conditions changed, made such information of sometimes doubtful usefulness. While of course deliberate misapplication of any of these standards would be a GAAP departure, the permitted and indeed necessary use of numerous assumptions does create the opportunity for management to deliberately influence the entity's reported earnings.

FASB's thoroughgoing review of accounting for pension and other postretirement benefits began in late 2005. The first phase of this project was intended to make pension and postretirement benefits information more useful and transparent for investors, creditors, employees, retirees, donors, and other users. The changes wrought by FAS 158 became effective on a phased basis, with the final phase-in occurring for years ending after December 15, 2008. While the changes imposed by FAS 158 have brought improvements to the statement of financial position, however, the FAS 87/106 requirements pertaining to income statement recognition of expense remain intact.

In the second, longer-term phase of this project, FASB expects to comprehensively consider a variety of issues related to the accounting for postretirement benefits. These include how the various elements that affect the cost of postretirement benefits (e.g., prior service costs, actuarial gains and losses) are best recognized and displayed in either earnings or other comprehensive income; how to measure the entity's benefit obligations, including whether more or different guidance should be provided about assumptions used in measuring benefit costs; and whether postretirement benefit trusts should be consolidated by the plan sponsor (i.e., treated as VIEs). Additional improvements to the financial statement disclosures about plan assets are also being considered.

| Sources of GAAP | | | |
|---|---|---|---|
| *APB* | *FAS* | *EITF* | *FSP* |
| 12, 16, 28, 30 | 5, 87, 88, 106, 112, 130, 132(R), 141(R), 144, 149, 157, 158,160 | 88-1, 88-5, 90-3, 91-7, 92-13, 93-3, 03-2, 03-4, 05-05, 06-4, 06-10, D-36 | FAS 106-2, FAS 158-1, APB 18-1 |

## DEFINITIONS OF TERMS

**Accrued pension cost.** Cumulative net pension cost accrued in excess of the employer's contributions.

**Accumulated benefit obligation.** Actuarial present value of benefits (whether vested or nonvested) attributed by the pension benefit formula to employee service rendered before a specified date and based on employee service and compensation (if applicable) prior to that date. The accumulated benefit obligation differs from the projected benefit obligation in that it includes no assumption about future compensation levels. For plans with flat-benefit or no-pay-related pension benefit formulas, the accumulated benefit obligation and the projected benefit obligation are the same.

**Accumulated postretirement benefit obligation.** The actuarial present value of benefits attributed to employee service rendered to a particular date. Prior to an employee's full eligibility date, the accumulated postretirement benefit obligation as of a particular date for an employee is the portion of the expected postretirement benefit obligation attributed to that employee's service rendered to that date. On and after the full eligibility date, the accumulated and expected postretirement benefit obligations for an employee are the same.

**Actual return on plan assets component (of net periodic pension cost).** Difference between fair value of plan assets at the end of the period and the fair value at the beginning of the period, adjusted for employer contributions and payments of benefits during the period.

**Actuarial present value.** Value, as of a specified date, of an amount or series of amounts payable or receivable thereafter, with each amount adjusted to reflect (1) the time value of money (through discounts for interest) and (2) the probability of payment (by means of decrements for events such as death, disability, withdrawal, or retirement) between the specified date and the expected date of payment.

**Amortization.** Usually refers to the process of reducing a recognized liability systematically by recognizing revenues or reducing a recognized asset systematically by recognizing expenses or costs. In pension accounting, amortization is also used to refer to the systematic recognition in net pension cost over several periods of previously unrecognized amounts, including unrecognized prior service cost and unrecognized net gain or loss.

**Annuity contract.** Irrevocable contract in which an insurance company[1] unconditionally undertakes a legal obligation to provide specified benefits to specific individuals in return for a fixed consideration or premium. It involves the transfer of significant risk from the employer to the insurance company. Participating annuity contracts provide that the purchaser (either the plan or the employer) may participate in the experience of the insurance company. The insurance company ordinarily pays dividends to the purchaser. If the substance of a participating annuity contract is such that the employer remains subject to all or most of the risks and rewards associated with the benefit obligation covered or the assets transferred to the insurance company, the purchase of the contract does not constitute a settlement.

**Assumptions.** Estimates of the occurrence of future events affecting pension costs, such as mortality, withdrawal, disablement and retirement, changes in compensation and national pension benefits, and discount rates to reflect the time value of money.

**Attribution.** Process of assigning pension benefits or cost to periods of employee service.

**Attribution period.** The period of an employee's service to which the expected postretirement benefit obligation for that employee is assigned. The beginning of the attribution period is the employee's date of hire unless the plan's benefit formula grants credit only for service from a later date, in which case the beginning of the attribution period is generally the beginning of that credited service period. The end of the attribution period is the full eligibility date. Within the attribution period, an equal amount of the expected postretirement benefit obligation is attributed to each year of service unless the plan's benefit formula attributes a disproportionate share of the expected postretirement benefit obligation to employees' early years of service. In that case, benefits are attributed in accordance with the plan's benefit formula.

**Career-average-pay formula.** Benefit formula that bases benefits on the employee's compensation over the entire period of service with the employer. A career-average-pay plan is a plan with such a formula.

**Contributory plan.** Pension plan under which employees contribute part of the cost. In some contributory plans, employees wishing to be covered must contribute. In other contributory plans, employee contributions result in increased benefits.

**Curtailment.** Event that significantly reduces the expected years of future service of present employees or eliminates for a significant number of employees the accrual of defined benefits for some or all of their future services. Curtailments include (1) termination of employee's services earlier than expected, which may or may not involve closing a facility or discontinuing a segment of a business and (2) termination or suspension of a plan so that employees do not earn additional defined benefits for future services. In the latter situation, future service may be counted toward vesting of benefits accumulated based on past services.

---

[1] *If the insurance company is controlled by the employer or there is any reasonable doubt that the insurance company will meet its obligation under the contract, the purchase of the contract does not constitute a settlement for purposes of FAS 88.*

**Defined benefit pension plan.** Pension plan that defines an amount of pension benefit to be provided, usually as a function of one or more factors such as age, years of service, or compensation. Any pension plan that is not a defined contribution pension plan is, for purposes of FAS 87, a defined benefit pension plan.

**Defined contribution pension plan.** Plan that provides pension benefits in return for services rendered, provides an individual account for each participant, and specifies how contributions to the individual's account are to be determined instead of specifying the amount of benefits the individual is to receive. Under a defined contribution pension plan, the benefits a participant will receive depend solely on the amount contributed to the participant's account, the returns earned on investments of those contributions, and forfeitures of other participants' benefits that may be allocated to such participant's account.

**Expected long-term rate of return on plan assets.** Assumption as to the rate of return on plan assets reflecting the average rate of earnings expected on the funds invested or to be invested to provide for the benefits included in the projected benefit obligation.

**Expected postretirement benefit obligation.** The actuarial present value as of a particular date of the benefits expected to be paid to or for an employee, the employee's beneficiaries, and any covered dependents pursuant to the terms of the postretirement benefit plan.

**Expected return on plan assets.** Amount calculated as a basis for determining the extent of delayed recognition of the effects of changes in the fair value of assets. The expected return on plan assets is determined based on the expected long-term rate of return on plan assets and the market-related value of plan assets.

**Explicit approach to assumptions.** Approach under which each significant assumption used reflects the best estimate of the plan's future experience solely with respect to that assumption.

**Fair value.** Amount that a pension or postretirement plan could reasonably expect to receive for an investment in a current sale between a willing buyer and a willing seller (i.e., in other than a forced or liquidation sale). Fair value of a plan investment is to be measured by its price in an active market, if available. If no active market exists for the investment, an active market price for an investment with similar characteristics may be used. Finally, if neither market exists, FAS 87 and FAS 106 permit the use of forecasted expected cash flows. FAS 149 clarifies that because these standards preceded the issuance of CON 7, the term "expected cash flows" as used to estimate fair value in this context does not require the use of the probability weighted expected cash flow model that FAS 7 introduced (although that model is based on sound estimation principles and is permitted to be used).

**Final-pay formula.** A plan with a benefit formula that bases benefits on the employee's compensation over a specified number of years near the end of the employee's service period or on the employee's highest compensation periods. For example, a plan might provide annual pension benefits equal to 1% of the employee's average salary for the last five years (or the highest consecutive five years) for each year of service.

**Flat-benefit formula.** A plan with a benefit formula that bases benefits on a fixed amount per year of service, such as $20 of monthly retirement income for each year of credited service.

**Full eligibility (for benefits).** The status of an employee having reached the employee's full eligibility date. Full eligibility for benefits is achieved by meeting specified age, service, or age and service requirements of the postretirement benefit plan.

**Full eligibility date.** The date at which an employee has rendered all of the service necessary to have earned the right to receive all of the benefits expected to be received by that employee (including any beneficiaries and dependents expected to receive benefits). Determination of the full eligibility date is affected by plan terms that provide incremental benefits expected to be received by or on behalf of an employee for additional years of service, unless those incremental benefits are trivial. Determination of the full eligibility date is not affected by plan terms that define when benefit payments commence or by an employee's current dependency status.

**Fund.** Used as a verb, to pay over to a funding agency (as to fund future pension benefits or to fund pension cost). Used as a noun, assets accumulated in the hands of a funding agency for the purpose of meeting pension benefits when they become due.

**Funding policy.** Program regarding the amounts and timing of contributions by the employer(s), participants, and any other sources (for example, state subsidies or federal grants) to provide the benefits a pension plan specifies.

**Gain or loss.** Change in the value of either the projected benefit obligation or the plan assets resulting from experience different from that assumed or from a change in an actuarial assumption. See also **Unrecognized net gain or loss**.

**Gain or loss component (of net periodic pension cost).** Sum of (1) the difference between the actual return on plan assets and the expected return on plan assets and (2) the amortization of the unrecognized net gain or loss from previous periods. The gain or loss component is the net effect of delayed recognition of gains and losses (the net change in the unrecognized net gain or loss) except that it does not include changes in the projected benefit obligation occurring during the period and deferred for later recognition.

**Interest cost component (of net periodic pension cost).** Increase in the projected benefit obligation due to passage of time.

**Market-related value of plan assets.** Balance used to calculate the expected return on plan assets. Market-related value can be either fair value or a calculated value that recognizes changes in fair value in a systematic and rational manner over not more than five years. Different ways of calculating market-related value may be used for different classes of assets, but the manner of determining market-related value must be applied consistently from year to year for each asset class.

**Measurement date.** Date at which plan assets and obligations are measured.

**Mortality rate.** Proportion of the number of deaths in a specified group to the number living at the beginning of the period in which the deaths occur. Actuaries use mortality tables, which show death rates for each age, in estimating the amount of pension benefits that will become payable.

**Net periodic pension cost.** Amount recognized in an employer's financial statements as the cost of a pension plan for a period. Components of net periodic pension cost are service cost, interest cost, actual return on plan assets, gain or loss, amortization of unrecognized prior service cost, and amortization of the unrecognized net obligation or asset existing at the date of initial application of FAS 87. The term "net periodic pension cost" is used instead of "net pension expense" because part of the cost recognized in a period may be capitalized as part of an asset such as inventory.

**Plan amendment.** Change in terms of an existing plan or the initiation of a new plan. A plan amendment may increase benefits, including those attributed to years of service already rendered. See also **Retroactive benefits**.

**Postemployment benefits.** Benefits provided to former and inactive employees after employment but before retirement. Postemployment benefits include, but are not limited to, salary continuation, supplemental unemployment benefits, severance benefits, disability-related benefits (including workers' compensation), job training and counseling, and continuation of benefits such as health care benefits and life insurance coverage.

**Postretirement benefits.** All forms of benefits, other than retirement income, provided by an employer to retirees. Those benefits may be defined in terms of specified benefits, such as health care, tuition assistance, or legal services, that are provided to retirees as the need for those benefits arises or they may be defined in terms of monetary amounts that become payable on the occurrence of a specified event, such as life insurance benefits.

**Prepaid pension cost.** Cumulative employer contributions in excess of accrued net pension cost.

**Prior service cost.** Cost of retroactive benefits granted in a plan amendment. See also **Unrecognized prior service cost**.

**Projected benefit obligation.** Actuarial present value as of a date of all benefits attributed by the pension benefit formula to employee service rendered prior to that date. The projected benefit obligation is measured using assumptions as to future compensation levels if the pension benefit formula is based on those future compensation levels (pay-related, final-pay, final-average-pay, or career-average-pay plans).

**Retroactive benefits.** Benefits granted in a plan amendment (or initiation) that are attributed by the pension benefit formula to employee services rendered in periods prior to the amendment. The cost of the retroactive benefits is referred to as prior service cost.

**Service.** Employment taken into consideration under a pension plan. Years of employment before the inception of a plan constitute an employee's past service. Years thereafter are classified in relation to the particular actuarial valuation being made or discussed. Years of employment (including past service) prior to the date of a particular valuation constitute prior service.

**Service cost component (of net periodic pension cost).** Actuarial present value of benefits attributed by the pension benefit formula to services rendered by employees during the period. The service cost component is a portion of the projected benefit obligation and is unaffected by the funded status of the plan.

**Settlement.** Transaction that (1) is an irrevocable action, (2) relieves the employer (or the plan) of primary responsibility for a pension benefit obligation, and (3) eliminates significant risks related to the obligation and the assets used to effect the settlement. Examples include making lump-sum cash payments to plan participants in exchange for their rights to receive specified pension benefits and purchasing nonparticipating annuity contracts to cover vested benefits. A transaction must meet all of the above three criteria to constitute a settlement.

**Substantive plan.** The terms of the postretirement benefit plan as understood by an employer that provides postretirement benefits and the employees who render services in exchange for those benefits. The substantive plan is the basis for the accounting for that exchange transaction. In some situations an employer's cost-sharing policy, as evidenced by past practice or by communication of intended changes to a plan's cost-sharing provisions, or a past practice of regular increases in certain monetary benefits may indicate that the substantive plan differs from the existing written plan.

**Transition obligation.** The unrecognized amount, as of the date FAS 106 is initially applied, of (1) the accumulated postretirement benefit obligation in excess of (2) the fair value of plan assets plus any recognized accrued postretirement benefit cost or less any recognized prepaid postretirement benefit cost.

**Unfunded accumulated benefit obligation.** Excess of the accumulated benefit obligation over plan assets.

**Unfunded accumulated postretirement benefit obligation.** The accumulated postretirement benefit obligation in excess of the fair value of plan assets.

**Unrecognized net gain or loss.** Cumulative net gain (loss) that has not been recognized as a part of net periodic pension cost. While not yet included in earnings, under requirements established by FAS 158 these will be displayed in the balance sheet once realized. Thus, these will no longer be unrecognized for balance sheet display purposes. See **Gain or loss**.

**Unrecognized prior service cost.** Portion of prior service cost that has not been recognized as a part of net periodic pension cost. While not yet included in earnings, under requirements established by FAS 158 this will be displayed in the balance sheet once realized (i.e., incurred). Prior service cost will no longer be unrecognized for balance sheet display purposes.

## CONCEPTS, RULES, AND EXAMPLES

The principal objective of FAS 87 is to measure the compensation cost associated with employees' benefits and to recognize that cost over the employees' service period. This statement is concerned only with the accounting aspects of pension costs. The funding (assets set aside to meet future payment obligations) of the benefits is not covered and is considered to be a financial management matter.

When an entity provides benefits that can be estimated in advance to its retired employees and their beneficiaries, the arrangement is a pension plan. The accounting for most types of retirement plans is covered by FAS 87 and 88. These plans include unfunded, insured, trust fund, defined contribution and defined benefit plans, and deferred compensation contracts, if equivalent. Independent deferred profit sharing plans and pension payments to selected employees on a case-by-case basis are not considered pension plans. The typical plan is written and the amount of benefits can be determined by reference to the associated documents. The plan and its provisions can also be implied, however, from unwritten but established past practices.

The establishment of a pension plan represents a commitment to employees that is of a long-term nature. Although some companies manage their own plans, this commitment usually takes the form of contributions made to an independent trustee. These contributions are used by the trustee to invest in plan assets of various types (treasury bonds and bills, certificates of deposit, annuities, marketable securities, corporate bonds, etc.). The plan assets are expected to generate a return generally in the form of interest, dividends, and/or appreciation in asset value. The return on the plan assets (and occasionally the proceeds from their liquidation) provides the trustee with cash to pay the benefits to which the employees are entitled. These benefits, in turn, are defined by the plan's benefit formula. The benefit formula incorporates many factors including employee compensation, employee service longevity, employee age, etc. and is considered to provide the best indication of pension obligations and costs. It is used as the basis for determining the pension cost recognized in the financial statements each fiscal year.

### Net Periodic Pension Cost

A pension plan creates long-term obligations. It is assumed that a company will continue to provide retirement benefits well into the future. The accounting for the plan's costs is reflected in the financial statements and these amounts are not discretionary. All pension costs incurred are recognized as expenses but, under the smoothing approach taken by FAS 87 and FAS 106, recognition of some elements of pension and postretirement benefit expense may be partially deferred until later periods.

Because pension obligations are long-term liabilities, there was a consensus of opinion, when FAS 87 was being written, that some current period effects should not be fully recognized in earnings as they occurred. Short-term fluctuations in interest rates, market prices of plan investments, and other factors could, if recognized as incurred, cause material swings in the net periodic pension cost and net income to be reported in the financial statements of the employer/sponsor. It was thought that such fluctuations would quite likely be offset by reversals in subsequent periods—for example, market declines in one period would be followed by market upward movements in later periods.

This possibility has traditionally been cited to justify the use of smoothing techniques in order to recognize certain of these changes in a systematic and rational manner (e.g., by amortization) instead of recognizing them immediately. This smoothing aspect has long been the object of criticism, and FASB has been active in its pursuit of a project that could curtail or eliminate that practice. As a first step, FAS 158 does increase on-balance-sheet disclosure of funding status and of the benefit expense elements subject to deferred recognition, but does not eliminate the practice of expense smoothing itself.

The benefits earned and costs recognized over the employees' service periods are computed by reference to the pension plan's benefit formula. Net periodic pension cost consists of the sum of the following six components:

1. Service cost
2. Interest cost on projected benefit obligation
3. Actual return on plan assets
4. Gain or loss
5. Amortization of unrecognized prior service cost
6. Amortization of unrecognized net assets or net obligation existing at date of initial application of FAS 87 (this last item is of historical interest only, since implementation of this standard was required in the late 1980s)

Pension plans may or may not be sensitive to future salary progression. The obligation, in present value terms, for future pension payments including the effects of future compensation adjustments is referred to as the *projected* benefit obligation, while the obligation computed without regard to salary progression is called the *accumulated* benefit obligation. For those plans that do not depend on salary progression, the accumulated and the projected benefit obligations are the same.

In order to calculate the net periodic pension cost, the accumulated benefit obligation (ABO) and the projected benefit obligation (PBO) must both be computed. Both of these obligation amounts are actuarially determined using the actuarial present value of benefits earned that are attributable to services rendered by the employee to the date of the computation. Under the provisions of most pension plans, PBO provides a more relevant measure of the estimated cost of the benefits to be paid upon retirement. This is because the benefit formula set forth in the plan normally results in increases in future pension benefits based on increases in the employee's compensation.

Pay-related, final-pay, or career-average-pay plans are examples of plans where future payments are based on future compensation levels. These plans measure benefits based on service performed to date but include assumptions as to future compensation increases, staff turnover rates, etc. In non-pay-related or flat-benefit plans, both obligations (ABO and PBO) are the same.

The following discussion employs a component-by-component analysis, providing a series of examples that cumulatively build to the comprehensive summary of net periodic pension costs and the sample pension disclosures that follow. Key amounts are cross-referenced between examples using parenthesized lowercase letters [(a), (b), etc.]. In accordance with accounting convention, obligations and increases thereto are presented in parentheses.

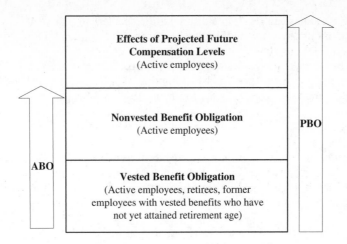

**Example**

| | *January 1, 2008* |
|---|---|
| Accumulated benefit obligation | $(1,500) |
| Progression of salary and wages | (400) |
| Projected benefit obligation | $(1,900) |

The expected progression of salary and wages is added to the accumulated benefit obligation to arrive at the projected benefit obligation. These amounts are provided by the actuary in a pension plan report.

Computation of the amounts to be presented on the balance sheet requires the determination of plan assets. Plan assets include contributions made by the employer that sponsors the pension plan (sponsor) plus the net earnings on the plan's investments (dividends, interest, and asset appreciation, less asset depreciation), less benefits paid to retired participants.

**Example**

| | |
|---|---|
| Plan assets, January 1, 2008 | $1,376 |
| Investment earnings during 2008 | 158 |
| Sponsor's contributions during 2008 | 145 |
| Benefits paid to retired participants | (160) |
| Plan assets, December 31, 2008 | $1,519 |

**Service costs.** This component of net periodic pension cost is the actuarial present value of benefits attributed during the current period. Under FAS 87, the plan's benefit formula is the key to attributing benefits to employee service periods. In most cases, this attribution is straightforward.

If the benefit formula is ambiguous, the accounting for pension service costs must be based on the substantive plan. In some cases, this means that if an employer has committed to make future amendments to provide benefits greater than those written in the plan, that commitment is the basis for the accounting. The relevant facts regarding that implicit commitment are disclosed.

Employers use pensions as a compensation tool to aid in the recruitment and long-term retention of employees. In order to provide incentives for employees to continue their employment with the company over time, plan participants' rights to receive present or future pension benefits are often conditioned on continued employment with the employer/plan sponsor for a specified period. As the conditions are satisfied, the employee is said to "vest" in that portion of the future benefits that become unconditional.

Vesting schedules can result in a disproportionate share of plan benefits being attributed to later years of employment. In this situation, instead of applying the benefit formula, proportions or ratios are used to attribute projected benefits to years of service in a manner that more equitably reflects the substance of timing of earning of the employee benefits. Normally, the actuary accomplishes this by attributing plan benefits to completed years of service by multiplying total benefits by the following ratio:

$$\frac{\text{Number of years of service completed by the employee}}{\text{Number of years of service required to be completed for full vesting}}$$

Certain types of benefits are not includable in vested benefits (e.g., death or disability benefit) and, thus, require a different allocation formula to attribute them to years of service. If the plan's benefit formula does not specify how to relate the benefit to years of service, the following formula is used by the actuary to attribute the benefits to years of service:

$$\frac{\text{Number of completed years of service}}{\text{Total projected years of service}}$$

FAS 87 actuarial assumptions must reflect plan continuation, must be consistent as to future economic expectations, and must be the best estimate in regard to each individual assumption. It is not acceptable to determine that the aggregate assumptions are reasonable if any of the individual assumptions are unreasonable.

The discount rate used in the calculation of service costs is the rate at which benefits could be settled. Examples include those rates in current annuity contracts, those published by the Pension Benefit Guaranty Corporation (PBGC), and those that reflect returns on high-quality, fixed-income investments.

Future compensation is considered in the calculation of the service cost component to the extent specified by the benefit formula. To the degree considered in the benefit formula, future compensation includes changes due to advancement, longevity, inflation, etc. Indirect effects, such as predictable bonuses based on compensation levels, and automatic increases specified by the plan also need to be considered. The effect of retroactive amendments is included in the calculation when the employer has contractually agreed to them. Service costs attributed during the period increase both the ABO and PBO since they result in additional benefits to be payable in the future.

**Example**

|  | *January 1, 2008* | *2008 Service cost* |
|---|---|---|
| Accumulated benefit obligation | $(1,500) | $ (90) |
| Progression of salary and wages | (400) | (24) |
| Projected benefit obligation | $(1,900) | $(114) (a)* |

\* *Component of net periodic pension cost*

The current period service cost component is found in the actuarial report.

**Interest on PBO.** The PBO is a discounted amount. It represents the discounted actuarial present value, at the date of the valuation, of all benefits attributed under the plan's formula to employee service rendered prior to that date. Each year, when the actuary calculates the end-of-year PBO, it is one year closer to the year in which the benefits attributed in prior years will be paid to participants. Consequently, the present value of those previously attributed benefits will have increased to take into account the time value of money. This annual increase, computed by multiplying the assumed settlement discount rate times the PBO at the beginning of the year, increases net periodic pension cost and PBO.

Since this "interest" cost is accounted for as part of pension cost it is not treated as interest for the purposes of computing capitalized interest under FAS 34.

**Example**

|  | January 1, 2008 | 2008 Service cost | 2008 Interest cost |
|---|---|---|---|
| Accumulated benefit obligation | $(1,500) | $ (90) | $(120) |
| Progression of salary and wages | (400) | (24) | (32) |
| Projected benefit obligation | $(1,900) | $(114) (a)* | $(152) (b)* |

\* *Component of net periodic pension cost*

The interest cost component is calculated by multiplying the start of the year obligation balances by an assumed 8% settlement rate. This amount is found in the actuarial report.

**Benefits paid.** Benefits paid to retirees are deducted from the above to arrive at the end of the year balance sheet amounts of the accumulated benefit obligation and the projected benefit obligation.

**Example**

|  | January 1, 2008 | 2008 Service cost | 2008 Interest cost | 2008 Benefits paid | December 31, 2008 |
|---|---|---|---|---|---|
| Accumulated benefit obligation | $(1,500) | $ (90) | $(120) | $160 | $(1,550) |
| Progression of salary and wages | (400) | (24) | (32) | -- | (456) |
| Projected benefit obligation | $(1,900) | $(114) (a) | $(152) (b) | $160 | $(2,006) |

Benefits of $160 were paid to retirees during the current year. This amount is found in the report of the pension plan trustee.

**Actual return on plan assets.** This component is the difference between the fair value of the plan assets at the end of the period and the fair value of the plan assets at the beginning of the period adjusted for contributions and payments during the period. Another way to express the result is that it is the net (realized and unrealized) appreciation and depreciation of plan assets plus earnings from the plan assets for the period.

**Example**

|  | January 1, 2008 | 2008 Actual return on plan assets | 2008 Sponsor funding | 2008 Benefits paid | December 31, 2008 |
|---|---|---|---|---|---|
| Plan assets | $1,376 | $158 (c)* | $145 | $(160) | $1,519 |

\* *Component of net periodic pension cost*

The actual return on plan assets of $158, cash deposited with the trustee of $145, and benefits paid ($160) are amounts found in the report of the pension plan trustee. These items increase the plan assets to $1,519 at the end of the year. The actual return on plan assets is adjusted, however, to the expected long-term rate (9% assumed) of return on plan assets ($1,376 × 9% = $124). The difference ($158 – $124 = $34) is a return on asset adjustment and is deferred as a gain (loss). The return on asset adjustment is a component of net periodic pension cost and is discussed in detail in the following section.

Under FAS 87, it was permissible to ascertain the fair value of plan assets as of a date other than the balance sheet date—but no greater than three months prior to year-end. This was a practical concession in recognition of the delay often encountered in receiving actuarial reports. However, FAS 158 deleted this provision, and requires that measurements of defined benefit plan assets and obligations must (with limited exceptions) be as of the balance sheet date of the respective reporting entity.

**Gain or loss.** Gains (losses) result from (1) changes in plan assumptions, (2) changes in the amount of plan assets, and (3) changes in the amount of the projected benefit obligation. As discussed previously, even though these gains or losses are economic events that impact the sponsor's obligations under the plan, immediately upon their occurrence, their instantaneous recognition in the sponsor's results of operations is not permitted by FAS 87. Instead, to provide "smoothing" of the effects of what are viewed as being short-term fluctuations, the net gain (loss) is amortized if it meets certain criteria specified below.

Note that under FAS 87, as originally promulgated, the gain or loss was referred to as *unrecognized* gain or loss, since there was no formal recognition until the amount reported in pension cost was recorded. However, FAS 158 requires that these actuarial gains and losses be given recognition in other comprehensive income as they occur, thus affecting balance sheet display in full, even as the expense recognition is deferred and amortized. If actuarial gains are realized, this will give rise to a pension- or other benefit plan-related asset (or reduction in a pension- or benefit plan-related liability); if actuarial losses are incurred, these will give rise to a benefit plan liability, or reduction in an extant plan asset.

Since actuarial cost methods are based on numerous assumptions (employee compensation, mortality, turnover, earnings of the pension plan, etc.), it is not unusual for one or more of these assumptions to be invalidated by changes over time. Adjustments will invariably be necessary to bring prior estimates back into line with actual events. These adjustments are known as actuarial gains (losses). The accounting issue regarding the recognition of actuarial adjustments is their timing. All pension costs must eventually be recognized as expense. Actuarial gains (losses) are not considered prior period adjustments since they result from a refinement of estimates arising from obtaining subsequent information. These are considered changes in an estimate, and are to be recognized in current and future periods (i.e., prospectively only).

Plan asset gains (losses) result from both realized and unrealized amounts. They represent periodic differences between the actual return on assets and the expected return. The expected return is generated by multiplying the expected long-term rate of return by the market-related value of plan assets. Market-related value is a concept unique to pension accounting. It results from the previously discussed actuarial smoothing techniques under FAS 87.

Market-related value consists of two components. The first component is the fair value of the plan assets. The second component is an adjustment for the unrecognized portion of previous years' market gains or losses that are being amortized over a period of five years or less using a consistently applied method. Consistently applied means from year to year for each asset class (i.e., bonds, equities), since different classes of assets may have their market-related value calculated in a different manner (i.e., fair value in one case, moving average in another case). Thus, the market-related value may be fair value, but it also may be other than fair value if all or a portion of it results from calculation.

Plan asset gains (losses) include both (1) changes in the market-related value of assets (regardless of definition) from one period to another and (2) any changes that are not yet reflected in market-related value (i.e., the difference between the actual fair values of assets and the calculated market-related values). Only the former changes are recognized and amortized. The latter changes are recognized over time through the calculated market-related values. Differences between the actual amount of PBO from the assumed amount will also result in gain (loss).

Irrespective of the income smoothing techniques used, if this unrecognized net gain (loss) exceeds a "corridor" of 10% of the greater of the beginning balances of the market-related value of plan assets or the projected benefit obligation, a minimum amount of amortization is required. The excess over 10% is divided by the average remaining service period of active employees and included as a component of net pension costs. Average remaining life expectancies of inactive employees may be used if that is a better measure due to the demographics of the plan participants. FAS 158 makes no change to the methodology set forth by FAS 87 for the deferred recognition of the income statement effects of actuarial changes pertaining to plan assets and obligations.

Net pension costs include only the expected return on plan assets. Any difference between actual and expected returns is deferred through the gain (loss) component of net pension cost. If actual return is greater than expected return, net pension cost is increased to adjust the actual return to the lower expected return. If expected return is greater than actual return, the adjustment results in a decrease to net pension cost to adjust the actual return to the higher expected return. If the unrecognized net gain (loss) is large enough, it is amortized. Conceptually, the expected return represents the best estimate of long-term performance of the plan's investments. In any given year, however, an unusual short-term result may occur given the volatility of financial markets.

The expected long-term rate of return used to calculate the expected return on plan assets is the average rate of return expected to be earned on invested funds to provide for pension benefits included in the PBO. Present rates of return and expected future reinvestment rates of return are considered in arriving at the rate to be used.

The use of estimates and smoothing are hallmarks of FAS 87 and may be reduced or eliminated when FASB completes the next phase of its comprehensive review of pension and other postretirement benefit plan accounting. No changes have been imposed by FAS 158, however.

To summarize, net periodic pension cost includes a gain (loss) component consisting of both of the following, if applicable:

1. As a minimum, the portion of the unrecognized net gain (loss) from previous periods that exceeds the greater of 10% of the beginning balances of the market-related value of plan assets *or* the PBO, usually amortized over the average remaining service period of active employees expected to receive benefits.
2. The difference between the expected return and the actual return on plan assets.

An accelerated method of amortization of unrecognized net gain (loss) is acceptable if it is applied consistently to both gains and losses, and if the method is disclosed in the notes to the financial statements. In all cases, at least the minimum amount discussed above must be amortized.

**Example**

| | January 1, 2008 | 2008 Return on asset adjustment | 2008 Amortization | December 31, 2008 |
|---|---|---|---|---|
| Unrecognized actuarial gain (loss) | $(210) | $34 (d)* | $2(d)* | $(174) |

\* *Components of net periodic pension cost*

The return on asset adjustment of $34 is the difference between the actual return of $158 and the expected return of $124 on plan assets. The actuarial loss at the start of the year ($210 assumed) is amortized if it exceeds a "corridor" of the larger of 10% of the projected benefit obligation at the beginning of the period ($1,900 × 10% = $190) or 10% of the fair value of plan assets ($1,376 × 10% = $138). In this example, $20 ($210 – $190) is amortized by dividing the years of average remaining service (twelve years assumed), with a result rounded to $2. The straight-line method is used, and it is assumed that market-related value is the same as fair value.

Note that the smoothing approach illustrated and discussed above, which is a fundamental defining characteristic of defined benefit plan accounting under FAS 87 (pensions) and also of FAS 106 (other postretirement benefit plans), continues at this time to represent GAAP. As noted above, as of mid-2008 FASB is continuing its reexamination of accounting for benefit plans, and one likely outcome of this project will be the revision or elimination of the various smoothing procedures incorporated in current standards.

**Amortization of unrecognized prior service cost.** Prior service costs are incurred when the sponsor adopts plan amendments that increase plan benefits attributable to services rendered by plan participants in the past. These costs are accounted for as a change in estimate. Prior service costs are measured at the amendment date by the increase in the projected benefit obligation. The remaining service period of every active employee expected to receive benefits is estimated, and an equal amount of prior service cost is assigned to each future period. This is called the years-of-service amortization method.

### Example of the years-of-service amortization method

The ABC Company amends its pension plan, granting $40,000 of prior service costs to its 100 employees. The employees are expected to retire in accordance with the following schedule:

| Group | Number of employees | Expected year of retirement |
|-------|---------------------|------------------------------|
| A | 10 | 2009 |
| B | 15 | 2010 |
| C | 20 | 2011 |
| D | 20 | 2012 |
| E | 35 | 2013 |
|   | 100 | |

The calculation of the service years to be recognized from this group is as follows:

|      |    |    | Service years |    |     |       |
|------|----|----|-----|----|-----|-------|
| Year | A | B | C | D | E | Total |
| 2009 | 10 | 15 | 20 | 20 | 35 | 100 |
| 2010 |    | 15 | 20 | 20 | 35 | 90 |
| 2011 |    |    | 20 | 20 | 35 | 75 |
| 2012 |    |    |    | 20 | 35 | 55 |
| 2013 |    |    |    |    | 35 | 35 |
|      | 10 | 30 | 60 | 80 | 175 | 355 |

Consequently, there are 355 service years over which the $40,000 prior service cost can be spread, which equates to $112.68 per service year. The following table shows the annual amortization expense based on the standard charge of $112.68 per service year.

| Year | Total service years | × | Cost per service year | = | Annual amortization |
|------|---------------------|---|-----------------------|---|---------------------|
| 2009 | 100 |  | $112.68 |  | $11,268 |
| 2010 | 90 |  | 112.68 |  | 10,141 |
| 2011 | 75 |  | 112.68 |  | 8,451 |
| 2012 | 55 |  | 112.68 |  | 6,197 |
| 2013 | 35 |  | 112.68 |  | 3,943 |
|      | 355 |  |  |  | $40,000 |

The foregoing example illustrates the years-of-service amortization method. Consistent use of an accelerated amortization method is also acceptable, and must be disclosed if used.

If most of the plan's participants are inactive, remaining life expectancy is used as a basis for amortization instead of estimated remaining service period. If economic benefits will be realized by plan participants over a shorter period than remaining service period, amortization of costs is accelerated to recognize the costs in the periods that the participants benefit. If an amendment *reduces* the projected benefit obligation, unrecognized prior service costs are reduced to the extent that they exist and any excess is amortized in the manner described above for benefit increases.

### Example

|  | January 1, 2008 | 2008 Amortization | December 31, 2008 |
|--|-----------------|-------------------|-------------------|
| Unrecognized prior service cost | $320 | $(27) (e)* | $293 |

\* *Component of net periodic pension cost*

Unrecognized prior service cost ($320) is amortized over the years of average remaining service (twelve years assumed) at the amendment date with a result rounded to $27. The straight-line method was used. These amounts are found in the actuarial report.

While the vast preponderance of changes to plans increase benefits with credit for prior service, there may be plan amendments that reduce benefits, also with reference to past service. In such instances, under FAS 158, the decreases to the projected benefit obligation are given immediate recognition. The reduction in benefits is to be recognized as a credit (referred to as a prior service credit) to other comprehensive income, which is to be used to offset any remaining prior service cost included in accumulated other comprehensive income (i.e., from previous plan amendments increasing benefits). Any remaining prior service credit is to be amortized as a component of net periodic pension cost on the same basis as the cost of a benefit increase.

Thus, under requirements established by FAS 158, changes in prior service costs (and in certain other components affecting pension and other postretirement benefit costs) arising in a given reporting period, but not included in current period pension or other benefit costs (e.g., due to the above-described amortization requirements) are fully reported in other comprehensive income. These formerly "off the books" amounts will now be formally displayed in the balance sheet, but the timing of their impact on reported benefit costs and on net income will remain as set forth by FAS 87 (for defined benefit pension plans) and FAS 106 (for other postretirement benefit plans). It is, however, widely anticipated that pension and other benefit cost recognition will be altered significantly as FASB continues with its ongoing examination of these matters. FAS 158 is addressed in greater detail below.

**Amortization of unrecognized amount at date of initial FAS 87 application.** FAS 87 has been GAAP for over twenty years, and few plans likely still remain with unamortized transition amounts. The difference between the PBO and the fair value of plan assets minus recognized prepaid or plus accrued pension cost at the beginning of the fiscal year of the initial FAS 87 application was to be amortized using the straight-line method over the average remaining active employee service period. If the average remaining service period was less than fifteen years, the employer could elect to use a fifteen-year period. If all or almost all of a plan's participants were inactive, the employer used the inactive participants' average remaining life expectancy.

*NOTE: Solely for purposes of illustrating amortization of an unrecognized amount at transition, implementation of FAS 87 is assumed to be currently taking place.*

**Example**

|  | *January 1, 2008* | *2008 Amortization* | *December 31, 2008* |
|---|---|---|---|
| Unamortized net obligation (asset) existing at FAS 87 application | $(6) | $3 (f)* | $(3) |

\* *Component of net periodic pension cost*

At initial adoption of FAS 87, the "transition amount" was computed as an asset of $48. This transition asset is being amortized using the straight-line method over sixteen years ($3 per year), which represents the average remaining service period of employees expected to receive benefits under the plan at transition. Thus, the unamortized balance at January 1, 2008, was $6 and the amortization for 2008 was $3. These amounts would be found in the actuarial report.

**Summary of net periodic pension cost.** The components that were identified in the above examples are summed as follows to determine the amount defined as net periodic pension cost:

|                                                                                              |     | 2008     |
| -------------------------------------------------------------------------------------------- | --- | -------- |
| Service cost                                                                                 | (a) | $114     |
| Interest cost                                                                                | (b) | 152      |
| Actual return on plan assets                                                                 | (c) | (158)    |
| Gain (loss)                                                                                  | (d) | 36       |
| Amortization of any prior service cost or credit                                             | (e) | 27       |
| Amortization of unrecognized net obligation (asset) existing at FAS 87 application           | (f) | (3)      |
| Total net periodic pension cost                                                              |     | $168     |

One possible source of confusion is the actual return on plan assets ($158) and the unrecognized gain of $36 that net to $122. The actual return on plan assets reduces pension cost because, to the extent that plan assets generate earnings, those earnings help the plan sponsor subsidize the cost of providing the benefits. Thus, the plan sponsor will not have to fund benefits as they become due, to the extent that plan earnings provide the plan with cash to pay those benefits. This reduction, however, is adjusted by increasing pension cost by the difference between actual and expected return of $34 and the amortization of the excess actuarial loss of $2, for a total of $36. The net result is to include the expected return of $124 ($158 – $34) less the amortization of the excess of $2 for a total of $122 ($158 – $36). In recognizing the components of net periodic pension costs, FAS 132(R) requires the disclosure of this expected return of $124 and the loss of $2.

Note that, while the components of periodic pension cost nominally remain the same under FAS 158 as under preamendement FAS 87, two of the components have changed in substance. Amortization of prior service cost previously meant the income statement recognition of what had in prior periods been an amount not given any financial statement recognition. Now, however, the prior service cost will be included in accumulated other comprehensive income, and then amortized, under the formula set forth by FAS 87, to pension cost.

Second, the amortization of gain or loss (which pertains to actuarially driven changes to the projected benefit obligation, as well as to asset valuation adjustments not recognized in current income), which under FAS 87 was not given financial statement recognition before the point in time when they were to be included in pension cost, now is associated with an item incorporated in accumulated other comprehensive income.

Thus, under FAS 158 there is *display* of both prior service costs and actuarial gains or losses immediately upon the occurrence or determination of the item, but there is still, as under the original FAS 87, *deferred recognition in expense* via the FAS 87-prescribed amortization process, set forth above.

If any transition amount dating from the adoption of FAS 87 still exists, that too must be recorded in accumulated other comprehensive income upon adoption of FAS 158, and amortization over any remaining period as originally determined when FAS 87 was adopted will continue as prescribed under that standard.

Under FAS 158, there will be *both* the componentized periodic pension expense *and* changes to the amounts reported in other comprehensive income, although for nonpublic entities the components of pension cost may be omitted. The suggested informative (i.e., footnote) form of disclosure consists of two tables, and is as follows for a publicly-held reporting entity (these amounts, which assume partial funding of other postretirement benefits, are not related to the earlier examples):

*Components of Net Periodic Benefit Cost and Other Amounts Recognized in Other Comprehensive Income*

|  | Pension benefits | | Other benefits | |
|---|---|---|---|---|
|  | 2007 | 2008 | 2007 | 2008 |
| **Net periodic benefit cost** | | | | |
| Service cost | $ 95 | $102 | $49 | $57 |
| Interest cost | 80 | 88 | 58 | 59 |
| Expected return on plan assets | (70) | (86) | (12) | (14) |
| Amortization of prior service cost | 11 | 12 | (3) | (5) |
| Amortization of net (gain) loss | 14 | 9 | 2 | 2 |
| Net periodic benefit cost | $130 | $125 | $94 | $99 |
| **Other changes in plan assets and benefit obligations recognized in other comprehensive income** | | | | |
| Net loss (gain) | $ 86 | $102 | $27 | $(46) |
| Prior service cost (credit) | 60 | 10 | (70) | (47) |
| Amortization of prior service cost | (11) | (12) | 3 | 5 |
| Total recognized in other comprehensive income | 135 | 100 | (40) | (88) |
| Total recognized in net periodic benefit cost and other comprehensive income | $265 | $225 | $54 | $11 |

Finally, the assumptions used in computing projected and accumulated benefits and expected return on plan assets must be disclosed. For postretirement health benefits, so-called sensitivity data must also be presented, since the amount of this often significant, and most commonly unfunded future obligation is highly responsive to changes in health care cost levels. The following tables set forth these key parameters:

*Assumptions*

*Weighted-average assumptions used to determine benefit obligations at December 31*

|  | Pension benefits | | Other benefits | |
|---|---|---|---|---|
|  | 2007 | 2008 | 2007 | 2008 |
| Discount rate | 6.75% | 7.25% | 7.00% | 7.50% |
| Rate of compensation increase | 4.25 | 4.50 | | |

*Weighted-average assumptions used to determine net periodic benefit cost for years ended December 31*

|  | | | | |
|---|---|---|---|---|
| Discount rate | 7.25% | 7.50% | 7.50% | 7.75% |
| Expected long-term return on plan assets | 8.00 | 8.50 | 8.10 | 8.75 |
| Rate of compensation increase | 4.50 | 4.75 | | |

*Assumed health care cost trend rates at December 31*

|  | 2007 | 2008 |
|---|---|---|
| Health care cost trend rate assumed for next year | 12% | 12.5% |
| Rate to which the cost trend rate is assumed to decline (the ultimate trend rate) | 6% | 5% |
| Year that the rate reaches the ultimate trend rate | 2009 | 2009 |

Assumed health care cost trend rates have a significant effect on the amounts reported for the health care plans. A one-percentage-point change in assumed health care cost trend rates (not required for nonpublic reporting entities) would have the following effects:

|  | 1-percentage-point increase | 1-percentage-point decrease |
|---|---|---|
| Effect on total of service and interest cost | $ 42 | $ (35) |
| Effect on postretirement benefit obligation | 185 | (176) |

## Reconciliation of Beginning and Ending ABO, PBO, and Plan Assets

The following table summarizes the 2008 activity affecting ABO, PBO, and Plan Assets and reconciles the beginning and ending balances per the actuarial report:

| | Accumulated benefit obligation | Progression of salaries and wages | Projected benefit obligation | Fair value of plan assets* |
|---|---|---|---|---|
| Balance, January 1, 2008 | $ (1,500) | $ (400) | $ (1,900) | $ 1,376 |
| Service cost | (90) | (24) | (114) (a) | |
| Interest cost | (120) | (32) | (152) (b) | |
| Benefits paid to retired participants | 160 | | 160 | (160) |
| Actual return on plan assets | | | | 158 (c) |
| Sponsor's contributions | | | | 145 |
| Balance, December 31, 2008 | $ (1,550) | $ (456) | $ (2,006) | $ 1,519 |

\* *Assumed to be the same as market-related value for this illustration.*

Expanded disclosure is now required regarding the portfolio assets maintained to pay future pension and other postretirement benefits. This information should be presented in a tabular format illustrated as follows:

**Plan assets.** The entity's pension plan weighted-average asset allocations at December 31, 2007, and 2008, by asset category are as follows:

| | Pension plan assets at December 31 | | Other benefit plan assets at December 31 | |
|---|---|---|---|---|
| | 2007 | 2008 | 2007 | 2008 |
| **Asset category** | | | | |
| Equity securities | 50% | 48% | 60% | 52% |
| Debt securities | 30 | 31 | 30 | 27 |
| Real estate | 10 | 12 | 5 | 13 |
| Other | 10 | 9 | 5 | 8 |
| Total | 100% | 100% | 100% | 100% |

The foregoing allocation information should be accompanied by an entity-specific narrative description of investment policies and strategies for plan assets, including weighted-average target asset allocations, where such are used as part of those policies and strategies. If the reporting entity holds its own shares in the trusteed assets of the plan(s), this fact, and the amounts held at each reporting date, should also be set forth.

### Employer's Liabilities and Assets under FAS 87 as Amended by FAS 158

Accounting for defined benefit plans remains a controversial topic. In particular, the fact that plan assets and liabilities are, with certain exceptions, not considered to be the employers' assets and liabilities, continues to be a contentious issue. When FAS 87 was first imposed, the FASB concluded that full imposition of accrual-basis recognition rules would have caused there to be unacceptably large adjustments to the financial statements of companies whose plans were materially underfunded. The adjustments would have been necessary to recognize previously unrecognized assets or liabilities representing the differences between PBO and the fair value of plan assets. To ease the perceived burden on these plan sponsors, FASB developed a compromise *minimum liability* approach for FAS 87. This minimum liability was computed by reference to the excess of the ABO (which is a smaller obligation than the PBO, since it does not recognize projected future compensation increases) over the fair value of the plan assets. Note that, for the purpose of this calculation, the fair value of the assets was used, rather than the market-related value that was used to calculate the expected return on plan assets. To the extent that there was a pension liability already recorded, the sponsor needed only to recognize the additional amount necessary to increase the recorded liability to the amount of the minimum liability.

The theory behind using the ABO was the fact that, if the pension plan were terminated at the balance sheet date, the future compensation increases would never occur and the pension obligation could be settled for the smaller amount. Some might argue that this approach conflicted with the underlying going concern assumption that is fundamental to financial accounting theory, of course. FAS 158 has eliminated the minimum liability approach of

FAS 87, and the full amount of over- or underfunding of pension plans must now be displayed in the balance sheet, as described later in this section.

Fair value is determined as of the financial statement date (prior to the effective date of FAS 158, this could be a date not more than three months prior to year-end, if used consistently). The amount is that which would result from negotiations between a willing buyer and seller not in a liquidation sale. Fair value is measured in preferred order by market price, selling price of similar investments, or discounted cash flows at a rate indicative of the risk involved.

Under FAS 87, an additional minimum liability was recognized by making an offsetting entry to recognize an intangible asset, but only up to the amount of unrecognized prior service cost. Any additional debit needed was considered a loss and was shown net of income tax benefits (subject to the restrictions on recognition of deferred tax assets per FAS 109) in other comprehensive income. This approach has now been made obsolete by the promulgation of FAS 158.

Regarding the additional minimum liability required under FAS 87 prior to being amended by FAS 158, there were several important matters impacting upon the actual computation of the amount to be displayed. First, an asset could not be recorded if the fair value of the plan assets exceeded the accumulated benefit obligation. Second, the calculation of the minimum liability required consideration of any already recorded prepaid or accrued pension cost. The net liability had to be equal to at least the unfunded accumulated benefit obligation. An already recorded prepaid pension cost would increase the amount of the recognized additional liability. An already recorded accrued pension cost would decrease it.

Third, the intangible asset was not subject to amortization. Fourth, at the time of the subsequent calculation, the amounts were to be either added to or reversed out with no effect on net income. These balance sheet entries were entirely independent of net income and would not affect the calculation of net pension costs. Fifth, unless a significant event occurred or measures of obligations and assets as of a more current date became available, interim financial statements were to show the year-end additional minimum liability adjusted for subsequent contributions and accruals. In such a case, previous year-end assumptions regarding net pension cost would also carry over to the interim financial statements.

The advent of FAS 158 has made the minimum liability recognition, together with the associated intangible asset, extinct. Under FAS 158 the full amount (measured by projected or accumulated benefit obligations, for pensions and other postretirement benefits, respectively) of over- or underfunding will be given balance sheet recognition, with the offsetting entry being to other comprehensive income. At the date of adoption of FAS 158, any remaining amounts arising from the now-superseded minimum liability rules under FAS 87 are eliminated and replaced by the amounts determined in accordance with FAS 158.

A schedule showing the variables of the above example in accordance with FAS 132(R), as amended by FAS 158, reconciling the balance sheet amounts with the funded status of the plan is shown below. Assumed activity for 2007 is provided for comparative purposes. This example is to illustrate the information required for publicly held entities; see comments below for reduced disclosure requirements applicable to nonpublicly held companies. Also, this example combines information about pension plans and other benefit plans, the latter of which are assumed data not detailed in the foregoing discussion.

| | Pension benefits | | Other benefits | |
|---|---|---|---|---|
| | 2007 | 2008 | 2007 | 2008 |
| ***Change in benefit obligation*** | | | | |
| Benefit obligation at beginning of year | $1,800 | $1,900 | $612 | $662 |
| Service cost | 111 | 114 | 22 | 30 |
| Interest cost | 144 | 152 | 35 | 43 |
| Plan participant's contributions | -- | -- | 33 | 13 |
| Amendments | -- | -- | -- | -- |
| Actuarial loss | -- | -- | -- | -- |
| Acquisition | -- | -- | -- | -- |
| Benefits paid | (155) | (160) | (40) | (60) |
| Benefit obligation at end of year | 1,900 | 2,006 | 662 | 688 |
| ***Change in plan assets*** | | | | |
| Fair value of plan assets at beginning of year | 1,241 | 1,376 | 87 | 206 |
| Actual return on plan assets | 150 | 158 | 24 | 5 |
| Acquisition | -- | -- | -- | 25 |
| Employer contribution | 140 | 145 | 152 | 137 |
| Plan participants' contributions | -- | -- | 13 | 20 |
| Benefits paid | (155) | (160) | (70) | (90) |
| Fair value of plan assets at end of year | 1,376 | 1,519 | 206 | 303 |
| Funded status [plan over (under) funded] | $(524) | $(487) | $(456) | $(385) |

Nonpublic reporting entities are not required to provide the information in the above tables. Instead, they are only required to disclose the employer's contributions, participants' contributions, benefit payments, and the funded status. Of course, expanded disclosures are not precluded under such circumstances.

Note that since this example disclosure addresses both pension and other postretirement plans, the captions are generically worded, but it is implicit that they refer to projected benefits for pension plans and accumulated benefits for other defined benefit plans.

Under prior GAAP (that is, FAS 87 prior to the amendments made by FAS 158), it was necessary to reconcile the funded status of the plans (the components of which were largely off-balance-sheet) to the amounts reported in the statement of financial position. However, given that FAS 158 requires the funded status of defined benefit plans to be reported in the statement of financial position, this reconciliation has been replaced by a simple table identifying the locations in the balance sheet were the net funded amounts are presented, as follows:

| | Pension benefits | | Other benefits | |
|---|---|---|---|---|
| | 2007 | 2008 | 2007 | 2008 |
| Noncurrent assets | $ 133 | $ 18 | $ -- | $ -- |
| Current liabilities | (225) | (125) | (150) | (99) |
| Noncurrent liabilities | (432) | (380) | (306) | (286) |
| Net amount recognized | $(524) | $(487) | $(456) | $(385) |

Amounts recognized in accumulated other comprehensive income must also be identified; for this example, these consist of

| | Pension benefits | | Other benefits | |
|---|---|---|---|---|
| | 2007 | 2008 | 2007 | 2008 |
| Net loss (gain) | $ 94 | $ 18 | $(11) | $(48) |
| Prior service cost (credit) | 210 | 160 | (92) | (22) |
| | $304 | $178 | $(103) | $(70) |

As set forth above, under the provisions of FAS 158 the *actual* underfunded or—for the first time—overfunded status of defined benefit pension plans will be reported without limitation in the balance sheets of reporting sponsoring entities. Under FAS 87 only a limited form of disclosure had been imposed for underfunded plans, with the definition of underfunding being based on the discrepancy between plan assets and the *accumulated* benefit obligations under the plans. By contrast, under FAS 158—for defined benefit pension arrangements—under- or overfunding will be defined by the differences between plan assets and the corresponding *projected* benefit obligations. Thus, the measure will now be derived from the (almost inevitably) larger projections of future benefit payments, including the effects of anticipated salary progressions.

## Additional FAS 87 Guidance

In situations not specifically addressed by FAS 87, EITF 88-1 states that the vested benefit obligation can be either (1) the actuarial present value of the vested benefits that the employee is entitled to if the employee separates immediately, or (2) the actuarial present value of the vested benefits to which the employee is currently entitled but based on the employee's expected date of separation or retirement. EITF's SEC observer indicated that the alternative selected is to be disclosed. This issue is most commonly applicable to foreign defined benefit pension plans.

Pension plans sometimes are coupled with life insurance plans with the employer as beneficiary. According to EITF 88-5, it is not appropriate for the purchaser of life insurance to recognize income from death benefits on an actuarially expected basis.

In recent years a trend has emerged for employers to terminate classic defined benefit pension plans and replace them with "cash balance" plans, the accounting for which has not been well understood. These hybrid plans typically describe the pension benefit by reference to an account balance rather than a monthly annuity at retirement. In Issue 03-4, EITF considered plans that are characterized by defined principal-crediting rates as percentages of salary, and offer defined, noncontingent interest-crediting rates that entitle participants to future interest credits at stated, fixed rates until retirement. The consensus reached was that "cash balance" plans with the foregoing attributes are to be deemed defined benefit plans, consistent with definitions set forth in FAS 87. This is true because an employer's contributions to a cash balance plan trust and the earnings on the invested plan assets may be unrelated to the principal and interest credits to participants' hypothetical accounts.

Given this consensus position, EITF also determined that the benefit promise in the cash balance arrangement is not pay-related as contemplated by FAS 87 and, accordingly, use of a projected unit credit method is neither required nor appropriate for purposes of measuring the benefit obligation and annual cost of benefits earned under FAS 87. The appropriate cost attribution approach, therefore, is the traditional unit credit method.

Transitioning to the accounting required under EITF 03-4 depended on how the plan had previously been dealt with by the sponsor. If a reporting entity had been accounting for a cash balance pension plan as a defined contribution plan, the effect of applying the consensuses (i.e., the difference between the funded status as a defined benefit plan and any existing prepaid or accrued pension cost) was to have been reported as the effect of adopting a new accounting principle (in a manner similar to a cumulative-effect-type adjustment) as of the beginning of the year containing the next reporting period beginning after May 28, 2003.

On the other hand, if an entity had been accounting for such a plan as a defined benefit plan, the effect of remeasuring the pension obligation using the guidance in this consensus was to have been calculated as of the above-mentioned measurement date. Any difference in the measurement of the obligation as a result of applying the consensus was to be reported as a component of actuarial gains and losses under FAS 87. For an entity that has an accounting policy of immediate recognition of all gains and losses, or all gains and losses outside the 10% corridor described in FAS 87, the component of such gain or loss that could be attributed to the adoption of the guidance in Issue 03-4, applying a with-and-without calculation, was to have been reported as the effect of adopting the consensus (in a manner similar to a cumulative-effect-type adjustment) as of the measurement date.

## Reporting Funded Status: Requirements under FAS 158

As suggested earlier in this chapter, the deferred recognition aspect of FAS 87 and FAS 106 have long been subject to harsh criticism, since real economic events (e.g., changes in fair values of plan assets) were being disguised and distorted in the financial statements, and the deviation from amounts reported and actual underlying facts could often be material in amount. For various reasons, the direct solution to this problem—using a pure fair value approach to measuring changes in plan assets and obligations, with changes being reported currently in operating income—is still not seen as feasible. As a compromise—but possibly only interim—solution, FAS 158 was issued in late 2006, with a phased implementation schedule.

FAS 158 has two major implications. First, it requires business entities having defined benefit plans (*other than* multiemployer plans) to display the funded status of those plans on the face of their balance sheets, instead of being reported, to greater or lesser degree, only in the informative disclosures. And second, it requires that actuarial gains and losses and prior service costs and credits arising in the reporting period, but not (under provisions of FAS 87 and FAS 106) reported in the current period's reported benefit cost, be included as items of other comprehensive income. These matters will be addressed in the following paragraphs.

Additionally, FAS 158 imposes a definitive requirement that the measurement date for plan assets and obligations be the end of the annual reporting period (that is, the balance sheet date). Previously, the measurement date could be either year-end or a date not more than three months prior to that date, if used consistently. This flexibility is no longer available.

Finally, the standard requires that additional information be presented in the notes to financial statements about certain effects on net periodic benefit cost for the upcoming fiscal year that arise as a consequence of the delayed recognition of actuarial gains or losses, prior service costs or credits, and transition asset or obligation.

FAS 158 does not change the accounting by employers participating in multiemployer defined benefit plans. For essentially practical reasons, FAS 87 provides that contributions made to such plans for the reporting period be recognized as net pension cost, and that any contributions due and unpaid be recognized as a liability. Thus, most of the complexities arising from smoothing were avoided in accounting for sponsors participating in multiemployer plans.

**Display of funded status.** The most important change wrought by FAS 158 is to move disclosure of the plan's funded status to the face of the balance sheet proper. Note that this is not a change in benefit cost recognition or measurement, since the fundamental and oft-criticized "smoothing" concepts of FAS 87 and FAS 106 were not altered by FAS 158. Nonetheless, by requiring that the amounts of net overfunding and underfunding of benefit plans be included in assets and liabilities, respectively, there will be a very substantial improvement in financial statement users' comprehension of the implications of the defined benefit plans under which the reporting entity is obligated. Previously, this was only revealed in the benefit plan footnotes, where the funded status was reconciled to the amount presented in the balance sheet proper.

Determination of funded status varies as between defined benefit pension plans and all other defined benefit arrangements (that is, those addressed by FAS 106). For the former, FAS 158 states that funded status is measured by the difference between the fair value of plan assets and the *projected* benefit obligation (explained earlier in this chapter). For the latter, it is the spread between the fair value of plan assets and the *accumulated* benefit obligation that measures funded status.

Whereas under FAS 87 the amount of pension plan liability to be reported by the employer (apart from current contributions payable) was limited to the difference between the value of plan assets and the *accumulated* benefit obligation, FAS 158 requires that the more meaningful measure—the difference between plan assets and the *projected* benefit obligation—be used to gauge the liability to be reported. Projected benefit obligation takes into account expected salary progression, while accumulated benefit obligation does not. For all defined benefit plans, other than those that do not take salary progression into account, a larger liability will now be recognized.

FAS 106 did not include a requirement that a measure analogous to minimum liability, as defined under FAS 87, be recognized by sponsors, in part because obligations under pension arrangements are subject to statutory enforcement whereas those under other promised postretirement benefits have been held not to be contractual commitments, and thus subject to revision or cancellation by the employer on a unilateral basis. For example, postretirement health care cost plans can be modified by employers without limitation.

More important, perhaps, was the fact that when FAS 106 was being deliberated, virtually all such arrangements were "pay as you go," with no assets whatsoever being set aside to satisfy these commitments. If FAS 106 had incorporated the same minimum liability reporting concept as did FAS 87, recognition of the underfunding would have required very substantial adjustments to sponsors' balance sheets—even to the extent of sharply reducing or eliminating reporting entities' net worth. The strongly voiced opposition to the FASB proposal (which did originally include a minimum liability provision) persuaded FASB to delete this requirement.

FAS 158, however, puts an end to this exemption. The net obligations associated with underfunded plans (which will likely describe virtually all postretirement benefit plans other than pensions, as well as some pension plans) will have to be displayed in the balance sheet. In contrast with the requirement for defined benefit pension plans, for these arrangements the measure is based on the *accumulated* postretirement benefit obligation, which is the actuarial present value of benefits attributed to employees as of the balance sheet date, which until full eligibility is achieved, will be a lesser amount than the *projected* benefit obligation. While it is likely that lower amounts of liability will be computed for other postretirement obligations than will be the case for otherwise similar defined benefit pension plans, it will nonetheless be a very substantial change from past practice under FAS 106, and could materially affect the financial statements of reporting entities offering such arrangements for their employees.

**Reporting when there are multiple plans.** When the reporting entity has multiple plans, it will not be acceptable to display one single net amount of over- or underfunding. Rather, all overfunded plans will have to be separately aggregated, as will all underfunded plans. The amount of overfunding is included in noncurrent assets, with no portion of the overfunding permitted to be displayed as a current asset. On the other hand, total underfunding is to be allocated between current and noncurrent liabilities, with the current portion being computed (on a plan-by-plan basis) as the sum of the actuarial present value of benefits included in the benefit obligation payable over the ensuing twelve months' time, to the extent that it exceeds the fair value of plan assets.

Conceivably, an employer may have the right to use the assets of an overfunded plan to pay the obligations of another, underfunded plan. Only in such circumstances would it be acceptable to offset the overfunding asset and the underfunding liability. Such a situation would be highly unlikely to occur, however.

To illustrate, if the reporting entity has three postretirement benefit plans, one of which is overfunded and two of which are underfunded, the amount of overfunding must be included in noncurrent assets. The amount of underfunding of the two other plans must be reported in liabilities, but a portion of this total might have to be included in current liabilities. This is illustrated in the following table:

|  | Overfunded plan | Underfunded plan #1 | Underfunded plan #2 | Balance sheet totals |
|---|---|---|---|---|
| FV of plan assets | $400,000 | $700,000 | $ 20,000 |  |
| PV of benefit obligation (total) | 340,000 | 874,000 | 240,000 |  |
| PV of benefit obligation (due in next twelve months) | 28,000 | 32,000 | 31,000 |  |
| Overfunding asset (noncurrent) | 60,000 |  |  | $ 60,000 |
| Underfunding liability (noncurrent) |  | 174,000 | 209,000 | 383,000 |
| Underfunding liability (current) |  |  | 11,000 | 11,000 |

In the table above, note that the overfunded plan results in the reporting of a noncurrent asset, and this is not mitigated by the simultaneous existence of underfunded plans. Also note that underfunded plan #1 has sufficient assets to satisfy the amounts due within one year, and therefore the sponsoring entity's balance sheet will not report any current liability with respect to this plan. However, plan #2, which is also underfunded, has benefit payments due over the twelve months following the balance sheet date that exceed the amount of plan assets, and thus the sponsor will have to provide additional funding in the current period. That amount must be reported as a current liability. Finally, observe that the noncurrent obligations pertaining to both underfunded plans are combined into a single balance sheet amount.

**Reporting of benefit plan transactions and events in comprehensive income.** FAS 158 requires an employer to recognize all transactions and events affecting the overfunded or underfunded status of a defined benefit postretirement plan in comprehensive income (or changes in unrestricted net assets, if the entity is a not-for-profit enterprise) in the year in which they occur. Previously, many delayed-recognition elements of pension and other postretirement benefit plan expense were "off-the-books," albeit subject to disclosure in the financial statement notes.

Under FAS 158, the reporting entity must recognize as a component of other comprehensive income the gains or losses and prior service costs or credits arising during that reporting period that are not recognized as components of net periodic benefit cost of the period pursuant to FAS 87 and FAS 106. For example, if a plan amendment is adopted which credits employees with prior service, this is not reflected immediately in benefit costs, but rather is subject to amortization (i.e., it is to be recognized as part of pension or other postretirement benefit plan cost over an extended period of time). The requirements established by FAS 158 do not alter the piecemeal recognition of expense (that is, smoothing) under current GAAP, but they do make it necessary to record in other comprehensive income, in the year the amendment is effected, the full amount of the prior service cost less what is recognized in pension cost in that period.

In other words, the methodology of expense measurement has not been affected by the issuance of FAS 158, but disclosure *on the face of the balance sheet* is now achieved. The effect of recording this debit in comprehensive income will be balanced by recording an additional underfunding liability. In accordance with FAS 109, this is to be treated as a temporary difference, since the liability has a different basis (carrying value) for financial reporting purposes than it does for tax purposes. Hence, it must be tax effected within accumulated other comprehensive income, and a deferred tax asset (in the normal circumstances) will be recorded. The tax asset, in turn, will be subject to the "more likely than not" test for realizability, in order to determine whether it needs to be reduced or offset fully by an allowance. (See Chapter 17 for full discussion of accounting for income taxes.)

**Example**

If Varga Corp., which is in the 30% tax bracket, grants its workers an amendment to a defined benefit pension plan which increases its obligation by $60,000, to be reflected in pension expense over fifteen years (i.e., amortized at $4,000 per year), under FAS 158 the following entry would be made (assuming the amendment is granted at year-end, and thus amortization will begin in the next period):

| | | |
|---|---|---|
| Accumulated other comprehensive income | 42,000 | |
| Deferred tax asset | 18,000 | |
| Pension liability | | 60,000 |

As noted earlier, the elements that will be reported in accumulated other comprehensive income, until taken into benefit expense as directed under FAS 87 or FAS 106, include gains and losses (i.e., those due to differences between expected and actual returns on plan assets, and those arising from actuarially determined adjustments), prior service cost or credits from plan amendments, and any remaining transition amounts deferred when FAS 87 was adopted. For new amounts (e.g., actuarial adjustment in the current period), there will be an entry similar to the above, whereby accumulated other comprehensive income is adjusted to reflect the full amount of the item, as well as the (offsetting) deferred tax effect thereof.

In subsequent periods, there will be opposite direction adjustments to the amount provided in other comprehensive income, as the normal, FAS 87-driven amortization occurs. For example, if the prior service cost recognized by Varga Corp. above is to be amortized based on average remaining service lives of current employees and the amount so determined for 2009, the first period after the amendment, is $5,000, the following entry would be recorded:

| | | |
|---|---|---|
| Pension cost | 5,000 | |
| Deferred tax asset | | 1,500 |
| Accumulated other comprehensive income | | 3,500 |

For each annual statement of income presented, these amounts are to be recognized in accumulated other comprehensive income, showing *separately* the amounts ascribed to net gain or loss and net prior service cost or credit. Those amounts are to be separated into amounts arising during the period and reclassification adjustments of other comprehensive income as a result of being recognized as components of net periodic benefit cost for the period.

**Measurement date for year-end financial statements.** For practical reasons, FAS 87 permitted the use of actuarial data (benefit obligations and plan asset value) that was up to several months stale in the preparation of the financial statements and accompanying notes, but this represented a departure from the general principal that balance sheet accounts represent amounts as of that very date. Since older actuarial data could sometimes result in misstatements of balance sheet amounts (such as the additional liability amount, based on the shortfall of fund assets compared to the accumulated benefit obligations under defined benefit pension plans), this rule was never theoretically sound, but rather was a concession to information availability. In the twenty-four years since FAS 87 was promulgated, information has become vastly more readily available. FAS 158 therefore eliminates this option, and requires that valuations be as of the balance sheet date.

The only exceptions to the foregoing general statement occur in the instance of plans sponsored by consolidated subsidiaries or equity-method investees. This is a practical concession, but given that under US GAAP subsidiaries and investees are permitted to report financial results using year-ends different than the parent's or investor's, the exception is a reasonable and logical one. In those situations, the determinations of the fair values of plan assets and obligations must be as of the subsidiaries' or investees' respective balance sheet dates.

**Measurement date for interim financial statements.** Publicly held entities must report quarterly, and private companies may choose to issue interim financial statements that are represented as being in accordance with GAAP. FAS 158 does not impose a requirement to evaluate plan assets and obligations more frequently than on an annual basis. Therefore, unless there has been an interim revaluation conducted—for example, because a plan amendment was adopted, or there had been a settlement or curtailment of a plan—it is prescribed that the funded status as of the most recent year-end be used in interim period reporting, with certain adjustments. The adjustments to be made are for subsequent accruals of service cost, interest, and return on plan assets included in current earnings (excluding, however, any amortization of amounts first recognized in other comprehensive income), subsequent contributions to the plan, and subsequent benefit payments from the plan. However, if there had been a revaluation subsequent to the prior year-end, the most recent valuation data would be used, again updated as just described, for any postvaluation accruals, contributions, and benefit payments.

**FAS 158 transition considerations.** Adjustments are necessary in order to initially place the underfunding or overfunding liability or asset onto the balance sheet, since these amounts formerly were disclosed only in the notes to the financial statements and reconciled by means of reference to various "off the books" amounts, such as unamortized prior service cost arising from plan amendments. FAS 158 provides different transition instructions relative to its recognition provisions for business entities and for not-for-profit organizations, which is made necessary by the fact that not-for-profits do not report other comprehensive income amounts.

FASB rejected retrospective revision of prior periods' financial statements upon adoption of FAS 158 due to concerns about cost. Thus, the adjustments necessary to recognize, in other comprehensive income, the elements previously not given formal financial statement recognition, are first recorded at the end of the year the standard is adopted.

Business entities must apply the recognition provisions of FAS 158 as of the *end* of the fiscal year of initial application. Retrospective application is not permitted. The amounts recognized in an employer's statement of financial position as of the end of the fiscal year before applying FAS 158, including amounts required to recognize any additional minimum pension liability, are to be adjusted so that gains or losses, prior service costs or credits, and transition assets or obligations that have not yet been included in net periodic benefit cost as of the end of the fiscal year in which FAS 158 is initially applied are recognized as components of the ending balance of accumulated other comprehensive income, net of tax. Any required adjustment shall be reported as an adjustment of the ending balance of accumulated other comprehensive income.

For not-for-profit enterprises, gains or losses, prior service costs or credits, and transition assets or obligations that have not yet been included in net periodic benefit cost as of the end of the fiscal year in which FAS 158 is initially applied are included in the ending balance of unrestricted net assets, net of tax, if any. Any required adjustment is to be reported in the statement of activities, in a separate line item or items within changes in unrestricted net assets, apart from expenses and outside a performance indicator or other intermediate measure of operations, if one is presented.

FAS 158 also specifies the transition methodology for its measurement date provisions. In fact, the standard offers two approaches for an employer to transition to a fiscal year-end measurement date, if an earlier date had previously been employed. In the first of these, the reporting entity remeasures plan assets and benefit obligations as of the beginning of the fiscal year that the measurement date provisions are applied. It then uses those new measurements to determine the effects of the measurement date change as of the *beginning* of the fiscal year that the measurement date provisions are applied.

Under this approach, for business entities, the net periodic benefit cost for the period between the measurement date that is used for the immediately preceding fiscal year-end and the beginning of the fiscal year that the measurement date provisions are applied, exclusive of any curtailment or settlement gain or loss, must be recognized, net of tax, as a separate adjustment of the opening balance of retained earnings. For example, assuming a calendar year and an actuarial valuation done three months before year-end, a catch-up adjustment will be needed for pension cost for the months of October, November, and December for the year prior to implementation of FAS 158's measurement provisions.

Put another way, this means that the pretax amount recognized as an adjustment to retained earnings is the net periodic benefit cost that without a change in measurement date otherwise would have been recognized on a delayed basis during the first interim period for the fiscal year that the measurement date provisions are applied.

Any gain or loss arising from a curtailment or settlement between the measurement date that is used for the immediately preceding fiscal year-end and the beginning of the fiscal year that the measurement date provisions are applied is to be recognized in earnings in that period and not as an adjustment to retained earnings. This provision is intended to prohibit a reporting entity from early application of the measurement date provisions (see discussion below) when the employer has issued financial statements for the prior year without recognition of such a settlement or curtailment.

For example, assume an entity with a June 30 year-end that used a March 31 measurement date curtailed its benefit plan on May 31, 2006, resulting in a curtailment loss. That employer would be able to apply early the measurement date provisions in fiscal year 2007 if it recognizes the May 31, 2006 curtailment loss in its financial statements for the year ending June 30, 2006. That would not be the case if its 2006 financial statements had been issued before it wished to early adopt for fiscal year 2007.

Other changes in the fair value of plan assets and the benefit obligations (for example, gains or losses) for the period between the measurement date that was used for the immediately preceding fiscal year-end and the beginning of the fiscal year that the measurement date provisions are first applied must be recognized, net of tax, as a separate adjustment of the *opening* balance of accumulated other comprehensive income for the fiscal year that the measurement date provisions are applied. Thus actuarial gains or losses, determined (for illustration purposes) as of October 31 for purposes of preparing the prior calendar year's financial statements, must be updated to December 31, with any computed differences used to adjust other comprehensive income as of January 1, beginning of the fiscal year when the FAS 158 measurement date requirements are first being applied.

For not-for-profit enterprises, the foregoing guidance also applies, except that the adjustments that would be made to the opening balances of retained earnings and accumulated other comprehensive income are instead to be recognized as a change in unrestricted net assets in the statement of activities, net of tax if applicable. Those amounts are to be reported in a separate line item or items apart from expenses and outside a performance indicator or other intermediate measure of operations, if one is optionally reported.

As an alternative to the foregoing methodology, to avoid the need to remeasure plan assets and obligations at year-end when an optional, earlier date had formerly been employed by the reporting entity, as was permitted under provisions of FAS 87 and FAS 106, FAS 158 allows for the use of another approach. Under this second approach, the reporting entity continues to use the measurements determined for the prior fiscal year-end reporting as the basis for estimating the effects of the change.

The net periodic benefit cost for the period between the earlier measurement date and the end of the fiscal year that the measurement date provisions are applied, exclusive of any curtailment or settlement gain or loss, is to be allocated proportionately between amounts to be recognized as an adjustment of retained earnings and net periodic benefit cost for the fiscal year that the measurement date provisions are applied.

For purpose of illustrating this approach, consider a calendar-year entity that formerly employed a September 30 measurement date, and has no settlement or curtailment during the period. Note that the change in asset and obligation values determined as of December 31, 2008, would actually gauge changes over fifteen months (since the immediately preceding determination date, which was September 30, 2007, was that long ago), and this must be proportionately assigned per FAS 158 guidance. Therefore, the entity would allocate, as an adjustment of retained earnings, three fifteenths of net periodic benefit cost determined for the period from September 30, 2007, to December 31, 2008. The remaining twelve-fifteenths would be recognized as net period benefit cost for the fiscal year that the measurement date provisions first are applied, which is the year ended December 31, 2008.

As under the first available method, explained above, any gain or loss arising from a curtailment or settlement between the measurement date that is used for the immediately preceding fiscal year-end and the beginning of the fiscal year that the measurement date provisions are applied is to be recognized in earnings in that period and not as an adjustment to retained earnings.

Any other changes in the fair value of plan assets and the benefit obligations (e.g., actuarial gains or losses) for the period between the earlier measurement date and the *end* of the fiscal year that the measurement date provisions are applied is to be recognized as other comprehensive income for the fiscal year that the measurement date provisions are applied.

**Effective dates.** The requirements set forth under FAS 158 were to be phased in, with different effective dates for the measurement and the recognition and disclosure provisions.

For the measurement provisions, the requirement to measure plan assets and benefit obligations as of the date of the employer's fiscal year-end balance sheet is to be effective for fiscal years ending after December 15, 2008 (e.g., for 2008 calendar years), and may not be applied retrospectively. Earlier application is encouraged, but only if effected for all of an employer's benefit plans. The requirement under FAS 132(R) to disclose the measurement date is eliminated, effective in the year the employer initially adopts the measurement date provisions of FAS 158, since it will be universally understood that year-end measurement is being applied.

The mandatory effective date for the standard's recognition and disclosure provisions depends on whether the reporting entity is publicly held or not. For a plan sponsor with publicly traded equity securities, initial application of the requirements to recognize the funded status of a benefit plan and the disclosure requirements was required as of the end of the fiscal year ending after December 15, 2006. Application as of the end of an earlier fiscal year had been encouraged, provided that it was applied to all of that entity's benefit plans.

For employers without publicly traded equity securities, application of the requirements pertaining to recognition of the funded status of a benefit plan and to the disclosure requirements was as of the end of the first fiscal year ending after June 15, 2007. Again, application as of the end of an earlier fiscal year was encouraged, but only if applied to all of that reporting entity's benefit plans.

FAS 158 provided that an employer without publicly traded equity securities was to disclose the following information in the notes to the financial statements for a fiscal year ending after December 15, 2006, but before June 16, 2007, unless it applied the recognition provisions of that standard in preparing those financial statements:

a.  A brief description of the provisions of FAS 158
b.  The date that adoption is required
c.  The date the employer planned to adopt the recognition provisions of the standard, if earlier

In the year that the *recognition provisions* of FAS 158 were initially to be applied, the reporting entity was required to disclose, in the notes to the annual financial statements, the incremental effect of applying the standard on individual line items in the year-end statement of financial position. In the year that the *measurement date provisions* of FAS 158 were initially applied, a reporting entity that is a business was to disclose the separate adjustments made to retained earnings and accumulated other comprehensive income. If the reporting entity was a not-for-profit, it was to disclose the separate adjustment made to unrestricted net assets.

## Disclosure Requirements

Disclosure requirements for defined benefit pension and other postretirement plans have, of necessity, always been rather voluminous and complex. In part, this has been caused by the "smoothing" (what FASB calls the "delayed recognition" of pension expense, as conceived by FAS 87 and FAS 106), and the resultant "off the balance sheet" nature of plan assets and obligations. What would have otherwise been distortions of the sponsor's (reporting entity's) financial position was arguably moderated via the footnote disclosures required first under FAS 87, then under FAS 132, and most recently (beginning in 2003) under FAS 132(R), which essentially remains in effect, as modified by FAS 158.

Under the provisions of FAS 158, a business entity that sponsors one or more defined benefit plans is required to disclose—separately for pension plans and for other postretirement benefit plans—the following information in the notes to its annual financial statements:

a.   For each *annual* statement of income presented, the amounts recognized in other comprehensive income, showing separately the net gain or loss and net prior service cost or credit. Those amounts are to be segregated into those amounts arising during the period and reclassification adjustments of other comprehensive income as a result of being recognized as components of net periodic benefit cost for the period.

b.   For each *annual* statement of income presented, the net transition asset or obligation recognized as a reclassification adjustment of other comprehensive income as a result of being recognized as a component of net periodic benefit cost for the period.

c.   For each *annual* statement of financial position presented, the amounts in accumulated other comprehensive income that have not yet been recognized as components of net periodic benefit cost, showing separately the net gain or loss, net prior service cost or credit, and net transition asset or obligation.

d.   The amounts in accumulated other comprehensive income expected to be recognized as components of net periodic benefit cost over the fiscal year that follows the most recent annual statement of financial position presented, showing separately the net gain or loss, net prior service cost or credit, and net transition asset or obligation.

e.   The amount and timing of any plan assets expected to be returned to the business entity during the 12-month period, or operating cycle if longer, that follows the most recent annual statement of financial position presented.

A significant change from the previously imposed disclosure requirements, which were set forth by FAS 132(R), is that these requirements apply consistently to both publicly held and nonpublicly held entities sponsoring defined benefit plans. Under prior practice, privately held companies were substantially exempted from many disclosure requirements.

While immediate income statement recognition of changes in defined benefit plan assets and obligations had been strongly opposed by reporting entities when FAS 87 was being developed in the mid-1980s, over the intervening years the severe deficiencies of GAAP have become well known, and this has been underlined in certain industries (e.g., airlines) as numerous entities have sought bankruptcy protection in part because of pension obligations that had been largely hidden from financial statement users, and perhaps underappreciated by entity management, as well. These defects include the use of an expected long-term rate of return on plan assets (rather than actual observed periodic returns), the deferral of actuarial gain and loss recognition, subject to the 10% corridor and amortization (instead of immediate recognition of actuarially-determined changes), and the delayed recognition of prior service cost associated with plan amendments (versus immediate recognition of the effects of plan amendments made by management). Criticism has also been directed at the combined reporting of service, interest, and other components of pension expense, although this is somewhat less of a concern than the previously noted matters. The latitude granted to preparers regarding the key assumptions affecting the computed pension obligation (salary progression, expected returns, discount rate) has been yet another area of concern.

FASB had for some time been contemplating, and slowly moving toward, a different model for accounting for pension and other postretirement benefit plan costs, which would reduce or eliminate the "smoothing" approach, but adoption of a full accrual approach remains controversial, particularly among critics citing the volatility introduced into measures of periodic performance as a result of the increasing usage of fair value measures. A big step was taken in 2006, with the promulgation of FAS 158, which requires that sponsors of such plans display in their balance sheets the funded status of the plans, effectively relocating certain former footnote disclosures to the body of the statement of financial position itself, as discussed above. This standard achieves a presentation and disclosure objective but does not, alas, ameliorate the fundamental recognition and measurement problems inherent in current GAAP for defined benefit plans.

FAS 132(R), as further amended by FAS 158, which sets forth the current disclosure requirements, establishes differential requirements for nonpublic companies, and also significantly expands requirements to interim period financial statements, bowing to concerns unique to public company financial reporting.

The FAS 158 amendments to FAS 132(R) continue the practice of exempting nonpublic reporting entities from significant portions of the following disclosure requirements. The specific exemptions are explicitly set forth in the next paragraphs.

**Reconciliation of plan benefit obligation.** This reconciliation must report, if applicable, the separate effects for the period of the service cost, interest cost, contributions by plan participants, actuarial gains and losses, foreign currency exchange rate changes, benefits paid, plan amendments, business combinations, divestitures, plan curtailments, settlements, and special termination benefits. In preparing this reconciliation for defined benefit pension plans, the plan benefit obligation equals the projected benefit obligation; for defined benefit postretirement plans, it equals the accumulated postemployment benefit obligation. *Nonpublic reporting entities remain exempt from this disclosure requirement.*

**Reconciliation of fair value of plan assets.** This reconciliation must report, if applicable, the separate effects for the period of the actual return on plan assets, foreign currency exchange rate changes, contributions made by the employer, contributions by the plan participants, benefits paid, business combinations, divestitures, and settlements. *Nonpublic reporting entities remain exempt from this disclosure requirement.*

**Funded status of the plan and the amounts recognized in the balance sheet.** This must separately report, as applicable, the assets and the current and noncurrent liabilities recognized. Other information formerly found in the notes to the financial statements (e.g., the amount of unamortized prior service cost) will now, under the requirements of FAS 158, be included in the balance sheet proper (e.g. in accumulated other comprehensive income), and are no longer footnote disclosure issues. *Nonpublic reporting entities remain exempt from this disclosure requirement.*

**Information about plan assets.** For each major category of plan assets, such as equities, debt instruments, and real estate, disclosure is required of the percentage of the fair value of total plan assets held as of the measurement date used for each balance sheet presented. A narrative description of investment policies and strategies employed is now required, which should address target allocations for major asset classes, presented on a weighted-average basis as of the measurement date, as well as other factors that are pertinent to an understanding, such as information about investment goals, risk management practices, permitted and prohibited investments (e.g., use of derivatives, diversification, and relationships between plan assets and benefit obligations). Also required is a narrative explanation of the basis upon which the expected long-term return on assets has been ascertained (e.g., the extent to which historical performance has been used to extrapolate from, what adjustments were made to anticipate future trends, etc.). The standard encourages expanded discussion and the use of greater asset categorization.

**Accumulated benefit obligation.** For defined benefit pension plans, disclosure is required of the accumulated benefit obligation, in addition to the aforementioned disclosures of the projected benefit obligation.

**Benefits to be paid.** The benefits expected to be paid in each of the next five fiscal years plus the aggregate of the five years thereafter. These estimated amounts are developed using the same assumptions that are used to measure the employer's benefit obligation, and should include benefits that will be attributable to estimated future employee service.

**Contributions to be received.** The amount of contributions expected to be paid into the plan during the next fiscal year; the aggregate of the amounts required by funding regulations or laws, discretionary amounts, and noncash contributions may be reported.

**Periodic benefit cost.** This must display separately the service cost component, interest cost component, expected return on plan assets, the gain or loss component, the prior service cost or credit component, the transition asset or obligation component, and the gain or loss recognized due to settlements or curtailments. *Nonpublic reporting entities remain exempt from this disclosure requirement.*

**Amounts reported in other comprehensive income.** Separately, the net gain or loss and net prior service cost or credit recognized in other comprehensive income for the period, and reclassification adjustments of other comprehensive income for the period, as those amounts, including amortization of the net transition asset or obligation, are recognized as components of net periodic benefit cost. Also required to be disclosed are the amounts in accumulated other comprehensive income that have not yet been recognized as components of net periodic benefit cost, showing separately the net gain or loss, the net prior service cost or credit, and the net transition asset or obligation.

**Assumptions.** There must be disclosure of various assumptions used in the accounting for plans: assumed discount rates, rates of compensation increase (for pay-related plans), and expected long-term rate of return on plan assets. These must be reported in a tabular format, identifying assumptions pertaining to the reported benefit obligation and to determine net benefit cost.

**Assumed health care cost trends.** For relevant plans, disclosure is required of the assumed health care cost trend rates for the following year used to measure the expected cost of benefits, as well as a general description of the direction and pattern of change in the assumed trend rates thereafter, together with the ultimate rate and when that terminal rate is expected to be achieved.

**Sensitivity data.** Disclosure of the effects of a one-percentage-point increase and decrease in the assumed health care cost trend rate on the aggregate service and interest cost components of the net periodic postretirement health care benefit cost, and on the accumulated postretirement benefit obligation for health care benefits. In computing these amounts all other assumptions must be held constant. *Nonpublic reporting entities remain exempt from this disclosure requirement.*

**Other information.** As applicable, other disclosures are also required. These include the amounts and types of securities of the employer and its related entities included in plan assets, the approximate amount of future annual benefits of plan participants covered by insurance contracts issued by the employer or its related entities, and any significant transactions between the employer or related entities and the plan, all of which are equally required for public and nonpublic reporting entities. Any commitment to future benefit increases used as a basis for computing the obligation, the cost of providing special or contractual termination benefits during the reporting period, and information about any changes not otherwise apparent, are also required disclosures, but only for publicly held reporting entities.

FAS 158 added a requirement to disclose the amounts in accumulated other comprehensive income expected to be recognized as components of net periodic benefit cost over the fiscal year that follows the most recent annual statement of financial position presented, showing separately the net gain or loss, net prior service cost or credit, and net transition asset or obligation. It further requires identification of the amount and timing of any plan assets expected to be returned to the employer during the 12-month period, or operating cycle if longer, that follows the most recent annual statement of financial position presented. These new disclosure requirements apply to all reporting entities.

Under FAS 132(R), as amended by FAS 158, nonpublic reporting entities must report (in lieu of disclosure items cited above as being exempted for such entities) as of each balance sheet date, benefit obligations, fair value of plan assets, and the funded status of the plan. For each period for which an income statement is presented, these entities must disclose employer contributions, participant contributions, and benefits paid. Regarding the composition of assets held by the plan, for each balance sheet the nonpublic reporting entity must reveal the percentage allocation across the major asset categories (e.g., equity securities, real estate, etc.), as well as narration about investment policies and strategies for each major investment category. A narration is also required of the basis for determining the assumed expected long-term rate of return on assets, including the reasons for any adjustments made to actual long-term historical-based expectations. Additional disclosures—if deemed useful in providing insights regarding risks attendant to various asset categories and to the long-term rates of return expected—are also encouraged.

Additionally, for defined benefit pension plans, the accumulated benefit obligation must be disclosed, as must the benefits expected to be paid in each of the following five fiscal years and over the aggregate for the next five years. The expected plan contributions to be received during the next fiscal year—inclusive of those required by statute or regulation, those that are discretionary, and those made as noncash contributions—are to be stated.

Furthermore the amounts in the financial statements, distinguishing benefit plan assets from current and from noncurrent benefit plan liabilities—must be identified, along with the amounts of net gain or loss and net prior service cost or credit recognized in other comprehensive income, and the related amounts as these elements are then recognized as components of periodic benefit expense. The amounts that are in accumulated other comprehensive income, not yet included in benefit expense, must be disclosed, classified into net gain or loss, net prior service cost or credit, and net transition asset or obligation.

The reporting entities must further disclose the weighted-average assumed discount rates, rate of assumed compensation cost increase (for pay-related plans), expected long-term returns on plan assets—the latter in a tabular format that identifies assumptions used to compute the benefit obligation and to determine benefit cost.

For postretirement health care plans, the assumed cost trend rate must be stated as it pertains to the following fiscal year, and a narrative discussion given regarding the pattern and direction of anticipated future changes, including the so-called ultimate trend rate (i.e., when all short-term perturbations affecting health care inflation have been resolved) that is expected, together with the timing of its achievement. (Cost trend assumptions are obviously of enormous importance in evaluating the adequacy of provisions made to accrue future benefit costs, but in practice it has proven to be extremely difficult to estimate even short-term cost changes in health care, let alone longer-term changes and the time until those changes might be expected to plateau.)

Postretirement benefit plan disclosures by private entities also must include information about the nature and impact of significant nonroutine events, such as plan amendments, curtailments, settlements, and the effects of any mergers or divestitures of parts of the reporting entity. Disclosure must be made of amounts included in accumulated other comprehensive income that are expected to flow into periodic pension benefit cost over the next fiscal year, with the portions attributable to net gain or loss, net prior service cost or credit, and the net transition asset or obligation. Similarly, the amount of plan assets expected to be returned to the sponsoring employer over the following fiscal year is to be identified.

For entities having multiple plans, the information required under FAS 132(R) is to be aggregated so that all defined benefit retirement plans are combined, and all other postretirement benefit plans are likewise combined. Disclosure of amounts recognized in the balance sheet must distinguish prepaid benefit costs from accrued benefit liabilities. However, disclosures about pension plans with assets in excess of the accumulated benefit obligation generally may be aggregated with disclosures about pension plans with accumulated benefit obligations in excess of assets. When aggregation is utilized, the financial statements must disclose separately the aggregate benefit obligations and aggregate fair value of plan assets for each of the pension plans and other benefit plans with accumulated obligations in excess of assets. The reporting entity may also combine disclosures about pension plans or other postretirement benefit plans outside the US with those for US plans unless the obligations of the plans outside the US are significant relative to the entity's total benefit obligation and the non-US plans use significantly different assumptions.

The simplified disclosures permitted for nonpublic entities are illustrated by the following tabulation of comparative data:

|  | *2007* | *2008* |
|---|---|---|
| **Funded status** |  |  |
| Projected benefit obligation at December 31 | $ 1,900 | $ 2,006 |
| Fair value of Plan assets at December 31 | 1,376 | 1,519 |
| Funded status | $ (524) | $ (487) |
| **Amounts recognized on the balance sheet** |  |  |
| Prepaid (accrued) benefit cost | $ -- | $ (23) |
| **Weighted-average assumptions** |  |  |
| Discount rate | 7.5% | 7.5% |
| Expected return on plan assets | 9.0% | 9.0% |
| Rate of compensation increase | 4.0% | 4.0% |
| **Additional pension data** |  |  |
| Net periodic pension cost | $ 163 | $ 168 |
| Employer contribution | 140 | 145 |
| Benefits paid | 155 | 160 |

Under FAS 87 and FAS 106, before the promulgation of FAS 158, most of the information used to determine the amounts in the foregoing disclosure was provided by the actuary or worksheet entries and did not appear in the entity's accounting records. Thus, accounts that reflect such events as the actuarial loss and prior service costs usually were not found in the employer's accounting records. However, FAS 158 requires that plans' under- or over-funded status and the "deferred recognition" gains and losses be formally recorded in the financial statements (the balance sheet, specifically). While FAS 158 does not alter the deferred recognition (i.e., smoothing) aspects of prior GAAP, it does mandate that essentially all the formerly off-balance-sheet defined benefit cost elements be included in the reporting entity's balance sheet.

**Interim Financial Reporting Requirements**

FAS 132(R) imposed new requirements affecting both public and nonpublic company interim financial reporting. Publicly traded entities must disclose, in interim financial statements that include a statement of income, details regarding both benefit cost and contributions paid. The amount of net periodic benefit cost recognized must be set forth, showing separately the service cost component, the interest cost component, the expected return on plan assets for the period, the amortization of the unrecognized transition obligation or transition asset, the amount of recognized gains or losses, the amount of prior service cost recognized, and the amount of gain or loss recognized due to a settlement or curtailment. Additionally, the total amount of the employer's contributions paid, and expected to be paid, during the current fiscal year, must be presented, if significantly different from amounts previously disclosed pursuant to the annual reporting requirements of the standard. It is permissible to present estimated contributions in the aggregate, combining contributions required by funding regulations or laws, discretionary contributions, and noncash contributions. FAS 158 has conformed these requirements to the newly imposed regime whereby the balance sheet fully discloses (in accumulated other comprehensive income) the deferred recognition items that formerly were "off-balance-sheet."

For nonpublic entities, disclosure is required—in interim periods when a complete set of GAAP-basis financial statements is being presented—of the total amount of the employer's contributions paid, and expected to be paid, during the current fiscal year, if significantly different from amounts previously disclosed pursuant to the annual reporting requirements of the standard. Estimated contributions may be presented in the aggregate combining contributions required by funding regulations or laws, discretionary contributions, and noncash contributions.

In developing FAS 158, FASB considered whether full or partial interim date remeasurement of pension and benefit plan assets and obligations should be mandated. It decided not to require this because of the additional costs that would be incurred by reporting entities to implement that change, and it would have raised additional issues not addressed by either FAS 87 or FAS 106. Furthermore, doing so would have represented a fundamental change in the measurement of net periodic benefit cost, and measurement issues were defined as being beyond the scope and objectives of this standard. Accordingly, remeasurement on an interim basis is neither required nor permitted under FAS 158.

**Reporting and Disclosure by Not-for-Profit Entities**

Not-for-profit entities sponsoring single-employer defined benefit plans are subject to FAS 158, but special rules are necessary to accommodate the fact that such entities do not report other comprehensive income as prescribed under FAS 130 for all other private sector entities. It is therefore necessary to analogize from the requirements of FAS 158. Rather than include the realized but as-yet-unrecognized net gains and losses, the unrecognized prior service cost or credit, and the unamortized transition amounts in accumulated other comprehensive income, these are to be reflected in changes in unrestricted net assets arising from a defined benefit plan. These changes will flow through the current period's statement of activities, since GAAP for not-for-profit organizations (FAS 117 and related standards—see discussion in Chapter 25) does not provide for an analogue to other comprehensive income, where nonstockholder changes in net worth are reported outside the income statement (statement of activities).

## Other Pension Considerations

**Annuity and insurance contracts.** If annuity contracts and other insurance contracts that are equivalent in substance are valid and irrevocable, if they transfer significant risks to an unrelated insurance company (not a captive insurer), and if there is no reasonable doubt as to their payment, they are excluded from plan assets and their benefits are excluded from the accumulated benefit obligation and from the projected benefit obligation. Most other contracts are not considered annuities for FAS 87 purposes. If a plan's benefit formula specifies coverage by nonparticipating annuity contracts, the service component of net pension costs is the cost of those contracts. In the case of a participating annuity contract, the cost of the participation right is recognized as an asset and measured annually at its fair value. If fair value is inestimable, the cost is systematically amortized and carried at amortized cost (not to exceed net realizable value). Benefits provided by the formula beyond those provided by annuities are accounted for in the usual FAS 87 manner. All other insurance contracts are considered investments and are usually measured at cash surrender value, conversion value, contract value, or some equivalent.

In certain circumstances, annuity benefits are paid by employers after the insurer fails to make required payments. According to EITF 91-7, a loss is recognized by an employer at the time the employer assumes the benefit obligation payments to retirees for an insolvent insurance company that held these pension obligations. The loss recognized is the lesser of any gain recognized in the original contract with the insurance company or the amount of benefit obligation payments assumed by the company. Any additional loss not recognized is accounted for as a plan amendment in accordance with FAS 87.

**Defined contribution plans.** In the typical defined contribution plan, the contribution is either discretionary or derived from a formula, and that amount is the expense to be reported in the sponsor's financial statements for the year. Benefits are generally paid from the pool of accumulated contributions and are limited to the plan assets available to pay them. If, however, the defined contribution plan has defined benefits, the provision is calculated as required under FAS 87.

**Multiemployer pension plans.** Participation in a multiemployer plan (two or more unrelated employers contribute such as in collectively bargained union-sponsored plans) requires that the contribution for the period be recognized as net pension cost and that any contributions due and unpaid be recognized as a liability. Assets of all the employers sponsoring this type of plan are usually commingled and not segregated or restricted. A Board of Trustees usually administers these plans. If there is a withdrawal of an employer from this type of plan and if an obligation to make up any funding deficiency is either probable or reasonably possible, FAS 5 applies.

Some plans are, in substance, a pooling or aggregation of single employer plans and are ordinarily without collective-bargaining agreements. Contributions are usually based on a specified benefit formula. These plans are not considered multiemployer, and the accounting is based on each employer's respective interest in the plan.

Per EITF 90-3, the existence of an executed agreement does not require recognition by an employer of a liability beyond currently due and unpaid contributions.

The foregoing accounting has not been affected by the promulgation of FAS 158.

**Non-US pension arrangements.** The terms and conditions that define the amount of benefits and the nature of the obligation determine the substance of a non-US pension arrangement. If they are, in substance, similar to pension plans, FAS 87 and FAS 88 apply.

**Business combinations.** When an entity that sponsors a single-employer defined benefit pension plan is purchased, the purchaser must assign part of the purchase price to an asset if plan assets exceed the projected benefit obligation, or to a liability if the projected benefit obligation exceeds plan assets. The projected benefit obligation includes the effect of any expected plan curtailment or termination as a result of the change in ownership of the sponsor. This assignment eliminates any existing unrecognized components, and any future differences between contributions and net pension cost will affect the asset or liability recognized when the purchase was initially recorded.

## FAS 88

FAS 88 was issued concurrently with FAS 87 and was meant to be applied within the framework of that standard. FAS 88 describes the accounting to be followed by obligors when all or part of defined benefit pension plans have been settled or curtailed. It establishes employer accounting procedures for benefits offered when employment is terminated.

Settlements include both the purchase of nonparticipating annuity contracts and lump-sum cash payments. The following three criteria must all be met in order to constitute a pension obligation settlement:

1. It must be irrevocable
2. It must relieve the obligor of primary responsibility for the obligation
3. It must eliminate significant risks associated with the obligation and the assets used to effect it

Transactions that do not meet these three criteria do not qualify for treatment as a settlement under FAS 88. For example, an obligor could invest in a portfolio of high-quality fixed-income securities that would provide cash flows of interest and return-of-principal payments on dates that approximate the dates on which settlement payments are expected to become due. This would not meet the above criteria, however, because the employer is still primarily liable for the pension obligation and the investment is not irrevocable. Such a defeasance strategy does not constitute a settlement.

Under an annuity contract settlement, an unrelated insurance company unconditionally accepts an obligation to provide the required benefits. The following criteria must be met for this type of settlement:

1. It must be irrevocable
2. It must involve a transfer of material risk to the insurance company

There can be no reasonable doubt as to the ability of the insurance company to meet its contractual obligation. The substance of any participating annuity contract must relieve the employer of most of the risks and rewards or it does not meet the criteria.

Curtailments include early discontinuance of employee services or cessation or suspension of a plan. Additional benefits may not be earned, although future service time may be counted towards vesting. Curtailments must meet the following criteria:

1. It must materially diminish present employees' future service or
2. It must stop or materially diminish the accumulation of benefits by a significant number of employees

A curtailment and a settlement can occur separately or together.

**Settlements.** If the entire projected benefit obligation is settled, any FAS 87 unrecognized net gain (loss) plus any remaining unrecognized net asset existing when FAS 87 was initially applied are immediately recognized. A pro rata portion is recognized in the case of partial settlement. If the obligation is settled by purchasing participating annuities, the cost of the right of participation is deducted from the gain (but not from the loss) before recognition.

If the total of the interest cost and service cost components of the FAS 87 periodic pension cost is greater than or equal to the settlement costs during a given year, the recognition of the above gain (loss) is not required, but is permitted. However, a consistent policy must be followed in this regard. The settlement cost is generally the cash paid, or the cost of nonparticipating annuities purchased, or the cost of participating annuities reduced by the cost of the right of participation.

### Example of a settlement

To use information from the previous baseline example, the company's pension plan settles the $1,150 vested benefit portion of its projected benefit obligation by using plan assets to purchase a nonparticipating annuity contract for $1,150. As a result of this settlement, nonvested benefits and the effects of projected future compensation levels remain in the plan. Also, a pro rata amount of the unrecognized net actuarial loss on assets, unrecognized prior service cost, and unamortized net asset at FAS 87 adoption are recognized due to settlement. Because the projected benefit obligation is reduced from $1,550 to $400, a drop of 74%, the pro rata amount used for recognition purposes is 74%. These changes are noted in the following table:

| | *Before settlement* | *Effect of settlement* | *After settlement* |
|---|---|---|---|
| Assets and obligations: | | | |
| Vested benefit obligation | $(1,150) | $1,150 | $0 |
| Nonvested benefits | (400) | | (400) |
| Accumulated benefit obligation | (1,550) | 1,150 | (400) |
| Effects of projected future compensation levels | (456) | | (456) |
| Projected benefit obligation | (2,006) | 1,150 | (856) |
| Plan assets at fair value | 1,519 | (1,150) | 369 |
| | | | |
| Items not yet recognized in earnings: | | | |
| Funded status | (487) | 0 | (487) |
| Unrecognized net actuarial loss on assets | 174 | (129) | 45 |
| Unrecognized prior service cost | 293 | (217) | 76 |
| Unamortized net asset at FAS 87 adoption | (3) | 2 | (1) |
| Prepaid (accrued) benefit cost | $(23) | $(344) | $(367) |

The entry used by the company to record this transaction does not include the purchase of the annuity contract since the pension plan acquires the contract with existing funds. The recognition of the pro rata amount of the unrecognized net actuarial loss on assets, unrecognized prior service cost, and unamortized net asset at FAS 87 adoption is recorded with the following entry:

| | | |
|---|---|---|
| Loss from settlement of pension obligation | 344 | |
| Accrued/prepaid pension cost | | 344 |

The foregoing provisions have been amended by FAS 158, necessarily, to state that the maximum gain or loss subject to recognition in earnings when an obligation is settled is the net gain or loss that is remaining in accumulated other comprehensive income, plus any transition asset remaining in accumulated other comprehensive income from the original application of FAS 87. The maximum gain or loss, first determined at the date of settlement, is fully reported in earnings only if the entire projected benefit obligation is settled; if it is only partially settled, only a pro rata portion of the maximum gain or loss can be recognized.

**Curtailments.** A curtailment results in the elimination of future years of service. The pro rata portions of any (1) unrecognized cost of retroactive plan amendments and (2) remaining unrecognized net obligation existing when FAS 87 was initially applied that is associated with the eliminated years of service are immediately recognized as a loss.

If curtailment results in a decrease in the projected benefit obligation, a gain is indicated. An increase in the projected benefit obligation (excluding termination benefits) indicates a loss. This indicated gain (loss) is then netted against the loss from unrecognized prior service cost recognized in accordance with the preceding paragraph. The net result is the curtailment gain or curtailment loss. This gain (loss) is accounted for as provided in FAS 5. A gain is recognized upon actual employee termination or plan suspension. A loss is recognized when both the curtailment is probable and the effects are reasonably estimable.

After the curtailment gain (loss) is calculated, any remaining unrecognized net asset existing when FAS 87 was initially applied is transferred from that category and combined with the gain (loss) arising after FAS 87 application. It is subsequently treated as a component of the new gain (loss) category.

### Example of a curtailment

To use information from the previous baseline example, the company shuts down one of its factories, which terminated the employment of a number of its staff. The terminated employees have nonvested benefits of $120 and projected benefit obligation of $261. As a result of this curtailment, 19% of the projected benefit obligation has been eliminated ($381 PBO reduction resulting from the curtailment, divided by the beginning $2,006 PBO). Accordingly, 19% of the unrecognized prior service cost and unamortized net asset at FAS 87 adoption are recognized due to the curtailment. In addition, the total projected benefit reduction of $381 is first netted against the unrecognized net actuarial loss on assets of $174, leaving $207 to be recognized as a gain. These changes are noted in the following table:

| | *Before curtailment* | *Effect of curtailment* | *After curtailment* |
|---|---|---|---|
| Assets and obligations: | | | |
| Vested benefit obligation | $(1,150) | | $(1,150) |
| Nonvested benefits | (400) | $120 | (280) |
| Accumulated benefit obligation | (1,550) | 120 | (1,430) |
| Effects of projected future compensation levels | (456) | 261 | (195) |
| Projected benefit obligation | (2,006) | 381 | (1,625) |
| Plan assets at fair value | 1,519 | 0 | 1,519 |
| Items not yet recognized in earnings: | | | |
| Funded status | (487) | 381 | (106) |
| Unrecognized net actuarial loss on assets | 174 | (174) | 0 |
| Unrecognized prior service cost | 293 | (56) | 237 |
| Unamortized net asset at FAS 87 adoption | (3) | 1 | (2) |
| Prepaid (accrued) benefit cost | $(23) | $152 | $129 |

The company records the recognition of the pro rata amount of the unrecognized prior service cost and unamortized net asset at FAS 87 adoption with the following entry, which is offset against the net gain of $207 resulting from the reduction in the planned benefit obligation:

| | | |
|---|---|---|
| Accrued/prepaid pension cost | 152 | |
| Gain from curtailment of pension obligation | | 152 |

FAS 158 has also revised the guidance on accounting for curtailments of defined benefit plans. To the extent that prior service costs are included in accumulated other comprehensive income under the new mandates, and this is associated with service years no longer expected to be rendered, this must be recognized currently as a loss. This would occur if prior service cost is being amortized over a term that no longer accurately reflects expected future service by the post-curtailment workforce. Prior service cost, in this context, includes that resulting from plan amendments and also any transition obligation remaining from the initial adoption of FAS 87.

Under FAS 158, curtailment gain or loss alters the projected benefit obligation. If such a gain exceeds any net loss included in accumulated other comprehensive income, or the entire gain if a net gain exists, it is reported as a curtailment gain. On the other hand, to the extent that such a loss exceeds any net *gain* included in accumulated other comprehensive income, or the entire loss if a net loss exists, this will be reported as a curtailment loss. Any transition asset remaining in accumulated other comprehensive income is to be treated as a net gain and combined with the net gain or loss arising subsequent to the FAS 87 transition.

**Termination benefits.** Termination benefits are accounted for in accordance with FAS 5. Special short time period benefits require that a loss and a liability be recognized when the offer is accepted and the amount can be reasonably estimated. Contractual termination benefits require that a loss and a liability be recognized when it is probable that employees will receive the benefits and the amount can be reasonably estimated. The cost of these benefits is the cash paid at termination and the present value of future payments. Termination benefits and curtailments can occur together.

**Example of termination benefits**

Again using the information from the previous baseline example, the company offers a one-time early retirement bonus payment, which is in addition to existing pension benefits. As a result of the offer, the company directly pays $200 in termination benefits. As a result of the employee retirements, the liability associated with projected future compensation levels drops by $60, while the pro rata portion of the unrecognized prior service cost associated with the retiring employees is $39. These changes are noted in the following table:

|  | *Before termination benefit* | *Effect of termination benefit* | *After termination benefit* |
|---|---|---|---|
| Assets and obligations: |  |  |  |
| Vested benefit obligation | $(1,150) |  | $(1,150) |
| Nonvested benefits | (400) |  | (400) |
| Accumulated benefit obligation | (1,550) |  | (1,550) |
| Effects of projected future compensation levels | (456) | $60 | (396) |
| Projected benefit obligation | (2,006) | $60 | (1,946) |
| Plan assets at fair value | 1,519 | 0 | 1,519 |
| Items not yet recognized in earnings: |  |  |  |
| Funded status | (487) |  | (427) |
| Unrecognized net actuarial loss on assets | 174 | (60) | 114 |
| Unrecognized prior service cost | 293 | (39) | 254 |
| Unamortized net asset at FAS 87 adoption | (3) | — | (3) |
| Prepaid (accrued) benefit cost | $(23) | (39) | $(62) |
| Cost of termination benefits |  | (200) |  |
| Total loss on terminations |  | $(239) |  |

The company nets the $60 gain on reduction of projected future compensation levels against the existing unrecognized net actuarial loss on assets. It then records the $39 loss caused by the increased amortization of the unrecognized prior service cost and the $200 cost of the termination benefits with the following entry:

| Loss on employee terminations | 239 |  |
|---|---|---|
| Accrued/prepaid pension cost |  | 39 |
| Cash |  | 200 |

**Component disposal.** Gains (losses), as calculated above, that result because of a disposal of a component of the entity are recognized according to the provisions of FAS 144.

## Postretirement Benefits other than Pensions

FAS 106 established the standard for employers' accounting for other (than pension) postretirement employee benefits (commonly, if misleadingly, called OPEB). This standard prescribes a single method for measuring and recognizing an employer's accumulated postretirement benefit obligation (APBO). It applies to all forms of postretirement benefits, although the most material such benefit is usually postretirement health care coverage. It uses the fundamental framework established by FAS 87 and FAS 88. To the extent that the promised benefits are similar, the accounting provisions are similar. Only when there is a compelling reason, is the accounting different.

FAS 106 requires accrual accounting and adopts the three primary characteristics of pension accounting as follows:

1. Delayed recognition (changes are not recognized immediately but are subsequently recognized in a gradual and systematic way)
2. Reporting net cost (aggregates of various items are reported as one net amount)
3. Offsetting assets and liabilities (assets and liabilities are sometimes shown net)

FAS 106 distinguishes between the substantive plan and the written plan. Although generally the same, the substantive plan (the one understood as evidenced by past practice or by communication of intended changes) is the basis for the accounting if it differs from the written plan.

FAS 106 focuses on accounting for a single-employer plan that defines the postretirement benefits to be provided. A defined benefit postretirement plan defines benefits in terms of (1) monetary amounts or (2) benefit coverage to be provided. Postretirement benefits can include tuition assistance, legal services, day care, housing subsidies, health insurance coverage (probably the most significant), and other benefits. The amount of benefits usually depends on a benefit formula. OPEB may be provided to current employees, former employees, beneficiaries and covered dependents. This standard applies to settlement of the APBO and to curtailment of a plan as part of a special termination benefit offer. It also applies to deferred compensation contracts with individuals. Taken together, these contracts are equivalent to an OPEB plan. FAS 106 does not apply to benefits provided through a pension plan. If part of a larger plan with active employees, the OPEB is segregated and accounted for in accordance with this standard. If not materially different, estimates, averages, and computational shortcuts may be used.

The basic tenet of FAS 106 is that accrual accounting is better than cash basis accounting. Recognition and measurement of the obligation to provide OPEB is required in order to provide relevant information to financial statement users. Although funding and cash flow information is incorporated into the statement, the overall liability is the primary focus.

The standard attempts, in accordance with the terms of the substantive plan, to account for the exchange transaction that takes place between the employer, who is ultimately responsible for providing OPEB, and the employee who provides services, in part at least, to obtain the OPEB. FAS 106 accounting requires that the liability for OPEB be fully accrued when the employee is fully eligible for all of the expected benefits. The fact that the employee may continue to work beyond this date is not relevant since the employee has already provided the services required to earn the OPEB.

OPEB are considered to be deferred compensation earned in an exchange transaction during the time periods that the employee provides services. The expected cost generally is attributed in equal amounts (unless the plan attributes a disproportionate share of benefits to early years) over the periods from the employee's hiring date (unless credit for the service is only granted from a later plan eligibility or entry date) to the date that the employee attains full eligibility for all benefits expected to be received. This accrual is followed even if the employee provides service beyond the date of full eligibility.

**Accounting for postretirement benefits.** The expected postretirement benefit obligation (EPBO) is the actuarial present value (APV) as of a specific date of the benefits expected to be paid to the employee, beneficiaries and covered dependents. This term is not used in FAS 87. Measurement of the EPBO is based on the following:

1. Expected amount and timing of future benefits
2. Expected future costs
3. Extent of cost sharing (contributions, deductibles, coinsurance provisions, etc.) between employer, employee and others (i.e., the government). The APV of employee contributions reduces the APV of the EPBO. Obligations to return employee contributions, plus interest if applicable, are recognized as a component of EPBO.

The EPBO includes an assumed salary progression for a pay-related plan. Future compensation levels represent the best estimate after considering the individual employees involved, general price levels, seniority, productivity, promotions, indirect effects, etc.

The APBO is the APV as of a specific date of all future benefits attributable to service by an employee to that date. It represents the portion of the EPBO earned to date. After full eligibility is attained, the APBO equals the EPBO.

The APBO also includes an assumed salary progression for a pay-related plan. Thus, this term is more comparable to the projected benefit obligation (PBO) under FAS 87. The accumulated benefit obligation in FAS 87 has no counterpart in FAS 106. (Note, however, that recently promulgated FAS 158 has amended FAS 87 and FAS 106. FAS 158 was discussed earlier in this chapter.)

Net periodic postretirement benefit costs include the following components:

1. Service cost—APV of benefits attributable to the current period (i.e., the portion of the EPBO earned this period)
2. Interest cost—Interest on the APBO
3. Actual return on plan assets
4. Gain or loss
5. Amortization of unrecognized prior service cost
6. Amortization of the transition asset or obligation

Note that return on plan assets is included in the periodic expense determination, consistent with accounting for defined benefit pension plans. However, in virtually all cases, OPEB plans are unfunded, and thus there will be no asset return. If a trust has been established to fund these benefits, it does not necessarily have to be "bankruptcy proof," or insulated completely from the claims of general creditors, in order to qualify as plan assets in accordance with FAS 106, per EITF 93-3. On the other hand, assets held in a trust that explicitly makes them available to the general creditors in bankruptcy do not qualify as plan assets under FAS 106. The funded status of other postretirement defined benefit plans will, under provisions of FAS 158, now be formally reported in the balance sheet, as described above.

The transition obligation was the unrecognized and unfunded APBO for all of the participants in the plan at the date of adoption of FAS 106. This obligation was either (1) recognized immediately as the effect of an accounting change, subject to certain limitations, or (2) elected to be recognized on a delayed basis over future service periods with disclosure of the unrecognized amount. The delayed recognition must have resulted in, at least, as rapid a recognition as would have been recognized on a pay-as-you-go (cash) basis. Under FAS 158 the transition obligation that was to be given deferred recognition will be included in accumulated other comprehensive income, with a corresponding liability.

Service costs and interest costs are defined and measured in the same manner by both FAS 106 and FAS 87. However, under FAS 106, interest increases the APBO while under FAS 87, interest increases the PBO.

Under FAS 106, a single method is required to be followed in measuring and recognizing the net periodic cost and the liability involved. That method attributes the EPBO to employee service rendered to the full eligibility date.

*Assumptions.* FAS 106 requires the use of explicit assumptions using the best estimates available of the plan's future experience, solely with regard to the individual assumption under consideration. Plan continuity is to be presumed, unless there is evidence to the contrary. Principal actuarial assumptions include: discount rates, present value factors, retirement age, participation rates (contributory plans), salary progression (pay-related plans) and probability of payment (turnover, dependency status, mortality). Present value factors for health care OPEB include cost trend rates, Medicare reimbursement rates and per capita claims cost by age.

Current interest rates, as of the measurement date, are used for discount rates in present value calculations. Examples include high-quality, fixed-income investments with similar amounts and timing and interest rates at which the postretirement benefit obligations could be settled. The EPBO, APBO, service cost and interest cost components use assumed discount rates.

The expected long-term rate of return on plan assets is an assumption about the average rate of return expected on contributions during the period and on existing plan assets. Current returns on plan assets and reinvestment returns are considered in arriving at the rate to be used. Related income taxes, if applicable, reduce the rate. Expected return on plan assets and the market-related value of plan assets use this rate in their calculation. Since ERISA does not require OPEB plans to be funded via the separate trust vehicles used for pension plans, OPEB plans are often unfunded. Thus, there are no "plan assets." Instead, the sponsor pays benefits directly, as they become due, from general corporate assets.

**Example**

A sample illustration of the basic accounting for OPEB as established by FAS 106 follows. Kinetic Corporation established a new OPEB plan as of January 1, 2008. Although the plan was new, it retroactively credited employees for their years of service to Kinetic prior to the establishment of the plan.

All employees had been hired at age 30 and become fully eligible for benefits at age 60. The plan is unfunded and, thus, there are no plan assets. The first calculation is the determination of the unrecognized transition obligation (UTO).

**Kinetic Corporation**
**December 31, 2007**

| Employee | Age | Years of service | Total years when fully eligible | Expected retirement age | Remaining service to retirement | EPBO | APBO |
|---|---|---|---|---|---|---|---|
| A | 35 | 5 | 30 | 60 | 25 | $ 14,000 | $ 2,333 |
| B | 40 | 10 | 30 | 60 | 20 | 22,000 | 7,333 |
| C | 45 | 15 | 30 | 60 | 15 | 30,000 | 15,000 |
| D | 50 | 20 | 30 | 60 | 10 | 38,000 | 25,333 |
| E | 55 | 25 | 30 | 65 | 10 | 46,000 | 38,333 |
| F | 60 | 30 | 30 | 65 | 5 | 54,000 | 54,000 |
| G | 65 | RET | -- | | -- | 46,000 | 46,000 |
| H | 70 | RET | -- | | -- | 38,000 | 38,000 |
| | | | | | 85 | $288,000 | $226,332 |

*Explanations*

1. EPBO (expected postretirement benefit obligation) is usually determined by an actuary, although it can be calculated if complete data is available.
2. APBO is calculated using the EPBO. Specifically, it is EPBO × (Years of service/Total years when fully eligible)

3. The unrecognized transition obligation (UTO) is the APBO at 12/31/07 since there are no plan assets to be deducted. The $226,332 can be amortized over the average remaining service to retirement of 14.17 (85/6) years or an optional period of 20 years, if longer. Kinetic selected the 20-year period of amortization.

4. Note that Employee F has attained full eligibility for benefits and yet plans to continue working.

5. Note that the above 2007 table is used in the calculation of the 2008 components of OPEB cost that follows.

After the establishment of the UTO, the next step is to determine the benefit cost for the year ended December 31, 2008. This calculation follows the framework established by FAS 87. The discount rate is assumed to be 10%.

**Kinetic Corporation**
**OPEB Cost**
**December 31, 2008**

| | | |
|---|---|---:|
| 1. | Service cost | $ 5,500 |
| 2. | Interest cost | 22,633 |
| 3. | Actual return on plan assets | -- |
| 4. | Gain or loss | -- |
| 5. | Amortization of unrecognized prior service cost | -- |
| 6. | Amortization of UTO | 11,317 |
| | Total OPEB Cost | $39,450 |

## Explanations

1. Service cost calculation uses only employees not yet fully eligible for benefits.

| Employee | [a]<br>12/31/07<br>*EPBO* | [b]<br>*Total years when*<br>*fully eligible* | [a ÷ b]<br>*Service cost* |
|---|---|---|---|
| A | $14,000 | 30 | $ 467 |
| B | 22,000 | 30 | 733 |
| C | 30,000 | 30 | 1,000 |
| D | 38,000 | 30 | 1,267 |
| E | 46,000 | 30 | 1,533 |
| | | | $5,000 |
| | Interest for 2006 ($5,000 × 10%) | | 500 |
| | Total service cost | | $5,500 |

2. Interest cost is the 12/31/07 APBO of $226,332 × 10% = $22,633.

3. There are no plan assets so there is no return.

4. There is no gain (loss) since there are no changes yet.

5. There is no unrecognized prior service cost initially.

6. Amortization of UTO is the 12/31/07 UTO of $226,332/20-year optional election = $11,317.

After calculation of the 2008 benefit cost, the next step is to project the EPBO and APBO for December 31, 2008. Assuming no changes, it is based on the December 31, 2007 actuarial measurement and it is calculated as shown earlier in the determination of the UTO.

**Kinetic Corporation**
**December 31, 2008**

| Employee | *Age* | *Years of*<br>*service* | *Total years when*<br>*fully eligible* | *EPBO* | *APBO* |
|---|---|---|---|---|---|
| A | 36 | 6 | 30 | $ 15,400 | $ 3,080 |
| B | 41 | 11 | 30 | 24,200 | 8,873 |
| C | 46 | 16 | 30 | 33,000 | 17,600 |
| D | 51 | 21 | 30 | 41,800 | 29,260 |
| E | 56 | 26 | 30 | 50,600 | 43,853 |
| F | 61 | 31 | -- | 59,400 | 59,400 |
| G | 66 | RET | -- | 44,620 | 44,620 |
| H | 71 | RET | -- | 36,860 | 36,860 |
| | | | | $305,880 | $243,546 |

Changes in experience or assumptions will result in gains (losses). The gain (loss) is measured by the difference resulting in the APBO or the plan assets from that projected. However, except for the effects of a decision to temporarily deviate from the substantive plan, these gains or losses have no impact in the year of occurrence. They are deferred and amortized as in FAS 87. Amortization of unrecognized net gain (loss) is included as a component of net postretirement cost for a year if, as of the beginning of the year, it exceeds 10% of the greater of the APBO or the market-related value of plan assets. The minimum amortization is the excess divided by the remaining average service period of active plan participants. A systematic method of amortization that amortizes a greater amount, is applied consistently to both gains and losses and is disclosed may also be used. If gains (losses) are recognized immediately, special rules of offsetting may be required.

**Effect of the prescription drug benefit on OPEB computations.** The Medicare Prescription Drug, Improvement and Modernization Act of 2003 introduced a prescription drug benefit under Medicare (Medicare Part D), as well as a federal subsidy to sponsors of retiree health care benefit plans that provide a benefit that is at least actuarially equivalent to Medicare Part D. FASB's initial attempt to address the accounting implications of the Act was FSP 106-1, which permitted sponsors of a postretirement health care plan that provide a prescription drug benefit to make onetime elections to defer accounting for the effects of the Act. More recently, FSP 106-2 has been promulgated, superseding FSP 106-1, and eliminating the deferral option. Under this guidance, the effects of the Act on current period measurements of postretirement benefit costs and the APBO must be accounted for, if defined criteria are met.

The guidance regarding accounting for the subsidiary set forth in FSP 106-2 applies only to sponsors of a single-employer defined benefit postretirement health care plan for which (1) the employers have concluded that prescription drug benefits available under the plan to some or all participants for some or all future years are "actuarially equivalent" to Medicare Part D and thus qualify for the subsidy under the Act and (2) the expected subsidiaries will offset or reduce the employers' shares of the cost of the underlying postretirement prescription drug coverage on which the subsidies are based. FSP 106-2 also provides guidance for disclosures about the effects of the subsidy for employers that sponsor postretirement health care benefit plans that provide prescription drug coverage but for which the employers have not yet been able to determine actuarial equivalency.

The central question raised has been whether a subsidy is substantively similar to other Medicare benefits that existed when FAS 106 was issued—and therefore to be accounted for as a reduction of the APBO and net periodic postretirement benefit cost—or whether the subsidy represents a payment to the employer that is determined by reference to its plan's benefit payments but is not, in and of itself, a direct reduction of postretirement benefit costs. A secondary issue pertains to the timing of accounting recognition of the subsidy.

FASB concluded that the former interpretation is the correct one. That is, measures of the APBO and net periodic postretirement benefit cost on or after the date of enactment are to reflect the effects of the Act. When an employer initially accounts for the subsidy, its effect on the APBO is to be accounted for as an actuarial experience gain. Additionally, the subsidy reduces service cost when it is recognized as a component of net periodic postretirement benefit cost. If the estimated expected subsidy changes, the effect is to be treated as an actuarial experience gain or loss.

Plan amendments will also affect the reporting of OPEB cost and the APBO. If prescription drug benefits currently available under an existing plan are deemed not actuarially equivalent as of the date of enactment of the Act, but the plan is later amended to provide actuarially equivalent benefits, the direct effect of the amendment on the APBO and the effect on the APBO from any resulting subsidy to which the employer is expected to be entitled as a result of the amendment are to be combined, and deemed to be an actuarial experience gain if it reduces APBO. On the other hand, if the combined effect increases the APBO, it is deemed to be prior service cost that is to be accounted for consistent with FAS 106.

Additionally, according to FSP 106-2, if a plan that provides prescription drug benefits that previously were deemed actuarially equivalent under the Act is subsequently amended to reduce its prescription drug coverage such that the coverage is not considered actuarially equivalent, any actuarial experience gain related to the subsidy previously recognized is unaffected. The combined net effect on the APBO of (1) the subsequent plan amendment that reduces benefits under the plan and thus disqualifies the benefits as actuarially equivalent and (2) the elimination of the subsidy is to be accounted for as prior service cost (credit) as of the date the amendment is adopted.

In the periods in which the subsidy affects the employer's accounting for the plan, this will have no effect on any plan-related temporary difference accounted for under FAS 109, because the subsidy is exempt from federal taxation.

There may be a time lag before the employer is able to determine whether the benefits provided by its plan are actuarially equivalent. During the interim period, it is required to disclose: the existence of the Act and the fact that measures of the APBO or net periodic postretirement benefit cost do not reflect any amount associated with the subsidy because the employer is unable to conclude whether the benefits provided by the plan are actuarially equivalent to Medicare Part D under the Act.

In interim and annual financial statements for the first period in which an employer includes the effects of the subsidy in measuring the APBO and the first period in which an employer includes the effects of the subsidy in measuring net periodic postretirement benefit cost, it is required to disclose the following:

a.  The reduction in the APBO for the subsidy related to benefits attributed to past service.

b.  The effect of the subsidy on the measurement of net periodic postretirement benefit cost for the current period. That effect includes (1) any amortization of the actuarial experience gain in (a) as a component of the net amortization called for by FAS 106, (2) the reduction in current period service cost due to the subsidy, and (3) the resulting reduction in interest cost on the APBO as a result of the subsidy.

c.  Any other disclosures required by FAS 132(R), as amended by FAS 158, specifically disclosure of an explanation of any significant change in the benefit obligation or plan assets not otherwise apparent in the other disclosures required by that standard.

When FSP 106-2 is initially adopted, a remeasurement of the plan's assets and APBO, including the effects of the subsidy, if applicable, as well as the other effects of the Act, is to be made as of the earlier of (1) the plan's measurement date that normally would have followed enactment of the Act or (2) the end of the employer's interim or annual period that includes the date of the Act's enactment. Alternatively, employers are permitted, but not required, to perform that remeasurement as of the date of enactment. The measurement of the APBO is to be based on the plan provisions in place on the measurement date (i.e., later amendments are not to be anticipated in the computation).

### Other Postemployment Benefits

FAS 112 applies the criteria set forth by FAS 43 to accrue an obligation for postemployment benefits other than pensions if services have been performed by employees, employees' rights accumulate or vest, payment is probable, and the amount can be reasonably estimable.

If these benefits do not vest or accumulate, FAS 5 applies. If neither FAS 43 nor FAS 5 is applicable because the amount is not reasonably estimable, this fact must be disclosed.

## Deferred Compensation Contracts

If the aggregate deferred compensation contracts with individual employees are equivalent to a pension plan, the contracts are accounted for according to FAS 87 and FAS 88. All other deferred compensation contracts are accounted for according to APB 12.

FAS 106 states that the terms of the individual contract will govern the accrual of the employee's obligation for deferred compensation and the cost is to be attributed over the employee service period until full eligibility is attained.

Per APB 12, the amount to be accrued is not to be less than the present value of the estimated payments to be made. This estimated amount is accrued in a systematic and rational manner. When elements of both current and future employment are present, only the portion attributable to the current services is accrued. All requirements of the contract, such as continued employment for a specified period, availability for consulting services, and agreements not to compete after retirement, need to be met in order for the employee to receive future payments. Finally, the total amount is amortized to expense over the period from the date the contract is signed to the point when the employee is fully eligible to receive the deferred payments.

One benefit that may be found in a deferred compensation contract is for periodic payments to employees or their beneficiaries for life, with provisions for a minimum lump-sum settlement in the event of early death of one or all of the beneficiaries. The estimated amount to be accrued is based on the life expectancy of each individual concerned or on the estimated cost of an annuity contract, not on the minimum amount payable in the event of early death.

### Example of a deferred compensation contract

The Clear Eye Corporation enters into a deferred compensation contract with its president, Dr. Smith. Under the terms of the agreement, Clear Eye will pay Dr. Smith an amount equal to twice his annual salary in a lump sum on the date of his mandatory retirement from Clear Eye, which is four years in the future. His salary is currently $120,000. In addition, Clear Eye will pay Dr. Smith an annual pension of $45,000 beginning on his mandatory retirement date, or a minimum $200,000 lump-sum payment in the event of his early death. However, these payments are contingent upon his working the remaining four years prior to his mandatory retirement. The actuarial present value of a lifetime annuity of $45,000 that begins at Dr. Smith's expected retirement date is $392,000.

Clear Eye makes the following entry each year to record its annual expense under the lump-sum payment agreement, which is based on a lump-sum payment of $240,000:

| | | |
|---|---|---|
| Deferred compensation expense | 60,000 | |
|    Deferred compensation liability | | 60,000 |

After two years, Dr. Smith receives a pay raise to $140,000, which increases the amount of his guaranteed lump-sum payment to $280,000. Since Clear Eye has thus far recognized a deferred compensation expense of $120,000, it must now increase its annual expense recognition to $80,000 in order to recognize additional expense totaling $160,000 over the remaining two years prior to the payment date. It makes the following entry to record the actual cash payment to Dr. Smith:

| | | |
|---|---|---|
| Deferred compensation liability | 280,000 | |
|    Cash | | 280,000 |

Clear Eye must also record the $392,000 present value of the lifetime annuity over the remaining four years of Dr, Smith's employment rather than the smaller $200,000 early death payment, which it does with the following annual entry:

| Deferred compensation expense | 98,000 | |
| Deferred compensation liability | | 98,000 |

Note that all of the foregoing entries assume that Clear Eye Corporation chooses to record the full (i.e., nondiscounted) amount of the estimated future liability pro rata each year. It would also have been acceptable under APB 12 to record the discounted present value amounts. In that case, while the charge for deferred compensation would have been lower in the earlier years, the accrued amounts would have to be further accreted to reflect interest on the obligation, so the overall charge over the four-year accrual for the lump-sum payment would have still equaled $280,000. The charge for the lifetime annuity over the four years until the payments commence would have been less than the estimated $392,000 obligation, since the amount recorded as of the inception of the annuity (i.e., retirement date) would be the present value of the future estimated payments.

## Employee Retirement Income Security Act of 1974

Congress passed the Employee Retirement Income Security Act (ERISA) in 1974. The principal objectives of ERISA were to provide statutory law for pension plan requirements, to strengthen the financial soundness of private pension plans, to safeguard employees' pension rights, and to create the Pension Benefit Guaranty Corporation (PBGC).

Prior to ERISA, the Internal Revenue Code was the principal source of law for governing and managing pension plans. Unfortunately, the thrust of the Code emphasizes tax considerations, and the important nontax aspects of pension plans, such as vesting, funding, and employee participation, were not addressed. ERISA filled the void by mandating minimum vesting, funding, employee participation, and other requirements. Virtually every private pension plan in the United States is affected by the provisions of ERISA.

ERISA, as subsequently amended by Congress and interpreted by regulations issued by the Internal Revenue Service (IRS), provides minimum vesting periods for participants. Amounts contributed by employees must, at all times, be 100% vested. Benefits derived from employer contributions must become nonforfeitable when the employee reaches normal retirement age. Normal retirement age is the earlier of the time a participant attains normal retirement age under the plan or the later of: (1) attainment of age sixty-five, or (2) the fifth anniversary of the individual's participation in the plan.

Plans must meet one of two alternative minimum vesting standards for benefits to be derived from employer contributions prior to normal retirement age.

1.  A five-year cliff schedule requiring full vesting after five years of service
2.  A three-to-seven-year graded schedule requiring 20% vesting after three years of service and 20% additional vesting in each of the following years (IRC § 1.411(a)-3T)

These vesting standards were liberalized by the Economic Growth and Tax Relief Reconciliation Act of 2001 (EGTRRA). EGTRRA provides accelerated vesting for participants with accrued benefits derived from employer matching contributions that complete an hour of service under the plan in a plan year beginning after December 31, 2001. Vesting of employer matching contributions under EGTRRA is under one of three alternative vesting schedules.

1.  Full and immediate vesting
2.  A three-year cliff schedule requiring full vesting after three years of service
3.  A six-year graded schedule requiring 20% vesting per year starting after completion of the second year of service

For plans that are determined, under a formula to provide a disproportionate share of benefits to highly compensated individuals (top-heavy plans), the minimum vesting is required to be even faster.

In addition, ERISA requires minimum funding, in accordance with an acceptable actuarial method, for private pension plans. ERISA also established standards for employee participation and has made defined contribution plans more popular.

All of the above requirements strengthen the financial soundness of employee pension funds. To further ensure the ability of a plan to pay pension obligations and to safeguard employee rights, ERISA amended the Internal Revenue Code to allow for the assessment of fines and the denial of tax deductions. The Act also requires that pension plans submit annual reports, provide a description of the plan, and make a full disclosure through the submission of various statements and schedules.

Prior to the enactment of ERISA, some employees lost pension benefits when plans were terminated because of bankruptcy or other reasons. In order to protect employee rights under these circumstances, ERISA created PBGC. The function of this agency is to guarantee employees, if the employer cannot pay, at least a minimum amount of benefits for their years of service. This guarantee is financed by an insurance premium charge that is levied on all employers with defined benefit plans. PBGC also has the right to administer terminated plans, to file liens on employers' assets, and to take over employers' assets under certain specified circumstances.

# 19 STOCKHOLDERS' EQUITY

## PERSPECTIVE AND ISSUES

CON 6 defines stockholders' equity as the residual interest in the assets of an entity after deducting its liabilities. Stockholders' equity is comprised of all capital contributed to the entity plus its accumulated earnings less any distributions that have been made. There are three major categories within the equity section: paid-in capital, retained earnings, and other comprehensive income. Paid-in capital represents equity contributed by owners. Retained earnings represents the sum of all earnings less that not retained in the business (i.e., what has been paid out as dividends). Other comprehensive income represents changes in net assets, other than by means of transactions with owners, which have not been reported in earnings under applicable GAAP rules (e.g., accumulated translation gains or losses). Accounting for paid-in capital and retained earnings are addressed in this chapter; comprehensive income was discussed in Chapter 3 and is not discussed here.

It is generally quite clear that liabilities differ from equity interests, since liabilities are claims against the assets of the reporting entity, while equity represents only residual claims to net assets, after all liabilities have been fully satisfied. While this conceptual distinction is straightforward enough, the evolution of complex financial instruments, some of which exhibit attributes of both liabilities and equity, has made it necessary that a formalized approach to distinguishing between these be developed. This has been receiving much attention for the past fifteen years, in fact, but a resolution is still not at hand.

FASB has been attempting to deal with this issue for years; a discussion memorandum, *Distinguishing between Liability and Equity Instruments and Accounting for Instruments with Characteristics of Both*, was issued in 1990, and an Exposure Draft, *Accounting for Financial Instruments with Characteristics of Liabilities, Equity, or Both,* was published in 2000. It was only in late 2001 that the FASB committed to the completion of this project, but to date that effort has culminated only in the promulgation of FAS 150, *Accounting for Certain Financial Instruments with Characteristics of Liabilities and Equity*. This is a "limited scope" statement, dealing only with mandatorily redeemable financial instruments and a few other situations. Other topics remain to be addressed, as does a promised revision to the definition of liabilities presented in CON 6, to facilitate and justify the newly mandated treatment for these instruments. This ongoing project is discussed later in this chapter.

Earnings are not generated by transactions in an entity's own equity (e.g., by the issuance, reacquisition, or reissuance of its common or preferred shares). Depending on the laws of the jurisdiction of incorporation, distributions to shareholders may be subject to various limitations, such as to the amount of retained (accounting basis) earnings.

A major objective of the accounting for stockholders' equity is the adequate disclosure of the sources from which the capital was derived. For this reason, a number of different paid-in capital accounts may be presented in the balance sheet. The rights of each class of shareholder must also be disclosed. Where shares are reserved for future issuance, such as under the terms of stock option plans, this fact must also be made known.

The long-standing controversy over accounting for stock-based compensation (e.g., employee stock options) heated up substantially in the wake of the financial reporting scandals of the late 1990s and early 2000s and the subsequent passage of the Sarbanes-Oxley Act. In the mid-1990s the FASB had concluded that the economic substance of such plans was to provide compensation, and that resulted in an expense that should logically be reported by the entity (the fair value method of accounting), in contradistinction to the intrinsic value method set forth by APB 25, which generally results in no compensation cost being associated with the option plans. Under intense political and constituent pressure, FASB produced a standard (FAS 123) in 1995 which, while extolling fair value accounting as preferable, permitted continued usage of the intrinsic value method with mere footnote disclosure of the effects that would have been obtained under FAS 123.

In late 2004 this standard was replaced by FAS 123(R), which also replaces APB 25 and FINs 28, 38 and 44, and finally imposed fair value accounting on almost all share-based payment plans.

SOP 93-6 revised the accounting for employers' contributions to employee stock ownership plans (ESOP). The major changes from the prior rules relate to the measurement of compensation cost and to the accounting for dividends paid on unallocated shares.

| | | | | | Sources of GAAP | |
|---|---|---|---|---|---|---|
| *ARB* | *APB* | *FAS* | *FIN* | *FTB* | *EITF* | *SOP* |
| 43, Ch. 1A, 1B, 7A, 7B, 13B; 46 | 6, 12, 15, 25, 29 | 5, 52, 87, 115, 123(R), 129, 130, 141(R) 150 | 31 | 85-6, 97-1 | 84-8, 84-40, 85-1, 85-2,85-46, 86-32, 89-11, 95-16, 96-18, 97-2, 97-14,98-2, 98-12, 99-7, 00-6, 00-8, 00-12, 00-16, 00-18, 00-19, 00-27, 01-1, 01-6, 02-8, 05-2, 06-11, D-42, D-43, D-60, D-72, D-83, D-90, D-98 | 90-7, 93-6 |
| | | | | | *FSP* 123(R)-1, 123(R)-2, 123(R)-3, 123(R)-4, 129-1, 150-5, EITF 00-19-2 | |

## DEFINITIONS OF TERMS

**Additional paid-in capital.** Amounts received at issuance in excess of the par or stated value of capital stock and amounts received from other transactions involving the entity's stock and/or stockholders. It is classified by source.

**Allocated shares.** ESOP shares assigned to individual participants. These shares are usually based on length of service, compensation or a combination of both.

**Appropriation (of retained earnings).** A segregation of retained earnings to communicate the unavailability of a portion for dividend distributions.

**Authorized shares.** The maximum number of shares permitted to be issued by a corporation's charter and bylaws.

**Blackout period.** A period of time during which exercise of an equity share option is contractually or legally prohibited.

**Broker-assisted cashless exercise.** The simultaneous exercise by an employee of a share option and sale of the shares through a broker.

**Calculated value.** A measure of the value of a share option or similar instrument determined by substituting the historical volatility of an appropriate industry sector index for the expected volatility of a nonpublic entity's share price in an option-pricing model.

**Callable.**  An optional characteristic of preferred stock allowing the corporation to redeem the stock at specified future dates and at specific prices.  The call price is usually at or above the original issuance price.

**Cliff vesting.**  A condition of an option or other stock award plan which provides that the employee becomes fully vested at a single point in time.

**Closed-form model.**  A valuation model that uses an equation to produce an estimated fair value.  The Black-Scholes-Merton formula is a closed-form model.

**Combination plans.**  Awards consisting of two or more separate components, such as options and stock appreciation rights, each of which can be exercised.  Each component is actually a separate plan and is accounted for as such.

**Committed-to-be-released shares.**  ESOP shares that will be allocated to employees for service performed currently.  They are usually released by payment of debt service.

**Compensatory plan.**  A stock option or similar plan including elements of compensation which are recognized over the service period.

**Comprehensive income.**  The change in equity of a business enterprise during a period from transactions and other events and circumstances from nonowner sources.  It includes all changes in equity during a period, except those resulting from investments by and distributions to owners.

**Constructive retirement method.**  Method of accounting for treasury shares which treats the shares as having been retired.  The shares revert to authorized but unissued status.  The stock and additional paid-in capital accounts are reduced, with a debit to retained earnings or a credit to a paid-in capital account for the excess or deficiency of the purchase cost over or under the original issuance proceeds.

**Contributed capital.**  The amount of equity contributed by the corporation's shareholders.  It consists of capital stock plus additional paid-in capital.

**Convertible.**  An optional characteristic of preferred stock allowing the stockholders to exchange their preferred shares for common shares at a specified ratio.

**Cost method.**  Method of accounting for treasury shares which presents aggregate cost of reacquired shares as a deduction from the total of paid-in capital and retained earnings.

**Cross-volatility.**  A measure of the relationship between the volatilities of the prices of two assets taking into account the correlation between movements in the prices of the assets.  (Refer to the definition of **volatility**.)

**Cumulative.**  An optional characteristic of preferred stock.  Any dividends of prior years not paid to the preferred shareholders must be paid before any dividends can be distributed to the common shareholders.

**Date of declaration.**  The date on which the board of directors votes that a dividend shall be paid.  A legal liability (usually current) is created on this date in the case of cash, property, and scrip dividends.

**Date of grant.**  The date on which the board of directors awards the stock to the employees in stock option plans.

**Date of payment.**  The date on which the shareholders are paid the declared dividends.

**Date of record.**  The date on which ownership of the shares is determined.  Those owning stock on this date will be paid the declared dividends.

**Deficit.**  A debit balance in the retained earnings account.  Dividends may not generally be paid when this condition exists.  Formally known as accumulated deficit.

**Derived service period.**  A service period for an award with a market condition that is inferred from the application of certain valuation techniques used to estimate fair value.  For example, the derived service period for an award of share options that the employee can exercise only if the share price increases by 10% at any time during a 4-year period can be inferred from certain valuation techniques. If the derived service period is three years, the estimated requisite service period is three years and all compensation cost would be recognized over that period, unless the market condition was satisfied at an earlier date. Also, an award of fully vested, deep out-of-the money share options has a derived service period that must be determined from the valuation techniques used to estimate fair value. (See also **explicit service period**, **implicit service period** and **requisite service period**.)

**Discount on capital stock.** Occurs when the stock of a corporation is originally issued at a price below par value. The original purchasers become contingently liable to creditors for this difference.

**Economic interest in an entity.** Any type or form of pecuniary interest or arrangement that an entity could issue or be a party to, including equity securities; financial instruments with characteristics of equity, liabilities, or both; long-term debt and other debt-financing arrangements; leases; and contractual arrangements such as management contracts, service contracts, or intellectual property licenses.

**Employee.** An individual over whom the grantor of a share-based compensation award exercises or has the right to exercise sufficient control to establish an employer-employee relationship based on common law as illustrated in case law and currently under US Internal Revenue Service Revenue Ruling 87-41.171. A grantee meets the definition of an employee if the grantor consistently represents that individual to be an employee under common law. The definition of an employee for payroll tax purposes under the US Internal Revenue Code includes common law employees. Accordingly, a grantor that classifies a grantee potentially subject to US payroll taxes as an employee for purposes of applying FAS 123(R) also must represent that individual as an employee for payroll tax purposes (unless the grantee is a leased employee). A leased individual is deemed to be an employee of the lessee for purposes of FAS 123(R) if all of a series of requirements are met. For purposes of FAS 123(R), and only for awards granted for service as directors, nonemployee directors acting in their role as members of a board of directors are treated as employees if those directors were (a) elected by the employer's shareholders or (b) appointed to a board position that will be filled by shareholder election when the existing term expires.

**Employee stock ownership plan (ESOP).** A form of defined contribution employee benefit plan, whereby the employer facilitates the purchase of shares of stock in the company for the benefit of the employees, generally by a trust established by the company. The plan may be leveraged by borrowings either from the employer-sponsor or from third-party lenders.

**Equity restructuring.** A nonreciprocal transaction between an entity and its shareholders—such as a stock dividend, stock split, spin-off, rights offering, or recapitalization through a large, nonrecurring cash dividend—that causes the per-share fair value of the shares underlying an option or similar award to change.

**Excess tax benefit.** The realized tax benefit related to the amount (caused by changes in the fair value of the entity's shares after the measurement date for financial reporting) of deductible compensation cost reported on an employer's tax return for equity instruments in excess of the compensation cost for those instruments recognized for financial reporting purposes.

**Explicit service period.** A service period that is explicitly stated in the terms of a share-based payment award. An award that vest after three years of continuous employee service from the grant date has an explicit service period of three years. (See also **derived service period**, **implicit service period**, and **requisite service period**.)

**Fair value.** The amount at which an asset (or liability) could be bought (or incurred) or sold (or settled) in a current transaction between willing parties, that is, other than in a forced or liquidation sale.

**Fixed options.** Options that grant the holder the rights to a specified numbers of shares at fixed prices. They are not dependent upon achievement of performance targets.

**Freestanding financial instrument.** A financial instrument that is entered into separately and apart from any of the entity's other financial instruments or equity transactions or that is entered into in conjunction with some other transaction and is legally detachable and separately exercisable.

**Graded vesting.** A vesting process whereby the employee becomes entitled to a stock-based award fractionally over a period of years.

**Grant date.** The date at which employer and employee reach a mutual understanding of the key terms and conditions of a share-based payment award. The employer becomes contingently obligated on the grant date to issue equity instruments or transfer assets to an employee who renders the requisite service. Awards made under an arrangement that is subject to shareholder approval are not deemed to be granted until that approval is obtained, unless approval is essentially perfunctory. Individual awards that are subject to approval by the board of directors, management, or both are not deemed to be granted until all such approvals are obtained. The grant date for an award of equity instruments is the date that an employee begins to benefit from, or be adversely affected by, subsequent changes in the price of the employer's equity shares. (See also **service inception date**.)

**Implicit service period.** A service period that is not explicitly stated in the terms of a share-based payment award but that may be inferred from an analysis of those terms and other facts and circumstances. For instance, if an award of share options vests upon the completion of a new product design, which is deemed probable in 18 months, then the implicit service period is 18 months. (See also **derived service period**, **explicit service period**, and **requisite service period**.)

**Intrinsic value.** The amount by which the fair value of the underlying stock exceeds the option exercise price. A nonvested share may be described as an option on that share with an exercise price of zero. Thus, the fair value of a share is the same as the intrinsic value of such an option on that share.

**Issuance costs.** The costs incurred in underwriting an equity offering, to be reported as reductions of paid-in capital.

**Issuance of equity instrument.** An equity instrument is issued when the issuing entity receives the agreed-upon consideration, which may be cash, an enforceable right to receive cash or another financial instrument, goods or services. An entity may conditionally transfer an equity instrument to another party under an arrangement that permits that party to choose at a later date or for a specified time whether to deliver the consideration or to forfeit the right to the conditionally transferred instrument with no further obligation. In that situation, the equity instrument is not issued until the issuing entity has received the consideration. FAS 123 (R) does not use the term issued for the grant of stock options or other equity instruments subject to vesting conditions.

**Issued stock.** The number of shares issued by the firm and owned by the shareholders and the corporation. It is the sum of outstanding shares plus treasury shares.

**Junior stock.** Shares with certain limitations, often as to voting rights, which are granted to employees pursuant to a performance compensation program. Such shares are generally convertible to ordinary shares upon achievement of defined goals.

**Lattice model.** A multiperiod model that produces an estimated fair value based on the assumed changes in prices of a financial instrument over successive periods. The binomial model is a lattice model. In each time period, the model assumes that at least two price movements are possible. The lattice represents the evolution of the value of either a financial instrument or a market variable for the purpose of valuing a financial instrument. In this context, a lattice model is based on risk-neutral valuation and a contingent claims framework. (Refer to closed form model for an explanation of the terms risk-neutral valuation and contingent claims framework.)

**Legal capital.** The aggregate par or stated value of stock. It represents the amount of owners' equity that cannot be distributed to shareholders. It serves to protect the claims of the creditors.

**Liquidating dividend.** A dividend distribution that is not based on earnings. It represents a return of contributed capital.

**Market condition.** A condition affecting the exercise price, exercisability, or other factors used in determining the fair value of an award under a share-based payment arrangement that relates to the achievement of either (a) a specified price of the issuer's shares or a specified amount of intrinsic value indexed solely to the issuer's shares, or (b) a specified price of the issuer's shares in terms of a similar (or index of similar) equity security (securities).

**Measurement date.** The date at which the equity share price and other factors, e.g., expected volatility, that enter into measurement of the total recognized amount of compensation cost for an award of share-based payment become fixed.

**Modification.** A change in any of the terms or conditions of a share-based payment award.

**Noncompensatory stock options.** Options which do not include an element of compensation. Under APB 25, many stock option plans meet the prescribed criteria and thus are deemed noncompensatory; under FAS 123(R) most stock plans will include an element of compensation to be measured and allocated over the service periods of the employees or to be disclosed as such in the notes to the financial statements.

**Nonpublic entity.** Any entity other than one (1) whose equity securities trade in a public market either on a stock exchange or in the over-the-counter market, including securities quoted only locally or regionally, (2) that makes a filing with a regulatory agency in preparation for the sale of any class of equity securities in a public market, or (3) that is controlled by an entity covered by (1) or (2). An entity that has only debt securities trading in a public market (or that has made a filing with a regulatory agency in preparation to trade only debt securities) is a nonpublic entity for purposes of FAS 123(R).

**Nonvested shares.** Shares that an entity has not yet issued because the agreed-upon consideration, such as employee services, has not yet been received.

**No-par stock.** Stock that has no par value. Sometimes a stated value is determined by the board of directors. In this case, the stated value is accorded the same treatment as par value stock.

**Outstanding stock.** Stock issued by a corporation and held by shareholders (i.e., issued shares that are not held in the treasury).

**Par value method.** A method of accounting for treasury shares which charges the treasury stock account for the aggregate par or stated value of the shares acquired and charges the excess of the purchase cost over the par value to paid-in capital and/or retained earnings. A deficiency of purchase cost is credited to paid-in capital.

**Participating.** An optional characteristic of preferred stock whereby preferred shareholders may share ratably with the common shareholders in any profit distributions in excess of a predetermined rate. Participation may be limited to a maximum rate or may be unlimited (full).

**Performance-based options.** Options that are granted to employees conditional on the achievement of defined goals, such as market price of the underlying stock or earnings of the entity.

**Performance condition.** A condition affecting the vesting, exercisability, exercise price, or other pertinent factors used in determining the fair value of an award that relates to both (1) an employee's rendering service for a specified (either explicitly or implicitly) period of time, and (2) achieving a specified performance target that is defined solely by reference to the employer's own operations (or activities). Attaining a specified growth rate in return on assets, obtaining regulatory approval to market a specified product, selling shares in an initial public offering or other financing event, and a change in control are examples of performance conditions for purposes of FAS 123(R). A performance target also may be defined by reference to the same performance measure of another entity or group of entities.

**Phantom stock plan.** A type of stock compensation arrangement that gives employees the right to participate in the increase in value of the company's shares (book value or market value, as stipulated in the plan), without being required to actually purchase the shares initially.

**Public entity.** An entity (1) with equity securities that trade in a public market, which may be either a stock exchange or an over-the-counter market, including securities quoted only locally or regionally, (2) that makes a filing with a regulatory agency in preparation for the sale of any class of equity securities in a public market, or (3) that is controlled by an entity covered by (1) or (2).

**Quasi reorganization.** A procedure that reclassifies amounts from contributed capital to retained earnings to eliminate a deficit in that account. All the assets and liabilities are first revalued to their current values. It represents an alternative to a legal reorganization in bankruptcy proceedings.

**Related party.** As defined by FAS 57.

**Reload feature and reload option.** A reload feature provides for automatic grants of additional options whenever an employee exercises previously granted options using the entity's shares, rather than cash, to satisfy the exercise price. At the time of exercise using shares, the employee is automatically granted a new option, called a reload option, for the shares used to exercise the previous option.

**Replacement award.** An award of share-based compensation that is granted (or offered to grant) concurrently with the cancellation of another award.

**Requisite service period.** The period or periods during which an employee is required to provide service in exchange for an award under a share-based payment arrangement. The requisite service period for an award that has only a service condition is presumed to be the vesting period, unless there is clear evidence to the contrary. If an award requires future service for vesting, the entity cannot define a prior period as the requisite service period. Requisite service periods may be explicit, implicit, or derived, depending on the terms of the share-based payment award.

**Restricted share.** A share for which sale is contractually or governmentally prohibited for a specified period of time. Most grants of shares to employees are better termed nonvested shares because the limitation on sale stems solely from the forfeitability of the shares before employees have satisfied the necessary service or performance condition(s) to earn the rights to the shares. Restricted shares issued for consideration other than employee services, on the other hand, are fully paid immediately. For those shares, there is no period analogous to a requisite service period during which the issuer is unilaterally obligated to issue shares when the purchaser pays for those shares, but the purchaser is not obligated to buy the shares. FAS 123(R) uses the term restricted shares to refer only to fully vested and outstanding shares whose sale is contractually or governmentally prohibited for a specified period of time. (See also **nonvested shares.**)

**Restriction.** A contractual or governmental provision that prohibits sale (or substantive sale by using derivatives or other means to effectively terminate the risk of future changes in the share price) of an equity instrument for a specified period of time.

**Retained earnings.** The undistributed earnings of a firm.

**Service condition.** A condition affecting the vesting, exercisability, exercise price, or other pertinent factors used in determining the fair value of an award that depends solely on an employee rendering service to the employer for the requisite service period. A condition that results in the acceleration of vesting in the event of an employee's death, disability, or termination without cause is a service condition.

**Service inception date.** The date at which the requisite service period begins. The service inception date usually is the grant date, but the service inception date may differ from the grant date.

**Service period.** The period over which a stock-based compensation award is earned by the recipient. If not otherwise defined in the plan, it is the vesting period. Under FAS 123(R), if performance conditions affect either exercise price or date, then the service period must be consistent with the related assumption used in estimating fair value.

**Settlement of an award.** An action or event that irrevocably extinguishes the issuing entity's obligation under a share-based payment award. Transactions and events that constitute settlements include (1) exercise of a share option or lapse of an option at the end of its contractual term, (2) vesting of shares, (3) forfeiture of shares or share options due to failure to satisfy a vesting condition, and (4) an entity's repurchase of instruments in exchange for assets or for fully vested and transferable equity instruments. The vesting of a share option is not a settlement as that term is used in FAS 123(R) because the entity remains obligated to issue shares upon exercise of the option.

**Share option.** A contract that gives the holder the right, but not the obligation, either to purchase (or call) or to sell (to put) a certain number of shares at a predetermined price for a specified period of time. Most share options granted to employees under share-based compensation arrangements are call options, but some may be put options.

**Share unit.** A contract under which the holder has the right to convert each unit into a specified number of shares of the issuing entity.

**Share-based payment (or compensation) arrangement.** An arrangement under which (a) one or more suppliers of goods or services (including employees) receive awards of equity shares, equity share options, or other equity instruments, or (b) the entity incurs liabilities to suppliers (1) in amounts based, at least in part, on the price of the entity's shares or other equity instruments, or (2) that require or may require settlement by issuance of the entity's shares. For purposes of FAS 123(R), the term shares includes various forms of ownership interest that may not take the legal form of securities (for example, partnership interests), as well as other interests, including those that are liabilities in substance but not in form. Equity shares refers only to shares that are accounted for as equity.

**Share-based payment (or compensation) transaction.** A transaction under a share-based payment arrangement, including a transaction in which an entity acquires goods or services because related parties or other holders of economic interest in that entity awards a share-based payment to an employee or other supplier of goods or services for the entity's benefit.

**Short-term inducement.** An offer by the entity that would result in modification or settlement of an award to which an award holder may subscribe for a limited period of time.

**Small business issuer.** A public entity that is an SEC registrant that files as a small business issuer under the Securities Act of 1933 or the Securities Exchange Act of 1934.

**Stock-based compensation.** Compensation arrangements under which employees receive shares of stock, stock options, or other equity instruments, or under which the employer incurs obligations to the employees based on the price of the company's shares.

**Stock options.** Enable officers and employees of a corporation to purchase shares in the corporation at a predetermined price for a defined period of time.

**Stock rights.** Enables present shareholders to purchase additional shares of stock of the corporation. They are commonly used if a preemptive right is granted to common shareholders by some state corporation laws.

**Suspense shares.** ESOP shares that usually collateralize ESOP debt. They have not been allocated or committed to be released.

**Tandem plans.** Compensation plans under which employees receive two or more components, such as options and stock appreciation rights, whereby the exercise of one component cancels the other(s).

**Terms of a share-based payment award.** The contractual provisions that determine the nature and scope of a share-based payment award. For example, the exercise price of share options is one of the terms of an award of share options. The written terms of a share-based payment award and its related arrangement, if any, usually provide the best evidence of its terms, but an entity's past practice or other factors may indicate that some aspects of the substantive terms differ from the written terms. The substantive terms of a share-based payment award as those terms are mutually understood by the entity and a party (either an employee or a nonemployee) who receives the award provide the basis for determining the rights conveyed to a party and the obligations imposed on the issuer, regardless of how the award and related arrangement, if any, are structured.

**Time value of an option.** The portion of the fair value of an option that exceeds its intrinsic value.

**Treasury stock.** Shares of a corporation that have been repurchased by the corporation. This stock has no voting rights and receives no cash dividends. Some states do not recognize treasury stock. In such cases, reacquired shares are treated as having been retired.

**Vesting.** Literally, to earn the rights to certain benefits. A share-based payment award becomes vested at the date that the employee's right to receive or retain shares, other instruments, or cash under the award is no longer contingent on satisfaction of either a service condition or a performance condition. Market conditions are not vesting conditions for purposes of FAS 123(R). The stated vesting provisions of an award often establish the requisite service period, and an award that has reached the end of the requisite service period is vested. However, the stated vesting period may differ from the requisite service period in certain circumstances.

**Volatility.** A measure of the amount by which a financial variable such as a share price has historically fluctuated or is expected to fluctuate during a period. Volatility also may be defined as a probability-weighted measure of the dispersion of returns about the mean. The volatility of a share price is the standard deviation of the continuously compounded rates of return on the share over a specified period. That is the same as the standard deviation of the differences in the natural logarithms of the stock prices plus dividends, if any, over the period. The higher the volatility, the more the returns on the shares can be expected to vary—up or down. Volatility is typically expressed in annualized terms.

## CONCEPTS, RULES, AND EXAMPLES

### Legal Capital and Capital Stock

Legal capital typically refers to that portion of the stockholders' investment in a corporation that is permanent in nature and represents assets that will continue to be available for the satisfaction of creditor's claims. Traditionally, legal capital was comprised of the aggregate par or stated value of common and preferred shares issued. In recent years, however, many states have eliminated the requirement that corporate shares have a designated par or stated value. States which have adopted provisions of the Model Business Corporation Act have eliminated the distinction between par value and the amount contributed in excess of par.

The specific requirements regarding the preservation of legal capital are a function of the business corporation laws in the state in which a particular entity is incorporated. Accordingly, any action by the corporation that could affect the amount of legal capital (e.g., the payment of dividends in excess of retained earnings) must be considered in the context of the relevant laws of the state where the company is chartered.

Ownership interest in a corporation is made up of common, and optionally, preferred shares. The common shares represent the residual risk-taking ownership of the corporation after the satisfaction of all claims of creditors and senior classes of equity.

**Preferred stock.** Preferred shareholders are owners who have certain rights superior to those of common shareholders. Preferences as to earnings exist when the preferred shareholders have a stipulated dividend rate (expressed either as a dollar amount or as a percentage of the preferred stock's par or stated value). Preferences as to assets exist when the preferred shares have a stipulated liquidation value. If a corporation were to liquidate, these preferred holders would be paid a specific amount before the common shareholders would have a right to participate in any of the proceeds.

In practice, preferred shares are more likely to have preferences as to earnings than as to assets. Although unusual, preferred shares may have both preferential rights. Preferred shares may also have the following optional features: participation in earnings beyond the stipulated dividend rate; the cumulative feature, ensuring that dividends in arrears, if any, will be fully satisfied before the common shareholders participate in any earnings distribution; and convertibility or callability by the corporation. Preferences must be disclosed adequately in the financial statements, either on the face of the balance sheet or in the notes thereto.

In exchange for the preferences, the preferred shareholders' other rights or privileges are often limited. For instance, the right to vote may be restricted to common shareholders. The most important right denied to the preferred shareholders, however, is the right to participate without limitation in the earnings of the corporation. Thus, if the corporation has exceedingly large earnings for a particular period, most of these earnings would accrue to the benefit of the common shareholders. This statement is true even if the preferred stock is participating (a fairly uncommon feature) because participating preferred stock usually has some upper limitation placed upon the extent of participation.

Occasionally, several classes of stock will be categorized as common (e.g., Class A common, Class B common, etc.). Since there can be only one class of shares that represents the true residual risk-taking ownership in a corporation, it is clear that the other classes, even though described as common shareholders, must in fact have some preferential status. Typically, these preferences relate to voting rights. An example of this situation arises when a formerly closely held corporation sells shares to the public but gives the publicly held shares a disproportionately small capacity to exercise influence over the entity, thereby keeping control in the hands of the former majority owners even as they are reduced to the status of minority owners. The rights and responsibilities of each class of shareholder, even if described as common, must be fully disclosed in the financial statements.

**Issuance of shares.** The accounting for the sale of shares by a corporation depends upon whether the stock has a par or stated value. If there is a par or stated value, the amount of the proceeds representing the aggregate par or stated value is credited to the common or preferred stock account. The aggregate par or stated value is generally defined as legal capital not subject to distribution to shareholders. Proceeds in excess of par or stated value are credited to an additional paid-in capital account. The additional paid-in capital represents the amount in excess of the legal capital that may, under certain defined conditions, be distributed to shareholders.

A corporation selling stock below par value credits the capital stock account for the par value and debits an offsetting discount account for the difference between par value and the amount actually received. If the discount is on original issue capital stock, it serves to notify the actual and potential creditors of the contingent liability of those investors. As a practical matter, corporations avoided this problem by reducing par values to an arbitrarily low amount. This reduction in par eliminated the chance that shares would be sold for amounts below par.

Where the Model Business Corporation Act has been adopted or where corporation laws have been conformed to the guidelines of that Act, there is often no distinction made between par value and amounts in excess of par. In those jurisdictions, the entire proceeds from the sale of stock may be credited to the common stock account without distinction between the stock and the additional paid-in capital accounts. The following entries illustrate these concepts:

**Facts:**   A corporation sells 100,000 shares of $5 par common stock for $8 per share cash.

| | | |
|---|---|---|
| Cash | 800,000 | |
|     Common stock | | 500,000 |
|     Additional paid-in capital | | 300,000 |

**Facts:**   A corporation sells 100,000 shares of no-par common stock for $8 per share cash.

| | | |
|---|---|---|
| Cash | 800,000 | |
|     Common stock | | 800,000 |

Preferred stock will often be assigned a par value because in many cases the preferential dividend rate is defined as a percentage of par value (e.g., 10%, $25 par value preferred stock will have a required annual dividend of $2.50).

If the shares in a corporation are issued in exchange for services or property rather than for cash, the transaction should be reflected at the fair value of the property or services received. If this information is not readily available, then the transaction should be recorded at the fair value of the shares that were issued. Where necessary, appraisals should be obtained in order to properly reflect the transaction. As a final resort, a valuation of the stock issued can be made by the board of directors (APB 29). Stock issued to employees as compensation for services rendered should be accounted for at the fair value of the services performed, if determinable, or the value of the shares issued. If shares are given by a major shareholder directly to an employee for services performed for the entity, this exchange should be accounted for as a capital contribution to the company by the major shareholder and as compensation expense incurred by the company. Only when accounted for in this manner will there be conformity with the general principle that all costs incurred by an entity, including compensation, should be reflected in its financial statements.

In certain instances, common and preferred shares may be issued to investors as a unit (e.g., one share of preferred and two shares of common sold as a package). Where both of the classes of stock are publicly traded, the proceeds from a unit offering should be allocated in proportion to the relative market values of the securities. If only one of the securities is publicly traded, then the proceeds should be allocated to the one that is publicly traded based on its known market value. Any excess is allocated to the other. Where the market value of neither security is known, appraisal information may be used. The imputed fair value of one class of security, particularly the preferred shares, can be based upon the stipulated dividend rate. In this case, the amount of proceeds remaining after the imputing of a value of the preferred shares would be allocated to the common stock.

The foregoing procedures would also apply if a unit offering were made of an equity and a nonequity security such as convertible debentures. Under proposed FASB guidelines, proceeds would be apportioned on the basis of relative fair values. (See the detailed discussion later in this chapter.)

Equity offerings generally involve the incurrence of various costs, such as legal and accounting fees and underwriting commissions. These are offset against the proceeds of the offering, generally reducing paid-in capital, which is thus reported net of costs. If a unit offering involves debt and equity, the offering costs should be allocated proportionally against equity and debt, possibly creating a discount on the debt issuance that will be amortized as additional interest expense in the usual manner. (See Chapter 15 for full discussion of accounting for premium or discount on debt.)

In certain situations, equity (or debt) is issued with a promise by the reporting entity to effect registration of the instruments by a defined date after issuance, or upon the occurrence of a contingent event. Per FSP EITF 00-19-2, such obligations are recognized and measured consistent with the requirements of FAS 5, which does not alter the accounting for the associated financial instrument itself.

### Stock Subscriptions

Occasionally, particularly in the case of a newly organized corporation, a contract is entered into between the corporation and prospective investors, whereby the latter agree to purchase specified numbers of shares to be paid for over some installment period. These stock subscriptions are not the same as actual stock issuances and the accounting differs.

The amount of stock subscriptions receivable by a corporation is occasionally accounted for as an asset on the balance sheet and is categorized as current or noncurrent in accordance with the terms of payment. However, in accordance with SEC requirements, most subscriptions receivable are shown as a reduction of stockholders' equity in the same manner as treasury stock. Since subscribed shares do not have the rights and responsibilities of actual outstanding stock, the credit is made to a stock subscribed account instead of to the capital stock accounts.

EITF 85-1 states that a contribution to a company's equity made in the form of a note receivable should generally not be reported as an asset unless circumstances indicate both the ability and intent to pay in a short period of time. EITF noted that the most widespread practice is to report these notes as a reduction of equity. However, if the cash is received prior to the issuance of the financial statements, the note may be reported as an asset.

If the common stock has par or stated value, the common stock subscribed account is credited for the aggregate par or stated value of the shares subscribed. The excess over this amount is credited to additional paid-in capital. No distinction is made between additional paid-in capital relating to shares already issued and shares subscribed for. This treatment follows from the distinction between legal capital and additional paid-in capital. Where there is no par or stated value, the entire amount of the common stock subscribed is credited to the stock subscribed account.

As the amount due from the prospective shareholders is collected, the stock subscriptions receivable account is credited and the proceeds are debited to the cash account. Actual issuance of the shares, however, must await the complete payment of the stock subscription. Accordingly, the debit to common stock subscribed is not made until the subscribed shares are fully paid for and the stock is issued.

The following journal entries illustrate these concepts:

1.  10,000 shares of $50 par preferred are subscribed at a price of $65 each; a 10% down payment is received.

| | | |
|---|---|---|
| Cash | 65,000 | |
| Stock subscriptions receivable | 585,000 | |
| Preferred stock subscribed | | 500,000 |
| Additional paid-in capital | | 150,000 |

2.  2,000 shares of no-par common shares are subscribed at a price of $85 each, with one-half received in cash.

| | | |
|---|---|---|
| Cash | 85,000 | |
| Stock subscriptions receivable | 85,000 | |
| Common stock subscribed | | 170,000 |

3.  All preferred subscriptions are paid and subscribed preferred shares are issued, and one-half of the remaining common subscriptions are collected in full.

| | | |
|---|---|---|
| Cash [$585,000 + ($85,000 × .50)] | 627,500 | |
| Stock subscriptions receivable | | 627,500 |
| Preferred stock subscribed | 500,000 | |
| Preferred stock | | 500,000 |

4.  The remaining common subscriptions are collected in full.

| | | |
|---|---|---|
| Cash ($85,000 × .50) | 42,500 | |
| Stock subscriptions receivable | | 42,500 |
| Common stock subscribed | 170,000 | |
| Common stock | | 170,000 |

When a subscriber defaults on an obligation under a stock subscription agreement, the accounting will follow the provisions of the state in which the corporation is chartered. In some jurisdictions, the subscriber is entitled to a proportionate number of shares based upon the amount already paid on the subscriptions, sometimes reduced by the cost incurred by the corporation in selling the remaining defaulted shares to other stockholders. In other jurisdictions, the subscriber forfeits the entire investment upon default. In this case, the amount already received is credited to an additional paid-in capital account that describes its source.

## Additional Paid-in Capital

Additional paid-in capital represents all capital contributed to a corporation other than that defined as par, stated value, no-par stock, or donated capital. Additional paid-in capital can arise from proceeds received from the sale of common and preferred shares in excess of their par or stated values. It can also arise from transactions related to the following:

1.  Sale of shares previously issued and subsequently reacquired by the corporation (treasury stock)
2.  Retirement of previously outstanding shares
3.  Payment of stock dividends in a manner that justifies the dividend being recorded at the market value of the shares distributed
4.  Lapse of stock purchase warrants or the forfeiture of stock subscriptions, if these result in the retaining by the corporation of any partial proceeds received prior to forfeiture

5. Warrants which are detachable from bonds
6. Conversion of convertible bonds
7. Other "gains" on the company's own stock, such as that which results from certain stock option plans

When the amounts are material, the sources of additional paid-in capital should be described in the financial statements.

### Examples of additional paid-in capital transactions

ABC Company issues 2,000 shares of common stock having a par value of $1, of a total price of $8,000. The following entry records the transaction:

| | | |
|---|---|---|
| Cash | 8,000 | |
| Common stock | | 2,000 |
| Additional paid-in capital | | 6,000 |

ABC Company buys back 2,000 shares of its own common stock for $10,000 and then sells these shares to investors for $15,000. The following entries record the buyback and sale transactions, respectively, assuming the use of the cost method of accounting for treasury stock:

| | | |
|---|---|---|
| Treasury stock | 10,000 | |
| Cash | | 10,000 |
| | | |
| Cash | 15,000 | |
| Treasury stock | | 10,000 |
| Additional paid-in capital | | 5,000 |

ABC Company buys back 2,000 shares of its own $1 par value common stock (which it had originally sold for $8,000) for $9,000 and retires the stock, which it records with the following entry:

| | | |
|---|---|---|
| Common stock | 2,000 | |
| Additional paid-in capital | 6,000 | |
| Retained earnings | 1,000 | |
| Cash | | 9,000 |

ABC Company issues a small stock dividend of 5,000 common shares at the market price of $8 per share. Each share has a par value of $1. The following entry records the transaction:

| | | |
|---|---|---|
| Retained earnings | 40,000 | |
| Common stock | | 5,000 |
| Additional paid-in capital | | 35,000 |

ABC Company previously has recorded $1,000 of stock options outstanding as part of a compensation agreement. The options expire a year later, resulting in the following entry:

| | | |
|---|---|---|
| Stock options outstanding | 1,000 | |
| Additional paid-in capital | | 1,000 |

ABC Company sells 2,000 of par $1,000 bonds, as well as 2,000 attached warrants having a market value of $15 each. Pro rata apportionment of the $2,000,000 cash received between the bonds and warrants results in the following entry:

| | | |
|---|---|---|
| Cash | 2,000,000 | |
| Discount on bonds payable | 29,557 | |
| Bonds payable | | 2,000,000 |
| Additional paid-in capital—warrants | | 29,557 |

ABC's bondholders convert a $1,000 bond with an unamortized premium of $40 and a market value of $1,016 into 127 shares of $1 par common stock whose market value is $8 per share. This results in the following entry:

| Bonds payable | 1,000 | |
| Premium on bonds payable | 40 | |
| Common stock | | 913 |
| Additional paid-in capital | | 127 |

When the amounts are material, the sources of additional paid-in capital should be described in the financial statements.

## Donated Capital

Donated capital can result from an outright gift to the corporation (e.g., a major shareholder donates land or other assets to the company in a nonreciprocal transfer) or may result when services are provided to the corporation. Under FAS 116, such nonreciprocal transactions are recognized as revenue in the period the contribution is received. Donated capital should be adequately disclosed in the financial statements.

Prior to the issuance of FAS 116, it was not uncommon for donations to be reported directly in a special paid-in capital account, donated capital. However, it is now required that donations be reflected in the income statement, which means that, after the fiscal period has ended and the books have been closed, the effect of donations will be incorporated in the reporting entity's retained earnings.

In the case of donations, historical cost is not adequate to properly reflect the substance of the transaction, since the historical cost to the corporation would be zero. Accordingly, these events should be reflected at fair market value (APB 29). If long-lived assets are donated to the corporation, they should be recorded at their fair value at the date of donation, and the amount so recorded should be depreciated over the normal useful economic life of such assets. If donations are conditional in nature, they should not be reflected formally in the accounts until the appropriate conditions have been satisfied. However, disclosure might still be required in the financial statements of both the assets donated and the conditions required to be met.

### Example of donated capital

A board member of the for-profit Adirondack Boys' Club (ABC) donates land to the organization that has a fair market value of $1 million. ABC records the donation with the following entry:

| Land | 1,000,000 | |
| Revenue—donations | | 1,000,000 |

The same board member donates one year of accounting labor to ABC. The fair value of services rendered is $75,000. ABC records the donation with the following entry:

| Salaries—accounting department | 75,000 | |
| Revenue—donations | | 75,000 |

The board member also donates one year of free rent of a local building to ABC. The annual rent in similar facilities is $45,000. ABC records the donation with the following entry:

| Rent expense | 45,000 | |
| Revenue—donations | | 45,000 |

Finally, the board member pays off a $100,000 debt owed by ABC. ABC records the donation with the following entry:

| Notes payable | 100,000 | |
| Revenue—donations | | 100,000 |

Following the closing of the fiscal period, the effect of all the foregoing donations will be reflected in Adirondack's retained earnings account.

## Retained Earnings

Legal capital, additional paid-in capital, and donated capital collectively represent the contributed capital of the corporation.  The other major source of capital is retained earnings, which represents the accumulated amount of earnings of the corporation from the date of inception (or from the date of reorganization) less the cumulative amount of distributions made to shareholders and other charges to retained earnings (e.g., from treasury stock transactions).  The distributions to shareholders generally take the form of dividend payments but may take other forms as well, such as the reacquisition of shares for amounts in excess of the original issuance proceeds.  The key events impacting retained earnings are as follows:

- Dividends
- Certain treasury stock resales at amounts below acquisition cost
- Certain stock retirements at amounts in excess of book value
- Prior period adjustments
- Recapitalizations and reorganizations

### Examples of retained earnings transactions

Merrimack Corporation declares a dividend of $84,000, which it records with the following entry:

| | | |
|---|---|---|
| Retained earnings | 84,000 | |
|    Dividends payable | | 84,000 |

Merrimack acquires 3,000 shares of its own $1 par value common stock for $15,000, and then resells it for $12,000.  The following entries record the buyback and sale transactions respectively, assuming the use of the cost method of accounting for treasury stock:

| | | |
|---|---|---|
| Treasury stock | 15,000 | |
|    Cash | | 15,000 |
| | | |
| Cash | 12,000 | |
| Retained earnings | 3,000 | |
|    Treasury stock | | 15,000 |

Merrimack buys back 12,000 shares of its own $1 par value common stock (which it had originally sold for $60,000) for $70,000 and retires the stock, which it records with the following entry:

| | | |
|---|---|---|
| Common stock | 12,000 | |
| Additional paid-in capital | 48,000 | |
| Retained earnings | 10,000 | |
|    Cash | | 70,000 |

Merrimack's accountant makes a mathematical mistake in calculating depreciation, requiring a prior period reduction of $30,000 to the accumulated depreciation account, and corresponding increases in its income tax payable and retained earnings accounts. Merrimack's income tax rate is 35%.  It records this transaction with the following entry:

| | | |
|---|---|---|
| Accumulated depreciation | 30,000 | |
|    Income taxes payable | | 10,500 |
|    Retained earnings | | 19,500 |

Retained earnings are also affected by action taken by the corporation's board of directors.  Appropriation serves disclosure purposes and restricts dividend payments, but does nothing to provide any resources for the satisfaction of the contingent loss or other underlying purpose for which the appropriation has been made.  Any appropriation made from retained earnings must eventually be returned to the retained earnings account.  It is not permissible to charge losses against the appropriation account nor to credit any realized gain to that account.  The use of appropriated retained earnings has diminished significantly over the years.

It is axiomatic that transactions in a corporation's own stock can result in a reduction of retained earnings (i.e., a deficiency on such transactions can be charged to retained earnings) but cannot result in an increase in retained earnings (any excesses on such transactions are credited to paid-in capital, never to retained earnings).

If a series of operating losses have been incurred or distributions to shareholders in excess of accumulated earnings have been made, and if there is a debit balance in retained earnings, the account is generally referred to as accumulated deficit.

### Dividends

Dividends are the pro rata distribution of earnings to the owners of the corporation. The amount and the allocation between the preferred and common shareholders is a function of the stipulated preferential dividend rate; the presence or absence of (1) a participation feature, (2) a cumulative feature, and (3) arrearages on the preferred stock; and the wishes of the board of directors. Dividends, even preferred stock dividends, where a cumulative feature exists, do not accrue. Dividends only become a liability of the corporation when they are declared by the board of directors.

Traditionally, corporations were not allowed to declare dividends in excess of the amount of retained earnings. Alternatively, a corporation could pay dividends out of retained earnings and additional paid-in capital but could not exceed the total of these categories (i.e., they could not impair legal capital by the payment of dividends). States that have adopted the Model Business Corporation Act grant more latitude to the directors. Corporations can now, in certain jurisdictions, declare and pay dividends in excess of the book amount of retained earnings if the directors conclude that, after the payment of such dividends, the fair value of the corporation's net assets will still be a positive amount. Thus, directors can declare dividends out of unrealized appreciation that, in certain industries, can be a significant source of dividends beyond the realized and recognized accumulated earnings of the corporation. This action, however, represents a major departure from traditional practice and demands both careful consideration and adequate disclosure.

Three important dividend dates are

1. The declaration date
2. The record date
3. The payment date

The declaration date governs the incurrence of a legal liability by the corporation. The record date refers to that point in time when a determination is made as to which specific registered stockholders will receive dividends and in what amounts. Finally, the payment date relates to the date when the distribution of the dividend takes place. These concepts are illustrated in the following example:

On May 1, 2008, the directors of River Corp. declared a $.75 per share quarterly dividend on River Corp.'s 650,000 outstanding common shares. The dividend is payable May 25 to holders of record May 15.

| | | | |
|---|---|---|---|
| May 1 | Retained earnings (or dividends) | 487,500 | |
| | Dividends payable | | 487,500 |
| May 15 | No entry | | |
| May 25 | Dividends payable | 487,500 | |
| | Cash | | 487,500 |

If a dividends account is used, it is closed to retained earnings at year-end.

Dividends may be made in the form of cash, property, or scrip. Cash dividends are either a given dollar amount per share or a percentage of par or stated value. Property dividends consist of the distribution of any assets other than cash (e.g., inventory or equipment).

Finally, scrip dividends are promissory notes due at some time in the future, sometimes bearing interest until final payment is made.

Occasionally, what appear to be disproportionate dividend distributions are paid to some, but not all, of the owners of closely held corporations. Such transactions need to be carefully analyzed. In some cases these may actually represent compensation paid to the recipients. In other instances, these may be a true dividend paid to all shareholders on a pro rata basis, to which certain shareholders have waived their rights. If the former, the distribution should not be accounted for as a dividend, but rather as compensation or some other expense category and included on the income statement. If the latter, the dividend should be "grossed up" to reflect payment on a proportional basis to all the shareholders, with an offsetting capital contribution to the company recognized as having been effectively made by those to whom payments were not made.

**Property dividends.** If property dividends are declared, the paying corporation may incur a gain or loss. Since the dividend should be reflected at the fair value of the assets distributed, the difference between fair value and book value is recorded at the time the dividend is declared and charged or credited to a loss or gain account.

**Scrip dividends.** If a corporation declares a dividend payable in scrip that is interest bearing, the interest is accrued over time as a periodic expense. The interest is not a part of the dividend itself.

**Liquidating dividends.** Liquidating dividends are not distributions of earnings, but rather a return of capital to the investing shareholders. A liquidating dividend is normally recorded by the declarer through charging additional paid-in capital rather than retained earnings. The exact accounting for a liquidating dividend is affected by the laws where the business is incorporated, and these laws vary from state to state.

**Stock dividends.** Stock dividends represent neither an actual distribution of the assets of the corporation nor a promise to distribute those assets. For this reason, a stock dividend is not considered a legal liability or a taxable transaction.

Despite the recognition that a stock dividend is not a distribution of earnings, the accounting treatment of relatively insignificant stock dividends (defined as being less than 20% to 25% of the outstanding shares prior to declaration) is consistent with it being a real dividend. Accordingly, retained earnings are debited for the fair market value of the shares to be paid as a dividend, and the capital stock and additional paid-in capital accounts are credited for the appropriate amounts based upon the par or stated value of the shares, if any. A stock dividend declared but not yet paid is classified as such in the stockholders' equity section of the balance sheet. Since such a dividend never reduces assets, it cannot be a liability.

The selection of 20% to 25% as the threshold for recognizing a stock dividend as an earnings distribution is arbitrary, but it is based somewhat on the empirical evidence that small stock dividends tend not to result in a reduced market price per share for outstanding shares. The aggregate value of the outstanding shares should not change, but the greater number of shares outstanding after the stock dividend should necessitate a lower per share price. As noted, however, the declaration of small stock dividends tends not to have this impact, and this phenomenon supports the accounting treatment.

On the other hand, when stock dividends are larger in magnitude, it is observed that per share market value declines after the declaration of the dividend. In such situations, it would not be valid to treat the stock dividend as an earnings distribution. Rather, it should be accounted for as a split. The precise treatment depends upon the legal requirements of the state of incorporation and upon whether the existing par value or stated value is reduced concurrent with the stock split.

If the par value is not reduced for a large stock dividend and if state law requires that earnings be capitalized in an amount equal to the aggregate of the par value of the stock dividend declared, the event should be described as a stock split effected in the form of a dividend, with a charge to retained earnings and a credit to the common stock account for the aggregate par or stated value. When the par or stated value is reduced in recognition of the split and state laws do not require treatment as a dividend, there is no formal entry to record the split but merely a notation that the number of shares outstanding has increased and the per share par or stated value has decreased accordingly. It should be noted that many companies account for stock splits as if they were a large stock dividend. By doing this, par value per share remains unchanged. The concepts of small versus large stock dividends are illustrated in the following examples:

Assume that stockholders' equity for the Wasatch Corp. on November 1, 2008, is as follows:

| | |
|---|---|
| Common stock, $1 par, 100,000 shares outstanding | $ 100,000 |
| Paid-in capital in excess of par | 1,100,000 |
| Retained earnings | 750,000 |

**Small Stock Dividend:** On November 10, 2008, the directors of Wasatch Corp. declared a 15% stock dividend, or a dividend of 1.5 shares of common stock for every 10 shares held. Before the stock dividend, the stock is selling for $23 per share. After the 15% stock dividend, each original share worth $23 will become 1.15 shares, each with a value of $20 ($23/1.15). The stock dividend is to be recorded at the market value of the new shares issued, or $300,000 (15,000 new shares at the postdividend price of $20). The entries to record the declaration of the dividend and the issuance of stock (on November 30) by Wasatch Corp. are as follows:

| | | | |
|---|---|---|---|
| Nov. 10 | Retained earnings | 300,000 | |
| | Stock dividends distributable | | 15,000 |
| | Paid-in capital in excess of par | | 285,000 |
| Nov. 30 | Stock dividends distributable | 15,000 | |
| | Common stock, $1 par | | 15,000 |

**Large Stock Dividend:** Because the focus of the Committee on Accounting Procedure was on reducing the number of small stock dividends, the accounting requirements for governing large stock dividends are less specific than those for small stock dividends. In practice, ARB 43 results in the par or stated value of the newly issued shares being transferred to the capital stock account from either retained earnings or paid-in capital in excess of par. To illustrate, assume that on November 10, 2008, Wasatch Corp. declares a 50% large stock dividend, a dividend of one share for every two held. Legal requirements call for the transfer to capital stock of an amount equal to the par value of the shares issued. Entries for the declaration on November 10 and the issuance of 50,000 new shares (100,000 × .50) on November 30 are as follows:

| | | | |
|---|---|---|---|
| Nov. 10 | Retained earnings | 50,000 | |
| | Stock dividends distributable | | 50,000 |
| | or | | |
| | Paid-in capital in excess of par | 50,000 | |
| | Stock dividends distributable | | 50,000 |
| Nov. 30 | Stock dividends distributable | 50,000 | |
| | Common stock, $1 par | | 50,000 |

## Treasury Stock

Treasury stock consists of a corporation's own stock which has been issued, subsequently reacquired by the firm, and not yet reissued or canceled. Treasury stock does not reduce the number of shares issued but does reduce the number of shares outstanding, as well as total stockholders' equity. These shares are not eligible to receive cash dividends. Treasury stock is not an asset although, in some very limited circumstances, it may be presented as an asset if adequately disclosed (ARB 43, Ch. 1A). Reacquired stock that is awaiting delivery to satisfy a liability created by the firm's compensation plan or reacquired stock held in a profit-sharing trust is still considered outstanding and would not be considered treasury stock. In each case, the stock would be presented as an asset with the accompanying footnote disclosure. Accounting for excesses and deficiencies on treasury stock transactions is governed by ARB 43, Ch 1B, and APB 6.

Three approaches exist for the treatment of treasury stock: the cost, par value, and constructive retirement methods.

**Cost method.** Under the cost method, the gross cost of the shares reacquired is charged to a contra equity account (treasury stock). The equity accounts that were credited for the original share issuance (common stock, paid-in capital in excess of par, etc.) remain intact. When the treasury shares are reissued, proceeds in excess of cost are credited to a paid-in capital account. Any deficiency is charged to retained earnings (unless paid-in capital from previous treasury share transactions exists, in which case the deficiency is charged to that account, with any excess charged to retained earnings). If many treasury stock purchases are made, a cost flow assumption (e.g., FIFO or specific identification) should be adopted to compute excesses and deficiencies upon subsequent share reissuances. The advantage of the cost method is that it avoids identifying and accounting for amounts related to the original issuance of the shares and is, therefore, the simpler, more frequently used method.

The cost method is most consistent with the one-transaction concept. This concept takes the view that the classification of stockholders' equity should not be affected simply because the corporation was the middle "person" in an exchange of shares from one stockholder to another. In substance, there is only a transfer of shares between two stockholders. Since the original balances in the equity accounts are left undisturbed, its use is most acceptable when the firm acquires its stock for reasons other than its retirement, or when its ultimate disposition has not yet been decided.

**Par value method.** Under the par value method, the treasury stock account is charged only for the aggregate par (or stated) value of the shares reacquired. Other paid-in capital accounts (excess over par value, etc.) are relieved in proportion to the amounts recognized upon the original issuance of the shares. The treasury share acquisition is treated almost as a retirement. However, the common (or preferred) stock account continues at the original amount, thereby preserving the distinction between an actual retirement and a treasury share transaction.

When the treasury shares accounted for by the par value method are subsequently resold, the excess of the sale price over par value is credited to paid-in capital. A reissuance for a price below par value does not create a contingent liability for the purchaser. It is only the original purchaser who risks this obligation to the entity's creditors.

**Constructive retirement method.** The constructive retirement method is similar to the par value method, except that the aggregate par (or stated) value of the reacquired shares is charged to the stock account rather than to the treasury stock account. This method is superior when (1) it is management's intention not to reissue the shares within a reasonable time period or (2) the state of incorporation defines reacquired shares as having been retired. In the latter case, the constructive retirement method is probably the only method of accounting for treasury shares that is not inconsistent with the state Business Corporation Act, although the state law does not necessarily dictate such accounting. Certain states require that treasury stock be accounted for by this method.

The two-transaction concept is most consistent with the par value and constructive retirement methods. First, the reacquisition of the firm's shares is viewed as constituting a contraction of its capital structure. Second, the reissuance of the shares is the same as issuing new shares. There is little difference between the purchase and subsequent reissuance of treasury shares and the acquisition and retirement of previously issued shares and the issuance of new shares.

Treasury shares originally accounted for by the cost method can subsequently be restated to conform to the constructive retirement method. If shares were acquired with the intention that they would be reissued and it is later determined that such reissuance is unlikely (due, for example, to the expiration of stock options without their exercise), then it is proper to restate the transaction.

### Example of accounting for treasury stock

1. 100 shares ($50 par value) that were originally sold for $60 per share are later reacquired for $70 each.
2. All 100 shares are subsequently resold for a total of $7,500.

To record the acquisition, the entry is

| *Cost method* | | | *Par value method* | | | *Constructive retirement method* | | |
|---|---|---|---|---|---|---|---|---|
| Treasury stock | 7,000 | | Treasury stock | 5,000 | | Common stock | 5,000 | |
| Cash | | 7,000 | Additional paid-in | | | Additional paid-in | | |
| | | | capital—common | | | capital—common | | |
| | | | stock | 1,000 | | stock | 1,000 | |
| | | | Retained earnings | 1,000 | | Retained earnings | 1,000 | |
| | | | Cash | | 7,000 | Cash | | 7,000 |

To record the resale, the entry is

| *Cost method* | | | *Par value method* | | | *Constructive retirement method* | | |
|---|---|---|---|---|---|---|---|---|
| Cash | 7,500 | | Cash | 7,500 | | Cash | 7,500 | |
| Treasury stock | | 7,000 | Treasury stock | | 5,000 | Common stock | | 5,000 |
| Additional paid- | | | Additional paid- | | | Additional paid- | | |
| in capital— | | | in capital— | | | in capital— | | |
| treasury stock | | 500 | common stock | | 2,500 | common stock | | 2,500 |

If the shares had been resold for $6,500, the entry is

| *Cost method* | | | *Par value method* | | | *Constructive retirement method* | | |
|---|---|---|---|---|---|---|---|---|
| Cash | 6,500 | | Cash | 6,500 | | Cash | 6,500 | |
| Retained earnings* | 500 | | Treasury stock | | 5,000 | Common stock | | 5,000 |
| Treasury stock | | 7,000 | Additional paid- | | | Additional paid- | | |
| | | | in capital— | | | in capital— | | |
| | | | common stock | | 1,500 | common stock | | 1,500 |

\* *"Additional paid-in capital—treasury stock" or "Additional paid-in capital—retired stock" of that issue would be debited first to the extent it exists.*

Alternatively, under the par or constructive retirement methods, any portion of or the entire deficiency on the treasury stock acquisition may be debited to retained earnings without allocation to paid-in capital. Any excesses will always be credited to an "Additional paid-in capital—retired stock" account.

The laws of some states govern the circumstances under which a corporation may acquire treasury stock and may prescribe the accounting for the stock. For example, a charge to retained earnings may be required in an amount equal to the treasury stock's total cost. In such cases, the accounting per the state law prevails. Also, some states (including those that have adopted the Model Business Corporation Act) define excess purchase cost of reacquired (i.e., treasury) shares as being "distributions" to shareholders that are no different in nature than dividends. In such cases, the financial statement presentation should adequately disclose the substance of these transactions (e.g., by presenting both dividends and excess reacquisition costs together in the retained earnings statement).

When a firm decides to formally retire the treasury stock, the journal entry is dependent on the method used to account for the stock. Using the original sale and reacquisition data from the illustration above, the following entries would be made if the cost and par value methods, respectively, were employed:

| _Cost method_ | | | | _Par value method_ | |
|---|---|---|---|---|---|
| Common stock | 5,000 | | Common stock | 5,000 | |
| Additional paid-in | | | Treasury stock | | 5,000 |
|   capital—common stock | 1,000 | | | | |
| Retained earnings | 1,000 | | | | |
|     Treasury stock | | 7,000 | | | |

\*   *"Additional paid-in capital—treasury stock" may be debited to the extent it exists.*

If the constructive retirement method were used to record the treasury stock purchase, no additional entry would be necessary upon the formal retirement of the shares.

After the entry is made, the pro rata portion of all paid-in capital existing for that issue (i.e., capital stock and additional paid-in capital) will have been eliminated. If stock is purchased for immediate retirement (i.e., not put into the treasury) the entry to record the retirement is the same as that made under the constructive retirement method.

In some circumstances, shares held by current stockholders may be donated back to the enterprise, possibly to facilitate a resale to new owners who will infuse needed capital into the business. In accounting for donated treasury stock, the intentions of management regarding these reacquired shares is key; if these are to simply be retired, the common stock account should be debited for the par or stated value (if par or stated value stock) or the original proceeds received (if no-par, no-stated-value stock). The current fair value of the shares should be credited to the "donated capital" account, and the difference should be debited or credited to a suitably titled paid-in capital account, such as "additional paid-in capital from share donations."

If the donated shares are to be sold (the normal scenario), variations on the par and cost methods of treasury stock accounting can be employed, with "donated capital" being debited and credited, respectively, when shares are received and later reissued, instead of the "treasury stock" account employed in the above illustrations. Note, however, that if the cost method is used, the debit to the donated capital account should be for the fair value of the shares, not the cost (a seeming contradiction). If the constructive retirement method is utilized instead, only a memorandum entry will be recorded when the shares are received; when reissued, the entire proceeds should be credited to "donated capital."

## Other Paid-in Capital Issues

**Takeover defense as cost of treasury stock.** In certain instances an entity may incur costs to defend against an unwelcome or hostile attempted takeover. In some cases, in fact, putative acquirers will threaten a takeover struggle in order to extract so-called "greenmail" from the target entity, often effected through a buyback of shares held by the acquirer at a premium over market value. FTB 85-6 states that the excess purchase price of treasury shares should not be attributed to the shares, but rather should be attributed to the other elements of the transaction and accounted for according to their substance, which could include the receipt of stated or unstated rights, privileges, or agreements. The SEC's position is that such excess is anything over the quoted market price of the treasury shares.

**Accelerated share repurchase programs.** EITF 99-7 pertains to accelerated share repurchase programs, which are combinations of transactions that permit an entity to purchase a targeted number of shares immediately, with the final purchase price determined by an average market price over fixed periods of time. Such programs are intended to combine the immediate share retirement benefits (boosting earnings per share, etc.) of tender offers with the market impacts and pricing benefits of disciplined open market stock repurchase programs. At issue were the implications of accelerated share repurchase programs on EPS calculations and entities' abilities to account for business combinations as (now obsolete) poolings of interests.

The consensus was that an entity should account for an accelerated share repurchase program as two separate transactions: first, as shares of common stock acquired in a treasury stock transaction recorded on the acquisition date, and second, as a forward contract indexed to its own common stock. Pursuant to EITF 99-3, an entity would classify the forward contract in the above example as an equity instrument because the entity will receive cash when the contract is in a gain position but pay cash or stock when the contract is in a loss position. Changes in the fair value of the forward contract would not be recorded, and the settlement of the forward contract would be recorded in equity.

The treasury stock transaction would result in an immediate reduction of the outstanding shares used to calculate the weighted-average common shares outstanding for both basic and diluted EPS. The effect of the forward contract on diluted EPS would be calculated in accordance with FAS 128, as interpreted by EITF Topic D-72.

**Freestanding derivatives indexed to, and potentially settled in, stock of a consolidated subsidiary.** EITF 96-13 establishes a framework for accounting for freestanding derivative instruments that are indexed to, and potentially settled in, a company's own stock. That consensus did not, however, provide guidance on how to account for freestanding derivative instruments that are indexed to, and potentially settled in, a subsidiary's stock. EITF 00-6 deals with how such contracts should be classified and measured in the consolidated financial statements.

A consensus exists that stock of a subsidiary is not equity of the parent; therefore, derivatives indexed to and to be settled in stock of a subsidiary do not meet FAS 133's exclusion criteria. If derivatives meet the criteria of FAS 133 (e.g., for net settlement, etc.), they must be accounted for under the provisions of FAS 133, and not of EITF 96-13. The consensus also discusses a number of exceptions based on the criteria set forth in FAS 133.

The EITF reached several consensuses regarding derivatives not within the scope of FAS 133, while also noting that option or forward strike prices and premiums could be indicative of impairments of the parent's investment in subsidiaries, to be assessed using FAS 121. A parent's contract to purchase a subsidiary's (minority held) common stock should not be recorded until settled; during the period of the contract, income should continue to be allocated to the minority interest. A contract to sell shares in a subsidiary, likewise, should be recorded when settled; until that time, income would not be allocated to outside interests (counterparties to the derivative).

A subsequent consensus, EITF 00-19, codified the EITF's position on this entire subject area. It applies to freestanding derivatives only—similar embedded derivatives are not covered. Also not covered are derivatives which are issued to compensate employees or to acquire goods and services from nonemployees, when performance has yet to occur. It does apply, however, to derivatives issued to acquire goods and services from nonemployees, when performance has occurred.

The issue for the EITF was how certain equity derivative contracts indexed to, and potentially settled in, a company's own stock should be accounted for. Such contracts could include written puts, written calls and warrants, purchased puts, purchased calls, forward sale contracts, and forward purchase contracts.

In its consensus, the EITF reached a number of conclusions. These are summarized as follows.

1. Initial balance sheet classification is to be guided by the principle that contracts which require net cash settlements are assets or liabilities, and those that require

settlement in shares are equity instruments. If the reporting entity has the choice of settlement modes, settlement in shares is to be assumed; if the counterparty has the option, net cash settlement is presumed. An exception occurs if the two settlement alternatives are not of equal value, in which case the economic substance should govern.

2. Initial measurement should be at fair value. Contracts classed as equity are accounted for in permanent equity, with value changes being ignored, unless settlement expectations change. For publicly held companies, under defined circumstances, guidance is provided by analogy from ASR 268. All other contracts would be classified as assets or liabilities, to be measured continuously at fair value. If settlement in shares ultimately occurs, already recognized gains or losses are left in earnings, not reclassified or reversed.

3. Events may necessitate reclassification of contracts from assets/liabilities to equity. If a contract first classed as equity is later reclassed to assets/liabilities, any value change to the date of reclassification will be included in equity, not earnings. Thereafter, value changes will be reported in earnings. If partial net share settlement is permitted, the portion that can be so settled remains in equity. Appropriate disclosure under APB 22 may be required, if more than one contract exists and different methods are applied to them.

4. All the following conditions must be satisfied in order to classify a contract in equity:

   a. The contract permits settlement in unregistered shares (the assumption being that the issuer cannot effectively control the conditions for registration, making cash settlement likely unless unregistered shares can be delivered);

   b. There are sufficient authorized, unissued shares to settle the contact, after considering all other outstanding commitments;

   c. The contract contains an explicit limit on the number of shares to be issued;

   d. There are no required cash payments to the counterparty based on the issuer's failure to make timely SEC filings;

   e. There are no "make whole" provisions to compensate the holder after he sells the shares issued in the market at a price below some defined threshold value;

   f. Requirements for net cash settlement are accompanied by similar requirements for existing shareholders;

   g. There are no provisions that indicate that the counterparties have rights greater than those of the actual shareholders; and

   h. There is no requirement for any collateral posting for any reason.

5. Contracts that are subject to this consensus cannot qualify for hedge accounting (this is based on the SEC's position on this matter).

6. Contracts offering multiple settlement alternatives that require the company to receive cash when the contract is in a gain position but pay either stock or cash at the company's option when in a loss position are to be accounted for as equity. Also, such contracts requiring payment of cash when in a loss position but receipt of either cash or stock at the company's option when in a gain position must be accounted for as assets/liabilities.

7. For EPS computation purposes, for those contracts that provide the company with a choice of settlement methods, settlement in shares is to be assumed, although this can be overcome based on past experience or stated policy. If the counterparty controls the choice, however, the more dilutive assumption must be made, irrespective of past experience or policy.

EITF 00-19 created some confusion regarding the accounting—as liability or equity—for certain freestanding financial instruments originally issued in compensation for employee services once the rights conveyed to the holder no longer were dependent upon employee status (e.g., after the options vest). An initial attempt to clarify this, FSP EITF 00-19-1, was quickly superseded by FSP FAS 123(R)-1, *Classification and Measurement of Freestanding Financial Instruments Originally Issued in Exchange for Employee Services under FASB Statement No. 123(R),* which holds that freestanding financial instruments issued to employees in exchange for past or future employee services that are subject to FAS 123(R), or were subject to FAS 123(R) upon initial adoption of that standard, will continue to be subject to the recognition and measurement provisions of FAS 123(R) throughout the life of the instruments, unless their terms are modified when the holder is no longer an employee. FSP FAS 123(R)-1 was subsequently amended by FSP FAS 123(R)-5, which addresses whether a modification of an instrument in connection with an equity restructuring should be considered a modification for purposes of applying FSP FAS 123(R)-1. The position holds that, for instruments originally issued as employee compensation and then modified, and where that modification to the terms of the instrument is made *solely* to reflect an equity restructuring that occurs when the holders are no longer employees, no change in the recognition or the measurement (due to a change in classification) of those instruments will result if *both* of the following conditions are met:

1. There is no increase in the fair value of the award (or the ratio of intrinsic value to the exercise price of the award is preserved—i.e., the holder is made whole), or the antidilution provision is not added to the terms of the award in contemplation of an equity restructuring; *and*
2. All holders of the same class of equity instruments (for example, stock options) are treated in the same manner.

Other modifications of the instrument (that is, any modification that fails to meet the dual tests above) that take place when the holder is no longer an employee, is subject to the modification accounting guidance set forth by FAS 123(R), as addressed above. Following modification, the accounting for such instruments, no longer held by employees, must follow GAAP, including FAS 150 if applicable.

FSP FAS 123(R)-6 makes certain technical corrections to FAS 123(R). It amends the standard to exempt nonpublic entities from disclosing the aggregate intrinsic value of outstanding fully vested share options (or share units) and share options expected to vest; revises the computation of the minimum compensation cost that must be recognized; makes a change to the examples to indicate that at the date that the illustrative awards were no longer probable of vesting, any previously recognized compensation cost should have been reversed; and amends the definition of *short-term inducement* to exclude an offer to settle an award.

These changes correct certain examples found in FAS 123(R) and amend one definition. As to the latter, the definition of short-term inducement in the glossary of terms included the phrase *or settlement of an award.* This reference raised a question about possible interaction between different provisions of the standard. FASB did not intend for a short-term inducement deemed to be a settlement to affect the classification of the award for the period it remains outstanding (for example, change the award from an equity instrument to a liability instrument). Therefore, an offer (for a limited time period) to repurchase an award should be excluded from the definition of a short-term inducement, and not be accounted for as a modification. However, if an entity has a history of settling its awards for cash, the entity should consider whether at the inception of the awards it has a substantive liability.

*Accounting for freestanding warrants and other instruments on shares that are redeemable.* Instruments having both liability-like and equity-like attributes have often been difficult to classify in the balance sheet. FAS 150 (see Chapter 15) requires liability categorization of many instruments which heretofore had been included in equity, or in some cases in a "mezzanine" capital section (which is countenanced by SEC rules although there is no such concept under GAAP). FSP FAS 150-1 holds that warrants for shares that are puttable are liabilities under FAS 150, because the warrants embody obligations to repurchase the issuer's shares and may require a transfer of assets, and likewise warrants for mandatorily redeemable shares are liabilities because they embody obligations to repurchase the issuer's shares that, if exercised, will require a transfer of assets.

In FSP FAS 150-5, *Issuer's Accounting under FASB Statement No. 150 for Freestanding Warrants and Other Similar Instruments on Shares That Are Redeemable,* this requirement is broadened somewhat further. It holds that both warrants on shares that are redeemable immediately after exercise of the warrants and also those that are redeemable at some date in the future are liabilities. The number of conditions that must be met before the warrants become exercisable is deemed to be irrelevant to the question, so that warrants to obtain either puttable or mandatorily redeemable shares are liabilities in all cases.

## Other Equity Accounts

In principle, modern financial reporting in conformity with GAAP subscribes to what was once known as the "all inclusive" or "clean surplus" concept, which means that all items of income, expense, gain or loss (other than transactions with owners) should flow through the income statement. In fact, however, a number of important exceptions have been imposed by specific GAAP standards, beginning with the market value declines recognized under the now superseded FAS 12 on noncurrent portfolios of marketable equity securities, and reported directly in shareholder equity. Later standards added translation gains or losses (FAS 52), certain adjustments for minimum pension obligations (FAS 87), and unrealized gains and losses on available-for-sale portfolios of debt or equity investments (FAS 115) to the litany of recognized economic events which escaped reporting in the income statement. Most recently, hedging gains and losses qualifying under FAS 133 are also deferred for income measurement purposes. As explained in Chapter 3, the FASB concepts project had foreseen the need for a flow statement analogous to the income statement to report all such changes for the reporting period, and this was finally mandated by FAS 130, which established the concept of comprehensive income (the term which now denotes normal earnings plus the change in these other equity accounts). Comprehensive income must now be reported either in a combined statement with the income statement, as a stand-alone statement, or in an expanded statement of changes in stockholders' equity.

In the balance sheet, the various elements of other comprehensive income (i.e., the current balances of such items as translation gains and losses and unrealized gains and losses from available-for-sale securities holdings) can be aggregated into a single caption, with details reserved to the notes, or the separate items can be grouped into a subsection of the equity section. Since items of other comprehensive income are neither paid-in capital nor retained earnings, this constitutes a third major classification within the equity section of the balance sheet. Many entities will have only minor amounts of such items or none at all.

Refer to Chapter 3 for a complete discussion of other comprehensive income.

## Accounting for Share-Based Payments

Explicit recognition of the imputed cost of compensation paid to executives and other employees via stock option and similar programs has been an objective of accounting standard setters for over a decade. While a few theorists argue that no cost is incurred when a company issues mere paper to employees, the mainstream recognizes that when employees accept lower cash compensation in exchange for stock-based compensation, which forms the basis for measuring compensation cost. Additionally, the issuance of shares to employees in lieu of some cash compensation (which is inevitably what is occurring, even though the employees are not given the choice of cash or stock) is no different than first paying cash compensation (which would be recognized as an operating expense) and then having the recipients use that cash to purchase company stock.

This simple point has been definitively settled by the promulgation of FAS 123(R). This standard replaces the failed and feeble attempt of a decade earlier, FAS 123, which held that, although fair value-based measures of stock-based compensation were preferable, it would nonetheless be permissible for companies to continue using the intrinsic value method of APB 25, under which employee options-related compensation cost was rarely recognized. While footnote disclosures of FAS 123-prescribed measures of fair value-based compensation cost was required, this was much less effective in providing users with an understanding of the cost of such programs and, in any event, failed to meet the requirement under GAAP to not substitute disclosure for actual recognition and measurement.

The most significant change from FAS 123 to FAS 123(R) is that now fair value must be used to measure the cost of all share-based payment plans, and the intrinsic value method as set forth under APB 25 has been eliminated entirely. There is still an optional exception available for nonpublic companies, where measures of stock price volatility required to apply the normal fair value approach simply do not exist, but under such circumstances a modified fair value model is prescribed, where an industry group-based surrogate for the entity's stock price volatility is employed. Thus, all stock-based compensation arrangements, where equity instruments are issued to employees, will result in compensation cost that is measured using a variant of the fair value model.

While the original FAS 123 was interpreted by many as having endorsed the "closed-form fair value model"—of which the Black-Scholes (now being called the Black-Scholes-Merton, or BSM) approach was the most widely recognized—financial statement preparers were free to select other fair value measurement methods. In the fourteen years since FAS 123 was issued, however, the differences between stock options granted to employees and those which are publicly traded (the actual objective of BSM and related models) have become better understood, and the features which give greater value to tradable options (exchangeability, public market pricing) and which are missing from most employee option grants have come to be appreciated as having major influence on option values. This led to some disaffection with the use of BSM models in the context of employee stock options, and a greater enthusiasm for what became known as lattice models.

Lattice models provide greater flexibility for including or excluding variables, or changing variable parameters, from one period to the other. FAS 123(R) does not require the use of lattice-type models, of which the binomial model is the most widely employed, but the advantages of such approaches are worthwhile.

In determining the fair value of share options, all the features and attributes of the options must be taken into consideration, including the expected volatility of the underlying equity instrument. The minimum value model allowed under FAS 123, which simply ignored expected volatility, has been rendered unacceptable by FAS 123(R).

The fair-value-based method required under FAS 123(R) is similar to the fair-value-based method first set forth by FAS 123. However, there are important differences that need to be understood by those who implemented original FAS 123 previously, even for disclosure purposes only. The following are the key differences between the original and revised standards:

1.  Under FAS 123(R), publicly held entities are required to account for awards of *equity instruments* using the fair-value-based method. This applies to recognition and measurement as well as to disclosure. It is no longer acceptable to maintain the APB 25-prescribed intrinsic value approach to recognition and measurement while relegating the FAS 123-based fair value measures to the footnote disclosures.

2.  Nonpublicly held entities are required to account for awards of *equity instruments* using the fair-value-based method unless it is not possible to reasonably estimate the grant-date fair value of awards of equity share options and similar instruments because it is not practicable to estimate the expected volatility of the entity's share price. In that situation, the entity will account for those instruments based on a value calculated by substituting the historical volatility of an appropriate industry sector index for the expected volatility of its share price. Former standard FAS 123 permitted a nonpublicly held entity to measure its equity awards using either the fair-value-based method or the minimum value method, with the latter being essentially the fair value model minus any factor for share price volatility. Thus, the "minimum value" alternative is no longer available. (And, as noted above, the APB 25-based intrinsic value method is now barred entirely.)

3.  Publicly held entities are required to measure *liabilities* incurred to employees in share-based payment transactions at fair value. Such liabilities arise when the share-based compensation scheme causes the reporting entity to recognize a liability rather than an equity item. FAS 150 identifies situations (e.g., when the obligation might have to be settled for cash at the option of the holder, or the shares issued have mandatory redemption features) where classification as a liability, rather than equity, will be required. Although FAS 150 does not apply, in general, to share-based compensation plans, it does serve to determine the classification of the instruments issued as either liabilities or equity.

4.  Nonpublicly held entities optionally may elect to measure their liabilities to employees incurred in share-based payment transactions at their intrinsic value. Intrinsic value, as used here, is not equivalent to intrinsic value as that term was used by APB 25. Under former standard FAS 123, all share-based payment liabilities were measured at their intrinsic value. If, under the provisions of FAS 123(R) the intrinsic value approach is elected, the liability must be remeasured at each reporting date, with a final measurement at the date of final settlement. This means that compensation cost-related charges (or credits) may be included in results of operations for some or all of the years from the date of grant until final settlement is made.

5.  Under FAS 123(R) reporting entities are required to estimate the number of instruments for which it is expected service will be rendered. That is, expense recognition is based on the estimated number of equity instruments that will be issued, with appropriate adjustments made as estimates of the rate of forfeitures change over time. The original FAS 123 permitted entities to accrue costs for all share options granted, without adjustment for expected forfeitures, and then to account for forfeitures as they later occurred.

6.  Incremental compensation cost for a modification of the terms or conditions of an award is measured by comparing the fair value of the modified award with the fair value of the award immediately before the modification. The original FAS 123 required that the effects of a modification be measured as the difference between the fair value of the modified award at the date it is granted and the award's value immediately before the modification determined based on the shorter of (1) its remaining initially estimated expected life or (2) the expected life of the modified award.

7. FAS 123(R) also clarifies and expands original FAS 123's guidance in several areas, including methods of measuring fair value, classifying an award as equity or as a liability, and attributing compensation cost to reporting periods. Most significantly, of course, FAS 123(R) does not prescribe an options-valuation model, but does propose use of "lattice-type" models as being more flexible and sensitive to peculiarities of employee stock options, versus the previously touted "closed-form" models exemplified by the well-known Black-Scholes(-Merton) model.

In addition, FAS 123(R) amends FAS 95 to require that excess tax benefits be reported as a financing cash inflow rather than as a reduction of taxes paid. This is more consistent with the view that the issuance of employee stock option shares is part of the capital raising process, and the tax advantages attendant to this are equivalently part of that same process. Previously (under original FAS 123, and under APB 25 as well) the tax reduction was to be included in tax expense and in operating cash flows.

The formerly employed term, stock-based compensation, has been replaced by the term share-based payment, partly to conform to IFRS usage, and partly to communicate the fact that FAS 123(R) is applicable to all such payments, whether to employees or to others for purchase of goods or services. For purpose of the discussion in this chapter, however, these will be taken as synonymous.

The most recent standard on business combinations, FAS 141 (R), reinforces FAS 123(R) by requiring that an acquiring entity use FAS 123 (R) to measure the liability associated with the replacement of an acquiree's share-based payment awards with its own share-based payment awards.

## FAS 123(R): Detailed Explanation

FAS 123(R) broadly addresses share-based payments. It covers plans for employees that convey shares of the employer's stock, derivatives (such as options) related to the employer's shares, or cash in amounts tied to the value of the employer's shares. All share-based plans are considered compensatory unless the benefit to employees is no greater than that which is available to shareholders generally. The benefit to recipients is assessed based both on the discount from market price and the number of shares they are eligible to buy. Consequently, virtually all plans will be considered compensatory for accounting purposes, including employee stock purchase plans that are noncompensatory under the federal tax laws. This represents a change from APB 25, under which noncompensatory plans for tax purposes were also noncompensatory for accounting proposes. The new rules are even somewhat stricter than those set forth under FAS 123.

Additionally, FAS 123 (R) modifies FAS 123 as to (1) the prescribed pattern of compensation cost recognition, (2) the accounting for employee stock purchase plans, and (3) accounting for the income tax effects of share-based transactions. It also amends FAS 95 to require that excess tax benefits be reported in the cash flow statement as a financing activity, rather than as an operating activity (these are currently reported as a reduction of income taxes paid).

**Scope.** FAS 123(R) was the result of a "limited scope" effort to address deficiencies in FAS 123. FAS 123(R) applies to

1. Public and nonpublic companies, and the
2. Accounting for all share-based awards to employees, including employee stock purchase plans

FAS 123(R) does not apply to

1. Accounting for employee stock ownership plan transactions (ESOP), or

2. Awards to nonemployees, with an exception made in the case of awards to nonemployee members of the board of directors in their capacity as directors, a distinction first established by the now-superceded FIN 44.

These exclusions will reportedly be taken up in a later phase of FASB's project on equity-based compensation arrangements.

**Overview of significant revisions made to FAS 123.** FAS 123(R) eliminates the alternative of continuing to account for share-based payment arrangements with employees under APB 25, which generally had resulted in having no reportable compensation cost associated with executive stock options. Because compensation cost will now be measured under the fair value approach and formally reported in the body of the income statement, FAS 123(R) also eliminates the requirement to provide a pro forma disclosure of the effect of applying fair-value-based accounting methods.

In the following paragraphs, the key features of FAS 123(R) will be explained, followed by examples of how the provisions of the standard would be applied. FAS 123(R) requires not merely a mandatory application of the formerly voluntary measurement requirements of FAS 123, but also certain changes in the required methodology itself. Therefore, in the following discussion, emphasis will be placed on the changes to the fair value methodology of FAS 123 that have been enacted, some of which are substantial.

**Measurement of compensation cost from share-based payment arrangements with employees.** The objective is to estimate, as of the grant date, the fair value of the award that an employee earns as a result of requisite service and satisfying vesting requirements. The estimate of fair value would reflect transferability and other restrictions if they are in effect when the award vests. Compensation cost is to be recognized only for those awards that vest (which obviously demands that estimates be made).

- **Classifying awards as liabilities or equity.** FAS 123(R) amended FAS 123 to require that the classification criteria of FAS 150 be applied in determining whether an instrument granted to an employee is a liability or equity. In particular, some stock-based compensation awards that call for settlement by issuing an entity's own equity instruments may be classified as liabilities if they meet the criteria of FAS 150. Under APB 25 there was no attempt to distinguish between awards creating equity instruments and those creating liabilities.

- **Valuation models.** In the absence of an observable market price for an award—often the reality for employee share options—reporting entities are now required to use a valuation method that takes into account the factors set forth in the standard. FAS 123 explicitly cited both the Black-Scholes and binomial approaches as being among the acceptable option pricing models, but the former was most widely used in practice, partially because it was less cumbersome, although still far from being intuitively obvious for most financial statement preparers. Since the promulgation of FAS 123 (1995), BSM has become the target of much criticism. It purportedly overstates compensation cost as a consequence of not reflecting the unique characteristics of nontradable employee options.

  While FAS 123(R) does not dictate a valuation model either, reportedly FASB believes and prefers that most companies will use the binomial, or other so-called *lattice* models of value, rather than a *closed-form* model such as the BSM. The binomial model is favored, however, because it accommodates more potential postvesting behaviors than the closed-form models.

  Binomial or other lattice models value options by constructing lattices or trees that represent different possible stock prices at different future points in time. The value of the option is determined at each node or branch of the tree. To determine these values, companies need to develop information about expected volatility, dividends, and risk-free rates that will apply at each of the possible branches or nodes of the model. In addition, information about employee postvesting behavior is needed to determine likely exercise dates. Note that under FAS 123(R) it will be necessary to use *expected volatility*, whereas under FAS 123 historical volatility of share prices were typically employed as a surrogate for future volatility.

- **Liability-classified awards.** The provisions dealing with share-based payments that involve liabilities, rather than equity, are affected by the issuance of FAS 150, which occurred after the original FAS 123 had been promulgated. Certain share-based payments create liabilities under FAS 150, (e.g., awards which result in the issuance of mandatorily redeemable shares, or those which require cash settlements or give the holders the right to demand cash, as do some stock appreciation rights). Liability-classified awards are to be remeasured at fair value each reporting period. Prior to vesting, the cumulative compensation costs would equal the proportionate amount of the award earned to date, and thus the periodic compensation cost would reflect both the passage of time (service period) and change in the fair value of the ultimate award. Subsequent to vesting, any further change in fair value would be recorded as a charge against earnings. This is similar to the result under FAS 123, but represents a fundamental change from APB 25, which required liability-classified awards be accounted for using the intrinsic value method, as were equity-based awards.

  The use of grant date to fix the value of equity-based awards, and settlement date to fix the value of liability-based awards, may seem inconsistent and/or confusing. FASB presents a rather detailed explanation for its decisions in the new standard, but essentially the logic is that to recognize changes in compensation based on post-grant-date changes to the value of the underlying equity would be equivalent to recognizing changes in the value of the entity's own equity shares in earnings, which is prohibited under GAAP. Also, grant date is when the parties (the entity and its employees) have fixed the terms of their arrangement, which provides a meaningful measure of the cost to be incurred by the entity. This differs importantly from the situation with equity-based compensation that is classified as a liability because it is to be settled for cash (e.g., cash SARs). In that scenario, the entity is obligated to distribute assets, and the relevant measure of compensation cost, ultimately, is the amount of assets disbursed.

- **Equity-classified awards.** Equity-classified awards that are publicly traded and have observable market prices are to be valued using the market price. Few, if any, employee stock compensation awards (i.e., employee stock options) would have this characteristic, however. If not publicly traded, equity-classified awards are valued using a model such as the binomial or the Black-Scholes-Merton.

- **Valuation for graded-vesting awards.** Companies that grant awards with graded vesting are to elect whether to measure the awards as if it were a cliff-vested award, or alternatively whether they are to be treated as several separate awards. If the former is chosen, the amount expensed each year would be the pro rata portion of compensation cost determined with reference to the entire package. If the latter approach is selected, each separately vesting portion will be valued and the associated compensation cost will be accrued over the term until that portion vests.

- **Measurement alternatives for nonpublic companies.** FAS 123 offered nonpublic companies choosing the fair value approach, broadly defined, the alternative of using a minimum value model, which eliminated the volatility variable from the valuation model of choice. This was done because for a nontraded stock there would be no historical record of volatility of prices, and hence (it was thought at the time) no reasonable way to estimate future volatility. FAS 123's minimum-value method for measuring fair value is no longer permitted. Nonpublic companies may now instead choose to use either continually updated intrinsic values or fair values to measure share-option or liability-classified awards. Note that no such choice would be available for nonvested or vested stock awards, which are to be measured using grant-date fair values.

If a nonpublic reporting entity chooses to use the intrinsic value alternative, the intrinsic value of an equity-classified award will have to be reestimated each reporting period. However, if a company uses the fair value alternative no reestimation is required, which could reduce fluctuations in reported earnings. If nonpublic companies choose the fair value approach, they will not later be able to return to the use of intrinsic value, because fair value is deemed preferable for purposes of applying APB 20 (accounting changes). These matters represent significant changes from FAS 123 as first promulgated. Furthermore, the intrinsic value method under FAS 123(R) differs dramatically from the intrinsic value method under APB 25: under the latter, intrinsic value is measured once, at grant date (generally), and typically was zero; under the former, it is remeasured at each balance sheet date and will be zero only under the unique situation where the market price never exceeds the exercise price, rendering the option, under this formulation, worthless from grant date to expiration date.

While fair value is to be determined as of grant date, in practice there has been some ambiguity regarding the precise definition of this term. FAS 123(R) does set forth criteria for determining that a share-based payment award has been granted. One of the criteria is a mutual understanding by the employer and employee of the key terms and conditions of a share-based payment award. However, the "mutual" aspect may not occur until some time after the formal grant, when actual communications between employer and employee are held, sometimes not until, for example, a regularly scheduled performance review that might not occur for weeks or months thereafter. To address these practical concerns, FSP FAS 123(R)-2, *Practical Accommodation to the Application of Grant Date as Defined in FASB Statement No. 123(R),* has held that, assuming all other criteria in the grant date definition have been met, a mutual understanding of the key terms and conditions of an award to an individual employee is presumed to exist at the date the award is approved in accordance with the relevant corporate governance requirements (that is, by the board or management with the relevant authority), if both the following conditions are met:

1. The award is a unilateral grant and, therefore, the recipient does not have the ability to negotiate the key terms and conditions of the award with the employer, and
2. The key terms and conditions of the award are expected to be communicated to an individual recipient within a relatively short time period from the date of approval.

**Recognizing compensation.** Vesting can be based on a service condition, performance condition, or a combination of both.

- Service conditions are requirements to achieve a specified duration of employment (e.g., number of years' continuous full-time service).
- Performance conditions are requirements to achieve company-specific operating or financial goals (e.g., net income over $3 million).

Compensation cost is to be recognized based on the actual number of awards that eventually vest. Estimates are used to make accruals each period and adjustments are made based on current estimates of expected future vesting until the actual number of awards that vest are known. This is a major change from FAS 123, which allowed companies to recognize compensation expense based on the assumption that all awards would vest, and then later adjust for actual forfeitures as they occurred. The formerly employed method is now barred.

Under provisions of FAS 123(R), compensation cost for equity-based awards is to be measured at the grant date, and not subsequently revised (apart from recognizing changed likelihood of forfeitures). Under APB 25, the measure was generally at grant date, but when either the amount the employee would be required to pay or the number of shares the employee would be entitled to were not known, compensation was measured at a later date (these were the so-called variable awards, the accounting for which was governed by FIN 28 and FIN 38, both of which have been superseded by the guidance in FAS 123[R]).

Market conditions affect the exercisability of an award, but not its vesting. FAS 123(R) defines a market condition as an exercisability requirement based on achieving a specified share price (e.g., reaching a market price of $22 per share before exercise is allowed). Market conditions can affect the grant-date fair value, and hence the compensation expense to be recognized by the reporting entity. If an employee forfeits an award because a market condition is not satisfied, compensation previously accrued is not reversed, unlike what is done in the event of ordinary forfeitures, which necessitate reversal of previously accrued compensation cost (or, equivalently, adjustment of compensation cost prospectively until the vesting date).

Under provisions of FAS 123(R), compensation cost for liability-based awards will be measured at the exercise or settlement date, but compensation is estimated at each reporting date from grant date to exercise or settlement date, much like variable accounting under APB 25 and its interpretations. This is similar to practice under the original FAS 123.

**Modified awards.** The incremental compensation cost resulting from a modification of an award will be measured as the excess of the fair value of the modified award over the fair value of the original award measured immediately prior to the modification. Modifications can occur because of repricing, extending the life, or changing the vesting condition of the award. Cancellations of existing awards and concurrent replacement with new ones have to be accounted for as modifications. In practice, modifications will rarely result in recognized compensation costs less than the fair value of the award at the grant date, but this could conceivably result if the original service or performance vesting conditions were not expected to be satisfied at the modification date.

## Accounting for Employee Stock Options under FAS 123(R)

FAS 123(R) does not permit public company accounting for stock-based compensation as had previously been provided under APB 25—which, together with associated interpretations, has been fully superseded by the new standard. Under FAS 123(R), fair value accounting must be applied in measuring compensation expense. Ideally, fair value would be market-observed. An observable market price, if available for an option with similar features, should be used as the estimate of fair value of the employee option. However, in most cases, due to the nature of employee stock options (which lack exchangeability, etc.), observable market prices will not be available. Therefore, the reporting entity will have to estimate the fair value of the employee share option using a valuation model that meets the requirements of FAS 123(R). The valuation model (which is very similar to that set forth under FAS 123) takes into account the following factors, at a minimum:

1. Exercise price of the option
2. Expected term of the option, taking into account several things including the contractual term of the option, vesting requirements, and postvesting employee termination behaviors
3. Current price of the underlying share

4. Expected volatility of the price of the underlying share
5. Expected dividends on the underlying share
6. Risk-free interest rate(s) for the expected term of the option

In practice, there are likely to be ranges of reasonable estimates for expected volatility, dividends, and option term. The closed-form models, of which Black-Scholes (now BSM) is the most widely regarded, are predicated on a set of deterministic assumptions, which remain invariate over the full term of the option. In the real world, of course, this condition is almost always not met. For this reason, current thinking is that a lattice model, of which the binomial model is an example, would be preferred. Lattice models explicitly identify nodes, such as the anniversaries of the grant date, at each of which new parameter values can be specified (e.g., expected dividends can be independently defined each period).

If a reporting entity changes from the BSM model to a binomial model, the change will be deemed a change in accounting estimate, not a change in accounting principle. A change from a binomial model back to a less desirable BSM model is to be discouraged, but apparently not prohibited if use of BSM or a similar closed-form model is supportable. The presumption is that moving from a binomial model to the BSM model would not be well received.

Other features that may affect the value of the option include changes in the issuer's credit risk, if the value of the awards contains cash settlement features (i.e., if they are liability instruments). Also, contingent features that could cause either a loss of equity shares earned or reduce realized gains from sale of equity instruments earned, such as a clawback feature (for example, where an employee who terminates the employment relationship and begins to work for a competitor is required to transfer to the issuing enterprise shares granted and earned under a share-based payment arrangement—see the illustrations in FAS 123[R]) would be factors affecting the valuation model.

**Market, performance, or service conditions** may affect vesting. An award becomes vested at the date the employee's right to receive or retain shares no longer has any of these conditions. Vesting may be conditional on satisfying two or more conditions. Regardless of the conditions that must be satisfied, the existence of a market condition requires recognition of compensation cost if service has been rendered, even if the market condition is never satisfied.

The definition of an employee used in FAS 123 (R) is that given by Internal Revenue Service Ruling 87-41. In addition, FAS 123(R) requires that nonemployee directors, acting in their role as members of the company's board of directors, be treated as employees if they were elected by the shareholders or appointed to the board and will be subject to election at the next shareholder election. Any awards granted to these individuals for their service as directors would be considered to be employee compensation.

The grant date is defined as the date when the employer and employee have a mutual understanding of the key terms and conditions of the share-based compensation arrangement and all necessary authorizations of those conditions have occurred. The service inception date is the first day of the requisite service period. Compensation cost is attributed over the service period.

If a given option plan involves the payment of compensation to the employees, such compensation cost should be recognized in the period(s) in which the services being compensated are performed. If the grant is unconditional, which means it effectively is in recognition of past services rendered by the employees and does not depend on the rendering of further service, then compensation is reported in full in the period of the grant. If the stock options are granted before the service inception date, compensation cost should be recognized over the periods in which the performance is scheduled to occur. Whether compensation cost is recognized ratably over the periods or not is a function of the vesting provisions of the plan. If the plan provides for cliff vesting, compensation will be accrued on an essentially straight-line basis, while if it provides for graded vesting, the pattern of recognition is subject to election and may be more complex. The accounting for graded vesting plans under FAS 123(R) represents a change from current practice.

Before presenting specific examples of accounting for stock options, simple examples of calculating the fair value of options using both the Black-Scholes-Merton and the binomial/lattice methods are provided. First, an example of the BSM, closed-form model is provided.

BSM actually computes the theoretical value of a so-called "European" call option, where exercise can occur only on the expiration date. "American" options, which include most employee stock options, can be exercised at any time until expiration. The value of an American-style option on dividend paying stocks is generally greater than a European-style option since preexercise the holder does not have a right to receive dividends that are paid on the stock. (For non-dividend-paying stocks, the value of American and European options will tend to converge.) BSM ignores dividends but this is readily dealt with, as shown below, by deducting from the computed option value the present value of expected dividend stream over the option holding period.

BSM also is predicated on constant volatility over the option term, which available evidence suggests may not be a wholly accurate description of stock price behavior. On the other hand, the reporting entity would find it very difficult, if not impossible, to compute differing volatilities for each node in the lattice model described later in this section, lacking a factual basis for presuming that volatility would increase or decrease in specific future periods.

The BSM model:

$$C = SN(d_1) - Ke^{(-rt)}N(d_2)$$

| | | |
|---|---|---|
| C | = | Theoretical call premium |
| S | = | Current stock price |
| t | = | time until option expiration |
| K | = | option striking price |
| r | = | risk-free interest rate |
| N | = | Cumulative standard normal distribution |
| e | = | exponential term (2.7183) |
| $d_1$ | = | $\dfrac{\ln(S/K) + (r + s^2/2)^t}{sv\,t}$ |
| $d_2$ | = | $d_1 - s$ |
| s | = | standard deviation of stock returns |
| ln | = | natural logarithm |

The BSM valuation is illustrated with the following assumed facts; note that dividends are ignored in the initial calculation but will be addressed once the theoretical value is computed. Also note that volatility is defined in terms of the variability of the entity's stock price, measured by the standard deviation of prices over, say, the past three years, which is used as a surrogate for expected volatility over the next twelve months.

### Example—Determining the fair value of options using the Black-Scholes model

Black-Scholes-Merton is a closed-form model, meaning that it solves for an option price from an equation. It computes a theoretical call price based on five parameters—the current stock price, the option exercise price, the expected volatility of the stock price, the time until option expiration, and the short-term risk-free interest rate. Of these, expected volatility is the most difficult to ascertain. Volatility is generally computed as the standard deviation of recent historical returns on the stock. In the following example, the stock is currently selling at $40 and the standard deviation of prices (daily closing prices can be used, among other possible choices) over the past several years was $6.50, thus yielding an estimated volatility of $6.50/$40 = 16.25%.

Assume the following facts:

$$S = \$40$$
$$t = 2 \text{ years}$$
$$K = \$45$$
$$r = 3\% \text{ annual rate}$$
$$s = \text{standard deviation of percentage returns} = 16.25\% \text{ (based on \$6.50 standard deviation of stock price compared to current \$40 price)}$$

From the foregoing data, all of which is known information (the volatility, s, is computed or assumed, as discussed above) the factors $d_1$ and $d_2$ can be computed. The cumulative standard normal variates (N) of these values must then be determined (using a table or formula), following which the BSM option value is calculated, *before the effect of dividends*. In this example, the computed amounts are

$$N(d_1) = 0.2758$$
$$N(d_2) = 0.2048$$

With these assumptions the value of the stock options is approximately $2.35. This is derived from the BSM as follows:

$$
\begin{aligned}
C &= SN(d_1) - Ke^{(-rt)}N(d_2) \\
&= 40(.2758) - 45(.942)(.2048) \\
&= 11.032 - 8.679 \\
&= 2.35
\end{aligned}
$$

The foregone two-year stream of dividends, which in this example are projected to be $0.50 annually, have a present value of $0.96. Therefore, the net value of this option is $1.39 ($2.35 – .96).

### Example—Determining the fair value of options using the binomial/lattice model

In contrast to the BSM, the binomial/lattice model is an open form, inductive model. It allows for multiple (theoretically, unlimited) branches of possible outcomes on a "tree" of possible price movements and induces the option's price. As compared to the BSM approach, this relaxes the constraint on exercise timing. It can be assumed that exercise occurs at any point in the option period, and past experience may guide the reporting entity to make certain such assumptions (e.g., that one-half the options will be exercised when the market price of the stock reaches 150% of the strike price, etc.). It also allows for varying dividends from period to period.

It is assumed that the common (Cox, Ross, and Rubinstein) binomial model will be used in practice. To keep this preliminary example relatively simple in order to focus on the concepts involved, a single-step binomial model is provided here for illustrative purposes. Assume an option is granted on a $20 stock that will expire in one year. The option exercise price equals the stock price of $20. Also, assume there is a 50% chance that the price will jump 20% over the year and a 50% chance the stock will drop 20%, and that no other outcomes are possible. The risk-free interest rate is 4%. With these assumptions there are three basic calculations.

1. Plot the two possible future stock prices.
2. Translate these stock prices into future options values.
3. Discount these future values into a single present value.

In this case, the option will only have value if the stock price increases, and otherwise the option would expire worthless and unexercised. In this simplistic example, there is only a 50% chance of the option having a value of $3.84, and therefore the option is worth $1.92 at grant date.

The foregoing was a simplistic single-period, two-outcome model. A more complicated and realistic binomial model extends this single-period model into a randomized walk of many steps or intervals. In theory, the time to expiration can be broken into a large number of ever-smaller time intervals, such as months, weeks, or days. The advantage is that the parameter values (volatility, etc) can then be varied with greater precision from one period to the next (assuming, of course, that there is a factual basis upon which to base these estimates). Calculating the binomial model then involves the same three calculation steps. First, the possible future stock prices are determined for each branch, using the volatility input and time to expiration (which grows shorter with each successive node in the model). This permits computation of terminal values for each branch of the tree. Second, future stock prices are translated into option values at each node of the tree. Third, these future option values are discounted and added to produce a single present value of the option, taking into account the probabilities of each series of price moves in the model.

### Example—Multiperiod option valuation using binomial model

Consider the following example of a 2-period binomial model. Again, certain simplifying assumptions will be made so that a manual calculation can be illustrated (in general, computer programs will be necessary to compute option values). Eager Corp. grants 10,000 options to its employees at a time when the market price of shares is $40. The options expire in 2 years; expected dividends on the stock will be $0.50 per year; and the risk-free rate is currently 3%, which is not expected to change over the 2-year horizon. The option exercise price is $43.

The entity's past experience suggests that, after 1 year (of the 2-year term) elapses, if the market price of the stock exceeds the option exercise price, one-half of the options will be exercised by the holders. The other holders will wait another year to decide. If at the end of the second year—without regard to what the stock value was at the end of the first year—the market value exceeds the exercise price, all the remaining options will be exercised. The workforce has been unusually stable and it is not anticipated that option holders will cease employment before the end the option period.

The stock price moves randomly from period to period. Based on recent experience, it is anticipated that in each period the stock may increase by $5, stay the same, or decrease by $5, with equal probability, versus the price at the period year-end. Thus, since the price is $40 at grant date, 1 year hence it might be either $45, $40, or $35. The price at the end of the second year will follow the same pattern, based on the price when the first year ends.

Logically, holders will rather exercise their options than see them expire, as long as there is gain to be realized. Since dividends are not paid on options, holders have a motive to exercise earlier than the expiration date, which explains why historically one-half the options are exercised after one year elapses, as long as the market price exceeds the exercise price at that date, even though the exercising holders risk future market declines.

The binomial model formulation requires that each sequence of events and actions be explicated. This gives rise to the commonly seen decision tree representation. In this simple example, following the grant of the options 1 of 3 possible events occur; either the stock price rises $5 over the next year, or it remains constant, or it falls by $5. Since these outcomes have equal *a priori* probabilities, p=1/3 is assigned to each outcome of this first year event. If the price does rise, one half the option holders will exercise at the end of the first year, to reap the economic gain and capture the second year's dividend. The other holders will forego this immediate gain and wait to see what the stock price does in the second year before making an exercise decision.

If the stock price in the first year either remains flat or falls by $5, no option holders are expected to exercise. However, there remains the opportunity to exercise after the second year elapses, if the stock price recovers. Of course, holding the options for the second year means that no dividends will be received.

The cost of the options granted by Eager Corp., measured by fair value using the binomial model approach, is computed by the sum of the probability-weighted outcomes, discounted to present value using the risk-free rate. In this example, the rate is expected to remain at 3% per year throughout the option period, but it could be independently specified for each period—another advantage the binomial model has over the more rigid BSM. The sum of these present value computations measures the cost of compensation incorporated in the option grant, regardless of what pattern of exercise ultimately is revealed, since at the grant date, using the available information about stock price volatility, expected dividends, exercise behavior and the risk-free rate, this best measures the value of what was promised to the employees.

The following graphic offers a visual representation of the model, although in practice it is not necessary to prepare such a document. The actual calculations can be made by computer program, but to illustrate the application of the binomial model, the computation will be presented explicitly here. There are four possible scenarios under which, in this example, holders will exercise the options, and thus the options will have value. All other scenarios (combinations of stock price movements over the 2-year horizon) will cause the holders to allow the options to expire unexercised.

First, if the stock price goes to $45 in the first year, one-half the holders will exercise at that point, paying the exercise price of $43 per share. This results in a gain of $2 ($45 − $43) per share. However, having waited until the first year-end, they lost the opportunity to receive the $0.50 per share dividend, so the net economic gain is only $1.50 ($2.00 − $0.50) per share. As this occurs after 1 year, the present value is only $1.50 × $1.03^{-1}$ = $1.46 per share. When this is weighted by the probability of this outcome obtaining (given that the stock price rise to $45 in the first year has only a 1/3 probability of happening, and given further that only one-half the option holders would elect to exercise under such conditions), the actual expected value of this outcome is [(1/3)(1/2)($1.46)] = $0.24. More formally,

$$[(1/3)(1/2)(\$2.00 - \$0.50)] \times 1.03^{-1} = \$0.2427$$

The second potentially favorable outcome to holders would be if the stock price rises to $45 the first year and then either rises another $5 the second year or holds steady at $45 during the second year. In either event, the option holders who did not exercise after the first year's stock price rise will all exercise at the end of the second year, before the options expire. If the price goes to $50 the second year, the holders will reap a gross gain of $7 ($50 − $43) per share; if it remains constant at $45, the gross gain is only $2 per share. In either case, dividends in both years 1 and 2 will have been foregone. To calculate the compensation cost associated with these branches of the model, the first-year dividend lost must be discounted for 1 year, and the gross gain and second-year dividend must be discounted for 2 years. Also, the probabilities of the entire sequence of events must be used, taking into account the likelihood of the first year's stock price rise, the proclivity of holders to wait for a second year to elapse, and the likelihood of a second-year price rise or price stability. These computations are shown below.

For the outcome if the stock price rises again

$$[(1/3)(1/2)(1/3)]\{[(\$7.00) \times 1.03^{-2}] - [(\$0.50) \times 1.03^{-1}] - [\$0.50 \times 1.03^{-2}]\} = [0.05544]\{\$6.59 - \$0.48 - \$0.47\} = \$0.31276$$

For the outcome if the stock price remains stable

$[(1/3)(1/2)(1/3)]\{[(\$2.00) \times 1.03^{-2}] - [(\$0.50) \times 1.03^{-1}] - [(\$0.50) \times 1.03^{-2}]\} = [0.05544]\{\$1.88 - \$0.48 - \$0.47\} = \$0.05147$

The final, favorable outcome for holders would occur if the stock price holds constant at \$40 the first year but rises to \$45 the second year, making exercise the right decision. Note that none of the holders would exercise after the first year given that the price, \$40, was below exercise price. The calculation for this sequence of events is as follows:

$[(1/3)(1/3)]\{[(\$2.00) \times 1.03^{-2}] - [(\$0.50) \times 1.03^{-1}] - [(\$0.50) \times 1.03^{-2}]\} = [0.1111]\{\$1.88 - \$0.48 - \$0.47\} = \$0.10295$

Summing these values yields \$0.709879 (\$0.2427 + \$0.31276 + \$0.05147 + \$0.10295), which is the expected value per option granted. When this per-unit value is then multiplied by the number of options granted, 10,000, the total compensation cost to be recognized, \$7,098.79, is derived. This would be attributed over the required service period, which is illustrated later in this section. (In the facts of this example, no vesting requirements were specified; in such cases, the employees would not have to provide future service in order to earn the right to the options, and the entire cost would be recognized upon grant.)

A big advantage of the binomial model is that it can value an option that is exercisable before the end of its term (an American-style option). This is the style that employee share-based compensation arrangements normally take. FASB prefers the binomial model because it can incorporate the unique features of employee stock options. Two key features that FASB recommends that companies incorporate into the binomial model are vesting restrictions and early exercise. Doing so, however, requires that the reporting entity had previous experience with employee behaviors (e.g., gained with past employee option programs) that would provide it with a basis for making estimates of future behavior. In some instances, there will be no obvious bases upon which such assumptions can be developed.

The binomial model permits the specification of more assumptions than does the BSM, which has generated the perception that the binomial will more readily be manipulated so as to result in lower option values, and hence lower compensation costs, than the BSM. But, this is not necessarily the case: switching from BSM to the binomial model can increase, maintain, or decrease the option's value. Having the ability to specify additional parameters, however, does probably give management greater flexibility and, accordingly, will present additional challenges for the auditors who must attest to the financial statement effects of management's specification of these variables.

To calculate option values using either the BSM or binomial models without the aid of computer software would be very difficult, but hardly impossible. Fortunately, reasonably priced software is now widely available to perform these calculations. What managers must do is determine the assumptions that should be used to create an unbiased, representative value of the options. We now turn to specific examples of accounting for share-based compensation as required under this FAS 123(R).

*NOTE: All examples ignore deferred tax effects for simplicity.*

### Example—Accounting for stock options for a publicly held entity

Options are granted to corporate officers to purchase 10,000 shares of $1 par stock at a price of $50 per share, which is equal to the current market price. The options may not be exercised until 3 years from the grant date(that is, they vest in three years). FAS 123(R) provides that public companies must use the fair value method to measure compensation cost associated with share-based equity programs. This means that it will be necessary to determine the expected volatility of the share price over the service period. Assume that either a lattice model or BSM has been used and that the fair value per option has been determined to be $7. Past experience suggests that forfeitures will be 4% per year, so that compensation cost under FAS 123(R) will be based on the net number of shares expected to vest, given as (.96 × .96 × .96 =).885. Total share-based compensation will be ($7 × .885 × 10,000 =) $61,932. The annual entries would be

| | | |
|---|---|---|
| Compensation cost | 20,644 | |
|     Additional paid-in capital | | 20,644 |

If all the options are subsequently exercised, the derived proceeds of the stock issuance will be $566,000. The entry would be

| | | |
|---|---|---|
| Cash | 500,000 (option price) | |
| Additional paid-in capital | 61,932 | |
|     Common stock | | 10,000  (par) |
|     Additional paid-in capital | | 551,932  (excess) |

**Example—Accounting for stock options for a nonpublic entity that is not an SEC registrant and elects the calculated value method**

Options are granted to corporate officers to purchase 10,000 shares of $1 par stock at a price of $50 per share, which is the current market price. The options may not be exercised until 3 years from the grant date (that is, they vest in three years). FAS 123(R) provides that nonpublic companies may use a surrogate measure of fair value, called calculated value, when it is not possible to determine the expected volatility of the share price over the service period. Essentially, this requires that a relevant industry sector-specific index be identified for use in place of the volatility factor in the normal BSM or lattice models.

In this case, the reporting entity identifies such an index and proceeds to compute a value of $6.60 per option. The total compensation cost thereby calculated, $66,000, is accrued over the three year period ratably. The annual entries would be

| | | |
|---|---|---|
| Compensation cost | 22,000 | |
|     Additional paid-in capital | | 22,000 |

If all the options are subsequently exercised, the derived proceeds of the stock issuance will be $566,000. The entry would be

| | | |
|---|---|---|
| Cash | 500,000 (option price) | |
| Additional paid-in capital | 66,000 | |
|     Common stock | | 10,000 (par) |
|     Additional paid-in capital | | 556,000 (excess) |

**Example—Accounting for stock options for a nonpublic entity that is not an SEC registrant and elects the intrinsic value method**

As discussed above, nonpublic companies are permitted to elect the intrinsic value method of accounting for the cost of share-based compensation plans. This methodology differs in important regards from the method used under now-defunct APB 25. Using this method, the intrinsic value must be measured at each reporting date, and used to accrue compensation cost for the period.

Assume again that options are granted to corporate officers to purchase 10,000 shares of $1 par stock at a price of $50 per share, which is the current market price. The options may not be exercised until 3 years from the grant date. These options have no intrinsic value ($50 – $50 = 0) at the grant date. The intrinsic value method and fair value method require the same measurement date (grant date) for shares and similar instruments whose fair value does not differ from their intrinsic value (and instruments with no time value). This example assumes there is no forfeiture before vesting occurs. Because of the company's decision to use the intrinsic value method, its share options are recognized at intrinsic value at each reporting date through the date of settlement, and the periodic adjustment in intrinsic value, prorated over the service period, is included in compensation cost for that period. Consequently, the compensation cost recognized each year of the 3-year requisite service period will vary based on changes in the share option's intrinsic value. For example, assume that at the end of year 1 stock is valued at $55 per share, resulting in a ($55 – $50) $5 intrinsic value per share—thus, a total value of $50,000 for the award. In year 1 the compensation cost would be 1/3 of $50,000. This entry would be

| | | |
|---|---|---|
| Compensation cost | 16,667 | |
|     Additional paid-in capital | | 16,667 |

Assume now that at the end of year 2 the stock is valued at $53 per share, and thus the intrinsic value is ($53 – $50 =) $3 per share option, for an intrinsic value of the award of $30,000 at that date. The intrinsic value of the award has declined by ($50,000 – $30,000 =) $20,000. Because services for 2 of the 3 years of service have now been rendered, the company must recognize *cumulative* compensation cost for two-thirds of the intrinsic value of the award, or ($30,000 × 2/3 =) $20,000. Because the company already recognized $16,667 in the first year, only $3,333 in further compensation cost is to be recognized in year 2.

| | | |
|---|---|---|
| Compensation cost | 3,333 | |
|     Additional paid-in capital | | 3,333 |

Note that, depending on the change in intrinsic value from the prior reporting date, the current period could be credited with *negative* compensation expense. To illustrate, assume instead that at the end of year 2 the stock is valued at $52 per share, for an intrinsic value of $20,000. Since 2 of the 3 year service period has elapsed, the cumulative compensation cost to be recognized is ($20,000 × 2/3 =) $13,333. Because the company already recognized $16,667 in the first year, *negative* $3,333 compensation cost is to be recognized in year 2.

| | | |
|---|---|---|
| Additional paid-in capital | 3,333 | |
| Compensation cost | | 3,333 |

### Example of fair value accounting for stock options with cliff vesting—measurement and grant date the same

Options are granted to corporate officers to purchase 10,000 shares of $1 par stock at a price of $50 per share, which is also the market price on the grant date. The options may not be exercised until 3 years from the grant date, and only if the employees remain employed through that date. The company has no reason to expect that any of the options will be forfeited by the employees to whom they are granted (i.e., after the completion of the service period). The company uses the following assumptions to apply the binomial model:

| | |
|---|---|
| Share options granted | 10,000 |
| Employees granted options | 100 |
| Expected forfeitures per year | 3.0% |
| Share price at the grant date | $50 |
| Exercise price | $50 |
| Par value per share | $1 |
| Number of years to vest | 3 years |
| Contractual term (CT) of options | 10 years |
| Risk-free interest rate over CT | 2 to 5% |
| Expected volatility over CT | 40 to 700% |
| Expected dividend yield | 1.0% |
| Suboptimal exercise factor | 2 |

Given these assumptions needed to construct a binomial model to value the options, a fair value estimate of approximately $6 per option is determined (details not presented). It is estimated that 3% of employees will turn over each year during the service period. The number of share options expected to vest is estimated at the grant date of (10,000 × .97 × .97 × .97 =) $9,127. The estimated fair value of the award on the grant date would be (9,127 × $6 =) $54,762. The entry to record the compensation cost [($54,762 ÷ 3) = $18,254] in each of the years 1, 2, and 3 is

| | | |
|---|---|---|
| Compensation cost | 18,254 | |
| Additional paid-in capital | | 18,254 |

If in year 1, the actual forfeiture rate is 6% instead of the 3% expected rate, and management determines that the forfeiture rate should change to 6%, then in year 2 an adjustment would be needed. The revised estimate of the number of options expected to vest is (10,000 × .94 × .94 × .94 =) 8,306. The revised cumulative compensation cost would be (8,306 × $6 =) $49,836. The cumulative adjustment to reflect adjustment of the forfeiture rate is the difference between two-thirds of the revised cost of the award and the cost already recognized in year 1. The related entries and computations are

| | |
|---|---|
| Revised total compensation cost | $49,836 |
| Revised cumulative cost as of the end of year 1 | $16,112 |
| Cost already recognized in year 1 | $18,254 |
| Adjustment to cost at the end of year 1 | $(2,142) |

The related journal entries are

| | | |
|---|---|---|
| Compensation cost | 2,142 | |
| Additional paid-in capital | | 2,142 |

Entries in years 2 and 3

| | | |
|---|---|---|
| Compensation cost | 16,112 | |
|     Additional paid-in capital | | 16,112 |

At the end of the third year, the company would examine actual forfeitures and make any necessary adjustments to reflect compensation cost for the number of shares actually vested. Assuming vesting equals expected, the journal entry at exercise of the options would be

| | | |
|---|---|---|
| Cash | 500,000 (option price) | |
| Additional paid-in capital | 49,836 | |
|     Common stock | | 10,000 (par) |
|     Additional paid-in capital | | 539,836 (excess) |

The difference between the market price of the shares and the exercise price at the date of exercise is deductible for tax purposes because the share options do not qualify as incentive stock options. The realized tax benefits result in a credit to additional paid-in capital and a reduction in the deferred tax asset.

The statement of cash flows, as amended by FAS 123(R), requires that the cash flow benefit that results from the tax benefit be classified as a cash inflow from financing activities and a cash outflow from operating activities.

### Example of accounting for stock options with graded vesting—measurement and grant date the same

In a shift from the position espoused in the exposure draft, FAS 123(R) requires each reporting entity to make a policy decision about whether to recognize compensation cost for an award with only service conditions that has a graded vesting schedule either (1) on a straight-line basis over the requisite service period for each separately vesting portion of the award as if the award was, in-substance, multiple awards, or (2) on a straight-line basis over the requisite service period for the entire award (that is, over the requisite service period of the last separately vesting portion of the award). However, FAS 123(R) requires that the amount of compensation cost recognized at any date must at least equal the portion of the grant-date value of the award that is vested at that date.

For this example, assume the basic facts from the prior example, but now the 10,000 options vest according to a graded schedule of 25% for the first and second years of service and 50% for the third year. Using the 3% annual employee turnover forfeiture rate, 300 options are expected to never vest, leaving 9,700 options expected to vest at 25% of the award—or 2,425 options vested. In the second year, another 3% are expected to be forfeited, leaving 9,409 to vest at 25% of the award—or 2,352 options vested. In the final year another 3% are forfeited and vesting occurs at 50% of the remaining—or 4,563 vested options. (Data upon which value per option amounts are derived are not presented in this example.)

| Year | Vested option | Value per option | Compensation cost |
|---|---|---|---|
| 1 | 2,425 | $5.00 | $12,125 |
| 2 | 2,352 | $5.50 | 12,936 |
| 3 | 4,563 | $6.00 | 27,378 |
| | 9,340 | | $52,439 |

The value of the option is determined separately for different vesting periods after which exercise might occur. Thus, the compensation cost associated with the options is less in the earlier years, as reflected in the table above. Compensation cost is recognized over the periods of requisite service during which each group of share options is earned. In year 1, therefore, compensation cost is [$12,125 + ($12,936 ÷ 2) + ($27,378 ÷ 3) = ] $27,719. The journal entry for year 1 would be

| | | |
|---|---|---|
| Compensation cost | 27,719 | |
|     Additional paid-in capital | | 27,719 |

## Accounting for Stock Appreciation Rights and Tandem Plans

**Background.** The accounting for variable stock plans is addressed by FAS 123(R). Under this standard, share-based compensation arrangements which provide for cash payments, or which give to grantees the choice of receiving stock or cash in settlement, are accounted for as liabilities, not equity, as compensation is accrued over the requisite service period. Publicly held entities are required to measure liabilities incurred to employees in share-based payment transactions at fair value. Nonpublic entities, on the other hand, may elect to measure their liabilities to employees incurred in share-based payment transactions at their intrinsic value.

Whether measured at fair value (using an option-pricing model such as BSM or binomial) or at intrinsic value (measured simply as the excess of market or other defined value over reference value as of the balance sheet date), these amounts are updated as of each financial reporting date. Thus, when share-based compensation plans give rise to liabilities, these are continually updated as to value, whereas under the fair value measurement approach to equity instruments arising from such compensation plans, value is assessed as of the grant date in most instances, never later to be revised.

Determining whether a share-based payment should be categorized as a liability requires close attention to the guidance of FAS 123(R), which invokes the requirements of SFAS 150. It states that, for example, a puttable share (giving the grantee the right to demand the issuer to redeem it) awarded to an employee as compensation is to be classified as a liability if either (1) the repurchase feature permits the employee to avoid bearing the risks and rewards normally associated with equity share ownership for a reasonable period of time from the date the requisite service is rendered and the share is issued, or (2) it is probable that the employer would prevent the employee from bearing those risks and rewards for a reasonable period of time from the date the share is issued. For this purpose, a period of six months or more is defined as a reasonable period of time.

Note that a share that is mandatorily or optionally redeemable upon the occurrence of a defined contingency, such as an initial public offering by the grantor entity, would not make this share-based payment a liability, unless the contingency were deemed probable of occurrence within a reasonable period of time. For example, if the entity had begun the regulatory approval and registration process, this might trigger liability classification.

FAS 123(R) had stipulated that options or similar instruments on shares were to be categorized as liabilities if the underlying shares were classified as liabilities (which was logical) or if the reporting entity was subject to a requirement to transfer cash or other assets under any circumstances (an extreme threshold condition, some believed) in order to settle the option. FSP 123(R)-4 moderates this position by holding that a cash settlement feature that can be exercised only upon the occurrence of a contingent event that is outside the employee's control does not meet the condition set forth by FAS 123(R).

Furthermore, an option or similar instrument that is first classified as equity, but subsequently becomes a liability because the contingent cash settlement event becomes probable of occurring, is to be accounted for similar to a modification from an equity to liability award. Accordingly, on the date the contingent event becomes *probable* of occurring (thus triggering reclassification of the award as a liability) the entity recognizes a share-based liability equal to the portion of the award attributed to past service (reflecting any provision for acceleration of vesting) multiplied by the award's fair value on that date. To the extent the liability equals or is less than the amount previously recognized in equity, that is the amount transferred from equity to the liability. To the extent that the liability exceeds the amount previously recognized in equity, the excess is recognized as additional compensation cost in that period. The total recognized compensation cost for an award with a contingent cash settlement feature must at least equal the fair value of the award at the grant date.

A puttable share that does not meet either of the foregoing conditions is to be classified as equity. Options or similar instruments on shares is to be classified as liabilities if (1) the underlying shares are classified as liabilities, or (2) the reporting entity can be required under any circumstances to settle the option or similar instrument by transferring cash or other assets. If the entity grants an option to an employee that, upon exercise, would be settled by issuing a mandatorily redeemable share, the option must be classified as a liability.

According to FAS 123 (R), a freestanding financial instrument ceases to be subject to this standard, and becomes subject to the recognition and measurement requirements of FAS 150 or other applicable GAAP when the rights conveyed by the instrument to the holder are no longer dependent on the holder being an employee of the entity. Thus, once the requisite service has been provided and the grantee has, say, elected to receive stock or another instrument, guidance on the appropriate accounting would be given by FAS 150. For example, a mandatorily redeemable share becomes subject to FAS 150 or other applicable GAAP when an employee (1) has rendered the requisite service in exchange for the instrument and (2) could terminate the employment relationship and receive that share. Similarly, a share option or similar instrument that is not transferable and whose contractual term is shortened upon employment termination continues to be subject to FAS 123(R) until the rights conveyed by the instrument to the holder are no longer dependent on the holder being an employee of the entity (generally, when the instrument is exercised).

An award may be indexed to a factor beyond the entity's share price. FAS 123(R) holds that, if that additional factor is not a market, performance, or service condition, the award is to be classified as a liability. In such a case, the additional factor is to be reflected in estimating the fair value of the award. An example of such a circumstance would be an award of options whose exercise price is indexed to the market price of the commodity (e.g., wheat or gold). Another example: a share award that will vest based on the appreciation in the price of that commodity; such an award is indexed to both the value of that commodity and the issuing entity's shares. If an award is so indexed, the relevant factors (expected commodity price change) should be included in the fair value estimate of the award. FAS 123(R) states that the award would be classified as a liability even if the entity granting the share-based payment instrument is a producer of the commodity whose price changes are part or all of the conditions that affect an award's vesting conditions or fair value.

**Stock appreciation rights and similar instruments.** SARs are a popular means of providing share-based compensation awards to employees. Essentially, the bonus arrangement is to pay employees the amount by which the share price at a defined date (say, three years hence) exceeds what it was at the measurement date. Depending on the plan, the award may be payable in the entity's shares, in cash, or in either at the option of the grantee. If the optionee has the right to demand cash or the SAR is payable in cash only, the grantor entity recognizes a liability for the accrued compensation.

If the entity is publicly held, measurement at fair value is required, with revaluation at each reporting date through final settlement. For nonpublicly held entities, an election must be made to use fair value or intrinsic value—but again, in either case, remeasurement at each reporting date until final settlement is required.

### Example of accounting for SAR—Share-based liabilities

The company grants SAR with the same terms and conditions used in the examples above. Each SAR entitles the holder to receive an amount in cash equal to the increase in value of one share of company stock over $50. Using the same assumptions and option-pricing model the fair value of the share options is computed to be $6 per SAR (details not presented). The awards cliff-vest at the end of 3 years. The forfeitures are expected to be 3% a year: thus, SAR expected to vest are (10,000 × .97 × .97 × .97 =) 9,127, and the fair value of the award at the beginning of year 1 is (9,127 × $6 =) $54,762. It is assumed that expected and actual forfeitures are the same. The share-based compensation liability at the end of year 1 is ($54,762 ÷ 3 =) $18,254. The journal entry for year 1 is

```
Compensation cost                                   18,254
    Share-based compensation SAR liability                      18,254
```

Under FAS 123(R), compensation arising in connection with share-based liabilities must be valued at fair value at each reporting date. At the end of year 2, the estimated fair value is assumed to be $10 per SAR. Therefore, the award's fair value is (9,270 × $10 =) $91,270, and the corresponding liability at that date is ($91,270 × 2/3 =) $60,847 because service has now been provided for 2 of the 3 years required. Compensation cost recognized for the award in year 2 is ($60,847 – $18,254 =) $42,593. The journal entry for year 2 is

```
Compensation cost                                   42,593
    Share-based compensation SAR liability                      42,593
```

At the end of year 3 the estimated fair value is assumed to be $9 per SAR. Therefore, the award's fair value is (9,270 × $9 =) $83,430 and the corresponding liability at that date is the same because the award is fully vested. Compensation cost for year 3 is ($83,430 – $42,593 – $18,254 =) $22,583. The journal entry for year 3 is

```
Compensation cost                                   22,583
    Share-based compensation SAR liability                      22,583
```

**Stock SARs.** If the SAR were to be redeemed (only) in common stock of the entity, "Stock rights outstanding" (a paid-in capital account) would replace the liability account in the above entries. Fair value would be assessed at the grant date (measurement date), and then not altered over the time to final settlement, consistent with how other equity compensation awards are measured under FAS 123(R).

**Tandem plans.** Often stock option plans and SAR are joined in tandem plans, under the terms of which the exercise of one automatically cancels the other. In the absence of evidence to the contrary, however, the presumption is that the SAR, not the options, will be exercised. If the SAR portion of the tandem plan is such that classification as a liability is required, as described above, then remeasurement through the settlement date is required.

### Modifications of Awards of Equity Instruments

In some instances awards previously issued but not yet settled are later modified in ways that may or may not change the classification (e.g., liability to equity). FAS 123(R) requires that modification of the terms or conditions of an equity award is to be treated as an exchange of the original award for a new award. In substance, the event is accounted for as if the entity repurchases the original instrument by issuing a new instrument of equal or greater value, incurring additional compensation cost for any incremental value.

Incremental compensation cost in such circumstances is to be measured as the excess, if any, of the fair value of the modified award—determined in accordance with the provisions of FAS 123(R)—over the fair value of the original award immediately before its terms are modified. These measures are to be based on the share price and other pertinent factors at the modification date. Any effect of the modification on the number of instruments expected to vest is also to be reflected in determining incremental compensation cost. The estimate at the modification date of the portion of the award expected to vest may also be subsequently adjusted, if necessary, as estimates or experience may dictate prior to final settlement.

The total recognized compensation cost for an equity award will at least equal the fair value of the award at the grant date, except for those instances when, at the date of the modification, the performance or service conditions of the original award are not expected to be satisfied. Accordingly, the total compensation cost measured at the date of a modification will be (1) the portion of the grant-date fair value of the original award for which the requisite service is expected to be rendered (or has already been rendered) at that date, plus (2) the incremental cost resulting from the modification.

The change in compensation cost for an equity award measured at intrinsic value (if elected for nonpublicly held companies) is to be measured by comparing the intrinsic value of the modified award, if any, with the intrinsic value of the original award, if any, immediately before the modification.

If a modification results in what had been a liability award becoming an equity award, the amount of the fair value (or implicit value, if such were elected as a measurement strategy by a nonpublic company), the amount becomes "fixed" as of the modification date, and this will differ from the amount that would have been recognized had the award been classified as equity at inception. On the other hand, if an award was originally equity and after modification becomes a liability, to the extent that the liability equals or is less than the amount recognized in equity for the original award, the offsetting debit is a charge to equity. To the extent that the liability exceeds the amount recognized in equity for the original award, the excess is recognized as compensation cost.

### Example of a liability to equity modification

Assume that a cash payment SAR plan is created, with features similar to earlier examples (10,000 SARs granted, with three-year term, 3% forfeiture per year expectation). The share-based compensation liability is (9,127 × $10 ÷ 3 =) $30,423, based on reporting date fair value measurement. On January 1 of year 2, the company modifies the SAR by replacing the cash-settlement feature with a net-share settlement feature, which converts the award from a liability award to an equity award, because there is no longer an obligation to settle for cash, or an obligation classified as a liability per FAS 150. For the equity award, fair value is to be measured at grant date only. Per FAS 123(R), when no other terms are altered by the modification, the fair value at the modification date is used to measure the amount of the total compensation to be awarded in equity instruments.

The journal entry to reclassify the liability to equity would be

| | | |
|---|---|---|
| Share based compensation SAR liability | 30,423 | |
|    Additional paid-in capital—SAR | | 30,423 |

Since no further remeasurement would be permitted, additional compensation cost of $30,423 per year will be recorded at the end of years 2 and 3, with credits to the additional paid-in capital account. In this example, total compensation cost was greater because the effective measurement date was the end of year 1, but it could also have happened that compensation cost was reduced for the same reason.

### Example of an equity to liability modification

Assume that a SAR plan, payable in shares, is created, with features similar to earlier examples (10,000 SARs granted, with three-year term, 3% forfeiture per year expectation). Using a valuation model, the amount of compensation is determined to be $40,000 in total, computed at grant date. At the end of the first year, compensation expense and additional paid-in capital of $13,333 is recorded, based on completion of 1 of the 3 years required service. At that date the fair value of the SARs amount to $45,000. If the plan is amended at the start of year 2 to offer grantees the right to a cash payout, the equity must be reclassified to liability and the value must be remeasured at each reporting date. At the time of modification, since the fair value exceeds what had been accrued, additional compensation cost must be recognized. The entry would be

| | | |
|---|---|---|
| Additional paid-in capital—SAR | 13,333 | |
| Compensation cost | 1,667 | |
|    Share-based compensation—SAR liability | | 15,000 |

On the other hand, if the fair value of the liability for the SAR at the modification date had been only $30,000, the difference between the amount accrued in year 1 and the modified value would have been left in the additional paid-in capital account. The entry follows:

| | | |
|---|---|---|
| Additional paid-in capital—SAR | 10,000 | |
|     Share-based compensation—SAR liability | | 10,000 |

A share-based payment award may also be modified as a result of an acquisition. FAS 141(R) describes the accounting for several instances where an acquirer exchanges its share-based payment awards for rewards held by the employees of an acquiree. If the acquiring entity replaces an acquiree's share-based awards when it is not obligated to do so, then all of the fair-value replacement cost is to be recognized as postcombination compensation expense. If the acquirer's replacement award requires some additional employee service, a portion of the replacement award's fair-value cost should be attributed to postcombination compensation expense. FAS 141(R) is covered in detail in Chapter 13.

### Accounting for Income Tax Effects of Share-Based Compensation

Under US income tax laws, the amount that is deductible in connection with a share-based compensation arrangement is limited to intrinsic value. This is generally defined by the amount by which the fair (market) value of the compensation exceeds the amount paid, if any, by the recipient. For example, if an option grant is made when the underlying stock is trading at $34, and the option is exercisable at that price, and it is later exercised when the stock is trading at $55, the deductible amount will be $21 per share, based on the *intrinsic value* of the option, which becomes observable only upon actual exercise. However, under FAS 123(R), compensation expense will have been recognized for the fair value of the option when granted, computed using either the BSM or lattice model as illustrated earlier in this section. Depending on other facts, that option value may have been $5, $10, or some other amount per share; it would not, however, be the same as the intrinsic amount other than by sheer coincidence.

Additionally, the timing of the compensation expense recognition will differ between tax and financial reporting. For financial reporting, expense is recognized over the expected service period, as explained above. For tax, the expense is deductible at the actual exercise date. Options not exercised (i.e., forfeited) thus never give rise to taxable deductions, whereas under GAAP the compensation cost would have been expensed.

It is thus inevitable that both the timing and the amounts of compensation expense related to share-based compensation will differ. To the extent that these are timing differences, interperiod tax allocation (deferred tax accounting) will be appropriate. The cumulative amount of compensation cost that will result in a tax deduction is to be considered a deductible temporary difference. This applies both for instruments classified as equity and for those categorized as liabilities. Any compensation cost recognized in the financial statements for instruments that will not result in a tax deduction should not be considered to result in a deductible temporary difference under FAS 109.

In general, the fair value of stock-based compensation, which is computed at grant date and recognized over the vesting period as compensation cost in the financial statements, will not be tax deductible currently, giving rise to deferred tax benefits measured with reference to the book compensation expense recognized. Ultimately, when the employee's options vest and are exercised, the company is able to deduct the intrinsic value, measured by the spread between fair value on exercise date and exercise price. To the extent this exceeds the fair value of the stock-based compensation recognized as GAAP-basis expense, the tax effect of that excess tax deduction is treated as a contribution to paid-in capital. If (less likely, but quite possible) the tax deduction is lower than the compensation already recognized for financial reporting purposes, this shortfall in tax benefits is additional compensation cost—in effect, the employer entity incurred higher compensation cost in connection with the share option program since it received less than the anticipated tax benefits related thereto.

If the exercise results in a tax deduction prior to the actual realization of the related tax benefit—because the entity, for example, has a net operating loss carryforward—then the tax benefit and the credit to additional paid-in capital for the excess deduction would not be recognized until that deduction reduces taxes payable.

However, to the extent that the excess stems from a reason *other* than changes in fair value of the entity's shares between the measurement date for accounting purposes (grant date, generally) and the later measurement date for income tax purposes (exercise date), that portion of the tax effect is to be reported in income (i.e., in the tax provision). For example, a change in the tax rate could result in such a difference.

Differences between the deductible temporary difference that arises and the tax deduction that would have resulted based on the current fair value of the entity's shares should not be considered either in measuring the gross deferred tax asset or in determining the need for a valuation allowance created by the application of FAS 123(R).

If there should be an excess of cumulative compensation cost recognized for financial reporting purposes over the tax deductible amount (e.g., due to options lapsing unexercised), the write-off of the deferred tax asset (net of valuation allowance, if any) is first to be offset against any remaining additional paid-in capital from previous awards accounted for under the fair value method (i.e., under either FAS 123 or FAS 123[R]); any remaining excess should be recognized in income (the tax provision). The additional paid-in capital available to absorb tax effects is referred to as the *APIC pool*.

If the reporting entity continued to use the APB 25 intrinsic value method, as had been permitted by original FAS 123, FAS 123(R) required that the entity is to calculate the amount available for offset against any remaining additional paid-in capital as the net amount of excess tax benefits that would have qualified as such had it instead adopted FAS 123 for recognition purposes as of that standard's original effective date and transition method. In making that determination, no distinction is to be made between excess tax benefits attributable to different types of equity awards (e.g., restricted shares vs. share options). The reporting entity is to exclude from that amount both excess tax benefits from share-based payment arrangements that are outside the scope of FAS 123(R) (e.g., ESOPs), and excess tax benefits that have not been realized pursuant to FAS 109.

FAS 123(R) stipulated that for purposes of calculating the "APIC pool" subsequent to adoption of that standard, the reporting entity was to include the net excess tax benefits that would have qualified as such had the entity adopted predecessor standard FAS 123 for recognition purposes (not merely for disclosure in the footnotes). FASB had assumed that this would have been readily determined from mandatory disclosure information, but apparently failed to fully appreciate the practical difficulties that would impact nonpublicly held companies which continued to apply intrinsic value accounting.

In response to these difficulties, the FASB staff has issued FSP 123(R)-3, *Transition Election Related to Accounting for the Tax Effects of Share-Based Payment Awards,* which offers an elective alternative to the accounting requirement originally imposed. Under this newly permitted alternative, the reporting entity, upon transitioning to FAS 123(R), is allowed to compute the beginning balance of the *APIC pool* as the sum of all net increases of additional paid-in capital recognized in an entity's annual financial statements related to tax benefits from stock-based employee compensation during fiscal periods subsequent to the adoption of FAS 123 but prior to the adoption of FAS 123(R), less the cumulative incremental pretax employee compensation costs that would have been recognized if FAS 123 had been used to account for stock-based employee compensation costs, multiplied by the entity's blended statutory tax rate upon adoption of FAS 123(R), inclusive of federal, state, local, and foreign taxes. Cumulative incremental compensation costs are the total stock-based employee compensation costs included in pro forma net income as if the fair-value-based method had been applied to all awards pursuant to the provisions of FAS 123, less the stock-based compensation costs included in the entity's determination of net income as reported.

FSP FAS 123(R)-3 states that in calculating cumulative incremental compensation costs, reporting entities must exclude compensation costs associated with an award that ordinarily does not result in tax deductions under existing tax law, unless the award has resulted in a tax deduction prior to the adoption of FAS 123(R) or the entity is unable to obtain the information necessary to determine the amount of such cost. In calculating cumulative incremental compensation costs, compensation costs associated with awards that are partially vested upon the adoption of FAS 123(R) are to be excluded.

Consistent with the treatment of excess tax deductions for share-based compensation as being essentially similar to capital contributions, FAS 123(R) amends FAS 95 to require that the realized tax benefit applicable to the excess of the deductible amount over the compensation cost recognized under GAAP be reported in the cash flow statement as both a cash inflow from financing activities and a cash outflow from operating activities. This is required whether the cash flow statement is being presented under the direct method or the indirect method.

It is possible that an entity has issued dividends to employees holding nonvested shares, nonvested share units, or outstanding options. If so, EITF 06-11 states that it should recognize the income tax benefit as an increase to additional paid-in-capital, but only if the deduction reduces income taxes payable.

## Other FAS 123(R) Matters

The most common share-based compensation arrangements have been presented. Other more complicated awards have been and will continue to be developed. Some of these are presented below. For a further discussion with examples refer to FAS 123(R).

**Share options with performance conditions and/or market conditions.** Some option arrangements provide grants of share options with a performance condition. These types of plans permit employees to vest in differing numbers of options depending on the increase in market value of one of the company's products (or other condition) over a vesting period. These performance conditions can include factors such as market share increases, passing clinical trials, and other performance goals.

In addition to performance conditions, market conditions may also affect the option arrangements. These would include such things as indexing share prices to an industry group and the exercise price of options tied to this index. Therefore, the exercise price could go up or down depending on how the index performs. Arrangements exist for share units to have both performance and market conditions. These are accounted for in the same way as other options. The difficulty is in determining the fair values, as there are more factors contributing to uncertainty. These factors can, however, be modeled in a binomial valuation model.

**Other modifications of share option awards.** A company may modify the vesting conditions of an award. The accounting treatment for these modifications depends on the probability of vesting under the original conditions or the modified conditions. Other modifications are whether SAR will be settled in cash or equity or some combination, different from the original plan assumptions. A modification of vesting conditions is accounted for based on the principles set forth in FAS 123(R). Illustrations of different potential modifications are illustrated in Appendix B of FAS 123(R).

**Other types of share-based compensation awards covered in FAS 123(R).** Other share awards that FAS 123(R) addresses are outlined below.

- Share award with a clawback feature: These are restrictions on the employee's subsequent employment with a direct competitor, which if violated cause the ex-employee to return the value of the share award to the company.
- Tandem plan—share options or cash SAR: Employees are granted awards with two separate components, in which exercise of one component cancels the other.
- Tandem plan—phantom shares or share options: Similar to the plan above, but the employee's choice of which component to exercise depends on the relative value of the components when the award is exercised.
- Look-back share options: Share options awarded under Section 423 of the Internal Revenue Code, which provides that employees will not be immediately taxed on the difference between the market price of the stock and a discounted purchase price if certain requirements are met.
- Employee share purchase plans: Employee share purchase plans are not compensatory if their terms are no more favorable than those available to all holders of the same class of shares and if all employees that meet limited employment qualifications may participate in the plan on an equitable basis.
- Book value share purchase plans (nonpublic companies only): Companies with two classes of stock—one of which is available to all employees and the price is based on book value.
- Voluntary (or involuntary) change to fair-value-based method (nonpublic companies only): A nonpublic company elects as accounting policy the intrinsic value method and grants share awards to employees. Subsequently, the accounting for the value of these awards is changed to fair value because it is preferable under GAAP. Estimating grant date values is very difficult in hindsight. Therefore, these companies do not have to retrospectively apply fair value methods to unvested awards at the date of change.
- Certain instruments become subject to FAS 150: Certain instruments will become subject to FAS 150 when an employee could terminate service and receive or retain the fair value of the instrument for the remaining contractual term of that instrument.

**Reload feature and reload option.** A reload feature provides for automatic grants of additional options whenever an employee exercises previously granted options using the entity's shares, rather than cash, to satisfy the exercise price. At the time of exercise using shares, the employee is automatically granted a new option, called a reload option, for the shares used to exercise the previous option.

**Example of reload options**

Mr. Jones has 6,000 shares of ABC Company's $1 par value common stock, as well as options to purchase an additional 8,000 shares at an exercise price of $12. It will cost Jones $96,000 to exercise the options. The current market price of ABC stock is $16, so he trades in his existing 6,000 shares, which have a market value of $96,000, to purchase 8,000 shares with his options. The option plan has a reload feature, so ABC issues 6,000 replacement options (matching the number of shares traded in), for which the exercise price is set at the current market value of $16. ABC records the stock sale with the following entry:

| | | |
|---|---|---|
| Treasury stock | 96,000 | |
| Common stock | | 8,000 |
| Additional paid-in capital | | 88,000 |

Jones elects to exercise his options when the market value of ABC Company's stock reaches $24. At an exercise price of $16, it will again cost Jones $96,000 to purchase shares. At the current market price of $24, Jones can trade in 4,000 of his existing shares to acquire new shares. However, he chooses to trade in only 3,000 shares and pay for the remaining options with cash. ABC records the stock sale with the following entry:

| | | |
|---|---|---|
| Cash | 24,000 | |
| Treasury stock | 72,000 | |
|     Common stock | | 6,000 |
|     Additional paid-in capital | | 90,000 |

The reload feature still applies, but now ABC only issues 3,000 replacement options, which matches the number of shares Jones traded in to acquire new shares. The new options are assigned at an exercise price of $24, to match the market value on the grant date.

**Effect of employer payroll taxes.** EITF 00-16 discusses (1) when a liability for employer payroll taxes on employee stock compensation should be recognized in the employer's financial statements and (2) how that liability should be measured. The consensus was that a liability for employee payroll taxes on stock compensation should be recognized and measured on the date of the event triggering the measurement and payment of the tax to the taxing authority (which would generally be the exercise date).

**Payments in lieu of dividends on options.** Normally dividends are not paid on shares that have not been issued; thus, unexercised options do not gain the benefit of any dividends declared on the underlying stock. However, an entity can choose to pay dividend equivalents on options. Under the provisions of original FAS 123, such dividends or dividend equivalents on options which vest are to be accounted for as other dividends, that is, charged against retained earnings. Those paid on options that do not vest are deemed to be compensation expense. FAS 23 provided that the reporting entity can either estimate what fraction of options will vest, and allocate such dividend equivalents between retained earnings and compensation expense accordingly, or else can charge all to retained earnings and account for forfeitures as they occur, by reversing the charge from retained earnings to compensation cost.

While FAS 123(R) is silent on this, it would appear that some of the foregoing guidance would still be valid. However, since the new standard requires, effectively, that forfeitures be estimated and accounted for over the service period, in the authors' view it would be consistent to likewise charge retained earnings only for the estimated number of options to be exercised (changing from period to period, if a lattice model is used), with the remainder of any payments in lieu of dividends charged currently to compensation expense.

**Example of payments in lieu of dividends on options**

Gary Ironworks declares dividends of $2 per share of common stock. Its president, Mr. Jones, has 5,000 unvested options. Gary's board of directors chooses to pay Mr. Jones dividends on the 5,000 shares represented by the unvested options, on the assumption that all the options will vest. The resulting entry follows:

| | | |
|---|---|---|
| Retained earnings | 10,000 | |
|     Dividends payable | | 10,000 |

There are several other employees who have 20,000 unvested options. The board also declares dividends for these options, with the provision that dividends paid can be retained even if the associated options do not vest. The controller expects that only 70% of the options will vest, so she creates the following entry to charge the other 30% of the dividends to compensation expense:

| | | |
|---|---|---|
| Retained earnings | 28,000 | |
| Compensation expense | 12,000 | |
|     Dividends payable | | 40,000 |

**Disclosure requirements under FAS 123(R).** For a company to achieve the objectives of FAS 123(R), the minimum information needed to achieve disclosure objectives are set forth below.

- A description of the share-based payment arrangements, including the terms of the awards. A nonpublic company should disclose its policy for measuring compensation cost.
- The most recent income statement should provide the number and weighted-average exercise prices of the share options and equity instruments.
- Each year for which an income statement is provided, a company should provide the weighted-average grant-date fair value of equity options and the intrinsic value of options exercised during the year.
- For fully vested share options and those expected to vest at the latest balance sheet date, the company should provide the number, weighted-average exercise price, aggregate intrinsic value, and contractual terms of options outstanding and currently exercisable.
- If more than one share-based plan is in effect, the information should be provided separately for different types of awards.
- For each year for which an income statement is provided, companies should provide the following:
  - Companies that do not use the intrinsic value method should provide a description of the method of determining fair value and a description of the assumptions used.
  - Total compensation cost for share-based payment arrangements, including tax benefits and capitalization of compensation costs should be stated.
  - Descriptions of significant modifications and numbers of employees affected should also be provided.
- On the latest balance sheet date the total compensation cost related to nonvested awards not yet recognized and the period over which they are expected to be recognized.
- The amount of cash received from exercise of share-based compensation and the amount of cash used to settle equity instruments should be disclosed.
- Description of the company's policy for issuing shares upon share options exercise, including the source of the shares.

### Making the Transition to FAS 123(R)

FAS 123(R) applies to all awards granted after the required effective date. It is not to be applied to awards granted in periods before the required effective date, except to the extent that prior periods' awards are modified, repurchased, or cancelled after the required effective date and as required by the modified prospective application method described below.

The cumulative effect of initially applying FAS 123(R), if there is any, is to be recognized as of the required effective date. Also as of the required effective date, all public entities and those nonpublic entities that used the fair-value-based method for *either* recognition or disclosure under original FAS 123 must apply the *modified prospective application transition method*. For periods before the required effective date, those entities may elect to apply the modified retrospective application transition method.

Nonpublic entities that used the (now banned) minimum value method under original FAS 123, for either recognition or pro forma disclosures, are required to apply the *prospective transition method* (see below) as of the required effective date.

**Modified prospective application.** As of the required effective date, all public entities and those nonpublic entities that utilized the fair-value-based method for either recognition or disclosure under FAS 123, including nonpublic entities that become public entities after June 15, 2005, were required to adopt FAS 123(R) using a modified version of prospective application (the *modified prospective application*). Under modified prospective application, FAS 123(R) applies to new awards and to awards modified, repurchased, or cancelled after the required effective date. In addition, compensation cost for the portion of awards for which the requisite service has not been rendered, and that are outstanding as of the required effective date, is to be recognized as the requisite service is rendered on or after the required effective date. Compensation cost for that portion of awards is to be based on the grant-date fair value of those awards as calculated for either recognition or pro forma disclosures under original FAS 123. It is not permitted to recognize changes to the grant-date fair value of equity awards granted before the required effective date of FAS 123(R).

The compensation cost for those earlier awards is to be attributed to periods beginning on or after the required effective date of FAS 123(R) using the attribution method that was used under original FAS 123, except that the method of recognizing forfeitures only as they occur, as prescribed under FAS 123, may not be continued. Also, any unearned or deferred compensation (contra equity accounts) related to those earlier awards has to be eliminated against the appropriate equity accounts.

**Modified retrospective application.** Public entities and those nonpublic entities that used the fair-value-based method for either recognition or disclosure under FAS 123 optionally can apply a modified version of retrospective application (the *modified retrospective application*) to periods before the required effective date. This may be applied either (1) to all prior years for which original FAS 123 was effective, or (2) only to prior interim periods in the year of initial adoption if the required effective date of FAS 123(R) does not coincide with the beginning of the entity's fiscal year. A reporting entity that elects to apply the modified retrospective method to all prior years for which FAS 123 was effective must adjust financial statements for prior periods to give effect to the fair-value-based method of accounting for awards granted, modified, or settled in cash in fiscal years beginning after December 15, 1994 (the date of original FAS 123), on a basis consistent with the pro forma disclosures required for those periods by FAS 123, as amended by FAS 148 and by paragraph 30 of APB 28. Accordingly, compensation cost and the related tax effects will be recognized in those financial statements as though they had been accounted for under FAS 123. Changes to amounts as originally measured on a pro forma basis are precluded, however.

When a reporting entity applies the modified retrospective application method to all prior years for which FAS 123 was effective, and it does not present all of those years in comparative financial statements, the beginning balances of paid-in capital, deferred taxes, and retained earnings for the earliest year presented shall be adjusted to reflect the results of modified retrospective application to those prior years not presented. The effects of any such adjustments is to be disclosed in the year of the adoption. If the reporting entity applies the modified retrospective application method only to prior interim periods in the year of initial adoption, there would be no adjustment to the beginning balances of paid-in capital, deferred taxes, or retained earnings for the year of initial adoption.

Finally, the amendments to FAS 95 made by FAS 123(R) must be applied to the same periods for which the modified retrospective application method is applied.

**Transition as of the required effective date for both modified prospective and modified retrospective transition methods.** Transition as of the required effective date for instruments that are liabilities under the provisions of FAS 123(R) is to be as follows:

1. For an instrument that had previously been classified as equity but is classified as a liability under FAS 123(R), recognize a liability at its fair value (or portion thereof, if the requisite service has not yet been fully rendered). If (1) the fair value (or portion thereof) of the liability is greater or less than (2) previously recognized compensation cost for the instrument, the liability shall be recognized first, by reducing equity (generally, paid-in capital) to the extent of such previously recognized cost and second, by recognizing the difference (that is, the difference between items [1] and [2]) in the income statement, net of any related tax effect, as the cumulative effect of a change in accounting principle.
2. For an outstanding instrument that previously was classified as a liability and measured at intrinsic value, net of any related tax effect, as the cumulative effect of a change in the accounting principle.

As of the required effective date, if the entity had a policy of recognizing the effect of forfeitures only as they occurred, it must estimate the number of outstanding instruments for which the requisite service is not expected to be rendered. Balance sheet amounts related to any compensation cost (excluding nonrefundable dividend payments), net of related tax effects, for those instruments previously recognized in income because of that policy for periods before the effective date of FAS 123(R) are to be eliminated and recognized in income as the cumulative effect of a change in accounting principle as of the required effective date.

Other than as might be required per the preceding paragraph, no transition adjustment as of the required effective date is to be made for any deferred tax assets associated with outstanding equity instruments that continue to be accounted for as equity instruments under FAS 123(R). For purposes of calculating the available excess tax benefits if deferred tax assets need to be written off in subsequent periods, the reporting entity should include as available for offset only the net excess tax benefits that would have qualified as such had the entity adopted FAS 123 for recognition purposes for all awards granted, modified, or settled in cash for fiscal years beginning after December 15, 1994. In making this determination, the entity should exclude excess tax benefits that have not been realized pursuant to FAS 109. Any entity that previously has recognized deferred tax assets for excess tax benefits prior to their realization is to discontinue that practice prospectively then follow the guidance in FAS 123(R) and FAS 109.

Outstanding equity instruments that are measured at intrinsic value under original FAS 123 at the required effective date (because it was not possible to reasonably estimate their grant-date fair value) are to continue to be measured at intrinsic value until they are settled.

**Nonpublic entities that used the minimum value method under FAS 123.** Nonpublic entities, including those that become public entities after June 15, 2005, that used the minimum value method of measuring equity share options and similar instruments for either recognition or pro forma disclosure purposes under original FAS 123 are to apply FAS 123(R) prospectively to new awards and to awards modified, repurchased, or canceled after the required effective date. Those entities are to continue to account for any portion of awards outstanding at the date of initial application using the accounting principles originally applied to those awards (either the minimum value method under FAS 123 or the provisions of APB 25 and its related interpretive guidance).

**Required disclosures in the period FAS 123(R) is adopted.** In the period that FAS 123(R) is adopted, any entity shall disclose the effect of the change from applying the original provisions of FAS 123 on income from continuing operations, income before income taxes, net income, cash flow from operations, cash flow from financing activities, and basic and diluted earnings per share. In addition, if awards under share-based payment arrangements with employees are accounted for under the intrinsic value method of APB 25 for any reporting period for which an income statement is presented, all public entities must continue to provide the tabular presentation of the following information that was required by FAS 123 for each of those periods:

1.   Net income and basic and diluted earnings per share as reported
2.   The share-based employee compensation cost, net of related tax effects, included in net income as reported
3.   The share-based employee compensation cost, net of related tax effects, that would have been included in net income if the fair-value-based method had been applied to all awards
4.   Pro forma net income as if the fair-value-based method had been applied to all awards
5.   Pro forma basic and diluted earnings per share as if the fair-value-based method had been applied to all awards

The required pro forma amounts are to reflect the difference in share-based employee compensation cost, if any, included in net income and the total cost measured by the fair-value-based method, as well as additional tax effects, if any, that would have been recognized in the income statement if the fair-value-based method had been applied to all awards. The required pro forma per-share amounts shall reflect the change in the denominator of the diluted earnings per share calculation as if the assumed proceeds under the treasury stock method, including measured but unrecognized compensation cost and any excess tax benefits credited to additional paid-in capital, were determined under the fair-value-based method.

For a nonpublic entity that used the minimum value method for pro forma disclosure purposes under the original provisions of FAS 123, it may not continue to provide those pro forma disclosures for outstanding awards accounted for under the intrinsic value method of APB 25.

### Accounting for Equity Instruments Issued to other than Employees

The now-superseded FAS 123 made it very clear that stock issuances to persons or entities other than employees (e.g., vendors providing goods or services to the enterprise) are to be measured at fair value (defined by either the value of the goods or services received or the value of the equity instruments delivered in exchange, whichever is subject to more reliable measurement), but it offered no specific guidance regarding measurement. FAS 123(R) likewise offers no specific instruction regarding such circumstances. However, the Emerging Issues Task Force supplemented the basic directive under FAS 123(R), with consensuses on EITF 96-18, dealing exclusively with those situations in which the fair value of the equity instruments delivered is more objectively ascertainable than is the value of goods or services received. EITF 96-18 is the foundation for the discussion that follows in this section.

**Measurement date.**  For purposes of ascertaining the amounts to be assigned for these transactions, the key concern is the determination of the measurement date. Essentially, the amount of expense or the value of the asset acquired through the issuance of equity instruments is fixed as of the measurement date, although, under certain circumstances as explained below, some subsequent adjustments may need to be made.

Per the consensus on EITF 96-18, the measurement date will be the earlier of the date at which a commitment for performance is made or when the performance is actually completed. Whether or not there has been a "performance commitment" by the party providing the goods or services is a question of fact and must be determined from the surrounding circumstances, but in general will be deemed to exist if there is a "sufficiently large disincentive for nonperformance" to make performance probable. This disincentive must derive from the relationship between the equity instrument issuer/recipient of the goods or services and its counterparty. Mere risk of forfeiture is not enough to qualify as a disincentive, nor is the risk of being sued for nonperformance. When a sufficiently large disincentive exists, however, the measurement date will precede the completion of performance and, accordingly, when accrual of the related expense or recognition of the asset would otherwise be required under GAAP, it will be necessary to include the value of the equity instruments in such cost.

For example, if the agreed-upon price for the construction of a new power plant includes options on the utility company's stock, subject to a completion date of no longer than three years hence, and the contract also contains substantial financial disincentives to late completion, such as a provision for liquidated damages, then it would be concluded that there was a "performance commitment" within the meaning of EITF 96-18. On the other hand, if the price agreed to were to be fully payable even in the event of late delivery, there would be no "performance commitment" as that term is used.

In many situations in which the compensation includes significant equity instrument components, there will still be no finding of a performance commitment because the payment arrangement provides for phases of work, with payment in full for work as it is completed. For example, if a contractor agrees to build a multiplicity of sales kiosks in various air terminals for a retailing chain, with payment to be made in cash and the retailer's stock upon the completion of each kiosk, the contractor could terminate the arrangement after any intermediate completion date without significant penalty. In such cases, the measurement date would be, for each subproject, the date on which the work is completed.

**When to recognize the fair value of the equity instruments.** In general, the normal rules of GAAP would apply in circumstances in which stock or other equity instruments were being granted as part, or all, of the consideration for the transaction. Thus, if the services provided represented an expense of the enterprise, the expense should be recognized when incurred, which could well precede the date on which the payment was ultimately to be made.

No specific guidance has been offered regarding timing or manner of recognition. However, an EITF consensus was reached that once recognized, an asset or expense would not later be reversed if a stock option issued as consideration were to expire unexercised. This is consistent with FAS 123(R)'s treatment of expirations of options granted to employees. (It is, however, in contrast to the accounting prescribed for forfeitures under both APB 25 and original FAS 123, which mandated that compensation be reversed under such circumstances.) Thus, an expense or asset measurement is made with the best information available at that time, and there is no "look back" based on subsequent events; the value assigned to the option would be credited to an appropriate paid-in capital account (e.g., "capital from expired options") if this becomes necessary.

**Accounting prior to measurement date.** If, under GAAP, it is necessary for the entity to recognize an expense or an asset related to the transaction involving the issuance of equity for goods or services prior to the measurement date, the then-current fair values of the equity instruments must be utilized to determine these amounts. If fair values change later, these variations are attributed to those later periods. Thus, for a transaction which calls primarily for cash payment but also, to a lesser extent, for the issuance of stock, a decline in the value of the equity portion in a later interim period would reduce the cost (or asset value) to be recognized in that period; if the stock portion is a significant component, a decline could largely eliminate the cost otherwise to be accrued or even, conceivably, cause it to become negative in a later reporting period. Of course, overall, the aggregate cost would be positive upon ultimate completion (at worst it could be zero, if the transaction were predicated only on the issuance of equity instruments, and these became worthless—an obviously unlikely scenario).

**Measurement of fair value of the equity instrument portion of the transaction when certain terms are not known at inception.** In some circumstances where there is a performance commitment there will also be a material uncertainty regarding the valuation of the equity instruments, either because of some question regarding the number of instruments to be delivered, the value of such instruments, or some factor dependent upon the performance of the party providing the service. For example, the arrangement may include a guarantee of the value of the instrument extending for some period subsequent to completion of performance that unless the underlying shares maintain a market price of $15 or greater for one year following delivery, or else a defined number of additional shares will be granted. This type of arrangement is referred to as a "market condition." In other circumstances there may be a condition based on the counterparty's performance, for example, when options are granted to a tax accountant structuring a tax shelter, in which the number of options ultimately deliverable depends upon successfully surviving an IRS audit. Situations such as this are denoted "counterparty performance conditions."

Where the arrangement contains market conditions, measurement of the equity instrument portion of the contracted price should be based on two elements: the first is the fair value of the basic equity instrument; the second is the fair value of the contingent commitment, such as the aforementioned promise to grant a specified number of extra shares if the market price falls below $15 during the one-year period. In practice, the valuation of these contingencies might prove to be challenging, but clearly any such promise has some positive value, and the standard requires that this be assessed. Changes in the value of the second (contingent) element subsequent to the performance commitment date would not be recognized since, per EITF 96-13, a derivative financial instrument to be settled in a company's own shares (as contrasted to a settlement in cash) is not to be remeasured.

Compared to market conditions, measurement when there are counterparty performance conditions is more complicated. At the measurement date, the equity instruments are valued at the lowest of the defined alternative amounts. For example, if the value of the option award to the tax accountant noted above is $20,000 (at the performance commitment date) assuming survival against IRS challenge, but only $5,000 if the IRS ultimately prevails, then the measurement of the value of the service would be based on the $5,000 amount. However, later, when the outcome of the performance condition is known, an additional cost would have to be recognized if a more favorable outcome occurred (in this example, successful defense of the tax shelter). The added cost would be based not on the values as of the performance commitment date, but rather as of the date of resolution of the condition. If the value of the options under the "success" outcome is $28,000 at that date, and the value of the "failure" outcome is $19,000, then an added cost of ($28,000 − 19,000 =) $9,000 would be recognized.

Where a given transaction involves both market and counterparty performance conditions, the accounting specified for situations involving only counterparty performance conditions is to be applied.

### Example of equity instruments issued to a third party

Carney Development Enterprises has engaged the services of Alfred Brothers Construction (ABC) to design an office tower. ABC agrees to accept 5,000 shares of Carney $1 par value common stock and 1,000 options on shares in exchange for this service, but it will only receive half the number of shares if it delivers completed drawings after the due date. Thus, there exists a sufficiently large disincentive for nonperformance. Also, if the value of Carney's stock declines below $15/share at any point during the six months subsequent to the issuance of shares to ABC, Carney agrees to issue additional shares to bring ABC's total compensation back up to the $15 level, which is capped at a maximum additional stock issuance of 2,000 shares.

Carney measures the value of its stock and options as of the performance commitment date for the initial 5,000 share payment, the 1,000 option grant, and the potential additional payment of 2,000 shares. At a price on the commitment date of $18/share, the initial share payment costs $90,000, while the additional payment costs $36,000. Carney appropriately values the stock options at $9 each, or $9,000 in total, using an option pricing model. During each of the 18 months of the design process, Carney recognizes 1/18 of the $90,000 cost of the initial stock grant and of the $9,000 option grant with the following entry:

| | | |
|---|---|---|
| Construction-in-progress | 5,500 | |
|     Stock options outstanding | | 500 |
|     Accrued liabilities | | 5,000 |

ABC successfully completes the drawings by the designated deadline, triggering a stock grant of 5,000 shares that Carney records with the following entry:

| | | |
|---|---|---|
| Accrued liabilities | 90,000 | |
|     Common stock | | 5,000 |
|     Additional paid-in capital | | 85,000 |

Carney's stock price drops below $18 immediately after the project is completed, so ABC never exercises the 1,000 stock options. Carney accounts for the stock options with the following entry:

| | | |
|---|---|---|
| Stock options outstanding | 9,000 | |
|     Additional paid-in capital—expired options | | 9,000 |

The value of Carney stock subsequently declines to $10/share, which represents a shortfall of $25,000 from the guaranteed minimum share price of $15. At the current market price of $10/share, Carney would have to issue an additional 2,500 shares to ABC to make up the shortfall. However, since this liability is capped at 2,000 shares, Carney only issues 2,000 shares, using the valuation of $18 set at the commitment date, and records the transaction with the following entry:

| | | |
|---|---|---|
| Construction-in-progress | 36,000 | |
|     Common stock | | 2,000 |
|     Additional paid-in capital | | 34,000 |

**Reporting prior to the measurement date when certain terms are not known.** When market conditions (e.g., the value of the stock underlying the options two years hence) are not known, and expenses must be accrued or assets recorded prior to the measurement date, the then-current fair values of the equity instruments at such dates should be used, with subsequent adjustments as necessary. When there are counterparty performance conditions, either alone or in conjunction with market conditions, then interim measurements should be based on the lowest of the alternative values as of each date, with subsequent changes in this same measure assigned to later periods.

**Reporting after the measurement date when certain terms are not known.** When market conditions (e.g., the value of the stock underlying the options two years hence) are not known, after the measurement date the principles of EITF 96-13 are to be applied, which generally would mean that changes in value would not be recognized. On the other hand, when there are counterparty performance conditions, with or without market conditions also being present, the principles of FAS 123, specifically the "modification accounting" procedures, are to be utilized. This results in reporting an adjustment in subsequent periods determined with reference to the difference between the then-current fair value of the revised equity instruments and that of the old instruments immediately prior to the recognition event. In all cases, the "then-current" values are to be determined with reference to the lowest aggregate fair values under the alternative outcomes specified by the contractual arrangement.

**Further guidance.** EITF 96-18 and EITF 00-8, which require "symmetrical accounting," do not address the period(s) or manner in which the fair value of the transactions should be recognized, other than to observe that a transaction should be recognized in the same period(s) and in the same manner as if cash were being exchanged in the transaction instead of the equity instruments. These matters were subsequently dealt with by EITF 00-18. The consensus is that where fully vested, exercisable, nonforfeitable equity instruments are issued at the date the grantor and grantee enter into an agreement, by eliminating any obligation on the part of the counterparty to earn the equity instruments, a measurement date has been reached. The majority held that the grantor should recognize the equity instruments when they are issued (in most cases, when the agreement is entered into), and generally agreed that whether the corresponding cost is an immediate expense or a prepaid asset (or whether the debit should be characterized as contra equity) depends on the specific facts and circumstances. No further consideration of this matter is planned.

Consensus was reached that, if an entity grants fully vested, nonforfeitable equity instruments that are exercisable by the grantee only after a specified period of time and the terms of the agreement provide for earlier exercisability by the grantee only after a specified period of time and the terms of the agreement provide for earlier exercisability if the grantee achieves specified performance conditions, the grantor should measure the fair value of the equity instruments at the date of grant and should recognize that measured cost under the same guidance as the foregoing. Change to EITF 96-18 should be made to eliminate a reference to immediate exercisability. A majority agreed that if, subsequent to the arrangement date, the grantee performs as specified and exercisability is accelerated, the grantor should measure and account for the increase in the fair value of the equity instruments resulting from the acceleration of exercisability using "modification accounting." Since, generally, option-pricing models are not sensitive to exercisability restrictions, it may be necessary to provide additional guidance on how to measure the discount attributable to the exercisability restriction.

For transactions that include a grantee performance commitment, there was general agreement that the grantee should account for the arrangement as an executory contract (that is, generally no accounting before performance) in the same manner as it would if the grantor had agreed to pay cash (upon vesting) for the goods or services. Further consideration will be directed to the accounting in cases in which the fair value at the date the equity instruments are earned is greater than or less than the fair value measured at the performance commitment date (measurement date).

**Consideration for future services.** EITF 96-18 discusses the appropriate balance sheet presentation of arrangements where unvested, forfeitable equity instruments are issued to an unrelated nonemployee (the counterparty) as consideration for future services. Per EITF Topic D-90, SEC staff has since addressed situations where the grantor is entitled to recover the specific consideration paid, plus a substantial mandatory penalty, as a minimum measure of damages for counterparty nonperformance. Fair value measurement under FAS 123(R) is required. In practice, however, it was found that some reporting entities have made no entries until performance occurs, while others have recorded the fair value of the equity instruments as equity at the measurement date and record the offset either as an asset (future services receivable) or as a reduction of stockholders' equity (contra equity).

The SEC staff believes that if the issuer receives a right to receive future services in exchange for unvested, forfeitable equity instruments, those equity instruments should be treated as unissued for accounting purposes until the future services are received (that is, the instruments are not considered issued until they vest). Consequently, there would be no recognition at the measurement date and no entry should be recorded. This does not apply to similar arrangements in which the issuer exchanges fully vested nonforfeitable equity instruments, as those types of arrangements are addressed in EITF 00-18.

## Convertible Preferred Stock

The treatment of convertible preferred stock at its issuance is no different than that of nonconvertible preferred. When it is converted, the book value approach is used to account for the conversion. Use of the market value approach would entail a gain or loss for which there is no theoretical justification since the total amount of contributed capital does not change when the stock is converted. When the preferred stock is converted, the "Preferred stock" and related "Additional paid-in capital—preferred stock" accounts are debited for their original values when purchased, and "Common stock" and "Additional paid-in capital—common stock" (if an excess over par or stated value exists) are credited. If the book value of the preferred stock is less than the total par value of the common stock being issued, retained earnings is charged for the difference. This charge is supported by the rationale that the preferred shareholders are offered an additional return to facilitate their conversion to common stock. Many states require that this excess instead reduce additional paid-in capital from other sources.

### Example of convertible preferred stock

Caspian Corporation issues 10,000 shares of $1 par value convertible preferred stock, and receives $1.25 per share. It records the initial sale with the following entry:

| | | |
|---|---|---|
| Cash | 12,500 | |
|     Convertible preferred stock | | 10,000 |
|     Additional paid-in capital—preferred stock | | 2,500 |

The terms of the convertible preferred stock allow Caspian's shareholders to convert one share of preferred for one share of common stock at any time. The preferred shareholders convert all of their shares to Caspian common stock, which has a par value of $2. This requires the following entry:

| | | |
|---|---|---|
| Convertible preferred stock | 10,000 | |
| Additional paid-in capital—preferred stock | 2,500 | |
|     Retained earnings | 7,500 | |
|     Common stock | | 20,000 |

## Mandatorily Redeemable Common and Preferred Stock

A mandatory redemption clause requires common or preferred stock to be redeemed (retired) at a specific date(s) or upon occurrence of an event which is uncertain as to timing although ultimately certain to occur. This feature is in contrast to callable preferred stock, which is redeemed at the issuing corporation's option. Mandatory redemption features are not uncommon in practice; closely held corporations, for example, have "buy-sell" agreements to redeem the shares of retiring or deceased owners at formula prices, often book value. Historically, the mandatory redemption feature has been ignored in determining balance sheet classification for nonpublic companies. On the other hand, for publicly held companies, mandatorily redeemable shares (which are almost always preferred stock in these situations) had to be displayed as either debt or as a "mezzanine equity" item separate from stockholders' equity.

Under FAS 150, which is discussed in greater detail later in this chapter, financial instruments with mandatory redemption features must be reported as liabilities. This means that "mezzanine" presentation of redeemable preferred stock is no longer appropriate. It also means that some entities, having "buy-sell" agreements with all of their respective shareholders, should report no equity at all and should display all of what formerly was equity within the liabilities caption of the balance sheet. This is a major change from previous GAAP practice.

The only exception to this requirement exists in the circumstance where the redemption is required to occur only upon the liquidation or termination of the reporting entity. Since financial statements are prepared under the assumption of a going concern, it would be inconsistent to classify this type of redeemable stock as a liability.

If the stock subject to mandatory redemption provisions represents the only shares in the reporting entity, it must, under FAS 150, report those instruments in the liabilities section of its balance sheet, and describe them as shares subject to mandatory redemption, so as to distinguish the instruments from other financial statement liabilities. Transition to this standard may create distress, particularly in those cases where there will be a need to modify loan agreements, restrictive covenants, and so forth, since these entities' debt/equity ratios and other financial indicators will change dramatically and in many instances immediately violate existing covenants. The use of the special caption above will serve to educate financial statements users regarding the substantive meaning of this new mode of financial statement presentation.

In some cases stock is issued which is not subject to mandatory redemption provisions currently, but which is contingently subject to such requirements once defined events occur. An assessment must be made each reporting period to ascertain whether the triggering event has yet occurred. If it has, reclassification of the conditionally mandatorily redeemable stock to liabilities must be effected.

FAS 150 offers two such examples. First, if shares are to become mandatorily redeemable upon a change in control of the issuing corporation, these remain classified within equity until that event occurs, if ever. When it does occur, the equity is reclassified to liabilities, measured at the fair value at that date, with no gain or loss recognized. Any disparity between the carrying value of the equity and the amount transferred to liabilities would therefore remain in equity, as additional paid-in capital or as a reduction to paid-in capital or to retained earnings.

Another example of conditional mandatory redemption would occur when preferred stock is issued with a mandatory redemption at a date certain, say ten years hence, conditioned on the failure of the preferred stockholders to exercise the right to convert to common stock before another defined date, say five years from issuance. For the first five years, the preferred stock would be displayed as equity, since the mandatory redemption feature has yet to become activated. If the shareholders elect to exchange the preferred stock to common stock, the usual accounting for such conversions would apply. If the five-year period elapses and the preferred shares are not exchanged, the mandatory redemption provision becomes effective, and the preferred stock is to be reclassified to liabilities, measured at fair value.

Accounting for mandatorily redeemable financial instruments of a nonpublic reporting entity must be conformed to the requirements outlined above, effective for existing or new contracts for fiscal periods beginning after December 15, 2004. For all other mandatorily redeemable financial instruments issued by nonpublic entities that are not SEC registrants, the classification, measurement, and disclosure provisions are deferred indefinitely. For mandatorily redeemable noncontrolling interests that would not be classified by the subsidiary as liabilities (because they are redeemable only upon liquidation) but would be classified by the parent as liabilities on the consolidated statements, the classification and measurement provisions of FAS 150 are deferred indefinitely. For other mandatorily redeemable noncontrolling interests, the measurement provisions of FAS 150 were deferred indefinitely, but the classifications provisions are not deferred. For financial instruments created before issuance date of FAS 150 and still existing at the beginning of the interim period of adoption, transition is to be achieved by reporting the cumulative effect of a change in an accounting principle by initially measuring the financial instruments at fair value or other measurement attribute required by the statement.

In addition to the requirement of FAS 150, expanded disclosure of mandatorily redeemable common or preferred stock is required by FAS 129. Specifically, the redemption requirements for each of the next five years must be set forth in the notes to the financial statements prepared in accordance with GAAP, if the amounts are either fixed or determinable on fixed or determinable dates. Thus, readers can interpret the cash requirements on the reporting entity in a manner similar to the drawing of inferences about other fixed commitments, such as maturities of long-term debt and lease obligations.

### Example of mandatorily redeemable stock

A major shareholder of the Atlantic Corporation swaps the company two tracts of prime real estate (Tract A and Tract B) in exchange for 10,000 shares and 5,000 shares, respectively, of $1 par value preferred stock. Each block of stock is mandatorily redeemable within one year if Atlantic ever sells the related tract of real estate. Tract A has a fair value of $400,000 and Tract B has a fair value of $200,000 on the initial transaction date. Since the shares are only conditionally redeemable at this time, Atlantic records a credit to equity accounts with the following entry:

| | | |
|---|---|---|
| Land | 600,000 | |
| Preferred stock | | 15,000 |
| Additional paid-in capital | | 585,000 |

Five years later, Atlantic sells Tract A for $550,000, which is the fair value of the land. Because the status of the shares has now changed to mandatorily redeemable, Atlantic reclassifies the related 10,000 shares as a liability, measured at their fair value on the reclassification date. Since the fair value has increased by $150,000, Atlantic shifts an additional $150,000 from the additional paid-in capital account to the liability account. It uses the following entry to do so:

| | | |
|---|---|---|
| Preferred stock | 10,000 | |
| Additional paid-in capital | 540,000 | |
| Liabilities—shares subject to mandatory redemption | | 550,000 |

Two years later, Atlantic sells Tract B for $125,000, which is the fair value of the land. The status of these shares has also now changed to mandatorily redeemable, so Atlantic reclassifies the related 5,000 shares as a liability, measured at their fair value on the reclassification date. Since the fair value has decreased by $75,000, Atlantic retains $75,000 in the additional paid-in capital account. It uses the following entry to do so:

| | | |
|---|---|---|
| Preferred stock | 5,000 | |
| Additional paid-in capital | 120,000 | |
| Liabilities—shares subject to mandatory redemption | | 125,000 |

## Put Warrant

A detachable put warrant can either be put back to the debt issuer for cash or can be exercised to acquire common stock. EITF 88-9 concluded that these instruments should be accounted for in the same manner as a mezzanine security. The proceeds applicable to the put warrant ordinarily are to be classified as equity and should be presented between the liability and equity sections in accordance with SEC ASR 268.

In the case of a warrant with a put price substantially higher than the value assigned to the warrant at issuance, however, the proceeds should be classified as a liability since it is likely that the warrant will be put back to the company.

### Example of a put warrant

Caspian Corporation issues 100 bonds with detachable put warrants, each of which allow holders, after two years have elapsed, to purchase one share of Caspian's $1 par value common stock from the company for $20 per share, and which are puttable for a cash payment of $5. Caspian apportions $5 of the bond sale price to the warrants. Caspian's share price on the issuance date is $23. At this price, warrant holders can purchase shares from Caspian for $20 and resell them for $23, yielding a net gain of $3. Since this is less than the $5 to be gained from the put feature of the warrants, this is classified as a liability, and is recorded as such with the following entry (the remaining entries for the issuance of the bond are not given here):

| | | |
|---|---|---|
| Cash | 500 | |
| Liabilities—puttable warrants | | 500 |

After two years, Caspian's stock price has declined to $20, so the warrant stock purchase feature clearly has no value. Instead, a warrant holder puts 30 warrants back to the company, which requires a cash payment of $5 for each warrant, and results in the following entry:

| | | |
|---|---|---|
| Liabilities—puttable warrants | 150 | |
| Cash | | 150 |

Caspian's stock price then increases to $30, which allows warrant holders to achieve a $10 gain if they acquire shares with their warrants for $20. Accordingly, another warrant holder acquires shares with 50 warrants, resulting in the following entry:

| | | |
|---|---|---|
| Cash | 1,000 | |
| Liabilities—puttable warrants | 250 | |
| Common stock | | 50 |
| Additional paid-in capital | | 1,200 |

In a separate bond issuance, Caspian again issues put warrants under the same terms, but now its stock price is $35 at the time of bond issuance, making the warrant feature more likely to be exercised than the put feature. Accordingly, Caspian records the proceeds in equity with the following entry (again, the remaining entries recording the bond issuance are omitted):

| | | |
|---|---|---|
| Cash | 500 | |
| Additional paid-in capital—warrants | | 500 |

Investors use all 100 warrants to acquire shares at the $20 exercise price. The entry follows:

| | | |
|---|---|---|
| Cash | 2,000 | |
| Paid-in capital—warrants | 500 | |
| Common stock | | 100 |
| Additional paid-in capital | | 2,400 |

The original classification should not be changed because of subsequent economic changes in the value of the put. The value assigned to the put warrant at issuance, however, should be adjusted to its highest redemption price, starting with the date of issuance until the earliest date of the warrants. Changes in the redemption price before the earliest put dates are changes in accounting estimates and changes after the earliest put dates should be recognized in income. If the put is classified as equity, the adjustment should be reported as a charge to retained earnings, and if the put is classified as a liability the adjustment is reported as interest expense.

Regardless of how the put is classified on the balance sheet, the primary and fully diluted EPS should be calculated on both an equity basis (warrants will be exercised) and on a debt basis (put will be exercised) and the more dilutive of the two methods should be used.

### Accounting for Stock Issued to Employee Stock Ownership Plans

For over thirty years, it has been a government policy to encourage employee ownership of corporations. To that end, tax laws have been adopted which make this prospect attractive to employer entities. Thus, there has been a steady increase in the number of corporations which are entirely or partially employee-owned under terms of employee stock ownership plans (ESOP). The accounting for ESOP was first set forth in AICPA Statement of Position (SOP) 76-3, which was later superseded by SOP 93-6, which remains the current source of GAAP.

Depending on what motivated the creation of the ESOP (e.g., estate planning by the controlling shareholder, expanding the capital base of the entity, rewarding and motivating the work force), the sponsor's shares may be contributed to the plan in annual installments in a block of shares from the sponsor, or shares from an existing shareholder may be purchased by the plan.

Employee stock ownership plans are defined contribution plans in which shares of the sponsoring entity are awarded to employees as additional compensation. Briefly, ESOP are created by a sponsoring corporation which either funds the plan directly (unleveraged ESOP) or, more commonly, facilitates the borrowing of money either directly from an outside lender (directly leveraged ESOP) or from the employer, which in turn will borrow from an outside lender (indirectly leveraged ESOP).

Borrowings from outside lenders may or may not be guaranteed by the sponsor. However, since effectively the only source of funds for debt repayment are future contributions by the sponsor, GAAP requires that the ESOP's debt be considered debt of the sponsor even absent a guarantee.

When recording the direct or indirect borrowings by the ESOP as debt in the sponsor's balance sheet, a debit to a contra equity account, not to an asset, is also reported. This is necessary since the borrowings represent a commitment (morally if not always legally) to make future contributions to the plan and this is certainly not a claim to resources. Significantly, this results in a "double hit" to the sponsor's balance sheet (i.e., the recording of a liability and the reduction of net stockholders' equity) which is often an unanticipated and unpleasant surprise to plan sponsors. This contra equity account is referred to as "unearned ESOP shares" in accordance with provisions of SOP 93-6. If the sponsor itself lends funds to the ESOP without a "mirror loan" from an outside lender, this loan should not be reported in the employer's balance sheet as debt, although the debit should still be reported as a contra equity account.

As the ESOP services the debt, using contributions made by the sponsor and/or dividends received on sponsor shares held by the plan, it reflects the reduction of the obligation by reducing both the debt and the contra equity account on its balance sheet. Simultaneously, income and thus retained earnings will be impacted as the contributions to the plan are reported in the sponsor's current statement of earnings. Thus, the "double hit" is eliminated, but net worth continues to reflect the economic fact that compensation costs have been incurred.

The interest cost component of debt service must be separated from the remaining compensation expense. That is, the sponsor's income statement should reflect the true character of the expenses being incurred, rather than aggregating the entire amount into a category which might have been denoted as "ESOP contribution."

In a leveraged ESOP, shares held serve as collateral for the debt and are not allocated to employees until the debt is retired. In general, shares must be allocated by the end of the year in which the debt is repaid. However, in order to satisfy the tax laws, the allocation of shares may take place at a faster pace than the retirement of the principal portion of the debt.

Under SOP 93-6, the cost of ESOP shares allocated is measured based upon the fair value on the release date for purposes of reporting compensation expense in the sponsor's income statements. This is in contradistinction to the actual historical cost of the shares to the plan.

Furthermore, dividends paid on unallocated shares (i.e., shares held by the ESOP) are not treated as dividends, but rather must be reported in the sponsor's income statement as compensation cost and/or as interest expense. Of less significance to nonpublic companies is the fact that under the new rules only common shares released and committed to be released are treated as being outstanding, with the resultant need to be considered in calculating both basic and diluted EPS.

### Example of accounting for ESOP transactions

Assume that Intrepid Corp. establishes an ESOP, which then borrows $500,000 from Second Interstate Bank. The ESOP then purchases 50,000 shares of Intrepid no-par shares from the company; none of these shares are allocated to individual participants. The entries would be

| | | |
|---|---|---|
| Cash | 500,000 | |
|     Bank loan payable | | 500,000 |
| Unearned ESOP shares (contra equity) | 500,000 | |
|     Common stock | | 500,000 |

The ESOP then borrows an additional $250,000 from the sponsor, Intrepid, and uses the cash to purchase a further 25,000 shares, all of which are allocated to participants.

| | | |
|---|---|---|
| Compensation | 250,000 | |
|     Common stock | | 250,000 |

Intrepid Corp. contributes $50,000 to the plan, which the plan uses to service its bank debt, consisting of $40,000 principal reduction and $10,000 interest cost. The debt reduction causes 4,000 shares to be allocated to participants at a time when the average market value had been $12 per share.

| | | |
|---|---|---|
| Interest expense | 10,000 | |
| Bank loan payable | 40,000 | |
|     Cash | | 50,000 |
| Compensation | 48,000 | |
|     Additional paid-in capital | | 8,000 |
|     Unearned ESOP shares | | 40,000 |

Dividends of $.10 per share are declared (only the ESOP shares are represented in the following entry, but dividends are paid equally on all outstanding shares)

| | | |
|---|---|---|
| Retained earnings (on 29,000 shares) | 2,900 | |
| Compensation (on 46,000 shares) | 4,600 | |
|     Dividends payable | | 7,500 |

Note that in all the foregoing illustrations the effect of income taxes is ignored. Since the difference between the cost and fair values of shares committed to be released is analogous to differences in the expense recognized for tax and accounting purposes with regard to stock options, the same treatment should be applied. That is, the tax effect should be reported directly in stockholders' equity, rather than in earnings.

## Financial Instruments with Characteristics of Both Liabilities and Equity

Standard setters have been struggling with the proper reporting for hybrid instruments—having characteristics of both liabilities and equity. Two needs had been perceived: first, to establish criteria for classification for certain instruments (e.g., mandatorily redeemable stock) that nominally are equity but have key characteristics of debt, but which will severely impact corporate balance sheets if a "substance over form" approach is strictly enforced; and second, to develop the methodology for disaggregating the constituent parts of compound instruments so that they may be accounted for as debt and as equity, respectively.

A discussion memorandum was issued in 1990; ten years later, FASB issued an Exposure Draft, *Accounting for Financial Instruments with Characteristics of Liabilities, Equity, or Both,* as well as a concomitant proposed amendment to CON 6 to revise the definition of liabilities. Later, FASB decided to restructure its efforts to engage in a multiphase project, the first part of which has come to fruition now with the recent issuance of FAS 150. This standard addresses only financial instruments issued in the form of shares that are mandatorily redeemable (i.e., that embody unconditional obligations requiring the issuer to redeem them by transferring its assets at a specified or determinable date or dates or upon an event that is certain to occur.)

According to FAS 150, the affected instruments include those, other than an outstanding share, that, at inception, embody an obligation to repurchase the issuer's equity shares, or are indexed to such an obligation, and that require or may require the issuer to settle the obligations by transferring assets (for example, a forward purchase contract or written put option on the issuer's equity shares that is to be physically settled or net cash settled). It also includes financial instruments that embody unconditional obligations, or financial instruments other than outstanding shares that embody conditional obligations, that the issuers must or may settle by issuing a variable number of equity shares, if, at inception, the monetary values of the obligations are based solely or predominantly on any of the following:

1. A fixed monetary amount known at inception, for example, a payable settleable with a variable number of the issuer's equity shares;
2. Variations in something other than the fair value of the issuer's equity shares, for example, a financial instrument indexed to the S&P 500 and settleable with a variable number of the issuer's equity shares; or
3. Variations inversely related to changes in the fair value of the issuer's equity shares, for example, a written put option that could be net share settled.

The requirements of FAS 150 apply to issuers' classification and measurement of freestanding financial instruments, including those that comprise more than one option or forward contract. It does not apply, however, to features that are embedded in financial instruments that are not derivatives in their entirety. For example, it does not alter the accounting treatment of conversion features (as found in convertible debentures), conditional redemption features, or other features embedded in financial instruments that are not derivatives in their entirety. It also does not affect the classification or measurement of convertible bonds, puttable stock, or other outstanding shares that are conditionally redeemable. FAS 150 also does not address certain financial instruments indexed partly to the issuer's equity shares and partly, but not predominantly, to another referent.

FAS 150 establishes requirements for only a limited range of financial instruments having characteristics of both liabilities and equity. FASB is now pursuing a second phase of its project and will address the accounting for various financial instruments with characteristics of both liabilities and equity not addressed in FAS 150. Guidance currently in effect under GAAP for those instruments remains in effect in the interim.

**Terminology of FAS 150.** This standard uses terminology that may not be familiar to most accountants but which is important to understanding when and how to apply FAS 150. Key terms include the following:

**Freestanding financial instrument**—A financial instrument that is entered into separately and apart from any of the entity's other financial instruments or equity transactions, or that is entered into in conjunction with some other transaction and is legally detachable and separately exercisable.

**Issuer**—The entity that issued a financial instrument or may be required under the terms of a financial instrument to issue its equity shares.

**Mandatorily redeemable financial instrument**—Any of various financial instruments issued in the form of shares that embody an unconditional obligation requiring the issuer to redeem the instrument by transferring its assets at a specified or determinable date (or dates) or upon an event that is certain to occur.

**Monetary value**—What the fair value of the cash, shares, or other instruments that a financial instrument obligates the issuer to convey to the holder would be at the settlement date under specified market conditions.

**Net cash settlement**—A form of settling a financial instrument under which the party with a loss delivers to the party with a gain cash equal to the gain.

**Net share settlement**—A form of settling a financial instrument under which the party with a loss delivers to the party with a gain shares of stock with a current fair value equal to the gain.

**Nonpublic entity**—Any entity other than one (a) whose equity securities trade in a public market either on a stock exchange (domestic or foreign) or in the over-the-counter market, including securities quoted only locally or regionally; (b) that makes a filing with a regulatory agency in preparation for the sale of equity securities in a public market; or (c) that is controlled by an entity covered by (a) or (b).

**Obligation**—A conditional or unconditional duty or responsibility to transfer assets or to issue equity shares.

**Physical settlement**—A form of settling a financial instrument under which (a) the party designated in the contract as the buyer delivers the full stated amount of cash or other financial instruments to the seller and (b) the seller delivers the full stated number of shares of stock or other financial instruments or nonfinancial instruments to the buyer.

In addition to the foregoing, the terms fair value and financial instrument are used as defined in other recent FASB standards.

**Applicability of FAS 150.** This standard only applies to three types of freestanding financial instruments: mandatorily redeemable financial instruments; obligations to repurchase the issuer's shares by transferring assets; and certain obligations to issue a variable number of shares. Mandatorily redeemable shares were addressed earlier in this chapter; the other classes of instruments affected by FAS 150 are discussed in the following paragraphs.

Obligations to repurchase the issuer's equity shares by transferring assets include financial instruments, other than outstanding shares, that, at inception, (a) embody obligations to repurchase the issuers' equity shares, or are indexed to such obligations, and (b) require or may require the issuers to settle the obligations by transferring assets. These must be classified as liabilities (or, rarely, as assets). Such obligations could include forward purchase contracts or written put options on an issuer's equity shares that are to be physically settled or net cash settled.

Certain obligations to issue a variable number of shares are financial instruments that embody unconditional obligations, or financial instruments other than outstanding shares that embody conditional obligations, that the issuers must or may settle by issuing variable numbers of equity shares. These obligations also must be classified as liabilities (or, rarely, as assets) if, at inception, the monetary values of the obligations are based solely or predominantly on any one of the following:

1. A fixed monetary amount known at inception (e.g., a payable settleable with a variable number of the issuer's equity shares);
2. Variations in something other than the fair value of the issuer's equity shares (e.g., a financial instrument indexed to the S&P 500 and settleable with a variable number of the issuer's equity shares); or
3. Variations inversely related to changes in the fair value of the issuer's equity shares (e.g., a written put option that could be net share settled).

FAS 150 only applies to freestanding instruments, which could include those that comprise more than one option or forward contract, as, for example, an instrument that consists of a written put option for an issuer's equity shares and a purchased call option. The standard does not apply to features embedded in another financial instrument, such as an option on the issuer's equity shares that is embedded in a nonderivative host contract.

If a freestanding instrument is composed of more than one option or forward contract and one of those contracts embodies an obligation to repurchase the issuer's shares that require or may require settlement by a transfer of assets, the financial instrument is a liability. In addition, if a freestanding instrument composed of more than one option or forward contract includes an obligation to issue shares, the various component obligations must be analyzed to determine if any of them would be obligations under FAS 150. If one or more would be obligations under this standard, then judgment must be used to determine if the monetary value of the obligations that would be liabilities is collectively predominant over the other component liabilities. If so, the instrument is a liability. If not, the instrument is outside the scope of FAS 150. Following is a list of examples of these types of financial instruments:

- Puttable warrants
- Warrant for shares that can be put by the holder immediately after exercise
- Warrant that allows the holder to exercise the warrant or put the warrant back to the issuer on the exercise date for a variable number of shares with a fixed monetary value
- Forward contract in which the number of shares to be issued depends on the issuer's share price on the settlement date
- Warrant with a "liquidity make-whole" put to issue additional shares to the holder if the sales price of the shares when later sold is less than the share price when the warrant is exercised
- Warrant that allows the holder to exercise the warrant or, if contingent event does not occur, put the warrant back to the issuer on the exercise date for a variable number of shares with a fixed monetary value

The standard does not apply to or affect the timing of recognition of financial instruments issued as contingent consideration in a business combination, nor the measurement guidance for contingent consideration, as set forth in FAS 141. It also does not affect accounting for stock-based compensation (FAS 123[R]), or ESOP plans (SOP 93-6), both of which were addressed earlier in this chapter.

**Initial and subsequent measurements.** As noted, mandatorily redeemable financial instruments, which are now to be reported as liabilities, are initially recognized at fair value. Mandatorily redeemable financial instruments are subsequently remeasured using fair value, with any adjustments to be included in the periodic determination of income. In general, the value of mandatorily redeemable financial instruments will be accreted over time and the accretion will be treated as interest expense. The method of determining subsequent fair values corresponds to that set forth in the following paragraph.

Forward contracts that require physical settlement by repurchase of a fixed number of the issuer's equity shares in exchange for cash are to be measured initially at the fair value of the shares, as adjusted for any consideration or unstated rights or privileges. Equity is reduced by this same amount. Fair value in this context may be determined by reference to the amount of cash that would be paid under the conditions specified in the contract if the shares were repurchased immediately. Alternatively, the settlement amount can be discounted at the rate implicit at inception after taking into account any consideration or unstated rights or privileges that may have affected the terms of the transaction.

Subsequent measurement can be effected by either accretion (which is feasible only if the amount to be paid and the settlement date are both fixed), or by determining the amount of cash that would be paid under the conditions specified in the contract if settlement occurred at the reporting date (useful when either the amount to be paid or the settlement date vary based on defined conditions and terms). In either case, the change from the amount reported in the prior period is interest expense. If accretion is appropriate, the instruments are to be measured subsequently at the present value of the amount to be paid at settlement, accruing interest cost using the rate implicit at inception.

Conditionally redeemable instruments, first classified as equity and transferred to liabilities when the condition is satisfied, are measured at fair value at that date, with no gain or loss being recognized from the reclassification. For earnings per share computation purposes, the amount of common shares that are to be redeemed or repurchased are excluded for both basic and diluted calculations.

**Gain or loss on retirement of redeemable instruments.** If mandatorily redeemable preferred or common stock is acquired prior to the mandatory redemption date, the financial statement implications are the same as when debt is retired. Since the mandatorily redeemable shares are categorized, for financial reporting purposes, as liabilities, not equity, the usual prohibition against reporting gain or loss on capital transactions (such as retirement of treasury stock) would not be applicable. Rather the guidance under GAAP (APB 26) governing debt retirement would be pertinent. Specifically, if the price paid to redeem the shares differs from the carrying value of the shares, the difference would be a gain or loss to be reported in the current period's earnings.

**Disclosure requirements.** The nature and terms of the financial instruments to which FAS 150 applies, and the rights and obligations embodied in those instruments, must be disclosed. That would include information about settlement alternatives, if any, in the contract, and would furthermore identify the entity that controls the settlement alternatives.

Additionally, for all outstanding financial instruments within the scope of FAS 150, and for each settlement alternative, issuers are required to disclose

1. The amount that would be paid, or the number of shares that would be issued and their fair value, determined under the conditions specified in the contract if the settlement were to occur at the reporting date;
2. How changes in the fair value of the issuer's equity shares would affect those settlement amounts;
3. The maximum amount that the issuer could be required to pay to redeem the instrument by physical settlement, if applicable;
4. The maximum number of shares that could be required to be issued, if applicable;
5. The fact that a contract does not limit the amount that the issuer could be required to pay or the number of shares that the issuer could be required to issue, if applicable; and
6. For a forward contract or an option indexed to the issuer's equity shares, the forward price or option strike price, the number of issuer's shares to which the contract is indexed, and the settlement date or dates of the contract, as applicable.

The definition of liabilities, set forth in CON 6 (see Chapter 1), was to have been revised in conjunction with the promulgation of new standards of accounting for instruments having characteristics of both liabilities and equity. That change will not be made at this time, however, but will be addressed in a subsequent phase of this FASB project. FASB also decided against imposing new requirements to bifurcate embedded derivatives. Furthermore, to prevent the provisions of the new standard from being circumvented by the insertion for nonsubstantive or minimal features into financial instruments, any such features are to be disregarded in applying FAS 150's classification provisions.

### Application of FAS 150

**Example 1: Obligations that require net share settlement—monetary value changes in the same direction as the fair value of the issuer's equity shares**

Tyler Corp. grants 10,000 stock appreciation rights that entitle the holder to receive a number of equity shares to be determined based on the change in the fair value of Tyler's equity shares. At the date of the grant, the fair value of Tyler's equity shares is $25 per share. Subsequently, the fair value of Tyler's equity shares increases to $28 per share. Tyler is thus required to issue shares worth $30,000 [($28 − $25) × 10,000], or 1,072 shares.

This financial instrument contains an obligation to issue a number of equity shares with a value equal to the appreciation of 10,000 equity shares. The number of shares to be issued, therefore, is not fixed. Classification will depend on whether the monetary value changes in the same direction as changes in the fair value of the equity shares. In this example, the monetary value changes in the same direction as changes in the fair value of the equity shares.

The increase in fair value of the equity shares from $25 to $28 resulted in an increase in the monetary value of the obligation from $0 to $30,000. If the fair value of the equity shares increases further, for example to $30 per share, the monetary value of the obligation increases as well to $50,000 [($30 – $25) × 10,000]. If the fair value of the equity shares then decreases, for example from $30 to $27, the monetary value of the obligation decreases to $20,000 [($27 –$25) × 10,000]. Because the monetary value of the obligation changes in the same direction as the change in fair value of the issuer's equity shares, this obligation does not qualify as a liability and the equity classification is prescribed. (Accounting for stock appreciation rights is discussed earlier in this chapter.)

**Example 2: Obligations that require net share settlement—monetary value changes in opposite direction as the fair value of the issuer's equity shares**

Harrison Corp. issues equity shares to Middleboro Co. for $5 million (1 million shares at $5 each). Simultaneously, Harrison enters into a financial instrument with Middleboro, under the terms of which, if the per share value of Harrison' shares is greater than $5 on a specified date, Middleboro will transfer shares of Harrison with a value of [(share price – $5) × 1,000,000] to Harrison. If the per share is less than $5 on a specified date, Harrison transfers shares of its own equity with a value of [($5 – share price) × 1,000,000] to Middleboro.

The 1,000,000 shares issued to Middleboro do not embody an obligation. They also do not convey to the issuer the right to receive cash or another financial instrument from the holder, or to exchange other financial instruments on potentially favorable terms with the holder. Therefore, the equity classification criteria are met and the component is classified as equity.

The financial instrument issued to Middleboro contains an obligation to issue a variable number of equity shares if the fair value of Harrison' equity shares is less than $5 on a certain date. As a result, the classification will depend upon whether the monetary value is equal to the change in fair value of a fixed number of equity shares, and whether the changes are in the same direction as the fair value of the equity shares.

The first criterion is met because the monetary value of the obligation is equal to the appreciation of a fixed number (1,000,000) of the issuer's equity shares. However, the monetary value of the obligation changes in a direction opposite to the changes in the fair value of the issuer's equity shares. If the fair value of the equity shares increases, the monetary value of the obligation decreases (and may in fact be reduced to zero or result in a receivable from the counterparty). If the fair value of the equity shares decreases, the monetary value of the obligation increases. Because the monetary value of the obligation does not change in the same direction as the fair value of the equity shares, criterion (b) is not met; therefore, the obligation is not classified as equity.

**Example 3: Written put options that require physical settlement**

Carlyle Corp. writes a put option that allows a holder, Yetta Co., to put 200 shares of Carlyle stock to Carlyle for $33 per share on a specified date. The put option requires physical settlement (delivery of the shares and payment therefore). Because the put option requires Carlyle to transfer assets (cash) to settle the obligation, the component is classified as a liability.

**Example 3a: Forward purchase contract that requires physical or net cash settlement**

In a fact pattern slightly at variance with the preceding example, Carlyle Corp. enters into a freestanding forward purchase arrangement with Yetta Co., under which Yetta is to transfer 200 shares of Carlyle stock to Carlyle for $33 per share on a specified date. The forward purchase agreement requires physical settlement (delivery of the shares and payment therefore). Because the forward purchase arrangement requires Carlyle to transfer assets (cash) to settle the obligation, the component is classified as a liability. The same result would hold if the contract called for a net cash settlement. While a put option (the preceding example) requires that the liability be initially recorded, and subsequently remeasured, at fair value, the forward purchase arrangement is to be recorded at fair value, and then accreted to the present value of the forward purchase price at each balance sheet date, using the implicit interest rate given by the initial fair value.

### Example 4:  Written put option that require net share settlement

Dragoon Corp. writes a put option that allows the holder, Zitti Corp., to put 200 shares of Dragoon stock to Dragoon for $44 a share on a specified date.  The put requires net share settlement (i.e., shares having a value equal to the spread between the option price and fair value must be delivered in settlement).  Assume the fair value of the shares at the date the put is issued is $44.  The monetary value of the obligation at that time is therefore zero.

Subsequently, the fair value of Dragoon's equity shares decreases to $36 and the put option is exercised.  At this point, the monetary value of the obligation is $1,600 [200 shares × ($44 – $36)].  Dragoon would be required to issue about 45 shares ($1,600 divided by $36).  The monetary value of the obligation increased because of a decrease in the fair value of Dragoon's equity shares.  Because changes in the monetary value of the obligation are not in the same direction as changes in the fair value of Dragoon's equity shares, the component is not classified as equity, but rather as a liability.  The contract is measured initially and subsequently at fair value, with changes in fair value recognized in current earnings.

### Example 5:  Unconditional obligation that must be either redeemed for cash or settled by issuing shares

If the reporting entity issues financial instruments which do not require the transfer of assets to settle the obligation, but instead, unconditionally require the issuer to settle the obligation either by transferring assets or by issuing a variable number of its equity shares, this may or may not create a liability.  Because such instruments do not require the issuer to settle by transfer of assets, they are not automatically classified as liabilities under FAS 150.  However, those instruments may still be classified as liabilities, if other stipulated conditions are met.

Assume that Zylog Corp. issues one million shares of cumulative preferred stock for cash equal to the stock's liquidation preference of $25 per share.  Under the terms, Zylog is required either to redeem the shares on the third anniversary of the issuance, for the issuance price plus any accrued but unpaid dividends, either in cash or by issuing sufficient shares of its common stock to be worth $25 per share.  This does not represent an unconditional obligation to transfer assets, and therefore the preferred stock is not a mandatorily redeemable financial instrument as that term is defined in FAS 150.  However, the stock is still a liability, because the preferred shares represent an unconditional obligation that the issuer may settle by issuing a variable number of its equity shares with monetary value that is fixed and known at inception.  Because the preferred shares are liabilities, payments to holders are reported as interest cost, and accrued but not-yet-paid payments are part of the liability for the shares.

If the redemption price of mandatorily redeemable shares is greater than the book value of those shares, the company should report the excess as a deficit (equity), even though the mandatorily redeemable shares are reported as a liability.

## Disclosure Requirements

Under FAS 129, which consolidates requirements previously set forth in APB 10, APB 15, and FAS 47, certain disclosures of an entity's capital structure are required.  Under this standard, the financial statements will be required to explain, in summary form, the pertinent rights and privileges of the various equity securities outstanding, including dividend and liquidation preferences, participation rights, call prices and dates, conversion and exercise prices or rates along with pertinent dates, sinking fund requirements, unusual voting rights, and significant terms of any contractual obligations to issue additional shares.

Furthermore, the number of shares issued upon conversion, exercise, or satisfaction of required conditions, during at least the most recent annual reporting period and any subsequent interim period that is presented, must be disclosed.  If preference shares have a liquidation preference considerably in excess of par or stated value in the event of involuntary liquidation, the aggregate amount must be disclosed. The amount that would be paid upon exercise of call privileges applicable to preferred shares must be disclosed also, but in this case either per share or aggregate data can be given. Any dividend arrearages on cumulative preferred shares must be stated, on both per share and aggregate bases. Finally, if redeemable preferred shares are outstanding, the amount of redemption requirements for each of the subsequent five years must be given, if fixed or determinable on fixed or determinable dates; if there are several series of such shares, this can be given in the aggregate.

In a staff position, FSP 129-1, FASB has noted that FAS 129 applies to all contingently convertible securities, including those containing requirements that are yet to be met, where the convertible shares are not otherwise required to be included in the computation of diluted EPS in accordance with FAS 128 (see Chapter 20). To comply, the significant terms of the conversion features of such security should be disclosed, in order for users of financial statements to be able to understand the circumstances of the contingency and the potential impact of conversion. The FSP identifies the following quantitative and qualitative terms as potentially being helpful in understanding both the nature of the contingency and the potential impact of conversion:

1. Events or changes in circumstances that would cause the contingency to be met, and significant features necessary to understand the conversion rights and the timing of those rights;
2. The conversion price and the number of shares into which the security is potentially convertible;
3. Events or changes in circumstances, if any, that could adjust or change the contingency, conversion price, or number of shares, including significant terms of those changes; and
4. The manner of settlement upon conversion and any alternative settlement methods (for example, cash, shares, or a combination).

In some instances the reporting entity may enter into derivatives transactions to hedge the impact of the written call option that implicitly is incorporated into contingently convertible instruments. FSP 129-1 states that disclosures of information about such derivative transactions may be useful in terms of fully explaining the potential impact of the contingently convertible securities. Such disclosure could include the terms of those derivative transactions (including the terms of settlement), how those transactions relate to the contingently convertible securities, and the number of shares underlying the derivatives. Of course, all the usual requirements for disclosures of derivatives and hedging activities also would apply.

### Corporate Bankruptcy and Reorganizations

**Entities operating under and emerging from protection of the bankruptcy laws.** The going concern assumption is one of the basic postulates underlying generally accepted accounting principles and is responsible for, among other things, the historical cost convention in financial reporting. For entities that have entered bankruptcy proceedings, however, the going concern assumption will no longer be of central importance.

Traditionally, the basic financial statements (balance sheet, income statement, and statement of cash flows) presented by going concerns were seen as less useful for entities undergoing reorganization. Instead, the statement of affairs, reporting assets at estimated realizable values and liabilities at estimated liquidation amounts, was recommended for use by such organizations. In more recent years, this is less frequently encountered in practice.

SOP 90-7 sets forth certain financial reporting standards for entities undergoing and emerging from reorganization under the bankruptcy laws. Under provisions of this SOP, assets are presented at estimated realizable values. Liabilities are set forth at the estimated amounts to be allowed in the balance sheet and liabilities subject to compromise are to be distinguished from those that are not. Furthermore, the SOP requires that in both the statements of income and cash flows, normal transactions be differentiated from those which have occurred as a consequence of the entity's being in reorganization. While certain allocations to the latter category are rather obvious, such as legal and accounting fees incurred, others are less clear. For example, the standard suggests that if the entity in reorganization earns interest income on funds that would normally have been used to settle obligations owed to creditors, such income will be deemed to be income arising as a consequence of the bankruptcy action.

Another interesting aspect of this standard is the accounting to be made for the emergence from reorganization (known as confirmation of the plan of reorganization). SOP 90-7 provides for "fresh start" financial reporting in such instances. This accounting is similar to that applied to purchase business combinations under APB 16, with the total confirmed value of the entity upon its emergence from reorganization being analogous to the purchase price in an acquisition. In both cases, this total value is to be allocated to the identifiable assets and liabilities of the entity, with any excess being allocated to goodwill. In the case of entities emerging from bankruptcy, goodwill (reorganization value in excess of amounts allocable to identifiable assets) is measured as the excess of liabilities existing at the plan confirmation date, computed at present value of future amounts to be paid, over the reorganization value of assets. Reorganization value is calculated with reference to a number of factors, including forecasted operating results and cash flows of the new entity.

SOP 90-7 applies only to entities undergoing formal reorganization under the Bankruptcy Code. Less formal procedures may still be accounted for under preexisting quasi reorganization accounting procedures.

**Quasi reorganizations.** Generally, this procedure is applicable during a period of declining price levels. It is termed "quasi" since the accumulated deficit is eliminated at a lower cost and with less difficulty than a legal reorganization.

Per ARB 43, Ch. 7A, the procedures in a quasi reorganization involve the

1. Proper authorization from stockholders and creditors where required
2. Revaluation of assets to their current values. All losses are charged to retained earnings, thus increasing any deficit.
3. Elimination of any deficit by charging paid-in capital

   a. First, additional paid-in capital to the extent it exists
   b. Second, capital stock when additional paid-in capital is insufficient. The par value of the stock is reduced, creating the extra additional paid-in capital to which the remaining deficit is charged.

No retained earnings may be created by a reorganization. Any excess created by the reduction of par value is credited to "Paid-in capital from quasi reorganization."

ARB 46 requires that retained earnings be dated for ten years (less than ten years may be justified under exceptional circumstances) after a quasi reorganization takes place. Disclosure similar to "since quasi reorganization of June 30, 20XX" is appropriate.

## Reporting by Limited Liability Companies and Partnerships

Accounting theory and practice have overwhelmingly developed within the context of businesses organized as normal corporations. Accordingly, there is little official guidance to entities organized as partnerships or other forms of business, which is generally not a serious concern given that most transactions entered into by such entities do not differ generically from those conducted by corporations. The primary differences relate to equity transactions and to the display of the equity section of the balance sheet.

AICPA Practice Bulletin (PB) 14 addresses certain issues pertaining to accounting and reporting by limited liability companies and partnerships. This pronouncement establishes that, when an entity restructures itself as a limited liability company or a limited liability partnership, the basis of all assets and liabilities from its predecessor entity are carried forward. Also, as suggested by FAS 109, if the new entity is not a taxable one, any deferred tax assets or liabilities existing previously are to be written off at the time the change in tax status becomes effective; with the elimination of any debit or credit balance being effected by a charge or credit to current period tax expense.

With regard to financial statement display issues, the practice bulletin establishes that the headings of each statement identify the entity as being a limited liability company or a limited liability partnership, similar to the common practice of identifying partnership entities. The apparent logic is that this alerts the user to certain anomalies, such as (most commonly) an absence of income tax expense and a related liability, and the use of somewhat distinctive captions in the equity section of the balance sheet. In the case of limited liability companies and partnerships, the term "members' equity" has been prescribed, and the changes in members' equity is to be communicated either in a separate financial statement, in a combined statement of operations and changes in members' equity, or in the notes to the financial statements.

The bulletin recommends that, where there are several classes of members' equity, these be set forth separately in the equity section of the balance sheet, although this is not a firm requirement. If not set forth in the balance sheet, however, the notes must provide adequate disclosure about the different classes of equity outstanding. This is entirely analogous to the existing GAAP requirements concerning disclosure about common and preferred stock of typical corporations, which has been analogized further to apply to classes of partnership equity in limited partnerships.

A deficit, if one exists, should be reported in the members' equity account(s), even if there is limited liability for the members. This is consistent with the "going concern" assumption that underlies GAAP. It is not required to disaggregate members' equity into separate components (undistributed earnings, unallocated capital, etc.) on the face of the balance sheet or in the notes, although this is of course permissible.

Amounts due from members for capital contributions, if any remain unpaid at the balance sheet date, should be shown as deductions from members' equity. This is entirely consistent with practice for unpaid stock subscriptions receivable.

GAAP presumes that comparative financial statements are more useful than those for a single period, and accordingly that comparative statements should normally be presented. However, for such financial statements to be meaningful, the information for the earlier period must be truly comparable to that of the more recent period. If the formation of the limited liability company or the limited liability partnership results in a new reporting entity being created, the guidance of FAS 154 dealing with changes in accounting entities should be consulted.

PB 14 sets forth certain disclosures to be made in the financial statements of limited liability companies or limited liability partnerships. There should be a description of any limitations on members' equity and of the different classes of members' interests and the respective rights, preferences, and privileges of each class and amounts thereof. If the entity will cease to exist at a stipulated date, this must be disclosed. As suggested above, any change in tax status, and the impact of eliminating any tax liability or benefit from the entity's balance sheet, must be adequately explained in the notes to the financial statements in the period the change in status occurs.

In the period in which a limited liability company or a limited liability partnership is formed by combining entities under common control, or by conversion from another type of entity, the bulletin requires disclosures about the assets and liabilities previously held by the predecessor entity or entities. Entities created by combining predecessors under common control are encouraged, but not required, to make disclosures set forth by APB 16 applicable to poolings.

## APPENDIX A

## FINANCIAL STATEMENT PRESENTATION

This appendix provides an illustration of the various financial statements that may be required to be presented and are related to the stockholders' equity section of the balance sheet.

### Stockholders' Equity Section of a Balance Sheet

| | | | |
|---|---|---:|---:|
| Capital stock: | | | |
| Preferred stock, $100 par, 7% cumulative, 30,000 shares authorized, issued, and outstanding | | | $ 3,000,000 |
| Common stock, no par, stated value $10 per share, 500,000 shares authorized, 415,000 shares issued | | | 4,150,000 |
|     Total capital stock | | | $ 7,150,000 |
| Additional paid-in capital: | | | |
| Issued price in excess of par value—preferred | | $ 150,000 | |
| Issued price in excess of stated value—common | | 845,000 | 995,000 |
|     Total paid-in capital | | | $ 8,145,000 |
| Donated capital | | | 100,000 |
| Retained earnings: | | | |
| Appropriated for plant expansion | | $2,100,000 | |
| Unappropriated | | 2,110,000 | 4,210,000 |
| Accumulated other comprehensive income | | | 165,000 |
|     Total capital, retained earnings, and accumulated other comprehensive income | | | $12,620,000 |
| Less 10,000 common shares held in treasury, at cost | | | (120,000) |
| Total stockholders' equity | | | $12,500,000 |

### Retained Earnings Statement

| | |
|---|---:|
| Balance at beginning of year, as reported | $ 3,800,000 |
| Prior period adjustment—correction of an error in method of depreciation (less tax effect of $77,000) | 115,000 |
| Balance at beginning of year, restated | $ 3,915,000 |
| Net income for the year | 583,000 |
| Cash dividends declared during the year | |
|     Preferred stock | (210,000) |
|     Common stock | (78,000) |
| Balance at end of year | $ 4,210,000 |

**Statement of Changes in Stockholders' Equity**

| | Preferred stock Shares | Amount | Common stock Shares | Amount | Additional paid-in capital | Donated capital | Retained earnings | Accumulated other comprehensive income* | Treasury stock (common) | Total stockholders' equity |
|---|---|---|---|---|---|---|---|---|---|---|
| Balance, 12/31/07, as reported | -- | -- | 400,000 | $4,000,000 | $840,000 | $100,000 | $3,800,000 | $ 56,000 | $(120,000) | $ 8,676,000 |
| Correction of an error in method of depr. | -- | -- | | | | | 115,000 | | | 115,000 |
| Balance, 12/31/07, restated | -- | -- | 400,000 | $4,000,000 | $840,000 | $100,000 | $3,915,000 | | $(120,000) | $ 8,791,000 |
| Preferred stock issued in public offering | 30,000 | $3,000,000 | -- | -- | 150,000 | -- | -- | | -- | 3,150,000 |
| Stock options exercised | -- | -- | 15,000 | 150,000 | 5,000 | -- | -- | | -- | 155,000 |
| Net income | -- | -- | -- | -- | -- | -- | 583,000 | | -- | 583,000 |
| Cash dividends declared: | | | | | | | | | | |
| Preferred, $7.00 per share | -- | -- | -- | -- | -- | -- | (210,000) | | -- | (210,000) |
| Common, $.20 per share | -- | -- | -- | -- | -- | -- | (78,000) | | -- | (78,000) |
| Unrealized holding gains on available-for-sale securities arising during period | | | | | | | | 85,000 | | |
| Less: Reclassification for adjustment of gains included in net income | | | | | | | | (12,000) | | |
| Foreign currency translation adjustments | | | | | | | | 36,000 | | |
| Total other comprehensive income | | | | | | | | 109,000 | | |
| Balance, 12/31/08 | 30,000 | $3,000,000 | 415,000 | $4,150,000 | $995,000 | $100,000 | $4,210,000 | $165,000 | $(120,000) | $12,500,000 |

* Comprehensive income for the period:

Net income $748,000
Other comprehensive income 109,000
$857,000

# 20 EARNINGS PER SHARE

## PERSPECTIVE AND ISSUES

Earnings per share (EPS) is an indicator widely used by both actual and prospective investors to gauge the profitability of a corporation. Its purpose is to indicate how effective an enterprise has been in using the resources provided by its common stockholders. In its simplest form, EPS is net income (loss) divided by the number of shares of outstanding common stock. The EPS computation becomes more complex with the existence of securities that are not common stock but have the potential of causing additional shares of common stock to be issued (e.g., convertible preferred stock, convertible debt, options, and warrants). Omission of an EPS number that takes into account the potential dilutive effects of such securities would be misleading. In addition, a lack of standardization in the way in which these securities are included in such an EPS computation would make comparisons among corporations extremely difficult.

In an effort to integrate with International Financial Reporting Standards and to simplify reporting practices on EPS, the FASB issued FAS 128 in 1997. FAS 128 established standards for computing and presenting EPS for public companies. If, however, a nonpublic company chooses to disclose EPS, it is required to do so in accordance with FAS 128.

Publicly traded corporations with a complex capital structure are obligated to report basic EPS and diluted EPS. The dual presentation is required on the face of the corporation's income statement even if both of these computations result in the same EPS amount. In addition, a reconciliation of the numerator and the denominator of the basic EPS computation to the numerator and denominator of the diluted EPS computation is required.

Basic EPS, which includes no dilution, is computed by dividing income available to common stockholders by the weighted-average number of shares outstanding for the period. In contrast, diluted EPS considers the potential dilution that could occur from other financial instruments that would increase the total number of outstanding shares of common stock.

FAS 129 established standards for disclosing information about an entity's capital structure. This statement consolidated the standards related to the disclosure of information about an entity's capital structure in one pronouncement. FAS 129 applies to all entities, public and nonpublic. Companies are required to disclose the rights and privileges of each type of security outstanding. Examples of disclosures include company policies on participation rights, on the liquidation of preferred stock, and on redeemable stock.

An amendment to FAS 128 is currently under deliberation, the stated purpose for which is to provide for convergence with the corresponding international standard, IAS 33, thereby improving comparability of EPS data on a global basis. In particular, provisions of this draft standard, if enacted, will do the following:

- Amend FAS 128 for calculating the number of incremental shares included in diluted shares when applying the treasury stock method.
- Eliminate the provisions of FAS 128 that allow an entity to rebut the presumption that contracts with the option of settling either in cash or stock will be settled in stock.
- Require that shares that would be issued as a result of conversion of mandatorily convertible securities would be included in the weighted-average number of ordinary shares outstanding used in computing basic earnings per share from the date that the conversion becomes mandatory.
- Contingently issuable shares would be included in diluted EPS from the beginning of the period during which the contingency has been satisfied.
- Retrospective application would be prohibited for contracts that were either settled in cash prior to adoption or modified prior to adoption to require cash settlement.
- Shares issuable upon conversion of a mandatorily convertible instrument would have to be included in the calculation of basic EPS, whether the effect is dilutive or antidilutive.
- Options and warrants with nominal exercise prices should be included in the computation of basic EPS if they are currently exercisable at minimal cost.
- A contract that may be settled in cash or shares would not be treated as being paid in shares if the share settlement only occurs under the legal bankruptcy of the issuer.
- When applying the treasury stock method to an instrument classified as a liability but potentially settled in shares, extinguishment of the liability upon share issuance would be included in proceeds in the computation of incremental shares.

The draft states that after the effective date, all prior period EPS data presented would be adjusted retrospectively. This retrospective adjustment would include interim financial statements, summaries of earnings, and selected financial statements, as well as the annual financial statements. The FASB expects to issue a third exposure draft on this topic during early 2008.

| Sources of GAAP | | | | |
|---|---|---|---|---|
| *APB* | *FAS* | *FIN* | *FTB* | *EITF* |
| 30 | 128, 129, 150, 160 | 28 | 79-8 | 92-3, 00-19, 03-6, 04-08, 05-2, D-42, D-53, D-62, D-72, D-82 |

## DEFINITIONS OF TERMS

There are a number of terms used in the discussion of earnings per share that have special meanings in that context. When used, they are intended to have the meanings given in the following definitions.

**Antidilution (antidilutive).** An increase in earnings per share or reduction in net loss per share resulting from the conversion, exercise, or contingent issuance of certain securities.

**Basic earnings per share (basic EPS).** The portion of net income available to each share of common stock outstanding during the reporting period.

**Call option.** A contract that allows the holder to buy a specified quantity of stock from the writer of the contract at a fixed price for a given period. Refer to **option** and **purchased call option**.

**Common stock.** A stock that is subordinate to all other stock of the issuer.

**Contingent issuance.** A possible issuance of shares of common stock that is dependent upon the exercise of conversion rights, options or warrants, the satisfaction of certain conditions, or similar arrangements.

**Contingent stock agreement.** An agreement to issue common stock (usually in connection with a business combination) that is dependent on the satisfaction of certain conditions.

**Contingently issuable shares (contingently issuable stock).** Shares issuable for little or no cash consideration upon the satisfaction of certain conditions pursuant to a contingent stock agreement.

**Conversion price.** The price that determines the number of shares of common stock into which a security is convertible. For example, $100 face value of debt convertible into five shares of common stock has a conversion price of $20 per share.

**Conversion rate.** The ratio of (1) the number of common shares issuable upon conversion to (2) a unit of convertible security. For example, a class of preferred stock may be convertible at the rate of three shares of common stock for each share of preferred stock.

**Convertible security.** A security that is exchangeable for another security based on a stated rate; for example, convertible preferred stock that is convertible into common stock on a two-for-one basis (two shares of common stock for each share of preferred stock).

**Conversion value.** The current market value of the common shares obtainable upon conversion of a convertible security, after deducting any cash payment required upon conversion.

**Diluted earnings per share (diluted EPS or DEPS).** The portion of net income available to each share of common stock outstanding during the reporting period and to each share that would have been outstanding assuming the issuance of common shares for all dilutive potential common shares outstanding during the reporting period.

**Dilution (dilutive).** A reduction in earnings per share or an increase in net loss per share resulting from assuming that convertible securities have been converted or that options and warrants have been exercised or other shares have been issued upon the fulfillment of certain conditions.

**Dual presentation.**  The presentation with equal prominence of two types of earnings per share amounts on the face of the income statement:  one is basic earnings per share (EPS), the other is diluted earnings per share (DEPS).

**Earnings per (common) share (EPS).**  The amount of net income attributable to each outstanding share of common stock.  For convenience, the term is used in FAS 128 to refer to either net income (earnings) per share or net loss per share.  The term is only permitted to be used without qualifying language when no potentially dilutive convertible securities, options, warrants, or other agreements providing for contingent issuances of common stock are outstanding during the period.

**Exercise price.**  The amount that must be paid for a share of common stock upon exercise of a stock option or warrant.

**If-converted method.**  A method of computing earnings per share that assumes conversion of convertible securities as of the beginning of the earliest period reported (or at the actual time of issuance, if later).

**Income available to common stockholders.**  Income (or loss) from continuing operations or net income (or net loss) adjusted by subtracting preferred stock dividends.

**Mandatorily redeemable instrument.**  A financial instrument, often issued in the form of a share, that requires the issuer to transfer assets to the holder in exchange for canceling the instrument on either a specified date (or dates), or upon occurrence of an event that is certain to occur.  In accordance with FAS 150, such instruments are considered liabilities and are not classified as equity in the issuer's balance sheet.

**Option.**  Unless otherwise stated in FAS 128, a call option that gives the holder the right to purchase shares of common stock in accordance with an agreement upon payment of a specified amount, including, but not limited to, options granted to and stock purchase agreements entered into with employees.  Options are considered "securities" in FAS 128. Refer to **Call option**.

**Potential common stock.**  A security or other contract that may entitle its holder to obtain common stock during the reporting period or after the end of the reporting period.

**Preferred stock.**  A class of capital stock, typically nonvoting, whose holders have rights to receive distributions (dividends or liquidating distributions) that have a higher priority than distributions to the common stockholders.  Common stockholders are not entitled to receive corporate distributions until all required higher-priority distributions to preferred stockholders have been made.

**Purchased call option.**  A contract that allows the reporting entity to buy a specified quantity of its own stock from the writer of the contract at a fixed price for a given period. Refer to **Call option**.

**Put option.**  A contract that allows the holder to sell a specified quantity of stock to the writer of the contract at a fixed price during a given period.

**Redemption price.**  The amount that the issuer of a security is required to pay to the holder at maturity or under a sinking fund arrangement.

**Reverse treasury stock method.**  A method of recognizing the dilutive effect on earnings per share of satisfying a put obligation.  It assumes that the proceeds used to buy back common stock (pursuant to the terms of the put option) will be raised from issuing shares at the average market price during the period.  Refer to **put option**.

**Rights issue.**  An offer to existing stockholders to purchase additional shares of common stock in accordance with an agreement for a specified amount (which is generally substantially less than the fair value of the shares) for a given period.

**Security.**  The evidence of a debt or ownership or related right.  For purposes of FAS 128, it includes stock options and warrants, as well as debt and stock.

**Treasury stock method.** A method of recognizing the use of proceeds that would be obtained upon exercise of options and warrants in computing diluted earnings per share. It assumes that any proceeds would be used to repurchase outstanding common stock at average market prices during the period.

**Two-class method.** A method employed for securities that cannot be accounted for by the if-converted method. This method computes earnings per share by treating participating securities as though they were common stocks with different dividend rates from that of the other common stock.

**Warrant.** A security issued by a corporation entitling the holder to purchase a specified number of shares of stock at a stated price, usually above the stock's market price at the time that the warrant is issued. Similar to call options, warrants are effective for a longer period of time. Warrants are often issued in tandem with another class of security (e.g., bonds or preferred stock) in order to provide an incentive to potential investors to purchase the other security.

**Weighted-average number of shares.** The number of shares outstanding determined by relating (1) the portion of time within a reporting period that a particular number of shares of a certain security has been outstanding to (2) the total time in that period. For example, if 100 shares of a certain security were outstanding during the first quarter of a fiscal year and 300 shares were outstanding during the balance of the year, the weighted-average number of outstanding shares would be 250 [(100 × 1/4) + (300 × 3/4)]. In computing DEPS, equivalent common shares are considered for all dilutive potential common shares.

## CONCEPTS, RULES, AND EXAMPLES

### Simple Capital Structure

Simple capital structures are those having no potential common shares (options, warrants, etc.). These entities will only have basic EPS. All other entities are considered to have a complex capital structure. Entities with a complex capital structure will have potential common stock in the form of potentially dilutive securities, options, warrants, or other rights that upon conversion or exercise would dilute earnings per common share. Dilutive securities have the potential upon their issuance to reduce earnings per share.

**Computational guidelines.** The basic EPS calculation is income available to common stockholders (the numerator) divided by the weighted-average number of common shares outstanding (the denominator) during the period. The objective of the basic EPS calculation is to measure the performance of the entity over the reporting period. Complexities arise because net income does not necessarily represent the earnings available to the common stockholder, and a simple weighted-average of common shares outstanding does not necessarily reflect the true nature of the situation.

**Numerator.** The income available to common stockholders used as the numerator in any of the EPS computations must be reduced by any preferential claims against it by other securities. The justification for this reduction is that the preferential claims of the other securities must be satisfied before any income is available to the common stockholder. These other securities are usually in the form of preferred stock, and the deduction from income is the amount of the dividend declared (whether or not paid) during the year on the preferred stock. If the preferred stock is cumulative, the dividend is deducted from income (added to the loss) whether or not declared. Dividends in arrears do not affect the calculation of EPS in the current period; such dividends have been included in prior periods' EPS computations. However, the amount in arrears is required to be disclosed, as well as the effects on the EPS calculation of the rights given to holders of preferential securities.

If an entity is presenting consolidated financial statements with less than wholly owned subsidiaries, then it should exclude from net income the income attributable to the noncontrolling interest in subsidiaries.

**Denominator.** The weighted-average number of common stock shares outstanding is "an arithmetical mean average of shares outstanding and assumed to be outstanding for EPS computations" (FAS 128). The difficulty in computing the weighted-average exists because of the effect that various transactions have on the computation of common shares outstanding. While it is impossible to analyze all the possibilities, FAS 128 provides discussion of some of the more common transactions affecting the number of common shares outstanding. By analogy, the theoretical model set forth in these relatively simple examples can be applied to situations that are not explicitly discussed.

If a company reacquires its stock (treasury stock), the number of shares reacquired is excluded from EPS calculations as of the date of reacquisition. The same theory holds for the issuance of common stock during the period. The number of shares newly issued is included in the computation only for the period after their issuance date. The logic for this treatment is that the proceeds from issuance of the shares were not available to the company to generate earnings until the shares were issued. This same logic applies to the reacquired shares because the cash paid to reacquire those shares was no longer available to generate earnings after the reacquisition date.

A stock dividend or split does not generate additional consideration, but it does increase the number of shares outstanding. FAS 128 states that the increase in shares as a result of a stock split or dividend, or decrease in shares as a result of a reverse split, is to be given retroactive recognition as an appropriate equivalent charge for all periods presented. Thus, even if a stock dividend or split occurs at the end of the period, it is considered outstanding for the entirety of each period presented. The reasoning is that a stock dividend or split has no effect on the ownership percentage of the common stockholder. As such, to show a dilution in the EPS reported would erroneously give the impression of a decline in profitability when in fact it was merely an increase in the shares outstanding due to the stock dividend or split. FAS 128 carries this principle one step further by requiring the retroactive adjustment of outstanding shares for stock dividends or splits occurring after the end of the period, but before the release of the financial statements. The rationale for this adjustment is that the primary interest of the financial statement user is considered to be the company's current capitalization. If this situation occurs, disclosure of both the end-of-year outstanding shares and those used to compute EPS is required.

When shares are issued in connection with a business combination that occurs during the period, they are treated as issued and outstanding as of the date of the acquisition.

| Weighted-Average (WA) Computation | |
|---|---|
| *Transaction* | *Effect on WA computation* |
| • Common stock outstanding at the beginning of the period | • Included in number of shares outstanding |
| • Issuance of common stock | • Increase number of shares outstanding by the number of shares issued times the portion of the year outstanding |
| • Conversion into common stock | • Increase number of shares outstanding by the number of shares converted times the portion of the year outstanding |
| • Reacquisition of common stock | • Decrease number of shares outstanding by number of shares reacquired times portion of the year since reacquisition |
| • Stock dividend or split | • Increase number of shares outstanding by number of shares issued for the dividend or resulting from the split retroactively as of the beginning of the earliest period presented |
| • Reverse split | • Decrease number of shares outstanding by decrease in shares retroactively as of the beginning of the earliest period presented |
| • Business combination | • Increase number of shares outstanding by number of shares issued times portion of year since acquisition |

The table does not provide for all of the possible complexities arising in the EPS computation; however, most of the others occur under a complex capital structure. The complications arising under a complex capital structure are discussed and illustrated in detail later in this chapter and in its Appendix. The illustration below applies some of the foregoing concepts to a simple capital structure.

### Example of EPS computation—Simple capital structure

Assume the following information:

| | *Numerator information* | | | | *Denominator information* | |
|---|---|---|---|---|---|---|
| a. | Income from continuing operations before extraordinary items | $130,000 | | a. | Common shares outstanding 1/1/09 | 100,000 |
| b. | Extraordinary loss (net of income tax) | (30,000) | | b. | Shares issued for cash 4/1/09 | 20,000 |
| c. | Net income | 100,000 | | c. | Shares issued in 10% stock dividend declared in July 2009 | 12,000 |
| d. | 6% cumulative preferred stock, $100 par, 1,000 shrs. issued and outstanding | 100,000 | | d. | Shares of treasury stock reacquired 10/1/09 | 10,000 |

When calculating the numerator, the claims related to the preferred stock are deducted to arrive at the income available to the common stockholders. In this example, the preferred stock is cumulative. Thus, regardless of whether or not the board of directors declares a preferred dividend, holders of the preferred stock have a claim of $6,000 (= 1,000 shares × $100 par × 6%) against 2009 earnings. Therefore, $6,000 must be deducted from the numerator to arrive at the income available to common stockholders. Note that any cumulative preferred dividends in arrears are ignored in computing this period's EPS since they would have been incorporated into previous periods' EPS calculations. Also note that this $6,000 would have been deducted for *non*cumulative preferred stock only if a dividend of this amount had been declared during the period.

The EPS calculations follow:

*Earnings per common share*

On income from continuing operations before extraordinary item $\dfrac{\$130,000 - \$6,000}{\text{Common shares outstanding}}$

On net income $\dfrac{\$100,000 - \$6,000}{\text{Common shares outstanding}}$

The computation of the denominator is based upon the weighted-average number of common shares outstanding. A simple weighted-average is not considered appropriate because of the various complexities. Table 1 illustrates one way of computing the weighted-average number of shares outstanding.

**Table 1**

| Item | Actual number of shares | Retroactive effects of July stock dividend | Subtotal number of shares deemed outstanding | Fraction of the year deemed outstanding | Shares times fraction of the year deemed outstanding |
|---|---|---|---|---|---|
| Number of shares as of beginning of the year | | 10,000 | | | |
| 1/1/09 | 100,000 | [10%(100,000)] | 110,000 | 12/12 | 110,000 |
| Shares issued 4/1/09 | 20,000 | 2,000 | 22,000 | 9/12 | 16,500 |
| | | [10%(20,000)] | | | |
| Treasury shares reacquired | | | | | |
| 10/1/09 | (10,000) | -- | (10,000) | 3/12 | (2,500) |
| Weighted-average number of common shares outstanding | | | | | 124,000 |

The stock dividend declared in July is treated as being retroactive to the beginning of the year. Thus, for the period 1/1 through 4/1, 110,000 shares are considered to be outstanding. When shares are issued, they are included in the weighted-average beginning with the date of issuance. The shares issued as a result of the stock dividend applicable to the 20,000 newly issued shares are also assumed to have been outstanding for the same period as the 20,000 shares. Thus, we can see that of the 12,000-share stock dividend, 10,000 shares relate to the beginning balance and 2,000 shares to the new issuance (10% of 100,000 and 20,000, respectively). The reacquisition of the treasury stock requires that these shares be excluded from the calculation for the remainder of the period after their reacquisition date. This amount is subtracted from the calculation because the shares were reacquired from shares outstanding prior to their reacquisition.

To complete the example, we divide the previously computed numerator by the weighted-average number of common shares outstanding to arrive at EPS.

*Earnings per common share:*

On income from continuing operations before extraordinary item $\dfrac{\$130,000 - \$6,000}{124,000 \text{ common shares}} = \$1.00$

On net income $\dfrac{\$100,000 - \$6,000}{124,000 \text{ common shares}} = \$0.76$

The numbers computed above are required to be presented on the face of the income statement. Reporting a $.24 extraordinary loss per share ($30,000 extraordinary item ÷ 124,000 common shares) is required either on the face of the income statement or in the notes to the financial statements.

**Preferred stock dividends payable in common shares.** All dividends represent distributions of accumulated earnings, and accordingly, are not reported as expenses on the income statement under GAAP. However, as illustrated above, for purposes of computing earnings per share, preferred dividends must be deducted in order to ascertain how much income is available for common stockholders. In some cases, preferred dividends are not payable in cash, but rather in common shares (based on market value as of the date of declaration, typically). In certain cases, the dividends may be payable in common shares or cash at the issuer's option.

FAS 128 defines income available to common stockholders as "income (or loss) from continuing operations or net income (or net loss) adjusted for preferred stock dividends." Logic suggests that this adjustment be made for all preferred stock dividends, regardless of the form of payment. This adjustment in computing income available to common stockholders is consistent with the treatment of common stock issued for goods or services.

**Example of preferred stock dividends payable in common shares**

Delta Corporation has three classes of preferred stock outstanding as noted in the following table:

| Stock type | Preferred stock description | Total $ issued |
|---|---|---|
| Series A | 7% preferred stock, $100 par value, 3,000 shares outstanding, payable in common stock priced at market value on declaration date | $300,000 |
| Series B | 5% preferred stock, $100 par value, 2,000 shares outstanding, payable in common stock at fixed price of $2.00/share | 200,000 |
| Series C | 8% preferred stock, $100 par value, 1,000 shares outstanding, payable in cash or in common stock at market price on declaration date, at Delta's option | 100,000 |

On the dividend declaration date, the price of a share of common stock is $2.50. Delta's Board of Directors approves the payment of the Series C dividend as 50% cash, 50% common stock. The following table shows the types and amounts of dividends due for all types of preferred stock:

| Stock type | Total dividend due | Applicable common stock price | Number of common shares issued | Cash issued |
|---|---|---|---|---|
| Series A | $21,000 | $2.50 | 8,400 | |
| Series B | 10,000 | 2.00 | 5,000 | |
| Series C | 8,000 | 2.50 | 1,600 | $4,000 |
| | $39,000 | | 15,000 | $4,000 |

Delta has net income of $110,000, from which the total dividend due, regardless of the form of payment, must be subtracted. The calculation follows:

$$\frac{\$110,000 \text{ net income} - \$39,000 \text{ dividend}}{\text{Common shares outstanding}}$$

Delta's fiscal year is the calendar year. Delta had 200,000 shares of common stock outstanding on January 1, issued an additional 30,000 common shares on May 1, and declared the previously described preferred stock dividends on 12/31. Based on this information, the weighted-average number of shares outstanding follows:

| Description | Number of shares | Fraction of the year deemed outstanding | Weighted-average shares outstanding |
|---|---|---|---|
| Number of shares as of 1/1 | 200,000 | 12/12 | 200,000 |
| Common stock issuance on 5/1 | 30,000 | 8/12 | 20,000 |
| Common stock issued on 12/31 as part of preferred stock dividend | 15,000 | 12/12 | 15,000 |
| Weighted-average number of common shares outstanding | | | 235,000 |

Delta divides the 235,000 common shares outstanding into the adjusted net income to arrive at the following earnings per share calculation:

$$\frac{\$110,000 - \$39,000}{235,000 \text{ common shares}} = \$0.30$$

**Effect of preferred stock dividends payable in common shares on computation of EPS.** At the option of the issuer, preferred stock dividends are sometimes payable in either cash or common stock. According to EITF D-82, the form of payment is not a determinant in accounting for the effect of the preferred dividend on net income available to common stockholders. Therefore, for the purposes of the numerator in EPS computations, net income or loss is adjusted to compute the portion available to common stockholders.

## Complex Capital Structure

The computation of EPS under a complex capital structure involves all of the complexities discussed under the simple structure and many more. A complex capital structure is one that includes securities that grant rights with the potential to be exercised and reduce EPS (dilutive securities). Any antidilutive securities (those that increase EPS) are not included in the computation of EPS. Note that a complex capital structure requires dual presentation of basic EPS and diluted EPS (DEPS). The common stock outstanding and all other dilutive securities are used to compute DEPS.

**Diluted earnings per share (DEPS).** DEPS represents the earnings attributable to each share of common stock after giving effect to all potentially dilutive securities which were outstanding during the period. The computation of DEPS requires that the following steps be performed:

1. Identify all potentially dilutive securities.
2. Compute dilution, the effects that the other dilutive securities have on net income and common shares outstanding.

**Identification of potentially dilutive securities.** Dilutive securities are those that have the potential of being exercised and reducing the EPS figure. Some examples of dilutive securities identified by FAS 128 are convertible debt, convertible preferred stock, options, warrants, participating securities, two-class common stocks, and contingent shares.

**Convertible securities.** A convertible security is one type of potentially dilutive security. A security of this type has an inherent dual nature. Convertibles are comprised of two distinct elements: the right to receive dividends or interest, and the right to potentially participate in earnings by becoming a common stockholder. This security is included in the DEPS computation due to the latter right.

**Options and warrants.** Options, warrants, and their equivalents generally derive their value from the right to obtain common stock at specified prices over an extended period of time.

**Participating securities and two-class common stocks.** The capital structure of some entities includes securities that may participate in dividends with common stocks according to a predetermined formula, or a class of common stock with different dividend rates from those of another class of common stock but without prior or senior rights. EITF 03-6 nullified the option of using the if-converted method for those securities that are convertible into common stock if the effect is dilutive. For these securities, participating securities and two-class commons stocks, the two-class method of computing EPS, as described below, is used.

**Financial instruments with characteristics of both liabilities and equity.** FAS 150 specifies that certain freestanding financial instruments (as distinguished from compound financial instruments) that may resemble equity are nevertheless required to be classified as liabilities on the issuer's balance sheet. (See Chapter 19.) Such instruments include mandatorily redeemable financial instruments (including mandatorily redeemable common or preferred stock) and certain forward contracts that require physical settlement by repurchase of a fixed number of the issuer's equity shares. Issuers of these instruments are required to (1) exclude any shares of common stock that are required to be redeemed or repurchased from the denominator of the EPS and DEPS computations, and (2) apply the two-class method described below to deduct from income available to common stockholders (the numerator of EPS and DEPS computations) any amounts that are attributable to shares that are to be redeemed or repurchased, including contractual dividends and participation rights in undistributed earnings. The deduction described in (2) is limited to amounts not recognized in the issuer's financial statements as interest expense.

**Contingent issuances of common stock.** Another consideration is contingent issuances of common stock (e.g., stock subscriptions). If shares are to be issued in the future with no restrictions on issuance other than the passage of time, they are to be considered issued and treated as outstanding in the computation of DEPS. Other issuances that are dependent upon certain conditions being met are to be evaluated in a different manner. FAS 128 uses as examples the maintenance of current earnings levels and the attainment of specified earnings increases. If the contingency is to merely maintain the earnings levels currently being attained, then the shares are considered outstanding for the entire period and considered in the computation of DEPS if the effect is dilutive. If the requirement is to increase earnings over a period of time, the DEPS computation includes those shares that would be issued based on the assumption that the current amount of earnings will remain unchanged if the effect is dilutive. Previously reported DEPS are not restated to give recognition to shares issued as a result of the earnings level attainment. If a contingent issuance is based upon the lapsing of time *and* the market price of the stock (which generally affects the number of shares issued), both conditions must be met to include the contingently issuable shares in the DEPS computation. FASB prohibits restatement of DEPS data should fluctuations in the market price occur in future periods.

**Example of the impact of contingent stock issuances on earnings per share**

Arturo Corporation offers its management team the following set of stock-based incentives that apply to the current year of operations:

- A stock grant of 25,000 common shares if the company attains full-year net income of at least $1 million.
- An additional stock grant of 1,000 common shares for every additional $100,000 of net income recorded above $1 million.
- A stock grant of 50,000 common shares if the company is granted ISO 9001 certification, to be issued immediately upon completion of the certification.

Arturo has 500,000 shares of common stock outstanding throughout the calendar year, which is its fiscal year. It obtains the ISO 9001 certification on April 1. Arturo's full-year net income is $1,300,000. It records the following basic EPS:

$$\frac{\$1,300,000 \text{ net income}}{537,500 \text{ common shares}} = \$2.42$$

The denominator incurs 3/4 of the 50,000 stock grant (e.g., 37,500 shares) associated with completion of the ISO 9001 certification, since the grant occurs after 1/4 of the fiscal year had been completed. The stock grant that is contingent on full-year earnings is not included in the basic earnings per share calculation, since the grant cannot occur until the last day of the year, and therefore has a negligible impact on the calculation

For the DEPS calculation, the contingent stock grant of 25,000 shares associated with the $1 million net income goal is included in the full-year weighted-average, as well as the 3,000 shares associated with the incremental increase in net profits above $1 million and the 50,000 shares associated with the ISO 9001 project completion. The calculation of shares to include in the DEPS denominator follows:

| | |
|---|---:|
| Common stock outstanding | $500,000 |
| Stock grant associated with ISO 9001 project completion | 50,000 |
| Stock grant associated with attainment of $1 million net income goal | 25,000 |
| Stock grant associated with attainment of incremental $300,000 net income goal | 3,000 |
| Total DEPS shares | $578,000 |

By including these shares in the denominator of the DEPS calculation, Arturo arrives at the following diluted earnings per share:

$$\frac{\$1,300,000 \text{ net income}}{578,000 \text{ common shares}} = \$2.25$$

**Computation of DEPS.** The second step in the process is the actual computation of DEPS. There are basically two methods used to incorporate the effects of other dilutive securities on EPS (excluding participating and two-class common securities for which the two-class method described above is used).

1. The treasury stock method, and
2. The if-converted method

**The treasury stock method.** The treasury stock method, which is used for the exercise of most warrants or options, requires that DEPS be computed as if the options or warrants were exercised at the beginning of the period (or actual date of issuance, if later), and that the funds obtained from the exercise were used to purchase (reacquire) the company's common stock at the average market price for the period. Note that the proposed amendment to FAS 128, which is outlined at the end of this chapter, would change this computation slightly. It stipulates that the number of incremental shares included in quarterly and year-to-date diluted EPS shall be computed using the average market price of common shares for the quarterly and year-to-date periods. For example, an entity with a calendar year-end would compute the number of incremental shares used for its second quarter DEPS using the average market price of common shares during the quarter ended June 30, 2009. The number of incremental shares used to calculate year-to-date DEPS at the end of the second quarter would be determined using the average market price of common shares for the year-to-date period ending June 30, 2009. These two average market prices would most likely differ since the one is the average market price for April–June and the other is the average market price for January–June.

An example of the existing requirements under FAS 128 follows. A corporation has warrants outstanding for 1,000 shares of common stock exercisable at $10 per share and the average market price of the common stock is $16 per share, the following would occur: the company would receive $10,000 (1,000 × $10) and issue 1,000 shares from the exercise of the warrants which would enable it to repurchase 625 shares ($10,000 ÷ $16) in the open market. The net increase in the denominator (which effects a dilution in EPS) is 375 shares (1,000 issued less 625 repurchased). If the exercise price is greater than the average market price, the exercise is not assumed since the result would be antidilutive. In that case, DEPS of prior periods presented in comparative form are not restated to reflect the change in market price.

| **Treasury Stock Method** | |
| --- | --- |
| Denominator must be increased by net dilution, as follows: | |
| Net dilution | = Shares issued – Shares assumed to be repurchased |
| *where* | |
| Shares issued | = Proceeds received ÷ Exercise price per share |
| Shares assumed to be repurchased | = Proceeds received ÷ Average market price per share |

**The if-converted method.** The if-converted method is used for those securities that are currently sharing in the earnings of the company through the receipt of interest or dividends as preferential securities, but that have the potential for sharing in the earnings as common stock (e.g., convertible bonds or convertible preferred stock). The if-converted method logically recognizes that the convertible security can only share in the earnings of the company as one or the other, not both. Thus, the dividends or interest less income tax effects applicable to the convertible security as a preferential security are not recognized in income available to common stockholders used to compute DEPS, and the weighted-average number of shares is adjusted to reflect the assumed conversion as of the beginning of the year (or actual date of issuance, if later).

---

**If-Converted Method**

*Numerator*

Income available to common stockholders recomputed to reflect assumed and/or actual conversion

- Add back interest expense less income tax effects
- Convertible preferred dividends are no longer subtracted
- Add back other expenses attributable to convertible issues

- - - - - - - - - - - - - - - - - - - - - - - - - - - - - - - - - - - - - - - - -

*Denominator*

Weighted-average number of shares of common stock outstanding adjusted to reflect the assumed and/or actual conversion of convertible securities at the beginning of the period or actual date of issuance, if later

---

**Exceptions.** Generally, the if-converted method is used for convertible securities, while the treasury stock method is used for options and warrants. There are some situations specified by FAS 128 for which this does not hold true.

1.  If options or warrants permit or require that debt or other securities of the issuer be tendered for all or a portion of the exercise price, the if-converted method is used.
2.  If options or warrants require that the proceeds from the exercise are to be used to retire existing debt, the if-converted method is used.
3.  If convertible securities require cash payment upon conversion, and are, therefore, considered equivalent to warrants, the treasury stock method is used.

**Dual presentation of earnings per share.** DEPS is a pro forma presentation which reflects the dilution of EPS that would have occurred if all contingent issuances of common stock that would individually reduce EPS had taken place at the beginning of the period (or the date actually issued, if later). The presentation of concept of dual earnings per share provides the reader with factually supportable EPS that range from no dilution to the maximum potential dilution. DEPS assumes that all issuances that have the legal right to become common stock exercise that right (unless the exercise would be antidilutive), and therefore anticipates and measures all potential dilution. The dual presentation of EPS and DEPS is prominently displayed on the face of the income statements. The underlying basis for the computation is that of conservatism. The DEPS considers all other potentially dilutive securities but only uses those securities which are dilutive. Thus, in most cases, the DEPS is less than the basic EPS. DEPS can never be greater than the basic EPS, but it could potentially be the same if all of the convertible securities were antidilutive.

*NOTE: The FASB concluded that an entity that reports a discontinued operation, an extraordinary item, or the cumulative effect of an accounting change in a period is to use income from continuing operations as the "control number" for determining whether including potential common shares in the diluted EPS computation would be dilutive or antidilutive. Income from continuing operations (or a similar line item above net income if it appears on the income statement) would be adjusted for preferred dividends. If necessary, refer to FAS 128, footnote 8, for an example.*

### Examples of EPS Computation—Complex Capital Structure

Each of the following independent examples is presented to illustrate the foregoing principles. The procedural guidelines are detailed to enable the reader to understand the computation without referring back to the preceding explanatory text.

#### Example of the treasury stock method

Assume that net income is $50,000 and the weighted-average number of common shares outstanding has been computed as 10,000. Additional information regarding the capital structure is

1.  4% nonconvertible, cumulative preferred stock, par value of $100 per share, 1,000 shares issued and outstanding the entire year

2. Options and warrants to purchase 1,000 shares of common stock at $8 per share were outstanding all year.
3. The average market price of common stock during the year was $10.

The first step in applying this method is the determination of basic EPS. This calculation appears as follows:

$$\frac{\text{Net income} - \text{Preferred dividends}}{\text{Weighted-average number of common shares outstanding}} = \frac{\$50,000 - \$4,000}{10,000 \text{ shares}} = \$4.60$$

The second step is the calculation of DEPS which is based upon outstanding common stock and other dilutive securities. The options and warrants are the only potentially dilutive securities in the example. However, remember that only dilutive options (Market price > Exercise price) are included in the computation. The treasury stock method is used to compute the number of shares to be added to the denominator as illustrated below.

| | |
|---|---|
| Proceeds from assumed exercise of options and warrants (1,000 shares × $8 per share) | $8,000 |
| Number of shares issued | 1,000 |
| Number of shares assumed to be reacquired ($8,000 ÷ $10 average market price per share) | 800 |
| Number of shares assumed issued and not reacquired | 200* |

\* *An alternative approach that can be used to calculate this number for DEPS is demonstrated below.*

$$\frac{\text{Average market price} - \text{Exercise price}}{\text{Average market price}} \times \text{Number of shares under options/warrants} = \text{Shares not reacquired}$$

$$\frac{\$10 - \$8}{\$10} \times 1,000 \text{ shares} = 200 \text{ shares}$$

DEPS can now be calculated as follows, including the effects of applying the treasury stock method:

$$\frac{\text{Net income} - \text{Preferred dividends}}{\substack{\text{Weighted-average number of} \\ \text{common shares outstanding} + \text{Number} \\ \text{of shares assumed issued and not reacquired} \\ \text{with proceeds from options and warrants}}} = \frac{\$50,000 - \$4,000}{10,200 \text{ shares}} = \$4.51$$

Note the dilutive effect of the options and warrants, as EPS of $4.60 is reduced to DEPS of $4.51.

### Table 2
### Computations of Basic and Diluted Earnings Per Share

| | EPS on outstanding common stock (Basic EPS) | | DEPS | |
|---|---|---|---|---|
| *Items* | *Numerator* | *Denominator* | *Numerator* | *Denominator* |
| Net income | $50,000 | | $50,000 | |
| Preferred dividends | (4,000) | | (4,000) | |
| Common shs. outstanding | | 10,000 shs | | 10,000 shs |
| Options and warrants | | | | 200 |
| Totals | $46,000 ÷ | 10,000 shs | $46,000 ÷ | 10,200 shs |
| EPS | | $4.60 | | $4.51 |

### Example of the if-converted method

Assume net income of $50,000 and weighted-average common shares outstanding of 10,000. Additional information regarding capital structure is

1. 7% convertible debt, 200 bonds each convertible into forty common shares. The bonds were outstanding the entire year. The income tax rate is 40%. The bonds were issued at par ($1,000 per bond). No bonds were converted during the year.
2. 4% convertible, cumulative preferred stock, par value of $100 per share, 1,000 shares issued and outstanding. Each preferred share is convertible into two common shares. The preferred stock was issued at par value and was outstanding the entire year. No shares were converted during the year.

The first step is to compute basic EPS. As in the previous example, this is $4.60. The next step is the computation of DEPS assuming conversion of the convertible debt in order to determine whether their conversion would be dilutive. The convertible bonds are assumed to have been converted to common stock at the beginning of the year since no bonds were actually converted during the year. The effects of this assumption are twofold. One, if the bonds are converted, interest expense would be reduced by $14,000 (= 7% × 200 bonds × $1,000 par value per bond); and two, there will be an additional 8,000 shares of common stock outstanding during the year (= 200 bonds × 40 common shares per bond). The effect of avoiding $14,000 of interest expense will increase net income, but it will also increase income tax expense due to the lost income tax deduction. Consequently, the net after-tax effect of avoiding interest expense of $14,000 is $8,400 [= (1 − .40) × $14,000]. DEPS is computed as follows:

$$\frac{\text{Net income} - \text{Preferred dividends} + \text{Interest expense (net of tax)}}{\begin{array}{c}\text{Weighted-average number of common shares}\\ \text{outstanding} + \text{Shares issued upon}\\ \text{conversion of bonds}\end{array}} = \frac{\$50,000 - \$4,000 + \$8,400}{10,000 + 8,000 \text{ shares}} = \$3.02$$

The convertible debt is dilutive because EPS of $4.60 is reduced to DEPS of $3.02.

To determine the dilutive effect of the preferred stock, the preferred stock is assumed to have been converted to common stock at the beginning of the year since no shares of preferred stock were actually converted during the year. The effects of this assumption are twofold. One, if the preferred stock is converted, there will be no preferred dividends of $4,000 for the year; and two, there will be an additional 2,000 shares of common stock outstanding during the year (the conversion rate is 2 for 1 on 1,000 shares of outstanding preferred stock). DEPS considering the preferred stock is computed, as follows, reflecting these two assumptions:

$$\frac{\text{Net income} + \text{Interest expense (net of tax)}}{\begin{array}{c}\text{Weighted-average number of common shares}\\ \text{outstanding} + \text{Shares issued upon conversion}\\ \text{of bonds and conversion of preferred stock}\end{array}} = \frac{\$50,000 + \$8,400}{10,000 + 8,000 + 2,000 \text{ shares}} = \$2.92$$

The convertible preferred stock is also dilutive because DEPS of $3.02 is reduced to DEPS of $2.92.

Together, the effect of the convertible bonds and preferred stock reduces EPS of $4.60 to DEPS of $2.92. In this example the convertible bonds must be considered first, prior to the inclusion of the convertible preferred stock in the computation. For a complete explanation of the sequencing process of including multiple dilutive securities in the computations of DEPS, see the comprehensive example in Appendix A. Table 3 summarizes the computations made for this example.

### Table 3
### Computations of Basic and Diluted Earnings Per Share

| Items | EPS on outstanding common stock (Basic EPS) Numerator | Denominator | DEPS Numerator | Denominator |
|---|---|---|---|---|
| Net income | $50,000 | | $50,000 | |
| Preferred dividend | (4,000) | | | |
| Common shs. outstanding | | 10,000 shs | | 10,000 shs |
| Conversion of preferred | | | | 2,000 |
| Conversion of bonds | | | 8,400 | 8,000 |
| Totals | $46,000 ÷ | 10,000 shs | $58,400 ÷ | 20,000 shs |
| EPS | $4.60 | | $2.92 | |

In the preceding example all of the potentially dilutive securities were outstanding the entire year and no conversions or exercises were made during the year. If a potentially dilutive security was not outstanding the entire year, then the numerator and denominator effects would have to be "time-weighted." For instance, suppose the convertible bonds in the above example were issued during the current year on July 1. If all other facts remain unchanged, DEPS would be computed as follows:

$$\frac{\text{Net income + Interest expense (net of tax)}}{\substack{\text{Weighted-average number of common shares outstanding +} \\ \text{Shares issued upon conversion of preferred stock and} \\ \text{conversion bonds}}} = \frac{\$50,000 + \tfrac{1}{2}(8,400)}{10,000 + 2,000 + \tfrac{1}{2}(8,000)} = \$3.39$$

Since the DEPS of $3.39 is still less than the EPS of $4.60, the convertible debt is dilutive whether or not it is outstanding the entire year.

If actual conversions or exercises take place during a period, the common shares issued upon conversion will be outstanding from their date of issuance, and therefore, will be included in the computation of the weighted-average number of common shares outstanding. These shares are then weighted from their respective dates of issuance. Assume that all the bonds in the above example are converted on July 1 into 8,000 common shares; the following effects should be noted:

1. For basic EPS, the weighted-average of common shares outstanding will be increased by (8,000 shares)(6 months outstanding/12 months in the period) or 4,000. Income will increase $4,200 net of income tax, because the bonds were only outstanding for the first half of the year.

2. For DEPS, the if-converted method is applied to the period January 1 to June 30 because it was during this period that the bonds were potentially dilutive. The interest expense, net of income tax, of $4,200 is added to the net income in the numerator, and 4,000 shares are added to the denominator.

3. Interestingly, the net effect of items 1. and 2. is the same for the period whether these dilutive bonds were outstanding the entire period or converted during the period.

## Participating Securities and the Two-Class Method

Reporting entities that issue securities that are entitled to participate in dividends with common shares will report lower EPS under the provisions of EITF 03-6. This issue addresses the computation of EPS by entities that have issued securities, other than common stock, that entitle the holder to participate in dividends when, and if, dividends are declared on common stock. In addition, EITF 03-6 provides further guidance on calculating EPS using a two-class method and requires companies to retroactively restate EPS amounts presented.

Participation rights are defined based solely on whether the holder is entitled to receive any dividends if the entity declares them during the period. The consensus also requires the use of the two-class method for computing basic EPS when participating convertible securities exist. The use of the two-class method was also expanded by EITF 03-6 to encompass other forms of participating securities, including options, warrants, forwards, and other contracts to issue an entity's common shares (except for unvested share-based compensation awards).

*Presentation and disclosure.* Presentation of participating securities' basic and diluted EPS is not required, but is permitted for other than common stock. What is required by EITF 03-6 is adjustment to the earnings that are used to compute EPS for the common stock.

*Participating security defined.* Determination of participating securities was difficult given the description in FAS 128, so the EITF 03-6 formally defined them as any "security that may participate in undistributed earnings with common stock, whether that participation is conditioned upon the occurrence of a specified event or not, regardless of the form of participation."

*Allocating earnings and losses.* In addition to the amount of dividends declared in the current period, net dividends must be reduced by the contractual amount of dividends or other participation payments that are paid or accumulated for the current period. The allocation of undistributed earnings for a period should be done for a participating security based on the contractual participation rights of the security to share in the current earnings assuming all earnings for the period are distributed. The allocation process is not based on a fair-value analysis, but is based on the term on the securities. For losses, an entity would allocate to the participating securities a portion of the net losses of the entity in accordance with the contractual provisions which may require the security to have an obligation to share in the issuing entity's losses. This occurs when the participating security holder has an obligation to share in the losses of the issuing entity if the holder is obligated to fund the issuing authority's losses or if losses incurred by the issuing entity reduce the security's principal or mandatory redemption amount.

*Two-class method.* This is an earnings allocation formula for computing EPS. It determines EPS for each class of common stock and participating securities according to dividends declared/accumulated and participation rights in undistributed earnings. This consensus requires that the two-class method be applied for participating convertible securities when computing basic EPS. This changes earlier guidance, which permitted reporting entities to make an accounting policy election to use the if-converted method, rather than the two-class method, in the basic EPS calculation, as long as the if-converted method was not less dilutive.

The FASB staff has issued a proposed FASB Staff Position (FSP FAS 128-a) in which it presents computational guidance for computing diluted EPS under the two-class method. The FASB currently expects to integrate this Staff Position into its planned FAS 128 update.

Their three-step process is as follows:

1. Compute the basic EPS using the two-class method.
2. Use the total earnings allocated to common stock in the first step to compute diluted EPS. Then determine the dilutive effect of any potential common shares under two scenarios, and use the more dilutive of the two.

   a. Assume the instrument has been exercised, and that all other dilutive potential common shares have been exercised.
   b. Add back undistributed earnings allocated to the participating security in calculating basic EPS and assume all other dilutive potential common shares have been exercised. Then reallocate undistributed earnings to the common shares and the participating security, including the impact of any additional common shares and income that would result from the exercise of potential common shares.

3. If diluted EPS should be presented, compute it for the second class of common stock by determining the incremental effect of reallocating undistributed earnings to the second class of common stock.

EITF 03-6 states that use of the two-class method is dependent upon having no unsatisfied *contingencies* or objectively determinable contingent events. Thus, if preferred shares are entitled to participate in dividends with common shareholders only if management declares the distribution to be "extraordinary," this would not invoke the use of the two-class computation of EPS. However, if classification of dividends as extraordinary is predetermined by a formula, then undistributed earnings would be allocated to common stock and the participating security based on the assumption that all of the earnings for the period are distributed, with application of the defined sharing formula used for the determination of the allocation to the participating security.

If the participating security participates with common stock in earnings for a period in which a specified event occurs, regardless of whether a dividend is actually paid during the period (e.g., achievement of a target market price or achievement of threshold earnings), then undistributed earnings would be allocated to common stock and the participating security based on the assumption that all of the earnings for the period are distributed. Undistributed earnings would be allocated to the participating security if the contingent condition would have been satisfied at the reporting date, even if no actual distribution was made.

### Example—Participating convertible preferred stock

Assume that Struthers Corp. had 20,000 shares of common stock and 5,000 shares of preferred stock outstanding during 2009, and reported net income of $65,000 for 2009. Each share of preferred stock is convertible into two shares of common stock. The preferred stock is entitled to a noncumulative annual dividend of $5 per share. After the common has been paid a dividend of $1 per share, the preferred stock then participates in any additional dividends on a 2:3 per share ratio with the common. For 2009, the common shareholders have been paid $26,000 (or $1.30 per share), and the preferred shareholders have been paid $26,000 (or $5.20 per share). Basic earnings per share under the two-class method for 2009 would be computed as follows:

|  |  |  |
|---|---:|---:|
| Net income |  | 65,000 |
| Less dividends paid: |  |  |
| Common | $26,000 |  |
| Preferred stock | 26,000 | 52,000 |
| Undistributed 2008 earnings |  | $13,000 |

Allocation of undistributed earnings

*To preferred*

$0.2(5,000) \div [0.2(5,000) + 0.3(20,000)] \times \$13,000 = \$1,857$

$\$1,857 \div 5,000$ shares = $0.37 per share

*To common*

$0.3(20,000) \div [0.2(5,000) + 0.3(20,000)] \times \$13,000 = \$11,143$

$\$11,143 \div 20,000$ shares = $0.56 per share

Basic earnings per share amounts

|  | *Preferred* | *Common* |
|---|---:|---:|
| Distributed earnings | $5.20 | $1.30 |
| Undistributed earnings | 0.37 | 0.56 |
| Total | $5.57 | $1.86 |

### Example—Participating convertible debt instrument

Assume that Wincomp, Inc. had 20,000 shares of common stock outstanding during 2009 and reported net income of $85,000 for the year. On January 1, 2009, Wincomp issues 1,000 30-year, 3% convertible bonds with an aggregate par value of $1,000,000. Each bond is convertible into 8 shares of common stock. After the common has been paid a dividend of $1 per share, the bondholders then participate in any additional dividends on a 2:3 per share ratio with common shareholders. The bondholders receive common stock dividends based on the number of shares of common stock into which the bonds are convertible. The bondholders do not have any voting rights prior to conversion into common stock. For 2009, the Wincomp common shareholders have been paid $20,000 (or $1.00 per share). Basic earnings per share under the two-class method for 2009 would be computed as follows:

|  |  |  |
|---|---:|---:|
| Net income |  | $85,000 |
| Less dividends paid: |  |  |
| Common | $20,000 | 20,000 |
| Undistributed 2008 earnings |  | $65,000 |

Allocation of undistributed earnings

*To convertible bonds*

$0.2(8,000) \div [0.2(8,000) + 0.3(20,000)] \times \$65,000 = \$13,684$

$\$13,684 \div 8,000 \text{ shares} = \$1.71 \text{ per share}$

*To common*

$0.3(20,000) \div [0.2(8,000) + 0.3(20,000)] \times \$65,000 = \$51,316$

$\$51,316 \div 20,000 \text{ shares} = \$2.57 \text{ per share}$

Basic earnings per share amounts

|  | Convertible bonds | Common |
|---|---|---|
| Distributed earnings | $ -- | $1.00 |
| Undistributed earnings | 1.71 | 2.57 |
| Total | $1.71 | $3.57 |

### Example—Participating warrants

Assume that SmithCo. had 15,000 shares of common stock and 1,000 warrants to purchase shares of common stock outstanding during 2009. SmithCo. reported net income of $75,000 for the year. Each warrant entitles the holder to purchase one share of common stock at $10 per share. In addition, the warrant holders receive dividends on the underlying common stock to the extent they are declared. For 2009, common shareholders have been paid $30,000 ($2.00 per share), and the warrant holders have been paid $2,000 (also $2.00 per share). Basic earnings per share under the two-class method for 2009 would be computed as follows:

|  |  |  |
|---|---|---|
| Net income |  | $75,000 |
| Less dividends paid: |  |  |
| Common stock | $30,000 |  |
| Warrants | 2,000 | 32,000 |
| Undistributed 2009 earnings |  | $43,000 |

Allocation of undistributed earnings

*To warrants*

$0.5(1,000) \div [0.5(1,000) + 0.5(15,000)] \times \$43,000 = \$2,687.50$

$\$2,687.50 \div 1,000 \text{ shares} = \$2.69 \text{ per share}$

*To common*

$0.5(15,000) \div [0.5(1,000) + 0.5(15,000)] \times \$43,000 = \$40,312.50$

$\$40,312.50 \div 15,000 \text{ shares} = \$2.69 \text{ per share}$

Basic earnings per share amounts

|  | Common | Warrants |
|---|---|---|
| Distributed earnings | $2.00 | $2.00 |
| Undistributed earnings | 2.69 | 2.69 |
| Total | $4.69 | $4.69 |

## Effect of Contracts That May Be Settled in Stock or Cash on the Computation of DEPS

EITF D-72 deals with the seeming conflict between guidance in EITF 00-19 and FAS 150, on the one hand, and FAS 128, on the other hand, regarding how the option to settle contracts (e.g., written puts on the reporting entity's shares) in stock or cash influences the computation of EPS. FASB staff concluded that in calculating EPS, adjustments should be made to the numerator for contracts that are classified, in accordance with the consensus codified in EITF 00-19, as equity instruments, but for which the company has a stated policy or for which past experience provides a reasonable basis to believe that such contracts will be paid partially or wholly in cash (in which case there will be no potential common shares included in the denominator). Thus, a contract that is reported as an equity instrument for accounting purposes may require an adjustment to the numerator for any changes in income or loss that would result if the contract had been reported as an asset or liability for accounting purposes during the period.

For purposes of computing diluted earnings per share, the adjustments to the numerator described above are only permitted for instruments for which the effect on net income (the numerator) is different depending on whether the instrument is accounted for as an equity instrument or as an asset or liability (e.g., those that are within the scope of FAS 150 or EITF 00-19). The provisions of FAS 128 require that for contracts that provide the company with a choice of settlement methods, the company will assume that the contract will be settled in shares. That presumption may be overcome if past experience or a stated policy provides a reasonable basis to believe that it is probable that the contract will be paid partially or wholly in cash.

EITF D-72 also states that, for contracts in which the holder controls the means of settlement, past experience or a stated policy is not determinative. In those situations, the more dilutive of cash or share settlement should be used.

Adjustment to the numerator in year-to-date diluted EPS calculations may be required in certain circumstances. EITF D-72 cites the example of contracts in which the holder controls the method of settlement and that would have a more dilutive effect if settled in shares, where the numerator adjustment is equal to the earnings effect of the change in the fair value of the asset/liability recorded pursuant to EITF 96-13 during the year-to-date period. In that situation, the number of incremental shares included in the denominator is to be determined by calculating the number of shares that would be required to settle the contract using the average share price during the year-to-date period.

EITF D-72 also notes that antidilutive contracts, such as purchased put options and purchased call options, should be excluded from diluted earnings per share.

FAS 150 requires entities that issue mandatorily redeemable financial instruments or that enter into forward purchase contracts that require physical settlement by repurchase of a fixed number of shares in exchange for cash to exclude the common shares that are to be redeemed or repurchased in calculating EPS and DEPS. Amounts attributable to shares that are to be redeemed or repurchased that have not been recognized as interest costs (e.g., amounts associated with participation rights) are deducted in computing the income available to common shareholders (the numerator of the earnings per share calculations) consistently under the "two-class" method. Therefore, FAS 150's requirements for calculating EPS partially nullify EITF D-72 for those financial instruments. For other financial instruments including those that are liabilities under FAS 150, the guidance in D-72 remains applicable.

### Inclusions/Exclusions from Computation of DEPS

Certain types of instruments and contracts having characteristics of both liabilities and equity require special treatment using the two-class method described previously, if under FAS 150, they are required to be classified as liabilities on the balance sheet of the issuer. Examples of these instruments include mandatorily redeemable common or preferred stock; and forward purchase contracts or written put options on the issuer's equity shares that require physical settlement or net cash settlement.

The computations of DEPS also does not include contracts such as purchased put options and purchased call options (options held by the entity on its own stock). The inclusion of such contracts would be antidilutive.

Sometimes entities issue contracts that may be settled in common stock or in cash at the election of either the issuing entity or the holder. The determination of whether the contract is reflected in the computation of DEPS is based on the facts available each period. It is presumed that the contract will be settled in common stock and the resulting common shares included in DEPS if the effect is dilutive. This presumption may be overcome if past experience or a stated policy provides a reasonable basis to believe that the contract will be paid partially or wholly in cash. The new standard described in the ED at the end of this chapter would preclude the assumption that the contract would be paid in cash, in whole or part. If during the reporting period the exercise price exceeds the average market price for that period, the potential dilutive effect of the contract on EPS is computed using the reverse treasury stock method. Under this method

1. Issuance of sufficient common shares is assumed to have occurred at the beginning of the period (at the average market price during the period) to raise enough proceeds to satisfy the contract.
2. The proceeds from issuance of the shares are assumed to have been used to satisfy the contract (i.e., to buy back shares).
3. The denominator of the DEPS calculation includes the incremental number of shares (the difference between the number of shares assumed issued and the number of shares assumed received from satisfying the contract).

### The Effect of Contingently Convertible Instruments on DEPS

In recent years contingently convertible securities have become more common. EITF 04-8 addresses the impact of the existence of such instruments on the computation of earnings per share. Contingently convertible instruments are those that have embedded conversion features that are contingently convertible or exercisable based either on a market price trigger or on multiple contingencies, if one of the contingencies is a market price trigger and the instrument can be converted or share settled based on meeting the specified market condition. A market price trigger is a condition that is based at least in part on the reporting entity's share price. Examples include contingently convertible debt and contingently convertible preferred stock. A typical trigger occurs when the market price exceeds a defined conversion price by a specified percentage (e.g., when the market price first equals or exceeds 20% more than the conversion price of $33 per share). Others have floating market price triggers for which conversion is dependent upon the market price of the reporting entity's stock exceeding the conversion price by a specified percentage(s) at specified times during the term of the debt. Yet other contingently convertible instruments require that the market price of the issuer's stock exceed a specified level for a specified period (for example, 20% above the conversion price for a 30-day period). In addition, these instruments may have additional features such as parity features, issuer call options, and investor put options.

EITF 04-8 holds that contingently convertible instruments are to be included in diluted earnings per share, if dilutive, regardless of whether the market price trigger has been met. The reasoning is that there is no substantive economic difference between contingently convertible instruments and conventional convertible instruments with a market price conversion premium. EITF 04-8 is to be applied to instruments that have multiple contingencies, if one of these is a market price trigger and the instrument is convertible or settleable in shares based on a market condition being met—that is, the conversion is not dependent on a substantive non-market-based contingency.

#### Example—Contingently convertible debt with a market price trigger

The holder of the Frye Corp. 4% interest-bearing bonds, amounting to $100,000 face value, may convert the debt into shares of Frye common stock when the share price exceeds the market price trigger; otherwise, the holder is only entitled to the par value of the debt. The conversion ratio is 20 shares per bond, or a total of 2,000 shares of stock. The implicit conversion price, therefore, is $50 per share.

At the time of issuance of the bonds, Frye common stock has a market price of $40. Frye's effective tax rate is 35%. Currently Frye has 20,000 shares of its common shares outstanding. The bonds become convertible when the average share price for the year exceeds $65 (130% of conversion price).

The contingently convertible bonds are issued on January 1, 2009. Income available to common shareholders for the year ended December 31, 2009, is $80,000, and the average share price for the year is $55. The issuer of the contingently convertible debt would apply the consensus in EITF 04-8, which requires the reporting entity to include the dilutive effect of the convertible debt in diluted earnings per share even though the market price trigger of $65 has not been met.

Basic EPS is ($80,000 ÷ 20,000 shares =) $4.00 per share. Applying the if-converted method to the debt instrument dilutes earnings per share to $3.77. (To compute diluted EPS, net income is increased by the after-tax effect of interest, and this is then divided by the total of outstanding plus potential common shares.)

## Consolidated DEPS

When computing consolidated DEPS entities with subsidiaries that have issued common stock or potential common shares to parties other than the parent company (minority interests) follow these general guidelines.

1. Securities issued by a subsidiary that enable their holders to obtain the subsidiary's common stock are included in computing the subsidiary's EPS. Per share earnings of the subsidiary are included in the consolidated EPS calculations based on the consolidated group's holding of the subsidiary's securities.

2. For the purpose of computing consolidated DEPS, securities of a subsidiary that are convertible into its parent company's common stock, along with subsidiary's options or warrants to purchase common stock of the parent company, are all considered among the potential common shares of the parent company.

## Partially Paid Shares

If an entity has common shares issued in a partially paid form and the shares are entitled to dividends in proportion to the amount paid, the common-share equivalent of those partially paid shares is included in the computation of basic EPS to the extent that they were entitled to participate in dividends. Partially paid stock subscriptions that do not share in dividends until paid in full are considered the equivalent of warrants and are included in the calculation of DEPS using the treasury stock method.

### Example of impact of partially paid shares on earnings per share

Orion Corporation has 200,000 shares of common stock outstanding. In addition, under a stock subscription plan, investors have paid $30,000 towards the purchase of 4,000 common shares at the fixed price of $15 per share. Investors purchasing shares under the plan are entitled to dividends in proportion to the amount paid. Thus, there are 2,000 shares in the stock subscription plan for the purpose of calculating basic earnings per share, calculated as follows:

$$\frac{4{,}000 \text{ common shares}}{(4{,}000 \text{ common shares} \times \$15/\text{share}) / \$30{,}000 \text{ paid}} = 2{,}000 \text{ shares}$$

Orion records net income of $50,000 for the fiscal year. Its calculation of basic earnings per share follows:

$$\frac{\$50{,}000 \text{ net income}}{2{,}000 \text{ existing common shares} + 2{,}000 \text{ stock subscription shares}} = \$0.25$$

Once the stock subscription plan is completed, with all shares paid for and issued under that earlier plan, Orion creates another plan, which is one that does not allow participants to share in dividends until all payments are completed. Again, participants have thus far paid $30,000 to acquire 4,000 common shares at a fixed price of $15 each. Orion has 204,000 shares of common stock outstanding, and its net income for the current fiscal year is $80,000. The average market price of Orion's stock during the period is $20. Orion calculates the number of additional common shares with the following calculation, which is the same approach used to calculate the number of shares associated with warrants:

| | |
|---|---:|
| Proceeds from assumed purchase of shares in subscription plan (4,000 shares × $15/share) | $60,000 |
| Number of shares to be issued | 4,000 |
| Number of shares assumed to be reacquired ($60,000 / $20 average market price) | 3,000 |
| Number of shares assumed issued and not reacquired | 1,000 |

Orion's DEPS calculation follows:

$$\frac{80,000 \text{ net income}}{204,000 \text{ existing common shares} + 1,000 \text{ shares from stock purchase plan}} = \$0.39$$

Note that Orion's basic EPS is not affected by the shares to be issued under this plan, since no right to dividends exists until the subscription has been fully paid.

## Effect of Certain Derivatives on EPS Computations

FAS 128 did not contemplate certain complex situations having EPS computation implications. In EITF 00-19, the accounting for derivative financial instruments that are indexed to, and potentially to be settled in, the reporting entity's own shares has been addressed. It establishes a model for categorization of a range of such instruments and deals with, *inter alia*, the EPS effects of each of these. The EITF approach assumes that when the entity can elect to settle these instruments by payment of cash or issuance of shares, the latter will be chosen; if the holder (counterparty) has that choice, payment of cash must be presumed. (Certain exceptions exist when the settlement alternatives are not economically equivalent; in those instances, accounting is to be based on the economic substance of the transactions.) As discussed in Chapter 19, balance sheet classification of such instruments is based on consideration of a number of factors, and classification may change from period to period if there are certain changes in circumstances.

For EPS computation purposes, for those contracts that provide the company with a choice of either cash settlement or settlement in shares, EITF 00-19 states that settlement in shares should be assumed, although this can be overcome based on past experience or stated policy. If the counterparty controls the choice, however, the more dilutive assumption must be made, irrespective of past experience or policy.

FAS 128 requires the use of the "reverse treasury stock method" to account for the dilutive impact of written put options and similar derivative contracts, if they are "in the money" during the reporting period. Using this method, an incremental number of shares is determined to be the excess of the number of shares that would have to be sold for cash, at the average market price during the period, to satisfy the put obligation over the number of shares obtained via the put exercise. EITF 00-19 states that, for contracts giving the reporting entity a choice of settlement methods (stock or cash), it should assume share settlement, although this can be overcome if past behavior makes it reasonable to presume cash settlement. If the holder controls settlement method, however, the more dilutive method of settlement must be presumed.

## Effect on EPS of Redemption or Induced Conversion of Preferred Stock

Companies may redeem shares of their outstanding preferred stock for noncash consideration such as by exchanges for other securities. Sometimes the company induces conversion by offering additional securities or other consideration to the holders. Such offers are sometimes referred to as "sweeteners." The accounting for "sweeteners" offered to convertible debt holders was addressed by FAS 84, and was explained in Chapter 15. EITF

Topic D-42 deals with the anomalous situation of "sweeteners" offered to induce conversion of convertible preferred shares.

The position of the SEC staff is that any excess of the fair value of consideration given over the book value of the preferred stock represents a return to the preferred stockholder and, consequently, is to be accounted for similar to dividends paid to the preferred stockholders for purposes of computing EPS. This means that the excess should be deducted from earnings to compute earnings available for common stockholders in the calculation of EPS.

If the converse is true, with consideration given being less than carrying value, including when there is an excess of the carrying amount of the preferred stock over the fair value of the consideration transferred, this should be added to net income to derive earnings available for common stockholders in the calculation of EPS.

If the redemption or induced conversion is effected by offering other securities, rather than cash, fair values would be the referent to determine whether an excess was involved.

Furthermore, per D-42, in computing the carrying amount of preferred stock that has been redeemed or been subject to an induced conversion, the carrying amount of the preferred stock is to be reduced by the related issuance costs irrespective of how those costs were classified in the stockholders' equity section of the balance sheet upon initial issuance.

Since FAS 150 defines mandatorily redeemable preferred stock as a liability, not as equity, the guidance in D-42 would not apply. Rather, any excess or shortfall offered in an induced conversion situation involving mandatorily redeemable preferred stock would be reported as gain or loss on debt extinguishment, not as a dividend.

In a related matter, EITF D-53 discusses the accounting required when a reporting entity effects a redemption or induced conversion of only a portion of the outstanding securities of a class of preferred stock. Reflecting an SEC staff position, any excess consideration should be attributed to those shares that are redeemed or converted. Thus, for the purpose of determining whether the "if-converted" method is dilutive for the period, the shares redeemed or converted should be considered separately from those shares that are not redeemed or converted. It would be inappropriate to aggregate securities with differing effective dividend yields when determining whether the "if-converted" method is dilutive, which would be the result if a single, aggregate computation was made for the entire series of preferred stock.

## EPS Impact of Tax Effect of Dividends Paid on Unallocated ESOP Shares

Accounting for ESOPs, discussed in Chapter 19, was significantly changed by SOP 93-6. Prior to its issuance, dividends paid on unallocated ESOP common stock held by an ESOP were to be charged to retained earnings. EITF 92-3 states that the tax benefits related to dividends paid on unallocated ESOP common stock held by an ESOP that are charged to retained earnings are not deducted from net income when calculating DEPS. EITF 92-3 also applies to convertible ESOP preferred stock when calculating the if-converted DEPS.

Under the provisions of SOP 93-6, dividends paid on unallocated shares are not charged to retained earnings. Since the employer controls the use of dividends on unallocated shares, these dividends are not considered dividends for financial reporting purposes. Consequently, the dividends do not affect the DEPS computation.

## Earnings Per Share Implications of FAS 123(R)

The revised standard FAS 123(R) mandates that share-based employee compensation arrangements must, with very few exceptions, be recognized as expenses over the relevant employee service period. FAS 128 requires that employee equity share options, nonvested shares, and similar equity instruments granted to employees be treated as potential common shares in computing diluted earnings per share. DEPS is to be based on the actual number of options or shares granted and not yet forfeited, unless doing so would be antidilutive. If vesting in or the ability to exercise (or retain) an award is contingent on a performance or market condition (e.g., as the level of future earnings), the shares or share options shall be treated as contingently issuable shares. If equity share options or other equity instruments are outstanding for only part of a reporting period, the shares issuable are to be weighted to reflect the portion of the period during which the equity instruments are outstanding.

FAS 128 provides guidance on applying the treasury stock method for equity instruments granted in share-based payment transactions in determining diluted earnings per share.

In the period of adoption of FAS 123(R), the reporting entity is required to disclose the effect of the change from applying the original provisions of FAS 123 on income from continuing operations, income before income taxes, net income, cash flow from operations, cash flow from financing activities, and basic and diluted earnings per share. In addition, if awards under share-based payment arrangements with employees had been accounted for under the intrinsic value method of APB 25 (see Chapter 19) for any reporting period for which an income statement is presented, all publicly held entities must continue to provide the tabular presentation of the following information that was required by FAS 123 for all those periods:

1.  Net income and basic and diluted earnings per share as reported
2.  The share-based employee compensation cost, net of related tax effects, included in net income as reported
3.  The share-based employee compensation cost, net of related tax effects, that would have been included in net income if the fair-value-based method had been applied to all awards
4.  Pro forma net income as if the fair-value-based method had been applied to all awards
5.  Pro forma basic and diluted earnings per share as if the fair-value-based method had been applied to all awards

The required pro forma amounts are to reflect the difference in share-based employee compensation cost, if any, included in net income and the total cost measured by the fair-value-based (FAS 123(R)) method, as well as additional tax effects, if any, that would have been recognized in the income statement if the fair-value-based method had been applied to all awards. The required pro forma per-share amounts is also to reflect the change in the denominator of the diluted earnings per share calculation as if the assumed proceeds under the treasury stock method, including measured but unrecognized compensation cost and any excess tax benefits credited to additional paid-in capital, were determined under the fair-value-based method.

### Presentation

The reason for the differentiation between simple and complex capital structures is that FAS 128 requires different financial statement presentation for each. FAS 128 mandates that EPS be shown on the face of the income statement for each of the following items (when applicable):

1.  Income from continuing operations
2.  Net income

An entity that reports a discontinued operation, an extraordinary item, or the cumulative effect of a change in accounting principle presents basic and diluted EPS amounts for these line items either on the face of the income statement or in the notes to the financial statements. These requirements must be fulfilled regardless of whether the capital structure is simple or complex. The difference in the two structures is that a simple capital structure requires presentation of only a single EPS number for each item, while a complex structure requires the dual presentation of basic EPS and DEPS for each item.

Earnings per share data is to be presented for all periods for which an income statement or summary of earnings is presented. If DEPS is reported for at least one period, it is to be reported for all periods presented, regardless of whether or not DEPS differs from basic EPS. However, if basic and diluted EPS are the same amounts for all periods presented, dual presentation may be accomplished in one line on the face of the income statement.

**Rights issue.** A rights issue whose exercise price at issuance is below the fair value of the stock contains a bonus element. If a rights issue contains a bonus element (somewhat similar to a stock dividend) and is offered to all existing stockholders, basic and diluted EPS are adjusted retroactively for the bonus element for all periods presented. However, if the ability to exercise the rights issue is contingent on some event other than the passage of time, this retroactive adjustment does not apply until the contingency is resolved.

**Restated EPS.** When a restatement of the results of operations of a prior period is required to be included in the income statement, EPS for the prior period(s) are also restated. The effect of the restatement, expressed in per share terms, is disclosed in the period of restatement. Restated EPS data is computed as if the restated income (loss) had been reported in the prior period(s).

**Year-to-date diluted earnings per share.** EITF D-62 addresses the matter of how to compute year-to-date diluted earnings per share (1) when a company has a year-to-date loss from continuing operations including one or more quarters with income from continuing operations, and (2) when in-the-money options or warrants were not included in one or more quarterly diluted EPS computations because there was a loss from continuing operations in those quarters.

FAS 128 directs that in applying the treasury stock method in year-to-date computations, the number of incremental shares to be included in the denominator is to be determined by computing a year-to-date weighted-average of the number of incremental shares included in each quarterly diluted EPS computation.

However, FAS 128 includes a prohibition against antidilution, which states that the computation of diluted EPS is not to assume conversion, exercise, or contingent issuance of securities that would have an antidilutive effect on earnings per share. There may be a conflict between these provisions when a period longer than three months has an overall loss but includes quarters with income. For period with year-to-date income (as in quarterly filings on Form 10-Q), in computing year-to-date diluted EPS, SEC staff believes that year-to-date income (or loss) from continuing operations should be the basis for determining whether or not dilutive potential common shares not included in one or more quarterly computations of diluted EPS should be included in the year-to-date computation.

According to D-62, (1) when there is a year-to-date loss potential common shares should never be included in the computation of diluted EPS, because to do so would be antidilutive, and (2) when there is year-to-date income, if in-the-money options or warrants were excluded from one or more quarterly diluted EPS computations because the effect was antidilutive (there was a loss from continuing operations in those periods), then those options or warrants should be included in the diluted EPS denominator (on a weighted-average basis) in the year-to-date computation as long as the effect is not antidilutive. Similarly, contingent shares that were excluded from a quarterly computation solely because there was a loss from continuing operations should be included in the year-to-date computation unless the effect is antidilutive.

**Other Disclosure Requirements**

The following additional items are required to be disclosed for all periods for which an income statement is presented:

1. A reconciliation of the numerators and the denominators of the basic and diluted EPS computations for income from continuing operations including the effects of all securities that affect EPS.
2. The effect of preferred dividends in arriving at income available for common stockholders in computing basic EPS.
3. Securities which could potentially dilute basic EPS in future periods but which were not included in DEPS for the period(s) presented since the results were antidilutive.

In addition, for the latest period for which an income statement is presented, a description is required for transactions occurring after the balance sheet date that result in a material change in the number of shares that were outstanding at the balance sheet date.

## APPENDIX

## COMPREHENSIVE EXAMPLE

The examples within the text used a simplified approach for determining whether or not options, warrants, convertible preferred stock, or convertible bonds have a dilutive effect on DEPS. If the DEPS number computed was lower than basic EPS, the security was considered dilutive. This approach is adequate when the company has only *one* potentially dilutive security. If the firm has *more than one* potentially dilutive security, a more complex ranking procedure must be employed (FAS 128).

For example, assume the following facts concerning the capital structure of a company:

1. Income from continuing operations and net income are both $50,000. Income from continuing operations is not displayed on the firm's income statement.
2. The weighted-average number of common shares outstanding is 10,000 shares.
3. The income tax rate is a flat 40%.
4. Options to purchase 1,000 shares of common stock at $8 per share were outstanding all year.
5. Options to purchase 2,000 shares of common stock at $13 per share were outstanding all year.
6. The average market price of common stock during the year was $10.
7. 7% convertible bonds, 200 bonds, each convertible into 40 common shares, were outstanding the entire year. The bonds were issued at par value ($1,000 per bond) and no bonds were converted during the year.
8. 4% convertible, cumulative preferred stock, par value of $100 per share, 1,000 shares issued and outstanding the entire year. Each preferred share is convertible into one common share. The preferred stock was issued at par value and no shares were converted during the year.

Note that reference is made below to some of the tables included in the body of the chapter because the facts above represent a combination of the facts used for the examples in the chapter.

In order to determine both basic EPS and DEPS, the following procedures must be performed:

1. Calculate basic EPS as if the capital structure were simple.
2. Identify other potentially dilutive securities.
3. Calculate the per share effects of assuming issuance or conversion of each potentially dilutive security on an individual basis.
4. Rank the per share effects from smallest to largest.
5. Recalculate EPS (step 1 above) adding the potentially dilutive securities one at a time in order, beginning with the security with the *smallest* per share effect.
6. Continue adding potentially dilutive securities to each successive calculation until all have been added or until the addition of a security increases EPS (antidilution) from its previous level.

Applying these procedures to the facts above

1. Basic EPS

$$\frac{\text{Net income} - \text{Preferred dividends}}{\text{Weighted-average number of common shares outstanding}} = \frac{\$50,000 - \$4,000}{10,000 \text{ shares}} = \$4.60$$

2. Identification of other potentially dilutive securities

     a. Options (two types)
     b. 7% convertible bonds
     c. 4% convertible cumulative preferred stock

## Diluted EPS (DEPS)

3. Per share effects of conversion or issuance of other potentially dilutive securities calculated individually

     a. Options—Only the options to purchase 1,000 shares at $8.00 per share are potentially dilutive. The options to purchase 2,000 shares of common stock are antidilutive because the exercise price is greater than the average market price. Thus, they are not included in the computation.

         Proceeds if options exercised:

$$1,000 \text{ shares} \times \$8 \text{ per share} = \underline{\$8,000}$$

         Shares that could be acquired:

$$\$8,000 \div \$10 = \underline{800}$$

$$\text{Dilutive shares: } 1,000 - 800 = \underline{200}$$

$$\frac{\text{Increase/decrease in net income}}{\text{Increase in weighted-average number of common shares outstanding}} = \frac{\$0}{200 \text{ shares}} = \$0$$

     b. 7% convertible bonds (see Table 3)

$$\frac{\text{Increase/decrease in net income}}{\text{Increase in weighted-average number of common shares outstanding}} = \frac{\$8,400}{8,000 \text{ shares}} = \$1.05$$

     c. 4% convertible cumulative preferred stock—The outstanding common shares increase by 1,000 when all shares are converted. This results in total dividends of $4,000 not being paid.

$$\frac{\text{Increase/decrease in net income}}{\text{Increase in weighted-average number of common shares outstanding}} = \frac{\$4,000}{1,000 \text{ shares}} = \$4.00$$

4. Rank the per share effects from smallest to largest

     a. Options                                      $ 0
     b. 7% convertible bonds                   1.05
     c. 4% convertible cumulative preferred stock     4.00

5. Recalculate the EPS in rank order starting from the security with the smallest per share dilution and adding one potentially dilutive security at a time

     a. DEPS—options added

$$\frac{\text{Net income} - \text{Preferred dividends}}{\text{Weighted-average number of common shares outstanding} + \text{Shares not acquired with proceeds of options}} = \frac{\$50,000 - \$4,000}{10,000 + 200 \text{ shares}} = \$4.51$$

b. DEPS—options and 7% convertible bonds added

$$\frac{\text{Net income} - \text{Preferred dividends} + \text{Interest expense (net of tax)}}{\substack{\text{Weighted-average number of common} \\ \text{shares outstanding} + \text{Shares not acquired} \\ \text{with proceeds of options} + \text{Shares issued} \\ \text{upon conversion of bonds}}} = \frac{\$50,000 - \$4,000 + \$8,400}{\substack{10,000 + 200 + \\ 8,000 \text{ shares}}} = \$2.99$$

c. DEPS—options, 7% convertible bonds and 4% convertible cumulative preferred stock added

$$\frac{\text{Net income} + \text{Interest expense (net of tax)}}{\substack{\text{Weighted-average number of common} \\ \text{shares outstanding} + \text{Shares not} \\ \text{acquired with proceeds of options} + \\ \text{Shares issued upon conversion} \\ \text{of bonds and preferred stock}}} = \frac{\$50,000 + \$8,400}{\substack{10,000 + 200 + \\ 8,000 + 1,000 \\ \text{shares}}} = \$3.04$$

### DEPS = $2.99

Since the addition of the 4% convertible cumulative preferred stock raises DEPS from $2.99 to $3.04, the preferred stock is antidilutive and is therefore excluded from the computation of DEPS.

A dual presentation of basic EPS and DEPS is required. The dual presentation on the face of the income statement would appear as follows:

| | |
|---|---|
| Net income | $50,000 |
| Earnings per common share* (Note X) | $4.60 |
| Earnings per common share, assuming dilution*(Note X) | $2.99 |

\* *The captions "Basic earnings per share" and "Diluted earnings per share" may be substituted, respectively.*

### Note X:  Earnings Per Share (illustrative disclosure based on facts from the Appendix)

The following adjustments were made to the numerators and denominators of the basic and diluted earnings per share computations:

| | Year Ended December 31, 2009 | | |
|---|---|---|---|
| | Income *(numerator)* | Weighted-average number of outstanding shares *(denominator)* | Amount *per share* |
| Net income | $50,000 | | |
| Less:  Preferred stock dividends | (4,000) | | |
| **Basic EPS** | | | |
| Income available to common stockholders | 46,000 | 10,000 | $4.60 |
| **Effects of Dilutive Securities** | | | |
| Options to purchase common stock | | 200 | |
| 7% convertible bonds | 8,400 | 8,000 | |
| **Diluted EPS** | | | |
| Income available to common stockholders adjusted for the effects of assumed exercise of options and conversion of bonds | $54,400 | 18,200 | $2.99 |

There were 1,000 shares of $100 par value, 4% convertible, cumulative preferred stock issued and outstanding during the year ended December 31, 2009, that were not included in the above computation because their conversion would not have resulted in a dilution of earnings per share.

# 21 INTERIM REPORTING

## PERSPECTIVE AND ISSUES

The term "interim reporting" refers to financial reporting for periods of less than a year. GAAP itself does not mandate interim reporting; however, the SEC requires public companies to file quarterly condensed financial information on Form 10-Q. The information required in those interim reports is substantially less than is specified under GAAP for annual financial statements, but the extent of informational content in interim financial statements is an evolving matter. For example, FAS 132(R), as amended by FAS 158, requires expanded disclosures about the costs of pension and other employee benefit plans and associated information in interim reports of both public and nonpublic companies (See Chapter 18 for details).

The basic objective of interim reporting is to provide current information regarding enterprise performance to existing and prospective investors, lenders, and other financial statement users. This enables these users to act upon relevant information in making informed decisions in a timely manner. The demand for timely information (e.g., SEC filings on Form 10-Q are due in no greater than 45 days after period end, whereas filings on Form 10-K are due, depending on entity size, as long as 90 days after year-end) means that interim data will often be more heavily impacted by estimates and assumptions.

There historically have been two competing views of interim reporting. Under the *integral* view, the interim period is considered to be an integral part of the annual accounting period. It thus follows that annual operating expenses are to be estimated and then allocated to the interim periods based on forecasted annual activity levels such as sales volume. The results of subsequent interim periods must be adjusted to reflect the effect of estimation errors in earlier interim periods of the same fiscal year. The APB indicated a preference for the integral view in APB 28, which remains the principal guidance on this topic.

Under the *discrete* view, the interim period is considered to be a discrete accounting period. Thus, estimations and allocations are to be made using the same methods used for annual reporting. It follows that the same expense recognition rules apply as under annual reporting, and no special interim accruals or deferrals would be necessary or permissible. Annual operating expenses are to be recognized in the interim period incurred, irrespective of the number of interim periods benefited (i.e., there would be no special deferral rules for interim periods).

Proponents of the integral view argue that unique interim expense recognition procedures are necessary to avoid fluctuations in period-to-period results that might be misleading to financial statement users. Using the integral view results in interim earnings which are indicative of annual earnings and, thus, arguably more useful for predictive purposes. Proponents of the discrete view argue that the smoothing of interim results for purposes of forecasting annual earnings has undesirable effects. For example, a turning point during the year in an earnings trend could be obscured if smoothing techniques implied by the integral view approach were to be employed.

In response to inconsistencies in interim reporting practices and problems in implementing GAAP in interim reporting, FASB had issued a Discussion Memorandum, *Interim Financial Accounting and Reporting*. A fundamental objective of this project was to resolve the integral/discrete debate. However, FASB made no recommendations and ultimately removed the project from its agenda. The current convergence efforts of FASB and IASB may result in changes to US GAAP for interim reporting, inasmuch as the APB 28 requirements lean toward the integral view (while nonetheless mandating certain discrete view procedures), but the corresponding IFRS (IAS 34) proclaims faithfulness to the discrete view (although certain aspects of that standard are closer to the integral view). Thus a "converged" standard could well differ from one or both of these current standards.

The debate between integral and discrete views of interim reporting is more than academic, and can result in very different interim measures of results of operations. This can occur, for example, because certain annual expenses may be concentrated in one interim period, yet benefit the entire year's operations. Examples include advertising expenses and major repairs and maintenance of equipment. Also, in the US (and many other jurisdictions) progressive (graduated) income tax rates are applied to total annual income and various income tax credits may arise, all of which are computed on annual pretax earnings, making the determination of quarterly income tax expense often complex.

Interim reporting is problematic for reasons other than the choice of an underlying measurement philosophy. As reporting periods are shortened, the effects of errors in estimation and allocation are magnified, and randomly occurring events which might not be material in the context of a full fiscal year could create major distortions in short interim period summaries of reporting entity performance. The effects of seasonal fluctuations and temporary market conditions further limit the reliability, comparability, and predictive value of interim reports.

Furthermore, the seemingly insatiable demand for information (particularly when in the consumers' view such information is available free of charge) is also changing how and how soon interim data is to be reported, and what level of assurance is to be provided by both preparers and independent attesting entities. With the advent of modernized accounting procedures such as the "virtual close," users will in the not-too-distant future be demanding to receive information from reporting entities on a real-time basis.

The spate of well-publicized audit failures in the late 1990s and early 2000s pressured the US Congress to pass the Sarbanes-Oxley Act of 2002 (SOX). Among its provisions is its Section 409, entitled "Real Time Issuer Disclosures" which charges the SEC with rule setting that would require issuers of public company financial statements to

> *...disclose to the public on a rapid and current basis...information concerning material changes in the financial condition or operations of the issuer, in plain English, which may include trend and qualitative information and graphic presentations...*

The issue of independent auditor association with interim financial reports is subject to continuing controversy. The assumption of standard-setting responsibility for audits of "issuers" (i.e., SEC registrants) by the Public Company Accounting Oversight Board

(PCAOB), as mandated by SOX, and the "real-time" demands of users described above, will intensify the pressure on the auditing profession to develop standards to provide real-time continuous assurance to users of financial data regarding its completeness, accuracy and relevance as well as the effectiveness of the design and operation of the reporting entity's internal controls.

Although much of the discussion that follows relates to quarterly reporting, the rules and concepts are equally applicable to reports covering monthly or other interim periods.

| *Sources of GAAP* | | | | |
|---|---|---|---|---|
| *APB* | *FAS* | *FIN* | *FTB* | *EITF* |
| 28 | 16, 69, 95, 109, 123(R) 128, 130, 131, 132(R), 154 | 18 | 79-9 | 86-13, 98-9, D-70 |

## DEFINITIONS OF TERMS

**Discrete view.** A philosophy for measuring interim period results that views each interim period separately without regard to the annual period to which it relates.

**Estimated annual effective tax rate.** The average annual tax rate which reflects the application of graduated income tax rates to estimates of annual earnings, adjusted for the effects of available tax credits.

**Integral view.** A philosophy for measuring interim period results that views each interim period as an integral part of the annual period. Expenses are recognized in proportion to revenues earned through the use of special accruals and deferrals.

**Interim reporting.** Financial reporting for a period of less than a year, (e.g., a month or quarter).

**Last-twelve-months reports.** Financial reporting that covers the twelve-month period ending on a given interim date.

**Liquidation of LIFO inventories.** A LIFO liquidation occurs in an interim period when units sold during that period exceed the number of units purchased during that same period. This results in costs associated with one or more previous years' LIFO layers being released into cost of goods sold.

**Seasonality.** The normal, expected occurrence of a major portion of revenues or costs in the same one or two interim periods (on a consistent basis from year to year).

**Year-to-date reports.** Financial reporting for the period beginning on the first day of the current fiscal year and ending on a given interim date during the year.

## CONCEPTS, RULES, AND EXAMPLES

### Revenues

As explained elsewhere in this book, revenue recognition practices have received a great deal of attention in recent years, largely because of aggressive reporting (including financial reporting fraud) that came to light in a number of restatements of previously issued financial statements and in SEC enforcement actions and private litigation. However, the underlying principles established by GAAP have not been altered and have remained essentially unchanged for many decades, notwithstanding the periodic issuance of certain interpretive literature (such as the SEC's Staff Accounting Bulletins 101 and 104).

Interim reporting GAAP follows the discrete view for revenue recognition. Revenues are recognized as earned during an interim period using the same principles followed in annual reports. This rule applies to both product sales and service revenues. For example, product sales cutoff procedures are applied at the end of each interim period in the same manner that they are applied at year-end, and revenue from long-term construction contracts is recognized at interim dates using the same method used at year-end.

With respect to contingent rental income of lessors, contingent rental income is not to be recognized during interim periods until the target that causes the contingent rental income to be earned is reached (EITF 98-9).

## Product Costs and Direct Costs

Product costs (and costs directly associated with service revenues) are treated in interim reports in the same manner as in annual reports. Thus, in general, the discrete view is followed. However, APB 28 provides for four integral view exceptions, described below.

1. The gross profit method may be used to estimate cost of goods sold and ending inventory for interim periods.
2. When inventory consists of LIFO layers and a portion of the base period layer is liquidated at an interim date, and it is expected that this inventory will be replaced by year-end, the anticipated cost of replacing the liquidated inventory is included in cost of sales of the interim period.
3. An inventory market decline reasonably expected to reverse by year-end (i.e., a decline deemed to be temporary in nature) need not be recognized in the interim period. The Emerging Issues Task Force (Issue 86-13) reached a consensus that there must be substantial evidence available to support the contention that the market value will recover before the inventory is sold which, in the view of members of the Task Force, generally limited this interim exception to seasonal price fluctuations. If an inventory loss from a market decline that is recognized in one period is followed by a market price recovery, the reversal is recognized as a gain in the subsequent interim period. Recognition of this gain in the later interim period is limited to the extent of loss previously recognized. This is in marked contrast to lower of cost or market write-downs in annual financial statements, which are not permitted to be restored in a later period.
4. Reporting entities using standard cost accounting systems ordinarily report purchase price, wage rate, and usage or efficiency variances in the same manner as year-end. Planned purchase price and volume variances are deferred if expected to be absorbed by year-end.

The first exception above eliminates the need for a physical inventory count at the interim date. The other three exceptions attempt to synchronize the quarterly financial statements with the annual report. For example, consider the LIFO liquidation exception. Without this exception, interim cost of goods sold could include low earlier year or base-period costs, while annual cost of goods sold would include only current year costs.

Several questions arise when using LIFO for interim reporting.

1. What is the best approach to estimate interim LIFO cost of sales?
2. As noted above, when an interim liquidation occurs that is expected to be replaced by year-end, cost of sales includes the expected cost of replacement. How is this adjustment treated on the interim balance sheet?
3. How is an interim liquidation that is not expected to be replaced by year-end recorded?

These problems are not addressed in APB 28. The only literature related to these problems is the AICPA Task Force Issues Paper, *Identification and Discussion of Certain Financial Accounting and Reporting Issues Concerning LIFO Inventories.* (See Chapter 9.)

The Issues Paper describes two acceptable approaches to measuring interim LIFO cost of sales. The first approach makes specific quarterly computations of the LIFO effect based on year-to-date amounts. This is accomplished by reviewing quarterly price level changes and inventory levels. The second approach projects the expected annual LIFO effect and then allocates that projection to the quarters. The allocation can be made equally to each quarter or can be made in relation to certain operating criteria per quarter.

The Issues Paper also describes two acceptable approaches to treating the interim liquidation replacement on the balance sheet. The first approach is to record the adjustment for the effect on pretax income of the replacement as a deferred credit in the current liabilities section. The second approach is to record the adjustment as a credit to an inventory valuation allowance.

When an interim LIFO liquidation occurs that is not expected to be reinstated by year-end, the effect of the liquidation is recognized in the period in which it occurs to the extent that it can be reasonably determined. A reporting entity using dollar-value LIFO may allocate the expected effect of the liquidation to the quarters affected.

### Example of interim reporting of product costs

Dakota Corporation encounters the following product cost situations as part of its quarterly reporting:

- It takes physical inventory counts at the end of the second quarter and end of the fiscal year. Its typical gross profit is 30% of sales. The actual gross profit applicable to the first six months of the year is 32%. The actual full-year gross profit is 29%.
- It carries one type of its inventory at LIFO and the remaining inventory at FIFO.
- It suffers a clearly temporary decline of $10,000 in the market value of a specific part of its FIFO inventory in the first quarter, which it recovers in the second quarter.
- It liquidates earlier-period, lower-cost LIFO inventories during the second quarter. The liquidation results in second quarter cost of goods sold being $90,000 less (and, of course, second quarter gross profit being $90,000 more) than it would have been absent the LIFO liquidation. Dakota expects to, and does, restore these inventory levels by year-end.
- It suffers a decline of $65,000 in the market value of its FIFO inventory during the third quarter. The inventory value increases by $75,000 in the fourth quarter.

Dakota computes interim cost of goods sold to reflect the effect of these situations as follows:

| | *Quarter 1* | *Quarter 2* | *First 6 months* | *Quarter 3* | *Quarter 4* | *Full year* |
|---|---|---|---|---|---|---|
| Sales | $10,000,000 | $8,500,000 | $18,500,000 | $7,200,000 | $11,800,000 | $37,500,000 |
| Complement of normal gross profit percentage | 70% | | | 70% | | |
| Cost of goods sold using gross profit method | 7,000,000 | | | 5,040,000 | | |
| Complement of year-to-date gross profit percentage based on actual count | | | 68% | | | 71% |
| Cost of goods sold based on actual count | | | 12,580,000 | | | 26,625,000 |
| Adjustment for effect of temporary LIFO liquidation[3] | | | 90,000 | | | |
| Decline in inventory value[4] | | | | 65,000 | | |
| Adjusted cost of goods sold | $7,000,000 | $5,670,000[1] | $12,670,000 | $5,105,000 | $8,850,000[2] | $26,625,000 |

| | Quarter 1 | Quarter 2 | First 6 months | Quarter 3 | Quarter 4 | Full year |
|---|---|---|---|---|---|---|
| Proof of 4th quarter cost of goods sold[5] | | | | | | |
| Q4 sales × Actual annual gross profit complement | | | | | $ 8,378,000 | |
| Difference between 68% complement based on Q2 count and 71% annual complement × 1st 6 mos sales | | | | | 555,000 | |
| Difference between 70% based on gross profit method used in Q3 and actual annual 71% × Q3 sales | | | | | 72,000 | |
| Q4 recovery of Q3 temporary decline | | | | | (65,000) | |
| Q4 recovery of Q3 temporary decline | | | | | (90,000) | |
| Reversal of Q2 temporary LIFO liquidation | | | | | $ 8,850,000 | |

[1]   *Calculated as adjusted cost of goods sold for first six months – Cost of goods sold recognized during the first quarter.*

[2]   *Calculated as (full year cost of goods sold of $26,625,000 – $12,670,000 cost of goods sold for first half of year – $5,105,000 cost of goods sold recognized during the third quarter).*

[3]   *Full recognition of replacement of earlier period layer in the period that the temporary liquidation was incurred.*

[4]   *No recognition is given to the first quarter temporary decline in value or the subsequent increase because, at the time it occurred, it was expected to be temporary. Full recognition is given to the third quarter market value decline assuming that it was not expected to be temporary. This is followed by recognition of the market value increase, but only to offset the amount of the initial decline.*

[5]   *The "proof" of the fourth quarter cost of goods sold illustrates that the fourth quarter reflects adjustments for the effects of applying the interim costing rules in the other quarters.*

## Other Costs and Expenses

The integral view is more clearly evident in how current US GAAP treats costs incurred in interim periods. Most other costs and expenses are recognized in interim periods as incurred. However, a cost that clearly benefits more than one interim period (e.g., annual repairs or property taxes) is allocated among the periods benefited. The allocation is based on estimates of time expired, benefit received, or activity related to the specific periods. Allocation procedures are to be consistent with those used at year-end reporting dates. However, if a cost incurred during an interim period cannot be readily associated with other interim periods, it is not arbitrarily assigned to those periods. The following parameters are used to account for certain types of interim expenses:

1. Costs expensed at year-end dates that benefit two or more interim periods (e.g., annual major repairs) are assigned to interim periods through the use of deferrals or accruals.
2. Quantity discounts given customers based on annual sales volume are allocated to interim periods on the basis of sales to customers during the interim period relative to estimated annual sales.
3. Property taxes (and like costs) are deferred or accrued at a year-end date to reflect a full year's charge to operations. Charges to interim periods follow similar procedures.

4. Advertising costs are permitted to be deferred to subsequent interim periods within the same fiscal year if the costs clearly benefit the later interim periods. Advertising costs may be accrued and allocated to interim periods on the basis of sales prior to actually receiving the service if the sales arrangement implicitly includes the advertising program. See Chapter 3 for a discussion of the specialized accounting for direct-response advertising prescribed by SOP 93-7. Those rules apply to both interim and annual reporting periods.

5. Lessees are to recognize contingent rental expense in the period before the end of the fiscal year when the achievement of the target that triggers the contingent rental expense becomes probable (EITF 98-9). If the assessment of probable target achievement changes during the year, previously recognized rental expense is reversed.

6. Planned major maintenance expenses must be accrued using the same method for both annual and interim financial reporting periods, while the accrue-in-advance method of accounting is prohibited in all periods (FSP AAG AIR-1).

Costs and expenses subject to year-end determination, such as discretionary bonuses and profit-sharing contributions, are assigned to interim periods in a reasonable and consistent manner to the extent they can be reasonably estimated.

Application of interim expense reporting principles is illustrated in the following examples:

### Example of interim reporting of other expenses

Dakota Corporation encounters the following expense scenarios as part of its quarterly reporting (for illustrative purposes, all amounts are considered to be material):

- Its largest customer, Floor-Mart, placed firm orders for the year that will result in sales of $1,500,000 in the first quarter, $2,000,000 in the second quarter, $750,000 in the third quarter, and $1,650,000 in the fourth quarter. Dakota gives Floor-Mart a 5% rebate if Floor-Mart buys at least $5 million of goods each year. Floor-Mart exceeded the $5 million goal in the preceding year and is expected to do so again in the current year.
- It incurs $24,000 of trade show fees in the first quarter for a trade show that will occur in the third quarter.
- It pays $64,000 in advance in the second quarter for a series of advertisements that will run during the third and fourth quarters.
- It receives a $32,000 property tax bill in the second quarter that applies to the following twelve-month period (July 1 to June 30).
- It incurs annual air filter replacement costs of $6,000 in the first quarter.
- Its management team is entitled to a year-end cash bonus of $120,000 if it meets an annual sales target of $40 million, prior to any sales rebates, with the bonus dropping by $10,000 for every million dollars of sales not achieved.

Dakota used the following calculations to record these scenarios:

| | Quarter 1 | Quarter 2 | Quarter 3 | Quarter 4 | Full year |
|---|---|---|---|---|---|
| Sales | $10,000,000 | $8,500,000 | $7,200,000 | $11,800,000 | $37,500,000 |
| Deduction from sales | (75,000)[1] | (100,000) | (37,500) | (82,500) | (295,000) |
| Marketing expense | | | 24,000[2] | | 24,000 |
| Advertising expense | | | 32,000[3] | 32,000 | 64,000 |
| Property tax expense | | | 8,000[4] | 8,000 | 16,000 |
| Maintenance expense | 1,500[5] | 1,500 | 1,500 | 1,500 | 6,000 |
| Bonus expense | 30,000[6] | 25,500 | 21,600 | 17,900 | 95,000 |

[1] *The sales rebate is based on 5% of actual sales to the customer in the quarter when the sale is made. The actual payment back to the customer does not occur until the end of the year when the $5 million goal is definitively reached.*

[2] *The $24,000 trade show payment is initially recorded as a prepaid expense and then charged to marketing expense when the trade show occurs in the third quarter.*

[3] *The $64,000 advertising payment is initially recorded as a prepaid expense and then charged to advertising expense when the advertisements run.*

[4] *The $32,000 property tax payment is initially recorded as a prepaid expense and then charged to property tax expense on a straight-line basis over the next four quarters.*

[5] *The $6,000 air filter replacement payment is initially recorded as a prepaid expense and then charged to maintenance expense over the one-year life of the air filters.*

[6] *The management bonus is recognized in proportion to the amount of revenue recognized in each quarter. Once it becomes apparent that the full sales target will not be reached, the bonus accrual is adjusted downward. In this case, the downward adjustment is assumed to be in the fourth quarter, since past history and seasonality factors made achievement of the full goal unlikely until fourth quarter results were known.*

*NOTE: With other fact patterns, quarterly accruals may have differed.*

## Income Taxes

At each interim date, the reporting entity is required to make its best estimate of the effective income tax rate expected to apply to the full fiscal year. This estimate reflects expected federal, state, local, and foreign income tax rates, income tax credits, and the effects of applying income tax planning techniques. However, changes in income tax legislation are reflected in interim periods only after the enactment date of the legislation. This process is necessary to avoid distortions that would result if early interim periods reflected the entire effect of lower income tax brackets, while later periods suffered from having all income taxed at higher bracket rates. Since income taxes apply to annual income, not to interim periods on stand-alone bases, an integral approach is clearly warranted.

The accounting for income taxes in interim periods is discussed extensively in Chapter 17.

## Discontinued Operations and Extraordinary Items

Extraordinary items and the effects of the disposal of a component of the entity (as defined by FAS 144) are reported separately in the interim period in which they occur. The same treatment is given to other unusual or infrequently occurring events. No attempt is made to allocate the effects of these items over the entire fiscal year in which they occur.

Materiality is evaluated by relating the item to the expected annual results of operations. Thus, an item to be reported in an early interim period may be judged material but later, when estimated results for the full fiscal year are known with greater precision, be found immaterial; the opposite pattern may also occur, with a presumed immaterial item being later found material to full-year results of operations. Either of such eventualities is inherent in the interim reporting process and would not be deemed an error requiring restatement.

### Example of discontinued operations and extraordinary items

Dakota Corporation's Helena, Montana, facility suffers a direct hit from a tornado during the second quarter. Dakota's management believes the loss warrants treatment as an extraordinary item since the state of Montana does not typically experience tornados. Dakota's insurance does not cover tornados and the loss resulting from cleanup costs and writing down the net book value of the damaged portion of the building is $620,000, or $403,000 net of applicable income taxes computed at a flat 35% rate. As required by FAS 144, Dakota's management estimates the expected future cash flows from the use and ultimate disposition of the property and determines that the building does not require any further write-down for impairment.

In the third quarter, before the tornado repairs are completed, this unfortunate facility is subjected to a flood; however, the unreimbursed damage is only $68,000, or $44,200 net of applicable income taxes. The flood damage is considered material in the third quarter, but subsequently, during the fourth quarter, is determined to be immaterial for annual reporting purposes.

Finally, in the fourth quarter, management declares the facility too damaged to repair, and reclassifies it as held-for-sale. The facility meets the criteria of FAS 144 to be classified as a component of the entity since its operations and cash flows are clearly distinguishable from the rest of Dakota Corporation. Activities conducted at the facility generated income from operations of $82,000 in the first quarter, followed by losses of $102,000, $129,000, and $104,000 in the succeeding quarters, prior to 35% income taxes. Upon classification of the facility as held for sale, the carrying value is written down to its fair value less cost to sell resulting in a further loss of $117,000, which is net of $63,000 in applicable income taxes.

Dakota includes these circumstances in its quarterly and annual financial statement in the following manner:

| | Quarter 1 | Quarter 2 | Quarter 3 | Quarter 4 | Full year |
|---|---|---|---|---|---|
| Income from continuing operations | $814,000 | $629,000 | $483,000 | $505,000 | $2,483,650[1] |
| Discontinued operations: | | | | | |
| Loss from operations of discontinued component, net of applicable income taxes of $36,400 | | | | (67,600)[2] | |
| Loss from operations of discontinued component, net of applicable income taxes of $88,550 | | | | | (164,450)[3] |
| Loss from reclassification of Montana facility as held for sale and adjusting the carrying value to fair value less costs to sell, net of applicable income taxes of $63,000 | | | | (117,000) | (117,000) |
| Loss from discontinued operations | | | | (184,600) | (281,450) |
| Extraordinary items: | | | | | |
| Tornado loss (less applicable income taxes of $217,000) | | (403,000) | | | (403,000) |
| Flood loss (less applicable income taxes of $23,800) | | | (44,200) | | 0[1] |
| Net income | $814,000 | $226,000 | $438,800 | $320,400 | $1,799,200 |

[1] *The full-year income from continuing operations does not match the total of quarterly income from continuing operations, because the third-quarter classification of flood damage is not considered extraordinary for annual reporting purposes, and so is added back into annual income from continuing operations. Annual income is also reduced by operating losses in the discontinued facility for the full year, which were retained in income from continuing operations for the first three quarters. Full-year income from continuing operations is computed as follows:*

| | |
|---|---|
| *Sum of operating income for four quarters* | *$2,431,000* |
| *– Extraordinary loss shifted back to operating income* | *(44,200)* |
| *+ After-tax effect of first three quarters of losses on discontinued operations* | *96,850* |
| *= Full-year income from continuing operations* | *$2,483,650* |

[2] *The facility is classified as discontinued in the fourth quarter; there is no requirement to restate prior interim statements to show the loss from operations of the facility in earlier quarters.*
[3] *The full-year financial statement reflects the full-year loss from discontinued operations.*

Note that classification as an extraordinary item is based on facts and circumstances, given the requirement under GAAP that the event be both infrequent in occurrence and unusual in nature. If the plant were located in Kansas, for example, and tornado damage did not qualify under both criteria given its location, then this would not have been presented as an extraordinary item.

## Accounting Changes

The following discussion relates to accounting changes made in interim financial statements of privately held companies. The special considerations that apply to public companies are discussed later in this chapter. The treatment of accounting changes in annual reports is covered extensively in Chapter 5.

**Change in accounting principle.** APB 28 requires disclosure in interim financial statements of any changes in accounting principles or the methods of applying them from those that were followed in

1. The prior fiscal year;
2. The comparable interim period of the prior fiscal year; and
3. The preceding interim periods of the current fiscal year.

The information to be included in these disclosures is the same as is required to be included in annual financial statements and is to be provided in the interim period in which the change occurs, subsequent interim periods of that same fiscal year, and the annual financial statements that include the interim period of change.

FAS 154 requires changes in accounting principle to be adopted through retrospective application to all prior periods presented. This accounting treatment is the same in both interim and annual financial statements. The impracticability exception provided by FAS 154 is only applicable to annual financial statements and may not be invoked for prechange interim periods occurring in the same fiscal year as the change is made.

**Change in accounting estimate.** Changes in accounting estimate are required by FAS 154 to be accounted for currently and prospectively. Retroactive restatement and presentation of pro forma amounts are not permitted. This accounting is the same whether the change occurs at the end of a year or during an interim reporting period.

**Change in reporting entity.** When an accounting change results in the financial statements presenting a different reporting entity than was presented in the past, all prior periods presented in the new financial statements, including all previously issued interim financial information, are to be retroactively restated to present the financial statements of the new reporting entity. In restating the previously issued information, however, interest previously capitalized under FAS 58 with respect to equity method investees that have not yet commenced their planned principal operations, is not to be changed.

**Restatements.** The term "restatement" is only to be used to describe a correction of an error from a prior period. Under FAS 154 and APB 9, when a restatement is made, the financial statements of each individual prior period presented (whether interim or annual) are to be adjusted to reflect correction of the effects of the error that relate to that period. Full disclosure of the restatement is to be provided in the financial statements of the

1. Interim period in which the restatement was first made;
2. Subsequent interim periods during the same fiscal year that includes the interim period in which the restatement was first made; and
3. Annual period that includes the interim period in which the restatement was first made.

## Contingencies

In general, contingencies and uncertainties that exist at an interim date are accrued or disclosed in the same manner required for annual reports. For example, contingent losses that are probable and subject to reasonable estimation are to be accrued. The materiality of the contingency is evaluated in relation to the expected annual results. Disclosures regarding material contingencies and uncertainties are to be repeated in all interim and annual reports until they have been removed, resolved, or become immaterial.

The following adjustments or settlements are accorded special treatment in interim reports if they relate to prior interim periods of the current fiscal year:

1. Litigation or similar claims
2. Income taxes (except for the effects of retroactive tax legislation enacted during an interim period)
3. Renegotiation proceedings associated with government contracts
4. Utility revenue under rate-making processes

If the item is material, directly related to prior interim periods of the current fiscal year in full or in part, and becomes reasonably estimable in the current interim period, it is reported as follows:

1. The portion directly related to the current interim period is included in that period.
2. Prior interim periods are restated to reflect the portions directly related to those periods.
3. The portion directly related to prior years is recognized in the restated first interim period of the current year.

### Example of interim reporting of contingencies

Dakota Corporation is sued over its alleged violation of a patent in one of its products. Dakota settles the litigation in the fourth quarter. Under the settlement terms, Dakota must retroactively pay a 3% royalty on all sales of the product to which the patent applies. Sales of the product are $150,000 in the first quarter, $82,000 in the second quarter, $109,000 in the third quarter, and $57,000 in the fourth quarter. In addition, the cumulative total of all sales of the product in prior years is $1,280,000. Dakota restates its quarterly financial results to include the following royalty expense:

|  | *Quarter 1* | *Quarter 2* | *Quarter 3* | *Quarter 4* | *Full year* |
|---|---|---|---|---|---|
| Sales related to lawsuit | $150,000 | $82,000 | $109,000 | $57,000 | $398,000 |
| Royalty expense | 4,500 | 2,460 | 3,270 | 1,710 | 11,940 |
| Royalty expense related to prior years' sales | 38,400 |  |  |  | 38,400 |

## Seasonality

The operations of many businesses are subject to recurring material seasonal variations. Such businesses are required to disclose the seasonality of their activities to avoid the possibility of misleading interim reports. APB 28 also recommends that such businesses supplement their disclosures with information for twelve-month periods ending at the interim date of the current and preceding year.

## Interim Reporting Considerations for Public Companies

**Quarterly reporting.** Condensed (summarized) unaudited interim financial statements are required to be filed with the SEC on a quarterly basis on Form 10-Q (Regulation S-X, Rule 10-01) or, for entities qualifying as small businesses, on Form 10-QSB. The minimum captions and disclosures required to be included in these financial statements are summarized in the Disclosure Checklist in Appendix A. Although such financial statements are informational tools used by investors, creditors, and analysts, they are not presented in sufficient detail to constitute a fair presentation of the reporting entity's financial position and results of operations in accordance with GAAP.

With the issuance of FAS 148 in December 2002, new interim disclosures were required regarding share-based employee compensation if the employer elected to use the APB 25 intrinsic value method in any period presented. FAS 123(R), issued in December 2004, ended the use of the APB 25 intrinsic value method and, accordingly, rescinded both APB 25 and FAS 148.

**Period of adoption disclosures.** In the interim period in which a new accounting principle is adopted, the SEC expects registrants to include in the quarterly condensed financial statements a complete set of the disclosures required to be included in annual financial statements. In addition, these complete disclosures are to be repeated in the interim condensed financial statements of the quarters immediately succeeding the quarter of adoption until an annual Form 10-K is filed that reflects the registrant's adoption of the new accounting principle. However, the SEC considers the reporting requirements of FASB Interpretation 48, *Accounting for Uncertainty in Income Taxes*, to be unduly burdensome for interim reporting, and so limits the Interpretation's disclosure requirements to the total amount of unrecognized tax benefits recorded, while excluding the tabular and other forms of the Interpretation from interim reporting.

**Fourth quarter adjustments.** When, as is typical, the fourth quarter results are not reported separately, the annual financial statements of publicly traded companies are required to include note disclosure of the effects on the fourth quarter of accounting changes made during the quarter; disposals of components of the reporting entity; extraordinary, unusual, or infrequently occurring items; and the aggregate effect of year-end adjustments having a material effect on the quarter's results.

**Earnings per share.** The same procedures used at year-end are used for earnings per share computations and disclosures in interim reports. Note that annual earnings per share generally will not equal the sum of the interim earnings per share amounts, due to such factors as stock issuances during the year and market price changes. No reconciliation requirements exist for such disparities.

**Accelerated reporting requirements.** In order to provide stakeholders with relevant, actionable information on a more timely basis, the SEC requires certain events that occur between regular quarterly reporting deadlines to be reported on its Form 8-K in accordance with an accelerated timetable. In response to the "real time issuer disclosure" mandate in Section 409 of the Sarbanes-Oxley Act of 2002, eight new items were added to the form and the 8-K filing deadline for most items was shortened to four business days after the occurrence of the triggering event. Events subject to accelerated reporting requirements are set forth below.

Form 8-K

| Item number | Event requiring disclosure |
| --- | --- |
| 1.01 | Entry into "material definitive agreement" that provides for rights or obligations material to and enforceable by or against the registrant |
| 1.02 | Termination of material definitive agreement |
| 1.03 | Bankruptcy or receivership |
| 2.01 | Completion of acquisition or disposition of significant amounts of assets (other than in the ordinary course of business) |
| 2.02 | Disclosure of material nonpublic information regarding a completed fiscal year or quarter |
| 2.03 | Creation of a direct financial obligation or an obligation under an off-balance-sheet arrangement |
| 2.04 | Triggering events that accelerate or increase a direct financial obligation or an obligation under an off-balance-sheet arrangement |
| 2.05 | Costs associated with exit or disposal activities |

Additional accelerated reporting requirements apply to issuers of asset-backed securities under Section 6 of the Form 8-K instructions.

# 22 SEGMENT REPORTING

## PERSPECTIVE AND ISSUES

With many companies organized as diversified holding companies or conglomerates, the presentation of basic consolidated financial statements on an aggregated basis does not provide users with sufficient information for decision-making purposes. The objective of segment reporting, as set forth in FAS 131, is to

*...provide information about the different types of business activities in which an enterprise engages and the different economic environments in which it operates to help users of financial statements:*

    *a. Better understand the enterprise's performance*
    *b. Better assess its prospects for future net cash flows [and]*
    *c. Make more informed judgments about the enterprise as a whole.*

The primary benefit of segment reporting is the release of "hidden data" from consolidated financial information. Different segments may possess different levels of profitability, risk, and growth. This important information is merged and thus "averaged out" in the consolidated amounts. Assessing future cash flows and their associated risks can be aided by segment data. For example, knowledge of the level of reporting entity operations in a growing or declining product line can help in the prediction of cash flow, while knowledge of the scope of reporting entity operations in an unstable geographic area can help in the assessment of risk. In general, information about the nature and relative size of an enterprise's various business operations is considered useful by decision makers.

Segment reporting is an important tool in analyzing companies that are diversified in terms of the types of businesses in which they engage or the geographic locations in which they operate. In addition, financial analysts have consistently requested that financial statement data be more disaggregated. Academic research has also demonstrated the value of disaggregated information for economic decision-making purposes.

FAS 131, *Disclosures about Segments of an Enterprise and Related Information,* currently governs the way publicly held businesses are required to report disaggregated information in financial reports to stockholders, including interim reports. The statement defines operating segments as distinct revenue-producing components of the reporting entity about which separate financial information is produced internally, and whose operating results are regularly reviewed by the reporting entity.

The approach used in FAS 131 is a "management approach," meaning it is based on the way management organizes segments internally to make operating decisions and assess performance. The management approach, in general, provides that external financial reporting will closely conform to internal reporting, thus giving financial statement users the ability to view the reporting entity's segments in the same manner as internal decision makers.

Financial information can be segmented in several ways: by types of products or services, by geography, by legal entity, or by type of customer. FAS 131 requires that each reportable segment report, among other items, its profit or loss, certain specific revenues and expenses, and its assets. Management is required to reconcile segment information with its consolidated general-purpose financial statements.

In addition, FAS 131 requires that all public companies report information on a company-wide basis about revenues for each product and service, about countries in which revenues are earned and assets are held, and about its major customers, even if this information is not used by management in making operating decisions.

The statement does not limit segment reporting to purely financial information. It also requires a description of the company's rationale or methods employed in determining the composition of the segments. This description includes the products or services produced by each segment, differences in measurement practices between segments and the consolidated entity, and differences in the segments' measurement practices between periods.

The corresponding international standard, which until recently was IAS 14, differed in some important respects from FAS 131, although as revised effective 1998 it did impose a management perspective to the definition of segments. With the replacement of IAS 14 by newly adopted IFRS 8, however, the IASB has now fully "converged" to the US GAAP approach. IFRS 8, which becomes mandatorily effective in 2009, requires that an entity report financial and descriptive information about its *reportable segments.* Reportable segments are defined as *operating segments* or aggregations thereof that meet certain defined criteria. Operating segments are components of an entity about which separate financial information is available that is evaluated regularly by the chief operating decision maker in deciding how to allocate resources and in assessing performance. Generally, segment financial information is required to be reported on the same basis as is used internally for evaluating operating segment performance and deciding how to allocate resources to operating segments.

## Recent Developments

The full convergence of the international standard, IFRS 8, with US GAAP's FAS 131, is the most significant recent development in segment reporting practice. It is furthermore important in demonstrating that, while an overall trend to universal utilization of IFRS is clearly discernible, IASB remains open to making changes to IFRS based on recognition of superior principles promulgated by other standard-setting bodies.

The Accounting Staff of the SEC's Division of Corporation Finance, in its periodically updated document, *Current Accounting and Disclosure Issues in the Division of Corporation Finance,* has as recently as November 2006 identified compliance with segment disclosure requirements as being a "significant focus of staff reviews." The principal concern was that foreign registrants were still making use of a "products and services" typology, rather than the "management approach" mandated by FAS 131. The Staff emphasized certain matters that had arisen as a result of those reviews and communicated the level of scrutiny that they were going to be applying to registrants' filings.

1. The chief operating decision maker (CODM) is not necessarily a single person. Rather, it is to be considered a function that may be carried out be several persons.

2. The Staff may challenge registrants' exclusion of components of the business from being considered operating segments when the CODM receives reports of that component's operating results on a quarterly or more frequent basis. In some cases, the Staff requested copies of all reports furnished to the CODM and reviewed internal documentation for its consistency with public statements made by members of the management and related press coverage. The Staff pointed out that there may be mitigating circumstances whereby the CODM receives reports on overlapping sets of components that are more representative of the way the reporting entity is managed.

3. As discussed later in this chapter, the Staff believes the aggregation of segments is a "high hurdle" and is appropriate only in situations when the user's understanding of the reporting entity's results and future prospects would not be enhanced by separate reporting.

4. The Staff reminded registrants to identify the products and services from which each reportable segment derives its revenues, and to report the total revenues from external customers for each product or service or each group of similar products and services. The Staff has observed that, based on their reviews of filings, registrants have taken "overly broad views" of what constitutes similar products. The Staff has, in some cases, reviewed public disclosures and marketing materials containing descriptions of the registrants' products.

5. Some registrants manage their segments based on geographic areas of operations and report accordingly. The Staff points out that, even when this is the case, the registrant is still required to provide separate disclosures with respect to each individual country in which revenues are material. This may be accomplished by providing material country disclosures as separate subtotals within each region.

6. Registrants must clearly quantify and explain each material reconciling item between the segment disclosures and the consolidated financial statements, including identification of measurement differences and asymmetrical allocations among segments.

7. The Staff provided interpretive guidance on the requirement that the registrant recast prior information for comparative purposes when changes are made (or are being contemplated) in the structure of the segments.

8. The Staff noted that, since the identification of reporting units can have a significant impact on the determination of goodwill impairment charges, registrants should disclose how goodwill is allocated to reporting units, and whether there have been changes in the manner in which goodwill is allocated.

| Sources of GAAP | | |
|---|---|---|
| *FAS* | *FTB* | *EITF* |
| 131 | 79-4, 79-5 | 04-10, D-70 |

## DEFINITIONS OF TERMS

**Assets test.** One of the three 10% tests; used to determine whether operating segments are separately reportable.

**Chief operating decision maker (CODM).** The person(s) at the reporting entity level whose general function (not specific title) is to allocate resources to, and assess the performance of, the segments. Within a reporting entity, this authority does not necessarily need to be vested in a single individual; rather, the responsibilities can be fulfilled by a group of individuals.

**Common costs.** Operating expenses incurred by the reporting entity for the benefit of more than one segment.

**Corporate assets.** Assets maintained for general corporate purposes and not used in the operations of any segment.

**Expenditures for segment assets.** Additions to a segment's long-lived assets; generally, property, plant, and equipment.

**Financial report.** Includes any aggregation of information that includes one or more complete sets of financial statements, such as an annual report to stockholders or a filing with the Securities and Exchange Commission.

**Foreign operations.** Operations located outside of the reporting entity's home country that generate either unaffiliated or intersegment revenues.

**General corporate expenses.** Expenses incurred for the benefit of the corporation as a whole, which cannot be reasonably allocated to any segment.

**Geographic area.** An individual country (domestic or foreign).

**Intersegment sales.** Transfers of products or services, similar to those sold to unaffiliated customers, between operating segments.

**Major customer.** A customer responsible for at least 10% of a reporting entity's revenues.

**Management approach.** The method chosen by FASB to determine the information to be reported; it is based on the way that management organizes the segments internally for making operating decisions and assessing performance.

**Nonpublic company.** A company other than one (1) whose debt or equity securities trade in a public market on a foreign or domestic stock exchange, or in the over-the-counter market (including securities quoted only locally or regionally) or (2) that is required to file financial statements with the US Securities and Exchange Commission. A company is no longer considered nonpublic when its financial statements are issued in preparation for the sale of any class of securities in a public market. Nonpublic companies include certain mutual associations, cooperatives, nonbusiness organizations, and partnerships that often make their financial statements available to a broad class, such as insurance policyholders, depositors, members, contributors, or partners.

**Operating segment.** A component of a reporting entity that earns revenues and incurs expenses, about which separate financial information is available that is evaluated regularly by the CODM in deciding how to allocate resources and in assessing performance.

**Profit center.** Those components of a reporting entity that sell primarily to outside markets and for which information about revenue and profitability is accumulated. They are the smallest units of activity for which revenue and expense information is accumulated for internal planning and control purposes.

**Profit and loss test.** One of the three 10% tests; used to determine whether operating segments are separately reportable.

**Reportable segments.** Segments considered to be significant to the operations of the reporting entity; a segment that has passed any one of the three defined 10% tests (assets, revenues, or profit and loss), or has been identified as being reportable through other criteria (e.g., aggregation, etc.).

**Revenues test.** One of three 10% tests; used to determine whether operating segments and major customers are reportable.

**Segment assets.** Those tangible and intangible assets directly owned or used by a segment, including any allocated portion of assets used jointly by more than one segment.

**Segment manager.** The person(s) accountable to the reporting entity's chief operating decision maker (CODM, as defined above) for one or more operating segment's activities, financial results, budgets, forecasts, and operating plans. The reporting entity's CODM can also serve as segment manager for one or more operating segments.

**Segment profit or loss.** All of a segment's revenues and gains minus its expenses and losses, including any similar items allocated to it by the reporting entity.

**Segment reporting.** Disclosure of information about different components of a reporting entity's operations, as well as information related to its products and services, geographic areas of operations, and major customers.

**Segment revenue.** Revenue from sales to unaffiliated customers and from intersegment sales or transfers.

**75% test.** A test used to determine whether the reportable segments of a reporting entity represent a sufficient portion of its total operations.

**Transfer pricing.** The pricing of products or services between segments or geographic locations.

## CONCEPTS, RULES, AND EXAMPLES

### Applicability of FAS 131

FAS 131 applies to public companies. The statement does not mandatorily apply to not-for-profit organizations or to nonpublic companies—which are, nevertheless, encouraged to voluntarily provide the segment disclosures prescribed by FAS 131.

### Operating Segments

In FAS 131, an operating segment is defined as a component of a reporting entity

a.  That engages in business activities that may generate revenues and incur expenses from transactions with external parties and/or with other components of the same reporting entity (intersegment transactions),
b.  About which discrete financial information is available, and
c.  Whose operating results are reviewed regularly by the reporting entity's chief operating decision maker (CODM) in order to assess the segment's performance and make resource allocation decisions.

Operating segments frequently have a segment manager function that communicates on an ongoing basis with the reporting entity's CODM. The segment manager is not necessarily a single individual but rather the segment management responsibility can vest functionally in a committee or group of designated individuals. Additionally, an operating segment is not necessarily revenue generating from its inception, as it may be in a start-up phase.

Not all activities that occur within the reporting entity are allocable to its operating segments. Activities that are non-revenue-producing or that are incidental to the reporting entity are not considered to be operating segments such as corporate headquarters or certain functional departments. FAS 131 specifies that the reporting entity's pension and other postretirement benefit plans are not considered to be operating segments.

This rather general definition means that management's judgment will be relied upon to determine operating segment classifications. However, FASB believes meaningful segment information will be provided in external financial reports because the externally reported segment information must conform with the segment information that is used internally.

### Reportable Segments

A segment is considered to be a reportable segment if it is significant to the enterprise as a whole because it satisfies one of the three quantitative 10% tests described below.

**Revenues test.** Segment revenue (unaffiliated and intersegment) is at least 10% of the combined revenue (unaffiliated and intersegment) of all operating segments.

**Profit and loss test.** The absolute amount of segment profit or loss is at least 10% of the greater, in absolute amount, of

1. Combined profits of all operating segments reporting a profit
2. Combined losses of all operating segments reporting a loss

EITF Topic D-70 clarifies that, if the CODM uses different measures of profit or loss to evaluate the performance of different segments (e.g. net income versus operating income), the reporting entity is to use a single, consistent measure for the purposes of this profit and loss test. This does not, however, affect the requirement that the reporting entity disclose the measure of profit or loss used by the CODM for the purposes of decision making regarding the segment's performance and resources to be allocated to the segment.

**Assets test.** Segment assets are at least 10% of the combined assets of all operating segments. Segment assets include those assets used exclusively by the segment and the allocated portion of assets shared by two or more segments. Assets held for general corporate purposes are not assigned to segments.

Interperiod comparability must be considered in conjunction with the results of the 10% tests. If a segment fails to meet the tests in the current reporting period, but has satisfied the tests in the past and is expected to in the future, it is considered as being reportable in the current year for the sake of comparability. Similarly, if a segment which rarely passes the tests does so in the current year as the result of an unusual event, that segment may be excluded to preserve comparability.

After the 10% tests are completed, a 75% test must be performed. The combined unaffiliated revenue of all reportable segments must be at least 75% of the combined unaffiliated revenue of all operating segments. If the 75% test is not satisfied, additional segments must be designated as reportable until the test is satisfied. The purpose of this test is to ensure that reportable segments account for a substantial portion of the entity's operations.

The following example illustrates the three 10% tests and the 75% test.

| Operating segment | Unaffiliated revenue | Intersegment revenue | Total revenue | Segment profit | Segment (loss) | Assets |
|---|---|---|---|---|---|---|
| A | $ 90 | $ 12 | $ 102 | $11 | $ -- | $ 70 |
| B | 120 | -- | 120 | 10 | -- | 50 |
| C | 110 | 20 | 130 | -- | (40) | 90 |
| D | 200 | -- | 200 | -- | -- | 140 |
| E | 140 | 300 | 440 | -- | (100) | 230 |
| F | 380 | -- | 380 | 60 | -- | 260 |
| G | 144 | -- | 144 | 8 | -- | 30 |
| Total | $1,184 | $332 | $1,516 | $89 | $(140) | $870 |

*NOTE: Because the $140 total segment losses exceed the $89 total segment profits, the $140 is used for the 10% test.*

**Summary of Test Results**

*x = Passed test – Reportable segment*

| *Operating segment* | *Total revenues (10% of $1,516 = $152)* | *Segment profit/loss (10% of $140 = $14)* | *Assets (10% of $870 = $87)* | *75% of unaffiliated revenues test* |
|---|---|---|---|---|
| A | | | | |
| B | | | | |
| C | | x | x | $110 |
| D | x | | x | 200 |
| E | x | x | x | 140 |
| F | x | x | x | 380 |
| G | | | | |
| | | | | 830 |
| | | | 75% of $1,184 | 888 |
| | | | Revenue shortfall | $ (58) |

Note that the aggregate revenues of the reportable segments that passed the 10% tests are $58 short of providing the required coverage of 75% of unaffiliated revenues. Consequently, an additional operating segment (A, B, or G) will need to be added to the reportable segments in order to obtain sufficient coverage.

Certain other factors must be considered when identifying reportable segments. Management may consider aggregating two or more operating segments if

1. They have similar economic characteristics,
2. Aggregation is consistent with the objective and basic principles of FAS 131, and
3. The segments are similar in all of the following areas:

    a. The nature of the products and services
    b. The nature of the production processes
    c. The type of customer for their products and services
    d. The methods used to distribute their products or provide their services
    e. The nature of the regulatory environment

This aggregation can occur prior to performing the 10% tests if management desires.

In their analyses, financial statement preparers have allegedly often ignored the second factor presented above in making aggregation decisions. The SEC, in particular, was quick to note that the paramount consideration should be the achievement of the financial reporting objectives of FAS 131 (i.e., providing useful information to financial statement users, allowing them to gain an understanding of management's decision making processes regarding operation of the business). With that in mind, the authors emphasize that aggregation decisions should be made carefully, and only after concluding that the information loss due to aggregation would not impede such understanding by financial statement users.

Management may *optionally* combine information on operating segments that do not meet any of the 10% tests to produce a reportable segment, but only if the segments being combined have similar economic characteristics and also share a majority of the five aggregation criteria listed above (EITF 04-10).

Note that information about operating segments that do not meet any of the 10% thresholds may still be disclosed separately. By utilizing the aggregation criteria and quantitative thresholds (10% tests) for determining reportable segments, FAS 131 uses what should be considered a modified management approach.

The number of reportable segments should not be so great as to decrease the usefulness of segment reporting. As a rule of thumb, FASB suggests that if the number of reportable segments exceeds ten, segment information may become too detailed. In this situation, the most closely related operating segments should be combined into broader reportable segments, again, however, subject to the objectives inherent in FAS 131's requirements.

Refer to the discussion of alternative balance sheet segmentation and the accompanying diagram in Chapter 2. It provides an example of the different components of a reporting entity used for various accounting and reporting purposes.

## Accounting Issues

Since segment revenue as defined by FAS 131 includes intersegment sales, transfer pricing becomes an issue. Rather than establishing a basis for setting transfer prices, FASB requires companies to use the same transfer prices for segment reporting purposes as are used internally. Since most segments are organizational profit centers, internal transfer prices would generally reflect market prices, but even if this is not the case, these same transfer prices must be used for segment disclosures. This is consistent with the management approach adopted by FAS 131.

Another issue in determining profit or loss is the allocation of common costs. Common costs are expenses incurred by the reporting entity for the benefit of more than one operating segment. Again, segment reporting is required to conform to internal management reporting. Accordingly, these costs are only allocated to a segment for external reporting purposes if they are included in the measure of the segment's profit or loss that is used internally by the CODM.

Difficulties can arise in distinguishing common costs from general corporate expenses. General corporate expenses are not direct expenses from the point of view of any operating segment; they are incurred for the benefit of the corporation as a whole and cannot be reasonably attributed to any operating segment. Common costs, on the other hand, benefit two or more segments and can be allocated to those segments in a manner determined by management to support internal decision making by the reporting entity.

Similarly, only those assets that are included internally in the measure of the segment's assets used to make operating decisions are reported as assets of the segment in external financial reports. If management allocates amounts to segment profit or assets internally and those amounts are used by the CODM, then those amounts are to be allocated on a reasonable basis and disclosed.

## Segment Disclosures

FAS 131 requires disclosures regarding the reporting entity's reportable segments that include

1. **General information**—An explanation of how management identified the reporting entity's reportable segments, including whether operating segments have been aggregated, is to be presented. Additionally, a description of the types of products and services from which each reportable segment derives its revenues is to be provided.
2. **Certain information about reported segment profit and loss, segment assets and the basis of measurement**—This will include certain revenue and expense items included in segment profit and loss, as well as certain amounts related to the determination of segment assets. Also, the basis of measurement for these items must be disclosed.
3. **Reconciliations**—Management must reconcile the segment amounts disclosed to the corresponding consolidated reporting entity amounts.
4. **Interim period information**—Although the interim disclosures are not as extensive as in the annual financial report, certain segment disclosures are required in interim financial statements.

See the comprehensive illustration of the disclosures required for segment reporting provided later in this chapter. Additionally, FAS 131 provides an illustrative example.

## Entity-Wide Disclosures

In addition to segment data, FAS 131 mandates that certain entity-wide disclosures be made. The entity-wide disclosures are required for all reporting entities subject to FAS 131, even those that have only a single reportable segment.

**Products and services.** Revenue from external customers for each product and service or each group of similar products and services is to be reported by the reporting entity unless impracticable. If deemed to be impracticable, that fact is to be disclosed. If the company's reportable segments have been organized around products and services, then this disclosure will generally not be required.

**Geographic areas.** A reporting entity separately discloses revenues from external customers and long-lived assets attributable to its domestic operations and foreign operations. If the reportable segments have been organized around geographic areas, then these disclosures will generally not be required because they would be duplicative.

Domestic operations are those operations located in the reporting entity's home country that generate either unaffiliated or intersegment revenues. Foreign operations are similar operations located outside of the home country of the reporting entity. For the purposes of these disclosures, US reporting entities' operations in Puerto Rico are not considered to be foreign operations although management is not precluded from voluntary disclosure regarding Puerto Rican operations (FTB 79-4).

If the reporting entity functions in two or more foreign geographic areas, to the extent revenues or assets of an individual foreign geographic area are material, then these amounts are separately disclosed. In addition, disclosure is required of the basis for attributing revenue to different geographic areas. A geographic area is defined as an individual country. If providing this information is impracticable, that fact is to be disclosed.

**Major customers.** If the reporting entity earns 10% or more of its revenue on sales to a single external customer, that fact and the amount of revenue from each such customer must be disclosed. Also, the segment making these sales must be disclosed. This disclosure provides information on concentrations of risk.

For the purpose of this disclosure, a group of customers under common control, such as subsidiaries of a common parent, is regarded as a single customer. Similarly the various agencies of a government are considered to be a single customer. An insuring entity (such as Blue Cross) is not considered to be the customer unless that entity (rather than the patient) controls the decision as to the doctor, type of service, etc.

## Restatement of Previously Reported Segment Information

Segment reporting is required on a comparative basis when the associated financial statements are comparative. Therefore, the information must be restated to preserve comparability whenever the reporting entity has changed the structure of its internal organization in a manner that causes a change to its reportable segments. Management must explicitly disclose that it has restated the segment information of earlier periods.

## Comprehensive Illustration

The following illustration is provided for a hypothetical company, Resources Unlimited. The illustration provides segment disclosures by legal entity.

*NOTE: FAS 131 provides illustrative segment disclosures by product line.*

**Description of the types of products and services from which each reportable segment derives its revenues.** Resources Unlimited has four reportable segments: Wholesale Corporation, Retail Corporation, Library Corporation, and Software Corporation. Wholesale Corporation buys and resells used elementary and college textbooks. Retail Corporation operates 200 college book stores and a related e-commerce Web site selling both new and used college textbooks, trade books, sports apparel, and other sundries. Library Corporation sells library books primarily to elementary school libraries. Software Corporation develops and sells library systems application software.

**Measurement of segment profit or loss and segment assets.** The accounting policies of the segments are the same as those described in the summary of significant accounting policies except the first-in-first-out (FIFO) method of inventory valuation is used for segment reporting. In addition, Resources Unlimited allocates interest expense to each segment based on the segment's average borrowings from the corporate office. However, the related debt is not allocated to the segments and remains on the corporate balance sheet. Resources Unlimited evaluates performance based on profit or loss before income taxes not including nonrecurring gains and losses.

Resources Unlimited accounts for intersegment sales and transfers as if the sales or transfers were transacted with third parties (i.e., at current market prices).

**Factors management used to identify reportable segments.** Resources Unlimited's business is conducted through four separate legal entities that are wholly owned subsidiaries. At the company's inception, each entity was founded and managed by a different Resources Unlimited stockholder/family member. Each corporation is still managed separately, as each business has a distinct customer base and requires different strategic and marketing efforts.

**Information about profit and loss and assets.** The amounts in the illustration are assumed to be the amounts in reports used by the CODM. Resources Unlimited allocates interest expense to the segments, however it does not allocate income taxes and unusual items to them.

|  | *($000 omitted)* | | | | |
| --- | --- | --- | --- | --- | --- |
|  | *Wholesale Corporation* | *Retail Corporation* | *Library Corporation* | *Software Corporation* | *Totals* |
| Revenues from external customers | $197,500 | $263,000 | $182,300 | $102,200 | $745,000 |
| Intersegment revenues | 23,000 | -- | -- | -- | 23,000 |
| Interest revenue | 250 | 150 | -- | -- | 400 |
| Interest expense | 1,570 | 2,150 | 1,390 | 2,700 | 7,810 |
| Depreciation and amortization* | 8,600 | 13,100 | 7,180 | 6,070 | 34,950 |
| Segment profit | 12,100 | 13,500 | 9,900 | 5,100 | 40,600 |
| Segment assets | 121,200 | 153,350 | 100,600 | 85,000 | 460,150 |
| Expenditures for segment assets | 7,200 | 12,700 | 5,600 | 6,700 | 32,200 |

\* *Depreciation and amortization are required to be disclosed for each operating segment even if the CODM evaluates segment performance using predepreciation measures such as earnings before income taxes, depreciation, amortization (EBITDA) (EITF D-70)*

**Reconciliations.** An illustration of reconciliations for revenues, profit and loss, assets, and other significant items is shown below. In general, this illustration assumes that there are no unreported operating segments, but there is a corporate headquarters, thus most reconciling items relate to corporate revenues and expenses.

As discussed previously, the company recognizes and measures inventory based on FIFO valuation for segment reporting. The consolidated financial statements are assumed not to include discontinued operations or the cumulative effect of a change in accounting principle.

|  | *($000 omitted)* |
|---|---|
| **Revenue** |  |
| Total revenues for reportable segments | $768,000 |
| Elimination of intersegment revenue | (23,000) |
| Total consolidated revenue | $745,000 |
| **Profit and loss** |  |
| Total profit for reportable segments | $40,600 |
| Elimination of intersegment profits | (6,100) |
| Unallocated amounts relating to corporate operations: |  |
| Interest revenue | 500 |
| Interest expense | (800) |
| Depreciation and amortization | (1,900) |
| Unrealized gain on trading securities | 1,865 |
| Income before income taxes and extraordinary items | $34,165 |
| **Assets** |  |
| Total assets for reportable segments | $460,150 |
| Corporate short-term investments, land and building | 25,100 |
| Adjustment for LIFO reserve in consolidation | (9,200) |
|  | $476,050 |

**Other significant items**

|  | *Segment totals* | *Adjustments* | *Consolidated totals* |
|---|---|---|---|
| Expenditures for segment assets | $32,200 | 800 | $33,000 |

The reconciling adjustment is the amount of expenditures incurred for additions to the corporate headquarters building, which is not included in the segment information.

**Products and services.**

| | |
|---|---|
| Used textbooks | $296,125 |
| New textbooks | 72,150 |
| Trade books | 45,700 |
| Sports apparel | 41,325 |
| Sundries | 5,200 |
| Library books | 182,300 |
| Library software | 102,200 |
| Total consolidated revenue | $745,000 |

**Geographic information.**

|  | *Revenues*[*] | *Long-lived assets* |
|---|---|---|
| United States | $687,400 | $253,200 |
| Foreign countries | 57,600 | 18,800 |
| Total | $745,000 | $272,000 |

[*] *Revenues are attributed to countries as follows: For Wholesale Corporation and Library Corporation, the country in which the customer takes delivery. For Retail Corporation, the country in which the retail store is located or, for internet sales, the country to which the merchandise is delivered. For Software Corporation, the country where the host server on which the software is installed is located.*

**Major customers.** No single customer represents 10% or more of the consolidated revenues. Consequently, management believes that the Companies' sales are appropriately diversified.

# 23 FOREIGN CURRENCY

## PERSPECTIVE AND ISSUES

Over the past half century, international activity by US corporations has increased enormously and the prospects are that this will only accelerate in the coming years. Not only are transactions consummated with independent foreign entities, but also with foreign subsidiaries or branches of US parents. In addition, foreign investment into the US has increased substantially, with acquisition of such venerable US companies as the former Amoco Corporation and Universal Studios.

To facilitate the proper analysis of foreign operations by financial statement users, transactions and financial statements denominated in foreign currencies must be expressed in a common currency (i.e., US dollars). The generally accepted accounting principles governing the translation of foreign currency financial statements and the accounting for foreign currency transactions are found primarily in FAS 52. Additional guidance in this area is provided by FIN 37. These principles apply to the translation of

1. Foreign currency transactions (e.g., exports, imports, and loans) that are denominated in other than a company's functional currency
2. Foreign currency financial statements of branches, divisions, subsidiaries, and other investees which are incorporated into the financial statements of a company reporting under US GAAP by combination, consolidation, or application of the equity method

The objectives of translation are to provide

1. Information relative to the expected economic effects of rate changes on an enterprise's cash flows and equity
2. Information in consolidated statements relative to the financial results and relationships of each individual foreign consolidated entity as reflected by the functional currency of each reporting entity

Companies sometimes use hedging strategies to attempt to manage their risk and minimize their exposure to fluctuations in the exchange rates of foreign currencies. Hedge accounting under FAS 133 is addressed at the end of this chapter.

| Sources of GAAP | | | |
|---|---|---|---|
| *FAS* | *FIN* | *DIG* | *EITF* |
| 52, 109, 130, 133, 159 | 37 | B4, B6, B37 | 92-4, 92-8, 93-9, 96-15, 97-7, |
| | | | 01-5, D-12, D-55, D-56, D-71 |

## DEFINITIONS OF TERMS

**Conversion.** The exchange of one currency for another.

**Current exchange rate.** The rate at which one unit of a currency can be exchanged for (converted into) another currency. For purposes of translation of financial statements in accordance with FAS 52, the current exchange rate is the rate at the end of the period covered by the financial statements or at the dates of recognition in those statements with respect to revenues, expenses, gains, and losses.

**Discount or premium on a forward contract.** The foreign currency amount of the contract multiplied by the difference between the contracted forward rate and the spot rate at the date of inception of the contract.

**Foreign currency.** A currency other than the functional currency of the reporting entity being referred to (for example, the US dollar could be a foreign currency for a foreign entity). Composites of currencies, such as the Special Drawing Rights on the International Monetary Fund (SDR), used to set prices or denominate amounts of loans, etc., have the characteristics of foreign currency for purposes of applying FAS 52.

**Foreign currency statements.** Financial statements that employ as the unit of measure a functional currency that is not the reporting currency of the enterprise.

**Foreign currency transactions.** Transactions whose terms are denominated in a currency other than the reporting entity's functional currency. Foreign currency transactions arise when an enterprise (1) buys or sells goods or services on credit whose prices are denominated in foreign currency, (2) borrows or lends funds and the amounts payable or receivable are denominated in foreign currency, (3) is a party to an unperformed forward exchange contract, or (4) for other reasons, acquires or disposes of assets or incurs or settles liabilities denominated in foreign currency.

**Foreign currency translation.** The process of expressing in the enterprise's reporting currency amounts that are denominated or measured in a different currency.

**Forward exchange contract.** An agreement to exchange at a specified future date currencies of different countries at a specified rate (forward rate).

**Functional currency.** The currency of the primary economic environment in which the entity operates; normally, the currency of the environment in which the entity primarily generates and expends cash.

**Local currency.** The currency of a particular country being referred to.

**Monetary items.** Cash, claims to receive a fixed amount of cash, and obligations to pay a fixed amount of cash.

**Nonmonetary items.** All balance sheet items other than cash, claims to cash, and cash obligations.

**Remeasurement.** If an entity's accounting records are not maintained in its functional currency, remeasurement is the process necessary to convert those records into the functional currency, with the objective of reflecting the same results as if the records had been maintained in the functional currency. Monetary balances are translated by using the current exchange rate, and nonmonetary balances are translated by using historical exchange rates. In the event that remeasurement into the functional currency is required, it must be done prior to translation into the reporting currency.

**Reporting currency.** The currency in which an enterprise prepares its financial statements.

**Reporting enterprise.** An entity or group of entities whose financial statements are being referred to. For the purposes of this discussion, those financial statements reflect (1) the financial statements of one or more foreign operations by combination, consolidation, or equity method accounting; (2) foreign currency transactions; or (3) both.

**Spot rate.** The exchange rate for immediate delivery of currencies exchanged.

**Transaction date.** The date on which a transaction (for example, a sale or purchase of merchandise or services) is recognized in accounting records in conformity with generally accepted accounting principles. A long-term commitment may have more than one transaction date (for example, the due date of each progress payment under a construction contract is an anticipated transaction date).

**Transaction gain or loss.** Transaction gains or losses result from a change in exchange rates between the functional currency and the currency in which a foreign currency transaction is denominated. They represent an increase or decrease in (1) the actual functional currency cash flows realized upon settlement of foreign currency transactions and (2) the expected functional currency cash flows on unsettled foreign currency transactions.

**Translation adjustments.** Translation adjustments result from the process of translating financial statements from the entity's functional currency into the reporting currency.

## CONCEPTS, RULES, AND EXAMPLES

### Translation of Foreign Currency Financial Statements

**Selection of the functional currency.** Before the financial statements of a foreign branch, division, or subsidiary are translated into US dollars, the management of the US company must make a decision as to which currency is the functional currency of the foreign entity. Once chosen, the functional currency cannot be changed unless economic facts and circumstances have clearly changed. Additionally, previously issued financial statements are not restated for any changes in the functional currency. The functional currency decision is crucial because different translation methods are applied which may have a material effect on the US company's financial statements.

FASB defines functional currency but does not list definitive criteria that, if satisfied, would with certainty result in the identification of an entity's functional currency. Rather, realizing that such criteria would be difficult to develop, FASB listed various factors that were intended to give management guidance in making the functional currency decision. These factors include

1. Cash flows (Do the foreign entity's cash flows directly affect the parent's cash flows and are they immediately available for remittance to the parent?)
2. Sales prices (Are the foreign entity's sales prices responsive to exchange rate changes and to international competition?)
3. Sales markets (Is the foreign entity's sales market the parent's country or are sales denominated in the parent's currency?)
4. Expenses (Are the foreign entity's expenses incurred primarily in the parent's country?)
5. Financing (Is the foreign entity's financing primarily from the parent or is it denominated in the parent's currency?)
6. Intercompany transactions (Is there a high volume of intercompany transactions between the parent and the foreign entity?)

If the answers to the questions above are predominantly yes, the functional currency is the reporting currency of the parent company (i.e., the US dollar). If the answers are predominantly no, the functional currency would most likely be the local currency of the foreign entity, although it is possible for a foreign currency other than the local currency to be the functional currency.

**Translation methods.** To deal with discrete circumstances, FASB chose two different methods to translate a company's foreign company's financial statements into US dollars: the *current rate* method and the *remeasurement* method. These are not alternatives, but rather are employed as circumstances dictate. The primary distinction between the methods is the classification of assets and liabilities (and their corresponding income statement amounts) that are translated at either the current or historical exchange rates.

The first method, known as the current rate method, is the approach mandated by FAS 52 when the functional currency is the foreign currency (e.g., the domestic currency of the foreign subsidiary or operation). All assets and liabilities are translated at the current rates while stockholders' equity accounts are translated at the appropriate historical rate or rates. Revenues and expenses are translated at rates in effect when the transactions occur, but those that occur evenly over the year may be translated at the weighted-average rate for the year.

Note that weighted-average, if used, must take into account the actual pace and pattern of changes in exchange rates over the course of the year, which will often not be varying at a constant rate throughout the period nor, in many instances, monotonically increasing or decreasing over the period. When these conditions do not hold, it is incumbent upon the reporting entity to develop a weighted-average exchange rate that is meaningful under the circumstances. When coupled with transactions (sales, purchases, et al.) that also have not occurred evenly throughout the year, this determination can become a fairly complex undertaking, requiring careful attention.

The theoretical basis for the current rate method is the "net investment concept," wherein the foreign entity is viewed as a separate entity in which the parent invested, rather than being considered part of the parent's operations. FASB's reasoning was that financial statement users can benefit most when the information provided about the foreign entity retains the relationships and results created in the environment (economic, legal, and political) in which the entity operates. Converting all assets and liabilities at the same current rate accomplishes this objective.

The rationale for this approach is that foreign-denominated debt is often used to purchase assets that create foreign-denominated revenues. These revenue-producing assets act as a natural hedge against changes in the settlement amount of the debt due to changes in the exchange rate. The excess (net) assets—which is the US parent company's net equity investment in the foreign operation—will, however, be affected by this foreign exchange risk, and this effect is recognized by the parent.

The second utilized method, the remeasurement method, has also been referred to as the monetary/nonmonetary method. This approach is required by FAS 52 when the foreign entity's accounting records are *not* maintained in the functional currency (e.g., when the US dollar is designated as the functional currency for a Brazilian subsidiary). This method translates monetary assets (cash and other assets and liabilities that will be settled in cash) at the current rate. Nonmonetary assets, liabilities, and stockholders' equity are translated at the appropriate historical rates. The appropriate historical rate would be the exchange rate at the date the transaction involving the nonmonetary account originated. Also, the income statement amounts related to nonmonetary assets and liabilities, such as cost of goods sold (inventory), depreciation (property, plant, and equipment), and intangibles amortization (patents, copyrights), are translated at the same rate as used for the related balance sheet translation. Other revenues and expenses occurring evenly over the year may be translated at the weighted-average exchange rate in effect during the period, subject to the considerations discussed above.

Thus, to summarize, if the foreign entity's local currency is the functional currency, FAS 52 requires use of the current rate method when translating the foreign entity's financial statements. If, on the other hand, the US dollar (or other nonlocal currency) is the functional currency, FAS 52 requires the remeasurement method when translating the foreign entity's financial statements. Both of these methods are illustrated below. All amounts in the following two illustrations, other than exchange rates, are in thousands. The trailing zeros have been dropped in order to focus on applying the concepts.

### Application of the Current Rate Method

Assume that a US company has a 100% owned subsidiary in Italy that commenced operations in 2009. The subsidiary's operations consist of leasing space in an office building. This building, which cost one million euros, was financed primarily by Italian banks. All revenues and cash expenses are received and paid in euros. The subsidiary also maintains its accounting records in euros. As a result, management of the US company has decided that the euro is the functional currency of the subsidiary.

The subsidiary's balance sheet at December 31, 2009, and its combined statement of income and retained earnings for the year ended December 31, 2009, are presented below in euros.

**Italian Company**
**Balance Sheet**
**At December 31, 2009**
**(€000 omitted)**

| Assets | | | Liabilities and Stockholders' Equity | | |
|---|---|---|---|---|---|
| Cash | € | 100 | Accounts payable | € | 60 |
| Accounts receivable | | 40 | Unearned rent | | 20 |
| Land | | 200 | Mortgage payable | | 800 |
| Building | | 1,000 | Common stock | | 80 |
| Accumulated depreciation | | (20) | Additional paid-in capital | | 320 |
| | | | Retained earnings | | 40 |
| | | | Total liabilities and | | |
| Total assets | | €1,320 | Stockholders' equity | | €1,320 |

**Italian Company**
**Statement of Income and Retained Earnings**
**For the Year Ended December 31, 2009**
**(€000 omitted)**

| | |
|---|---|
| Revenues | €400 |
| Expenses (including depreciation of €20) | 340 |
| Net income | 60 |
| Retained earnings, January 1, 2009 | -- |
| Less dividends declared | (20) |
| Retained earnings, December 31, 2009 | € 40 |

Various exchange rates for 2009 are as follows:

€1 = $1.50 at the beginning of 2009 (when the common stock was issued and the land and building were financed through the mortgage)
€1 = $1.55 weighted-average for 2009
€1 = $1.58 at the date the dividends were declared and paid and the unearned rent was received
€1 = $1.62 at the end of 2009

Since the euro is the functional currency, the Italian Company's financial statements must be translated into US dollars by the current rate method. This translation process is illustrated below.

**Italian Company**
**Balance Sheet Translation**
**(The euro is the functional currency)**
**At December 31, 2009**
**(€/$000 omitted)**

| *Assets* | *Euros* | *Exchange rate* | *US dollars* |
|---|---|---|---|
| Cash | € 100 | 1.62 | $ 162.00 |
| Accounts receivable, net | 40 | 1.62 | 64.80 |
| Land | 200 | 1.62 | 320.00 |
| Building, net | 980 | 1.62 | 1,587.60 |
| Total assets | €1,320 | | $2,138.40 |
| *Liabilities and Stockholders' Equity* | | | |
| Accounts payable | € 60 | 1.62 | $ 97.20 |
| Unearned rent | 20 | 1.62 | 32.40 |
| Mortgage payable | 800 | 1.62 | 1,296.00 |
| Common stock | 80 | 1.50 | 120.00 |
| Additional paid-in capital | 320 | 1.50 | 480.00 |
| Retained earnings | 40 | See income statement | 61.40 |
| Translation adjustments | -- | See computation below | 51.40 |
| Total liabilities and stockholders' equity | €1,320 | | $2,138.40 |

**Italian Company**
**Statement of Income and Retained Earnings**
**Statement Translation**
**(The euro is the functional currency)**
**For the Year Ended December 31, 2009**
**(€/$000 omitted)**

| | *Euros* | *Exchange rate* | *US dollars* |
|---|---|---|---|
| Revenues | €400 | 1.55 | $620.00 |
| Expenses (including depreciation of €20 [$31.00]) | 340 | 1.55 | 527.00 |
| Net income | 60 | 1.55 | 93.00 |
| Retained earnings, January 1 | -- | -- | -- |
| Less dividends declared | (20) | 1.58 | (31.60) |
| Retained earnings, December 31 | € 40 | | $ 61.40 |

**Italian Company**
**Statement of Cash Flows**
**Statement Translation**
**(The euro is the functional currency)**
**For the Year Ended December 31, 2009**
**(€/$000 omitted)**

| | *Euros* | *Exchange rate* | *US dollars* |
|---|---|---|---|
| *Operating activities* | | | |
| Net income | € 60 | 1.55 | $ 93.00 |
| Adjustments to reconcile net income to net cash provided by operating activities | | | |
| Depreciation | 20 | 1.55 | 31.00 |
| Increase in accounts receivable | (40) | 1.55 | (62.00) |
| Increase in accounts payable | 60 | 1.55 | 93.00 |
| Increase in unearned rent | 20 | 1.58 | 31.60 |
| Net cash provided by operating activities | 120 | | 186.60 |
| *Investing activities* | | | |
| Purchase of land | (200) | 1.50 | (300.00) |
| Purchase of building | (1,000) | 1.50 | (1,500.00) |
| Net cash used by investing activities | (1,200) | | (1,800.00) |

|  | Euros | Exchange rate | US dollars |
|---|---|---|---|
| *Financing activities* | | | |
| Proceeds from issuance of common | 400 | 1.50 | 600.00 |
| Proceeds from mortgage payable | 800 | 1.50 | 1,200.00 |
| Dividends paid | (20) | 1.58 | (31.60) |
| Net cash provided by financing activities | 1,180 | | 1,768.40 |
| Effect of exchange rate changes on cash | N/A | | 7.00 |
| Increase in cash and equivalents | 100 | | 162.00 |
| Cash at beginning of year | 0 | | 0 |
| Cash at end of year | € 100 | 1.62 | $ 162.00 |

Note the following points concerning the current rate method:

1. All assets and liabilities are translated using the current exchange rate at the balance sheet date (€1 = $1.62). All revenues and expenses are translated at the rates in effect when these items are recognized during the period. Due to practical considerations, however, weighted-average rates can be used to translate revenues and expenses (€1 = $1.55).

2. Stockholders' equity accounts are translated by using historical exchange rates. Common stock was issued at the beginning of 2009 when the exchange rate was €1 = $1.50. The translated balance of retained earnings is the result of the weighted-average rate applied to revenues and expenses and the specific rate in effect when the dividends were declared (€1 = $1.58).

3. Translation adjustments result from translating all assets and liabilities at the current rate, while stockholders' equity is translated by using historical and weighted-average rates. The adjustments have no direct effect on cash flows. Also, the translation adjustment is due to the net investment rather than the subsidiary's operations. For these reasons, the cumulative translation adjustments balance is reported as a component of accumulated other comprehensive income (AOCI) in the stockholders' equity section of the US parent company's consolidated balance sheet. This balance essentially equates the total debits of the subsidiary (now expressed in US dollars) with the total credits (also in dollars). It also may be determined directly, as shown next, to verify the translation process.

4. The translation adjustments credit of $30.70 is calculated as follows for the differences between the exchange rate of $1.62 at the end of the year and the applicable exchange rates used to translate changes in net assets:

| | | | |
|---|---|---|---|
| Net assets at inception (Land and building of $1,200,000 – Portion financed by mortgage of $800,000) | $400 \times (\$1.62 - \$1.50)$ | = | $48.00 credit |
| Net income | $60 \times (\$1.62 - \$1.55)$ | = | 4.20 credit |
| Dividends declared | $20 \times (\$1.62 - \$1.58)$ | = | 0.80 debit |
| Translation adjustment | | | $51.40 credit |

5. The translation adjustments balance that appears as a component of AOCI in the stockholders' equity section is cumulative in nature. Consequently, the change in this balance during the year is disclosed as a component of other comprehensive income (OCI) for the period. In the illustration, this balance went from zero to $51.40 at the end of 2009. (The financial statement presentation of other comprehensive income is covered in Chapter 3.) In addition, assume the following occurred during the following year, 2010:

**Italian Company**
**Balance Sheet**
**At December 31**
**(€000 omitted)**

| Assets | 2010 | 2009 | Increase/(Decrease) |
|---|---|---|---|
| Cash | € 200 | € 100 | €100 |
| Accounts receivable, net | -- | 40 | (40) |
| Land | 300 | 200 | 100 |
| Building, net | 960 | 980 | (20) |
| Total assets | €1,460 | €1,320 | €140 |
| **Liabilities and Stockholders' Equity** | | | |
| Accounts payable | € 100 | € 60 | € 40 |
| Unearned rent | 0 | 20 | (20) |
| Mortgage payable | 900 | 800 | 100 |
| Common stock | 80 | 80 | 0 |
| Additional paid-in capital | 320 | 320 | 0 |
| Retained earnings | 60 | 40 | 20 |
| Total liabilities and stockholders' equity | €1,460 | €1,320 | €140 |

**Italian Company**
**Statement of Income and Retained Earnings**
**For the Year Ended December 31, 2010**
**(€000 omitted)**

| | |
|---|---|
| Revenues | €440 |
| Operating expenses (including depreciation of €20) | 340 |
| Net income | 100 |
| Retained earnings, Jan. 1, 2010 | 40 |
| Less: Dividends declared | (80) |
| Retained earnings, Dec. 31, 2010 | € 60 |

Exchange rates were

€1 = $1.62 at the beginning of 2010
€1 = $1.65 weighted-average for 2010
€1 = $1.71 at the end of 2010
€1 = $1.68 when dividends were declared in 2010 and additional land bought by incurring mortgage

The translation process for 2010 is illustrated below.

**Italian Company**
**Balance Sheet Translation**
**(The euro is the functional currency)**
**At December 31, 2010**
**(€/$000 omitted)**

| Assets | Euros | Exchange rate | US dollars |
|---|---|---|---|
| Cash | € 200 | 1.71 | $ 342.00 |
| Land | 300 | 1.71 | 513.00 |
| Building, net | 960 | 1.71 | 1,641.60 |
| Total assets | €1,460 | | $2,496.60 |
| **Liabilities and Stockholders' Equity** | | | |
| Accounts payable | € 100 | 1.71 | $ 171.00 |
| Mortgage payable | 900 | 1.71 | 1,539.00 |
| Common stock | 80 | 1.50 | 120.00 |
| Additional paid-in capital | 320 | 1.50 | 480.00 |
| Retained earnings | 60 | See income statement | 92.00 |
| Translation adjustments | -- | See computation below | 94.60 |
| Total liabilities and stockholders' equity | €1,460 | | $2,496.60 |

**Italian Company**
**Statement of Income and Retained Earnings**
**Statement Translation**
**(The euro is the functional currency)**
**For the Year Ended December 31, 2010**
**(€/$000 omitted)**

|  | Euros | Exchange rate | US dollars |
|---|---|---|---|
| Revenues | €440 | 1.65 | $726.00 |
| Expenses (including depreciation of €10 [$12.50]) | 340 | 1.65 | 561.00 |
| Net income | 100 | 1.65 | 165.00 |
| Retained earnings, 1/1/10 | 40 | -- | 61.40 |
| Less: Dividends declared | (80) | 1.68 | (134.40) |
| Retained earnings, 12/31/10 | € 60 | | $ 92.00 |

**Italian Company**
**Statement of Cash Flows**
**Statement Translation**
**(The euro is the functional currency)**
**For the Year Ended December 31, 2010**
**(€/$000 omitted)**

|  | Euros | Exchange rate | US dollars |
|---|---|---|---|
| *Operating activities* | | | |
| Net income | €100 | 1.65 | $165.00 |
| Adjustments to reconcile net income to net cash provided by operating activities | | | |
| Depreciation | 20 | 1.65 | 33.00 |
| Decrease in accounts receivable | 40 | 1.65 | 66.00 |
| Increase in accounts payable | 40 | 1.65 | 66.00 |
| Decrease in unearned rent | (20) | 1.65 | (33.00) |
| Net cash provided by operating activities | 180 | | 297.00 |
| *Investing activities* | | | |
| Purchase of land | (100) | 1.68 | (168.00) |
| Net cash used by investing activities | (100) | | (168.00) |
| *Financing activities* | | | |
| Mortgage payable | 100 | 1.68 | 168.00 |
| Dividends | (80) | 1.68 | (134.40) |
| Net cash provided by financing activities | 20 | | 33.60 |
| Effect of exchange rate changes on cash | N/A | | 17.40 |
| Increase in cash and equivalents | 100 | | 180.00 |
| Cash at beginning of year | 100 | | 162.00 |
| Cash at end of year | €200 | 1.71 | $342.00 |

Using the analysis presented before, the **change** in the translation adjustment attributable to 2010 is computed as follows:

| | | | | | |
|---|---|---|---|---|---|
| Net assets at January 1, 2010 | €440 | ($1.71 – $1.62) | = | $39.60 | credit |
| Net income for 2010 | €100 | ($1.71 – $1.65) | = | 6.00 | credit |
| Dividends for 2010 | € 80 | ($1.71 – $1.68) | = | 2.40 | debit |
| Total | | | | $43.20 | credit |

The balance in the cumulative translation adjustment component of accumulated other comprehensive income (AOCI) at the end of 2010 is $94.60. ($51.40 from 2009 and $43.20 from 2010.)

6.  The use of the equity method by the US parent company in accounting for the subsidiary would result in the following journal entries (in $000s), based upon the information presented above:

|  | *2009* | *2010* |
|---|---|---|
| **Original investment** | | |
| Investment in Italian subsidiary | 600* | -- |
| Cash | 600 | -- |

\* *€80 of common stock + €320 of additional paid-in capital = €400 translated at €1. 50 = $600.*

|  | | |
|---|---|---|
| **Earnings pickup** | | |
| Investment in Italian subsidiary | 93.00 | 165.00 |
| Equity in subsidiary income | 93.00 | 165.00 |
| **Dividends received** | | |
| Cash | 31.60 | 134.40 |
| Investment in Italian subsidiary | 31.60 | 134.40 |
| **Translation adjustments** | | |
| Investment in Italian subsidiary | 51.40 | 43.20 |
| OCI—Translation adjustments | 51.40 | 43.20 |

Note that in applying the equity method to record this activity in the US parent company's accounting records, the parent's stockholders' equity should be the same whether or not the Italian subsidiary is consolidated. Since the subsidiary does not report the translation adjustments on its financial statements, care should be exercised so that it is not forgotten in the application of the equity method.

7. If the US company disposes of its investment in the Italian subsidiary, the cumulative translation adjustments balance becomes part of the gain or loss that results from the transaction and is eliminated. For example, assume that on January 2, 2011, the US company sells its entire investment for €465 thousand. The exchange rate at this date is €1 = $1.71. The balance in the investment account at December 31, 2010, is $786,600 as a result of the entries made previously.

| | Investment in Italian Subsidiary | |
|---|---|---|
| 1/1/09 | 600.00 | |
| | 93.00 | 31.60 |
| | 51.40 | |
| 1/1/10 balance | 712.80 | |
| | 165.00 | |
| | 43.20 | 134.40 |
| 12/31/10 balance | 786.60 | |

The following entries would be made by the US parent company to reflect the sale of the investment:

| | | |
|---|---|---|
| Cash (€465 × $1.71 conversion rate) | 795.15 | |
| Investment in Italian subsidiary | | 786.60 |
| Gain from sale of subsidiary | | 8.55 |
| AOCI—Translation adjustments | 94.60 | |
| Gain from sale of subsidiary | | 94.60 |

If the US company had sold only a portion of its investment in the Italian subsidiary, only a pro rata portion of the accumulated translation adjustments balance would have become part of the gain or loss from the transaction. To illustrate, if 80% of the Italian subsidiary was sold for €372 on January 2, 2011, the following journal entries would be made:

| | | |
|---|---|---|
| Cash (€372 × $1.71 exchange rate) | 636.12 | |
| Investment in Italian subsidiary (80% × $786.60) | | 629.28 |
| Gain from sale of subsidiary | | 6.84 |
| AOCI—Translation adjustments (80% × $94.60) | 75.68 | |
| Gain from sale of subsidiary | | 75.68 |

An exchange rate might not be available if there is a temporary suspension of foreign exchange trading. This occurred, for example, when Israel announced, on December 30, 1988, that it would devalue its currency, the shekel, on January 2, 1989, at which time it would resume settling unexecuted foreign currency transactions. EITF Topic D-12 provides that, if exchangeability between two currencies is temporarily lacking at a transaction date or the balance sheet date, the first subsequent rate at which exchanges could be made is to be used to implement FAS 52. While this circumstance has been rare, it could happen again.

**Application of the Remeasurement Method**

In the previous situation, the euro was the functional currency because the Italian subsidiary's cash flows were primarily in euros. Assume, however, that the financing of the land and building was denominated in US dollars instead of euros and that the mortgage payable is denominated in US dollars (i.e., it must be repaid in US dollars). Although the rents collected and the majority of the cash flows for expenses are in euros, management has decided that, due to the manner of financing, the US dollar is the functional currency. The accounting records, however, are maintained in euros.

The remeasurement of the Italian financial statements is accomplished by use of the remeasurement method (also known as the monetary/nonmonetary method). This method is illustrated below using the same information that was presented before for the Italian subsidiary.

**Italian Company**
**Balance Sheet (Remeasurement)**
**(The US dollar is the functional currency)**
**At December 31, 2009**
**(€/$000 omitted)**

| *Assets* | *Euros* | *Exchange rate* | *US dollars* |
|---|---|---|---|
| Cash | € 100 | 1.62 | $ 162.00 |
| Accounts receivable, net | 40 | 1.62 | 64.80 |
| Land | 200 | 1.50 | 300.00 |
| Building, net | 980 | 1.50 | 1,470.00 |
| Total assets | €1,320 | | $1,996.80 |
| **Liabilities and Stockholders' Equity** | | | |
| Accounts payable | € 60 | 1.62 | $ 97.20 |
| Unearned rent | 20 | 1.58 | 31.60 |
| Mortgage payable | 800 | 1.62 | 1,296.00 |
| Common stock | 80 | 1.50 | 120.00 |
| Additional paid-in capital | 320 | 1.50 | 480.00 |
| Retained earnings | 40 | (See income statement) | (28.00) |
| Total liabilities and stockholders' equity | €1,320 | | $1,996.80 |

**Italian Company**
**Statement of Income and Retained Earnings (Remeasurement)**
**(The US dollar is the functional currency)**
**For the Year Ended December 31, 2009**
**(€/$000 omitted)**

| | *Euros* | *Exchange rate* | *US dollars* |
|---|---|---|---|
| Revenues | € 400 | 1.55 | $620.00 |
| Expenses (not including depreciation) | (320) | 1.55 | 496.00 |
| Depreciation expense | (20) | 1.50 | (30.00) |
| Remeasurement loss | -- | See analysis below | (90.40) |
| Net income (loss) | 60 | -- | (3.60) |
| Retained earnings, January 1 | -- | -- | -- |
| Less dividends declared | (20) | 1.58 | (31.60) |
| Retained earnings, December 31 | € 40 | | $(28.00) |

**Italian Company**
**Remeasurement Loss**
**(The US dollar is the functional currency)**
**For the Year Ended December 31, 2009**
**(€/$000 omitted)**

| | Euros | | Exchange rate | US dollars | |
|---|---|---|---|---|---|
| | Debit | Credit | | Debit | Credit |
| Cash | € 100 | | 1.62 | $ 162.00 | |
| Accounts receivable, net | 40 | | 1.62 | 64.80 | |
| Land | 200 | | 1.50 | 300.00 | |
| Building, net | 980 | | 1.50 | 1,470.00 | |
| Accounts payable | | € 60 | 1.62 | | $ 97.20 |
| Unearned rent | | 20 | 1.58 | | 31.60 |
| Mortgage payable | | 800 | 1.62 | | 1,296.00 |
| Common stock | | 80 | 1.50 | | 120.00 |
| Additional paid-in capital | | 320 | 1.50 | | 480.00 |
| Retained earnings | | -- | -- | | -- |
| Dividends declared | 20 | | 1.58 | 31.60 | |
| Revenues | | 400 | 1.55 | | 620.00 |
| Operating expenses | 320 | | 1.55 | 496.00 | |
| Depreciation expenses | 20 | | 1.50 | 30.00 | |
| Totals | €1,680 | €1,680 | | $2,554.40 | $2,644.80 |
| Remeasurement loss | | | | 90.40 | |
| Totals | | | | $2,644.80 | $2,644.80 |

**Italian Company**
**Statement of Cash Flows (Remeasurement)**
**(The US dollar is the functional currency)**
**For the Year Ended December 31, 2009**
**(€/$000 omitted)**

| | Euros | Exchange rate | US dollars |
|---|---|---|---|
| *Operating activities* | | | |
| Net income (loss) | € 60 | See income statement | $ 3.60 |
| Adjustments to reconcile net income to net cash provided by operating activities | | | |
| Remeasurement loss | -- | See income statement | 90.40 |
| Depreciation | 20 | 1.50 | 30.00 |
| Increase in accounts receivable | (40) | 1.55 | (62.00) |
| Increase in accounts payable | 60 | 1.55 | 93.00 |
| Increase in unearned rent | 20 | 1.58 | 31.60 |
| Net cash provided by operating activities | 120 | | 186.60 |
| *Investing activities* | | | |
| Purchase of land | (200) | 1.50 | (300.00) |
| Purchase of building | (1,000) | 1.50 | (1,500.00) |
| Net cash used by investing activities | (1,200) | | (1,800.00) |
| *Financing activities* | | | |
| Proceeds from issuance of common | 400 | 1.50 | 600.00 |
| Proceeds from mortgage payable | 800 | 1.50 | 1,200.00 |
| Dividends paid | (20) | 1.58 | (31.60) |
| Net cash provided by financing activities | 1,180 | | 1,768.40 |
| Effect of exchange rate changes on cash | N/A | | 7.00 |
| Increase in cash and equivalents | 100 | | 162.00 |
| Cash at beginning of year | 0 | | 0 |
| Cash at end of year | €100 | 1.62 | $162.00 |

Note the following points concerning the remeasurement method:

1. Assets and liabilities which have historical cost balances (nonmonetary assets and liabilities) are remeasured by using historical exchange rates (i.e., the rates in effect when the transactions giving rise to the balance first occurred). Monetary assets and

monetary liabilities, cash and those items that will be settled in cash, are remeasured by using the current exchange rate at the balance sheet date. In 2010, the unearned rent from year-end 2009 of €10 would be remeasured at the rate of €1 = $1.58. The unearned rent at the end of 2009 is not considered a monetary liability. Therefore, the $1.58 historical exchange rate is used for all applicable future years. See the appendix at the end of this chapter for a listing of accounts that are remeasured using historical exchange rates.

2.  Revenues and expenses that occur frequently during a period are remeasured, for practical purposes, by using the weighted-average exchange rate for the period. Revenues and expenses that represent allocations of historical balances (e.g., depreciation, cost of goods sold, and amortization of intangibles) are remeasured using historical exchange rates. Note that this is a different treatment as compared to the current rate method.

3.  If the functional currency is the US dollar rather than the local foreign currency, the amounts of specific line items presented in the reconciliation of net income to net cash flow from operating activities will be different for nonmonetary items (e.g., depreciation).

4.  The calculation of the remeasurement gain (loss), in a purely mechanical sense, is the amount needed to make the dollar debits equal the dollar credits in the Italian company's trial balance.

5.  The remeasurement loss of $90.40 is reported on the US parent company's consolidated income statement because the US dollar is the functional currency. When the reporting currency is the functional currency, as it is in this example, it is assumed that all of the foreign entity's transactions occurred in US dollars (even if this was not the case). Accordingly, remeasurement gains and losses are taken immediately to the income statement in the year in which they occur as they can be expected to have direct cash flow effects on the parent company. They are not deferred as a translation adjustments component of AOCI as they were when the functional currency was the euro (applying the current rate method).

6.  The use of the equity method of accounting for the subsidiary would result in the following entries by the US parent company during 2009:

**Original investment**

| | | |
|---|---|---|
| Investment in Italian subsidiary | 600.00 | |
| Cash | | 600.00 |

**Earnings (loss) pickup**

| | | |
|---|---|---|
| Investment in Italian subsidiary | 3.60 | |
| Equity in subsidiary income | | 3.60 |

**Dividends received**

| | | |
|---|---|---|
| Cash | 31.60 | |
| Investment in Italian subsidiary | | 31.60 |

Note that remeasurement gains and losses are included in the subsidiary's net income (net loss) as determined in US dollars before the earnings (loss) pickup is made by the US company.

7.  In economies in which—per EITF Topic D-55—cumulative inflation is greater than 100% over a three-year period, FASB requires that the functional currency be the reporting currency, that is, the US dollar. Projections of future inflation cannot be used to satisfy this threshold condition. The remeasurement method must be used in this situation even though the factors indicate the local currency is the functional currency. FASB made this decision in order to prevent the evaporation of the for-

eign entity's fixed assets, a result that would occur if the local currency was the functional currency.

**Cessation of highly inflationary condition.** Per EITF 91-24, when a foreign subsidiary's economy is no longer considered highly inflationary, the entity converts the reporting currency values into the local currency at the exchange rates on the date of change on which these values become the new functional currency accounting bases for nonmonetary assets and liabilities.

Furthermore, the consensus in EITF 92-8 was that when a change in functional currency designation occurs because an economy ceases to be highly inflationary, the deferred taxes on the temporary differences that arise as a result of a change in the functional currency are treated as an adjustment to the cumulative translation adjustments portion of stockholders' equity (accumulated other comprehensive income).

**Applying FAS 109 to foreign entity financials restated for general price levels.** APB Statement 3 (the portion not rescinded by SOP 93-3) states that price-level-adjusted financial statements are preferred for foreign currency financial statements of entities operating in highly inflationary economies when those financial statements are intended for readers in the United States. If this recommendation is heeded, the result is that the income tax bases of the assets and liabilities are often restated for inflation. EITF 93-9 provides guidance on applying the asset-and-liability approach of FAS 109 as it relates to such financial statements. A consensus was reached on (1) how temporary differences are to be computed under FAS 109 and (2) how deferred income tax expense or benefit for the year is to be determined.

With regard to the first issue, temporary differences are computed as the difference between the indexed income tax basis amount and the related price-level restated amount of the asset or liability. The consensus reached on the second issue is that the deferred income tax expense or benefit is the difference between the deferred income tax assets and liabilities reported at the end of the current year and those reported at the end of the prior year. The deferred income tax assets and liabilities of the prior year are recalculated in units of the current year-end purchasing power.

On a related matter, EITF Topic D-56 states that, when the functional currency changes to the reporting currency because the foreign economy has become highly inflationary, FAS 109 prohibits recognition of deferred income tax benefits associated with indexing assets and liabilities that are remeasured in the reporting currency using historical exchange rates. Any related income tax benefits would be recognized only upon their being realized for income tax purposes. Any deferred income tax benefits that had been recognized for indexing before the change in reporting currency is effected are eliminated when the related indexed amounts are realized as income tax deductions.

## Summary of Current Rate and Remeasurement Methods

1.  Before foreign currency financial statements can be translated into US dollars, management of the US parent company must select the functional currency for the foreign entity whose financial statements will be incorporated into theirs by consolidation, combination, or the equity method. As the examples illustrated, this decision is important because it may have a material effect upon the financial statements of the US company.

2.  If the functional currency is the local currency of the foreign entity, the current rate method is used to translate foreign currency financial statements into US dollars. All assets and liabilities are translated by using the current exchange rate at the balance sheet date. This method insures that all financial relationships remain the same in both local currency and US dollars. Owners' equity is translated using historical

rates, while revenues (gains) and expenses (losses) are translated at the rates in existence during the period when the transactions occurred. A weighted-average rate can be used for items occurring frequently throughout the period. The translation adjustments (debit or credit) which result from the application of these rules are reported in other comprehensive income and then accumulated and reported as a separate component of stockholders' equity of the US company's consolidated balance sheet (or parent-only balance sheet if consolidation is not deemed appropriate).

3.  If the functional currency is the parent company's reporting currency (the US dollar), the foreign currency financial statements are remeasured in US dollars. All foreign currency balances are restated in US dollars using both historical and current exchange rates. Foreign currency balances which reflect prices from past transactions are remeasured using historical rates, while foreign currency balances which reflect prices from current transactions are remeasured using the current exchange rate. Remeasurement gains/losses that result from the remeasurement process applied to foreign subsidiaries that are consolidated are reported on the US parent company's consolidated income statement.

The above summary can be arranged in tabular form as shown below.

| Functional currency | Functional currency determinants | Translation method | Reporting and display |
|---|---|---|---|
| Local currency of foreign company | a. Operations not integrated with parent's operations<br>b. Buying and selling activities primarily in local currency<br>c. Cash flows not immediately available for remittance to parent<br>d. Financing denominated in local currency | Current rate (all assets/liabilities translated using current exchange rate; revenues/expenses use weighted-average rate; equity accounts use historical rates) | Accumulated translation adjustments are reported in equity section of the US parent company's consolidated balance sheet as part of accumulated other comprehensive income (AOCI).<br>Changes in accumulated translation adjustments reported as a component of other comprehensive income (OCI).<br>Effect of exchange rates on cash included in reconciliation of beginning and ending cash balances on statement of cash flows. |
| US dollar | a. Operations integrated with parent's operations<br>b. Buying and selling activities primarily in the US and/or US dollars<br>c. Cash flows immediately available for remittance to parent<br>d. Financing denominated in US dollars | Remeasurement (monetary assets/liabilities use current exchange rate; historical cost balances use historical rates; revenues/expenses use weighted-average rates and historical rates, the latter for allocations like depreciation expenses). | Remeasurement gain/loss is reported on the US company's consolidated income statement.<br>Remeasurement gain/loss shown as a reconciliation item between net income and cash flows from operations in the statement of cash flows.<br>Effect of exchange rates on cash included in reconciliation of beginning and ending cash balances on statement of cash flows. |

**Application of FAS 52 to an investment to be disposed of that is evaluated for impairment.** Under FAS 52, accumulated foreign currency translation adjustments are reclassified to net income only when realized upon sale or upon complete or substantially complete liquidation of the investment in the foreign entity. EITF 01-5 addresses whether a reporting entity is to include the translation adjustments in the carrying amount of the investment in assessing impairment of an investment in a foreign entity that is held for disposal if the planned disposal will cause some or all of the translation adjustments to be reclassified to net income. The consensuses were that an entity that has committed to a plan that will cause the translation adjustments for an equity-method investment or consolidated investment in a foreign entity to be reclassified to earnings is to include the translation adjustments as part of the carrying amount of the investment when evaluating that investment for impairment. An entity would also include the portion of the translation adjustments that represents a gain or loss from an effective hedge of the net investment in a foreign operation as part of the carrying amount of the investment when making this evaluation.

## Foreign Operations in the US

With the world economy as interconnected as it is, entities in the US are sometimes the subsidiaries of parent companies domiciled elsewhere in the world. The financial statements of the US company may be presented separately in the US or may be combined as part of the financial statements in the foreign country.

In general, financial statements of US companies are prepared in accordance with US generally accepted accounting principles. However, adjustments may be necessary to conform these financial statements to the accounting principles of the foreign country of the parent company where they will be consolidated.

## Translation of Foreign Currency Transactions

According to FAS 52, a foreign currency transaction is a transaction " ... denominated in a currency other than the entity's functional currency." Denominated means that the amount to be received or paid is fixed in terms of the number of units of a particular foreign currency regardless of changes in the exchange rate. From the viewpoint of a US company, a foreign currency transaction results when it imports or exports goods or services to or from a foreign entity or makes a loan involving a foreign entity and agrees to settle the transaction in currency other than the US dollar (the functional currency of the US company). In these situations, the US company has "crossed currencies" and directly assumes the risk of fluctuating exchange rates of the foreign currency in which the transaction is denominated. This risk may lead to recognition of foreign exchange transaction gains or losses in the income statement of the US company. Note that transaction gains or losses can result only when the foreign transactions are denominated in a foreign currency. When a US company imports or exports goods or services and the transaction is to be settled in US dollars, the US company is not exposed to a foreign exchange gain or loss because it bears no risk due to exchange rate fluctuations.

### Example of foreign currency transaction translation

The following example illustrates the terminology and procedures applicable to the translation of foreign currency transactions. Assume that US Company, an exporter, sells merchandise to a customer in Italy on December 1, 2009, for €10,000. Receipt is due on January 31, 2010, and US Company prepares financial statements on December 31, 2009. At the transaction date (December 1, 2009), the spot rate for immediate exchange of foreign currencies indicates that €1 is equivalent to $1.30. To find the US dollar equivalent of this transaction, the foreign currency amount, €10,000, is multiplied by $1.30 to get $13,000. At December 1, 2009, the foreign currency transaction is recorded by US Company in the following manner:

| | | |
|---|---|---|
| Accounts receivable—Italy (€ denominated) | 13,000 | |
| Sales | | 13,000 |

The accounts receivable and sales are measured in US dollars at the transaction date using the spot rate at the time of the transaction. While the accounts receivable is measured and reported in US dollars, the receivable is denominated or fixed in euros. This characteristic may result in foreign exchange transaction gains or losses if the spot rate for the euro changes between the transaction date and the date the transaction is settled (January 31, 2010).

If financial statements are prepared between the transaction date and the settlement date, all receivables and liabilities denominated in a currency other than the functional currency (the US dollar) must be restated to reflect the spot rates in effect at the balance sheet date. Assume that on December 31, 2009, the spot rate for euros is €1 = $1.32. This means that the €10,000 are now worth $13,200 and that the accounts receivable denominated in euros has increased by $200. The following adjustment is recorded on December 31, 2009:

| | | |
|---|---|---|
| Accounts receivable—Italy (€ denominated) | 200 | |
| Foreign currency transaction gain | | 200 |

Note that the $13,000 credit to sales recorded on the transaction date is not affected by subsequent changes in the spot rate. This treatment exemplifies the two-transaction viewpoint adopted by FASB. In other words, making the sale is the result of an operating decision, while bearing the risk of fluctuating spot rates is the result of a financing decision. Therefore, the amount determined as sales revenue at the transaction date is not altered because of the financing decisions to wait until January 31, 2010, for payment of the account and to accept payment denominated in euros. The risk of a foreign exchange transaction loss can be avoided by (1) demanding immediate payment on December 1, 2009, (2) fixing the price of the transaction in US dollars instead of in the foreign currency, or (3) by entering into a forward exchange contract to hedge the exposed asset (accounts receivable). The fact that, in the example, US Company did not take any of these actions is reflected by recognizing foreign currency transaction gains or losses in its income statement (reported as financial or nonoperating items) in the period during which the exchange rates changed. This treatment has been criticized, however, because earnings will fluctuate because of changes in exchange rates and not because of changes in the economic activities of the enterprise. The counterargument, however, is that economic reality is that earnings *are* fluctuating because the management chose to commit the reporting entity to a transaction that exposes it to economic risks and, therefore, the case can be made that the volatility in earnings faithfully represents the results of management's business decision.

On the settlement date (January 31, 2010), assume the spot rate is €1 = $1.31. The receipt of €10,000 and their conversion into US dollars is recorded as follows:

| | | |
|---|---|---|
| Foreign currency (€) | 13,100 | |
| Foreign currency transaction loss | 100 | |
|     Accounts receivable—Italy (€ denominated) | | 13,200 |
| Cash | 13,100 | |
|     Foreign currency (€) | | 13,100 |

The net effect of this foreign currency transaction was to receive $13,100 in settlement from a sale that was originally measured (and recognized) at $13,000. This realized net foreign currency transaction gain of $100 is reported on two income statements—a $200 gain in 2009 and a $100 loss in 2010. The reporting of the gain or loss in two income statements causes a temporary difference in the basis of the receivable for income tax and financial reporting purposes. This results because the 2009 unrealized transaction gain of $200 is not taxable until 2010, the year the transaction was ultimately completed or settled. Accordingly, deferred income tax accounting is required to account for the effects of this temporary difference.

It is important to note that all monetary assets and liabilities of US Company that are denominated in a currency other than US Company's functional currency (the US dollar) are required to be remeasured at each balance sheet date to the extent that they are affected by increases or decreases in the exchange rate. For example, a US Company whose functional currency is the US dollar holds a bank account in France that is denominated in euros. At each balance sheet date, by reference to the spot rate for the euro, US Company would remeasure the carrying amount of its French bank account and record any resulting transaction gains and losses in the same manner as above.

## Intercompany Transactions and Elimination of Intercompany Profits

Gains or losses from intercompany transactions are reported on the US company's consolidated income statement unless settlement of the transaction is not planned or anticipated in the foreseeable future. In that case, which is atypical, gains and losses arising from intercompany transactions are reflected in the accumulated translations adjustments component of accumulated other comprehensive income in stockholders' equity of the US entity. In the typical situation (i.e., gains and losses reported on the US entity's income statement) gains and losses result whether the functional currency is the US dollar or the foreign entity's local currency. When the US dollar is the functional currency, foreign currency transaction gains and losses result because of one of the two situations below.

1.  The intercompany foreign currency transaction is denominated in US dollars. In this case, the foreign subsidiary has a payable or receivable denominated in US dollars. This may result in a foreign currency transaction gain or loss that would appear on the foreign subsidiary's income statement. This gain or loss would be translated into US dollars and would appear on the US entity's consolidated income statement.

2.  The intercompany foreign currency transaction is denominated in the foreign subsidiary's local currency. In this situation, the US entity has a payable or receivable denominated in a foreign currency. Such a situation may result in a foreign currency transaction gain or loss that is reported on the US parent entity's income statement.

The above two cases can be easily altered to reflect what happens when the foreign entity's local currency is the functional currency. The gain or loss from each of these scenarios would be reflected on the other entity's financial statements first (i.e., the subsidiary's rather than the parent's and vice versa).

The elimination of intercompany profits due to sales and other transfers between related entities is based upon exchange rates in effect when the sale or transfer occurred. Reasonable approximations and averages are allowed to be used if intercompany transactions occur frequently during the year.

### Example of intercompany transactions involving foreign exchange

Cassiopeia Corporation buys an observatory-grade telescope from its Spanish subsidiary for €850,000, resulting in a profit for the subsidiary of €50,000 on the sale date at an exchange rate of $1:€0.6 (euros). The profit is eliminated at $1:€0.6. The payable to the subsidiary is due in 90 days, and is denominated in euros. On the payment date, the exchange rate has changed to $1:€0.65 Thus, rather than paying $1,416,667 to settle the payable, as would have been the case on the sale date, Cassiopeia must now pay $1,307,692 on the payable date. Cassiopeia presents the $108,975 exchange gain in its income statement in the following manner:

| | |
|---|---|
| Sales | $20,000,000 |
| Cost of sales | (14,000,000) |
| Gross profit | 6,000,000 |
| Operating expenses | (5,500,000) |
| Other revenues/gains (expenses/losses) | |
| Gain on translation of foreign currencies | (108,975) |
| Net income | $608,975 |

In a separate series of transactions, the subsidiary sends a weekly shipment of telescope repair parts to Cassiopeia, totaling €48,000 of profits for the entire year. For these transactions, the exchange rate varies from $1:€0.6 to $1:€0.75. A reasonable estimate of the average exchange rate for all the transactions is $1:€1.67. Consequently, the €48,000 profit is eliminated at the $1:€1.67(= $71,642) average exchange rate.

## Foreign Currency Hedging

FAS 133, *Accounting for Derivative Instruments and Hedging Activities*, provides complex hedging rules that permit the reporting entity to elect to obtain special accounting treatment relative to foreign currency risks with respect to the following items:

1. Recognized assets or liabilities
2. Available-for-sale debt and equity securities
3. Unrecognized firm commitments
4. Foreign-currency-denominated forecasted cash flows
5. Net investment in a foreign operation

Chapter 8 provides a detailed discussion of derivatives and hedging. The table on the next page provides a high-level summary of the complex provisions that apply to hedges related to foreign currency exposures.

**Measuring hedge effectiveness.** While any entity may utilize hedging strategies, under the provisions of FAS 133 the transaction must meet a number of important conditions in order to qualify for hedge accounting. Among these conditions (discussed in greater detail in Chapter 8) are the establishment, at inception, of criteria for measuring hedge effectiveness and ineffectiveness. Periodically, each hedge must be evaluated for effectiveness, using the preestablished criteria, and the gains or losses associated with hedge ineffectiveness must be reported currently in earnings, and not deferred to future periods. In the instance of foreign currency hedges, FAS 133 states that reporting entities must exclude from their assessments of hedge effectiveness the portions of the fair value of forward contracts attributable to spot-forward differences (i.e., differences between the spot exchange rate and the forward exchange rate).

In practice, this means that reporting entities engaging in foreign currency hedging will recognize changes in the above-described portion of the derivative's fair value in earnings, in the same manner that changes representing hedge ineffectiveness are reported, but these are not considered to represent ineffectiveness. These entities must estimate the cash flows on forecasted transactions based on the current spot exchange rate, appropriately discounted for time value. Effectiveness is then assessed by comparing the changes in fair values of the forward contracts attributable to changes in the dollar spot price of the pertinent foreign currency to the changes in the present values of the forecasted cash flows based on the current spot exchange rate(s).

### Example

On October 1, 2009, Braveheart Co. (a US company) orders from its European supplier, Gemutlicheit GmbH, a machine that is to be delivered and paid for on March 31, 2010. The price, denominated in euros, is €4,000,000. Although Braveheart will not make the payment until the planned delivery date, it has immediately entered into a firm commitment to make this purchase and to pay €4,000,000 upon delivery. This creates a euro liability exposure to foreign exchange risk; thus, if the euro appreciates over the intervening six months, the dollar cost of the equipment will increase.

To reduce or eliminate this uncertainty, Braveheart desires to lock in the purchase cost in euros by entering into a six-month forward contract to purchase euros on the date when the purchase order is issued to and accepted by Gemutlicheit. The spot rate on October 1, 2009, is $1.40 per euro and the forward rate for March 31, 2010 settlement is $1.44 per euro. Braveheart enters into a forward contract on October 1, 2009, with the First Intergalactic Bank to pay US $5,760,000 in exchange for the receipt of €4,000,000 on March 31, 2010, which can then be used to pay Gemutlicheit. No premium is received nor paid at the inception of this forward contract.

The transaction is a firm commitment consistent with the requirements of FAS 133, and fair value hedge accounting is used in accounting for the forward contract.

# Hedging Foreign Currency Exposures

*Hedges of foreign currency (FC) exposures (where FC is not the reporting entity's functional currency)*

| | A | B | C |
|---|---|---|---|
| | Fair value (FV) hedges | Cash Flow (CF) hedges | C. Hedges of a net investment in a foreign operation |
| Types of items that may qualify to be hedged | A1. Recognized assets or liabilities<br>A2. Available-for-sale debt securities<br>A3. Available-for-sale equity securities<br>A4. Unrecognized firm commitments (UFC) | B1. Forecasted CF from recognized assets or liabilities<br>B2. Forecasted external transactions<br>B3. Forecasted intercompany transactions<br>B4. Unrecognized firm commitments (UFC) | |
| Risk being hedged | Changes in FV of the hedged item that result from changes in the exchange rate (ER) of the FC in which it is denominated (which, by definition, is not the functional currency of the reporting entity) | The FC exposure to variability in the "equivalent functional currency cash flows" associated with the hedged item | Exposure of the net investment to changes in the exchange rate applicable to the functional currency of the investee |
| Type of instruments that qualify for use as hedging instruments | A1, A2, A3—Required to be derivatives A$ can be a derivative instrument or nonderivative financial instrument | Required to be derivatives | Can be derivative instrument or a nonderivative financial instrument; Nonderivative financial instruments, to be designated, cannot be subject to GAAP that requires that they be presented at FV since that accounting treatment would not result in foreign currency transaction gains or losses under FAS 52 |
| Summary of accounting treatment | General Rule: When the ER changes, recognize in current earnings: (1) changes in FV of hedged item caused by the hedged risk, (2) gain or loss on changes in FV of the designated hedging instrument, and (3) hedge ineffectiveness, if any<br><br>AFS securities: Change in FV of the security attributable to FC risk is reported in earnings; other changes in FV of the security, not attributable to the comprehensive risk continue to be reported in other comprehensive income | General Rule: The effective portion of the gain or loss on a derivative designated as a cash flow hedge is reported in other comprehensive income (OCI) and the ineffective portion is reported currently in earnings. In the period or periods during which a hedged forecasted transaction affects earnings, amounts in accumulated other comprehensive income (AOCI) are reclassified to earnings.<br><br>Additional complex accounting provisions are provided by FAS 133, ¶30 through ¶35 | To the extent of hedge effectiveness, gains or losses on the hedging derivative instrument (or FC transaction gains or losses on the hedging nonderivative instrument) are accounted for in the same manner as a FC translation adjustment (i.e., reported as other comprehensive income and as a change in accumulated other comprehensive income); The hedged net investment is accounted for consistent with FAS 52 as described in this chapter; Any hedge ineffectiveness is reflected as a transaction gain or loss in earnings of the period in which it arises |
| Applicable conditions, criteria limitations or exceptions | **Fair value hedges**<br>a. Fair value hedges are required to meet the requirements of FAS 133, ¶20 and ¶21 with respect to such matters as timely hedge designation, tests of hedge effectiveness at inception and on an ongoing basis<br>b. A3(i) The AFS equity security cannot be traded on an exchange or market where transactions are denominated in the investor's functional currency, and (ii) Dividends and all other cash flows associated with holding or selling the security must be denominated in the same foreign currency.<br>c. A2, A4—The hedged transaction must be denominated in a FC other than the hedging unit's functional currency, and if consolidated financial statements, the party to the hedging instrument must be either (i) the operating unit with the FC exposure or (ii) another member of the consolidated group (subject to certain specified restrictions and meeting certain conditions) with the same functional currency as that operating unit.<br>d. FC derivatives entered into with another member of the consolidated group can be designated as hedging instruments in all fair value hedge transaction types (A1-A4) only if that member has entered into an offsetting contract with an unrelated third party to hedge the exposure it acquired from issuing the derivative instrument to the affiliate that initiated the hedge.<br><br>**Cash flow hedges and hedges of net investments in foreign operations**<br>e. Cash flow hedges must meet the requirements of FAS 133, ¶28 and ¶B40-¶B40C<br>f. Cash flow hedges of forecasted transactions must additionally meet the requirements of FAS 133, ¶29<br>g. Cash flow hedges of forecasted transactions (B1), and hedges of net investments in foreign operations (C) must also meet the criteria in d. above. | | |
| Eligibility for FAS 159 Fair Value Option (FVO) | A4—Limited eligibility when the UFC involves only financial instruments | Not eligible | Not eligible |

Assume the relevant time value of money is measured at 1/2% per month (a nominal 6% annual rate). The spot rate for euros at December 31, 2009, is $1.45, and at March 31, 2010, it is $1.48. The forward rate as of December 31 for March 31 settlement is $1.46.

Entries to reflect the foregoing scenario are as follows:

| | | | |
|---|---|---|---|
| 10/1/09 | *No entries, since neither the forward contract nor the firm commitment have value on this date* | | |

| | | | |
|---|---|---|---|
| 12/31/09 | Forward currency contract | 78,818 | |
| |     Gain on forward contract | | 78,818 |

*To record present value (at 1/2% monthly rate) of change in value of forward contract [= change in forward rate (1.46 – 1.44) × €4,000,000 = $80,000 to be received in three months, discounted at 6% per annum]*

| | | |
|---|---|---|
| Loss on firm purchase commitment | 197,044 | |
|     Firm commitment obligation | | 197,044 |

*To record present value (at 1/2% monthly rate) of change in amount of firm commitment [= change in spot rate (1.45 – 1.40) × €4,000,000 = $200,000 to be paid in three months, discounted at 6% per annum]*

| | | |
|---|---|---|
| Gain on forward contract | 78,818 | |
|     Loss on firm purchase commitment | | 197,044 |
|     P&L summary (then to retained earnings) | 118,226 | |

*To close the gain and loss accounts to net income and thus to retained earnings*

| | | | |
|---|---|---|---|
| 3/31/10 | Forward currency contract | 81,182 | |
| |     Gain on forward contract | | 81,182 |

*To record change in value of forward contract {[= (1.48 – 1.44) × €4,000,000 = $160,000] – gain previously recognized ($78,818)}*

| | | |
|---|---|---|
| Loss on firm commitment | 122,956 | |
|     Firm commitment obligation | | 122,956 |

*To record change in amount of firm commitment {[= (1.48 – 1.40) × €4,000,000] less loss previously recognized ($197,044)}*

| | | |
|---|---|---|
| Firm commitment obligation | 320,000 | |
| Machinery and equipment | 5,600,000 | |
|     Cash | | 5,920,000 |

*To record purchase of machinery based on spot exchange rate as of date of contractual commitment (1.40) and close out the firm commitment obligation (representing effect of change in spot rate during commitment period)*

| | | |
|---|---|---|
| Cash | 160,000 | |
|     Forward contract | | 160,000 |

*To record collection of cash on net settlement of forward contract [= (1.48 – 1.44) × €4,000,000]*

| | | |
|---|---|---|
| Gain on forward contract | 81,182 | |
| P&L summary (then to retained earnings) | 41,774 | |
|     Loss on firm purchase commitment | | 122,956 |

*To close the gain and loss accounts to net income and thus to retained earnings*

Observe that in the foregoing example the gain on the forward contract did not precisely offset the loss incurred from the firm commitment. Since a hedge of an unrecognized foreign currency denominated firm commitment is accounted for as a fair value hedge, with gains and losses on hedging positions and on the hedged item both being recorded in current earnings, it may appear that the matter of hedge effectiveness is of academic interest only. However, according to FAS 133, even if both components (that is, the net gain or loss representing hedge ineffectiveness, and the amount charged to earnings which was excluded from the measurement of ineffectiveness) are reported in current period earnings, the distinction between them is still of importance.

With respect to fair value hedges of firm purchase commitments denominated in a foreign currency, FAS 133 directs that "the change in value of the contract related to the changes in the differences between the spot price and the forward or futures price would be excluded from the assessment of hedge effectiveness." As applied to the foregoing example, therefore, the net credit to income in 2009 ($118,226) can be further analyzed into two constituent elements: the amount arising from the change in the difference between the spot price and the forward price, and the amount resulting from hedge ineffectiveness.

The former item, not attributed to ineffectiveness, arose because the spread between spot and forward price at hedge inception, (1.44 − 1.40 =) .04, fell to (1.46 − 1.45 =) .01 by December 31, for an impact amounting to (.04 − .01 =) .03 × €4,000,000 = $120,000, which, reduced to present value terms, equaled $118,227. The net credit to earnings in December 2009, ($78,818 + 118,226 =) $197,044, relates to the spread between the spot and forward rates on December 31 and is identifiable with hedge ineffectiveness.

## Forward Exchange Contracts

Foreign currency transaction gains and losses on assets and liabilities that are denominated in a currency other than the functional currency can be hedged if a US company enters into a forward exchange contract. The following example shows how a forward exchange contract can be used as a hedge, first against a firm commitment and then, following delivery date, as a hedge against a recognized liability.

A general rule for estimating the fair value of forward exchange rates under FAS 133 is to use the changes in the forward exchange rates, and discount those estimated future cash flows to a present-value basis. An entity will need to consider the time value of money if significant in the circumstances for these contracts. The following example does not apply discounting of the future cash flows from the forward contracts in order to focus on the relationships between the forward contract and the foreign currency denominated payable.

### Example

Durango, Inc. enters into a firm commitment with Dempsey Ing., Inc. of Germany, on October 1, 2009, to purchase a computerized robotic system for €6,000,000. The system will be delivered on March 1, 2010, with payment due sixty days after delivery (April 30, 2010). Durango, Inc. decides to hedge this foreign currency firm commitment and enters into a forward exchange contract on the firm commitment date to receive €6,000,000 on the payment date. The applicable exchange rates are shown in the table below.

| Date | Spot rates | Forward rates for April 30, 2009 |
|---|---|---|
| October 1, 2009 | €1 = $1.55 | €1 = $ 1.57 |
| December 31, 2009 | €1 = $1.58 | €1 = $1.589 |
| March 1, 2010 | €1 = $1.58 | €1 = $1.585 |
| April 30, 2010 | €1 = $1.60 | |

The example on the following pages separately presents both the forward contract receivable and the dollars payable liability in order to show all aspects of the forward contract. For financial reporting purposes, most companies present just the net fair value of the forward contract that would be the difference between the current value of the forward contract receivable and the dollars payable liability. Note that the foreign currency hedges in the illustration are not perfectly effective. However, for this example, the degree of ineffectiveness is not deemed to be sufficient to trigger income statement recognition per FAS 133. (Hedge effectiveness is discussed in Chapter 8.)

The transactions that reflect the forward exchange contract, the firm commitment and the acquisition of the asset and retirement of the related liability appear below. The net fair value of the forward contract is shown below each set of entries for the forward exchange contract.

In the case of using a forward exchange contract to speculate in a specific foreign currency, the general rule to estimate the fair value of the forward contract is to use the forward exchange rate for the remainder of the term of the forward contract.

## The Fair Value Option

In 2007, FASB issued FAS 159, *The Fair Value Option for Financial Assets and Financial Liabilities*. FAS 159 encourages reporting entities to voluntarily elect to use fair value to measure eligible financial assets and financial liabilities in their financial statements. This election is referred to as the Fair Value Option (FVO). Changes in the fair values of these assets and liabilities would be reflected in earnings as they occur.

In issuing FAS 159, FASB indicated that, among the reasons it decided to permit this election was that the election would "enable entities to achieve consistent accounting and, potentially, an offsetting effect for the changes in the fair values of related assets and liabilities without having to apply complex hedge accounting provisions, thereby providing greater simplicity in the application of accounting guidance."[1]

As noted in the table, Hedging Foreign Currency Exposure, presented earlier in this chapter, the provisions of FAS 159 have limited applicability with respect to foreign currency risks. The election does not affect cash flow hedges or hedges of a net investment in a foreign operation. With respect to fair value hedges, the reporting entity may elect the FVO for eligible nonderivative financial assets or liabilities. An unrecognized firm commitment (UFC) may qualify as a financial instrument if it only involves financial assets and liabilities. FAS 159 provides, as an example, a forward purchase contract for a loan that is not readily convertible to cash. This instrument would qualify for the FVO. In order to achieve the desired economic offsetting that would resemble hedge accounting, the reporting entity would also have to hold assets denominated in the same foreign currency (which is not the entity's functional currency) that give rise to foreign currency transaction gains or losses that would partially or fully offset changes in the fair value of the forward purchase contract during its term and at settlement.

Elections made under the FVO are irrevocable and, if made by early adopting FAS 159, also require the reporting entity to early adopt the disclosure provisions of FAS 157 that otherwise would not be effective until the same date as FAS 159.

---

[1] *Statement of Financial Accounting Standards No. 159, **The Fair Value Option for Financial Assets and Financial Liabilities**. Norwalk, CT: Financial Accounting Standards Board, 2007.*

(1)  10/1/08 (forward rate for 4/30/09 €1 = $1.57)
Forward contract receivable                    9,420,000
   Dollars payable                                           9,420,000

This entry recognizes the existence of the forward exchange contract using the gross method. Under the net method, this entry would not appear at all, since the fair value of the forward contract is zero when the contract is initiated. The amount is calculated using the 10/1/08 forward rate for 4/30/09 (€6,000,000 × $1.57 = $9,420,000).

Net fair value of the forward contract = $0

Note that the net fair value of the forward exchange contact on 10/1/08 is zero because there is an exact amount offset of the forward contract receivable of $9,420,000 with the dollars payable liability of $9,420,000. Many companies present only the net fair value of the forward contract on their balance sheets, and therefore, they would have no net amount reported for the forward contract at its inception.

(2)  12/31/08 (forward rate for 4/30/09 €1 = $1.589)
Forward contract receivable                    114,000
   Gain on hedge activity                                  114,000

The dollar values for this entry reflect, among other things, the change in the forward rate from 10/1/08 to 12/31/08. However, the actual amount recorded as gain or loss (gain in this case) is determined by all market factors.

Net increase in fair value of the forward contract = (1.589 − 1.57 = .019 × €6,000,000 = $114,000).

The increase in the net fair value of the forward exchange contract on 12/31/08 is $114,000 for the difference between the $7,134,000 ($7,020,000 plus $114,000) in the forward contract receivable and the $7,020,000 for the dollars payable liability. Many companies present only the net fair value on their balance sheet, in this case as an asset. And, this $114,000 is the amount that would be discounted to present value, if interest is significant, to recognize the time value of the future cash flow from the forward contract.

(4)  3/1/09 (forward rate for 4/30/09 €1 = $1.585)
Loss on hedge activity                              24,000
   Forward contract receivable                        24,000

These entries again will be driven by market factors, and they are calculated the same way as entries (2) and (3) above. Note that the decline in the forward rate from 12/31/08 to 3/1/09 resulted in a loss against the forward contract receivable and a gain against the firm commitment [1.585 − 1.589 = (.004) × €6,000,000 = ($24,000)].

(3)  12/31/08
Loss on hedge activity                              114,000
   Firm commitment                                       114,000

The dollar values for this entry are identical to those in entry (2), reflecting the fact that the hedge is highly effective (100%) and also the fact that the market recognizes the same factors in this transaction as for entry (2). This entry reflects the first use of the firm commitment account, a temporary liability account pending the receipt of the asset against which the firm commitment has been hedged.

(5)  3/1/09
Firm commitment                                      24,000
   Gain on hedge activity                               24,000

*Forward contract entries*

Net fair value of the forward contract = $90,000
The net fair value of the forward exchange contract on 3/1/09 is $90,000 for the difference between the $9,510,000 ($9,420,000 plus 114,000 minus $24,000) in the forward contract receivable and the $9,420,000 for the dollars payable liability. Another way of computing the net fair value is to determine the change in the forward contract rate from the initial date of the contract, 10/1/08, which is $1.585 – $1.57 = $.015 × €6,000,000 = $90,000. Also note that the amount in the firm commitment temporary liability account is equal to the net fair value of the forward contract on the date the equipment is received.

(7) 4/30/09 (spot rate €1 = $1.60)

| | | |
|---|---|---|
| Forward contract receivable | 90,000 | |
|     Gain on forward contract | | 90,000 |

The gain or loss (gain in this case) on the forward contract is calculated using the change in the forward to the spot rate from 3/1/09 to 4/30/09 [€6,000,000 × ($1.60 – $1.585) = $90,000]

Net fair value of the forward contract = $180,000

The net fair value of the forward exchange contract on 4/30/09 is $180,000 for the difference between the $9,600,000 ($9,510,000 plus $90,000) in the forward contract receivable and the $9,420,000 for the dollars payable liability. The net fair value of the forward contract at its terminal date of 4/30/09 is based on the difference between the contract forward rate of €1 = $1.57 and the spot rate on 4/30/09 of €1 = $1.60. The forward contract receivable has reached its maturity and the contract is completed on this date at the forward rate of €1 = $1.57 as contracted on 10/1/08. If the entity recognizes an interest factor in the forward contract over the life of the contract, then interest is recognized at this time on the forward contract, but no separate accrual of interest is required for the accounts payable in euros.

(9) 4/30/09

| | | |
|---|---|---|
| Dollars payable | 9,420,000 | |
|     Cash | | 9,420,000 |
| | | |
| Foreign currency units (€) | 9,600,000 | |
|     Forward contract receivable | | 9,600,000 |

This entry reflects the settlement of the forward contract at the 10/1/08 contracted forward rate (€6,000,000 × $1.17 = $7,020,000) and the receipt of foreign currency units valued at the spot rate (€6,000,000 × $1.20 = $7,200,000).

*Hedge against a recognized liability entries*

(6) 3/1/09 (spot rate €1 = $1.58)

| | | |
|---|---|---|
| Equipment | 9,390,000 | |
| Firm commitment | 90,000 | |
|     Accounts payable (€) | | 9,480,000 |

This entry records the receipt of the equipment, the elimination of the temporary liability account (firm commitment), and the recognition of the payable, calculated using the spot rate on the date of receipt (€6,000,000 × $1.58 = $9,480,000).

(8) 4/30/09

| | | |
|---|---|---|
| Transaction loss | 120,000 | |
|     Accounts payable (€) | | 120,000 |

The transaction loss related to the accounts payable reflects only the change in the spot rates and ignores the accrual of interest. [€6,000,000 × ($1.60 – $1.58) = $120,000]

(10) 4/30/09

| | | |
|---|---|---|
| Accounts payable (€) | 9,600,000 | |
|     Foreign currency units (€) | | 9,600,000 |

This entry reflects the use of the foreign currency units to retire the account payable.

## APPENDIX

## ACCOUNTS TO BE REMEASURED USING HISTORICAL EXCHANGE RATES

1.  Marketable securities carried at cost (equity securities and debt securities not intended to be held until maturity).
2.  Inventories carried at cost
3.  Prepaid expenses such as insurance, advertising, and rent
4.  Property, plant, and equipment
5.  Accumulated depreciation on property, plant, and equipment
6.  Patents, trademarks, licenses, and formulas
7.  Goodwill
8.  Other intangible assets
9.  Deferred charges and credits, except policy acquisition costs for life insurance companies
10. Deferred income
11. Common stock
12. Preferred stock carried at issuance price
13. Revenues and expenses related to nonmonetary items

    a.  Cost of goods sold
    b.  Depreciation of property, plant, and equipment
    c.  Amortization of intangible items such as goodwill, patents, licenses, etc.
    d.  Amortization of deferred charges or credits, except policy acquisition costs for life insurance companies

*Source: FAS 52.*

# 24 PERSONAL FINANCIAL STATEMENTS

## PERSPECTIVE AND ISSUES

AICPA Statement of Position (SOP) 82-1, *Personal Financial Statements,* addresses the preparation and presentation of personal financial statements, or, more specifically, financial statements of individuals or groups of related individuals (i.e., families). Personal financial statements are generally prepared to organize and plan an individual's financial affairs on a more formal basis. Specific purposes that might require the preparation of personal financial statements include the obtaining of credit, income tax planning, retirement planning, gift and estate planning, or the public disclosure of financial affairs. Third-party recipients of personal financial statements use them in deciding whether to grant credit, in evaluating the financial condition of individuals, in assessing the financial affairs of public officials and candidates for public office, and for other purposes. Estimated current values of assets and liabilities are almost always specified for use in the preparation of personal financial statements as this information is more relevant to users than historical cost.

| Sources of GAAP |
|---|
| *SOP* |
| 82-1 |

## DEFINITIONS OF TERMS

**Estimated current value of an asset.** The amount for which an item could be exchanged between a buyer and a seller, each of whom is well informed and willing, and neither of whom is compelled to buy or sell.

**Estimated current amount of liabilities.** Payables and other liabilities are to be presented at the discounted amounts of future cash to be paid. The interest rate used to discount the debt is the rate implicit in the transaction in which the debt was incurred. If, however, the debtor is able to repay the debt currently at a lower amount, the debt is to be presented at that reduced figure.

**Net worth.** The difference between total assets and total liabilities, after deducting estimated income taxes on the differences between the estimated current values of assets and the estimated current amounts of liabilities and their income tax bases.

## CONCEPTS, RULES, AND EXAMPLES

Personal financial statements can be prepared for an individual, jointly for a husband and wife, or collectively for a family.

Personal financial statements consist of

1. **Statement of financial condition**—The only required financial statement, the statement of financial condition presents the estimated current values of assets and the estimated current amounts of liabilities. A liability is recognized for estimated income taxes on the difference between the asset and liability amounts set forth in the statement of financial condition and their respective income tax bases. Naturally, the residual amount after deducting the liabilities (including the estimated income tax liability) from the assets is presented as net worth at that date.

2. **Statement of changes in net worth**—An optional statement that presents the primary sources of increases and decreases in net worth over a period of time.

3. **Comparative financial statements**—The inclusion of a comparison of the current period's financial statements with one or more previous period's financial statements is optional.

**Basis of presentation.** The accrual basis, rather than the cash basis of accounting, is used in preparing personal financial statements. The presentation of personal financial statements does not require the classification of assets and liabilities as current and noncurrent. Instead, assets and liabilities are presented in order of liquidity and maturity.

**Measurement.** In personal financial statements, assets are presented at their estimated current values. This is defined by SOP 82-1 as the amount at which the item could be exchanged between a buyer and a seller, assuming both parties are well informed, and neither party is compelled to buy or sell. Disposal costs, if material, are deducted to arrive at current values. It is important to note that this definition has not been amended to conform to the definition of fair value as set forth in FAS 157, which is discussed in detail in Chapter 6. The definition of estimated current value in SOP 82-1 more closely resembles the definition of fair value less cost to sell that is used in FAS 144, *Accounting for the Impairment or Disposal of Long-Lived Assets* (See Chapter 11). Futhermore, SOP 82-1 specifically provides for adjustment of the current value of securities for the effects of transferability restrictions or the effects of the investor holding a large block of securities (blockage factor). Adjustments for blockage factors are specifically prohibited by FAS 157.

A specialist may need to be consulted in the determination of the current value of certain types of assets (e.g., works of art, jewelry, restricted securities, investments in closely held businesses, and real estate). If property is held in joint tenancy, as community property, or through a similar joint ownership arrangement, the finanacial statement preparer may require the advice of an attorney to determine, under applicable state law, the portion of the property interest that should be included in the indiviual's assets.

Liabilities are presented at the lesser of the discounted amount of cash to be paid or the current cash settlement amount. The discount rate should be the rate implicit in the transaction that gave rise to the liability. As a practical matter, the preparer may decide to use the individual's incremental borrowing rate at the inception of the transaction to discount the remaining cash flows.

The use of information about recent transactions involving similar types of assets and liabilities, in similar circumstances, constitutes a satisfactory means of determining the estimated current value of an asset and the estimated current amount of a liability. If recent transactional information cannot be obtained, it is permissible to use other methods (e.g., capitalization of past or prospective earnings, the use of liquidation values, the adjustment of historical cost based on changes in a specific price index, the use of appraisals, and the use of the discounted amounts of projected cash receipts and payments). The methods used should be followed consistently from period to period unless the facts and circumstances dictate a change to different methods.

Income taxes payable are to include unpaid income taxes for completed tax years and the estimated amount for the elapsed portion of the current tax year. Additionally, personal financial statements are required to include estimated income tax on the difference between the current value (amount) of assets (liabilities) and their respective income tax bases as if they had been realized or liquidated.

The table below summarizes the methods of determining "estimated current values" for assets and "estimated current amounts" for liabilities.

| *Assets and liabilities* | *Discounted cash flow* | *Quoted market price* | *Appraised value* | *Other* |
|---|---|---|---|---|
| • Receivables | x | | | |
| • Marketable debt and equity securities | | x | | If traded on valuation day: closing price. If not traded: valuation must fall in range (between bid and ask price); Adjustments may be required for factors such as the holding of a large block of equity securities in an enterprise (blockage factor) or for restrictions on transfer of the securities |
| • Options—securities | | x | | If a quoted market price for the option is not available, compute based on the value of the asset subject to option considering factors such as the exercise price and length of option period |
| • Options—other assets* | | | | Difference between the exercise price and the current value of the contracted asset, discounted at the interest rate that would be available to the indivisual to borrow with the asset under option as collateral |
| • Investment in life insurance | | | | Cash surrender value less outstanding loans |
| • Investment in closely held business | x | | x | Liquidation value, multiple of earnings, reproduction value, adjustment of book value or cost |
| • Real estate (including leaseholds) | x | | x | By reference to sales of comparable property, appraisals used for the purpose of borrowing, by reference to assessed values used for property tax purposes, and to the relationship of assessed value to current value of properties in the geographic area |
| • Intangible assets | x | | | Net proceeds from current sale or discounted cash flows from asset; otherwise, may use cost of purchasing a similar asset, if available |
| • Future interests (nonforfeitable rights)** | x | | | |
| • Payables and other liabilities | x | | | Discharge amount if lower than discounted amount |
| • Noncancelable commitments*** | x | | | |
| • Income taxes payable | | | | Unpaid income tax for completed tax years and estimated income tax for elapsed portion of current tax year to date of financial statements |

| | |
|---|---|
| • Estimated income tax on difference between current values of assets and current amounts of liabilities and their respective tax bases | Computed as if current value of assets and liabilities had been respectively realized or liquidated considering applicable tax laws and regulations, recapture provisions and carryovers. |
| • Uncertain obligations* | Not covered by SOP 82-1; follow recognition, measurement, and disclosure guidance in FAS 5 |

  * *Adapted from: "Personal Financial Statements: Valuation Challenges and Solutions," Michael D. Kinsman, CPA, PhD, and Bruce Samuelson,CPA, DBA,* **Journal of Accountancy***, September 1987, pp. 138-148.*
  ** *Rights have all of the following attributes: (1) are for fixed or determinable amounts; (2) are not contingent on holder's life expectancy or occurrence of a particular event (e.g., disability/death), and (3) do not require future performance of service by holder.*
*** *Commitments have all of the following attributes: (1) are for fixed or determinable amounts; (2) are not contingent on others' life expectancies or occurrence of a particular event (e.g., disability/death); and (3) do not require future performance of service by others.*

**Business interests** that comprise a large portion of a person's total assets should be presented separately from other investments. An investment in a separate entity that is marketable as a going concern (e.g., a closely held corporation) should be presented as one amount. If the investment is a limited business activity, not conducted in a separate legal entity, separate asset and liability amounts should be shown (e.g., investment in real estate and related mortgage; only the person's beneficial interest in the investment is included in his/her personal financial statements).

The preparer must decide whether to value the net investment him/herself or to engage a qualified specialist. The possible valuation methods available are discounted cash flow, appraised value, liquidation value, multiple of earnings, reproduction value, adjustment of book value (e.g., equity method), or cost. In some cases it is appropriate to use a combination of approaches to reasonably estimate the current value.

The following disclosures are typically made in either the body of the financial statements or in the accompanying notes. (This list is not all-inclusive.) Source: SOP 82-1.

1. A clear identification of the individuals covered by the financial statements
2. That assets are presented at their estimated current values and liabilities are presented at their estimated current amounts
3. The methods used in determining the estimated current values of major assets and the estimated current amounts of major liabilities or major categories of assets and liabilities, and changes in methods from one period to the next
4. If assets held jointly by the person and by others included in the statements, the nature of the joint ownership
5. If the person's investment portfolio is material in relation to his or her other assets and is concentrated in one or a few companies or industries, the names of the companies or industries and the estimated current values of the securities
6. If the person has a material investment in a closely held business,
   a. The name of the company
   b. The person's percentage of ownership
   c. The nature of the business
   d. Summarized financial information about assets, liabilities, and results of operations for the most recent year based on the businesses' own financial statements as well as the basis of presentation (e.g. GAAP, cash basis, income tax basis, etc.), and any significant loss contingencies
7. Description of intangible assets and their estimated useful lives

8.   The face amount of life insurance the individual owns
9.   Certain nonforfeitable rights, such as pensions based on life expectancy
10.  The methods and assumptions used to calculate estimated income taxes on the differences between the estimated current values of assets and the estimated current amounts of liabilities and their tax bases as well as a statement that the provision will probably differ from the amounts eventually paid as the timing and method of disposal as well as changes in the tax laws and regulations will affect the actual taxes to be paid
11.  Unused operating loss and capital loss carryforwards and any other unused deductions or credits and, if applicable, the tax year in which they expire (under the current income tax code, there will frequently be unused alternative minimum tax credit carryfowards)
12.  The differences between the estimated current values of major assets and the estimated current amounts of major liabilities or categories of assets and liabilities and their tax bases
13.  Maturities, interest rates, collateral, and other pertinent details relating to receivables and debt
14.  Certain noncancellable commitments such as operating leases

# APPENDIX

## HYPOTHETICAL SET OF PERSONAL FINANCIAL STATEMENTS

**Marcus and Kelly Imrich**
**Statements of Financial Condition**
**December 31, 2009 and 2008**

|  | 2009 | 2008 |
|---|---|---|
| *Assets* | | |
| Cash | $ 381,437 | $ 207,621 |
| Certificate of deposit | 20,000 | 10.000 |
| Securities | | |
|    Marketable (Note 2) | 128,787 | 260,485 |
|    Tax-exempt bonds (Note 3) | 1,890,222 | 986,278 |
| Loans receivable (Note 4) | 262,877 | 362,877 |
| Partnership and joint venture interests (Note 5) | 935,000 | 938,000 |
| Real estate interests (Note 6) | 890,000 | 2,500,000 |
| David Corporation (Note 7) | 2,750,687 | 2,600,277 |
| Cash surrender value of life insurance (Note 8) | 388,000 | 265,000 |
| Personal residences (Note 9) | 2,387,229 | 2,380,229 |
| Deferred losses from partnerships | 68,570 | 60,830 |
| Vested interest in David Corporation benefit plan | 545,960 | 530,960 |
| Personal jewelry and furnishings (Note 10) | 513,000 | 6,700 |
|    Total assets | $11,161,769 | $11,109,257 |
| | | |
| *Liabilities* | | |
| Mortgage payable (Note 11) | $ 254,000 | $ 267,000 |
| Security deposits—rentals | -- | 5,700 |
| Income taxes payable—current year balance | 9,800 | 10,680 |
|    Total liabilities | 263,800 | 283,380 |
| | | |
| Estimated income taxes on difference between estimated current values of assets and estimated current amounts of liabilities and their tax bases (Note 12) | 555,400 | 731,000 |
| *Net Worth* | 10,342,569 | 10,094,877 |
|    Total liabilities and net worth | $11,161,769 | $11,109,257 |

**Marcus and Kelly Imrich**
**Statement of Changes in Net Worth**
**For the Years Ended December 31, 2009 and 2008**

|  | 2009 | 2008 |
|---|---|---|
| *Realized increases in net worth* | | |
| Salary and bonus | $ 200,000 | $ 175,000 |
| Dividends and interest income | 184,260 | 85,000 |
| Distribution from limited partnerships | 280,000 | 260,000 |
| Gain on sales of marketable securities | 58,240 | 142,800 |
| | 722,500 | 662,800 |
| *Realized decreases in net worth* | | |
| Income taxes | 180,000 | 140,000 |
| Interest expense | 25,000 | 26,000 |
| Real estate taxes | 21,000 | 18,000 |
| Personal expenditures | 242,536 | 400,000 |
| | 468,536 | 584,000 |
|    Net realized increase in net worth | 253,964 | 78,800 |
| *Unrealized increases in net worth* | | |
| Marketable securities (net of realized gains on securities sold) | 37,460 | 30,270 |
| Benefit plan—David Corporation | 15,000 | 14,000 |
| Personal jewelry and furnishings | 20,000 | 18,000 |
| | 72,460 | 62,270 |

*Unrealized decreases in net worth*

| | | |
|---|---:|---:|
| Estimated income taxes on the difference between the estimated current values of assets and the estimated current amounts of liabilities and their tax bases | 78,732 | 64,118 |
| Net unrealized decrease in net worth | (6,272) | (1,848) |
| Net increase in net worth | 247,692 | 76,952 |
| Net worth at the beginning of year | 10,094,877 | 10,017,925 |
| Net worth at the end of year | $10,342,569 | $10,094,877 |

**Marcus and Kelly Imrich**
**Notes to Financial Statements**

**Note 1:** The accompanying financial statements include the assets and liabilities of Marcus and Kelly Imrich. Assets are stated at their estimated current values, and liabilities at their estimated current amounts.

**Note 2:** The estimated current values of marketable securities are either (1) their quoted closing prices or (2) for securities not traded on the financial statement date, amounts that fall within the range of quoted bid and asked prices.

Marketable securities consist of the following:

| | December 31, 2009 | | December 31, 2008 | |
|---|---|---|---|---|
| | *Number of* | *Estimated current* | *Number of* | *Estimated current* |
| *Stocks* | *shares* | *values* | *shares* | *values* |
| Susan Schultz, Inc. | | | 1,000 | $122,000 |
| Ripley Robotics Corp. | 500 | $ 51,927 | 1,000 | 120,485 |
| L.A.W. Corporation | 300 | 20,700 | 100 | 5,000 |
| Jay & Kelly Corp. | 300 | 20,700 | 200 | 5,000 |
| J.A.Z. Corporation | 200 | 35,460 | 200 | 8,000 |
| | | $128,787 | | $260,485 |

**Note 3:** The interest income from state and municipal bonds is generally not subject to federal income taxes but is, except in certain cases, subject to state income tax and federal alternative minimum tax.

**Note 4:** The loan receivable from Carol Parker, Inc. matures January 2016 and bears interest at the prime rate.

**Note 5:** Partnership and joint venture interests consist of the following:

| | *Percent owned* | *Cost* | *Estimated current value 12/31/2009* | *Estimated current value 12/31/2008* |
|---|---|---|---|---|
| East Third Partnership | 50.0% | $ 50,000 | 100,000 | 100,000 |
| 631 Lucinda Joint Venture | 20.0 | 10,000 | 35,000 | 38,000 |
| 27 Wright Partnership | 22.5 | 10,000 | 40,000 | 50,000 |
| Eannarino Partnership | 10.0 | 40,000 | 60,000 | 50,000 |
| Sweeney Joint Venture | 30.0 | 100,000 | 600,000 | 600,000 |
| Kelly Parker Group | 20.0 | 20,000 | 100,000 | 100,000 |
| 707 Lucinda Joint Venture | 50.0 | (11,000) | -- | -- |
| | | | $935,000 | $938,000 |

**Note 6:** Mr. and Mrs. Imrich own a one-half interest in an apartment building in DeKalb, Illinois. The estimated current value was determined by Mr. and Mrs. Imrich. Their income tax basis in the apartment building was $1,000,000 for both 2009 and 2008.

**Note 7:** Kelly Imrich owns 75% of the common stock of the David Corporation. A condensed statement of assets, liabilities, and stockholders' equity (income tax basis) of David Corporation as of December 31, 2009 and 2008 is summarized below.

| | *2009* | *2008* |
|---|---:|---:|
| Current assets | $2,975,000 | $3,147,000 |
| Investments | 200,000 | 200,000 |
| Property and equipment (net) | 145,000 | 165,000 |
| Loans receivable | 110,000 | 120,000 |
| Total assets | $3,430,000 | $3,632,000 |

| | | |
|---|---:|---:|
| Current liabilities | $2,030,000 | $2,157,000 |
| Other liabilities | 450,000 | 400,000 |
| Total liabilities | 2,480,000 | 2,557,000 |
| Stockholders' equity | 950,000 | 1,075,000 |
| Total liabilities and stockholders' equity | $3,430,000 | $3,632,000 |

**Note 8:**  At December 31, 2009 and 2008, Marcus Imrich owned a $1,000,000 whole life insurance policy. Mrs. Imrich is the sole beneficiary under the policy.

**Note 9:**  The estimated current values of the personal residences are their purchase prices plus their cost of improvements. Both residences were purchased in 2007.

**Note 10:**  The estimated current values of personal effects and jewelry are the appraised values of those assets, determined by an independent appraiser for insurance purposes.

**Note 11:**  The mortgage (collateralized by the residence) is payable in monthly installments of $2,479, including interest at an annual rate of 6% through 2021.

**Note 12:**  The estimated current amounts of liabilities at December 31, 2009, and December 31, 2008, equaled their income tax bases. Estimated income taxes have been provided on the excess of the estimated current values of assets over their tax bases as if the estimated current values of the assets had been realized on the dates of the statements of financial condition, using applicable income tax laws and regulations. The provision will probably differ from the amounts of income taxes that eventually will be paid because those amounts are determined by the timing and the method of disposal or realization and the income tax laws and regulations in effect at the time of disposal or realization.

The excess of estimated current values of major assets over their income tax bases are

| | December 31 | |
|---|---:|---:|
| | *2009* | *2008* |
| Investment in David Corporation | $1,400,000 | $1,350,000 |
| Vested interest in benefit plan | 350,000 | 300,000 |
| Investment in marketable securities | 100,000 | 120,300 |
| | $1,850,000 | $1,770,300 |

# 25 SPECIALIZED INDUSTRY GAAP

# BANKING AND THRIFT

## PERSPECTIVE AND ISSUES

In 2004 the AICPA issued a new AAG, *Depository and Lending Institutions: Banks and Savings Institutions, Credit Unions, Finance Companies and Mortgage Companies.* This replaced former, separate guides for each of these industries and reflects the new, unified set of financial reporting requirements applicable to all such institutions. Among other things, this AAG incorporates requirements set forth by FAS 150, FIN 46(R), FTB 01-1, and various FSP and EITFs.

While at one time regulator-imposed financial reporting rules (regulatory accounting principles, commonly called RAP) were mandated for official filings and were also often utilized for general purpose reporting, this is no longer true. Today, financial reporting by banks and thrifts must comply with GAAP, although some specialized industry guidance does exist within that body of standards. In general, certain characteristics unique to financial services entities do demand that certain accounting and financial reporting matters be given more elaboration and interpretation than do these same principles when applied to less specialized entities. These more complex areas are summarized in this section of Chapter 25.

The thrift and (to a lesser degree) banking industries endured difficult times in the 1980s and early 1990s, largely due to very difficult interest rate environments, and a record number of banks and thrifts failed. The formal insolvencies of the thrift insurance fund (FSLIC) and, to a lesser extent, of that for the banks (FDIC) seemed possible, and extraordinary steps were taken by government regulators to avert such events. Mergers were encouraged, and in some cases effectively insolvent institutions (i.e., those having liabilities in excess of assets, when both were adjusted to fair values) were acquired by healthier banks or thrifts. In some instances, acquisitions were encouraged by an unorthodox accounting treatment, whereby the net deficit was accounted for as "supervisory goodwill," to be amortized over an agreed-upon period (typically, fifteen to twenty-five years), with the net unamortized goodwill being considered a "valid asset" for purposes of computing regulatory capital (rather than being deducted from net assets, as would otherwise have been the case).

The accounting profession objected to this treatment, since this supervisory goodwill failed to meet the usual definition of goodwill as being related to excess future earnings potential. However, the profession was ultimately forced to acquiesce, albeit setting some constraints in FAS 72. That standard was later largely eliminated by FAS 147, discussed in this section. Supervisory goodwill was eliminated as an acceptable asset for banks and thrifts by controversial government legislation, spawning a wave of litigation against the federal government which continues to the present time.

Under current GAAP (FAS 142), any goodwill remaining is no longer subject to amortization, but is to be tested for impairment at least annually, more often under defined circumstances (see general discussions in Chapters 11 and 13.

Banks and savings institutions are exempted from the need to present certain cash flow information by FAS 104. Specifically, gross amounts for such high-volume transaction categories as deposits and withdrawals need not be disclosed. Banks and thrifts are not exempt from presenting cash flow statements, however.

Lenders often incur significant costs directly related to the origination or purchase of loans and normally receive different nonrefundable fees at the inception of the loans. Historically, disparate accounting procedures had been applied in the reporting of these costs and fees. FAS 91, *Accounting for Nonrefundable Fees and Costs Associated with Originating or Acquiring Loans and Initial Direct Costs of Leases,* eliminated this diversity. This standard enumerated various categories of costs and fees and set forth the required accounting for each of them. Most fees previously recognized at inception of the loan are now deferred and amortized, via the effective yield method, over the term of the arrangement.

FAS 114 requires loss recognition whenever loans are restructured, unless these involve only an extended payment schedule with full contractual rates of interest being applied to the new due dates. Apart from loan restructurings, however, the issue of when to provide loss reserves, and how these are to be determined, continues to receive a good deal of attention from accounting standard setters and regulatory authorities. The banking regulators and the SEC have indicated that heightened scrutiny is to be applied to loan loss provisions, and interpretative guidance has been offered on the interplay between FAS 5 and 114.

Two AICPA Statements of Position heavily impact accounting by banks. The first of these, SOP 01-6, *Accounting for Certain Entities (Including Entities with Trade Receivables) That Lend to or Finance the Activities of Others,* reconciles and conforms the accounting and financial reporting provisions of AICPA AAG applicable to banks and saving institutions, credit unions, and finance companies. It provides revised accounting guidance for sales of loan servicing rights and makes other recommendations, although it does not establish new GAAP. The provisions for this SOP are discussed in detail in this chapter.

AICPA SOP 03-3, *Accounting for Certain Loans and Debt Securities Acquired in a Transfer,* addresses the accounting for the differences between contractual and expected future cash flows of acquired loans when these differences are attributable, at least in part, to credit quality. Under this standard, when loans are acquired with evidence of deterioration in credit quality since origination, the acquirer must estimate the cash flows expected to be collected on each loan; this is to be done both at the purchase date and periodically over the lives of the loans. Cash flows expected to be collected in excess of the purchase price will be recognized as yield, while contractual cash flows in excess of expected cash flows will not be so recognized, since to do so would probably cause later recognition of bad debts. This SOP is also addressed in detail later in this section.

| | | | | Sources of GAAP | | |
|---|---|---|---|---|---|---|
| *APB* | *FAS* | *FIN* | *FTB* | *EITF* | *SOP* | *AAG* |
| 23 | 72, 91, 104, 109, 114, 115, 118, 134, 140, 147, 150, 156 | 9, 46(R) | 85-1, 87-3, 01-1 | 84-4, 84-9, 84-19, 84-20, 84-21, 84-22, 84-31, 85-7, 85-8, 85-13, 85-18, 85-20, 85-24, 85-26, 85-31, 85-41, 85-42, 85-44, 86-21, 86-31, 86-38, 87-22, 87-34, 88-17, 88-19, 88-20, 88-25, 89-3, 89-19, 90-18, 90-21, 92-5, 93-1, D-2, D-4, D-21, D-34, D-35, D-47, D-49, D-54, D-57, D-67, D-74, D-78, D-80 | 01-6, 02-1, 03-3 | *Depository and Lending Institutions: Banks and Savings Institutions, Credit Unions, Finance Companies and Mortgage Companies* |

## DEFINITIONS OF TERMS

**Accretable yield.** In the context of loans acquired in transfers, the cash flows expected to be collected in excess of the initial investment.

**Carrying amount.** The face amount of the interest-bearing asset plus (or minus) the unamortized premium (or discount).

**Commitment fees.** Fees charged for entering into an agreement that obligates the enterprise to make or acquire a loan or to satisfy an obligation of the other party under a specified condition. For purposes of this Statement, the term commitment fees includes fees for letters of credit and obligations to purchase a loan or group of loans and pass-through certificates.

**General reserve.** Used in the context of the special meaning this term has in regulatory pronouncements and in the US Internal Revenue Code.

**Incremental direct costs.** Costs to originate a loan that (1) result directly from and are essential to the lending transaction and (2) would not have been incurred by the lender had that lending transaction not occurred.

**Long-term interest-bearing assets.** For purposes of this section, these are interest-bearing assets with a remaining term to maturity of more than one year.

**Net-spread method.** Under this method, the acquisition of a savings and loan association is viewed as the acquisition of a leveraged whole rather than the acquisition of the separate assets and liabilities of the association.

**Nonaccretable difference.** In the context of loans acquired in a transfer, the excess of contractual cash flows over the amount of expected cash flows.

**Origination fees.** Fees charged to the borrower in connection with the process of originating, refinancing, or restructuring a loan. This term includes, but is not limited to, points, management, arrangement, placement, application, underwriting, and other fees pursuant to a lending or leasing transaction and also includes syndication and participation fees to the extent they are associated with the portion of the loan retained by the lender.

**Pretax accounting income.** Represents income or loss for a period, exclusive of related income tax expense, determined in conformity with generally accepted accounting principles.

**Reserve for bad debts.** Term is used in the context of the special meaning this term has in regulatory pronouncements and in the US Internal Revenue Code.

**Separate-valuation method.** Under this method, each of the identifiable assets and liabilities (assumed) of the acquired savings and loan association is accounted for in the consolidated financial statements at an amount based on fair value at the date of acquisition, either individually or by types of assets and types of liabilities.

**Servicing asset or liability.** A contract to service financial assets under which the estimated future revenues from contractually specified servicing fees, late charges, and other ancillary revenues are expected (asset) or not expected (liability) to adequately compensate the entity for providing the servicing.

**Taxable income.** Represents pretax accounting income (1) adjusted for reversal of provisions of estimated losses on loans and property acquired in settlement of loans, gains or losses on the sales of such property, and adjusted for permanent differences and (2) after giving effect to the bad debt deduction allowable by the US Internal Revenue Code assuming the applicable tax return were to be prepared based on such adjusted pretax accounting income.

## CONCEPTS, RULES, AND EXAMPLES

### Justifying a Change in Accounting Principle

The following sources are preferred for banking and thrift industries that must justify a change in accounting principle:

1. AAG, *Depository and Lending Institutions: Banks and Savings Institutions, Credit Unions, Finance Companies and Mortgage Companies* (2004)
2. Statement of Position 83-1, *Reporting by Banks of Investment Securities Gains or Losses*
3. Statement of Position 01-6, *Accounting for Certain Entities (Including Entities with Trade Receivables) That Lend to or Finance the Activities of Others*
4. Statement of Position 03-3, *Accounting for Certain Loan and Debt Securities Acquired in a Transfer*

### Acquisition of a Banking or Thrift Institution

The following discussion applies not only to the acquisition of a savings and loan association, but also to acquisition of savings and loan holding companies, commercial banks, mutual savings banks, credit unions, and other depository institutions with assets and liabilities of the same type.

**Purchase method.** In accounting for the acquisition of a banking and thrift institution, the fair value of the assets and liabilities acquired must be determined using the separate-valuation method. Under this method, each of the identifiable assets and liabilities acquired are accounted for individually, or by type, at its fair value at the date of acquisition. The total amount is reported in the consolidated financial statements.

Note that use of the net-spread method is not considered appropriate for this type of business combination. The net-spread method, which views acquisition of the institution as a leveraged whole, does not appropriately recognize the fair value of individual, or types of, assets and liabilities.

Liabilities acquired are accounted for at their present value at the date of acquisition. The present value of savings deposits due on demand equals the face amount plus interest accrued or accruable at the acquisition date. The present value of other liabilities assumed is calculated by using interest rates for similar liabilities in effect at the date of acquisition.

**Identified intangible assets.** The purchase price of a banking or thrift institution may include intangible benefits from the purchase, such as the capacity of acquired assets to generate new business. Intangible assets that can be separately identified at a determinable fair value are to be assigned a portion of the total purchase price and are to be amortized over their estimated lives. Any portion of the purchase price that cannot be identified with specific tangible and intangible assets (less liabilities assumed) is assigned to goodwill.

**Unidentifiable intangible asset.** An unidentifiable intangible asset arises when the fair value of liabilities assumed exceeds the fair value of tangible and identified intangible assets acquired. This asset is amortized over a period no greater than the estimated remaining life of any long-term interest-bearing assets acquired. Amortization is applied to the carrying amount of the interest-bearing assets expected to be outstanding at the beginning of each subsequent period. If, however, the assets acquired do not include a significant portion of long-term interest-bearing assets, the unidentifiable intangible asset is amortized over a period not exceeding the estimated average remaining life of the existing customer base acquired. The amortization period may not exceed forty years.

In the sale or liquidation of a large segment, or separable group, of the operating assets of an acquired banking or thrift institution, the portion of the unidentifiable intangible asset identified with that segment, or separable group, shall be included in the cost of the assets sold. If the sale or liquidation of a large portion of the interest-bearing assets significantly reduces the benefits of the unidentifiable intangible asset, any reduction shall be recognized as a charge to income.

**Regulatory-assisted combinations.** Bank regulatory authorities may grant financial assistance to encourage a bank acquisition. Generally, this is done when a failing bank is sold to a solvent one and the amount of any such direct assistance is less than the cost that would have been incurred honoring the deposit insurance commitment, net of recoveries on assets held by the failing bank. Under GAAP, the assistance should be accounted for as part of the combination if receipt of the assistance is probable and the amount to be received is reasonably estimable. Otherwise, assistance should be reported as a reduction of the unidentifiable asset (goodwill), with any excess over that amount being reported in income. If the grantee is required to repay all or a portion of the assistance, a liability would be recognized, together with a charge against income. Assistance received must be disclosed in the financial statements.

Of primarily historical interest now is another form of assistance that had been offered by regulatory authorities during the "thrift crisis" of the mid-1980s (and which also affected some banks). This was the right to treat the excess of acquired liabilities over acquired assets as an asset (called "supervisory goodwill"), which was permitted for purposes of computing regulatory capital. During that era, the objective was to avoid having the large numbers of thrift and bank failures deplete the insurance funds (FSLIC and FDIC). Later this was seen as having created other problems, and subsequent laws effectively eliminated this accounting treatment, which in turn contributed to another wave of institutional failure when formerly technically solvent banks were judged insolvent.

Many of the institutions which failed or were forced to shrink operations due to the change in federal policy sued for breach of contract. The result of some of these lawsuits was for the government to make some restitution to the savings institutions. EITF Topic D-78, *Accounting for Supervisory Goodwill Litigation Awards or Settlements,* states that any settlements received should be accounted for not as governmental financial assistance (as described in FAS 72), but rather in the same manner as other litigation awards would normally be reported. These are not to be deemed extraordinary gains, but rather are to be included in operating income, with adequate disclosure made to avoid the drawing of misleading inferences regarding possible recurrence. Unsettled claims should be accounted for as only contingent gains (i.e., these should be disclosed, if material, but may not be accrued until and unless realized).

**Elimination of special accounting for goodwill associated with bank and thrift mergers.** The thrift, and later, banking crises of the 1980s gave rise to a number of unusual and often unwise practices. One of these was the invention of "supervisory goodwill," which sometimes was used as an inducement to relatively stronger institutions to acquire those that were, on a mark-to-market (i.e., fair value) basis, already insolvent. The net liabilities assumed, in such instances, was recognized as the intangible asset goodwill, although this would not have generally qualified as such under existing GAAP, since it often did not imply excess future earnings potential, the usual working definition for goodwill. However, thrift and banking regulators permitted the combined institutions to present this asset on their balance sheets, subject to amortization over agreed-upon periods, and to treat the unamortized balance as a qualified asset for capital computation purposes (whereas goodwill was otherwise to be deducted from equity for purpose of making this calculation).

The accounting profession objected to the recognition of supervisory goodwill for GAAP-basis reporting purposes, but ultimately had to acquiesce. In FAS 72, certain parameters were established for the amortization periods to be applied to such supervisory goodwill (referred to as an "unidentifiable intangible asset" in that standard). Thus, the intangible was to be amortized over a period no longer than the estimated remaining life of interest-bearing assets (loans and investments) acquired, which would typically be shorter than the agreed-to terms under the various acquisition agreements then being encouraged by the regulators. FAS 72 was an attempt to mitigate, but not eliminate, the distortions caused by the regulatory recognition of supervisory goodwill.

Beginning in 1989, supervisory goodwill was eliminated from regulatory filings, and although this did not require that such goodwill be deleted from GAAP-basis financial statements, this was largely the consequential effect. More recently, accounting for purchase business combinations has been revised by FAS 141, and the accounting for goodwill has been materially altered by FAS 142.

In light of the foregoing, FASB promulgated FAS 147, because special accounting for goodwill of financial institutions is no longer needed. The requirements of FAS 141 deal with the assignment of purchase price to the various acquired assets and assumed obligations, and FAS 142 specifies the accounting for goodwill. FAS 147 also specifies that acquisitions of branches are to be accounted for as business combinations, if a branch meets the definition of a business, with the possibility of recognizing goodwill in such a transaction. If the branch does not meet the definition of a business, the transaction is to be accounted for as merely the acquisition of assets, and goodwill cannot be recognized. (The definition of a business is set forth in EITF 98-3.)

The guidance in FAS 147 does not apply to combinations of mutual associations, which remain governed by previous literature, including FAS 72. It stipulates that the guidance of FAS 144 must be applied to the long-term customer relationship intangibles often recognized in acquisitions of financial institutions—including depositor-relationship intangibles, borrower-relationship intangibles, and credit cardholder intangibles. The impairment testing of servicing assets, another commonly encountered bank or thrift intangible, is set forth by FAS 140, rather than by FAS 144.

Under FAS 147's transition provisions, intangibles recognized previously continue to be accounted for under FAS 72 if they arose in transactions other than business combinations.

However, for those that arose in business combinations, the remaining unamortized balances are to be transferred to goodwill unless they can be identified as other specific intangibles (e.g., customer relationships). Amounts reclassified to goodwill are to be prospectively accounted for in accordance with FAS 142 (i.e., no longer subject to amortization, but tested at least annually for impairment). The standard provides guidance on transitional testing for impairment of goodwill, as well as for certain acquired long-term customer relationship intangibles to be held and used.

**Bad-Debt Reserves**

Both stock and mutual savings and loan associations are required by regulatory authorities to place a portion of their earnings into a general reserve as protection for depositors. Savings and loan associations are allowed by the IRS to maintain a bad-debt reserve and to deduct any additions to their reserve in determining taxable income. Since this method differs from the method for determining bad debt expense, pretax accounting income and taxable income will differ.

**Accounting by Creditors for Impairment of a Loan**

A persistent practice problem has been in the proper determination of loan loss provisions. Since such reserves are necessarily matters of judgment, the possibility of manipulation (by either understatement or overstatement) in order to manage reported earnings or otherwise bias perceptions about the thrift's or bank's performance has always existed. In more recent years, this has received greater attention, first by the issuance of a detailed standard on accounting for impaired loans (FAS 114), and later by several FASB, SEC and banking regulatory authority policy announcements.

Under FAS 114, loans are deemed impaired when it is probable that a creditor will be unable to collect all amounts contractually due, including both principal and interest. This determination is made by applying normal loan review procedures. Once impairment has been identified, the creditor institution must compute the present value of all the estimated future cash flows, using the loan's effective interest rate as the discount factor. The effective rate is defined as the loan's contractual rate as adjusted for any deferred loan fees, premiums, or discounts. It is this effective rate, and not the market rate at the time of determination of impairment, which must be used to compute the loss provision.

If the computed present value of the expected future cash flows is less than the carrying amount of the loan, an impairment will be recognized and recorded in a valuation allowance. Significant changes in the amount and/or timing of future estimated cash flows require that the creditor recalculate the amount of the loan's impairment. Adjustments, subject to the LCM criteria, will be reflected through changes in the valuation allowance.

In the event of a formal loan restructuring through a troubled debt restructuring, the loan is remeasured at the fair market value at the date of the restructuring. This treatment differs from an impairment because it is assumed that a new, formally restructured loan reflects current market conditions; therefore, no impairment is deemed to exist.

The standard, as amended, provides that impairment losses be recognized as bad debts when measured; however, no guidance is provided on the recognition and measurement of amounts later recovered.

More recently, new attention has been given to the relationship between FAS 5 and 114 as definitive guidance for the provision of loss reserves. In several articles and an EITF Topic (D-80, *Application of FASB Statements No. 5 and No. 114 to a Loan Portfolio*), the FASB has indicated that loss provisions must be based only on probable losses which have occurred as of the balance sheet date, even if the individual loan which may have been impaired cannot be identified. Predictions of likely future losses to be incurred, even if such predictions have been historically highly accurate, cannot be used to anticipate losses that have not yet occurred.

There is no conflict between FAS 5, in force since 1975, and FAS 114, which became effective in 1995. Losses are to be provided when it is probable that the asset has been impaired and the amount is subject to reasonable estimation. FAS 114 is more specific than FAS 5 in that it requires certain methods of measurement for loans that are individually considered impaired, but it does not fundamentally change the recognition criteria for loan losses. FAS 114 provides guidance on measurement and disclosure for loans that are identified for evaluation and that are individually deemed to be impaired (because it is probable that the creditor will be unable to collect all the contractual interest and principal payments as scheduled in the loan agreement). It also includes all loans that are restructured in a troubled debt restructuring involving a modification of terms, except for those loans that are excluded from the scope of the standard.

In determining the existence and extent of impairment, "environmental" factors such as existing industry, geographical, economic, and political factors, should be given consideration. Obviously, the distinction between existing environmental factors and forecasts of changes in these factors over the near-term horizon is a subtle one, but it is one which must be maintained, since the latter cannot be used to justify current period loan loss provisions. For example, even if the consensus economic forecast is for a recession (which normally results in greater loan losses being experienced as current debtors face financial difficulties) if that downturn is not being experienced at the balance sheet date, loss reserves cannot be boosted to anticipate loan quality deterioration that has not yet occurred.

FASB has noted that some loans specifically identified for evaluation may be individually impaired, while other loans that are not impaired individually pursuant to FAS 114 may have specific characteristics that indicate that there would be probable loss in a group of loans with those characteristics. Loans in the first category must be accounted for under FAS 114, and loans in the second category should be accounted for under FAS 5. Under FAS 5, a loss is accrued if characteristics of a loan indicate that it is probable that a group of similar loans includes some losses even though the loss could not be identified with a specific loan. Characteristics or risk factors must be specifically identified to support an accrual for losses that have been incurred but that have not yet reached the point where it is probable that amounts will not be collected on a specific individual loan. A creditor should not ignore factors and information obtained in the evaluation of the loan's collectibility.

For example, if an individual loan specifically identified for evaluation is fully collateralized with risk-free assets, then consideration of that loan as sharing characteristics with a group of uncollateralized loans is inappropriate. Under FAS 5, a loss is recognized if characteristics of a loan indicate that it is probable that a group of similar loans includes some losses even though the loss could not be identified to a specific loan. However, a loss would be recognized only if it is probable that the loss has been incurred at the date of the financial statements and the amount of loss can be reasonably estimated.

If a creditor concludes that an individual loan specifically identified for evaluation is impaired, an allowance in addition to one measured under FAS 114 may not be established. That is, the FAS 114 allowance should be the sole measure of impairment for that loan. This is equally true if the measurement of impairment under FAS 114 results in no allowance. For example, a creditor might conclude that a given collateral-dependent loan is impaired, because it is probable that the creditor will be unable to collect all the contractual interest and principal payments as scheduled in the loan agreement. The creditor might, however, measure the impairment using the fair value of the collateral, which could result in no allowance if the fair value of the collateral is greater than the recorded investment in the loan. Further consideration of the need for a loss reserve by applying FAS 5 to these facts would not be legitimate.

Particularly objectionable is the practice of increasing (or not decreasing) the allowance for loan losses in "good" economic times to provide for losses expected to occur in the future. This income smoothing technique is invalid under all circumstances, and cannot be rationalized by citing the historical cyclicality of the economy and the reasonable likelihood that higher losses will follow periods having lower loss experience.

## Nonrefundable Loan Fees and Costs

**Loan origination fees.** These fees should be deferred and recognized over the life of the loan as an adjustment of interest income. If there are any related direct loan origination costs, the origination fees and origination costs should be netted, and only the net amount should be deferred and amortized via the interest method. Origination costs include those incremental costs such as credit checks and security arrangements, among others, pertaining to a specific loan.

The only exception to the foregoing rule would be in the instance of certain loans that also qualify as debt instruments under FAS 115. For those carried in the "trading securities" portfolio, related loan origination fees should be charged to expense when incurred; the requirement that these be carried at fair value would make adding these costs to the asset carrying amounts a useless exercise.

### Example 1

Debtor Corp. wishes to take out a loan with Klein Bank for the purchase of new machinery. The fair value of the machinery is $614,457. The loan is for ten years, designed to give Klein an implicit return of 10% on the loan. The annual payment is calculated as follows:

$$\text{Annual payment} = \frac{\$614,457}{PV_{10},\,10\%} = \frac{614,457}{6.14457} = \$100,000$$

Unearned interest on the loan would be $385,543 [(10 × $100,000) − $614,457].

Klein also is to receive a "nonrefundable origination fee" of $50,000. Klein incurred $20,000 of direct origination costs (for credit checks, etc.). Thus, Klein has *net* nonrefundable origination fees of $30,000. The new net investment in the loan is calculated below.

| | |
|---|---:|
| Gross investment in loan (10 × $100,000) | $1,000,000 |
| Less: Unamortized net nonrefundable origination fees | (30,000) |
| | 970,000 |
| Less: Unearned interest income (from above) | 385,543 |
| Net investment in loan | $ 584,457 |

The new net investment in the loan can be used to find the new implicit interest rate.

$$\frac{100,000}{(1+i)^1} + \frac{100,000}{(1+i)^2} + \ldots + \frac{100,000}{(1+i)^{10}} = \$584,457$$

*where i = implicit rate*

Thus, the implicit interest rate is 11.002%. The amortization table for the first three years is set up as follows:

| (a)<br>Loan payments | (b)<br>Reduction in<br>unearned interest | (c)<br>Interest revenue<br>(PV x implicit<br>rate of 11.002%) | (d)<br>Reduction in net<br>orig. fees (c-b) | (e)<br>Reduction in PV<br>of net invest (a-c) | (f)<br>PV of net loan<br>investment |
|---|---|---|---|---|---|
| | | | | | $584,457 |
| $100,000 | $61,446* | $64,302 | $2,856 | $35,689 | 548,759 |
| 100,000 | 57,590** | 60,374 | 2,784 | 39,626 | 509,133 |
| 100,000 | 53,349*** | 56,015 | 2,666 | 43,985 | 465,148 |

\* ($614,457 x 10%) = $61,446
\*\* [$614,457 − ($100,000 − $61,446)] x 10% = $57,590
\*\*\* [$575,900 − ($100,000 − $57,590)] x 10% = $53,349

**Commitment fees and costs.** Often fees are received in advance in exchange for a commitment to originate or purchase a loan. These fees should be deferred and recognized upon exercise of the commitment as an adjustment of interest income over the life of the loan, as in Example 1 for origination costs and fees. If a commitment expires unexercised, the fees should be recognized as income upon expiration.

As with loan origination fees and costs, if both commitment fees are received and commitment costs are incurred relating to a commitment to originate or purchase a loan, the net amount of fees or costs should be deferred and recognized over the life of the loan.

If there is a remote possibility of exercise, the commitment fees may be recognized on a straight-line basis over the commitment period as "service fee income." If there is a subsequent exercise, the unamortized fees at the date of exercise shall be recognized over the life of the loan as an adjustment of interest income, as in Example 1.

In certain cases, commitment fees are determined retroactively as a percentage of available lines of credit. If the commitment fee percentage is nominal in relation to the stated rate on the related borrowing, with the borrowing earning the market rate of interest, the fees shall be recognized in income as of the determination date.

### Example 2

Glass Corp. has a $2 million, 10% line of credit outstanding with Ritter Bank. Ritter charges its annual commitment fee as 0.1% of any available balance as of the end of the prior period. Ritter will report $2,000 ($2 million × 0.1%) as service fee income in its current income statement.

**Fees and costs in refinancing or restructurings.** (Assume this is not a troubled-debt restructuring.) When the terms of a refinanced/restructured loan are as favorable to the lender as the terms for loans to customers with similar risks who are not in a restructuring, the refinanced loan is treated as a new loan, and all prior fees of the old loan are recognized in interest income when the new loan is made.

When the above situation is not satisfied, the fees or costs from the old loan become part of the net investment in the new loan.

### Example 3

Jeffrey Bank refinanced a loan receivable to $1,000,000, at 10% interest, with annual interest receipts for ten years. Jeffrey's "normal" loan in its portfolio to debtors with similar risks is for $500,000 at 9% interest for five years. Jeffrey had loan origination fees from the original loan of $20,000. These fees are recognized in income *immediately* because the terms of the restructuring are as favorable to Jeffrey as a loan to another debtor with similar risks.

### Example 4

Assume the same facts as in Example 3 except that the refinanced terms are $500,000 principal, 7% interest for three years. Since the terms of the restructuring are not as favorable to Jeffrey as a loan to another debtor with similar risks, the $20,000 origination fees become part of the new investment in the loan and recognized in interest income over the life of the new loan, as in Example 1.

**Purchase of a loan or group of loans.** Fees paid or fees received when purchasing a loan or group of loans should normally be considered part of the initial investment; to be recognized in income over the lives of the loans. However, if the loans qualify as debt securities under FAS 115 and are held in the lender's "trading securities" portfolio, these fees should be reported in income when paid or received, and not added to the cost of the loans.

**Special arrangements.** Often lenders provide demand loans (loans with no scheduled payment terms). In this case, any net fees or costs should be recognized on a straight-line basis over a period determined by mutual agreement of the parties, usually over the estimated length of the loan.

Under a revolving line of credit, any net fees or costs are recognized in income on a straight-line basis over the period that the line of credit is active. If the line of credit is terminated due to the borrower's full payment, any unamortized net fees or costs are recognized in income.

### Example 5

Green Bank received $50,000 as a nonrefundable origination fee on a $2 million demand loan. Green's loan dictates that any fees are to be amortized over a period of ten years. Therefore, $5,000 (= $50,000 × 1/10) of origination fees will be recognized as an addition to interest income each year for the next ten years.

**Financial statement presentation.** The unamortized balance of origination, commitment, and other fees/costs that are recognized as an adjustment of interest income shall be reported on the balance sheet as part of the loan balance to which they relate. Except for any special cases as noted in the above paragraphs, the amount of net fees/costs recognized each period as an adjustment will be reported in the income statement as part of interest income.

## Accounting for Loans Acquired by Transfer

Banks commonly acquire loans originated by other financial intermediaries. In some cases, these are impaired when first acquired. That is, due to changes in the borrowers' credit risks since loan inception, the expected cash flows from the purchased loans may not equal the contractual cash flows. (Note that the differences in expected cash flows versus contractual cash flows arising from changes in interest rates during the interval from loan inception to loan acquisition is a separate issue; the resulting discount or premium would be amortized by the effective yield method over the expected term of the loan.)

SOP 03-3, *Accounting for Certain Loans and Debt Securities Acquired in a Transfer,* addresses the accounting for the differences between contractual and expected future cash flows of acquired loans when these differences are attributable, at least in part, to credit quality.

Under the provisions of SOP 03-3, purchased loans are to be displayed at the initial investment amount on the balance sheet. The amount of any discount is not to be displayed in the balance sheet nor should the acquirer carry over an allowance for loan losses established by the seller. This prohibition applies equally to stand-alone purchases of loans and to those which occur as part of purchase business combinations. Expanded disclosure requirements have also been established.

When loans are acquired with evidence of deterioration in credit quality since origination, the acquirer will be required to estimate the cash flows expected to be collected on the loan. This exercise is to be done both at the purchase date and again periodically over the lives of the loans. Cash flows in excess of the initial investment (purchase price) expected to be collected should be recognized as yield; this is referred to as "accretable yield." On the other hand, contractual cash flows in excess of expected cash flows (the nonaccretable difference) should not be recognized as yield. (Accretion of this amount would necessitate, in most instances, later recognition of bad debt expense, and thus would distort multiple periods' results of operations.)

Changing expectations of future cash flows are to be handled differently, depending on whether these are decreases or increases. If, subsequent to acquisition, there are decreases in the probable cash flows, impairments are to be recognized. In other words, such a development cannot be handled prospectively as a yield adjustment over the remaining lives of the loans.

By contrast, probable increases in subsequent cash flows expected to be collected should be recognized prospectively as a yield adjustment. In cases where a new, higher yield on a loan is established (due to a probable increase in cash flows to be collected), that yield should be used as the effective interest rate in any later test for impairment.

If loans are refinanced or restructured after acquisition, these cannot be accounted for as new loans, unless these are troubled debt restructurings (as addressed by FAS 15, 114, and 115).

Under the provisions of the SOP, acquired loans are not to be aggregated for purposes of determining evidence of postorigination credit deterioration. Rather, each loan, even if purchased in a pool, must be individually evaluated. However, subsequent pooling or aggregation of smaller-balance homogeneous loans is allowed for purposes of recognition, measurement, and disclosure. To be accounted for in the aggregate, loans must have a common credit risk (such as past due status or credit score) and have a common predominant risk characteristic (such as type of loan or date of origination). Furthermore, aggregation is limited to loans purchased in the same fiscal quarter.

The SOP does not provide general guidance as to the recognition of income, because that guidance does not exist for originated loans. However, income recognition will still be prohibited on loans for which an investor expects to substantially improve the collateral for resale or expects to use the collateral in operations.

Variable loans with index rate decreases, contractual cash flow decreases, and expected cash flow decreases should be evaluated based on the change in expected cash flows attributable to the decrease in index rates. Those changes should be recognized prospectively, rather than as impairments. The decrease in expected cash flows due to index rate decreases must be ascertained, and those changes are to be evaluated against the loan's contractual payments receivable, which must be calculated based on the index rate as it changes over the life of the loan.

### Conforming Practice by all Financial Institutions

SOP 01-6, *Accounting for Certain Entities (Including Entities with Trade Receivables) That Lend to or Finance the Activities of Others,* reconciled and conformed the accounting and financial reporting provisions of the former AICPA AAG applicable to banks and saving institutions, credit unions, and finance companies. It furthermore added mortgage companies and corporate credit unions to the scope of coverage. The standard applies, additionally, to all entities which finance other entities, even via normal trade credit arrangements, and thus directs the accounting to be employed by manufacturers, retailers, wholesalers, and other business enterprises. The provisions of SOP 01-6 have been incorporated into the current AAG, *Depository and Lending Institutions: Banks and Savings Institutions, Credit Unions, Finance Companies and Mortgage Companies.*

SOP 01-6 provides revised accounting guidance for sales of loan servicing rights, in order to comply with the revenue recognition model set forth in EITF Issue 95-5, *Determination of What Risks and Rewards, if Any, Can Be Retained and Whether Any Unresolved Contingencies May Exist in a Sale of Mortgage Loan Servicing Rights.* It also adopts the basis allocation approach set forth in FAS 140. It made it clear that all entities which lend to or finance the activities of others are subject to the accounting guidance found in the Guide, *Audits of Finance Companies,* including insurance companies to the extent they engage in lending activities, notwithstanding that the finance companies Guide explicitly excluded such enterprises from its scope.

The SOP eliminated differences in accounting and disclosure established by the respective AAG and carried forward that accounting guidance for transactions determined to be unique to certain financial institutions. The formerly separate AAG have now been superseded by the new, combined AAG, *Depository and Lending Institutions.*

SOP 01-6 requires that, to the extent management has the intent and the ability to hold them for the foreseeable future or until maturity or payoff, loans should be reported on the balance sheet at outstanding principal adjusted for any charge-offs, the allowance for loan losses, any deferred fees or costs on originated loans, and any unamortized premiums or discounts on purchased loans. Nonmortgage loans held for sale should be reported at the lower of cost or fair value. When a decision is made to sell loans not previously held for sale, those loans should be reclassified as held-for-sale and carried at the lower of cost or fair value.

With regard to credit losses, these are to be deducted from the allowance. Loan balances should be charged off in the periods in which the loans are deemed uncollectible. Recoveries of amounts previously charged off should be recorded when received. Credit losses on off-balance-sheet instruments should be reported separately from valuation accounts for recognized instruments.

Under SOP 01-6, standby commitments to purchase loans are reported in one of two ways, depending on whether the settlement date is within a reasonable time and whether the entity has the intent and ability to accept delivery without selling assets. If both conditions are met, the entity should record the loans purchased at cost, net of the standby commitment fee received, on the settlement date. If one or both conditions are not met, or if the entity does not have the intent and ability to take delivery without selling assets, the standby commitment fee (which is essentially a written put option premium) should be reported as a liability. Thereafter, the liability should be reported at the greater of the initial standby commitment fee or the fair value of the written put option, with the unrealized gains or losses included in current operations.

A transfer of servicing rights should only be accounted for as a sale if the transfer qualifies as a sale under EITF 95-5, *Determination of What Risks and Rewards, If Any, Can Be Retained and Whether Any Unresolved Contingencies May Exist in a Sale of Mortgage Loan Servicing Rights,* and if (1) the seller has written approval from the investor (if required), (2) the buyer is a currently approved seller/servicer, (3) if a seller-financed sale, the nonrefundable down payment is large enough to demonstrate the buyer's commitment to complete the transaction, and (4) the transferor receives adequate compensation for any temporary servicing it performs. Sales of servicing rights previously sold should be recognized in income consistent with this provision and the requirements under FAS 140.

The SOP also addresses a number of other issues. Thus, Federal Home Loan Bank and Federal Reserve Bank stock is to be classified as a restricted investment security, carried at cost, and evaluated for impairment. Also, any delinquency fees are to be recognized in income when chargeable, assuming collectibility is reasonably assured. Prepayment fees are not recognized in income until the loans or trade receivables are prepaid, except as set forth by FAS 91. Finally, accrual of interest income should not be affected by the possibility that rebates may be calculated using a method different than the interest method, except as set forth in FAS 91.

With regard to financial statement disclosures, the SOP requires that the summary of significant accounting policies state the basis of accounting for loans, trade receivables, and lease financings; the method used to determine the lower of cost or market of nonmortgage loans held for sale, the classification and method of accounting for interest-only strips, loans, and other receivables or retained interests in securitizations; and the method for recognizing interest income on loan and trade receivables, including the method of amortizing net deferred fees or costs. The accounting policies note should also describe the criteria for placing loans on nonaccrual status, for charging off uncollectible loans and trade receivables, and for determining past due or delinquency status.

The financial statement notes should include a description of the accounting policies and methodology used to estimate the allowance for loan losses, and any liability for off-balance-sheet credit losses, as well as the related charges for loan, trade receivable, or other credit losses. Aggregate gains or losses on sales of loans or trade receivables should be presented separately in the financial statements or disclosed in the notes thereto. Major categories of loans or trade receivables should be presented separately either in the balance sheet or the notes, as should the allowance for credit losses, the allowance for doubtful accounts, and any unearned income. Receivables held for sale should be separately reported.

The SOP also requires that foreclosed and repossessed assets be reported separately on the balance sheet or disclosed in the notes. The recorded investment in loans and trade receivables on nonaccrual status should be disclosed, as should the amount of loans and trade receivables past due ninety days or more and still accruing.

The amount of securities deposited with state regulatory authorities (if required) should be disclosed. The carrying amount of loans, trade receivables, securities, and financial instruments that serve as collateral for borrowings should also be disclosed.

FAS 133 requires disclosure of the extent, nature, terms, and credit risk of financial instruments, not limited to derivatives with off-balance-sheet credit risk.

Previously, GAAP for banks and savings institutions did not require disclosure of capital requirements for branches of foreign banks, because those branches do not have capital. However, branches are subject to requirements to maintain certain levels of capital-equivalent deposits and may be required to maintain other specified reserves. Since failure to comply with those requirements potentially has an adverse impact on the reporting entity, disclosures about the balance requirements and a branch's compliance are required under SOP 01-6. Similarly, capital requirements for trust operations are unpublished, are subject to variations of interpretation as between regulatory agencies, and may not be uniformly applied to the trust operations of all institutions. Nonetheless, to the extent that an institution has been advised of an expectation that certain trust-related capital levels be maintained, its compliance with those expectations should be disclosed.

### Servicing Assets and Liabilities

Financial institutions often acquire, or retain, servicing rights to financial assets, such as for loans originated and subsequently sold to other institutions or to qualified special-purpose entities. FAS 156 has significantly altered the accounting for retained or acquired servicing rights, which are now to be recorded, at acquisition, at fair value. If the contractually expected fees and other revenues are expected to exceed the cost of providing the servicing, a servicing asset is recorded; if a shortfall of revenue is expected, a liability is recognized. Subsequent accounting for servicing assets and liabilities can be either by the amortization or the fair value method, with the option to elect one or the other for a given class of financial asset being serviced.

The accounting for servicing is described in detail in Chapter 8.

### Cash Flow Statement

Banks, savings institutions, and credit unions are not required to report gross cash receipts and payments for the following:

1. Deposits placed with other financial institutions
2. Withdrawals of deposits
3. Time deposits accepted
4. Repayments of deposits
5. Loans made to customers
6. Principal collections of loans

If an enterprise is part of a consolidated enterprise, net cash receipts and payments of the enterprise should be reported separate from the gross cash receipts and payments of the consolidated enterprise.

**Other Accounting Guidance**

FTB 01-1 granted financial institutions extended mandatory implementation dates for several provisions of FAS 140. These pertain exclusively to isolation criteria under FAS 140 (which determine whether transfers are to be accounted for as sales or as secured borrowings). (FAS 140 is addressed in Chapters 7 and 8.)

The Emerging Issues Task Force (EITF) has addressed a number of matters that arise solely or primarily in the context of financial reporting by lending institutions. In EITF 84-4, it addressed whether ADC (acquisition, development and construction) loans were to be accounted for as loans, investments, or interests in a joint venture. It also considered the accounting for a partial sale of an arrangement. These issues were resolved by the issuance of the AICPA Notice to Practitioners, *ADC Arrangements*, which covers ADC arrangements in which the lender expects to participate in residual profit and gives guidance on accounting and reporting concerns.

In EITF 84-9, it was agreed that to allow banks to delay recording assets and liabilities for checks deposited until collection is made from the drawee bank would constitute an accounting change. However, a consensus was reached that the change would be difficult to justify because this approach is conceptually flawed.

EITF 84-19 concluded that, for situations where a lender allows a borrower to make larger payments for some number of periods (at least twelve payments), after which the borrower is then relieved of any remaining obligation, the loss related to the forgiven portion should be accrued over the period of the larger payments.

EITF 84-20 stated that forward commitment GNMA "dollar rolls" should be marked to market. Other issues discussed in EITF 84-20 were resolved by SOP 85-2, which was subsequently amended by SOP 90-3.

In some instances, a reporting entity may sell a loan but retain a share in the interest income, as well as the servicing rights for that loan. EITF 84-21 debated whether the present value of the future interest inflows should be recognized immediately or over the life of the loan. It was agreed that the accounting treatment specified in the AICPA AAG, *Savings and Loan Associations*, should be followed. Separately, EITF 85-13 mandated that a gain should be recognized upon the sale of mortgage service rights that include participation in the future interest stream of the loans. On yet another related topic, FTB 87-3 states that servicing fee rates set by secondary market makers (GNMA, FHLMC, FNMA) should be considered normal for transactions with those agencies.

Yet another question pertaining to servicing rights was addressed by EITF 86-38. In particular, it dealt with the implications of mortgage prepayments on the amortization of servicing rights. The consensus held that an excess service fee receivable (resulting from a higher than normal servicing fee) must be written down to the present value of the remaining future excess service fee revenue discounted with the same factor used to calculate the original receivable.

In EITF 87-34, the Task Force discussed events in which a mortgage loan servicer (transferor) transfers the servicing rights and related risks to an unaffiliated enterprise (transferee), which then makes a subservicing agreement whereby the transferor services the loans for a fixed fee. Income recognition should be deferred, and treatment as a sale or a financing depends on the circumstances surrounding the transaction. However, this consensus does not apply to temporary subservicing agreements. In addition, a loss should be recognized currently if loan prepayments may result in future servicing losses. When there is such a sale of mortgage servicing rights with a subservicing agreement, EITF 90-21 states that this should be accounted for as a sale if substantially all the risks and rewards of ownership have been transferred to the buyer. If substantially all the risks and rewards have not been transferred, then the transaction must be accounted for as a financing.

Normal servicing fee rates for mortgage loans are those set by federally sponsored secondary market makers (GNMA, FHLMC, FNMA). For transactions with those agencies or for mortgage loans sold to private sector investors where the seller retains servicing rights, normal servicing rates should be considered. In the latter case, a stated servicing fee rate that differs from the normal rate requires adjustment to the sales price to yield the normal rate. In either case, according to FTB 87-3, a loss should be accrued if expected servicing costs exceed anticipated fees based on the stated servicing fee rate. If the servicer refinances a mortgage loan and actual prepayments differ from any anticipated payments, then the servicing asset must be adjusted.

In EITF 84-22, the Task Force agreed that when a mutual savings and loan association converts to stock ownership and pools with another S&L, its EPS should be excluded from the restated combined EPS for years before the date of conversion. The method of presentation must be disclosed.

EITF 84-31 addressed equity certificates of deposit, stating that contingent interest expense resulting from equity certificates of deposit be recognized concurrently with gains relating to the assets upon which the equity is given.

When a bank or thrift institution is acquired, the excess of the fair value of liabilities over the fair value of assets, if any, should be amortized to expense in accordance with FAS 72, according to EITF 85-8. Any other goodwill resulting from the combination was to have been amortized according to APB 17, which has since been replaced by FAS 142, prohibiting amortization of goodwill but requiring annual impairment testing.

EITF 85-18 mandates that neither equity commitment notes nor equity contract notes should be included in earnings per share computations.

EITF 85-20 holds that a guarantor should recognize loan guarantee fees as revenue over the term of the guarantee. Any direct costs related to the guarantee must be recognized in the same manner. If material, footnote disclosure is required, and the probability of loss should be continually assessed. Subsequently, FIN 45 was issued, requiring that a liability be recognized, at the inception of a guarantee, for the fair value of the obligation undertaken by the guarantor.

Regarding distribution fees paid by mutual funds not having front-end charges (loads), the Task Force concluded that the cost deferral method should continue to be employed. Under this method, fees expected to be received over some future period should be recognized upon receipt. Deferred incremental direct costs are amortized while indirect costs are expensed as incurred.

RAP basis accounting is no longer used in general-purpose financial statements. EITF 85-31 states that the Comptroller's Banking Circular 202, which limits the net deferred tax debits allowable on a bank's statement of condition, applies only for regulatory purposes and does not affect GAAP financial statements.

EITF 85-42 established that, when a financial institution is acquired by purchase, the excess of the fair value of liabilities over the fair value of assets (FAS 72 goodwill) was to have been amortized over a period up to the remaining life of the long-term interest-bearing assets acquired. Any other goodwill resulting from the combination was to have been amortized according to APB 17, which has been superseded by FAS 142 which uses an impairment approach rather than periodic amortization.

EITF 86-21 states that AICPA Notice to Practitioners, *ADC Arrangements*, which deals with real estate ADC arrangements of financial institutions, should also be considered in relation to ADC arrangements transacted by nonfinancial institutions, shared appreciation mortgages, and loans on operating real estate. The Task Force also reached consensus that paragraphs 3-5 of that Notice should be consulted in determining the nature of expected residual profit on the arrangement.

During the 1980's, many thrifts failed, and some of these were then acquired by banks. EITF 86-31 dealt with the tax effects of a required reduction in bad-debt reserves (for tax purposes) in a merger of a savings and loan association and a banking, insurance, or other financial institution. The tax effects should be accounted for as an expense in the current period's combined financial statements of the merged entity.

Also, after the bad-debt reserves were adjusted for the merger transaction, deferred taxes were to be recorded for the difference between bad-debt reserves for tax and financial purposes.

Lenders often spread risk by creating loan syndications or participations. EITF 88-17 concluded that there are no material differences between loan syndications and some loan participations, and thus both should receive the same accounting treatment. In addition, it found that a transaction structured legally as a participation, but which actually constitutes an in-substance syndication, should be accounted for as a syndication. A transaction structured legally as a syndication must also meet certain criteria to be accounted for as such by the lead syndicator.

EITF 88-20 addressed purchased credit card portfolios involving premiums paid to the seller. It held that the excess of the purchase price of a credit card portfolio including cardholder relationships over the amounts due should be allocated between the credit card loans acquired and the cardholder relationships acquired. The premium related to cardholder relationships is an identifiable intangible asset and is amortized over the period of benefit. The premium related to the loans is amortized over the life of the loans.

In EITF 89-3, the Task Force agreed that the savings accounts deposited in a credit union must be unequivocally listed as a liability if the financial statements of the credit union are to comply with the (now superseded) AICPA Credit Union Guide. The statement of financial condition must present savings accounts either as the first item in the liabilities and equity section or as a separate subtotal before total liabilities. This guidance is consistent with other GAAP literature, including FAS 150.

Lending institutions often utilize what formerly were called special-purpose entities (SPEs), and which now may or may not qualify as qualified SPEs (QSPEs) or might be simply variable interest entities (VIEs). A fairly common transaction involves securitizations of credit card receivables, which sometimes have a feature called a "removal of accounts provision" (ROAP) that allows certain accounts to be withdrawn and replaced by other receivables. EITF 90-18 concluded that credit card securitizations with such a provision should be recognized as sales transactions under FAS 77 as long as the removal meets any specified terms, doesn't reduce the interests of the investor in the pool, and doesn't reduce the seller's percentage interest below a contractually specified level. FAS 77 was later superseded by FAS 125, and then by FAS 140, under which the accounting implications of a ROAP depend on whether it results in the transferor maintaining effective control over the transferred assets. Unconditional ROAPs and those conditioned on a transferor's decision would preclude sale accounting when the receivables are transferred.

On a related topic, EITF 92-5 stipulated that credit card origination costs that qualify for deferral in accordance with FAS 91 should be netted against the credit card fee charged, if any, and the net amount should be amortized on a straight-line basis over the term of the credit card or one year, depending on the significance of the fee.

Additionally, for both purchased and originated credit cards, the accounting policies, the net amount capitalized, and the amortization period should be disclosed.

EITF 93-1 mandates that credit card accounts acquired individually should be accounted for as originations under FAS 91 and EITF Issue 92-5.

# BROADCASTING

## PERSPECTIVE AND ISSUES

FAS 63 sets forth accounting and reporting standards for the broadcasting industry. A broadcaster is an enterprise or an affiliated group of enterprises that transmits radio or television program material. Broadcasters acquire program exhibition rights through license agreements. A typical license agreement for program material (e.g., features, specials, series, or cartoons) covers several programs (a package) and grants a television station, group of stations, network, pay television, or cable television system (licensee) the right to broadcast either a specified number or an unlimited number of showings over a maximum period of time (license period) for a specified fee. Ordinarily, the fee is paid in installments over a period generally shorter than the license period. The agreement usually contains a separate license for each program in the package. The license expires at the earlier of the last telecast allowed or the end of the license period. The licensee pays the required fee whether or not the rights are exercised. If the licensee does not exercise the contractual rights, the rights revert to the licensor with no refund to the licensee.

| Sources of GAAP | |
| --- | --- |
| *FAS* | *EITF* |
| 63 | 87-10 |

## DEFINITIONS OF TERMS

**Barter.** The exchange of unsold advertising time for products or services.

**Broadcaster.** An enterprise or an affiliated group of enterprises that transmits radio or television program material.

**Daypart.** An aggregation of programs broadcast during a particular time of day (e.g., daytime, evening, late night) or programs of a similar type (e.g., sports, news, children's shows).

**License agreement for program material.** A typical license agreement for program material (e.g., features, specials, series, or cartoons) covers several programs (a package) and grants a television station, group of stations, network, pay television, or cable television system (licensee) the right to broadcast either a specified number or an unlimited number of showings over a maximum period of time (license period) for a specified fee.

**Network affiliation agreement.** A broadcaster may be affiliated with a network under a network affiliation agreement. Under the agreement the station receives compensation for the network programming that it carries based on a formula designed to compensate the station for advertising sold on a network basis and included in the network programming.

## CONCEPTS, RULES, AND EXAMPLES

### Accounting for License Agreements

A broadcaster accounts for a license agreement for program material as a purchase of rights. Thus, an asset and a liability are recorded for the program rights purchased and the liability incurred when the license period begins and the broadcaster has met the following requirements:

1. Knows or can reasonably determine the cost of each program
2. Has accepted the program material according to the license agreement
3. Has access to the program for the first telecast (unless an agreement with another licensee prevents the telecast)

The asset is capitalized and the liability reported at either the gross amount of the liability for program rights or, alternatively, at the fair value of the liability. If a present value technique is used to measure fair value, the difference between the gross and net liability must be accounted for as interest. Under either method, the capitalized costs are allocated to each program within a package based on the relative value of each program to the broadcaster.

The asset is separated into current and noncurrent portions based on expected time of program usage. The liability is likewise segregated according to the payment maturities.

## Amortizing Capitalized Costs

The capitalized costs are amortized to expense as the program rights are used; generally based on the estimated number of program telecasts. However, licenses granting the right to unlimited broadcasts of programs such as cartoons are amortized over the license period, since the number of telecasts may be indeterminable.

Feature programs and program series require specific treatment. Feature programs are amortized program-by-program, unless amortization as a package produces approximately the same result. Syndicated programs are amortized as a series. If the broadcaster considers the first showing to be more valuable than reruns, the series is amortized using an accelerated method. If each showing is equally valuable, straight-line amortization is used.

### Example of accounting for program license agreements

On July 31, 2009, Lakie Media Company executed a license agreement for three movies, which it plans to televise on its local television station. The agreement allows the broadcast of each movie twice during the license period. Lakie is a calendar year-end company. The appropriate rate for imputing interest is 12%. Additional facts and assumptions are as follows:

| | *License Period* | | | *First telecast* | | *Second telecast* | |
| | | | *Film* | | *% of Total* | | *% of* |
| *Film* | *From* | *To* | *availability date* | *Date* | *revenue* | *Date* | *Total revenue* |
| A | 10/1/09 | 9/30/11 | 9/1/09 | 3/1/10 | 60% | 6/1/11 | 40% |
| B | 10/1/09 | 9/30/11 | 9/1/09 | 5/1/10 | 70% | 7/1/11 | 30% |
| C | 11/1/09 | 8/31/11 | 10/1/09 | 6/1/10 | 75% | 8/1/11 | 25% |

Payment terms and discounted present value data are as follows (Films A and B were acquired as a package):

| | | *Payment* | | *Discount period*[*]* | |
| *Film(s)* | *Date* | *Amount* | *From* | *To* |
| A & B | 7/31/09 | $1,000 | | |
| | 12/31/09 | 6,000 | 10/1/09 | 12/31/09 |
| | 12/31/10 | 6,000 | 10/1/09 | 12/31/10 |
| | | 13,000 | | |
| C | 12/31/10 | 3,750 | 11/1/09 | 12/31/10 |
| | | $16,750 | | |

[*] *Discounted from the first day of the license period to the date of payment.*

Based on management's estimates of expected advertising revenues, Film A represents 70% and Film B 30% of the total package A and B.

**Present value approach.** When each film's license period begins, an asset and a liability are recorded at the present value of the liability. Since the first three payments apply to the package of films A and B, the $12,027 combined present value (see the amortization schedule below) must be allocated to these films according to the 70%/30% assumption stated above.

| Film | Asset and liability recognized | |
|------|-------------------|----------------|
| A | $ 8,419 | ($12,027 × 70%) |
| B | 3,608 | ($12,027 × 30%) |
| | 12,027 | |
| C | 3,283 | |
| | $15,310 | |

In this case, all costs are capitalized in 2009 because all of the films' licensing periods begin in that year (assuming the three conditions are met).

The amount capitalized as an asset is amortized according to the percentage of revenues to be earned each year from each film. Interest is accrued on the unpaid balance of the liability for each film. Note that for films A and B, the unpaid balance at December 31, 2009, is $11,027 ($12,027 – the $1,000 downpayment).

### Amortization Schedules—Annual Compounding

| Description | Date | Payment | Interest at 12% | Principal | Balance |
|-------------|------|---------|-----------------|-----------|---------|
| Films A and B | | | | | |
| Down payment | 7/31/09 | $ 1,000.00 | -- | $ 1,000.00 | -- |
| Discounted obligation | 10/1/09 | | | | $11,027.23 |
| Payment | 12/31/09 | 6,000.00 | $ 329.91 | 5,670.09 | 5,357.14 |
| Payment | 12/31/10 | 6,000.00 | 642.86 | 5,357.14 | -- |
| | | 13,000.00 | 972.77 | 12,027.23 | |
| Film C | | | | | |
| Original obligation | 11/1/09 | | | | 3,283.44 |
| Accrued interest | 12/31/10 | -- | 64.77 | (64.77) | 3,348.21 |
| Payment | 12/31/10 | 3,750.00 | 401.79 | 3,348.21 | -- |
| | | 3,750.00 | 466.56 | 3,283.44 | |
| | | $16,750.00 | $1,439.33 | $15,310.67 | |

| | 2009 | 2010 | 2011 | Total |
|---|------|------|------|-------|
| Amortization of film rights | | | | |
| Film A | | | | |
| ($12,027 × 70% =) $8,419 × 60% | | $ 5,051 | | |
| ($12,027 × 70% =) $8,419 × 40% | | | $3,368 | $ 8,419 |
| Film B | | | | |
| ($12,027 × 30% =) $3,608 × 70% | | 2,526 | | |
| ($12,027 × 30% =) $3,608 × 30% | | | 1,082 | 3,608 |
| | | | | 12,027 |
| Film C | | | | |
| $3,283 × 75% | | 2,462 | | |
| $3,283 × 25% | | | 821 | 3,283 |
| Total amortization of film rights | | $10,039 | $5,271 | 15,310 |
| Interest expense per amortization schedule | | | | |
| Films A and B | $330 | $ 643 | | 973 |
| Film C | 65 | 402 | | 467 |
| | $395 | $ 1,045 | | 1,440 |
| | | | | $16,750 |

**Gross method.** Costs are capitalized at the gross amount of the liability.

| Film | Asset and liability recognized | |
|------|-------------------|----------------|
| A | $ 9,100 | ($13,000 × 70%) |
| B | 3,900 | ($13,000 × 30%) |
| C | 3,750 | |
| | $16,750 | |

Again, since the license period for all the films begins in 2009, the assets and liabilities are recognized in that year.

Under the gross approach, no interest is accrued on the unpaid liability. Thus the only expense recognized is the amortization of the program cost.

| Film | Year of expense recognition | | | | Total |
| --- | --- | --- | --- | --- | --- |
| | *2010* | | *2011* | | *Total* |
| A | $5,460 | (1) | $3,640 | (4) | $ 9,100 |
| B | 2,730 | (2) | 1,170 | (5) | 3,900 |
| C | 2,813 | (3) | 937 | (6) | 3,750 |
| | $11,003 | | $5,747 | | $16,750 |

| | |
| --- | --- |
| (1) $9,100 × 60% | (4) $9,100 × 40% |
| (2) $3,900 × 70% | (5) $3,900 × 30% |
| (3) $3,750 × 75% | (6) $3,750 × 25% |

## Accounting for Network Affiliation Agreements

A broadcaster may be affiliated with a network under a network affiliation agreement. Under the agreement, the station receives compensation for the network programming that it carries based on a formula designed to compensate the station for advertising sold on a network-wide basis and included in the network programming. Program costs, a major expense of television stations, are generally lower for a network affiliate than for an independent station because an affiliate does not incur program costs for network programs.

Upon termination of a network affiliation agreement, immediate replacement, or an agreement to replace the affiliation, the broadcaster will recognize a loss measured by the unamortized cost of the previous affiliation less the fair value of the new affiliation. No gain is recognized if the fair value exceeds the unamortized cost. If the terminated affiliation is not replaced, its unamortized cost is charged to expense.

## Accounting for Barter Transactions

Broadcasters may exchange unsold advertising time for products or services. The broadcaster benefits (providing the exchange does not interfere with its cash sales) by exchanging otherwise unsold time for such things as programs, fixed assets, merchandise, other media advertising privileges, travel and hotel arrangements, entertainment, and other services or products. Such transactions are reported at the fair value of the services or products (except when advertising time is exchanged for programs).

Barter revenue is recognized (EITF 87-10) when all of the following conditions are met:

1. Persuasive evidence exists of the advertising arrangement in the form of a noncancelable contract signed by both the broadcaster and the advertiser.
2. The production of the advertising is complete and has been delivered or is available for immediate and unconditional delivery in accordance with the terms of the arrangement.
3. The period of the arrangement has begun and the advertiser is entitled to use the advertising time.
4. The terms of the agreement and any fees involved are fixed and determinable.
5. Collectibility of any cash portion of the arrangement is reasonably assured.

If all of these conditions are satisfied except for the existence of a noncancelable contract, then the advertising revenue is not recognized until the advertising is aired.

The products or services received in exchange for the advertising time are reported when received or used. A liability results if products or services are received in advance of advertising revenue recognition and a receivable results if the advertising revenue is recognized prior to receipt of the products and services.

## Reporting and Disclosure

The capitalized cost of program rights is reported in the balance sheet at the lower of unamortized cost or net realizable value. Net realizable value is estimated on a package, series, program-by-program, or daypart basis. Daypart is an aggregation of programs broadcast during a particular time of day (e.g., daytime, evening, late night) or programs of a similar type (e.g., sports, news, children's shows). Broadcasters generally sell access to viewing audiences to advertisers on a daypart basis. If the broadcaster expects the usefulness of a program to diminish, the program may have to be written down from unamortized cost to estimated net realizable value. This establishes a new cost basis for the program. The write-down is not permitted to be restored in future periods.

Network affiliation agreements are reported in the balance sheet as intangible assets.

## CABLE TELEVISION

### PERSPECTIVE AND ISSUES

FAS 51 sets forth accounting and reporting standards for the cable television industry. These standards apply to cable television systems in the prematurity period. During the prematurity period, the cable television system is partially under construction and partially in service. The prematurity period begins with the first earned subscriber revenue. Its end will vary with the system's circumstances but will be determined based on plans for completion of the first major construction period or achievement of a specified predetermined subscriber level at which no additional investment will be required for other than cable television plant. The length of the prematurity period varies with the franchise development and construction plans. Except in the smallest systems, programming is usually delivered to portions of the system, and some revenues are obtained before construction of the entire system is complete. Thus, virtually every cable television system experiences a prematurity period during which it is receiving some revenue while continuing to incur substantial costs related to the establishment of the total system.

| Sources of GAAP |
|:---:|
| *FAS* |
| 34, 51, 142, 144 |

### DEFINITIONS OF TERMS

**Cable television plant.** The cable television plant refers to the equipment required to render service to subscribers including:

*Head-end.* This includes the equipment used to receive signals of distant television or radio stations, whether directly from the transmitter or from a microwave relay system. It also includes the studio facilities required for operator-originated programming, if any.

*Cable.* This consists of cable and amplifiers (which maintain the quality of the signal) covering the subscriber area, either on utility poles or underground.

*Drops.* These consist of the hardware that provides access to the main cable, the short length of cable that brings the signal from the main cable to the subscriber's television set, and other associated hardware, which may include a trap to block particular channels.

*Converters and descramblers.* These devices are attached to the subscriber's television sets when more than twelve channels are provided or when special services are provided, such as "pay cable" or two-way communication.

**Direct selling costs.** Direct selling costs include commissions, the portion of a salesperson's compensation other than commissions for obtaining new subscribers, local advertising targeted for acquisition of new subscribers, and costs of processing documents related to new subscribers acquired. Direct selling costs do not include supervisory and administrative expenses or indirect expenses, such as rent and other facilities costs.

**Subscriber-related costs.** Costs incurred to obtain and retain subscribers including costs of billing and collection, bad debts, and mailings; repairs and maintenance of taps and connections; franchise fees related to revenues or number of subscribers; general and administrative system costs, such as salary of the system manager and office rent; programming costs for additional channels used in the marketing effort or costs related to revenues from, or number of subscribers to, per channel or per program service; and direct selling costs.

## CONCEPTS, RULES, AND EXAMPLES

### Accounting during the Prematurity Period

Before the first subscriber revenue is earned by the cable company, the beginning and end of the prematurity period must be established by management. This period generally will not exceed two years. Once the prematurity period has been established, it may not be changed except in extraordinary circumstances.

Separate accounting is required for any portion[1] of a cable television system that is in the prematurity period and that is distinct from the rest of the system. This distinction is made if the portion is characterized by a majority of the following differences:

- Accountability (e.g., separate forecasts, budgets, etc.)
- Investment decisions (e.g., separate ROI, breakeven, etc.)
- Geographical (e.g., separate franchise area)
- Mechanical (e.g., separate equipment)
- Timing (e.g., separate inception of construction or marketing)

If the portion meets these requirements, it will be charged costs of the entire system only if these costs are directly traceable to that portion. Separate projections are also developed for that portion.

During the prematurity period, costs incurred for the plant are capitalized as usual. General and administrative expenses and subscriber-related costs are considered period costs. Subscriber-related costs are costs incurred to obtain and retain subscribers to the cable television system.

System costs that will benefit the cable system upon completion (e.g., programming costs), and that will remain fairly constant despite changes in the number of subscribers, are separated into amounts benefiting current operations (which are expensed currently) and amounts allocable to future operations (which are capitalized). The amount to be currently expensed is determined by multiplying the total monthly system costs by a fraction calculated each month during the prematurity period as follows:

$$
\begin{array}{l}
\text{Current portion} \\
\text{of system costs} \\
\text{benefiting future} \quad = \\
\text{periods}
\end{array}
\dfrac{
\begin{array}{l}
\text{Greatest of} \\
\text{a)} \quad \text{Average \# of subscribers expected that month as estimated at prematurity period,} \\
\text{b)} \quad \text{Average \# of subscribers assuming straight-line progress towards estimated \# of subscribers at end of prematurity period, or} \\
\text{c)} \quad \text{Average \# of actual subscribers}
\end{array}
}{
\text{Total \# of subscribers expected at end of prematurity period}
}
$$

During the prematurity period, interest cost is capitalized using an interest capitalization rate as described in FAS 34. The amount of interest cost to be capitalized is determined as follows:

---

[1] *The word "segment" has been used by some television enterprises. However, since FAS 131 uses segment in a different context, the FASB uses the word "portion" instead of "segment" to refer to the part of a cable television system that is still in the prematurity period.*

$$\frac{\text{Interest cost}}{\text{capitalized}} = \frac{\text{Interest}}{\text{capitalization rate}} \times \text{Average amount of qualifying assets during the period}$$

FAS 34 defines qualifying assets. The amount of capitalized interest cost may not exceed actual interest cost for the period.

Depreciation and amortization during the prematurity period are determined as follows:

$$\frac{\text{Depreciation and}}{\text{amortization}} = \frac{\substack{\text{Monthly depreciation and amortization, of total} \\ \text{capitalized costs expected on completion of the} \\ \text{prematurity period (using depreciation method to be} \\ \text{used at completion of prematurity period)}}}{} \times \substack{\text{Fraction used to determine} \\ \text{monthly system costs to be} \\ \text{expensed currently}}$$

### Amortization

**Amortizable life for portions built at different times.** Costs that have been capitalized for a portion of a cable television system that is in the prematurity period and that are clearly distinguishable on the basis of differences in timing between construction of that portion and the rest of the system are amortized over the same depreciation period used by the main cable plant.

**Installation revenues and costs.** A cable television system recognizes initial hookup revenue to the extent of the direct selling costs associated with that revenue. Any excess over the direct selling costs is deferred and amortized to income over the average period that subscribers are expected to be connected to the system.

Initial installation costs are capitalized and depreciated over a period that does not exceed the period used to depreciate the cable plant. After the initial installation, any costs incurred to disconnect or reconnect subscribers are charged to expense as incurred.

**Franchise application costs.** A cable television franchise is a right granted by a municipality to provide service to its residents. The treatment of franchise application costs depends upon whether or not the application is successful. If successful, the application costs are capitalized and amortized as intangible assets over the life of the franchise agreement. If unsuccessful or abandoned, all application costs are charged to expense.

**Impairment.** Capitalized plant and amortizable intangible assets are subject to the impairment provisions outlined in FAS 144 (discussed in detail in Chapter 11). Any of the system's intangible assets deemed to have an indefinite life are tested for impairment at least annually under the provisions of FAS 142. A separate evaluation is made for portions of the cable television system that are in their prematurity period. If total capitalized costs reach the maximum recoverable amount, capitalization continues. However, the provision to record an impairment loss to reduce capitalized costs to recoverable value is increased.

## COMPUTER SOFTWARE DEVELOPERS

### PERSPECTIVE AND ISSUES

As technology has come to play a more important role in businesses, increasing levels of activity have been devoted to the development of computer software. This involves a number of undertakings.

- Software licensed, purchased, or leased from others for internal use
- Software obtained from others for resale in the normal course of business (either on a stand-alone basis or as part of a larger product)
- Software developed internally for sale to others
- Software developed internally for the developer's own use

Software can be licensed, purchased, or leased and can reside on the user's hardware or be "hosted" by an application service provider (ASP) and leased to the user for remote use over the Internet. A growing set of accounting standards deal with some, but not all, of these issues.

The accounting for the cost of software developed internally for sale (or lease, etc.) to others is addressed by FAS 86; it provides that costs incurred prior to the point at which technological feasibility has been demonstrated are to be expensed as research and development costs, but specified costs incurred subsequently are capitalized, and later amortized or expensed (e.g., as cost of sales) as appropriate.

The cost of software acquired from others for resale in the normal course of business is not separately addressed by GAAP, but would be handled as are any other inventory costs. The usual inventory costing methods (LIFO, FIFO, etc.) and financial reporting concerns (lower of cost or market, etc.) are applicable to such situations.

SOP 98-1 addresses accounting for the costs of software acquired from others, or developed internally, for internal use. Internal-use software and the related rules regarding costs of developing Web sites are discussed in connection with the discussion of intangible assets in Chapter 11. This standard establishes the conditions that must be met before internal use software costs are capitalized. To qualify for capitalization, costs must have been incurred subsequent to the completion of the conceptual formulation, design and testing of possible project alternatives (including the process of vendor selection for purchased software). In addition, management at the appropriate level of authority must have authorized funding for the development project and conclude that it is probable that the project will be completed and the software will be used to perform the intended functions. This prerequisite is roughly analogous to the "technological feasibility" threshold prescribed by FAS 86 for software to be sold or leased to customers. Costs that are eventually capitalized under SOP 98-1 will be amortized over the period of expected economic benefit, as is the case with all other long-lived assets used in the business.

The increasingly central role of technology has received the attention of accounting standard setters in another arena as well. For enterprises that sell computer software and associated goods and services (program upgrades, maintenance agreements, etc.), complicated issues of revenue recognition arise. A series of Statements of Position provide guidance regarding the recognition of revenue on software sales including multiple-element arrangements that can include the cost of the software bundled with elements of training, upgrades, and postcontract customer support (PCS).

| Sources of GAAP | | |
|---|---|---|
| *FAS* | *EITF* | *SOP* |
| 2, 86 | 96-6, 97-13, 00-3, 03-5 | 97-2, 98-4, 98-9 |

## DEFINITIONS OF TERMS

**Coding.** Generating detailed instructions in a computer language to carry out the requirements described in the detail program design. The coding of a computer software product may begin prior to, concurrent with, or subsequent to the completion of the detail program design.

**Customer support.** Services performed by an enterprise to assist customers in their use of software products. Those services include any installation assistance, training classes, telephone question and answer services, newsletters, on-site visits, and software or data modifications.

**Detail program design.** The specifications of a computer software product that take product functions, features, and technical requirements to their most detailed, logical form and enables coding of the product.

**Maintenance.** Activities undertaken after the product is available for general release to customers to correct errors (commonly referred to as "bugs") or keep the product updated with current information. Those activities include routine changes and additions.

**Product design.** A logical representation of all product functions in sufficient detail to serve as product specifications.

**Product enhancement.** Improvements to an existing product that are intended to extend the life or improve significantly the marketability of the original product. Enhancements normally require their own product design and may require a redesign of all or part of the existing product.

**Product masters.** A completed version, ready for copying, of the computer software product, the documentation, and the training materials that are to be sold, leased, or otherwise marketed.

**Testing.** Performing the steps necessary to determine whether the coded computer software product meets function, feature, and technical performance requirements set forth in the product design.

**Working model.** An operative version of the computer software product that is completed in the same software language as the product to be ultimately marketed, performs all the major functions planned for the product, and is ready for initial customer testing (usually referred to as **beta testing**).

## CONCEPTS, RULES, AND EXAMPLES

### Costs of Software Developed Internally for Sale or Lease

A separate set of accounting issues arise in connection with the costs of computer software developed internally for lease or sale to others. The principal issue relates to the point in the development process at which development efforts are no longer characterized as research and development (R&D). The costs of R&D activities are required to be expensed currently as discussed in Chapter 11. The determination of this milestone has important accounting significance because specified costs incurred subsequent to the completion of R&D may be deferred (i.e., inventoried) and later reclassified as cost of sales as the finished products are sold or leased.

FAS 86 established the concept of technological feasibility to demarcate the point at which it is proper to begin to defer costs. According to this standard, all costs of development are considered research and development costs until technological feasibility has been established. This point is reached when all the necessary planning, designing, coding, and testing activities have been completed, to the extent these activities are necessary to establish that the product in question can meet its design specifications. Design specifications, in turn, may include such product aspects as functions, features, and technical performance requirements.

If the process of creating the software involves a detail program design, evidence of having achieved technological feasibility includes having performed these steps

1.  The product design (the logical representation of the product) and detailed program design have been completed. This step includes having demonstrated that the necessary skills, hardware, and software technologies are accessible to the entity for completion of product development.

2.  The detailed program design has been documented and traced to product specifications, thus demonstrating completeness and consistency.

3. The detailed program design has been reviewed for any high-risk elements, such as unproven functions or product innovations, and any such high-risk elements have been resolved through coding and testing.

If the software development effort does not involve creation of a detailed program design, then the following steps would require completion to demonstrate technological feasibility:

1. A product design and working model of the software have been completed.
2. The completeness of the working model and its consistency with the product design have been confirmed by testing.

If all the foregoing steps in either of the above listings have been completed as applicable, then technological feasibility has been demonstrated, and qualifying costs of producing product masters incurred thereafter are capitalized as production costs. Such costs include additional coding and testing activities that occur after the establishment of technological feasibility. The costs of producing product masters include not only the master copy of the software itself but also related user documentation and training materials. In the nonauthoritative opinion of the FASB Staff, capitalized production costs may include allocated indirect costs (e.g., occupancy costs related to programmers). This practice is inconsistent, however, with GAAP for software developed for internal use which prohibits such allocations (see Chapter 11).

Capitalization of software costs ceases once the product is available for general release to customers of the entity. Period costs, such as maintenance and ongoing customer support efforts, are expensed as incurred.

The capitalized production costs must be amortized, beginning when the product is first available for general release to customers. Amortization is computed on a product-by-product basis, which means that costs related to development of earlier products cannot be "rolled forward" into the costs of newer products, thereby delaying expense recognition. Periodic amortization must be the greater of (1) an amount determined with reference to total estimated revenues to be generated by the product, or (2) an amount computed on a straight-line basis with reference to the product's expected life cycle.

#### Example of amortization of capitalized computer software development costs

Assume total costs of $30,000 have been capitalized at the point product sales begin. Management estimates that the product will eventually generate revenues of $5,100,000 over a period of four years. For the current period (1/2 of a year), revenues of $600,000 have been earned. Capitalized costs of $3,750 must be amortized, which is the greater of the pro rata amount based on estimated total revenues to be derived from product sales [($600,000 ÷ $5,100,000) × $30,000 = $3,529] or the amount determined on a straight-line basis ($30,000 ÷ 4 × 1/2 = $3,750).

Other costs, such as product duplication, training material publication, and packaging, are capitalized as inventory on a unit-specific basis and expensed as cost of sales when product sales revenues are recognized.

Capitalized production costs are subject to annual evaluation for net realizable value; if impairment adjustments are recognized, the written-down amount becomes the new cost basis for further amortization purposes, as well as for comparison to net realizable value in the following period.

Capitalized inventory costs are subject to the same lower of cost or market evaluation as is required for inventories of tangible goods (see Chapter 9).

### Software Revenue Recognition

The basic principles underlying SOP 97-2 are set forth in the following paragraphs.

**Licensing vs. sales.** AcSEC was concerned that transfers of rights to software by licenses rather than by outright sales (a technique widely employed to provide vendors with legal recourse when others engage in unauthorized duplication of their products) were being accounted for differently. It concluded that any legal distinction between a license and a sale should not cause revenue recognition to differ.

**Product may not equate with delivery of software.** Arrangements to deliver software, whether alone or in conjunction with other products, often include services. Services to be provided in such contexts commonly involve significant production, modification, or customization of the software. Thus, physical delivery of the software might not constitute the delivery of the final product contracted for, absent those alterations, resulting in the requirement that such arrangements be accounted for as construction-type or production-type contracts in conformity with ARB 45 and SOP 81-1. However, if the services do not entail significant production, modification, or customization of the software, the services are accounted for as a separate element.

**Delivery is the key threshold issue for revenue recognition.** This is consistent with the principles set forth in CON 5, *Recognition and Measurement in Financial Statements of Business Enterprises*, which states that

> *An entity's revenue-earning activities involve delivering or producing goods, rendering services, or other activities that constitute its ongoing major or central operations, and revenues are considered to have been earned when the entity has substantially accomplished what it must do to be entitled to the benefits represented by the revenues. . . [t]he two conditions (being realized or realizable and being earned) are usually met by the time the product or merchandise is delivered. . . to customers, and revenues. . . are commonly recognized at time of sale (usually meaning delivery).*

**Revenue must be allocated to all elements of the sales arrangement, with recognition dependent upon meeting the criteria on an element-by-element basis.** Under prior GAAP, the accounting for vendor obligations remaining after delivery of software was dependent upon whether or not the obligation was deemed to be significant. Under SOP 97-2, however, all obligations are accounted for and revenue is allocated to each element of the arrangement, based on vendor-specific objective evidence (VSOE) of the fair values of the elements. Revenue associated with a particular element is not recognized until the revenue-recognition conditions established by the SOP are met, as the earnings process related to that element will not be considered complete until that time.

**Fair values for revenue allocation purposes must be vendor-specific.** When there are multiple elements of an arrangement, revenue is generally recognized on an element-by-element basis as individual elements are delivered. Revenue is allocated to the various elements in proportion to their relative fair values. Under SOP 97-2, this allocation process requires that VSOE of fair value be employed, regardless of any separate prices stated in the contract for each element, since prices stated in a contract may not represent fair value and, accordingly, might result in an unreasonable allocation of revenue. This approach is consistent with the accounting for commingled revenue as set forth in the current standard on accounting for franchise fee revenue. The use of surrogate prices, such as those published by competitors or industry averages, was rejected because of the wide differences in products and services offered by vendors. Separate transaction prices for the individual elements comprising the arrangement, if they are also being sold on that basis, would be the best such evidence, although under some circumstances (such as when prices in the arrangement are based on multiple users rather than the single user pricing of the element on a stand-alone basis) even that information could conceivably be invalid for revenue allocation purposes. Relative sales prices of the elements included in the arrangement are to be used whenever possible.

**The earnings process is not complete if fees are subject to forfeiture.** Even when elements have been delivered, if fees allocated to those elements are subject to forfeiture, refund, or other concession if the vendor does not fulfill its delivery responsibilities relative to other elements of the arrangement, those fees are not treated as having been earned. The potential concessions are an indication that the customer would not have licensed the delivered elements without also licensing the undelivered elements. For that reason, there must be persuasive evidence that fees allocated to delivered elements are not subject to forfeiture, refund, or other concessions before revenue recognition can be justified. Thus, for example, in determining the persuasiveness of the evidence, the vendor's history of making concessions that were not required by the provisions of an arrangement is more persuasive than are terms included in the arrangement that indicate that no concessions are required.

### Operational Rules Established by SOP 97-2

1. If an arrangement to deliver software or a software system, either alone or together with other products or services, requires significant production, modification, or customization of software, the entire arrangement is accounted for in conformity with ARB 45, *Long-Term Construction-Type Contracts*, and SOP 81-1, *Accounting for Performance of Construction-Type and Certain Production-Type Contracts*.

2. If the arrangement does not require significant production, modification, or customization of software, revenue is recognized when all of the following criteria are met:

    a. Persuasive evidence of an arrangement exists;
    b. Delivery has occurred;
    c. The vendor's fee is fixed or determinable; and
    d. Collectibility is probable.

3. For software arrangements that provide licenses for multiple software deliverables (multiple elements), some of which may be deliverable only on a when-and-if-available basis, these deliverables are considered in determining whether an arrangement includes multiple elements. The requirements with respect to arrangements that consist of multiple elements are applied to all additional products and services specified in the arrangement, including those described as being deliverable only on a when-and-if-available basis.

4. For arrangements having multiple elements, the fee is allocated to the various elements based on VSOE of fair value, regardless of any separate prices stated for each element within the contract. VSOE of fair value is limited to the following:

    a. The price charged when the same element is sold separately; or
    b. For an element not yet being sold separately, the price established by management, if it is probable that the price, once established, will not change before the separate introduction of the element into the marketplace.

The revenue allocated to undelivered elements cannot later be adjusted. However, if it becomes probable that the amount allocated to an undelivered element of the arrangement will result in a loss on that element, the loss must be immediately recognized. When a vendor's pricing is based on multiple factors such as the number of products and the number of users, the amount allocated to the same elements when sold separately must consider all the relevant factors of the vendor's pricing structure.

SOP 98-9 amended the guidance of SOP 97-2 with regard to multiple-element arrangements not accounted for as long-term construction contracts when (1) there is VSOE of the fair values of all undelivered elements, (2) VSOE does not exist for one or more of the delivered elements, and (3) all other revenue recognition criteria have been satisfied. In such cases, the newly defined "residual" method of allocation of selling price is to be utilized. This results in deferral of the aggregate fair value of the undelivered elements of the arrangement (to be recognized later as delivery occurs), with the excess of the total arrangement fee over the deferred portion being recognized in connection with the delivered components. This change was made to accommodate the situation whereby software is commonly sold with one "free" year of support, where additional years of support are also marketed at fixed prices; in this case, the fair value of the "free" support is deferred (and amortized over the year), while the software itself is assigned a revenue amount which is the difference between the package price and the known price of one year's support.

5. If a discount is offered in a multiple-element arrangement, a proportionate amount of the discount is applied to each element included in the arrangement, based on each element's fair value without regard to the discount. However, no portion of the discount is allocated to any upgrade rights.

6. If sufficient VSOE does not exist for the allocation of revenue to the various elements of the arrangement, all revenue from the arrangement is deferred until the earlier of the point at which (1) such sufficient VSOE does exist, or (2) all elements of the arrangement have been delivered. The exceptions to this guidance, provided in SOP 97-2, are as follows:

   a. If the only undelivered element is postcontract customer support (PCS), the entire fee is recognized ratably over the contractual PCS period, or when the PCS rights are implicit in the arrangement, over the period that PCS is expected to be provided to the customer.

   b. If the only undelivered element is services that do not involve significant production, modification, or customization of the software (e.g., training or installation), the entire fee is recognized over the period during which the services are expected to be performed.

   c. If the arrangement is in substance a subscription, the entire fee is recognized ratably over the term of the arrangement, if stated, otherwise over the estimated economic life of the products included in the arrangement.

   d. If the fee is based on the number of copies delivered, how the arrangement is accounted for depends on whether the total fee is fixed, and on whether the buyer can alter the composition of the copies to be received, as follows:

      (1) If the arrangement provides customers with the right to reproduce or obtain copies of two or more software products at a specified price per copy (not per product) up to the total amount of the fixed fee, an allocation of the fee to the individual products generally cannot be made, because the total revenue allocable to each software product is unknown at inception and depends on subsequent choices to be made by the customer and, sometimes, on future vendor development activity. Nevertheless, certain arrangements that include products that are not deliverable at inception impose a maximum number of copies of the undeliverable product(s) to which the customer is entitled. In such arrangements, a portion of the arrangement fee is allocated to the undeliverable product(s). This allocation is made assuming that the customer will elect to receive the maximum number of copies of the undeliverable product(s).

      (2) In arrangements in which no allocation can be made until the first copy or product master of each product covered by the arrangement has been de-

livered to the customer, and assuming the four conditions set forth above are met, revenue is recognized as copies of delivered products are either (a) reproduced by the customer, or (b) furnished to the customer if the vendor is duplicating the software. Once the vendor has delivered the product master or the first copy of all products covered by the arrangement, any previously unrecognized licensing fees are recognized, since only duplication of the software is required to satisfy the vendor's delivery requirement and such duplication is incidental to the arrangement. Consequently, the delivery criterion is deemed to have been met upon delivery to the customer of the product master or first copy. When the arrangement terminates, the vendor recognizes any licensing fees not previously recognized. Revenue is not recognized fully until at least one of the following conditions is met: either (a) delivery is complete for all products covered by the arrangement, or (b) the aggregate revenue attributable to all copies of the software products delivered is equal to the fixed fee, provided that the vendor is not obligated to deliver additional software products under the arrangement.

(3) The revenue allocated to the delivered products is recognized when the product master or first copy is delivered. If, during the term of the arrangement, the customer reproduces or receives enough copies of these delivered products so that revenue allocable to the delivered products exceeds the revenue previously recognized, the additional revenue is recognized as the copies are reproduced or delivered. The revenue allocated to the undeliverable product(s) is reduced by a corresponding amount.

7. The portion of the fee allocated to a contract element is recognized when the four revenue recognition criteria are met with respect to the element. In applying those criteria, the delivery of an element is considered not to have occurred if there are undelivered elements that are essential to the functionality of the delivered element, because functionality of the delivered element is considered to be impaired.

8. No portion of the fee can be deemed to be collectible if the portion of the fee allocable to delivered elements is subject to forfeiture, refund, or other concession if any of the undelivered elements are not delivered. If management represents that it will not provide refunds or concessions that are not required under the provisions of the arrangement, this assertion must be supported by reference to all available evidence. This evidence may include the following:

a. Acknowledgment in the arrangement regarding products not currently available or not to be delivered currently;

b. Separate prices stipulated in the arrangement for each deliverable element;

c. Default and damage provisions as defined in the arrangement;

d. Enforceable payment obligations and due dates for the delivered elements that are not dependent on the delivery of future deliverable elements, coupled with the intent of the vendor to enforce rights of payment;

e. Installation and use of the delivered software; and

f. Support services, such as telephone support, related to the delivered software being provided currently by the vendor.

## Other Accounting Guidance

As a complex and still evolving area, the use of technology in general, and computer software in particular have created many accounting concerns. EITF has addressed a number of these, and its positions are summarized in the following paragraphs.

Both software developers and motion picture companies engage in development of software products that combine entertainment (e.g., including well-known cartoon characters and film storylines in the software) and education. The term "edutainment" has been coined to refer to these hybrid products. Diversity in accounting practice had arisen whereby different companies engaged in edutainment development were using different combinations of GAAP to account for the same activities.

While no EITF consensus exists, in EITF 96-6 the SEC staff announced that

1. Edutainment products developed for sale or lease, or that are otherwise marketed are to be accounted for under FAS 86.
2. Costs subject to FAS 86 accounting include film costs incurred in the development of the product that would otherwise be accounted for under FAS 53 (subsequently superseded and replaced by SOP 00-2, *Accounting by Producers and Distributors of Films,* discussed later in this chapter).
3. Exploitation costs (marketing, advertising, publicity, promotion, and other distribution expenses) are to be expensed as incurred unless they qualify for capitalization as direct response advertising under SOP 93-7, *Reporting on Advertising Costs.*

In the absence of an EITF consensus on this issue, the SEC announcement should be deemed the most meaningful guidance on this topic.

In EITF 97-13, a consensus was reached that all expenditures incurred for business process reengineering activities (either by insiders or outsiders) are to be expensed immediately. This guidance also applies when business process reengineering activities are part of development or implementation of internal-use software. Finally, the accounting for internal-use software development and acquisition of property, plant, and equipment are not affected by this consensus.

Another consensus in EITF 97-13 was that, in cases where a third party is engaged for a business process reengineering project, the entire consulting contract price is to be allocated to each activity on the basis of the relative fair values of the separate components.

Some software users do not actually receive and load applications software on their computers, but instead merely access and use it via the Internet, on the vendor's or a third party's server, on an as-needed basis. (Commonly, the applications are "hosted" by companies known as application service providers, or ASPs.) In such arrangements, the customer is paying for two elements—the right to use the software and the storage of the software (and sometimes, the customer's proprietary data) on the provider's hardware. EITF 00-3 has addressed certain concerns arising in such circumstances.

When a vendor provides hosting, several revenue recognition issues may arise. First, the relationship between the customer and the ASP may be structured in the form of a service agreement providing Internet access to the specified site, without a corresponding software license. In such instances, the application of SOP 97-2 to the arrangement was unclear. Second, when the transaction is structured as a software license with a service element, evaluation of how the arrangement meets the delivery requirement of SOP 97-2 was unclear.

In its consensus on this issue, the EITF found that SOP 97-2 only applies if the customer has the right to take possession of the software at any time during the hosting period, without significant penalty, and install the software on its own hardware or contract with another service provider to host it. Most, if not all, ASP arrangements would not provide this option to the customer and therefore SOP 97-2 would not apply. The EITF notes that hosting arrangements might involve multiple elements to be accounted for in a variety of ways.

For those few hosting arrangements meeting the foregoing criteria, and thus subject to SOP 97-2, software delivery is deemed to have occurred when the customer first has the option to take possession. The criteria of SOP 97-2 must be met in order for the ASP to recognize revenue allocable to the software element; revenue relating to the hosting element is recognized as that service is provided.

Finally, the EITF has addressed the matter of nonsoftware deliverables included in arrangements containing more-than-incidental software. SOP 97-2, *Software Revenue Recognition*, provides authoritative guidance regarding the amounts and timing of revenue recognition in transactions involving the sale or license of computer software. Such transactions are often structured to bundle other software-related "elements" with the software such as future upgrades, postcontract customer support (PCS), training, customization, or other services. Those bundled arrangements are referred to as multiple-element arrangements (MEA).

EITF 03-5 states that in an MEA that includes software that is "more than incidental" to the arrangement, SOP 97-2 applies to the software-related elements enumerated above as well as any nonsoftware element for which the software element is essential to its functionality.

# EMPLOYEE BENEFIT PLANS, INCLUDING PENSION FUNDS

## PERSPECTIVE AND ISSUES

Employee benefit plans have become increasingly important and diverse. Using assets that are segregated from the plan sponsor, they provide benefits to employees and former employees in accordance with a plan agreement. The provisions of the plan agreement deal with such matters as eligibility, entitlement to benefits, funding, plan amendments, operation and administration, allocation of responsibilities among the fiduciaries, and fiduciaries' ability to delegate duties. A few examples of employee benefit plans are pension plans, profit-sharing plans, stock bonus plans, 401(k) plans, 403(b) plans, disability plans, health care plans, life insurance plans, unemployment benefit plans, tuition assistance plans, dependent care plans, and cafeteria/flexible benefit plans. For accounting and reporting purposes, the plans are divided into three major types: defined benefit pension plans, defined contribution pension plans, and health and welfare benefit plans.

Employee benefit plans that are sponsored by and provide benefits to the employees of state and local governmental entities[2] are outside of the scope of this publication. Readers instead should refer to the Wiley publication, *GAAP for Governments*.

All authoritative pronouncements in the GAAP hierarchy apply to employee benefit plans unless the pronouncement specifically excludes them from its scope. Certain authoritative pronouncements apply specifically to employee benefit plans. Because those pronouncements are particularly relevant to the transactions of employee benefit plans, they are discussed in this chapter.

FAS 35, *Accounting and Reporting by Defined Benefit Pension Plans*, is the principal standard involving the accounting and reporting of employee benefit plans. Although FAS 35's provisions apply only to defined benefit pension plans, the AICPA AAG, *Audits of Employee Benefit Plans*, requires defined contribution plans and employee health and welfare benefit plans to apply specialized accounting principles and practices that are similar to

---

[2] *See Chapter 1, Researching GAAP Matters, for a definition of "governmental entity."*

those prescribed by FAS 35. FAS 35 applies only to ongoing plans, not to plans that are terminated or expected to be terminated. The Statement describes the objectives of plan financial statements and the necessary components of a complete set of plan financial statements.

FAS 102, *Statement of Cash Flows—Exemption of Certain Enterprises and Classification of Cash Flows from Certain Securities Acquired for Resale*, exempts defined benefit pension plans and certain other employee benefit plans from FAS 95's requirement to present a statement of cash flows.

FAS 110, *Reporting by Defined Benefit Pension Plans of Investment Contracts*, requires defined benefit pension plans to report all investment contracts, including guaranteed investment contracts issued by insurance companies, at fair value. Only contracts that incorporate mortality or morbidity risk (insurance contracts) may be reported at contract value.

The Audit Guide (AAG) mentioned above is the primary AICPA pronouncement that sets standards for employee benefit plans. In addition to providing accounting and reporting guidance for the plans, it provides summaries of statutory rules and regulations applicable to employee benefit plans and illustrative financial statements.

SOP 92-6 and SOP 01-2, both entitled, *Accounting and Reporting by Health and Welfare Benefit Plans,* provide the standards for health and welfare benefit plans. They divide the diverse universe of plans into two major types: defined benefit health and welfare plans and defined contribution health and welfare plans. They require defined benefit health and welfare plans to use certain provisions of FAS 106, *Employer's Accounting for Postretirement Benefits other than Pensions,* to measure benefit obligations. In addition, they apply many of the measurement and disclosure provisions of FAS 35 to health and welfare plans.

SOP 94-4, *Reporting of Investment Contracts Held by Health and Welfare Benefit Plans and Defined Contribution Pension Plans,* requires defined contribution plans and health and welfare benefit plans to report insurance and investment contracts in a manner similar to the requirements of FAS 110.

SOP 99-2, *Accounting for and Reporting of Postretirement Medical Benefit 401(h) Features of Defined Benefit Pension Plans,* specifies the accounting for and disclosure of 401(h) features of defined benefit pension plans that offer medical benefits to retirees in addition to the normal retirement benefits.

SOP 99-3, *Accounting for and Reporting of Certain Defined Contribution Plan Investments and Other Disclosure Matters,* amended the AAG and SOP 94-4 to simplify the required disclosures about investments.

This section presents a highly summarized discussion of accounting and reporting standards by employee benefit plans. Readers who desire a more in-depth discussion should refer to the Wiley publication, *GAAP for Employee Benefit Plans.*

This chapter does not describe an employer's requirements for reporting information about employee benefit plans. That information is described in Chapter 18.

| Sources of GAAP | | |
|---|---|---|
| *FAS* | *AAG* | *SOP* |
| 35, 102, 110 | *Audits of Employee Benefit Plans* | 92-6, 94-4, 99-2, 99-3, 01-2 |

## DEFINITIONS OF TERMS

**Accumulated plan benefits** or **benefit obligations.** Benefits that are attributable to services rendered by employees before the date at which the actuarial present value of the plan obligation is computed.

**Defined benefit plan.** A plan that promises stated or otherwise determinable benefits to participants based on factors such as compensation, years of service, and age.

**Defined contribution plan.** A plan in which benefits are based on amounts contributed, investment experience, and allocated forfeitures, net of administrative expenses. Each participant's benefits are computed based on his or her individual account.

**Health and welfare benefit plan.** Plans that provide benefits such as medical, dental, visual, or other health care, insurance, disability, vacation, education, or dependent care.

**Net assets.** The residual interest in the assets of an employee benefit plan that remains after deducting its liabilities. The liabilities of a plan do not include its accumulated plan benefits (defined benefit pension plans) or its benefit obligation (defined benefit health and welfare plans).

**Plan sponsor.** The company, association, employee group, or other group of representatives that established or maintains the plan.

## CONCEPTS, RULES, AND EXAMPLES

In addition to varying by basic type (defined benefit plan, defined contribution plan, and health and welfare benefit plan), employee benefit plans vary by operating and administrative characteristics. Plans established by one employer or a group of controlled corporations are referred to as single employer plans. Alternatively, they can include the employees of many employers who are related in some way, often by all being parties to a collective-bargaining agreement. Those plans are referred to as multiemployer plans. A plan can be either contributory or noncontributory. A contributory plan requires both the employer and the participants to fund (contribute to) the cost of the future benefits. In a noncontributory plan, the participants do not fund any part of the cost of the future benefits. Insured plans are funded through insurance contracts. Self-funded plans are funded through contributions and investment return. Split-funded plans are funded by a combination of insurance contracts, contributions, and investment return.

### Complete Set of Financial Statements

The primary objective of a plan's financial statements is to provide the information necessary to assess the plan's ability to pay benefits when due. Thus, financial statements are to include information about the plan's resources, the results of transactions and events that changed the plan's resources, the stewardship of management over the plan's resources, and any other facts necessary to understand the information provided.

A complete set of financial statements includes a statement of net assets available for benefits as of the end of the plan year (balance sheet equivalent), a statement of changes in net assets available for benefits for the plan year ended (income statement equivalent), and notes to the financial statements. In addition, defined benefit plans must include information about the actuarial present value of accumulated benefits and changes in the accumulated benefits. That information can appear either as additional financial statements or in the notes to financial statements.

FAS 102 exempted defined benefit pension plans from the requirement that a statement of cash flows be provided. Other employee benefit plans were also exempted if they report similar to defined benefit pension plans, including FAS 35's requirement to report plan investments at fair value. Although not required, presentation of a statement of cash flows is encouraged if it would provide useful information about the plan's ability to pay future liabilities, as would be the case if the plan either holds illiquid investments or purchases investments using borrowed funds.

FAS 130, *Reporting Comprehensive Income,* requires that changes in equity other than transactions with owners be reported in financial statements in the period in which they are recognized. The statement of changes in net assets available for benefits is a comprehensive income statement because all changes in net assets available for benefits are reflected in that statement. Thus, although it did not specifically exempt employee benefit plans from its provisions, FAS 130 did not change the reporting for employee benefit plans.

## Statement of Net Assets Available for Benefits

Most investments of the plan are reported at fair value. If there is an active market, quoted market prices are used. If market quotations are not available, investments are valued "in good faith" by the plan's trustees and administrator. The selling price of similar investments or discounted cash flows can be useful in estimating fair value. The use of an independent expert may be necessary for the valuation of certain investments. Investment contracts with an insurance company, bank, or other financial institution are reported at fair value. Only insurance contracts—contracts that incorporate mortality or morbidity risk (defined benefit pension plans) or that are fully benefit-responsive (defined contribution plans and health and welfare plans)—may be reported at contract value, and then only if the plan reports at contract value in its annual report filed with government agencies. The financial statements are to identify plan investments by type of investment and indicate how fair value was determined. It is not necessary to disclose the original cost of investments in the basic financial statements. Plans are to disclose in the notes to the financial statements any investments representing 5% or more of the net assets available for benefits as of the end of the year.

Contributions receivable include those due as of the reporting date from participants, employers, withdrawing employers of a multiemployer plan, and other sources (such as a state or federal government in the case of a grant or subsidy). Receivables arise from formal commitments of an employer, legal requirements, or contractual requirements. The receivables are to be reduced by an allowance for uncollectible amounts if warranted.

Long-lived assets (such as buildings, equipment, furniture and fixtures, and leasehold improvements) that are used in the plan's operations are presented at cost less accumulated depreciation or amortization.

## Statement of Changes in Net Assets Available for Benefits

The statement of changes in net assets available for benefits is a comprehensive income statement that includes all recognized transactions and events that change the net assets available for benefits. At a minimum, the statement is to include separate amounts for

1.  Contributions from

    a.  Employer(s)—separating cash from noncash contributions
    b.  Participants, including those transmitted by the plan sponsor
    c.  Other identified sources

2.  Net appreciation or depreciation (realized and unrealized amounts may be combined) in fair value for each significant class of investment, presented by

    a.  Investments measured by quoted market prices
    b.  Investments measured by some other means

3.  Investment income (not including appreciation or depreciation in fair value)
4.  Payments to plan participants for benefits, excluding amounts paid by insurance contracts that are not included in plan assets

5.  Payments to insurance companies to purchase contracts that are excluded from plan assets
6.  Administrative expenses
7.  Other changes, if necessary, with appropriate description(s)

## Transactions with Related Parties (FAS 57)

Transactions between a plan sponsor and its employee benefit plans are subject to the disclosure requirements of FAS 57, *Related-Party Disclosures*. The required disclosures include

1.  The nature of the relationship
2.  A description of the transactions for each of the periods in which a statement of changes in net assets available for benefits is presented
3.  The dollar amounts of transactions for each of the periods in which a statement of changes in net assets available for benefits is presented
4.  The effects of any change from the prior period in the method of establishing terms of the transaction
5.  The amounts due from related parties at the date of each statement of net assets available for benefits

The disclosures are not permitted to represent that transactions were made at arm's length unless such representations can be substantiated.

## Risks and Uncertainties

Employee benefit plans must disclose the information required by SOP 94-6, *Disclosures of Certain Significant Risks and Uncertainties*. Risks that are unique to employee benefit plans include

1.  A significant industry downturn that could cause employees to retire early in order to avoid being laid off, especially if the plan's participants are concentrated within a particular industry or with a single employer
2.  Likelihood that an employer will significantly increase pension or health and welfare benefits in order to avoid a union walkout
3.  A planned downsizing that is expected to offer early retirement to employees
4.  Investments in the stock of the employer

## Defined Benefit Plans

In addition to the statement of net assets available for benefits and the statement of changes in net assets available for benefits, defined benefit pension plans must provide information about the actuarial present value of accumulated plan benefits and changes in the actuarial present value of accumulated plan benefits. The information can be included as separate financial statements or as schedules in the notes to the financial statements.

Accumulated plan benefits include the present value of future benefits to retired or terminated employees or their beneficiaries, to beneficiaries of deceased employees, and to present employees or their beneficiaries. Whenever possible, plan provisions are to govern the measurement of accumulated plan benefits. If the benefits earned in each year are not determinable from the plan's provisions, a formula for measurement is provided in FAS 35. When calculating accumulated plan benefits, an ongoing plan is to be assumed, analogous to the going concern assumption used in preparing GAAP financial statements of other types of entities. Thus, interest rates used for discounting expected future payments are based on rates of return on investments for the benefit deferral period, and employee turnover and employee mortality are considered.

At a minimum, the information provided in the financial statements for accumulated plan benefits is to include

1.  Vested benefits of participants currently collecting benefits
2.  Other vested benefits
3.  Nonvested benefits
4.  Accumulated contributions of active employees in contributory plans, if applicable

Either a reconciliation or a narrative description is to identify significant factors affecting the accumulated plan benefits from the beginning of the year to the end. The information is to include

1.  Effects of plan amendments
2.  Changes in the nature of the plan, such as a merger or a spin-off
3.  Changes in actuarial assumptions
4.  Benefits accumulated during the year
5.  Benefits paid during the year
6.  Interest component (from amortizing the discount)
7.  Other changes

The last four items can be combined into a single "other changes" category.

If the provisions of the defined benefit plan include a postretirement medical benefit component that is funded in accordance with IRC §401(h), SOP 99-2 specifies the accounting and disclosure rules with respect to the §401(h) component. These specialized rules are necessary due to legal requirements regarding the separate accounting for and funding of these arrangements.

## Defined Contribution Plans

The three general types of defined contribution plans are profit-sharing plans, money purchase pension plans, and stock bonus plans. A profit-sharing plan is a plan that is neither a pension plan, as defined in the Internal Revenue Code, nor a stock bonus plan. Employer contributions to a profit-sharing plan are to be either discretionary or based on a fixed formula. Although the plan is called a profit-sharing plan, the contributions need not be made from the profits of the plan sponsor. A money purchase plan is a benefit plan that bases employer contributions on a fixed formula that is unrelated to profits. A stock bonus plan is a plan that makes its distributions to participants in the stock of the employer unless the participant chooses otherwise. Within these three categories of plans are more specialized plans, such as 401(k) plans, 403(b) plans, savings plans, employee stock ownership plans, target benefit plans, and Keogh plans.

The three primary attributes that distinguish a defined contribution plan from a defined benefit plan are

1.  Employer contributions are determined at the discretion of the employer or according to a contractual formula, rather than being actuarially determined.
2.  Individual accounts are maintained for each plan participant, rather than a single account in which all participants partake.
3.  Benefits are determined based on the amount accumulated in a participant's account at the time he or she retires or withdraws from the plan, rather than being defined in the plan agreement. If vested, the account's value is either paid to the participant or used to purchase an annuity for the participant.

The liabilities of a defined contribution plan include accounts payable, amounts owed for securities purchases, and borrowings. The liabilities are not to include amounts that have not been paid to withdrawing participants. Those amounts are included in net assets available for benefits (representing the participants' equity in the plan net assets) and disclosed in the notes to the financial statements. Because those amounts are liabilities for regulatory purposes, a note to reconcile the financial statements to the Form 5500 may be necessary to comply with the Employee Retirement Income Security Act of 1974 (ERISA), as amended.

FSP AAG INV-1 and SOP 94-4-1 specify that, if the net assets of an investment company contain fully benefit-responsive investment contracts, those assets shall be reported at their contract values, because that is the amount participants in the fund would receive if they were to initiate withdrawals under the terms of the plan. An asset is considered fully benefit-responsive if (1) the investment contract is between the fund and the issuer and prohibits the fund from assigning or selling the contract without issuer permission, (2) the issuer is obligated to repay principal and interest, or a financially responsible third party assures that the interest rate will not drop below zero, (3) all permitted participant-initiated transactions occur at contract value, and (4) an event that would limit the fund's ability to transact at contract value with the issuer is not probable. The FSP also specifies disclosure requirements for this scenario.

### Employee Health and Welfare Benefit Plans

Defined benefit health and welfare plans stipulate a determinable benefit amount, which may take the form of a payment directly to the participant or a payment to a third party (such as a service provider or an insurance company) on the participant's behalf. These benefits may be provided upon retirement of the participant or during the postemployment period between termination of employment and retirement. Factors such as length of employment, age, and salary level determine the level of benefits to be provided. The contributions from the employer may be determined actuarially, by actual claims paid, or by a formula established by the plan sponsor. Regardless of the manner in which the plan is funded, the plan is a defined benefit health and welfare plan if its purpose is to provide a defined benefit.

Like defined benefit pension plans, defined benefit health and welfare plans must include information in their financial statements about the actuarial present value of benefit obligations earned by having performed past service. A benefit obligation exists if all of the following conditions are met:

1. The participants' rights to receive benefits are attributable to services already rendered.
2. The participants' benefits vest or accumulate.
3. Payment of benefits is probable.
4. The amount can be reasonably estimated.

If conditions 1. and 2. are not met, the obligation exists if the event that gives rise to the liability has already occurred and the amount can be reasonably estimated. The benefit obligations are measured as of the end of the plan year and include the actuarial present value of

1. Claims payable
2. Claims incurred but not reported (IBNR)
3. Insurance premiums due
4. Accumulated eligibility credits and postemployment benefits, net of amounts currently payable

5. Postretirement benefits for retired participants and their beneficiaries, other plan participants who are eligible to receive benefits, and participants who are not yet eligible to receive benefits.

Benefit obligations of defined benefit health and welfare plans, similar to accumulated plan benefits of defined benefit pension plans, do not appear as liabilities on the statement of net assets available for benefits. Instead, they are presented either as a separate financial statement, on the face of another financial statement, such as the statement of net assets available for benefits, or in the notes to the financial statements. Regardless of the location selected, the information about benefit obligations is required to be presented in its entirety in the same location.

A reconciliation, presented as a separate statement, on the face of another financial statement, or in the notes to the financial statements, is to identify significant factors comprising the change in the benefit obligation from the beginning of the year to the end. The changes are classified into at least three categories: (1) amounts currently payable, which includes claims payable, claims IBNR, and premiums due insurance companies, (2) accumulated eligibility credits and postemployment benefits, net of amounts currently payable, and (3) postretirement benefit obligations, net of amounts currently payable and claims IBNR. The information for each category is to include, at a minimum, the effects of

1. Plan amendments
2. Changes in the nature of the plan, such as a merger or a spin-off
3. Changes in actuarial assumptions
4. Benefits accumulated during the year
5. Benefits paid during the year
6. Interest component (from amortizing the discount)
7. Other changes

The last four items can be combined into a single "other changes" line.

SOP 01-2 requires the following additional disclosures:

1. The weighted-average assumed discount rate used to measure the obligation for postemployment benefits
2. Investments representing 5% or more of the net assets available for benefits as of the end of the plan year and
3. The portion of the plan's estimated cost of providing postretirement benefits that is funded by contributions from retirees.

Defined contribution health and welfare plans, like other defined contribution plans, maintain an account for each participant that determines the amount of benefits that the participant will eventually receive. The terms of a defined contribution health and welfare plan agreement determine the contribution that will be made by the employer or participant into each account. Defined contribution health and welfare plans do not report information about benefit obligations because a plan's obligation is limited to the amounts accumulated in the participants' accounts.

### Government Regulations

Pursuant to the requirements of ERISA, the federal government oversees the operating and reporting practices of employee benefit plans. ERISA establishes minimum standards for participation, vesting, and funding. It defines the responsibilities of plan fiduciaries and standards for their conduct. It requires plans to annually report summarized plan information to plan participants.

The Department of Labor (DOL) and the Internal Revenue Service (IRS) are authorized to issue regulations establishing reporting and disclosure requirements for employee benefit plans that are subject to ERISA. Each year, plans are required to report certain information to the DOL, the IRS, and the Pension Benefit Guaranty Corporation (if applicable). For many plans, the information is reported using Form 5500, which includes financial statements prepared in conformity with GAAP and additional supplementary financial schedules.

Various provisions of the Internal Revenue Code apply to employee benefit plans. If an employee benefit plan qualifies under Section §401(a) of the Code, certain favorable tax treatments apply. For example, if a plan is qualified, the plan sponsor receives current deductions for contributions to the plan, and the plan participants do not pay income taxes on those contributions or the accumulated earnings on them until benefits are distributed to them. In addition, plan participants may receive favorable tax treatment on the distributions. Qualified plans are exempt from income taxes, except for taxes on unrelated business income. Nonqualified plans, which generally provide benefits selectively only to a few key employees, are not entitled to those favorable treatments.

### Terminating Plans

If a decision has been made to terminate a plan, the plan is a terminating plan, even if another plan will replace the terminated plan. A terminating plan may continue to operate for as long as necessary to pay accrued benefits. Prominent disclosure of the relevant circumstances is necessary in all financial statements issued by the plan after the decision to terminate is made. Financial statements of a terminating plan are prepared on the liquidation basis of accounting for plan years ending after the termination decision. For plan assets, the change to the liquidation basis may have little or no effect, since many assets are already reported at current fair value. However, the liquidation basis for accumulated plan benefits (defined benefit pension plans) and benefit obligations (defined benefit health and welfare plans) may differ from the actuarial present value of benefits for an ongoing plan. For example, certain or all benefits may become vested upon plan termination.

## FINANCE COMPANIES

### PERSPECTIVE AND ISSUES

The unified AAG, *Depository and Lending Institutions: Banks and Savings Institutions, Credit Unions, Finance Companies and Mortgage Companies*, was issued in early 2004. Previously, GAAP for the finance industry was largely to be found in *Audits of Finance Companies* (AAG, 1999) and SOP 92-3, *Accounting for Foreclosed Assets*.

Finance companies provide lending and financing services to consumers (consumer financing) and to business enterprises (commercial financing). Some financing companies engage solely in consumer or commercial financing activities; others engage in both types.

Manufacturers, retailers, wholesalers and other business enterprises may provide financing to encourage customers to buy their products or services. Such financing is known as captive financing activity and may be provided by those companies or affiliated companies. Although most companies originally financed only their own products and services, many have expanded their financing activities to include a wide variety of products and services sold by unaffiliated businesses.

Consumer financing activities include direct consumer loans, retail sales contracts, and insurance services.

Commercial financing enterprises often provide a wide range of services, including factoring arrangements, revolving loans, installment and term loans, floor plan loans, and lease financing.

SOP 01-6, *Accounting by Certain Entities* (*Including Entities with Trade Receivables*) *That Lend to or Finance the Activities of Others*, conformed the accounting by various institutions such as banks, thrifts, credit unions, finance companies, corporate credit unions, and mortgage companies. It also is applicable to the financing activities of manufacturers, retailers, wholesalers, and other business enterprises. It eliminated differences in accounting and disclosure established by the respective financial institution AAGs, but carried forward accounting guidance for transactions determined to be unique to certain financial institutions.

The AAG, *Depository and Lending Institutions,* has the following features:

- Mortgage companies and corporate credit unions are explicitly included in the scope of the combined Guide.
- Regulatory capital disclosures are required for mortgage companies, credit unions, banks, and thrifts.
- Credit unions report amounts placed in their deposit insurance fund as an asset if such amounts are fully refundable, due to unique legal and operational aspects of the credit union share insurance fund. Banks and thrifts expense payments to their deposit insurance fund as incurred. Both practices have been preserved because of differences in how the funds operate.
- Finance companies record purchases and sales of securities on the settlement date, whereas banks, thrifts, and credit unions follow trade date accounting. Under the SOP, finance companies follow trade date accounting.
- FAS 114, *Accounting by Creditors for Impairment of a Loan,* and 118, *Accounting by Creditors for Impairment of a Loan—Income Recognition and Disclosures,* address loan impairment measurement and disclosure requirements, but they do not specify how to recognize income on impaired loans. The AAG for finance companies gives specific guidance on the recognition of interest income on impaired loans. Under the SOP, such guidance for finance companies is eliminated.
- Certain disclosures for credit unions will be eliminated. These disclosures include, for example, additional information about repurchase agreements, servicing assets, and deposit liabilities.

| **Sources of GAAP** | | | | |
|---|---|---|---|---|
| *FAS* | *FIN* | *SOP* | *EITF* | *AAG* |
| 91, 124, 127, 140 | 41, 42 | 92-3, 96-1, 01-6, 02-1, 03-3 | 95-22 | *Depository and Lending Institutions: Banks and Savings Institutions, Credit Unions, Finance Companies and Mortgage Companies* |

## DEFINITIONS OF TERMS

**Accounts receivable loan.** A loan collateralized by the accounts receivable of the borrower.

**Dealer reserves.** Finance company liabilities for dealers' shares of finance charges on retail contracts purchased from dealers.

**Direct consumer loan.** A two-party transaction in which the finance company lends funds directly to the borrower; such a loan may or may not be collateralized.

**Discount.** Amount deducted from the face value in advance as a charge for the loan or a deduction for interest at the time of the loan or any charge for credit that is precomputed and included in the face of the instrument.

**Discount loan.** A loan that is written with the interest or finance charges included in the face amount of the note. Discount loans are also called *precompute* or *add-on* loans.

**Effective interest rate.** The implicit rate of interest based on the amount advanced and the amount and timing of the specified repayments over the period of the contract.

**Factor.** A company that engages primarily in factoring.

**Factoring.** Purchase, usually without recourse, of individual accounts receivable arising in the client's ordinary course of business. Under a factoring agreement, the finance company also provides credit checking, collection, and recordkeeping services.

**Floor plan checking.** Physical inspection of dealer's inventories that are collateral for advances to the dealer to be repaid from the proceeds from sale of specific items. Sometimes referred to as floor plan auditing.

**Floor planning.** Financing of dealers' inventories, particularly automobiles and other consumer goods, sometimes referred to as wholesaling. The dealers are obliged to repay the supplier or manufacturer from proceeds of sale of specific items, or after an elapsed period even though inventory is not sold.

**Interest-bearing loan.** A loan that is written at the principal amount advanced to the borrower and bearing interest computed monthly on the unpaid balance.

**Interest method.** A method of computing income under which interest income on a fixed-rate obligation is accrued over the life of the loan based on a constant rate (percent) of interest applied to the outstanding loan balance. As a result, the amount of income recognized at a given time is directly proportional to the outstanding loan balance. Also called the **actuarial method**.

**Inventory loan.** A loan collateralized by inventory of the borrower.

**Nonrefundable fee.** Any charge made in connection with a loan that does not have to be refunded to the borrower when the loan is prepaid.

**Origination fee.** An amount charged by finance companies for originating, refinancing, or restructuring a loan. The amount may be intended to cover costs such as underwriting, loan application processing, and reviewing legal title to property involved.

**Overadvance (in factoring).** An amount advanced to a client in excess of the amount of uncollected receivables purchased by the factor.

**Points.** Amounts, generally expressed as a percent of the loan, charged for granting loans, that primarily are adjustments of yield but also may be intended to cover costs such as underwriting, loan application processing, and reviewing title to collateral.

## CONCEPTS, RULES, AND EXAMPLES

### Finance Receivables

Finance receivables include both interest-bearing and discount loans. The face amount of an interest-bearing or simple interest loan is equal to the amount of cash loaned; unearned interest is not computed. Conversely, for discount loans the amount of cash loaned is less than the face value of the loan. This difference represents unearned interest income to the borrower, and as such, is recognized by the lender over the life of the loan.

### Allowance for Loan Losses

A finance company should maintain an allowance for loan losses that is adequate to cover estimated losses. The allowance for loan losses decreases the carrying amount of loans receivable to net realizable value. FAS 5 and 114 provide guidance for the recognition of estimated losses from the uncollectibility of receivables. FAS 5 requires that an allowance for loan losses be established when it is probable that a loan has been impaired and the amount can be reasonably estimated. FAS 114 requires that impairment of a loan be based on the present value of expected future cash flows discounted at the loan's effective interest rate or at the loan's market price or at the fair value of the collateral of the loan if applicable.

## Interest Income and Nonrefundable Loan Fees

The interest method should be used to account for interest income in accordance with FAS 91, *Accounting for Nonrefundable Fees and Costs Associated with Originating or Acquiring Loans and Initial Direct Costs of Leases.* Under this method, often called the actuarial method, interest on installment loans is computed and accrued over the lives of the loans to arrive at constant interest rates throughout the loans' lives. Use of this method produces loans that are carried at amounts equal to future receipts discounted at original implicit interest rates. The accounting for nonrefundable loan fees is also covered in FAS 91. (See the treatment of this area under the section on Banking and Thrift.)

## Accounting for Loans Acquired by Transfer

Finance companies may acquire loans originated by other financial intermediaries. In some cases, these will have been impaired at the date they are acquired, due to changes in the borrowers' credit risks occurring subsequent to origination. SOP 03-3, *Accounting for Certain Loans and Debt Securities Acquired in a Transfer,* addresses the accounting for the differences between contractual and expected future cash flows of acquired loans when these differences are attributable, at least in part, to credit quality.

SOP 03-3 is discussed under the Banking and Thrift section of this chapter.

## Other Items

**Factoring commissions.** The amount a finance company charges as a factoring commission is dependent on such variables as sales volume, number of invoices issued, collection activities, and patterns of returns and chargebacks. Finance companies should recognize factoring commissions over the periods in which services are rendered. A finance company is considered as rendering services from the time a customer's credit is approved until the customer's account is settled.

**Advances and overadvances to factoring clients.** Finance companies generally do not treat advances to clients as receivables. Instead, advances are applied against amounts owed to clients from the purchase of the client's receivables. Finance companies generally limit advances to percentages of the unpaid amounts of factored receivables. Overadvances, which are amounts in excess of outstanding receivables purchased, should be recorded as loans receivable.

**Repossessed assets acquired in liquidation of receivables.** Finance companies may repossess goods or other property that collateralize loans when they foreclose on uncollectible loans. Repossessed assets are typically sold as soon as possible to minimize losses from defaulted loans. Certain types of collateral, such as automobiles, may be readily salable in wholesale or other markets. Repossessions of such collateral are fairly common. Repossessions on commercial loans can result in significant losses because of the bargain prices associated with reselling inventories, plant, property, and equipment.

Terms of recourse arrangements include the following:

1. Full recourse—The dealer is required to pay off the uncollected receivable balance to the finance company at the date of repossession.
2. Partial or limited recourse—The dealer is liable for repossession losses up to an agreed amount.
3. Nonrecourse—Loss is borne entirely by the finance company.

**Dealer reserves and holdbacks.** Finance companies account for dealer reserves and holdbacks as liabilities. Dealer reserve accounts are credited for the dealers' share of the finance charges. Dealer reserve accounts may be charged as the result of customers paying off contracts early, losses on full or partial recourse contracts, and from payments to dealers in excess of minimum requirements.

**Sales of receivables.** A finance company may decide to sell a portfolio of receivables to another finance company or financial institution. FAS 140, *Accounting for Transfers and Servicing of Financial Assets and Extinguishment of Liabilities*, controls whether such transactions should be accounted for as sales of receivables or as loans collateralized by receivables. Generally, a transfer is treated as a sale if the transferor surrenders control of the receivables. The provisions of FAS 140 are addressed in Chapters 7 and 8.

# GOVERNMENT CONTRACTORS

## PERSPECTIVE AND ISSUES

ARB 43 governs the accounting and income recognition issues concerning cost-plus-fixed-fee and fixed-price supply contracts. The fees under government cost-plus-fixed-fee contracts are recognized as income on the basis of partial performance if there is reasonable assurance of realization. Fees are also accrued as they become billable unless this accrual is not reasonably related to the proportionate performance of total work to be performed.

This pronouncement also covers renegotiation (refunds of excessive profits) and contracts terminated for the convenience of the government.

| Sources of GAAP |
| --- |
| *ARB* |
| 43 (Chapter 11) |

## DEFINITIONS OF TERMS

**Contractors.** In the context of this discussion, contractors are enterprises that sell products or services to the US government pursuant to a formal contract. The relationship to the government can be direct (a prime contract between the enterprise and the government) or indirect ( a subcontract between the enterprise and a prime contractor).

**Contract.** A legal agreement obligating a contractor (referred to as the "general contractor" or "prime contractor") to provide products or services to the US government. The term also refers to subcontracts obligating subcontractors to indirectly perform in a similar manner under the supervision and control of the prime contractor.

**Cost-plus-fixed-fee contracts.** An agreement that provides for contractors to receive a specified fixed fee and to be reimbursed for their allowable costs. Because title passes to the government and the contractor obtains an unconditional right to partial payment prior to delivery, delivery of the finished product is not necessarily evidence of performance.

**Disposal credits.** Deductions from the termination claim receivable for approved retention or sale of inventory previously included in the claim.

**No-cost settlements.** Settlements in which the contractor waives the right to make a claim. No sale is recorded and applicable costs retain their usual classification.

**Service contracts.** Contracts in which the contractor acts only as an agent.

**Supply contracts.** Contract in which the contractor's services extend beyond that of an agent. Contracts include services such as the use of the contractor's own facilities and the contractor assumes responsibility to creditors for material and services, and to employees for salaries.

**Subcontractor's claims.** Claims made in conjunction with a terminated contract resulting from costs incurred under the terminated contract that did not result in the transfer of billable materials or services to the contractor before termination.

## CONCEPTS, RULES, AND EXAMPLES

Cost-plus-fixed-fee contracts (CPFFC) are used for the manufacture and delivery of products, the construction of plants and other facilities, and for management and other services. The amount of the flat-fee payment is usually determined by the ratio of the actual expenditures to the total estimated expenditures. CPFFC may be cancelled and terminated by the government. If this occurs, the contractor is entitled to reimbursement for expenditures and an appropriate portion of the fixed fee.

Normally, profits are recognized when the right to full payment is unconditional. However, revenues can be accrued and profits recognized for partial performance when total profit can be reasonably estimated and realization is reasonably assured. The fees are usually accrued as they become billable. Because risk is minimal and there is no credit problem, billable amounts are indicative of realization. The contractor's fee is considered earned when it is billable and when the related costs are incurred or paid. Accrual based on billable amounts is an application of the percentage-of-completion method, rather than a deviation from the accrual method. The fee is considered billable when approved by the government. An alternative date is used when a determination is made that estimated and final costs are significantly different. Accrual of the fee upon delivery or based on percentage of completion is more appropriate when excess costs are substantial.

For supply contracts, reimbursable costs and fees are included in sales. For service contracts, only fees are included in sales. Unbilled amounts are included in the balance sheet as a receivable but are to be captioned and presented separately from billed receivables. Advances in CPFFC are generally intended to assist the contractor in financing its costs. Thus, in general, advances are treated as liabilities and are not offset against contract receivables. Advances are permitted to be offset against contract receivables only when there is an expectation that the advances will be applied against those specific charges. Any such offsets require disclosure in the financial statements.

### Renegotiation

Renegotiation typically addresses a refund to the government of "excessive" profits. In reality, it is more of an adjustment of the selling price. The financial statements are to disclose situations when a substantial portion of a contractor's business consists of contracts that are subject to renegotiation. When a reasonable estimate of renegotiation refunds can be made, a provision is shown as a deduction from revenue in the income statement and as a current liability on the balance sheet. Deferred income taxes are adjusted accordingly. When a reasonable estimate cannot be made, disclosure is required along with the reasons for the inability to make an estimate. Footnote disclosure is also required regarding material uncertainties and their significance, and regarding the basis for determining the renegotiation provision.

### Terminated Defense Contracts

These contracts are contracts terminated for the convenience of the government. Profits accrue as of the effective date of termination and are included in financial statements after the termination. Disclosure is made of all material facts and circumstances. Termination claims are recorded as a single amount even if they consist of several different types of cost reimbursements. Material termination claims are to be captioned separately from other receivables and such claims receivable directly from the government are to be presented separately from related claims against other contractors. Claims receivable are classified as current assets unless there is an indication of extended delay, such as a serious disagreement indicative of probable litigation. Pretermination contract advances are shown as a deduction from claims receivable and adequately explained. Termination loans are classified as current liabilities and cross-referenced to the related claims receivable.

Material termination claims are separately captioned in the revenues section of the contractor's statement of income. When inventory is reacquired by the contractor after including it in a termination claim, it is recorded as a purchase. The credit is applied against the termination claim receivable.

# INSURANCE

## PERSPECTIVE AND ISSUES

The two major types of insurance companies are life and property and casualty. Each category is further subdivided into stock companies and mutual associations. Due to the regulated nature of the insurance industry, financial reporting may be in conformity to statutory accounting principles (SAP) or GAAP. Furthermore, publicly held companies subject to SEC accounting rules will account for certain transactions and events in other manners dictated by those requirements. While accounting principles under GAAP are broadly applicable to all types of insurance companies (including those dealing in such specialized products as mortgage insurance, title insurance, and reinsurance), the nature of the estimation process (such as for claims liabilities) differs substantially depending upon the character of the risks assumed.

The main contrasts between SAP and GAAP arise from the more conservative nature of SAP, which is a reflection of the insurance regulatory agencies' concern with protection of the policyholders' interests, and hence with the liquidity and solvency of the insurance companies. Accordingly, under SAP certain costs, such as policy acquisition expenses, are written off as incurred; certain nonliquid assets, such as property and furniture, are not recognized; and claims liabilities are very conservatively estimated. In contrast to this essentially short-term perspective, financial statements prepared on the GAAP basis are more concerned with the value of the companies' investments and net worth on a going concern basis.

The primary source of insurance industry GAAP is FAS 60. Although mutual insurance companies and certain other organizations had initially not been required to apply this standard, FAS 120 later extended its requirements to these enterprises. Insurance contracts are categorized as short duration (which includes most property and liability insurance) or long duration (which includes most life, mortgage, and title insurance). Nominal insurance contracts that are effectively investment contracts, however, are not accounted for as insurance. The AAG, *Audits of Property and Liability Insurance Companies*, was issued in 1998.

Current industry-specific guidance can be found in the AICPA's AAG, *Life and Health Insurance Entities*, which was revised in 2001. This Guide discusses those aspects of accounting and auditing unique to life and health insurance entities, and contains significant discussions of statutory accounting practices (SAP), which comprise laws, regulations, and administrative rulings adopted by various states that govern the operations and reporting requirements of life insurance entities. It does not reflect SAP under the National Association of Insurance Commissioners (NAIC) codification project, but AcSEC subsequently issued SOP 01-5, *Amendments to Specific AICPA Pronouncements for Changes Related to the NAIC Codification*, which requires insurance enterprises to disclose, at the date of each balance sheet presented, a description of the prescribed or permitted statutory accounting practice and the related monetary effect on statutory surplus of using an accounting practice that differs from either state-prescribed statutory accounting practices or NAIC statutory accounting practices. Retroactive application of these provisions is not permitted.

AcSEC issued SOP 03-1, *Accounting and Reporting by Insurance Enterprises for Certain Non-Traditional Long-Duration Contracts and for Separate Accounts,* which addresses the classification and valuation of liabilities, as well as disclosures for nontraditional annuity and life insurance contracts issued by insurance enterprises. Several of the conclusions reached on these topics are discussed later in this section.

An Invitation to Comment was issued in 2007 by FASB on the subject of separating insurance contracts into risk transfer and financing segments, so that these contract segments may be appropriately accounted for.

| Sources of GAAP | | | | |
|---|---|---|---|---|
| *FAS* | *FIN* | *SOP* | *EITF* | *AAG* |
| 5, 60, 91, 97, | 40 | 92-5, 94-5, | 92-9, 93-6, | *Audits of Property and* |
| 109, 113, 114, | | 95-1, 97-3, | 93-14, 99-4 | *Liability Insurance* |
| 115, 120, 124 | | 98-7, 00-3, | | *Companies, Life and Health* |
| | | 01-5, 03-1, | *FSP* | *Insurance Entities* |
| | | 05-1 | FAS 97-1 | |

## CONCEPTS, RULES, AND EXAMPLES

### Premium Income

Premium income is recognized differently for short and long duration contracts. For short duration contracts, premium income is recognized over the contract term in proportion to the amount of insurance provided. In the case of long duration contracts, revenue is accrued as the premiums become due from policyholders, except for contracts that provide benefits over a term longer than the premium payment term (such as twenty-year life policies), in which case income is recognized over the longer period during which benefits may be provided.

### Claim Cost Recognition

Costs of benefits are recognized when insured events such as property damage occur. Estimated costs are accrued for as claims incurred but not yet reported. For long duration contracts, the present values of estimated future benefits are accrued, net of the present values of future net premiums to be collected. Accrual of these benefit obligations generally involves actuarial determinations. Accountants may be dependent on the services of specialists in such cases, as they are in computing costs related to defined benefit pension plans. Recognition of other expenses is governed by the matching concept. For example, costs that vary with acquisition activity are capitalized and amortized over the period during which premium income is earned. Catastrophic losses (as from natural disasters such as hurricanes) are accrued under the guidelines of FAS 5: when impairment of the asset or incurring of a liability is probable and the amount is reasonably estimable.

### Investments

The other major concern of GAAP for insurance enterprises relates to the presentation of investments held. FAS 115 established the accounting requirements for investments in debt and marketable equity securities. Briefly, those investments must be categorized as being either held-for-trading, available-for-sale, or held-to-maturity. Investments falling within the first two categories should be reported at fair value, with value changes affecting the trading securities portfolio being reflected in income, while changes in the available-for-sale portfolio are reported in a separate equity account. Securities to be held to maturity are accounted for at amortized historical cost, absent a permanent decline in value. Equity securities that do not meet the definition of "marketable" are also to be reported at fair value, with gains or losses reported in stockholders' equity. In addition, real estate acquired in settling mortgage guaranty and title insurance claims is to be reported at fair value.

### Deferred Income Taxes

GAAP requires that deferred income taxes be provided for temporary differences. An exception was previously provided under the "indefinite reversal criterion," for stock life insurance companies only, for differences designated as policyholders' surplus. However, FAS 109 holds that deferred taxes must be provided, consistent with the accounting prescribed for all other temporary differences.

### Other Matters

**Reinsurance.** Another specialized topic area pertinent to insurance companies is that of reinsurance, which is addressed by FAS 113. This standard, which amends FAS 60, eliminates the former practice of reporting assets and liabilities net of the effects of reinsurance. It requires that reinsurance receivables, including amounts related to claims incurred but not reported, be reported as assets, consistent with the manner in which liabilities relating to the underlying reinsured contracts are accounted for. The standard also establishes criteria for recognition as reinsurance, and sets forth detailed accounting for long and short duration contracts, as well as new disclosure requirements. FIN 40 clarifies that GAAP applies equally to mutual insurance companies as it does to stock companies, unless explicit exceptions are established. Regulatory reporting can no longer, therefore, be deemed to be in accordance with GAAP.

**Loss reserves.** SOP 92-4 addressed matters relating to estimation of loss reserves, and a number of auditing concerns relating to reserves, reinsurance, loss adjustment expenses, and other topics. SOP 92-5 concerns accounting for foreign property and liability reinsurance, and concludes that except for special circumstances, only the periodic method is acceptable in accounting for foreign reinsurance premiums. SOP 94-5 requires disclosures where permission was received from the National Association of Insurance Commissioners to use different accounting practices. SOP 95-1 covers capitalization and amortization costs and several other matters for mutual life insurance companies. FAS 120 requires that the provision of this SOP be applied to assessment enterprises, fraternal benefit societies, and stock life insurance companies.

**Guaranty funds.** SOP 97-3 addresses matters pertaining to guaranty funds and certain other insurance-related assessments. Existing practice has been quite diverse, but SOP 97-3 essentially applies the criteria of FAS 5, *Accounting for Contingencies*, to these matters, with the exception that practice can be substantially conformed. The key elements of this standard are discussed in the following paragraphs.

Under the standard, guaranty fund and similar assessments would be recognized when (1) it has been imposed or is deemed probable of being imposed, (2) the event obligating an entity to pay the assessment has occurred, and (3) the amount of the assessment can be reasonably estimated. All three conditions would have to be fulfilled before a liability could be accrued. Discounting to present value will be permitted. The SOP offers specific guidance regarding the ability to reasonably estimate the liability for assessments.

Guaranty funds are essentially state-mandated insurance funds used to settle claims against insolvent insurers and, typically, all licensed insurers are assessed premiums based on the volume of defined lines of business they conduct in the given state. A variety of methods have been applied in determining the amounts of guaranty fund assessments (e.g., retrospectively, based on premiums written over the past two years; or prospectively, based on business written over the next several years following an insolvency of a failed insurer), with the result that entities upon which assessments are being levied have been inclined to use different methods of recognizing the cost and related obligation. In general, to warrant accrual under SOP 97-3, an insolvency of another insurer would have to have occurred, since the presumption would be that the assessments would become probable (the threshold criterion) when there has been a formal determination of another entity's insolvency. An example of an exception would be when the state uses prospective premium-based guaranty fund assessments; if the reporting entity cannot avoid the obligation by ceasing to write policies, the obligating event would be the determination of insolvency, but if it could avoid the assessment, the obligating event is the writing of premiums after the insolvency.

**Surplus notes.** AICPA Practice Bulletin 15, *Accounting by the Issuer of Surplus Notes*, affects accounting by certain insurance companies that issue a security known as surplus notes. It requires that these instruments be accounted for as debt and included in the liabilities caption of the balance sheet. Furthermore, interest must be accrued over the term of the notes, whether or not payment of interest and/or principal has been approved by an insurance company. However, disclosure is required as to the status of the request for approval.

**Deposit accounting.** SOP 98-7 applies to entities entering into short duration insurance and reinsurance contracts that do not transfer insurance risk, or multiple year contracts that either do not transfer insurance risk or for which insurance risk transfer is not determinable. Insurance risk is comprised of timing risk and underwriting risk, and one or both of these may not be transferred to the insurer (assuming entity in the case of reinsurance) under certain circumstances. For example, many workers' compensation policies provide for "experience adjustments" which have the effect of keeping the underwriting risk with the insured, rather than transferring it to the insurer; in such instances, deposit accounting would be prescribed.

Under the provisions of SOP 98-7, for contracts that transfer only significant timing risk, or that transfer neither significant timing nor underwriting risk, a deposit asset (from the insured's or ceding entity's perspective, respectively, for insurance and reinsurance arrangements) or liability (from the insurer's or assuming entity's perspective, respectively, for insurance and reinsurance arrangements) should be recognized at inception. The deposit asset or liability should be remeasured at subsequent financial reporting dates by calculating the effective yield on the deposit to reflect actual payments to date and expected future payments. Yield is to be determined as set forth in FAS 91, using the estimated amounts and timings of cash flows. The deposit is to be adjusted to that which would have existed at the balance sheet date had the new effective yield been applied since inception of the contract; thus, expense or income for a period will be determined by first calculating the necessary amount in the related balance sheet account.

For contracts that transfer only significant underwriting risk, a deposit asset or liability is also established at inception. However, subsequent remeasurement of the deposit does not occur until such time as a loss is incurred that will be reimbursed under the contract; instead, the deposit is reported at its amortized amount. Once the loss occurs, the deposit should be remeasured by the present value of expected future cash flows arising from the contract, plus the remaining unexpired portion of the coverage. Changes in the deposit arising from the present value measure are to be reported in the insured's income statement as an offset against the loss to be reimbursed; in the insurer's income statement, the adjustment should be reported as an incurred loss. The reduction due to amortization of the deposit is reported as an adjustment to incurred losses by the insurer. The discount rate used to compute the present value is to be the rate on government obligations with similar cash flow characteristics, adjusted for differences in default risk, which is based on the insurer's credit rating. Rates are determined at the loss date(s) and not revised later, absent further losses.

For insurance contracts with indeterminate risk, the procedures set forth in SOP 92-5 (the open-year method) should be applied. This involves balance sheet segregation of amounts that have not been adjusted due to lack of sufficient loss or other data. When sufficient information becomes available, the deposit asset or liability is adjusted, which is to be reported as an accounting change per FAS 154.

**Demutualizations.** SOP 00-3, *Accounting by Insurance Enterprises for Demutualizations and Formations of Mutual Insurance Holding Companies and for Certain Long-Duration Participating Contracts,* addressed the increasingly common phenomenon of demutualizations (whereby formerly mutually owned insurers issue stock), as well as the formation of insurance holding companies (MIHC). A key concern is the accounting for the "closed block" of assets and liabilities, and of earnings allocable to the closed block. This pertains to mechanisms designed to protect the adjustable policy features and dividend expectations of participating life insurance policyholders from the competing interests of stockholders. Typically, the plan of demutualization describes how the closed block will operate. The closed block assets and cash returns on those assets will not inure to the stockholders of the demutualized company; instead, all cash flows from these assets will be used to benefit the closed block policyholders. The insurance enterprise remains obligated to provide for minimum guarantees under the participating policy, and it is consequently possible under certain circumstances that additional "stockholder" funds will have to be used to meet the contractual benefits of the closed block policyholders. The assets designated to the closed block are subject to the same liabilities, with the same priority in the case of insolvency or in liquidation, as assets outside the closed block. In many situations, commissions and other expenses (including management expenses) of operating and administering the closed block will not be charged to the closed block. Unless the state insurance department consents to an earlier termination, the closed block will continue in effect until the date on which none of the policies in the closed block remains in force.

Alternatives to the closed block have arisen in practice encompassing, for a number of types of contracts, various mechanisms believed by the insurance enterprise and state insurance regulators to be appropriate in the specific circumstances. Closed block alternative mechanisms have been used in lieu of closed blocks for certain participating life contracts to commit to the insurance regulator that the insurance company will continue to follow its established dividend practices. Closed block alternative mechanisms also have been used to protect nonguaranteed elements of participating and nonparticipating insurance contracts such as interest credits on deferred annuities and adjustable premiums on adjustable premium term business. In some instances, the methodology and limitations defined in the agreements with the state insurance regulators have considered only specific profit components, such as mortality experience on a block of term insurance or investment spreads on a block of annuities, and in other instances have considered virtually all components of product profitability. Where there is a limitation on the profits that may inure to the stockholders, there generally is a formal agreement between the insurance company and the insurance regulators that defines (1) the contracts covered by the limitation, (2) the profit limitation calculation, and (3) the timing and manner (for example, as policy dividends, reduced premiums, or additional benefits) in which amounts that may not be distributed to stockholders are to be distributed to policyholders.

Some of the more important conclusions reached by AcSEC were as follows:

1. The classification of expenses related to a demutualization and the formation of an MIHC should be considered other than extraordinary expense.
2. Closed block assets and liabilities from the closed block should be included with the corresponding financial statement items of the insurance enterprise.
3. AcSEC has concluded that SOP 95-1, *Accounting for Certain Insurance Activities of Mutual Life Insurance Enterprises*, should continue to be applied after conversion to a stock company. However, provisions of FAS 60, *Accounting and Reporting by*

*Insurance Enterprises*, relating to dividends on participating contracts should apply to such contracts sold before the date of demutualization or date of formation of the MIHC.

4. The maximum future contribution of the closed block to the earnings of the company is typically the excess of the GAAP liabilities over the GAAP assets at the date of demutualization. Under FAS 60, a dividend liability should be established for current earnings that will be paid to policyholders through future benefits. From a shareholder perspective, excess earnings of the closed block that will never inure to the shareholders should be set up as a liability. AcSEC decided upon establishment of a dividend liability for excess earnings due to policyholders that cannot inure to shareholders.

5. For a "distribution-form" demutualization, an insurance enterprise should reclassify all of its retained earnings as of the date of demutualization to capital stock and additional paid-in capital accounts. A "subscription-form" demutualization should not, in and of itself, result in reclassification of retained earnings. AcSEC concluded that the equity accounts of the MIHC at the date of formation should be determined using the principles for transactions of companies under common control with the amount of retained earnings of the demutualized insurance enterprise, before reclassification to the capital accounts, being reported as retained earnings of the MIHC.

## Nontraditional Long-Duration Contracts

SOP 03-1, *Accounting and Reporting by Insurance Enterprises for Certain Nontraditional Long-Duration Contracts and for Separate Accounts*, addresses the classification and valuation of liabilities as well as disclosures for nontraditional annuity and life insurance contracts issued by insurance enterprises. The requirements under this standard are set forth in the following paragraphs.

The portion of separate account assets representing contract holder funds are to be measured at fair value and reported in the insurance enterprise's financial statements as a summary total, with an equivalent summary total for related liabilities, if the separate account arrangement meets all the specified criteria. If the arrangement does not meet the criteria, assets representing contract holder funds should be accounted for as general account assets, and any related liability should be accounted for as a general account liability.

Assets underlying an insurance enterprise's proportionate interest in a separate account do not represent contract holder funds, and thus are not to be separately reported and valued. If a separate account arrangement meets the criteria in SOP 03-1 and (1) the terms of the contract allow the contract holder to invest in additional units in the separate account or (2) the insurance enterprise is marketing contracts that permit funds to be invested in the separate account, the assets underlying the insurance enterprise's proportionate interest in the separate account should be accounted for in a manner consistent with similar assets held by the general account that the insurance enterprise may be required to sell.

If the enterprise's proportionate interest in the separate account is less than 20% of the separate account, and all of the underlying investments of the separate account meet the definition of securities under FAS 115 or FAS 60, or the definition of cash and cash equivalents, the enterprise may report its portion of the separate account value as an investment in equity securities classified as trading under FAS 115.

Assets transferred from the general account to a separate account should be recognized at fair value to the extent of third-party contract holders' proportionate interest in the separate account if the separate account arrangement meets the criteria set forth in the SOP. Any gain related to the third-party contract holder's proportionate interest should be recognized immediately in earnings of the general account of the insurance enterprise, if the risks and rewards of ownership have been transferred to contract holders using the fair value of the asset at the date of the contract holder's assumption of risks and rewards. A guarantee of the asset's value or minimum rate of return or a commitment to repurchase the asset would indicate that the risks of ownership have not been transferred, and no gain can be recognized. If the separate account arrangement does not meet the criteria in the SOP, the transfer generally should have no financial reporting effect (that is, general account classification and carrying amounts should be retained). In certain situations loss recognition may be appropriate.

The basis for determining the balance that accrues to the contract holder for a long-duration insurance or investment contract that is subject to FAS 97 is the accrued account balance. The accrued account balance equals

1. Deposit(s) net of withdrawals;
2. Plus amounts credited pursuant to the contract;
3. Less fees and charges assessed;
4. Plus additional interest (for example, persistency bonus); and
5. Other adjustments, such as appreciation or depreciation recognized under this SOP, to the extent not already credited.

For contracts that have features that may result in more than one potential account balance, the accrued account balance should be the highest contractually determinable balance that will be available in cash or its equivalent at contractual maturity or the reset date, without reduction for future fees and charges. The accrued account balance should not reflect any surrender adjustments (for example, fair value annuity adjustments, surrender charges, or credits). For contracts in which amounts credited as interest to the contract holder are reset periodically, the accrued balance should be based on the highest crediting rate guaranteed or declared through the reset date.

For a contract not accounted for under FAS 133 that provides a return based on the total return of a contractually referenced pool of assets either through crediting rates or termination adjustments, the accrued account balance should be based on the fair value of the referenced pool of assets (or applicable index value) at the balance sheet date, even if the related assets are not recognized at fair value.

To determine the accounting under FAS 97 for a contract that contains death or other insurance benefit features, the enterprise should first determine whether the contract is an investment or universal-life-type contract. If the mortality or morbidity risks are other than nominal and the fees assessed or insurance benefits are not fixed and guaranteed, the contract should be classified as a FAS 97 universal-life-type contract. A rebuttable presumption is that a contract has significant mortality risk where the additional insurance benefit would vary significantly in response to capital markets volatility. The determination of significance should be made at contract inception, other than at transition, and should be based on a comparison of the present value of expected excess payments (that is, insurance benefit amounts and related incremental claim adjustment expenses in excess of the account balance) to be made under insurance benefit features to the present value of all amounts expected to be assessed against the contract holder (revenue).

For contracts classified as insurance contracts that have amounts assessed against contract holders each period for the insurance benefit feature that are assessed in a manner that is expected to result in profits in earlier years and subsequent losses from that insurance benefit function, a liability should be established in addition to the account balance to recognize the portion of such assessments that compensates the insurance enterprise for benefits to be provided in future periods in accordance with the guidance in the SOP.

If a reinsurer assumes the insurance benefit feature, it should assess the significance of mortality and morbidity risk within the reinsurance contract according to the guidance in SOP 03-1, regardless of whether there is an account balance. The reinsurer should determine the classification of the reinsurance contract as an investment contract or as an insurance contract at the inception of the reinsurance contract. For reinsurance contracts, the mortality or morbidity risk could be deemed other than nominal even if the original issuer did not determine mortality or morbidity to be other than nominal. Similarly, the issuer of a contract that provides only an insurance benefit feature that wraps a noninsurance contract, for example, a guaranteed minimum death benefit related to a mutual fund balance, should evaluate its contract in the same manner. A reinsurer or issuer of the insurance benefit features of a contract should calculate a liability for the portion of premiums collected each period that represents compensation to the insurance enterprise for benefits that are assessed in a manner that is expected to result in current profits and future losses from the insurance benefit function. That liability should be calculated using the methodology described in SOP 03-1.

Contracts may provide for potential benefits in addition to the account balance that are payable only upon annuitization, such as annuity purchase guarantees, guaranteed minimum income benefit (GMIB), and two-tier annuities. Insurance enterprises should determine whether such contract features should be accounted for under the provisions of FAS 133. If the contract feature is not accounted for under the provisions of FAS 133, an additional liability for the contract feature should be established if the present value of expected annuitization payments at the expected annuitization date exceeds the expected account balance at the expected annuitization date in accordance with the guidance in SOP 03-1.

Sales inducements provided to the contract holder, whether for investment or universal-life-type contracts, should be recognized as part of the liability for policy benefits over the period for which the contract must remain in force for the contract holder to qualify for the inducement or at the crediting date, if earlier, in accordance with the SOP. No adjustments should be made to reduce the liability related to the sales inducements for anticipated surrender charges, persistency, or early withdrawal contractual features.

Sales inducements that are recognized as part of the liability under SOP 03-1, that are explicitly identified in the contract at inception, and that meet the criteria specified in the SOP should be deferred and amortized using the same methodology and assumptions used to amortize capitalized acquisition costs.

The financial statements of an insurance enterprise should disclose information about the following:

1. Separate account assets and liabilities; the nature, extent, and timing of minimum guarantees related to variable contracts; and the amount of gains and losses recognized on assets transferred to separate accounts.
2. An insurance enterprise's accounting policy for sales inducements, including the nature of the costs capitalized and the method of amortizing those costs; the amount of costs capitalized and amortized for each of the periods presented; and the unamortized balance as of each balance sheet date presented.
3. The nature of the liabilities and methods and assumptions used in estimating any contract benefits recognized in excess of the account balance pursuant to the SOP.

### Deferred Acquisition Costs for Insurance Contract Modifications or Exchanges

SOP 05-1, *Accounting by Insurance Enterprises for Deferred Acquisition Costs in Connection with Modifications or Exchanges of Insurance Contracts*, addresses the accounting for deferred acquisition costs related to the internal replacement of selected insurance and investment contracts. An internal replacement is a modification of an insurance product's benefits, features, rights, or coverages (described hereafter as "benefits") by a variety of means, including the extinguishment and replacement of a contract.

If an internal replacement occurs and the rights and obligations of the parties are essentially unchanged, then the replacement contract is considered a continuation of the replaced contract. In this case, the replaced contract's unamortized deferred acquisition costs, unearned revenue liabilities, and deferred sales inducement assets should continue to be recognized as part of the replacement contract. Also, cost incurred in connection with such a replacement are charged to expense as incurred.

A contract change must meet all of the following criteria in order to be considered a continuation of the replaced contract—if any condition is not met, the change is treated as a substantially changed contract:

1. The insured event, risk, or period of coverage has not changed.
2. The contract holder's investment return rights have not changed.
3. Either there is no change in the insurance premium, or a premium reduction is matched by a corresponding reduction in benefits.
4. Net of distributions, there is no net reduction in contract value.
5. There is no change in contractual participation or dividend features.
6. There is no change in the contract's amortization method or revenue classification.

If benefits replacement results in a substantially changed contract, then the replaced contract is considered extinguished, in which case unamortized deferred acquisition costs, unearned revenue liabilities, and deferred sales inducement assets from the replaced contract should not be deferred as part of the replacement contract.

If a contract is accounted for under FAS 97 and FAS 120 (long-duration participating contracts), the estimated gross profit of the replacement contract is treated as a revision of the replaced contract's gross profit when determining the amortization of deferred acquisition costs, deferred sales inducement assets, and the recognition of unearned revenues. If a contract is accounted for under FAS 91 (nonrefundable fees), the cash flows of the replacement contract revise the cash flows of the replaced contract for purposes of calculating the interest rate amortization of unamortized deferred acquisition costs and deferred sales inducement assets.

This SOP does not apply to contract modifications resulting from an election by the contract holder that was within the original contract, as long as (1) the election followed the terms of the original contract, (2) the election is not subject to any underwriting, (3) the insurance provider cannot decline the coverage or adjust contract pricing, and (4) the benefit had been accounted for since the contract inception. The SOP also does not apply if a contract feature is nonintegrated (it provides coverage that is priced solely for the incremental benefits coverage, and does not alter other components of the contract), in which case it should be accounted for as a separately issued contract.

### Other Accounting Guidance

In EITF 92-9, it was noted that industry practice is to amortize the present value of future profits (PVP) using an interest method with accrual of interest added to the unamortized balance. In the past, there has been some diversity in the application of this method in practice, and so the EITF mandates that the interest rate used to amortize PVP should be the liability or contract rate. It also states that changes in estimates of future gross profits on FAS 97 contracts should be accounted for as a catch-up adjustment. And finally, PVP and any related liability should be subject to the premium deficiency test required in FAS 60 and 97.

A number of issues involving retrospective rating provisions contained in reinsurance contracts were resolved by EITF 93-6, including criteria for the recognition and amounts of assets and liabilities by the assuming and ceding enterprises, respectively, and accounting for changes in coverage during the reinsurance period. A number of conditions were identified, satisfaction of which are necessary for a contract to be treated as reinsurance, and in their absence such contracts are to be accounted for by the deposit method.

EITF 93-14 addresses how enterprises other than insurance companies should account for contracts with insurance companies covering various types of risks such as product and environmental liability risks. This EITF also addresses "pooled risk" contracts and reinsurance contracts entered into by a captive insurer. In order for a contract to be considered insurance it must indemnify the insured party as this would result in a transfer of risk. If no transfer of risk exists (FAS 5), then the contract is not considered insurance, and the balance of the premium less any amount to be retained by the insurer should be accounted for as a deposit.

EITF 99-4 provided guidance on the accounting for those formerly mutual insurance companies that have undergone demutualization transactions and converted to stock enterprises. In order to effect a demutualization, a company may be required to issue consideration, often in the form of stock, to existing participating policyholders in exchange for their current membership interests. The receipt of such stock has no direct effect on the policyholders' contractual interests of their insurance policies (for example, it does not alter the cash surrender value of their life insurance policies). However, the governance of the mutual insurance company and, in particular, the participating policyholders' interest in that governance are modified. Thus, stock received from a demutualization should be accounted for at fair value with a gain recognized in income from continuing operations.

SOP 92-5 addressed the lack of uniformity of practices among foreign reinsurers, and in particular how US insurers were to account for property and liability reinsurance assumed from foreign companies.

SOP 94-5 supplements the disclosure requirements in other FASB and SEC pronouncements. Required disclosures are set forth for insurance enterprises that have received permission by the insurance department in their domiciliary states to use accounting practices other than those prescribed by state laws, regulations, and rules and by the National Association of Insurance Commissioners (NAIC). This SOP also defines liability for unpaid claims and claims adjustment expenses and lists the related disclosures required.

Another SOP, 95-1, provides guidance on applying FAS 60, 97, and 113 in accounting for mutual life insurance contracts. Capitalization and amortization of acquisition costs is discussed. Premiums are to be reported as revenue when due from policyholders. Death and surrender benefits are reported as expenses, and annual dividends are reported separately as expenses. The calculation of estimated gross margin and liability for future policy benefits is described.

SOP 97-3 was promulgated in order to address the diversity in practice of accounting for assessments made by government agencies against insurance activities such as workers' compensation second injury funds, this SOP imposed accrual accounting requirements and set forth the conditions that must be met before a liability may be recognized.

Recently in the news have been so-called insurance policies which did not involve the actual transfer of risk, and the fact that accounting requirements governing these situations may not have been adequate. SOP 98-7 provided guidance on how to account for insurance and reinsurance contracts that do not have the effect of transferring insurance risk. It applies to all entities and all types of insurance or reinsurance contracts, other than long duration life and health insurance contracts. The method prescribed by this SOP is "deposit accounting."

SOP 00-3 provided necessary guidance to the proper accounting for demutualization transactions and also for the formation of mutual insurance holding companies. It also provides guidance to stock insurers that choose to apply SOP 95-1 to account for participating policies within the scope of that SOP.

SOP 01-5 amended SOP 94-5 to require disclosure of the entity's prescribed or permitted statutory accounting practice and the related monetary effect on statutory surplus of using accounting methods that differ from either the state-prescribed statutory practices, or the NAIC statutory practices.

A FASB Staff Position, FSP 97-1, has clarified that recognition of an unearned revenue liability representing amounts that have been assessed to compensate insurers for services to be performed over future periods is a requirement under FAS 97. This requirement is absolute and was not amended by SOP 03-1, as some had inferred incorrectly. Importantly (given recent alleged abuses by some insurers), this liability is not to be used to inappropriately level or smooth out gross profit over the term of the contract or produce a level gross profit from the mortality benefit over the life of the contract.

The staff of the SEC's Division of Corporate Finance has issued guidance in its "Current Accounting and Disclosure Issues" publication regarding the proper disclosures required of publicly held property-casualty insurance companies. The disclosure about the policies and methodologies for estimating the liability for unpaid claims and claim adjustment expenses should (1) separately address each material line of business, (2) identify and describe the actuarial method used, (3) describe any policy for adjusting the liability for unpaid claims and claim adjustment expenses to an amount differing from the amount calculated by its actuaries, and (4) describe any difference in the annual and interim procedures for determining the liability for unpaid claims and claim adjustment expenses. Further, the disclosure of the reasons for incurred claims and claim adjustment expenses in the current income statement that are attributed to insured events in prior years should (1) quantify the amount by line of business and by accident year within each line, (2) describe the new events or information obtained since the last reporting period that led to any changes in estimate, and (3) explain why recognition occurred in the current period, rather than in earlier periods.

The SEC staff also requires disclosure about reserving assumptions. For each material line of business, disclosure should include (1) the key assumptions affecting the estimate of liability for unpaid claims and claim adjustment expenses, and (2) a quantification of any material assumption changes from the preceding period. Finally, registrants should disclose whether the liability for claims and claim adjustment expenses is likely to change in the future. This disclosure should include, for each material line of business, (1) the identification of key assumptions that are reasonably likely to change, (2) an explanation of why management believes each change is likely, and (3) quantification of the effect that these changes may have on future financial position, liquidity, and results of operations.

# INVESTMENT COMPANIES

## PERSPECTIVE AND ISSUES

An investment company pools shareholders' funds to provide shareholders with professional investment management. Investment companies' activities include selling capital shares to the public, investing the proceeds in securities, and distributing net income and net realized gains to its shareholders.

The AAG, *Audits of Investment Companies,* discusses those aspects of accounting and auditing unique to investment companies, and provides guidance on accounting for offering costs, amortization of premium or discount on bonds, liabilities for excess expense plans, reporting complex capital structures, payments by affiliates, and financial statement presentation and disclosures for investment companies and nonpublic investment partnerships.

| Sources of GAAP | | |
|---|---|---|
| *FSP* | *FAS* | *SOP* |
| EITF 85-24-1 | 102, 126 | 93-1, 93-2, 93-4, 95-2, 95-3, 01-1, 07-1 |

## DEFINITIONS OF TERMS

**Closed-end fund.** An investment company having a fixed number of shares outstanding, which it does not stand ready to redeem. Its shares are traded similarly to those of other public corporations.

**Closed-up fund.** An open-ended investment company that no longer offers its shares for sale to the general public but still stands ready to redeem its outstanding shares.

**Equalization.** An accounting method used to prevent a dilution of the continuing shareholders' per share equity in undistributed net investment income caused by the continuous sales and redemptions of capital shares.

**Ex-dividend or ex-distribution.** Synonym for shares being traded without dividend or without capital gains distribution. The buyer of a stock selling ex-dividend does not acquire a right to receive a previously declared but not-yet-paid dividend. Dividends are payable on a fixed date to shareholders recorded on the stock transfer books of the disbursing company as of a previous date of record. For example, a dividend may be declared as payable to holders of record on the books of the disbursing company on a given Friday. Because five business days are allowed for delivery of the security in regular-way transactions on a stock exchange or over-the-counter, the exchange or the National Association of Securities Dealers (NASD) declares the stock ex-dividend as of the opening of the market on the preceding Monday or on one business day earlier for each intervening nontrading day. Therefore, anyone buying the stock on and after Monday is not entitled to the dividend. In the case of nontraded shares of mutual funds, the ex-dividend date is the same as the record date.

**Open-end investment company.** A mutual fund that is ready to redeem its shares at any time and that usually offers its shares for sale to the public continuously.

## CONCEPTS, RULES, AND EXAMPLES

Several types of investment companies exist: management investment companies, unit investment trusts, collectible trust funds, investment partnerships, certain separate accounts of life insurance companies, and offshore funds. Management investment companies include open-end funds (mutual funds), closed-end funds, special purpose funds, venture capital investment companies, small business investment companies, and business development companies.

All of the investment companies mentioned have the following characteristics:

1. Investment activity—Investing in assets, usually in securities of other entities, for current income, appreciation, or both.
2. Unit ownership—Ownership in the investment company is represented by stock or other units of ownership, to which proportionate shares of net assets can be attributed.
3. Pooling of funds—The funds of the investment company owners are pooled together to take advantage of professional investment management.
4. Reporting entity—The investment company is the primary reporting entity.

### Accounting Policies

The accounting policies for an investment company result from the company's role as a vehicle through which investors can invest as a group. These policies are largely governed by the SEC, Small Business Administration, and specific provisions of the Internal Revenue Code relating to investment companies.

Investment companies report all investment securities at market value, or if quoted market values are not available, at fair values as determined by management. Along with other industry groups for which specialized GAAP already existed, calling for presentation of all investments at market value (a group that includes broker-dealers and defined benefit pension plans), investment companies were exempted from the provisions of FAS 115.

Security purchases and sales are generally recorded at the trade date; therefore, the effects of all securities trades entered into by the investment company to the date of the financial statements are included in the financial report.

Investment companies record dividend income on the ex-dividend date, not on the later record or payable date. The rationale for this treatment is that the market price of market securities may be affected by the exclusion of the declared dividend. Additionally, investment companies record a liability for dividends payable on the ex-dividend date because mutual fund shares are purchased and redeemed at prices equal to or based on net asset value. If investors purchase shares between the declaration and ex-dividend dates they are entitled to receive dividends; however, investors purchasing shares after the ex-dividend date are not entitled to receive dividends.

Open-end investment companies often employ the practice of equalization. This theory states that the net asset value of each share of capital stock sold comprises the par value of the stock, undistributed income, and paid-in capital and other surplus. When shares are sold or repurchased, the investment company calculates the amount of undistributed income available for distribution to its shareholders. Based on the number of shares outstanding, the investment company determines the per share amount; this amount is credited to an equalization account when shares are sold. Conversely, the equalization account is charged when shares are repurchased.

### Accounting for High-Yield Debt Securities

The accounting by creditors for investments in "step interest" and "PIK" debt securities, if these qualify as "high-yield" securities, is addressed by the Guide. Step interest bonds are generally unsecured debentures that pay no interest for a specified period after issuance, then pay a stipulated rate for a period, then a higher rate for another period, etc., until maturity. Thus, they combine some of the characteristics of zero-coupon bonds with some features of current interest bonds. PIK (payment in kind) bonds pay some or all interest in the form of other debt instruments ("baby" or "bunny" bonds), which in turn may also pay interest in the form of baby bonds. All babies mature at the due date of the parent bond.

The Guide, as amended, requires that the effective interest method should be used for step interest bonds; to the extent that interest income is not expected to be realized, a reserve against the income should be established. A previously employed technique, the bifurcation method, is no longer acceptable. For PIK bonds, the effective interest method is also required; the market value method, which was widely used in the past, can no longer be employed.

### Exemptions from the Requirement to Provide a Statement of Cash Flows

The following conditions must be met for an investment company to be exempted from providing a statement of cash flows:

1. Substantially all of the entity's investments were highly liquid.
2. The entity's investments are carried at market value.

3. The entity had little or no debt, based on average debt outstanding during the period, in relation to average total assets.
4. The entity provides a statement of changes in net assets.

## Taxes

Investment companies that distribute all taxable income and taxable realized gains qualifying under Subchapter M of the Internal Revenue Code are not required to record a provision for federal income taxes. If the investment company does not distribute all taxable income and taxable realized gains, a liability should be recorded at the end of the last day of the taxable year. The rationale for recording on the last day of the year is that only shareholders of record at that date are entitled to credit for taxes paid.

## Commodity Pools

SOP 01-1, *Amendment to Scope of Statement of Position 95-2, "Financial Reporting by Nonpublic Investment Partnerships," to Include Commodity Pools,* stipulates that investment partnerships which are commodity pools subject to regulation by the CFTC are subject to the guidance of SOP 95-2. Thus, notwithstanding the rapid turnover common among such pools, the financial statements must include a schedule of investments.

In adopting this requirement, AcSEC rejected arguments that disclosure of investments would result in competitive harm or provide adversaries with the knowledge to enter into positions that might harm the reporting entity, such as by creating a "short squeeze." It determined that the information needs of the investors in these partnerships would be paramount to concerns over competitive risks that could be exacerbated by such disclosures.

## Other Accounting Guidance

SOP 93-1 concludes that for PIK and step bonds, (1) the effective-interest method should be used to determine interest income; (2) a reserve against income should be established for interest income not expected to be realized; (3) the cost plus any discount should not exceed undiscounted future cash collections; (4) SEC yield-formula calculations must be made; and (5) all high-yield and restricted debt securities whose values were estimated should be indicated in the portfolio. For defaulted debt securities, any interest receivable written off that had been recognized as income constitutes a reduction of income. Write-offs of purchased interest increase the cost basis and represent an unrealized loss until the security is sold. "Capital infusions" are accounted for as an addition to the cost basis, while related "workout expenditures" are recorded as unrealized losses. Any ongoing expenditures to protect the value of the investment are recorded as operating expenses. Auditors should consider additional pricing valuation audit procedures.

SOP 93-2 was developed to clarify the reporting of shareholder distributions that exceed the tax-basis current and accumulated earnings and profits in GAAP financial statements. The statement recommends that the caption "tax return of capital" be used to report such distributions.

In SOP 93-4, it was concluded that transactions denominated in a foreign currency must originally be measured in that currency. Reporting exchange rate gains and losses separately from any gain/loss on the investment due to changes in market price is allowable but not required.

SOP 95-2 pertains to investment partnerships that are exempt from SEC registration under the Investment Company Act of 1940. Specifically, the statement requires that the financial statements include a condensed schedule of securities that categorizes investments by type, country or geographic region, and industry; discloses pertinent information concerning investments comprising greater than 5% of net assets; and aggregates any securities holdings less than the 5% of net assets threshold. The statement of operations for nonpublic investment companies shall be presented in conformity with requirements for public investment companies per the AAG so as to reflect their comparable operations. The financial statements shall also present management fees and disclose their computation.

SOP 95-3 requires investment companies with enhanced 12b-1 plans or board-contingent plans for which the board has committed to pay costs to recognize a liability and the related expense, for the amount of excess costs. This liability should be discounted at an appropriate current rate if the amount and timing of cash flows are reliably determinable and if distribution costs are not subject to a reasonable interest charge. Excess costs are recorded as a liability as the fund has assumed an obligation to pay the 12b-1 fee after the termination of the plan to the extent that the distributor has excess costs.

In a related matter, FSP EITF 85-24-1 specifies the accounting for cash received from a third party for a distributor's right to future cash flows relating to distribution fees for previously sold shares. Revenue recognition is deemed proper when cash is received from a third party if the distributor has no continuing involvement nor recourse; any deferred costs related to the sale of shares is to be expensed concurrently. It further defines absence of continuing involvement and recourse.

The disclosure requirements under SOP 95-2 were extended to commodity pools regulated by the CFTC by SOP 01-1.

SOP 07-1 (whose implementation had been indefinitely delayed as of February 2008) concludes that an entity falls within the guidelines of the AAG *Investment Companies* if the entity is regulated by the Investment Company Act of 1940, such as a management investment company, unit investment trust, small business investment company, business development company and certain offshore funds. It also notes that investment company accounting should be retained in the financial statements of the parent company of an investment company or equity method investor in an investment company if (1) the subsidiary is an investment company, (2) the consolidated group follows policies distinguishing the nature and type of investments made by the investment company from the nature and type of investments made by other entities within the consolidated group that are not investment companies, and (3) the parent company or equity method investor should be investing for current income, capital appreciation, or both, rather than for strategic operating purposes.

In a related matter, FASB Staff Position FSP FIN 46(R)-7 holds that investments accounted for at fair value are not subject to consolidation.

**Amendment to AAG *Investment Companies* for certain guaranteed investment contracts.** FASB Staff Position FSP AAG INV-01 and SOP 94-4-1 affect the required display of certain contracts held by investment companies if these are fully benefit-responsive. Both the fair values of the contracts, segregated between guaranteed investment contracts and so-called wrapper contracts, and the contract (guaranteed) values, must be displayed in the investment company's balance sheet.

A contract is deemed fully benefit-responsive if *all* five conditions set forth by the FSP are met. These conditions are defined as

1. The contract is negotiated directly between the fund and the issuer, and it prohibits the fund from assigning or selling the contract or its proceeds to another party without the consent of the issuer.

2. Either (a) the repayment of principal and interest credited to participants in the fund is guaranteed by the issuer of the investment contract, or (b) the fund provides for prospective interest crediting rate adjustments to participants in the fund on a designated pool of investments held by the fund, provided that the terms of the agreement

with participants in the fund specify that the crediting interest rate cannot be less than zero. The risk of decline in the interest crediting rate below zero must be transferred to a financially responsible third party through a "wrapper" contract. If an event (e.g., decline in creditworthiness of the contract issuer or wrapper provider) has occurred that may affect the realization of full contract value for a particular investment contract, the contract no longer is to be considered fully benefit-responsive.

3. The terms of the contract require all permitted participant-initiated transactions with the fund to occur at contract value with no conditions, limits, or restrictions. Permitted participant-initiated transactions are those transactions allowed by the underlying defined-contribution plan, such as withdrawals for benefits, loans, or transfers to other funds within the plan.

4. Events that limit the ability for the fund to transact at contract value with the issuer (e.g., premature termination of the contracts by the plan, plant closings, layoffs, plan termination, bankruptcy, mergers, and early retirement incentives) must be *probable* of *not* occurring.

5. The fund itself must allow participants reasonable access to their funds.

This FSP requires that balance sheets of investment companies report separately investments, including guaranteed investment contracts, at fair value, and wrapper contracts, also at fair value. The balance sheet must also display an additional account to bring the total assets being reported to contract amounts—that is, the amounts at which participants can transact with the fund.

Additionally, the following information must be disclosed in footnotes to the financial statements for each investment contract, and be reconciled to corresponding line items on the balance sheet:

1. The fair value of the wrapper contract and the fair value of each of the corresponding underlying investments;

2. Adjustment from fair value to contract value (if the investment contract is fully benefit-responsive); and

3. Major credit ratings of the issuer or wrapper provider.

Other expanded disclosures are mandated for investment companies having fully benefit-responsive contracts, as follows:

1. A description of the nature of the investment contracts, how they operate, and the methodology for calculating the crediting interest rate, including the key factors that could influence future average crediting interest rates, the basis for and frequency of determining credit interest-rate resets, and any minimum crediting interest rate under the terms of the contracts. This disclosure should explain the relationship between future crediting rates and the amount reported on the balance sheet representing the adjustment of the portion of net assets attributable to fully benefit-responsive investments from fair value to contract value.

2. A reconciliation between the beginning and ending balance of the amount presented on the balance sheet that represents the difference between net assets at fair value and net assets for each period in which a statement of changes in net assets is presented. This reconciliation should include

   a. The change in the difference between the fair value and contract value of all fully benefit-responsive investment contracts, and

   b. The increase or decrease due to changes in the fully benefit-responsive status of the fund's investment contracts.

3. The average yield earned by the entire fund (without regard to the interest rate credited to participants in the fund) for each period for which a balance sheet is presented.

4. The average yield earned by the entire fund with an adjustment to reflect the actual interest rate credited to participants in the fund covering each period for which a balance sheet is presented.

5. Two different sensitivity analyses

   a. The effect on the weighted-average crediting interest rates calculated at the latest balance sheet date and the next four reset dates, under two or more scenarios where there is an immediate hypothetical increase or decrease in interest rates, with no change to the duration of the underlying investment portfolio and no contributions or withdrawals. These scenarios should include, at a minimum, immediate hypothetical changes in market yields equal to one-quarter and one-half of the current yield.

   b. The effect on the weighted-average crediting interest rates calculated at the latest balance sheet date and the next four reset dates, under two or more scenarios where there are the same immediate hypothetical changes in market yields in the first analysis, combined with an immediate hypothetical 10% decrease in the net assets of the fund due to participant transfers, with no change to the duration of the portfolio.

6. A description of the events which limit the ability of the fund to transact at contract value with the issuer (for example, premature termination of the contracts by the plan, plant closings, layoffs, plan termination, bankruptcy, mergers, and early retirement incentives), including a statement that the occurrence of such events is probable or not probable.

7. A description of the events and circumstances that would allow issuers to terminate fully benefit-responsive investment contracts with the fund and settle at an amount different from contract value.

To be considered within the scope of the foregoing guidance, all, or essentially all, of the investment company's net assets will need to be held by participants in one or more qualified employer-sponsored defined-contribution plans. In order to be considered within the scope of the guidance in this FSP, any portion of the net assets of the investment company that is not held by participants in qualified employer-sponsored defined-contribution plans as of the effective date are not permitted to increase due to gross contributions, loan repayments, or transfers into the fund.

# MORTGAGE BANKING

## PERSPECTIVE AND ISSUES

Mortgage banking comprises two activities.

1. The origination or purchase of mortgage loans and subsequent sale to permanent investors, and

2. Long-term servicing of the mortgage loan.

To the extent that mortgage banking activities discussed in this section may be undertaken by subsidiaries or divisions of commercial banks or savings institutions, the same accounting and reporting standards apply. Normal, nonmortgage lending of those enterprises, however, is accounted for in accordance with the lender's normal accounting policies for such activities.

Mortgage loans held for sale are valued at the lower of cost or market. Mortgage-backed securities are reported under FAS 115 as held-to-maturity, trading, or available-for-sale, depending on the entity's intent and ability to hold the securities.

Loan origination fees and related direct costs for loans held for sale are capitalized as part of the related loan and amortized, using the effective yield method. However, fees and costs associated with commitments to originate, sell, or purchase loans are treated as part of the commitment, which is a derivative accounted for under FAS 133.

Loan origination fees and costs for loans held for investment are deferred and recognized as an adjustment to the yield.

SOP 01-6, *Accounting by Certain Entities (Including Entities with Trade Receivables) That Lend to or Finance the Activities of Others,* provides uniform and consistent guidance for the accounting and reporting practices for similar transactions by various types of depository and lending institutions, and has now been incorporated in a unified AAG. The SOP includes in its scope, corporate credit unions and mortgage companies and, in fact, affects disclosure practices for any entity that extends credit to customers. (See the summary under the Banking and Thrift Institutions section of this chapter for a discussion of the general disclosure requirements for all enterprises. These general requirements also apply, when applicable, to mortgage banking enterprises and are not repeated in this section.) In addition, the SOP prescribes required disclosures for mortgage banking enterprises regarding their regulatory capital and net worth requirements.

| Sources of GAAP | | | |
|---|---|---|---|
| *FAS* | *FTB* | *SOP* | *AAG* |
| 65, 91, 115, 133, 134, 140, 149 | 87-3 | 01-6 | *Depository and Lending Institutions: Banks and Savings Institutions, Credit Unions, Finance Companies and Mortgage Companies.* |

## DEFINITIONS OF TERMS

**Affiliated enterprise.** An enterprise that directly or indirectly controls, is controlled by, or is under common control with another enterprise; also, a party with which the enterprise may deal if one party has the ability to exercise significant influence over the other's operating and financial policies.

**Current (normal) servicing fee rate.** A servicing fee rate that is representative of servicing fee rates most commonly used in comparable servicing agreements covering similar types of mortgage loans.

**Federal Home Loan Mortgage Corporation (FHLMC).** Often referred to as "Freddie Mac," FHLMC is a private corporation authorized by Congress to assist in the development and maintenance of a secondary market in conventional residential mortgages. FHLMC purchases and sells mortgages principally through mortgage participation certificates (PC) representing an undivided interest in a group of conventional mortgages. FHLMC guarantees the timely payment of interest and the collection of principal on the PC.

**Federal National Mortgage Association (FNMA).** Often referred to as "Fannie Mae," FNMA is an investor-owned corporation established by Congress to support the secondary mortgage loan market by purchasing mortgage loans when other investor funds are limited and selling mortgage loans when other investor funds are available.

**Gap commitment.** A commitment to provide interim financing while the borrower is in the process of satisfying provisions of a permanent loan agreement, such as obtaining a designated occupancy level on an apartment project. The interim loan ordinarily finances the difference between the floor loan (the portion of a mortgage loan commitment that is less than the full amount of the commitment) and the maximum permanent loan.

**Government National Mortgage Association (GNMA).** Often referred to as "Ginnie Mae," GNMA is a US governmental agency that guarantees certain types of securities (mortgage-backed securities) and provides funds for and administers certain types of low-income housing assistance programs.

**Internal reserve method.** A method for making payments to investors for collections of principal and interest on mortgage loans by issuers of GNMA securities. An issuer electing the internal reserve method is required to deposit in a custodial account an amount equal to one month's interest on the mortgage loans that collateralize the GNMA security issued.

**Mortgage-backed securities.** Securities issued by a governmental agency or corporation (e.g., GNMA or FHLMC) or by private issuers (e.g., FNMA, banks, and mortgage banking enterprises). Mortgage-backed securities generally are referred to as mortgage participation certificates or pass-through certificates (PC). A PC represents an undivided interest in a pool of specific mortgage loans. Periodic payments on GNMA PC are backed by the US government. Periodic payments on FHLMC and FNMA PC are guaranteed by those corporations and are not backed by the US government.

**Mortgage banking enterprise.** An enterprise that is engaged primarily in originating, marketing, and servicing real estate mortgage loans for other than its own account. Mortgage banking enterprises, as local representatives of institutional lenders, act as correspondents between lenders and borrowers.

**Permanent investor.** An enterprise that invests in mortgage loans for its own account, for example, an insurance enterprise, commercial or mutual savings bank, savings and loan association, pension plan, real estate investment trust, or FNMA.

**Repurchase financing.** A repurchase agreement that relates to a previously transferred financial asset between the same counterparties, and which is entered into contemporaneously with, or in contemplation of, the initial transfer.

**Securitization.** The transformation of a pool of financial assets (e.g., mortgages) into securities (asset-backed securities).

**Servicing.** Mortgage loan servicing includes collecting monthly mortgagor payments, forwarding payments and related accounting reports to investors, collecting escrow deposits for the payment of mortgagor property taxes and insurance, and paying the taxes and insurance from the escrow funds when due.

**Standby commitment.** A commitment to lend money with the understanding that the loan probably will not be made unless permanent financing cannot be obtained from another source. Standby commitments ordinarily are used to enable the borrower to obtain construction financing on the assumption that permanent financing will be available on more favorable terms when construction is completed. Standby commitments normally provide for an interest rate substantially above the market rate in effect when the commitment is issued.

## CONCEPTS, RULES, AND EXAMPLES

### Mortgage Banking Activities

A mortgage banking enterprise (MBE) acts as an intermediary between borrowers (mortgagors) and lenders (mortgagees). MBE activities include purchasing and originating mortgage loans for sale to permanent investors and performing servicing activities during the period that the loans are outstanding. The mortgage loans offered for sale to permanent investors may be originated by the MBE (in-house originations); purchased from realtors, brokers, or investors; or converted from short-term, interim credit facilities to permanent financing. The common technique used by the MBE to market and sell the loans is referred to as securitization because the mortgage loans receivable are pooled and converted to mortgage-backed securities and sold in that form.

MBEs customarily retain the rights to service the loans that they sell to permanent investors in exchange for a servicing fee. The servicing fee, normally a percentage of the mortgage's outstanding principal balance, compensates the MBE for processing of mortgagor payments of principal, interest and escrow deposits, disbursing funds from the escrow accounts to pay property taxes and insurance on behalf of the mortgagor, and remitting net proceeds to the permanent investor along with relevant accounting reports.

**Mortgage loans.** The MBE is required to classify mortgage loans that it holds as either (1) held-for-sale, or (2) held for long-term investment.

*Loans held-for-sale.* Mortgage loans held for sale are reported at the lower of cost or market as of the balance sheet date. Any excess of cost over market is accounted for as a valuation allowance, changes in which are to be included in income in the period of change.

*Determination of cost basis.* The following matters must be considered with respect to the cost basis used for the purposes of the lower of cost or market value determination:

1. If a mortgage loan has been identified as a hedged item in a fair value hedge under FAS 133, the cost basis used reflects adjustments to the loan's carrying amount for changes in the loan's fair value attributable to the risk being hedged.
2. Purchase discounts on mortgage loans reduce the cost basis and are not amortized as interest revenue during the period that the loans are held for sale.
3. Capitalized costs attributable to the acquisition of mortgage servicing rights associated with the purchase or origination of mortgage loans are excluded from the cost basis of the mortgage loans.

*Determination of market value.* The market value of mortgage loans held for sale is determined by type of loan; at a minimum, separate determinations are made for residential and commercial loans. Either an aggregate or individual loan basis may be used in determining the lower of cost or market for each type of loan. Market values for loans subject to investor purchase commitments (committed loans) and loans held for speculative purposes (uncommitted loans) must be determined separately as follows:

1. For committed loans, market value is defined as fair value.
2. For uncommitted loans, market value is based on quotations from the market in which the MBE normally operates, considering
   a. Market prices and yields sought by the MBE's normal market outlets,
   b. Quoted Government National Mortgage Association (GNMA) security prices or other public market quotations of rates for long-term mortgage loans, and
   c. Federal Home Loan Mortgage Corporation (FHLMC) and Federal National Mortgage Association (FNMA) current delivery prices.

*Loans held for long-term investment.* Mortgage loans may be transferred from the held-for-sale classification to the held-for-long-term investment classification only if the MBE has both the intent and ability to hold the loan for the foreseeable future or until maturity. The transfer to the long-term investment classification is recorded at the lower of cost or market value on the date of transfer. Any difference between the loan's adjusted carrying amount and its outstanding principal balance (e.g., purchase discounts as discussed above) is recognized as a yield adjustment using the interest method.

If recoverability of the carrying amount of a mortgage loan held for long-term investment is doubtful and the impairment is judged to be other than temporary, the loan's carrying amount is reduced by the amount of the impairment to the amount expected to be collected with the related charge recognized as a loss. The adjusted carrying value becomes the loan's new cost basis and any eventual gain on recovery may only be recognized upon the loan's sale, maturity, or other disposition.

**Mortgage-backed securities.** The securitization of mortgage loans held-for-sale is accounted for as a sale of the mortgage loans and purchase of mortgage-backed securities.

*Classification and valuation.* After the securitization of a held-for-sale mortgage loan, any mortgage-backed securities retained by the MBE are classified as (1) trading, (2) available-for-sale, or (3) held-to-maturity under the provisions of FAS 115, as amended by FAS 134. As is the case with the MBE's mortgage loans held for investment, the MBE must have both the intent and ability to hold the mortgage-backed securities for the foreseeable future or until maturity in order to classify them as held-to-maturity. If the MBE had committed to sell the securities before or during the securitization process, the securities are required to be classified under the trading category. Mortgage-backed securities held by a not-for-profit organization are stated at fair value under FAS 124.

The fair value of uncommitted mortgage-backed securities collateralized by the MBE's own loans is ordinarily based on the market value of the securities. If the trust holding the loans may be readily terminated and the loans sold directly, fair value of the securities is based on the market value of either the loans or the securities, depending on the entity's intentions. Fair value for other uncommitted mortgage-backed securities is based on published yield data.

**Repurchase agreements.** Mortgage loans or mortgage-backed securities held for sale may be temporarily transferred by an MBE to another financial institution under a formal or informal agreement which serves as a means of financing these assets. Such agreements are accounted for as collateralized financing arrangements; the loans and securities transferred under the agreements are still reported by the MBE as held for sale.

A formal repurchase agreement specifies that the MBE retains control over future economic benefits and also the risk of loss relating to the loans or securities transferred. These assets are subsequently reacquired from the financial institution upon the sale of the assets by the mortgage banking enterprise to permanent investors.

An informal repurchase agreement exists when no formal agreement has been executed but loans or securities are transferred by an MBE that does all of the following:

1. Is the sole marketer of the assets
2. Retains any interest spread on the assets
3. Retains risk of loss in market value
4. Reacquires uncollectible loans
5. Regularly reacquires most or all of the assets and sells them to permanent investors

When mortgage loans held for sale are transferred under a repurchase arrangement, they continue to be reported by the transferor as loans held for sale. Mortgage-backed securities sold under agreements to repurchase are reported as trading securities as defined in FAS 115.

## Servicing Mortgage Loans

Rights to service mortgage loans for others are recognized as separate assets by an MBE. If the enterprise acquires such rights through purchase or origination of mortgage loans and retains them upon sale or securitization, the total cost of the mortgage loans must be allocated between the rights and the loans (without the rights) based on their relative fair values. If it is impossible to determine the fair value of the mortgage servicing rights apart from the mortgage, the MBE/transferor records the mortgage servicing rights at zero value (FAS 140). Otherwise, mortgage servicing rights are capitalized at their fair value and recognized as a net asset if the benefits of servicing the mortgage are expected to be more than adequate compensation to the servicer for performing the duties. If the benefits of servicing the mortgage are not expected to adequately compensate the servicer, the servicer recognizes a liability. The asset Mortgage Servicing Contract Rights is initially measured at its fair value. Subsequent impairment is recognized as follows:

1. The mortgage servicing assets are stratified based on predominant risk characteristics.
2. Impairment is recognized through a valuation allowance for an individual stratum. The amount of impairment equals the carrying amount for a particular stratum minus its fair value.
3. The valuation allowance is adjusted to reflect changes in the measurement of impairment after the initial measurement of impairment.

**Servicing fees.** Servicing fees are usually based on a percentage of the outstanding principal balance of the mortgage loan. When a mortgage loan is sold with servicing rights retained, the sales price must be adjusted if the stated rate is materially different from the current (normal) servicing fee rate so that the gain or loss on the sale can be determined. The adjustment is

$$\text{Adjustment} = \begin{array}{c}\text{Actual}\\ \text{Sales}\\ \text{Price}\end{array} - \begin{array}{c}\text{Estimated sales price}\\ \text{obtainable if normal}\\ \text{servicing fee rate}\\ \text{had been used}\end{array}$$

This adjustment allows for recognition of normal servicing fees in subsequent years.

The adjustment and any recognized gain or loss are determined as of the sale date. If estimated normal servicing fees are less than total expected servicing costs, then this loss is accrued on the sale date as well.

## Repurchase Financing

A repurchase financing involves the transfer of a previously transferred financial asset back to the lender as collateral for a financing between the borrower and the lender. The lender usually returns the financial asset to the borrower when the financing is repaid. The borrower and lender cannot separately account for an asset transfer and related repurchase financing unless the two transactions have a valid business purpose for being entered into separately, and the repurchase financing does not result in the lender retaining control over the financial asset. If a transaction meets these criteria, then evaluate the initial transfer without the repurchase financing to see if it meets the requirements for sale accounting (FAS 140). If the transaction does not meet these criteria, then the arrangement is probably a forward contract.

## Sales to Affiliated Enterprises

When mortgage loans or mortgage-backed securities are sold to an affiliated enterprise, the carrying amount of the assets must be adjusted to lower of cost or market as of the date that management decides that the sale will occur. This date is evidenced by formal approval by a representative of the affiliated enterprise (purchaser), issuance of a purchase commitment, and acceptance of the purchase commitment by the seller. Any adjustment is charged to income.

If a group of (or all) mortgage loans are originated specifically for an affiliate, then the originator is an agent of the affiliated enterprise. In this case, the loans are transferred at the originator's cost of acquisition. This treatment does not apply to "right of first refusal" or similar contracts in which the originator retains all risks of ownership.

## Issuance of GNMA Securities

An issuer of GNMA securities who elects the internal reserve method must pay one month's interest cost to a trustee. This cost is capitalized (at no greater than the present value of net future servicing income) and amortized.

## Loan and Commitment Fees and Costs

Mortgage bankers may pay or receive loan and commitment fees as compensation for various loan administration services. These fees and costs are accounted for as described in the following paragraphs.

**Loan origination fees received.** Loan origination fees and related direct costs are deferred and amortized, using the effective yield method. Fees and costs associated with commitments to originate, sell, or purchase loans, however, must be considered part of the commitments, which are deemed to be derivatives under FAS 133. FAS 149 amended FAS 133 to remove the accounting for such fees and costs from the guidance of FAS 91. Previously, these fees were capitalized and FAS 149 indicates that these previous transactions are not to be recharacterized. If the loan is held for investment, loan origination fees and costs are recognized as an adjustment of yield using the effective interest method.

**Services rendered.** Fees for specific services rendered by third parties as part of a loan origination (e.g., appraisal fees) are recognized when the services are performed.

**Commitment fees paid to investors on loans held for sale.** Residential or commercial loan commitment fees paid to permanent investors are recognized as expense when the loans are sold or when it is determined that the commitment will not be used. Since residential loan commitment fees typically cover groups of loans, the amount of fees recognized as revenue or expense relating to an individual transaction is calculated as

$$\begin{matrix} \text{Revenue or expense} \\ \text{recognized on} \\ \text{individual transaction} \end{matrix} = \begin{matrix} \text{Total} \\ \text{residential loan} \\ \text{commitment fee} \end{matrix} \times \frac{\text{Amount of individual loan}}{\text{Total commitment amount}}$$

Loan placement fees (fees for arranging a commitment directly between investor and borrower) are recognized as revenue once all significant services have been performed by the MBE. In some cases, an MBE secures a commitment from a permanent investor before or at the same time a commitment is made to a borrower and the latter commitment requires

1. Simultaneous assignment to the investor, and
2. Simultaneous transfer to the borrower of amounts paid by the investor.

The fees related to such transactions are also accounted for as loan placement fees.

**Expired commitments or early repayment of loans.** At the time that a loan commitment expires unused or is repaid before repayment is due, any related fees that had been deferred are recognized as revenue or expense.

## Reporting

An MBE must, on its balance sheet, distinguish between mortgage loans and mortgage-backed securities that are held for sale and those that are held for long-term investment. The notes to the financial statements are to disclose whether the MBE used the aggregate method or the individual-loan method to determine the lower of cost or market.

SOP 01-6, *Accounting by Certain Entities (Including Entities with Trade Receivables) That Lend to or Finance the Activities of Others,* contains specific capital disclosure requirements including, at a minimum

1.  A description of the minimum net worth requirements related to

    a.  Secondary market investors, and
    b.  State-imposed regulatory mandates.

2.  The actual or possible material effects of noncompliance with those requirements.
3.  Whether the entity is in compliance with the regulatory capital requirements including, as of the date of each balance sheet presented, the following measures:

    a.  The amount of the entity's required and actual net worth
    b.  Factors that may significantly affect adequacy of net worth such as potentially volatile components of capital, qualitative factors, or regulatory mandates

4.  If the entity is not in compliance with capital adequacy requirements as of the most recent balance sheet date, the possible material effects of that condition on amounts and disclosures in the financial statements.
5.  Loan servicers with net worth requirements imposed by more than one source are to disclose the new worth requirements of

    a.  Significant servicing covenants with secondary market investors with commonly defined servicing requirements,
    b.  Any other secondary market investor where violation of the net worth requirement would have an adverse effect on the business, and
    c.  The most restrictive third-party agreement if not already included in the above disclosures.

The SOP points out that noncompliance with minimum net worth requirements may trigger substantial doubt about the entity's ability to continue as a going concern.

## MOTION PICTURES

### PERSPECTIVE AND ISSUES

The production, sale, licensing, and distribution of motion pictures (and television series) are fraught with uncertainties. The industry is speculative in nature with studios routinely investing multimillion dollar sums in the hope that the production will achieve critical acclaim and that moviegoers will flock to the box office, purchase licensed merchandise tied to the film and its characters, and purchase and rent videos and DVDs. Due to the uncertainties involved in estimating the revenues that will be earned and costs that will be incurred over a film's life, an acceptable estimation methodology is required to achieve proper matching of costs and revenues and accurately reflect the results of the film's financial performance. This methodology is provided in SOP 00-2, *Accounting by Producers or Distributors of Films*.

| Sources of GAAP | |
| --- | --- |
| *SOP* | *EITF* |
| 00-2 | 96-6 |

### DEFINITIONS OF TERMS

**Cross-collateralized.** A contractual arrangement granting distribution rights to multiple films, territories and/or markets to a licensee. In this type of arrangement, the exploitation results of the entire package are aggregated by the licensee in determining amounts payable to the licensor.

**Distributor.** The owner or holder of the rights to distribute films. Excluded from this definition, for the purposes of applying SOP 00-2, are entities that function solely as broadcasters, retailers (such as video stores), or movie theaters.

**Exploitation costs.**  All direct costs incurred in connection with the film's distribution. Examples include marketing, advertising, publicity, promotion, and other distribution expenses.

**Film costs.**  Film costs include all direct negative costs incurred in the physical production of a film, including allocations of production overhead and interest capitalized in accordance with FAS 34.  Examples of direct negative costs include costs of story and scenario; compensation of cast members, extras, directors, producers, and miscellaneous staff; costs of set construction and operations, wardrobe and accessories; costs of sound synchronization; rental facilities on location; and postproduction costs such as music, special effects, and editing.

**Film prints.**  The materials containing the completed audio and video elements of a film which are distributed to a theater to exhibit the film to its customers.

**Firm commitment.**  An agreement with a third party that is binding on both parties. The agreement specifies all significant terms, including items to be exchanged, consideration, and timing of the transaction.  The agreement includes a disincentive for nonperformance that is sufficiently large to ensure the expected performance.  With respect to an episodic television series, a firm commitment for future production includes only episodes to be delivered within one year from the date of the estimate of ultimate revenue.

**Market.**  A distribution channel located within a certain geographic territory for a certain type of media, exhibition, or related product.  Examples include theatrical exhibition, home video (laser disc, videotape, DVD), pay television, free television, and the licensing of film-related merchandise.

**Nonrefundable minimum guarantee.**  Amount to be paid by a customer in a variable fee arrangement that guarantees an entity a minimum fee on that arrangement.  This amount applies to payments paid at inception, as well as to legally binding commitments to pay amounts over the license period.

**Overall deal.**  An arrangement whereby an entity compensates a creative individual (e.g., producer, actor, or director) for the exclusive or preferential use of that party's creative services.

**Participation costs.**  Frequently, persons involved in the production of a film are compensated, in part or in full, with an interest (referred to as a "participation") in the financial results of the film.  Determination of the amount of compensation payable to the participant is usually based on formulas (participations) and by contingent amounts due under provisions of collective bargaining agreements (residuals).  The recipients of this compensation are referred to as participants and the costs are referred to as participation costs.  Participations may be paid to creative talent (e.g. actors or writers), or to entities from whom distribution rights are licensed.

**Producer.**  An individual or enterprise that is responsible for all aspects of a film.  Although the producer's role may vary, his or her responsibilities include administration of such aspects of the project as initial concept, script, budgeting, shooting, postproduction, and release.

**Revenue.**  Amounts earned by an entity from its direct distribution, exploitation, or licensing of a film, before deduction for any of the entity's direct costs of distribution.  In markets and territories where the entity's fully or jointly owned films are distributed by third-party distributors, revenue is the net amount payable to the entity by the distributor.  Revenue is reduced by appropriate allowances, estimated returns, price concessions, or similar adjustments, as applicable.

**Sale.**  The transfer of control of the master copy of a film and all of the associated rights that accompany it.

**Set for production.** A film qualifies as being set for production when all of the following conditions have been met: (1) management with relevant authority authorizes (implicitly or explicitly) and commits to funding the film's production; (2) active preproduction has begun; and (3) the start of principal photography is expected to begin within six months.

**Territory.** A geographic area in which a film is exploited, usually a country. In some cases, however, a territory may be contractually defined as countries with a common language.

## CONCEPTS, RULES, AND EXAMPLES

SOP 00-2, *Accounting by Producers or Distributors of Films,* provides the authoritative guidance with respect to accounting for arrangements to sell, license, or exhibit films. The term "film" is generic and includes intellectual property produced on traditional celluloid film as well as videotape, digital, or other video-recording formats. The content or format of films includes (1) feature films, (2) television series, (3) television specials, and (4) similar products (including animated films and television programming). The guidance in the SOP applies to producers and distributors who own or hold rights to distribute or exploit films. The SOP does not apply to the following specialized industries or applications that have their own specialized GAAP:

1. The recording industry (FAS 50)
2. Cable television (FAS 51)
3. Broadcasters (FAS 63)
4. Computer software to be sold, leased, or otherwise marketed (FAS 86)
5. Software revenue recognition (SOP 97-2)
6. Entertainment and educational software products (EITF 96-6)

There are many varieties of contractual sales or licensing arrangements governing the rights or group of rights to a single or multiple films. The film's producer (referred to in the SOP and in this discussion as "the entity") may license it to distributors, theaters, exhibitors, or other licensees (referred to in the SOP and in this discussion as "customers") on an exclusive or nonexclusive basis in a particular market or territory. The terms of the license may be for a fixed (or flat) fee or the fee may be variable based on a percentage of the customer's revenue. If the arrangement is variable, it may include a nonrefundable minimum guarantee payable either in advance or over the licensing period.

### Revenue Recognition

An entity recognizes revenue from a sale or licensing arrangement only when all of the following conditions are met:

1. Persuasive evidence exists of a sale or licensing arrangement with a customer.
2. The film is complete and, in accordance with the terms of the arrangement, has been delivered or is available for immediate and unconditional delivery.
3. The license period for the arrangement has started and the customer can begin exploitation, exhibition, or sale.
4. The arrangement fee is fixed or determinable.
5. Collection of the arrangement fee is reasonably assured.

If any of the above conditions has not been met, the entity defers recognizing revenue until all of the conditions are met. If the entity recognizes a receivable on its balance sheet for advances under an arrangement for which all of the above conditions have not been met, a liability for deferred revenue of the same amount is to be recognized until such time as all of the conditions have been met.

**Persuasive evidence of an arrangement.** This condition is met solely by documentary evidence that sets forth, at a minimum, the following terms: (1) the license period, (2) the film or films covered by the agreement, (3) a description of the rights transferred, and (4) the consideration to be exchanged. If the agreement is ambiguous regarding the parties' rights and obligations, or if there is significant doubt as to the ability of either party to perform under the agreement, revenue is not recognized. Acceptable documentary evidence must be verifiable (e.g., a contract, a purchase order, or an online authorization).

**Delivery.** The delivery condition may be satisfied by an arrangement providing the customer with immediate and unconditional access to a film print held by the entity. The customer may also receive a lab access letter that authorizes it to order a film laboratory to make the film immediately and unconditionally available for its use. Under these conditions, the delivery condition is satisfied if the film is complete and available for immediate delivery.

Some licensing arrangements require the entity to make significant changes to the film after it becomes initially available. Significant changes are changes that are additive to the film and that result from the entity creating additional content after the film becomes initially available. The changes can consist of the reshooting of selected scenes or adding additional special effects. When such changes are required to be made to the film, the arrangement does not meet the delivery condition. The costs incurred for these significant changes are added to film costs and subsequently recorded as expense when the related revenue is recognized.

Changes that are not considered to be significant changes include insertion or addition of preexisting film footage, addition of dubbing or subtitles to existing footage, removal of offensive language, reformatting to fit a broadcaster's screen dimensions, or adjustments to allow for the insertion of television commercials. Such insignificant changes do not alter the film's qualification to meet the delivery condition. The expected costs of these insignificant changes are accrued and charged directly to expense by the entity at the time that revenue recognition commences even if they have not yet been incurred.

**Commencement of exploitation.** Some arrangements impose on the customer a release date or "street date" before which the film may not be exhibited or sold. Such a date defines the commencement date of the exploitation rights. The entity does not begin to recognize revenue on the arrangement until this restriction has expired.

**Fixed or determinable arrangement fee.** When there is a flat fee that covers a single film, the amount of the fee is, of course, considered fixed and determinable and the entity recognizes the entire license fee as revenue when all of the conditions set forth above have been satisfied.

If the flat fee applies to multiple films, some of which have not been produced or completed, the entity allocates the fee to each individual film by market or territory based on relative fair values of the rights to exploit each film under the licensing arrangement. The entity bases the allocations to a film or films not yet produced or completed on the amounts that would be refundable if the entity did not ultimately complete and deliver the films to the customer. The entity allocates the remaining flat fee to completed films based on the relative fair values of the exploitation rights to those films under the arrangement. These allocations may not be adjusted subsequently even if better information becomes available. After making the allocations described above, the entity recognizes revenue for each film when all of the above conditions are met with respect to that film by market and territory. If the entity is not able to determine relative fair values for the exploitation rights, then the fee is not fixed or determinable and the entity may not recognize revenue until such a determination can be made and it meets all five of the conditions.

An entity's arrangement fees may be variable based on a percentage of the customer's revenue from exploitation of the film. When all five conditions have been met, the entity commences revenue recognition as the customer exploits or exhibits the film.

Certain variable fee arrangements include a nonrefundable minimum guarantee whereby the customer guarantees to pay the entity a nonrefundable minimum amount that is applied against the variable fees on a film or group of films that are not cross-collateralized. In applying the revenue recognition conditions, the amount of the nonrefundable minimum guarantee is considered to be fixed and determinable and is recognized as revenue when all of the other conditions have been met. If the nonrefundable minimum guarantee is applied against variable fees from a group of films on a cross-collateralized basis, the amount of the minimum guarantee attributable to each individual film cannot be objectively determined. In this situation, the entity recognizes revenue as described in the preceding paragraph (i.e., when all five of the conditions have been met as the customer exhibits or exploits each film). Under this scenario, if there is a remaining portion of the nonrefundable minimum guarantee that is unearned at the end of the license period, the entity recognizes the remaining guarantee as revenue by allocating it to the individual films based on their relative performance under the arrangement.

**Returns and price concessions** can affect whether the arrangement fee meets the condition of being fixed and determinable. The factors to consider include the provisions of the arrangement between the entity and its customer and the entity's policies and past actions related to granting concessions or accepting product returns. If the arrangement includes a right-of-return provision or if its past practices allow for such rights, the entity must meet all of the conditions in FAS 48, in order for it to recognize revenue. Among those conditions is a requirement that the entity be able to reasonably estimate the amount of future returns. FAS 48 is discussed in detail in Chapter 10.

**Barter revenue.** If an entity licenses programming to television stations in exchange for a specified amount of advertising time on those stations, the exchange is accounted for as a nonmonetary exchange in accordance with APB 29 (as interpreted by EITF 93-11) and FAS 153. See the discussion of nonmonetary transactions in Chapter 11.

**Modifications of arrangements.** If, during the term of a licensing arrangement, the entity and its customer agree to extend an existing arrangement for which all of the revenue recognition conditions have been met, the accounting follows the same rules cited above for flat-fee arrangements, variable fee arrangements, and variable fee arrangements with minimum guarantees.

For modifications that are not extensions of an existing arrangement, the modification is accounted for as a new arrangement and a termination of the former arrangement. At the time the former arrangement is terminated, the entity accrues and expenses all costs associated with the arrangement or reverses previously reported revenue to reflect refunds and concessions that result from the new arrangement. In addition, the entity adjusts accumulated film cost amortization and accrued participation costs attributable to the excess revenue. The new arrangement fee is accounted for by applying the provisions of the SOP.

#### Example

Eva Enterprises produced a film that did not meet revenue expectations. The film was originally projected to gross $9,500,000 and to date has only earned $2,300,000.

The original arrangement called for a fixed fee of $150,000. Eva had previously met all five criteria for recognizing the $150,000 fixed fee as revenue. To placate its customers, Eva negotiated a new arrangement that reduced the original fixed fee from $150,000 to $80,000 and substituted a variable component based on 1% of the customers' revenues from exploiting the film. The effects of the new arrangement on Eva's revenue are computed as follows:

**Revenue recognizable under new arrangement**

| | |
|---|---|
| Fixed fee | $ 80,000 |
| Variable fee earned to date (1% of $2,300,000) | <u>  23,000</u> |
| | 103,000 |
| **Original fixed fee recognized as revenue** | <u>150,000</u> |
| **Reduction in revenue due to new arrangement** | $<u>(47,000)</u> |

In addition to the adjustment above, Eva also must adjust its previously recorded accumulated amortization of film costs and accrued participation costs attributable to the excess revenue previously recorded. Prospectively, the new arrangement is accounted for in accordance with the provisions of the SOP.

**Product licensing.** Any revenue from licensing arrangements to market film-related products is deferred until the release date of the film.

**Present value.** Revenue that an entity recognizes in connection with licensing arrangements is recorded at the present value of the license fee computed in accordance with APB 21 as of the date that the entity first recognizes the revenue.

### Costs and Expenses—Components

Costs associated with the production and bringing to market of a film can be categorized as one of the following:

1. Film costs
2. Participation costs
3. Exploitation costs
4. Manufacturing costs

**Film costs.** Film costs are presented separately on the entity's balance sheet. They consist of direct negative costs, production overhead, and production period interest capitalized in accordance with FAS 34. Direct negative costs include costs to acquire the rights to intellectual property (e.g., film rights to books or stage plays, or original screenplays); the cost of adaptation or development of the property; compensation of the cast, directors, producers, extras, and other staff members; costs of set construction and operations, wardrobe and accessories; costs of sound synchronization; on-location rental facilities; and postproduction costs such as music, special effects, and editing. Production overhead includes allocation of costs of individuals or departments with exclusive or significant responsibility for the production of films. However, production overhead does not include general and administrative expenses, the costs of certain overall deals, or charges for losses on properties sold or abandoned. If the entity presents a classified balance sheet, unamortized film costs are presented as a noncurrent asset. The amortization of film costs is explained later in this section.

**Participation costs.** Participation costs are contingent compensation paid to creative talent such as actors or writers, or to entities from whom the distribution rights are licensed, such as the publisher of a novel on which a screenplay is based (these recipients are referred to as participants). The costs are computed (accrued) based on contractual formulas (participations) and by contingent amounts due under provisions of collectively bargained union agreements (residuals). The accrual of these costs is discussed later in this section.

**Exploitation costs.** Exploitation costs are the direct costs associated with the film's distribution. The advertising cost component of exploitation costs is accounted for in accordance with SOP 93-7 which is discussed in Chapter 11. All other exploitation costs, including marketing costs, publicity, promotion, and other distribution expenses, are expensed as incurred.

**Manufacturing costs.** The cost of making theatrical film prints is charged to expense over the period benefited. The cost of manufacturing and/or duplication of products to be held for sale such as videocassettes and digital video discs is charged to expense on a unit-specific basis when the related product revenue is recognized. Unsold inventories are to be evaluated at each balance sheet date, for net realizable value and obsolescence.

## Costs and Expenses—Amortization of Film Costs and Accrual of Participation Costs

Amortization of capitalized film costs and accrual (expensing) of participation costs commences when the film is released and the entity begins to recognize revenue from the film. The method used to compute the amortization of film costs and the accrual of participation costs is called the individual-film-forecast-computation method. This method amortizes film costs using the following formula:

$$\frac{\text{Current period actual revenue}}{\substack{\text{Estimated remaining unrecognized} \\ \text{ultimate revenue as of the beginning} \\ \text{of the fiscal year}}} \times \substack{\text{Unamortized film} \\ \text{costs at the} \\ \text{beginning of the} \\ \text{fiscal year}} = \substack{\text{Film cost amortization} \\ \text{for the fiscal year}}$$

Similarly, participation costs are accrued and expensed using the following formula:

$$\frac{\text{Current period actual revenue}}{\substack{\text{Estimated remaining unrecognized} \\ \text{ultimate revenue as of the beginning} \\ \text{of the fiscal year}}} \times \substack{\text{Unaccrued ultimate} \\ \text{participation costs} \\ \text{at the beginning of} \\ \text{the fiscal year}} = \substack{\text{Amount of} \\ \text{participation costs to} \\ \text{be accrued (expensed)} \\ \text{for the fiscal year}}$$

Irrespective of the above calculation, participation costs are subject to special rules. The liability is only accrued if it is probable that there will be a sacrifice of assets to settle the entity's obligation under the participation agreement. In addition, at each balance sheet date, accrued participation costs must at least equal the amounts that the entity is obligated to pay at that date.

Using this formulaic approach, if the actual results from the exploitation of the film are realized as originally estimated, the entity would earn a constant rate of profit over the ultimate period for each film before considering exploitation costs, manufacturing costs and other period costs.

It is, of course, likely that the actual results will vary from the estimates and that the estimates will require review and refinement. At each reporting date, the entity reviews and revises estimates of ultimate revenue and ultimate participation costs to reflect the most current information available to it. As a result of this review, the denominator is revised to include only the remaining ultimate revenue at the beginning of the fiscal year of change. In this way, these changes in estimate are accounted for prospectively as of the beginning of the fiscal year of the change. The numerator is unaffected by the change since it is based on actual results. The entity uses this revised denominator in the fraction applied to the net unamortized film costs and to the film's unaccrued ultimate participation costs. The difference between expenses determined using the new estimates and any amounts previously recorded as expense during that fiscal year are charged (or credited) to the income statement in the period (e.g., quarter) during which the estimates are revised.

**Ultimate revenue.** In general, ultimate revenue to be included in the denominator of the fraction includes estimates of revenue to be recognized by the entity from the exploitation, exhibition, and sale of a film in all markets and territories. There are, however, certain limitations that apply to the determination of ultimate revenue.

1. The period over which ultimate revenue for a film may be estimated is limited to ten years following the date of the film's initial release.
2. For previously released films acquired as part of a film library, the period over which ultimate revenue may be estimated is limited to twenty years from the date of

acquisition of the library. A film must have been initially released at least three years prior to the acquisition date of the film library in order to be categorized as part of the library for the purposes of applying this limitation.

3. Ultimate revenue includes estimates of revenue for a market or territory only if persuasive evidence exists that the revenue will be earned, or if an entity can demonstrate a history of earning revenue in that market or territory. Ultimate revenue includes estimates of revenue from newly developing territories only if an existing arrangement provides persuasive evidence that the entity will realize the revenue.

4. Ultimate revenue includes estimates of revenue from licensing arrangements with third parties to market film-related products only if there is persuasive evidence that the revenue from that arrangement will be earned for that particular film (e.g., a signed contract to receive a nonrefundable minimum guarantee or nonrefundable advance) or if the entity can demonstrate a history of earning revenue from that form of arrangement.

5. Ultimate revenue includes estimates of the portion of the wholesale or retail revenue from an entity's sale of peripheral items (such as toys and apparel) attributable to the exploitation of themes, characters, or other contents related to a particular film only if the entity can demonstrate a history of earning revenues from that form of exploitation in similar kinds of films. Under this limitation, the amount of revenue to be included in ultimate revenue is an estimate of the amount that would be earned by the entity if rights for such a form of exploitation had been granted under licensing arrangements with third parties. Thus, the entity's estimate of ultimate revenue does not include the entire gross wholesale or retail revenue from the sale of peripheral items, but rather, the amount that it would realize in net license fees from the sales.

6. Ultimate revenue excludes estimates of revenue from unproven or undeveloped technologies.

7. Ultimate revenue excludes estimates of wholesale promotion or advertising reimbursements to be received from third parties. These reimbursements are accounted for as an offset against exploitation costs.

8. Ultimate revenue excludes estimates of amounts related to the sale of film rights for periods after those identified in 1. and 2. above.

With respect to episodic television series, the following rules apply:

1. The period over which ultimate revenue for an episodic television series may be estimated is limited to ten years from the date of delivery of the first episode or, if the series is still in production, five years from the date of delivery of the most recent episode, if later.

2. Ultimate revenue includes estimates of secondary market revenue (revenue from syndication of the series to markets other than the initial market) for produced episodes only if the entity can demonstrate through its experience or industry norms that the number of episodes already produced, plus those for which a firm commitment exists and the entity expects to deliver, can be licensed successfully in the secondary market.

3. Ultimate revenue excludes estimates of amounts related to the sale of rights for periods after those identified in 1. above.

Ultimate revenue is a gross undiscounted amount and does not include amounts representing projections of future inflation. The portion of ultimate revenue that is expected to be received in a foreign currency is valued at current spot rates.

**Ultimate participation costs.** The estimate of unaccrued ultimate participation costs to be used in the individual-film-forecast-computation method is made using assumptions consistent with the entity's estimates of film costs, exploitation costs, and ultimate revenue subject to the limitations set forth above. If, at any balance sheet date, the recognized participation costs liability exceeds the estimated unpaid ultimate participation costs for an individual film, the excess liability is first applied to reduce unamortized film costs with any remaining excess credited to income. If the entity continues to incur participation costs after the film costs have been fully amortized, the participation costs are accrued and expensed as the related revenues are recognized.

### Example of individual film forecast computation method

Paula Pictures incurred film costs and earned revenues from its motion picture, Arachno-Man, as follows:

|  | Year 1 | Year 2 |
|---|---|---|
| 1. Film cost, including capitalized interest (FC) | $15,000 | |
| 2. End-of-year estimate of ultimate revenue (UR) | 36,000 | $30,000 |
| 3. Remaining ultimate revenue at beginning of year* (RUR) | -- | 11,000 |
| 4. Actual earned revenues for the year (ER) | 19,000 | 5,000 |
| 5. End-of-year estimate of ultimate participation costs (UPC) | 3,600 | 3,000 |
| 6. Actual participation costs for the year (APC) | 1,600 | 500 |

\* *Revised estimate of ultimate revenue less actual revenue earned from date of release through the beginning of the year.*

The individual film forecast computation method is applied as follows:

### Year 1

Film cost amortization:

$$\frac{\$19,000 \text{ ER}}{\$36,000 \text{ UR}} \times \$15,000 \text{ FC} = \$7,917 \text{ Film cost amortization}$$

Accrual of participation costs:

$$\frac{\$19,000 \text{ ER}}{\$36,000 \text{ UR}} \times \$3,600 \text{ UPC} = \$1,900 \text{ Accrued participation costs}$$

### Year 2

Film cost amortization:

$$\frac{\$5,000 \text{ ER}}{\$11,000 \text{ RUR}^*} \times \$7,083^{**} \text{ Unamortized film costs} = \$3,220 \text{ Film cost amortization}$$

\* *Computed as Year 2 revised estimate of ultimate revenue of $30,000 less actual revenue recognized in prior year of $19,000.*
\*\* *Computed as film cost of $15,000 less prior amortization expense recognized of $7,917.*

Accrual of participation costs:

$$\frac{\$5,000 \text{ ER}}{\$11,000 \text{ RUR}} \times \$1,100 \text{ Remaining ultimate participation costs}^{***} = \$500$$

\*\*\* *Computed as Year 2 revised estimate for ultimate participation costs of $3,000 less the prior year accrued amount of $1,900.*

## Valuation of Unamortized Film Costs

Consistent with the rules for recognizing impairment of long-lived assets in FAS 144, the SOP sets forth examples of events or changes in circumstances that indicate that the entity must assess whether the fair value of the film (whether it has been completed or is still in production) is less than the carrying amount of its unamortized film costs.

1.  An adverse change in the expected performance of the film prior to its release
2.  Actual costs substantially in excess of budgeted costs

3. Substantial delays in completion or release schedules
4. Changes in release plans, such as a reduction in the initial release pattern
5. Insufficient funding or resources to complete the film and to market it effectively
6. Actual performance subsequent to release fails to meet prerelease expectations

Upon making the comparison between the film's fair value and its unamortized costs, any excess of the unamortized costs over the fair value is to be written off as an operating expense on the income statement. Amounts written off may not be subsequently restored.

The fair value of a film is often estimated using a traditional discounted cash flow model. The limits regarding the number of years of revenue to include in the determination of ultimate revenue do not apply to the estimation of future cash flows associated with the film for the purpose of determining the film's fair value. Factors to be considered by management in estimating future cash inflows for a film include

1. The film's performance in prior markets, if previously released
2. The public's perception (the popularity and market appeal) of the film's story, cast, director, or producer
3. Historical results of similar films
4. Historical results of the cast, director, or producer on prior films
5. The running time of the film

In addition to estimating the film's cash inflows, management must estimate future costs to complete the film (if any), future exploitation and participation costs, and other necessary cash outflows necessary to achieve the estimated cash inflows.

When using the traditional discounted cash flow method to estimate fair value, the estimates of future cash inflows and outflows represent management's best estimates of the most likely cash flows. The discount rate used is adjusted to consider the level of risk inherent in investing in a project of this nature.

When using the expected cash flow approach to estimate fair value (which is preferred and encouraged by FAS 144), all possible relevant future cash inflows and outflows are probability-weighted by period and the estimated average for each period used. In employing this method, the discount rate is risk-adjusted as described above only if the probable expected cash flows have not already been risk-adjusted. Guidance for applying these two estimation techniques is contained in CON 7, discussed in detail in Chapter 1 and illustrated in Chapter 11.

**Subsequent events.** When evidence of the possible need for a write-down of unamortized film costs arises after the date of the balance sheet but before the entity issues its financial statements, a rebuttable presumption exists that the conditions leading to the write-off existed at the balance sheet date. When this situation arises, whether the film was released before or after the balance sheet date, the entity uses this subsequent evidence to compute the adjustment necessary to record a change in estimate in its financial statements. If management is able to demonstrate that the conditions leading to the write-down did not exist at the balance sheet date, the presumption can be overcome, and the recognition of the effects of the change in estimate can be postponed until the subsequent period. However, full disclosure of the circumstances and amounts is required in the current financial statements.

# NOT-FOR-PROFIT ORGANIZATIONS

## PERSPECTIVE AND ISSUES

Not-for-profit organizations have several characteristics that distinguish them from business enterprises. First, and perhaps foremost, not-for-profit organizations exist to provide goods and services without the objective of generating a profit. Rather than obtaining resources by conducting exchange transactions at a profit or from capital infusions from owners, a not-for-profit organization obtains most resources from others that share its desire to serve a chosen mission—an educational, scientific, charitable, or religious goal. Although not-for-profit organizations can be "owned" or controlled by another, the ownership interest is unlike that of business enterprises because the "owner" cannot remove resources from the entity for personal use or gain; the resources must be used for a mission-related purpose. Examples of not-for-profit organizations are: churches and religious organizations, colleges and universities, health care organizations, libraries, museums, performing arts organizations, civic or fraternal organizations, federated fund-raising organizations, professional and trade associations, social clubs, research organizations, cemeteries, arboretums, and zoos.

Specifically excluded from the list of not-for-profit organizations are organizations that exist to provide dividends, lower costs, or other economic benefits directly and proportionately to their members, participants, or owners, such as mutual insurance companies, credit unions, farm or utility cooperatives, and employee benefit plans. Further, some not-for-profit organizations are governmental[3] and are required to follow the standards of the Governmental Accounting Standards Board (GASB). Governmental organizations are outside of the scope of this publication. Readers instead should refer to the Wiley publication, *GAAP for Governments.*

All authoritative pronouncements in the GAAP hierarchy, including EITF consensuses, apply to not-for-profit organizations unless the pronouncement specifically excludes not-for-profit organizations from its scope. Certain authoritative pronouncements apply specifically to not-for-profit organizations. Because those pronouncements are particularly relevant to the transactions of not-for-profit organizations they are discussed in this chapter.

FAS 93, *Recognition of Depreciation by Not-for-Profit Organizations,* issued in 1987, was the first standard issued by the FASB that applied specifically to not-for-profit organizations. It requires not-for-profit organizations to depreciate their long-lived assets and to disclose balances for the major classes of assets, depreciation for the period, accumulated depreciation, and the organization's policy for computing depreciation.

FAS 116, *Accounting for Contributions Received and Contributions Made,* establishes standards for recognition and display of contributions received and contributions made. It requires all contributions received and made to be measured at fair value and recognized in the period the gift is made. It applies to any contribution of assets, including contributions of cash, securities, supplies, long-lived assets, use of facilities or utilities, services, intangible assets, or unconditional promises to give those items in the future.

FAS 117, *Financial Statements of Not-for-Profit Organizations,* establishes standards for the general-purpose financial statements issued by not-for-profit organizations. It defines a complete set of financial statements for most organizations as a statement of financial position, a statement of activities, a statement of cash flows, and accompanying notes. It requires an organization's net assets and its revenues, expenses, gains, and losses to be classified based on the existence or absence of restrictions imposed by donors.

FAS 124, *Accounting for Certain Investments Held by Not-for-Profit Organizations,* establishes standards for investments held by not-for-profit organizations. It requires equity securities with readily determinable fair values and debt securities to be reported at fair value with the resulting holding gains and losses reported in the statement of activities. It also establishes standards for reporting investment return, including losses on donor-restricted endowment funds.

---

[3]   *See Chapter 1, Researching GAAP Matters, for a definition of "governmental entity."*

FAS 136, *Transfers of Assets to a Not-for-Profit Organization or Charitable Trust That Raises or Holds Contributions for Others,* establishes standards for transfers of assets to a not-for-profit organization or a charitable trust that raises or holds contributions for others. Although it primarily affects federated fund-raising organizations, community foundations, and institutionally related foundations, all organizations are subject to its standards because they can be the beneficiaries of the contributions raised by those organizations.

Combinations in which the acquiring entity is a not-for-profit organization, unlike combinations in which the acquiring entity is a business enterprise, cannot be assumed to be an exchange of commensurate value. Acquired not-for-profit organizations lack owners who are focused on receiving a return on and return of their investment. Moreover, the parent or governing body of an acquired organization may place its mission effectiveness ahead of achieving maximum price when negotiating a combination agreement. Thus, when two not-for-profit organizations combine, it will be necessary to determine if there was an exchange of commensurate value (in which case, standards similar to FAS 141 would be applied) or if there is a contribution inherent in the transaction that would be reported in accordance with FAS 116.

If there is a contribution inherent in the transaction, it would be measured as the excess of the net fair values of the identifiable assets acquired and the liabilities assumed over the fair value of the consideration exchanged. If the acquired entity is a business enterprise, the contribution inherent in a combination would be measured as the excess of the fair value of the acquired business enterprise over the cost of that business enterprise. The primary difference is that no goodwill would be recognized in most contributions of not-for-profit organizations, although it would be in the contributions of business entities.

In the rare cases in which the sum of the fair values of the liabilities assumed exceeds the sum of the fair values of the identifiable assets acquired, the acquiring organization would initially recognize that excess as an unidentifiable intangible asset (goodwill).

Two AICPA AAG provide standards for not-for-profit organizations. *Health Care Organizations* applies to providers of health care services, including hospitals, nursing homes, medical clinics, continuing care retirement communities, health maintenance organizations, home health agencies, and rehabilitation facilities. *Not-for-Profit Organizations* applies to all other nongovernmental not-for-profit organizations. Both Guides discuss the aspects of financial statement preparation and audit particularly relevant to the organizations within their scope. In addition, each provides a helpful listing of all category A GAAP pronouncements and their applicability to not-for-profit organizations.

SOP 94-3, *Reporting of Related Entities by Not-for-Profit Organizations,* establishes standards for consolidation by not-for-profit organizations of investments in for-profit entities and other not-for-profit organizations. It also describes the disclosures required when related entities are not consolidated because the relationship does not meet the criteria of control and economic benefit.

SOP 98-2, *Accounting for Costs of Not-for-Profit Organizations and State and Local Governmental Entities That Include Fund-Raising,* establishes standards for the functional classification of expenses incurred in activities that combine program or management and general components with fund-raising. It requires that all costs of the combined activity be classified as fund-raising expenses unless three criteria—purpose, audience, and content— are met.

SOP 02-2, *Accounting for Derivative Instruments and Hedging Activities by Not-for-Profit Health Care Organizations, and Clarification of the Performance Indicator,* clarifies that the performance indicator required to be reported in the financial statements of a not-for-profit health care organization is analogous to income from continuing operations of a business (for-profit) enterprise.

This chapter contains a highly summarized discussion of accounting and reporting standards for not-for-profit organizations. Readers who desire a more in-depth discussion should refer to the Wiley publication, *Not-for-Profit GAAP*.

| Sources of GAAP | | |
|---|---|---|
| *FAS* | *AAG* | *SOP* |
| 93, 116, | *Not-for-Profit Organizations,* | 94-3, |
| 117, 124, 136 | *Health Care Organizations* | 98-2, 02-2 |

## DEFINITION OF TERMS

**Agent.** An entity that acts for and on behalf of another. For example, a not-for-profit organization acts as an agent for and on behalf of a donor if it receives resources from the donor and agrees to transfer the resources or the return generated by investing those resources to another entity named by the donor. Similarly, a not-for-profit organization acts for and on behalf of a beneficiary if it agrees to solicit contributions in the name of the beneficiary and distribute any contributions thereby received to the beneficiary.

**Collections.** Works of art, historical treasures, or similar assets that meet the following three criteria: (1) they are held for public exhibition, education, or research in service to the public rather than for financial gain; (2) they are protected, kept unencumbered, cared for, and preserved; and (3) they are subject to a policy requiring that the organization use the proceeds from the sale of an item to acquire another item for the collection.

**Contribution.** A voluntary and unconditional transfer of assets to an entity (the donee) from another entity that does not expect to receive equivalent value in exchange and does not act as an owner (the donor). A contribution can also take the form of a settlement or cancellation of the donee's liabilities.

**Donor-imposed restriction.** A donor stipulation that specifies a use for contributed resources that is narrower than the limitations that result from the nature of the organization, the environment in which it operates, and the purposes specified in its articles of incorporation, bylaws, or similar documents. A restriction may be temporary or permanent. A temporary restriction is a restriction that will expire (be satisfied) either by an action of the organization (such as spending the resources for the purpose described by the donor) or by the passage of time. A permanent restriction never expires. Instead, it requires that the contributed resources be maintained permanently, although it allows the organization to spend the income or to use the other economic benefits generated by those resources.

**Donor-imposed condition.** A donor stipulation that specifies a future and uncertain event whose occurrence (or failure to occur) gives the donor the right of return of resources it has transferred or releases the donor from the obligation to transfer assets in the future. For example, "I will contribute one dollar for each dollar raised during the month of July in excess of $10,000," includes a donor-imposed condition. If only $9,000 is raised, the donor has no obligation to transfer assets.

**Endowment fund.** A fund of cash, securities, or other assets held to provide income for the support of a not-for-profit organization. A donor-restricted endowment fund is a fund established by a donor, specifying that the gift must be invested permanently to generate support (a permanent endowment fund) or invested for a specified period of time (a term endowment fund). A quasi endowment fund is a fund established by an organization's governing board to provide income for a long, but usually unspecified, period of time. A quasi endowment fund may be created from unrestricted resources or from resources that are for a restricted purpose but not required by the donor to be invested.

**Intermediary.** An organization that acts as a facilitator for the transfer of resources between two or more other parties. An intermediary generally does not take possession of the assets transferred.

**Net assets.** The residual interest in the assets of a not-for-profit organization that remains after deducting its liabilities. Net assets are divided into three categories—permanently restricted, temporarily restricted, and unrestricted—based on the nature and existence (or absence) of donor-imposed restrictions. Permanently restricted net assets are the portion of net assets that result from contributions and other inflows of resources that are subject to permanent donor-imposed restrictions. Permanently restricted net assets are not permitted to be expended or used up. Temporarily restricted net assets are the portion of net assets that result from contributions and other inflows of resources that are subject to temporary donor-imposed restrictions. They are permitted to be expended or used up as long as their use is consistent with the limitations imposed by the donor. Unrestricted net assets are the portion of net assets that are neither permanently nor temporarily restricted by donors. The use of unrestricted net assets is subject only to the limitations imposed by the nature of the organization, its articles of incorporation or bylaws, and the environment in which it operates.

**Promise to give.** A written or oral agreement to contribute resources to another entity at a future date. A promise to give can be either conditional or unconditional. The obligation of the donor who makes a conditional promise to give is dependant on the occurrence (or failure to occur) of a donor-imposed condition. An unconditional promise to give depends only on the passage of time or demand by the donee for payment of the promised assets.

**Trustee.** An entity that holds and manages assets for the benefit of a specified beneficiary in accordance with a charitable trust agreement.

**Voluntary health and welfare organization.** An organization formed for the purpose of attempting to prevent or solve health and welfare problems of society, and in many cases, of particular individuals.

## CONCEPTS, RULES, AND EXAMPLES

### The Reporting Entity

Not-for-profit organizations were exempted from the provisions of FAS 141 and FAS 142. Consequently the financial statement preparer must consider the applicability of SOP 94-3, *Reporting of Related Entities by Not-for-Profit Organizations*, in determining the reporting entity. SOP 94-3 provides guidance on reporting investments in majority-owned for-profit subsidiaries, investments in common stock in which the not-for-profit organization owns a 50% or less voting interest, and certain relationships with other not-for-profit organizations.

If a not-for-profit organization has a controlling financial interest in a for-profit organization (generally a majority voting interest), it follows the standards in ARB 51, *Consolidated Financial Statements,* as amended by FAS 94, *Consolidation of All Majority Owned Subsidiaries.* Not-for-profit organizations as defined in FAS 117 are specifically exempted from following the consolidations provisions of FIN 46(R), *Consolidation of Variable Interest Entities.* FIN 46(R) does, however, include an anti-abuse provision that provides that the scope exemption does not apply if the not-for-profit organization is being used by a business enterprise in a manner similar to a variable interest entity in order to circumvent FIN 46(R). Variable interest entities are discussed at length in Chapters 13 and 16.

If a not-for-profit organization has significant influence over the operating and financial policies of the investee (generally owns 20% or more but less than 50% of the voting stock), it either follows the standards in APB 18, *The Equity Method of Accounting for Investments in Common Stock,* or, if permitted by the AAG, reports the investment at fair value.

Different combinations of control and economic interest determine the appropriate accounting for relationships with other not-for-profit organizations, as shown in the following table. Control is defined for this purpose as the direct or indirect ability to determine the direction of management and policies through ownership, contract, or otherwise. Economic interest is defined as an interest in another entity that exists if (1) the other entity holds or utilizes significant resources that must be used for the purposes of the reporting organization, either directly or indirectly by producing income or providing services or (2) the reporting organization is responsible for the liabilities of the other entity.

| *Control?* | *Economic interest?* | *Standards* |
|---|---|---|
| Yes, via ownership of a majority voting interest | Yes | Consolidate. |
| Yes, via ownership of a majority voting interest | No | Consolidate. |
| Yes, via majority voting interest in the board of the other entity, as a majority owner | Yes | Consolidate. |
| Yes, via majority voting interest in the board of the other entity, as a majority owner | No | Consolidation is prohibited, and disclosure required. |
| Yes, via a contract or an affiliation agreement | Yes | Consolidation is permitted, but not required. |
| Yes, via a contract or an affiliation agreement | No | Consolidation is prohibited, and disclosure required. |
| No | Yes | Consolidation is prohibited, and disclosure required. |
| No | No | Consolidation is prohibited. No disclosure required. |

In all cases, consolidation is prohibited if control is likely to be temporary or does not rest with the majority owner. If consolidation is prohibited but consolidated financial statements were presented in accordance with SOP 78-10, *Accounting Principles and Reporting Practices for Certain Nonprofit Organizations* (otherwise superseded), organizations may continue to consolidate the other organizations.

Certain disclosures are necessary if consolidated statements are not presented. If consolidated statements are not presented when consolidation is permitted, but not required, the not-for-profit organization must disclose the identity of the other organization, the nature of the relationship, and summarized financial data in addition to the information required by FAS 57, *Related-Party Disclosures*. If consolidation is prohibited, the not-for-profit organization must disclose the information required by FAS 57.

## Complete Set of Financial Statements

Financial statements are intended to help donors, creditors, and others who provide resources to a not-for-profit organization assess the services provided by the not-for-profit organization and its ability to continue to provide those services. The statements should also help them assess whether management has properly discharged its stewardship responsibilities and whether it has performed satisfactorily in its other management duties.

FAS 117, *Financial Statements of Not-for-Profit Organizations,* requires all not-for-profit organizations to present a statement of financial position, a statement of activities, a statement of cash flows, and notes to the financial statements any time it purports to present a complete set of financial statements. In addition, voluntary health and welfare organizations are required to present a statement of functional expenses as an additional basic financial statement. In most ways, the content and format of those financial statements are similar to the financial statements prepared by business enterprises.

However, three major differences between not-for-profit organizations and business enterprises cause differences in the content and format of financial statements of not-for-profit organizations. First, there is no profit motive in the nonprofit sector, and thus no single indicator of performance comparable to a business enterprise's net income or bottom line. In fact, the best indicators of the performance of a not-for-profit organization are generally not measurable in dollar amounts but rather in the reader's qualitative judgment about the effectiveness of the organization in achieving its mission. Nevertheless, dollars are the language of financial reporting. Information to help assess performance is provided in financial statements (1) by reporting revenues and expenses gross rather than net and (2) by classifying expenses based on the mission-related programs and supporting activities they sustain, rather than by their natural classifications (salaries, utilities, depreciation, etc.).

Second, because the bottom line of a not-for-profit organization's statement of activities is not a performance measure, but simply a change in net assets for the reporting period, there is no need for not-for-profit organizations to distinguish between components of comprehensive income as business enterprises do. All revenues, expenses, gains, and losses are reported in a single statement rather than being divided between an income statement and a statement of other comprehensive income.

Third, not-for-profit organizations receive contributions, a type of transaction that is without counterpart in business enterprises. Those contributions often are subject to donor-imposed restrictions which can affect the types and levels of service that a not-for-profit organization can offer. Because donor-imposed restrictions are prevalent, recurring, and, in some cases, permanent, financial reporting by not-for-profit organizations needs to reflect the nature and extent of donor-imposed restrictions and changes in them that occur during the reporting period.

If the reporting entity is a not-for-profit health care organization, the AAG requires it to include within its statement of activities an intermediate subtotal called a performance indicator. SOP 02-2 clarifies that the performance indicator is analogous to income from continuing operations of a business (for-profit) enterprise, and thus would exclude items that are required to be reported in or reclassified from other comprehensive income, extraordinary items, the effect of discontinued operations, the cumulative effect of accounting changes, transactions with owners acting in that capacity, and equity transfers from entities that control the reporting entity, are controlled by the reporting entity, or are under common control with the reporting entity. The performance indicator also excludes restricted contributions, contributions of and reclassification related to gifts of long-lived assets, unrealized gains and losses on investments not restricted by donors or law (except for investments classified as trading), and investment returns restricted by donors.

### Net Assets and Changes in Net Assets

The nature and extent of donor-imposed restrictions are reported in the statement of financial position by distinguishing between the portions of net assets that are permanently restricted, temporarily restricted, and unrestricted. Separate line items on the face of that statement or details in the notes to the financial statements are used to meet the requirement to disclose the amounts for different types of permanent and temporary restrictions.

Changes in donor-imposed restrictions are reported in the statement of activities. The organization's revenues, expenses, gains, and losses for the period are classified into the three classes of net assets so that the statement of activities reports amounts for the change in permanently restricted net assets, the change in temporarily restricted net assets, and the change in unrestricted net assets, as well as the change in net assets in total. Transactions and events that do not change the net assets of the organization as a whole, but only their classification, are reported separately as reclassifications. Reclassifications are events that simultaneously increase one class of net assets and decrease another. For example, unrestricted net assets increase and temporarily restricted net assets decrease when the purchase of a long-lived asset fulfills a donor-imposed restriction to acquire long-lived assets with the gift (sometimes referred to as a release of restrictions).

Not-for-profit organizations often use fund accounting as a tool for tracking compliance with donor-imposed restrictions and internal designations. Fund accounting is a system of recording resources whose use is limited either by donors, granting agencies, governing boards, law, or legal covenants. A separate fund (a self-balancing group of accounts composed of assets, liabilities, and net assets) is maintained for each purpose limitation. For external reporting, a fund may be classified entirely in one net asset class or it may need to be allocated among two or three classes. (For an example of the allocations necessary to restate a fund balance to net asset classes, see the discussion of endowment funds in "Investments" in this section.)

## Reporting Revenues

Revenues are reported in the statement of activities as increases in unrestricted net assets unless the use of the resources received is subject to a donor-imposed restriction. Thus, contribution revenues increase unrestricted net assets, temporarily restricted net assets, or permanently restricted net assets, depending on the existence and nature of donors' restrictions. Revenues from most exchange transactions (such as sales of goods or services) are classified as unrestricted.

Revenues from exchange transactions only increase restricted net asset classes if a pre-existing donor-imposed restriction limits the use of the resources received. For example, if a donor contributes a car to the local library and requires that the proceeds from the sale of the car be used to purchase children's books, the proceeds from the sale of the car (an exchange transaction) increase temporarily restricted net assets. Investment income and gains (which are also exchange transactions) increase unrestricted net assets unless a donor required that the gift be invested and the investment return used for a restricted purpose. For example, assume a donor contributes securities worth $85,000 to a zoo, requires that all dividends and gains be retained and reinvested until the accumulated value is $100,000, and states that the $100,000 must be maintained as a permanent endowment fund, the income of which is to be used for the purchase of animals. In the early years of the endowment, before the accumulated value reaches $100,000, investment income and gains increase permanently restricted net assets. Investment income and gains earned after the accumulated value of the fund reaches $100,000 increase temporarily restricted net assets with the restriction expiring upon use of those funds to purchase animals.

FAS 116, *Accounting for Contributions Received and Contributions Made*, requires contributions to be recognized as revenue at the time of the gift and measured at the fair value of the contributed assets regardless of the form of the assets contributed. Donor-imposed restrictions do not change the timing of recognition of a contribution. Donor-imposed restrictions, or the absence of them, affect only a contribution's classification as an increase in permanently restricted net assets, temporarily restricted net assets, or unrestricted net assets. Donor-imposed conditions, however, affect the timing of recognition. Because a contribution is an unconditional transfer, a transfer of assets subject to donor-imposed conditions is not a contribution yet, although it may become one at a future date. Conditional transfers are not recognized as contribution revenues until the conditions are substantially met. Thus, the distinction between donor-imposed restrictions and donor-imposed conditions is very important to the timing of recognition. If a donor's stipulations do not clearly state whether a gift depends on meeting a stated stipulation and the ambiguity cannot be resolved by communicating with the donor or by examining the circumstances surrounding the gift, a transfer is presumed to be conditional.

Unconditional promises to give cash or other assets are recognized in financial statements when the promise is made and received, provided that there is sufficient evidence in the form of verifiable documentation (written, audio, or video). If payments of the promises are due in future periods, the promise has an implied time restriction that expires on the date the payment is due. Thus, unless circumstances surrounding the receipt of the promise indicate that the donor intended the gift to support the current period's activities, unconditional promises increase temporarily restricted net assets. A present value technique is used to measure unconditional promises to give, although short-term promises (due in less than one year) may be reported at net realizable value. Conditional promises are not recognized as revenue until the conditions are substantially met; however, they are required to be disclosed in notes to the financial statements.

In a manner similar to recognizing promises to give, a beneficiary recognizes contributions held on its behalf by an agent, trustee, or intermediary. For example, if the assets held by the agent were transferred subject to a condition that is not yet met, the beneficiary does not recognize its potential rights to the assets held by the agent. If a beneficiary has an unconditional right to receive cash flows from a charitable trust or other pool of assets, the beneficiary recognizes its rights when the beneficial interest is created and measures the rights using the present value of the estimated expected cash flows. However, if the beneficiary and the agent, trustee, or intermediary are financially interrelated organizations, the beneficiary reports its rights to the assets held using a method similar to the equity method of accounting for investments. (For further discussion, see "Transfers received as an agent, trustee, or intermediary" in this section.)

The value of volunteer services received by the organization is recognized in certain circumstances. Contributed services that create or improve a nonfinancial asset (such as building a shed or replacing a roof) are recognized as revenue as contributions either by valuing the hours of service received or by measuring the change in the fair value of the nonfinancial asset created or improved. Other contributed services are recognized only if they meet all three of the following criteria: (1) they require specialized skills, (2) they are provided by persons possessing those skills, and (3) they would typically need to be purchased if not provided by donation. If volunteer services neither meet those three criteria nor create or improve nonfinancial assets, they cannot be recognized in the organization's financial statements. However, organizations are required to describe the programs or activities for which contributed services are used, the nature and extent of services received for the period (regardless of whether those services are recognized), and disclose the amount recognized as revenues.

An organization that maintains works of art, historical treasures, and similar assets in collections, as defined, does not recognize gifts of items that are added to its collections unless it also capitalizes its collections. However, gifts that are not added to collections or items given to organizations that do not maintain collections in accordance with the definition are recognized as revenues and measured at the fair value of the assets received.

## Reporting Expenses

Expenses are recognized in the statement of activities as decreases in unrestricted net assets. Financing an expense with donor-restricted resources does not make the expense restricted; instead, it releases the restriction on the restricted resources, causing a reclassification to be reported in the statement of activities.

Expenses must be reported by functional classifications either on the face of the statement of activities or in the notes to the financial statements. The functional classifications describe the major classes of program services and supporting activities of an organization. Program services are the mission-related activities of the organization that result in goods and services being distributed to clients, customers, or members. They are the activities that are the major purpose of and the major output of the organization. For example, a not-for-profit organization with the mission of enhancing the lives of the community's senior citizens might have senior center, home visits, transportation services, and home maintenance as its program expense classifications. Supporting activities are all activities of a not-for-profit organization other than program services. Fund raising expenses and management and general are two common supporting activity classifications.

FAS 117 encourages, but does not require, most not-for-profit organizations to provide an analysis of expenses by natural classification. Information about expenses by natural classifications (salaries, benefits, rent, depreciation, and so forth) can help readers of the financial statements understand the mix of fixed and discretionary costs incurred by the organization. Only voluntary health and welfare organizations are required to report information about expenses by both functional and natural classification. Those organizations must provide that information in a matrix format in a statement of functional expenses.

FAS 93, *Recognition of Depreciation by Not-for-Profit Organizations,* requires the depreciation of land, buildings, and equipment used by not-for-profit organizations. An exception to that requirement is provided for certain works of art, historical treasures, and similar assets. If a not-for-profit organization can demonstrate both (1) that an asset individually has cultural, historical, or aesthetic value worth maintaining in perpetuity and (2) that the organization has the ability to protect and preserve that value essentially undiminished and is doing so, depreciation need not be recognized. Depreciation expense is a natural expense classification that must be allocated to programs and supporting activities in reporting expenses by functional classification.

Many not-for-profit organizations solicit contributions as part of conducting activities that also serve their program or management and general functions. For example, an organization that has a mission of reducing the incidence of cancer might conduct a direct mail campaign and include in an envelope a listing of lifestyle changes that will lessen the risks of cancer and a request for contributions. When a fund-raising activity is conducted in conjunction with an activity that serves a program or other support purpose, the activity is referred to as a joint activity. Users of the financial statements of not-for-profit organizations are particularly interested in the extent to which the organization is able to minimize its fundraising and management and general costs. Because neither of these types of costs directly benefit the beneficiaries of the organization's programs, successful organizations attempt to minimize them as a percent of the organization's support and revenue. Since the effectiveness of the management of a not-for-profit organization is often judged on operating metrics of this nature, there is a natural incentive for management to maximize the portion of the costs of these joint activities that is characterized as program expenses.

SOP 98-2 established standards for reporting the costs of joint activities. It begins with the presumption that the costs of a joint activity are reportable as fund-raising expenses. To overcome that presumption, three criteria must be met: purpose, audience, and content. If all three of the criteria are met, the costs of a joint activity are to be charged as follows:

- Costs identifiable with a particular function are charged to that function.
- Joint costs are allocated between fund-raising and the appropriate program or management and general function.

Joint costs are the costs of conducting joint activities that are not directly identifiable with a particular component of the activity. Joint costs might include the costs of salaries, professional fees, paper, printing, postage, event advertising, telephones, broadcast airtime, and facility rentals.

Determining whether all three criteria are met is complicated because the purpose and audience criteria have additional tests within them. The purpose test includes a call to action test, a compensation or fees test, a similar scale and same medium test, and an other evidence test. The audience criteria includes a prior donor test, an ability and likelihood to contribute test, and a need to use or reasonable potential for use test. Failure of one of the additional tests often causes the activity to fail the criterion.

If any of the three criteria is not met, all costs of the joint activity must be reported as fund-raising expense. "All costs" includes the costs that would have been considered program or management and general if they had been incurred in a different activity. There is an exception to the rule that all costs are charged to fund-raising expense if one or more of the criteria is not met. The costs of goods or services provided in an exchange transaction (sometimes referred to as a quid pro quo contribution) that is part of the joint activity are charged to cost of goods sold rather than fund-raising expense. For example, the costs of direct donor benefits, such as the value of items sold at a fund-raising auction or meals served at a fund-raising dinner, are not charged to fund-raising expenses.

SOP 98-2 requires that the method used to allocate the joint costs be rational and systematic and that it result in a reasonable allocation of costs. The method selected is to be applied consistently given similar facts and circumstances. No particular method of allocation is required by the SOP, but three allocation methods are illustrated: the physical units method, the relative direct cost method, and the stand-alone joint-cost-allocation method.

Organizations that allocate joint costs are required to disclose the types of activities in which joint costs have been incurred, a statement that the costs have been allocated, and the total amount of joint costs allocated, and the portion of joint costs allocated to each functional expense category. The SOP also encourages disclosure of the amount of joint costs for each type of joint activity.

### Transfers Received as an Agent, Trustee, or Intermediary

FAS 136, *Transfers of Assets to a Not-for-Profit Organization or Charitable Trust That Raises or Holds Contributions for Others,* establishes standards for transactions in which a donor makes a contribution by using an agent, trustee, or intermediary. (Agents, trustees, and intermediaries are referred to as recipient organizations.) The donor transfers assets to the recipient organization. The recipient organization accepts the assets from the donor and agrees to use the assets on behalf of or transfer the assets, their investment return, or both to another entity—the beneficiary—named by the donor. FAS 136 also establishes standards for transactions that take place in a similar manner but are not contributions because the transactions are revocable, repayable, or reciprocal. FAS 136 does not set standards for recipient organizations that are trustees.

In general, a recipient organization reports a liability if it accepts assets from a donor and agrees to use those assets on behalf of or transfer those assets to another organization or individual specified by the donor. When it subsequently spends the assets on behalf of the beneficiary or transfers the assets, their return, or both to the beneficiary, the nonprofit organization reduces the liability it recorded earlier. If the assets received from the donor are donated materials, supplies, or other nonfinancial assets, the recipient organization may choose either to (1) report the receipt of the assets as liability to the beneficiary concurrent with recognition of the assets received or (2) not to report the transaction at all. The choice is an accounting policy that must be applied consistently from period to period and disclosed in the notes to the financial statements.

If the donor explicitly grants the recipient organization variance power, the recipient organization, rather than the beneficiary, recognizes contribution revenue. Variance power is the unilateral power to direct the transferred assets to an entity other than the specified beneficiary. Unilateral power means that the recipient organization does not have to contact the donor, the beneficiary, or any other interested party in order to substitute a different beneficiary. Variance power must be granted by the instrument transferring the assets.

If the recipient organization and the specified beneficiary are financially interrelated organizations, the recipient organization reports contribution revenue and the specified beneficiary recognizes its interest in the net assets of the recipient organization using a method similar to the equity method of accounting for investments in common stock. Organizations are financially interrelated if the relationship between them has both of the following characteristics: (1) one organization has the ability to influence the operating and financial decisions of the other and (2) one organization has an ongoing economic interest in the net assets of the other. The ability to influence the operating and financial decisions of the other can be demonstrated in several ways: (1) the organizations are affiliates as defined in FAS 57, *Related-Party Disclosures*, (2) one organization has considerable representation on the governing board of the other, (3) the charter or bylaws of one organization limit its activities to those that are beneficial to the other, or (4) an agreement between the organizations allows one organization to actively participate in the policymaking processes of the other. An ongoing economic interest in the net assets of another is a residual right to the other organization's net assets that results from an ongoing relationship. A common example of financially interrelated organizations is a foundation that exists to raise, hold, and invest assets for a specific beneficiary that it supports.

In addition to establishing standards for contributions transferred to beneficiaries via agents, trustees, and intermediaries, FAS 136 sets standards for transfers that take place in a similar manner but are not contributions because the terms of the transfer or the relationships between the parties make the transfer revocable, repayable, or reciprocal. Transfers are recognized by the recipient organization as liabilities if one or more of the following situations are present: (1) the transfer is subject to the transferor's right to redirect the transferred assets to another beneficiary, (2) the transfer is accompanied by the transferor's conditional promise to give, (3) the transferor controls the recipient organization and specifies an unaffiliated beneficiary, or (4) the transferor specifies itself or its affiliate as the beneficiary of a transfer that is not an equity transaction. An equity transaction is a transfer that has all of the following terms: (1) the transferor specifies itself or its affiliate as beneficiary, (2) the transferor and the recipient organization are financially interrelated organizations, and (3) neither the transferor nor its affiliate expects payment of the transferred assets (although payment of investment return is allowable). Equity transactions are reported by the recipient organization as a separate line item in the statement of activities.

### Investments and Endowment Funds

FAS 124, *Accounting for Certain Investments Held by Not-for-Profit Organizations*, requires investments in equity securities with readily determinable fair values and all debt securities to be reported at fair value. Although the standard applies to the same securities that FAS 115 covers for business enterprises, accounting for the resulting gains and losses is different than specified by that standard. Gains and losses (both realized and unrealized) are reported in a not-for-profit organization's statement of activities.

The AAG establishes standards for reporting other investments. The appropriate standards to apply depend on whether the not-for-profit organization is a college or university, a voluntary health and welfare organization, a health care organization, or another type of not-for-profit organization. Most organizations have the option of reporting their other investments at either cost or at the lower of cost or market.

Not-for-profit health care organizations are required to apply the provisions of FAS 133, *Accounting for Derivative Instruments and Hedging Activities*, in the same manner as business enterprises, including the provisions pertaining to cash flow hedge accounting. The gain or loss items that affect a business enterprise's income from continuing operations similarly affect the not-for-profit health care organization's performance indicator, and the gain or loss items that are excluded from a business enterprise's income from continuing operations (such as items reported in other comprehensive income) are to be excluded from the performance indicator.

Not-for-profit health care organizations are to provide disclosures similar to those required by paragraphs 45 and 47 of FAS 133. When applying paragraph 47, they are to disclose the activity affecting the amount of accumulated derivative gains or losses that have been excluded from the performance indicator (because they do not report accumulated other comprehensive income).

Many of the investments held by not-for-profit organizations are held as the investments of endowment funds. Endowment funds generally are established by gifts from donors who desire to provide support for the organization permanently (a permanently restricted endowment fund) or for a specified period of time (a term endowment fund). In addition, a governing board may determine that certain resources be invested and that only the return generated be spent by the organization. These board-designated amounts are referred to as quasi endowment funds or funds functioning as endowment. The net assets of an endowment fund are classified in accordance with the restrictions placed on the resources by donors, if any. Because a donor can place different restrictions on each source of the net assets (original gift, investment gains and losses, and investment income), each source must be examined separately to achieve the proper classification.

Each source is unrestricted unless its use is temporarily or permanently restricted by the donor or by a law that extends the donor's restriction to the source. Thus, the net assets of an endowment fund created by the governing board from a large unrestricted bequest (or from unrestricted net assets) are classified as unrestricted because no donor was involved in the transaction of creating the endowment fund and all amounts transferred to that fund are free of donor-imposed restrictions.

In contrast, assume that a donor contributes $50,000 to a museum and stipulates that the gift be invested in perpetuity and the investment income be used to purchase works of art. The donor further stipulates that any gains on the investment be added to the original gift and invested in perpetuity. The donor's original gift ($50,000) increases permanently restricted net assets because of the stipulation that the gift be invested in perpetuity. The income earned by the investment of the gift increases temporarily restricted net assets. When works of art are purchased, the restriction on net assets resulting from the income is fulfilled and the net assets are reclassified to unrestricted net assets. The realized and unrealized gains from investment of the gift increase permanently restricted net assets because the donor required that those gains also be reinvested in perpetuity.

In most cases, the classification of the original gift and the investment income is straightforward because donors explicitly state the time and purpose restrictions on them. Classification of gains and losses on the investments is not as clearly determinable unless the donor explicitly states how gains are to be used and whether losses must be restored immediately from other sources, from future gains on the investments, or not at all. However, donors are often silent in their agreements about those matters.

In the absence of explicit donor restrictions, the law in most states provides some direction about the restrictions on investment gains of donor-restricted endowment funds. The Uniform Management of Institutional Funds Act (UMIFA) extends certain donor restrictions to the net appreciation (accumulated net gains) of donor-restricted endowment funds. In states that have adopted UMIFA, net appreciation is expendable unless the donor states otherwise. UMIFA provides that the net appreciation can be spent for the uses and purposes for which the endowment fund was established. Thus, unless the donor specifies otherwise, gains increase unrestricted net assets if the endowment's income is not restricted by the donor, and gains increase temporarily restricted net assets if the endowment's income is temporarily restricted by the donor. Assume in the earlier example of the $50,000 gift to the museum that the donor was silent about the use of gains earned by investing the original gift. In a state that has adopted UMIFA, the accumulated gains on the endowment fund would be restricted to the purchase of artwork because the law requires that the donor's restriction be extended to those gains. The restrictions on those temporarily restricted net assets expire when the museum purchases works of art even if the money to purchase the work of art is not withdrawn from the fund. Thus, this single endowment fund can be composed of permanently restricted net assets (the original $50,000 gift), temporarily restricted net assets (the gains on which restrictions have not yet been met), and unrestricted net assets (the gains on which restrictions have been met).

FAS 124 requires that losses on the investments of an endowment fund reduce temporarily restricted net assets to the extent that temporary restrictions on net appreciation have not yet been met before the loss occurs. The remainder of the loss, if any, reduces unrestricted net assets. If the losses reduce the value of the fund below the level required by the donor or by law, future gains that restore the value to the required level are classified as unrestricted net assets.

Expanding on the previous example, assume that several years after the fund was established, the assets of the fund have increased in value to $65,000. Assume also that the classification of the net assets in the fund is: $50,000 permanently restricted (the original gift), $10,000 temporarily restricted (accumulated gains on which the restrictions have not been met), and $5,000 unrestricted (gains on which the restriction was met by purchasing a work of art with unrestricted funds in years after the inception of the fund). A market correction causes the value of the investments to fall to $58,000. The $7,000 loss decreases temporarily restricted net assets from $10,000 to $3,000. Assume that a further market correction reduces the value of the investments another $9,000 from $58,000 to $49,000. The $9,000 loss reduces temporarily restricted net assets by $3,000 (the amount remaining after the $7,000 loss decreased the original $10,000) and reduces unrestricted net assets by $6,000. After recording the loss, the classification of the $49,000 value of the endowment fund would be: $50,000 permanently restricted (the original gift) and ($1,000) deficit in unrestricted net assets. A not-for-profit organization is required to disclose the amount by which the value of the endowment fund is less than the level required by the donor.

Continuing the example, assume that the next year the value of the investments increases from $49,000 to $53,000. The $4,000 gain increases unrestricted net assets by $1,000 (the restoration of the deficit) and increases temporarily restricted net assets by $3,000. After the gain, the net assets of the endowment fund are $50,000 permanently restricted (the original gift) and $3,000 temporarily restricted for the purchase of works of art.

## Collections

Not-for-profit organizations are allowed an exception to the normal requirement to capitalize purchases of property, plant, and equipment. If a not-for-profit organization maintains collections of works of art, historical treasures, or similar assets in the manner defined in FAS 116, it can choose whether it will capitalize and report those collections in its statement of financial position. To qualify for the exception, an organization must (1) hold the items for public exhibition, education, or research in service to the public rather than for financial gain, (2) protect the items, keep them unencumbered, care for them, and preserve them, and (3) use the proceeds from the sale of any items to acquire other items for the collection. If an organization meets those criteria, it can choose one of the following policies: (1) capitalize its collections, (2) capitalize only collection items acquired after the adoption of FAS 116, or (3) not capitalize any collections. An organization cannot selectively choose to capitalize only certain collections.

If an organization does not capitalize its collections, transactions involving collection items must be reported separately on the face of its statement of activities. Similarly, if an organization chose to capitalize its collections prospectively when it adopted FAS 116, it would separately report transactions involving collection items not previously capitalized. Descriptions of the collections, including information about stewardship policies and items deaccessed (removed from the collection), must be included in notes to the financial statements by organizations that do not capitalize their collections or that capitalize them prospectively.

Capitalization is required of works of art, historical treasures, and similar assets that are not collection items, even if those items are held by organizations that regularly maintain collections. Thus, if a museum does not capitalize its collections and it is given a work of art that it does not to add to its collection (perhaps because it duplicates other collection items), the museum would recognize that contribution and report the asset in its statement of financial position as a work of art held for sale.

## Split-Interest Agreements

A split-interest agreement is an arrangement in which a donor transfers assets to a not-for-profit organization or to a charitable trust and requires the benefits of ownership of those assets be split among two or more beneficiaries. Charitable gift annuities, annuity trusts, charitable remainder unitrusts, charitable lead trusts, and pooled (or life) income funds are examples of split-interest agreements. The AAG provides standards for reporting the initial gifts that create these funds and the annual adjustments necessary to report them properly. Accounting for split-interest gifts is a complex area; the following discussion is highly summarized and overly simplified.

Not-for-profit organizations are required to report their interests in irrevocable split-interest agreements. If another party, such as a bank, holds the assets, a not-for-profit organization recognizes its interest as a contribution and measures its interest at fair value, usually based on the present value of the cash flows to be received. If the not-for-profit organization holds the assets and is also a beneficiary of the agreement, it reports the fair value of the assets received from the donor as its assets and reports the actuarially computed present value of the payments to be made to other beneficiaries as its liability. The difference between the two amounts is the contribution received by the not-for-profit organization. Each year thereafter, the liability to the beneficiaries is recomputed based on revaluations of the amounts to be paid, the expected lives of the beneficiaries, and other relevant actuarial assumptions.

The net assets resulting from most split-interest agreements are classified as temporarily restricted because they are subject to time restrictions and purpose restrictions. The net assets are time-restricted either because the distributions are not yet due (when amounts are held by a third party) or because the contribution amount cannot be used by the not-for-profit organization until the death of the beneficiary or some other future specified date. However, the net assets are classified as permanently restricted if the donor has permanently restricted the organization's use of the assets. (For example, the donor requires that the not-for-profit organization use the remaining assets to create a permanent endowment fund at the end of the agreement.) Similarly, if upon the establishment of the agreement the organization can immediately spend the contribution portion without restriction, as is the case for some gift annuities, the net assets would be classified as unrestricted.

Revocable split-interest agreements are not recorded unless the not-for-profit organization holds the assets. Assets received by a not-for-profit organization that acts as trustee under a revocable agreement are recognized as refundable advances at their fair value.

# OIL AND GAS PRODUCERS

## PERSPECTIVE AND ISSUES

Oil and gas producing activities are those activities that involve the acquisition of mineral interests in properties, exploration, development, and production of crude oil, including condensate and natural gas liquids, and natural gas. Specialized GAAP does not address refining, marketing, or transportation issues. The successful efforts method of accounting adheres to a traditional historical cost basis. Property acquisition costs, whether the property is proved or unproved, are capitalized as incurred. For other costs incurred under this method, a direct relationship between the costs incurred and specific reserves discovered is required before costs are permitted to be capitalized. Under the successful efforts method, costs that cannot be directly related to the discovery of specific oil and gas reserves are expensed immediately as incurred, analogous to research and development. Oil and gas producing companies are also subject to the requirements of FAS 143 regarding the recognition of asset retirement obligations.

The use of the successful efforts method is preferred, but not required by GAAP. An oil and gas producing company is permitted to use, as an alternative to the successful efforts method, a prescribed form of the full cost method permitted by the SEC. All enterprises are required to disclose the method used for accounting for costs incurred and the method of disposition used for capitalized costs. The SEC requires additional disclosures for publicly traded companies and also provides guidance (SAB 106) on ensuring that the expected cash flows associated with asset retirement obligations are not double-counted in making computations under the full cost method.

For an enterprise that uses the full cost method of accounting, assets being depreciated, depleted, or amortized are considered to be in use in the earning activities of the enterprise and, consequently, do not qualify for interest capitalization. However, assets employed in ongoing exploration or development activities but that are not yet engaged in earning activities and not presently being depreciated, depleted or amortized, are subject to interest capitalization.

Exploratory wells or tests that are in progress at the end of the period present unique accounting issues. If, subsequent to the end of the period, but before the financial statements are issued, a well or test is found to be unsuccessful, the incurred costs, less salvage value, are expensed. Retroactively restated financial statements are not permitted.

| Sources of GAAP | | | |
|---|---|---|---|
| *FAS* | *FIN* | *FSP* | *SAB* |
| 19, 25, 69, 144 | 33, 36 | FAS 19-1, FAS 142-2 | 106 |

## CONCEPTS, RULES, AND EXAMPLES

The following is a discussion of the recommended treatment of oil and gas activities as per FAS 19. (Note that this treatment is recommended, but not required.)

The costs of the special types of assets used in oil and gas producing activities are capitalized when incurred. Some examples include

1. Mineral interests in properties

   a. Unproved—Properties with no proved reserves
   b. Proved—Properties with proved reserves

2. Wells and related equipment and facilities
3. Support equipment and facilities
4. Uncompleted wells, equipment, and facilities

Costs associated with drilling exploratory wells or exploratory-type stratigraphic wells are capitalized until it is determined that the well has proved reserves at which time the capitalized costs are reclassified to wells and related equipment and facilities. If, however, proved reserves are not found, the capitalized drilling costs of the well are charged to expense. When drilling is completed if it is determined that the well has reserves but those reserves cannot be classified as proved, the reporting enterprise will continue to capitalize drilling costs if (1) the reserves found are sufficient to justify completion of the well as a producing well and, (2) the reporting enterprise is making sufficient progress assessing the reserves and the economic and operating viability of the project.

These costs are amortized as reserves are produced and, along with lifting (production) costs, are classified as costs of production. Periodically, unproved properties are evaluated for impairment. The impairment model used for drilling and mineral rights is not the same model set forth in FAS 142 for intangible assets, but rather, is based on the level of established reserves (FSP FAS 142-2). If impaired, a loss is recognized.

Acquisition costs incurred to obtain oil and gas properties through purchase, lease, etc., are capitalized.

Geological and geophysical costs, unproved properties' carrying costs, and the costs of dry hole and bottom hole contributions are expensed. Drilling costs are capitalized until a determination has been made as to the success of the well. If successful, these costs are transferred to uncompleted wells, related equipment, and facilities. The cost of drilling, less residual value, is charged to expense if proved reserves are not found.

Development costs are incurred in order to

1. Get access to and prepare well locations
2. Drill and equip development wells
3. Set up production facilities
4. Provide better recovery systems

These costs are capitalized as uncompleted equipment and facilities until drilling or construction is completed.

The cost of support equipment is capitalized and depreciated. This depreciation, along with other operating costs, is allocated to exploration, development, or production costs, as appropriate.

Production involves different costs ranging from lifting to field storage. These costs, together with depreciation, depletion, and amortization of capitalized acquisition, exploration, and development costs, are part of the cost of the oil and gas produced.

Unproved properties are reclassified to proved properties upon discovery of proved reserves. When proved reserves are found, the costs capitalized as uncompleted wells, equipment, and facilities are reclassified as completed wells, equipment, and facilities. Capitalized costs are amortized or depleted by the unit of production method. Estimated residual values must be considered when determining amortization and depreciation rates.

Any information that becomes available between the end of the period and the date when the financial statements are issued is to be considered in the evaluation of conditions existing at the balance sheet date. With respect to the costs of a company's wells, related equipment, facilities, and the costs of related proved properties, the provisions for impairment as outlined in FAS 144 are applicable.

# RECORDING AND MUSIC

## PERSPECTIVE AND ISSUES

FAS 50 sets forth accounting and reporting standards for the recording and music industry. In this industry, business is transacted through license agreements, contractual arrangements entered into by an owner (licensor) of a music master or copyright. License agreements are modifications of the compulsory provisions of the copyright law. The licensor grants the licensee the right to sell or distribute recordings or sheet music for a fixed fee paid to the licensor or for a fee based on sales. This section presents the proper accounting by both the licensor and the licensee for license agreements in the recording and music industry.

The industry is currently attempting to adapt its business models for copyright protection, product distribution, and artist compensation to new electronic distribution channels. The new business models that inevitably evolve may require additional accounting guidance.

| Sources of GAAP |
| :---: |
| *FAS* |
| 50 |

## DEFINITIONS OF TERMS

**Advance royalty.** An amount paid to music publishers, producers, songwriters, or other artists in advance of their earning royalties from recording or sheet music sales. These amounts are based on contractual terms and are generally nonrefundable.

**License agreements.** Contractual arrangements entered into by an owner (licensor) of a master or music copyright and a licensee that grant the licensee the right to sell or distribute recordings or sheet music for a fixed fee paid to the licensor or for a fee based on sales.

**Minimum guarantee.** An amount paid in advance by a licensee to a licensor for the right to sell or distribute recordings or sheet music.

**Recording (or record) master.** The master tape resulting from the performance of the artist. It is used to produce tapes for use in making cartridges, cassettes, and compact discs.

**Royalties.** Amounts paid to producers, songwriters, or other artists for their participation in making recordings and to sheet music publishers for their copyright interest in music.

## CONCEPTS, RULES, AND EXAMPLES

### Accounting by Licensors

**Revenues.** A license agreement is considered an outright sale when the licensor has

1. Signed a noncancelable contract
2. Agreed to accept a specified fee
3. Transferred the music rights to the licensee, who is able to use them
4. Fulfilled all significant duties owed the licensee

When all of these conditions are met, the earnings process is complete and revenue is recognized if there is reasonable assurance that the license fee is fully collectible.

In some cases the licensee pays a minimum guarantee, which is an amount paid in advance to a licensor for the right to sell or distribute recordings or sheet music. A minimum guarantee is first recorded by the licensor as a liability and then amortized to income as the license fee is earned. If the amount of the fee that is earned is indeterminable, then straight-line recognition of revenue from the guarantee is required over the license period.

**Example**

A licensor receives a $10,000 minimum guarantee under a five-year license agreement. The entry to record the receipt of cash is

| | | |
|---|---|---|
| Cash | 10,000 | |
|     Liability under license agreement | | 10,000 |

The licensor recognizes revenue from the guarantee on a straight-line basis. At the end of each year of the license period, the licensor records the following entry:

| | | |
|---|---|---|
| Liability under license agreement | 2,000 | |
|     License fees earned (revenue) | | 2,000 |

A licensor may charge fees for such items as free recordings beyond a certain number given away by a recording club. The amount of such fees is not determinable when the license agreement is made. Therefore, the licensor can recognize revenue only when the amount can be reasonably estimated or when the license agreement expires.

**Cost of artist compensation.** Royalties are paid to producers, songwriters, or other artists for their participation in making recordings and to music publishers for their copyright interest in music. Amounts for artists are determined by the terms of personal service contracts negotiated between the artists and media companies and usually are determined based upon a percentage of sales activity and license fee income, adjusted for estimated sales returns. Publishing royalties are generally based on copyright or other applicable laws. Royalties are recorded as a period expense of the licensor.

Advance royalties are amounts paid to music publishers, producers, songwriters, or other artists in advance of their earning royalties. Such royalties are based on contractual terms and are generally nonrefundable. Advance royalties are recorded as assets if the licensor expects that the artist's recording will be successful enough to provide for full recovery of the advance from future royalties due the artist. As royalties are subsequently earned by the artist, the capitalized advance is charged to expense. The advance must be apportioned between current and noncurrent assets according to how soon each portion is expected to be charged to expense. If it later appears that the advance will not be fully recovered from subsequent royalties earned by the artist, then the unrecoverable portion is charged to expense in the period in which the loss becomes apparent.

**Cost to produce masters.** A master is the media that contains the recording of the artist's performance. The costs of producing a master include (1) the cost of the musical talent (musicians, vocal background, and arrangements); (2) the cost of the technical talent for engineering, directing, and mixing; (3) costs for the use of the equipment to record and produce the master; and (4) studio facility charges. Under the standard type of artist contract, the media company bears a portion of the costs and recovers a portion of the cost from the artist out of designated royalties earned. However, either party may contractually agree to bear all or most of the cost.

The portion of the cost that is paid by the media company is recorded as an asset if the company expects that sales of the artist's recording will be successful enough to provide for full recovery of the accumulated costs. If this is not the case, then these costs are expensed. Any amount capitalized is amortized over the useful life of the recording in a manner that relates the costs to estimated net revenue to be realized. Costs to produce masters that are recoverable from the artist's royalties are treated as advanced royalties by the media company.

## Accounting by Licensees

When a licensee pays a minimum guarantee in advance, the guarantee is recorded as an asset and then amortized to expense according to the terms specified in the license agreement. If it later appears that the minimum guarantee is not fully recoverable through use of the rights received under the agreement, then the unrecoverable portion is charged to expense.

Fees for which the amount is indeterminable before the agreement expires are sometimes stipulated in the license agreement. An example is a fee charged to a recording club for free recordings beyond a certain number given away. The licensee must estimate the amount of such fees and accrue them on a license-by-license basis.

# REGULATED OPERATIONS

## PERSPECTIVE AND ISSUES

Although various businesses are subject to regulatory oversight to greater or lesser degrees, as used in GAAP the term regulated operations refers primarily to public utilities, whose ability to set selling prices for the goods or services they offer is constrained by government actions. Generally, the regulatory process has been designed to permit such enterprises to recover the costs they incur, plus a reasonable rate of return to stockholders. However, given the political process of rate-setting by regulatory authorities, and the fact that costs such as those for plant construction have escalated, the ability to recover all costs through rate increases has become less certain. For this and other reasons, specialized GAAP has been promulgated.

| Sources of GAAP | | |
|---|---|---|
| *FAS* | *FTB* | *EITF* |
| 71, 90, 92, 98, 101, 143, 144 | 87-2 | 92-7, 92-12, 93-4, 97-4 |

## CONCEPTS, RULES, AND EXAMPLES

These accounting principles apply to regulated enterprises only if they continue to meet certain criteria, which relate to the intended ability to recover all costs through the rate-setting process. When and if these conditions are no longer met, due to deregulation or a shift to rate-setting which is not based on cost recovery, then application of the specialized GAAP is to terminate.

## Asset Recognition

If certain costs are not recognized for current rate-setting purposes, but it is probable that the costs will be recovered through future revenue, then these costs can be capitalized even though a nonregulated enterprise would be required to expense these costs currently. Deferred costs can include an imputed cost of equity capital, if so accounted for rate-setting purposes, even though this would not normally be permitted under GAAP. Thus, the regulatory process can result in the accounting recognition of an asset that would not otherwise be recognized by a commercial enterprise. If at any time it becomes apparent that the incurred cost will not be recovered through generation of future revenue, that cost is to be charged to expense. If a regulator subsequently excludes specific costs from allowable costs, the carrying value of the asset recognized is to be reduced to the extent of the excluded costs. Should the regulator allow recovery of these previously excluded costs or any additional costs, a new asset is to be recognized and classified as if these costs had been initially included in allowable costs.

## Imposition of Liabilities

In other situations, the regulatory process can result in the accounting recognition of a liability. This usually occurs when regulators mandate that refunds be paid to customers, which must be accrued when probable and reasonably estimable, per FAS 5, *Accounting for Contingencies.* Furthermore, regulatory rates may be set at a higher level, in order to recover costs expected to be incurred in the future, subject to the caveat that such amounts will be refunded to customers if it later becomes apparent that actual costs incurred were less than expected. In such cases, the incremental rate increase related to recovery of future costs must be accounted for as a liability (unearned revenue), until the condition specified is satisfied. Finally, regulators may stipulate that a gain realized by the utility will be returned to customers over a specified future period; this will be accounted for by accrual of a liability rather than by recognition of the gain for accounting purposes.

## Phase-in Plans

Special rules apply to phase-in plans, as defined in FAS 92, *Regulated Enterprises— Accounting for Phase-in Plans.* If a phase-in plan was ordered by regulators for a plant that had been substantially constructed before 1988, then all allowable costs which are deferred for regulatory purposes, subject to the phase-in plan, are also deferred for financial reporting purposes. However, the imputed cost of capital permitted by regulators (in effect, interest on the deferred costs) cannot be capitalized for financial reporting. Specific criteria must be met in order to utilize phase-in accounting, and the method cannot be employed for plants not constructed until after 1987.

## Abandonment

Accounting for abandonments is also stipulated for regulated enterprises. If an abandonment occurs or becomes probable, any costs which are probable of not being recovered are required to be written off as a loss. Furthermore, if the return on the investment that will be recoverable will not be equal to the normal rate of return, then an additional loss accrual must be recognized currently. This loss is measured by the difference between the projected future revenues, discounted at the enterprise's incremental borrowing rate, and the remaining costs to be recovered. The amount of loss to be recognized obviously depends on the enterprise's estimate of time to elapse until rate increases are effective, and the length of time over which the increases will remain in effect. These estimates may change over time, and the effect of revisions in the estimate will be reflected in earnings in the periods the new estimates are made.

The carrying value of the costs of an abandoned plant is increased during the period from the abandonment until recovery occurs through rate increases as promised by the regulatory authorities. If full return of investment is anticipated, the cost of abandoned assets is accreted at the rate (the enterprise's overall cost of capital) permitted for rate-setting purposes. If partial or no return on investment is expected, the asset value is accreted at the same rate that was used to compute the loss accrual, which is the enterprise's incremental borrowing rate. During the recovery period, the costs of the abandoned plant are amortized. If full return on investment is expected, this amortization is to be computed on the same basis as is permitted for rate-setting purposes. If partial or no return is expected, amortization is recognized in amounts that provide a constant rate of return on the unamortized balance of the investment in the costs of the abandoned plant.

## Accounting for Liabilities Related to Asset Retirement Obligations

Historically, and particularly since the advent of nuclear energy generation, public utilities have faced the problem of accounting for costs which are expected to be incurred attendant upon the retirement from service of the generating facilities. Environmental and other laws and regulations typically mean that very substantial costs have to be borne, in order to dispose of waste, restore the land (not merely the power generating facility site, but, in the case of coal-fired plants, restoration of the strip mining locations) and ameliorate other problems. These issues are addressed by FAS 143, *Asset Retirement Obligations.*

Chapter 11 presents a detailed examination of FAS 143, and that discussion is not duplicated here. In brief, this pronouncement establishes standards for measuring the future cost to retire an asset and recognizing it in the financial statements as a liability and correspondingly, as part of the depreciable cost of the asset. FAS 143 applies to legal obligations associated with the retirement of tangible long-lived assets that result from their acquisition, construction, development and/or normal operation. It does not apply to situations where moral suasion is to be applied to encourage cleanup efforts, even if the reporting entity has a history of making such voluntary gestures. However, the principle of "promissory estoppel" does create legal obligations even absent contractual or statutory requirements, in some cases.

If costs, such as those related to nuclear decommissioning, are legal obligations, the present value of the future expenditures is recognized as an added cost of the asset, and as a liability, at acquisition. Further cost accretion is required due to the passage of time. Depreciation charges are based on the recorded cost of the asset, including the estimated future retirement costs. Changes in estimates, which are inevitable, are handled differently if they are increases versus decreases, as described in Chapter 11.

## Accounting for Asset Impairments

While not unique to regulated industries (public utilities, in particular), the issue of asset impairment will often be dealt with in these operations, due to the large investment in very long-lived fixed assets and the potential impact of changes in technology over time. FAS 144 addresses this issue. Briefly, under defined conditions, assets must be reviewed to determine whether their carrying value will be fully recovered from future cash flows from using and disposing of them. If the future estimate of cash flows over the asset's (or group of assets') remaining estimated useful life, undiscounted, is less than the carrying value, the asset is considered impaired, and the carrying value is reduced to the fair value of the asset with the impairment loss being charged to expense in the current period. Typically, a projected cash flows approach is used in estimating value, although in some instances a more direct approach, relying on market prices, might be usable. FAS 144 is discussed in detail in Chapter 11.

## Accounting for Deregulation and "Stranded Costs"

In recent years the utilities industries have undergone varying degrees of deregulation. This will have significant effects on the financial reporting of many of the entities operating in these industries, since under GAAP many had recognized regulatory assets and regulatory liabilities which will no longer be recognizable once full deregulation occurs. Also, certain costs may no longer be recoverable in a deregulated environment, transforming certain assets into "stranded costs."

A consensus in EITF 97-4 has addressed the matter of deregulation. When deregulation legislation has been enacted affecting all or a portion of the entity's operations, it is to cease applying FAS 71 to the affected operations. In cases in which the effects of deregulation are imposed by means of a rate order, such an order would have to be sufficiently detailed so that the entity would be able to determine how it will be affected. Regulatory assets would not, however, be immediately written off; instead, an evaluation of regulatory cash flows would be conducted to determine whether an impairment had occurred and to determine whether the portion of the business from which the regulatory cash flows are derived is still subject to FAS 71. Only if the asset is impaired (applying FAS 144 criteria) or if FAS 71 is no longer applicable would the asset be written off before being recovered. Similarly, regulatory liabilities would not be reclassified into income until the obligation is eliminated by the regulatory authority.

A related concern is whether the new regulatory assets or liabilities must be given recognition to reflect expenses and obligations that will arise from the portion of the business being deregulated. The same "source of cash flow" type of analysis noted above is to be applied to make these determinations. Thus, a cost or obligation is recognized as a regulatory asset or liability, respectively, once it is expensed or incurred after FAS 101 is applied to that portion of the operations, if it has been designated for recovery or settlement, respectively, via regulated cash flows.

### Other Accounting Guidance

In EITF 91-6 a consensus was reached that Nonutility Generators (NUG) are to recognize the lesser of (1) the amount billable under the contract or (2) a formula-based pricing arrangement, as revenue. The formula-based pricing arrangement is determined by the kilowatt-hours (kwhs) made available during the period multiplied by the estimated average revenue per kwh over the term of the contract for the fixed or scheduled price period of the contract. Revenue is not to be recognized utilizing the formula-based pricing arrangement if its only purpose is to establish liquidating damages. Additionally, a receivable arises when the amounts billed are less than the amount computed pursuant to the formula-based pricing arrangement and if the contract requires a payment, probable of recovery, to the NUG at the end of the contract term.

EITF 92-7 addresses the treatment of additional revenues of rate-regulated utility companies that are to be billed in the future under alternative revenue programs. The EITF abstract identifies two types of alternative revenue programs, defined as Type A and Type B. The revenues from alternative revenue programs are to be recognized when the events permitting billing of the revenues have occurred and three specific criteria that are discussed in the abstract are met.

Also, rate-regulated utilities recognizing revenues from an alternative revenue program that do not meet the conditions of this consensus must amend the plan or change the program to meet the conditions.

In EITF 92-12, it was held that, if the regulator includes other postemployment benefits, (OPEB), costs in rates on a pay-as-you-go basis, the regulatory asset relating to the cost under FAS 106 is not to be recognized. Further, the regulatory asset for a rate-regulated enterprise is to recognize the difference between FAS 106 costs and the OPEB costs if future revenue will at least offset the deferred cost and meet four specific criteria, which are discussed in the EITF.

Regarding the accounting for regulatory assets, EITF 93-4 determined that a rate-regulated enterprise that fails to initially meet the asset recognition criteria can recognize a regulatory asset for other postemployment benefits costs in a future period when applicable criteria are met. This consensus applies also to all regulatory assets recognized pursuant to FAS 71 criteria.

Additionally, it was noted that the carrying amount of the regulatory asset to be recognized is to be reduced by any impairment that may have occurred.

The consensus of EITF 91-6 was extended by EITF 96-17. Fixed price arrangements are to be handled in accordance with EITF 91-6. Variable price arrangements in which the rate is at least equal to expected costs are to recognize revenue as billed, in accordance with the provisions of the contract for that variable price period. A long-term power sales contract is to be reviewed periodically to determine whether it is a loss contract, in which case the loss is to be recognized immediately. Finally, any premium related to a contractual rate in excess of the current market rate is to be amortized over the remaining portion of the contract for long-term power sales contracts acquired in a purchase business combination.

# TITLE PLANT

## PERSPECTIVE AND ISSUES

FAS 61, *Accounting for Title Plant*, presents accounting and reporting standards for costs relating to the construction and operation of title plants. A title plant comprises a record of all transactions or conditions that affect titles to land located in a specified area. The length of time spanned by a title plant depends upon regulatory requirements and the time frame required to gather sufficient information to efficiently issue title insurance. Updating occurs frequently as documentation of the current status of a title is added to the title plant.

This pronouncement applies to enterprises such as title insurance companies, title abstract companies, and title agents that use a title plant in their operations. The standard provides that costs directly incurred to construct a title plant are to be capitalized when the entity can use the title plant to do title searches and that such capitalized costs are not normally depreciated. The statement also requires that the costs of maintaining a title plant and of doing title searches be expensed as incurred.

| Sources of GAAP |
| :---: |
| *FAS* |
| 61, 144 |

## DEFINITIONS OF TERMS

**Title plant.** Consists of (1) indexed and catalogued information for a period concerning the ownership of, and encumbrances on, parcels of land in a particular geographic area; (2) information relating to persons having an interest in real estate; (3) maps and plats; (4) copies of prior title insurance contracts and reports; and (5) other documents and records. In summary, a title plant constitutes a historical record of all matters affecting title to parcels of land in a particular geographic area.

## CONCEPTS, RULES, AND EXAMPLES

### Acquisition Costs

The cost of constructing a title plant includes the cost of obtaining, organizing, and summarizing historical information pertaining to a particular tract of land. Costs incurred to assemble a title plant are to be capitalized until the record is usable for conducting title searches. Costs incurred to construct a backplant (a title plant that predates the time span of an existing title plant) must also be capitalized. However, an enterprise may capitalize only those costs that are directly related to and traceable to the activities performed in constructing the title plant or backplant.

The purchase of a title plant or backplant, or an undivided interest therein (the right to its joint use) is recorded at cost as of the date acquired. If the title plant is acquired separately, it is recorded at the fair value of consideration given.

Capitalized title plant costs are not amortized or depreciated unless an impairment in the carrying amount of the title plant occurs. The following events or changes in circumstances can indicate that the carrying amount may not be recoverable. An impairment may be indicated by the following circumstances (not intended to be an exhaustive list):

1. Changing legal or statutory requirements
2. Economic factors, such as changing demand
3. Loss of competitive advantage
4. Failure to maintain an up-to-date title plant
5. Circumstances that indicate obsolescence, such as abandonment of title plant

The provisions of FAS 144 apply to any such impairment. See Chapter 11 for a complete discussion of this topic.

### Operating Costs

Costs of title plant maintenance and of conducting title searches are required to be expensed currently. A title plant is maintained through frequent, often daily, updating which involves adding reports on the current status of specific real estate titles and documentation of security or other ownership interests in such land. A title search entails a search for all information or documentation pertaining to a particular parcel of land. This information is found in the most recently issued title report.

Once a title plant is operational, costs may be incurred to convert the record from one storage and retrieval system to another or to modify the current storage and retrieval system. These costs may not be capitalized as title plant. However, they may be separately capitalized and amortized using a systematic and rational method.

### Reporting Title Plant Sales

The sale of a title plant is to be reported separately. The amount to be reported is determined by the circumstances surrounding the sale as follows:

| *Terms of sale* | *Amount reported* |
| --- | --- |
| Sale of title plant and waiver of all rights to future use | Amount received less adjusted cost of title plant |
| Sale of undivided ownership interest (rights to future joint use) | Amount received less pro rata portion of adjusted cost of title plant |
| Sales of copies of title plant or the right to use it | Amount received |

Note that in the last instance the amount reported is simply the amount received. In this case, no cost is allocated to the item sold unless the title plant's value drops below its adjusted cost as a result of the sale.

# APPENDIX A

## DISCLOSURE CHECKLIST FOR COMMERCIAL BUSINESSES

The disclosure checklist presented below provides a quick reference to those disclosures that are common to the financial statements of most commercial business enterprises. Selected references to items required by the SEC, for public companies only, are also incorporated as many private company financial statement preparers believe these to be "best practices" to be emulated, but this checklist does not purport to be suitable for use as a comprehensive SEC disclosure checklist, nor is it designed to be used for reporting entities that are not-for-profit organizations, state or local governments, or that are engaged in other industries that are subject to specialized accounting and reporting rules.

*Notes to the Financial Statement Preparer:*

FAS 141(R), *Business Combinations,* and FAS 160, *Noncontrolling Interests in Consolidated Financial Statements,* are to become effective for fiscal years, and interim periods within those fiscal years, beginning on or after December 15, 2008, with early adoption prohibited. Due to the pervasiveness of the disclosure required by these standards and the fact that they will be effective shortly after the expected release of this publication, these have been included in the accompanying checklist.

The most effective way to use this checklist to document the preparer's thought process is to use a standardized tickmark or letter key such as the following:

✓– Disclosure made;  IM– Disclosure considered and judged to be immaterial;
NA– Disclosure not applicable  X– Disclosure not made (For each item marked X, append an explanation)

## CONTENTS

## GENERAL

### A.  Basis of Reporting

1.  Name of entity for which statements are being presented (if d/b/a different name than legal name, indicate both).

2.  Titles of statements should be appropriate (certain titles denote and should be reserved for GAAP financial statements; other titles denote other comprehensive basis of accounting [OCBOA] financial statements).

3.  Dates and periods covered should be clearly stated.

4.  If one or more consolidated subsidiaries have different fiscal periods than the parent (not to exceed 3 months), disclose any intervening events that materially affect financial position or results of operations.

5.  If comparative statements are presented, repeat footnotes from prior years to extent appropriate.

6.  Differences between "economic" entity and legal entity being presented should be noted (e.g., consolidated or not? subsidiaries included and excluded, combined statements?, etc.)  Disclose summarized financial information for previously unconsolidated subsidiaries.

7.  Identify new accounting principles not yet adopted and expected impact of adoption.

**B.  Accounting Policies**

*Chapter 5 includes a listing of accounting policies frequently disclosed by reporting entities (the listing is not intended to be all-inclusive)*

1.  Description of business unless otherwise apparent from statements themselves.     _____
2.  Identify and describe significant accounting principles followed and methods of applying them that materially affect statements; disclosures should include principles and methods that involve

   a.  Selection from acceptable alternatives.     _____
   b.  Principles and methods peculiar to the company's industry.     _____
   c.  Unusual or innovative applications of generally accepted accounting principles.     _____
   d.  Consolidation or combination policy.     _____

3.  If there have been any material changes in classifications made to previously issued financial statements, these should be noted.     _____

**C.  Accounting Changes**

1.  Nature and justification of change in accounting principle.     _____

   a.  The nature of and reasons for making the change, addressing preferability of the newly adopted principle.     _____
   b.  Descriptions of prior period items that have been restated.     _____
   c.  The effects of the change for both current period and prior period(s) being presented; specific quantification of the effects on income from continuing operations, net income, any other financial statement caption materially affected, and corresponding per share amounts for each.     _____
   d.  The cumulative effect on retained earnings at the beginning of the earliest period's financial statements presented.     _____
   e.  If FAS 154 requirement to restate prior periods is not adhered to, based on impracticability criterion, explain and provide details regarding method of accounting applied.     _____
   f.  When indirect effects of change in accounting principle are included, describe these effects and state the amounts recognized in the current reporting period, together with per share amounts.  If possible, also state the indirect effects of the change in each of the prior periods being presented.     _____

2.  For change in reporting entity, nature of change and reason for it; also, effect of change on income before extraordinary items and net income for all periods presented (also per share amounts).     _____
3.  For a change in entity not having material effect currently but anticipated to have such effect in later periods, the nature of the change and reason the change was made.     _____
4.  For a change in accounting estimate, if the change affects several future periods (e.g., for change in useful lives of fixed assets), disclose the effect on income from continuing operations and net income of current period (and related per share amounts).     _____
5.  For a change in estimate not having material effect in the current period, but which is deemed likely to have material effects on later periods, describe the change.     _____
6.  For the correction of an error, disclose the nature of the error in previously issued statements and the effect of its correction on income before extraordinary items and net income (only in period of discovery and correction), with per share equivalents.     _____

**D.   Related Parties**

1.   Nature of relationship and amounts due to or from related parties with significant terms and manner of settlement.

2.   For each income statement presented, a description of and dollar amounts of transaction, including those to which no or nominal amounts are assigned, as well as guarantees or other terms which are needed for understanding of financial statement impact, and description of any change in terms.

3.   Economic dependency (e.g., major customer, supplier, franchisor, franchisee, distributor, general agent, borrower, or lender) should be described and amount of transactions disclosed.

4.   Nature and extent of related-party leases.

5.   The nature of control relationship, even absent any transactions, of companies under common ownership or management control, if such could lead to operating results or financial position significantly different than what would have resulted if entities were autonomous.

6.   Amount of investments in related parties.

**E.   Contingencies and Commitments**

1.   When accruals are not made because probable loss could not be estimated, describe the nature of the contingency.

2.   Report the upper limit of range of estimates for cases in which lower limit is accrued because no best estimate exists.

3.   The nature of reasonably possible losses and either the estimated amount of the loss or a statement that no estimate is possible.

4.   Describe unasserted claims for which it is both probable that a claim will be asserted, and reasonably possible that an unfavorable outcome will result.

5.   Report events occurring after balance sheet date that may give rise to a loss contingency, either via a footnote or by means of a pro forma presentation.

6.   Gain contingencies may be disclosed (but not accrued), if described such that the likelihood of realization is not overstated.

7.   Disclose about guarantees, including guarantees of the indebtedness of others

   a.   The nature of the guarantee, including the approximate term, how the guarantee arose, and the events or circumstances that would require the guarantor to perform under the guarantee.

   b.   The maximum potential amount of the future payments (undiscounted) that the entity would be required to make, or if the guarantee provides no limitation on future payments, that fact.

   c.   The reasons why the maximum future payments cannot be estimated, if the entity is unable to estimate that amount.

   d.   The current carrying amount of the liability.

   e.   The nature of any recourse provisions that would enable the entity to recover from third parties any amounts paid under the guarantee, and the extent to which the proceeds are expected to cover the amount in b. above.

   f.   A description of any assets (collateral) that can be liquidated to recover amounts paid under the guarantee, and the extent to which the proceeds from liquidation are expected to cover the amount in b. above.

8.   Disclose material commitments and purchase obligations.

9.   Describe any pending renegotiation of government contracts.

10.  Pending litigation in which the entity is involved should be described, with gross potential losses and potential recovery (e.g., from insurance) separately identified.

11.  Tax contingencies or disputes to which the entity is a party should be noted.

12.  Unused letters of credit.

13.  Environmental risks and liabilities should be described.

14. Accounts or notes receivable sold with recourse; other guarantees to repurchase receivables.                                                                                                    _____

15. Unusual purchase or sales commitments.                                              _____

16. Compensated absences or postemployment benefits that cannot be reasonably estimated but that otherwise meet criteria for accrual should be described.                       _____

## F.  Risks and Uncertainties

1. Nature of operations including description of major products, services, principal markets served, locations, and relative importance of operations in various businesses and basis for determination of relative importance (e.g., sales volume, profits, etc.).                                                                                     _____

2. Explanation that the preparation of financial statements requires the use of management's estimates.                                                                             _____

3. Significant estimates used in the determination of the carrying amounts of assets or liabilities or in the disclosure of gain or loss contingencies when, based on information known to management prior to issuance of the financial statements it is at least reasonably possible that the effect on the financial statements of a condition, situation, or set of circumstances existing at the balance sheet date for which an estimate has been made will change in the near term due to one or more future confirming events and the effect of the change would be material to the financial statements. (If the estimate involves a loss contingency covered by FAS 5, include an estimate of the possible loss or range of loss, or state such estimate cannot be made.)                                                                                      _____

4. Vulnerability due to concentrations in the volume of business with a particular customer, supplier, or lender; revenue from particular products or services; available sources of supply of materials, labor, or other inputs; and market or geographic area. (For concentrations of labor subject to collective bargaining agreements, disclose both the percentage of the labor force covered by a collective bargaining agreement and the percentage of the labor force covered by a collective bargaining agreement that will expire within one year. For concentrations of operations located outside of the entity's home country, disclose the carrying amounts of net assets and the geographic areas in which they are located.)                            _____

## G.  Nonmonetary Transactions

1. Nature of transaction.                                                              _____

2. Gain or loss and basis of accounting for assets transferred.                        _____

3. For advertising barter transactions

    a. Amount of revenue and expense recognized from advertising barter transactions.                                                                                  _____

    b. Volume and type of advertising surrendered and received (e.g., number of equivalent pages, broadcast minutes) that was not recognized in the income statement because the fair value was not determinable.

## H.  Subsequent Events

1. Adjust financial statements for conditions existing at balance sheet date.            _____

2. Disclose for conditions subsequent to balance sheet (consider pro forma presentation); examples are: for sale of a bond or capital stock issue, purchase or sale of a business, settlement of litigation when event giving rise to claim occurred subsequent to balance sheet date, loss of plant or inventories as a result of fire or flood, losses on receivables resulting from conditions (such as a customer's major casualty) arising subsequent to balance sheet date, significant net realized and unrealized marketable equity security gains and losses after the date of the financial statements, substantial loans to insiders or affiliates, significant long-term investments, substantial dividends not in the ordinary course of business, loss contingen-

cies arising after the date of the financial statements, or significant foreign currency rate changes after the balance sheet date and their effects on unsettled balances pertaining to foreign currency transactions. _____

**I. Rights and Privileges of Various Equity Securities Outstanding**

1. Show each class separately and any changes during the period.
2. Par value, assigned or stated value should be disclosed. _____
3. Liquidation preferences are to be stated. _____
4. Participations (for preferred classes) are to be disclosed. _____
5. Call, conversion, and exercise data are to be noted. _____
6. Redeemable preferred stock should be described. _____

**J. Business Combinations and Variable Interest Entities (VIEs)**

**Notes to the preparer:**

- Disclosures required by FAS 140 regarding a VIE are to be included in the same note to the financial statements as the information required by this section.
- Information regarding VIEs may be aggregated for similar entities if separate reporting would not provide the user with additional material information.

1. Business combinations *occurring during the reporting period* or after the reporting date but before the financial statements are issued, **including variable interest entities** (VIEs) where the VIE is a business.

    *The acquirer is to disclose the following information for each business combination that occurs during the reporting period*

    a. The name and a description of the acquiree.
    b. The acquisition date. _____
    c. The percentage of voting equity interest acquired. _____
    d. A description of how the acquirer obtained control over the acquiree. _____
    e. The primary reasons for the business combination. _____
    f. The amounts recognized as of the acquisition date for each major class of assets acquired and liabilities assumed. _____
    g. Receivables acquired not subject to AICPA SOP 03-3, *Accounting for Certain Loans or Debt Securities Acquired in a Transfer,* such as trade receivables with repayment terms of one year or less:

    *The following disclosures are to be provided by major class of receivable such as loans, direct finance leases under FAS 13, and any other class of receivables*

    (1) The fair value of the receivables.
    (2) The gross contractual amount of the receivables. _____
    (3) The best estimate at the acquisition date of the contractual cash flows not expected to be collected. _____

    h. Contingent consideration arrangements and indemnification assets

    (1) Amounts recognized as of the acquisition date. _____
    (2) A description of the arrangements and the basis for determining the amount of payment. _____
    (3) An estimate of the range of outcomes (undiscounted) or, if a range cannot be estimated, that fact and the reasons why. _____
    (4) If the maximum amount potentially due under the arrangement is unlimited, the acquirer is to disclose that fact. _____

    i. Assets and liabilities arising from acquiree contingencies

    *The acquirer is permitted to aggregate these disclosures for assets and liabilities that are similar in nature*

   (1) The amounts recognized at the acquisition date or an explanation of why no amount was recognized.     _____

   (2) The nature of recognized and unrecognized contingencies.     _____

   (3) An estimate of the range of outcomes (undiscounted) for contingencies (recognized and unrecognized) or, if a range cannot be estimated, that fact and the reasons why a range cannot be estimated.     _____

j.    Goodwill

   (1) A qualitative description of the factors that make up goodwill recognized (e.g., expected synergies from combining acquiree operations with those of the acquirer, intangible assets that do not qualify for recognition separately from goodwill, or other factors).     _____

   (2) The total amount of goodwill that is expected to be deductible for tax purposes.     _____

   (3) If the assignment of goodwill to reporting units (as required by FAS 142 has not been completed on the financial statements' issuance date, the acquirer is to disclose that fact.     _____

k.    Bargain purchases

   (1) The amount of gain recognized.     _____

   (2) The line item in the income statement in which the gain is recognized.     _____

   (3) A description of the reasons why the transaction resulted in a gain.     _____

l.    Transactions recognized separately from the acquisition of assets and assumption of liabilities in the business combination (e.g., settlement of preexisting acquirer/acquiree relationships, arrangements to compensate employees or former owners of the acquiree for future services, acquirer reimbursements made to the acquiree or its former owners for paying acquisition-related costs of the acquirer)

   (1) A description of each transaction.     _____

   (2) How the acquirer accounted for each transaction.     _____

   (3) The amounts recognized for each transaction and the line item in the financial statements in which each amount is recognized.     _____

   (4) If the transaction effectively settled a preexisting relationship, the method used to determine the settlement amount.     _____

m.    Acquisition-related costs

   (1) The amount recognized as expense and the line item or items in the income statement in which recognized.     _____

   (2) Amount of issuance costs not recognized as an expense and how they were recognized.     _____

n.    Step acquisitions (business combinations achieved in stages)

   (1) The fair value at the acquisition date of the equity interest in the acquiree held by the acquirer immediately preceding the acquisition date.     _____

   (2) The amount of gain or loss recognized from the remeasurement to fair value of the equity interest in the acquiree held by the acquirer prior to the business combination and the line item in the income statement in which that gain or loss is recognized.     _____

o.    Business combinations where the acquirer holds less than 100% of the equity interests of the acquiree at the acquisition date

   (1) The fair value of the noncontrolling interest in the acquiree at the acquisition date.     _____

(2) The valuation technique or techniques used to measure the fair value of the noncontrolling interest and the significant inputs used. _____

p. Acquirers that are public business enterprises (defined in FAS 131 as amended by FSP FAS 126-1)

(1) The amounts of revenue and the net income of the acquiree since the acquisition date included in the consolidated income statement for the reporting period.

(2) The following supplemental pro forma information. _____

*If the acquirer believes disclosure of any of the information required by this section is impractical, the acquirer is to disclose that fact accompanied by an explanation of why management believes this to be the case*

(a) The amounts of revenue and net income of the consolidated entity for the current reporting period as though the acquisition date for all business combinations that occurred during the year had been as of the beginning of the annual reporting period. _____

(b) If comparative financial statements are presented, the revenue and net income of the consolidated entity for the comparable prior reporting period as though the acquisition date for all business combinations that occurred during the current year had occurred as of the beginning of the comparable prior annual reporting period. _____

(3) If the acquirer is required to disclose segment information, the amount of goodwill by reportable segment. _____

q. The primary beneficiary of a VIE that is not a business is to disclose the amount of gain or loss recognized on the initial consolidation of the VIE. _____

r. For business combinations occurring during the reporting period that are deemed immaterial individually but that are considered collectively material, the acquirer is to disclose the information required by items 1f. through 1p. in the aggregate. _____

s. Subsequent business combinations—If the acquisition date of a business combination is after the reporting date but before issuance of the financial statements, the acquirer is to disclose the information required by items 1a. through 1q. unless the initial accounting for the business combination is incomplete at the time the financial statements are issued. If this is the case, the acquirer is to indicate which disclosures it is unable to make and the reasons why. _____

2. Adjustments to current and prior period business combinations, **including variable interest entities** (VIEs) where the VIE is a business

*The following disclosures are to be made for each material business combination or, in the aggregate for individually immaterial business combinations that collectively are material*

a. *Provisional amounts recognized during measurement period*—If the initial accounting for the business combination is incomplete with respect to certain assets, liabilities, noncontrolling interests, or items included in the consideration transferred and the amounts recognized in the financial statements for the business combination are considered to be provisional

(1) The reasons why the initial accounting is incomplete. _____

(2) The assets, liabilities, equity interests, or items included in the consideration transferred for which the initial accounting is incomplete. _____

(3) The nature and amount of any measurement-period adjustments recognized during the reporting period. _____

  b.   *Contingent consideration assets/liabilities*—For each reporting period after the acquisition date until the entity collects, sells, or otherwise loses the right to an asset representing contingent consideration, or until the entity settles a contingent consideration liability or the liability is cancelled or expires

    (1)   Any changes in the recognized amounts, including any difference arising upon settlement.     \_\_\_\_\_

    (2)   Any changes in the range of outcomes (undiscounted) and the reasons for those changes.     \_\_\_\_\_

    (3)   The disclosures required to be made in each interim and annual reporting period by FAS 157, ¶32 regarding recurring fair value measurements subsequent to initial recognition. These disclosures are to be made separately for each major category of assets and liabilities that represents contingent consideration:

      (a)   The fair value measurements at the reporting date.     \_\_\_\_\_

      (b)   The level within the fair value hierarchy in which the fair value measurements fell in their entirety, segregating fair value measurements by classification as Level 1 (using quoted prices in active markets for identical assets or liabilities), Level 2 (using significant other observable inputs), or Level 3 (using significant unobservable inputs).     \_\_\_\_\_

      (c)   For Level 3 fair value measurements, a reconciliation of the beginning and ending balances, separately presenting changes during the period attributable to the following:

        1]   Total gains or losses for the period (realized and unrealized) segregating those gains or losses included in net income and a description of where those gains or losses included in net income are reported in the statement of income     \_\_\_\_\_

          a]   Separate disclosure of the portion attributable to changes in unrealized gains or losses related to those assets and liabilities still held at the reporting date and a description of where those gains or losses are reported in the statement of income.     \_\_\_\_\_

        2]   Purchases, sales, issuances, and settlements (net).     \_\_\_\_\_

        3]   Transfers in and/or out of Level 3 (e.g., due to changes in the observability of inputs significant to the valuation).     \_\_\_\_\_

      (d)   In annual reporting periods only: The valuation techniques used to measure fair value and a discussion of changes in valuation techniques, if any, during the period.     \_\_\_\_\_

  c.   *Acquiree contingencies*—For each reporting period after the acquisition date, until the acquirer collects, sells, or otherwise loses the rights to recognized assets arising from contingencies, or the acquirer settles recognized liabilities or its obligation to settle them is cancelled or expires

    (1)   Any changes in the recognized amounts of assets and liabilities arising from contingencies and the reasons for those changes.     \_\_\_\_\_

    (2)   Any changes in the range of outcomes (undiscounted) for both recognized and unrecognized assets and liabilities arising from contingencies and the reasons for those changes.     \_\_\_\_\_

  d.   *Goodwill reconciliation*—The reconciliation of the carrying amount of goodwill at the beginning and end of the reporting period required by FAS 142, as amended by FAS 141(R) (See *Goodwill and Identifiable Intangibles* under "Balance Sheet" disclosures).     \_\_\_\_\_

3.   Any additional information necessary to meet the overarching disclosure objectives with respect to business combinations, **including variable interest entities** (VIEs) where the VIE is a business, to enable users of the financial statements to

- Evaluate the nature and financial effects of business combinations occurring either during the current reporting period, or after the reporting date but before issuance of the financial statements.
- Evaluate the financial effects of adjustments recognized in the current reporting period that relate to business combinations that occurred in the current or previous reporting periods.

4.   Disclosures to be made by the primary beneficiary of a variable interest entity (unless that party also holds a majority voting interest)

a.   The nature, purpose, size, and activities of the VIE.
b.   The carrying amount and classification of consolidated assets that are collateral for the VIE's obligations.
c.   Any lack of recourse by creditors (or beneficial interest holders) of a consolidated VIE to the general credit of the primary beneficiary.

5.   Disclosures to be made by an enterprise that holds a significant variable interest in a VIE but is *not* the primary beneficiary

a.   The nature of its involvement with the VIE and when that involvement began.
b.   The nature, purpose, size, and activities of the VIE.
c.   The enterprise's maximum exposure to loss as a result of its involvement with the VIE.

6.   An enterprise that does not apply FIN 46(R) to one or more VIE or potential VIE because after exhaustive efforts it is unable to obtain the necessary information is to make the following disclosures:

a.   The number of entities to which FIN 46(R) is not being applied and the reason why the information required to apply FIN 46(R) is not available.
b.   The nature, purpose, size (if the information is available), and activities of the VIE or potential VIE and the nature of the enterprise's involvement with those entities.
c.   The enterprise's maximum exposure to loss as a result of its involvement with the entity or entities.
d.   The amount of income, expense, purchases, sales, or other measure of activity between the reporting enterprise and the entity (entities) for all periods presented. (If not practicable to present the prior period information in the first set of financial statements to which this requirement applies, that prior period information may be omitted.)

## K.   Consolidations

1.   A parent with one or more less-than-wholly-owned subsidiaries is to disclose for each reporting period

a.   Separately on the face of the consolidated financial statements, the amounts of consolidated net income and consolidated comprehensive income and the related amounts of each attributable to the parent and the noncontrolling interest.
b.   Either on the face of the consolidated income statement or in the notes, amounts attributable to the parent for the following items, if reported in the consolidated financial statements

      (1)  Income from continuing operations.     \_\_\_\_\_

      (2)  Discontinued operations.     \_\_\_\_\_

      (3)  Extraordinary items.     \_\_\_\_\_

  c.  Either in the consolidated statement of changes in equity if presented, or in the notes, a reconciliation of beginning of period and end of period carrying amounts of total equity, equity attributable to the parent, and equity attributable to the noncontrolling interest separately disclosing

      (1)  Net income.     \_\_\_\_\_

      (2)  Transactions with owners acting in their capacity as owners, separately showing contributions and distributions.     \_\_\_\_\_

      (3)  Each component of other comprehensive income.     \_\_\_\_\_

  d.  A separate schedule in the notes to the consolidated financial statements showing the effects of any changes in the parent's ownership interest in a subsidiary on the equity attributable to the parent.     \_\_\_\_\_

2.  If a subsidiary is deconsolidated during the reporting period, the parent is to disclose

  a.  The amount of gain or loss recognized.     \_\_\_\_\_

  b.  The caption in the income statement in which the gain or loss is recognized unless presented separately on the face of the income statement.     \_\_\_\_\_

  c.  The portion of any gain or loss that relates to the remeasurement to fair value of any investment retained by the former parent in its former subsidiary.     \_\_\_\_\_

**L.  Collaborative Arrangements**—In the initial interim or annual period and all annual periods thereafter, a participant to a collaborative arrangement (EITF 07-1) is to disclose the following information. This information is to be disclosed separately for each individually significant collaborative arrangement

1.  Information regarding the nature and purpose of its collaborative arrangements.     \_\_\_\_\_

2.  The entity's rights and obligations under the arrangements.     \_\_\_\_\_

3.  The accounting policy for collaborative arrangements.     \_\_\_\_\_

4.  The amounts attributable to transactions arising from the collaborative arrangement between participants for each period an income statement is presented and their classification in the income statement.     \_\_\_\_\_

5.  Upon initial application of 07-1, the following is to be disclosed:

  a.  A description of the prior period information that was retrospectively adjusted, if any.     \_\_\_\_\_

  b.  The effect of the change on revenue and operating expenses (or other appropriate captions of changes in the applicable net assets, and on any other affected financial statement line item.     \_\_\_\_\_

**M.  Fair Value and the Fair Value Option**

**Notes to the preparer:**

- While not required, preparers are encouraged to combine the disclosures associated with FAS 157 and 159 with fair value disclosures required by other pronouncements such as FAS 107, FAS 115, APB 18, FAS 133, FAS 155, etc.

- Unless otherwise indicated, the disclosures included in this section are required to be presented in interim and annual financial statements.

Disclosures required to be made separately for each major category of assets and liabilities measured at fair value on a recurring basis in periods subsequent to initial recognition.

1.  The amount of the fair value measurements at the reporting date.     \_\_\_\_\_

2. The level within the fair value hierarchy in which the fair value measurements fall within their entirety; separately disclosing the amounts of fair value measurements that use quoted prices in active markets for identical assets or liabilities (Level 1), significant other observable inputs (Level 2), and significant unobservable inputs (Level 3).

3. For those fair value measurements using significant unobservable (Level 3) inputs, a reconciliation of the beginning and ending balances, separately stating changes during the period attributable to[1]

    a. Total realized and unrealized gains or losses for the period segregating those gains or losses included in income (changes in net assets) and a description of where those gains or losses are reported in the statement of income (statement of activities)

        (1) The unrealized gains or losses included in this disclosure that relate to assets and liabilities still held at the balance sheet date.

        (2) A description of where, in the statement of income, those unrealized gains or losses are reported.

    b. Purchases, sales, issuances, and settlements (net).

    c. Transfers in and/or out of Level 3 (e.g., due to changes in the observability of significant inputs).

4. In the first interim period of the fiscal year of adoption and subsequently in annual financial statements, the valuation techniques used to measure fair value and discussion of changes in valuation techniques, if any, during the period.

Separate disclosures required for each major category of assets and liabilities measured at fair value on a nonrecurring basis in periods subsequent to initial recognition.

5. Fair value measurements recorded during the period and the reasons for the measurements.

6. The level within the fair value hierarchy in which the fair value measurements fall; in their entirety; separately disclosing the amounts of fair value measurements in Level 1, Level 2, and Level 3.

7. For Level 3 fair value measurements, a description of the inputs and the information used to develop them.

8. In the first interim period of the fiscal year of adoption and subsequently in annual financial statements, the valuation techniques used to measure fair value and a discussion of changes in valuation techniques used to measure similar assets and/or liabilities in prior periods.

9. Any entity that has not applied the provisions of FAS 157 in interim or annual financial statements is to disclose the following until that Statement is applied in its entirety to all assets and liabilities within its scope:

    a. The fact that, pursuant to the deferral provided by FSP FAS 157-2 for certain nonfinancial assets and nonfinancial liabilities, except those that are recognized or disclosed at fair value in the financial statements on a recurring basis (at least annually), the entity has only partially applied FAS 157.

    b. Each major category of assets and liabilities that are recognized or disclosed at fair value for which the entity has not applied the provisions of FAS 157.

Fair Value Option (FVO) disclosures required by FAS 159

*Disclosures required as of each interim and annual balance sheet date*

10. The reasons that management elected the FVO for each eligible item or group of similar eligible items.

11. If management elected the FVO for some but not all of the eligible items within a group of similar items

---

[1] *For the purposes of this reconciliation, derivative assets and liabilities are permitted to be presented net.*

    a.    A description of the items in the group and the reasons for the partial election.     \_\_\_\_\_

    b.    Information sufficient to enable users to understand how the group of similar items relates to the individual line items presented on the balance sheet.     \_\_\_\_\_

12.   For each balance sheet line item that includes one or more items for which the FVO was elected

    a.    Information sufficient to enable users to understand how each balance sheet line item relates to major categories of assets and liabilities presented in accordance with the fair value disclosure requirements of FAS 157 (see above) that provide the reader with information with respect to the level or levels within the fair value hierarchy in which the assumptions used to measure fair value (referred to as "inputs") are derived.     \_\_\_\_\_

    b.    The aggregate carrying amount of items included in each balance sheet line item, if any, that are not eligible for the FVO.     \_\_\_\_\_

13.   The difference between the aggregate fair value and the aggregate unpaid principal balance of

    a.    Loans and long-term receivables (other than securities subject to FAS 115) with contractual principal amounts and for which the FVO has been elected.     \_\_\_\_\_

    b.    Long-term debt instruments that have contractual principal amounts and for which the FVO has been elected.     \_\_\_\_\_

14.   For loans held as assets for which the FVO has been elected

    a.    The aggregate fair value of loans on nonaccrual status if the entity's policy is to recognize interest income separately from other changes in fair value.     \_\_\_\_\_

    b.    The aggregate fair value of loans that are 90 or more days past due.     \_\_\_\_\_

    c.    The difference between the aggregate fair value and the aggregate unpaid principal balance for loans that are 90 or more days past due, in nonaccrual status, or both.     \_\_\_\_\_

15.   For investments that, absent election of the FVO, would have been accounted for under the equity method, the following disclosures from APB 18 are to be made. The extent of disclosures necessary to inform the reader of the financial position and results of operations of an investee is based on management's evaluation of the significance of an investment to the financial position and results of operations of the reporting entity.

    a.    Parenthetical disclosure, or disclosure in the notes to the financial statements or in separate statements or schedules of

        (1)   The name of each investee and the percentage of ownership of its common stock held by the reporting entity.     \_\_\_\_\_

        (2)   The accounting policies of the investor with respect to investments in common stock.     \_\_\_\_\_

    b.    When investments in common stock of corporate joint ventures or other investments accounted for under the equity method are, in the aggregate, material to the investor's financial position and results of operations, it may be necessary to present in the notes, or in separate statements, either individually or in groups, summarized information as to assets, liabilities, and results of operations of the investees.     \_\_\_\_\_

*Disclosures required in each interim and annual period for which an income statement is presented about items for which the FVO has been elected*

16.　For each line item in the balance sheet, the amounts of gains and losses from changes in fair value included in net income during the period and the specific line in the income statement on which those gains and losses are reported. FAS 159 permits management to meet this requirement by aggregating these disclosures with respect to items for which the FVO was elected with the amounts of gains and losses from changes in fair value with respect to other items measured at fair value as required by other authoritative literature.

17.　A description of how interest and dividends are measured and where they are reported in the statement of income.

18.　With respect to gains and losses included in net income during the period attributable to changes in instrument-specific credit risk associated with loans and other receivables held as assets

    a.　The estimated amount of such gains or losses.
    b.　How the gains or losses were determined.

19.　For liabilities with fair values that have been significantly affected during the reporting period by changes in instrument-specific credit risk

    a.　The estimated amount of gains and losses from changes in fair value included in net income attributable to changes in the instrument-specific credit risk.
    b.　How the gains and losses were determined.
    c.　Qualitative information regarding the reasons for those changes.

*Other required disclosures*

20.　In annual financial statements only, the methods and significant assumptions used to estimate the fair value of items for which the FVO was elected.

21.　If management elects the FVO upon the occurrence of an event where (1) an investment newly becomes subject to the equity method, (2) a subsidiary or a variable interest entity that the investor previously consolidated ceases to qualify for consolidation but the investor continues to hold common stock in the entity, or (3) an eligible item is required to be measured or remeasured at fair value at the time of the event but is not required to be subsequently remeasured at each succeeding reporting date, the following disclosures are required in the financial statements covering the period of the election

    a.　Qualitative information about the nature of the event.
    b.　Quantitative information by balance sheet line item indicating which line items in the income statement include the effect on net income of initially electing the FVO for the item.

## N.　Other Disclosures

1.　Asset valuation allowances.
2.　Pledged and encumbered assets.
3.　Current and noncurrent classifications, if so utilized.
4.　For derivatives, the hedging or trading objectives and policy.

## BALANCE SHEET

## A.　Cash and Cash Equivalents

1.　Segregate and classify the amount of restricted cash according to the nature of the restriction.
2.　Compensating balances disclosed as to their nature and amount (if use of cash on balance sheet is not restricted, separate presentation on balance sheet is not required).
3.　Classify cash to be used to settle long-term liability as noncurrent.
4.　Classify cash to be used to acquire long-lived assets as noncurrent.
5.　Overdrafts are to be presented as a current liability.

6. If uninsured balances are material, concentration of credit risk must be disclosed. \_\_\_\_\_
7. For SEC, foreign bank balances are to be distinguished. \_\_\_\_\_

## B. Accounts, Notes, and Loans Receivable

1. Separately report each major category of loans and trade receivables. \_\_\_\_\_
2. Separately report receivables involving officers, employees, and other related parties and disclose amount and nature of transactions. \_\_\_\_\_
3. State the allowance for doubtful accounts or loan losses and the current period provision. \_\_\_\_\_
4. Disclose any unearned income, unamortized premiums or discounts, and any net unamortized deferred fees and costs related to loans or trade receivables. \_\_\_\_\_
5. If unbilled receivables (work in process) are reported, distinguish from billed receivables. \_\_\_\_\_
6. The recorded investment in loans (and trade receivables, if applicable) on nonaccrual status, as of each balance sheet presented is stated. \_\_\_\_\_
7. State the recorded investment in loans (and trade receivables, if applicable) on accrual status that are past due ninety days or more, as of each balance sheet presented. \_\_\_\_\_
8. The carrying amount of financial instruments that serve as collateral for borrowings. \_\_\_\_\_
9. The amount of receivables held for sale. \_\_\_\_\_
10. The amount and nature of receivables sold without recourse. \_\_\_\_\_
11. The amount of foreclosed or repossessed assets, which can be included in the other assets category if the notes to the financial statements disclose the amount. \_\_\_\_\_
12. Credit balances reclassified as a current liability. \_\_\_\_\_
13. Concentrations of risk. \_\_\_\_\_
14. Transfers of receivables with recourse. \_\_\_\_\_
15. For impaired loans, disclose

    a. For each balance sheet

        (1) Investment in impaired loans. \_\_\_\_\_
        (2) Amount of allowance for credit losses. \_\_\_\_\_
        (3) Policy of income recognition for interest. \_\_\_\_\_

    b. For each income statement, disclose the average investment in impaired loans, interest income recognized and activity in the allowance for credit losses account. \_\_\_\_\_

16. For noninterest-bearing notes or inappropriate stated interest rates, disclose the discount or premium, the effective rate of interest and face amount, amortization for the period, and issue costs. \_\_\_\_\_
17. All other nontrade receivables (e.g., tax refunds, contract claims, etc.) are separately presented. \_\_\_\_\_
18. The basis for accounting for trade receivables, loans receivable, and lease financings, including those held for sale. \_\_\_\_\_
19. The method for recognizing interest income on loan and trade receivables, including related fees and costs, and the method of amortizing net deferred fees or costs. \_\_\_\_\_
20. The accounting policies and methodology used to estimate the allowance for doubtful accounts and/or loan losses, including the factors that influenced management's judgment (such as existing economic conditions and historical losses). \_\_\_\_\_
21. The accounting policies and methodology used to estimate any liability for off-balance-sheet credit losses, including the factors that influenced management's judgment. \_\_\_\_\_
22. The policy for placing loans (and trade receivables, if applicable) on nonaccrual status. \_\_\_\_\_
23. The policy for recording payments received on loans (and trade receivables, if applicable) that are on nonaccrual status. \_\_\_\_\_

24. The policy for resuming interest accruals on loans that are on nonaccrual status. _____
25. The policy for charging off uncollectible trade receivables and loans. _____
26. Whether past due or delinquency status is based on how recently payments have been made or on contractual terms. _____
27. Whether aggregate or individual asset basis is used in determining the lower of cost or fair value of nonmortgage loans held for sale. _____
28. The aggregate amount of gains or losses on sales of loans or trade receivables (including the amounts of adjustments to record receivables held for sale at the lower of cost or fair value) separately presented in the financial statements or disclosed in the notes. _____
29. The classification and method of accounting for receivables that can be contractually prepaid or otherwise settled in a way that the entity would not recover substantially all of its recorded investment. _____
30. For certain loans or debt securities acquired in a transfer (per SOP 03-3), the following disclosures are required:

    a. How prepayments on loans receivable are accounted for. _____
    b. For loans acquired through purchase, including in a business combination, separately for loans accounted for as debt securities and for those not accounted for as debt securities

        (1) The outstanding balance (undiscounted cash flows owed). _____
        (2) The carrying amount at the beginning of the period. _____
        (3) The carrying amount at the end of the period. _____
        (4) A reconciliation of the amount of accretable yield at the beginning of the period to the amount of accretable yield at the end of the period. _____
        (5) For loans acquired in the current period

            (a) The contractually required payments receivable. _____
            (b) The cash flows expected to be collected. _____
            (c) The fair value at acquisition. _____
            (d) The carrying amount of any acquired loans in nonaccrual status. _____

        (6) The carrying amount of all loans in a nonaccrual status. _____
        (7) For loans not accounted for as debt securities

            (a) The amount of any expense recognized for impairment. _____
            (b) The amount of any reduction in a valuation allowance for losses that results from an increase in cash flows previously expected to be collected. _____
            (c) The amount of the allowance for uncollectible loans at the beginning of the period. _____
            (d) The amount of the allowance for uncollectible loans at the end of the period. _____

## C. Short-Term Investments

For all classifications (trading, available-for-sale, or held-to-maturity), disclose the following information:

1. Fair value. _____
2. Gross unrealized gains. _____
3. Gross unrealized losses. _____
4. Amortized cost for each major security type. _____
5. Maturity date for those debt instruments held to maturity. _____
6. For each period for which the results of operations are presented, disclose

    a. Proceeds from sales of available-for-sale securities and gross realized gains and gross realized losses on those sales.
    b. Basis on which cost was determined in computing realized gain or loss. _____

    c.   Gross gains and gross losses included in earnings from transfers of securities from available-for-sale category into trading category.    \_\_\_\_\_

    d.   Change in net realized holding gain or loss on available-for-sale securities that has been included in separate component of shareholders' equity during the period.    \_\_\_\_\_

    e.   Change in net unrealized holding gain or loss on trading securities that has been included in earnings during the period.    \_\_\_\_\_

  7.   For any sales/transfers from held to maturity classification, disclose

    a.   Cost of security.    \_\_\_\_\_
    b.   Realized or unrealized gain or loss.    \_\_\_\_\_
    c.   Circumstances leading to decision to sell or transfer the security.    \_\_\_\_\_

  8.   For SEC reporting—Substantial post-balance-sheet market decline.    \_\_\_\_\_

## D.  Inventories

  1.   Basis of valuation (cost, lower of cost or market, etc.).    \_\_\_\_\_
  2.   Cost flow assumptions employed (FIFO, LIFO, etc.).    \_\_\_\_\_
  3.   Classification (materials, work in process, etc.), with amounts of inventory in each.    \_\_\_\_\_
  4.   Inventory accounting principles peculiar to a particular industry.    \_\_\_\_\_
  5.   Pledging of inventories in borrowing agreements.    \_\_\_\_\_
  6.   Product financing arrangements.    \_\_\_\_\_
  7.   Accrued net losses on firm purchase commitments.    \_\_\_\_\_
  8.   Liquidation of LIFO inventories and effects on income.    \_\_\_\_\_
  9.   Amount of revenue and costs associated with inventory exchanges recognized at fair value.    \_\_\_\_\_
  10.   Lower of cost or market "losses," if material.    \_\_\_\_\_

## E.  Investments—Equity Method

  1.   Name of each investee and the percentage of ownership of common stock.    \_\_\_\_\_
  2.   Accounting policies with respect to each of the investments.    \_\_\_\_\_
  3.   Difference between the carrying amount for each investment and its underlying equity in the investee's net assets and the accounting treatment of the difference between these amounts.    \_\_\_\_\_
  4.   For those investments which have a quoted market price, the aggregate value of each investment.    \_\_\_\_\_
  5.   If investments in investees are considered to have a material effect on the investor's financial position and operating results, summarized data for the investor's assets, liabilities, and results of operations.    \_\_\_\_\_
  6.   If potential conversion of convertible securities and exercise of options and warrants would have material effects on the investor's percentage of the investee.    \_\_\_\_\_

## F.  Other Investments

  1.   For equity and debt securities

    a.   Classification as a held-to-maturity or an available-for-sale investment.    \_\_\_\_\_
    b.   Basis of accounting.    \_\_\_\_\_
    c.   Any valuation accounts in stockholders' equity which reflect unrealized gains and losses and any income statement effects.    \_\_\_\_\_

  2.   In the reporting entity's annual financial statements: For all investments for which there is an unrealized loss where impairment has not been recognized because the loss is not considered "other than temporary"

    a.   Quantitative disclosure in tabular form and aggregated by category of investment under FAS 115 and 124, and cost-method investments, as of the date of each balance sheet presented    \_\_\_\_\_

*NOTE: The disclosures in (1) and (2) below are to be segregated by those investments that have been in a continuous unrealized loss position for less than 12 months and those that have been in a continuous unrealized loss position for 12 months or longer.*

(1)   The aggregate amount of unrealized losses.

(2)   The aggregate related fair value of investments with unrealized losses.   _____

b.   A narrative as of the date of the most recent balance sheet that provides sufficient information to enable the reader of the financial statements to understand the disclosures in a. above, as well as both the positive and negative information that the investor considered in reaching the conclusion that the impairment is not other than temporary.   _____

*NOTE: These disclosures may be aggregated by investment category; however, individually significant unrealized losses should not be aggregated.*

Examples of relevant information that could be included in this narrative are

- The nature of the investments
- The causes(s) of the impairment(s)
- The number of investment positions in an unrealized loss position
- The severity and duration of the impairment(s)
- Other evidence considered by the investor in concluding that the impairment is not other than temporary (e.g., reports from industry analysts, sector credit ratings, volatility data regarding the fair value of the security, and/or any other relevant information that the investor considered)

c.   For investments valued using the cost method, as of the date of each balance sheet presented in the annual financial statements

(1)   The aggregate carrying amount of all investments valued using the cost method.   _____

(2)   The aggregate carrying amount of cost-method investments not evaluated for impairment by the investor.   _____

(3)   The fact that the fair value of a cost-method investment is not estimated by management if no events or changes in circumstances have been identified that potentially would have a significant adverse effect on the investment's fair value, and either

a.   The investor determined that it is not practicable to estimate the fair value of the investment, or   _____

b.   The investor is exempt from estimating fair value.   _____

## G.   Property, Plant, and Equipment

1.   Classes of assets, including separate identification of

a.   Assets held and used.   _____
b.   Assets held for sale.   _____
c.   Assets under construction and not in service.   _____
d.   Idle assets.   _____

2.   The bases of valuation.   _____
3.   The methods of computing depreciation.   _____
4.   The amount of accumulated depreciation either by classes of assets or in total.   _____
5.   A description of and the amount of any assets pledged as collateral.   _____
6.   Capitalized interest cost

a.   The total amount of interest cost incurred during the period.   _____
b.   The amount which has been capitalized.   _____

7.   Estimated costs to complete, for major construction.   _____
8.   Capitalized preproduction costs related to long-term supply agreements. Aggregate amount of assets recognized

    a.   Pursuant to agreements providing for contractual reimbursement of pre-production design and development costs. _____

    b.   Molds, dies, and other tools that the supplier *owns*. _____

    c.   Molds, dies, and other tools that the supplier *does not own*. _____

9.    Asset retirement obligations (ARO)

    a.   General description of ARO and the related long-lived assets. _____

    b.   Description of how the fair value of the liability for ARO was determined. _____

    c.   Funding policy, if any, for ARO. _____

    d.   Fair value of assets, if any, that are legally restricted to satisfy the liability. _____

    e.   Reconciliation of the beginning and ending aggregate carrying amount of the liability separately showing the changes resulting from

        (1)   Additional liability incurred during the current period. _____

        (2)   Settlements of the liability during the current period. _____

        (3)   Accretion expense. _____

        (4)   Revisions in expected cash flows. _____

        (5)   Explanation of any significant changes in ARO not otherwise apparent. _____

10.    Impairment of assets classified as held and used

    a.   Description of impaired assets (asset groups) and situation surrounding the impairment. _____

    b.   Amount of the impairment loss and the method used to determine fair value. _____

    c.   If impairment losses are not reported separately or parenthetically, the caption that includes the losses. _____

    d.   For SEC registrants: the business segment affected. _____

    e.   Disclosures required for exit and disposal activities, and discontinued operations (including lessee's early termination of leases and early termination of other executory contracts) are included in Income Statement (O) in this Appendix [RN1]. _____

## H.  Goodwill, Identifiable Intangibles, and Other Assets

1.    For goodwill, a reconciliation of changes in the carrying amount during the period, showing separately

    a.   The gross amount and accumulated impairment losses at the beginning of the period. _____

    b.   Additional goodwill recognized during the period, except goodwill that is included in a disposal group that, upon acquisition, meets the criteria in FAS 144 to be classified as held for sale. _____

    c.   Adjustments resulting from the subsequent recognition of deferred income tax assets during the period (FAS 109, ¶30 and ¶30A as amended by FAS 141[R]). _____

    d.   Goodwill included in a disposal group classified as held for sale. _____

    e.   Goodwill derecognized during the period without having previously been reported in a disposal group classified as held for sale. _____

    f.   Impairment losses recognized during the period. _____

    g.   Net foreign exchange differences arising during the period. _____

    h.   Any other changes in carrying amounts during the period. _____

    i.   The gross amount and accumulated impairment losses at the end of the period. _____

2.    Goodwill impairment losses recognized during the period

    a.   The facts and circumstances causing the impairment. _____

    b.   The method of determining fair value of the associated reporting unit (whether based on quoted market prices; prices of comparable businesses; or present value or other valuation techniques; or a combination of these methods). _____

c.   If the amount recognized is an estimate that has not yet been finalized, that fact and the reasons why the estimate is not yet complete.                    _____

3.   Goodwill impairment losses that had been estimated in prior periods

a.   In periods subsequent to recognition of an estimated goodwill impairment loss, disclose the nature and amount of any significant adjustments made to the initial estimate.                    _____

4.   For each major class of intangible asset, for each period-end for which a balance sheet is presented

a.   For amortizable intangibles

(1)   Gross carrying amount and accumulated amortization, in total and by major class of intangible asset.
(2)   Amortization expense for the period.                    _____
(3)   Estimated aggregate amortization expenses for each of the five succeeding fiscal years as of the date of the latest balance sheet presented.                    _____

b.   For intangible assets not subject to amortization, the total carrying amount and the carrying amount for each major intangible asset class.                    _____

c.   The entity's accounting policy on the treatment of costs incurred to renew or extend the term of a recognized intangible asset.                    _____

d.   For intangible assets that have been renewed or extended in the period for which the balance sheet is presented

(1)   For entities that capitalize renewal or extension costs, the total amount of costs incurred in the period to renew or extend the term of a recognized intangible asset, by major intangible asset class.                    _____
(2)   The weighted-average period prior to the next renewal or extension (both explicit and implicit), by major intangible asset class.                    _____

5.   For each impairment loss recognized related to an intangible asset (other than goodwill), the following disclosures are to be made in financial statements that include the period the loss is recognized:

a.   A description of the impaired intangible asset.                    _____
b.   The facts and circumstances that caused the impairment.                    _____
c.   The amount used to determine fair value.                    _____
d.   The amount of the impairment loss, and the caption of the income statement in which it is included.                    _____

6.   In the period of acquisition either individually or in a group of assets, as part of an asset acquisition transaction or a business combination, the following information as of acquisition date. This information is to be disclosed separately for each material business combination or in the aggregate for individually immaterial business combinations that are material collectively if the aggregate fair values of the intangible assets acquired, other than goodwill, are significant.

a.   For each class of intangible asset subject to amortization

(1)   The total amount assigned and the amount assigned to any major intangible asset class.                    _____
(2)   The amount of any significant residual value, in total and by major intangible asset class.                    _____
(3)   The weighted-average amortization period, in total and by major intangible asset class.                    _____

b.   For intangible assets *not* subject to amortization, the total amount assigned and the amount assigned to any major intangible asset class.                    _____

c.   For intangible assets with renewal or extension terms, the weighted-average period prior to the next renewal or extension (both explicit and implicit) by major class of intangible asset.                    _____

7. For entities subject to segment reporting requirements under FAS 131, as amended by FSP FAS 126-1

   a. The disclosures regarding goodwill in H.1. above are to be provided in total and for each reportable segment along with any significant changes in the allocation of goodwill by reportable segment. _____

   b. If any portion of goodwill has not yet been allocated to a reporting unit at the date the financial statements are issued, disclosure is to be made of that amount and the reasons it has not yet been allocated. _____

   c. For any impairment losses recognized with respect to intangible assets other than goodwill, disclose the reportable segment in which the impaired intangible asset is reported. _____

8. Research and Development (R&D) Activities

   a. The amount of R&D assets acquired in a transaction other than a business combination and written off in the period and the line item in the income statement in which the amounts written off are included. _____

   b. The total research and development costs charged to expense for each period for which an income statement is presented. _____

   c. For contractual agreements

      (1) The terms of significant agreements under the R&D arrangements as of the date of each balance sheet presented. _____

      (2) The amount of compensation earned and costs incurred under contract for each period for which an income statement is presented. _____

9. Deferred charges and other assets

   a. Charges, segregated by type. _____
   b. Carrying value of capitalized computer software. _____

10. Computer software

    a. Capitalized value. _____
    b. Amortization. _____
    c. Write-downs to realizable value. _____

11. Capitalized direct-response advertising. _____
12. For obligations to service financial assets

    a. Amounts of servicing assets/liabilities recognized and amortized. _____
    b. Fair value of items (methods and assumptions). _____
    c. Risk and amounts of impairment. _____

I. **Accounting for Transfers and Servicing of Financial Assets**

   1. For all servicing assets and liabilities

      a. The amounts recognized and amortized during the period. _____
      b. Fair value of such recognized items including methods and assumptions. _____
      c. Risk characteristics of assets used to measure impairment. _____
      d. Activity in the valuation allowance for impairment. _____

   2. For securitizations accounted for as a sale

      a. Accounting policies for initially and subsequently measuring retained interests, including how fair value was determined. _____

      b. A description of the entity's continuing involvement with the transferred assets. _____

      c. The gain or loss from the securitizations. _____

      d. The key assumptions used in measuring the fair value of retained interests, both initially and subsequently. _____

e.  A sensitivity analysis or stress test showing the hypothetical effect on the fair value of retained interests for two or more variations from the expected level for each key assumption used in measuring the fair value of retained interests. _____

f.  Cash flows between the securitization SPE and the entity. _____

3.  For securitized assets that the entity continues to service

a.  The total principal amount outstanding of the securitized assets and any other financial assets that the entity manages with them, the portion that has been derecognized, and the portion that continues to be recognized for each category reported on the balance sheet. _____

b.  Delinquencies at the end of the period. _____

c.  Credit losses, net of recoveries, during the period. _____

4.  Other disclosures

a.  Security required for repurchase agreements or security lending transactions. _____

b.  Fair value of assets transferred, or description and reasons why fair value cannot be measured. _____

c.  Any assets pledged as collateral that are not separately reported on the face of the balance sheet. _____

d.  Fair value of any assets accepted as collateral, and the amount that has been sold or repledged. _____

## J. Current Liabilities

1.  For accounts payable, disclose amounts that are

a.  Trade. _____

b.  Nontrade. _____

c.  Related parties (affiliates; investees for which the equity method is used; employee trusts; principal owners; management, immediate families of owners and management; or any party capable of significantly influencing a transaction). _____

2.  Callable obligations:
For long-term obligations which have become callable due to a violation of the debt agreement, report

a.  A description of covenants violated. _____

b.  In unclassified balance sheet, include surrounding circumstances with disclosure of long-term debt maturities. _____

c.  Obligation that will be classified as noncurrent because it is probable that a violation of debt agreement will be cured within a grace period or a waiver has been obtained. _____

3.  Income taxes payable

a.  Current portion. _____

b.  Deferred portion. _____

4.  Notes payable

a.  Description of note. _____

b.  Classified by type

    (1)  Trade creditors. _____
    (2)  Bank. _____
    (3)  Factors or other financial institutions. _____
    (4)  Holders of commercial paper. _____
    (5)  Related parties (see Accounts Payable, 1.c.). _____
    (6)  Employees, underwriters, and promoters (other than related parties). _____

c.  Describe assets used as security. _____

      d.   Interest rate.                                   \_\_\_\_\_

      e.   Aggregate maturities and maturities for next five years.    \_\_\_\_\_

5.   Product warranties

      a.   The nature of the product warranty, including how the warranty arose and the events or circumstances in which the entity must perform under the warranty.   \_\_\_\_\_

      b.   The entity's accounting policy and methodology used in determining its liability.   \_\_\_\_\_

      c.   A reconciliation of the beginning and ending liability balances showing separately the changes during the period attributable to warranties issued, claims paid or otherwise settled, and any adjustments to the liability.   \_\_\_\_\_

      d.   The nature and extent of any recourse provisions or available collateral that would enable the entity to recover the amounts paid under the warranties.   \_\_\_\_\_

      e.   The disclosures required by FAS 57 if the warranties are made to benefit related parties.   \_\_\_\_\_

6.   Other current liabilities

      a.   Accruals.   \_\_\_\_\_

      b.   Advances or deposits.   \_\_\_\_\_

      c.   Current portions of long-term liabilities.   \_\_\_\_\_

      d.   Compensated absences.   \_\_\_\_\_

      e.   Liabilities not recorded because amounts could not be estimated.   \_\_\_\_\_

      f.   Short-term debt expected to be refinanced

          (1)   Terms of new obligation incurred or expected to be incurred.   \_\_\_\_\_

          (2)   Terms of equity securities issued or expected to be issued.   \_\_\_\_\_

      g.   Bank overdrafts.   \_\_\_\_\_

      h.   Special termination benefits.   \_\_\_\_\_

      i.   Credit balances in accounts receivable.   \_\_\_\_\_

      j.   Terms, interest rates, collateral, and other significant information about the underlying obligation.   \_\_\_\_\_

## K.  Current and Deferred Income Tax Assets and Liabilities

1.   Classify as current if related to asset or liability that is current or will result in net taxable or deductible amounts next year. Otherwise classify as noncurrent.   \_\_\_\_\_

2.   Total of deferred income tax liabilities.   \_\_\_\_\_

3.   Total of deferred income tax assets.   \_\_\_\_\_

4.   Report the valuation allowance for deferred income tax assets, allocated pro rata between current and noncurrent deferred income tax assets, and changes in the allowance during the year.   \_\_\_\_\_

5.   Deferred income tax liabilities and assets attributable to different taxpaying components or to different tax jurisdictions are not permitted to be offset.   \_\_\_\_\_

6.   The approximate income tax effect of each type of temporary difference and carryforward that gives rise to a significant portion of deferred income tax liabilities and assets. For non-SEC reporting, disclose the types of temporary differences and carryforwards but may omit disclosure of the income tax effects of each type.   \_\_\_\_\_

7.   The amounts and expected timing of reversals of deductible temporary differences.   \_\_\_\_\_

8.   Any portion of the valuation allowance for deferred income tax assets for which subsequently recognized income tax benefits will be allocated to reduce goodwill or other noncurrent intangible assets of an acquired entity or directly to contributed capital.   \_\_\_\_\_

9.   The amounts and expiration dates of net operating loss and income tax credit carryforwards for income tax purposes.   \_\_\_\_\_

10.   The reporting entity's accounting policy on classification of interest and penalties.   \_\_\_\_\_

11.   At the end of each annual reporting period

a. A tabular reconciliation of the total amounts of unrecognized income tax benefits at the beginning and end of the period including, at a minimum

    (1) The gross amounts of the increases and decreases in unrecognized income tax benefits as a result of income tax positions taken during a prior period. _____

    (2) The gross amounts of increases and decreases in unrecognized income tax benefits as a result of income tax positions taken during the current period. _____

    (3) The amounts of decreases in the unrecognized income tax benefits relating to settlements with taxing authorities. _____

    (4) Reductions in unrecognized income tax benefits resulting from a lapse of the applicable statue of limitations. _____

b. The total amount of unrecognized income tax benefits that, if recognized, would affect the effective tax rate. _____

c. The total amounts of interest and penalties recognized in the statement of income and the total amounts of interest and penalties recognized in the balance sheet. _____

d. For income tax positions for which it is reasonably possible that the total amounts of unrecognized income tax benefits will significantly increase or decrease within 12 months of the reporting date

    (1) The nature of the uncertainty. _____

    (2) The nature of the event that could occur in the next 12 months that would cause the change. _____

    (3) An estimate of the range of the reasonably possible change or a statement that an estimate of the range cannot be made. _____

e. The tax years that remain subject to examination by major income tax jurisdictions. _____

## L. Long-Term Debt and Debt Extinguishment

1. Notes and bonds

a. The aggregate amount of debt shown as a long-term liability on the face of the financial statements net of the current portion due within one year and any discount or premium. _____

b. The detail relating to each debt issue, including

    (1) Nature of the liabilities. _____

    (2) Maturity dates. _____

    (3) Interest rates (effective and stated). _____

    (4) Call provisions. _____

    (5) Conversion privileges. _____

    (6) Restrictive covenants (i.e., sinking fund requirements, restrictions on retained earnings, etc.). _____

    (7) Assets pledged as collateral (these assets are shown in the asset section of the balance sheet). _____

    (8) Amounts due to related parties including officers, directors, and employees, and terms of settlement. _____

    (9) Disclosure of notes or bonds issued subsequent to the balance sheet date. _____

  (10) Amounts of unused letters of credit. _____

c. The current portion of the long-term debt is shown as a current liability unless other than current assets will be used to satisfy the obligation. _____

d. Long-term debt is classified as current if the debtor is in violation of a debt covenant at the balance sheet date which

    (1) Makes the obligation callable within one year, or _____

      (2)  Will make the obligation callable within one year if the violation is not cured within a specified grace period. _____

  e.  The debt referred to in d. above need not be reclassified if either of the following conditions are met:

      (1)  The creditor has waived or has subsequently lost the right to demand repayment for one year (or, if longer, the operating cycle) from the balance sheet date, or _____

      (2)  It is probable (likely) that the violation will be cured by the debtor within the grace period stated in the terms of the debt agreement, thus preventing the obligation from being called. _____

2.  For the extinguishment of debt the following information provided either on the face of the financial statements or in the notes:

  a.  A description of the extinguishment transaction, including the sources of the funds used, if practicable. _____

  b.  The income tax effect of the transaction. _____

  c.  The amount and the per share amount of the aggregate gain or loss, net of tax. _____

  d.  For debt considered to be extinguished by an in-substance defeasance, a general description of the transaction and the amount of debt that is considered extinguished at the end of the period so long as that debt remains outstanding. _____

  e.  A description of the restrictions on assets set aside solely for satisfying scheduled payments on a specific debt obligation. _____

3.  Troubled debt restructurings

  a.  Disclosures by the debtor

      (1)  A description of the changes in terms and/or major features of the settlement. _____

      (2)  The aggregate gain on restructuring and the related tax effect. _____

      (3)  The aggregate net gain or loss on the transfer of assets recognized during the period. _____

      (4)  The per share amount of the aggregate gain or loss, net of tax. _____

  b.  Disclosures by the creditor

      (1)  For the outstanding restructured receivables, the aggregate recorded investment. _____

      (2)  The amount of commitments to lend additional funds to debtors owing receivables whose terms have been modified by restructurings. _____

      (3)  The recorded investment amount for which impairment has been recognized, including the total allowance for credit losses related to those impaired loans, and recorded investments not requiring an allowance. _____

      (4)  The activity in the allowance for credit losses account, including the balance in the allowance for credit losses account at the beginning and end of each period, additions charged to operations, direct write-downs charged against the allowance, and recoveries of amounts previously charged off. _____

      (5)  The creditor's interest income recognition policy on impaired loans, including how cash receipts are recorded. _____

      (6)  For each period of operation, the amount of interest income related to impaired loans, the average investment impaired and if practical, the amount of interest income using a cash-basis method. _____

4.  Unconditional purchase obligations are to be disclosed, if all the following criteria are met:

  a.  It is noncancelable, or cancelable only

(1) Upon the occurrence of some remote contingency. _____

(2) With the permission of the other party. _____

(3) If a replacement agreement is signed between the same parties. _____

(4) Upon payment of a penalty in an amount such that continuation of the agreement appears reasonably assured. _____

b. It is negotiated as part of a supplier's product financing arrangement for the facilities that will provide the contracted goods or services or for costs related to those goods or services (e.g., carrying costs for contracted goods); and _____

c. It has a remaining term in excess of one year. _____

d. If the obligation fulfills the foregoing criteria and is recorded on the balance sheet, the following disclosures are required:

(1) Aggregate amount of payments to be made. _____

(2) Aggregate amount of maturities and sinking fund requirements for all long-term borrowings. _____

e. If the obligation is not recorded on the balance sheet, then the following footnote disclosures are required:

(1) The nature and term of the obligation(s). _____

(2) The total amount of the fixed or determinable portion of the obligation(s) at the balance sheet date in the aggregate and for each of the next five years, if determinable. _____

(3) The nature of any variable components of the obligation(s). _____

(4) The amounts purchased under the obligation(s) (as in take-or-pay or through-put contracts) for each period for which an income statement is presented. _____

5. For contingently convertible debt securities, disclose the qualitative and quantitative terms that users need to understand the potential impact of conversion, including: events or changes in circumstances that would cause the contingency to be met and features necessary to understand the conversion rights, the conversion price and number of shares, events or changes that could adjust or change any features of the securities, and the manner of settlement upon conversion. _____

6. The following disclosures are to be made in annual financial statements with respect to convertible debt instruments that were outstanding during any of the periods presented and that are within the scope of FSP APB 14-1, *Accounting for Convertible Debt Instruments That May Be Settled in Cash upon Conversion (Including Partial Cash Settlement)*:

a. As of each date for which a balance sheet is presented

(1) The carrying amount of the equity component. _____

(2) The principal amount of the liability component, its unamortized discount, and its net carrying amount. _____

b. As of the date of the *most recent* balance sheet presented

(1) The remaining period over which any discount on the liability component will be amortized. _____

(2) The conversion price and the number of shares on which the aggregate consideration to be delivered on conversion is determined. _____

(3) For public entities (as defined in FAS 123[R], ¶E1), the amount by which the if-converted value of the instrument exceeds its principal amount, irrespective of whether the instrument is currently convertible. _____

(4) Information about derivative transactions entered into in connection with the issuance of the instruments, including the terms of those derivative transactions, how those transactions relate to the instruments, the number of shares underlying the derivative transactions, and the reasons for entering into those derivatives transactions. This disclosure is required

regardless of whether the related derivative transactions are accounted for as assets, liabilities, or equity instruments.     _____

   c.   For each period for which an income statement is presented

      (1)  The effective interest rate for the period on the liability component.     _____

      (2)  The amount of interest cost recognized in the period relating to both the contractual interest coupon and amortization of the discount on the liability component.     _____

## M.  Financial Instruments and Derivatives

*Note that for the purposes of these disclosures, the term "financial instruments" includes derivative instruments accounted for under FAS 133.*

1.  The method and significant assumptions used to estimate fair value.     _____
2.  If not practicable to estimate fair value, disclose pertinent information such as carrying amount, effective interest rate, and maturity and the reason why it is not practicable.     _____
3.  Disclose all significant concentrations of credit risk arising from all financial instruments (except financial instruments of a pension plan and certain other financial instrument identified in FAS 107), whether from an individual counterparty or groups of counterparties, including

   a.   Information about the (shared) activity, region, or economic characteristic that identifies the concentration.     _____

   b.   The maximum amount of loss due to credit risk that, based on the gross fair value of the financial instrument, the entity would incur if parties to the financial instruments that make up the concentration failed completely to perform according to the terms of the contracts and the collateral or other security, if any, for the amount due proved to be of no value to the entity.     _____

   c.   The company's policy of requiring collateral or other security to support financial instruments subject to credit risk, information about the entity's access to that collateral or other security, and the nature and a brief description of the collateral or other security supporting those financial instruments.     _____

   d.   The company's policy of entering into master netting arrangements to mitigate the credit risk of financial instruments, information about the arrangements for which the entity is a party, and a brief description of the terms of those arrangements, including the extent to which they would reduce the entity's maximum amount of loss due to credit risk.     _____

4.  Entities with derivative instruments are to disclose information that will enable users of the financial statements to understand

   a.   How and why the entity uses derivatives.     _____
   b.   How derivatives and related hedged items are accounted for.     _____
   c.   How derivatives and related hedged items affect the entity's financial position, financial performance, and cash flows.     _____

*Quantitative disclosures about derivative instruments may be more useful and less likely to be considered out of context or otherwise misunderstood, if similar information is disclosed about other financial instruments or nonfinancial assets and liabilities to which the derivative instruments are related by activity. In those situations, management is encouraged, but not required, to present a more complete picture of its activities by disclosing that information.*

5.  For derivative instruments that are not designated or qualifying as hedging instruments, if the entity's policy is to include these derivative instruments in its trading activities (such as part of a trading portfolio that includes derivative and nonderivative or cash instruments), management can elect not to separately disclose gains

and losses as required by 6.d. (5) below, provided all of the following information is disclosed

  a.   A description of the nature of the entity's trading activities and related risks and how the entity manages those risks.

  b.   The gains and losses on its trading activities (including both derivative and nonderivative instruments) recognized in the income statement, separately by major types of items (e.g., fixed income/interest rates, foreign exchange, equity, commodity, and credit).

  c.   The line items in the income statement that include gains and losses from trading activities.

6.   Companies that hold or issue derivative instruments (or nonderivative instruments that are designated and qualify as hedging instruments) are to disclose the following information for every interim and annual reporting period for which a balance sheet and income statement are presented:

*If information about derivative instruments (or nonderivative instruments that are designated and qualify as hedging instruments) is disclosed in more than a single note, the entity is to cross-reference from the derivative note to other notes in which derivative-related information is disclosed.*

*The amounts required to be reported for nonderivative instruments designated and qualifying as hedging instruments are to be the carrying value of the nonderivative hedging instrument, including the adjustment for the foreign currency transaction gain or loss on that instrument.*

  a.   The objectives for holding or issuing those instruments within a context needed to understand those objectives and its strategies for achieving those objectives.

*Information regarding these instruments is to be disclosed in the context of each instrument's underlying risk exposure (e.g., interest rate, credit, foreign exchange rate, or overall price). These instruments are also to be distinguished between those used for risk management purposes and those used for other purposes.*

*Qualitative disclosures regarding management's objectives and strategies for using derivatives are more meaningful if described in the context of the entity's overall risk exposures related to interest rates, foreign currency exchange, commodity prices, credit risk, and equity price risk. Additional qualitative disclosures, if made, are to include a discussion of those exposures even if the entity does not manage some of those exposures by using derivatives. Management is encouraged, but not required, to provide these additional qualitative disclosures about these risks and how they are managed.*

*Derivatives used for risk management purposes include those designated as hedging instruments as well as those used as economic hedges for other purposes with respect to the risk exposures of the entity. The description is to distinguish between hedging instruments designated as fair value hedges, cash flow hedges, and hedges of foreign currency exposure in a net investment in a foreign operation. For derivatives not designated as hedging instruments, the description is to indicate the purpose of the derivative activity for which the derivatives are held or issued.*

  b.   Information to enable users of the financial statements to understand the volume of the entity's derivative activity. Management is to select the format and specifics of these volume-related disclosures that are most relevant and practical for their individual facts and circumstances.

  c.   Present, in a tabular format, all of the following information regarding the location and fair value amounts of derivative instruments reported in the balance sheet

    (1)  The fair value of derivative instruments is to be presented on a gross basis even when the instruments are subject to master netting arrangements and qualify for net presentation in the balance sheet under FIN 39, *Offsetting of Amounts Related to Certain Contracts.* Cash collateral payables and receivables associated with derivative instruments are not to be added to or netted against the fair value amounts.

    (2)  Fair value amounts are to be presented as separate asset and liability values segregated between derivatives designated and qualifying as hedging instruments and those that are not. Within each of these two broad categories, fair value amounts are to be presented separately by type of derivative contract (e.g., interest rate contracts, foreign exchange contracts, equity contracts, commodity contracts, credit contracts, etc.).

    (3)  The disclosure is to identify the line item or items in the balance sheet in which the fair value amounts for these categories are included.

d.   Present, in a tabular format, all of the following information, except item (1), regarding the location and amount of the gains and losses on derivative instruments and related hedged items reported in the income statement (or, when applicable in the balance sheet, such as in the case of gains or losses initially recognized in other comprehensive income [OCI]). Gains and losses are to be separately presented for the following items:

*This information is to be presented separately by type of derivative contract (e.g., contracts relating to interest rates, foreign exchange, equity, commodities, credit, etc.). The disclosures are to identify the line item or items in the income statement in which the gains or losses for these categories of derivative instruments are included. Information about hedged items can be presented in a tabular or nontabular format.*

    (1)  Derivative instruments designated and qualifying as fair value hedges and the related hedged items.

    (2)  The effective portion of gains and losses on derivative instruments designated and qualifying in cash flow hedges and net investment hedges that was recognized in OCI during the current period.

    (3)  The effective portion of gains and losses on derivative instruments designated and qualifying as cash flow hedges and net investment hedges recorded in accumulated other comprehensive income (AOCI) during the term of the hedging relationship and reclassified to earnings during the current period.

    (4)  The portion of gains and losses on derivative instruments designated and qualifying in cash flow hedges and net investment hedges representing

        (a)  The amount of the hedges' ineffectiveness, and

        (b)  The amount, if any, excluded from the assessment of hedge effectiveness.

    (5)  Derivative instruments not designated or qualifying as hedging instruments.

e.   The existence and nature of credit-risk-related contingent features and the circumstances that could trigger the features in derivative instruments that are in a net liability position at the end of the reporting period.

f.   The aggregate fair value amounts of derivative instruments that contain credit-risk-related contingent features that are in a net liability position at the end of the reporting period.

g.   The aggregate fair value of assets that are already posted as collateral at the end of the reporting period, and

    (1)  The aggregate fair value of additional assets that would be required to be posted as collateral and/or

      (2) The aggregate fair value of assets needed to settle the instrument immediately, if the credit-related contingent features were triggered at the end of the reporting period. _____

7. Disclosures for every interim and annual reporting period for which a balance sheet and income statement are presented are also to include the following:

    a. For fair value hedges

      (1) For derivative instruments as well as nonderivative instruments that may give rise to foreign currency transaction gains or losses under FAS 52, that have been designated and have qualified as fair value hedging instruments and for the related hedged items

        (a) The net gain or loss recognized in net income during the reporting period representing _____

          1] The amount of the hedges' ineffectiveness, and _____

          2] The component of the derivative instrument's gain or loss, if any, excluded from the assessment of hedge effectiveness. _____

        (b) The amount of net gain or loss recognized in net income when a hedged firm commitment no longer qualifies as a fair value hedge. _____

    b. For cash flow hedges

      (1) For derivative instruments that have been designated and have qualified as cash flow hedging instruments and for the related hedging transactions

        (a) A description of the transactions or other events that will result in the reclassification into earnings of gains and losses that are reported in accumulated other comprehensive income (AOCI), and the estimated net amount of the existing gains or losses at the reporting date that is expected to be reclassified into earnings within the next 12 months. _____

        (b) The maximum length of time over which the entity is hedging its exposure to the variability in future cash flows for forecasted transactions excluding those forecasted transactions related to the payment of variable interest on existing financial instruments. _____

        (c) The amount of gains or losses reclassified into earnings as a result of the discontinuance of cash flow hedges because it is probable that the original forecasted transactions will not occur by the end of the originally specified time period or within the additional period of time as specified by FAS 133, ¶33. _____

8. Except for those financial instruments specifically exempted under FAS 107, as amended by FAS 133, disclose (except for small, nonpublic entities as set forth in FAS 133)[2]

    a. The fair value of financial instruments and related carrying amount for which it is practicable to estimate that value. _____

    b. The methods and significant assumptions used to estimate fair value of financial instruments. _____

9. If not practicable to estimate the fair value of a financial instrument or classes of financial instruments, provide

    a. Information pertinent to estimating fair value of that financial instrument or class of financial instruments, such as carrying amount, effective interest rate, and maturity date. _____

---

[2] *The preparer should consult with FSP FAS 126-1 which expanded the definition of a public entity to include entities that are "conduit bond obligors." As a result of this expanded definition, certain reporting entities that were previously considered to be private companies are not considered public companies and, consequently, are no longer exempt from the fair value disclosures required by FAS 107.*

    b.    The methods and significant assumption used to estimate fair value of financial instruments.     \_\_\_\_\_

10.    For forward sales contracts, forward purchase contracts, purchased put options, and purchased call options that are indexed to, and potentially settled in, a company's own stock, disclose the gains and losses that are included in earnings.   \_\_\_\_\_

11.    Disclose any gains or losses on written put options that require net cash settlement or give the counterparty a choice of net cash settlement or settlement in the company's stock.   \_\_\_\_\_

12.    Disclose the accounting policy for the premium paid (time value) to acquire an option that is classified as held-to-maturity or available-for-sale.   \_\_\_\_\_

## N.   Pensions and Other Postretirement Benefits

*An employer that sponsors one or more defined benefit pension plans or one or more other defined benefit postretirement plans is to provide the following information, separately for pension plans and postretirement plans. Amounts related to the employer's results of operations are to be included for each period for which an income statement is presented. Amounts related to the employer's financial position are to be disclosed as of the date of each balance sheet presented.*

*Note that the term "changes in foreign currency exchange rates" as used herein is applicable to plans of a foreign operation whose functional currency is not the reporting currency, as those terms are defined in FAS 52.*

1.    Defined benefit plans and other postretirement plans

    a.    Schedule reconciling beginning and ending balances of the benefit obligation, (for defined benefit pension plans, the benefit obligation is the projected benefit obligation; for defined benefit postretirement plans, the benefit obligation is the accumulated postretirement benefit obligation) separately showing if applicable, the effects during the period attributable to each of the following (not required for nonpublic entities)

        (1)    Service cost.   \_\_\_\_\_
        (2)    Interest cost.   \_\_\_\_\_
        (3)    Contributions by plan participants.   \_\_\_\_\_
        (4)    Actuarial gains and losses.   \_\_\_\_\_
        (5)    Changes in foreign currency exchange rates.   \_\_\_\_\_
        (6)    Benefits paid including prescription drug benefits.   \_\_\_\_\_
        (7)    Plan amendments.   \_\_\_\_\_
        (8)    Business combinations.   \_\_\_\_\_
        (9)    Divestitures.   \_\_\_\_\_
      (10)    Curtailments.   \_\_\_\_\_
      (11)    Settlements.   \_\_\_\_\_
      (12)    Special termination benefits.   \_\_\_\_\_
      (13)    Gross amount of subsidy receipts from prescription drug benefits from the benefits provided by the Medicare Prescription Drug, Improvement and Modernization Act of 2003 (for employers sponsoring postretirement health care plans that provide prescription drug benefits).   \_\_\_\_\_

    b.    Schedule reconciling beginning and ending balances of the fair value of plan assets, separately showing if applicable (not required for nonpublic entities)

        (1)    Actual return on plan assets.   \_\_\_\_\_
        (2)    Changes in foreign currency exchange rates.   \_\_\_\_\_
        (3)    Employer contributions.   \_\_\_\_\_
        (4)    Employee or retiree contributions.   \_\_\_\_\_
        (5)    Gross benefit payments including prescription drug benefits, if applicable.   \_\_\_\_\_

    (6)  Gross amount of subsidy receipts under the Medicare Prescription Drug, Improvement and Modernization Act of 2003.

    (7)  Business combinations.              \_\_\_\_\_

    (8)  Divestitures.                   \_\_\_\_\_

    (9)  Settlements.                    \_\_\_\_\_

c.  Information on the funded status of the plan(s), and amounts recognized in the balance sheet, separately presenting the assets and current and noncurrent liabilities recognized (not required for nonpublic entities).   \_\_\_\_\_

d.  The following information regarding assets of the plan:

    (1)  The percentage of the fair value of the total plan assets held as of the measurement date used for each balance sheet presented, by each major category of plan assets including, but not limited to

        (a)  Equity securities.            \_\_\_\_\_

        (b)  Debt securities.             \_\_\_\_\_

        (c)  Real estate.               \_\_\_\_\_

        (d)  All other assets.             \_\_\_\_\_

    (2)  A narrative description of investment policies and strategies, including target allocation percentages or ranges of percentages for each major category of plan assets presented on a weighted-average basis as of the measurement date(s) of the latest balance sheet presented, if applicable, and other factors pertinent to an understanding of the policies or strategies such as investment goals, risk management practices, permitted and prohibited investments including the use of derivatives, diversification, and the relationship between plan assets and benefit obligations.   \_\_\_\_\_

    (3)  A narrative description of the basis used to determine the overall expected long-term rate-of-return-on-assets assumption, such as the general approach used, the extent to which the overall rate-of-return-on-assets assumption was based on historical returns, the extent to which adjustments were made to those historical returns to reflect expectations of future returns, and how those adjustments were determined.   \_\_\_\_\_

    (4)  Disclosure of additional asset categories and additional information about specific assets within a category is encouraged if such information is expected to be useful to understand the risks associated with the each asset category and the overall expected long-term rate of return on assets.   \_\_\_\_\_

e.  Defined benefit pension plans: The accumulated benefit obligation.   \_\_\_\_\_

f.  The benefits, as of the date of the latest balance sheet presented, that are expected to be paid in each of the next five fiscal years, and in the aggregate for the five fiscal years thereafter. The estimate of expected benefits is to be based on the same assumptions used to measure the entity's benefit obligation at the end of the year and is to include benefits attributable to estimated future service by employees. The estimate is also to include in the expected benefit payments, the gross benefit payments expected for prescription drug benefits, if applicable. Separate disclosure is also to be made of the gross amount of expected subsidy receipts under the Medicare Prescription Drug, Improvement and Modernization Act of 2003.   \_\_\_\_\_

g.  The best estimate of the employer, as soon as reasonably determinable, of contributions expected to be paid to the plan during the next fiscal year that begins after the date of the latest balance sheet presented. Estimated contributions are permitted to be presented in the aggregate combining

    (1)  Contributions required by funding laws and regulations.   \_\_\_\_\_

    (2)  Discretionary contributions.        \_\_\_\_\_

    (3)  Noncash contributions.           \_\_\_\_\_

h. Net periodic benefit cost recognized, separately showing (not required for nonpublic entities)

   (1) Service cost. _____

   (2) Interest cost. _____

   (3) Expected return on plan assets for the period. _____

   (4) Amortization of unrecognized transition asset or obligation. _____

   (5) Recognized gains or losses. _____

   (6) Recognized prior service costs or credits. _____

   (7) Transition asset or obligation. _____

   (8) Recognized settlement or curtailment gain or loss. _____

i. Separate disclosure of the net gain or loss and net prior service cost or credit recognized in other comprehensive income (OCI) for the period and reclassification adjustments of OCI for the period, as those amounts, including amortization of the net transition asset or obligation, are recognized as components of net periodic benefit cost. _____

j. The amounts in accumulated other comprehensive income (AOCI) not yet recognized as components of net periodic benefit cost, separately presenting the net gain or loss, net prior service cost or credit, and net transition asset or obligation. _____

k. The following assumptions used in the accounting for the plans, on a weighted-average basis:

   (1) Assumed discount rates. _____

   (2) For pay-related plans, rates of compensation increase. _____

   (3) In a tabular format, expected long-term rates of return on plan assets, specifying the assumptions used to determine

      (a) The benefit obligation. _____

      (b) Net benefit cost. _____

l. Assumed health care cost trend rate(s) for the next year used to measure the expected cost of benefits covered by the plan (gross eligible charges), and a general description of the direction and pattern of change in the assumed trend rates thereafter, along with the ultimate trend rate(s) and when that rate is expected to be achieved. _____

m. The effect of both a 1% increase and a 1% decrease in the assumed health care cost trend rates on each of the following: (not required for nonpublic entities)

   (1) Service and interest cost components (aggregated) of the net periodic postretirement health care benefit costs. _____

   (2) Health care accumulated postretirement benefit obligation for health care benefits (APBO) (based on the substantive plan and while holding all other assumptions constant). _____

n. Other, if applicable

   (1) Amounts and types of employer and related-party securities included in plan assets. _____

   (2) Approximate amount of future annual benefits covered by insurance contracts by the employer and related parties. _____

   (3) Any significant transactions between the employer and related parties with the plan during the period. _____

o. Alternative amortization method used to amortize prior service amounts or net gains and losses, if applicable (not required for nonpublic entities). _____

p. Existence and nature of substantive commitments, such as past practice or a history of regular benefit increases, used as the basis for accounting for the benefit obligation, if applicable (not required for nonpublic entities). _____

q.  Special or contractual termination benefits recognized during the period (not required for nonpublic entities) including a description of the

    (1)  Nature of the event.                                     \_\_\_\_
    (2)  Cost.                                                        \_\_\_\_

r.  If not otherwise apparent, an explanation (not required for nonpublic entities) of matters of significance in regard to changes in

    (1)  Benefit obligation.                               \_\_\_\_
    (2)  Plan assets.                                         
    (3)  Unamortized prior service cost amount.         \_\_\_\_

s.  The amounts in AOCI expected to be recognized as components of net periodic benefit cost during the fiscal year following the most recent annual balance sheet presented, separately presenting

    (1)  Net gain or loss.                                 \_\_\_\_
    (2)  Net prior service cost or credit.               \_\_\_\_
    (3)  Net transition asset or obligation.              \_\_\_\_

t.  The amount and timing of any plan assets expected to be returned to the business entity during the 12-month period, or operating cycle if longer, that follows the most recent annual balance sheet presented.

2.  Employers with two or more defined benefit plans (pension, postretirement, or both) are, in general, to separately aggregate all of the employer's defined benefit pension plans and all of the employer's defined benefit postretirement plans.

a.  Disaggregate into groups if otherwise required or if it would provide useful information.                                               \_\_\_\_
b.  Disclosures are to be made as of the date of each balance sheet presented.   \_\_\_\_
c.  Generally, the entity is permitted to aggregate disclosures regarding pension plans with assets in excess of the ABO with disclosures regarding pension plans with ABO in excess of assets. The same aggregation is permitted for other postretirement benefit plans. If the disclosures are aggregated, however, the employer is to disclose

    (1)  For plans where the ABO is in excess of plan assets as of the measurement date of each balance sheet presented, disclose the

        (a)  Aggregate benefit obligation.                   \_\_\_\_
        (b)  Aggregate fair value of plan assets.        \_\_\_\_

    (2)  For pension plans where the ABO is in excess of plan assets, disclose the

        (a)  Aggregate pension accumulated benefit obligation.   \_\_\_\_
        (b)  Aggregate fair value of plan assets.        \_\_\_\_

d.  US pension and OPEB plans and plans outside the US may be combined unless benefit obligations outside the US are significant relative to the total benefit obligation and those plans use significantly different assumptions.   \_\_\_\_

3.  For postretirement health care plans that provide prescription drug benefits

a.  Until management has determined whether benefits provided by the plan are actuarially equivalent, the following disclosures are to be included in interim and annual financial statements of the reporting entity/plan sponsor.   \_\_\_\_
b.  The existence of the Medicare Prescription Drug Improvement and Modernization Act of 2003 (the Act).   \_\_\_\_
c.  The exclusion from APBO or net periodic postretirement benefit cost of amounts associated with the subsidy due to the fact that management is unable to reach a conclusion as to whether the benefits provided by the plan are actuarially equivalent to Medicare Part D under the Act.   \_\_\_\_

   d.   In interim and annual financial statements for the first period in which the reporting entity/plan sponsor includes the effects of the subsidy in measuring net periodic postretirement benefit cost

      (1)  The reduction in the APBO for the subsidy related to benefits attributed to past service.    \_\_\_\_\_

      (2)  The effect of the subsidy on the current period net periodic postretirement benefit cost including

         (a)  Amortization, if any, of the actuarial experience gain in (a) as a component of the net amortization called for by FAS 106, ¶59.    \_\_\_\_\_

         (b)  The reduction of current period service cost resulting from the subsidy.    \_\_\_\_\_

         (c)  The reduction in interest cost on the APBO resulting from the subsidy.    \_\_\_\_\_

      (3)  Pursuant to FAS 132(R), ¶5(r), if not otherwise apparent, an explanation of any significant change in the benefit obligation or plan assets.    \_\_\_\_\_

4.   Streamlined disclosure requirements applicable to nonpublic entities

*A nonpublic entity sponsoring one or more defined benefit pension plans or one or more other defined benefit postretirement plans is to provide the following information, separately for pension plans and other postretirement benefit plans. Amounts related to the employer's results of operations are to be disclosed for each period for which an income statement is presented. Amounts related to the employer's financial position are to be disclosed at the date of each balance sheet presented.*

   a.   Benefit obligation, fair value of plan assets, funded status of plan.    \_\_\_\_\_

   b.   Employer contributions, participant contributions, benefits paid.    \_\_\_\_\_

   c.   Information about plan assets

      (1)  For each major category of plan assets (including but not limited to equity securities, debt serurities, real estate, and all other assets), the percentage of the fair value of total plan assets held as of the measurement date used for each balance sheet presented.    \_\_\_\_\_

      (2)  A narrative description of the plan's investment policies and strategies, including target allocation percentages or range of percentages for each major category of plan assets, presented on a weighted-average basis as of the measurement date(s) of the latest balance sheet presented, if applicable, and other factors pertinent to understanding the policies and strategies, such as investment goals, risk management practices, permitted and prohibited investments including the use of derivatives, diversification, and the relationship between plan assets and benefit obligations.    \_\_\_\_\_

      (3)  A narrative description of the basis used to determine the overall expected long-term rate-of-return-on-assets assumption, such as the general approach used, the extent to which the assumption was based on historical returns, the extent to which adjustments were made to those historical returns to reflect expectations of future returns, and how those adjustments were determined.    \_\_\_\_\_

      (4)  Disclosure of additional asset categories and additional information about specific assets within a category is encouraged if the information is expected to be useful in understanding the risks with respect to each asset category and the overall expected long-term rate of return on assets.    \_\_\_\_\_

   d.   For defined benefit plans, the accumulated benefit obligation (ABO).    \_\_\_\_\_

   e.   As of the date of the latest balance sheet presented, the benefits expected to be paid in each of the next five fiscal years, and in the aggregate for the five fiscal years thereafter. The expected benefits are to be estimated using the same assumptions used to measure the entity's end-of-year benefit obligation and are to include benefits attributable to estimated future service by employees. _____

f. The employer's best estimate, as soon as it can be determined reasonably, of contributions expected to be paid to the plan during the next fiscal year beginning after the date of the latest balance sheet presented. Estimated contributions may be presented in the aggregate, combining

(1) Contributions required by funding laws or regulations. _____
(2) Discretionary contributions. _____
(3) Noncash contributions. _____

g. The amounts recognized in the balance sheets, showing separately the postretirement benefit assets and current and noncurrent postretirement benefit liabilities. _____

h. Separate disclosure of the net gain or loss, and the net prior service cost or credit recognized in OCI for the period, and reclassification adjustments of OCI for the period as those amounts, including amortization of the net transition asset or obligation, are recognized as components of net periodic benefit cost. _____

i. The amounts in AOCI that have not yet been recognized as components of net periodic benefit cost, separately presenting the net gain/loss, net prior service cost/credit, and net transition asset/obligation. _____

j. The amount included within OCI for the period that results from a change in the additional minimum pension liability recognized. _____

k. The assumed health care cost trend rate(s) for the next year used to measure the expected cost of benefits covered by the plan (gross eligible charges), and a general description of the direction and pattern of change in the assumed trend rates thereafter, together with the ultimate trend rate(s) and when the rate is expected to be achieved. _____

l. The amounts and types of securities, if applicable, of the employer and related partied included in plan assets, the approximate amount of future annual benefits of plan participants covered by insurance contracts issued by the employer or related parties, and any significant transactions between the employer or related parties and the plan during the period. _____

m. The nature and effect of significant nonroutine events, such as amendments, combinations, divestitures, curtailments, and settlements. _____

n. The amounts in AOCI expected to be recognized as components of net periodic benefit cost over the fiscal year following the date of the most recent annual balance sheet presented, with separate presentation of the net gain/loss, net prior service cost/credit, and net transition asset/obligation. _____

o. The amount and timing of any plan assets expected to be returned to the employer during the 12-month period (or operating cycle, if longer) following the most recent annual balance sheet presented. _____

5. Defined contribution plans

a. Separately from disclosures regarding defined benefit plans, the employer is to disclose the following information for all periods presented:

(1) Cost recognized for defined contribution pension plans. _____
(2) Cost recognized for other defined contribution postretirement benefit plans. _____
(3) Description of the nature and effect of any significant changes during the period affecting comparability, such as a change in the employer contribution rate, a business combination, or a diversiture. _____

6. Multiemployer plans

a.   Total amount of contributions for each annual period for which an income statement is presented, without disaggregating amounts with respect to pension plans and other postretirement benefit plans.     _____

b.   Description of nature and effect of any significant changes affecting comparability, such as a change in the employer's contribution rate, a business combination, or a divestiture.     _____

c.   Apply the accounting and disclosure provisions of FAS 5, *Accounting for Contingencies,* in situations where it is either reasonably possible or probable that

   (1)   The employer would withdraw from the plan under circumstances resulting in an obligation to the plan for a portion of the unfunded pension plan benefit obligation, *or*     _____

   (2)   The employer's contributions to the fund would be increased during the remainder of the contract period to make up for a shortfall in the funds needed to maintain the negotiated level of benefit coverage (referred to as a "maintenance of benefits" clause).     _____

## O.   Leases—General Disclosures and Disclosures of Lessees

1.   For capital leases, disclose

   a.   The gross amount of assets recorded under capital leases presented by major classes according to function or nature.     _____

   b.   Future minimum lease payments in the aggregate and for each of the next five fiscal years with separate deductions made for executory costs (including any profit thereon) included in the minimum lease payments, and the amount of imputed interest needed to reduce the net minimum lease payments to present value.     _____

   c.   Total of minimum sublease rentals to be received in the future under noncancelable subleases.     _____

   d.   Total contingent rentals actually incurred for each period for which an income statement is presented.     _____

   e.   Depreciation on capital leases should be separately disclosed.     _____

2.   For sale-leaseback transactions, disclose

   a.   In addition to requirements of FAS 13 and 66, financials of seller-lessee shall describe terms of sale-leaseback transaction, including future commitments, obligations, provisions, or circumstances requiring or resulting in seller-lessee's involvement.     _____

   b.   Where seller-lessee has accounted for transaction by deposit method or as a financing

   (1)   The obligation for future minimum lease payments as of the date of the latest balance sheet presented in the aggregate and for each of the five succeeding fiscal years.     _____

   (2)   The total of minimum sublease rentals, if any, to be received in the future under noncancelable subleases in the aggregate and for each of the five succeeding fiscal years.     _____

3.   For operating leases having a remaining noncancelable term in excess of one year, disclose

   a.   Future minimum lease payments in the aggregate and for each of the next five fiscal years.     _____

   b.   Total of minimum rentals that will be received under noncancelable subleases.     _____

4.   For all operating leases

a.  Present rental expense disclosing separately the amount for minimum rentals, contingent rentals, and sublease rentals. _____

b.  Rental payments for leases with terms of a month or less that were not renewed may be excluded. _____

5.  General description required of lessee's leasing arrangements including, but not limited to

   a.  Basis of computing contingent rental payments. _____

   b.  Existence and terms of renewal or purchase options and escalation clauses. _____

   c.  Restrictions imposed by leasing agreements such as on dividends, additional debt, and further leasing arrangements. _____

6.  For reporting entities that engage in the purchase or sale of tax benefits under the leasing provisions of the Economic Recovery Tax Act of 1981 (tax leases), the accounting policies followed including the method of accounting for tax leases and the methods of recognizing revenue and allocating income tax benefits and asset costs to the current period and future periods. _____

## P.  Leases—Lessors

1.  For sales-type and direct financing leases, disclose

   a.  Components of the net investment in leases including the following:

      (1)  Future minimum lease payments to be received with separate deductions for amount representing executory costs (including any profit thereon), and the accumulated allowance for uncollectible lease payments. _____

      (2)  Unguaranteed residual values accruing to benefit of lessor. _____

      (3)  For direct financing leases only, initial direct costs. _____

      (4)  Unearned interest revenue. _____

   b.  Future minimum lease payments to be received for each of the next five fiscal years. _____

   c.  Total contingent rentals included in income for each period for which an income statement is presented. _____

2.  For operating leases, disclose

   a.  The cost and carrying amount (if different) of property leased or held for leasing, segregated by major classes of property according to function or nature, and the total amount of accumulated depreciation. _____

   b.  Minimum rentals on noncancelable leases in the aggregate and for each of the next five fiscal years. _____

   c.  Total contingent rentals included in income for each period for which an income statement is presented. _____

3.  A general description of the lessor's leasing arrangements. _____

4.  For an investment in leveraged leases recorded net of the nonrecourse debt, the net of the balances of following accounts shall represent the initial and continuing investment in leveraged leases:

   a.  Rentals receivable, net of portion of rental applicable to principal and interest on nonrecourse debt. _____

   b.  A receivable for amount of investment tax credit to be realized on transaction. _____

   c.  Estimated residual value of leased asset. _____

   d.  Unearned and deferred income consisting of

      (1)  Estimated pretax income (or loss), after deducting initial direct costs, remaining to be allocated to income over the lease term. _____

      (2)  Investment tax credit remaining to be allocated to income over lease term. _____

    e.    For leverage leases, for each income statement presented, disclose

        (1)   Pretax income from leveraged leases.       \_\_\_\_\_

        (2)   Tax effect of that pretax income.       \_\_\_\_\_

        (3)   Amount of investment tax credit recognized as income.       \_\_\_\_\_

## Q.   Equity-Like Instruments Classified as Liabilities

   1.   Issuers of financial instruments within the scope of FAS 150 must disclose

      a.   The nature and terms of the financial instruments.       \_\_\_\_\_

      b.   The rights and obligations embodied therein.       \_\_\_\_\_

      c.   Information about settlement alternatives, if any, in the contract.       \_\_\_\_\_

      d.   The entity that controls the settlement alternatives.       \_\_\_\_\_

   2.   For all outstanding financial instruments and for each settlement alternative, issuers disclose

      a.   The amount that would be paid, or the number and fair value of shares that would be issued, determined under the conditions specified in the contract, if the settlement were to occur at the reporting date.       \_\_\_\_\_

      b.   How changes in the fair value of the issuer's equity shares would affect those settlement amounts.       \_\_\_\_\_

      c.   The maximum amount that the issuer could be required to pay to redeem the instrument by physical settlement, if applicable.       \_\_\_\_\_

      d.   The maximum number of shares that could be required to be issued, if applicable.       \_\_\_\_\_

      e.   That a contract does not limit the amount that the issuer could be required to pay or the number of shares that the issuer could be required to issue, if applicable.       \_\_\_\_\_

      f.   For a forward contract or an option indexed to the issuer's equity shares, the forward price or option strike price, the number of issuer's shares to which the contract is indexed, and the settlement date or dates of the contract, as applicable.       \_\_\_\_\_

   3.   For entities having no equity instruments outstanding but having financial instruments in the form of shares, all of which are mandatorily redeemable financial instruments required to be classified as liabilities, disclose the components of the liability that would otherwise be related to shareholders' interest and other comprehensive income (if any) subject to the redemption feature.       \_\_\_\_\_

## R.   Stockholders' Equity

   1.   The following should be disclosed:

      a.   The sources of capital supplied to the firm.       \_\_\_\_\_

      b.   The legal restrictions on the distribution of invested capital.       \_\_\_\_\_

      c.   The legal, contractual, managerial, and financial restrictions on the distribution of dividends to stockholders.       \_\_\_\_\_

      d.   The priorities of the classes of stockholders in a partial or final liquidation.       \_\_\_\_\_

   2.   Capital stock and additional paid-in capital

      a.   For each class of stock, disclose

        (1)   Par, stated, or assigned value.       \_\_\_\_\_

        (2)   Number of shares authorized, issued, and outstanding.       \_\_\_\_\_

        (3)   Number of shares held in treasury.       \_\_\_\_\_

        (4)   Conversion terms of preferred, if applicable, including call prices, rates, and dates. Additionally, the amount of redemption requirements for all issues of stock that are redeemable at fixed or determinable prices on fixed or determinable dates must be disclosed for each of the five years following the date of the latest balance sheet presented.       \_\_\_\_\_

(5) Changes in the number of shares authorized, issued, and outstanding during the year and changes in the equity accounts. _____

(6) Liquidation values, if different than par, in the aggregate for preferred. _____

(7) For preferred classes of stock, any dividend preferences, special privileges, etc. _____

(8) Any unusual voting rights. _____

b. The amount of cumulative dividends in arrears, per share and in aggregate. _____

c. Aggregate securities issuable under rights or warrants, as well as their prices, and exercise and expiration dates. _____

d. Any discount on capital stock. _____

e. The amount of subscribed shares not yet issued. _____

f. Deferred compensation expense offset against the paid-in capital account, "Stock options outstanding." _____

g. Stock dividends distributable in total or at par or stated value with the excess included in additional paid-in capital. Also acceptable is deferment of their recording until issuance. However, disclosure is necessary in the notes. _____

h. The amount of capital stock issued in business combinations (purchase or pooling) or agreements to issue additional shares at a later date. _____

i. Transactions affecting equity subsequent to the date of the financial statements (recapitalization, sales of stock, etc.). _____

j. Additional paid-in capital, listed by source, along with any changes during the period. _____

k. Any changes in the capital accounts of partners or sole proprietors. _____

3. Retained earnings

a. Appropriation and segregation of retained earnings, as well as their nature, cause, and amount. Changes in these accounts should be disclosed. _____

b. Nature and dollar amounts of restrictions on retained earnings (treasury stock, lease covenants, etc.). _____

c. Date retained earnings for ten years following quasi reorganization. _____

d. Increase/decrease results from combination by pooling of interests (revenues, expenses, extraordinary items, and net income). _____

e. Prior period adjustments, net of tax and in gross. For correction of an error, in the period discovered, disclose

(1) Nature of the error on previous statements.

(2) Effect of correction on income before extraordinary items, net income, and related per share amounts. _____

4. Dividends

a. Dividends in aggregate and per share as well as the nature and extent of any restrictions on retained earnings limiting availability of dividends. _____

b. The amount of dividends in arrears, per share and in aggregate. _____

c. Dividends declared after balance sheet date, prior to opinion date, unless a long-established history of regular payment dates exists and the dividend is not abnormal in amount. _____

d. For stock dividends and stock splits, disclosure of the amounts capitalized, per share and in total. Historical presentations of earnings per share should be restated in an equivalent number of shares so the figures are presented on a comparable basis. _____

5. Treasury stock

a. If treasury stock is accounted for by the cost method, present total cost of treasury stock as a deduction from total stockholders' equity. Disclose number of shares held in treasury. _____

b.    If treasury stock is accounted for by the par value method, present par value of treasury stock as a deduction from par value of issued shares of same class. Any related additional paid-in capital from treasury stock is netted with corresponding additional paid-in capital without separate disclosure. Disclose number of shares held in treasury.    \_\_\_\_\_

c.    If treasury stock is accounted for by the constructive retirement method, disclose number of shares held in treasury.    \_\_\_\_\_

6.   Share-based payment arrangements

*NOTE: If the reporting entity grants equity or liability instruments under multiple share-based payment arrangements with employees, the information specified in a. through e. is to be provided separately for each different type of award to the extent that differences in the awards' characteristics make separate disclosure important to understanding the way the reporting entity uses share-based compensation.*

a.    Plan description, including general terms of awards such as requisite service period(s) and other substantive conditions including vesting requirements, maximum contractual term of equity (or liability) share options or similar instruments, the number of shares authorized for awards of equity share options or other equity instruments, and the method used to measure compensation cost under share-based payment arrangements with employees.    \_\_\_\_\_

b.    For the most recent year for which an income statement is provided    \_\_\_\_\_

    (1)   The number and weighted-average exercise prices (or conversion ratios) for each of the groups of share options or share units

       (a)   Outstanding at the beginning of the year.    \_\_\_\_\_
       (b)   Granted during the year.    \_\_\_\_\_
       (c)   Exercised or converted during the year.    \_\_\_\_\_
       (d)   Forfeited during the year.    \_\_\_\_\_
       (e)   Expired during the year.    \_\_\_\_\_
       (f)   Exercisable or convertible at the end of the year.    \_\_\_\_\_
       (g)   Outstanding at the end of the year.    \_\_\_\_\_

    (2)   The number and weighted-average grant-date fair value (or calculated value or intrinsic value when permitted to be used) of equity instruments not specified in (1) above (such as shares of nonvested stock) for each of the following groups of equity instruments:

       (a)   Nonvested at the beginning of the year.    \_\_\_\_\_
       (b)   Granted during the year.    \_\_\_\_\_
       (c)   Vested during the year.    \_\_\_\_\_
       (d)   Forfeited during the year.    \_\_\_\_\_
       (e)   Nonvested at the end of the year.    \_\_\_\_\_

c.    For each year for which an income statement is provided

    (1)   Weighted-average grant-date fair value (calculated value or intrinsic value for those reporting entities permitted to use those methods) of equity options or other equity instruments granted during the year.    \_\_\_\_\_

    (2)   The total intrinsic value of options exercised (or share units converted), share-based liabilities paid, and the total fair value of shares vested during the year.    \_\_\_\_\_

d.    For fully vested share options (or share units) and share options expected to vest at the date of the latest balance sheet

    (1)   The number, weighted-average exercise price (or conversion ratio), the aggregate intrinsic value (except for nonpublic entities), and the weighted-average remaining contractual term of options (or share units) outstanding.    \_\_\_\_\_

(2)  The number, weighted-average exercise price (or conversion ratio), the aggregate intrinsic value (except for nonpublic entities), and the weighted-average remaining contractual term of options (or share units) currently exercisable (or convertible).                                     _____

e.  For awards not accounted for using the intrinsic value method, for each year for which an income statement is presented

(1)  A description of the method used during the year to estimate the fair value (or calculated value) of awards under share-based payment arrangements.                                                       _____

(2)  A description of the significant assumptions used during the year to estimate the fair value (or calculated value) of share-based compensation awards including, where applicable

(a)  Expected term of share options and similar instruments, including a discussion of the method used to incorporate the contractual term of the instrument and the employees' expected exercise and postvesting employment termination behavior into the fair value (or calculated value) of the instrument.                               _____

(b)  Expected volatility of the entity's shares and the method used to estimate it.                                                         _____

(c)  If the entity uses a valuation method that employs different volatilities during the contractual term

1]  The range of expected volatilities used.                    _____
2]  The weighted-average expected volatility.                   _____

(d)  If the entity is a nonpublic entity that uses the calculated value method

1]  The reasons why it is not practicable for it to estimate the expected volatility of its share price.                         _____
2]  The appropriate industry sector index it has selected and the reasons for selecting that particular index.                _____
3]  How it has calculated historical volatility using that index.   _____

(e)  Expected dividends and, if the entity uses a method employing different dividend rates during the contractual term, the range of expected dividends used and the weighted-average expected dividends.                                                             _____

(f)  Risk-free rate(s) and, if the entity uses a method employing different risk-free rates, the range of risk-free rates used.            _____

(g)  The discount for postvesting restrictions and the method used to estimate it.                                                       _____

f.  For each year for which an income statement is presented

(1)  Total compensation cost for share-based payment arrangements recognized in income, the associated income tax benefit recognized, and the total compensation cost capitalized as part of the cost of an asset.      _____

(2)  A description of significant modifications, including the terms of the modifications, number of affected employees, and the total incremental compensation cost resulting from the modifications.                _____

g.  As of the latest balance sheet date presented, the total compensation cost related to nonvested awards not yet recognized and the weighted-average period over which it is expected to be recognized.                         _____

h.  The amount of cash received from exercise of share options and similar instruments granted under share-based payment arrangements and the tax benefit realized from stock options exercised during the annual period.    _____

     i.     The amount of cash used to settle equity instruments granted under share-based payment arrangements.    \_\_\_\_\_

     j.     A description of the reporting entity's policy (if any) for issuing shares upon share option exercise (or share unit conversion), including the source of the shares (i.e., newly issued shares or treasury shares). If, as a result of this policy, the entity expects to repurchase shares in the following annual period, an estimate of the amount (or range, if more appropriate) of shares to be repurchased during that period.    \_\_\_\_\_

7.   Employee stock ownership plans (ESOP)

     a.    Description of the plan, including basis for determining contributions, groups covered, nature and effect of matters affecting comparability of information across periods.    \_\_\_\_\_

     b.    The basis for releasing shares by leveraged and pension reversion ESOP.    \_\_\_\_\_

     c.    Accounting policies pertinent to ESOP transactions.    \_\_\_\_\_

     d.    Compensation cost recognized during the period.    \_\_\_\_\_

     e.    Numbers of shares allocated, committed to be released, and held in suspense by the ESOP.    \_\_\_\_\_

     f.    Fair value amount of unearned compensation at year-end.    \_\_\_\_\_

     g.    Nature of any repurchase obligations and aggregate fair value thereof.    \_\_\_\_\_

8.   Contingently convertible securities

     a.    The significant terms of the conversion features in sufficient quantitative and qualitative detail to enable the financial statement reader to understand the nature and circumstances of the contingency and the potential impact of conversion including

        (1)  Events or changes in circumstances that would cause the contingency to be met.    \_\_\_\_\_

        (2)  Features of the securities that significantly affect the conversion rights and their timing (e.g., the periods in which the contingency could potentially be met and the fact that the securities may be converted if the contingency is met).    \_\_\_\_\_

        (3)  The conversion price and number of shares into which the security is potentially convertible.    \_\_\_\_\_

        (4)  Events or changes in circumstance, if any, that could adjust or change the contingency, conversion price, or number of shares, including significant terms of those changes.    \_\_\_\_\_

        (5)  The manner of settlement upon conversion and any alternative settlement methods (e.g., cash, shares, or a combination of both).    \_\_\_\_\_

     b.    For companies required to report earnings per share (EPS): Whether the shares that would be issued upon conversion are included in diluted EPS and the reasons why or why not.    \_\_\_\_\_

     c.    Information regarding derivative transactions entered into in connection with the issuance of the contingently convertible securities including the terms of the transactions including settlement, how the derivative transactions relate to the contingently convertible securities, and the number of shares underlying the derivatives.    \_\_\_\_\_

9.   The issuer of a registration payment arrangement shall disclose the following information about each registration payment arrangement or each group of similar arrangements. These disclosures are incremental to the disclosures that may be required under other applicable GAAP and are required even if the likelihood of the issuer having to make any payments under the arrangement is remote.

a. The nature of the registration payment arrangement, including the approximate term of the arrangement, the financial instrument(s) subject to the arrangement, and the events or circumstances that would require the issuer to transfer consideration under the arrangement.

b. Any settlement alternatives contained in the terms of the registration payment arrangement, including the party that controls the settlement alternatives.

c. The maximum potential amount of consideration, undiscounted, that the issuer could be required to transfer under the registration payment arrangement (including the maximum number of shares that may be required to be issued). If the terms of the arrangement provide for no limitation to the maximum potential consideration (including shares) to be transferred, that fact shall be disclosed.

d. The current carrying amount of the liability representing the issuer's obligations under the registration payment arrangement and the income statement classification of any gains or losses resulting from changes in the carrying amount of that liability.

10. For SEC only, disclose

a. Dividend payout restrictions.
b. Stock subscriptions.
c. Redemption requirements on redeemable stock.
d. Separate classification for redeemable preferred stock.

## INCOME STATEMENT

### A. Basic Disclosures

1. Revenues and related costs with the following categories separately stated, if applicable

a. Product sales net of discounts, returns, and allowances.
b. Rental revenues.
c. Service revenues including billings for out-of-pocket costs.
d. Other revenue.

2. Income or loss before extraordinary items.
3. Extraordinary items.
4. Income taxes.
5. Discontinued operations.
6. Depreciation.
7. Interest expense.
8. Gain or loss from extinguishment of debt.
9. Foreign currency realized gains and losses.
10. Marketable securities gains and losses.
11. Research and development expenses.
12. S Corporation election—No income tax effect.

### B. Short-Term Investments

1. Proceeds from sales of available-for-sale securities and the gross realized gains and gross realized losses on those sales.
2. Basis on which cost was determined in computing realized gain or loss.
3. The gross gains and gross losses included in earnings from transfers of securities from the available-for-sale category into the trading category.
4. The change in net unrealized holding gain or loss on available-for-sale securities that has been included in other comprehensive income during the period.
5. The change in net unrealized holding gain or loss on trading securities that has been included in earnings during the period.

## C.   Income Taxes

1. State if entity is not subject to income taxes because income is taxed directly to owners. State the net difference between tax and book bases of assets and liabilities. _____

2. State amounts allocated to

   a. Current tax expense or benefit. _____
   b. Deferred tax expense or benefit (exclusive of the effects of other components listed below). _____
   c. Investment tax or other credits. _____
   d. Government grants (to the extent recognized as a reduction of income tax expense). _____
   e. The benefits of operating loss carryforwards. _____
   f. Tax expense that results from allocating certain tax benefits directly to contributed capital. _____
   g. Adjustments of a deferred tax liability or asset for enacted changes in tax laws or rates or a change in the tax status of the enterprise. _____
   h. Adjustments of the beginning-of-the-year balance of a valuation allowance because of a change in circumstances that causes a change in judgment about the realizability of the related deferred tax asset in future years. _____

3. Amounts allocated to

   a. Continuing operations. _____
   b. Discontinued operations. _____
   c. Extraordinary items. _____
   d. Cumulative effect of accounting changes. _____
   e. Prior period adjustments. _____
   f. Gains and losses included in comprehensive income but excluded from net income. _____
   g. Capital transactions. _____

4. Reconcile statutory tax rates to actual rates for significant items (nonpublic enterprises need only disclose the nature of significant reconciling items). _____

5. Amounts and expiration dates of operating loss and tax credit carryforwards for income tax purposes. _____

6. If consolidated return filed, separately issued financial statements should state

   a. Amount of current and deferred tax expense for each income statement. _____
   b. Tax-related balances due to or from affiliates for each balance sheet. _____
   c. The method of allocating consolidated amounts of current and deferred tax expense and effects of any change in that methodology. _____

7. Cumulative effect of change (similar to change in accounting principle) for earliest restated financial statements. _____

8. When a deferred tax liability is not recognized because of the exceptions to comprehensive recognition of deferred taxes, the following information shall be disclosed:

   a. A description of the types of temporary differences for which a deferred tax liability has not been recognized and the types of events that would cause those temporary differences to become taxable. _____
   b. The cumulative amount of each type of temporary difference. _____
   c. The amount of the unrecognized deferred tax liability for temporary differences related to investments in foreign subsidiaries and foreign corporate joint ventures that are essentially permanent in duration if determination of that liability is practicable or a statement that determination is not practicable. _____
   d. The amount of the deferred tax liability for temporary differences other than those in c. above (i.e., undistributed domestic earnings, the bad-debt reserve

for tax purposes of a US savings and loan association or other qualified thrift lender, the policyholders' surplus of a life insurance enterprise, and the statutory reserve funds of a US steamship enterprise) that is not recognized.

**D.  Extraordinary Items**

1.  Segregated and shown net of tax.
2.  Adequate explanations of nature of extraordinary item(s).
3.  Infrequent or unusual items shown separately although not extraordinary; not shown net of tax.
4.  For adjustment of amounts reported in prior period that do not qualify as prior period adjustments, classify separately in same manner as original item, with year of origin, nature and amount.

**E.  Interim Financial Information**

1.  Provide, at a minimum, the captions and disclosures required when publicly traded entities report summarized interim financial information. These required disclosures are

    a.  Sales or gross revenues, provision for income taxes, extraordinary items, cumulative effect of a change in principle, net income, and comprehensive income.
    b.  Basic and diluted earnings per share for each period presented.
    c.  Seasonal revenues, costs, and expenses.
    d.  Significant changes in income tax estimates.
    e.  Disposal of a component of an entity and extraordinary, unusual, or infrequently occurring items.
    f.  Contingencies.
    g.  Effect of changes in accounting principles or estimates.
    h.  Significant changes in financial position.
    i.  Information regarding reportable operating segments including provisions related to restatement of segment information in previously issued financial statements.

        (1)  Revenues from external customers.
        (2)  Intersegment revenues.
        (3)  A measure of segment profit or loss.
        (4)  Total assets for which there has been a material change from the amount disclosed in the last annual report.
        (5)  A description of differences from the last annual report in the basis of segmentation or in the measurement of segment profit or loss.
        (6)  A reconciliation of the total of the reportable segments' measures of profit or loss to the enterprise's consolidated pretax income, extraordinary items, discontinued operations, and the cumulative effect of changes in accounting principles.
        (7)  The following information regarding defined benefit pension plans and other defined benefit postretirement benefit plans, disclosed for interim statements that include an income statement:

            (a)  The amount of the net periodic benefit cost recognized, for each period for which a statement of income is presented, separately showing the

                1]  Service cost component.
                2]  Interest cost component.
                3]  Expected return on plan assets for the period.
                4]  Gain or loss component.
                5]  Prior service cost or credit component.

        6]   Transition asset or obligation component.     \_\_\_\_\_

        7]   Gain or loss recognized due to a settlement or curtailment.     \_\_\_\_\_

    (b)   The total amount of the employer's contributions paid, and expected to be paid during the current fiscal year, if significantly different from amounts previously disclosed. Estimated contributions may be presented in the aggregate, combining contributions required by funding laws or regulations, discretionary contributions, and non-cash contributions.     \_\_\_\_\_

  (8)   Information about the use of fair value to measure assets and liabilities recognized in the balance sheet as required by FAS 157.     \_\_\_\_\_

  (9)   Information about derivative instruments required by FAS 161, *Disclosures about Derivative Instruments and Hedging Activities.*     \_\_\_\_\_

2.   When summarized financial information is reported on a regular quarterly basis, the above captions and disclosures included in 1a. through 1i. (7) are presented for the current quarter and the current year-to-date (or the preceding twelve months to date), along with comparable data for the preceding year.     \_\_\_\_\_

## F.   Segment Data

1.   General information on segments including

    a.   Factors used to identify the enterprise's reportable segments, including the basis of organization (e.g., whether management has chosen to organize the enterprise around differences in products and services, geographic areas, regulatory environments, or a combination of factors and whether operating segments have been aggregated).     \_\_\_\_\_

    b.   Types of products and services from which each reportable segment derives its revenues.     \_\_\_\_\_

2.   The following about each reportable segment if the specified amounts are included in the measure of segment profit or loss reviewed by the chief operating decision maker:

    a.   Revenues from external customers.     \_\_\_\_\_

    b.   Revenues from transactions with other operating segments of the same enterprise.     \_\_\_\_\_

    c.   Interest revenue.     \_\_\_\_\_

    d.   Interest expense.     \_\_\_\_\_

    e.   Depreciation, depletion, and amortization expense.     \_\_\_\_\_

    f.   Unusual items.     \_\_\_\_\_

    g.   Equity in the net income of investees accounted for by the equity method.     \_\_\_\_\_

    h.   Income tax expense or benefit.     \_\_\_\_\_

    i.   Extraordinary items.     \_\_\_\_\_

3.   Disclose the following about each reportable segment if the specific amounts are included in the determination of segment assets reviewed by the chief operating decision maker:

    a.   The amount of investment in equity method investees.     \_\_\_\_\_

    b.   Total expenditures for additions to long-lived assets other than financial instruments, long-term customer relationships of a financial institution, mortgage and other servicing rights, deferred policy acquisition costs, and deferred tax assets.     \_\_\_\_\_

4.   An explanation should be provided of the measurements of segment profit or loss and segment assets for each reportable segment; at a minimum, these shall include the following:

    a.   The basis of accounting for any transactions between reportable segments.     \_\_\_\_\_

b.   The nature of any differences between the measurements of the reportable segments' profits or losses and the company's consolidated income before income taxes, extraordinary items, discontinued operations, and the cumulative effect of changes in accounting principles (if not apparent from the reconciliations); for example, accounting policies and policies for allocation of centrally incurred costs that are necessary for an understanding of the reported segment information.

c.   The nature of any differences between the measurements of the reportable segments' assets and the company's consolidated assets (if not apparent from the reconciliations); for example, accounting policies and policies for allocation of jointly used assets that are necessary for an understanding of the reported segment information.

d.   The nature of any changes from prior periods in the measurement methods used to determine reported segment profit or loss and the effect, if any, of those changes on the measure of segment profit or loss.

e.   The nature and effect of any asymmetrical allocations to segments; for example, an enterprise might allocate depreciation expense to a segment without allocating the related depreciable assets to that segment.

5.   Reconciliations of the totals of segment revenues, reported profit or loss, assets, and other significant items to corresponding company amounts, as follows:

a.   The total of the reportable segments' revenues to the enterprise's consolidated revenues.

b.   The total of the reportable segments' measures of profit or loss to the company's consolidated income before income taxes, extraordinary items, discontinued operations, and the cumulative effect of changes in accounting principles.

c.   The total of the reportable segments' assets to the company's consolidated assets.

d.   The total of the reportable segments' amounts for every other significant item of information disclosed to the corresponding consolidated amount.

6.   Company-wide disclosures (required for all companies subject to FAS 131 including those companies that have a single reportable segment)

a.   Revenues from external customers for each product and service or each group of similar products and services unless it is impracticable to do so. (The amounts of revenues reported shall be based on the financial information used to produce the enterprise's general-purpose financial statements. If providing the information is impracticable, that fact shall be disclosed.)

b.   Revenues from external customers

(1)  Attributed to the enterprise's country of domicile.

(2)  Attributed to all foreign countries in total from which the enterprise derives revenues unless it is impracticable to do so. (If revenues from external customers attributed to an individual foreign country are material, those revenues shall be disclosed separately. Also disclose the basis for attributing revenues from external customers to individual countries.)

c.   Long-lived assets other than financial instruments, long-term customer relationships of a financial institution, mortgage and other servicing rights, deferred policy acquisition costs, and deferred tax assets

(1)  Located in the enterprise's country of domicile.

(2)  Located in all foreign countries in total in which the enterprise holds assets unless it is impractical to do so. (If assets in an individual foreign country are material, those assets shall be disclosed separately.)

    d.   If providing the geographic information is impracticable, that fact shall be disclosed.       _____

7.   Major customers

If revenues from transaction with a single external customer amount to ten percent or more of an enterprise's revenues, disclose that fact, the total amount of revenues from each such customer, and the identity of the segment or segments reporting the revenues.       _____

8.   Earnings before income tax disclosures

Depreciation and amortization expense for each reportable segment, when the chief operating decision maker evaluates the performance of its segments based on earnings before interest, taxes, depreciation, and amortization.       _____

## G.  Development Stage Enterprises

1.   The financial statements should be identified as those of a development stage company and should include a description of the nature of the development stage activities.       _____

2.   The financial statements for the first fiscal year in which the company is no longer considered to be in the development stage should disclose that in prior years it had been in the development stage. If financial statements for prior years are presented for comparative purposes, the cumulative amounts and other additional disclosures required below need not be shown.       _____

3.   On the balance sheet, any cumulative net losses should be reported with a descriptive caption such as "deficit accumulated during the development stage" in the stockholders' equity section.       _____

4.   Report the cumulative amounts of revenue and expenses since inception.       _____

5.   Report the cumulative amounts of sources and uses of cash since inception.       _____

6.   Present in the statement of stockholders' equity all transactions since inception.       _____

7.   Disclose the date of each stock issuance in the statement of changes in stockholders' equity.       _____

8.   Disclose the basis for stock issued for other than cash.       _____

## H.  Long-Term Construction Contracts

1.   The method of recognizing income (percentage-of-completion or completed-contract).       _____

2.   If the percentage-of-completion method is used, the method of computing percentage of completion (e.g., cost-to-cost, efforts-expended).       _____

3.   If the completed-contract method is used, the justification for its use should be indicated.       _____

4.   Length of the operating cycle; if greater than one year, the range of contract durations should be disclosed.       _____

5.   The basis of recording inventory.       _____

6.   The effect of changes in estimates.       _____

7.   The accounting for deferred costs.       _____

8.   The accounting for general and administrative expenses.       _____

9.   Criteria for determining substantial completion (e.g., compliance with specifications, acceptance by customer).       _____

10.   Information on revenues and costs arising from claims.       _____

## I.  Research and Development

1.   Expenditures.       _____

2.   R&D arrangements.

    a.   Terms including royalties, purchase provisions, license agreements and funding.       _____

b.　Amounts earned and costs incurred each period for which an income statement is presented. _____

## J.　Sales Where Collection Is Uncertain

1.　Method and justification of accounting for installment basis sales. _____
2.　Yearly gross profit rates. _____
3.　Contractual terms such as interest and repossession provisions. _____
4.　Average length of installment contracts. _____

## K.　Revenue Recognition

1.　Basis for recognizing revenue and cost of sales for each material type of transaction. _____
2.　If the company is a party to multiple-deliverable arrangements (MDA)

　　a.　The nature of the company's MDA. _____
　　b.　The company's accounting policies regarding recognition of revenue on MDA including provisions relative to performance, cancellation, termination, or refund. _____
　　c.　Whether deliverables are separable into units of accounting. _____
　　d.　The method of accounting for each element. _____
　　e.　The method used to determine each element and value it. _____

3.　When a right of return exits

　　a.　Description of return privilege granted to customers. _____
　　b.　Length of time covered by the return privilege. _____
　　c.　Estimated amount of returns. _____
　　d.　Material changes in estimates of returns. _____

## L.　Other Reporting

1.　Financing arrangements—Real estate and product financing. _____
2.　Real estate sales. _____
3.　Futures contracts. _____
4.　Service sales transaction

　　a.　The revenue recognition method used and its justification. _____
　　b.　Information concerning unearned revenues. _____
　　c.　Information concerning deferred costs. _____
　　d.　Periods over which services are to be performed. _____

5.　Time-sharing transactions

　　a.　The seller's policies regarding meeting the FAS 66 criteria for buyer's commitment (¶5[b])and collectibility of sales price (¶37[d]). _____
　　b.　Maturities of notes receivable for each of the five years following the financial statement date, and in the aggregate for all years thereafter, with the total in agreement with notes receivable presented on the face of the balance sheet. _____
　　c.　The weighted-average and range of stated interest rates on notes receivable. _____
　　d.　The estimated cost to complete improvements and promised amenities. _____
　　e.　The activity in the allowance for uncollectible accounts including

　　　　(1)　Beginning allowance. _____
　　　　(2)　Additions associated with current period sales. _____
　　　　(3)　Amounts written off against the allowance. _____
　　　　(4)　Changes in estimate associated with prior period sales. _____
　　　　(5)　Ending allowance. _____

　　f.　If the developer sells receivables with recourse, the seller is to provide the same disclosures regarding activity related to receivables sold. _____

## M.  Foreign Currency

1.  Aggregate transaction gain or loss that is included in the entity's net income.   _____
2.  Analysis of changes in accumulated translation adjustments which are reported as other comprehensive income.  At a minimum, the disclosures should include

    a.  Beginning and ending amounts of the translation adjustments account.   _____
    b.  Aggregate adjustment for the period resulting from translation adjustments, and gains and losses from certain hedges and intercompany balances.   _____
    c.  Amount of income taxes for the period allocated to translation adjustments.   _____
    d.  Amounts transferred from the translation adjustments account and included in determining net income as a result of the (partial) sale or liquidation of the foreign operation.   _____

3.  Significant rate changes subsequent to the date of the financial statements including effects on unsettled foreign currency transactions.  Rate changes subsequent to the balance sheet date are not incorporated into the financial statements for the period just ended.   _____

## N.  Exit and Disposal Activities, and Discontinued Operations

1.  For assets (or disposal groups) either sold or reclassified from held-and-used to held-for-sale during the period

    a.  The facts and circumstances leading to the expected disposal.   _____
    b.  The expected manner and timing of the disposal.   _____
    c.  If not separately presented on the face of the balance sheet, the carrying amounts of the major classes of assets and liabilities included as part of the disposal group.   _____
    d.  Gain or loss recognized for initial or subsequent write-downs to fair value less cost to sell, and, if not separately stated, the income statement caption in which included.   _____
    e.  Amounts of revenue and pretax profit or loss reported as discontinued operations, if applicable.   _____
    f.  In the period of disposal, the actual gain or loss on disposal (either on the face of the income statement or in the notes to the financial statements).   _____
    g.  For public companies, the segment in which the long-lived asset or disposal group is reported.   _____

2.  For assets (or groups) reclassified from held-for-sale to held-and-used during the period, including the removal of individual assets or liabilities from a disposal group to be sold

    a.  The facts and circumstances leading to the decision to change the plan to sell the long-lived asset (disposal group).   _____
    b.  The effect of the changed decision on the results of operations for the period in which the decision was made and any prior periods presented.   _____

3.  If assets held-and-used meet the criteria for reclassification to held-for-sale after the date of the balance sheet but before issuance of the financial statements

    a.  The facts and circumstances leading to the expected disposal.   _____
    b.  The expected manner and timing of the disposal.   _____
    c.  The carrying amount of the major assets and liabilities included as part of the disposal group.   _____

4.  In the period in which an exit or disposal activity is initiated and any subsequent period until the activity is completed, a description of the exit or disposal activity, including the facts and circumstances leading to the expected activity and the expected completion date.   _____

5. For each major type of cost associated with the exit or disposal activity (for example, onetime termination benefits, contract termination costs, and other associated costs), disclose

     a. The total amount expected to be incurred in connection with the activity.     _____

     b. The amount incurred in the period.

     c. The cumulative amount incurred to date.     _____

     d. A reconciliation of the beginning and ending liability balances showing separately the changes during the period attributable to costs incurred and charged to expense, costs paid or otherwise settled, and any adjustments to the liability with an explanation of the reason(s) therefor.     _____

     e. The line item(s) in the income statement or statement of activities in which the costs are aggregated.     _____

6. For each reportable segment of a public company, the total amount of costs expected to be incurred in connection with the activity, the amount incurred in the period, and the cumulative amount incurred to date, net of any adjustments to the liability with an explanation of the reason(s) therefor.     _____

7. If a liability for a cost associated with the exit or disposal activity is not recognized because its fair value cannot be reasonably estimated, disclose that fact and the reasons why the fair value cannot be reasonably estimated.     _____

8. Discontinued operations

     a. For each discontinued operation that generates continuing cash flows

        (1) The nature of the activities from which the cash flows originate.     _____

        (2) The period of time that the cash flows are expected to continue.     _____

        (3) The principal factors that led to the conclusion that the expected continuing cash flows are not direct cash flows of the disposed component.     _____

     b. For all periods presented, amounts of intercompany revenues and expenses that previously eliminated in consolidation for each discontinued operation which

        (1) The ongoing entity will engage in a continuation of activities with the disposed component after its disposal.     _____

        (2) After the disposal transaction, amounts are presented in income from continuing operations that represent a continuation of revenues and expenses that were intercompany transactions prior to the disposal transaction.     _____

     c. In a period in which operations are first classified as discontinued, the types of postdisposal continuing involvement that the entity is expected to have.     _____

     d. If amounts previously reported in discontinued operations directly related to the disposal of a component of an entity in a prior period are subsequently adjusted, those amounts are to be classified separately in the current period discontinued operations with disclosure in the notes to the financial statements of the nature and amount of the adjustments.     _____

## O. Earnings Per Share

1. For each income statement presented

     a. Reconciliation of the numerators and the denominators of the basic and diluted per share computations for income from continuing operations.     _____

     b. Effect that has been given to preferred dividends in arriving at income available to common stockholders in computing basic EPS.     _____

     c. Securities (including those issuable pursuant to contingent stock agreements) that could potentially dilute basic EPS in the future that were not included in the computation of diluted EPS because to do so would have been antidilutive for the period(s) presented.     _____

2.  Earnings per share amounts for income from continuing operations and net income, shown on the face of income statement for all periods presented.     \_\_\_\_\_

3.  If applicable, per share amounts for discontinued operations, extraordinary items, and cumulative effect of an accounting change, presented either on face of income statement or in notes to financial statements.     \_\_\_\_\_

4.  For latest income statement, provide a description of any transaction that occurs after end of the period but before issuance of financial statements that would have changed materially the number of common shares or potential common shares outstanding at end of period if transaction had occurred before end of period.     \_\_\_\_\_

5.  Amounts should be restated when stock dividends, splits, or reverses occur after close of period but before statements are issued with appropriate disclosure.     \_\_\_\_\_

6.  When operations of a prior period have been restated, earnings per share data also should be restated; the effect of the restatement, expressed in per share terms, should be disclosed in year of restatement.     \_\_\_\_\_

7.  Disclose EPS for income from continuing operations when there are discontinued operations of a segment of a business.     \_\_\_\_\_

## STATEMENT OF CASH FLOWS

**A.  Basis**

1.  Definition of cash and cash equivalents adopted.     \_\_\_\_\_
2.  Summarize noncash investing and financing activities.     \_\_\_\_\_

**B.  Format**

1.  Reconcile net income to net cash flow.     \_\_\_\_\_
2.  If direct method used, display major categories of gross cash receipts and cash payments

    a.  Cash receipts

    (1) Cash receipts from sale of goods or services.     \_\_\_\_\_
    (2) Interest and dividends received.     \_\_\_\_\_
    (3) Other operating cash receipts.     \_\_\_\_\_

    b.  Cash payments

    (1) Payments to employees and other suppliers of goods or services.     \_\_\_\_\_
    (2) Income taxes paid.     \_\_\_\_\_
    (3) Interest paid.     \_\_\_\_\_
    (4) Other operating cash payments.     \_\_\_\_\_

    c.  Reconcile net income or loss to net cash flow from operating activities.     \_\_\_\_\_

3.  If indirect method used

    a.  Present reconciliation of net income or loss to cash flow from operating activities, separately reporting all major items, either within the statement or in a separate schedule.     \_\_\_\_\_
    b.  Disclose both interest and income taxes paid in a schedule following the statement or in the notes.     \_\_\_\_\_

4.  Report cash flows from purchases and sales or maturities of trading securities under operating activities.     \_\_\_\_\_

5.  Report cash flows from investing activities

    a.  Report separately cash inflows and outflows.     \_\_\_\_\_
    b.  Report gross for each security classification in the statement of cash flows, the cash flows from purchases, sales and maturities of available-for-sale securities, and separately for held-to-maturity securities.     \_\_\_\_\_

6.  Report cash flows from financing activities

  a. Report separately cash inflows and outflows.   _____

  b. Effect of exchange rate changes on cash balances held in foreign currencies shown separately on statement of cash flows.   _____

  c. Cash payments for debt issue costs.   _____

## STATEMENT OF COMPREHENSIVE INCOME

**A. Format Options**

 1. Continuation of income statement (preferred by FASB).   _____

 2. Separate statement starting with net income.   _____

 3. Part of statement of stockholders' equity.   _____

**B. Disclosures**

 1. Total amount for comprehensive income.   _____

 2. Amounts of other comprehensive income by type.   _____

 3. Reclassification adjustment(s) for items included in net income also included in other comprehensive income in this period or prior period

  a. Face of financial statement in which comprehensive income reported.   _____

  b. Notes to financial statements.   _____

  c. Gross display on face of financial statement or net display on face of financial statement and gross display in notes to financial statements except for minimum pension liability which does not have reclassification adjustments.   _____

 4. Cumulative amounts of other comprehensive income by type

  a. Face of balance sheet.   _____

  b. Statement of changes in stockholders' equity.   _____

  c. Notes to financial statements.   _____

# APPENDIX B

## INTERNATIONAL VS. US ACCOUNTING STANDARDS

The International Accounting Standards Committee was founded in 1973 by representatives of professional bodies in Australia, Canada, France, Germany, Japan, Mexico, the Netherlands, the United Kingdom, Ireland, and the United States, and grew to include representatives from ninety-one countries. From 1973—by coincidence, the birth year of the current US accounting standard setter, the FASB—until December 2000, the IASC's members had included all the professional accountancy bodies that are members of the International Federation of Accountants (IFAC). As of mid-2008, these comprised 157 member bodies in 123 countries, representing over two and one-half million professional accountants.

From its formation, the IASC endeavored to create a set of financial reporting standards that would receive truly worldwide recognition. It now appears to be on the verge of achieving that long-held goal, perhaps as early as 2011. Prior to IASC's transition into the IASB (discussed below), it had issued forty-one international accounting standards (IAS), of which, after a series of revisions, thirty remain in effect. Thirty-three Interpretations of these standards had also been issued by the former Standing Interpretations Committee (SIC) as of that transition date, of which eleven remain in force.

From its inception and for many years thereafter, IASC labored in relative obscurity, its pronouncements being viewed as of importance mainly to less developed nations lacking their own standard-setting capabilities. The organization itself was seen as something of a "debating society" which over time had the potential to reduce, but not fully eliminate, differences among the major financial reporting standards regimes established by national bodies. The best hope at the time was said to be that through its efforts there would come about a *harmonization* among the standards. A major impediment was (and remains) a lack of enforcement authority; unlike national bodies, which have the support of national auditing standard setters and securities regulatory bodies, which attempt to impose discipline on the preparer and auditor communities, the IASB has no such capabilities.

The IASC achieved a higher profile in the mid-1990s, when it undertook several major standards improvement programs, resulting in substantially reducing available alternative methods of recording identical economic transactions or events. The first of these, the *Comparability/Improvements Project*, culminated with the promulgation of ten revised standards that took effect in 1995. More importantly, IASC embarked on its *Comprehensive Core Set of Standards* program that year, motivated by a historic agreement with the International Organization of Securities Commissions (IOSCO), which committed IASC to revisions of the standards that IOSCO deemed essential for its consideration of possible endorsement of the IAS for purposes of cross-border securities registrations. IASC completed these changes and promulgation of the required new standards occurred at year-end 1998, with about eleven standards being revised or newly issued, setting forth important new rules dealing with financial instruments and hedging activities, which remain controversial today.

The completion of the core set of standards was a major achievement. IASC had hoped that, having essentially performed its part of the bargain, IOSCO would likewise deliver on its explicit and implied commitments—namely, full and unqualified support for cross-border registrations including financial statements compliant with IAS standards. The endorsement that came after several years' delay, however, was tentative and tepid. To an extent, this was a consequence of the rivalry between the IASC and the FASB, which opposed granting endorsement to what it claimed was an inferior set of standards that was the product of an inadequate standard-setting process. Many believe that FASB at the time harbored its own hopes of becoming the de facto worldwide standard setter.

The US SEC, arguably the most important member of IOSCO, permitted it to ratify the core set of standards, provided that "supplemental treatments," which could be imposed by national securities regulators, were defined. (IOSCO cannot mandate acceptability of IFRS-based financial reporting, but rather can only recommend this to the sovereign regulators, which are charged with protecting investors in their respective jurisdictions.) The supplemental treatments suggested included reconciliations, added disclosures, and interpretations. Scores of such reconciling items, expanded disclosures, and interpretive matters were identified, although it was not expected that any jurisdiction would mandate all or even most of these. It is clear now that little or nothing came of these recommendations, which became irrelevant as further developments unfolded.

IASB, the successor to the IASC, reached formal agreements with FASB in 2002 and 2006, committing both to a program of convergence of their respective sets of financial reporting standards. This late-2002 memorandum of understanding (the "Norwalk Agreement") had the two bodies pledging their best efforts to (1) make their existing financial reporting standards fully compatible as soon as is practicable, and (2) coordinate their future work programs to ensure that once achieved, compatibility is maintained. The 2006 *Memorandum of Understanding* restated this commitment and introduced a *roadmap* for the achievement of convergence. The SEC promised to consider accepting filings by foreign registrants reporting in accordance with IFRS, without the heretofore required reconciliation of key measure to US GAAP.

Meanwhile, largely as a consequence of widely reported financial reporting frauds and audit failures of the late 1990s and early 2000s, there arose a spirited debate over whether US GAAP-style rules-based accounting standards (i.e., with copious, detailed guidance on how implementation is to be effected) or IASB-style principles-based standards (setting forth only general guidance, leaving interpretation to the judgment of preparers and auditors) would be more effective in restraining financial reporting fraud. This debate was based on what seems to have been the misguided perception (largely promoted by IASB advocates) that the two sets of standards really are located at diametrically opposed positions on a continuum, which they are not. In fact, all valid standards are based on conceptual foundations and all standards, including IFRS, include some implementation guidance.

The debate about principles-based versus rules-based accounting standards seems destined to fade away without any resolution. The SEC, directed by Sarbanes-Oxley to study this matter, concluded that both rules and principles are necessary, and essentially endorsed a comprehensive compromise position, which it dubbed *objectives-based* standards. Standards promulgated under US GAAP since this debate arose show no signs of being any less prescriptive, but a number of former differences between US GAAP and IFRS have now been eliminated, with FASB now committed to completion of the convergence effort by 2011.

While a modest number of nominal differences between the IFRS and US GAAP currently persist, but any proposed listing of truly substantive discrepancies is much shorter. FASB published (first in 1996, then in revised form in 1999) a study setting forth over 250 of these apparent differences, motivated partly by its desire to forestall SEC acceptance, without reconciliation, of financial statements of foreign filers prepared in conformity with IFRS. A closer look, however, reveals that

1. The number of meaningful differences was then and remains much lower, and
2. In many instances where substantive differences do exist (e.g., permitting revaluations of long-lived assets to current value amount), the related disclosure requirements are extensive enough to minimize the risk that users could be misled.

In fact, with regard to some of the cited differences, it is arguable (e.g., in the case of accounting for certain financial instruments under IAS 39 vs. under FAS 133) that the IFRS approach is in fact superior to that under corresponding US standards.

As of mid-2008, the "convergence" of the major sets of financial reporting standards is an ongoing process, but the odds of US GAAP's supersession by IFRS within a very few years have increased substantially since mid-2007, making convergence less of an issue than it was only recently.

Following the Norwalk Agreement, the two boards began a "short-term convergence" project to remove as many impediments to convergence as possible, although new ones have managed to arise: witness IASB's amendment of IAS 2 to ban LIFO accounting for inventories, which FASB would be loathe to do unless the IRS' conformity rule were to be dropped, since a significant fraction of corporate taxpayers enjoy tax deferrals under LIFO. The organizations concurrently made a commitment to undertake longer-term projects for any remaining incompatibilities, among which were: accounting for disposal of noncurrent assets and presentation of discontinued operations; costs associated with exit or disposal activities; accounting for government grants; inclusion of costs of idle capacity and spoilage in inventory costs; presentation of accounting policy and estimate changes and corrections of errors; depreciation on assets held for disposal or otherwise idled; interperiod tax allocation methodology; accounting for long-term construction contracts; reporting under hyperinflationary conditions; and joint venture accounting (use of the proportionate consolidation method).

As to FASB's efforts to date, a number of convergence activities have been undertaken, mostly addressing rather detailed technical issues that have separated US GAAP from IFRS. At least one change to US GAAP—requiring fair value accounting for nonmonetary exchanges of productive assets now recorded as book value swaps—was a clear admission of the superiority of the IASB's position on the issue, and the more recent adoption by FASB of IASB's "fair value option" is similarly an acknowledgement of the logic of IFRS's more comprehensive embrace of fair value accounting. On some matters, FASB has decided to maintain divergent positions, based on its perception that its current rules are superior to those adopted by IASB. On the whole, however, convergence appears to have been a process to which both boards were sincerely committed, and over a very short time many former differences have been eliminated, so that, as of mid-2008, while there are still two distinct sets of standards, they are rapidly losing the former sharp distinctions that separated them from each other. Still, some major hurdles (e.g., optional use of revalued amounts under IFRS for plant assets, prohibited under US GAAP) will have to be overcome for full convergence to ultimately transpire.

In 2006, FASB promulgated a comprehensive standard setting forth a hierarchy of fair value measurement strategies, and IASB has since proposed a very similar new standard. FASB and IASB are working together on major new pronouncements, including a conceptual framework and standards on consolidated financial statements and revenue recognition. These could well result in major changes to existing requirements under both FASB and IASB standards, effectively converging to new and different standards than either body has yet produced.

IASB has directed its staff to develop proposals that would serve to eliminate differences from FASB standards in the areas of impairment of property, plant, and equipment; intangible assets; liabilities and equity; purchase method accounting, consolidation of special-purpose entities; and accounting for income taxes (deferred taxes). Many of the IFRS standards published after 2003 (IFRS 2 through 8) have also, in effect, reflected convergence efforts, most recently with IFRS 8's adoption of US GAAP approach to segment disclosures.

The FASB has now completed a number of convergence projects and has, as of mid-2008, only a very few projects it has not completed. Major projects completed in 2008 relate to applications of the purchase accounting method, and accounting for noncontrolling (formerly, minority) interests. Still on the agenda are projects to address revenue recognition, distinguishing liabilities from equity, and several matters pertaining to financial instruments.

**Developments favorable to wider use of IFRS.** Several significant events have occurred over the past decade or so, the effect of which has been to improve the standing of IFRS and to raise the probability that full acceptance of IFRS-based financial reporting by international capital markets will ultimately be achieved. First, the European Commission's (EC) Single Market Commissioner announced in 1995 that the European Union had abandoned its previously expressed goal of developing unique European standards of accounting. This gave a clear boost to the IASB's efforts, by removing the specter of yet another layer of national and supranational accounting standards.

In 2000, the EU published *EU Financial Reporting Strategy: The Way Forward*, which stated that companies within the EU seeking listings on EU stock market would no longer have the free choice of preparing their consolidated financial statements in accordance with either their own national accounting standards or US GAAP. Beginning in 2005, these entities have been required to employ only IFRS, and the transition to IFRS-based reporting by some 7,000 companies received a great deal of attention and brought unprecedented interest in these standards. The proclamation of support for the IASB standards by the EU was regarded as a major breakthrough for the IASB. While it was necessary to make certain minor changes to the financial instruments standards to gain European acceptance, and the EU imposed two controversial "carve-outs," dealing with financial instruments, implementation has now been accomplished by all affected entities.

More recently, the US SEC in 2007 adopted a rule that permits foreign private issuers (i.e., non-US companies which have registered securities in the US), which formerly were permitted to use foreign GAAP or IFRS but were required to reconcile net income and stockholders' equity to parallel amounts under US GAAP, to no longer do so, provided that the financial statements conform to "full" IFRS (i.e., as promulgated by IASB). This is expected to facilitate cross-listing of shares, encourage wider adoption of IFRS (since filers using other national GAAP will not receive this exemption), and add to pressure for full convergence between US GAAP and IFRS. In response to this action by SEC, domestic private issuers asked the SEC for permission to elect to report under IFRS, instead of US GAAP. As of mid-2008, this is deemed quite likely to be accepted by the SEC, which will provide a substantial boost to the status of IFRS and add to the already significant pressure to adopt IFRS for at least public company reporting in the US.

Some of the most highly technical standards under IFRS (and, generally too, under US GAAP), are those addressing financial instruments, impairment of assets, business combinations, segment reporting, income taxes, earnings per share, and interim financial reporting. Convergence of certain of these may prove to be difficult because of the underlying subject matter and legitimately diverse philosophical beliefs (e.g., interim reporting can be viewed as integral to the full fiscal year of which they are a constituent part, or alternatively as stand-alone periods to be reported upon).

Other standards under IFRS (and, to an extent, under US GAAP) suffer from weak writing in the standards themselves. For example, the standards dealing with related-party disclosures, provisions and contingencies, and investments in associates all suffer from this flaw. The related-party disclosure standard (IAS 24, for which minor simplifications were proposed in 2007, which remain pending as of mid-2008) contains an essentially circular definition of "close members of the family," defined as: "those that may be expected to influence, or be influenced by, that person in their dealings with the enterprise." The standard on provisions, contingent liabilities, and contingent assets (IAS 37, for which substantial revisions were proposed in 2005, which remain outstanding) uses terms such as "probable outflow of resources" and "prejudicial to interest," which resist mechanical definition. The standard on accounting for investments in associates (IAS 28) prescribes the use of the "equity method" when there is "significant influence," which is evidenced by, for example, "participation in policy making processes" and "material transactions between the investor and investee."

Finally, under IFRS (but much less so under US GAAP) some standards offer radically different alternative methods of accounting that remain equally acceptable for financial reporting purposes. The standard on property, plant, and equipment allows either the use of historical cost or of "revaluation"—and there is substantial diversity in terms of frequency of updating values among enterprises which elect the revaluation option. (US GAAP prohibits revaluation.) Cash flow statements can use either the direct or indirect methods of presenting operating cash flows (the same choice is offered under US GAAP), and also gives the choice, regarding the presentation of interest and dividend income, of including this in operating or investing cash flows (no choice given in the US). Finally, investment property may be accounted for under the fair value or the cost model (again, no choice offered under US GAAP).

Thus, in reporting under IFRS, the concern must be not merely for the existing (but rapidly diminishing) differences between US GAAP and IFRS, per se, but also about the *methods elected* by the parent entity to report under IFRS. Of lesser concern, but still important, under IFRS there are often *optional* disclosure recommendations, in addition to the mandatory ones (under US GAAP, all disclosure requirements should be deemed mandatory). Finally, both US GAAP and IFRS are dynamic sets of standards, subject to refinement, revision, and supersession. Neither offers a fixed reference point over more than a short time horizon.

*Wiley IFRS 2009* discusses all existing IFRS requirements in great detail, but given the great and growing interest in these matters, the following table sets forth a comparison between US GAAP and IFRS as it exists in mid-2008. The comparisons have been organized consistent with the chapters in this book.

| GAAP 2009 chapter | Topic | US GAAP treatment | IFRS treatment |
|---|---|---|---|
| 1 | Researching GAAP Matters (General guidance) | No comprehensive guide to statement presentation is offered; however, basic financial statements are the same under both sets of standards | Comprehensive guidance on presentation of financial statements provided; minimum line items identified for all financial statements |
| | | FASB's *Conceptual Framework* is similar to IASB's *Framework for the Preparation and Presentation of Financial Statements*; convergence with IFRS is likely to occur as result of joint project to replace both sets of conceptual standards | FASB's *Conceptual Framework* is similar to IASB's *Framework for the Preparation and Presentation of Financial Statements*; latter is less detailed; convergence with US GAAP expected to occur |
| | | Comparative financials urged, not mandatory (but required for SEC filings); greater specificity as to location of disclosures in body of statements or in notes | Comparative financials are required, including footnote data; disclosure can often be optionally in financials or in notes |
| | | Formal GAAP hierarchy now defined by accounting standards, with changes forthcoming to simplify hierarchy and move to GAAP | No hierarchy established beyond IFRS |
| | | Justification for GAAP departure previously was found in the auditing literature but was very rarely invoked; this has been eliminated under new GAAP hierarchy, FAS 162 | "True and fair" override of IFRS permitted |
| | | No special rules for small or medium-sized entities or nonpublicly held reporting entities, although this has been debated for many years | IFRS for SMEs proposal (actually for nonpublicly accountable entities) likely to be enacted by year-end 2008 with publication of self-contained set of simplified rules |
| 2 | Balance Sheet | Limited guidance on offsetting of assets and liabilities; classified balance sheet not required, but definition of current/noncurrent differs from IFRS somewhat | Specific guidance on offsetting of assets and liabilities; classified balance sheet required unless liquidity ordering is more meaningful, some difference from GAAP definitions of current/noncurrent |
| | | Some differences from IFRS re: exclusion of long-term debt being refinanced, etc. | Some differences re: exclusion of long-term debt from current liabilities, etc. |
| | | No offsetting of assets and liabilities with different counterparties; offsetting with same counterparties only permitted if intention is to settle "net" and right to offset is enforceable under law | Some offsetting of assets and liabilities with different counterparties permitted when legal provision exists |
| | | Adjustment made for post-balance-sheet date events only if they bear upon existence or valuation at the balance sheet date; other material information relegated to disclosures | Conforms to US GAAP requirements |
| | | GAAP does not specify the accounts to be presented in the balance sheet | Minimum balance sheet classifications are prescribed under IFRS |

| GAAP 2009 chapter | Topic | US GAAP treatment | IFRS treatment |
|---|---|---|---|
| 2 | Balance Sheet | Joint project with IASB to require presentation of both beginning and ending balance sheets | Joint project on financial statement presentation with FASB ongoing |
| 3 | Statements of Income and Comprehensive Income | No required income statement captions, and either single-step or multiple-step format can be used | Minimum captions in income statement are prescribed under IFRS |
| | | Little specific guidance as to form, but expenses are to be classed by function (e.g., cost of sales, administrative, etc.) | Expenses can be classed by function (e.g., selling) or by nature (e.g., salaries, cost of goods sold, etc.) |
| | | Under FAS 141(R), noncontrolling interest's share in net income is displayed as a split-out of earnings "below the line" rather than as a deduction in arriving at net income | Same as current US GAAP |
| | | Extraordinary items classification permitted under limited circumstances, with net-of-tax presentation, and unusual items can also be segregated within operating income (but not tax effected); will be revised to mirror IFRS | Extraordinary classification is no longer permitted, but unusual items can be segregated for display purposes, on a pretax basis |
| | | Estimated operating results of a discontinuing operation are included in the measurement for the expected gain or loss on disposal; timing of segregation of discontinuing operations from continuing operations may differ from that under IFRS; direct continuing cash flows or involvement in operations preclude discontinuing operations display | Actual operating results of a discontinuing operation are reported as incurred; timing of recognition of gain or loss in discontinuance and income or loss from activities of the discontinuing operation may differ from US GAAP |
| | | Broader definition of discontinued operations than under IFRS, either a reportable business or geographical segment, or reporting unit, subsidy, or asset group | Narrow definition of discontinued operations as being reportable business or geographical segment or major component |
| | | Total comprehensive income and accumulated other comprehensive income can be reported in various ways; total comprehensive income can be presented in a statement combined with income statement, in separate statement, and in statement of changes in stockholders' equity | Total recognized income and expense can be presented in a statement of changes in equity, which would also include items that are recognized directly in equity; or, alternatively, a statement of recognized income and expense can be used, with other changes in equity relegated to disclosures in the notes (only) |
| | | Restructuring costs recognized when there is little discretion to avoid costs; most costs are only recognized when later incurred | Restructuring costs recognized when announced or commenced, which is earlier than under US GAAP |
| | | Joint financial reporting project with IASB in progress, which may require inclusion of changes in other comprehensive income in income statements | Join project with FASB; decision to require single statement of recognized income and expense, replacing two separate statements under current IFRS |

| GAAP 2009 chapter | Topic | US GAAP treatment | IFRS treatment |
|---|---|---|---|
| 4 | Statement of Cash Flows | Required for most entities, but limited exemptions exist | Required for all reporting entities |
| | | Direct and indirect methods for operating cash flows permitted, direct is urged but rarely seen | Direct and indirect methods for operating cash flows permitted |
| | | Interest paid and dividends received must be classified as operating cash flows, and dividends paid must be classified as financing cash flows | Choice allowed in classifying 1. Dividends and interest paid or received as operating cash flows, or 2. Interest or dividends paid as financing cash flows and interest or dividends received as investing cash flows |
| | | Overdrafts cannot be included in cash (show as financing source of cash) | Overdrafts can be included in cash under defined conditions |
| 5 | Accounting Policies, Changes and Restatements | A first-time adoption of US GAAP would normally require retrospective restatement | First-time application of IFRS requires retrospective restatement to standards effective as of beginning of current period |
| | | Corrections of errors require retrospective restatement of prior periods' financials | Corrections of errors require retrospective restatement of prior periods' financials |
| | | Changes in estimate accounted for prospectively | Changes in estimate accounted for prospectively |
| | | Voluntary change in accounting policies require restatements of prior periods' financials | Voluntary change in accounting policies require restatements of prior periods' financials |
| 6 | Fair Value | Comprehensive standard established a three-level hierarchy of fair value methods, but does not dictate further application of fair value measures. | No comprehensive guidance issued by IASB, but current project promises ultimately the issuance of a standard very similar to US GAAP |
| 7 | Cash, Receivables and Prepaid Expenses | No specific guidance offered under US GAAP or IFRS | No specific guidance offered under either set of standards |
| | | Industry specific guidance for acquired loans and receivables | Loans and receivables measured at amortized cost |
| | | Accounting for pledging, factoring similar to that under IFRS | Accounting for pledging, factoring similar to that under US GAAP should be acceptable |
| 8 | Short-Term Investments and Financial Instruments | Stricter definition of "sales" resulting in more recognition of secured borrowing transactions | Slightly looser definition of "sales" of financial assets |
| | | Basis adjustment arising from firm commitments and forecasted transactions may not be included in initial measurement of hedged item | Hedging gains and losses from cash flow hedges of firm commitments and of forecasted transactions can be included as part of the initial measurement of the cost basis of the related hedged item (basis adjustment) |

| GAAP 2009 chapter | Topic | US GAAP treatment | IFRS treatment |
|---|---|---|---|
| 8 | Short-Term Investments and Financial Instruments | Nonderivative instruments can be used to hedge currency risk associated with net investment in foreign entity or a fair value hedge of unrecognized firm commitment | Nonderivative instruments can be used to hedge foreign currency risk |
| | | Hedging of portion of cash flows of hedged item not permitted | Hedging of portion of cash flows of hedged item is permitted |
| | | Hedging gains and losses on cash flow hedges recorded in other comprehensive income when they occur, then reclassify to income with hedged item | Similar to US GAAP |
| | | Hedging for part of term of hedged item not permitted | Hedging for part of term of hedged item permitted if effectiveness can be shown |
| | | Hedging effectiveness can be assumed in limited circumstances (using "shortcut method") | Hedging effectiveness must be demonstrable; new option to designate any financial asset or liability for measurement at fair value with changes in current income |
| | | "Macrohedging" not permitted | "Macrohedging" is permitted |
| | | Gain/loss on hedging net investment in foreign subsidiary taken to income upon complete liquidation of investment | Gain/loss on hedging net investment in foreign subsidiary taken to income upon partial or complete disposal or liquidation of investment |
| | | Reclassifications to "trading" required under certain conditions, but reclassification from trading not permitted | Reclassifications to or from "trading" prohibited |
| | | Derecognition of financial assets based on loss of control, which requires isolation from transferor, transferee ability to pledge or sell, and absence of repurchase obligation by transferor | Derecognition of financial assets based primarily on risks and rewards criterion; also, on loss of control, as a secondary test |
| 9 | Inventory | Allowable costing methods include FIFO, average cost, and LIFO | LIFO costing is now banned |
| | | No special rules for biological inventory (e.g., growing crops, livestock) | IAS 41 on agriculture specifies use of fair value less estimated selling costs for biological assets, with changes in value reported in income |
| | | Presentation at lower of cost or market required | Presentation at lower of cost or net realizable value |
| | | Only in rare instances (mining of gold, etc.) is presentation at fair value in excess of cost permitted | Certain defined situations, including agricultural products, for reporting at fair value in excess of actual cost |
| | | Certain costs (idle capacity, spoilage) cannot be added to overhead charge in inventory cost, conforming to IFRS rule | Certain costs (idle capacity, spoilage) cannot be added to overhead charge in inventory cost |

| *GAAP 2009 chapter* | *Topic* | *US GAAP treatment* | *IFRS treatment* |
|---|---|---|---|
| 9 | Inventory | Lower of cost or market adjustments cannot be reversed | Lower of cost or market adjustments must be reversed under defined conditions |
| | | Recognition in interim periods of inventory losses from market declines that reasonably can be expected to be restored in the fiscal year are not required | Recognition in interim periods of inventory losses from market declines that reasonably can be expected to be restored in the fiscal year is required; guidance in the areas of disclosure and accounting for inventories of service providers offered |
| 10 | Revenue Recognition—Evolving Principles and Specialized Applications | Conceptual framework offers guidance (major project in process to provide revised standard for revenue recognition based on balance sheet changes); specific guidance on limited matters (e.g., software development; construction) | Some specific guidance offered under IFRS (a separate standard on revenue recognition exists, unlike US GAAP); cooperating with FASB on project expected to result in exposure of new approach late 2008 |
| | | Generally must recognize revenue ratably over service period, no up-front recognition under GAAP | More possibility for up-front revenue recognition when some performance has occurred |
| | | Revenue recognition deferred on delivered part of multielement contract if refund would be triggered by failure to deliver remaining elements | Revenue generally recognized on delivered part of multielement contract even if refund triggered by failure to deliver remaining elements, if delivery is probable |
| | | Revenue-cost and gross-profit approaches to percentage-of-completion both allowed for long-term construction contracts; use of completed contract method under certain circumstances is required | If percentage cannot be reliably estimated, use of cost recovery method required; "revenue-cost" approach to percentage of completion mandatory; completed contract method banned |
| 11 | Long-Lived Assets (Tangible assets) | Cost components similar to IFRS except that hedging gain/loss from qualifying cash flow hedges are not includable | Cost components similar to US GAAP, but gain/loss from effective cash flow hedging can be added to basis of asset |
| | | Change in depreciation method now handled prospectively | Change in method accounted for prospectively |
| | | Mandatory capitalization of construction period interest costs, only interest costs are subject to capitalization (but no ancillary costs can be included) | Capitalization of construction period interest is now mandatory; ancillary costs also can be capitalized |
| | | Costs of major overhauls generally expensed | Costs of major overhauls added to asset |
| | | Cost basis required | Alternatively can use cost basis or revaluation to fair value (entire classes of assets must be accounted for under revaluation method) |

| GAAP 2009 chapter | Topic | US GAAP treatment | IFRS treatment |
|---|---|---|---|
| 11 | Long-Lived Assets (Tangible assets) | Impairments recognized in current income | If cost method used, impairments are recognized in income; if revaluation employed, impairment treated as reversal of revaluation unless it exceeds former write-up, in which case excess impairment taken to current income |
| | | Impairment suggested when book value exceeds gross expected future cash flows; second step prescribed to measure amount of impairment uses discounted present value of cash flows | Impairment suggested when book value exceeds greater of value in use (discounted cash flows) or fair value less cost to sell, single step to test and measure impairment |
| | | Impairments, once recognized, cannot be reversed | Recognized impairments reversed under defined conditions |
| | | Component-level depreciation expected; asset retirement obligations recognized as part of asset cost; changes in estimated amount of obligation effectively amortized over remaining term | IFRS has been brought into closer conformity with US GAAP as to component depreciation, accrual of asset retirement obligations, although IFRS guidance on retirement obligations is more general; changes in estimated amount of the obligation recognized over remaining term if cost model is used (if revaluation model, impact is immediately felt in earnings) |
| | | Like-kind exchanges of productive assets measured at fair value, with gain or loss recognized, similar to procedures under IFRS | Like-kind exchanges measured at fair value, with gain or loss recognized |
| | | Investment property must be carried at depreciated cost | Investment property can be carried at depreciated cost or fair value |
| | | Segregate asset held for sale, write down to lower of amortized cost or fair value less estimated costs to dispose, cease depreciating assets; comparative balance sheet reclassified to report disposal group separately | Similar to US GAAP approach, except comparative balance sheet is not restated |
| 11 | Long-Lived Assets (Intangible assets) | Internally generated goodwill not recognized (although, implicitly, indirectly given recognition in limited circumstance of replacement for impaired acquired goodwill) | Internally generated goodwill not recognized |
| | | Research and development expenditures all expensed as incurred, included in operating cash flows | Research costs expensed as incurred, but development costs capitalized and amortized, with portion capitalized in period included in investing cash flows |
| | | Amortization required if identifiable intangibles have finite lives, with testing for impairment also required under defined circumstances | Similar to US GAAP |

| GAAP 2009 chapter | Topic | US GAAP treatment | IFRS treatment |
|---|---|---|---|
| 11 | Long-Lived Assets (Intangible assets) | Measurement of impairment done with reference to fair value (often operationalized using discounted cash flows) | Measurement of impairment done with reference to higher of value in use or fair value less costs to sell |
| | | Estimated residual often defined by present value of expected disposal proceeds | Estimated residual value defined by current net selling price assuming asset is age, condition as of expected end of useful life |
| | | Measurement of goodwill impairment uses special method, requires first comparing fair value of cash generating unit to book value including goodwill, then comparing implied goodwill to carrying value; measured at level of business segment or one level below that | Measurement of goodwill impairment similar to other long lived assets, requires only single-step computation; measured at lowest level goodwill can be assigned (cash generating unit) |
| | | Impairment testing at segment or lower level, except that indefinite life intangibles are tested separately from business unit | Impairments tested at cash generating unit level |
| | | No reversals of impairments once recognized for intangible assets | Impairments of intangible, once recognized, can be reversed, under defined conditions, except for goodwill |
| | | Revaluations never permitted (only amortized cost is permitted) | Revaluation of intangibles permitted under limited circumstances where prices from active markets are available |
| | | Decommissioning (asset retirement) obligations not recomputed after initial computation, generally | Decommissioning (asset retirement) obligations recomputed at current risk-adjusted rate each balance sheet date |
| 12 | Investments (Passive) | Classification as trading, available-for-sale, or held-to-maturity limited to securities; equity method required for investee accounting | Classification as trading, available-for-sale, or held-to-maturity applies to all types of financial assets, not just to securities; choice of equity, cost, fair value methods for some investees |
| | | US GAAP adopted "fair value option" similar to that available under IFRS | "Fair value option" allows any financial asset or liability to be designated at inception to be accounted for at fair value with changes reported in current earnings |
| | | If held-to-maturity securities are sold, use of this category is prohibited thereafter | If held-to-maturity securities are sold, use of this category is prohibited for next two years |
| | | Investment in unlisted securities valued at cost | Investments in unlisted securities can be valued at fair value, if reliable measure available |
| | | Derecognition of financial assets based on risks-and-rewards analysis; partial derecognition prohibited; Qualifying SPEs permitted as vehicle for nonconsolidation if conditions met | Derecognition of financial assets based on risks-and-rewards and control analyses; partial derecognition permitted; no parallel to QSPE rules under US GAAP |

| *GAAP 2009 chapter* | *Topic* | *US GAAP treatment* | *IFRS treatment* |
|---|---|---|---|
| 12 | Investments (Equity method and other) | Use of equity method based on significant influence being wielded by investor | Same as under US GAAP (but equity method investees are referred to as associates under IFRS) |
| | | Extensive disclosures required of investees' balance sheet and income statement data | Extensive disclosures required of associates' balance sheet and income statement data |
| | | Impairment of equity-method investment required when impairment is "other than temporary" | More complex consideration of impairment required; if certain criteria met, value in use (based on expected cash flows from earnings distributions and ultimate disposition) or recoverable amount, whichever is greater, is to be reported as lower carrying value than equity method amount |
| | | Joint ventures generally accounted for by equity method, but some industries (e.g., construction) use proportional consolidation is traditional | Joint ventures accounted for by equity method or proportionate consolidation, but IASB is expected to ban proportionate consolidation and conform with US GAAP treatment |
| | | No need to conform investor and investee accounting policies | Need to conform investor and investee accounting policies |
| | | Investment property must be accounted for by cost (and depreciation) method | Investment property can be accounted for by cost (and depreciation) method, or by fair value method with changes reported in income |
| 13 | Business Combinations and Consolidated Financial Statements | Acquisition method required for all business combinations under FAS 141(R); consolidation rules effectively based on majority ownership criterion; closing date generally used for recognizing acquisitions | Acquisition method of accounting required by IFRS 3; consolidation rules based on control criterion; control date used for recognizing acquisitions; revised IFRS 3 closely follows FAS 141(R) except gross-up for 100% goodwill (i.e., including noncontrolling interest share) is optional, not required |
| | | Special consolidation requirements apply to Variable Interest Entities (VIE), consolidation by primary beneficiary generally required | VIEs not yet addressed by IFRS, but Special Purpose Entities are consolidated under concept of control |
| | | Recognize postacquisition obligations at fair value | Recognize postacquisition obligations only for provisions that had been recognized by acquired entity |
| | | "Qualifying" SPEs to be consolidated if QSPE exceptions not satisfied, but elimination of QSPE accounting is under consideration | No concept of QSPE under IFRS |
| | | Consolidation of majority owned subsidiaries required unless control is not exercised by parent | Consolidation required unless control is not exercised by parent, or unless control is temporary (to lapse within twelve months) |

| GAAP 2009 chapter | Topic | US GAAP treatment | IFRS treatment |
|---|---|---|---|
| 13 | Business Combinations and Consolidated Financial Statements | Recognize all assets and liabilities at fair value, for both majority (controlling) and noncontrolling interests' shares | Assets and liabilities recorded at full fair value, including minority interest's share |
| | | Acquiree deferred tax recognized only after date of acquisition (i.e., having full valuation allowance at acquisition date) used to offset goodwill, then offset intangible assets, finally to offset tax expense | Acquiree deferred tax recognized only after date of acquisition (i.e., having full valuation allowance at acquisition date) is effected as current period credit to tax expense and also goodwill adjustment as if adjustment occurred at acquisition date |
| | | Subsequent creation of allowance for tax asset recognized in acquisition transaction effected via charge to tax expense | |
| | | No promulgated rules governing "parent company only" financial statements, but use of equity method would be acceptable | In "parent company only" financials, the investment in subsidiaries, equity investees, and joint ventures may be presented at cost or under rules for investments in securities, but equity method cannot be used |
| | | Not necessary to conform parent and subsidiary accounting policies if some entities use specialized industry practices | Need to conform parent and subsidiary accounting policies |
| | | Noncontrolling interest in consolidated subsidiary must now (under FAS 141[R]) be presented in equity | Minority interest included in equity |
| | | Acquired in-process R&D now to be capitalized; postacquisition-date expenditures on IPR&D are expensed | Purchased in-process R&D capitalized, and subsequent expenditures generally are also capitalized and amortized, if "development" costs |
| | | Negative goodwill reported as gain, with no offsetting against acquired assets | Negative goodwill reported as gain, with no offsetting against acquired assets |
| | | The fair value of contingent consideration and other contractual contingencies are now to be recognized at date of acquisition; noncontractual contingencies are recognized only if "more likely than not" threshold is met | Fair value of contingent consideration included in purchase price allocation process, if probable of occurrence and subject to reliable estimation |
| | | Goodwill not amortized, but is annually tested for impairment | Similar to US GAAP, but different impairment testing procedures |
| | | One year permitted to finalize purchase price allocation process, including resolution of preacquisition contingencies | Similar to US GAAP |
| | | Combinations of entities under common control ("brother sister" mergers) accounted for at book value, like former poolings of interest | No specific rules for "brother sister" mergers, so either purchase accounting or book value (pooling) accounting is acceptable per parent entity's policy choice |

| GAAP 2009 chapter | Topic | US GAAP treatment | IFRS treatment |
|---|---|---|---|
| 13 | Business Combinations and Consolidated Financial Statements | Revalue previous steps in acquisition to fair value at each step in acquisition process | Similar to US GAAP (would be affected by currently proposed changes to both US GAAP and IFRS) |
| | | Expected restructuring or similar postacquisition costs, if not contractually obligated at acquisition date, are not accrued but are only recognized subsequently as period costs | Restructuring reserves generally not allowed, unless acquiree had recorded contingent liability before transaction. |
| 14 | Current Liabilities and Contingencies | Short-term debt refinanced before statement issuance date can often be shown as noncurrent | Short-term debt refinanced before balance sheet date can be shown as noncurrent; if later (but still before issuance of financials) disclosure only |
| | | Contingent liabilities generally recognized only if deemed probable and subject to reasonable estimation | Similar to US GAAP, but threshold for recognition is somewhat lower, using "more likely than not" criterion |
| | | Provisions (estimated liabilities) measured by reference to low end of range of amounts needed to settle, sometimes but not always discounted to present value | Provisions measured by reference to best estimate to settle (often the midpoint in range), discounted to present value |
| | | Strict criteria must be met to accrue restructuring costs, and mere intent to incur such costs is not sufficient to justify accrual; must meet definition of a liability at balance sheet date | Somewhat more flexibility to accrue restructuring charges if plans have been announced and/or actions have been undertaken as of balance sheet date, even if definition of liability is not met |
| | | Specific rules for certain provisions (e.g., for environmental liabilities) | Only general guidance provided under IFRS |
| | | Contingent gains not recognized, although contingent assets acquired in business combination are recognized at fair value under FAS 141(R) | IFRS provides for some recognition of contingent gains |
| 15 | Long-Term Liabilities | Convertible debt classified as liability | Convertible debt assigned to both debt and equity based on relative fair values |
| | | Embedded derivatives generally must be bifurcated and accounted for separately | Embedded derivatives generally must be bifurcated and accounted for separately |
| | | Noncurrent presentation of defaulted debt if waiver granted before statement issuance date | Noncurrent presentation of defaulted debt if waiver granted before balance sheet date only |
| | | Equity-like instruments giving holder right to demand cash settlement, or with defined cash settlement terms, must be classed as liabilities | Similar to US GAAP |
| | | Joint project with IASB to address instruments with attributes of both liabilities and equity is ongoing | Joint project with FASB to address instruments with attributes of both liabilities and equity is ongoing |

| GAAP 2009 chapter | Topic | US GAAP treatment | IFRS treatment |
|---|---|---|---|
| 16 | Leases | Capital lease accounting is required if one of four defined conditions are met; otherwise, operating lease | Similar to US GAAP; finance lease treatment if risks and rewards are transferred to lessee; also if property is special purpose for lessee use |
| | | No additional factors that parallel those under IFRS for determination of financing (capital) treatment by lessor | If lessee to bear lessor's loss upon lease cancellation, or lessee will shoulder gain or loss from change in residual value of leased asset, or lessee has bargain renewal right, then lease may be deemed financing transaction for lessor |
| | | Third-party guarantees cannot be included in minimum lease payments to determine whether capital lease criteria are met | Third-party guarantees must be included in minimum lease payments to determine whether capital lease criteria are met |
| | | Present value of lease payments computed using incremental borrowing rate, unless practical to determine implicit rate that is lower than incremental borrowing rate | Present value of lease payments computed using implicit rate (if unknown, incremental rate can be used) |
| | | More guidance provided on specialized topics; deferral of profit on sale-leasebacks is required | Only general guidance; profit recognition on sale-leasebacks permitted if fair value priced |
| | | Separate accounting for land and building in combined lease depends on terms and materiality of land | Separation of land and building components of lease is mandatory under recent provisions |
| | | Output contracts are leases | Output contracts are not leases |
| | | Leasehold interest in land accounted for as prepayment | Leasehold interest in land can be accounted for as investment property, valued at fair value with changes reported in current earnings; or else as a prepayment |
| | | Gain on sale/leaseback not recognized in current earnings, but deferred and amortized, unless seller retains use of much of asset, in which case gain is recognized (immediate recognition of loss also commonly required) | Gain on sale/leaseback amortized over term of financing lease, but recognized at once if operating leaseback |
| | | Lease obligations disclosures more extensive than under IFRS | Lease obligations disclosures less than under GAAP |
| | | Joint convergence project with IASB has now been limited to lessee issues | Same as US GAAP |
| 17 | Income Taxes | Comprehensive interperiod allocation using liability method (balance sheet orientation) required under US GAAP | Comprehensive interperiod allocation using liability method (balance sheet orientation) required under IFRS, very similar to US GAAP |
| | | Exemptions from interperiod allocation rules found under IFRS not present under US GAAP | Exemptions provided for nontaxable goodwill, certain asset/liability acquisitions that are not business combinations and that do not immediately affect book or tax income, and permanent differences |

| GAAP 2009 chapter | Topic | US GAAP treatment | IFRS treatment |
|---|---|---|---|
| 17 | Income Taxes | Tax effects of all temporary differences are recognized, subject to allowance for tax assets that are not "more likely than not" to be realized | Tax effects of all temporary differences are recognized, subject to allowances for tax assets that are not "more likely than not" to be realized |
| | | Recognize effect of rate changes when enacted | Recognize effects of rate changes when "substantively enacted" which may precede US GAAP recognition |
| | | Prohibits recognition of effects of temporary differences related to 1. Foreign currency nonmonetary assets when the reporting currency is the functional currency, and 2. Intercompany transfers of inventory or other assets remaining within the company | |
| | | Deferred tax assets and liabilities are current or noncurrent based on related asset or liability, net current and net noncurrent amounts are displayed | Deferred tax assets and liabilities are noncurrent, and are to be reported net |
| | | Post-business-combination recognition of deferred tax asset eliminates goodwill, then other intangible assets, with any excess taken to income | Post-business-combination recognition of deferred tax asset eliminates goodwill with any excess taken to income |
| | | Several specific exemptions to general requirement to provide deferred tax on all temporary differences are set forth | No exceptions to general principle that all temporary differences in carrying amount of assets and liabilities require deferred taxes |
| | | Recognize deferred tax asset in all cases, provide reserve when realization is not "more likely than not" | Recognize deferred tax asset when realization is probable, which means "more likely than not" per IFRS 3 |
| | | Effect of change in rates or change in assessed likelihood of realization on deferred tax related to item originally recognized in stockholders' equity must be reported in current earnings | Effect of change in rates or change in assessed likelihood of realization on deferred tax related to item originally recognized in stockholders' equity must be reported in equity using "backward tracing" (may soon be changed to conform with US GAAP method) |
| | | Subsequent year realization of tax benefit from business combination reduces goodwill, then other tangible assts, and only then excess reported in current earnings | Subsequent year realization of tax benefit from business combination reduces goodwill, then excess reported in current earnings |
| | | Rate reconciliation based on domestic federal rate time pretax profit from continuing operations only | Rate reconciliation based on applicable rates times accounting profit |
| | | Tax effect of intercompany transactions recognized at seller entity's tax rate | Tax effect of intercompany transactions recognized at buyer entity's tax rate |

| *GAAP 2009 chapter* | *Topic* | *US GAAP treatment* | *IFRS treatment* |
|---|---|---|---|
| 17 | Income Taxes | Benefit of uncertain tax positions can only be recognized to the extent that there is at least a 50% likelihood of being sustained on exam. | No specific guidance on uncertain tax positions (apply general approach for contingent losses) |
| | | | Convergence with FASB approach likely, with exposure document due in late 2008 |
| 18 | Pensions and Other Postretirement Benefits | Defined benefit plans; use of projected unit credit method required to match expense to periods of service; smoothing is accomplished by deferred recognition of actuarial gains and losses, amortization of prior service costs, et al. | Methodology very similar to that under US GAAP, with deferred recognition of actuarial gains or losses. However, past service costs are recognized immediately, not deferred |
| | | Past service costs amortized over service period or life expectancy of workers | Past service costs expensed immediately |
| | | Actuarial gains and losses cannot be recognized in equity; are to be deferred and amortized to pension expense over expected term of plan participants to the extent that defined "corridor" is exceeded | Actuarial gains and losses can be recognized in equity rather than earnings under amendment to IAS 19 effective in 2006; if in earnings, either immediate recognition or amortization similar to US GAAP is permissible |
| | | Recognition of a minimum liability on the balance sheet to at least the unfunded accumulated pension benefit obligation | No minimum liability to be reported in the balance sheet |
| | | No limitation on recognition of pension assets | Limitation on recognition of pension assets |
| | | Curtailment gains recognized only when employees terminate or plan suspension is adopted, computed differently than under IFRS | Curtailment gains or losses recognized when announced; computed differently than US GAAP |
| | | Anticipating changes in the law that would affect variables such as state medical or social security benefits expressly prohibited | Anticipate changes in future postemployment benefits based on its expectations in the law |
| | | Termination benefits expensed when employees accept and amount can be estimated, recognize contractual benefits when it is probable that employees will accept | Termination benefits expensed when employer is committed to pay these |
| | | Expense recognition for certain types of equity compensation benefits; opposed to mandatory stock compensation expensing; prior service cost to be amortized over the expected service life of existing employees; contributions to multiemployer plans expenses | Expense for equity compensation benefits not recognized, but current agenda item; prior service cost related to retirees and active vested employees to be expensed; benefit obligation for multiemployer recognized |
| | | No limitation on amount of pension plan asset (in connection with overfunding) that can be presented on balance sheet | Balance sheet asset recognition limited by complex rules |

| GAAP 2009 chapter | Topic | US GAAP treatment | IFRS treatment |
|---|---|---|---|
| 18 | Pensions and Other Postretirement Benefits | Joint convergence project with IASB, with late-2007 discussion document promised, has many complex issues to be addressed. | Joint convergence project with FASB, with late-2007 discussion document promised, has many complex issues to be addressed. |
| 19 | Stockholders' Equity | Mandatorily redeemable preferred shown as liability with dividends deducted as expense | Mandatorily redeemable preferred shown as liability with dividends deducted as expense |
| | | Fair value method required for share-based compensation plans; special simplified method prescribed for nonpublic companies | Mandatory income statement recognition of effect of stock-based compensation measured at fair value; no special rules for nonpublic entities |
| | | Fair value measurement of goods and services acquired for stock from nonemployees using counterparty's commitment or actual performance date | Fair value measurement of goods and services acquired for stock from nonemployees using modified grant date method |
| | | Income tax benefits related to share-based payment (measured by spread between current fair value and exercise price) credited to equity; any payroll taxes recognized in expense at time of exercise | Tax benefits related to share-based payments credited to equity only if in excess of compensation expense; any payroll taxes recognized in expense over same period as recognition of option plan cost (vesting period) |
| | | Tax benefits related to share-based payments based on GAAP expense, later adjusted when actual tax effects are realized | Tax benefits related to share-based payments based on expected applicable tax deduction |
| | | Modifications of awards require new measurement based on date of modification | Modifications do not trigger new measurement of fair value |
| | | Joint project with IASB to address instruments with features of both liabilities and equity | Joint project with FASB to address instruments with features of both liabilities and equity |
| 20 | Earnings Per Share | Very similar to IFRS, but with more detailed guidance on calculations | Similar to US GAAP. Calculation of year-to-date EPS (versus previously reported interim date) varies from US GAAP |
| | | Report basic and diluted EPS on continuing operations, discontinued operations, extraordinary items, cumulative effect of change in accounting and net income | Report basic and diluted EPS on continuing operations and net income |
| | | For interim reporting, average the interim periods' incremental shares to compute EPS | For interim reporting, use treasury stock method on year-to-date results, unlike US GAAP approach |
| | | Proposed changes would converge with IFRS | |
| 21 | Interim Reporting | Some timing differences in recognition of interim revenues and expenses vs. IFRS | Some timing differences in recognition of interim revenues and expenses vs. US GAAP |

| GAAP 2009 chapter | Topic | US GAAP treatment | IFRS treatment |
|---|---|---|---|
| 21 | Interim Reporting | Basic principle is that interim period is integral to full year, but actual requirements depart from this in many instances; net result is mixed approach not unlike IFRS | Basic principle is that interim period is discrete period, but actual requirements depart from this in many instances; net result is mixed approach not unlike US GAAP |
| 22 | Segment Reporting | "Management approach" provides flexibility in defining segments; segment results using internal managerial approach OK, even if these differ from financial statements | Approach very similar to US GAAP recently adopted |
| | | Disclosures based on primary classification (either geographic or product-based), with some additional "entity-wide" items (major customers, etc.)—not necessarily lines of business or geographical areas, however | Defines segments based on components of the entity that are businesses, having operating results reviewed by the chief operating decision maker, and having discrete financial information; these are reportable if one of three threshold criteria (sales, profit, or assets) are met |
| | | No segment result definition given, no requirement for capital expenditures, liabilities disclosure by segments | Segment result defined, also require capital expenditures and liabilities segment disclosures; entity-wide and some geographic analyses are also required |
| 23 | Foreign Currency | Selection of functional currency is open to judgment, but in practice there is a greater emphasis on cash flows than on currency that influences pricing of output | Greater emphasis placed on the currency of the economy that influences sales prices for goods and services |
| | | Choice of reporting (presentation) currencies, and if other than functional currency translate assets and liabilities at balance sheet date exchange rate, income and expense at rate at dates of transactions (or average for period, if not materially different) | Very similar to US GAAP |
| | | Exchange losses to be expensed in all instances | Exchange losses on a liability for the recent acquisition of an asset invoiced in a foreign currency either as<br><br>1.  Charge to expense, or<br>2.  Add to the cost of the asset when the related liability cannot be settled and there is no practical means to hedge |
| | | Current exchange rate use to translate all balance sheet items, including goodwill and fair value adjustments | Same as under US GAAP |
| | | In highly inflationary economy (having cumulative three-year price change of 100%), parent's currency (US dollar) must be used as functional currency | In hyperinflationary economy, an entity cannot avoid restatement under IAS 29 by adopting stable currency (e.g., that of parent company) as functional currency |

| GAAP 2009 chapter | Topic | US GAAP treatment | IFRS treatment |
|---|---|---|---|
| 23 | Foreign Currency | Equity accounts are translated at historical rates | Translation of equity accounts not specified under IFRS |
| 24 | Personal Financial Statements | Current value reporting required | No published guidance |
| 25 | Specialized Industry GAAP | No primary guidance for government grants, agriculture, but there are specific requirements for certain industries, such as oil and gas | Guidance provided for government grants, agriculture, reporting by banks, extractive industries, insurance |
|  |  | Specialized guidance on various industries, including insurance; banking and thrifts; motion pictures, computer software, and agricultural industries, and others, found in "secondary" GAAP sources such as AICPA Guides, SOP, etc. | No such guidance offered; there is no "secondary" source for GAAP guidance |

# APPENDIX C

## PROPOSED FASB ACCOUNTING CODIFICATION CHAPTER CROSS-REFERENCE

FASB has proposed replacing all currently authoritative accounting standards with a reorganized, authoritative accounting codification. According to the currently planned timetable, this would occur in April 2009. During the field-testing verification phase, constituents are encouraged to register and use the online Codification Research System free of charge and provide feedback to FASB regarding its accuracy. The test Web site is found at http://asc.fasb.org/home.

This appendix illustrates the basic organization of the codification by topic and subtopic and provides a cross-reference to the relevant chapter of this publication in which the content is covered.

| *Topic # and title* | *Subtopic # and title* | *GAAP 2009 chapter number and title* |
|---|---|---|
| **I. General Principles and Objectives** | | |
| 105 Generally Accepted Accounting Principles | | 1 Researching GAAP Matters |
| 110 Conceptual Framework | | 1 Researching GAAP Matters |
| **II. Overall Financial Reporting, Presentation, and Display Matters** | | |
| **A. Overall Presentation of Financial Statements** | | |
| 205 Presentation of Financial Statements | | |
| | 205-20 Discontinued Operations | 3 Statement of Income and Comprehensive Income |
| | | 11 Long-Lived Assets |
| | | 21 Interim Reporting |
| 210 Balance Sheet | | 2 Balance Sheet |
| | 210-20 Offsetting | 2 Balance Sheet |
| 215 Statement of Shareholder Equity | | 19 Stockholders Equity (Appendix A) |
| 220 Comprehensive Income | | 3 Statement of Income and Comprehensive Income |
| 225 Income Statement | | 3 Statement of Income and Comprehensive Income |
| | 225-20 Extraordinary and Unusual Items | 3 Statement of Income and Comprehensive Income |
| | | 4 Statement of Cash Flows |
| | | 21 Interim Reporting |
| | 225-30 Business Interruption Insurance | |
| 230 Statement of Cash Flows | | 4 Statement of Cash Flows |
| 235 Notes to Financial Statements | | 5 Accounting Policies, Changes, and Restatements |
| **B. Various Financial Reporting, Presentation, and Display Matters** | | |
| 250 Accounting Changes and Error Corrections | | 5 Accounting Policies, Changes, and Restatements |
| 255 Changing Prices | | 23 Foreign Currency |
| 260 Earnings Per Share | | 20 Earnings Per Share |
| 270 Interim Reporting | | 21 Interim Reporting |
| 275 Risks and Uncertainties | | 2 Balance Sheet |
| 280 Segment Reporting | | 22 Segment Reporting |

| *Topic # and title* | *Subtopic # and title* | *GAAP 2009*<br>*chapter number and title* |
|---|---|---|
| | 350-50 Web Site Development Costs | 11 Long-Lived Assets |
| 360 Property, Plant, and Equipment | | 11 Long-Lived Assets |
| | 360-20 Real Estate Sales | 10 Revenue Recognition—Evolving Principles |
| 405 Liabilities | | 14 Current Liabilities and Contingencies |
| | | 15 Long-Term Liabilities |
| | 405-20 Extinguishment of Liabilities | 15 Long-Term Liabilities |
| | 405-30 Insurance-Related Assessments | |
| 410 Asset Retirement and Environmental Obligations | | |
| | 410-20 Asset Retirement Obligations | 11 Long-Lived Assets |
| | 410-30 Environmental Obligations | 11 Long-Lived Assets |
| | | 14 Current Liabilities and Contingencies |
| 420 Exit or Disposal Cost Obligations | | 3 Statement of Income and Comprehensive Income |
| 430 Deferred Revenue | | 10 Revenue Recognition—Evolving Principles |
| | | 14 Current Liabilities and Contingencies |
| 440 Commitments | | 2 Balance Sheet |
| 450 Contingencies | | 14 Current Liabilities and Contingencies |
| | 450-20 Loss Contingencies | 14 Current Liabilities and Contingencies |
| | 450-30 Gain Contingencies | |
| 460 Guarantees | | 14 Current Liabilities and Contingencies |
| 470 Debt | | 15 Long-Term Liabilities |
| | 470-20 Debt with Conversion and Other Options | 15 Long-Term Liabilities |
| | 470-30 Participating Mortgage Loans | 15 Long-Term Liabilities |
| | 470-40 Product Financing Arrangements | 9 Inventory |
| | 470-50 Modifications and Extinguishments | 6 Fair Value |
| | | 15 Long-Term Liabilities |
| | 470-60 Troubled Debt Restructurings by Debtors | 7 Cash, Receivables, and Prepaid Expenses |
| | | 12 Long-Term Investments |
| | | 15 Long-Term Liabilities |
| | | 25A Banking and Thrift |
| 480 Distinguishing Liabilities from Equity | | 15 Long-Term Liabilities |
| | | 19 Stockholders' Equity |
| 505 Equity | | 19 Stockholders' Equity |

| *Topic # and title* | *Subtopic # and title* | *GAAP 2009*<br>*chapter number and title* |
|---|---|---|
| | 718-30   Awards Classified as<br>Liabilities | 19   Stockholders' Equity |
| | 718-40   Employee Stock<br>Ownership Plans | 19   Stockholders' Equity |
| | 718-50   Employee Stock Purchase<br>Plans | 19   Stockholders' Equity |
| | 718-740 Income Taxes | |
| 720   Other Expenses | | |
| | 720-15   Start-Up Costs | 3   Statement of Income and<br>Comprehensive Income |
| | 720-20   Insurance Costs | |
| | 720-25   Contributions Made | |
| | 720-30   Real and Personal Property<br>Taxes | 14   Current Liabilities and<br>Contingencies |
| | 720-35   Advertising Costs | 3   Statement of Income and<br>Comprehensive Income |
| | | 5   Accounting Policies,<br>Changes, and Restatements |
| | 720-40   Electronic Equipment<br>Waste Obligations | 11   Long-Lived Assets |
| | 720-45   Business and Technology<br>Reengineering | 25D   Computer Software<br>Developers |
| 730   Research and<br>Development | | 11   Long-Lived Assets |
| | | 13   Business Combinations and<br>Consolidated Financial<br>Statements |
| | 730-20   Research and Development<br>Arrangements | |
| 740   Income Taxes | | 17   Income Taxes |
| | 740-20   Intraperiod Tax Allocation | 17   Income Taxes |
| | 740-30   Other Considerations or<br>Special Areas | 17   Income Taxes |
| | 740-270 Interim Reporting | 17   Income Taxes |
| | | 21   Interim Reporting |

**B.**   **Broad Transactional Categories**

| | | |
|---|---|---|
| 805   Business Combinations<br>and Reorganizations | | 13   Business Combinations and<br>Consolidated Financial<br>Statements |
| | 805-20   Reorganizations | 19   Stockholders' Equity |
| | 805.xx   Superseded by Bus. Comb.<br>2 Project | 13   Business Combinations and<br>Consolidated Financial<br>Statements |
| | 805-718 Compensation—Stock<br>Compensation | |
| | 805-740 Income Taxes | |
| 810   Consolidation | | |
| | 810-20   Control of Partnerships and<br>Similar Entities | 12   Long-Term Investments |

| *Topic # and title* | *Subtopic # and title* | *GAAP 2009*<br>*chapter number and title* |
|---|---|---|
| | 860-40 Transfers to Qualifying<br>Special-Purpose Entities | 7 Cash, Receivables, and<br>Prepaid Expenses |
| | 860-50 Servicing Assets and<br>Liabilities | 7 Cash, Receivables, and<br>Prepaid Expenses |

**IV. Industry/Unique Topics**

| | |
|---|---|
| 905 Agriculture | |
| 908 Airlines | |
| 910 Contractors—<br>Construction | 10 Revenue Recognition |
| 912 Contractors—Federal<br>Government | 25G Government Contractors |
| 915 Development Stage<br>Entities | 3 Statement of Income and<br>Comprehensive Income |
| 920 Entertainment—<br>Broadcasters | 25B Broadcasting |
| 922 Entertainment—Cable<br>Television | 25C Cable Television |
| 924 Entertainment—Casinos | |
| 926 Entertainment—Films | 25K Motion Pictures |
| 928 Entertainment—Music | 25N Recording and Music |
| 930 Extractive Activities—<br>Mining | |
| 932 Extractive Activities—<br>Oil and Gas | 25M Oil and Gas Producers |
| 940 Financial Services—<br>Brokers and Dealers | |
| 942 Financial Services—<br>Depository and<br>Lending | 25A Banking and Thrift |
| 944 Financial Services—<br>Insurance | 25H Insurance |
| 946 Financial Services—<br>Investment<br>Companies | 25I Investment Companies |
| 948 Financial Services—<br>Mortgage Banking | 25J Mortgage Banking |
| 950 Financial Services—<br>Title Plant | 25P Title Plant |
| 952 Franchisors | 10 Revenue Recognition |
| 954 Health Care Entities | |
| 956 Limited Liability Entities | 19 Stockholders' Equity |
| 958 Not-For-Profit Entities | 25L Not-For-Profit Organizations |
| 960 Plan Accounting—<br>Defined Benefit<br>Pension Plans | 25E Employee Benefit Plans,<br>Including Pension Funds |
| 962 Plan Accounting—<br>Defined Contribution<br>Pension Plans | 25E Employee Benefit Plans,<br>Including Pension Funds |
| 965 Plan Accounting—<br>Health and Welfare<br>Benefit Plans | 25E Employee Benefit Plans,<br>Including Pension Funds |

| *Topic # and title* | *Subtopic # and title* | *GAAP 2009*<br>*chapter number and title* |
|---|---|---|
| 970  Real Estate—General | | 10  Revenue Recognition |
| 972  Real Estate—Common<br>     Interest Realty<br>     Associations | | |
| 974  Real Estate—Real Estate<br>     Investment Trusts | | |
| 976  Real Estate—Retail<br>     Land | | 10  Revenue Recognition |
| 978  Real Estate—Time-<br>     Sharing Activities | | 10  Revenue Recognition |
| 980  Regulated Operations | | 25O  Regulated Operations |
| 985  Software | | 25D  Computer Software<br>      Developers |
| 995  US Steamship Entities | | |

**V.     Glossary**                                                           "Definition of Terms" in each
                                                                                                        chapter

**VI.    Postcodification Standards (including Basis for Conclusions)**

**VII.   Precodification Standards**

**VIII.  Proposed Standards**